SO-EFN-275

Stephen Birnham Travel Guides

Canada
Caribbean, Bermuda, and the Bahamas
Disneyland
Europe
Europe for Business Travelers
Florida for Free
France
Great Britain and Ireland
Hawaii
Mexico
South America
United States
USA for Business Travelers
Walt Disney World

CONTRIBUTING EDITORS

Duncan Anderson	Andrew Gillman	Martina Norelli
Melvin Benarde	Agnes Gottlieb	Ottar Odland
Gunnar Berj	Patricia Graves	Carol Offen
Paolo Braghieri	Jessica Harris	Pat Patricof
Mark Brayne	Jack Herbert	A. E. Pedersen
John Buskin	Marilyn Bruno Herrera	Samuel Perkins
Ron Butler	Ritva Hildebrandt	Susan Pierres
Ann Campbell-Lord	Brian Hill	Fred Poe
Linda Carreaga	Elva Horvath	Colin Pringle
Rik Cate	Julian Isherwood	Carol Reed
Stacey Chanin	Mark Kalish	Allen Rokach
Vinod Chhabra	Leslie F. Kauffmann	Margery Safir
Roger Collis	Virginia Kelley	George Semmler
Karen Cure	André Leduc	Hella Sessoms
Jeff Davidson	Richard Lee	Janet Stobbart
Martha de la Cal	Alan Levy	Phyllis Stoller
Claire Devener	Theodora Lurie	Bruce Thorstad
Thomas S. Dyman	Sirrka Makelainen	Nancy Patton Van Zant
Bjorn Edlund	Thomas C. Marinelli	Betty Vaughn
Bonnie Edwards	Carol Martin	Florence Vidal
Donna Evleth	Alexandra Mayes	Richard Walbleigh
Jackie Fierman	Mack McBean	Dennis Weber
Ted Folke	Virginia McCune	Jennifer Wright
Lois Gelatt	Anne Millman	Derrick Young
Norman Gelb	Tamara K. Mitchell	Eleni Ziogas
Jerry Gerber	Jack Monet	Sonia Zalubowski

ADVISORY EDITOR David Walker   DIVERSIONS EDITOR Jeff Davidson

SYMBOLS Gloria McKeown   MAPS General Cartography Inc.

COVER Paul Posnick

A Stephen Birnbaum Travel Guide

Birnbaum's EUROPE 1986

Stephen Birnbaum
EDITOR

Claire Hardiman
EXECUTIVE EDITOR

Kristin Moehlmann
Associate Editor

Denise DeGennaro
Assistant Editor

Ellen Rapp
Editorial Assistant

HOUGHTON MIFFLIN COMPANY BOSTON 1985

For Alex, who merely makes this all possible

This book is published by special arrangement
with Eric Lasher and Maureen Lasher.

ISBN: 0-395-39398-1 (pbk.)
ISSN: 0749-2561 (Stephen Birnbaum Travel Guides)
ISSN: 0883-2498

Printed in the United States of America

Q 10 9 8 7 6 5 4 3 2 1

Contents

GETTING READY TO GO

A mini-encyclopedia of all the practical travel data you need to plan your vacation down to the final detail.

When and How to Go

Preparing

On the Road

FACTS IN BRIEF

A compilation of pertinent tourist information such as entry requirements and customs, sports, language, currency, clothing requirements, and more for 32 European countries.

DIVERSIONS

A selective guide to 21 active and cerebral vacations including the places to pursue them where your quality of experience is likely to be highest.

For the Mind

For the Experience

THE EUROPEAN CITIES

Thorough, qualitative guides to each of the 34 cities most often visited by vacationers and businesspeople. Each section, a comprehensive report of the city's most appealing attractions and amenities, is designed to be used on the spot. Directions and recommendations are immediately accessible because each guide is presented in a consistent form.

DIRECTIONS

Europe's most spectacular routes and roads, most arresting natural wonders, most magnificent châteaux and castles, all organized into over 100 specific driving tours.

A Word from the Editor

There is no record of the specific guidebook that Hannibal and his Carthaginian hordes used to chart the route for their elephant trek through the Alps, but you can be sure that they had the help of at least a rudimentary work describing the basics of European geography. Indeed, guides to Europe have existed literally for centuries, and one might logically ask why another one is necessary amid this plenty.

Our answer is that the nature of European travel and even the travelers themselves have changed dramatically of late. For the past 2,000 years or so, travel on the Continent was an extremely elaborate undertaking, one that required extensive planning. Even as recently as the 1950s, a person who had actually been to Europe could dine out on his or her experiences for years, since such adventures were quite extraordinary and usually the province of the privileged alone. With the advent of jet air travel in the late 1950s, however, and of increased-capacity, wide-body aircraft during the 1960s, travel to and around Europe has become extremely common. In fact, in two decades of nearly unending inflation, air fares may be the only commodity in the world that have actually gone down in price. And, as a result, international travel is now well within the budgets of mere mortals.

Attitudes as well as costs have changed significantly. Beginning with the so-called flower children and hippies of the 1960s, international travel lost much of its aura of mystery. Whereas their parents might have chosen a superficial sampling of Europe — a 14-countries-in-14-days tour, for example — these young people, motivated as much by wildly inexpensive "youth fares" as by the inclination to see the world, simply picked up and settled in various parts of Europe for an indefinite stay. While living as cheaply as possible, they usually adopted with great gusto the language and lifestyle and generally immersed themselves in things European.

Thus began an explosion of travel to and in Europe. And, over the years, the development of inexpensive charter flights and packages fueled and sharpened the new American interest in and appetite for more extensive exploration of the Continent.

Now, as we move deeper into the 1980s, those same young people who were in the forefront of the modern travel revolution have undeniably aged. While it may be impolite to point out that they are probably well into their untrustworthy 30s (and mostly firmly enmeshed in establishment activities), their original zeal for travel remains unabated. For them it's hardly news that the way to get to Switzerland is to head for France, take a left, and then wait for snow-capped mountains to appear. Such experienced and knowledgeable travelers have decided precisely where they want to go and are more often searching for ideas and insights to expand their already sophisticated travel consciousness. And — reverting to their youthful instincts and habits — they are after a deeper understanding and fuller assimilation of the European milieu. Typically, they visit single countries (or even cities) several times and may actually do so more than once in a single year.

Obviously, any European guidebook must keep pace with and answer the real needs of today's travelers. That's why we've tried to create a guide that's specifically organized, written, and edited for this more demanding audience, for whom qualitative information is infinitely more desirable than mere quantities of unappraised data. We think that this book, as well as the other guides in our series, represent a new generation of travel guides, ones that are especially responsive to modern needs and interests.

For years, dating back as far as Herr Baedeker, travel guides have tended to be encyclopedic, seemingly much more concerned with demonstrating expertise in geography and history than in any analysis of the sorts of things that genuinely concern a typical tourist. But today, when it is hardly necessary to tell a traveler where London is, it is hard to justify devoting endless pages to historical perspective. As suggested earlier, it's not impossible that the guidebook reader may have been to Europe nearly as often as the guidebook editor, so it becomes the responsibility of that editor to provide new perceptions and to suggest new directions to make his guide genuinely valuable.

That's exactly what we've tried to do in our *Get 'em and Go* series. I think you'll notice a different, more contemporary tone to the text as well as an organization and focus that are distinctive and more functional. And even a random examination of what follows will demonstrate a substantial departure from the standard guidebook orientation, for we've not only attempted to provide information of a different sort, but we've also tried to present it in a context that makes it particularly accessible.

Needless to say, it's difficult to decide precisely what to include in a guidebook of this size — and what to omit. Early on, we realized that giving up the encyclopedic approach precluded the inclusion of every single route and restaurant, which helped define our overall editorial focus. Similarly, when we discussed the possibility of presenting certain information in other than strict geographical order, we found that the new format enabled us to arrange data in a way that we feel best answers the questions travelers typically ask.

Large numbers of specific questions have provided the real editorial skeleton for this book. The volume of mail I regularly receive seems to emphasize that modern travelers want very precise information, so we've tried to address these needs and have organized our material in the most responsive way possible. Readers who want to know the best restaurant in Paris or the best beach on the Côte d'Azur will have no trouble whatever extracting that data from this guide.

Travel guides are, of course, reflections of personal taste, and putting one's name on a title page obviously puts one's preferences on the line. But I think I ought to amplify just what "personal" means. I do not believe in the sort of personal guidebook that's a palpable misrepresentation on its face. It is, for example, hardly possible for any single travel writer to visit thousands of restaurants (and nearly as many hotels) in any given year and provide accurate appraisals of each one. And even if it were possible for one human being to survive such an itinerary, it would of necessity have to be done at a dead sprint, and the perceptions derived therefrom would probably be less valid than those of any intelligent individual visiting the same establishments. It is, therefore, impossible (especially in an annually revised and updated guidebook *series* such as we offer) to have only one person provide all the data on the entire world.

I also happen to think that such individual orientation is of substantially less value to readers. Visiting a single hotel for just one night or eating one hasty meal in a given restaurant hardly equips anyone to provide appraisals that are of more than passing interest. No amount of doggedly alliterative or oppressively onomatopoeic text can camouflage a technique that is specious on its face. We have, therefore, chosen what I like to describe as the "thee and me" approach to restaurant and hotel appraisal and, to a somewhat more limited degree, to the sites and sights we have included in the other sections of our text. What this really reflects is personal sampling tempered by intelligent counsel from informed local sources, and these additional friends-of-the-editor are almost always residents of the city and/or area about which they have been consulted.

Despite the presence of several editors, a considerable number of writers and researchers, and numerous insightful local correspondents, very precise editing and tailoring keep our text fiercely subjective. So what follows is purposely designed to be the gospel according to Birnbaum, and it represents as much of my own taste and insight as is humanly possible. It is probable, therefore, that if you like your cities distinctive and your mountains uncrowded, prefer small hotels with personality to huge high-rise anonymities, and can't tolerate fresh fish that's been relentlessly overcooked, we're likely to have a long and meaningful relationship. Readers with dissimilar tastes may be less enraptured.

I also should point out something about the person to whom this guidebook is directed. Above all, he or she is a "visitor." This means that such elements as restaurants have been specifically picked to provide the visitor with a representative, enlightening, stimulating, and above all pleasant experience. Since so many extraneous considerations can affect the reception and service accorded a regular restaurant patron, our choices can in no way be construed as a definitive guide to resident dining. We think we've listed all the best places, in various price ranges, but they were chosen with a visitor's viewpoint in mind.

Other evidence of how we've tried to tailor our text to reflect changing travel habits is most apparent in the section we call DIVERSIONS. Where once it was common for travelers to spend a European visit nailed to a single spot, the emphasis today is more likely to be directed toward pursuing some active enterprise or special interest while seeing the surrounding countryside. Such is the amount of perspiration regularly stimulated by today's "leisurely" vacationer that a common by-product of a typical modern holiday is often the need to take another vacation to recover from the first. So we've selected every activity we could reasonably evaluate and organized the material in a way that is especially accessible to activists of either an athletic or cerebral bent. It is no longer necessary, therefore, to wade through a pound or two of extraneous prose just to find the very best golf course or the clearest snorkeling spot within a reasonable radius of your destination.

If there is a single thing that best characterizes the revolution in and evolution of current holiday habits, it is that Americans now consider travel a right rather than a privilege. No longer is a trip to the far corners of the world necessarily a once-in-a-lifetime thing, nor is the idea of visiting exotic, faraway places in the least worrisome. Travel today translates as the enthusiastic desire to sample all of the world's opportunities, to find that elusive quality of experience that is not only enriching but comfortable. For that reason, we've tried to make what follows not only helpful and enlightening, but the sort of welcome companion of which every traveler dreams.

Finally, I should point out that every good travel guide is a living enterprise; that is, no part of this text is cast in bronze. In our annual revisions, we expect to refine, expand, and further hone all our material to serve your travel needs even better. To this end, no contribution is of greater value to us than your personal reaction to what we have written as well as information reflecting your own experiences while using the book. We earnestly and enthusiastically solicit your comments on this book *and* your opinions and perceptions about places you have recently visited. In this way, we will be able to provide the most current information — including the actual experiences of the travel public — and to make those experiences more readily available to others. So please write to us at 60 E 42nd St., New York, NY 10165.

We sincerely hope to hear from you.

STEPHEN BIRNBAUM

How to Use This Guide

A great deal of care has gone into the organization of this guidebook, and we believe it represents a real breakthrough in the presentation of travel material. Our aim has been to create a new, more modern generation of travel books and to make this guide the most useful and practical travel tool available today.

Our text is divided into five basic sections, in order to best present information on every possible aspect of a European vacation. This organization itself should alert you to the vast and varied opportunities available on this continent as well as indicating all the specific, detailed data necessary to plan a trip in Europe. You won't find much of the conventional "quaint villages and beautiful scenery" text in this guide; we've chosen instead to use the available space for more useful and purposeful information. Prospective European itineraries tend to speak for themselves, and with so many diverse travel opportunities, we feel our main job is to explain them and to provide the basic information — how, when, where, how much, and what's best — to allow you to make the most intelligent choices possible.

What follows is a brief summary of the five sections of this book and what you can expect to find in each. We believe that you will find both your travel planning and en route enjoyment enhanced by having this book at your side.

GETTING READY TO GO

This mini-encyclopedia of practical travel facts is a sort of know-it-all companion that provides all the precise information you need to go about creating a trip to Europe. There are entries on more than two dozen separate topics, including how to travel, what preparations to make before you leave, what to expect in the different countries of Europe, what your trip is likely to cost, and how to avoid problems. The individual entries are specific, realistic, and cost-oriented.

We expect that you will use this section most in the course of planning your trip, for its ideas and suggestions are intended to facilitate the often confusing planning period. Entries are intentionally concise in an effort to get directly to the meat of the matter. This information is further augmented by extensive lists of sources for more specialized information and some suggestions for obtaining travel information on your own.

FACTS IN BRIEF

Here is a compilation of pertinent tourist information such as entry and customs requirements, languages, currencies, and clothing and climate data on 32 European countries. This section provides easy and immediate access to crucial information to be used at the planning stage as well as on the road.

DIVERSIONS

This very selective guide is designed to help travelers find the very best places in which to pursue a wide range of physical and cerebral activities without having to wade through endless pages of unrelated text. With a list of more than 20 theme vacations — for the body, the mind, and the experience — DIVERSIONS provides a guide to the special places in Europe where the quality of experience is highest. Whether you seek golf or tennis, fishing or skiing, Europe's chicest hotels or most esoteric museum, each entry is the equivalent of a comprehensive checklist of the absolute best in Europe.

THE EUROPEAN CITIES

Individual reports on the 34 cities most visited by tourists and businesspeople have been researched and written by professional journalists on their own turf. Useful at the planning stage, THE EUROPEAN CITIES is really designed to be taken with you and used on the spot. Each report offers a short-stay guide to its city within a consistent format: an essay, introducing the city as a historic entity and a contemporary place to live; *At-a-Glance,* a site-by-site survey of the most important (and sometimes most eclectic) sights to see and things to do; *Sources and Resources,* a concise listing of pertinent tourist information, meant to answer a myriad of potentially pressing questions as they arise — from the address of the tourist office to where to find the best night spot, to see a show, to play tennis, or to get a taxi; and *Best in Town,* our cost-and-quality choices of the best places to eat and sleep on a variety of budgets.

DIRECTIONS

Here are a series of more than 100 European itineraries, from the green counties of Ireland to the Greek islands, covering 32 European countries. These itineraries take you along Europe's most beautiful routes and roads, past its most spectacular natural wonders, through its most historic cities and countryside. DIRECTIONS is the only section of the book to be organized geographically, and its itineraries cover the touring highlights of Great Britain and Ireland and the entire Continent in short, independent journeys of one to three days' duration. Itineraries within each country can be connected for longer trips or used individually for short, intensive explorations.

Each entry includes a guide to sight-seeing highlights; a cost-and-quality guide to accommodations and food along the road (small inns, pensions, paradores, castle hotels, hospitable farms, country hotels, campgrounds, and off-the-main-road discoveries); and suggestions for activities.

Although each of the sections of the book has a distinct format and a special function, they have all been designed to be used together to provide a complete package of travel information. To use this book to full advantage, take a few minutes to read the table of contents and random entries in each section to give you an idea of how it all fits together.

Pick and choose information that you need from different sections. Assume, for example, that you have always wanted to take that typically English vacation, a walking tour through rural England, but you never really knew how to organize it or where to go. Turn first to the hiking section of GETTING READY TO GO as well as the chapters on planning a trip, eating out and hotels in Europe, and climate and clothes. These short, informative entries provide plenty of practical information. For specific information on entering and getting around Britain, shopping, currency, and the like, see FACTS IN BRIEF. But where to go? Turn next to *Exploring Great Britain,* DIRECTIONS. Perhaps you choose to walk the 100-odd-mile Cotswold Way. Your trip will certainly begin and end in London, and for a complete rundown on that fabulous city, you should read the London chapter of THE EUROPEAN CITIES. Finally, turn to DIVERSIONS to peruse the chapters on sports, hotels, antiques, and other activities in which you are interested to make sure you don't miss anything in the neighborhood.

In other words, the sections of this book are building blocks to help you put together the best possible trip. Use them selectively as a tool, a source of ideas, a reference work for accurate facts, and a guide to the best buys, the most exciting sights, the most pleasant accommodations, the tastiest food — *the best travel experiences* that you can have in Europe.

GETTING READY
TO GO

When and How to Go

What's Where

Europe is the world's second smallest continent, encompassing a relatively spare 3.7 million square miles, but with a comparatively dense population of 725 million (an average of 196 people per square mile). It is shaped vaguely like a triangle bounded by Arctic waters and the Atlantic Ocean on the west, the Mediterranean, Aegean, and Black seas to the south, and an eastern border that follows a somewhat imprecise line through the Soviet Union along the Caucasus Mountains, the Caspian Sea, and then north along the Ural Mountains.

Actually, Europe does not conform to the traditional geographical concept of a continent. It is not a self-contained land area surrounded on all sides by water. It is the western fifth of what is commonly known as Eurasia, the giant landmass that stretches from the Atlantic Ocean to the Japanese islands in the Pacific. In the course of its 3,000 years of recorded history, however, cultural, religious, political, and economic influences — along with a sometimes turbulent intermingling of ethnic groups — have defined Europe as an entity, no matter how diverse its parts or geography.

Its dominant influence in Western civilization is due to its location in the North Temperate Zone and the wealth and diversity of its natural resources. The continent is divided into northern and southern sections by an immense mountain chain — really a series of mountains and valleys — that includes, west to east, the Pyrenees Mountains, the Rhone Valley, the French-Swiss-Austrian Alps, and the curving Carpathian Mountains that in Romania recede toward Bucharest and the Black Sea. Below this mountainous demarcation line are countries with generally warmer climates and coasts on the southern seas; north of it are countries of highlands and plains with coasts on the northern seas that separate the main body of the continent from Scandinavia.

Turmoil has never spared Europe, and this century has been as devastating as any. But time and time again, the resourcefulness of its people and the richness of its natural resources — farming, mining, and industrial development — have helped it recuperate from the ravages of natural and man-made disaster. And these same strengths gave birth to the amalgam of cultures that forged Western civilization and shaped the world.

Herein, a short survey of the geography of Europe's nations, starting in the far north and moving east and south.

SCANDINAVIA

Scandinavia refers to the entire segment of Europe consisting of Norway, Sweden, and Denmark — which share close cultural and historical ties and which, today, all have at least titular monarchies; Finland; and Iceland, a separate island northeast of mainland Europe. Norway, Sweden, and Finland are separated from central Europe by several straits that wind from the Atlantic Ocean into the Baltic Sea and adjacent gulfs. The northernmost quarter of these countries is in the Arctic Circle, which also touches the northern fringes of Iceland.

ICELAND: This North Atlantic island was settled by Norwegians ten centuries ago, and its Norwegian character is still strong; Icelanders today speak a language that is basically Old Norse. The 40,000-square-mile island lies east of Greenland just touching the Arctic Circle, and, not surprisingly, fishing and the canning and export of fish products are major industries. The population is sparse (225,000), but has a nearly 100% literacy rate, the highest in the world. Summers are damp and cool; the winters are harsh but made habitable by the tempering influence of the Gulf Stream. Features of particular interest to visitors are the natural hot springs flowing beneath the island's surface, providing an abundance of thermal heat.

NORWAY: Continental Europe's northwesternmost country, Norway's most dramatic topographic feature is its fjord-splintered Atlantic coast, lined with sheer and awesome cliffs. The North Cape, uppermost tip of the country that reaches deep into the Arctic Circle, is a popular summer cruise destination. Most of the northern region is mountainous and a quarter of the country is forested. Necessarily, most of the country's four million people live in the south, the majority in the coastal region extending from Bergen along the southern Atlantic coast to Oslo, the capital. Some 25,000 Laplanders live in the far north. One of Norway's most important resources is the sea, and the Atlantic Ocean supports much of the country's important fishing industry. These same waters are warmed by the Gulf Stream, which moderates the coastal climate all year.

SWEDEN: This is the central of Europe's three most northerly countries, between Norway, with which it shares the Scandinavian Peninsula, and Finland, which borders it on the north but is otherwise separated from it by the Baltic Sea. Sweden is one of the world's most prosperous countries and its resources are highly visible: timberlands that cover half the country; mountains of ore along the Norwegian border; and vast northern glacial fields that melt during summer and send water coursing through the country's carefully dammed rivers and lakes, providing an ample and reliable source of cheap power. In the center and south of the country are highly productive farms and most of the country's eight million people. Most visited is the historic triangle bounded by the coastal cities of Gothenburg on the west, Malmo near the southern tip of the country, and Stockholm, the capital, on the Baltic Sea. Sweden is spattered with numerous lakes, rivers, and waterways.

DENMARK: The most southern and also the smallest of the Scandinavian countries covers a total area of 16,600 square miles, extending over several little islands off the coast of north central Europe and most of the peninsula known appropriately as Jutland, since it actually juts into the straits leading from the North Sea to the Baltic Sea. Because Denmark is made up of flatlands with meager agricultural resources, its people have traditionally depended on trade and conquest for their livelihoods, choices made easy by the country's excellent sea connections. Today it is a highly industrialized nation with a population of just over five million, famous for chinaware and fine furniture design. A major resource, and worldwide attraction, is Copenhagen, its capital, known for its convivial and spirited atmosphere. Denmark's possessions include the Faeroe Islands (midway between Scotland and Iceland) and Greenland.

FINLAND: Although Finland shares northern borders with both Norway and Sweden, it is culturally and even topographically distinct from the rest of Scandinavia. It covers a relatively flat area of 130,120 square miles. The northern Lapland region within the Arctic Circle is comprised of treeless plains, the central region of the country is forested, and the coastal areas extending along its Baltic Sea gulfs are fertile and most populous. Unlike Norway, Denmark, or Sweden, it has no monarchy, and visitors will observe that the country's almost five million citizens take fierce pride in their democracy, perhaps because the country had been dominated for centuries first by Sweden and later by Russia (which flanks Finland's eastern border), only becoming a republic after World War I. Major cities — Helsinki (the capital), Turku, Tampere — are highly modern, and Helsinki is a popular jumping-off point (notably by cruise ship) for visits to Leningrad and other places in the neighboring Soviet Union.

GREAT BRITAIN AND IRELAND

The islands that make up Great Britain and the Republic of Ireland — which used to be known as the British Isles — lie in the North Atlantic immediately off the northwest coast of France, separated from the Continent by the English Channel, the Strait of Dover, and the North Sea. Dover, on the southwest tip of England, and Calais, in the northwestern corner of France, are only 25 miles apart. Included in the scattering of tiny islands nearby that belong to Great Britain are the Channel Islands; the Isle of Man; the Orkneys, Hebrides, and Shetlands off the coast of Scotland; and others.

GREAT BRITAIN: England, Scotland, and Wales, are the major entities that compose Great Britain; together with Northern Ireland, they make up what is officially referred to as the United Kingdom of Great Britain and Northern Ireland. The first three of these countries cover the entire area of the island nearest the Continent — the largest island in Europe. Northern Ireland is situated in the northeastern quarter of the island immediately to the west, the rest of which belongs to the Republic of Ireland. In total, the United Kingdom covers some 94,000 square miles and has a population of 56 million. Physically, England dominates its island, covering well over half the area that extends from the southern coast fronting the English Channel to Newcastle, at the edge of the Scottish Lowlands. Wales abuts England on the west, projecting into St. George's Channel, which separates it from Ireland. Scotland forms the northern third of the island. The entire island is characterized by hilly terrain, as distinct from mountainous, although the celebrated Scottish Highlands occasionally rise 3,000 to 4,000 feet above sea level. The island has been able to draw upon its own resources for livestock breeding, mining, energy, and industry, with large oil reserves in the North Sea (shared with Norway). The climate is subject to prevailing southwesterly winds that account for its frequently cloudy and damp — but essentially mild — weather all year. These generally inviting physical characteristics complement Great Britain's enormous historical, political, and cultural appeal and continue to make it one of the most pleasant countries in the world to visit.

Northern Ireland is primarily an agricultural region with many lakes, although much of the land is actually volcanic. Otherwise, Northern Ireland's geographical and physical characteristics are similar to those of Ireland.

IRELAND: The Republic of Ireland covers some 27,000 square miles, the lion's share of the island it shares with Northern Ireland; it has a population of 3.5 million. Highland outcroppings rise to 3,500 feet in places along the country's coasts, but most of Ireland is characterized by fertile plains, scenic lakes, and bays, especially along its Atlantic coastline. The famed River Shannon in the southwest is the longest river in Ireland or Great Britain. Ireland is essentially an agricultural country, and the same damp, moist air that tempers Great Britain's climate is responsible for the renowned green associated by song and legend with the country. Irish Gaelic is the official language, although traditionally English is the predominant spoken tongue. Dublin, the capital, is centrally located on the island's east coast facing the Irish Sea and Wales.

THE BENELUX COUNTRIES

The Benelux countries, so named for the acronym formed by the first letters of BELgium, the NEtherlands, and LUXembourg, form a wedge of lowland terrain in the northwest corner of continental Europe between Germany and France and the waters of the North Sea. The three small countries are all monarchies and have high standards of living.

BELGIUM: Directly north of France, Belgium is heavily industrialized for a country of its modest size (11,781 square miles and just under ten million people), but is probably best known as one of Western Europe's major international business and economic centers. Brussels, the capital, is a beautiful city of medieval and Renaissance architecture, with a cosmopolitan atmosphere considerably enhanced by its being the administrative center of the European Economic Community (the EEC or the Common Market). Because of its geographic position in Europe, Belgium has been the battleground in more than its fair share of wars, and many, many Europeans and Americans make pilgrimages to the cemeteries and former battlegrounds throughout the country that mark some of the worst confrontations of World Wars I and II.

THE NETHERLANDS: Much of the Netherlands, or Holland as it is more commonly known, is actually below sea level, protected from the ravages of the sea by dikes surrounding the country's coast. Extending north from Belgium, with an irregular coastline that shelters numerous fishing villages, Holland has had to reclaim much land from the North Sea in order to add needed farmland (it has an area of 15,700 square miles and a population of just over 14 million people). Amsterdam, the country's capital, is one of the Continent's liveliest cities, with networks of canals lined by historically and architecturally distinctive Dutch homes and numerous museums housing works of the Dutch masters and other great European artists.

LUXEMBOURG: Surrounded by Belgium, Germany, and France almost like an afterthought, Luxembourg is one of Europe's tiniest independent nations (999 square miles and 360,000 people) and one of its most fortunate. For not only is it a popular tourist destination, but it also makes a comfortable living from forests in the north and iron mines and prosperous farms in the south. The capital, also called Luxembourg, is a walled town built around a tenth-century castle. The country is one of the few in the world known officially as a grand duchy, a territorial designation bestowed on it by France and dating back to the early nineteenth century, although Luxembourg has long since been independent.

ATLANTIC EUROPE

France and Spain, two of the giants of Europe, have substantial coastlines on both the Atlantic Ocean and the Mediterranean Sea, and act as virtual dikes by separating those two very distinct bodies of water. Sharing Spain's Atlantic coast is Portugal, and thoroughly landlocked high in the Pyrenees Mountains between France and Spain is tiny Andorra. Another tiny country, Gibraltar, sits at the southernmost tip of the Iberian Peninsula, overlooking the straits that connect the Mediterranean to the Atlantic, guarding the entrance to Mediterranean Europe.

FRANCE: Its strategic position between the Atlantic and the Mediterranean has made it the historic crossroads of Europe, bearing a constant traffic of goods and people. With an area of 211,208 square miles, France is the largest country in Western Europe, a land exceptionally varied and richly productive, with major mountain ranges in the south (the Pyrenees on the border with Spain, the Alps reaching from the Riviera to Switzerland) and a rich basin of farmland in the center of the country. Its famed vineyards are ubiquitous and grow throughout the country, but are only one item in what may be the most diverse range of agricultural and dairy products on the Continent. France has a population of more than 53 million people, almost 2.5 million of whom live in Paris, the capital.

ANDORRA: Sheep raising and tourism are the mainstays of this small country of 175 square miles (31,000 people) high in the Pyrenees. The major community is Andorra la Vieja.

SPAIN: The second largest country in Western Europe, Spain's 194,883 square miles cover the major portion of the Iberian Peninsula, the Continent's southwesternmost segment of land, and includes the Canary and Balearic islands. Spain shares borders with France (and Andorra), Portugal, which occupies a long rectangle of land separating most of Spain's western border from the ocean, and Gibraltar. The Atlantic Ocean borders the country along the northwest and southwest; the entire eastern coast of the country faces the Mediterranean, and Spain's southern Andalusian region is popular for its warm climate and for "sun and fun" resorts along the extended coast. Much of the interior of the country consists of relatively arid, high valleys within ranges of mountains that offer limited areas of arable land. Spain has a total population of 37.7 million people and Madrid, at the very center of the country, is one of Europe's largest capitals.

PORTUGAL: This southwestern corner of Continental Europe occupies a 35,553 square-mile segment of the Iberian Peninsula, bordered by Spain to the north and east and the Atlantic Ocean to the south and west. Much of the northern part of the country is mountainous, notably above the Tagus River, which bisects the country and flows into the Atlantic at Lisbon, the capital. Below the Tagus, Portugal is warm and more agricultural, particularly along the growing resort area of the Algarve, the province that lines the country's southern Atlantic coast. The country has a moist and moderate climate, which is partly responsible for the olives and port wine that are among its most famous products, and for the vivid blooms of its trees and plants. Its population is 10 million. In addition to Lisbon and the resort regions, the numerous fishing villages along the coast are popular and colorful tourist attractions.

GIBRALTAR: This 2.25-square-mile piece of land at the southern tip of Spain, creating the passage from the Atlantic into the Mediterranean, is best known for its much-photographed physical landmark, the Rock of Gibraltar, and has served primarily as a military fortress since it became an official British possession in 1713. Gibraltar is a free port.

MEDITERRANEAN EUROPE

The countries listed below — Monaco, Italy (and San Marino, the tiny country in north central Italy), Malta, Yugoslavia, Albania, and Greece — all have extensive coasts on the Mediterranean or its tributary seas, the Tyrrhenian, Adriatic, Ionian, and Aegean.

MONACO: Covering an area of 468 acres, this tiny principality situated within France's Riviera coast close to the Italian border is smaller than New York City's Central Park. From the late nineteenth century until World War II, it developed and sustained a reputation as a winter social center for royalty and wealthy families. Today, however, the visitor profile has a much more diverse social and economic base, although Monte Carlo — the district that encompasses the famed casinos and several elegant turn-of-the-century hotels, as well as several extremely new luxury hostelries — still caters to a chic, international clientele. Monaco's beautiful locale, overlooking the Mediterranean and rising sharply toward the Maritime Alps of France, which completely surround Monaco on the north, east, and west, contributes to its popularity.

ITALY: Italy is the most central European nation of the Mediterranean, with northern borders on France, Switzerland, Austria, and Yugoslavia. It is a boot-shaped peninsula, the second longest in the world (after Baja California), extending into the sea. It covers an area of 116,318 square miles. It is an essentially mountainous country, but several of the most historic port cities of the Western world are along its coastline, including Naples, Genoa, and Venice. The capital, Rome, is midway down the peninsula a few miles inland from the western coast and encompasses Vatican City, a sovereign entity within Rome's municipal boundaries. Except for traditional winter weather in the Alpine region of the north and whipping winds along the coasts in colder months, the climate is moderate to very warm throughout the year. Its cities are among the world's most historic. Two major islands — Sicily, at the toe of the peninsula, and Sardinia, west of the mainland across the Tyrrhenian Sea — are a part of Italy. The country has a population of 56.7 million.

SAN MARINO: Figuratively, this smallest republic in the world (23 square miles and 21,500 people) could be papered over with the postage stamps that, along with tourism, represent its major industry. San Marino is an enclave within the Apennines, a few miles south of Rimini on Italy's Adriatic coast. The capital, also called San Marino, is the site of a church dating back to the tenth century.

MALTA: This speck of an island country 60 miles south of Sicily is actually composed of three islands, of which the largest is also named Malta. It is flat and hot in summer, but its strategic locale along the Mediterranean trade routes has subjected it to invading conquerors since the time of the Carthaginians. Its most recent occupants were the British, who maintained it as an important naval base. Malta became an independent republic in 1874. As a tourist destination, it is notable for remnants of fortifications and other structures built during the many centuries of foreign occupancy.

YUGOSLAVIA: The country's long Adriatic coast and the sprinkling of beaches and islands along it have made Yugoslavia a prime vacation spot within the Communist world, equally popular with European and international visitors. The coast stretches from Italy to Albania and the country also borders Austria, Hungary, Romania, Bulgaria, and Greece. Though much of the country is hilly or mountainous and not especially productive farmland, the northeastern region is flatter and has rich soil. Yugoslavia covers a total area of 99,000 square miles. The coastal region is speckled with fishing villages and resorts. The Danube River runs through Belgrade, the capital, in the west central part of the country. Its population of 22.4 million includes people of numerous ethnic backgrounds, but Serbs predominate.

ALBANIA: This is the recluse of the Balkan nations, a country of small villages and state farms that even fellow Eastern Europeans find hard to visit. About the size of Maryland — 11,100 square miles, with an estimated population of 2,875,000 — the country has a long Adriatic coast and lies in relation to Yugoslavia and Greece much as Portugal does to Spain. Westerners know it best as the most outspoken of the Eastern European Communist nations, the country that broke relations with the Soviet Union in 1961 to establish close ties with China. After the death of Mao, these relations cooled, and Albania now trades with Greece Yugoslavia, Italy, and others. Its post–World War II history, however, is only the most recent warp in a historic tapestry that has been woven by a series of conquering and invading cultures. By 800 AD Albania was under the control of Bulgaria and then, with the rest of the Balkan Peninsula, was swept into the Ottoman Turkish Empire from 1478 until 1912, when for a very brief period (until Italy invaded in 1939) it was first a republic and then a monarchy. Sadly, this rich history is inaccessible to most foreign visitors, for Albania does not welcome Western tourists. We do not, therefore, cover it in this guide.

GREECE: This ancient nation is the land terminus of southeastern Europe. Its mountainous mainland borders Albania, Yugoslavia, Bulgaria, and the small continental portion of Turkey; the seas that surround the countries on three sides are the setting for the nation's more than 450 historically celebrated islands, of which the largest and most famous are Crete and Rhodes. Including all its islands, the country has a total land area of 50,960 square miles and a population of nearly ten million. The overall climate is moderate, which, as in most coastal Mediterranean spots, provides the country with a longer than average tourist season. Once outside Athens, the capital, visitors will see that this is not a prosperous country since most of the land does not lend itself to agriculture, although half the working population is engaged in farming. Shipping, shipbuilding, and tourism are the most lucrative industries in Greece.

CENTRAL EUROPE

In defining central Europe, we throw our net as wide as possible to include all those Continental European countries east of France and west of the Soviet Union that do not have coasts on the Mediterranean. Included are West Germany, East Germany, and Poland; the landlocked nations of Switzerland, Liechtenstein, Austria, Hungary, and Czechoslovakia; and the Balkan countries of Romania and Bulgaria, both with eastern coastlines on the inland Black Sea. Many of the countries on this list didn't exist as distinct political entities 80 years ago, and we have swept up in one catch countries and cultures that have been in conflict or alliance dozens of times in the past 1,000 years. But ours may not be as arbitrary a distinction as it appears. Most of the countries mentioned here — the exceptions are Romania and Bulgaria — were at one time, in some form, part of the Hapsburg Empire, which ruled much of Europe for nearly 700 years. The Hapsburgs started as a minor ruling family in Switzerland and Alsace in the eleventh century, but from 1278 until 1918 the seat of their power was Austria.

WEST GERMANY: This segment of the nation that was divided after World War II extends south from the North Sea and Denmark into the center of the continent, covering a total area of 96,000 square miles. It borders six other Western European nations — the Netherlands, Belgium, Luxembourg, France, Switzerland, and Austria — as well as East Germany and Czechoslovakia. The most populous country of Europe (62 million) outside the Soviet Union, it is also one of the richest, thanks to heavy industrialization, with particular concentration in the Ruhr Valley near the border with the Netherlands and Belgium. Much of the rest of the northern region, however, is a plain devoted to agriculture, and the south of the country is touched by the Bavarian Alps and other mountains in that long chain that bisects the continent. Southern Germany is a land of considerable charm and beauty, which escaped the fate of many of Germany's modern cities, most of which have been rebuilt after heavy damage during World War II. Bonn, the capital, is situated about midway between the southern and northern boundaries along the Rhine.

EAST GERMANY: Like northern West Germany, East Germany is essentially a plains area. Half the size of West Germany (with a population of just under 17 million), it is nonetheless the most industrially productive of the Eastern European countries outside the Soviet Union. The country, officially known as the German Democratic Republic, is bounded by the Baltic Sea on the north, Poland to the east, Czechoslovakia to the south, and West Germany. The people here, like the West Germans, are Teutonic, with more Slavic influence. East Berlin, the capital, is considerably more modern than other cities in the country, having been extensively rebuilt in the past 20 years.

POLAND: This north central European state is characterized by relatively even terrain that extends across the northern part of the Continent, although the country's southern border rises into the Carpathian Mountains that separate it from Czechoslovakia. Poland, bounded by East Germany on the west, the Soviet Union on the east, and the Baltic Sea on the north, covers an area of 120,000 square miles with a population of 35 million people. Poland has firm ethnic and historic roots in central Europe dating from the ninth century, although the country went through periods in the eighteenth century when it virtually disappeared after being divided among Russian, Prussian, and Austrian empires. Firmly part of the Eastern European bloc today, it is generally more receptive to Western visitors than many of its neighbors.

CZECHOSLOVAKIA: It's hard not to read something of the labyrinthian history of central Europe in Czechoslovakia, which is surrounded by Poland, Austria, Hungary, Russia, and East and West Germany. The centuries of wars that carved its shape and decided its borders are the history of Europe. Down its center run the Carpathian Mountains; in the west is its capital, Prague, surrounded by good farm country and lined by mineral-rich mountains; in the east are the Tatra Mountains, a continuation of the Carpathian chain. The country covers a total of 49,000 square miles and has a population of 15 million people. As a nation, Czechoslovakia is relatively young, having been created as a republic at the end of World War I out of provinces of the former Austro-Hungarian Empire.

SWITZERLAND: This country is aptly referred to as the crest of Europe, with mountain peaks as high as 15,000 feet above sea level. Surrounded by Italy on the south, France on the west, Germany on the north, and Liechtenstein and Austria on the east, Switzerland is completely landlocked, but its glaciers feed the major rivers of the Continent that flow to the North and Baltic seas and the Mediterranean. Switzerland covers an area of 16,000 square miles. The country's deep and fertile valleys are not only scenic, but a source of the nation's important dairy products. Its 6.4 million people are for the most part German, French, and Italian, and all three of these languages are spoken in the country, though the dominant language is Swiss-German, which about 65% of the people speak natively. Needless to say, most citizens are at least bilingual; English is widely spoken as well. In the eastern canton of Grison the Latin language of Romansh is still spoken.

LIECHTENSTEIN: Nestled at the eastern border of Switzerland along the Rhine River, Liechtenstein is one of the several small (62 square miles; 25,000 people) principalities of Western Europe that fascinate visitors with their charm and beauty. Despite its small size and essentially Alpine topography, there is some farming in the country, though tourism is a far more significant part of the economy. Liechtenstein's principal business, however, is business itself; a carefully maintained tax haven, it attracts a variety of banking and corporate operations to Vaduz, its capital. Today its diplomatic and communications services are provided by Switzerland, but it has a long and proud history that goes back to the fourteenth century.

AUSTRIA: Like its western neighbor, Switzerland, Austria is totally surrounded by mountains, but the valleys created by its three Alpine ranges extend the length of the country (its total area is 32,375 square miles). Also like Switzerland, Austria is a major ski resort center and has exceptional scenery, both of which give it year-round tourist appeal. Austria's 7.5 million people are predominantly German, and German is the official language, though very small minorities in the country speak Slovenian, Croatian, and Hungarian. This is an accurate reflection of history as well as contemporary geography, for Germany is the country's northwestern neighbor, and it has borders with Czechoslovakia, Hungary, and Yugoslavia. In many ways, Austria is at the center of the confused history of central Europe; for more than 600 years it served as the center of power of the Hapsburgs, whose dynasty extended from the Netherlands to the Ottoman Empire and gave the Holy Roman Empire the bulk of its emperors.

HUNGARY: One of several fully landlocked nations of central Europe, Hungary lies below southeastern Czechoslovakia and also borders, from west to east, Austria, Yugoslavia, Romania, and a tip of the Soviet Union. Most of Hungary's 36,000 square miles is highly productive agricultural plains, although industry has absorbed most of the working population (total population is about 10.7 million people) since the end of World War II. Hungarians are the product of a mixture of races, notably those ethnic groups from what is now the south central region of the USSR and Turkey, who pushed northwest nearly 2,000 years ago. Budapest, the capital, straddles the Danube and is one of Europe's most historic and romantic cities.

ROMANIA: Legendary mountain ranges — the Transylvanian Alps and Carpathians — are key physical features of this country, joining into an arc that divides west and east. Most of Romania's northern border is along the Ukrainian district of the Soviet Union; the Black Sea is to the east, Bulgaria to the south, and Yugoslavia and Hungary to the west. In total, the country covers 91,700 square miles. Visitors will see pronounced Hungarian and German influences among its 22 million people, although the country's history goes back to the time of the Romans. Bucharest, the capital, is a major tourist attraction for foreign visitors as well as the local populace, and the Black Sea resort city of Constanta draws visitors from throughout the eastern part of the Continent.

BULGARIA: Like Romania, its northern neighbor, Bulgaria borders the Black Sea on the east and is physically bisected by a mountain range, the Balkans, which runs east to west through the center of the country. Its other borders are with Turkey, Greece, and Yugoslavia. Covering 43,000 square miles with a population of just under nine million, Bulgaria is one of the poorest of the Eastern European countries: It is primarily a Slavic country and nearly 1,000 years ago dominated the region that extends from the Black Sea west to the Adriatic. The two world wars during this century depleted many of its resources. Sofia is its capital.

EURASIA

THE SOVIET UNION: The entire Soviet Union has a land area larger than all of the rest of Europe, about 8.65 million square miles, and its European section alone is just about half of Europe's total area. It has a total population of 260 million people. Its western boundary extends along the length of the Continent, from the Barents Sea in the north where it borders the northeastern tip of Norway and Finland, along the Baltic Sea, Poland, Czechoslovakia, Hungary, and Romania to the Black Sea, Caucasus, and Caspian Sea. The Ural Mountains are traditionally considered the dividing line between the European and the eastern (Asian) republics that make up the complete federation of Soviet states. As might be expected for a landmass of this size, the terrain is exceptionally diverse. It ranges from glacial fields within the Arctic Circle, huge forests, a great central plain (incorporating the famed Kirghiz Steppe, a fertile agricultural area), to subtropical pockets along certain coastal areas of the Black and Caspian seas. The Caspian is actually the world's largest lake, totally enclosed by land. Unlike the rest of Europe, however, the climate of Soviet Europe tends to be more humid and cold, lacking the warmth from the Gulf Stream. The Dnieper River, which empties into the Black Sea, and the Volga River, which is the longest in Europe and extends from the center of the country to the Caspian Sea, are the major waterways of the European part of the USSR. Moscow, the capital, with a population of more than 7.5 million, and Leningrad, the former capital, at the easternmost corner of the Baltic Sea, are the major cities.

When to Go

 It may be superfluous to point out that Europe is not a single-season vacation area. Europeans, of course, are their own best source of travel and vacation traffic, and they long ago established patterns of travel around the Continent on a year-round basis. But since summer is traditionally vacation time, in Europe as in North America, the heaviest traffic period (and generally the most expensive) is mid-May to mid-September.

Europe's appeal in other than the traditional peak season has broadened considerably during the past decade. This is the by-product of lower air fares in combination with relatively inexpensive package tours. Europe is not, however, a destination like the Caribbean, where hotel rates and fares drop automatically on a particular date, and where high season and off-season are precisely defined. There are, however, three tourist seasons in Europe, honored as much in the breach as in fact: high season, mid-May to mid-September; off-season, December to mid-March; and the "shoulder seasons," the months between these periods.

Off-season Europe can be less expensive — by as much as 20% in some resort hotels — than summer, and it is becoming an extremely popular time to travel, as savvy North Americans learn to take advantage of discounts on flights and accommodations. Autumn to spring is the well-defined social and cultural season in Europe. It is also ski season in the Swiss, Austrian, French, and Italian Alps, and in any of these places winter means high season and high prices across the board. For the most part, off-season savings will be in effect in those places that are traditional summer destinations, such as Copenhagen, Stockholm, and Helsinki, Madrid and central Spain, and the northern Italian cities, including Venice.

It should be noted that what the travel industry refers to as shoulder seasons — the 1½ to 2 months preceding and following the peak summer months — are often sought out because they offer reasonably good weather and fewer crowds. But be warned that high-season prices can prevail in many places during these periods, notably in certain popular areas of the Mediterranean — the Greek Islands, several of the more "social" communities of the French Riviera, Spain's Costa del Sol, and Portugal's Algarve. Most major cities in Europe hold at least one international business or industrial show each year (the Frankfurt Book Fair each fall is one example, as are the annual fall and spring fashion shows in Paris, Milan, and Florence), and these are sure to affect the availability of discounts on accommodations. In countries with harvest festivals (mostly wine countries like Germany, France, and Italy), off-season discounts also may not exist.

In short, Europe's vacation appeal, like many other popular destinations, has become multiseasonal. But it's a big continent, and the noted exceptions notwithstanding, most travel destinations are decidedly less trafficked and less expensive during the winter.

CLIMATE: Since the travel plans of most North American visitors are traditionally affected by the availability of vacation time and a desire to travel when the weather's best (or at some other specific time, as when sports are involved), here is a brief breakdown of appealing destinations by month and/or season.

January, February, March – Ski season, of course, and the central European Alps are the place to be both in terms of challenge and social activity (slopes in Spain, Eastern Europe, and Scandinavia are good destinations for less chic — and cheaper — skiing). During the coldest months, try the southern side of the Alps, which is warmer. Late March and even April skiing can be surprisingly good in the traditional ski centers, which are likely to be less crowded after Easter and offer better service and perhaps even lower prices.

April – Early travelers, particularly Scandinavians on charter flights, head for the Mediterranean, notably Spain's Costa del Sol and the Greek Islands. Tulips, hyacinths, and daffodils are blooming in Holland — until about mid-May.

May – The month can be nippy or warm, depending on where you are. If the season isn't too windy or damp, the English countryside can be an attractive destination for a week's drive. Other comfortable spring destinations include Hungary, Italy, and Greece.

June – Most of the Continent has warmed into the 70s, and June is also the first full month of Europe's peak season. Take your pick of any place from the Greek Islands (low 80s) to Copenhagen (upper 60s), and don't overlook Iceland, islands in the lower Baltic Sea, and the Scandinavian capitals, which are fairly well protected from the North Atlantic winds.

July to early August – It's hot in the Mediterranean, but the best time to visit Scandinavia. This is the best period for cruises to Norway's North Cape and for visits to Moscow and Leningrad, as well as for tours of Scotland, the Low Countries (Holland, Belgium, Luxembourg), and France. Central Spain can be surprisingly comfortable since much of it is on an elevated plateau. This is traditional vacation time for Europeans, especially the French, who clear out of Paris in droves in August.

September – North Americans traditionally empty out of the Continent after Labor Day, although increasingly greater numbers of visitors are timing their arrivals for the week or two following the first Monday of the month, since the weather remains excellent and many retail establishments on the Continent reopen after summer closings. The Riviera weather is very good, as are resorts on the Black Sea.

October – This is the period for manufacturers' exhibitions, fashion shows, international trade fairs, and food festivals. It's also harvest season throughout much of central Europe, and the fairs and festivals that celebrate these events draw heavy crowds of regional visitors as well as vacationers. Take along a sweater.

November and December – Temperatures throughout the Continent are wet and chilly, but not the marrow-freezing cold of the northern US and Canada, except in the northernmost reaches of Europe.

Below is a chart of seasonal temperature ranges in the countries of Europe. For more climate information, see *Climate and Clothes* (by country) in FACTS IN BRIEF and the individual city reports in THE EUROPEAN CITIES.

AVERAGE TEMPERATURES (in °F)

	January	April	July	October
Albania	35°–55°	45°–65°	60°–90°	50°–75°
Andorra	40°–55°	50°–70°	70°–90°	45°–65°
Austria	25°–35°	40°–55°	60°–75°	40°–55°
Belgium	30°–40°	40°–60°	55°–75°	45°–60°
Bulgaria	30°–45°	45°–60°	65°–85°	50°–70°
Czechoslovakia	20°–35°	40°–60°	55°–80°	40°–60°
Denmark	25°–35°	35°–50°	55°–70°	45°–55°
Finland	15°–30°	30°–45°	55°–70°	35°–50°
France	30°–45°	45°–60°	60°–80°	45°–60°
Germany (East)	25°–35°	40°–55°	60°–75°	45°–55°
Germany (West)	30°–40°	40°–60°	60°–80°	45°–60°
Gibraltar	40°–55°	50°–70°	70°–90°	45°–65°
Great Britain	35°–45°	40°–60°	50°–70°	45°–60°
Greece	40°–55°	50°–70°	70°–90°	45°–65°
Hungary	20°–35°	50°–70°	60°–80°	35°–50°
Iceland	30°–35°	35°–45°	50°–60°	35°–45°
Ireland	35°–50°	40°–60°	50°–70°	40°–60°
Italy	40°–50°	50°–65°	65°–80°	55°–70°
Liechtenstein	35°–45°	40°–60°	55°–75°	40°–55°
Luxembourg	30°–40°	40°–60°	55°–75°	45°–55°
Malta	50°–60°	55°–70°	70°–85°	65°–75°
Monaco	45°–55°	55°–60°	70°–80°	60°–70°
Netherlands	30°–40°	45°–55°	60°–70°	50°–60°
Norway	20°–30°	35°–50°	55°–70°	35°–50°
Poland	25°–35°	35°–55°	55°–75°	40°–55°
Portugal	40°–55°	35°–45°	70°–90°	45°–65°
Romania	20°–35°	40°–65°	60°–80°	45°–65°
San Marino	40°–50°	50°–65°	65°–80°	55°–70°
Soviet Union	below 0°	25°–50°	50°–70°	20°–40°
Spain	40°–55°	50°–70°	70°–90°	45°–65°
Sweden	20°–30°	35°–45°	60°–70°	40°–50°
Switzerland	35°–45°	40°–60°	55°–75°	40°–55°
Yugoslavia	25°–35°	45°–65°	60°–80°	45°–65°

For specific information on weather, contact the International Association for Medical Assistance to Travelers, which provides climate charts for most countries in both Western and Eastern Europe; for a minimum donation of $20 they will provide their entire set of 24 charts. Its address in the US is 736 Center St., Lewiston, NY 14092 (phone: 716-754-4883). The European Travel Commission offers an extensive listing of events during the entire calendar year for its 23 member countries and islands; these lists are available free with a stamped, self-addressed envelope. 630 Fifth Ave., Room 610, New York, NY 10111 (phone: 212-307-1200).

Traveling by Plane

The air space between North America and Europe is the most heavily trafficked in the world. It is served by dozens of scheduled airlines, almost all of which sell seats at a variety of prices under widely different terms. It is not uncommon for passengers sitting side by side on the very same wide-body jet flight to have paid fares varying by hundreds of dollars for their respective seats, and all too often the traveler paying more would have been just as happy with the terms of a cheaper ticket.

You probably will spend more for your air fare than for any other single item in your European travel budget. To find the least expensive seat, there are certain facts you should know about the kinds of flights available, bargain arrangements, and the latest wrinkles in the scheduled and charter airline scene.

SCHEDULED AIRLINES: Dozens of national European airlines serve Europe from North America, and though they concentrate on destinations in their home countries, most serve other parts of Europe as well. They offer fares that are competitive with national and international privately owned carriers, and usually have an interesting array of package tours that emphasize their countries' special attractions. (British Airways' year-round London Show tours are an example; they include, in addition to round-trip air fare from the US, a week of hotel accommodations in London, and tickets to a selection of London plays and musicals.) Private airlines and package-tour companies offer competing programs, so compare prices and terms carefully.

Some American airlines serving Europe are: American, Delta, Northwest Orient, Pan American, People Express, Tower Air, TWA, and World.

Gateways – Cities that have direct air service to European destinations are Anchorage, Atlanta, Baltimore, Boston, Chicago, Dallas/Fort Worth, Detroit, Honolulu, Houston, Los Angeles, Miami, Minneapolis/St. Paul, New York, Newark, Philadelphia, St. Louis, San Francisco, Seattle, Tampa, and Washington, DC. This list is hardly final, as new gateways are constantly being added.

Fares – Perhaps the most common misconception about fares on scheduled airlines is that the cost of the ticket determines how much service you'll receive on the flight. This is true to a very limited extent. A far more realistic definition is that the *less* you pay for your ticket, the more restrictions and qualifications you'll be subject to *before* you get on the plane (as well as after you get off).

These qualifying aspects usually relate to the months in which you travel, how far in advance you purchase your ticket, the minimum and maximum time you remain abroad, your willingness to decide on a return date at the time of booking — and your ability to stick to your decision. Currently, scheduled carriers are offering a number of ticket categories. These are first class, business class, economy, and excursions or advance purchase excursion (APEX).

In a class by itself is the Concorde, the supersonic jet developed by France and

Britain that cruises at speeds of 1,350 miles per hour and makes transatlantic crossings in half the time of subsonic jets. Air France offers Concorde service from New York to Paris; BA flies from New York, Washington, DC, and Miami to London. Service is one class (lavish care, with champagne and caviar all the way) and expensive: The fare is well above first-class fare on a subsonic carrier, but for some the gift of time — only 3½ hours to cross the Atlantic — is worth its relatively high price.

1. *First Class:* More than twice the cost of a conventional economy ticket, and quite a price to pay for free earphones and a glass of subpar champagne. But the atmosphere is certainly classier — especially on the wide-body jets — and there is the added comfort of more leg room, more spacious and plusher seats, and, increasingly, "sleeper" seats — and the service is much more attentive. No advance booking is required, there is no minimum or maximum length of stay, nor is there a cancellation penalty. Unlimited free stopovers are allowed — that lets you stop in any number of cities en route to your most distant destination provided that certain set, but generous, maximum permitted mileage limits are respected. Note that it is not easy to inform yourself of stopover possibilities. It takes a good travel agent, working with the airline's rate desk (to which the public doesn't have access) to apprise you fully of stopover privileges.

2. *Business Class:* Not too long ago, there were only two classes of air travel: first class and all the rest (called economy). But because passengers paying full economy fares traveled in the same compartment as passengers flying for considerably less on various discount fares, the airlines introduced special frills to compensate those paying the full price. Thus, business class came into being, though many airlines have their own names for it, such as Clipper Class on Pan Am and Ambassador Class on TWA. Seating is in the forward part of the economy class compartment; the section may be separated by an actual partition. Liquor and headsets are free, and there may be a greater number of selections on the menu as well as a separate counter for speedier check-in. Like first class, you travel on any scheduled flight you wish, and your one-way or round-trip ticket is valid for a year. There are no minimum- or maximum-stay requirements, no advance booking is necessary, and you are not subject to any cancellation penalties. In addition, the fare allows the same unlimited free stopover privileges as first class.

3. *Economy:* The terms of this fare vary slightly from airline to airline. Those that transformed part of their original economy class compartment into business class tend to offer economy tickets for substantially less than business class, the saving effected by limiting the frills (you pay for liquor and headsets, you check in with the masses) and by reducing the stopover privileges. Not all airlines have adopted the two-tiered system, however; many have retained a single economy fare that may resemble either of the two newer classes in price and flexibility. But common to all economy fares is their relative convenience. As is the case with the higher-priced tickets, they can be bought for a flight up to the minute of takeoff if seats are available, and if the ticket is round trip, the return reservation can be made anytime you wish — months before you leave or the day before you return. They are valid for a year, after which they can be renewed if not used (but you must pay any price increase that may have occurred in the meantime). If you ultimately decide not to fly at all, your money will be refunded.

4. *Excursion and Advance Purchase Excursion (APEX):* Excursion fares have long been the traditional bargain fares. Passengers sit with and receive the same services as economy-class passengers even though they have paid as much as a third less for their seats. Excursions apply to round-trips only and have minimum and maximum stay requirements, but generous ones — you can stay abroad as much as a year in some cases. In the past, excursions had neither advance booking

requirements nor cancellation penalties, they often permitted one stopover (which had to be paid for) in each direction, and they had "open jaws," which meant that you could fly to one city and depart from another, arranging and paying for your own transportation between the two. Traditional excursion fares still exist on air routes to some European countries, especially southern ones, but a newer, cheaper (as much as 50% off economy fares) type of excursion, the advance purchase excursion (APEX) is now more common. The ticket is usually good for a minimum of 7 days and a maximum of 2, 3, or 6 months abroad, and, as its name implies, it must be paid for in its entirety a certain number of days (usually 21) before departure. The drawback to the APEX is that it severely penalizes travelers who change their minds. The return flight must be reserved at the time you buy the ticket, and if for some reason you are forced to change it while abroad, you pay the difference between the round-trip APEX fare and the round-trip economy fare. In other words, by changing your return reservation after travel has begun, you change your entire round-trip ticket from the APEX to the economy category. There is also a penalty of $50 or more (up to 10% of the amount of the fare) for changing or canceling a reservation before travel begins. No stopovers are allowed on the APEX, but it is sometimes possible to create an open-jaw effect by buying an APEX on a split-ticket basis; that is, flying to one city and returning from another. The total price will be half the price of an APEX to the first city plus half the price of an APEX to the second. Excursion fares are sold at basic and peak season rates; APEX fares usually have three price seasons, a low, an off-peak, and a high season, and there may be a surcharge for weekend travel.

A type of fare available only between the US and France is the Vacances or Visite fare, introduced by Air France some years ago and quickly copied by other airlines. It is slightly cheaper than an APEX, requires no advance purchase, has minimum and maximum stay requirements (14 days to 2 months) and penalties for cancellation, and is sold at basic and peak rates, often with a weekend surcharge.

Standby fares, once the rock bottom fares to Europe, are elusive, but they may be available from time to time. Although the definition of standby varies somewhat from airline to airline, it generally means that one buys a ticket for the desired flight usually no sooner than the day of anticipated departure, and then one literally "stands by" at the airport on the chance that a seat will be available. This clearly makes most sense in the low season, when flights are frequently not sold out. Something else to look into are GIT (group inclusive tour) and ITX (independent tour excursion) fares. These "tour basing" fares are for group or independent travelers prepurchasing a minimum of ground arrangements at their destination. In the past, they were among the least expensive fares, but with the advent of discount fares such as the APEX, they have all but disappeared from some air routes or their price tags are the equivalent of other discount fares. They reappear at times, however, as in winter "ski group" fares to Europe.

Another way to fly for less is with one of the smaller airlines that consistently manage to offer bargain rates. You will note early in your research that there is little, if any, difference in the prices charged by the main carriers in the same fare category between the same two cities; in addition to other factors, the economics of the marketplace tends to rule, with airlines rushing to match any new package of fares and conditions proposed by a competitor. But some airlines — often those that were once strictly supplemental, or charter, airlines — can provide a lot for less because of lower overhead, uncomplicated route networks, and other limitations in their service.

One of the newest airlines in this group, Virgin Atlantic, flies from Newark to London's Gatwick Airport twice weekly off-season and daily in summer. At press time, the round-trip high season fare for the flight was $438. For information and reservations, call 201-623-0500. People Express also flies from Newark to Gatwick, five times weekly off-season and daily in summer; its round-trip fare for the flight at the same time was even cheaper: $398. People Express lists a tieline in the phone book, or call 201-596-6000. World Airways flies daily year-round from Honolulu via Los Angeles and Baltimore/Washington, DC, to London and Frankfurt. Its reservation system's toll-free telephone number is 800-772-2600. Tower Air schedules flights from New York to Brussels twice a week in the off season and more frequently in peak season. Tower's telephone number in New York State is 718-917-8500; elsewhere in the US, dial 800-221-2500.

Also among the airlines to be considered for budget air travel is Icelandair (formerly Icelandic), which has long been known as a source of low-cost scheduled flights to Europe. Its round trip to Luxembourg (from New York, Baltimore/Washington, Chicago, Detroit, and Orlando), coupled with free bus service or a "thru-fare" abroad Luxembourg's Luxair to any one of a number of major cities in Europe, makes a very attractive package. Call Icelandair at 212-757-8585 or 800-223-5500.

Discount fares can appear and disappear quickly. Special promotional fares may be offered when an airline inaugurates a new route, for example, or to encourage travel in slow seasons. Check with all the airlines serving your intended destination and call each one several times; you may receive varying quotes from different clerks. When you think you've obtained a good deal, make your booking, but be sure to read the fine print for specifications about duration of stay, cancellations, and so on.

Reservations – When making plane reservations through a travel agent, ask the agent to give the airline your home phone number as well as a daytime business number. All too often the agent uses the agency number as the official contact for ticket and flight plans. The airlines are pretty good about getting departure delay information to passengers if they can reach them, but often they can't if the agency is closed for the night or the weekend. Specify to your travel agent that you want a home phone contact provided to the airline, and if you've got any doubts, call the airline and do it yourself.

Most return reservations from international destinations are automatically canceled after the required reconfirmation period (usually 72 hours) has passed. If you look at the back of your airline ticket, you'll see the need to reconfirm specifically spelled out. Don't let yourself be lulled into a false sense of security by the "OK" on your plane ticket next to the number and time of a returning flight. That only means that a reservation has been entered: *A reconfirmation is still necessary.*

Seating – Where you sit can make a real difference in your comfort on the flight. Airline seats are usually assigned on a first come–first served basis at check-in time. That argues for getting to the airport early. Prereserved seats arranged through travel agents are often ignored, or airlines may require that passengers arrive at the departure gate at least 30 minutes (or more) before departure to hold them. A better strategy is to visit an airline ticket office (or one of a select group of travel agents) to secure an actual boarding pass for the flight. Once this has been issued, airline computers show you as "checked in," and you effectively own the seat you have selected (this is also good insurance against being bumped from an overbooked flight and is, therefore, an especially valuable tactic for travel at peak holiday times).

You must decide whether to sit in a window seat, aisle seat, or middle seat. You won't ordinarily have much choice about the kind of plane you fly, but remember that for long flights 747s and 1011s are more comfortable than DC10s. For shorter hops, a DC10 will be perfectly comfortable. Some other hints: Generally speaking, seats in the middle of the economy section, over the forward part of the wing, give you the smoothest ride on a 747, and seats toward the front of the aircraft are the quietest. Seats immediately behind the exits and in the front rows of each section offer the most leg room, and be careful of seats in the last row, since they seldom recline all the way.

Sleeper seats, found in first class on many airlines, allow passengers to stretch out for long flights.

Smoking – Regulations regarding smoking on airplanes require that nonsmoking sections must be enlarged to accommodate all passengers who want to sit in them, provided they have confirmed reservations and do not arrive late for the flight. Cigar and pipe smoking are banned even from the smoking sections. These regulations apply to domestic flights and to flights by US carriers departing from or returning to the US. They do not apply to flights by foreign carriers into or out of the US.

Flying with Children – Portable bassinets are usually available, and they work best when used at the very front of the aircraft. On longer flights, the bulkhead seats generally are reserved for families traveling with small children. As a general rule, a child under 2 years of age (and not occupying a seat) flies at 10% of whatever fare the accompanying adult is paying. A second child without a second adult pays the fare applicable to children age 2 through 11, usually 50% of an adult economy fare and two-thirds an adult APEX fare.

Seat Size – If you have a weight problem, you may face the prospect of a long plane ride with trepidation. Be aware, therefore, that center seats in the three-seat alignments of wide-body 747s and DC10s are about 1½ inches wider than those on either side. Overweight travelers should also be aware that if the standard seat belt doesn't span their girth, all airlines have belt extensions.

Meals – It is possible to order many special kinds of meals for your flight if you give the airline 24 hours' notice. The range of available diets includes high protein, vegetarian, kosher, low calorie, and low sodium.

Getting Bumped – A special air travel problem with scheduled flights is the threat that an airline will accept more reservations than there actually are seats on a given flight. This is entirely legal and is done to compensate the airlines for prospective passengers who don't show up for a flight for which they have reservations. If the airline has oversold the flight and everyone does show up — either on a domestic flight or on your way overseas *from* the US — the airline is subject to stringent rules.

The airline must first seek ticketholders willing to be bumped voluntarily from their seats for a negotiable sum paid by the airline. If there are not enough volunteers, the airline may bump passengers involuntarily according to a priority seating plan available at all ticket counters. Unless the carrier can put them on an alternate flight that will get them to their planned destination within 1 hour of the original arrival time, these passengers must be paid denied-boarding compensation equivalent to the one-way fare to their destination (subject to a maximum of $200). If the airline cannot get them there within 2 hours of the original arrival time on a domestic flight or 4 hours on an international flight, the compensation must be doubled. These rules do *not* apply to inbound flights from abroad, even on US carriers. The airline may also offer bumped travelers a voucher for a free flight instead of the denied-boarding compensation. The passenger can choose either the money or the voucher (the dollar value of which may be no less than the monetary compensation to which the passenger would be entitled). The voucher is not a substitute for the bumped passenger's original ticket — the airline continues to honor that as well.

Baggage – Travelers from the US may face two different kinds of regulations. Flying to Europe on a US flag airline or on a major international carrier, each passenger is allowed only one carry-on bag, of which the total combined dimensions of length, width, and depth must be less than 45 inches. That is to say, it must fit easily under a seat on the plane. Each first-class or business passenger is also allowed to check two bags, neither of which may exceed a total of 62 inches when length, width, and depth are combined. Economy and discount passengers are also allowed two bags in the cargo hold, the total combined dimensions of *both* bags not to exceed 107 inches, and no single bag to exceed 62 inches (nor, usually, 70 pounds). Children paying 50% or more of an adult fare have the same baggage allowance as full-fare passengers, but infants traveling at 10% of an adult fare are entitled to one piece of baggage, whose combined dimensions may not exceed 45 inches. Charges for additional, overweight, or outsize bags are assessed at a flat rate.

On European local or trunk carriers, however, you may find your luggage subject to the old weight determination, under which economy or discount passengers are allowed only 44 total pounds of luggage without additional charge. First-class or business passengers are allowed 66 total pounds.

Luggage should be clearly labeled, and all tags from previous trips should be removed. If your luggage is not in the baggage claim area after your flight has arrived or if it's damaged, report the problem to the airline personnel *immediately*. Fill out a report form on your lost or damaged luggage, and hold on to your claim check until you receive your baggage. There are regulations permitting later filing for unnoticed damages, but at least claim what's apparent. By no means should you sign any paper indicating you'll accept an offered settlement at that moment. Since the airline is responsible for the value of your bags within certain statutory limits, you should take time to assess the extent of your loss (see *Insurance*, GETTING READY TO GO).

CHARTER FLIGHTS: By actually renting a plane or at least booking a block of seats on a specially arranged flight, charter operators can offer travelers air transportation — often coupled with a hotel room, meals, and other arrangements in a charter package — at costs lower than most economy or excursion fares. Although charters were once the very best air bargain available, numerous discount fares on scheduled airlines are now often just as low, especially on the more competitive routes, and their terms are usually more flexible.

Charter travel once required that an individual be a member of a club or other "affinity" group whose main purpose was not travel, but newer "public charters" are more flexible. Public charters are open to anyone, they have none of the advance booking requirements of the traditional forms of charters, and they also have no minimum-stay requirements. They allow the traveler to book one flight to cross the Atlantic and to book another one-way passage coming back. (Note: These are American regulations, and they do not control charter laws in other countries. For example, if you want to book a one-way foreign charter back to the US, you may find advance booking rules are in force.) Some things to keep in mind about the charter game:

1. If you are forced to cancel your trip, you can lose most and possibly all of your money unless you have cancellation insurance, which is a *must* (see *Insurance*, GETTING READY TO GO).
2. Most charters have little of the flexibility of regularly scheduled flights regarding refunds and rescheduling flights; if you book a return flight you must be on it, and if you miss the flight you lose the flight and your money.
3. By virtue of the economics of charter flights, your plane will almost always be full; so you will be crowded, though not necessarily uncomfortable.
4. Charter flights can be canceled by the operator for any reason (usually underbooking) up to 10 days before departure. Your money is returned in two weeks in this event, but it may leave you little time to make new arrangements.
5. Charter operators are permitted to assess a surcharge of up to 10% of the air fare if rising fuel or other costs warrant it, up to 10 days before departure. No price increases are allowed within 10 days of departure.

Bookings – If you do take a charter, read the contract carefully and note:

1. When you are to pay the deposit and the balance, and to whom the check is to be made payable. Ordinarily checks are made out to an escrow account, which means the charterer can't spend your money until your flight has been completed.

The charter company should be bonded (usually by an insurance company), and you should know the name of the bonding agent. If you want to file a claim against the charter company, the claim should be sent to the bonding agent.

2. Stipulations regarding cancellation by the consumer. You may forfeit some or all of your payment if you cancel. Frequently, if you cancel well in advance, you may forfeit only a $25 or $50 fee; if you cancel even 2 or 3 weeks before the flight, there may be no refund at all (unless you can provide a substitute passenger).

3. Stipulations regarding cancellation and changes made by the charterer. Flights may not be canceled within 10 days of departure except for circumstances — such as natural disasters or political upheavals — making it physically impossible to fly. Charterers may make "major changes," however, such as in the date or place of departure or return, but you are entitled to cancel and receive a refund if you don't accept these changes.

DISCOUNT TRAVEL SOURCES: A source of information about money-saving travel opportunities is *Travel Smart,* a monthly newsletter (Communications House, 40 Beechdale Rd., Dobbs Ferry, NY 10522; $37 a year). Another useful idea, if you have a flexible travel schedule, is to join one of the organizations that routinely keep in touch with airlines, charter operators, cruise lines, and tour packagers to help them dispose of unsold inventory at discounts of between 15% and 60%. They charge an annual fee, for which members receive the toll-free number of a telephone hot line to call for information on imminent trips and, in some cases, periodic mailings on upcoming trips for which there is more advance notice. Among these are:

1. Stand Buys Ltd., 26711 Northwestern Hwy., Suite 420, Southfield, MI 48034 (phone: in Michigan, 313-352-4876; elsewhere, 800-821-3695). Annual fee, $45.

2. Discount Travel International, 7563 Haverford Ave., Philadelphia, PA 19151 (phone: 215-878-8282). Annual fee, $40.

3. Moment's Notice, 40 E 49th St., New York, NY 10017 (phone: in New York State, 212-486-0503; elsewhere, 800-221-4737). Annual fee, $35.

4. Worldwide Discount Travel Club, 1674 Meridian Ave., Miami Beach, FL 33139 (phone: 305-534-2082). Annual fee, $45.

5. On Call to Travel, PO Box 11622, Portland, OR 97211 (phone: 503-287-7215). Annual fee, $45.

CONSUMER PROTECTION: Consumers who feel they have not been dealt with fairly by an airline should make their complaints known. Begin with the customer service representative at the airport where the problem occurs, and if he or she cannot resolve the complaint, write to the airline's consumer office, attaching copies (never the originals) of any tickets, receipts, or other documents that back up your claims.

Until December 31, 1984, travelers with problems could also contact the Civil Aeronautics Board, which was responsible for overseeing the airline industry in a number of areas important to passengers. The Airline Deregulation Act of 1978, however, mandated the gradual phasing out of the CAB, though the law that abolished it did not abolish the consumer protection regulations it had established, nor its consumer assistance responsibilities. These responsibilities, along with many former CAB employees, were transferred intact to the Department of Transportation. Although it was still too early at press time to tell just how smoothly procedures for dealing with consumer complaints would function in the new surroundings, passengers with problems that formerly fell under the CAB's jurisdiction — lost baggage, compensation for getting bumped, smoking rules, charter regulations, deceptive practices by an airline — should now write to the Consumer Affairs Division, Room 10405, Office of Community and Consumer Affairs, Office of Governmental Affairs, US Department of Transportation, 400 Seventh St., SW, Washington, DC 20590, or call the office at

202-755-2220. Even so, consumer complaints should still be addressed initially to the airline that provoked them.

BUCKET SHOPS: Flights between European cities are among the most expensive anywhere. This cost can occasionally be avoided by careful use of stopover rights on the higher-priced transatlantic airline tickets, but if your ticket doesn't allow them, take heart. Discounts have recently been introduced on some intra-European routes, between Great Britain and the Netherlands and between Great Britain and Germany, for instance. The discount fares may go by such names as PEX, APEX, and Euro-Budget, and some can be bought in the US, while some must be bought overseas (either way, always ask about the restrictions and cancellation penalties that govern them). Another source of savings is the European airline ticket outlet known as the "bucket shop." The name notwithstanding, there's nothing shady here. You may be asked to fly on an airline whose name is unfamiliar, but a little checking will reveal that Balair is another name for Swissair and that British Air Tours is the discount service of British Airways. The advantage of using a bucket shop is the very low price; disadvantages involve some inflexibility in departure dates and departure points. Bucket shops are found in greatest profusion in London and can be located most easily in London's Sunday newspapers — the *Times, Express, Observer,* and *Telegraph* are best. There's also a new magazine that's a very valuable aid in uncovering inexpensive worldwide air fares. It's called *Discount Traveller,* and it's available on most newsstands in London. If you could use a copy before you arrive overseas, write to the publisher: Pierwest UK, Ltd., 17 Praed St., London W2.

A selected list of London bucket shops follows:

Bestways Travel & Tours, 56/58 Whitcomb St., London WC2H 7DN (phone: 930-3985).
Buckingham Travel, 79 Long Acre, London WC2E 9NG (phone: 836-8622).
London Flight Centre, 131 Earl's Court Rd., London SW5 9RH (phone: 370-6332).
London Travel Mart, 33 Marshall St., London W1V 1LL (phone: 734-4412).
Prinja Travel, 170 New Bond St., London W1 (phone: 499-7203).
Sage Travel, E Finchley Station, High Rd., London N2 0NW (phone: 444-7202, 444-8554, and 883-2284).
Trailfinders, 48 Earl's Court Rd., London W8 6EJ (phone: 937-5400).
Travel Bazaar, 221 Westbourne Park Rd., London W11 1EA (phone: 221-1729).
Travelworld Olympic, 36 Kensington High St., London W8 4PL (phone: 937-1512).

A few words of warning may be in order. If you are quoted a price that is dramatically lower than other bucket shop offerings to the same city, the ticket may be stolen and may not be honored by the airline. Always check with the carrier that a confirmed reservation exists in your name for the specific flight and date of the ticket, and never part with any cash until a ticket is firmly in your hand.

Traveling by Ship

 Alas, the years when steamships reigned as the primary means of transatlantic transportation are gone; when Italy, France, Sweden, Germany, Norway, the Netherlands, and England — and the US — had fleets of liners that offered sometimes luxurious week-plus trips across the North Atlantic.
But one ship remains for this type of service: Cunard's *Queen Elizabeth 2.* For

seagoing enthusiasts, the *QE2* is the most luxurious vessel on the seas — as well as one of the largest. Transatlantic crossing between New York and Southampton, England (sometimes via Cherbourg, France), are scheduled frequently from April through December, and they do not come cheap. Last year the one-way, per-person (double-occupancy) cost for the 5-day trip ranged from $950 to $6,850.

Somewhat longer transatlantic crossing prospects for travelers who have the time are what are referred to in the industry as "positioning" cruises. These are the sailings of US-based cruise vessels from their winter season berths (usually Fort Lauderdale, Miami, or San Juan) to cities in Europe from which they'll be offering summer cruise programs. Eastbound positioning cruises take place at particular times in the spring; westbound ones in the fall. Since ships do not make the return trip until ready to position themselves for the next season, most lines have an arrangement that allows you to fly home economically — though the cruises themselves are not an inexpensive way to travel. Cunard's recently acquired *Vistafjord* is among the ships regularly offering positioning cruises. Its 1985 eastbound crossing was a 15-day voyage from Fort Lauderdale — via Bermuda, the Azores, Madeira, and Cadiz — to Genoa for prices ranging between $2,050 to $8,190 per person, double occupancy. For information on its future cruises, write to Cunard/NAC, 555 Fifth Ave., New York, NY 10017 (phone: in New York State, 212-880-7531; elsewhere in the US, 800-221-2400.)

Royal Viking Line also has cruises between the US and Europe. In 1985, the *Royal Viking Sea* went from Fort Lauderdale to Barcelona in a 15-day spring crossing at prices ranging from $2,280 to $9,225 per person, double occupancy, and returned in the summer from London to New York; its sister ship, the *Royal Viking Sky*, made a 21-day Venice to Fort Lauderdale crossing in the fall (2,961 to $12,831). For information on positioning cruises, write to Royal Viking Line, One Embarcadero Center, San Francisco, CA 94111 (phone: in California, 415-398-8000; elsewhere in the US, 800-422-8000).

For travelers who want to ride the waves but find the above prices too steep, another possibility exists — but the departure is from Montréal. Polish Ocean Lines' *Stefan Batory* makes roughly a half-dozen round trips a year between Montreal and Gdynia, Poland, calling at London and Rotterdam en route. In 1985, the one-way fare to London ranged from $775 to $1,365 (per person, double occupancy). And for the person willing to travel in one of the three- or four-berth cabins, the prices are lower still. For future sailing dates, prices, and reservations, contact McLean Kennedy Passenger Services, 410 St. Nicolas St., Montréal, Québec H2Y 2P5, (phone: 514-849-6111).

For travelers seeking cruises out of British and continental European ports, the opportunities are limitless. Northern European waters are particularly popular in summer, with Copenhagen and Amsterdam major embarkation centers, notably for sailings along Norway's fjord-lined coast as well as to major Baltic ports that include Leningrad, Helsinki, and Stockholm. Travelers to this region are also advised that July is the month of the midnight sun; cruises to witness this phenomenon are available out of Bergen, Norway.

Still other major ports for summer cruises in Europe are Calais and Nice in France; Genoa and Venice in Italy; Mainz, Germany and Basel, Switzerland, for Rhine boat trips; and of course Piraeus, the famed port city of Athens, from which there are innumerable sailings each day for single-day or week-plus cruises to the beautiful Aegean Islands (see *Europe's Classic Cruises and Wonderful Waterways,* DIVERSIONS).

Freighters – An alternative to cruise ships is travel by freighter. These are cargo-carrying ships that also take a limited number of passengers (usually about 12) in reasonably comfortable accommodations. The idea has romantic appeal, but there are a number of things to keep in mind. Though freighters are usually cheaper than cruise ships, they are not the cheapest means of crossing the Atlantic (excursion or even economy air fare is cheaper). Accommodations and recreational facilities vary, but freighters are not designed to amuse passengers, so it is important to enjoy the idea of the freighter itself. Schedules are erratic, and the traveler must fit his or her schedule to the ship's (freighter passengers have found themselves waiting as much as a month for a promised sailing, a serious drawback). In 1985 there were only a few passenger cabins available for crossings to northern European ports — Le Havre, Rotterdam, Bremerhaven, and Gdynia. Service to Mediterranean ports was less limited, but travelers frequently found they had to book all of a very long trip (40 to 60 days is not unusual) or nothing. *Pearl's Freighter Tips* (175 Great Neck Rd., Suite 303-B, Great Neck, NY 11021; phone: 516-487-8351) is run by the knowledgeable Pearl Hoffman, who finds sailings for her customers and provides background advice. *TravLtips Cruise and Freighter Travel Association* (163-07 Depot Rd., Flushing, NY 11358; phone: 718-939-2400) publishes a freighter and cruise magazine in addition to booking passage.

Touring by Car

Europe is ideally suited for driving tours. Distances between major cities are usually reasonable, and a visitor can use the flexibility of a car to maximum advantage. (See DIRECTIONS for our choices of the most interesting European driving itineraries.)

But driving isn't a cheap way to travel. Gas prices are higher in Europe than in North America, and car rentals are no cheaper. It is therefore important to explore every possibility for the best alternative for your plans.

RENTALS FROM THE US: Travel agents can arrange foreign rentals for clients, but it is just as easy to do it yourself by calling the international divisions of such familiar car rental firms as Hertz (phone: 800-654-3001), Avis (phone: 800-331-2112), Budget (phone: 800-527-0700), National (known in Europe as Europcar; phone: 800-CAR-RENT), or Dollar Rent a Car (known in Europe as InterRent; phone: 800-421-6868). All publish directories listing the foreign locations in which they operate and the rates for various types of cars, and all quote weekly flat rates based on unlimited mileage with the renter paying for gas. Some also offer time and mileage rates (i.e., a basic per-day or per-week charge, plus a charge for each mile, or kilometer, driven), which are generally only to the advantage of those who plan to do very little driving.

It is also possible to rent a car before you go by contacting any of a number of smaller, less well known US companies that do not operate worldwide but specialize in European auto travel, including leasing and car purchase in addition to rental. These firms (some addresses are given below) act as agents for a variety of European suppliers, offer unlimited mileage almost exclusively, and frequently manage to undersell their larger competitors. Comparison shopping is always necessary, however, because the company that has the cheapest rentals in one country may not necessarily have the cheapest in another, and even the international giants offer discount plans whose conditions are easy for most travelers to fulfill. Hertz's Affordable Europe, Avis's Supervalue Rates Europe, and similar plans offered by Budget, National, and Dollar allow discounts of anywhere from 15% to 30% off their usual rates provided the car is reserved a certain number of days before departure, is rented for a minimum period, and, in some cases, is returned to the same location that supplied it.

The first factor influencing cost is, naturally, the type and size of car. Rentals are based on a tiered price system, with different sizes of cars often listed as A (the smallest and cheapest) through F, G, or H (the largest and most expensive). The larger the car, the more it costs to rent in the first place and the more gas it consumes, of course, but for some people, the greater comfort and extra luggage space may be worth it. Be warned, too, that very few European cars have automatic transmission, and those that do are more likely to be in the F group than the A group. Cars with automatic shift must be specifically requested at the time of booking, and, again, they cost more and consume more gas.

Other costs to be added to the price tag include dropoff charges or one-way services fees, which may be charged if the car is returned to a different city — or country — from the one in which it was picked up. The cost of optional collision damage waiver protection, if you want it, must also be added. Rates for rental cars include public liability, property damage, fire, and theft coverage and collision coverage with a deductible. In the event of an accident, you are responsible for the deductible amount, but you can dispense with the obligation to pay it by buying the offered waiver at a cost of approximately $4 to $8 a day. A further consideration: Car rentals are subject to value-added taxes in Europe. The rate varies from a low of 5% in Spain to a high of 33.33% in France, and rates between 15% and 25% are common (Switzerland charges no tax). Even if you intend to visit only France, you may want to consider a nearby country as the pickup and dropoff point. Bear in mind also that one-way rentals bridging two countries are frequently exempt from tax.

There are legitimate bargains in car rentals provided you shop for them. Call all the familiar car rental names whose toll-free numbers are given at the beginning of this section (don't forget to ask about their special discount plans) and call the smaller companies listed below. Begin early, because the best deals may be booked to capacity quickly and may require payment 14 to 21 days before delivery.

Auto-Europe, PO Box 500, Yorktown Heights, NY 10598 (phone: in New York State, 800-942-1309; elsewhere, 800-223-5555).

Europe by Car, 1 Rockefeller Plaza, New York, NY 10020, or 9000 Sunset Blvd., Los Angeles, CA 90069 (phone: in New York State, 212-581-3040; in California, 800-252-9401; elsewhere, 800-223-1516).

Kemwel, 106 Calvert St., Harrison, NY 10528 (phone: in New York State, 800-942-1932; elsewhere, 800-468-0468 or 800-431-1362).

Fly/Drive – Airlines, car rental companies, tour operators, and even independent travel agents offer fly/drive packages. Typically, they used to include round-trip airfare and a car waiting at the airport, plus a night's free lodging in the gateway city. Increasingly, in place of the night's lodging, a block of prepaid accommodations vouchers, one for each night of the stay, is included, along with a list of hotels that accept them. Tour prices vary according to the category of cars and hotels used. Naturally, the greater the number of hotels participating in the scheme, the more freedom you have to range at will during the day's driving and still be near a place to stay for the night. Most packages allow you to make day-to-day advance reservations en route, but there are less flexible car tours that provide a car, a hotel plan, and a prearranged itinerary that permits no deviation because the hotels are all booked in advance.

Local Rentals – It has long been commonplace that the least expensive way to rent a car is to do it in Europe. This is less true than before. Many medium to large European car rental companies have become the overseas suppliers of stateside companies such as those mentioned above, and often the stateside agency, by dint of sheer volume, has been able to negotiate more favorable rates for its US customers than the European firm offers its own. Lower rates can certainly be found by searching out small, strictly local car rental companies overseas, whether at less than prime addresses in major cities or in more remote areas. But to find them you must be willing to invest a sufficient amount of vacation time comparing prices on the scene. You must also be prepared to return the car to the location that rented it — dropoff possibilities are likely to be limited.

DRIVING IN EUROPE: Anyone driving in Europe must have a valid driver's license from the state in which the driver resides and proof of liability insurance. This will be included as part of any car rental contract, but if the driver is in his or her own car, he or she must carry an International Insurance Certificate, known familiarly as a Green Card. Your insurance carrier can arrange for a special policy to cover you in Europe, and will automatically issue your Green Card at this time. An International Driver's Permit is currently *required* only for driving in Spain, Greece, and several Eastern European countries. Elsewhere, an American driver's license will suffice, but in certain countries — such as Austria, Italy, and West Germany — it must be accompanied by a certified translation into the language of that country. Many national tourist boards *strongly* recommend that American drivers obtain an International Driver's Permit, especially if they plan to do a lot of driving. You can obtain your International Driver's Permit before you leave from most branches of the AAA. The application must be accompanied by two passport-size photos, and a fee of $5.

Roads, Rules, and Maps – Western Europe's network of highways is as well maintained as any in North America, with a system comparable to the American highway system: expressways, first-class roads, and well-surfaced secondary roads (which in outlying areas like Scandinavia's Arctic region may be dirt or gravel but will be carefully maintained in any case). Three decades ago, a pan-European commission established standards for international European routes, called E roads. Most European maps note E-route numbers together with national route numbers. Single-country maps generally use only a national number. Every European country maintains its own highway system. The pictorial direction signs are standardized under the International Roadsign System and their meanings are indicated by their shapes — triangular signs indicate danger; circular signs give instructions; and rectangular signs are informative.

Driving is on the right side of the road in most of Europe and the basic rule of the road is "priority to the right"; that is, those coming from the right at intersections have the right of way. Exceptions are priority roads, marked by a sign with a yellow diamond on it; these have the right of way until the diamond reappears with a black bar and the right of way reverts to those coming from the right. Another exception is the limited form of "priority to the left" that has recently been introduced in Paris. Bound to be confusing, it initially applies only to selected traffic circles. In Great Britain, Ireland, and Malta, driving is on the left side of the road and all rules are reversed. On Swiss mountain passes, traffic going up has priority over traffic coming down.

European countries are most zealous in prosecuting offenders of driving laws, especially in the matter of drinking before driving. The Scandinavian countries, those of Eastern Europe, and Great Britain and Ireland routinely administer breath tests and are rigorous in imposing fines and jail sentences. If you've been drinking, do as the natives do and walk home, take a cab, or make sure that a licensed member of your party sticks strictly to seltzer water. In many European countries, the use of seat belts is compulsory for the driver and front seat passenger (and in France, children under 10 may not sit in the front seat unless the car has no back seat). Zebra stripes on city streets give pedestrians the right of way and cars must stop for them. In many cities, use of the horn is restricted.

Three particularly good sources of maps, atlases, and travel information are the American Automobile Association, Rand McNally, and Kummerley & Frey, whose maps are available in bookstores and map shops around the country. The American Automobile Association publishes regional maps of Europe and an overall Europe planning map that are available to members from the travel agencies in most AAA offices. Rand McNally atlases and maps are available in most bookstores or can be bought directly from the publisher (PO Box 7600, Chicago, IL 60680). All Michelin publications — red and green guides as well as road maps — are available from their US headquarters (Michelin Guides and Maps, PO Box 1007, New Hyde Park, NY

11042) and are distributed extensively throughout the US. Road maps are also sold at gas stations throughout Europe.

Automobile Clubs – Most European automobile clubs offer emergency service to any breakdown victim, whether a club member or not. To signal for help, pull over to the side of the road and raise your hood. Motor patrols usually drive small cars painted a uniform color. In Northern European countries, they are likely to be yellow. Call boxes are located on many major routes and numerous countries have a single national number to dial for roadside assistance. Though it isn't necessary to belong to an automobile club to qualify for emergency assistance, service is cheaper, or even free, if you're a member. Due to reciprocal arrangements, AAA members are automatically entitled to a number of foreign clubs' services.

Gasoline – Petroleum is sold by the liter on the Continent and by the imperial gallon in Britain. A liter is slightly more than 1 quart, and 3.75 liters equal a US gallon. One imperial gallon equals 1.2 US gallons.

Gas prices everywhere rise and fall depending upon the world supply of oil, and the American traveler in Europe is further affected by the prevailing rate of exchange for the dollar. Gas prices are considerably higher in Europe, so check the current prices abroad just before you go and budget accordingly.

Touring by Train

 Perhaps the most economical, and for sophisticated travelers often the most satisfying, way to see a lot of Europe in a relatively short time is by rail. It is the quickest means of transportation between two city centers up to 300 miles apart — but time isn't really the point. Travel by Europe's excellent train system is a way to keep moving and to keep seeing at the same time. With the many special fares and discounts available, it is an almost irresistible bargain, especially for anyone traveling around Europe for a month or longer.

Some of the special trains you may encounter in Europe include the Trans-Europ Express (TEE) trains, which came into being in the 1950s to provide the European Economic Community with fast, efficient, not to mention luxurious, service between major cities. Some are indeed international; others operate within one country exclusively. TEEs are first-class only and supplements must be paid for all departures. The supplement includes the price of a reserved seat, which is obligatory on any TEE crossing a border but not on those remaining in one country. If there is no TEE on a route, the next best train is likely to be an Intercity (IC) train. There are both international and national IC trains. Some, in fact, are former TEEs to which second-class cars have been added in recent years to help curb high operating costs, a problem aggravated by low ridership. A great many more already existed as part of the rail networks of certain countries (Germany, for instance, has a highly developed IC system). Supplements must be paid to ride all Continental IC trains except the Swiss ones (other exceptions are the IC trains of Great Britain, whose railway system has never been integrated with the Continental system), while reservations are obligatory only on those crossing borders. Another train of the same high quality is the Trans-Europ Night (TEN), an overnight train with sleeping quarters. For summer travel, early reservations are recommended.

France's TGV's (*trains à grande vitesse,* "very high speed trains") represent the state of the art in train technology. They run fastest (170 mph in commercial operation, though the record is 237.5 mph) on their own track, which has so far been laid between Paris and Lyon. But they can run at slower speeds on conventional track, so you can take a TGV to other destinations, including Paris to Switzerland. TGVs carry first- and second-class passengers, supplements must be paid for rush-hour departures, and reservations are obligatory.

All the above are but a small part of Europe's highly developed rail service. Hundreds of towns across the Continent are served by "regular" express and local trains. These trains have first- and second-class cars and meal service (and on those that make long overnight trips, various sleeping facilities, which must be reserved during peak travel periods).

Accommodations, Fares, Services – Fares on European trains are based on the quality of accommodations the passenger enjoys. You pay on the basis of traveling first class or second class, and on TEE, IC, some TGV trains, and other expresses such as Rapidos in Italy and Talgos in Spain, first or second class plus a supplement. Traditionally, seating is arranged in compartments, with three or four passengers on one side facing a like number on the other side, but increasingly in the newer cars, compartments have been replaced by a central-aisle design.

Tickets can be purchased through travel agents or national railway offices in the US (addresses below) or abroad, as well as at train stations, where domestic and international tickets are usually sold separately and lines can be long. The fare structure differs from country to country, but short hauls are always more expensive on a per-mile basis than longer runs. Most ticket and reservations systems are computerized and efficient. There is a flat fee of $4 for European reservations made in the US. Normally reservations can be made up to 2 months prior to the travel date. You can ask for a window seat as well as for a smoking or nonsmoking section.

European trains carry two basic kinds of sleeping quarters: *couchettes,* the coach seats of a compartment converted to sleeping berths; and *wagons-lits,* or sleepers, individual bedrooms that compare favorably with the slumber coaches on transcontinental American trains. First-class couchettes have four berths per compartment; second class have six. The berth is narrow, with a pillow, blanket, and sheet provided. Couchettes cost a standard surcharge ($13 per person if bought in the US) added to the basic first- or second-class fare. Wagon-lits, or sleepers, cost more.

The wide range of dining facilities runs the gamut from prix fixe menus served in dining cars or at your seat through self-service cafeteria-style cars to vendors hawking their wares through the aisles and corridors. In-seat lunch and dinner reservations can be made in advance, but dining car arrangements are made after boarding either by visiting the dining car or through the train steward.

A standardized pictorial code has been fashioned to indicate the many amenities offered at train stations. These include showers as well as restaurants, post and telegraph offices, exchange bureaus, and diaper changing facilities. Most large cities have two or more stations, with service to different parts of the country leaving from different stations. Do make sure you know the name of the station from which your train departs.

Baggage can often be checked through to your destination; French and German railways offer door-to-door delivery (which must be arranged locally) in larger towns or cities within the country. (Your luggage may not go on the same train you do and may not arrive until the next day.) Baggage can be checked overnight at most stations, but it is a good idea to travel as light as possible: You will find porters in short supply at most stations, and self-service carts are frequently scarce as well.

Drivers should be aware that all European railways have some form of auto ferry — called Motorail in Britain and Auto-Couchette on the Continent — that allows car owners to take to the rails for long distances while their car travels with them on a flatcar. However, this service can only be booked in Europe, and you can expect great difficulty because it is quite popular with the Europeans.

Passes – Rail passes offer unlimited train travel within a set period of time for a flat purchase price. They save you money and, because they are validated by a clerk on the day of your first trip, they save you the trouble of standing in ticket lines each time you want to take a train. The Eurailpass offers unlimited first-class travel over the rail networks of 16 countries — Austria, Belgium, Denmark, Finland, France, Germany, Greece, Holland, Ireland, Italy, Luxembourg, Norway, Portugal, Spain, Sweden, and Switzerland — for periods of either 15 or 21 days or 1, 2, or 3 months. Children under 4 travel free and children under 12 for half price. With the Eurailpass you don't pay the supplement ordinarily charged for TEEs, ICs, and other special express trains. The only extras are the nominal reservation fee, and sleeper and couchette costs. The Eurail Youth passes are designed for those under 26 and are good for 1 or 2 months of unlimited second-class travel; supplements must be paid for upgrading your ticket and for any of the special express trains. Eurailpass also includes free travel or substantial reductions on many Danube and Rhine river trips, lake steamers, ferry crossings, auxiliary bus routes as well as scheduled Europabus services, and airport to city center rail connections.

BritRail passes are issued for either first-class or economy travel in England, Wales, and Scotland for periods of 7, 14, or 21 days or 1 month. Children age 5 through 15 travel half fare in each of the eight categories. BritRail Youth passes, good only in economy accommodations, are sold at four rates to those aged 16 through 25. A senior citizen's pass allows persons 65 and up to travel first class at economy rates. BritRail also sells the BritRail Seapass for travel to the Continent and/or Ireland and a special train and car travel package, the Rail-Drive package, available for 7, 14, or 21 days. This includes 4 days' car rental for each 7-day period, and the car can be picked up and delivered at over 260 locations, including some 73 rail stations throughout Great Britain.

The Eurail and BritRail passes must be purchased *before* going abroad from a travel agent or the five offices listed below.

If you're going to tour one country extensively, inquire about national discount plans (before leaving the US in case the plan requires purchase abroad). Many countries issue passes similar to Eurail that allow unlimited travel for defined periods of time over the national transportation network. In addition, there is an endless array of special discount tickets, rail and bike plans, rail and road plans, and other bargains. Most national railroads also offer discounts to those over 60 or 65 and those under 26. Areawide programs also exist: The Benelux Tourail ticket allows unlimited travel in Belgium, the Netherlands, and Luxembourg for 8 days of your choice during a 16-day period from the beginning of April to the end of October. The Scandinavian Rail Pass is good for 21 days of first- or second-class travel on trains throughout Denmark, Finland, Norway, and Sweden and over certain ferry routes as well.

Further Information – *The Eurail Guide,* by Marvin L. Saltzman ($10.95), discusses routes, rates, and ins and outs of Eurailpasses and other special rail deals around the world in complete detail, and is an excellent buy for the serious rail traveler. The most revered and most accurate worldwide railway book is *The Thomas Cook Continental Timetable,* issued monthly; $15.95. Cook's also publishes an excellent *Rail Map of Europe;* $6.95. All are sold by the Forsyth Travel Library, PO Box 2975, Shawnee Mission, KS 66201 (phone: 913-384-0496), at the above prices plus a $1 handling charge.

Addresses for the national railway offices in the US that sell tickets and passes and make reservations are:

BritRail Travel International, 630 Third Ave., New York, NY 10017 (phone: 212-599-5400); 510 W Sixth St., Los Angeles, CA 90014 (phone: 213-626-0088); 333 N Michigan Ave., Chicago, IL 60601 (phone: 312-263-1910); Plaza of the Americas, North Tower, Suite 750, Dallas, TX 75201 (phone: 214-748-0860). French National Railroads, 610 Fifth Ave., New York, NY 10020 (phone: 212-

582-2110); 2121 Ponce de Leon Blvd., Coral Gables, FL 33134 (phone: 305-
445-8648); 11 E Adams St., Chicago, IL 60603 (phone: 312-427-8691); 9465
Wilshire Blvd., Beverly Hills, CA 90212 (phone: 213-274-6934); 360 Post St.,
San Francisco, CA 94108 (phone: 415-982-1993).

German Rail, 747 Third Ave., New York, NY 10017 (phone: 212-308-3100); 1121
Walker St., Houston, TX 77002 (phone: 713-224-8781); 520 Broadway, Suite
320, Santa Monica, CA 90401 (phone: 213-394-0293); 104 S Michigan Ave.,
Chicago, IL 60603 (phone: 312-263-2958); 625 Statler Office Building, Boston,
MA 02116 (phone: 617-542-0577); 1 Hallidie Plaza, Suite 250, San Francisco,
CA 94102 (phone: 415-981-5548); 8000 E Gerard Ave., Suite 518 South, Den-
ver, CO 80231 (phone: 303-695-7715).

Italian State Railways, 666 Fifth Ave., New York, NY 10103 (phone: 212-397-
2667); 765 Rt. 83, Suite 105, Bensonville, IL 60106 (phone: 312-860-1090);
15760 Ventura Blvd., Encino, CA 91436 (phone: 213-783-7245).

Swiss Federal Railways, 608 Fifth Ave., New York, NY 10020 (phone: 212-
757-5944); 250 Stockton St., San Francisco, CA 94108 (phone: 415-362-2260).

Package Tours

Package tours are one of the best of travel buys. They are economical and
convenient, save the purchaser an immense amount of planning time, and
offer so many variations in destinations and arrangements that it's virtually
impossible for the Europe-bound traveler not to find one that fits at least the
bulk of his or her travel preferences.

In essence, a package tour is a combination of travel arrangements and services that
may be purchased as a single booking. It may include any or all of the following:
transatlantic transportation, local transportation (and/or car rentals), accommodations, some or all meals, sight-seeing, entertainment, transfers to and from hotel at each
destination, taxes, tips, escort service, and a variety of incidental features that might
be offered as options at additional cost.

In other words, a package may be any combination from a fully escorted tour offered
at an all-inclusive price to a simple fly/drive booking allowing purchasers to do exactly
as they please. The principal advantage of a package is that it saves you money: The
cost of the combined arrangements invariably is well below the price that would be paid
if all the elements included were bought individually. An important additional feature
is that you may purchase all of these elements at the same time.

Lower prices are made possible because tour packages are designed for high-volume
participation. The tour packager negotiates for services in wholesale quantities —
blocks of hotel rooms, group meals, busloads of ground transportation, and so on
— and thus purchases them at a lower per-person price. Even after markups and
commissions are added, the tour price to retail customers is still reasonably below what
they would pay if planning such a trip as individuals. Most packages, however, are
subject to various restrictions governing the duration of a trip and require full payment
by a given time before departure.

Aside from the cost-saving advantages of package arrangements, Europe itself is
ideally suited to package travel. The reason is that, essentially, Europe is a multiple
country, see-and-do destination as distinct from, say, the Caribbean, where most visitors go to a single island or country for a week or two of vacation and unpack everything
until they're ready to return home. To be sure, many visitors to Europe do seek out
a single city or country for a concentrated visit, booking themselves in a hotel, apart-

ment, home, or villa that serves as a stationary base from which they make regional tours and visits. But for the bulk of North American travelers, Europe remains a destination for cramming in as much travel and sight-seeing as possible with the time and money the visitor has available. Hence the popularity — and practicality — of package tours.

Packages are put together by tour operators or wholesalers, some retail travel agencies, airlines, charter companies, hotels, and even special interest organizations, and what goes into them depends on who is organizing them. The most common type, assembled by tour wholesalers and sold through travel agents, run the gamut from deluxe everything to simple tourist-class amenities or even bare necessities. Fly/drive and fly/cruise packages are usually the joint planning efforts of airlines and, respectively, car rental companies and cruise line operators. Charter flight programs may range from little more than air fare and a minimum of ground arrangements to full-scale tours. There are also hotel packages organized by hotel chains or associations of independent hotels and applicable to stays at any combination of member properties; resort packages covering arrangements at a specific hotel; and, of course, special interest tours, which can be once-only programs organized by particular groups through a retail agency or regular offerings packaged by a tour operator. They can feature food, arts festivals, sporting activities, a commemorative occasion, even scientific exploration. A good travel agent will be able to provide information not only on packages of general interest but also on the specialized ones, even though the latter can sometimes be booked either through an agent or the packager, particularly if the program caters to a small number of people and is limited to one or a few departures annually.

One of the consumer's biggest problems is finding enough information to judge the reliability of a tour operator, since individuals very seldom have direct contact with the firm putting the package together. Usually, a retail travel agent intervenes between customer and tour operator and much depends on the candor and cooperation of the agent.

You should ask your travel agent a number of questions about the tour he or she is recommending. For example: Has the agent ever before used the packages provided by this tour operator? How long has the tour operator been in business? Which and how many companies are involved in the package? If air travel is by charter flight, is there an escrow account in which deposits will be held, and, if so, what is the name of the bank?

This last question is very important. The law requires that tour operators deposit every charter passenger's deposit and subsequent payment in a proper escrow trust account. Money paid into such an account cannot legally be used except to pay for the costs of a particular package or as a refund if the trip is canceled. So to best ensure the safe handling of your money, make out your check to the escrow bank account. The law requires that the account number appear on any tour brochure, and it is usually found in that mass of minuscule type on the back. On the face of your check, write the details of the charter, including the destination and dates; on the back, print the words "For Deposit Only." Your travel agent may prefer that you make your check out to him, saying that he will then pay the tour operator the fee minus his commission. But it is perfectly legal to write your check this way and if your agent objects too vociferously, consider taking your business elsewhere. If you don't make your check out to the escrow account, you lose your escrow protection should the trip be canceled or the tour operator or travel agent fail. (Even the protection of escrow may not be enough to safeguard a traveler's investment, as recent bankruptcies and defaults by travel suppliers have shown. For information on insurance against such eventualities, see *Insurance.*)

To determine whether or not a package — or more specifically *which* package — fits your own travel plans, start by evaluating your own interests and needs, deciding how much you want to see and do. Then gather together whatever package tour information is available on programs that fit your schedule.

Read the package brochures carefully and check for the following: what exactly is included in the tour price — and what isn't; are tour prices guaranteed for the duration of the tour program; departure dates; variation in price and itinerary at different times of the year; how much is the supplement for a single room; what meals are included in the price; class of hotels; amount of refund in case of cancellation before departure; can the operator cancel the tour if too few people sign up; can the operator unilaterally increase the price?

Read the responsibility clause (usually at the end of the descriptive literature) carefully. Here the tour operator usually expresses the right to change services or schedules as long as you are offered equivalent service; this clause also absolves the operator of responsibility for circumstances beyond human control that may affect the tour.

European Packages Booked in Europe – Those who may want to add on a tour or package arrangement after they are in Europe should know that package tours can be booked at all major capitals and other metropolitan areas. Besides the excitement of adding a vacation within a vacation to your itinerary, these Europe-based packages represent an economical way of getting from one point in Europe to another (and back). The most popular center in which to book while abroad is London. North American travelers find British-organized tours particularly attractive because they're mostly for English-speaking groups and are often accompanied by English-speaking escorts and/or guides. In addition, many British tour operators cater to the budget end of the market. Once upon a time, the smart shopper could pick up a flight from London to Athens and back, plus a week's worth of adequate, if spartan, accommodations, for less than half the price of an air ticket alone. These days, the bargains are not quite as enticing, though the British still manage to put together a good deal that becomes even better when the exchange rate is favorable to Americans.

The following are some of Britain's major high-volume or economy-minded tour operators. Some have become familiar names in this country recently because they have opened US offices and begun to market some or all of the tour offerings in their British catalogues directly to the American public; i.e., booking one of their packages is no different from booking the package of an American tour operator. Almost all of the rest have at least a representative in the US to handle American bookings. Note that most of these offices or representatives prefer to deal with travel agents rather than individuals. Note also that because of the extra costs involved in making arrangements from this end, packages booked here can run 5% to 15% more than if booked in Britain; and if you attempt to book through the British office by mail, your request will most likely be referred to the US representative. Clearly, you will save money by waiting until you are in England to book, but you will be taking a chance that the package you want will still be open at the last minute.

Cosmos of London: In 1985, this firm specializing in low-cost motorcoach tours of Europe offered 46 tour series, visiting countries from Scandinavia to Eastern Europe and the Mediterranean. For information or brochures, contact Cosmos Tours, 69-15 Austin St., Forest Hills, NY 11375 (phone: in New York State, 718-268-7000; elsewhere, 800-221-0090). Bookings must be made through a travel agent. The London office is at 180 Vauxhall Bridge Rd., London SW1V 1ED (phone: 834-7412).

Frames National: Reasonably priced coach tours of Europe, Great Britain, and Ireland, including a series of low-cost minitours of England, Scotland, and

Wales, are available through Frames. The company's US agent, Tourpak International, The Kemwel Group, 106 Calvert St., Harrison, NY 10528 (phone: in New York State, 800-942-1807; elsewhere, 800-431-1491), prefers bookings through travel agents. The London office is at 33 Elizabeth St., London SW1W 9RR (phone: 730-8691).

Glenton Tours: This long-established company is a specialist in first-class but relatively inexpensive motorcoach tours of Great Britain (over 30 itineraries), and it also has two tours visiting Ireland. The US representative is BTC, 19 W 44th St., New York, NY 10036 (phone: in New York State, 212-719-1223; elsewhere, 800-225-6577), which accepts bookings directly from the public. Head offices in London are at 114 Peckham Rye, London SE15 4JE (phone: 639-9777).

Globus-Gateway: Probably the British tour operator used most by Americans, Globus-Gateway in 1985 had some 40 motorcoach tours of Scandinavia and the Continent as well as 10 of Great Britain and Ireland. Bookings through travel agents only. Globus-Gateway's US and London addresses and phone numbers are the same as those for Cosmos (see above).

Thomson Holidays: Great Britain's largest tour operator owns its own airline, Britannia Airways, and its coach tours travel from home turf to Europe and as far afield as the Himalayas. Thomson is also known for a broad selection of Mediterranean holiday packages that include round-trip air fare (from Britain) and a week or two or more of villa or apartment rental. The US office offers US-originating (from Chicago, Detroit, Los Angeles, and San Francisco) motorcoach tours to Europe (and a London city package), but the bulk of the company's hefty travel offerings are still based in Britain and booked through London. For information on packages originating in the US, contact Thomson Vacations, 401 N Michigan Ave., Chicago, IL 60611 (phone: 312-467-4200 or 800-222-6400), but book through a travel agent. For everything else, write to Thomson Holidays, Rochester House, 2 Belvedere Rd., London SE19 2HQ (phone: 653-8899).

Townsend Thoresen: Best known as the major ferry service for crossings from Great Britain to the Continent, this firm also has short motorcoach tours of Europe ranging in duration from 2 to 5 days. Bookings in the US are handled by the company's agent, Express International, PO Box A, Main St., Saltillo, PA 17253 (phone: in Pennsylvania, Alaska, or Hawaii, 814-448-3945; elsewhere, 800-458-3606), which will deal with the public. The London office is at 127 Regent St., London W1R 8LB (phone: 437-7800, 734-4431).

Trafalgar Tours: It offered more than 25 motorcoach itineraries of the Continent and Great Britain and Ireland in 1985, plus a group of budget-conscious Cost-Saver tours on which savings were realized by scheduling a number of nights in hotels without private baths. Bookings are made through travel agents or Trafalgar Tours, 21 E 26th St., New York, NY 10010 (phone: in New York City, 212-689-8977; elsewhere, 800-854-0103). In London, the main office is at 9-11 Bressenden Pl., London SW1E 5DF (phone: 828-4388).

Not to be discounted is Thomas Cook, the best known of all London tour operators. Its name is practically synonymous with the Grand Tour of Europe, but Cook's tours span the world, with itineraries ranging from deluxe to moderate, including some of the budget variety as well. You can book a tour directly through any of its offices in major cities in North America or through any travel agency. Thomas Cook's headquarters are in London at 45 Berkeley St., Piccadilly, London W1A 1EB (phone: 499-4000).

Camping, Recreational Vehicles, Hiking, and Biking

CAMPING AND CARAVANNING: In Europe, sites for camping and caravans (as campers and other recreational vehicles are called) are run by government tourist agencies, automobile associations, provinces and municipalities, and private companies. Most are open from Easter through October and they fill quickly at the height of the summer season, so it is a good idea to arrive early in the day if you haven't been able to reserve a pitch in advance. Caravanning is extremely popular with European vacationers, and many parks cater more to the caravanner than to the tent dweller. If you get into difficulty, remember that tourist offices throughout Europe can direct you to sites in the areas they serve.

In the US, camping maps and lists of sites are distributed by the tourist offices of individual European countries. Some comprehensive guides to sites are also available. The AA guide, *Camping and Caravanning in Europe* ($12.95), published by the Automobile Association of Great Britain, Fanum House, Basingstoke, Hampshire RG21 2EA, England, is sold by bookstores that specialize in travel. It lists about 4,000 sites inspected and rated by the AA and provides other information of interest to campers. The AA's *Camping and Caravanning in Britain,* listing about 1,000 sites, is available from travel bookstores or from the British Travel Bookshop (40 W 57th St., New York, NY 10019, phone: 212-765-0898; $8.50 plus $1.95 handling charge). The *Camping Caravanning France* guide, published by Michelin (in French but with an introduction in English on how to use the book) is readily available from bookstores in France.

The international camping organization Fédération Internationale de Camping et Caravanning issues a pass, called a carnet, that entitles the bearer to a modest discount at many camping grounds around the Continent. It is available in the US from the National Campers and Hikers Association, 7172 Transit Rd., Buffalo, NY 14221 (phone: 716-634-5433), for a fee of $20, which includes camping information and membership in the association. If you are already a member of AAA, the carnet can be obtained through them for $7.50; for $14, you will receive a copy of the AA's *Camping and Caravanning in Europe* along with the carnet; for $12, *Camping and Caravanning in Britain* along with your carnet; for $20, the carnet and both guides.

Camping equipment is available for sale or rent throughout Europe, and rentals can be booked in advance through any number of outfitters. National tourist offices in the US can supply information on reliable dealers. Rentals of recreational vehicles can also be arranged from the US through several companies, including:

Auto-Europe, PO Box 500, Yorktown Heights, NY 10598 (phone: in New York State, 800-924-1309; elsewhere, 800-223-5555).

Europe by Car, 1 Rockefeller Plaza, New York, NY 10020, or 9000 Sunset Blvd., Los Angeles, CA 90069 (phone: in New York State, 212-581-3040; in California, 800-252-9401; elsewhere, 800-223-1516).

Foremost Euro-Car, 5430 Van Nuys Blvd., Van Nuys, CA 91401 (phone: in California, 800-272-3299; elsewhere, 800-423-3111).

Kemwel, 106 Calvert St., Harrison, NY 10528 (phone: in New York State, 800-431-1362; elsewhere, 800-468-0468 or 800-942-1932).

Reservations should be made well in advance, as the supply is limited and the demand great. The vehicles offered range from small buses customized in various ways for camping, often including elevated sun roofs, to larger coach-type motorhomes. Towed vehicles can be hired overseas but are not usually offered by companies in the US.

Make sure that whatever you drive is equipped to deal with the electrical and gas standards of all countries on your itinerary. There are differences between the bottled stove gas supplied in Britain and that on the Continent. You should either have a sufficient supply of the type your camper requires or equipment that can use either. If you're towing a camper, note that nothing towed is automatically covered by liability insurance and that the primary vehicle's Green Card must carry an endorsement for the towed vehicle. As towing is an additional strain on car and driver, both should be in top physical condition.

Whether driving a camper or towing, it is essential to have some idea of the terrain you'll be encountering en route. Not only are numerous mountain passes closed in winter, but grades are often too steep for certain vehicles to negotiate. Car tunnels, or piggyback services on trains, usually bypass those summits too difficult to climb, but they also impose dimension limitations and often charge high fees. The AA guides provide detailed information on the principal passes and tunnels, as do tourist offices.

Packaged camping tours are available for those who wish to avoid the problems of advance planning and day-to-day organizing yet still reap the savings that shoestring travel affords. Be aware, however, that these packages are usually geared to the young, with ages 18 to 35 as common limits. Transfer from place to place is by bus, as on other sightseeing tours, but overnights are in tents and meal arrangements vary. Often there is a food fund that covers meals in restaurants or in the camps; sometimes there is a chef and sometimes the cooking is done by the participants themselves. An organization called Camping Tours of Europe, 40 Underhill Blvd., Syosset, NY 11791 (phone: 516-496-7400), markets the camping tours of several British tour operators.

BIKING: For young or energetic travelers, the bicycle offers a marvelous way of seeing Europe, especially those countries where terrains are especially conducive to easy cycling like the Benelux nations and parts of Scandinavia. Long and short rentals are available throughout Europe, and cities such as Amsterdam, where biking is a way of life, provide complete cycling services. Certain national railways, including those in Belgium, France, Switzerland, Germany, Austria, and the Netherlands, have bicycles for rent at many train stations, often at a discount for ticketholders. Many also feature "rent it here, leave it there" programs, allowing you to take your bike on the train to another town without returning it to the station from which it was rented. Almost all European trains have facilities for bike transport at nominal fees.

Detailed maps will infinitely improve a biking tour, and are available from a number of sources. Bartholomew maps of the National or GT series provide excellent coverage of Britain and Ireland. If you cannot find them, write to John Bartholomew & Son Ltd., 12 Duncan St., Edinburgh EH9 1TA, Scotland, for a price list. Detailed Michelin maps (1:200,000) covering France and other parts of Europe are available from Michelin Guides and Maps, PO Box 1007, New Hyde Park, NY 11042 (phone: 516-488-4477). The ANWB (Royal Dutch Touring Club), PO Box 93200, 2509 BA, The Hague, publishes a series of detailed maps charting Holland's excellent bike paths.

A valuable book for planning a trip is *Bicycle Touring in Europe,* by Karen and Gary Hawkins (Pantheon Books; $5.95). National tourist offices in the US can provide information specific to their countries or direct you to European organizations promoting cycling. Frequently, these are automobile clubs, as many national cycling federations promote racing, not touring.

Membership in the American Youth Hostels organization is a prerequisite for staying at most youth hostels abroad. There is no age limit for membership, although hostels in Switzerland and Bavaria, Germany, give priority to members age 26 and under (meaning that in summer and on holidays, there probably will not be space available for older travelers). The *International Youth Hostel Handbook, Volume One: Europe and the Mediterranean,* which can be purchased with an AYH membership, describes over 2,500 hostels and includes a map of their locations. For those preferring not to travel alone, AYH and some of its local chapters, or councils, sponsor a number of biking (and hiking) trips to Europe each year. Departures are geared to various age groups and levels of skill; overnights are spent in hostels and hotels. For information, contact the national organization (1332 I St., NW, Suite 800, Washington, DC 20005; phone: 202-783-6161) or your local council. The Metropolitan New York Council of the American Youth Hostels (132 Spring St., New York, NY 10012; phone: 212-431-7100) is an affiliate with a particularly broad tour program of its own, and its free store catalogue, *Information & Equipment,* is another useful planning aid for cyclists as well as hikers and campers.

One of the attractions of a bike tour is that shipment of equipment — your bike — is handled by organizers and the shipping fee is included in the total tour package. Travelers simply deliver the bike to the airport, already disassembled and boxed; shipping boxes can be obtained from most bicycle shops with little difficulty. Bikers not with a tour must make their own arrangements with the airline, and there are no standard procedures for this. Some international carriers provide shipping cartons for bikes and charge only a nominal fee. Other airlines don't provide cartons and may charge as much as $50 or more. A further attraction of some tours is the existence of a "sag wagon" to carry extra luggage or you and your bike when you tire.

The International Bicycle Touring Society (IBTS) is another nonprofit organization that regularly sponsors low-cost bicycle tours around the US and Canada and overseas. Participants must be over 21 and are usually between 30 and 60 years old. A sag wagon accompanies the tour group, and accommodations are in inns and hotels. The IBTS is at 2115 Paseo Dorado, La Jolla, CA 92037 (phone: 619-459-8775). Numerous other organizations, non-profit and commercial, sponsor bicycle tours of the US and abroad. For an annually published list of sponsors, send a stamped, self-addressed #10 envelope and $2 to the League of American Wheelmen (Bicycle USA, Suite 209, 6707 Whitestone Rd., Baltimore, MD 21207; phone: 301-944-3399). You may also want to investigate the tours of Britain and the Continent offered to members of Britain's Cyclists Touring Club (CTC). For information, write to the CTC at Cotterell House, 69 Meadrow, Godalming, Surrey GU7 3HS, England, and join early if you decide to participate.

HIKING: Marked hiking trails abound in Europe. Germany alone has some 80,000 miles of them in addition to 9,000 Alpine trails. On Britain's Pennine Way, one of the country's official long-distance footpaths and its roughest, you can walk 270 lonely miles up the backbone of England to the Scottish border, a trip recommended only for experienced hikers equipped with maps and compass to steer them through remote moorland and probable bad weather. Less practiced but more gregarious hikers can join the weekend crowds for a short stretch of one of France's easiest *sentiers de grande randonnée,* the Sentier de l'Île de France, a 375-mile circular route ringing Paris. Equally popular (lodging along the way for July and August is booked months in advance) but much more difficult is the spectacularly scenic Tour du Mont-Blanc, a 100-mile route around the mountain massif taking in three countries — France, Italy, and Switzerland.

Preliminary information on where to hike is available from many tourist offices in the US. The British Tourist Authority's information sheet, *Walking,* describes national parks, long-distance footpaths, and other walking areas in England, Wales, Scotland, and Northern Ireland. The Irish Tourist Board can supply a general information sheet on walking and climbing or a specific one on the Wicklow Way and the South Leinster

Way. The Swiss National Tourist Office distributes *Postbus: The Best High-Altitude and Panoramic Walks,* a booklet detailing various scenic routes whose jumping-off points can be reached via the Swiss postbus service. But even those tourist offices that do not have literature on hand (or have little in English) can direct you to associations in their countries that supply maps, guides, and further information. For long visits, membership in a local club is suggested.

All you need to set out on a simple hike are a pair of sturdy shoes and socks; jeans or long pants to keep branches, nettles, and bugs off your legs; a canteen of water; a hat for the sun; and, if you like, a picnic lunch. It is a good idea to dress in layers, so that you can peel off a sweater or two to keep pace with the rising sun and put them back on as the sun goes down. Make sure, too, to wear clothes with pockets or bring a pack to keep your hands free. Some useful and important pocket or pack stuffers include a jackknife, waterproof matches, a map, and a compass.

To make your outing safe and pleasant, find out about the trails you plan to hike in advance and know your own limits. Unless you are in good shape, choose an easy route. Stick to the defined route unless you are an experienced hiker or know the area well. And *always* let someone know where you are going and when you expect to be back, at least by leaving a note on your car if the hike is impromptu. If you prefer to travel as part of an organized group, see the January/February issue of *Sierra* magazine for the Sierra Club's annual list of foreign outings, or contact the Sierra Club Outing Department, 530 Bush St., San Francisco, CA 94108 (phone: 415-981-8634). Each year the club sponsors a number of foreign outings, including several to Europe, usually about 2 weeks in length. Trips vary from year to year, but in 1985 you could hike the Lake District and Cotswold Hills of England, the Scottish Highlands, the German Black Forest, the mountains of Corsica, the Pyrenees in Spain, the Dolomites of Italy and Austria, the Swiss Alps, and the Tour du Mont-Blanc. Other trips combined hiking with biking (as in Ireland and on the Dalmatian Coast of Yugoslavia). Some trips are backpacking trips, moving to a new camp each day; others make day hikes from a base camp. Overnights can be in small hotels, inns, or guest houses, in campgrounds or mountain huts. American Youth Hostels (see address above) also sponsors foreign hiking trips, though fewer than its foreign biking trips. In 1985, participants on its Alpine Ramble spent 42 days backpacking through the mountains of France, Switzerland, Austria, and Italy, staying in hostels and camping. Mountain Travel, a company specializing in adventure trips around the world, offers a great variety of trips ranging from easy walks that can be undertaken by anyone in good health to those that require basic or advanced mountaineering experience. Its trips take in the Alps, the Dolomites, and the Pyrenees as well as the mountains of Scandinavia, Eastern Europe, Greece, and the Soviet Union. In 1985, it even offered a 15-day tour of Greenland — dogsledding. For information, contact Mountain Travel, 1398 Solano Ave., Albany, CA 94706 (phone: in California, 415-527-8100; elsewhere, 800-227-2384). Note that Mountain Travel also customizes itineraries for independent travelers.

Preparing

Calculating Costs

After a few lean years, travel to Europe from North America has burgeoned once again, in response, no doubt, to the lusty rebound of the US dollar abroad and the generally improving economy. Many Americans are choosing this year to take the trip they've been postponing, and they are finding that in addition to the advantageous exchange rate, a number of factors make travel to Europe affordable. Discount fares and the availability of charter flights can greatly reduce the cost of transportation. Package tours can further reduce the price because the group rates obtained by the tour packager are usually much less than the tariffs paid by someone traveling à la carte; that is, paying for each element — hotel, car rental, meals, airfare — separately.

Prices, inflation, and exchange rates are not uniform across Europe. Traditionally, northern and central European countries — Scandinavia, the Benelux nations, Germany, Switzerland, Austria — are more expensive and have less favorable exchange rates for the dollar than do the Mediterranean and Eastern European countries. However, the dollar has increased in strength all across Europe, and even the "expensive" countries — in particular, France and Great Britain — have become a better buy. Additionally, both countries have a saving grace: though their capitals — like our major cities — suffer from a high cost of living, travel in the surrounding countryside can be more reasonable, and even inexpensive (depending on your choice of accommodations and means of transport). The dollar goes further than ever in Yugoslavia, Greece, Italy, Spain, and Portugal, the traditionally cheaper European countries. Ireland also is still relatively a good buy, whether you plan to stay in Dublin or to ramble around the countryside.

There are many variables that affect the cost of a European vacation, but the major expenses are transportation, accommodations, and food, the latter two of which are especially affected by fluctuations in the daily and weekly exchange rate — that is, how much of a given foreign currency the dollar will buy. Below are the ways we suggest to put a price tag on these major items, but all your budgeting will be enhanced if you first consider some basic questions about how you intend to travel.

1. Will you go on your own? With friend(s) on an independent itinerary of your own planning? On loosely organized tour arrangements in which some features (transatlantic transportation, rooms, transfers) are included as prepaid items, but which permit you to arrange sight-seeing, dining, and other things on your own? Or on a totally preplanned escorted tour with almost all transportation, rooms, meals, sight-seeing, local travel, tips, and the like, included and prepaid? (See *Package Tours,* GETTING READY TO GO.)
2. How much are you willing to spend? This, in turn, breaks down into two alternatives: Do you have a specific budget into which your trip must fit, or will you adjust your expenditures to the cost of the tour you want to take? (Most travelers start with a budget range, but as arrangements progress, are inclined to

extend this amount if related or additional travel possibilities fit into their itineraries.)

3. When do you plan to travel? Timing can be a key to saving money if you're willing to visit Europe during the less-trafficked off-season months (usually winter) when transatlantic air fares are lower and so are the prices of resort hotels, except in the winter ski resorts and those cities with fashion showings, special exhibitions, and so on. In this connection, keep in mind those times that are generally referred to as the shoulder months, the periods between the traditional low and high seasons (approximately late March to mid-May and late September through November). Costs are only a little lower than in high season, but you won't be bucking the crowds of the peak months and the weather should be agreeable. (See *When to Go,* GETTING READY TO GO.)

These component travel arrangements — transportation, hotel accommodations, and food — are the three basic cost elements of all tour and travel arrangements, but there are a number of other expenses you must allow for: local transportation (particularly when traveling on your own with a rented car, Eurailpass on trains, and so on); sight-seeing; shopping; local taxes (a frequently annoying extra when affixed by city and country governments on your hotel rooms and purchases); miscellaneous services (laundry, drinks); and tips.

Transportation – Air fare to Europe is really the easiest cost to pin down, though the range and variety of flights available may be confusing initially. A detailed explanation of the various categories is given in *Traveling by Plane,* GETTING READY TO GO. Essentially the traveler can choose from one of several categories of scheduled flights — ranging in expense from first class, which presumably no vacation traveler needs, to standby — or charters.

In earlier sections of GETTING READY TO GO we have discussed and compared the various alternatives of travel within Europe: rented car, bus, train, or air. The most important factor in determining which of these to use is the amount of time you will be abroad. If more than 2 weeks, and you plan to do a great deal of traveling, a Eurailpass is likely to be the most economical form of transport between cities. If road touring is your object, you should look into fly/drive arrangements versus straight rentals and compare the rates offered by some of the smaller US firms specializing in European car travel with those of the large international chains (see *Touring by Car,* GETTING READY TO GO).

Accommodations – Room costs in Europe run a very wide gamut, but for purposes of making an estimate, expect to pay in Europe about what you would pay in a major American city for equivalent accommodations. And figure on the high side if you're visiting major tourist centers during high season.

Most expensive will be international hotels with a full complement of business services. There is no sacred edict stating that travelers must put up at deluxe hotels in Europe, and, in fact, you might be missing a good deal of the European experience by insisting on international standards and skipping over the great small hotels. Especially in Europe, hotels in the first-class range usually are available at about one-third less than their deluxe counterparts, and second-class hotels offer clean, comfortable accommodations. For a detailed discussion of the range and variety of accommodations available in Europe, see *Hotels, Pensions, and Special Places in Europe,* GETTING READY TO GO.

There are two options for cheaper accommodations for anyone staying for an extended period of time in one place in Europe. One is renting an apartment, called holiday lets in Britain. These are available in most European cities and can be arranged through travel agents. The other is a house exchange, in which you and a European family exchange houses for an agreed-upon period of time. Both are discussed in *Hotels, Pensions, and Special Places in Europe,* GETTING READY TO GO.

Food – Restaurant dining in Europe — particularly in the better eating establishments of major tourist destinations — is, comparatively speaking, going to hit your purse, wallet, or credit card hardest. If you're an independent traveler and taking all your meals out (although many hotels still provide Continental breakfast with the cost of your accommodations), allow anywhere from $35 to $50 per person per day for food. This should cover taxes and the service charge, and perhaps a small carafe of table wine with a fixed menu dinner — and you won't be splurging. (An à la carte dinner in one of any city's finest restaurants can almost double this estimate, as can heavy consumption of alcohol.) To estimate this portion of your travel expenses, see *Eating Out*, THE EUROPEAN CITIES, for the cities you plan to visit. If you are a budget traveler, the wonderful meals to be had in the pubs, bistros, trattorias, tavernas, etc., of the country you are in can greatly reduce your outlay.

Local Taxes – The ones that most affect foreign visitors are those affixed by governments to overnight room accommodations and to items purchased at local stores, called VAT (value added tax). The room tax may or may not be specified at the time of booking, so do be sure to ask in advance. VAT on purchases can be avoided in certain countries — Great Britain and Ireland, for example — by having the purchase sent directly to your home in the US. Moreover, many countries have methods (always cumbersome, by the way) for getting a refund. Check with the national tourist offices of the countries on your itinerary for details (see *National Tourist Offices in the US* in SOURCES AND RESOURCES). For a more complete discussion of the VAT, see *Shopping*. In essence, VAT taxes on purchases are frequently reimbursed if visitors ask the sales clerk for refund forms and submit them to a customs inspector at departure while showing the item to prove that it is being taken out of the country. The refund arrives later, as a check in the mail.

Service Charges – Increasingly, hotels and restaurants include a 10% to 15% charge on the cost of rooms and food to cover gratuities. Again, this may not be specified at the time of making reservations, so ask in advance. At restaurants, visitors should ask if a service charge is included in the bill submitted at the end of a meal. Even when such charges are included, a few coins or additional tip is appropriate if the service has been exceptional or if the service charge is a minimal amount.

Other expenses, such as the cost of local sight-seeing tours, will vary from city to city, country to country. Most of the better European hotels will have a *concierge* or a person with information on services available at the front desk. He or she should be able to provide a rundown on the cost of local tours and full-day excursions in and from the city.

Entry Requirements and Documents

A valid US passport is the one document that all countries require for travel in Western Europe and, of course, you must have one for reentry into the US. As a *general* rule (see the country-by-country listings in FACTS IN BRIEF for specifics) possession of a US passport entitles the bearer to remain in Western European countries for up to 3 months as a tourist; for study, residency, or work completely different documents and considerably more laborious procedures are required. Almost all Eastern European countries require that visitors have visas, which can be obtained from the consulate of the country before leaving the US or, in some cases, at the border. In addition, all except Yugoslavia and Hungary require some form of prepaid travel arrangements. In one or two instances these can be made at the border, but most require advance planning. See FACTS IN BRIEF for details.

Vaccination certificates are required by European authorities only if the traveler is entering from an area listed as contagious by the World Health Organization. Because smallpox is considered eradicated from the world, only a very few countries continue to require visitors to have a smallpox vaccination certificate. You will certainly not need one for travel between Europe and the US.

New passports are now valid for 10 years from the date of issue (5 years for travelers under 18 years of age). The passport itself is not renewable; passport holders must turn in their expired passports to receive new and valid ones. This can take as little as 2 weeks or as much as a month, and certainly, anyone applying for a passport for the first time should allow at least 4 weeks for delivery — even 6 weeks in high season, from approximately mid-March to mid-September. Normal passports contain 24 pages, but frequent travelers can request a 48-page passport at no extra cost.

Passport renewal can be done by mail, but if you are applying for the first time or are under 18 and renewing your passport, you must do so in person at one of the following places:

1. The State Department Passport Agencies in Boston; Chicago; Honolulu; Houston; Los Angeles; Miami; New Orleans; New York City; Philadelphia; San Francisco; Seattle; Stamford, CT; and Washington, DC.
2. A federal or state courthouse.
3. Any of the 1,000 post offices across the country with designated acceptance facilities.

Application blanks are available at all these offices and must be presented with:

1. Proof of US citizenship. This can be a previous passport or one in which you were included. If you are applying for your first passport and you were born in the United States, your birth certificate is all the proof required. If you were born abroad, a Certificate of Naturalization, a Certificate of Citizenship, a Report of Birth Abroad of a Citizen of the United States, or a Certification of Birth is necessary.
2. Proof of identity. Again, this can be a previous passport, or a driver's license, a Certificate of Naturalization or of Citizenship, or a government ID card with a physical description or a photograph. Failing any of these, you should be accompanied by a friend of at least 2 years' standing who will testify to your identity. Credit cards or social security cards do not suffice as proof of identity.
3. Two 2 × 2-inch front-view photographs in color or black and white not more than 6 months old. These must be taken by a photographer rather than by a machine.
4. Cash, check, or money order for the $7 execution fee (not required if you are renewing a passport) and the $35 passport fee ($20 for travelers under 18).

Passports can be renewed by mail on forms obtained at designated locations only if the expired passport was issued no more than 8 years before the date of the application for renewal and if it was not issued before the applicant's 18th birthday. Send the completed form with two photos (signed on the back), $35 (no execution fee required here), and the expired passport to the nearest passport agency office.

Every individual, regardless of age, must have his or her own passport. A "family" passport is no longer issued although those issued before Jan. 1, 1981, remain valid until their printed expiration date.

■ **SHOULD YOU LOSE YOUR PASSPORT ABROAD:** Immediately report the loss to the nearest US consulate. You can get a 3-month temporary passport directly from the consulate, but you must fill out a "loss of passport" form and follow the same application procedure — and pay the same fees — as you did for the original. It's likely to speed things up if you have a record of your passport number and the place and date of its issue.

■**IF YOU NEED AN EMERGENCY PASSPORT:** Although a passport application normally takes several weeks to process, it is possible to be issued a passport in a matter of hours. Go directly to your nearest passport office — there is no way, however, to avoid waiting in line — and explain the nature of the emergency, which does not have to be dire in the conventional sense: a ticket in hand for a flight the following day will suffice. Should the "emergency" occur outside of business hours, all is not lost! There's a 24-hour telephone number in Washington, DC (phone: 202-634-3600), that can put you in touch with a State Department duty officer who may be able to expedite your application.

Planning a Trip

123 For most travelers, a week-plus trip to Europe and back means at least $1,000 (and often lots more) of personal expense, which is too much to permit an "I'll take my chances" type of vacation. Hence a little advance planning is crucial. This is not to suggest that you have to work out the details of your stay or itinerary in minute detail in advance, but that by considering where you want to go, what you want to do, and how much you want to spend, you'll find it much easier to avoid delays and unexpected expenses and eliminate the need to alter your plans because of unforeseen developments.

In thinking out your trip, start with the following basics:

1. How much time will you have for your trip?
2. Do you want to visit one, a few, or several different places?
3. During what time of the year do you plan to travel? (It can make a considerable difference in what's open and functioning at your destination as well as in the cost of transportation and accommodations.)
4. How much money do you have to spend on your trip?
5. Do you want an unstructured trip (in which you'll be be on your own when you get to your destination), or would you prefer the company and schedule of an escorted tour?

With firm answers to these major questions, start reviewing literature on the places in which you're most interested. Almost all European countries have tourist offices in North America that are ready sources for brochures or other information on features of their respective countries (their addresses are listed in *National Tourist Offices in the US*, GETTING READY TO GO). For those few that don't (likely to be in Eastern Europe), contact their consulates, embassies, or missions to the United Nations. Still other good sources of information are airlines, hotel representatives, and travel agents, who should be well supplied with literature from wholesalers and tour operators who organize packages and other travel arrangements to Europe. (Many of the major airlines, car rental services, and other travel businesses have toll-free (800) telephone numbers that can be obtained by dialing 800-555-1212 and asking for the companies' toll-free numbers for your area. In other words, up-to-date travel information on almost all the countries of Europe is plentiful and you should be able to accumulate not only everything you want to know about the places you want to visit, but also about the tours and packages that are available to each.

You can now make almost all of your own travel arrangements if you have the time to follow through with hotels, airlines, tour operators, and so on. But you'll probably save considerable time and energy if you have a travel agent make reservations and arrangements for you. The agent also should be able to advise you of alternative arrangements of which you may not be aware. A travel agent's services won't cost you any money and may even save you some (see *How to Use a Travel Agent,* GETTING READY TO GO). Well before departure (depending on how much in advance you make your reservations) the agent will supply you with a packet that includes all your tickets and hotel confirmations, and often a day-by-day outline of where you'll be when, along with a detailed list of whatever flights or trains you're taking.

Before your departure, find out what the weather is likely to be at your destinations at the time of year you'll be visiting. And if you're planning an extended stay in any city or country, you'll find it useful to read a bit about the country's history, its food specialties, people, and places of interest, especially if you are visiting for the first time.

Before you leave, put your house in order: Pay all the bills, cancel newspapers, and arrange for mail to be held at the post office; have a good friend check the pipes and water the plants; and generally don't advertise your departure.

Make a list of any valuable items you are carrying with you, including credit card numbers and the serial numbers of your traveler's checks. Put copies in your luggage to facilitate identification in case of loss. Put your name and business address — *but never your home address* — on a label on the exterior of your luggage.

Review your travel documents. If you are traveling by air, check to see that your ticket has been filled in correctly. The left side of the ticket should have a list of each stop you will make (even if you are only stopping to change planes), beginning with your departure point. Be sure that the list is correct, and count the number of carbons to see that you have one for each plane you will take. If you have confirmed reservations, be sure that the column marked "status" says "OK" beside each flight (but don't forget to reconfirm 72 hours before flight time). Have in hand vouchers or proof of payment (preferably from the hotels themselves) for any reservations for which you've paid in advance; this includes hotels, transfers to and from the airport, sightseeing tours, car rentals, special events, and so on.

How to Pack

 The goal is to remain perfectly comfortable, neat, and clean, and adequately fashionable wherever you go, but actually to pack as little as possible. The main obstacle to achieving this end is habit: Most of us wake each morning with an entire wardrobe hanging in our closets, and we assume that our suitcase should offer the same variety and selection. Not so; only our anxiety about being caught short makes us treat a suitcase like a mobile closet, and you can eliminate even the anxiety (and learn to travel lightly) by following two firm packing principles:

1. Organize your travel wardrobe around a single color — blue or brown, for example — that allows you to mix and match clothes. Holding firm to one color scheme will make it easy to eliminate items of clothing that don't harmonize. Pick clothes for their adaptability and compatibility with your basic color; you will put together the widest variety of wardrobe with the fewest pieces of clothing.
2. Use laundries to renew your wardrobe. Never overpack to ensure a supply of fresh clothing — shirts, blouses, underwear — for each day of a long trip. Businesspeople routinely use hotel laundries to wash and clean clothes and, if these prove too expensive, there are self-service laundromats in most towns of any size.

Climate and Clothes – The real determinant of what to pack for a trip to Europe is where and when you are going. There are few useful generalities to be made about weather on a continent as disparate as Europe, because most of it is farther north than most of the United States and yet its weather, in the main, is milder. London, for example, sits astride latitude 51° 30′, about even with Québec's Gaspé Peninsula. But Great Britain and Ireland are warmed by the Gulf Stream, and it is a cold winter indeed that brings to London more than a few days below 25°F (about −4°C). Every country in Europe has distinct seasonal changes (including Greece and Spain), but the degree, duration, and drama of the changes vary widely.

Such general observations serve to tell you that in all probability your current winter or summer wardrobe contains everything you will need for a trip to Europe. It's unlikely you'll encounter unique or extreme weather conditions that require new clothes. But to pick and choose from your wardrobe appropriately you will need weather information on your specific destinations. This is available in the *Climate and Clothes* sections of FACTS IN BRIEF and the individual city reports in THE EUROPEAN CITIES, as well as in the chart of European temperature ranges that accompanies *When to Go*, GETTING READY TO GO. Other sources of specific information are European tourist authorities with offices in the US; airlines that serve your destination; and your travel agent, who should be able to provide useful, personal tips on clothing requirements at the time of year you are traveling.

The key to meeting a variety of weather and climate changes *and* still traveling light is the "layered look." In terms of travel, it means a shirt on top of a T-shirt, with possibly a couple of sweaters on top of both, topped off by a jacket or a Windbreaker over all. The idea of layering is to permit you to stay warm while allowing you to strip off layers in response to temperature changes. It is also adapted to the ruling principle of dressing according to a single color scheme. Individual items in layers can mix and match, to be used together or independently.

Fashion – Be guided by your own taste. Europe is no more formal than North America, and whatever makes you feel comfortable probably will be accepted. Certainly the lucky fellow attending an opening night at Milan's La Scala opera house should be wearing formal attire, but on any other night he'd be perfectly comfortable and acceptable in a jacket, tie, and trousers. (And European students have been attending opera for years in blue jeans, so don't make yourself crazy.) A blazer, trousers, and tie will also get a man into the finest restaurants in Europe. Of course, there will be diners at other tables more formally dressed, but you won't be turned away or made to feel self-conscious.

If you'll be touring several countries, select clothing on the basis of what can serve several functions. Coordinates are an easy way for a woman to vary her wardrobe without adding to luggage content. For a man, one dark suit will suffice when coupled with sports jackets and several pairs of slacks. Synthetics are immensely practical for this type of trip. Added musts for men and women alike are a sweater and walking shoes.

Packing – A recommended packing procedure is the so-called layer method, designed to get everything in and out of a bag with as few wrinkles as possible. Heavy items go on the bottom and sides, and corners are stuffed with such articles as socks, underwear, shoes, handbags, and bathing suits. Then layer on the more easily wrinkled items, such as shirts and slacks, dresses and skirts, even jackets. Pack them with as few folds as possible. On the top layer put the immediate needs, such as bed clothing, sweater, raincoat, and the like. Make the layers even and the total content as full and firm as possible to keep the contents from shifting around during transit.

Traveling Wrinkle-Free – While packing, interleave each layer of clothes with plastic cleaning bags, which will help preserve pressed clothes while they are in the suitcase. Unpack your bags as soon as you get to a hotel. Nothing so destroys clean and pressed clothes as sitting for days in a suitcase. Finally, if something is badly wrinkled and can't be professionally pressed before you must wear it, hang it overnight in a bathroom where the bathtub has been filled with very hot water; keep the bathroom door closed so the room becomes something of a steam room. It really works miracles.

Some Final Packing Hints – Try to select toiletries and cosmetics that come in plastic containers. Bottled liquids should be placed in plastic bags. If traveling overnight, put a few necessary toiletry items in a purse, the aforementioned shoulder bag, or some other small, easily carried case. Add an emptied airline bag to your suitcase; you'll find it handy for overnight trips, beach outings, or for carrying purchases home. Don't ever put necessities such as medicine, travel documents, cash, or credit cards in your luggage; keep them in a piece of hand luggage that you carry.

How to Use a Travel Agent

 A reliable travel agent remains your best source of service and information for planning a trip abroad, whether you have a specific itinerary that only requires reservations or need extensive help in sorting through the maze of air fares, tour offerings, hotel packages, and the scores of other arrangements required for a trip to the Continent.

You should know what you want from a travel agent to evaluate what you are getting. It is perfectly reasonable to expect your travel agent to be a thorough travel specialist, with information about your destination, and, even more crucial, a command of current air fares, package tours, charters, ground arrangements, and other details.

To make the most intelligent use of a travel agent's time and expertise, you should know something of the economics of the industry. As a client, you traditionally pay nothing for the services performed by the agent; it's all free, from the booking of hotels to general advice on the best alpine lodges. Any money that the travel agent makes on the time spent arranging your itinerary — booking hotels, resorts, or flights, or suggesting activities — comes from commissions paid by the suppliers who provide these services — the airlines, hotels, and so on. These commissions generally run anywhere from 7% to 15% of the total cost of the booking. In some cases an agent may ask you to pay a fee for exceptional service such as planning a lengthy, personal itinerary or making reservations at places that do not pay commissions. In most instances, however, you'll find that agents provide their traditional services at no charge.

This system implies two things about your relationship with any travel agent.

1. You will get better service if you arrive at the agent's desk with your basic itinerary already planned. Know roughly where you want to go, what you want to do, and how much you want to spend. Use the agent to make bookings for you (which pay commissions) and to advise you on facilities, activities, and alternatives within the parameters of the basic itinerary you have chosen. You get the best service when you are requesting commissionable items. There are few commissions on camping or driving-camping tours; an agent is unlikely to be very enthusiastic about helping to plan one.
2. There is always the danger that an incompetent or unethical agent will send you to a place offering the best commission rather than the best facilities for your purposes, so be watchful.

You should choose a travel agent with the same care with which you would choose a doctor or lawyer. You will be spending a good deal of money on the basis of the agent's judgment, and you have a right to expect that judgment to be mature, informed, and interested. At the moment, unfortunately, there are no real standards within the travel agent industry to help you gauge an agent's competence or expertise. The quality of individual agents varies enormously. While several states are in the process of drawing up legislation for licensing agents — which would at least ensure that anyone acting as a travel agent has met some minimum standards — only four states at present have any form of registration on their books. However, one industry organization, the American Society of Travel Agents (ASTA) requires its member agencies, which must be accredited to a major airline association, such as the International Air Transport Association, to adhere to its strict Principles of Professional Conduct and Ethics code. If you feel you have been improperly or unfairly dealt with, complaints can be made to ASTA's Consumer Affairs Department, 4400 MacArthur Blvd., NW, Washington, DC 20007 (phone: 202-965-7520). The Association of Retail Travel Agents (ARTA) is a smaller but very highly respected trade organization similar to ASTA, and its member agencies and agents similarly agree to abide by a Code of Ethics. Complaints about an ARTA member's service can be made to ARTA's Grievance Committee, 25 S Riverside Ave., Croton-on-Hudson, NY 10520 (phone: 914-271-9000). More useful is the knowledge that any travel agent who has been in the business for at least 5 years and has completed the 18-month course of study conducted by the Institute of Certified Travel Agents in Wellesley, Massachusetts, will carry the initials CTC (Certified Travel Counselor) after his or her name. This indicates a relatively high level of expertise.

Perhaps the best way to find a travel agent is by word of mouth. If the agent (or agency) has done a good job for friends over a period of time, it probably indicates a level of commitment and concern. But always ask for the name of the specific agent within an agency, for it is that individual who will serve you, and quality can vary widely within a single agency.

Insurance

 It is unfortunate that most decisions to buy travel insurance are impulsive and are usually made without any real consideration of the traveler's existing insurance policies. Too often the result is the purchase of needlessly expensive short-term policies that duplicate existing coverage and reinforce the tendency to buy coverage on a trip-by-trip basis rather than to work out a total and continuing travel insurance package that might well be more effective and economical.

Therefore, the first person with whom you should discuss travel insurance is your own insurance broker — not a travel agent or the clerk behind the airport insurance counter. You may well discover that the insurance you already carry — homeowner's policies and/or accident, health, and life insurance policies — protect you adequately while you travel, and that your real needs are in the more mundane areas of excess value insurance for baggage, or trip cancellation insurance.

To make insurance decisions intelligently, however, you should first understand the basic categories of travel insurance and what they are designed to cover. Then you can decide what you need in the broader context of your personal insurance needs, and you can choose the most economical way of getting the desired protection — through riders on existing policies; with one-shot short-term policies; through a special program put together for the frequent traveler; through coverage that's a part of various travel club benefits; or with a combination policy sold by insurance companies through brokers, tour operators, and even travel agents.

There are five basic categories of travel insurance: baggage and personal effects; personal accident and sickness; trip cancellation and interruption; flight (to cover death or injury); automobile (driving one's own car or a rental).

Baggage and Personal Effects Insurance – If baggage and personal effects are included in your current homeowner's policy, check with your broker about the necessity of a special floater to cover you for the duration of a trip. The object is to protect your bags and their contents in case of damage or theft anytime during your travels, not just while you're in flight and covered by the airline's policy. Furthermore, only limited protection is provided by the airline. For most international flights, including domestic portions of international flights, the airline's liability limit is approximately $20 per kilo ($9.07 per pound) for checked baggage and $400 per passenger for unchecked baggage. (On domestic flights, the limit of liability on most airlines is $1,250 per passenger.) But these limits, which should be specified in the fine print of your ticket, represent maximums, and to be awarded even this amount, you'll have to provide an itemized list of lost property. If you're including new and/or expensive items, be prepared to back up your claim with sales receipts or other proofs of purchase.

If you are carrying goods worth more than the maximum protection offered by the airline, you should consider excess value insurance, available from the individual airline. Currently, a typical charge is 50¢ per $100 of protection. Insurance can be purchased at the airline counter when you check in, though you should arrive early to fill out the necessary forms and to avoid keeping other checking-in passengers waiting while you transact your insurance purchase. Excess value insurance is also included in certain of the combination travel insurance policies discussed below.

■ **ONE NOTE OF WARNING:** Be sure to read the fine print of any excess value insurance policy; there are often specific exclusions, such as money, tickets, furs, gold and silver objects, art, and antiques. And remember that insurance companies ordinarily will pay only the depreciated value of the goods rather than their replacement value. To best protect the items you're carrying in your luggage, have photos made of valuables, and keep a record of all serial numbers of such items as cameras, typewriters, radios, and so on. (Original purchase receipts can also be useful in later litigation with the airlines.) This will establish that you do, indeed, own the objects. If your luggage disappears en route or is damaged, deal with the situation immediately, at the airport, train station, or bus station. If an airline loses your luggage, you will be asked to fill out a Property Irregularity Report before you leave the airport. If your property disappears elsewhere, make a report to the police at once.

Personal Accident and Sickness Insurance – This insures you in case of illness on the road (hospital and doctor's expenses, lost income, and so on). In most cases it is a standard part of existing health insurance policies, though you should check with your broker to be sure that your policy will pay for medical expenses incurred abroad.

Trip Cancellation Insurance – Most package tours, cruises, and charter flights require full payment a substantial period of time before departure. Although cancellation penalties vary, rarely will you get more than 50% of this money back if forced to cancel within a few weeks of leaving. Any refund of money paid for a charter flight canceled even well in advance may depend on your being able to supply a substitute passenger. Therefore, if you take a package tour or charter, you should have cancellation insurance to guarantee full refund of your money should you, a traveling companion, or a member of your immediate family get sick and force you to cancel your trip or *return home early.* The key here is *not* to buy just enough insurance to guarantee full reimbursement in the case of cancellation. The proper amount of coverage should be sufficient to cover the cost of having to catch up with a tour after its normal departure date or having to return home at the full economy air fare if you have to forgo the return portion of a discounted flight (such as an excursion with advance purchase requirements), and especially if you have to forgo the return portion of a charter flight.

Cancellation insurance designed to cover a specific package is frequently offered by tour operators. Otherwise, it can be bought through travel agents or from insurance companies or their agents as part of a combination travel insurance policy. Read any policy carefully before you buy it. Be sure it provides enough money to get you home from the farthest point on your itinerary. Also, be sure to check the specific definition of "family members" and "pre-existing medical condition." Some policies will not pay if you become ill from a condition for which you have received treatment in the past.

Note that trip cancellation insurance usually protects you in the event that you, the traveler, are unable to take — or complete — your trip. A recent innovation is coverage in the event of default and/or bankruptcy on the part of the tour operator, airline, or other travel supplier. In some travel insurance packages, this contingency is included in the trip cancellation portion of the coverage; in others, it is a separate feature. Either way, it is becoming increasingly pertinent. Whereas most travelers have long known to beware of the possibility of default or bankruptcy when buying a charter flight or tour, in recent years, more than a few respected scheduled airlines have unexpectedly revealed their shaky financial condition, sometimes leaving stranded ticketholders in their wake. Moreover, the value of escrow protection of a charter passenger's funds has lately come into question. While default/bankruptcy insurance will not ordinarily result in reimbursement in time for you to pay for new arrangements, it can assure that you will eventually get your money back, and even independent travelers buying no more than an airplane ticket may want to consider it.

Flight Insurance – Airlines have carefully established limits of liability for the death or injury of passengers. For international flights these are printed right on the ticket: a maximum of $75,000 in case of death or injury. But remember, these limits of liability are not the same thing as insurance policies; they merely state the *maximum* an airline will pay in the case of death or injury, and every penny of that is usually subject to a legal battle.

This may make you feel that you are not adequately protected. But before you buy last-minute flight insurance from an airport vending machine, as many passengers do, consider the purchase in light of your total existing insurance coverage. A careful review of your current policies may reveal that you are already amply covered for accidental death, sometimes up to three times the amount provided for by the specific flight insurance you're buying in the airport.

Be aware that airport insurance, the kind you typically buy from a counter or a vending machine, is among the most expensive forms of life insurance coverage available anywhere, and that even within a single airport, rates for approximately the same coverage can vary. Often the vending machines are more expensive than coverage sold over the counter, even when policies are with the same national company.

If you buy your ticket with an American Express, Diners Club, or Carte Blanche credit card, you are issued automatic accident and accidental death insurance at no extra cost. American Express automatically provides $100,000 in free accidental death insurance; Diners Club and Carte Blanche, $150,000. Each of these cards offers additional coverage at extremely reasonable prices. For $3, holders of any of these cards can buy $250,000 of flight insurance (or $500,000 for $5.50).

Combination Policies – A number of insurance companies offer all-purpose travel insurance packages that include baggage, personal accident and sickness, trip cancellation insurance, and, sometimes, default and bankruptcy protection. They cover you for a single trip and are sold by travel agents, insurance agencies, and others. One such policy available through travel agents is Travel Guard, endorsed by the American Society of Travel Agents.

Automobile Insurance – Public liability and property damage (third party) insurance are compulsory in Europe, and whether you drive your own car or a rental, you must carry insurance. Every car rental contract has optional insurance (it adds only a few dollars to the total price of the contract); you must take it to drive in Europe. Your contract (with appropriate insurance box ticked off) will suffice as proof of insurance. If you drive your own car you must carry an International Insurance Certificate (called a Green Card), available through insurance brokers in the US.

Hints for Handicapped Travelers

Roughly 35 million people in the US alone suffer from some sort of disability. At least half this number are physically handicapped. Like everyone else today, they — and the uncounted disabled millions around the world — are on the move. More than ever before the disabled are demanding facilities they can use comfortably, and they are being heard. Accessibility, both here and abroad, is being brought up to more acceptable standards every day. Although the US travel industry has only recently awakened to these needs, service in many European countries — especially in Switzerland, Great Britain, the Netherlands, and Scandinavia — has been provided with the disabled in mind for some time.

Planning – It is essential to make travel arrangements in advance and to specify to all services involved the degree of your disability or restricted mobility. There are some excellent organizations to help you. Rehabilitation International/USA (RIUSA) is a national organization that provides information and services to the disabled and is affiliated with similar organizations in more than 75 countries. RIUSA publishes the *International Directory of Access Guides,* a free listing of over 450 access guides both domestic and international with information on where to write for them. For the latest edition of the directory, send $1 to cover postage to RIUSA, Travel Survey Department, Rehabilitation/World, 1123 Broadway, Suite 704, New York, NY 10010 (phone: 212-620-4040).

Another organization, Mobility International, has contacts in some 45 countries and offers advice and assistance to the disabled, including information on accommodations, access guides, and organized tours. Write Mobility International USA (MIUSA), PO Box 3551, Eugene, OR 97403 (phone: 503-343-1284, voice and TTY).

The Travel Information Center at Moss Rehabilitation Hospital is a free service designed to help handicapped people plan trips. To obtain information about particular cities or countries or any special interests you have, write to the Travel Information Center, Moss Rehabilitation Hospital, 12th St. and Tabor Rd., Philadelphia, PA 19141 (phone: 215-329-2468).

To keep abreast of developments in travel for the handicapped as they occur, you may want to join the Society for the Advancement of Travel for the Handicapped (SATH), an organization devoted exclusively, as its name implies, to promoting and servicing handicapped travelers. Tax-deductible membership costs $40 per year ($20 to students) and includes a quarterly newsletter. Contact SATH, 26 Court St., Brooklyn, NY 11242 (phone: 718-858-5483).

An excellent book to consult is Louise Weiss's *Access to the World: A Travel Guide for the Handicapped* (Facts on File; $14.95). Weiss provides extensive information on transportation and hotels and offers sound tips for the disabled traveler abroad. Mary Meister Walzer's *A Travel Guide for the Disabled: Western Europe* (Van Nostrand Reinhold; $11.95) gives a country-by-country listing of hotels and restaurants along with their access ratings and provides other useful information. Frommer's *A Guide for the Disabled: The United States, Canada, & Europe* (Simon & Schuster; $10.95), by Frances Barish, contains chapters on London, Paris, Amsterdam, and Vienna. Another book of note, *TravelAbility* by Lois Reamy (Macmillan; $13.95), is mainly for travel in the US but useful to handicapped travelers whatever their destination. There is also a travel magazine, *The Itinerary,* for people with disabilities. It comes out every other month with information on accessibility, listings of tours, news of devices, travel aids, and special services as well as numerous general hints. To sub-scribe ($7 a year), write to *The Itinerary*, PO Box 1084, Bayonne, NJ 07002 (phone: 201-858-3400).

Other good sources of information are the tourist offices of the particular countries you plan to visit. Many publish brochures specifically for the handicapped, although not always in English. The Danish Tourist Board's *Access in Denmark — A Tourist Guide for the Disabled* and the Netherlands National Tourist Office's *Holiday in Holland for the Handicapped* are two particularly comprehensive publications, both available in English. The Norwegian Tourist Board publishes a guide to accessible accommodations, and the Irish Tourist Board, to accommodations and restaurants. The British Tourist Authority's *Britain for the Disabled* booklet lists the names and addresses of numerous British organizations serving the disabled in a variety of capaci-ties. For the US addresses of these and other government tourist authorities, see *National Tourist Offices in the US*, GETTING READY TO GO.

Air Travel – Disabled passengers should make reservations well in advance and provide the airline with all relevant details of their condition when doing so. These include information on mobility, toileting, whether or not you use oxygen, and whether airline-supplied equipment such as a wheelchair or portable oxygen will be necessary. Be sure that the person you speak with understands fully the degree of your disability. Then, the day before the flight, call back to make sure that all arrangements have been taken care of, and on the day of the flight, arrive early so that you can board before the rest of the passengers. Carry with you a medical certificate stating your specific disability or the need to carry particular medicines (some airlines require the certifi-cate). In most cases, you can be wheeled as far as the plane, and sometimes right onto it, in your own wheelchair; if not, a boarding chair may be used. Your own wheelchair will be folded and put in the baggage compartment and should be tagged as escort luggage to assure that it's available at planeside immediately upon landing rather than in the baggage claim area.

The Airport Operators Council International puts out a guide to the accessibility of more than 470 airports here and abroad called *Access Travel: Airports*. For a free copy, write to Access America, Washington, DC 20202. Useful information on every stage of air travel from planning to arrival is provided in *Incapacitated Passengers Air Travel Guide*, a booklet published by the International Air Transport Association (IATA). To receive a copy, also free, write to Senior Manager, Passenger Services, IATA, 2000 Peel St., Montréal, Québec H3A 2R4, Canada (phone: 514-844-6311).

Travel by Ship – The best-equipped ship for the handicapped is the Cunard's *Queen Elizabeth II*. All but the top deck is accessible. Be sure to provide the ship's manage-ment with details of your condition and a physician's letter.

Travel by Train – Though many European railways are accessible to the handi-capped, information in English varies. Check with tourist offices or a travel agent.

Tours – The following travel agencies and tour operators specialize in group tours or independent travel arrangements for the handicapped. Their tour packages are thoroughly researched in advance to make sure that hotels, restaurants, and places of interest present no insurmountable obstacles.

Evergreen Travel Service/Wings on Wheels Tours, 19505 L, 44th Ave. W, Lynn-wood, WA 98036 (phone: 206-776-1184; 800-562-9298 in Washington State). Handles cruises, group tours, and individual arrangements for the physically disabled and the blind.

Flying Wheels Travel, Box 382, Owatonna, MN 55060 (phone: 507-451-5005 or 800-533-0363). Handles tours and individual arrangements for the physically disabled and the elderly.

The Guided Tour, 555 Ashbourne Rd., Elkins Park, PA 19117 (phone: 215-

782-1370). Offers group tours for the physically handicapped as well as trips for the developmentally disabled.

Interpretours, Encino Travel Service, 16660 Ventura Blvd., Encino, CA 91436 (phone: 818-788-4118 or 818-788-4515, voice and TTY). Arranges independent travel, cruises, and tours for the deaf, with an interpreter as tour guide.

Travel Horizons Unlimited, 11 E 44th St., New York, NY 10017 (phone: 212-687-5121). Arranges cruises, group tours, and independent travel for those who require hemodialysis.

Hints for Traveling with Children

 What better way to be receptive to the experiences you will encounter than to take along the young, wide-eyed members of your family? Their company does not have to be a burden or their presence an excessive expense. Discount air fares can even make a flight to Europe a plausible alternative to a good summer camp. Furthermore, the trip will be an investment in your children's futures, making geography come alive to them, and a sure memory that will be among the fondest you will share with them someday. Their insights will be refreshing to you; their impulses may take you to unexpected places with unexpected dividends. At whatever age, the experience will be invaluable to them. It is necessary, however, to take some extra time beforehand to prepare for the trip.

Here are several hints for making a trip with children easy and fun.

1. Children should be part of the planning of the trip, and preparations should begin about a month before you leave, using maps, atlases, travel magazines, and travel books to make clear exactly where you are going and how far away it is. Part of the excitement of the journey will be associating the tiny dots on the map with the very real places children visit a few weeks later. You can show pictures of streets and scenes in which they will stand within a month. Don't shirk history lessons, but don't burden them with dates. Make history light, anecdotal, and pertinent.
2. Children should be in on the planning of the itinerary, and where you go and what you do should reflect some of their ideas. If they know enough about architecture and geography before they go, they will have the excitement of recognition when they arrive, and the illumination of seeing how it is or is not like what they expected.
3. Before you leave, eat some traditional foods of the countries you plan to visit. This will familiarize children and excite them about what is to come. They may be surprised by the differences in the same dishes prepared absolutely authentically.
4. Learn the language with your children — a few basics like "hello," "good-bye," and "thank you." You need no other motive than a perfectly selfish one: Thus armed, your children will delight Europeans and help break the ice wherever you go.
5. Give children specific responsibilities. They should always carry their own flight bag and look after their own personal things, and some other light travel responsibility will give them a stake in the journey.

Packing – Choose your own and your children's clothes wisely. Take only drip-dry, wrinkle-resistant articles, comfortable shoes — sneakers or sandals — and a few things to keep warm and dry. But keep packing to a minimum. No one likes to carry added luggage, and you'll be surprised that clothes, when abroad, are about the last thing on your mind.

It is a good idea to take along as many handy snacks as you can squeeze into the corners of your suitcases. These should include things like raisins, nuts, sucking candy, and crackers (especially for the tots). Don't worry if your supply is quickly depleted — European airports and train stations are well stocked with such items. Along with these few edibles, pack a special medical kit (see *Medical and Legal Aid Abroad*, GETTING READY TO GO), and some wash-and-dry towellettes for dirty fingers. Have your children take along a few favorite toys. Pens, crayons, and paper take up the least amount of room and can be put to use during long car trips or train rides.

Planning – No matter what the reading level of your children, there are books to prepare them for a trip. The very youngest may enjoy *Babar Loses His Crown* (Random House), in which Babar the elephant sightsees in Paris. Miroslav Sasek's travel series for children (Macmillan) includes *This Is Greece* and *This Is Ireland*, geared to readers grades 3 through 6. The delightful Artstart series by Ernest Raboff (Doubleday), designed to introduce children ages 5 to 12 to famous artists and their works, may help to lengthen their attention span in museums; Piero Ventura's beautifully illustrated *Great Painters* (Putnam) is an excellent introduction to Italian, Flemish, English, and French painting for older children (ages 12 and up). David Macaulay's *Cathedral: The Story of Its Construction* (Houghton Mifflin; kindergarten to grade 5), in which line drawings explain the process to those who cannot read the text, may stimulate an interest in medieval architecture; *Castle* is by the same author. James Giblin's *Walls: Defenses Throughout History* (Little, Brown), discusses the walled city of Carcassonne, Hadrian's Wall in England, and the great defensive walls of World Wars I and II, among others, and will appeal to teenage readers.

Getting There and Getting Around – Take time to investigate all available discount and charter flights as well as any package deals and special rates offered by the major airlines. Sometimes booking is required up to 2 months in advance. Are there special reductions for children? The answer, happily, is almost always yes. Children under 2 usually travel at 10% of the accompanying adult's fare on airplanes as long as you keep them on your lap. (Don't despair, though. If there are empty seats around you, no one will object to your putting your child down. Armrests on airplanes are generally removable.) Children ages 2 through 11 usually travel at one-half to two-thirds the adult fare. Given advance notice, airlines will provide special infant seats and children's meals. For landings and takeoffs, have a bottle or pacifier on hand for the infants and some gum or sucking candy for older children. This will keep everyone swallowing properly and ensure against earaches caused by rapid changes in air pressure. Newborn babies, whose lungs may not be able to adjust to the altitude, should not be taken aboard an airplane. (Note: Some airlines refuse to carry pregnant women in their eighth or ninth month, for fear something could go wrong with an in-flight birth. Check with the airline ahead.)

By ship, children usually travel at a considerably reduced fare. Train travel in many European countries is free for very young children (sometimes provided they do not occupy a seat) and half price for older children. If you are considering buying a Eurailpass, good for unlimited train travel throughout Europe, note that it, too, is half price for those under 12 (under 4, free). Many countries, among them France, Germany, Italy, Switzerland, Great Britain, and Ireland, have their own national rail passes, and most of them feature 50% discounts for children. Rail passes must usually be bought in the US; inquire at the tourist offices of the countries you plan to visit.

Accommodations and Meals – Often a cot will be placed in a hotel room at little or no extra charge. If you wish to sleep in separate rooms, special rates are sometimes available for families in adjoining rooms. You might want to look into accommodations along the way that will add to the color of your trip. For instance, there are many country inns, farms, and villas throughout Europe that will be a treat for the whole family. (See *Hotels, Pensions, and Special Places in Europe*, GETTING READY TO GO.)

And don't forget castles, many of which double as hotels. Your children will love them. Camping facilities throughout Europe are generally excellent and are often situated in beautiful, out-of-the-way spots. They are usually well equipped and cheaper than any hotel you will come across.

As far as food goes, don't deny yourself or your children the delights of a new cuisine. Encourage them to try new things and don't forget about picnics. There are many small grocery shops throughout the Continent which sell fresh bread, cheese, and cold cuts. There's nothing lovelier than stopping in your tracks at a beautiful view, eating lunch as you muse on the surroundings.

What to See and Do – For specific suggestions on what to see and do, see the individual city reports in THE EUROPEAN CITIES. Here are some general things to remember: First and foremost, don't forget that a child's attention span is far shorter than that of an adult. Children don't have to see every museum to learn something from their trip. Watching, playing with, and talking to other children can be equally enlightening experiences. Try to break up the day into short, palatable segments: no more than a morning or afternoon dedicated to any one activity, be it travel or sight-seeing. Also, remember the places that children the world over love to visit: zoos, of which there are many in Europe; country fairs and small amusement parks; beaches and nature trails. Let your children lead the way sometimes: You are bound to see things you would never have noticed on your own.

Hints for Single Travelers

 Just about the last trip in human history in which the participants were neatly paired was the voyage of Noah's Ark. Ever since, passenger lists and tour groups have reflected the same kind of asymmetry that occurs in real life, as countless individuals set forth to see the world unaccompanied (or unencumbered, depending on your outlook) by spouse, lover, friend, or relative.

There are very significant attractions to traveling alone. It forces you to see more; it requires that you be self-reliant, independent, and responsible. Traveling alone necessitates that you be more outgoing, and, therefore, you tend to meet more people than you would have had you been traveling in a pair. And unfortunately, it also turns you into a second-class citizen.

For the truth is that the travel industry is not yet prepared to deal fairly with people who vacation by themselves. Most travel bargains, including package tours, hotel accommodations, resort packages, and cruises, are based on *double-occupancy* rates. This means that the per-person price is offered on the basis of two people traveling together and sharing a double room. For exactly the same package, the single traveler will have to pay a surcharge, called the "single supplement," which can add 30% to 55% to the basic per-person rate.

Don't despair, however. Throughout Europe, there are scores of inexpensive guesthouses and small hotels. In addition to a more cozy atmosphere, prices (which usually include a delicious breakfast) are still quite reasonable for the single traveler. If you prefer to have your arrangements taken care of for you, a number of options have emerged. Cosmos, the British tour operator specializing in budget motorcoach tours of Europe, offers a plan whereby singles who wish to share rooms are matched with like-minded individuals and charged the basic tour price. Those wishing to stay on their own, of course, pay the single supplement. Cosmos tours can be booked through travel agents. Singleworld, which organizes its own packages and also books singles on the cruises and tours of others, similarly arranges shared accommodations if requested, charging a one-time surcharge that is much less than the single supplement would be. Singleworld — actually a club joined through travel agents for a yearly fee of $18, paid at the time of booking — is one of the many organizations catering solely to single vacationers of all ages. Some charge membership fees; others offer their services free. But the basic service offered by all is to match the unattached person with a compatible travel mate. The Travel Companion Exchange (PO Box 833, Amityville, NY 11701; phone: 516-454-0880) is one that functions on a membership basis ($29 for 6 months; $53 for a year). Members fill out a questionnaire to establish a personal profile and also write a small listing much like an ad in a personal column. This listing is circulated to other members, who can request the complete questionnaire and then make contact to plan a joint vacation.

Another organization that heartily welcomes singles is Club Méditerranée, an attractive option for those wishing to meet people of other nationalities. Of Club Med's 100 or so vacation villages in countries around the world, approximately half are in Europe — and their clientele is predominantly European. Activities include tennis, scuba diving, snorkeling, yoga, bridge, sailing, swimming, and skiing; there are no televisions, telephones, or newspapers — it's a vacation from everything. For further details, contact Club Méditerranée, 3 E 54th St., New York, NY 10022 (phone: in Alaska or Hawaii, 602-948-9190, collect; in Arizona, 800-352-3103; elsewhere, 800-528-3100).

Two specific groups of single travelers deserve special mention: women and students. There are countless women who travel alone in Europe. Such a venture need not be feared. Traveling alone is no different from living alone at home. A woman eating alone in a restaurant is neither an uncommon sight nor scorned. Unwanted admirers can usually be best dealt with by ignoring them. In fact, most European cities are generally regarded as safer than American cities — for everyone, including single women.

A large number of single travelers, needless to say, are students. There are many benefits for students abroad, and the place to begin is by applying for an International Student Identity Card (ISIC) before you leave home. Reductions on train and air fares, and free entry to most museums and other exhibits are only some of the advantages of this card — it includes medical and accident insurance for overseas travel. Application requires an $8 fee, a passport-size photograph, and proof that you are a full-time student (this means a letter or bill from your school registrar with the school's official seal; high school and junior high school students can use their report cards). To apply, write to the Council on International Educational Exchange (CIEE) at 205 E 42nd St., New York, NY 10017 (phone: 212-661-1414), or at 312 Sutter St., San Francisco, CA 94108 (phone: 415-421-3473). There is no maximum age limit, but you must be at least 12 years old. This organization, which administers a variety of work, study, and travel programs for students, also sponsors charter flights to Europe that are open to the public.

You need not be a student to be eligible for the Eurail Youthpass. It entitles young people under 26 who are not permanently residing in Western Europe or North Africa to unlimited second-class rail travel throughout 16 participating European countries. This must be purchased while still in the US. To obtain the pass, contact the national tourist office of one of the participating countries. Eurailpasses are also honored on many boats, steamers, and ferries; inquire before you buy your ticket. (See *Travel by Rail*, GETTING READY TO GO.)

Students should also keep in mind that youth hostels exist in many cities throughout Europe. Hostels are a sure place to meet people your own age. They are generally clean, well located, and always cheap. To get a hostel card for hostels run by the International Youth Hostel Federation (IYHF), write to the American Youth Hostels, 1332 I St., NW, Suite 800, Washington, DC 20005 (phone: 202-783-6161). Membership costs $20 for people between 18 and 59; $10 for anyone outside those limits. (If joining through the mail add a $1 handling fee to the price of membership.)

Hints for Older Travelers

Reduced air fares, special package deals, and more free time are just some of the factors that have helped bring the world closer to the some 28 million Americans over age 65. Senior citizens are an ever-growing segment of the travel population. The trend among them is to travel more frequently and for longer periods of time. Retired travelers can also take advantage of off-peak travel, escaping from high prices and crowds. To top it off, discounts are available for senior citizens in countries throughout Europe.

Planning – When packing, bear in mind that you will not always find central heating in European guesthouses, restaurants, and other public places. Only a few warm articles of clothing are necessary, however — remember, one secret to happy traveling is to *pack lightly*. Most common toilet articles, in familiar brands, are available throughout Europe. Be sure to take with you any medication you need, enough to carry you through without a prescription for the duration of your trip; pack it separately in a carryall in case your luggage is lost or detoured, along with a note from your doctor for the benefit of airport authorities. It is also wise to bring a few common medications with you — aspirins and something for stomach upset may come in handy. If you are diabetic or have cardiac problems, carry your medical records with you. Two organizations that provide listings of qualified, English-speaking doctors throughout Europe are the International Association for Medical Assistance to Travelers (IAMAT) and Intermedic. (For information about these services, and other medical services, see *Medical and Legal Aid Abroad,* GETTING READY TO GO.) A word of caution — don't overdo it. Allow time for some relaxing period each day to refresh yourself for the next scheduled sight-seeing event. Traveling across time zones can be exhausting. Plan on spending at least one full day resting before you start touring.

In the US, many hotel and motel chains, airlines, car rental companies, and bus lines offer discounts to older travelers. Some of these discounts, however, are extended only to members of certain senior citizens organizations. Because the same organizations frequently offer package tours at home and abroad, the benefits of membership are twofold. Members can take advantage of discounts as individual travelers and also reap the savings that group travel affords. Age requirements for some of these organizations are quite low or nonexistent. Among them are:

1. *American Association of Retired Persons (AARP):* Travel programs for members cover the globe and include a broad range of escorted motorcoach tours, extended vacations in European cities and resorts, and cruises. Membership is open to anyone age 50 and above, whether retired or not; dues are $5 a year or $12.50 for 3 years. 1909 K St., NW, Washington, DC 20049 (phone: 202-872-4700).
2. *National Council of Senior Citizens:* The roster of tours offered by this organization is different each year, but the emphasis is always on keeping costs low. There is no age requirement, but most members are over 50. The membership fee is an annual $8 per individual or $10 per couple. 925 15th St. NW, Washington, DC 20005 (phone: 202-347-8800).
3. *National Association of Mature People:* Membership is open to anyone age 40 and up at $9.95 per year for either an individual or a couple. PO Box 26792, Oklahoma City, OK 73126 (phone: 405-848-1832).

Many tour operators specialize in group travel for older persons. Gadabout Tours, operated by Lois Anderson, runs escorted trips to Europe. Write to 700 E Tahquitz-McCallum Way, Palm Springs, CA 92262 (phone: 619-325-5556). Grand Circle Travel, which caters exclusively to the over-50 traveler, packages a huge variety (no continent is left untrod) of escorted tours, cruises, and extended vacations in one spot. Contact Grand Circle at 555 Madison Ave., New York, NY 10022 (phone: in New York City, 212-688-5900; elsewhere, 800-221-2610).

Educational travel is another option for older people. Interhostel, sponsored by the Division of Continuing Education of the University of New Hampshire, sends travelers (50 and up) back to school for 2-week sessions at cooperating institutions in various European countries. Contact Interhostel, UNH Division of Continuing Education, Brook House, Rosemary La., Durham, NH 03825 (phone: 603-862-1147). Another organization, Elderhostel, runs programs (for those age 60 and up) from 1 to 3 weeks in length at a vast number of schools in the US, Canada, and overseas. Contact Elderhostel, 80 Boylston St., Suite 400, Boston, MA 02116 (phone: 617-426-7788).

Discounts – Before you go, inquire about discounts for senior citizens at the national tourist offices of the countries you plan to visit. You may be surprised at the number available. Admission to many museums in Austria, for instance, is half-price for seniors, and many Swiss hotels reduce rates off-season or even year-round for seniors (ask the Swiss National Tourist Office for the *Season for Seniors* booklet listing the hotels).

Transportation discounts are particularly plentiful. They frequently go into effect at age 65 (sometimes at age 60 for women and 65 for men) and they may be valid only at certain hours or on certain days, but since they are as high as 50%, they mean significant savings. Among them are France's Carte Vermeil, which allows 50% off rail fares during off-peak hours. It can be obtained by filling out a form at major French railroad stations and presenting it, along with a passport and a fee (about $10), to the designated official at the station. Germany's Senioren-Pass, purchased in a similar fashion for a higher fee, does not restrict travel to specified hours, nor does Switzerland's Senior Half-Fare Travel Card, which can be used on postal motorcoaches and lake boats in addition to trains. It can be bought through travel agents or the Swiss National Tourist Office in the US as well as at stations in Switzerland (a recent passport photo is required). All three of the above cards are valid for a year.

Medical and Legal Aid and Consular Services

 MEDICAL AID ABROAD: The surest way to return home in good health is to be prepared for common medical concerns en route. So before we describe the health facilities available overseas, here are some tips to consider while still in the US.

Prepare a compact and personal medical kit including Band-Aids, first-aid cream, nose drops, suntan cream, insect repellent, aspirins, an extra pair of prescription glasses or sunglasses if you wear them, Lomotil or an equivalent for diarrhea, Dramamine or an equivalent for motion sickness, a thermometer, and a supply of those medicines you take regularly. In the corner of your kit, keep a list of all the drugs you have brought and their purpose as well as a copy of your doctor's prescriptions (or a note from your doctor). This could come in handy if you are ever questioned by police or airport authorities about why you are carrying drugs. It is also a good idea to ask your doctor to prepare a medical identification card that includes such information as your blood type, your social security number, any allergies or chronic health problems you have, and your medical insurance number.

Be sure to check with your insurance company about the applicability of your policy while you're abroad; many policies do not apply, and others are not accepted in Europe.

(Older travelers should note that Medicare does *not* make payments for medical care obtained out of the country.) International Underwriters/Brokers has developed two programs that provide comprehensive coverage for travelers: For only $1 per day (but there is a 25-day minimum) their program, *HealthCare Abroad,* includes a $2,000 blanket sickness and accident benefit (with a $50 deductible), a $15,000 major medical benefit, a $5,000 medical evacuation benefit, and more. There is an age limit of 70, but no medical examination is required. For $2.50 per day (minimum 12 days, maximum 60 days), HealthCare Abroad offers significantly better coverage in terms of dollar limits, and the age limit is 85 (a doctor's certificate is required from age 75). For further information, write to HealthCare Abroad, 923 Investment Bldg., 1511 K St., NW, Washington, DC 20005 (phone: in Virginia, 703-790-5655; elsewhere, 800-336-3310).

Other organizations provide a variety of medical services for travelers. *The International Health Care Service* provides information about health conditions in various foreign countries, advice on immunizations recommended, and treatment if necessary. A pre-travel counseling and immunization package costs $125; a post-travel screening $75 (lab work extra). A list of English-speaking doctors in Europe is available for $1 (and a stamped, self-addressed envelope). The International Health Care Service, New York Hospital–Cornell Medical Center, 440 E 69th St., New York, NY 10021 (phone: for appointments, 212-472-4284).

Membership (individual $6; family $10) in *Intermedic* will bring you a directory of English-speaking physicians in over 90 countries who have indicated a willingness to respond to traveling Intermedic members and agreed to a ceiling on fees for an initial visit. Contact Intermedic, 777 Third Ave., New York, NY 10017 (phone: 212-486-8900). Membership in the *International Association for Medical Assistance to Travelers* — IAMAT — brings a directory of affiliated medical centers in over 100 countries to be called for a list of participating English-speaking doctors who have also agreed to a set payment schedule. Membership costs a minimum donation of $5; for $20, a set of worldwide climate charts detailing weather and sanitary conditions will be included. To join, write well in advance of your trip to IAMAT, 736 Center St., Lewiston, NY 14092 (phone: 716-754-4883).

Medic Alert Foundation International sells identification tags that specify that the wearer has a medical condition — such as a heart condition, diabetes, epilepsy, or severe allergies — that may not be readily apparent to a casual observer. These are conditions that, if unrecognized at a time when emergency treatment is necessary (a time, incidentally, when you may be unable to speak for yourself), can result in tragic treatment errors. In addition to the identification emblems, a central file is maintained (with the telephone number clearly inscribed on the ID) where your complete medical history is available 24 hours a day via a telephone call. The one-time membership fee of $15 to $38 depends upon the type of emblem — stainless steel to 10K gold-filled. For information, contact: Medic Alert, PO Box 1009, Turlock, CA 95381 (phone: in California, 209-668-3333 or 800-468-1020; elsewhere, 800-228-6222).

Assist-Card International provides a number to call — 24 hours a day, 365 days a year — where complete emergency medical assistance can be arranged, including ambulance or air transportation to the proper treatment facilities, local lawyers for a case that is the by-product of an accident, and up to $5,000 in bail bonds for a judicial proceeding that is similarly the result of an accident. They will arrange for a flight home if the traveler is unable to complete the trip because of illness or an accident and will pay any necessary fare differential. This organization also pays the first $3,000 in medical expenses and $500 in prescriptions. Fees for the Assist-Card vary according to the length of the trip abroad, ranging from $30 for a 5-day card to $180 for a 90-day itinerary. For information, contact: Assist-Card Corporation of America, 347 Fifth Ave., New York, NY 10016 (phone: in New York, 212-752-2788; elsewhere, 800-221-4564).

International SOS Assistance also offers a program that covers medical emergencies while traveling. Members are provided with telephone access — 24 hours a day, 365 days a year — to a worldwide monitored multilingual network of medical centers. A phone call brings assistance ranging from telephone consultation to transportation home by ambulance or aircraft, and in some cases transportation of a family member to the place where you are hospitalized. The first $1,000 of sickness or accident bills are insured ($25 deductible). The service can be purchased for a week ($15; each additional day, $2), a month ($45), or a year ($195). For information, contact: International SOS Assistance, Inc., PO Box 11568, Philadelphia, PA 19116 (phone: 215-244-1500 in Pennsylvania; elsewhere, 800-523-8930).

Americans will find drugs available over the counter in Europe that are sold only by prescription in the US, and though this can be very handy be aware that common cold drugs or aspirins that contain codeine or other controlled substances will not be allowed into the US. To make the most effective use of European drugstores, ask your doctor for the generic names of drugs you use so that you can ask for an equivalent medicine abroad. Do not expect European drugstores to fill US prescriptions automatically. Many do, but in Scandinavia, Holland, Great Britain, Ireland, and a few other countries, you may have to have a local doctor rewrite it. There is usually never any problem finding a 24-hour drugstore in any major city throughout Europe.

Medical care abroad is generally less expensive than in North America. In those countries with free public health systems — Great Britain, for example — visitors qualify for free emergency medical aid in certain circumstances only. Emergency dental services are also available through National Health Service dentists. But a word about foreign dentists in general: In many countries, the tendency is to pull out a tooth as soon as it gives the least bit of trouble, so you'd best see your dentist before you leave home.

Generally, water is clean and potable throughout Europe. Still, microbes to which the natives are accustomed may cause newcomers stomach and intestinal upsets. You may wish to stick to bottled mineral water, at least at the beginning of the trip and especially in Eastern Europe and in Mediterranean countries. Similarly, because of Mediterranean pollution and the risk of infectious hepatitis, eat only cooked fish and shellfish.

For further information on medical assistance and facilities in the major European countries, read *Traveling Healthy,* by Sheilah M. Hillman and Robert S. Hillman, MD. Unfortunately out of print, it may be found in the library.

LEGAL AID ABROAD: It is far more serious to be arrested abroad than at home for an infringement of the law, because you are alone and punishment can be more severe. Granted, the American consulate can advise you of your rights and provide a list of English-speaking lawyers, but it cannot interfere with local due process.

The best advice is to be honest and law abiding. If you are issued a traffic ticket, pay it. If you are approached by drug hawkers, ignore them. Penalties for possession of marijuana and other narcotics are generally far more severe than in the US. Also, you may be approached in Eastern Europe by natives eager to buy your American dollars at a profit to you. Again, don't take any risks. You can easily be caught.

CONSULAR SERVICES: There is one crucial place to keep in mind when outside the US — namely, the United States consulate. If you are injured or become seriously ill, the consulate will direct you to medical assistance and notify your relatives. If, while abroad, you become involved in a dispute that could lead to legal action, the consulate, once again, is the place to turn to. And in case of a natural disaster or local civil unrest, the consulate will handle evacuation procedures if called for. Keep in mind, though, that the consulate cannot act as an arbitrator or ombudsman on an American citizen's behalf. The consul has no power, authorized or otherwise, to subvert, alter, or contravene the legal processes, however unfair, of the country in which he or she serves. Nor can a consul oil the machinery of a foreign bureaucracy or provide legal advice. The consul's responsibilities do include providing a list of English-speaking lawyers, information on local sources of legal aid, assignment of an interpreter if the police have none, informing relatives in the US, and the organization and administration of any defense monies sent from home. If a case is tried unfairly or the punishment seems unusually severe, the consul can make a formal complaint to the authorities. In a case of what is called "legitimate and proven poverty," the consul will contact sources of money (such as family or friends in the US), make application for aid to agencies in foreign countries, and, in the last resort, arrange for repatriation at government expense. Consuls will not lend money.

Do not expect the consulate to help you with trivial difficulties such as canceled reservations or lost baggage. The consulate is primarily concerned with the day-to-day administration of services such as issuing passports and visas; providing notarial services; the distribution of VA, social security, and civil service benefits to resident Americans; depositions; extradition cases; and reports to Washington of births, deaths, and marriages of US citizens. A list of US embassies and consulates in Europe follows. The first address listed is always that of the US Embassy; remaining addresses are of consulates in cities other than the one in which the embassy is located.

AUSTRIA: A-1091 Boltzmanngasse 16, Vienna (phone: 222-31-55-11); A-5020 Giselakai 51, Salzburg (662-28-601)

BELGIUM: 27 blvd. du Régent B-1000 Brussels (phone: 02-513-3830); Rubens Center, Nationalestraat 5, B-2000 Antwerp (phone: 03-232-1800)

BULGARIA: 1 A Stamboliiski Blvd., Sofia (phone: 88-45-01 through -05)

CZECHOSLOVAKIA: Trziste 15-12548, Prague (phone: 53-66-41)

DENMARK: Dag Hammarskjölds Alle 24, Copenhagen (phone: 01-42-31-44)

FINLAND: Itainen Puistotie 14A, Helsinki (phone: 17-19-31)

FRANCE: 2 av. Gabriel, 75382 Paris Cedex 08 (phone: 01-296-1202); 22 Cours du Maréchal Foch, 33080 Bordeaux Cedex (phone: 56-52-65-95); 7 Quai Général Sarrail, 69454 Lyon Cedex, 3 (phone: 7-824-6849); 9 rue Armeny, 13006 Marseilles (phone: 91-54-9200); 1 rue du Maréchal Joffre, 06000 Nice (phone: 93-88-89-55 or 93-88-87-72); 15 ave. d'Alsace, 67082, Strasbourg, Cedex (phone: 88-35-31-04 through -06)

GERMANY, EAST: Neustaedtische Kirchstrasse 4–5, 108 Berlin (phone: 220-2741).

GERMANY, WEST: Deichmanns Aue, 5300 Bonn 2 (phone: 0228-339-3390); Cecilienallee 5, 4000 Dusseldorf 30 (phone: 0211-49-00-81); Siesmayerstrasse 21, 6000 Frankfurt Am Main (phone: 0611-74-00-71); Alsterufer 27/28, 2000 Hamburg 36 (phone: 040-44-10-61); Koeniginstrasse 5, 8000 Munich 22 (phone: 089-2-30-11); Urbanstrasse 7, 7000 Stuttgart (phone: 0711-21-02-21)

GREECE: 91 Vasilissis Sophias Blvd., Athens (phone: 721-29-51); 59 Leoforos Nikis, GR-546-22 Thessaloniki (phone: 31-266-121)

HUNGARY: V. Szabadsag Ter. 12, Budapest (phone: 12-64-50)

ICELAND: Laufasvegur 21, Reykjavik (phone: 2-9100)

IRELAND: 42 Elgin Rd., Ballsbridge, Dublin 4 (phone: 68-87-77)

ITALY: Via Veneto 119/A, 00187 Rome (phone: 06-46-74); Banca d'America e d'Italia Bldg., Piazza Portello 6, Genoa (phone: 010-282-741 through 5); Piazza Repubblica 32, 20124 Milan (phone: 02-652-841 through 5); Piazza della Repubblica, 80122 Naples (phone: 081-660-966); Via Vaccarini 1, 90143 Palermo (phone: 091-291-532 through 5); Lungarno Amerigo Vespucci 38, Florence (phone: 055-298-276)

LUXEMBOURG: 22 blvd. Emmanuel Servais, Luxembourg 2535 (phone: 4-0123)

NETHERLANDS: Lange Voorhout 102, The Hague (phone: 070-62-49-11); Museumplein 19, Amsterdam (phone: 020-79-03-21); Baan 50 1, Rotterdam (phone: 010-117-560)

NORWAY: Drammensveien 18, Oslo 2 (phone: 44-85-50)

POLAND: Aleje Ujazdowskie 29/31, Warsaw (phone: 28-30-41 through -49)

PORTUGAL: Av. das Forcas Armadas, 1600 Lisbon (phone: 72-56-00)

ROMANIA: Str. Tudor Arghezi 7–9, Bucharest (phone: 12-40-40)

SPAIN: Serrano 75, Madrid (phone: 276-3400 or -3600); Via Layetana 33, Barcelona (phone: 3-319-9550); Paseo de las Delicias 7, Seville (phone: 54-23-18-85)

SWEDEN: Strandvagen 101, Stockholm (phone: 08-63-05-20)

SWITZERLAND: Jubilaeumstrasse 93, 3005 Bern (phone: 031-43-70-11); Zollikerstrasse 141, 8008 Zurich (01-552-566)

UNITED KINGDOM: 24/31 Grosvenor Sq., London W1A 1AE (phone: 01-499-9000); Queen's House, 14 Queen St., Belfast BT1 6EQ (phone: 228239); 3 Regent Terr., Edinburgh EH7 5BW (phone: 031-556-8315)

USSR: Ulitsa Chaykovskogo 19/21/23, Moscow (phone: 096-252-2451 through -2459); Ulitsa Petra Lavrova 15, Leningrad (phone: 812-274-8235)

YUGOSLAVIA: Kneza Milosa 50, Belgrade (phone: 011-64-56-55); Brace Kavurica 2, Zagreb (041-44-48-00)

If your itinerary includes any country not on the above list, its national tourist office will tell you which consulate or embassy abroad is charged with responsibility for Americans there.

On the Road

Traveler's Checks, Credit Cards, and Foreign Exchange

It may seem hard to believe, but one of the greatest (and least understood) costs of travel is money itself. If that sounds simplistic, consider the fact that you can lose as much as 30% of your dollars' value simply by changing money at the wrong place or in the wrong form. So your one single objective in relation to the care and retention of your travel funds is to make them stretch as far as possible. And when you do spend money, it should be on things that expand and enhance your travel experience, not on unnecessaries. This requires more than merely ferreting out the best air fare or the most charming budget hotel. It means being canny about the management of money itself. Herewith, a primer on making your money go as far as possible.

TRAVELER'S CHECKS: Most people understand the necessity of protecting travel funds from loss or theft by carrying them in the form of replaceable and/or refundable traveler's checks rather than cash. An equally good reason is that traveler's checks invariably get a better rate of exchange than cash does — usually by at least 1%. The reasons for this are rather technical, but it is a fact of travel life that you should not ignore.

That 1% won't do you much good, however, if you have already spent it buying your traveler's checks. Several of the major traveler's check companies charge 1% for the privilege of using their checks; others don't — but the issuing institution (i.e., the particular bank at which you purchase them) may itself charge a fee. Thomas Cook checks issued in US currency are free if you have made your travel arrangements through their travel agency, for example; and if you purchase traveler's checks at a bank in which you maintain significant accounts (especially commercial accounts of some size), you might also find that the bank will absorb the 1% fee as a courtesy to an important customer.

The traveler's checks listed below are readily recognized and convertible in all of the Western European and most of the Eastern European countries covered in this guide. However, don't assume that restaurants, smaller shops, or other establishments in remote locations are going to have change for checks in large denominations. And don't expect change in US currency except at banks and international airports.

We cannot overemphasize the importance of knowing how to replace lost or stolen checks. All of the traveler's checks companies have selling agents around the world, both in their own name and at other associated agencies (usually, but not necessarily, banks), where refunds can be obtained during business hours. Most of them also have 24-hour toll-free telephone lines, and some will even provide emergency funds to tide you over a Sunday. Be sure to make a photocopy of the refund instructions that will be given to you by the issuing institution at the time of purchase. Keep one list in your wallet, but keep the copy with other "emergency information," stashed away in the bottom of your luggage. This emergency packet should include an accurate list of the serial numbers of your traveler's checks, the purchase receipt, your passport number and date of issue, the numbers of any credit cards you have with you, and any other bits of information you can't bear to be without. The serial numbers and purchase receipt will certainly facilitate refund arrangements if the checks are lost or stolen. Here is a list of the major companies issuing traveler's checks and the number to call for refunds.

American Express: To report lost or stolen checks in the continental US, call 800-221-7282; in Alaska and Hawaii, 800-221-4950; from Europe, 801-968-8300, collect.

Bank of America: To report lost or stolen checks in the US except Hawaii, Alaska, and California, 800-227-3460; from those states or outside the US, 415-622-3800, collect.

Citicorp: To report lost or stolen checks anywhere in the US, call 800-645-6556; from Europe, 813-623-1709, collect.

Thomas Cook MasterCard: To report lost or stolen checks anywhere in the US, 212-974-5696, collect. From Europe and Ireland, call this London number collect: 733-502995; from the United Kingdom, dial operator and ask for "free phone 4194," which is toll-free. In Europe, you can also call the nearest branch of Thomas Cook. (*Note:* If you have no success reaching any of these, try calling 212-974-5696, collect, from anywhere in the world; it just won't be as efficient.)

MasterCard: To report lost or stolen checks in the US except New York State, Alaska, and Hawaii, 800-223-9920; from those states or outside the US, 212-974-5696, collect.

Visa: To report lost or stolen checks in California, 800-632-0520; in Alaska or Hawaii, 800-227-6830; elsewhere in the US, 800-227-6811; outside the US, 415-574-7111, collect. From Europe, you can also call this London number collect: 937-8091

TIP PACKS: It's not a bad idea to buy a *small* amount of coins and banknotes of every country you plan to visit in advance of your departure. But note the emphasis on small, because exchange rates for these "tip packs" are uniformly vile. Their advantages are threefold: You become familiar with the currencies (really the only way to guard against being cheated during your first few hours in a new country); you are guaranteed some money should you arrive when a bank or exchange counter isn't open or available; and you don't have to depend on hotel desks, porters, or taxi drivers for change.

A "tip pack" is the only foreign currency you should buy before you leave. Although foreign currency traveler's checks are available from American Express, Thomas Cook, and Deak-Perera (41 E 42nd St., New York, NY 10017; phone: 212-883-0400), the exchange rates are usually worse than you will get in banks abroad, and it is generally better to carry the bulk of your travel funds abroad with you in US dollar traveler's checks.

CREDIT CARDS: There are two different kinds of credit cards available to consumers in the US, and travelers must decide which kind best serves their interests. Convenience cards — American Express, Diners Club, Carte Blanche, are the most widely accepted — cost the cardholder a basic membership fee but put no limit on the amount that may be charged to the card in any month. However, the entire balance must be paid in full at the end of each billing period, so the cardholder is not actually extended any credit — although deferred payment plans can usually be arranged for some types of purchases.

Bank cards, on the other hand, are often issued free, although some banks now charge a fee. They are real credit cards in the sense that the cardholder has the privilege of paying a minimum amount of the total balance in each billing period. For the privilege, an interest rate is charged on the balance owed. In addition, a maximum is set on the amount the cardholder can charge, which represents the limit of credit the card company is willing to extend. Major bank cards are Visa and MasterCard (formerly Master Charge). In Europe, MasterCard goes under the name Eurocard; in Great Britain it's Access; your MasterCard is good wherever these European equivalents are accepted. Visa is Carte Bleue in France and Barclaycard in Great Britain. (Credit cards are rarely accepted in the Federal Republic of Germany, although a few of the major hotels may honor one or another.)

One of the thorniest problems of using credit cards abroad has to do with the rate of exchange at which any purchase is charged. The fact is that the exchange rate in effect on the date that you make a foreign purchase has nothing to do with the rate of exchange at which your purchase is billed to you when you get the invoice months later in the US. The amount American Express charges is ultimately a function of the exchange rate in effect on the day your charge is received at an American Express service center, and there is a one-year limit on the time a shop can take to forward its charge slips. The rate Visa uses to process an item is a function of the rate the shop's bank used to process it. Thus, though up to 60 days may pass between the date of your purchase and the date Visa converts it, the conversion rate usually varies little from the one prevailing about 2 weeks after your purchase, assuming the foreign merchant makes deposits weekly and that his bank processes them in 3 to 5 days.

The principle at work in this credit card–exchange rate roulette is simple, but very hard to predict. You make a purchase at a particular dollar versus local currency exchange rate. If the dollar gets stronger in the time between purchase and billing, your purchase actually costs you less than you anticipated. If the dollar drops in value during the interim, you pay more than you thought you would. There isn't much you can do about these vagaries except to follow one very broad, very clumsy rule of thumb: If the dollar is doing well at the time of purchase, its value increasing against the local currency, use your credit card on the assumption it will still be doing well when billing takes place. If the dollar is doing badly, assume it will continue to do badly and pay with traveler's checks. If you get badly stuck, your only recourse is to complain.

In any case, all types of credit cards are handy additional means to avoid carrying a lot of cash. However, establishments that you may encounter in Europe may not honor *all* the major cards. Therefore, you'll find it helpful if you have several different credit cards with you on your trip to cover some of the costs of shopping, outside meals, or other expenses. Following is a list of credit cards that have wide international use, with some of their key features of greatest significance to travelers and a telephone number for further information:

American Express — Emergency personal check cashing at American Express or representatives' offices (up to $200 cash in local currency, $800 in traveler's checks). Emergency personal check cashing for guests at participating hotels (up to $250 in the US or Canada; $100 elsewhere), and, for holders of airline tickets, at participating airlines in the US (up to $50). Extended payment plan for cruises, tours, and plane tickets. $100,000 free travel accident insurance on plane, train, bus, and ship if ticket was charged to card; up to $1,000,000 additional low-cost flight insurance available. Contact: American Express Card, PO Box 39, Church St. Station, New York, NY 10008 (phone: 800-528-4800).

Carte Blanche — Emergency personal check cashing at participating Hilton hotels in the US (up to $1,000) and for guests at other participating hotels and motels (up to $250 per stay). Extended payment plan for airline tickets. $150,000 free travel accident insurance on plane, train, and ship if ticket was charged to card; up to $500,000 additional low-cost flight insurance available. Contact: Carte Blanche, PO Box 5824, Denver, CO 80217 (phone: 800-525-9135).

Diners Club — Emergency personal check cashing at participating Citibank branches worldwide (up to $1,000, with a minimum per check of $50 in the US and $250 overseas); emergency personal check cashing for guests at participating hotels and motels (up to $250 per stay). Extended payment plan for all charges can be arranged. $150,000 free travel accident insurance on plane, train, and ship if ticket was charged to card; up to $500,000 additional low-cost flight insurance available. Contact: Diners Club, PO Box 5824, Denver, CO 80217 (phone: 800-525-9135).

MasterCard — Cash advance at participating banks worldwide. Interest charge on unpaid balance and other details are set by issuing bank. Check with your bank for information.

Visa — Cash advance at participating banks worldwide. Interest charge on unpaid balance and other details are set by issuing bank. Check with your bank for information.

FOREIGN EXCHANGE: Rule number one is as simple as it is inflexible: Only change your money at banks, where your dollars always buy the greatest amount of foreign currency. Unless someone holds a gun to your head, never, repeat never, exchange dollars for foreign currency at hotels, restaurants, or retail shops, where you are sure to lose a significant amount of your dollar's buying power.

Rule number two: Estimate your money needs carefully; if you overbuy you lose twice — buying and selling back. Every time you exchange money, someone is making a profit, and rest assured, it isn't you. In countries with foreign exchange restrictions (most Eastern European countries), you may be forced to turn in local currency when you leave (and in extreme cases, without the opportunity to sell it back). Use up foreign notes before leaving, saving just enough for airport departure taxes (that often must be paid in local currency) and tips.

Rule number three: Don't buy money on the black market. The exchange rate will be better, but it is a common practice to pass off counterfeit bills to unsuspecting foreigners who aren't familiar with the local currency. If you buy in a country with strict currency control, you also will have no exchange slips that allow you to re-exchange any remaining currency or to account for expenses and purchases you have made. It's usually a sucker's game, and you are almost always the sucker; it also can land you in jail.

Rule number four: Learn the local currency quickly and keep aware of daily fluctuations in the exchange rate. These are listed in every major newspaper in Europe and in the English-language *International Herald Tribune* daily for the preceding day. Rates change to some degree every day. For rough calculations it is quick and safe to use round figures, but for purchases and actual currency exchanges, you should carry a small pocket calculator that allows you to use the exact rate.

Dining Out in Europe

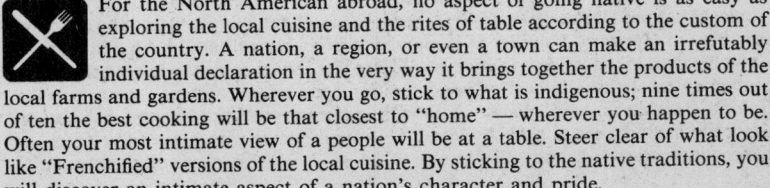

For the North American abroad, no aspect of going native is as easy as exploring the local cuisine and the rites of table according to the custom of the country. A nation, a region, or even a town can make an irrefutably individual declaration in the very way it brings together the products of the local farms and gardens. Wherever you go, stick to what is indigenous; nine times out of ten the best cooking will be that closest to "home" — wherever you happen to be. Often your most intimate view of a people will be at a table. Steer clear of what look like "Frenchified" versions of the local cuisine. By sticking to the native traditions, you will discover an intimate aspect of a nation's character and pride.

There is no better example of this than the food of Britain. The unjustly maligned British cuisine can be excellent if you stick to what the country does best: roasted meats (beef and mutton), grilled chops (pork, lamb, and veal), and meat pies and puddings. Perhaps the best of British cooking comes at breakfast and teatime. As antidote to the cold wet mornings, your bed-and-breakfast may (and should) begin with eggs, bacon, grilled sausages, maybe a grilled kidney and tomato, kippered herring, and, of course, toast, tea, and marmalade. Teatime brings a comforting procession of tea cakes and sandwiches of countless description, crumpets, scones, and Sally Lunns (sweet tea cakes served hot, named for a woman in Bath who first created the recipe 200 years ago), served with dollops of fresh cream and black currant jam. Somerset Maugham reckoned that the only way to survive in England (he lived out his days in the Côte d'Azur) was to have breakfast and tea three times a day. Do not forget that a ready source of satisfying and inexpensive sustenance is the Ploughman's Lunch served in pubs, consisting of (real) English Cheddar cheese, York ham, dark bread, and beer.

In non-English-speaking countries, of course, you will often have the frustrating experience of being presented with a menu that might be written in Martian, for all the information it gives you. An excellent pocket-sized guide available in bookstores is the Berlitz *European Menu Reader,* which will help you decode menus in 14 European languages. It also deals with the differences in American and British terminology.

Moving across the water, to speak of *a* Scandinavian cuisine as though there were only one would offend Danes, Swedes, Finns, and Norwegians alike. However, some elements are shared by these countries: dill, sour cream, herring, and aquavit, of course. Along with the dozen-odd recipes for herring — smoked, pickled, creamed — there are the pickled and smoked versions of salmon from Sweden and Norway. The Finns have over 10,000 lakes so their catch comes equally from fresh and salt water. The lobsterlike freshwater crayfish is particularly prized. Denmark is blessed with an intensive dairy industry and concomitantly fine local blue Tybo (with and without caraway) and, of course, Jarlsberg cheese. You can try them all, if you like, on the national munchie, the Danish open-face sandwich. The Swedish smorgasbørd should be experienced at least once if only to know how to do it properly: Begin with herring, change plates for the salmon, and so on right through the Swedish meatballs. When in Norway head straight for the salmon and the boiled cod with buttered potatoes — the fewer adornments, the better.

The Nordic influence has pervaded northern Germany, where herring is also a staple. Like British cooking, that of Germany is hearty and straightforward. The German people retain an affection for the cakes, tarts, and other confections that accompany afternoon coffee at the local *Konditorei* (pastry shop). Their two staffs of life — and this is true from the Rhine nearly to the Volga — are potatoes and beer. The potatoes are usually boiled, garnished with parsley and butter, and served with the sauerbraten and roast pork and countless boiled and grilled wursts. As for the beers, the Germans are only outdone by the British in their available variety of brews. Though it is less true now than in the past, nearly all towns of any size have breweries. Sauerkraut is not a ubiquitous dish, as it is far more important in southern Germany than northern. Excellent breads of a dozen types — dark, light, rye, *Vollkorn* (whole grain), *Bauernbrot* (peasant bread) — make excellent sandwiches.

Eastern European dishes are characterized by the superb food of Hungary. *Gulyas* (goulash) has put Hungarian cuisine in the global spotlight, but you'll find the real thing only here in Hungary. Familiar as it may be, it probably will not be what you expect if you have eaten it outside its native land. Here it is served as a soup (a very thick one) containing meat (usually beef or pork), onions, sour cream, and, of course, paprika. *Halázlé* (Hungarian bouillabaisse), although indigenous to Lake Balaton, has become a favorite in Budapest as well. A clear soup, usually made with *fogas* (pike perch) or bream, it is seasoned with onions and an ocean of spices — one of them paprika, naturally. *Kolozsuári rakotikáposzia* translates as "layered cabbage," but the dish loses something in the translation. Between the layers of cabbage, you'll find eggs and sausages and an acre of sour cream. Crisp pork chops top off everything. Don't be intimidated by the idea that paprika dishes might be too incendiary. Any restaurant in town can temper its cooking to conform to your particular taste.

The natural gastronomic foil to this Slavic richness, and one central Europeans themselves flock to, is the sun-baked cooking of the Mediterranean. This cuisine of the sun and sea crosses national boundaries from Málaga, Spain, to Athens, Greece, and derives its appeal from an array of flavorful ingredients simply prepared and presented. Olive oil, garlic, tomato, basil, anchovies, wild thyme, and fish and shellfish of every description are the staples. *Pissaladière Niçoise,* the tart of onion, tomatoes, olives, and anchovies, is only slightly less famous than the Marseille fish soup (it's more than that) of saffron, garlic, tomato, and seafood, called bouillabaisse. Not surprisingly, Mediterranean fish soups come with many names: In Barcelona they call it *zarazuela;* in southern France the generic name is *bourride;* in Italy, depending where you are, you find it as *buridda, zuppa di pesce,* or *cacciuco.* Greece and Yugoslavia have a profusion of fish and shellfish dishes — oysters, mussels, and shrimp especially — usually simply grilled or fried or done up into stews and soups. Their lamb and goat dishes retain the same seaborne tang, roasted or grilled with garlic and oil.

There is more to the kitchens of Spain, France, and Italy than the Mediterranean Sea. The best and easiest entrée into the amenities of Spanish life would be a visit to a *tapas* bar, where the dozens of appetizers *(tapas),* ranging from bits of sausage and cheese to stewed game birds and pickled vegetables, are downed with slices of the dry-cured ham called *serrano* and *copitas* full of *fino* (dry) sherry. Spanish cooking at its best is a matter of fresh ingredients simply prepared; two examples are the garlic soup of central Spain and *gazpacho,* made from the early ripening tomatoes, peppers, and other vegetables. The expensive golden spice, saffron, though not exactly a staple, appears with rice in the national chicken and rice dish *arroz con pollo* and in the traditional dish of shellfish and chicken on a bed of saffron rice known as *paella.*

Of all the countries of Europe, Italy is perhaps the most compartmentalized when it comes to food. Dishes and ingredients we regard as Italian national heritage are often restricted to a single region. *Pesto,* the pungent paste made of basil, garlic, pine nuts, Parmesan, and olive oil, is found in Genoa and not in Venice. The Milanese favorite *risotto alla milanese* (rice cooked with saffron and Parmesan) and minestrone are not native to Naples, which in turn is home to spaghetti with a fish and tomato sauce and delicious fish-garnished pizza. One or two rules to remember are that from Tuscany south olive oil is used increasingly instead of butter, and Tuscany is the heart of the country for the purest, and some would say best, Italian cooking. The best place to sample it is outside of the larger cities in one of the small town inns called *bucas.* Here the Tuscan staples of beans, beef, and Chianti will be given their best showing. Venice has made the word *scampi* universally recognized as shrimp broiled in butter. More strictly Venetian is the luxurious combination of oysters and caviar — the caviar from sturgeon fished from the Po River. Wherever you go in Italy, keep in mind that the *caffès* serve more than just coffee: Chocolate truffles and small pastries make for a pleasant way to kill an hour and watch the world go by.

Which brings us at last to France. All that pertains to eating and drinking in the land of the Gauls is a matter of great concern, and any visit to the country, however short, will be enriched immensely by your getting into the spirit of the place. Though it is less true than it used to be, France remains a country of regional cooking, and the savvy traveler will explore the specialties wherever he or she goes. Burgundy (Bourgogne), stretching from Lyon northward, is home to the wine-rich beef stew *boeuf bourguignon,* a boggling array of sausages and pâtés, which go perfectly with cool Beaujolais and Pouilly-Fuissé, and delectably tender roast chickens from Bresse. In the southwest between Bordeaux and Périgueux, roast duck, preserved goose, and the fattened liver of each — *foie gras* — are local prizes, and farther south in Bayonne they make a raw cured ham, *jambon de Bayonne.* Following the specialties of the region is important not only because they are what the local chefs know and make best, but also because in partaking of the local *plats,* you will deepen your understanding of the local differences in character and attitude. They might make a terrific *cassoulet* — the bean and meat casserole famous in Toulouse — in some restaurant in Colmar in the Alsatian wine country, but why dilute your Alsatian experience with that hearty southern dish when you could have *choucroute garnie,* the native rendition of sauerkraut, sausages, and pieces of smoked ham and pork? By experiencing first hand, so to speak, the Alsatian synthesis of French finesse with hearty German ingredients, you will have made a big step toward understanding the makeup of that beautiful region on the Rhine. When in the Mediterranean Pyrenees your appreciation of the rugged country and the bluff, resilient people can only be increased when eating a leg of mountain lamb, roast partridge in cabbage, or the redoubtable wild boar stew *civet de sanglier.*

There is one type of French cooking that is, in a sense, national, and this is *haute cuisine* as practiced in the best and most expensive restaurants of the country. Whether of the rich and elaborate *cuisine classique* or the lighter, more fantasy-inspired *cuisine nouvelle* variety, the best practitioners of this cooking, because of the expense and artistry involved, transcend the limits of their region. No matter how slim your budget, you should try to indulge yourself at least once at one of France's best *haute cuisine* temples. Think of it as an experience that will live far beyond the few pleasant hours you spend at table.

But aside from a few comparatively rare gastronomic highs in France and Italy, where great and elaborate dining is part of the national temper, your best meals will be found in the *bistros, trattorias, tavernas,* and pubs of Europe, wherever the fare is simple and catered to local tastes. Seeking these places out will do much to enhance your enjoyment of a European trip, for it is by an accumulation of these intimacies that you look into a nation's heart. For our list of Europe's finest restaurants, see *The Shrines of European Gastronomy,* DIVERSIONS.

Hotels, Pensions, and Special Places in Europe

 From elegant, centuries-old resorts to modest and inexpensive guesthouses, you can be comfortable and well cared for on almost any budget in Europe. It is this diversity that makes a trip to and through Europe such fun, and travelers should learn to use it to their best advantage.

Our choice of hotels, pensions, guesthouses, bed-and-breakfasts, international first-class hotels, and unique hostelries are included in the *Best in Town* section of the individual city reports of THE EUROPEAN CITIES; the *Best en Route* section of DIRECTIONS reports; and for Europe's finest, most historic, and most elegant hotels, *Europe's Most Memorable Hostelries,* DIVERSIONS. The hotels in these sections represent our cost-and-quality choices for a variety of traveling budgets, but the lists are selective, not comprehensive, and with some diligent searching — before you leave and on the road — you will turn up an equal number of "special places" that are uniquely yours.

Costs – On the whole, deluxe and first-class accommodations in Europe, especially in the large metropolitan centers (London, Paris, and so on) are just as expensive as the same type of accommodations in the US. To some extent, the strong position of the dollar abroad in recent years has helped to bring such top-of-the-line establishments within the range of a great number of travelers who previously would not have been able to afford them. But it is not necessary to keep an eye on the rate of exchange to know whether a European trip will be possible for you, because affordable alternatives to the top-rated establishments have always been available. Once upon a time, such things as the superiority of New World plumbing made many of these alternatives unthinkable for North Americans. Today, the gap has closed considerably, and in most countries the majority of hostelries catering to the tourist trade are likely to be at least adequate in their basic facilities.

One way to help you select the type of hotel that fits your finances and personal needs is to become familiar with the official hotel grading system used in the countries you plan to visit. Not all European governments grade hotels — Great Britain, for example, doesn't — but most do. Many use a system of five categories, assigning a letter or a certain number of stars to each according to specific criteria, among them the number of rooms, the percentage of rooms with private bathrooms, and the presence of other amenities. While the results of these assessments may not tally with your own judgments, and while the five-star (deluxe) or one-star (plain but comfortable) hotels of one country may not measure up to those of another country, by knowing the rating in advance you'll have a reasonable idea of the type of accommodations to expect — and their price. The national tourist offices of countries that grade hotels should be able to furnish you with a general price range for each category in their system.

Even with a rough idea of what accommodations are going to cost, you may still be annoyed at the gang of taxes and surcharges that can be added to the final hotel bill. The most common include the Value Added Tax, a government tax on certain purchases and services (in some places, as high as 18% on hotels) and an obligatory service charge (typically 10% to 15%) in lieu of optional tips. In some countries, the practice is to quote room prices inclusive of such extras; in others, they may come as a surprise. Thus, if you're traveling on a tight budget, it's best to check in advance what the *total* tab is going to be.

Room prices, of course, vary according to season, and visitors should expect to pay a premium for traveling in Europe during the peak summer months. However, not even a willingness to pay for top accommodations will guarantee you a room if you don't have reservations. This also can be the case in smaller cities and villages, where the number of rooms, not the price, is likely to be the qualifying factor. Regardless of the city, keep in mind that the larger hotels are the ones most frequently prebooked as 2- and 3-day stopover centers for the thousands of tour groups ranging the Continent. Thus individual reservations should be made as far in advance as possible. Remember also that a confirmed reservation often must be secured with a deposit in the height of season. Reservations and deposits can be handled readily by any travel agent.

SPECIAL PLACES: Among the most interesting accommodations in Europe are those truly distinctive and frequently historic facilities whose ambience and style reflect something special of the country they are in. Examples of these are the country inns and manor houses of Britain and Ireland; the famed *relais* of France; converted castles in Germany; the architecturally distinctive *paradores* of Spain; the resort health spas of southeastern Europe; and Italy's *pensiones,* virtually a cultural institution within that country, although this style of accommodation has long been available throughout the Continent. Many of these unique hostelries are included in the individual reports in THE EUROPEAN CITIES and in *Best en Route* in DIRECTIONS.

British Castles and Country House Hotels – Located throughout the British Isles and neighboring islands, these inns specialize in the traditional atmosphere, service, and hospitality of the great English country estates. Many once were country homes, manor houses, or castles, and a number are noteworthy for architectural features, gardens or parklands, riverside or lake settings, or locations in dell, dale, and mountain. The real attraction, however, is the history associated with so many of these establishments and their antique decors. Most have modern facilities (televisions, private baths) along with traditional features such as fireplaces and sitting rooms. They are much sought out by the British themselves as weekend retreats. Weekend reservations are a must; midweek reservations are strongly recommended during high season. Prices range roughly from $20 to $50-plus per person, including breakfast. For information, contact the British Town Authority.

Relais et Châteaux – Most members of this association are located in France, but the group does extend to many other countries. There are three types of members: Châteaux-Hôtels, Relais de Campagne, and Relais Gourmands. Some properties are actually ancient castles or palaces — dating back more than 1,000 years — which have been converted to hotels. Others — the *relais* — are old inns, manor houses, even converted mills, convents, and monasteries. A few well-known city and resort establishments are included, such as the *Crillon* in Paris and the *Marbella Club* in Spain, but most are in quiet country surroundings, graced with parks and flowering gardens. (The third group of association members, *Relais Gourmands,* is composed of especially fine restaurants.) *Relais et Châteaux* hotels are frankly expensive, but no more so than you would expect to pay for deluxe and frequently elegant accommodations and service anywhere in the world. All have good restaurants, and the properties themselves adhere to uniformly high standards. The *Relais* catalogue ($10) is available, in travel bookshops or by mail from David Mitchell & Company, 200 Madison Ave., New York, NY 10016, (phone: 212-696-1323).

Gast im Schloss – Germany's contribution to high style and historic accommodations is this association of hotels and restaurants in castles, mansions, and historic buildings. Most of these properties have exceptionally picturesque settings and surroundings — on hills overlooking the Rhine, alongside lakes, or in densely wooded parks and parklands. Though stylish and often grand, there is nonetheless a prevailing sense of informality in most of the hotels. All have modern facilities and many offer numerous leisure activities — tennis, riding, hunting, fishing, swimming, golf — either on the property or nearby. Prices are moderate to expensive, the atmosphere friendly and hospitable, and many of the properties offer the frankly romantic appeal of dinner before an open fireplace and a room in a castle turret. Special itineraries have been designed for motorists who want to visit several hotels in the association. An illustrated *Gast im Schloss* booklet is available from the German National Tourist Office.

Paradores and Pousadas – Since 1928 the Spanish government has been renovating abandoned castles, old inns, and historic structures — and raising some modern buildings — to create its excellent system of *paradores*. Guests can stay in Moorish castles or splendidly ornate hunting chalets completely fitted out with modern facilities, and yet prices are often incredibly low. Within the Spanish system of grading hotels, *paradores* range from two- to four-star establishments, with prices for a double room in 1985 ranging from approximately $30 to $60. Tax and tip, but not breakfast, are excluded in such figures, which vary little from low to high season. Portugal has a similar network of state-operated inns called *pousadas.* Some are newly built; others are converted historic buildings, palaces, and monasteries; all have modern conveniences. In 1985, the rates for a room for two ranged from about $20 to $30 in the low season and from about $30 to $50 in the high season, tax, tips, and breakfast included. For further information contact the Spanish and Portuguese National Tourist Offices, or get in touch with Marketing Ahead, Inc., 515 Madison Ave., New York, NY 10022 (phone: 212-759-5170).

Pensiones (The anglicized spelling is *Pensions*) – Italy's contribution to Continental accommodations happily remains part of the entire European travel scene. *Pensiones* are ideal for the visitor wishing to spend some time getting to know a city.

Their chief attractions are family-style quarters for a limited number of visitors, home meals for those who wish to dine in-house, and more reasonable prices than one would pay at a hotel. In other words, *pensiones* offer a more personalized type of living — and economy — for those who are traveling on their own. Whatever may be sacrificed in the way of front desk and other services at regular hotels is usually compensated for at *pensiones* by an element of charm. Prices of these establishments in Italy last year ranged from about $15 to $85 (including taxes, without meals) for a double room with private bath, although it must be pointed out that few of the cheaper establishments have private bath facilities. The more expensive *pensiones* serve two or three meals a day and some — as in seaside resorts in summer — require that you take one or more of them. The cheaper may serve only breakfast. A list of *pensiones* in main tourist centers of Italy is available directly from the Italian Government Travel Office (ENIT).

HOME EXCHANGES: An alternative for families who are content to stay in one place during their vacation is a home exchange. Several companies publish directories of individuals and families willing to trade homes with people for a specified period of time; the Jones family from Chicago moves into the home of the Chabrol family in Paris, while the Chabrols enjoy a stay in the Joneses' home. It is an exceptionally inexpensive way to ensure comfortable, reasonable living quarters with amenities that no hotel could possibly offer. Often the trade includes a car; almost always it means living in a new community in a way the average hotel guest never manages. In some cases, you must be willing to list your home in the directory; in others, you can subscribe to the directory without listing your own home and negotiate directly with the owners of the home you want. There is no guarantee that you will find a listing in the area of Europe in which you are interested, but each of the directories listed below has hundreds or thousands of listings in the US, in other parts of North America, and in Europe.

1. *Vacation Exchange Club:* Some 6,000 listings, about one-half of which are foreign. For $22.70, the subscriber is listed in one directory and receives two, one in late winter, one in the spring. For $15, the subscriber receives both directories but is not listed in either. 12006 111th Ave., Suite 12, Youngtown, AZ 85363 (phone: 602-972-2186).
2. *Adventures in Living:* Listing in an annual directory and two annual supplements, $35. A few rental properties are also listed. PO Box 278, Winnetka, IL 60093.
3. *Holiday Exchanges:* 6 back issues, a listing, and a monthly issue for the next 6 months ($25) or the next 12 months ($32). PO Box 5294, Ventura, CA 93003 (phone: 805-642-4879).

APARTMENT RENTAL ABROAD: Another alternative to hotels for the visitor content to stay in one spot for a week or more is actually to rent an apartment — called a flat in Europe — for the duration of your stay. Called holiday lets in Britain, a flat has both the advantages and the disadvantages of living "at home" abroad. It is certainly cheaper than a luxury or first-class international hotel for the same period of time; it has the comforts of home (vacation rentals are always furnished), including a kitchen, which means savings on food; it gives a sense of the country that a large hotel often does not. But beware: If you don't eat out, you have to cook in. And though some flats come with a cleaning person, most don't.

Most tourist authorities have information on rental agencies in their respective countries. In addition, a number of companies arrange rentals of European houses and flats from the US. They handle booking and confirmation paperwork, generally for a fee included in the rental price.

AAD Associates: Apartments and cottages in England, Scotland, and Wales, including London. Seasonal accommodations in university residences (rooms or self-catering flats) also available. Minimum rental period is usually 1 week. PO Box 3927, Amity Station, New Haven, CT 06525 (phone: 203-387-4461).

At Home Abroad: Has numerous rental listings in Western Europe. Minimum rental period is usually 2 weeks or one month. Photographs provided by mail after payment of $50 registration fee. 405 E 56th St., #6H, New York, NY 10022 (phone: 212-421-9165).

Villas International Ltd.: Lists apartments, cottages, castles, châteaux, chalets, and some windmills for rent in Europe; specify exact location of interest when requesting a brochure. Minimum rental, 1 week. 71 W 23 St., NewYork, NY 10010 (phone: in New York State, 212-929-7585; elsewhere, 800-221-2260).

RESERVATIONS: It is best to make reservations for accommodations in the major European cities, even if you are traveling off-season. Several European cities have convention centers, and hotel space can be limited if a large convention is being held at the same time you visit. All the hotel entries in the *Best in Town* section of the individual listings in THE EUROPEAN CITIES have phone numbers for reservations.

The advice to make reservations early is woven into every travel article; making a *late* reservation may be almost as good advice. For it's not at all unusual for hotel rooms, totally unavailable as far as 6 months in advance, suddenly to become available 6 days — or even 6 hours — before your arrival. Cancellations tend to occur closer to rather than farther from a designated date, and somewhat flexible travelers recognize that there will almost always be some cancellation in one hotel or other on the date they plan to arrive.

Although it is not a problem unique to Europe, the international travel boom has brought with it some abuses in the hotel trade that are pretty much standard operating procedure in any industry facing demand that outstrips supply. Hotels overbook rooms on the assumption that a certain percentage of no-shows is inevitable. When cancellations don't occur and everybody with a reservation arrives as promised, you can find yourself in the position of holding a valid reservation for which no room exists.

There's no sure way to avoid all the pitfalls of hotel overbooking, but there *are* some ways to minimize the risks. First, always carry evidence of your confirmed reservation with you when you travel. In order to have the greatest impact, this evidence should be a direct communication from the hotel to you or your travel agent. A letter or computer reservation slip should specify the exact dates and duration of your accommodations and the price. Make sure your travel agent, if you use one, passes on to you any official information received from the hotel. Absolutely the weakest form of confirmation is that voucher slip a travel agent routinely issues, since it carries no official indication that the hotel has verified your reservations.

Even better is the increasing opportunity to guarantee hotel reservations, and this is becoming the only practice to ensure that a hotel will keep a room waiting for you. This guarantee is accomplished by giving the hotel (or its reservation system) the number of your American Express, Diners Club, MasterCard, or Visa credit card, and agreeing that the hotel is authorized to charge you for that room no matter what. Even with a guaranteed reservation, it's still possible to cancel if you do so before 6 PM of the day of your reservation (it's sometimes 4 PM in resort areas). But when you do cancel under this arrangement, make sure you get a cancellation number to protect you from being billed erroneously.

What if you can't get reservations in the first place? This is a problem that annoys business travelers who can't plan months ahead. The word from savvy travelers is that a bit of currency (perhaps attached discreetly to a business card) will sometimes increase your chances with recalcitrant desk clerks. There are less venal ways of improving your odds, however. If you are making reservations for business, ask an associate at the destination to make reservations for you.

There is a good reason to do this above and beyond the very real point that a resident has the broadest knowledge of local hotels. Often a hotel will show as being "sold out" on the international computer when in reality there are a few rooms available. This is because local managers of chains hold suddenly canceled rooms for local use.

The computerization of reservations has made it unwise for a hotel to indicate that it suddenly has five rooms available (the result of cancellations), when there might be 30 or 40 travel agents lined up in the computer waiting for them. That small a number of vacancies is much more likely to be held by the hotel for its own (local) sale, so a local associate is an invaluable conduit to these otherwise unknown vacant rooms.

Tipping

Tipping in FACTS IN BRIEF includes information on tipping in the various countries of Europe, but throughout Europe you will find the custom of including some kind of service charge as part of a meal more common than in North America. If *service compris* (or *incluso* or *eingeschlossen*) is printed on the menu, followed by a percentage figure, you will know that the noted amount of your bill will be automatically added as a service charge (in some cases, it is already calculated in the menu prices). Unfortunately, not every restaurant notes that the charge is added, but you should feel no embarrassment about asking a waiter. *Service compris* generally ranges from 10% to 15%. If it isn't added, a 15% tip — just as in the US — is usually a safe figure although one should never hesitate to penalize poor service or reward excellent and efficient attention by leaving less or more.

Theoretically, if service is included, no further gratuity is necessary or expected. In practice, in many countries it is customary to leave something on the table for the waiter above and beyond the service charge. Diners in Great Britain, Ireland, France, and West Germany, for instance, frequently leave the small change after the check has been paid — provided the service has been good. In Italy and Spain, the "accepted" amount of this additional gratuity ranges from 5% to 10%. The maître d' is rarely tipped, except by regulars or if he has performed some particular favor. The sommelier (wine steward) is not tipped simply for serving the wine, although if he has selected it for you, it is customary to leave 10% of the price of the bottle.

Hotel bills in many European countries also include service, but there are situations in which tips are appropriate. For unloading your car, the doorman receives no less than $1 or 50¢ per bag, whichever is greater. For carrying your luggage, bellhops or porters should get a minimum of 50¢ per bag; up to $1 in large cities. For any special service you receive in a hotel, a tip is expected — 50¢ for a small service, ranging upward to $1 or more depending on whether someone has really gone out of his or her way to help you. Chambermaids are taken care of by the service charge, but you might want to leave an additional small tip. If no service charge has been included in the bill, then leave about $1 a day.

Shopping

Several sections of this book are devoted to shopping. For a general idea of what goods are special in the various European countries, see the short *Shopping* section of FACTS IN BRIEF. Every city report in THE EUROPEAN CITIES includes an extensive list of specific shops, markets, department stores, and boutiques, as well as descriptions of special shopping streets where they exist. And in DIVERSIONS, chapters on antiques, shopping, and auctions offer a where and how-to of the very best shopping opportunities and experiences in Europe.

How to Shop Abroad – The goods are enticing as ever, and their prices are enhanced by a dollar that has been consistently strong overseas in recent years. Even so, quality European-made goods are not necessarily cheaper in a fashionable boutique in the capital city of the country from which they come than they are in an equally fashionable US store. To know if the price is an improvement on the available US price, it is necessary to do some homework before you go. You should arrive in Europe with a list of the goods you want — as specific as possible, with brands or labels — and the cost of each in the US. With this in hand, you are armed for major European purchases. In some cases you will find it cheaper to buy abroad, but almost as often you will find it is not, and knowing the difference exactly is crucial to a successful shopping trip.

Duty-Free Shops – If intuition and common sense tell you that it is always cheaper to buy goods in an airport duty-free shop than at home or in the streets of a foreign city, you'd better inform your common sense with some very basic facts. Consider, first, exactly what duty-free means. It does *not* mean that the goods you buy in the shop are free of duty when you return to the US. It means that the shop has paid no import tax on goods of foreign make because the goods bought in the shop are not to be used in the country (that is why duty-free goods are available only in the restricted passengers' area of international airports or, if not, goods bought in the shops are delivered to departing passengers' planes). You save money only on goods of foreign make in a duty-free store, because they are the only items on which import tax would be charged in any other store. There is usually no saving on locally made items, although in countries that impose VAT taxes (see below) that are refundable to foreigners, the prices in airport duty-free shops are also minus this tax, sparing travelers the bother of taking steps to obtain the refund. Beyond this, there is little reason to delay buying local souvenirs until you reach the airport. In fact, because airport duty-free shops usually pay high airport rents, the locally made goods sold in them may well be more expensive than they would be in a downtown store. The real bargains are foreign goods, but let the buyer beware — not all foreign goods are automatically cheaper in an airport duty-free shop.

Spirits, smoking materials, and perfumes are pretty standard bargains, but when buying cameras, watches, clothing, chocolates and other foods, and luxury items, be sure to know what they cost elsewhere. Terrific savings do exist (they are the reason such shops exist, after all), but just as many overpriced, over-rated items line duty-free shelves.

Two of Europe's best known duty-free shops are at Ireland's Shannon Airport, the oldest, and at Amsterdam's Schiphol Airport, the largest. You can get a catalogue of the Amsterdam shop — useful for price comparisons — through KLM Royal Dutch Airlines offices or by writing to the Amsterdam Airport Shopping Centre, PO Box 7501, 1118 ZG Schiphol Airport, Holland. Shannon Airport also operates a mail-order service that can be used long after you've left Ireland; pick up the catalogue as you pass through Shannon or request it from Shannon Development, 590 Fifth Ave., New York, NY 10036 (phone: 212-581-0480).

Value Added Tax – Commonly abbreviated as VAT, this tax is levied by various European countries. It is added to the purchase price of most merchandise, somewhat like a sales tax, but it is already included in the price tag. Although intended for residents, visitors must pay it (in some cases, it can be avoided by having the store ship purchases to an address abroad), but they can then take steps to obtain a refund. The procedure — similar in most countries that allow rebates to foreigners — is cumbersome, but considering that the tax is as high as 33% on luxury articles in France, it can mean substantial savings. This is how you do it: Ask the salesperson for a form that indicates the total cost of your purchase and the amount of the VAT included in it. (Some shops have a minimum cost of purchase before VAT will be rebated, but you can find that out as you enter.) Later, as you leave the country, your forms will be validated at a customs desk that usually adjoins passport control. They are then mailed back to the store at a post box that usually adjoins the Customs desk. If your purchases were paid for with a credit card, the VAT refund will usually appear as a credit (in dollars) to your account. If they were paid for in cash, your refund will arrive in the mail in the form of a check in the currency of the country in which the purchase was made. Your own US bank will assess a fee, anywhere from $5 to $15, for converting that check into dollars. Far less costly is sending it (after endorsing it) to Ruesch International, 1140 19th St., NW, Washington, DC 20036 (phone: 800-424-2923), whose flat fee for converting foreign currency checks to US dollars is only $2. Note that a variation of the above procedure occurs in Sweden, where the store will give you a check that can be cashed at the airport (or other point of departure) provided you take your purchases out of the country no more than 7 days after buying them.

Time Zones and Business Hours

TIME ZONES: The countries of Europe fall into three time zones: Greenwich Mean Time — measured from Greenwich, England, at longitude 0°0′ — is the base from which all other time zones are measured. Areas in zones reenwich have earlier times and are called Greenwich Minus; those to the east have later times and are called Greenwich Plus. For example, New York City is 5 hours earlier than Greenwich, England (Greenwich Minus 5); when it is noon in Greenwich it is 7 AM in New York. Greenwich Mean Time includes Ireland, Great Britain, and Portugal. All other Western European countries, including Spain, Czechoslovakia, East Germany, Hungary, and Yugoslavia, fall into Central European Time, and are an hour later than Greenwich Mean Time (Greenwich Plus 1). When it is noon in Greenwich it is 1 PM in East Berlin. The remaining Eastern European countries, as well as Greece, Turkey, Finland, and western Russia, are Greenwich Plus 2; Moscow is Greenwich Plus 3.

Almost all European nations move their clocks an hour ahead in late spring and an hour back in the fall, corresponding to daylight saving time in the US; therefore the same differential between time zones is maintained year-round.

European timetables use a 24-hour clock to denote arrival and departure times, which means that hours are denoted sequentially from 1 AM. A train leaving at 6 AM will be noted as leaving at 6:00; but a train leaving at 6 PM will be noted as leaving at 18:00. Midnight is 24:00.

BUSINESS HOURS: Businesses open Mondays through Fridays between 8 and 9 AM and, in the northern European countries, continue through the day until 4 or 5 PM. The central and southern European countries tend to close for a 2- to 2½-hour lunch break and therefore close later in the evening — between 5:30 and 7. There are variations, of course. For instance, offices in Yugoslavia open at 7 AM or even earlier and remain open to 2:30 PM or so, although stores and other types of businesses keep more familiar hours.

Banks close an hour or two earlier than businesses as a rule but tend to open on Mondays through Fridays at about the same time. If it's vital to you, check in advance because there are some exceptions: in West Germany, for example, banks are open from 9 AM to 12:30 PM, and then open again from 1:30 or 2:30 to 3:30 or 4:30 PM (and some, but not all, are open Saturday mornings until noon); in Italy, they close at 1:30 PM and do not reopen.

Holidays also vary within countries but if generalization can be attempted it is that (1) all businesses close down for a national day once a year and (2) religious holidays are more widely celebrated in Europe than in the US. Easter is often a 4-day celebration — Good Friday through Easter Monday — and Ascension Day, Whitmonday or Pentecost, the Assumption, All Saints' Day, and December 26 are all observed.

Mail, Telephone, and Electricity

MAIL: Europe's Poste Restante is our general delivery and is probably the best way to have your mail sent if you do not have a definite address. The central or main post office in each city or town handles Poste Restante, so make sure you call at the correct office when inquiring after your mail.

American Express has instituted a policy of holding mail free of charge only for clients. You must be able to show an American Express card, traveler's checks, or a voucher proving you are on one of the company's tours to avoid paying for mail privileges. Those who aren't clients must pay a nominal fee each time they ask if they have received mail whether they actually have a letter or not. There is also a forwarding charge for clients and nonclients alike. A list of American Express addresses in Europe is contained in the pamphlet "Services and Offices" available from the nearest US branch of American Express.

US embassies and consulates abroad do not accept mail for tourists. They will, however, help out in emergencies, if you need to receive important business documents or personal papers, for example. It is best to inform them either by separate letter or cable, or by phone if you are in the country already, that you will be using their address.

TELEPHONE: Direct dialing within a country, between nations, and overseas is the rule rather than the exception in Europe. There are a lot of digits involved once you start dialing outside one country, but by avoiding operator-assisted calls, costs are cut considerably and rates are reasonable.

Except for calls made through hotel switchboards. One of the most unpleasant surprises foreign travelers encounter is the amount they find tacked on to their hotel bill for telephone calls, for foreign hotels routinely add surcharges that can be the equivalent of a daily room rate. It's not at all uncommon to find 300% or 400% added on for telephone charges.

Until recently, the only recourse against this unconscionable overcharging was to call collect when phoning from abroad, or to use a telephone credit card (available through a simple procedure from any local phone company). But now American Telephone & Telegraph, which was unjustifiably blamed for these overcharges, has put together *Teleplan,* to set limits on surcharges on calls made by hotel guests from their rooms. *Teleplan* is currently in effect in virtually all the hotels in Ireland and Portugal; in all Hilton International hotels; and in all Marriott properties in Europe. *Teleplan* agreements stipulate a flat amount for credit card or collect calls (currently between $1 and $6) and a flat percentage (between 20% and 100%) on calls paid for at the hotel. For further information, contact the International Information Service, AT&T Communications, 500 Amsterdam Ave., NE, Atlanta, GA 30306 (phone: 800-874-4000) and ask for the Teleplan brochure.

Until *Teleplan* becomes universal, it's wise to ask the surcharge rate *before* calling from any foreign hotel. Similarly, it's still a good idea to use your telephone credit card, if you have one, and if not, to place your call collect. If none of these devices is open to you, make your international calls from the local post office or special telephone center to avoid the surcharges, which seem to be restricted to international hotels. You can always place a call abroad and ask the party to call you right back.

ELECTRICITY: A useful, free brochure, *Foreign Electricity Is No Deep Dark Secret*, will be mailed to you if you send a stamped, self-addressed envelope to the Franzus Company, 352 Park Ave. S, New York, NY 10010. It provides information about adapter plugs and converters for electrical appliances to be used abroad but manufactured for the 110-volt, 60-cycle alternating current used in the US. Most of the world (including Europe) uses 200- to 250-volt, 50-cycle alternating current. The motor of a US appliance used in Europe therefore runs at twice the speed it's meant to and quickly burns out. You can solve the problem by buying a lightweight converter to transform foreign voltage into the domestic kind (there are two types of converters, depending on the wattage of the appliance) or by buying dual-voltage appliances. The difference between the 50- and 60-cycle currents will cause no problem — the appliance will simply run more slowly — but you will still have to deal with differing socket formations. Many European sockets require two long round prongs rather than the thin rectangular ones used here. Sets of adapter plugs for use worldwide can be bought at hardware stores.

Drinking and Drugs

DRINKING: It is more than likely that some of the warmest memories of your European trip will be moments of conviviality shared in a pub, a *Weinstube*, or a sunlit café. European beers and ales, wines, aperitifs, and liquors are bound to be a source of interest and pleasure and should heighten many a moment. With the exception of European beer, which at around 5% has a slightly higher alcoholic content than that of North America, European beverages are no stronger than those found in the US: Wines and champagne contain a standard 12% alcohol; fortified wines such as sherry, port, and the aperitifs have anywhere between 12% and 18%; and brandies and hard liquor between 40% and 50% (80 to 100 proof). The potency of such famed liquors as Russian vodka, Scandinavian aquavit, and Yugoslavian slivovitz derives from the fact that they are often taken fast and neat rather than that they have high alcoholic content.

Europe offers a wide variety of alcoholic drinks, and you should taste as many as you can. A short survey of some of the favorites:

Austria – Here the classic drink combination (especially in summer) is a shot of schnapps followed by a chaser of beer. Schnapps is a general term for a wide range of liquors, distilled from grain at about 80 proof. Enjoyed in a *Gasthaus,* schnapps is served straight up.

Britain – Scotch whisky and English ale are the favorites in England's pubs. Whisky may be tempered with a little water (never ice), and ale comes cellar-chilled rather than refrigerated.

Bulgaria – In Bulgaria, a bar is a *bar* (same spelling), and the favorite drink is a small, chilled glass of slivovitz, a flavorful spirit made from plums.

France – Wine, of course, by the glass or carafe is the trademark of Parisian cafés, where the house choice *(vin maison)* is usually reasonably priced and palatable.

Germany – The size of many German waistlines testifies to the overriding popularity of *Bier,* served by the *viertel liter* (one-quarter liter) in a *Taverne* or *Bier Keller* (beer cellar).

Greece – High-proof ouzo is the drink of Greece. The best is made from grapes, tasting faintly of licorice (it's flavored with anise), and is served on the rocks or with water in a *kafenio* (coffeehouse).

Ireland – In the pubs of Ireland, Guinness stout, a dark, syrupy ale with a thick, creamy head and a pronounced bitterness from hops, is the favorite.

Italy – Along with wine, the popular drink at a local *caffè* is Campari, usually served on the rocks with soda and a twist.

Poland – Polish vodka, traditionally served neat and slightly chilled in a liqueur glass, is distilled from grain. Available in *bars* (same spelling), Polish vodka often comes with a grind of fresh pepper or a twist of lemon.

Scandinavia – Without a doubt, the national drink of Scandinavia is aquavit, a flavored neutral spirit, sometimes derived from potatoes, sometimes from grain. Served icy cold in a tulip-shaped glass, occasionally with a side of beer, aquavit is almost always imbibed with meals. In fancy restaurants, the bottle is brought to the table encased in a jacket of ice.

Spain – In addition to a glass of red wine *(a tinto),* the people of Spain enjoy a wide range of excellent sherries. Most people will order a glass of sherry *(a fino),* served in a small glass to be sipped leisurely in an outdoor *café* or *bar* (same spelling).

Switzerland – On the French side, drinking habits run along Gallic lines; that is, wine is preferred. On the German side, a cup of coffee with schnapps or a mug of beer is popular.

Yugoslavia – Once again, the taste is for plums, and slivovitz, served in a *gostina* (bar), is considered the national drink.

National taxes on alcohol in the Common Market countries affect the prices of liquor there, not — as used to be the case — the fact that they are manufactured in other countries. Any alcoholic beverage is expensive in Denmark because it is highly taxed. In France if a drink costs a lot it's because the café prices it that way. Gin is as cheap in Italy as it is in Great Britain. However in Austria, for example, not a Common Market country, taxes make imported liquor exorbitant and it is best to stick with whatever is produced locally.

Whiskey and gin are not indigenous to the Continent and as a general rule, mixed drinks are expensive. If you like a drop before dinner, a good way to save money is to buy a bottle of your favorite brand at the airport before leaving the US and enjoy it in your hotel before setting forth. European countries allow a quart or more of hard liquor and at least one bottle of wine to be brought in duty-free.

The legal age for drinking varies between 18 and 21 and there's a generally relaxed attitude about who gets served in cafés and pubs. But there are strict laws, rigorously enforced in some countries, about driving after drinking, with breath tests commonplace. Be extremely cautious before getting behind the wheel if you've had something to drink. There are alternative ways to get home, and you can always retrieve the car at a later time.

DRUGS: There is a ready supply of hashish and other drugs in most of the capitals and major cities of Europe, but don't be deluded into believing that this easy access denotes a casual attitude on the part of authorities. The moderate legal and social acceptance that marijuana has won in the US has no counterpart in Europe, and the border police of just about every European country will pounce on any suspect. The best advice is not to take any risks; and for heaven's sake never cross a border carrying any illegal or controlled substance. Customs officials make routine, random searches and will throw the book at any offender, which can mean imprisonment for the smallest amount of a drug. (If you carry medicines that contain a drug, make sure you have a current doctor's prescription.) There isn't much that the US government through its consular representative will do for drug offenders beyond providing a list of English-speaking lawyers. Having broken a local law, your fate is in the hands of the local authorities.

Ironically, you can get in almost as much trouble coming through US customs with over-the-counter drugs picked up in Europe that contain substances that are controlled in the US. European cold medicines, pain relievers, and the like, often have codeine or codeine derivatives that are illegal except by prescription in the US. Throw them out before you leave Europe.

Customs and Returning to the US

 Customs exemptions for US citizens returning from abroad have been revised once again. The most meaningful change for the tourist is the increase in the individual duty-free allowance to $400 on accompanying items. A flat 10% duty based on the "fair retail value in country of acquisition" is assessed on the next $1,000 worth of merchandise brought in for personal use or as gifts. Any amounts over $1,400 are dutiable at a variety of rates.

Families can now pool purchases dutiable under the flat rate amount. For example, a family of three would be eligible for up to a total of $3,000 at the 10% flat duty rate (after each family member had used up his or her $400 duty-free exemption) rather than three separate $1,000 allowances. This grouping of purchases is extremely useful when considering the duty on the purchase of a high-tariff item, jewelry or a fur coat, for example. Individuals are allowed 1 carton (200) cigarettes and 1 liter of alcohol if over 21. Alcohol above the allowance is liable for both duty and an Internal Revenue tax. Antiques that are 100 or more years old and accompanied by proof from the seller of that fact are duty-free, as are paintings and drawings if done entirely by hand (frames, however, are dutiable).

Personal exemptions can be used once every 30 days and in order to be eligible an individual must have been out of the country for more than 48 hours. If any portion of the exemption has been used once within any 30-day period, or if your trip is less than 48 hours long, the duty-free allowance is cut to $25. The allotment for individual gifts mailed from abroad (one per day per recipient) has been raised to $50 retail value per gift. These gifts do not have to be declared and are not included in your duty-free exemption.

Clearing customs is a simple procedure. Forms are distributed by airline or ship personnel before arrival. If your purchases total no more than the duty-free $400 limit, you need only fill out the identification part of the form and can make your declaration orally to the customs inspector. If entering with more than $400 worth of goods, a written declaration must be submitted. It is illegal not to declare dutiable items; you are smuggling, and the penalty can be anything from stiff fines and seizure of the goods to prison sentences. It simply isn't worth doing.

Just as you wouldn't exchange money for foreign currency in the back alleys of foreign cities, so should you avoid the suggestions of foreign merchants to *help* you secure a bargain by deceiving customs officials. Such transactions are frequently a setup using the foreign merchant as an agent of US customs. Another tool of US customs is TECS, the Treasury Enforcement Communications System, a computer that is being used to store all kinds of information pertinent to returning citizens.

There is a basic rule to buying goods abroad, and you should never contravene it: If you can't afford the duty on it, don't buy it. Your list or verbal declaration should include all items purchased abroad as well as gifts received abroad, purchases made for others, repairs, and anything brought in for sale. Do not include in the list items that do not accompany you; i.e., purchases that you have had shipped home. These are dutiable in any case, even if for your own use and even if the items that accompany your return from the same trip do not exhaust your $400 duty-free exemption. In fact, it is a good idea, if you have accumulated too much while abroad, to mail home any personal effects (made and bought in the US) that you no longer need rather than your foreign purchases. These personal effects pass through customs as "American Goods Returned" and are not subject to duty.

Gold, gold medals, and bullion may be brought into the US and up to $5,000 in currency or negotiable instruments as well without being declared in writing, but you must declare them verbally to the customs agent as you enter. Sums over $5,000 must be declared in writing. Drugs are totally illegal with the exception of physician-prescribed medication. It's a good idea to travel with no more than you actually need of any medication and to have the prescription on hand in case any question arises either abroad or re-entering the US.

Customs implements the rigorous Department of Agriculture regulations concerning the importation of vegetable matters, seeds, bulbs, and the like. Living vegetable matter may not be imported without an import permit and everything must be inspected, permit or not. Processed foods and baked goods are usually okay. Regulations on meat products generally depend on the country of origin and manner of processing.

Customs agents are businesslike, efficient, and not unkind. During the peak season, clearance can take time, but this is generally due to the strain put on capacity by a number of jumbo jets disgorging their passengers at the same time, not unwarranted zealousness on the part of the customs people.

Duty-Free Craft Items – In order to help developing nations improve their economy through export, the US has adopted a Generalized System of Preferences (GSP). In effect since 1976, the GSP entitles US citizens to bring home some 2,800 items from dozens of developing countries duty-free. The only European countries currently on the GSP list are Gibraltar, Malta, Portugal, Romania, and Yugoslavia. The Generalized System of Preferences allows you to bring in products worth more than the $400 duty-free exemption discussed above. The list of goods eligible for GSP status includes cameras, candy, bone and nonbone china, cigarette lighters, cork, earthen tableware or stoneware, china figurines, artificial flowers, furs, wood or plastic furniture, games, golf equipment, ivory, jewelry, precious metal or stones, musical instruments, perfume, printed matter, records and tapes, electric shavers, silverware, toys, and wood carvings.

The US Customs Service publishes a free kit of pamphlets with customs information, including *Know Before You Go,* a basic discussion of customs requirements pertaining to all travelers; *International Mail Imports; Pets, Wildlife; Traveler's Tips on Bringing Food, Plant, and Animal Products into the United States; GSP and the Traveler; Pocket Hints; Currency Reporting; Importing a Car;* and *Trademark Information for Travelers.* For the entire kit or individual pamphlets, write or call the US Customs Service, PO Box 7407, Washington, DC 20044 (phone: 202-566-8195), or contact any of the seven regional offices: in Boston, Chicago, Houston, Los Angeles, Miami, New Orleans, and New York.

Sources and Resources

National Tourist Offices in the US

Below is a list of European tourist authorities in the United States. These organizations can provide travel and entry information on their respective countries. Literature is usually available at no charge. Remember that different countries have different entry requirements, so if your plans include a multiple country tour, contact each country's tourism office. For more foreign entry information, see FACTS IN BRIEF and *Entry Requirements and Documents,* GETTING READY TO GO. When requesting travel brochures and maps, state your particular areas of interest regarding hotels, restaurants, and tourist attractions.

The best places for tourist information in each European city are listed in the individual city reports in THE EUROPEAN CITIES.

ANDORRA: Sindicat d'Iniciativa de les Valls d'Andorra, 1923 W Irving Park Rd., Chicago, IL 60613 (phone: 312-472-7660).

AUSTRIA: Austrian National Tourist Office, 500 Fifth Ave., New York, NY 10110 (phone: 212-944-6880); 3440 Wilshire Blvd., Suite 906, Los Angeles, CA 90010 (phone: 213-380-3309); 500 N Michigan Ave., Suite 544, Chicago, IL 60611 (phone: 312-644-5556); 4800 San Felipe St., Suite 500, Houston, TX 77056 (phone: 713-850-8888).

BELGIUM: Belgian National Tourist Office, 745 Fifth Ave., New York, NY 10151 (phone: 212-758-8130).

BULGARIA: Bulgarian Tourist Office, 161 E 86th St., New York, NY 10028 (phone: 212-722-1110).

CZECHOSLOVAKIA: ČEDOK, Czechoslovak Travel Bureau, 10 E 40th St., Suite 1902, New York, NY 10016 (phone: 212-689-9720); Embassy of Czechoslovakia, 3900 Linnean Ave., NW, Washington, DC 20008 (phone: 202-363-6308).

DENMARK: Danish Tourist Board, 655 Third Ave., New York, NY 10017 (phone: 212-949-2333); 150 N Michigan Ave, Suite 2110, Chicago, IL 60601 (phone: 312-726-1120); 8929 Wilshire Blvd., Suite 300, Beverly Hills, CA 90211 (phone: 416-823-9620).

FINLAND: Finnish Tourist Board, 655 Third Ave., New York, NY 10017 (phone: 212-949-2333).

FRANCE: French Government Tourist Office, 610 Fifth Ave., New York, NY 10020 (for mail inquiries only); 628 Fifth Ave., New York, NY 10020 (phone: 212-757-1125); 9401 Wilshire Blvd., Beverly Hills, CA 90212 (phone: 213-271-6665); 645 N Michigan Ave., Chicago, IL 60611 (phone: 312-337-6301); 103 World Trade Center, PO Box 58610, Dallas, TX 75258 (phone: 214-742-7011).

GERMANY, EAST: Embassy of the German Democratic Republic, 1717 Massachusetts Ave., NW, Washington DC 20036 (phone: 202-232-3134); Koch Travel Bureau, 157 E 86th St., New York, NY 10028 (phone: 212-369-3800).

GERMANY, WEST: German National Tourist Office, 747 Third Ave., New York, NY 10017 (phone: 212-308-3300); 444 S Flower St., Suite 2230, Los Angeles, CA 90071 (phone: 213-688-7332).

GREAT BRITAIN: British Tourist Authority, 40 W 57th St., New York, NY 10019 (phone: 212-581-4700); 612 S Flower St., Los Angeles, CA 90017 (phone: 213-623-8196); John Hancock Center, Suite 3320, 875 N Michigan Ave., Chicago, IL 60611 (phone: 312-787-0490); Plaza of the Americas, North Tower, Suite 750, Dallas, TX 75201 (phone: 214-720-4040).

GREECE: Greek National Tourist Organization, Olympic Tower, 5th fl., 645 Fifth Ave., New York, NY 10022 (phone: 212-421-5777); 611 W Sixth St., Suite 1998, Los Angeles, CA 90017 (phone: 213-626-6696); 168 N Michigan Ave., Chicago, IL 60601 (phone: 312-782-1084). National Bank of Greece Bldg., 31 State St., Boston, MA 02109 (phone: 617-227-7366).

HUNGARY: Hungarian Travel Bureau (IBUSZ), 630 Fifth Ave., Room 520, New York, NY 10111 (phone: 212-582-7412).

ICELAND: Iceland Tourist Board, 655 Third Ave., New York, NY 10017 (phone: 212-949-2333).

IRELAND: Irish Tourist Board, 590 Fifth Ave., New York, NY 10036 (phone: 212-869-5500); 230 N Michigan Ave., Chicago, IL 60601 (phone: 312-726-9356); 625 Market St., San Francisco, CA 94105 (phone: 415-957-0985).

ITALY: Italian Government Travel Office, 630 Fifth Ave., Suite 1565, New York, NY 10111 (phone: 212-245-4822); 500 N Michigan Ave., Chicago, IL 60611 (phone: 312-644-0990); 360 Post St., San Francisco, CA 94108 (phone: 415-392-6206).

LIECHTENSTEIN: Swiss National Tourist Office, 608 Fifth Ave., New York, NY 10020 (phone: 212-757-5944); 250 Stockton St., San Francisco, CA 94108 (phone: 415-362-2260); 104 S Michigan Ave., Chicago, IL 60603 (phone: 312-641-0050).

LUXEMBOURG: Luxembourg National Tourist Office, 801 Second Ave., New York, NY 10017 (phone: 212-370-9850).

MALTA: Malta Tourist Information Office, c/o Consulate of Malta, 249 E 35th St., New York, NY 10016 (phone: 212-725-2345); 2017 Connecticut Ave. NW, Washington, DC 20008 (phone: 202-462-3611).

MONACO: Monaco Government Tourist and Convention Bureau, 845 Third Ave., New York, NY 10022 (phone: 212-759-5227).

NETHERLANDS: Netherlands National Tourist Office, 576 Fifth Ave., New York, NY 10036 (*for mail inquiries only*); 437 Madison Ave., New York, NY 10022 (phone: 212-223-8141).

NORWAY: Norwegian Tourist Board, 655 Third Ave., New York, NY 10017 (phone: 212-949-2333).

POLAND: Polish National Tourist Office, 500 Fifth Ave., Suite 328, New York, NY 10110 (phone: 212-391-0844).

PORTUGAL: Portuguese National Tourist Office, 548 Fifth Ave., New York, NY 10036 (phone: 212-354-4403).

ROMANIA: Romanian National Tourist Office, 573 Third Ave., New York, NY 10016 (phone: 212-697-6971).

SAN MARINO: San Marino Government Tourist Office, 1685 E Big Beaver Rd., Troy, MI 48084 (phone: 313-528-1190, Saturdays only).

SPAIN: Spanish National Tourist Office, 665 Fifth Ave., New York, NY 10022 (phone: 212-759-8822); 845 N Michigan Ave., Chicago, IL 60611 (phone: 312-944-0215); 1 Hallidie Plaza, San Francisco, CA 94102 (phone: 415-346-8100); 4800 The Galleria, 5085 Westheimer, Houston, TX 77056 (phone: 713-840-7411).

SWEDEN: Swedish Tourist Board, 655 Third Ave., New York, NY 10017 (phone: 212-949-2333); 150 N Michigan Ave., Suite 2110, Chicago, IL 60601 (phone: 312-726-1120); 8929 Wilshire Blvd., Suite 300, Beverly Hills, CA 90211 (phone: 416-823-9620).

SWITZERLAND: Swiss National Tourist Office, 608 Fifth Ave., New York, NY

10020 (phone: 212-757-5944); 250 Stockton St., San Francisco, CA 94108 (phone: 415-362-2260); 104 S Michigan Ave., Chicago, IL 60603 (phone: 312-641-0050).

USSR: Intourist Travel Information Office, 630 Fifth Ave., New York, NY 10111 (phone: 212-757-3884).

YUGOSLAVIA: Yugoslav National Tourist Office, 630 Fifth Ave., Suite 280, New York, NY 10111 (phone: 212-757-2801).

Table of Weights and Measures

 When you are traveling in Europe, you'll find that just about every quantity, whether it is length, weight, or capacity, will be in a figure unfamiliar to the average US citizen. In fact, this is true for travel almost everywhere in the world, since the US is one of the last countries to make its way to the metric system. It will happen soon in the US, and your trip to Europe may serve to familiarize you with what will one day be the weights and measures at your grocery store.

There are some specific things to keep in mind during your trip. Fruits and vegetables at a market are weighed in kilos (kilograms), as is your luggage at the airport and your body weight. This latter is particularly pleasing to people of large builds, who instead of weighing 220 pounds hit the scales at a mere 100 kilos. A kilo is 2.2 pounds and 1 pound is .45 kilos. Body temperature is measured in degrees Centigrade or Celsius rather than Fahrenheit, so that a normal body temperature reading is 37°, not 98.6°, and freezing is 0° rather than 32°. Gasoline stations sell gas by the liter (approximately four to a gallon), but machines measuring air for tires are in pounds, just as in the United States, so no conversion is necessary. Highway signs are written in kilometers rather than miles (1 mile equals 1.6 kilometers; 1 kilometer equals .62 miles). And speed limits are in kilometers per hour, so think twice before hitting the gas when you see a speed limit of 100. That means 62 miles per hour.

Although mathematics is not a popular subject, the tables and conversion factors listed below should give you all the information you will need to understand any transaction, road sign, or map you encounter on your travels.

APPROXIMATE EQUIVALENTS		
Metric Unit	**Abbreviation**	**US Equivalent**
LENGTH		
meter	m	39.37 inches
kilometer	km	.62 mile
millimeter	mm	.04 inch
CAPACITY		
liter	l	1.057 quarts
WEIGHT		
gram	g	.035 ounce
kilogram	kg	2.2 pounds
metric ton	MT	1.1 ton
ENERGY		
kilowatt	kw	1.34 horsepower

CONVERSION TABLES
METRIC TO US MEASUREMENTS

Multiply:	by:	to convert to:
LENGTH		
millimeters	.04	inches
meters	3.3	feet
meters	1.1	yards
kilometers	.6	miles
CAPACITY		
liters	2.11	pints (liquid)
liters	1.06	quarts (liquid)
liters	.26	gallons (liquid)
WEIGHT		
grams	.04	ounces (avoir.)
kilograms	2.2	pounds (avoir.)

US TO METRIC MEASUREMENTS

LENGTH		
inches	25.	millimeters
feet	.3	meters
yards	.9	meters
miles	1.6	kilometers
CAPACITY		
pints	.47	liters
quarts	.95	liters
gallons	3.8	liters
WEIGHT		
ounces	28.	grams
pounds	.45	kilograms

TEMPERATURE

$$°F = (°C \times 9/5) + 32 \qquad °C = (°F - 32) \times 5/9$$

Camera and Equipment

 Vacations are everybody's favorite time for taking pictures. After all, most of us want to remember the places we visit — and show them off to others — through spectacular photographs. Here are a few suggestions to help you get the best results from your travel picture-taking.

BEFORE THE TRIP: If you're just taking your camera out after a long period in mothballs, or have just bought a new one, check it thoroughly before you leave to prevent unexpected breakdowns and disappointing pictures.

1. Shoot at least one test roll, using the kind of film you plan to take along with you. Use all the shutter speeds and f-stops on your camera, and vary the focus to make sure everything is in order. Do this well in advance of your departure so there will be time to have film developed and to make repairs, if they are necessary. If you're in a rush, most large cities have custom labs that can process film in as little as 3 hours.

2. Clean your camera thoroughly, inside and out. Dust and dirt can jam camera mechanisms, spoil pictures, and scratch film. Remove surface dust from lenses and camera body with a soft camel's-hair brush. Next, use at least two layers of crumpled lens tissue and your breath to clean lenses and filters. Don't rub hard and don't use compressed air on lenses or filters because they are so easily damaged. Persistent stains can be removed by using a Q-tip moistened with liquid lens cleaner. Anything that doesn't come off easily needs professional attention. Once your lens is clean, protect it from dirt and damage with an inexpensive skylight or ultraviolet filter.

3. Check the batteries in the light meter, and take along extra ones just in case yours wear out during the trip.

EQUIPMENT TO TAKE ALONG: Keep your gear light and compact. Items that are too heavy or bulky to be carried with you will likely stay in your hotel room.

1. Most single lens reflex (SLR) cameras come with a conventional 50mm lens, a general purpose lens good for street scenes taken at a distance of 25 feet or more and full body portraits shot at normal distances. You can expand your photographic options with a wide-angle lens such as a 35mm, 28mm, or 24mm. These are especially handy for panoramas, cityscapes, and large buildings or statuary from which you can't step back. For close-ups, a macro lens is best, but a screw-on magnifying lens is an inexpensive alternative. Telephoto and zoom lenses are bulky and not really necessary unless you are shooting animals in the wild. If you want one such lens that gives a range of options, try a 35mm to 80mm zoom; it is relatively light, though expensive. Protect all lenses with a 1A or 1B skylight filter, which should be removed for cleaning only. And take along a polarizing filter to eliminate glare and reflection, and to saturate colors in very bright sunlight.

2. Travel photographs work best in color. The preferred and least expensive all-around slide films are Kodachrome 64, Fujichrome, and Agfachrome. For very bright conditions, try slower film, like Kodachrome 25. In places that tend to be cloudy, or indoors with natural light (as in museums), use a fast film such as Ektachrome 400, which can be "pushed" to ASA 800 or 1600. Films tend to render color in slightly different ways. Kodachrome brings out reds and oranges. Agfachrome mutes bright tones and produces fine browns, yellows, and whites. Fujichrome is noted for its yellows, greens, and whites. Anticipate what you are

likely to see, and take along whichever types of film will enhance your results.

If you choose film that develops into prints rather than slides, try Kodacolor 100 or 400 for bright, sunny days. For environments where there isn't much contrast — in the shade or on dark, overcast days — use Kodak Vericolor. Remember that multiple prints made from slide transparencies are generally better than those made from print negatives.

How much film should you take? If you are serious about your photography, pack one roll of film (36 exposures) for each day of your trip. Film is especially expensive abroad, and any leftovers can be bartered away or brought home and safely stored in your refrigerator. Processing is also more expensive abroad and not as safe as at home. If you are concerned about airport security X-rays damaging your undeveloped film (X-rays do not affect processed film), store it in lead-lined bags sold in camera shops. This possibility is not as much of a threat as it used to be, however. In the US, incidents of X-ray damage to unprocessed film (exposed or unexposed) are minimal because low-dosage X-ray equipment is used virtually everywhere. As a rule of thumb, photo industry sources say that film with speeds up to ASA 400 can go through security machinery in the US five times without any noticeable effect. Overseas, the situation varies from country to country, but at least in Western Europe, the trend is also toward equipment that delivers less radiation. While it is doubtful that one exposure would ruin your pictures, if you're traveling without a protective bag, you may want to ask to have your photo equipment inspected by hand, especially on a prolonged trip with repeated security checks. In the US, Federal Aviation Administration regulations require that if you request a hand inspection, you get it, but overseas, the response may depend on the humor of the inspector. Naturally, a hand inspection is only possible if you're carrying your film and camera on board with you; it's a good idea anyway, because it helps to preclude loss or theft or the possibility, especially at Eastern European airports, that checked baggage will be X-rayed more heavily than hand baggage. *A note of warning:* The new very high speed film with an ASA rating of 1,000 should never be subjected to X-rays, even in the US. If you're taking some of this overseas, note that there are lead-lined bags made especially for it.

3. A small battery-powered electronic flash unit is handy for very dim light or at night, but only if the subject is at a distance of 15 feet or less. Flash units cannot illuminate an entire scene, and many museums do not permit flash photography, so take such a unit only if you know you will need it. If your camera does not have a hot-shoe, you will need a PC cord to synchronize the flash with your shutter.

4. Invest in a broad camera strap if you now have a thin one. It will make carrying the camera much more comfortable.

5. A sturdy canvas or leather camera bag — not an airline bag — will keep equipment organized and easy to find.

6. For cleaning, bring along a camel's-hair brush that retracts into a rubber squeeze bulb. Take plenty of lens tissue as well, and plastic bags to protect cameras against dust.

7. Pack some extra lens caps — they're the first things to get lost.

SOME TIPS: For better pictures, remember the following pointers:

1. *Get close* — Move in to get your subject to fill the frame.
2. *Vary your angle* — Get down, shoot from above, look for unusual perspectives.
3. *Pay attention to backgrounds* — Keep the background simple or blur it out.
4. *Look for details* — Not just a whole building, but a decorative element; not just an entire street scene, but a single remarkable face.
5. *Don't be lazy* — Always carry your camera gear with you, loaded and ready for those unexpected moments.

FACTS IN BRIEF

Facts in Brief

Tourist authority addresses listed below are for information within each country. For US addresses of national tourist authorities, see *National Tourist Offices in the US*, GETTING READY TO GO.

Andorra

TOURIST INFORMATION: The center for assistance is the Sindicat d'Iniciativa de les Valls d'Andorra, Plaça Príncep 1, Andorra la Vieja (phone: 2-0214).

ENTRY REQUIREMENTS: Andorra has none, but France and Spain have checkpoints on their sides of the border and will request a valid US passport.

CLIMATE AND CLOTHES: All 175 square miles of Andorra are tucked into a few folds high up in the eastern Pyrenees between Spain and France. The altitude assures snow-capped mountains and chilly evenings the year round, but the temperature on June, July, and August days can easily reach 80°F (25°C) before plunging at nightfall, so pack cottons as well as heavy sweaters.

MONEY: The French franc, which equals 100 centimes, and Spanish peseta, which equals 100 centimos, are both legal tender.

LANGUAGE: Catalán, spoken in neighboring Spain, is the official tongue but French and Spanish are equally common. Shopkeepers and hoteliers speak English.

GETTING THERE/GETTING AROUND: Train – Andorra is one of the few countries in Europe without an inch of train track on its territory. The nearest train station in Spain is at Puigcerdá, from which bus connections are available to Andorra la Vieja.

From France, the French railway stops at Ax-les-Thermes and l'Hospitalet and the Société-Franco-Andorrane de Transports runs buses from these two towns to Andorra la Vieja.

Buses – Seasonal bus service between Latour-de-Carol, France, and the main centers in Andorra is provided by Autos Víuda Pujol Huguet. There are also daily buses from Barcelona, Spain. Microbuses serve the principal Andorran villages from Andorra la Vieja.

Cars – Winter snows can close the main French Rte. 20 to Andorra. The alternate, all-weather route is Spain's Rte. C1313 from Puigcerdá to Seo de Urgel, where it connects with Rte. C145 to Andorra.

SPECIAL EVENTS: The *Feste de Andorra la Vieja* is the first Saturday, Sunday, and Monday in August.

SHOPPING: On weekends, the roads leading through Andorra la Vieja are as clogged with shoppers as Macy's aisles during Christmas. Tax-free merchandise (often a euphemism for smuggled goods) is the goal, and cars bulging with purchases can barely pass one another on the narrow thoroughfare. Cigarettes, sheepskin jackets, liquor, Parisian fashions, gasoline, canned goods, and perfume are just a few of the bargains that lure the shopper. Most stores are open 7 days a week.

TIPPING: Sometimes restaurants and hotels include service charges, sometimes not. From 10% to 15% is the expected tip.

Austria

TOURIST INFORMATION: Literature can be obtained from the Austrian National Tourist Office (Oesterreichische Fremdenverkehrswerbung), Margaretenstr. 1, A 1040 Vienna (phone: 222-56-16-66). Regional information is provided by state tourist offices found in the capital cities of the nine states and called either *Landesfremden-verkehrs-verband* or *Fremdenverkehrsverband.*

ENTRY REQUIREMENTS: US citizens with valid US passports need no visas for visits of 3 months or less.

CLIMATE AND CLOTHES: Mountains cover over 70% of the country and altitude rather than latitude determines temperature. Be prepared for summer showers. On the whole, the climate is moderate with summer daytime averages in the 70s F (20°C) and nights cooling to the 50s F (10°C). Winter days are in the 30s F (0°C) and 40s F (5°C). Comfortable sporting gear is standard. For Vienna, you'll want something chic for a gala evening on the town.

MONEY: The Austrian Schilling (AS internationally, S in Austria) is divided into 100 Groschen.

LANGUAGE: German *(Hochdeutsch)* is the written language and is taught in the schools but numerous and pronounced regional dialects exist. English is taught as the second language and is understood in major tourist areas.

GETTING THERE/GETTING AROUND: Airlines – Royal Jordanian Airlines (ALIA) and Romanian Air (TAROM) are the only airlines with nonstop service to Vienna from New York. (Royal Jordanian also offers direct flights from Los Angeles.) Austrian Airlines, as well as many other European airlines, connect most major European cities with Vienna and other Austrian destinations. Austrian Airlines offers daily domestic service from Vienna to Graz, Klagenfurt, Linz, and Salzburg; Tyrolean Airways has daily service from Vienna to Innsbruck, Frankfurt, and Zürich.

Trains – Austrian Federal Railways (OeBB) offers the Austrian Network Pass (for passengers ages 27 to 60) and the Austria Ticket (a youth pass for those between 6 and 26), which provide unlimited travel on trains, postal buses, certain steamers, and cogwheel railways. 50% discounts are available to travelers over 60 (women) and 65 (men).

Cars – European makes can be rented from the usual array of international and local firms in all major Austrian cities. Rates are based on a 24-hour period. Rentals in increments of 5, 12, and 24 hours are available through the OeBB's Car at the Station plan. Road condition information in English can be obtained daily from 6 AM to 10 PM in Vienna by phoning 72997 and from other areas by dialing 0222-7-2997.

SPECIAL EVENTS: Austria's most famous musical festivals are: *International Music Festival of Vienna,* May and June, reservations from the Austria Travel Agency, Opernring 3-5, A-1010 Vienna (phone: 5-6000); the *Carinthian Summer Festival* in Ossiach and Villach, June through August; the *Bregenz Festival on Lake Constance* in July and August; and the *Salzburg Festival* also in July and August. Tickets for all of these are available in the US through Mrs. Rosemarie Fliegel, 500 Fifth Ave., New York, NY 10110 (phone: 212-944-6891).

SHOPPING: Dirndls, lederhosen, alpine hats with a rakish feather or enameled emblem, and fabric printed with folkloric patterns are all evocative of provincial Austria and can be purchased regionally at *Heimatwerk* shops, which generally have the best selection of local artisans' work. Other specialties include the ubiquitous enamelware, loden cloth coats and jackets, well-designed sweaters, Viennese petit-point articles, precious jewelry, porcelain, and glassware. Sleek Austrian skiwear is a bargain only for those paying top dollar. The form-fitting outfit that costs $350 in the US can be had for about $200 at shops near the slopes.

Stores are open between 8 AM and 6 PM; some close for 2 hours at noon for lunch. Most close Saturdays at noon, and all day Sundays.

TIPPING: Service charges run between 10% and 15% on restaurant and hotel bills, with the higher percentage included in luxury establishment bills. Porters and bellmen should receive 10 schillings per bag, doormen about 5, and taxi drivers 10% of the fare.

Belgium

TOURIST INFORMATION: Rue Marche aux Herbes 61, 1000 Bruxelles (Brussels), is the address for Tourist Information Brussels (TIB), 513-8940. Tourist offices in all other cities are called either Syndicat d'Initiative or Dienst voor Toerisme.

ENTRY REQUIREMENTS: A valid US passport is good for visits of 3 months or less by US citizens.

CLIMATE AND CLOTHES: The sea is the predominant influence on the weather and the gently undulating hills that cover a good part of the country's interior don't stop the prevailing westerlies. In the Ardennes morning fogs near the shore turn into evening mists. The climate is temperate with few extremes. Temperatures reach 70°F (21°C) in summer and drop to the low 40s (near 0°C) in winter. Dress is cosmopolitan and French in style. Bikinis are much in evidence on Belgium's west coast beaches, but none are St.-Tropez style, and whatever swimming attire you wear you must keep on.

MONEY: The Belgian franc (BF) equals 100 centimes.

LANGUAGE: French is spoken by inhabitants of the Walloon area south of Brussels — about 32% of the population. Brussels itself is primarily French-speaking but lies in Flanders, where the language is Flemish, an accented version of Dutch. German is the third national language but is spoken by less than 1% of the inhabitants. English is widely understood.

GETTING THERE/GETTING AROUND: Airlines – Sabena flies nonstop from Boston, Chicago, Detroit, Atlanta, and New York to Brussels. Pan Am, TWA, and Tower Air also fly to Brussels from New York.

Trains – Belgium's rail network is said to be the world's most comprehensive. The Société Nationale Chemin de Fer Belge (SNCB) offers three reduced-fare plans and also the Benelux Tourail season ticket, good for 10 consecutive days of unlimited travel between March 1 and September 30 on the Belgian, Dutch, and Luxembourg railways.

Cars – Motoring information as well as breakdown service is provided by the Touring Club de Belgique, rue de la Loi 44, 1040 Brussels (phone: 513-8240), and the Royal Automobile Club de Belgique, which also has an SOS breakdown number (phone: 736-5959). The small yellow cars of the touring *secours* (literally, "help") patrol offer assistance to motorists in need.

SPECIAL EVENTS: Belgian folkloric pageants and processions are famed and numerous. *Carnival* in Binche climaxes on Shrove Tuesday with costumed and ostrich-plumed "Gilles" pummeling the crowds with oranges. Ascension Day in May is celebrated in Bruges by the famed *Procession of the Holy Blood;* and also in May, the *Cat Festival* of Iper features costumes, floats, and the tossing of plush cats from the town's belfry.

SHOPPING: Chocolate is a Belgian specialty. *Godiva* has its own stores in Belgium, but is by no means the only source for fine chocolates. The true maven should also seek out the *Neuhaus, Corne de la Toison d'Or,* and *Wittamer* brands.

Pewter, manufactured by *Les Potstainiers Hugo* in Huy and *Meestertingieters* in Tongeren, and *Val St. Lambert* crystal are good buys. Belgian linen and laces are justifiably famous.

The beautifully balanced sporting guns of the *Fabrique Nationale* in Herstal, among the aristocracy of shotguns, can be specially ordered with scenes hand etched by local craftsmen.

Larger Belgian stores are open from 9:15 AM to 6 PM. Smaller shops that close for lunch usually remain open until 8 PM.

TIPPING: A 16% service charge is added to most restaurant bills and is also included on taxi meters.

Bulgaria

TOURIST INFORMATION: Balkantourist, the state travel agency, has headquarters at 1 Vitoša Blvd. in Sofia (phone: 84-131, ext. 284). Local tourist information offices throughout the country provide maps and other materials and assistance.

ENTRY REQUIREMENTS: US citizens require a visa to enter the country unless they are traveling with a tour group or with a group of six or more and possess a voucher indicating they have prepaid for tourist services. People entering on business or without prearranged accommodations must obtain visas from the Bulgarian embassy or consulate before leaving the US. When applying for a business visa, you must present a "letter of invitation" from the company you are visiting. Both tourist and business visas cost $14 and are available within 7 business days of filling out the appropriate forms. Contact the Bulgarian Embassy, 1621 22nd St. NW, Washington, DC 20008 (phone: 202-387-7969).

CLIMATE AND CLOTHES: The Balkan Mountains (highest range is the Rila Dagh, at more than 9,000 feet) crisscross the country to reach straight to the edge of the Black Sea and its golden beaches. Summers are dry but not oppressively hot (80s F, high 20s C) and winters cold, dry, and relatively windless with temperatures in the 30s F (around 0°C). Informality is the keynote in summer dress. Jackets and ties (and warm coats) are best for fall and winter in Sofia, the capital.

MONEY: The lev equals 100 stotinki. *Note:* The exchange rate is 80% higher for tourists.

LANGUAGE: Bulgarian, a South Slavic tongue, is similar to Russian and uses a Cyrillic alphabet. You can just navigate the tourist circuit with English (Russian is the second language) and should consider the use of English-speaking guides if you wish to communicate in the countryside.

GETTING THERE/GETTING AROUND: Airlines – There's no direct US-Bulgaria service but Balkanair and other international carriers connect Sofia to all European capitals. Within Bulgaria, Balkanair flies between the major cities at reasonable rates. Bus-Tours run by Balkantourist are accompanied by multilingual guides, alleviate the language problem, and are suggested for sight-seeing.

Trains – The BDG (Bulgarian State Railway) service between Sofia and Varna on the Black Sea is frequent and efficient but most other trains are locals and crowded.

Cars – Probably the best bet for the tourist, with rentals of Russian Zhigulis, Mercedes-Benz, Volkswagens, and Toyotas available through Shipka, the touring agency of the Bulgarian Motorists Union, 6 St. Sofia St., Sofia (phone: 87-99-21). It also issues gas coupons that can save travelers between 20% and 30%. Free emergency assistance is provided by road aid cars that patrol the highways or can be called (phone: 146).

SPECIAL EVENTS: Bulgaria is the world's leading exporter of attar of roses and one of the biggest festivals occurs the first Sunday in June celebrating the harvest of the huge rose crop, which covers a 20-mile swath in the Kazanlŭk area.

Slunchev Bryag, best known as Sunny Beach, on Bulgaria's Riviera hosts a pop music festival called *Golden Orpheus* in early June, which brings entertainers and groups from all over the world. In a more serious vein, Sofia's continuous musical weeks in May and June concentrate on the classical, and Plovdiv has chamber music concerts throughout the month of June. Humor is the focus of Gabrovo's biannual (odd years only) comedic extravaganza, which brings tourists from all over the world to this centrally located town for 10 days in mid-May.

SHOPPING: Attar of roses in hand-carved wooden containers is the most popular Bulgarian souvenir, but larger purchases could include leathergoods or the rugs made in Kotel (in general, a center for crafts), which come in a variety of colorful designs, or those of Chiprovtsi. The *Bulgarian Artists Union* runs shops around the country featuring products of the membership, and the state-run foreign currency *Corecom* stores are a good source for other Bulgarian products including silks and sheepskin coats. Normal store hours are 8:30 AM to 7 PM Mondays through Saturdays.

TIPPING: In theory tips are not accepted; in practice they are. About 10% of a restaurant bill.

Czechoslovakia

TOURIST INFORMATION: Čedok's blue sign with the white bird in flight signifies general tourist services at some 150 locations throughout the country. Its main branch is at Na příkopě 18, Prague (phone: 212-7111), and its accommodations service is at Panská 5, Prague. Larger cities also have tourist information centers.

ENTRY REQUIREMENTS: US tourists require a visa good for visits of up to 30 days. Czechoslovak consulates and embassies abroad issue visas within 48 hours upon receipt of an application, two passport photos, and a fee of $12. In order to obtain a visa, proof of prepaid land arrangements or Čedok vouchers amounting to $15 per person per day must be submitted. This foreign exchange requirement can be handled at the border.

CLIMATE AND CLOTHES: Czechoslovakia is really three contiguous areas snaking across central Europe, and temperatures are about the same in all three — Bohemia, Moravia, and Slovakia. Average temperatures are around 70°F (21°C) in summer, and the low 20s F (a little below 0°C) in winter, although mountains are chillier in both seasons.

Dress is casual but conservative. Evenings at luxury resorts such as Karlovy Vary (Carlsbad) and Mariánské Lázně (Marienbad) call for reasonably dressy clothes.

MONEY: One koruna (Kčs.) is comprised of 100 halers. It is illegal to import or export Czechoslovak currency.

LANGUAGE: Czech is spoken by about two thirds of the population — those living in the Czech Socialist Republic — a combination of the Bohemian and Moravian countries. Slovak, the native language of the rest of the population, is spoken in the eastern Slovak Socialist Republic. Both languages are Slavic and very similar. Those engaged in tourism speak English.

GETTING THERE/GETTING AROUND: Airlines – CSA, the Czechoslovak airline, flies the New York–Prague route with Iljusin 62s nonstop in summer and from Montreal year-round. Prague is the hub from which domestic flights on CSA radiate to 13 airports, including Brno, Bratislava, Košice, Ostrava, Piešťany (for spas), and Poprad in the Tatras (for skiing and mountaineering).

Bus – Express bus service to East Germany, Austria, Poland, Russia, Yugoslavia, and Hungary as well as domestic service aboard CSAD coaches, next to the airlines, is probably the fastest way of traveling in Czechoslovakia.

Trains – There's frequent service aboard trains of the Československé Státní Dráhy (CSD) and various European expresses stop at Prague, Bratislava, and Brno.

Cars – The Yellow Angels in four-wheel vehicles of the Ustredni Automotoklub provide emergency service for motorists. Gas coupons are sold at frontier crossings or at the automobile club office in Prague at Opletalova 29 (phone: 22-35-44).

SPECIAL EVENTS: Fine international performances are part of Prague's annual spring music festival, *Prague Spring (Pražské Jaro)*, beginning May 12, the anniversary of the Czech composer Bedřich Smetana's death, and continuing through June 4. Two colorful folk festivals offer grand displays of typical costumes, music, and dances of the republic's two states, the *Moravian Fete* held in Strážnice in June, and the *Slovakian Festival* in Východná in July.

SHOPPING: Antiques are a lure, and the small shops in Prague delight the collector and window-shopper alike. However, antiques must be purchased at *Tuzex*-approved shops to be eligible for export. State-supported *Tuzex* shops sell a wide range of crafts and tourist goods, such as Bohemian glass and porcelain and fine quality records, for foreign currency. Modern applied arts are sold at *Art Centrum* in Prague and special folk art outlets for hand-painted Easter eggs, straw Christmas ornaments, jewelry, woven linens, and the like, are found in many towns. Long store hours facilitate shopping. Shops are open Mondays through Fridays from 9 AM to 6 PM, Saturdays from 9 AM to 1 PM.

TIPPING: Restaurant bills don't include service charges, and at least 10% should be added; taxi drivers also expect 10% tips; 5 korunas should be given to porters and doormen.

Denmark

TOURIST INFORMATION: The central office of Denmark's Turistråd, across the street from Copenhagen's Town Hall at Hans Christian Andersen Blvd. 22, Copenhagen V (phone: 11-14-15), has maps, brochures, and literature on touring the entire country as well as Greenland and the Faeroe Islands; its 12 regional offices in Denmark's major cities are equally well stocked. Innumerable local *turistbureaus* and regional offices of the *Turistråd* are distinguished by the international tourist logo, a green sign carrying a lowercase *i*.

ENTRY REQUIREMENTS: A valid US passport is good for visits of 3 months or less.

CLIMATE AND CLOTHES: Thanks to the Gulf Stream, winters are relatively mild with daytime temperatures averaging 34°F (about 0°C) in February, the coldest month. The changeable summer weather often includes rainstorms and the long summer nights can be chilly but summer days average about 70°F (21°C). The casual Danish lifestyle is reflected in an equally casual attitude about clothes.

MONEY: The Danish krone (DKr) equals 100 øre.

LANGUAGE: Danish, but English has been compulsory in secondary schools since World War II and is spoken and understood throughout the country.

GETTING THERE/GETTING AROUND: Airlines – SAS flies directly to Copenhagen from Anchorage, Chicago, Los Angeles, New York, and Seattle. Northwest serves Copenhagen from its gateway cities of Boston, Detroit, Minneapolis, New York, and Seattle. Icelandic Airlines has regularly scheduled flights from Baltimore, Chicago, and New York to Copenhagen (all with stops in Reykjavík); Finnair has weekly flights to Copenhagen from New York. Danair's domestic flights leave Copenhagen's Kastrup Airport for Bornholm, Fünen, and nine airports in Jutland and the Faeroe Islands. SAS has service to Greenland. Cheap charters carry sun-starved Scandinavians to warmer Mediterranean shores such as Greece, Israel, and Majorca.

Trains – The modern Intercity and L (Lyntog) expresses crisscross the country at great speeds, navigating the crossing between Zealand and Fünen aboard huge, handsome ferries. At other junctions, you leave the train, cross by boat, and board another train to continue. The Danish State Railway, Dansk Statsbaner (DSB), is one of the sponsors of the new Scandinavian Rail Pass, and also honors the Eurailpass.

Ferries – The DSB ferries are an integral part of the highway and rail system and, though they have been supplemented by bridges, they are still an essential part of the major crossing between Fünen and Zealand, called the Store Baelt (Great Belt).

SPECIAL EVENTS: In July and August, Odense recreates local boy Hans Christian Andersen's fairy tales. Frederikssund's *Viking Festival* in June and July is a fine historical pageant. An array of first-class cultural events is held all summer long at Copenhagen's *Tivoli* amusement park, open from May to mid-September.

SHOPPING: Shopping in Copenhagen is a trip in itself. *Bing & Grøndahl* and *Royal Copenhagen* porcelain, *Holmegaard* glass, *Georg Jensen* silver, and furs from *A. C. Bang* and *Birgir Christensen* are but a few of the products that make the dedicated shopper shiver with delight. Some better buys are *Bornholm* ceramics, handmade woolens from Tönder and the Faeroe Islands, and *Lego* toys. Herring, ham, and the national drink, aquavit, can always cheer you up when you contemplate your empty wallet back home. Denmark has a stiff sales tax (MOMS), but the 22% MOMS can be saved by having stores send purchases to your Danish point of exit or home. (Any item costing $75 or more is exempt from the tax.)

There are no firmly fixed national store hours but generally they're open weekdays between 9 AM and 5:30 PM and on Saturday mornings.

TIPPING: Railway porters and washroom attendants receive tips, but otherwise they are not expected unless a special service has been provided. Service charges are always included in restaurant bills and taxi meters.

Finland

TOURIST INFORMATION: The Finnish Tourist Board (MEK) has a regional office in Rovaniemi and is headquartered in Helsinki at Asemapäällikönkatu 12B, 00530 Helsinki (phone: 144-511). All cities and towns have city tourist offices (Matkailutoimisto), identified by the lowercase *i* on a green background.

ENTRY REQUIREMENTS: A valid US passport is required for visits of 3 months or less by US citizens.

CLIMATE AND CLOTHES: In the south, snow covers the country from December to mid-April, when it begins melting. Winter comes earlier to the north, around the end of October, and stays later, until mid-May. Midday temperatures in Helsinki average 72°F (22°C) in July, the warmest month, and 25°F (−4°C) in February, the coldest. At Ivalo, to the far north, warm July days average 66°F (18°C) and cool February days, 17°F (−8°C).

Informal dress is frowned upon in the better restaurants, where jackets and ties are expected. In general, the tenor is slightly more conservative than in other Scandinavian countries.

MONEY: The Finnish markka (FIM) equals 100 pennis.

LANGUAGE: Finland's two official tongues are Finnish, spoken by 93% of the Finnish people, which like Hungarian and Estonian is a Finno-Ugric language; and Swedish, an Indo-European language spoken by about 6.5% of the people. Lappish, also Finno-Ugric, is the native speech of about 2,000 citizens. English is found in the major tourist centers and is the country's most widely spoken foreign language.

GETTING THERE/GETTING AROUND: Airlines – Only Finnair flights link New York, Seattle, and Los Angeles with Helsinki directly. SAS flies from New York to Helsinki via Copenhagen and Stockholm. Domestically, they serve 21 cities at some of the cheapest fares in Europe. Finnair offers a Holiday Ticket good for 15 days of unlimited domestic air travel, as well as family and senior citizen discounts.

Trains – Valtionrautatiet (VR) provides excellent equipment and service relatively inexpensively and offers a selection of discount tourist plans including the Finnrail Pass, for various periods of unlimited travel; the Tourist Ticket, which includes bus, boat, air, and train travel, valid for a year; and the Scandinavian Rail Pass.

Cars – The 519-mile trip between Helsinki and Rovaniemi, the capital of Lapland on the Arctic Circle, takes 2 days by car over well-maintained, year-round roads. Car rentals are readily available in Helsinki.

Ferries, Ships, and Other Transport – The series of interconnecting lakes in western, central, and southeastern Finland seems to take up more room than the landmass there. A varied fleet, from hydrofoils to small lake steamers, provides service in this unique area. The railroad's northern terminus is Kemijarvi, just above the Arctic Circle. As a result, buses are the primary surface transport as well as being a major means of transit in the northern region of Lapland. Contact Oy Matkahuolto Ab, Lauttasaarentie 8, 00200 Helsinki (phone: 692-20-88), for overseas bus depots, reservations, and ticket sales in Finland.

SPECIAL EVENTS: All Finland is a festival between June and September, with many diverse cultural events. Music is the theme of most, with the performing arts celebrated in Helsinki throughout the summer.

In mid-February the *Salpausselkä Skiing Championships* feature cross-country ski races at Lahti. The beginning of March brings the *Kuopio Skating Marathon* in Kuopio. Also in Feburary is the 75-kilometer *Finlandia Ski Race* between Hämeenlinna and Lahti. Reindeer roundups in Lapland are in progress from October to February.

SHOPPING: The Finnish genius for modern design has made *Marimekko* fabrics, *Arabia* ceramics, and *Iittala* glassware international household names. *Lapponia* jewelry, fusing gold and silver in stylized replicas of natural forms, is highly regarded, as is the *Aarikka* line of wooden jewelry. Multicolored patterned rya rugs come from Finland as do the orange-handled scissors made by *Fiskars,* which also makes a fine line of steel cutlery. Traditional decorated *Puukko* sheath knives make perfect presents for outdoor people. For an overall view of Finnish products, stop at Helsinki's *Design Center* at Kasarminkatu 19.

The Finnish 14% sales tax (VAT) can be avoided by having stores send purchases to your departure point or directly home. Summer shopping hours are generally 8:30 AM to 5 PM on weekdays and 9 AM to 3 PM on Saturdays.

TIPPING: Restaurants add a 14% service charge during the week and 15% on Sundays and holidays, but you can leave a bit extra for the waiter, and make sure to tip about 3 Fmks to the restaurant doorman. Hotel bills also include the service. Porters receive 3 Fmks but others, including cab drivers, don't expect tips.

France

TOURIST INFORMATION: The Office of Tourism is headquartered at 127 Champs-Élysées, Paris (phone: 723-6172), and has branches at the major train stations such as the Gare du Nord, Gare de l'est, Gare de Lyon, and Gare d'Austerlitz. Local Syndicats d'Initiative (SI) supply literature in cities and towns. Regional information is available in Paris from the more than 20 provincial tourist bureaus, called collectively Maisons de Province à Paris, scattered around the city.

ENTRY REQUIREMENTS: For visits of less than 3 months US citizens need only a valid passport.

CLIMATE AND CLOTHES: It's generally fair and warm in the summertime, particularly in the south. Winters are mild, with overall daytime averages in the 40s F (about 5°C), rising to highs of around 55°F (12°C) in January and February along the Riviera.

The celebrated French sense of style is best illustrated by the manner of dress. Visitors will certainly not feel ill at ease dressed casually and comfortably, but you may find a visit to Paris the perfect opportunity to practice a little Parisian chic.

MONEY: The French franc (F) equals 100 centimes.

LANGUAGE: French is spoken with verve and pride and, while you can get by with English, you're well advised to use whatever French words and phrases you know. Residents of Paris have a reputation for dealing coldly with non-French speakers. This is only partially justified, and in the provinces visitors will find few who speak English but an enormous amount of cordiality and patience.

GETTING THERE/GETTING AROUND: Airlines – Air France has daily Concorde flights between New York and Paris. Concorde flights take 3 hours 45 minutes from New York to Paris. Tickets cost about 20% more than subsonic first-class fares. Air France flies nonstop to Paris from Anchorage, Chicago, Houston, Los Angeles, New York, and Washington, DC; TWA flies nonstop from Boston, New York, St. Louis, and in high season from Washington, DC; Pan Am flies nonstop from New York to Orly Airport in Paris, nonstop from New York to Nice, and one-stop from Los Angeles to Paris. Delta, American, and Aeroméxico fly nonstop from Atlanta, Dallas/Fort Worth, and Miami respectively.

Air Inter, the national domestic carrier, serves approximately 30 French cities as well as Corsica.

Trains – With over 22,000 miles of track, France has the largest rail network on the Continent, and, with crack Corail and turbotrains and the new TGV (train à grande vitesse), the fastest trains. The TGV has set records, but its maximum speed in commercial operation is 170 mph. It cuts the trip from Paris to Lyon to 2 hours, and there are numerous round trips daily.

The *France Vacances* rail pass offers unlimited travel over the entire Société Nationale des Chemins de Fer Français (SNCF) French railway system. Available for either first- or second-class travel, for periods of 7 or 15 days or 1 month, it must be purchased before going abroad, either from a travel agent or from French National Railroads offices in the US.

For train information in English in Paris, call 380-5050.

Cars – French toll roads, called *autoroutes*, are well patrolled and breakdown service is readily available. Emergency call boxes are being installed on other routes.

SPECIAL EVENTS: The *Festival d'Avignon*, a theater festival held annually in July and August, has no peer in France. Some wonderful, purely musical festivals take place each summer, among them the Strasbourg *International Music Festival* in early June, the *International Music and Opera Festival* in mid-July in Aix, and the *Berlioz Festival* in September in Lyon.

Famous sporting events include the *Le Mans* 24-hour race in mid-June and the *Tour de France,* the world's premier bicycle race, the first 3 weeks in July. The *Air Show* at Le Bourget takes place in June of odd-numbered years and the *Auto Show* in Paris in October of even years. The *Cannes Film Festival* is held annually in May.

Dijon's *Gastronomic Fair* in early November is followed by the *Three Days of Glory* in Nuits-Saint-Georges, Beaune, and Meursault nearby.

SHOPPING: Boutiques, no matter how beautiful, are pricey. You might have to work harder to find wholesale outlets or stores that carry seconds, discontinued lines, and overstocks, but they exist and the savings are significant. Decent prices on housewares can be found in large Parisian department stores or their branches as well as at the usually cheaper *Prisunic* and *Monoprix* chains.

For the ultimate in bric-a-brac shopping stop at any hamlet, no matter how small, on market day. Regional products include pottery from Quimper and Vallauris and porcelain from Limoges, as well as truffles from Périgord, mustards from Dijon, and herbs from Provence, also the home of lovely printed fabrics, exemplified by the Souleido cottons.

Most department stores are open Mondays through Saturdays from 9 AM to 6:30 PM, with one or two late-night closings. Boutiques close on Mondays as well as Sundays and for a 2-hour lunch break between noon and 2 PM.

TIPPING: Hotel and restaurant bills include a 12% to 15% service charge. The doorman should receive 5F per piece, for help with suitcases; the room service waiter 10F; the chambermaid is covered by the hotel's overall service charge. Taxi drivers are rarely tipped by the French but may expect it from an American; 10% will suffice.

East Germany

TOURIST INFORMATION: The Reisebüro der GDR (Travel Agency of the German Democratic Republic) is charged with all tourist-related matters. The central office in East Berlin is at Alexanderplatz 5 (phone: 215-4402). There are Reisebüro offices throughout the country and at all international border crossings as well. Most cities also have their own information bureaus.

ENTRY REQUIREMENTS: In order to obtain a visa you need the dates and itinerary for your visit and must then obtain prepaid hotel reservations for each night. Necessary application forms may be had directly from the Reisebüro in East Berlin, from US travel agents, Reisebüro-appointed agencies in Western Europe, and Reisebüro offices in Eastern Europe. Once processed (processing can take 8 to 10 weeks), the GDR issues a visa entitlement certificate that entitles the holder to the required visa either at the border or from the embassy in Washington. Transit visas are issued at the border with proof of a visa for the next country. Day passes for visits to East Berlin (visits must end at midnight) are issued in West Berlin at Checkpoint Charlie or for pedestrians only at the Bahnhof Friedrichstrasse.

CLIMATE AND CLOTHES: The primarily flat topography stretches as far south as Leipzig, where the foothills of the Thuringian Mountains begin. Climatic changes can be abrupt as a result of the combination of the moist northern Baltic maritime climate with that of the mountains to the south and west. The average temperature in July is

62°F (16°C) although it can rise as high as 85°F (29°C). The January average is 20°F (−6°C) but it can plunge to 0°F (−18°C). Casual, informal dress is fine.

MONEY: The ostmark (OM) is comprised of 100 pfennigs. There's no limit to the amount of foreign currency that can be brought in, but it must be declared upon entering. It's illegal to import or export ostmarks.

LANGUAGE: *Hoch Deutsch* or High German is the official language but *Platt* (or low) *Deutsch* is spoken in the north and the Saxon dialect is common in the south. About 300,000 Sorbs (Wends) live in Lusatia and speak a Slavic tongue. Many engaged in tourism speak English.

GETTING THERE/GETTING AROUND: Airlines – Pan Am flies from New York to West Berlin's Tegel Airport via London; LOT, the Polish airline, has nonstop service from New York to Warsaw with connections to East Berlin's Schönefeld Airport; Interflug, the GDR line, has flights from major European cities to East Berlin.

Trains – Deutsche Reichsbahn (DR) trains run frequently and many have automobile transport facilities, particularly useful if you're making connections with the car and passenger ferries crossing the Baltic between Warnemünde and Gedser, Denmark, or Sassnitz and Trelleborg, Sweden.

Cars – Travel in locally available rental cars, or your own, is unrestricted although you must have prearranged overnight accommodations that must be honored. A valid driver's license is required and GDR insurance must be purchased even if you have a Green Card. Autobahns are toll roads, unless you are in transit to and from West Germany. You can pay for gas in foreign currency or with discount gas coupons purchased at the border at Intertank stations.

SPECIAL EVENTS: Leipzig's industrial fairs originated over 800 years ago and are held semiannually in the spring and fall. Hotel space is limited and reservations should be made 6 months in advance.

The cultural scene is lively year-round. Advance ticket reservations can be made with US travel agents or Reisebüro offices for performances of popular attractions such as operas at the *Deutsche Staatsoper* or for plays by the Brecht-created *Berliner Ensemble.*

SHOPPING: Porcelain manufacturing began in Meissen and you can buy the products as well as tour the plant, *Staatliche Porzellan-Fabrik,* there. Craft articles include stoneware, hand-carved wood products, and embroidery. Goose-down bedding has traditionally kept the population warm and can do the same for you if you care to carry some home. Stores are generally open 9 AM to 7 PM weekdays and 9 AM to noon on Saturdays.

TIPPING: Not officially encouraged, but accepted; a tip of 10%, or a minimum of 3 OMs for small services, is the norm.

West Germany

TOURIST INFORMATION: The German National Tourist Board (Deutsche Zentrale für Tourismus, DZT) is located at D-6000 Frankfurt am Main, Beethovenstrasse 69 (phone: 069-7572-0). A small charge is usually made for regional publications, available at local tour offices, called *Verkehrsverein,* located in train stations, city halls, tourist kiosks, and storefronts throughout the country.

ENTRY REQUIREMENTS: No visa is necessary for periods of 3 months or less for US citizens with valid US passports.

CLIMATE AND CLOTHES: Generally moderate temperatures prevail from the shores of the North Sea south over the forests and river valleys to the slopes of the Bavarian Alps. Summer days average a comfortable 70°F (21°C), but be prepared for chilly evenings that sometimes dip to the low to mid-50s F (about 10°C).

Dress is conservative in the cities, though not forbiddingly so. Ties for men are absolutely required only in the casinos and better restaurants; jackets will suffice in most first-class establishments. There are some nude beaches; except for these, keep your suits on.

MONEY: The deutsche mark (DM) equals 100 pfennigs.

LANGUAGE: High German is the written language and the one that's commonly spoken, albeit with different accents, throughout the country. Regional dialects, Bavarian for one, are on the wane but are still found in small towns and rural areas.

English, mandatory in German schools since World War II, is common among the younger generations and is the second language of the country today.

GETTING THERE/GETTING AROUND: Airlines – Lufthansa regularly schedules direct flights between New York and Frankfurt, Hamburg, and Düsseldorf; between Atlanta, Boston, Chicago, Dallas, Miami, Los Angeles, San Francisco, and Frankfurt; and between Miami and Düsseldorf. Pan Am now offers direct flights to Frankfurt from New York and Miami and also flies from New York to Munich, Berlin, Hamburg, Düsseldorf, and Stuttgart. TWA flies directly to Frankfurt from New York. World Airways flies to Frankfurt from Baltimore/Washington International Airport.

Delta has direct service from Atlanta to Frankfurt. Northwest Orient has flights to Hamburg from New York, and Air Florida connects Miami with both Frankfurt and Düsseldorf.

Trains – The Germanrail Tourist Card is good for 9 or 16 days of unlimited travel over the Deutsche Bundesbahn's (DB) 15,000-mile rail network. Included is a discount for travel to West Berlin. The tourist card is only available outside Germany. DB also sells youth tickets and offers discounts to senior citizens. (The Eurailpasses are valid on the DB.)

Cars – The exceptionally large range of models available for rent runs the gamut from VWs to a selection of motor homes. Money-saving rentals of 30 days or more, called leases, are good values.

Cruises – Advance reservations are essential for the exceedingly popular 2-, 3-, and 4-day Rhine cruises run by the Koln-Düsseldorfer German Rhine Line (K-D), 170 Hamilton Ave., White Plains, NY 10601 (phone: 914-948-3600).

SPECIAL EVENTS: The *Richard Wagner Opera Festival* in Bayreuth takes place in July and August every year. The prudent will order direct from Bayreuth at least a year in advance. Write: Festspielleitung Bayreuth, Postfach 2320, 8580 Bayreuth 2. The German National Tourist Office's *Calendar of Events* is insurance against missing any of the fairs, folk festivals, concerts, and the like, that take place throughout the country each year.

SHOPPING: So, he's promised you a Mercedes-Benz. You can save something like $2,000 to $4,000 on the US purchase price of any Mercedes diesel model, if you order it in advance from a US dealer or overseas delivery specialist to be picked up in Germany. Making a more modest dent in your wallet are excellent German steel cutlery, goose-down comforters, Rosenthal china and glassware, cameras, optical goods, and toys (wooden ones for the younger set or, for the more sophisticated, multicomponent structural types such as *Fischer technik*).

Inquire locally about rebates on the German 14% VAT sales tax. Stores are open weekdays from 9 AM to 6:30 PM with some closing for lunch. They follow the same hours the first Saturday of every month but close at 2 PM the other three Saturdays.

TIPPING: A 10% to 12% service charge is customarily included in restaurant checks. Superior service may warrant something in addition. Porters receive 1 deutsche mark a bag. Taxi drivers should get about 15% of the fare.

Gibraltar

TOURIST INFORMATION: The Gibraltar Tourist Information Center is at Cathedral Square (phone: 76400) on the Rock; write for literature to PO Box 303, Gibraltar.

ENTRY REQUIREMENTS: US citizens can enter this British colony with a valid US passport and can stay for up to 3 months.

CLIMATE AND CLOTHES: Hot summer temperatures in the high 80s and low 90s (mid 20s to low 30s C) are kept comfortable both by southeasterly sea breezes and by dips in the Mediterranean. Lightweight, light-colored clothes are pro forma. The rainy season is during the cooler — mid-60s (16°C), low-70s (22°C) — winter months.

MONEY: The pound sterling (£) is comprised of 100 pence. Gibraltar prints its own bank notes, which can only be used locally; the British pound sterling is also valid.

LANGUAGE: The Gibraltar residents are British subjects and English is the official language, but Spanish is commonly spoken.

GETTING THERE/GETTING AROUND: Gibraltar Airways and British Airways fly from London in 2½ hours. Gibair Viscounts make the 20-minute trip from Tangiers to Gibraltar twice a day and the Mons Calpe car and passenger ferry takes 2½ hours one way. There is summer hydrofoil service.

On the Rock, touring is done on foot or by minibus, taxi, or rental car.

SPECIAL EVENTS: A self-governing British colony, Gibraltar celebrates a few anniversaries like the *Battle of Trafalgar Day,* in October, and *Remembrance Day,* in November.

The most prominent religious festival in this predominantly Catholic colony is *Holy Week,* when outdoor processions and special services are held.

Deep-sea and pier fishing competitions take place year-round, and the *Shark Angling Festival* is held in April.

SHOPPING: Gibraltar is a very good shopping place for tourists, with duty-free facilities at the air terminal and at a few shops. Also, there is no VAT. It's a bargain bonanza for British products such as whiskey, woolens, and linens, as well as such international goods as gold jewelry, pearls, leathergoods, fishing tackle, sporting goods, and watches. North African mementos including camel saddles and djellabas can be picked up at one of the raffish bazaars that coexist with the more stately boutiques. Cigarettes, tobacco and, yes, Havana cigars are very nicely priced.

Normal shopping hours are 9 AM to 1 PM and 3 PM to 7 PM weekdays and 9 AM to 1 PM on Saturdays. However, whenever a cruise ship is in port the stores are open.

TIPPING: Most restaurant bills include service. If not, 10% to 15% is expected.

Great Britain

TOURIST INFORMATION: Over 700 Tourist Information Centres (TICs) provide accommodations listings, as well as literature, throughout England, Wales, Scotland, and Northern Ireland. The central London office is the National Tourist Information Centre, Victorian Station Forecourt, London, SW 1 (phone: 730-3488).

ENTRY REQUIREMENTS: A valid US passport is the only requirement for stays of 3 months or less by US citizens.

CLIMATE AND CLOTHES: Daily temperatures average in the low 60s F (about

16°C) in summer and hover around 40°F (6°C) in December, January, and February. Winter is wetter than summer, with 15 or 16 rainy days a month as opposed to summer's 12 or 13. The seasons are well defined though not as extreme as those in our northeastern states. Dress accordingly. A finely tuned sense of fashion is terrific in London but not necessary in the country.

MONEY: The pound sterling (£) is divided into 100 pence.

LANGUAGE: English is the national language, but Welsh is widely spoken in Wales, as is Gaelic in the Outer Islands in Scotland. Regional dialects are often heard in Scotland, Yorkshire, and Cornwall.

GETTING THERE/GETTING AROUND: Airlines – British Airways flies to London from 15 US cities — Anchorage, Boston, Chicago, Detroit, Los Angeles, Miami (Concorde and subsonic service), New Orleans, New York (Concorde and subsonic service), Philadelphia, Pittsburgh, Orlando, San Francisco, Seattle, Tampa, and Washington, DC (Concorde and subsonic service). US carriers with direct service to London are Pan Am out of Detroit, Houston, Los Angeles, Miami, New York, San Francisco, Seattle, and Washington, DC; Delta, from Atlanta; TWA flies from Boston, Chicago, Los Angeles, New York; and British Caledonian departs from Houston, Dallas, Atlanta, Los Angeles, and St. Louis. Pan Am also has one-stop flights to London from Detroit and Houston. Additional service is also provided by American Airlines, Northwest Airlines, Air India, Air New Zealand, and World Airways.

At least 10 domestic airlines have schedules to major cities and islands. British Airways runs many shuttle flights daily between Glasgow, Edinburgh, Belfast, and London.

Trains – British Rail's 125 new intercity trains offer superb service, and BR's numerous bargain plans for travelers couldn't be more tempting: BritRail pass, BritRail Youth pass for those under 26; and the BritRail Seapass, which includes travel on Sealink ships and Hoverspeed hovercraft to Ireland and the Continent (all of which must be purchased outside Britain).

Cars – Yes, they still drive on the left-hand side of the road. If you're a member of the AAA in the US, reciprocal membership can be obtained with the RAC or AA, two British automobile clubs, to take advantage of their publications, emergency, and other services.

SPECIAL EVENTS: A mind-boggling array greets the visitor, with the theater perhaps the first goal of most. Royal Shakespeare Company performances begin in Stratford in late March or early April and continue through January. The National Theatre on London's South Bank has performances year-round. *The Edinburgh Festival,* Scotland's all-cultural bash, which coincides with the *Military Tattoo,* runs for 3 weeks in August. Opera at Glyndebourne, East Sussex, from the end of May to early August is an elegant, dressy occasion.

Dates for some of the more famous sporting events? June for the *Derby* in Epsom, Surrey, and the *Royal Ascot* races in Ascot, Berkshire; late June to early July for the *Wimbledon Lawn Tennis Championships* in London, and for the *Henley Regatta* in Henley-on-Thames; July for the *British Grand Prix* and early August for *Cowes' Sailing Week,* on the Isle of Wight; and every 2 years in September for the *Farnborough Air Show* in Hampshire.

The Queen's Official Birthday is saluted by mounted guards "Trooping the Color" in London, second Saturday in June.

SHOPPING: There are still a few antiques left, in spite of the shiploads consigned US dealers, and it's fun to hunt for them. In London try Tower Bridge Rd. (New Caledonian Market) — a dealer's market — early Friday mornings. However, you don't have to look far to find new and unused china from quality suppliers such as *Minton, Royal Doulton, Staffordshire, Aynsley* and *Wedgwood.*

Harris tweeds, *Liberty* prints in cotton and silk, and ancestral tartans are sold by the yard and are made up into fashionable clothes. *Burberry* and *Jaeger* are good labels, and there are lesser-priced durable sport clothes at *Marks & Spencer* stores around the country. Main sale months are January and July.

Sales tax (VAT) is 15%. Some stores can refund VAT to foreign buyers who take the goods out of the country.

Shops open weekdays and Saturdays from 9 AM to 5:30 PM. Hours may differ in small towns, where shops sometimes close at noon one day a week, and in London, where most shops open and close later.

TIPPING: Service charges of between 10% and 15% are usually included in hotel bills but make sure. Otherwise the tipping standard is between 10% and 15% in restaurants and taxis, and 50 pence per bag for bellmen and porters.

Greece

TOURIST INFORMATION: The National Tourist Organization of Greece has its main office at 2 Amerikis St. in Athens (phone: 322-3111). There are ten regional branches and four bureaus at frontier crossings. In most cities and towns special tourist police provide information as well as assistance.

ENTRY REQUIREMENTS: A valid US passport is good for visits of up to 3 months.

CLIMATE AND CLOTHES: The country boasts of over 3,000 hours of sunshine a year. Hot summers, with averages in the high 80s F (about 30°C), are mitigated somewhat by the *meltemia* breezes. Winters are mostly mild; January averages about 55°F (13°C) in Athens and ten degrees less to the north.

Lightweight white and pastel clothes are appropriate summerwear. Pack something dressy for the captain's dinner if planning a cruise; ties are required for men only for admittance to one of the country's three gambling casinos.

MONEY: The drachma (Dr) is divided into 100 lepta.

LANGUAGE: Greek; English is spoken on the tourist circuit.

GETTING THERE/GETTING AROUND: Airlines – Olympic Airlines and TWA have nonstop service from New York to Athens. Domestic flights radiate from Olympic's Hellinikon Airport near Athens to about 20 cities and islands at the season's height.

Trains – Three international expresses reach Athens through Belgrade. However, because Yugoslavia is not included in the Eurail system, those with Eurailpasses enter Greece via ferry from Brindisi, Italy. The Hellenic State Railway (OSE) uses buses as well as trains to offer frequent service throughout the country. These routes are supplemented by privately run bus companies.

Cars – The Automobile and Touring Club (ELPA) mans road patrols and highway stations as well as an emergency number (phone: 104) good within a 60-kilometer range of major cities.

SPECIAL EVENTS: The annual *Athens Festival* is held in the Odeon, built by Herod Atticus in AD 161, from June through September. Superb Greek dramas are presented outdoors at Epidaurus from July until the end of September. Schedules and tickets for both are available from the Athens Festival Box Office, 4 Stadiou St., Athens (phone: 322-1459 or 3223-111, ext. 240), which also sells tickets to the daily sound and light shows in English at the Acropolis from April through October.

SHOPPING: To educate yourself in the range and variety of crafts produced in Greece before making a purchase, visit one of the *EOMMEX* (National Organization of Greek Handicrafts) showrooms in Athens and 13 other major Greek cities. Unfortunately they display but don't sell handmade wares. There's also a permanent exhibit of ceramics at Maroussi, where Greek pottery is sold as well as displayed.

Caftans, shirts, and dresses made from striped and textured *sedoni* cotton, which was originally used as sheeting, as well as from the heavier grades of colored cloth are widely available. Traditional fishermen's clothes, including lacy wool undershirts and navy blue hats, are trendy additions to a wardrobe. Two small items in great favor with the incurably anxious are worry beads and evil eyes.

During the summer, gift and craft shops are open 6 days a week from 8 AM to 9 PM, closed Sundays. Regular stores are open Mondays, Wednesdays, and Saturdays from 8 AM to 2:30 PM and Tuesdays, Thursdays, and Fridays from 8 AM to 1:30 PM and 5 to 8:30 PM.

TIPPING: The minimum tip for a small service is 10 drachmas. Service charges are included in most bills, but it is customary to add 5% to 10%.

Hungary

TOURIST INFORMATION: Branches of Ibusz, the state tourist board, are found in all major cities. The central office is at Felszabadulás-tér 5, H–1364 Budapest V (phone: 180-617). Ibusz also has a 24-hour accommodation service at Petöfi-tér 3 in Budapest. Tourist offices in smaller cities and towns are called *Idegenforgalmi Hivatal*.

ENTRY REQUIREMENTS: Tourist visas good for 30 days (and valid only for 3 months from the date of issue) are required and must be applied for with two passport photos and a valid US passport. They're obtained from Hungarian consulates abroad as well as at highway border crossings and the Budapest airport, but are not available on the Vienna-Budapest hydrofoil or on trains.

CLIMATE AND CLOTHES: Hungary is a small — 35,910-square-mile — nation bisected by the Danube River. Lake Balaton to the west is Europe's second largest lake and a good place to cool off during the typically hot summers, with temperatures averaging 86°F (30°C). Winters are cold (about 30°F, −1°C) and dry. Hungarians take pains to look their best. Casual, tacky dress usually indicates a tourist.

MONEY: The forint (Ft) equals 100 fillér.

LANGUAGE: Hungarian, a Finno-Ugric tongue, is the native language of 95% of the population. German is the second language (a heritage of the Austro-Hungarian Empire) but English is becoming increasingly common.

GETTING THERE/GETTING AROUND: Airlines – No commercial airlines fly directly from the US to Budapest. Indirect flights to Budapest are offered by KLM, via Amsterdam; Lufthansa, via Frankfurt; SAS, via Copenhagen; British Airways, via London; Air France, via Paris; and Pan Am, via Frankfurt or Zürich. Malev has frequent service between Ferihegy Airport, Budapest, and Zürich, Madrid, Frankfurt, London, Copenhagen, and Paris.

Trains – Budapest is a transfer point for some 25 international expresses including the Nord Orient Express and the Wiener Walzer. Nationally the MÁV (Magyar Államvasutak) diesel or electric express trains run often and are comfortable.

Cars – International firms and Ibusz rent European models. Some words of caution: The law against driving after drinking is carefully enforced.

SPECIAL EVENTS: Feasts and gaiety are traditional when the wine harvest begins in the fall. Important vineyard areas include Tokay; the Badacsony mountain slopes near Balaton; Eger (where the red "Bulls' Blood" is made); Sopron; and parts of the Puszta. Fall also starts the season at Budapest's opera house, the Academy of Music.

During the summer you can hear music of native sons Franz Liszt, Béla Bartók, or Franz Lehár in Budapest's Margaret Island open-air theater.

SHOPPING: Embroidery patterns and techniques, startling in their color and complexity, vary from region to region, and those of the Kalocsa, Mezökövesd, Pálóc, and Sárköz areas are highly regarded. Painted and carved wooden vessels and objects originally made by shepherds are still fashioned today, also true of peasant earthenware. Village potters produce local as well as more modern styles. Sándor Kántor working today in Karcag exemplifies this trend. *Folkart and Handicraft Cooperatives* around the country sell these products for forints or they can be bought with foreign exchange from Intertourist shops.

Stores are open weekdays from 10 AM to 6 PM; on Saturdays from 10 AM to 2 PM.

TIPPING: Add 10% to 15% to restaurant bills; 20 forints is the usual small tip for taxi drivers, porters, and hairdressers.

Iceland

TOURIST INFORMATION: The Iceland Tourist Board's head office is at Laugarvegur 3, Reykjavík (phone: 2-7488).

ENTRY REQUIREMENTS: US citizens need only a valid passport for visits of 3 months or less.

CLIMATE AND CLOTHES: While far more temperate in winter than might be expected — 31°F (0°C) is the average January temperature in Reykjavík — summers are cool, with July averages in the low 60s F (10°C).

Daylight is continuous from mid-May through August but gradually lessens until there are only 3 or 4 hours of daylight in each 24-hour period from November through January. Careful attention is paid to fashion. High-styled jeans are fine for Saturday night disco clothes but won't do for dinner in the more staid restaurants.

MONEY: The Icelandic krona (IKr) equals 100 aurar.

LANGUAGE: Present-day Icelandic hasn't changed much from the Old Norse spoken by the ancient Vikings who colonized the island 1,100 years ago. Danish is the second language and English is compulsory in high school and is widely spoken, particularly by the younger generation.

GETTING THERE/GETTING AROUND: Airlines – Icelandair has nonstop service from Baltimore/Washington International Airport, Chicago, and New York to Keflavík Airport, about 45 minutes from the capital. There is also service from Detroit. Reykjavík is the hub of Icelandair's domestic flights to 16 cities in the nation. These flights, by the way, cost very little more than bus service to the same destinations.

Trains – There are no trains in Iceland.

Buses – BSI (Bifreidastod Island, or Iceland Coach Company) is the umbrella group for most of the national bus companies and is headquartered at the Umferdarmidstodin (bus station) in Reykjavík (phone: 2-2300). There's a total of about 8,000 miles of road, about 4,500 of which are covered by the coaches. In 1974 the road encircling the island known as the "ring route" was completed. Coach passes for this road, as well as passes good for unlimited travel anywhere in the country, are available from BSI.

Cars – There are plenty of car rental firms, with most supplying VW beetles and four-wheel-drive wagons. Be advised that roads are mostly unpaved and surfaced in dirt or crushed volcanic matter.

SPECIAL EVENTS: June 17 heralds the widely celebrated *National Day.* In early August the Westman Island holds a summer festival featuring bonfires and open-air entertainment. One of the most famous events is the biennial *Reykjavik Arts Festival* (the next is in 1986), featuring top artists in opera, ballet, and theater, as well as famous sculptors and painters from around the world.

SHOPPING: The fluffy, earth-colored *Lopi* wool blankets, outerwear, and accessories are synonymous with Iceland. Sheep are also the source of the shearling coats, jackets, and hats made here.

Several fine potters hand-throw earthenware containers in natural colors. Crushed lava is a common addition to highly glazed ceramic pieces popular as souvenirs.

The duty-free shop at Keflavík Airport sells all of these products.

Stores are open weekdays from 9 AM to 6 PM and some, but not all, from 10 AM to noon on Saturday.

TIPPING: Service charges are added to most bills and extra tips are not expected.

Ireland

TOURIST INFORMATION: The lowercase *i* identifies tourist information offices in some 70 locations around the country. The Irish Tourist Board (Bord Failte) publications are also available on a regional basis and in Dublin at 14 Upper O'Connell St., Dublin 1 (phone: 74-77-33).

ENTRY REQUIREMENTS: US citizens require only a valid passport.

CLIMATE AND CLOTHES: Summer highs are in the mid-60s F (around 18°C) and winter averages in the 40s F (around 4°C). This is partially explained by the chilling east winds. Make sure you have a warm wool sweater or jacket even in summer. Tweeds are worn year-round and lend a conservative cast to what is essentially a casual mode of dress.

MONEY: The Irish pound (£IR) equals 100 pence. Be aware that the Irish pound (punt) and the British pound are no longer related and are not interchangeable. Each has its own value in relation to world currencies.

LANGUAGE: Though Irish, or Gaelic, is the national language, English is spoken more widely today except in those few areas where Gaelic is still dominant.

GETTING THERE/GETTING AROUND: Airlines – Aer Lingus flies into Ireland's Shannon International Airport from Boston and New York and also provides domestic service between Dublin and Cork. Aer Arann schedules flights between Galway and the Aran Islands in Galway Bay.

Trains – Coras Iompair Eireann (CIE), with its new supertrain intercity service, manages railroads as well as bus routes. Rambler tickets good for 8 or 15 days are an inexpensive way to cover Erin and the 15-day Overlander ticket includes travel in Northern Ireland. Both tickets can be used for either bus or train travel.

Cars – Mobile homes as well as cars can be rented here and the Irish Tourist Board has mapped out a number of scenic tours for the motorist.

Ferries – Car- and passenger-carrying ferries connect Great Britain with Ireland. The ferries run between Holyhead and Dun Laoghaire; Holyhead and Dublin; Liverpool and Dublin; Fishguard and Rosslare; and Pembroke and Rosslare. The Irish Continental Line's ships sail between Rosslare and Le Havre, Rosslare and Cherbourg, and Le Havre and Cork; Brittany Ferries operate between Cork and Roscoff, France.

SPECIAL EVENTS: The Royal Dublin Society organizes the *Dublin Horse Show* in August, an outstanding sporting and social event, as well as the *Spring Show and Industries Fair* in May, a trade and livestock exhibition. Traditional Irish ballads are celebrated in the *Fleadh Cheoil na h-Eireann,* Ireland's premier cultural festival, in August. Other major festivals are the *Rose of Tralee Festival* in early September at Tralee and the *Cork Choral and Folk Dance Festival* in early May. Rarely performed eighteenth- and nineteenth-century operas are presented at the *Wexford Festival Opera,* a must if you're near Wexford in late October. Also in late October is the *Cork International Jazz Festival,* drawing talented musicians from around the world. St. Patrick gets his due during a week of celebrations throughout the country in mid-March. New plays by Irish authors feature in the Dublin Theatre Festival, held during late September.

September culminates both of Ireland's most popular spectator sport seasons in Dublin with the *All Ireland Hurling Finals* followed by the *All Ireland Football Finals.*

SHOPPING: Crafts are thriving in Ireland. Products in the traditional and modern international styles and combinations of the two are found in craft centers, workshops, and stores throughout the country. Details are in the *Craft Hunters Pocket Guide* from the Irish Tourist Board. The traditional and highly prized white wool Aran sweaters and hats, earthenware in modern but natural shapes, and exceedingly well executed jewelry in contemporary styles are typical of the work currently being done.

Pearly *Belleek* china, luminous *Waterford* crystal, and Irish lace endow any table with elegance. Irish smoked salmon goes well in such a setting.

Irish sales tax (VAT) varies; it is charged at varying rates — from 8% to 35% on most items. Avoid it by having products shipped directly home, or reclaim the VAT by having your invoice stamped at customs.

Stores are open between 9:30 AM and 5:30 PM Mondays through Saturdays with one early closing day in rural areas — usually either Mondays or Wednesdays.

TIPPING: Check to make sure the customary 10% to 15% service charge is added to restaurant bills. If so, no further tip is necessary. Taxi drivers usually get 10% and porters about 20 pence per case.

Italy

TOURIST INFORMATION: Publications and assistance are provided on a region-by-region basis by various Assessorati Regionali al Turismo (ART) offices; in provinces by the Ente Provinciale per Il Turismo (EPT); and in towns and resort areas from assorted Aziende Autonome di Soggiorno e Turismo (AAST) offices.

ENTRY REQUIREMENTS: US citizens require only a valid US passport for visits of 3 months or less.

CLIMATE AND CLOTHES: Hot summers get hotter the farther south you go (high 80s F or about 30°C), but are mitigated by shore breezes along Italy's 5,000-mile coastline.

Northern Alpine areas are exceedingly cold in winter as are the Apennines, but temperatures are in the relatively mild 40s F (around 7°C) and even warmer along the Italian Riviera and the Amalfi and Sicilian coasts.

Residents of Milan, Italy's fashion capital, dress chicly, though they are more conservative than Romans, who follow every fashion fad. It's fun to shop in either city and you'll fit right in as you shoulder the latest in Gucci bags. Stylishly casual resort wear is perfect for the beach areas and jeans are fine for the hill country.

MONEY: The Italian currency unit is the lira (Lit); the plural of lira is lire.

LANGUAGE: Italian is universally spoken but Italy's original city-states each had their own dialect and literature and in some places these dialects — Sardinian, Sicilian, Neapolitan, Venetian, and Milanese — are still spoken.

GETTING THERE/GETTING AROUND: Airlines – Alitalia flies nonstop from Boston, Chicago, Los Angeles, and New York to Milan; it also provides direct flight service from these cities to Rome. Pan Am has service between Rome and New York; and

TWA from Boston and New York to Rome and Milan. Service within Italy is provided by Alitalia and ATI. Alisarda has flights between the mainland and Sardinia.

Trains – Travel is quick on the Rapidos and TEE expresses and will be even quicker between Rome and Florence when a new line for high-speed trains is completed. Until then, the trip takes about 3 hours.

Cars – Italy's toll roads are excellent, but be prepared for the speed of traffic.

SPECIAL EVENTS: Summer outdoor performances of Italian operas are held in July and August in Rome's *Terme di Caracalla;* from mid-July through August in Verona's *Arena;* and in July at the *Arena Sferisterio* in Macerata. The regular opera season at such notable houses as *La Scala* in Milan, *San Carlo* in Naples, and the *Opera* in Rome runs from December to June. Two festivals of note that feature concerts, ballet, opera, and drama are Spoleto's *Festival of Two Worlds,* between mid-June and mid-July, and Florence's *Maggio Musicale Fiorentino* in May, June, and July.

Colorful pageants that feature medieval costumes include Gubbio's *Race of the Candles* in mid-May; Siena's *Il Palio,* a horse race and flag-throwing contest in medieval garb, held on July 2 and August 16; Venice's *Il Redentore,* a gondola procession and race the third Sunday in July; and every other September, the *Living Chess Game* at Marostica.

SHOPPING: Italian leathergoods, textiles, jewelry, and ceramics are fine buys. Most elegantly hand-stitched sheets, carefully worked boots, stunningly designed silk ties and scarves, and subtly knit fabrics fill the boutiques of Rome and Milan. *Upim, Standa, Coin,* and *Rinascente* chain stores are great for locally made finds from bras to ceramics. Baskets from the straw market in Florence are terrific to tote your purchases around in, including perhaps rolls of the gorgeous Florentine papers, appropriate for lining drawers or covering notebooks.

Store hours are generally from 9 AM to noon and 3:30 or 4 to 7:30 or 8 PM; stores in northern Italy have shorter lunch hours and earlier closing times.

TIPPING: Keep a handful of lire notes ready. In spite of 15% to 18% service charges at your hotel and 15% usually added to restaurant bills, you'll be expected to give about 1000 to 1500 lire or more to chambermaids for each night you stay, and 700 lire or more to bellhops for each bag they take, and so on. Waiters and wine stewards get an extra 10% of the bill. Taxi drivers receive 15% of the meter, hairdressers 15% of the bill. Even service station attendants expect about 700 or more lire for cleaning windshields and giving directions.

Liechtenstein

TOURIST INFORMATION: Locally available at the Liechtenstein Tourist Office, Städtle 37, FL-9490 Vaduz (phone: 2-1443).

ENTRY REQUIREMENTS: If entering from Switzerland, there are no border formalities whatsoever. US citizens can visit the country as tourists for up to 3 months with a valid US passport.

CLIMATE AND CLOTHES: This tiny country is a land of mountains and valleys. The eastern two thirds of its 61 square miles are covered by mountains of moderate height; these drop to the beautiful and fertile Rhine Valley in the west, and the entire country, like its neighbors Switzerland and Austria, is cooled and made temperate by the *Föhn,* the famous south wind of this section of central Europe. Travelers will feel perfectly comfortable in informal clothes throughout Liechtenstein.

MONEY: The Swiss franc (sfr) equals 100 centimes.

LANGUAGE: Liechtenstein's official language is German, but many citizens speak

Alemannic, a dialect similar to that of southwestern Germany and Alsace, and accents vary from village to village. Most people involved in any way with tourists speak English.

GETTING THERE/GETTING AROUND: There are no flights into this tiny country simply because it has no airport. After flying into Zurich on Swissair, you travel by train to Buchs, Switzerland. The rail line between Zurich and Vienna passes through Liechtenstein, but not Vaduz, the capital. Express trains make stops at Buchs and at Feldkirch, Austria, with postal buses providing the link between these stations and Vaduz.

SPECIAL EVENTS: The prince's birthday in August is celebrated as a national holiday. The first Sunday of Lent signals *Bonfire Sunday* with the lighting of fires and torches followed by traditional pancake suppers.

SHOPPING: Beautiful postage stamps and prestamped postcards are collector's items, inexpensive souvenirs, and also a leading local industry. Swiss watches, optical goods, and music boxes are reasonably priced. Shops are open weekdays from 8 AM to noon and from 1:30 to 6:30 PM, with Saturday closings at around 4 PM.

TIPPING: A 15% service charge is included in all hotel and restaurant bills.

Luxembourg

TOURIST INFORMATION: The Office de Nationale du Tourisme (ONT), with general information on the country, is in Luxembourg City next to the train station at the place du Gare (phone: 48-11-99) and has an office at Findel Airport (phone: 48-79-93). The Syndicat d'Initiative, located in most towns, provides local information. It is headquartered at the place d'Armes (phone: 2-2809). ONT and Syndicat offices are identified by the national information logo of a blue knight on a white background.

ENTRY REQUIREMENTS: US citizens can stay in Luxembourg for up to 3 months with a valid US passport.

CLIMATE AND CLOTHES: Hilly and forested in the north, Luxembourg has a storybook look, with pastoral farms stretching in the south along the banks of the Moselle River, which separates the country from neighboring Germany. Temperatures are moderate: summer days in the low 70s F (20s C) and winter days in the 40s F (around 5°C). Dress for the weather, not for society, and carry a wool sweater or jacket in the summer in the Ardennes and sturdy shoes for hiking in the mountains.

MONEY: The Luxembourg franc (Lux. F.) equals 100 centimes. Belgian and Luxembourg francs can be used interchangeably with Luxembourg currency, but the Luxembourg franc is not widely accepted outside the country. Change them for Belgian francs or other currencies before leaving.

LANGUAGE: It's a trilingual country: French is the official language, but German is spoken by most people, and Letzeburgesch, a Low German dialect, by all. English, compulsory in high school, is understood everywhere.

GETTING THERE/GETTING AROUND: Airlines – Icelandair provides direct service from New York; direct and nonstop service from Detroit, Chicago, and Baltimore/Washington. There are also nonstop flights from Orlando. Findel Airport is just outside Luxembourg City.

Trains – The Chemin de Fer Luxembourgeois (CFL) offers a number of reduced-fare plans, including weekend excursion rates, flat-fee 1-day, 5-day, and 1-month network passes, and senior citizen half-fare tickets. The Benelux Tourail ticket, good for 10 consecutive days of travel in Belgium, Luxembourg, and the Netherlands, is available at railway stations.

Cars – Luxembourg car rental fleets probably have the cheapest rates on the Continent for periods of a week or more. If you pick up and deliver your car there, you will probably pay less than the rate for the same car (for example, a Ford Fiesta) rented in Belgium and dropped off in Paris.

SPECIAL EVENTS: The *Octave,* an annual pilgrimage to Our Lady of Luxembourg, takes place the fifth Sunday after Easter in both Luxembourg City and Diekirch, with the royal family of Luxembourg participating in the closing procession; the *St. Willibrord's Dancing Procession* is held on Whitsun Tuesday about a month later in Echternach. *Remembrance Day* honors General George Patton, Jr., early each July in Ettelbrück; and Grevenmacher holds its *Grape and Wine Festival* (one of the many towns along the Moselle to do so) in mid-September.

SHOPPING: The beautiful porcelains and crystal of *Villeroy and Boch* are produced in Septfontaines, where the factory is open to visitors. A regional specialty is the earthenware pottery of Nospelt, northwest of Luxembourg City, where there's a 2-week exhibit of local work each August. They are sold locally in leading shops.

Stores are open Tuesdays through Saturdays from 8 AM to noon and from 2 to 6 PM; Mondays from 2 PM to 6 PM; closed Sundays. VAT varies between 7% and 12% and can be avoided by having purchases sent directly to the airport for collection before boarding the plane. Some stores will reimburse the VAT if the customer returns with an invoice cleared by customs authorities.

TIPPING: A 15% service charge is included in hotel, restaurant, and bar bills. Porters and bellmen receive about 20 francs per bag and taxi drivers 15% of the meter charge.

The Maltese Islands

TOURIST INFORMATION: The Malta National Tourist Office is located in Valletta (phone: 2-4444) on the main island of Malta.

ENTRY REQUIREMENTS: US citizens require a valid US passport for visits of up to 3 months.

CLIMATE AND CLOTHES: Vibrantly clear and sunny weather makes Malta very appealing to tourists. What rain there is falls between November and February, also the period of highest winds. Temperatures climb into the 90s F (30s C) in the heat of the Mediterranean summer, but otherwise hover in the 70s F (20s C). A holiday mood prevails throughout the country and informality is the keynote, though bikinis, fine for the beach, should not be worn off the sands.

MONEY: The Maltese pound (£M) equals 100 cents.

LANGUAGE: Maltese is a Semitic language derived from Phoenician and uses the Latin alphabet instead of the Arabic in its printed form. It is influenced by Italian (Sicily is only 60 miles to the north) and English (Malta was a British colony for some 160 years). Today, both Italian and English are spoken by almost all inhabitants.

GETTING THERE/GETTING AROUND: Airlines – Air Malta has nonstop daily flights from London and Rome (twice daily during the summer) to Luqa Airport outside Valletta. There is no longer air service connecting the island of Malta to Gozo; they are linked by frequent car and passenger ferries. The third Maltese island, Comino, is less than a square mile in area, has only one hotel, no cars, and is connected by scheduled boat service to the island of Malta in the summer.

Cars – A variety of cars can be rented in Malta as well as in Rabat, the capital of the island of Gozo. Driving on the left-hand side of the road is a custom inherited from the British.

SPECIAL EVENTS: Two-day *festas,* honoring the patron saint of different Maltese villages, provide plenty of local color and gaiety in this exceedingly Catholic republic. They're concentrated in the summer months and feature processions of saints' images through village streets, accompanied by bands and marchers. Valletta's *Carnival* is celebrated by the whole country on the second weekend in May with a float parade and enormous papier-mâché characters as well as much merrymaking.

SHOPPING: An overview of the country's typical handcrafts can be obtained from a visit to the *Centru Snajja Maltim* (Malta Crafts Center) opposite St. John's Cathedral in Valletta. However, you shouldn't miss the *Crafts Village,* at Ta Qali near Mdina, where you can see the products being made as well as purchase them on the spot. The heavy lacework is in the traditional mode. Decorative glass is manufactured here and so are Persian-style rugs. Maltese gold and silver filigree jewelry is beautiful. Stores open at 9 AM and close at 7 PM (8 PM on Saturdays) with a 2-hour lunch break.

TIPPING: The norm is 10%. Sometimes it is included in restaurant bills.

Monaco

TOURIST INFORMATION: The National Office of Tourism is at 2a blvd. des Moulins, Monte Carlo, 98030 Monaco (phone: 30-87-01).

ENTRY REQUIREMENTS: There is no frontier between France and Monaco and French regulations (for US citizens, a valid US passport for visits of up to 3 months) pertain.

CLIMATE AND CLOTHES: Monaco claims 305 days of sun every year, with averages for water temperature and air temperature about the same: in the high 70s F (20s C) in summer, dropping to the mid-50s F (around 10°C) in winter. For clothes, what goes on the French Riviera is appropriate here but topless is allowed only at the Beach Club. Casual dress suffices in the casino's American Room, but coat and tie are required in the other rooms. You can always dress up more if you wish.

MONEY: The French franc (F), which equals 100 centimes. French bank notes are legal tender here, but Monégasque coins bearing Prince Rainier's likeness are circulated domestically and are fully convertible in France.

LANGUAGE: French is spoken, but the singular Monégasque dialect, a mixture of Italian and Nicois, is officially encouraged and mandatory in grade school. English is also taught in the schools and is spoken in hotels, restaurants, and at the casinos.

GETTING THERE/GETTING AROUND: With the exception of two local bus routes, Monaco relies on France for transportation and other services.

Airlines – Pan Am flies nonstop from New York to Nice. British Airways provides service to Nice via London. Air France, Sabena, and Iberia have flights via Paris into Nice–Côte d'Azur Airport. Heli Air, Monaco's helicopters, connect Monte Carlo with the airport as well as with other destinations on the Riviera. There's also bus service between the airport and Monaco.

Trains – The Gare de Monaco/Monte Carlo is on the SNCF's (Société Nationale des Chemins de Fer Français) Riviera line. Several international trains make stops there such as the overnight Train Bleu from Paris. SNCF's Métrazur shuttles along the Côte d'Azur between Cannes and Menton, stopping at Monaco every 30 minutes. Both the Eurailpass and SNCF's France Vacances pass include Monaco.

Cars – The principality is easily reached from Autoroute A8 or from the scenic Route de la Moyenne Corniche. The Automobile Club of Monaco, 23 blvd. Albert I, Monte Carlo (phone: 30-27-72), provides information for motorists as well as details on the Grand Prix.

SPECIAL EVENTS: April is the month for the *International Tennis World Championships.* The *Grand Prix de Monaco* is held in May, when futuristic Formula 1 racing cars take to the Belle Époque streets of Monte Carlo. Several nights in late July and early August are enlivened by the *International Fireworks Festival;* the elegant *Monégasque Red Cross Gala* usually coincides with this festival. The *International Circus Festival* comes in December, and January brings sports cars in abundance for the *Monte Carlo Rallye.*

SHOPPING: All the international names in perfume, jewelry, and clothes are carried by the chic shops surrounding the casino. Local embroidery, ceramics, and other handcrafted products are sold at *Boutique du Rocher,* the proceeds of which go to charity. Monégasque stamps are highly prized by collectors.

TIPPING: All bills — hotel, restaurant, and taxi — include a 15% service charge. Tips are not expected, but if you consider the service extraordinary, they are accepted.

The Netherlands

TOURIST INFORMATION: The ubiquitous VVV (Vereniging voor Vreemdelingen Verkeer) is headquartered at Rokin 5, Amsterdam (phone: 020-26-64-44). Offices are easily identified throughout the country by a triangular logo of three Vs, and provide lists of accommodations as well as information services.

ENTRY REQUIREMENTS: US citizens require only a valid US passport for stays up to 3 months.

MONEY: The guilder (also called florin; both are abbreviated Fl.), which is 100 cents.

CLIMATE AND CLOTHES: The influence of the surrounding North Sea results in a temperate, if damp, climate. June through September are the warmest months, with daytime highs around 70°F (21°C), and July through November is the rainiest time. Winter lows are in the 30s F (around 0°C). Dress is casual.

LANGUAGE: The national language is Dutch, but English is spoken by many people.

GETTING THERE/GETTING AROUND: Airlines – KLM flies to Amsterdam's Schiphol Airport from Chicago, Houston, Los Angeles, and New York. Domestically, KLM's City Hoppers connect Amsterdam and Enschede, Groningen, Rotterdam, and Maastricht.

Trains – Service is extensive and frequent. The claim is made that all towns in Holland have trains in both directions at least once an hour. Discount plans offered by the Nederlandse Spoorwegen (NS) include single Rover Tickets good for 1 and 8 days; Teenage Rover tickets for those under 20; and Multi-Rovers for small groups. The NS also sells the Benelux Tourrail pass for 10 days of consecutive travel in the three-country area.

Cars – Emergency road service is provided by the yellow cars of the Royal Dutch Touring Club's (ANWB) Wegenwacht service.

Cruises – Rhine River trips of 2 days or more begin and end in Amsterdam. Schedules and reservation information are available from K-D Line headquarters, Frankenwerft 15, 5000 Cologne, Germany; or Rhine Cruise Agency, D. Neuhold Corp., 170 Hamilton Ave., White Plains, NY 10601 (phone: 914-948-3600). VVV has details on local boat trips.

SPECIAL EVENTS: Bulbs flower in awesome profusion at the famed *Keukenhof* (kitchen garden) of the castle near Lisse in April and May, with crocuses, daffodils, tulips, and hyacinths. The equally colorful displays of commercial bulb growers are free for the looking in areas east, north, and south of Amsterdam.

Famous cheese auctions are held at Alkmaar on Friday mornings from May through

September and at Gouda from 9 to 10 AM on Thursdays from mid-June through August. The second Saturday in May is *Windmill Day,* with some 400 mills testing their sails; in July and August, 17 mills near Kinderdijk are in operation on Saturday afternoons. *The Holland Festival,* the nation's cultural bash, is held the first 3 weeks of June with various cities hosting events. The Holland Culture Card, available from Netherlands tourist offices in the US for $7.50, provides free access to more than 200 of Holland's museums and exclusive reservations for performing arts events (including the *Holland Festival*) with only 24 hours notice.

SHOPPING: Amsterdam is one of the world's diamond cutting centers, but before you purchase, a few words of caution: Not only have diamond prices skyrocketed because of speculation in recent years, but there is often a dramatic difference between Dutch and US appraisals of the same diamond, with US estimates of value often lower than Dutch. Less controversial purchases? Dröste chocolates, with the ever-popular sectioned apple, makes a nice small gift. Equally delicious and long-lasting are the whole (unsectioned) Edam and Gouda cheeses. Art prints are reasonable here and Dutch reproductions are of high quality. Blue Delftware is produced by *Porceleyne Fles* in Delft. A softer hued blue porcelain is made in Makkum in Friesland. Check the *Vroom en Dreesman* (V en D) chain of stores throughout the country for locally manufactured goods in a wide range of prices. Shops are generally open from 8:30 or 9 AM to 5:30 or 6 PM. They're closed Sundays and another half-day during the week, usually Monday mornings or Wednesday afternoons.

TIPPING: A 15% service charge is included in hotel and restaurant bills. The porters at train stations get 65 (Dutch) cents per bag by law; bellmen expect less. A guilder is the usual tip for small services.

Norway

TOURIST INFORMATION: The central organization is the Norwegian Tourist Board, H Heyerdahlsgate 1, Oslo 1 (phone: 42-70-44). Regional tourist offices called Turisttrafikkomiteen (TTKs) are in major towns, and tourist information offices are in smaller towns and villages.

ENTRY REQUIREMENTS: US citizens require a valid US passport for stays of up to 3 months.

CLIMATE AND CLOTHES: Above the Arctic Circle in Kirkenes near the Russian border, round-the-clock days in summer and long winter nights average in the mid-50s F (10°C) and mid-teens F (−0° to −10°C) respectively. Oslo's southern summer temperatures average in the low 70s F (about 20°C). The fjords are warm enough for summer swimming. Plan on some pretty dresses and spiffy jackets for the 14-day North Cape cruises but otherwise dress is casual and comfortable.

MONEY: The Norwegian krone (NOK), which is 100 øre.

LANGUAGE: Norwegian is the national language. English is commonplace among the younger generation and those in the tourist industry. However, don't expect to chat with northern farmers and fishermen unless you speak Norwegian.

GETTING THERE/GETTING AROUND: Airlines – SAS has direct service from New York to Oslo. Flights are also available on Northwest Orient from Minneapolis and New York and on Icelandic from Chicago and New York. Plane travel is common in this long, narrow land and three lines, Widerøe's Flyveselskap, Braathen's SAFE, and SAS, cover the routes.

Trains – The routes are well engineered and magnificently scenic with modern equipment and a notably comfortable second class. The Oslo-Bergen trip across the

Hardanger plateau is particularly breathtaking. Norges Statsbaners (NSB) participates in the Scandinavian Railpass and has discounts for senior citizens and families.

Cars – The Arctic Highway runs 1,564 miles from Oslo to Kirkenes but is hardly an expressway. Hard-surfaced, winding roads are fine for exploring but not for covering a lot of ground in a short time. Snow closes certain passes in winter, making May through September prime driving time.

Cruises – Ships provide three kinds of coastal travel: among one or several fjords on an areawide basis; coastal trips with steamers calling at various ports between Bergen and Kirkenes; and 14-day North Cape cruises. Inquire locally about the first, with the Bergen Line for information on the second, and either Royal Viking Lines or Norwegian American Cruises for North Cape cruise schedules.

SPECIAL EVENTS: The century-old *Holmenkollen Cross-Country and Ski-Jumping Competition* outside Oslo at the beginning of March attracts top talent and underscores Norway's role as the cradle of modern skiing. Other leading cross-country races include downtown Oslo's *Monolith* in January and Lillehammer's *Birkebeiner* in March. Jazz is a mania for many in Scandinavia and for none more so than the Norwegians, who hold three international festivals annually: at Kongsberg the end of June; Molde the end of July; and Voss in March. Classical music, together with ballet, opera, and drama, composes the *Bergen Cultural Festival* in late May and early June. The Nobel Peace Prize is presented in Oslo in December.

SHOPPING: The colorful, intricately patterned hand-knit Norwegian sweaters never wear out. Wood-handled, stainless steel Norwegian cutlery is exceptionally stylish, as are blond bentwood chairs of impeccable design. Sports equipment is well known and well made: Rods, spools, hand-tied flies, and *O. Mustad & Son* hooks for the fisherman; *Bonna, Epoke, Skilom,* and *Asnes* cross-country skis, and *Rottefella* bindings for cross-country skiers. Stores are open weekdays from 8:30 AM to 5 PM (Thursday nights until 7 PM) and Saturdays until 1 or 2 PM.

TIPPING: Between 2 and 3 NOK is the usual small tip for bellmen, porters, chambermaids (per night), and cloakroom personnel. A 15% service charge is usually added to restaurant bills.

Poland

TOURIST INFORMATION: Informacja Turystyczna (IT) centers are everywhere: hotels, gas stations, at the frontier, along highways and at airports, railway stations, and seaports. Orbis, the state tourist board, has its headquarters at ul. Bracka 16, Warsaw (phone: 26-02-71).

ENTRY REQUIREMENTS: A regular visa, issued for periods of up to 90 days (or a transit visa good for 2 days) must be obtained from a consular office before reaching Poland (allow 2 to 3 weeks for processing). Travel vouchers or exchange orders amounting to $15 per person per day must be in hand before applying for the visa, which also necessitates a valid passport, two photos, and a visa fee of $16. Details from Orbis, 500 Fifth Ave., New York, NY 10110 (phone: 212-391-0844).

CLIMATE AND CLOTHES: Autumn, normally crisp and sunny, is a long, lovely season, especially in the forests and hills that cover about a third of the country. Snow covers the Carpathian Mountains by mid-December and lasts until April. Winter temperatures hover around 26°F (−3°C), while summers are warm and dry, with an average temperature of 68°F (20°C). Blue jeans are okay for daytime touring and shopping but evenings at the theater and best restaurants call for dresses and ties.

MONEY: The zloty (Zl), which is 100 groszy. No import or export of Polish currency is allowed. Unused zlotys must be left at the border, where a receipt for the amount is issued. When you return to the US, any Orbis office will refund your money upon presentation of this receipt. There is a mandatory daily exchange rate of $15 for pleasure and business travelers; $7 per day if you are either of Polish origin and visiting friends or relatives or between the ages of 16 and 21.

LANGUAGE: Polish, Slavic in origin, is the official language, but French, German, and English are all spoken.

GETTING THERE/GETTING AROUND: Airlines – At press time there were still no direct flights to Warsaw from the US, as ordered by the Reagan administration. However, LOT does fly direct to Warsaw from Montréal. Within Poland, LOT's reasonably priced flights connect Warsaw with ten cities and also Cracow and Katowice to Gdansk and Szczecin.

Trains – The Polskie Koleje Panstwowe or PKP's Polrailpass for 8, 15, 21, or 30 days of unlimited rail travel is a bargain. The modern expresses providing frequent intercity service are the best-equipped trains.

Cars – Both self-drive and chauffered Fiats are rented by PZM (the Polish Automobile and Motorcycle Federation), the people to contact for routings, reservations, and emergency assistance. PZM border offices as well as those in cities sell gas coupons for foreign exchange, which save 20% over zloty prices. The address for their Foreign Touring Office is ul. Sandomierska 19, 02-567 Warsaw (phone: 49-56-42).

SPECIAL EVENTS: The *Chopin Piano Competition* is held every 5 years in Warsaw (the next is in fall 1985). Orbis can advise on ticket procurement. If you can't make it, there are spring and summer Chopin concerts in Warsaw's lovely Lazienki Park and a month devoted to his music at the Duszniki Spa each August. More music? Warsaw hosts an internationally famous *Modern Music Festival* each September and in August organists from all over the world come to Oliwa on the Baltic to give concerts on the cathedral's superb organ. Warsaw's *Jazz Jamboree* is an October event drawing fans from everywhere.

The *Poster Biennale* — a competition of graphic art posters depicting various events, people, and places, held in Warsaw's largest art galleries in June of even years — is one of the most prestigious contests of its kind. *CEPELIA,* the national folk art cooperative, has an enormous display and sale of regionally made products in Warsaw each June.

In March, Zakopane, a resort in the Tatra Mountains, holds the most important Nordic and Alpine ski races of the season. And in May all attention is focused on the big, international *Berlin-Warsaw-Prague Bicycle Race.*

SHOPPING: State-run foreign currency shops include *DESA,* which specializes in fine arts and quality merchandise such as crystal and *Wloclawkek* pottery, and *CEPELIA,* the craft co-op with the best regional wares, including Baltic amber beads and jewelry, kilim-style flat weave rugs, sheepskin outerwear — especially those decorated with Zakopane embroidery — and Silesian lace.

Shops are usually open weekdays from 9 AM to 7 PM, Saturdays till 5 PM.

TIPPING: The usual tip is 10% of hotel, restaurant, hairdresser, and taxi bills. Service charges are not included in most bills.

Portugal

TOURIST INFORMATION: Postos do Turismo, Tourist Posts, provide tourist information at offices throughout the country. In Lisbon, there are branches at the Palácio

Foz on the Praça dos Restauradores (phone: 36-70-31), at the airport, and at train stations.

ENTRY REQUIREMENTS: US citizens need only a valid US passport for stays of up to 60 days.

CLIMATE AND CLOTHES: Lacking in extremes, the weather is mostly sunny and mild, ranging between 60° and 80°F (15° to 26°C) year-round on the mainland and in the Azores. Madeira, off the African coast to the southwest, is a bit warmer and attracts sun and sand lovers in all seasons, but the tourist trade peaks December through April. Resort wear, including long skirts for evenings, is de rigueur here in the winter just as it is during the summer season in the Algarve.

MONEY: The escudo is abbreviated with a dollar sign, which is placed where the decimal point in our currency normally lies (for example, 8$50), and equals 100 centavos.

LANGUAGE: Portuguese, though English is spoken in major tourist areas.

GETTING THERE/GETTING AROUND: Airlines – Transportes Aereos Portugueses (TAP–Air Portugal) and TWA both fly from New York to Lisbon. Some TAP planes stop at Terceira in the Azores. Domestically, TAP has jet service to Oporto and Faro, Terceira and San Miguel in the Azores, and Funchal and Porto Santo in Madeira. Scheduled five-passenger Beechcrafts fly to Bragança, Faro, and Vila Real.

Trains – Because the track gauge is an unusually wide 9 inches (in Spain as well) the cars on the efficient and modern CP (Companhia dos Caminhos de Ferro Portugueses) are wider and extremely comfortable. The CP's small electric trains make frequent runs from Lisbon to Sintra and Cascais. Reservations are suggested on the express trains to Pôrto and the Algarve, the International Sud-Expresso to Paris, and the twice-daily trains to Madrid.

The CP sells economical Tourist Tickets good for unlimited travel for periods 5, 10, or 15 days and has other discount plans for groups.

Cars – Services for the stranded motorist include call boxes, a frequent sight along major routes, and a nationwide emergency number (115) for assistance and to reach round-the-clock ambulance crews.

SPECIAL EVENTS: The streets erupt with color and pageantry during celebrations commemorating various saints. Tradition calls for folk dancing, fireworks, processions, and bullfights. Of particular note is the *Festa do Santo Antonio* held in mid-June in Lisbon's Moorish Alfama section and the *Festa do Santo Sylvestre* on New Year's Eve in Madeira, where elaborate fireworks are set off from barges in the harbor. A running of the bulls is part of the festivities at Villa Franca de Xira in July. And for local color nearer Lisbon, Mercês, just outside Sintra, holds a fair annually at the end of October featuring food and crafts.

SHOPPING: Hand-painted *azulejos* were once used as ballast for ships crossing the Atlantic — they now weigh down suitcases on international jets. Tiles in myriad designs are made by Sant'Anna, Víuva Lamego, and Sacavem in or near Lisbon. Vista Alegre makes exquisite porcelain in both antique and modern designs. Craftsmen's skills are considered a precious resource in Portugal, where apprentices are carefully nurtured in order to retain this shopper's paradise for tin and copperware, wrought-iron products, the hand-stitched rugs called Arraiolos, and filigree in silver and gold.

White port wine, difficult to find in the US, as well as red port and fine old Madeiras are elegant and warming souvenirs.

Stores are open from 9 AM to 1 PM and 3 to 7 PM weekdays and 9 AM to 1 PM on Saturdays. Shopping center hours are 10 AM to midnight daily.

TIPPING: Tips in the 10% to 15% range are expected even though a 10% service charge is normally included on hotel and restaurant bills. Porters and bellmen should receive from 20$00 to 25$00 per bag.

Romania

TOURIST INFORMATION: Carpati, the national tourist office, embraces all phases of travel and is in Bucharest at 7 Magheru Blvd. (phone: 14-51-60). In towns where there is no Carpati office, county tourist offices (Oficiul Judetean de Turism) provide travel assistance.

ENTRY REQUIREMENTS: Tourist visas, good for visits of up to 60 days, cost $12 and require a valid US passport for documentation. They're available at Romanian diplomatic offices abroad, at the border, or at Otopeni Airport in Bucharest. If accommodations are not arranged in advance, you will be required to change $10 for each day of your visit, and you will not be able to refund this amount when you leave the country. This guarantees a minimum expenditure of $10; amounts over that will be refunded when you leave.

CLIMATE AND CLOTHES: The mode of dress reflects the atmosphere: It's relaxed and casual. Black Sea bathing resorts are informal — suitable for summer heat — and daytime temperatures average around 82°F (28°C) in July and August. Carpathian ski resorts, usually blanketed in 3 feet of snow during the high season (December to March), have temperatures in the mid to upper 30s F (about −1°C). Overall, the four seasons are clearly defined and the climate is similar to New York's.

MONEY: The leu (L), which is 100 bani. Romanian currency is not convertible and it is illegal to enter or leave the country with it.

LANGUAGE: Romanian, a Romance language derived directly from Latin, shows some Slavic influences. French, the second language until the post–World War II era, is not spoken much now; English is becoming more common.

GETTING THERE/GETTING AROUND: Airlines – TAROM, Romanian Air Transport, has direct flights from New York to Bucharest with a 1-hour stopover in Vienna or Amsterdam; Pan Am also flies direct from New York. Other major airlines have connecting flights from Europe. Domestically, TAROM has one or more flights a day between Bucharest and 14 destinations.

Trains – Căile Ferate Române (CFR), the Romanian Railway Company, with diesel and electrically equipped trains, accepts Interail passes but not Eurail. International expresses connect Romania with both Eastern and other European countries.

Cars – Car rentals (limited to the nationally produced Dacia 1300 and 2000), accommodations, itineraries, and road assistance are provided by the touring section of the Romanian Automobile Club (ACR). ACR also sells discount gas coupons at border crossings. The club is headquartered at 27 Nikos Beloiannis St., Bucharest (phone: 13-42-60).

Cruises – The Danube (Dunărea) River enters the Black Sea from southern Romania, forming a natural boundary with Yugoslavia and Bulgaria. River cruises from Vienna to the Black Sea and the Danube Delta, and shorter trips between Romanian towns are run by NAVROM.

SPECIAL EVENTS: Centuries-old folk customs are very much alive today and festivals are colorful displays of dances, costumes, and folk art. Carpati publishes a calendar with histories of major celebrations. Most noteworthy are the *Simbra Oilor* at Oas (the first Sunday in May), marking the return of the sheep to the pasture; the *Girls Fair* at Mount Gaina, originally more of a mating game for singles than a fair, has grown into a major folk festival on the third Sunday in July; and the *Hora de la Prislop*, with a galaxy of dances and costumes, the second Sunday in August at Mount Prislop.

SHOPPING: Given the continuing strength of folkloric traditions it's not surprising that crafts are carefully nurtured and products highly prized. Pottery is produced at over 200 locations: the black pottery of Marginea in Bukovina, the Corund near Moldavia, the Vama in Oas, and particularly the pottery of the Oltenia provinces. Potters fairs provide grand selections from a variety of craftsmen and regions. Rugs run the gamut from the flatwoven or *scoarta* style exemplified by Moldavian and Banat rugs to Persian hand-knotted, high-pile rugs. Glass paintings from the eighteenth and nineteenth centuries have inspired a modern generation of glass painters. The best examples of Romanian art can be viewed and purchased at government-sponsored *Galeriile de Arta* boutiques. Keep an eye out for silk dresses in subdued, abstract patterns hand-painted by leading artists, a scarce but stunning find. *COMTURIST* shops sell a wide range of products for foreign exchange, including caviar from sturgeon caught in the Danube Delta.

Smaller shops have shorter hours of 9 AM to 1 PM and again from 4 to 8 PM; department stores stay open from 9 AM to 10 PM. Stores are closed on Sundays.

TIPPING: Though not expected, tips are accepted for special services.

San Marino

TOURIST INFORMATION: The Government Tourist Board is located near the walls of the city at the Palazzo del Turismo, San Marino, SM (phone: 99-21-02).

ENTRY REQUIREMENTS: There are no border formalities between San Marino and Italy; your valid US passport is all that is required for 3 months or less.

CLIMATE: Summer days average around 82°F (28°C) in spite of the republic's setting on craggy peaks high above the Romagna plain. Relatively mild winters in the 40s F (4° to 9°C) are chilled by the constant presence of the somewhat unsettling *garbino* wind blowing from the south.

MONEY: The Italian lira (Lit) circulates in San Marino, but some local coins and medallions are minted as souvenirs.

LANGUAGE: The Sammarinese dialect is commonly used but Italian is the official tongue. English is spoken by about 30% of the population.

GETTING THERE/GETTING AROUND: Airlines – Rimini, Italy, 14 miles (22 km) to the east, has the nearest airport to the republic and is the closest stop for trains and express buses. Local buses make frequent connections between Rimini and San Marino.

Cars – Take the Rimini exit off autostrade A14 and proceed about 11 miles (18 km) west. Drive right up Monte Titano to the capital or leave your car below and take the cable car *(funivia)* to the ramparts.

SPECIAL EVENTS: September 3 celebrates the day of Patron Saint Marino with a crossbow contest among members of the Crossbowmen's Corps, who dress in traditional Renaissance costumes.

Two captain's regents rule San Marino for periods of only 6 months at a time and their investiture ceremonies, every April 1 and October 1, are elaborate affairs with costumed guards and foreign representatives in attendance.

Every other summer the *International Art Biennale* takes place in San Marino.

SHOPPING: San Marino stamps are a major source of revenue and have considerable value among collectors. Both modern and traditional ceramic pieces are popular and unique souvenirs. And even this minuscule land produces its own wine — a tasty Muscatel *(Moscato)*.

TIPPING: Service charges are usually added but check to make sure. Tips of between 500 and 1000 lira should be given for small services.

The Soviet Union

TOURIST INFORMATION: Intourist is the Soviet Travel Bureau and arranges through its appointed travel agents in the US all trips to the USSR. The head office is 16 Marx Prospekt, Moscow 103009 (phone: 203-6962). Intourist offices are located in most cities.

ENTRY REQUIREMENTS: Visas are required and there are three kinds: tourist, "ordinary" (for business or family visits), and transit. All need advance planning. Once your trip has been confirmed by Intourist in Moscow, your travel agent must file an application with a consular office in the US a minimum of 14 days before departure. An itinerary complete with dates must be submitted along with a $10 processing fee and other documents. Intourist offices furnish procedural details. Contact Intourist at 630 Fifth Ave., Suite 868, New York, NY 10111 (phone: 212-757-3884).

CLIMATE AND CLOTHES: Make no mistake, it's warm in summer and very, very cold in winter, but Moscow is at least dry, crisp, and often sunny even when your breath steams the air. This guide deals exclusively with the European portion of the USSR, where winter temperatures average 20°F (-7°C), usually lower, and summers rarely get above the 70s F (20s C). Boots, warm socks, heavy coats, and lined gloves are essential in winter. You'll also want something festive for the inevitable farewell gala if you're part of a group tour.

MONEY: 1 rouble (Rbl.) equals 100 kopecks. Roubles cannot be taken into or out of the Soviet Union. When initially exchanging currency, a customs certificate is issued that must be presented to exchange roubles for dollars. Money can be exchanged only through outlets of the State Bank of the USSR. When you leave the country any remaining Russian currency can be changed into dollars at the bank of the last border point — providing that you have bank receipts of previous transactions.

LANGUAGE: More than 100 ethnic groups live in the Soviet Union's 15 republics. Russian, an East Slavic language, is the official one. Intourist personnel and workers in the hotel and restaurant industries speak English.

GETTING THERE/GETTING AROUND: Precious little flexibility in travel arrangements is allowed. Predetermined itineraries are required and routes and modes of transportation are restricted. Once you arrive, it's possible to extend your stay by about 2 days.

Airlines – Aeroflot flies Ilyushin 62s to Moscow from Montréal, Canada (no direct flights are available from the US). Planes are clearly a boon for travel in the world's largest country — 6,800 miles east to west and 2,800 miles north to south. Aeroflot has thousands of domestic flights to cities in all the republics at reasonable rates.

Trains – The Moscow to Leningrad route is quickly traveled on the Soviet railway's Sovyetskaya Zheleznaya Doroga (SZD) and the Trans-Siberian Railroad covers 6,250 miles of the USSR and stops in over 65 towns and villages. The entire Trans-Siberian trip — from Moscow to Nakhodka — takes about 8 days. Overall, the trains aren't terribly fast but most are comfortable. Passage is arranged through Intourist.

Cars – You can drive a rental car or your own automobile into the Soviet Union at certain border points and may also rent Russian makes from Intourist in certain cities. The restricted driving routes in the country are determined and fully arranged through Intourist, which also provides the necessary papers for car touring and insurance. One word to the wise motorist: Obey Russian rules of the road — they're strictly enforced.

SPECIAL EVENTS: Among a number of government-sponsored cultural events,

Moscow's *Russian Winter Festival* from Christmas Day through the first week in January offers the repertoire of the country's finest ballet, opera, symphonic, and theatrical companies; the spectacular Moscow circus with its dancing bears; and horse-pulled sleigh *(troika)* rides. Other folk and classical music festivals include *White Nights* in Leningrad in June, Kiev's *Spring Fete* in late May and June, and Riga's *Song Festival* in July.

SHOPPING: Fine performances by Soviet virtuosos and orchestras are captured on the technically excellent *Meloydia* records. Good-quality opera glasses make appropriate gifts for the culturally inclined and fur hats and lined gloves for those living in cold climes.

Caviar's not only an antidote to Socialist austerity but a luxurious memento. Exquisitely painted and lacquered *palekh* boxes, reputedly a dying art, represent the height of refinement and are lovely souvenirs. Purchases can be made with foreign currency at the *Beryozka* shops in major hotels or with roubles at stores such as *GUM, Detsky Mir (Child's World),* and *Melodia.*

Shopping hours for department stores are from 8 AM to 9 PM, and in smaller shops from 10 AM to 7 PM; most shops are open 6 days a week.

TIPPING: Tipping is not officially sanctioned; however, it is usually appreciated. Doormen or porters should receive a ruble or two; cab drivers 10% of the fare; waiters 10% of the bill; and checkroom attendants, 50 kopecks.

Spain

TOURIST INFORMATION: Oficinas de Información y Turismo are found in all major cities, train stations, and airports. In addition to dispensing literature and giving travel assistance, they sell inexpensive tourist insurance policies covering medical expenses, accidents, and baggage theft.

ENTRY REQUIREMENTS: A valid US passport is good for visits of 6 months or less.

CLIMATE AND CLOTHES: Surrounded by the sea, the Iberian Peninsula is dominated by the vast interior central plateau where river valleys have formed lateral depressions interspersed with mountain ranges. In Spain, the result of this diversity is a varied climate: Coolest and most humid along the north Mar Cantábrico coast, with winters averaging 26°F (−3°C) and summer temperatures of around 77°F (25°C); dry and arid in the central regions; tremendously hot during summers in Andalusia to the south (up to 95°F, 35°C); and year-round temperate (66°F, 19C), sunny days abound on the Costa del Sol and in the Balearic and Canary islands.

The fashionable Spanish dress with enviable panache, so in leading cities wear your most chic clothing. Generally, casual clothes, suitable for the climate, are acceptable tourist attire, and in the resorts, most anything goes.

MONEY: The peseta (Pta) equals 100 centimos, which are seldom used.

LANGUAGE: Castillian Spanish is the official tongue but other regional languages are: Catalán (Barcelona), Basque (Pyrenees), Gallego (Galicia), Valenciano (Valencia), and Mallorquín (the Balearic Islands). English is understood in principal resorts, hotels, restaurants, and shops but not too far off the tourist track.

GETTING THERE/GETTING AROUND: Airlines – Iberia has direct flights from New York to Barcelona, Madrid, and Málaga; from Miami to Madrid; from Boston to Madrid and Málaga; and also summer-only nonstops from New York to Santiago de Compostela, and winter-only nonstops from New York to Las Palmas and Tenerife; TWA from Los Angeles and New York to Madrid and Málaga. Air Florida and Aero Mexico have service from Miami. Spain is the third largest country in Europe and, domestically, Iberia and Aviaco serve some 30 cities. There are reasonably priced Visit Spain passes offering unlimited travel for 45 days over all routes. They must be purchased in the US.

Trains – It is now possible to take high-speed, air-conditioned trains like the Talgo to Paris, Marseille, Geneva, and Rome without changing at the borders. RENFE's (Spanish National Railways) best equipment is usually found on the longer distance runs between major cities and are widely recommended. However, some second-class trains can be slower, more crowded, and often poorly equipped. Buses are best for short hauls and excursions.

Cars – Rental rates are particularly reasonable and one-way Iberian rentals that allow pickup in Spain and dropoff in Portugal (or vice versa) are useful for touring.

SPECIAL EVENTS: All cities and towns in Spain hold fairs or fiestas *(ferias),* some more colorful and exciting than others. Undoubtedly the three most famous are: Valencia's *Fallas de San José* in mid-March, when groups of huge figures *(ninots)* are composed into satirical groups *(fallas),* paraded, and finally set on fire; the *Feria de Sevilla* in late April, with the citizenry parading on horseback in elegant regional dress to the accompaniment of music and flamenco dancing; and the *Feria de San Fermín* in Pamplona the second week of July, with the historic running of the bulls.

The most splendid Holy Week *(Semana Santa)* observances take place in Andalusia, with particularly notable processions in Seville and Málaga. The sherry wine harvest is celebrated in Jerez de la Frontera in mid-September.

SHOPPING: Leathergoods, from supple suede gloves and elegant calf handbags to wineskins that require careful curing *(botas),* are excellent purchases, with perhaps the best selection found in Madrid. Designer clothes, including those of Pertegaz and Balenciaga, are the height of fashion. Costume jewelry is imaginative and black and white pearls labeled Perlas Majórica are world famous.

Other exceptional buys are shoes, from classical calf pumps to provincial cloth espadrilles; porcelain by *Lladro* and pottery by regional craftsmen; and wool rugs using technologies translated from tapestry makers or simple cotton-rag throws. Spanish sherry is unequaled and *fino* is a fine buy, as are brandies. Saffron flavoring is a tasty addition to your Spanish recipes.

Shops are usually open from 9:30 AM to 1 PM and from 4:30 to 8 PM on weekdays and are closed Saturday afternoons and Sundays. Department stores now stay open through the traditional 3-hour siesta, and most are open all day Saturday, from 9:30 AM to 7:30 or 8 PM.

TIPPING: Though service charges of 15% are included in restaurant bills, extra tips of between 5% and 10%, depending on the attention you receive, are expected. Taxi drivers receive 5% of the meter and in most cases, 25 to 50 pesetas is enough for porters, bellmen, and per night for chambermaids.

Sweden

TOURIST INFORMATION: The identifying logo of the over 200 "Turistbyrå" is the international lowercase white *i* against a green background. Regional information is provided by the Swedish Tourist Board, which is located in Stockholm at Sverigehuset, Hamngatan 27 (phone: 08-789-2000).

ENTRY REQUIREMENTS: For visits of 3 months or less a valid US passport is all that is necessary.

CLIMATE AND CLOTHES: July and August temperatures range in the low to mid 60s F (about 18°C) around the sea-level cities of Malmö, Gothenburg, and Stockholm.

January and February, the coolest months, average 26°F (−3°C) in Stockholm, slightly warmer in the south. The well-styled, yet comfortable and functional, clothing of the Swedes mirror their refined sense of design and informal, outdoor orientation. Casual dress is fine in summer but in fall and winter, you'll want a more cosmopolitan look.

MONEY: The Swedish krona (SEK), which equals 100 øre.

LANGUAGE: Swedish, but people with a firm command of English are common.

GETTING THERE/GETTING AROUND: Sweden is about 1,000 miles long from top to toe. Transportation on clean, modern equipment with an enviable on-time record makes all areas, from Malmö in the south to beyond the Arctic Circle, easily accessible.

Airlines – SAS flies direct to Gothenburg and Stockholm from New York and has connecting flights via Copenhagen from Chicago, Los Angeles, and Seattle. Northwest Orient's new service runs from Detroit, Minneapolis, and New York to Stockholm. Thirty-two cities in Sweden are connected by the domestic airline, Linjeflyg.

Trains – Staten Järnvägar (SJ) diesel and electric trains are comfortable and fast. Service in the north is augmented by postal buses that carry passengers to outlying areas. The SJ network is part of the new Scandinavian Railpass, good for 21 days of unlimited travel in first or second class on all trains, the Helsingør-Malmö ferry, and also for 50% discounts on other specified ferry runs.

Cars – Most major US car rental firms are represented in Sweden. For a motoring map with suggested itineraries, contact the Swedish Tourist Board, 655 Third Ave., New York, NY 10017 (phone: 212-949-2323).

SPECIAL EVENTS: Midsummer is greeted with great gaiety the weekend closest to the summer solstice in late June. Maypoles, garlands, flower-decked houses, dancing, and special midsummer dishes typify this most popular festival. *Santa Lucia's Day,* December 13, ushers in Christmas with young girls and women wearing crowns of candles and distributing traditional pastries at dawn.

The rococo Drottningholm Court Theater outside Stockholm presents primarily eighteenth-century operas, ballets, and classical music mid-May to mid-September.

SHOPPING: The famed crystal of *Orrefors, Kosta,* and *Boda* can be bought in Stockholm or you can visit the glass district near Växjo, where 36 of the nation's 44 glassworks are concentrated. "Seconds" are sold at shops adjoining the factories.

Swedish cotton and woolen fabrics are used to advantage by designers such as *Katja.* If you're thinking mink, it's a good buy here.

Beautifully designed kitchenware and utensils, in a variety of materials, are quality items, as is furniture. Avoid the 20% VAT (called MOMS) by having the store send merchandise directly to your home. Also, many stores throughout Sweden participate in the Scandinavian Taxfree program. An export receipt is issued at the time of purchase and is then presented at designated airport and ferry terminals for a partial VAT refund.

Shops are generally open weekdays between 10 AM and 6 PM and on Saturdays from 10 AM until anywhere between 1 and 4 PM.

TIPPING: A 13% service charge is automatically tacked on to restaurant tabs and hotels add 15%. Taxi drivers expect a 15% tip.

Switzerland

TOURIST INFORMATION: The headquarters of the Swiss National Tourist Office (Schweizerische Verkehrszentrale) is at Bellariastrasse 38, CH-8027 Zürich (phone: 202-3737). All but the tiniest Swiss towns have efficient and well-prepared tourist offices, and regional centers have region-wide information.

ENTRY REQUIREMENTS: A valid US passport. No visa is required for visits of less than 3 months.

CLIMATE AND CLOTHES: Famous for its snow-capped mountains — at 15,217 feet the Dufourspitze on Monte Rosa is the highest — Switzerland also boasts a sun belt along Lake Maggiore (890 feet above sea level) complete with palm trees. These contrasts indicate not only a variety of climates but also abrupt changes in the weather. However, normal summer daytime highs average in the mid-70s F (24°C).

The citizen's dress is generally conservative in color and style. However, you'll be at ease if you dress according to the activities you pursue.

MONEY: The Swiss franc (SFr) equals 100 centimes (French) or rappen (German).

LANGUAGE: There are four. German, used by 65% of the population; French by 19%, Italian by 12%, and Romansh, derived from Latin, by less than 1%. Swiss dialects, called collectively Schweizerdeutsch, vary from region to region. English is widely understood.

GETTING THERE/GETTING AROUND: The transportation network is beautifully integrated and famed for the punctuality of its moving parts. The key to its workings is the *Official Timetable* available from the Swiss National Tourist Office (SNTO) branches in the US or abroad. Note that anyone driving in Switzerland must buy a special car sticker, now used in lieu of tolls. Rental cars usually have these stickers; if you're driving into the country, they can be purchased for 30 SFr. ($10 to $15) at border crossings.

Airlines – Swissair has daily nonstop service to Zürich and Geneva from New York, Boston, and Chicago. Pan Am and TWA fly direct to Zürich on a daily basis from New York.

Trains – This small country has 2,000 miles of electrified track covering its terrain. The SBB (Schweizerische Bundesbahnen) offers the Swiss Holiday Card, allowing unlimited trips on trains, boats, and postal buses and discounts of up to 50% on mountain railways and cable cars. Other transportation bargains include Half-Fare Cards for the general public, senior citizens, and those between 16 and 26. For information on all discount cards contact any of the SNTO branches in the US before you go.

Cars – Road service and information are provided by the Automobile Club de Suisse, Laupenstrasse 2, Berne, and the Touring Club Suisse, 9 rue Pierre-Fatio, Geneva. For breakdown service, phone 140, and for road conditions, 163 from anywhere in the country. The national Swiss number for English-language information is 111.

SPECIAL EVENTS: The list of Swiss festivals goes on and on whether your interest lies in music, history, industry, or sports. World-renowned occasions, such as Geneva's 10-day *International Motor Show* in March and the *Lucerne Festival* of musical events in August are most enjoyable, but don't overlook the patriotic and folkloric observances that give a clear sense of Swiss culture. The major national event of this kind is celebrated all around Switzerland on August 1, when fireworks light the sky to commemorate the founding of the Swiss Confederation. A complete roster of special events is available at SNTO offices.

SHOPPING: Switzerland is synonymous with watches and the wondrous array awaiting your choice is overwhelming. The watchmaker's sweetest rival in Switzerland is the chocolatier. Be sure to try many a chocolate connoisseur's favorite — *Lindt.* Not surprisingly, music boxes, precision tools, optical goods, and drafting sets are high-quality, interesting buys. Multibladed and multipurpose red *Swiss Army* knives are universally popular.

Caran d'Ache pastels, crayons, colored pencils, and pens are treasured by children as well as professional artists. Also art books, most notably the *Skira* series — an exemplary collection — are published here.

Stores are open from 8 AM to 12:15 PM and from 1:30 to 6:30 on weekdays except for Monday mornings, when they are often closed. Stores close at 4 PM on Saturdays and all day on Sundays.

TIPPING: A 15% service charge is added to hotel, restaurant, and bar bills as well as automatically included in taxi fares, so that only porters and bellmen require tipping, about one franc per bag.

Yugoslavia

TOURIST INFORMATION: Major cities have Tourist Information Offices, identified by the internationally recognized green sign with the white *i*. The two main centers in Belgrade are located at the railway station and in the subway at Terazije Street next to the Albania building (phone: 63-53-43). In small towns, the words *Turist Biro* and *Drustvo* denote information locations.

ENTRY REQUIREMENTS: Visas good for visits of up to 90 days can be obtained at all Yugoslavian border points, embassies, and consulates abroad. Permits for 30-day visits are issued at any point of entry for a 25¢ fee. A valid US passport is the only document needed for a visa.

CLIMATE AND CLOTHES: Swimming is comfortable along the Adriatic coast from May through October, when water temperatures hit the mid-60s F (about 18°C) (at least from Dubrovnik south). They rise to the mid-70s F (24°C) in summer, when air temperatures hit the low 80s F (28°C). Inland summers are hot; winters in the mountains are cold, with snows beginning in December and lingering through April.

Dressing or undressing is your choice on the many nude beaches found along the Istrian Peninsula. Zagreb requires the most conservative clothes and Dubrovnik and Sveti Stefan are scenes of the more chic looks.

MONEY: The dinar (Din) equals 100 paras. Only 1,500 dinars may be taken in or out of Yugoslavia.

LANGUAGE: Serbo-Croatian is the official language in four of the six republics: Croatia, Bosnia-Herzegovina, Montenegro, and Serbia. Although all citizens speak the same language, it has two written versions: The Serbs, affiliated with the Eastern Orthodox Church, use the Cyrillic alphabet and the Croats, mostly Roman Catholics, use a modified Latin version. Macedonian and Slovenian are the languages of Macedonia and Slovenia. More and more students are choosing English as their second language and it is frequently spoken by the young as well as those associated with the tourist industry.

GETTING THERE/GETTING AROUND: The Jugoslovenski Zeljeznice (JZ) rail line runs inland from north to south with occasional spurs east to cities along the coast. Planes, the Adriatic Highway, and the sea are the best ways to get to and between points on the Istrian and Dalmatian coasts and islands and to the southern Adriatic coast.

Airlines – The national airline JAT (Jugoslovenske Aerotransport) flies direct from New York to Ljubljana, Zagreb, and Belgrade throughout the year and, in summer, nonstop to Dubrovnik. The extensive domestic service is rated a bargain by European standards.

Trains – The jewel in the JZ's crown is the new 325-mile line between Belgrade and Bar on the Montenegro coast. It's an engineering tour de force — 254 tunnels and 234 bridges had to be built in order to complete the line. The fastest, most comfortably equipped are the business trains *(Poslovni voz)*.

Cars – Probably the best way to view the scenic Adriatic coast. Rentals are readily available and gas coupons — available at border crossings — save 10% over regular prices but only if your car has foreign plates. If a breakdown occurs, call 987, an emergency number manned by the SPI (local automobile club).

SPECIAL EVENTS: Summer here is a festival of culture and folklore. The most elaborate event is Dubrovnik's artistic extravaganza in mid-July through August, with performances set in historical locales and parks. Others include: Zagreb's *International Review of Original Folklore* in July, with over 80 groups the world over plus Yugoslavian troupes competing in a stunning exhibition of regional dances and costumes; Split's *Melodies of the Adriatic* festival in early July and every Thursday from April through September; and Korcula's celebration featuring the *Moreska Sword Dance.*

SHOPPING: Yugoslavia is well known for primitive art. The works of leading artists are widely reproduced and internationally acclaimed. The delicate, colorful, and detailed paintings on glass are exquisite. Check the major cities for exhibitions and dealers.

Many stores specialize in the fine native handcrafts such as embroidery, sweaters, leatherware, wood carvings, ceramics, and the bright and cheerfully colored Bosnian and Serbian rugs.

The town of Samobor near Zagreb lends its name to the country's finest crystal.

Shops are open from 7 AM to noon and 2 or 3 PM to 7 or 8 PM on weekdays and are closed Sundays.

TIPPING: Discretionary at hotels and restaurants as service charges are put on the bills, but it's best to give a few dinars extra. Porters receive 50 dinars per bag.

DIVERSIONS

DIVERSIONS

Introduction

If you could read the minds of a random selection of passengers on any transatlantic flight, the impression you would gather of the attractions of Europe would be diverse indeed. The sportsman — mind lingering affectionately on a favorite rod stored carefully in the cargo hold — thinks of salmon fishing in Ireland or Scotland; the culture maven, of the most incredible collection of art and architecture in the world; the gourmand, of the restaurants of Alfred Giradet, Paul Bocuse, and Michel Guérard; the hedonist, of the beaches lining the Mediterranean from Gibraltar to Turkey; the mountaineer, of the Alps; and the rest of the passengers, of a combination of all these things and, perhaps, if it is a second or third visit, of the guest room of a favorite château in the Loire Valley or the view from a particular hill in southern Italy or a mountain in the Peloponnese.

What best characterizes Europe is not simply its diversity, but its density. Three quarters of a continent and some 2,000 miles lie between America's highest mountains and the great urban cultural centers of the East Coast; but Basel, Switzerland, tucked between Germany's Black Forest and the foothills of the Alps, has one of Europe's finest small museums and is less than half a day's drive from Strasbourg, France, and the exquisite villages of Alsace. The number of activities one can enjoy and never be more than a day from Basel is simply staggering. And Basel is just one city in the center of Europe.

The unparalleled proximity of Europe's great cities and historic countryside offers a variety of experience that couldn't be better suited to contemporary travelers. Certainly North Americans would travel to Europe under almost any conditions; to some degree we are all Europeans, and every trip carries with it something of a small celebratory homecoming. But today travelers are uniquely willing to take advantage of the range of activities Europe offers, and of the fact that museum and mountain, ski slope and opera house, are virtually cheek by jowl.

But the sheer density of Europe poses a challenge. Combining the right place with the right activity is an art even in one's own country, and facing a continent of 33 nations, an equal number of major cities, and hundreds of regions, districts, and areas all with distinct cultural features, even the most savvy traveler can be forgiven some trepidation.

The pertinent queston is: Where is the quality of experience highest? In the following pages we suggest the best places in Europe to pursue 21 different activities — from tennis, golf, and fishing to experiencing the wildernesses of this most civilized of continents, enjoying most accomplished theatrical and operatic performances, or ferreting out auctions, flea markets, antique shops, and Europe's finest shopping streets. Each section represents a distillation of the best in Europe, a selective guide to Europe at its most intriguing, to make your homecoming an unparalleled adventure.

For the Body

Europe's Unparalleled Ski Scene

 Skiing is one of the most memorable activities you can enjoy on a European vacation. In the first place, no other mountains in the world are quite like the Alps and their surrounding ranges. America has peaks as high, but the valleys in Europe are lower, so that the ski runs in Europe are generally longer and more diverse. And most of the European ski resorts possess an atmosphere that you simply don't find elsewhere.

Europe's ski centers come in all sizes and shapes. There are giants like St.-Moritz, Kitzbühel, and Chamonix, which offer vast assortments of runs and lifts, multilingual instructors, and facilities for a score of other winter sports, including — increasingly — cross-country skiing, now often called ski touring, plus well-equipped shops, fine hotels, lively nightlife, and all the other accouterments required by the glossy good life of Europe's leisure classes.

Then there are the small resorts, with only a handful of lifts — but runs that go on and on, and an atmosphere that is less chaotic and more *gemütlich* (comfortable and cozy) than that of the majors. A good many of these smaller areas (and larger as well) have teamed up with similar ones nearby and installed a couple of extra lifts that enable guests to ski from one area to the other. These multiresort combinations often offer you the ski facilities of far bigger areas, but with the pleasant, intimate après-ski life found only in small villages. It is also not unknown — as at Zermatt — literally to ski from one European country to another, and then back again.

Almost everywhere you go in Europe, it's possible to arrange for powder tours. There is now helicopter skiing in many parts of Switzerland, for instance; the tours around Lauterbrunnen and Zermatt are especially beautiful. And a number of mountain tours are accessible via the various ski lifts. A cable car will get you to the top of the Aiguille du Midi, near Chamonix, in the French Alps, where you can begin the endless run down the glacier known as the Vallée Blanche — full of crevasses and melted-snow pools, surrounded by high peaks. The Jungfraujochbahn, the railroad that ascends Switzerland's highest mountain, the Jungfrau, puts you at the start of a number of runs that will take you to the Concordiaplatz, where four glaciers cross. You can take your pick. Best of all, you don't have to be a superexpert (just a strong intermediate whose knees will not go wobbly crossing over a crevasse on a snow bridge scarcely wider than a pair of skis). Good skiers can tackle the Haute Route from Chamonix to Zermatt, over-nighting on the way in mountain huts. (Information: École Suisse d'Alpinisme, Bureau des Guides, La Fouly/Verbier, CH-1936, Verbier, Switzerland; phone: 74825.) These excursions are mainly spring flings.

In summer, you can ski on the tip-tilted glaciers — among others — at Corvatsch, in the Upper Engadine above the towns of St.-Moritz and Silvaplana, and at Les Diablerets in the Suisse Romande above the town of Gstaad.

The list of ski resorts that follows includes some of the best of the Continent's offerings in all departments.

But first, some general hints for enjoying skiing in Europe:

If you possibly can, avoid skiing in Europe at Christmas time. Not only are there miserably long lift lines but the weather conditions are also unreliable enough so that you might well end up with a mastery of the art of making parallel turns on grass and mud. If you have no choice about when you go, at least try to get your skiing in before December 26, while European families are still sitting around their Christmas trees. Late January usually offers the best combination of good snow, longer sunny days, off-peak prices, and manageable crowds.

Try, also, to hold out for a half-pension arrangement with your hotel. European skiers take lunch seriously and there is lots of fine, uncrowded skiing to be done while they are banqueting.

In virtually all the ski centers on our roster, the choice of hotels is large, and even the most modest little *gasthaus* usually offers cozy pine-paneled rooms, fluffy eiderdowns, and handsome Tyrolean furniture. Just to give you a place to start, we've included the names of a few favorites in each price range: Expensive (E), Moderate (M), Inexpensive (I) – or, at least, more moderate. Each town, no matter how tiny, has a tourist office that can provide you with up-to-date information about hotel availability, unusual tours, ski schools, and so on. Take their reports of snow conditions with a grain of salt, however.

KITZBÜHEL, Austria: Don't be put off by the comparatively low altitude (2,642 feet): The region is a famous snowbowl that often has better ski conditions than resorts with twice its base elevation. The movie star of Austrian skiing, Kitzbühel is colorful, animated, international. The town is a kind of Tyrolean showpiece with white peaks rising behind brightly painted buildings. Cable cars and chair lifts connect its ski areas with those of four neighboring towns to give you fantastic skiing possibilities. If you prefer less glitter, lodge a little way down the road in charming St. Johann-in-Tyrol, convenient to all Kitzbühel's facilities. Lodgings: *Die Postkutsche* (E); *Weisses Rössl* (M); *Pension Klausnerhof* (I).

OBERGURGL, Austria: One of the highest villages in the Alps, Obergurgl is far less known as a ski resort than a mountaineering center. At the end of the 31-mile Ötztal Road (off the main Innsbruck highway), it has a pleasant Shangri-La quality. The 6,232-foot base elevation means both later sunlight and higher wind, and you will return to the flatland a healthy-looking bronze. Evening pleasures are simpler than at the more cosmopolitan centers, but a day on the Gaisberg–Hohe Mut will send you to bed by 9:15 anyway. Lodgings: *Hotel Hochfirst* (E); *Hotel Burger* (M); *Gasthof Gamper* (I).

ST. ANTON-AM-ARLBERG, Austria: Halfway between Innsbruck and Zürich on the main Arlberg road, St. Anton is a rather ordinary, heavily trafficked town. But the mountains above, rising from a 4,264-foot base, offer a vast network of lifts and superb skiing, ideal for vigorous skiers who like to spend most of the day on the slopes (as most St. Anton skiers do). The village is not the best for nonskiers. St. Christoph, about 4 miles away near the top of the Arlberg Pass, is small, cheerful, and convenient to the high-altitude beginners' slopes. Lodgings: *Hotel Schwarzer Adler* (E); *Hotel Tannenhof* (M); *Fremdenheim Fallesin* (I).

ZÜRS-LECH, Austria: Lech, a friendly, sunny mountain village on the shores of the River Lech, and Zürs, which grew up as a sort of hotel colony when skiing boomed in the Vorarlberg, share excellent, lift-linked slopes and broad snowfields that make intermediates look like experts. There's a wonderful run all the way down to St. Anton, and you can make the return trip by bright yellow Austrian postal bus. With a base elevation of 4,756 feet, this is a good area to try in early winter when the rest of the countryside is still patched with green and brown. Lodgings: *Gasthof Post,* Lech (E); *Zürserhof,* Zürs (E); *Central,* Lech (M); *Ulli,* Zürs (M); *Fremdenheim Katharina,* Lech (I); *Gasthof Schweizerhaus,* Zürs (I).

STARÝ SMOKOVEC, Czechoslovakia: Eastern Europe's best skiing is found in the heart of the High Tatras, in a national park of a region full of deep woods, frozen lakes, and craggy peaks. For skiing, there are jumps and slalom runs and long, gentle cross-country trails. The base elevation is 3,280 feet, and compared to the big centers of capitalist decadence in the West, the mood is pastoral and low key; you won't feel out of place in last season's stretch pants. Lodgings: the fine old *Grand Hotel Starý Smokovec* (E); and at Novy Smokovec, the *Parkhotel* (M) and the *Bystrina* (I).

CHAMONIX, France: The presence of towering Mont-Blanc, the highest mountain in Europe, has made Chamonix, with a base elevation of 3,280 feet, the most famous resort in the French Alps (which are now connected to Courmayeur in Italy by the Tunnel du Mont-Blanc). The snowscapes amid the spires and glaciers of a whole range of 13,000-foot mountains are spectacular, and the *téléphérique* ride to the Aiguille du Midi is one of the great European experiences — with or without skis. The expert skiing is unexcelled anywhere, though even competent intermediates can make the magical 12.4-mile glacier run down the Vallée Blanche from the Aiguille. The lively nightlife, the fine French cuisine, and the busy gambling casino all make the resort a delight for nonskiers; the clientele is definitely sporty. Lodgings: *Mont-Blanc* (E); *Richemond* (M); *Roma* (I).

VAL-D'ISÈRE, France: Once a mountain resort and hunting village of the duke of Savoy, this town built around a quaint sixteenth-century church lies on the Col de l'Iseran, the highest pass in the Alps; the base elevation is 6,068 feet. France's top skiers come here in preference to more chic centers like Mégève and Chamonix, and most of the evening talk at the town's modern, comfortable ski hotels is about trails and boots and bindings. The ski school has a fine reputation for serious, systematic instruction, and when the snow is deep or conditions are icy, the big runs are best left to the experts. Val-d'Isère is an ideal place for a long stay devoted to real improvement in the sport. Lodgings: *Christiania* (E); *Santons* (M); *Bellevue* (I).

VALLOIRE, France: A great deal of new lift building and trail making has taken Valloire dramatically out of the "Sleepy Alpine hamlet" class — the base elevation is now 4,592 feet. But it's still less international and far less congested than many centers with comparable facilities. Just near the Galibier Pass, the old part of the village centers around a large, friendly ice-skating rink and an old church. There is a fine cross-country run through the Col du Mt. Tabor to the Italian town of Bardonecchia. Lodgings: *Rapin* (E); *Les Carrettes* (M); *Centre* (I).

GARMISCH-PARTENKIRCHEN, Germany: Americans first got to know this Alpine ski resort back in the days when it was chiefly the US military that occupied the powdery slopes and a few dollars bought all the snow you could ski. The town itself is large, modern, and busy, and offers a whole range of winter sports activities including curling and bobsledding. High above is the 9,840-foot Zugspitze, Germany's tallest mountain, whose peak, miraculously, is accessible by cog railway and cable car. There is a fine assortment of lifts and trails for every grade of skier, and the facilities are scrupulously maintained by a large local staff. Lodgings: *Wittelsbach* (E); *Bellevue* (M); *Aschenbrenner* (I); or, glamorously perched at 8,692 feet on the Zugspitzplatt, just under the summit, the *Schneefernerhaus* (I).

REIT IM WINKL, Germany: A picturesque Bavarian town in the middle of a wide-open valley, with a base elevation of 2,296 feet, this is not the kind of place you're likely to see represented on bumper stickers and ski parka patches. Yet, with some two dozen tows and chair lifts fanned out on a cluster of broad plateaus and mild peaks under 6,560 feet, it's ideal for beginners and intermediates; the ski circus between Winklmoos-Alm, Dürnbachhorn, and Kammerköhr-Steinplatte is immensely satisfying and only of medium difficulty. There is a 2.5-mile toboggan trail, with a smaller version for children, and a fleet of horse-drawn sleighs for drives in the country, Dr. Zhivago style — that is, with fur blankets wrapped around your knees. Evenings, you stuff yourself on sausage and sauerkraut piled into small mountains on your dinner plate at any of the nearby restaurants. Lodgings: *Unterwirt* (E); *Altenburger Hof* (M); *Edelweiss* (I).

CORTINA D'AMPEZZO, Italy: The country's number one ski resort, which attracts a stylish, predominantly Italian crowd, held Italy's first Winter Olympics back in 1956 and subsequently boomed, so that it is now one of the best-equipped ski towns in the Alps. One of its special pleasures is ice skating in the huge open shell of its Olympic Stadium, which you can have to yourself on virtually any early January morning. But whatever your sport, you'll always be surrounded here by the toothy spikes of the Dolomites. A lift network that links a series of high passes allows you to cover a great deal of terrain without ever doubling back, and a powerful sun is always there even in February and March to remind you that Venice and the Mediterranean are only a few hours away. Lodgings: *Cristallo* (E); *Concordia Parc* (M); *Menardi* (I).

LIVIGNO, Italy: The characteristic wooden houses of this curious, little-known village are strung out along about 7.5 miles of a valley near the Italian and Swiss frontiers. Not so long ago, cross-country skiers had these broad snowfields, the pretty lake, the gentle landscape, and the limitless horizons almost all to themselves. Now there's downhill skiing as well. The region's development has been enthusiastic but not excessive, and the area offers several hostelries and a number of attractive slopes with a base elevation of 6,068 feet. Lodgings: *Du Lac* (E); *Palú* (M); *Alpina* (I).

SESTRIERE, Italy: Like Courchevel in France, this development of the Fiat Company was built — expressly as a ski resort — on once-empty snowfields, and there's little of the cozy sense of a real village that you find in older ski towns. Nonetheless, there's a great deal of life here in season, along with superb high-altitude runs — rising from a base of about 6,560 feet — for every level of skier (it's possible to ski here for a week without ever repeating a run); a fine ski school (though a number of the instructors speak only rudimentary English); and lots of sun, evenly distributed between the slopes and the large terraces with deck chairs and umbrella tables. Sestriere is a marvelous place on weekdays, but impossible on weekends in high season when big tour buses arrive by the score from Torino (Turin), about 56 miles away. Lodgings: *Cristallo* (E); *Belvedere* (M), a local landmark; *Olimpic* (I).

KLOSTERS, Switzerland: Davos, some 7.5 miles away by road, is one of the Alps' finest ski centers, but it's a big, citified, not always attractive spot. By far the nicest place to stay in the region is the charming animated village of Klosters, which is connected to Davos by the ski lifts of the great Parsenn area. The Parsenn snowfields, with a base elevation of about 4,000 feet, are wonderfully varied, and while there are a number of areas that are rewarding for beginners, the area is also rich in challenging runs that are so long they make you feel as if you're crossing most of Switzerland. The Klosters Valley gets early shade — but its brisk nightlife starts just after twilight and seems to keep going until the tows open in the morning. Not a village of cowbells and milkmaids, Klosters is cosmopolitan, expensive — and great fun. Lodgings: *Vereina* (E); *Walserhof* (M); *Pension Soldanella* (I).

MÜRREN, Switzerland: Famous in the annals of ski racing as the site of the great Alpine-Kandahar course and the founding place of the Kandahar Ski Club, this sunny, romantic village, on a kind of balcony overhanging the Lauterbrunnen Valley, is little known among vacation skiers and can still be a discovery to Alpine veterans. Some of the toughest, most exciting slopes in Switzerland, as well as countless simpler trails, rise above the 5,412-foot base; many runs end up within a few minutes' walk of your hotel. There's a spectacular revolving restaurant on the peak of the Schilthorn. Lodgings: *Hotel Mürren* (E); *Sporthotel-Edelweiss* (M); *Alpina* (I).

ST.-MORITZ, Switzerland: St.-Moritz has such a long-standing, far-reaching reputation for being elegant, expensive, and sophisticated that a number of serious skiers spend years avoiding it — and years regretting their boycott when they finally do break down and go. The sheiks and the furs and the Lamborghinis are all there, of course — but so are some of the finest, most exciting, best-maintained ski runs in Europe. It would take several days just to ski them all once. There is not just something for everybody — there's everything for everybody. The base elevation is 6,068 feet. The town has grown into a small ski city, and you can easily pick up a mink or a Matisse along with your boot wax. Make sure to have coffee and pastry at *Hanselmann*. Lodgings: *The Palace* (E), if you can afford it; *Neues Post* (M); *Languard* (I).

WENGEN, Switzerland: Like Zermatt, Wengen, in the middle of the Bernese Oberland, is car-free (with the nearest garages and parking lots a 15-minute train ride away at Lauterbrunnen). The town, which extends along a sheltered plateau at the foot of the imposing Jungfrau at 4,264 feet, shares a vast ski terrain with nearby Scheidegg and Grindelwald. There is a choice of mountain railways (including the renowned Jungfraujochbahn), which offer newer, higher ski trails at every stop. And the unparalleled Jungfrau Glacier runs are open from the middle of February until the end of May. In addition to all this skiing, there is a great deal of hockey, skating, curling, and just plain walking on well-packed, breathtakingly scenic snowy mountain paths. Lodgings: *Regina* (E); *Bellevue* (M); *Schweizerheim* (I).

ZERMATT, Switzerland: As the world's oil supply runs out, there will be fewer and fewer cars everywhere. But, for the moment, the no-autos-at-all policy in Zermatt, at 5,248 feet, is delightful. And despite the town's heavy international traffic, it maintains a rustic village flavor. Zermatt also has that unique Alpine monument, the Matterhorn, and a dazzling fishnet of cog railways, cable cars, gondolas, T-bars, and pommel lifts that serve an enormous variety of runs across snowfields and through the trees. And when you've done all that, there's a famous tour over the Theodule Pass to Breuil-Cervinia in Italy. In addition, there's fine springtime skiing and regular town-to-glacier helicopter service. All things considered, Zermatt probably offers Europe's most complete skiing experience. Lodgings: *Monte Rosa* (E); *Alpenblick* (M); *Chesa Valese* (I).

Tennis in Europe

 Most American passions eventually sweep Europe as well, and tennis is no exception. The population of courts, players, clubs, and cute little robin's-egg blue outfits has soared in the last decade, so that tennis is now as much the sport of European butchers and bakers as it once was of barons. However, the groundswell started from a far narrower base than in America, and the sport still has a long way to go. Facilities aren't as extensive as in the US, instruction isn't as expert, and there is still a shortage of high-powered accessories like videotape units, ball machines, and the like. And the organized tennis vacation is still a comparative rarity.

Tennis etiquette is similarly primitive, particularly in the Mediterranean countries. If you were brought up in a world of tennis whites, "sorry, partner," and "take two, please," you may be put off by the noise level both on and off the courts, and by the general lack of reverence for the game. Nonetheless, a tennis match is still a fine, rapid way to escape the standard tourist circuit and get into local life. Travel with your tennis gear — and be sure to bring it all, so that your day need not be marred by the exorbitant cost of a Swiss T-shirt or a pair of German socks. Many clubs welcome brief visits by foreigners and you may suddenly find yourself with a circle of Dutch or Danish friends. Like French in the gambling casino, English is the lingua franca of the tennis court, particularly among the well-to-do.

Synthetic court surfaces are still uncommon in Europe, so you can also arrange to enjoy the pleasures of English grass courts and well-kept clay ones — and often in spectacularly beautiful settings.

A cultural parenthesis: When Europeans kick back stray balls, it's not out of rudeness or impatience, but instead because of their early soccer training.

Here are some good places to make a foray onto European tennis courts:

COPENHAGEN, Denmark: Ever since the success of Bjorn Borg, tennis has taken a great leap forward all over Scandinavia. The climate in Copenhagen in spring and summer is delightful for court capers and a number of clubs offer temporary membership to visiting foreigners, including: *Boldklubben af 1893,* Per Henrik Lings Allé, 10 (phone: 38-18-90); *Hellerup Idraetsklub,* Hartmannsvej 37, Hellerup (phone: 62-14-28); and *Kjøbenhavns Boldklub,* Peter Bangsvej 147 (phone: 71-41-80). You can get additional information about facilities, tournaments, and the like from the courteous *Dansk Tennis Vorbund, Brøndby Stadion,* 20 Idraettens Hus, 2600 Glostrup, Copenhagen, Denmark (phone: 45-55-55).

IPSWICH, England: Open all year, the *Fulcher School of Tennis* is situated in 10 acres of parkland just north of Ipswich. Individual and group instruction, as well as special late July tennis camps for children aged 10 to 14. Three indoor courts are good insurance against the English climate; there are also three all-weather courts. Simple accommodations are available; other amenities include a heated swimming pool, badminton, video analysis, and a pro shop. Information: *Fulcher School of Tennis,* Thurleston Tennis Centre, Henley Rd., Ipswich, Suffolk IP1 6TD, England (phone: 21-09-03).

SOUTHAMPTON, England: *The Southampton School of Lawn Tennis Coaching* has a beautiful new rural center between Winchester and Southampton. This school specializes in courses for adults on every level from beginner to expert. Besides the grass and hard-surfaced tennis courts, first-class accommodations are also available along with a swimming pool, squash court, and badminton hall. Although summer is the prime time for attending, the school runs weekend and 5-day courses during the off season at various centers in Dorset and Hampshire. Information: *The Southampton School of Lawn Tennis Coaching,* 35 Cobden Ave., Bitterne Park, Southampton SO2 4FU, England (phone: 55-64-15).

BODMIN, England: *Tennisville Holidays* in Cornwall is very British and very family oriented with a cheerful atmosphere and excellent coaching. Courses are usually a week, but many guests stay longer. Both private and group instruction. Open from Easter to September, with simple but companionable accommodations. Housing with families available for kids — who can stay on their own while parents travel. *Tennisville* runs another center in the picturesque seaside town of Looe. Information: *Tennisville,* Sunny Banks Farm, Fletchers Bridge, Bodmin, Cornwall, England PL30 4AN (phone: 5048).

HAILSHAM, England: *The Windmill Hill Place Residential Tennis Centre* is 50 miles from London and 10 minutes from the sea, near the resort town of Eastbourne. There are 8 grass, 6 all-weather, and 4 indoor courts amid 20 acres of wooded grounds, and the main residence is an elegant Georgian mansion. Weekend and week-long sessions year-round. Information: *Windmill Hill Place Residential Tennis Centre,* Windmill Hill, Hailsham, Sussex, England (phone: 83-25-52).

L'ALPE D'HUEZ (ISÈRE), France: A number of French towns, particularly in the mountain districts, organize summer tennis courses *(stages de tennis)* — week-long tennis holidays that package room and board along with intensive tennis instruction and court time. This one is among the best, with 5 businesslike weekdays devoted to physical preparation and 5 hours daily to instruction and training. Offered mid-July to mid-August. Information: Stage de Tennis, Office de Tourisme, Maison de l'Alpe, 38750 L'Alpe d'Huez, France (phone: 80-35-41); or *Club des Sports,* 38750 L' Alpe·d' Huez, France (phone: 80-34-42).

CAP D'AGDE, France: The *Club Pierre Barthès* is one of Europe's most dazzling complexes. Sixty-two courts (6 covered and 14 lighted), just a forehand away from one of the Mediterranean's choicest beaches. A lovely colony of guest-villas and apartments and a small hotel. Open year-round; book well in advance, especially for summer months. Information: *Club Pierre Barthès,* 34300 Cap d'Agde, France (phone: 26-00-06).

CARGÈSE, France: One of the very best spots to play tennis in Europe is at one of the 76 "vacation villages" of the *Club Méditerranée. Le Club,* as it's known in its native France, is founded on the formula Leisure=Sport so the villages' facilities are extensive, their instruction first rate, and their settings consistently attractive and maintained with ecological fervor. The *Cargèse Club Med,* located on the Gulf of Chioni in Corsica, is a fine place to mix tennis and the sea. There are ten courts with the green Corsican hills on one side and a rocky bay and wide, blond beach on the other. Accommodation is in very comfortable separate bungalows. And the Club organizes various excursions around the most inviting parts of Corsica. Open from late May to mid-September. Information: *Club Méditerranée,* 20130 Cargèse, France; or contact the Club's New York office at 3 E 54th St., New York, NY 10019 (phone: 212-750-1670).

LES RESTANQUES, France: This *Club Méditerranée* village, close to the Riviera beaches of St.-Tropez and Grimaud, has eight gorgeous courts, with green all around and blue all above. Four are lighted, so you can keep playing until bedtime. You can go swimming in the sea or in the village pool — or try your hand at sailing, provided you can tear yourself away from the courts for an hour. And the village is sufficiently protected so that you're not oppressed by the proximity of the heavily beaten Riviera track. Information: *Club Méditerranée,* 83360 Les Restanques, St.-Pons-les-Mûres, France; or in the US (see above).

VITTEL, France: This *Club Méditerranée* village — in the green French countryside — is the best of them all for tennis: There are 20 courts (12 clay), frequent tournaments, and instruction at all levels — and you'll never have any trouble finding partners on short notice. Accommodation is available in several of the gracious old spa hotels that went up here in the days when taking the waters was an indispensable interlude for the Parisian upper classes. Open May through September. Information: *Club Méditerranée,* 88000 Vittel, France; or in the US (see *Cargèse, France*).

BADEN-BADEN, Germany: The main tennis club of Germany's most elegant spa has nine carefully groomed courts in the middle of the lush Lichtentalerallée promenade. Giant ancient trees surround you and fine stately hotels like the *Bellevue* and the *Brenner's Park* are just a hard forehand away. Information: *Tennis Club Rot-Weiss,* Sekretariat, Lichtentalerallée 5, D-7570 Baden-Baden, Germany (phone: 2-4141) — and this is only one of half a dozen clubs in town. Visitors' Bureau offers special all-inclusive tennis weeks, including instruction. General information: Baden-Baden Verkehrsverein, Augustaplatz 8, D-7570 Baden-Baden, Germany (phone: 27-52-00).

BERNKASTEL-KUES and OBERLAHR, Germany: A highly professional setup split between two handsome resort hotels, *Hans Pötter's Tennis School* has videotape recorders, backboards, ball machines, and indoor and outdoor courts that are open for both day and night play through the year. You can sign up for special intensive weekend courses, or for more leisurely vacation weeks that leave you time for excursions in the hill and lake country of the Rhine River valley. The *Alpha* has a brand-new 4-court *halle* that opens like a convertible, and there are 4 more at the *Westerwald Treff.* Information: Tennisschule Potter, *Westerwald Treff,* 5231 Oberlahr, Germany (phone: 870); or *Alpha Hotelpark,* 5550 Bernkastel-Kues, Germany (phone: 2011).

ATHENS, Greece: Athens is one of those enviable Mediterranean capitals where the weather is good for tennis all year long; though it's sometimes breezy and sometimes hot, it's always worth bringing your gear. Play and instruction are pleasantly inexpensive by US standards, and a strong American player is often treated as a kind of visiting apostle in Greek clubs. Courts and clubs to sample include the *Athens Tennis Club,* 2 Vas. Olgas Ave. (phone: 923-2872); *Attic Tennis Club,* Dafni and Kalliga St., Filothei (phone: 682-5649); *Kifissia Athletic Club,* 45 Tatoiou Rd., Strofyli, Kifissia (phone: 803-8100); and the *Glyfada Tennis Club,* Diadochou Pavlou Ave., Glyfada (phone: 895-3012). More detailed information is available from the *Greek Tennis Federation,* 89 Patission St., Athens 104 (phone: 821-0478).

CORFU, Greece: Of the myriad Greek islands, this is the one where tennis has made the deepest inroads. The *Club Méditerranée* has a seaside village at Ipsos with 16 courts that start to function in early May and attract a large assortment of first-class vacation players. Accommodation is in simple but charming thatched huts, with communal dining areas. The sea is all around, and water skiing is also popular. Information: *Club Méditerranée,* Corfu, Ipsos-Corfu, Greece, or contact the *Club Med* in New York (see *Cargèse, France*). Another spot where you'll find good players is the *Corfu Tennis Club* (4 Romanou St., Corfu, Greece; phone: 3-7021). The club, which has been around since 1896, retains its gracious, tennis-is-all-that-counts air. Good courts are also available at the *Hilton Hotel,* the *Roda Beach,* and the *Nissaki.*

CORTINA D'AMPEZZO and VENICE, Italy: Nicola Pietrangeli, of Italian Davis Cup fame, offers a series of summer-long tennis clinics that shift locations every few weeks from the elegant alpine resort of Cortina to the Lido of Venice. Several of the sessions are also held in the lovely Tuscan town of Siena. Groups are kept small, and the tennis is serious and intense, despite the magnificent frivolity of the settings. An inclusive package can be arranged with accommodations at Cortina's *Albergo Cristallo* or either of the two *grandes dames* of the Lido — the *Excelsior* and the *Hotel des Bains* — where the courts are. The clinics begin in late May and run until the end of September. Information and reservations: Write *Tennis Clinics Nicola Pietrangeli,* CIGA Hotels, Viale S Maria Elisabetta, Lido 44, Venice, Italy; or phone the CIGA office in Milan at 657-1351. If you're in Venice when Pietrangeli isn't, there's always lots of top-drawer tennis at both of the Lido hotels mentioned above; and at two Lido clubs with seven courts each: the *Henkell Club,* Via Malamocco Lido (phone: 76-01-22), and the *Tennis Club Lido,* Via Sandro Gallo 163 (phone: 76-09-54).

ROME, Italy: The town has been tennis mad ever since Italy won its Davis Cup, and there are some 50 clubs and centers, with a preponderance of clay courts. Among those that welcome transient players are the *Circolo Tennis Belle Arti,* Via Flaminia 158 (phone: 360-6529); the *Circolo Tennis della Stampa,* Piazza Mancini at the Duca d'Aosta Bridge (phone: 396-0792); the *CRAL Ministero Lavori Pubblici,* Lungotevere Thaon de Revel 3 (phone: 39-33-11); and the *Oasi di Pace,* Via degli Eugenii 2, Appia Antica (phone: 799-4550). For complete information and a list of every court in town contact the *Federazione Italiana Tennis,* Via B. Eustachio 9, Rome, Italy (85-82-50).

MONTE CARLO, Monaco: The *Monte Carlo Country Club* (actually on French soil) has 23 splendid clay and synthetic courts, set into the rich surrounding greenery like precious stones. You'll also find a panoramic view of the bay and skilled multilingual instructors. The club belongs to the Société des Bains de Mer, and if you stay at one of the SBM's hotels (the *Paris,* the *Hermitage,* the *Mirabeau,* or the *Monte Carlo Beach*), you'll be provided with a complimentary discount card. Four courts are lighted; and from mid-April to mid-September, you can sign up for special 5-day courses. Two squash courts are available as well. Information: *Monte Carlo Country Club,* BP 49, Monte Carlo, Monaco (phone: 78-20-45).

VALE DO LOBO, Portugal: The *Roger Taylor Tennis Center,* run by Britain's former top star, is in the middle of an enticing resort area on the sunny Algarve coast. There are 12 courts (6 lighted; 2 covered) and a 5-hour daily clinic that starts off with seaside jogging. Superb golf and swimming are also available. Guest accommodations are in *Vale do Lobo* villas or the luxurious *Dona Filipa Hotel.* The complex is only 9 miles (15 km) from Faro Airport. Information and reservations through the London office: *Roger Taylor Tennis Center,* Urbanizaçao de Luxo, 8100 Vale do Lobo, Algarve, Portugal (phone: 94-779); or *Roger Taylor Tennis Holidays Ltd.,* 85 High St., Wimbledon, London SW19 5EG (phone: 947-9727).

MARBELLA, Spain: Lew Hoad — remember Hoad and Rosewall? — runs one of the best-known tennis schools in Europe here on the heavily developed Costa del Sol, with courses and programs for all kinds of players. You can lodge in apartments near the school, or, some 15 miles away, at the deluxe *Los Monteros Hotel* complex by the sea, whose spacious grounds are full of lawns, swimming pools, palm trees, and tropical foliage. There are also 10 additional tennis courts here along with 5 squash courts. Information: *Lew Hoad's Campo de Tenis,* Apartado 111, Fuengirola, Marbella (Málaga), Spain (phone: 47-48-58). The area is also home to one of the biggest tennis operations of the *Club Med,* with 16 courts, 4 of them lighted, and accommodations in a large, comfortable hotel about 6 miles from the beach. Shuttle service is provided. Open year-round. Information: *Club Méditerranée,* Don Miguel, Marbella (Málaga), Spain; or contact the Club's New York office (see under *Cargèse, France*).

GSTAAD, Switzerland: The dowager *Palace Hotel,* the tennis hot spot in Switzerland, features the Roy Emerson Tennis Weeks in June and July as its main offering, back to back with the Swiss Championships. Emerson is not just a big name, his instruction is as exciting as his demonstrations. The prices are high, but the hotel and the tennis facilities are all spectacular — so if you can afford it, by all means go. Information: *Palace Hotel,* 3780 Gstaad, Switzerland (phone: 8-3131). A number of other Swiss resort towns organize special tennis weeks in summer and offer packages that include rooms, meals, instruction, and unlimited play. Among those that combine the best facilities with the most attractive settings are the *Derby Hotel, CH* 7260, Davos Dorf, Switzerland (phone: 611-66); and the *Tennisschule Laax, Sporthotel Signina,* 7032 Laax (GR), Switzerland (phone: 081-39-01-51). Similar packages are also available in the lovely towns of Grindelwald and Lenk. For details, contact the Verkehrsbüro at 3818 Grindelwald, Switzerland (phone: 53-12-12), or at 3775 Lenk, Switzerland (phone: 3-1595).

THE GREAT EUROPEAN TOURNAMENTS

WIMBLEDON, Wimbledon, England: Still a magnet to players good enough to compete for much bigger cash prizes elsewhere, this tourney, held in late June or early July, is an experience even if you've never held a racket. Grass courts, strawberry teas, and the legendary Centre Court are all high points, and the world-class matches going on quietly on all the outlying lawns end up being merely side shows. Good seats for late-round matches are completely sold out months in advance, as are a good many seats throughout the tourney; and there are long lines for the tickets that are available. However, patience is generally rewarded. Centre Court and Court Number One seats are allocated by lottery. Send a stamped, self-addressed envelope with your request for an allocation form in October, and you should receive the forms early in the new year. Information: *All-England Lawn Tennis Club,* Church Road, Wimbledon, London, SW19 5AE (phone: 946-2244). Tickets are available in the US through Keith Prowse & Co., 234 W 44th St., New York, NY 10036 (212-398-1430 or 800-223-4446, toll-free outside New York), or through the Abbey Box Office, 1775 Broadway, Suite 530, New York, NY 10019 (212-265-7800).

THE FRENCH OPEN, Paris, France: Held at *Roland Garros Stadium,* generally in early June, this tournament has traditions that go back to the great days of La Coste, Borotra, and Lenglen. It is a good notch above Rome in prestige and professionalism. Information: Le Secrétaire Général, *Fédération Française de Tennis,* Stade Roland Garros, 2 av. Gordon Bennett, 75016 Paris, France (phone: 743-9681).

THE ITALIAN INTERNATIONAL CHAMPIONSHIPS, Rome, Italy: Generally held in late May, this event has a pleasant Tiber-side setting among the cypresses, but attracts noisy, soccer-style crowds that deter some world-class players from participating. For exact dates and ticket information, contact the *Federazione Italiana Tennis,* Viale Tiziano 70, Rome, Italy (phone: 396-2300).

Great Golf Courses of Europe

There is a fair amount of controversy between the Scots and the Dutch as to who actually invented the game of golf, but there's little doubt as to who has been most instrumental in advancing it around the world. Golf is now almost universally conceded to be a game of primarily British origin, and the expansion of the number of places to play around the globe follows a track that almost exactly mirrors the expansion of the British Empire. And even where the Britons did not actually annex territory, their vacation preferences clearly affected the construction of golf courses, as evidenced by the courses that exist in such exotic Eastern European locations as Karlovy Vary and Mariánské Lázně. Non-Czechs know them better as the historic spas of Carlsbad and Marienbad, the favorite haunts of the Hanoverian kings of England who were returning to visit their then-German homelands.

It will come as no surprise that the finest courses in Europe are found in England, Scotland, and Ireland, but what *is* surprising is the fact that these courses are almost always hospitable to visiting golfers. (See also *Scotland's Fabled Golf Courses,* DIRECTIONS.) For the few private clubs among the best in Europe, it's always a wise idea to carry your home club membership card and a letter from your own club president or golf professional asking for hospitality. Europeans put great store in interclub reciprocity and will almost always honor such an official request.

Herewith, the best and most accessible golf courses in Europe:

SUNNINGDALE, Sunningdale, England: While the Old Course is considered the championship layout here, the New is probably the harder of the two. When you play them, you will discover that the decision on difficulty is an arbitrary one at best. Fairways and greens are meticulously maintained, and this is perhaps the finest single set of courses in England. Private but persuasible. Information: Sunningdale Golf Club, Ridgemount Rd., Sunningdale, Berkshire, England (phone: 2-1681).

WENTWORTH, Virginia Water, England: The East Course at Wentworth is generally considered the prettiest of the three courses and can do wonders for a shaky backswing. (There's also a par three layout here.) But it's the West Course that is sometimes not so affectionately called the Burma Road. For a high-handicap player, the West is not unlike putting an innocent head into the mouth of an unfriendly lion. Again, it's a private club that's likely to offer access to traveling players on weekdays upon presentation of your own club membership card and a letter from your club president. Information: Wentworth Golf Club, Virginia Water, Surrey, England (phone: 2201).

BALLYBUNION, Ballybunion, Republic of Ireland: No less an authority than Herbert Warren Wind calls this one of the ten toughest courses in the world, and you will have no reason to disagree. The course is laid out at the point where the Shannon River estuary meets the Atlantic Ocean, and you should be not the least concerned that the out-of-bounds area beside the fourteenth hole is a graveyard. A new Robert Trent Jones 18-hole course has recently been added. Information: Ballybunion Golf Club, County Kerry, Republic of Ireland (phone: 27146).

KILLARNEY GOLF AND FISHING CLUB, Killarney, Republic of Ireland: There are now two courses here beside the legendary lakes, and it's the older course that is better. The scenery is startling in this fabled spot, and it may take an act of will to keep your head down, though it may not be worth the effort. The sight of the lakes framing the purple mountains is a once-in-a-lifetime experience. Information: Killarney Golf and Fishing Club, Mahoney's Point, Killarney, County Kerry, Republic of Ireland (phone: 064-3-1034).

PORTMARNOCK, Portmarnock, Republic of Ireland: This fabled layout (just outside Dublin) is perhaps the best single course in the Republic. The short flag sticks, which are set on springs to let them swing freely in the breeze, tell you something about the wind hazards here, though again the quality of the course is superb. Be prepared for soaring scores but a bracing outing. Information: Portmarnock Golf Club, Portmarnock, County Dublin, Republic of Ireland (phone: 32-30-82).

ROYAL DUBLIN, Dollymount, Republic of Ireland: The "other" Dublin area golfing magnet that, though second to Portmarnock, still deserves a place among the Continent's best. Again, the winds blow here and the rough grows to a size not normally known in the New World. Information: Royal Dublin Golf Club, Dollymount, County Dublin, Republic of Ireland (phone: 33-63-46).

LAHINCH, Lahinch, Republic of Ireland: This extraordinary course has been known to inflict players with every plague save famine and flood. It has one short par 5 that has been lengthened a bit by putting something that looks like the Great Wall of China in the middle of the fairway, and to add a little extra spice to your round, there's a 145-yard par 3 that's completely blind. Would you like to guess how they managed that? Our pick for the best in the west of Ireland. Information: Lahinch Golf Club, Lahinch, County Clare, Republic of Ireland (phone: 81003).

ROYAL PORTRUSH, Portrush, Northern Ireland: Though the troubles in Northern Ireland persist, the golf remains above the internecine disputes. The *Dunluce Course* is the championship layout here and is named after the striking old castle that is perched on the white cliffs above the fairways. Information: Royal Portrush Golf Club, Bushmills Rd., Portrush, County Antrim, Northern Ireland (phone: 822311).

ROYAL COUNTY DOWN, Newcastle, Northern Ireland: This is "where the Mountains of Mourne meet the sea." They played the British Amateur championship here a few years ago, and there are hazards in certain places that can prove rather startling to weak-kneed players. The minutes of the founding club meeting in 1889 reported that "the Secretaries were empowered to employ Tom Morris to lay out the course at a cost not to exceed £4." God alone only knows how old Tom hacked this course out of the rough sandhills for that price, but he sure made a beauty. Information: Royal County Down Golf Club, Newcastle, County Down, Northern Ireland (phone: 23314).

PENINA GOLF CLUB, Algarve, Portugal: Designed by Henry Cotton, who was three times the British Open champion, the course has managed to overcome the disadvantage of being set on very flat terrain. Literally hundreds of thousands of trees and shrubs were planted to provide a frame for the golf holes, and this former rice field is now a fine test of golfing skill. The large *Penina Golf Hotel* adjoins the golf course. Information: Penina Golf Club, Algarve, Portugal.

THE OLD COURSE, St. Andrews, Fife, Scotland: This is the prime magnet that draws all of the world's golfers, for this course dates, they say, from the fifteenth century. Its aura is only slightly diminished by the bathers and strollers who consistently cross the first and eighteenth fairways of the Old Course — it's the shortest route to the beach — though once out on the course, its extreme difficulty and careful design become more readily apparent. There are three other courses on the same site — the Eden, Jubilee, and New (which was opened in 1894) — but it's the Old that you must play. Plan your play date here carefully because there's no golfing on the Old

Course on Sunday. Information: Links Management Committee, Golf Pl., St. Andrews, Fife, Scotland.

GLENEAGLES, Auchterarder, Scotland: The Scots tend to denigrate this superb quartet of courses here because they do not conform to the treasured linksland tradition. But visiting golfers will fall prey to no such prejudice, and the King's Course in particular is an absolute joy to play. It's also consistently in the best condition of any Scottish course and the extraordinary hotel here is reason enough for a visit. Information: Gleneagles Hotel Golf Course, Auchterarder, Perthshire, Scotland (phone: 35-43).

CARNOUSTIE, Carnoustie, Scotland: Just 5 miles from St. Andrews is this site of a half dozen British Open golf tournaments. If the Championship Course (the better of the two tracks here) is the least impressive of the championship Scottish courses at first glance, it takes only one round of play to appreciate its true value. It encompasses the very essence of what's best about playing golf in Scotland, and the back nine in particular — with the famous fourteenth hole called Spectacles — and the three backbreaking finishing holes will leave you with memories (not necessarily pleasant) that you will not soon forget. Information: Carnoustie Golf Club, Links Parade, Carnoustie, Tayside, Scotland (phone: 5-3249).

ROYAL TROON, Troon, Scotland: Laid out along the beach, with the outgoing nine heading virtually straight down the strand, and the closing nine paralleling it only a few yards inland, the only distraction is the fact that the course lies directly below the flight path into Prestwick Airport. So it sometimes seems as though players are about to be sucked up into the jet wash. Another classic British Open layout (and site of the 1982 tournament), it is one of the few private clubs in Scotland that is open to visitors; playing privileges are usually made available to members of clubs in the US who can produce a respectable certificate of handicap. Women are allowed to play the Championship links only on Mondays, Wednesdays, and Fridays. Information: Royal Troon Golf Club, Craigend Rd., Troon, Ayrshire, Scotland (phone: 31-15-55).

TURNBERRY, Turnberry, Scotland: The two courses here, the Ailsa and the Arran, are quite close in quality, but it's the Ailsa on which the British Open was played in 1977. The wind blows in from the sea, and it sometimes takes an act of courage just to stand up on the craggy tees and hit out into the teeth of what occasionally seems like a gale. The beautiful *Turnberry Hotel* — now being completely refurbished — provides some respite from the elements, but the golfing challenge is the real lure here. Information: Turnberry Hotel Golf Course, Turnberry, Ayrshire, Scotland (phone: 202).

LA MANGA CAMPO DE GOLF, Los Belones, Spain: The home of the Spanish Open, it's the "most superbly maintained" course in the world according to Gary Player. The two 18-hole championship layouts offer tantalizing views of the Mediterranean from nearly every tee, and the sights and scenery provide a sort of ancillary hazard. Information: La Manga Campo de Golf, Los Belones, Cartagena, Murcia, Spain (phone: 56-35-00/04).

European Beaches:
Sun and Sand on Six Seas

When you look down on a teeming Riviera beach in the middle of July, it's hard to believe that it wasn't so many decades ago that the great Riviera hotels closed down for the season with the first searing rays of the midsummer sun. Nothing can turn back the clock, however, or dismantle the seafront condominiums and cement-block hotels, or banish the sun-seeking Scandinavian hordes.

But Europe has many beaches of great natural beauty, whatever their man-made garnish: beaches that offer a vast assortment of marine pleasures, beaches where the people are more fun to watch than the fish ever were.

Some caveats: The crowds during the first 3 weeks of August, when Europe's entire population seems bent on cramming in vacation, are too much of a good thing (late June and early September are the ideal times).

Also, though you will find surf far tamer here than in America, you will also find far less in the way of skilled lifeguard protection. And, though the waves are gentle, the sun is fierce: Take it in carefully measured doses and keep smearing on that fancy French suntan goo.

KNOKKE, Belgium: The North Sea has a wintry sound to it, and, indeed, the water is briskly unlike that of the bathtubby Mediterranean. Nonetheless, the broad beaches along the Royal Road that is the Belgian coastline are beautifully kept and ideal for summer vacationing. Knokke, in the corner by the Dutch border, is the most complete of resorts: You'll find fine cuisine, ample sports facilities, gracious garden-rimmed villas, a gambling casino, and the country's most inviting hotel, *La Réserve* — lapped about by the sea, the swimming pool, and little Victoria Lake. But there are simpler pleasures as well, among them less-developed southerly beaches such as Blankenberge and Wenduine. You can walk along the dikes and the great empty dunes, go on pony rides and ride the traditional sail carts on the beach, or take in any number of the colorful folk festivals that take place all along the coast. And, in case of a cloudy day, there is a varied choice of easy excursions: the fish market at Zeebrugge, the bird reserve at Het Zwin, the lovely old village of Damme, and beautiful, canal-crossed Bruges.

LE CAP D'AGDE, France: The ancient Greeks used to anchor their ships off this jutting promontory. And a lot of modern French prefer its wide sandy beaches and deep calm coves to the overbuilt, overrun, overpriced Côte d'Azur. Unlike the Riviera, the development of this coastline from St.-Cyprien to Port Camargue has been carefully controlled to retain its natural beauty. There are good facilities for boating and for tennis (at the *Club Pierre Barthès*) and hills nearby that offer many wonderful walks. And the surrounding region is one of France's most attractive and least visited: You can day-trip to the walled towns of Carcassonne and Aigues-Mortes, the Roman theater at Nîmes, and the horse farms of Camargue; and, at Béziers, take in bloodless bullfights.

PORTO-VECCHIO, Corsica, France: According to our First Law of Beaches, islands have the best ones, and the best of these are the least accessible. Witness Porto-Vecchio. A 5.5-mile-long bay that gives its name to the small fishing port at its head, Porto-Vecchio plunges into the eastern coast of Corsica, just opposite the side where most boats and planes arriving from the French mainland discharge their passengers. The beaches predicted by the First Law are here in force — fine-sand strands like La Marine, Golfo di Sogno, St.-Cyprien, Pinarello, and Palombaggia, which flank the port town. The vegetation is subtropical; umbrella pines and conifers peculiar to the area line the coast. Other local specialties are lobsters and nudism. For information about the latter, contact: Syndicat d'Initiative, 20210 Porto-Vecchio, 2 Rue Maréchal Juin, Corsica, France. (phone: 70-09-58). For off-beach entertainment, you can fly or sail to Bonifacio, a medieval fortress town at the southern tip of the island that is still entered by drawbridge. And from there, it's only 7.5 miles by ferry to Sardinia.

THASSOS, Greece: A Greek island, but not one of *the* Greek islands, Thassos lies in the northernmost part of the country, about an hour's ferry ride off the coast of Macedonia. Cooler than its sunbaked southern cousins, Thassos is also heavily wooded and its landscape is a study in greens — the silvery sage of the olive groves, the dark greens of the towering firs. Makriamos, a few kilometers south of Limenas, the principal town, is the island's best beach, but if you drive the circular shore road, you'll find a dozen more: Skala Panagia, Kinira, Skala Marion, Skala Sotiros, Skala Rahoniou, and others. The quiet bays of Arhangelos and Agios Ioanis are also idyllic. The tree-covered ruins of the acropolis of ancient Thassos will remind you you're in Greece. Should there be a cloudy day, you can take the ferry back to Kavala and amble around the Byzantine fortress and the Imaret, a center of the country's Moslem culture.

THE GULF OF MIRABELLO, Crete, Greece: Crete's choicest beaches are located on either side of the town of Agios Nikolaos, which lies at the head of this deep bay (Kólpos Mirampelou in Greek) on the far eastern end of the island. Along with the beaches are some of the island's choicest beach hotels: the *Minos Beach,* the *Mirabello,* the *Elounda Beach,* the *Elounda Gulf Villas;* their most attractive accommodations are in Cretan-style bungalows right on the beachfront. Agios Nikolaos is full of animated taverns and fish restaurants, mainly along the docks and on the banks of Voulismeni, a tiny volcanic lake. Between sunbaths, you can hire a little boat to go out to the islet of Spinalonga, where you can explore a charming Venetian castle; drive or stroll to the village of Kritsa to have an ouzo, a game of backgammon, and a look at the frescoes in its thirteenth-century church.

FORTE DEI MARMI, Italy: The Italian Riviera is really like a gigantic seaside café, and the chief amusement is watching the passing (or sprawling) parade: the phalanxes of multicolored umbrellas, deck chairs, and sentry-box cabins; the fleets of pedalboats; the sippers of Campari, builders of sand castles, players of volleyball, and scantily clad waders — out more to be seen than to enjoy the warm surf. The whole expanse between the Lido di Camaiore and the bustling resort town of Viareggio is really one long marina. Patrician families from Rome, Florence, and Milan have been coming here every summer for a century, though in recent years, many of their pined and palmed seafront villas have been transformed into small hotels. Never expect romantic solitude, and remember that all of Italy vacations in mid-August.

COSTA SMERALDA, Sardinia, Italy: In the space of only a few years, $200 million and the Aga Khan transformed a rocky, primitive wasteland between the port of Olbia and La Maddalena at Sardinia's tip into the country's most glamorous beach complex. The boulders are still there and the water is a cloudless cobalt blue, but scattered from cove to cove are four elegant hotels, cleverly designed so that they seem to have grown out of the rocks: the *Romazzino,* the *Cervo,* the *Pitrizza,* the *Cala di Volpe.* The crowd can get very fancy, particularly when the yacht fleet is in — but the sun-and-sea life is superbly simple. Boats connect the area with Genoa and Civitavecchia on the mainland, and Alisarda flies from Rome, Milan, and Nice. However you go, remember to reserve well in advance for a midsummer visit.

THE LIDO, Venice, Italy: Just a reminder that while you are visiting the most beautiful city in the world you can also swim, sunbathe, and eat shrimp on the Lido, a long, skinny island bordered on one side by the sea and, on the other, by the lagoon, just a short boat ride from downtown Venice. There is golf, tennis, riding, boating, and plenty of beach life on the wide strands (some of them public, and some — immaculately groomed — the private reserves of the great seafront hotels). When you've had enough of the sun, you can go for a stroll along the Venetian canals or sip an *aperitivo* in piazza San Marco.

PRAIA DE ROCHA, Portugal: Some of Europe's finest beaches are along a 100-kilometer stretch of Portuguese coastline between Faro and the Sagres promontory in the country's southernmost province, the Algarve. The strands face south toward Africa, and both the air and the water stay temperate most of the year. The heavy development that the area has undergone in recent years has taken its toll on the coast's raw natural beauty, but, in exchange, has provided it with an array of fine shorefront hotels: the *Algarve* at *Praia de Rocha,* the *Golf da Penina* at *Penina,* and the *Alvor Praia* at *Prainha,* to name just a few. Praia de Rocha has a beige yellow beach set against craggy red cliffs that erosion has sculpted into strange, exotic shapes: Rock spires, arches, and hollows make a kind of natural labyrinth on the sand. In the old fortress of St. Catherine, there is a good seafood restaurant (grilled sardines and *vinho verde* are local specialties) and stunning lookout point; the nearby port of Portimâo gets a steady traffic of colorful fishing craft. The golf links at *Penina* offer 27 holes on 360 acres that roll across the foothills of the Monchiquo Mountains.

MAMAIA, Romania: The Black Sea is one of those bodies of water that Americans learn about in geography class but never consider for swimming. Yet, the Romanian and Bulgarian Black Sea coasts are to Eastern Europe what the Riviera is to France. Dr. Ana Aslan's discovery of the supposed wonder drug Gerovital has attracted a score of health-cure seekers to Romania. But there's still an immense gap between Techirghiol and St.-Tropez. Mamaia, a 5-mile strip of beach and rich vegetation between the Black Sea and Lake Siutghiol, offers a wide choice of hotels that — though the architecture is uniformly Moscow Modern — boast rooms and facilities fully as satisfactory as those of their Western counterparts. The crowd is international (with a preponderance of Eastern Europeans), and the nightlife and sports facilities are as abundant and varied as in the West — but prices are quite reasonable, and there's a refreshing plenitude of rustic Romanian restaurants serving wines and meals you'd never in an eon encounter in the Hamptons.

FORMENTOR, Majorca, Spain: First find the Balearic Islands, three and a half clumps of land about 100 miles off the eastern coast of Spain. The largest clump is Majorca; the thin tongue of land that runs off the top is Cape Formentor. Though honky-tonk Palma de Mallorca, its urbanized beaches, and its tour-bus traffic jams may mar the idyllic green countryside, the almond groves and wild flowers and the high shoreline cliffs that you see as you make the 40-mile drive northward from the capital to Formentor will give you entirely different feelings. Formentor's beaches — and those of Cala de San Vincente — are superb, and so is the *Hotel Formentor*, surrounded by pine woods and looking majestically toward the sea, the bay, the mountains, the rust-colored bluffs. The cape ends with a dramatically positioned lighthouse. Not far away is the village of Puerto de Pollehsa, where you can ingest a bowl of seafood stew and an *ensaimada* (the Majorcan pastry specialty), take a boat ride on the bay, and have a look at the hilltop Notre Dame de Puig.

KUŞADASI, Turkey: About 65 miles (105 km) south of Izmir, this lovely old town founded in the seventeenth century by Genoese traders occupies the site of an ancient Greek settlement on a sandy peninsula across the protected bay from the Greek island of Samos. The little beaches all around the town and along the road to Selçuk are among the prettiest in the Aegean, and the area is famous for the variety of wild birds and flowers that soften the glare of sand, sun, and whitewashed houses. Near the port is *Öküz Mehmet Paşa,* an old traders' inn transformed into a luxury hotel and restaurant (information from *Ninotour,* Kuşadasi). Just keep saying *karides, çipura, barbunya,* and *trança şiş,* and the waiters will keep bringing you the four freshest fish in Turkey. A 15-minute drive away is Ephesus, the ruins of the Ionian city that was the capital of all Asia Minor — one of the Mediterranean's most enthralling archaeological sites. The skin diving around Kuşadasi is particularly rewarding: The water is crystalline, and there are as many brightly colored fish in the sea as there are birds in the air and flowers on land.

DUBROVNIK, Yugoslavia: Far down the Dalmatian coast, not far from the Albanian border, this walled and turreted city is one of Europe's best preserved and most captivating — and it would be worth a visit even if it were in the middle of a desert. Instead, it juts out dramatically into the gleaming blue Adriatic. Inside the medieval walls is a collection of fine Renaissance palaces and churches, many dating from the great period of Venetian domination of the sea. The feeling of antiquity is heightened by the absence of cars and there's a wide flagstone main promenade that teems with life in summer, especially in July and August during a 6-week-long music festival. Out on both sides of the town are the beaches — long and bright, some of sand and others of scrubbed white pebbles; just across from the port is the tiny island of Lokrum, a wooded national park with fine swimming and skin diving and, hidden among the pines, a splendid outdoor restaurant installed in an ancient structure that began its life as a monastery. Big ferries, tiny dinghies, and just about any other kind of boat you can name putter up and down the coast in season, and you have a choice of a variety of maritime excursions from an hour's fishing offshore to a weekend cruise to Venice.

CLUB MÉDITERRANÉE: *Club Med* isn't really a club at all, but a chain of some 76 vacation villages sited strategically on some of the most pleasurable parts of the planet. The idea started in France, and the head office is in Paris — but the clientele is, by now, thoroughly international. Guests are usually on the young side and interested in active vacations. There's always a variety of sports to enjoy, everything from judo to water skiing, and a *Club Med* vacation can be an exceptionally good deal for those who take advantage of the activities, because there's no extra charge. But the Club's settings are protected and beautifully landscaped and friendly (like a summer camp for big kids) and the outside world is kept at a distance, so you can enjoy yourself just as much if you do nothing more active than snooze in the sun. Accommodation at the Club's beach and seaside villages is usually in attractive, functional bungalows, and there are communal dining facilities. Some of the best Clubs for beach life include *Santa Giulia* in Corsica, *Pakostane* in Yugoslavia, *Corfu* in Greece, and *Foça* in Turkey. You can get a complete list and information from the US office: *Club Med*, 3 E 54th St., New York, NY 10022 (phone: 212-750-1670).

The European Mountain Experience

Maybe in another decade Europe's mountains will look like its beaches, with vacationers climbing shoulder to shoulder with little men hawking alpenstocks and chocolate bars at the peaks. But at least for now, the mountain country — often no more than a morning's drive from the subway and the stock exchange — is still a wilderness paradise and has something to offer both pick-and-crampon types bound to scale the murderous North Wall of the Eiger and weekend enthusiasts accustomed to nothing more strenuous than strolls in the Vienna Woods.

There is a sense of good fellowship in the mountains: While beach people more often than not resent each other's territorial encroachment, mountain people share a sense of physical accomplishment that makes the trails and the Alpine huts very friendly places to be.

Though mountains are mountains — dangerous if you don't know what you're about — the Alps are for the most part as accommodating as the Continent itself. Europeans are great hikers, and there are miles and miles of well-signposted trails. Most good European mountain areas are liberally scattered with huts and refuges where you can get meals that, at the end of a day on the trail, taste better than a banquet at *Maxim's* and bunk on a mattress that feels as good as any at the *Ritz*. When the sun goes down, there's usually plenty of mulled wine and lusty singing. Many hikers spend weeks just trekking from one hut to the next. Some areas, especially in Teutonic countries, are so geared to entertaining hikers that they hand out small cards listing all the main huts, each of which is provided with a rubber stamp so that you can brand your card in the appropriate space. The goal, of course, is to end up with a stamp after the name of every hut.

Whether you go out walking for a week or just a day, there are some precautions to observe. You don't have to outfit yourself for the conquest of Everest on your first stroll, but stout boots will certainly enhance the experience and a knapsack will come in handy. In it you should stuff a pocket flashlight and — no matter how hot the sun and cloudless the sky when you embark — a lightweight rain parka and a sweater. Alpine weather is enormously capricious and you can easily experience four seasons in a day. If you'll be out longer than that, you may want to bring a good long book. (Picking an area where excursions to the valleys are a possibility is a good idea if you're easily daunted by rain.)

And don't fail to buy a good map before you set out; take it to the local tourist office to find out about the relative hazards and pleasures of the local trails. Never start out knowing nothing.

Here we've assembled a list of areas that will provide you with the most satisfying mountain experiences. Each item is keyed according to the activities you can enjoy there: Rambling (R), on walking paths that are easy enough to be pleasurable to children and beginning hikers; Trudging (T), on longer and steeper trails that will challenge intermediate hikers and adults; and Dangling (D), rope-and-crampon mountain goat stuff, suitable for trained climbers.

GROSSGLOCKNER and GROSSVENEDIGER, Austria: Austria's two star peaks both rise out of craggy ranges that offer a mountaineer's paradise of challenging climbs. The graves in the little mountain cemetery in the churchyard of Kals are grisly reminders of the perils of the Glockner, the tougher of the two. Experts can commence the ascent to its peak and to Grossvenediger's summit from a number of well-placed refuges throughout the area. For everyone else, there are *hütte*-to-*hütte* hikes that last several days and cover some of the Alps' most dramatic terrain. For information: Tiroler Fremdenverkehrswerbung, Bozner Platz 6, A-6010 Innsbruck, Austria (phone: 2-0777); or Fremdenverkehrsbüro, Postfach 90, 9900 Lienz, Austria (phone: 47-47). A good way to make either climb is under the auspices of the *Hochgebirgsschule Tyrol,* an Innsbruck-based climbing school and guide operation. To find out more, contact *Hochgebirgsschule Tyrol,* Anichstrasse 34, A-6020 Innsbruck, Innrain 67 (phone: 2-5986). **T, D**

OBERGURGL, Austria: On a wide, sunny plain at 6,560 feet in the middle of the Ötztaler Alps, this town — one of the highest in Europe — offers a choice of accommodations that range from luxury hotels to simple wooden chalets, and the surrounding mountains are dotted with *hüttes* — refuges where hikers can find simple food and shelter. A great ring of glaciers and towering peaks and an abundance of high Alpine flora make for startling scenery, which you can view from afar along easy trails a half hour from town or conquer if you have the inclination and the skills. Obergurgl is a ski resort in winter; the town of Vent, on the other side of the Ramolkogl, is quieter and far less developed. It is also the jumping-off point for the ascent of the 12,464-foot Wildspitze. For information about instruction and guided climbs: *Hochgebirgsschule Obergurgl,* Haus Schönblick, A-6456 Obergurgl 53, Tyrol, Austria (phone: 251). **R, T**

THE HIGH TATRAS, Czechoslovakia: Like most of Eastern Europe, this magnificent mountain district is generally overlooked by Americans, though the resort areas are less developed and less expensive than their Western cousins, and there is a century-old tradition of climbing and a well-maintained network of húts and hotels. Starý Smokovec (3,280 feet), Strbske Pleso (4,428 feet), and Tatranská Lomnica (2,788 feet) are the main starting points for area excursions. The hotel at Popradské Pleso (4,920 feet) is located right by the lake, and is a fine springboard for trips into the popular Pic Rysy group. The *Sliezsky Dom,* a comfortable, modern hotel at 5,576 feet, has easy access to the Gerlachovský Stít and the whole Tatra range. Among the best high *chata* (mountain huts) are the *Zbojnícka,* the *Terryho,* the *Iames Pod Solískom,* and the *Pod Rysmi,* which at 7,380 feet is the highest *chata* in Czechoslovakia. Information: Čedok,

Na Příkopě 18, 111 35 Prague, Czechoslovakia (phone: 22-42-51); or Čedok, Room 1902, 10 E 40th St., New York, NY 10016 (phone: 212-689-9720). **R, T**

CUMBRIA and LANCASHIRE, England: From April through October, fell-walking and rock-climbing are favorite sports among the crags and crests of the Lake District counties, but it's certainly more Albion than Alpine. Centers for guided jaunts, rock-climbing courses, wildlife observation, and bird-watching are: *The Mountain Goat*, Victoria St., Windermere, Cumbria LA23 1AD (phone: 5161); *Countrywide Holidays*, Birch Heys, Cromwell Range, Manchester M14 6HU (phone: 225-1000). For more information on climbing in Britain: British Mountaineering Council, Crawford House, Precinct Centre, Manchester University, Booth St. E, Manchester M13 9RZ (phone: 273-5835). **R, T**

MONT-BLANC, France and Italy: Though the highest mountain in the Alps is now pierced by a two-country tunnel that obviates the necessity for climbing over its majestic summit, it still provides some of the most challenging mountaineering in Europe. Chamonix — a classy, chichi, ski resort town that attracts everyone from sun-deck loungers to helmeted, pick-toting rock climbers — is the principal center of the French side; the Compagnie des Guides (Maison de la Montagne, 190 Pl. de l'Église, 74400 Chamonix, France; phone: 53-00-88) is the best source of information and assistance. Courmayeur on the Italian side is less developed: It basks in a great natural amphitheater bisected by the Dora River and sprinkled with picture-postcard Alpine hamlets. For details: Azienda di Soggiorno, Piazzale Monte Bianco, Courmayeur, Italy (phone: 842-060). If the taming of Mont-Blanc by tunnel and cable car takes the romance out of the mountain for you, try going farther afield in the Valle d'Aosta to lesser-known centers like Paquier, Valtournanches, Cogne, and Valsavaranche in the Gran Paradiso National Park. For information on the whole area: Ufficio Informazioni Turistiche della Valle d'Aosta, Piazza E Chanoux 8, Aosta, Italy (phone: 3-5655). **R, T, D**

THE DOLOMITES, Italy: The hard hiking in this vast range south of the Brenner Pass — long a favorite region of expert and experienced climbers — has remained largely uncharted. Yet its jagged peaks, rising like giant rusty pink fangs above smooth snow meadows, are one of the most awesome natural sights in Europe, and if you ever cross the Sella, the Falzarego, the Pordoi, and the Pellegrino passes under a full moon, the rest of your life will seem anticlimactic. Cortina d'Ampezzo — once the site of the Winter Olympics and now a favorite summer resort of affluent Italians from the flatlands — is the classiest of a number of towns where you can begin your mountain rambles; Corvara, Ortisei, and Canazei are equally beautiful and just as well placed. And, because a large chunk of the Dolomites once belonged to Austria, you are likely to find the atmosphere — as well as the language — in all these towns far more Teutonic than Latin. The Marmolada and the Gruppo Sella are the major peaks, but there are dozens more. For information: The Azienda Autonoma per il Turismo, Via Matteotti, 3, Belluno, Italy (phone: 2-4077); Azienda di Soggiorno e Turismo, Piazza Walter 28, Bolzano, Italy (phone: 2-5656); Azienda Autonoma per il Turismo, 4 Via Alfieri, 4, Trento, Italy (phone: 983-880). **R, T, D**

THE MATTERHORN and MONTE ROSA, Switzerland: The car-free town of Zermatt, accessible only by railway, offers access to a dozen peaks of the "4,000 Club" — a sobriquet which refers to those mountain peaks that are over 4,000 meters (13,120 feet) high — representing five of the six highest mountains in Europe. If you don't want to be bothered this year with the Andes or the Himalayas, this area of the Swiss Alps will furnish you with nine lives' worth of advanced climbing. The *High Alpine School*, which runs summer courses for experts, can also locate guides for you — advisable on these treacherous trails no matter how many times you have hopped up Mt. McKinley. Information: Hochalpine Bergsteigerschule Zermatt and Bergführerverein, 3920 Zermatt, Switzerland (phone: 67-34-56); and Verkehrsverein, 3920 Zermatt, Switzerland (phone: 671-031). **D**

PONTRESINA, Switzerland: The Swiss take even their strolling seriously, and scores of footpaths are scrupulously marked by destination and estimated hiking time. That is especially true in the glorious Engadine Valley — one of those places that has everything for everybody. The 4.3-mile walk from Alp Languard to Muottas Muragl is a novice's dream: High but level, it gives you spectacular vistas of the Engadine lakes and the whole Bernina Range. The area is also supplied with Alpine gardens and a game reserve, a choice of chair lifts and railways so that you can start your tour up high, plus huts with panoramic views, where you can savor three-star lunches. For experts, there's plenty of ice and rock climbing on the Piz Palu; and some of the most exciting climbing in Switzerland is on the 13,120-foot Piz Bernina. The fine *Mountain School* has a large team of expert guides and offers a variety of courses for aspiring mountaineers. Information: Schweizer Bergsteigerschule, Chesa Hotel Engadinerhof, CH-7504 Pontresina, Switzerland (phone: 6-6444); and Kur und Verkehrsverein, CH-7504 Pontresina, Switzerland (phone: 6-6488). **R, T, D**

STRADA ALTA LEVENTINA, Switzerland: Much to the delight of Alpine hikers, the Swiss government (which is never neutral about nature) has recently refurbished the old St. Gotthard High Road, a medieval mule track and pilgrim's way. The whole trail, which runs 27.9 miles, makes a comfortable 3-day excursion, and there's plenty of fine food and comfortable shelter along the way. You start from Airolo, 3,772 feet, and on the first day travel via Brugnasco, Cresta, and Lurengo to Osco. The second day, you pass through Targuel, Rossura, Sorsello, Gianón, and Anzonico; and on the third day through Segno, Sobrio, Diganengo, and Pollegio Biasca. Just follow the red and white signs. Information: Ente Turistico di Leventina, 6760 Faido, Switzerland (phone: 38-16-16); or Swiss National Tourist Office, 608 Fifth Ave., New York, NY 10020 (phone: 212-757-5944). **R**

Going for Game: Hunting and Fishing in Europe

With the growth of the environmental movement in Europe, fishing and hunting aren't the wide-open free-for-alls that they were as recently as a decade ago. Nevertheless, the possibilities for pursuing these sports are rich and extensive. From the Scottish Highlands to Poland's Mazur Lakes, from the Tatra Mountains of Czechoslovakia to the coasts of Brittany, there is an abundance of wildlife — often in spectacular settings.

THE HUNT

In the last 10 years, seasons have been shortened and are more rigorously observed. At the same time license costs have risen sharply: In Greece, for example, a 15-day hunting permit that cost $25 not long ago now sells for over $200. In some countries — Germany, Belgium, and Holland among them — you can hunt only as the guest of the owner of a private game reserve. (Foreigners may make contact through sporting magazines and clubs, but hired hospitality has a hefty price tag.) Here are some of your best bets for unparalleled European hunting adventures:

ŽIDLOCHOVICE, Southern Moravia, Czechoslovakia: This Eastern European country, practically one giant game reserve, offers some of the finest hunting in Europe; the pheasant preserve at Židlochovice, near Brno, is one of its unique and richest areas, attracting hunters from all over the Continent by the hundreds every autumn. Northern

Moravia also has two excellent reserves in the Jeseniky and Beskydy districts. Either way, you must go in one of the groups organized by Čedok, the national travel bureau. For information: Čedok - Lovy, Na Příkopě 18, Prague, Czechoslovakia; or Čedok, 10 E 40th St., New York, NY 10016 (phone: 212-689-9720). Prague, incidentally, has a number of specialty shops where you can buy excellent hunting equipment.

THE WEST COUNTRY, England: When the English say "hunting" they mean for fox, on horseback, with hounds; it is an activity as British as taking high tea. Two hotels in Devon specialize in arranging fox-hunting holidays: the *Kings Arms Hotel,* Fore St., Kingsbridge TQ7 1AB, England (phone: 2071), and the *Glazebrook House,* South Brent TQ10 9JE, England (phone: South Brent 3322). You will surely need to be a proficient horseman to keep up with the Tallyho-Joneses. For information on hunting and shooting in Britain, contact: The British Tourist Authority, 40 W 57th St., New York, NY 10019 (phone: 212-581-4700); or British Field Sports Society, 59 Kennington Rd., London SE1 (phone: 928-4742).

ORCHAPE, France: This isn't a place but an organization that arranges wild fowl shoots in Ireland, Red-leg partridge shoots in Spain, and big-game expeditions in Hungary and Czechoslovakia. Information: *Orchape,* 6 rue d'Armaillé, 75017 Paris, France (phone: 380-3067).

CRETE, Greece: Quail and partridge hunting is a special experience in the wild and primitive parts of the island of Dia, across from Heraklion, but a far cry from the busy north shore beaches. This terrain is typical of the savage regions that served partisans so well during the island's German occupation. You will need a guide. The season begins on September 15 and lasts until the end of November. Hare and rabbit until the end of January. For more information: Greek National Tourist Organization in Crete, Xanthoudidou 1, Herakleion, Crete (phone: 22-24-87); or the Forestry Office, Dassarchio Iraklion Dedalou ST. 22, Herakleion, Crete (phone: 282-776).

THE HIGHLANDS, Scotland: August 12, the "Glorious Twelfth," is the opening day of the 4-month grouse season, a national ceremony of sorts that takes place annually inside the triangle determined by Aberdeen, Perth, and Inverness. Braemar, Ballater, and Aboyne are among the more colorful spots. Hunters in the area also stalk roe, fallow, sika, and red deer at this time of year. The list of Scottish hotels that arrange for both grouse-shooting and deer-hunting expeditions for their guests includes: *Raemoir House Hotel,* Banchory, Kincardineshire; *Tullich Lodge,* Ballater, Aberdeenshire; and *Knockie Lodge,* Whitebridge, Inverness-shire. Contact them well in advance, since you may need to write directly to the estates with hunting grounds. See if you can arrange to be there for one of the gatherings of the clans, Scottish ceremonies that also enliven the Highlands. For detailed information: Highlands and Islands Development Board, Bridge House, 27 Bank St., Inverness IV1 1QR, Scotland (phone: 3-4171).

THE *COTOS* OF THE PYRENEES, Spain: Under the administration of its National Institute for the Conservation of Nature, Spain has an extensive network of *cotos* — national hunting reserves. A number of the choices are clustered in the Pyrenees: Alto Pallars, Arán, Los Circos, Fresser, Cadí, Cerdaña, Vall Ferrera. Wild boar are profuse, and the Spanish specialize in tracking these harvest-plunderers; chamois, deer, roebuck, and grouse are also taken in the October to January season. Most big hunting areas have their *Parador Nacional* — a picturesque state-run country hotel. All foreigners planning to hunt in Spain should contact: Administración Turistica Española, Sección de Caza, Calle Velasquez 25, Madrid, Spain (phone: 435-6641). More information: *Federación Española de Caza* (National Hunting Federation), José O. Gasset 5, Madrid, Spain (phone: 276-9184); or travel agencies that specialize in hunting trips, such as *Cacerias Conde,* Princesa 7, Madrid, Spain (phone: 247-1804); or *Promoción de Caza y Pesca,* Duque de Sexto 41, Madrid, Spain (phone: 276-3661).

NOVI SAD, Vojvodina, Yugoslavia: The fertile wooded Vojvodine, north of Belgrade, is the nation's least exploited tourist area — and its richest hunting land. Near

Novi Sad and the banks of the Danube, the Odzaci, Karavukovo, Bagremara, and Ristovaca reserves shelter a superabundance of wild hare, pheasant, and partridge. Information: Lovoturs, Dr. Salvadora Allendea 26, Novi Sad 21000, Yugoslavia (phone: 61-62-42); and the Yugoslav National Tourist Office, Rockefeller Center, Suite 210, 630 Fifth Ave., New York, NY 10020 (phone: 212-757-2801).

FISHING HOLES

The best of Europe's fishing is some of the best on the planet. There are swordfish on the Costa Cantábrica in Spain, and carp and pike on Poland's Mazur lakes. The beaches of Brittany in France make for superb surfcasting. Britain lures anglers with the proximity of ancient hotels and quaint inns to its best fishing streams. (The booklet called *Fishing,* available from the British Tourist Authority, 40 W 57th St., New York, NY 10019; phone: 212-581-4700, can provide the details.) Switzerland's fishing centers cater to novices as well as to longtime fly-tiers with special summer fishing courses. The Swiss National Tourist Office, 608 Fifth Ave., New York, NY 10020, (phone: 212-757-5944), can tell you more, as can Schweizerischer Sportfischer-Verband, 4657 Dulliken Dorfstrasse 16, Switzerland (phone: 35-35-05). Even the cities have their contributions: There's hardly a better way to spend a lazy Sunday than angling in the Belgian canals at Damme, near Bruges. The Pan Angling Travel Service, Room 730, 180 N Michigan Ave., Chicago, IL 60601 (phone: 312-263-0328), specializes in putting together fishing trips outside the US.

Here are some of the Old World's most celebrated fishing spots — worth every bit of the traveling you'll have to do to experience them.

MARIAGER FJORD-KATTEGAT, Denmark: Fishing boats leave regularly from the fjord's three main towns — Hobro, Mariager, and Hadsund — to make for the open sea of the Kattegat, where cod, flounder, mackerel, sea trout, and plaice can be hauled out in an abundance as satisfying as the good fellowship aboard the ship. Information: Turistbureauet (Office of Tourism), Vestergade 2, Hobro, DK-9500 Mariagerfjord, Denmark (phone: 52-22-88). Other fine fjords for fishing are Roskildefjord, just west of Copenhagen, and Limfjorden, up north in Himmerland. Information about Roskildefjord: the Office of Tourism, Fondens Bro 3, Box 278, DK-4000 Roskilde, Denmark (phone: 35-27-00); or the Office of Tourism, Østergade 3, DK-3600 Frederikssund, Denmark (phone: 31-06-85). Information about the Limfjorden: the Office of Tourism, Havnen 4, DK-7900 Nynøbing, Mors, Denmark (phone: 72-04-88). For general information: Danish Tourist Board, 75 Rockefeller Plaza, New York, NY 10019 (phone: 212-582-2802).

ITCHEN and TEST RIVERS, near Nether Wallop, Hampshire, England: For the outsider, topnotch fishing can be hard to find in Izaac Walton's home country: Most of the fishing rights to the best streams are controlled by associations and private citizens. However, there are also many country hotels that own equally productive fishing waters, and these establishments are British institutions. The Test River is a carefully managed, world-famous stream stocked with special fast-growing brown and rainbow trout. Information: National Anglers' Council, 11 Cowgate, Peterborough PE1 1LZ, England (phone: 54-084). In the same district, there is exceptional angling on a number of local rivers (practically in the shadow of Winchester Cathedral and Izaak Walton's burial place). The celebrated Itchen produces small, extra-wily wild trout; wild and unspoiled Itchen feeder streams are spring fed and good for large and exceptionally active trophy fish. Other well-known streams in the area include the Avon, the Derwent, the Dove (where Walton fished), the Eden, the Kennet, the Lune, the Ribble, and the Wharfe. They're all clear, fast flowing, and, because of their origins in Britain's chalk hills, highly alkaline; conditions, in other words, are ideal for nurturing big native brown trout that rise freely even when they reach 4 pounds or more. The British Tourist Authority's booklet *Fishing,* cited above, provides information on a number of country hotels in the area.

CÔTE D'AZUR, France: The Riviera bathing beaches are crowded, pebbly, and shadowed by high-rise condominiums. But past the 3-mile limit, the Mediterranean is as deep and blue and challenging as ever, and the tuna fishing is superb. Information about lining up a seagoing craft and the necessary equipment: *Fédération Départementale des Associations de Pêche,* 37 av. St. Augustin, 06000 Nice (phone: 72-06-04); also *Club de Pêche Sportive de Cannes* (Thon), Hotel Sofitel, blvd. Jean-Hibert, 06400 Cannes (phone: 39-00-84); *Syndicat d'Initiative,* av. Martyrs de la Résistance, 06220 Vallauris (phone: 63-82-58); *Office de Tourisme,* 5 av. Gustave V, 06000 Nice (phone: 87-60-60). *La Pêcherie,* 244 av. de la Californie, Nice-Carras (phone: 83-34-57), is a shop that specializes in scuba diving and underwater fishing gear and is also a filling station for oxygen tanks.

LAKE CONSTANCE, Germany: One of the great lakes of Europe, the lovely Bodensee, as this body of water is called in German, is filled with a dozen different kinds of fish, including the prized *forelle* (trout). Ample facilities for boat hire are available both in Switzerland and in Germany (both of which touch the lake's shoreline); picturesque Lindau, a medieval German town on an island connected by bridge to the mainland, is a good place to base yourself. Information: *Verkehrsverein-Lindau* 8890, Ludwigstrasse, 68, Bodensee, Germany (phone: 5022); or the *Verband Deutscher Sportfischer* (German Fishing Association), Bahnhofstrasse 37, D-6050 Offenbach, Germany (phone: 885-187).

BALLYNAHINCH RIVER, near Connemara, Ireland: Irish game-fishing waters are among the finest in Europe, and the 3-mile-long Ballynahinch ranks among the nation's best salmon streams. As in the rest of the British Isles, fishing rights are privately held, but guests at the *Ballynahinch Castle,* a cozy, 20-room country hotel that was, in the seventeenth century, the ancestral home of a family of Connemara chieftains named O'Flaherty, have access to its seven beats. The season for salmon, which average 10 pounds and sometimes exceed 20, runs from May through September, peaking in June and early July and again in September. Good-size sea trout are also taken during a late June through September season. The Ballynahinch is part of an extensive complex of lakes, tributaries, and connecting rivers draining into Bertraghboy Bay. Information: *Ballynahinch Castle,* Ballinafad, County Galway, Ireland (phone: Clifden 135); or *Bord Failte* (Irish Tourist Board), Baggot St. Bridge, Dublin 2, Ireland (phone: 76-58-71).

BLACKWATER RIVER, near Youghal, Ireland: One of Ireland's most famous salmon rivers, rising near the border of Cork and Kerry, the Blackwater takes in 85 miles of long glides and deep pools. Salmon above 20 pounds are sometimes taken in the upper reaches; sea trout are taken lower down, closer to Youghal, where the river empties into the sea. Brown trout, weighing in at an average of about a half-pound each, are fairly active on both wet and dry flies on the upper portion. Information: *Inland Fisheries Trust,* Portmahon House, 77 Strand Rd., Sandymount, Dublin, or Bord Failte (above).

SHANNON RIVER, Ireland: The 240-mile-long Shannon, the longest river in all of Britain and Ireland, drains a fifth of Ireland (about 6,060 square miles); its tributaries are 1,130 miles in length. It is slow moving, punctuated by numerous large lakes, and, for coarse fish (as bream, rudd, pike, perch, tench, and rudd/bream hybrids are collectively known), the Shannon has few equals anywhere; when the fish are biting, a catch of over a hundred pounds (mostly bream) is not unusual. On the Upper Shannon — that is, from the source to Athlone — Carrick-on-Shannon in County Leitrim is one of the best-organized fishing centers, and Strokestown, in County Roscommon, is a favorite destination of specimen rudd hunters. Particularly exciting lakes include Ree, which shelters all varieties of coarse fish; Lough Allen, which offers the best northern pike angling in all of Europe; and Lough Patrick, where, in 1970, two anglers caught over 500 pounds of tench in one short session. On the Lower Shannon, Lough Derg is productive for pike, and the Plassey River — as the Shannon is called where it flows by Limerick City — is a coarse fisherman's dream. The Clare Lakelands, centered on the village of Tulla, are a must for the serious angler looking for a quiet vacation. Information: *Bord Failte* (above).

TROMS COUNTY, Norway: This is a place for serious fishermen to settle in for a month — or a summer. A hundred different rivers and watercourses, churning across a wild landscape, teem with salmon, sea trout, and sea char. You can fish in the lakes as well or in the saltwater fjords. June to early September is the season. The *International Sea-Fishing Festival,* which includes 3 days of competition, takes place every mid-July in Harstad. Information: Turisttrafikkomiteen, Postboks 1077, 9001 Tromsø, Norway (phone: 8-2169); Harstad Tourist Office, Torvet 7C, Box 447, 9401 Harstad, Norway (phone: 63-235); or the Norwegian Tourist Board, 75 Rockefeller Plaza, New York, NY 10019 (phone: 212-972-0799). (The book *Angling in Norway,* available from the Norwegian Tourist Board, is detailed and helpful.) The *Fly-spesialisten Reisebyrå,* Kronprinsesse Märthas Pl. 1, N-0160 Oslo, Norway (phone: 41-38-70), specializes in setting up and booking salmon fishing trips and boat rentals.

Wild Europe

The air of the cities is polluted almost beyond hope, and the great monuments are crusted over with the grime of progress. Cement spreads along the seashores and through the countryside like a cancer; crowds throng the museums, the ski slopes, and the beaches; and the seas are, it seems, indelibly stained with oil. But there are still places in Europe where times haven't changed: forests that are still dark and silent; Mediterranean coves that are still deserted; country roads that are still only dirt; high mountain paths where you can walk for hours without meeting another soul — or encountering a chewing gum wrapper. Germany's Wildpark Altenfelden-Mühltal; the plains of the Puszta and the great horse-farming area of Hungary; Italy's National Park of Abruzzo; and Krkonoše, Czechoslovakia's Mountain of the Giants National Park, are only a few examples.

To get away from it all, you can also go on the 4-day International Walking Tour in July, from Apeldoorn, Holland; the group hike organized by Nederlandse Wandelsport Bond takes in dunes, canals, and major tulip-growing areas. For information, contact them at Catharÿnesingel 114, 3511 NH Utrecht, Holland (phone: 31-94-58).

Or you can go pony trekking in the beautiful countryside around Scotland's Loch Trool and the Forest of Galloway. Information: Dumfries and Galloway Tourist Association, Douglas House, Newton Stewart, DG8 6DQ Scotland (phone: 2549).

In Greenland you can go on dogsled expeditions and drive with hunters and dogs across frozen fjords and lakes and through mountain passes to tiny hunting settlements. Information: Ilulissat Tourist Office, Knud Rasmussens Hus, Box 99, DK-3952 Ilulissat, Denmark (phone: 4-3079); or the Danish Tourist Board, 75 Rockefeller Plaza, New York, NY 10019 (phone: 212-582-2802).

Or, in France, you can take bicycle tours through the château-dotted Loire Valley. Information: Fédération Française de Cyclotourisme, 8 rue Jean-Marie-Jégo, 75013 Paris, France (phone: 580-3021). Or the Bicyclub de France, 8 place de la Porte de Champerret, 75017 Paris, France (phone: 766-5592).

You can even sit around on an empty beach in the altogether: There are scores of places for that, among them the sunny coast of Corsica, near San Nicolao or Porto-

Vecchio. For details, contact the Délégation Régionale du Tourisme, 38 Cours Napoléon, 20178 Ajaccio, France (phone: 21-55-31); or the Fédération Française de Naturisme, 4 av. du Coq, 75009 Paris, France (phone: 280-0521).

And that's only the beginning. Here are some more ideas for savoring the wilder side of Europe.

THE ARDENNES, Belgium: These deep, mysterious forests flanking the River Meuse, the picturesque valleys, and the lacy network of sparkling streams haven't changed all that much since Shakespeare wrote about them as the idyllic Forest of Arden in *As You Like It*. The man-made attractions are equally unspoiled: Dinant and Durbuy are the quaintest of villages; and the castles at Bouillon, Annevoie, and Spontin look like models for fairy-tale illustrations. You can explore underground grottoes at Han-sur-Lesse and Remouchamps or paddle a kayak down the Lesse or the Amblève, flanked by wild high cliffs. Namur is a good base of operations. For information: Fédération du Tourisme de la Province de Namur, 3 rue Notre-Dame, B-5000 Namur, Belgium (phone: 22-29-98); or the Belgian National Tourist Office, 745 Fifth Ave., New York, NY 10022 (phone: 212-758-8130).

THE CAMARGUE, France: A marshy triangle on the southern coast, bounded by the two branches of the Rhone and the sea, the Camargue is the closest thing in Europe to the Wild West: On some fifty *manades,* or ranches, cowboys called *gardians* ride herd on black bulls and wild white horses, who thunder across the swampy plains and salt flats and startle hundreds of pink-winged flamingoes into flight over the Étang de Vaccarès, the largest sanctuary of its kind in Europe. In Arles, the nearest large town, the bulls of the Camargue do bloodless combat in an ancient Roman amphitheater. And a little sea village called Stes.-Maries-de-la-Mer is the destination of a pilgrimage of Gypsies from all over Europe every May 24 and 25. Information: Syndicat d'Initiative d'Arles, 35 pl. de la République, 13200 Arles, France (phone: 96-29-35); and Parc de la Camargue, Le Mas du Pont-de-Rousty, 13200 Arles, France (phone: 97-10-40).

NATIONAL PARK OF THE PYRENEES, France: A mountain range rising as high as the 10,820-foot summit of Mt. Vignemale, the Pyrenees are one of the wildest of Europe's uncharted landscapes; this national park, established in 1967 by the French government, covers a huge area extending from Mt. Lariste to Port Vieux and makes a common boundary on the south with the Spanish National Park of Ordesa. The French park teems with exotic wildlife, including brown bears, ibex, chamois, griffon, and the rare lammergeier, with its huge 9-foot wing span. There are information centers at Arrens, Cauterets, and Arundy, and a well-maintained network of high mountain refuges. Information: Parc National des Pyrénées, BP 300, 65013 Tarbes, France (phone: 93-30-60).

WALES, Great Britain: The Pembrokeshire Coast National Park, extending from Amroth to Cardigan, takes in a breathtaking 150 miles of rocky cliffs, remote bays, sandy inlets, wild headlands, and, offshore, tranquil islets. You can walk the length of the coastline on a marked footpath. Or, to the north, explore Snowdonia National Park's 1,000 square miles of rugged mountains and moors, limpid lakes, and rolling green countryside speckled with hewn-stone hamlets. You'll want to see the Gower Peninsula, the Mawddach Estuary, and the great monolithic castles of Caernarvon, Caerphilly, Conwy, Harlech, and take one of Wales's eight narrow-gauge steam railways. (Try Llanberis to the summit of Mt. Snowdon.) Go pony trekking in Brecon Beacons National Park. And see if you can llearne just thryye llyttle wyrdds of ancient Welsh. Information: Wales Tourist Board, 3 Castle St., Cardiff CF1 2R5, Wales (phone: 2-7281). Ask for the booklets *Wales Walking* (hundreds of different routes) and *Where to Stay in Wales* (farmhouses, country inns, campsites).

THE ISLAND OF IOS, Greece: One of the outermost of the Cyclades island group, Homer's reported burial place, and a pirates' lair, Ios has the dazzling Aegean beauty of its sister islands Mykonos and Paros, but 50 years' less development. Gleaming white churches and chapels and windmills perch on rolling green hills high above secluded, sand-rimmed bays. There's a sleepy harbor village, a fine bathing beach in Milokotos Bay, the remains of a temple of Apollo at Psathi. Life is very simple. Information: Greek National Tourist Organization, 645 Fifth Ave., New York, NY 10022 (phone: 212-421-5777). For hotel reservations: Hellenic Chamber of Hotels, 6 Aristidou St., Athens, Greece (phone: 323-6962).

FINNMARK COUNTY, Norway: The northernmost province of the northernmost country in Europe, Finnmark is well above the Arctic Circle and even shares an odd 100-mile-long border with the top of Russia; though temperatures rise in summer to a temperate 86°F (30°C), they plunge in winter to a glacial −60°F (−51°C). Yet it is a beautiful land, full of peaceful fishing villages, great fjords, vast snowfields that you can cross on sleds, craggy cliffs teeming with wild birds. The Alta may be the best salmon river in the world. Go in midsummer, when the days are warm and the sun never drops below the horizon; or at Easter when, following a picturesque age-old custom, the Lapps who tend the country's 130,000 reindeer drive the animals down to the seacoast. Information: Turist-trafikkomitéen for Finnmark, Postboks 223, 9501 Alta (phone: 35040); or Turist-trafikkomitéen, Postboks 1077, 9001 Tromsø (phone: 8-2169), which is the general information office for the entire north and remains open all year.

PUSZCZA BIOLOWIESKA, Poland: One of the last strongholds of the majestic bison, this deep wilderness — the largest forest area in central Europe — also shelters wild boars, stags, lynxes, wolves, elk, and over 200 species of birds. Giant 500-year-old trees still flourish here, and in late September, during the mating season, the deer put on an enthralling spectacle. Culinary highlights of a visit to the area include mushrooms, wild blueberries, and Zubrowka, an aromatic vodka made from a local grass. Information: Office of Foreign Tourism, Orbis, ul. Stawki 2, 00193 Warsaw, Poland (phone: 39-71-23); or from the Polish National Tourist Office, 500 Fifth Ave., New York, NY 10036 (phone: 212-391-0844).

PLITVICE LAKES NATIONAL PARK, Yugoslavia: Just 62 miles from Zagreb, in the valley between the wooded mountains of the Mala Kapela and the Plješevica, 16 stunning emerald and turquoise lakes arranged in a series of terraces linked by churning cascades have left immense deposits of tufa and travertine, shaped into marvelous dams and stalactites. The primeval forests around them are fragrant with evergreens, and the sparkling lakes are filled with trout. And in the winter the ice skating can be a mystical experience. Local information is readily available from park attendants or hotel staff members. Or contact Nacionalni Park, Plitvička Jezera, 48231 Yugoslavia (phone: 7-6314); or the Yugoslav State Tourist Office, Rockefeller Center, Suite 210, 630 Fifth Ave., New York, NY 10020 (phone: 212-757-2801).

For the Mind

Twenty-Five Centuries of History: Europe's Great Museums

 Museum-going is a fine art — one essential to travel enjoyment, but one that few people seem able to master. On the one hand there are the camera-toting tourists like the one in the old *New Yorker* cartoon who accosts a Louvre guard: "Quick — where's the Mona Lisa? I'm double-parked." Then there are the "serious" tourists in sensible shoes and glasses who plod through the cluttered halls of the Uffizi, Baedecker in hand, trying to absorb 600 years of European paintings in an afternoon. Both groups would probably rather be somewhere else.

But museum-going can be a great pleasure if you follow a few simple guidelines. First, make several short visits to a large museum rather than one long one. Stay just an hour and take in no more than a dozen really fine works. (You wouldn't try to skim 70 novels in a morning.)

There is no fatigue like aching, yawny museum fatigue — best described as the dread "Museum Foot" — and once it sets in, merely sitting for 3 minutes in front of a Rubens won't cure it. So go when you're fresh — preferably as soon as the museum opens, before the crowds have arrived.

If possible, know what you want to see before beginning your rounds, so that you don't clutter your senses with bleeding saints and blustery seascapes. At the very least, stop on your way *in* to thumb the catalog and finger the postcards to get an idea of what there is to see and where you'll find it. And when you look at the paintings, don't look at the nameplate first (you'll find out quickly enough what *you* really like as opposed to what you're *supposed* to like).

Remember that a very personal experience of a minor museum can be more satisfying than a endless ramble through one of Europe's great warehouses of beauty. There is something essentially deadening about the format in which we are obliged to view the world's greatest art. Break away in any way you can: Take an hour's drive in the country just to see Piero della Francesca's *Madonna del Parto* in the cemetery of tiny Monterchi, 70 miles southeast of Florence. Don't forget that single altarpiece in the empty village church, the grouping of portraits adorning the fireplace of the ancient mansion — art in the environment for which it was created. And visit a gallery or an auction house occasionally, just to remind yourself that once it was *all* for sale.

KUNSTHISTORISCHES MUSEUM, Vienna, Austria: The heart of the great Hapsburg collection, opened to the public by Joseph II, the People's Emperor, survived two world wars intact and appears here today in most of its imperial glory. If you had an hour to devote to just one museum in Europe, you couldn't do better than to spend it in the room that this museum devotes to the work of Pieter Breughel, that dark Flemish Renaissance genius who executed the grotesque *Peasant Wedding*, the icily beautiful *Hunters in the Snow,* and the lunatic *Battle of Carnival and Lent.* Elsewhere, you'll find a roomful of works by Rubens, including the famous portrait of a nude, fur-swathed Helene Fourment, and the Ildefonso altar painting as well as a stunning assortment of Albrecht Dürers and Jan van Eyck's *Cardinal of Santa Croce,* Giorgione's *Three Philosophers,* Titian's *Gypsy Madonna,* plus fine works by Cranach, Velázquez, Rembrandt, Holbein, Van Dyck, and Tintoretto. Open Tuesdays through Fridays from 10 AM to 6 PM, and on Saturdays and Sundays from 9 AM to 6 PM; on Tuesday and Friday evenings parts of the museum are also open from 7 to 9 PM, when illumination gives the paintings a special glamour. Information: Kunsthistorisches Museum, Maria-Theresien-Platz 1, Vienna, Austria.

THE BRITISH MUSEUM, London, England: Trying to knock off this gigantic storehouse of world culture in a single visit is like trying to master nuclear physics while in the barber's chair. The crown jewels of the collection, mainly devoted to archaeology and human history, are the renowned Elgin Marbles — the massive sculpture and relief saved from the ruins of the Parthenon and carted off to safe, civil England. Here, too, you'll find the Rosetta Stone, the black basalt tablet that provided the key to Egyptian hieroglyphics; the Royal Gold Cup; the Portland Vase; the Sutton Hoo Ship Burial. The collections of Greek, Roman, and Egyptian antiquities are unrivaled anywhere in the world, and a new permanent display is devoted entirely to Etruscan civilization. "Man Before Metals" gives you an enthralling look at the art and technology of the Stone Age. The Near and Far Eastern departments are magnificent reminders of the time when Britannia ruled the waves. And at the library's check-out desk, you can ask to inspect one of Shakespeare's first folios. Open Mondays through Saturdays, 10 AM to 5 PM, and on Sundays from 2:30 to 6 PM. Information: British Museum, Great Russell St., London WC1B 3DG, England.

THE NATIONAL GALLERY, London, England: Started by the British Government in 1824 with the purchase of 38 paintings, the National Gallery now houses one of the finest representative collections of European painting from the thirteenth to the nineteenth centuries. Among its masterpieces are the *Arnolfini Wedding* of Jan van Eyck; Piero della Francesca's *Baptism of Jesus;* Caravaggio's *Christ at Emmaus;* Botticelli's *Nativity;* Goya's *Dr. Peral;* and a moving, pitiless self-portrait by Rembrandt. Save for a rainy day the very best of British painting, from Hogarth to Turner, though even on your first visit you might catch a glimpse of Constable's *Hadleigh Castle* and Turner's *Fighting Téméraire.* Open weekdays 10 AM to 6 PM (and several evenings a week during the summer); and on Sundays from 2 to 6 PM. Information: National Gallery, Trafalgar Sq., London WC2N 5DN, England.

THE TATE GALLERY, London, England: A gift of Sir Henry Tate, built in 1897 on the site of Millbank Prison, the Tate is the national collection of modern painting and sculpture, but also contains British painting of the past. It boasts one of the world's best collections of French Impressionist and post-Impressionist works as well as excellent examples of the sculpture of Rodin, Maillol, Mestrovic, Moore, and Epstein. The British Department is the best place to see the work of William Blake. And the Tate is also very energetic about mounting vast special exhibitions of work on loan from abroad. Open weekdays 10 AM to 6 PM and Sundays 2 to 6 PM. Information: The Tate Gallery, Millbank, London SW1P 4RG, England.

CENTRE GEORGES POMPIDOU, Paris, France: Known as the *Beaubourg* (after the plateau on which it is built), the most arresting thing here is the building itself — a multicolored carnival of tubes, girders, and transparent escalators that looks as though it were built with a giant Erector set. A modern Parisian landmark, this potpourri of ever-changing exhibitions spans world culture, covering everything from an Einstein memorial to the history of the jukebox. Crowded with visitors all day until its closing at 10 PM, it is probably the most successful attempt at museum-making in years. Open weekdays except Tuesdays from noon to 10 PM; weekends from 10 AM to

10 PM. Information: Centre Georges Pompidou, Rue Rambuteau at the corner of Rue St.-Martin, Paris, France (phone: 277-1233).

MUSÉE DU JEU DE PAUME, Paris, France: At the end of the Tuileries Gardens, this elongated rectangle of a museum is really an outbuilding of the Louvre, whose collection of late-nineteenth- and early-twentieth-century French painting it houses. You have the feeling here of being at the nerve center of modern art, as you inspect works by Corot and Manet, Degas, Monet, Sisley, Pissarro, the incomparable Renoir, Cézanne, Van Gogh, Gauguin, Seurat, and Toulouse-Lautrec. The setting is appropriately green and airy, and far from the heavy respectability of Mother Louvre. When you've seen the Tate and the Jeu de Paume, you're ready for the rest of the twentieth century. Open 9:45 AM to 5:15 PM weekdays except Tuesdays; 11:30 AM to 5:15 PM on weekends. Information: Musée du Jeu de Paume, Pl. de la Concorde, Paris, France (phone: 260-1207).

THE LOUVRE, Paris, France: This colossal haystack crammed with needles was initiated by François I in the sixteenth century with 12 paintings and the casts of a few of his favorite Greek sculptures. Today, a one-way stroll through each of its treasure-laden rooms would cover over 8 miles — and if you never saw the inside of another museum, you could still form a very complete picture of European, Oriental, and ancient art from a study of its collection. You couldn't miss the *Mona Lisa* or the *Venus de Milo* if you were dead set on doing so. But a few delights are easily overlooked in the lavish confusion: van Eyck's *Madonna of Chancellor Rolin;* Albrecht Dürer's *Self-Portrait;* Rigaud's portrait of the narcissistic *Louis XIV;* Ingres's *Turkish Bath;* Frans Hals's *Bohemian;* Memling's *Portrait of an Old Woman;* a small medieval gilded wood statuette of St. Stephen; and the *Handmaiden of the Dead,* a 4,000-year-old Egyptian wood carving of a young girl bearing food and wine for the banquet after death. Open 9:45 AM to 5:15 PM every day except Tuesdays; certain sections open until 6:30 PM. Information: The Louvre, Palais du Louvre, Paris, France (phone: 260-3926).

THE DEUTSCHES MUSEUM, Munich, Germany: A change of pace, from the aesthetic to the technical. Unique in Europe, this huge complex on an islet in the Isar River covers the entire history of the development of man's knowledge of the natural sciences and his mastery of technology. Displays include everything from ancient compasses to modern aircraft. Some items are original, others are "faithful to the last detail" reconstructions. There are plenty of hands-on exhibits that can be activated by the spectator, and so children generally go gleefully out of their minds here. But even to diehards who ordinarily prefer Titian to fission, the museum is fascinating and you don't have to be a scientist to enjoy it. Open daily 9 AM to 5 PM. Information: Deutsches Museum, Isarinsel, 8000 Munich 22, Germany (phone: 21791).

THE NATIONAL ARCHAEOLOGICAL MUSEUM, Athens, Greece: The nation's largest museum houses archaeological treasures found all over the country and representing every period of ancient Greek history. Without a certain amount of scholarly preparation, you are not likely to be able to distinguish the Neolithic from the Cycladic from the Mycenaean — so just allow yourself to be overwhelmed by this matchless legacy of the most gifted civilization on record. You'll see sculptured bronze shields right from the pages of the *Iliad;* golden mortuary masks; Cycladic idols; Thessalian ceramics; the frescoes recently unearthed on the island of Santorini; and vast quantities of sculpture, including the *Philosopher of Antikythira,* the grave shrine of Aristonautes, the *Poseidon of Artemission,* and the *Dipylon Head.* Open daily except Mondays, 8 AM to 7 PM, Sundays 9 AM to 7 PM. Information: The National Archaeological Museum, Patission 44, Athens, Greece.

THE GALLERIA DEGLI UFFIZI, Florence, Italy: While you are hiking through the glowing rooms of the Uffizi, awash in the golden tides of the Italian Renaissance, just reflect on the fact that over 90% of Italy's artistic patrimony is stacked in dingy storerooms, hanging in museum wings permanently closed for lack of personnel, and adorning the offices of petty bureaucrats in obscure ministries and consulates out of public view. Consequently, what you see here is the *crema della crema della crema* by Botticelli, Leonardo, Raphael, Piero della Francesca, Giotto, Caravaggio, and virtually every other major Italian artist. Particularly beautiful, and often overlooked, are the thirteenth- and fourteenth-century religious paintings on wood panels. Recent hours were from 9 AM to 7 PM, Tuesdays through Saturdays, 9 AM to 1 PM on Sundays, closed on Mondays. But the Uffizi's schedule is frequently shuffled by personnel shortages, labor disputes, and artistic excess. Best to check just before a visit. Information: Galleria degli Uffizi, Loggiato degli Uffizi 6, Florence, Italy.

THE VATICAN MUSEUMS, Rome, Italy: The Vatican Museums attract not only the usual population of museum-goers, but also pilgrims and Vatican visitors — so crowding can be a problem, and the Sistine Chapel, in particular, often has an aura of the subway in rush hour. The morning is probably the best time to go: Grab your ticket and dash past the papal robes, old maps, and tomb inscriptions, and you'll leave the school groups and convent delegations far behind. Your goals are the Raphael rooms, the classical statuary (including the *Apollo Belvedere* and the *Laocöon*), the tapestry gallery, and the works of Fra Angelico, Giotto, and Filippo Lippi in the Pinacoteca. This is a difficult museum, and so a catalogue is a good investment. One more word to the weary: Don't combine the museums with a visit to St. Peter's. Open Mondays through Saturdays, and the last Sunday of every month, from 9 AM to 2 PM (but you won't be admitted after 1 PM); and until 5 PM (admission until 4 PM) from July to September. Information: The Vatican Museums, Viale Vaticano, Rome, Italy.

THE RIJKSMUSEUM, Amsterdam, The Netherlands: The huge red brick building is one of a complex of three museums clustered around Museumplein. (The others are the Van Gogh Museum and the Stedelijk, devoted to modern art.) The star attraction at the Rijksmuseum is the incomparable Rembrandt collection, which includes *Night Watch,* the *Anatomy Lesson,* the *Jewish Betrothal,* the *Drapers' Guild,* and a magnificent self-portrait. Here, there are Rembrandts by the roomful. But you'll also find lovely Vermeers, including the famous *Milkmaid,* along with works by Frans Hals, whose *Married Couple* ranks among northern Europe's greatest paintings. There's more — but stick with the Dutch masters on your first visit. Open daily, except Mondays, 10 AM to 5 PM and Sundays 1 PM to 5 PM. Information: Rijksmuseum, Stadhouderskade 42, Amsterdam, Holland. Also visit Rembrandt's house at Jodenbreestraat 4. Open daily 10 AM to 5 PM and Sundays 1 PM to 5 PM.

THE PRADO, Madrid, Spain: The heart of the Prado is the regal collection assembled by Spain's Bourbon and Hapsburg kings. Concentrate first on works by the four great Spanish masters: Velázquez, El Greco, Murillo, and Goya, whose progression from fashionable court painter to embittered madman is documented in breathtaking detail. Then turn to an excellent selection of works by another genius, Hieronymus Bosch, and to the fine Van Dycks, Titians, and Tintorettos — all hanging here as a result of Spain's royal ties with Flanders and Italy. Goya's *Maja Desnuda* is here, as is Velázquez's great *Las Meninas* (which you can view in a mirror, just as it was painted), and a delightful statue of a reclining Hermaphrodite. Thirteen new rooms of Flemish masterpieces have opened up. (Picasso's fabled *Guernica* is housed nearby, in the Casón del Buen Retiro.) Open 10 AM to 5 PM Tuesdays through Saturdays in the winter, until 5:30 PM in the spring and fall and 6 PM in the summer. The museum closes at 2 PM on Sundays and is closed on Mondays year-round. Information: The Prado, Paseo del Prado, Madrid, Spain.

THE HERMITAGE, Leningrad, USSR: For a long time after its founding, the czars made the opulent Hermitage the private preserve of themselves and their friends, and it was only with the revolution that the public got a look at the splendid contents — works on the order of Gainsborough's *Duchess of Beaufort;* Renoir's *Girl with a Fan;*

Ingres's *Portrait of Count Guriev;* Breughel's *Fair;* Rembrandt's *Old Man in Red;* Titian's *Danaë;* Holbein's *Portrait of a Young Man;* and a wonderful, little-known Michelangelo sculpture, the *Crouching Boy.* As you might expect, a great deal of space is allotted to Russian history and culture, and exhibits run the gamut from exquisite antique silver and a map of the Soviet Union in semiprecious stones to "The Heroic Military Past of the Russian People" and turn-of-the-century paintings with fetching titles like *The Dairymaid Spurned* and *The Volunteer Shall Return No More.* The Indian and Oriental art collections are first rate — but unless you are wintering in Leningrad, stick to the magnificent European collection. Open daily from 10:30 AM to 6 PM (summer months: 10 AM to 5 PM); closed on Mondays. Information: The Hermitage, Dvortsovaya Naberezhnaya 36, Leningrad, USSR.

MORE GREAT PAINTINGS

A number of the Continent's finest works of art will be found outside the museums listed above. Here's where you'll find a selection of the standouts.

CATHEDRAL OF ST. BAVON, Ghent, Belgium – *The Adoration of the Mystical Lamb,* by Jan and Hubert van Eyck.
MUSÉE DES BEAUX ARTS, Ghent, Belgium – *The Carrying of the Cross,* by Hieronymus Bosch.
NY CARLSBERG GLYPTOTEK, Copenhagen, Denmark – Paul Gauguin's *Vahine No Te Tiare.*
GEMÄLDEGALERIE DAHLEM, West Berlin, Germany – Rembrandt's *Man in the Golden Helmet.*
ALTE PINAKOTHEK, Munich, Germany – Pieter Paul Rubens's *Rubens and Isabella Brant* and Albrecht Dürer's *Portrait of Osvolt Krel.*
STAATSGALERIE, Munich, Germany – Edouard Manet's *Lunch in the Studio.*
PINACOTECA COMUNALE, Borgo San Sepolcro, Italy – Piero della Francesca's *The Resurrection.*
MUSEO DIOCESANO, Cortona, Italy – Fra Angelico's *The Annunciation.*
PALAZZO DUCALE, Mantova, Italy – *La Camera degli Sposi,* by Mantegna.
CENACOLO VINCIANO, Milan, Italy – Leonardo da Vinci's *Last Supper.*
VILLA DEI MISTERI, Pompeii, Italy – The frescoes.
CATHEDRAL OF SIENA, Siena, Italy – Duccio di Boninsegna's *The Maestá.*
MUSEO CORRER, Venice, Italy – *The Courtesans,* by Vittore Carpaccio.
KUNSTMUSEUM, Basel, Switzerland – Holbein's *Portrait of Boniface Amerbach.*
VILLA FAVORITA, Lugano, Switzerland – Tiziano's *Portrait of the Doge Francesco Venier.*

On the Boards: Theater and Opera in Europe

London, of course, should be a first — and prolonged — stop on any theatergoer's itinerary; the stages here are some of the liveliest in the world — and, of course, there's no language barrier. Yet even on the Continent, there are several old, established English-language companies: the *English Theater* (Josefsgasse 12, Vienna, Austria; phone: 42-12-60); the *English-Speaking Theater of Paris* (55 rue de Seine; phone: 326-63-51); and the *ABC Theater of Oslo,* which performs Scandinavian classics in English during the summer at a variety of locations. The *Café*

Theater in Frankfurt (Hamburgerallée 45; phone: 77-74-66) has even sent a play to New York's off-Broadway; and the *English Speaking Theater Amsterdam* plays the *Bellevue*, Leidsekade 90, in winter months and the *Suikerhof*, Prinsengracht 381, in summer.

Besides which, some theatricals — among Europe's best — are largely nonverbal. And even when the language barrier does portend problems, you may encounter acting so compelling that you end up forgetting that you're not supposed to be understanding what's going on. In addition, many of Europe's great companies often perform international classics whose content is familiar. If you don't know the play, it's simple enough to search a city's largest bookstore for an English copy of the plays that are on. (Oddly enough, the simultaneous-translation earphone setups provided by some major theaters seem to create, rather than remove, a barrier between you and the players.)

What about tickets? Before you leave the US, pick up a copy of the local newspaper — the *London Times* or the *Sunday Observer* is the best for London goings-on — and figure out what to see. You can buy tickets in advance for productions of the *Royal Shakespeare Theatre* in Stratford-on-Avon, and for the *Edinburgh Festival*, in the US at *Keith Prowse & Co., Ltd.*, 234 W 44th St., New York, NY 10036 (phone: 212-398-1430 or 800-223-4446, toll-free outside New York). Tickets for London shows are also available through *KPI*. For tickets to performances in other cities, wait until you get there.

THE BURGTHEATER, Vienna, Austria: Over 200 years old, this is one of Europe's great theaters and most accomplished companies. The repertory has a decidedly classical flavor, and sooner or later, every important play written in German for the last 300 years crosses the stage. The building, at Dr. Karl-Lueger Ring 2, is an imposing, colonnaded baroque palace, and a première is a glittering Viennese social occasion. The same company performs a somewhat flashier repertory at the *Akademie Theater*. Tickets for both are available from 2 months to 15 days in advance from the Österreichischer Bundestheaterverband, Bestellbüro, Goethegasse 1, A-1010 Vienna, Austria. Seven days or less in advance, try the central box office at Hanuschgasse 3, behind the opera house (phone: 5324-2656).

STEIRISCHER HERBST, Graz, Austria: This is a young, electric, eclectic arts festival (whose name translates "Styrian Autumn"); it generally plays from early October through early November. You'll encounter a good deal of experimental theater, nonverbal theater, and film; and the performing groups are from all over Europe and America, so language is not a constant problem. The festival is increasingly important as a place to see what's fresh in European theater. Information: Steirischer Herbst, Palais Attems, Sackstrasse 17/I 8010 Graz, Austria (phone: 7-3007).

LATERNA MAGIKA, Prague, Czechoslovakia: This amalgam of cinema, opera, theater, and circus offers you one of the most fascinating spectacles on the Continent; the name, which translates as "Magic Lantern," attempts to convey the swirling, kaleidoscopic style. Now you know less about it than you did before, so just go — and take children. Information: Laterna Magika, Narodni 40, Prague, Czechoslovakia (phone: 26-00-33). Prague also has a long tradition of mime, and a genius named Fialka, the Marcel Marceau of the Second World, performs regularly at *Na Zabradli*.

THE NATIONAL THEATRE, London, England: If English-speaking theater is your religion, the *National Theatre* should be your temple. It is, in fact, a complex of three theaters (the *Olivier*, the *Lyttleton*, and the *Cottesloe*) on the South Bank of the Thames. And it is the direct descendant of the nearby *Old Vic*, which was, for decades, London's crown jewel. Gielgud, Richardson, Ashcroft, Plowright, Scofield, Guinness, Finney, and all the other English theater greats have performed here — and the repertory knows no bounds of time, nationality, or style. Information: National Theatre, South

Bank, London SE1 9PX, England (phone: 928-2252; or, for recorded ticket information, 928-8126, 24 hours a day).

THE ROYAL SHAKESPEARE COMPANY, Stratford and London, England: This splendid company, which also picks its stars from the roster of English acting greats, performs in the splashy new $280 million Barbican Arts Centre. In Stratford-on-Avon, its home is the *Royal Shakespeare Theatre,* set beautifully alongside the river, as well as the tiny 150-seat *The Other Place.* The Stratford season runs from April through January. (Be warned that in midsummer, busloads of holidaymakers fresh from visits to see Ann Hathaway's chamber pot turn the atmosphere a trifle frantic.) In London, you can generally buy tickets to a production with the same confidence that you'd pick up a Rolls or a Burberry. The company's specialty is breathing life into period pieces so obscure that even the boys at Eton don't have to read them. Information: Royal Shakespeare Theatre, Stratford-on-Avon, Warwickshire CV37 6BB, England (phone: 29-56-23; or, for 24-hour booking information, 6-9191). In London: Barbican Theatre, 13 Cromwell Tower, Barbican EC2 (phone: 628-8795).

THE ROYAL COURT, London, England: Once termed experimental and even avant-garde, the *Royal Court* was where John Osborne introduced *Look Back in Anger,* where the Arnold Wesker trilogy was first performed, and where Harold Pinter vented his wrath on the English language. The audience is now very proper British and intermission crowds are indistinguishable from those, say, at the Royal Ballet. But the *Royal Court* is still *the* place to watch young England on stage. Information: The Royal Court Theatre, Sloane Sq., London SW1, England (phone: 730-1745).

THE CHICHESTER FESTIVAL THEATRE, Chichester, England: Launched in 1962, this drama festival offers four plays between May and September, with topflight casts on a par with anything you'd see in London's West End. The theater, a striking hexagonal structure in the middle of a 40-acre parkland, lies just an hour and a half train ride from Victoria Station. And during the main season, trains don't leave Chichester until the final curtain has fallen. Information: Chichester Festival Theatre Office, Oaklands Park, Chichester, West Sussex, PO19 4AP England (phone: 78-13-12).

COMÉDIE-FRANÇAISE, Paris, France: As much a part of Paris as the Louvre, its next-door neighbor, and as French as the Académie Française, the *Comédie-Française* is as totally dedicated as either to the preservation of Gallic language and culture and its productions run to Racine and Corneille, frothy Molière, *Cyrano de Bergerac* done in the grand manner, and even *Waiting for Godot,* now that it's a classic. All the great names of French theater do a turn at the *Comédie,* and even if you know no more French than "La plume de ma tante," go. (Just think of it as a visit to another national monument.) Information: Comédie-Française, 2 rue de Richelieu, Paris, France (phone: 296-1020).

L'ODÉON, Paris, France: One of France's richly endowed (talent and money) national theaters, the Odéon's style is more streamlined and flashy than some of its conventional cousins. Guest productions from the best French theatrical companies, as well as glittering foreign attractions such as the Peking Art Theater, the Greek National Theater performing *Euripides,* and Ingmar Bergman directing Shakespeare. Information: L'Odéon, pl. de l'Odéon, Paris, France (phone: 325-7032).

MARCEL MARCEAU, Paris, France: Just as the world had only one Edith Piaf and only one Maurice Chevalier, there is only one Marcel Marceau — and if you've never seen him, you're missing a treat. After a long struggle with the forces of anticreation, he has opened his own school of mime, the *École Internationale de Mimodrame,* and, though much of the year sees him gesturing and grimacing his way around the world, he can be found here when he's in Paris. Information: École Internationale de Mimodrame, rue René Boulanger 17, Paris, France (phone: 209-6586).

THÉÂTRE DU ROND-POINT, Paris, France: Better known as the Compagnie

Renaud-Barrault, this is the new home theater of the reigning king and queen of the French stage — Jean-Louis Barrault and Madeleine Renaud. The repertory is diverse and far-ranging, but there's a good, steady diet of Beckett and Ionesco, as well as important new foreign plays. The theater is also a gathering place for stage personalities from all over Europe. Information: Théâtre du Rond-Point, av. Franklin Roosevelt, Paris, France (phone: 256-7080).

THE SCHILLER-THEATER, West Berlin, Germany: With one of Europe's richest theatrical traditions, the Berlin stage nurtured half a dozen actors and actresses who later became major stars on Broadway and in Hollywood. The *Schiller,* the prince of German theaters, specializes in lavish, highly styled productions of the classics. Information: Schiller-Theater, Bismarckstrasse 110, West Berlin, Germany (phone: 319-5236). While you're in town, try to catch a political cabaret, another staple of the German theater scene. Best bets are *Die Stachelschweine* in the Europa-Center (phone: 261-4795) and *Die Wühlmause,* at Nürnbergerstrasse 33 (phone: 213-7047). And don't miss the famous *Berliner Ensemble* of Brecht-Weill-Lenya fame; it's well worth crossing the Wall for. Information: Berliner Ensemble, Bertolt-Brecht Platz, East Berlin, East Germany (phone: 282-3160).

THE NATIONAL THEATER OF GREECE, Athens and Epidaurus, Greece: Productions here take you as close as you can get to the mysterious, ritualistic origins of the theater: where the national Greek company performs ancient Greek plays in their original settings. The Athens Festival runs throughout the summer in the Odeon of Herod Atticus at the foot of the Acropolis. The Epidaurus Festival spans July and August, set in the spectacular theater of Epidaurus, about 90 miles southwest of Athens. Information and tickets for both: Greek National Tourist Organization, 2 Spirou Miliou Arcade, Athens, Greece (phone: 322-1459). Tickets are on sale at the Epidaurus amphitheater only on the day of the performance (phone: 2-1005).

THE ABBEY THEATRE, Dublin, Ireland: The history of Ireland's national theater goes back into the last century, but its current $2.5 million home (the original "Shabby" having burned in 1951) was built in 1966. The pride of Dublin and the cradle of spirited Irish rhetoric, the Abbey is still home to Synge, Yeats, O'Casey, Behan — and the best in modern Irish drama as well. Catch an evening of *Playboy of the Western World* or *Juno and the Paycock,* have a quick whiskey around the corner on O'Connell Street, and, in the space of 3 hours, you can pretty much sense the essence of Ireland. Information: Abbey Theatre, Lower Abbey St., Dublin 1, Ireland (phone: 74-45-05).

PICCOLO TEATRO, Milan, Italy: When Italy's best company was founded just after World War II under the aegis of Giorgio Strehler, the idea was to take theater out of the hands of the idle elite and make it a vital instrument of popular culture; and though furs and jewels are often seen in the theater's modest foyer, nowadays the spirit still survives. There is always talk about moving to more ample quarters — and, at the same time, about keeping the *Piccolo* pure. The repertory is international and imaginative, the production style original and intense. Along with La Scala, this is the city's principal cultural institution. Information: Piccolo Teatro, Via Rovello 2, Milan, Italy (phone: 869-0631).

THE EDINBURGH FESTIVAL, Edinburgh, Scotland: Part music and part theater, this mid August to early September event gets much of its enormous vitality from the Fringe, a ragtag collection of a hundred-odd new productions that arrive in the city every year like a convention of sidewalk artists. Some are scruffy, low-budget, op-pop-punk improvisations. Others — remember *Beyond the Fringe?* — are out-of-town previews for big-time productions. For regular festival information and tickets: Edinburgh International Festival of Music and Drama, 21 Market St., Edinburgh, Scotland (phone: 226-4001). The Fringe has separate quarters: Festival Fringe Society, 170 High St., Edinburgh EH1 1QS, Scotland (phone: 226-5259).

OPERA

Unlike theater, the great opera houses of Europe share a common pool of talent and music. A case in point was *Carmen* (French) at the Vienna Staatsoper (Austrian), conducted by Kleiber (German), directed by Zeffirelli (Italian), and sung by Domingo (Spanish) and Obrazova (Russian).

However, operas are generally best seen on their own home territory — Wagner in Germany, Verdi in Italy, Bizet in France. Even if the soloists are of mixed nationalities, there is something about most productions that doesn't travel quite as well as you might expect. At any rate, if you are seeing a visiting team, ask what language the performance will be sung in: You might prefer not to see a Sicilian Brunhilde or a Tyrolean Carmen.

The finely tuned tentacles of the German opera world extend far beyond the city limits of Munich, Berlin, and Frankfurt, and while it's risky to be out of earshot of avenue de l'Opéra in France, in Germany, a sort of vast, well-managed farm system makes it possible to hear first-rate performances in any one of a dozen provincial centers.

Meanwhile, opera is most fun in Italy (even when questionably performed): Rather than the reverent silence of Teutonic audiences, you'll find zestful participation, and, in the south and the provinces, opera-goers sound catcalls for clinkers and hum along the rest of the time. And — either because of training methods or government subsidies or unpolluted air — the most exciting new voices are turning up in Eastern Europe; and the unknown with the unpronounceable name you may hear in Prague or Warsaw may soon be getting top billing in London or New York.

In general, however, you'll see the best performances at the festivals of Salzburg, Wiener Festwochen, Bayreuth, Berliner Festwochen, Munich, and the Maggio Musicale Fiorentino. (See *Music Festivals* for descriptions.) From mid-July to late August, try the festival at the *Arena of Verona*. Information: Ente Autonomo Spettacoli Lirici Arena di Verona, Piazza Bra 28, 37100 Verona, Italy (phone: 2-3520). And, of course, don't miss these great European opera houses:

The *Staatsoper,* Opernring 2, Vienna, Austria (phone: 5324-2655). Great for Richard Strauss.

The *Volksoper,* Wahringerstrasse 78, Vienna, Austria (phone: 5324-2657). Good for Johann Strauss; specializes in Viennese operetta.

English National Opera Company, at the Coliseum, St. Martin's La., London WC2, England (phone: 836-3161). Great opera classics performed in English.

The *Royal Opera House,* at Covent Garden, Floral St., London WC2, England (phone: 240-1066, box office; 240-1911, other information).

L'Opéra, Pl. de l'Opéra, Paris, France (phone: 742-5750). For advance bookings, write the Service Location par Correspondance, 8 rue Scribe, 75009 Paris, France.

The *Bayerische Staatsoper,* in the National Theater, Max-Joseph-Platz 2, 8000 Munich 2, Germany (phone: 22-13-16).

The *Deutsche Oper,* Bismarckstrasse 34-37, 1000 Berlin, Germany (phone: 341-4449).

La Scala, Via dei Filodrammatici 2, Milan, Italy (phone: 88-791 or 80-70-41).

San Carlo, Via Vittorio Emanuele, Naples, Italy (phone: 41-82-66).

Teatro La Fenice, San Fantin, 2549, Venice, Italy (phone: 2-3954).

Gran Teatro del Liceu, Rambla Caputxins 65, Barcelona, Spain (phone: 318-9122; box office, 301-6787).

Bolshoi Opera, Bolshoi Theater, Sverdlov Square 1, Moscow, USSR.

Europe's Magnificent Music Festivals

 Every summer, Europe bursts into garlands of music festivals, looped in bright tones across the Continent in every direction. Some — like those at Salzburg and Bayreuth — are distinguished old celebrations of musical genius. Others are Ludwig-come-latelies whose thinly disguised purpose is to drum up tourist trade for otherwise quaint but hardly notable old villages. Still, they can make for a pleasant end to a day at the beach, and there will be plenty of last-minute tickets (or space for your blanket on the village green), though the major ones, serious musical pilgrimages, sell out months in advance.

Most of the festivals make inspired use of their home city's finest monuments — ducal palaces, castle courtyards, and Gothic cathedrals — so that concert-going becomes sight-seeing. Moreover, music often acquires a new power outside the concert hall.

SALZBURG FESTIVAL, Salzburg, Austria: Tickets to concerts of this generally recognized king of European festivals are high — but requests outnumber places by about four to one, and hotel accommodations during the run of the event, between late July and late August, are scarcer still. Still, if you can swing it and if you can afford it, there's nothing else quite like Salzburg. The performers are the best in the world, the audiences are distinguished and reverent, and you can't help but feel as if you are hearing Mozart for the first time. If you can manage only one concert, make it Von Karajan conducting a Mozart opera in the large Festspielhaus. To do this, write for a program in the fall and for tickets by Christmas. Bring dressy clothes: To Austrians, the marriage of Figaro is almost more important than their own. And if you happen to be cruising in the area, without any advance planning, give the festival a try anyway: Tickets for some of the delightful morning chamber concerts are often available. Or the concierge of the *Goldener Hirsch* may slip you one for *Don Giovanni* if you slip him back $200; and if somebody dies, he may even let you share a room. Information: Salzburger Festspiele, Postfach 140, 5010 Salzburg, Austria (phone: 4-2541).

WIENER FESTWOCHEN, Vienna, Austria: Music, as every schoolchild knows, was invented in Vienna; and for 5 weeks every year between early May and early June, the city holds a melomanic orgy to commemorate the event. Bernstein, Levine, and Abbado come to town, with theater groups from all over Europe; and there are new productions at the Staatsoper, premières of new plays, art exhibitions, symposia, colloquia, and plain old songfests. And every one of the city's 23 *Bezirke* (districts) sponsors special district programs. Spring is a nice time to see the city. Information: Wiener Festwochen, Friederich Schmidt-Platz, 4, A-1080 Vienna, Austria (phone: 4256).

FLANDERS FESTIVAL, Brussels, Belgium: The most important collection of musical events in Belgium, this festival is celebrated from spring into October in a number of Belgian towns — Ghent, Bruges, Mechelen, Antwerp, Leuven, and Brussels. Often concerts take place in the towns' most beautiful buildings. There is a strong emphasis on dance, and Belgium's renowned Ballet du XXème Siècle always appears. Information: Festival van Vlaanderen, Eugeen Flageyplein 18, B-1050, Brussels, Belgium (phone: 648-1484).

PRAGUE SPRING, Prague, Czechoslovakia: This doyen of European festivals has been around since 1945. Conductors and soloists from Eastern Europe are always on the program, along with some fine Russian artists whose performances usually sell out by the time they reach Carnegie Hall. Mid-May to early June. Information: International Music Festival "Prague Spring," Dum Umelcu, Alsovo Nabrezi 12, CS-11001, Prague 1, Czechoslovakia (phone: 231-9307).

BATH FESTIVAL, Bath, England: The weeks between mid-May and early June are beautiful ones in this lovely Georgian town, and the festival offers music to match — a splendid selection of choral works that pays homage to composers like Glück, Monteverdi, and Purcell, and a variety of interesting chamber performances, plus walking tours, film shows, art exhibitions, and garden tours. Information (from January through June): Bath Festival Office, Linley House, 1 Pierrepont Pl., Bath, England BA1 1JY (phone: 6-2231).

CHELTENHAM FESTIVAL, Cheltenham, England: Founded just after World War II in this gracious Regency spa, the Cheltenham Festival exploits majestic settings like the Pittville Pump Room and the Victorian Town Hall to enhance a musical menu that can run from ancient madrigals to the best in British contemporary. You may also hear the world premiere of works specially commissioned for the festival. Two weeks in July, with the enchanting Cotswold Hills and Severn Vale a short drive away. Information: Cheltenham Festival Office, Town Hall, Cheltenham, Gloucestershire GL50 1QA, England (phone: 21-621).

INTERNATIONAL FESTIVAL OF LYRICAL AND MUSICAL ARTS, Aix-en-Provence, France: This is one of the most attractive towns in the south of France, and the festival, which takes place from mid-July to early August, makes use of several locations, including two cloisters, the Cathedral of St. Sauveur, the courtyard of the Archbishop's Palace, and the lovely place des Quatres Dauphins. There is a strong emphasis on what the festival committee calls "the most beautiful instrument" — the human voice — but you'll hear works of all vintages, from early Corelli to late Stockhausen to Negro spirituals. Information: Festival International d'Art Lyrique et de Musique, Palais de l'Ancien Archevêché, 13100 Aix-en-Provence, France (phone: 23-37-81).

INTERNATIONAL CHAMBER MUSIC FESTIVAL, Divonne-les-Bains, France: Held in a sleepy little village, a 15-minute drive across the border from Geneva, the site of France's most profitable casino, this connoisseur's festival presents chamber music (and only chamber music) of the highest caliber in the jewel-like Théâtre de Divonne, whose whimsical decor would enliven even an amateur bassoon recital. At the end of June or the beginning of July, an excursion to this event can be delightful, so delightful in fact that some particularly faithful patrons come all the way from Paris for a single concert. Information: Festival International de Musique de Chambre, Syndicat d' Initiative, 01220 Divonne-les-Bains, France (phone: 50-01-22). (See also *Gambling.*)

FESTIVAL DE STRASBOURG, Strasbourg, France: This 2-week event has been held annually in early June since 1938 and takes place mostly in the Palais de la Musique et des Congrès, but some events are also held in the town's majestic cathedral as well as at other venues; succeeding days in one recent year saw performances by pianists Claudio Arrau and Vladimir Ashkenazy, violinist Itzhak Perlman, conductor Leonard Bernstein, singers Pilar Lorengar and Marilyn Horne, and the Juilliard Quartet. Between concerts, you can eat yourself under the harpsichord: Strasbourg is generally acknowledged to serve more luscious food than any other town in France (see *The Shrines of European Gastronomy*). Information: Festival de Strasbourg, 24 rue de la Mésange, 67081 Strasbourg, France (phone: 32-43-10).

BAYREUTH FESTIVAL, Bayreuth, Germany: This is the festival that Wagner built. A month-long orgy of Teutonic splendor that occupies the town every year beginning in late July, it features half a dozen Wagner operas presented in the theater that Wagner himself designed for this purpose, just down the road from a museum devoted to him. In their way, the audiences are as devoted as those who worshipped at Woodstock — different god, though, and a different crowd. Information: Bayreuth Festival, Postfach 2320, D-8580 Bayreuth, Germany (phone: 2-0221).

BERLINER FESTWOCHEN, Berlin, Germany: Held every September during the crisp Berlin autumn, this eclectic festival offers a wide range of opera, orchestral music, chamber music, theater, mime, dance, and an assortment of circus performances. The roster of conductors who appeared here in one 30-day stretch not long ago — Böhm, Solti, Inbal, Stockhausen, Leinsdorf, Giulini, Abbado, Von Karajan — reads like the list of graduates of Mount Olympus Conservatory. Information: Berliner Festspiele, Budapesterstrasse 48-50, D-1000 Berlin 30, Germany (phone: 2-6341).

MUNICH OPERA FESTIVAL, Munich, Germany: In early July, while most of Europe's opera houses sleep, Munich explodes for a melodious month with the music of Wagner, Strauss, Mozart, and, occasionally, the works of hot-blooded Latins like Verdi and Donizetti as well. Performances are held in the monumental *National Theater* and the miraculous *Cuvilliés Theater* (also known as the *Altes Residenztheater*), perhaps the most beautiful auditorium in Europe. Information: Münchner Opernfestspiele, Postfach 745, D-8000, München 1, Germany (phone: 2-1851).

MAGGIO MUSICALE FIORENTINO, Florence, Italy: Italy's answer to Salzburg presents artists just as fine, but programs so much more diverse that it seems a conscious attempt is being made to avoid musical chauvinism; you are as likely to hear Berg and Stravinsky as Rossini and Puccini. Some of the concerts are held in the magical Boboli Gardens — lovely and quintessentially Italian on a June evening. Despite its name, which translates "Florentine Musical May," the festival continues right through the month of June as well. Information: Maggio Musicale Fiorentino, Teatro Comunale, Via Solferino 15, 50123 Florence, Italy (phone: 26-28-41).

INTERNATIONAL FESTIVAL OF THE TWO WORLDS, Spoleto, Italy: Founded in 1957 by Maestro Gian Carlo Menotti, this celebrated event, which begins in mid-June every year, brings together performers from both sides of the Atlantic for 3 weeks of dance, poetry readings, concerts, drama, opera, and art exhibits; the festival is celebrated for the diversity and high quality of its concerts and for the sizable number of premières of new works on its programs. However, the setting is equally noteworthy. Spoleto, which was the capital for the dukes of Lombard between the sixth and eighth centuries, is a picturesque place, full of narrow vaulted passages and interesting nooks and crannies, quaint old shops and colorful markets. The final concert is traditionally held in front of the twelfth-century cathedral, with the audience sitting on the majestic stairway that overlooks it — in the shadow of handsome palaces and hanging gardens. Menotti himself is still actively involved. Information: Festival dei Due Mondi, 17 Via Margutta, Rome (phone: 361-4009).

EDINBURGH FESTIVAL, Edinburgh, Scotland: Between late August and early September, the *Edinburgh Festival* presents a diverse, jampacked program of music and theater that includes everything from the Scottish Chamber Orchestra playing in the stately eighteenth-century Hopetoun House to pop-rock multimedia happenings on the steps of the post office to old-fashioned British military tattoos. An assemblage of innovative, low-budget productions known as the Fringe gives the festival its color. The substance derives from the first-rate program of superb operas, concerts, and recitals; and the Edinburgh Festival is one of Europe's major musical events. Information: Edinburgh International Festival of Music and Drama, 29 St. James's St., London SWI A 1HA England (phone: 839-2611); or 21 Market St., Edinburgh, Scotland (phone: 226-4001).

MENUHIN FESTIVAL, Gstaad, Switzerland: Staged in August in the town of Gstaad-Saanen, among the towering peaks of the Bernese Oberland, this most personal of European music festivals is the work of the master violinist Yehudi Menuhin. The dozen-odd chamber concerts by celebrated virtuosos are held in the ancient church at Saanen. The rehearsals are open to the public, and one of the concerts is given by the top students of London's Menuhin School. Daytimes, you can enjoy spectacular Alpine rambles. Information: Menuhin Festival, Bureau de Renseignements, 3780 Gstaad, Switzerland (phone: 4-1055).

INTERNATIONAL MUSIC FESTIVAL, Lucerne, Switzerland: Switzerland's major festival, held from mid-August to early September, has brought the likes of Rostropovitch, Richter, Milstein, Pollini, Von Karajan, Fischer-Dieskau, Barenboim, Arrau, and Dorati to this flowered, serene, lakeside town. (One recent festival featured appearances by all of them.) A special feature is the intensive program of advanced instrumental courses given by festival performers in collaboration with the Lucerne Conservatory. For program information: Internazionale Musikfestwochen, Luzern, Pilatusstrasse 14, 6002 Lucerne, Switzerland (phone: 23-35-62). For course information: Sekretariat der Meisterkurse im Konservatorium Luzern, Dreilindenstrasse 93, CH-6006 Lucerne, Switzerland (phone: 36-76-86).

MONTREUX-VEVEY MUSIC FESTIVAL and THE INTERNATIONAL JAZZ FESTIVAL, Montreux, Switzerland: Montreux has two international festivals a month apart: the blaring, rocking *International Jazz Festival* in July, which attracts everyone from the likes of Herbie Hancock and Dave Brubeck to the Brockville Junior High Half Time Stompers; and, in September, the elegant *Festival de Montreux-Vevey,* featuring some of the world's major musical personalities — Weissenberg, Rostropovich, Milstein, Ashkenazy, and the Soloisti Veneti all took part in the recent fortieth anniversary program in the shadow of the legendary lakeside Château de Chillon. The festival is also the site of the prestigious Clara Haskil Competition. Information: Festival de Jazz, Gd. Rue, 42, CH-1820 Montreux, Switzerland (phone: 61-33-84); or the Festival de Musique Montreux-Vevey, 14 ave. des Alpes, CH-1820 Montreux, Switzerland (phone: 63-54-54 or 63-12-12).

DUBROVNIK SUMMER FESTIVAL, Dubrovnik, Yugoslavia: From mid-July to late August some 100 performances are presented in over 40 different locations in this enthralling medieval walled city on the Adriatic. You can enjoy everything from Beethoven symphonies in the courtyard of the Rector's Palace to Bosnian folk dances on the ramparts. Musically, it's not on a par with its Western cousins, but the setting can't be beat. Information: Dubrovnik Summer Festival, Od Sigurate 1, Dubrovnik, Yugoslavia (phone: 2-7996).

Learning the Language

Americans, in their splendid isolation, have always had reputations as poor learners of foreign languages, and we walk the world expecting universal mastery of English to have preceded us. If the natives didn't understand, the popular wisdom went, you were supposed to say it again, louder. In the years since World War II, this daydream has been approaching some kind of reality, with English emerging as the international language of trade and tourism. But no matter how many sales managers or desk clerks or headwaiters can answer your questions, there is no substitute for some knowledge of the local language as a way into a foreign culture. Without it, you only skim the surface of the country you visit; you read its dust jacket but never open the book.

The best method to acquire the language skills that will so greatly enhance your travel experience is an academic program in the country whose language you're trying to learn. The sounds and the rhythms of local speech will become a part of your thought processes; every shop, every market, every street corner, is soon a language lab. Most European countries offer foreigners special courses lasting anywhere from 2 weeks to a full year in settings as diverse as metropolitan capitals and Alpine castles. Here's *la crème de la crème:*

FRENCH

ALLIANCE FRANÇAISE: Exams at this venerable institution dedicated to the diffusion of French culture are a universal standard of French proficiency. The school is located in the heart of the Parisian student quarter, and it has a clientele of all colors and tongues. Information: Alliance Française, 101 blvd. Raspail, 75270 Paris Cedex 06, France (phone: 544-3828).

SORBONNE: The *University of Paris* offers a variety of courses, during both the summer and the academic year, in French language and civilization. The *cours de civilisation française* — a potpourri of grammar, literature, history, and fine arts studies — is a model for courses at a number of other French universities that offer special programs for foreigners. Information: Cour de Civilisation Française, Galerie Richelieu, 47 rue des Écoles, 75005 Paris, France (phone: 329-1213).

ÉCOLE FRANCE LANGUE: Courses at all levels in French language and civilization, with considerable use of audiovisual methods. Information: École France Langue, 2 rue de Sfax, 75116 Paris, France (phone: 500-40-15).

EUROCENTRE: An international foundation with head offices in Zürich, twenty-two schools distributed in seven European countries — and an outpost at Columbia University in New York City. The Paris branch — sixteen classrooms, two language labs, a film room, and a library, set in the middle of the Latin Quarter — offers a program that blends excursions with course work. Information: Eurocentre, 131 passage Dauphine, 75006 Paris, France (phone: 325-8140). For a complete list of all the Eurocentres, programs, and fees, contact Eurozentren, Seestrasse 247, CH-8038 Zürich, Switzerland (phone: 482-50-40).

CHAMBRE DE COMMERCE ET D'INDUSTRIE: The Chamber of Commerce sponsors programs in commercial French, with emphasis on understanding the life of the French business world. For details: Chambre de Commerce et d'Industrie, Direction de l'Enseignement, 14 rue Chateaubriand, 75008 Paris, France (phone: 561-9900).

COURS POUR ÉTUDIANTS ÉTRANGERS, UNIVERSITÉ DE PROVENCE: A course in French civilization specifically designed for foreign students, under the auspices of the university, in one of the most gracious and charming towns in the south of France. University-age students tend to dominate, and the town is one large, animated campus. Information for both year-round and intensive summer courses: Institut d'Etudes Françaises pour Étudiants Étrangers, 23 rue Gaston-de-Saporta, 13625 Aix-en-Provence, France (phone: 23-28-43).

UNIVERSITÉ LIBRE DE BRUXELLES: Courses all year long — designed for everyone from the rank beginner to the college French instructor — with a Belgian accent. Information: Université Libre de Bruxelles, 50 av. Franklin-Roosevelt, Brussels, Belgium (phone: 649-0030).

GERMAN

GOETHE INSTITUT: Perhaps the most respected school of German language, the institute has some 16 centers in Germany and a number of foreign countries, promoting German culture abroad. Courses, which come in 4- and 8-week packages, are intensive and include nearly 24 hours a week of instruction. Special new courses combine sports like sailing, riding, and skiing with language study. For complete information, contact the central office, Goethe Institut, Postfach 201009, Lenbachplatz 3, 8000 Munich 2,

Germany (phone: 599-9200). Or write directly to either of the two big city centers at Knesebeckstrasse 38-48, 1000 Berlin 15, Germany (phone: 881-3051); or at Sonnenstrasse 25, 8000 Munich 2, Germany (phone: 592-421).

DEUTSCHER AKADEMISCHER AUSTAUSCHDIENST: This central office handles special courses for foreigners at a variety of German universities. The most desirable university towns are Munich, Hamburg, Augsberg, and Heidelberg (which offers a unique course in German literature, film and theater). Information: DAAD, Kennedyallee 50, D-5300 Bonn 2, Germany (phone: 8821), or German Academic Exchange Service, 535 Fifth Ave., Suite 1107, New York, NY 10017 (212-599-0464).

HUMBOLDT INSTITUT: In the sixteenth-century castle of Ratzenried, deep in the Allgäu district, at the foot of the German Alps. Beautiful countryside, accommodations at the castle or in nearby private houses. Main courses start on first Monday of each month, with special sessions available in summer and holiday periods. Summer programs in the ancient towns of Meersburg and Constance, on Lake Constance. Information: Humboldt Institut, Schloss Ratzenried, 7989 Argenbühl/Allgäu, Germany (phone: 3041).

SALZBURG INTERNATIONAL LANGUAGE CENTER and IFK-INTERNATIONALE FERIENKURSE: Salzburg, Austria, where the courses at these two schools are held, is one of the most charming towns in all of Europe, and so, though you may end up speaking the Austrian dialect, the experience is worth it for the mountains, the music, and the *mohn strudel*. Information: Salzburg International Language Center, Moosstrasse 106, A-5020 Salzburg, Austria (phone: 44-485); and IFK-Internationale Ferienkurse, Franz-Josef-strasse 19, A-5020 Salzburg, Austria (phone: 76-595).

GREEK

THE ATHENS CENTRE: Located in a residential area of Athens, the center offers year-round courses devoted to the intensive study of modern Greek as well as a special Translators' Seminar. Courses provide an insight into aspects of Greek culture, art, and history. The center assists students from abroad in finding accommodations, including summer sublets. Information: The Athens Centre, Greek Language Programs, 48 Archimidous St., 11636 Athens, Greece (phone: 701-2268).

HELLENIC-AMERICAN UNION: Popular with Athens' resident American community as well as with locals who come to use the English library and read the *New York Times* on microfilm, the *Hellenic-American Union* offers courses in modern Greek for students of all proficiencies. Information: The Registrar, Academic Section, Hellenic-American Union, Massalias 22, Athens, Greece (phone: 362-9886).

ITALIAN

UNIVERSITÀ ITALIANA PER STRANIERI: Founded in 1925 by the Italian government, this "University for Foreigners" is housed in the eighteenth-century Palazzo Gallenga of Perugia. Well run, with a diverse student body and nominally priced courses in subjects as varied as elementary Italian and Etruscology, it puts much of the country's regular university system to shame. Courses of varying lengths — from 2 weeks to 9 months — are offered throughout the year. Information: Università Italiana per Stranieri, Palazzo Gallenga, Piazza Fortebraccio, Perugia, Italy (phone: 6-4344).

SOCIETÀ DANTE ALIGHIERI: The Dante is a worldwide organization for the diffusion of Italian culture, with some 400 branches teaching Italian to 50,000 students a year. The Rome branch offers courses in art, music, theater, furniture, and interior decoration; and sponsors films, concerts, lecture series, and assorted excursions. There are four 2-month terms from October to May, plus 2-month-long summer terms in June and July. Fees are quite low and instruction first-rate. Information about instruction in Rome and other Italian cities: Società Dante Alighieri, Piazza Firenze 27, 00186 Rome, Italy (phone: 678-1105).

EUROCENTRO: Eurozentren's sole center in Italy is located in a Renaissance *palazzo* in the heart of Florence. In addition to providing first-rate Italian language instruction, the center puts a great deal of emphasis on teaching its students about Italian art and architecture, some of the finest of which can be seen from the school's windows. Information: Eurocentro, Piazza Santo Spirito 9, 50125 Firenze, Italy (phone: 29-46-05).

SPANISH

ESCOLA OFICIAL DE IDIOMES: Because this school is located in Barcelona, you will hear a lot of the local Catalán dialect in the city's shops and markets rather than the Castilian, which is spoken around Madrid and is the national language. Intensive month-long summer courses are offered as well as two leisurely semesters that begin in October and end in June. Lodging with private families is available. Information: Escola Oficial de Idiomas, Av. de les Drassanes, s/n, Barcelona, Spain (phone: 329-3412).

CENTRO DE ESTUDIOS DE ESPAÑOL: Founded in 1945, well before the Costa del Sol boom, and situated in a pleasant villa on a suburban street in Málaga, this school limits its classes to six students each, and offers month-long courses at four skill levels throughout the year. Dandy for keeping a winter visit to the sea from descending entirely into frivolity — but the beach is never more than an irregular verb away. Information: Centro de Estudios de Español, Av. J. S. Elcano 110, Málaga, Spain (phone: 29-05-51).

UNIVERSITY OF MADRID: Through its philology department, Spain's largest university, like many others around the country, offers special courses for foreigners — everything from beginners' summer programs to advanced seminars for teachers of Spanish. Information: Secretaria de los Cursos para Estranjeros, Facultad de Filosofía y Letras, Edificio A, Ciudad Universitaria, 28040 Madrid 3, Spain.

COLEGIO DE ESPAÑA: In the noble and lively university town of Salamanca, the Colegio offers Spanish language and literature at every level, with special month-long immersion courses in the summer. Frequent excursions add color to the classroom routine. The university itself also offers excellent courses for foreign students in Spanish language and civilization. Information: Colegio de España, Calle Compañia 65, 37008 Salamanca (phone: 21-47-88); and Cursos Internacionales de la Universidad, Patio de Escuelas, 37008 Salamanca (phone: 21-66-89).

TIPS ON OVERSEAS LANGUAGE PROGRAMS

Whether you're learning French or German, Italian or Spanish, be diligent about exposing yourself to the language you're studying. Read signs religiously, muddle through the newspaper daily, listen to the radio constantly, and eavesdrop on conversations. Stay with good solid lowbrow material — the local tabloid newspaper, not the local *Times*. Follow the latest murder and the hottest rock star romance. Watch the soap operas on television. Go back to comic books. Then hit the movies: Start with dubbed American films — even ones you've seen in English — where your familiarity with the settings, gestures, and lip movements will provide you with clues to the meaning of the lines. Then try out local films: If they're incomprehensible, see them again. And read books on subjects that really interest you; improve your tennis in German, or your love-making in French.

Speak with courage and without fear of error. Be zealous about putting yourself in situations that will demand that you communicate, and don't rely on friends who know the language better to help you do your daily business. Go shopping, talk to the chambermaid about her liver trouble, tell strangers the story of your life. The more you speak, the better you'll do it; 10 minutes in the street is worth an hour at home with chapter 6, exercise 17. Everybody is an expert in his own language, and most people are delighted to give free lessons in grammar or vocabulary while they repair your shoe or show you the way to the zoo.

Finally, remember that *accent* is as much a part of a language as its vocabulary. Listen to sounds and imitate them, and insofar as your ear and your tongue permit, try not to say everything as if you were reading from the Pittsburgh phone book.

And if they still don't understand, damn it, say it again, louder.

The Antiquer's Guide to Europe

 Whether you're at Piccadilly Circus, on a dirt road in Andalusia, or in the throbbing heart of downtown Bratislava, sooner or later you'll see a sign that says "Antiques," and sooner or later you'll find yourself pawing over relics of the past as if in search of a gracious way to drain off excess capital. Europe has plenty to entice you — English silver, Persian rugs, fine painting and sculpture, and antique china, not to mention Venetian glass and French and English furniture.

For the most part, you'll do better buying such items in their country of origin — and at auction. Although every once in a while a dealer will underprice an item he doesn't love or understand, it's generally true that most will do the opposite, so that you're likely to pay unnecessarily high prices for Georgian sterling in Italy and Spanish paintings in Scandinavia. Antique hunting in the auction houses ordinarily saves you about 30% — but only so long as you know the market. If you don't, stick to the shops, and just as auctiongoers are best advised to patronize the first-echelon salerooms and to avoid auction rings and other questionable operations, so should the less-than-expert buyer stick to reputable dealers, particularly when it comes to high-ticket items. With the booming of the art market, the forgery business has taken on the proportions of an industry. Conscientious dealers will usually guarantee in writing the authenticity of your purchase and will often accept its return, for the original price, if you change your mind. At the same time, a good dealer can advise novices about imperfections.

Ideally, of course, you should always buy only the best example you can find of a particular genre, in the best condition: Whether an item is damaged or not is a major factor in determining its market price (and should matter to you if you're buying as a potential investment); and in any case, a stain, a chip, or a warp will probably annoy you in the long run. Helpful antique dealers can give you some feedback on the matter, can also provide you with the name of a good restorer, and, sometimes, can even arrange for you to pay the trade price for a restoration. Before you buy something that has already been restored, ask the dealer to explain what catchwords like "remodeled," "renewed," and "restyled" actually mean when applied to an item. You don't want to buy a Renaissance Tuscan closet whose only original part is the keyhole.

You can learn something of what the dealers know at a number of courses that are available throughout the year at *Earnley Concourse,* Chichester, Sussex PO20 7JI, England (phone in Bracklesham Bay: 67-03-92). *Christie's London* offers a fine arts course that covers the subject in a year. Information: Director, Christie's Fine Arts Course, 63-B Old Brompton Rd., London SW7 3JS, England (phone: 581-3933).

To find out where to buy, consult the *Weltkunst* (a world art review), published twice monthly and available at well-stocked newsstands in Germany (or through the magazine's office at Nymphenburgerstrasse 84, 8000 Munich 19, Germany (phone: 18-

10-91); it contains a good Europe-wide auction calendar. So do the *Antiques Trade Gazette,* available at 116 Long Acre, London WC2 (phone: 836-0323), and *Art and Auction* magazine, 250 W 57th St., New York, NY 10019 (phone: 212-582-5633). Also see the art and auction page of the weekend edition of the *International Herald Tribune;* the *Guide Émer,* a specialized French publication aimed at the art and antiquity trade available from Émer Publicité, 50 rue-quai de l'Hôtel de Ville, 75004 Paris (phone: 277-8344); and *A Guide to the Antique Shops of Britain,* by R Ferguson and S King, published by the *Antique Collectors Club,* 5 Church St., Woodbridge, Suffolk (phone: 5501).

Some of the best hunting grounds are in Vienna, London, Paris, Berlin, and Rome; along a number of streets full of antique shops in other cities; and at a number of antique fairs that take place all over Europe throughout the year. Here are some details.

ANTIQUE CAPITALS

VIENNA, Austria: Go straight to the Dorotheergasse, a lovely old street off the Graben where antique shops have proliferated in the shadow of the great *Dorotheum* auction house at Number 17. The shops flow out into the side streets — the Braüner-strasse, the Spiegelgasse, and the Stallburggasse — and they devote themselves to every imaginable genre of antique. There are generalists who carry furniture, painting, and rugs; and specialists that stock only brocades, or crystal, or music boxes, or clocks and watches, or toy soldiers, and — because this is Vienna — a number that deal exclusively in collectors' instruments, manuscript pages of musical scores, composers' autographed letters, and the like. (Have a look at *Doblinger Musikhaus* at Dorotheergasse 10.) Also, call at the strongholds of the *Hofstätters,* Vienna's leading antique dynasty: *Reinhold,* at Dorotheergasse 15, is the sculpture and furniture branch; *Wolfgang,* at Spiegelgasse 14, has fine medieval pieces; and there's the *Galerie Hofstätter* at Brauner-strasse 7 that seems to have tidied up after the Hapsburgs. Arrange also to attend at least one auction at the *Dorotheum,* a major source for dealers, which is always an education even if you never lift a finger. On Saturday, try the less rarefied end of the spectrum: The flea market at Naschmarkt in the 6th district is easily reached from the Stadtbahn's Kettenbrückengasse station. And the city's big annual antique fair, the *Wiener Kunst Und Antiquitätenmesse,* runs for a week in November in the Hofburg. If you still haven't found anything, you're not really interested in antiques.

LONDON, England: The British Empire is the world's largest antique, but in its heyday the sun never set on the loot that flowed into its prosperous capital. And before that, during the French Revolution, the city was also a safe haven for things of value. Consequently, London has long been the unquestioned center of the antique trade. Anything can be bought here, and everything has a market value and instant liquidity. The 10-day *Grosvenor House Antiques Fair,* held annually in June is a sun in the antique dealer's solar system; you'll find everything from Etruscan heads to Victorian bustles, and every piece has been authenticated by independent experts. The great auction houses, *Christie's* on King Street and *Sotheby's* on Bond Street, are instrumental in setting market prices; they're superb places to develop a feel for the market. Then there are the street markets that blossom and thrive in Camden Passage, Islington, Mondays through Saturdays (Wednesdays are best for antiques); at Bermondsey Square and Tower Bridge Road (the New Caledonian), held on Fridays beginning at 7 AM (the best time); and, on Saturdays, on Portobello Road, Westbourne Park, where you'll recognize as sellers the buyers of the previous day's Caledonian. All week long, you can browse in the *Kensington Antique Hypermarket,* 26-40 Kensington High St., the *Chelsea Antique Market,* 253 King's Road or *Gray's Antique Market,* Davies Mews. London's two renowned department stores, *Harrods* and *Fortnum and Mason,* both have excellent antique departments that stock only the finest quality items. Antique shops also can be found in quantity along Kensington Church Street, Fulham Road, Bond Street, Mount Street, Jermyn Street, Brompton Road, and King's Road. Buy silver at the *Silver Vaults* under Chancery Lane; porcelain at the *Antique Porcelain Company Ltd.,* 149 New Bond Street; prints at *Colnaghi's,* 14 Old Bond Street, or at *Craddock and Barnard,* 32 Museum Street; books at *E. Joseph,* 1 Vere St.; Oriental rugs at the *Vigo-Sternberg Galleries,* 37 South Audley Street, or at *Alexander Juran,* 74 New Bond Street; and Russian icons at the *Temple Gallery,* 4 Yeoman's Row (phone: 589-6622). *Mallett and Sons,* 40 New Bond St., is a miniature museum. Incidentally, if you've bought — or taken on approval — something you'd like an expert to examine, try the British Museum (where you'll never be quoted a value) or *Sotheby's* (where you'll be reminded that the house will be happy to sell it).

PARIS, France: Despite the ravages of the Revolution, you can still do some productive antique hunting in Paris. The most fruitful market is the giant *Biennale Internationale des Antiquaires,* a marathon fair held in even-numbered years in midautumn at the Grand Palais. The rest of the time, visit the venerable *Hôtel Drouot* auction house in its new modern quarters at 9 rue Drouot on the Right Bank. In addition, on the site of the old Magasins du Louvre there's a new antiques shopping center with 250 shops: *Le Louvre des Antiquaires,* 2 pl. du Palais Royal; phone: 297-2720 (open Tuesdays through Sundays, 11 AM to 7 PM). Two other important antique centers are *Le Village Suisse* at 78 av. de Suffren and av. de la Motte-Picquet (open every day except Tuesday and Wednesday; phone: 306-2639) and *La Cour aux Antiquaires* at 54 rue du Faubourg-St.-Honoré (open daily except Saturday, Sunday, and Monday mornings). Don't worry: Saturday, Sunday, and Monday are the days to hit the *Marché aux Puces,* the huge flea market between the porte de St.-Ouen and the porte de Clignancourt, where some 3,000 shops, stalls, and blankets display everything from Renoir watercolors to 78 rpm records. The *Porte de Vanves* and the *Porte de Montreuil* markets are also in business on weekends only; you'll find more blankets, fewer shops, and better prices. And if you're in Paris in March or September, don't miss the semiannual *Foire à la Ferraille* at the Parc Floral, Bois de Vincennes, where all the dealers stock up (phone: 262-44-44, for information). A number of streets are heavily populated with antique shops. On the Right Bank, they include the rue du Faubourg-St.-Honoré, rue La Boétie, rue de Miromesnil (especially for armor and toy soldiers), avenue Victor-Hugo, rue St.-Honoré, and rue du Faubourg-St.-Antoine. On the Left Bank, prowl the quai Voltaire, rue de Grenelle, boulevard St.-Germain, rue Bonaparte, rue de Beaune (scientific instruments), rue du Bac (dolls, toys), rue des Saints-Pères, rue de Seine, and rue Jacob. *Galerie Nikolenko,* 220 blvd. St.-Germain, specializes in Russian and Greek icons. In addition, between the two banks, you'll find some pleasant shops in even more pleasant surroundings on the Île St.-Louis. If you're a stamp fancier, don't miss the open-air stamp market — held on Thursdays, Saturdays, and Sundays at the corner of avenue Gabriel and avenue Marigny — or the countless shops along the rue Drouot and in the arcades of the Palais Royal. Finally, to keep abreast of Parisian auction activities, write for a free copy of *La Gazette de l'Hôtel Drouot,* 99 rue de Richelieu, 75002 Paris.

WEST BERLIN, Germany: Berlin dealers have a long-cultivated and prized reputation for expertise and honesty, and you are likely to have a 30-year guarantee and an item's complete pedigree pressed upon you, even if you're running to catch a plane. And if you ever have any complaints, you can take it to a special court of arbitration established solely to handle antique matters. The Keithstrasse is virtually one long row of antique shops with a variety of specialties. Some of the best include *Galerie Eva Lohmaier* (for silver and jewelry), *Hagen Jung* (for porcelain), *Karin Sonnenthal* (for Biedermeier furniture), *Helgard Kramer* (for miniatures), and *Ruth Schmidt* (for really fine East Asian pieces). The area around Kurfürstendamm and Fasanenstrasse is also productive, as are Eisenacherstrasse, Winterfeldstrasse, Motzstrasse, and Fugger-strasse. *(Joachim Schröder,* at number 4, has fine silver and furniture). Bleibtreustrasse and Mommsenstrasse are the places to hunt for Jugendstil and art deco pieces. The *Berliner Flohmarkt* (flea market) inhabits an old U-Bahn station at Nollendorfplatz, and is open from 11 AM to 7:30 PM every day except Tuesdays; you'll find a number of shops in the nearby Wilmersdorf and Charlottenburg sections of the city. Another sprawling secondhand market is on Saturdays and Sundays, 8 AM to 3:30 PM, in the Tiergarten, Strasse des 17 Juni. Among other reputable and well-stocked dealers are the *Galerie Pels-Leusden,* on the Kurfürstendamm (for drawings and watercolors); *Wilhelm Weick,* on the Eisenacherstrasse (for paintings); *Werner Wormuth,* also on Eisenacherstrasse (for old frames and fine restoration); *Herbert Klewer,* on Viktoria-Luiseplatz (for furniture); and *Seidel und Sohn,* on Eisenacherstrasse (for eighteenth-century furniture and art). Berlin's giant department store, *Ka-De-We,* also has a first-rate antique section.

   ROME, Italy: The main artery for antique hunters is the via del Babuino; for junking, there's the sprawling Sunday morning flea market at porta Portese; and for items in between are middlebrow streets like via dei Coronari (on the pricey side), via del Governo Vecchio, via di Panico, and via Margutta (the site of an annual open-air art show). There is also an annual autumn fair in via dei Coronari; all the shops are open at night and the strolling is delightful. And all week long throughout the year there is a pleasant collection of stands and stalls in piazza Borghese. On the aristocratic via del Babuino, the nobility includes *Di Giorgio, Amedeo di Castro, Apolloni, Olivi, Fallani* (for sculpture), *Luciano Coen* (for rugs), and *Sestieri* at piazza di Spagna (for paintings). Two other fine Rome shops are *Tanca* on the Salita dei Crescenzi, for antique jewelry and silver; and *Lukacs-Donath* on via Veneto, for porcelain. It should be noted that Italy's antique trade is lively in the provinces, as well. The most important event is the *Mostra d'Antiquariato* held in Florence's Palazzo Strozzi in September and October of odd-numbered years. And there are shops of national importance in Florence *(Bartolozzi, Bellini);* Milan *(Longari, Brunelli, Schubert);* Turin *(Rossi, Accorsi);* and Venice *(Barozzi, Trois, Casellati).* The best auction houses in Rome are *Antonina* on via del Babuino and the branch of *Christie's* at piazza Navona. *Finarte* is tops in Milan. As a general rule, the antique market in Italy is less richly international than in other European countries, and you should stick to local creations. Also tread with extreme caution when you inspect classical Roman and Greek pieces: There are enough of them around to fill the Roman Empire six times over.

MORE GREAT STREETS FOR ANTIQUE HUNTING

   BRUSSELS, Belgium – Rue Watteau, rue Lebeau, rue Ernest Allard, Chaussée d'Ixelles, and the place du Grand Sablon, which has a Saturday- and Sunday-morning antique market.
   COPENHAGEN, Denmark – All the side streets adjacent to Strøget, a kilometer-long pedestrians-only thoroughfare that runs through the city's center.
   NICE, France – Village Segurane, at rue Pierre Gautier, near the harbor.
   MUNICH, Germany – The Ottostrasse, near Stachus.
   ATHENS, Greece – Pandrossou, Solonos, Kriezotou, and Balaritou streets, and Kolonaki Square.
   DUBLIN, Ireland – Grafton Street, Dawson Street, Liffey Street, Bachelor's Walk, and Ormond Quay.
   NAPLES, Italy – Via Domenico Morelli and via Santa Maria di Constantinopoli, near the Museo Nazionale; Via Chiaia.
   AMSTERDAM, The Netherlands – Nieuwe Spiegelstraat, near the Rijksmuseum. And nearly everywhere in the Hague; there are some 150 antique shops in the city.
   WARSAW, Poland – Nowy Świat, Krakowskie Przedmieście.

MADRID, Spain – Calle del Prado, Plaza de las Cortés, Carrera de San Jerónimo, and the Rastro, a huge Sunday market.

BERNE, Switzerland – The Kramgasse.

GENEVA, Switzerland – Rue de la Cité, rue de l'Hôtel de Ville, la Grande Rue.

LAUSANNE, Switzerland – Cheneau de Bourg.

ZÜRICH, Switzerland – The Schlüsselgasse, Schipfe, Neumarkt, Rindermarkt, and the Oberdorf.

MOSCOW, USSR – The state-run thrift shops, Komissionyj — try the one at 46 Gorky Street — where you'll find everything from a piece of chipped crockery with a picture of a waving cosmonaut to a seventeenth-century icon of St. Dmitri (though most of the best items have been in London and Paris since 1917).

ANTIQUE FAIRS

THE SALZBURGER MESSE, Salzburg, Austria – Generally held in late March or early April in the Residenz, with dealers coming from all over the country.

LA FOIRE DES ANTIQUAIRES DE BELGIQUE, Brussels, Belgium – Held 2 weeks in March at the Palais des Beaux Arts.

THE AUER DULT, Munich, Germany – A week-long flea market that takes place three times annually, in April or May, July or August, and October. Mariahilfplatz.

THE IRISH ANTIQUE DEALERS' FAIR, Dublin, Ireland – Held in August, at about the same time as the chichi Royal Dublin Society Horse Show.

THE ANTIQUE FAIR, Delft, The Netherlands – Held for 3 weeks every autumn in the Prinsenhof Museum.

THE INTERNATIONAL ANTIQUE DEALERS FAIR, Lausanne, Switzerland – A November annual at the Palais de Beaulieu.

ANTIC: INTERNATIONAL ART AND ANTIQUES FAIR, Zürich, Switzerland – An annual exposition generally held in the spring at the Zuspa Exhibition Centre.

For the Experience

Europe's Most Memorable Hostelries

 Europe is full of fascinating places to get a good night's sleep. In fact, some of the grandest of the world's grand hotels are here; they have the refinement and cachet that you'll find only in establishments that have spent centuries serving royalty and the cream of society. Other hostelries, as quaint as these grandees are luxurious, seem more like country homes; their atmosphere depends on whether you're in Sicily or Slovenia, the Cotswolds or Crete. A number of other lodging places are to be found in what were once spare monasteries or towering castles. The caravansaries we list below, by category, are sure to give you sweet dreams — and plenty of happy memories to look back on when your trip is over.

THE GRANDEST OF THE GRAND HOTELS

Like the great transatlantic liners that were once the centerpiece of European travel, the great hotels of Europe seem destined to disappear, to be gradually replaced by more practical concrete palaces. And when the world has finally been transformed into one gigantic *Holiday Inn,* we will look back longingly on the grand hotels' shimmering chandeliers, their lordly tail-coated concierges, the neat rows of shoes in their corridors awaiting morning massages. Already, these hotels belong more to the past than the present — still extant only by some strange quirk of fate. So enjoy them while you can, these gracious temples of excess, and damn the expense — which is usually monstrous. But don't think of it as just the cost of a hot bath, a night's sleep, a morning's coffee. A stay at a hotel such as Paris's *Ritz* is a concert, a visit to a museum, an evening at the theater, an experience seldom duplicated in the modern world. When you start your day with a turn in those historic revolving doors, you somehow see the whole of the surrounding city from a different, far more glittering perspective.

Some notes on getting the most from your stay: First, opt out of American Plan (AP; full pension, or three meals a day) and Modified American Plan (MAP; half pension, or two meals) in favor of Continental Plan (CP; breakfast only) at urban hotels; apart from the fact that working your way through a capital's hundred best restaurants is a pleasure, many great city hotels serve remarkably ordinary meals. Second, remember that the more princely a hotel, as a rule, the more regal the surcharges applied to telephone calls (300% is not unheard of) — so call collect when you can or telephone from the nearest post office. You can dine out on the difference. Third, remember the story of the irascible New Yorker, a guest at one of the Continent's most fabulous hostelries, who refused to pay the automatic 18% service charge because he said he hadn't had any service. And he won.

Here are some of the world's finest dormitories, on whose crested stationery there will be a good deal to write home about.

HOTEL SACHER, Vienna, Austria: The quintessential European hotel experience, this rococo monument to good living stands opposite the Vienna State Opera House and is a kind of "mission control" for Vienna's rich musical life. The rooms are not all elegant, but the service is uniformly superb, and the resident concierge is Vienna's prime source of otherwise unavailable opera and concert tickets. Its restaurant serves some of the finest food in Europe; the hotel's clientele has remained unchanged since, it seems, the rise of the Hapsburgs. Information: Hotel Sacher, Philharmonikerstrasse 2, Vienna, Austria (phone: 52-55-75).

THE IMPERIAL, Vienna, Austria: Built more than a century ago as a private palace for the duke of Württemberg, this establishment manages to be at once majestic and modern and the impeccable, heel-clicking service that has always been a tradition here is not at all hard to get used to. The *Imperial* was, incidentally, a favorite of such discriminating egoists as Hitler and Wagner. Information: The Imperial, Kartner-ring 16, Vienna, Austria (phone: 65-17-65).

LA RÉSERVE, Knokke-Heist, Belgium: In the country's finest beach resort, both on the shore of little Lake Victoria and a 2-minute stroll from Knokke's broad, sweeping beach, this is a model vacation hotel: Swimming pool, tennis courts, golf, horseback riding, sailing, and water skiing are on the property, and the large bird sanctuary (to which the hotel's name refers) and a gambling casino are nearby. The food is wonderful, and an extensive art collection adorns the rooms. Information: La Réserve di Knokke-Heist, Elizabethlaan 160, 8300 Knokke-Heist, Belgium (phone: 60-06-06).

CLARIDGE'S, London, England: With India and Aden gone, here is the final bastion of the British Empire — though it often looks more like an Arabian caravansary these days. Its supreme, traditional elegance is as much a part of the London experience as the horse guards and the crown jewels. Information: Claridge's, Brook St., London W1A 2JQ, England (phone: 629-8860).

THE CONNAUGHT, London, England: Another stronghold of nineteenth-century Britain, luxurious and intimate, that will soon have you feeling like a distinguished guest at Lord Hyphen's town house. Small — with a tenaciously faithful clientele — it sometimes seems to be booked several generations in advance. Information: The Connaught, Carlos Pl., Mayfair, London W1Y 6AL, England (phone: 499-7070).

THE SAVOY, London, England: This hostelry is to theater what the *Sacher* is to music. In the heart of London's West End, the lobby is often a *Who's Who* of the international entertainment world. The atmosphere is gently Edwardian, but the management is contemporary — and adept at catering to the demands of plutocrats from every part of the planet. Tea here is as vital a British ritual as the coronation. Information: The Savoy, The Strand, London WC2R OEU, England (phone: 836-4343).

LA RÉSERVE, Beaulieu, France: If thoughts of the French Riviera and Côte d'Azur awaken longings in you, you can get some satisfaction here at this luxurious seaside establishment graced by plenty of sun and surf, plus a sauna and swimming pool — and one of France's most renowned restaurants. The *Monte Carlo Casino* is just minutes away. Information: La Réserve, 5 Blvd. Général-Leclerc, 06310 Beaulieu-sur-Mer, France (phone: 01-00-01).

HÔTEL DU CAP, Cap d'Antibes, France: Over a hundred years old, this Riviera landmark stands at the end of the Antibes peninsula in a lovely, semitropical park, looking out over the sea. An immaculately kept private beach, wisteria-rimmed tennis courts, and dinners on the patio of the patrician *Eden Roc* restaurant are highlights. Open from Easter to the end of October. Information: Hôtel du Cap, Blvd. Kennedy, 06604 Antibes, France (phone: 61-39-01).

THE NORMANDY, Deauville, France: A great Norman mansion facing the sea in an urbane resort that is often called the "Twenty-first Arrondissement of Paris," this hotel is a 5-minute walk from the *Deauville Casino*, which still has Europe's classiest casino clientele, most of whom catch a few hours' sleep at the *Normandy* between wagers. Fine at the height of the August racing season, and fine, too, for a winter weekend, when the rain and wind lash the Norman coast. Information: The Normandy, Rue Jean-Mermoz, 14800 Deauville, France (phone: 88-09-21).

THE NÉGRESCO, Nice, France: Something of an anachronism on the heavily trafficked and highly developed Riviera, this beautiful white Belle Époque cream puff is still one of the shrines of European hotelkeeping. Its charming period rooms give you views over the ultramarine Baie des Anges and the long and lively promenade des Anglais. Information: The Négresco, 37 promenade des Anglais, 06000 Nice, France (phone: 88-39-51).

THE RITZ, Paris, France: Perhaps the world's most famous hotel, the *Ritz* is beautifully positioned on place Vendôme like the national monument it is. A recent overhaul has attempted to ease it out of French literature and into the twentieth century with notable success and its name is still synonymous with luxury. Even its sale to an "English" group that seems largely Arab does not appear to have diminished its aura. Information: The Ritz, 15 pl. Vendôme, 75001 Paris, France (phone: 260-3830).

HÔTEL DE CRILLON, Paris, France: Only the understated gold "C's" on its doors identify this grand example of Louis XV style, wonderfully situated right on place de la Concorde. Once a private mansion, its interior is a regal assembly of eighteenth-century marble, carved and gilt-covered ornamentation, tapestries, and crystal chande-liers — luxe of the sort usually protected behind velvet cordons, but here eminently approachable. The *Crillon* has 180 large rooms and 30 suites. Those on the square have the best views; those on the courtyards are the quietest. Information: Hôtel de Crillon, 10 pl. de la Concorde, 75008 Paris, France (phone: 265-2424).

THE GEORGE V, Paris, France: On the avenue of the same name that bisects the Champs-Élysées, this has been a favorite address of American travelers since the days of the Grand Tour. There is a prosperous, worldly air about its bustling halls, a feeling that things of continental importance are going on in the bar or under the sun lamps. The breakfast room serves some of the best hot croissants in town. Information: The George V, 31 av. George V, Paris 75008 (phone: 723-5400).

THE PLAZA-ATHÉNÉE, Paris, France: The most exquisitely French of Paris's major hotels, this one — Paris at its suave and urbane best — and has attained such heights that among its regular guests are a few who look down their noses at the *Ritz*. Information: The Plaza-Athénée, 25 av. Montaigne, 75008 Paris, France (phone: 723-7833 or 723-4636).

BRENNER'S PARK HOTEL, Baden-Baden, Germany: On the lushly pastoral Lich-tentalerallée, this hotel has a setting like that of a Hapsburg summer palace and a wealth of balconies that make the most of it, offering views of particularly lordly trees and a romantic stream. The opulent *Baden-Baden Casino* and the wooded tennis club are an idyllic stroll away, as are all the other pleasures of this playground spa. Informa-tion: Brenner's Park Hotel, An der Lichtentalerallée, D-7570 Baden-Baden, Germany (phone: 35-30).

THE VIER JAHRESZEITEN, Hamburg, Germany: That rare combination of urban efficiency and countrified serenity, this fine hotel has a lovely lakefront setting with a view of the waterways that are so characteristic of the city, and all around are flowered promenades, gleaming yachts, and handsome villas. The hotel grill has a friendly fireplace and fine food. Among hotel people, this jewel is known as "the best Swiss hotel outside Switzerland." Information: The Vier Jahreszeiten, Neuer Jungfernstieg 9-14, 2000 Hamburg 36, Germany (phone: 3-4941).

CALA DI VOLPE, Costa Smeralda, Italy: The crown jewel of the complex devel-oped by the Aga Khan on once-remote Sardinia, one of the Mediterranean's most fascinating islands. Rustic in style, like a Sardinian village, but deluxe in its comfort, it is discreetly tucked into a magnificent bright blue bay, just at the water's edge. Tennis, boating, swimming and skin diving, and glamorous nightlife are just outside your door, and it has served as the elegant background for some typical excess in a James Bond film. Open May through September. Information: Cala di Volpe, Costa Smeralda, Arzachena (Sassari), Italy (phone: 9-6083).

THE HASSLER, Rome, Italy: "Position is everything," said General von Clausewitz — and that is the distinction of this Roman classic, perched at the top of the Spanish Steps and at the edge of the Villa Borghese and its gardens. You'll enjoy its splendid sunset views over the city, its celebrated roof garden, and its quiet, understated luxury, a dramatic contrast to Rome's brouhaha. Information: The Hassler, 6 piazza Trinità dei Monti, 00187 Rome, Italy (phone: 679-2651).

THE GRITTI PALACE, Venice, Italy: Dramatically situated on the Grand Canal, this Renaissance *palazzo,* a compact version of the Doge's Palace, has a dining terrace that floats on the water in the midst of the gondola traffic. If you just hang out of your window, you will see most of Venice float by in the course of a day. Information: The Gritti Palace, Campo Santa Maria del Giglio, Canal Grande 30100, Venice, Italy (phone: 2-6044).

THE DUE TORRI, Verona, Italy: A magnificent living museum fitted out entirely with antiques, this deluxe centuries-old inn is *the* place to be during the opera festival that takes place in the summer at the Arena di Verona. The management and the mood are highly personal, and exquisite good taste has governed the selection of the least important accessory — even the ashtrays are lovely. Information: The Due Torri, Piazza S. Anastasia 4, Verona, Italy (phone: 59-50-44).

HÔTEL DE PARIS, Monte Carlo, Monaco: Across the square from the great *Monte Carlo Casino,* this newly refurbished grand symbol of the era when money still bought happiness has been the winter palace for Russian grand dukes and English lords who have been coming to this petit principality for 3-month doses of sun and roulette for over a century. The hotel's elaborately painted and chandeliered dining room is an opera set — as is the whole regal, truly glamorous building. Information: Hôtel de Paris, Pl. du Casino, Monte Carlo, Monaco (phone: 50-80-80).

REID'S, Funchal, Portugal: On the island of Madeira, this immensely gracious resort hotel, the perfect place to recover from a difficult year, has something of an old British colonial flavor about it. Set on a promontory above the sea, it's surrounded by a veritable jungle of the flowers and foliage for which the island itself is so famous. The hotel has a private beach, private boats, tennis, two pools, and great charm. Information: Reid's, Estrada Monumental 139, Funchal, Madeira, Portugal (phone: 2-3001).

THE RITZ, Madrid, Spain: A multimillion-dollar refurbishing by Trust House Forte has returned this lavish landmark to the aristocracy of European hotels. Although this white castle is just a Goya's throw from the Prado, its marble terrace and chiaroscuro summer garden may be all you'll ever want to see of Madrid. Information: Hotel Ritz, Plaza de la Lealtad 5, Madrid 14, Spain (phone: 221-2857).

BÜRGENSTOCK HOTELS, Bürgenstock, Switzerland: This complex of three luxurious hotels (the *Grand,* the *Palace,* the *Park*) is located in a 500-acre natural park that sprawls along a massive, wooded ridge some 1,500 feet above Lake Lucerne. Views from the hotel windows seem to take in half of Switzerland; rooms are hung with tapestries and Old Masters and furnished with lovely antiques. Information: The Bürgenstock Estate, CH-6366 Bürgenstock, Switzerland (phone: 64-13-31).

LE BEAU RIVAGE, Lausanne, Switzerland: A giant, queenly Victorian manor set on 10 acres of lush private park on the shore of Lac Leman in Lausanne-Ouchy. The constantly tended grounds are like a botanical garden — with tennis courts — and you can come and go by boat to the front door. Information: Beau Rivage, 1006 Ouchy, Lausanne (phone: 26-38-31).

THE PALACE, St.-Moritz, Switzerland: Apprentices from all over the world come to this legend of Swiss hotelkeeping to learn to do things as perfectly as only the Swiss can. Stand on your sun-washed balcony on a crisp February morning, look out on the dazzling snows of the Engadine Valley and its high Alpine backdrop, and you will feel like the King of the Golden Mountain. Information: The Palace, CH-7500 St.-Moritz, Switzerland (phone: 2-1101).

THE DOLDER GRAND, Zürich, Switzerland: A romantic old Gothic fantasy on a forested mountainside 6 minutes by hotel car from downtown Zürich. Golf, tennis, woodland pathways, panoramic views over city and lake, world-class cuisine, an ice rink, and an open-air pool with man-made waves are only a few of the delights that will make you want to settle down forever in the hotel's tower suite. Information: The Dolder Grand, Kurhausstrasse 65, CH-8032 Zürich, Switzerland (phone: 251-6231).

CASTLE HOTELS

Some of Europe's most fascinating hostelries started their lives as abbeys, baronial mansions, castles and châteaux, monasteries, and palaces. Most national tourist offices can tell you about those within their borders; the book *Castle Hotels of Europe* by Robert P. Long ($6.95) pinpoints hundreds of others in 18 countries on the Continent and in Britain. Also see *Relais et Châteaux,* published by the French organization of the same name, as a guide to a group of castle hotels, restaurants, and inns devoted to maintaining high standards of personalized service and cuisine. Here's our selection of some of the choicest:

SCHLOSS DÜRNSTEIN, Dürnstein, Austria: In northeast Austria, on a rocky plateau above the Danube, this baroque castle has been deftly transformed into a gracious modern hostelry. Formerly the summer residence of the Starhemberg princes, it now features a heated swimming pool, sauna and solarium, and first-class Austrian cuisine. Open mid-March to mid-November. Information: Schloss Dürnstein, A-3601, Dürnstein, Austria (phone: 212).

HOTEL-PALAIS SCHWARZENBERG, Vienna, Austria: Small and exclusive, this establishment occupies a wing of a palace still owned by one of Austria's oldest families, at the center of a 37-acre park close to the center of the city. The hotel is beautifully furnished, partly with antiques, and the atmosphere is perfectly sedate, totally calm. Information: Hotel-Palais Schwarzenberg, Schwarzenberg Place 9, Vienna, Austria (phone: 78-45-15).

CHÂTEAU DE NAMUR, Namur, Belgium: This 31-room château occupies a deep green private park at the summit of La Citadelle above Namur, overlooking the entire Meuse River valley. Swimming in the hotel pool and playing tennis on its courts will keep you busy between excursions to the Ardennes Forest. Information: Château de Namur, ave. de l'Ermitage, Namur 1, Belgium (phone: 22-25-46).

STEENSGAARD HERREGARDSPENSION, Millinge, Denmark: This half-timbered manor on the island of Fünen dates from the late thirteenth century and looks every bit of its age, from the armor hall and the library to the ancient park that surrounds it and the vaulted cellar, now set up for billiards. You can play tennis, take horseback or carriage excursions in the wild countryside, or just enjoy the mile-long private beach. Each of the 14 rooms has a view of the lake or the park. Information: Steensgaard Herregardspension, Steensgard 4, DK-5642, Millinge, Fünen, Denmark (phone: 61-94-90).

EASTWELL MANOR, Ashford, Kent, England: Set in some 3,000 acres of parkland picturesquely speckled with fluffy white sheep, this elegant, rambling stone country house was opened as a hotel just in 1980, but though the present house was rebuilt in 1926, its history can be traced back to the Norman Conquest; over the years it has had twenty owners, and Queen Victoria once made a visit here. The lavish use of space and splendid service reminds guests of an earlier, grander age: one visitor called it "the world's best twenty-room hotel." Though the rooms are absolutely huge, they are so cleverly decorated with sitting areas, soft colors, and pretty fabrics, that they seem positively inviting. An oak-paneled bar lures guests down for drinks before dinner, which is served in a baronial dining room. The menu is French, with an emphasis on nouvelle cuisine; you can order such delicacies as *aspèrges feuilletées au beurre fondu* and *fricassée de fruits de mer*. There is also a short menu of local specialties — among them smoked eel and roast English lamb (which, like the beef, comes from the estate). Details: Eastwell Manor, Eastwell Park, Ashford, Kent TN25 4HR, England (phone: 35751).

CHÂTEAU D'AUDRIEU, Audrieu, France: This magnificent eighteenth-century country house, preserved over the years by a single family, is set among lovely gardens in a 50-acre park crisscrossed by graveled pathways and scattered with trees that are almost as old as the house itself. The 18 sleeping rooms, which have retained their original paneling despite the ravages of the World War II D-day battles fought in the area, are furnished with antiques, and the bathrooms are modern. Audrieu is located halfway between Caen and Bayeux, just a few miles from the historic beaches and just 2 hours' drive from Paris. Information: Château d'Audrieu, 14250 Audrieu (Calvados), France (phone: 80-21-52).

CHÂTEAU D'ARTIGNY, Montbazon, France: François Coty, the celebrated French perfumer, spent two decades building this opulent, mansard-roofed château on the site of another that had existed there since 1769 — so it isn't the oldest of castles. However, Coty had style and taste, and the château reflects this: The ceilings are almost as ornate as those you've seen at Versailles, and the bathtubs are real marble. There are 32 rooms in the main château; but the establishment's most notable sleeping quarters are located on the top floor of the adjacent Pavilion Ariane, accessible via a lovely curved staircase. Information: Château d'Artigny, 37250 Montbazon, Route d'Azay-le-Rideau (Indre-et-Loire), France (phone: 26-24-24).

DOMAINE DES HAUTS DE LOIRE, Onzain, France: Here is a Loire Valley château where you can spend the night. Once a hunting pavilion for a French count, this cozy country-French establishment, its rooms papered with wonderful toiles and full of giant hand-hewn beams, feels like someone's home; everywhere there are gleaming antique copper pots and pans, often filled with fresh flowers, and the dining room is elegant and airy, so that you can watch the sun set as you wait for your supper. Information: Domaine des Hauts de Loire, 41150 Onzain (Loir-et-Cher), France (phone: 79-72-57).

SCHLOSSHOTEL KRONBERG, Kronberg, Germany: One of the finest castle-hotels in a country that is full of them, this fairy-tale structure in the woods about a half-hour from Frankfurt was built in 1888 by the German Empress Friedrich, who was daughter to Queen Victoria and mother to Kaiser Wilhelm II. It has also housed French army officers, American soldiers and civilians, and assorted European blue-bloods, and, in 1945, was invaded by jewel thieves who made a celebrated haul of heirlooms stored there. Though a relative newcomer on the hotel scene, it is lovely — full of nineteenth-century furnishings and priceless paintings and tapestries. Information: Schlosshotel Kronberg, Hainstrasse 25, 6242 Kronberg/Taunus, Germany (phone: 7011). If you acquire the *schlosshotel* (translation: "castle-hotel") habit, write the Vereinigung der Burg und Schlosshotels, an association of similar establishments, c/o "Gast. im Schloss," 3526 Trendelburg 1, Germany (phone: 331).

DROMOLAND CASTLE, Newmarket-on-Fergus, Ireland: The former seat of the O'Brien clan, this sixteenth-century conglomeration of turrets and towers — just a short drive from Shannon Airport — is stuffed with huge oil paintings and ornamented by handsome paneling, elaborate stone carvings, and picture windows that give out onto 500 acres of soft greenness; the chandeliered restaurant gleams sumptuously with its silk curtains and upholstery. Though owned by a West Virginian, the establishment makes you feel that you've come to the heart of Ireland. Riding is a favorite activity, along with tennis, golf (on a nine-hole course), and fishing for trout and salmon. Information: Dromoland Castle, Newmarket-on-Fergus, County Clare, Ireland (phone in Shannon: 7-1144).

VILLA D'ESTE, Lake Como, Italy: To visit Villa d'Este is to fall gently into a life lined with silk: The public rooms at this vast 400-year-old villa seem as fresh and opulent as when the villa was the home of a Renaissance cardinal, awash with antique chairs upholstered in deep blue brocaded silk, polished marble pillars, crystal chandeliers, winged staircases ascending to a balcony, handloomed carpeting, and arched leaded windows that open out to the cliffs and cypresses of the Como countryside. Breakfasts served at the lakeside dining room are a special treat: fresh grapefruit or orange juice (natural or mixed with champagne); freshly baked breads, rolls, brioches, and croissants; strong black coffee; cheeses; and hot baked Parma ham. Days are leisurely, filled with ambling along the marina, sitting in the sun, bathing in the lake, and sipping a drink on the terrace. Information: Villa d'Este, 22010 Cernobbio, Lake Como, Italy (phone: 51-14-71).

GLENEAGLES HOTEL, Auchterarder, Scotland: Staying at this immense Regency stone hostelry is a travel experience of a lifetime, akin to seeing the Taj Mahal for the first time. The lofty columned lounge, with its ornate ceilings, plus the cocktail bar, the glittering ballrooms, and the other public rooms are impressive; bedrooms, which range in size from large to cavernous, add to the effect. And there are amenities of all sorts — a swimming pool, tennis and squash courts, playgrounds, billiard rooms, and even facilities for game fishing. However, at this hotel, golf is the king, and, on the 700-acre grounds, you'll find not one 18-hole course, but three. As if that's not enough, the four courses at St. Andrews — owned by the townspeople so that anyone can play them — are an easy drive across the meadows of Strathearn. The opulent dining room offers a good choice of classical French as well as Scottish entrées. Information: Gleneagles Hotel, Auchterarder, Tayside, Perthshire, Scotland (phone: 22-31).

INVERLOCHY CASTLE, Fort William, Scotland: At the foot of the mountain Ben Nevis, this century-old Scottish Highland castle — splendidly Victorian inside, with a magnificently frescoed great central hall — is surrounded outside by 50 acres of woods and a dramatic landscape. You can fish, golf, go riding, play tennis — or just sit around and sip the castle's private-label whisky. Queen Victoria slept here. Information: Inverlochy Castle, Fort William, Inverness-shire PH33 68N, Scotland (phone: 2177).

SON VIDA, Palma de Mallorca, Spain: This spectacular thirteenth-century castle sits serenely atop a hill overlooking the Bay of Palma, with a breathtaking view of bustling Palma (15 minutes away) and the sea beyond. Tennis courts, a golf course, and riding stables spread out over the 1,400 acres of lavishly landscaped grounds. Information: Son Vida, Palma de Mallorca, Spain (phone: 45-10-11).

CHÂTEAU GÜTSCH, Lucerne, Switzerland: A few minutes by private cable car above Lucerne and its gleaming lake, this lovely turn-of-the-century mansion at the edge of the Gütsch woods has a heated swimming pool, public rooms decorated with suits of armor and old Swiss chests, a candlelit dining room in the wine cellar, and rooms fitted out with four-poster beds. The views from this elevation are spectacular — and in some rooms you can enjoy them from the bathtub. Information: Château Gütsch, Kanonenstrasse, CH-6003 Lucerne, Switzerland (phone: 22-02-72).

COZY INNS AND SMALL HOTELS

If your tastes run toward the rustic, you will be glad to know that Europe can lay claim to a superabundance of small hotels and inns with the charm and ambience that only years of operation can produce. You can stay at Tuscan villas, half-timbered taverns, Swiss chalets, and Scottish country houses, where the owners take in guests so often that they've come to call their homes inns. These places are decidedly unhomogenized — as quaint as familiar American inns, but far more varied in their styles. Should you get hooked, you will want to buy a copy of *Europe's Wonderful Little Hotels and Inns,* edited by Hilary Rubinstein (Congdon & Weed/St. Martin's Press; $14.95). It was compiled from the recommendations of the editor's fellow travelers and describes about

900 of the kind of cozy places we've culled from our own experiences — and listed below. A few — the last word in luxurious simplicity — will cost you as much as their five-star urban cousins; at others, a night's lodging is quite reasonably priced.

JAGDSCHLOSS GRAF RECKE, Wald-im-Pinzgau, Austria: This lovely mountain lodge on the edge of the Hohe Tauern National Park makes a fine jumping-off spot for hunting, Alpine touring, and riding excursions in the Oberpinzgau. Information: Jagdschloss Graf Recke, 5742 Wald-im-Oberpinzgau, Austria (phone: 417).

HUBERTUSKROEN, Feldballe, Denmark: A fine example of *kroer,* Danish country inns, this half-timbered building in the middle of a vast estate was built in 1710 on the site of a thirteenth-century castle and is today an important center of horse breeding and the preparation (for eating) of guinea fowl. Information: Hubertuskroen, Mollerup Gods, DK-8410 Ronde, Denmark (phone: 37-10-03).

THE LYGON ARMS, Broadway, England: In the heart of the Cotswolds, this fine specimen of a sixteenth-century English inn has a guest list that includes Charles I and Oliver Cromwell. Information: The Lygon Arms, Broadway, Worcestershire, England WR12 7DU (phone: 85-22-55).

OUSTAU DE BAUMANIÈRE, Les Baux-de-Provence, France: Famed primarily for its restaurant, one of the very finest in France, the inn is beautifully set on an abandoned quarry in a wild Provençal valley and is elegantly furnished with local antiques; it offers tennis, swimming, and horseback riding to fill your time between the three-star meals. Closed February. Information: Oustau de Baumanière, 13520 Les Baux-de-Provence, France (phone: 97-33-07).

LE VIEUX LOGIS, Trémolat, France: France's beautiful Dordogne River valley is the setting for this unprepossessing inn, a former farmhouse that has welcomed guests only since 1952, but has been in the family of the present owner, Mme. Giraudel-Destord, since it was built. It's a comfortable place: The beds are covered with pristine white or bright floral spreads and vast down-filled comforters (a rarity in this area); the cooks are generous with the ebony truffles that are sold in Scarlat, not far away. The proprietors — physicians all — make the raising of geese for *foie gras* their avocation. Information: Le Vieux Logis, 24510 Trémolat, France (phone: 22-80-06).

VILLA SAN MICHELE, Fiesole, Italy: Formerly a Renaissance monastery with a façade designed by Michelangelo, this hotel (and Italian National Trust Monument) in the hills above Florence is surrounded by lovely gardens and seems like a gracious Tuscan villa. Information: Villa San Michele, Via di Doccia 4, Fiesole, Italy (phone: 5-9451).

POUSADA DO INFANTE, Sagres, Portugal: On the western end of the sunny, sandy Algarve coast, this small establishment is a handsome representative of the many official Portuguese inns *(pousadas).* Its 15 rooms must be reserved long in advance. Information: Pousada do Infante, 8650 Sagres, Algarve, Portugal (phone: 6-4222).

PARADOR NACIONAL DE GIL BLAS, Santillana del Mar, Spain: The state-run Spanish *paradors* occupy elegantly restored old convents and castles along the sea, in the mountains, or on the outskirts of ancient villages. The *Gil Blas,* located in the region of the beautiful Costa Cantábrica, is typical, with its heavy stone walls and arches, wood-beamed ceilings, tile floors, and gracious rustic furnishings. Information: Parador Nacional de Gil Blas, Santillana del Mar, Santander, Spain (phones: 81-80-00). The central Parador office also handles bookings: Red de Paradores del Estado, Calle Velasquez 25, Madrid, Spain (phone: 435-9700). For a complete list of all the Spanish *paradors,* write the Spanish National Tourist Office, 665 Fifth Ave., New York, NY 10022 (phone: 212-759-8822).

CHESA GRISCHUNA, Klosters, Switzerland: This establishment in the charming Alpine town of Klosters is as near perfect an Alpine chalet as you'll find: Riotous pink flowerfalls cascade over dark wooden balconies; pine-paneled rooms are warmed with crackling fires; fondue and *glühwein* are standard fare in the cozy dining room; and the eiderdown on your bed is as light as a dollop of whipped cream. Information: Chesa Grischuna, CH-7250 Klosters, Switzerland (phone: 4-2222). The Swiss National Tourist Office (608 Fifth Ave., New York, NY 10020; phone: 212-757-5944) has a listing of other Swiss inns and castle hotels.

AND NOW FOR SOMETHING REALLY RUSTIC

The Alps have their hikers' and climbers' huts, but for getting away from it all in the most styleless style, you can't beat:

THE ARCTIC HOTEL, Narssarssuaq, Denmark: At the southern tip of Greenland, this no-frills establishment occupies an old World War II air base. There are ancient Norse settlements to explore, fjords for boating, the great ice glaciers for hiking adventures — so it doesn't really matter that you won't find a discotheque within 500 miles. Information: The SAS Arctic Hotel, DK-3923 Narssarssuaq, Greenland, Denmark (phone: 3-5253; telex: 90336 — often the only way to make contact).

The Shrines of
European Gastronomy

 In Europe, even ordinary food is very good by stateside standards; and the best attains an excellence only possible where the freshest and most flavorful ingredients are available to culinary artists who, working with the accumulated wisdom of centuries, cook with a religious devotion.

Such are the chefs behind the 29 restaurants we've listed here, the places we prize most among European dining spots. They are not, we must emphasize, the kinds of places where you could eat three meals a day, every day. (That would be a bit like subjecting yourself to three consecutive Wagnerian operas without respite.) Nor are these shrines of European gastronomy meant for grabbing a quick bite on your way to another event; dinners are productions, worth planning for and taking the appropriate time to enjoy.

Reservations should be made several days in advance whenever possible, and in many cases, writing ahead is the only way to secure a table. But it's also a good idea (where realistic) to pass by the restaurant, choose a table, and have a look at the menu.

Acquiring at least a rudimentary knowledge of wine also takes a little advance preparation, but is almost a prerequisite for eating in this type of establishment, since wines are as important as the food itself in the composition of your meal. The wine steward (sommelier) and the captain will help (so don't be afraid to ask), and afterward will monitor your bites and sips lest some selection fall short of the celestial. (If this happens, don't be bashful about returning it to the kitchen.)

A few more words of advice: Order what appeals to you, and don't be bullied into a rigid menu no matter how zealously it is pressed upon you. Daily specialties are usually good choices, and you should not be frightened off by multicourse epicurean feasts. In fact, these are very small samplings of the many dishes of which the chef is most proud, and can be an unforgettable treat. Prices will, inevitably, be high, but this is a once-in-a-lifetime thing. You should treat it (and enjoy it) as such.

Finally, a note on our choices. Nothing is quite so much fun (or as difficult) as putting together a list of Europe's most appealing restaurants. Actually, little could be more brazen. We could, of course, have played it safe by including only those establishments that hold multistar recognition from other appraisers of haute cuisine, but we thought that was misleading at best. It would give short shrift to the enormous variety of cuisines that exist across Europe and to the many world-class restaurants that operate across the Continent and that serve meals worth wandering for — but aren't French. So our reach is considerably wider, though we've noted our picks of the best Gallic tables; what follows is a true Europe-wide selection of restaurants that are, quite simply, nonpareil.

ZU DEN DREI HUSAREN (The Three Hussars), Vienna, Austria: This quintessentially Viennese establishment, in the heart of the old city just off the bustling Kärntnerstrasse, offers a whole range of epicurean entrées and a vast selection of hors d'oeuvres. There's not a better place in the world to sample a classic wiener schnitzel. Open for dinner only; closed all day Sundays. Information: Zu den Drei Husaren, Weihburggasse 4, Vienna, Austria (phone: 52-11-92).

HOTEL SACHER, Vienna, Austria: The venerable hotel-restaurant has changed little since its kitchen confected the first Sacher torte — a rich, justly celebrated chocolate cake filled with apricot jam and coated with an equally sinful chocolate icing that is always served with a generous dollop of fresh whipped cream. The clicking of heels and the tinkling of crystal blend as naturally as ever into the harmonies of the Vienna Opera across the street, and only the ancient waiters belie the establishment's age. Epic *tafelspitz* (boiled beef) has been served for a century; don't miss it. And for dessert — since you can buy a Sacher torte to take out around the corner — have some *palatschinken* — thin pancakes rolled around jam or chocolate and sprinkled with powdered sugar. Information: Hotel Sacher, Philharmonikerstrasse 4, Vienna, Austria (phone: 52-55-75).

ROMEYER, Brussels, Belgium: Despite its rustic surroundings on the edge of the Soignes Forest about 6 miles (10 km) outside the city, this grand lodge offers one of the most cosmopolitan menus you'll find anywhere on the Continent: The restaurant's genial owner and namesake, Belgium's foremost chef, is wont to daub his Ostend oysters with caviar or to shape a mousse of *pâté de foie gras* like a porcupine and stud it profusely with black truffle "needles." Closed Sunday evenings, Mondays, and the month of August. Information: Romeyer, 109 chaussée de Groenendael, 1990 Hoeilaart, Belgium (phone: 657-0581).

COMME CHEZ SOI, Brussels, Belgium: As an alternative to the very grand country lodge above, we offer this very intimate urban restaurant, distinguished by a kitchen wholeheartedly devoted to modern culinary delights. The talented young chef here considers the "new" in nouvelle cuisine an invitation to experiment, and almost any one of his adventures will provide an evening's repast you will remember long and lovingly. Elegantly decorated and quietly friendly, nothing here will disappoint you. Closed Sundays and Mondays, and all of July. Information: Comme Chez Soi, 23 pl. Rouppe, Brussels, Belgium (phone: 512-2921).

THE CONNAUGHT GRILL, London, England: The *Connaught* is to London what the *Sacher* is to Vienna, and its *Grill* is every bit as well mannered as you'd expect of a place so thoroughly steeped in British tradition. The best dishes on the menu are those on which the Empire was founded: roast beef and Yorkshire pudding, Lancashire hot pot, gooseberry pie. After dinner, you will feel as if the gentlemen should retire to the library with a glass of port and a cigar. Information: The Connaught Hotel, Carlos Pl., London W1, England (phone: 499-7070 or 492-0668).

LE GAVROCHE, London, England: After over 70 years of rating restaurants, the *Guide Michelin* gave its first three-star rating in Britain to this most French of restaurants. It is owned and run by Albert Roux, a former chef for the Rothschild family and once the chef in the royal household. The wine card is exceptionally long and inviting (listing some 235 items, including a 1945 Château Lafite Rothschild for about $250, though many modest vintages are available for less than $20). Start with crab vahiné, a house specialty — fresh chopped crab served in the shell with a garnish of herbs. Information: Le Gavroche, 43 Upper Brook St., London W1, England (phone: 408-0881).

AUBERGE DE L'ILL, Illhaeusern (Alsace), France: There are those who claim that Alsace, not Paris, is France's culinary capital, and this establishment is their strongest piece of evidence. As run by the Haeberlin brothers — Jean-Pierre and Paul (the chef) — and Paul's son, Marc, the restaurant's menu is superbly Alsatian and impeccably prepared: wild hare salad, terrine of crayfish, peach salad with Burgundy. Closed Mondays and Tuesdays, most of February, and the first week in July. Information: Auberge de l'Ill, Rue de Collanges, Illhaeusern, 68150 Ribeauvillé, France (phone: 71-83-23).

MOULIN DE MOUGINS, Mougins (Côte d'Azur), France: If your vision of the Riviera is dining in distinguished (or at least glamorous) company in a beautiful garden flooded with sunlight in an elegant country setting, what you've experienced is precognition, not hallucination. Just such romantic trances are regularly accomplished hereabouts, often accompanied by the smell of oranges; though far more likely in this case is the wafting aroma of heavenly fish soup, lobster grilled in basil butter, or fowl braised in port. Happy dreams. Closed Mondays and from October 25 to December 20. Information: Moulin de Mougins, 424 chemin du Moulin, Mougins, France (phone: 75-78-24).

ALAIN CHAPEL, Mionnay (Lyon), France: In the flash and sizzle of the new style of cuisine and the chefs perfecting it, don't fail to seek out the unfalteringly fine food at chef Alain Chapel's namesake. The chef is himself self-effacing, perhaps because the dishes speak so well for him: lobster with noodles, stuffed calf's ear, a fabulous lobster salad. Closed Mondays, Tuesday afternoons, January, and half of February. Information: Alain Chapel, Mionnay 01390, France (phone: 891-8202).

PAUL BOCUSE, Lyon, France: Out of the way though it may be, this city in what Parisians disdainfully label the provinces is home to one of the country's most honored restaurants, and travelers come from all over the world to sample its specialties — *soupe au potiron, loup au four, cassolette d'écrevisses.* In point of fact, the absence of large-scale tourism keeps Bocuse purer than its three-star *confrères* in the capital, which serve so many clients who barely know a *coquille St.-Jacques* from a cheeseburger. Closed most of February and August. Information: Paul Bocuse, 50 quai Plage, Collonges-au-Mont d'Or, France (phone: 822-0140).

HOTEL DES FRÈRES TROISGROS, Roanne (Lyon), France: More than any other restaurant in France, this splendid house celebrates the land, changing the dishes on its menu season by season to use only the area's fresh vegetables, poultry, shrimp, and snails to best advantage. Pierre Troisgros rejoices in the natural flavor of foods delicately enhanced and underscored. A shopping trip with him is something of a lesson in local ecology, wildlife, biology, and topography all rolled into one. Closed Tuesdays, Wednesday afternoons, most of January, and most of August. Information: Hotel des Frères Troisgros, 22 cours de la République, Roanne, France (phone: 71-66-97).

GRAND VÉFOUR, Paris, France: At the far end of Palais-Royal's serene courtyard, this lovely, lavishly ornamented relic of old Paris is perhaps the most classically French of the great Parisian temples of gastronomy. Specialties of the house include *ballotine de canard* and a fluffy frog soufflé. Closed Saturdays and Sundays and the month of August. Information: Grand Véfour, 17 rue de Beaujolais, Paris, France (phone: 296-5627).

RESTAURANT LASSERRE, Paris, France: A friend once described a meal at *Lasserre* as similar to dining in one of those fabulous Fabergé music boxes, and so it is. The atmosphere in the plush upstairs dining room is very elegant, with waiters in white tie and tails. Service is swift and impeccable, and the cuisine sublime. Some special dishes include crab pâté *au Richard;* terrines of veal, duck, and chicken (served as one dish); eel pâté; frogs' legs in garlic; *rouget en julienne;* and saddle of hare. Restaurateur René Lasserre recommends writing at least a month in advance for reservations, offering a couple of possible dates; his replies are prompt and this slight inconvenience will ensure a table in the elite center section of the dining room. Closed Sundays, Mondays, and the month of August. Information: Restaurant Lasserre, 17 av. Franklin-Roosevelt, Paris, France (phone: 359-5343).

LA TOUR D'ARGENT, Paris, France: Located in a corner building on the Left Bank with a stunning view of Notre-Dame, this restaurant serves a *soufflé Valtesse* that seems to hover several inches above the plate and a duck concoction, *caneton Tour d'Argent,* that is as much a symbol of Paris as the Eiffel Tower. A sort of gastronomical Louvre, the restaurant is also fitted out with a small museum of grand cuisine and, in the cellars, a small exhibit about the history of wine. Try to go in the off-season. Closed Mondays. Information: La Tour d'Argent, 15 quai de la Tournelle, Paris, France (phone: 354-2331).

THE RITZ, West Berlin, Germany: The restaurant's unusual menu offers specialties from several continents, all exquisitely prepared and exotically served. The Oriental dishes are especially breathtaking. Knowledgeable patrons order in advance. Closed Saturdays, Sundays, and the month of August. Information: The Ritz, Rankestrasse 26, 1000 West Berlin 30, Germany (phone: 24-72-50).

WALTERSPIEL, Munich, Germany: Everything about the *Walterspiel* is tastefully discreet, from its half-lit glow to its creamy decor and hushed carpeting. This restaurant in the *Vierjahreszeiten Hotel* offers Bavaria's most elegant and sophisticated cuisine, and when you've had the *Auszug aus schwarzen Trüffel* (essence of black truffles), or the *Seewolf mit Crevettenschaum soufliert Orangensahne* (seawolf with shrimp foam in orange cream sauce), you'll forget all about the last time you saw Paris. Information: Walterspiel, Maximilianstrasse 17, 8000 Munich, Germany (phone: 230-39-0 or 22-88-21).

TAVERNA TA NISSIA, Athens, Greece: One of the best restaurants in all of Greece is in the basement of the *Hilton* hotel. The decor and the music are Greek, and so is the food. Notable on the menu are the *kakavia,* a lavish bouillabaisse, and the spit-roasted Olympia lamb. The exotic Greek hors d'oeuvres and salads are also worth making room for. Information: Taverna Ta Nissia, Vassilissis Sofias 46, Athens, Greece (phone: 722-0201).

HUNGÁRIA, Budapest, Hungary: If the name is unfamiliar to those who knew Budapest in its golden era, that's because the restaurant gained international fame as *Café New York.* When it opened in 1894, it was the most famous address in the city, and its destruction during World War II was an international tragedy. The city lovingly restored it to all its former splendor — gilt columns, glittering mirrors, glass globe lights — an outrageous temple of art nouveau spoiled only by a few incongruous Soviet chandeliers. The scene looks like something out of the MGM back lot. Information: Hungária, Lenin Kórút 9, Budapest, Hungary (phone: 22-38-49).

DANTE, Bologna, Italy: This restaurant is the *crema della crema* of a number of fine ones in a city widely known as the mecca of Italian *bongustaii* (gourmets). On a quiet back street among the ocher porticoes of Bologna, with just a handful of tables in its small dining room. The menu stars exotic delights like *risotto mille e una notte* (1001 Nights rice) and *scaloppa di fegato d'oca al tartufo nero* (black-truffled goose liver cutlet). The perfect complement to them is a bottle of the region's simple, sparkling Lambrusco. Information: Dante, Via Belvedere 2/b, Bologna, Italy (phone: 22-44-64).

TREDICI GOBBI, Florence, Italy: The restaurant's name means "thirteen hunch-backs," and here you will find the essence of the tastes of Tuscany. Try *bistecche alla fiorentina* — Florentine steaks — in giant slabs that lean out over the edges of the plate; pungent Tuscan *fagioli* (beans) and a dark, velvety chianti that easily goes down by the liter. Closed Sunday evenings, Mondays, and the month of August. Information: Tredici Gobbi, Via del Porcellana 9, Florence, Italy (phone: 29-87-69).

GIANNINO, Milan, Italy: Despite its Lombard location, this is a Tuscan restaurant. The menu now includes exotic international specialties — but the restaurant first made its name in the nineteenth century with a simple plate of beans, and homegrown delicacies like *olivette di vitello tartufate, panzerotti* (mozzarella in grilled pasta), and *tortelloni al basilico,* which are still the best offerings. Before you leave, make sure you see the spectacular kitchen. Closed Saturdays, Sundays, and the month of August. Information: Giannino, Via Amatore Sciesa 8, Milan, Italy (phone: 545-2948).

EL TOULÀ, Rome, Italy: Completely unlike the plain, brightly lit restaurants that are so typical of Rome, this one has a decor that is plush and subtle and a menu that takes you through Venice, Paris, Vienna, and other European capitals. The clientele is aristocratic and well traveled. Closed Saturday lunch, Sundays, and the month of August. Information: El Toulà, Via della Lupa 29b, Rome, Italy (phone: 678-1196).

BALI, Amsterdam, The Netherlands: The best place in Europe to enjoy the Indonesian *rijsttafel* that the Dutch brought with them from their former colony, this restaurant lays out a spectacular spread that includes some 25-odd dishes of chicken, shrimp, fish, veal, coconut, almonds, peanuts, ginger, chutney, pickles, kumquats, sieved eggs, onion rings, and fried bananas to spoon over (and garnish) mountains of rice. The meal — a unique experience by any standard — is even more fun when you do it with a group of friends. Closed Sundays and Mondays. Information: Bali, Leidsestraat 95, Amsterdam, Holland (phone: 22-78-78).

AVIZ, Lisbon, Portugal: You will find Portuguese specialties on the menu of this Lisbon landmark, but the best dishes on the menu include *shashlik au riz,* smoked mallard, and other specialties that had their genesis all over the Continent. The restaurant's management and many of the staff are the legacy of the late, great *Hotel Aviz,* once the Waldorf of Lisbon. Information: Aviz, Rua Serpa-Pinto 12B, Lisbon, Portugal (phone: 32-83-91).

HORCHER, Madrid, Spain: At this legendary establishment transplanted from prewar Berlin, game and fish are the specialties, but the ever-changing menu usually glitters with fanciful creations like asparagus mousse Cantabrica, pineapple lobster Titus, and crêpes Sir Holten, and no two meals here are ever quite alike. In Madrid, ten in the evening is considered a fine time to start dinner, and the service at *Horcher* is leisurely — so be sure to do enough cocktail-hour snacking beforehand to keep body and soul together. Closed Sundays. Information: Horcher, Alfonso XII 6, Madrid, Spain (phone: 222-0731).

OPERAKÄLLAREN, Stockholm, Sweden: Sunday — the traditional day to eat smorgasbørd — is the best time to visit this large, beautifully designed dining palace facing the sea from inside the Royal Opera House. This is the particular smorgasbørd, piled with seafood from all the waters of the North, that is the pride of Scandinavia. Information: Operakällaren, Box 1616, Stockholm S-11186 (phone: 11-11-25 or 24-27-00).

GIRARDET, Crissier (just northwest of Lausanne), Switzerland: Merely the best restaurant in the world. Alfred Girardet (known as Fredy) is simply one of the greatest culinary geniuses ever to put saucepan to fire, a master whose art is not wasted in pretensions of any sort, which makes a visit to his informal, comfortable restaurant a special joy. Girardet looks a little like a young, blond Orson Welles, and the only thing more attractive than he is his food. Closed Sundays and Mondays, the first 3 weeks of August, and from Christmas until January 10. Information: Girardet, Hôtel de Ville, 1 rue d'Yverdon, Crissier, Switzerland (phone: 34-15-14).

ARAGVI, Moscow, USSR: One of the last oases of even moderate luxury left in the Soviet Union, this bustling Georgian restaurant crowded with commissars, foreign journalists, ballerinas, diplomats, and the like, does a booming business in caviar (*ikra* in Russian) and icy vodka. The best dishes are hot and spicy, like *tsiplyata tabaka,* roast chicken pressed between scalding stones, and *shashlik po kharski,* skewered roast Georgian mutton. Sturgeon roasted on a spit is also excellent. Information: Aragvi, 6 Gorky St., Moscow, USSR.

Shopping Spree: Europe for the Savvy

Shopping and Europe used to go hand in hand. You could buy things in Europe that you couldn't buy at home — or at least at prices far lower than you paid stateside. This is no longer quite so true nowadays, after years of galloping inflation and waltzing currencies. For although the value of the dollar has greatly increased recently, making hotels and restaurants much more afford- able, the prices of European goods have not been as favorably affected. The extraordi- nary bargains of yore can be hard to find, though it is indeed still true that the most famous foreign merchandise — the coveted goods that bear the labels of such posh purveyors as Gucci, Vuitton, Burberry, Lanz, and the like — still costs about half the price it brings in US shops.

Duty-free shops are another institution of which a wise shopper should beware: The only connection we have ever been able to see between *duty* and *airports* is that people feel they have a duty to buy something in them. One thing they certainly are is mostly bargain-free.

Furthermore, goods travel a great deal more than they used to, and a lot of the standard items that people used to stalk on the Champs-Élysées is available on Main Street. By the time you've traipsed, lugged, crammed, and declared, you're better off picking up Twining's tea and other such imports at the corner drugstore.

The moral of the story is this: Shop as part of the *experience* of travel. Buy because it brings you into contact with people and places, customs and creation. Shop for things you couldn't find elsewhere, things that will remind you of those people and places when you are back home. Shop for things of very good quality, things you will use often. Then your purchase becomes like an expensive snapshot, and the pleasure of the experience lingers.

BEST BUYS

What follows is a list of some of the great shopping experiences of Europe — its finest shops, its special products, small museums of commerce that will interest you even if you're not out to buy. We've indexed them not by place but by item on the theory that you may prefer to look for these purchases when you need them. Similar, more specific shopping lists are part of each individual city chapter in THE EUROPEAN CITIES.

Antiques – The *Dorotheergasse* in Vienna; *Sotheby's* and *Christie's* auction houses in London; the giant *Louvre des Antiquaires* on the site of the old Magasins du Louvre in Paris; *Via del Babuino,* Rome.

Birds – *Le Marché aux Oiseaux* — the bird market — held Sundays on place Louis- Lépine, Paris.

Books – The *Dorotheum* auction house, Vienna; *Blackwell's* in Oxford, England; *Foyle's* and a number of other stores on Charing Cross Rd., London; the *Dom Knigi,* 26 Kalinin Prospekt, Moscow.

Buttons – You'll find 10,000 different designs at *La Boutique à Boutons,* 110 rue de Rennes, Paris.

Cameras – *Foto-Radio Wegert,* Kurfürstendamm 26-A and 188, and other branches in West Berlin; the stores of the *Weber* chain in Lucerne (among them *Victoria Ltd.,* Pilatusstrasse and *Weber Bahnhof,* across from the main railroad station).

China – Augarten porcelain at the *Schloss Augarten* in Vienna; *Bing & Grøndahl,* Amagertorv 4, Copenhagen; *Rosenthal,* Kaiser 63, Frankfurt and all over Germany; Delftware from *Focke and Meltzer,* Kalverstraat 176, Amsterdam; *Richard Ginori,* in major Italian cities; *Vista Alegre* porcelain at Largo do Chiado 18, Lisbon.

Coats – *House of Burberry,* 18 Haymarket, London; *Loden-Frey,* Maffeistrasse 7, Munich (for loden coats); *Roland's* on piazza di Spagna, Rome.

Copperware – "Dinanderies," hammered copper, from Dinant, Belgium. Villedieu-les-Poëles, a small farm town in Normandy, is wall-to-wall copper; *poëles* — frying pans — have been made there since the seventeenth century.

Crystal – You'll find Bohemian Moser crystal at *Na Příkopě 12,* Prague; Waterford crystal all over Ireland and at *Ireland House Shop,* 150 New Bond St., London; Val St. Lambert crystal at the *Cristallerie Dena-Select,* 12 Shopping-Centre Bascule, Brussels; Venetian glass at *Pauly,* ponte dei Consorzi, Venice.

Cutlery – *Henckels* at Rossmarkt 11, Frankfurt, Kurfürstendamm 33, Berlin, and in all other major German cities.

Diamonds – *Amsterdam Diamond Center,* Rokin 1-5, Amsterdam.

Eiderdowns – *Fru Lyng,* Akersgaten 47, Oslo.

Embroidery and Needlework – *Madeira Superbia,* Av. Duque de Loulé 75-a, Lisbon (for Madeiran embroidery); *Casa Bonet,* Puig Dorfila 3, Palma de Mallorca, Spain.

Enamelware – *David Andersen,* Karl Johansgate 20, Oslo.

Fabrics – *Athos Maestosi,* Via Cesare Balbo 39-41, Rome.

Food and Liquor – *Fortnum and Mason,* Piccadilly, London; *Fauchon,* place de la Madeleine, Paris; *Alois Dallmayr,* Dienerstrasse 14-15, Munich; *Charlot,* José O. Gasset 8, Madrid; *Gastronom,* Gruzinskaya 62, Moscow (for caviar and vodka).

Furniture and Furnishings – *Illums Bolighus,* Amagertorv 10, Copenhagen.

Furs – *Birger Christensen,* Østergade 38, Copenhagen; *Revillon,* 42 rue La Boétie, Paris; *Balzani,* Via del Corso 475, Rome; *Sistovaris and Sons,* Voulis 14, Athens; *Granlund and Paulsen,* Storgt. 27, Oslo; *GUM* on Red Square or at Profsoyuznaya 16, Moscow. (In Russia, a *shapka,* the characteristic fur hat, is your best purchase.)

Gloves – *Perrone,* 92 Piazza di Spagna, Rome.

Guns – *Holland and Holland,* Bruton St., London.

Hats – *James Lock — The Hatters* (since 1759), 6 St. James's St., London.

Haute Couture – The great Paris houses include *Christian Dior,* 30 ave. Montaigne; *Saint Laurent,* 5 ave. Marceau; *Pierre Cardin,* 27 av. de Marigny; *Courréges,* 40 rue François-I; plus *Givenchy,* at 3 av. George-V, and *Chanel,* 31 rue Cambon. In Rome, there's *Valentino,* Via Gregoriana 24.

Jewelry – *A. E. Köchert,* Neuer Markt 15, Vienna; *Chaumet,* 82 ave. Louise, Brussels (especially for diamonds); *Asprey,* 165 New Bond St., London; *Cartier,* 7 pl. Vendôme and *Van Cleef and Arpels,* 22 pl. Vendôme, both in Paris; the necklace of shops on the Ponte Vecchio in Florence; *Bulgari,* Via Condotti 10, Rome; *Nardi,* Piazza San Marco 69, Venice; *Bonebakker,* Rokin 86-90, Amsterdam; and various stores in Perth, Scotland, for River Tay pearls.

Kitchenware – The premises of *E. Dehillerin,* 18 rue Coquillière, Paris, draws the great French chefs. (No matter where you go, it's always nice to bring home the special utensil used for national dishes — a fondue pot and forks from Switzerland; *paelleleros* from Spain; *escargot* sets from France; and *moka express* from Italy.)

Knitwear – *Westaway and Westaway,* 29 Bloomsbury Way, London; *Albertina,* Via

Lazio 10, Rome; *William Schmidt and Co.,* Karl Johansgate 41, Oslo (for Scandinavian hand-knitted sweaters).

Lace – *Manufacture Belge de Dentelles,* 68 galerie de la Reine (near the Grand Place), Brussels; many stores in the towns of Bruges and Malines; *Jesurum* at Ponte Canonica, Venice; and, for Dalmatian lace, stores on the islands off the coast of Yugoslavia.

Leather Goods – *Hermès,* 24 rue du Faubourg-St.-Honoré, Paris; *Ottino,* Via Cerretani 60, Florence; *Fendi,* Via Borgognona 39, Rome; *Loewe,* on Gran Via 8 or Serrano 26 in Madrid and in other major cities in Spain; and *Gucci,* in Rome, Milan, and Montecatini. Suedes are a good purchase in Yugoslavia: Try *Jugoexport,* Terazije 2 in Belgrade.

Lenses – Contact, telescopic, binocular, or otherwise: *Söhnges,* at Briennerstrasse 7 in Munich, as well as in other German cities.

Linen – *Brown Thomas Department Store,* 15 Grafton St., Dublin.

Menswear – For something solid and English, try *Simpson's,* 203 Piccadilly, London. *Brioni* at via Barberini 79 and *Carlo Palazzi* at via Borgognona 7, both in Rome, sell typically Italian garments — at the former are more classic, at the latter are flashier. Style at its highest: *Giorgio Armani,* 102 via del Babuino, Rome.

Music – *J. Votruba,* 1070 Lerchenfelder Gurtel 4, or *Doblinger,* Dorotheergasse 10, both in Vienna; *Ricordi,* Via Montenapoleone 2, Milan. You'll find Russian records at *Melodye,* 40 Kalinin Prospekt, Moscow — but the sound quality is disappointing. Or get a harmonica from Trossingen, Germany; or a violin from Mittenwald, Germany, or Cremona, Italy — where it all began.

Paintings Works by contemporary artists will be found in Paris, at galleries along rue du Faubourg-St.-Honoré, avenue Matignon, rue La Boétie (on the Right Bank), and scattered throughout the area around the rue de Seine, rue Bonaparte, and rue des Beaux-Arts (on the Left Bank). Berlin, as vital an art center nowadays as Paris, is liveliest on and around the Kurfürstendamm; a complete directory of galleries isavailablefrom*Arbeitsgemeinschaft Berliner Kunstamtsleiter,* Leibnitzstrasse 56, Berlin, Germany (phone: 882-7020). In Rome do your browsing along the via Margutta. *Kreisler,* at Serrano 19, and *Kreisler Dos,* Hermosilla 8, are your best bets in Madrid. The Royal Society of Portrait Painters (17 Carlton House Terrace, London, England; phone: 930-6844) will help you choose an artist to execute your family's portrait.

Perfumes – *Floris,* 89 Jermyn St., and *Penhaligon's,* 41 Wellington St. (both in London); *Galéries Lafayette,* in Paris; and throughout the town of Grasse in the south of France, where you can sometimes visit the great perfume factories.

Pewter – Throughout the town of Huy, Belgium; *The Pewter Shop,* 18 Burlington Arcade, London; Nurnberg, Germany; and *N. M. Thune,* Ø. Slottsgate 12, Oslo.

Pharmaceuticals – The *Boots* chain all over England and *Savory and Moore,* 13 Curzon St. in London; the *Pharmacie Principale,* 11 rue du Marché, Geneva.

Prints – In London: *Colnaghi,* 14 Old Bond St.; *Craddock and Barnard,* 32 Museum St.; *Weinreb and Douwma,* 93 Great Russell St. (fine maps as well). In Paris: the *Calcographie* department of the Louvre.

Riding Equipment – *Der Reiter,* Heinestrasse, 43, Vienna.

Rugs – For *flokati* rugs in Athens: *Greco-Floc* at Adrianou 9 and *Karamichos* at Mitropoleos 3. For Orientals, *Alexander Juran,* at 74 New Bond St. in London, and *Luciano Coen,* Via Margutta 65 in Rome. Also, the island of Sardinia in Italy and in the souks of Istanbul — if you want to take your chances.

Shoes – Still in Italy, and still *Ferragamo,* Via Condotti 66 and 74, Rome. Bring gold. *Gucci* has branches in Rome, Milan, and Montecatini.

Silver – *Georg Jensen,* at Østergade 40, and *Hans Hansen* at Amagertorv 16, in Copenhagen; *The Silver Vaults,* Chancery La., London; *Armaos,* at Akadimias 22, and

Argiriou Bros., at Kiffissias 103, in Athens; *Kurt Decker,* at Biblioteksgatan 12, Stockholm.

Ski Equipment – All along the Maria-Theresienstrasse in Innsbruck; and *Steen and Strøm,* Kongensgate 23, Oslo.

Sporting Goods – *Lillywhite's,* Piccadilly Circus, London.

Stamps – In London at the stamp auctions held by *Christie's;* in Paris at the outdoor stamp market at the corner of avenues Gabriel and Marigny (on Thursdays, Saturdays, and Sundays), or at the shops along the rue Drouot; in Madrid on the Plaza Mayor, every Sunday from 10 AM to 2 PM, or the shops on Calle Felipe III; in Moscow at Dzerzhinsky 16; and at the *Ufficio Filatelico* of the Republic of San Marino.

Sweets – *Fortnum and Mason,* Piccadilly, London; *Au Duc de Praslin,* 33 rue Vivienne, Paris; the *Confiserie Sprüngli,* Bahnhofstrasse 21, Zürich.

Tea – *King's Teagarden,* Kurfurstendamm 217, Berlin, has 170 different varieties to either take home or drink on the spot.

Tobacco – *Dunhill,* 30 Duke St., London. Cigar specialists: *James J. Fox,* 2 Burlington Gardens, London; *Davidoff,* 2 rue de Rive, Geneva.

Toys – The *Christkindlmarkt* on the Rathausplatz, at Christmastime, and *Mühlhauser,* 28 Kärtnerstrasse, in Vienna; *Hamley's,* 200 Regent St., London; *Puppen König,* Gangolfstrasse 8, Bonn; the city of Nürnberg in Germany (electric trains, Christmas tree ornaments, Steiff animals); port towns like Bremen and Lübeck (for ships in bottles); *Dom Igrushki,* Kutuzovsky Prospekt 8, Moscow (for the nesting wooden dolls, *matrioshkas*).

Tweeds – *Irish Cottage Industries,* 44 Dawson St., Dublin; and *Magee* in Donegal.

Umbrellas – And canes, handles, pommels: *Madeleine Gély,* 218 blvd. St.-Germain, Paris.

Watches – *Bucherer,* Schwanenplatz 5, in Lucerne, but also sold all over Switzerland. (And don't look for any bargains in Swiss watches: The several million handsome phonies ground out every year in Singapore and Taiwan are the only cheapies along the streets of Geneva.) Excellent Russian Slava watches are available at the factory in Moscow. And if you're interested in knowing a little bit more than the time, don't miss Vienna's great *Uhrenmuseum* (translation: the "clock museum").

Wine – The wine auctions at *Sotheby's* and *Christie's* in London; *Fauchon* at place de la Madeleine in Paris; *Weinhaus Schulmeister,* Langestrasse 9, Baden-Baden, Germany; *Buccone,* Via Ripetta 19, Rome; the *Madeira Wine Association* on Av. Arriaga in Funchal, and the wine lodges in Vila Nova de Gaia, across the river from Oporto, Portugal.

Wood Carvings – All through the Tyrol district of Austria; in the town of Spa, Belgium; and in the town of Oberammergau, Germany.

HANDICRAFTS

Some countries now have exposition centers to exhibit their handicrafts; often, the goods must be approved by a design board. For the best in Europe:

Den Permanente, Vesterbrogade, 8 Copenhagen.

The Finnish Design Center, Kasarmikatu 19, Helsinki.

Gobelins looms, 42 av. des Gobelins, Paris (open Tuesdays, Wednesdays, and Thursdays, 2 to 4 PM).

National Organization of Hellenic Handicrafts, Mitropoleos 3, or Xenias and Evron St., Athens.

Forum, Rosenkrantzgate 7, Oslo; *Husfliden,* Møllergate, 4, Oslo, and Vågsalmenning, 3, Bergen.

Highland Home Industries, 53 George St., Edinburgh.
Artespaña (Empresa Nacional de Artisania), Hermosilla 14, Plaza de las Cortés 3, or Gran Via 32, Madrid.
Svensk Hemslöjd, Sveavägen 44, Stockholm.
Schweizer Heimatwerk, Rudolf Brun-Brücke, Zürich.
Craftcentre Cymru, in towns throughout Wales.
Narodna Radinost, throughout Yugoslavia.

DEPARTMENT STORES

Europe's greatest and grandest:

Harrods and *Selfridges,* London
Stockmann, Helsinki
Au Printemps, Paris
Galeries Lafayette, Paris
Kaufhaus des Westens, West Berlin
Brown Thomas, Dublin
Switzer, Dublin
GUM, Moscow
NK, Stockholm
El Corte Inglés, Madrid
De Bijenkorf, Amsterdam

SHOPPING STREETS

They vary in size and style — but are all worth a stroll. Take your shopping bag.

The Kärtnerstrasse and Graben, Vienna
Strøget, Copenhagen
Bond Street, London
Rue du Faubourg-St.-Honoré, Paris
The Kurfürstendamm, Berlin
The Ponte Vecchio and via Tornabuoni, Florence
Via Condotti, Rome
The Rialto Bridge markets, Venice
The Flower Market along Singel Canal, Amsterdam
The Marktgasse, Bern
The Nevsky Prospekt, Leningrad

FLEA MARKETS

A country's junk is its life. And its past. And as a result, the myriad flea markets that you find scattered across the Continent are intensely direct experiences of the culture. Some do a thriving trade in semifine antiques; others offer everything from torn inner tubes to inner tubes that are only punctured. Bargain like a Bedouin whether you're in Sicily or Switzerland. Go when it's raining, hang around until closing time, and you'll pay almost fair prices. Here are a few of the liveliest:

The Flohmarkt, Vienna – Open Saturday mornings, Naschmarkt in the Sixth District, Vienna.
Marché des Antiquités et du Livre, Brussels – The antique and book market, as

this market on the place du Grand Sablon is called. Open all day Saturdays and Sunday mornings.

Marché de la Brocante, Brussels – At place du Jeu de Balle. Open every morning; busiest on Sundays.

Israels Plads, Copenhagen – Open Saturdays from 8 AM to 2 PM, May through September.

Camden Lock, London – Open Saturdays and Sundays. Near Chalk Farm.

Camden Passage, London – Open Mondays through Saturdays, with open-air market on Wednesdays, Thursdays, and Saturdays all day. Islington.

New Caledonian, London – Open Fridays from 7 AM to noon. Bermondsey Sq. and Tower Bridge Rd.

Petticoat Lane, London – Open Sunday mornings until 2 PM. Middlesex St.

Portobello Road, London – Open Mondays through Saturdays (the best day); mornings only on Thursday. Located near Westbourne Park.

Place de la Banque, Dijon – No town in France is without its *marché aux puces* (literally, "flea market"), and Dijon is no exception. This one is open on Tuesday and Friday mornings.

Villeurbanne, Lyon – Open all day Thursdays and Saturdays, Sunday mornings, and all day the first Sunday of every month, at Chemin de la Feyssine. Also, *Brocante Stalingrad* is open Thursdays and Saturdays all day and Sunday mornings; 115 blvd. Stalingrad, Villeurbanne.

Boulevard Risso, Nice – Every day except Sundays from 8 AM to 5 PM.

Brocante de la Porte de Montreuil, Paris – Open all weekend and Mondays; Saturday morning is best. This and the next market on the list are Paris's more rough-and-tumble *marchés*.

Brocante de la Porte de Vanves, Paris – Open Saturdays and Sundays all day. Porte de Vanves.

Le Marché aux Puces, Paris – Spread out over a vast area at the porte de Clignancourt, this market is open all day on Saturdays and Sundays, as well as on Mondays (which is the best time).

The Flohmarkt, West Berlin – Located in an abandoned subway station at Nollendorfplatz, with the stalls set up in old railway cars. A mandatory beer stop is the famous *Zur Nolle* tavern. Open from 11 AM to 7:30 PM every day except Tuesday.

The Auer Dult, Munich – Held thrice annually in April or May, July or August, and October, for a full week each time on the Mariahilfplatz.

Monastiraki, Athens – Open all day every day, with a special open-air bazaar — *Youssouroum* — on Sunday mornings. Althinas St. and Monastiraki Sq.

Via Pietrapiana, Florence – Open every day during shopping hours.

Piazza Grande, Arezzo – On the first Saturday and Sunday of every month.

Porta Portese, Rome – Off viale Trastevere on Sunday mornings. Surrounded by old car parts and mounds of Calabrian country furniture, Russian refugees hawk chess sets and balalaikas.

Valkenburgerstraat, Amsterdam – Just off Waterlooplein and open daily, except Sundays, from 10 AM to 4 PM. Also the colorful secondhand book market, *Oudemanhuispoort,* in the arcade at the entrance to the university; open Mondays through Saturdays, 10 AM to 4 PM. There's also a flea market every Thursday during the summer in the Hague.

Feira da Ladra, Lisbon – This Thieves' Market is held Tuesdays and Saturdays, near the Church of St. Vincent.

Los Encantes, Barcelona – Open Monday, Wednesday, Friday, and Saturday mornings. Near the plaza de las Glorias. Also try the Thursday all-day antique market in Plaza de la Catedral.

El Rastro, Madrid – Held on Sunday mornings from 10 AM to 2 PM (but some sections are open mornings all week long). At Plaza Cascorro and Ribera de Curtidores. There's also a stamp market from 10 AM to 2 PM on Sundays at the plaza Mayor.

Marché aux Puces, Geneva – Held on Wednesday and Saturday, on the Rondpoint de Plainpalais from 8:30 AM to 4:30 PM.

Flohmarkt, Zürich – Every Saturday from May to October, 7 AM to 4 PM on the Bürkliplatz. (Also try the *Rosenhof market* in the Niederdorf, open all day Thursdays and Saturdays from May to October.)

Auctions in Europe:
Going, Going, Gone

The auction world has always been something of a private club, where dealers stocked up in order to mark up and amateurs dared not tread. But during the inflation-ridden 1970s, the art market caught the public eye, and auction action became livelier than ever before. (At *Phillips* — London's number three firm — the year-end sales have increased fivefold in a decade.) Many dealers are now so sure of attracting consistently buy-happy crowds that they are also *selling* through the salerooms. So it goes without saying that the days when you could pick up an unnoticed Rembrandt for a song are long gone.

Nonetheless, there are still plenty of reasons to go to auctions: Aside from the fact that auction salerooms are among the best places in the world to learn about art, they are also great theater — high drama at low cost. The bidding has a seductive rhythm, and the tension has a way of catching you up even if you're not faintly interested in the lot on the block. The auctioneer — now more often a sedate gentleman in a business suit than the sort of fast-talking spieler who (as the American satirist Ambrose Bierce once noted) "proclaims with a hammer that he has picked a pocket with his tongue" — becomes a pied piper, with the bidders winking, blinking, and nodding in time to his music. As any addict will tell you, an auction is stock market, gambling casino, and living theater all rolled into one — the perfect answer to rainy day blues, more fun than watching the ticker tape, less decadent than an afternoon movie.

And though you can no longer expect to make a killing at an auction, there are good values to be found. Sales held when the weather is unspeakably foul may keep down the crowds — and the prices. Similarly, there are sometimes a few bargains at the beginning of a sale, before the bulk of the potential buyers have arrived and before the bidders have warmed up. In addition, prices can be low at the smaller London firms in August, when, because the big houses are closed for holiday, many dealers are on vacation. And in any event, you can usually buy an item on the block for about 30% off its price in a store — providing you know how to go about it.

Seasoned auctiongoers follow some important rules, the most important of which is to visit the exhibition of merchandise that takes place 2, 3, 4 days or more before the sale. ("If you can't be at the sale, you can leave a commission bid with the auctioneer, or even place an order by telephone — but if you can't be at the exhibition, you have no business buying," noted one aficionado.) Only there will you have the chance to examine the lots at close range, to inspect them for nicks, cracks, and other flaws that can affect their value and for signs that what you're paying for is what you're getting. Caveat emptor is the order of the day, and disclaimers are made by the score by nearly every auction house in the business. (A recent *Christie's* catalog warned: "Each lot is sold by the Seller thereof, and with all faults and defects therein and with all errors of description, and is to be taken and paid for whether genuine and authentic or not, and no compensation shall be paid for same.") Consequently, it behooves you to make a pest of yourself: Have paintings moved so that you can look at them close up, and objects under lock and key removed from their cases. If you anticipate buying furniture, you'll have to know the dimensions of the empty spaces you intend to fill; take a measuring tape to the exhibition. If you're contemplating a large purchase, get an expert to accompany you.

Reputable houses, of course, make every effort to help their customers avoid mistakes, and publish lists of prices they estimate the lots will fetch — and, often, whole illustrated catalogs, full of carefully worded descriptions that can give you a great deal of information about the house's opinion of a lot's age and authenticity. (Here, too, there are disclaimers — that, for instance, the "origin, date, age, attribution, genuineness, provenance, or condition of any lot is a statement of opinion, and is not to be relied upon as a statement or representation of fact." But catalog descriptions are usually accurate and in some cases are regulated by law.)

An elaborate lexicography prevails, and the catalog can tell you that a phrase like "style of the eighteenth dynasty" in a sale of Egyptian statues denotes a fake, whereas a simple "eighteenth dynasty" identifies the real McCoy. "Signed" means that the house believes that the signature on a painting is the artist's own, while "bears signature" indicates only the possibility. "Dated" means that the lot bears a date and that the date may be accurate. Even the typography of the catalog can help you out. Descriptions that commence with capital letters refer to items that the house considers particularly valuable — but not so valuable as items allotted a whole page. Names of previous owners are also a clue to an item's value: Having belonged to a well-known collector is, for instance, a very fine pedigree indeed.

Once you've digested the catalog and looked over the goods, you're ready for the auction. Based on your inspection, decide on your top bid (remembering to figure in the house's commission, up to 20%, and Value Added Tax where applicable) and don't allow yourself to be pushed beyond it. (It *can* happen, and often does, that in the excitement of the fray, people bid far out of their price range: Witness the poor Viennese student who, entranced by the bidding, kept raising his hand until he'd bought a Holbein; or the Swiss banker who attended the sale of his jade collection and ended up repurchasing every item from himself.) You will not, however, be held to a bid you regret if you call out promptly "withdrawn" in the appropriate language.

For all of its other troubles, London is still the world's auction capital, and the "market price" of a work of art or antique generally refers to what it (and others of its genre) have fetched in the London salerooms. Everyone knows about *Sotheby's* and *Christie's*, both over 200 years old and not far behind the Changing of the Guard and the red double-deckers as visitor attractions and symbols of the city. But fingers are rising and hammers are falling all over Europe. Here's a selection of the famous houses.

THE DOROTHEUM, Vienna: Founded by the Emperor Joseph I in 1707 as a pawnshop for the poor, the *Dorotheum* was already middle aged when *Sotheby's* and *Christie's* were born, and it's been in the Dorotheergasse, the center of Vienna's antique district, since 1785. You should see it as a sort of national monument, even if you're not in the market. Besides the repertory of art and antique auctions that are standard fare at all European auction houses, the *Dorotheum* stages eight major coin auctions a year and, after ignoring the twentieth century for years, is rapidly expanding its modern art department. Branches of the *Dorotheum* can now be found in seven other Austrian cities. For details: Dorotheum, Dorotheergasse 17, Vienna 1, Austria (phone: 528-5650).

GALERIE MODERNE, Brussels: This is the aristocrat among the many galleries in this city at the heart of the global art market. You'll find Oriental rugs by the kilometer, small pieces of sculpture, and ornate eighteenth-century furniture — all of consistently high quality. *Galerie Moderne* has three salerooms; the headquarters is at 3 rue du Parnasse, Brussels, Belgium (phone: 513-9010). Another Brussels auction house to inspect is *Nova,* with sales of jewelry, stamps, silver, and pianos, 35 rue du Pepin, Brussels, Belgium (phone: 512-2494).

KØBENHAVENS AUKTIONER, Copenhagen: Spread out over approximately 7,000 square yards, this amalgamation of three old-city firms runs 200 sales a year of everything from heavy-duty machinery and motorboats to paintings and samovars. Items are displayed in the settings in which they'll end up: Machine tools in simulated workshops, Old Masters in elegantly furnished salons. Not on the regular circuit of Continental dealers, Københavens Auktioner attracts just a small number of foreign buyers. Information: Københavens Auktioner, Aebelogade 4, 2100 Copenhagen, Denmark (phone: 29-90-00).

ARNE BRUUN RASMUSSEN, Copenhagen: This is strictly a fine arts house, with a large trade in Scandinavian valuables, antique Danish silver and bronze, rare books, rugs, fine wines, and a number of the sort of Russian items that tend to surface in all the Scandinavian salerooms. Ten-day sales take place every 2 months, generally by category. Information: Arne Bruun Rasmussen, Bredgade 33, DK-1260 Copenhagen, Denmark (phone: 13-69-11).

CHRISTIE'S, London: *Christie's* was founded in 1766, so that today an object's whole lineage can often be traced through the records of its appearances in *Christie's* sales; the motherhouse on King Street is a national landmark. Sales take place daily, and the exhibition rooms are a constantly changing museum. There are also branches in a dozen countries. The South Kensington saleroom handles items of recent vintage and generally lower value, such as toys, telescopes, and top hats. In Geneva, sales are generally at the *Hôtel Richemond;* the major emphasis is on more valuable silver, jewelry, clocks. In Rome, not a few sale items come from the hoards of Count X and Princess Y, and there's an air of studied elegance about the salerooms in the glamorous Palazzo Lancellotti on piazza Navona. For information: contact Christie's at 8 King St., St. James's, London SW1Y 6QT, England (phone: 839-9060); at 85 Old Brompton Rd., South Kensington, London SW7 3JS, England (phone: 581-2231); at 8 pl. de la Taconnerie, CH-1204 Geneva, Switzerland (phone: 28-25-44); or at piazza Navona 114, 00186 Rome, Italy (phone: 654-1217).

SOTHEBY PARKE BERNET, London: When the city's oldest auctioneer, *Sotheby's* merged with another royal auction house, New York's *Parke-Bernet,* in 1972, a sort of multinational corporation of art was born. Although you'll find Sotheby sales in many countries, their little white building on Bond Street is a kind of art world nerve center, with a roster of experts in every field that rivals that of the British Museum; an important sale of Old Masters, with hundreds of thousands of dollars riding on every twitch, beats an evening at the National Theatre. But they also do a thriving trade in lower-priced objects, Victoriana, and collectibles of every sort, from illustrated biscuit tins to yacht fittings. Branch salerooms in London, across Britain, and on the Continent ensure that the sun never sets on a Sotheby auction. Information: Sotheby Parke Bernet, 34–35 New Bond St., London W1A 2AA, England (phone: 493-8080).

PHILLIPS, London: Currently number three and trying harder and harder, it is the only one of the top London houses to maintain a full program of sales in the summer months, while its rivals are on holiday. It operates an extensive program of estate sales, often sparsely attended by the general public, so there's a good chance you'll find dealer-level prices. *Phillips* does a large volume in modestly priced lots; its employees are extremely helpful to auction novices. Information: Phillips, 7 Blenheim St., London W1Y 0AS, England (phone: 629-6602).

HÔTEL DROUOT, Paris: This venerable establishment now occupies startling steel and glass quarters on the Right Bank street that was named for it and has 16 salerooms on three levels and parking space for 400 cars. Some 60 *commissaires-priseurs* (government-authorized auctioneers) form a kind of cooperative that handles the 600,000-odd lots that are sold here each year. In addition to the whole range of art objects, you can buy third-hand TV sets, bottles of Château d'Yquem, and even an occasional horse. French auctioneers offer a unique, legal, 30-year guarantee on the authenticity of all purchases. Their Sunday sales are becoming a Parisian institution. For information: Hôtel Drouot, 9 rue Drouot, 75009 Paris, France (phone: 246-1711).

KARL UND FABER, Munich: Once auctioneers of antiquarian books and prints, *Karl und Faber* deals extensively in prints and drawings by the Old Masters, modern paintings and graphics, and top-class nineteenth-century art. There are two principal sale periods annually, in June and November. This is a good place to start a collection of Dürer or Rembrandt etchings. Information: Karl und Faber, Amiraplatz 3, 8000 Munich 2, Germany (phone: 22-18-65).

NEUMEISTER, Munich: This house's sales, which take place about once every 6 weeks, offer particularly good buys in faïence (a special kind of crockery) and silver, German furniture, and nineteenth-century paintings. The catalogs are excellent and detailed and the subscription service efficient enough that you can prepare for the sales well in advance. Information: Neumeister Münchner Kunstauktionshaus, Bärerstrasse 37, 8000 Munich 40 (phone: 28-30-11).

KUNSTHAUS LEMPERTZ, Cologne: This fourth-generation family business, founded in 1845 and situated in one of Germany's richest cities, specializes in Chinese, Japanese, and Southeast Asian art and also offers medieval work, sculpture, paintings by the Old Masters, and even twentieth-century applied arts. New York's Metropolitan Museum is a customer at its sales (three in the spring and three in the fall). *Lempertz* maintains a stateside representative, Mr. Ernest Werner, 17 E 96th St., New York, NY 10028 (212-289-5666), to handle relations with its steady US customers. Information: Kunsthaus Lempertz, 1 Neumarkt 3 D-5000, Cologne 1, Germany (phone: 21-02-51).

L'ANTONINA, Rome: The auctions at this house on piazza di Spagna are also cocktail-hour social events, presided over by superbly suited auctioneers and patronized by suntanned women in fancy jeans and simple mink. When you go, you'll find some good buys (primarily in Italian furniture and religious art) — and plenty of overpriced junk. The saleroom is small; arrive early or you'll be listening from the corridor. *L'Antonina* also occasionally auctions the contents of an entire villa, on location. The crowd is smaller, more professional — and the trip to the old estates can be a picturesque excursion into Italy's patrician past. Information: L'Antonina, Piazza di Spagna, 93 Rome, Italy (phone: 679-4009).

DURAN SUBASTAS DE ARTE, Madrid: Not really in the European big league — but then, Spanish art has a way of staying in Spain. You'll find attractively priced silver and porcelain items, a lot of ivory, and much early Spanish furniture that goes for considerably less than comparable Italian pieces — plus some of the world's most hideous paintings. Information: Duran Subastas de Arte, Serrano 12, Madrid, Spain (phone: 401-3400 or 276-3000).

BUKOWSKI, Stockholm: Over 100 years old and highly respected in the trade, Scandinavia's foremost saleroom stages nine sales annually — in spring and autumn for Old Master Art and Antiquities and in December for modern works. They also run two annual sales in Helsinki, spring and autumn. Third-rate French and Italian canvases are often knocked down at vastly inflated figures. But you'll also encounter a good selection of Scandinavian paintings, which rarely drift south of the Baltic Sea — a refreshing change of scenery to auction eyes trained in London, Paris, or Rome. Information: Bukowski, Wahrendorffsgaten 8, 11147 Stockholm, Sweden (phone: 24-81-65); or Bukowski, Forchstrasse 239, CH-8029 Zürich, Switzerland (phone: 55-22-70).

PETER INEICHEN, Zürich: The *Ineichen* salerooms, a Swiss national institution, are a carnival of antique watches and clocks, automatons, weapons, cameras, toys, and various and sundry other things Swiss: miniature Prussian cavalry officers, jeweled poignards, bioscopes, daguerreotypes, nickelodeons, and once, a ballerina clock that chimed the hour by cuckooing *Swan Lake*. Record price for a pocket watch: 650,000 Swiss francs; for a clock: 700,000. That's just in case you're cleaning out your closets. Information: Peter Ineichen, C. F. Meyer-Strasse 14, CH-8002 Zürich, Switzerland (phone: 201-3017).

GALERIE KOLLER, Zürich: As efficient, ethical, and expensive as Switzerland itself, *Koller* stages two 2-week-long series of auctions annually, one in fall and one in spring, plus a small sale on the first Tuesday of every month. Jewelry — an immense assortment of it — is a consistent highlight. As a sideline, *Koller* also maintains the twelfth-century Château de Lucens, a vast living gallery in Lucens, with all furnishings for sale. Commissions charged to both buyer and seller are a hefty 18%. Information: Galerie Koller, Rämistrasse 8, CH-8024 Zürich, Switzerland (phone: 47-50-40).

Spas: Europe's Unique Watering Spots

Long before travelers even dreamed of the pleasures of sea bathing and sun-tanning, spas like *Vichy* and *Badgastein,* blessed with mineral-rich waters thought to have healing powers, were important stops on the Grand Tour — every bit as important as Paris and Rome. Consequently, they all developed such a wide range of facilities over the years — fine hotels, golf courses and tennis courts, racetracks and bridle paths, gambling casinos, and elegant shops — that you can have a splendid spa vacation without taking so much as a sip of the waters that were their original raison d'être.

On the other hand, taking a cure — a favorite pastime of so many historic and fictional folk — is still a possibility, and you'll find baths of every tint and temperature, power showers, steam rooms and saunas, whirlpools and sprays, masseuses, mud tubs, paraffin packs, salt and honey rubs, infrared and ultraviolet treatments, facilities for vapor inhalations and gymnastics. And fountains — so that you *can* drink the water. Every resort has its specialty: Some specialize in water cures. (Some waters are good for arthritis, some for ailments of the liver.) Thalassotherapy — practiced at St.-Malo, Pornichet, Quiberon, and Tréboul-Douarnenez, all in Brittany — is a kind of marine approach to thermalism that emphasizes the benefits of salt water and sea air. (Grilled shrimp and oysters on the half shell are the extra added attractions.) Gerovital, a procaine derivative developed by a Romanian doctor named Ana Aslan and used in therapy centers like Constanta, Eforie, Mamaia, and Mangalia along the Romanian Black Sea coast, is claimed to retard the aging process dramatically. True or not, many health insurance plans will cover the cost of a doctor-prescribed spa visit. While there is good deal of controversy about the real medical value of taking the waters, a visit to a spa is usually at least rejuvenating. All the national tourist offices of countries that boast major spas also maintain detailed lists of their countries' facilities, indexed by the ailments that the waters are thought to cure. You can make your arrangements à la carte, or, through your hotel, you can buy a package that will allow you access to most spa facilities throughout your stay. You will, however, generally be required to have a checkup by a local doctor before being submerged, steamed, and pummeled.

Here's a selection of spots at which to sample the spa experience. The tourist offices in all these towns are active and informed, and a note to them should produce ample material on hotels and facilities.

BADGASTEIN, Austria: High in the Alps, some 50 miles from Salzburg, this fine old spa was visited by Holy Roman Emperor Frederick III as early as the fifteenth century and eventually became known as the Spa of Kings. All the patrician elegance of the days of royalty is still very much in evidence, but there are all the facilities of this era as well: three swimming pools, tennis courts, golf courses, pathways for solitary rambles through the lush Alpine countryside. And sooner or later, everyone in *Badgastein* takes the flatcar rail ride through the galleries of the old Bockstein gold mine.

SPA, Belgium: Like a cathedral, the great bathhouse dominates the main square of this town, which lent its name to all of the world's watering spots, and the healthful waters of its mineral springs flow freely from fountains at every turn. The city of Liège is less than an hour away, and the road that takes you there leads past dozens of stately country mansions and lovely forests ribboned with scores of well-marked trails. You can go horseback riding in the woods, or swimming in the tranquil lake. Every August 15, there's the colorful, traditional Battle of Flowers. Long a favorite with the English, *Spa* retains a pleasant Anglo-Saxon air.

MARIENBAD, Czechoslovakia: *Marianské Lazné,* as this spa is called today, and *Carlsbad* (now *Karlovy Vary*) are the Eastern European spa-dom's two centers, and the grandiose Esplanade, the pastel facades, the palms, and the crystal are all from another, more gracious period that is somehow at odds with the communized monotony of postwar Bohemia. There are beautiful tours in the nearby hills, and you can visit Prince Metternich's superb castle — though you'll have to go to Schloss Nymphenberg near Munich if you want to see where *Last Year at Marienbad* was really filmed. Bookings in Czechoslovakia are necessary well in advance since hotel facilities are limited. The most practical approach is to sign up for one of the comprehensive tours that includes air fare, full room and board, and access to all health facilities, and which can be arranged through Čedok, 10 E 40th St., New York, NY 10016 (212-689-9720). Prices are extremely reasonable when compared to those at other major European spas.

ÉVIAN-LES-BAINS, France: On the south shore of Lac Leman, *Évian* attracts a large number of visitors from nearby Geneva — at least in part for the gambling in its busy casino. But there are also boat excursions and water sports of every sort on the great lake, and the high Alps and Italy are but an easy afternoon away. Like that of its thermal cousin, *Vichy, Evian's* mineral water has been exported around the world, spreading the fame of the spa. Convalescent vacationers guarantee return trips by gorging on *pâté de foie, fondue savoyarde,* and *mousse au chocolat;* most of the dieting is done between meals. Try to stay at the *Royal,* one of France's most luxurious hotels.

BADEN-BADEN, Germany: Since the Romans discovered the springs, which are so hot they are used in the town's central heating systems, this town, equidistant from Stuttgart and Frankfurt, has become so international that it's often called the "summer Paris." And it's still dotted with Russian chapels and villas from the high-living czarist days. The superbly tended Lichtentaler Allée (walkway) is one of the Continent's loveliest strolling places, and the glittering casino is an ancestor of Monte Carlo's. At cocktail hour in the high season, everyone who is anyone — and everyone *is* — gathers in the great frescoed *Trinkhalle* for a glass of warm water.

MONTECATINI, Italy: In the heart of Tuscany, *Montecatini* has a grandeur that makes it look more like a relic of the last days of the Roman Empire than a modern health resort. Its eight separate mineral springs feed into a cluster of buildings amid a vast area of parks and gardens, full of imperial-sized pools, graceful colonnades and portals, and marble statuary and high domes. The *Grand Hotel e La Pace* is a venerable hostelry on the same regal scale as the town. Montecatini is also an art center, with a colony of active galleries and antique shops; in summer, it plays host to a roster of famous trotting races; and high-fashion boutiques line its prosperous streets. If that's not enough, Florence is only an hour away.

SATURNIA, Italy: This tiny place in the Tuscan hills, between the Aurelia coast road and the via Cassia, near a less tiny place named Manciano (Rte. 74), is not really a spa but a warm thermal waterfall with sitting places smoothed and hollowed out of the rocks by 2,000 years of bathers. You can swim and soak here comfortably even on a crisp day in February, as long as you can make it from the car to the springs.

Wheels of Fortune: Gambling in Europe

 An old Napoleonic edict, still in force, forbids roulette within 100 kilometers (62 mi) of Paris. Consequently, the casino of Forge-les-Eaux is exactly 101 kilometers (about 62.5 mi) from the city. Most other European governments take a similar stance: Gambling is generally not tolerated in cities, where citizens are expected to be hard at work, but is permitted in spas, seaside towns, and other resorts, which are presumed to be frivolous by nature. In London — one exception to the rule — gaming is allowed only in private clubs and only to members of 48 hours' duration.

Restrictions notwithstanding, gambling is booming — and the whole casino scene is changing. Though splendid old dowager queens like Monte Carlo, Deauville, and Baden-Baden have retained their enormous cachet, they are as much national monuments as after-dark hotspots. Elsewhere, dress rules have eased or disappeared. Glossy new casinos are multiplying like rabbits, and slot machines, craps, and junkets are being imported from America.

Casinos are almost but not quite like those in the US, and there are some things to remember:

When you go, be on the safe side, and — despite the new populism — dress with decorum or you may be turned away at the door (albeit with exquisite courtesy).

Take your passport. Most casinos require identification.

Don't be shocked when you're asked to pay an admission fee — it's customary in Europe. The sum may be small and usually includes a few free chips. Or it may be hefty and buy you a whole year's membership in a private club.

Remember that European casinos generally don't open until a discreet midafternoon hour and close at around 3 or 4 AM. Marathon games of Chemin-de-Fer, which can go on around the clock, are the only exceptions. The casinos are, however, open on Sundays and holidays.

If you're new to the games or their foreign terminology, ask at the admission desk for an explanatory booklet. And don't be shy about cross-examining the *chefs de partie* (the floor men). They are there specifically to provide you with every possible assistance in losing your money.

French is still the lingua franca of most Continental roulette wheels. Remember the following: *faites vos jeux* (place your bets); *rien ne va plus* (no more bets); *rouge-noir* (red-black); *pair-impair* (even-odd); *passe-manque* (high-low); *jeton* (chip); *mise* (bet); *en plein* (single number, pays 35 times the *mise*); *à cheval* (two numbers, pays 17 to 1); *transversale* (three numbers, pays 11 to 1); *carré* (four numbers, pays 8 to 1).

With the exception of England, where it's forbidden by law, tipping is usually the croupiers' prime source of income. In roulette, the custom is to leave one of the 35 chips when you hit a number *en plein*. (You will not, however, be expected to tip for smaller wins or for a long period of residence at the table.)

Government regulation of gaming is particularly strict in France and England, less so elsewhere. But avoid semiprivate, semilegal, and uncontrolled clubs, lest you lose your shirt (and bankroll). For most games, the best odds are offered in England — thanks to the British Gaming Board.

Here's where you'll find the best and the brightest of the European casinos:

BADEN-BEI-WIEN, Austria: Vienna is one of the few European capitals that does have a casino. (You'll find it at the *Palais Esterhazy* on the Kärntnerstrasse.) But for the Viennese, who are forbidden to gamble there, a favorite evening's entertainment is the half-hour trip to nearby Baden — which has more space, more atmosphere, and fewer tourists.

LONDON, England: One of the few European capitals to offer gambling, London has a number of fine old clubs. *Crockford's,* one of the most distinguished, occupies a beautiful Georgian mansion in the middle of Mayfair. Once the private reserve of half the aristocracy of England, it now boasts a membership that is overwhelmingly foreign. The membership fee, about £150 annually, gives you access to one other London casino, the *International Sporting Club.* Unless you can arrange to go as the guest of a member, 48 hours must pass between your application for membership and admission to the club. The same goes for admission to London's newest major casino, *The Ritz,* in the basement of the *Ritz Hotel* on Piccadilly. It has an exclusive membership, an elegant atmosphere, and an excellent restaurant. As at many London casinos, there are female croupiers, as deft as they are decorative; they wear burgundy-colored designer gowns and rake in chips and deal blackjack decks with feline grace. Remember, the odds are better for the player in England, and the prohibition on tipping means that you can lose your money more slowly.

CANNES, France: The classiest of the Côte d'Azur casinos and a favorite haunt of vacationing sheiks and oil barons, the *PalmBeach* casino is owned by the great Barrière chain. Its gross receipts always rank among the highest in Europe. Open summer and early fall only.

DEAUVILLE, France: Sometimes known as Paris's 21st Arrondissement, this attractive town on the coast of Normandy has been a playground of European royalty since the nineteenth century, when Napoleon III's half-brother brought horse racing here and put the place on the map. The casino is a great, glittering wedding cake by the sea, sumptuously decorated, and is host to various social and cultural events during the fashionable summer season, which peaks with the August racing weeks. At that time, formal dress is still required in certain rooms. Stay in the beautiful casino-owned *Hôtel Normandy,* stroll the boardwalk, and spend your winnings on lobster at the seaside *Ciro's,* also a casino property.

DIVONNE-LES-BAINS, France: Just outside wealthy, gambling-free Geneva, in a sleepy little border village, this most profitable of French casinos attracts very big players from the foreign business and numbered-account community, and the sums that change hands on a single spin of the wheel in the handsome, hospitable casino could buy beach houses and thoroughbred race horses. Just alongside the gambling tables, there's an excellent restaurant where you can dine until breakfast time.

SEINE-MARITIME, France: Just outside the 100-kilometer roulette-free zone that Napoleon decreed must surround the country's capital, *Forges-Les-Eaux* attracts Parisians who would rather not risk the wheels in that city's various clandestine gaming dives. The casino complex includes the *Grand Hôtel du Parc,* a delightful place to stay if you're dreading the predawn drive back to Paris.

BADEN-BADEN, Germany: The biggest, oldest, richest, and most beautiful casino in Germany, it has been around for over 200 years. Its rooms are stunning and there is outdoor roulette on a vine-covered patio in summer; the casino also boasts a famous double-wheel table where the betting, at the height of the season, is with real gold chips.

The town is one of Europe's most fashionable spas as well, and the casino is the site of countless business congresses and chamber music concerts. Every Friday morning, two master croupiers provide basic instruction in the casino games. Free admission.

BAD HOMBURG, Germany: A short distance northwest of Frankfurt, this casino occupies a special place in European gaming history: An early venture of the celebrated brothers Blanc, who went on to Monte Carlo 20 years later, it was the setting of that famous novelette of compulsive gambling, *The Gambler,* whose author, the great Russian master Feodor Dostoyevsky, managed to run through a nonfictional fortune of his own.

ATHENS, Greece: Fifteen miles (24 km) north of the city atop Pamitha Mountain, the *Mont Parnes* casino can justly claim a location more spectacular than any other on the Continent. There's also fine Greek food, a nightclub, and, for those who don't feel like making the return trip to Athens, a hotel. Its more convenient to go by car, but public transportation is available from Syntagma. Some hotels provide a private minibus link.

CAMPIONE D'ITALIA, Italy: The casino (whose name translates to "sample of Italy") is a delightful 20-minute boat ride across the lake from Lugano in Switzerland. The ferries operate at frequent intervals both day and night — to assure the Swiss of plenty of opportunity to sin on someone else's soil. Otherwise the crowd is largely Italian.

VENICE, Italy: In the summer, the *Municipal Casino* is quartered out at the Lido, by the beach. But connoisseurs prefer its winter setting on the Grand Canal, in the majestic *Palazzo Vendramin-Calergi,* where the composer Wagner died. At night in the off-season, the streets of Venice can be quiet and bleak, but the *Palazzo* is always warm, gracious, and animated. There are several first-class restaurants and a nightclub.

MONTE CARLO, Monaco: The queen of European casino cities now has three separate gaming establishments: the beautiful old *Palais* on the town's main square, with its fabulous, ornate decor and its sea-view picture windows; the *Monte Carlo Sporting Club,* set on a spectacular man-made promontory by the shore; and the Nevada-style *Loews* in the lobby of the flashy new *Loews Hotel* — a joint undertaking between the American hotel company and the staid old Société des Bains de Mer, owner of most of Monaco. During the winter, the high rollers crowd the old *salons privés* of the main casino, and in the summer the Rolls and yacht crowd moves down to the *Sporting* complex. Try dining at its park-view Polynesian restaurant. The *Loews,* which offers free admission, teems with American junketeers, and the steady din from the neon-lit slots and crap tables is miles away from the hushed elegance of the *salons privés.* Make the rounds of all three for a total picture of the European gambling scene today.

SCHEVENINGEN, The Netherlands: Holland's most attractive casino is in the gigantic old *Kurhaus,* a nationally protected monument.

ESTORIL, Portugal: This is certainly the gaudiest, flashiest, shiniest casino in Europe. There is a big, slick floor show on double revolving stages and a marvelous seafood restaurant; the clientele is so well groomed and glittering that you can't help but wonder what they all do from 9 to 5. Probably nothing.

PONTEVEDRA, Spain: Gambling has only recently been legalized in Spain, and the *Casino de la Toja* at El Grove is the best of the country's many new gaming houses. On an island near Pontevedra. A glamorous second is the *Casino Castillo de Perelada,* dramatically set in the imposing Perelada castle, near Gerona. The *Casino Gran Madrid* is at Torrelodones, about 17 miles (27 km) outside the capital on the highway to La Coruña.

SVETI STEFAN, Yugoslavia: There's plenty of capitalist decadence on this jewel-like promontory jutting into the royal blue Adriatic. Try the new *Maestral* hotel for raking in the dinars and for lovely swimming when you've had enough.

Offshore Europe:
Islands of Every Kind

 With today's efficient transportation networks, it's getting harder to spot any difference between the center of Majorca and the center of Madrid. But there are still many landfalls where you can find the solitude and isolation that have always characterized islands — and have, throughout the ages, constituted their main attractions. Herewith a selection of some of our favorites:

BORNHOLM, Denmark: The country's most easterly island is more like a part of Sweden — and, in fact, it takes less time to get to that nation's town of Ystad than it does to the homeland. A cross between a modern Scandinavian summer resort and a medieval Viking shrine, the island is full of attractions: one of Denmark's largest forests, at Almingden; the spectacular National Trust white dunes at Dueodde; the mysterious grove of monoliths at Gryet; the great coastal cliffs of Helligdommen; plus peaceful old fishing villages like Hasle and Helligpeder, full of half-timbered houses; early medieval round churches like Østerlars near Gudhjem and Nylars near Akirkeby, Viking castles; and herring smokehouses. Rønne, an attractive old merchants' port, is the main town; you can get boats to Copenhagen (7 hours away) as well as Sweden and Germany. While you're there, visit one of the area's ceramic factories and the Rønne Theater, the oldest playhouse in Denmark. Clustered off the mother island are some 20 baby islands known as Ertholmene: Christiansø is well worth the 1¼-hour ferry ride it will take you to get there from the beautifully preserved old market town of Svaneke. Information: Bornholm Tourist Office, Havnen, DK-3700 Rønne, Denmark (phone: 95-08-10), or the North Bornholm Tourist Office, 2 Hammershusvej, Sandvig, DK-3770 Allinge, Denmark (phone 98-00-01).

THE FAEROES, Denmark: Forty thousand fiercely independent Faeroese (and twice that number of sheep) inhabit the 18 rugged islands of this umbrella-shaped archipelago 300 miles from Iceland and 185 miles north of the Shetlands in the middle of the wild North Atlantic. A population of several million wild sea birds of every species — guillemots, gannets, fulmars, oystercatchers, and the tjaldun (the national symbol) — inhabit the towering shoreline cliffs. One startling island sight is the gathering of the prized guillemot eggs by Faeroese, who dangle by ropes over cliffside nests hundreds of feet above the swirling sea. Another is the *grindadráp*, a midsummer whale-slaughtering expedition, which turns the sea a violent red and ends with an all-night celebration. July 29 is the Feast of St. Olav, a gala event that has all the islanders converging on Torshavn for banquets of whale steak, parades, concerts, and contests in ancient island skills. To get there, you can take the 3½-hour flight from Copenhagen to Vagar Airport — 2 hours by road from the capital of Thorshavn. Or go by sea: The romantic voyage lasts 33 hours; DFDS Danish Seaways has sailings about once a week from Esbjerg between June and September. And bring your own liquor: The islands went dry a year before American Prohibition and never remoistened. Another sea route is from Scotland via the P & O Ferry, Orkney, and Shetland Services, PO Box 5, Jamieson's Quay, Aberdeen AB9 8DL, Scotland (phone: 2-9111); or P & O Ferries, Smyril Passenger Dept., Strandfaraskib Landsins, 3800 Torshavn, Faroe Islands (phone: 14-550). Information: Danmarks Turistråd, Turistinformationen, Hans Christian Andersens Blvd. 22, DK-1553, Copenhagen V, Denmark (phone: 11-13-25).

CORSICA, France: Most people can't remember anything more about Corsica than the fact that it used to belong to Italy (only 7.5 miles north of Sardinia, it is also half as far from the Italian mainland as it is from France) and that Napoleon was born on the island in Ajaccio. "By the fragrance of its soil alone," wrote Napoleon, "I would know Corsica with my eyes closed." Since the French discovered it in force about a decade ago, however, it has become the country's classiest summer resort, and it's jammed in July and August. Yet in other months, and throughout the year when you get away from the main beach centers, Corsica is still a place of savage Mediterranean beauty and startling contrasts: There are deep forests covering more than half the island; a thousand kilometers of coastline to explore; alpine landscapes like those at Monte Rotondo, Conte Cintro, and the little-known Ponte-Leccia; medieval cliff towns like Bonifacio; and a beautiful old port called Bastia. The dialect is a strange amalgam of French and Italian; the bouillabaisse is the fishiest and spiciest in France; and the *paghiella*, a haunting ancient harmony for three male voices, is still sung at all the island's religious festivals and by Corsican shepherds in the fields. Boat crossings from Nice, Toulon, and Marseille take 5 to 12 hours, and there are frequent 35-minute flights from Paris, Marseille, and Nice. Information: Centre d'Information, La Maison de la Corse, 82 blvd. Haussmann, 75008 Paris (phone: 293-4550); or Délégation Régionale du Tourisme, 38 Cours Napoléon, BP 162, 20178 Ajaccio (phone: 21-55-31).

MONT-ST.-MICHEL, France: This spectacular granite monument about 2,000 yards off the coast of Normandy was, centuries ago, part of the mainland forest of Scissy. When the forest yielded to the sea, it became an island twice a day with the tides, and the rest of the time guides led visitors across the sodden shoals, between treacherous patches of quicksand. In the eighth century, the bishop of Avranches built a shrine to celebrate a dream vision of the Archangel Michael, and in the eleventh century, a Benedictine monastery was carved out of the natural granite. After the revolution, the Mont did a stretch as a state prison, and in 1877 a causeway — all that remains above water during the exceptionally high tides of the spring and fall equinoxes — was built to connect the island to the mainland. The Benedictines are in charge again, and Mont-St.-Michel is one of France's most stunning sights. Walk the single main street, flanked by timbered houses, to the abbey gate; lunch on one of the area's special plump, moist omelettes; and see both the original Romanesque monastery church and La Merveille, the Gothic thirteenth-century marvel. Rennes, 37 miles away, is the closest large town. If you're at the Mont during low tide, there's also fine shrimping in the shallows.

ANDROS, Greece: Picking out just one of the magnificent islands of Greece is a little like trying to choose your favorite gold ingot at the Central Bank of Zürich. Lush, verdant Andros seems a fair compromise, situated, as it is, roughly in the middle of the three great island clusters: the Cyclades, the Sporades, and the Dodecanese. More wooded than some of its barren southern cousins and less touristy than crossroads like Rhodes and Mykonos, Andros has all of their magnetic Aegean virtues: a limpid sea and honey-colored beaches (Batsi, Korthion, Gavrio, Kapparia); evocative archaeological remains (ancient Palaeopolis); high mountain slopes (Mt. Petalo); plus pine woods and the fig and lemon groves of the valleys. A grilled *barbounia* (Aegean red mullet), a glass of ouzo, and the lilting music of a *bouzouki* in a *taverna* in the capital town of Andros, built on a promontory and capped with an old Venetian castle, and you will soon be mulling early retirement. Good reading matter for your visit: Thornton Wilder's beautiful novel, *The Woman of Andros*. Daily boats from Rafina and Karistos are available, and there are plenty of possibilities for island-hopping trips to Tinos, Siros, and Naxos. Information: Greek National Tourist Organization, 2 Amerikis St., Athens, Greece (phone: 322-3111); or the Greek National Tourist Organization, 645 Fifth Ave., Olympic Tower, New York, NY 10022 (phone: 212-421-5777).

LIPARI, Italy: Italy's islands are places of summer and sun and sea — and many can be seriously overcrowded, not only by foreign tourists, but also by natives, who seem to prefer vacationing in throngs, and all on the 2 or 3 days around August 15. Altogether different are the Aeolian Isles — a dramatic, volcanic cluster of eight landfalls off the northern coast of Sicily a little more bothersome to get to, and consequently a lot less frequently gotten to. (You may remember an old Roberto Rossellini–Ingrid Bergman film called *Stromboli,* which brought the islands some short-lived notoriety.) Lipari is the center of most activity — now as it once was, long ago, for the ancient Greeks, Romans, and Carthaginians — and the island is rich in archaeological relics, volcanic craters, and thermal springs. You can easily rent a boat to explore the empty coves that scallop the island's rocky shoreline, and regular ferry services are available from Messina, Milazzo, and Naples; during the summer you can hire a super-speedy hydrofoil from Messina, Taormina, Cefalú, or Palermo. Information: Ente Provinciale per il Turismo, Via Calabria, Isolato 301-bis, 98100 Messina, Italy (phone: 77-53-56); or Azienda Autonoma di Soggiorno e Turismo, Via Vittorio Emanuele 239, 98050 Lipari (Messina), Italy (phone: 981-1580).

CAPRI, Italy: The most famous, most expensive, and most crowded of all the Italian islands, Capri (CApri, not CaPREE) is also one of the most beautiful places in the world. To be sure, in July and August the little main square and the Marina Piccola beach are like cans of Mediterranean sardines, so you'd be wise to keep your distance if you're looking for peace and quiet. But Capri can be breathtaking with its sapphire sky and sea, its soft air scented with the heady aroma of the hillside lemon groves, and lush purple explosions of wisteria nearly everywhere you turn. Whenever you go, there's plenty to keep you busy: lazy morning orange juice in one of the Piazzetta cafés, funicular rides from the boat dock, afternoon jaunts down to the marina; rowboat rides around the grottoes; hair-raising minibus trips back up the hairpin road to town; and spooky moonlight rambles to the pagan shrine of the Matromania cave. The Roman Emperor Tiberias built 12 villas here to honor the 12 Olympian deities, and the area around his Villa Jovis — from which he ruled the whole empire for a decade — is a wonderful place to walk for fine views. A wide variety of boats, including the higher-priced, higher-speed hydrofoil, ply the waters between the island and Naples or Sorrento. Information: Ente Provinciale per il Turismo, Via Partenope 10 A, 80121 Napoli, Italy (phone: 41-89-88); or the Azienda Autonoma di Soggiorno e Turismo, 1 Piazza Umberto I, 80073 Capri, Italy (phone: 837-0686).

MADEIRA, Portugal: About 600 miles and an hour's plane ride southwest of Lisbon, this semitropical paradise and former British colony has not been a "discovery" since the inauguration in the mid-1960s of the airport at Funchal, but it is still a flowered and forested place of enormous serenity. The climate is a travel agent's fantasy, and there's year-round sea bathing, exciting skin diving, and fine mountain climbing. You can pluck bananas and nibble the sugarcane that grows in the fertile valleys; then drown any remaining sorrows in the fabled Madeira wine. Funchal, the island's capital, is a gracious, manicured seaside city, where the flowers, the fruit, and the fish from all over the island tend to end up; *Reid's Hotel* here is a splendid old relic of another era. You will also find a glittering new casino. There is a good deal of ship traffic from Lisbon and points east. The spectacular Funchal fireworks display is one of Europe's great New Year's Eve celebrations. Information: Direcção Regional de Turismo, Av. Arriaga 18, Funchal (Madeira) 9000, Portugal (phone: 2-9057).

ARRAN, Scotland, and ARAN, Ireland: Arran is a lovely clump of old Scotland set gently into the Firth of Clyde, about 13 miles from Ardrossan on the mainland; the Aran Islands are three rugged outposts of Ireland strung gently across the mouth of Galway Bay, about 35 miles from the mainland port of Galway. Yet, despite their relative proximity to their home countries, both Arran and the Arans have changed very little over the centuries, and their timeless landscapes and stubborn adherence to age-old traditions set the islands apart from their mainlands in time, if not space. In

Brodick, Arran's fair city, you can visit baronial Brodick Castle; watch the Highland Games with the island athletes in their tartan kilts; join the bidding at the annual Highland sheep auction; fish for trout in the icy Goens; or cross moors where red deer roam to the mysterious, prehistoric Standing Stones of Tormore. On the largest of the three Arans, Inishmore, there is Dun Aengus, a cyclopean fort with a circular tower that dates from the first century. The women there still wear red skirts and raw cowhide moccasins called *pampooties;* the men have retained their vests and peaked caps; and Gaelic is spoken in the home. The farming islanders grow potatoes in a homemade soil of sand and seaweed, while the fishing population sets out in wicker-framed, hide-covered *curraghs* (boats) to go lobstering and cockle picking. For information about Arran, write to the Information Center, The Pier, Brodick, Isle of Arran, Scotland (phone: 2140). For details about the Aran Islands, contact Ireland West Tourism, Áras Fáilte, Galway City, Ireland (phone: 6-3081); or the Irish Tourist Board, 590 Fifth Ave., New York, NY 10036 (phone: 212-869-5500).

IBIZA, Spain: A hundred miles from both Alicante and Valencia, Ibiza is the smallest of the three principal Balearic Islands and the least affected by the burgeoning of everything that fuses Spain and the sea. Founded by the Carthaginians in the seventh century BC, you can feel the proximity of Africa in the baking sun, the tropical vegetation, the warm southern winds, the whitewashed Moorish houses, the green palms and pines, and the golden crescents of beach. The 1¼-hour boat trip to Ibiza's satellite, Formentera, is a pleasant way to get away from being away from it all. Boats leave regularly for Barcelona as well as for the two closer ports of Valencia and Alicante. Or you can fly from Barcelona (an hour away) or Valencia (a half-hour distant); the flight is especially pleasant for the view it gives you of the island, looking almost incandescent from on high. Information: Oficina de Información de Turismo, Vara del Rey 13, Ibiza, Spain (phone: 301-900).

HVAR, Yugoslavia: An elongated lobster claw of an island off the Dalmatian coast, Hvar has long been a haven for nudists, who control some of the best of the many splendid beaches. It is also known for having the highest percentage of cloudless days per year in the Adriatic, a statistic of which the natives are so proud that they will reimburse you for your room and board on days that it rains for 3 straight hours — and provide full refunds in the event of fog, snow, or subzero temperatures. The city, also called Hvar, is rich in architectural treasures from the palmy days of Venetian rule, and the lovely beaches face even lovelier beaches on tiny splinter islands like Palmiž an and Biševo. Split is the closest port, though during the summer, a great variety of boats ply the Adriatic, from Venice on down, and many call in at the busy harbor. Information: Tourist Office, 58460 Stari Grad, Hvar, Yugoslavia (phone: 75-821); or Yugoslav State Tourist Office, Rockefeller Center, Suite 210, 630 Fifth Ave., New York, NY 10020 (phone: 212-757-2801).

The Quintessential Europe

You've waited in line at the Eiffel Tower, and you've heard Big Ben. You've trekked through the Louvre to admire Mona Lisa's greenish complexion (duly noting the permanent traffic jam around it), and you've admired the Colosseum. No one who fancies himself a traveler could tour Europe and omit visits to these great monuments; their grandeur prevails — despite the tourist hordes and twentieth-century tarnish. Yet there are scores of other spots in Europe that are not so celebrated and in their way deserve to be: Though not giants like the Eiffel Tower and the Colosseum, these somewhat lesser-knowns do offer an experience that is quintessentially European; here, the foreignness of the Continent and its traditions will come resoundingly home to you.

You will doubtless encounter dozens of these wonders on your own — but to get you started, here is our selection.

DINNER AT THE *SACHER* AND A PREMIERE AT THE STATE OPERA, Vienna, Austria: This is the happiness that money can buy — the most gracious, elegant, worldly evening in Europe. The *Sacher Hotel,* aptly placed on Philharmonikerstrasse, has been the rendezvous of musicians, artists, and all Vienna since (it seems) the time of the Pharaohs; and its *Hotel Restaurant* may just be the best on the Continent. In the world of the *Sacher*, everything is just as it has always been — the decor as rich, the service as perfect, the clientele as brilliant, and the wiener schnitzel, the *palatschinken,* and the Sacher torte as delectable as ever. Music is still an Austrian national religion, and the glittering Staatsoper is its temple. The frothy *Der Rosenkavalier* is the most Viennese of its productions, and if you can arrange it, *the* opera to see (Beethoven's *Fidelio* is a close second choice). The black-tie New Year's Eve performance of *Die Fledermaus* is Europe's hardest ticket, though the concierge at the *Sacher* has been known to work even this miracle.

CHRISTCHURCH COLLEGE MEADOW, Oxford, England: A beautiful, manicured English greensward, with the soft, rain-nurtured texture of a hill in the Cotswolds or the lawn at Wimbledon, this meadow was a greenhouse for the British Empire, and eight centuries of the finest young people of England have strolled through the stone portals of the Great Quadrangle here and listened to the tolling of the evening bells from Tom Tower. Bolingbroke was at Christchurch before he became king; William Penn before he was expelled for "nonconformity"; Gladstone before he was prime minister; Lewis Carroll before he wrote *Alice in Wonderland.* Walk slowly down the High Street. Two debating dons may sweep by you in their flowing black robes. Or there may be a game on Merton Cricket Ground, the players' uniforms a crisp white against the green velvet pitch. Have a pint of bitter and a pork pie at the *Turf Tavern.* Browse in renowned *Blackwell's Book Store.* And you, too, will listen to the bells of Tom Tower.

THE BOULEVARD ST.-MICHEL, Paris, France: Essentially, this seething, vibrant merry-go-straight has changed very little since Ernest Hemingway and James Joyce and Co. discovered it in the 1920s. You will still find the endless ebb and flow of laughing, arguing students; the Africans and Orientals of every shade, height, and costume; the smells — of street-corner crêpes, roasting chestnuts, nougat, and steaming *pommes frites;* the impromptu concerts by guitarists, bongo drummers, solo trumpeters, string quartets, their open instrument cases your invitation to drop in a franc. And there are art movie theaters showing four films in four basements in four different languages — and cafés by the score, their neat rows of seats the orchestra to the stage that is the Boul' Mich'. If you can manage to make the scene for Bastille Day — July 14 — by all means do so: The French really do dance in the streets.

OMAHA BEACH, Normandy, France: After the D-day invasion, everything was different. One world ended, another world began. June 6, 1944, will come to be one of those watershed dates, like 1066 and 1775, that divide eras in human history. Here are the pyramids of the twentieth century: the German pillboxes on the murderous cliff at Pointe du Hoc (recently dedicated as US soil), the landing craft and giant bulkheads sunk in the sands of Arromanches, the white crosses and silent chapel at St.-Laurent-sur-Mer. Save a gray, blowy late afternoon. You can see it all panoramically, scanning the whole expanse of the coastline that was the site of the greatest mass military operation in history. Or you can find a way down to the beach somewhere along the peninsula, roll up your trousers, and wade through the shallow waters breaking on the sand flats. Whether you're twenty and read about Omaha Beach in a book or eighty and lost a son on these bloodied shoals, a visit here is the most strangely moving experience in all of Europe. In some way, we were all here.

THE ACROPOLIS OF LINDOS, Rhodes, Greece: Every day, the baking sun and corroding salt reclaim one more tiny particle of this ancient marble memory, a temple to Athena, set 30 miles south of the island city of Rhodes, on a soaring promontory 400 feet above the sea. But below, and all around in every direction, the elements of the Greek islands that neither nature nor man has succeeded in eroding endure: the silent, craggy coves; the sweeping blond beaches, the white cottages gleaming against the cloudless sky; the olive groves and vineyards sloping down to the cobalt sea. A fishing boat cuts a momentary ripple in the glassy surface, the waters fold back into the timeless Aegean, and you think of Theseus skin diving and Sophocles grilling sardines. This is a place for dawns, for sunset, for solitude.

THE ACCADEMIA DELLE BELLE ARTI, Florence, Italy: On the quiet side street of via Ricasoli, in a pleasant but uninspired building, are three of the greatest works of art of the Renaissance. Most famous, of course, is Michelangelo's stunning *David,* a colossus and a hymn to youth and power in its glorification of the human body. The *Prisoners* — a group of half-finished figures contorted as if to wrench their massive bodies free of the great marble blocks that imprison them — are among Michelangelo's most mature and disturbing works, as dark and yearning as the *David* is sunny and serene. They flank the corridor that leads to the *David.* And in the next room is the splendid *Cassone Adimari,* a fifteenth-century Tuscan wedding chest delicately embellished with paintings of lavishly robed and coiffed gentlewomen and graceful courtiers. Together, these three masterpieces embody the very spirit of the Renaissance: its boundless optimism and faith in man, its struggle toward freedom from the oppressive past, its festive joy in sheer physical beauty.

THE GRAND CANAL, Venice, Italy: The best way to come in is by train on the causeway across the lagoon. Walk out of the Santa Lucia Station to the head of the wide steps that lead down to the water. Stand still. And look. The whole lavish length of the Grand Canal is lined with a royal flush of Renaissance palaces that make you feel as though all human endeavor that followed has been more or less superfluous. Take a gondola — a trite, overpriced, touristy gondola — and have your driver pull over at the landing stage of the *Gritti Palace Hotel,* and see it all again from the Byzantine windows of your own top-floor suite. If it's the first time and you don't have a lump in your throat, you have a stone for a heart. Didn't anyone ever say "See *Venice* and die"?

THE BULLFIGHT IN SEVILLE, Spain: "Sunday in Andalusia" is the title of this scenario. The morning is cool and quiet, with the southern sun and the heady odor of orange blossoms sliding in through the shutters, but you can feel the heat settling over the city, the excitement building. Follow the crowd: to late morning mass in the Gothic cathedral — one of the largest in Christendom — spectacular with its soaring columns, majestic vaults, rich stone-and-iron lacework; to the exotic tropical gardens of the Alcazar; to the shade of the riverside for an alfresco lunch of chilled *gazpacho* and *manzanilla;* and finally to the bullring at plaza de la Maestranza. All your senses are assailed by the scene before you: the ocher turf glaring in the late afternoon sun; the tinny blare of the band; the procession's gaudy, spangled costumes; the *bandilleros'* ballet; the coarse, feverish crowd watering its passion with warm wine squirted from bulging skins; the black bull's thundering fury; the arrogant grace of the matador; the swirl of the red *muleta;* the flash of the sword blade. Death, triumph, idle amusement; blood, manhood, music, and sun: an age-old ritual, the core of Spain. At its worst, the *corrida* is a slaughterhouse. At its best, it can be a spectacle of unparalleled glory. Afterward, follow the crowd again: the evening *paseo* — the promenade — on the Sierpes, where all of Seville takes the air, arm in arm. And at night, somewhere in the maze of whitewashed walls and flowered patios in the Barrio de Santa Cruz, heels clack the torrid rhythms of the *flamenco* to the quivering sound of Spanish guitars.

GRINDELWALD, in the Bernese Oberland, Switzerland: At an altitude of 3,500 feet, the village of Grindelwald is the center stage for a great Alpine amphitheater. In the foreground are the sunny plateaus of the Grosse and Kleine Scheidegg and the ice-blue waters of the gleaming Bachsee. In the high distance, in a snowy military row, stand the five great rocky guards: the Wetterhorn, the Schreckhorn, Eiger, Monch, and — at 13,642 feet — the fabled Jungfrau: The rack railway of the Jungfraujoch is Europe's most spectacular transportation experience.

Like so many of the great Swiss and Austrian mountainscapes, this scene shades from the fairyland to the forbidding: from the charming town full of wooden chalets, puffing chimneys, and gaily splurging window boxes, to the craggy peaks and the ominous North Wall of the Eiger, which has taken the lives of so many climbers. If you visit in summer, trudge through the woods to the Bachsee or up the summit of the Faulhorn; from there, it seems that you can see the entire planet. If it's winter, step into your skis and swoop across the great snowfields of the Scheideggs. In any season, when the sun drops behind the peaks and a twilight chill comes over the town, have a steaming glass of *glühwein* and a languid nap under the feathery softness of a Swiss eiderdown.

THE COVERED MARKET, Istanbul, Turkey: At Europe's outer edge, over 4,000 separate shops and stalls cluster together in a gigantic covered labyrinth that is the Continent's most exotic, most chaotic shopping center — *Kapali Çarşi,* the souks of Constantinople. Jewelry, carpets, perfumes, lace, porcelain, silks, skins, gold and silver, copper and tin, wood and straw, ancient daggers, and modern fezzes crowd this direct descendant of the great Oriental bazaars. The Spice Market — *Misir Çarşisi* — is lined with great open sacks of red pepper, yellow turmeric, silvery thyme, and the air is heady with the smell of mint, clove, and cinnamon. Vendors shout, buyers haggle, itinerant juice sellers bang away on their brass jugs. Deep in the market, difficult to find, is the great vaulted court of the Bedestan. You can buy a Turkish carpet, nibble a Turkish delight, sip a Turkish coffee in one of the exotic little cafés where the men play *tric-trac* and smoke the *nargile* (a Turkish bubble pipe). And afterward, have yourself steamed and scrubbed in an ancient *hammam,* Turkish bath.

THE WHITE NIGHTS OF LENINGRAD, USSR: Once a year, during the last half of June, the sun leaves the horizon over the most beautiful of man-made cities for only a few brief hours, and in place of the night, a mysterious chalky haze hangs over the horizon. The stolid Russians go giddy and sentimental, and in a sort of metropolitan tribal rite that celebrates the return of the White Nights, they flock to Strelka, at the prow of Vassilyevsky Island. The delicate pastel façades of structures put up along the entrancing canals of the Neva in the brilliant heyday of the court of St. Petersburg positively glow in this eerie light; and the great past of Mother Russia comes splendidly alive: the opulence of the czars' Winter Palace, the brooding mystery of Dostoyevsky in the Peter and Paul Fortress, the excitement of the revolution, the romance of Tchaikovsky.

Europe's Classic Cruises and Wonderful Waterways

Whether you're dangling your hand from a dinghy or sitting at the captain's table on a transatlantic liner, being on a boat is something special. People wave and sing and talk to each other, the winds whip your hair, the waves rock you — gently or not — like a baby in a cradle. The pace seems closer to man's own than that of the Concorde.

The flip side is that ship or boat travel takes a relatively long time; that all water looks the same in the deep; that your fellow passengers aren't always congenial; and that the romantic winds can chill you to numbness while the waves make you sick. So it's always a good idea to bring a Windbreaker, a pile of great books, and Dramamine. And if you're the restless type, don't set out on a long voyage until the sea has you hooked.

Here's an assortment of cruises in all styles and lengths that will put you in touch with the delights of putting out to sea:

ATLANTIC CROSSINGS: The days when the Atlantic could be crossed only by boat, when people talked about things like outside cabins and tipping the purser and sitting at the captain's table, and got a lump in their throats on seeing the white cliffs of Dover or the Statue of Liberty are not altogether past. There are at least three ways to enjoy all the things that made the *Île de France* and the *Queen Mary* such legends: The *Queen Elizabeth 2* makes the crossing from Southampton or Cherbourg to New York in 5 days; Cunard Lines, which runs her, offers a special package, in conjunction with British Airways, that includes return air fare — just in case you decide the sea voyage is really a *once*-in-a-lifetime experience. Some arrangements also include much-reduced fares for spouses and hotel accommodations in New York or London. Information: Cunard Lines, South Western House, Canute Rd., Southampton SO9 1ZA, England (phone: 341-66); or 8 Berkeley St., London W1X 6NR (phone: 491-3930); or Cunard, 555 Fifth Ave., New York NY 10017 (phone: 212-880-7500). The *Royal Viking Line* occasionally offers a longer New York–Copenhagen run that includes a swing through the Norwegian fjords and stops in Amsterdam, Southampton, and Dublin. Information: Royal Viking Line, One Embarcadero Center, San Francisco, CA (phone: 415-398-8000 or 800-422-8000, toll free). The Polish Ocean Lines operates a ship that crosses between Rotterdam or London and Montréal in 9 days. Contact Gdynia America Shipping Lines, Stelp and Leighton, 238 City Rd., London EC1V 2PR (phone: 251-3389); or McClean Kennedy Ltd., 410 St. Nicholas St., PO Box 1086, Montréal H2Y 2P5, Canada (phone: 514-849-6111).

NORWAY'S NORTH CAPE: This is the kind of scenery that inspired Sibelius's sweeping scores: There are shimmering fjords; angular, towering glaciers; deep ever-green forests; Arctic panoramas palely, eerily illuminated by the midnight sun. A typical cruise starts from Copenhagen or Oslo, takes in the magnificent Romsdalsfjord and Geirangerfjord, crosses the Arctic Circle, and eventually goes as far as Honningsvaag on Norway's North Cape, Europe's northernmost point. Shorter runs leave from Bergen on Norway's western coast for Kirkenes at the top of the cape (which is also accessible by air). Cruises of a variety of durations to the finest, deepest, and steepest fjords are offered by the *Royal Viking Line* (Ruseløkkveien 14, N-0251 Oslo 2, Norway; phone: 41-93-90); *Det Bergenske Dampskibsselskab* (Passasjeravdelingen, Bradbenken 1, 5000 Bergen, Norway; phone: 21-00-20); *Bennett Travel Bureau* (Karl Johansgate 3, N-0154 Oslo 1, Norway; phone: 20-90-90). More information: Norwegian Tourist Board, 75 Rockefeller Plaza, New York, NY 10019 (phone: 212-972-0799).

THE MEDITERRANEAN: A Mediterranean cruise can be nothing more than a 30-minute hydrofoil ride between Naples and Capri — or a languid 14-day odyssey that includes every center of civilization in the ancient world from Alexandria to the Balearic Islands. One typical seven-country, three-continent cruise touches down at Dubrovnik, Kuşadasi, Rhodes, Cyprus, Haifa, Alexandria, and Venice. Another variety takes in the Dalmatian coast, Corfu, Malta, Tunis, Sardinia, Elba, Portofino, and Nice. *Sun, Chandris,* and *Costa* are three good, reliable lines with sleek ships and cheerful, accommodating staff. When you pick a cruise, don't be unduly influenced by mere quantity of ports on the itinerary: four leisurely and sharply distinct courses usually beat eight hurried appetizers (and anyway, after a while, all handmade rugs, dockside taverns, and burly old seamen look the same). Most cruise space is booked through travel agents, but you can also write directly to the lines: *Sun Lines,* 2 Karageorgi Servias St., Athens, Greece (phone: 322-8883) or 1 Rockefeller Plaza, New York, NY 10020 (phone: 212-397-6400); *Chandris Shipping Lines,* 95 Akti Miaouli, Piraeus, Greece (phone: 412-6757); and *Costa Armatori,* via Gabriele D'Annunzio 5, Genova (phone: 54-831), or their *Costa Cruises* office in the US, 1 Biscayne Tower, Suite 3190, Miami, FL 33131 (phone: 800-462-6782; in Miami, 305-358-7330).

THE GREEK ISLANDS: Greek Islands cruises, which come in myriad styles, degrees of luxury (or not), and durations, show you a fascinating section of the marvel-filled Mediterranean. From Piraeus, you can make a quick run out to Aegina and Poros, or you can spend a week drifting out into the Dodecanese. Or you can sail from one wash-white-and-olive-green haven to the next until *you* have become a burly old seaman hawking handmade rugs at a dockside stand. Most cruises come as 3-, 4-, and 7-day packages, with the commonest ports of call being Santorini, Mykonos, Delos, Crete, Patmos, Rhodes, Kuşadasi, and Lindos. (If you're undecided about the detour Crete requires, remember that the Palace of Knossos is one of the great wonders of the Mediterranean.) Among the best companies are *K-Lines Hellenic Cruises* (Kavounides Shipping Company, 33 Akti Miaouli, Piraeus, Greece; phone: 452-2011); and *Epirotiki Lines* (87 Akti Miaouli, Piraeus, Greece; phone: 452-6641 in Athens, 360-1919); or in the US at 551 Fifth Ave., New York, NY 10017 (phone: 212-599-1750). *Sun Lines* and *Chandris* are both fine for the islands as well (see above). Alternatively, you can take a toothbrush, a bathing suit, and a copy of the *Odyssey* and do the whole thing on one of the hundreds of local ferries that link all the islands — or even charter your own yacht. You'll never want for bread and wine.

THE RHINE: The cruise down (or up) the Rhine, once an integral part of every American's Grand Tour, has gone a little out of fashion of late — perhaps when the German mark came so belligerently into ascendency. But if you can afford it, this journey is still an experience of a lifetime. The banks of this *Alter Mann* ("Old Man River") as it cleaves Europe from Rotterdam to Basel are lined with ancient castles and villages that come straight from the fairy tales of the Brothers Grimm. The 150-year-old *KD German Rhine Line* has 19 ships, some functioning as waterborne buses and others (like floating hotels) that cover five countries in as many days. Information: *KD German Rhine Line,* Frankenwerft 15, 5000 Cologne, Germany (phone: 2-0880); *Rhine Cruise Agency,* D. Neuhold Corp., 170 Hamilton Ave., White Plains, NY 10601 (phone: 914-948-3600).

THE DANUBE: While it is certainly not blue, this celebrated waterway is long — twice as long as the Rhine — and immeasurably historic: When you've grasped the geography of the Danube and the Rhine, you've acquired the key to understanding much of the movement of European history. Meanwhile, the Danube offers an enormous variety of cruising possibilities. You can nip around Vienna waters for a mere 2½ hours; or you can ride a Hungarian torpedo for 5 hours to Budapest. You can make a leisurely overnight trip from Vienna on the *Theodor Körner,* where some versions of the voyage allot 5 hours for sipping wine in the harbor before anyone even turns on the motor. Or you can go through Yugoslavia and Romania and out into the Black Sea, where you make the first right turn for Istanbul or your first left for Yalta. (There are ships that do both.) The best operation is that of the *DDSG* (*D*onaud*amp*fs*chi*ffahrts *g*esellschaft!), Handelskai 265, 1020 Vienna (phone: 26-65-36); or Hint. Zollamtstrasse 1, Vienna (phone: 72-51-41). The company also books passage on Hungarian, Czech, or Russian boats.

CANAL AND RIVER CRUISING BY BOAT OR BARGE: There are two ways to cruise Europe's canals and rivers — by self-skippered boat or by joining a chartered cruise. We'll begin by describing self-skippered boat rentals. It works like this: You get a boat — a simple cabin cruiser. Someone shows you how to work the thing and tells you whom to call if you break down. You buy a pile of groceries, some fishing tackle, and a book of folk songs — and cast off for a floating holiday that will take you along as many of the hundreds of miles of the waterways that crisscross England, Wales, Holland, and France as you choose. There are plenty of places to moor, to walk and bicycle in the countryside (bring your own bike), to buy fresh piles of groceries (including local beer, ale, or wine). If you fear you'll feel as if you're driving at Indy after only an hour of Driver's Ed., hire a skipper to do the piloting. And if you don't feel like cooking, hire a whole crew (or stop in restaurants along the way). It's simple, idyllic, and expensive. And everyone who does it comes back talking about next year. For more information on self-skippered rentals (address of rental firms listed below): *British Waterways Board,* Melbury House, Melbury Terrace, London NW1 6JX, England (phone: 723-3700), to find out about inland waterways in England, Scotland, and Wales; *Inland Waterways Association,* 114 Regent's Park Rd., London NW1 8UQ (phone: 586-2510); *Anglo-Welsh Narrow Boats,* Canal Basin, Leicester Rd., Market Harborough LE16 7BJ, Leicestershire, England (phone: 6-6910); *Nautic Voyages,* 8 rue de Milan, Paris IX, France (phone: 526-6080); *Frisia,* Oude Oppenhuizerweg 79, 8606 JC Sneek, Holland (phone: 128-14). And you might be interested in a weekend course called "Introduction to Canals" offered from time to time at the Earnley Concourse, near Chichester PO20 7JL, Sussex, England (phone in Bracklesham Bay: 67-03-92).

If self-skippering sounds too intimidating or simply too troublesome, consider joining a charter barge along the canals and small rivers of England, Scotland, the Netherlands, or France. The sailing is handled by captain and crew and the most important person on the entire boat is the cook — ah, the cook. There has been a proliferation of luxury barges and boats in the past 5 years cruising the rivers of England's Cotswolds, across the best "eating" provinces of France, along Holland's wide, interconnecting system of canals. Usually barges are owned by the captain, who intimately knows the area being cruised, and bookings are arranged through larger companies. (Names and addresses of firms offering both self-skippered rentals and charter cruises are listed below.)

Barges are uniformly small — accommodating from 6 to 28 passengers and anywhere from 3 to 8 crew members, not counting dogs that regularly accompany such expeditions — and when not downright luxurious, they are always comfortable. They are also slow, cruising in a week of slow floating the distance a car would cover in a couple of hours of determined driving. They average about five miles an hour, but that doesn't account for the many planned and unplanned stops along the way while passengers shop in villages, explore nearby sites, bicycle along the towpath, or help with a lock — all of which happen all the time on any cruise.

And that leisurely pace, really, is the point of the cruise. Passengers see a small section of foreign countryside with an intimacy and warmth simply impossible through any other means of conveyance. Days are leisurely, punctuated by excellent meals (all food but drinks and wine are included in the price of most cruises) cooked from provisions picked up along the way. Passengers can join the cook on shopping forays or spend their time wandering through villages, reading, sketching, biking, visiting nearby historic sites, or making longer half-day or day trips arranged by the captain, with the promise of a fine meal back on board at day's end.

Certainly some of the most luxurious and intimate cruises are those offered by *Continental Waterways* and *Floating Through Europe* (addresses below), but numerous companies have charter cruises through the most inviting waterways of Western Europe. When reading a brochure, keep an eye on itinerary and routes as well as the boat's facilities (most have private cabins but shared bathrooms) and length of the cruise (3 days to a week is standard). The brochure should be specific about the kind of cruise it is (some are specifically "gourmet" fests, with emphasis on food; others make quite a point to visit historic sites along the river or canal or stop at the most beautiful châteaux; some seek out antique areas for shopping) and give some idea of the activities possible along the route. And most important, the captain and crew should know well the area being cruised, and it should be an area you want to know well, for you will spend the duration of the cruise immersed in a riverside view of provincial life.

Some favorite English itineraries: The River Avon, from Stratford-on-Avon to Tewkesbury, through a string of delicious sixteenth-century villages, with stops for performances of the Royal Shakespeare Company in Stratford and antiquing in nearby Cotswolds' towns; the Thames, from Oxford to Windsor; and the Norfolk Broads, through John Constable country, with more than 200 miles of rivers, lakes, and connecting waterways.

In the Netherlands, cruises generally begin at Rotterdam, that active seaport, and proceed through the country's incredible system of canals to Gouda (home of the famous cheese) and Delft.

Favorite French routes are the canals and rivers of Burgundy, the province prized by lovers of good food and wine, the Canal du Midi in the Mediterranean province of Languedoc, and the canals and rivers of Brittany and Alsace.

These are only a few routes of the dozens offered by the cruise charterers listed below. Whether you do it yourself or join a well-skippered barge, it is the most intimate way to get to know Europe.

Anglo Welsh Waterways Holidays, The Canal Basin, Market Harborough, Leicester LE16 7BJ, England (phone: 66-910).

Bargain Boating, Morgantown Travel Service, 127 High St., Morgantown, WV 26505 (phone: 304-292-8471). Self-skippered, chartered boats and cruisers in England, Holland, France, Ireland, and Scotland.

Blake's Holidays, Wroxham, Norwich NR12 8DH, England (phone: 3584). Chartered boats in England, Scotland, Ireland, Holland, Greece.

Blue Line Cruisers, BP 21, le Grand Bassin, 11400 Castlenaudary, France (phone: 23-17-51). Chartered cruises in France, Italy, Greece, Turkey, Yugoslavia.

Continental Waterways, 127 Albert Bridge Rd., London SW11, England (phone: 228-8671). Chartered boats in France and southern England.

Emerald Star Line Ltd., St. James's Gate, Dublin 8, Ireland (phone: 720-244). Chartered boats in Ireland.

Europ Yachting, 7 rue St. Lazare, 75009 Paris, France (phone: 526-1031). Chartered and self-skippered boats in France.

Floating Through Europe, 271 Madison Ave., New York, NY 10016 (phone: 212-685-5600). Hotel barge cruises in Belgium, England, France, Germany, and Holland.

Hobby Voyage, 8 rue de Milan 75009, Paris, France (phone: 526-60-80). Self-skippered cruises in Burgundy and the south of France.

Hoseasons Holidays Ltd., Sunway House, Lowestoft, Suffolk NR32 3LT, England (phone: 622-11). Self-skippered boats in England, Wales, Scotland, France, Greece, and Ireland.

Quiztour, 19 rue d'Athenes, 75009 Paris (phone: 874-7530), or *Salt & Pepper Tours,* 7 W 36th St., Suite 1500, New York, NY 10018-7911 (phone: 212-736-8226). Chartered boats in France.

Reisedienst, 1020 Wien, Handelskai 265, Austria (phone: 26-65-36). Booking agents for chartered boats in Hungary, Czechoslovakia, and Russia.

Skipper Travel, 210 California Ave., Palo Alto, CA 94306 (phone: 415-321-5658). Self-skippered and chartered boats in Ireland, France, Holland, and England.

World Yacht Enterprises, Ltd., 14 W 55th St., New York, NY 10019 (phone: 212-246-4811). Private yacht cruises in France, Italy, Spain, Greece, Turkey, and Yugoslavia.

THE LAKE OF LUCERNE: The German name of this body of water in central Switzerland — *Vierwaldstättersee,* or "Lake of the Four Cantons" — refers to the way the lake's angular, bizarrely shaped arms and bays reach into a quartet of the tiny nation's 23 states. Seen from the sky, the lake looks like a missing piece in a jigsaw puzzle. Boats leave from the main landing stage near the railroad station in Lucerne and wander across deep blue green coves, so tiny they look like toys, and friendly open meadows, and up to the edge of some of the most breathtaking landscapes in the Alps. A full-day trip will give you time to stop for lunch and a cable car ride up the Rigi-Kulm that will give you a chance to look down on the lake and the mountains around it. Information: *Schiffahrtsgesellschaft (SGV) des Vierwaldstättersees,* Werftestrasse 5, CH-6002 Lucerne, Switzerland (phone: 44-34-34).

THE CANALS OF VENICE: It's hard to reconcile yourself to doing anything aimed so expressly at the gawking tourist as hiring a gondola. But once you overcome your scruples, you're in for an experience that is poetic, mysterious — and worth every one of the vast number of lira that you are required to spend, particularly at night, when the pale moonlight silvers the city's medieval palaces, the island of San Giorgio Maggiore, and the Giudecca, and turns Venice into a heart-stopping stage that calls to mind Robert Browning's *In a Gondola* and Thomas Mann's *Death in Venice.* Rates — 30% higher after dark — vary little from one gondolier to another; choose one who is pleasant (and perhaps not overly talkative, since twisting around to keep up your end of the conversation can get uncomfortable). Should you opt against the gondola for reasons of price or principle, the *vaporetto* — the Venetian equivalent of a public bus — provides much the same experience at a fraction of the cost. Or take a turn in one of the *traghetti* — gondola ferries — that make 2-minute, 10-cent trips across the Grand Canal at points that are far from a bridge.

THE
EUROPEAN
CITIES

AMSTERDAM

More than any other major city in Europe, Amsterdam seems to have been designed with people in mind. It is a city built to human scale, refreshingly free of high-rise monuments to corporate egotism. It does not overawe or oppress. Its small streets, graceful canals, and narrow buildings invite exploration. Even its mansions — the elegant seventeenth-century canal houses built by earlier generations of the great and wealthy — are grand without being grandiose.

Emerging from Amsterdam's Central Station to face a welter of taxis, trams, boats and bridges, commuters and traffic, one might not believe that it is a soothing city. But cross the traffic and follow any of the canals that lace the city like the concentric tiers of a football stadium, and you will discover its serenity. The four largest and most historic canals — Singel, Herengracht, Keizersgracht, and Prinsengracht — pass near almost everything worth seeing at some point in their grand perambulation around the city.

These canals and the buildings that line them were the heart of Holland's thriving trade for centuries, and as you walk your eye will begin to pick out the details that distinguish the city's singular traditional architecture — unique gables and spires atop the attenuated and tipsy houses that delineate seventeenth- and eighteenth-century Amsterdam from the modern city. The finest old houses, built by rich traders, are along Herengracht (aptly, "Gentlemen's Canal"). On Singel, at the Munt, is the flower market, with flower-burdened boats and barges moored along the canal. And a few blocks from where Singel leaves the port are two cat boats, filled with Amsterdam's stray cats. And most canals are picturesquely dotted with houseboats. Walking the canals is not only unavoidable in Amsterdam, it is one of the chief joys of city life. And being a sensible lot, when Amsterdammers are in a hurry, they prefer to navigate the narrow canal streets by bicycle. Where cars get stuck for hours behind vans and trucks, bikes whiz through. (Of a population of 687,000, some 500,000 people have bicycles, and any visitor can join them for the price of a rental and the will power to ignore hectic traffic.)

Amsterdam has plenty of historical structures — more than 7,000 on the protected list — but few monuments as such. And though its beautiful seventeenth-century central area has been preserved largely intact, and the city must rank among the world's tops in museums per capita — 44 at last count — it is no architectural mausoleum. You will find that most of these protected seventeenth- and eighteenth-century buildings are carrying on business pretty much as usual today. They house small firms, families, cluttered shops, cafés, prostitutes — or all of these together. This is the genius of Amsterdam. In a word, the city has soul.

The Dutch call it *gezelligheid,* a very special quality that translates inade-

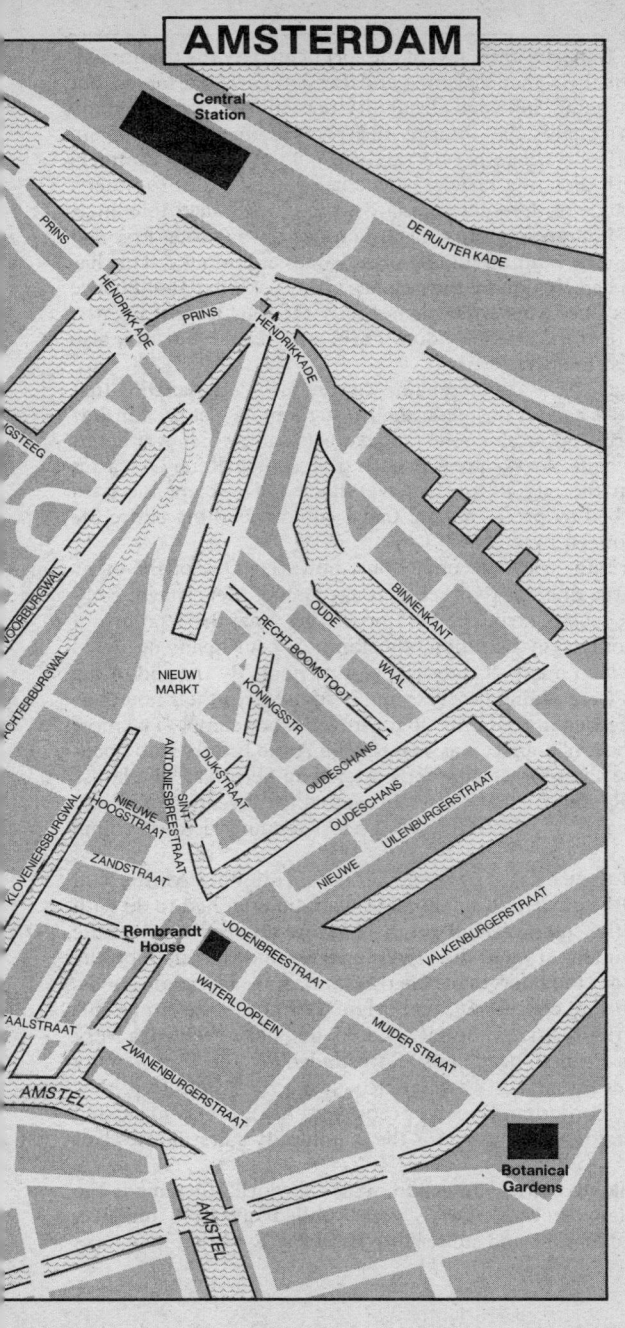

AMSTERDAM

Central Station

DE RUIJTER KADE

PRINS

HENDRIKKADE

PRINS

HENDRIKKADE

GSTEEG

VOORBURGWAL

BINNENKANT

OUDE

RECHT BOOMSTOOT

WAAL

ACHTERBURGWAL

NIEUW
MARKT

KONINGSSTR

OUDESCHANS

DIJKSTRAAT

SINT
ANTONIESBREESTRAAT

OUDESCHANS

NIEUWE
HOOGSTRAAT

KLOVENIERSBURGWAL

ZANDSTRAAT

UILENBURGERSTRAAT

NIEUWE

Rembrandt
House

JODENBREESTRAAT

WATERLOOPLEIN

VALKENBURGERSTRAAT

AALSTRAAT

ZWANENBURGERSTRAAT

MUIDER STRAAT

AMSTEL

Botanical
Gardens

AMSTEL

quately as "coziness." It means intimacy, of the sort offered by the traditional, dark-walled cafés with their shaded lamps and Persian-carpeted tables, but also openness, the easygoing, informal sociability that characterizes so many Amsterdammers. It is a quality that informs all aspects of life in the city, from dress — which almost everywhere is eclectic — to politics. Amsterdammers are not concerned with dictating beliefs, behavior, or appearance to others.

This casual acceptance of different standards, the city's famed tolerance, is firmly rooted in its bourgeois past. Amsterdam has always been first and foremost a mercantile city, built on middle-class values and money. This has by no means proved a bad thing, and the city has always exerted an influence disproportionate to its size. Amsterdam is not only the fourth most favored tourist destination in Europe after London, Paris, and Rome, but it is also Europe's fourth largest financial center.

The city's early "regent" class of merchants was unique in appreciating that intolerance of any kind is bad for business, and throughout its history Amsterdam has displayed a truly admirable reluctance to persecute whichever heretics were currently in vogue. As the great French philosopher René Descartes put it, while living in the city in 1631, "Everybody here except me is in business and so absorbed by profit-making that I could spend my entire life here without being noticed by a soul."

Amsterdammers are not without convictions, however. One of the city's few monuments, a statue of a dockworker at Jonas Daniël Meijerplein, commemorates the heroic general strike of 1941 protesting Nazi deportations of the city's Jews — the only demonstration of its kind to occur in any occupied country, and one in which many of the strikers were shot. By the end of the war, Amsterdammers were hiding nearly as many fugitives in their homes as the Germans had succeeded in rounding up for forced labor camps. The most famous of these fugitives, of course, was 14-year-old Anne Frank, who documented her experience so unforgettably for posterity in her diary; the house where the Frank family and friends were sequestered for 2 years is now one of the major tourist sights in Amsterdam — a heart-rending visit for young and old alike.

But it is fitting that the earliest known document mentioning Amsterdam by name, from which the city traditionally dates its founding, had to do with commerce. Issued by the count of Holland in 1275 and on view today at the city archives, the document granted the inhabitants around the "dam on the Amstel" exemption from toll charges on the transport of locally made goods.

In spite of this important concession, that original dam, the site of present-day Dam Square in the heart of the city, could not have seemed a very promising location to its first occupants. Surrounded by the flat, marshy swampland of the river estuary, it was regularly swept by storms that blew in unimpeded from the bordering Zuiderzee (Southern Sea). It was so lacking in resources of any kind that the wood for the community's first houses had to be imported.

But, as the Dutch like to boast, while God made the world, they made the Netherlands, and today the Zuiderzee is gone, walled out by a massive, 19-mile dike completed in 1932 and supporting Highway E-10 that now links the provinces of North Holland and Friesland. In the sea's place is the reclaimed Flevoland polder and the immense freshwater Ijsselmeer. And the uninviting landscape has disappeared beneath the capital itself, most of whose buildings are supported by an estimated five million wooden piles driven deep into the soggy ground.

Amsterdam's convenient central location for trade was virtually its only natural resource and Amsterdammers, who soon became known for their acute (and frequently ruthless) business practices, were quick to take advantage of the fact. By the dawn of the sixteenth century, the early settlement had grown into a thriving city of about 12,000. This original city center, still referred to locally as the *walletjes* for the early walls surrounding it, is better known nowadays as the famous red-light district, with prostitutes, porno shops, and sex clubs incongruously housed in a picturesque quarter of preserved seventeenth- and eighteenth-century homes and warehouses.

Amsterdam reached the peak of its fortune during the Golden Age of the seventeenth century, when it became the center of a worldwide maritime empire and the base of the country's emergence as a major world power in spite of (in fact, largely because of) an almost perpetual state of war. With characteristic aplomb, the city carried on a highly profitable trade with both its enemies and allies, even going so far at one point as to insure enemy ships against destruction by Dutch forces. It also offered sanctuary to a stream of skilled refugees from other cities — again to its own considerable profit — and it was during this period that work was completed on the rapidly expanding city's crowning glory: the elegant network of canals ringing it, along which the great and newly rich constructed magnificent homes. Today Amsterdam has more canals than Venice — about 100 — containing more than 60 miles of waterways and spanned by some 1000 bridges.

The period following the Golden Age was one of decline for both the city and the country. By the dawn of the nineteenth century, Holland was a French province under Napoleon. After the emperor's defeat, it became a Dutch monarchy for the first time in 1815 under King Willem I. World War I bypassed the country, and by the time it was invaded by Nazi forces in World War II, Holland had become one of the most backward nations in Europe.

Today it is one of the most progressive, and much of the credit for this must go to Amsterdam. For this great and unique city, which even the Dutch themselves don't really understand and tend to dismiss as "difficult," has never lost its sense of pride or determined independence. Today, thanks largely to its opportunistic burghers and the liberal traditions they helped to establish, Amsterdam remains a city, more than anything else, of possibilities. It is open, *gezellig,* vibrant, amoral, fascinating, and — above all — alive. Certainly it is a city to be seen but, even more, a city to settle into, if only for a few days.

AMSTERDAM AT-A-GLANCE

SEEING THE CITY: During summer months, the towers of two of Amsterdam's most historic churches offer the best views of the old city center areas. The *Oude Kerk* (Old Church), which dates from the early fourteenth century, is located in the heart of the *walletjes* district in the oldest part of the city at Oudekerksplein. The church is open daily except Sundays from 10 to 5 (phone: 25-82-84). The *Westerkerk* (Western Church), Rembrandt's burial place, was completed in 1631 and is situated amidst Amsterdam's Golden Age canals in the most beautiful part of the city at the Westermarkt. Boasting the city's tallest church tower at more than 250 feet, it can be visited from 2 to 5 PM on Tuesdays, Wednesdays, Fridays, and Saturdays from June 1 until September 15 (phone: 84-27-05).

At the harbor next to Central Station is the modern Harbor Building housing the *MartInn* restaurant, from which you can enjoy a panoramic view of the harbor and canals in comfort. Open on weekdays for lunch and dinner until 10 PM. Reservations required. De Ruiterkade 7 (phone: 25-62-77). For a spectacular view of Amsterdam's newer southern fringe area, visit the elegant *Ciel Bleu* French restaurant atop the 23-story luxury *Okura Hotel*. Open every day from 6 PM to 1 AM. Reservations recommended. Ferdinand Bolstraat 175 (phone: 78-71-11).

SPECIAL PLACES: The major sights of Amsterdam are grouped conveniently around a few principal areas, all within walking distance of one another. The city's central landmark and natural focal point is Dam Square, or simply, "the Dam." At the end of the Damrak — a short street leading from the harbor and Central Station — the busy square is dominated by the distinctive war memorial constructed there in 1956. In good weather, the steps ringing the monument are a sea of young people — residents and tourists — resting, singing, making plans. The open plaza of the square opposite the monument often attracts a variety of spontaneous and organized activities, and free puppet shows are staged there on most Wednesday and Saturday afternoons in the summer.

Taking a boat tour of Amsterdam's canals has become a virtual tourist cliché, but it's still the best way to make a first acquaintance with the city. Several operators along the Rokin, the Damrak, and the Nassaukade run the tours, which last about an hour. The best tour is run by *Kooij,* near the Dam on the Rokin at the intersection with Spui. Tours depart every few minutes (phone: 23-38-10).

Royal Palace – Although hailed as the "eighth wonder of the world" after its completion in 1662 because of the 13,659 wooden piles holding it up, the queen hardly ever uses it and its regal interior, decorated by the leading artists of the time can be viewed during the summer on weekdays from 12:30 to 4 PM; and on some Wednesdays in winter at 1:45 PM. Small admission charge. On Dam Square, opposite the war memorial across the plaza (phone: 24-86-98).

Nieuwe Kerk (New Church) – An imposing late Gothic church dating from around 1500 and the traditional place of inauguration of new monarchs. Following two decades of restoration, the church was reopened just in time for the installation of Queen Beatrix in 1980. On Dam Square, next to the Royal Palace. Open weekdays 11 AM to 4 PM, Sundays noon to 5 PM, with an organ concert at 3 PM; closed January and February (phone: 23-64-32).

De Drie Fleschjes (The Three Bottles) – A historic, cask-lined tasting house unchanged since it first opened for business in 1650. Make sure you sample some of the traditional "old Holland" liqueurs (the best-known brands are Bols and Hoppe) that are its specialty. Open daily except Sundays from 12 PM to 8:30 PM. Behind the Nieuwe Kerk at Gravenstraat 18 (phone: 24-84-43).

Wynand Fockink – Another atmosphere-saturated tasting house notable for its 1679 interior, collection of hand-painted mugs, and illustrated bottles immortalizing all of Amsterdam's mayors since 1800 (irreverently known as turkeys). Sample the mellow, aged gin *(oude jenever)* or taste a liqueur or two. Seeing one of these splendid establishments should not stop you from visiting the other as well. Each is special in its own way and they're well within crawling distance of each other. Open daily except Sundays from 11 AM to 8 PM. Directly behind the Dam monument at Pijlsteeg 31 (phone: 24-39-89).

Canals – More than any other, Amsterdam is a city to stroll through. Not to be missed is its most beautiful section — the concentric rings of canals known as the Singel (Moat), Herengracht (Gentlemen's Canal), Keizersgracht (Emperor's Canal), and Prinsengracht (Prince's Canal). To see what the elegant homes lining the canals originally looked like on the inside, pay a visit to the *Willet-Holthuysen Museum,* open Tuesdays through Saturdays from 10 AM to 5 PM; Sundays from 1 to 5 PM. Admission charge. Herengracht 605 (phone: 26-42-90).

Anne Frank House – A short way west of the Dam and just around the corner from the Westerkerk is the house containing the secret annex where the Frank family and their friends hid from the Nazis for 2 years. No matter how prepared you are, you will be shocked by the size and vulnerability of the quarters that housed 14-year-old Anne, her parents, their friends the Van Daans, their teenaged son Peter, and a dentist named Dussel. You'll go in behind a bookcase that disguised the entrance to the upstairs hideout and see the simple artifacts, photos, and newspaper clippings that speak so mutely and eloquently of tragic times.

Anne's father, Otto Frank (who was the lone survivor of the Gestapo raid in August 1944 that sent the whole group to extermination camps), found Anne's diary, which has become one of the great cultural documents of this century.

Downstairs there is an excellent exhibit on the city and its Jews during the war, a tale of heroism and cowardice. A visit to Anne's house is an excellent way to introduce young people to the horrors of the Holocaust. Open daily from 9 AM to 5 PM, Sundays from 10. Admission charge. Prinsengracht 263 (phone: 26-45-33).

Jordaan – Amsterdam's colorful working-class district. You should devote a day to simply exploring the maze of narrow streets and alleys with their innumerable small boutiques and arts and crafts shops sprinkled among the more traditional businesses . . . and several nights to experiencing the Jordaaners themselves in their characteristic neighborhood cafés — unlike any others in Amsterdam (see *Nightclubs and Nightlife*). The major part of the Jordaan is bordered by the Rozengracht, Lijnbaansgracht, Brouwersgracht, and Prinsengracht, with the most interesting shops concentrated on the 2e Anjeliersdwarsstraat, 2e Tuindwarsstraat, and 2e Egelantiersdwarsstraat. Try to catch the Saturday market on the Lindemarkt.

Walletjes – Immediately to the east of the Dam is the picturesque old-city center named for the medieval walls that once surrounded it. This attractive area includes a number of purely historic sites, described in the entries that follow, and is worth a daytime walk. Ironically, perhaps, the old-city center is now best known as the red-light district, a European capital of public sex. And it really is public; everything is out in the open, with no effort at concealment. (Once Paris was the world's sex capital; now it looks tame in comparison with once-puritanical cities like Copenhagen and Amsterdam). Almost 1,000 "girls," many of them extremely attractive, line OZ Voorburgwal, the Oudezijds Achterburgwal, and the small neighboring streets, standing in windows with real red lights, on the streets, and even riding bicycles. There are live sex shows and sex shops all along OZ Voorburgwal. The Zeedijk, as it is popularly known, is not a good area to walk around in alone; visit with a large group or by taxi.

Amstelkring Museum (Our Lord in the Attic) – The seventeenth century was a period of repression of Catholics, and at least 26 clandestine churches were built in city attics by 1681. This one, extending through the joined attics of three houses, is equipped with everything from organ to baroque altar. The entry house was set up in 1663 and has one of the few completely preserved classical seventeenth-century living rooms still existing in Amsterdam. Open daily from 10 AM to 5 PM, Sundays from 1 PM. Guided tours by appointment. Admission charge. In the heart of the walletjes district at Oude Zijds Voorburgwal 40 (phone: 24-66-04).

Waag (Weigh-House) – Part of a gate and a fragment of the old city walls dating from 1488, the Waag was later converted into a weighing house. Anatomy lessons were given here from 1619 until 1939, an early one of which was the subject of Rembrandt's famous painting *The Anatomy Lesson of Dr. Tulp*. The Waag now houses the Jewish Historical Museum. On the edge of the walletjes district at Nieuwmarkt 4 (phone: 24-22-09).

Schreierstoren (Weepers' Tower) – Dating from 1569, this is another fragment of the original city walls. Henry Hudson departed from here on his voyage to the New World in 1609. Tradition has it that the tower got its name from the sailors' wives who used to see off their husbands from here. It is located between the walletjes district and Central Station at the corners of Prins Hendrikkade and Geldersekade.

Flea Market – This is Amsterdam's famous open-air secondhand market. A major part of the fun used to be haggling over the price of treasures unearthed from the random mounds, but a surfeit of overaffluent visitors has spoiled the dealers somewhat. Still, you can try. On the Valkenburgerstraat near the Waterlooplein (for which the market was originally named). Open daily except Sundays from 10 AM to 4 PM.

Rembrandt House – The house where Rembrandt lived and worked from about 1639 to 1658 is fully restored and furnished much as it must have appeared to him. Virtually all of his 250 etchings are on display here. Open weekdays from 10 AM to 5 PM, Sundays from 1 PM. Admission charge. Near the flea market at Jodenbreestraat 4–6 (phone: 24-94-86).

Munt (Mint) – A short street called the Rokin leads to the Munt. Although named for the money-coining use it was put to after the French occupation, this monument, which dates from 1490, is interesting as another piece of the original city walls.

Rembrandtsplein – Turning left at the Munt takes you into the Reguliersbreestraat, which leads directly into the concentration of bars and nightclubs around the Rembrandtsplein. Once the city's butter market, Rembrandtsplein is now one of the centers of its nightlife, known particularly for striptease. If you enter the Rembrandtsplein from Amstelstraat, a street on your right, called Engelse Pelgrimsteeg, is where some of the English Pilgrims lived before leaving for the New World. Farther along the right-hand side of number 1, at the corner of Halve Maan Steeg, is the smallest police station in the world, now used for people who've had too good a night.

Try to catch a film at the Tuschinski, just before the square. This ornate art deco theater is worth seeing for its own sake, regardless of what's playing. Reguliersbreestraat 26 (phone: 26-26-33).

Begijnhof – The best known of the 75 *hofjes* (enclosed courtyards) still scattered around Amsterdam and unobtrusively concealed behind ordinary doors in the walls of residential buildings. Founded in 1346 as a cloister, it is now, like the other *hofjes,* an idyllic inner-city residential block for the elderly, but anyone may take advantage of the oasis of tranquillity provided by the courtyard. The Begijnhof also contains Amsterdam's English church as well as its oldest surviving house at number 34, constructed in about 1470 (not open to the public). The easy-to-miss entrance is on a short street called Spui leading from the Rokin.

Flower Market – Amsterdam's famous floating flower market, on a string of barges moored along the Singel between the Munt and the Leidsestraat, is a delight for flower lovers. You can board the barges and shop, and you can also get good prices for cut flowers as well as dried and silk blooms. The flower market is especially lovely on summer nights, when it is illuminated by hundreds of lights reflected in the canals.

Leidseplein – One of the city's major centers of nightlife; in the summer its open terrace is also a favorite daytime gathering place for dedicated people watchers and beer drinkers; in winter, its open-air ice skating rink is popular. Next door to the terrace is the Stadsschouwburg, home of the Netherlands Opera and the world-famous National Ballet. Leidseplein 26 (phone: 24-23-11).

Vondel Park – Amsterdam's beautiful main park, with 120 acres of woodland, waterways, grassy fields, and one of the best jogging tracks in town. In summer, it is transformed into just the kind of colorful human zoo Amsterdam would be expected to produce, with a number of open-air events presented on an almost daily basis (see *Special Events*). Bordered by Constantijn Huygensstraat, Overtoom, Amstelveenseweg, Koninginneweg/Willems Parkweg.

Rijksmuseum – This world-famous museum is probably best known for its possession of Rembrandt's *Night Watch*, but it also has the world's greatest collection of Dutch masters and other painters from the fifteenth to the nineteenth century. Open weekdays (except Mondays) from 10 AM to 5 PM, Sundays from 1 PM. Admission charge. Stadhouderskade 42 (phone: 73-21-21).

Stedelijk Museum – Amsterdam's museum of modern art, with paintings and sculptures dating from the mid-nineteenth century as well as changing exhibitions of contemporary international artists. Open Tuesdays through Saturdays from 10 AM to 5 PM; Sundays, 1 to 5 PM. Admission charge. Paulus Potterstraat 13 (phone: 73-21-66).

Van Gogh Museum – Grouped with the Rijksmuseum and the Stedelijk along Amsterdam's appropriately named Museumplein, this newest of the city's big three museums only opened in 1972. Its ultramodern facilities feature an unrivaled collection of 200 paintings and 400 drawings by the famous Dutch artist. On Sundays from 1:30 to 4 PM, adults can take art lessons, complete with live models. (Most Dutch museums charge admission fees, but some museums — including the Van Gogh Museum and Rijksmuseum — are free on Wednesdays.) Open weekdays (except Mondays) from 10 AM to 5 PM, Sundays from 1 PM. Paulus Potterstraat 7 (phone: 76-48-81).

Rai – Amsterdam's modern congress and exhibition center, with a regularly changing schedule of major international trade fairs, exhibitions, and expositions. Europaplein 8 (phone: 541-1411).

Albert Cuyp Market – Amsterdam's largest and most colorful street market, with rows of stalls selling food, clothing, books, and practically everything else imaginable. It extends for blocks along the street for which it is named, starting at the Ferdinand Bolstraat, not far from the Museumplein. Open daily except Sundays and not to be missed whether or not you buy.

Aviodome Museum – A perfect way to fill in waiting time at Schiphol Airport, with exhibits on everything to do with flight, from the first flying reptile of 150 million years ago to a replica of the Wright Brothers' plane, a mockup of a modern jet cabin, and a half-scale model of the Apollo Moon Lander. Kids who visit on their birthdays receive a flying lesson in the working Link trainer. Open every day except Mondays. Admission charge. At Schiphol International Airport, about 6 miles from Amsterdam on Highway E-10 to The Hague (phone: 17-36-40).

Maritime Museum – This collection pays tribute to the country's three centuries of globe-girdling exploits. Displays include ship models, nautical paintings, and charts. Open Tuesdays through Saturdays, 10 AM to 5 PM; Sundays from 1 PM to 5 PM.

Arts and Crafts Center – This is a complex of 16 shops where you can see traditional Dutch craftsmen at work — and buy their finished handmade products. It's also a good place to sample typical Dutch sweet treats. Special presentations are featured on weekends. Open Tuesdays through Sundays from 10 AM to 5 PM, Nieuwendijk 16 (phone: 246501).

World Trade Center – This colossal complex of offices, shops, and exhibition halls caters to the international businesses that are the lifeblood of the city. Stravinskylaan 1 (phone: 461166).

■**EXTRA SPECIAL:** If you're feeling romantic, or would like to be, take a candlelit evening wine and cheese tour of the canals, May to mid-September. Tours last about 2 hours and reservations are necessary. Bergmann, Tesselsekade opposite Central Station (phone: 22-77-88).

SOURCES AND RESOURCES

For brochures, general information, maps showing all the major sights, lists of many of the city's hotels and restaurants, and similar materials, go to the city tourist offices (VVV) in the Old Dutch Coffee House opposite the front of the Central Station. Leidseplein 15. Open daily, 9 AM to 8:30 PM, except Sundays 10 AM to 5:30 PM (phone: 26-64-44).

In the US, contact the Netherlands Tourist Office, Information Dept., 437 Madison Ave., New York, NY 10022 (phone: 212-223-8141).

Avoid paying for most commercial "tourist" maps, as these simply repeat information the VVV is happy to supply for free. Worth the expense for its detail (which includes the entire public transport system) is the *Falkplan,* available at any newsstand.

For Local Coverage – The best guide to what's on is the weekly *Amsterdam This Week,* free from the VVV. Current films, which are shown in their original language, are also listed. Don't take the bar, club, and restaurant listings as definitive, however, since they pay to be included. *This Week* and the *Amsterdam Times* also contain listings of museums and other sights as well as general information and useful tips.

The English-language monthly magazine *Holland Herald* covers activities of interest to visitors throughout the country and frequently runs features on restaurants, shopping, special attractions, and Dutch life in general. It is available on KLM flights and at major newsstands in the city center.

The following recommended books are available in Amsterdam bookstores; most are not available in the US: An outstanding photographic souvenir of Amsterdam, as well as an excellent and knowledgeable survey of the city and its people, is the Time-Life *Amsterdam* book in the Great Cities series, written by expatriate Dutch author Hans Koning. For the very serious reader, another book of the same name by Roelof van Gelder and Rene Kistemaker presents a solid history of the Dutch capital from its birth around 1200 to its Golden Age in the 17th century. Many of the city's most colorful aspects are well showcased in *The Glory of Amsterdam,* by a talented trio of photographers, A. van der Heyden, B. Kroon, and T. Land. A companion for exploring another side of life in Amsterdam is Ben ten Holter's splendid guide, *Amsterdam Pub,* subtitled with perfect accuracy *A Pub Crawler's Delight.* The entire country is in focus with *Insight Holland,* Max Dendermonde's liberally photographed and lively look at the quirks and charms of his native land. Other fascinating insights are offered by Helen Colijn, a Dutch-born American, in *Of Dutch Ways.*

Before leaving home, pick up a Culture Card. This will guarantee you access to many of Holland's otherwise sold-out concert and dance performances as well as free admission to the country's museums and other valuable concessions. For details, contact one of the Netherlands National Tourist Offices (see *National Tourist Offices in the US,* GETTING READY TO GO).

CLIMATE AND CLOTHES: Amsterdam winters tend to be mild, with the minimum average temperature in the coldest months of January and February at about 31°F (0°C). The sunniest month is June, and peak average temperature throughout the summer is about 70°F (21°C). A useful accessory is an umbrella — if you can keep it from blowing away.

GETTING AROUND: Bus and Tram – The workhorse of Amsterdam's exemplary system is its network of frequently running trams (streetcars), supplemented by bus routes and a metro (subway) line. The city is divided into tariff zones. Buy a multiple "strip card" from the driver, tell him your destination, and he will stamp the appropriate strip for that zone. Most places in the city center require two strips. Cards can also be purchased at reduced prices from the GVB (city transport) office in front of Central Station, where simplified maps of the system are available as well. All cards are good for unlimited transfers within the same zone for one hour after being stamped. If transferring, you can enter trams by the rear door. Another money saver is the *dagkaart* (day card), which permits unlimited travel on the date purchased. Persons over 65 and under 10 travel at half-fare. After the normal system shuts down (around midnight), the night bus network *(nachtbus),* covering the main routes through the city, is in service.

Taxi – Service is expensive, and taxis don't normally cruise, although you can sometimes flag down an empty one. The easiest way to get one is through a hotel porter or by calling 77-77-77.

Car Rental – *Hertz, Avis,* and many smaller firms are well represented at Schiphol Airport and in the city, but driving in Amsterdam is no way to have a happy holiday. If you do, here are some basic survival tips: (1) Trams have absolute right-of-way and enjoy exercising it; (2) all other traffic coming from the right usually has priority and the Dutch regard yielding as a matter of dent before dishonor; (3) stay out of marked cycle lanes and watch out for kamikaze cyclists; (4) keep a good book handy to spare your blood pressure. Rules of the road are contained in the *Welcome to Holland* brochure published by the National Tourist Office and available from most VVVs.

Bicycle – If you have nerves of steel, do as the Dutch do and rent a bike, but make sure you leave it securely locked! One source is *Rent-a-Bike* at Central Station, Stationsplein 33 (phone: 25-38-45).

Boat – A boat tour of the canals is the best way to get the feel of the city. In addition to the glass-topped sightseeing boats already mentioned under *Special Places,* canal bikes (pedal boats) for 2 to 4 persons can be rented at various locations around town, April 1 to October 1 (phone: 26-55-74).

MUSEUMS: Amsterdam has about 40 altogether. Additional museums of interest not mentioned under *Special Places* include:

Amsterdam Historical Museum, housed in a former orphanage dating from 1414, with changing exhibitions as well as permanent displays about the history of Amsterdam. Kalverstraat 92 (phone: 25-58-22).

Netherlands Industrial and Technical Institute, Tolstraat 129 (phone: 64-60-21).

Madame Tussaud's Waxworks Museum, Kalverstraat 156 (phone: 22-99-49).

Theater Museum, Herengracht 168 (phone: 23-51-04).

Museum of Biblical Antiquities, Herengracht 368 (phone: 24-79-49).

Fodor Museum, contemporary Dutch artists, Keizersgracht 609 (phone: 24-99-19).

't Kromhout, exhibition and demonstration of nineteenth-century shipbuilding, Hoogte Kadijk 147 (phone: 27-67-77).

Allard-Pierson Museum, an archaeological collection spanning several thousand years of classical culture. Oude Turfmarkt 127 (phone: 525-2556).

Royal Tropical Museum, 2 Linneausstraat (phone: 92-49-49).

Additional monuments include: *Noorderkerk* (Northern Church), from 1623, at the Noordermarkt; *Zuiderkerk* (Southern Church), 1611, Zandstraat; *Portuguese Synagogue,* Jones Daniël Meijerplein, dating from 1675; *Montelbaanstoren,* a city wall fragment dating from 1512, at the corner of Oude Schans and Oude Waal.

 SHOPPING: The world's largest duty-free shopping center is located at Amsterdam's Schiphol Airport. City shops are closed Sundays and Monday mornings, some all day Mondays. Normal hours are from 9 AM to 5:30 or 6 PM, with a slightly earlier closing time on Saturdays. Large stores and many smaller shops, especially in the center, remain open until 9 PM on Thursdays.

Amsterdam has three major shopping streets; the pedestrian-only Kalverstraat extending from the Dam to the Munt; the Leidsestraat lined with specialty shops between the Spui and the Leidseplein; and P.C. Hooftstraat for high-fashion apparel, elegant china, and gems.

Amsterdam has had a long history as a center of the diamond industry, and a number of old firms are happy to show visitors around their works. Whether you can afford to buy diamonds or not, you may want to see how the precious gems are polished to perfection. Contact Coster Diamonds at Paulus Potterstraat 2–4 (phone: 76-22-22) or A. Van Moppes and Zn, Albert Cuyptstraat 2 (phone: 76-12-42). You can pick up an introductory brochure about diamonds from the city tourist office.

Other good buys besides diamonds are famous Delftware, handicrafts, tulip bulbs, and antiques (watch out, however, for abundant fake diamonds or fake antiques; to be safe, stick to recommended merchants). The greatest concentration of antique shops is to be found along the Nieuwe Spiegelstraat and adjoining Spiegelgracht, near the Rijksmuseum. There is also a covered antique market at Looiersgracht 38, near the main police station between the Leidseplein and Jordaan, open Mondays through Thursdays 11 AM to 5 PM; Saturdays 9 AM to 5 PM (24-90-38), and a Sunday antique market during the summer at the Nieuwmarkt. Stamps and coins are featured every Wednesday and Saturday afternoon on the Nieuwe Zijds Voorburgwal between the Dam and the Spui and old books are on daily offer at the historic Oudemanhuispoort between Oude Zijds Achterburgwal and Kloveniersburgwal. For other Amsterdam markets, the Jordaan, and the new arts and crafts center, see *Special Places.*

The following shops are especially recommended:

Hajenius – Supplying "everything for the smoker" since 1826, including custom-rolled cigars. Rokin 92–96.

De Bijenkorf (The Beehive) – Amsterdam's renowned emporium concentrates on the finest in contemporary fashions and furnishings.

Bonebakker – This is the place for diamonds; the oldest and most respected gem merchant in the Netherlands, founded in 1792. Although their premises are elegant, prices aren't a bit higher than anywhere else. Rokin 88.

Authentic Ship Models – A fascinating array of wooden model ships and maritime antiques. A variety of "do-it-yourself" model kits featuring windmills and da Vinci machinery as well as ships. Bloemstraat 191.

Klompenboer – You can watch wooden shoes being made here. Nieuw Zijds Voorburgwal 20.

Maison de Bonneterie – This elegant, chandelier-hung Amsterdam institution, dating from the nineteenth century, specializes in high-quality fashion. Kalverstraat 183.

Metz – Designer clothes and decorative items plus an excellent selection of English imports. Keizersgracht 455.

Proceleyne Fles – Good for Delft blue. Muntplein 12 at the base of the Munt.

Fong Leng – For the latest in haute couture. P.C. Hooftstraat 77.

Tesselschade – Handmade dolls and typical crafts. Leidseplein 33.

Vroom and Dreesman – Amsterdam's second department store, carrying a wide range of goods. Kalverstraat 201.

Wijs and Zoon – For gift tulip bulb parcels. Opposite the flower boats at Singel 508.

 SPECIAL EVENTS: Art and antiques share the spotlight during *Amsterdam Art Weeks,* from early to late March. *The Queen's Birthday,* on April 30, is a time of uninhibited celebration throughout the land. In Amsterdam, festivities include a fireworks display, a fair on the Nieuwmarkt, cafés open all night, street music, and a huge open-air market in the city center. During the first 3 weeks of June is the annual *Holland Festival,* a day-and-night cultural extravaganza crammed with dance, music, and theater performances by top Dutch and foreign companies. During this period also is the alternative *Festival of Fools,* which attracts hundreds of fringe and experimental theater groups and troupes from all over the world. Throughout the summer, various music, mime, dance, theater, and special children's programs for all tastes are presented free on most days of the week in the Vondel Park. At the beginning of September the world's largest *floral procession* departs from Aalsmeer, site of the world's biggest flower auction, winding its way to Dam Square by late afternoon. In mid-September Jordaaners celebrate their own district and way of life with markets, fairs, cabarets, and other festivities during the 2-week *Jordaan Festival,* and on September 15, the 10-day *Art Festival* starts, during which time all concert and theater performances offer special, extra-low, fixed prices to introduce the new season. Tickets, which go on sale the last week of August (and disappear fast), can be obtained from the CISCA (Cultural Information and Service Center, Amsterdam) office at the side of the Stadsschouwburg at Leidseplein 26 (phone: 22-90-11). In about mid-November, St. Nicholas, the original Santa Claus, makes his grand entry into Amsterdam.

 SPORTS: Sports facilities within the city are much in demand and largely restricted to members. Those listed here are open to everyone, but phone ahead first to make sure there's a place for you. Additional facilities outside Amsterdam are included in *Exploring the Netherlands,* DIRECTIONS.

Bowling – *Knijn,* Scheldeplein 1 (phone: 64-22-11).

Cycling – There are special cycle paths for exploring the Amsterdamse Bos woodland park south of the city, where bikes can also be rented (phone: 44-54-73).

Fishing – At the *Bosbaan* in the Amsterdamse Bos, but you have to go through the formality of getting a license first, obtainable from any post office (phone: 43-14-14).

Golf – *Amsterdam Golf Club,* Zwarte Laantje 4, Duivendrecht (phone: 94-36-50).

Horseback Riding – *Amsterdamse Manege,* Nieuwe Kalfjeslaan 25, Amsterdam (phone: 43-13-42), has indoor and ring riding only.

Skating – *Jaap Eden Rink,* Radioweg 64 (phone: 94-98-94). Dutch artificial ice rinks are open only in the winter months.

Soccer – Amsterdam is, of course, the home of the world-famous championship *Ajax* soccer team. It's easier to get tickets to heaven than to home games, but if you're feeling blessed, you can always try at Olympic Stadium, Stadionplein 20 (phone: 71-11-15).

Tennis – *Park Tennis,* Stadionstraat 10 (phone: 62-87-67).

 THEATER: The *Mickery,* Rozengracht 117 (phone: 23-67-77), specializes in importing foreign avant-garde drama — usually performing in English — and mime groups. There are several resident English-language companies presenting contemporary plays in Amsterdam. The best are *ESTA,* which performs at the Centrum Bellevue Theater, Leidsekade 90 (phone: 24-72-48), and the

American Repertory Theater, Kerkstraat 4 (25-94-95). The *Shaffy Theater,* Keizersgracht 324 (phone: 23-13-11), also occasionally hosts English groups on tour. The *Carré,* Amstel 115–125 (phone: 22-52-25), frequently has top international performers and groups. Current schedules are listed for all of these in the *This Week* guide, and the VVV will also accept bookings (in person only).

MUSIC: The dry months for high culture are July and August, when the great orchestras are touring or taking a well-earned rest. At other times of the year, the best in classical music is usually at the *Concertgebouw,* Van Baerlestraat 98 (phone: 71-83-45). However, during the part of the 1985–86 season when this venerable edifice will be undergoing structural repairs, its world-famous orchestra will be performing at other venues around town. There is a regular series of concerts, on Saturday afternoons at the *English Church* in the Begijnhof (phone: 24-96-65), as well as frequent concerts of all kinds at the *Waalse Church,* Oude Zijds Achterburgwal 157 (phone: 23-20-74), and at the *Mozes & Aaron Church,* Waterlooplein 57 (phone: 22-13-05). Sunday morning coffee concerts and other entertaining events take place at the *Round Lutheran Church,* now a cultural annex of the *Sonesta Hotel,* Kattengat 1 (phone: 21-22-23). Pop concerts, featuring top international groups, are held at the *Jaap Edenhal* on the Radioweg (phone: 94-96-52). Popular jazz clubs are *BIM-Huis,* Oude Schans 73–77 (phone: 23-33-73); and *De Kroeg,* Lijnbaansgracht 163 (phone: 25-01-77). The cozy *Piano Bar Le Maxim,* Leidsekruisstraat 35 (phone: 24-19-20), features a variety of music. Current performances are listed in *This Week.* For bookings and further information, contact the VVV.

NIGHTCLUBS AND NIGHTLIFE: The greatest concentration of nightclubs and discotheques is around the Leidseplein, Rembrandtsplein, and adjoining Thorbeckeplein. Two of Amsterdam's best-known nightclubs are the *Blue Note,* Leidsedwarsstraat 71 (phone: 24-69-52), and *Piccadilly,* Thorbeckeplein 6–10 (phone: 26-84-94). For sex clubs, see *Sins.* A popular disco is *Zorba the Buddha,* Oude Zijds Voorburgwal 216 (phone: 25-96-42). For a late nightcap, stop in at the *Marriott Hotel*'s *Windjammer,* Stadhouderskade 21 (phone: 83-51-51), and the *Sonesta*'s *Club Boston,* Kattengat 1 (phone: 21-22-23). Young, informal, Dutch, and licensed to swing all night are *societeiten* like the *Dansen by Jansen,* Handboogstraat 15 (phone: 22-88-22), and *Stinx,* Kerkstraat 50 (phone: 26-37-00). To get into these places, you have to show your passport and take out a membership, which costs a few dollars.

What really distinguishes Amsterdam's nightlife is its unique cafés (highly recommended is the *Amsterdam Pub Guide* — see *Sources and Resources*). A full listing of the best would fill this volume by itself, but the representative sample that follows will get you started well. For other recommended places, see the jazz cafés listed under *Music* and those serving food under *Eating Out. Hoppe,* dating from 1670, is the most famous and most "in" of the traditional "brown" (small, dark, old-world, intimate, lively, convivial) cafés, at Spui 18–20 (phone: 24-07-56); *Gollum,* a minuscule place especially famed among those in the know for its wide variety of Belgian Trappist beers, Raamsteeg 4 (phone: 25-46-34); *Kalkhoven,* a relaxed, comfortable, classic Amsterdam café with the traditional carpeted tables, at Prinsengracht 283 (phone: 24-86-49); *De Englebewaarder,* a favorite haunt of artist and journalist types and popularly known as "the literary café," Kloveniersburgwal 59 (phone: 25-37-72); *Papeneiland,* tracing its ancestry back to a coffin-maker who sold drinks at the beginning of the seventeenth century, claims to be the oldest café in Amsterdam. It is distinguished by a tunnel entrance in its cellar that formerly led under the canal and was used by seventeenth-century Catholics as a secret way of getting together for worship, Prinsengracht 2 (phone: 24-19-89). *Chris,* a 1629 cafe, is probably best known for its toilet, which is flushed (to the discomfiture of innumerable victims) from the bar, Bloemstraat 42 (phone: 24-59-42); *Nol,* which resembles the preceding two, is a typical Jordaan café that comes alive nightly in a special Jordaan way. Not to be missed if you enjoy people uninhibitedly enjoying themselves, at Westerstraat 109 (phone: 24-53-80). For drinks mixed with music, visit *De Twee Zwaantjes,* where for several generations the local brew has been served accompanied by a song, Prinsengracht 114 (phone: 25-27-29). Note that most Amsterdam cafés normally close at 1 AM on weekdays (some later), an hour later on weekends. Many serve an important function as congenial daytime gathering places as well, and quite a few start the day (with excellent coffee, if you prefer) at 9 AM or earlier.

For the best guide to Amsterdam's extensive gay scene, pick up the *Man to Man* map, available at major central newsstands. You can also order it directly by sending $3 in cash (no checks) to: *Man to Man,* PO Box 10419, Amsterdam. In spite of the sexist title, this comprehensive listing of bars, coffee shops, clubs, hotels, and so on, also includes places catering to lesbians as well as help and advice centers. For information in Amsterdam, you can go directly to *Man to Man* at Spuistraat 21 (also a bookshop and film club) (phone: 25-87-97) or COC, Rosenstraat 8 (phone: 23-45-96).

 SINS: The center of erotic activity is the famous red-light district immediately east of the Damrak, bordered by the Warmoestraat, Zeedijk, and Damstraat as far as the Kloveniersburgwal. Here you will find rows of prostitutes on display behind street-level windows as well as hard-core sex clubs, films, porno shops, and the like. Most famous of the sex clubs is the three-floor *Casa Rosso,* at Oude Zijds Voorburgwal 108 (phone: 26-22-21). The most exclusive, which caters to the rich and famous, is not in the district at all. This is *Yab-Yum,* at Singel 295 (phone: 24-95-03). Other well-established clubs outside the district include *Satyricon,* Roompotstraat 1 (phone: 76-24-20), and *Bayadera,* Westeinde 18 (phone: 25-11-23). The city's major transvestite club is *Madame Arthur's,* Warmoesstraat 131 (phone: 26-25-79). A long-established and reputable escort agency is *Escort Guide Service,* Oude Zijds Voorburgwal 233 (phone: 24-77-31). There are also major "sex supermarkets" with books, films, and sex devices scattered throughout the center, such as *Christine le Duc,* at Spui 6 (phone: 24-82-65), Reguliersdwarsstraat 107 (phone: 23-13-21), and Leidsekruisstraat 33.

BEST IN TOWN

 CHECKING IN: If you arrive without reservations (not recommended), go to the VVV, which, for a nominal fee (a little over a dollar), will locate a room for you in one of Amsterdam's more than 200 hotels. Note that while the larger hotels and restaurants accept major international credit cards (primarily Diners Club and American Express), cards are not used widely in Holland.

Rates in most hotels vary according to time of year and individual rooms. In determining our classifications, we used as a standard the price of the most inexpensive double room with toilet and bath or shower during the summer season. Amsterdam hotels are not cheap. Expect to pay $75 or more in those places listed as expensive and $40 to $60 for those we have rated moderate. Rock bottom is $30 in those hotels in our inexpensive category unless you're prepared to share toilet facilities or put up with dormitory accommodations.

The big international hostelries will sell you the breakfast of your choice, but the more traditional Dutch hotels still include it as part of the room charge. It may be either Continental (coffee and rolls) or Dutch (heartier, with bread and cheese).

Americain (or American) Hotel – It is difficult to explain precisely what makes this landmark hotel, built in 1882, so special, but its ornate art nouveau café-restaurant, protected as a historical monument, is certainly part of the answer. Both Dutch and visiting celebrities find their way here eventually — as does everyone else in Amsterdam. A glass of beer, served by black-suited waiters, costs about the same as anywhere else in town and the clientele ranges from jeans-clad students to the jet set. More than any other hotel, the *Americain* captures the indefinable essence of the city. There is also a handy reading table with the major foreign papers. Open every day from 9 AM until 1 AM. Leidseplein 28 (phone: 23-48-13). Expensive.

Hilton – This ultramodern and luxurious 276-room canal-side hotel is decorated with original Dutch paintings. Its bar and disco offer evening entertainment. Apollolaan 138 (phone: 78-07-80). Expensive.

Sonesta – A new hotel incorporates 13 seventeenth-century houses and an ancient Lutheran church with its modern structure — 720 beds in all. *Rib Room,* coffee shop, and a brown café. Kattengat 1 (phone: 21-22-23). Expensive.

Apollo – Recently enlarged (230 rooms), its lobby fronts the water. Its special feature is a waterside bar with panoramic views of five canals. British management. Apollolaan 2 (phone: 73-59-22). Expensive.

Okura – A 23-story hotel with 768 beds, this Japanese-owned and operated hotel includes the *Blue Sky Penthouse Restaurant* with a panoramic view and French food; Japanese restaurant; a coffee shop; sauna; and shopping arcade. At Ferdinand Bolstraat 175 (phone: 78-71-11). Expensive.

Amstel Hotel – The grand old dame of Amsterdam hotels since it opened in 1866. Celebrities and royalty stay here, and so should you if you want to find out what old-world opulence and service are really all about. It has 118 rooms. Professor Tulpplein 1 (phone: 22-60-60). Expensive.

Hotel de l'Europe – An honorable alternative if you can't get into the *Amstel.* This elegant, 81-room hotel can trace its origins back to a fortress built in 1481 to defend the city. It was completely rebuilt in 1895 and has retained the grandeur of that extravagant period. Nieuwe Doelenstraat 2–4 (phone: 23-48-36). Expensive.

Grand Hotel Krasnapolsky – The *Kras* has grown over the years from a unique coffee shop begun by a Polish immigrant to an Amsterdam institution, and the complete renovation of its 380 rooms has not destroyed its character or its atmosphere. The only hotel actually located on the Dam, at number 9 (phone: 55-49-111). Expensive.

Hotel Pulitzer – An attractive mix of old and new, with 200 rooms built into a group of 19 interconnected historic canal houses. The rooms are modern but by no means uniform, since their layout is necessarily determined by the original architecture. The original roof beams have also been retained. Prinsengracht 315–331 (phone: 22-83-33). Expensive.

Jan Luyken Hotel – In the heart of the concert and museum quarter, this first-class 65-room hotel combines modern amenities with traditional Dutch hospitality. Jan Luykenstraat 54–58 (phone: 76-41-11). Moderate.

Ambassade Hotel – A pleasant, old-fashioned, traditional Dutch hotel whose 42 rooms are in a historic, antique-furnished canal house. Herengracht 341 (phone: 26-23-33). Moderate.

De Roode Leeuw – There are 86 recently modernized rooms in this long-standing Amsterdam hotel just off the Dam. Damrak 93–94 (phone: 24-03-96). Moderate.

Mikado – There are only nine rooms in this tiny modern hotel, but each one is immense and all are on the ground floor. If you like the personal touch, this is the place for you. Not only will the staff have no difficulty remembering who you are, but they will serve you breakfast in bed. No phones in the rooms. Amstel 107–111 (phone: 23-70-68). Moderate.

Wiechmann – Owned by a former Oklahoman, a Mr. Boddy, this 30-room hotel (only 12 have bath or shower) is friendly, comfortable, and reasonable. It has a bar and a breakfast room; no elevator. Prinsengracht 328–330 (phone: 26-33-21). Moderate.

Canal House Hotel – It has 16 cozy and comfortable rooms, most overlooking the canal, set in a homey, antique-furnished seventeenth-century merchant's house. No phones in the rooms. Keizersgracht 148 (phone: 22-51-82). Moderate.

Hotel Trianon – Just around the corner from the concert hall and major museums, this attractive hotel has 60 rooms, all with bath or shower, plus a restaurant overlooking an enclosed garden. J. W. Brouwersstraat 3 (phone: 73-20-73). Moderate.

Kabul – This hotel in the heart of the red-light district mainly attracts the young, but its four rooms with baths are the cheapest in the city. There are also 15 double rooms without toilets and showers as well as dormitory accommodations. Room phones only for contacting the desk. Warmoestraat 38–42 (phone: 23-71-58). Inexpensive.

Wijnnobel – Small, with only 12 rooms, none with bath or shower, no phones and no elevators, this hotel features prewar European atmosphere, a warm host, and breakfast served in rooms. There is a small gold sign outside, a marble entrance, and formidable stairs (nonclimbers, beware!). Vossiusstraat 9 (phone: 72-22-98). Inexpensive.

 EATING OUT: Amsterdam is justly famed for its restaurants — more than 200 specializing in foreign food alone — and especially famed for its Indonesian import, *rijsttafel* (rice table). Don't miss the chance to experience this 20-course gourmet extravaganza.

In a traditional *rijsttafel* — the ceremonial feast of the Dutch colonists in Indonesia — a large dish of rice is surrounded by up to 20 smaller dishes of meat and chicken with a variety of sauces, prawns, kebabs in peanut sauce, roast pork on sticks, fried bananas, cucumber in sour sauce — and many, many others, some spicy and some bland. It is a treat. If you are in the mood for lighter fare, try *bami goreng,* buttered noodles with strips of meat, or *nasi goreng,* a plate of rice with meat. All are served in Amsterdam's ubiquitous Indonesian restaurants.

Traditional Dutch foods and drinks should also be sampled. You will probably be familiar with Gouda and Edam, the popular Dutch cheeses, already. Many open-air stalls around the city hawk salted raw herring, a Dutch favorite, for about $2.

Meals in Holland are designed to stick to your ribs and to warm you in winter. Especially good in cold weather (if you need an excuse) is classic Dutch split-pea soup, or *erwtensoep.* Also good are *capucijners,* an indigenous Dutch bean; Dutch beef stew *(hutspot);* and broccoli or kale with potatoes and sausage *(boerenkool met rookworst).*

Dutch beer, particularly Amstel or Heineken, is excellent. Gin is the native liquor, called *jenever* in Dutch; *oude jenever* is aged gin, milder and mellower; *jonge jenever* is stronger and plainer in taste.

For the best in cheap eating, try one of our recommended cafés ($10 or less) or a traditional *broodjeswinkel* (sandwich shop, not to be confused with modern junk-food snack bars).

At the restaurants we have rated as expensive, be prepared to part with $70 or more for a complete dinner for two, including wine, drinks, and coffee. You can get away with considerably less, however, if you choose carefully from the varied menus. Places in the moderate category range between $30 and $50 for everything; at those listed as inexpensive, expect to pay about $20 (with the simplest about half that).

Note that any restaurant displaying the blue Tourist Menu sign (there are several in Amsterdam) must provide a three-course meal for the fixed price of about $7 (not including drinks). In Amsterdam, service charges and local taxes are usually included

in the bill. Reservations are necessary unless otherwise stated. Credit cards are accepted
only where specifically mentioned.

Dikker & Thijs – An elegant, refined restaurant long famed among the Dutch for
the high standard of its French cuisine. Closed on Sundays. Major credit cards.
Prinsengracht 444 (phone: 26-77-21). Expensive.

't Swarte Schaep (The Black Sheep) – Popular for its specialty — filet steak
mouton noir — this restaurant is best appreciated from an upstairs table overlooking the lively Leidseplein. Korte Leidsedwarsstraat 24 (phone: 22-30-21). Expensive.

Dorrius – Authentic Dutch food in an authentic Dutch setting; the place to try the
Dutch pea soup, for which Holland is famous. Closed Sundays. Major credit cards.
Nieuwe Zijds Voorburgwal 342 (phone: 23-58-75). Expensive.

Dikkert – French cuisine featuring specialties of pheasant, venison, and rabbit in a
300-year-old windmill south of Amsterdam in bordering Amstelveen. Major credit
cards. Amsterdamseweg 104a (phone: 41-13-78). Expensive.

De Kersentuin – Quintessential nouvelle cuisine (with many ingredients flown in
daily from France) served in the lush surroundings of an indoor Oriental garden.
Food, service, and decor are among the most distinctive in town. Reservations
advised. Major credit cards. Dijsselhofplantsoen 7 (phone: 64-21-21). Expensive.

Miranda Paviljoen – A romantic, century-old teahouse on the banks of the Amstel
River featuring both Dutch and French specialties. Major credit cards. Amsteldijk
223 (phone: 44-57-68). Expensive.

Le Papillon – Most Amsterdam kitchens close at about 11 PM, but if your appetite
is jet-lagged, this cosmopolitan French restaurant is the place to go. It doesn't open
until 10 PM and doesn't close until 4 AM (5 AM on weekends). Frans Halsstraat
2–4 (phone: 64-13-23). Expensive.

D'Vijff Vlieghen (Five Flies) – It's a bit of an adventure just finding this place: The
main door doesn't open, so you must enter by way of a side street, called D'Viff
Vliaghen. There are a series of delightful dining rooms connected by steep little
sets of stairs. Try shellfish, fish, or the typically Dutch noisette of veal with
cherries. Spuistraat 294 (phone: 24-83-69). Expensive to moderate rate.

Bali – An Indonesian restaurant well known for its *rijsttafel*, this place is pricy for
its kind and a bit westernized, but still awfully good. Leidsestraat 89-97. Expensive
to moderate.

Oesterbar – This is the place for serious fish eaters: nothing fancy, just remarkably
fresh fish and shellfish of all kinds cooked simply, but to perfection. Enjoy your
meal seated at the counter near the ovens or one near the fish tanks. (Note that
the restaurant does not welcome solo diners.) Leidseplein 10 (phone: 23-29-88).
Moderate.

Keijzer – Comfortable, old-fashioned (in the best sense of the word) Dutch restaurant especially famed for its sole *à la meunière*. Closed Sundays. Major credit
cards. Van Baerlestraat 56 (phone: 71-14-41). Moderate.

Indonesia – One of Amsterdam's best *rijsttafels* is served in this elegant but friendly
restaurant overlooking the Munt. Major credit cards. Singel 550 (phone: 23-
20-35). Moderate.

Petra Van Niftrik – An intimate place with a muted interior of light gray, blue, and
rose. Entrées change monthly, though typical dishes include smoked eel soup and
rabbit with green pepper in cognac sauce. Reestraat 7. Moderate.

Silveren Spiegel – Picturesque and charming are the only words to describe this
intimate, antique-furnished restaurant located in two very crooked houses dating
from 1614. The food is international. Closed Sundays. Major credit cards. Kattengat 4 (phone: 24-65-89). Moderate.

Sea Palace – Amsterdam's only floating restaurant captures the flavor of the Far

East with Pekinese and Shanghai specialties served in a reconstructed Chinese pagoda overlooking the inner harbor. Reservations. Oosterdokskade 8 (phone: 26-47-77). Moderate to inexpensive.

Türkiye – Belly dancers and Turkish food are the attractions of this entertaining restaurant. Major credit cards. No reservations. Nieuwe Zijds Voorburgwal 169 (phone: 22-91-10). Inexpensive.

Brasserie 404 – A pleasant, informal place specializing in fish dishes and the best soups in town. Closed Sundays. No reservations. Singel 404 (phone: 23-35-22). Inexpensive.

New Peking – Near the museums and concert hall, this is one of the best of Amsterdam's many good Chinese restaurants. No reservations. Van Baerlestraat 166 (phone: 79-16-91). Inexpensive.

El Pacifico – One of many lively and informal restaurants packed into the red-light district's main thoroughfare, specializing in outstanding Mexican food. You can't reserve and you may be in for a long wait standing around the crowded bar at this popular place, so go easy on the tequila. Warmoestraat 31 (phone: 24-29-11). Inexpensive.

Scheltema – Long famed as the favorite watering hole of Amsterdam's journalists, this traditional café is highly regarded by its regulars for the quality, quantity, and reasonable prices of its food. No reservations. Nieuwe Zijds Voorburgwal 242 (phone: 23-23-23). Inexpensive.

't Smackzeyl – A typical neighborhood café on the edge of the Jordaan, mainly patronized by younger students living in the area. Ask the friendly barman to translate the menu scrawled on the wall. It's worth it. No reservations. Brouwersgracht 101 (phone: 22-65-20). Inexpensive.

Klein Kalfje – A lovely, old-Dutch café-restaurant beautifully situated on the Amstel. A great place to spend a sunny afternoon is the café's waterside terrace across the road. Closed Saturdays. No reservations. Amsteldijk 355 (phone: 44-53-38). Inexpensive.

Keuken van 1870 – Amsterdam's civic kitchen and the cheapest meal you will find in the city. The food is plain but filling, the service blurringly fast, and the decor nonexistent. The most interesting thing about this place is the other customers, and it has, in fact, become something of a minor tourist attraction. You may find it worth a visit . . . once. Closed weekends. Definitely no reservations. Spuistraat 4 (phone: 24-89-65). Inexpensive.

Broodje van Kootje – The most famous of Amsterdam's traditional sandwich shops. The decor is antiseptic but the food is varied, wholesome, and cheap. Recommended for a quick lunch or snack. For breakfast, try an *uitsmijter* — the Dutch version of ham and eggs. Leidseplein 20 (phone: 23-20-46), Rembrandtsplein 12 (phone: 23-65-13), and Spui 28 (phone: 23-74-51). Inexpensive.

Restaurant Split – This Yugoslavian restaurant has three long, narrow dining rooms decorated with folk crafts such as wood carvings and woven wall hangings. The menu features a variety of hearty multi-course dinners, but don't miss dessert — the whipped cream-filled *palacinka* is out of this world. Amsteldijk 53-55 (phone: 72-46-43). Inexpensive.

Sluizer – The good, solid fish served in this Old World restaurant with marble-topped tables and fringed lampshades makes it popular with Amsterdammers and visitors alike. No reservations. *Note:* Don't confuse this place with the restaurant of the same name next door. Utrechtsestraat 45 (phone: 26-35-57). Inexpensive.

ATHENS

Athens is the site of the greatest achievements of the classical age of Greece. Its architectural, social, artistic, and political triumphs have become a universal legacy. Against its ancient standards are measured the cultural, intellectual, and spiritual development of all Western civilizations.

And in Athens the units of this measure are everywhere apparent. Drive down a wide thoroughfare and you pass the Temple of the Olympian Zeus, masterfully carved Corinthian columns still intact, honoring the highest of Greek gods. Turn a corner in Monastiraki, the flea market, and you come upon the Agora, the ancient marketplace crowned by the Theseion, one of the best-preserved Doric temples, sacred to blacksmiths, who worked here 2,000 years ago; follow the Panathenaic Way, the grand ceremonial path of Ancient Athens, and like centuries of Athenians before you, you approach the Acropolis, the crown of Greek culture high on a rock above Athens.

For more than 2,000 years the Acropolis has dominated the city — first as a spiritual center and fortress; later as the site of the Parthenon, a temple honoring Athena, the patron goddess of Athens; still later as the locus of churches, mosques, and even harems as it was transformed by different conquerors. Today, stripped of the many statues that once lined the way, with drums and columns strewn about, the Acropolis remains even in ruins majestic and monumental.

The setting inspires contemplation, its starkness somehow appropriate. Bared to its essentials, you can only imagine the golden age of Greece (in the middle of the fifth century BC) when Pericles had the Parthenon built — every column curving slightly inward in order to appear perfectly straight at a distance — when the dramas of Aeschylus and Sophocles were performed for the first time in the Theater of Dionysus below; when democracy first brought all citizens together to decide their common fate on the Pnyx hill to the west.

The Acropolis commands an excellent view of the surrounding Attic plain and overlapping layers of Western civilization. Immediately below the walls lies the Agora; adjacent is Plaka, the nineteenth-century area frequented by Lord Byron when he lived in Athens. In the distance to the north rises Mt. Parnes, the highest mountain in Attica, and Mt. Pentelikon where Pentelic marble is quarried. Between the mountains spreads the Mesogheia Valley where grapes for resinated wine (*retsina*) are harvested. To the south lies the Saronic Gulf; slightly west of there a smokestack marks the offshore island of Salamis where the Greeks defeated the Persians in the famous naval battle of 480 BC.

To the east lies the modern city, spread out around the Acropolis almost like an afterthought. Planned for King Otto in 1840 by German architects,

Athens was designed to accommodate a maximum of 200,000 people. Today some 3.6 million people inhabit Greater Athens, which extends to the port of Piraeus. Roads are narrow and inadequate for the ever-increasing number of automobiles. Traffic is horrendous, with streets congested during seemingly interminable rush hours. The indefatigable breeze blowing in from the sea doesn't even manage to keep the air fresh, for Athens is blanketed, winter and summer, with a hazy cloud of pollution.

These intransigently modern problems have not been able to dim the city's splendid natural advantages. Athens' perfect Mediterranean climate — the sun shines brilliantly most of the year and the air is dry even in midsummer — endows the city with a relaxed atmosphere and outlook.

Athenians embrace their environment with relish. The cream-colored, terraced marble homes built into the hills are sunny and airy. Athenians take to the beaches lining the coasts year-round for sun, sea, and vigorous noisy games. As early as April, a few leathery-looking old men paddle around in the water — and are joined by everyone else quite comfortably from May to October. In Syntagma and Kolonaki squares, residents spend hours over cups of coffee — the thick, muddy Greek variety — discussing life and politics or just people-watching. Athenian workers break in the afternoons for a few hours, return to work, and head out to dinner quite late, about 10 PM. Even on weeknights, *tavernas* — informal restaurants — are full past midnight. In many *bouzoukia* — nightclubs in which traditional bouzouki music is played — the entertainment does not really start until midnight. Despite the big-city veneer, people take their time.

Travelers will find this both engaging and perplexing. The lifestyle is quite pleasant, but it takes its toll on the economy. Greece has mastered a few industries — its shipping fleet is the largest in the world and tourism is a well-organized business — but still Greece is one of the least productive of the major countries in Europe. A member of the European Common Market only since January 1, 1981, Greece entered as its tenth and poorest member. Greek economic analysts hoped that Greece's entry into the Common Market would boost the economy. But Greek industries and workers, previously sheltered by import restrictions, now face stiffer competition from Common Market countries, and the government is balking at conforming to standing EEC regulations, many of which favor the Northern European members. However, some benefits are beginning to roll in, and Greece stands to obtain billions of dollars' worth of agricultural and regional development subsidies.

The most populous and advanced city in Greece, Athens is caught between the incongruities of a valiant past and a problematic present. The dilemma is in part historic. After the classical age of Greece, Athens was conquered and dominated by foreign powers. Though the early rulers were relatively benign, Athens lost the freedom and democratic structure that nurtured its greatest cultural achievements. First conquered by the Macedonians and later by the Romans, Athens remained an important seat of learning until the Edict of Justinian closed the schools of philosophy in AD 529. Under Byzantine rule, many temples were modified to Christian use, and Athens became just another provincial city. After the fall of Constantinople in 1453, the Ottomans

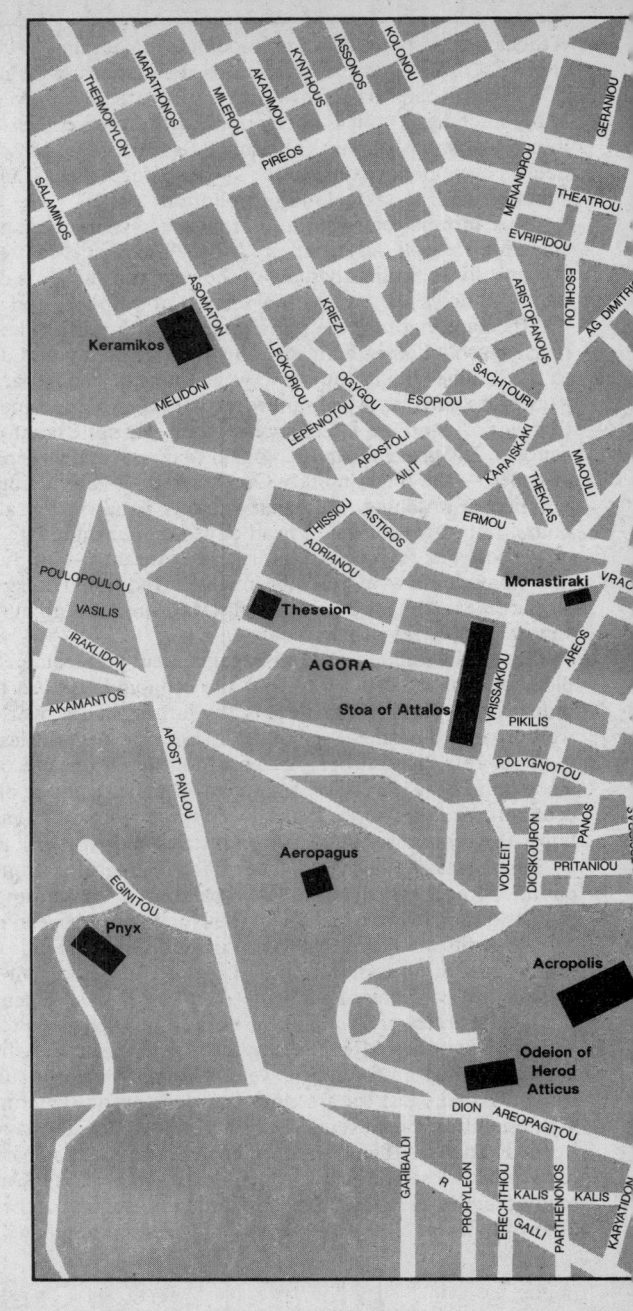

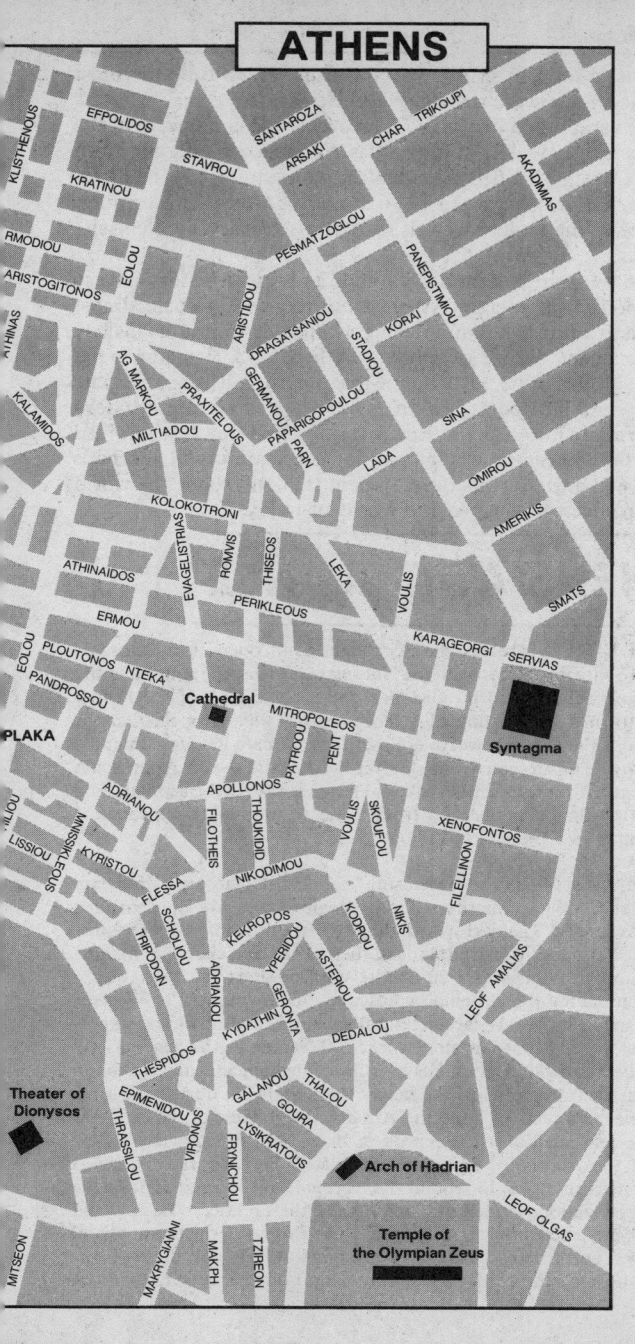
ATHENS

EFPOLIDOS
KLISTHENOUS
KRATINOU
STAVROU
SANTAROZA
ARSAKI
CHAR TRIKOUPI
AKADIMAS
EOLOU
RMODIOU
ARISTOGITONOS
PESMATZOGLOU
ARISTIDOU
DRAGATSANIOU
PANEPISTIMIOU
KORAI
STADIOU
GERMANOU
PAPARIGOPOULOU
PARN
SINA
AG. MARKOU
PRAXITELOUS
MILTIADOU
KALAMIDOS
LADA
OMIROU
AMERIKIS
KOLOKOTRONI
EVAGELISTRIAS
ROMVIS
THISEOS
LEKA
VOULIS
SMATS
ATHINAIDOS
PERIKLEOUS
KARAGEORGI
SERVIAS
ERMOU
PLOUTONOS
NTEKA
EOLOU
PANDROSSOU
Cathedral
MITROPOLEOS
PATHOOU
PENT
Syntagma
PLAKA
ADRIANOU
APOLLONOS
FILOTHEIS
THOUKIDID
VOULIS
SKOUFOU
XENOFONTOS
ILLIOU
LISSIOU
MNISIKLEOUS
KYRISTOU
NIKODIMOU
FILELLINON
FLESSA
SCHOLIOU
TRIPODON
KEKROPOS
ADRIANOU
YPERIDOU
KODROU
NIKIS
ASTERIOU
LEOF AMALIAS
KYDATHIN
GERONTA
DEDALOU
THESPIDOS
GALANOU
THALOU
EPIMENIDOU
SONOU
VIRONOS
GOURA
**Theater of
Dionysos**
THRASSILOU
FRYNICHOU
LYSIKRATOUS
Arch of Hadrian
LEOF OLGAS
MITSEON
MAKRYGIANNI
MAKPH
TZIREON
**Temple of
the Olympian Zeus**

seized the city and ruled for almost 400 years, during which time the most sacred sites of the Acropolis were damaged and desecrated.

Athens became the capital of a liberated Greece after the conclusion of the War of Independence in 1829. The country was ruled as a monarchy until 1967, when ex-King Constantine fled Greece after failing to topple the dictatorship established earlier in the year. In 1974, 5 months after the restoration of democracy in Greece, the monarchy was formally abolished by plebiscite in favor of a republic.

Athens has, in a sense, gone full circle. Though its ancient history is very ancient indeed, as a modern democracy Athens is entirely new, with an almost burdensome history and a future still unmade. Perhaps this split in its history has created the ambivalent nature of modern Athens — a city somewhat overshadowed by the glories of its past. But at this juncture, it is appropriate to begin again, as a young democracy in an especially rich setting. Modern Athens needs time to come into its own. But with the spirit that has survived centuries of foreign domination and subjugation, it certainly will. Perhaps here modern Greeks will bring forth a development that will shape the world of the future as their ancestors shaped the world of today.

ATHENS AT-A-GLANCE

 SEEING THE CITY: Lycabettus, the city's highest hill, opens up a panorama of Athens — Syntagma Square and the National Gardens, the Acropolis and its surrounding hills, and in the distance, the Saronic Gulf. The 912-foot summit is crowned by the tiny nineteenth-century chapel of St. George, visible from other parts of the city and worth a closer look. A café halfway up and a restaurant at the top provide unsurpassed views, refreshments, and meals. Approaches to the summit include footpaths that afford ever-expanding views of Athens, roads, and funicular. Open daily (the funicular operates from 8 AM to midnight). Entrance at Ploutarchou and Aristipou in Kolonaki (no phone).

 SPECIAL PLACES: Most of the interesting sights of Athens are within easy walking distance of one another. Archaeological sites are concentrated around the Acropolis. The narrow, winding streets of the immediately adjacent areas of Plaka and Monasteraki lend themselves to walking. Syntagma Square, the center of modern Athens, is a 20-minute walk or short cab ride away.

The Acropolis – Dominating the Athenian landscape, this monument of Western civilization is unsurpassed in its beauty, architectural splendor, and historical importance. Situated on a massive 512-foot limestone rock, 300 feet above the general level of the city, this naturally strategic location has been inhabited since Neolithic times. Circa 1500 BC, a Mycenean ruler crowned the height with a citadel; during the same period, the first in a series of a temples honoring Athena, the goddess of the city, was built — a tradition that continued over the centuries. In 480 BC, the Persians sacked the city and destroyed the Acropolis. Some 35 years later, Pericles, the renowned Athenian statesman, conceived a plan to rebuild the Acropolis on a grand scale as the true capital of Greek civilization. Under the direction of the architects Iktinos and Kallikrates, structures were erected that endure today. The Propylea, the monumental entrance on the west, was constructed between 449 and 444 BC. Though the roof was destroyed by thunder in 1645, the rows of columns, Doric on the outside (without bases) and Ionic on the inside (with bases and more elaborately designed capitals), still line the way. On the south side of the Propylea stands the temple of the Wingless Victory, Athena Nike, built between 425 and 422 BC in monolithic Ionic columns. On the north side of the entrance is a Roman tower built in the first century AD as a votive offering by Agrippa, nephew of Emperor Augustus.

Beyond the Propylea, on the highest part of the hill, stands the Parthenon, the main temple of the Acropolis, built between 447 and 432 BC of white Pentelic marble. This is the virgin Athena's most sacred temple, and everything about it is a celebration of perfect order, from its Doric columns to the *metopes* — friezes with reliefs of mythological battles — that decorate it (many of which now, alas, are in the British Museum in London). From a distance the columns appear perfectly parallel and straight, an illusion that is sustained only by a minor miracle of engineering, the turning of each column slightly inward to create an image of perfect harmony. To the north is the Erechtheion, a temple honoring both Athena and Poseidon, god of the sea, who in ancient times lost the battle to Athena for the worship of the Athenians. The Ionic structure contains several novelties in architecture, including the Karyatids, sculptures of lovely maidens that support a porch and stylized sculptural decor of little friezes of palm flowers between the capitals and columns that influenced the later Corinthian style. Because of environmental damage, five of the six original Karyatids have been replaced by copies. Four of the originals can now be seen at the Acropolis Museum. Athena is the patron of Athens because she gave men the gift of the olive, and her olive tree stands at the west side of the temple; a saltwater spring to represent Poseidon is said to have sprung inside the temple in ancient times. Close inspection of the supporting wall directly north of the Erechtheion reveals several drums that survive from the first Acropolis; their purpose is to keep alive the memory of the catastrophic sack of Athens by the Persians.

Over the years, the Acropolis has undergone many alterations at the hands of conquerors. The Parthenon and the Erechtheion were converted into churches during the Byzantine era. During the Turkish occupation, the Parthenon was used as a mosque and the Erechtheion as a harem. The roof was blown off in a battle between the Turks and the Venetians in 1687, yet the majesty of the Parthenon has proved indestructible.

Even today, air pollution and a high content of sulfur in the rain water are turning the once-tough marble to soft gypsum. The work of reconstruction is under way. Rehabilitation of the Erechtheion was recently completed; the limestone Acropolis rock base is being stabilized; and architects began a 10-year renovation of the Parthenon in 1983 and will soon follow with the reconstruction of the Propylea. Despite all hardships, the Acropolis has endured thousands of years as one of the highest accomplishments of Western civilization.

The Acropolis Museum houses most of the works of art discovered in the Acropolis since excavation began in 1835. Highlights of the collection include fragments of the Parthenon frieze and numerous sculptures — the *Kritian Boy,* the *Calf Bearer,* the *Rider and the Running Hound,* and the *Korai* maidens. Open daily. Admission charge. Entrance on Areopagitou St. (museum phone: 323-6665).

Pnyx – This hill on the west side of the Acropolis, which now serves as the theater for the sound and light show, is the true cradle of Athenian democracy. Here, in classical times, Athenians assembled to decide issues. All free male citizens were summoned to the hill. Officers carrying ropes covered with fresh paint would round up those who didn't come and mark them so that they could be identified and fined. No such penalties are incurred today for those who don't attend the sound and light show. The script delivers a dramatized history of the Acropolis in ridiculously overblown language. But the view of the Acropolis is spectacular. Shows in English are held nightly at 9 PM from April 1 to October 31. Admission charge. Entrance on Areopagitou St. opposite the Acropolis.

Areopagus – The highest court of ancient Athens convened on this hill below the Acropolis. According to Aeschylus, Orestes was tried here for the murder of his mother, Klytemnestra. The jury split and Athena broke the tie by throwing her support behind Orestes. Legend has it that he had been chased by the Furies — mythological creatures with women's heads and birds' bodies. In AD 51, St. Paul delivered his Sermon of the Unknown God from this site. Open daily. Free. Just below the west slope of the Acropolis.

Mouseion Hill – In 1687, a Venetian cannon fired from this hill severely damaged the Parthenon. At the top, there's a monument of Philopappos, a prominent Athenian of the second century AD. Open daily. Free. Aeropagitou west of the Acropolis.

Agora (Stoa of Attalos) – The commercial and public center of ancient Athens spreads out below the Acropolis, which was the town's spiritual and military center. Situated at the junction of the three main roads of the time — from Piraeus, the Mesogheia Valley, and the mountains — the Agora was the main marketplace. Leaders, philosophers, and common people gathered here to discuss current events and metaphysics. During the classical age of Greece, Sophocles taught here, and the plays of Aeschylus were performed in the theater. Much of what remains — columns, statues — is in ruins, but you can recreate the scene imaginatively. You needn't work too hard on the reconstructed Stoa of Attalos. Originally built in the second century BC by Attalos II, king of Pergamon, the marble-colonnaded structure was rebuilt with funds from private American donors. Once an arcade of shops, the Stoa is now a museum housing artifacts excavated from the site, including early plans for the building and the Acropolis and a collection of marble statues and sculptures. The Theseion, or Temple of Hephaistos and Athena, sits atop the highest point of the Agora. These two were patron saints of the blacksmiths and coppersmiths who worked nearby and continue to do so today. Built between 444 and 442 BC, the Theseion is one of the best preserved Doric temples in existence. In the seventh century AD, the temple was adapted to Christian use as a church sacred to St. George. Most of the ruins are scattered between the Stoa and the Theseion. Open daily; museum closed Tuesdays. Admission charge. Entrance on Adrianou.

Keramikos – The cemetery of ancient Athens has some original graves in place, including the Memorial of Dexilos, honoring a knight killed in action at Corinth in the fourth century BC. Other graves are in the Oberlaender Museum, just beside the cemetery entrance. Open daily; museum closed Tuesdays. Admission charge. Off Ermou below Monastiraki (phone: 346-3552).

Theater of Dionysos – Built in the fourth century BC, this is the oldest of the Greek theaters. The plays of Sophocles, Euripides, Aristophanes, and Aeschylus were first performed here. Open daily. Admission charge, except on Sundays. On the slope of the Acropolis (phone: 321-0219).

Odeion of Herod Atticus – Athens's other ancient theater was built in AD 160 by a rich Athenian philosopher. The structure illustrates the Roman influence on later Greek architecture. This theater is now the setting of the annual, summer-long Athens Festival, which features opera, ballet, and concerts performed by first-rate companies from Europe and the US. Open daily. Free. On the southern slope of the Acropolis (phone: 922-6330).

Temple of the Olympian Zeus – Honoring Zeus, the supreme god of heaven and earth, this massive temple was built over a 700-year period beginning in the sixth century BC. The temple was the largest constructed in the elaborate Corinthian style; only 14 columns remain intact; one is fallen — all are beautifully carved. Open daily. Admission charge. Queen Olga and Amalias.

Arch of Hadrian – Roman Emperor Hadrian had this arch constructed in AD 132 to demarcate the city he built from the earlier city said to be built by the mythological King Theseus. Open daily. Free. Queen Olga and Amalias. (phone: 922-6330).

Olympic Stadium – On the site of the ancient Panathenean Stadium, this white marble structure was the stadium for the first modern Olympic games in 1896. Open daily. Free. Vasileos Konstantinou and Agras.

Plaka – Hugging the north and northeast slopes of the Acropolis, this section of nineteenth-century Athens retains its essential nature. The narrow, winding streets are lined with restored one- and two-story houses, shops selling popular Greek art, and lively *tavernas*. One of the best places to go for dinner and evening entertainment is *Xynos*, 4 Agelou Geronta (for a full description of this and several other Plaka restaurants, see *Eating Out*). At the west side of Plaka is the Roman Agora and the unusual Tower of the Winds Monument. Dating from the first century BC, this marble octagonal-shaped structure has eight reliefs, each personifying a wind blowing from a different direction. Open daily. Free. Between Ermou and the north slope of the Acropolis.

Monastiraki – Traditions of leatherworking and metalsmithing first carried on in the adjacent Agora continue here today. Numerous shops carry a wide variety of items, including antiques, jewelry, leathergoods, copper, and bronze. You can see coppersmiths work in the back of their shops. Sometimes you can bargain for goods. For more information, see *Shopping*. Open daily. Free. Off Monastiraki Square, on and around Ifestou.

Greek Orthodox Cathedral – Since 1864, this has been the headquarters of the Greek Orthodox Church. The structure is actually composed of stones from 72 demolished cathedrals. The interior is impressively ornate. Note the lovely twelfth-century Byzantine church immediately to the south. Open daily. Free. Mitropoleos, between Syntagma and Monastiraki.

Syntagma Square – The center of modern Athens, this is prime territory for watching the world go by. Sitting at one of the cafés, you can watch foreign businesspeople rushing in and out of the luxurious *NJV Meridien* and *Grande Bretagne* hotels, office workers heading home for their lunch break, and Greek men trying to pick up female tourists. The House of Parliament and Memorial to the Unknown Soldier flank the east side of the square. Twenty minutes before every hour, *evzones*, soldiers in traditional dress, perform the Changing of the Guard ceremony; Sundays at 11 AM the entire regiment comes out in full regalia. Free. Between Georgiou and Othonos.

National Gardens – These shady gardens provide pleasant relief from the summer sun. Queen Amalia, wife of King Otto, had them designed some 140 years ago. Peacocks and waterfowl are at home here and nightingales sing in the spring. Open daily. Free. Entrances on Amalias, Vasilissis Sofias, and Irodou Attikou.

Benakis Museum – Just a short walk from Syntagma, this collection from the private holdings of Antonios Benakis has an eclectic display — costumes, ceramics, furniture, and arms. Some of the highlights are a writing desk of Lord Byron, Moslem wood carvings, and delicate Byzantine miniatures. Closed Tuesdays. Admission charge, except on Sundays. 1 Koumbari (phone: 361-1617).

National Archaeological Museum – One of the world's greatest museums, this institution houses a treasure of art spanning 2,500 years of ancient Greek civilization. The scope and breadth of the collection are staggering — rooms and rooms of Greek vases, statues, and sculpture. Some of the highlights are the Death Mask of Agamemnon; a statue of Anavissos Kouros, the finest of the tradition of *kouroi,* beautiful youths represented nude in a rigid stance with their left feet slightly forward and their arms at their sides; the bronze statue of Poseidon, god of the sea, discovered at Cape Artemision in 1928; the statue of the Youth from Marathon; and the sculpture of the bronze Jockey and Horse of Artemision. Closed Mondays. Admission charge. Patission between Tositsa and Irakliou (phone: 821-7717).

■**EXTRA SPECIAL:** When you've had your fill of the city, head for Sounion and the Temple of Poseidon, 40 miles (64 km) south of Athens along the southwest coast. Though the road is somewhat congested in the summer, the route follows the Saronic Gulf, and the view is Greece at its most elemental — sun, rock, and sea. The closer you get to Sounion, the better it gets, as the road winds around steep cliffs overlooking spectacular vistas.

High on a cliff above the sea stands the Temple of Poseidon. Only 15 Doric columns remain, but the temple of the sea god is beautiful in all its starkness. The setting, the ever-changing light, the crashing waves, inspired no less a personage than Byron to engrave his name in the marble. Later he wrote in *Don Juan,* "Place me on Sunium's marble steep/Where nothing save the waves and I/May hear our mutual murmurs sweep . . ." Open daily. Admission charge (phone: 292-39363).

En route you can stop off for a swim in the little town of Vouliagmeni, home of the *Astir Palace,* one of Europe's great resorts. Built on a hill above Vouliagmeni Beach, the hotel has a marble terrace with a spectacular view, luxury bungalows on the beach, and a variety of fine restaurants.

SOURCES AND RESOURCES

The National Tourist Organization of Greece (NTOG) provides all manner of information — free maps, brochures, and pamphlets — and supervises tourist-related services, from the classification of hotels and restaurants to the operation of public beaches. 2 Karageorgis Servias on Syntagma Square (phone: 322-2545 or 322-3111). The NTOG also runs an information desk at Hellinikon, Athens's international airport. Another source of tourist information and aid is the Tourist Police, a branch of the Metropolitan Police that helps travelers find accommodations. For information 24 hours a day in several languages, call the special number — 171. The headquarters of the Tourist Police is at 7 Syngrou (phone: 923-9224); other offices are at Larissa Railway Station (phone: 821-3574) and Hellinikon Airport (phone: 981-9730).

The Complete Guide to Greece, by John and Maureen Freely (George Phillip & Son Ltd.; $3.50), has an extensive section on Athens. The book is available in Athens bookstores, hotels, and some kiosks.

For Local Coverage – The *Athens News* is the only English-language daily. *The Athenian* is an English-language monthly magazine with articles on contemporary Greece and thorough listings of entertainment events, points of interest, and restaurants. *This Week in Athens,* distributed by the NTOG, is a weekly pamphlet with information on what's going on currently as well as more general information. American newspapers and magazines are sold at kiosks around Syntagma or in Kolonaki.

For Food – Check the Restaurants and Night Life section in *The Athenian* and the *Athens News.*

 CLIMATE AND CLOTHES: Athens has an almost ideal climate — plenty of sunshine and dry air most of the year. In summer, Athens is at its most basic — rocky hills, sun-drenched streets, and long beaches. Even during July and August when the temperatures exceed 90°F (32°C) cool evening breezes make the heat bearable. During May, June, September, and October, days are somewhat cooler, with temperatures ranging from 60° to 80° F (between 16° and 31° C). The beaches are less crowded and the water is still warm enough for swimming. In spring, the hills come to life with gentle hues of green and colorful wild flowers. Winters are mild, with temperatures in the 40s and 50s F (between 5° and 13° C), damper air, and more rain than any other season. If you're visiting during the summer, lightweight clothes are essential — shorts, loose shifts, cotton suits. Summer evenings are cooler and call for sweaters or light jackets. For the spring and fall, a light jacket or coat is advisable. You can use a winter coat during the cold months, but another good way to counter the penetrating dampness is by wearing a few layers of sweaters. Seeing the city any time of year makes demands on your feet — bring comfortable walking shoes.

 GETTING AROUND: Bus – There are some 40 bus and trolley routes serving central Athens and the outlying areas. Buses and electric trolleys run from 5 AM to 12 or 12:30 AM. They afford a convenient, inexpensive, and fairly comfortable way to get around, provided you avoid them during rush hours: 7 to 9 AM, 2 to 3 PM, 5 to 6 PM, and 8 to 10 PM. The fare is 20 drachmas (about 18¢) to any point in the Athens-Piraeus area, provided there is no transfer. Bus routes are outlined on the NTOG map of Athens, but you can always check with the NTOG or Tourist Police for information (phone: 171).

Subway – Athens's only underground line passes through central Athens, linking Piraeus, the major port, with the suburb of Kifissia. The line actually goes underground only downtown and emerges outside of town. The fare is 20 drachmas (18¢), no matter how far you go. Trains run frequently between 5:30 AM and midnight.

Taxi – Cab fares in Athens are inexpensive when compared to those in other major European cities. Most cabs are individually owned, but rates are standardized, so if you want to avoid being taken for a ride, ask the hotel desk or tourist office how much your trip usually costs. You can pick up a cab at stands near the main squares, major hotels, or railway stations, or hail one in the street though it's difficult to find one during rush hours. To hail one, you must clearly yell your destination (hotel or area) and stand on a street with traffic going in that direction. Sharing a cab is a common practice, but you pay the full fare even if you share.

Car Rental – All major car rental companies have offices in Athens. A valid international driver's license is required for Americans. Some of the most reliable agencies are: *Avis,* 48 Amalias (phone: 322-4951); *Budget,* 90 Syngrou (phone: 921-9555); *Hellascars,* 7 Stadiou (phone: 923-5353); and *Hertz,* 12 Syngrou (phone: 922-0102).

Tours – Various companies offer sight-seeing tours of Athens by air-conditioned bus, as well as half- and full-day excursions to attractions within a few hours of the city — Cape Sounion, Delphi, Corinth, Mycenae, Epidaurus, and so on. Some of the best companies are *Chat Tours,* 4 Stadiou (phone: 322-2886, 322-3137), and *Key Tours,* 2 Ermou (phone: 323-2520, 323-3756). If you are interested in hiring a government-trained guide, contact the NTOG, a travel agent, or the hotel concierge.

 MUSEUMS: For a complete description of the National Archaeological Museum, the Acropolis Museum, the Benaki Museum, and the Agora Museum (Stoa of Attalos) see *Special Places.* Other interesting museums are:

Byzantine Museum, 22 Vasilissis Sofias (phone: 721-1027).
Goulandris National History Museum, 13 Levidou in Kifissia (phone: 801-5870).
Kanellopoulos Museum, Theorias and Panos in Plaka (phone: 321-2313).
Museum of Greek Folk Art, 17 Kydathinaion in Plaka (phone: 321-3018).
National History and Ethnological Museum, Stadiou on Kolokotronis Square (phone: 323-7617).
War Museum, Vasilissis Sofias and Rizari (phone: 723-9560).

 SHOPPING: Goods from all over Greece are available in stores in Athens. Specialties include handicrafts, gold and silver jewelry, embroidered shirts and dresses, fabrics, *flokati* rugs of fluffy sheep wool, pottery, onyx, marble, alabaster, and leathergoods. These are available in the main shopping area downtown around Syntagma, Omonia, and Kolonaki squares as well as in Monastiraki, the flea market, where shopping sometimes involves bargaining. The best pottery is available in Maroussi at shops along Kifissias Blvd.

Before you buy handicrafts, you can visit the *National Organization of Hellenic*

Handicrafts, 9 Mitropoleos, where items are exhibited to give some standard notions of quality and price. Goods are not for sale.

Another thing to keep in mind is where the regional specialties originate. Some of the best jewelry comes from Ioannina; interesting ceramics from Sifnos and Skopelos; and highly original embroidery from Skyros, Crete, Lefkas, and Rhodes. The Thessaly and Epirus regions specialize in *flokati* rugs.

Downtown stores are open six days a week and are usually open Mondays, Wednesdays, and Saturdays from 8 AM until 2:30 PM; Tuesdays, Thursdays, and Fridays from 8 AM until 1:30 PM and from 5 PM until 8 PM. Shops around Monastiraki remain open on Sundays from 8 AM to 12:30 PM.

Benaki Museum – This is the place to pick up prints and jewelry with reproductions of themes and designs found in the museum's collection. A wide variety of items from matchbooks, scarves, tablecloths, and needlepoint kits are also available. 1 Koubari at the corner of Vasilissis Sofias.

Greek Women's Institution – Exquisite embroideries and handwoven fabrics from the islands are on sale here, along with reproductions of old embroidered patterns from the Benaki Museum collection. 13 Voukourestiou.

Lalaounis – This internationally known jeweler does original and traditional Greek designs in gold and silver. Voukourestiou and Panepistimiou.

Lyceum of Greek Women – Woven fabrics, embroidery, bedspreads, rugs, curtains, and pillowcases are sold along with ceramics and jewelry. 17 Dimokritou.

Monastiraki – This flea market section is a bargainer's heaven where you can find just about anything for any price, depending on your bargaining skills. A myriad of small stalls carry everything from first-class junk to quality copper, brass, antique jewelry, icons, old books, and leathergoods, sandals and embroidered shirts and dresses. Open daily, but Sunday is really a field day, with an open-air bazaar from 8 AM to noon. Off Monastiraki Square, on and around Ifestou.

National Welfare Organization – This nonprofit organization runs two shops that carry a wide variety of crafts, from moderately priced copper and woven products to embroideries, jewelry, and rugs. 8 Karageorgi Servias and 24 Voukourestiou.

Parthenis – This new star among Greek designers is the first to export Greek women's fashions successfully on a large scale. His designs are avant-garde and medium-priced. Dimokritou and Tsakalof in Kolonaki or Nikis near Plaka.

Periptero – These small kiosks at street corners carry an eclectic assortment of goods — newspapers, chocolate, pens, pencils, film, cosmetics, books, dolls, and pharmaceutical items. For 5 drachmas you can use the telephone.

XEN – The YWCA store has a small but attractive collection of embroideries. 11 Amerikis.

Zolotas – This renowned jeweler does both original and traditional designs in silver and gold. 10 Panepistimiou.

 **SPECIAL EVENTS:** The *Athens Festival* is an international arts festival presenting a full summer of theater, music, opera, and ballet performed by renowned artists from Greece, Europe, and the US. Most of the events are held in the *Herod Atticus Odeion,* a Roman amphitheater built in AD 160 at the foot of the rock of the Acropolis — a setting that enhances the contemporary entertainment by creating links with the rich artistic heritage of Greece. Tickets are available at Voukourestiou in the arcade (phone: 322-3111, ext. 240, or 322-1459), or at the theater just before the performance.

The *Athens Wine Festival* offers a really good time for both Athenians and tourists from mid-July to mid-September. Held in a lovely pine-wooded park at Daphni, 7 miles (11 km) from Athens, admission entitles you to unlimited access to wine produced in all different regions of Greece. Inexpensive drinking glasses are for sale that make nice souvenirs when the partying is over. A few concessions and *tavernas* provide snacks and meals — barbecued chicken and souvlaki. Groups perform traditional and popular music and dances that get pretty merry as the night wears on.

On *Good Friday,* one of the most solemn religious holidays (usually in April), an impressive candlelight *Epitaph Procession* leads from the Greek Orthodox Cathedral on Metropoleos to Syntagma Square and back.

 SPORTS: The Mediterranean climate, a long coastline, and well-organized beaches combine to make Athens good territory for those who enjoy sports.

Golf – At the *Glyfada Golf Club,* 8 miles from the center of Athens (phone: 894-6820), you can challenge 72 par on a gradually sloping course set in the foothills of Mt. Hymettus, overlooking the Saronic Gulf. The 6,808-yard course has well-maintained fairways lined with pine trees. Clubs and carts are available for rent and a city bus links the course with downtown.

Horseback Riding – The *Tatoi Riding Club* welcomes travelers to its three open-air tracks. Varimbopi (phone: 808-1844).

Sailing – Quite popular, particularly in Piraeus, where many residents maintain private boats in Mikrolimano, the small harbor. Many sailing regattas are held throughout the year. For information: Sailing Clubs Federation, 15A Xenofontos (phone: 323-6813 or 323-5560).

Swimming – The beaches to the north of Athens are some of the cleanest you'll find so close to any major city. Within a one-hour bus or cab ride from downtown, you can swim and sunbathe at attractive beaches that have lovely natural settings and complete facilities — changing rooms; refreshment stands; tennis, basketball, and volleyball courts; playgrounds; canoe and paddleboat rentals. The National Tourist Organization of Greece operates beaches at Alimos, 6 miles from downtown (phone: 982-7064), which is the most crowded; Alipedou Voulas, farther south (phone: 895-3248); and Vouliagmeni, 16 miles from the center (phone: 896-0906), a long and popular beach jutting out between sea and bay; and Varkiza, 24 miles (38 km) from town, where bungalows are available (phone: 897-2102). Glyfada, 10 miles (16 km) from Athens, is a fashionable resort area with good beaches. Beaches are open year-round, though most people swim between May and October. There's a small admission charge at the NTOG beaches. Bear in mind that because of Greece's lack of treatment plants for sewage and industrial waste, the farther away from the city, the cleaner the water.

Tennis – The NTOG beaches have outdoor tennis courts at Alipedou Voulas (phone: 895-3248) and Vouliagmeni (phone: 896-0906) that are open daily year-round. No equipment is provided and a modest fee is charged. The *Athens Tennis Club,* 2 Vasilissis Olgas (phone: 923-2872), is open to nonmembers.

Water Skiing – Several training centers in Vouliagmeni provide instruction for beginners and equipment for those with experience: *Naval Club,* Vouliagmeni Bay (phone: 896-2416); *Lypiterakou School,* Vouliagmeni Beach (phone: 896-0743); and *G. Kasidokosta School,* Astir Vouliagmeni Beach (phone: 896-0820).

 THEATER: Athens has a fairly active theater scene, but plays are presented almost exclusively in Greek. The state theatrical company, the *National Theater* in Athens, 20 Agiou Constantinou (phone: 522-3243), performs modern and classical plays as well as works by foreign playwrights (translated into Greek). During the summer, the company performs in the ancient *Epidauros* theater as part of the *Athens Festival.*

Language is no barrier to appreciating the folk dances performed by the renowned *Dora Stratou Dance Company* of Athens. Performances are held nightly from early May until the end of September at the theater on Philopappou Hill (phone: mornings, 322-4861; afternoons, 91-46-50).

MUSIC: The *Athens State Orchestra* gives classical concerts during the winter and spring, and *Lyriki Skini,* the National Opera Company, performs operas with foreign guest stars during the winter and spring at the *Olympia Theater,* 59 Akadimias (phone: 361-2461). During the summer, both groups participate in the *Athens Festival. Parnassos Hall,* 8 Agion Georgiou Karits (phone: 323-8745), has regular recitals throughout the year which offer a look at Greek musical culture. For traditional Greek bouzouki music, see *Nightclubs and Nightlife.*

 **NIGHTCLUBS AND NIGHTLIFE:** Athens has an active nightlife. Athenians tend to dine late, so very often things don't get rolling until after 10 PM. Whether you're interested in a simple evening sitting around a café watching the world go by or more elaborate dining and entertainment, which can get rather costly, you'll find numerous places to go and plenty of company. Bars and other night spots close at 2 AM.

The most celebrated of Greek social institutions are the *tavernas* — restaurant-cafés that come in all sizes and styles, with or without entertainment. The emphasis is on eating, but there's often a variety of entertainment: clubs featuring local singers or groups that generally perform folk songs and popular music (the Plaka section is one of the most lively, with a profusion of *tavernas* and *boites*). Among the most popular *tavernas* are *Xynos,* 4 Agelou Geronta in Plaka (phone: 322-1065), which features guitarists performing Greek songs; *Myrtia,* 35 Markou Moussourou in Pangrati (phone: 751-1686); and *Epestrefe,* in Nea Kifissia, west of the National Rd. (phone: 246-8166), for bouzouki and balalaika music. Best bets for *boites* are concentrated in the Plaka area: *Apanemia,* 4 Tholou (phone: 324-8580); *Diagonios,* 111 Andrianou (phone: 323-3644); *Esperides,* 6 Tholou (phone: 322-5482); and *Zoom,* 37 Kydathineon (phone: 322-5920).

If you're interested in a frenetic nightlife scene, try *bouzoukia* (establishments where the emphasis is on traditional bouzouki music) or nightclubs. As the volume of the music increases, so does the pace: People burst balloons, toss flowers, throw plates, and break into impromptu dances as the level of energy becomes almost as high as the tab for drinks, dinner, entertainment, and broken plates. For classic bouzouki by renowned composers and singers and *rembetika* — traditional folk songs — try *Harama,* Endos Skopeftiriou in Kesariani (phone: 766-4869). *The Galaxy Supper Club* in the *Athens Hilton* puts on a sophisticated show with a live orchestra and dancing (phone: 722-0201, ext. 348). Reservations are necessary at both places; and though the doors open at about 10 PM, the excitement really starts around midnight and keeps building.

For a more subdued evening, you can spend hours over coffee, drinks, and pastry at *Zonar*'s and *Floka,* two well-known cafés off Syntagma.

If you're interested in trying your luck, the *Mount Parnes Casino,* 22 miles from Athens (phone: 322-9412) in the *Mount Parnes Hotel,* operates games of chance — baccarat, chemin de fer, blackjack, and roulette. There's also a club for dining and dancing. You may drive to the top of the mountain or leave your car at the parking lot and reach the hotel entrance by cable car.

Saturday night fever has come to Athens. Among the classiest discos are *Barbarela,* 253 Syngrou (phone: 942-5601); *Can Can Disco,* Kifissou and Petrou Ralli (544-4440); *Papagayo,* 37 P. Ioakim (phone: 724-0736); and *Make Up*, beginning of Panepistimiou, in an arcade just west of Voukourestiou (phone: 364-2160). Make reservations in advance. Less exclusive, but still hot, is *Athens, Athens,* 253 Syngrou Ave., in Nea Smyrni (phone: 942-5602).

 SINS: Whatever your sexual preference, bars and street corners on Akadimias Street and Syngrou Avenue are the big pickup spots at night after the stores close down; during the day, it's Syntagma.

BEST IN TOWN

CHECKING IN: Athens has a wide variety of hotels. The chic *Athenaeum Inter-Continental* and the renowned *Grande Bretagne* top the list, which also includes less plush but still pleasant accommodations. The NTOG divides hotels into five categories — Deluxe, A, B, C, and D. Listed below are our choices for the best hotels in all categories from the most posh to less expensive though comfortable rooms. Hotel prices in Greece compare favorably with those in other European countries and the US. In all categories, Greek hotels generally offer good value; many moderately priced and inexpensive hotels have lots of class — swimming pools and rooftop sundecks, gardens, or bars with panoramic views of the city. Expect to pay $70 to $120 a night for a double room in the expensive category (deluxe hotels); around $30 to $40 in the moderate; and $25 or below in the inexpensive. A number of hotels lower their rates by as much as 20% in the off-season from November 1 to March 31.

The Athenaeum Inter-Continental – This luxury hotel is a study in space and light: A massive glass atrium fills the huge, beige marble lobby with light, and picture windows illuminate separate living and sleeping areas in all 630 guest rooms. Furnishings are modern and comfortable. French and Continental food is served at *La Rôtisserie;* across the way, the *Café Pergola,* which opens onto a terrace with a free-form swimming pool, serves the best Sunday brunch in Athens. Other amenities include a pub, tea lounge, and disco. 89–93 Syngrou Ave. (phone: 902-3666). Expensive.

The Athens Hilton – The *Hilton* is something of a landmark, if not of Greek history, of luxury, comfort, and services. At the *Byzantine Café* Greek teenagers and homesick Americans can buy real American milk shakes for more than American prices; *Ta Nissia Taverna* serves excellent Greek specialties (see *Eating Out*), and there's also a supper club and bar. In the warm months, an international set hangs out around the large outdoor swimming pool, the best in Athens. The 480 rooms are modern and nicely appointed, and have views of the Acropolis or the mountains to the north. 46 Vasilissis Sofias (phone: 722-0201). Expensive.

Grande Bretagne – This grand old hotel, built in 1826 and currently undergoing a major overhaul, retains its old-fashioned elegance. The lobby and public rooms are spacious, with marble floors, Oriental carpets, valuable paintings, and mahogany armchairs. Right on Syntagma Square, in the heart of the city, the hotel is still the scene of state receptions and its guest list includes the most prominent personalities of the last 150 years. Among the facilities are an elegant dining room, an American-style bar, restaurants, and coffee shop. The hotel is air-conditioned throughout; 400 rooms and 25 palatial suites. Syntagma Square (phone: 323-0251). Expensive.

Astir Palace – Opened in 1983, this property faces the House of Parliament and is within an easy walk of the smart shops of Kolonaki. One of the most tastefully decorated hotels in Athens, it caters mainly to a well-heeled business clientele. The 78 beautiful rooms, all air-conditioned, look onto a small sunken garden studded with ruins of ancient Athens that were uncovered during the excavation. The hotel also has a restaurant and a coffee shop. Syntagma Sq. (phone: 364-3113). Expensive.

Park – This deluxe hotel is in a quiet section of town convenient to the Archaeological Museum. The building is topped off with a swimming pool and a roof garden bar that offer good views of the Acropolis and Lycabettus Hill. The 146 rooms are fully equipped with radios and TVs, private baths, and refrigerator bars. The *Latina Restaurant* serves Italian specialties; snacks are available 24 hours a day at the coffee shop; there's another restaurant, boutiques, shops, and a bank. 10 Alexandras (phone: 883-2711). Expensive.

St. George Lycabettus – At the foot of Lycabettus stands another fashionable hotel, complete with black marble floors, a rooftop pool, and plush rooms — brass trimmings, thick carpets, and balconies with beautiful views. Plushest of all are the corner suites that have balconies on two sides and lots of space. There's an attractive restaurant serving international cuisine, a grill, bar, beauty parlor, and sauna; 154 rooms. 2 Kleomenous (phone: 729-0711). Expensive.

Attika Palace – This modern eight-story hotel in the heart of town is a convenient and comfortable place to stay. Though the lobby is small, the 78 rooms are large, airy, and nicely furnished. Many have balconies, and the rooms on the seventh and eighth floors have sweeping views of the city and the Acropolis. Hallways and lounges are spacious, and there's also a restaurant and bar. All rooms have private baths and telephones. 6 Karageorgi Servias, off Syntagma Square (phone: 322-3007). Moderate.

Electra – Another first-rate hotel in the center of the city, the 110 rooms are simply and comfortably furnished and air-conditioned. The bar is good for a quick drink or a more leisurely cocktail after a day's sight-seeing. The restaurant serves both Greek and international specialties. Service is top rate. 5 Ermou, just off Syntagma Square (phone: 322-3223). Moderate.

Divani Zafolia-Alexandras – This fairly new hotel has a neo-Byzantine decor, a much-frequented swimming pool, and a roof garden. Near the Archaeological Museum, the 206 rooms have private baths, balconies, and air-conditioning. The *Grand Byzantine* is a large bar; the restaurant serves international cuisine, and there's also a lively nightclub and an underground garage. 87–89 Alexandras (phone: 692-5112). Moderate.

Athens Gate Hotel – Overlooking the Arch of Hadrian and the Temple of the Olympian Zeus, this modern, brightly furnished hotel offers excellent value. Rooms have balconies, private baths, and good views. The rooftop sundeck commands a panoramic view of Athens — from the Parliament, Lycabettus, the Olympic Stadium, the Acropolis, to the Saronic Gulf in the distance. The *Athenian Restaurant* serves traditional Greek dishes and international specialties, too. There's also a well-appointed bar done in marble, leather, and chrome; 106 rooms. 10 Syngrou (phone: 923-8302). Moderate.

Titania Hotel – Located between the city's two main squares, Syntagma and Omonia, this 400-room hotel is stylish both inside and out. Atop the eight-story structure there's a bar and terrace with stunning views. Rooms are done in bright colors and contemporary designs. All are equipped with phones and bathrooms. Other facilities include a 24-hour coffee shop, a restaurant, and a lounge. 52 Panepistimiou (phone: 360-9612). Moderate.

Hotel Stanley – Popular with northern European travelers, this 400-room hotel has a quiet atmosphere, reasonable prices, and functional if undistinguished accommodations. Extras here include a pool, sundeck, and roof garden. Rooms are air-conditioned; there are three bars, a cafeteria, restaurant, and TV room. The rooms are rather small (particularly singles, which can be cramped), but most have nice views. 1 Odysseos, Karaiskaki Square (phone: 524-9519). Moderate.

Athenian Inn – Very little traffic passes by this exceptionally clean and attractive 10-year-old pension on a side street in the chic Kolonaki quarter. The 28 rooms, as well as the small bar and dining room, are outfitted with the dark rustic furniture and fabrics of the Greek countryside. 22 Haritos (phone: 723-9552). Moderate to inexpensive.

Nefeli – In the shadow of the Acropolis, this attractive hotel has 18 contemporarily furnished rooms with private baths and telephones. Other facilities include a coffee shop and roof garden facing the Acropolis. Iperidou in Plaka (phone: 322-8044). Inexpensive.

Museum Hotel – This new hotel right near the Archaeological Museum has 58 clean and comfortable rooms, a large lobby, a bar, and a recreation room. 16 Bouboulinas and Tositsa (phone: 360-5612). Inexpensive.

Niki – Another excellent value, this small hotel near Syntagma Square has 24 clean, standard rooms. 27 Nikis (phone: 322-0913). Inexpensive.

EATING OUT: Visitors to Athens from Chicago, New York, Toronto, and other places with large Greek communities soon will understand why transplanted Greeks take to restaurateuring. In Greece, eating out is a way of life. Restaurants are more than places to have a bite before the evening's entertainment; very often they are the entertainment. Whether in a local *taverna* or one of the more elegant restaurants in town, Greeks take their time over food. Breakfast is light; lunch is eaten in the midafternoon; and dinner usually doesn't start until 9 PM. Then the parade of Greek food begins: appetizers — *horiatikisalata* (tomato, cucumber, olives, and feta cheese salad), *taramosalata* (a fish roe spread), *plaki* (a bean dish), *melitsanosalata* (eggplant salad), *dolmadakia* (grape leaves stuffed with meat, rice, and onions, served with a lemon sauce). Next is the entrée: There's a choice of grilled meats — baby lamb or beef, veal, or chicken — and a wide assortment of seafood — octopus, squid, red snapper, lobster, or *youvetsi* (a casserole). *Retsina,* a resinated wine, either white or red, traditionally accompanies *taverna* meals, although locally brewed beers have become popular. Greeks indulge their love for rich pastries and thick, strong coffee at cafés. What makes all this even more attractive is the relatively modest tab. Expect to pay around $30 and up for a dinner for two in the places listed as expensive; $20 in those listed as moderate; and $10 and under in the inexpensive category. Prices don't include drinks or tips. Many restaurants are open only for dinner, so telephone beforehand.

Ta Nissia – Spacious and elegant, the restaurant has all the trimmings — high redwood ceiling, marble floors, and brass ornaments with traditional designs. The atmosphere is quite pleasant, complete with wandering troubadours singing Greek songs. The food maintains a high style from the *mezedakia* (delicious hors d'oeuvres), through the main course — leg of lamb, and roast suckling pig prepared in its own juices — to the rich desserts. Open daily. Reservations. 46 Vasilissis Sofias, in the *Hilton* (phone: 722-0201). Expensive.

L'Abrevoir – The oldest French restaurant in Athens, it is also one of the best, serving marvelously light soufflés, snails, and tender swordfish steak. In summer, dine in the garden under mulberry trees. It is the perfect spot for a secluded lunch for two. Open daily. Reservations at night only. 51 Xenokratous, Kolonaki (phone: 722-9061).

Gerofinikas – Run by Greeks from Istanbul, the specialties here are Greek and Turkish. A wide variety of *mezedakia* and seafood specialties are on display in the showcase up front. Old favorites are shrimp wrapped in smoked salmon, extraordinarily light *taramosalata,* smoked trout, rice orientale, a wide assortment of salads, and such entrées as lobster thermidor, swordfish on a skewer, and grilled meats. Don't pass up dessert — strawberries with cream, baklava, or *ekmek kadayifi* (super-rich bread pudding). Service is good, and dining is leisurely. Open daily for lunch and dinner. Reservations. 10 Pindarou (phone: 362-2719, 363-6710). Expensive.

Dionyssos – The two restaurants by this name have similar menus and different, though equally splendid, views — one, a panorama from the top of Lycabettus, the other, the Acropolis. Such views make the visit worthwhile, but the food, including baby lamb, Adriatica charcoal-grilled shrimp, and veal mignonette is usually mediocre. The waiters at both are multilingual. Open daily. Reservations. Dionisiou Areopagitou, just opposite the Acropolis (phone: 923-1936), and Mt. Lycabettus, accessible by the funicular that starts at the top of Ploutarchou, above Kolonaki Square (phone: 722-6374). Expensive to moderate.

Mikrolimano – This is a little port in Piraeus that harbors a row of seafood restaurants. Fishermen get up at 3 AM to catch the sweet and succulent daily fare, such as *garides* (prawns), *octapodi* (octopus), *astako* (crawfish, lobster, or langouste), *barbounia* (red mullet), and *garides yiovetsi* (a shrimp, cheese, wine, and tomato casserole that most of the restaurants along the port claim to have invented). The usual procedure here is to go into a restaurant and make your selection straight from the refrigerator. In summer, you would then saunter back outside and dine beside the small yachts right on the quay where musicians and flower vendors stroll.

A few good restaurants right on the small port are *Kuyu and Kaplanis* (phone: 411-1623) for red snapper baked with shrimp, mushrooms, and whiskey; *Zorba No. 1* (phone: 412-5501) for a stunning variety of *mezedakia, kasemburek* (pastries filled with cheese and tomatoes), shellfish in delicate sauces, and stuffed eggplant; and *The Black Goat* for its great selection of fresh, fresh fish (this last is a popular yachtsmen's rendezvous (phone: 42-76-26). Reservations not necessary at any of the Mickrolimano fish *tavernas.* Expensive to moderate.

Myrtia – If you want a spirited Greek atmosphere, head for the hill behind the Olympic Stadium. Here, serenading guitarists play all the popular Greek tunes, some of which you may recognize. The menu is fixed: plate after plate of *mezedakia*, meat, salad, potatoes, and fruit. Excellent food and service and a warm ambience have long attracted Greece's best known celebrities. Closed Sundays. Reservations. 35 Markou Mousouri (phone: 701-2276). Expensive to moderate.

Vasilena – Farther into Piraeus, another unusual dining experience is available. Here, in a renovated grocery store, you pay a flat price and feast on a parade of Greek delicacies. There's no menu, but the food keeps coming anyway. Take it slowly — there are twenty courses, and the faster you eat, the sooner you get more. In the summertime, dine on a terrace. Closed Sundays. Reservations. 72 Etolikou, Akti Kondili (phone: 461-2457). Moderate.

Act I – Right in the center of town, this cozy restaurant/cocktail lounge is reminiscent of a New York piano bar. Evenings, a pianist plays old American favorites as well as contemporary Greek hits. The food is plentiful and good, including Greek and American specialties.18 Akademias (phone: 360-2492). Moderate.

Corfu – Just off Syntagma Square, this unpretentious restaurant is frequented by businesspeople and government officials for its attentive service and hearty food. The extensive menu has all the Greek favorites but specializes in dishes from the island of Corfu — beef *pastitsada,* beef *sofrito,* and prawn and lobster. Open daily. Reservations not necessary. 6 Kriezotou (phone: 361-3011). Moderate.

Lotofagos – This homey restaurant is actually a cottage in Kifissia, one of Athens' highest-income suburbs. Surrounded by a fireplace, copper pots, and earthenware, diners order from a menu that includes chicken with mangoes, spaghetti primavera, and fresh salad vegetables. The key is always left in the door so that customers can enter like one of the family. Closed Tuesdays and Wednesdays. Reservations. Aghias Lavras 4, Kifissia (phone: 801-3201). Moderate.

Ta Kalamia – One of the most famous tavernas in Greece, Ta Kalamia (which means bamboo) recently moved from polluted central Athens to a breezy northern suburb. The first course here, a mixture of wonderful *mezedakia,* is followed by a variety of imaginative meat dishes. In summer, dine al fresco in a garden lined with live bamboo. Open daily. Reservations not necessary. Aghiou Georgiou and Aiskilou 26, Halandri (phone: 681-0529). Moderate.

Stagecoach – This American steakhouse is renowned in Athens as a center of expatriate life. Its huge mahogany bar is frequented by many a homesick traveler, and its restaurant offers hearty American fare such as steaks, apple pie, and perked coffee. Open daily. Reservations. Loukianou 6, Kolonaki (phone: 723-7902). Moderate.

Ellinikon – This sophisticated little place is said to be "where the elite meet." Indeed, fashionable young men and women as well as visiting executives from the US and around the Continent are the usual clientele. The restaurant serves a variety of Continental and local dishes, the best of which are blanketed with a rich egg and lemon sauce spiked with wine. The pastries are also quite good. Open daily. Reservations not necessary. Kolonaki Sq. 19-20 (phone: 361-5866). Moderate.

Zafiris – Off the beaten track in Plaka, this little restaurant serves fine game dishes and attracts the likes of Greek presidents, present and past. Open daily. Reservations. Thespidos 4, Plaka (phone: 322-5460). Moderate.

Xynos – Though much of the rest of the Plaka has become highly commercialized, this old, well-known *taverna* retains a fair measure of authenticity. The place is always lively with guitarists playing popular Greek songs and plenty of good retsina to go around. Food is typically Greek and good — veal *hasapi,* lamb *yiovetsi,* Greek salads, shish kebab, and spicy appetizers. In the summer the action takes place in the garden; in winter, inside where the walls are lined with amusing murals of Greek life. Closed Sundays. Reservations. 4 Angelou Gerondos (phone: 322-1065). Moderate to inexpensive.

Aerides – Also in Plaka, right across the street from the Tower of the Winds, this appealing little restaurant displays its daily specials in the window. There's a full menu of Greek dishes from appetizers to meat, fish, and dessert. You can dine outdoors in nice weather and contemplate the Tower beside or the Acropolis above. Open daily. Reservations not necessary. On Markourelous (phone: 322-6266). Inexpensive.

Bouillabaisse – One of the best *tavernas* in Athens in which to enjoy the famous French fish soup that gave this restaurant its name. There's also a variety of other well-prepared seafood. Attentive waiters serve meals on a large pebbled terrace overhung with trailing vine leaves. Zisimopoulou 28, Amphithea, just behind the Athens Planetarium (phone: 941-9082). Moderate. Inexpensive.

O Platanos – One of the oldest *tavernas* in the Plaka, this place is located off a small street away from the hectic crowd. It is simply decorated, but has a large and well-prepared selection of Greek foods and unbeatable prices. Closed Sundays. 4 Diogenous (phone: 322-0666). Inexpensive.

Apotsos – This cozy indoor *ouzerie* is popular with writers, professors, models, and actors who enjoy the simple but tasty Greek dishes and the low prices. The atmosphere is casual and cluttered and the taverna's walls a collage of old signs, photographs, and other memorabilia. Open daily. Reservations not necessary. In an arcade on Panepistimiou, just west of Voukourestiou. Inexpensive.

Socrates' Prison – The owners of this unpretentious taverna — a former prison — claim it really was the site of Socrates' internment. Good food, house wine, and boisterous conversation make it a jolly spot. Open daily. Reservations not necessary. Across from Herod Atticus theater (phone: 922-3434). Inexpensive.

If you're interested in a unique gastronomic experience, head a few miles east out of Athens on the road that leads up Mt. Hymettus. You'll come to Kareas, a small town on the mountain, which is inhabited predominantly by Romanian refugees. They have set up several restaurants along the road serving unusual dishes — *stiphado* (hare stew with small onions in tomato sauce) and charcoal-grilled meats including baby lamb and goat. As you eat, you can enjoy the cool mountain air, which provides welcome relief on hot summer days, and an excellent view of Athens.

BARCELONA

Seeing a circle of men and women move in simple, slow-paced steps to the music of flute and drum in a bright square on a Sunday afternoon can give you an almost visceral understanding of Barcelona and its people. This regional dance, the *sardana* — once described by a poet as a dance "of people going forth holding hands" — is indicative of the sense of community and passion for music that is typical of Barcelona.

The *sardana* seems to begin spontaneously. You first notice that people walking back from mass or a Sunday stroll have begun to linger in the cathedral square. Seemingly from nowhere, a band gathers and begins to play what sounds like rhythmic dirges. The people set aside purses, prayer books, and hymnals and join hands to form large circles. Slowly the circles revolve as the dancers step out the intricately counted measures on tiptoe. Soon the dancers are captured by the intensity of the music. They hold their hands high, some close their eyes. The music continues in hauntingly mournful tones. Then, almost abruptly, the *sardana* is over. The dancers nod to their neighbors, gather up their belongings, and continue on their way home.

You have seen the soul of Barcelona, witnessed the strong community feeling of the Catalonian region that tempers the proverbial Spanish individualism. Indeed, Catalán clannishness has frequently set this region at odds with the rest of Spain. There is a strong feeling of regional pride here and use of the Catalán language has become a symbol of the struggle for regional autonomy. Since the death of Francisco Franco, the government of King Juan Carlos has accorded more autonomy to the region.

Located across the Pyrenees from France, south of the Costa Brava (literally, "wild coast") along the Mediterranean Sea, Barcelona's history and language link it as much to France as to Spain. Catalán, the lilting language of the region, is derived from the French *langue d'oc* and is spoken in French Catalonia as well.

The Romans developed the port of Barcelona in about 200 BC, and the city flourished under both the Romans and the Visigoths before being overrun by the Moors. The powerful counts of Barcelona were able to drive the Moors from the lands to the south in the tenth century, and by 1100, Barcelona had dominion over all of Catalonia.

At one point, it was said that "even fish in the Mediterranean wore the red and yellow stripes of the kingdom led by Catalonia." Barcelona was a major Mediterranean power, a force whose might and grandeur can be felt even today in the medieval streets of the city's old quarter, the Barrio Gótico. In the 1400s, it rivaled Genoa and Venice in Mediterranean trade. But the discovery of the New World proved disastrous for Catalonia, and as the ports of Seville and Cádiz rose in importance, Barcelona declined.

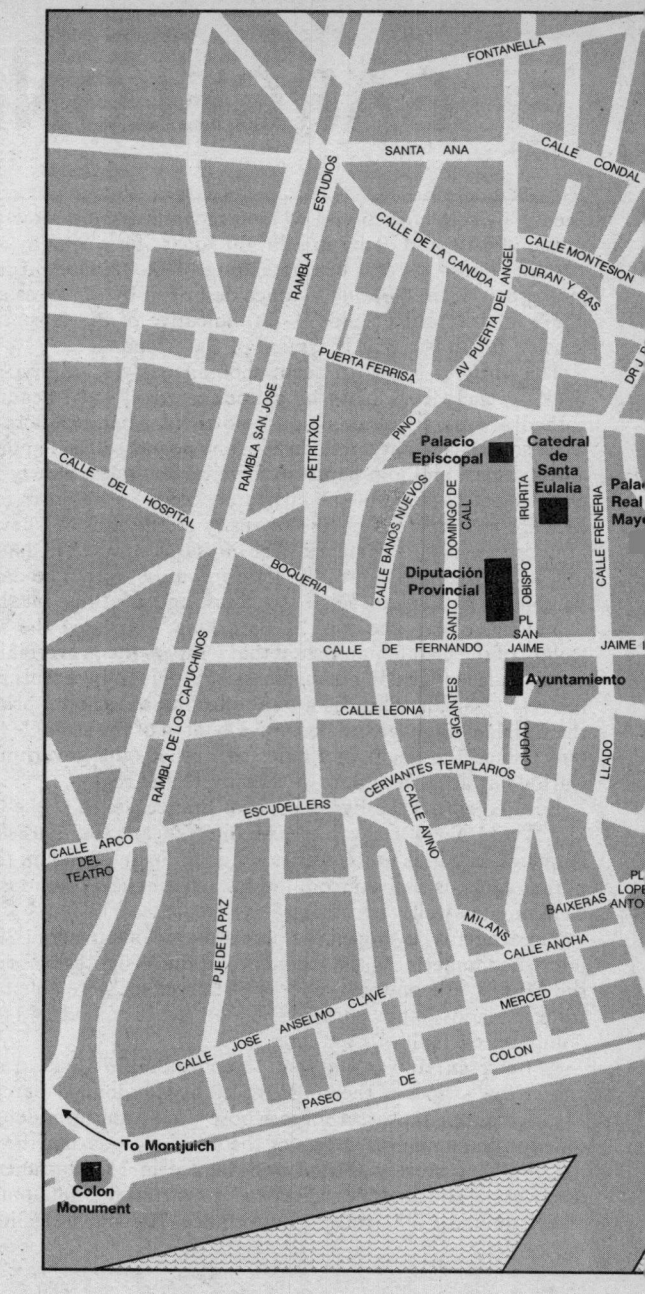

FONTANELLA

SANTA ANA

CALLE CONDAL

CALLE DE LA CANUDA

CALLE MONTESION

DURAN Y BAS

AV PUERTA DEL ANGEL

ESTUDIOS

RAMBLA

PUERTA FERRISA

DR J

RAMBLA SAN JOSE

PETRITXOL

PINO

**Palacio
Episcopal**

**Catedral
de
Santa
Eulalia**

**Pala
Real
Maye**

CALLE DEL HOSPITAL

CALLE BAÑOS NUEVOS

DOMINGO DE CALL

IRURITA

CALLE FRENERIA

BOQUERIA

**Diputación
Provincial**

SANTO

OBISPO

PL
SAN
JAIME

JAIME

CALLE DE FERNANDO

RAMBLA DE LOS CAPUCHINOS

CALLE LEONA

GIGANTES

Ayuntamiento

CIUDAD

LLADO

CERVANTES TEMPLARIOS

ESCUDELLERS

CALLE AVIÑO

CALLE ARCO
DEL
TEATRO

PJE DE LA PAZ

MILANS

BAIXERAS

PL
LOPE
ANTO

CALLE ANCHA

CALLE JOSE ANSELMO CLAVÉ

MERCED

COLON

PASEO DE

⬅ **To Montjuich**

🔳
**Colon
Monument**

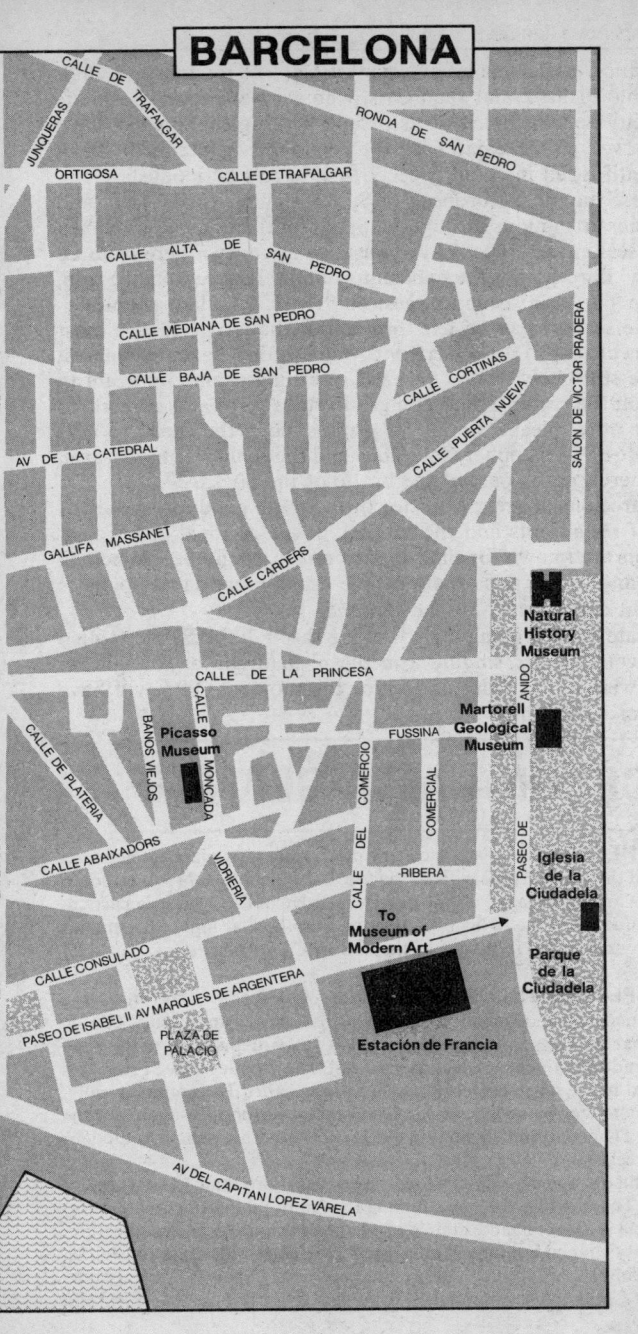

BARCELONA

CALLE DE TRAFALGAR

JUNQUERAS

RONDA DE SAN PEDRO

ORTIGOSA

CALLE DE TRAFALGAR

CALLE ALTA DE SAN PEDRO

CALLE MEDIANA DE SAN PEDRO

CALLE BAJA DE SAN PEDRO

CALLE CORTINAS

CALLE PUERTA NUEVA

SALON DE VICTOR PRADERA

AV DE LA CATEDRAL

GALLIFA MASSANET

CALLE CARDERS

Natural History Museum

CALLE DE LA PRINCESA

CALLE MONCADA

BANOS VIEJOS

Picasso Museum

CALLE DEL COMERCIO

FUSSINA

Martorell Geological Museum

CALLE DE PLATERIA

ANIDO

CALLE ABAIXADORS

VIDRIERIA

COMERCIAL

PASEO DE

RIBERA

Iglesia de la Ciudadela

To Museum of Modern Art

CALLE CONSULADO

PASEO DE ISABEL II AV MARQUES DE ARGENTERA

Parque de la Ciudadela

PLAZA DE PALACIO

Estación de Francia

AV DEL CAPITAN LOPEZ VARELA

Early in this century, Barcelona became a meeting place for artists, including Joan Miró, Pablo Picasso, and Juan Gris, who were attracted to the life and color of this city and the spirit of its people. During the Spanish Civil War, Barcelona served as the capital for the republican government from November 1937 until it fell in January 1939 to Franco's nationalists.

Today, Barcelona, the most European of Spanish cities, is big, rich, and commercial. Cataláns are famous throughout Spain for their business acumen and young people seeking advancement in business are drawn here from all parts of the country. Barcelona is the publishing and literary capital of Spain, as well as its major port and second largest city (with 4 million people).

The flavor of the seaport can be felt throughout the city, but it is most apparent in the area closest to the waterfront. With all the charms of the rest of the city, you are still likely to find yourself returning again and again to the harbor: to watch the comings and goings of cruise ships and tankers; to hire motorboats or other pleasure craft for cruises along the coast; to take pictures of the statue of Christopher Columbus and the replica of his caravel, *Santa María;* or merely to be part of the bustle of the docks.

The people of Barcelona are renowned for their love of good food, attested by the profusion of restaurants and the subtlety of the regional dishes. But most of all, Cataláns are known for their love of music. Many people belong to choral societies and choirs and young people usually join dance societies to learn old Catalán dances, such as the *sardana.*

If you are fortunate some evening to be walking through the Barrio Gótico at dusk and hear voices softly singing a medieval madrigal as though the spirits of the past were alive, pause and savor the moment: You will have found the essence of Barcelona.

BARCELONA AT-A-GLANCE

SEEING THE CITY: There are excellent panoramic views of Barcelona, its harbor, and the Mediterranean from the top of Tibidabo, a 1,745-foot mountain in the Collcerola range on the northwest edge of the city. It is particularly beautiful to see the lights of Barcelona from here at night. The mountain can be reached by car or by funicular at the end of Calle Balmes.

SPECIAL PLACES: The old medieval area of Barcelona, known as the Barrio Gótico, is a hodgepodge of streets that throw up a spiky Gothic silhouette against the sea. It is in this area that you will find most of the chief buildings and monuments of historic interest and artistic value. From this hub, the city expanded in the nineteenth century in an area called Ensanche (literally, "enlargement"), characterized by wide, tree-shaded avenues. Beyond Ensanche are the modern suburbs. La Diagonal and Gran Via de las Cortes Catalanas are modern Barcelona's major streets.

Barrio Gótico – The old quarter of Barcelona represents more than 15 centuries of architectural history. The Catedral de Santa Eulalia (begun in the fourteenth century) on Calle de Santa Lucía is an excellent example of Mediterranean Gothic architecture. The inside of the county council building (Diputación Provincial), Plaza de San Jaime, is one of the finest examples of Gothic civil architecture in the Spanish Levant style. And legend has it that Christopher Columbus was presented to Ferdinand and Isabella on his return from America in the magnificent banqueting hall, Salón de Tinell, of the Great Royal Palace (Palacio Real Mayor) in the Plaza del Rey. You can also see ruins of the old Roman Temple of Augustus in a patio on the nearby Calle del Paradís. West of the harbor.

Montjuich Park (Parque de Montjuich) – Buildings to house exhibits for the 1929 World's Fair scale the slopes of Montaña de Montjuich, a huge fortress hill overlooking the sea, south of Barrio Gótico. One exhibit was a group of houses comprising a Spanish village (Pueblo Español), and this still exists. Here you can see the different local styles of Spanish architecture and watch artisans and craftsmen at work. The Museum of Catalonian Art (Museo de Arte de Catalunya), housed in what was the Spanish exhibition pavilion, contains many beautiful Romanesque and Gothic artifacts from small churches in Catalonia. The museum and the village are open daily; small admission fees. The hill also has beautiful gardens, a large amusement park, and a fort built in 1640, when the Catalans rebelled against Philip IV. Reached by funicular railway from the harbor. South of Calle del Marqués del Duero, along Paseo de Colón.

The Ramblas – This collection of streets, once the bed of a mountain torrent, is the heart and soul of the city. This is where Catalans gather during the day to read a favorite newspaper or magazine at a sidewalk café, shop in the bird and flower markets, or merely chat and stroll with friends. The Ramblas are full of color and movement and sound and light. The area begins near the harbor.

Gaudí's Works – Antonio Gaudí was a leader in the art nouveau movement in architecture, and although he was killed in a tram accident before he could complete it, his Church of the Holy Family (Templo de la Sagrada Familia) in the Plaza de la Sagrada Familia, begun in 1884, is one of Spain's most extraordinary buildings. Its famous Nativity facade has four tall spires and a porch filled with naturalistic sculpture. Two luxury apartment buildings on the Paseo de Gracia — one at number 43 and the other at the corner of Calle de Provenza, both begun in 1905 — are good examples of Gaudí's style. Güell Park was to have been a garden city of 60 dwellings, but the project was curtailed by Gaudí's death and only two houses, a park entrance, and some walks were constructed in the park near Calle Olot.

■**EXTRA SPECIAL:** The Montserrat Sierra lies northwest of Barcelona in the geographical and spiritual heart of Catalonia. Wagner set his opera *Parsifal* here. Located in these impressive mountain peaks is the Benedictine monastery whose Marian shrine has attracted pilgrims for over 700 years. The *Black Madonna (La Moreneta)* is a twelfth-century polychrome wooden statue of the Virgin Mary, which represents the spiritual life of the province. To hear the members of the Escolanía, one of the oldest boys' choirs in Europe, sing morning mass is to understand the religious spirit of Barcelona and Catalonia. Take the number 2 funicular from near the monastery, then walk another half hour from the top to reach the San Jerónimo belvedere, 4,061 feet above sea level. From this spot, on a clear day, you will see a panorama from the Pyrenees to the Balearic Islands. The monastery is 38 miles (60.8 km) from Barcelona, via Route NII.

SOURCES AND RESOURCES

Brochures, maps, and general information are available from the Tourist Information Office, Gran Vía de las Cortes Catalanas 658 (phone: 301-7443), and Plaza de San Jaime (phone: 302-2420).

For Local Coverage – The best local guide to the city is *Barcelona* (Editorial Everest; about $4.50).

There is no English-language paper published in Barcelona, but with the help of a pocket dictionary, non-Spanish speakers should be able to decipher the listings of local events published in *Guía de Ocio: La semana de Barcelona* and *A Donde Ir.*

CLIMATE AND CLOTHES: Although Barcelona is a Mediterranean port, it can be a bit cold in winter. Temperatures range from a low of 44°F (7°C) in January to a high of 83°F (28°C) in August. Barcelona is a formal city. If you are planning to attend the opera, for instance, virtually all of the audience will be in formal dress. For daytime, casual attire will suffice.

GETTING AROUND: Bus – There are more than 50 bus lines in Barcelona. You board some buses from the rear and buy a ticket from a conductor.

Subway – A *Metro* sign indicates an entrance to Barcelona's subway system, comprised of five lines that crisscross the city.

Taxi – Taxis can be hailed while they cruise the streets. Fares are moderate. Remember to enter the cab from the curb side; entering from the street side is illegal.

MUSEUMS: Barcelona has several important museums in addition to those listed in *Special Places.*

Federico Marés Museum (Museo Federico Marés), sculpture, including medieval, wooden religious statuary, Calle de los Condes de Barcelona (phone: 310–5800).

Picasso Museum (Museo Picasso), Calle de Montcada 15 (phone: 319-6902).

Maritime Museum (Museo Marítimo), Reales Atarazanas, Puerta de la Paz (phone: 301-1871).

Martorell Geological Museum (Museo de Geología "Martorell"), Parque de la Ciudadela (phone: 319-9312).

Contemporary Arts Research Center (Centro Estudios de Arte Contemporaneo), Parque de Montjuich (phone: 329-1916).

Museum of Modern Art (Museo de Arte Moderno), Parque de la Ciudadela (phone: 319-5728).

Costume Museum (Museo de Indumentaria), Palacio del Marqués de Llío, Calle de Montcada 12 (phone: 310-4516).

City History Museum (Museo de Historia de la Ciudad), Veguer s/n (phone: 315-1111).

SHOPPING: As a port city, Barcelona is filled with more than its share of tacky souvenir shops, but it also is a good place to shop for leather and other Spanish goods. Stores are open Mondays through Saturdays from 9 AM to 8 PM, although some smaller shops may close between 1:30 and 4 PM.

Corte Inglés – A department store where you can buy anything from Maja soap to Spanish leather gloves. Plaza de Catalunya.

Pueblo Español – Typical folk crafts are made and sold here. Montjuich.

Loewe – This is a branch of Spain's best-known and most expensive purveyor of fine leathergoods. Paseo de Gracia 35.

SPECIAL EVENTS: Religious holidays and saints' days are the occasion of numerous festivals in Barcelona. The feast of *Our Lady of Mercy,* the city's patron, is celebrated during the last week of September with bullfights, folk dancing, and general gaiety that includes men building human pyramids. There are bonfires, fireworks, dancing, and revelry on the nights before the feast days of *St. John* and *St. Peter* (June 23 and 28, respectively).

SPORTS: Bullfighting – Cataláns pride themselves on being different from the rest of Spain: They claim they abhor bullfighting, and in fact most of the faces you will see in the stadium are those of tourists. However, you can catch a rousing bullfight, usually held between 5 and 6 PM, at one of the two rings: *Las Arenas,* near the Plaza de Espana, and *Monumental,* on Av. Carlos I.

Golf – There are several golf courses in Barcelona and its environs, including the *Real de Golf el Prat,* Caspe 35 (phone: 318-9190); *Club de Golf San Cugat,* San Cugat del Vallés (phone: 674-3958); and *Club de Golf Vallromanos,* Vía Augusta 59 (phone: 568-0362).

Tennis – Courts may be available at the *Royal Tennis Club Barcelona,* Bosch I Gimpera 5 (phone: 203-7758); and *Turó,* La Diagonal 687 (phone: 203-8958).

THEATER: Barcelona has a lively theater life, with everything from satirical reviews to *Oh! Calcutta!* Most work is performed in Spanish or Catalán. Two of the many theaters are *Apolo,* Paralelo 61 (phone: 241-4006); and *Victoria,* Paralelo 65 (phone: 241-3985).

MUSIC: Churches and musical groups offer recitals and concerts at various places all year long. The opera season opens in November at the *Gran Teatro Liceo,* San Pablo 1 (phone: 318-9122). There are concerts by the *Municipal Orchestra* and visiting orchestras at the *Palau de la Música,* Amadeo Vives 1 (phone: 301-1104). Each October, Barcelona hosts the *International Festival of Music* featuring classical concerts at the Palau de la Música and at other locations throughout the city.

NIGHTCLUBS AND NIGHTLIFE: For flamenco try *El Cordobes,* Ramblas Capuchinos 35 (phone: 301-5700), or *Los Tarantos,* Plaza Real 17 (phone: 317-8098). *Bocaccio,* Muntaner 505 (phone: 247-3136), is a popular discotheque, and *Camoa,* Corts Catalanes 322 (phone: 325-3870), has a floor show.

SINS: El Barrio Chino, off Ramblas near the docks, is notorious for its haunts, dives, and joints. Now that censorship has been relaxed, however, other areas are giving the Barrio Chino competition with porno shows and *espactaculos sexy.*

BEST IN TOWN

CHECKING IN: Expect to pay between $65 and $95 a night for a double room at one of Barcelona's expensive hotels; $30 to $65 at a moderately priced hotel; and under $30 at an inexpensive one.

Princesa Sofía – Part of the European HUSA chain, this is one of Barcelona's newest hotels. Rooms are large, standard, decorated in contemporary style, and have large, tiled bathrooms. The hotel is fully air-conditioned. It has an indoor swimming pool, gym, and sauna, and four restaurants. Plaza Papa Pío XII (phone: 330-7111). Expensive.

Ritz Hotel – Some of the old-world charm has sagged, but the *Ritz* remains a favorite with those who appreciate the finer things and gracious hotel management. There are some high-ceilinged doubles in fine period style, but all the rooms are attractive and comfortable. Gran Vía de las Cortes Catalanas 668 (phone: 318-5200). Expensive.

Avenida Palace – Polished brass and fancy carpets lend a tasteful, old-world atmosphere to this deluxe hotel next to the Iberia ticket office. Fair-sized rooms are cheerful and quiet. There is a split-level grill among the well-kept public rooms. Gran Vía de las Cortes Catalanas 605 (phone: 301-9600). Moderate.

Colón – An ideal location just across the street from the cathedral is the main selling point for this hotel, but it is also recommended for its clean, pleasantly decorated, high-ceilinged rooms. Rooms on the sixth floor have large open terraces. Av. de la Catedral 7 (phone: 301-1404). Moderate.

Gala Placidia Hotel – Particularly suitable for families or long visits, the *Gala Placidia* has 28 suites of varying size. The suites have sitting rooms with fireplaces, dining areas, and refrigerators, as well as small bedrooms. Vía Augusta 112 (phone: 217-8200). Moderate.

Regencia Colón – This is a sister of the more expensive *Colón* around the corner. It offers good beds, large bathrooms, and air-conditioning at bargain prices. Calle Sagristans 13–17 (phone: 318-9858). Inexpensive..

 EATING OUT: Cataláns eat late. Lunch is from 1 to 3:30 PM in most restaurants, and dinner is served between 8:30 and 11 PM. Check for the daily special — *menu del dia,* usually a three-course meal with bread and wine — which restaurants are required by law to offer at a set price. Try the soup of lobster, crayfish, squid, mussel, and white fish of various types called *zarzuela.* The most basic Catalán dish is a hearty stew of sausage, beans, meatballs, and spices, *escudella i carn d'olla.* The ubiquitous caramel custard, *crema catalana,* made with eggs, milk, sugar, and cinnamon, usually tops off the meal. Expect to pay $40 to $80 for a dinner for two in restaurants classified as expensive, $25 to $40 in the moderate range, and under $25 in inexpensive places.

Amaya – This has the best Basque food in Barcelona, but what a price you pay for the experience: The restaurant is chaotic and the menu simply mad, a printed sheet of dozens and dozens of items, many handwritten in margins, which the non-Spanish-speaker will find a struggle to translate. To simplify matters, focus on the restaurant's excellent vegetable entrées — beans à la Catalán, mushrooms, fresh peas with ham. Open daily except Mondays and July and August. Ramblas Santa Mónica 24 (phone: 302-1037). Expensive.

Quo Vadis – Muted paneling, soft lights, and harmonious decor provide a pleasing ambience at this top-rated establishment. Service is solicitous and the international cuisine is excellent. Open daily, except Sundays. Reservations essential. Carmen 7 (phone: 302-4072). Expensive.

Agut d'Avignon – This beautiful multilevel restaurant in the old Barrio Gótico has whitewashed walls, oak plank floors, and antique furnishings. Its traditional Catalán food — especially the duck — is excellent. Open daily, except Sundays. Closed in August. Reservations recommended. Trinidad 3 (phone: 302-6034). Expensive.

La Bota del Recó – Gigantic portions of savory Catalán specialties served in a rustic atmosphere. Always crowded, but worth the usually short wait. Try the *parrilladas* (assorted grilled meat or fish). Virgen de Montserrat 232 (phone: 256-6002). Moderate.

Los Caracoles – At first glance, this restaurant looks like a tourist trap, but you'll be impressed by the good solid Catalán cooking. *Los caracoles* means snails, so try some; the languostinos are also fresh and delicious. Reservations needed (but even so, you'll have to wait during rush hours). Open daily. Escudellers 14 (phone: 302-3185). Moderate to inexpensive.

Casa Costa – Barceloneta, the peninsula protecting the port from the sea, is noted for its narrow streets, colorful atmosphere, and seafood restaurants such as the *Casa Costa.* Fresh, fresh fish is served picnic-style at this delightful establishment. Open daily. Balnard 124 (phone: 319-5028). Inexpensive.

EAST BERLIN

Most foreign visitors coming here for the first time find the short trip through the Berlin Wall an adventure full of the Cold War drama one has read about in such books as Len Deighton's *Funeral in Berlin* and John le Carré's *The Spy Who Came In from the Cold*. Once you are past the border formalities, however, the feeling of excitement gives way to the intriguing observation that East Berlin, though full of surprises, has little similarity to Cold War fictional fantasies. For this is a vigorous, multifaceted city, and if some of it lives in the past, it is more likely to be the past of bygone Prussian glory than the cloak-and-dagger drama of the recent Cold War.

Strangely enough, it was the Wall, that sad reminder of Europe's political division, that brought about the condition of normalcy one finds everywhere in this metropolis of 1.1 million people. After the war, East Germany was slowly bleeding to death. Thousands were escaping daily to the West, using the relatively unguarded route from East to West Berlin. Since the Wall went up in 1961, however, escape has become not only virtually impossible but gradually unnecessary as well, as more and more East Germans become content with the quality of their lives in this Communist country of which East Berlin has been the capital since 1949.

Though the ugly barbed wire is still very much of a raw wound on both sides of the Wall, the Iron Curtain is no longer as savagely impenetrable as it once was, with 1-day visas to visit East Berlin readily available to Westerners of all nationalities. Whatever the rights and wrongs of the division of both Germany and Berlin, people in central Europe and especially Berlin have had to make their peace with a state of affairs that is in the hands of statesmen in far-off Moscow and Washington. And nowhere has this process of coping with the immutable laws of history affected people's lives more than in East Berlin. The effects can be seen and felt in every nook and cranny, but most especially in East Berliners' determined conviction that this is their home.

They are proud of what they have accomplished in the short span of years since 1945, when the ruins of war were the only sights to be seen in a city virtually bombed flat by the Allies. To some extent, this pride is justified, in view of the many material achievements of the past decades. There is no poverty in East Germany, no unemployment, and everyone has enough to eat. The people of East Germany are also proud of their highly industrial state whose production ranks about tenth in the world. They boast greater productivity per capita than the USSR; a higher per capita income than Italy, Ireland, and socialist Eastern Europe; and oddly enough, more television sets per capita than France. Most unbiased observers attribute East Germany's outstanding progress to a combination of party discipline and the traditional German habit of hard work.

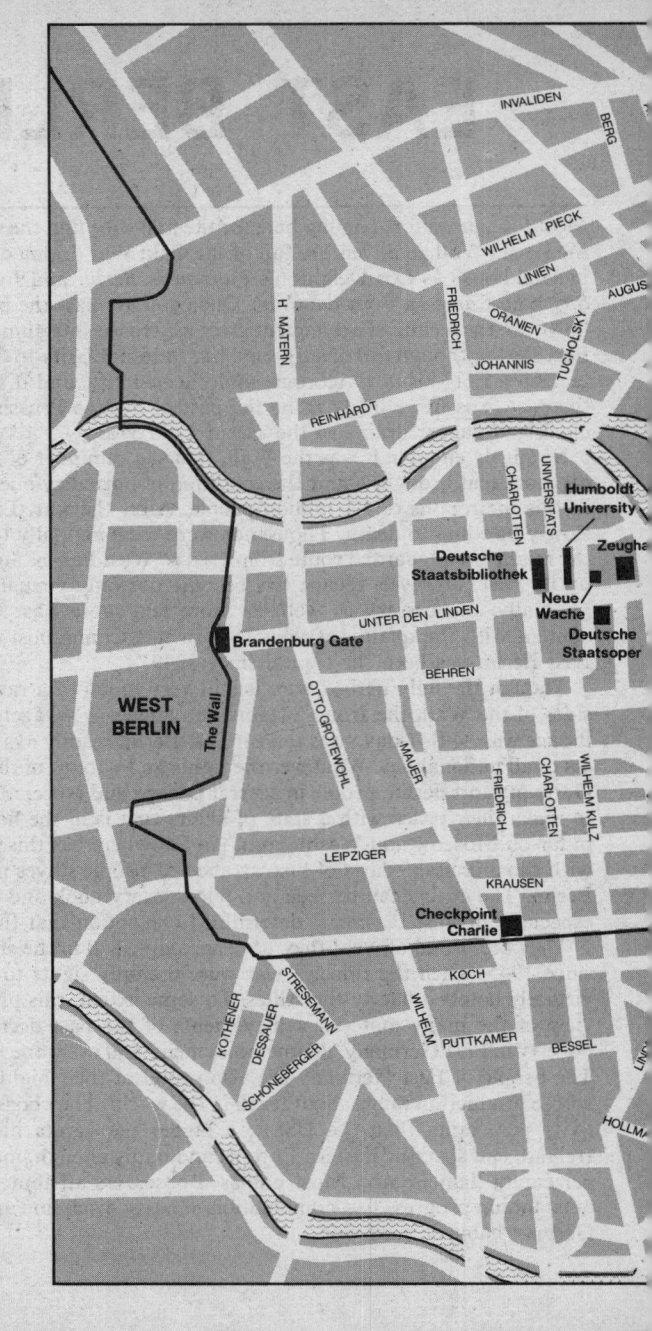

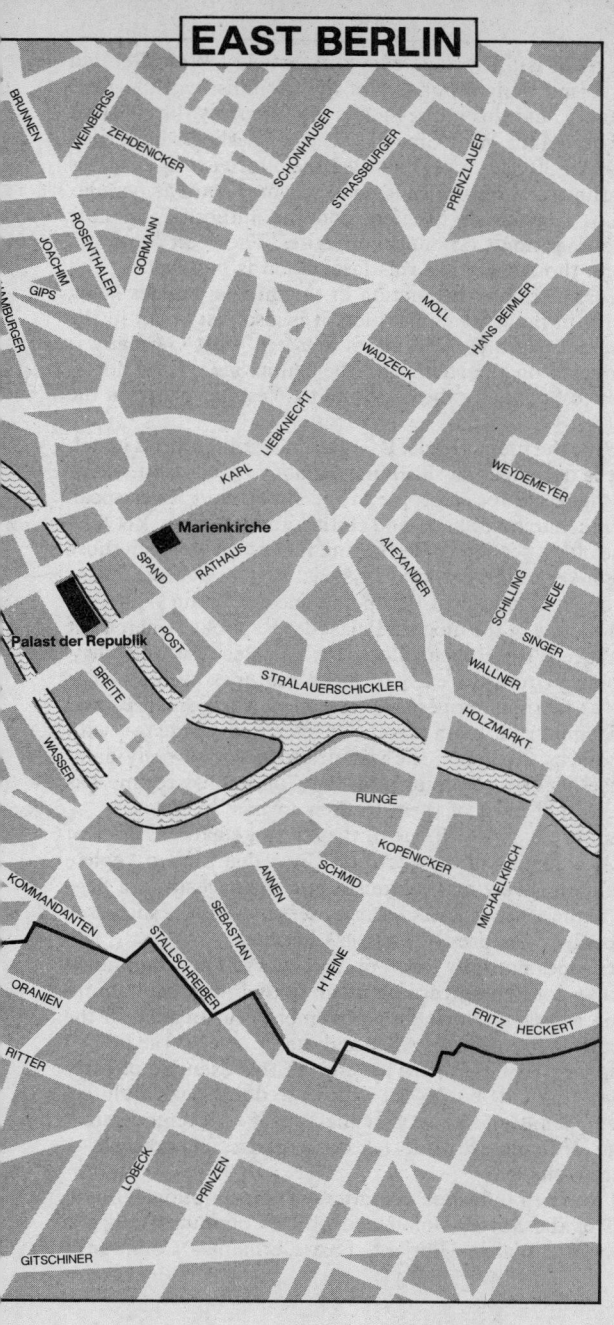

EAST BERLIN

BRUNNEN

WEINBERGS

ZEHDENICKER

SCHONHAUSER

STRASSBURGER

PRENZLAUER

ROSENTHALER

JOACHIM

GORMANN

HAMBURGER

GIPS

MOLL

HANS BEIMLER

WADZECK

LIEBKNECHT

KARL

WEYDEMEYER

Marienkirche

RATHAUS

SPAND

ALEXANDER

SCHILLING

NEUE

Palast der Republik

POST

SINGER

BREITE

STRALAUERSCHICKLER

WALLNER

WASSER

HOLZMARKT

RUNGE

KOPENICKER

SCHMID

MICHAELKIRCH

KOMMANDANTEN

ANNEN

SEBASTIAN

STALLSCHREIBER

ORANIEN

H HEINE

FRITZ HECKERT

RITTER

LOBECK

PRINZEN

GITSCHINER

On the other hand, there is a shortage of luxury articles. West German radio and television transmit daily reminders of the capitalist world's great wealth and cultural vitality, and this impression is reinforced by the constant stream of visitors from across the Wall. Since 1972, West Berliners have been making extensive use of the 30 days a year allotted them for visiting relatives and friends in East Berlin. As a result, jeans and rock music are as popular here as they are in Los Angeles or Munich, and the authorities in East Germany actually encourage non-Communist appetites. The West continues to fascinate people here, though little of this fascination is political.

In many respects, East Germany is a nation in the middle; besides being the westernmost country in the Communist bloc, it is also just about in the middle of Europe, where Eastern Europe meets Western. East Germany is bounded by Czechoslovakia on the south and the Baltic Sea on the north. Berlin is actually closer to Poland on the east than to West Germany on the west.

Recently spruced up for the tourist trade, East Berlin is still hardly a match for West Berlin, but it is no longer so shockingly shabby by contrast. Compared to West Berlin, there are fewer people in the streets and fewer speak English, nightlife isn't much to rave about, and clothes aren't as chic. Yet East Berlin encompasses the oldest section of Berlin, and it is a city in which those interested can glimpse a very different kind of social system at work.

The two cities — modern Communist Berlin and ancient Berlin — are curiously intermixed. On the site of the modern Palast der Republik, where East Germany's parliament meets, the Hohenzollerns built a palace and ruled first as electors of Brandenburg (from the early fifteenth century), then as kings of Prussia, and finally as German emperors. They made their small capital an architectural jewel, lining the main street — Unter den Linden — with magnificent baroque palaces. Although the war destroyed or severely damaged every one of these historical monuments, the Communist regime has spared no efforts in restoring most of them to their former splendor.

The old Prussian military flair is still one of the striking characteristics of East Berlin. The weekly changing of the guard on Unter den Linden, replete with goose-stepping soldiers, lively martial music, and the pageantry of flags and banners, is a clear reminder that East Germany sees itself as the successor to what it calls the "benign" features of Prussia's heritage.

East Berlin, however, does not only dwell on past glory. The Communist authorities here have also gone about turning much of their new capital into a showcase modeled on Moscow. Nowhere is this more evident than in the Karl-Marx-Allee. Formerly Frankfurter Allee and Stalin Allee ("rue de Debâcle" is the nickname wry East Berliners have given this example of early postwar reconstruction), this wide boulevard with its wedding-cake architecture represents the remodeling of the city in the "spirit of Communism." However, more recent architecture — at Alexanderplatz, for example — is much more pleasing to the eye.

Despite widespread Western influence in matters of consumption and culture, the strong hand of the Soviet Union and other Communist allies is omnipresent. For 20 years, Walter Ulbricht, East Germany's Communist leader until 1971, ran a tight ship. No doubt about it: This is the capital of a linchpin Eastern bloc country, and one of Eastern Europe's economic giants. Communist banners and slogans are no longer as omnipresent as they once were, but free enterprise is almost nonexistent. Hotels, restaurants, shops, theaters, and just about everything else are state owned. Uniformed police, soldiers, and other representatives of the "first German workers' and farmers' state" are highly visible, and serve to reinforce the impression that although East Berlin may tolerate jeans and rock, it is well on the way to creating a new society, based on Communist principles and closely allied to the Soviet Union.

There is opposition to the regime, even among young people, but it is rarely open. The small number of dissidents consists almost entirely of artists and intellectuals who most resent restrictions on free speech, assembly, and travel to the West. Another sore point is the government's policy regarding consumerism. A point at issue is the countrywide chain of Intershop stores, in which anyone may come to shop for Western goods, but only with Western currency. Only those East Germans with access to Western currency can buy the luxury items offered to Western tourists at a discount. (It is not uncommon for visitors to be approached by East Berliners wanting to purchase dollars or deutsche marks.) Because its priorities lie elsewhere, East Germany is unable to satisfy the consumer demands of its citizens. With Western propaganda concentrating on the restrictive situation in East Berlin and Communist propaganda significantly ignoring it, the truth is hard to know. One of the purposes of a visit is to judge the situation for yourself.

But that is hardly the only reason to visit. Unlike West Berlin, which has had to substitute economic prosperity for the loss of its hinterland, East Berlin is closely linked to the quiet, lake-studded and forested countryside surrounding it, the Mark of Brandenburg. The people, although not quite as well dressed as their counterparts on the other side of the Wall, are pleasant, polite, and infused with a heartening sense of camaraderie. Wherever one goes — museums, restaurants, hotels — one is treated with friendly courtesy.

The Cold War political division of the city means that you can use West Berlin as a base for discovering this fascinating "other" Berlin. And the Four Power Agreement of 1971 gives you the assurance that your visit will take place in an atmosphere relatively free of political tension. (Since 1974, the US has maintained an embassy in this world capital.) John le Carré notwithstanding, you would do well to come in from the cold to East Berlin.

You can travel to East Berlin either with a West Berlin sight-seeing bus or on your own. Should you choose the latter, take the subway or elevated S-Bahn to the border control at the East Berlin train station, Bahnhof Friedrichstrasse.

Another way to enter East Berlin is by car or by foot via Checkpoint Charlie, an elaborate "hole in the Wall" that has been in operation ever since 1961. It can only be used by non-German nationals, and the formalities are exactly like the ones you have to go through at Bahnhof Friedrichstrasse (see below). The one difference is the customs check if you come by car. On the

West Berlin side of the Wall, manned by members of the Allied Forces, Checkpoint Charlie is at the corner of Friedrichstrasse and Kochstrasse.

To go to East Berlin, you will need a valid US passport and 5 deutsche marks for a day's visa, and you will have to exchange at least 25 deutsche marks to get in — at the manipulated rate of one deutsche mark for one East German mark — but you can exchange any amount above that minimum. Remember that you are never allowed to leave East Germany with East German marks in your pocket; you have to exchange money at the border control point when entering East Berlin, and you are required to spend at least the minimum amount before leaving. (The rest can be exchanged back to Western currency at the border.) No Western printed matter is allowed into East Berlin, and there are strict rules regarding the amount and kind of Western goods you can bring with you as gifts.

SPECIAL NOTE: You must leave East Berlin by midnight unless you get a special entry visa. Information and application forms are available from the Reisebüro in East Berlin (the East German government's official travel agency; see *Sources and Resources*), from US travel agents, the East German Embassy in Washington, Reisebüro-appointed agencies in Western Europe, and Reisebüro offices in Eastern Europe. Processing can take up to 8 weeks. Once the application is processed, the government issues a Visa Entitlement Certificate, which allows you to obtain a visa at the border or from the embassy in Washington. (Transit visas are issued at the border if you present a visa for the next country.)

EAST BERLIN AT-A-GLANCE

SEEING THE CITY: The slender spire of the Fernsehturm (television tower) climbs to a height of 1,209 feet above the city and the Wall. Built in 1969, it is Europe's second tallest tower. A revolving sphere at the 655-foot level is decked out with studio and transmission facilities as well as with a restaurant and café, from which there is a magnificent view of both Berlins. Open daily. Between Alexanderplatz and Marx-Engels-Platz (phone: 212-3333).

SPECIAL PLACES: Most of the city has been laid out in a grid pattern, making it easy to get around. Orient yourself on the important downtown streets: Friedrichstrasse runs north to south, Unter den Linden and Karl-Marx-Allee, east to west. The center of the city is on an island in the Spree River. You can negotiate most of the downtown area by foot. For outlying areas, use the U-Bahn (subway), buses, streetcars, or S-Bahn (aboveground trains). See *Getting Around*.

DOWNTOWN

Unter den Linden – Some 1,500 yards long and almost 70 yards wide, this avenue is in the very heart of East Berlin. Originally laid out to connect the royal palace with the hunting preserve, the Tiergarten, it got its name from the rows of linden trees that were planted on both sides and in the center of the wide boulevard. In the eighteenth and nineteenth centuries, a number of magnificent structures were built along the boulevard. Although they were bombed in the last war, the government has faithfully restored them. We will look first at the north side of the street, gradually working our way to the west.

Zeughaus (Arsenal) – Built between 1695 and 1706, this lovely baroque structure is the oldest on Unter den Linden. Set on the Spree, it overlooks historic Museum Island (Museumsinsel). Originally an arsenal (hence the name), the building now houses the Museum of German History (Museum für Deutsche Geschichte), which is devoted to a Marxist view of German history. Closed Fridays. Unter den Linden 2 (phone: 200-0591).

Neue Wache (The New Guard House) – Built in 1818, this has been a monument to the victims of fascism and militarism since 1960. It is guarded by members of the People's Army, and there is a colorful ceremonial changing of the guard every Wednesday at 2:30 PM. Unter den Linden 4.

Humboldt University – Erected in the mid-eighteenth century, it became Friedrich Wilhelm University in 1810. Since 1949, this, the largest university in East Germany, has been known by its present name. Famous teachers included Hegel, Max Planck, and Einstein; Marx and Engels were students here. Unter den Linden 6.

Deutsche Staatsbibliothek (The German State Library) – Built in the early twentieth century, the library occupies the site of the former Prussian State Library; the latter's stock of books that remained in East Berlin during the war has been stored here. The rest are at the new Staatsbibliothek in West Berlin. Unter den Linden 8.

Brandenburger Tor (Brandenburg Gate) – There is very little of historical interest between the Deutsche Staatsbibliothek and this massive Berlin landmark at the western end of Unter den Linden. The Brandenburg Gate has been inaccessible to cars and pedestrians since August 1961, when the Wall was erected only a few yards away. The closest you can get to the gate is the corner of Otto-Grotewohl-Strasse (formerly Wilhelmstrasse), which is about 100 yards away. This late-eighteenth-century triumphal arch is brilliantly lit up at night. Pariser Platz.

Altes Palais (Old Palace) – On the south side of Unter den Linden, the first historic structure one sees is the Old Palace. Built in 1836, it was the residence of Emperor William I during the last 50 years of his life. It is now used by Humboldt University. Unter den Linden 9.

Alte Bibliothek (Old Library) – The Prussian State Library was here until 1914. Built in the late eighteenth century, it is now part of Humboldt University. Set back from Unter den Linden, on Bebelplatz. (Formerly Opernplatz, made famous during the Nazi burning of books in 1933.)

St. Hedwigs Kathedrale – This Roman Catholic cathedral dates from the late eighteenth century and was built according to plans laid down by Frederick the Great (who was by all appearances impressed by the Pantheon in Rome). Gutted in the war, it has been just as carefully restored as most other Unter den Linden landmarks. Bebelplatz.

Deutsche Staatsoper (The German State Opera) – The opera house was built in 1743 and burned down a hundred years later. Rebuilt, it was twice destroyed by bombs during the last war. Almost 1,500 people can attend performances here, and it is also used by the renowned orchestra, the Staatskapelle Berlin, for concerts (for ticket information see Music, *Sources and Resources*). Unter den Linden 7.

Palais Unter den Linden – Originally built in the seventeenth century, it was known as the Kronprinzenpalais until 1945. The rebuilt facade, however, is modeled on the one added in 1857. Two German emperors were born here, and during the Weimar Republic, it was used as a museum of contemporary art; today the government maintains it as an official guesthouse. Unter den Linden 1.

Palast der Republik – Past Unter den Linden, on the island in the Spree. This was the site of the former royal palace, which was severely damaged during the war. The Hohenzollerns resided here from 1451 to 1918. Dismantled in 1950, it is now a multipurpose building, housing, among other things, the East German parliament, theaters, and restaurants and cafés. The architecture is extremely modern. Marx-Engels-Platz.

Staatsratsgebäude – The East German government, the State Council, meets in this modern structure. The centerpiece is one of the portals from the former royal palace. South side of Marx-Engels-Platz.

Museumsinsel – On the north side of Marx-Engels-Platz, surrounded on three sides by the Spree River, is one of the world's largest and most magnificent museum complexes. The buildings date back to the nineteenth and early twentieth centuries. The Altes Museum accommodates contemporary paintings and the Cabinet of Engravings, containing 135,000 prints by German and foreign masters (fifteenth to eighteenth century); among the latter treasures are Botticelli's illustrations to Dante's *Divine Comedy*. Across the street is the National Gallery, which houses nineteenth- and twentieth-century art. Behind this is the Pergamon Museum, whose collection of antique art is one of the most important of its kind in the world. Its showpieces are the Pergamon Altar and the Market Gate of Miletus, both second century BC. In this building are also the Far Eastern Collection, the Museum of Ethnography, the Near Eastern Museum, and the Islamic Museum.

At the northernmost tip of this island of museums is the Bode Museum, once the famed Kaiser Friedrich Museum. It now houses the Egyptian Museum, the Early Christian and Byzantine Collection, the Picture Gallery, the Sculpture Collection, the Cabinet of Coins and the Museum of Pre- and Proto-History. Among the treasures here are such masterpieces of German sculpture as the twelfth-century Naumburg Crucifix and the Winged Altarpiece from Minden Cathedral (fifteenth century).

Except for the Near Eastern Museum and part of the Antique Collection, both at the Pergamon Museum, the Museumsinsel is closed Mondays and Tuesdays.

Marienkirche (St. Mary's Church) – Just past the Museumsinsel, within the shadow of the Fernsehturm, is St. Mary's, Berlin's second oldest church. First erected in 1240, it is a pleasant combination of Gothic and neoclassical styles. Karl-Liebknecht-Str.

SUBURBS

Sowjetisches Ehrenmal – Within the confines of verdant Treptower Park, not far from the left bank of the Spree, is this huge Soviet War Memorial. Dedicated in 1949, it honors more than 5,000 Soviet soldiers who fell in the battle for Berlin in 1945. Much of the material used came from the ruins of Hitler's Reich Chancellery. Open daily. Entrance from Puschkinallee and Am Treptower Park.

Tierpark – East Berlin's zoo was opened in 1955 on the grounds of Friedrichsfelde Palace. The animals are shown as far as possible in herds or family groups, in spacious enclosures that blend with the landscape. Open daily. Am Tierpark 125.

■ **EXTRA SPECIAL:** Much of East Berlin's area is water; the Spree River and its tributaries flow through the city for a total of 20 miles before joining the Havel in West Berlin. The extensive forests in the outlying areas to the south combine with the waterways to form a vacationer's paradise. You might enjoy a scenic boat ride with the *Weisse Flotte,* a fleet of 60 white excursion ships that ply these waters every day from March to September (phone: 2-7120). Boats depart eight times a day from the piers on the Spree at the Treptower Park S-Bahn station. (This trip is mostly for Berliners, so English is rarely spoken on board.)

You can get on and off these boats as often as you wish. Along the way you might want to stop off at these sights: the Müggelturm, a 98-foot-high tower near Berlin's largest lake; the Rathaus of Köpenick; and the Mecklenburger Dorf in Köpenick, a replica of a north German village of the last century, featuring typical north German snacks and beverages at very reasonable prices.

The sights may be approached by land (subway, streetcar, S-Bahn, or bus) as well as by water; they are closed Mondays and Tuesdays.

SOURCES AND RESOURCES

General information, brochures, and maps can be obtained at the Fernsehturm. Open daily. Between Alexanderplatz and Marx-Engels-Platz (phone: 212-4675).

By the way, all telephone numbers in East Berlin can also be reached from West Berlin by first dialing the area code 0372. The best detailed local map, *Berlin Stadtatlas,* is available at bookstores in West Berlin only. The East German Travel Agency (Reisebüro) maintains a special Tourist Service Bureau for foreign visitors on the first floor of its skyscraper at Alexanderplatz 5 (phone: 215-4402). Open daily.

For Local Coverage – A calendar of events, entitled *Wohin in Berlin,* is published twice a month. It is available at the Fernsehturm and at most newsstands in East Berlin and it is in German only. Information in English can be obtained both at the Fernsehturm and at the Tourist Service Bureau on Alexanderplatz. Listings of cultural events can also be requested from the tourist office in West Berlin. There is no food guide. We suggest that you buy a helpful volume (in German) entitled *Berlin von 7 bis 7;* it is available in West Berlin only and contains listings for East Berlin.

 CLIMATE AND CLOTHES: The weather is very similar to that in the northeastern US, although it is not as hot in summer or as cold in winter. The temperature is rarely above 70°F (19°C) or below freezing. Rain can fall at any time of the year. Wear whatever you would wear in the US.

 GETTING AROUND: Subway and Bus – Equipped with the same kind of yellow cars as in West Berlin, East Berlin's two subway (U-Bahn) lines will get you to many places in the city. There is a good network of buses and streetcars, as well as an extensive interurban railroad system, the S-Bahn, which reaches most parts of the city and beyond. Keep in mind that you may not leave the city limits if you only have a day's visa. Maps are available at the Fernsehturm or at the East German Travel Agency (see above).

Taxi – Do not hail taxis in the streets. There are taxi stands all over town. To call a taxi in the downtown area, dial 3646.

Car Rental – The major American firms are represented. You can get information at the East German Travel Agency (see above).

 MUSEUMS: In addition to the Zeughaus and the museums in the Museums-insel complex, described in *Special Places,* there is one additional institution you ought to visit: *Märkisches Museum,* Am Köllnischen Park (phone: 275-4902), which surveys Berlin's local history, is one of the best of its kind in Europe (closed Mondays and Tuesdays).

 SHOPPING: The opportunities are limited. Most stores belong to the state-owned chains and offer items whose quality often leaves much to be desired. However, Western goods at low prices can be had at the Intershop stores at the *Metropol, Palast, Unter den Linden, Berolina,* and *Stadt Berlin* hotels, as well as at Schoenefeld Airport. At the Intershops you must pay in Western currency.

Keep in mind that the West Berlin customs authorities will not allow you to bring back more than 200 cigarettes or one bottle of liquor if you have spent only a day in

East Berlin. The Intershops and the following recommended stores honor Diners Club and American Express credit cards, except for *Haus des Kindes:*

Glas/Porzellan – Crystal and china. Karl-Marx-Allee 62.

Haus des Kindes – Department store for children's clothing and toys. South side of Strausberger Platz.

Pelzmoden – Furs. Unter den Linden 37–39.

Uhren/Schmuck – Watches and jewelry. Unter den Linden 14.

 SPECIAL EVENTS: Every autumn, the city puts on an ambitious theater and music festival. Another venerable traditional event, and one that appeals to people of all ages, is the annual *Christmas Fair.* It is held at the open area between Alexanderplatz and Jannowitz Brücke from the end of November to a week before Christmas.

 THEATER: Berlin's noble theater tradition continues unabated under the postwar East German regime. The classical repertoire holds sway at the *Deutsches Theater,* Schumannstr. 13a (phone: 287-1225), and — at the same address — at the intimate *Kammerspiele,* which was founded more than 60 years ago by Max Reinhardt (phone: 287-1226). Another small stage, the *Maxim Gorki Theater,* also performs plays from the classical repertoire as well as dramas by the late Russian playwright. For Brecht fans, a visit to the *Berliner Ensemble* — which the late German dramatist founded in 1948 — is a must, at Am Bertolt-Brecht-Platz (phone: 282-3160). Genuine, albeit slightly muted, political and social satire can be enjoyed at the *Distel,* whose shows are performed at two small theaters at Friedrichstr. 101 (phone: 207-1291) and Degnerstr. 9 (phone: 376-5174). Tickets to all theater performances in the city can be bought directly at the box offices; they can also be ordered at the ground-floor theater and concert ticket counter of the theaters' visitors service at the *Palast Hotel* (closed Sundays), Spandauer Str. (phone: 212-5258/5902).

 MUSIC: Some of the world's best opera is performed at the 200-year-old *Deutsche Staatsoper,* which also accommodates concerts by the opera's famed orchestra, the *Staatskapelle Berlin,* Unter den Linden 7 (phone: 205-4556). The *Komische Oper,* no less renowned than the *Staatsoper,* is much more modern in its approach to opera, at Behrenstr. 55–57 (phone: 229-2555). In two concert halls in the newly restored Schauspielhaus (built in 1820), some of the world's best orchestras perform, Platz der Akademie (phone: 227-2306, 227-2122). International pop and folk music stars perform at the theater in Palast der Republik, Marx-Engels-Pl. (phone: 248-2354). If you are lucky enough to get tickets, you can also enjoy some of Europe's best pop and rock music in East Berlin, performed by such East German groups as the Puhdys, at the new Friedrichstadtpalast, Friedrichstr. 107 (phone: 283-64-74). Tickets at box offices or at the government travel agency.

 NIGHTCLUBS AND NIGHTLIFE: For obvious reasons, East Berlin's nightlife is nothing to write home about. There are two relatively lively night spots, each featuring dancing to live music as well as stage shows. There is a cover charge at the *Moskva-Bar,* Karl-Marx-Allee 34 (phone: 279-4052). At the *Lindencorso,* you can not only dance to live music in the *Konzertcafé* (closed Mondays), you can also enjoy interesting musical shows and revues in the first-floor *Nachtbar Havanna* (cover charge; open daily), at Unter den Linden 17 (phone: 220-2461). If it is just a quiet time you want, with drinks and snacks, two interesting publike places in historic settings can be recommended: *Raabediele* (open daily), in Ermeler Haus, Märkisches Ufer 10–12 (phone: 229-4037); and *Zur letzten Instanz* (closed Saturdays), Waisenstr. 16–17 (phone: 212-5528). After dark, singles gather at the *Pinguin Bar*, Rosa-Luxemburg-Str. 39, for dancing.

EAST BERLIN / Best in Town 277

 SINS: On a 1-day tourist visa, you must leave East Berlin by midnight. Spend your evening at the *Staatsoper,* and then make your date with Checkpoint Charlie by midnight. Sin in East Berlin you don't need.

BEST IN TOWN

 CHECKING IN: Compared to most Western European cities, East Berlin offers a small choice of comfortable hotel accommodations. Largely to blame for this situation is the widespread destruction of World War II and the fact that the East German authorities gave greater priority to other problems, like housing and industry. Nevertheless, increased prosperity in the entire Eastern bloc and the country's need for foreign exchange — especially from the West — have resulted in a recent spate of hotel construction. Our offerings, though meager, include a number of those hotels, which are certainly among the best you can find anywhere.

Remember: You will need a special entry visa (valid for more than a day) if you want to stay overnight in East Berlin. For information on this and for listings of more modest, although much less comfortable accommodation, consult the government travel agency (see *Sources and Resources*).

The hotels in our listings have a bath or shower in every room, and the rooms are all equipped with telephones. Each hotel has a restaurant on the premises as well as an Intershop (see *Shopping*), and they are all equipped for guests in wheelchairs. Reservations must be made in advance. Hotel rates are high; in fact, they are double the price charged to guests from Communist countries. For a double room in those hotels we have classed as expensive, expect to pay $80 and up; $50 to $80 in the moderate category; under $50 in the inexpensive class. Payment must be made in Western currency or by credit card.

Metropol – This handsome high-rise was built in the mid-1970s by a Swedish firm and is without doubt one of the best hotels in town. Extras are a sauna and a garage. There are 340 rooms, and the rooms and the service are bound to appeal to those used to Western European luxury hotels. Friedrichstr. 150–153 (phone: 2-2040). Expensive.

Palast – This new 600-room hotel provides first-class service, luxurious accommodations, and a good view of the city. Its restaurants serve a variety of cuisines — from Asian to French. Karl Liebknecht Str. 5 (phone: 2410). Expensive.

Berolina – Pleasantly set back from bustling Karl-Marx-Allee, this 300-plus-room hotel offers first-class service and comfort. Restaurant and cozy grill/bar on the premises. Karl-Marx-Allee 31 (phone: 210-95-41). Moderate.

Stadt Berlin – In the middle of East Berlin's downtown area, its 994 rooms make it the largest in the city. Right behind the hotel is Alexanderplatz; closed off to automobile traffic, the square is ringed by restaurants, stores, the Fernsehturm, and other public buildings. It has a sauna and a garage. Alexanderplatz (phone: 2190). Moderate.

Hospiz am Bahnhof Friedrichstrasse – Near the rail entry to East Berlin, this clean, well-run hospice has no frills but is comfortable and reasonably priced. Albrechtstr. 8 (phone: 282-5396). Inexpensive.

 EATING OUT: Continuing an old Berlin tradition, East Germany's capital offers a large number of good restaurants. Most of them are in the downtown area, and the food ranges from native German to Continental to ethnic (chiefly Eastern European). In general, though, restaurants here are inferior to those of West Berlin.

Prices are quite reasonable. A dinner for two, with drinks and wine, costs about $25 or more at restaurants in the expensive category; between $15 and $25 in the moderate range; and less than $15 at places classified as inexpensive. Tips are included in the bill.

Panorama-Restaurant – A fitting name for a restaurant on the 37th floor of the Hotel Stadt Berlin. The food almost equals the marvelous view. Try the daily specialties. Reservations necessary. Open daily. Alexanderplatz (phone: 2190). Expensive.

Ganymed – On the Spree, near Bahnhof Friedrichstrasse (handy if you arrive by subway or S-Bahn). As at many restaurants here, there is background music. The atmosphere is comfortable and intimate. Continental food and good wines. Open daily; supper only on Mondays. Reservations suggested. Schiffbauerdamm 5 (phone: 282-9540). Expensive to moderate.

Stockinger – Simply furnished, but still one of the city's finest restaurants. Along with traditional German fare, the menu features several exotic Oriental dishes. The big hit, though, is the 2-ounce can of Molossol caviar for under $30. Closed Sundays and Mondays. Reservations suggested. Schönhauser Allee 61 (phone: 448-3110). Expensive to moderate.

Metropol – This hotel dining room, tastefully decorated, features rustic Gemütlichkeit. The food is Continental and of the best standard. Open daily. Reservations accepted. Friedrichstr. 150–153 (phone: 2-2040). Expensive to moderate.

Fernsehturm – Europe's second largest tower (described in *Seeing the City*) has a revolving café-restaurant from which, at a height of 655 feet, you get a breathtaking all-around view of East and West Berlin. The food is also good. There is a $2.50 admission charge, and you have to be finished within an hour. Open daily. Reservations accepted. Situated between Alexanderplatz and Marx-Engels-Platz (phone: 210-4232). Moderate.

Zum Stilbruch – Once a traditional Berlin tavern, now a small and cozy restaurant. The Continental dishes are well prepared and efficiently served at prices that prevailed in West Germany 20 years ago. The specialties are the Eastern European dishes (upon request). Closed Saturdays and Sundays. Reservations suggested. Florastr. 84 (phone: 483-0494). Moderate.

Offenbach Stuben – This intimate, cozy restaurant is one of the few eateries here that is privately run. The German and Continental cuisine are fine, as are the beverages. Closed Sundays and Mondays. Reservations suggested. Stubbenkammerstr. 8 (phone: 448-4106). Moderate.

Operncafé – This historic eighteenth-century building was formerly a palace and now houses a number of gastronomic establishments. The restaurant's specialty is Bulgarian food. Next door is the famed *Staatsoper*. Closed Sundays and Mondays. Reservations accepted. Unter den Linden 5 (phone: 200-0256). Moderate.

Palast der Republik – On the site of the former Prussian royal palace the authorities — in the mid-1970s — put up this huge multipurpose building (see *Special Places*). Three large-capacity restaurants offer good Continental food. The *Spree Restaurant* is closed Mondays; the *Palast Restaurant* is closed Tuesdays; and the *Linden Restaurant* closes Wednesdays. Reservations suggested. No credit cards. Marx-Engels-Platz (phone: 238-2364). Moderate.

Moskva – Worth a visit just to sample its Russian specialties. Open daily. Reservations suggested. Karl-Marx-Allee 34 (phone: 279-2869). Moderate.

Ermeler Haus – If you prefer to avoid the hustle and bustle of the immediate downtown area, this is for you. The baroque structure, built in 1703, is one of the few historic buildings left, aside from those on Unter den Linden. The interior is all rococo, as is the restaurant, which offers good Continental dishes in intimate surroundings. Open daily. Reservations suggested. Märkisches Ufer 10–12 (phone: 229-4037). Inexpensive.

Möwe – Across the Spree from Bahnhof Friedrichstrasse and down the road a bit is this intimate, tastefully appointed grill-restaurant. *Möwe,* German for dove, is the symbol of the local artists' association, whose club this is. It is, however, open to the public. This pleasant place is frequented by an intelligent, wide-awake crowd. The kitchen is praiseworthy: Continental cuisine, with an eye to the East. Closed Mondays. Reservations accepted. No credit cards. Hermann-Matern-Str. 18 (phone: 282-5741). Inexpensive.

Müggelsee-Perle – Recently rated as one of East Germany's top restaurants. The fish, fowl, and game dishes are best; also try the Berlin pea soup. On the shore of East Berlin's largest lake, Grosser Muggelsee, the restaurant is accessible by excursion ship (see *Extra Special*) as well as by bus and car. Open daily. Reservations accepted. Am grossen Muggelsee (phone: 657-3044). Inexpensive.

WEST BERLIN

The first fact of life in West Berlin is location — not geography, but location. West Berlin is smack in the heart of East Germany — 110 miles from the West German border, and the same distance from the Baltic Sea in the north and Czechoslovakia to the south. It is only 52 miles from the Polish border at the Oder River. West Berlin is closer to Warsaw than it is to Munich. The city has had only four decades to get used to the sobering reality that after 300 years it is no longer the center of Germany. There is no city in the world so isolated from its political and cultural center as West Berlin — this well-spring of German life so far from the rest of West Germany.

In 1963, when John F. Kennedy told thousands of cheering Germans that he, too, was a Berliner, he made a political statement of rare depth and resonance. Not only did it sum up the current state of the Cold War — very frigid, indeed, since the building of the Berlin Wall 2 years before — but its unspoken promise of a worldwide community of sympathy for the plight of West Berliners managed to touch and soothe the profound anxiety of the city and its residents. For 15 years West Berliners had lived in an isolation made more desolate by the overpowering cultural and historic importance of their city before World War II. Long gone was the imperial Berlin that ruled Germany until World War I; gone was the devil-may-care Berlin of the 1920s and early 1930s so admirably captured by Christopher Isherwood in its mad gaiety and decadence; gone even were the days of terrible power of the Third Reich. Berlin was a capital city without a country. And then in 1961 the city was irreversibly truncated, and West Berliners saw the few treasured historic buildings that had survived the war disappear behind the blank and pitiless concrete face of the Wall. As the Wall went up, they lost family, friends, city, and heritage overnight. This radical surgery left a wake of shock, an anger that had hardly begun to dissipate when President Kennedy visited in 1963. It also left a stubborn determination to remain free, which more than any other emotion from that dark period still drives the city today.

The division of Berlin, now an everyday fact of life for West Berlin's 1.9 million and East Berlin's 1.1 million people, began in 1944, when the US, Great Britain, and the Soviet Union, meeting in London, divided not only the city, but all of Germany, into occupied zones.

Because no written Soviet guarantee of access from West Germany existed, the Western Allies were unable to prevent Moscow from launching a land blockade on West Berlin in 1948. It took a whole year of a massive Allied airlift to force the Soviets to back down. West Berlin had been saved from slow starvation, but 70 Allied airmen and 8 German workers died trying to keep West Berlin's lifeline open. The city divided along Cold War political lines into two separate municipal entities. Soviet threats against West Berlin, which continued throughout the 1950s, culminated in the overnight building of the Wall by the East German Communist regime on August 13, 1961. The concrete barrier effectively sealed off the 185 square miles of West Berlin from the 156 square miles of East Berlin. That ugly 9-foot-tall symbol of what ails Europe's body politic kept the people of West Berlin separated from East Berlin. Nevertheless, thousands of Berliners on either side of the dividing line continued to maintain bonds of blood and friendship.

This effort was made easier in 1971 when the three Western Allies met with the Soviet Union and produced the Four Power Agreement on Berlin to reduce East-West tension over the city. Since then, access to West Berlin from West Germany has been assured, and both halves of the city have settled down to a relatively normal existence. Nevertheless, West Berlin continues to be the only city in Europe under military occupation. In the Western sectors, sovereignty is still exercised by the Americans, the British, and the French; and the 13,000 Allied troops here are a visible reminder for the West Berliners that Western guarantees enable them to live and work in freedom. Although they have the last word, the occupying powers have delegated civil authority in the city to the West Berliners and have allowed West Berlin to enter into close legal, monetary, and economic ties with West Germany. Political democracy is now deeply entrenched in West Berlin.

World War II and its aftermath gave the heart of the old city to East Berlin, and the new, truncated West Berlin, rising from the ashes of the war, has had to create its own urban essence. That it has succeeded in this massive enterprise is an understatement.

Since the war devastated Berlin, construction of new buildings has greatly changed the appearance of the city. Some of the architecture of the past — the majestic Charlottenburg and Bellevue palaces, for example — has managed to survive war and change. But Tegel Airport as well as numerous hospitals, schools, factories, businesses, and housing projects have all been built in a kind of anonymous contemporary style — many of the buildings are high-rises — and at a pace that continues unabated. The sparkle and the glitter of Kurfürstendamm, West Berlin's prestigious international thoroughfare, have become its trademark.

But what makes West Berlin an outstanding place to live in and to visit is its culture. Continuing its prewar role, the city remains a cultural center of the very first order. It has 18 theaters, and one company, the Schaubühne, is said by critics to be the world's best German-speaking troupe. Also of international rank are the famed Berlin Philharmonic Orchestra and its conductor, Herbert von Karajan, and numerous museums like the great Dahlem Museum, the National Gallery, and the Bauhaus Museum. There is a kind of creative ferment here and a cult of quality that has attracted many writers, artists, composers, architects, and actors.

West Berlin is not only a cultural but an educational center, and one of the finest in Europe. The Free University and the Technical University, where many young Germans study, enjoy excellent reputations. Despite the great many older citizens living in West Berlin, this is a city of — and for —

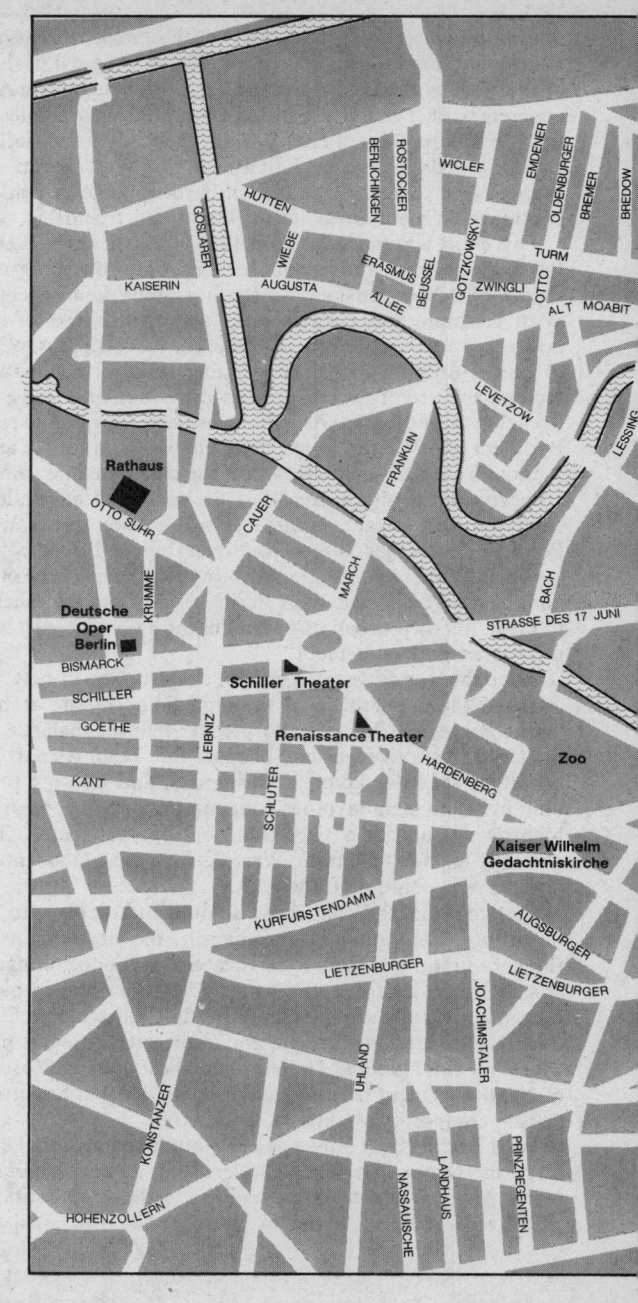

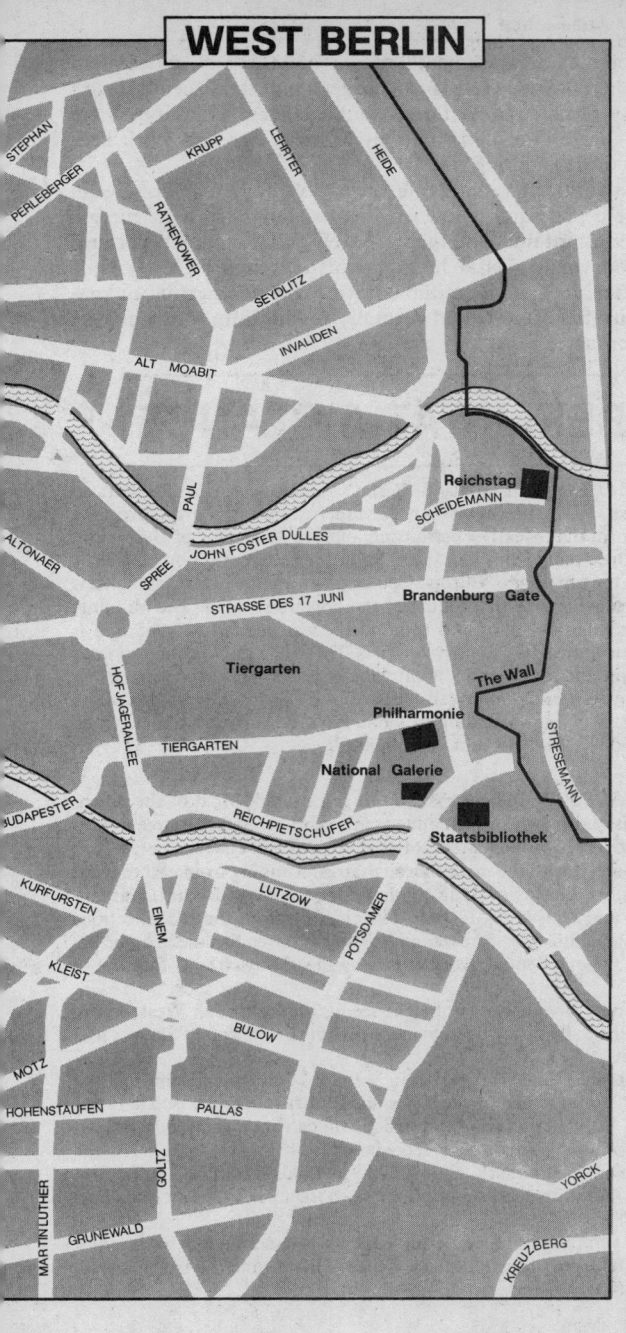

WEST BERLIN

STEPHAN

PERLEBERGER

RATHENOWER

KRUPP

LEHRTER

HEIDE

SEYDLITZ

INVALIDEN

ALT MOABIT

ALTONAER

PAUL

SPREE

JOHN FOSTER DULLES

SCHEIDEMANN

Reichstag

STRASSE DES 17 JUNI

Brandenburg Gate

HOF JAGERALLEE

Tiergarten

The Wall

TIERGARTEN

Philharmonie

STRESEMANN

National Galerie

BUDAPESTER

REICHPIETSCHUFER

Staatsbibliothek

KURFURSTEN

EINEM

LUTZOW

POTSDAMER

KLEIST

BULOW

MOTZ

HOHENSTAUFEN

PALLAS

GOLTZ

YORCK

MARTIN LUTHER

GRUNEWALD

KREUZBERG

the young, a city of pop music, experimental movies and theaters, and student hangouts. West Berlin is West Germany's largest industrial center, with headquarters of many firms such as Borsig and Siemens. The city's large foreign population — more than 200,000 non-Germans live and work here — adds special spice to the melting pot.

It is hard to do justice to the remarkable variety of life here. West Berlin is for people who like islands and who thrive on exchanges of high energy. Things seem to be in constant flux, and there is rarely a dull moment. Perhaps Christopher Isherwood would feel at home in this new and highly sophisticated West Berlin after all. The indomitable spirit of the courageous, pugnacious, and worldly-wise Berliners would certainly remind him of the city he wrote about half a century ago.

WEST BERLIN AT-A-GLANCE

SEEING THE CITY: The Funkturm, Berlin's radio tower, is a steel-latticed tower 453 feet above the town. An elevator ascends the structure to a viewing platform that, weather permitting, offers a good view of Germany's largest city. Open daily from 10 AM to 11 PM. Messedamm (phone: 3-0381).

Although not as high, the top floor of Europa-Center offers a more breathtaking view of this fascinating city, since it is in the middle of the downtown area. The building, a business center with numerous shops and restaurants, was erected in 1965 and is grouped around two courtyards. Its 22-story tower is 270 feet high. On the top floor are the *I-Punkt* restaurant and a café and a nightclub. The roof terrace commands an extensive panoramic view, especially impressive after dark. The sparkling lights of the broad Kurfürstendamm give you an inkling of what West Berlin is all about. Open daily. Breitscheidpl. (phone: 261-1014 and 261-6968).

SPECIAL PLACES: West Berlin is easy to get around. Most of the downtown area was laid out in the late nineteenth century, and the streets form a sensible grid. You can see much of that part of the city by foot, if you familiarize yourself with the main thoroughfares. Running from east to west, these are Kurfürstendamm (the closest thing to Main Street in West Berlin), Hardenbergstrasse, Kantstrasse and Strasse des 17 Juni. The chief north to south connections are Potsdamer Strasse, Joachimstaler Strasse, and Wilmersdorfer Strasse. To get beyond the city center, use the excellent network of buses and subways (the U-Bahn). See *Getting Around.*

Three tour operators offer a wide range of sight-seeing tours through West Berlin. For times and places of the daily departures, consult the tourist office (see *Sources and Resources*) or your hotel.

The Wall and East Berlin – The Wall snakes its way for 30 miles right through the center of Greater Berlin, and it is one of the city's main tourist attractions. There are wooden pedestals on the West Berlin side from which you can get a good view of East Berlin. The best sites for doing this are at Potsdamer Platz and across from the Brandenburg Gate. (The latter landmark, almost 200 years old, is actually on the East Berlin side of the Wall; for a detailed description, see THE EUROPEAN CITIES, *East Berlin.*)

You will probably not want to miss East Berlin, which is fascinating for two reasons: It offers Westerners easy access to a firsthand experience of life behind the Iron Curtain, and it is the site of the older, historic section of Berlin.

You can travel to East Berlin as many do, with a West Berlin sight-seeing bus. For information, consult the tourist office (see *Sources and Resources*). To go on your own, either take the subway or S-Bahn to the border control point at the East Berlin train station, Bahnhof Friedrichstrasse, or drive or walk to Checkpoint Charlie, manned by members of the Allied Forces, located at the corner of Friedrichstrasse and Kochstrasse. Checkpoint Charlie can only be used by non-German nationals, and the formalities are exactly like the ones you have to go through at Bahnhof Friedrichstrasse.

In order to get in to East Berlin for 1 day (you must return by midnight), you will need a passport, and five deutsche marks for a 1-day visa. You must also exchange at least 25 deutsche marks into East German marks at the rate of one for one, and you must spend at least this amount in East Berlin. If you wish, you can exchange and spend more than the 25 marks, but you are not allowed to cross the border with East German currency. (Any extra currency can be converted back to deutsche marks at the border.) No Western printed matter is allowed and there are strict rules about what and how much you can bring into East Berlin as gifts. For a detailed report on the city, see THE EUROPEAN CITIES, *East Berlin.*

Kaiser Wilhelm Gedächtniskirche – This huge neo-Romanesque church was built toward the end of the nineteenth century, but was almost completely destroyed by Allied bombing during World War II, and has been only partially rebuilt. New are its hexagonal bell tower and the octagonal church. The old west tower, 207 feet tall, was preserved in its ruined state. Partially new, partially old, partially preserved, and partially destroyed, it has become a symbol of the city and Berliners consider it the focal point. Breitscheidpl.

Zoo – One block north of the Gedächtniskirche is West Berlin's zoo. When Berlin's zoological gardens were laid out in 1841, the site was well outside the city; today, it is in the heart of West Berlin. This was Germany's first zoo, and it still has more species than any other zoo in the world. Open daily. Admission charge. Hardenbergpl. 8 (phone: 261-1101).

Aquarium – Next door to the zoo, with the most comprehensive collection in the world. The prewar building has been completely renovated, but it still has the tropical hall in which you can watch large numbers of alligators and crocodiles in their own environment; your vantage point is a bridge, a mere 10 feet or so above the bloodthirsty creatures. Open daily. Admission charge. Budapester Str. 32 (phone: 261-1101).

Tiergarten – This beautiful public park — far more extensive than the zoological gardens, which are at its western fringe — was originally the royal hunting preserve. It is now one of the world's largest and most beautifully landscaped urban parks and is dotted with charming lakes and ponds. The Tiergarten extends from the zoo to the Wall at the Brandenburg Gate, about 2 miles away.

Reichstag – At the eastern edge of the Tiergarten, just north of the Brandenburg Gate, is Germany's former parliament building. It was built in the late nineteenth century in Italian High Renaissance style. Gutted by fire in 1933, it has been rebuilt since the war and is now used for political conclaves. The Wall runs right next to the building; there is a good view of East Berlin and the Brandenburg Gate. A permanent display is devoted to recent German history. Open daily. Free. Pl. der Republik.

Philharmonie – The home of the world-renowned Berlin Philharmonic Orchestra and its permanent conductor, Herbert von Karajan, is a few blocks south of the Reichstag, at the southern fringe of the Tiergarten. The building's asymmetrical architecture has been controversial ever since it was completed in 1963. The concert hall can accommodate an audience of 2,200, seated in "terraces" surrounding the stage. Group visits are permitted daily from 1:30 to 3 PM (Sundays from 2:30 to 3:30 PM), provided no concert or rehearsal is in progress. Free. Matthäikirchpl. (phone: 26-92-51).

National Galerie – Only a short distance behind the Philharmonie, in what is still under development as the city's new cultural center, is this imposing modern museum.

Designed by Ludwig Mies van der Rohe, it houses West Berlin's collections of nine-
teenth- and twentieth-century art. Jazz concerts are held during the summer months
in the sculpture garden. Closed Mondays. Free. Potsdamer Str. 50 (phone: 2666).

Staatsbibliothek – Directly opposite the National Gallery is the new State Library,
West Berlin's successor to the Prussian State Library that is now in East Berlin. This
starkly modern structure was opened in 1978. Its collection of more than 3 million
volumes makes it one of the world's largest. Closed Sundays. Free. Potsdamer Str. 33
(phone: 2661).

War Memorial – Plaques and impressive statuary are grouped in the courtyard of
this building near the Tiergarten and National Gallery, which housed the German
Armed Forces' Supreme Command during World War II, to honor the German officers
who were shot here for the ill-fated anti-Hitler uprising on July 20, 1944. There is a
historical documentary center on the second floor. Open daily. Free. Stauffenbergstr.
14 (phone: 261-6015).

Rathaus Schöneberg – More than a mile due south is West Berlin's city hall, which
also functions as the seat of local government for the borough of Schöneberg. There
is a good panoramic view from the top of the spireless tower, which contains a replica
of the American Liberty Bell, presented to the Berliners by General Lucius Clay in
1950. On June 26, 1963, President John F. Kennedy made his famous "Ich bin ein
Berliner" speech to a gathering of over 450,000 Berliners from the balcony here. The
tower can be ascended Wednesdays, Saturdays, and Sundays, from April to September.
Free. John-F.-Kennedy-Pl. (phone: 7831).

Schloss Charlottenburg – A few miles to the northwest is this truly majestic palace,
the best example of royal Prussian architecture in Berlin. Begun in 1695, it took 100
years to build. The historic royal chambers, completely restored since the massive
destruction of the last war, are open to the public daily, except Mondays, for a small
admission fee. The palace also houses the Museum of Arts and Crafts and the Pre-
Historic Museum (both free). Closed Fridays. The beautifully laid out park behind the
palace is one of the nicest areas in the city. Luisenpl. (phone: 3-2011).

International Congress Center and Fairgrounds – About a mile and a half
southwest of the palace is West Berlin's most modern structure, the recently opened
ICC, as it is called. Across the street from this looming building, and connected to it
by a covered pedestrian walkway, are the rambling fairgrounds, the site of the year-
round fairs and exhibitions, which include international *Green Week* (an agricultural
exhibition) and the German Radio and TV exhibition. Situated within the fairgrounds
area is the Funkturm or radio tower (see *Seeing the City*). Masurenallee and Messedamm (phone: 3-0381).

Olympic Stadium – Another 2 miles to the west, this huge sports arena casts its
shadow over the low-lying houses of a pleasant residential area. It was built for the 1936
Olympic Games, and if you look hard, you can still make out the "royal" box, from
which Hitler and his cohorts took in the spectacle. It is open daily to the public when
no sports events are on. There is no admission fee, except for the ascent by elevator
to the top of the adjacent bell tower. Olympischer Pl. (phone: 304-0676).

Spandau Citadel – Even farther to the west, on the Havel River, is the historic
Spandau Citadel. The oldest edifice on the grounds, the Julius Tower, dates from the
fourteenth century. The citadel, which had been used variously as a fortification, a
prison, and the royal treasury, is now a local history museum. The Nazi war criminals were not housed here but at the prison in Wilhelmstrasse, in the middle of
Spandau. The citadel is open to the public, for an admission fee, except Mondays.
Am Juliusturm.

Museum Center in Dahlem – To the south, in the fashionable and lovely section
of Dahlem, is West Berlin's largest museum complex. Its extensive buildings accommodate several institutions, and you can spend at least a full day going through them:

the Painting Gallery, an important collection of European painting from the Middle Ages to the eighteenth century, with good pieces of fanciful rococo art; the Sculpture Department, with Byzantine and European sculpture from the third to the eighteenth century; the Ethnographic Museum, with one of the world's most complete collections; Museums of Islamic, Indian, and Far Eastern Art; and a Department of Prints and Engravings. All are closed Mondays and admission is free. Lansstr. 8 (phone: 8-3011).

Botanical Gardens – No more than half a mile to the east are the largest botanical gardens in Germany and one of the world's most significant collections of flora. Of special interest in the 104-acre gardens are the geographical gardens, where plants from various parts of the world flourish in carefully maintained native environments. There is a fascinating botanic display at the museum, next to the entrance of the gardens. The gardens are open daily; however, the museum closes Mondays. Admission fee to both museum and gardens. Königin-Luise-Str. 6 (phone: 831-4041).

■**EXTRA SPECIAL:** Largely unknown to most tourists, who rarely leave the downtown area, the western sections of West Berlin are mostly forests and waterways. The Havel River, Tegeler See, and Wannsee as well as the Grunewald, Tegel, and Spandau forests make up at least one-fourth of West Berlin's total area. To see it all, you can board one of the 70 ships that make daily trips on the Havel. Boats leave eight times a day from Easter until the end of September. There are many Havel shiplines; the largest of them is Stern and Kreisschiffahrt, Sachtleben Str. 60 (phone: 803-8750).

Along the way, you can get off at any number of points and explore to your heart's content, then reboard a boat. Stopping-off points include Grunewald Tower, formerly Kaiser Wilhelm Tower, dating from the nineteenth century and affording a good view from the top; Lindwerder Island, with restaurants offering snacks of beer, coffee, and cake; and Pfaueninsel (Peacock Island), a beautiful example of an eighteenth-century formal garden with small pavilions, ponds, and a château dating from 1796 that is open to the public. All stops on this trip are well provisioned with restaurants and beer gardens. (The only catch is that since these boats are mostly for Berliners and rarely cater to foreign visitors, English is usually not spoken by the guides).

SOURCES AND RESOURCES

The Tourist Office (Verkehrsamt) will supply you with all sorts of free information in English about West Berlin. This includes a general tourist map and numerous brochures. For the best detailed local map, go to a bookstore and ask for *Berlin Stadtatlas,* which costs the equivalent of $6. The Tourist Office is in the large complex of shops and restaurants at Europa-Center, at the foot of Kurfürstendamm (phone: 2123-4). It also maintains branches at Tegel Airport and on the ground floor of Europa-Center (entrance on Budapesterstr.), both of them open daily until 10:30 PM.

For Local Coverage – There is no English-language newspaper, but a monthly calendar of events called *Berlin Programm* can be bought at the Tourist Office and at newsstands; some of the information is in English.

CLIMATE AND CLOTHES: Although Berlin is farther north than any city in the US (except those of Alaska), its climate is very temperate. Though more temperate in both summer and winter, you will find weather conditions here very similar to those prevailing in the northeastern US. Temperatures rarely go above 70°F (21°C) and seldom slip below freezing. Rain can fall at any time of the year, but experts say that Berlin's air tends to be fresher and less damp than West Germany's because of the lake-studded woodlands surrounding the city.

 GETTING AROUND: Subway and Bus – Berlin has one of the world's most efficient public transportation systems. The subway, or U-Bahn, with its snappy little yellow cars, has been a fact of life here since 1902, and its nine lines serve almost every part of the city. The U-Bahn is fast, clean, convenient, and one of the cheapest in Germany. The 100-year-old S-Bahn "el," with three lines, was taken over by West Berlin's public transit authority in 1984. A ticket, costing 70 cents, is valid for a trip from one end of the city to the other, and you can transfer as often as you wish within the U-Bahn system, the elevated S-Bahn, and to any of the 84 bus lines that ply West Berlin's streets. A carnet, valid for five rides, is available. The West Berlin Transport Authority also sells a tourist ticket, valid for 4 consecutive days on all U-Bahn, S-Bahn, and bus lines, which costs $11. (A 2-day tourist ticket sells for $5.50; a 1-day ticket for $3.)

Taxi – Taxis can be hailed in the streets, and there are cabstands all over town and at the major hotels. (To call a cab, dial 6902 or 26-10-26.)

Car Rental – The major American firms are represented as well as several European companies. Information can be had at any hotel.

 MUSEUMS: The Prussian State Museums in Dahlem, at Charlottenburg Palace, and at the National Gallery are described in *Special Places.* West Berlin is also the home of two unusual art collections, each of them dating from the late eighteenth century. Directly opposite Charlottenburg Palace is the *Egyptian Museum,* whose priceless treasures include the world-renowned bust of Queen Nefertiti and the magnificent Kalabsha Gate. Closed Fridays. Free. Schlossstr. 70 (phone: 3-2011). West Berlin's *Museum of Local Art and History* is in a beautiful eighteenth-century rococo building, the former Prussian Supreme Court, which has been lovingly restored. Visit the beer cellar, which features traditional Berlin snacks and beverages. Closed Mondays. Admission fee. Lindenstr. 14 (phone: 251-4015).

 SHOPPING: West Berlin, this capitalist jewel in a Communist setting, is a shopper's paradise. There is hardly anything you cannot buy here, and some of the items offered for sale are truly unique. If you just want to browse before making up your mind, go through Europa-Center, at the foot of Kurfürstendamm in the middle of the downtown area. This city within a city has scores of small shops and boutiques offering a variety of typical German specialties. German cameras, including those by Leica, Rollei, and Zeiss, are available here, but it is necessary to do very careful comparison shopping. The same brands are often cheaper in the US. Optical goods such as binoculars, telescopes, and microscopes are also German specialties, and there are good buys in china and porcelain; great names in the latter are Meissen, Rosenthal, and KPM (Imperial Porcelain Manufactory). Women's and men's fashions, toys, cutlery, and clocks are good buys too. Although you might want to do some exploring on your own, here is a small sample of recommended stores:

Altkunst – Porcelain, crystal, and pewter. Keithstr. 8.

Dürlich – Antique furniture. Keithstr. 5.

J. A. Henckels – Cutlery. Kurfürstendamm 33.

Horn's – The latest in women's fashions. Kurfürstendamm 213 (phone: 881-4055).

Ka De We – Germany's largest and best-stocked department store with simply everything, including an enormous food shop (6th floor). Tauentzienstr. 21–24 (phone: 24-01-71).

Marga Schoeller – For English and American books. Knesebeckstr. 33.

Staatliche Porzellan Manufaktur Berlin – Beautiful china. The factory is at Wegelystrasse 1 and the salesroom at Kurfürstendamm 205.

Greta Verhoek – Antiques. Keithstr. 12.

 SPECIAL EVENTS: *Green Week,* an annual agricultural fair, takes place at the fairgrounds toward the end of January. The *Berlin Film Festival,* another annual fixture, is in February. A *Festival of German Drama* is performed every May, and once a year in September the city puts on its ambitious *Festival of the Arts.* A *Jazz Festival* attracts international soloists to West Berlin every year during the first week of November.

 SPORTS: Bicycling – You can rent a bicycle by the hour for a jaunt through the expansive Grunewald forest from *F. Damrau,* Schmetterlingspl. (phone: 811-5829; call before 9 AM).

Golf – The *Golf und Landclub,* Berlin-Wannsee, has a nine-hole golf course. Stölpchenweg (phone: 805-3055).

Ice Hockey – From November through April, you can see professional games at the *Eissporthalle.* Jafféstr. (phone: 3-0381).

Ice Skating – In the winter, there are various public rinks in the city. Consult the tourist office for locations and skating hours.

Jogging – There are special trails in Grunewald forest, but you can jog just about anywhere.

Soccer – *Hertha,* West Berlin's entry in the West German professional soccer leagues, plays Saturdays at the Olympic Stadium. Olympischer Pl. (phone: 304-0676).

Swimming – Aquatic sports can be enjoyed at a number of indoor and outdoor pools; each of West Berlin's 12 boroughs has at least one public facility. There is a sandy beach — *Wannseebad* — on the shores of the Havel River at Strandbadweg.

Tennis – In addition to several private clubs, the city has a number of public courts. For locations and hours of admission, consult the tourist office.

Trotting Races – Every Wednesday and Sunday there is racing at the trotting race course in *Mariendorf.* Mariendorfer Damm 222 (phone: 7-4011).

 THEATER: Theater in West Berlin, still Germany's theatrical metropolis, is an all-German affair. For a look at the classical repertoire, attend a performance at the *Schiller Theater,* Bismarckstr. 110 (phone: 319-5236). What is probably the most important German-language theater in the world is a new, three-stage complex, *Schaubühne am Lehniner Platz,* Kurfürstendamm 153 (phone: 89-00-23). Other prominent theaters are: *Renaissance Theater,* Hardenbergstr. 6 (phone: 312-4202); *Freie Volksbühne,* Schaperstr. 24 (phone: 884-20-80); *Theater am Kurfürstendamm,* Kurfürstendamm 206 (phone: 881-2489); *Komödie,* Kurfürstendamm 206 (phone: 882-7893); *Tribüne,* Otto-Suhr-Allee 18–20 (phone: 341-2600). One of Europe's most successful children's theaters is *Grips,* Altonaer Str. 22 (phone: 391-4004). Consult the monthly calendar of events, *Berlin Programm,* for complete listings of all performances.

MUSIC: West Berlin is one of the world's musical centers, with performances of everything from classical to pop and rock. The Berlin Philharmonic Orchestra, conducted by Herbert von Karajan, performs at the *Philharmonie,* Matthäikirchpl. 1 (phone: 261-4383). The Radio Symphony

Orchestra gives most of its concerts at one of West Berlin's two broadcasting stations, *Sender Freies Berlin,* at Masurenallee 8–14 (for tickets, dial 302-7242). Concerts and recitals of classical music can be heard at the *Hochschule der Künste* (College of Arts), Hardenbergstr. 33 (phone: 3185-2374). One of the world's leading opera houses, the *Deutsche Oper,* has daily performances (once a week ballet is scheduled) at Bismarckstr. 34–37 (phone: 341-4449). Operettas and musicals are launched at *Theater des Westens,* Kantstr. 12 (phone: 312-1022). Pop concerts, many by visiting international stars, are performed at the *Philharmonie* (above) and at the *Deutschlandhalle,* Messedamm (phone: 3-0381). For the latest in jazz and rock music, attend one of the concerts that are frequently given at *Quartier Latin,* Potsdamer Str. 96 (phone: 261-37-07). For all the latest listings, consult the *Berlin Programm.*

NIGHTCLUBS AND NIGHTLIFE: For live music and dancing, try some of these popular places: *Loretta,* Lietzenburger Str. 89 (phone: 882-7863); *Big Eden,* Kurfürstendamm 202 (phone: 323-5849); *Jazz Keller,* Breitenbach Pl. 8 (phone: 824-4144). It is not only the young crowd that likes to dance at these clubs: *Café Keese,* Bismarckstr. 108 (phone: 312-9111); *Big Apple,* Bundesalle 13 (phone: 881-2887); *Buccaneer,* Rankestr. 32 (phone: 24-50-57); *Bristol-Bar,* in *Hotel Kempinski,* Kurfürstendamm 27 (phone: 88-10-91). Discotheques hit this city with a big splash in the late 1970s and are still the latest thing. For the youngsters, *Space* is really "in" at Bismarckstr. 90 (phone: 313-4044). The following discos, however, are popular with people from all age groups: *Zorba, the Buddha,* Kurfürstendamm 156 (phone: 892-68-34); *Subway,* Kurfürstendamm 105 (phone: 891-13-05); *Salsa,* Wielandstr. 13 (phone: 324-16-42); *Château,* Uhlandstr. 25 (phone: 882-2646); *Annabell's,* Fasanenstr. 64 (phone: 883-52-20); *Metropol,* Nollendorfpl. 5 (phone: 216-4122); *VIP-Club,* top of the Europa-Center, Breitscheidpl. (phone: 261-2452). A gay club featuring music, dancing, and an occasional show is *KC,* at Kleiststr. 34 (phone: 24-70-48). Talking about shows, one cannot forget West Berlin's cabarets. Both *Stachelschweine,* Europa-Center (phone: 261-4795), and *Wühlmäuse,* Lietzenburgerstr. corner of Nürnberger Str. (phone: 213-7047), put on interesting performances, devoted chiefly to literary and political satire. Nightclubs featuring transvestite shows have long been a German specialty. If you like this sort of thing — and even if you do not — you will be pleasantly surprised; visit *Dollywood's,* Welser Str. 24 (phone: 24-89-50), or *Chez Nous,* Marburger Str. 14 (phone: 213-1810). Jazz buffs have two very popular clubs at their disposal, each of them featuring live music: *Quasimodo,* Kantstr. 12A (phone: 312-80-86), and *Eierschale,* Podbielskiallee 50 (phone: 832-7097). For live rock, try *Flöz,* Nassauische Str. 37 (phone: 861-1000). Folk music from all over the world reigns supreme at *Folkpub,* Leibnizstr. 56 (phone: 883-6111), and at *Go In,* Bleibtreustr. 17 (phone: 881-7218). West Berlin is known for its multitude of small, intimate, publike bars, which offer no more than excellent drinks, a few snacks, and lots of Gemütlichkeit (congeniality). Three of them are worthy of mention: *Die Kleine Weltlaterne,* which caters to an arty crowd, at Nestorstr. 22 (phone: 892-6585); *Lutter & Wegener,* a wine cellar of note, Schlüterstr. 55 (phone: 881-3440); and *Zwiebelfisch,* a favorite haunt for journalists and students, Savignypl. 7–8 (phone: 31-73-63).

SINS: If gambling is one of your sins, pay a visit to the city's one and only licensed gambling casino. It is on the ground floor at the Budapester Str. side of Europa-Center, and it is open daily from 3 PM to 3 AM (phone: 261-1501). The games on the premises are roulette, baccarat, and blackjack. As in most Continental cities, some of the more popular night spots in West Berlin are devoted to striptease shows. Two of the best are: *New Eden Saloon,* Kurfürstendamm 71 (phone: 323-5849), and *Crazy Horse,* Marburger Str. 2 (phone: 211-5350).

BEST IN TOWN

CHECKING IN: Visitors to the city can choose from one of the best assortments of hotels in all of Germany. Since there always seems to be something happening in this scintillating city, overnight accommodations are often hard to find and it is advisable to make reservations — either directly with the hotel of your choice or through the city's efficient Tourist Office (see *Sources and Resources*). Our selection includes some of the luxury hotels as well as establishments that can be classified as moderate and inexpensive. Many of the latter are exciting little houses, noted for their charm. A word of caution: Hotel accommodations are extremely expensive in West Germany, and West Berlin follows suit. Should you prefer more modest although somewhat less comfortable rooms, the Tourist Office is the place to turn to. The hotels in our selection have a bath or a shower in every room, and in almost every case the rooms have telephones. For a double room in those hotels we have classed as expensive, expect to pay $50 or more; from $30 to $50 in the moderate category; under $30 in the inexpensive class.

Kempinski – As West Berlin's most traditional hostelry, the newly renovated *Kempinski*'s motto is noblesse oblige. Formerly located on Unter den Linden, a street which is now in East Berlin, it is the classiest hotel in West Berlin. Its present location in the middle of West Berlin's golden mile — the Kurfürstendamm — makes it ideal for sight-seeing. The 358-room *Kempinski* also boasts a renowned restaurant, a grill room, and the *Bristol Bar*. Breakfast is extra. Kurfürstendamm 27 (phone: 88-10-91). Expensive.

Inter-Continental – The *Hilton*, as it was known for twenty years until the end of 1978, was a trademark in West Berlin. *Inter-Continental* has now assumed the management of this 600-room establishment, but it continues to offer luxurious accommodations in an area a bit removed from West Berlin's hustle and bustle. Although only a stone's throw from the center of activities, it overlooks the Tiergarten. There are several restaurants on the premises (especially good is *Zum Hugenotten*) as well as a popular ballroom. Breakfast is extra. Budapester Str. 2 (phone: 2-60-20). Expensive.

Schweizerhof – With 441 rooms, this establishment is located opposite the *Inter-Continental*. The ongoing motif is Swiss, as the name implies, and the service is excellent. There is a restaurant, where breakfast is extra. Budapester Str. 25 (phone: 2-6961). Expensive.

Steigenberger – One of West Germany's largest hotel chains recently opened this new luxury establishment with 400 rooms, several restaurants and bars, a swimming pool, sauna, and shopping arcade. Downtown, facing lovely Los Angeles Platz. Ranke Str. 30 (phone: 2-1080). Expensive.

Am Zoo – When Thomas Wolfe came to Berlin in the early 1930s, he stayed at this 145-room hotel, one of the traditional downtown establishments. Breakfast is included in the price of a room. Kurfürstendamm 25 (phone: 88-30-91). Expensive.

Penta – With 425 rooms, this new hotel is one of West Berlin's largest and most modern. On the premises are such amenities as a restaurant, bar, beer cellar, swimming pool, sauna, solarium, and an underground parking garage. Centrally located at Nürnberger Str. 65 (phone: 24-00-11). Expensive.

Berlin Excelsior – Another brand-new luxury hotel. Just off Kurfürstendamm in the center of town, the *Excelsior* is planned for conventions as well as pleasure; thus it offers typing and secretarial service in addition to the usual amenities. All

325 rooms have refrigerators, and public rooms include a breakfast room, restaurant, bar, and banquet room. Hardenbergstr. 13–14 (phone: 3-1991). Expensive.

Seehof – Only 2½ miles down the road from the downtown area, on the Lietzensee lake. The 77-room hotel overlooks a small park. Lietzensee Ufer 11 (phone: 32-00-20). Expensive.

Gehrhus – This charming 34-room hotel looks like the palace it was in 1912; its very first guest was Kaiser Wilhelm. This romantic atmosphere is heightened by the quiet location, 20 minutes from downtown West Berlin. Breakfast is included in the price. Brahmsstr. 4–10 (phone: 826-2081). Expensive to moderate.

Börse – This small, 38-room hotel is right in the middle of town, so don't expect too much peace and quiet. But here you are surrounded by shops, cafés, restaurants, theaters, and movie houses. Kurfürstendamm 34 (phone: 881-3021). Moderate.

Novotel – This new 187-room hotel next to Tegel Airport provides efficiency without any sacrifice of comfort. Sauna, solarium, and swimming pool on premises. Kurt-Schumacher Damm 202 (phone: 41-060). Moderate.

Am Studio – A modern hotel offering a magnificent view of the city from each of its 78 rooms. Kaiserdamm 80 (phone: 30-20-81). Moderate.

Plaza – Just around the corner from Kurfürstendamm is this 131-room alternative to higher-priced accommodations. Knesebeckstr. 63 (phone: 884-13-0). Moderate.

Econtel – Midway between the airport and downtown and near the opera house and Charlottenburg Palace, this new hotel puts its accent on comfort rather than luxury, but it doesn't sacrifice modern facilities. Sömmeringstr. 24-26 (phone: 34-40-01). Inexpensive.

Sachsenhof – This 65-room hotel is a well-run establishment right in the middle of Christopher Isherwood's Berlin. He and Sally Bowles lived around the corner in Nollendorfstrasse 17. Motzstr. 7 (phone: 216-2074). Inexpensive.

Stuttgarter Hof – Do not be fooled by the war ruins that greet your eye. In the courtyard is one of the city's more pleasant lower-priced hotels. This is far from the city center but nearby are the Wall and Checkpoint Charlie. Breakfast is included in the price. Anhalter Str. 9 (phone: 261-1466). Inexpensive.

 EATING OUT: German food is hearty and can be very good or, at its worst, as heavy as lead. Main courses usually consist of roasted or stewed meat with boiled potatoes or dumplings (called *Knödel* — which are very heavy) and sauerkraut, cabbage or other vegetables, like string beans. Wiener Schnitzel and Sauerbraten, of course, are well-known specialties.

Like other Continentals, Germans like rolls for breakfast, occasionally the sweet, cruller-like pastries called *Krapfen* and *Berliner Pfannkuchen*. Then at mid-morning they often have a snack of sausages and bread called *Brotzeit* or "breadtime."

Sausages are the specialty in Germany at any time of day or night; they are made from pork, veal, and game. The frankfurter, which originated in Vienna, is longer, slimmer, and better than the American variety. *Weisswurst* is white sausage made mostly of veal; *Bratwurst* is pork sausage; a *Regensburger* is a spicy pork sausage.

Interesting appetizers are herring, which is very popular and comes in many varieties, and *Hase im Topf*, a delicious rabbit pâté. Soups are popular and very substantial: *Leberknödelsuppe* (liver dumpling soup), *Erbsensuppe* (pea soup), and *Kohlsuppe* (cabbage soup) are just a few. *Schwarzbrot*, or dark bread, is very tasty, especially Westphalian pumpernickel.

For a typical Berlin treat, try a *Konditorei*, a little shop that offers excellent cakes and pastries with coffee or tea. Special desserts are *Schwarzwälder Kirschtorte*, a Black Forest cherry cake with whipped cream; *Baumkuchen*, a towering cake with icing; *Gugelhupf*, a marvelous coffee cake; *Käsekuchen*, or cheesecake; special *Berliner Pfannkuchen* or cruller; and many others.

And of course Germans are famous for their beer and wine. In South Germany, light beer *(helles)* and dark *(dunkles)* come in many sizes and varieties. Most beers come from Munich, but you might want to try *Berliner Weisse* in the summer, a whitish beer made from wheat and often served *mit Schuss,* or raspberry juice. North Germans drink *pilsener* beer. *Bierkeller* (beer restaurants) serve food as well as beer.

Germany produces a lot of wine, some of it very good. You may be disappointed in *Liebfraumilch,* which is not a place name (it means "Milk of Our Lady") and thus not reliable. Best bets are the Moselles — light, pleasant, and often cheap — like *Wehlener Sonnenuhr, Piesporter,* or *Zeltinger.* Rhine wines, of course, are famous — some of the best are *Niersteiner, Oppenheimer,* and *Schloss Johannisberger.*

Expect to pay $30 or more at restaurants in the expensive category; between $20 and $30 in the moderate range; and less than $20 at places classed as inexpensive. Prices are for a dinner for two, not including drinks and wine. Tips are included in the bill.

Rockendorf's – Although a bit off the beaten track, this restaurant is well worth the trip. It's in a turn-of-the-century villa in the suburb of Waidmannslust. Nostalgia is trump here, as well as imaginatively prepared Continental dishes and a very good choice of wines. Closed Sundays, Mondays, and three weeks in August. Reservations suggested. Düsterhauptstr. 1 (phone: 402-3099). Expensive.

Maître – After a year's absence, one of West Berlin's best restaurants has reopened in a lovely villa in suburban Dahlem. It still maintains the high standards that led to its reputation as a bastion of haute cuisine in its former downtown location. Good wine list and fine service. Dinner only from Tuesdays through Fridays; lunch and dinner, Saturdays; lunch only, Sundays. Closed Mondays. Reservations suggested. Podbielskiallee 31 (phone: 832-60-04). Expensive.

Ritz – Small and unpretentious with a menu of Continental dishes that are pure culinary poetry. This is definitely not a restaurant for those who want to see and be seen; its intimate atmosphere is for good food and privacy. Closed Saturdays, Sundays, and August. Reservations suggested. Rankestr. 26 (phone: 24-72-50). Expensive.

Hotel Berlin – One of the best hotel restaurants in town, though its accommodations are so-so; its excellent Continental dishes are served amid elegant surroundings. You can dine either in the restaurant or in the smaller grill room. Lunch is cheaper than dinner. Closed Sundays. Reservations accepted. Kurfürstenstr. 62 (phone: 26-92-91). Expensive to moderate.

Hotel Kempinski – Restaurant and grill room with top-quality dishes, both Continental and non-European. This is a favorite among city VIPs. Open daily. Reservations accepted. Kurfürstendamm 27 (phone: 88-10-91). Expensive to moderate.

Kardell – Specialties are leg of lamb, game, steak, and fish. Herr Kardell, the owner, still runs the place with obsessive detail. Open daily; supper only Saturdays. Reservations accepted. Gervinusstr. 24 (phone: 324-1066). Expensive to moderate.

Conti Fischstuben – As the name implies, this is for lovers of seafood. A small restaurant in the *Hotel Ambassador* with an exclusive flair. Closed Sundays, Mondays, and four weeks in July or August. Reservations accepted. Bayreuther Str. 42 (phone: 219-02-0). Expensive to moderate.

Daitokai – This genuine Japanese haunt is close to Kurfürstendamm. The food is good, the service friendly, and you can sit on the floor in Japanese style. Closed Mondays. No reservations. Europa-Center (phone: 261-80-99). Moderate.

I-Punkt – The international menu is adequate, but most people come here for the spectacular view. Located on the 20th floor of the Europa-Center complex, the restaurant offers one of the best panoramic views of West Berlin. Especially impressive after dark (described in *Seeing the City*). Open daily. Reservations not necessary. Europa-Center at Breitscheidpl. (phone: 261-1014). Moderate.

Ax-Bax – The beautiful people often hang out in this nicely designed bar that has no identifying sign on the door. In addition to the drinks and glitter, it also has good food. Open daily from 7:30 PM. Closed Saturdays. Leibnizstr. 34 (phone: 313-8594). Moderate.

Restaurant im Reichstag – One wing of this late-nineteenth-century building, formerly the seat of the German parliament (see *Special Places*), has been set aside as a restaurant. Solid German food in a historic German setting. Closed Mondays. Reservations accepted. Platz der Republik (phone: 3977-2172). Moderate.

Florian – A finely tuned crew maintains this admirable restaurant. The menu emphasizes south German, Austrian, and Bohemian cuisines, and the wines and the service are as good as the food. The neighborhood is "in" and so *Florian* is frequented by artists, film people, and the so-called New Wave set. Supper only. Reservations suggested. Grolmanstr. 52 (phone: 313-91-84). Moderate.

Paris-Bar – This traditional bistro is a magnet for students and artists drawn by the French cuisine as well as the paintings on the walls. Reservations possible. Closed Sundays. Kantstr. 152 (phone: 313-80-52). Moderate.

Anselmo – A must for devotees of Italian cuisine. This intimate restaurant features an imaginative and well-run kitchen, rustic decor, and a pleasant atmosphere. Closed Mondays. Reservations suggested. Damaschkestr. 17 (phone: 323-3094). Moderate.

Hongkong – The kitchen staff here knows how to make the tantalizing most of basic Cantonese cooking, with an extensive menu and excellent service. This conveniently located restaurant is open daily. Reservations accepted. Kurfürstendamm 210 (phone: 881-5756). Moderate.

Giraffe – It has a clublike atmosphere, a sylvan setting, and Continental food. Dine on the terrace, weather permitting. Open daily. Reservations suggested. Klopstock Str. 2 (phone: 391-4717). Moderate.

Churrasco – If you are nostalgic for a good steak, this is the place. The beef, atmosphere, and decor are Argentine. The only main dish available is steak, charcoal broiled, the price depending on which of three sizes you order. The excellently prepared salads are extra. Open daily. No reservations. Kurfürstendamm 177 and 214 (phone: 881-3321 and 883-4900). Moderate.

Schipkapass – A rustically decorated Czech restaurant, featuring those two mainstays of every good Bohemian kitchen: Prague ham and Pilsner beer. You can feast on the large portions. Open daily, supper only; Sundays and holidays, lunch too. Reservations accepted. Hohenzollerndamm 185 (phone: 87-19-41). Moderate.

Exil – This out-of-the-way place is well worth the trip. Located on a canal in a section called Kreuzberg, it features well-prepared Viennese dishes. You can dine at the bowerlike terrace, weather permitting. The service is also charmingly Viennese. Supper only; closed Mondays. Reservations suggested. Paul-Lincke-Ufer 44a (phone: 612-7037). Moderate.

Blockhaus Nikolskoe – For fans of German history and good Continental food, this restaurant, high above the wide Havel River, looks like a Russian dacha. It was built in log cabin fashion in 1819 by Prussian King Friedrich Wilhelm III for his daughter, Charlotte, and her husband, Grand Duke Nicholas (later Russian Czar Nicholas I). Closed Thursdays. Reservations accepted. It is in a forested area, with no street address; ask directions when you make reservations (phone: 805-2914). Moderate.

Hardtke – Two traditional restaurants with traditionally hearty German food such as fresh *Leberwurst* and *Blutwurst*. All meat dishes come from its own butcher shops. Rustic, friendly atmosphere. Open daily. No reservations. Meinekestr. 26–27 (phone: 881-9827). Inexpensive.

Brasserie – You will find a true French bistro here. The decor, food, and wine are typical of the Gallic provinces. Try the cold buffet lunch on Sundays. There is also a small enclosed terrace. Open daily. Reservations accepted. Wittenbergpl. 3 (phone: 24-57-86). Inexpensive.

El Bodegón – This lively Spanish *finca,* featuring a wide range of Iberian dishes, is much frequented by students, musicians, and artists. The atmosphere is genuinely Spanish, including guitar music, chiefly flamenco. Open daily, supper only. Reservations accepted. Schlüterstr. 61 (phone: 312-4497). Inexpensive.

Hollandstüb'l – Dutch cuisine, with the accent on dishes from the East Indies (*nasi goreng, rijsttafel,* and so on). The decor is something for nostalgia fans: a leftover from the 1920s, when one of Berlin's more popular restaurants was located here. Closed Mondays. No reservations. Martin-Luther-Str. 11 (phone: 24-85-93). Inexpensive.

Gottlieb – This plainly appointed restaurant is somewhat off the beaten track, but is worth a visit. The menu features southern German, Austrian, and Czech dishes. Youngish crowd and friendly atmosphere. Open daily for supper; open Sundays at 10:30 AM (closed for 2 weeks in August). No reservations. Neue Steinmetzstr. 6 (phone: 782-3943). Inexpensive.

Einstein – The high-ceilinged and mirrored dining room in this turn-of-the-century villa is a perfect setting for an afternoon's Viennese coffee and pastry. Open daily until 2 AM. No reservations. Kurfürstenstr. 58 (phone: 261-5096). Inexpensive.

Café Möhring – This traditional German *Konditorei* has three locations on the city's magnificent Kurfürstendamm. Here you can enjoy rich cakes, light Danish pastry, and other wonders from their own bakery to go along with your coffee or tea. Light hot meals are also available. Kurfürstendamm 161, 213, and 234 (phone: 892-50-75, 881-20-75, and 881-32-44). Inexpensive.

BRUSSELS

The headquarters of NATO, the Common Market, the Benelux Union, and the European Atomic Energy Community, Brussels is not only the capital of Belgium and of the Belgian province of Brabant, it is in many ways the capital of all Europe. Three distinct sets of ambassadors reside in the city: one for Belgium; one for NATO; and one for the Common Market. It is a common joke that if someone were to yell "Fire!" in a Brussels theater, half the audience would run out to safety, and the other half would call their home governments for further instructions.

Brussels is a fast-paced modern city of 1.2 million people (including suburbs), rivaling New York in its often ruthless destruction of the old in favor of the new. There are skyscrapers, traffic problems, and broad avenues with underpasses and overpasses. Much of the city is starkly modern; what is not modern is frankly medieval, and of that, happily, much remains.

The Grand' Place, the magnificent square that justly is the city's pride and joy, was a prosperous marketplace in the Middle Ages, when it was known as the Grote Markt. Splendid old baroque guild houses, with facades ornately decorated in gold, line the square, its noble fifteenth-century Gothic Hôtel de Ville in the southwest facing the palatial eighteenth-century Maison du Roi, now the municipal museum. Nearby, the still narrow and cobbled streets bear quaint medieval names reminiscent of the market that was held there: Bread Street, Pepper Street, Street of the Herb Market, and Little Street of the Butchers. Besides produce, goods such as lace, tapestries, jewelry, crystal, and leather are, as they have always been, the staples of the city's trade. The heart of the city is enclosed by a rough hexagon of boulevards that run along its fourteenth-century ramparts. Within this belt of ancient streets lies almost all of historic Brussels. Much of the history of the city — and to some degree, the very history of all Europe — can be traced in its growth from Grote Markt to Common Market.

Brussels lies just northeast of the geographic center of Belgium, surrounded by vast forests. Sitting on the crucial intersection of a north-south river (the Senne River now runs underground through the city) and an east-west land route (between Bruges and Cologne), Brussels's destiny as a marketplace was inevitable. Today's city, which celebrated its millennium in 1979, traces its origins to the earliest known written records of the area, which date from 979; but on the eastern edge of town, near the Common Market headquarters, excavations have uncovered Stone Age burial mounds that reveal that a thriving community was on the spot in 5000 BC. The historic town was known as Bruocsella, a bustling Christian community in the seventh century that within 200 years had become an established market for produce from the Senne River valley. The city's character as a center of trade and business was already established. By 1288 Brussels was important enough to be the object of a pitched battle by the duke of Brabant, Jean le Victorieux, who won the battle of Woeringen against Renalt the Bellicose in order to protect the city. As nobles of the city married into the ruling houses of Europe, Brussels seesawed between the great powers of Europe — sometimes in one sphere of influence, sometimes in another. In the course of its long and troubled history, it was allied with or controlled by Spain, Austria, Burgundy, France, and Holland.

Although dominated by foreign powers for most of its history and subject to wars, rebellions, and invasions for centuries, the canny Belgian burghers learned early on to prosper even in adversity. This knack of riding the tides of history came to fruition in the fifteenth and sixteenth centuries under the political domination of Philip of Burgundy and Charles V of Spain. This was the golden age of Flemish painting, tapestry, and lace.

Finally in 1830, after centuries of foreign rule, the people of Brussels began the revolution against the Hollanders that made them an independent nation. It happened in a strange way: During a performance of an opera, *La Muette de Portici* by Daniel François Auber, at the Theatre Royal de la Monnaie (Mint Theatre), a patriotic song aroused the audience to leave the opera house, take to the streets, and begin the fight. After independence, the first king of Belgium was Leopold of Saksen-Koburg, a naturalized Englishman and Queen Victoria's "dearest uncle" and confidant. He was followed by Leopold II, who is often remembered for his many mistresses and for the fact that the Congo was his personal property, but who was determined to make Brussels a truly royal capital. Town planning, not painting or music, fascinated him and he dedicated himself to what he called "outside art." His nephew, Albert I, was Belgium's great hero during World War I. Next came the controversial Leopold III, who was king during World War II and abdicated in favor of his son, Baudouin, the present king.

Brussels has known little tranquillity in its long history. For centuries Spain, Austria, France, and Holland made Belgium an arena for their power politics; in this century, Germany invaded Belgium during both world wars and used it as a highway for its armies. Twice in this century the Germans have set up field kitchens for their troops in the Grand' Place.

Like many European cities, Brussels has thrived despite such vicissitudes. Its people have not only endured, but have amassed great fortunes while doing it, and garnered the sophistication and taste to use their money to best advantage. The result is an unusually rich tapestry of a city, well endowed with good food and good art — two passions that most Belgians share. The food of Brussels rivals that of France, from which it is derived. And it is said that if a resident of Brussels loses wife or job, he neither gets drunk nor calls out his rival. He goes out for a good dinner.

A clue to the Belgian character can be found in Flemish art. The greatest Belgian artists are the Breughels, elder and younger; Hans Memling; and Peter Paul Rubens. And the worlds that these men portrayed — the peasant simplicity of the Breughels' lusty canvases; the mysticism of Memling; and

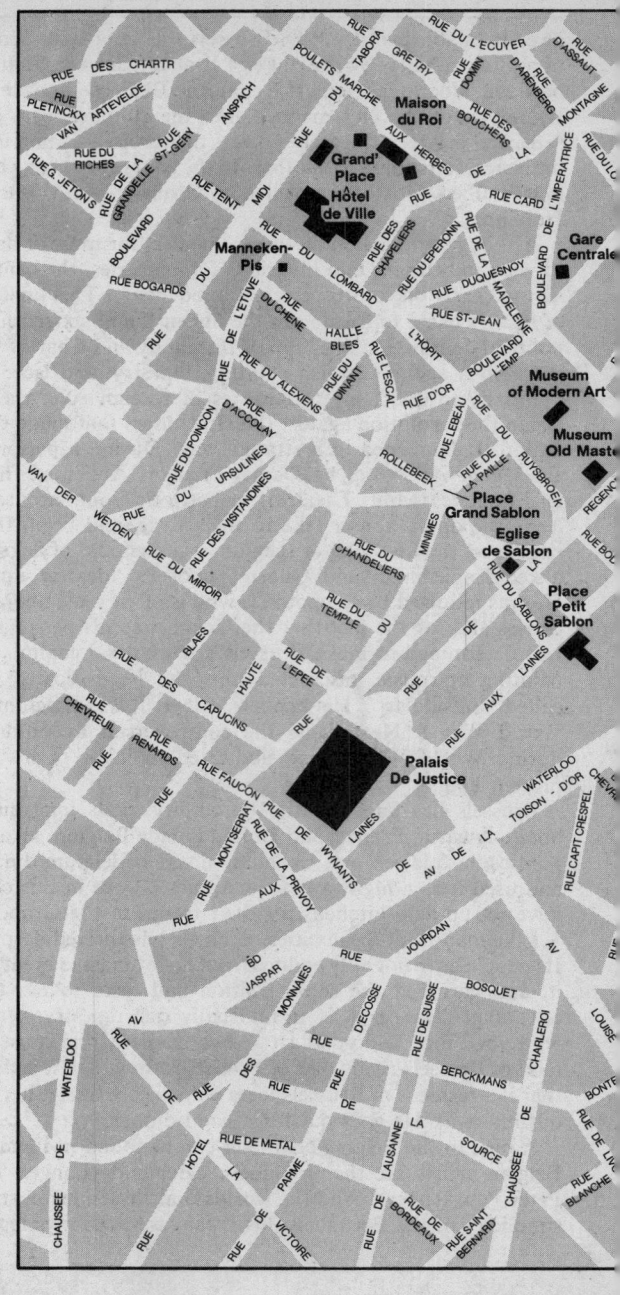

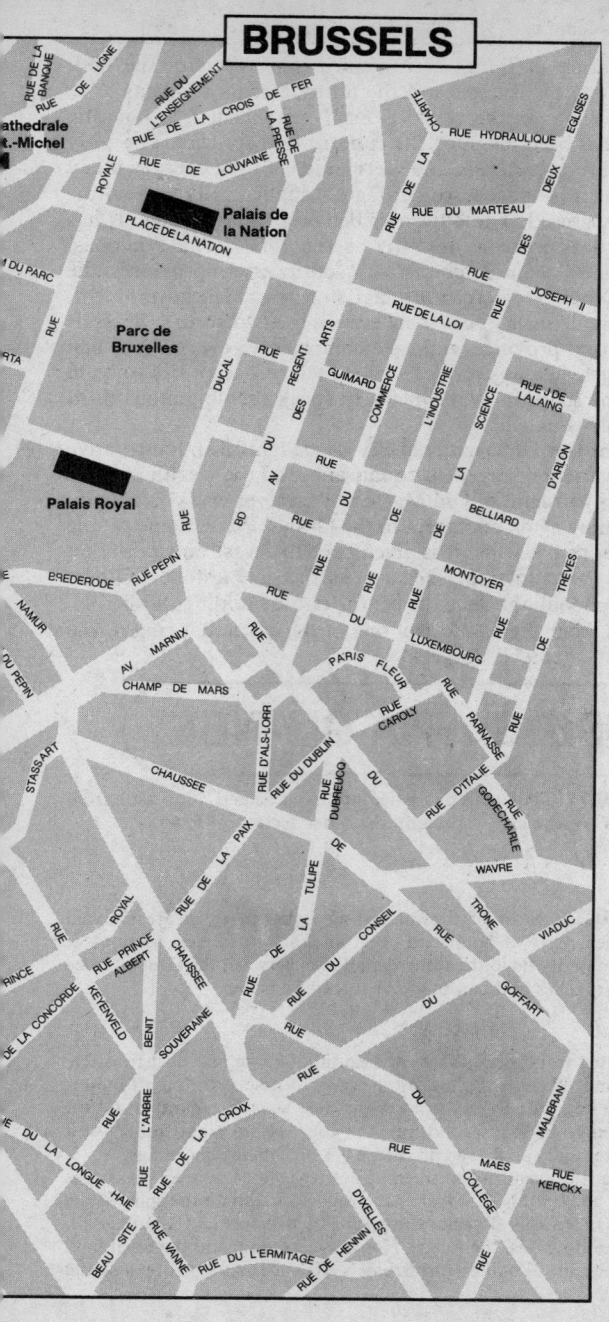

BRUSSELS

Cathedrale
St.-Michel

RUE DE LA BANQUE
RUE DE LIGNE
RUE DU L'ENSEIGNEMENT
RUE DE LA CROIS DE FER
RUE DE LA PRESSE
RUE DE LOUVAINE
ROYALE
RUE DE LA CHARITÉ
RUE HYDRAULIQUE
DEUX EGLISES
RUE DE LA
RUE DU MARTEAU

Palais de
la Nation

PLACE DE LA NATION

RUE DES
RUE JOSEPH II

DU PARC

Parc de
Bruxelles

RTA

RUE DE LA LOI

DUCAL
DES
REGENT
ARTS
GUIMARD
COMMERCE
L'INDUSTRIE
SCIENCE
RUE J DE
LALAING
DU
RUE
AV
D'ARLON

Palais Royal

BD
RUE
DE
DE
BELLIARD

RUE PEPIN

BREDERODE
RUE PEPIN
RUE
RUE
RUE
RUE
MONTOYER
DE TREVES

NAMUR
RUE
DU
LUXEMBOURG

DU PEPIN

AV MARNIX
RUE
PARIS FLEUR
RUE

CHAMP DE MARS
RUE CAROLY
PARNASSE

STASSART
CHAUSSEE
RUE D'ALS-LORR
RUE DU DUBLIN
RUE DUBRHEUQ
DU
RUE D'ITALIE
RUE
GODECHARLE

WAVRE

RUE DE LA PAIX
DE
LA TULIPE
DE
CONSEIL
TRONE
VIADUC

ROYAL
RUE PRINCE ALBERT
CHAUSSEE
RUE
DU
RUE
GOFFART

PRINCE
KEYENVELD
BENIT
SOUVERAINE
RUE
DU
MALIBRAN

DE LA CONCORDE

RUE
L'ARBRE
RUE DE LA CROIX
RUE

DU LA LONGUE HAIE
RUE VANNE
RUE DU L'ERMITAGE
RUE DE HENNIN
DU
RUE
MAES
COLLEGE
RUE KERCKX

BEAU SITE
D'IXELLES
RUE

Rubens's deft combination of things of the spirit and things of the flesh — reflect an aspect of life in Brussels and the attitude of its residents.

Although Belgium's place in the world is firmly established, a domestic problem remains that has been plaguing the country for centuries. The early tribes that settled Belgium were Latin and Germanic, and the country today is a mixture — not a blend — of the two heritages. Linguistically and culturally, the two have never fused. The bitterness between the two factions has led to a series of political crises as recently as the 1960s. The Walloons, French-speaking Belgians, live in Belgium's four southwestern provinces; the Flemings, who speak Dutch, are in the north and northeast. The government, a democratic republic, is an uneasy coalition between the two groups. Brussels sits in Brabant, the central province, and, as a compromise, every street sign here is in both languages, just as every official speech or decree has to be in French and Dutch. One solution for people is to speak the ubiquitous third language, a good British English.

This 1,000-year-old modern international city is a delightful and restorative place to visit, with its variety of excellent restaurants and the wealth of great Flemish paintings in its Museum of Old Masters. Whatever else you do, you will find yourself returning again and again to the Grand' Place. Some people prefer it in the early morning, when it is given over to a vast flower market and the sun drenches the colors splashed across the cobblestones. Others prefer it at night, when floodlights lace the centuries-old buildings with gold. Day or night, taken in from the comfort of one of the cafés that ring it, the Grand' Plàce is a sight one never forgets.

BRUSSELS AT-A-GLANCE

SEEING THE CITY: The Palais de Justice, at place Poelaert, is on a hill from which you can see the city, especially the older section of town.

SPECIAL PLACES: Most of the interesting sights in town are situated within the inner circle of boulevards that enclose the central sections of town; a great majority lie in the rather small area between the Grand' Place and Parc de Bruxelles and can easily be covered on foot.

IN TOWN

Grand' Place – Reputed to be Europe's most beautiful square and an irresistible magnet to everyone, Grand' Place is the historic heart of Brussels. It doesn't matter whether you see it for the first time by day or by night. Just wander around it and get the feel of the place. Then go back a second time for your serious sight-seeing. And don't miss the bird market and the flower market, both on Sunday mornings.

It is hard to believe that this beautiful square was destroyed by Louis XIV's armies in 1695 during a 35-hour bombardment. Most of the square, including the spire of the town hall, burned down, but within 3 years, the people of Brussels had rebuilt it all.

In the square are the guild houses, the King's House (see below), and the town hall, unquestionably the most beautiful building in Brussels. Its spire is topped by a statue of St. Michael, patron saint of Brussels. Construction was begun in the fifteenth century and its style is pure Gothic. Inside is an excellent collection of tapestries. The building is considered a symbol of the city's freedom and it is rated as one of Europe's finest examples of fifteenth-century architecture. Closed Saturdays and Mondays. Small admission fee (phone: 512-7554).

The other buildings around the square are guildhalls built between 1696 and 1698, after the originals were destroyed in the 1695 bombardment. Among the guilds represented are the bakers, coopers, archers, boatmen, haberdashers, butchers, and brewers.

Wander through the narrow, medieval streets leading off the Grand' Place. Their names are straight out of the Middle Ages: Street of the Herring, Stove Street, Pepper Street, Butter Street, Street of the Cheese Market — all dating back to the days when this area was one vast marketplace *(broodhuis)*.

King's House (Maison du Roi) – This historic building, on the site of a thirteenth-century bread market, was rebuilt in the 1870s. It houses the Municipal Museum of the City of Brussels (Musée Communal), which has exhibits on the history and archaeology of the city. There are also examples of the applied arts of Brussels, such as tapestries, lace, and goldsmiths' work, and here are displayed the clothing and uniforms for the *Manneken-Pis* (see below). Closed weekend afternoons. Grand' Place (phone: 511-2742).

Brewery Museum (Maison des Brasseurs) – Set in the building of the ancient brewers' guild, right in the Grand' Place, is a collection of old beer-making equipment. Next door is a charming drinking house where you can taste the various beers. Closed weekends and the first 2 weeks in September. Small admission fee. 10 Grand' Place (phone: 512-2696).

The Manneken-Pis – Southwest of the Grand' Place is the small bronze seventeenth-century statue by Jerôme Duquesnoy. This impudent little boy making water is considered symbolic of the city's irreverent spirit. There are many guesses as to its origin, but all that anybody knows for sure is that it has been here since 1619. Periodically, he is stolen and then returned safely. His dazzling wardrobe, which he sometimes wears, is on display at the King's House. He has over 396 suits of clothing, given to him by everybody from Louis XV of France to the Boy Scouts of America and the Allied Armies of World War II. Rue de l'Étuve, just off the Grand' Place.

Galeries St.-Hubert – Built in 1847, just north of the Grand' Place, this is the oldest arcade in Europe and has been a fashionable promenade since it was built. There are elegant shops and restaurants here, and the surrounding streets, such as the quaint and narrow Petite rue des Bouchers, are known for their many fine restaurants. Rue du Marché-aux-Herbes.

Brussels Park (Parc de Bruxelles) – Near the fine arts complex, this historic park was originally the hunting ground of the dukes of Brabant. It was laid out in the formal French manner during the eighteenth century, when it was a fashionable promenade. In 1830, the park was the scene of heavy fighting between Holland troops and patriots. The Palais du Roi, the office of the sovereign, overlooks the park just east of the place Royale. The rue Ducale boasts a row of aristocratic mansions. Byron lived in number 51 when he composed the Waterloo stanzas of *Childe Harold*.

Royal Square – Between the palace and the fine arts complex is the elegantly proportioned neoclassical square built in the eighteenth century. The statue of Charles of Lorraine was removed by anti-Royalists during the French Revolution and replaced by one of Godfrey of Bouillon, leader of the first Crusade.

Museum of Old Masters (Musée d'Art Ancien) – This is a very large collection of paintings, mostly Flemish, from the fourteenth to the seventeenth century. Included are the works of Rubens, the Breughels, and Van Dyck, among others. It's open for a small fee; closed Mondays. 3 rue de la Régence (phone: 513-9630).

Museum of Modern Art – Next to the Musée d'Art Ancien, this new building

— with underground levels — is a dramatic showcase for an extensive collection of Belgian and foreign art dating from 1880 to the present. Closed Mondays. Pl. Royale (phone: 513-9630).

Church of Notre-Dame-du-Sablon – Right near the fine arts complex, this fifteenth-century church is an outstanding example of late Gothic architecture. According to tradition, a Brussels woman had a vision that she should bring a statue of the Virgin Mary from Antwerp to Brussels; when she did so, her boat was guided by angels. She presented the statue to the crossbowmen, and their chapel became a popular place for pilgrimage. So many people crowded the chapel that in 1400 work began on the present church. Pl. du Petit Sablon.

Grand Sablon Square – Below the church, the heart of the antiques center of Brussels is the scene of a book and antiques market on Saturdays and Sundays.

Petit Sablon Square – This square is dotted with 48 small bronze statues representing the medieval trade guilds. A formal garden slopes down the square from the church above and contains statues of the counts of Egmont and Hoorn, two of Brussels's martyrs of independence. In 1568 these great Flemish (Catholic) noblemen were beheaded in the Grand' Place for protesting to Philip II of Spain about persecution of Protestants. Egmont's courage was celebrated in a play by Goethe and an overture by Beethoven. Nearby, his home, the sixteenth-century Egmont Palace, is now the scene of many international receptions. Off the place du Petit Sablon is the rue des Six Jeunes Hommes, which has some lovely old houses.

St. Michael's Cathedral – Majestically situated on top of a hill near the center of town, the national cathedral of Belgium is one of the oldest buildings in Brussels. Begun in the thirteenth century, it's in typical Belgian Gothic style. Its sixteenth-century stained-glass windows were donated by Emperor Charles V. The baroque pulpit and the mausoleums are also worthy of note. Blvd. de l'Imperatrice.

Congress Column (Colonne du Congrès) – Near the cathedral, the column was built in 1859 to honor the national congress that promulgated the Belgian constitution, after the 1830 revolution. On top of the column is a statue of King Leopold I. In front is the eternal flame that burns in memory of the unknown soldiers from both world wars. From the esplanade there is a good view of the entire city. Rue Royale, north of St. Michael's Cathedral at rue du Congrès.

Royal Museum of Art and History – Situated in the Parc du Cinquantenaire at the eastern end of town, this is one of the largest museums of its kind. Its exhibits include ancient civilizations, particularly Egyptian and Greco-Roman, Belgian history and folklore, and the useful and decorative arts in Europe. It's open daily except Mondays. Admission fee, except on Wednesday and Saturday afternoons, Sundays, and holidays. Av. des Nerviens (phone: 733-9610).

OUT OF TOWN

Since Belgium is such a small country (only 11,750 square miles), even its major cities of Bruges, Antwerp, and Ghent are within a short distance of Brussels.

Erasmus's House (Maison d'Erasme) – Located in the southwestern suburb of Anderlecht, this was not, in fact, Erasmus's house, but the home of a friend where the "Prince of Humanists" stayed in about 1521. Nevertheless, this is a beautiful patrician residence, immensely evocative of the personality of the man. Rooms are richly furnished in sixteenth-century style; there's a library, a quiet walled garden, and documents to illustrate the life and work of Erasmus. The house also includes a small but excellent collection of Renaissance paintings, including Hans Holbein's portrait of Erasmus and works by Roger van der Weyden and Hieronymus Bosch. Closed Tuesdays and Fridays. Admission fee. 31 rue du Chapitre, Anderlecht (phone: 521-1383).

Church of St. Pierre and St. Guidon – Also in Anderlecht, not far from Erasmus's House, you might want to look at the fifteenth-century Gothic Church of St. Pierre and

St. Guidon with its ancient crypt and Renaissance wall paintings. Just north of the church on the rue du Chapelain is a small, interesting Flemish convent *(béguinage),* founded in 1252 and restored in 1956 to its original appearance, with the mother superior's room, kitchen, courtyard, and so on. 4 rue du Chapelain, Anderlecht.

Atomium – The Parc du Centenaire, in a northern suburb of Brussels, was the site of the 1958 World's Fair. The symbol of the fair is the Atomium, which represents the molecule of a crystal of iron magnified 65 billion times. There's an elevator to a restaurant at the top and escalators to various spheres that contain exhibits on the peaceful uses of atomic energy. Admission fee.

In the park there is a vast group of exhibition halls dating from the 1935 and 1958 World's Fairs. Heysel (phone: 478-3008).

Waterloo – On the night before the battle, the duchess of Richmond gave a huge ball on Brussels's rue Royale that was immortalized in Lord Byron's *Childe Harold's Pilgrimage* and Thackeray's novel *Vanity Fair.* The site of the famous battle is only 12 miles (19.2 km) south of the city and is accessible by public bus and by coach excursions. If you climb the lion monument (Butte du Lion), you can see a somewhat obstructed view of the battlefield itself. There is a museum of battle nearby. Chemin des Vertes Bornes 90 (phone: 384-3139).

A better sense of the battle can be had from a visit to another museum in the town of Waterloo, which is 1.8 miles (3 km) north of the battlefield and was once Wellington's headquarters. Wellington Museum (closed Mondays from September through June). Admission fee. 147 Chaussée de Bruxelles (phone: 354-7806).

Beersel Castle – This early-fourteenth-century château-fort is 16 kilometers south of Brussels. The brick building, with three towers and set in the middle of a moat, has no furnishings but does have the obligatory torture room. Visitors (especially those with small children) should be careful around the castle since there are lots of open windows and few safety rails. Open daily in summer; weekends only in winter. Admission charge.

Gaasbeek Castle – This historic thirteenth-century castle (many times restored) is 6 miles (10 km) southwest of Brussels. Though its exterior, with seven round towers, is medieval, its interior contains Renaissance furnishings and valuable tapestries, furniture, and objets d'art. There's a 100-acre park. The view from the terrace in the garden was painted by Pieter Breughel the Elder. It's open to the public daily except Mondays and Fridays from April through October, daily except Fridays in July and August. Admission is free.

■**EXTRA SPECIAL:** Take a 1¼-hour train ride to Bruges (in Dutch, Brugge), often called Die Scone, "the beautiful." This is one of Europe's best-preserved medieval cities, a place of rare charm: narrow cobbled streets with picturesque canals spanned by more than 50 bridges. The maze of winding streets makes driving difficult, but most of the places in town can be reached on foot.

Everything centers around the Grote Markt, or main square; you can enjoy a 40-minute tour of the city by the canal boats that are anchored just southeast of the Grote Markt or rent a horse-drawn carriage right in the square. Also on the Grote Markt is the tourist office. Don't miss the famous belfry, very tall — 353 feet — with a carillon of 49 bells. Concerts are held year-round..

Bruges is famous as a lacemaking center, and the finest examples of the art are exhibited in the Gruuthuse Museum, a fifteenth-century palace with fine furniture and a superb collection of old Flemish lace. Other outstanding places are the Groeninge Museum, containing a great many fine examples of Flemish art; the graceful thirteenth-century Gothic cathedral; the Memling Museum at St. Jans Hospital, containing the oldest pharmacy in the world as well as many important works of the great fifteenth-century painter.

Bruges has many other sights, not least of which are the streets themselves, narrow and winding and lined with gabled houses. You can see the town in one rather strenuous day or, if you choose, stay overnight at one of the charming hotels, such as the *Duc de Bourgogne* at 12 Huidenvettersplaats (phone: 33-20-38).

SOURCES AND RESOURCES

Basic information about Brussels is available in the US from the Belgian National Tourist Office, 745 Fifth Ave., New York, NY 10151 (212-758-8130). In Brussels, be sure to visit the main office at 61 rue Marché-aux-Herbes (phone: 513-8940) for excellent maps and leaflets, calendars of tourist events, and aid of any sort.

For Local Coverage – The best English-language publication is *The Bulletin,* a weekly with the format of a news magazine. It's available at local newsstands.

For Food – The tourist office publishes a booklet, *Gourmet Restaurants,* which may be purchased for a small fee. The guide includes a gastronomic rating of more than 100 restaurants as decided by "five of the best food critics in Brussels."

 CLIMATE AND CLOTHES: Brussels has a temperate climate, much like that of the northeast corner of the US. But the stormy North Sea is not far away, so rain and wind often batter the capital. Take a raincoat or umbrella, just to be safe. Summer weather is variable, with mean temperatures in the 70s F (21°–26°C); winter temperatures are rarely below freezing and hover around 40°F (4.4°C).

Dress as you would in any world capital. Dress up for dinner at the more fashionable restaurants.

 GETTING AROUND: Most of the important sights in Brussels are within the central section of the city and can easily be explored on foot.

Bus, Tram, and Métro – A clear and detailed map is available at the tourist office. Rides are inexpensive, and you can buy a ten-ride card at a savings. There is a special 1-day unlimited ticket for about $2.25.

Taxi – Taxis are plentiful but quite expensive. The tip is included in the fare. You can order a cab from *Taxis Verts* (Green Taxis) by calling 511-2244, or pick one up at a taxi stand.

Car Rental – *Avis* is at 145 rue Américaine (phone: 537-2121); *Hertz* at 8 blvd. Maurice Lemonnier (phone: 513-2886); or try *ABC Service Rent-a-car* at 133 rue d'Anderlecht (phone: 513-1954).

MUSEUMS: Besides those mentioned in *Special Places,* some of the more interesting museums include:

Museum of Natural Science, 29 rue Vautier (648-0475), is noteworthy for its collection of well-preserved dinosaur skeletons, unearthed in western Belgium in 1878. Open daily.

Royal Library, Mont des Arts (phone: 513-6180), which has more than 3 million volumes as well as coins, maps, and splendid illuminated manuscripts. Closed Sundays.

Museum of Musical Instruments, 17 place du Petit Sablon (phone: 512-0848), has 4,000 musical instruments from the Bronze Age to the present. The museum is open Sunday mornings, Tuesday, Thursday, and Saturday afternoons, and Wednesday evenings.

Royal Museum of Central Africa, Leuvensesteenweg 13, Tervuren (phone: 767-5401) has an interesting art gallery and a panorama of African life. Open daily.

Chinese Pavilion, 44 av. Van Praet Laeken (phone: 268-1608), with a first-rate collection of seventeenth- and eighteenth-century Chinese and Japanese porcelains. Closed Mondays. Admission fee.

Museum of Fine Arts of Ixelles, 71 rue Jean-Van-Volsem, Ixelles (phone: 511-9084), houses splendid Dürers, Toulouse-Lautrec posters, and works of French and Belgian Impressionists. Closed Mondays.

Galerie Ravenstein Design Center, Galerie Ravenstein 51 (phone: 511-6235), has a permanent exhibit of Belgian designs and products. Closed Saturday afternoons and Sundays.

 SHOPPING: Brussels is not a city for bargain hunters, but you will get top quality for the price you pay. It *is* the home of *Val St. Lambert,* one of the world's finest crystals. Pewter and linen are also excellent values. Leather-goods and women's clothing are terribly chic and equally *cher.*

Lace is the product you will see most often, especially in the souvenir shops around the Grand' Place. Some of the little old ladies who made Brussels lace world famous are still working, but alas, much of the lace is now machine-made in Hong Kong. This lace is usually used on cocktail napkins and place mats, which make small, inexpensive gifts to take home. Look carefully at tags to know what you are buying.

Antiques are usually of excellent quality. Try the Saturday and Sunday market at the place du Grand Sablon. You will usually see some lovely things there, even if you are only "just looking." There is also a book market at the same place.

Although there are fine shops all over the city, there are two main shopping districts. One is the area including the boulevard Adolphe Max, the boulevard Anspach, rue Neuve, rue Marché-aux-Herbes, and Galeries St.-Hubert. The other is the avenue Louise, avenue de la Toison d'Or, and the boulevard de Waterloo. Anderlecht, a suburb of Brussels, has one of the largest covered suburban shopping centers in Europe.

A good place to get a sampling of everything is at *L'Innovation* (also known as *Inno*), Brussels's finest department store (111 rue Neuve). A few other recommended stores include:

Art et Selection – Famous Val St. Lambert crystal. 83 rue Marché-aux-Herbes.

Biot-Believre – Linen tablecloths and the like, hand embroidered on request. 8 rue de Naples.

Chaudoir – Brussels tapestries, made with sixteenth-century techniques and modern designs. 56 rue des Ailes.

Delvaux – This is the *Gucci* of Brussels, *the* place for leathergoods. 31 Galerie de la Reine.

Manufacture Belge de Dentelles – Lace and lacemaking. 6–8 Galerie de la Reine.

Nina Meert – A boutique for dresses, blouses, and lingerie made of Belgian lace and linen. 5 rue de Florence.

Le Potier d'Étain – Modern pewter. 43 rue de Rollebeek.

 SPECIAL EVENTS: The *Ommegang* pageant takes place in the Grand' Place on the first Thursday in July at 9 PM. It is a centuries-old spectacle commemorating the miraculous arrival of a statue of the Virgin Mary in the Sablon church. The word *ommegang* means, literally, "to walk around," which is done much as it was in the sixteenth century for Charles V and his court. The oldest and noblest families take part in the procession, representing their ancestors who took part in the original pageant. This colorful, splendid tradition is one of Belgium's most popular attractions.

During August, September, and early October, Brussels is part of the *Festival of Flanders,* one of Europe's major music festivals, featuring internationally known orchestras, soloists, operas, and dance companies — and tickets are reasonably priced. For information write the Festival of Flanders, Eugeen Flageyplein 18, 1050 Brussels (phone, in Flanders: 015-20-17-66). There's also a month-long fair in summer (mid-July to mid-August) on the boulevard du Midi, featuring rides and local foods.

SPORTS: Golf – The *Royal Golf Club of Belgium (Royale Golf Club de Belgique),* Château de Ravenstein, Tervuren (phone: 767-5801), is the diplomats' golf club. The clubhouse is in one of the buildings belonging to the Ravenstein Château property. The facilities are excellent and it is only 7 miles (11 km) from downtown Brussels.

Horseback Riding – Try *Royal Etrier Belge,* 19 champs du Vert Chasseur (phone: 374-2860), or get a booklet called *Belgium on Horseback* from the tourist office.

Jogging – The best runs are in Woluwé Park off avenue Tervuren, Cinquantenaire Park, and Bois de la Cambre off avenue Roosevelt.

Soccer (known as *football*) – This is the most popular spectator sport. Major games are played at *Heysel Stadium,* 135 av. de Marathon (phone: 478-9300).

Swimming – At *Bains de Bruxelles,* 28 rue du Chevreuil (phone: 511-2468); *Calypso,* 60 av. L. Wiener (phone: 673-3929); and *Poseidon,* 2 av. des Vaillants (phone: 771-6655).

Tennis – Try the *Lawn Tennis Federation,* 164 av. Louise (phone: 648-0934; 648-7468).

THEATER: The marionette theater, *de Toone,* is a must. Popular plays are performed by puppets in Brussels slang nightly except Sundays, at 21 Petite rue des Bouchers (phone: 511-7137). Most modern plays are in French or Dutch, though occasionally there is some amateur theater in English. Brussels's 17 theaters, which present a variety of plays, are listed in the daily newspapers.

MUSIC: One of the world's most prestigious music competitions is the *Concours Reine Elisabeth,* named for the grandmother of the present king. It takes place in May and is usually covered by TV and radio. Brussels is the home of the internationally known *Béjart Ballet du Vingtième Siècle.*

The *Theatre Royal de la Monnaie,* pl. de la Monnaie (phone: 218-1211), is the home of opera and ballet in Brussels, but it is also an important part of its history. The original building dated from the late seventeenth century and was built on the site of the old mint (hence the name). The present building goes back to 1817. In 1830, at a performance of Auber's opera *La Muette de Portici* at the *Monnaie,* one of the patriotic songs ("Sacred love of the fatherland, give us courage and pride") so inflamed the audience that they streamed out of the opera house and unleashed the rebellion that led ultimately to Belgium's independence. Recitals and concerts by world-famous musicians are given throughout the year, usually in the *Palais des Beaux-Arts,* 23 rue Ravenstein (phone: 512-5045).

NIGHTCLUBS AND NIGHTLIFE: As in most large cities, the nightclubs are tourist traps, so be prepared to spend a lot of money if you go to them. *Maxim's,* 22 rue Capitane Crespel (phone: 511-3617), is an old favorite. It has a floor show, so reservations are necessary. *Crazy,* 15 rue Capitane Crespel (phone: 511-8731), is based, more or less, on the *Crazy Horse* in Paris. It advertises itself as having "20 super beauties in extra nudity." Reservations are recommended. *En Plein Ciel,* 38 blvd. de Waterloo (phone: 513-8877), the rooftop restaurant of the Hilton Hotel, has a small dance floor. The atmosphere is pleasant; the view, on a starry night, impressive. Reservations are necessary. *Mozart,* at 541 Chaussée d'Alsemberg (phone: 344-0809), is a pub that serves jazz as well as food until 4 AM. You can have dinner up until 6 AM at *Safir,* the classic all-night spot at 23 Petite rue des Bouchers (phone: 511-8478). Reservations are not necessary.

For a pleasant nightcap, try the *Café de la Grand' Place* (phone: 513-0807), the *Hotel Metropole Café* (phone: 219-2384), or *Au Bon Vieux Temps,* 12 rue Marché-aux-Herbes (phone: 219-5309). Reservations are unnecessary. Beer lovers might stop by *La Houblonnière,* 4 pl. de Londres (phone: 513-1483), where scores of Belgian beers are available for sampling.

 SINS: This is a city full of lonely businessmen, and many of its bars are clip joints, with very high prices and ladies who are out to "take" you for your money. The expensive spots are on the rue Stassard near avenue Louise; the cheaper ones are in the Gare du Nord area and in the St. Catherine district, where muggings are on the increase. Recent competition between much more expensive imported (Dutch and French) ladies and Belgian ones has occasionally sparked violent incidents — so watch out.

BEST IN TOWN

 CHECKING IN: A double room and bath in an expensive Brussels hotel usually runs from $80 to $100; a moderately priced hotel charges between $50 and $70; an inexpensive hotel can be $20 to $40. Rates include a 16% service charge and VAT.

The Amigo – Gracious and comfortable, this hotel is in an ideal location, only one street away from the Grand' Place. It has the charm, but not the noise, of the square and an aristocratic interior with velvet upholstery and silk wainscoting. There's a garage, a restaurant, a bar, and 183 spacious rooms and suites. Best are the sixth-floor apartments with terraces. 1–3 rue de l'Amigo (phone: 511-5910). Expensive.

Royal Windsor – Also in the Grand' Place area, this 300-room hotel is Tudor style and its restaurants offer a variety of menus. Its atmosphere is British; its ambience modern and quite pleasant, with soundproofed rooms, TV, various room sizes, interesting paneling, and handwoven fabrics. Underground parking garage. 5–7 rue Duquesnoy (phone: 511-4215). Expensive.

Brussels Hilton – This skyscraper is one of Brussels's largest hotels (369 rooms) and it's close to the avenue Louise shopping area. There is a superb view of the city from the roof garden restaurant. The *Hilton* is where the international business set hangs out. All rooms have TV and air-conditioning. There are duplexes with balconies and full kitchens, an authentic French restaurant, an English pub, and a bar-discotheque patronized by locals. 38 blvd. de Waterloo (phone: 513-8877). Expensive.

Hyatt Regency – One of the more gracious of the newer hotels, the *Regency* has 322 rooms. It has many deluxe suites, a gourmet restaurant, meeting facilities, and a 24-hour coffee shop. 250 rue Royale (phone: 219-4640). Expensive.

Brussels Sheraton – This is Brussels's largest hotel (526 rooms), with several dining rooms and a coffee shop. It's a sleek, modern, 31-story affair with a handsome lobby, well-appointed, good-size rooms, a discotheque, and a pool. 3 pl. Rogier (phone: 219-3400). Expensive.

Holiday Inn – This large (288-room) hotel is like any other in the chain — clean, convenient, and standardized. It has tennis courts, a pool, and a sauna. Courtesy buses run to the airport and into town. 7 Holiday St., near the airport in Diegem (phone: 720-5865). Expensive.

Jollyhotel Atlanta – Recently redone, this hotel takes its name from the heyday of *Gone With the Wind.* There is a dining room–roof garden with a good view of the city. The hotel is downtown and some of the 242 rooms can be noisy. 7 blvd. Adolphe Max (phone: 217-0120). Expensive.

Arcade Stephanie – Close to one of the best shopping districts in Brussels, this 142-room hotel is convenient for shoppers, but its front rooms can be noisy. 91–93 Ave. Louise (phone: 538-8060). Moderate.

Astoria – A smaller hotel (125 rooms) with a lovely staircase and quiet, comfortable rooms, the *Astoria* is a souvenir of the Belle Époque. The bar is decorated to represent a Pullman compartment. 103 rue Royale (phone: 217-6290). Moderate.

City Garden – Modern, spacious, and comfortable, this 96-room hotel offers kitchenettes and proximity to the metro and Common Market headquarters. 59 rue Joseph II (phone: 230-0945). Moderate.

La Legende – This small (32-room) hotel is centrally located in the city; a short walk takes you by the Manneken-Pis. Rue de l'Etuve 33 (phone: 512-8290). Inexpensive.

Noga – Although close to the interesting rue Neuve shopping district, this small hotel is very quiet. Rue du Béguinage 38 (phone: 218-6763). Inexpensive.

Marie Jose – This small, pleasant hotel is not far from a metro stop and has a very good restaurant. 73 rue du Commerce (phone: 512-0843). Inexpensive.

 EATING OUT: Brussels's pride in good food extends from the most fashionable to the simplest restaurants, from the most elaborate haute cuisine to the freshest produce. A good restaurant in Brussels goes to exceptional lengths to please a patron who enjoys good food. If you order pâté, for example, you won't get by without sampling several varieties, while the restaurateur beams at every sign of pleasure that you show. Belgium's cooks are some of the best in the world and Belgian food, a stepchild of French cuisine, has developed its own specialties. These include Brussels sprouts, of course; and asparagus from Malines, red cabbage prepared with apple called *à la flamande; carbonnades flamandes,* or beef braised in beer; blood and white sausage called *boudin; waterzooi de volaille,* or chicken in a vegetable and cream soup; *anguilles au vert,* or eels, served with herbs; and mussels served in a variety of ways. Belgian pastries are excellent, especially *pain à la grecque,* a very light, sweet rusk; *gaufres,* or waffles, and tarts made with custard, sugar, or rice. And don't miss *pralines,* the famous Belgian chocolate with a variety of fillings. Brussels people will tell you that their chocolate is the best in the world — and they may be right. Beers are special here, including, among others, Geuze-Lambiek, Kriek-Lambiek, and Trappiste.

There are 1,500 restaurants in Brussels and the best rate almost as national monuments. You can spend a small fortune for a good meal, but you don't have to. It is almost impossible to have a bad meal anywhere. A dinner for two, including wine (and remember, the wine is imported), in a luxury restaurant averages $80 to $90; in a moderately priced restaurant, it comes to between $45 and $55; and in an inexpensive restaurant, $35 or less. Unless otherwise noted, Brussels's restaurants take major credit cards.

Villa Lorraine – This is probably Belgium's most famous restaurant and one of the few three-star restaurants (according to *Michelin*) outside France. The setting is a lovely villa just outside the Brussels city limits; the service is impeccable, the decor sumptuous, the food such French-style stuff as dreams are made of. Try the hot lobster pâté or the sole. Closed Sundays and most of July. Reservations required. 75 av. du Vivier d'Oie (phone: 374-3163). Expensive.

Comme Chez Soi – From the outside, this small restaurant in a small townhouse looks inconsequential. Inside is one of the best restaurants in Belgium, also with three Michelin stars. Try the mussels, fish, venison, foie gras, and pastries. Closed Sundays, Mondays, and all of July. Reservations required. 23 pl. Rouppe (phone: 512-2921). Expensive.

Romeyer – The most recent Belgian restaurant to earn a third Michelin star, it's actually a country lodge in the Forêt de Soignes, just a few miles outside the city. Specialties include lobster sausage and stuffed crayfish. Closed Sunday evenings, Mondays, and all of February and August. Reservations necessary. 109 Steenweg op Groenendaal, Hoeilaart (phone: 657-0581). Expensive.

L'Écailler du Palais Royal – Unpretentious from the outside, this is a superb seafood restaurant in a sixteenth-century guild house. Try turbot, lobster, and oysters in season. Closed Sundays, public holidays, and all of August. Reservations required. 18–20 rue Bodenbroek (phone: 512-8751). Expensive.

Bernard – When you come in here, you may think that you have wandered into a grocery store by mistake. But go up one flight to the small dining room with tables tucked nose to nose. It looks unpretentious, but it caters mostly to knowledgeable Belgians. Closed Saturday evenings and Sundays and all of July. Reservations required. 93 rue de Namur (phone: 512-8821). Expensive.

Auberge de Boendael – Although this restaurant isn't downtown, it's definitely worth the ride for its delicious meat and fish specialties that are grilled over a wood fire. Try to save room for a dessert of homemade coffee ice cream *(cafe glacé)* and sorbets. Closed Saturdays and Sundays. Reservations necessary. 12 Sq. du Vieux Tilleul (phone: 672-7055). Expensive.

La Cravache d'Or – Here, the varied culinary repertoire includes smoked salmon *à la vinaigrette de framboise,* oysters in champagne, and truffles in broth. Closed late July to late August. 10 pl. Albert-Leemans (phone: 538-3746). Expensive.

De Bijgaarden – Imaginative cuisine combines with superb management at this impeccable suburban restaurant. *Pheasant Smitane* and *sole Hôtellerie* share the menu with other creative house specialties. Closed Sundays. Isidoor-Van-Beveren Straat 20, Groot Bijgaarden (phone: 466-4485). Expensive.

Chez Jean – Usually packed with regulars, this simple establishment just off the Grand' Place serves tasty Belgian fare. Daily specials are scrawled in soap on wall mirrors. Closed Sundays and Mondays. Reservations advisable. 6 rue Chapeliers (phone: 511-9815). Moderate.

Duc d'Arenberg – A seventeenth-century house with white walls and lots of paintings is the setting for this cheerful restaurant, best known for duck and Normandy crêpes. Open daily. Reservations recommended. At 9 pl. du Petit Sablon (phone: 511-1475). Moderate.

Henry – A popular tavern with a restaurant in the back that's informal and inviting. Try the steaks or the lamb chops. Dixieland jazz on weekend nights. 8 blvd. de Waterloo (phone: 512-1090). Moderate.

Le Cheval Blanc – Popular among the fashionable crowd in Brussels, its nouvelle cuisine menu often includes the vegetables, seafood, and game available in season. There's also a very good dessert trolley. Reservations a must. Closed Sunday nights. 204 rue Haute (phone: 512-3771). Moderate.

Le Gantier Glouton – Translated as "The Gluttonous Glovemaker," this quaint eatery is located in an old glove shop in the heart of town. It features basic Belgian cuisine; save room for the delicious *gâteau au chocolat,* a rich chocolate and cream cake. Closed Sundays and Mondays. No credit cards. 60–62 rue des Eperonniers (phone: 512-7511). Moderate.

Taverne du Passage – Decorated in 1900s style, this is a popular restaurant. Open daily. Reservations recommended. 30 Galerie de la Reine (phone: 512-3732). Moderate.

Maison du Boeuf – In the *Brussels Hilton* overlooking the gardens of the Egmont Palace, this restaurant specializes not only in beef but also in shellfish. Open daily. Reservations recommended. 38 blvd. de Waterloo (phone: 513-8877). Moderate.

La Maison d'Attila – En route to Waterloo, this restaurant features a popular

Mongolian Barbecue, with all you can eat, do-it-yourself shishkabobs, exotic salad concoctions, and unlimited wine. Reservations recommended. No credit cards. 38 av. du Prince de Ligne (phone: 375-3805). Inexpensive.

Vincent – On one of the narrow, cobblestone streets near the Grand Palace, this is the place to go for Belgian specialties. *Moules à l'Escargot* (mussels cooked in a butter and garlic sauce) is a tasty starter; steaks are a good main course. Closed all of August. No reservations. 8 rue des Dominicains (phone: 511-2302). Inexpensive.

Au Vieux Saint-Martin – This is a favorite place for artists. It is bright and cheerful, with newspapers and magazines that you can read if you are dining alone. The menu is simple and the specialties are Belgian. Open daily. No reservations. No credit cards. 38 pl. du Grand Sablon (phone: 512-6476). Inexpensive.

Aux Armes de Bruxelles – This is one of the old Brussels restaurants on one of the narrow little streets leading off the Grand' Place. Its specialty is fish. Closed Mondays and all of June. Reservations advised. 13 rue des Bouchers (phone: 511-5598). Inexpensive.

BUDAPEST

The Danube, central Europe's great river — which flows for 1,770 miles from the Black Forest to the Black Sea, through Ulm, Regensburg, Linz, and Vienna — is particularly wide and beautiful when it reaches Budapest. And if you can arrive on the hydrofoil from Vienna — a 4½-hour trip — you will see Budapest at its most splendid. Buda and Pest, the city's two component parts, both face that mighty river, the city's physical and spiritual center.

Sprawling over the rolling hills of Buda and the almost endless plain of Pest, the two halves of the city form strophe and antistrophe around the Danube. Buda rises and falls along its hills in a swelling reprise of medieval cobblestoned streets and ancient buildings, crowned by the Gothic spires of the thirteenth-century Matthias Church. The streets of Pest — the governmental and commercial center of the city — run in rings and radials around grand squares of monumental buildings and dramatic statues and memorials. The two cities have been united only since 1873, and one has the feeling that the marriage has not settled into comfortable middle age yet. From the river one sees the two buildings that characterize Budapest's two halves: Matthias Church in Buda, where generations of Hungarian kings were crowned; and Pest's baroque Houses of Parliament, towering like a huge wedding cake on the banks of the river. It is as if both parts of the city relate to the Danube more comfortably than to each other.

So beautiful is this city of 2.2 million people that visitors might not suspect that Budapest, like other central European cities, has suffered a history of recurrent invasion, destruction, and reconstruction that only intensified in this century, with a siege and heavy bombing in World War II that demolished 33,000 buildings and all the city's bridges. Witnesses of the revolutionary uprising in 1956 report that Budapest's citizens — who justly adore their city — took to the streets with tears of helplessness streaming down their cheeks as Russian tanks smashed across the boulevards.

The Hungarian nation was founded by Árpád, a semi-legendary chief of the Magyars, who brought his people from the Urals in the ninth century. Before this time, Budapest had been a Roman town of considerable size called Aquincum. The Magyar cities of Buda and Pest grew as trade and craft centers, thriving especially under Hungary's first king, St. Stephen (1001–38). A bloody invasion in 1241, by the Mongols, destroyed both Buda and Pest. The cities were rebuilt and became more and more splendid until the Osmani Turks arrived in the sixteenth century, bringing 150 years of decay, poverty, and captivity to Budapest. (Two positive Turkish contributions were the Turkish baths that remain in Buda to this day and the name Hungary, which comes from the Turkish word *on-gur,* meaning "ten tribes.") The country fell into the Hapsburg Empire in 1686 and stayed there — though with growing

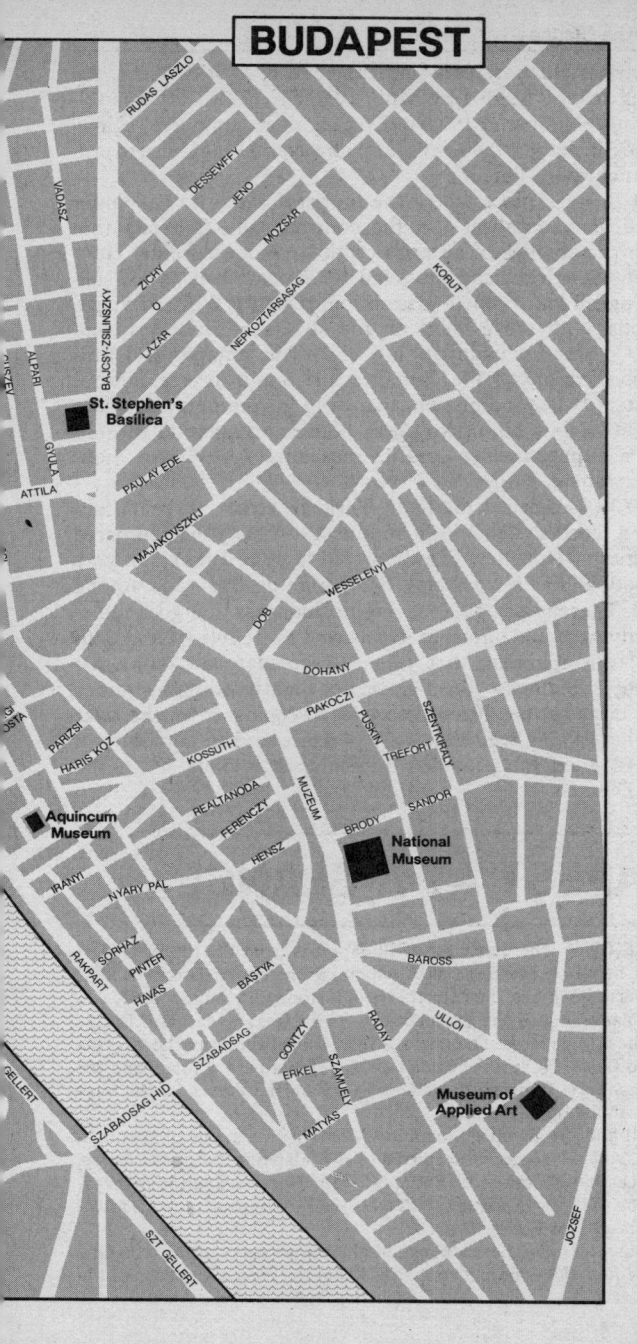

BUDAPEST

RUDAS LASZLO
VADASZ
DESSEWFFY
JENO
MOZSAR
ZICHY
O
LAZAR
NEPKOZTARSASAG
KORUT
BAJCSY-ZSILINSZKY
ALPARI
GYULA
ATTILA

St. Stephen's Basilica

PAULAY EDE
MAJAKOVSZKU
WESSELENYI
DOB
DOHANY
RAKOCZI
PUSKIN
SZENTKIRALY
PARIZSI
HARIS KOZ
KOSSUTH
TREFORT
REALTANODA
MUZEUM
FERENCZY
BRODY
SANDOR

Aquincum Museum

IRANYI
HENSZ

National Museum

NYARY PAL
SORHAZ
PINTER
BASTYA
HAVAS
RAKPART
BAROSS
SZABADSAG
GONTZY
RADAY
ULLOI
ERKEL
SZAMUELY
GELLERT
SZABADSAG HID
MATYAS

Museum of Applied Art

SZT GELLERT
JOZSEF

restiveness on the part of Hungarians — until the end of World War I. An oppressive right-wing regime headed by Miklós Horthy (1918–44) was followed by the disastrous bombing in 1945 and yet another oppressive regime, this time Communist. Since the 1956 revolution, however, Hungary's government has become much more liberal.

Today's Budapest is not a place where the tourist is likely to encounter the rigors of dialectical materialism. On the contrary, this is a city that loves good living. In the absence of an aristocratic or moneyed elite, Hungary worships its artists, writers, and musicians. Rock and roll, jeans, suggestive T-shirts in English and French, a tradition of satire, Western magazines, fads, and foods — all are evident on the streets of Budapest, and visitors from other Communist countries are said to be amazed and titillated by the permissiveness of city life. Budapest's rich and diverse cultural life includes 25 theaters (where admission, thanks to government subsidies, is often the equivalent of only 50¢), two opera houses, an operetta theater, three concert halls, a puppet theater, and 43 museums. And Gypsy violinists seem to be everywhere.

Hungarian cuisine has absorbed German, Turkish, Greek, French, and other influences into a blend so deliciously unique that it has been compared with the French. Wines of Hungary, like the world-famous Tokay, are very popular and very good, and as for desserts, Hungarian pastries rank among the best in the world. There is a popular saying in Budapest that goes something like this: "If only we could afford to live as well as we live — how well would we live." It is an aphorism that seems ill suited to a Communist country, but it fits life in Budapest like a glove. Its slightly mordant humor is characteristic of a city that has listened to tales sweeping down the river for centuries, and where living well is in part pleasure and in part duty, a tribute to centuries of good life provided by Budapest and its sister, the ancient, untroubled Danube.

BUDAPEST AT-A-GLANCE

 SEEING THE CITY: The best view of Budapest is from the top of Gellért Hill (Gellért hegy) on the Buda side, which can be climbed from Gellért Square (Gellért tér). From the balustrades of a stone fort built in 1851, you will enjoy a panorama of the Danube with its bridges — Margaret Bridge to Margaret Island in the middle of the Danube, the recreational center of the city; the historic Chain Bridge to Castle Hill on the Buda side, the oldest part of town; and the Elizabeth Bridge that connects Buda with the Inner City on the Pest side, the busy downtown commercial and shopping center.

Near the fort you will find the gigantic Liberation Monument, a statue of a woman holding an olive branch, which is sometimes referred to as Budapest's Statue of Liberty; it commemorates the Russian liberation of Budapest from Nazi occupation in 1945.

You may wish to enjoy the view at leisure, with a cocktail or dinner at the *Citadella Restaurant* on Gellért hegy (see *Eating Out*).

Since Buda is built on seven hills, there are several alternative views of the city. One of the best is from the *Hilton Hotel,* atop Castle Hill. From the *Hilton* you can see the

Danube, Margaret Island, and the flat Pest side of the river, including the spectacular facade of the Parliament of Hungary.

 SPECIAL PLACES: Budapest, once actually three cities — Buda, Óbuda, and Pest — sprawls on two sides of the Danube River and is difficult to explore on foot because of the distances involved. To make matters worse, the streets of Pest run in circles; Buda's streets are hilly and cobbled. A map is strongly advised (see *Sources and Resources*). Public transportation in Budapest, however, is good, with plenty of trams and buses available at low fares.

Castle Hill (Vár hegy) – Topped by monuments, this hill is the heart of medieval Budapest, with cobbled streets, narrow alleys, and lovely squares. Its baroque and classical buildings, painted in lovely pastel shades, now house famous restaurants, writers' houses, a student quarter, and many landmarks of old Budapest. Much of Castle Hill, badly damaged during World War II, has been painstakingly restored.

Budapest Hilton – It is not even faintly ironic that the first sight to see in medieval Budapest is the magnificent new *Hilton*. It has taken 10 years to build, primarily because it occupies one of the most historic sites in Buda, high on Castle Hill, looking down on the Danube. As excavation for the hotel proceeded, archaeologists kept uncovering the ruins of cultures that had lived on this site since the thirteenth century, and in the end, the hotel elected — in response to strong local pressure — to include many of these historic ruins in its own design.

As a result, its modern stone and glass facade includes the walls and tower of a thirteenth-century Dominican church and a Jesuit monastery. Part of the front of the hotel is a seventeenth-century baroque building, once a Jesuit college. Inside, the thoroughly modern decor has been adapted to incorporate Gothic columns, Roman milestones, bas reliefs, and shards found during excavation. An integral part of the hotel is the famous Fishermen's Bastion, a neoclassical citadel overlooking the Danube (see below). Adjoining is the Church of Matthias.

Fishermen's Bastion – So named because the fishermen of the city had to protect this northern side of the Royal Castle from siege in medieval times, the bastion is now a twentieth-century version of Romanesque ramparts and turrets that afford yet another place from which to view the Danube and the city.

Matthias Church – This Gothic edifice atop Castle Hill dates from the thirteenth century, although it has been rebuilt many times, most recently after severe damage during World War II. Its name translates as "Church of Our Lady." With Gothic spires and colored tile roof, this coronation church of Hungarian kings has one of Europe's most memorable silhouettes. During the Turkish occupation of Hungary in the sixteenth and seventeenth centuries, the church served as a mosque.

Especially noteworthy are the baroque gilt and splendor of the nave and the baroque and Renaissance chalices and vestments in the treasury. There are concerts at the church on Friday evenings. 1, Szentháromság tér.

Ruszwurm – Just down the block from Matthias Church is this fabulous seventeenth-century pastry shop, still serving the best baked goods in central Europe. With displays of old utensils once used by pastry cooks, nineteenth-century signs, and Biedermeier cherrywood furniture with striped silk upholstery, *Ruszwurm* has been designated a historic monument.

Its pastries, known all over Europe, are miraculously light and rich. You can hardly go wrong: try *rétes,* or strudel; vanilla slices; or Ruszwurm cake, a chocolate cake filled with chocolate cream and seasoned with orange peel and rum. 1, Szentháromság utca 3 (phone: 16-14-31).

Royal Palace – Reduced to rubble by bombs in 1944–45, the palace has been carefully reconstructed to incorporate all the styles of its historic past. That was not its first reconstruction. When bombed out, it existed primarily as an eighteenth-century building with some baroque touches; before that it had been destroyed and rebuilt several times since it was first constructed as a castle. It now houses the Historical Museum of Budapest and the National Gallery. 1, Szent Györgytér 2.

Historical Museum of Budapest – In the southern wing of the Royal Palace, the museum contains archaeological remains of the ancient town and the history of the construction of the palace. It displays splendid furniture, sculpture, ceramics, glass, and china; the halls, dating from the fifteenth century, have Renaissance doorcases carved in red marble. 1, Szent György tér 2 (phone: 16-06-07).

Hungarian National Gallery – Newly housed in the Royal Palace, this museum displays the works of the greatest Hungarian artists of the nineteenth and twentieth centuries. English-language guides are available. Budavari Palota (phone: 16-00-30).

Aquincum Museum – One of the most significant excavations of a Roman urban area outside Italy, Aquincum (meaning "ample waters") in its heyday had almost 100,000 inhabitants. Its streets, homes, temple, and amphitheater have been unearthed 4 miles upstream on the right bank of the Danube. The museum on the site has mosaics, jewelry, glass, and inscribed stones. 103 Szentendrei út, Budapest III (phone: 68-76-50).

Margaret Island (Margitsziget) – This resort and recreation island lies right in the middle of the river, accessible from both banks by the Margaret Bridge (Margit híd). Cars and trains enter from Árpád Bridge to the north. The whole island is a park, with a sports stadium, a large municipal swimming pool, a rose garden, a fountain, several hotels, restaurants, and spas. During the summer months, when theaters close, the performances move to outdoor quarters here; you can see plays, concerts, films, and sports events. For specific programs, inquire at the national tourist office, Ibusz (see *Sources and Resources*).

Parish Church of the Inner City (Belvárosi Templom) – This is the oldest church in Pest, dating back to the twelfth century. It shows evidence of many styles of construction, including a Romanesque arch, a Gothic chancel, a Muslim prayer niche, and a Roman wall. Március 15 (March 15) Square.

St. Stephen's Basilica – With its large dome and two tall spires, the basilica dominates the flat landscape of Pest. Built during the nineteenth century, its murals and altarpieces are by leading Hungarian painters and sculptors. 5, Bajcsy-Zsilinszky utca.

Hungarian National Museum – This is the oldest and most important museum in Budapest. The first collections were bequeathed to the museum in 1802, and the buildings were erected between 1836 and 1846. Here are the greatest historical and archaeological collections of the country. One of the prehistoric exhibitions displays the most ancient remnant of European man, the skull from Vértesszölös. There are also Roman ceramics, Avar gold and silver work, and the famous Hungarian Crown of St. Stephen and other historic crown jewels. Among the gold objects are a chiseled Byzantine crown (called the Crown of Monomachos) and the gold baton of Franz Liszt. There is also an exhibition of minerals. 5, Múzeum körút 14–16 (phone: 13-44-00).

Museum of Applied Art – Another one of the great museums of Budapest, the most important collections of which are European and Hungarian ceramics, the work of goldsmiths and silversmiths from the fifteenth to seventeenth century, Italian Renaissance textiles, Turkish carpets, and Flemish tapestries from the seventeenth century. 9, Üllöi út 33–37 (phone: 17-52-22).

Parliament – Mirrored in the Danube, these impressive buildings on the Pest side are reminiscent of the London Houses of Parliament. Finished in 1904, they were built over a period of 20 years. A maze of 27 courtyards, 27 staircases, and 88 statues, Parliament is a favorite haunt for lovers after dark. Along Széchenyi rakpart and backed by Kossuth Lajos tér.

Népköztársaság Útja (People's Republic Road) – This noble avenue, which extends from the basilica to Heroes Square, has known many names that reflect Budapest's stormy past, among them Stalin Avenue and, in 1956, Avenue of Hungarian Youth. It is lined with palaces on both sides, many of which were designed by the architect Miklós Ybl at the end of the nineteenth century; among these buildings are the State Opera House and several theaters. Number 60 once housed the Gestapo, then the Communist secret police.

Heroes Square (Hősök Tere) – At the end of Népköztársaság is a large square marked with the Millennary Monument, which was built in 1896 to celebrate Hungary's millennium. A semicircular colonnade displays a pantheon of Hungarian historical figures. On this square are the Museum of Fine Arts and the Exhibition Hall.

Museum of Fine Arts – Here is the greatest collection of its kind in the country. The building is at the entrance of Városliget (City Park) on the right side of the Hősök Tere. From the beginning of the nineteenth century, more than 100,000 works of art were collected and housed in this neoclassical structure. Among the masterpieces are seven paintings by El Greco and five by Goya. The Italian and Dutch sections have many world-famous paintings, including the *Madonna Esterházy* by Raphael and the *Sermon of St. John the Baptist* by Pieter Breughel, the Elder. The museum also has permanent exhibitions of Egyptian antiquities, Greco-Roman antiquities, and modern European painting and sculpture. Dózsa György út 41 (phone: 42-97-59).

City Park (Városliget) – This large park just northeast of Heroes Square contains an artificial lake; a public spa, Széchenyi Baths; a zoo; a botanical garden; an amusement park; and Vajdahunyad Castle, a 21-building conglomeration of Hungarian architectural styles.

Vörösmarty Pastry Shop (Cukrászda) – In the heart of the city of Pest, adjacent to the airline terminal, this shop was formerly called the Gerbeaud and was famous for its chocolates. *Vörösmarty* is no mere pastry shop; it is an institution. The coffee houses of Budapest are social and literary centers, akin to the eighteenth-century coffee houses of London, and Vörösmarty, with its decadent pastries and its leisured atmosphere reminiscent of days gone by, is the best in town. V, Vörösmarty tér 7 (phone: 18-13-11).

Korona – Another, rather new pastry shop with old-fashioned furniture, *Korona* is a gathering place for literary types and sometimes features poetry readings and other literary events. Hungarian, of course. 1, Disz tér 16 (phone: 16-15-91).

Wine Sampler (Gresham Borkóstoló) – Located near the Houses of Parliament, this is a place where you can taste fine Hungarian wines such as Tokay, which is often sweet; Egri Bikavér (Bull's Blood), a marvelous dry red wine believed to have medicinal value; and Leányka, a good white wine. 2 Mérleg utca (phone: 17-25-02).

Tokay Sampler (Tokaji Borkóstoló) – This is another wine-sampling house located on Pest's grandest avenue, at 20 Népköztársaság út (phone: 12-33-48).

Spas – Hungary is famous for its thermal spas. Budapest spas — there are some 20 in the city today — date from the Roman era and from the Turks, who built several baths in the city in the sixteenth century, among them the Rudas and Király spas in Buda, both still functioning. Although these spas treat people who are suffering from respiratory, rheumatic, and circulatory ailments, they are restorative for almost anyone, especially anyone suffering from obesity or simple fatigue. Treatments include drinking cures (mineral waters), baths in lukewarm or very hot mineral pools, mud packs, and massages, all directed by specialists under the direction of doctors. However, there is a large caveat about Budapest spas: They are not all hygienic. For this reason the spas around Hungary's Lake Balaton are more famous and more widely patronized by Westerners. If you are interested in Budapest spas, try the newly opened *Thermal Hotel Margitsziget* on Margaret Island or contact the tourist office, Ibusz, for help in making a judicious selection (see *Sources and Resources*).

■**EXTRA SPECIAL:** A boat trip on the beautiful Danube is an experience you will not soon forget. Ibusz offers several full-day tours to the Danube Bend area, the spot 12 miles north of Budapest where the Danube makes a hairpin turn that changes its west to east course to a north to south course. This is an area rich in scenery — with limestone hills and volcanic mountains — and in Hungarian history, with river communities that date from Roman times.

For information about boat tours, which are available from May to September for about $23, inquire at Ibusz (see *Sources and Resources*).

SOURCES AND RESOURCES

For general information, brochures, and maps, contact Ibusz (the Hungarian travel bureau), Felszabadulás tér 5 (phone: 18-68-66). City maps, booklets on Budapest attractions, and other information are available from the New York headquarters of Ibusz, 630 Fifth Ave., New York, NY 10020 (phone: 212-582-7412).

For Local Coverage – A comprehensive monthly bulletin, *Coming Events in Budapest*, is available at hotel desks in German, English, and French. An illustrated daily paper in English and German, the *Daily News*, is available at newsstands and hotels.

Major international newspapers, such as the *London Times* and the *International Herald Tribune*, are also available.

 CLIMATE AND CLOTHES: The wooded Buda hills protect the city against extremes of heat and cold. In summer the average temperature is about 72°F (22°C); in winter it is about 34°F (1°C). Dress in Hungary tends to be more informal than in the US. Men usually wear open-necked shirts, except in theaters and good restaurants, where they always wear ties and dark suits.

 GETTING AROUND: Bus, Tram, and Underground – Public transportation is efficient and very cheap. Tickets are sold at tobacco shops, kiosks, and ticket offices, but not on the vehicles. Each ticket, valid for one trip, must be punched in the machines inside the vehicles.

Bus Tours – You might wish to get acquainted with Budapest by taking the 3-hour tour of the city offered daily by Ibusz (see above).

Taxi – There are taxi stands throughout the city; rates are cheap and a 20% tip is customary.

Car Rental – *Ibusz-Avis*, Martinelli tér 18 (phone: 18-41-58); *Hertz* (c/o Cooptourist), Kossuth ter 13–15 (phone: 11-88-03); *Budget* (phone: 34-25-40), are at the airport, as are branches of *Avis* and *Hertz*.

 MUSEUMS: Besides the museums listed in *Special Places*, you may wish to visit the *Museum of Postage Stamps*, 7, Dob utca 75–81, to see an extensive collection that includes some very rare stamps or the *Museum of Medical Science*, 1, Apród utca 1–3, which traces the history of European and Hungarian medicine from Roman times to the present.

 SHOPPING: Many shops are state owned. As in other Communist countries, high-quality consumer goods are not available to Hungarians. Thus the items in a Budapest department store would appear shabby by Western standards. However, the *Intertourist Shops* sell a considerably better array of gifts for foreign currency only. Here you can find colorful pottery, Herend and Alföldi porcelain, Matyó and Kalocsa embroideries, which can be used for wall hangings or even framed as folk art. The country is famous for its peasant blouses, dolls in regional costumes, and embroidered sheepskin jackets. There are also herdsmen's carvings on wood and horn. There are *Intertourist Shops* in all the major hotels and on Kigyó utca in Pest. Budapest also has shops and cooperatives devoted exclusively to folk art: these are at 5, Kecskeméti út 4; 5, Váci utca 14; 5, Régiposta út 12; 5, Kossuth Lajos út 2; and 13, Szent István krt. 26.

A big bargain in Budapest is custom-made clothing, both suits for men and dresses for the ladies. The workmanship and style are excellent, but it is best to bring your own material, as there is little high-quality fabric around. Ask your hotel porter for the nearest custom tailor or dressmaker or try the *Klára Rothschild Salon* on Váci utca.

At any grocery store you can buy an authentic, inexpensive, and easy-to-carry souvenir — a packet of Hungarian paprika, the real stuff, not the red dust generally sprinkled on as a decorative touch in the US. Or get some Hungarian wine at one of the many delicatessens.

 SPECIAL EVENTS: *Budapest Music Weeks,* in early fall, includes international competitions for various types of musicians and many concerts. For information about this and other special events, contact Ibusz (see above).

Besides *Christmas, Boxing Day* on December 26, *New Year's Day,* and *Easter Monday,* Hungarians celebrate political anniversaries on April 4 *(Liberation from the Nazis),* May 1 *(Labor Day),* August 20 *(St. Stephen's Day,* for the first king of Hungary; now *Constitution Day),* and November 7 (the *Russian Revolution*).

 SPORTS: Boating – By arrangement with Ibusz (see above), you can rent a sailboat, sailing dinghy, motorboat, small hydrofoil, and even water skis by the hour or by the day. It is the very best way to enjoy the Danube.

Golf – The *Vöröscsillag Hotel* (see *Checking In*) has a mini-golf link.

Greyhound Racing – On the Danube embankment, just outside Budapest, there are races from May to September. Inquire at Ibusz for details (see above).

Horse Racing – There are trotting races at the track at Kerepesi út 9–11, Budapest 8, and flat racing at the track at Albertirsai út 9, Budapest 10.

Skating – There is a large outdoor ice-skating rink in City Park, near Vajdahunyad Castle.

Skiing – The Buda hills right in and around Budapest, accessible by bus and funicular, have several slopes, the most popular of which is the Szabadsághegy.

Soccer – As in many European countries, soccer (called football) is the most popular spectator sport. There are many sports stadiums in Budapest, of which the largest is the *People's Stadium (Népstadion)* near City Park in Pest, seating 96,000 spectators. Istvánmezei út 3–5 (phone: 63-64-30).

Swimming – Budapest has many indoor and outdoor pools. People swim in the Danube, but it is not too clean (though not nearly as dirty as, say, the Hudson) and sometimes has strong currents. The largest public facility — both indoor and outdoor — is the *National Sports Swimming Pool* on Margaret Island. In addition, many hotels have pools, both ordinary and thermal.

Tennis – There are tennis courts near Dózsa Stadium on Margaret Island and at *FTC Sporttelep (Sports Grounds)* at 129 Üllöi út.

 **THEATER:** In Budapest everyone goes to the numerous theaters that are subsidized by the state and are very cheap. Most performances are, of course, in Hungarian, but you might enjoy seeing a Shakespearean or some other familiar play in Hungarian. If not, the *Municipal Operetta Theater* at 17 Nagymezö utca in Pest has performances of Kálmán, Lehár, Romberg, and other great musicians whose works need no translation. The *Main Puppet Theater,* at Népköztársaság út 69, presents programs for both children and adults, with everything from the

Three Little Pigs to *The Miraculous Mandarin* for children and revues and satires for adults. The *Budapest Grand Circus* is at Állatkerti körút 7.

For tickets and more detailed information see the current *Coming Events in Budapest,* contact Ibusz (see above), or call the *Central Booking Agency for Theaters,* at 18 Népköztársaság út (phone: 12-00-00).

 MUSIC: Budapest has a rich musical life; this city of Bartók and Kodály has two opera houses, several symphony orchestras, and a great many chamber groups. The *Hungarian State Opera House,* at Népköztársaság út 22, and the *Erkel Theater,* at Köztársaság tér 30, offer operas and ballets. Concerts are given at the *Academy of Music* at Liszt Ferenc tér 8. The Matthias Church also has concerts.

In the summer, the music goes outdoors to Margaret Island. For tickets and information contact Ibusz or the Central Booking Agency (see *Theater*).

 NIGHTCLUBS AND NIGHTLIFE: Though much more lively than that of other Eastern European cities, Budapest's nightlife is somewhat limited. There are great cabarets in such hotel spots as the *Bellevue* in the *Duna Inter-Continental* and the *Troubadour* in the *Budapest Hilton* (see *Checking In*). Others worth a visit are the *Maxim,* Akácta utca 3; *Moulin Rouge,* Nagymezö utca 17; *Casanova,* Batthyány tér 4; and the *Szép Ilonka* at Fö utca 20, Budapest 1. All stay open until at least 4 AM, most until 5 AM. After that there is always a Turkish bath or a sauna.

For a unique evening out, you might want to see some Hungarian folk dancing. The national dance, the *csárdás,* created in the mid-nineteenth century, is still danced at village weddings and festivities and at the *Folklore Center* at Fehérvári út 47. Also the *Korona Pastry Shop* in the Buda Castle district at Disz tér 16, Budapest 1, has become a popular evening spot for Hungarians and foreign visitors who like poetry, prose, and music. A selection from the best Hungarian contemporary and classical literature, is occasionally presented in foreign languages.

 SINS: It's gluttony, of course — those fabulous pastries at places like *Vörösmarty* and *Korona.* Sample them, compare them, wash them down with strong coffee, and then have some more. There's *dobos torta,* a cake of many layers and many fillings; just plain strudel *(rétes)* filled with fruit, nuts, cheese, or poppy seeds; the *Indiáner,* a light pastry filled with fresh whipped cream and glazed with chocolate; and so many others.

BEST IN TOWN

 CHECKING IN: Although new hotels are constantly being built, there is often a shortage of hotel rooms in Budapest, especially during the summer. It is advisable to make reservations in advance, either through your travel agent or Ibusz (see *Sources and Resources*).

Hotel prices in Budapest, however, are quite reasonable in comparison with those of other European cities. We have listed as expensive hotels that charge from $70 to $85 and up for a double; $45 to $65 as moderate; and $20 to $40 as inexpensive. Note that Ibusz rents rooms in private homes (usually with shared bath) from $12 per day.

Budapest Hilton – This 323-room hotel sits on Castle Hill in Buda, next to historic Fishermen's Bastion overlooking the Danube, adjacent to the Matthias Church. The hotel includes ruins of a thirteenth-century church of the Dominican Order and a Jesuit monastery. A walkway with a glass wall allows guests to see the restored cloisters. The hotel has a restaurant called *Halászbástya* (see *Eating Out*); a coffee shop with rustic decor; a two-level espresso bar with an outdoor terrace; the *Troubadour Dancing Bar,* which is a riot of purple with a false-chain ceiling imitating the armors of medieval knights; and the *Codex Bar,* which occupies the site of the country's first print shop, opened in the fifteenth century. Hess András tér 1–3 (phone: 16-01-15). Expensive.

Duna Inter-Continental – This deluxe 349-room hotel is on the Belgrade Rampart along the Danube in Pest, between the Chain and Elizabeth bridges. It has been one of the grand hotels of Europe since its opening in 1970. It has three restaurants, the peasant-inn-style *Csárda,* the *Rendezvous,* and the *Bellevue.* In addition it offers the *Intermezzo* terrace café and the *Tokaj* wine cellar. Apáczai Csere János utca 4 (phone: 17-51-22). Expensive.

Atrium Hyatt Hotel – The newest in town, this 356-room luxury hotel has a top-floor VIP Regency Club, a swimming pool, and a health club. Its *Old Timer Restaurant* has international cuisine, the *Tokaj* has Hungarian fare and gypsy music, the *Atrium Terrace* is its coffee shop, and the rustic *Clark Brasserie* is very popular for snacks accompanied by draft beer (see *Eating Out*). Roosevelt tér 2 (phone: 38-30-00). Expensive.

Forum Hotel – This attractive 408-room hotel is next to the *Hyatt* and opened at about the same time. It boasts a swimming pool with a great view of Castle Hill, and there's also a health club with a bar. For dining, you can choose between the elegant *Silhouette Restaurant* and the informal *Forum Grill* (open from 6 AM to 2 AM). For dessert — pastries and coffee — stop by the *Viennese Café.* Apáczai Csere János utca 12–14 (phone: 17-80-88). Expensive.

Gellért – This 240-room old-world hotel is on the Buda side of the Danube near Liberation Memorial Park at the foot of Gellért Hill. It has a swimming pool with medicinal waters, a thermal bath, and sun terrace. The hotel is famous for its Magyar (Hungarian) cuisine. It has a restaurant with Gypsy music, espresso bar, cocktail bar, and nightclub. Gellért tér 1 (phone: 46-07-00). Expensive to moderate.

Thermal Hotel Margitsziget – This 340-room luxury spa hotel has health facilities with diagnostic and treatment centers and equipment for hydrotherapy and physiotherapy. It has a swimming pool, solarium, sauna, and fitness rooms and offers special inclusive packages with spa treatments and diet plans. Margaret Island (phone: 11-10-00). Expensive to moderate.

Hotel Buda Penta – Another new hotel in Buda, it's near the Southern Railway Station and Underground Terminal. There are 400 comfortable rooms, a swimming pool and health club, a restaurant, coffee shop, and nightclub. Krisztina körút 41–43 (phone: 25-00-60). Moderate.

Hotel Novotel – There are 324 rooms, a swimming pool, tennis courts, restaurants, and bars. Alkotás utca 63–67 (phone: 86-95-88). Moderate.

Hotel Olympia – Somewhat on the outskirts of town in the residential Buda hills, this is a pleasant hotel with a swimming pool, health club, tennis court, and restaurants. There's also a nightclub with floor shows. Eötvös út 40 (phone: 16-64-56). Inexpensive.

 EATING OUT: The justly celebrated cuisine of Hungary dates from ancient times and can be traced to the dining habits of specific tribes, such as the Voguls, Kalmuks, and Turkomans. Enriching these styles are ingredients from Persia, France, Austria, Greece, Turkey, and Yugoslavia. The most celebrated ingredient, of course, is paprika, the red pepper that comes in different strengths and is used copiously, most notably in *paprikás csirke* (paprika chicken) and in sauces. (Don't worry about paprika dishes being too hot; any restaurant will be glad to spice to your taste.) Various Magyar (Hungarian) dishes have become world famous, particularly goulash *(guylás),* which will not be what you expect if you have eaten it outside Hungary. Here it is a very thick soup with meat (usually beef or pork), onions, sour cream, and paprika. If you like fish, try Hungarian bouillabaisse *(halászlé),* a clear soup made with *fogas* (a unique pike perch caught only in Lake Balaton) or bream, seasoned with onions and many spices including paprika. *Kolozsvári rakott Káposzta,* or layered cabbage, includes eggs and sausage, heaps of sour cream, and crisp pork chops.

Hungarian rye bread is superb, and a biscuit called *pogácsa,* a flaky pastry strewn with bits of crackling pork, is delicious. And of course Hungarian pastries are absolutely fabulous; Budapest is the place to let that diet go. You might start with *rétes* (strudel) or *dobos torta,* the famous many-layered cake — but the sky is the limit. Filled with apricot preserves and *lekvár* (prune preserves), walnuts, hazelnuts, crushed poppy seeds, and chocolate, they are all sinfully delectable.

Hungarian wines are wonderful, especially Tokay, which is often sweet; even better is Egri Bikavér (Bull's Blood), a dry, red wine. Leányka is a delicious white wine.

Hungarians love to linger over small cups of strong coffee called *eszpresszó,* or over *dupla,* which is strong double mocha brew. These are to be had everywhere — in pastry shops, cafés, and the *Mackó* shops whose symbol is a bear cub.

Budapest has over 2,000 restaurants, cafés, pastry shops, wine and beer cellars, and taverns. A few of the highlights are listed below. For a dinner for two with wine, expect to pay $50 to $60 in restaurants listed as expensive; $20 to $30 in those categorized as moderate; and $10 to $20 in inexpensive places.

Hungária – For that big night on the town, the *Hungária* (known as the *New York Café* prior to World War II) wins the laurels. A Budapest institution since 1894, it's a palatial establishment in every respect. The opulent art nouveau decor, gilt columns, frosted glass globes, and glittering mirrors will probably remind you more of an opera house or a royal palace than a restaurant. The *Hungária* is not only a top restaurant, but a coffee house, café, and nightclub. Among its specialties are *kengurufarokleves* (kangaroo-tail soup), *crêpes à la Hortobágy* (crêpes stuffed with meat and served with a paprika sauce), *sertésborda magyarovári módra* (pork cutlet with mushrooms, ham, and cheese), and a dessert called *omlette surprise* (parfait in sponge cake baked in a froth of egg white). 7, Lenin Körút 9 (phone: 22-38-49). Expensive.

Gundel – Perhaps the most famous chef in Budapest's history was Gundel, and his restaurant is still the center of grand style in Budapest. If the gorgeous turn-of-the-century atmosphere doesn't attract you, come for one reason only — the crêpe filled with hazelnuts and cream, over which is poured a bittersweet chocolate sauce. Your mouth throws a party for your whole body. Állatkerti út 2 (phone: 22-10-02). Expensive.

Alabárdos – This restaurant is located in one of the most beautiful Gothic buildings in the old royal palace district. Try the house specialty, meat flambé served with great ceremony on a sword. 1, Országház utca 2 (phone: 16-08-28). Expensive.

Mátyás Pince – Tourists are not the only people drawn to this romantic beer cellar in central Pest where the real commodities are copious quantities of wine and even richer servings of Gypsy music and old Budapest spirit. If you actually get hungry, its fish dishes are well known around the city. Március 15 (phone: 18-06-08). Moderate.

Ménes Csárda – This small, cozy establishment with a folk art decor became an instant hit after it opened in 1982. It serves unusual Hungarian specialties — often prepared at your table — in attractive ceramic dishes made for the restaurant by an artist. Try the stuffed filet of pork with *tápióbicskei hozzávaló* and the cherry or cottage cheese *(túrós)* strudel. Good, light wines are available. While you dine, a Gypsy cimbal player performs. Apáczai Csere János utca 15 (phone: 17-08-03). Expensive.

Halászbástya – This restaurant is part of the *Hilton* hotel, in the vaults of the Fisherman's Bastion (see *Special Places*). It has a fabulous view of the Parliament and town, and good Gypsy music. Halászbástya (phone: 16-15-33). Expensive.

Vadrózsa – In a private villa with a shady garden, this restaurant features charcoal-broiled specialties like goose liver and perch pike, and other tempting dishes. Very friendly service. Pentelei Molnár utca 15 (phone: 35-11-18). Expensive to moderate.

100-éves – The restaurant is actually 50 years older than the 100 years its name indicates. In a lovely baroque town palace in the center of the city, its atmosphere is intimate and the food enjoyable. Service can be slow at lunchtime when it's very crowded. Pesti Barnabás utca 2 (phone: 18-36-08). Moderate.

Régi Országház – This is an old inn on the north side of the castle in Buda. It offers many rooms with different decors, a wine cellar, Gypsy music, and jazz. 1, Országház út 17 (phone: 16-02-25). Moderate.

Pilvax – This old café-restaurant in the heart of the old inner city of Pest is noted for its chicken broth, pastries, and cakes. Gypsy music accompanies the meal. 5, Pilvax Köz 1. Moderate to inexpensive.

Apostolok – Recently renovated, this old brasserie is centrally located and very popular, especially for lunch. Kigyó utca (phone: 18-37-04). Moderate to inexpensive.

Clark Söröző – Stop here for a glass of beer or wine and a light meal, such as a bowl of mushroom soup *(vargánya leves)*. The strudel *(káposztás rétes)* is a must. Apáczai Csere János utca 15 (phone: 17-08-03). Inexpensive.

Pest-Buda – This restaurant has been operating in the same building on Castle Hill since 1880. All the houses in this area are protected historic buildings and represent the architecture of seven centuries. Though, sadly, a good number of the medieval houses in the neighborhood were almost destroyed during World War II, all have been carefully restored. When it was first opened, the *Pest-Buda* had a local carriage trade and attracted visitors from as far away as Vienna. It is not suited for big functions or balls, but rather is a place for family suppers, with romantic, vaulted dining rooms and period furnishings. Try the *Wiener schnitzel* and *pommes frites*. 1, Fortuna utca 3 (phone: 36-07-68). Inexpensive.

Citadella – This restaurant is located within the ancient fortress walls built by the Hapsburgs to dominate Budapest. From the terrace you can enjoy their panoramic view of the city. During the summer in the large courtyard, which was formerly a prisoners' exercise area, there are open-fire dinners of goulash, bacon, and steaks. 11 Gellérthegy (phone: 45-13-62). Inexpensive.

COPENHAGEN

In the early mornings of 1848 in Copenhagen's old waterfront district, Nyhavn, a tall, top-hatted figure could often be seen emerging from the elegant portals of number 67B. A few books underneath his arm, the figure would walk in the direction of the docks, with the apparent intention of inspecting the wooden sailing ships moored there. However, he had other things on his mind.

The figure was Hans Christian Andersen, Denmark's beloved raconteur of fairy tales and the country's most famous citizen. A poor shoemaker's son who allegorized the remarkable tale of his own life in *The Ugly Duckling,* Andersen often found inspiration during these morning walks around Nyhavn, where he lived for some 20 years. The stately old merchants' townhouses, the shabby sailors' bars, the tattoo parlors, and all the other assorted arcana of dockside life — so much of which is the same today — must have provided good soil for his fertile imagination. Once, when questioned about his literary methods, he replied, "It came without incentive — while I was walking on the street the thought came to me."

Thus it is no surprise to discover that Andersen's first literary success, a fantastic tale in the E. T. A. Hoffmann tradition, bore the title, *A Walk from Holmen's Canal to the East Point of the Island of Amager in the Years 1828 and 1829.*

During that same period, a mere ten blocks away from Andersen, one might find that dour theologian and progenitor of existentialism, Søren Kierkegaard, out taking *his* morning constitutional. Kierkegaard and Andersen were literary contemporaries, and although they had about as much in common as Hamlet and Victor Borge, their writings bear witness to the fact that they both loved their walks in Copenhagen.

The largest city in Scandinavia, with a population of 1.4 million, Copenhagen is situated on the northeastern shore of Zealand, the largest of Denmark's approximately 500 islands. Here the Danes have somehow managed to synthesize the urban sophistication of a large Continental city with the friendly charm of a small village. And Copenhagen remains a pedestrian's paradise. The famed walking street Strøget is still the backbone of the city, linking Kongens Nytorv, the largest square in the harbor, with Rådhuspladsen, the largest square in the downtown area. You can find just about anything you could want on Strøget — with its modern department stores, tiny boutiques, ice cream stands, bars, theaters, sex shops, and infinite opportunities for idle conversation — just about anything, that is, except cars and automotive pollution.

This congenial and idyllic atmosphere might lead the casual observer to believe that Copenhagen has been lucky enough to occupy some turgid backwater of history, far from the dynamic fury of world events. On the contrary, Copenhagen has had a rich and dramatic history, a history of which the Danes are justly proud. Because of its strategic location on the Øresund, a narrow seaway connecting the North and the Baltic seas, Copenhagen has been besieged by the Swedes, leveled by the English, and occupied by the Germans.

According to Danish tradition, Copenhagen (literally, "the merchants' harbor") was founded in 1167 by a Bishop Absalon during the reign of Valdemar the Great. Absalon built a fortress on the island of Slotsholmen to protect the port, and the ruins of this fortress are still visible in the cellars of the parliament building Christiansborg.

In 1416, King Erik of Pomerania made Copenhagen the capital of Denmark, but it was not until the reign of Christian IV (1588–1648) and the Danish Renaissance that Copenhagen acquired some of the features one associates with it today. Christian IV was a great builder, and many of his contributions still stand — the Stock Exchange, Rosenborg Palace, the Round Tower, Kongens Have Park, and the districts of Nyboder and Christianshavn.

Disaster struck Copenhagen during the following century: The great fire of 1728 destroyed two-fifths of the houses in the city. Its construction materials of wood and straw thatch were particularly combustible, and the narrow streets and alleys made fire-fighting all but impossible. A second great fire in 1795 reduced another fifth of the city to ashes.

Efforts at reconstruction were delayed by war. In 1801, the Danes found themselves confronted by a large English fleet under the command of Lord Nelson. Legend has it that the Danes hoisted a cease-fire flag after a heavy bombardment, whereupon Nelson raised his telescope to his blind eye and ordered the attack intensified. The subsequent Danish resistance was a high-water mark in the patriotic lore of Copenhagen. The English retired, only to send a larger fleet in 1807 to finish the job. A fierce rocket assault left most of Copenhagen in flames, and the city capitulated — for the first time in modern history.

Displaying their remarkable recuperative powers, the Danes quickly rebuilt Copenhagen. The Danish golden age of the mid-nineteenth century followed, a time in which social progress, as evidenced by the parliamentary constitution of 1849, was accompanied by a flourishing of the arts. Many of the buildings one sees today are remnants of the Danish golden age. Fittingly, the old ramparts were removed during this era and replaced with a lush and verdant belt of parks.

Denmark lost its border provinces to Prussia in a war in 1864 but managed to steer clear of any other major conflicts until the 5-year German occupation during World War II. From April 9, 1940, to May 5, 1945, the heroic resistance of the Danish people to the Nazis was nearly unanimous. When the Danish merchant fleet was ordered by the Germans to make for a neutral port at the time of the occupation, more than 90% of the seamen (about 5,000 men) chose to answer the appeal of London radio to sail to an Allied port and join the war. Of the 5,000, 600 died and 60% of the ships were sunk. Back

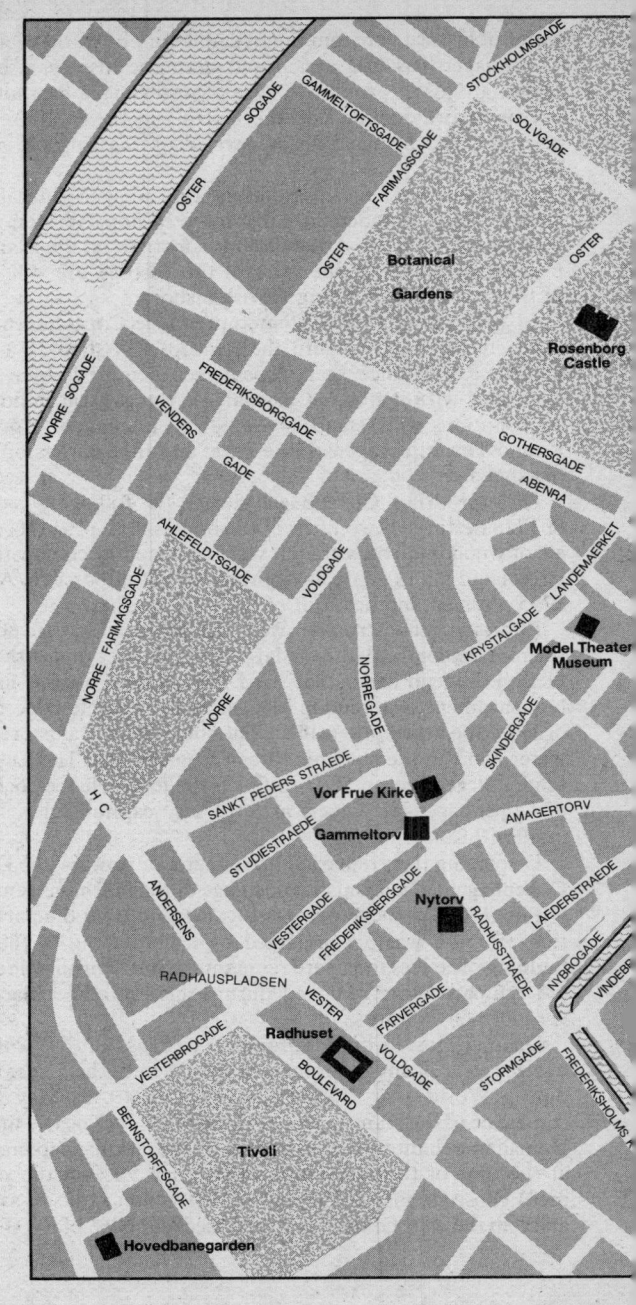

COPENHAGEN

VOLDGADE

DELFINGADE

ELSDYRSGADE

SUENSONSGADE

GRØNNINGEN

HAREGADE

RIGENSGADE

ESPLANADEN

FREDERICIAGADE

ADELGADE

Museum of
Decorative Art

BORGERGADE

KRONPRINSESSEGADE

DRONNINGENS TVAERGADE

STORE KONGENSGADE

BREDGADE

Amalienborg
Castle

ADELGADE

BORGERGEADE

AMALIENGADE

NY ØSTERGADE

BREMERHOLM

PILESTRAEDE

KONGENS
NYTORV

NYHAVN

NYHAVN

ØSTERGADE

HERLUF TROLLES GADE

KØBMAGERGADE

NIKOLAJGADE

HEIBERGSGADE

PEDER

ADMIRALGADE

KAN

HOLBERGSGADE

SKRAMS

VED STRANDEN

HOLMENS

NIELS JUELS GADE

HAVNEGADE

Thorvaldsen
Museum

TORDENSKJOLDGADE

Christiansborg
Castle

KNIPPELS BRO

BRYGGE

CHRISTIANS

INDERHAVNEN

in Copenhagen, the underground press flourished and isolated incidents of resistance were numerous, reaching a climax on August 29, 1943, when the Danish government unanimously and unqualifiedly said "no" to German ultimatums. Open resistance began: sabotage by underground groups, arms supplies, intelligence activities, and, most dramatically, escape routes for Jews and other war victims. About 7,000 persons were successfully evacuated to Sweden, and only 450 arrested and taken to Germany. The Danes paid a price for their courageous actions: Their resistance was met with violent Nazi countermeasures such as arrests, deportations, executions, and random shootings. Yet the Danes remained so active in resisting Hitler that Denmark was generally recognized as a de facto ally.

Postwar Copenhagen is a unique blend of historical charm and modern efficiency. Enlightened social reform and respect for aesthetic and sentimental values make Copenhagen one of the most delightful cities in Europe. The brutal new skyscrapers that loom over the horizon of many European cities have been exiled to the suburbs here, and one is hard pressed to find any symptoms of urban blight.

Denmark is a highly advanced country politically and socially. Its government, which resembles England's, is a constitutional monarchy with Queen Margrethe II on the throne and a parliament of 179 members called the Folketing. Widely known as a nation that provides for its citizens, Denmark has a comprehensive social security system and national health insurance. Its standard of living ranks among the highest in the world, as does its cost of living, which in 1980 was higher than that of the US or West Germany. In recent years, Denmark has had a serious deficit in its balance of payments, due in large part to dependence on foreign oil. This deficit was accompanied by high unemployment and inflation of about 10%. In an effort to deal with these problems, the government instituted wage and price controls.

Aside from its political prominence as the capital of Denmark, Copenhagen is also the site of a major shipyard and design center, and is the home of the Carlsberg and Tuborg breweries, which produce one of Denmark's leading exports — beer.

The Danish people enjoy a reputation for being masters of recreational pursuits; in fact, Copenhagen is known among more reserved Scandinavians as a den of sex, drugs, and rock 'n' roll — in short, a Valhalla of vice. This reputation is not entirely unjustified, as Copenhagen is a place to have a good time, sinful or otherwise.

Ever since the Vikings left their women responsible for the farms when they went out on plundering raids, Danes have had an unusually liberal attitude toward sex. In 1967, Denmark became the first country in the world to abolish all restrictions on the sale of pornographic literature to adults. After an initial boom, the sales of pornography actually went down, as did the number of sex crimes. Male tourists who expect Danish women to be especially promiscuous may be disappointed; there is probably no great difference in promiscuity from country to country.

Whatever your pleasure, whether it be pornography or the Royal Danish Ballet, you will find much to enjoy in Copenhagen. A statue of the town's symbol, the *Little Mermaid,* rises green and sleek from the waterfront to greet all visitors. Commissioned by Carlsberg magnate Carl Jacobsen in 1913, the statue was completed in 1915 and has survived the repeated humiliations of having been soaked in red paint, then in blue paint, and even decapitated. The *Mermaid* was erected by the Danes to express their gratitude to Hans Christian Andersen for his love of fantasy and of his fellow man.

In Andersen's tale, a mermaid falls hopelessly in love with a mortal prince who, alas, loves another. Begging to have feet so she can walk like a human, the mermaid suffers great physical pain whenever she takes a step as well as emotional anguish when she finds that her prince is otherwise inclined. In the end she must pay the penalty of dissolving into an incorporeal spirit whose function is to help mortals navigate in perilous waters.

The spirits of the mermaid, the snow queen, the nightingale, and the ugly duckling seem to haunt the picture-book streets of the Copenhagen that Hans Christian Andersen loved so dearly. And no wonder. Even today, in spite of its dominant role as Denmark's political and commercial center, Copenhagen's skyline is still much the same as it was in his day — a fairy-tale conglomeration of ancient church steeples, spiraling golden towers, massive domes, and staircased gables.

COPENHAGEN AT-A-GLANCE

SEEING THE CITY: There are no World Trade Centers or Eiffel Towers in Copenhagen, but a far more authentic alternative exists in the Round Tower. Built in 1642 by the monarch Christian IV as an observatory, it offers a panorama of the spires and steeples of the old town of Copenhagen. Peter the Great of Russia reportedly drove a carriage containing the Czarina Catherine to the top of the Round Tower in the eighteenth century, but today's visitors will unfortunately have to climb the 687-foot spiral walkway. Be advised, however, that the observatory on the roof is open only in clear weather. Open daily for a small fee, the Round Tower (Rundetårn) is on Købmagergade.

Several of Copenhagen's churches also provide views of the city, including the bizarre baroque tower of Vor Frelsers Kirke on Prinsessegade, which is also open to visitors. Here the spiral stairway is on the outside of the tower, so bring a sweater if it's chilly.

SPECIAL PLACES: Copenhagen is a pedestrian's paradise, and it is relatively easy to get oriented after locating Strøget, the walking street. The medieval street plan of the old town is irregular, however, and once you leave the downtown area and familiar landmarks, it is possible to get lost. Danes are generally very helpful, and, as nearly everyone seems to speak English, it is very difficult to get hopelessly lost.

DOWNTOWN

Slotsholmen Island and Christiansborg Castle – In the central part of Copenhagen it is possible to visit the island where Absalon built his fortress in 1167, founding the city. The best way to get there is to walk from Rådhuspladsen down Vester Voldgade, left on Stormgade, and across the bridge leading into Porthusgade, where you will be confronted with Thorvaldsen's Museum to your left and Christiansborg Castle to your right. Thorvaldsen was the most famous Danish sculptor; in 1838 he donated all of his work to the city of his birth, and in turn, the city built the museum to house his variations on classical themes (museum closed Tuesdays in winter).

Christiansborg was completed in 1740, burned in 1794, and then rebuilt in new classical style in 1828 by the architect C. F. Hansen. When this castle burned down in 1884, the present castle was built by Thorvald Jorgenson and features a mixed baroque rococo design. Closed Mondays all year and Saturdays in winter.

Copenhagen's Cathedral (Vor Frue Kirke) – Using Rådhuspladsen as a starting point, you reach the old section of Copenhagen by taking a left down Vester Voldgade and then taking a right on Studiestraede. Up ahead you will see Vor Frue Kirke, Copenhagen's neoclassic cathedral, which was completed in 1829. The cathedral is open to visitors daily.

Gammeltorv – If you take a right on Nørrebrogade in front of the cathedral, you will enter the oldest part of the city — the marketplace of Gammeltorv, which the fortress on Slotsholmen was built to defend in 1167. In addition to being the first marketplace in Copenhagen, Gammeltorv has been the site of jousting tournaments and public executions and is still a center for social activity. Nytorv was added in 1606 as an extension of Gammeltorv, and a statue at the corner of Nytorv and Frederiksberggade identifies Nytorv as the birthplace of Søren Kierkegaard as well as the place where he spent most of his life.

Model Theater Museum (Dukketeatermuseet) – Located at the end of Skindergade, the street that runs through the Latin Quarter, Copenhagen's university area, this museum houses a historical collection of toy theaters. Open daily. Købmagergade 52.

Botanical Gardens (Botanisk Have) – This includes a park and greenhouses that grow tropical and subtropical plants. Open daily. Entrance at Gothersgade and Sø lvgade. Gothersgade 128.

Rosenborg Castle (Rosenborg Slot) – This Renaissance castle was built by Christian IV in 1603–33. Its fine interiors contain the crown jewels and treasures of the Danish royal family from the fifteenth to the nineteenth century. Open daily May until late October; Tuesdays and Fridays only in winter. Øster Voldgade 4A.

Amalienborg Castle – The residence of the Danish royal family since 1794. Amalienborg is another spectacular example of Danish rococo, with four identical palaces perfectly situated against the harbor background. Unfortunately, Amalienborg can only be seen from the outside.

In the basement there is a museum with collections of nineteenth-century royal dress, but it is closed temporarily for repairs.

The Harbor – The harbor area, or Nyhavn, favorite haunt for sailors from around the world and home of Hans Christian Andersen for many years, is a fascinating area where you can run into all manner of characters ranging from sleek fashion models walking their Afghan hounds to the proverbial drunken sailors who may have just been decorated at Tattoo Jack's. For an interesting tour, start at the Royal Danish Theater at Kongens Nytorv, then follow the left-hand side of Nyhavn Canal toward the water. En route you can look at the sturdy fishing boats and sailing ships. The right-hand side of Nyhavn, also known as the Charlottenborg side, has been an elegant residential area for many years. It was here, in number 67, that Andersen lived between 1845 and 1864 and wrote his famous fairy tales. In recent years, a number of good, small restaurants have emerged on both sides of Nyhavn; the sailors' bars here — *Cap Horn,* the *Brooklyn,* and others — may seem exotic, but are generally no bargain, and seem to survive by enticing inebriated Swedes on their way to the ferry back to Sweden.

Museum of Decorative Art (Kunstindustrimuseet) – Founded in 1890, the museum contains European and Oriental applied art from the Middle Ages to modern times, including a fine collection of contemporary decorative art. Open from 1 to 4 PM daily except Mondays. Bredgade 68.

Resistance Museum (Frihedsmuseet) – This museum is located in Churchill

COPENHAGEN / At-a-Glance 331

Park just outside the entrance to Kastellet, Copenhagen's old harbor fortifications that are open to the public between 6 AM and 10 PM. The Frihedsmuseet contains relics from the resistance movement during the German occupation of 1940–45. Open daily except Mondays. Churchill Park at Langelinie.

Langelinie Pavilion and Promenade – One of the loveliest spots in Copenhagen is just opposite the citadel, overlooking the harbor — the Langelinie *Pavilion* and Promenade. The *Pavilion* is an elegant restaurant where you can gaze at the moonlit waters and dine and dance until the wee hours. Should you want a breath of fresh air, you can always suggest a walk along the promenade to take a look at *Den Lille Havfrue,* or the *Little Mermaid,* erected in 1913 thanks to a grant from Carlsberg Brewery magnate Carl Jacobsen.

Carlsberg Brewery – In case you're wondering how they make the stuff that everybody seems to be drinking, you will be happy to learn that guests are welcome at the Carlsberg Brewery, a 20-minute walk from Rådhuspladsen, or take the No. 6 bus. Danes take their beer as seriously as the Irish take Guinness stout, and be advised that Elephant Beer, the world-famous Danish brew by Carlsberg, is about twice as strong as regular American beer (or even the Elephant Beer marketed in the US); closed weekends. Ny Carlsbergvej 140 (phone: 21-12-21, extension 1312).

Tuborg Brewery – Tuborg, which can be reached by taking bus 1, also welcomes visitors on weekdays. Strandvejen 54 (phone: 29-33-11, extension 2212).

Tivoli – On the south side of Rådhuspladsen you will find the fabled Tivoli, Copenhagen's favorite summer recreation facility. Built in 1843 on top of old city ramparts, Tivoli is a dazzling hybrid of gardens (160,000 flowers), lakes, theaters, dance halls, and restaurants, illuminated at night by over 100,000 colored lights. Whether you are looking for a first-class restaurant such as *Belle Terasse* or *Divan I and II* or the tawdry company of a one-armed bandit, Tivoli has it all.

The season starts on May 1 and runs through the third Sunday in September, and the hours are 10 AM to midnight daily. Internationally known artists perform on an outdoor stage every night. The concert hall features nightly concerts with orchestras, conductors, and soloists, often free of charge. Other entertainment includes the Tivoli Boy Guard marching band, a pantomime theater, children's theater, promenade concerts every night around the gardens, and amusement park facilities. Especially recommended are the fireworks at 11:45 PM Wednesdays, and 11:15 PM on weekends. Rådhuspladsen.

Christiania – The dreams of the 1960s may have died sometime in the early 70s, and the media would have us believe that the Age of Love has become the Age of Punk; however, the news has not yet reached Copenhagen. Christiania, a sprawling section of Copenhagen that covers about ten square blocks in the Christianshavn district, can easily be found by walking toward the towering golden spire of the aforementioned Vor Frelser Kirke. The casual visitor will be assaulted by a helter-skelter patchwork of theatrical spectacles, conceptual art pieces, strung-out hippies, stray children and dogs, psychedelic paintings, and, yes, whatever you want to smoke, if such is your bent. Although this community has been the subject of hot debate in Copenhagen, its very existence is symptomatic of the Danes' civic tolerance.

OUT OF THE CITY

Dragør – Dragør is an enchanting fishing village south of Copenhagen that dates from the sixteenth century and is still in vintage condition. Its streets are paved with cobblestones, and 65 of its quaint, old, red-roofed houses are protected historical sites. On the tip of the island of Amager, Dragør is about a 30-minute ride from Rådhuspladsen on buses No. 30 or 33, and worth the trip if you want to see a village straight from the pages of Hans Christian Andersen.

The oldest house in the village is the home of the *Dragør Museum,* open daily in summer only, except Mondays. There is a small admission charge. There are also ferry connections from Dragør to the town of Limhamn in Sweden, and the boat is the most pleasant way to get there.

Open-Air Museum (Frilandsmuseet) – This is a half-hour ride outside of the city on the No. 84 or No. 384 bus, and is an elaborate tribute to the joys of being down on the farm in the Danish countryside. (Just more proof that the Danes are incurable romantics.) Old houses from the various regions of Denmark have been dismantled and moved here, piece by piece, and efforts have even been made to recreate the ecological environment of each kind of farm. Interiors have also been recreated, and during the summer the visitor can watch sheep being sheared, wool being carded, garments being spun, and other examples of agrarian toil. There is a modern restaurant, but if you have not had your fill of pastoral splendor, there are also picnic tables and benches. The Open-Air Museum is open all year, though only weekends in winter. (A winter visit will make it easy for you to understand why so many Danes live in Copenhagen.) Closed on Mondays, with folk dancing on weekends during the summer; open weekends only in winter. Small admission fee. Kongevejen 100, Sorgenfri, Kgs. Lyngby.

Louisiana Modern Art Museum – In the town of Humlebaek, 22 miles (about 35 km) north of Copenhagen, pleasantly situated in a park overlooking the sea, Louisiana is a museum that has the most important collection of modern Danish art in Europe. Originally the private collection of art patron Knud W. Jensen, Louisiana was opened to the public in 1958. If you like well-displayed modern art, and if you are planning to go to Helsingør, stop en route at Humlebaek and see Louisiana. Open daily. Admission fee for adults. Gammel Strandvej 13, Humlebaek.

Roskilde – About 19 miles (30 km) west of Copenhagen is an ancient city that was the capital of Denmark until 1445. The site of the first Danish church (a short-lived wooden affair erected by Harald Bluetooth in 960), Roskilde is a treasure trove of Viking artifacts and other items of archaeological interest. Roskilde Cathedral was built in the 1170s by Bishop Absalon on top of Harald's church, and aside from being the first Gothic cathedral in Denmark, it is the burial place of 38 Danish kings and queens. The tour in the cathedral will lead you from one spectacular marble sarcophagus to another — if that's your cup of tea. The cathedral, or Domkirke, is open daily for a small admission fee. The church is, of course, closed to visitors during religious services (phone: 02-35-27-00).

The pièce de résistance of Roskilde, however, is a relic of heathen culture, the Viking Ship Museum (Vikingeskibshallen) — a museum containing five reconstructed Viking ships that had been sunk off Roskilde around 1000 AD. Aside from this magnificent bit of salvage work, the museum offers detailed descriptions of Viking seafaring techniques and life on board ship. When seeing the boats, it is somewhat awe inspiring to remember that they sailed those things across the Atlantic to Greenland and New-foundland. The museum is open daily. Inquiries may be addressed to Viking Ship Museum, 4000 Roskilde (phone: 35-65-55).

Oldtidsbyen – In Lejre, 7½ miles (about 12 km) west of Roskilde, the Oldtidsbyen is a reconstruction of an old Iron Age village, not to be missed if you are interested in archaeology. Run by the Historical Archaeological Experimental Center, the Old-tidsbyen was created with grants from the Carlsberg Foundation and the government for the purpose of studying Iron Age life. The village is open daily May through September for a small admission fee.

Bornholm – Should the summer weather be extremely warm or should you just be suffering from a stiff dose of the urban blues, why not follow the example of the Danes and beat a retreat to Bornholm, a beautiful island in the Baltic between Denmark and Sweden. A 1-night ferry trip from Copenhagen, Bornholm is the secret summer para-dise for the nature-loving Swedes and Danes, and offers over 200 Viking burial mounds, 40 rune stones, and four round churches from the early Middle Ages. There are also several spectacular beaches. If interested, write to the Bornholm Tourist Office, Havnen, DK-3700 Rønne (phone: 03-95-08-10).

■**EXTRA SPECIAL:** About a 45-minute train ride north of Copenhagen lies the site of Hamlet's famous castle, Helsingør (Elsinore). In case you had been looking forward to roaming the ramparts in search of the ghost, you may be disappointed to learn that the present castle, Kronborg, is not the original but was built in the sixteenth and seventeenth centuries. The Danes insist that Hamlet did exist, however, and refer the curious to the medieval Danish historian Saxo Grammaticus's epic work, *Gesta Danorum,* for further details. The best thing about the castle is the magnificent view of the sound from the ramparts. Occasionally, visiting theatrical groups perform *Hamlet* in the courtyard.

SOURCES AND RESOURCES

For general information, brochures, and maps, contact the Danish National Tourist Office, 75 Rockefeller Plaza, New York, NY 10019 (phone: 212-582-2802). In Copenhagen, contact the Danish Tourist Board, H. C. Andersens Blvd. 22, 1553 Copenhagen V, at the Tivoli entrance by Town Hall (phone: 11-14-15); or the Tourist Association of Copenhagen, in the Magasin du Nord department store, Kongens Nytorv (phone: 11-44-33).

For Local Coverage – The Copenhagen Tourist Office should be able to keep you abreast of events of interest. *Copenhagen This Week,* available at hotels and the tourist offices, is also helpful. Unfortunately, there are no English-language newspapers in Copenhagen. If you miss English, buy the traveler's daily blessing, the *International Herald Tribune* (about 75¢), or listen to the 8:15 AM English news on Radio Denmark.

For Food – As far as food is concerned, a detailed list of restaurants is available, free of charge, from the Danish Tourist Office.

CLIMATE AND CLOTHES: Thanks to the Gulf Stream, Denmark has a rather mild, if somewhat undramatic, climate. The average daytime temperature from June to August is 70°F (20°C). Due to its northerly latitude, Copenhagen gets sunshine long into the evenings during the summer months, but once the sun goes down, it does get chilly, so bring sweaters. In recent years there has also been a good deal of rain and fog in the summer, so bring raincoats as well. The winters have much less sun but have an average temperature just above 32°F (0°C) and snow is infrequent. Hence you will not need Arctic gear, only warm winter clothes.

As far as dress is concerned, the Danes do not stand on ceremony, and generally, informal attire is acceptable in most theaters and restaurants. Men should bring a tie and jacket if they are planning to dine at the more exclusive restaurants.

GETTING AROUND: Bus – As mentioned previously, Copenhagen is small enough to be seen on foot but the bus system offers a cheap and efficient alternative if your feet are weary from the cobblestones. The city bus system is excellent. Local buses and S-trains start running at 5 AM (6 on Sundays), and the last regular departures from downtown are at about 1 AM. All buses and railways in Copenhagen and environs are in a collective fare system, meaning that all tickets and discount cards are good for a full hour's travel within defined zones.

The bus driver will ask you where you are going, and charge you accordingly. You can purchase special tourist tickets at your hotel or at the train station. When you board the bus with a ticket, you must stamp your ticket or discount card yourself by running it through the automatic machine at the front of the bus; when taking the train, you will see the machine on the platform. This is important, as an invalid or unstamped ticket can cost you up to $15, and they are checked now and again.

Taxi – Taxis are expensive but fast, and can be hailed on the streets. They are unoccupied when the green light is on, and the tip is included in the fare. If you want to order a taxi, call 35-35-35 or 35-14-20.

Car Rental – To rent a car, you must be at least over 20, although some firms require 25. Reputable companies include *Avis,* Kampmannsgade 1 (phone: 15-22-99), *Hertz,* Hammerichsgade 1 (phone: 12-77-00), *Europcar,* Gammel Kongevej 70 (phone: 24-66-77), and *Inter Rent* at Jernbanegade 6 (phone: 11-62-00).

Bicycle – If you want your own means of transport, why not follow the example of the Danes and get a bicycle? Nearly all streets have separate lanes for bicycle traffic, and except for the worst winter months, it is often easier to ride a bicycle than drive a car on Copenhagen's narrow streets. Bicycles can be rented at *Københavns Cykelbørs,* Gothersgade 159 (phone: 14-07-17), for $3 a day with a deposit of $5 or $10.

 MUSEUMS: In addition to the museums mentioned in *Special Places,* Copenhagen boasts a number of well-organized museums, the most notable of which are:

The Stock Exchange (Børsen), built in 1624, Børsgade.

The Danish Film Museum (Det Danske Filmmuseum), Store Søndervoldstraede.

The Geological Museum (Geologisk Museum), Øster Voldgade 7.

The New Carlsberg Glyptotek, Egyptian, Greek, Etruscan, and Roman art; also nineteenth-century French and Danish works, Dantes Plads.

The National Museum (Nationalmuseet), prehistoric Denmark from the Ice Age to the Vikings, 12 Frederiksholms Kanal.

Royal Museum of Fine Arts (Statens Museum for Kunst), Danish and European works of art, including a Matisse collection, Solvgade at Oster Voldgade.

Copenhagen's City Museum and the Søren Kierkegaard Collection (Københavns Bymuseum og Søren Kierkegaard-Samlingen), the city's 800 years in pictures and mementos; also Søren Kierkegaard curios, Vesterbrogade 59.

Toy Museum (Legetøjsmuseet), Teglgårdstraede 13.

Zoological Museum, Universitetsparken 15.

 SHOPPING: With all the walking streets, Copenhagen is ideal for the consumer. You should bear in mind that the 22% sales tax in Denmark is included in the price. You can avoid this tax by having the goods sent to you in the US. Make a note of the store's name and address, keep your receipt, and insure all goods against damage.

Denmark is world famous for beautifully designed wares for the home — furniture, of course; sterling silver by *Georg Jensen* and others; and porcelain by *Bing & Grøndahl,* and *Royal Copenhagen.* Also, Copenhagen is northern Europe's main fur trading center. It might be wise to check the prices of these items before you leave home, as savings may not be substantial in Denmark.

You might wish to stroll down Strøget, the most famous of the city's shopping streets, three-quarters of a mile in length, which is made up of five interconnecting streets, none of them named Strøget. From Rådhuspladsen the names are Frederiksberggade, Nygade, Vimmelskaftet, Amagertorv, and Østergade. This stretch abounds in department stores and specialty shops. And take a look at the side streets as well.

Other walking streets are Fiolstraede and Købmagergade in the old Latin Quarter, once the student quarter and now more cosmopolitan, the place to go for antiques and rare books as well as boutiques and specialty shops.

A. C. Bang – Furs. Ostergade 27.

Bing & Grøndahl – World-famous porcelain. Amagertorv 4.

Birger Christensen – Also for furs. Ostergade 38.

C. Danel – Furniture. Gammel Kongevej 124.

Den Kongelige Porcelainsfabrik – Royal Copenhagen Porcelain Factory, next door to Bing & Grøndahl. Amagertorv 6.

Den Permanente – Permanent exhibit of Danish arts and crafts has 260 member craftsmen. Vesterbrogade 8.

Hans Hansen Silver – Similar quality and lower prices than *Georg Jensen.* Amagertorv 16.

Illum – Large department store with selections of all typical Danish wares; also a fine restaurant. Østergade 52.

Illums Bolighus – World-renowned furnishings center of modern design. Amagertorv 10.

Georg Jensen Silver – Needs no introduction. Østergade 40.

Magasin du Nord – Largest and best-known department store; every variety of Danish merchandise well displayed. Kongens Nytorv 13.

A. Michelsen – High-quality silver. Bredgade 11.

Rosenthal Studio Haus A/S – Porcelain. Frederiksberggade 21.

 SPECIAL EVENTS: The advent of spring in Copenhagen is heralded by the *Bakken,* a festive amusement park located in the Deer Park north of Copenhagen (mid-April) and in Tivoli (May 1). The *Benneweis Circus*, Jernbanegade (phone: 14-21-92), begins its season on or about April 1. Each summer Copenhagen holds an international festival in June. The theme alternates between the Festival of Fools (focusing on theater) and the Copenhagen Carnival, the largest pre-Lent celebration in northern Europe.

 SPORTS: Copenhagen does not have the variety of sports facilities that are found in many American metropolises, but the few sports popular in Denmark are *very* popular. They are:

   Bicycle Racing – Due to the Danish mania for bicycles, this is one of Denmark's biggest international sports. Ordrup Cykelbane, Brannersvej, Charlottenlund. From May to September, usually Tuesdays and Sundays.

   Horse Racing – Not many horses in Denmark, but the Danes enjoy gambling. Klampenborg Galopbane, Klampenborgvej, Klampenborg. Races are on Saturdays between mid-April and mid-December.

   Soccer – Known in Denmark as *fodbold,* there are matches every weekend from April to June and August to November. The Danish national team also plays World Cup matches in Copenhagen at Idraetsparken, Østerbro.

   Swimming – The coast north of Copenhagen has many beaches, and the water is relatively warm in the latter part of the summer. Klampenborg, in the northern part of Copenhagen, is the city beach, and very popular. South of Copenhagen, Køge Bay Strandpark is an area of beaches, marinas, and dunes. Nude or topless bathing is tolerated in Denmark, but exhibitionism is frowned upon. There are also a number of excellent olympic-sized public pools, both indoor and outdoor. Between May 15 and August 31, try Bavnehøj Friluftsbad, Enghavevej 90 (phone: 21-49-00).

THEATER: Winter is the theater season in Copenhagen, and the famous *Royal Theater* at Kongens Nytorv is closed June, July, and August. In the summer there are lighter diversions, like cabarets at Tivoli, beer hall entertainment at Bakken, and international acts at the Benneweis Circus. The well-organized and friendly Tourist Information Office can give you information about shows that do not require a knowledge of Danish. In summer, the *Mermaid Theater*, Nyvestergade 70 (phone: 11-43-03), performs Danish plays in English.

If you are in Copenhagen in the winter, the *Royal Theater* is worth a visit. Opera and ballet alternate with plays on its stages, and the *Royal Danish Ballet* is one of high international caliber. Kongelige Teater, Kongens Nytorv (phone: 14-17-65, 14-17-66).

 MUSIC: Classical music concerts are performed by the *Radio Symphony Orchestra* in Radio Concert Hall and *Sealand Symphony Hall* in Tivoli. During the winter season there are also modern music concerts at Ny Carlsberg Glyptotek (see *Museums*) and Louisiana Museum (see *Special Places*). Excellent jazz is often available at *Montmartre,* the northern European jazz capital, Nørregade 41 (phone: 12-78-36). The world's best rock bands often give extraordinary performances in Copenhagen, as the audiences tend to be very responsive, at Falkonér Teatret, Falkonér Allé (phone: 86-85-01). If you want to make bookings for musical or theatrical events and you can't make it to the theater, these ticket agents may help: *City,* Mikkel Bryggers Gade 9 (phone: 11-24-65); *Wilhelm Hansen,* Gothersgade 9 (phone: 15-54-57).

 **NIGHTCLUBS AND NIGHTLIFE:** Popular traditional night spots with food, live music, and dancing are the *Hotel Scandinavia's Artilleri Bar,* Amager Blvd. 70 (phone: 11-23-34); *Nautilus,* Toldbodgade 24-28 (phone: 11-82-82), in the *Copenhagen Admiral Hotel;* and *Reine Pédauque–Hotel d'Angleterre,* Kongens Nytorv 34 (phone: 12-00-95).

More informal are *Den Røde Pimpernel,* H. C. Andersens Blvd. 7 (phone: 12-20-32); *HongKong,* Nyhavn 7 (phone: 12-92-72). If you like discotheques, there are several alternatives, but nothing that measures up to New York's finest. Most of them require specific dress, and their pretensions of exclusivity often extend to asking you to buy a phony membership card at the door. The best of the lot are the *Penthouse Club,* in the Sheraton Hotel, Vester Søgard 6; *Annabel's,* Lille Kongensgade 16; and *On the Rox,* Pilestraede 12-14.

The music cafés are a much better deal, and are much friendlier. The best are, in addition to the aforementioned *Montmartre, Daddy's Dance Hall* (rock and punk), Axeltorv 9 (phone: 11-46-79), and *La Fontaine,* Kompagnistraede 11 (phone: 11-60-98). (This place specializes in jazz, but is perhaps best known for being the place *everyone* goes to for morning coffee after a night on the town.) For folk music and a younger crowd, try *Vognhjulet*, Thorsgade 67 (phone: 83-15-70).

 SINS: As mentioned previously, Copenhagen has a reputation among fellow Scandinavians for being a Valhalla of vice. And many tourists do indeed come to Copenhagen seeking satisfactions that they think they cannot find elsewhere. Indeed, there are a lot of bizarre things going on behind some of those quaint rococo facades, but probably none that could parallel the frustrated fantasies of tourists. Be that as it may, a perusal of any sex shop will confirm Copenhagen's status as the pornographic Hollywood — the Danes proudly note that since they abolished censorship, violent sexual crimes like rape have been considerably less frequent, and there is a certain logic to keeping potential miscreants in the theaters rather than in the streets. In line with this philosophy, there is no street prostitution to speak of in Copenhagen. If you are seeking female companionship, a few bars are recommended: *Alcazar,* Vesterbrogade 97; *Wonder Bar,* Studiestraede 69. If you are seeking male companionship, try *Kakadu Bar,* Colbjørnsensgade 6.

BEST IN TOWN

CHECKING IN: There are a few large luxury hotels in Copenhagen, and they are unfortunately a bit expensive by American standards, particularly since too often service is bad. Prices range from $95 to $125 per diem for a double room with shower and bath at a luxury hotel to $30 to $35 for the same facilities at a less pretentious establishment. When booking rooms, you should check on whether breakfast is included and whether you have a shower or a bath. Also, look for off-season discounts. Expect to pay $65 or more for a double in those hotels we classify as expensive; between $50 and $60 for hotels in our moderate category; and under $50 in the inexpensive range. Remember to book in advance, if possible, during summer months.

Hotel d'Angleterre – Built in 1795 and renovated most recently in 1980 by new British owners, the 246-bed *Hotel d'Angleterre* is the oldest and most fashionable hotel in town. The old-fashioned wood-paneled rooms and the location near Nyhavn give something of the sensation of being on a very classy ocean liner. The *Hotel d'Angleterre* also has a good, reasonably priced French restaurant and the *Reine Pédauque* nightclub. Kongens Nytorv 34 (phone: 12-00-95). Expensive.

Copenhagen Admiral Hotel – In an old warehouse on the waterfront near *d'Angleterre* and a good deal less expensive, the *Admiral* is one of the largest and newest hotels in Copenhagen. In the evening, the congenial *Nautilus* nightclub opens downstairs. Toldbodgade 24 (phone: 11-82-82). Expensive.

Grand Hotel – A few blocks away from Tivoli and Rådhuspladsen and right near the Central Railway Station, the 175-bed *Grand* is a conveniently located hotel with a wide variety of rooms. Vesterbrogade 9 (phone: 31-36-00). Expensive.

Hotel Scandinavia – A modern skyscraper run by SAS, this 1,065-bed hotel is the largest in town. Like the *Sheraton Copenhagen,* it caters basically to the needs and tastes of businesspeople on the move. The *Artilleri Bar* is downstairs. Amager Blvd. 70 (phone: 11-23-24). Expensive.

Sheraton Copenhagen – An alternative to the above, the 846-bed *Copenhagen* has a pleasant view of the city and the *King's Court Bar.* Vester Søgade 6 (phone: 14-35-35). Expensive.

Plaza – If finely wrought antique furnishings, mahogany paneling, and luxurious comfort appeal to you, consider getting one of the 106 rooms here. Because of the unusually high quality of accouterments and service, you need to make reservations months ahead of your intended visit. Bernstorffsgade 4 (phone: 14-92-62). Expensive.

Avenue Hotel – A 128-bed hotel, the *Avenue* is in western Copenhagen, about 20 blocks from Rådhuspladsen. Closed between December 23 and January 1. Room and board available. Åboulevarden 29 (phone: 37-31-11). Moderate.

Hotel Østerport – Though this long low hotel built alongside the railroad tracks looks rather odd, it provides comfortable accommodations and a good smørgasbørd lunch. Oslo Plads 5 (phone: 11-22-66). Moderate.

Hotel Cosmopole – A block south of Tivoli, the 245-bed *Cosmopole* has a wide variety of rooms and pension rates. A good bargain for the single tourist. Colbjørnsensgade 11 (phone: 21-33-33). Moderate.

Hotel Viking – An honorable old salt's hotel near Nyhavn, this 159-bed hotel provides an address in the heart of the city's harbor section. Bredgade 65 (phone: 12-45-50). Moderate to inexpensive.

Absalon Hotel – A clean little hotel in the harbor for those on a limited budget, the *Absalon* has 300 beds with a wide variety of prices. Helgolandsgade 19 (phone: 24-22-11). Inexpensive.

Ibsens Hotel – A decent alternative to the *Absalon,* this is an 86-bed hotel on a quiet side street near the Botanical Gardens. Vendersgade 25 (phone: 13-19-13). Inexpensive.

Hotel Ry – If you are running short of cash and you are feeling adventurous, this 57-bed hotel might be just the thing for you. Some 1½ miles north of Rådhuspladsen, the *Ry* has no bathing facilities, but is by far the cheapest hotel in town. Ryesgade 14 (phone: 37-69-61). Inexpensive.

 EATING OUT: The Danes enjoy good food as well as good beer, and there are a number of classy old restaurants with capital Continental cuisine — especially French. There are also many small taverns, or *kro,* with Danish specialties like open-face sandwiches or *smørrebrød.* Reservations are not usually a problem, but it is always wise to call. Be advised that liquor is heavily taxed and likely to be about 50% more expensive than at home — your bill in general may seem a bit high, but remember that the 15% service charge is included in the price. Expect to pay at least $60 for a meal for two at a restaurant in our expensive category; $40 to $60 in the moderate range; and $30 to $40 in any restaurant listed as inexpensive. Prices don't include wine and drinks.

Baron of Beef/Flora Danica – A fine French-Danish restaurant right behind Tivoli in the *Plaza Hotel.* Danish food especially recommended for samples of local specialties. Bernstorffsgade 4 (phone: 14-92-62). Expensive.

Langelinie Pavillonen – In the harbor north of Amalienborg Castle, with a magnificent view of the waterfront. Music, dancing, decent food . . . and the *Little Mermaid.* Langelinie (phone: 12-12-14). Expensive.

Belle Terrasse – The most elegant restaurant in Tivoli. Lush gardens, live music, very romantic ambience. An experience, though an expensive one. Reservations needed. Tivoli (phone: 12-11-36). Expensive.

La Cocotte – Good French cuisine and wines characterize this restaurant, tucked away at the rear of the *Hotel Richmond.* Vester Farimagsgade 33 (phone: 14-04-07). Expensive.

Copenhagen Corner – Ask for a window table for a good view of pedestrian traffic past Rådhuspladsen (City Hall Square). The food seems to be slipping lately, but the surroundings are still pleasant (phone: 14-45-45). Expensive to moderate.

Påfuglen – If you want to dine in Tivoli for more reasonable rates, try this place. Tivoli (phone: 12-95-40). Moderate.

Wessels Kro – Want to partake of the famous Danish *store kolde bord* ("the great cold table")? Wide assortment of Danish hams and other cold cuts at this quaint old tavern. Svaertegade 7 (phone: 12-67-93). Moderate.

Dahua – Chinese food in Copenhagen is not bad, and this is the best. Gammel Torv 8 (phone: 15-78-55). Moderate.

Fiskehusets Restaurant – Across the canal from Christiansborg, the best seafood restaurant in Copenhagen. Try also *Krogs Fiskerestaurant* next door. Gammel Strand 34 and 38 (phone: 14-79-16 and 15-89-15). Moderate.

Parnas – A crazy place with live piano bar and hash with Béarnaise sauce. Friendly artists' bar otherwise. Lille Kongensgade 16 (phone: 11-49-10). Inexpensive.

Peder Oxe – This restaurant has a little something for everybody's tastes, but the specialties are meat dishes and serve-yourself salads. Reservations necessary. Grabrodre Torv 11 (phone: 11-00-77). Moderate to inexpensive.

DUBLIN

This friendly city is steeped in a history often troubled, sometimes splendid; a city of wide Georgian streets, elegant squares, magnificent doorways; of memorable sunsets that bathe the eighteenth-century red brick facades until the houses seem to glow with their own fire and the very windows seem made of gold; a city of ancient churches and cathedrals thrusting their hallowed spires and towers against the skyline; a city where the English language acquires a unique dimension, and where the dark, creamy-headed Guinness stout flows abundantly in companionable pubs. This is a city like no other European capital; set like a jewel in the sweep of Dublin Bay; behind, to the south, rise the Dublin hills and the Wicklow Mountains. Through the city the River Liffey — James Joyce's Anna Livia Plurabelle — wends its leisurely way to the sea, spanned, as it passes through Dublin, by eleven bridges.

Once, there was only one bridge. Indeed, it was not so much a bridge as a mere ford in the river, and it stood approximately where the Father Matthew Bridge stands today. It was built by the first Celtic inhabitants of what is now Dublin. When they came here, we cannot be sure; what is certain is that, by AD 140, they were well established on this site. The Celts themselves probably referred to the spot by a name that endures to this day in the official Gaelic Baile Atha Cliath, the Town of the Ford of the Hurdles.

It was not, however, until the coming of the Vikings, or Norsemen, that Dublin as we now know it began to take shape. The old Celtic settlement had at no time been a place of national importance; its significance was as a ford of the Liffey en route to the ancient royal capital of Tara. In the year AD 837, 65 Viking longboats sailed into Dublin harbor and up the mouth of the River Liffey. These early Viking settlers established themselves a little downstream from the old Celtic settlement, on a spot where the Poddle, which now flows underground, entered the Liffey, causing it to form a dark pool, or *dubh linn*. The Vikings referred to their settlement by these two Gaelic words, and the anglicized version became the city's modern English name. Dublin rapidly became the focal point of the Viking invasion of Ireland. Then, as the Vikings began to see that trading was ultimately more profitable than plunder and as they began to settle and intermarry in their new homeland, Dublin became a major center for their extensive European trade. Not long after their arrival they were converted to Christianity and in 1034 erected a cathedral, which became the nucleus of present-day Christ Church. The cathedral stood in the center of Viking Dublin and allows us to place the ancient city accurately.

Just over three centuries after the coming of the Vikings, new invaders swept Ireland. In 1169 the first contingent of Normans landed on the beach of Bannow, in County Wexford. Two years later, the powerful baron Richard Gilbert de Clare, otherwise known as Strongbow, arrived at the gates of

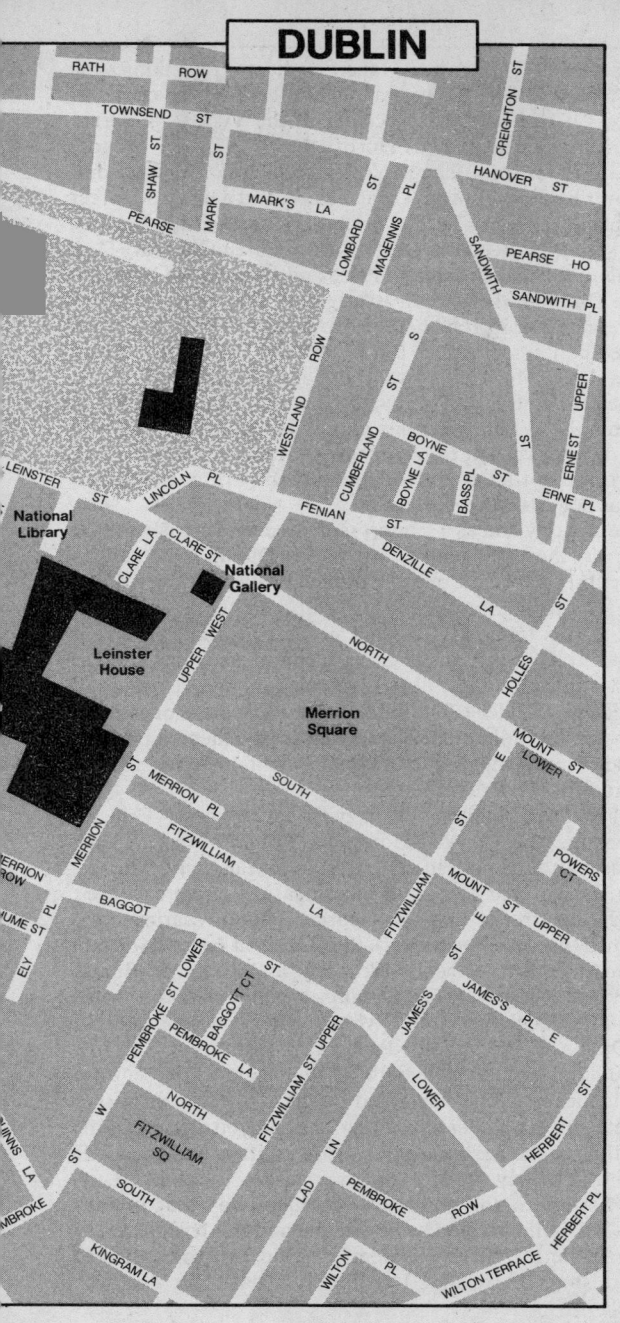

DUBLIN

RATH ROW

TOWNSEND ST

CREIGHTON ST

SHAW ST

MARK ST

MARK'S LA

ST

HANOVER ST

PEARSE

LOMBARD

MAGENNIS PL

SANDWITH

PEARSE HO

SANDWITH PL

WESTLAND ROW

S ST

BOYNE

BOYNE LA

ERNE ST UPPER

LEINSTER ST

LINCOLN PL

CUMBERLAND ST

BASS PL

ST

ERNE PL

FENIAN ST

National Library

CLARE LA CLARE ST

National Gallery

DENZILLE LA

ST

UPPER WEST

NORTH

HOLLES

Leinster House

Merrion Square

MOUNT ST LOWER

ST E

ST

MERRION PL

SOUTH

MERRION

FITZWILLIAM

POWERS CT

MERRION ROW

BAGGOT

LA

FITZWILLIAM

MOUNT ST UPPER

HUME ST PL

PEMBROKE ST LOWER

BAGGOTT CT

ST

ST E

JAMES'S

JAMES'S PL E

PEMBROKE LA

FITZWILLIAM ST UPPER

LOWER

ELY

INNS LA

NORTH

FITZWILLIAM SQ

HERBERT ST

ST W

SOUTH

LAD LN

PEMBROKE

ROW

HERBERT PL

MBROKE

KINGRAM LA

WILTON

PL

WILTON TERRACE

Dublin with a thousand men. The city was taken by storm; its Viking king and inhabitants were forced to flee. Thereafter Dublin became the center of the English conquest, as it had become the center of the Viking conquest.

Not long afterward, it became necessary to fortify the city. For this purpose Dublin Castle was built not far from the old Viking cathedral. The cathedral itself had been taken over by Strongbow not long before, and a new and larger edifice erected in its place. The city walls were built along with the castle. (Their remains can be seen at St. Audeon's Arch, below Christ Church.) Thus medieval Dublin began to take shape, small in size and surrounded by walls.

In shape and in size Dublin did not alter greatly until the arrival of a new viceroy, or king's representative, in 1662 heralded Dublin's rise to a definitive national importance. Dublin, under James Butler, duke of Ormonde, became and remained the central arena for Ireland's social, political, and cultural life.

Butler, believing that the stability of a government should be reflected in public works, began municipal improvements almost immediately. The solitary, medieval Dublin Bridge was joined by four new bridges across the river; the Phoenix Park (to this day the largest enclosed urban park in the world) was walled and several new streets were built.

Dublin's importance as a city and as a seaport increased enormously in that time. It was, however, in the eighteenth century that Dublin was truly to flourish. During this century it became one of the most brilliant and sparkling capitals in all Europe. The strong movement toward parliamentary independence that took place at this time was reflected in the splendid Parliament House (now the Bank of Ireland in College Green), commenced in 1729, the first in a series of great public buildings. Extensive rebuilding was carried out on Dublin Castle and Trinity College. The Wide Streets Commission was set up. It was as if the city were proudly preparing for the unprecedented position of importance it would occupy when, in 1782, parliamentary independence was conceded to Ireland by the British Parliament.

Great buildings followed one another in dizzying succession — Leinster House, the Royal Exchange, the Mansion House, the Four Courts, the Custom House. Irish classical architecture, in all its gravity, beauty, and balance, reached full maturity. It flowered in public buildings and private houses, spacious squares and elegant streets. This was Georgian Dublin (various king Georges sat on the British throne in the period): the Dublin of Henry Grattan, Oliver Goldsmith, Jonathan Swift, Bishop Berkeley and Edmund Burke, David Garrick and Peg Woffington. Handel himself conducted the world première of his *Messiah* in this glittering city, whose center was concentrated in the area between Dublin Castle and the Parliament House.

Architecturally, Dublin reached its zenith in the eighteenth century. Henceforward, its brilliance was to be sculpted in the written word rather than in stone. The nineteenth century saw an end to the halcyon days of Home Rule; with the dismantling of the Parliament, Dublin's political and social life suffered a blow from which it was not to recover easily. By contrast, its literary life began to flower. In the nineteenth century two great literary movements were born in Dublin — the Gaelic League and the Irish Literary Renaissance. Between them, the two movements revived and romanticized the early legends and history of Ireland. The literary renaissance — spearheaded by William Butler Yeats, Lady Augusta Gregory, Douglas Hyde, and John Millington Synge, to name but a few — placed a splendid and indelible mark on twentieth-century English literature. (Equally renowned are Irish or Ireland-born writers not directly associated with the Gaelic League renaissance, men like Samuel Beckett, who won the Nobel Prize for Literature in 1969 and who was born in Dublin in 1906; George Bernard Shaw, who wrote in England but was born in Dublin; and Brendan Behan.) The movement found its greatest expression in the creation of the Abbey Theatre, associated forever with the brilliant plays of Sean O'Casey; for many years the Abbey was the most famous theater in the world. The Gaelic League, on the other hand, had more popular appeal; with its dream of the restoration of the Gaelic language and the reestablishment of a separate Irish cultural nation, it provided a great deal of the inspiration for the Easter Rebellion of 1916.

This uprising was concentrated in Dublin. It sparked the 5-year War of Independence, which culminated in the Anglo-Irish Treaty of 1921 (whereby Ireland gained the status of Free State). The signing of the treaty was followed by Civil War in 1922–23, during which many buildings that had escaped damage in 1916 suffered badly. Today, happily, all the heirlooms of the eighteenth century have been restored to their original grandeur.

Dublin today, with a population of 422,786, is far larger than it has been at any other stage of its history. Nevertheless, it is still an eminently walkable city. The crossroads of medieval and eighteenth-century Dublin remain the center of interest. Within a half-mile radius of the Bank of Ireland on College Green lie the cathedrals, the museums, Dublin Castle, the great Georgian public buildings, the parks, and the shops. All are neatly enclosed by the Royal Canal to the north and the Grand Canal to the south.

Besides sight-seeing, a visitor should sample Dublin's abundant cultural offerings, especially its theaters. But the true focal point of Dubliners' social life is the pub, and it is there you must go to find them. Dublin can be a comfortable, "down home" place to visit, so slow down and enjoy it. If you do, you will find that there is an endearing earthiness about Dublin, a quality which inspired James Joyce to refer to his native city in off-color, though affectionate, terms as "strumpet city in the sunset" and "dear, dirty Dublin."

DUBLIN AT-A-GLANCE

SEEING THE CITY: Views of this essentially flat city are best from a number of restaurants in the surrounding hills; particularly nice is *Killakee House* in Rathfarnham (phone: 906645/906917). Or see Dublin from afar in the neighboring Wicklow Mountains.

SPECIAL PLACES: Central Dublin is very compact. Since traffic can be slow moving, by far the best way to see the city is on foot. A good idea is to take one of the CIE (Coras Iompair Eireann, National Transport Company) city sight-seeing tours. These last for about 3 hours and are an excellent and enjoyable way of getting one's bearings. They leave from the Central Bus Station, Store St. (phone: 74-63-01). Then, armed with Dublin Tourism's splendid, signposted *Tourist Trail,* the determined sight-seer should set off on foot to see and experience as much of Dublin as time allows.

SOUTH DOWNTOWN

Merrion Square – This is the loveliest of all Dublin's Georgian squares, a study in balance and elegance, evoking the graciousness of a vanished age. Note particularly the variety of fan-lighted doorways. Have a look at number 1, where the young Oscar Wilde lived with his celebrated parents, the surgeon Sir William Wills Wilde and poetess "Speranza"; number 42, home of Sir Jonah Barrington, eighteenth-century barrister and raconteur; number 58, where Daniel O'Connell lived, "the Liberator" who won Catholic Emancipation in 1829; number 70, home of tragic Sheridan Le Fanu, author of sinister tales such as *Uncle Silas* and *Through a Glass Darkly* — after his wife's death in 1858 he shut himself up there, appearing only after nightfall to walk in the shadows of Merrion Square; number 82, where William Butler Yeats, poet and Nobel Prize winner, lived. Today, the only house in the square used as a private dwelling is number 71, where well-known couturiere Sybil Connolly has her home and studio.

Leinster House – When young Lord Kildare, earl of Leinster, chose to build a mansion here in 1745, all of fashionable Dublin protested, for at that time the north side of the city was the fashionable side. Undaunted, he went ahead with his plan, asserting that "Where I go, fashion will follow." His prophecy came true. The house Lord Kildare built is said to resemble the White House, whose architect, James Hoban of Carlow, studied in Dublin after the completion of Leinster House. The building was purchased in the nineteenth century by the Royal Dublin Society, and in 1921 the Parliament of the new Irish Free State chose the building as its meeting place. Leinster House continues to be the meeting place of the Dail (House of Representatives) and Seanad (Senate). When the Dail is in session, you may watch from the visitors' gallery. Apply for tickets at the main gate. Kildare St., Merrion Square (phone: 78-99-11).

The National Museum – When Leinster House belonged to the Royal Dublin Society, it became the nucleus of a complex of cultural buildings — the National Gallery, the National Library, the Museum of Natural History, and the National Museum. These are all worth visiting, but the National Museum especially should not be missed. There is a collection of gold objects dating from the Bronze Age to early Christian times almost without parallel in Western Europe. No admission charge. Kildare St. (phone: 76-55-21).

St. Stephen's Green – Not far from Merrion Square lies St. Stephen's Green, one of the loveliest of Dublin's many public parks. It is on 22 acres with gardens, a waterfall, and an ornamental lake. It's an excellent place to come in summer, to sit and watch working Dublin take its lunch; bands play on the bandstand in July and August.

The Mansion House – Dublin preceded London in building a Mansion House for its lord mayor in 1715. In the Round Room the Declaration of Irish Independence was adopted in 1919, and the Anglo-Irish Treaty of 1921 was signed there. The Round Room is normally open to visitors. Dawson St. (phone: 76-28-52).

Trinity College – Dawson Street descends to meet Trinity College, the oldest university in Ireland, founded by Elizabeth I of England on the site of the twelfth-century Monastery of All Hallows. Alumni of the college include Oliver Goldsmith, Edmund Burke, Jonathan Swift, Bishop Berkeley (pronounced "bark-lee," who also lent his name to incorrectly pronounced Berkeley in California), William Congreve, Thomas Moore, Sheridan Le Fanu, and Oscar Wilde, to name but a few. No trace of the original Elizabethan structure remains; the oldest surviving part of the college dates from 1700. The Long Room, Trinity's famous library, is the longest single chamber library in existence. It contains a priceless collection of 800,000 volumes and 3,000 ancient manuscripts and papyri. The library's chief treasure is the *Book of Kells,* an eighth-century manuscript transcription of the four Gospels described as the "most beautiful book in the world." Admission charge April to October. Closed Saturday afternoons and all day Sundays. College Green (phone: 77-29-41).

Parliament House – Facing Trinity College is the monumental Parliament House, now the Bank of Ireland. Built in 1729 and regarded as one of the finest examples of the architecture of its period, this was the first of the great series of eighteenth-century public buildings in Dublin. As its name implies, it was erected to house the Irish Parliament in the century that saw the birth of Home Rule. College Green (phone: 77-68-01).

Dublin Castle – As you move away from College Green, Dame Street leads westward toward the older part of the city, where the early Viking and Norman settlers chose to establish themselves.

Castles have gone up and down on the site of the present castle. A Celtic *rath* was almost certainly followed by a wooden Viking fortress and this in turn was supplanted by the great stone castle erected by John of England in the thirteenth century. The castle was for 400 years the center of English rule in Ireland; for much of this time it had as grim a reputation as the Tower of London. Although the present building is essentially eighteenth century, one of the four towers that flanked the original moated castle survives as the Record Tower. Fifteenth-century Bedford Tower was the state prison; today it houses the Heraldic Museum and the unique Genealogical Office, where visitors with Irish ancestry can (for a fee) have their family tree traced. The Georgian State Apartments, formerly the residence of the English viceroys, were beautifully restored between 1950 and 1963 and are now used for state functions. St. Patrick's Hall in the State Apartments was the scene of the inauguration of Ireland's first president, Douglas Hyde; here, too, President John F. Kennedy was made a freeman of Dublin.

The Bedford Tower, the Chapel Royal, and the State Apartments can be visited for a small admission charge. Dublin Castle (phone: 71-17-77).

Christ Church Cathedral – Not far from Dublin Castle, the massive shape of Christ Church Cathedral crowns the hill on which the ancient city stood. Founded in 1038 by Viking King Sitric Silkenbeard of Dublin, Christ Church was demolished in the twelfth century and rebuilt by the Norman Richard Gilbert de Clare (Strongbow), who is buried within its walls. The cruciform building has been much restored through the centuries, but the beautiful pointed nave and the wonderful stonework remain virtually unchanged. These walls have witnessed many dramatic scenes in the course of Irish history. Christ Church today is the Church of Ireland (Protestant) Cathedral for the Diocese of Dublin. The vaulted crypt remains one of the largest in Ireland. In front of this cathedral Dubliners traditionally gather to ring in the New Year. The cathedral and crypt can be visited. Christ Church Pl. (phone: 77-80-99).

St. Audeon's Arch and the City Walls – The thirteenth-century church of St. Audeon is Dublin's oldest parish church. It was founded by early Norman settlers, who gave to the church the name St. Ouen, or Audeon, after the patron saint of their native Rouen. Close to the church is a flight of steps leading down to St. Audeon's Arch, the sole surviving gateway of the medieval city walls.

St. Patrick's Cathedral – Christ Church stood within the old walled city. One of her twelfth-century archbishops, John Comyn, felt that while he remained under municipal jurisdiction he could not achieve the temporal power for which he thirsted. Accordingly, he left the city walls and built a fine palace within a stone's throw of Christ Church. Today St. Patrick's is the national cathedral of the Church of Ireland. By the nineteenth century both cathedrals were in a state of considerable disrepair. Henry Roe, a distiller, came to the aid of Christ Church, restoring it at his own expense; Sir Benjamin Lee Guinness of the famous brewing family came to the assistance of St. Patrick's — hence the saying in Dublin that "Christ Church was restored with glasses, St. Patrick's with pints!"

The early English interior of St. Patrick's is very beautiful; the nave is the longest in Ireland. The cathedral's particular fascination, however, lies in its wealth of monuments, especially the Geraldine Door, the Cork Memorial, and the monument to Dame St. Leger. The greatest interest of all, though, is in the long association with St. Patrick's of Jonathan Swift, author of *Gulliver's Travels* and dean of the cathedral for 32 years. Within these walls he is buried, beside his loving Stella. On a slab near the entrance is carved the epitaph he composed for himself, which Yeats described as the greatest epitaph in literature. Open to visitors. St. Patrick's Cathedral (phone: 75-48-17).

Guinness Brewery – Founded in 1759 by Arthur Guinness with the sum of £100, Guinness's today is the largest exporting stout brewery in the world. Visitors are welcomed although, due to major reconstruction, they are no longer invited on a tour of the brewery. An audiovisual presentation is offered instead, after which visitors can sample the Dark Fantastic to their hearts' content. No admission charge. St. James's Gate (phone: 75-67-01).

NORTH DOWNTOWN

The Four Courts – Almost across the river from Guinness's lies the stately Four Courts of Justice, dating from the apogee of the eighteenth century. The building was begun by Thomas Cooley and completed by James Gandon, the greatest of all the Georgian architects. Court sittings (Supreme and High) are open to the public. No admission charge. Inns Quay (phone: 72-55-55).

St. Michan's Church – Not far from the Four Courts is St. Michan's, a seventeenth-century church built on the site of a tenth-century Viking church. The eighteenth-century organ is said to have been played by Handel when he was in Dublin for the first ever public performance of the *Messiah*.

Of more immediate interest, perhaps, is the extraordinary crypt, with its remarkable preservative atmosphere: Bodies have lain here for centuries without decomposing and you can, if you feel so inclined, shake the hand of an 8-foot-tall Crusader! Open Mondays through Fridays and Saturday mornings. Small admission charge. Church St.

Moore Street – A left turn past the historic General Post Office leads down Henry Street; the second turn to the right off Henry Street is Moore Street. In this street, among the fruit and flower sellers, you can hear the true voice of Dublin — lively, warm, voluble, speaking an English that is straight Sean O'Casey.

The Municipal Gallery of Modern Art – Beyond the Garden of Remembrance (a memorial to those who died for Irish freedom), on the north side of Parnell Square, is Charlemont House, designed by Sir William Chambers in 1764. Lord Charlemont, for whom the house was designed, was a great patron of the arts; it is fitting that his house became, in recent times, the Municipal Gallery of Modern Art. The gallery should not be missed; it has an outstanding collection of Impressionist paintings, and more recent artists such as Picasso, Utrillo, and Bonnard are well represented, to say nothing of such prominent Irish painters as Sir William Orpen, John B. Yeats (the poet's father), and Jack Yeats. Closed Mondays and Sunday afternoons. No admission charge. Parnell Square (phone: 74-19-03).

The Abbey Theatre – Alas, the original Abbey Theatre, founded by Yeats and Lady Gregory on the site of the old city morgue, is no more. In 1951, at the close of a performance of O'Casey's *The Plough and the Stars* — a play that ends with Dublin blazing in the aftermath of rebellion — the theater itself caught on fire and was burned to the ground. The New Abbey, designed by Michael Scott, one of the country's foremost architects, opened in 1966 on the site of the original building. The lobby, which can be seen daily (except Sundays), contains interesting portraits of those connected with the theater's early successes. Performances nightly (except Sundays). Abbey St. (phone: 74-45-05).

The Custom House – This masterpiece of Georgian architecture adorns the north bank of the Liffey, to the east of O'Connell Street. It was the chef d'oeuvre of James

Gandon and is one of the finest buildings of its kind in Europe. The Custom House is occupied by government offices and is not open to the public; it should, nonetheless, be seen at close range: the carved riverheads that form the keystones of the arches and entrances are splendid. Custom House Quay (phone: 74-29-61).

THE SUBURBS

The Phoenix Park – Lying northwest of the city center, the Phoenix Park is the largest enclosed urban park in the world. Within its walls are the residences of the president of the republic and the US ambassador. The park covers 1,760 acres, beautifully planted with a great variety of trees. Among the attractions are the lovely People's Gardens, the herd of fallow deer, the horse-race course, and the Zoological Gardens. Dublin Zoo is said to be the most beautiful zoo in Europe; it also has a most impressive collection of animals and holds several records for lion breeding. The park and zoo are open daily.

The Chester Beatty Library – Founded by an American, naturalized British resident in Ireland, this library is considered to be the most valuable and representative private collection of Oriental manuscripts and miniatures in the world. The "copper millionaire with a heart of gold," Chester Beatty willed his marvelous library to the people of Dublin. Open Tuesdays through Fridays. No admission charge. 20 Shrewsbury Rd., Ballsbridge (phone: 69-23-86).

Malahide Castle – In a north city suburb of Dublin, Malahide Castle has only recently been opened to the public. For eight centuries this was the home of the Talbots of Malahide. Magnificently furnished in period style (mostly eighteenth century) with part of the very valuable National Portrait Collection on view, it is well worth a visit. Malahide, County Dublin (phone: 45-23-37).

■**EXTRA SPECIAL:** Until you have been in a pub, you have not experienced Dublin. Here Dubliners come to pursue two serious occupations: drinking and conversation. Many pubs are ugly modern, complete with Muzak and plastic, but plenty of traditional pubs remain — noisy, companionable places where you can pursue friendly ghosts of bygone Dublin in an unhurried atmosphere. Some favorites are the *Horseshoe Bar* in the *Shelbourne Hotel,* St. Stephen's Green (phone: 76-64-71), favored by the uppity, horsey set; the *Bailey,* at 2 Duke St. (phone: 77-30-55), a literary pub which actually displays the door of nearby 7 Eccles St., where Joyce's Molly and Leopold Bloom lived; *O'Donoghue's,* off St. Stephen's Green, for Irish ballads; and for plain drinking and gab the *Stag's Head* at 1 Dame Ct. (phone: 77-93-07), or *Davy Byrne's* at 21 Duke St. (phone: 77-52-17). And incidentally, though many would have it otherwise, it is now quite acceptable for women to go pub crawling.

SOURCES AND RESOURCES

For general information, brochures, and maps before your visit, contact the Irish Tourist Board, 590 Fifth Ave., New York, NY 10036 (phone: 212-869-5500). For on-the-spot information and assistance, call the Dublin Tourism Tourist Information Offices at Dublin Airport and 14 O'Connell St. (phone: 74-77-33). The Tourist Information Offices will advise you on all aspects of your stay in Ireland and will make theater bookings and hotel reservations anywhere in the country. They also sell *Dining in Ireland* (also available at most bookstores).

The *Tourist Trail,* published by Dublin Tourism and available at their offices, is an excellent walking guide to the city. Another invaluable Dublin Tourism publication is

Dublin — Useful Information. The best city map is the Ordnance Survey Dublin Map; less-detailed, but generally adequate maps are also available.

For Local Coverage – *In Dublin,* published fortnightly, covers every conceivable activity in Dublin, including theater, cinema, music, exhibitions, sports, and cabarets. *What's On in Dublin* is published monthly by Dublin Tourism and is available at their offices. Main daily newspapers are: the *Irish Times,* the *Irish Independent,* and the *Irish Press;* main evening papers are the *Evening Herald* and the *Evening Press.*

For Food – *Dining in Ireland* contains listings of the majority of established restaurants; categories covered range from economy to haute cuisine. It is available in Tourist Information offices and most bookstores.

 CLIMATE AND CLOTHES: Dublin has a maritime climate, with cool summers and mild winters. Average winter temperatures range from 39° to 45°F (4° to 7°C), January being the coldest month; average summer temperatures range from 61° to 70°F (16° to 21°C), July being the warmest month. The most useful clothes are casuals, lightweight wools, extra sweaters for cold spells, comfortable walking shoes, and, indispensably, a light raincoat.

 GETTING AROUND: Bus – *CIE (Coras Iompair Eireann, National Transport Company)* operates rail and bus transport not only in Dublin but nationwide. Cross-city bus routes are extensive. Fares are not paid on entering; they are collected after the passenger is seated. Exact fares are not required. Although Dublin has no subway, a new commuter rail system, *Dublin Area Rapid Transport (DART),* runs from central Dublin along the bay as far north as Howth and as far south as Bray.

Day tours from Dublin are operated by *CIE* from the Central Bus Station, Store St. There is a wide range of tours available (phone: 74-63-01).

All information regarding bus and rail travel throughout the republic can be obtained by telephoning 78-77-77. An official bus and rail timetable is available at newsstands.

Taxi – There are stands at many points throughout the city, especially near main hotels, and cabs can also be hailed in the streets. Your first conversation with a Dublin cabdriver will assure you that you are in fact in Ireland. Among the companies that operate a 24-hour radio service are *Blue Cabs* (phone: 76-11-11), *Irish Taxi Co-op.* (phone: 76-66-66), and *National Radio Cabs* (phone: 77-22-22).

Car Rental – Many Dublin firms offer excellent self-drive facilities. Advice and brochures are available from tourist offices.

 MUSEUMS: The National Museum and the Heraldic Museum have already been mentioned in *Special Places.* Dublin is also the home of the *Dublin Civic Museum,* South William St., and the *Museum of Childhood,* The Palms, 20 Palmerstown Park, Rathmines (private collection of antique dolls and toys). The latter has a small admission charge (phone: 97-32-23).

 **SHOPPING:** Neatly balanced on two banks of the Liffey, Dublin has two downtown shopping areas: one around O'Connell and Henry streets, and the other centered in Grafton Street and its environs (stores on the south side are more elegant). Powerscourt House Centre, just off Grafton Street, has a number of clothes, antiques, and craft shops in a courtyard built around a pretty town house. Good buys are the chunky Aran sweaters, Donegal tweed, Waterford and Galway crystal, and Belleek china. *Brown Thomas* and *Switzer's* are the main department stores on Grafton Street; *Arnott's, Roche's,* and *Clery's* are fine stores in the O'Connell and Henry streets area. The famous *Kilkenny Design Centre* has a marvelous store on Nassau Street, with a wide range of Irish goods. Some other recommended shops are:

Sybil Connolly – Ireland's reigning couturière. 71 Merrion Sq.

Paul Costelloe – Designer of ready-to-wear for women. 42 Drury St.

Eason & Son Ltd. – Jammed with tomes and paperbacks, maps, records, and stationery. 40–42 Lower O'Connell St.

Pat Flood – Silver and gold jewelry in traditional Irish designs. 12 Fade St. and also at Powerscourt House Centre.

Irish Cottage Industries – Sweaters, tweeds, and anything else handknit, handwoven, or handbraided. 44 Dawson St.

H. Johnston Ltd. – Traditional blackthorne walking sticks. 11 Wicklow St.

Kapp and Peterson – Tobacco and handcarved pipes. 55 Grafton St.

Kevin & Howlin Ltd. – Clothing for men, ready and custom made. 31 Nassau St.

Mullins of Dublin – For coats of arms emblazoned on parchments, plaques, even door knockers. 36 Upper O'Connell St.

Waltons Musical Instrument Galleries – Bagpipes and Irish harps as well as records. 2–5 N Frederick St.

The Weavers Shed – Handwoven fabrics, by the yard or made up. 9 Duke La.

 SPECIAL EVENTS: Outstanding annual events include *St. Patrick's Day* on March 17, of course, with a parade and many other events; an *Irish Music Festival (Feis Cheoil)* in May; the *Festival in Great Irish Houses* in June, for concerts by international celebrities in Georgian mansions near Dublin; *Bloomsday,* June 16, when fans of James Joyce gather from around the world to follow the circuitous path through Dublin that takes Leopold Bloom from morning until late at night in *Ulysses;* the *Horse Show,* the principal sporting and social event of the year, in August; and the *Dublin Theatre Festival* in October, featuring new plays by Irish authors in a series of exciting first nights. For details about these and other events, inquire at the Tourist Office (see above).

 SPORTS: Gaelic Games – Football and hurling are two fast and enthralling field sports; important matches are played at *Croke Park.* For details, see the calendar of events in *In Dublin* or call Croke Park (phone: 74-31-11).

    Golf – There are over 30 courses within easy reach of Dublin; visitors are welcome at all clubs on weekdays, but gaining admission can be more difficult on weekends. Two of the finest courses in the world, *Portmarnock* and *Royal Dublin,* are just north of the city, and these should not be missed.

    Horse Racing – *Phoenix Park* is the site of races in the city, but the course is straight, not circular, which makes for frustrating viewing. You may see the start, the middle, or the end, but you won't see the whole race. Better is the very famous racecourse, *Curragh,* about a mile outside the town of Kildare in County Kildare. It's less than an hour's drive from Dublin. Six miles south of the city, Leopardstown has a very modern racecourse.

    Horseback Riding – A list of riding establishments registered with the Irish Horse Board and located close to Dublin is available at Tourist Offices.

 **THEATER:** For complete program listings see the publications under *For Local Coverage.* There are eight main theaters in the city center; smaller groups perform in the universities, in suburban theaters, and occasionally in pubs and hotels. The main theaters are the *Abbey* and the *Peacock,* both at Lower Abbey St. (phone: 74-45-05); the *Gate* (the theater of Michael MacLiammoir and Hilton Edwards), Cavendish Row (phone: 74-40-45); the *Gaiety,* South King St. (phone: 77-17-17), mostly for revues, musicals, and opera; the *Olympia,* Dame St. (phone: 77-89-62), for everything from revues to straight plays; the *Eblana,* Store St. (phone: 74-67-07), a small theater offering mostly modern comedy; the *Focus,* Pem-

broke Pl. (phone: 76-30-71) for Russian and Scandinavian works; the *Project Arts Centre,* 39 E Essex St. (phone: 71-33-27), very avant-garde.

For children, the *Lambert Puppet Theatre* in the suburb of Monkstown will prove irresistible. Clifton La., Monkstown (phone: 80-09-74).

It is always advisable to reserve in advance for theater in Dublin. You can make bookings at theaters, tourist offices, the information desks of *Switzer's* and *Brown Thomas* stores, Grafton St., and the central ticket bureau (phone: 79-44-55). Most of the theaters accept telephone reservations.

 MUSIC: The National Concert Hall, Earlsfort Terrace, off St. Stephen's Green (phone: 71-18-88), is the center of Dublin's active musical life and the new home of the *RTE (Radio Telefis Eireann) Symphony Orchestra. RTE* performances are held regularly as are a variety of other concerts. For a schedule, phone the concert hall or check local publications. In April and September the *Dublin Grand Opera Society* holds its spring and winter seasons at the Gaiety Theatre. Traditional Irish music is a must. Sessions are held at many places around town by an organization called *Comhaltas Ceoltoiri Eireann* (phone: 80-02-95); ballad sessions are held nightly except Sundays in the *Abbey Tavern,* Howth, 10 miles north of the city on the coast (phone: 32-20-06). Many pubs have music on an informal basis — *O'Donoghue's* in Merrion Row is one of the most famous (and least comfortable). Try also *Toner's* and the *Baggot Inn,* both in Lower Baggot St., *Slattery's* in Capel St., and *The Merchant* in Merchant's Quay. There are many other listings in *In Dublin.*

 NIGHTCLUBS AND NIGHTLIFE: There is little in the way of large-scale cabaret-cum-dancing in Dublin; swinging Dublin tends to congregate on the discotheque scene. Premises range from the large, lively places where an escort is not necessarily required to small, intimate clubs. Most discotheques only have wine licenses.

Among the more established discotheques on a rapidly changing scene are the large and lively *Annabel's* in the *Burlington Hotel; Raffles* in the *Sachs Hotel; Barbarella's* and *Jules,* both off Merrion Row; *Flamingo's* in *Parkes Hotel* on Stillorgan Rd.; *Blinkers* at Leopardstown racecourse. Smaller, more intimate clubs are mainly to be found in the Leeson Street area: try *Maxwell Plums, Bojangles, Samantha's, Styx,* and *Aphrodite's.* The most famous traditional cabaret in Dublin is the long-established *Jury's Cabaret;* nightly, except Mondays (phone: 60-50-00). Also good are the *Braemor Rooms,* Churchtown (phone: 98-86-64), and the *Irish Cabaret* at the *Burlington Hotel* (phone: 60-52-22).

 SINS: Drinking is the pet vice of the Irish; local sources say the Liffey runs dark with Guinness and "even the damned island is shaped like a diseased liver!"

Dublin's "sin strip," Leeson Street, is not outstandingly — but perhaps sufficiently — sinful.

BEST IN TOWN

 CHECKING IN: Dublin has something for everyone in every price range. There are a few truly deluxe, first-class hotels, a plethora of streamlined, modern places (low on warmth but efficiently run), and some really inexpensive grade-A guest houses on the edge of town (about $20 for a room and full Irish breakfast).

Because the value of the pound fluctuates considerably, our price estimates can only be approximate. Expect to pay between $60 and $80 for a double room in hotels classified as expensive; $30 to $60 is moderate; below $30 is inexpensive.

Note: The Tourist Board offers a list of hotels they have inspected and graded; they also have a computerized reservation service all over Ireland (see *Sources and Resources*).

The Berkeley Court – This new baby of the P. V. Doyle Group has proved itself outstanding since it opened in 1978. Situated close to the city in the leafy suburb of Ballsbridge, the *Berkeley* combines old-world graciousness with modern efficiency. Contemporary and antique are blended in an impeccable decor. Service is exceptionally warm. There are 200 rooms, an excellent dining room, and a good coffee shop. Lansdowne Rd. (phone: 60-17-11). Expensive.

The Shelbourne – This venerable hotel, a nice mixture of the dignified and the lively, is now more polished than ever. Some rooms are truly splendid — particularly front rooms on the second floor. Many are supremely comfortable if compact. But the sense of history you get in the creaky-floored hallways and the glittering function rooms and the varied clientele, which ranges from socialites to literati, make this establishment especially appealing. The *Horseshoe Bar* is one of the livelier fixtures of Dublin pub life. St. Stephen's Green (phone: 76-64-71). Expensive.

The Westbury – The newest luxury addition to the Doyle Hotel Group, it has a fashionable location as the centerpiece of a chic new mall of shops and restaurants. The management emphasizes elegance, and the 132 guest rooms have canopied beds and an abundance of mahogany and brass furnishings. Private suites with Jacuzzis are also available. Among the restaurants here, the most noteworthy is the grand *Russell Room.* Grafton St. (phone: 79-11-22). Expensive.

The Burlington – Just outside the city center, this is Ireland's largest hotel with 420 bedrooms. Amenities include a hairdressing salon and nightclub. There are several restaurants: the *Rooftop Carvery,* commanding fine views over Dublin; the luxurious *Sussex Room,* serving high-quality Irish and international cuisine; the *Georgian Grill,* offering fast-service snack meals. Upper Leeson St. (phone: 60-52-22). Expensive.

Jury's – Another modern hotel, in Ballsbridge, its 314 bedrooms are large and well appointed, although bathrooms are rather small. Despite the hotel's size, there are nice personal touches, such as an Alka-Seltzer left beside the bathroom glass for guests who have dined too well in one of the excellent restaurants. The *Embassy Room* offers Irish and international cuisine; the *Kish* restaurant, within the *Pavilion,* has a very extensive seafood menu. The *Pavilion* also has a cocktail bar, indoor swimming pool, and spacious lounge area. There is also the 23-hour *Coffee Dock.* For entertainment, *Jury's* offers Ireland's longest-running and most famous cabaret. The *Dubliner Bar* is particularly pleasant. Northumberland Rd. (phone: 60-50-00). Expensive.

Bloom's – Centrally located, this intimate and elegant hotel has a high commitment to service. There are 86 rooms with color TV, air-conditioning, trouser pressing, free mixers and ice, and direct-dial telephones. Every corridor has an ice cabinet and a shoeshine. There is a tea lounge decorated with plants, the *Anna Livia Gourmet Restaurant,* the *Blazes Boylan Coffee House,* and *Bloom's Bar* (note the names from Joyce). Anglesea St. (phone: 71-56-22). Expensive.

The Tara Tower – Ten minutes' drive from the city center, on a well-serviced bus route, this modern hotel is comfortable and very reasonably priced. The 100 bedrooms are all well equipped, with radio, television, and telephone; many overlook Dublin Bay. The lobby is small, but there is a good restaurant and a grill that's open until midnight. Merrion Rd. (phone: 69-46-66). Moderate.

The Montrose – Similar to but larger than the *Tara Tower,* the *Montrose* is near the National Radio and Television Studios and across the road from the new Belfield campus of University College, Dublin. About 10 minutes' drive from the city center, on a well-serviced bus route. Its 190 bedrooms are comfortable, and there is a good restaurant. Amenities include a grill, bars, health center, hairdressing salon, and souvenir shop. Stillorgan Rd. (phone: 69-33-11). Moderate.

The Clarence – This centrally located hotel is on the Liffey and near shopping areas. It has 70 comfortable bedrooms, most with baths, and a restaurant. 6–8 Wellington Quay (phone: 77-61-78). Moderate.

The Mount Herbert – Close to the city center, the *Mount Herbert* is a well-run family-owned guesthouse. It has 88 bedrooms (77 with bath); the restaurant is quite good. No bar (wine license only). Very pleasant atmosphere. 7 Herbert Rd. (phone: 68-43-21). Inexpensive.

The Ariel – Most of the 15 rooms of this homey guesthouse have baths. 52 Lansdown Rd. (phone: 68-55-12). Inexpensive.

Egan's Montrosa – With 19 rooms, all with baths, this is another comfortable guesthouse. 7 Iona Park (phone: 30-36-11). Inexpensive.

Iona House – Another guesthouse with eight rooms, all with baths. 5 Iona Park (phone: 30-62-17). Inexpensive.

 EATING OUT: Where food is concerned, Ireland, first and foremost an agricultural country, has outstanding raw materials, but truly distinctive and extensive Irish cuisine really does not exist. There are, of course, traditional dishes such as Irish stew, Dublin coddle, bacon and cabbage, but this kind of dish is a rara avis on the menu of most of the better restaurants, being looked down upon as too common to prepare for discriminating diners.

Where the serving of its enviable agricultural produce is concerned, Ireland has nothing to be ashamed of — top restaurants can compare with the best anywhere. Dublin offers a wide range of first-class restaurants, a somewhat more restricted range of moderately priced establishments, and a number of fast-service, inexpensive eating places.

Dinner for two with wine will cost between $40 and $55 in expensive restaurants; $20 to $40 is moderate; below $20 is inexpensive.

Berkeley Court – One of the best of the hotel restaurants, this is a truly elegant, lavishly appointed room; its prize-winning chef produces highly satisfactory cuisine. Lansdowne Rd. (phone: 60-17-11). Expensive.

Snaffles – Tucked away in the basement of one of Dublin's most elegant old Georgian houses, with less the air of a restaurant than that of the private dining room of some comfortable country house. The cooking is vintage Irish country house, simple and excellent. Superbly prepared game and fowl, including such rarities as plover, are specialties. Don't miss the spinach. Major credit cards. Reservations essential. 47 Lower Leeson St. (phone: 76-22-27). Expensive.

The Lord Edward – Strictly for seafood lovers (no meat on the menu), this restaurant is located in a tall, Victorian building opposite historic Christ Church Cathedral, in the older part of the city. The seafood is prepared and served in the classic French style. Closed Sundays and bank holidays. Reservations are essential. Major credit cards. 23 Christ Church Pl. (phone: 75-25-57). Expensive.

King Sitric – A superb small restaurant, right on the bay, serves perfectly cooked fish and excellent wines in a tastefully restored old house. The service is also very good. They also specialize in game birds such as grouse and snipe. East Pier, Howth (phone: 32-52-35). Expensive.

Le Coq Hardi – Run by owner/chef John Howard, twice Gold Medal winner in the prestigious Hotelympia/Salon Culinaire contest, this is a gracious Georgian estab-

lishment. Its extensive à la carte menu offers many house specialties such as Mr.
Howard's renowned *caneton à l'orange*. Closed Sundays and closed for lunch
Saturdays. Reservations essential. Major credit cards. 35 Pembroke Rd., Balls-
bridge (phone: 68-90-70). Expensive.

The Grey Door – Opened in 1978, this restaurant has already achieved an enviable
reputation for fine Russian and Finnish cuisine. The wine list is good and the more
adventurous imbiber can sample such rarities as Russian champagne. The setting
behind this elegant doorway in the heart of Georgian Dublin is intimate, rather
like dining in a private home. Closed Sundays. 23 Upper Pembroke St. (phone:
76-32-86). Expensive.

Restaurant Patrick Guilbaud – This trendy place for French nouvelle cuisine draws
an equally stylish crowd. 46 James Pl., off Baggot St. (phone: 76-41-92). Expensive.

Locks Restaurant – This provincial-style restaurant is on the banks of the Grand
Canal near Portobello Bridge. Only the freshest produce is used for the French
and Scandinavian dishes served here. 1 Windsor Terrace, Portobello (phone:
75-20-25). Expensive.

Oliver's – In the harbor town of Dun Laoghaire, just south of Dublin, this is one
of the few restaurants in the area that is open on Sundays. Small and friendly, it
features fresh seasonal food. Reservations advised. 62 Upper Geroge's St., Dun
Laoghaire (phone: 80-22-04). Expensive.

Restaurant na Mara – The name means "restaurant of the sea," and, unsurpris-
ingly, this long-established eatery specializes in seafood. The building itself is an
elegantly converted railway station (owned by the National Transport Company).
Closed Sundays and Mondays. 1 Harbour Rd. in Dun Laoghaire, just south of
Dublin (phone: 806767 or 800509). Expensive.

Coffers – Around the corner from *Bloom's* hotel, this small, comfortable restaurant
specializes in steaks — varying from a plain fillet to a pork steak cooked in fresh
apples and Pernod. This is another of the few restaurants open on Sundays; it also
has a special pre-theater dinner daily. 6 Cope St. (phone: 71-59-00/71-57-40).
Moderate.

Rudyards – It occupies three floors of a tall, narrow house in Crown Alley and offers
a combination of mildly exotic Continental dishes. No reservations. 15 Crown
Alley, off Dame St. (phone: 71-08-46). Moderate to inexpensive.

Casper & Giumbini's Drink and Food Emporium – A really lively restaurant with
some traditional Irish dishes, such as Irish stew (not always easy to come by in
Irish restaurants!). There's also an exotic range of cocktails to choose from and
a selection of international beers. 6 Wicklow St. (phone: 77-51-22). Inexpensive.

Unicorn Minor – Run by an Italian family, but the menu features international
cuisine. Closed Sundays and bank holidays. Close to St. Stephen's Green at Merrion Court, off Merrion Row (phone: 68-85-52). Inexpensive.

The Bad Ass Cafe – One of the newest, brightest, and liveliest restaurants to hit
town in some time. Famed as much for its (loud!) rock music and videos as for
its great pizza. Steaks are another specialty. Crown Alley, behind the Central Bank
on Dame St. (phone: 71-25-96). Inexpensive.

Murph's – Irish-American food served at reasonable prices in this chain of lively
restaurants, owned by two Irish-American brothers. À la carte throughout the day
until midnight (2 AM in Baggot Street). Interesting decors. Closed Sundays and
public holidays. 99 Lower Baggot St. (phone: 68-12-05); 18 Suffolk St. off Grafton
St. (phone: 71-10-38); 21 Bachelor's Walk (on the waterfront, near O'Connell St.)
(phone: 74-57-69). All inexpensive.

Captain America's Cookhouse – Specializes in "genuine American hamburgers."
Open daily. 1st Fl., Grafton Court, Grafton St. (phone: 71-52-66). Inexpensive.

Pancake HQ – The emphasis here is on salads, seafood, hamburgers, and steaks, and lavish dessert pancakes are a specialty of the house. The atmosphere is cheerful, and the clientele tends to be fairly young and lively. Closed Sundays. 5 Beresford Pl. (phone: 74-46-57). Inexpensive.

Kilkenny Kitchen – This bright, self-service restaurant in the Kilkenny Design Centre makes a perfect stop for morning coffee, lunch, or afternoon tea (no dinner) during a day of shopping. There's a limited but tasty choice of dishes and very good salads. Closed Sundays. Kilkenny Shop, Nassau St. (phone: 77-70-66). Inexpensive.

EDINBURGH

Beautiful and famous metropolises like Rome or San Francisco may be built on hills, but Edinburgh, a stark and in some ways still medieval city whose streets have often flowed with blood, has the distinction of being built on extinct volcanoes.

Astride one of these, high above the houses where Edinburgh's 450,000 inhabitants dwell, looms Edinburgh Castle, a portentous fairy-tale structure that often causes visitors to gasp for breath the first time they see it. It seems almost supernatural, with ancient stonemasonry rising out of volcanic rock as if there were no dividing line between the two.

From the seventh century onward there was a fortress where Edinburgh Castle now stands, and as life in the Middle Ages became more civilized, life within the fortress spilled over onto the long sloping ridge — carved by glaciers ages after the volcanic era — that runs downward from Edinburgh Castle to the foot of Arthur's Seat, another extinct volcano, crowning Edinburgh's central park. The ridge, with its clusters of high stone and wood tenements, its one thin, snakelike public street, its cathedral, and its tollbooth, was and still is the securing knot at the center of Scotland's legal, commercial, and artistic fiber.

Walking around central Edinburgh today is sheer joy. You don't even need a map; you can't go wrong. Every time you come to a hilltop you see a glorious, sweeping fusion of earth, sky, and sea, and every time you look up an alley you see fantastic steeples, jagged, smoking, chimney-potted skylines, or beauteous rotund domes. The city lights its most imposing public buildings at night, and they are legion, spread out over a series of precipices and valleys. Nature provides incredible sunsets, the product of Scotland's unique slowly fading evening light (the "gloaming") and rapid change in the evening temperature. Legend and romance are at every hand. Somebody famous lived in almost any residence you pass.

At the head of the legend-and-romance brigade are arch-Presbyterian John Knox and Mary, Queen of Scots, who together dominated life in the Edinburgh of the late sixteenth century. (Not that they dominated it together. When Mary arrived in Edinburgh in the autumn of 1561 as Scotland's very young and very Catholic new queen, Knox described the event in his diary as God having fouled the air with black fog and seeping rain.) The political and religious strife attendant upon Mary's reign is notorious, as are her two marriages and the three deaths associated with them, the last of these her own (she was beheaded by her cousin Queen Elizabeth I of England, to whom she had fled for asylum). Mary lived in Holyrood Palace, by the abbey at the base of Arthur's Seat. John Knox lived up the ridge from her near St Giles's Cathedral within the city gates. Both residences are extant and open to the public today.

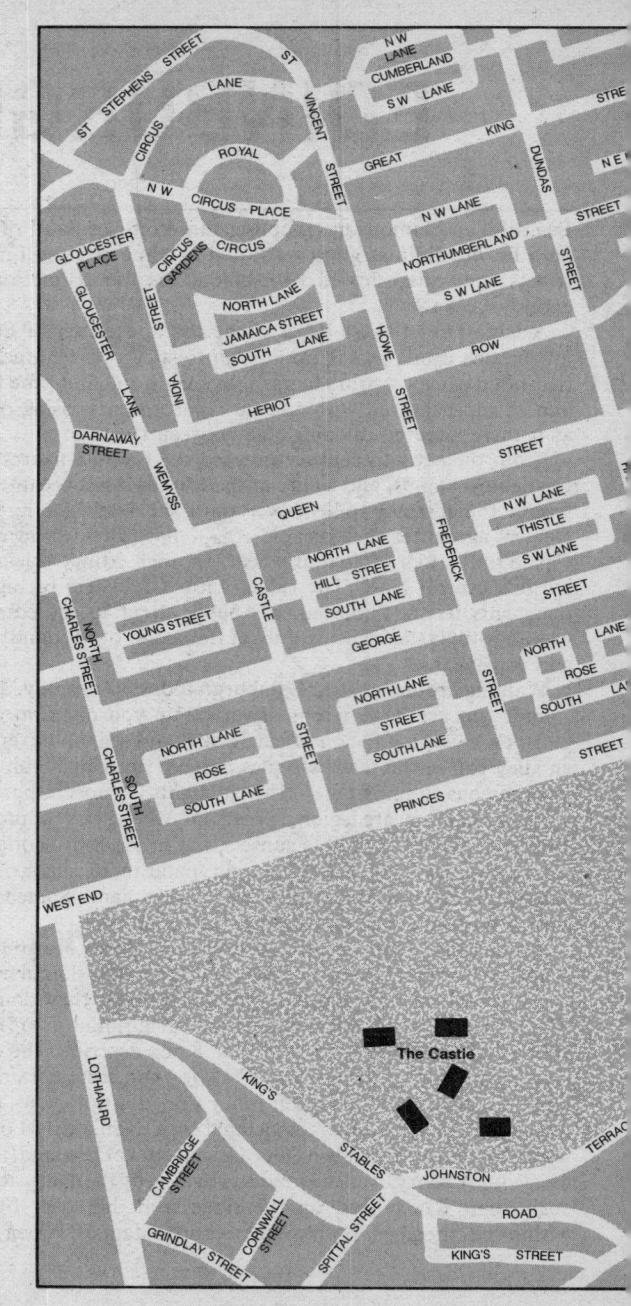

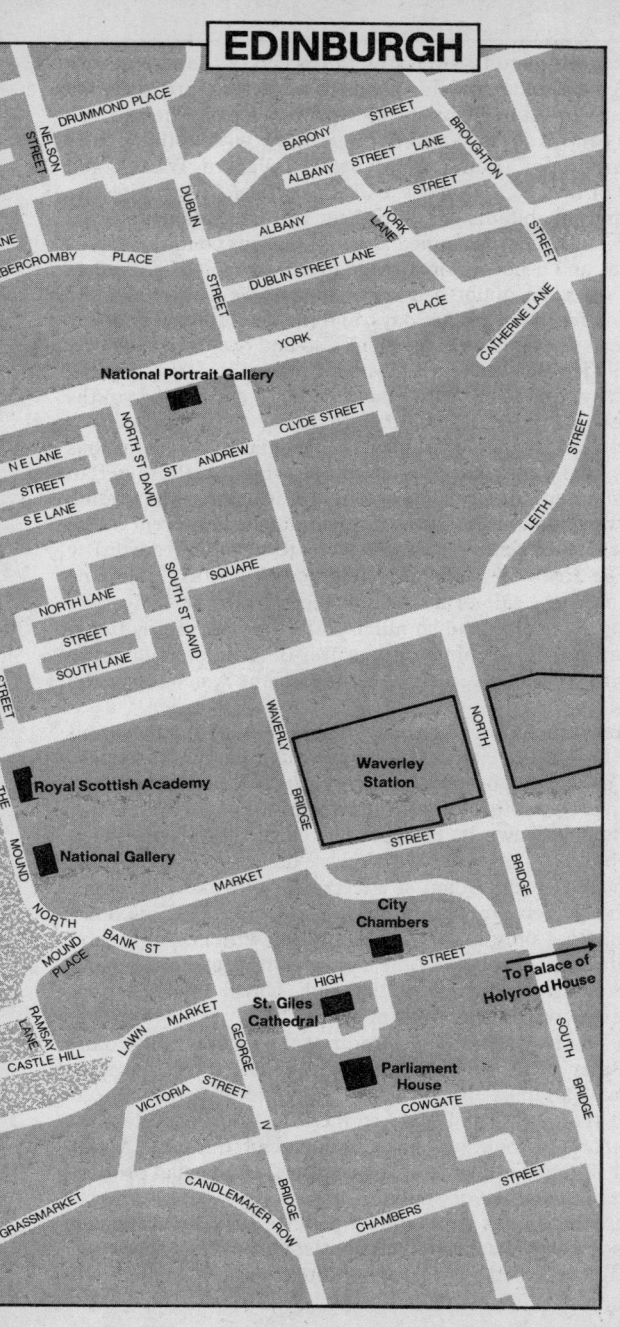

EDINBURGH

DRUMMOND PLACE

NELSON STREET

BARONY STREET

ALBANY STREET LANE

STREET

BROUGHTON

DUBLIN STREET

ALBANY

YORK LANE

STREET

BERCROMBY PLACE

DUBLIN STREET LANE

PLACE

CATHERINE LANE

YORK

LEITH STREET

National Portrait Gallery

CLYDE STREET

N E LANE

NORTH ST DAVID

ST ANDREW

STREET

SQUARE

SOUTH ST DAVID

S E LANE

NORTH LANE

STREET

SOUTH LANE

WAVERLEY BRIDGE

NORTH

Waverley Station

THE MOUND

Royal Scottish Academy

STREET

National Gallery

MARKET

BRIDGE

NORTH MOUND PLACE

BANK ST

City Chambers

STREET

To Palace of Holyrood House

RAMSAY LANE

CASTLE HILL

LAWN MARKET

HIGH

St. Giles Cathedral

GEORGE

Parliament House

SOUTH BRIDGE

VICTORIA STREET

COWGATE

GRASSMARKET

CANDLEMAKER ROW

BRIDGE

CHAMBERS

STREET

Their Edinburgh reached its full flower around the end of the seventeenth century, when the tenements along the ridge had grown 15 (or more) tottering stories high and housed uncounted numbers of people, all of whom threw their garbage into the central street, warning those below with nothing more than the terse cry *"Gardez-loo!"* Buildings frequently collapsed. Water could be had only from one of the city's six wells, called *pennywells* (their sites are still marked today), and inhabitants would line up with buckets from 3 AM on to be sure of some water. These cramped and malodorous conditions, plus a plethora of alehouses and a police force made up of decrepit Highlanders back from European wars, no doubt had something to do with the locals' favorite sport, rioting on fete days, parade days, and the king's birthday. Riots occasioned by more serious events were frequent also and occurred regularly in every age up to the Victorian and even beyond. Famous instances are the assassination of a wealthy councillor, John MacMorran, by dissatisfied youths at the Royal High School (sixteenth century); "Cleanse the Causeway," a battle in the streets between two noble families, the Douglases and Hamiltons (seventeenth century); the Jenny Geddes affair, in which a Presbyterian fishwife caused pandemonium by throwing a stool at a dean who was reading the new Episcopal service book in St. Giles's Cathedral (the first event in the British Civil War, seventeenth century); the Porteous Riots, immortalized by Sir Walter Scott in *The Heart of Midlothian* (eighteenth century); and the trial of William Burke, whose sale of his victims' corpses to the University of Edinburgh's medical luminaries did so much to further the international reputation of that great institution (nineteenth century). Religious riots have scarred the city's history repeatedly, although the last one was back in the 1930s.

Obviously this wizened medieval town had to spread out somehow, and luckily, in the second half of the eighteenth century, its by now thoroughly Protestant God sent it an increase in trade and prosperity. City fathers erected a wealth of new buildings on another ridge to the north — known as the New Town, connected to the Old Town by bridges. The classically proportioned beauty of New Town buildings, many of which were designed by the world-renowned British architect Robert Adam, is a testament to what is generally regarded as Edinburgh's golden age, part of the so-called Scottish Enlightenment. It was a great age not only for architects but for writers, publishers, philosophers, and politicians. Throughout the city, taverns became seminars. Among many other well-known people of the time, David Hume, Adam Smith, and James Boswell were Edinburgh men.

Today's Edinburgh has lost some of its traditional vibrancy and color, though it is certainly safer and cleaner. The near stranglehold the Presbyterian Church of Scotland attained on the social institutions during Queen Victoria's reign meant that industriousness, temperance, and respectability — the middle-class virtues — took supreme command of the city. About 60% of the present inhabitants are white-collar workers, an unusual proportion which helps keep the local flavor staid.

Nonetheless, signs are that things are livening up. Since 1979, an avalanche of flashy pubs, nightspots, and restaurants has shattered the city's sober air. Edinburgh has always been favored by geography, situated as it is on the Firth of Forth, an inlet in the North Sea, and surrounded by woods, rolling hills, and lochs (lakes). It is not only a national capital but a port whose chief exports include whisky, coal, and machinery; a large brewing center; and a center for nuclear and electronics research. And though the idea of a Scottish Assembly at Edinburgh — favored by a majority of Scottish voters — was set aside on a technicality a few years ago, a groundswell of agitation for Scotland's greater control of its own affairs remains. Who can say whether Edinburgh's second golden age is at hand? Perhaps not all its volcanoes are extinct.

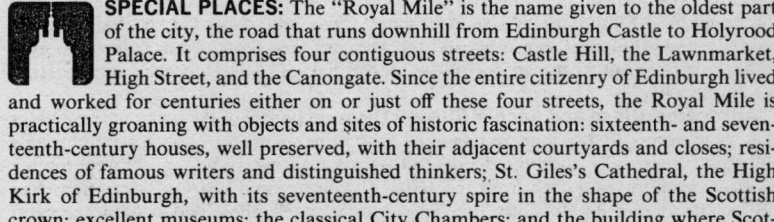

EDINBURGH AT-A-GLANCE

SEEING THE CITY: Edinburgh has many wonderful views; on a clear day you can see for miles in all directions from the top of any of its extinct volcanoes. To the north lies the sparkling Firth of Forth and, beyond it, the ancient kingdom of Fife. To the south are the lovely Pentland Hills and surrounding plowed farmlands. Look eastward, where the giant Bass Rock, off the coast of Berwickshire, meets your eye. Look westward, and you can see across the whole nation to Ben Lomond, nearly on the west coast of Scotland! If you have a car, drive up Arthur's Seat (the road begins just by Holyrood Palace), park at Dunsapie Loch, and walk to the uppermost height (a steep and furzy climb — wear flat shoes and watch out for falling sheep). If you have no car, see the city from Edinburgh Castle.

SPECIAL PLACES: The "Royal Mile" is the name given to the oldest part of the city, the road that runs downhill from Edinburgh Castle to Holyrood Palace. It comprises four contiguous streets: Castle Hill, the Lawnmarket, High Street, and the Canongate. Since the entire citizenry of Edinburgh lived and worked for centuries either on or just off these four streets, the Royal Mile is practically groaning with objects and sites of historic fascination: sixteenth- and seventeenth-century houses, well preserved, with their adjacent courtyards and closes; residences of famous writers and distinguished thinkers; St. Giles's Cathedral, the High Kirk of Edinburgh, with its seventeenth-century spire in the shape of the Scottish crown; excellent museums; the classical City Chambers; and the building where Scotland's Parliament met from 1639 until union with England's in 1707.

THE ROYAL MILE

Edinburgh Castle – The oldest building in Edinburgh is part of the castle structure, a tiny ethereal chapel built by Queen Margaret, the wife of the Malcolm who features in *Macbeth*. King James VI of Scotland (later James I of England) was born here. The Scottish Regalia, including Sceptre and Crown, are on display. These disappeared after the union of Scotland with England and were found, over a hundred years later, by Sir Walter Scott (who was leading a government commission appointed to look for them) in an old locked box. Emotion ran so high that his daughter, who was present on the occasion, fainted when he lifted the lid. Also in the castle is the Scottish National War Memorial, honoring Scots who died in the two world wars.

Outlook Tower Visitor Centre – A short distance east of the castle, climb up 98 steps, walk outside, and find yourself face to face with church spires. The camera obscura, actually a periscope, throws a revolving image of nearby streets and buildings onto a circular table, while one of the tower's denizens gives an excellent historical talk. Downstairs is a very good book shop carrying everything from Lady Antonia Fraser's best-selling biography of Mary, Queen of Scots, to gleaming coffee-table volumes about one of the national obsessions, Scotch whisky. Open daily, 9:30 AM to early evening. Admission charge. Castle Hill (phone: 226-3709).

Parliament House – Built from 1632 to 1640, after Charles I suggested that it replace the Collegiate buildings of St. Giles's Cathedral, this historic sanctum once housed Scotland's Parliament and is today the country's supreme court. Until 1982, tourists could enter only by written request. Its showpiece is the Great Hall, with a fine hammer-beam roof and walls laden with portraits by Raeburn and other famous Scottish artists. Closed Saturdays through Mondays. Upper High St. (phone: 225-2595).

St. Giles's Cathedral – A church of some sort has stood here for over 1,000 years. The medieval building here was named for the Athenian saint Egidius (Giles). St. Giles's has often been showered by flying religious fur, especially at the time of the Reformation. In 1559–60 soldiers were put on guard at the church and many of its treasures hidden in private Catholic homes; Protestant nobles nonetheless ravaged the altars. Later, English troops came to their aid and stripped St. Giles's from top to bottom. It was at this stage that John Knox, a prime mover in this sequence of events, was made minister of St. Giles's. His unmarked grave is believed to be under Parliament Square, just outside St. Giles's. Open daily. Upper High St. (phone: 225-4363).

The Mercat Cross, or Market Cross – Near the east door of St. Giles's stands a monument erected by W. E. Gladstone, prime minister of Britain off and on from 1868 to 1894. Here was the crossroads at which proclamations were read out and public hangings took place, until well into the nineteenth century. It was also the commercial focal point of old Edinburgh, the place being so thick with butchers, bakers, merchants, burgesses, lawyers, tinkers, tailors, farmers, drovers, and fishmongers that the town council issued ordinances requiring each trade to occupy its own separate neighboring street or close (hence the names you see on the entrances to the closes as you go down the Royal Mile: Fleshmarket Close, Advocates' Close, and so on). City tradesmen never obeyed these ordinances, however, and the Mercat Cross remained as colorful as ever until the city began to spread out in the second half of the eighteenth century. High St., by St. Giles's.

Advocates' Close and Anchor Close – These are typical of the many narrow alleys that gave access to the inns and taverns that were so much a part of Edinburgh's eighteenth-century cultural life. Doors to these places (taverns no longer) were topped by stone architraves dating from the sixteenth century and bearing inscriptions like "Blissit Be God of Al His Gifts" or "Spes Altera Vitae" (these two examples are still in Advocates' Close today). In Anchor Close was Douglas's, where the poet Robert Burns habitually drank. Entrances of both closes are from High St.

Acheson House – When King Charles I was crowned at Edinburgh in 1633, Sir Archibald Acheson, baronet, was his secretary of state. Acheson built this house, a small courtyard mansion, the only one of its kind in Edinburgh, in the same year. It was the height of elegance in its day, yet 100 years later it had become a popular brothel and 200 years after that was inhabited by 14 families, though it had been built to house one. It was bought and restored by the marquess of Bute in 1935, whereupon, despite its history, it was leased to the Canongate Kirk for a manse! Today it houses the Scottish Craft Centre, where you can buy all sorts of attractive, handmade items. Closed Sundays. Free. 140 the Canongate (phone: 556-8136).

Canongate Kirkyard – Opposite Acheson House. Pause long enough to read the long list — mounted on a plaque — of notables buried there. The Canongate.

Scottish Stone and Brass Rubbing Centre – You can rub any of the brasses or stones on show. Materials are provided for a fee that probably won't come to over

£4. The brass commemorating Robert Bruce, king of Scotland from 1306 to 1329, is very impressive. In addition to being nice souvenirs, your own finished products will make beautiful gifts. Open daily except Sundays. Canongate Tollbooth Annex, 163 Canongate (phone: 225-1131).

Holyrood Palace – A royal retreat since the beginning of the sixteenth century, the palace is where Queen Elizabeth II stays when she is in residence in Edinburgh today. It is made of stone, a huge, imposing round-towered edifice befitting kings and queens. Most of what you see of it now was built by Charles II from 1671, but it is chiefly associated with Mary, Queen of Scots, who lived in it well before that for six contentious, sensational years. The old part, still extant, contains her bedroom and the supper room in which David Riccio, her secretary, was brutally murdered before her very eyes by a gang of armed men that included her jealous husband, her cousin Lord Darnley. By the side of the palace, within its spacious grounds, are the picturesque ruins of Holyrood Abbey and the lodge known as Queen Mary's Bath House, where she reputedly bathed in red wine. A guide will take you through it all, sparing no gory details. Closed Sundays from November through April, and when the queen is in town. Admission charge. At the bottom of the Canongate (phone: 556-7371).

BEYOND THE ROYAL MILE

Princes Street Gardens – Princes Street is modern Edinburgh's Main Street, its Broadway, and its Fifth Avenue. The gardens stretch nearly the street's whole length on the south side, where the old Nor' Loch, which was used in medieval times as the castle moat, once stood. The city spends thousands of pounds every year to keep the gardens opulent with flowers. In summer months (June–September) there are concerts, children's shows, variety acts, and do-it-yourself Scottish country dancing (to professional bands) here. Gates close at dusk. Princes St.

National Gallery of Scotland – Smack in the middle of Princes Street Gardens, on a man-made embankment called the Mound, is this exquisite museum, opened in 1859. It contains paintings by British and European masters from the fourteenth century to Cézanne. Open daily. Free. The Mound (phone: 556-8921).

Scott Monument – Sir Walter Scott is certainly one of Edinburgh's favorite sons — his face even decorates all Bank of Scotland notes, even though he was the most famous bankrupt in Scottish history. The elaborate 200-foot Gothic-style monument on the east end of Princes Street Gardens helps make Edinburgh's skyline the ornamental marvel it is. Its 287 steps take you to the summit. (Don't attempt it if you suffer vertigo.) Closed weekends. Admission charge. Princes St. (phone: 225-2424, ext. 6596).

The New Town – To the north of Princes Street lies the largest neoclassical townscape in Europe, built between the 1760s and 1830s. Assiduous conservation means that little has changed externally in these streets, squares, and crescents. Three of the more interesting ones are Charlotte Square (designed by Robert Adam), Moray Place, and Ann Street. The New Town Conservation Centre, 13A Dundas St. (phone: 556-7054), arranges guided tours of the area; closed weekends.

The Georgian House – On the most gracious square in the elegant New Town, the National Trust for Scotland has furnished a house in period style and opened it to the public. The kitchen is a wonderland of now-defunct utilitarian objects that would have belonged to a typical high-income late-eighteenth-century ménage. Fascinating audiovisual sessions on the history and topography of the New Town come with the admission price. Open daily April through October; weekends only November to mid-December; closed mid-December through March. 7 Charlotte Square (phone: 225-2160).

Edinburgh Zoo – Opposite the Pentland Hills, away from the city center, en route to the western suburb of Corstorphine, you'll find a zoo with a view and the world's most famous penguins, the largest colony in captivity. Every afternoon at 2:30, from

April to October, they perform their delightful Penguin Parade through the park grounds. Open daily. Admission fee. Corstorphine Rd., Murrayfield (phone: 334-9171).

The Grassmarket – This ancient street is flanked by many cozy eateries, elegant shops, and seedy-looking flophouses. The West Bow, off the street's east end, has some intriguing boutiques. Leading from the Grassmarket is Cowgate, with the sixteenth-century Magdalen Chapel (phone the Scottish Reformation Society to see it: 225-1836).

Dean Village – This 800-year-old grain milling town on the Water of Leith is over 100 feet below the level of much of the rest of the city and a good place to soak up local color. In summer the woodland walk along the river is popping with bohemians who live in the next village, Stockbridge. End of Bell's Brae (turn left off Queensferry St. onto Bell's Brae as you approach Dean Bridge from the west end of Princes St.).

■ **EXTRA SPECIAL:** The Edinburgh International Festival is held every year during the last three weeks of August. It features the best-known, most highly regarded performers of our time in opera, music, theater, and dance. Each year brings different orchestras, soloists, theater and opera companies — all are absolutely top-notch.

Accompanying the festival proper is the phenomenal Edinburgh Festival Fringe, an orgy of over 300 productions by amateur and lesser-known professional companies from Europe, Britain, and the US who come to Edinburgh at their own expense to strike a blow for art and for themselves.

And the Edinburgh Military Tattoo, a spectacular concert in full Highland dress by the massed pipe bands of Her Majesty's Scottish regiments, blasts forth most nights during the festival on the Castle Esplanade.

Those interested are advised to reserve tickets — and hotel space — as far in advance as possible, especially for the most popular attractions such as the Tattoo. A detailed festival brochure is available at the British Tourist Authority in New York (see *Sources and Resources*) by April. You can book reservations through a travel agent or write directly to the individual events. For the international festival, it's the Festival Box Office, 21 Market St. Edinburgh EH1 1BW (phone: 226-4001); for the Tattoo, the Tattoo Office, 1 Cockburn St., Edinburgh EH1 1BP (phone: 225-1188); and the Edinburgh Festival Fringe Society is at 170 High St. (phone: 226-5257).

SOURCES AND RESOURCES

For information in the US, contact the British Tourist Authority, 40 W 57th St., New York, NY 10036 (phone: 212-581-4700); in Edinburgh the City of Edinburgh Tourist Bureau, 5 Waverley Bridge (phone: 226-6591), offers information, maps, and leaflets. The Edinburgh office stocks all City of Edinburgh publications. On sale there is the *Edinburgh Official Guide,* updated annually. In it is a reasonable working map of downtown areas, with places of interest marked. A good, more detailed map is the Edinburgh number of the *Geographia Street Atlas and Index* series, on sale at most local bookshops. The pamphlets on Edinburgh history and legend at the *Camera Obscura* bookshop (see *Special Places*) will add greatly to your appreciation of what you see of the city. Each costs about $3.

For Local Coverage – The *Scotsman,* morning daily; the *Edinburgh Evening News,* evening daily; *What's On,* published monthly by the city, listing forthcoming happenings; another *What's On,* a free, privately owned monthly, is available in most hotel lobbies; *Teletourist Service,* recorded daily telephone prospectus from May through

September (phone: 246-8041). Also see the *Festival Times,* during the Edinburgh Festival.

For Food – See *Restaurants in Edinburgh,* sold by the Tourist Board.

CLIMATE AND CLOTHES: A day with no rain is a rarity, even in summer. When the wind blows, put millstones in your shoes. Mists are not unknown either. Temperatures usually don't go below freezing in winter or over 70°F (21°C) in summer. A mackintosh with a zip-in wool lining that fits over everything you own is a recommended survival kit.

GETTING AROUND: You can walk from the Royal Mile into the Grassmarket or to Princes Street and from there to Dean Village and the New Town.

Bus – City Transport Headquarters is at 14 Queen St. (phone: 554-4494), parallel to Princes St. two blocks away. Route maps and timetables are available from their information office at the Air Terminal on Waverley Bridge. You can go anywhere by bus from Princes Street — if you have exact fare. The Tourist Board office has details of bus tours of the city and countryside. Longer-distance buses go from St. Andrew Square Bus Station, St. Andrew Square (phone: 556-2126).

Taxi – There are cabstands at St. Andrew Square Bus Station and in Waverley Station, off Princes St. Or phone City Cabs (phone: 228-1211), Central Radio Taxis (phone: 229-5221), or Radiocabs (phone: 225-6736).

Car Rental – All major national firms are represented.

MUSEUMS: The city runs three museums of local history: *Huntly House,* the Canongate (phone: 225-2424, ext. 6689); *Canongate Tollbooth,* the Canongate (phone: 225-2424, ext. 6638); and *Lady Stair's House* (a Burns, Scott, and Stevenson museum), Lawnmarket (phone: 225-2424, ext. 6593). The *Scottish National Gallery* is described in *Special Places.* Other museums are:

The Scottish National Portrait Gallery/The National Museum of Antiquities – These museums are on two sides of one building. 1 Queen St. (phone: 556-8921).

The Scottish National Gallery of Modern Art – Matisse to Picasso. Belford Rd. (phone: 556-8921).

The Royal Scottish Museum – A museum of natural history, science, and technology, great for kids. Chambers St. (phone: 225-7534).

The Edinburgh Wax Museum – With every notorious Scot from Macbeth to Billy Connolly. 142 High St. (phone: 226-4445).

Museum of Childhood – Antique toys, games, dolls, and costumes, all beautifully explained and arranged. 38 High St. (phone: 225-1131, ext. 6645).

The DeMarco Gallery – Headquarters for avant-garde art. 10 Jeffrey St. (phone: 557-0707).

Lauriston Castle – A sixteenth-century home decorated entirely with Edwardian antiques. Off Cramond Rd. S (phone: 336-2060).

SHOPPING: Princes Street is Edinburgh's main shopping street, chock-a-block with a variety of stores. In addition, at the east end of Princes Street is Waverley Market, a large, modern mall with even more shops. The best buy is in Scottish tartans and woolens. Also worth a look are antiques — particularly Victoriana — in the area around St. Stephen's Street in Stockbridge. Bone china and Scottish crystal are attractive, and don't miss the shortbread, which is on sale everywhere. We especially recommend the following shops:

Jenner's Department Store – Sells everything, especially bone china and Scottish crystal. Princes and St. David's sts. (phone: 225-2442).

Janet Lumsden – Antique silver, jewelry, glass, and porcelain. 51A George St. (phone: 225-2911).

The Scotch House – Classy, expensive woolens such as kilts, sweaters, tweeds, scarves, shawls, and mohairs. 60 Princes St. (phone: 226-5271).

The Woollen Mill – A good, inexpensive alternative to the Scotch House at 139 Princes St. (phone: 226-3840); 62 Princes St. (phone: 225-4966); 453 Lawnmarket (phone: 225-1525); and 51 High St. (phone: 556-9786).

Debenham's – A branch of the London firm with clothes, accessories, cosmetics, and more. 109–112 Princes St. (phone: 225-1320).

Pitlochry Knitwear – Bargains in Scottish products, especially sweaters, kilts, and ladies' suits. 28 North Bridge (phone: 225-3893).

 SPECIAL EVENTS: The *Edinburgh International Festival* and its overflow the *Edinburgh Festival Fringe* are held every year during the last three weeks in August. (For details, see *Extra Special.*) The *Edinburgh Folk Festival* occurs in early spring (for details, contact the Folk Festival office, 170 High St., Edinburgh EH1 1QS; phone: 226-3645).

 SPORTS: Golfing – Golfing is Scotland's national mania. A letter from your home club president or pro will get you into any of the city's 22 courses (you'll only need it for the posh, private ones like *Royal Burgess, Bruntsfield,* both in suburban Barnton, and *Muirfield* in nearby Gullane). Clubs can be rented. Full details on public courses are listed in the *Edinburgh Official Guide* and in the free leaflet "Golf in Scotland," both available at the tourist office.

Skiing – *Hillend Ski Center* on the Pentland Hills is the largest artificial slope in Britain. Equipment for hire. Open daily 9:30 AM to 9 PM, weekends May through August 9:30 AM to 5 PM (phone: 445-4433).

Swimming – Have a dip in the luxurious *Royal Commonwealth Pool,* built for the 1970 Commonwealth Games. Open weekdays 9 AM to 9 PM, Saturdays and Sundays 10 AM to 4 PM. Dalkeith Rd. (phone: 667-7211). For other sports, consult your Edinburgh *Official Guide.*

 THEATER: The *King's,* 2 Leven St. (phone: 229-1201), and the *Royal Lyceum,* Grindlay St. (phone: 229-9697), are Edinburgh's two main venues. Although productions at the *King's* are considered mediocre, the *Royal Lyceum* has been gaining a reputation for its fine work. The *Playhouse,* 20 Greenside Pl. (phone: 557-2590), is a converted cinema where musical productions are staged. *The Traverse,* 112 West Bow (phone: 226-2633), a private theater club with an avant-garde image and a much higher standard, sometimes opens its doors to the public. *The Netherbow,* 43 High St. (phone: 556-9579), and *Theatre Workshop,* 34 Hamilton Pl. (phone: 225-7942), mount small-scale, artistic productions. Schedules are in the dailies.

 **MUSIC:** Classical music is the city's overriding passion. Highbrow musical events are held at *Usher Hall,* Lothian Rd. (phone: 228-1155), where the *Scottish National Orchestra* holds performances on Friday nights at 7:30. The *Scottish Opera Co.,* which has excellent standards, has seasons at the *Playhouse* (see *Theater* for address), where other famous names in both classical and nonclassical music give concerts. For chamber music and occasional jazz, try *Queen's Hall,* Clerk St. (phone: 668-2117). At *St. Mary's Cathedral,* Palmerston Pl. (phone: 225-6293), evensong is sung on weekdays at 5:15 by a trained choir with boy sopranos. Also, countless amateur groups swell the city's halls and churches. Details are available

in the dailies. The *Magna Carta,* 20 Abercromby Pl., mainly features jazz; open every night but Sunday.

NIGHTCLUBS AND NIGHTLIFE: Edinburgh isn't exactly Las Vegas; it isn't even Philadelphia. Discos here are usually filled with a very young crowd, but you could risk the following if you're under thirty: *Annabel's,* 3 Semple St. (phone: 229-7733); *Cinderellas Rockerfellas,* 99 St. Stephen St. (phone: 556-0266); and *Outer Limits* (teenagers leave at 11 PM so others can roll up to an after-hours bar), W Tollcross (phone: 228-3252). Jazz and folk music can be heard at bars and hotels around the city; check the *Evening News'* "Nightlife" page or *What's On* magazine. *Caley Palais,* 31 Lothian Rd. (phone: 229-7670), draws a younger crowd with its brand of live music. *Fire Island,* 127 Princes St. (no phone), is the city's gay (male) disco.

SINS: You have to know somebody.

BEST IN TOWN

CHECKING IN: In Scotland it is practically impossible to get a room without an accompanying kippers-to-nuts Big Scottish Breakfast (you pay for it whether you eat it or not). Expect to shell out $90 and up for a double with breakfast in the hotels listed below as expensive; $70 to $90 for those in the moderate category; between $40 and $60 for the cheapies-but-goodies in the inexpensive range. Unless otherwise noted, hotels accept all major credit cards. Should you find it impossible to get into any of our selected hotels, City of Edinburgh District Council at the airport, and in town at 5 Waverley Bridge (phone: 226-6591), has an accommodations service covering all of Edinburgh and district.

The George – The best in town. It is in the New Town between Charlotte and St. Andrew squares and is known for its comfort. It has 212 bedrooms, two dining rooms, two bars. Phones in rooms. 19–21 George St. (phone: 225-1251). Expensive.

The Caledonian – An elephantine Edwardian railroad hotel with 212 rooms, three dining rooms, and three bars. Recently completely refurbished, it boasts great views of Edinburgh Castle. Celebrities love it. Phones in rooms. West end of Princes St. (phone: 225-2433). Expensive.

Dalhousie Castle – Originally built in the twelfth century and added onto ever since (Queen Victoria once stayed here). Now it's a luxury country-house hotel with 25 rooms. About 8 miles south of Edinburgh (phone: Gorebridge 2-0153). Expensive.

The Carlton – This building has been remarkably transformed from an old department store into a grand and sophisticated Victorian hotel. Recently opened with 120 guest rooms, two dining rooms, and one bar, more rooms and facilities are scheduled to open this year. North Bridge, off Princes St. (phone: 556-7277). Expensive.

The Edinburgh Sheraton – This brand-new, honey-colored hotel just off Princes Street seems architecturally inappropriate for the neighborhood, but it can't be beat for its range of modern amenities: 263 very well equipped rooms, a health club and gym, sauna and whirlpool, swimming pool, parking, bar, and restaurant. 1 Festival Sq. (phone: 229-9131). Expensive.

The Post House – An ultramodern, all-conveniences affair, this is a good place to be if you have a car (it's beside the zoo, out of the city center). Its low-priced coffee house is less stuffily British than almost anywhere else. Breakfast optional. It has 208 rooms, all with phones. Corstorphine Rd. (phone: 334-8221). Expensive to moderate.

Braid Hills Hotel – Muriel Spark fans will remember that this is where Miss Jean Brodie, by then past her prime, took tea. An old established family-run hotel in the southern suburbs toward the Pentland Hills. 134 Braid Rd. (phone: 447-8888). Moderate.

The Howard – Its flower-filled window boxes are the last word in winsomeness. It has 26 rooms, with phones (and, surprisingly for a hotel this size, private baths). 32–36 Great King St. (phone: 557-3500). Moderate.

Melville Castle – This was the family seat of "King Harry the Ninth" or Henry Dundas, the first Viscount Melville, the Tory Lord Advocate who ruled Scotland from Westminster by a system of patronage in the late eighteenth and early nineteenth centuries. It's superbly romantic and highly historic. It has 23 rooms, most with phones. In the village of Lasswade, about 6 miles (10 km) south of Edinburgh (phone: 663-6634) — ask for directions. Inexpensive.

The Donmaree – This sweet little family hotel in a respectable suburb has 20 rooms. 21 Mayfield Gardens (phone: 667-3641). Inexpensive.

Galloway Guest House – Not as well equipped as the *Donmaree*, but more centrally located, just off the panoramic Dean Bridge. Guests have limited access to the kitchen; the nine rooms have no phones. No credit cards. 22 Dean Park Crescent (phone: 332-3672). Inexpensive.

 EATING OUT: Reports on Scottish food vary from calling it a joke to claiming it is at least superior to the English. You might want to try some of the following specialties: cock-a-leekie soup (chicken and leek), salmon, haddock, trout, and Aberdeen Angus steak. Scones originated in Scotland, and shortbread shouldn't be missed. Restaurants usually keep the city's formal hours (lunch until 2:30, dinner anywhere from 6:00). Expect to pay $50 and up for dinner for two, excluding wine and tips, in establishments listed as expensive; $25 to $50 in moderate establishments; and $30 and under in inexpensive places.

Prestonfield House – A 300-year-old country estate within its own peacock-laden park grounds. Candlelit dinners in rooms with tapestries, paintings, and blazing open fires. French cooking. Accepts major credit cards. Reservations necessary. Off Priestfield Rd. (phone: 667-8055). Expensive.

Mermans – This small immensely popular seafood restaurant changes its menu seasonally. The décor is French provincial, but the crowd is a mixed bag — artists, tourists, and businesspeople. Reservations recommended. Closed Mondays and Saturday lunch; closed Sundays September to April. 8–10 Eyre Pl. (phone: 556-1177). Expensive.

Cosmo's – Edinburgh's link to Rome. Everybody who works here is sunnily Italian, as is the menu. Fabulous seafoods and veal, and a cocktail bar made of imported Italian marble. Major credit cards. Reservations necessary. Closed Sundays and Mondays. 58A Castle St. (phone: 226-6743). Expensive.

Beehive Inn – Among the fittings in this Old Town restaurant is a cell door from the very old town jail. Steaks and fish are served from an open charcoal grill and are followed by luscious desserts. Major credit cards. Closed Sundays. 18 Grassmarket (phone: 225-7171). Expensive.

The Howtowdie – White tablecloths and glass cases full of taxidermists' birds set the tone at this Highland-style establishment long famed for its ritzy image and traditional Scottish cooking. Reservations necessary. Closed Sundays. 27a Stafford St. (phone: 225-6291). Expensive.

The Pompadour – The facinating lunch menu here is a steadily unfurling history of Scots cooking, while dinners feature French cuisine. In the Caledonian Hotel, Princes St. (phone: 225-2433). Expensive.

Denzler's – Swiss staff and cuisine, the finest wines, ultramodern decor, and droll menu (try their luscious Black Forest Gâteau — no, it isn't baked trolls with cream, it's chocolate cake). No credit cards. Reservations necessary. 80 Queen St. (phone: 226-5467). Moderate.

Shamiana – Tandoori (Indian) food at its finest. Everything is cooked from scratch with delicate spices. Pale pink tablecloths, bone china, waitresses in saris, give the place a rarefied air. Major credit cards. Reservations necessary. Open evenings only, closed Sundays. 14A Brougham St. (phone: 229-2265). Moderate.

Edinburgh Rendezvous – Lovers of Chinese cooking should make for this pleasant, dimly lit dining parlor. American Express and Diners Club only. Reservations necessary. 10A Queensferry St. (phone: 225-3777 or 225-2023). Moderate.

Nimmo's – The bistro here serves homemade steak pies for lunch and has candlelit Continental meals at night. There's a charming wine bar for pub lunchers, too. Reservations necessary for the bistro. Closed Sundays. 101 Shandwick Pl. (phone: 229-6119). Moderate to inexpensive.

Madogs – Here you'll find American fare (and some Mexican dishes) in a setting of wicker chairs, potted palms, pop music, and big glossy photos of Hollywood heroes. Reservations necessary at lunchtime and Friday and Saturday nights. Major credit cards. Closed Sundays October to May. 38a George St. (phone: 225-3408). Inexpensive.

Henderson's Salad Table – This cafeteria-style vegetarian's heaven-on-earth may keep you standing in line for as long as 15 minutes, but it's worth it. Piles of salads, hot pots, opulent desserts available continuously day and evening. Closed Sundays, except during Festival. 94 Hanover St. (phone: 225-2131). Inexpensive.

Duncan's Land – This unexpected little oasis, in a lovely seventeenth-century house, has light country French cooking. Closed Sundays and Mondays. 8 Gloucester St. (phone: 225-1037). Inexpensive.

FLORENCE

Florence, city of the arts, jewel of the Renaissance, symbol of the Tuscan pride in grace and refinement, is for many an acquired taste. Rome has romance, Venice intrigue, and Naples a poignant gaiety — Florence may seem too austere, too serious, too severe. The elegance that is Florence does not seize you immediately — not like the splashing fountains of Rome, the noisy laughter and song of Naples, the pastel-colored chandeliers peeking out of patrician palaces along Venice's Grand Canal.

Next to the mellow tangerine hues of Rome, the pinks of Venice, and the orgy of color that is Naples, Florence is a study in neutral shades: blacks and whites, beiges and browns, a splattering of dark green. Its people seem less spontaneous and exuberant than Romans or Neapolitans, more hard-working and reserved, with a sort of innate sense of dignity and pride.

Florentine palaces are more like fortresses, at first glance rather forbidding and uninviting to the visitor; the city's somber streets are lined with solid, direct architecture; its civic sculpture is noble and restrained. But this is only a superficial view of Florence. Step into the palaces and you will be awed by the beauty of fine details as well as some of the world's great art treasures. Look at the fine Florentine crafts in gold and leather and exquisite fabrics in the elegant but classically serious shops. Then you will understand why the culture and art of Florence have attracted people from around the world through the centuries, and why it is as much a favorite of artists, students, and expatriates today as it was during its apogee under the Medicis in the fifteenth century.

Florence was the home of Cimabue and Giotto, the fathers of Italian painting; of Brunelleschi, Donatello, and Masaccio, who paved the way for the Renaissance; of the della Robbias, Botticelli, Leonardo da Vinci, and Michelangelo; of Dante Alighieri, Petrarch, and Boccaccio; of Machiavelli and Galileo. Art, science, and life found their finest, most powerful expression in Florence, and records of this splendid past fill the city's many galleries, museums, churches, and palaces, demanding attention.

Florence — Firenze in Italian — was founded by the Romans in the first century BC on the banks of the Arno River amidst the fertile Tuscan hills. It was probably named after Florinus, the Roman general who besieged the nearby Etruscan hill town of Fiesole in 63 BC. Roman Florence became a thriving military and trading town, but few architectural monuments of that time have survived.

After the fall of the Roman Empire, the town sank into the decadence of the Dark Ages. It wasn't until the late eleventh century that Florence gave signs of new life. It was then that the great guilds were developed, the florin-based currency appeared, and Florence became a powerful, self-governing republic. Interfamily feuds were widespread, and over 150 square stone towers — built for refuge next to the houses of influential families — dominated the city's skyline during the twelfth century. None, unfortunately, remains today.

As a free city-state or *comune,* Florence managed to maintain a balance between the authority of the Germanic emperors and that of the popes, overcoming the difficulties of internal struggles between the burgher Guelphs who supported the pope and the aristocratic Ghibellines who were for the Holy Roman Emperor. Eventually, by the late thirteenth century, the Guelphs won power and a democratic government was inaugurated with the famous Ordinances of Justice. So began Florence's ascent over 3 centuries, reaching its height and greatest splendor under the Medici family.

It was due in large measure to the patronage of the Medicis that Florence became the liveliest and most creative city in Europe. Giovanni di Bicci founded this illustrious dynasty of art patrons and Cosimo the Elder, the Grand Merchant of Florence, continued to gather artists around him. But it was Cosimo's grandson, Lorenzo the Magnificent (1449–92), who put Florence in the forefront of the Italian Renaissance. In the eighteenth century, the grand duchy of the Medici was succeeded by that of the house of Lorraine, until Tuscany became part of the kingdom of Italy in 1860. From 1865 to 1871, Florence reigned as temporary capital of the kingdom. With the capital's transfer to Rome, the history of Florence merges with that of the rest of Italy.

Two catastrophes in this century have caused inestimable damage to Florence's art treasures. In 1944, all the beloved bridges crossing the Arno — except for the Ponte Vecchio — were blown up by the Nazis. Reconstruction began as soon as the Germans retreated. Then, two decades later, in November 1966, the Arno burst its banks, covering the historic center with a muddy slime. Over 1,400 works of art, two million volumes of valuable books, and countless homes were damaged by floodwaters that reached depths of 23 feet. The people of Florence, with help from all over the world, rose to the challenge. Before the floodwaters had receded, they began the painstaking chore of rescuing their treasures from 600,000 tons of mud, oil, and debris.

Today, the city of Florence — with a population of more than half a million — is still a vital force in the arts, in culture, and in science, as well as an industrial, commercial, and university center. The tremendous creative tradition of the Florentines has also kept them in the forefront in the fields of fashion and handicrafts, making this one of Italy's most attractive cities for shoppers as well as for art lovers . . . and gastronomes.

FLORENCE AT-A-GLANCE

SEEING THE CITY: The Piazzale Michelangelo, on the left bank of the Arno, offers a wonderful panorama of the city. Just follow the Viale Michelangelo up the flank of the hill. (Or take bus 13 from the railway station.) For a special view of Florence and the entire Arno Valley, visit the Convent of St. Francis, perched on a hill studded with cypress and sumptuous villas in neighboring Fiesole (see *Special Places*).

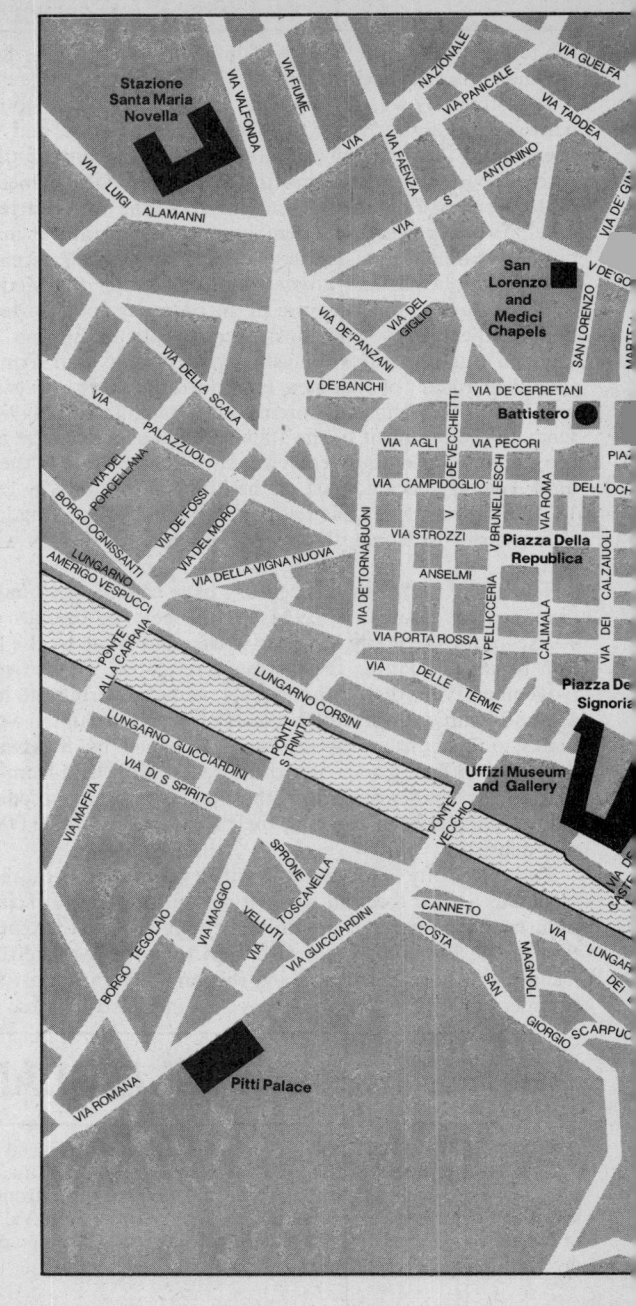

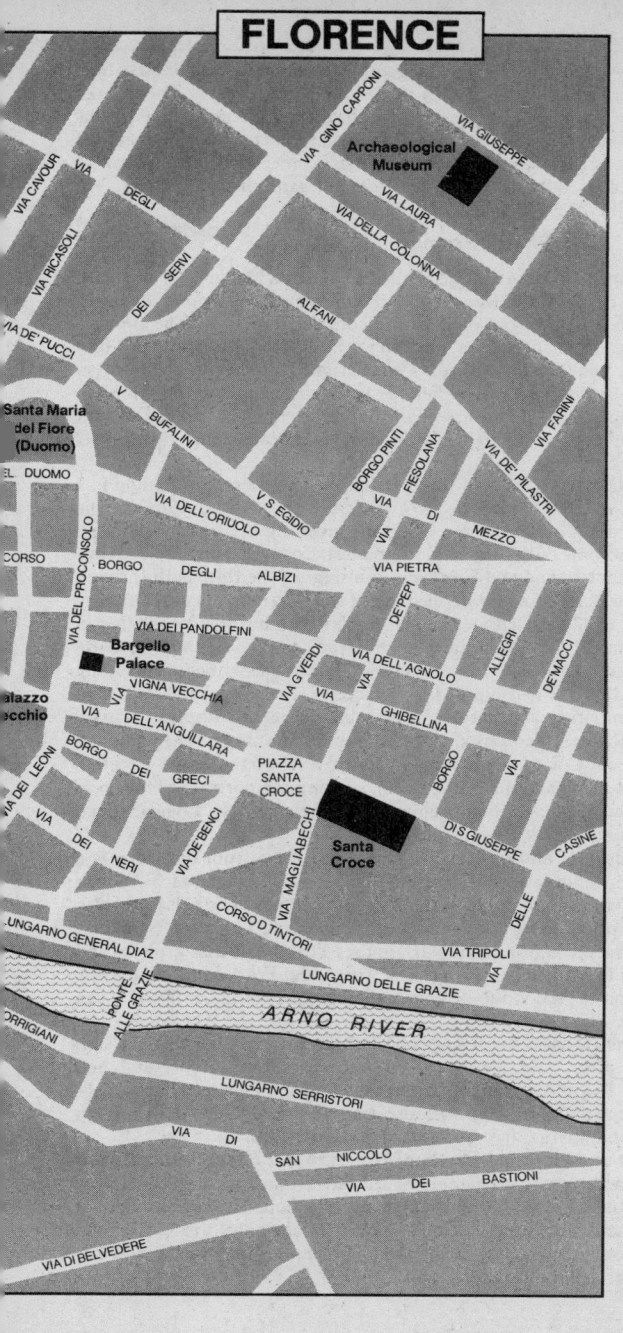

FLORENCE

Archaeological Museum

VIA GINO CAPPONI
VIA GIUSEPPE
VIA LAURA
VIA DELLA COLONNA
VIA CAVOUR
VIA
DEGLI
SERVI
DEI
ALFANI
VIA RICASOLI
VIA DE'PUCCI
V
BUFALINI
VIA FARINI

Santa Maria
del Fiore
(Duomo)

EL DUOMO
VIA DELL'ORIUOLO
V S EGIDIO
BORGO PINTI
VIA FIESOLANA
VIA DE'PILASTRI
VIA
DI
MEZZO
CORSO
BORGO
DEGLI
ALBIZI
VIA PIETRA
VIA DEL PROCONSOLO
VIA DEI PANDOLFINI
DE PEPI
Bargello
Palace
VIA DELL'AGNOLO
ALLEGRI
DE MACCI
VIGNA VECCHIA
VIA G VERDI
VIA
alazzo
ecchio
VIA
DELL'ANGUILLARA
GHIBELLINA
BORGO
VIA
BORGO
DEI
GRECI
PIAZZA
SANTA
CROCE
VIA DEI LEONI
VIA
DEI
NERI
VIA DE BENCI
VIA MAGLIABECHI
Santa
Croce
DI S GIUSEPPE
CASINE
DELLE
CORSO D'TINTORI
VIA TRIPOLI
UNGARNO GENERAL DIAZ
VIA
LUNGARNO DELLE GRAZIE
PONTE
ALLE GRAZIE
ORRIGIANI

ARNO RIVER

LUNGARNO SERRISTORI
VIA
DI
SAN
NICCOLO
VIA
DEI
BASTIONI
VIA DI BELVEDERE

372 FLORENCE / At-a-Glance

SPECIAL PLACES: The Arno is a good orientation point for first-time visitors to Florence. Most of the city sits on the north, or right, bank of the river. The city's principal squares are the Piazza del Duomo, the religious heart of Florence; the Piazza della Repubblica, its bustling commercial center, and the Piazza della Signoría, the ancient political center and today a favorite meeting place because of its outdoor cafés. The most elegant shopping street, Via Tornabuoni, runs from the Arno to the Piazza Antinori.

DOWNTOWN

The Cathedral (Duomo) Complex – The Cathedral of Santa Maria del Fiore, with its magnificent red dome designed by Brunelleschi, dominates a large double square 10 blocks north of the Arno. It was begun in 1296 and completed in 1434. The cupola's 138-foot diameter is greater than that of St. Peter's in Rome. The slim, 269-foot campanile to the right as you face the cathedral was designed and begun by Giotto in 1334. The Romanesque baptistry nearby is famous for its bronze doors by Ghiberti. All three structures are open daily. There are small charges to enter the campanile, visit the top of the cathedral dome, and light the baptistry's mosaic dome. Piazza del Duomo.

Uffizi Museum and Gallery (Galleria degli Uffizi) – The museum building is a Renaissance palace designed by Vasari in 1574 to house the offices, *uffizi*, of the Medicis' administration. In 1581, Francesco I began converting the top floor into an art museum destined to become one of the world's greatest. Today the palazzo contains many of the most important Italian and European paintings of the thirteenth through eighteenth centuries, as well as a fine new collection of self-portraits of contemporary artists (many donated in 1982 to celebrate the museum's 400th birthday) exhibited in the Niobe Room. The Botticelli Room contains his *Birth of Venus* and *Spring* (recently restored). Fifteen rooms are devoted to Florentine and Tuscan masterpieces, including the work of Cimabue, Giotto, Fra Filippo Lippi, Uccello, Fra Angelico, Da Vinci, Michelangelo, not to mention such other non-Florentine masters as Raphael, Titian, Tintoretto, Caravaggio, Rubens, Van Dyck, and Rembrandt. Special arrangements can be made to visit the Vasari Corridor (actually an upper level of the Ponte Vecchio, connecting the Palazzo Vecchio and the Pitti Palace), housing self-portraits of the great Renaissance artists. Closed Mondays. Small admission fee; free Sundays. Loggiato degli Uffizi 6, between the Piazza della Signoria and the Arno.

Pitti Palace and Gallery (Palazzo Pitti) – Across the Arno from the Uffizi is a rugged, austere, fifteenth-century palace built to the plans of Brunelleschi, which became the seat of the Medici grand dukes in the sixteenth century. The palace, a work of art itself, is filled with priceless frescoes and stucco decoration. Its Palatine Gallery, devoted to sixteenth- and seventeenth-century art, houses 11 Raphael masterpieces and fine paintings by Rubens in addition to the work of Titian and Fra Filippo Lippi. The Gallery of Modern Art on the second floor houses mainly nineteenth-century Tuscan works. Closed Mondays. Piazza dei Pitti.

The Museum of Gems (Museo degli Argenti) – On its ground floor this museum has 16 rooms filled with silver, gold, jewels, cameos, tapestries, furniture, crystal, and ivory of the Medicis. The Royal Apartments (Appartamenti Monumentali) once inhabited by the Medici, Lorena, and Savoy families also may be visited. Open daily, except Mondays. Small admission charge; free Sundays. Piazza dei Pitti.

The Bargello Palace and National Museum (Palazzo del Bargello ed Museo Nazionale) – The Bargello is a fine example of thirteenth- and fourteenth-century medieval architecture, housing an important sculpture collection. The entire school of Florentine and Tuscan sculpture is represented — from Michelangelo to Cellini and Donatello. Open daily, except Mondays. Small admission charge; free Sundays. A few blocks north of the Uffizi. Via del Proconsolo 4.

The Academy (Galleria dell'Accademia) – Michelangelo's original *David* was brought here from the Piazza della Signoria in 1873. Since then, millions of visitors have come just to see this monumental sculpture. But don't ignore the rich collection of Florentine paintings — from thirteenth-century Primitives to sixteenth-century Mannerists. Closed Mondays. Small admission charge; free Sundays. Via Ricasoli 6.

Palazzo Vecchio – This palace, built between 1299 and 1314, was the residence of the Medicis until Cosimo I moved the seat of government to the Pitti Palace in 1550. The severe Gothic exterior of the palace contrasts with the sumptuous apartments inside. The Salon of the Five Hundred (Sala dei Cinquecento) on the first floor is painted with frescoes by Vasari and others and contains *The Genius of Victory* by Michelangelo. On the third floor is a new permanent exhibition of 140 works of art removed from Italy by the Nazis and recovered by famed Italian sleuth Rodolfo Siviero. Closed Saturdays. Small admission charge; free Sundays. Piazza della Signoria.

Church of St. Lawrence (Chiesa di San Lorenzo) – A Renaissance building designed by Brunelleschi and his students during the fifteenth century, this was the parish church of the Medicis. Most of the Medicis are buried here. The Laurentian Library, a Michelangelo masterpiece with 10,000 precious volumes, can be entered through the church cloisters or from the square. Closed Sundays. Piazza San Lorenzo.

Medici Chapels (Capelle Medici) – The famous tombs of the Medici designed by Michelangelo are in the new sacristy of the Medici Chapels. The chapels were once a part of the Church of St. Lawrence, but are now separate. Open daily except Mondays. Small admission charge; free Sundays. Piazza Madonna degli Aldobrandini.

Medici Palace (Palazzo Medici-Riccardi) – Typical of the Renaissance style, this palace was the residence of the Medicis from 1460 to 1540. A tiny chapel on the first floor is decorated with wonderful frescoes by Benozzo Gozzoli. The Medici Museum on the ground floor contains one of Filippo Lippi's *Virgin and Child* paintings, the death mask of Lorenzo the Magnificent, and a series of Medici portraits by Bronzino. The palace is open daily, but the museum is closed Wednesdays. Small admission fee; free Sundays. Near the Church of San Lorenzo. Via Cavour.

Ponte Vecchio – This was the only one of Florence's bridges to survive destruction in 1944. Built in 1345, it is famous for the rows of shops lining both sides reserved almost exclusively for gold- and silversmiths since the late sixteenth century.

Straw Market (Mercato Nuovo) – This covered market dates back to the sixteenth century. You'll find an amazing assortment of handbags, sun hats, and place mats in traditional Florentine straw and raffia; wonderful embroidery work; typical gilt-pattern wooden articles, and other souvenirs. The symbol of the market is a delightful bronze statue of a wild boar, called *Porcellino*. Rub its nose and toss a coin into the nearby fountain to ensure a return trip to Florence. Near Piazza della Signoria.

Boboli Gardens (Giardino di Boboli) – Behind the Pitti Palace, this delightful Italian-style terraced garden is studded with cypress, unusual statuary, grottoes, and fountains. It was laid out for Cosimo I's consort, Eleonora of Toledo, in the sixteenth century. Open daily.

ENVIRONS

Fiesole – This beautiful village on a hill overlooking Florence and the Arno was an ancient Etruscan settlement and, later, a Roman city. Stop to enjoy the view of Florence from the terrace before visiting the fourteenth-century cloisters and tiny cells of the Convent of St. Francis. Below the convent is an eleventh-century cathedral surmounted by a battlemented campanile. Nearby is a Roman theater, built about 80 BC, where classical plays are sometimes performed, especially during the annual festival (*L'Estate Fiesolana*), which is devoted primarily to music. Fiesole is 5 miles (8 km) north of Florence, and can be reached by bus 7 from the city.

The Villas – Scattered about the surrounding countryside are a number of stately villas of the historic aristocracy of Florence, some of which are open to the public during certain hours. Three associated with the Medicis are the sixteenth-century Villa della Petraia, with its impressive fountain by N. Tribolo, 4 miles (6 km) north of the city; the fifteenth-century Villa di Castello, surrounded by terraced gardens, 6 miles (10 km) north of Florence in Castello; and the Villa Medici Poggia a Caiano, built for Lorenzo the Magnificent in 1485, 21 miles (34 km) northwest of Florence in Poggia a Caiano. *Agriturist* runs organized excursions into the countryside and to the villas; for information, contact the local tourist office or phone 287838.

  ■**EXTRA SPECIAL:** Florence is a convenient place from which to visit Pisa. The main reason people come to Pisa, of course, is to see the Leaning Tower (Torre Pendente). The twelfth-century white marble tower serves as a campanile or belfry for the cathedral, which is also of architectural interest. Climb up the 294 steps of the tower for a wonderful panorama of the town. Pisa is the birthplace of Galileo, and the astronomer-physicist used the Leaning Tower in working out his theory of the laws of gravity. The tower leans because of a slight slipping of land that occurred early during its construction.
  Another interesting side trip from Florence is to Siena. Originally an Etruscan city, Siena has many splendid gothic structures, including the Palazzo Comunale and the Cathedral. Siena is also famous for its colorful Corsa del Palio festival. Held twice during the summer (July 2 and August 16) in the Campo, the main piazza of Siena, this is a celebration of the city's heritage and features a parade, medieval costumes, and a traditional horse race.

SOURCES AND RESOURCES

The Azienda Autonoma di Turismo (Tourist Information Office), Via Tornabuoni 15 (phone: 217459), will provide general information, brochures, and maps of Florence and the surrounding area, as will Ente Provinciale per il Turismo, Via A. Manzoni 16 (phone: 678841). For information on Tuscany, contact the Regional Tourist Office, Via di Novoli 26. Helpful for younger travelers are the Association of Youth Hostels, Viale A. Righi 2, and the Student Travel Service (STS), Via Zannetti 18r. Numerous maps and pocket-size guidebooks to Florence, such as the *Storti Guides,* are published locally and are available at newsstands throughout the city.

For Local Coverage – Check the brochure *Florence Concierge Information,* usually available at your hotel, or pick up a copy of the monthly *Calendar of Events in Florence and Its Province* at the Tourist Information Office.

CLIMATE AND CLOTHES: Florence's climate can be rather severe: cold and damp in winter and stifling in summer. Spring and fall are the best times to visit, particularly if it doesn't happen to rain. The hottest season is from mid-June to mid-September, when temperatures range from 60°F (15°C) to 90°F (32°C). Temperatures rarely drop below freezing in winter — the range is 36°F (2°C) to 52°F (11°C) from December through mid-March, but the cold is often gripping. Heavy overcoats are advisable, and an umbrella is a necessity.

GETTING AROUND: Most visitors find Florence one of the easiest European cities to get around in. Although it is fairly large, the scale is rather intimate, and you can get just about anywhere by foot. The Arno is a good orientation point. Most of the city lies on the north, or right, bank.
  Buses – ATAF is the city bus company, running about 40 city and suburban routes. A free bus route map is available from the ATAF office, Piazza del Duomo

57R. Tickets can be bought at tobacco counters, in bars, and at some newsstands and cost 400 lire. A 500-lire ticket, also available, can be used more than once, with a 1½-hour time limit.

Taxi – You can hail a taxi that is cruising (it's available if the light on top is lit) or pick one up at one of the numerous cabstands around the city. You can call for a taxi by dialing 4798 or 4390. Fares are calculated by meters, but there are extra charges for night rides, luggage, station pickups, and the like. It is customary to leave a small tip. A general rule is to round off the fare to the nearest 500 or 1,000 lire.

Car Rental – *Hertz,* Via M. Finiguerra 33 (phone: 282260); *Avis,* Borgo Ognissanti 128r (phone: 213629); *Europcar,* Borgo Ognissanti 120r (phone: 294130); and *Maggiore,* via M. Finiguerra 11 (phone: 294578).

MUSEUMS: Since museums are possibly the city's top attraction, quite a few have been listed in *Special Places.* In all, there are 40 museums in Florence. A few churches and palaces also are listed here, because the artwork in them makes them, in effect, museums, too. The Superintendent of Monuments (phone: 214856 and 218341) can provide information about hours.

Museum of Anthropology and Ethnology (Museo di Antropologia ed Etnologia), Via del Proconsolo 12.

Archaeological Museum (Museo Archeologico), Via della Colonna 36.

Bardini Museum, Piazza dei Mozzi.

Museum of the Works of the Duomo (Museo Opera del Duomo), Piazza del Duomo.

Church of Santa Maria Novella (Chiesa di Santa Maria Novella), Piazza Santa Maria Novella.

Church of the Holy Trinity (Chiesa della Santa Trinita), Pianna Santa Trinita.

Church of Santa Maria del Carmine, Piazza del Carmine.

Church of the Holy Cross (Chiesa di Santa Croce), Piazza Santa Croce.

Orsanmichele, Via Arte della Lana 1.

Stibbert Museum (Museo Stibbert), Via Frederick Stibbert 26.

Museum of the History of Science (Instituto e Museo di Storia della Scienza), Piazza del Giudici 1.

Florence "As it Was" (Firenze com'era), Via dell' Oriuolo 24.

Horne Museum (Museo Horne), Via de Benci 6.

Museum of St. Mark (Convento di San Marco), Piazza San Marco.

Strozzi Palace (Palazzo Strozzi), Piazza Strozzi.

Bandini Museum (Museo Bandini), Via G. Dupre, Fiesole.

Michelangelo Buonarroti's House (Casa Buonarroti), Via Ghibellina 70.

Davanzati Palace (Palazzo Davanzati), Via Porta Rossa.

SHOPPING: Shopping is absolutely wonderful in Florence, Italy's center for handicraft and fashions. The smartest streets for fashions are via Tornabuoni, via della Vigna Nuova, via Calzaiuoli, and via Roma. The shops lining the Ponte Vecchio sell beautiful gold and silver jewelry. Antiques, leathergoods, and handmade lingerie are other specialties of shops here. Stores are open from 9 AM to 1 PM (except Mondays) and from 3:30 to 7:30 PM Mondays through Saturdays. Food stores also close on Wednesday afternoons (but are open Monday mornings). During the summer, afternoon opening and closing are a half-hour later.

Alex – The best in designer clothes for women — Gianni Versace, Kansai Yamamoto, Byblos, Claude Montana, Basile, Thierry Mugler. Via Vigna Nuova 19r.

Antico Setificio Fiorentino – Fabulous fabrics, all hand-loomed. Via Vigna Nuova 97.

BM – English-language bookstore. Borgo Ognissanti 4r.

Beltrami – Chain of elegant, expensive leatherwear shops: shoes, bags, jackets, pants, etc. Via Calzaiuoli 31r, 44r, and 101r; Via dei Pecori 16r; Via Calimala 11r.

Bijoux Cascio – Moderately priced jewelry, particularly in gold; the designs are the shop's own. Via Tornabuoni 32.

Corsellini – Handmade pipes and accessories. Via Panzani 49r.

David – Leather bags, luggage, shoes, clothes. Via Roma 11-13r.

Emilio Paoli – Straw market with class. Articles produced locally and imported. Wonderful gifts. Via Vigna Nuova 24-28r.

Feltrinelli – Art books. Via Cavour.

Franco Maria Ricci Libreria – Fine books selected by the producers of a fine magazine. Via delle Belle Donne 41r.

Gants – Gloves of the highest quality; *Gants* makes its own. Via Porta Rossa 78.

Gerard – Way-out, punk, and exotic fashion for men and women. Via Vaccereccia 18-20r.

Giannini – Stationers with class. Piazza Pitti 47r.

Gucci – Parent store of Italy's most chic leather and fashion purveyor. Less expensive than in the US, but expensive nonetheless. Via de Tornabuoni 73.

Happy Jack – Fine men's boutique; alterations done quickly. Via Vigna Nuova 7-13r.

Il Papiro – *Papier à cuve*, or marbelized paper, a method of hand decoration invented in the seventeenth century; lovely stationery. Via Cavour 55.

Inmarket – Benetton sweaters in latest colors and styles. Via Calimala 6.

Libreria Salinnbeni – Specializing in art books. Via M. Palmieri 14.

Lily of Florence – American sizes in shoes. Borgo S. Jacopo 20.

Mario Buccellati – Fine jewelry and table silver in traditional Florentine designs. Via Tornabuoni 69.

Melli – Antique jewelry, ivory, silver, clocks. Ponte Vecchio.

Mercato Nuovo (Straw Market) – Covered market with all sorts of items made from straw. Near Piazza della Signoria.

Mercato San Lorenzo – Open-air market selling everything from used clothing to hot tripe sandwiches. Mohair sweaters are a good buy here.

Mujer – Original fashions for the adventurous woman. Via Vaccereccia 6r.

Neuber – British and Italian wools. Via Strozzi 32r.

Parson – Trendy women's boutique. Via Tosinghi 16-18r.

Pineider – Italy's most famous stationers. Piazza della Signoria 13r, Via Tornabuoni 76r, Via dei Cerretani 9r.

Pollini – Fashionable shoes and boots. Via Calimala 12r.

Pratesi – Elegant linens. Lungarno A. Vespucci 8-10.

Primi Mesi – Embroidered crib and carriage sets; maternity, infants', and toddlers' wear. Via dei Cimatori 23r.

Principe – Small but elegant department store. Piazza degli Strozzi.

Santa Croce Church – Top-quality leather boxes, wallets, and handbags from the school and retail shop operated by the church. Piazza Santa Croce.

Schwicker – Quality gifts by Florentine artisans. Piazza Pitti.

Seeber – English-language bookshop. Via Tornabuoni 68.

Ugo Poggi – Florentine handicrafts in silver, china, glass. Via Strozzi 26.

Ungaro Parallele – High fashion for women. Via Vigna Nuova 30r.

UPIM – Large, moderately priced department store. Piazza della Repubblica.

Zanobetti – Classical clothing for men and women. Via Calimala 22r.

 SPECIAL EVENTS: Florence is bathed in medieval splendor each year for festivities surrounding *St. John the Baptist's Day*, June 24 and 28. Part of the tradition for the past 500 years has been for more than 500 men, wearing sixteenth-century costumes, to play a very rough traditional soccer game,

Partita di Calcio. On Easter Sunday, a centuries-old ceremony called *Scoppio del Carro,* literally, "Bursting the Cart," takes place in the Piazza del Duomo, culminating in a great fireworks display. The *Festa delle Rificolone,* September 7, is celebrated with a procession along the Arno and across the Ponte San Nicolo with colorful paper lanterns and torches. On *Ascension Day* each May, Florentines celebrate the *Festa del Grillo* by buying crickets in cages at the Cascine Gardens and setting them free.

SPORTS: Check with your hall porter to find out which sports facilities are currently open to the public. Most are private clubs.

Golf – There is a good course at *Golf dell'Ugolino* in nearby Impruneta at Via Chiantigiana 3 (phone: 205-1009).

Tennis – You can play tennis at *Circolo del Tennis,* Viale Visarno 1 (phone: 490164, 356651); Piazzale Michelangelo, Viale Michelangelo 61 (phone: 681-1880); *Il Poggetto,* Via Michele Mercati 24B (phone: 46012); and *Ass. Sportiva Assi,* Viale Michelangelo 64 (phone: 6811967).

THEATER: If you'd like to see a play in Italian, the principal theaters in Florence are the *Teatro Comunale,* Corso Italia 16 (phone: 216253); *Teatro della Pergola,* Via della Pergola 32 (phone: 272690); *Teatro Verdi,* Via Ghibellina 99 (phone: 29-62-42); and *Teatro Niccolini,* Via Ricasoli 5 (phone: 213282). *Cinema Astro,* Piazza S. Simone (near Santa Croce), has films in English every night except Mondays.

MUSIC: The *Teatro Comunale* (see *Theater*) is the principal opera house and concert hall. The *Maggio Musicale Fiorentino* festival, which attracts some of the world's finest musicians and singers, is held there each May and June. The opera season is January and February and July. *Teatro della Pergola* (see *Theater*) is the scene of Saturday afternoon concerts autumn through spring. Open-air concerts are held in the *Boboli Gardens* (see *Special Places*) and in the cloisters of the *Badia Fiesolana* and of the *Ospedale degli Innocenti* on July and August evenings.

NIGHTCLUBS AND NIGHTLIFE: A Florentine evening usually begins with an *aperitivo* at one of the cafés on piazza della Signoria or piazza della Repubblica or at *Harry's Bar,* Lungarno Amerigo Vespucci 22R (phone: 296700), or at the bar in the *Excelsior Hotel* (see *Checking In*). Among the more popular discos are *Papillon,* Via Porta Rossa 15R (phone: 262808); *Jackie O',* Via dell'Erta Canina 24/6 (phone: 216146); *Full-up,* Via della Vigna Vecchia 21R (phone: 293006); *Divina Club,* Borgo degli Albizi 66R (phone: 214406); *Yab Yum,* Via Sassetti 5R (phone: 282018); and the *Space Electronic,* Via Palazzuolo 37 (phone: 293082). *Tabasco,* Piazza Santa Cecilia 3, is gay. The *Loggia Tornaquinci* is an elegant piano bar on the top floor of a sixteenth-century Medici building, Via Tornabuoni 6 (phone: 219148). Other piano bars include the *Caffè,* Piazza Pitti 9 (phone: 296241); the *Octopus,* Via del Parione 50 (phone: 294122); *Oberon,* Via dell'Erta Canina 12R (phone: 216516); and *Arcadia,* Via Pandolfini 26 (phone: 210013). There are also piano bars at some of the hotels such as the *Majestic, Savoy, Anglo-American,* and the *Londra.* Popular for drinks is *Caffè Strozzi,* Piazza Strozzi 16-19R (phone: 212574).

SINS: The family that runs the Santa Maria Novella Pharmacy (Officina Profumo Farmaceutica di Santa Maria Novella), Via della Scala 16, takes great *pride* in the frescoes by Giotto and Spinello Aretino that decorate their shop, and the fact that it has operated continuously as a drugstore since it was founded by monks in 1612. The best place to satisfy your *lust* for that marvelous Italian ice cream is *Vivoli,* at Via Isole delle Stinche 7. The flavors are as traditional as chocolate and strawberry and as exotic as grapefruit or tea. More typical *lustful* urges are being satisfied these days in the shadows along the Via del Porcellana.

-BEST IN TOWN

CHECKING IN: The city is well organized for visitors, with over 400 hotels and pensions, *pensioni,* to accommodate some 20,000 people. At an expensive hotel, plan on spending from $100 to $300 a night for a double room. Moderate-priced hotels cost between $55 and $100 a night, and the price for hotels or pensions listed as inexpensive will be $30 to $55.

Excelsior Italie – Overlooking the Arno, just a short walk from the city center, the *Excelsior* is classic both in style and service. The excellent terrace restaurant has a splendid view when the stained-glass windows are opened. It's a favorite of the Florentines. Major credit cards. Piazza Ognissanti 3 (phone: 294301). Expensive.

Villa Medici – Halfway between the railway station and the River Arno, the *Villa Medici* is a reconstruction of the nineteenth-century Sonnino de Renzis Palace. In addition to the charming, spacious rooms, there is a roof garden restaurant and pool. Major credit cards. Via del Prato 42 (phone: 261331). Expensive.

Savoy – Conveniently situated in the heart of Florence, the *Savoy* is a classical gem with most rooms in Venetian style. It also has a popular piano bar. Major credit cards. Piazza della Repubblica 7 (phone: 283313). Expensive.

Grand Hotel Baglioni – Another traditional hotel in refined Tuscan taste: parquet floors, solid furnishings, handsome carpets. Sober — even somber — atmosphere and service. Near the railway station and a short walk from the best shopping. Major credit cards. Piazza Unitá Italiana 6 (phone: 218441). Expensive to moderate.

Villa San Michele – This beautiful little villa-hotel, partly designed by Michelangelo, is on the slopes of the Fiesole hill. Major credit cards. Via Doccia 4, Fiesole (phone: 59451). Expensive to moderate.

Hotel de la Ville – Dark, quiet, and somber, this is the perfect hotel for light sleepers. Its double doors and storm windows provide a peaceful oasis in the center of Florence, just off the elegant via Tornabuoni. Major credit cards. Piazza Antinori 1 (phone: 261805). Expensive to moderate.

Hotel Regency – This small Florentine villa in a quiet residential area has a charming garden and a very good restaurant. Major credit cards. Piazza Massimo d'Azeglio 3 (phone: 245247). Expensive to moderate.

Lungarno – Comfortable, functional, and cheerful, this modern hotel has some rooms with terraces and balconies overlooking the Arno between Ponte Vecchio and Ponte Santa Trinità. Major credit cards. Borgo San Jacopo 14 (phone: 264211). Moderate.

Grand Hotel Minerva – The 110 rooms here are large and comfortably furnished, all with private modern baths; the staff is pleasant; and the hotel is very nicely situated near the train station as well as shopping and museums. Piazza Santa Maria Novella 16 (phone: 284555). Moderate.

Beacci Tornabuoni – This delightful *pensione* occupies the top floors of a fourteenth-century palace on Florence's most elegant street. It's traditional yet cheerful and sunny, provides excellent service, and has a charming terrace. Via Tornabuoni 3 (phone: 212645). Inexpensive.

Pensione Bencistà – This fifteenth-century villa, now a small hotel, is a beautiful bargain among the olive trees between Fiesole and San Domenico. There are no phones in the rooms. Closed November to mid-March. Fiesole (phone: 59163). Inexpensive.

EATING OUT: Tuscan food is considered to be the best regional cuisine in the country by many Italians. Indeed, two Florentine women, Maria and Catherine de' Medici, often are credited with introducing fine cooking to France via the French court in the sixteenth century. A full meal for two including the house wine or the low-priced but excellent local Chianti at an expensive restaurant will cost between $45 and $90. Expect to pay between $25 and $45 at a moderate restaurant; between $15 and $25 at an inexpensive one.

Enoteca Pinchiorri – Possibly Italy's best restaurant and most impressive wine collection (60,000 bottles), in the fifteenth-century Ciofi-Iacometti Palace, with a delightful courtyard for dining al fresco. The four chefs, who have all apprenticed with the "greats" in France, prepare exquisite nouvelle dishes such as mosaic of sweet and sour fish, sweetbread salad with shrimp sauce, and medallions of veal with capers and lime. Closed Sundays and Mondays all day, and lunch on Tuesdays. Reservations required. Via Ghibellina 87 (phone: 242777). Expensive.

Il Barrino – Originally opened by renowned singer Gino Paoli, this tiny, luxurious restaurant has changed hands often and lost some of its glamour, but it continues to offer an interesting, albeit brief, menu and has the advantage of staying open later than most. Closed Sundays, Mondays, and August. Reservations required. Via de' Biffi 2r (phone: 215180). Expensive.

Sabatini – Thoroughly outclassed since the arrival of *Pinchiorri*, it's still quiet, dignified, and noted for its well-prepared traditional cuisine. Some may find the classical menu far less interesting than those of less expensive *trattorie*. Closed Mondays and the first half of July. Reservations recommended. Via Panzani 9a (phone: 211559). Expensive.

Coco Lezzone – Another Florentine favorite serving authentic local food using the best ingredients and no pretenses. Try the *pappa al pomodoro,* a thick soup made of fresh tomatoes, herbs, and bread. This restaurant is crowded and hurried; don't expect to linger. Closed Sundays, summer Saturdays, and August. Via del Parioncino 26R (phone: 287178). Expensive to moderate.

Cantinetta Antinori – Not quite a restaurant, but a typically rustic yet fashionably chic cantina, with food designed to accompany the Antinori wines. Perfect for a light lunch of salami or *finocchiona* with fine bread, *crostini* (chicken liver canapés), soup, or a modest hot dish such as tripe or *bollito* (mixed boiled meats). Closed Saturday nights, Sundays, and August. Piazza Antinori 3 (phone: 292234). Expensive to moderate.

Da Noi – Currently *di moda* (in fashion), this small restaurant offers a cuisine that's extremely imaginative yet traditional at the same time. Try the *crespelle* (crêpes) stuffed with spinach and ricotta cheese in a sweet pepper sauce, or fresh fish prepared with sage and rosemary or with tarragon. Delicious desserts. Closed Sundays, Mondays, and August. Reservations recommended. Via Fiesolana 40r (phone: 242917). Expensive to moderate.

Osteria Natalino – Predominantly a fish restaurant, with a famous artist client or two whose works adorn the limited wall space. The catch of the day is temptingly displayed in its tiny entrance. Specialties include spicy seafood and rice, *risotto di mare.* Closed Sundays. Reservations advised. Via Borgo degli Albizi 17 (phone: 26-34-04). Expensive to moderate.

Otello – It's busy and modern, walls lined with paintings and courtyard open in fine weather. Florentine specialties include grilled meats and *costola di vitello alla zingara* (veal in piquant sauce). Closed Tuesdays and August. Reservations required. Via degli Orti Oricellari 28R (phone: 215819). Expensive to moderate.

Harry's Bar – An island of American-style calm on the banks of the Arno, where every English-speaking visitor is obliged to stop at least once. Italian specialties are best, though it's also the place to find a hamburger and french fries. The bar is a favorite of journalists and other expatriots. Closed Sundays and mid-December to mid-January. Lungarno Vespucci 22R (phone: 296700). Expensive to moderate.

Garga – Unusual specialties include *zuppa di cavoli neri* (soup of bitter green local vegetable), *risotto* of leeks and bacon, and *gnocchetti verdi* (pasta of spinach and ricotta) — all exquisitely prepared. Only five tables. Closed Sundays. Reservations required. Via del Moro 40 (phone: 218094). Moderate.

Hosteria Ganino – A longtime Florentine favorite, this typically tiny Tuscan trattoria has recently changed hands and surpassed its former glory. Now run by a family of enthusiastic nonrestaurateurs, the Ganino provides few comforts (five marble-topped tables covered with plain brown paper for tablecloths) but the best of Florentine cuisine, including fresh mushrooms and truffles in season and a justifiably famous cheesecake. Al fresco dining on the small piazza in good weather. Closed Sundays and August. Reservations advisable. Piazza dei Cimatori 4r (phone: 214125). Moderate.

La Crêperie – As the name suggests, the specialty here is a vast assortment of crêpes, salads, and desserts. Closed Sundays. Reservations advised. Via Vecchietti 6-8-10r (phone: 294470). Moderate.

Il Giardinetto – Fine Florentine and Bolognese cuisine, with a small courtyard for al fresco dining. Open later than most. Closed Mondays. Reservations required. Viale Giannotti 62r (phone: 680640). Moderate.

La Loggia – The most spectacular site in Florence, with a view over the entire city, is run by some ex-*Sabatini* waiters who have transformed a once-mediocre restaurant into a Florentine favorite — especially pleasant during the summer for the panorama from the terrace. Closed Wednesdays. Reservations advised. Piazzale Michelangelo 1 (phone: 28-70-32). Moderate.

Il Latini – Lodged in the former stables of the historic Palazzo Rucella, this popular Florentine eatery serves such solid and abundant fare as hardy Tuscan soups, unpretentious meat platters, grilled fish, fresh vegetables, and traditional desserts. A very good value. Closed Tuesdays for lunch and Mondays. Via Palchetti 6R (phone: 210916). Moderate to inexpensive.

Fagioli – A cheery, rustic ambience and a full bar. Enjoy the thick white bean soup with pasta, *passato di fagioli con pasta*. Closed Saturdays, Sundays, and August. Corso Tintori 47R (phone: 244285). Inexpensive.

Angiolino – On the Pitti Palace side of the river, with a cozy ambience. There is no menu posted outside, just a sign that, translated, reads: "Only full meals served." It's very good potluck, and very economical. Closed Mondays. Via Santo Spirito 36R (phone: 298976). Inexpensive.

Le Mossacce – Still largely frequented by habitués, it's filled with long paper-covered tables and serves excellent country-style cooking. Try a *ribollita*, fresh, thick vegetable soup. Closed Saturday nights, Sundays, and August. Via del Proconsolo 55R (phone: 294361). Inexpensive.

Vecchia Bettola – A typical Tuscan trattoria with quality home-style cooking and marble tabletops. Closed Tuesdays and Monday dinner. Viale Ariosto 32–34r (phone: 224158). Inexpensive.

FRANKFURT

Trade and traffic have formed Frankfurt's destiny since its earliest existence as a community, more than 1,200 years ago. Its location on the Main River at the heart of the European continent made it the crossroads of prehistoric trade routes linking northern Europe with the Mediterranean areas, and Eastern with Western Europe. The city grew, spreading out to meet the imperial forest of Dreieich in the south and the wooded Taunus Mountains encircling the broad plain formed by the Main as it flows toward the Rhine. Frankfurt today is a bustling commercial city with a genuine international flair. It is also a city with many parks and museums. Look behind the imposing glass and steel of modern Frankfurt and you will find lovingly restored landmarks that highlight the city's long history.

The Celts were here first, but were forced west across the Rhine by migrating German tribes. Romans had settled along the Main by the first century AD, but they fled the Saxon tribes, who, in turn, were driven out by the Franks in 496. The little settlement on the Main became the site of the Franks' ford — where Saxons from south of the river could cross over to trade.

Ludwig the German, first ruler of the German Empire and a grandson of Charlemagne, made Frankfurt his capital, and from 1356 to 1792 Frankfurt was where the Holy Roman emperors were elected. Frankfurt was granted the right to mint money in the sixteenth century and since that time finance and trade have been synonymous with it. The Rothschild financial dynasty started here with Meyer Amschel Rothschild (1743–1812); his sons who succeeded him were known as "the five Frankfurters."

Frankfurt also claims Germany's greatest poet, Johann Wolfgang von Goethe, as its own. Goethe was born here in 1749. St. Paul's Church, where Germany's first National Assembly met in 1848, has become a symbol of German liberalism.

In this century, Frankfurt once again earned a reputation as a center of liberalism, as pockets of opposition to the Nazis were centered here. Although a massive Allied air attack during World War II destroyed much of the city, Frankfurt was quick to rebuild after the war and never really stopped. The city has made a conscious attempt to relieve the coldness of modern skyscrapers with attractive pedestrian precincts for shopping and strolling or simply relaxing in an outdoor café. The city's parks and forest and neighboring green belts are much used by Frankfurt's urban population.

Around 600,000 people live in Frankfurt proper, but the greater Frankfurt area, extending across the fertile Main valley and up into the Taunus Mountains, has a population of more than a million. Frankfurt's citizens work in its financial center and in the chemical, electronics, machine tool, and printing industries. They are cosmopolitan and used to sampling the world's best

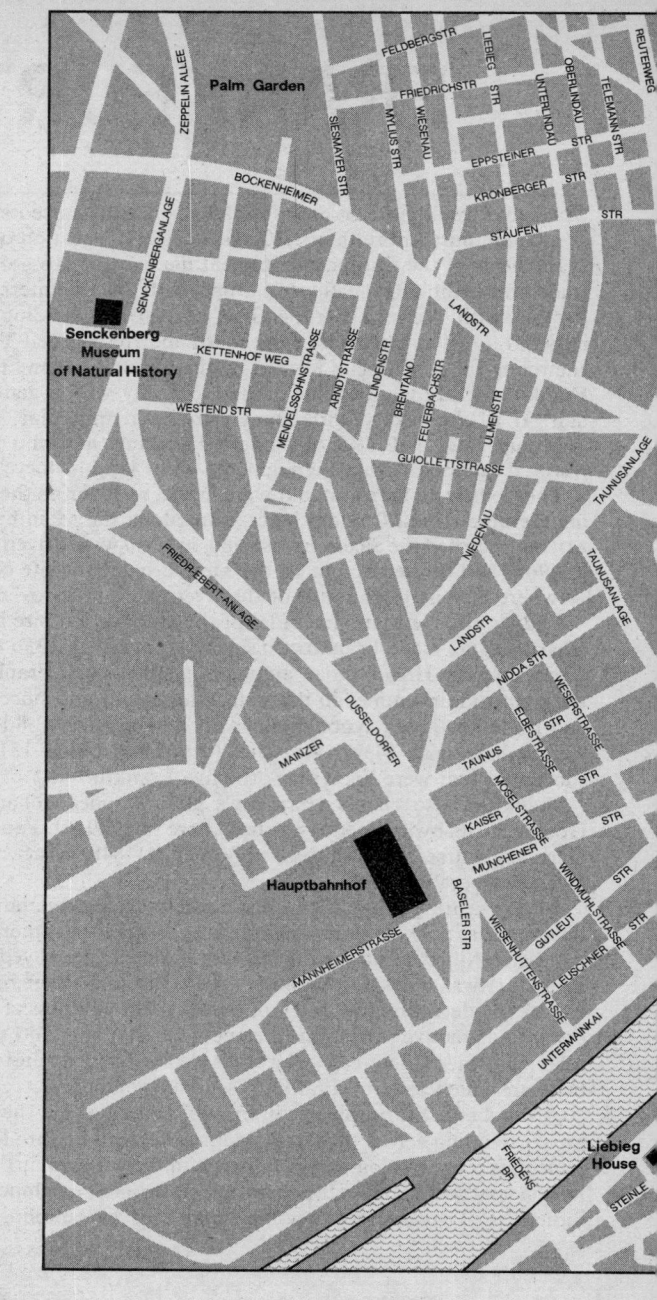

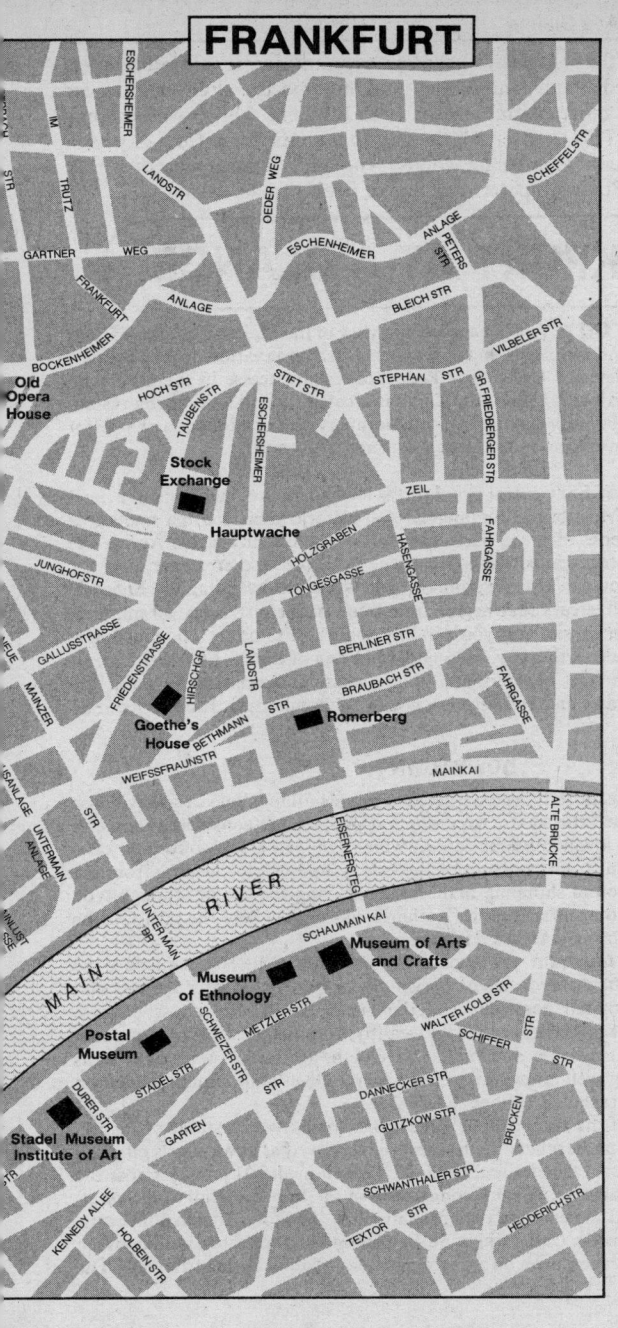

FRANKFURT

Old Opera House

Stock Exchange

Hauptwache

Goethe's House

Romerberg

Museum of Arts and Crafts

Museum of Ethnology

Postal Museum

Stadel Museum Institute of Art

RIVER

MAIN

ESCHERSHEIMER LANDSTR

OEDER WEG

ESCHENHEIMER

ANLAGE

PETERS STR

SCHEFFELSTR

GARTNER

WEG

FRANKFURT

ANLAGE

BOCKENHEIMER

BLEICH STR

VILBELER STR

HOCH STR

STIFT STR

STEPHAN STR

GR FRIEDBERGER STR

TAUBENSTR

ESCHERSHEIMER

ZEIL

FAHRGASSE

HOLZGRABEN

JUNGHOFSTR

TONGESGASSE

HASENGASSE

GALLUSSTRASSE

FRIEDENSTRASSE

HIRSCHGR

BERLINER STR

MANZER

LANDSTR

STR

BRAUBACH STR

FAHRGASSE

BETHMANN

WEIFSSFRAUNSTR

MAINKAI

ALTE BRUCKE

ISANLAGE

UNTERMAIN ANLAGE

STR

EISERNERSTEG

WALLIST

UNTER MAIN BR

SCHAUMAIN KAI

METZLER STR

SCHWEIZER STR

WALTER KOLB STR

SCHIFFER STR

STADEL STR

STR

DANNECKER STR

GARTEN

STR

GUTZKOW STR

BRUCKEN

DUBER STR

SCHWANTHALER STR

HEDDERICH STR

KENNEDY ALLEE

HOLBEIN STR

TEXTOR STR

TRUTZ

M

STR

goods as the result of the role Frankfurt plays as an international trade center. Still, despite all the efficiency, the money-making, and the slightly smug air of success, there is a more casual approach to life here than exists in some other German cities. This is, after all, the city that shuts down for a day each spring so its citizens can walk in the woods. And a city whose mascot is that bumbling little kid, Struwwelpeter, can't take itself too seriously.

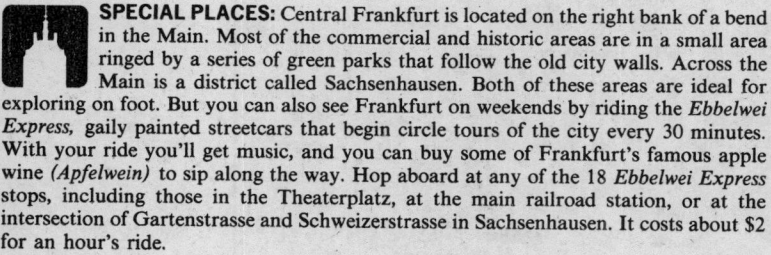

FRANKFURT AT-A-GLANCE

SEEING THE CITY: You get a sweeping view of the Main valley, the Taunus Mountains, and the city from the glass-enclosed observation deck of the new 1,086-foot television tower near Rosa Luxemburgstrasse in the Ginnheim section of northwest Frankfurt. There is a cafeteria and a revolving restaurant in the tower — the tallest structure in West Germany. Small admission charge for the observation platform. Open daily, March through September.

SPECIAL PLACES: Central Frankfurt is located on the right bank of a bend in the Main. Most of the commercial and historic areas are in a small area ringed by a series of green parks that follow the old city walls. Across the Main is a district called Sachsenhausen. Both of these areas are ideal for exploring on foot. But you can also see Frankfurt on weekends by riding the *Ebbelwei Express,* gaily painted streetcars that begin circle tours of the city every 30 minutes. With your ride you'll get music, and you can buy some of Frankfurt's famous apple wine *(Apfelwein)* to sip along the way. Hop aboard at any of the 18 *Ebbelwei Express* stops, including those in the Theaterplatz, at the main railroad station, or at the intersection of Gartenstrasse and Schweizerstrasse in Sachsenhausen. It costs about $2 for an hour's ride.

DOWNTOWN

Hauptwache – This beautifully reconstructed baroque building, once a sentry house dating from 1730, and the little square over which it presides are considered the heart of Frankfurt. There is a lovely outdoor café in which you can enjoy coffee and cake while you get your bearings. Just in front of the café is an escalator leading from the street to a huge underground shopping mall. Before leaving the square, though, you may want to visit St. Katharine's Church (Katharinenkirche), where the poet Goethe was christened and confirmed. An der Hauptwache.

Goethe's House and Museum – A few blocks southwest of the Hauptwache is the boyhood home of Frankfurt's favorite son. Faithfully reconstructed after the war and furnished with many original possessions of the poet's family, the house offers a fascinating peek at eighteenth-century life in a wealthy, commercial city. In a museum adjoining the house, you can see documents on Goethe's life and work as well as pictures and sculpture by well-known artists of his era. Open daily. Small admission charge. Grosser Hirschgraben 23 (phone: 28-28-24).

Römerberg – South of the Hauptwache, on a broad square with a statue of Justice, you will see three adjoining burghers' houses that have served as Frankfurt's city hall since 1405. The three gabled facades and the row of seven medieval houses across the street are the symbol of this city. History comes alive in the Imperial Hall (Kaisersaal) where banquets were held to celebrate the coronations of the Holy Roman Emperors. East of Römerberg Platz is the Cathedral of St. Bartholomew (the Dom), built between the thirteenth and fifteenth centuries on a Carolingian foundation dating from 852. The cathedral's outstanding feature is a tall fifteenth-century dome and lantern tower. Römerberg Pl.

Alt-Sachsenhausen – A few steps from Römerberg, near where the ancient Franks forded the river, the Eiserner Steg footbridge leads you across the river into another old section of the city. (*Sachsenhausen* means "Saxons' houses.") Here you can enjoy the jumble of half-timbered houses and rough cobbled streets with their inviting pubs and restaurants, and the charming little squares and pretty fountains that are particularly lively meeting places at night and on weekends.

Palm Garden (Palmengarten) – One of Europe's most famous botanical gardens, these 55 acres of trees, meadows, ponds, gardens, and footpaths offer a welcome sanctuary from the bustling city. Over 12,000 varieties of plants grow in the park and thousands of orchids and cacti are displayed in its conservatories. A traditional Sunday afternoon entertainment in Frankfurt is a stroll through the flower gardens, perhaps, pausing to listen to one of the concerts, followed by an elaborate ice cream sundae on the flower-bedecked terrace of the *Palmengarten Restaurant.* Small admission charge. Open daily. Entrance at Palmengartenstr. (phone: 212-3382).

The Frankfurt Zoo (Zoologischer Garten) – This is one of Europe's oldest, but nonetheless one of its most up-to-date. Founded in 1858, the zoo is noted for its beautifully landscaped open-air enclosures and for its success in breeding rare species. Open daily. Small admission fee. Alfred-Brehm-Pl. 16 (phone: 212-3731).

The Frankfurt Stock Exchange (Frankfurter Wertpapierbörse) – Frankfurt is one of the most important financial centers in the world. More than 270 German and overseas banks have headquarters or subsidiaries in the city. No tour of the financial district would be complete without a visit to the spectators' gallery to watch the activity on the floor of the Stock Exchange. Open Mondays through Fridays, 10:45 AM to 1:30 PM. Free. Börsenpl. (phone: 219-7383).

Städel Museum Institute of Art and Municipal Gallery (Städelsches Kunstinstitut und Städtische Galerie) – Famous works of Flemish Primitives and German masters of the sixteenth century are on display in the second-floor picture gallery. Open daily, except Mondays, 10 AM to 5 PM. Small admission charge. Schaumainkai 63 (phone: 61-70-92).

Old Opera House (Alte Oper) – A victim of wartime bombing, this 100-year-old landmark was finally rebuilt in 1981. Although no opera performances are held here, the ultra-modern complex of rooms and halls is now used for concerts and conferences. The facade and the vestibule (now a café) were fully restored. Opernplatz (phone: 134-0400).

SUBURBS

The Leather Museum (Deutsches Ledermuseum) – Exhibits recording the history of shoe fashions and the history of the handbag are displayed in a wonderfully fragrant museum in Offenbach just 5 miles (8 km) southeast of Frankfurt. Open daily. Small admission charge. Frankfurterstr. 86, in Offenbach (phone: 8-3982).

■**EXTRA SPECIAL:** The charming old town of *Marburg an der Lahn,* remarkable for its university, its castle, and the first Gothic church ever built in Germany (between 1235 and 1285), is 59 miles (94 km) north of Frankfurt in the Hesse region. The church is dedicated to St. Elizabeth of Hungary, who lived and performed good works here. The university is a center for Protestant theology. On the market square in the old quarter of town, you can see several old half-timbered houses dating from the mid-sixteenth century. As you wander the twisting alleys of the old quarter, you may meet country people in traditional costume, particularly if your visit coincides with marketdays, Wednesdays and Saturdays.

SOURCES AND RESOURCES

For information, maps, brochures, hotel and restaurant listings, plus special sight-seeing tours and tickets to local events, see the Frankfurt Tourist Association (Frankfurter Verkehrsverein). It has information bureaus on the north side of the main train station, opposite track 23 (phone: 212-8849 or 212-8851), and on level B of the Hauptwache underground mall (phone: 212-8708). The office at the train station is open daily; the one at Hauptwache closes on Sundays.

For Local Coverage – The travel association publishes a bimonthly guide to events in the city, *Frankfurter Wochen Schau,* and *Seven,* an English-language weekly that carries a calendar of events throughout Germany, is available at newsstands. *Frankfurt Guide of the City,* by Franz Lerner, is the best guide published in English. It is filled with city history and interesting facts as well as a variety of walking tours. It is available at bookstores and some newsstands.

CLIMATE AND CLOTHES: Frankfurt's climate is similar to San Francisco's — seldom very hot or very cold. However, it is often overcast and frequently foggy and rainy, so a raincoat is recommended in all seasons. Late spring and fall are apt to be the most pleasant times to visit. There is very little air-conditioning — so some visitors may find it uncomfortable during the occasional summer week when temperatures climb into the 80s F (around 26°–32° C).

GETTING AROUND: Frankfurt has a clean, efficient, and quiet rapid transit system of buses, streetcars, subways, and trains. The trip from the Rhine-Main Airport to Frankfurt's main railway station takes only 12 minutes by train. You use the same kind of ticket for the entire system. Buy tickets from automatic dispensers before boarding or purchase a special 1-day, cut-rate ticket at the tourist information bureaus. Maps and timetables are conveniently posted throughout the system.

Buses and Streetcars – City buses, *Stadtbus,* and streetcars, *Strassenbahn,* will take you, inexpensively, to all parts of the city and to many suburbs.

Subways and Trains – The subway system, called the *U-Bahn,* and the new fast trains, *S-Bahn,* to outlying areas get you where you want to go quickly and comfortably. The main stops are at Hauptwache and the railway station.

Taxi – There are stands near major hotels, stations, and at some intersections. Most public telephone booths have a taxi call-number posted. But taxis are expensive.

Car Rental – Major international firms are represented.

MUSEUMS: In addition to those mentioned in *Special Places,* Frankfurt has a number of interesting museums (most of which charge no admission). They are all open daily, except Mondays. The best of these are:

The History Museum (Historisches Museum), Saalgasse 19 am Römerberg (phone: 212-3370).

The Museum of Arts and Crafts (Museum für Kunsthandwerk), Schaumainkai 15 (phone: 212-4037).

The Museum of Ethnology (Museum für Völkerkunde), Schaumainkai 29 (phone: 212-5390).

The Liebieg House (Liebieghaus), ancient and modern sculpture, Schaumainkai 71 (phone: 63-89-07).

The Postal Museum (Bundespostmuseum), Schaumainkai 53 (phone: 60601).

Senckenberg Museum of Natural History, Senckenberganlange 25 (phone: 7-5421).

 SHOPPING: Frankfurt is filled with the world's goods, so bring plenty of money. It is said that more money passes through the cash registers of the well-stocked department stores on the Zeil than on any other street in Europe. The best-known department stores are *Kaufhof,* Zeil 116, and *Hertie,* Zeil 90. There are several pedestrian streets besides the Zeil, including Grosse Bockenheimerstrasse, with its chic boutiques and elegant apparel shops. Incidentally, this street is known locally as Fressgasse (a rough English equivalent is "Gluttony Alley") because it is lined with so many restaurants, wine bars, and delicatessens. The best buys are the well-known German cutlery, expensive but superbly made leather clothing, and Frankfurt's distinctive blue and gray pottery.

Bellak – For the best in German handicrafts. Goethestr. 20.

Rosenthal am Kaiserplatz – Porcelain. Friedensstr. 10.

Mädler – Expensive leathergoods. Kaiserpl. 18 and Zeil 105.

Nikolaus Franz – Hummel, Meissen, and Rosenthal figurines. Steinweg 5.

 SPECIAL EVENTS: Frankfurt is at its busiest during the more than a dozen trade fairs that draw some 1.2 million visitors to the city each year. The biggest of these are the *International Frankfurt Fairs* held in spring and fall and the *Book Fair* in October. Most of these events are held at the fairgrounds *(Messegelände),* a huge exhibition center near the main railway station. The tradition of trade fairs in Frankfurt dates back 800 years. There are also numerous public fairs, such as the *Main Fair,* in August, in the streets between the river and St. Paul's Church; and *Dippemess,* a big country fair held in April with colorful stalls of crockery the main attraction. One other very special local holiday deserves mention: *Wäldchestag.* On the Tuesday following Whitmonday, most Frankfurters leave the city to walk in the neighboring woods, eat sausages and drink beer, and dance in the Forest House (Oberforsthaus).

 SPORTS: One out of every six Frankfurt residents belongs to some type of sports club, and walking and jogging along the river or the marked paths in the city forest and in the nearby Taunus Mountains has reached epidemic proportion. Physical fitness is even sponsored by the state government, which maintains *Trimm Dich* facilities ("keep yourself trim"), a 1.5-mile (2.5-km) illustrated course of exercises and jogging in the city forest. Frankfurt is a major soccer city, with professional matches held in the *Wald Stadium,* Mörfelder Landstr. (phone: 670-80-11). There's also a 6-day bicycle race each year at the *Festhalle* at the fairgrounds.

Bicycling – Besides the 6-day race, numerous cycling events are scheduled during summer months, and there are paths in the city parks and the forest.

Golf – Germany's largest golf course is the *Frankfurter Golfclub.* West of *Wald Stadium,* Golf Str. 41 (phone: 666-23-18).

Ice Skating – You can skate or just watch other people at various rinks, including one at the *Wald Stadium.*

Racing – Flat races and steeplechase races are held at *Racecourse Frankfurt-South* in suburban Niederrad, Schwarzwaldstr. (phone: 67-24-29).

Soccer – *Eintracht* is Frankfurt's local professional club. You can join the enthusiastic supporters at *Wald Stadium* nearly every other weekend during the season.

Swimming – Several hotels have swimming pools and there are numerous indoor and outdoor pools throughout the city. *Stadtbad Mitte,* Hochstr. 4–8, has warm and cold pools as well as saunas (phone: 212-5238).

Tennis – Exhibition matches are played at *Wald Stadium* and the *Festhalle*. It is difficult for visitors to get court time at parks and clubs because of local demand.

THEATER: Frankfurt has 20 theaters, but performances generally are in German, so they may be of limited interest unless you know the language. *The City Theater (Städtische Bühnen)* on Theaterplatz contains the opera house, a large theater, and a smaller stage for more intimate productions. The *Fritz Rémond-Theater* is at the Frankfurt Zoo, Alfred Brehm Pl. 76 (phone: 43-51-66), and often produces current British and American hits in German. Drama is offered at the *Theater am Turm (TAT)*, Oederweg 1 (phone: 1545-100), and you'll find light comedy the specialty at *Die Kömodie*, Theaterpl. (phone: 28-45-80).

MUSIC: Whatever your taste in music, from opera and jazz to punk, you'll hear it in Frankfurt. The *City Opera* performs in an elegant new home in the arts complex on Theaterplatz (phone: 256-2335). There are frequent choral, symphony, and chamber music concerts at *Hessischer-Rundfunk*, Bertramstr. 8 (phone: 1551), at the huge *Jahhunderthalle* in suburban Höchst (phone: 31-91-84), and at the *Old Opera House*, Opernplatz (phone: 134-0400). Jazz lovers will love Frankfurt, which is purported to have more than 100 daily performances, ranging from traditional New Orleans to modern jazz. *Der Jazzkeller*, Kleine Bockenheimerstr. 18a (phone: 28-85-37), is the best-known club, but you should also try *Jazz-Kneipe*, Berlinerstr. 70 (phone: 28-71-73); *Sinkkasten Arts Club*, Brönnerstr. 5 (phone: 28-03-85); *Jazzhaus*, Kleine Bockenheimerstr. 12 (phone: 28-77-94); and *Jazz-Life Podium*, Kleine Rittergasse 22 (phone: 62-63-46).

NIGHTCLUBS AND NIGHTLIFE: All of the city's big hotels offer music and dancing, and discotheques are cropping up all over the city. *Why Not*, on Hauptwache Pl., doesn't really get going until after midnight, then stays open until 4 AM. *Tangenta*, Bockenheimer Landstr. 89, features a pub upstairs and a disco in the cellar. One of the trendiest discos is *Dorian Gray*, at the airport, modeled after New York's Studio 54. *Blue Infinitum* in the *Plaza* hotel, Hamburger Allee 2-10 (phone: 77-07-21), features floor shows as well as dancing. Pub-hopping in Sachsenhausen gets merrier and merrier as the night wears on. Look for the traditional green wreath hanging over the door to identify taverns that serve Frankfurt's special apple wine. Among the most authentic are *Zum Fichtekraenzi*, Wallstr. 5; *Zum Gemalten Hause*, Schweizerstr. 67; and *Zum Grauen Bock*, Grosse Rittergasse 49.

SINS: The side streets off Kaiserstrasse and Münchnerstrasse, going away from the train station, are lined with sex shops, strip clubs, and "sex discos," and many hotel concierges will accommodate their guests with a list of brothels. But, in case your transgressions tend more toward the tummy, *Café Christine*, Eschersheimer Landstr. 319, near the Hessischer-Rundfunk concert hall, will tempt you with its delicious hot chocolate and a fantasy of pastry.

BEST IN TOWN

CHECKING IN: Although Frankfurt has a total of 200 hotels and pensions with over 14,000 beds, only the most confident traveler comes without reservations. Space is always tight and is nearly impossible during the big trade fairs, when, incidentally, maximum prices apply. At an expensive hotel you'll pay from $65 to more than $120 a night for a double room. Moderate hotels charge from $25 to $65; anything below must be considered inexpensive. Virtually all hotels in Frankfurt, regardless of price, share the German virtue of cleanliness.

Frankfurter Hof – In the tradition of grand European hotels, the *Frankfurter Hof* was refurbished and restored to its prewar charm after serving as headquarters for the Allied occupation forces. You can always find an attractive spot in its public rooms where a waiter will bring you a drink, a newspaper, or a message. In the *Restaurant Français,* you're apt to see international movers and shakers from the political and financial worlds. The less expensive *Grill* has an extensive menu and offers excellent service. Bethmannstr. 33 (phone: 2-0251). Expensive.

Frankfurt Inter-Continental – One of Europe's largest, the *Inter-Continental* provides American-style hotel service. It has a swimming pool, sauna, and solarium, a glittering nightclub, and several restaurants, including one on the roof with an enchanting view of the Main and Frankfurt's skyline. Ask for a room on the river side. Wilhelm-Leuschnerstr. 43 (phone: 23-05-61). Expensive.

Canadian Pacific Frankfurt Plaza – Frankfurt's newest luxury hotel is conveniently located near the fairgrounds, but its decor is more sophisticated than you might expect from a hotel — the tallest in West Germany — that caters to conventioneers. There is a bakery on the premises, a small disco, and a seductive piano bar, *Die Biblio Theke.* Hamburger Allee 2-10 (phone: 77-07-21). Expensive.

Frankfurt-Sheraton – You can walk right into the *Sheraton* from the airport's central terminal. A recent extension has made this one of West Germany's largest hotels, with 820 rooms. In addition to the usual amenities, there is a comfortable restaurant, *Maxwell's,* with an extensive menu and good wine list. The hotel's *Red Baron* nightclub is a popular late night spot. Central terminal, Rhine-Main Airport (phone: 697-70). Expensive.

Parkhotel Frankfurt – Typical of small European-style luxury hotels, the *Parkhotel* offers what many Frankfurters consider "the best table in town" in its restaurant, *la Truffe.* The hotel is conveniently located near the main train station. Wiesenhüttenpl. 26 (phone: 2-6970). Expensive.

Palmengarten – A small, 20-room hotel right next to the lovely Palm Garden. Closed in December. Palmengartenstr. 8 (phone: 75-20-41). Moderate.

Haus Hübner – This small hotel is in a pleasant neighborhood not far from the main train station. Westendstr. 23 (phone: 74-60-44). Moderate.

Hotel am Holzhausenpark – The charm of this small hotel is its location on a quiet street facing a small park north of the city center. Seven languages are spoken here, making it a favorite of international visitors. Holzhausenstr. 62 (phone: 59-08-01). Moderate.

Hotel am Dom – This smallish hotel, although in the historic downtown area, is an oasis of quiet. Kannengiessergasse 3 (phone: 28-21-41). Moderate.

Mozart – This charming 35-room hotel is next to the US military headquarters. Note that the quieter rooms are in the back. Parkstr. 17 (phone: 55-08-31). Moderate.

Saloniki – No breakfast is served here, but reasonably priced hotels like this small one very near the train station are hard to find in Frankfurt. Moselstr. 46 (phone: 23-10-61). Inexpensive.

 EATING OUT: Though Frankfurt is not noted for its culinary arts, local specialties are as good in restaurants as you would find them in private homes, and the large population of foreign-born residents of the city ensures a wide choice of European and Asian cuisine. You'll pay $30 or more for two, not including drinks or extras, at restaurants in the expensive category; $10 to $30, in the moderate range; and under $10 at inexpensive places. Lunch is often the main meal, and in most places it is served between 11 AM and 3 PM. Restaurants then close until about 5:30 PM. Except in big hotel restaurants, you cannot just drop in anywhere for a late lunch. However, there is a late afternoon *Kaffee* ritual, at which Frankfurters brace themselves with coffee and pastry or a snack at a *Konditorei*. A local specialty that is a perfect nosh with beer or wine is *Handkäs mit Musik:* soft Limburger cheese mixed with vinegar, oil, a bit of onion, and a few caraway seeds. And whether the frankfurter originated here or not, you can buy the best franks in Frankfurt, on the freshest rolls, from a cart right outside the *Kaufhof* department store.

Restaurant Français – Game and French cuisine and excellent service have made this dining room at the *Frankfurter Hof* a particular favorite of people used to having the best. Reservations recommended. Bethmannstr. 33 (phone: 2-0251). Expensive.

Rôtisserie – This elegant restaurant in the *Inter-Continental Hotel* is a first-class eating establishment, especially when game is in season. Reservations recommended. Wilhelm Leuschnerstr. 43 (phone: 23-05-61). Expensive.

Erno's Bistro – This is a French bistro with checked tablecloths and superior French cooking. It's apt to be crowded, but worth the wait for a table. Closed weekends and mid-June to mid-July. Liebigstr. 15 (phone: 72-19-97). Expensive.

La Truffe – Number one in Frankfurt, say locals. This recently redone restaurant, the dining room of the *Park Hotel,* has a decor that's almost as classically elegant as its traditional French cuisine. Try the truffle dishes, the delicious cheeses, and the fine wines. Closed Sundays and mid-July to mid-August. Reservations recommended. Wiesenhuttenpl. 36 (phone: 269-78-82). Expensive.

Humperdinck – Not your typical Hansel and Gretel atmosphere nor your typical German fare. Instead, this new establishment in the fashionable Westend district concocts wonderful nouvelle cuisine dishes, with an emphasis on seafood and lamb. Closed Sundays, and Saturdays until 7 PM. Reservations recommended. Grüneburgweg 95 (phone: 72-21-22). Expensive to moderate.

Firenze – Appearances can be misleading, for what looks like an ordinary pizzeria is really a topnotch Italian restaurant. Specialties are baked artichokes, stuffed scampi, gnocchi, and fresh fish. Closed Mondays. Reservations recommended. Berger Str. 30 (phone: 43-39-56). Expensive to moderate.

Börsenkeller – Located in the financial district, the *Börsenkeller* serves delicious roast pork and other local specialties in a large rustic room decorated with wood tables, wrought-iron lamps, and candles. Reservations advised for midday. Schillerstr. 11 (phone: 28-11-15). Expensive to moderate.

Frankfurter Stubb – German specialties are beautifully prepared in this well-appointed cellar restaurant at the *Frankfurter Hof.* When white asparagus *(Spargel)* from the Schwetzinger area south of Frankfurt is in season, in May, you'll find it presented here in an imaginative array of dishes, served with wine chosen to complement its delicate flavor. Bethmannstr. 33 (phone: 21-56-79). Moderate.

Dippegucker – Decorated in typical Frankfurt style with hanging brass lamps and bright tablecloths, this restaurant is popular with families for Sunday afternoon dinner. Hearty portions of good German food, including Frankfurt's famous smoked pork chops with sauerkraut, *Rippchen mit Kraut,* are served here. Reservations advised. Eschenheimer Anlage 40 (phone: 55-19-65). Moderate.

Knoblauch – The name of this restaurant is German for garlic, an ingredient used with a deft hand in the fragrant, hearty, delicious food served here. A warm, noisy, cheerful place, *Knoblauch* is actually a pub-restaurant and art gallery. Closed Saturdays. Staufenstr. 39 (phone: 72-28-28). Moderate.

Künstlerkeller – In the cellar of a former Carmelite monastery dating back to the thirteenth century. Modern central heating, hearty food, and the convivial patrons will make you feel both comfortable and welcome. Be sure to ask the hostess for her wine recommendations. No reservations. Closed Mondays. Seckbächer Gasse 2 (phone: 29-22-42). Inexpensive.

Hahnhof – True German *Gemütlichkeit* reigns supreme here: This traditional restaurant draws its food, wines, and atmosphere from the sun-drenched Rhine valley southwest of Frankfurt. Open daily for dinner only. Berliner Str. 64 (phone: 28-78-33). Inexpensive.

GENEVA

Probably the most international of all cities, Geneva is where world leaders have often gathered in order to negotiate agreements and dream of peace. It is the birthplace and headquarters of the International Red Cross, founded in 1863 by Henri Dunant, a native son. The Geneva Convention, binding nations to care for all sick and wounded in war, was signed here in 1864. Home to the defunct League of Nations, center of the European United Nations, Geneva has hosted Big Four foreign ministers' conferences in 1954 and 1959 and has been the site of the nuclear disarmament talks.

Geneva's international role is a historical one, certainly due in part to its central location at one of Europe's crossroads. Near the French border and not far from Italy, where the Rhône River flows into its 45-mile-long lake, called Lake Geneva in English and Lac Léman in French, the city has had a very long and distinguished history. "Gen-eva," a Ligurian word that is the same as "Genoa," means "emerging from the waters." Waters were important in the city's history, since Geneva was the location of the only bridge across the Rhône for many centuries, a bridge that had been built and rebuilt many times even before the Romans took the city from the Celts in 58 BC.

Because of its strategic location, Geneva was also the site of many feuds and wars, from the rivalry between its prince bishop and the duke of Savoy during the fifteenth century to Napoleon's occupation from 1798 to 1815. The year 1815 marked Geneva's entry into the Swiss Confederation to protect its long-fought-for independence and peace.

During the Middle Ages, Geneva, as host to a series of international fairs, took up its international vocation. The Protestant Reformation left a deeper mark on Geneva than on any other city, since John Calvin himself chose it as his headquarters, earning for Geneva the title of "the Rome of the Protestants." Here Calvin preached and prayed but also acted as a dictatorial ruler, building new ramparts, creating his own laws, and even burning his enemy, Miguel Serveto, at the stake for his incompatible religious opinions. Calvin's most influential move was the founding of the University of Geneva in 1559: For 2 centuries thereafter Geneva became schoolmaster for all of Protestant Europe. So austere and rigid was the tone of this Calvinist city that many of its own citizens, the most famous of whom was Jean-Jacques Rousseau, opted to flee. Rousseau, the great eighteenth-century philosopher, never returned to his birthplace after his books were burned there.

Other celebrities found Geneva more congenial, notably Rousseau's great rival philosopher Voltaire and that great Swiss writer and personality Madame de Staël. And virtually all the romantics flocked to the city and its surrounding lake: Chateaubriand, Byron, Dostoyevsky, Goethe, and Victor Hugo were just a few.

Today, with 170,000 inhabitants, Geneva is rather small for a major city. Human in scale, its sights can easily be seen on foot. Its two most characteristic landmarks are the Jet d'Eau, said to be the tallest fountain in the world, rising to a height of between 400 and 500 feet from May to October; and the Flower Clock in the Jardin Anglais, with its face made of flowers and its hands keeping perfect time — as befits a city that is the home of the leading watchmakers of the world.

Whether you want to buy a watch; walk along the quais, particularly the quai du Mont-Blanc with its panoramic view of the Alps; visit this capital of the Reformation with its old town clustered in narrow streets around the Cathedral of St. Pierre; or, as many do, use Geneva as a base for exploring the Alps or the lake — Geneva, the international city, will warmly extend toward you its traditional hospitality.

GENEVA AT-A-GLANCE

SEEING THE CITY: The best view of the town and its surroundings is from the North Tower of Cathédrale St.-Pierre; on a clear day it is well worth the 153 steps and the admission charge; the panorama of city, lake, Alps, and Jura Mountains is spectacular. Another superb view — and the most-often-photographed one — is from the quai du Mont-Blanc near the bridge; on the sailboat-dotted lake you can see the famous Jet d'Eau, pride of Geneva, with the Alps as background.

SPECIAL PLACES: The old town, built on a hill around its famous Reformation Cathedral, was important in medieval times as the site of international fairs. The few streets in the immediate vicinity of the Bourg de Four are easily explored on foot. Just stroll down the narrow, cobblestoned streets, discovering delightful corners like place Bourg de Four, the former market square, have coffee or snacks in one of the cafés, and browse in the antique stores. In summer there are regular walks in the old town with English-speaking guides: ask at the Tourist Office (see *Sources and Resources*) for details.

DOWNTOWN

Cathédrale St.-Pierre – Built in the twelfth to thirteenth century on the site of earlier churches, Cathédrale St.-Pierre was reconstructed later; John Calvin preached here, and his chair can be seen in the austere interior.

Calvin Auditorium – Next door to Cathédrale St.-Pierre is a Gothic church where John Knox used to preach; it was restored in 1959 for John Calvin's 450th anniversary.

Maison Tavel – A few steps from Calvin Auditorium is the oldest house in Geneva, already in existence by 1303. After restoration is completed, the Museum of Old Geneva will be established here.

Old Arsenal – Across the street from the Maison Tavel is the arsenal dating from the days of Napoleon. (Its cannons were seized by the Austrians in 1814.) On the wall are three modern mosaics by Cingria.

Hôtel de Ville – This is Geneva's town hall, where the Geneva Convention was signed in 1864 in the Alabama Court. (This room may be visited by applying to the guardian.) Its oldest part is Baudet Tower, erected in 1455.

St. Germain Church – On the site of an early Christian basilica, with beautiful

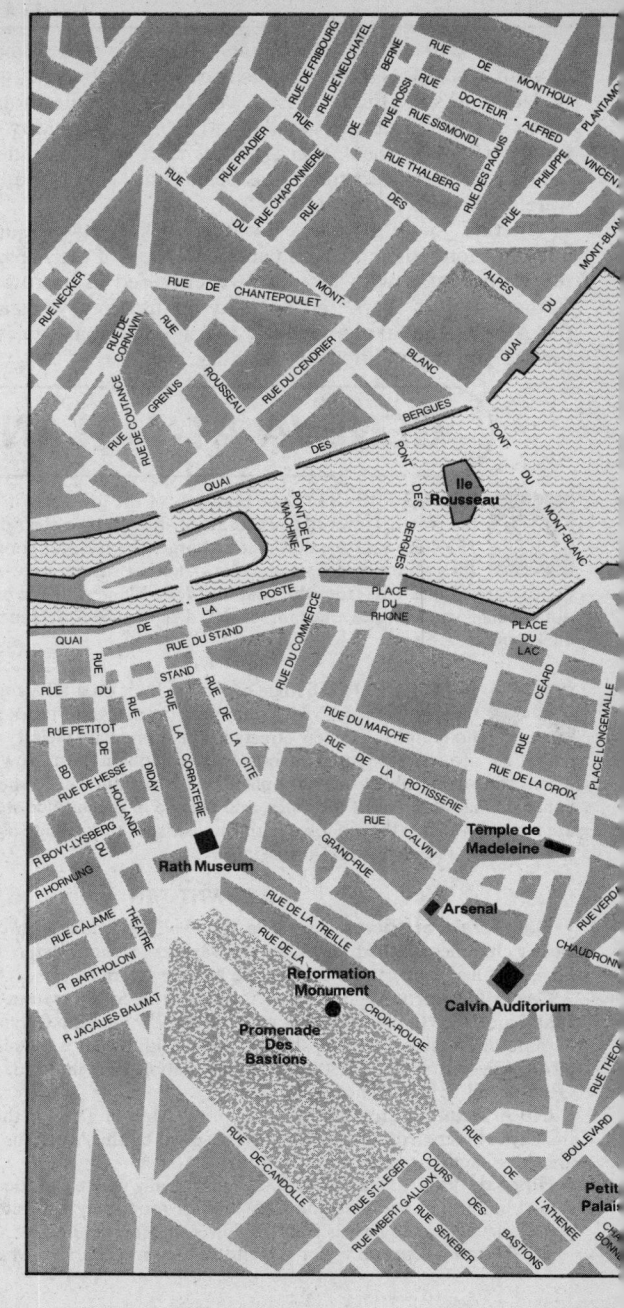

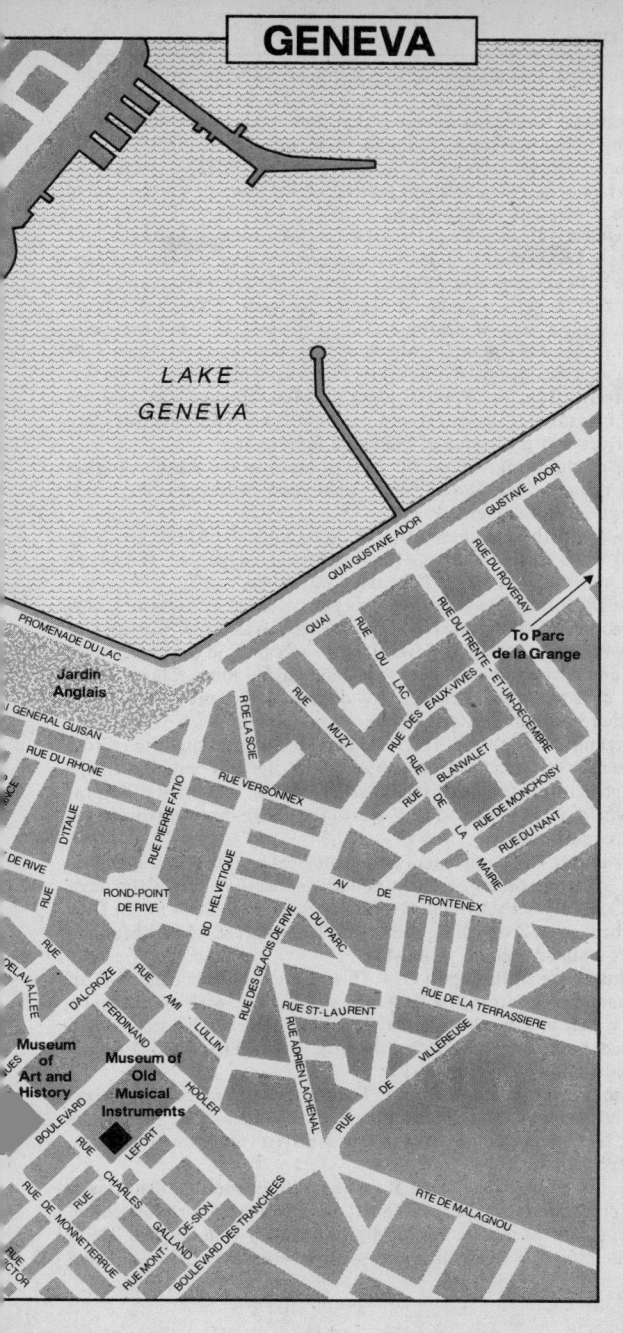

GENEVA

LAKE
GENEVA

PROMENADE DU LAC

QUAI GUSTAVE ADOR

GUSTAVE ADOR

RUE DU ROVERAY

To Parc
de la Grange

Jardin
Anglais

I GENERAL GUISAN

QUAI

RUE DU LAC

RUE DU TRENTE-ET-UN-DÉCEMBRE

RUE DU RHONE

RUE DE LA SCIE

RUE

MUZY

RUE DES EAUX-VIVES

RUE VERSONNEX

RUE PIERRE FATIO

RUE DE RIVE

D'ITALIE

RUE

RUE DE

LA

RUE BLANVALET

RUE DE MONCHOISY

RUE DU NANT

MAIRIE

ROND-POINT
DE RIVE

BD HELVETIQUE

AV

DE

FRONTENEX

RUE

DELAVALLEE

DALCROZE

RUE AMI

LULLIN

FERDINAND

HODLER

RUE ADRIEN LACHENAL

RUE DES GLACIS DE RIVE

DU PARC

RUE ST-LAURENT

RUE DE LA TERRASSIERE

RUE

DE

VILLEREUSE

Museum
of
Art and
History

Museum of
Old
Musical
Instruments

BOULEVARD

RUE

LEFORT

CHARLES

GALLAND

RUE DE SION

RUE MONT-

BOULEVARD DES TRANCHEES

RTE DE MALAGNOU

RUE DE MONNETIERRUE

VICTOR

modern stained-glass windows, this church is an example of fifteenth-century Gothic architecture.

Reformation Monument – Under the ramparts that used to surround the town, in a pleasant park belonging to the university, is a long, plain wall, erected in 1917, with statues of the main Reformation leaders — Calvin, Knox, Farel, de Bèze — flanked by other, less prominent personages; bas-reliefs and tablets tell the story of Calvin, one of the world leaders of the Protestant Reformation.

Promenade on the Quais – Both sides of the lake are interesting. You might start at quai du Mont-Blanc (see *Seeing the City*). Here are several top hotels, a landing pier, a monument to the duke of Brunswick who left his fortune to the town about 100 years ago (with the condition that he get a monument like the Scaligeri in Verona); see the panoramic table on the quai, a map of nearby and distant peaks that are especially beautiful in the afternoon when the sun sets on the Alps. If you go north, the quai ends at the Botanical Garden, in a succession of beautifully manicured city parks. However, following the river westward from the Pont (Bridge) du Mont-Blanc is the quai des Bergues, with the charming, small Rousseau Island just off it. This is a wonderful place for a rest, under large trees and the statue of Geneva's famous son.

On the opposite side of the bridge (Pont du Mont-Blanc) is the Jardin Anglais (English Garden), with a huge clock whose face is composed of flowers, the hands giving the exact time — typically Genevois!

Parc de la Grange – From the Jardin Anglais, the quai Gustave-Ador eventually runs into the delightful Parc de la Grange, with the finest rose garden of Europe (overpowering in June) and the even larger Parc des Eaux-Vives.

Palais des Nations – The former League of Nations palace, as big as Versailles, now houses the European section of the United Nations as well as a small museum of diplomatic history and a Philatelic Museum. Several impressive halls in the palace were decorated by European and African artists. There are daily guided tours. Closed at the end of December for 14 days. Admission charge. Av. de la Paix (phone: 34-60-11). In surrounding buildings there are other international offices, such as:

The World Health Organization (phone: 91-21-11) and the International Red Cross (phone: 34-60-01). Especially striking is the new building of the International Labor Office. This impressive structure has a luxurious marble interior and artistic decorations from all over the world (phone: 99-61-11). Visits to the above three organizations are possible on special request only.

Museum of Art and History – The important archaeological section features medieval furniture, sculpture, armory, and an excellent fine arts collection; one of the most interesting paintings is Conrad Witz's *Miraculous Fishing,* painted in 1444 for an altar of the cathedral with a background depicting medieval Geneva. Free; closed Monday mornings. 2 rue Charles-Galland (phone: 29-00-11).

Watch Museum (Musée de l'Horlogerie) – This is an exquisite collection of watches, clocks, and enamelworks from the sixteenth century on, with emphasis on artisans from Geneva, which is a worldwide watchmaking center. The setting is a charming townhouse and park, now owned by the city. Free, but closed Monday mornings. 15 rte. de Malagnou (phone: 36-74-12).

Ariana Museum – One of three great museums in Europe that specialize in porcelain and pottery — mainly European but also some Chinese and Japanese. The museum is in a large villa near the UN. Closed October to March or April (it varies) and Mondays; free. 10 av. de la Paix (phone: 33-39-44).

Baur Collection – In the home of the original owner, with a small garden, this is a private collection of superb Chinese and Japanese ceramics. It is open in the afternoon only. Admission charge; closed Mondays. 8 rue Munier-Romilly (phone: 46-17-29).

Carouge – Within the city limits is a little old town where time stands still and people live their quiet lives independently of busy Geneva, between its low houses, shady squares, fountains, and pubs. Enchanting! Carouge is becoming more and more popular after dark, though, when its cafés and small theaters fill up.

Museum of Old Musical Instruments (Musée d'Instruments Anciens de Musique) – This private collection was bought by the city, but its former owner is still the curator. All the instruments, however old, are still good enough to play, and on occasion, visiting musicians do just that. Open Tuesday, Thursday, and Friday; check opening hours. Admission charge. 23 rue Lefort (phone: 46-95-65).

Museum of the History of Science (Musée de l'Histoire des Sciences) – A collection of instruments and souvenirs mainly of Swiss scientists (mathematical, medical, astronomical, physics, and other items) is in a lovely setting. It is closed in the morning and from November to April. The museum is open to the public free of charge. Villa Bartholoni, 128 rue de Lausanne (phone: 31-69-85).

Institut et Musée Voltaire – The beautiful residence of Voltaire, with his furniture, art objects, manuscripts, correspondence, and works, is open every afternoon except Saturday and Sunday at no charge. 25 rue des Délices (phone: 44-71-33).

Jean-Jacques Rousseau Museum – The manuscripts, letters, pictures, and death mask of Rousseau can be seen here daily, except for Saturday afternoons and Sundays, at no charge. The Public and University Library, Salle Lullin, promenade des Bastions (phone: 20-82-66).

OUT OF TOWN

Bodmerian Library – In the bewitching setting of the luxurious villa of Zürich millionaire Martin Bodmer, in the suburb of Cology, with a panoramic view of the lake and the town, this is a unique private collection of rare manuscripts, first editions, and incunabula; the villa also houses a research institute. The exhibits of the collection change occasionally. Open Thursday afternoons only; admission charge. Chemin du Guignard, Cology (phone: 36-23-70).

Boat Ride on the Lake and the Rhône – Beautiful Lake Geneva (Lac Léman), a 45-mile-long lake with Geneva on its western end, Lausanne in the middle, and Vevey and Montreux to the east, has been popular with nature lovers at least since the days of Rousseau. Its southern shore is in France; the northern shore in Switzerland is the more famous part. The romantics loved Lake Geneva, particularly the area around Vevey and Montreux, and the list of greats who've lived there is formidable: Byron, Goethe, Victor Hugo, and Balzac are just a few.

The Castle of Chillon — celebrated by Byron in "The Prisoner of Chillon" in 1816 — can be visited by boat. This ninth-century castle held François Bonivard prisoner; he was chained to a pillar for 4 years (1532–36) for delivering Protestant sermons.

A trip on the lake is a must, with its vineyards, châteaux, and old towns. Cruises of varying lengths are offered several times a day by three different companies — except in winter. There are also daily trips down the unspoiled, wooded shores of the Rhône. For details, inquire at the Tourist Office (see *Sources and Resources*) or at Company Mouettes Genevoises (phone: 32-29-44).

Château de Coppet – About 6 miles (10 km) from Geneva, on the lake, in the charming little town of Coppet, is the castle and park of the famous Madame de Staël, the meeting place of some of the greatest minds of the eighteenth and early nineteenth centuries. Madame de Staël led a complicated and unconventional life, which is described in her famous autobiography; she was separated from her husband for the love of the novelist Benjamin Constant. She wrote several successful novels and a study of German romanticism that so enraged Napoleon that he destroyed an entire edition as "un-French," and she was forced to flee to England and Russia. Closed November to February and Mondays. Admission charge (phone: 76-10-28).

■**EXTRA SPECIAL:** Mount Salève, the "house mountain" of Geneva, is only about 4 miles (6 km) away, but it is in France, so you must have your passport ready at the border. Salève's peak is 4,000 feet high; in fall and winter, when the city is often deep in fog, Salève towers above it all.

Go by car or by the No. 8 bus from Geneva to Veyrier, where the cable car affords a magnificent view at any time of the Valley of the Arve, Geneva, and Mont-Blanc. There are scores of walks, including the steep Pas de l'Échelle from Veyrier to Monnetier, a picturesque village with a number of good restaurants. If you wish, you can continue to Rocher-de-Faverges.

In warm weather — for the more daring or just for spectators — Mount Salève is a center for hang gliding.

SOURCES AND RESOURCES

For general information, brochures, and maps, contact the Office du Tourisme, 2 rue des Moulins-en-l'Île (phone: 28-72-33). In the US, contact the Swiss National Tourist Office, 608 Fifth Ave., New York, NY 10020 (phone: 212-757-5944).

The Tourist Office in Geneva publishes a little booklet called *Geneva au feminin* which is excellent for history and comprehensive sightseeing and is available in English. Another small booklet called *Geneva* (Editions Panoramic), with pictures and short text, captures the spirit of the town well.

For Local Coverage – *This Week in Geneva,* a bilingual publication, is helpful for practical information, cultural programs, and advertisements for restaurants and shops; it also contains a concise "guided tour" of the city. (You can also get this separately in a pamphlet without advertising.)

There are no local newspapers in English, but the daily (Paris) *International Herald Tribune* is available for world news.

 CLIMATE AND CLOTHES: The temperature in Geneva is never very hot or very cold; the average in summer is 65°F (18°C), 34°F in winter (1°C). When the cold north wind called the *bise* blows, it goes through your bones, sunshine or not; it also clears the air of fog, dust, and germs.

Rain rarely lasts long, but in winter, fog can persist for days. Bring a raincoat and a sweater in any season, and a scarf or a hat for that *bise.* People dress fashionably in Geneva, as in New York or any cosmopolitan city. The Swiss tend to be on the conservative side. Jackets and ties are required for men in some restaurants.

GETTING AROUND: Most places can be reached on foot, as everything is relatively close by.

Taxi – They are expensive, with the additional tip included.

Bus – There are many buses and they run frequently. You must buy a ticket from a vending machine at all stops. (You cannot buy it on the bus, and you are fined if found without one.) Information booklets with bus routes are available for a small fee. On number 1 at Cornavin (railroad station) you can take a complete, circular sight-seeing tour, returning as number 11 to the same spot.

Car Rental – All major firms are represented at the airport and in the city. (The rates are among the highest in Europe.) *Avis* has offices at 44 rue Lausanne (phone: 31-90-00) and the airport; *Budget* at 36 rue de Zürich (32-04-07); and *Bucher* at 4 rue Fendt (phone: 34-62-10).

MUSEUMS: In addition to the museums described in *Special Places,* the following are also interesting:

Musée d'Histoire Naturelle – The most modern natural history display in Europe. 11 rte. de Malagnou (phone: 35-91-30).

The Petit Palais – Exhibits modern art from 1890 to the present, especially Renoir and Picasso. 2 terr. St.-Victor (phone: 46-14-33).

Musée d'Etnographie – Offers a rich worldwide collection. 65 blvd. Carl-Vogt (phone: 28-12-18).

Musée Rath – Temporary exhibits. Its watch and jewelry exhibition is one of Switzerland's finest. Pl. Neuve (phone: 28-56-16).

The Museum of the Reformation – In the University Library. Promenade des Bastions (phone: 20-82-66).

SHOPPING: The main shopping area, offering the best and most expensive stores, is around rue du Rhône and its parallel and side streets. Other shopping streets are *les rues basses,* literally "downhill streets," so called because their names change every few blocks: A few include rue du Marché, rue de la Confédération, and rue de Rive. Also, many new (and expensive) boutiques and gift shops have recently opened up in the small streets around place du Bourg-de-Four in Old Town.

Geneva's best buys are watches — the most famous in the world — jewelry, toys, clothes, and the nearly ubiquitous Swiss Army knives. There is a flea market on Wednesdays and Saturdays on the plain de Plainpalais and a flower and vegetable market on Saturday mornings on the streets of *les rues basses.*

To sample everything, try Geneva's best-known department stores, *Placette* at rue Grenus and *Grand Passage* at 50 rue du Rhône.

Here is a small selection of recommended stores:

À La Bonbonnière – Geneva's best chocolates. 11 rue de Rive.

Aux Mille Cadeau – Lovely gifts, music boxes, cuckoo clocks. 11 rue Céard.

Bon Génie – Fashion. Pl. du Molard.

Bucherer – Watches and jewelry. 26 quai Général Guisan.

Davidoff – The original home of these famous cigars. 2 rue de Rive.

Gübelin – More fine watches and jewelry. 1 pl. du Molard.

Hermès – Fine fashion in expensive ties, leathergoods, scarves, and saddlery. 43 rue du Rhône.

La Cage – An antique store in the old town, specializing in medieval art. 10 rue du Vieux Collège.

Schmitt – An antique store in the old town. 3 rue de l'Hôtel de Ville.

Spengler – An excellent big store with reasonably priced clothes for men, women, and children (not designer names). 26 blvd. Georges Favon.

Sturzenegger – Fine Swiss embroidery and linens. 3 rue du Rhône.

Uniprix – The Woolworth's of Geneva. 4 rue Croix-d'Or.

SPECIAL EVENTS: The *Escalade,* the most typically Genevois celebration, commemorates the city's victory over the Savoyard enemy in 1602, on or around December 11, with a colorful evening pageant by torchlight in the darkened streets, with medieval costumes and all-night living it up. *Fête de Genève* is a long weekend in mid-August, with fairs and processions, culminating in magnificent fireworks on the lake. The *First of August* is a national holiday commemorating the founding of the Swiss Confederation, with bonfires on the hills. The *International Motor Show* here is one of the most important in Europe, keeping all Geneva excited and its hotels packed; the show lasts for 10 days in early March. The

Watch and Jewelry Show (Montres et Bijoux), with a display of the latest products, is every other October.

SPORTS: Golf – The 18-hole *Golf Club of Geneva,* in a magnificent setting in Cologny, is private, but accepts guests. Geneva has no public courses.
    Sailing – The most obvious sport in Geneva; rentals are all along the quais, especially quais Mont-Blanc, Wilson, and Gustave-Ador.

Ice Skating – Indoor and outdoor skating is only in winter, at *Vernets* skating rink at quai des Vernets.

Skiing – There are excellent runs, which are very crowded on weekends, within 1 hour of Geneva in the marvelous resorts of Haute Savoie in France. The best known are Chamonix and Megève, about an hour away; the new resort, Flaine, is even closer. The closest good skiing in Switzerland is in Champéry or on the Glacier of Les Diablerets, about an hour and a half away.

Soccer – Called football in Europe, soccer is very popular. Games are in different stadiums, including *Stade des Charmilles.*

Swimming – Beaches on the lake are open in summer, like the Geneva Beach on Quay Gustave Ador and Pâquis Beach on the quai du Mont-Blanc (and two beaches on the rte. de Lausanne).

Tennis – There are several clubs; courts must be reserved in advance. Try the *Geneva Tennis Club* at Parc des Eaux-Vives.

THEATER: The major theaters are the *Théâtre de Carouge,* rue Joseph-Girard; *Le Caveau,* av. Ste.-Clotilde; and the *Casino Theater,* rue de Carouge. Performances are in French except for some visiting companies. International shows are presented at the *Grand Casino* at the *Hilton Hotel,* 19 Quai du Mont-Blanc.

MUSIC: Operas are performed in the *Grand Théâtre* from October to May (not daily), with one production per month and greatly varying quality. The opera is located at pl. Neuve (phone: 21-23-11). There are also excellent popular and classical concerts. The *Orchestre de la Suisse Romande* gives regular performances with many renowned guest artists. Tickets are somewhat difficult to get. Most performances are at *Victoria Hall,* rue Hornung (phone: 28-33-80 or 28-82-21). There are also frequent concerts and recitals in churches. There are open-air concerts in season.

NIGHTCLUBS AND NIGHTLIFE: Geneva has the most active nightlife in Switzerland (which does not mean all that much) — enjoyed mainly by visiting and resident foreigners. The best are the private clubs: *Griffins,* which is private, is good if you can get in, blvd. Helvétique. Among a dozen places with shows, the most popular and international are *Ba-Ta-Clan,* the best-known striptease spot at 15 rue de la Fontaine (phone: 29-64-98); or *Pussy Cat Saloon,* another striptease spot (in the same building as *Club 58*), at 15 Glacis de Rive (phone: 35-15-15); *Maxim's,* with music hall show and dining run by Bob Azzam, 2 rue Thalberg (phone: 32-99-00); and *La Garçonnière,* which offers a transvestite show at 22 pl. Bémont at Cité (phone: 28-21-61). *Régine's,* a member of the chic, international discotheque chain, is attached to the *Hilton Hotel's* Grand Casino at 19 Quai du Mont-Blanc (phone: 31-57-35). Several of the good hotels have dancing in their restaurants (*Richemond,* Jardin Brunswick). For gambling you have to go to Divonne in France, 12.5 miles (20 km) away, as Swiss casinos allow only minimum bets.

SINS: Strangely enough, prostitution is not as obvious here as in Zürich; however, call girls are readily available at the *Pussy Cat Saloon* and *Club 58.*

BEST IN TOWN

 CHECKING IN: There are many hotels, but *the* small, charming, inexpensive one with atmosphere is almost nonexistent; it's either old-time luxury or functional modern. Most hotels are around the main railroad station, which is only a few minutes from the lake. Continental breakfast is included in the room price everywhere. All the hotels listed here have telephones in rooms; most also have radios. Reservations are highly recommended. The range for a double with a bath and/or shower in the expensive category is from $105 to $170; moderate, $45 to $73; inexpensive, $35 to $48 ($28 to $30 without bath). In the outskirts you will find more moderate rates.

NOGA Hilton – This sleek, modern hostelry with 300 rooms right on Lake Geneva is currently the most expensive in the city. Guests can enjoy a sauna, heated pool, boutiques, nightclub, discotheque, and numerous restaurants. Parking available. 19 Quai du Mont-Blanc (phone: 31-98-11). Very expensive.

Le Richemond – This is the most prestigious hotel in town, full of understated elegance; its 139 rooms are generally full. The restaurant *Le Gentilhomme* is one of the best in town, with dance music at night. Major credit cards. Jardin Brunswick (phone: 31-14-00). Expensive.

Beau-Rivage – This hotel has retained its old-world charm in spite of recent total renovations; there are 120 rooms, some with superb lakefront views. Its famous restaurant is called *Chat Botté.* Major credit cards. 13 quai du Mont-Blanc (phone: 31-02-21). Expensive.

Le Chandelier – This hotel is in the old town, with 25 renovated rooms loaded with atmosphere. From the higher floors there is a view of roofs and the lake. Major credit cards. 23 Grand Rue (phone: 21-56-88). Moderate. (The candlelit restaurant in the same building is not part of the hotel but has the same name.)

Du Midi – A pleasant, modern hotel with 80 comfortable rooms, *Du Midi* has an excellent location, higher floors with views of the river, cafés, and restaurants. Major credit cards. Pl. Chevelu (phone: 31-78-00). Moderate.

La Tourelle – If you don't mind being out of town, this is *the* place, about 10 minutes from the center of town (direct bus service) in luxurious, residential Vésenaz, with 24 attractive, comfortable rooms in a villa with a garden and a view of the lake. Closed December and January. American Express, Diners Club (discouraged). 23 rte. d'Hermance, Genève-Vésenaz (phone: 52-16-28). Moderate.

Époque – Another good buy, *Époque* is modern and central, has 60 rooms, a snack bar, and a restaurant. Major credit cards. 10 rue Voltaire (phone: 45-25-50). Moderate to inexpensive.

Le Grenil – Connected with the YMCA, this modern hotel is not far from the center, with a snack restaurant; an excellent value. Most of its 48 rooms have showers but few have toilets. American Express, Diners Club. 7 av. Ste.-Clotilde (phone: 28-30-55). Inexpensive.

Des Tourelles – (No connection with *La Tourelle!*) This is a family-type, centrally located hotel with 24 rooms, *without* private showers (or toilets), but these are available free on every floor. The place is pleasant and sunny and offers a view of the river. No credit cards. 2 blvd. James Fazy (phone: 32-44-23). Inexpensive.

Lido – A "best buy," this is an excellently run 32-room, no-frills hotel in a central location. Major credit cards. 8 rue Chantepoulet (phone: 31-55-30). Inexpensive.

 EATING OUT: Geneva has more than 1,100 eating establishments in all categories. Strangely, there are not as many different cuisines as one might expect — French cooking dominates all other varieties, with Italian second. Definitely try the French-Swiss cheese dishes, like fondue and *raclette* (delicious cheese, melted on an open fire in individual portions, to be eaten with potatoes) served in special inexpensive pubs. Also, try the excellent lake fish, like *perche* (perch) and, if available, the rare *omble chevalier* (grayling), found only in Lac Léman. When ordering, ask for the *carte*, as *menu* applies only to the daily set meal. Tips are included in bills, but it is customary to add a bit. Our price range is for a three-course dinner for two, without drinks, wine, or coffee. Count on $70 to $100 and up for expensive places, $35 to $65 for moderate, and $15 to $25 and down for inexpensive.

Girardet, Hotel de Ville, Crissier – *Extra special:* Some 37.5 miles (60 km) from Geneva, just outside Lausanne, young, talented chef Fredy Girardet has created a restaurant that is the best in Europe. Be sure to write for dinner reservations months ahead; call for lunch weeks ahead. If you splurge only once during your European stay, do it here. Closed Sundays, Mondays, parts of August, Christmas. No credit cards. 1 rte. d'Yverdon, Crissier (phone: 021/34-15-14). Expensive.

La Perle du Lac – On the lake, in Parc Mon Repos; in summer you can dine outside with the ravishing view; in winter it is intimate, elegant, and candlelit. Closed Mondays. Some credit cards. 128 rue de Lausanne (phone: 31-35-04). Expensive.

Le Duc – It's said to be one of the best fish restaurants in the country. Closed Sundays and Mondays. Some credit cards. 7 quai du Mont Blanc (phone: 31-73-30). Expensive.

Tse Fung – In *Hôtel la Réserve* at the city limits, this is one of the best Chinese restaurants in Europe. Credit cards. 301 rte. de Lausanne, Bellevue (phone: 74-17-36). Expensive.

Auberge à la Mère Royaume – A cozy, wood-paneled "old Geneva style" place with French specialties. Closed Saturday lunch and Sundays. Credit cards. 9 rue des Corps-Saints (phone: 32-70-08). Moderate.

Chez Valentino – A lively Italian place with fabulous hors d'oeuvres; flowery terrace in season; 3 miles (5 km) from the center. Closed August, Monday and Tuesday lunch. Some credit cards. 63 rte. de Thonon, Vésenaz (phone: 52-14-40). Moderate.

Restaurant Edelweiss – A Swiss chalet with folk music and regional specialties. 2 place Navigation (phone: 31-49-40). Moderate.

Hostellerie de la Vendée – With a functional, sober interior, but outstanding service and food, frequented by chic local clientele; it offers seasonal specialties. On the outskirts of town. Closed Sundays. Credit cards. 28 Chemin de la Vendée, Petit Lancy (phone: 92-04-11). Moderate.

Olivier de Provence – One of Geneva's most popular French restaurants is in the charming setting of Carouge. In summer it has a big, tree-shaded garden. Closed Sundays. Credit cards. 13 rue Jacques-Dalphin (phone: 42-04-50). Moderate.

Café des Beaux-Arts – This modest but very lively bistro is near Carouge (cheese/potato au gratin a specialty). Closed Mondays and the second Sunday of the month. No credit cards. 32 rue de Carouge (phone: 29-15-01). Inexpensive.

Café du Centre – This pleasant *brasserie* is on historic place du Molard, with a huge variety of dishes served till well after midnight. (The more expensive restaurant is upstairs.) No credit cards. 5 pl. du Molard (phone: 21-85-86). Inexpensive.

Les Armures – This is a good place for raclette, fondue, or even pizza, in the heart of the old town. It has atmosphere. Closed Sundays, Monday lunch. Credit cards. 1 rue du Puits-St.-Pierre (phone: 28-34-42). Inexpensive.

Restaurant du Palais de Justice – An unassuming little place with lots of local color, on the romantic square of the old town. Closed Sundays and Monday lunch. No credit cards. 8 pl. Bourg-de-Four (phone: 20-42-54). Inexpensive.

HELSINKI

The Daughter of the Baltic, Helsinki is surrounded by water on three sides. Its gleaming white buildings, many of which were designed by distinguished architects and built of local light-colored granite, have earned Helsinki the additional title of White City of the North. Almost as close geographically and culturally to Russia as to Scandinavia, the city reflects both Eastern and Western influences in the sharp contrast, for instance, between the purely classical Lutheran cathedral in Empire style and the red brick Uspenski cathedral with its golden cupolas.

Helsinki is on the southern coast of Finland, overlooking the Gulf of Finland on the Baltic Sea; the city is bounded to the north by green fields, forests, and lakes. Across the Gulf of Finland lie the Soviet republics of Estonia and Latvia, and at the farthest eastern end of the gulf is Leningrad. Helsinki's natural seaport, kept open most of the winter by icebreakers, was once protected by the fortifications on Suomenlinna, a group of five rocky islands south of the city's center.

Helsinki lies midway between Stockholm to the west and Leningrad to the east. So hemmed in by Sweden and Russia, it is no wonder that Finland became the buffer and the buffeted in wars between the two great rival powers. The Finnish people and their language are not really Scandinavian; originally, nomadic Finnish-speaking fishermen and hunters migrated to the area from Eastern Europe during the first century AD. (The language will be entirely unfamiliar to most Americans unless one knows Estonian, which is related.) At this time, the Lapps, the original inhabitants of the area, were forced to move northward to Lapland. From the thirteenth century, when Finland was conquered by the Swedes, through the nineteenth century, when Russia took over — and until the Finnish nation declared its independence from Russia in 1917 — Finland suffered in the recurring wars between the two countries.

In 1812, shortly after the Russians conquered Finland in the Napoleonic Wars, Helsinki was made the capital by Czar Alexander I. Until then Turku, a city on the west coast, had held the title. In 1828, the university was moved from Turku to Helsinki, making it an intellectual as well as a political center.

During the same period, in 1808, the city had been ravaged by a fire that totally demolished its crowded wooden buildings. When Helsinki was subsequently rebuilt as the nation's capital, the city was well planned and deliberately spacious. Carefully charted by Johan Albrecht Ehrenström and executed by the noted architect Carl Ludvig Engel, the reconstruction was completed by 1840. The neoclassical buildings in the old center of town date from this period. Due to the efforts of a five-year renovation program begun in 1984, these buildings are beginning to house new shops, restaurants, and cafés. About half of these structures are already bustling with activity.

The city is well laid out, with wide streets, plenty of parks, and buildings designed by distinguished architects. The skyline of this pollution-free city is accented by the imposing dome of the Lutheran cathedral and the onion domes of the Russian Orthodox church. Helsinki is a place to see modern architecture at its best; the Finnish nation, world renowned for its achievements in modern design, has produced such notables as Eliel Saarinen and Alvar Aalto — and many striking examples of their work can be seen here. Surely the most dramatic of Helsinki's many fine specimens of modern architecture is Temppeliaukio Church, blasted from solid rock, designed by two Finnish brothers, Timo and Tuomo Suomalainen. In addition to finely designed buildings, Helsinki is noted for its parks and squares, which are often graced by magnificent sculptures.

Helsinki's harbor, Finland's largest, handles the bulk of the nation's maritime activity. Finland's imports of petroleum products, vehicles, and consumer goods just exceed its exports of paper, wood, metal products, and machinery. The government of Finland is a parliamentary republic headed by a president who is elected for six years. As the only capitalist nation bordering on the Soviet Union, Finland is fanatically neutral. Its standard of living (with a per capita income of $10,200 in 1982) is higher than the Soviet Union's but still much lower than that of neighboring Sweden or the US. Sixty percent of its people live in cities — with half a million, over 10% of Finland's total population, in Helsinki — making their living from manufacturing and service industries.

Finland, ostensibly something of an out-of-the-way place to visit, can be especially hospitable to Americans. Many Finns speak English, which has replaced Swedish as the second language taught in schools. Like other Scandinavians, Finns are culturally advanced; illiteracy is unknown, social welfare is well provided, and all the proceeds from gambling are allocated to public charity. Though by nature — or because of the climate — Finns seem shy and reserved, sometimes a brooding people, they are passionate underneath. Jean Sibelius's music expresses this hidden passion, and so perhaps does Finland's well-publicized high incidence of alcoholism. Finns are far from gloomy: They can surprise you with their wry humor. They are lovers of pleasure, dining out as much as their budgets allow. They are also great music lovers — mad about dancing, whether it be disco or cheek to cheek (mostly to American tunes).

Finns love nature and the outdoors. With 62,000 lakes in the country, everyone swims and many families have a boat, whether it be a canoe or a luxury yacht. Summer, from June to September, finds the bulk of the population at the family cottage along a waterfront of lake, river, or sea, often commuting to work when not on vacation. And naturally in winter everyone — young and old — skis.

One Finnish quality the visitor will appreciate is cleanliness. The streets, homes, shops, hotels, and restaurants are spotless. The Finns themselves are a well-scrubbed people, hardly surprising when you consider that one of the great Finnish pastimes is the sauna.

Don't leave Finland without enjoying a sauna. There are plenty of saunas

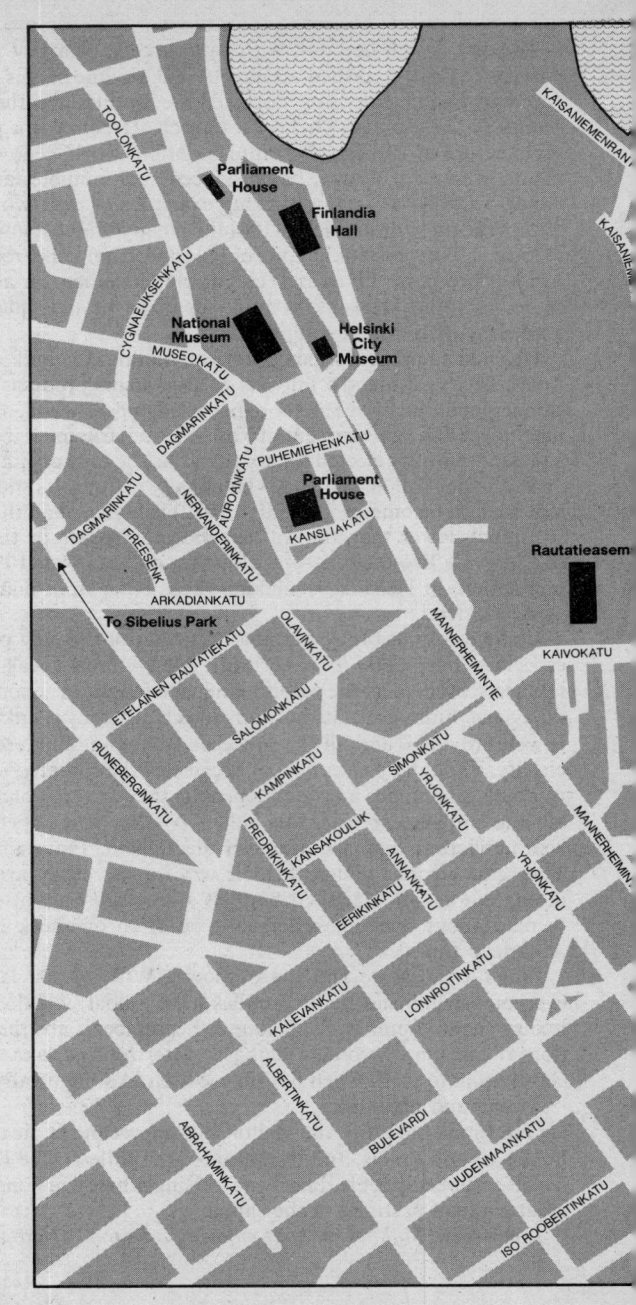

TOOLONKATU

Parliament
House

Finlandia
Hall

KAISANIEMENRAN

KAISANIEM

CYGNAELUKSENKATU

National
Museum

Helsinki
City
Museum

MUSEOKATU

DAGMARINKATU

PUHEMIEHENKATU

AUROANKATU

NERVANDERINKATU

Parliament
House

DAGMARINKATU

FREESENK

KANSLIAKATU

Rautatieasem

MANNERHEIMIN TIE

ARKADIANKATU

To Sibelius Park

OLAVINKATU

KAIVOKATU

ETELAINEN RAUTATIEKATU

SALOMONKATU

RUNEBERGINKATU

KAMPINKATU

SIMONKATU

YRJONKATU

MANNERHEIMIN.

FREDRIKINKATU

KANSAKOULUK

ANNANKATU

YRJONKATU

EERIKINKATU

LONNROTINKATU

KALEVANKATU

ALBERTINKATU

BULEVARDI

ABRAHAMINKATU

UUDENMAANKATU

ISO ROOBERTINKATU

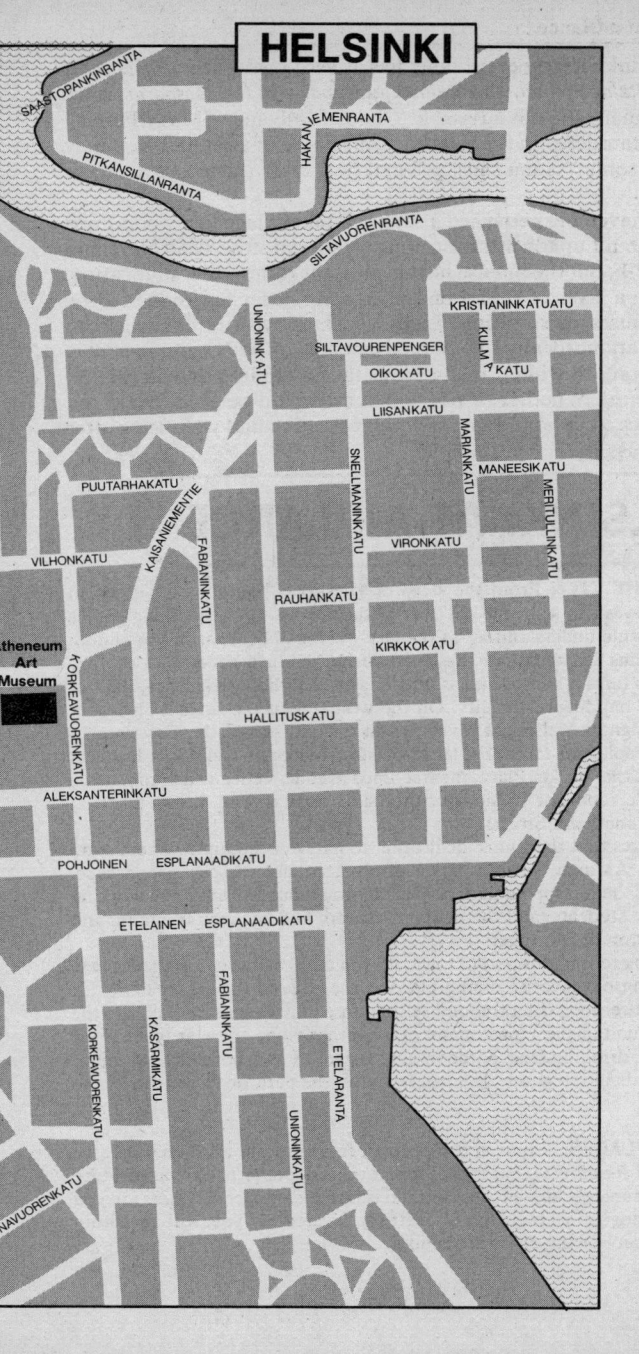

HELSINKI

SAASTOPANKINRANTA

PITKANSILLANRANTA

HAKANIEMENRANTA

SILTAVUORENRANTA

UNIONINKATU

KRISTIANINKATUATU

SILTAVOURENPENGER

KULMA KATU

OIKOKATU

LIISANKATU

PUUTARHAKATU

SNELLMANINKATU

MARIANKATU

MANEESIKATU

MERITULLINKATU

KAISANIEMENTIE

VILHONKATU

FABIANINKATU

VIRONKATU

RAUHANKATU

Atheneum
Art
Museum

KORKEAVUORENKATU

KIRKKOKATU

HALLITUSKATU

ALEKSANTERINKATU

POHJOINEN   ESPLANAADIKATU

ETELAINEN   ESPLANAADIKATU

FABIANINKATU

KASARMIKATU

ETELARANTA

KORKEAVUORENKATU

KASARMIKATU

UNIONINKATU

INAVUORENKATU

in and around Helsinki; nearly every hotel has at least one. Three of the most popular are at the *Palace Hotel,* the *Kalastajatorppa,* and the *Hesperia;* since anyone can go and many do, it is advisable to book in advance. (Many Finnish business deals are transacted in the relaxed atmosphere of a sauna.) You may wish to partake of some "sauna sausage" and beer after the event, as many Finns do.

Just in case you haven't experienced a sauna, it takes place in a wood-lined room with benches built up toward the ceiling. A special stove heats the room to about 176° to 212°F, but the intense heat is pleasant rather than suffocating. Water is thrown on a layer of stones on the stove in order to produce *löyly,* or steam, which causes perspiration. Light whisking with birch twigs can increase the perspiration. Ideally the sauna user cools off with a dip in a lake, sea, or swimming pool. In winter, many Finns take a dip in a hole in the ice, which they call *avanto.* Whether or not you are a would-be polar bear, you will surely experience a euphoric sense of total relaxation and well-being after the sauna. Don't miss it.

HELSINKI AT-A-GLANCE

 SEEING THE CITY: From the steps of Helsinki's majestic cathedral, an observer's eyes can span the old part of the city and in a sweeping glance draw a capsule understanding of the city's history. In front of the church is the spacious Senate Square, designed during the early nineteenth century in neoclassical style to form a homogeneous whole. The Sederholm residence, built in 1755–57, is the oldest building in the city. On the west side of the square, always in harmony with the design, is Helsinki University; on the east side is the Government Building. Nearby is Esplanadi Park (Esplanadipuisto), center of Helsinki's business activities. Beginning at the Market Place, the tree-lined avenue, with a wide promenade for strollers and ample room for traffic on either side, ends several blocks north at Mannerheimintie (Mannerheim Street).

A tourist soon realizes that the Finns' dedication to nature is no myth. There is no crowding in Helsinki. As many as 240 parks, of all sizes, dot the city's landscape, leaving almost 30% of the metropolitan area open. Throughout Helsinki, the working people, the retired, the students, and the newcomers, too, find squares, triangles, and parks of all kinds to stop at for a rest.

On a summer walking tour in this part of town, it's fun to take time out at the *Kappeli Restaurant,* a charming old favorite dining place at the edge of Esplanadi Park, for lunch or coffee in the afternoon. In a tranquil setting, foreign visitors soon fall into the casual, lighthearted mood of the Finns, many of whom gravitate there at lunch hour to enjoy the leisure of drinking beer outdoors and listening to a potpourri of music played by modern bands in the gazebolike bandstand in the park or to watch passing parade.

 SPECIAL PLACES: Trams and buses run frequently in all directions (see *Sources and Resources*), but most foreign visitors prefer to explore the city by foot. Fortunately, downtown Helsinki is rather compact. Chances are you will be staying in a hotel that is centrally located, so you will be within walking distance of many of the city's attractions.

DOWNTOWN

Finlandia Hall – Either as part of a sight-seeing tour or, even better, to attend a performance, you should not miss this $9 million marble edifice, the last architectural triumph of the country's late, great Alvar Aalto, world acclaimed for his simple yet elegant design. The sleek, white concert and congress hall is set in Hesperia Park on Mannerheimintie, almost directly across from the National Museum. You can't miss it. Check at your hotel desk for a free copy of *Helsinki This Week* to learn the program schedule. Karamzininkatu 4 (phone: 4-0241).

Sibelius Monument – Dedicated in 1967 to Finland's revered composer, Jean Sibelius, this monument is a giant sculpture of tubular steel pipes. To the side of this impressive work, which dwarfs visitors, the sculptress Eila Hiltunen molded a head of the composer. Lighted at night, the bold monument is a gripping sight. Sibelius Park.

Temppeliaukio Church – Known as the "Rock Church," this unique house of worship was designed by two brothers, Timo and Tuomo Suomalainen. Carved out of solid rock, it is topped with a copper dome that spans 70 feet. It occupies most of a block and from the street or air only the dome is visible. The interior is pink and gray granite with vertical glass strips cut into the ceiling that allow light to enter in dramatic shafts. Breathtakingly beautiful in its simplicity. Open daily from 10 AM to 9 PM; Sundays, 12:30 to 4 PM and 6 to 9 PM. Lutherinkatu 3 (phone: 49-46-98).

Parliament House – Visitors are welcome except when Parliament is in session and on holidays. You can join a guided tour at certain hours or attend plenary sessions in the galleries. Admission is free. Mannerheimintie 30 (phone: 4321).

National Museum – Founded in 1893, this large museum also includes an extensive library. The government-owned building was designed in 1910 by the noted Finnish architects Saarinen, Gesellius, and Lindgren. Collections include archaeological, historical, and ethnological items. There are 19,000 archaeological items from the Stone, Bronze, and Iron ages in Scandinavia and the Soviet Union; 80,000 historical items include Finnish interiors, costumes, textiles, weapons, metals, and coins; Finnish, Ugric, and Lapp ethnic collections include 15,300 items on hunting, textiles, folk art, and furniture. Mannerheimintie 34 (phone: 402-5229).

Art Museum of the Ateneum – Due to repairs scheduled to be completed in 1988, the collections of paintings, sculptures, drawings, and etchings — mostly modern Finnish but also foreign and classical — are now housed in temporary facilities. Open daily. Small admission fee; free on Saturdays. Kaivokatu 2–4 (phone: 62-54-42).

Seurasaari – This charming national park and open-air museum provides a representative picture of early Finland, complete with farm and manor houses that were transferred from all over the country and reassembled here. You might want to picnic outdoors. The museum, which sits on an island, offers some entertainment in the summer, mostly folk dancers in colorful native garb. Bus number 24 will take you there, and you enter by a footbridge. Open daily, May 15 to August 31. Small admission charge; free on Wednesdays. Seurasaari Island (phone: 48-47-12).

Korkeasaari Zoo – In 1988, this largest of Finland's zoos will mark its 100th birthday. Most animals are housed in their natural environment. Besides northern animals, the collection includes llamas, bison, bears, and lions, and a number of endangered species, among them the rare snow leopards. Guests can take lunch in an open-air restaurant and gaze out to sea toward Helsinki's skyline and South Harbor. The zoo is about a 10-minute ferry ride from the lower end of Aleksanterinkatu in North Harbor. The boat leaves every hour. Open daily (phone: 17-00-77).

Suomenlinna Sveaborg – An intriguing island, one of a group of five rocky islands to the south of the city center, only a 15-minute boat ride from South Harbor. This eighteenth-century fortification, reputed to be the largest sea fortress in the world, is well worth a visit. Built in 1748, when Finland was part of Sweden, the fortress was planned and directed by Marshal Augustin Ehrensvärd. Called the Gibraltar of the North, the fortress capitulated to the Russians in 1808 and defended itself successfully against an Anglo-French fleet in 1855, during the Crimean War.

A visitor can explore the fortifications of Susisaari (Wolf Island) and Kustaanmiekka (Gustav's Sword) with their forts and casements, parks and walks.

Nearby, on the island of Susisaari, the Ehrensvärd Museum exhibits Suomenlinna's history. The Armfelt Museum on the island of Kustaanmiekka shows the life of the nineteenth-century Finnish gentry; also on Kustaanmiekka are the Coast Defense Artillery Museum and the submarine *Vesikko.*

The islands also have art exhibitions and a restaurant open in the summer.

The ferry from Market Square to Suomenlinna leaves half-past every hour and takes about 15 minutes. In summer, tours start at the information kiosk (phone: 66-81-54).

Market Square – At the foot of Esplanade at South Harbor is Helsinki's open-air marketplace, one of the most visited spots in all of the capital. From 7 AM to 2 PM and in summer also from 3:30 to 8 PM daily, except Sundays, the brightly colored stalls, manned by old and young alike, sell everything from fresh-cut flowers and farm-grown vegetables and fruit to trinkets and freshly hauled in fish. Bustling and bursting with color, it's a place to see and a place to mingle with the Finns. Browse or buy, but be sure to stop long enough to taste the freshly brewed coffee and munch on the delicate Finnish pastries.

Linnanmäki – Helsinki's answer to Copenhagen's Tivoli is patronized by Finns from all parts of the country as well as local residents and tourists. It's more than an amusement park; only 30% of its visitors are children. Founded in the mid-1940s, the park includes 28 different rides, an indoor and an open-air theater, restaurants, two small cafés, a dancing pavilion, and assorted kiosks. Special rides are the gigantic Big Dipper and a carousel built in 1892 with hand-carved animals. The Peacock Theater seats 906 indoors and features internationally known comedians, clowns, acrobats, musicians, and marionettes. The open-air auditorium offers similar entertainments plus high-wire acrobatic acts.

A special aspect of Linnanmäki is that its proceeds, often exceeding $250,000 a year, are donated to various children's charities, hence the title "the park with the heart." Open daily from May 1 until the end of August. Small admission fee; rides extra.

SUBURBS

Tapiola – Called "Garden City of Finland," it's a utopian suburb designed in the 1950s to emphasize the quality of living in harmony with the surrounding nature. The name Tapiola, taken from the Finnish national epic *Kalevala,* was an imaginary place where the fabled people lived. Tapiola was built step-by-step by a group of private nonprofit organizations, and it still is not considered complete. About 17,000 people share the 670 acres, which include their own newspapers, clubs, shopping centers, a marina, a sports arena, libraries, and an outdoor glassed-in swimming pool.

Tapiola will be a revelation to American visitors. You might want to check with Helsinki City Tourist Office (see *Sources and Resources*) for a sight-seeing tour. Tapiola is a short but expensive cab ride from downtown Helsinki, or take a bus marked Tapiola from the terminal on Simonaukio.

■**EXTRA SPECIAL:** Since Finland is a country of 62,000 lakes and 30,000 islands, it would be sheer folly to make it to this land and not experience some part of the visit on water. Get another perspective on the capital from a boat. There are leisurely paced sight-seeing and lunch cruises and Archipelago tours that depart daily from Market Square from June 1 to August 31, taking you past innumerable little islands and around peninsulas. You can choose between a ride that lasts 1¼

hours or one that runs for 5 hours, including lunch. You'll enjoy this respite on
a warm summer day.

SOURCES AND RESOURCES

For general information, brochures, and maps, contact the Finland National Tourist
Office, 655 Third Avenue, New York, NY 10017 (phone: 212-949-2333), or the Helsinki City Tourist Office, Pohjoisesplanadi 19 (phone: 169-3757 and 17-40-88). "Helsinki Today" (phone: 058) gives recorded programs of events in the city.

 CLIMATE AND CLOTHES: Weather in Helsinki can be cold and gray in
winter. The cold is no different from that of the US Great Lakes area in
winter. A heavy coat and sweater (wool dresses and/or a suit, for women),
a pair of lined boots, and good wool- or silk-lined gloves will see you through
the outdoors in fine shape. Don't worry about the heating indoors; hotels and restaurants are more than comfortable.

Casual clothes are in order, but ties and jackets are required for men in most hotel
dining rooms. Women can use a couple of cocktail dresses. In summer or winter, pants
suits are popular here.

For hot weather, lightweight cotton or drip-dry clothes are ideal. Bring a bathing
suit or two; add a sweater and a raincoat, to play safe. The thermometer in summer
can rise from a coolish 50° to 60°F (10° to 16°C) to the hot 90s (about 30° to 32°C). At
this time of year tourists are treated to a bonus — almost 19 hours of daylight.

A note on the midnight sun and the winter darkness: The area of northern Finland
that lies within the Arctic Circle has 2 months of midnight sun (June and July) and
2 of winter darkness (December and January). In southern Finland (which includes
Helsinki), midsummer offers about 5 hours of nocturnal twilight.

 GETTING AROUND: Tram and Bus – Trams 3T and 3B, which can be
mounted anywhere along their route, offer a tour of the business and residential areas of the capital, with a taped commentary in English during the
summer months. In addition, a 24-hour tourist ticket, which can be bought
from the City Tourist Office, entitles you to unlimited travel on trams and buses for
about $5. "The Helsinki Card" ($8 to $13) entitles you to unlimited travel as well as
to free entry to museums.

Taxi – Cab stations, clearly marked "Taksi," are at every few corners, with plenty
of cabs waiting their turns. Cabs are plentiful but not cheap; the meters start at about
$2.20 (no tipping). You can hail a cab when the sign is illuminated.

Car Rental – Besides *Hertz* and *Avis*, there are *InterRent, Europcar*, and others.

 MUSEUMS: In addition to the museums described in *Special Places*, the
following are noteworthy:
Gallen Kallela – The castlelike studio-home of painter Akseli Gallen-
Kallela. Tarvaspää (phone: 51-33-88).

City Museum – Where you'll find history of the city. Karamzinkatu 2 (phone:
169-3444).

Mannerheim Museum – The home of Finland's great war hero and president
Marshal Mannerheim, Kalliolinnantie 14 (phone: 63-54-43).

Museum of Applied Arts – Finnish industrial design and native handicrafts. Korkeavuorenkatu 23 (phone: 7-44-55).

SHOPPING: Shopping can be fun and profitable in Finland. You'll run into some of the best buys in Europe if you're interested in textiles, ceramics, glassware, jewelry, handicrafts, or toys. Jewelry includes gold items fashioned after centuries-old ornaments as well as bold modern designs in silver and wood. Famed rya rugs woven in fine wools are everywhere. There are bargains in furs — mink, lynx, red fox, and others. *Marimekko* clothes and fabrics, Arabia pottery, and Finnish wooden toys are also exceptional items. Note: Before you go shopping, visit the Finnish Design Center at Kasarminkatu 19 (phone: 62-63-88), which is a permanent exhibition of Finnish handicrafts and industrial design.

The main shopping area in Helsinki is in the vicinity of the large hotels, particularly along Aleksanterinkatu and Esplanadi Park and their side streets.

Special tip: Department stores will ship your purchases home — with a 16% deduction of sales tax.

Aarikka – Toys and other design articles in wood and silver. Pohjoisesplanadi 27.

Arabia – Ceramics, crystal, and exquisite china. Pohjoisesplanadi 25.

I-Shop – Designer glassware and interesting articles in wood. Pohjoisesplanadi 27.

Marimekko – Fabric and clothing. Pohjoisesplanadi 31.

Metsovaara – Wonderful variety of textiles. Pohjoisesplanadi 23.

Pentik – The newest creations in fashionable leather wear. Pohjoisesplanadi 27.

Stockmann's – The leading department store. Aleksanterinkatu/Mannerheimintie/Keskuskatu.

Vuokko – Bold new fashions. Pohjoisesplanadi 25.

Forum – A brand-new shopping plaza packed with boutiques and shops displaying novelty items. On its four floors there are also restaurants, cafés, and a delicatessen. Mannerheimintie/Simonkatu.

Senate Center – A complex of bazaars, art galleries, shops, restaurants, and cafés in the revived old town Empire buildings. Handicrafts, fashions, furs, and articles for the home. Aleksanterinkatu/Unioninkatu/Sofiankatu.

SPECIAL EVENTS: More than a decade ago, Finland introduced over 800 summer festivals, produced and presented in various sections of the country. The idea was to attract foreign visitors and to familiarize them with the Finnish people and their achievements and, at the same time, to entertain them with local professional talent and international luminaries. The events run from symphonic concerts and opera performances given in a fifteenth-century castle courtyard to rock, folk, jazz, and pop music; to art exhibits; to seminars on world problems — cultural fare for everyone, including the small fry. For information, contact Finland Festivals, Aleksanterinkatu 19A (phone: 66-96-96).

The Finland Festival chain of dozens of programs generally starts in mid-June and run till mid-August. These are followed by the big *Helsinki Festival*, which includes as many as 100 presentations between late August and early September. For complete program information, contact *Helsinki Festival*, Unioninkatu 28 (phone: 65-96-88).

Visitors might also like to catch the *Changing of the Guard* at the Main Guard Post, behind the President's Palace every day at 3 PM.

SPORTS: Because of its climate, Finland is a paradise for all varieties of winter sports. Lovers of nature and the outdoors, Finns go in for boating and bicycling as well as skiing.

Bicycling – Finland is big on bicycling. There are prescribed routes, but you can plan out your own by using maps. Those around Helsinki and other cities run partly on special bicycle lanes. There are also some old country roads in good cycling condition. Check with the Helsinki Tourist Office for details, including where to rent a bike.

Boating – There are many yachting clubs on the islands right outside Helsinki. A boat can be rented, but the reefy waters are rather tricky. Check with the Yachting Association or the Motor Boat Association, both at Topeliuksenkatu 41a (phone: 4-7371).

Golf – The best part of golfing in this country in summer is that you can tee off as late as 10 PM, in daylight, and finish 18 holes later in daytime because there are almost 24 hours of light. Try *Helsinki Golf Club,* a short cab ride away, for the best 18-hole course. Tali Manor. Open May to October. Greens fee, $6 to $9 a day. Caddy carts available (phone: 55-02-35; 55-78-99).

Jogging – Finns are health oriented and are on the jogging kick, too. Americans dedicated to the daily ritual will find paths close to Olympic Stadium and in the Kaivopuisto park in the southern part of the city.

Horseback Riding – You won't have trouble finding a horse to ride. Check with the *Finnish Equestrian Federation,* Topeliuksenkatu 41A (phone: 4-7371).

Hunting – Finland's big game is moose. Three- to four-day packages, including tests at shooting areas, licenses, insurance, comfortable accommodations, and full board are available to those who want to join in the sport. The season runs from late October to December. Contact Kaleva Travel Agency, Lönnrothinkatu 5 (phone: 60-27-11).

Skiing – Skiing is to Finns as baseball is to Americans. In Finland skiing means mostly cross-country skiing, for which its terrain is ideal. All over the country there are marked and often illuminated ski trails of varying lengths and difficulty. There are also numerous downhill slopes with ski lifts. The peak season for skiing in south and central Finland is from January to March; in Lapland it runs from late autumn through May. (A bonus for skiers in May is a deep suntan, which is produced by 14 to 16 hours of sunshine.)

Ski equipment can be rented at all ski centers.

You can — and many Finns do this on weekends — just put on your skis and follow tracks on the Gulf of Finland to the islands. There are ski tracks all around Helsinki. Or you may prefer a weekend or week-long ski package at one of the many winter sports centers all over Finland. Resorts offer cross-country skiing, of course, as well as ski lifts, downhill slopes, marked and illuminated ski trails, keep-fit rooms, guided excursions, saunas, evening entertainment, and ski instruction. Two popular areas near Helsinki are Messilä (65 mi/100 km) near the site of international skiing competitions in February, and Hyvinkää (about 40 mi/64 km).

Further information about skiing is available from the local sports association, Suomen Latu, Korkeavuorenkatu 25A (phone: 17-01-01); the Helsinki City Tourist Office (see above); or from any travel agent in Helsinki.

Veteran skiers may enter the *Finlandia Ski Race* (cross-country) in early March or any of a number of ski races. Inquire at the Finland National Tourist Office.

Soccer – In summer there are games between Finland and other countries. Check *Helsinki This Week* for schedules.

Tennis – There's tennis fever in Scandinavia too. Helsinki alone has 26 clubs. It's best to bring your own racket. For booking a court and other information, call the *Finnish Tennis Association,* Topeliuksenkatu 41A (phone: 4-7371).

Winter Sports and Activities – And a unique experience in Lapland is a reindeer safari, often complete with a Lapp guide; participants travel by reindeer sledge across the fells and spend the night in a modern log cabin. For information about such winter tours, contact Kaleva Travel Agency, Lönnrothinkatu 5 (phone: 60-27-11).

THEATER: The top three theaters in town are: *Finnish National Theater (Suomen Kansallisteatteri)* at Asema-aukio (railway station plaza) (phone: 17-18-26); *City Theater (Kaupunginteatteri)* Eläintarhantie 5 (phone: 71-70-11), and the *Swedish Theater (Svenska Teatern)* Erottaja (phone: 17-04-38). You may not understand Swedish or Finnish, which are the languages of practically all productions, but you might want to take in one performance just for fun. In summer there are only open-air performances.

 **MUSIC:** There's always an excellent choice of concerts by symphony orchestras, chamber groups, and jazz artists. Many name performers from Europe, the US, and other countries can be seen, so don't be surprised if you find a group of Japanese instrumentalists playing one concert and the New York Philharmonic at another. Major concert halls include: Finlandia Hall; Karamzininkatu 4; House of Culture (Kulttuuritalo), Sturenkatu 4; Sibelius Academy, P. Rautatiekatu 9; House of Nobility (Ritarihuone), Aleksanterinkatu 3; and Finnish National Opera, Bulevardi 23–27 (phone: 60-85-54). (Operas are sung in their original languages.) Musiikki-Fazer, Aleksanterinkatu 11 (phone: 63-39-37), is the main agency for concert and opera tickets.

 NIGHTLIFE AND NIGHTCLUBS: Finns are nightlifers, especially the under-50 segment of the population, who are endowed with limitless endurance. The disco has won points in this city, and the proof is in the crowds that flock to the night spot on the lower level of the swank *Hesperia Hotel*, 50 Mannerheimintie (phone: 44-13-11).

Another dance spot that features international orchestras and floorshows is a grand hotel located on the Gulf of Finland, called *Kalastajatorppa*, Kalastajatorpantie 2 (phone: 48-80-11). Roulette, live entertainment, and dancing are also featured at *Kaivohuone*, Kaivopuisto (phone: 17-78-81); dancing also at *M Club*, Mannerheimintie 10 (phone: 64-17-17). *Groovy*, Ruoholahdenkatu 4 (phone: 694-5718), is a popular jazz pub with good performances by Finnish and international guests. For a jumping disco that attracts a youngish crowd, try *The Old Baker's*, Mannerheimintie 12 (phone: 60-56-07).

 SINS: Roulette, which is restricted to a limit of 25¢ per chip, is quite popular in Finland. You will find roulette wheels in many hotels and night spots. You can feel good about sinning in this enlightened country, because gambling proceeds in Finland support charities for the handicapped and invalids.

BEST IN TOWN

 CHECKING IN: Most of the city's accommodations are centrally located, modern, and equipped with all the amenities to make for comfort during a stay (and all of the hotels listed below have a sauna). Although there is a hotel boom in Helsinki, reservations should be made in advance, especially in the peak of the summer season. For those traveling to Finland in summer, seasonal discount accommodations coupons, called Finncheques, are available. These coupons (you have to buy at least four) reduce hotel rates considerably and are good at 160 hotels across the country; a full breakfast is also included. Finncheques can be purchased in the US from Holiday Tours of America, 40 E 49th St., New York, NY 10017 (212-832-9072). Expect to pay from $60 to $100 a night for a double room in a hotel in the expensive category; $40 to $60 in the moderate category; and $40 and under in the inexpensive category.

Hesperia Hotel – This 380-room luxury hotel is across the street from Hesperia Park and a stone's throw from Finlandia Hall. Its good location, fine service, steak room, restaurant, boutiques, disco, and swimming pool make it a popular spot. There's also roulette in the lobby for those who follow the sportin' life. Suites available. Mannerheimintie 50 (phone: 44-13-11). Expensive.

Inter-Continental – With 555 rooms, this is Helsinki's largest hotel. A few luxury suites are available. Several dining rooms, a banquet hall, and a ballroom serve convention groups. The sauna on the top floor gives you a chance to look out over the city from the adjoining terrace. Roulette is near the *Ambassador Room* on the eighth floor. Take time to saunter through the shopping arcade in the lobby. Mannerheimintie 46 (phone: 44-13-31). Expensive.

Kalastajatorppa – In the perfect setting of a park, bordered by the blue waters of the Gulf of Finland, "Fisherman's Cottage," as the hotel's name translates into English, is a spacious and ultramodern hotel. Its newest annex is designed so that windows from double rooms overlook the sea. Several handsome suites are available. This latest addition to the hotel connects to the older section via a white-washed rock tunnel, brilliantly lighted for walking. A romantic formal garden invites a stroll between dancing sessions in the main dining room or *Red Room* disco. Lots of activity in this hotel, including tennis courts. Kalastajatorpantie 1 (phone: 48-80-11). Expensive.

Marski – In the center of town, across from *Stockmann's* department store. Check in on the main floor of the hotel, which is in an office building. Hotel rooms begin on the third floor. It's a little more like a businessman's hotel but equipped with most desired facilities, including the traditional sauna. *The Clock* bar behind the reception desk is popular for cocktails in the late afternoon. Mannerheimintie 10 (phone: 64-17-17). Expensive.

Palace – This gracious hotel is near the South Harbor and the Market Place. An older hotel with only 59 rooms, it has been beautifully renovated and the accommodations are most comfortable and the service fine. The Italian *La Vista* restaurant on the second floor and the dining room on the tenth floor serve excellent fare, and the *American Bar* on the top floor is a delight. In summer you can take your drinks and lunch on the terrace and enjoy the wide expanse of sea, watching ships come and go. Eteläranta 10 (phone: 17-11-14). Expensive.

Presidentti – A luxurious establishment that's centrally located with 500 rooms. Among its restaurants is one specializing in vegetarian food and a 24-hour café. Etelä Rautatienkatu 4 (phone: 69-11). Expensive.

Socis-Seurahuone – Across from the Railway Station, this hotel has traditional Old World charm and has been beautifully renovated. It also has a good restaurant, the *Viennese Café,* and 114 rooms with modern conveniences. Kaivokatu 12 (phone: 17-04-41). Expensive to moderate.

Rivoli Jardin – A charming and cozy hotel well run and centrally located. Bar, café, and winter garden. Fitness room. Snacks are available through room service, but there's no full-service restaurant. Kasarminkatu 40 (phone: 17-78-80). Moderate.

Torni – In the heart of town, this hotel is known for its different restaurants, ranging from Balkan to Spanish. The small bar on the 13th floor has a spectacular view of the city and the sea. *Torni* has 150 rooms with modern conveniences. Yrjönkatu 26 (phone: 64-46-11). Moderate.

Vaakuna – One of the older hotels belonging to the Helsinki Hotels chain, it has a friendly and gracious ambience, is centrally located in the same building as the *Sokos* department store, and has a total of 290 rooms plus seven suites. Three saunas. On the ninth floor there's the noted *Sky Bar* and an adjoining terrace, unfolding a panoramic view of the city. Asema-aukio 2 (phone: 17-18-11). Moderate.

Klaus Kurki – A centrally situated hotel frequented by business people. Comfortable rooms, a quiet bar, a pleasant restaurant, and an unpretentious Mexican grill for lunch. Bulevardi 2 (phone: 60-23-22). Moderate.

Hospiz – This YMCA hotel near the center of town has 144 rooms and an unlicensed restaurant. It's at Vuorikatu 17 (phone: 17-99-58). Moderate to inexpensive.

Marttahotelli – A quiet 44-room hotel run by the Finnish Housewives' Association, it's near the business district and has an unlicensed restaurant. Uudenmaankatu 24 (phone: 64-62-11). Inexpensive.

Note: During June, July, and August, the university's student quarters are for rent. They offer more modest accommodations and services than ordinary hotels, but are quite comfortable and reasonably priced. For general hotel bookings in Finland contact the Hotel Booking Center, Railway Station, 00100 Helsinki 10 (phone: 17-11-33) or the Finland National Tourist Office (see *Sources and Resources*).

 EATING OUT: Although Finnish cuisine shows Eastern (Russian) and Western (French and Swedish) influences, there are some dishes that are uniquely Finnish. You will see Swedish smørgasbord with Finnish variations (called *voileipäpöytä* by the Finns), especially for lunch. Of course, fish dishes are big in Finland, especially salmon, whitefish, and Baltic herring. Not to be missed are the delicious little native crayfish, which taste like American lobster but are even more delicate; they are in season from about July 20 until September.

You might want to try reindeer meat, which is served in many forms — as steaks, chops, and stews, for example — but especially tasty is reindeer tongue, served smoked or in Madeira sauce.

One typical dish is *piirakka,* a pastry dough of rye flour (rye bread is big in Finland), filled with rice or potato; also *kalakukko,* a fish and pork pie.

The national dessert is Finnish crêpes, called *ohukainen.* Also delicious are fresh berries: strawberries and cloudberries (yellowish raspberries).

Finns drink their own high-quality beer and vodka (often served, as the Russians do, ice cold with hors d'oeuvres); also brandy, Scotch, and Campari. Try Finnish after-dinner liqueurs made with berries, particularly *mesimarja* (from brambleberries), *lakka* (from cloudberries), and *karpalo* (from cranberries).

For a quick bite, try places called *grilli*.

Dress is informal, but in the evening jackets and ties are required for men. Women can wear casual or cocktail dresses. If you feel like dressing up, do. You won't be alone.

Note: There are a number of charming, strictly summer restaurants in Helsinki that are near water or on small islands; great for dinner and dancing. The Valhalla on the island fortress of Suomenlinna is one of the most charming. Check the reception desk at your hotel or get a list from the Helsinki City Tourist Office.

Remember, there is no tipping in restaurants; a service charge is included in your bill. However, leaving a small added gratuity is a common practice. The obligatory cloakroom fee to restaurant doormen is usually clearly indicated; if not, it is about $1.

Restaurant prices are comparable to those in other European countries; expect to pay $70 to $100 for dinner for two with one cocktail at an expensive restaurant; $45 to $60 is moderate; $25 to $35 is inexpensive (with beer).

Adlon – Intriguing restaurant, with entrance through a medieval courtyard to a posh room, mirrored walls, interesting lighting effects. In the same complex is the less expensive, cozy *Vine Bar*, good for lunch or a snack. Good dance band. Reservations suggested. Fabianinkatu 14 (phone: 66-46-11). Expensive.

Havis Amanda – Cellar restaurant with charming atmosphere. Table d'hote menu and a la carte. Specializes in seafood and enjoys a reputation for excellence. Luscious desserts. Unioninkatu 23 (phone: 66-68-82). Expensive. A moderately priced steak house belongs to the same complex just behind the corner at Pohjoisesplanadi 17.

Palace – The hotel's two restaurants are considered among the city's best. The second-floor *La Vista* is notable for its Italian delicacies while the *Gourmet* restaurant on the ninth floor highlights international and Finnish cuisine. For predinner cocktails, try the *American Bar,* with a breathtaking view of the harbor. Reservations. Eteläranta 10 (phone: 17-11-14). *Gourmet,* expensive; *La Vista,* moderate.

Kalastajatorppa – In the hotel by same name ("Fisherman's Cottage," in English), set in a park along the Gulf of Finland, a 15-minute cab ride from the center of Helsinki. The *Red Room* is a swinging nightclub downstairs. A fine menu served table d'hôte or à la carte. Dancing any night; an international floor show and folk dancing groups are an added attraction in summer. Open 6 PM to 1 AM. Reservations a must. Kalastajatorpantie 2 (phone: 48-01-00). Expensive.

Svenska Klubben – After entering a pleasant, castlelike hall, surrounded by beautifully decorated rooms and salons, diners will be delighted by the cuisine and distinguished service. Maurinkatu 6 (phone: 62-87-06). Expensive.

Savoy – In the center of town at the top of an office building. One of the better patronized dining places for intimate luncheons. Continental, international menus, Finnish specialties. Eteläesplanadi 14 (phone: 17-65-71). Expensive.

Kappeli – This large establishment has several dining rooms, a coffeehouse, and a beer cellar, with outdoor service in summer. Its atmosphere is part of its attraction. Located near the colorful Market Square. A lively concert from the bandstand across the adjoining park accompanies your lunch. Dancing at night. Reservations advisable. Esplanadipuisto (Esplanadi Park) (phone: 17-92-42). Moderate to expensive.

Parilla Espagnola – For a change of pace, try this charming little place specializing in Latin atmosphere and cuisine. Reservations recommended for lunch. Eerikinkatu 4 (phone: 60-33-05). Moderate.

Hamlet – This cellar restaurant with a theatrical motif is, quite fittingly, a popular meeting place for young actors. There's good solid food and delicious salads. Vilhonkatu 6 (phone: 63-02-05). Moderate.

Bellevue – Not too far from Market Square near the Russian Orthodox church. Decor in quiet oak motif. Unpretentious but very good food. Seafood and a choice of Eastern-influenced dishes. Russian specialties, better-than-average steaks. Rahapajankatu 3 (phone: 17-95-60). Moderate.

Hesperia Steak Room – On lobby floor of the *Hesperia Hotel,* many American visitors like to take à la carte dinners from the open-hearth grill, especially the steaks and french fries. Pleasant, cheerful atmosphere. Mannerheimintie 50 (phone: 44-13-11). Moderate.

Kala Rivoli and Rivoli-Chèri – The city's best French and seafood restaurants. These two, owned by the same proprietor and side by side, are considered choice. Fresh seafood served (other dishes too). Accent of decor is nautical in the seafood room, Art Deco in the French salon. Reservations recommended. Albertinkatu 38 (phone: 64-34-55). Moderate.

Mikado – In the very heart of Helsinki, it's delightfully furnished in art deco style and serves fine salmon dishes and tasty Finnish specialties. Mannerheimintie 6 (phone: 60-74-63). Moderate.

Brasserie Grill Room – On the lobby floor of the *Inter-Continental* hotel, this cheerful room serves lunch from 11 AM to 3 PM. Choice of set lunch or à la carte.

Wide variety of dishes. Background music. Mannerheimintie 46–48 (phone: 44-13-31). Moderate.

Torni – At this popular place for both lunch and dinner, you can choose from a variety of good dishes in three dining rooms, each featuring a different cuisine. Kalevankatu 5 (phone: 64-46-11). Moderate.

Välskärin Kellari – At this arched-ceilinged, cellar dining room in the old center of town, dishes are prepared over a genuine charcoal grill. Corner Hallituskatu and Ritarikatu 3 (phone: 17-43-95). Moderate.

Säkkipilli and The Old Baker's – A busy downtown spot with two restaurants, a pub, and a disco. Corner of Kalevankatu 2 and Mannerheimintie 12 (phone: 60-56-07). Moderate.

Sea Corner – One of *Hotel Vaakuna*'s restaurants, popular for lunches and snacks and featuring seasonally fresh delicacies. Asema-aukio 2 (phone: 1718-11). Moderate to inexpensive.

Happy Days – A complex of cheerful restaurants: a steak joint; a Viennese coffeehouse; an Italian restaurant and a snack bar. Popular meeting spot. Pohjoisesplanadi 2 (phone: 62-40-23). Moderate to inexpensive.

Kellarikrouvi – Ratskeller-style restaurant. Features assorted casseroles among other dishes. Good three-course lunch. Pohjois Makasiininkatu 6 (phone: 65-51-98). Inexpensive.

China – Good Cantonese-style Chinese food, if you're in the mood. Set menu, but à la carte, too. Annankatu 25 (phone: 64-02-58). Inexpensive.

LENINGRAD

Imperial Russia: music, art, theater, ballet, literary salons, glittering court life. This city was the center of the lavish, reckless social milieu immortalized by Pushkin, Dostoyevsky, Tolstoy, and Turgenev. Almost inevitably, it was also the Cradle of the Revolution: Bloody Sunday, the storming of the Winter Palace, and Lenin's triumphant return from exile. Leningrad is relatively young for a European city of such rich cultural and political heritage — less than 280 years old — but what happened here has changed the course of world history.

In a city of such great beauty, where virtually every downtown building displays a plaque noting its historical significance, it is sometimes difficult to focus on the people who live here and the life of the city today. But Leningrad is also a city where a visitor is immediately comfortable. When the days lengthen and dusk comes late, it is hard to resist walking among the people strolling arm in arm in the streets or relaxing in the parks in the fading light that casts its strange glimmer over the city. These glorious White Nights of summer are a consequence of Leningrad's location on the Gulf of Finland at about the same latitude as Helsinki. Leningrad is built on a series of islands, 403 miles (645 km) northwest of Moscow. Although its climate is less harsh than the capital's, this city's harbor is frozen 3 or 4 months of the year.

The hundreds of islands near the mouth of the Neva River, at a point where the Baltic Sea penetrates deepest into its eastern shore, were disputed for centuries by a succession of Finns, Swedes, and Russians. The Neva was an important early trade artery between Europe and Asia. In 1703, after defeating Sweden, Peter the Great built a fortress here to ensure against future invasions. Within 9 years, Peter had built a new city, his "window on Europe," and had moved the capital from Moscow.

St. Petersburg — Petrograd — as the new capital was originally called, was designed from the first to rival the beauty of Western Europe's finest cities. It developed in well-planned stages, acquiring an elegant facade as government buildings, cathedrals, and private residences of the nobility took their places along the Neva and the Fontanka and Moika rivers. Many of the most beautiful palaces were built in the last half of the eighteenth century under the direction of Catherine the Great's favorite French and Italian architects. As the excessive indulgence of the gentry increased, the lives of the czars' subjects became even more intolerable. Serfs were in semislavery. In St. Petersburg itself, overcrowded hovels where workers lived in miserable poverty surrounded the beautiful palaces, the lovely parks, and the great squares and avenues. This incredible contrast between the lifestyle of the nobility and the daily oppression of the workers was impossible to ignore. Change was inevitable.

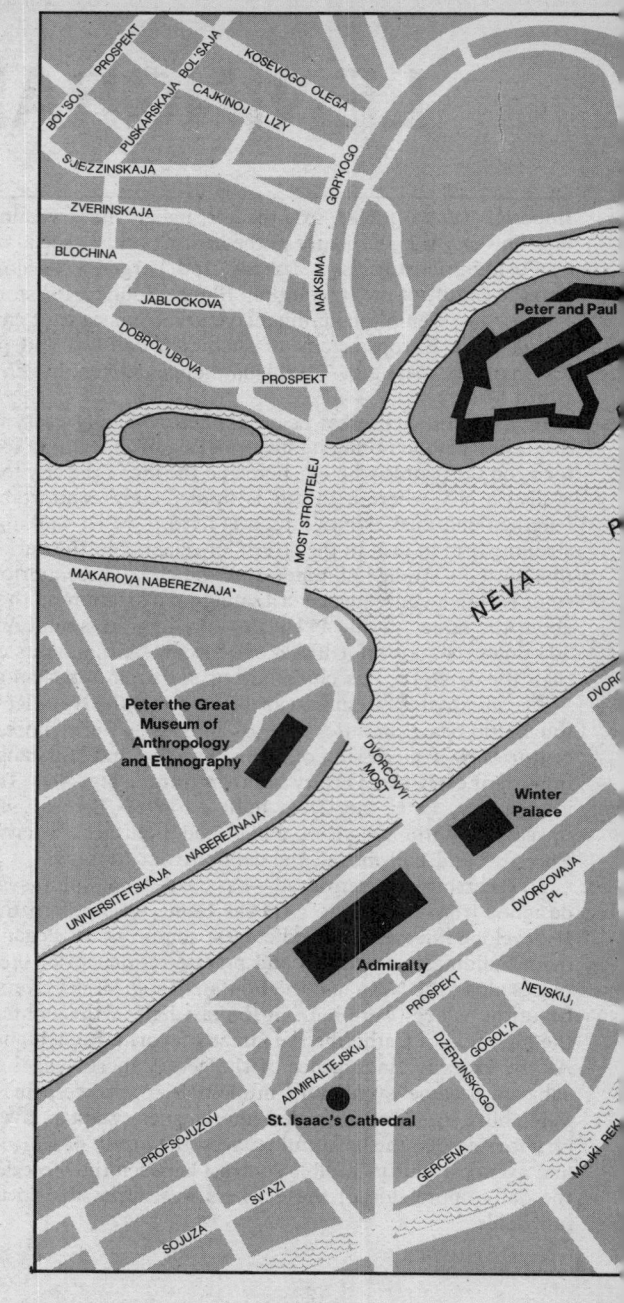

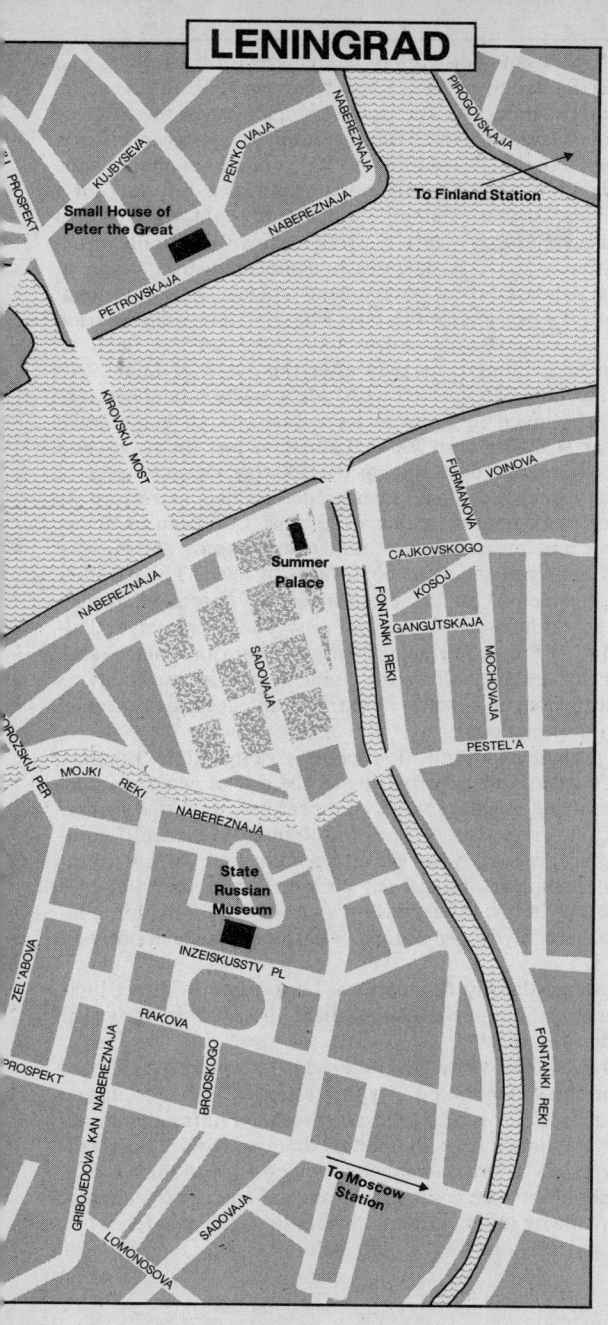

LENINGRAD

Small House of Peter the Great

To Finland Station

KUJBYSEVA

PENKOVAJA

NABEREZNAJA

NABEREZNAJA

PROGOVSKAJA

PROSPEKT

PETROVSKAJA

KIROVSKIJ MOST

NABEREZNAJA

FURMANOVA

VOINOVA

Summer Palace

CAJKOVSKOGO

KOSOJ

FONTANKI REKI

GANGUTSKAJA

SADOVAJA

MOCHOVAJA

PESTEL'A

DROZSKIJ PER

MOJKI REKI

NABEREZNAJA

State Russian Museum

ZEL'ABOVA

INZEISKUSSTV PL

RAKOVA

PROSPEKT

BRODSKOGO

FONTANKI REKI

GRIBOJEDOVA KAN NABEREZNAJA

SADOVAJA

LOMONOSOVA

To Moscow Station

On January 9, 1905, thousands of workers marched with their wives and children to the Winter Palace to petition Czar Nicholas II to intervene on behalf of better working conditions. The czar's troops opened fire at close range. The resulting massacre, known as Bloody Sunday in Russian history, was the spark that ignited the Revolution of 1905. Nicholas made some concessions that allowed him to survive the popular uprising, but only for a time. His inability to rule, further economic hardship brought on by World War I, and continued revolutionary activity brought down the whole structure of czardom in March 1917. A new era in Russian history began in November of that year when a Soviet government replaced the provisional government. It also meant a new era for this city: The capital was moved back to Moscow.

The city was renamed Leningrad in 1924 after the death of Lenin. Although its political importance diminished when Moscow became the seat of government, the city continued to grow as an industrial and commercial center until World War II. More than 700,000 Russians lost their lives and some 10,000 buildings were destroyed during the 900-day German siege of Leningrad. But the city emerged from the war determined to restore its former beauty, and today Leningrad remains the most European of Soviet cities. The canals, rivers, and low buildings remind one of Venice, and Nevsky Prospekt has much of the air of the great boulevards of Paris. The parallels are reinforced by the eighteenth- and nineteenth-century baroque and neoclassical architecture that dominates the central city. The Sheremetyev Palace, Count Orlov's Marble Palace, Prince Potemkin's Taurida Palace, and, of course, the Winter Palace are among the noble homes in use today as museums, offices, meeting houses — restored to the grandeur of their original state but eminently more functional.

Even Leningrad's present modernization plan is designed to preserve the beauty of the city's past. New construction in the downtown area must be completed within existing facades. No skyscrapers are permitted to mar the horizon; glass and concrete structures are prohibited in central Leningrad. Modern building is allowed beyond the city center, however, and numerous large apartment complexes have been built to house the city's 4.5 million people. Most of the industrial expansion — from the shipbuilding industry to factories producing hydrogenerators — has taken place in outlying areas.

Leningrad has an extraordinarily rich cultural heritage, with direct links to the most fundamental changes in Russian political history. It is a city that speaks most eloquently of its past.

Possibly the only drawback to visiting Leningrad is its water. You should not drink tap water or the water served at your restaurant table because a parasite, called *Giardia Lamblia,* is believed to be prevalent in the Leningrad water system. It can cause violent intestinal illness that can require hospitalization if not properly treated. There is an incubation period of about 2 weeks; therefore, this illness should not be confused with usual travelers' maladies. You can avoid this parasite by taking minimal precautions; cooked food, tea, coffee, bottled water, and soft drinks are quite safe.

LENINGRAD AT-A-GLANCE

 SEEING THE CITY: There is no one vantage point that will afford you a good view of the entire city. Peter the Great's decree that no structure should be taller than the spires of the Cathedral of Saints Peter and Paul (about 400 feet), along with the fact that the city is built on marshland, has created a relatively low skyline. However, if you stand beside the Neva opposite the Peter and Paul Fortress, you can get a sense of where and how the city began. At the Admiral Building, where the city's three major avenues converge, you can grasp Leningrad's layout and planning. In Palace Square, site of czarist splendor and bloody revolution, you can get in touch with the city's history; on Nevsky Prospekt at Griboyedov Canal, you can feel the contemporary pulse of the city.

 SPECIAL PLACES: The major sites of Leningrad are spread out over a number of the 101 islands that interconnect to form the city, but all are easily reached by public transportation. If you don't want to visit them on your own, tours of the major sites can be arranged with the Intourist Travel Service bureau (see *Sources and Resources*).

DOWNTOWN

Peter and Paul Fortress (Petropavlovskaya Krepost) – Before Peter the Great chose this location to build a new capital for Russia, he had ordered a fortress built to bar the Swedish fleet's approach. As St. Petersburg became secure from attack, the fortress, established in May 1703, came to be used more as a prison for opponents of the czarist regime. The list of political prisoners included Peter the Great's own son, the Czarevich Alexei; Dostoyevsky, before his exile to Siberia; and the anarchist Mikhail Bakunin. The Cathedral of Saints Peter and Paul (Petropavlovsky Sobor), with its tall, extremely slender golden spire, stands in the center of the fortress. It is the burial place of all the Russian czars from Peter I to Alexander III, with the exception of Peter II. In 1924, the Peter and Paul Fortress became a museum. Open daily, except Wednesdays. Small admission fee. Reached from Revolutsii Pl. on Peter and Paul Fortress Island.

Summer Palace; Garden of Peter I (Letny Sad; Dvorets-Musei Petra I) – Across the Neva from the fortress, on the Kutuzov Embankment (Naberezhnaya Kutuzova), is a 30-acre park, laid out in 1704, and an unpretentious summer palace built in the Dutch style for Peter the Great. The park, filled with classical sculptures, is a favorite open space with Leningraders, particularly during the summer's long White Nights. The palace is open daily, except Tuesdays, May through November. The park is open year round, although the sculpture is covered during the winter. The park is entered at Pestelya Ul. 2.

State Hermitage; Winter Palace (Godudarstvenni Ermitazh; Zimnniy Dvoryets) – Built as a home for the czars and czarinas during the eighteenth-century reigns of Elizabeth and Catherine the Great, the Winter Palace was designed by the Italian architect Rastrelli. The grandiose, baroque palace and four adjacent buildings now house the Hermitage collection, one of the finest art collections in the world. The splendor of the room decorations — patterned parquet floors, molded and painted ceilings, furniture, and decorative objects of malachite, lapis lazuli, and jasper — dazzle the eye as much as the Da Vincis, Raphaels, Titians, Rembrandts, and the Impressionist and post-Impressionist paintings. When you think you have already seen every richness and extravagance imaginable, arrange to take the special tour of the Gold

Treasure Room. The exquisite jewels of Catherine the Great are housed here along with a spectacular collection of Scythian gold. Open daily, except Thursdays. Small admission charge. Dvortsovaya Nab. 36 (phone: A2-0G–32).

Palace Square (Dvortsovaya Pl.) – Between the Winter Palace and the great curve of the Admiralty Building, the former general staff headquarters, is the central square of the city. The red granite Alexander Column in the center was erected in 1834 as a monument to the victory over Napoleon in 1812. This square, the site of Bloody Sunday in 1905, is closely associated with the revolutionary movement. The climax of the October Revolution in 1917 was the storming of the Winter Palace from this square. Each year there are parades and demonstrations in the square to mark the event.

Peter the Great Monument – The famous bronze statue of Peter the Great, designed by the French sculptor E. M. Falconet, stands in the center of the grassy Decemberists Square (Dekabristov Pl.) to the west of the Admiralty Building. The statue, commissioned by Catherine the Great, depicts Peter astride a horse whose hoofs are trampling a writhing snake (said to be a symbolic representation of Sweden).

St. Isaac's Cathedral Museum (Isaakievsky Sobor) – Leningrad's largest church — and one of the world's largest domed structures — stands to the south of Decemberists Square. The cathedral is filled with mosaic and painted ceiling murals, decorated with 14 kinds of minerals and semiprecious stones. Malachite and lapis lazuli columns form a part of the massive gilded iconostasis before the altar. A Foucault pendulum that moves 13 degrees each hour is suspended from the central dome. Open daily, except Tuesdays. Isaakievskaya Pl.

Alexander Nevsky Monastery (Aleksandr Nevskaya Lavra) – The monastery's Trinity Cathedral (Troitsky Sobor) was built in 1724 to house the remains of St. Alexander Nevsky, which had been brought here from Vladimir. In 1922, the silver sarcophagus containing the saint's ashes was moved to the Hermitage. The monastery also has ten other churches, four cemeteries, known as necropolises, a seminary, and the Museum of Urban Sculpture. The eighteenth-century necropolis includes the graves of Peter I's sister and Mikhail Lomonosov, the scientist who founded Moscow University. The nineteenth-century necropolis includes the graves of Dostoyevsky, Tchaikovsky, Moussorgsky, Rimsky-Korsakov, and Borodin. You must buy a ticket to enter these cemeteries, but you may visit the interesting modern necropolis opposite the cathedral without charge. Here you will find unusual grave markers, such as the propeller of the plane in which a buried pilot met his death and a miniature oil rig, designating the burial site of three oil-field workers. The Museum of Urban Sculpture has models and site photographs of most of the city's monuments. It is open daily, except Thursdays. Small admission charge. Near the Aleksandra Nevskovo Metro stop. Aleksandra Nevskovo Pl. 1.

Russian State Museum (Gosudarstvenni Russky Musei) – Next to the Tretyakov Gallery in Moscow, this museum has the largest collection of Russian art in the world. There are some 300,000 exhibitions of Russian painting, sculpture, decorative arts, and folk arts in this museum in the former Mikhailovsky Palace. Open daily, except Tuesdays. Small admission charge. Inzhenernaya Ul. 4/2 (phone: A4-73-54).

Ethnographical Museum of the Peoples of the USSR (Gosudarstvenni Musei Etnografii Narodov USSR) – In a wing of the Russian State Museum but with its own entrance, this museum houses a beautiful collection of clothing, household goods, and folk articles associated with the daily life and customs of the peoples of the 15 constituent republics that make up the USSR. Open daily, except Mondays. Small admission charge. Inzhenernaya Ul. 4/1 (phone: A0-36-52).

Church of the Blood of the Savior (Chram Spasa na Krovi) – Built in the Old Russian style similar to St. Basil's in Moscow, this church was erected at the end of the nineteenth century on the spot where Alexander II was assassinated. The exterior is covered with mosaics. Open daily. Just north of the Russian State Museum. Gribovedova Kan. Nab. 1.

The Bridges of Leningrad – From the ironwork of the large, impressive Kirov Bridge over the Neva to the multitude of small bridges connecting the islands, these structures are a natural museum of the city. The stone turrets and chains of the Lomonosov Bridge over the Fontanka are an example of the earliest bridges. This heavy style soon gave way to light, airy ironwork decorated with lions, gilded griffins, sphinxes, and other delightful creatures. There are hundreds of these bridges, large and small, and they create one of the unifying aspects of the city. The most famous, perhaps, is the Anichkov, which spans the Fontanka River at Nevsky Prospekt and has four sculptures by Peter Klodt.

Smolny Monastery and Institute – The cathedral and convent of the monastery were built in the eighteenth century by Czarina Elizabeth, and the institute was founded during the reign of Catherine II as a school for young ladies of the nobility. The room at the institute where Lenin later lived and worked is now a museum. Tours of the buildings' interiors are available by special arrangement, but the park may be visited at any time. Along the Neva between Smolnovo Ul. and Smolny Prospekt, about seven blocks east of the Cernysevskaya Metro stop.

Piskarevskoye Memorial Cemetery – An eternal flame and small museum are at the entrance of these memorial grounds commemorating the 900-day siege of Leningrad during World War II. Some 500,000 of those who died before the ring of the blockade was broken in 1943 were buried in mass graves here. The museum contains photographs and documents relating to the heroism of the city's residents during the blockade. North of the Smolny Monastery, across the Neva in the northeast sector of the city. Piskarevsky Prospekt.

Lenin Monument at the Finland Station (Pom'yatnik Leninu u Finlandskiya Vokzal) – Lenin arrived at the Finland Station after 10 years in exile, and it was here, on April 3, 1917, that he spoke to workers from the turret of an armored car. In 1926, a statue of Lenin standing on an armored car was erected in a square in front of the railway station to commemorate the event and to mark the ninth anniversary of the revolution. Near the Lenina Pl. Metro stop. Lenina Pl.

Cruiser Aurora *(Creiser Avrora)* – A blank shot fired from this cruiser signaled the beginning of the October Revolution. The cruiser is now permanently moored in the Neva, opposite the *Hotel Leningrad* (see *Checking In*). Open daily, except Wednesdays and Saturdays. Small admission charge. Petrogradskaya Nab.

ENVIRONS

Pushkin – Once known as the Czar's Village, this town is worth a visit because it is the site of the Yekaterinsky Palace, named for Peter the Great's wife, Catherine I. Built during the reigns of Elizabeth and Catherine II, the palace has a stunning aqua facade, decorated with gold and white ornaments. Part of the palace is now open as a museum with exhibits of furniture, china, and the palace's history. There's also a museum with manuscripts, rare books, and the personal belongings of Alexander Pushkin, who studied at the school for the nobility attached to the palace. The village was renamed for the poet in 1937, on the 100th anniversary of his death. The palace is set in a 1,482-acre park. The museums are open daily, except Tuesday. Train service is available from the Vitebsky Station in Leningrad, with buses and taxis available at the station here. Fourteen miles (22 km) south of Leningrad along Moscow Prospekt.

Pavlovsk – One of the most beautifully restored palaces in the Soviet Union is less than 2 miles (3 km) from Pushkin. Originally hunting grounds that belonged to the Czar's Village, the palace grounds constitute one of the largest landscaped parks in Europe. The land and palace were a gift from Catherine II to her son Paul in 1777. You enter the 1,500-acre park on a road from Pushkin through cast-iron gates and over a wooden bridge. The palace is open daily, except Thursdays and Fridays. Fifteen miles (24 km) south of Leningrad along Moscow Prospekt.

■ **EXTRA SPECIAL:** On the southern shore of the Gulf of Finland, Peter the Great built the Grand Palace, which he hoped would rival Versailles. He personally drafted the layout of the 300-acre park and gave detailed instructions on the design of the spectacular system of fountains that cascade through the park and gardens. The buildings were badly damaged during World War II but have been restored carefully, according to the original plans. Some 129 of the fountains in the system that begins on the Ropshinskiye Heights 13 miles (21 km) away are working today. The most impressive of these is the Samson Fountain, directly in front of the Grand Palace, which portrays Samson ripping open the jaws of a lion as a spray of water rises 65 feet in the air from the lion's mouth. The fountains are said to use nearly 7,500 gallons of water a minute. Petrodvorets is about 20 miles (32 km) southwest of the city. It can be reached by leaving the city along Stacek Prospekt or, in summer, by hydrofoil down the Neva into the gulf.

SOURCES AND RESOURCES

It is best to buy comprehensive guides to Leningrad before you leave the US. One of the most useful is *The Complete Guide to the Soviet Union,* by Victor and Jennifer Louis (St. Martin's Press; $9.95). A good guide to the city and its museums is *Next Time You Go to Russia,* by Charles A. Ward (Charles Scribner's Sons; $8.95). *Leningrad: Art and Architecture,* by V. Schwartz (Moscow: Progress Publishers), is especially good and may be obtained in the US through stores that import Russian publications. *Leningrad, Its Monuments and Architectural Complexes* (Leningrad: Aurora Art Publishers) is a beautifully illustrated book sold in *Beriozka* stores (see *Shopping*) in Leningrad.

Although good transportation and city maps are available in hotels at news or book kiosks for very reasonable prices, it would be helpful to take along a Falkplan map for *Leningrad* (Hamburg: Falk-Verlag; $6.95). This is a pocket map designed to be used in sections and includes a street name index and gazetteer for monuments, museums, hotels, and theaters. It is available in the US. *Intourist* deals with all adult foreign travel within the USSR and provides local English-speaking guides. The main *Intourist* office in Leningrad is at St. Isaac's Sq. 3. Although you will have an English-speaking guide with you during tour activities, it would be helpful if you learned the Russian (Cyrillic) alphabet and the sound for each of its characters. Many Russian words have English or French cognates, so once you sound out the words, life can become much simpler. Especially helpful is the Berlitz book *Russian for Travellers;* $1.95.

For Local Coverage – You can buy the *Moscow News,* an English-language weekly newspaper, or you may find the *International Herald-Tribune* on sale in Intourist hotels occasionally. If neither of the above is sufficient, the American Consulate General is at Petra Lavrova Ul. 15 (phone: 75-45-48).

Phone books are nearly impossible to find in Leningrad, but you can get directory assistance from the hotel desk or service bureau. Telephones in hotel rooms are connected to the city system. To use a public pay phone, deposit a 2-kopek coin in the pay slot before lifting the receiver, then dial when you hear a continuous buzzing sound. For long-distance calls, book them at least an hour ahead of time through the service bureau in your hotel.

 **CLIMATE AND CLOTHES:** Leningrad is near the Gulf of Finland and the Baltic Sea and, although farther north, tends to be warmer than Moscow. The temperatures average 16° to 19°F (−9° to −7°C) during January and in the mid-60s F (16° to 18° C) during July, with about 6 to 13 days of precipitation per month. During the late spring and summer, the days are very long,

but in December, when the canals and rivers are frozen over and the cold is intense, the short days make life something of an endurance test. Even so, this winter weather does not daunt the Walrus Club, whose members swim in the Neva beside the Peter and Paul Fortress in an area cleared of ice just for them. The river is frozen from mid-November to April.

If you travel during these cold months, a fur hat, heavy coat, boots, gloves, and scarves are essential, but tour buses and building interiors are well heated, so tourists normally are not unduly distressed by the cold. In Russia, one must check one's coat at restaurants, museums, and theaters, so a heavy loop or chain should be sewn into the collar. (The check rooms have only coat hooks, no hangers.)

In warmer weather, a raincoat with a removable lining or a sweater and raincoat will suffice. Winter is a good 6 months long, so it can still be quite cool in early fall and late spring. Even in the summertime a sweater is welcome for evenings. A travel umbrella is essential in this city.

 GETTING AROUND: Leningrad has a small but exceedingly good subway system, called the Metro, which is supplemented by a network of bus, trolley, and tram routes that enable you to move about the city with relative ease. Fares on each are less than a dime. Good, inexpensive, transportation maps are generally available in the hotels.

Bus, Trolley, and Tram – These vehicles all have self-service cash boxes and require exact change. You deposit your fare when you get on, and get a ticket by turning a knob on the side of the cash box. If it is crowded, you will be expected to pass your money to whoever is standing next to the cash box. If you happen to be standing near the cash box during the rush hour, you may end up feeling just like a native after dispensing 15 or 20 tickets.

Metro – Since Leningrad is built on marshy land, the stations for the 25-mile Metro are exceptionally deep. In fact, some escalator rides from the surface take 2 minutes — and escalators here move much more rapidly than they do in the US. Be forewarned: Stand to the right on down escalators; the left lane is for "runners." Coming up, however, you can stand on either side.

Taxi – Taxis are available at taxi stands or through hotel service bureaus, but they are expensive compared to other forms of transportation. Taxis and taxi stands can be recognized by a green "T" and a checkered pattern.

Car Rentals – You can rent automobiles, with or without chauffeurs, through Intourist. Rentals must be paid for in foreign currency.

Boats – In summer, hydrofoils and excursion boats ply the Neva River, the canals, and the smaller rivers. The fare can range from 25¢ to 75¢, depending on the length of the trip.

 MUSEUMS: Leningrad is a major art center; many of the best-known museums are listed in *Special Places*. In addition, you may enjoy visiting — either individually or with an Intourist guided tour — some of the following:

State Museum of the History of Leningrad (Gosudarstvenni Musei Istorii Leningrada), Krasnovo Flota Nab. 44 (phone: 22-77-98).

Peter the Great Museum of Anthropology and Ethnography (Musei Antropologii i Etnografii im. Petra Velikovo), Universitetskaya Nab. 3 (phone: 28-14-12).

Zoological Museum (Zoologichesky Musei), Universitetskaya Nab. 1 (phone: 28-01-12).

Museum of History of Religion and Atheism of the USSR (Gosudarstvenni Musei Istorii Religii i Ateizma), Kazanskaya Pl. 2 (phone: A1-27-05).

Central Naval Museum (Tsentralny Voenno-Morskoi Musei), Pushkinskaya Pl. 4 (phone: A8-25-02).

House Museum of Peter I (Musei "Domik Petra I"). Dwelling used by Peter the Great while the Peter and Paul Fortress was being constructed. Petrovskaya Nab. 2 (phone: B3-90-70).

Pushkin Apartment Museum (Musei Kvartira A. S. Pushkina). House where Pushkin lived during the last months of his life. R. Moiki Nab. 12 (phone: 22-32-82).

Brodsky House Museum (Musei-Kvartina I. I. Brodskovo). Home of the portrait-ist of Lenin. Iskusstv Pl. 3 (phone: 21-20-00).

Leningrad Branch of the Central Lenin Museum (Leningradsky Filial Tsental-novo Muzeya V. I. Lenina), Khalturina Ul. 5/1 (phone: 21-28-97).

Zoological Park, Park Lenina 1 (phone: 24-66-87).

SHOPPING: For foreigners, the best buys will usually be found at the government-run hard-currency shops known as *Beriozka* (literally, "Little Birch Tree"). These shops sell just about anything Russia is noted for: furs, amber, jewelry, silver, balalaikas, vodka, caviar, wooden toys, and samovars. There are *Beriozkas* in most hotels and at two downtown locations: Nevsky Prospekt 9 and Gertsena Ul. 26. Payment in these shops must be made in foreign currency or with traveler's checks or credit cards.

You can also shop where the locals do, using Soviet currency. If you do, select the item you want and take it to a clerk, who will give you a sales slip, which you take to the cash desk, the *Kacca.* When you pay, you'll receive a receipt, which you return to the clerk, who will give you your merchandise, already wrapped.

Gostiny Dvor – A huge, sprawling department store. Leningrad's answer to Moscow's *GUM.* Nevsky Prospekt 35.

Dom Knigi – The largest bookstore in Leningrad, with shops selling posters, repro-ductions, and postcards on the second floor. The building itself is of interest because it was the Russian headquarters of the Singer Sewing Machine Co. during the early years of this century; it has some wonderful art nouveau details as well as distinctive metalwork sculpture on its roof. Nevsky Prospekt 28.

SPECIAL EVENTS: The major annual arts festival in Leningrad is called *White Nights,* and is held June 21–29, when days here are so long that there is only a brief period of dusk each night. During the festival, there are performances by the *Kirov Opera and Ballet,* the *Maly Theater Opera and Ballet,* and by various top Soviet singers and musicians. *Leningrad Spring,* March 31–April 3, is a week of festivities celebrating the end of winter. Here, as in Moscow, major celebrations are held on *International Labor Day,* May 1; *Victory Day,* May 9; *Constitution Day,* October 7; and *Revolution Day,* November 7.

SPORTS: Hundreds of sporting events are held each year in Leningrad's two major sports arenas: *Kirov Stadium,* Morskoi Prospekt, and *Yubileini Sports Palace,* Dobrolyubova Prospekt 18. Leningraders are particularly fond of soccer and ice hockey. Schedules for current matches and events and tickets are available through your hotel service bureau.

THEATER: Your hotel service bureau will have tickets and information on performance schedules. Even for popular companies, such as the renowned *Kirov Ballet,* tickets are surprisingly inexpensive. Performances begin early; usually 7 PM for the theater and 7:30 PM for the circus and puppet shows. Be sure to try the theater buffet during intermission. All manner of consumables, from salami to champagne, are available. Besides the *Kirov Academic Theater of Opera and*

Ballet (Akademichesky Teatr Operi i Baleta im S. M. Kirova), Teatralnaya Pl. 1, the major theaters in Leningrad include the *Maly Theater of Opera and Ballet (Akademichesky Mali Teatr Operi i Baleta),* Iskusstv Pl. i; *Bolshoi Puppet Theater (Bolshoi Teatr Kukol),* Nekrasova Ul. 10; *Leningrad State Circus (Leningradsky Gosudarstvenni Tsirk),* R. Fontanki Nab. 3; *Pushkin Academic Drama Theater (Akademichesky Teatr Drami im. A. S. Pushkina),* Ostrovskovo Pl. 2; *Gorky Academic Bolshoi Drama Theater (Akademichesky Bolshoi Dramatichesky Teatr im. M. Gorkovo),* R. Fontanki Nab. 65; *Academic Theater of Comedy (Akademichesky Teatr Komedii),* Nevsky Prospekt 56; and *Theater of Musical Comedy (Teatr Muzikalnoi Komedii),* Rakova Ul. 13.

MUSIC: Tickets and performance schedules for concerts can be obtained through your hotel service bureaus. Concerts usually begin at 7:30 PM. The major concert halls are the *Leningrad Philharmonia (Leningradskaya Philarmoniya),* Brodskovo Ul. 2, and *Glinka State Academic Chorus Kapella (Gosudarstvennaya Akademicheskaya Khorovaya Kapella im. M. I. Glinki),* R. Moiki Nab. 20.

NIGHTCLUBS AND NIGHTLIFE: There are no nightclubs of the Western type, but at restaurants, dancing is as much a part of the evening as the meal. Most nighttime activity here centers on one of the many theater or concert hall performances. There are late night, foreign-currency bars on the tenth floor of the *Hotel Leningrad,* on the lower floor of the *Hotel Moskva,* and in the hotels *Astoria* and *Evropeiskaya* (see *Checking In*). There are also several buffets in the *Moskva* and *Leningrad,* which stay open late, serving both food and drink. In terms of big-city nightlife, this may be scant fare, but considering the range and quality of early evening entertainment, most visitors find it a more than acceptable trade-off.

SINS: Moscow may be the capital of this country, but Leningrad had that honor for more than 200 years and remains the cultural and artistic *pride* of the Soviet Union. Leningraders claim their city is one of the most beautiful in the world. Cleanliness is one of the hallmarks of this city, so you can raise the *anger* of local residents by carelessly littering. Someone will probably scurry to retrieve your trash, muttering as he or she deposits it in a nearby receptacle. An army of older women, affectionately called grandmother, *babushka,* sweep the city with their twig brooms each morning, a sight worth taking a 6 AM walk to witness. With so much to keep you busy here, there is little time for *sloth,* but at least once just sit on a park bench in the Summer Garden or in front of Kazan Cathedral to watch the children at play and enjoy the rhythms of the city.

BEST IN TOWN

CHECKING IN: Hotel accommodations in the Soviet Union are handled somewhat differently than in Western Europe. Before you enter Russia you must have confirmed and paid hotel reservations, arranged through Intourist. You must apply for a visa listing all proposed stops and their duration, and once approved, deviations from your itinerary are not usually permitted. Visa applications also can be handled by your travel agency. Changes in your program can be requested at the Intourist service bureau in your hotel after you arrive, but do not count on the requests being approved. Normally you will not be told which hotel you have been assigned until you arrive in the city. Accommodations can be purchased in any available class, but in Leningrad Deluxe Suite, Deluxe, and First Class are usually the only available rates unless you are traveling with a group. The top rate is about $190 for double occupancy in a Deluxe Suite. A Deluxe room runs close to $100, and a First-Class double will cost $60. Rates for travelers requesting single rooms are about twice the rate for double occupancy. No meals are included in the advance payment plan. The hotels have banks, *Beriozkas,* postcard and stamp kiosks, service bureaus, beauty parlors, barber shops, and newsstands to serve most tourists' needs.

Leningrad – Completed in 1970, this fine hotel overlooks the Neva River and has accommodations for 1,300 guests. Clean lines and lots of light reveal the Finnish source of the building plans. It has a good restaurant, a late night bar on the tenth floor, and buffets on every other floor. Pirogovskaya Nab. 5/2 (phone: 48-91-23). Deluxe.

Moskva – Leningrad's newest hotel is a mammoth in the Russian style. Even though it was opened in 1977, it is not as modern in appearance or facilities as the *Leningrad.* Still, the staff is noted for its helpfulness and it is ideally located for connections with public transportation. The hotel has a restaurant and bar as well as buffets in the central portion of the building on each floor. Alexandra Nevskovo Pl. 2. (phone: 274-2051). Deluxe.

Astoria – Some people call this the most civilized hotel in Russia. Built in 1912 in the heart of downtown Leningrad, this fine old hotel has only 260 rooms. It is noted for its restaurant and late night bar and supposedly is where Hitler planned to hold his victory banquet after his armies captured Leningrad. Gertsena Ul. 39 (phone: 96-26-84). Deluxe.

Evropeiskaya – Another of Leningrad's small but grand old hotels, the *Evropeiskaya* has not been kept up as well as the *Astoria* but it is still has charm. Located off Nevsky Prospekt, the hotel has 268 rooms, a good restaurant, and a late night bar. Next door is the *Sadko,* one of Leningrad's best restaurants (see *Eating Out*). Brodskovo Ul. 1/7. Deluxe.

Sovetskaya – A city-owned hotel sometimes used by Intourist to handle overflow bookings, the *Sovetskaya* is large and comfortable and has the largest *Beriozka* in the city. However, it is somewhat less conveniently located in the southwestern part of the city. Lermontovsky Prospekt 43.

EATING OUT: Meals at major restaurants in Leningrad can be booked in advance through your hotel service bureau. You will receive a prix fixe menu, obviating the need to speak Russian. Dinner prices range from $30 to $50 for two. Any drinks ordered in addition to the vodka and wine included in the prix fixe dinner must be paid for in Soviet currency. Most of the Leningrad hotels have dining rooms with live bands, dancing and, occasionally, a floor show. Reservations for hotel restaurants also should be made in advance with your hotel service bureau. There are also many cafés in Leningrad, providing a good opportunity to mix with local residents. The service bureaus won't make reservations for these cafés, so arrive early in case there's a wait. Payment in the cafés must be in Soviet currency.

And do sample the street cuisine. Venders sell tasty meat-, mushroom-, or cabbage-filled fried pastries, *pirozhki,* and ice cream, *morozhenoye,* here is delicious. Try some *Kvass,* a drink made from fermented black bread and sold from small tanks on the sidewalks. Flavored mineral water is sold from automatic dispensers. Here they use community glasses instead of paper cups, but you can wash the glass by pressing down on the spit in the machine. Put the clean glass under the spout, drop in your coins, and return the glass to the washing spot when you've finished your drink.

Sadko – One of the best restaurants in Leningrad with traditional Russian fare, such as beef Stroganoff, skewered meatballs, called *Lyulya Kebab,* and blinis: crêpes stuffed with caviar, smoked salmon, or other delicacies. A balalaika orchestra, singers, and, occasionally, folk dancers provide entertainment. Next to the *Hotel Evropeiskaya* (see *Checking In*). Brodskovo Ul. and Nevsky Prospekt.

Neva Café – A popular restaurant that can seat 1,000 people. Also at this address is the *Sever Café*, famous for tortes and other desserts. Intourist will not prebook for this restaurant, so go early to secure a table. Nevsky Prospekt 44.

Kavkazky – Specializing in Caucasian dishes, such as the shish kebab, known as Caucasian *shashlik*. Nevsky Prospekt 25.

Baku – An Azerbaijani restaurant with an upstairs room for dancing. Reservations necessary. Sadovaya Ul. between Rakova Ul. and Nevsky Prospekt.

LISBON

Lisbon is a city where the sun plays beautiful tricks. At certain times of the day, it casts a golden reflection so intense that the broad expanse of estuary facing the city seems to live up literally to its popular name, *Mar da Palha*, or "Sea of Straw." And as the sun moves across a violet blue sky still unspoiled by pollution, the pastel buildings, tree-lined boulevards, cobblestone streets, and mosaic sidewalks of this city built in tiers on seven hills are bathed again and again in new perspectives of light.

It is a city that, legend tells us, was founded by Ulysses — although less romantic historians say it was the Phoenicians — a city from which explorers embarked to find India (led by Vasco da Gama) and to discover Brazil (under the command of Pedro Álvares Cabral). A city where a giddy night on the town can mean sitting in a dimly lit café listening to a woman draped in black sing sad songs. A city that further hints of a strain of melancholia by calling its cemetery the Pleasures. A city where *obrigado*, "thank you," is the most frequently heard word. It is, in short, one of the most pleasant cities in the world.

The westernmost capital in Europe, Lisbon has grown up along the northern bank of the Tagus, where it broadens into one of the best harbors in Europe, then narrows again in its rush to the Atlantic Ocean, some 5 miles away. Aloof from the rest of Europe for centuries, Lisbon was barely touched by the Renaissance, the Reformation, or the Industrial Revolution, and it remained neutral in World War II. Its history has been shaped by the Moors, the 1755 earthquake, the revolution of 1974, and the sea — above all, by the sea.

From the days of the Phoenicians in 1200 BC, the city has been an important port of call for Mediterranean ships sailing to northern Europe. Lisbon was conquered repeatedly by Greeks, Carthaginians, Romans, and Visigoths before the Moors made it their citadel in AD 716. The Arab occupation ended in 1255, but even today the Moorish influence can be perceived in the architecture of the city's old houses and in the manners and features of the Portuguese people.

During the centuries when the seas were uncharted and darkness and superstition ruled men's imaginations, Lisbon was sending forth missionaries and caravels into the unknown, and her explorers were bringing the world's riches back from Africa, Brazil, India, and China. By the sixteenth century, Lisbon was a great commercial and maritime power, the "Queen of the Tagus," ruling from an unparalleled site where ocean routes converged.

Then, on All Saints' Day morning, November 1, 1755, while most of Lisbon was at mass, a violent earthquake shook the city like a straw in the wind. Within 10 minutes, two-thirds of Lisbon was in ruins. Forty-foot tidal waves rose on the Tagus and slammed into the city. Fires, started by tapers lighted in the churches for the feast day and fanned by a violent windstorm, burned for 6 days. As many as 60,000 people perished; the "Queen of the Tagus" was a charnel house. Only the old Moorish quarter, the Alfama, snuggled against one of the city's highest hills, survived the disaster and, on the rubble of the valley floor below it, Lisbon was rebuilt. The straight lines and eighteenth-century proportions of the quarter called *a Baixa* — the lower town — grew up in place of the medieval jumble, and the stately plan of the city's classical squares and boulevards was traced out. The modern city has continued to spread east and north along the Tagus, and more than 1.6 million people live in Lisbon and its environs today. Until a few years ago, this was the capital of the world's last great colonial empire, and yet it was essentially a small town. Social circles were tight; no one strayed beyond his or her station.

Portugal's monarchy fell in 1910 when Manuel II abdicated and a republic was proclaimed. But the country lived under the tight reins of the dictatorship of Antonio Salazar from 1932 to 1968. When he retired, however, his successors could not retain control of the country, and during a revolution in 1974 a democratically inspired military junta took control of the government. It was a revolution in which few lives were lost, but one that altered the face of Lisbon. Once-pristine buildings were spray-painted with political slogans, mosaic sidewalks that used to be scoured daily became grubby, and, with the breakup of the colonial empire, refugees from Angola poured into the city. The government housed some in hotels; others lived in shanties — even at the airport, their crated belongings lining the banks of the Tagus for miles.

Within a few years, however, the situation stabilized, allowing Lisbon's beauty to reemerge and captivate the visitor once more. A parliament, then a president, was elected; refugees were resettled; hotels and public buildings were renovated; and new accommodations for visitors added each year. The delights of Lisbon are again apparent, and tourism is flourishing.

LISBON AT-A-GLANCE

SEEING THE CITY: A city built on hills frequently surprises its visitors with lovely views that emerge without warning around unexpected corners. Lisbon has 17 natural balconies — called *miradouros* — from which to view the city. Foremost of these is the hilltop near St. George's Castle. From this vantage point, the sun often gives the Tagus the golden reflection that has earned it its sobriquet. Across one of Europe's longest suspension bridges, renamed the April 25th Bridge, Ponte 25 do Abril, after the revolution, you can get a marvelous panorama of the Tagus estuary from the top of the statue *Christ the King, Cristo Rei.* There is a small entrance fee. If you don't have a car, you can cross the river by ferry from Praça do Comércio and take the bus from Cacilhas to the statue.

SPECIAL PLACES: The central shopping and commercial district of Lisbon is the quarter known as the *Baixa*. It stretches from Rossio Square south to the Praça do Comércio at the river's edge. The Rua Garrett and the Rua do Carmo, which link the Rossio to the Praça Luís de Camões, are two of

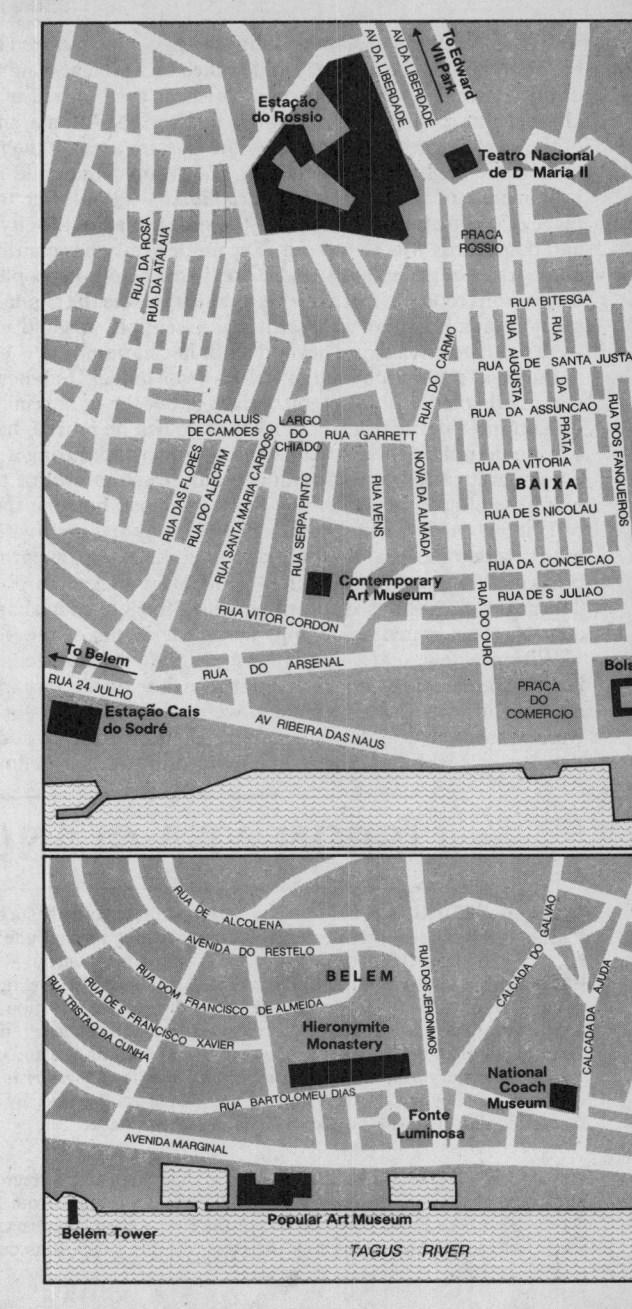

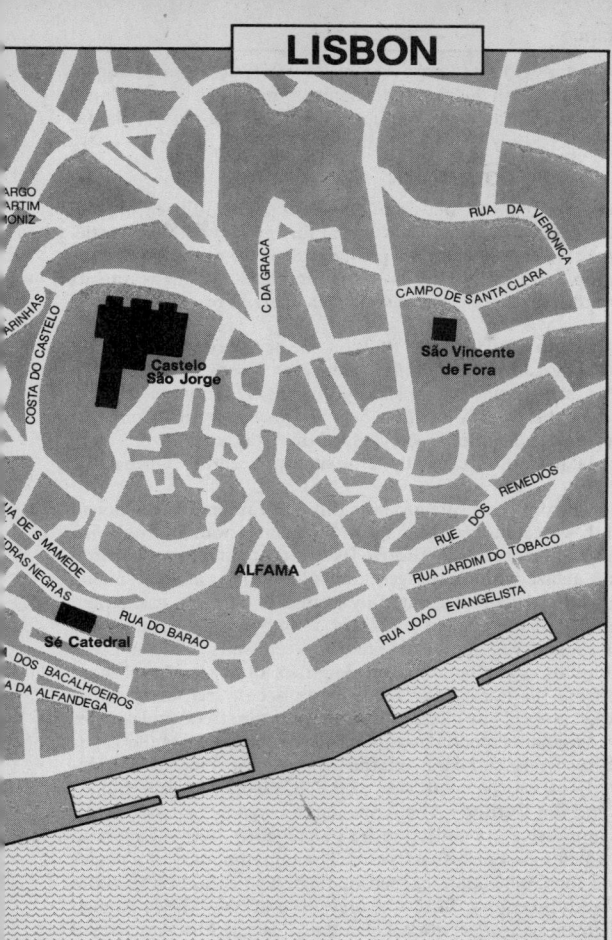

LISBON

ARGO
ARTIM
IONIZ

RUA DA VERONICA

C DA GRACA

CAMPO DE SANTA CLARA

COSTA DO CASTELO

ARINHAS

Castelo
São Jorge

São Vincente
de Fora

RUE DOS REMEDIOS

IA DE S MAMEDE

RAS NEGRAS

ALFAMA

RUA JARDIM DO TOBACO

RUA DO BARAO

RUA JOAO EVANGELISTA

Sé Catedral

DOS BACALHOEIROS

A DA ALFANDEGA

TAGUS   RIVER

the busiest streets in Lisbon, and with the Largo do Chiado constitute the area known locally as the Chiado. The old Moorish quarter, the Alfama, is to the east of this central section, and the Belém section with its many museums lies along the river at the far western reaches of the city.

DOWNTOWN

Sé Cathedral – Lisbon's principal Catholic church, built in the twelfth century and remodeled following two violent earthquakes, is a typical fortress-church with battlements, towers, and solid massive construction. Its plain facade is Romanesque, but the burial chapel, the ambulatory, and the cloister are pure Gothic. Religious vestments and ecclesiastical gold are displayed in a museum. Open daily. Free. Largo de Sé (phone: 86-76-52).

St. George's Castle (Castelo São Jorge) – Built on one of Lisbon's highest hills, this castle with ten towers is considered the cradle of the city. Taken as a whole, St. George's Castle is made up of the building constructed by the Visigoths in the fifth century and modified during the twelfth century, a lovely garden with flamingoes, swans, and rare white peacocks, and the Arabic Palace that was used as the royal residence by kings of Portugal from the fourteenth to the sixteenth century. Open daily. Free. Rua Costa do Castelo.

The Alfama – Walk down from the castle grounds through Lisbon's most ancient section. A cobbled labyrinth with some streets so narrow you must walk in single file, the Alfama is one of the most colorful spots in Europe. Its streets are lit by wrought-iron lamps, lined with balconies ablaze with scarlet geraniums harboring canaries singing in the sun, and lined with little taverns decorated by strings of peppers, garlic, and cheese. On washday — Friday — the ancient buildings of the area are strung with clotheslines, and the week's laundry is hung out to dry between walls that could well have been built by the Visigoths. Some buildings are Moorish, others medieval mansions. The youngest date from the late 1800s. The Alfama is best seen early in the morning when the fish market is open, late in the afternoon when the streets and squares are alive with people, or on a romantic moonlit evening. Between the banks of the Tagus and the castle in the area between the cathedral and the Church of St. Vincent Outside-the-Walls (São Vicente de Fora) on the south side of the St. George's Castle hill.

Gulbenkian Museum and Art Center – The Armenian oil tycoon Calouste Sarkis Gulbenkian donated the impressive art collection he put together over 40 years to Portugal, the country in which he spent his last years. The museum, part of a center for arts and culture named for Gulbenkian, opened in 1969. The collection includes paintings, sculpture, eighteenth-century furniture and decorations, Greco-Roman coins, Chinese vases, and Japanese lacquerwork. Open daily, except Mondays. Small admission charge; free on weekends. Av. de Berna 45 (phone: 73-51-31).

Lisbon Zoo – Set in a 65-acre park north of the city center, the zoo houses some 3,500 animals. There are elephant and pony rides for children, rowboats, a roller-skating rink, a small train, and puppets and clowns in the children's playground. Open daily. Small admission charge. Easily reached by subway to the Sete Rios station. Between Parque das Laranjeiras and Estrada de Benfica (phone: 78-20-41).

Tower of Belém (Torré de Belém) – This quadrangular tower, which looks like a huge chess piece, is the second of Lisbon's great landmarks and is considered by the Portuguese to be representative of their brave past. Its image is often used on official papers as a symbol of the country. This masterpiece of Manueline architecture was built on an island in the middle of the Tagus between 1515 and 1521, but the river has changed course since medieval times and the tower now stands on the north bank of the river. On a terrace atop the five-story tower is a statue of Our Lady of Safe Homecoming, a beacon for Portuguese seamen. Open daily. Small admission charge. Off the av. da Marginal, Belém.

Hieronymite Monastery (Mosteiro dos Jerónimos) – Begun in 1502 to commemorate the great voyages of Portuguese explorers such as Vasco da Gama, who is buried here, the monastery is considered an outstanding example of sixteenth-century Portuguese architecture. It is often said that the monastery was "built by pepper" because the riches brought by the spice trade paid for it. The richly sculpted cloisters, the two portals, and the extremely slender columns and characteristic network-vaulting are details of exceptional beauty. Tombs of Portuguese kings and da Gama line the great nave of the church. Open daily. Praça do Império, Belém.

House of Pointed Stones (Casa dos Bicos) – Although the upper part of the façade of this interesting sixteenth-century building was destroyed in the 1755 earthquake, its restoration was finally completed in 1983. It is an archaeological curiosity because the entire facade is covered by a facing of pyramid-shaped stones. Only two similar constructions are known to exist: Casa de los Picos in Segovia, Spain, and Palazzo dei Diamanti in Ferrara, Italy. Rua da Alfândega.

ENVIRONS

Estoril – This seaside suburb 16 miles (25 km) west of Lisbon became internationally famous during World War II when both Allied and Axis spies were tripping over each other, notably at the *Hotel Palacio* (see *Checking In*). Since Portugal was neutral, there was a gentlemen's agreement: Allied diplomats could play golf at the local clubs on certain days, Axis diplomats could have it on the others. Immediately after the war, Estoril became home for numerous members of Europe's exiled royalty. Only Queen Sofia of Bulgaria and the count of Barcelona are still here. Nonetheless, Estoril, with its gambling casino, nightclubs, and the new Autodrome for auto racing enthusiasts, still has more than a touch of glamour and intrigue. The main resort hotels are clustered around Parque Estoril, a lovely park of stately palm trees and purple red bougainvillea, which faces the esplanade and the beach. Easily reached by suburban train from Lisbon's Cais do Sodré station.

Cascais – Once a simple fishing village 4 miles (6 km) west of Estoril, Cascais now rivals St.-Tropez as a chic beach resort. Its summer Sunday bullfights attract numerous visitors, and its Handicraft Fair (Feira de Artesanato), where handicrafts from all over Portugal are sold, is held not far from the Cascais railway station. The town is famous for its seafood restaurants overlooking a bay often crowded with sailboats. Also served by suburban railway from Lisbon's Cais do Sodré station.

Queluz – This town is known for its lovely pink rococo palace, where official guests of the Portuguese government usually are housed. The palace, built in 1747 and restored after being partially destroyed by a fire in 1934, is filled with Portuguese antiques and tapestries, Italian glassware and marble, Dutch tiles, Chinese screens, and Austrian porcelain. In summer, music lovers can attend chamber music concerts in the palace. Open daily, except Tuesdays. Small admission fee. 8.5 miles (14 km) northwest of Lisbon; reached by suburban railway from Rossio station.

■**EXTRA SPECIAL:** The beauty of the Sintra Mountain range (Serra de Sintra) has been sung by the poets, most notably by Lord Byron in *Childe Harold* and by Portugal's most famous poet, Camões, in *Lusiads.* The town of Sintra, some 20 miles (32 km) northwest of Lisbon, is one of the oldest in Portugal. It is noted for its National Palace, once the summer residence of the royal family, and Pena Palace and park, which stand on the highest peak of the range. The palace is a rambling conglomeration of several styles and is entered via a drawbridge. The 500-acre park contains more than 400 kinds of trees and many rare plants. Nearby is a Capuchin monastery dating from the sixteenth century and Monserrate Park, landscaped on the slope of a steep hill. The parks and buildings are open daily, except Tuesdays. Small admission charges. There are good views of the whole region from various *miradouros* in the Sintra range. Sintra can be reached by suburban train from Lisbon's Rossio station. A pleasant alternative for the return trip to Lisbon is to take a bus to the coast through Cascais to the Estoril station, where you can continue to the city by train.

SOURCES AND RESOURCES

Maps and general tourist information can be obtained from the Lisbon tourist posts at Palácio Foz in the Praça dos Restauradores (phone: 36-36-24); Lisbon Airport (phone: 88-59-74); the Rocha Conde de Óbidos Dock Passenger Station (phone: 66-50-18); the Alcântara Docks Passenger Station (phone: 60-07-56); and at the Santa Apolónia Railway Station (phone: 86-78-48). The Lisbon Tourist Council also provides tourist information, in English, by telephone (phone: 36-94-50).

For Local Coverage – Most hotel desk clerks can provide maps of the city.

The Portuguese Government publishes two handy guides: *Portugal Welcomes You,* which contains an excellent map, a food glossary, and details about places of interest, and *Lisbon and the Lisbon Coast.* Both are available free from the office of the Directorate General for Tourism (Direcção-Geral do Turismo), Av. António Augusto de Aguiar 86 (phone: 57-50-91).

CLIMATE AND CLOTHES: April in Portugal is not always as nice as it sounds in the song: it's usually one of the rainiest months. But the climate generally is pleasant, with temperatures ranging from 59°F (15°C) to 82°F (28°C) in summer and 48°F (9°C) to 59°F (15°C) in winter. A sweater will come in handy for cool summer evenings, and low-heeled shoes are recommended if you plan to do much walking on Lisbon's cobblestoned streets.

GETTING AROUND: Although the various sections of the city, such as Alfama, are ideal for strolling, remember Lisbon is built on seven hills. You'll probably want to ride from one section to another. Parking is problematical, so public transportation and taxis are your best bet.

Bus and Tram – Maps and other information about Lisbon's buses and tram services can be obtained at the side of the Santa Justa Lift, the public elevator just off rua do Carmo. Rossio Square is a central point of departure.

Taxi – You can hail a taxi on the street or pick one up at stands conveniently scattered throughout the city. (You should know that by law you must get in and out of a taxi on the pavement side, not on the street side.) Cabs are metered and inexpensive in the city. For trips outside Lisbon or the taxi's area, you pay a set rate per kilometer, and you must pay the return journey whether or not you make it.

Subway – The underground system serving Lisbon is called the Metropolitano. You'll see a large "M" aboveground designating each station. Rossio and Restauradores are the most central stations of the Metropolitano network.

Train – Frequent fast electric trains connect Lisbon with the tourist towns to the west: Belém, Estoril, and Cascais. These commuter trains leave from the Cais do Sodré station. The Lisbon-Sintra line operates from Rossio station.

Car Rental – Most major car rental firms have offices in Lisbon. (A word of caution: Normally polite and helpful while on foot, the Portuguese can turn into fiends when they sit behind the wheel of a car; be careful when you are crossing streets or driving.)

MUSEUMS: Lisbon's museums are closed on Mondays; when they're open, a small admission fee is charged. In addition to the Gulbenkian, described in *Special Places,* notable museums in Lisbon include:

National Art Museum (Museu Nacional de Arte Antiga), Rua das Janelas Verdes 95 (phone: 67-27-25).

National Coach Museum (Museu Nacional dos Coches), Praça Alfonso de Albuquerque at Belém (phone: 62-80-22).

Museum of Folk Art, Praça do Império at Belém (phone: 61-16-75).

Museum of Modern Art (Museu de Arte Contemporânea), Rua Serpa Pinto 6 (phone: 36-80-28).

Naval Museum (Museu de Marinha), Praça do Imperio at Belem (phone: 61-25-43).

Military Museum, Largo do Museu de Artilharia (phone: 86-71-35).

National Costume Museum, Largo Julio Castilho 2 (phone: 79-03-64 or 79-07-25).

 **SHOPPING:** The most important shopping area is the *Baixa* quarter between Rossio Square and the river. Some of the city's most fashionable shops are in the streets leading to the *Largo do Chiado,* or *Praça Luis de Camoes,* as the square is more formally known. Antique shops are scattered throughout the city, but there are nearly a dozen on rua Dom Pedro V alone. Shops in the downtown area are open weekdays from 9 AM to 1 PM and from 3 to 7 PM except Saturdays, when some stores are closed and others are only open till 1 PM. Decorative tiles, *azulejos,* and hand-embroidered linens are particularly good buys here. If you like to poke around for unusual bargains, try browsing through the *Thieves Market (Feira da Ladra)* held on Tuesdays and Saturdays in the Largo de Santa Clara near the Alfama district.

American Visitors Bureau – A wide display of Portuguese arts and crafts. The bureau will help you ship your purchases to the US. Rua Castilho 61.

Casa Quintão – Handmade rugs that are works of art. Rua Ivens 30.

Lavores – Specializing in linen for bridal trousseaus, including hand-embroidered items in original old Portuguese designs. Rua Aurea 175–179.

Madeira Gobelins – Hand-embroidered table linens. Rua Castilho 77A.

Portico – Crystal, pewter, and porcelain. Rua da Misericordia 37.

Fábrica Sant'Anna – Wonderful tiles made from seventeenth- and eighteenth-century patterns. Rua do Alecrim 95.

Vista Alegre – Superb porcelain and bisque. Largo do Chiado 18.

 SPECIAL EVENTS: *The Feast of St. Anthony,* June 13, and the night before are a bit like New Year's Eve and New Year's Day. Although most people identify the saint with Italy, he was born here and the people of Lisbon make much ado about it. The old Alfama quarter comes alive on St. Anthony's night. Dances are held in streets festooned with colored lanterns, and throughout the night, gallons of good, rough wine are drunk to wash down mountains of sardines roasted on open barbecues. Lisbon's St. Anthony is a powerful matchmaker, and this is the night when the city's young girls hope to meet their future husbands. Street stalls sell little pots of a spicy-smelling green herb called *manjerico,* each holding a message of advice or consolation for lovers. Parades are held down the Avenida da Liberdade, in which neighborhood associations bedecked in traditional costumes attempt to outdo each other in their displays. After St. Anthony, homage is paid to two other saints, St. John (June 23–24) and St. Peter (June 28–29) and, in between, the festivities smoulder on. This is the *Festas dos Santos Populares* (festivals of the popular saints), and although they don't know it, Lisboners are in fact carrying on a tradition that is rooted in ancient celebrations of the summer solstice.

 SPORTS: Soccer – This is Portugal's most popular sport by far, and it is ruled by a triumvirate of three top-class clubs: *Sporting* and *Benfica,* both from Lisbon, and *Porto,* from the northern capital of Oporto. Any game in which one of these teams takes part should be worth watching, as the rivalry is very intense. Matches are played Sundays, and tickets can be obtained with the help of your hotel desk.

Bullfighting – Portuguese bullfighting is quite different from the Spanish version. Bulls are never killed in the ring here; and the mounted horsemen, *cavaleiros,* wear magnificent eighteenth-century costumes as they ride against the bulls. The season lasts from Easter to October, with contests usually held on Thursdays and Sundays. The most important fights take place at the *Praça de Touros,* Campo Pequeno in the av. República.

Fishing – Boats can be rented for deep-sea fishing from local fishermen at Sesimbra, a fishing village 19 miles (30 km) south of Lisbon, or at Cascais.

Golf – Caddies and clubs can be hired at the 18-hole *Estoril Golf Club,* Av. República, Estoril (phone: 268-01-76 or 268-13-76); the 14-hole *Lisbon Sports Club,* Casal de Carregueria, at Belas (phone: 96-00-77); and the 9-hole *Estoril Sol Golf Club,* Estrada de Estoril-Sintra (phone: 923-24-61).

Horseback Riding – Equestrians can be accommodated at the *Lisbon Country Club* near Sesimbra, *Clube de Campo Dom Carlos I* at Cascais, and the *Estribo Clube* at Birre-Cascais.

Swimming – The whole coast west of Lisbon and across the river from the city is banded with sandy beaches, and many of the hotels have private swimming pools.

Tennis – Courts are available at *Clube de Tênis* at Estoril; *Clube de Campo Dom Carlos I* at Cascais; and at the *Lisbon Sports Club* at Belas.

 THEATER: Classical and contemporary plays are performed in Portuguese year-round except during July at the *Teatro Nacional de D. Maria II,* Praça Dom Pedro IV (phone: 37-10-78). The revue *(revista)* is a popular Lisbon tradition. Topical sketches, satire, music, and dancing make for a lively evening even if you don't understand the language. The best revues are presented in small theaters in Lisbon's Parque Mayer on avenida Liberdade.

 MUSIC: *São Carlos Opera House,* built in the eighteenth century, is one of Europe's prettiest, with its apricot-colored interior set off by touches of green and gold. The season is from mid-December until May. Various ballet companies also perform here. Largo de São Carlos (phone: 36-85-64). Symphony concerts and chamber music can also be heard at the *São Luis Municipal Theater,* Rua António Maria Cardoso (phone: 32-71-72), and at the *Gulbenkian Arts Center,* Av. de Berna 45 (phone: 77-91-31).

 NIGHTCLUBS AND NIGHTLIFE: The most popular night spots are the *fado* restaurants scattered throughout the old districts of Alfama and Bairro Alto. *Fado,* which means "fate" or "destiny," is the name given to songs sung, usually by a woman called a *fadista,* to the accompaniment of one or more 12-stringed guitars. The songs can be anecdotal, satirical, sentimental, or sometimes gay. Although *fado* has become commercialized and many restaurants beef up their shows with folk dancing and popular music, you may be lucky enough to be on hand some night when the singers and guitarists are in the mood to revive authentic Portuguese *fado.* You'll never forget it. The *fado* is particularly good at *Senhor Vinho,* Meio-a-Lapa 18 (phone: 67-26-81); *Lisboa à Noite,* Rua das Gaveas 69 (phone: 36-85-57); and *A Severa,* Rua das Gaveas 51–61 (phone: 36-40-06). Reservations are essential. Go after 10 PM. There is a huge, Las Vegas–style nightclub at the *Casino Estoril,* on Parque Estoril in the resort (phone: 26-45-21).

Good discos in Lisbon are sometimes difficult to get into unless you're a regular customer and many have expensive cover charges. However, if you really want to disco, two of the best are *Ad Lib,* Rua Barata Saigueiro 18 (phone: 56-17-17); and *Stone's,*

Olival 1 (phone: 66-45-45), with a staggering cover charge. Other good places are *Whispers,* Av. Fontes Pereira de Melo 35 (phone: 57-54-89), and *Trumps* (huge dance floor), Imprensa Nacional, 104-B (phone: 67-10-59).

 SINS: Estoril has one of the largest *gambling* casinos in Europe. *Casino Estoril,* on Parque Estoril (phone: 26-45-21), is the top attraction for many of the tourists who flock to the resort. In addition to the huge glittering main hall where blackjack, roulette, and chemin de fer are a few of the ways to risk money, there are separate gaming rooms for all the high-roller specialties.

The *pride* of Portugal is its port wine, made from grapes grown along the Upper Douro in the north of the country. Port can be ruby, tawny, or white, according to the color of the wine, and can be dry, medium, or sweet. You can sample the various kinds at the *Port Wine Institute,* which is open from 10 AM to midnight daily, Rua S. Pedro de Alcântara 45 (phone: 32-33-07).

BEST IN TOWN

 CHECKING IN: Your first decision may be whether to stay right in Lisbon or to commute with thousands of others from the seaside resorts of Estoril and Cascais by the clean, inexpensive trains that run about every 20 minutes. Whichever you choose, a double room and bath will cost $70 to $95 a night at a hotel in the expensive category; $30 to $45 in the moderate range; and $20 to $30 in the inexpensive category.

IN TOWN

The Ritz – On a hill overlooking Eduardo VII Park, this 290-room hotel is known for its dazzling appointments: silks, satins, and suedes. The public rooms overlooking the park are the largest; those on the lower front can be noisy. Despite its increasingly commercial aspects, the *Ritz* remains one of Portugal's best hotels, and its *Grill Room* (see *Eating Out*) is one of the city's most fashionable restaurants. Rua Rodrigo da Fonseca 88 (phone: 68-41-31). Expensive.

Lisboa-Sheraton – One of the best European Sheratons, this 400-room hotel offers comfortable rooms, marbled baths, and elegant public areas and lounges. All the rooms are air-conditioned and there is a heated, open-air swimming pool. The 30-story *Sheraton* is a bit away from the city center. Rua Latino Coelho 1 (phone: 57-57-57). Expensive.

Altis – This nine-story ultramodern hotel of steel, glass, and concrete is doing so well it's adding 80 more rooms to the 225 it already has. There's a nice view from its rooftop grill. Rua Castilho 11 (phone: 56-00-71). Expensive.

Príncipe Real – Relatively unknown to most tourists, this tiny hotel on a quiet street a few blocks from the avenida da Liberdade is quite charming and has very good service. It is attractively decorated with lovely antiques and good reproductions. Rua de Alegria 53 (phone: 36-01-16). Moderate.

Tivoli – The lobby of this large hotel is on the busy, and noisy, avenida Liberdade and is used as a meeting place by many tourists. Rooms vary in size but are comfortable, with standard modern furnishings. Av. Liberdade 185 (phone: 53-01-81). Moderate.

Tivoli Jardim – Located on a quieter street behind its sister hotel, the *Tivoli,* the *Jardim* is less noisy, although it, too, has a huge lobby. Many of its 120 rooms have balconies. The service is first rate. Rua Júlio Cesar Machado 7–9 (phone: 53-99-71). Moderate.

York House – This is one of the most attractive places to stay in Lisbon, but it is located some distance west of the heart of the city. Once a sixteenth-century convent, *York House* is a lovely small hotel filled with antiques. It is a particular favorite with British visitors and writers. You might easily miss it, since there is no sign outside. You enter the hotel grounds by a gate and then pass through a garden cloister to the reception room. Rua das Janelas Verdes 32 (phone: 66-25-44). Moderate.

Lisboa-Plaza – The cozy rooms in this centrally located hotel have been redecorated in art nouveau style. The *Edwardian Bar* is a popular meeting place. Av. Liberdade, Park Mayer (phone: 36-39-22). Moderate.

Fenix – Run by the Spanish HUSA chain, this 125-room hotel near Eduardo VII Park is modern without being garish. It has a cheery bar and an excellent restaurant that serves Spanish dishes. Praça Marques de Pombal 8 (phone: 53-51-21). Moderate to inexpensive.

Diplomático – Just down the hill from the *Ritz,* this ultramodern hotel offers small but cheerfully bright rooms with balconies. Rua Castilho 74 (phone: 56-20-41). Moderate to inexpensive.

Rex – Portuguese tile decor lends a special flavor to this small hotel near Eduardo VII Park. The rooms are fairly large and comfortable, and the top-floor terrace restaurant has a splendid view of the city. Rua Castilho 169 (phone: 68-21-61). Inexpensive.

SUBURBS

Hotel Palacio – The renowned *Palacio* is a lovely, gracious old hotel, whose staff seems to have been here forever and to remember anyone who has ever stayed here. There's a bar that's small and pretty with a pianist who plays not very up-to-date music and a bartender who always remembers what you drink. The reception rooms and the dining room are majestic, the service is excellent, and the sommelier is a fountain of knowledge. There are gardens, a swimming pool, and cabana apartments behind the hotel. Temporary membership in the local golf club is available (and hotel guests don't pay greens fees); there are tennis courts next door, and the Atlantic Ocean is a 5-minute walk from the lobby. Parque Estoril, Estoril (phone: 268-0400). Expensive.

Estoril Sol – This is Portugal's biggest hotel and it is geared to convention, group-tour, and gambling-junket visitors. The huge lobby has numerous shops and there are five bars as well as a rooftop restaurant, a pool, and a gymnasium. The beach is across the railway tracks from the hotel, but there's an underground passage for guests. Parque Palmela, Cascais (phone: 28-28-31). Expensive.

Palacio de Seteais – This is one of the loveliest and most romantic hotels in Europe. Converted from a formal eighteenth-century French villa, it is situated in a lovely garden. There are only 18 rooms, but each is beautifully furnished with antique furniture, rugs, and tapestries. The only drawback to this dream hotel is that a car is essential. Rua Barbosa du Bocage 8, Sintra (phone: 293-3200). Moderate.

 **EATING OUT:** Portuguese food offers a surprising variety of tastes. Over the centuries, this sea-trading nation's cuisine has come under the influence of such far-flung countries as Asia, Africa, and the Americas as well as neighboring Spain and nearby France. Seafood is the staple — Lisbon residents are said to consume ten times as much fish as meat — and sometimes is found in unlikely combination with meats, such as in the local specialty of pork marinated in wine and garnished with clams, *carne de porco à alentejana.* Dinner for two, with a local wine, can average about $40 to $60 at expensive restaurants; from about $25 to $35 at a moderate establishment; and from $15 to $25 at inexpensive restaurants. It

is the custom here to dine no earlier than 7:30 PM; but many restaurants close their kitchens at 11 PM.

Avis – When the old *Hotel Avis* was torn down some years ago, Alberto Rapetti and some of his staff opened this restaurant just off Largo do Chiado, bringing with them all the elegance and flair that had made the old place an international favorite. The restaurant is very Belle Époque. The food is excellent; the service, flawless. This is Lisbon's best. Open daily; closed Saturdays and Sundays for lunch. Reservations recommended. Rua Serpa Pinto 12B (phone: 32-83-91). Expensive.

Tavares – Lisbon's well-born bachelors did much of their frolicking here at the turn of the century. Today the lovely mirrors, crystal, gilt, and brocades provide a perfect setting for excellent food and wine. *Tavares,* which began as a café in the eighteenth century, is Lisbon's oldest restaurant. Closed for lunch on Sundays and all day Saturdays. Reservations recommended. Rua da Misericordia 37 (phone: 32-11-12). Expensive.

Tagide – There's a small dining room on the first floor here, and a beautiful staircase leads up to a second-floor dining area with a great view of the Tagus. *Tagide* serves fine food, and the service is excellent. Open daily; closed Sundays and for lunch on Saturdays. Reservations recommended. Largo da Biblioteca Pública 18 (phone: 32-07-20). Expensive.

Ritz Grill – The restaurant of the *Hotel Ritz* (see *Checking In*) prepares unusually good food and is a fashionable gathering place for Lisbon businesspeople. Open daily. Reservations recommended. Rua Rodrigo da Fonseca 88 (phone: 68-41-31). Expensive.

Gambrinus – This restaurant, famous for its fish and shellfish, has numerous small dining rooms that fan out from the open, blue-tile kitchen. Located in the heart of the city, it is usually jammed with businessmen at lunchtime. Open daily. Reservations recommended. Rua das Portas de Santo Antão 25 (phone: 32-14-66). Expensive.

Pavilhão de Caça – One of Lisbon's finest game restaurants, it serves fine pheasant, partridge, duck, quail, venison, and wild boar. Rua do Seculo 138 (phone: 37-22-19). Expensive.

Cozinha Velha – This is the former royal kitchen of the palace at Queluz (see *Special Places*), now turned into a restaurant with much atmosphere. It has high stone arches, a gigantic walk-in fireplace, enormous spits, and walls lined with more gleaming copper utensils than you ever thought existed. The menu includes fine Continental cooking as well as Portuguese specialties. Open daily. Reservations recommended. Palacio de Queluz, Queluz (phone: 95-02-32). Expensive.

Casa da Comida – A discreetly elegant restaurant with tables set around a charming enclosed garden. Reservations recommended. Travessa das Amoreiras 1 (phone: 68-53-76). Expensive.

Conventual – One of Lisbon's most unusual menus, with delicacies based on old Portuguese convent and monastery recipes, some of which date back to the sixteenth century. Reservations recommended. Praça Flores 44 (phone: 60-91-96). Expensive to moderate.

Restaurante 33 – Good food and unstarchy comfort can be found behind an elegant clapboard façade. Alexandre Herculano 33 (phone: 54-60-79). Expensive to moderate.

Seteais – An eighteenth-century palace makes a lovely setting for lunch on a sunny day, especially a leisurely Sunday. If you have a car, by all means make the trip to this exquisite restaurant in the *Hotel Palacio de Seteais* (see *Checking In*). Sintra (phone: 293-3200). Expensive to moderate.

Tia Matilde – It specializes in the cuisine of the Ribatejo, the region where Portugal's fighting bulls are bred. Rua Dr. Alvaro Castro 12 (phone: 77-21-72). Inexpensive.

Porto do Abrigo – Although not too imposing in appearance, the tiny *Porto* is one of Lisbon's culinary landmarks. Famous for its Portuguese specialties, it's usually very crowded at lunchtime. Reservations recommended. Rua dos Remolares 16 (phone: 36-08-73). Inexpensive.

Xico Carreira – It's owned by a former bullfighter, and posters and mementos of the sport decorate this popular restaurant full of local color and off the beaten track for most tourists. Crowded for lunch. Closed Sundays. Parque Mayer (phone: 36-38-05). Inexpensive.

Bota Alta – Exceptionally good Portuguese cooking is served in a cheery bistro atmosphere. In the midst of the Bairro Alto quarter, the scene of Lisbon's bohemian nightlife, it's usually very busy. Travessa da Queimada 3 (phone: 32-79-59). Inexpensive.

Bonjardim – Considered tops in the field of preparing *frango na brasa,* chicken that's charcoal broiled on a grill or a rotating spit and accompanied by a fiery chile sauce, which you can (thankfully) brush on yourself. This is one of Lisbon's most popular — and cheapest — culinary delights. There are two *Bonjardim* restaurants; they face each other in Travessa de Santo Antao, just off the central Restauradores square. Noisy and crowded at lunchtime, but a wonderful value. Travessa de Santo Antao 10 and 11 (phone: 32-74-24 and 32-43-89). Inexpensive.

LONDON

British author and journalist V. S. Pritchett noted that the essence of London was contained in the very sound of its name: *Lon-don,* a weighty word, solid, monumental, dignified, even ponderous. London is a shapeless city without a center; it sprawls over 620 square miles and brims over with a variety of neighborhoods and people. One of its sharpest observers, Daniel Defoe, portrayed London in the eighteenth century much as it could be described today: "It is . . . stretched out in buildings, straggling, confused . . . out of all shape, uncompact and unequal; neither long nor broad, round or square."

London can best be understood not as one city but as a conglomeration of villages that were incorporated whole, one by one, as the monster expanded — Chelsea, Battersea, Paddington, and Hampstead are just a few. Fortunately, all of its important parks and squares have remained inviolate, but not without a struggle, for London's merchant class — its backbone and its pride — has always resisted and defeated town planners, ever since Parliament turned down Sir Christopher Wren's splendid plan to rebuild after the fire of 1666. It was royalty and aristocracy that created and preserved the parks — St. James's Park, Hyde Park, Kensington Gardens, Regent's Park, and Kew Gardens were all royal parks — and their enthusiasm became contagious. The passionate regard of Londoners for their green spots has been one of the city's saving graces as it grew so helplessly and recklessly, more in the spirit of commerce than of urban planning.

Today's London — though marred by soulless high-rise intruders of glass and concrete — boasts more greenery than any other metropolis can hope to display these days. Aside from its many garden squares and the meticulously tended gardens of so many Londoners' homes, the city is punctuated by a series of large parks and commons; besides those already mentioned, there are Wimbledon Common, Highgate Wood, Primrose Hill, Hampstead Heath — the list goes on and on. And to make even more certain that citification does not intrude too far into London life, a green belt, almost 100 square miles of forest and grassland, virtually encircles the city and, to the chagrin and impatience of "developers," is meticulously preserved by law.

London's other natural resource, the River Thames, has not been so fortunate. As any glance at a map will show, London follows the serpentine meanderings of the Thames, England's principal river. Nearly everything of interest in London is on or near the Thames, for London is London because it is a natural port. The river has always been London's mainstay, for centuries its only east-west road. But the Thames, with its tributary the Fleet, is a working river; it is no longer — as it was in the heyday of Elizabeth I — also used for ornament or for pleasure. In miles of wharves and dockland, there is little beauty to behold. Yet it has rightly been said that "every drop

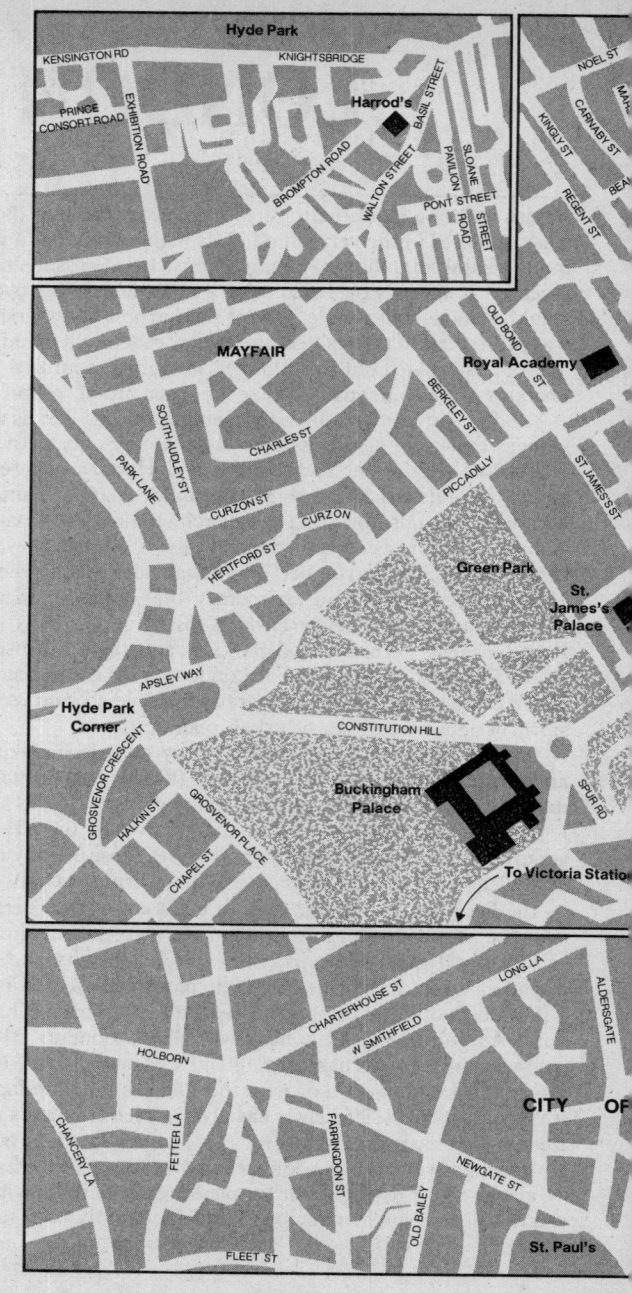

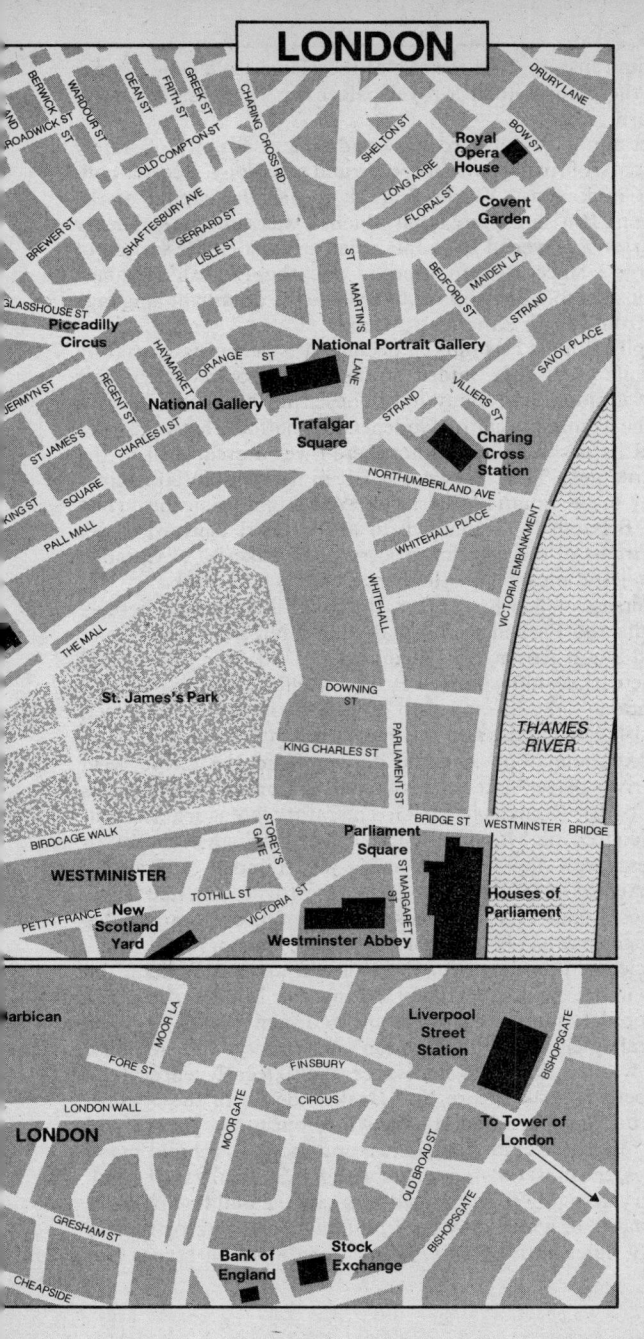

LONDON

DRURY LANE

Royal Opera House

BOW ST

Covent Garden

SHELTON ST

LONG ACRE

FLORAL ST

MAIDEN LA

STRAND

BEDFORD ST

SAVOY PLACE

GREEK ST

FRITH ST

DEAN ST

CHARING CROSS RD

OLD COMPTON ST

SHAFTESBURY AVE

GERRARD ST

LISLE ST

WARDOUR ST

BERWICK ST

BROADWICK ST

GLASSHOUSE ST

Piccadilly Circus

National Portrait Gallery

ST MARTIN'S LANE

ORANGE ST

National Gallery

HAYMARKET

REGENT ST

JERMYN ST

Trafalgar Square

STRAND

VILLIERS ST

Charing Cross Station

ST JAMES'S

CHARLES II ST

KING ST

SQUARE

PALL MALL

NORTHUMBERLAND AVE

WHITEHALL PLACE

WHITEHALL

VICTORIA EMBANKMENT

THE MALL

St. James's Park

DOWNING ST

PARLIAMENT ST

THAMES RIVER

KING CHARLES ST

BIRDCAGE WALK

STOREY'S GATE

BRIDGE ST

WESTMINSTER BRIDGE

Parliament Square

WESTMINSTER

TOTHILL ST

VICTORIA ST

ST MARGARET ST

Houses of Parliament

PETTY FRANCE

New Scotland Yard

Westminster Abbey

Barbican

MOOR LA

Liverpool Street Station

BISHOPSGATE

FORE ST

FINSBURY

CIRCUS

LONDON WALL

MOOR GATE

LONDON

OLD BROAD ST

To Tower of London

GRESHAM ST

BISHOPSGATE

Bank of England

Stock Exchange

CHEAPSIDE

of the Thames is liquid history." At the site of the Naval College in Greenwich, for example, there once stood a royal palace where Henry VIII and Elizabeth I were born.

A great river port and a city of gardens, London is also a city of stately squares and monuments, of royalty with its pomp and ceremony, a cosmopolitan city of the first rank. Until World War II, it was the capital of the mammoth and far-flung British Empire upon which, it was said, the sun never set. For many centuries, a powerful Britannia ruled a considerable section of the globe — the largest since Roman times — and the English language spread from the inconsiderable British Isles to become the dominant language all over the world, from North America to India.

If the British Empire is most certainly in decline, it is declining gracefully among memories of its great days; and if once-subject peoples hated their oppressor, they love London, and many have chosen to live there. London is still the center of the Commonwealth of independent nations that were once British colonies, and its cosmopolitan atmosphere owes a great deal to the ubiquity of former colonials. Their presence is felt in the substantial Indian-Pakistani community in the Southall district of West London; in the strong Caribbean flavor in Brixton; in Chinatown in and around Gerrard Street — near Piccadilly Circus; in the Cypriot groceries and bakeries of Camden Town; and in the majestic mosque on the fringe of Regent's Park.

A tantalizing diversity of accents flavors the English language here — accents from Australia and Barbados, Bangladesh and Nigeria, Canada and Malaysia, Kenya and South Africa, Sri Lanka and Ireland, Hong Kong and the US. And then the various inflections of Britain itself are also to be heard in the streets of London — the lilt and rasp of cockney, Oxford, Somerset, Yorkshire, the Scottish Highlands, and the Welsh mining towns.

London's somewhat onomatopoeic name derives from the Celtic term *Llyn-din,* meaning "river place," but little is known of London before it was renamed *Londinium* by the Romans in AD 43. The rather fantastical twelfth-century historian Geoffrey of Monmouth may have originated the myth widespread in Shakespeare's day — that London was founded by Brute, a direct descendant of Aeneas in 1108 BC, who named it Troynovant, new Troy. Even in medieval times, London had grandiose notions of its own importance — a prideful self-image that has been amply justified by history.

The city was sufficiently prominent for the Norman invader William the Conqueror to make it his capital in 1066. During the Middle Ages, the expansion of trade, population growth, and the energetic activities of its guilds of merchants and craftsmen promoted London's prosperity. Indisputably, London's golden age was the English Renaissance, the sixteenth century, the time of Queen Elizabeth I, Shakespeare, and Drake's defeat of the Spanish Armada. The Tudor buildings of London were wiped out in the great fire of 1666. Christopher Wren, the architect of genius, undertook to rebuild many buildings and churches, the most outstanding of which is St. Paul's Cathedral. The eighteenth century, a highly sophisticated age, saw the building of noble homes and stately squares, of which only Bedford Square and Fitzroy remain complete. In the early nineteenth century, interest continued in homes and squares; and only in the Victorian age, the height of the Empire, were public buildings like the Houses of Parliament redesigned, this time in grand and fanciful neo-Gothic style.

London has seen whole catalogues of heroes and villains, crises and conflagrations, come and go, sometimes swallowed whole in the passage of time, sometimes leaving relics. Still on elegant display is stately Hampton Court Palace, the most magnificent of England's palaces, where Henry VIII lived now and again with five of his six wives. There is a spot downtown — in front of the Banqueting House on Whitehall — where another king, Charles I, was beheaded by his subjects, who were calmly committing dreaded regicide 150 years before the more explosive French across the English Channel even contemplated such a gesture.

London has lived through the unbounded permissiveness of the flamboyantly royal Restoration period (1660–85), when even King Charles II frequented brothels and didn't care who knew it, and it has survived the stern moral puritanism of the Victorian era, when it was downright rude to refer to a *breast* of a chicken or a piano *leg*. And most recently, London stood up with exemplary courage under the devastating effects of the Nazi bombings, which destroyed a great many buildings and killed thousands of people.

Many of our images of London, taken from old movies, actually mirror its realities: Big Ben rises above the Houses of Parliament, somberly striking the hour; ramrod-straight scarlet-uniformed soldiers half hide their faces in towering black bearskin hats; waiters at the Bank of England still sport the kinds of top hats and tailcoats their predecessors wore for a century; lawyers in court still don wigs and black robes. A few images, however, are outdated: The bowler hat has been slipping out of fashion for years, and rigid environmental regulations have made London's once-famous pea-soup fogs rare.

London's nearly infinite variety of urban moods includes the sturdy edifices lining Whitehall, center of the British government, with Trafalgar Square at its head and Parliament at its foot; the elegant shopping areas of Knightsbridge, Bond Street, and the Burlington Arcade; suburban chic in Barnes and Blackheath; handsome squares in Bloomsbury; melancholy mystery in Victoria and Waterloo train stations with their spy-movie atmosphere; the vitality of East End street markets; and the riparian tranquillity of Thames-side towpaths in Putney and along Hammersmith Mall.

The British have a talent that amounts to genius for government — for democracy and political tolerance — a talent that has been developing ever since the Magna Carta was signed in 1215, and one that makes London's ambience easy and relaxed for individualists and eccentrics of all sorts. It is no wonder that the eccentric and inveterate Londoner of the eighteenth-century heyday, Dr. Samuel Johnson, once declared, "When a man is tired of London, he is tired of life, for there is in London all that life can afford."

Johnson's opinion, though somewhat overblown, was essentially shared by one of several modern American writers who chose to live in London. Disillusioned with New York, Boston, and Paris, Henry James decided in favor of London in 1881. Somehow he concluded that London was a place eminently suited to human life: "It is not a pleasant place; it is not agreeable, or cheerful, or easy, or exempt from reproach. It is only magnificent. You can draw up a tremendous list of reasons why it should be unsupportable. The fogs, the smoke, the dirt, the darkness, the wet, the distances, the ugliness, the brutal size of the place, the horrible numerosity of society . . . but . . . London is on the whole the most possible form of life."

LONDON AT-A-GLANCE

 SEEING THE CITY: London has, for the most part, resisted the temptation to build high. Aside from a handful of modest gestures toward sky-scraping, there aren't many towering structures to obscure panoramic overviews of the city from its higher vantage points, which include:

London Hilton Hotel – There were discreet noises of disapproval from Buckingham Palace when it was realized that the view from the roof bar of the *Hilton* included not only the palace grounds but, with high-powered binoculars, the insides of some of the royal chambers as well. In fact, the view over Mayfair, Hyde Park, and Westminster is breathtaking. Park La. (phone: 493-8000).

Westminster Cathedral – Not to be confused with Westminster Abbey. The top of the bell tower of London's Catholic cathedral looks down on a broad expanse of the inner city. There is an elevator to take you up for a token charge (from April through September only). Off Victoria St. near the station, at Ashley Pl. SW 1.

Hampstead Heath – Climb to the top of Parliament Hill, on the southern rim of this "wilderness" in north London. On a clear day, the view south from the Heath makes the city look like a vast village.

South Bank Arts Center – On the south bank of Waterloo Bridge, the bunkerlike complex of cultural buildings is an attraction in itself, including as it does Royal Festival Hall, the National Theatre, the National Film Theatre, the Hayward Gallery, and other cultural attractions. For a view of London, look across the Thames — upriver to the Houses of Parliament, downriver to St. Paul's Cathedral.

Tower Bridge Walkway – The upper part of one of London's famous landmarks is now open to visitors. In addition to the viewing gallery, there is an exhibition on the history of London's bridges and a museum that includes the bridge's Victorian steam pumping engines. Open daily.

St. Paul's Cathedral – The reward for climbing the 600 steps into the dome of this cathedral — the largest in the world after St. Peter's in Rome — is a panoramic view of London.

SPECIAL PLACES/ATTRACTIONS: Surveying London from the steps of St. Paul's Cathedral at the turn of the nineteenth century, a visiting Prussian general commented to his English host: "What a place to plunder!" Even those who are less rapacious will appreciate the extraordinary wealth of sights London displays for visitors to inspect. Though some are dispersed in various corners of this vast city, most are clustered reasonably close together in or near the inner districts of Westminster, the City, and Kensington.

London A–Z or *Nicholson's Street Finder,* inexpensive pocket-sized books of street maps (available in bookstores and from most "newsagents"), are very useful for finding your way. Also helpful are maps of the subway system and bus routes — both available free from the London Transport information centers at several stations including Victoria, Piccadilly, Charing Cross, Oxford Circus, and Heathrow Central, and at the ticket booths of many other stations.

WESTMINSTER

Changing of the Guard – An American who lived in London once said, "There's just no better way to convince yourself that you're in London!" At 11 AM every day (from April through August, every other day in winter), this famous ceremony takes place in the Buckingham Palace forecourt.

The Horse Guards – If you haven't had enough, you can see a new guard of 12 members of the Household Cavalry troop in with trumpet and standard, daily at 11:15 AM; alternate days in winter; 10 AM on Sundays. On the west side of Whitehall.

Buckingham Palace – The royal standard flies from the roof when the monarch is in residence at her London home. Although George III bought the palace in 1762, no sovereign lived here until 1837, when Queen Victoria moved in. The palace, unfortunately, is open only to invited guests. Its interior contains magnificently decorated apartments, a superb picture gallery, and a throne room (66 feet long), where foreign ambassadors are received and knights are knighted. The palace grounds contain the largest private garden in London (40 acres). And the gate that was built for the entrance, too narrow for the coaches of George IV, now marks an entrance to Hyde Park and is known as Marble Arch. Buckingham Palace Rd.

State Visits – If you aren't going to be in London for the Queen's official birthday in June, you might want to see her greet a foreign dignitary in full regalia. This happens quite frequently; it is announced in the royal calendar in the London *Times*. The Queen meets her guest at Victoria Station, and they ride to Buckingham Palace in a procession of horse-drawn coaches, followed by colorful Horse Guards. Meanwhile, at Hyde Park Corner, the cannoneers on horseback perform elaborate maneuvers before their salute thunders through the whole city.

Queen's Gallery – Treasures from the royal art collection are on display to the public only in this room of the palace. Exhibitions change about once a year. It is open daily; closed Mondays. Admission charge. Buckingham Palace Rd. SW1.

Royal Mews – The mews is a palace alley where the magnificent state coaches and the horses that draw them are stabled. The public is admitted on Wednesdays and Thursdays, from 2 to 4 PM. Buckingham Palace Rd. SW1.

St. James's Park – Parks are everywhere in London and Londoners love them. This is one of the nicest. With its sizable lake inhabited by pelicans and other wild fowl, St. James's was originally a royal park, laid out by Henry VIII in 1532.

The Mall – The wide avenue parallel to Pall Mall and lined with lime trees and Regency buildings leads from Trafalgar Square to Buckingham Palace. This is the principal ceremonial route used by Queen Elizabeth and her escort of Household Cavalry for the State Opening of Parliament (October/November) and the Trooping of the Color (mid-June). It is closed to traffic on Sunday afternoons.

Trafalgar Square – One of London's most heavily trafficked squares is built around the towering Nelson's Column, a 145-foot monument that honors Lord Nelson, victor at the naval Battle of Trafalgar in 1805. At the base of the monument are four huge bronze lions and two fountains. Flanked by handsome buildings, including the National Gallery and the eighteenth-century church of St. Martin in the Fields, the square is a favorite gathering place.

Piccadilly Circus – Downtown London finds its center here in the heart of the theater district and on the edge of Soho. The traffic island in the center of the busy "circus," or circle, serves as a meeting place for young people during the summer. The famous statue popularly known as Eros (removed temporarily for renovation) was actually designed in 1893 as *The Angel of Christian Charity,* a memorial to the charitable earl of Shaftesbury — the archer and his bow were meant as a pun on his name. The Trocadero, a recently converted three-story shopping and entertainment complex, is also here. Two of its more popular exhibitions are the *Guinness World Book of*

Records display, with re-creations of some of the more dramatic entries in the best-selling book, and the London Experience, for a look at the city's history.

The National Gallery – One of the world's great art museums, this is an inexhaustible feast for art lovers. In the vast collection on display are works by such masters as Uccello, Da Vinci, Titian, Rembrandt, Rubens, Cranach, Gainsborough, El Greco, Renoir, Cézanne, and Van Gogh. Open daily. Trafalgar Sq. WC2 (phone: 839-3321).

The National Portrait Gallery – Right behind the National Gallery is this delightful museum. Nearly every British celebrity you have ever heard about is pictured here, with the earliest personalities at the top and the twentieth-century notables at the bottom. 2 St. Martin's Pl. WC2 (phone: 930-1552).

Whitehall – This broad boulevard stretches from Trafalgar Square to Parliament Square, lined most of the way by government ministries and such historic buildings as the Banqueting House (completed in 1622, with a ceiling painted by Rubens) and the Horse Guards (whose central archway is ceremonially guarded by mounted troopers).

Downing Street – Off Whitehall, a street of small, unpretentious Georgian houses includes the official residences of the most important figures in the British government, the Prime Minister at number 10 and the Chancellor of the Exchequer (secretary of the treasury) at number 11.

Cabinet War Rooms – Constructed to resemble its wartime appearance, this underground complex of 20 rooms was Winston Churchill's auxiliary command post during World War II, which he used most often during the German Luftwaffe's "blitz" on London. Of special note are the map room, with maps pinpointing the positions of Allied and German troops in the final stages of the war, and the cabinet room, where the prime minister met with his staff. Open daily. Admission charge. Beneath the government building on Great George St.

Westminster Abbey – You can easily get lost among the endlessly fascinating tombs and plaques and not even notice the Abbey's splendid architecture, so do look at the structure itself, and don't miss the cloisters, which display its Gothic design to advantage. Note also the fine Tudor chapel of Henry VII, with its tall windows and lovely fan-tracery vaulting, and the thirteenth-century chapel of St. Edward the Confessor, containing England's Coronation Chair.

Ever since William the Conqueror was crowned here in 1066, the Abbey has been the traditional place where English monarchs are crowned, married, and buried. You don't have to be an Anglophile to be moved by the numerous tombs and memorials with their fascinating inscriptions — here are honored (not necessarily buried) kings and queens, soldiers, statesmen, and many other prominent English men and women. Poets' Corner, in the south transept, contains the tombs of Chaucer, Ben Jonson, Tennyson, Browning, and many others — plus memorials to nearly every English poet of note and to some Americans, such as Longfellow and T. S. Eliot.

The Abbey is itself a lesson in English history. A church has stood on this site since at least AD 170; in the eighth century, it was a Benedictine monastery. The current early English Gothic edifice, begun in the thirteenth century, took almost 300 years to build.

Guided tours of the Abbey offered six times a day (phone: 222-5152). Broad Sanctuary SW1.

The Houses of Parliament – The imposing neo-Gothic, mid-nineteenth-century buildings of the Palace of Westminster, as it is sometimes called, look especially splendid from the opposite side of the river. There are separate chambers for the House of Commons and the House of Lords, and visitors are admitted to the Strangers' Galleries of both houses by lining up at St. Stephen's Entrance, opposite Westminster Abbey. Big Ben, the world-famous 13.5-ton bell in the clock tower of the palace, still strikes the hours. The buildings themselves are closed to the public. Westminster Hall, with its magnificent hammer-beam roof, and the gold and scarlet House of Lords are well worth seeing. St. Margaret St. SW1 (phone: 219-3000).

The Tate Gallery – London's fine art museum includes an impressive collection of British sculpture and art. It has recently been extended to include a permanent display of modern art. Best of all are the masterpieces by Turner, Hogarth, and Blake. Millbank SW1 (phone: 821-7128).

Soho – This area of London is full of character: lively, bustling, and noisy by day; discreetly enticing by night. Its name comes from the ancient hunting cry used centuries ago when the area was parkland. The hunting, in a way, still goes on, but there's not much to shout about nowadays. Soho lacks the sophistication and glamour of its counterparts in Europe, but it's not sleazy either. The striptease clubs vie for customers with numerous restaurants serving usually inexpensive (mostly Italian and Chinese) food. Soho offers a diversity of entertainments: Shaftesbury Avenue is lined with movie theaters. Gerrard Street abounds with Chinese restaurants, and it is the place to go for Chinese New Year celebrations. London's liveliest fruit and vegetable market is on Berwick Street (if you shop here, never touch the produce, as the vendors will get furious). Old Compton Street has several good delicatessens, where you could buy a picnic lunch to take to — of course — Soho Square.

Covent Garden – Tucked away behind the Strand, Covent Garden was the site of London's main fruit, vegetable, and flower market for more than 300 years. The area was immortalized in the musical *My Fair Lady* by the scene in which young Eliza Doolittle sold flowers to the ladies and gents emerging from the Royal Opera House. The Opera House is still there but the market moved out in 1974, and the Garden has since undergone extensive redevelopment. The central market building has been converted into London's first permanent late-night shopping center with emphasis on all-British goods. In the former flower market is the London Transport Museum, whose exhibits include a replica of the first horse-drawn bus and a steam locomotive built in 1866. Boutiques selling good-quality clothes for men and women are springing up all over, along with discos, wine bars, and restaurants. Just to remind everyone of the old Covent Garden, there are around 40 of the original wrought-iron trading stands from which the home-produced wares of English craftsmen and women are sold.

Bloomsbury – Well-designed squares — Bloomsbury Square, Bedford Square, Russell Square, and others — surrounded by pretty, terraced houses, form this aristocratic district. Within its confines are the British Museum and the University of London, with its Courtauld Gallery, renowned for its impressionist collection. The Bloomsbury group included Virginia Woolf, her husband Leonard Woolf, her sister Vanessa Bell and her husband Clive Bell, Lytton Strachey, E. M. Forster, Roger Fry, and Maynard Keynes. Living nearby and peripheral to this central group were D. H. Lawrence, Bertrand Russell, and others. Unfortunately, none of the original buildings in Bloomsbury Square has survived, but the garden is still there, and nearby Bedford Square remains complete. Virginia Woolf lived at 46 Gordon Square before her marriage.

The British Museum – One of the world's largest museums offers a dazzling array of permanent exhibitions — including the legendary Elgin Marbles (from the Parthenon) and the Rosetta Stone — and an equally impressive parade of temporary displays. The Egyptian and Mesopotamian galleries are especially stunning. The manuscript room of the British Library, within the museum, displays the original Magna Carta together with the signatures of a great many famous authors and numerous original manuscripts, including *Alice in Wonderland.* To take a look at the gigantic Reading Room where so many books — Marx's *Das Kapital,* for example — were written, you must write to the library for tickets. Great Russell St. WC1 (phone: 636-1555).

Oxford and Regent Streets – London's main shopping streets include large department stores *(Selfridges, Debenhams, John Lewis, Liberty, D. H. Evans),* chain stores offering good value in clothes *(Marks and Spencer, C & A, British Home Stores, Littlewoods),* and scores of moderately priced clothing stores. The sidewalk has recently been widened, and one section of the road is open only to taxis and buses at certain times.

The Burlington Arcade – A charming covered shopping promenade dating from the Regency period (early nineteenth century), the arcade contains elegant, expensive shops selling cashmere sweaters, antique jewelry, and other costly items. Off Piccadilly (the street, not the circus) near Bond St. W1.

Hyde Park – London's most famous patch of greenery (361 acres) is particularly well known for its "Speakers' Corner" at Marble Arch, where crowds gather each Sunday afternoon to hear impromptu diatribes and debates. Among the park's other attractions are sculptures by Henry Moore; an extensive bridle path; a cycle path; the Serpentine lake, where boats for rowing and sailing can be rented and where there's swimming in the summer; a bird sanctuary; and vast expanses of lawn.

Madame Tussaud's – The popularity of this wax museum is undiminished by the persistent criticism that its effigies, besides being hideous, do not resemble the illustrious personalities they are supposed to replicate. Moved to London from Paris in 1802 when Madame was 74, the current museum includes many modern and historical personalities, and the gory Chamber of Horrors, with its murderers and hangmen. Open daily. Admission charge. Marylebone Rd. (phone: 935-6861).

THE CITY

The difference between London and the City of London can be confusing to a visitor. They are, in fact, two different entities, one within the other. The City of London, usually called only the City, covers the original Roman London. It is now the "square mile" financial and commercial center of the great metropolis. With a lord mayor (who only serves in a ceremonial capacity), a police force of its own, and a resident population of 6,000 due to rapidly growing new developments — it is the core of Greater London. The latter, with its governing body, the Greater London Council, administers 32 boroughs including the City.

St. Paul's Cathedral – The cathedral church of the London Anglican diocese stands atop Ludgate Hill and is the largest church in London. This Renaissance masterpiece by Sir Christopher Wren took 35 years to build (1675–1710). Its domed exterior is majestic and its sparse decorations are gold and mosaic. The interior contains particularly splendid choir stalls, screens, and, inside the spectacular dome, the "whispering gallery," with its strange acoustics. Nelson and Wellington are buried below the main floor, and there is a fine statue of John Donne, metaphysical poet and dean of St. Paul's from 1621 to 1631 — he stands looking quite alive on an urn in an up-ended coffin which, typically, he bought during his lifetime and kept in his house. Wren himself was buried here in 1723, with his epitaph inscribed beneath the dome in Latin: "Reader, if you seek his monument, look around you."

A gorgeous monument it remains; though damaged by bombs during World War II, it became a rallying point for the flagging spirits of wartime Londoners. More recently, St. Paul's raised British spirits as the site for the royal wedding of Prince Charles and Lady Diana Spencer in July 1981. The Golden Gallery at the top of the dome, 542 steps from the ground, offers an excellent view of the city. St. Paul's Churchyard EC4.

Old Bailey – This is the colloquial name for London's Central Criminal Court, located on the site of the notorious Newgate Prison. Visitors are admitted to the court, on a space-available basis, to audit the proceedings and to see lawyers and judges clad in wigs and robes. Old Bailey EC4 (phone: 248-3277).

The Museum of London – Exhibits depict London history from the Roman occupation to modern times. The museum is in the Barbican, the modern building complex that was constructed in a part of London devastated by bombers during World War II. Closed Mondays. 150 London Wall EC2 (phone: 600-3699).

The Bank of England – Banker to the British government, holder of the country's gold reserves in its vaults, controller of Britain's banking and monetary affairs, "the Old Lady of Threadneedle Street" is the most famous bank in the world. Bathed in tradition as well as the mechanics of modern high finance, its porters and messengers are attired in traditional livery. Visits by appointment only. Threadneedle St. EC2 (phone: 601-4444).

Mansion House – The official residence of the lord mayor of London, containing the mayor's private apartments, built in the eighteenth century in Renaissance style. Visits by appointment only, Mondays through Thursdays. Mansion House St. EC4 (phone: 626-2500).

Lloyd's – A palatial building houses the world's most important place for international high-risk insurance. True to tradition, the Lutine Bell, salvaged from a sunken frigate, sounds out whenever a mishap occurs that is covered by Lloyd's insurers. Visits by appointment only (but a public gallery is scheduled to open sometime in 1986). Leadenhall St. EC3 (phone: 623-7100, ext. 3733).

The Stock Exchange – The second largest exchange in the world can be seen from the viewing gallery on weekdays from 9:45 AM to 3:15 PM. Old Broad St. EC 2 (phone: 588-2355).

The Monument – A fluted Doric column — topped by a flaming urn — was designed by Sir Christopher Wren to commemorate the Great Fire of London (1666) and stands 202 feet tall, allegedly 202 feet from the bakery on Pudding Lane where the fire began. The view from the top is partially obstructed by new buildings. Admission charge. Monument St. EC 3 (phone: 626-2717).

The Tower of London – The foundations of the infamous tower were built by William the Conqueror in the eleventh century. Originally conceived as a fortress to keep "fierce" Londoners at bay and to guard the river approaches, it has served as a palace, a prison, a mint, and an observatory as well. Today the main points of interest are the Crown Jewels; the White Tower (the oldest building), with its exhibition of ancient arms, armor, and torture implements; St. John's Chapel, the oldest church in London; the Bloody Tower, where the two little princes were murdered in 1485 and Sir Walter Raleigh languished from 1603 to 1615; an exhibit of old military weapons; Tower Green, where two of Henry VIII's queens — and many others — were beheaded; and Traitors' Gate, through which boats bearing prisoners entered the castle. The yeoman warders still wear historic uniforms. They also give excellent recitals of that segment of English history that was played out within the tower walls. You can see the wonderful Ceremony of the Keys here every night at 9:30 PM; you'll have to reserve tickets several months ahead. Send a stamped, self-addressed envelope to: Resident Governor, Constable's Office, HM Tower of London EC3N 4AB (phone: 709-0765). Closed Sundays in winter. Admission charge.

Fleet Street – Most native and foreign newspapers and press associations have their offices here — in the center of London's active newspaper world. The street also boasts two seventeenth-century pubs, the *Cheshire Cheese* (just off Fleet St. at 5 Little Essex St.) and the *Cock Tavern* (number 22). The *Cheshire Cheese* is the tavern where Dr. Samuel Johnson held court for the literary giants of his day — Goldsmith, Boswell, and others.

Johnson's House – In nearby Gough Square is the house where Johnson wrote his *Dictionary;* it's now a museum of Johnsoniana. Admission charge. 17 Gough Sq., EC 4 (phone: 353-3745).

The Inns of Court – Quaint and quiet precincts house the ancient buildings, grounds, and gardens that mark the traditional center of Britain's legal profession. Only the four Inns of Court have the right to call would-be barristers to the bar to practice law. Especially charming is the still-Dickensian Lincoln's Inn, where young Dickens worked as an office boy. In its great hall the writer later set his fictional case of *Jarndyce* v. *Jarndyce* in *Bleak House.* John Donne once preached in the Lincoln's Inn chapel designed by Inigo Jones. Both hall and chapel can be seen on weekdays if you apply at the Gatehouse in Chancery Lane, WC 2 (phone: 405-1393). Also lovely are the gardens of Lincoln's Inn Fields, laid out in 1618 by Inigo Jones.

OTHER LONDON ATTRACTIONS

Regent's Park – The sprawling 472-acre park just north of the city center has beautiful gardens, vast expanses of lawns, a pond with paddleboats, and one of the finest zoos in the world (admission charge). Bordering the park are elegant terraced homes.

Camden Passage – This quaint pedestrian alleyway lined with antique and specialty shops has an open-air market — pushcarts selling curios and antiques — on Tuesdays, Wednesday mornings, and Saturdays. Islington, north of the city, N1.

Hampstead Heath – The north London bucolic paradise of wild heathland, meadows, and wooded dells is the highest point in London. Kenwood House, an eighteenth-century estate on the heath, is open to the public.

Kew Gardens – Here are the Royal Botanic Gardens, with tens of thousands of plants and trees. The gardens' primary purpose is to serve botany by researching, cultivating, experimenting, and identifying plants. There are shaded walks, floral displays, and magnificent Victorian glass greenhouses — especially the Temperate House, with some 3,000 different plants, including a 60-foot Chilean Wine Palm.

Portobello Road – This area is famous for its antique shops, junk shops, and outdoor pushcarts; it is one the largest street markets in the world. The pushcarts are out only on Saturdays, the most crowded day for the market. Less well known is Bermondsey Market, Long Lane at Tower Bridge Rd. SE1, on Fridays from 7 AM on; this is where the antiques on Portobello Road or Camden Passage were probably purchased.

Victoria and Albert Museum – Born of the 1851 Exhibition, the museum contains a vast collection of fine and applied arts (probably the largest collection of the latter in the world) — an amalgam of the great, the odd, and the ugly. Especially delightful are the English period rooms. There are superb collections of paintings, prints, ceramics, metalwork, costumes, and armor in the museum, which also contains English miniatures and famous Raphael cartoons. The museum's new Henry Cole Wing (named after its founder) houses a broad selection of changing exhibitions as well as an interesting permanent display of printmaking techniques. Closed Fridays. Cromwell Rd. SW7 (phone: 589-6371).

Greenwich – This Thames-side borough is traditionally associated with British seapower, especially when Britain "ruled the waves"; it includes such notable sights as: the National Maritime Museum on Romney Rd. (phone: 858-4422), containing superb exhibits on Britain's illustrious nautical past; the Old Royal Observatory, with astronomical instruments; *Cutty Sark,* a superbly preserved nineteenth-century clipper ship that's open to visitors; Royal Naval College, with beautiful painted hall and chapel; and Greenwich Park, 200 acres of greenery sloping down toward the river.

Richmond Park – The largest urban park in Britain is one of the few with herds of deer roaming free. (Hunting them is illegal, though this was once a royal hunting preserve.) It also has large oaks and rhododendron gardens. From nearby Richmond Hill you can enjoy a magnificent view of the Thames Valley.

Manor Houses – Five beautifully maintained historic homes are located in the Greater London area. Notable for their architecture, antique furnishings, lovely grounds, and, in the case of Kenwood, an eighteenth-century art collection, these homes are all accessible by subway: Kenwood (Hampstead), Ham (Richmond), Chiswick (Turnham Green or Chiswick Park), Syon (Osterley), and Osterley (Gunnersbury).

Hampton Court – Situated on the Thames, this sumptuous palace and gardens are in London's southwest corner. Begun by Cardinal Wolsey in 1515, the palace was appropriated by Henry VIII and was a royal residence for two centuries. Its particular attractions include a picture gallery, tapestries, state apartments, Tudor kitchens, the original tennis court, a moat, a great vine (two centuries old), gardens, and a maze. You can go to Hampton Court by bus, by train, or, best of all, in summer take the boat from Westminster Pier. Hampton, Middlesex (phone: 977-8441).

■ **EXTRA SPECIAL:** For a spectacular side trip out of London, there is nothing quite like Oxford and Stratford-on-Avon, Shakespeare's birthplace — both of which can be seen in a 1-day organized bus tour. Otherwise you can choose one; the regular bus to Stratford (90 mi/144 km) travels via Oxford (65 mi/105 km), so you can catch a glimpse of the ancient colleges if you try hard.

Shakespeare's birthplace is still an Elizabethan town, and even if you don't have a chance to see a play at the Shakespeare Memorial Theatre, you will enjoy the Tudor houses with overhung gables and traditional straw roofs. The poet's birthplace is a must, as is the grave at charming Holy Trinity Church. You might also enjoy the "Great Garden of New Place," said to contain every flower that Shakespeare mentioned in his plays, and Anne Hathaway's Cottage.

Oxford is England's oldest university town; its fine Gothic buildings have cloistered many famous Englishmen. Most of the great colleges are on High Street (the High) or Broad Street (the Broad). See Queen's College, Christ Church, Trinity College, the Bodleian Library, and the marvelous Ashmolean Museum of Art; be sure to look in a bookstore too — and *Blackwell's* on Broad Street is one of the finest in the world. Students guide the university tours.

Another highly recommended day trip, which is less ambitious than Stratford and Oxford, is Cambridge, only 1 hour and 20 minutes from London by train. Cambridge is even more delightful than Oxford because the town takes full advantage of the River Cam. So don't fail to walk along "the Backs," the stretch of greenery beside the river; or better yet, rent a canoe or a punt, a flat-bottomed boat that is propelled by a long pole. (It's easier than it sounds.) The town has two parallel main streets that change their names every two blocks; one is a shopping street and the other is lined with colleges. Don't miss *Heffer's* on Trinity Street; it's the best bookstore in Cambridge. Stroll through the famous colleges — King's College, Trinity, Queens, Jesus, Magdalene, and Clare. King's College Chapel is a fifteenth-century Gothic structure that is a real beauty. Also see at least one garden and one dining hall.

SOURCES AND RESOURCES

In the US, contact the British Tourist Authority, 40 W 57th St., New York, NY 10019 (phone: 212-581-4700). The National Tourist Information Centre at Victoria Station, open daily (phone: 730-3488), is one of the best local sources of information, as is the London Visitor and Convention Bureau at Westgate, Tower of London EC3 (phone: 730-3488 weekdays), open daily. A wide range of leaflets and brochures on the city's landmarks and events are available as well as a staff to answer questions on what to do, how to do it, and when. Suboffices are at Heathrow Travel Centre (open 7 days a week) and in *Selfridges* and *Harrods* department stores. For recorded information on the day's events, telephone 246-8041; call 246-8007 for another recording on children's events. One of the most comprehensive guidebooks is the *Blue Guide to London* (Benn).

For Local Coverage – Of London's several newspapers, the *Guardian, The Times, The Standard,* and *The Daily Telegraph* are most useful. Also helpful are the weekly magazines, *What's On and Where to Go, City Limits, Time Out*, and *London Events and Entertainment.*

For Food – The annual *Good Food Guide* ($16.95) and *Egon Ronay's* hotel and restaurant guide ($13.95) are available in most bookstores (prices are slightly lower in the UK).

 CLIMATE AND CLOTHES: Conventional wisdom has it that Britain doesn't have climate — it only has weather. The truth is that the weather in London is often unreliable and unpredictable, with beautiful mornings turning into dreary afternoons and vice versa. But legends about incessant rain are exaggerated (though having a raincoat or umbrella and waterproof footwear handy is advisable). In fact, London has less rain than Rome, which is known as a sunny city. It just spreads its rain out over more days. The British capital is very much a city of the temperate zone. With occasional exceptions, summers tend to be moderately warm, with few days having temperatures above 75°F (24°C), and winters moderately cold, with few days dropping below 30°F (− 1°C). Spring and autumn tend to be comfortable, with little more than a sweater or light overcoat required (and a raincoat ready for contingencies). In this age of informality, no place still requires formal evening dress, though nightclubs and a few haute cuisine restaurants may insist that men wear jackets and ties and women not be scandalously attired.

 GETTING AROUND: Bus and Underground – The London public transport system is still reasonably efficient. Its subway, called the "underground" or "tube," and its bus lines cover the city pretty well, though buses suffer from traffic congestion, and the underground is notoriously thin south of the river. The tops of London's famous, red double-decker buses do, however, offer some delightful views of the city and its people. The underground is easy to understand and to use, with clear directions and poster maps in all stations. Pick up free bus and underground maps from tourist offices or underground station ticket booths. The fares are set according to length of the journey. On most buses, conductors take payment after you tell them where you're going; some require that you pay as you enter. Underground tickets are bought on entering a station. Retain your ticket: You'll have to surrender it when you get off (or have to pay again), and bus inspectors make spot checks to see that no one's stealing a free ride. There are also Red Arrow express buses, but check stops before you get on. With just a few exceptions, public transport comes to a halt around midnight, though it varies according to underground line and bus route. If you're traveling late, check out available facilities.

A London Explorer ticket, which can be bought at the London Tourist Board or at any underground station — at about £8.50 for 3 days, £11 for 4 days, and £16 for 7 — provides unlimited travel on bus and underground within a specified area.

The underground links Heathrow, London's main airport, with downtown. The Piccadilly Line zips from Piccadilly Circus to the airport in about 45 minutes. (The underground does not connect with Gatwick Airport, but there are trains to Victoria Station every 15 minutes.) Buses also link Heathrow with the city. For bus and underground information, call 222-1234.

Taxi – Those extremely comfortable, fine old London cabs are scheduled to be replaced soon with more "practical" models. Taxi fares in London are increasingly expensive (we didn't mind the prices so much for a ride in the old cabs), and a 15% tip is customary. You should tell the cabbie where you're going *before* entering the cab. When it rains or late at night, an empty cab (identifiable by its roof light being on) is often very difficult to find, so it is wise to carry the telephone number of one or more of the cab companies that respond to calls by phone. There are many "minicab" companies that do not respond when hailed on the street nor use meters. They operate on the basis of a fixed fare between their home base and your destination. Hotel porters or reception desks usually can make arrangements to have such a car pick you up at a specified time and place. You should also be aware that taxi rates are higher after 8 PM and on holidays.

Car Rental – Several agencies, including *Hertz,* at 35 Edgware Rd. W2 (phone: 402-4242) and *Avis,* 35 Headford Pl. SW1 (phone: 245-9862) are represented in London. *Swan National,* 305 Chiswick High Rd. W4 (phone: 995-4665) is cheaper, or try *Guy Salmon Car Rentals,* 7-23 Bryanston St., Marble Arch (phone: 408-1255), or *Godfrey Davis,* Davis House, Wilton Rd. SW1 (phone: 834-8484). And for riding in style, call *Avis Luxury Car Services* (phone: 235-3235) for chauffeur-driven Rolls-Royces and Daimlers.

Walking Tours – A trained guide can show you Shakespeare's London or that of Dickens or Jack the Ripper — many different tours are offered. These reasonably priced tours last up to 2 hours, generally in the afternoon or evening. *Time Out* magazine and the city's information centers have listings of tour companies.

Bus Tours – London Transport's 2-hour unconducted tour (leaflets describe the sights you pass) leaves every hour from three spots: Marble Arch, Piccadilly Circus, and Grosvenor Gardens (phone: 222-1234). It's the cheapest and most comprehensive tour of London. Among other good bus tours are those run by American Express (phone: 930-4411), Thomas Cook (phone: 499-4000), and Frames' (phone: 837-6311).

Taxi Tours – Several firms and taxi drivers offer guided tours of London; details are available at information centers. You can make arrangements for the personal services of a member of London's Guild of Guides by phoning the London Tourist Board's Guide Department (phone: 730-3450).

Boat Excursions – See London from the Thames. Boats leave roughly every half-hour from Westminster Pier at the foot of Westminster Bridge and from Charing Cross Pier on Victoria Embankment; they sail downriver to the Tower of London and Greenwich or upriver to Kew. Also available is a journey along Regent's Canal through north London (summer only): Jason's Trip, opposite 60 Blomfield Rd., Little Venice W9 (phone: 286-3428). For further information about these and other boat trips, contact the London Tourist Board's River Boat Information Service (phone: 730-4812).

 SPECIAL EVENTS: Dates vary marginally from year to year and should be checked — together with details — with the London Tourist Board. In early June you can enjoy the annual *Trooping of the Color,* England's most elaborate display of pageantry — a Horse Guards' parade, with military music and much pomp and circumstance — all in celebration of the queen's official birthday. You can see some of the parade without a ticket, but for the ceremony you must book before March 1 by writing to the Brigade Major, Headquarters, Household Division, Horse Guards, Whitehall, SW1 (do not send money; tickets cost £2 and £5). Late June heralds the *Wimbledon Lawn Tennis Championship* — the world's most prestigious — complete with a member of the royal family presenting the prizes. The *Henley Royal Regatta,* which takes place in early July (at Henley-on-Thames, a 1-hour train ride from London), is an international rowing competition and one of the big social events of the year. The Royal Tournament, a military pageant, takes place at Earls Court for 3 weeks in July. October/November is the time for the *State Opening of Parliament; Guy Fawkes Day* is on November 5, when fireworks and bonfires mark the anniversary of the plot to blow up both houses of Parliament and King James I in 1605; and on the second Saturday in November, an inaugural procession for the new lord mayor, who rides in a golden carriage, followed by floats and bands, takes place.

 MUSEUMS: Many of London's museums are described in *Special Places.* Other noteworthy museums include:
The Natural History Museum, Cromwell Rd. SW7 (phone: 589-6323).
Science Museum, Exhibition Rd. SW7 (phone: 589-3456).

Planetarium, Marylebone Rd. NW1 (phone: 486-1121).
Dickens's House, 48 Doughty St. WC1 (phone: 405-2127).
Jewish Museum, Woburn House, Upper Woburn Pl. WC1 (phone: 388-4525).
Wallace Collection, Lady Wallace's fine collection of European paintings, sculpture, and armor, at Hertford House, Manchester Sq. W1 (phone: 935-0687).
Dulwich College Picture Gallery, works by European masters in one of England's most beautiful art galleries, College Rd. SE21 (phone: 693-5254).
Courtauld Institute Galleries, a remarkable collection of French Impressionist paintings, Woburn Sq. WC1 (phone: 636-2095).
Institute of Contemporary Arts, The Mall, SW1 (phone: 930-6393).
The Museum of Mankind, ethnographic exhibits, 6 Burlington Gardens W1 (phone: 437-2224).
Sir John Soane's Museum, its collection, includes Hogarth's series *The Rake's Progress,* 13 Lincoln's Inn Fields WC2 (phone: 405-2107).
The London Toy and Model Museum, October House, 23 Craven Hill, W2.

SHOPPING: Although London is considered one of the most expensive cities in the world, savvy shoppers can still find good buys. The lure, however, is more for fine workmanship and style than low prices.

The favorite items on a tourist's shopping list in London are cashmere and Shetland woolen knitwear; fabric (tweeds, blends, men's suitings); riding gear; custom-made men's suits, shoes, and hats; shotguns; china and crystal; umbrellas; antiques; sporting goods; English food specialties (jams, marmalade, various blended teas, Stilton cheese, shortbread, and others). Books published by British houses, once a fine buy, are now sky high in price, and you'll do better to buy the US editions.

Devoted bargain hunters recognize that the best time to buy British is during the semiannual sales that occur around New Year's Day and again in early July. The Christmas/New Year's sales offer by far the best bargains in the city, and the crowds are the equal of the low prices. Many stores remain open on New Year's Day to accommodate the crowds, and the best publicized single sale is that offered at *Harrod's* for three weeks beginning the first Saturday in January. That opening day is an event in itself.

Be sure to bring your passport along when you shop and always inquire about the VAT refund application forms when you make a large (over $25) purchase. The VAT (Value Added Tax) is a 15% surcharge which you must pay at the sales counter, but for which you may be reimbursed when you return home. Though scattered about the city, shopping tends to center in the West End area, particularly along Bond Street, Oxford Street, South Moulton Street, Piccadilly, Regent Street, and Jermyn Street. Other good places for shopping are Kings Road, Kensington High Street, and Kensington Church Street, along with Knightsbridge and Covent Garden.

This is a city of markets; we have already described Portobello Road and Camden Passage in *Special Places.* Also of note are Camden Lock Market, Camden High St. NW1, on Saturdays and Sundays, for far-out clothes, leather items, antiques, and trinkets; and the very famous Petticoat Lane, Middlesex St. E1, on Sunday mornings for food, cheap clothes, crockery, and many other used and new items.

The following list of stores is only a sampling of London's treasure houses.

Anderson and Sheppard – A reputable "made-to-measure" tailor for men's clothes, 30 Savile Row W1.
Antiquarius – A good place for antiques. 135-141 King's Rd. SW3.
Aquascutum – Needs no introduction; famous for raincoats and jackets for men and women. 100 Regent St. W1.
Laura Ashley – A relatively inexpensive women's boutique specializing in romantic styled skirts, dresses, and blouses. 183 Sloane St. SW1; plus other branches along Sloane St., on Fulham Rd., and in Covent Garden.

Asprey – Fine jewelry, silver, and leather. 165 New Bond St. Wl.

Browns – Beautiful but expensive women's clothes. 23-27 S Molton St. W1.

Burberrys – Superb but expensive men's and women's raincoats and traditional clothes, and home of the now nearly ubiquitous plaid that began life as a raincoat lining, at 18 Haymarket SW1.

Church & Co. – For fabled men's shoes. 58-59 Burlington Arcade W1; Old Bond St.

Crocodile – For chic and expensive women's clothes. 57 Beauchamp Pl. SW3.

Justin De Blank – For excellent quality specialty foods, especially cheese and take-out dishes. 42 Elizabeth St. SW1.

Dillon's – A good bookstore, London's most scholastic, partly owned by London University. 1 Malet St. WC1.

Fenwick – Sells trendy, moderately priced women's clothes. 63 New Bond St. W1.

Fortnum and Mason – Boasts designer originals (usually of the rather dowdy variety), a soda fountain, and one of the most elegant grocery departments in the world (the staff wears striped trousers and morning coats). 181 Piccadilly Wl.

Foyle's – London's largest bookstore. 119 Charing Cross Rd. WC2.

Gidden's of London – For riding gear. 15 Clifford St. W1.

Thomas Goode and Company – London's best china and glass shop first opened in 1827. Even if you don't plan to buy anything, you may want to look at their beautiful 1876 showroom. 19 S Audley St. W1.

Grays Market – The hundreds of stalls here and at the annex down the street sell everything from antique playing cards to sixteenth-century furniture. 1-7 Davies Mews W1 and 58 Davies St. W1.

Harvie and Hudson – Men's shirts made to order. 77 and 97 Jermyn St. SW1.

Harrods – The ultimate department store, although quite expensive. It has everything, even a mortuary and a bank, and what it doesn't stock, it will get for you. The "food halls" particularly fascinate visitors, and traditional British merchandise is available in abundance. For those interested in trendy styles, it has the Way In boutique. Brompton Rd., Knightsbridge SW1.

Douglas Hayward – A reputable tailor. 95 Mount St. W1.

Hamley's – The largest toy shop in the world, with 5 floors. 200 Regent St. W1.

Jaeger – For tailored (and expensive) women's clothes. 204 Regent St. W1.

Herbert Johnson – Sells men's hats. 13 Old Burlington St. W1.

Peter Jones – Another good, well-stocked department store, offering moderately priced, tasteful goods. Sloane Square, SW1.

John Keil – Lovely, expensive antiques. 25 Mount St. W1.

John Lewis – Yet another good, moderately priced department store, particularly noted for its fabrics department and household goods. 278 Oxford St. W1.

Liberty – Famous for print fabrics. Scarves and ties a specialty. 210 Regent St. W1.

Lillywhites – For the whole gamut of sporting goods. Piccadilly Circus SW1.

John Lobb – World-famous for made-to-order shoes that will last ten years or more with proper care. 9 St. James's St. SW1.

Marks and Spencer – Locally nicknamed "Marks and Sparks," this is a chain of stores specializing in clothes for the whole family, made to high standards and sold at reasonable prices. Its linens and sweaters (especially cashmere and Shetland) are among the best buys in Britain. 458 Oxford St. W1 (and many other outlets).

Harvey Nichols – A luxury department store specializing in fashion and household goods. Knightsbridge SW1.

Partridge Ltd. – Fine (but expensive) antiques. 144 New Bond St. W1.

James Purdey and Sons – The place for shooting gear. 57 S Audley St. W1.

Reject China Shop – Good buys in slightly irregular, name brand china are sometimes available here. For a fee, the shop will ship your purchases back home. 33-35 Beauchamp Pl. SW3.

Peter Robinson Top Shop – For young, trendy, moderately priced women's clothing. 216 Oxford St. W1.

Scotch House – Famous for Scottish wools, sweaters, tartans — a wide selection of well-known labels. 2 Brompton Rd. SW1, and many other branches.

Selfridges – This famous department store offers somewhat less variety than *Harrods,* but it has just about everything too — only a little less expensive. The china and crystal department carries most patterns available. Oxford St. W1.

Simpson – Has elegant garments for men and women. 203 Piccadilly W1.

James Smith and Sons – This is the oldest umbrella shop in Europe. 53 New Oxford St. WC1.

Sotheby Parke Bernet – The world's oldest art auctioneer, *Sotheby*'s is interesting to look at even if you don't plan to buy. They auction books, porcelain, furniture, jewelry, and works of art; at times, even such odd items as vintage cars and wines. Viewing hours are between 9:30 AM and 4:30 PM on weekdays, at Bloomfield Pl. W1 (phone: 493-8080).

Smythson of Bond Street – The world's best place to buy diaries, note pads, calendars, and exotic ledgers. 54 New Bond St. W1.

Swaine, Adeney, Brigg, and Sons – For riding gear and their famous silk umbrellas. 185 Piccadilly W1.

Turnbull and Asser – Marvelous men's shirts made to order. 71 Jermyn St. SW1.

Wedgwood – For porcelain, of course. 266 and 270 Regent St. W1.

Westaway and Westaway – Cashmere and Shetland wool kilts, sweaters, scarves, and blankets. 65 Great Russell St. WC1 and 29 Bloomsbury WC1.

 SPORTS: Soccer (called football hereabouts) and cricket are the most popular spectator pastimes, but London offers a wide variety of other sports.

Cricket – The season runs from mid-April to early September. The best places to watch it are at Lord's Cricket Ground, St. John's Wood Rd. NW8 (phone: 289-1615), and The Oval, Kennington SE11 (phone: 582-6660).

Fishing – Several public ponds right in London are accessible to the angler. A permit is required from Royal Parks Department, the Storeyard, Hyde Park W2 (phone: 262-5484). The department can also provide information on where to fish.

Golf – Aside from private clubs, for which membership is required, there are several municipal courses, some of which rent out clubs. Try *Pickett's Lock Center,* Pickett's Lock La. N9 (phone: 803-3611), *Addington Court,* Featherbed La., Addington, Croydon (phone: 657-0281), and *Beckenham Place Park,* Beckenham, Kent (phone: 650-2292). *Wentworth,* Virginia Water, Surrey (phone: Wentworth 2201), and *Sunningdale,* Ridgemount Rd., Sunningdale, Berkshire (phone: Ascot 21681), are the best courses within driving distance of London, and a letter from your home club pro or president may give you access to their links.

Greyhound Racing – Empire Stadium, Empire Way, Wembley (phone: 902-1234), and others. Check afternoon newspapers for details.

Horse Racing – Nine major racecourses are within easy reach of London, including Epsom, where the "Derby" (pronounced Darby) is run, and Ascot, where "Royal Ascot" takes place — both in June. The flat racing season is from March to November; steeplechasing, August to June. Call the Jockey Club, 42 Portman Sq., W1 (phone: 486-4921) for information.

Horseback Riding – Try *Bathurst Riding Stables,* 63 Bathurst Mews, W2 (phone: 723-2813), and *Ross Nye's Riding Establishment,* 8 Bathurst Mews, W2 (phone: 262-3791).

Ice Skating – There is the *Queen's Ice Skating Club,* 17 Queensway W2 (phone: 229-0172), and *Silver Blades Ice Rink,* 386 Streatham High Rd. SW16 (phone: 769-7861). Skates are for rent at both rinks.

Rugby – An autumn-through-spring spectacle at Rugby Football Ground, Whitton Rd., Twickenham (phone: 892-8161).

Soccer – *The* big sport in Britain. The local football season is autumn to spring and the most popular clubs are *Arsenal,* Highbury Stadium, Avenell Rd. N5 (phone: 359-0131); *Chelsea,* Stamford Bridge, Fulham Rd. SW6 (phone: 381-0111); *West Ham United,* Boleyn Ground, Green St. E13 (phone: 470-1325).

Swimming – Several excellent indoor public pools include: *Swiss Cottage Center,* Adelaide Rd. NW3 (phone: 586-5989), *Putney Swimming Baths,* 376 Upper Richmond Rd. SW15 (phone: 789-1124), and *The Oasis,* 167 High Holborn, WC 1 (phone: 836-9555). There is outdoor swimming in the Hyde Park Serpentine and on Hampstead Heath in the summer.

Tennis – More than 50 London public parks have tennis courts available to all. Get information from the London Tourist Board (phone: 730-3488).

 THEATER: London remains the theater capital of the world, with about 50 theaters regularly putting on plays in and around its West End theater district and a vigorous collection of "fringe" theaters in various parts of town. Best known, and most accomplished, are the two main repertory theater companies — the *National Theatre Company* at the National Theatre, South Bank SE1 (phone: 928-2252), and the *Royal Shakespeare Company,* at the new Barbican Centre, The Barbican EC2 (phone: 628-8795), both present dazzling productions of classics and new plays. Shakespearean plays are also performed in summer at the open-air theater in Regent's Park NW1 (phone: 486-2431).

In the West End, presentations include both first-class and second-rate drama and comedy, a fair sprinkling of farce (for which the British have a particular fondness), and the best of imports from the American stage. Visitors from the US often find attending theater in London easier — and somewhat cheaper — than it is at home. Except for the small handful of runaway box office successes, tickets are usually available for all performances and you can reserve by telephone, but tickets must be picked up well before curtain time. In a recent effort to revive failing attendance, the West End Theatre Society opened a half-price ticket kiosk in Leicester Square. Modeled after the TKTS booth in New York's Times Square, it posts a list of shows for which the remaining seats may be purchased at half-price on the day of performance.

The quality of London's fringe theater varies from accomplished and imaginative to amateurish. Theaters in pubs are at the *King's Head* in Islington, 115 Upper St. N1 (phone: 226-1916), and at the *Bush* in the Bush Hotel, Shepherd's Bush Green (phone: 743-3388); the *Riverside Studios* in Hammersmith, Crisp Rd. W6 (phone: 748-3354), and the *New End Theatre* in Hampstead, 27 New End NW3 (phone: 435-6054), have established reputations for the excellence of their productions, which often move on to the West End and sometimes even directly to Broadway. Lunchtime fringe theater presentations offer an alternative to sight-seeing on rainy days.

Check *Time Out* for comprehensive lists, plot summaries, and theater phone numbers. Daily papers list West End performances. If you don't have the time or inclination to go to the box office, you can buy theater tickets through a ticket broker, who will charge a fee for this service.

Show tours to London are very popular in season; if you are interested, see your travel agent for package deals. If you want to reserve individual tickets in advance, there are agencies that keep a listing of what's on in London. For a service charge of $5 per ticket, they will sell you the best seats only. Contact *Edwards & Edwards,* One Times Square Plaza, New York, NY 10036 (phone: 212-944-0290 or 800-223-6108), or *Keith Prowse & Co.,* 234 W 44th St., New York, NY 10036 (phone: 212-398-1430 or 800-223-4446).

MUSIC: Few cities offer a greater variety of musical performances — both classical music and the many varieties of popular music. For classical music, the focus of attention is the *South Banks Arts Center* with its three concert halls — Royal Festival Hall, Queen Elizabeth Hall, and the Purcell Room — (phone: 928-3191 for all three) and Royal Albert Hall, Kensington Gore SW7 (phone: 589-8212). *Wigmore Hall,* Wigmore St. W1 (phone: 935-2141), is best known for recitals of chamber music and performances by some of the world's most accomplished instrumental and vocal soloists. Concerts are also often held in the dignified, splendid setting of St. John's Church, Smith Square SW1 (phone: 222-1061). The *London Symphony Orchestra* performs in its own concert hall at Barbican Centre, The Barbican EC2. During the summer there are outdoor concerts given at Kenwood, Crystal Palace, and Holland Park, and bands play in many of London's parks.

Operas at Covent Garden Royal Opera House, Floral St., WC2 (phone: 240-1066), are internationally famous. The *English National Opera Company* offers its performances at the London Coliseum, St. Martin's La. WC2 (phone: 836-3161). The best of London's ballet performances are presented at Covent Garden, the Coliseum and at Sadler's Wells, Roseberry Ave. EC1 (phone: 837-1672) as well as at *The Place,* 17 Duke Rd. WC1 (phone: 387-0161), home of the London Contemporary Dance Theatre and the London School of Contemporary Dance. Details about concert, recital, opera, and ballet performances can be found in the arts sections of the Sunday newspapers.

Although some superstar popular musicians and vocalists make occasional appearances in converted movie houses, parks, and even deserted airfields outside town, much good live popular music can be heard in London's music pubs. Among the best of them are the *Bull's Head,* 373 Lonsdale Rd. SW13 (phone: 876-5241); *Two Brewers,* Clapham High St. SW4 (phone: 874-4128); *Kensington,* 54 Russell Gardens, Holland Rd. W14 (phone: 603-3245); and *Hope and Anchor,* 207 Upper St. N1 (phone: 359-4510).

NIGHTCLUBS AND NIGHTLIFE: Not two decades ago, they virtually rolled up the sidewalks in London at 11 PM. Now there's a very lively and often wild nightlife, including nightclubs, jazz clubs, historical feast entertainments, and gambling casinos. Some wind up around midnight; most go on until well into the early morning hours. In Covent Garden and still-trendy-after-all-these-years Chelsea, particularly along King's and Fulham roads you'll find the latest fads and most fashionable pubs, wine bars, and restaurants. Two nightclubs with floor shows are the *London Room,* Drury La. (phone: 831-8863); and *Omar Khayyam,* 177 Regent St. W1 (phone: 734-7675). There is dancing at both. There's a show but no dancing at *Madisons,* Camden Lock, Chalk Farm Rd. NW1 (phone: 485-6044). The best jazz clubs are *Ronnie Scott's,* 47 Frith St. W1 (phone: 439-0747), and *The 100 Club,* 100 Oxford St. W1 (phone: 636-0933). *Dingwalls,* Camden Lock, Chalk Farm Rd. NW1 (phone: 267-4967) and the *Marquee,* 90 Wardour St. W1 (phone: 437-6603), have a continually changing program of much-acclaimed performers of rock music.

A special nighttime treat is called a *historical feast entertainment,* complete with traditional meals served by costumed waiters and waitresses. Menus resemble those of traditional Elizabethan feasts, and there is period music, horseplay, occasional mock sword fights, Shakespearean playlets, and other light entertainment. Try *Tudor Rooms,* 80 St. Martin's La. WC2 (phone: 240-3978); *Beefeater,* St. Katherine Dock E1 (phone: 408-1001); *Shakespeare's Tavern,* Blackfriar's La. EC4 (phone: 408-1001); and *King Arthur's Court,* Northumberland Ave., WC 2 (phone: 408-1001).

As for discos, the scene is a rapidly changing one, and many places are open only to members, such as *Annabel's,* 44 Berkeley Square (phone: 629-3558). At the moment, the most popular discos are: the *Hippodrome,* Charing Cross Rd. WC2 (phone: 437-4311); *Palace,* 1a Camden Rd. NW1 (phone: 387-0428); *Stringfellows,* 16-19 Upper St. Martin's La. WC2 (phone: 240-5534); and *Legend's,* 29 Old Burlington St. (phone:

437-9933). *Tramp,* 40 Jermyn St. SW1 (phone: 734-0565), is where up-and-coming starlets and the chic social set meet to disco (members only).

Comedy based on female impersonation is a major theme in British popular humor, as reflected in the number of pubs where female impersonators regularly perform. These include: *Union Tavern,* 146 Camberwell New Rd. SE5 (phone: 735-3605); and *Black Cap,* 171 Camden High St. NW1 (phone: 485-1742). Phone for details.

Information on gay clubs and pubs is contained in the biweekly *Gay News,* sold at larger newsstands.

 SINS: London has a reputation for free and easy gambling, but over the last year or so, the gaming laws have been enforced more rigorously and many clubs have had to shut down. It is best to check the current situation at your hotel desk when you arrive. Gambling club membership is usually available within 48 hours upon presentation of your passport. Card games, roulette, and dice are featured in most of the clubs.

By reputation, Soho is the sin center of London, but being ripped off is often the only sin visitors experience there. Soho striptease clubs usually give very little or no value for the money. Some of the worst are touted by street barkers or men who sidle up to passersby in the street, promising exotic and erotic pleasures. An exception that tries to redeem the good name of striptease is *Raymond's Revue Bar,* 8 Brewer St. W1 (phone: 734-1593).

Soho does, however, boast a goodly number of prostitutes, some walking the street looking for customers, some advertising their services discreetly on nameplate cards in doorways — "Celeste, French lessons, second floor" — that sort of thing. Street walkers are also much in evidence in the Shepherd's Market district at night, and when the police aren't cracking down, on Park Lane, near the *London Hilton* and *Dorchester* hotels. Many of the "massage parlours" that have sprouted in various parts of town (there are several in Soho) offer clients more than massages.

Blue movies are shown in many movie houses — advertisements for them appear in *What's On and Where to Go.* And the *Gay Switchboard* (phone: 837-7324) offers telephone information and advice to visiting gays of both sexes.

BEST IN TOWN

 CHECKING IN: Between early spring and midautumn hotel reservations are a must. If you arrive without them, go to the National Tourist Information Centre at Victoria Station Forecourt; for a small fee, the people here will try to help you find a room. Expect to pay $110 to $160 and up for a double room in an expensive hotel; $65 to $100 is moderate; and $40 to $60 is inexpensive.

Claridges – Even the bathrooms and clothes closets are immense in this lush outpost for visiting royalty, heads of state, and other distinguished and/or affluent foreigners. The line of chauffered limousines outside the main entrance sometimes makes traffic there impenetrable. Wrought-iron balconies and a sweeping foyer staircase help provide a stately setting for one of London's most elegant hostelries. Brook St. W1 (phone: 629-8860). Expensive.

Connaught – A touch too sober for high livers; a trifle too formal for the rough-and-ready crowd. But there aren't many hotels left in the world that can rival this old London fixture in providing welcome, elegance, and comfort — particularly in its luxurious suites. Carlos Pl. W1 (phone: 499-7070). Expensive.

Dorchester – Next to the *Hilton,* overlooking Hyde Park, this very luxurious hotel, now under Arab ownership, maintains its traditional British atmosphere, with

Georgian and Regency furnishings and elegant service. Its Terrace Restaurant serves fine food and has recently been awarded a Michelin star. Rooms are tastefully furnished, and there is 24-hour room service and central air-conditioning, among the hotel's amenities. Park La. W1 (phone: 629-8888). Expensive.

Montcalm – A smaller, elegant hotel with a lovely facade, a warm-toned and understated interior, and top-notch service. Its rooms have all the usual comforts, and many of its suites are especially luxurious. There's a bar and a small French restaurant. Great Cumberland Pl. W1 (phone: 402-4288). Expensive.

London Hilton on Park Lane – Well situated off Hyde Park corner, near shopping and theater, this contemporary high-rise hotel offers luxury accommodations and views of the park and the city. Special attention to business executives includes a multilingual switchboard, secretarial staff, office equipment, and private dining rooms. The rooms here have all the amenities plus space for reading and writing. There's every conceivable service plus a few more — the *Roof Restaurant* with a view, the *Polynesian Restaurant*, the *British Harvest Restaurant*, serving traditional British food, and a pub, disco, and snack bar. 22 Park La. W1 (phone: 493-8000). Expensive.

Ritz – The fellow who was heard to mutter snootily, "Nobody stays at the *Ritz* anymore," was off-base, especially since the recent renovation restored much of the old luster and certainly got the "bugs" out. While the fare offered in the *Ritz* dining room is just acceptable, the decor is splendid and the service impeccable. Piccadilly W1 (phone: 493-8181). Expensive.

Savoy – A favorite of film and theater performers, some of whom check in for months and have nothing but praise for the accommodations and service. Once one of London's top addresses, it is just coming back into vogue. It's a 200-room hotel with armies of chambermaids and porters to keep things running. The Strand WC2 (phone: 836-4343). Expensive.

Churchill – A turn-of-the-century palatial mood is reflected in the discreet, impressive decor and the marble lobby. This is a well-run, efficient place, with a pleasant restaurant and a snack room that serves the best bacon and eggs in London. Very popular with Americans looking for accommodations somewhere between the old world and the new. Portman Sq. W1 (phone: 486-5800). Expensive.

Berkeley – Remarkably understated, this 150-room hotel manages to preserve its impeccably high standards while keeping a low profile. Soft-spoken service complements the tastefully lavish, traditional English decor. Wilton Pl. SW1 (phone: 235-6000). Expensive.

Dukes – Despite the small size of its 55 rooms, this is an establishment where nobility and prestige shine through. It even extends to the rooms' being named for former peers. 35 St. James's Pl. SW1 (phone: 491-4840). Expensive.

Grosvenor House – This 478-room grande dame facing Hyde Park has a health club, some interesting shops, three restaurants (the *Pavilion Coffee Shop, Ninety Park Lane* with French cuisine, and *Pasta Vino e Fantasia* with an Italian menu), the *Park Lounge*, which serves traditional afternoon teas, and the exclusive Crown Club on the top floor for members only — usually businesspeople who require special services — with rooms, suites, a lounge, and other complimentary extras. Park La. W1 (phone: 499-6363). Expensive.

Park Lane – If you don't mind the noise of the city streets, the location of this hotel in the heart of London should appeal to you. All rooms have recently been redecorated, and some have views of Green Park across the street. Piccadilly W1 (phone: 499-6321). Expensive.

Inter-Continental – Smack-dab in the middle of town, right on Hyde Park Corner, with windows overlooking the route of the mounted troops as they go cantering off for the Changing of the Guard each morning. Its well-proportioned rooms are equipped with refrigerated bars. Modern, comfortable, but the location's the main allure. 1 Hamilton Pl., Hyde Park Corner W1 (phone: 409-3131). Expensive.

Stafford – In a surprisingly quiet side street in the city center, this is where many American television and newspaper organizations put up visiting correspondents to give them efficient, friendly, British small-hotel management at its best. Many visitors think of it as their own personal secret, but it's been out for some time. 16 St. James's Pl. SW1 (phone: 493-0111). Expensive.

St. James's Club – For about $150 you can become a member of this exclusive residential club in the heart of London (though you don't need to join for your first stay). You have full use of club facilities, and pay relatively modest rates for one of the 45 rooms and suites. The club's Rolls Royce fetches you from the airport and some of the best food available in London is served in the magnificent art deco dining room. 7 Park Pl., SW1 (phone: 629-7688). Expensive.

Selfridges – Just behind the department store of the same name, this hotel is modern both in furnishings and tone, with a refreshing, unaffected courtesy that seems often to escape some of London's midtown establishments. Conveniently located for shopping. Orchard St. W1 (phone: 408-2080). Expensive.

Brown's – As English as you can get, retaining pleasing, quaint, Victorian charm, and not at all marred by heavy, sturdy furniture or the somewhat hushed atmosphere. Strong on service. If it's an English tea you're after, this is the place. Dover St. W1 (phone: 493-6020). Expensive.

London Marriott – Conveniently close to the American Embassy and West End shopping is this modern hotel. It's bright and busy, and it has everything — lounge, bar, restaurant, shop, very comfortable rooms, and good service. Grosvenor Sq. W1 (phone: 493-1232). Expensive.

Cavendish – Immortalized as the *Bentinck,* the hotel run by Louisa Trotta (in real life, Rosa Lewis) in the TV series *The Duchess of Duke Street,* this modern replacement offers one of the most attractive locations in central London, near Piccadilly. Its 255 rooms are comfortable, if not elegant. Jermyn St. SW1 (phone: 930-2111). Expensive.

Britannia – Mahogany furniture, velvet armchairs, rooms painted in colors you might choose at home — all very tasteful and solid, despite the anonymity of its spacious foyer with its pretentious chandeliers. This is where the American Embassy — also on the square — often puts up visiting middle-ranking State Department officials. Grosvenor Sq. W1 (phone: 629-9400). Expensive.

Cadogan – Very comfortable older place, redolent of Edwardian England. Oscar Wilde was arrested here, and Lillie Langtry, who was having an affair with the Prince of Wales (later Edward VII), lived next door. The furniture and decor are original, but modern conveniences are offered as well — phone, TV, refrigerator in every room, bar, and restaurant. The hotel has 66 rooms. 75 Sloane St. SW1 (phone: 235-7141). Expensive to moderate.

Royal Court – Clean, comfortable, and recently refurbished, the hotel has a courteous, helpful staff, at the head of London's fashionable Chelsea shopping and residential district and within quick, easy reach of the rest of the action in town. Sloane Sq. SW1 (phone: 730-9191). Expensive to moderate.

Basil Street – A relic with a reputation for graceful, old-fashioned service and beautiful antique furnishings to match. It draws a faithful international clientele who, if they can get reservations, prefer staying here to patronizing any of the modern, impersonal, newer hotels. Down the street from *Harrods* department store. 8 Basil St. SW3 (phone: 581-3311). Moderate.

Kensington Hilton – A bit out of the way, this modern hotel offers a great deal of comfort at prices cheaper than those of most Hiltons. Services include a restaurant, piano bar, and a lavish brunch on Sundays. Rooms are well designed and well maintained. 179–199 Holland Park Ave. (phone: 603-3355). Moderate.

Durrants – This elegant Regency-style hotel has a splendid location behind the Wallace Collection and is only a few minutes' walk from the shopping on Oxford Street. It has been family-run for more than 50 years and all the rooms have retained their character while being kept comfortably up-to-date. George St. W1 (phone: 935-8131). Moderate.

Gatwick Hilton International – Part of the airport's expansion program, this hotel has been built to provide much-needed accommodations for the ever-increasing number of visitors using the Gatwick gateway. Connected to the terminal by an enclosed walkway, amenities include many services for business travelers, bars, health club, 24-hour room service, and more. Gatwick Airport (phone: 51-80-80). Moderate.

Ebury Court – A small hotel with smallish but cozy rooms. Its faithful clientele testifies to its comfort and suitability. Hard to beat — all things considered — in a town where hotel prices tend to be unreasonable. 26 Ebury St. SW1 (phone: 730-8147). Moderate.

Harewood Hotel – This small modern hotel is well maintained by a pleasant and efficient staff. Some of the rooms have private terraces. Restaurant and wine bar. Harewood Ave., NW1 (phone: 262-2707). Moderate to inexpensive.

Pastoria Hotel – In the very center of the West End, near all the theaters, this pleasant, comfortable little hotel has 53 rooms, most with baths and TV; it has a bar and a restaurant. St. Martin's St. WC2 (phone: 930-8641). Moderate to inexpensive.

Diplomat Hotel – Small, with no restaurant and only 26 rooms — all with baths — it is nonetheless comfortable, friendly, and inexpensive. In Belgravia at 2 Chesham St. SW1 (phone: 235-1544). Inexpensive.

EATING OUT: Few London restaurants were ever known for the excellence of their cuisine — and some visitors of times past might call that a charitable understatement. But there's been a notable transformation in recent years. While restaurants offering really good English cooking — and not simply "chips with everything" — are still not easy to find (some are listed below), there has been a veritable explosion of good foreign restaurants in town (some of which are also noted below).

To sample something typically English, order roast beef or lamb and Yorkshire pudding; Dover sole, plaice, and oysters in season are also good. Other specialties include small meat pies; kedgeree, a kind of stew with fish, onion, and egg; Scotch eggs, hard boiled, covered with sausage meat, fried, and served cold; oxtail stew, eel pies, and sausages. For dessert try berries and berry pies. And special English cheeses include Stilton, good Cheddar, Caerphilly (it's Welsh), and Cheshire.

English beer, stout, and ale are fine, especially Guinness and Whitbread's; if you like gin, try Plymouth or Tanqueray; and hard cider is quite popular and quite good. Don't miss Pimm's Cup, a drink served in better pubs, made up of gin in a tall, iced pewter tankard, with borage or mint, a slice of cucumber, orange, and apple. The fact that a restaurant has fancy prices on its menu does not guarantee the excellence of its food, but most of the best restaurants in town are expensive — which means about $100 for two, including wine but not service; moderate restaurants, $50 to $75; inexpensive restaurants, less than $30. Some London restaurants have developed the Continental habit of automatically adding a service charge to the bill, so make certain you're not tipping twice. Reservations are necessary in all restaurants below.

Le Gavroche – Probably the best restaurant in London and, according to *Guide*

Michelin, one of the best in the entire country, with three stars to its credit (only one other establishment in Britain has received such a high rating). The cuisine is classic French, with many dishes that qualify as genuine masterpieces. Closed Saturdays and Sundays. 43 Upper Brook St. W1 (phone: 408-0881). Very expensive.

Capital Hotel Restaurant – The elegant, comfortable, small dining room in this hotel near *Harrods* department store offers well-chosen, admirably, and richly prepared French dishes. It is considered the best place in town by some discriminating Londoners. Avoids the aren't-you-lucky-to-get-a-table attitude flaunted by some other better London restaurants. 22-24 Basil St. SW3 (phone: 589-5171). Expensive.

Tante Claire – Run by chef Pierre Koffman and his wife, Annie, this place has been awarded two Michelin stars as well as many other honors. While fish dishes are the chef's specialty, everything — especially the duck, calf's liver, and *pied de cochon farci aux morilles* (pig's foot stuffed with foie gras and mushrooms) — is excellent. Closed Saturdays and Sundays. Major credit cards. 68 Royal Hospital Rd. SW3 (phone: 352-6045). Expensive.

Wilton's – Good food, elegantly served in a plush, rather formal Victorian setting. Game, oxtail, steak and kidney pie — what the best of English cooking can be all about. Closed Saturdays, Sundays, and three weeks in July/August. 55 Jermyn St. SW1 (phone: 629-9955). Expensive.

Connaught Hotel Restaurant – Very dignified and very proper, this distinguished restaurant with one Michelin star has a fine reputation for both its cuisine and impeccable service. It's not a place for loud conversation or outlandish attire, but for appreciation of masterful culinary performance. The setting — lots of rich wood paneling and crystal chandeliers — matches the distinction of the menu. Carlos Pl., W1 (phone: 499-7070). Expensive.

Leith's – A fine Continental restaurant in an out-of-the-way Victorian building northwest of Kensington Gardens, *Leith's* serves very good hors d'oeuvres, main courses, and desserts as part of a fine prix fixe dinner. Its wine selection is also very good. 92 Kensington Park Rd. W11 (phone: 229-4481). Expensive.

The Guinea Grill – Down an alley off Berkeley Square, this unimposing pub-cum-restaurant serves the best beef in Britain. It also substitutes displays of its fresh food — steaks, chops, fresh vegetables, and fruit — for a menu. It's as good as it looks, cooked with care. Closed Sundays. 30 Bruton Pl. W1 (phone: 629-5613). Expensive.

The Savoy Grill – Renowned as a celebrity-watching ground, but with a stiff, mostly male, business clientele. Although the menu features some classic French dishes, the English grills and roasts are its specialty. The lovely decor resembles a luxurious ship's dining room (first class, of course) of 50 years ago. At the *Savoy Hotel,* The Strand WC2 (phone: 836-4343). Expensive.

Langan's Brasserie – Still trendy after all these years, and still a popular haunt for celebrities (probably because one of the owners is actor Michael Caine). Ask for a table downstairs and take your time studying the lengthy menu. Reservations necessary. 1 Stratton St. W1 (493-6437). Expensive to Moderate.

Poons of Covent Garden – This Cantonese restaurant has built a reputation for good authentic cooking and specializes in wind-dried food. You can even watch the chefs at work through a glass partition. Closed Sundays. 41 King St. WC2 (phone: 240-1743). Expensive to moderate.

Gay Hussar – Perhaps the best Hungarian restaurant this side of Budapest. Its substantial menu offers a varied selection; goulash, of course, but much else. The food here has the unfortunate distinction of being extremely filling as well as delicious. Informal atmosphere, with a regular clientele drawn from London's newspaper and publishing world. Make reservations early. Closed Sundays. 2 Greek St. W1 (phone: 437-0973). Moderate.

Sweetings – A special experience, this very traditional fish restaurant is one of the great lunchtime attractions in the financial district. You may have to sit at a counter with your lobster, brill, or haddock — but it will be fresh and perfectly prepared. Weekday lunchtime only; no reservations, and expect a wait. 39 Queen Victoria St. EC4 (phone: 248-3062). Moderate.

Hungry Horse – This is the place to discover what a properly made English meat pie and Yorkshire pudding should taste like, as well as other English goodies. Don't be put off by having to pass under an archway and climb down a flight of stairs to get there — if anything, the inside looks a touch too tidy. 196 Fulham Rd. SW10 (phone: 352-7757). Moderate.

Tate Gallery Restaurant – Who would expect one of London's better restaurants to be in a fine art museum? But there it is — a genuine culinary outpost (leaning toward French cuisine) with a very good wine list, not just another museum eat-and-run hangout. Lunch only. Closed Sundays. Tate Gallery. Millbank SW1 (phone: 834-6754). Moderate.

Shezan – This quiet, brick-and-tile restaurant is just below street level, and prepares some very fine Pakistani food. Specialties include marinated-in-yogurt *murg tikka Lahori* (chicken cooked in *tandoori*, or clay ovens) and *kabab kabli* (minced spiced beef). An enthusiastic staff will explain the intricacies of tandoori cooking, help with your order, and lavish you with excellent service. Closed Sundays. 16-22 Cheval Place SW7 (phone: 589-7918). Moderate.

Wheeler's – Of the chain of London seafood restaurants with the same name, this is the original and it's also the best of the lot. It's an old-fashioned establishment which specializes in the many ways of preparing Dover sole, most of them delicious. Closed Sundays. 19 Old Compton St. W1 (phone: 437-2706). Moderate.

Chuen Cheng Ku – At this huge restaurant in the heart of Chinatown, the overwhelming majority of the clientele is Chinese. The specialty here is dim sum, served every day until 6 PM. Also try the pork with chili and salt, duck webs, steamed lobster with ginger, and shark fin soup. 17 Wardour St. W1 (phone: 734-3281). Moderate.

123 – One block away from the Japanese embassy, this is where its diplomatic staff eats, a sure sign of quality. But be warned that there are two menus — one in English, the other in Japanese — and they are vastly different. The latter offers a far more extensive array of sashimi. Ask the waiter to translate. Closed Sundays. 27 Davies St. W1 (phone: 499-3911). Moderate.

Bombay Brasserie – At lunchtime there is an Indian buffet; at dinner, classic cooking from the Bombay region. Parsi dishes, rarely found outside India itself, are also included. And the setting is lovely, with lots of wicker, plants, and ceiling fans. Courtfield Close, Courtfield Rd. SW7 (phone: 370-4040). Moderate.

Chicago Pizza Pie Factory – A little while ago, an American advertising executive turned his back on the ad world to bring London deep-dish pizza Windy City style, along with Budweiser beer and chocolate cheesecake. Londoners beat a path to his door and haven't yet stopped clamoring to get in. Open Daily. 17 Hanover Sq. W1 (phone: 629-2669). Inexpensive.

The Standard Indian Restaurant – Possibly the best Indian restaurant for the money in London, it tends to get crowded quickly. There are no reservations, so if you're headed here, dine early to beat the rush. 23 Westbourne Grove W2 (phone: 727-4818). Inexpensive.

Hard Rock Café – An American-style place, with a loud jukebox and good burgers. It's always crowded. 150 Old Park La. W1 (phone: 629-0382). Inexpensive.

The Widow Applebaum – Not an authentic "New York Jewish" delicatessen, but this place serves pretty good herring, cold cuts, chopped liver, potato salad, dill pickles, and apple pie. Outdoor tables. Closed Sundays. 46 S Molton St., W1 (phone: 629-4649). Inexpensive.

Dumpling Inn – This Peking-style restaurant serves excellent Oriental dumplings, and most of the other dishes are equally good. Try the fried seaweed; it's got lots of vitamins and tastes terrific. The service, though efficient, is a little brisk. 15A Gerrard St., W1 (phone: 437-2567). Inexpensive.

Calabash – West African cuisine gives this restaurant a unique position on London's restaurant map, especially since it's located in the bubbling Covent Garden district. The service is accommodating and helpful and the food is both good and different. Closed Sundays. Downstairs at London's "Africa Center," 38 King St., WC2 (phone: 836-1976). Inexpensive.

The Bangkok – Known for its *saté* — small tender slices of beef marinated in a curry and soy sauce and served with a palate-destroying hot peanut sauce. From your table you can watch your meal being prepared by chefs in the windowed kitchen. Closed Sundays. 9 Bute St. SW7 (phone: 584-8529). Inexpensive.

Geale's – This place serves up truly English — and fresh — fish and chips in a setting that looks like a 1930s tearoom. Go early, because *Geale's* is no secret. Closed Sundays, Mondays, and three weeks in July. 2 Farmer St. W8 (phone: 727-7969). Inexpensive.

Cranks – There are three branches of this self-service vegetarian restaurant. All are popular and serve good homemade desserts as well as salads, quiches, and other hot food. Drop in for coffee or afternoon tea. Closed Sundays. 8 Marshall St. W1 (phone: 437-9431); 11 The Market, Covent Garden WC1 (phone: 379-6508); Tottenham St. W1 (phone: 631-3912). Inexpensive.

Cosmoba – A small and friendly family-run Italian restaurant that is basic in every respect — except its food. Tucked down a tiny alley and always packed with regulars. 9 Cosmo Pl. WC1 (phone: 837-0904). Inexpensive.

A NOTE ON PUBS: There are several thousand pubs in London, the vast majority of which are owned by the six big brewers. Most of these pubs fall into two categories: the "public," which is for the working man who wants to get on with the business of drinking, and the "saloon" or "lounge," which makes an attempt at providing comfort and may serve good food and wine as well as beer. Liquor at the latter may cost more. Eating in a crowded pub is not always easy because the few tables are barely large enough to hold all the empty beer glasses, let alone food. Pub food is hearty but not especially imaginative: a ploughman's lunch, which is a hunk of bread and cheese plus pickle; cottage pie, which is ground meat with mashed potato on top baked in the oven; sausages; and sandwiches.

These are some of the best pubs: *Dirty Dick's,* 202 Bishopsgate EC2, is offbeat but popular, with fake bats and spiders hanging from the ceilings, sawdust on the floor, and good bar snacks; *Admiral Codrington,* 17 Mossop St. SW3, is large and Victorian, with brass beer pumps, engraved mirrors, and good food; *Dickens Inn* by the Tower, St. Katherine's Way E1, is a converted warehouse overlooking a colorful yacht marina and serving shellfish snacks; *George Inn,* 77 Borough High St. SE1, dates from 1676 and retains the original gallery for viewing Shakespearean plays in the summer; *The Flask,* 77 Highgate West Hill N6, serves drinks at three wood-paneled bars and on its outside patio; *The Lamb,* 94 Lamb's Conduit St. WC1, is also wood paneled and hung with photos of past music-hall performers; *Museum Tavern,* 49 Gt. Russell St. WC1, is across the road from the British Museum and decorated with hanging flower baskets; *Princess Louise,* 208 High Holborn WC1, has live music, cabaret, and a wine bar upstairs with good food; *Salisbury,* 90 St. Martin's La. WC2, is vintage late Victorian with ornate mirrors and a marble counter and has a gay clientele; *Bull and Bush,* North End Way NW3, dates to the seventeenth century and has a garden; *Prospect of Whitby,* 57 Wapping Wall E1, was once the haunt of thieves and smugglers, as the oldest riverside pub in London (now it draws jazz lovers); *Sherlock Holmes,* 10 Northumberland St. WC2, is dedicated to Holmesiana and excellent, made-to-order meat sandwiches; *Ye Olde Cheshire Cheese,* 145 Fleet St. EC4, is a seventeenth-century pub with paneled walls and sawdust floors popular with the Fleet Street set.

MADRID

Cobblestone plazas. Open-air cafés along shaded sidewalks. Late-night suppers. Classic art. Sensuous music. The lyrical Castilian tongue. Elegance and, most of all, the warmth of the *madrileños*. These are the things that give form to Madrid, the capital of Spain, center of the Iberian Peninsula, heart of the castle country, and home of the Prado, one of the world's most important art museums.

Madrid and the region of Castile have dominated the rest of Spain for five centuries, and Castilian is equated with Spanish when referring to the language, although other regional languages are used in the country. As is frequently true of a major metropolitan area, Madrid continually draws talent from other regions of the country with its glamour, its high standard of living, and its opportunities for success. (Per capita incomes in Madrid are twice the national average of about $4,000.) As a result, there is a lively mix of people who animate this strikingly handsome city, making capital life gay and charging it with energetic currents.

Madrid is a young city. What is considered Old Madrid actually dates only from the sixteenth and seventeenth centuries, from the reign of the Hapsburgs. According to legend, the city, called Mantua, was founded by Iberians and settled by Romans. Chronicles of the Middle Ages report that the Moors built a large fortress, Alcázar, here as a foreguard of the Arab kingdom of Toledo. But Madrid did not become important until the Hapsburg King Philip II moved the capital to this geographic crossroads in 1561.

This period of Hapsburg domination was also Spain's golden age in the arts, when such literary and artistic giants as Cervantes, Lope de Vega, Calderón, and Velázquez were attracted to the flourishing new cultural capital of the Spanish Empire. The spirit of this golden age is palpable in Old Madrid today. A walk through its winding, gaslit streets evokes memories of the days of courtiers with Walloon collars, long black capes, and flashing swords.

With the decline of the Hapsburg dynasty at the end of the seventeenth century, King Philip V, grandson of French King Louis IV, was entitled to the throne of Spain. After a brief war of succession, he established the Bourbon dynasty as the legitimate heir to the kingdom in 1700. The Bourbon monarchs systematically converted Madrid into a model city of the Enlightenment. A geometric pattern of wide avenues and streets was laid out, relieved by regular parks and fountains; museums and libraries were built; public works initiated; and cultural and scientific academies founded.

This steady progress of city and country foundered, though, in 1808, when the French were encouraged to invade Spain because of the weakness of Spain's Bourbon King Charles IV; Napoleon's bid for power was successful, and he was able to force the crowning of his brother, Joseph, as king of Spain.

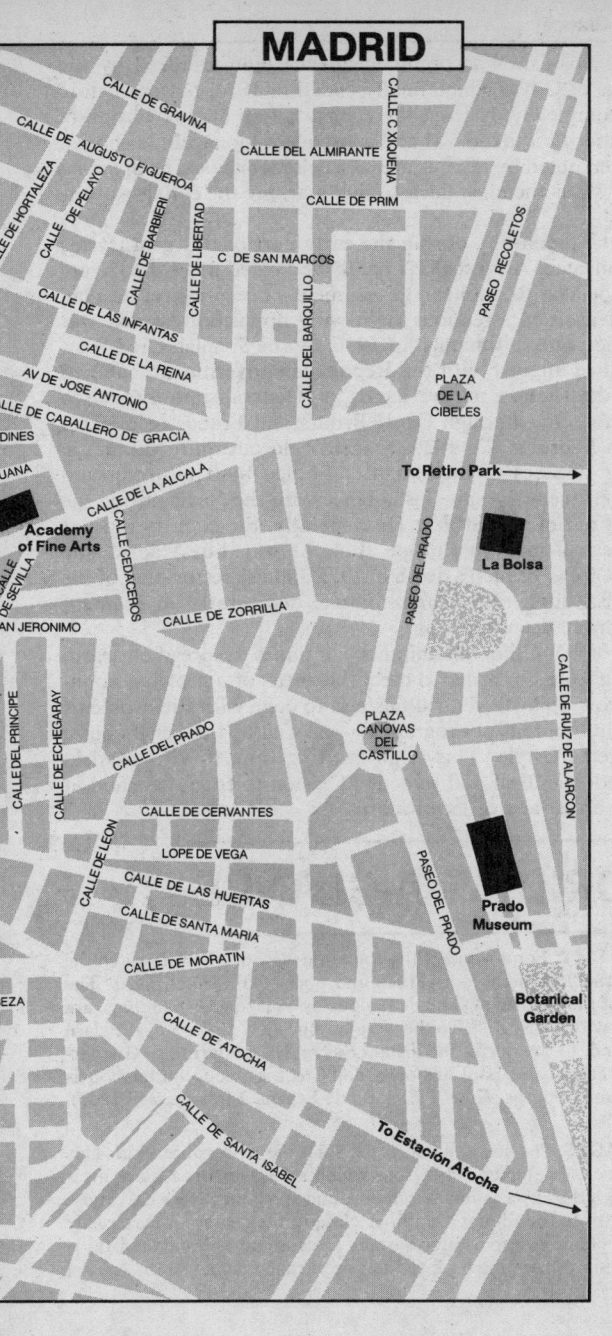

MADRID

CALLE DE GRAVINA

CALLE C XIQUENA

CALLE DEL ALMIRANTE

CALLE DE AUGUSTO FIGUEROA

CALLE DE PRIM

CALLE DE HORTALEZA

CALLE DE PELAYO

CALLE DE BARBIERI

CALLE DE LIBERTAD

C DE SAN MARCOS

PASEO RECOLETOS

CALLE DE LAS INFANTAS

CALLE DEL BARQUILLO

CALLE DE LA REINA

AV DE JOSE ANTONIO

PLAZA DE LA CIBELES

CALLE DE CABALLERO DE GRACIA

DINES

JUANA

CALLE DE LA ALCALA

To Retiro Park ⟶

CALLE CEDACEROS

PASEO DEL PRADO

Academy of Fine Arts

La Bolsa

CALLE DE SEVILLA

AN JERONIMO

CALLE DE ZORRILLA

CALLE DEL PRINCIPE

CALLE DE ECHEGARAY

PLAZA CANOVAS DEL CASTILLO

CALLE DE RUIZ DE ALARCON

CALLE DEL PRADO

CALLE DE CERVANTES

CALLE DE LEON

LOPE DE VEGA

CALLE DE LAS HUERTAS

CALLE DE SANTA MARIA

PASEO DEL PRADO

CALLE DE MORATIN

Prado Museum

BEZA

Botanical Garden

CALLE DE ATOCHA

CALLE DE SANTA ISABEL

To Estación Atocha ⟶

This gave rise to the Spanish War of Independence, immortalized by the paintings and etchings of Goya, which finally ended in 1814, but not before Madrid was almost completely destroyed. Reconstruction and expansion of the city proceeded under Ferdinand VII and subsequent monarchs, although it was periodically interrupted by revolutions and colonial wars. The Spanish-American War of 1898 was the most devastating, marking the collapse of the Spanish Empire.

The instability of the monarchy during the early part of this century led to further political upheaval. Alfonso XIII finally abdicated in 1931 to avoid a civil war. But the Socialist Republican government's decentralization plan and reform measures aroused strenuous right-wing opposition, which was followed by insurrection and, ultimately, in 1936, by the Spanish Civil War. Madrid, which remained aligned with the Republican government, suffered mass privation and destruction at the hands of Generalísimo Francisco Franco's Nationalist forces. Although Great Britain and France recognized the Franco regime on February 27, 1939, Madrid held out until March 28.

During nearly four decades of dictatorship, Franco built a strong and repressive central government. Despite his alliance with the Nazis during the Civil War, Spain kept out of World War II. Generally, the country did not keep pace with the rest of modern Europe after the war, but Madrid, the capital, prospered and grew. Franco's death in 1975 and the restoration of the monarchy and the institution of a representative, democratic government have been events of dramatic proportion.

Madrid, now a city of 4.5 million inhabitants, continues to spread outward, absorbing surrounding towns in order to meet the needs of a growing populace. In its effort to grow up fast, Madrid has had to cope with the problems — such as crime, pollution, and pornography — as well as the benefits of a modern, more liberated lifestyle. This is an exciting time to visit Madrid — as it attempts to redefine itself and refocus its vision to the future and at the same time preserve the best of its proud past.

MADRID AT-A-GLANCE

SEEING THE CITY: For a wonderfully romantic view of Madrid, watch the sun set from the 25th-floor roof garden and pool of the *Hotel Plaza*. The fluffy clouds of the Madrid sky, made famous by Velázquez's paintings, are usually tinted with a rosy hue. To the west is a fine view of the Royal Palace and its formal gardens and, to the north, the distant Sierra de Guadarrama (Guadarrama Mountains). The terrace and pool are open daily to the public (admission is charged) during the summer months. *Hotel Plaza,* Pl. de España 2 (phone: 247-1200).

SPECIAL PLACES: The bustling Puerta del Sol is the center of Madrid. This square is the zero kilometer mark from which all Spanish roads are measured. Although the city's radius is immense and spreading every day, those places of interest to the tourist are rather close to the center and are easily reached by the excellent public transportation system. Because post-Franco reform is in full swing, street names are changing back to their pre-Franco names; thus, Av. del

Generalísimo has become Paseo de la Castellana, Calle del General Mola is now Calle del Príncipe de Vergara, and so on. Check with hotel personnel or a taxi driver if you have doubts about an address or street name.

Prado Museum – The Prado is one of the three or four greatest museums in the world and the most important stop in Madrid for many visitors. It is magnificently rich in Spanish paintings and has a renowned collection of Flemish works collected by Spain's Catholic monarchs as well as a notable collection of Italian paintings. You enter the neoclassical building on the first floor, where a large central gallery is hung with major works of the painters of Spain's golden period (from the late sixteenth century to the eighteenth century): José Ribera's renowned *Martyrdom of St. Bartholomew;* Murillo's religious paintings; Velázquez's masterpieces, *The Spinners* and *Maids of Honor;* and the *Adoration of the Shepherds* and other religious paintings of El Greco. With Goya, Spanish painting regained its reputation in the eighteenth and nineteenth centuries. His work, including his strikingly honest portraits of royalty and the famous *Naked Maja* and *Maja Clothed,* is displayed in a gallery to the left of the Murillo collection. There are also special rooms devoted to Rubens and the Venetian school, including works by Titian, Veronese, and Tintoretto; and a fine collection of Renaissance art, represented by Raphael; and Flemish primitives such as Hieronymus Bosch and Hans Memling. The Prado owns one of Bosch's finest creations, *The Garden of Delights,* whose theme is sexuality and the transience of sexual pleasure.

On the ground floor, a special section is devoted to the tapestry cartoons designed by Goya for the Escorial (see *Extra Special*) and to his extraordinary *Disasters of War* etchings, which represent his thoughts and comments on the War of Independence. You will also find Goya's stunning *Second of May* and *Third of May* canvases. Opposite the Goya gallery is a gallery devoted to Spanish primitive and Renaissance painting. There are additional galleries devoted to less well known painters of Spain's golden period and to the Dauphin's Treasures: Greek, Roman, and Spanish sculpture and precious enamels, jewelry, and gold pieces that belonged to Louis XIV. The Prado has recently been expanded to provide additional space for exhibition of paintings formerly in storage and seen only on a rotating basis. As with any of the great museums, it is impossible to savor its wonders in a single visit. If time is limited, it is best to select a few galleries of special interest and devote yourself to them. Reproductions from the museum's collection, post cards, and fine art books are for sale at moderate prices at the shop near the exit. There's a cafeteria on the premises, which is open during museum hours. Closed Mondays. Small admission charge. Paseo de Prado (phone: 468-0950; 230-6204).

Retiro Park – The splendid trees of this large public park have been preserved for generations as a retreat. The 130-acre park shelters the Crystal Palace of the Bourbon kings. It has dozens of fountains, statues, formal flowerbeds, and a large rowing lake, Estanque, with a monument to Alfonso XII. On late summer evenings (at 11 PM) outdoor ballet performances are held in the park's theater. East of the Prado, along Alfonso XII and Alcalá.

Madrid's Squares – The most famous fountain in Madrid, and possibly in all of Spain, is in *Cibeles Square* a few blocks north of the Prado, once the crossroads of eighteenth-century Madrid. The fountain features a sculpture of the Greek goddess of fertility, Cybele, riding in a lion-drawn chariot, and is particularly impressive when lit up at night. A famous statue of Don Quixote, Sancho Panza, and Rocinante embellishes the *Plaza de España,* just north of the Royal Palace. To the east of the palace is *Plaza de Oriente,* dominated by one of the finest pieces of sculpture in Spain: a statue of Philip IV cast from a design by Velázquez. Between the Royal Palace and the Puerta del Sol is the large, cobblestoned *Plaza Mayor,* surrounded by seventeenth-century balconied buildings with graceful arches. This is an ideal spot for a refreshing glass of sangría.

Royal Palace – The neoclassic palace, built on the spot where the Alcázar once stood, was first occupied by Bourbon King Charles III in 1764. In addition to the fine paintings and furniture in the royal apartments, the Royal Armory (Real Armería) has one of the world's best collections of medieval arms and armor. There is also a museum of royal horse-drawn carriages that includes a black ebony vehicle from the seventeenth century. There are guided tours in English and, during summer months, a sound and light show in the Sabatini Gardens in the north part of the palace grounds. Open daily. Small admission fee. West of Plaza Mayor, on Calle de Bailén (phone: 248-7404).

Casa de Campo – *Madrileños* love to spend Sundays boating on the central lake of this huge park across the Manzanares from the Royal Palace. It has a zoo and an amusement park, *Parque de Atracciones,* with rides and entertainment at an outdoor theater rife with a gay carnival atmosphere. The amusement park can be reached by bus or by cable car, called the *teleférico,* from the station at Paseo del Pintor Rosales. Bring picnic food or eat at the park's restaurant. The zoo is open daily from April through September, and on Saturdays, Sundays, and holidays only from October through March. There is a small admission fee. Casa de Campo.

Streets of Old Madrid – The labyrinth of narrow lanes that constitute the oldest part of the city lies between Puerta del Sol and the Royal Palace. Each street or lane or alleyway is marked by a sign with its name and a descriptive picture, originally an aide for an illiterate seventeenth-century populace. *Elbow Street (Calle del Codo)* is marked by a picture of an armored elbow and the tiny *Bread Passageway (Pasadizo del Panecillo)* shows friars of the adjacent St. Michael's Basilica distributing bread to the poor. If you descend the stairway at the southwest corner of the Plaza Mayor, you'll pass through the *Archway of Knivesmen (Arco de Cuchilleros)* and enter an area of taverns and inns that evoke a past era of bandits and their hideouts. At night this area is alive with people "*tasca*-crawling," *madrileños* roaming from one pub *(tasca)* to another, enjoying different specialty tidbits and appetizers — from glorious mushrooms to squid cooked in their ink — that accompany your drinks at each little pub.

Archaeological Museum (Museo Arqueológico Nacional) – Among the Iberian and classical antiquities of special interest are the *Dama de Baza,* a goddess figure from the fourth century BC, and the *Dama de Elche,* an impressive polychrome stone head of a woman in a splendid headdress. The National Library is in the same building. Closed Mondays. A few blocks north of Pl. de la Cibeles. Calle Serrano 13 (phone: 403-6559).

■**EXTRA SPECIAL:** The massive monastery-palace of *San Lorenzo de El Escorial* was built on a foothill of the Sierra de Guadarrama by order of Philip II in the sixteenth century to celebrate his victory over France at St.-Quentin, Flanders. It took more than 1,500 workmen 21 years to complete this extraordinary, austere monument designed by Juan de Herrera. The gray granite edifice has hundreds of rooms and thousands of windows. While its architectural style is not to everyone's taste, El Escorial is, nevertheless, a sight never to be forgotten. The guided tour includes visits to the royal apartments, the museums, the royal pantheon with its tombs of Spanish monarchs, the library, and the church. Open daily, small admission charge. About 30 miles (48 km) northwest of Madrid. If you drive, take Route A6 to Guadarrama, then head south on Route C600. There is frequent train service to El Escorial from Madrid's Atocha and Recoletos stations.

En route, you may also want to visit the *Valley of the Fallen (Valle de los Caídos),* a spectacular memorial to those who died in the Spanish Civil War. A huge church, containing the coffins of soldiers from both sides who died in the war, has been hollowed into a mountain. Franco is also buried here. A cross stands 500 feet in the air atop the mountain peak. Open daily. Small parking charge. A few miles west off Rte. C600 near Guadarrama.

SOURCES AND RESOURCES

All Madrid hotels distribute street maps and magazines listing current events. Further information can be obtained from the Tourist Information Office (Oficina de Turismo), Princesa 1 (phone: 241-2325), and the special tourist volume of the telephone book.

For Local Coverage – Two English-language publications, *Guidepost Magazine* and the *Iberian Daily Sun,* are available at newsstands throughout the city. *Guidepost* carries the events of the week, indicates movies in English, and publishes its own list of Madrid's 100 best restaurants. For Spanish-speakers, Madrid's *Guía del Ocio* is the most complete weekly guide for food, entertainment, and sports.

CLIMATE AND CLOTHES: The average daily temperature in Madrid in August is 75°F (24°C), but days can be very hot and dry, and evenings cool from June to September. In January, the average daily temperature dips to 40°F (4°C). However, damp winds and inadequately heated buildings make sweaters and other warm clothes a necessity.

GETTING AROUND: Bus – Excellent, inexpensive bus service is available in Madrid. Signs clearly marking the routes are located at each bus stop. Some buses are entered from the rear. Microbuses cost a bit more — though still less than 50¢ — and are equipped with plush seats and airconditioning.

Subway – Madrid's Metro is rapid and efficient. Stops along all ten subway lines are clearly marked, and color-coded Metro maps are easy to read. Metro tickets purchased from booths or machines are put into electronic turnstiles as you enter the system. Do not discard your ticket until the end of the ride.

Taxi – Metered cabs are white with a diagonal red line. If a cab is available it will have a windshield sign that says *libre* or an illuminated green light on its roof. Fares are moderate.

Car Rental – All major international firms are represented.

MUSEUMS: Madrid has a number of interesting museums in addition to those described in *Special Places*. A morning visit is recommended, since many museums close in the early afternoon.

Folk Museum (Museo del Pueblo Español), Atocha 106 (phone: 228-5039).

Lázaro Galdiano Museum. Exquisite enamels, ivories, and paintings. Serrano 122 (phone: 261-6084).

Lope de Vega's House (Casa Museo de Lope de Vega). Recreation of the home and garden of the great Spanish dramatist. Calle Cervantes 11 (phone: 429-9216).

The Americas Museum (Museo de América). Pre-Columbian artifacts and American and Philippine crafts. Av. R. Católicos 6 (phone: 243-9437).

Colón Waxworks Museum (Museo Cera Colón), Plaza Colón (phone: 419-2282).

Descalzas Reales Convent (Convento de las Descalzas Reales), Pl. de las Descalzas Reales (phone: 222-0687).

Royal Tapestry Factory (Real Fábrica de Tapices), Fuenterrabía 2 (phone: 251-3400).

Museo Panteon de Goya (Ermita de San Antonio). Cupola fresco by Goya. Paseo de la Florida (phone: 247-7921).

Bullfighting Museum (Museo Taurino), Pl. de Toros Monumental (phone: 255-1857).

San Francisco el Grande Church, Calle de Bailén, 44.

Contemporary Art Museum (Museo de Arte Contemporáneo), Av. Juan de Herrera 2 (phone: 449-7150).

SHOPPING: Fine Spanish leathergoods, Lladró porcelains, silver jewelry, and needlework are particularly good buys in Madrid. Shops generally open at 9:30 AM, close from 1:30 to 4:30 PM for lunch and siesta, and close for the night at 8:30 PM. Madrid's two main department stores, *El Corte Inglés,* Preciados 3 (phone: 232-8100), and *Galerías Preciados,* Arapiles 10–12 (phone: 446-3200), do not close in the afternoon and are particularly helpful to tourists, even providing interpreters who accompany you while you shop.

Herrero – High-quality shearling, leather, suede, and fur goods. Gran Vía 51. *Rodero,* down the street at number 80, carries the same type and quality of merchandise.

El Rastro – The flea market behind the Plaza Mayor (it starts at the Plaza Cascorro) is fun to visit, especially on Sunday mornings, even if you're only browsing for copper, brass, ironwork, embroidery, china, or tiles. Don't pay the first price asked, and watch your wallet.

ESE – Favorite tourist souvenirs at discount prices. Juan Hurtado de Mendoza 5.

Loewe – The renowned leather house. Gran Vía 8 and Serrano 26.

National Handicraft Center – Top-quality Spanish handicrafts. Gran Vía 32.

Zurro – Gloves made to order. Preciados 16.

SPECIAL EVENTS: Most festivals in Madrid center around celebrations of favorite saints' days. The *Festival of San Isidro* begins May 15 and ushers in Madrid's bullfight season. On June 13, young women make a colorful pilgrimage to the Hermitage of San Antonio de la Florida to light a candle and pray to this matchmaking saint for a boyfriend. Madrid's biggest celebration is the festival of *La Paloma,* July 15 to August 15, which is characterized by an outdoor carnival and dancing. On *New Year's Eve,* crowds gather at the Puerta del Sol and eat a grape at every stroke of the clock at midnight to ensure good luck.

SPORTS: Bullfighting – Although not universally appreciated, bullfighting is the most renowned sport of Spain — Spaniards insist it is an art — and the largest bullfighting ring in Madrid is *Las Ventas,* Pl. de Toros Monumental, which seats 22,300 people. There is also a smaller ring, *Vista Alegre,* near the Metro stop Vista Alegre. The season runs from May 15 through October 1. Tickets may be purchased a day in advance at a counter at Calle Victoria 9, near the Puerta del Sol.

Golf – Three fine private 27-hole golf courses are found at the *Club Deportivo Las Lomas–El Bosque* in Boadilla del Monte (phone: 633-0899); *Club de Campo,* Carretera de Castilla (phone: 207-0395); and *Puerta de Hierro Club,* La Coruña Highway (phone: 216-1745). Hotels can provide information regarding private entry into these clubs.

Horse Racing – The *Hipódromo de la Zarzuela,* La Coruña Highway, 4 miles (7 km) north of the city, features Sunday afternoon races during spring and fall meetings. Buses for the track leave from Calle Princesa and Hilarión Eslava.

Jai Alai – Matches are scheduled twice daily, at 5 PM and 11 PM at the *Frontón Madrid,* Dr. Cortezo 10 (phone: 239-1037). Betting action is lively and the stakes consistently high.

Swimming – Madrid has 20 public swimming pools, including *Stella,* Arturo Soria 231; *El Lago,* Av. de Valladolid 37.

THEATER: Theater productions are in Spanish only, but ballets, operas, and operettas, *zarzuelas,* have universal appeal and are inexpensive. Check local listings for the *Teatro de la Zarzuela,* Jovellanos 4 (phone: 429-8216), and the *Centro Cultural de la Villa,* Pl. de Colón (phone: 275-6080).

MUSIC: *Bolero* and *fandango* are the typically Castilian dances and *flamenco* is Andalusian, but it is the latter most tourists want to see, so there are numerous flamenco cabarets in Madrid. Two of the best are *Café de Chinitas,* Torija 7 (phone: 248-5135), and *Torres Bermejas,* Mesonero Romanos 11 (phone: 232-3322). Classical music concerts are held Saturdays and Sundays at the *Teatro Real,* Plaza de Oriente 4 (phone: 241-9739), and there are free recitals on certain weekdays at *Fundación Juan March,* Castelló 77 (phone: 435-4240, 435-4840), and *Sala Fénix,* Castellana 37.

NIGHTCLUBS AND NIGHTLIFE: Nightlife in Madrid used to go on all night, but many clubs close at 2 or 3 AM, these days. Cover charges at cabarets and nightclubs include one drink, dancing, and floor shows that are becoming more risqué by the night. Top choices include *Scala-Meliá Castilla,* Capitán Haya 43 (phone: 450-4400), and *Pasapoga,* Gran Vía 37 (phone: 221-5027). Discotheques and boîtes run two sessions a night, at 7 PM and 11 PM. Among the more popular are *Pachá,* Barceló 11 (phone: 446-0137); *Boccaccio,* Marqués de la Ensenada 16 (phone: 419-1008); and *Cleofa's,* Goya 7 (phone: 276-4523). Striptease shows are the attraction at *Alazán,* Castellana 24 (phone: 276-4058). Among the popular gay bars are *Gay Club,* Paseo del Prado 48 (phone: 468-3344); *Rey Fernando,* Prim 9 (phone: 231-5561); and *Los Centauros,* Santa Barbara 10 (phone: 232-6523).

SINS: Whether mortal or venial, the sins of Madrid are always of the flesh. High jinks are had for a price in select bars along the streets of Capitán Haya and Dr. Fleming, and "special" messages are advertised in the classified ad section of the daily newspapers and telephones numbers are listed in *Guía del Ocio.* Topless bars are back again, and "suggestive" floor shows can be seen at *Montmatre Boite Club,* Libertad 28 (phone: 231-8580), and at *Don "Q,"* Paseo de la Castellana 83 (phone: 455-7769).

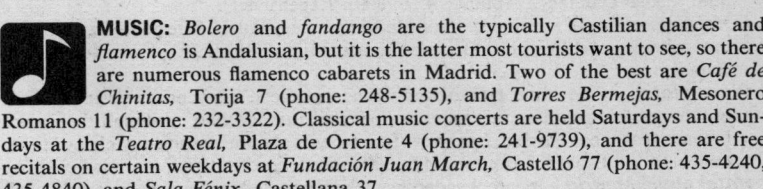

BEST IN TOWN

CHECKING IN: As of 1979, the Spanish government deregulated fixed prices in all hotels. Expect to pay $65 to $95 a night for a double room in an expensive hotel; from $30 to $60 in a moderately priced hotel; and from $20 to $30 in the inexpensive category. Double rooms in *pensiones* and *residencias,* without baths, are available at less than $20 a night.

Villa Magna – A tower of glass and marble with landscaped gardens in the heart of aristocratic Madrid, this hotel offers luxury service and spacious rooms. The hotel's *Rue Royale* restaurant is run by *Maxim's* of Paris. Paseo de Castellana 22 (phone: 261-4900). Very expensive.

Hotel Ritz – Old world graciousness, impeccable service, and sumptuously decorated rooms. The hotel, which still requires men to wear jackets and ties in most of its public areas, is quite near the Prado. Plaza Lealtad 5 (phone: 221-2857). Very expensive.

Eurobuilding Hotel – An extremely well designed modern hotel that manages to serve two masters without strain. In its 150-room tower are single and double rooms for individuals; another wing, with 400 units, is designed for group tour travel. The twain rarely meet, and when they do (usually around one of the hotel's two pools), there is little of the friction that is generated in less well designed hotels. Other facilities include complete business and convention services and a health club. Padre Damián 23 (phone: 457-7800). Expensive.

Hotel Miguel Angel – The newest of Madrid's luxury hotels. The good-sized rooms are well appointed, and most have balconies. Miguel Angel 29 (phone: 442-8199). Expensive.

Plaza Hotel – The same mix of individual travelers, convention business, and businesspeople populate this hotel as does the *Eurobuilding,* although the mood is somewhat more harried. But views from rooms are fine despite any chaos in the lobby. Pl. de España 2 (phone: 247-1200). Moderate.

Hotel Meliá Madrid – Ideally located near the Plaza de España and extremely well run. Rooms in this gleaming white, modern hotel are tastefully decorated in various styles. The dining room, grill, bar, and *Bong Bing* discotheque are popular meeting places. Princesa 27 (phone: 241-8200). Expensive to moderate.

Hotel Suecia – Friendly management and pleasant ambience, a few blocks from Plaza de Cibeles. In addition to comfortably redecorated rooms, the hotel offers excellent dining in its *Bellman Restaurant,* where a prix fixe smørgasbord is the main attraction. Major credit cards. Marqués de Casa Riera 4 (phone: 231-6900). Moderate.

Hotel Mayorazgo – Excellent service and well-appointed rooms just a step from the city's heartbeat at Gran Vía. The decor provides a retreat to a pleasant Castilian past. Flor Baja 3 (phone: 247-2600). Moderate.

Hotel Arosa – Although it has 126 rooms, it retains the atmosphere of a small hotel. The rooms, no two of which are exactly alike, are small and very elegant; and the bathrooms, with built-in hair dryers and lidded bidets, are the most luxurious in any smallish Madrid hotel. There's also a full-service restaurant around the corner. Calle Salud, Gran Via 29 (phone: 232-1600). Moderate.

Hotel Serrano – Refined and immaculate, its marble-floored lobby is richly decorated with antiques, including a large seventeenth-century tapestry, comfortable furnishings, and huge arrangements of fresh flowers. No restaurant, but snacks and sandwiches are available at the bar. 34 rooms. Marques de Villamejor 8 (phone: 435-5200). Moderate.

Hotel Calatrava – Contemporary couches and antique desks in the lobby are set off by prints of English fox hunting and horse racing scenes. The 99 rooms are brightly decorated with green bedspreads and matching headboards, and all have air-conditioning, color TV, and minibars. The hotel has a full-service restaurant and bar. Tutor 1 (phone: 241-9880). Moderate.

Hotel Londres – This well-scrubbed hostelry, just a short walk from Madrid's major department stores, has 57 rooms. Be warned: some have only shower stalls, with sinks and toilets down the hall. Only breakfast is served, though with a little notice, owner Milagros (her name means "miracles") will prepare a tasty assortment of sandwiches for lunch. Galdo 2 (phone: 231-4105). Inexpensive.

Hostal Jamyc – A small deluxe pension centrally located near the Prado and Parliament. Pl. de las Cortés 4 (phone: 429-0068). Inexpensive.

Hostal Don Diego – A well-kept pension near the Retiro Park. Several rooms have ample balconies. Velázquez 45 (phone: 435-0760). Inexpensive.

 EATING OUT: *Madrileños* eat the main meal of their day during the 2 to 4 PM work break. An early evening snack such as wine and appetizers or coffee and sweets takes the edge off appetites until a light supper is eaten after 10 PM. If you can't adjust to the Spanish schedule, there are always cafeterias and snack bars, and many restaurants start serving dinner at about 8:30 PM to accommodate non-Spaniards. Expensive restaurants will charge from $45 to $80 for a dinner for two with wine; expect to pay between $25 and $45 for similar fare at moderately priced restaurants; and something under $25 at inexpensive restaurants.

Jockey – This intimate, 18-table restaurant is internationally recognized for its outstanding French cuisine and impeccable service. Open daily, except Sundays and the month of August. Amador de los Ríos 6 (phone: 419-2435). Expensive.

Horcher – Although the original owner, Otto Horcher, has died, the Continental cuisine, service, and above all else, taste and style of this grand restaurant have not faltered or failed. Eating here is an experience in luxury, an indulgence that should include such excesses as baby lamb à la Castilian, endive salad (with truffles), and crêpes Sir Holten for dessert. Reservations are a must. Open daily; closed Sundays. Alfonso XII 6 (phone: 222-0731). Expensive.

Cabo Mayor – This is a current favorite in town, and deservedly so. The menu is primarily *montanes* — from northern Spain — with tasty fish and other seafood dishes served in a very pleasing setting. Closed Sundays. Reservations necessary. Juan Hurtado de Mendoza 11-13 posterior (phone: 250-8776). Expensive.

Gure-Etxea – This is the best Basque cuisine in Madrid, with specialties such as *porrusalda*, a leek and potato soup with cod, and a variety of fish dishes. Not to be missed. Reservations suggested. Pl. de la Paja 12 (phone: 265-6149). Expensive.

Principe de Viana – Basque cuisine is served in a relaxed, elegant atmosphere. Closed Saturday lunch and Sundays. Manuel de Falla 5 (phone: 259-1448). Expensive.

La Dorada – Fresh seafood of every imaginable variety is flown in daily to this mammoth establishment, but you must be willing to ignore the noise, crowds, and rushed service in order to enjoy it. Reservations essential. Closed Sundays. Orense 64-66 (phone: 270-2002). Expensive.

Antigua Casa Sobrino de Botín – A favorite with celebrities from Hemingway to top bullfighters, this fine restaurant is known for its roasts of baby lamb and suckling pig. Ask for a table in the cellar, or *bodega*, for atmosphere. If you are still here at about 11 PM, you can enjoy a serenade by the strolling minstrels clad in traditional seventeenth-century dress. They are really a local college group called the Tuna. Open daily. Calle Cuchilleros 17 (phone: 266-4217). Moderate.

Casa Paco – The steaks served in this old tavern are the best in town. Closed Sundays and the month of August. Puerta Cerrada 11 (phone: 266-3166). Moderate.

La Ribera del Ebro – Cuisine from the Rioja region of Spain and wine in *porrones* (glass bottles with long drinking spouts) make this charmingly decorated restaurant a tasteworthy experience. Daily specials are recited by the waiters, and after-dinner *pacharán* (sloe liqueur) and chocolate-covered fruits are on the house. You may catch the Tuna (strolling minstrels) here too. Capitán Haya 51 (phone: 279-7080). Moderate.

Darío's – A true "find," known primarily to *madrileños*. The Castilian decor is simple, but the menu is extensive and the portions, giant-sized. Joaquín María Lopéz 30 (phone: 243-3043). Inexpensive.

Casa Gallega – Huge portions of top-quality meats and seafood make this Galician restaurant a favorite with local residents. Bordadores 11 (phone: 241-9055). Inexpensive.

El Callejón – A favorite Hemingway haunt, this restaurant is not the least bit fancy, but it serves excellent Castilian fare and is conveniently located just off the Gran Vía. Callejón Ternera 6 (phone: 222-5401). Inexpensive.

Foster's Hollywood – Serves the chicest hamburgers in town. If you're craving familiar food, right down to apple pie, this is the place. Magallanes 1 (phone: 448-9165). Inexpensive.

MARSEILLE

Some cities pass through a chrysalis stage as important ports before they emerge into greatness as commercial centers or industrial powers. Not so Marseille. As it has been for 25 centuries, since before the Greeks controlled the wine-dark seas of the Mediterranean, modern Marseille is above all else a port city. In 600 BC, Phocaean Greeks from Asia Minor founded the city, calling it Massalia, and then, as now, it acted as port of entry for goods, people, ideas, and most of all, history. (A commemorative block near Marseille's thriving Vieux Port proclaims with perfect accuracy and stunning lack of modesty: "They founded Marseille, from which civilization reached the West.")

With a population just brushing one million, Marseille is among France's largest cities. But that may say more about the importance of the Mediterranean to France than of France's influence on Marseille. Landlocked Paris, so gay in springtime and so gray in winter, is another country, 500 miles away, every mile of which must be traveled on land. It is a journey that traditional Marseillais, otherwise so effusive and warm, are reluctant to make. Marseille and its people face steadfastly toward the sea, from which they have always drawn such strength.

When the city provisioned the Crusaders and welcomed back their booty, it was trading with Africa, the Near East, and the Far East. Today the names have changed, but France's major port does business with the same countries, and a lot more besides. Marseillais have as much in common with Italians and Greeks — fellow Mediterraneans — as they do with Parisians.

Unlike Paris, which has become predictable and bourgeois by comparison, Marseille is France's connection to the sensuous world of the Mediterranean. Sailors from all over the world roam the Canebière, the famous street leading up from the Vieux Port (old port) in search of women, excitement, or perhaps a little bit of smuggling on the side on their next tour of duty. And occasionally violence still erupts, as it did in the gangland murder at the *Bar du Téléphone* not too many years ago. The milieu of the French underworld endures as a presence, for Marseille remains, as both Interpol and Hollywood would have it, "the French connection." Even though many of the drug middlemen have gone to Amsterdam, perhaps, or to Berlin, Gene Hackman would still recognize the place. But an odd question lingers: Do we consider port cities wicked because of Marseille, or do we feel such thrilling wickedness in Marseille because it is so much the port city of our dreams?

As in all great port cities, numerous foreigners and immigrants have settled in Marseille — particularly industrial workers from the island of Corsica and a large number of North Africans. Often poor, Algerians, Tunisians, and Moroccans live in slums around the Porte d'Aix and the rue Ste.-Barbe, where shops sell North African items so cheaply, but where few people feel comfortable wandering after dark.

Life is lived boisterously in the Marseille streets, particularly in the area around the Vieux Port, which is now a harbor for pleasure boats and for sidewalk restaurants offering bouillabaisse. Although German bombs knocked out much of the picturesque but seedy old quarter during World War II, some reminders of Marseille's tradition still survive.

From the beginning, the city prospered at the hands of the Greek traders, declined under Roman rule, and was revived by the Crusaders, whom Marseille supplied with food and weapons. Devastated by the great plague in 1720, in which 50,000 of its citizens perished, Marseille rose again to support the French Revolution with enthusiasm. In 1792, 500 volunteers marched to Paris, singing a new war song composed at Strasbourg by a young officer named Rouget de Lisle. All the way to Paris, the Marseillais sang the new song with Mediterranean exuberance. Practice improved their performance, so that when the troops reached Paris, their expert chorus electrified all listeners. The song caught on and became France's stirring national anthem, named not for the city but for those staunch choristers: *La Marseillaise.*

One hundred years later, the opening of the Suez Canal virtually assured Marseille's continued maritime supremacy, and commercial traffic abandoned the small Vieux Port for a new one directly to the north. The new port was also destroyed during World War II, but it was rebuilt and expanded. Flat, nondescript, and soulless buildings have risen on the once vibrant site of the old quarter. Ironically, every new groundbreaking brings the possibility of unearthing still more traces of earlier civilizations, like the Roman docks discovered in the 1940s or the Greek ramparts found in 1967. Medieval churches now stand side by side with steel and glass apartment buildings.

Many of Marseille's visitors are heading off to the Côte d'Azur and are in the city only to change trains at the newly rebuilt Gare St.-Charles or planes at the modern Aéroport de Marignane. But there's sufficient reason to linger. Step into a café on the Vieux Port as the burning Mediterranean sun starts to sink in the sky and order a milky white *pastis,* an aniseed-flavored aperitif. Around you are spectacular white limestone hills and in front, a harbor filled with the cries and accents of far-off lands. Drink it all in, along with your *pastis.* Who knows? You may, like the American writer M. F. K. Fisher, fall in love with Marseille and stay longer, soaking in its rich Mediterranean atmosphere and exploring its abundant historic remains.

MARSEILLE AT-A-GLANCE

SEEING THE CITY: Take the number 60 bus up to this hilly city's most imposing height, a 531-foot limestone bluff that is crowned by the Basilica of Notre-Dame-de-la-Garde. There's an extraordinary view — particularly at sunset — from the church's terrace: The boats on the Vieux Port, the white rocky islands, and the densely built city stretch out below. The half-Roman,

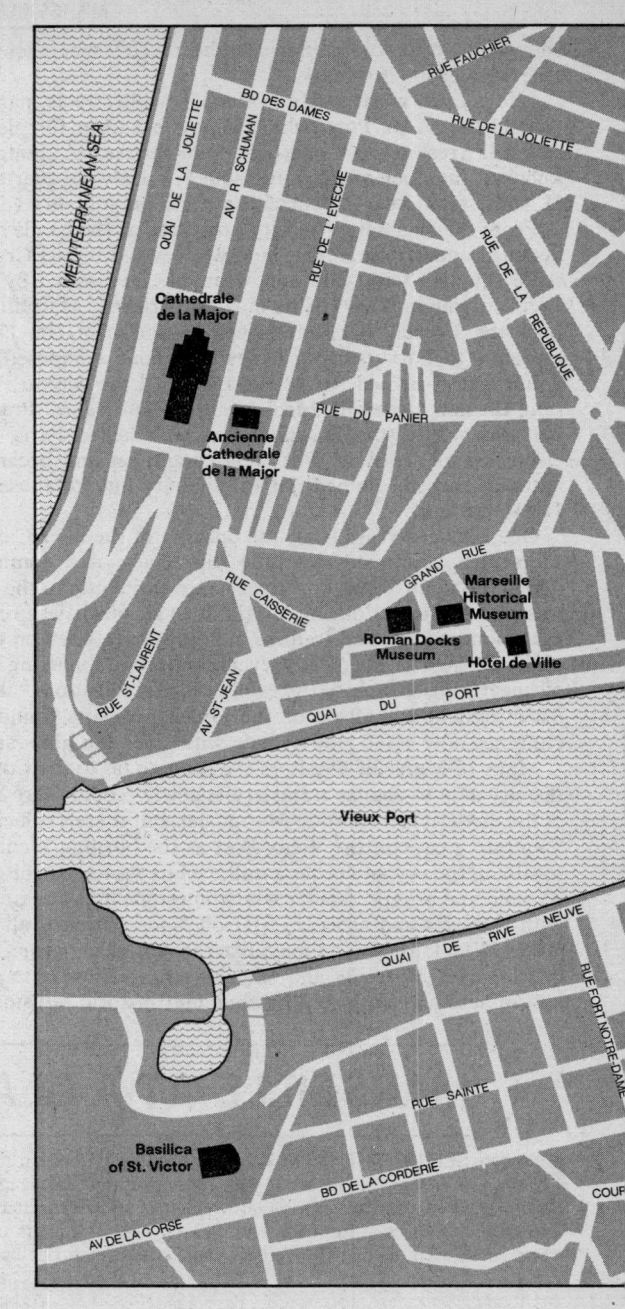

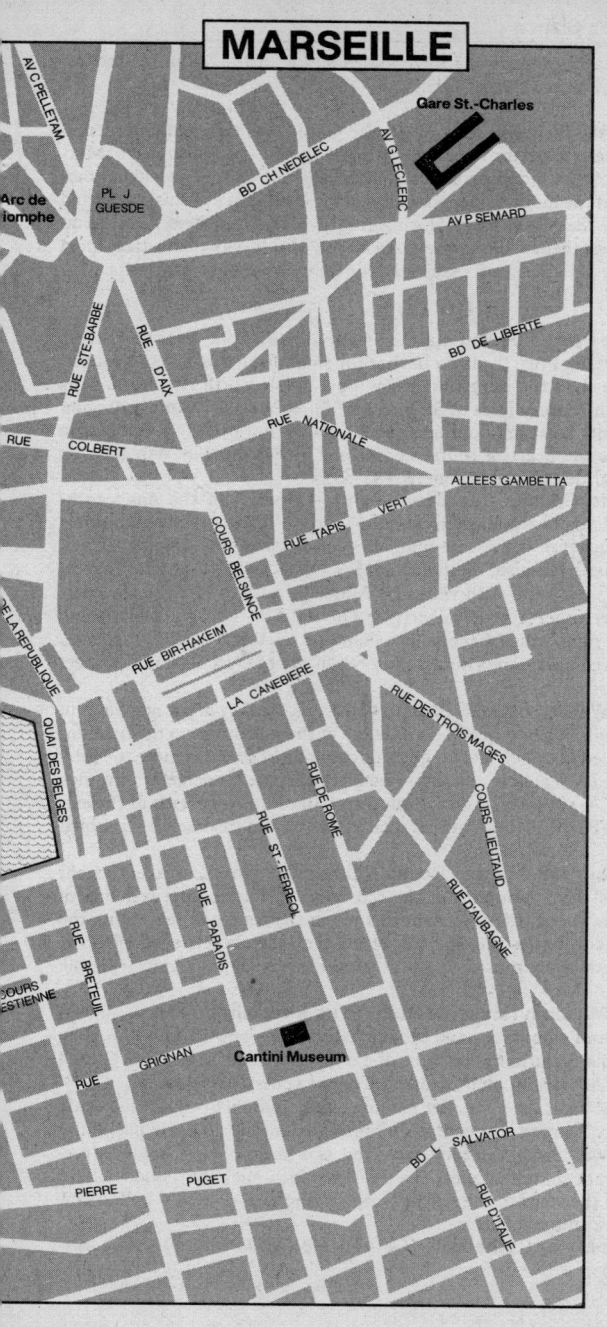

MARSEILLE

Gare St.-Charles

AV C PELLETAM

Arc de iomphe

PL J GUESDE

BD CH NEDELEC

AV G LECLERC

AV P SEMARD

RUE STE-BARBE

RUE D'AIX

BD DE LIBERTE

RUE COLBERT

RUE NATIONALE

ALLEES GAMBETTA

RUE

VERT

COURS BELSUNCE

RUE TAPIS

DE LA REPUBLIQUE

RUE BIR-HAKEIM

QUAI DES BELGES

LA CANEBIERE

RUE DES TROIS MAGES

RUE DE ROME

COURS LIEUTAUD

RUE ST-FERREOL

RUE D'AUBAGNE

RUE PARADIS

RUE BRETEUIL

COURS ESTIENNE

GRIGNAN

Cantini Museum

RUE

PIERRE

PUGET

BD L SALVATOR

RUE D'ITALIE

half-Byzantine basilica itself, topped by a huge gilded statue of the Virgin, is far less
of a draw than its view. Pl. du Colonel Eden.

 **SPECIAL PLACES:** If you walk down the Gare St.-Charles's monumental
staircase and continue on the boulevard d'Athènes, you'll come to Mar-
seille's busy central shopping street, the Canebière. Visitors are sometimes
disappointed at the modern, occasionally tacky appearance of this celebrated
boulevard that runs into the Vieux Port. During the Middle Ages there were hemp
fields here, or *chénevières* (hence the name Canebière); the broad plane tree–lined
concourse is still the key artery — and essential reference point — of Marseille.

IN THE CITY

The Old Port (Vieux Port) – Follow the Canebière down to the quai des Belges
and you'll arrive at the Vieux Port. Today a harbor for small fishing boats and yachts,
it's far more picturesque than the burgeoning new port to the north. Its entrance is
framed by the seventeenth-century forts of St. Jean and St. Nicholas (a Foreign Legion
base). Terraced restaurants hawking bouillabaisse (at staggering prices) overlook the
animated marina. This is the heart of Marseille. A tour of the entire harbor area by
boat leaves from the quai des Belges (phone: 90-47-33).

Museum of Fine Arts (Musée des Beaux-Arts) – Housed in the nineteenth-
century Palais de Longchamp — noteworthy in its own right for impressive fountains
and gardens (and even a zoo) — the museum offers a considerable display of art.
Paintings from the Italian, Flemish, Dutch, and French (David, Courbet, Ingres)
schools share the palace's left wing with works by Marseille natives Honoré Daumier
and Pierre Puget and by other Provençal artists. On the first floor is a charming
children's museum. The right wing of the palace contains a natural history museum.
Closed Tuesdays and Wednesday mornings. Admission charge. Pl. Bernex (phone:
62-21-17).

Outdoor Markets – Wander through the city's raucous market areas and take in
their vivid sights and smells. They're particularly alive in the mornings on the quai des
Belges, where the fishermen and their wives sell their catch directly. Also, note the food
market on rue Longue des Capucins (at rue Vacon, near the Canebière); the flea
markets near the Porte d'Aix (that is, the triumphal arch in pl. Jules-Guesde at the end
of rue d'Aix); and rue St.-Barbe in the Algerian quarter (but avoid this racially troubled
area after dark).

Roman Docks Museum (Musée des Docks Romains) – An unexpected benefit
came from the Germans' 1943 bombing of the old quarter. Fascinating remains of
long-buried Roman docks and statuary were unearthed in the course of rebuilding the
area, and the museum incorporates the original setting plus objects retrieved offshore.
Closed Tuesdays and Wednesday mornings. Admission charge. 28 pl. Vivaux. (phone:
73-21-60).

Marseille Historical Museum (Musée d'Histoire de Marseille) – Excavations of
the ancient Greek port and ramparts have become Marseille's newest museum. The
open-air archaeological dig features the remains of a boat excavated on the site. Closed
Sundays and Mondays. Admission charge. 3 rue Colbert (phone: 90-42-22).

Le Panier – From the quai du Port, the narrow streets climb toward what little
remains of Old Marseille. Reminiscent of Paris's Montmartre (and likewise beginning
to suffer the same "renewal" fate), the Panier quarter is a maze of tiny streets rever-
berating with the exuberant sounds of daily life in a Provençal neighborhood. Behind
the Hôtel de Ville, climb the steps to the left of Notre-Dame des Accoules' bell tower,
the remains of a twelfth-century church.

La Major and Old La Major Cathedrals (Cathédrales de la Major) – Reminiscent of Moslem mosques, the cathedrals' domes and cupolas dominate the quai de la Tourette. The sadly battered *Ancienne (Old) Major* was built in the twelfth century in pure Romanesque style on the ruins of the Roman Temple of Diana. The huge, ostentatious cathedral next to it was built in the nineteenth century in a Romanesque/ Byzantine style. Pl. de la Major.

Basilica of St. Victor (Basilique St.-Victor) – The present fortified Gothic church dates from the eleventh to the fourteenth century, but the real interest lies below, in its crypt, which is actually an ancient basilica founded in the fifth century in honor of the third-century martyr St. Victor. This basilica contains a chapel and the tomb of two third-century martyrs in addition to pagan and early Christian catacombs. Crypt closed Sundays. Admission charge. Pl. St.-Victor (phone: 33-25-86).

Cité Radieuse – Designed by the renowned Le Corbusier, the seventeen-story housing development — or *unité d'habitation*—was avant-garde for its time (1947–52) and is still a landmark in modern functional architecture. 280 blvd. Michelet.

Parc Borély – This is a lovely stretch of greenery where you can take some sun by the lake, rent a bicycle, or visit three museums on the premises: the Château Borély, the Archaeological Museum in the château, or the Lapidary Museum in an adjoining annex (see below for details about each museum). There's also a quaint racetrack on the same site. The park itself closes after dark. Promenade de la Plage and ave. Clot-bey.

Château Borély – Built by a rich businessman between 1767 and 1778, the château contains fine eighteenth-century salons. Closed Tuesdays and Wednesday mornings. Admission charge. Parc Borély (phone: 73-21-60).

Archaeological Museum (Musée d'Archéologie) – This museum, located in the Château Borély, has Egyptian, Greek, and Roman pieces, including ceramics, bronzes, and antique glass. Parc Borély (phone: 73-21-60).

Lapidary Museum – In a structure adjacent to the Château Borély with an archaeological garden, this museum contains Greek, Roman, and Christian art, including sarcophagi and marine antiquities. Parc Borély (phone: 73-21-60).

OUT OF TOWN

Promenade de la Corniche – This scenic coast road that winds for some 3 miles south of the Vieux Port passes in its course Marseille's most spectacular homes and a breathtaking view of the sea and the islands, including the Château d'If and the Frioul Islands (see below). Also known as the Corniche Président-J.-F.-Kennedy, it passes a picture-postcard fishing port, Vallon des Auffes, and lovely rocky coves before it becomes the promenade de la Plage (with Parc Borély) and continues toward Cassis, a beautiful fishing town, now also a summer resort, that was celebrated by Derain, Vlaminck, Matisse, and Dufy. Cassis is 14 miles (22 km) from Marseille; pick up Corniche J.-F.-Kennedy, at rue des Catalans.

Château d'If – Set on a rocky island, this beautiful castle was built in the sixteenth century for defense and then turned into a state prison, whose most famous "guest" was Alexander Dumas's count of Monte Cristo. Inside some cells are carvings by Huguenot prisoners. The château is open daily for a small admission charge and can be reached by boats that leave about every 15 minutes for a 20-minute ride from the quai des Belges (phone: 90-47-33).

Frioul Islands – These islands southwest of Marseille have sparkling creeks that provide an idyllic retreat from the city's sometimes torrid atmosphere. Boats leave for the islands from the quai des Belges every 15 minutes (phone: 90-47-33).

■**EXTRA SPECIAL:** For unsurpassed and unspoiled natural beauty, don't leave the region without seeing its spectacular *calanques* along the coast between Marseille and Cassis. The *calanques* are crystal-clear narrow creeks running between stark white limestone cliffs that soar up to 650 feet, much like small fjords. They can be approached only by foot (about an hour and a half each way) or by boat, thereby ensuring a minimum number of tourists. The closest *calanques* — Sormiou and Morgiou — can be reached from Roy d'Espagne (take bus number 44) and Les Baumettes (number 22), respectively. For information on organized hiking ventures, visit Les Excursionnistes Marseillais, 33 Allées Léon Gambetta, from 6 to 8 PM daily except Sundays and Mondays. Otherwise, leave by boat from quai des Belges (phone: 90-47-33).

SOURCES AND RESOURCES

The English-speaking staff of the Office du Tourisme, 4 La Canebière (phone: 54-91-11), provides hotel reservations, maps, guides, and advice. For information in the US, contact the French Government Tourist Office, 610 Fifth Ave., New York, NY 10020 (phone: 212-757-1125).

For a closer look at Marseille, read *A Considerable Town,* by the American M. F. K. Fisher — a charming and personal account of a city she loves.

A good street-indexed map is the *Carte et Plan Fréjet,* which you can buy at major bookstores along the Canebière. They also carry general English-language guidebooks, but no local English publications exist.

For Local Coverage – If you read French, pick up *Le Mois à Marseille* or *Poche Soir* for current events.

 CLIMATE AND CLOTHES: The Mediterranean climate is dry and joyously sunny 300 days a year, with warm summer temperatures in the high 80s F (30° to 32°C) and mild winter temperatures that rarely go below 40°F (4°C). It rains in spring and fall in brief but heavy downpours. The city can be windy, with the capricious *Mistral* whipping down the Rhône at up to 65 miles an hour and lasting anywhere from a few hours to a few days.

 GETTING AROUND: Bus and Métro – Marseille's attractive new subway system is coordinated with the buses, allowing easy — and free — transfers between systems. Buy a *carnet* of six tickets instead of the single ticket. The Métro shuts down each night at 12:30 AM and most buses earlier. (For information phone: 47-48-60.)

Taxi – There are cabstands around the city or you can phone 95-92-50 or 02-20-20.

Car Rental – Major international firms are represented.

Ferry – For ferries to Corsica, inquire at SNCM, 61 blvd. des Dames (phone: 91-92-20).

 MUSEUMS: Besides those described in *Special Places,* other notable Marseille museums are:

   Musée Cantini – Provençal ceramics and contemporary art exhibits. 19 rue Grignan (phone: 54-77-75).

Musée Grobet-Labadié – Louis XV and XVI furniture, antique musical instruments, Delacroix paintings. 140 blvd. Longchamp (phone: 62-21-82).

Musée du Vieux Marseille – A folklore museum set up in a sixteenth-century house, the Maison Diamamtée, and best known for its *santon* collection (see *Shopping*). Rue de la Prison (phone: 55-10-19).

All museums have an admission charge (except Sunday mornings) and are closed Tuesdays, Wednesday mornings, and at midday (noon to 2 PM).

SHOPPING: Major department stores and elegant couturier and gift shops are clustered in the frenetic area around the Canebiére (rue de Rome and rue St.-Ferréol). The new Centre Bourse shopping center is north of the Canebiére. Cheaper shops, usually selling North African items, are in the vicinity of the Porte d'Aix (Arc de Triomphe).

Typical Marseillais souvenirs include clay *santons,* which can be found in tourist shops or at numerous booths set up for the Christmas Santons Fair. The word *santon* is derived from the Italian *santibelli,* meaning "the beautiful saints." These small, naively modeled and brightly colored figurines represent both biblical figures and traditional characters of Provence life such as the gypsy, the shepherd, and the milkmaid.

Or try some *navettes* (half-bread, half-cake loaves that stay fresh for months) from a remarkable 200-year-old bakery, *Le Four des Navettes,* 136 rue Sainte.

 SPECIAL EVENTS: From late June through mid-August, the *Théâtre aux Étoiles* presents outdoor theater, concerts, and ballet at Palais du Pharo, the palace and gardens set panoramically above the harbor entrance at blvd. Charles Livon (phone: 31-04-99). There's also an *International Folklore Festival* in early July at the Château Gombert, pl. des Héros. The best events during the rest of the year are the *Santons Fair,* during which the traditional hand-painted clay statuettes fill Christmas crêches all over the city (December 1–January 6); *La Fête de Mai,* when the cours Julien and place Carli are closed to cars and open to circus acts, theater troupes, and singers (late May); and the *Garlic Fair,* when mounds of garlic cover the sidewalks of blvd. Garibaldi (June).

 SPORTS: Professional sports include auto racing, basketball, horse racing, ice hockey, rugby, and soccer. (Inquire at the tourist office.)

Bicycling – *Locacycle,* 6 rue J. Critofol (phone: 64-13-17), rents bikes and motorbikes as does *Mattei,* 121 av. du Prado (phone: 79-90-10).

Fishing – Notably for gilt-head and mackerel: off the Corniche, in the *calanques,* the Frioul Islands, and in nearby fishing villages.

Golf – The nearest 18-hole course is 14 miles away at *Domaine de Riquetti,* Les Milles, Aix-en-Provence (phone: 24-20-41).

Horseback Riding – Inquire at the *Société Sportive,* near the Jardin Puget, cours Pierre-Puget (phone: 33-11-78).

Sailing – Contact *Centre Municipal de Voile,* Plage du Roucas-Blanc (phone: 76-31-60).

Tennis – There are 12 courts behind the Municipal Stadium, Allée Ray-Grassi (phone: 77-83-89). The *Raquette Club Marseille* offers 6- to 10-day instruction sessions with room and board provided, at pl. de St.-Tronc (phone: 75-19-33). *Set-Squash Marseille,* 265 av. de Mazargues (phone: 71-94-71), provides facilities for both tennis and squash.

 **THEATER:** In addition to the summertime *Théâtre aux Étoiles* (phone: 31-04-99), there's a surprisingly good choice of theater activity year-round. The choices range from the intimate *Centre Culturel* (theater and music), 33 cours Julien (phone: 47-09-64); the *Café-Théâtre de la Plaine,* 10 rue Vian (phone: 94-12-66); and the *Théâtre de Poche,* 2 av. Maréchal-Foch (phone: 86-37-61), to the more ambitious *Théâtre Nationale de Marseille,* 4 rue du Théâtre Français (phone: 48-53-23), and *Théâtre Axel Toursky,* 22 av. Edouard Vaillant (phone: 02-58-35). (Note: Non-French speakers will of course find no handicap with operettas or mime, which are frequently presented.)

MUSIC: The Marseillais know good opera and ballet as well as they know bouillabaisse. The *Opéra de Marseille,* pl. Ernest-Reyer (phone: 54-29-29 or 33-03-58), the recently launched *Théâtre de Recherche de Marseille* (TRM), Espace Massalia, 60 rue Grignan (phone: 33-70-85), both have devoted followings. In addition, the *Opéra de Marseille* is the home of the Compagnie Roland Petit, France's well-known ballet company. Chamber music and organ recitals are frequent at major churches and occasionally outdoors on the Vieux Port. Popular music doesn't fare nearly as well. There are occasional acts at *Théâtre Toursky.*

 NIGHTCLUBS AND NIGHTLIFE: The most "in" night spots include *Bunny's Club,* 2 rue Corneille, with a packed dance floor and an excellent sound system; *La Commanderie,* 20 rue Corneille (phone: 33-45-56), a cabaret that draws its neighbor's overflow with a *sympathique* evening of nonstop songs; *London Club,* 73 corniche Kennedy (phone: 52-64-64), a friendly nightclub/discotheque. For good jazz: *La Cave du Gaulois,* 42 rue Francis Davso.

 SINS: The area around the *Opéra* (between it and the Vieux Port) is filled with sailors' haunts. The seamy cabarets and strip clubs beckon with Pigalle-style nightlife and attractions. And dangers.

BEST IN TOWN

 CHECKING IN: Marseille traditionally has had a meager selection of good hotels. With a recent spurt of hotel construction there's now an overabundance of ultramodern luxury rooms, but no improvement in the lower price ranges. Expect to pay $50 or more for a double room (including breakfast) in expensive hotels; $30 to $50 for moderate; and under $30 for inexpensive.

Concorde Palm Beach – This is a supermodern hotel by the sea with an outdoor pool, health and sports center, and a good restaurant, *La Réserve.* 2 Promenade de la Plage (phone: 76-20-00). Expensive.

Frantel – One of the city's newest hotels, it has a very central location 5 minutes' walk from the Old Port, It belongs to a major French chain, but distinguishes itself by its elegance, its pleasant piano bar, and an outstanding restaurant, *l'Oursinade* (see Eating Out). The 200 rooms have all the luxury hotel amenities. Rue Neuve-St.-Martin (phone: 91-91-29). Expensive.

Grand Hôtel Noailles – Still the classic Marseille hotel, this stylish old building has undergone a recent renovation, after losing 90 of its 160 rooms to office space. It now features steel and Plexiglas decor, with luxury appointments and direct-dial phones in many rooms. 66 La Canebière (phone: 54-91-48). Expensive.

Le Petit Nice – This small (20 rooms and suites), gracious hotel, built in the nineteenth century as a private villa, has a shaded garden and a two-star Michelin restaurant to recommend it, both of them looking out over the Mediterranean from a magnificent position on the Corniche. The restaurant is closed Mondays and at lunch on winter Tuesdays; the hotel is closed January and the first week in February. 160 Corniche Président-J.-F.-Kennedy (phone: 52-14-39). Expensive.

Sofitel Vieux Port – A magnificent modern hotel with a splendid view from its perch above the entrance to the Old Port, near the Palais du Pharo. It has some 200 rooms, air-conditioning, a heated outdoor pool, a cozy bar, and a fine restaurant, *Les Trois Forts* (see Eating Out). 36 blvd. Charles-Livon (phone: 52-90-19). Expensive.

Résidence Bompard – In a quiet park on a hill not far from the sea, the *Bompard* is nevertheless only a 5-minute drive on the coastal road from the bustle of the Vieux Port. Some of its 40-plus rooms — in the main building or surrounding bungalows — have kitchenettes. No restaurant. 2 rue des Flots-Bleus (phone: 52-10-93). Moderate.

Esterel – This hotel is small, quiet, and comfortable. Rooms are air-conditioned, with color TV, and it's very convenient to the Metro and shopping. No restaurant. 124 rue Paradis (phone: 37-13-90). Inexpensive.

Hotel de Genève – Old, now modernized, in a quiet pedestrian precinct just behind the Old Port. No restaurant. 3 *bis* rue Reine-Elizabeth (phone: 90-51-42). Inexpensive.

EATING OUT: What it has traditionally lacked in hotels, Marseille has always made up for in restaurants; they are among France's finest, and that is saying a lot. Besides classic French cuisine, be sure to try Provençal (from Provence — the southernmost region of France) specialties. The city is virtually synonymous with bouillabaisse, a dish not to be missed. In its classical form, this soup is based on Mediterranean rockfish, but other fish and shellfish are usually added, particularly lobster and crab. The seasoning (cayenne, garlic, tomatoes, herbs) is very special, but the star ingredient is saffron, which gives bouillabaisse its golden color. It is often served with *rouille,* a relish made of red pepper, garlic, and fish broth, as well as with aïoli, a delicious olive-oil-based garlic mayonnaise. Another dish common on menus in Marseille is *bourride,* a fish stew that some prefer to bouillabaisse.

You may wish to sample *pastis,* the aniseed-flavored aperitif that tastes something like licorice. Usually colorless, *pastis* is served diluted with ice water, which turns it cloudy white. Also try wines from Provence, particularly the dry, pleasant rosé.

Expect to pay $50 and considerably higher in the expensive category (for two with wine and service included); from $30 to $50 in the moderate range; and under $30 in the inexpensive category.

Michel (Les Catalans) – Across the street from the *Calypso.* The menu is short, the prices are right, and the seafood is succulent, rating one Michelin star. Don't miss the bouillabaisse. Closed Tuesdays, Wednesdays, and July. 6 Rue des Catalans (phone: 52-64-22). Expensive.

Chez Brun (Aux Mets de Provence) – At this venerable family-run restaurant, you'll eat in the *ancienne* style. Up to 20 dishes of the true Provençal cuisine, which means fish and olive specialties. Closed Sundays, Mondays, and holidays. Reservations necessary. (On the second floor, the entrance is hard to find — watch closely!) 18 quai du Rive-Neuve (phone: 33-35-38). Expensive.

Calypso – This outstanding restaurant offers a classic sea view and Marseille's best bouillabaisse. No meat or vegetables here, just impeccably served seafood. But the quality and quantity leave nothing to be desired. Its twin and peer — *Michel* — is across the street. Closed Sundays, Mondays, and the month of August. Reservations essential. 3 rue des Catalans (phone: 52-64-00). Expensive.

L'Oursinade – In the *Frantel,* this serves very fine Provençal cuisine in an atmosphere of understated elegance. Closed Sundays and late July through August. Rue Neuve-St.-Martin (phone: 91-91-29). Expensive to moderate.

Les Trois Forts – Here you'll find a panoramic view of the Old Port and such inventive dishes as lamb's liver braised with melon and honey. *Sofitel Vieux Port,* 36 blvd. Charles-Livon (phone: 52-90-19). Expensive to moderate.

Les Platanes (Restaurant des Abattoirs) – By the slaughterhouse, at the city's northern extreme, this immense old café is where the butchers themselves eat. Choose among beef, pork, veal, and a great selection of sausages. Lunch only.

Closed Sundays. Weekday reservations advised. 7 av. Journet (phone: 60-93-17). Moderate.

New York – For seafood again, try this restaurant in the old harbor area. Especially good are the fish terrine and the *bourride*. Closed Sundays. 7 quai des Belges (phone: 33-60-98). Moderate.

Chez Caruso – This is where the locals go when they crave some delicious Italian food. Closed October 10 to November 10, Sunday nights, and Mondays. 158 quai du Port (phone: 90-94-04). Moderate.

Au Pescadou – On entering you'll immediately be dazzled by the spectacular array of fresh oysters, clams, mussels and other seafood delicacies. With ingredients like these, only the simplest preparation is needed. Open daily. Closed July and August. Reservations advised. 19 pl. Castellane (phone: 78-36-01). Moderate to inexpensive.

Le Tonneau – This colorful, tiny place is right off the Canebière. Its copious, family-style meals of rabbit or *fricassé de volaille* are often served in front of the TV set. Closed Saturdays, Sundays, and 3 weeks in August. No reservations needed. 9 rue Beauvau (phone: 33-63-92). Inexpensive.

MILAN

Milan is the financial and commercial hub of Italy and one of the most important business centers in the world. At first glance, it is a city of cold, uninspired skyscrapers, a city whose energizing force is money. Even the museum devoted to Leonardo da Vinci here is a testament to his scientific and technical genius rather than to his artistic spirit. The people of Milan are industrious, sophisticated, chic, serious — not inclined to watch the world pass by from a sunny café table.

Although with nearly two million people Milan is second in size to Rome, many Milanese think of their city as Italy's real capital; it is arguably more powerful than Rome. There are over 400 banks in Milan. As a silk market, it rivals Lyon. Its International Trade Fair each spring draws tens of thousands of businesspeople from all over the world. Still, Milan's economic preoccupation is tempered by an appreciation of less mundane pursuits. It is La Scala, with its perfect acoustics and grand traditions, not the Milan Stock Exchange (Borsa Valori), that is the pride of the city. The opening of the opera season each December is an important event for all of Milan. And the delicate Gothic spires of Milan's magnificent cathedral seem to soar in defiance of the stolid buildings around it.

Milan has had a tumultuous history. Invading armies continually descended upon it from the time it was a Celtic settlement called Mediolanum. The Romans subdued the city in 222 BC, and it eventually grew to rival Rome for primacy of the West. In AD 313, Constantine the Great officially recognized Christianity in the famous Edict of Milan, and with the coming of Christianity, Milan found a spiritual father in Bishop Ambrose (later proclaimed a saint), who accomplished the seemingly impossible task of conciliating church and state. This period was followed, however, by barbarian invasions by Attila, the Franks, and the Burgundians that shaped the fifth and sixth centuries.

Under the tyranny of civil rulers, the people of Milan turned even more toward the religious authorities to protect them and represent their interests. By the mid-eleventh century, Milan had developed into one of the first Italian city-states and was ruled by bishops until Frederick Barbarossa invaded from Germany. When Barbarossa tried to extend his despotic rule to the surrounding Lombardian cities, however, the entire region united in the Lombard League to defeat him and won recognition of its independence.

In 1260, the Torriani became the first of the powerful families to rule Milan, but the Visconti seized power away from them in 1277. Under the Visconti, particularly under Gian Galeazzo (1345–1402), Milan grew in wealth and splendor. When the Visconti died out in 1447, Milan experienced three years of republican government before Francesco Sforza proclaimed himself duke.

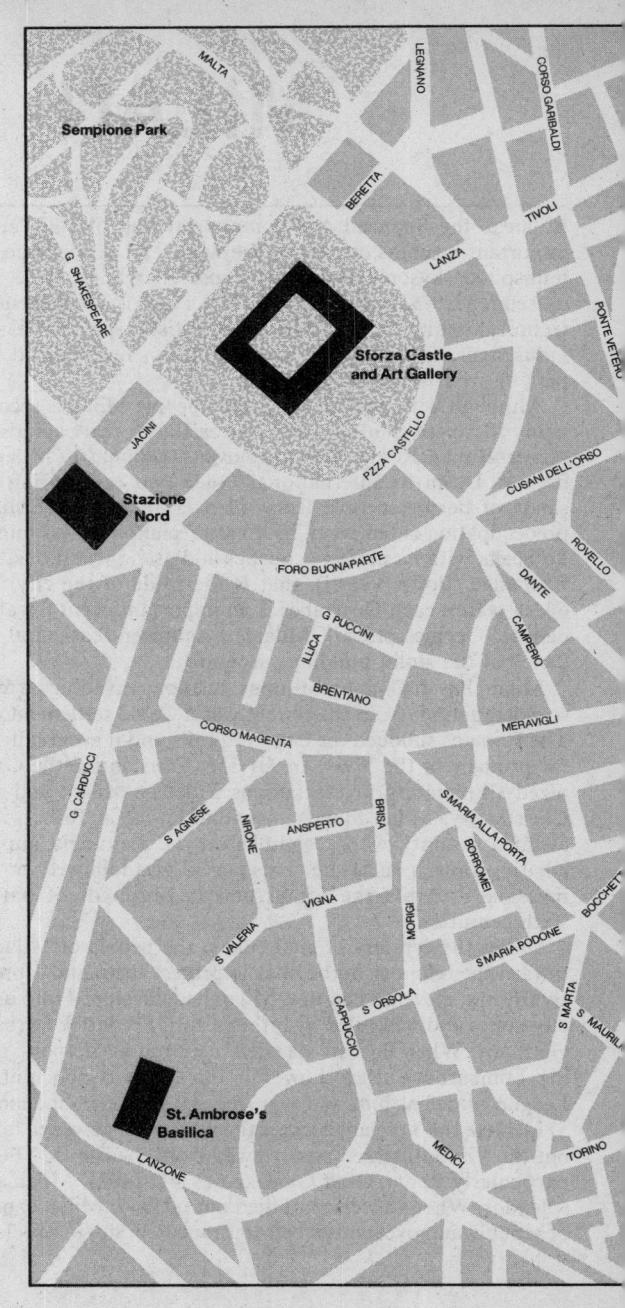

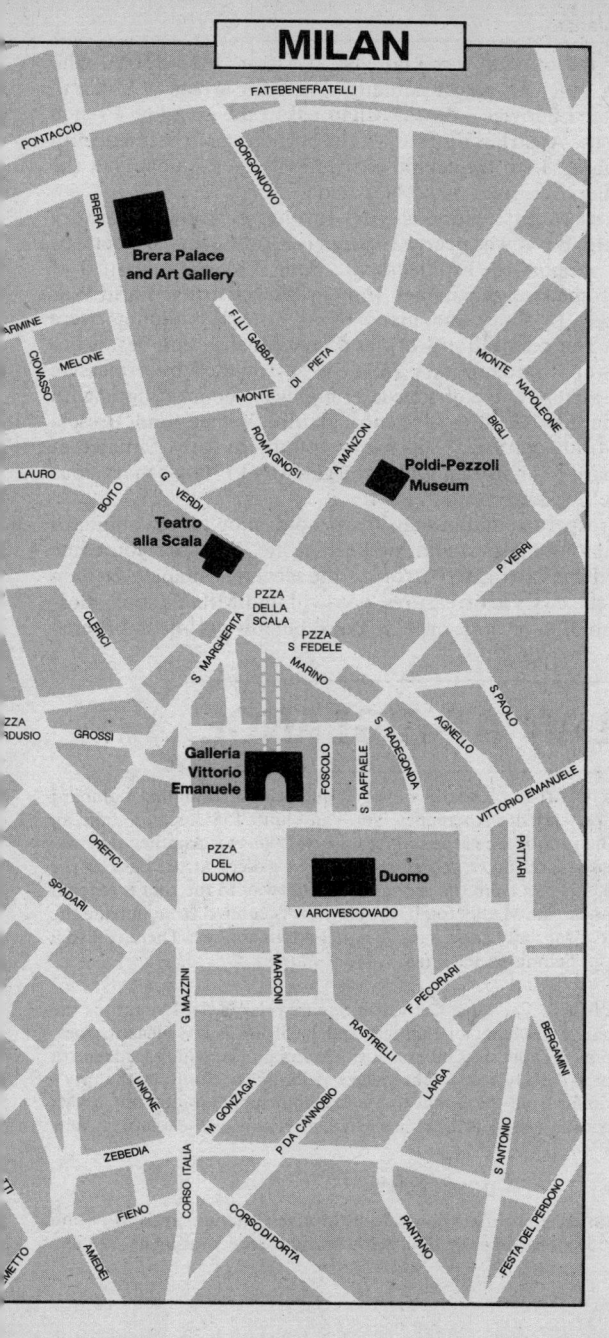

MILAN

FATEBENEFRATELLI

PONTACCIO

BORGONUOVO

BRERA

**Brera Palace
and Art Gallery**

ARMINE

CIOVASSO

MELONE

F.LLI GABBA

DI PIETA

MONTE

MONTE NAPOLEONE

LAURO

BOTTO

G. VERDI

ROMAGNOSI

A. MANZONI

BIGLI

**Poldi-Pezzoli
Museum**

**Teatro
alla Scala**

CLERICI

S. MARGHERITA

PZZA
DELLA
SCALA

PZZA
S FEDELE

MARINO

P. VERRI

S. PAOLO

PZZA
RDUSIO

GROSSI

**Galleria
Vittorio
Emanuele**

FOSCOLO

S RAFFAELE

S RADEGONDA

AGNELLO

VITTORIO EMANUELE

OREFICI

SPADARI

PZZA
DEL
DUOMO

Duomo

PATTARI

V ARCIVESCOVADO

G MAZZINI

MARCONI

F PECORARI

BERGAMINI

RASTRELLI

UNIONE

M GONZAGA

P DA CANNOBIO

LARGA

ZEBEDIA

CORSO ITALIA

S ANTONINO

FIENO

CORSO DI PORTA

PANTANO

FESTA DEL PERDONO

AMEDEI

The most famous of the Sforzas was Ludovico il Moro (1451–1508), who brought Leonardo da Vinci, Donato Bramante, and other artists to Milan to enhance the city. After Ludovico's death, Milan fell to the invading French and, then, in 1713, to the Austrian Empire. At the beginning of the nineteenth century, Napoleon made Milan the capital of the Cisalpine Republic, but the tyrannic Austrian rulers returned when Napoleon fell.

In 1848, the Milanese staged a glorious 5-day revolution, known in history as the Cinque Giornate. But it was nearly 10 years before Milan was liberated and could throw its support to the Piedmonte King Victor Emmanuel of Savoy who would become king of a unified Italy in 1860. During World War II, Milan was bombed 15 times and many of its historic buildings were damaged extensively. But restoration work and new construction began immediately after the war. Contemporary Milan is surrounded by a massive industrial belt and a virtual maze of four-lane highways connecting it with the other northern industrial cities — Genoa, Turin, Venice, and Brescia — and, by the Autostrada del Sole, to Rome and southern Italy. Situated at the head of the Lombard plain, Milan is also the gateway to Italy's marvelous lake region along the Swiss border.

The city itself is prosperous and elegant; its people enjoy a high standard of living and a stimulating cultural and intellectual life. Whether you come on business, to attend the opera, to patronize the elegant Milanese fashion houses, or to admire the city's art treasures, you will find Milan's sophistication equal to that of London or Paris or New York, but always uncompromisingly Italian.

MILAN AT-A-GLANCE

SEEING THE CITY: For a grand view of Milan, the surrounding Lombard plain, the Alps, and the Apennines, you can climb 158 steps, or take an elevator, to the roof of the cathedral (see *Special Places*). Another stairway to its northeast turret takes you to the topmost gallery at the base of the cathedral's central spire, 354 feet from the ground. The stairway to the roof is entered from the south transept near the Medici tomb; the elevator is entered from outside the south transept. Both are open daily and charge a small admission fee. There is also a 350-foot viewing tower in Sempione Park (see *Special Places*).

SPECIAL PLACES: The huge Cathedral Square (piazza del Duomo) is the heart of Milan. The center of political and local life is the elegant glass-domed shopping arcade, the Galleria Vittorio Emanuele, which leads north from the piazza del Duomo to the piazza della Scala. Some of the city's tourist attractions are too far from the center to reach comfortably on foot, but ATM, the local bus and tram system, connects these sites efficiently, as does the relatively new subway system.

DOWNTOWN

The Cathedral (Duomo) – The most magnificent Milanese monument is the white marble cathedral with 135 spires and more than 2,200 sculptures decorating its exterior.

Take the time to go up to the roof, a vantage point from which you can study the fine details of its pinnacles and flying buttresses. The interior of the cathedral, divided into five main aisles by an imposing stand of 58 columns, contains another 2,000 sculptures. The cathedral is considered the finest example of Gothic architecture in northern Italy, although its own architectural peculiarities — it was begun in 1386 but not completed until 1813 — prevent it from being pure Gothic. Only St. Peter's in Rome is larger. Piazza del Duomo.

La Scala (Teatro alla Scala) – The most famous opera house in the world was built between 1776 and 1778 on the site of the church of Santa Maria della Scala. It was here that works by Donizetti, Rossini, Bellini, and Verdi were first acclaimed and where Arturo Toscanini conducted and was artistic director for many years. The neoclassic building was damaged extensively during World War II, but was rebuilt and reopened in 1946. Its acoustics are perfect. The adjacent Scala Museum (Museo della Scala) has a rich collection of manuscripts, costumes, and other memorabilia documenting the theater's history. The museum is open daily. Small admission fee. Theater and museum are north of the piazza del Duomo, through the Galleria Vittorio Emanuele, on the piazza della Scala (phone: 80-53-418).

Poldi-Pezzoli Museum (Museo Poldi Pezzoli) – The Milanese nobleman Gian Giacomo Poldi-Pezzoli bequeathed his home and exquisite private art collection to the city in 1879. It includes some prime examples of Renaissance to seventeenth-century paintings and sculpture, Oriental porcelains, Persian carpets, and tapestries. There is also a Botticelli portrait of the Madonna, frescoes by Giovanni Battista Tiepolo, and Giovanni Bellini's *Pietà*. Open daily; closed Mondays. Small admission fee. A short walk from La Scala. Via Manzoni 12 (phone: 79-48-89).

Brera Palace and Art Gallery (Palazzo e Pinacoteca di Brera) – One of the most important state-owned galleries in Italy, and Milan's finest, is housed in the seventeenth-century Brera Palace. Its 38 rooms contain a broad representation of Italian painting, with particularly good examples from the Venetian and Lombard schools. The palace also has an important library of incunabula, manuscripts and books representing the printed output of Lombardy since 1770. In the courtyard, there is a monumental statue of Napoleon I, depicted as a conquering Caesar. The art gallery is open daily, except Mondays. There is a small admission charge every day except Sundays. The library is open daily; closed Sundays. A few blocks north of La Scala. Via Brera 28 (phone: 80-83-87).

Sforza Castle and Art Gallery (Castello Sforzesco e Museo d'Arte) – In the mid-fifteenth century, Duke Francesco Sforza built this large, square brick castle on the site of a castle of the Visconti that had been destroyed. It became a fortress after the fall of the Sforzas and was damaged repeatedly in sieges before restoration began in the nineteenth century. Further damage from World War II has been repaired and today the quadrilateral building contains the Museum of Antique Art (Museo d'Arte Antica). Among its treasures is the unfinished *Rondonini Pietà*, the last work of Michelangelo. The museum is entered from the courtyard of the residential part of the castle, the Corte Ducale. Closed Mondays and at lunchtime. Small admission charge. West of the Brera. Piazza Castello (phone: 62-36, ext. 3940).

Beyond the castle is the beautiful, 116-acre Sempione Park (Parco Sempione), with its aquarium, sports arena, and neoclassic Arch of Peace (Arco della Pace), a triumphal arch with statues and bas-relief. The arch, on the model of Septimio Severus at Rome, marks the beginning of the historic Simplon Road (Corso Sempione) through the Alps to France, which was built by order of Napoleon.

St. Ambrose's Basilica and Museum (Basilica e Museo di Sant'Ambrogio) – The basilica was founded in the fourth century by Bishop Ambrose (later St. Ambrose), who baptized St. Augustine here. The bas-relief on the doorway dates from the time of St. Ambrose and the two bronze doors are from the ninth century. The basilica was enlarged in the eleventh century, and its superb atrium was added in the twelfth century. Two other early Christian saints — Gervase and Protasius — are buried with St. Ambrose in the crypt. The ceiling of the apse is decorated with tenth-century mosaics. Above the portico is the Museum of St. Ambrose (Museo di Sant-Ambrogio), where you can see a twelfth-century cross, a missal of Gian Galeazzo Visconti, and other religious treasures. The museum is open daily, except Tuesdays. Small admission charge. South of the Sforza Castle. Piazza Sant'Ambrogio 15 (phone: 87-20-59).

The Church of St. Mary of Grace (Santa Maria delle Grazie) – The interior of this brick and terra cotta church, representing a period of transition from the Gothic to the Renaissance, is decorated with some fine fifteenth-century frescoes. But the church, though beautiful in itself, is usually visited because Leonardo da Vinci's *The Last Supper* is on a wall of the refectory of the former Dominican convent next to it. *The Last Supper* was painted in tempera, which is not particularly known for its durability, and though it has been restored several times, it is in a state of considerable deterioration. Another attempt at restoration is under way. The convent is closed Mondays. Small admission charge. A few blocks northwest of Sant'Ambrogio. Piazza Santa Maria delle Grazie.

ENVIRONS

The Carthusian Monastery (Certosa di Pavia) – Gian Galeazzo Visconti founded this monastery in 1396 as a family mausoleum. With its facade of multicolored marble sculpture and its interior heavily decorated with frescoes, baroque grillwork and other ornamentation, the monastery is one of the most remarkable buildings in Italy. It is conveniently reached from Milan by coach excursion or by road. Open daily; closed Mondays. Sixteen miles (26 km) from Milan, just off the Milan-Pavia Rd.

Monza – The world-famous Monza *Autodromo* is the scene of the Italian Grand Prix Formula One race early in September each year. It is possible for visitors to drive around the course with its well-known seven corners for a small fee. The *Autodromo* is in a splendid park that was once part of the Royal Villa (Villa Reale) and now has golf courses, a racecourse, and a swimming pool as well as the auto track. The cathedral at Monza is also worth a visit. It was built in the thirteenth and fourteenth centuries and has a facade of white, green, and black marble, notable for its harmonious proportions and decorations. Monza is easily reached by bus from via Jacini Piazza Quattro Novembre in Milan or by train. By road, it is 7 miles (11 km) northeast of Milan on Route 36.

■**EXTRA SPECIAL:** The Italian *commedia dell'arte,* a comedy of improvisation that had a strong influence on French theater, began in the sixteenth century in Bergamo, a small hill town close to the first foothills of the Alps. This beautiful old city also holds interest for music lovers as the birthplace of the composer Donizetti. The modern lower town was only laid out early in this century, but the upper town, connected by a funicular railway, is a step back into the Middle Ages. Its Palazzo della Ragione in the piazza Vecchia is the oldest communal palace in Italy. (It dates from 1199, but was rebuilt in the sixteenth century.) The Church of St. Mary Major (Santa Maria Maggiore) in the piazza del Duomo, begun in 1137, has beautiful details inside and out. The Instituto Musicale Donizetti, Via Arena 9, is a small museum of Donizetti memorabilia. In the lower town, the Galleria dell'Accademia Carrara has a fine collection of paintings, with the Venetian school well represented. Bergamo is 30 miles (48 km) from Milan along the Autostrada 4. It also is reached easily by train or by bus from Milan's piazza Castello.

SOURCES AND RESOURCES

General tourist information is available at the Palazzo del Turismo of the Provincial Tourist Board, EPT, Via Marconi 1 (phone: 80-96-62).

For Local Coverage – The tourist board can provide copies of *Tutta Milano*, a useful guide to activities, facts and phone numbers, and listings of restaurants and discos. The biweekly *Night & Day Milano* has bulletins on special events.

The Milan Trade Fair Center is at Largo Domodossola 1 (phone: 499-7336).

 CLIMATE AND CLOTHES: Milan temperatures are generally moderate, although the city occasionally suffers extremes of heat or cold. Summer can be hot and airless, with temperatures as high as 85°F (29°C); winter can be cold, wet, and foggy, with temperatures below 10°F (-12°C) and occasional snow. The Milanese are fashion conscious, so you may want to bring something special for evenings. Opening night at La Scala is strictly formal, after that informal dress is acceptable.

 GETTING AROUND: Much of the center of Milan has been closed to traffic, so it is far more convenient for visitors to use public transportation. Inexpensive day tickets that allow unlimited travel on the public transportation system are available.

Bus and Tram – The local bus and tram service, ATM, efficiently connects various points of this widespread city. Tickets are sold at tobacconists and newsstands throughout the city and must be purchased in advance.

Subway – The Metropolitana Milanese (MM) has two lines. The most useful for tourists is line 1, which runs south from near the main railway station, through the Piazza del Duomo, and west beyond the Piazza Santa Maria delle Grazie. Tickets are sold at coin-operated machines in each station.

Taxi – Taxis can be hailed while cruising or picked up at a cabstand.

Car Rental – Most international firms are represented.

 MUSEUMS: In addition to those listed in *Special Places*, there are several other museums in Milan worth a visit.

Leonardo da Vinci National Museum of Science and Technology (Museo Nazionale della Scienza e della Tecnica "Leonardo da Vinci"), Via San Vittore 21 (phone: 46-27-09).

Museum of Milan, Via Sant'Andrea 6 (phone: 70-62-45).

Modern Art Gallery of the Villa Reale, Via Palestro 16 (phone: 70-28-19).

National Museum of the Risorgimento (Museo del Risorgimento Nazionale), Via Borgonuovo 23 (phone: 80-53-598).

Ambrosiana Library (Biblioteca Ambrosiana). Including the picture gallery. Piazza Pio XI 2 (phone: 80-01-46).

Manzoni Museum and Manzoni's House (Museo e Casa di Manzoni), Via Morone 1 (phone: 87-10-19).

Basilica di San Lorenzo Maggiore, Corso di Porta Ticinese.

Milan also has scores of art galleries with interesting shows. The following offer an excellent selection of contemporary and early-20th-century Italian art: *Ariete Grafica*, Via Sant'Andrea 5 (phone: 79-55-73); *Galleria Philippe Daverio*, Via Monte Napoleone 6/a (phone: 79-86-95); and *Centro Annunciata*, Via Manzoni 44 (phone: 79-60-26).

SHOPPING: Milan is an international fashion center and is full of enticing, if expensive, shops. The main shopping area comprises the streets near the Piazza del Duomo and La Scala, particularly the elegant Via Monte Napoleone, Via della Spiga, and Via Sant'Andrea. Here you'll find the boutiques of top Italian designers (*Giorgio Armani* at Via Sant'Andrea 9, *Ferragamo* at Via Monte Napoleone, and *Krizia* at Via della Spiga 23), most of whom are based in Milan. In addition, many other elegant shops sell unusual, high-quality goods. Boutiques offering modern fashions and antique clothes are scattered throughout the old Brera quarter and around St. Ambrose's Basilica. Early in December, there is a flea market near the basilica, where you can rummage through a wide selection of clothes, antiques, old books, and knickknacks. Shop hours generally are from 9 AM to 12:30 PM and 3:30 to 7:30 PM. Most shops are closed on Monday mornings.

Accademia – Fine menswear and accessories. Via Solferino 11.

Arte Antica – One of the city's best-known antique stores, with French porcelain, clocks, and furniture. Via Sant'Andrea.

L'Artisan Parfumeur – A new shop specializing in perfumes and home scents. Via Francesco Sforza 3.

Guanti Berni – Beautiful leather gloves for men and women. Via Sant'Andrea.

Brigatti – Considered Milan's finest men's sportswear shop. Also has a ski boutique for the entire family. Corso Venezia 15.

Calderoni – Exquisite jewelry and silver. Via Monte Napoleone 8.

Cose – Chic and trendy women's clothing. Via della Spiga 8.

Decomania – Art deco objects and furniture. Via Fiori Chiari 5/9.

Erreuno – Elegant women's fashions. Via della Spiga 15.

Franco and Aldo Lorenzi – Elegant travel and smoking accessories for men. Via Monte Napoleone 9.

Provera – Top-quality wines (and free tasting). Corso Magenta 7.

Rubinacci – Top French designers and the store's own elegant line of women's fashions. Via Sant'Andrea 10.

Vittorio Siniscalchi – One of Milan's best custom shirtmakers for men. Via Gesu 8.

Stationery – The city's best-stocked stationery store, with interesting gadgets and office accessories. Via Solferino 3.

 SPECIAL EVENTS: The *International Trade Fair* held in late April is one of the most important commercial fairs in the world. Although this is the city's biggest, there are various other trade fairs and exhibitions almost every month except July and August, often making advance hotel reservations essential. In July and August, the city sponsors a variety of outdoor cultural events; sometimes restaurants join in by serving regional specialties in the parks. The opening of the opera season at *La Scala* each year on December 7 is the city's major cultural event.

 **SPORTS: Golf** – The *Golf Club Milano*'s 27-hole course is located at the park in nearby Monza (phone: 70-30-81).

Horse Racing – Thoroughbred and trotting races are run at the internationally famous *Ippodromo San Siro* on the eastern outskirts of Milan. For information, contact the Municipal Sports and Tourism Department (Ripartizione Sport-Turismo), Via Marconi 2 (phone: 86-52-94).

Soccer – Home matches of Milan's crack soccer teams, *Milan* and *Internazionale,* are played at the *San Siro Stadium* in the same complex as the racecourse.

Swimming – Public indoor pools include *Cozzi,* Viale Tunisia 35; *Mincio,* Via Mincio 13, and *Solari,* Via Montevideo, 11. Open-air pools include *Lido,* Piazzale

Lotto 15, near the San Siro Stadium; *Romano,* Via Ponzio 35; and *Piscina Olimpica* in the park at Monza.

Tennis – Public courts should be booked well ahead of time. Some of the main courts are at *Bonacossa,* Via Mecenate 74 (phone: 506-1277); *Centro Polisportivo,* Via Valvassori Peroni 48 (phone: 236-6254); *Lido di Milano,* Piazzale Lotto 15 (phone: 39-16-67), and *Ripamonti,* Via Iseo 4 (phone: 645-9253).

THEATER: You can take in classical Italian theater productions at the *Piccolo Teatro,* Via Rovello 2 (phone: 87-76-63); at the *Manzoni,* Via Manzoni 40 (phone: 79-05-43); or at the *Salone Pier Lombardo,* Via Pierlombardo 14 (phone: 54-571-74). For avant-garde and experimental theater, try *Teatro dell'Elfo,* Via Menotti 11 (phone: 71-67-91); the *Centro Ricerca Teatro,* Via Piliziano 11 (phone: 31-821-15); or the *Frigoriferia Suburbana,* Via Donatello 8.

MUSIC: The renowned La Scala (see *Special Places*) is an obvious must for any opera fan, but there are also ballets and concerts held here, Piazza della Scala (phone: 80-70-41). Concerts also are held at the *Auditorium Angelicum,* Piazza Sant'Angelo 2 (phone: 63-27-48), and the Conservatorio di Musica, Via Conservatorio 12 (phone: 701-755). Tickets to the Angelicum are sold at Via Gustavo Favo 4 or at Ricordi Music Shop, via Berchet 2.

NIGHTCLUBS AND NIGHTLIFE: Popular nightclubs include *Caffè Roma,* Via Ancona 4 (phone: 87-69-60), and *Amnesie,* Via B. Cellini 2 (phone: 70-29-38). Top discos include *Good Mood,* Via Turati 29 (phone: 655-93-49); *Rolling Stone,* Corso XXII Marzo 32 (phone: 73-31-72); *Odissea,* Via Besenzanica 3 (phone: 476-56-53); and *Plastic,* Via Umbria 120 (no phone). Jazz can be heard at *Scimmie,* Via Ascania Sforza 49 (phone: 839-18-74), and at *Ca'Bianca Club,* Via Ludovico il Moro 117.

Milan has many cozy piano bars that are ideal for a late drink and snack. Try *Golden Memory,* Via Lazzaro Papi 22 (phone: 54-842-09); *Gershwin's,* Via Corrado il Salico 10 (phone: 84-977-22); or *Don Pub,* Via Arco 1 (phone: 89-58-46).

SINS: There are striptease shows at *Teatrino,* Corsia dei Servi 3 (phone: 79-37-16), *Maschere,* Via Borgogna 7 (phone: 70-55-84), and *Smeraldo,* Piazza 25 Aprile (phone: 66-27-68). Prostitutes solicit only at night on downtown streets. There are several soft-porn movie theaters, found under "Luci Rosse" in newspaper film listings.

BEST IN TOWN

CHECKING IN: As an international business center, Milan offers a wide range of accommodations for the visitor, from traditional, old-fashioned hotels to efficient, modern, commercial ones. Expensive hotels here will cost from $150 to $270 a night for a double room; moderate-priced hotels charge $75 to $150 for a double; and inexpensive hotels will charge between $40 and $50. Unless otherwise noted, all Milan hotels accept major credit cards.

Principe and Savoia Hotel – A classic European deluxe hotel with marble baths, antiques, thick rugs, air-conditioning, and attractive dining and drinking facilities. There are kitchenette apartments with balconies in the new wing. The location is excellent: just north of the cathedral on a fashionable street away from the busy main road. Piazza della Repubblica 17 (phone: 6230). Expensive.

Palace Hotel – Recently transformed by a $2.5-million renovation. Each floor has a different color scheme and the rooms have been decorated in ultramodern style. The smaller new wing is more conventional than the renovated old wing. Dining on the roof garden. Piazza della Repubblica 20 (phone: 6336). Expensive.

Milano Hilton – An attractive contemporary hotel in the new commercial center facing the main railway station about a mile north of the center and the cathedral. Tastefully decorated in a mixture of Italian provincial and modern styles. There is also a colorful, moderately priced Italian restaurant and a discotheque. The service is first rate. Via Galvani 12 (phone: 6983). Expensive.

Executive Hotel – Conveniently next to the airport bus terminal, about a mile from downtown Milan, this is an American-style hotel with a pleasant staff, deluxe rooms, and a good restaurant and bar as well as saunas and a swimming pool that's covered in winter. Via Don Luigi Sturzo 45 (phone: 6294). Expensive to moderate.

Jolly President – This centrally located deluxe hotel has 201 comfortable rooms and a restaurant. Largo Augusto 10 (phone: 77-46). Expensive to moderate.

Marino alla Scala – A friendly hotel, favored by opera-goers and other artistic types, next to La Scala. Rooms are small but comfortable, and some have balconies. Piazza della Scala 5 (phone: 86-78-31). Moderate.

Europeo – Not far from the center of town, this fine hotel has its own peaceful garden, all the modern conveniences, and very good service. Via Canonica 38 (phone: 34-40-41). Moderate.

Manin Hotel – This small, first-class hotel is about a half mile from La Scala. Some of the rooms have been renovated in a modern style; the older rooms are not impressive but are spacious and comfortable. There's also a very good restaurant and bar. Via Manin 7 (phone: 659-6511). Moderate.

Nasco – On the city's outskirts, this new, American-style hotel is an excellent choice when downtown hotels are full. Via Spallanzani 40 (phone: 204-38-41). Moderate.

Lord Internazionale Hotel – A tiny, budget hotel on a busy little shopping street near the cathedral. Rooms are quite small, but colorful and clean. It is most suitable for short stays. There is no restaurant, but the lobby is cheerful and the management accommodating. Via Spadari 11 (phone: 86-24-20). Moderate.

Manzoni – A small, pleasant hotel right in the city's center. Via Santo Spirito 20 (phone: 70-57-00). Moderate to inexpensive.

Centro – An attractive budget hotel in the heart of downtown Milan. Via Broletto 46 (phone: 87-52-32). Inexpensive.

Antica Locanda Solferino – A delightful small hotel in the old Brera quarter a few blocks north of La Scala. This was once an old tavern and retains much of the old-world fin-de-siècle charm in its furniture and decor. No credit cards. Must be booked far in advance. Via Castel Fidardo 2 (phone: 659-2706). Inexpensive.

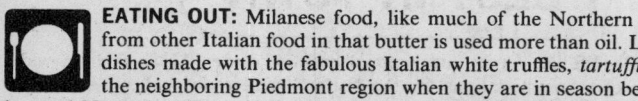 **EATING OUT:** Milanese food, like much of the Northern cuisine, differs from other Italian food in that butter is used more than oil. Look for special dishes made with the fabulous Italian white truffles, *tartuffi bianchi,* from the neighboring Piedmont region when they are in season between September and November. Expect to pay $75 or more for dinner for two at one of Milan's expensive restaurants — the most expensive in Italy; $50 to $65 at a moderately priced restaurant; and $30 to $45 at an inexpensive one. Prices don't include drinks, wine, or tips. It is a good idea to have reservations at any Milanese restaurant.

Gaultiero Marchesi – Milan's only two-star restaurant provides an elegant setting for an Italian nouvelle cuisine that is considered the best in Italy. Reservations necessary. Closed Sundays and August. Via Bonvesin della Riva 9 (phone: 74-12-46). Very expensive.

Savini – Everything here, from the food to the decor, is classic and exquisite. There is ultraprofessional service in the height of nineteenth-century elegance: crystal chandeliers and red silk lampshades. The traditional northern Italian dishes are even better than the more Continental cuisine. Closed Sundays, August. Reservations recommended. Galleria Vittorio Emanuele 11 (phone: 805-8343). Expensive.

Biffi Scala – This large elegant restaurant is the traditional spot for supper after the opera. It is known for good food and good service. Closed Sundays, August. Have reservations by all means. Piazza della Scala (phone: 87-63-32). Expensive.

Saint Andrews – This elegant downtown restaurant with dark-paneled walls and plush upholstery is a favorite of Milanese executives. Closed Sundays and August. Via Sant'Andrea 23 (phone: 79-30-32). Expensive.

Al Porto – The specialties at this family-run restaurant are fresh fish and friendly service. Closed Sundays and August. Piazza Cantore (phone: 832-1481). Expensive to moderate.

Rigolo – A large, friendly place that's a favorite of local journalists and businessmen, this restaurant serves Tuscan specialties (such as thick, grilled steaks) and a superb selection of homemade desserts. Closed Mondays and August. Via Solferino 11 (phone: 805-97-68). Moderate.

Alfio-Cavour – It has a central location, an enclosed winter garden, and very good risotto and fish and meat dishes. Closed Saturdays and August. Via Senato 31 (phone: 70-06-33). Moderate.

Le Colline Pisane – This lively trattoria serves fine food in pleasant surroundings. Closed Sundays and August. Reservations recommended. Largo La Fobba 5 (phone: 65-991-36). Moderate.

Osteria del Vecchio Canneto – It's definitely the place to try for wonderful fish. Sample the baked clams au gratin, the mixed fish grill, and the fine Abbruzzi wine. Closed Sundays and August. Via Solferino 56 (phone: 659-84-98). Moderate.

Gran San Bernardo da Alfredo – Some of the best regional cooking in town is served in this large and friendly restaurant. Try the classic Lombardy stew of pork, sausages, carrots, and white wine, *casseoeula,* served with cornbread, or *polenta.* Closed Sundays and August. Via Borgese 14 (phone: 38-90-00). Moderate.

Bottega del Vino – This charming restaurant is part of Peck's, an elegant food specialty shop, and probably has the best wine list in town. Closed Sundays and August. Via V. Hugo 4 (phone: 87-67-74). Moderate.

Giardino – Near the banks of the Naviglio River, this restaurant in the nineteenth-century courtyard spreads out under surrounding trees in summer and is enlivened by passing musicians. The food is simple but delicious and the atmosphere is reminiscent of a nineteenth-century Milanese tavern or *Osteria.* Closed Tuesdays. Alzaia Naviglio Grande 36 (phone: 839-9321). Moderate to inexpensive.

Quattro Mori – At this comfortable, family-run trattoria serving traditional Milanese food, try the fresh antipasto, veal cutlets, and grilled meats. Closed Sundays and August. Via San Giovanni sul Muro 2 (phone: 87-06-17). Moderate to inexpensive.

MOSCOW

For many Westerners, Moscow is so closely associated with Soviet hegemony that it seems as much a political philosophy as a place. Come to Moscow, the city, however, and you will be exposed to a feast of sights, a rich selection of cultural activities, and contact with warm, generous, and responsive people.

Moscow has always been on the periphery of Europe. Situated on the Moskva River deep in the northwestern region of what is the world's largest state in area (the Soviet Union encompasses 8.65 million square miles), it was impervious to outside cultural and economic influences for centuries. The original Moscow architecture, for example, developed in the fifteenth century when imported Byzantine traditions were forced into conformity with the native arts of northwestern Russia. The bulbous domes that are a characteristic feature of Russian churches are apparently a native Russian form.

A bit of history may help you to understand the city better. There is archaeological evidence that people occupied this area along the Moskva as early as the Neolithic period, but the first mention of the tiny village of Moscow is found in Russian chronicles of 1147. Yuri Dolgoruky, a prince of Suzdal, had established a small wooden fortress on a hill overlooking the river, in the same vicinity as the present-day Kremlin. (The word *kremlin* is a transliteration of the Russian word for fortress.) At first merely a stop on the river trade route between the Baltic Sea and the Black Sea, Moscow became the capital of the principality in the thirteenth century and was the center of power in the northern area when Mongol Tartars overran the Russian lands.

The present brick walls of the Kremlin were firmly in place by the late fifteenth century, but they could not prevent the town growing up outside the fortress from being destroyed by the Crimean Tartars in 1571 and again by the Poles in the seventeenth century. Following these troubled times, Moscow began to expand and establish itself as a powerful city under a long line of Romanov czars. The most famous Romanov was Peter I, called Peter the Great, who was much enamored of France and Western Europe. In 1714, Peter the Great moved the capital from Moscow to a new city he was building on the Gulf of Finland to reflect the taste and culture of the West.

Although the capital was moved to St. Petersburg (now Leningrad), Moscow remained an important center of the Orthodox Church and, as they had done since the reign of Ivan the Terrible, Russian czars continued to return to the Assumption (Uspensky) Cathedral in the Kremlin for their coronations. During the eighteenth and nineteenth centuries, Moscow established its university and its major theaters and continued to expand its boundaries. As the city spread out from the Kremlin complex, the ring of fortress monasteries and convents that had served as Moscow's protective perimeter became an integral part of the city itself. A contemporary city map reflects this gradual expansion in ever-widening rings from the Kremlin–Red Square center.

In his zeal to ensure that his new capital would have no rival, Peter the Great had decreed that no stone buildings be erected anywhere in Russia except in St. Petersburg. So, even though Napoleon's armies failed to conquer Moscow in 1812, nearly three-quarters of the city was destroyed in the fires in the wake of the French occupation. A special commission was set up by Alexander I to reconstruct Moscow in 1825, and several magnificent buildings were constructed in the imperial style, including the renowned Bolshoi Theater.

After the 1917 Revolution, the new Bolshevik government returned the capital to Moscow, and the Kremlin once again was the seat of power. Since then, Moscow has undergone a series of transformations. Between 1926 and 1939, the population doubled; today it exceeds 7.5 million. New offices, and later skyscrapers, filled in the city's modern skyline. Streets were widened and old areas of the city were razed to make way for modern hotels and offices. In 1935, the first part of Moscow's extensive Metro system was completed. During World War II, 75 Nazi divisions massed against the city but were unable to conquer it. Moscow handed the German armies their first major defeat as the Russian people bore the brunt of the most ferocious German attacks while the Western Allies organized their strategy with the US.

Moscow today is about three-quarters the size of Los Angeles. A circular bypass highway about 16 miles from the city's center marks its present boundaries. Beyond the circular highway you will pass miles of slender white birch trees and, occasionally, one of the quaint wooden houses with intricately carved facades typical of this area. The generally flat country surrounding Moscow has facilitated construction and maintenance of a railway network that makes Moscow a manufacturing and industrial hub as well as the government center. It is, indeed, the heart of the USSR; its most powerful and important city. You can comprehend the ethnic diversity of the Soviet Union merely by walking along Moscow's streets. Ukrainians, Lithuanians, Caucasians, Georgians, central Asians — they all come here, as tourists, to shop or to bring their goods to sell at farmers' markets throughout the city.

The first-time visitor should not be put off by the stoic facade of the Muscovite's public demeanor. Eavesdrop on a wedding reception in your hotel or visit the circus or racetrack or dine at one of the local restaurants and you will find the zest and exuberance with which Russians celebrate life. The bureaucratic complexity of dealing with everyday existence may dampen enthusiasm during working hours, but when it's time to play, Russian spirits revive rapidly.

To the Western eye, Moscow may always be more impressive than beautiful. Its appearance may change with new construction or the shift in seasons, but its character never varies: It is a city that exudes energy, a city pulsating with power.

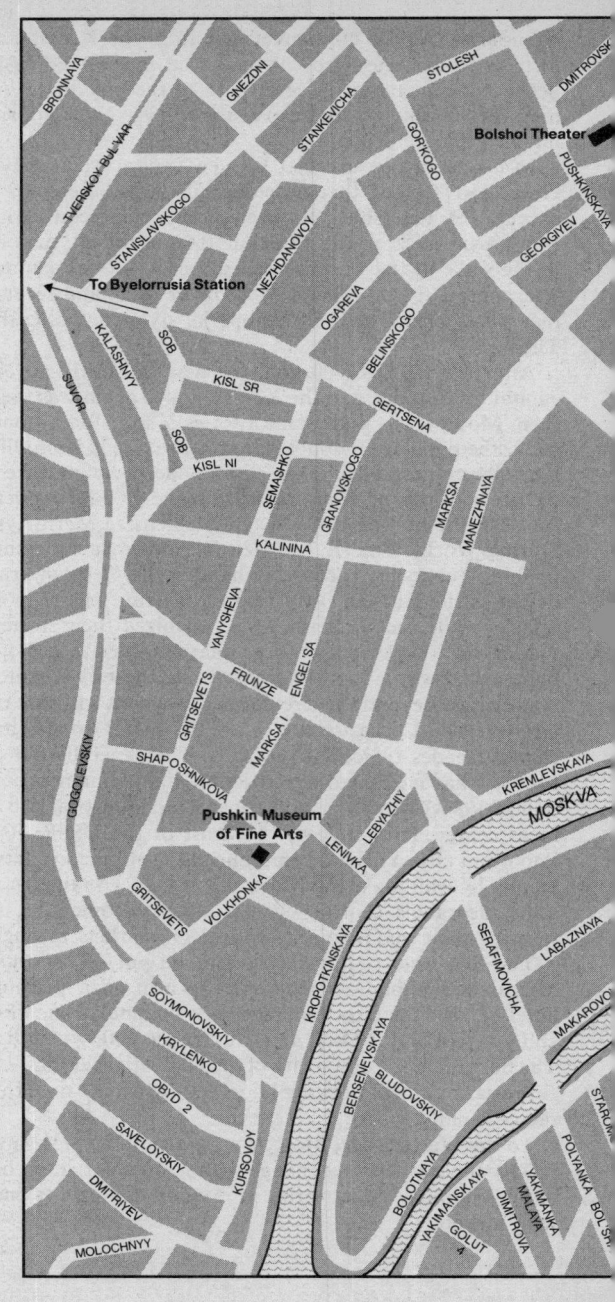

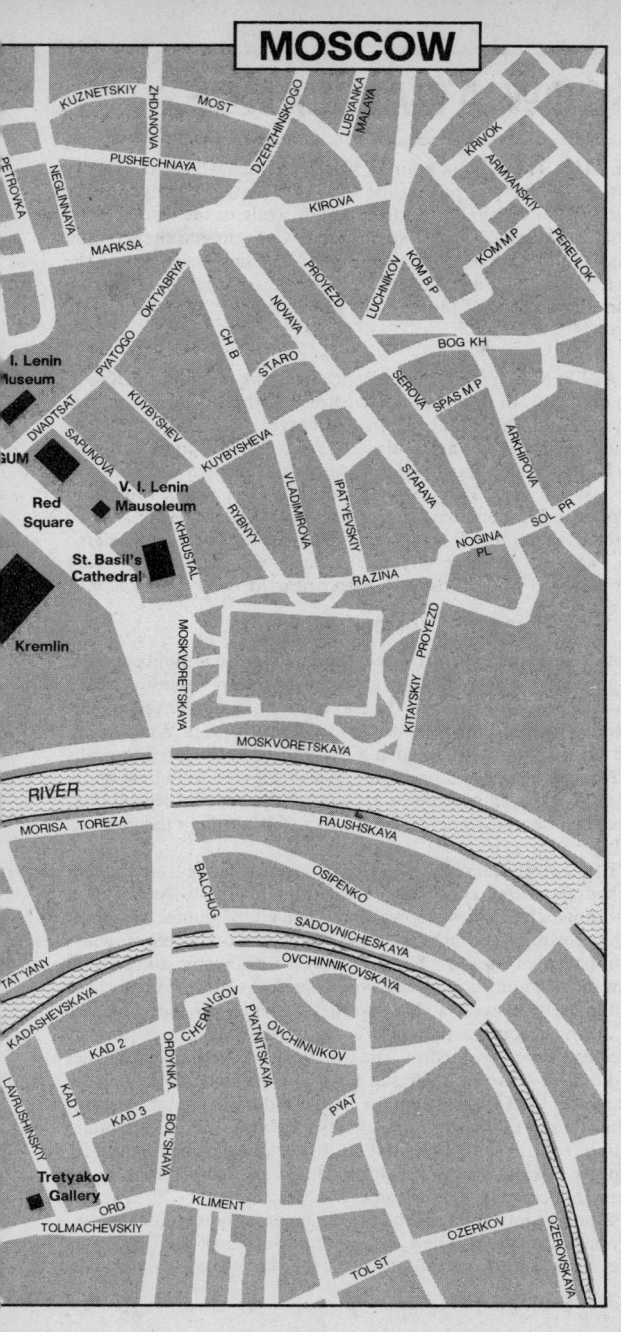

MOSCOW

KUZNETSKIY
ZHDANOVA
MOST
DZERZHINSKOGO
LUBYANKA MALAYA
KRIVOK
PETROVKA
NEGLINNAYA
PUSHECHNAYA
ARMYANSKIY
KIROVA
KOMM P
PEREULOK
MARKSA
PROYEZD
LUCHNIKOV
KOM B P
NOVAYA
BOG KH
I. Lenin Museum
PYATOGO OKTYABRYA
CH B
STARO
SEROVA
SPAS M P
GUM
SAPUNOVA
KUYBYSHEV
KUYBYSHEVA
ARKHIPOVA
Red Square
V. I. Lenin Mausoleum
VLADIMIROVA
IPATYEVSKIY
STARAYA
SOL PR
St. Basil's Cathedral
KHRUSTAL
RYBNYY
NOGINA PL
Kremlin
RAZINA
MOSKVORETSKAYA
KITAYSKIY PROYEZD
MOSKVORETSKAYA
RIVER
MORISA TOREZA
RAUSHSKAYA
BALCHUG
OSIPENKO
SADOVNICHESKAYA
OVCHINNIKOVSKAYA
TAT'YANY
KADASHEVSKAYA
KAD 2
ORDYNKA
CHERNIGOV
PYATNITSKAYA
OVCHINNIKOV
LAVRUSHINSKIY
KAD 1
KAD 3
BOL'SHAYA
PYAT
Tretyakov Gallery
ORD
KLIMENT
TOLMACHEVSKIY
TOL ST
OZERKOV
OZEROVSKAYA

MOSCOW AT-A-GLANCE

SEEING THE CITY: The lookout point in front of Moscow State University in Lenin Hills affords the best panoramic view of the city. Below you is the Moskva River and the Luzhniki sports complex, while in the distance you can see the gold and silver domes of Novodevichy Convent and the Kremlin complex (see *Special Places*) and six look-alike skyscrapers. The university is near the Leninskie Gory Metro stop. There's a fine view of Red Square and the Kremlin from the *Rossia Restaurant* on the top floor of the 21-story tower wing of the *Hotel Rossia*. Razina Ul. 6 (phone: 298-5401).

SPECIAL PLACES: Moscow grew up in concentric rings around the Kremlin and much of what is of interest to the visitor is within the area bounded by the Boulevard Ring, Bulvarnoye Koltso. However, there is also much to explore in the area between the Boulevard Ring and the more outlying Garden Ring, Sadovoye Koltso, which roughly duplicates an old earthen wall that was demolished early in the last century. Gorky Street (Gorkovo Ul.), which runs from Revolution Square (Revolyutsii Pl.) northwest to Byelorusskaya Square (Belorusskovo Vokzala Pl.) and the railway terminus for trains from Western Europe, is considered Moscow's main street. The new 265-acre Olympic Village with eighteen 16-story apartment houses is not far from Michurinsky Prospekt near Moscow University.

INSIDE THE KREMLIN

The Kremlin Complex – Kremlins, or fortresses, can be found in a number of old Russian towns. None, however, is as well known as the Moscow Kremlin, which occupies 69 acres overlooking the Moskva and is the seat of the Soviet government. The entire complex is surrounded by a red fortress wall studded with towers. Atop five of these towers are gigantic red stars that are lighted at night. Buried in the Kremlin walls are the ashes of various Russian heroes and one American — John Reed, whose book, *Ten Days That Shook the World,* is an eyewitness account of the Russian Revolution. There are guided tours of the Kremlin complex, or you can walk through the grounds on your own. Open daily.

Cathedral Square – The central square in the Kremlin takes its name from the fact that three principal cathedrals are situated here. The largest of these, Assumption (Uspensky) Cathedral, with its white limestone walls and five gilded domes, was built around 1475. This was the private cathedral of the czars, many of whom were crowned here, but when Napoleon occupied Moscow his men used it for a stable and burned some of its icons for firewood. Annunciation (Blagoveshchensky) Cathedral had three cupolas when it was built in early-Moscow style between 1484 and 1489. But when six new domes were added during reconstruction after a fire in the sixteenth century, it became known as the "golden-domed" cathedral. The five domes of Archangel Michael (Arkhangelsky) Cathedral, built between 1505 and 1509, are painted silver. All the czars from Ivan Kalita to Peter the Great, except for Boris Godunov, are buried here. Also on the square is the Palace of Facets (Granovitaya Palata), the oldest public building in Moscow, dating from 1473 to 1491; the Belltower of Ivan the Great, and several other early cathedrals. A kiosk sells tickets for the major cathedrals, which now function only as museums, not as religious institutions. Open daily.

The Great Kremlin Palace – Once the residence of the imperial family in Moscow, the palace today is a government building where the Supreme Soviets of the USSR and of the Russian Federation meet. Built from 1838 to 1849, the yellow-and-white-walled palace appears from the outside to have three floors. Actually, there are only two; the second floor has two tiers of windows. Not open to the general public, except by special tour.

The Armory (Oruzheinaya Palata) – The luxury of court life in czarist Russia is manifest in the halls of this museum next to the Great Kremlin Palace. Wonderful treasures of gold and silver, Fabergé eggs, royal carriages, ball gowns, and other royal regalia are preserved here. If you are lucky, you may be able to join one of the very small tour groups admitted to the Diamond Fund (Almasmovo Fondo SSSR) on Mondays, Wednesdays, and Saturdays. This section of the armory holds Catherine II's diamond-encrusted crown, her scepter with its Orlov diamond, and her golden orb, as well as other precious gems. Advance arrangement for this tour must be made through Intourist (see *Sources and Resources*).

OUTSIDE THE KREMLIN

Red Square (Krasnaya Ploshchad) – This enormous square — 2,280 feet long and 426 feet wide — is the heart of Moscow and the Soviet Union. It is bounded on the west by the Kremlin wall and the Lenin Mausoleum, on the south by St. Basil's Cathedral, on the east by the mammoth department store, *GUM,* and on the north by the State History Museum. The chief festivals — May Day on May 1 and Revolution Memorial Day on November 7 — take place amidst much flag waving in this square.

V. I. Lenin Mausoleum (Mausolei V. I. Lenin) – The body of V. I. Lenin, the Russian revolutionary and founder of Bolshevism, is displayed in its glass sarcophagus in this huge red and black, stepped mausoleum in front of the Kremlin wall. An impressive changing of the guard ceremony takes place in front of the mausoleum every hour. New guards goose-step out of the Kremlin through the main gate at 2 minutes before the hour and replace the old guards in front of the tomb as the clock in the Kremlin's Spassky Tower chimes the hour. Incredible numbers of people pass through the mausoleum each week to view Lenin's body. Open daily; closed Mondays and Fridays. On Red Square.

St. Basil's Cathedral (Pokrovsky Sobor) – St. Basil's is to Moscow what the Eiffel Tower is to Paris and the Statue of Liberty is to New York — a symbol uniquely expressive of the city. The gay colors and fanciful patterns of the cupolas of the cathedral's nine chapels have fascinated visitors since St. Basil's was built at the bidding of Ivan the Terrible in the mid-sixteenth century to celebrate the liberation of the Russian state from the Tartar yoke. Legend has it that terrible Ivan had the architects blinded when it was finished, so that they could never build a finer church. Take time to go inside and wander through the narrow passages to the tiny but extensively frescoed chapels. St. Basil's no longer has a religious function; it is a museum. Open daily; closed Tuesdays. Small admission charge. On Red Square.

GUM – One of the best-known — and largest — department stores in the world, *GUM* (an acronym, pronounced "goom") was built in the late nineteenth century as an arcade for nearly 1,000 small shops. It is said that some 350,000 shoppers wander through the three levels of this government-operated store each day. Open Mondays through Saturdays, 8 AM to 9 PM. On Red Square.

Central V. I. Lenin Museum (Tsentralny Musei V. I. Lenin) – Photographs of early revolutionary leaders and documents relating to Lenin's rise to power are housed in this red brick parliament (Duma) building on Revolution Square, just north of Red Square. Among the thousands of exhibits in the museum's 22 halls are many of Lenin's manuscripts, letters, and personal belongings, including a 1920 Rolls-Royce. Open daily; closed Mondays. Small admission charge. Revolution Square 4 (Revolyutsii Pl. 4) (phone: 295-4808).

Central Market (Tsentralny Rynok) – Flowers and produce are available year-round at this open-air market. Farmers from the southern republics fly to Moscow weekly to sell their goods in the free-enterprise markets here and elsewhere around the city. A few blocks west of the Kolchoznata Metro stop. Tsvetnoi Prospekt 15.

The Metro – Moscow's subway system is one of the city's most interesting museums in addition to being a clean, efficient means of transportation. Each of its more than 80 stations has its own aesthetic scheme: stained-glass windows, mosaics set with gold, crystal chandeliers, marble and stainless steel columns, bronze statues. The first line of the Metro was opened in 1935; the newer the station, the less ornate it is likely to be. Some of the station platforms, reached by fast escalators, are as much as 300 feet underground. For a single, very small fare you can ride the entire system, getting off at every station for a look. Since trains arrive every 2 to 4 minutes, you can cover much of the system in a short time. The most central station is at Revolution Square. Open daily, 6 AM to 1 AM.

New Maiden Convent (Novodevichy Monastyr) – Founded in 1524 to commemorate the liberation of Smolensk, this richly endowed convent was part of a ring of fortress-monasteries and convents that formed a protective circle around the Kremlin. Boris Godunov was proclaimed czar from this convent; Peter I's sister, Sophia, was imprisoned here when she encouraged rebellion against him; noble families sent their unmarried daughters and widowed, or unwanted, wives to live here. There is a functioning Russian Orthodox church here, but the convent's Smolensk Cathedral now serves as a museum of Russian applied arts from the sixteenth and seventeenth centuries. Chekhov, Gogol, Prokofiev, Stanislavski, Khrushchev, and other famous Russians are buried in a cemetery to the south of the convent, but it can only be visited by special permit (through Intourist). The convent is open daily; closed Tuesdays. Near the Sportivo Metro station. Also reached by trolleys 11 and 15 or buses 108 and 132. Between Novodevichy Proyed and Bolshaya Pirogovskaya.

Moscow State University – South of the convent, across the Moskva, the monumental Moscow State University towers above the city from its 415-acre site in Lenin Hills. Statistics offer the best summary of the world's largest university. The new buildings put up during the late Stalinist period between 1949 and 1953 contain 45,000 rooms connected by some 90 miles of corridors. The main building is 787 feet tall and its facade is 1,470 feet long. The university was founded in 1755 by Russian scientist Mikhail Lomonosov and officially bears his name. Near the Universitet and Leninskije Gory Metro stops. Also reached by bus and trolley. Universitetskij Prospekt.

Tretyakov Gallery (Gosudarstvennaya Tretyakovskaya Galereya) – An exceptional range of Russian art from tenth-century religious works to modern works is displayed in this turn-of-the-century gallery built to house the collections of Pavel and Sergei Tretyakov. Of special interest is the nineteenth-century collection and an icon exhibit that includes the historic *Virgin of Vladimir* and Andrei Rublev's masterpieces, *Trinity* and *Savior*. Open daily, except Mondays, 10 AM to 8 PM. Small admission fee. Across the Moskva from the Kremlin, near the Novokuzneckaja Metro station. Also reached by trolleys 1 and 8 and buses 6, 115, and K. Lavrushinsky Pereulok 10 (phone: 231-1362, 231-0565).

Pushkin Museum of Fine Arts (Gosudarstvenni Musei Izobrazitelnikh Iskusstv im. A. S. Pushkina) – Originally built as an educational museum, the Pushkin still has a large study collection of plaster casts of world sculpture. However, its most important works are in its rich collection of ancient Oriental and Renaissance art and its collection of nineteenth- and early-twentieth-century French paintings, including the work of Paul Cézanne, Claude Monet, and Pierre Auguste Renoir. Open daily, except Tuesdays, 10:30 AM to 8 PM. Small admission fee. A few blocks southwest of the Kremlin's Borovitsky Tower, near the Kropotkinskaya Metro stop. Volkhonka Ul. 12 (phone: 203-7998, 203-6973).

The Moscow Circus – Actually, there are two versions of this famous Moscow entertainment. The new circus is noted for its music, lights, breathtaking aerial acts, and spectacular finales; the old circus is folksier and includes special animal acts. The master clown, Oleg Popov, and the clown duo, Mikhail Sakharov and Igor Pavlov, are extremely popular with Moscow audiences. The role of the clowns in the Russian circus is central to the entire evening. The master clown is seen between each act, filling time with silly skits and riotous routines while equipment is being rearranged. Performances start at 7:30 PM, and tickets can be arranged through Intourist. The old circus performs at Tsvetnoi Prospekt 13; the new Moscow Circus, at Vernadskovo Prospekt 17, Lenin Hills.

USSR Exhibition of Economic Achievements (Vistavka Dostizheny Narod-nono Khozyaistva SSSR-VDNC) – This is sort of the Smithsonian Institution of the Soviet Union. All aspects of Soviet life — agriculture, industry, culture, and science — are detailed by the exhibits at this 553-acre park and pavilion site in northwest Moscow. The park, which has a zoo and a circus, is a popular place for Muscovites to spend a free day. In winter there is skiing, skating, and riding in a *troika,* the Russian horse-drawn sleigh. Outside the main entrance is an impressive monument to the Soviet space effort, a gleaming rocket trail in titanium called *Conquerors of Space.* The famous sculpture *The Worker and the Collective Farm Woman,* created by Vera Mukhina for the Paris Fair of 1937, stands at the North Gates entrance. The various buildings have different hours and closing days. The VDNKH Metro stop is just beside the main entrance. Mira Prospekt.

ENVIRONS

Kolomenskoye Estate-Museum – Established as a country estate for the ruling family in the fourteenth century, Kolomenskoye is on a hill beside the Moskva River about 10 miles (16 km) southeast of the Kremlin. The first stone church in the Russian "tent roof" style was erected here by Ivan Kalita in 1532, and several churches and buildings from the sixteenth and seventeenth century can also be seen here. The museum has interesting exhibits of door locks and keys, ceramic tiles and stones, and carved-wood architectural details. The museum is open daily; closed Mondays and Tuesdays. Small admission charge. The buildings can be seen from the main road, but the entrance is from a dirt road off the Kashirskoye Chaussée (Highway).

Kuskovo Estate – One of the best collections of eighteenth-century Russian art can be found in the palace of this estate that once belonged to the Sheremetiev family, one of the oldest Russian noble families. The palace has pine-log walls faced with painted boards and was built by serf craftsmen. Since 1932, it has been known as the State Museum of Ceramics, housing collections of Russian porcelain, glass, china, and majolica. A 70-acre formal French garden completes the ensemble. Open daily; closed Tuesdays. Small admission charge. The estate is about 6 miles (10 km) from central Moscow, along the Ryazanskoye Highway.

Arkhangelskoye Estate – The museum in the palace on this estate contains a collection of European painting and sculpture, but a visit is recommended primarily because of the grounds and the pleasant setting beside the Moskva. The park is in the French style, with statues and monuments lining the avenues. The museum is open daily; closed Mondays and Tuesdays. Small admission charge. Arkhangelskoye is 10 miles (16 km) from Moscow and can be reached by taking Leningradsky Prospekt to the Volokolamskoye Highway and then taking the left fork onto Petrovo-Dalniye Highway.

■**EXTRA SPECIAL:** There are two old cities northeast of Moscow that hold special attraction for the visitor. Arrangements to visit them are best made well in advance through Intourist.

Zagorsk: This little town on the Koshura and Glimitza rivers is the center of the handmade toy industry. Its Toy Museum (Krasnoi Armiyi Prospekt 136) has a wonderful collection of toys from the Bronze Age to the present. The reason most visitors come here, however, is to see the Trinity Monastery of St. Sergius (Troitskio-Sergievskaya Lavra), one of the most important surviving medieval monasteries in the Soviet Union. Founded by St. Sergius in 1340, the monastery has important historical significance as well as importance as a center of art and learning. During the Time of Troubles, it withstood a 16-month siege by Polish troops. Today it is the center for Russian Orthodoxy and a major pilgrimage site.

The monastery's Trinity Cathedral (Troitsky Sobor), built between 1422 and 1427, holds the tomb of St. Sergius and many beautiful icons. Assumption (Uspensky) Cathedral is best known for its stunning blue domes decorated with gold stars. Boris Godunov and members of his family are buried in tombs beside this cathedral. In the museum housed in other monastery buildings you can see rich collections of Russian ecclesiastical art, portraits, rare fabrics, and Russian handicrafts. The museum is open daily; closed Fridays. Zagorsk is about 45 miles (72 km) from central Moscow. Follow Mira Prospekt onto the Jaroslavskoje Highway, which will take you to Zagorsk.

Suzdal: A settlement since at least the tenth century, Suzdal has become a museum-city of ancient monasteries, churches, and convents and secular buildings spanning the centuries. Inside the walls of the Suzdal Kremlin beside the River Kamenka, you'll find the Nativity of the Virgin (Rozhdestvensky) Cathedral, built between 1222 and 1225. Its star-studded blue domes are similar to those at the Assumption Cathedral in Zagorsk. The Suzdal Local Museum is housed in the Archbishop's Palace near the cathedral and features collections of early Russian icons, clothing, and jewelry. Recently, representative eighteenth- and nineteenth-century buildings have been brought to Suzdal from various regions of the country and installed in the open-air Museum of Wooden Architecture beside the river.

Suzdal is 22 miles (35 km) due north of Vladimir, another ancient city worth a visit. You may want to make a 2-day excursion from Moscow and use Vladimir as a base for your trip to Suzdal. If you leave Moscow by Entusiastov Prospekt, it runs into Kazansky Highway, which will take you to Vladimir, 114 miles (182 km) to the northeast. If you plan to go directly to Suzdal, drive north along the Klasma River out of Vladimir. There also are frequent trains from Moscow's Kurst railway station to Vladimir.

SOURCES AND RESOURCES

Intourist is the largest travel agency in the Soviet Union. It owns hotels and restaurants and deals with all types of foreign travel. In Moscow, the Intourist office is at Marx Prospekt 15 (phone: 292-2768). There are two other travel agencies in the Soviet Union: the Tourist Council of the Trade Unions, which organizes visits by trade union delegations, and Sputnik, Lebyazhny Pereulok 4 (phone: 223-9512), which organizes group tours for young people. Intourist provides English-speaking guides for general and specific sight-seeing, but for your own enjoyment, take the time to learn the Russian (Cyrillic) alphabet and the sound of each of its characters. When you sound out the signs you see, you will recognize many English and French cognates.

Although good transportation and city maps are available at hotel kiosks in Moscow, comprehensive travel guides in English should be purchased before you leave the US. One of the most useful general guides is *The Complete Guide to the Soviet Union*, by Victor and Jennifer Louis (St. Martin's Press; $9.95). A good guide to Moscow and its museums is *Next Time You Go to Russia*, by Charles A. Ward (Charles Scribner's Sons, $8.95).

The *Falkplan City Map of Moscow* (Hamburg: Falk-Verlag; $6.95) is a valuable backup for local maps and is available in bookstores throughout the US. It is an excellent, handy pocket map with a street name index, public transportation routes, and lists of hotels, museums, and theaters.

For Local Coverage – An English edition of the weekly paper *Moscow News* is usually available at the hotels, and in Intourist hotels the *International Herald Tribune* is sometimes available, although not on a regular basis. If you are desperate for news of the world, stop by the American Embassy, Chaikovskovo Ul. 19/23 (phone: 252-0011), for an update. Otherwise, bring along a shortwave radio or be content with blissful ignorance.

A word about telephones: Telephone directories seem to be one of Russia's rarest commodities, but you can get assistance at your hotel's desk or service bureau. The service bureau can book long-distance calls for you, but it is advisable to arrange the call at least an hour before you wish to make connections. To use the pay phones, deposit a 2-kopek coin in the slot before lifting the receiver. Dial when you hear a continuous buzzing sound.

 CLIMATE AND CLOTHES: The harshness of the Moscow winter has sent shivers from the pages of a hundred Russian novels. Snow begins to fall as early as October, and by December the city is usually covered with snow and ice. So it's true that winter can be excruciating for the uninitiated — it defeated Napoleon, after all — but it is also true that the overcast winter half-days give way each spring to a glory of lilacs and tulips and that summer in this city is wonderfully mild. Temperatures can range from 10° F (−12° C) in January to about 65° F (18° C) in July. Boots, a heavy coat, scarf, warm hat, and gloves are essential in winter. Layered clothing is the best approach, since the interiors of buildings are well heated. It rains an average of 8 to 12 days a month, so bring a travel umbrella.

One need not dress up in Moscow, but on the other hand, shorts are in poor taste and blue jeans are inappropriate for evenings out. You are expected to check your coat when entering any public building or restaurant. (It is simply not cultured, *neh kulturni,* to take your coat with you.) All garments are hung on hooks, so it is a good idea to sew a chain or heavy loop into your coat collar in order to prevent damage — and dark looks from the cloakroom attendant.

It is preferable to pack clothes made of washable fabrics. Laundry service is available in hotels, but it is often slow, and dry cleaning is questionable at best.

 GETTING AROUND: Moscow has a very efficient and exceptionally inexpensive public transportation system. From late spring through early fall, you might also take one of the low-priced boats that cruise along the Moskva River, stopping in different parts of the city.

Bus, Tram, and Trolley – These transport lines operate from 6 AM to 1:30 AM and cost only a few kopeks — less than a dime. Exact change is required. You deposit your fare in a cash box that produces a ticket when you turn a knob at the side of the box. When the bus is especially crowded, you will be expected to pass your fare along to the person standing by the cash box, who makes the transaction for you and passes back your ticket. Maps showing the routes for all lines are available at hotel kiosks.

Metro – The subway has several interconnected lines. One runs in a rough circle; the others radiate out to different parts of the city. Trains arrive and depart at the various stations frequently and operate from 6 AM to 1 AM.

Taxi – Prices have risen sharply for Moscow's taxis. Normally, they can only be found at cabstands — marked with a "T" and a checkered pattern similar to the one on taxi doors — or at hotels. They can be ordered in advance, however, through your hotel service bureau or, if you speak Russian, by calling 225–0000 or 225–0006.

Car Rental – Automobiles, with or without chauffeurs, may be rented through Intourist for use in the city. Rentals must be paid for in foreign currency.

 MUSEUMS: Besides the museums mentioned in *Special Places,* Moscow has numerous museums devoted to Russian art and folk craft, the work of famous writers and composers who lived here, and various aspects of Russian history.

State History Museum, Red Square 1/2 (phone: 228-8452).
Museum of the Revolution (Tsentralni Musei Revolyutsii SSSR), Gorkovo Ul. 21 (phone: 299-9633).
Doestoyevsky Apartment-Museum, Doestoyskovo Ul. 2 (phone: 281-1085).
Pushkin Fine Arts Museum (Musei Izobrazitelnikh Iskusstv im A. S. Pushkina), Volkhonka Ul. 12 (phone: 203-7993).
Leo Tolstoy Museum (Gosudarstvenni Literaturni Musei L. H. Tolstovo), Kropokinskaya Ul. 11 (phone: 202-2190).
Leo Tolstoy Home (Filial Museya L. H. Tolstovo), Leva Tolstovo Ul. 21 (phone: 246-9444).
Glinka State Central Museum of Musical Culture (Gosudarstvenni Tsentralni Musei Musikalnoi Kulturi im. M. I. Glinki), Georgievsky Pereulok 4 (phone: 292-6669).
Chekhov Museum, Sadovaya-Kudrinskaya Ul. 6 (phone: 291-3837).
State Museum of Oriental Art (Gosudarstvenni Musei Iskusstv Narodov Vostoka), Obukha Ul. 16 (phone: 227-3411).
Museum of Folk Art (Musei Narodnovo Iskusstva), Stanislavskovo Ul. 7 (phone: 290-2114).
Andrei Rublev Museum of Old Russian Art, Pryamikova Pl. 10 (phone: 278-1429).
Lenin Funeral Train Pavilion-Museum, Lenina Pl. 1 (phone: 231-7300).
Darwin Museum, Malaya Pirogovskaya Ul. 1 (phone: 246-6470).
Gorky Museum, Vorovskovo Ul. 25A (phone: 290-0535).
Central Exhibition Hall (Tsentralni Vistavochni Sal), Oktyabrya Pl. 50-letiya (phone: 202-9304).

 SHOPPING: There are wonderful things to buy here: amber, furs, samovars, lacquer boxes, balalaikas, caviar, vodka, and that ultimate Russian souvenir, Matroska dolls, a family of gaily painted wooden dolls hidden one inside the other. Tourists usually can find the widest variety of goods and the best prices at the special government stores, *Beriozkas.* These stores only accept foreign currency, traveler's checks, or credit cards. Most Intourist hotels have such shops, although they vary in size and variety of stock. The largest is in the *Rossia Hotel.* If you decide instead to use Russian currency and shop where the Muscovites do, here are some suggestions:

Detsky Mir – The name translates to "Children's World," and this shop is particularly noted for its wonderful toys. Marksa Prospekt 2.
Dom Knigi – Beautiful souvenir books about Moscow and the Soviet Union and colorful Russian posters and post cards can be purchased at this House of Books. Kalinina Prospekt 26.
Melodia – As its name suggests, this is the place to buy records of some of those marvelous Russian folk songs you've been hearing since you arrived. Kalinina Prospekt 40.

 SPECIAL EVENTS: Because pictures of the ceremonies in Red Square are transmitted around the world, the *International Labor Day* celebration, with its parades and demonstrations every May 1, and the anniversary of the *1917 Russian Revolution,* celebrated November 7 and 8, are probably the best-known special events in Moscow. There are also two major festivals of the arts: *Russian Winter Festival,* December 25–January 5, and *Moscow Stars Festival of Folk and Classical Dance,* May 5–13. *International Women's Day,* March 8, commemorates the Second International Conference of Socialist Women, which took place in Copenhagen in 1910. April 22 is *Lenin's birthday.*

 SPORTS: Muscovites are avid sports fans, particularly of ice hockey, soccer, and horse racing. Attending such events is a good way to see Soviet citizens at leisure, enjoying themselves with exuberance and spirit. Schedules and tickets are available through the Intourist service bureaus. In addition to the new Olympic sports complex, there is a major sports facility across the Moskva River from Moscow State University: Luzhniki Park. The *Central Lenin Stadium,* Luzhniki E3, seats 103,000 people and is used primarily for various international competitions. This stadium was the scene of the opening and closing of the 1980 Olympic Games and the principal athletic center for the games. A totally new sports complex built near Mir Prospekt for the Olympics has the largest indoor stadium in Europe.

Horse Racing – Harness and thoroughbred racing with low-stake pari-mutuel betting takes place each Wednesday, Saturday, and Sunday at the *Hippodrome Racecourse,* Begovaya U1. 22. Post time is 5 PM, with an additional program at 1 PM on Sundays. In winter, there are also exciting *troika* races held on the snow or ice.

Ice Hockey – The most popular ice hockey teams in Moscow are *Spartak, Dinamo* and *TSSKA.* Ticket and schedule information is available from Intourist.

Soccer – This sport is a passion with many Muscovites. The *Dynamo Stadium,* Leningradskii Prospekt 36, holds 60,000 people and was built for one of Moscow's powerhouse teams.

Swimming – The water for the *Moskva Open-Air Swimming Pool,* Kropotkinskaya nab. 37, is heated so the pool can be used all year round. In winter, when the steam gathers over the pool, it may look like something from Dante's *Inferno,* but this steam layer protects the swimmers from the cold. There also are other pools and several bathing beaches in Moscow. Swimming competitions take place at the *Palace of Water Sports,* Mironovskaya 27.

 THEATER: Intourist service bureaus can provide schedules and tickets, but don't expect to get tickets for popular companies, such as the *Bolshoi Ballet,* unless you book well ahead of time. One special treat in attending theater performances in Moscow is the buffet available during intermissions. You can have champagne, sandwiches, chocolates, or delectable Russian ice cream. The most famous theater here is, of course, the *Bolshoi Theater* (Gosudarstvenni Akademichesky Bolshoi Teatr Soyuza SSR), Sverdlova Pl. 2. The *Bolshoi Opera* and the *Bolshoi Ballet* also perform at the 6,000-seat *Palace of Congresses Theater (Kremlevsky Dvorets Syezdov)* inside the Kremlin complex. (Enter through Kutafia-Troitsky Gate on Prospekt Marksa at Prospekt Kalinina.) Other major theaters here are: *Maly Theater (Gosudarstvenni Akademichesky Mali Teatr),* Sverdlova Pl. 1/6, which stages Russian classics; *Moscow Drama* and *Comedy Theater,* Taganka *(Moskovsky Teatr Drami i Komedii na Taganke),* Chkalova Ul. 76, considered this city's most avant-garde theater; *State Central Puppet Theater (Gosudarstvenni Tsentralni Teatr Kukol),* Spartakovskaya Ul. 26; *Stanislavsky and Nemirovich-Danchenko Academic Musical Theater (Moskovsky Akademichesky Muzikalni Teatr im K. S. Stanislavskovo i V. I. Neimirovicha-Danchenko),* Pushkinskaya Ul. 17, which presents ballets as well as musical events.

 MUSIC: Ticket and schedule information is available from Intourist. The three most important concert halls for music lovers in Moscow are the *Moscow State Conservatoire,* Gertsena Ul. 13; the *Tchaikovsky Concert Hall (Konsertni Sal im P. I. Chaikovskovo),* Sadovaya Bolskaya Ul. 20 in Mayakovsky Pl.; and the *Hall of Columns (Kolonnyi Sal)* in the Trade Unions House, Pushkinskaya Ul. 1. Opera is performed at the *Bolshoi Theater* and the *Stanislavsky and Nemirovich-Danchenko Academic Musical Theater* (see *Theater*). For something a bit lighter, try the *Moscow Operetta Theater,* Pushkinskaya Ul. 6.

 NIGHTCLUBS AND NIGHTLIFE: Nightlife in Western terms really doesn't exist here. Restaurants do have dancing each night and some foreign-currency bars stay open late for drinkers. With the rich selection of theater, ballet, opera, music, the circus, and sports to choose from, your evenings need never be boring. At any hour of the night, a walk in floodlight-lit Red Square is a very special experience.

 SINS: Biggest! Best! First! The intense *pride* of the Soviets in their accomplishments in all phases of their lives is often astounding. *Anger* is instantly directed at anyone who shows a lack of respect for the city — particularly anyone who litters. You will notice the cleanliness of the streets and the lack of graffiti or trash in the Metro stations and trains. You can also raise the ire of guards within the Kremlin by stepping off the sidewalk into the street where there are no crosswalks. When they blow their whistles, they mean business! Join the locals for an afternoon of *sloth* in one of Moscow's many green spots. The Alexander Garden in the shade of the Kremlin wall is a convenient downtown setting when you incline toward indolence.

BEST IN TOWN

 **CHECKING IN:** Whether traveling with a group or as an individual, you must have paid-in-advance reservations for accommodations before entering the Soviet Union. These reservations can be made through Intourist. You may request a particular hotel when you make your reservation, but normally you will not be advised of your assigned hotel until you arrive. There are three types of tourist accommodation: Deluxe Suite, Deluxe, and First Class. Double occupancy in a Deluxe Suite costs as much as $165; in Deluxe rooms, $100; and in First Class, about $50. No meals are included in these prices.

Intourist – Completed in 1970, this 22-story hotel is on Gorky Street, a short walk from Red Square. Rooms are quite comfortable and you leave your room key at the front desk rather than with the floor matron, which is the typical procedure at hotels in Moscow. There's a floor show and dancing in the *Stars Sky* restaurant on the ground floor and a late-night, foreign-currency bar on a lower level. The Intourist Central Excursion Bureau is right next door. Gorkovo Ul. 3 (phone: 203-4008).

National – A Deluxe rating for this fine old hotel could be granted solely on the view of the Kremlin it offers. Opened in 1903, the *National* provides elegant surroundings, an excellent restaurant on the ground floor, and a late-night, hard-currency bar on the second floor. Prospekt Marksa 14/1 (phone: 203-6539).

Metropol – The facade of this beautiful turn-of-the-century hotel is decorated with a marvelous majolica relief that reproduces Mikhail Vrubel's *Dream Princess*. It is close to the *Bolshoi* and *Maly* theaters on Sverdlova Pl. (see *Theaters*) and has a friendly outdoor café during warm weather. The public rooms here are elegantly appointed, and its restaurants — particularly the *Russian Tea Room (Russkaya Chainaya)* — serve very good food. One of the few places in Moscow where you can sometimes find Pepsi-Cola. Prospekt Marksa 1/4 (phone: 225-6673).

Rossia – This is Europe's largest hotel, capable of accommodating 6,000 guests. It is so large that it has four separate wings, each with its own entrance and dining facility. On the top floor of the 21-story tower wing, the *Rossia Restaurant* provides a great view of the Kremlin and Red Square (see *Seeing the City*). The south wing has its own 3,000-seat concert hall and two cinemas. On the corner of the east wing is the entrance to an enormous foreign-currency *Beriozka* shop (see *Shopping*). Near St. Basil's Cathedral, the *Rossia* was completed in 1967 for the 50th anniversary of the Revolution. North Wing, Razina Ul. 6 (phone: 298-5401); East Wing, Moskvoretskaya Nab. 1 (phone: 298-1442).

Ukraina – One of the seven look-alike skyscrapers built during the late Stalinist period (Moscow State University is the largest), the *Ukraina* is a large, comfortable hotel on the banks of the Moskva. It is some distance from the center of the city, however. Kutuzovsky Prospekt (phone: 243-3030).

 EATING OUT: You may book prix fixe menu meals through the Intourist service bureaus for many Moscow restaurants. Payment to the service bureau usually is in foreign currency and may range from $15 to $25 per person. However, this includes appetizers, entrée, dessert, vodka, wines, fruit drinks, and coffee as well as music and dancing. If you go to the cafés or restaurants on your own, you must pay in Russian currency; no credit cards are accepted. These restaurants will not fall into the gourmet category, but they do offer a wide variety of national foods from the various regions of the Soviet Union. If you like black caviar (called *ikra*), indulge yourself. If you like vegetables, you'll be disappointed; even in summer, vegetables are puny compared to what is available at home.

Aragvi – This bustling Georgian restaurant is the closest you'll get to luxury dining in Moscow. As a result, it's usually filled with diplomats, ballerinas, commissars, and foreign journalists who have sampled the best in Europe's more glittering capitals. Georgian food is highly seasoned; specialties include a spicy meat soup called *kharcho;* skewered roast Georgian mutton, *shashlik po kharski;* and roast chicken pressed between scalding stones, *tsiplyata tabaka.* Reservations are necessary. Gorkovo Ul. 6 (phone: 229-3762).

Baku – Azerbaijan cuisine and music. The cuisine is similar to Turkish food. Try meatballs in vine leaves, *golubtsy,* or the sour milk and meat soup, *dovta.* Gorkovo Ul. 24 (phone: 299-9426).

Uzbekistan – Uzbek cuisine and music. Sample the large meat-filled dumplings, *muntyi,* or the soup made of minced meat, eggs, and dumplings. Neglinnaya Ul. 29 (phone: 294-6053).

National Restaurant – Good food and an excellent view of the Kremlin. Located on the ground floor of one of Moscow's fine old hotels, the *National* (see *Checking In*). A late-night bar on the second floor serves whiskey and other drinks for hard currency. Gorkovo Ul. 1 (phone: 203-9555).

Salvyansky Bazar – Traditional Slav cuisine and music. Originally opened in 1870, this has always been a favorite dining spot of writers and musicians. 25-vo, Oktyabrya Ul. 17 (phone: 228-4845).

Tsentralynyi – Traditional Russian food, such as beef Stroganoff and skewered mutton and onions, *shashlik.* Originally opened in 1865 as *Filippov's.* Gorkovo Ul. 10 (phone: 229-7235).

Arbat – Seats 2,000 people. Almost always filled with tourists, the *Arbat* offers a floor show as well as music and dancing. Kalinina Prospekt (phone: 291-1403).

MUNICH

To many people, Bavaria is a place apart from the rest of West Germany; gayer, more rosy-cheeked, less Teutonic. And Munich, the principal city of this southern region in the lap of the Bavarian Alps, is one of the jolliest cities in all Europe. It is, of course, renowned for two of the wildest, noisiest, fun-filled festivals anywhere. During Oktoberfest each year (held in September, oddly enough), hundreds of thousands of Germans and tourists celebrate the wedding of Crown Prince Ludwig to Princess Therese von Sachsen-Hildburghausen. The fact that the wedding took place in 1810 doesn't deter the crowd's enthusiasm one bit. Then, less than 4 months later, Müncheners go on another binge, called Fasching. Traditionally, all sorts of bizarre behavior is acceptable — and usually takes place — during this carnival season, preceding Lenten abstinence.

Even when there is no formal festival taking place, this is the beer capital of the world. Germans guzzle more beer than the people of any other country: 150 liters per person per year. But the Bavarians do even better, downing 250 liters apiece annually.

The thing that makes Munich so special, however, is that it is able to combine this earnest lust for life with modern sophistication. There is a pleasing blend of elegance and rustic charm, the naughty and the nice, here. Bavarian beer gardens and folk art coexist with Paris fashion, grand opera, and astrophysics, giving rise to such nicknames as "Village of a Million," and "Metropolis with a Heart."

As a cultural center, Munich has produced the largest number of German Nobel Prize winners; it is the home of the respected Bavarian State Opera, more than 20 legitimate theaters and cabarets, and important scientific institutes; and it is the largest university city in Germany, with more than 30,000 students in residence.

Statistics show that only one in three of Munich's 1,297,000 citizens was born here, and one in ten is foreign-born. There is little wonder, though, that a cosmopolitan center that manages to retain a strong Alpine village flavor is so attractive to outsiders.

During the past 800 years, Munich has grown up along the banks of the Isar River, which flows down from the Bavarian Alps through forest and farmland before cutting a determined path through the eastern part of the city on its way to meet the Danube. On very clear days, the Alps, some 50 miles away, provide a stunning backdrop for the city.

Munich takes its name from the monks, *Munichen* in High German, who founded a Benedictine monastery in this area in the ninth century. The city itself was established beside the Isar River in 1158 by Henry the Lion, duke of Saxony, who had been ceded part of Bavaria by Emperor Friedrich Barbarossa. But in 1180 Barbarossa replaced Duke Henry with the Palatine

Count Otto von Wittelsbach. From that time, the House of Wittelsbach was closely linked to Bavaria's and Munich's fortunes until the monarchy was replaced by a republic after World War I.

Toward the middle of the nineteenth century, Bavarian King Ludwig I put much of his energy into making Munich the most beautiful city in Europe. It was during his reign that many of the city's great buildings were erected and Ludwigstrasse was built. However, the king was forced to abdicate in 1848 when the scandal of his liaison with the Spanish dancer Lola Montez lent fuel to a revolutionary movement. His 18-year-old grandson, Ludwig II, became king in 1864. and carried out an even more grandiose building scheme. He ordered the construction of three extravagant castles and commissioned an array of phantasmagoria ranging from a boat in the shape of a huge shell to furniture, porcelain, and robes. Often called the Dream King, Ludwig II was much loved by his subjects, but court doctors declared him to be in an "advanced stage of mental disorder" and he was stripped of his powers shortly before he died by drowning at the age of 40.

After Germany's defeat in World War I, Munich was the center of the Nazi movement. Adolf Hitler and his National Socialists made an abortive attempt to seize power here in 1923 during the infamous Beer Garden Putsch. In 1938, Mussolini, Chamberlain, and Daladier met here with Hitler and agreed to let Germany annex the Sudetenland.

Much of the city was destroyed in bombing raids during World War II, but unlike some of its sister cities, Munich eschewed the modern and reconstructed its past. Except for the space-age architecture of the suburban Olympic Village, built for the 1972 summer games, Munich looks like a typical old European city. In some cases, original plans were used in the reconstruction or restoration of Munich landmarks. Today the city's public buildings reflect the many styles in which they were built over the centuries: late Gothic, Venetian Renaissance, neoclassical, rococo, and baroque. Church spires and bell towers, rather than high-rise office buildings, dominate the skyline.

Modern Munich is many things: an old-world city, a center of culture and sophistication, a city of gaiety, an intellectual center, and, with all its beer, *Wurst,* and *Gemütlichkeit,* a carnival of life.

MUNICH AT-A-GLANCE

 SEEING THE CITY: An exceptional view of Munich and the Bavarian Alps is available from the television tower (Olympiaturm) located just northwest of the city at Olympic Village. The 943-foot tower was erected to facilitate televising the 1972 Summer Olympics. A $1.20 elevator ride will take you to the tower terrace at 623 feet, with its impressive panorama of the city. There is also a dining room, the *Tower Restaurant,* which revolves for a 360° view.

 SPECIAL PLACES: Marienplatz, with its tall white column of the Virgin, the city's patron, is the heart of Munich. Many of the streets leading from it have been closed to traffic and turned into a pedestrian zone called *Fussgängerbereich.* About eight blocks west of Marienplatz is the central square,

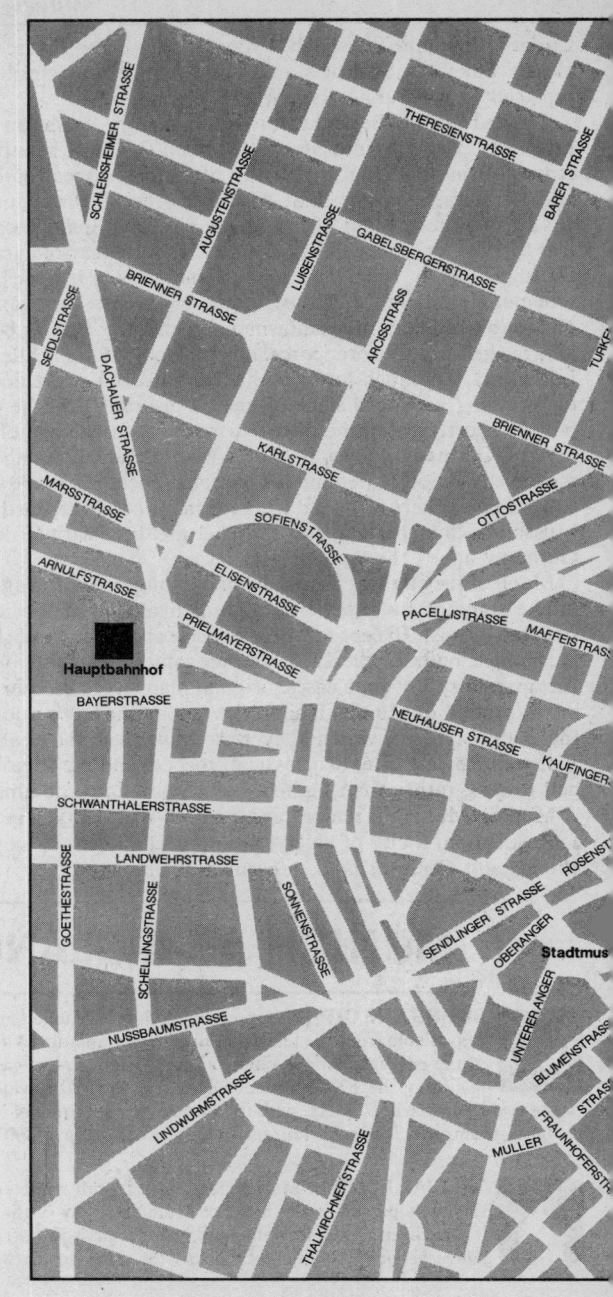

MUNICH

AMALIENSTRASSE

LUDWIGSTRASSE

KAULBACHSTRASSE

KONIGINSTRASSE

SKAR VON MILLER RING

VON DER TANN STRASSE

Bavarian
National
Museum

PRINZREGENTEN STR

WEINSTR THEATINERSTR

Frauenkirche Residenz

National
Theater

KARL SCHARNGL RING

MARSTALL STR

MAXIMILIANSTRASSE

Rathaus

Hofbrauhaus

tualienmarkt

WESTENRIEDERSTR

FRAUENSTRASSE

ZWEIBRUCKENSTR

STEINSDORFSTRASSE

KLENZESTRASSE

BAADERSTRASSE

KOHLER STR

LUDWIGSBRUCKE

REICHENBACHSTRASSE

CORNELIUSSTRASSE

ERHARDTSTRASSE

Karlsplatz, known locally as Stachus, where buses, trams, and subways to all parts of the city arrive and depart. Visitors are often confused because street names change abruptly in central Munich for no apparent reason. You can always get back to the center again, though, because there are numerous signs pointing the way and the spires and towers of landmark churches stand out above the lower red-roofed buildings that constitute the heart of Munich. The Isar River cuts through the city's eastern section, and a walk north along its banks will lead to a huge, lovely park, the English Garden. On the west side of the park lies the Schwabing district. Munich has a superbly integrated system of buses, trams, and subways to help you enjoy the city.

DOWNTOWN

Schwabing – At the turn of the century, Schwabing had a reputation as an artistic and intellectual center. Today this district to the north of the University of Munich is known to most visitors as the place "where the action is" in Munich. By day Schwabing resembles any other German residential district, but about six in the evening people swarm into its streets looking for a good time. The sidewalks along Leopoldstrasse, Schwabing's main street, and on Amalienstrasse and Türkenstrasse, take on a festive air. You'll see a confusion of sights: painters displaying their art, street musicians, poets offering their latest verses, barbers giving haircuts on the sidewalk, palm readers, quick-sketch artists. You can buy sandals, copper jewelry, ceramics, beads, belts — just about anything, in fact, including genuine and bogus antiques. Schwabing has more than 200 restaurants, with Greek, Yugoslavian, Italian, and Bavarian the most popular. There are countless discotheques, jazz *kellers,* cafés, and boutiques.

Old Pinakothek (Alte Pinakothek) – One of the world's great art galleries, this huge Renaissance building contains large and important collections of Dutch and Flemish painting from the fourteenth to the eighteenth century. The museum was built from 1826 to 1836 to house paintings gathered by the dukes of Wittelsbach. Ludwig I made numerous other acquisitions that enhanced the museum's reputation. Among its treasures are important works by Albrecht Dürer and Peter Paul Rubens. Open daily; closed Mondays. Small admission charge. Barer Str. 27 (phone: 2380-5216).

German Museum (Deutsches Museum) – Considered the largest technical museum in the world, the German Museum is housed on an island in the Isar River to the southeast of the city center. Included in its massive displays are the original 139-foot U-boat built in 1906, locomotives from the Bavarian State Railway, a collection of antique pianos and organs, a Messerschmitt 267 jet fighter from 1944, a planetarium, salt and coal mining exhibits in actual caverns, the new aeronautical and space center, and much, much more. Unfortunately, detailed descriptions are only available in German, but it's still very much worth a visit. Open daily. Small admission charge. Reached by subway or by walking across one of several bridges connecting the island with the city. Isar Island (phone: 2-1791).

The English Garden (Englischer Garten) – This eighteenth-century garden, one of the oldest landscaped parks on the Continent, is a favorite meeting place. It has lakes and pavilions, such as the Chinese pagoda; riding trails; a Japanese teahouse; and outdoor cafés from which you can enjoy the passing scene. If you want to splurge, a pleasant carriage ride through the park will cost about $10 for a half hour. The park is northeast of the city's center, between Schwabing and the Isar River.

Cathedral of Our Lady (Frauenkirche) – The onion domes atop two 325-feet symmetrical towers have made this late Gothic cathedral Munich's most distinctive landmark. The dull red brick facade of the cathedral was damaged extensively during air raids in 1944, but it has been rebuilt. The cathedral contains a rich depository of religious works of art, relics, sacred tombs, and the mausoleum of Emperor Ludwig IV. An elevator inside the south tower takes visitors to the top of one of the towers, from which there is a good view of the city. Frauenpl. 1.

The Palace (Residenz) – Although damaged during World War II, the royal palace has regained much of its glory. Built for the dukes of Wittelsbach, the palace has been extended over the centuries to form a complex of buildings with seven inner courts. There are state rooms and royal suites in Renaissance, rococo, and neoclassical styles and displays of royal treasures. Open daily except Mondays. Small admission charge. Entrance Max-Joseph-Pl. 3 (phone: 22-46-41).

Bavarian National Museum (Bayerisches Nationalmuseum) – The vast array of art and historical memorabilia from the Middle Ages to the nineteenth century on display here should give you an excellent introduction to Bavarian culture. The museum has what may be the most extensive collection of arts and crafts in the world. Along with its tapestries and wood carvings, the museum is best known for its unique Krippenschau Collection of Christmas cribs and nativity scenes. Closed Mondays. Small admission charge. Prinzregentenstr. 3 (phone: 21681).

Hofbräuhaus – This immense beer hall is a dance palace, a restaurant, and a national monument to the good life. In the beer garden, you'll be part of a scene people around the world associate with Munich: cheerful fräuleins carrying as many as 10 steins of beer at once, waitresses and waiters in peasant costumes moving through a noisy crowd selling pretzels stacked on long sticks, or white radishes cut into fancy spirals — both suitably salty to help you work up a thirst. It's not expensive, and is a must on any visitor's sight-seeing agenda. Am Platz 9 (phone: 22-16-76).

The New City Hall (Neues Rathaus) – Munich's new city hall dominates Marienplatz. Each day throngs of people peer up at its famous carillon (Glockenspiel), waiting to see the mechanical knights and their squires joust while the carillon signals to the city that it is 11 AM. It is a delightful diversion, not to be missed. Marienpl.

The Victuals Market (Viktualienmarkt) – A few blocks south of Marienplatz, farmers, butchers, bakers, and other purveyors of food specialties set out their wares in an open-air market Mondays through Saturdays. It's the perfect place to browse, take pictures, and buy a snack or picnic fixings. Viktualienmarkt.

SUBURBS

Olympic Village (Olympiapark) – Built for the 1972 Olympic Games, the scene of the terrorist massacre of Israeli athletes. The modern sports complex includes swimming pools, tracks, and gymnasiums. The park also has an 80,000-seat stadium — under an extraordinary skinlike roof — and an artificial lake. The housing built for Olympic athletes and officials now constitutes a major residential suburb. Guided tours are available and you can even swim in one of the pools that Mark Spitz made famous in his successful pursuit of five gold medals. Small admission charge. It can be reached easily by bus or subway. Oberwiesenfeld (phone: 306-13-423, 306-13-424).

Nymphenburg Palace and Park (Schloss Nymphenburg) – Just west of the Munich city limits stands a splendid 495-acre park with lakes and hunting lodges and Nymphenburg Palace, once the residence of the Bavarian kings. The great hall of the palace is decorated with frescoes by Johann Baptist Zimmermann, and a museum (Marstallmuseum) in the south wing of the palace houses state carriages and sleighs. The Nymphenburg China Factory, with showrooms open to the public, is on the north crescent of the grounds. Concerts are presented on the grounds during summer months, and it is a particularly lovely spot to visit when rhododendron are in bloom from May through June. Open daily; closed Mondays. Small admission charge. Entrance from Menzingerstr (phone: 1-2081).

Hellabrunn Zoo (Tierpark Hellabrunn) – Europe's largest zoo, Hellabrunn keeps its extensive collection of animals in a 173-acre natural setting of forestland and rivers. The zoo is famous for breeding rare animals and for its anthropoid ape section. Guided tours on Wednesdays. Open daily. Small admission charge. There is regular bus service from Marienpl. Four miles (6 km) south of Munich at Siebenbrunnerstr. 6 (phone: 66-10-21).

Dachau – The name Dachau has evoked nothing but horror since this first Nazi concentration camp was built in 1933. Some 200,000 prisoners and deportees were received here. The number who died or disappeared is uncertain, although it is estimated that 32,000 may have perished. The magnitude of the atrocities committed is compounded by the natural beauty of the area: Dachau itself is a charming terraced town near a misty heath. The old administration building is now used as a museum where photos, memorabilia, and exhibits document what transpired here. A film about the camp is shown twice daily in English. Open daily; closed December 24 and the afternoons of December 31 and Shrove Tuesday. No admission charge. Dachau, 14 miles (22 km) northwest of Munich, can be reached by Petershausen commuter train from the main railway station. There is a direct bus from the station to the camp. (phone: 08131-1741)

■**EXTRA SPECIAL:** It's said that over 650 kinds of beer are brewed in Bavaria, including those made privately. Munich is home to six of Germany's major producers, and one of these, Spaten (which alone makes nine different labels), will arrange tours upon request. During a half-hour walk through the plant, accompanied by an English-speaking guide, guests learn the various steps of beer-making — from germination of the barley to bottling the brew. The tour is an essential preliminary to enlightened imbibing. Spaten is located at Marsstr. 46; to make reservations, call 5122.

SOURCES AND RESOURCES

The Munich Tourist Office has information counters at the main railway station, Hauptbahnhof, Bayerstr. entrance 2 (phone: 239-1256), and at the Arrivals Hall of Riem Airport (phone: 90-72-56). Both are open daily until late evening.

For Local Coverage – The tourist office publishes an official monthly program, *München,* that lists theater, museum, and concert schedules, special exhibitions, hotels, camping facilities, and other useful information, but it is only published in German. However, many hotels provide literature in English focusing on Munich's activities and entertainment programs. The *Munich Times,* a newspaper in English, comes out twice a week.

CLIMATE AND CLOTHES: Because of the proximity to the shifting air currents of the Alps, Munich's weather can be unpredictable. Except in summer, come prepared for extremes. You'll need solid shoes, rain boots, warm underwear, a Windbreaker, and a hat or cap. Temperatures can range from a high of 74°F (23°C) in July to a chilly 26°F (−3°C) in January. Munich is a very fashion-conscious city, so you'll probably want to dress up for evening unless your nights on the town are going to be in informal Schwabing.

GETTING AROUND: Munich has an integrated rapid transit system, and the tickets that you buy from the blue dispensers at stations, streetcar stops, and on those vehicles bearing a white and green "K" sign can be used on buses, streetcars, subways, and local trains. You can cancel the tickets yourself in automatic canceling machines at the barriers of stations and in streetcars and buses bearing a yellow and black "E" sign. There is a reduced-rate ticket for about $2 that permits you to ride as much as you care to during a 24-hour period. These special tickets are sold at the Tourist Information offices and all ticket offices.

Bus and Streetcar – The Karlsplatz is the main junction for Munich's streetcars, and the East Railway Station (Ostbahnhof) across the Isar from central Munich is the terminal for many of the city's blue and white buses.

Subway and Train – Munich's subway is called the U-Bahn. It crosses the city in a north-south direction and has its central stops at Marienplatz and Hauptbahnhof. Like most European underground rail systems, the U-Bahn is clean, modern, and efficient. The S-Bahn, which connects with the U-Bahn at Marienplatz and Hauptbahnhof, is the interurban express line. It runs underground across the city in an east-west direction. Outside the city, it branches out over the whole federal railway network.

Taxi – Munich's taxis are high-priced. It will cost you nearly $2 just to have the driver flip down the arm of the meter. Taxis can be hailed on the street, or you can get one radio-dispatched by dialing 2-1611.

Car Rental – There are international and local rental firms in downtown Munich and at the airport. If you do drive, you should know that in some areas of Munich traffic-light poles contain two sets of lights: one on top for cars and a bottom set for bicycles. Munich also employs "motorbike" women, easily recognized by their light blue jumpsuits, who patrol the highways to aid lost or stranded motorists. Fluent in several languages, these women carry maps, tourist information, and other helpful material.

 **MUSEUMS:** Besides those mentioned in *Special Places,* notable museums in Munich are:

The State Museum of Modern Art (Staatsgalerie Moderner Kunst). Twentieth-century sculpture and painting. Prinzregentenstr. 1 (phone: 29-27-10).

Gallery in Lenbachhaus (Städtische Galerie im Lenbachhaus). Kandinsky and the Blue Rider School. Luisenstr. 33 (phone: 52-10-41).

BMW-Museum, Petuelring 130 (phone: 38-95-33-07).

Valentin Museum, Gate Tower, Isartorpl. (phone: 22-32-66).

Neue Pinakothek, Nineteenth- and early-twentieth-century art. Barerstr. 29 (phone: 238-05-195).

City Museum (Münchner Stadtmuseum), St.-Jakobs-Pl. 1 (phone: 233-2370).

Glyptothek. Greek and Roman sculpture. Königspl. 3 (phone: 28-61-00).

Antikensammlungen, Königspl. 1 (phone: 59-83-59).

Museum in Stuck-Villa, Prinzregentenstr. 60 (phone: 47-12-60).

 **SHOPPING:** Munich is such an elegant shopping city that some visitors confess to losing all sense of proportion once turned loose in the pedestrian zone. Shops tempt you with Bavarian beer steins, wonderful antiques, marvelous German porcelain, and items of German steel as well as Parisian fashions. Munich's most elegant shops can be found along Maximilianstrasse and Briennerstrasse and the small streets between Marienplatz and Odeonsplatz. Most of the antique shops are concentrated along Ottostrasse near Karlsplatz. The city's leading department stores are *Kaufhof* on Marienplatz and *Karstadt,* near Karlsplatz. Most stores are open from 9 AM to 6:30 PM on weekdays, but close at 2 PM on Saturdays.

Alois Dallmayr – A world-famous gourmet food store. Dienerstr. 14–15.

Anglia English Bookstore – The biggest selection of English-language paperbacks in southern Germany. Schellingstr. 3.

Auer Dult – A wonderful flea market for secondhand goods, antiques, and curiosities. Set up three times a year — usually in April or May, August, and October. Mariahilfpl., across the Isar in the southeastern district of Au.

Beck – Famous for textiles, women's wear, and Bavarian handicrafts. Marienpl.

Dirndl-Ecke – An interesting display of Bavarian handicrafts, including Hummel figurines. Near the Hofbräuhaus. Platzl 4.

Franz Widmann – *Solingen* carving sets and other items made of this renowned German steel. Karlspl. 10.

Loden-Frey – Men's and women's loden coats in great variety. Maffeistr. 7–9.

Ludwig Mory – A huge and varied stock of interesting beer steins. Located in the new city hall. Marienpl. 8.

Rosenthal – Home of the marvelous china, crystal, and cutlery. Theatinerstr. 8.

Seitz – Wax art candles typical of this region. Pacellistr. 2.

Staatliche Porzellan Manufaktur – The main distributor of *Nymphenburg* porcelain. Odeonspl.

Wallach Haus – Dirndls and peasant dresses. Residenzstr. 3.

Walter – Leather clothing for men and women. Amalienstr. 9.

 SPECIAL EVENTS: Munich is famous the world over for *Oktoberfest,* celebrated from late September through the first Sunday in October, and the pre-Lenten carnival, *Fasching,* which engulfs the entire city during the month preceding *Ash Wednesday* each February or March. *Oktoberfest* is 16 riotous days of beer-drinking, sausage-eating, and merry-making at Theresa's Meadow, a fairgrounds on which local breweries set up gaily decorated beer gardens, brass bands oom-pah-pah continuously, and oxen are roasted on open spits. Unbelievable quantities of beer are drunk: some 750,000 kegs are tapped. *Fasching,* which has been celebrated in Munich since the fourteenth century, hints more of indulgence in forbidden pleasures of the flesh (there is a traditional agreement that husbands and wives overlook one another's indiscretions during Fasching), but it, too, is characterized by lots of drinking and endless fun-seeking. The nonstop street reveling is all the more colorful for the outlandish costumes the celebrants don for fancy balls and an enormous parade through the city.

 SPORTS: The excellent facilities built for the 1972 Summer Olympics are used by a variety of professional teams in Munich, providing visitors with an opportunity to see everything from European soccer and basketball to ice hockey and track and field events. Sports schedules are listed in the monthly Tourist Office program, *München.* If you are a swimmer, you might enjoy using the *Olympic Swimming Hall* in Olympic Village. It's open to the public daily.

 THEATER: Munich has been known for centuries as a theater city. You can see everything from Greek tragedy to classical ballet to modern experimental drama in the numerous theaters here. The chief theaters are the *Opera House, National Theater,* Max-Joseph-Pl. (phone: 22-13-16); the *Cuvilliés Theater* in the Royal Palace, Residenzstr. 1 (phone: 22-13-16); *Theater in Marstall,* Marstallpl. (phone: 22-13-16); *Residenz Theater,* Max-Joseph-Pl. 1 (phone: 22-57-54); *Münchner Kammerspiele* in Schauspielhaus, Maximilianstr. 26 (phone: 23-72-1328); the *Munich Puppet Theater (Münchner Marionettentheater),* Blumenstr. 29a at Sendlinger-Tor-Pl. (phone: 26-57-12); and the *Munich Theater for Children (Münchner Theater für Kinder),* Dachauer Str. 46 (phone: 59-54-54 and 59-38-58).

 MUSIC: The first opera was performed in Munich in 1650, and the names of Wagner, Mozart, and Strauss (Strauss was born in Munich) are closely linked with the *Bavarian State Opera,* which performs in the *National Theater.* Opera also can be heard at the *Staatstheater an Gärtnerplatz,* Gärtnerpl. 3 (phone: 260-3232). Hardly a day passes without a concert of classical music at one of the museums or theaters; jazz can be heard at clubs such as *Allotria,* Türkenstr. 33 (phone: 28-73-42); *Domicile,* Leopoldstr. 19 (phone: 39-94-51); *Musicland,* Siegesstr. 19 (phone: 34-33-34, 39-39-33); Unterfahrt, Kirchenstr. 96 (phone: 448-27-94); and Schwabinger Podium Sieges-Wagnerstr. 7 (phone: 39-94-82)

NIGHTCLUBS AND NIGHTLIFE: Nightlife and Schwabing are almost interchangeable terms. You can dance over an aquarium filled with sharks at the *Yellow Submarine* in the *Holiday Inn* (see *Checking In*), Leopoldstr. 194 (phone: 34-09-71), disco at *Crash*, Lindwurmstr. 88 (phone: 77-32-72), or rock the night away at the club in the *Hotel Bayerischer Hof* (see *Checking In*), Promenade pl. 2–6 (phone: 212-09-94). Music and other entertainment is offered at *Marienkäfer*, a youngish hangout, Schraudolphstr. 44, and *Domicile*, on Leopoldstr. near Franz-Joseph-Str., offers jazz and rock. One of the oldest Schwabing disco cellars is *Rumpelkammer*, Trautenwolfstr. 1 (phone: 34-47-93). *Cittá 2000* at Leopoldstr. 28a is an open, multilevel restaurant and nightclub that shares a blockwide building with fashionable boutiques. You can also combine dining, dancing and smart shopping at *The Drugstore*, Feilitzschstr. 12 (phone: 34-75-31). Biting humor and satire are the offerings at the literary cabaret, *Lach und Schiessgesellschaft*, Ursulastr. (phone: 39-19-97).

 SINS: Most visitors look for sin in Schwabing, and that is where you are likely to find prostitutes cruising in their Mercedeses and BMWs, blinking their headlights at prospective clients. Many inexpensive pensions in the district rent space for such liaisons.

If you prefer gambling, take the *Garmisch Casino's Blitz Bus* or one of the other buses the casinos run to bring players from Munich to the Garmisch area at the foot of the Alps, 54 miles (87 km) away. The buses leave from the north side of the main railway station at 5 PM on weekdays and at 2 PM Sundays. They leave Garmisch at 11 PM for the return to Munich. The trip takes about 1 hour and 35 minutes each way.

BEST IN TOWN

 CHECKING IN: Except during Oktoberfest and Fasching, there is plenty of hotel space in Munich, but prices are high any time of the year. Top hotels will cost a minimum of $65 a night for a double, and most of their rooms are much higher; moderate-priced hotels charge between $30 and $65 a night; and anything below $30 must be considered inexpensive. And just so you don't forget, make reservations ahead if you're coming for Oktoberfest or Fasching. Munich also has many delightful, inexpensive pensions. They don't have all the modern conveniences of a hotel, but they do have *Gemütlichkeit*, and that warmth and geniality is probably one of the things you came to Munich for.

Four Seasons (Hotel Vier Jahreszeiten) – Only a few blocks away from the glittering National State Opera. Another of the great hotels of Europe, the *Four Seasons* exudes opulence and elegance, right through to its recently added ultramodern wing and a new rooftop swimming pool. Its *Walterspiel* restaurant is wonderful (see *Eating Out*). Owned by Inter-Continental. Maximilianstr. 17 (phone: 23-03-90). Expensive.

Munich Hilton – Close to the picturesque English Garden, the 500-room *Hilton* is designed to meet the particular needs of the international business traveler. There are several restaurants, a pool, a sauna, a shopping arcade, and a massive underground garage. Am Tucherpark 7 (phone: 34-00-51). Expensive.

Munich Sheraton – East of the center of town and clearly geared to the convention trade, the *Sheraton* has a 1,500-seat meeting hall with sophisticated sound and translating units. The hotel has 650 rooms. Arabellastr. 6 (phone: 92-40-11). Expensive.

Königshof – Despite its central location, this traditional and comfortable establishment is quiet. It also boasts one of Munich's best hotel restaurants, which has a great view of busy Karlsplatz. Karlsplatz 25 (phone: 55-84-12). Expensive.

Holiday Inn Munich – This 360-room hotel is on Schwabing's main thoroughfare and is the home of the *Yellow Submarine* (see *Nightclubs and Nightlife*). Leopoldstr. 194 (phone: 34-09-71). Expensive.

Continental – A favorite of those who know the city well, located close to the center of town and known affectionately as *The Conti.* Filled with flowers and space and priceless antiques. The hotel is part of a group of buildings known as the *Kunstblock,* the center of the Munich art and antique market. Max-Joseph-Str. 5 (phone: 55-79-71). Expensive.

Bayerischer Hof-Palais Montgelas – Long considered Munich's landmark hotel, the 442-room *Bayerischer Hof* has recently drawn criticism for poor service and declining standards. In the past, however, the hotel always had a top-drawer clientele, including Ludwig I, who favored it because the royal palace didn't have bathtubs, while the hotel did. More recent amenities include a *Trader Vic's* restaurant and a rooftop pool. Promenadepl. 2–6 (phone: 2-1200). Expensive.

Penta – Part of a European chain and designed to cut down on rapidly soaring hotel prices, the *Penta* caters to a predominantly business clientele. Guests carry their own baggage to their rooms. A unit in each room dispenses drinks, snacks, and even Continental breakfast (eliminating the need for room service). There is an extensive shopping arcade and restaurant complex under the hotel, which is near the German Museum. Hochstr. 3 (phone: 448-5555). Expensive.

Hotel Uhland – A charming little hotel in a lovely old building on a street near Theresa's Meadow. Uhlandstr. 1 (phone: 53-92-77). Moderate.

Biederstein – Charming, probably Munich's quietest hotel. It's on the fringe of Schwabing, next to the English Garden park. Keferstr. 18 (phone: 39-50-72). Moderate.

Bundesbahn Hotel – Located in the main railway station building, but surprisingly quiet and comfortable. Bahnhofspl. 2 (phone: 55-85-71). Moderate.

Mariahilf – A particular favorite with English tourists. This pension is located in a quiet sector of the city across the Isar from central Munich. Lilienstr. 83 (phone: 48-48-34). Moderate.

Lettl – Centrally located with breakfast included in the tariff. When reserving, ask for a room in the new wing. Amalienstr. 53 (phone: 28-30-26). Moderate.

Hotel Daniel – It offers a very good buy: breakfast; plain, but clean and comfortable quarters; and a great location near the train station, subway, and within walking distance of most shopping. Sonnenstr. 5 (phone: 55-49-45). Moderate.

Theresia – Located in Schwabing, very close to the museums, is this well-run establishment. Luisenstr. 51 (phone: 52-12-50). Inexpensive.

Pension am Bahnhofsplatz – What could be more convenient than this reasonably priced pension, just off the main station? No breakfast available. Bahnhofsplatz 5, fourth fl. (phone: 59-50-45). Inexpensive.

 EATING OUT: Like everything else in Munich, dining out can be very expensive. Even beer hall fare, once the staple of budget-minded students, can add up quickly to $10 to $15 or more. At expensive restaurants expect to pay a minimum of $40 for a meal for two; $15 to $40 should be considered in the medium price range; and anything below that, inexpensive. Unless otherwise noted, make reservations.

Bavarian cuisine is hearty and heavy, and most of it seems created to make you consume inordinate amounts of beer. Liver dumplings, *Leberknödel,* is the most famous of more than four score Bavarian dumplings. *Leberkäse* translates as livercheese but is neither; it's a baked pâté of beef and bacon. Pork sausages and sauerkraut, *Schweinswürstl mit Kraut,* is another unforgettable local dish. Munich is the sausage,

Wurst, capital of the world. *Weisswurst,* a veal-based sausage, is sold throughout the city by street vendors as well as in beer gardens. You'll also want to taste some of the local pretzels and salt rolls and sticks sold under such names as *Brez'n, Römische,* and *Salzstangerl.* Another specialty here is the large, tasty white radish, *Radi,* cut in spirals and sold with plenty of salt. If all of this makes you very thirsty, order *ein Mass Bier;* that's a liter. Otherwise, a half liter, *eine Halbe,* should suffice. If Bavarian food is too much for you every day, you'll have a wide variety of other ethnic foods to choose from, especially in the conglomeration of foreign restaurants in Schwabing.

Aubergine – This is Munich's and West Germany's first three-star restaurant. Chef Eckart Witzigmann insists on only the freshest of ingredients and his menu is sprinkled with dishes like venison with wild berries. Also try the lobster fricassee. Closed Sundays. Maximilianspl. 5 (phone: 59-81-71). Expensive.

Käfer Schänke – This started out as a corner grocery store, worked itself up to one of Europe's largest delicatessens and Germany's biggest catering service, and now includes a popular restaurant upstairs over the sprawling store. You can get anything from homemade head cheese, *Presskopf,* to bass from the Mediterranean. Closed Sundays. Prinzregentenstr. at Schumannstr. 1 (phone: 4-1681). Expensive.

Boettner – *Boettner* is a tiny wine restaurant in a high-ceilinged, paneled room behind a caviar-lobster shop. It has only about ten tables and is always crowded. The specialty here is lobster. Theatinerstr. 8 (phone: 22-12-10). Expensive.

Sabitzer – A favorite of Munich's beautiful people, decorated all in white with turn-of-the-century art hung on the walls, this fine, small restaurant serves nouvelle cuisine. Closed Sundays and Saturdays in July and August. Reservations suggested. Reitmorstr. 21 (phone: 29-85-84). Expensive.

Tantris – This highly rated restaurant is located in Schwabing. *Tantris* serves some of the best of modern, light French cuisine outside France. Closed Sundays. Johann-Fichte-Str. 7 (phone: 36-20-61, 36-20-62). Expensive.

Walterspiel – In the *Four Seasons* hotel, this restaurant is quiet and ultra elegant, and its delicious Bavarian cuisine is among the finest in Germany. If you try the *Auszug aus schwarzen Trüffel* (essence of black truffles), you're sure to agree. Maximilianstr. 17 (phone: 23-03-90). Expensive.

Eaton Place – Despite the somewhat thick English decor, this downtown restaurant has a famed Continental kitchen. Try one of the luscious salads or a succulent seafood platter. Closed Sundays. Mariannenstr. 3 (phone: 29-31-00). Expensive.

Goldene Stadt – Bohemian dishes are served in the four adjoining dining rooms here. A photomural of a bridge over the Moldau in central Prague dominates the main dining room. Closed Sundays. Oberanger 44 (phone: 26-43-82). Moderate.

Mifune – Ever since actor Toshiro Mifune opened this restaurant, it's been a must for lovers of Japanese food. Closed Sundays. Ismaninger Str. 136 (phone: 98-75-72). Moderate.

Weisses Brauhaus – Perhaps the most traditional of Munich's restaurants, this inn has been serving hearty food and wheat beer at the same site for over 400 years. A best bet is the roast pork with dumplings. No reservations. Tal 10 (phone: 29-98-75). Moderate.

Spatenhaus – This is a fine example of a typical Bavarian *Gaststatte* (inn), with its whitewashed walls, pine tables and chairs, and many cozy niches. A delicious dinner here might include roast duck, suckling pig, or hare with mushrooms in cream sauce; dessert could be the flaky apple strudel or crisp apple fritters. No reservations. Residenzstr. 12 (phone: 22-78-41/2). Moderate.

Spöckmeier – This popular *Gasthaus* — which some say serves the best veal sausages in town — has two dining rooms: The vast, whitewashed and raftered hall downstairs bustles with shoppers and sightseers, and the smaller, wood-paneled room upstairs hums with the quiet conversation of elegant drinkers. Closed Sundays in the summer. No reservations. On Rosenstr., just off Marienpl. (phone: 26-80-88). Moderate.

Zum Alten Markt – Just a stone's throw from the colorful Viktualienmarkt, this new downtown restaurant is a must for lovers of good but reasonably priced Continental food with an emphasis on fish and veal dishes. Closed Sundays. Reservations suggested. Dreifaltigkeitsplatz 3 (phone: 29-99-95). Moderate.

Pfälzer Weinprobierstube – This tradition-laden wine cellar, in the former royal Residenz (see *Special Places*), features vintages from the Palatinate (Pfälz). The hearty food is also from that former Bavarian region. Open daily. No reservations. Residenzstr. 1 (phone: 22-56-28). Inexpensive.

Augustiner Bräu – Stop in for a draft of Augustiner and a look at this beer hall's remarkable interior: Its three rooms are richly ornamented with seashell mosaics, carved wood paneling and columns, brass chandeliers, plasterwork, and a glass-paned ceiling dome. Newly renovated, its Old World charm is hard to resist. No reservations. Closed Sundays. Neuhauserstr. 16 (phone: 260-4106). Inexpensive.

Zum Bögner – For hearty Bavarian dishes, you couldn't do better than this centuries-old traditional restaurant. Try the liver-dumpling soup, the pot roast with onions, or the sauerbraten. Im Tal 72 (phone: 22-67-50). Inexpensive.

NAPLES

Naples, Gothic and baroque under an azure sky, intellectual capital of the Mezzogiorno, and Italy's third most populated city with nearly 1.5 million inhabitants, has often been described as one of the world's most beautiful seaports. Indeed, the magnificent Bay of Naples has long been lauded by its many illustrious visitors for its gently curving shoreline and palm-lined seaside avenues, its mild climate, sunny beaches, and romantic islands.

But Naples has always had a darker side. The brooding Mt. Vesuvius, "its terror and its pride," ever hovering over the city, buried neighboring Pompeii and Herculaneum when it erupted in AD 79. And the eerie Phlegrean Fields (Campi Flegrei), a steaming volcanic area just north of here whose violent beauty inspired both Homer and Virgil, was regarded by the ancients as the entrance to the Underworld. More recently, the earthquake that devastated southern Italy in November 1980 took a tragic toll even in Naples, adding yet another major problem to the city's permanent ills of unemployment, crime, and disease.

For some visitors today, Naples is a disappointment. The old quarter, Spacca-Napoli, is among the most densely populated areas in the world; infant mortality and unemployment rates here are the highest in Italy — almost a third of the city's labor force is unemployed, and another estimated 40,000 persons derive their livelihood from smuggling. When a cholera outbreak in 1973 revealed that Naples had no sewers and was living on a beautiful but poisoned bay, "See Naples and die," once a popular saying beckoning visitors to the seductive charms of the city, suddenly acquired a morbid and foreboding significance. But the poor of Naples survive with a surprising stoicism, and the people themselves are one of the attractions of Naples.

They can make Naples a special experience. Stroll along the via Caracciolo and watch the fishermen pulling in their nets, oblivious to the traffic behind them; buy lemons and oranges or sulfur water from men and women who transact their business across seventeenth-century marble tabletops; give in to the importuning of pizza vendors hawking their wares; or, when the jostling of the small, crowded streets becomes too much to bear, retire to a café table in the elegant Galleria Umberto I and watch well-dressed Neapolitans socialize over an afternoon coffee or aperitif.

Naples, of course, is famous for its songs, its festivals, and its gaiety. There is a particular style of Neapolitan singing called *bel canto,* which is accompanied by guitar or mandolin and can be joyful or melancholy. The city's opera house, built in 1737, is among the world's finest. A Neapolitan school of painting, characterized by realism and warm colors based on chiaroscuro, flourished in the eighteenth and nineteenth centuries.

The city, probably founded by the Greeks in the seventh century BC, was

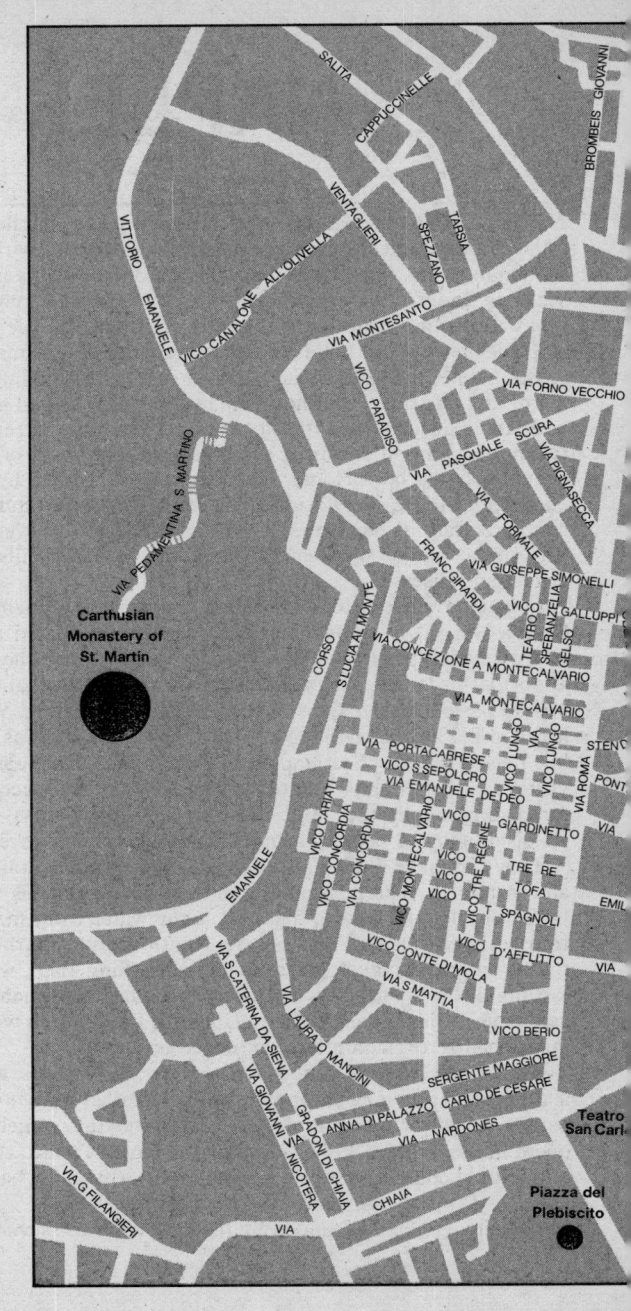

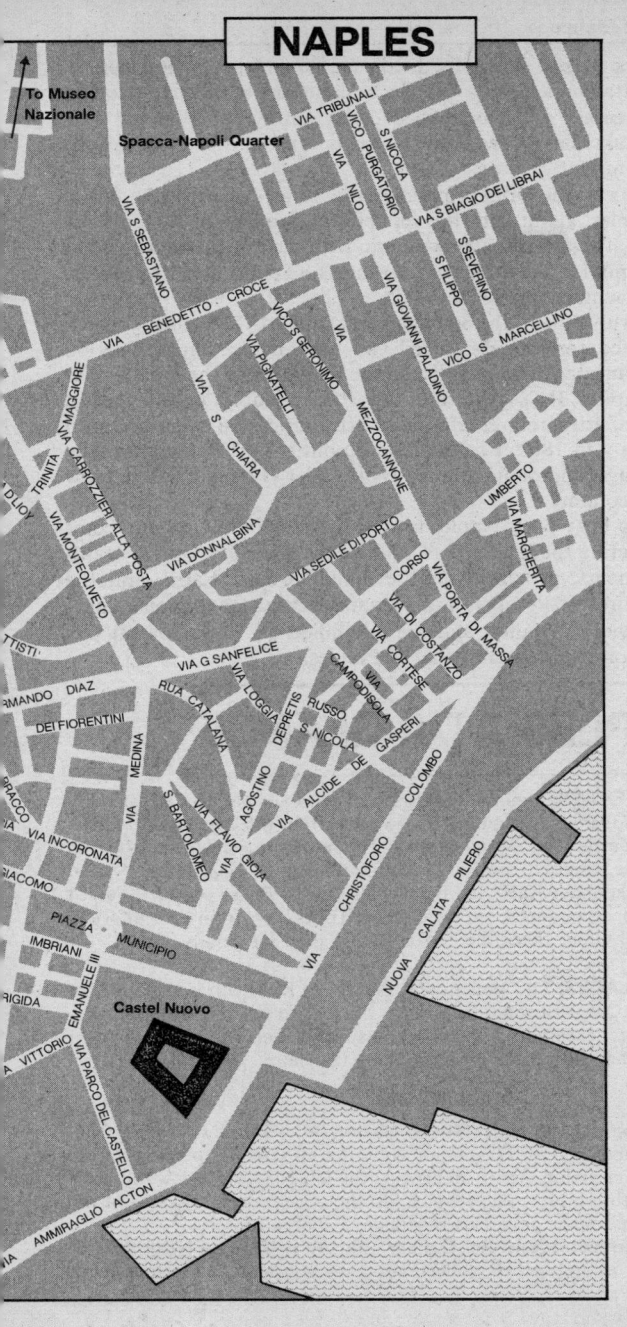

NAPLES

To Museo Nazionale

Spacca-Napoli Quarter

VIA TRIBUNALI
VICO PURGATORIO
S NICOLA
VIA NILO
VIA S BIAGIO DEI LIBRAI
S SEVERINO
S FILIPPO
VIA S SEBASTIANO
VIA GIOVANNI PALADINO
VICO S MARCELLINO
VIA BENEDETTO CROCE
VICO S GERONIMO
VIA PIGNATELLI
VIA S MAGGIORE
TRINITA
VIA CARROZZIERI ALLA POSTA
D'LOY
VIA S CHIARA
MEZZOCANNONE
UMBERTO
VIA MARGHERITA
VIA MONTEOLIVETO
VIA DONNALBINA
VIA SEDILE DI PORTO
CORSO
VIA PORTA DI MASSA
TTISTI
VIA G SANFELICE
VIA DI COSTANZO
VIA CORTESE
RMANDO DIAZ
RUA CATALANA
VIA LOGGIA
CAMPANISOLA
VIA RUSSO
DEI FIORENTINI
DEPRETIS
S NICOLA
VIA MEDINA
AGOSTINO
ALCIDE DE GASPERI
SPACCO
VIA INCORONATA
S BARTOLOMEO
VIA FLAVIO GIOIA
VIA
COLOMBO
GIACOMO
CHRISTOFORO
PIAZZA MUNICIPIO
IMBRIANI
EMANUELE III
NUOVA CALATA PILIERO
RIGIDA
A VITTORIO
VIA PARCO DEL CASTELLO
Castel Nuovo
VIA AMMIRAGLIO ACTON

first called Parthenope, later Neapolis. Little remains of its earliest period. With the rest of the Italian peninsula, Naples became part of the great Roman Empire, and its intensely green countryside and sunny shores were soon studded with palatial villas of wealthy Romans who chose to spend the winters in Naples's milder climate.

But the tranquillity of the Roman period came to an end with the fall of the empire, and Naples, along with the rest of Italy, sank into the abyss of the Dark Ages. The city came into its own again with the rule of the Angevins, who made it their capital in the thirteenth century, and continued its progress under the Aragons, who took over in 1442.

Following the corrupt rule of the Spanish from 1503 to 1734, during which time the heavily taxed commoners staged two uprisings, a happier period followed with the Bourbons, who established the Kingdom of the Two Sicilies with Naples as its capital. Its ancient dignity restored, Naples became one of Europe's major cities, attracting great men of art, music, and literature until the unification of Italy in 1860. Economic and political problems gradually diminished her prestige, and damage from World War II dealt a severe blow to an already sick economy.

Today, thanks to a busy port, Naples is an important industrial and commercial center, attracting tourists, artists, and lovers of beauty with a wealth of historical monuments, proximity to the Amalfi Coast, Capri, and the archaeological treasures of Pompeii and Herculaneum, a contagious gaiety and exuberant, if chaotic, vitality; and the magnificent — if somewhat tarnished — splendors on the romantic Bay of Naples.

NAPLES AT-A-GLANCE

 SEEING THE CITY: Panoramic views of Naples and the bay are at every turn. Within the city, the outstanding view is from the Carthusian Monastery of St. Martin (see *Special Places*). The most spectacular view is from Mt. Vesuvius, some 15 miles (24 km) southeast of Naples (see *Special Places*). Every Sunday at about 10:30 AM, the Naples Tourist Board conducts guided tours of one church, palace, or another in the old city. Tours leave from their information office at Piazza del Gesù; check the booklet *Qui Napoli* for details.

 SPECIAL PLACES: The semicircular Piazza del Plebiscito is the center of public life in Naples, while the narrow winding streets of the old Spacca-Napoli Quarter exemplify its colorful, noisy heart. Santa Lucia, to the west of the port, has a lovely promenade along the shore.

DOWNTOWN

National Archaeological Museum (Museo Nazionale) – Priceless bronzes from Herculaneum and Pompeii and an exceptional collection of Greco-Roman sculpture make this one of the most important archaeological museums in the world. The museum is in a sixteenth-century palace, which also houses precious artworks of the Farnese family. Open mornings only; closed Mondays. Piazza Museo.

The Capodimonte Museum and Art Gallery (Museo e Galleria Nazionale di Capodimonte) – One of Italy's best collections of paintings from the fourteenth through sixteenth century is displayed in the palace of this former royal estate in the northeastern part of the city. Among the masters represented are Simone Martini, Bellini, Masaccio, Botticelli, Correggio, and Titian. The royal apartments on the first floor include a marvelous parlor, the *Salottino of Maria Amalia,* completely built and decorated in Capodimonte ceramics (some of which were shattered in the 1980 earthquake). Off Corso Amedeo di Savoia, Parco di Capodimonte. Open mornings, all day on Sundays; closed Mondays.

National Museum and Carthusian Monastery of St. Martin (Certosa di San Martino) – This enormous monastery founded by the Anjou dynasty is beautifully situated on the Vomero Hill, near the Corso Vittorio Emanuele III. The marvelous view from the belvedere of room 25 is said to have inspired the saying, "See Naples and die." Also, of special interest is the lavish baroque monk's chancel. Open mornings only; closed Mondays. St. Elmo Hill.

The New Castle (Castel Nuovo) – Deep moats surround this imposing castle built between 1278 and 1292 for Charles I of Anjou and rebuilt in the fifteenth century for the Aragons. It is famous for the triumphal arch that adorns its entrance. Built from designs by Francesco Laurana, the arch bears the arms of Aragon and is ornamented with elaborate sculpture. Open daily. Piazza Municipio.

ENVIRONS

The Phlegrean Fields – Hot springs and sulfurous gases rise from this dark, violent volcanic area which extends in an arc along the Gulf of Pozzuoli. The Solfatara crater, which may be visited, is still active. Lakes have formed in some of the craters of the extinct volcanoes. From Capo Posillipo to Capo Miseno, west of Naples.

Mt. Vesuvius – Vesuvius last erupted in 1944, and has averaged one eruption every 35 years over the past 300. The mountain has two summits: Monte Vesuvius proper, 4,189 feet high, and Monte Somma, 3,713 feet high. You can drive or take a bus from Herculaneum to the Vesuvius Observatory and take a chair lift or walk from there to the crater. You must be accompanied by a guide and there are small fees for the ascent to the crater. Open daily. About 15 miles (24 km) southeast of Naples on Autostrada Napoli. The volcano is accessible by train (the Circumvesuviana line from Stazione Vesuviana, near the central station in Naples) and by bus.

Pompeii – In AD 79, one of the most disastrous volcanic eruptions in history occurred when Mt. Vesuvius spewed forth molten lava and cinders, burying the towns of Stabiae, Herculaneum, and Pompeii. Pompeii, south of the great volcano, had been a favorite resort of rich Romans, and the excavation of its marvelously preserved ruins has provided a virtually complete picture of Roman life in the first century AD. About two-thirds of the city has been uncovered, including the Forum, where religious services and public meetings were held; the Stabian Baths (Terme Stabiane); the Casa dei Vettii, a house with remarkable frescoes; and the Villa of the Mysteries (Villa dei Misteri), a grand patrician villa that also has wonderful frescoes. A good view of the excavations is available from the Tower of the God Mercury (Torre di Mercurio) on the town wall. The 1980 earthquake took its toll here too, but nearly all sites previously open to the public have been restored and reopened. Open daily except Mondays from 9 AM to 1½ hours before sunset. Small admission charge. About 9 miles (14 km) south of Mt. Vesuvius on the Autostrada Napoli. It is also reached easily by train from Naples. Take the Circumvesuviana line from the Stazione Vesuviana near the central station.

■**EXTRA SPECIAL:** Although Capri is better known, the island of Ischia is also popular with Italians. The beaches are beautiful, the white cottages of the villages have a slightly Moorish look, and the slopes are dressed with pine, chestnut, vines, olives, and tropical vegetation. The climate is one of the best in the Mediterranean, and its numerous hot springs are said to be beneficial for various maladies. Cafés, restaurants, and smart shops line the Corso Vittoria Colonna in the town of Ischia Porto. There is frequent daily service to both islands by boat and hydrofoil from Naples. For information about steamers and hydrofoils, contact *Caremar,* Molo Beverello, Piazza Municipio (phone: 31-38-82). Also for hydrofoils: *SNAV,* Via Caracciolo 10 (phone: 66-04-44), and *Alilavro,* Via Caracciolo 13 (phone: 68-10-41).

SOURCES AND RESOURCES

For general information, brochures, and maps of Naples and its environs, contact the tourist office, EPT (Ente Provinciale per il Turismo), Via Partenope 10/A (phone: 40-62-89); other offices are at the central railway station, the Mergellina railway station, and at the Capodichino airport. The City of Naples Tourism Office (Azienda Autonoma di Turismo) is in the Royal Palace at Piazza Plebiscito (phone: 41-87-44). The Europa Youth and Student Travel Service is at Via Mezzocannone 119 (phone: 20-64-56), and the Association of Youth Hostels (AIG) is at Via del Chiostro 9 (phone: 32-00-84).

For Local Coverage: The tourist office publishes a useful monthly booklet, *Qui Napoli,* which is distributed to the better hotels. Listings are in Italian and English.

CLIMATE AND CLOTHES: June and September are the best months to visit Naples. Summer is hot, with average highs of 84°F (29°C). Winters, though milder than in more northerly parts of Italy, can be rainy. Temperatures stay well above freezing. Light summer clothes are in order from May through September. Women may want a light wrap for evenings (and for covering bare shoulders when visiting churches). A raincoat or light overcoat is useful in winter.

GETTING AROUND: Bus and Tram – Main routes and schedules are listed in *Napoli, Carnet del Turista.* Fares are inexpensive.

    Railway – The Metropolitana is inexpensive and runs from Napoli Gianturco to Pozzuoli Solfatara.

Taxi – Taxis can be hailed while they cruise or may be picked up at any cabstand. For a radio-dispatched taxi call 36-44-44 or 36-43-40.

Car Rental – Major international firms are on Via Partenope.

MUSEUMS: In addition to those mentioned in *Special Places,* a number of other museums and churches are impressive. Check opening hours with your hotel hall porter or EPT offices before setting out. Most are open 9 AM to 2 PM weekdays and 9 AM to 1 PM holidays; and closed on Mondays.

    Catacombs of St. Janarius (San Gennaro), Church of the Buon Consiglio, Tondo di Capodimonte.

    Filangieri Civic Museum (Museo Civico G. Filangieri), Via Duomo.

    New Church of Jesus (Gesù Nuovo), Piazza del Gesù.

    Church of St. Lawrence Major (San Lorenzo Maggiore), Via Tribunali and Piazza San Gaetano.

    Church of St. Dominick Major (Chiesa di San Domenico Maggiore), Piazza San Domenico.

    Villa Floridiana, Via Cimarosa, Vomero.

    St. Clara's Church (Chiesa di Santa Chiara), Via Benedetto Croce.

    Royal Palace (Palazzo Real), Piazza del Plebiscito.

SHOPPING: Naples is commonly divided into two central areas, the Zona Elegante (Elegant Zone) and the Zona Commerciale (Commercial Zone). The most fashionable shopping area is now centered around the Piazza dei Martiri, the Elegant Zone, along Via Calabritto, Via Filangieri, Via dei Mille, and Via Chiaia, which leads to the Commercial Zone between Piazza Trieste e Trento and Piazza Dante along the still fashionable Via Roma/Via Toledo and toward the main railway station along Corso Umberto I.

Galleria Umberto I – A favorite meeting place of Neapolitans and the perfect spot to sample the delicious Neapolitan ice cream.

Coin – Good department store at Via Scarlatti 10.

Giovanni Apa Co. – One of several factory wholesalers for coral and cameos. In Torre del Greco, 15 miles (24 km) from Naples, off the Naples-Pompeii Highway. (Note that "Mediterranean" coral now comes mostly from Southeast Asia.)

La Rinascente – National department store. Via Roma 343.

 **SPECIAL EVENTS:** Twice a year (on September 19 and the first Sunday in May) Neapolitans crowd into the Cathedral of St. Januarius (Duomo San Gennaro) and its square on via Duomo, praying for "the miracle." On these days the dried blood of the saint is supposed to liquify. If it does not — and it doesn't always — some disaster is supposed to befall the city. Other important festivals celebrate the feast of *Santa Maria del Carmine,* July 16, and the *Madonna di Piedigrotta,* which lasts several days in early September.

 SPORTS: Most sports facilities belong to private clubs, so check with your hall porter about which may be currently open to the public.

Swimming – The polluted Bay of Naples is not the best spot for water sports, but there are fine seaside resorts on the islands and along the Amalfi Coast.

Tennis – Courts at several tennis clubs including *Tennis Club Vomero,* Via Rossini 8 (phone: 65-89-12), and *Tennis Club Napoli,* Villa Comunale (phone: 38-48-01).

 THEATER: Even if you don't understand the Neapolitan dialect, you may enjoy a performance by the renowned *Repertory Group of Eduardo de Filippo* at the *San Ferdinando Theatre,* Piazza Teatro San Ferdinando (phone: 44-49-00).

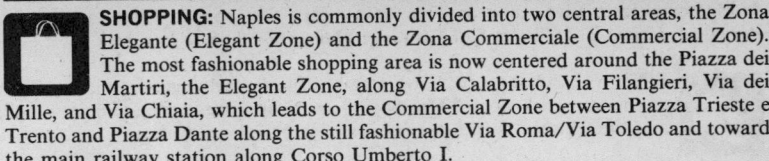 **MUSIC:** The season at the *Teatro San Carlo,* Via San Carlo (phone: 41-71-44), one of the finest opera houses in the world, generally begins in December; the famed concert hall and foyer may be visited by the public between 9 AM and noon daily. Concerts are scheduled frequently at the *RAI-TV Auditorium,* Via G. Marconi (phone: 61-01-22), and at the *San Pietro a Maiella Conservatory of Music,* Via S. Pietro a Maiella (phone: 45-92-55), and in the church or cloisters of Santa Chiara, Via Benedetto Croce. (phone: 20-76-97, 32-05-82).

 NIGHTCLUBS AND NIGHTLIFE: Like most port towns, Naples has a number of seedy bars and rip-off joints to be avoided. Currently OK discotheques are: *Shaker,* Via Nazario Sauro 24; and *Damiani,* Via Domiziana. Some good places on Via Manzoni are *Papillon* and the *Zeppelin Club. Harry's Bar,* Via Lucilio, is the spot for a quiet drink in an elegant setting. *Il Gabbiano,* near the principal hotels at Via Partenope 26, is a piano bar that serves late snacks (phone: 41-16-66). A new addition to the late-night bar scene is *Ipanema,* a small establishment with live Brazilian music on weekends, a weekly review by Brazilian showman Celso Karan, exotic drinks from Rio's favorite *caipirinha* to the all-American whiskey sour, and informal food. Live music on Thursdays during the summer. Closed in August. Riviera di Chiaia 217 (Piazza San Pasquale; phone: 68-09-06, 2 to 6 PM).

SINS: You'll find people hawking many black market goods, but buy them at your own risk: Some "Marlboros" are Neapolitan-made and quite rough, and the whiskey bottles may contain tea or colored water.

BEST IN TOWN

CHECKING IN: An expensive hotel in Naples will charge from $100 to $200 a night for a double; moderately priced hotels range from $60 to $100; and in the inexpensive category you'll be charged $30 to $60.

Excelsior – Naples' only truly deluxe hotel, part of the reliably luxurious CIGA chain, the *Excelsior* dominates Santa Lucia, its terraced seaside rooms overlooking the eleventh-century Castel dell'Ovo and old fishing village of Borgo Marinaro. The *Casanova Grill* takes some prizes, too (see *Eating Out*). Via Partenope 48 (phone: 41-71-11). Expensive.

Vesuvio – Close to the *Excelsior*, facing the picturesque port of Santa Lucia. The *Vesuvio* has medium-sized rooms and good baths. The decor ranges from period style to modern. Via Partenope 45 (phone: 41-70-44). Expensive to moderate.

Royal – Modern and busy, this waterfront hotel with a rooftop pool is Naples' biggest, and still expanding. Via Partenope 38 (phone: 40-02-44). Moderate.

Britannique – Swiss management and efficiency; hospitable and very clean. Most rooms in this old converted villa are large and have views. Near *Parker's*. Corso Vittorio Emanuele III 133 (phone: 66-09-33). Moderate to inexpensive.

San Germano – A few miles drive from the center of Napoli at the crossroads for the *Ippodromo di Agnano* racecourse. Pleasant rooms, a lovely garden, swimming pool, and nearby tennis courts. Via Beccadelli 41 (phone: 760-5422). Inexpensive.

Mediterraneo – Conveniently located in the Commercial Center, but not very romantic. Via Nuova Ponte di Tappia (phone: 31-22-40). Inexpensive.

Miramare – Reputable and conveniently located with comfortable, recently renovated rooms, this small hotel offers good service and a pleasant atmosphere. No restaurant, but very near *La Cantinella* (see below). Via N. Sauro 24 (phone: 41-67-75). Inexpensive.

EATING OUT: Naples is the home of pizza and spaghetti with tomato sauce, called *spaghetti c'a pummarola*. (One piece of advice: don't eat raw seafood that's come from the polluted Bay of Naples.) Dinner for two with a house wine will run between $60 and $90 at an expensive restaurant; $30 and $60 at a moderate one; and $15 and $30 at an inexpensive one.

Casanova Grill – A delightfully intimate restaurant for such a grand hotel as the *Excelsior*, the *Casanova* offers a wide selection of enticing antipasti, plenty of fresh fish, Neapolitan specialties like pasta with seafood, a remarkable fish soup, and roast baby lamb with rosemary and garlic — all prepared and served with care and refinement. Hotel Excelsior, Via Partenope 48 (phone: 41-71-11). Expensive.

La Cantinella – A current favorite of Neapolitans, visiting dignitaries, and tourists staying nearby along the picturesque port of Santa Lucia. Fresh fish, as everywhere, is at a premium, but local clams and mussels when mated with a hint of garlic, fresh parsley, and *pummarola* or tomato, and lavished on a steaming plate of linguine constitute one of the great pleasures of southern Italian life within reach of everyone's pocket. Friendly and efficient service. Closed Sundays. Via Cuma 42 (corner of Via N Sauro) (phone: 40-48-84, 40-53-75). Expensive to moderate.

La Sagrestia – Dine al fresco here on delicious Neapolitan dishes such as homemade pasta stuffed with ricotta cheese, *scazzette di Fra' Leopoldo,* or any of their fresh fish dishes. Closed Wednesdays (but Sundays in July and August). Via Orazio 116 (phone: 66-41-86). Expensive to moderate.

Il Gallo Nero – Elegant dining in an antique-filled nineteenth-century villa or on a terrace with a splendid view of Mergellina. Classical favorites as well as sensible innovations, plus fresh fish and imaginative meat dishes. Closed Mondays and August. Via Tasso 466 (phone: 643-012). Moderate.

La Fazenda – Very Neapolitan, serving homemade garlic bread and fresh fish and chicken in rustic surroundings. Closed Sundays and 2 weeks in August. Calata Marechiaro 58 (phone: 769-7420). Moderate.

Ciro a Santa Brigida – One of the best and busiest of Naples' *trattorie-pizzerie* since the 1920s. Sample the great variety of fresh fish or pastas such as *lasagna imbottita* and *maccheroni alla siciliana.* This is also a good place for the typical Neopolitan dessert, *pastiera,* made of ricotta cheese and wheat. Closed Sundays. Via Santa Brigida 71/74 (phone: 32-40-72). Moderate.

Bersagliera – For local color in fine weather, the Borgo Marinaro facing the Castel dell'Ovo can't be beat. And this is the only one of the "made for tourists" portside restaurants that almost makes it: sometimes a dose of sun in a spectacular setting is worth more than a flawless meal. A mixed grill of seafood at only about $6 includes a surprisingly tender and tasty fresh squid — a dish certainly worth a repeat visit. Naples' famous *scugnizzi* (streetwise waifs) ask for pieces of bread as they pass by between swims in the polluted Bay of Naples. Closed Tuesdays. Borgo Marinaro 10-11, Santa Lucia (phone: 41-56-92). Moderate to inexpensive.

Dora – The ambience here is that of a small fishing boat and the fish served is first class. Try the *linguine all' aragosta* (pasta with crayfish). Closed Sundays and August. Via Ferdinando Palasciano 30 (phone: 68-41-49). Moderate.

Pizzeria Bellini – This is one of the city's oldest *pizzerie.* Besides a vast assortment of pizza (with fresh basil and tomatoes, the most famous), there are pasta, fish, and meat dishes as well. Closed Wednesdays. Via S. Maria di Constantinopoli 80 (phone: 549774). Inexpensive.

Vini e Cucina – A place to enjoy real home cooking, Neapolitan style, this little restaurant is increasingly popular and often impossibly crowded, but the food is delicious. Closed Sundays. Corso Vittorio Emanuele 762. Inexpensive.

NICE

Those who remember the halcyon days of ornate villas, swaying palms, and languid luxury under an azure sky may shake their heads sadly at the Côte d'Azur of today: a symphony in cement, a real estate speculator's orgy of high-rise apartment blocks, pillbox hotels, and honky-tonk pizza parlors. Its once-quaint little marinas are linked by a permanent shoreline traffic jam, and some of its renowned beaches now look more like a horde of people dangling their feet from the edge of a freeway.

Nice, somehow, has managed to keep its head above the concrete and retain its special flavor — a mixture of Marseille, the Mardi Gras, and the Mediterranean. Even in the dead of winter, there is always something faintly festive about Nice: Perhaps it's all that city strung along all that sea. And at the first shine of sun, the café tables come out, the awnings unfurl, and strollers in sandals are back clacking along the promenade des Anglais. In the summer, the population of 400,000 burgeons with holiday-makers from Paris, Piccadilly, and Peoria — though no longer from St. Petersburg — and an empty or moderately priced hotel room is harder to find than a winning lottery ticket. And a lot more scarce than a movie star.

The Greeks founded the city in 350 BC as a little market town and auxiliary port. The stolid Romans, too, discovered the pleasures of the Riviera, and the remains of their lavish colonization are evident today in the Arena and the Baths on the hill at Cimiez — the city's elegant residential section. In the fourteenth century, the House of Savoy wrested the growing city from the counts of Provence and retained almost unbroken possession of it for close to 500 years. Napoleon lived for a time at number 6 on what is today the rue Bonaparte, later on rue St.-François-de-Paule by the opera house. In 1860, the head of the House of Savoy and king of newly unified Italy, Victor Emmanuel II, ceded the region to France in return for military support against an Austrian invasion. Giuseppe Garibaldi, the Italian patriot, was born here, as was Masséna, the general Wellington admired most after Napoleon. In modern times, the beauty and climate of Nice have made it the amusement park of the European aristocracy, an off-season refuge from harsh northern climes and irritating revolutions.

The city, between Cannes and Monte Carlo, is one big easy-to-scan color post card: the lapis lazuli of the Bay of Angels (Baie des Anges), the activity of the Vieux Port, and the timelessness of the towering Castle (Château) — the name given to the hill with the ruins of an old fortress that looms over the harbor. Along the bay runs the fabled promenade des Anglais, a broad seafront avenue that resembles a mile-long outdoor café. At one end of the promenade is the city's pulse, place Masséna: semitropical gardens set against crimson buildings and cool graceful arcades. Avenue Jean-Médecin is Main Street, bisecting the city with a straight line from place Masséna to the railroad station. The old city, La Vieille Ville, is a little piano-shaped quarter — all narrow and cobbled and noisy, and pungently southern — that huddles in the shadow of the Château. La Vieille Ville's boundaries are the quai des États-Unis and the boulevard Jean-Jaurès beside the Paillon River, which is covered in parts by esplanades and divides the old town from modern Nice to the west.

NICE AT-A-GLANCE

SEEING THE CITY: The long azure sweep of the bay, the compact jumble of red-tiled roofs in La Vieille Ville, the foothills of Provence, and the Maritime Alps rising sharply just outside the city are best seen from a viewing platform at the summit of the 300-foot Château. It can be reached by an elevator — or a 300-step climb — at the end of the quai des États-Unis, where the quay joins the rue des Ponchettes.

SPECIAL PLACES: Nice is a city to be seen casually, to be ambled through under a morning sun, with no particular purpose. Let your discoveries be guided by casual occurrences: the repair of a sandal strap, the purchase of a peach in an open market, a cold glass of Corsican white wine at a portside café.

IN THE CITY

Promenade des Anglais – If you only have an hour in Nice, spend it strolling along this promenade from the place Masséna to the *Hotel Négresco* (see *Checking In*). Ornate hotels grace one side, and a narrow, crowded strip of pebbled beach separates you from the brilliant blue of the bay. The promenade takes its name from the city's English colony, which constructed the path that was the predecessor of this one. You can lunch in your bathing suit on several excellent private beaches along the promenade des Anglais. Prices are moderate and carafe wines are good.

La Vieille Ville – Old Nice is a tight labyrinth of winding streets and alleys, steep ascents between medieval buildings, and balconies festooned with rainbows of drying laundry. The character of the city as it grew down the slopes of the Château from the fourteenth to the eighteenth century is in striking contrast to the city of expansive patrician promenades that developed in more modern times. Explore the rue Rossetti, the rue de la Boucherie, or the rue du Collet. Crowd your way through the teeming street markets. Stop in at the Cathedral of Sainte Réparate and the seventeenth-century Church of St. James.

The Flower Market (Le Marché aux Fleurs) – On the edge of the old city, just behind the quai des États-Unis, you'll find the wholesale flower market that offers one of Nice's most colorful spectacles. The varieties of blossoms are dazzling, the aromas heady, and there are a few well-placed cafés, where you can see, sniff, and sip, all at the same time. Open weekdays. Cours Saleya.

Palais Lascaris – A splendid private palace of the seventeenth century in Genoese style, this is the former residence of the Count Lascaris-Ventimiglia. It is noted for its frescoed ceilings, its decorative woodwork, and its regal staircase. Close Mondays in summer; Mondays, Tuesdays, and some public holidays in winter; and the month of November. 15 rue Droite (phone: 62-05-54).

The Vieux Port – To the east of the Château, the harbor of Nice is an artful array of multicolored boats from one-man dinghies and kayaks to the white steamers that

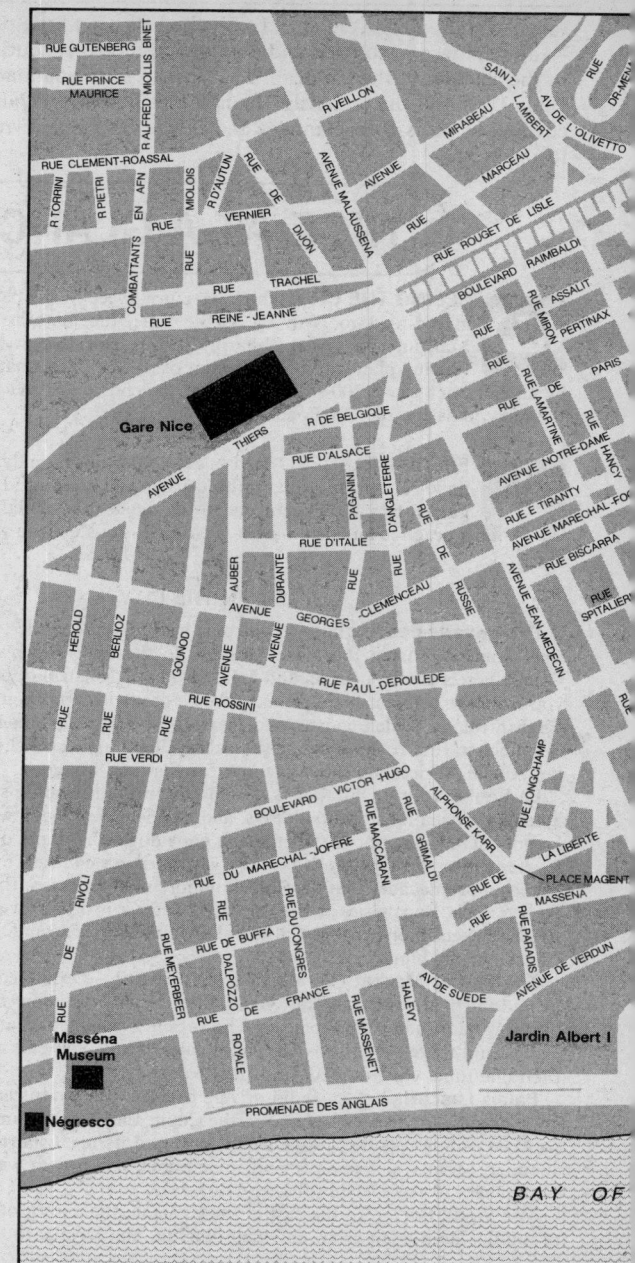

RUE GUTENBERG
RUE PRINCE MAURICE
R ALFRED MIOLLIS BINET
RUE CLEMENT-ROASSAL
R TORRINI
R PIETRI
COMBATTANTS EN AFN
RUE MIOLLIS
R D'AUTUN
RUE DE VERNIER
RUE DIXON
RUE TRACHEL
RUE REINE - JEANNE
R VEILLON
AVENUE MALAUSSENA
AVENUE
RUE
MIRABEAU
SAINT - LAMBERT
AV DE L'OLIVETTO
RUE
DR MENT
MARCEAU
RUE ROUGET DE LISLE
BOULEVARD RAIMBALDI
RUE MIRON
ASSALIT
RUE
PERTINAX
RUE LAMARTINE
RUE DE
PARIS
RUE
Gare Nice
THIERS
R DE BELGIQUE
RUE D'ALSACE
RUE D'ANGLETERRE
PAGANINI
RUE D'ITALIE
AUBER
DURANTE
RUE
RUE DE
RUSSE
AVENUE
AVENUE GEORGES -CLEMENCEAU
AVENUE
AVENUE NOTRE-DAME
HANCY
RUE E TIRANTY
AVENUE MARECHAL-FOC
RUE BISCARRA
AVENUE JEAN-MEDECIN
RUE SPITALIERI
HEROLD
BERLIOZ
GOUNOD
AVENUE
AVENUE
RUE PAUL-DEROULEDE
RUE
RUE
RUE
RUE ROSSINI
RUE VERDI
BOULEVARD VICTOR -HUGO
RUE MACCARANI
RUE GRIMALDI
ALPHONSE KARR
RUE LONGCHAMP
RUE
LA LIBERTE
PLACE MAGENT
RUE DE MASSENA
RUE DU MARECHAL -JOFFRE
RUE DE BUFFA
RUE DU CONGRES
RUE DALPOZZO
RUE PARADIS
AVENUE DE VERDUN
RUE DE RIVOLI
RUE MEYERBEER
RUE
DE FRANCE
ROYALE
AV DE SUEDE
HALEVY
RUE MASSENET
Jardin Albert I
Masséna Museum
Négresco
PROMENADE DES ANGLAIS

BAY OF

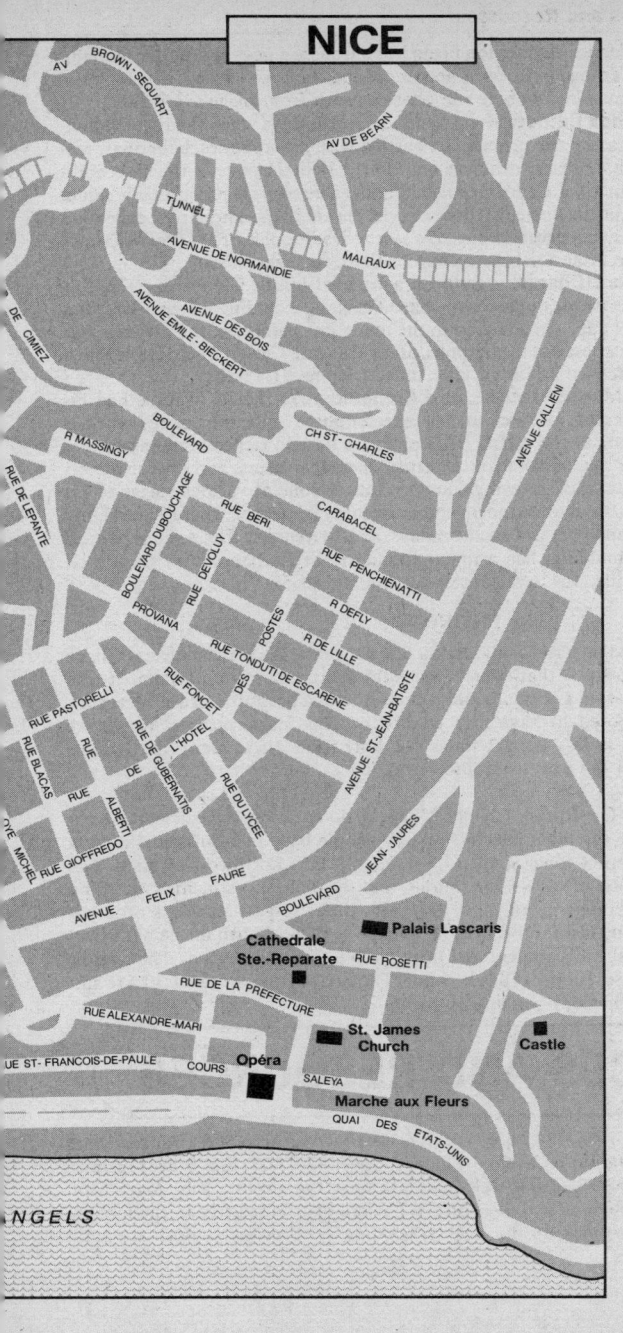

NICE

AV BROWN-SÉQUART

AV DE BEARN

TUNNEL

MALRAUX

AVENUE DE NORMANDIE

AVENUE DES BOIS

AVENUE EMILE-BIECKERT

DE CIMIEZ

BOULEVARD

CH ST-CHARLES

AVENUE GALLIENI

R MASSINGY

RUE DE LEPANTE

BOULEVARD DUBOUCHAGE

RUE BERI

CARABACEL

RUE DEVOLUY

RUE PENCHIENATTI

PROVANA

DES POSTES

R DEFLY

R DE LILLE

RUE TONDUTI DE ESCARENE

RUE FONCET

RUE PASTORELLI

RUE DE GUBERNATIS

L'HOTEL

AVENUE ST-JEAN-BATISTE

RUE BLACAS

RUE

DE

RUE DU LYCEE

CRE MICHEL

RUE

ALBERTI

RUE GIOFFREDO

FELIX

FAURE

JEAN-JAURES

AVENUE

BOULEVARD

Palais Lascaris

Cathedrale
Ste.-Reparate

RUE ROSETTI

RUE DE LA PREFECTURE

RUE ALEXANDRE-MARI

St. James
Church

Castle

UE ST-FRANCOIS-DE-PAULE

COURS

Opéra

SALEYA

Marche aux Fleurs

QUAI DES ETATS-UNIS

NGELS

make the crossing to Corsica. Excursion boats leave from the port and putter along to nearby Riviera towns. To reach the port, go out around the base of the Château at the far end of quai des États-Unis or take rue Cassini south from place Garibaldi.

The Russian Orthodox Cathedral – A reminder of the days when the royal Romanovs roamed the Riviera and the promenade bustled with grand dukes, ballerinas, and an occasional Bolshevik, the cathedral was built in the Belle Époque of the nineteenth century, under the auspices of Czar Nicholas himself. The church supports a bouquet of ornate onion domes in the ancient Russian style. Inside you'll find a rich collection of icons and an impressive, carved iconostasis — the traditional screen that separates the altar from the nave in an Orthodox church. Blvd. du Tzarewitch.

Musée National Marc Chagall – Built on a wooded hill in Cimiez in 1972, this modern museum houses work donated by Marc Chagall, including 17 canvases that make up his *Biblical Message.* In addition to the many fine paintings, the museum has sculptures, mosaics, sketches, and lithographs, all by Chagall. Closed Tuesdays. Admission fee. Av. du Dr. Menard and blvd. de Cimiez (phone: 81-75-75).

Matisse Museum (Musée Matisse et d'Archéologie) – Henri Matisse had his studio in the Cimiez section of Nice and a representative collection of his work is installed on the first floor of the Arena Villa opposite the old Benedictine monastery gardens in Cimiez. You can see some of the artist's personal effects and his private art collection, as well as canvases, drawings, and sculpture done at various stages of his career. The tomb of Matisse is at the north end of a nearby cemetery, where Raoul Dufy is also buried. Closed Sunday mornings, Mondays, and November. The Archaeological Museum, in the same building, has artifacts found at the Roman site of Cimiez. It follows the same schedule. 164 Av. des Arènes (phone: 81-59-57).

ENVIRONS

Eze Village – Perched on a rock spike 1,550 feet above the sea is this unusual village — once a medieval fortress — that offers a splendid panorama of the Riviera. It also has a tropical garden (Jardin Exotique) and a church with a beautiful fifteenth-century font. Nietzsche is supposed to have first worked out his masterpiece, *Thus Spake Zarathustra,* here. Eze is less than 7 miles (11 km) from Nice, along the Middle (Moyenne) Corniche on the way to Monte Carlo.

■**EXTRA SPECIAL:** The Rosary Chapel (Chapelle du Rosaire), designed and decorated by Matisse, is the main reason so many people have rediscovered *Vence,* a picturesque old market town some 13.5 miles (22 km) northwest of Nice. The stunning stained-glass windows, the murals, and the church vestments created by Matisse may bring you here, but you'll also enjoy the setting — on a rock promontory, sheltered by the last foothills of the Alps — and the charm of the old town, enclosed in elliptical walls and entered through five arched gateways. The chapel, on av. Henri Matisse, is open Tuesdays and Thursdays from 10 to 11:30 AM and 2:30 to 5:30 PM; other days by appointment.

SOURCES AND RESOURCES

The Nice Office de Tourisme–Syndicat d'Initiative has two branches to assist you: Alongside the railway station on avenue Thiers (phone: 87-07-07) and 5 av. Gustave V (phone: 87-60-60). There's also a welcome desk near the airport. *Sept Jours–Sept Nuits* is a monthly directory of activities on the Riviera distributed free in the lobbies of most Nice hotels. Also pick up the weekly *Semaine des Spectacles.* Both are published in French only, but they're easy to decipher, as is *Nice-Matin,* the daily newspaper of the area. You can get tourist information in English by calling 85-65-83.

CLIMATE AND CLOTHES: Hot summer days in Nice are tempered by fresh breezes off the bay, and winter months are mild. The average temperature in January is 48°F (9°C). But there is a lot more rain than the tourist officials like to admit (Nice averages 66 days of rain a year), and sudden bouts of the whipping *mistral* — cold gusts of wind from the northwest — in spring. So bring something warm and something waterproof, even if you are coming to soak up the sun. Dress is casual just about everywhere, though you'll want something special for the evenings at the more elegant restaurants.

GETTING AROUND: It's a good thing that central Nice is compact and easily accessible by foot, because traffic becomes ludicrous during the tourist seasons. Many areas have become pedestrian zones, such as rue Masséna and some of its cross streets, as well as numerous streets in the Vieille Ville. If you want to move faster, rent a motorbike at *Motorent,* 3 rue Barralis (phone: 87-48-78) or at *Locomoto,* 12 rue Bottero (phone: 96-80-73).

Bus – You can hop on a bus for outlying districts, such as Cimiez, at the place Masséna.

Taxi – Cabs are expensive, so watch the meter and remember streets often are clogged with traffic at certain hours. You'll find plenty of cabs at stands, and they can be hailed in the streets; or phone a taxi at 82-32-32 or 88-89-93.

Car Rental – Major international firms are represented, and most of them stock convertibles for conspicuous cruising. Check the phone book's yellow pages.

Boats – *Gallus* boats cruise along the Riviera. Apply to SATAM, 24 quai Lunel (phone: 55-33-33). For ferries to Corsica, inquire at SNCM, 3 av. Gustave (phone: 89-89-89).

MUSEUMS: The Chagall and Matisse museums described in *Special Places* are the most impressive in Nice, but there are several others of interest:

Natural History Museum (Musée d'Histoire Naturelle) – Exhibitions on marine life. 60 *bis* blvd. Risso (phone: 55-15-24).

Masséna Museum – Memorabilia of Napoleon's trusted marshal and exhibitions on the history of Nice. 65 rue de France (phone: 88-11-34).

Jules Chéret Museum – Nice's municipal art museum, with works by Fragonard, Renoir, Degas, Picasso. 33 av. des Baumettes (phone: 44-50-72).

Musée de Terra Amata – Artifacts from this excavated prehistoric site. 28 blvd. Carnot (phone: 55-59-93).

Musée International d'Art Naïf Anatole Jakovsky – Jakovsky's collection of almost 600 paintings documenting naive art from the eighteenth century to the present. Château Ste.-Hélène, av. Val-Marie (phone: 71-78-83).

SHOPPING: Street market shopping in the Vieille Ville is the least expensive and the most fun. Rue Masséna, place Magenta, and rue Paradis are the pedestrian zone of shops and cafés, with rue Paradis noted for its elegant shops. There's also a flea market on boulevard Risso every day except Sunday. Some Nice shops of note:

Alziari – An olive mill that sells oils, spices, rustic wooden kitchenware, and olive oil soap. 14 rue St.-François-de-Paule.

Comtesse du Barry – For French food delicacies of every description; 57 varieties of *foie gras.* 7 rue Halévy.

Confiserie du Vieux Nice – A sweets factory with Provence specialties such as candied fruits and flowers. Watch the stuff being made downstairs, then buy it upstairs. Quai Papacino and rue Robilante.

Riviera Bookshop – A wide choice of books in English. 10 rue Chauvain (phone: 85-84-61).

Vuitton – Handbags, luggage, and other items with the status LVs. 2 av. de Suède.

 SPECIAL EVENTS: The Nice event par excellence is *Carnival,* which begins three weekends before Lent and ends when His Majesty, King Carnival, is burned in effigy on Shrove Tuesday. The festivities include parades and floats, confetti and flower battles, fireworks, and masked balls. The *Fête des Mais* is a month of Sundays in May, with special merriment in the gardens of the Roman Arena at Cimiez. In July, the 10-day *Grande Parade du Jazz*, also in the Cimiez gardens, is the biggest jazz festival in Europe. To find out more about special events in Nice, contact *Comité des Fêtes, des Arts et des Sports,* 5 Promenade des Anglais (phone: 87-16-28).

 SPORTS: Boating – Various kinds of small boats are available for hire in the Vieux Port. Windsurfing craft, *planches à voile,* can be rented at bathing establishments along the promenade.

　　　　Golf – The most spectacular course is at Mont-Agel in the hills above Monte Carlo. There are also good courses at Biot and Valbonne.

Horse Racing – Thoroughbred racing takes place at the *Hippodrome de Côte d'Azur* in nearby Cagnes-sur-Mer.

Riding – Horses can be rented at *Club Hippique de Nice,* 368 rte. de Grenoble (phone: 29-81-10).

Skiing – From November to April, you can ski on the slopes at Valberg, Isola, Esteng d'Entraunes, Auron, and Gréolières-les-Neiges in the Alps, only an hour or two away.

Swimming – The Ruhl Plage is the most central of Nice bathing beaches. Castel Plage is set right into the rock of Pointe de Rauba Capeù below the Château. In winter, you can swim at *Piscine Municipale J. Médecin,* 178 rue de France (phone: 86-24-01).

Tennis – Contact the *Nice Lawn Tennis Club,* Parc Imperial (phone: 96-17-70).

 THEATER: In summer, all of Nice's best theatrical experiences take place outdoors: cabaret-type shows at the *Théâtre 12,* 12 av. St.-Jean-Baptiste (phone: 85-40-28); concerts and theatrical and folkloric shows at the *Théâtre de Verdure* in the Albert I Garden just off place Masséna (phone: 82-38-68) and at the Roman Arena at Cimiez. The tourist office can provide ticket information. The *Nouveau Théâtre de Nice,* Esplanade des Victoires (phone: 56-86-86), presents a season of plays in French from October through April.

 MUSIC: In addition to musical performances outdoors in summer, there is an opera season at the *Théâtre de l'Opéra,* quai des États-Unis, from November through April. The box office is at 4 rue St.-François-de-Paule (phone: 80-59-83, information; 85-67-31, reservations). The *Nice Philharmonic Orchestra* plays a musical spring and a musical autumn at the opera house.

 NIGHTCLUBS AND NIGHTLIFE: The hottest disco in town, attracting a young crowd, is *La Camargue,* 5 pl. Charles-Felix (phone: 85-74-10). *Au Pizzaiolo,* 4 *bis* rue du Pont Vieux (phone: 62-34-70), in the old city, is cozier, less expensive, and offers an Italian-Niçois menu along with dancing and a modest cabaret. *Superstar*, 3 pl. de L'Armée du Rhin (phone: 56-84-05), is a popular and lively disco.

NICE / Best in Town 549

SINS: With the recent closing of Nice's *Casino Ruhl,* gamblers now have to go to Cannes or Monte Carlo to pursue their vice. But you don't have to travel far to indulge in *gluttony* at some of Nice's opulent restaurants.

BEST IN TOWN

CHECKING IN: Nice hotels can be divided into those along the promenade des Anglais, with a view of the bay — and the traffic — and those set back on quieter streets. At an expensive hotel you will pay $85 or more per night for a double; $50 to $80 at a moderately priced hotel; less than $50 a night is inexpensive. However, expect prices to leap by one-half in summer, and perhaps double on the expensive end. Do not show up in the summer high season without a reservation unless you want to become an expert in Riviera hotel lobbies.

Négresco – One of those Côte d'Azur landmarks where everyone should stay at least once before the revolution comes. A great wedding-cake hotel overlooking the promenade, with beautifully appointed rooms, a fine restaurant called *Chantecler* (see *Eating Out*), and staff in eighteenth-century costume. The building itself has been designated a national monument. 37 promenade des Anglais (phone: 88-39-51). Expensive.

Beach Regency – Formerly the *Hyatt Regency Nice,* this is a deluxe, modern, fully air-conditioned hotel of seven stories. With the new management there's now a very fine restaurant, *Le Rendez Vous,* and such lively activities as *thés dansants* (tea dances) and festive buffet lunches held on Sundays. And there's still a swimming pool on the roof as well as a good terrace restaurant overlooking the bay. The location is a bit away from the center, toward the airport, but the street address is still right. 223 promenade des Anglais (phone: 83-91-51). Expensive.

Méridien – Above the now-defunct Ruhl Casino near the Albert I Garden, this shiny, modern hotel has lots of glass and escalators, and it is luxurious in a more streamlined way than the Victorian dowager hotels that gave the Riviera its reputation. There's a good restaurant, piano bar, and health club. The hotel also has an underground parking lot that offers access to the pedestrian zone. 1 promenade des Anglais (phone: 82-25-25). Expensive.

Napoléon – A typical, gracious Niçois building on a quiet corner a few streets back from the beachfront, near the pedestrian zone. The owner is also the manager and the atmosphere is warm and welcoming. Bar, but no restaurant. 6 rue Grimaldi (phone: 87-70-07). Moderate.

La Pérouse – A charming small hotel at the far end of the quai des États-Unis with a view of the entire bay. It offers gardens, pool, sauna. One drawback: traffic noise on an uphill curve outside. No restaurant. 11 quai Rauba-Capeù (phone: 62-34-63). Moderate.

West End – Here is traditional elegance of a somewhat British type. A faithful clientele seems to have been coming back each year since the Crimean War. Seafront, but no restaurant. 31 promenade des Anglais (phone: 88-79-91). Moderate.

New York – An old white building with tropical flora in its entrance court on a side street off the busy avenue Jean-Médecin. Centrally located and recently remodeled despite its elderly appearance. 44 av. Marechal-Foch (phone: 92-04-19). Moderate to inexpensive.

Georges – Only 18 rooms, but each is comfortable, clean, well cared for, and looks as if it's been decorated with surplus *Négresco* furnishings. Rooms are understandably hard to come by in the summer, but it's well worth the necessary advance planning. 3 rue Henri-Cordier (phone: 86-23-41). Inexpensive.

 EATING OUT: The cuisine in Nice is a curious mixture of Parisian, native Provençal, and neighboring Italian. However, the city can claim specialties of its own. They include *pissaladière,* a kind of pizza topped with black olives, onions, and anchovies; *stocaficada,* a ragoût of stockfish, served with potatoes, tomatoes, peppers, and zucchini; and *pan bagnat,* a loaf of French bread split down the middle, soaked in olive oil, and garnished with tomatoes, radishes, peppers, onion, hard-boiled egg, black olives, and parsley. *Socca,* a popular dish in bars of the old town and port, is an enormous pancake made from chickpea flour and olive oil, baked like pizza or fried in oil. It is usually washed down with a solid red wine or a little glass of *pointu* (chilled rosé). Nice's Bellet reds, whites, and rosés, Appellation Contrôlée wines grown within the city limits, should be tried during your stay. At expensive restaurants, expect to pay $100 or more for dinner for two (without drinks or wine), $50 to $100 at moderately priced restaurants, and a minimum of $50 at inexpensive restaurants.

Le Moulin de Mougins – One of the most extraordinary dining experiences on the Côte d'Azur awaits you in Roger Vergé's converted sixteenth-century mill in the charming market town of Mougins. The cuisine has three Michelin stars and among the specialties to be enjoyed are braised slivers of Provençal duck in honey and lemon sauce, escalope of fresh salmon, lobster *fricassée,* pâté of sole, and for dessert, cold wild strawberry soufflé. Closed Mondays, Thursdays at lunch, mid-November to mid-December, and mid-February to mid-March. Reservations essential. About 20 miles (32 km) west of Nice in Mougins (phone: 75-78-24). Expensive.

Chantecler – If you don't stay at the *Négresco,* at least have a meal here on the outdoor terrace facing the sea. Prize-winning chef Jacques Maximin creates such specialties as *gourmandise de foie gras*, a luxurious pâté, and *charlotte de St.-Pierre,* a fish fantasy. The *menu dégustation* features tiny, elegant portions of a dozen different dishes. Reservations at this two-star restaurant are a must in summer; closed November. 37 promenade des Anglais (phone: 88-39-51). Expensive.

La Poularde chez Lucullus – Very elegant French dining in the solid bourgeois tradition with plenty of rich cream sauces; turn-of-the-century decor with lots of wrought iron. Try the veal kidneys flambéed in champagne, the grilled lobster, or the roast lamb. Closed Wednesdays and mid-July to mid-August. Reserve, even a few days ahead. 9 rue Gustave-Deloye (phone: 85-22-90). Expensive.

Château de la Chèvre d'Or – For a special treat, drive east out of Nice on the Moyenne Corniche to Eze (see *Special Places*), where you will find this excellent restaurant in a restored medieval manor house with a garden. (It's also a hotel.) You can dine on lobster mousse or rack of lamb, while enjoying a spectacular panorama of the sea. Closed from November 15 to February 15 and on Wednesdays from October to Easter. Reservations required. Moyenne Corniche, Eze (phone: 41-12-12). Expensive.

L'Ane Rouge – Fine seafood specialties include oysters, lobster, *bourride* (fish stew) — or try the sweetbreads. One Michelin star. Closed mid-July to September, Saturday evenings, and Sundays. 7 quai des Deux-Emmanuel (phone: 89-49-63). Expensive.

Colombe d'Or – This gallery-restaurant in a small hotel (with pool) just outside the gates of the old town in St.-Paul-de-Vence is most noted for its collection of post-Impressionist art. Matisse and other artists sometimes paid their bills in the 1920s and 1930s with the paintings that now decorate the walls. The restaurant specializes in grills and roasts, and there is a lovely view from its terrace in summer. Reservations recommended; closed early November to mid-December. About 14 miles (22 km) northwest of Nice in St.-Paul-de-Vence (phone: 32-80-02). Expensive.

Rôtisserie de Saint-Pancrace – Here you can dine on prawn stew, quenelles of salmon, roast pigeon, or ravioli stuffed with foie gras, among other dishes that have earned the restaurant its Michelin star. A lovely view from the garden terrace. Closed Mondays and early January to early February. In the village of Saint-Pancrace, 8 km north of Nice on D914 (phone: 84-43-69). Expensive to moderate.

Petit Brouant – Also known as *Chez Puget,* this family restaurant of great class and gracious surroundings serves classic French cuisine. Specialties include bouillabaisse. Reservations required. Closed in June. 4 *bis* rue Gustave-Deloye (phone: 85-25-84). Moderate.

Chez Don Camillo – A tranquil, intimate place, this restaurant offers an appetizing taste of Italy (in case you're not going to make it across the border), but with a Niçois accent. Closed Sundays and the month of July. Reservations necessary. 5 rue des Ponchettes (phone: 85-67-95). Moderate.

Chez les Pêcheurs – The specialties of this seafood restaurant in the Old Port include fish pâté and grilled deep sea bass *(loup de mer).* Closed Wednesdays and November through mid-December. 18 quai Docks (phone: 89-59-61). Moderate.

Les Pléiades – Located in the *Hotel Aston* terrace garden, this restaurant is noted for its lunchtime buffet of hors d'oeuvres, made up of all the things that tempted you this morning in the market. 12 av. Félix-Faure (phone: 80-62-52). Moderate.

Michel – This restaurant has very good seafood dishes, especially the fish soup, stuffed mussels, and the sole meunière. Closed Mondays and the month of July. 12 rue Meyerbeer (phone: 88-77-42). Moderate.

La Méranda – A tiny, crowded place near the flower market, run by a husband and wife team. Service is a bit slow, as each dish is prepared to order. Tripes niçoises and pâté *au pistou* are splendid choices. Closed February, August, Saturday evenings, Sundays, and Mondays. 4 rue de la Terrasse (no phone). Inexpensive.

La Nissarda – A good place to try an assortment of Niçois specialties: ratatouille, *pissaladière,* and *stocaficada.* Closed Tuesday evenings, Wednesdays and the month of July. Reservations advised. 17 rue Gubernatis (phone: 85-26-29). Inexpensive.

OSLO

The capital of Norway sits at the head of a 60-mile fjord on the country's southeastern coast, framed by a vast expanse of lakeland, woods, and moors, where fir-treed hills rise 2,000 feet. The oldest of the Scandinavian capitals, Oslo is enormous: 172 square miles, only a tenth of which is urban and town districts. The rest is a marvelous outdoor playground for Oslo's approximately 450,000 residents and its visitors from around the world.

Oslo today is a jumble of architectural styles, but each year more modern concrete and glass buildings replace old wooden structures. Along with its attempts at modernization in this century, the city of Oslo has made a conscious effort to integrate art into the daily lives of its citizens. Frescoes and wood carvings decorate public and private buildings, and sculpture is an integral part of public squares and parks. In spring and summer, all this colorful art, the small malls and shopping streets, and outdoor cafés give the center of the city the feeling of a medieval festival.

People are believed to have lived at the head of the Oslo fjord 7,000 years ago. But the history of Oslo as we know it dates from 1050, when the Viking King Harald, called "Harald Hard Rule," built a commercial town in what is now east Oslo.

During the reign of Harald's successor, Olav Kyrre (1066–93), Oslo became an ecclesiastical center, its principal cathedral named after the city's patron saint, St. Hallvard. The foundation stones are all that remain today of this once mighty cathedral that served as the burial place of so many Viking kings.

Medieval Oslo reached its zenith during the reign of King Haakon V Magnusson (1299–1319), who built the majestic Akershus Castle and Fortress and decreed Oslo the capital of Norway. After Haakon's death the city went into decline. Many of its people were killed by the Black Death in 1349, and when Norway united with Denmark, Oslo lost its importance as a capital. Several times the city was devastated by fire, and in 1624 all of its wooden buildings succumbed to flames.

King Christian IV, who ruled Norway and Denmark at the time, ordered a new capital built somewhat farther west, behind the walls of Akershus. He named it Christiana, a name that was used until 1925, when the ancient name of Oslo was reintroduced. The streets laid out by Christian IV are still the main streets of central Oslo. And a few of the stone and half-timbered buildings from this era can be seen today.

In 1814, during the Napoleonic wars, Norway and Denmark were separated and there followed a 90-year union with Sweden. Oslo's main street, the hub of the city today, is named for the first of the Swedish-Norwegian kings, Karl Johan. After the union with Sweden was dissolved in 1905, the Norwegian capital entered a period of expansion, interrupted only by World War

I and the German Occupation during World War II. Since 1917, Oslo has been Norway's most important maritime city as well. Its harbor has more than 8 miles of quays, and world's largest tourist ships can dock in Oslo.

Norway is a constitutional monarchy with a parliamentary government. King Olav V lives in the Royal Palace at one end of Karl Johans Gate and the parliament meets in the century-old National Assembly building (Stortingsbygningen) a few blocks away.

The king, like virtually all Norwegians, is an avid cross-country skier and can occasionally be seen heading for one of the thousands of trails within the city limits. Oslo residents often ski at night after work, and many of the city's most festive events are connected with skiing and other winter sports.

Ski jumping originated near Oslo in 1879. The 100th anniversary of the sport was celebrated by close to 100,000 people during the *Holmenkollen Ski Festival* in March 1979. The Holmenkollen Ski Jump, which can be seen from most parts of Oslo, has been a landmark since it was built for the 1952 Winter Olympics. The jumping tower itself is 184 feet high and its summit is 1,350 feet above the fjord overlooking Oslo. It is the combination of such man-made sights with an extraordinary natural beauty that makes Oslo a very special place to visit.

OSLO AT-A-GLANCE

 SEEING THE CITY: Spectacular views of the city and the Oslo fjord are available from several vantage points in the hilly, wooded area, *Oslomarka,* on the east, north, and west of the city. Perhaps the best panorama is from Tryvannstårnet, a 390-foot observation tower atop the 1,600-foot-high Tryvann Hill on the outskirts of Oslo. It is reached by a 25-minute walk from the Frognerseteren Station at the end of the Holmenkollen suburban rail line, 30 minutes from the city center. The *Scanorama Bar* on the top of the *Hotel Scandinavia* offers the best view of the city from downtown between 3 PM and midnight, but you'll need reservations. Holbergs Gate 30 (phone: 11-30-00).

 **SPECIAL PLACES:** The Vika area of the city, with its colorfully decorated buildings and public squares and several closed-to-traffic pedestrian streets, is perfect for sight-seeing on foot. East of the main harbor area within walking distance is what remains of the oldest parts of the city, an area called Gamlebyen, which you can also reach by bus or tram. Expensive homes and swimming beaches, as well as several important museums, are on the Bygdøy peninsula, which juts into the fjord southwest of the harbor. You can reach the peninsula by bus or, in summer months, by one of the ferries that leave from near city hall. Suburban trains provide easy access to the outer districts of Oslo, where you will find what is undoubtedly the widest network of ski trails in the world, with some 1,364 miles to choose from.

DOWNTOWN

Oslo Harbor – Stroll along this busy, modern waterfront and you will see graceful white cruise ships that ply the fjords, small ferries, and private boats. Don't miss the chance to snack on tasty, tiny shrimp sold by fishermen who catch them at sea and cook them aboard their boats as they head back to the pier in front of city hall.

Oslo City Hall (Rådhus) – A spacious square with fountains and sculpture separates

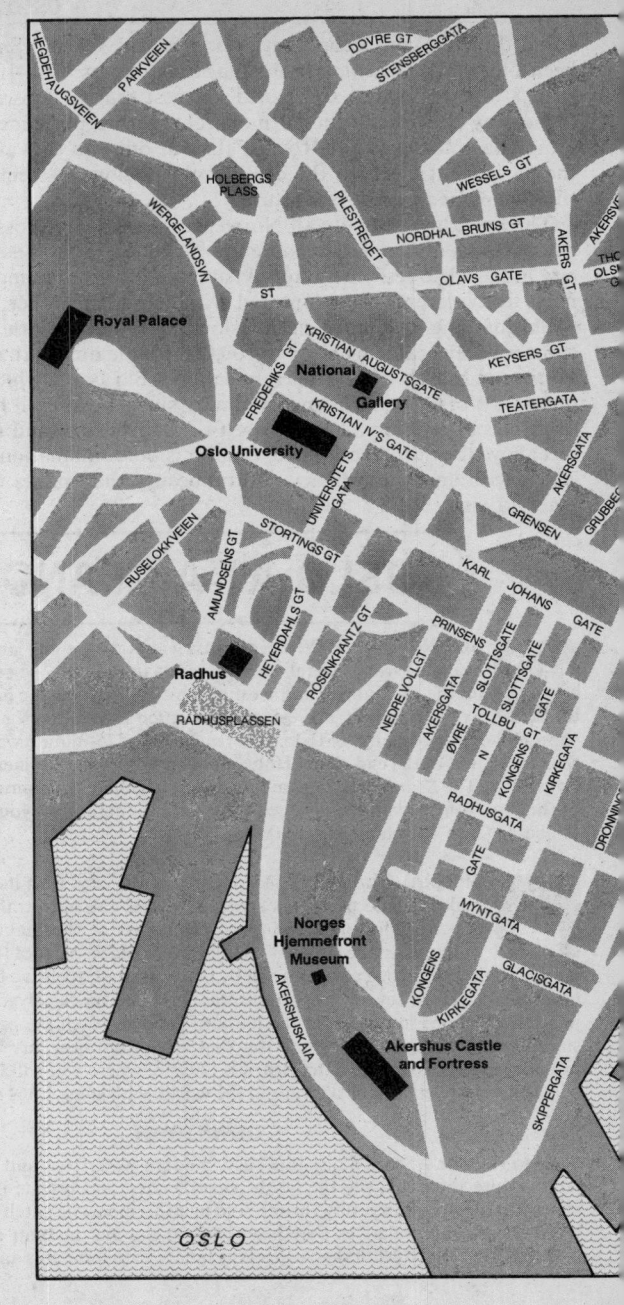

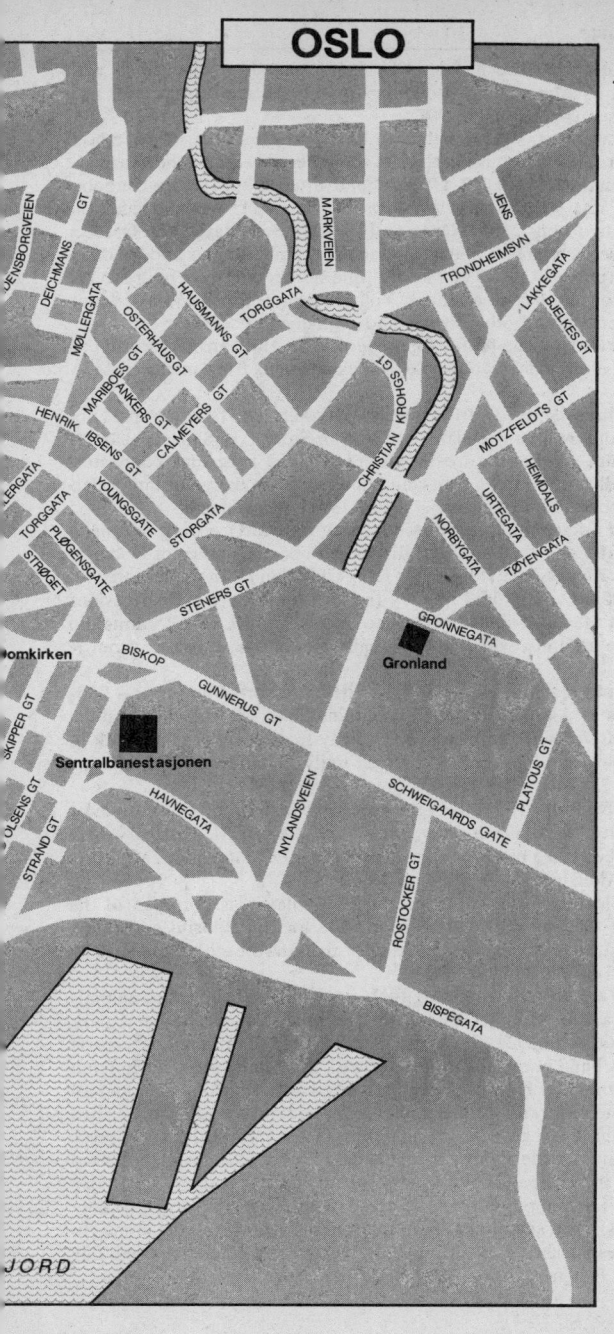

OSLO

JENSBORGVEIEN

GT

DEICHMANNS

MØLLERGATA

OSTERHAUS GT

HAUSMANNS GT

TORGGATA

MARKVEIEN

JENS

TRONDHEIMSVN

LAKKEGATA

BJELKES GT

MARIBOES GT

ANKERS GT

CALMEYERS GT

CHRISTIAN KROHGS GT

MOTZFELDTS GT

HENRIK IBSENS GT

HEIMDALS

URTEGATA

LLERGATA

YOUNGSGATE

STORGATA

NORBYGATA

TØYENGATA

TORGGATA

PLØGENSGATE

STRØGET

STENERS GT

GRONNEGATA

omkirken

BISKOP

Gronland

GUNNERUS GT

SKIPPER GT

Sentralbanestasjonen

PLATOUS GT

OLSENS GT

HAVNEGATA

NYLANDSVEIEN

SCHWEIGAARDS GATE

STRAND GT

ROSTOCKER GT

BISPEGATA

JORD

this outstanding landmark from the harbor. City hall is lavishly embellished with contemporary Norwegian sculpture, wood carvings, paintings, and tapestries. Open daily. Free. Rådhusplassen (phone: 41-00-90).

Oslo Cathedral (Domkirken) – Although both its exterior and interior have been restored since the cathedral was first built in the late seventeenth century, the altarpiece and pulpit are original, dating from 1699. Of particular interest are the bronze doors by Dagfin Werenskiold, the stained-glass windows by Emanuel Vigeland, and the ceiling decorations by Hugo Lous Mohr. Open daily, except Saturdays from October through April. Regular services are held at 11 AM and 6 PM on Sundays and Wednesdays at noon. Stortorvet (phone: 41-27-93). The old-time stables that were built around the cathedral have been converted to small shops. You can browse for antiques or watch silversmiths, weavers, potters, and other artists and craftsmen at work.

Ruin Park (Minneparken) – The foundation stones of St. Hallvard Cathedral can be seen in this park with a number of archaeological excavations from medieval Oslo. Oslo gate at Bispegata.

Oslo's Markets – Three large, colorful outdoor markets are favorite spots for picture taking. Garden and greenhouse plants are sold in Stortorvet Square, near the cathedral; vegetables, fruits, and flowers are on sale in Grønland Torg; and Youngstorget, for handicrafts as well as vegetables, fruits, and flowers. Open daily until midafternoon; March 15 to October 14 and December 17 to 23; closed Sundays.

Akershus Castle and Fortress (Akershus Festning og Slott) – Built originally by King Haakon V about 1300, this is one of the most important relics of medieval Norway. It was rebuilt in Renaissance style under King Christian IV in the seventeenth century. It has been restored and is used now by the government for state occasions and festivities. Buildings are open daily, May 2 to September 15. Small admission charge. Admission to the grounds, which are open all year, is free. Entrance from R ådhus Gate.

The Norwegian Resistance Museum (Norges Hjemmefront Museum) – This museum, on the grounds of Akershus Fortress, contains materials and memorabilia that will give you a picture of what happened in Norway from the German attack in 1940 until the end of the occupation in 1945. Open daily. Small admission charge. Akershus (phone: 41-43-79).

Gamle Aker Kirke – Built in 1100, this is the oldest stone church in Scandinavia. It is still used as a parish church. Open daily, May 15 to August 31. During winter months, the church may be visited by appointment between 10 AM and noon, Mondays through Fridays. Free. Akersbakken 26 (phone: 46-11-68).

The Royal Palace (Slottet) – The residence of King Olav V is not open to the public, but you can visit the grounds. Get there in time for the colorful ceremony, complete with brass band, that marks the changing of the guard each day from 1:30 to 2 PM. At the west end of Karl Johans Gate.

Vigeland Sculpture Park (Vigelandsanlegget) – A world of people and animals sculpted in granite, iron, and bronze by Gustav Vigeland inhabit a lovely 80-acre park in the western section of Oslo. In 1921, the city of Oslo offered the brilliant, egocentric Norwegian sculptor a free hand in carving his masterwork in Frogner Park, a depiction of the whole cycle of human life. He was given a studio, workmen, assistants, and all the funds he needed — the cost ran into the millions by the time the job was finished in 1943. Vigeland takes on birth, growth, joy, suffering, and death in the 1,150-piece collection of huge, writhing, nude figures in metal and stone. The result has been variously called obscene, inspired, and mindless by critics. On the grounds, you'll also find a statue of Abraham Lincoln presented to Norway by the people of North Dakota on July 4, 1914. The park has a swimming pool, tennis courts, and a sports arena. In summer, there are two restaurants in addition to the year-round cafeteria. Open day and night all year. Free. Frogner.

The Vigeland Museum (Vigeland Museet) – Just across from the southern end of Frogner Park is Vigeland's former residence and studio. It contains 1,650 sculptures, 3,700 woodcuts, hundreds of plates for woodcuts, and some 11,000 sketches by the eminent Norwegian artist. During summer months, concerts are held in the museum's courtyard. Closed Mondays. Free. Nobels Gate 32 (phone: 44-11-36).

Munch Museum (Munch Museet) – Edvard Munch, the expressionist painter and graphic artist who died in 1944, bequeathed all his art treasures to the city of Oslo. This light, airy, spacious museum was built in the eastern section of the city to house the almost 1,000 oil paintings, 4,500 drawings, 15,000 prints, and notes, letters, sketches, and other materials in the collection. Open daily; closed Mondays. Free. Tøyen Gate 53 (phone: 67-37-74).

The National Gallery (Nasjonalgalleriet) – This is where you'll find Norway's principal art collection. The emphasis is on Norwegian artists, but there is a representative sample of international artists, particularly the French Impressionists. Munch's much-reproduced *Girls on the Bridge* is here. Open daily. Free. Universitets Gate 13 (phone: 20-04-04).

Oslo University (Universitas Osloensis) – The main attraction here for tourists is the old festival hall, called the *Aula,* with its Munch murals. This is where the award ceremony for the Nobel Peace Prize (the only Nobel Prize awarded here; the rest are awarded in Stockholm) normally takes place. Open June 21 to August 8. During the winter season, admittance is upon request by telephoning 42-90-10, ext. 756. Free. Karl Johans Gate.

Sigrun Berg's Weaving Studio (Sigrun Berg's Vevstue) – Sigrun Berg is one of Scandinavia's most famous weaving experts. She welcomes visitors to her 200-year-old studio. Damstredet 20 (phone: 20-80-41).

THE PENINSULA

Viking Ship House (Vikingskiphuset) – Three longships, the *Gokstad ship,* the *Tune ship,* and the *Oseberg ship,* from the period AD 800–900, will transport you back to the days when Vikings roamed the seas. The upswept prow of the *Oseberg ship* with a stunning pattern of carved animals is an excellent example of the workmanship and beauty that characterized these ships. The museum also has collections of utensils, gold and silver jewelry, and accouterments from the Viking period. Open daily. Small admission charge. Huk Aveny 35 (phone: 55-86-36).

Norwegian Folk Museum (Norsk Folkemuseum) – Some 150 wooden buildings from all over Norway have been located in a picturesque park near the Viking Ship House to provide a representative picture of Norway's past. One of the museum's treasures is a unique hand-hewn, wooden stave church from 1200. You can also see the last apartment of Norwegian playwright Henrik Ibsen and a group of buildings from Lapp communities in Norway's extreme north. Open daily. Small admission charge. Museumveien 10 (phone: 55-80-90).

Kon-Tiki Museum (Kon-Tiki Museet) – The balsa raft *Kon-Tiki,* used by Thor Heyerdahl and his friends on their 1947 voyage across the Pacific Ocean from Peru to Polynesia, is preserved here along with Easter Island statues and an underwater display. Also on display is the papyrus boat *Ra II,* on which Heyerdahl traveled across the Atlantic Ocean from North Africa to Barbados in 1970. Open daily. Small admission charge. Bygdøy (phone: 55-65-52).

Norwegian Maritime Museum (Norsk Sjøfartsmuseum) – Norway's long maritime traditions are recalled by the collections inside this museum, a short walk from the *Kon-Tiki.* Outside the building, you can see Roald Amundsen's Polar ship, *Gjoa,* the first vessel to navigate a northwest passage in 1903–06. Guided tours. Open daily. Small admission charge. Bygdøy (phone: 55-63-95).

Fram Museum (Polarskipet Fram) – The third ship museum in the area houses the *Fram*, built for Fridtjof Nansen's Polar Expedition, 1893–96 and also used by Amundsen on his expedition to the South Pole in 1910–12. Open daily. Small admission charge. Bygdøy (phone: 55-84-00).

SUBURBS

Ski Museum (Ski Museet) – The world's oldest ski museum is situated inside the takeoff structure on the giant Holmenkollen ski-jumping hill. The collection outlines the history of skiing from the well-preserved tip of a ski found in a bog and believed to be some 2,500 years old to skis used in early Polar expeditions as well as modern equipment. Small admission charge. A 20-minute ride by the Holmenkollen railway from central Oslo and a 15-minute walk from the Holmenkollen Station. Holmenkollen (phone: 14-20-19).

Frognerseteren – A 20-minute walk up the hill from the Ski Museum will take you 1,460 feet above sea level to a panoramic view of Oslo and the fjord. You can also stop in at the cozy lodge and restaurant here. If you have the stamina, another 10 minutes of uphill walking will lead you to the 390-foot Tryvannstarnet, the highest lookout tower in Scandinavia.

The Sonja Henie–Niels Onstad Arts Center (Sonja Henie–Niels Onstads Kuntsenter) – The arts center, 7 miles west of Oslo near Fornebu Airport, was opened in 1968. It houses the permanent collection of twentieth-century art donated by the international skating star and her husband. Included are works by Picasso, Miró, Villon, and Munch. Exhibitions and other events illustrating current trends and ideas in film, music, architecture, literature, and the applied arts are scheduled regularly. Open daily, 11 AM to 10 PM. Restricted hours during Christmas and Easter holidays. Reached by bus from central Oslo. Høvikodden, 1322 Hovik (phone: 54-30-50).

Ekeberg Park – You'll have a fine view of Oslo and the fjord from the 685-foot hill in this lovely park just southeast of the city. It was on this hill that the oldest works of art in Oslo, Stone Age carvings some 3,000 years old, were found in 1915. These rock carvings can be seen between the Merchant Navy Academy here and Kongsveien. The park is easily reached by the Ljabru tram. For a unique experience, the Oslo Travel Association (see *Sources and Resources*) may be able to arrange a torchlit sleigh ride through the Ekeberg woods.

■**EXTRA SPECIAL:** In the ancient fortress town of Fredrikstad, 60 miles (96 km) south of Oslo, you can watch craftsmen and designers at work in their quaint workshops, weaving and printing textiles, blowing glass, making silver jewelry, pottery, and furniture. *Plus Organization* operates a permanent exhibition and sales room for the arts and crafts produced there.

SOURCES AND RESOURCES

The Oslo Tourist Board has its headquarters in Oslo's oldest buildings, Rådmannsgården, circa 1628, at Rådhus Gate 19. It provides free information and maps and arranges tours and guide service at its tourist office, which is open daily except Sundays. Oslo Town Hall (phone: 42-71-70).

For Local Coverage – The association publishes *Oslo This Week,* which you'll want to check for special attractions. It's available at most hotels and at the tourist office. And, if you're going to be here for 4 or more days, the travel association can make an appointment for you to meet with an English-speaking Norwegian who shares your business, cultural, or hobby interests. Oslo doesn't have an English-language newspaper, but American and British periodicals are sold at many kiosks.

CLIMATE AND CLOTHES: From April to September, the nights are very short in Oslo. Since the sun shines 24 hours a day during midsummer above the Arctic Circle, some visitors may want to bring a sleeping mask or some other device to prevent the brightness from disturbing their rest. Summers are short but pleasant, although it can be quite rainy along the coast. So medium-weight clothing and a light raincoat will be useful during the summer. The Gulf Stream keeps Norway's climate temperate. Temperatures range from about 20°F (−6°C) in January to just about 70°F (21°C) in July. Be sure to bring boots, gloves, and other warm gear in winter to take advantage of Oslo's beautiful outdoors.

 GETTING AROUND: Bus and Tram – The most important terminal stop is Grønlands Torg. Most of the buses running through the city center stop at Wessels Plass and by the University Square or at the National Theater. For information about timetables and fares, telephone 56-00-10.

Underground (T-Banen) and Suburban Tram lines – The National Theater is the central stop for most electrified trams and the subway to the forested park areas on the outskirts of Oslo. If you're planning to be in the city for one month, check with Oslo Sporveiers office in Kirkeristen (by the cathedral) about its universal card, to be used for travel on various buses, trams, the underground, and even some ferries. You'll need a photograph for the card, which costs about $27 (phone: 68-95-80).

Taxi – You can call a taxi by dialing 348 or find one at any taxi stand. Taxi stand locations are listed in part 1A of the telephone directory under the heading *Drosjer*. You can also hail a taxi on the street, but drivers are not allowed to pick up passengers within 328 feet of a taxi stand. To order a taxi for a prearranged time, you must call at least an hour before you need it (phone: 38-03-86).

Ferry and Local Boats – Boats and ferries leave from various piers along the harbor. For information on timetables, call 41–62–08 or 42–50–39.

Car Rental – Major American and European firms are represented.

 MUSEUMS: As well as the museums listed in *Special Places,* other notable Oslo museums are:

Museum of Applied Art (Kunstindustrimuseet), St. Olavs Gate 1 (phone: 20-35-78).

Norwegian Customs Museum (Norsk Tollmuseum), Schweigaards Gate 15 (phone: 41-49-60).

Historical Museum (Historisk Museum), Fredriks Gate 2 (phone: 41-63-00).

Natural History Museum, the university's Sars Gate 1, Toyen (phone: 68-69-60).

Norwegian Science and Industry Museum (Norsk Teknisk Museum), Frystik-kalléen 1, Etterstad (phone: 67-51-95).

 SHOPPING: Like other Scandinavian cities, Oslo is not a haven for bargain hunters. Prices are high, but you can get good value for your dollar if you concentrate on typically Norwegian items: arts and crafts, ski sweaters, and, if you are buying furs, Norwegian blue fox and black saga mink. Several exhibition and sales centers have a wide range of Norwegian products on display, so you can get a good idea of what is available. Shops generally are open 9 AM to 5 PM, Mondays through Fridays, but close at 1 PM on Saturdays and remain open until 6 or 7 PM on Thursdays. Some of the larger stores have longer hours.

Arts and Crafts Center (Brukskunstsentret i Basarhallene) – This is a permanent sales exhibition, representing the best of Norwegian arts and crafts. Located in the arcades behind the Oslo Cathedral, the center is surrounded by small workshops. Karl Johans Gate 11 (phone: 42-43-70).

Marjatta Butikk og Galleri A/S – A permanent sales exhibition of high-quality jewelry and art crafts from throughout Scandinavia and many other countries. The gallery also has changing exhibitions of contemporary art. Kongens Gate 14 (phone: 42-31-67).

David-Andersen's Sterling and Enamelware – This firm has won a number of the highest awards in international exhibitions. Karl Johans Gate 20 (phone: 41-69-55).

Forum – The Oslo Crafts and Industrial Association operates this permanent sales exhibition of Norwegian contemporary arts and crafts just opposite the *Hotel Bristol*. Exhibits have been selected because of their quality and design. Rosenkrantz Gate 7 (phone: 42-38-70).

Homecrafts (Husfliden) – Handknit winter sportswear, hand weavings, sealskin slippers, wood carvings, and other Norwegian souvenirs are specialties at this exhibition and sales center near Oslo Cathedral. It is operated by the Norwegian Home Arts and Crafts Association. Møllergaten 4 (phone: 42-10-75).

Norway Designs A/S – You'll find the biggest displays of fine-quality arts and crafts in Oslo here. Items for sale include furniture, fabrics, ceramics, and jewelry. Stortings Gate 28 (phone: 42-70-50).

Oslo Sweater Shop – In the *Hotel Scandinavia*, this shop has the largest selection of Norwegian sweaters. Holbergs Gate 30 (phone: 11-29-22).

Steen & Strom – Norway's largest department store. Kongens Gate 23 (phone: 41-68-00).

J. Tostrup – This is the oldest silversmith in Oslo, established in 1832. *J. Tostrup* creations of enamel on sterling silver won the Grand Prix in Paris in 1900 and in Milan in 1954. A branch is located in the *Hotel Scandinavia* shopping arcade. The main store is at Karl Johans Gate 25 (phone: 42-30-90).

SPECIAL EVENTS: On *Constitution Day*, May 17, everyone in Norway is in a festive mood. The colorful pageantry of students in traditional Norwegian costumes and brass bands will delight visitors. The annual *Holmenkollen Ski Festival*, which attracts the cream of the world's cross-country skiers and ski jumpers, takes place in early March. *Holmenkollen Day* is the last Sunday of the festival, when up to 100,000 spectators make their way to the Holmenkollen Ski Jump for a special jumping program. In January, the *Monolith Meet*, a major cross-country race, takes place in the Vigeland Sculpture Park. The sporting calendar for January and February each year features a number of international speed-skating events, which often include the European or World Championships.

SPORTS: Oslo considers itself the world skiing capital, but the city provides a natural playground for sports enthusiasts of all stripes.

Boating – Sailing or boating on the Oslo fjord can be a delightful experience. For boat rentals, contact Baatformidlingen, Aarvollveien 38 (phone: 15-47-86), or *Peder Farmen A/S*, Strand Gate 7, 3250 Larvik (phone: 034-81-473).

Camping – The Norwegian Automobile Association operates two campsites close to the city. *Ekeberg Camping* at Ekebergs-letta is adjacent to Oslo's largest natural park and less than 2.5 miles (4 km) from the center of Oslo. It has a riding school, a children's wading pool, a recreation and sports ground, a kiosk, and a shop and is open from June 1 to September 1. *Bogstad Camping*, near Bogstad Lake about 6 miles (10 km) from the city, is open all year and has winter-insulated cabins for rent. It also has shops, a cafeteria, a post office, and other conveniences (phone: 50-76-80).

Curling – There are several curling clubs in Oslo, and members of foreign clubs are welcome to use their rinks. For information apply to *Oslo Curlingkrets*, attn. Odd Hagen, Geitmyrsveien 7 (phone: 60-23-83).

Cycling – It is possible to enjoy cycling in the Oslomarka area without being unduly bothered by auto traffic. Suggested cycle tours of the area can be obtained from the Ski Association, *Skiforeningen,* Skippergt. 40 (phone: 20-42-90). Many local tourist offices and hotels rent bicycles for a modest fee.

Golf – The best-known links are the *Bogstad Golf Course* near Bogstad Lake and the Bogstad camping grounds.

Hiking – In summer, there is a network of about 1,860 miles (3,000 km) of footpaths for hikers in the Oslo area. July and August are the best months for mountain walking. Midtstuen and Frognerseteren stations on the Holmenkollen Railway are good starting points. *Den Norske Turistforening* (DNT), at Stortings Gate 28, publishes several maps covering the mountain areas with suggested tour routes. If you'd prefer to hike with a group, conducted tours with guides are organized by the *Norwegian Mountain Touring Club* (phone: 41-80-20).

Fishing – There are trout in all the lakes in Oslo and salmon abound in nearby rivers. You can obtain a fishing license at the post office. Pimpling, or ice fishing, is popular in the Oslomarka area and on the Oslo fjord whenever the ice is safe. You can't rent equipment, but if you have your own, you are in for a wonderful time. On the fjord ice, you'll find marked trails to follow.

Ice Skating – The skating season lasts from mid-November until mid-March. Oslo prepares and maintains ice-skating rinks in some 137 locations. There is also an artificial frozen rink open to the public at *Valle Hovin.* Admission to Oslo skating rinks is free, but there is a small fee for the use of changing rooms. Ice hockey, speed skating, and figure skating competitions are held frequently at the *Bislett, Frogner,* and *Jordal Amfi stadiums.* Details of such events are listed in *Oslo This Week.*

Skiing – Skiing is the national pastime in Norway, and the Oslo municipality maintains more than 1,300 miles of ski trails through the surrounding woods and hills of Oslomarka. These are primarily for cross-country skiing, but slalom tracks and hills for ski jumping and alpine skiing are available, too. Night skiing along one of the 54 floodlight-lit tracks in the area can be particularly exhilarating. There are even a few ski trails specifically for the blind. The best part is that all of the best spots are only a short ride by bus or suburban railway from downtown Oslo. Rødkleiva, a favored alpine center near the Voksenkollen station, is 30 minutes away on the Holmenkollen railway. Guided rambling tours start from the same station each day at 10 AM, January 2 to approximately March 5. Reservations should be made 1 day in advance by calling 20-42-90. The Sognsvann railway line goes to Lake Sognsvann, another popular starting point for ski tourers. Buses leave Grønlands Torg about every hour for Skansebakken in Sørkedalen district and Skar in the Maridalen district, two other convenient starting points for ski tourers. There are also buses to such slalom centers as Kirkerudbakken in neighboring Baerum and Ingierkollen at Kolbotn. Tomm Murstad's ski school at Øvreseter, close to the upper terminal of the Holmenkollen railway, is one of several that provide instruction in cross-country and slalom during the winter months (phone: 14-46-65). Information on skiing and related activities in the Oslo area is available from the *Ski Association,* Skippergt. 40 (phone: 20-42-90).

If you want to be the envy of your more sedentary friends, earn a badge for long-distance ski touring from the Association for the Promotion of Skiing (Skiforeningen). Skiers between the ages of 13 and 55 get a gold badge for doing 310 miles (500 km), a silver badge for 186 miles (300 km), and a bronze badge for 124 miles (200 km). If you're over 55, you can earn the same badges for tours of 186, 124, or 62 miles, respectively. Control cards, available from sports stores, the ski association, and tourist offices, can be stamped at various checkpoints in the area.

Swimming – Besides several beaches on the Bygdøy peninsula, where you can swim in the Oslo fjord, there are a number of public swimming pools, including an outdoor pool at Vigeland Park (see *Special Places*). Three public baths and swimming pools near the center of the city are *Tøyenbadet,* Helgesens Gate 90 (phone: 67-18-87), *Bislet bad,*

Pilestredet 60 (phone: 46-48-51), and *Vestkantbadet,* Sommerogaten 1 (phone: 44-07-26). All have saunas.

THEATER: Programs are published in the daily press and in *Oslo This Week.* Most performances start at 8 PM. The *National Theater (Nationaltheatret)* is Norway's principal theater, Storgings Gate 15 in Studenterlunden Park (phone: 41-27-10). *Amfiscenen,* the experimental stage of the *National Theater,* is in the same building (with the same phone number), but up five flights of stairs. The *Puppet Theater (Dukketeatret),* in the same building as the Oslo City Museum, is a delight not only for children, at Frognerveien 67 (phone: 42-11-88, 42-07-43); *Det Norske Teatret* produces foreign plays and musicals in the Norwegian language known as *ny norsk* or new Norwegian; *Oslo nye teater* features classic and modern comedy, Rosenkrantzgt. 10 (phone: 42-11-88); *Chat Noir* presents cabaret acts, Klingenberggaten 5 (phone: 42-31-84, 41-60-46), and *ABC-teatret* is the place for light comedy and cabaret, St. Olavsplass 1 (phone: 11-21-66, 11-48-30).

MUSIC: Music has deep roots in Oslo's cultural life. Concerts are played outside the Royal Palace whenever King Olav V is in residence between October 1 and June 24, and museums and libraries arrange public concerts regularly. *The Philharmonic Society Orchestra* gives numerous concerts during the autumn and winter season. Many of the concerts are held in the university's festival hall or at the new *Oslo Concert Hall (Oslo Konserthus),* Munkedamsveien 14 (phone: 20-93-33); *Den Norske Opera* produces ballets as well as operas at the *Folketeaterbygningen,* Youngstorget (phone: for advance sales, 42-79-32 or 42-78-98).

NIGHTCLUBS AND NIGHTLIFE: The *Leopard* at the *Hotel Bristol* (see *Checking In*) is a discotheque on one floor and has orchestras playing for dancing on two other floors (phone: 41-58-40). Other discos are *Hetlands Juballong* in the *Hotel Scandinavia,* the *Bonanza* at the *Grand Hotel,* and *Casablanca,* Klingenberg Gate 4 (phone: 42-39-90). Lodges high above the city at Forgnersetern often have discotheques that are popular rendezvous for the younger set. After an evening zipping down the floodlight-lit Trysvannskleiva ski run, skiers gather around the blazing log fire at the lakeside *Trysvannstua Lodge* (phone: 14-41-34).

SINS: Spirits are not served on Sunday, but one must take care not to become *inebriated* on the other 6 days of the week. Drinks are about twice the size Americans are used to, and more expensive, too. To be safe rather than sorry, order the 2.5-centiliter size.

BEST IN TOWN

CHECKING IN: Oslo has a more than adequate number of good modern hotels. But reservations should be made early if you plan to visit during the busiest ski periods: February, March, and Eastertime. If you do arrive without a place to stay, Innkvartering, the accommodations center at the Oslo East Railway Station, Jernbanetorget, makes room reservations for hotels, pensions, and private homes for a small fee and a refundable deposit. However, no advance bookings are made, and you must show up at the center in person on the day you require the room. You will pay about $80 to $100 a night at expensive Oslo hotels; from $45 to $80 for those in the moderate range. Anything under $45 a night falls into the inexpensive category. For budget travelers there are some simple pensions and a youth hostel, and six of Oslo's best hotels offer special weekend rates during the period between September 23 and May 14.

Hotel Scandinavia – Norway's largest and Oslo's tallest hotel near the Royal Palace has many rooms with lovely views of the city and the fjord. Service is excellent; facilities include a swimming pool and five restaurants (see *Eating Out*) and bars, the most notable of which is the *Scanorama Bar* on the 22nd floor. Holbergs Gate 30 (phone: 11-30-00). Expensive.

Grand Hotel – This dignified and traditional establishment offers excellent service. It has several elegant restaurants, including *The Mirror Room* (see *Eating Out*). There's also a swimming pool. Karl Johans Gate 31 (phone: 42-93-90). Expensive.

Bristol Hotel – Smaller, very modern, and English style, the *Bristol* has an inappropriate but very good Spanish restaurant, a dance bar, and a popular grill room. Kristian IV's Gate 7 (phone: 41-58-40). Expensive.

Continental Hotel – This centrally located, top-quality hotel has excellent service and two restaurants worth noting: *The Second Floor,* an Oslo favorite, and *Theatercaféen,* one of the city's most popular old-fashioned cafés (see *Eating Out*). Stortings Gate 24/26 (phone: 41-90-60). Expensive.

Holmenkollen Park Hotel – Storybook, timber-beamed, comfortable, the *Holmenkollen* is distinguished by an excellent view of Oslo from its lovely setting on Holmenkollen Hill on the outskirts of the city. A huge fireplace dominates its public salon; some rooms have terraces, and its popular restaurant features Norwegian specialties. Reached by car or the Holmenkollen suburban tram line. Kongeveien 26, Holmenkollåsen (phone: 14-60-90). Expensive.

KNA-Hotellet – Not far from the Royal Palace, west of the city center, is this hotel owned by the Royal Norwegian Automobile Club. Good restaurant and bar. Parkveien 68 (phone: 56-26-90). Expensive.

Sara Hotel Oslo – Recently remodeled, Oslo's second largest hotel is near the east railroad station. The main attraction is an old Viking-style pub. B. Gunnerus Gate 3 (phone: 42-94-10). Expensive.

Ambassadeur Hotel – This charming, small hotel with suites and demisuites is situated in the west end of the city. Camilla Collettsvei 15 (phone: 44-18-35). Expensive.

Stefanhotellet – The newest and most modern of several clean, modest hotels operated by the local Mission society has a renowned restaurant (see *Eating Out*), but no liquor, wine, or beer served on the premises. Rosenkrantz Gate 1 (phone: 42-92-50). Moderate.

Nobel Hotel – Convenience is a keynote here. The *Nobel* is small, centrally located, and near the *Grand Hotel.* Karl Johans Gate 33 (phone: 42-74-80). Moderate.

Gabelshus Hotel – The guests of this small hotel have been coming here for years. Gabels Gate 16 (phone: 56-25-90). Moderate.

Hall Hotel-Pension – This small west end establishment caters to visitors who stay for several weeks or even months. Fritzners Gate 21 (phone: 56-44-80). Moderate.

Forbundshotellet – Modest, newly modernized, this is another hotel operated by the Mission society. Holbergs Plass 1 (phone: 20-88-55). Moderate.

Scandic Hotel – This hotel west of Oslo is very modern and quite comfortable. Hövik (phone: 12-17-40). Moderate.

Hotell Munch – All the conveniences you would expect from a hotel in a higher price range, but no restaurant. Munchsgt. 5 (phone: 42-42-75). Moderate.

 EATING OUT: As you might expect, Norwegian cuisine centers on a wide range of fish and seafood specialties. The trout from Norway's lakes and the salmon from its rivers are not to be missed. You also will find delicious meals of cod, haddock, and coalfish. *Gravlax* is one type of smoked salmon you should try, but if smoked salmon is too hard on your pocketbook, sample another Norwegian delicacy: warm smoked mackerel. With your food, you may want some beer: *brigg* is the weakest, lager is called *pils,* and *export* is the strongest. *Akevitt* (the Norwegian spelling of aquavit), which is made from potatoes and herbs and spices, is usually drunk with a meal. But many restaurants are only licensed to sell beer and wine. Breakfast can vary from the Continental coffee, rolls, butter, and marmalade to the traditional Norwegian *Koltbord,* a buffet of cold meats, fish, cheese, salads, porridge, and cereals. Dining out in Oslo is reasonable. A full dinner at an expensive restaurant will cost $25 or more; moderately priced establishments charge about $12 for a meal. Credit cards are welcomed at large restaurants, but smaller ones generally don't accept them. It is not usually necessary to make reservations.

The Second Floor (Annen Etage) – On the second floor of the *Hotel Continental* is this exclusive Norwegian member of *Tradition et Qualité,* featuring French and Norwegian cuisine. Open Mondays through Fridays for lunch and dinner; Saturdays, 5 PM to midnight; Sundays, 3 to 7 PM. Stortings Gate 24/26 (phone: 41-90-60). Expensive.

Étoile – On the top floor of the *Grand Hotel* with a beautiful view of the city, the *Étoile's* first-class kitchen serves French and Norwegian food. Open Mondays through Saturdays, noon to midnight; Sundays 3 PM to midnight. Lunch table from noon to 2:30 PM. Karl Johans Gate 31 (phone: 43-93-90). Expensive.

Molla – This fine fish and game restaurant is in an old textile mill on the banks of the River Akerselva, which was the setting for Oskar Braaten's novels about factory workers' lives in the beginning of the century. Reservations advised. Sagvn. 21 (phone: 37-54-50). Expensive.

Blom, the artists' restaurant – Recently reopened, the old wooden building has been replaced by a new, modern building complex. The tradition of good cooking continues. Karl Johans Gate 41B (phone: 42-73-00). Expensive.

Bagatelle – Fine French cuisine and a distinguished wine cellar. Open for lunch from 11:30 AM to 1:30 PM and for dinner from 5:30 to 9:30 PM. Closed Saturdays and in July. Bygdøy allé 3-5 (phone: 44-63-97). Expensive.

La Mer – Perhaps the best fish and seafood restaurant in Oslo. Closed on Sundays. Pilestredet 31 (phone: 20-34-45). Expensive.

Tre Kokker – Some critics call this restaurant, run by celebrated gourmet Hroar Dege, the finest in the country. It's intimate and elegant and decorated with much modern Norwegian art. The traditional Norwegian menu specializes in fish and game. Dancing nightly, from 12 to 2:30 AM. Reservations required. Drammensveien 30 (phone: 44-26-50). Expensive.

Frascati Restaurant – The French rotisserie has an international menu. Open Mondays through Saturdays, 11 AM to 12:30 AM. Closed Sundays. Stortings Gate 20 (phone: 41-68-76). Expensive.

Tostrupkjelleren Restaurant – This is the best of Oslo's basement restaurants, a meeting place for politicians, journalists, and businesspeople. Open weekdays. Karl Johans Gate 25 (phone: 42-14-70). Expensive.

Holberg Restaurant – A first-class gourmet grill restaurant with an international à la carte menu, it holds special gastronomical weeks in autumn and spring. Its decorations are from the Holberg époque by Bjorn Winblad. In the *Hotel Scandinavia.* Open daily. Holbergs Gate 30 (phone: 11-30-00). Expensive.

Casablanca – This big, old-style music hall features floor shows and dancing to international orchestras with dinner. Open weekdays. Klingenberg Gate 4 (phone: 42-39-90). Expensive.

Najaden – In the Maritime Museum is this first-class restaurant with pleasant atmosphere. It offers a special tourist's lunch with assorted herrings, hot dishes, and cheeses. Bygdøynes, Bydøy peninsula (phone: 55-44-90). Expensive.

Folk Museum Restaurant – Dining on Norwegian specialties is an experience in this open-air restaurant. Outdoors is a stage where folk dancers entertain. Open from May 4 to September 15 during museum hours. Bygdøy Peninsula (phone: 55-82-11). Expensive.

Theatercaféen – In the *Hotel Continental* is this unrivaled Oslo favorite, much frequented by artists. Music, but no dancing. Open weekdays. Stortings Gate 24/26 (phone: 41-90-60). Expensive to moderate.

Holmenkollen Restaurant – This first-class kitchen specializes in Norwegian dishes, the dining room specializes in a spectacular view of the city and fjord. Open Monday to Saturday, 11 AM to 11 PM. Reached by the Holmenkollen line. Holmenkollveien 119, Holmenkollåsen (phone: 14-62-26). Moderate.

The Old Town Hall (Det Gamle Raadhus) – Originally built as the city's town hall in 1641, the place is filled with old Christiana atmosphere. Open weekdays. Nedre Slotts Gate 1 (phone: 42-01-07). Expensive.

The Market Square Guest House (Stortorvets Gjaestgiveri) – Meat balls, cured meats, and other traditional Norwegian dishes are served in the dining rooms of this early-eighteenth-century building. Grensen 1 (phone: 11-33-64). Moderate.

Engebret's Café – This popular meeting place is a hodgepodge of small dining rooms, retaining the original interior of the 1857 restaurant. It is considered by many to serve the best fish in Oslo. Closed Sundays. Bankplassen 1 (phone: 42-12-62). Moderate.

Christian – A charming restaurant on the third floor of *Christiania Glas Glasmagasin*, a department store near the Oslo cathedral. It serves typical Norwegian specialties. Open during business hours, 9 AM to 4:30 PM. Atortorget 10 (phone: 11-40-80). Moderate.

Statholdergaarden – This seventeenth-century building was made into a restaurant in the mid-nineteenth century. Note especially its impressive rococo ceiling. Said to have Oslo's best "eat as much as you want" luncheon buffet. Open weekdays. Radhus Gate 11 (phone: 41-48-25). Moderate.

Håndverkeran Bar and Grill – A meeting place for artists and journalists, who flock to its special sandwich buffet from 11 AM to 2 PM each day. Open Mondays through Saturdays. Rosenkrantz Gate 7 (phone: 41-83-58). Moderate.

Stefanhotellet – The top-floor restaurant in one of the Mission hotels. Serves excellent Norwegian food and an interesting selection of nonalcoholic wines. Rosenkrantz Gate 1 (phone: 42-92-50). Moderate.

Storyville – A Creole restaurant, Storyville, named for the famous New Orleans district, also serves French specialties. Universitetsgaten 26 (phone: 42-96-35). Moderate.

Ming Wah Kro – The decor is not particularly appealing, but the well-priced Chinese food is. Open daily from 1 to 10 PM. Parkvn. 13 (phone: 46-80-96). Moderate.

Grand Café – The busy but cozy restaurant in the *Grand Hotel* has large murals of life in Old Christiana at the turn of the last century as well as excellent food. Music after 7 PM. Open daily until 11:30 PM. Karl Johans Gate 31 (phone: 43-93-90). Moderate.

PARIS

It was Victor Hugo, the great French poet and novelist, who captured the true spirit of his native city when he called it "the heir of Rome, the mundane pilgrim's home away from home." For if Rome is the spiritual home of the West, Paris — with its supreme *joie de vivre* and its passion for eating, drinking, and dressing well — belongs unabashedly to this world. Like a magnet, Paris has always attracted visitors and exiles from all over the world. At the same time it remains, not so much an international city, but very French, even provincial at that. Paris has its own argot, and each neighborhood retains its peculiar character, so that the great capital is still very much a city of 20 villages.

But the parochialism aside — and forgetting about the consummate haughtiness of Parisians (someone once remarked that Parisians didn't even like themselves) — the main attraction of the "City of Light" is its beauty. When you speak of the ultimate European city, it must be Paris, if only for the view from the place de la Concorde or the Tuileries toward the Arc de Triomphe or sights beside the Seine. Here is the fashion capital of the world and the center of gastronomic invention and execution. Here the men all seem to swagger with the insouciance of privilege, and even the humblest of shopgirls dresses with the care of a haute couture mannequin. Paris is the reason "foreign" means "French" to so many travelers.

Paris is in the north central part of France, in the rich agricultural area of the Seine River valley. With a population of 2.5 million people, it is France's largest city, an industrial and commercial center, and an important river port. Roughly elliptical in shape, the city has more than doubled in size in the last century. Its limits now are the ring of mid-nineteenth-century fortifications that once were well beyond its boundaries. At its western edge is the vast Bois de Boulogne and to the east the Bois de Vincennes — two enormous parks. Curving through Paris, the Seine River divides the city into its northern Right Bank (Rive Droite) and southern Left Bank (Rive Gauche). The Right Bank extends from the Bois de Boulogne on the far west, through the place Charles-de-Gaulle (l'Étoile), which surrounds the Arc de Triomphe, and farther east to the Tuileries Gardens and the fabulous Louvre. North of the Louvre is the area of the Grands Boulevards, centers of business and fashion; farther north is the district of Montmartre, built on a hill and crowned by the domed Church of the Sacré-Coeur, an area that has attracted great artists (and many of markedly less greatness) since the days of Monet and Renoir.

The Left Bank of the Seine sweeps from the Eiffel Tower on the west through the Latin Quarter, with its university and its bohemian and intellectual community. South of the Latin Quarter is Montparnasse, once inhabited jointly by artists and intellectuals and laborers, now a large urban renewal project that includes a suburban-style shopping center around the Tour Montparnasse.

In the middle of the Seine are two islands, the Île de la Cité and the Île St.-Louis, the oldest parts of Paris. It was on the Île de la Cité (in the third century BC) that Celtic fishermen known as Parisii first built a settlement they named Lutetia, "place surrounded by water." Caesar conquered the city for Rome in 52 BC, and, in about AD 300, Paris was invaded by Germanic tribes, the strongest of which were the Franks. In 451, when Attila the Hun threatened to overrun Paris, a holy woman named Geneviève promised to defend the city by praying. She succeeded — the enemies decided to stay away from the capital — and Geneviève became the patron saint of Paris. Clovis I, first Christian king of the Franks, made Paris his capital in the sixth century. Relentless Norman sieges, famine, plague, and the Hundred Years' War curtailed the city's development, but at the end of the tenth century, peace and prosperity came with the triumph of Hugues Capet over the Carolingians. Capet ascended the throne, the first of a long line of Capetian kings, and Paris became the "central jewel of the French crown," a great cultural center and seat of learning.

The Capetian monarchs contributed much to the growth of the city over the next few centuries. A defensive wall was begun in 1180 by Philip Augustus to protect the expanding Right Bank business and trading center as well as the intellectual quarter around the newly formed university on the Left Bank. He then built a new royal castle, the Louvre, just outside these ramparts, but he never lived there. Medieval Paris was a splendid city and a leader in the arts and in the intellectual life of Europe. The Sorbonne attracted such outstanding scholars as Alexander of Hales, St. Bonaventure, Albertus Magnus, and Thomas Aquinas.

The Île de la Cité remained a warren of narrow streets and wood and plaster houses, but the banks of the Seine continued to be built up in both directions. Renaissance kings, patrons of the arts, added their own architectural and aesthetic embellishments to the flourishing city. Major streets were laid out; some of Paris's most charming squares were constructed; the Pont Neuf, the first stone bridge spanning the Seine, was completed; and the royal gardener, Le Nôtre, introduced proportion, harmony, and beauty with his extraordinary Tuileries.

Louis XIV, who was responsible for many of the most notable local landmarks, including Les Invalides, moved the court to Versailles in the late seventeenth century. Paris nevertheless continued to blossom, and it was under the Sun King's rule that France and Paris first won international prestige. Visitors were drawn to the city, luxury trades were begun, and the Panthéon, Champ-de-Mars parade ground, and École Militaire were built. At age 16, Napoleon Bonaparte graduated from this military school in 1785 with the notation in his report: "Will go far if circumstances permit!"

French history reflects the conflict between two extremes of the French character, both equally strong: the penchant for aristocracy and the penchant for revolution. To the French aristocracy we owe magnificent palaces like the Louvre, the Luxembourg Palace, and Versailles, with their typical French

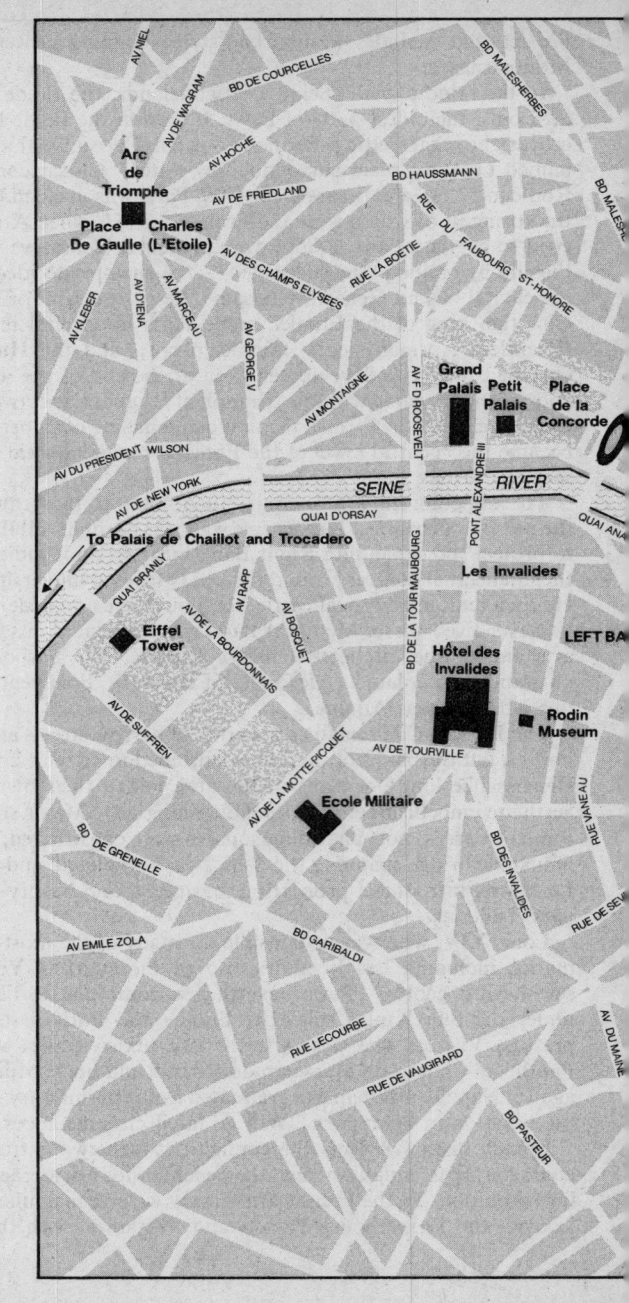

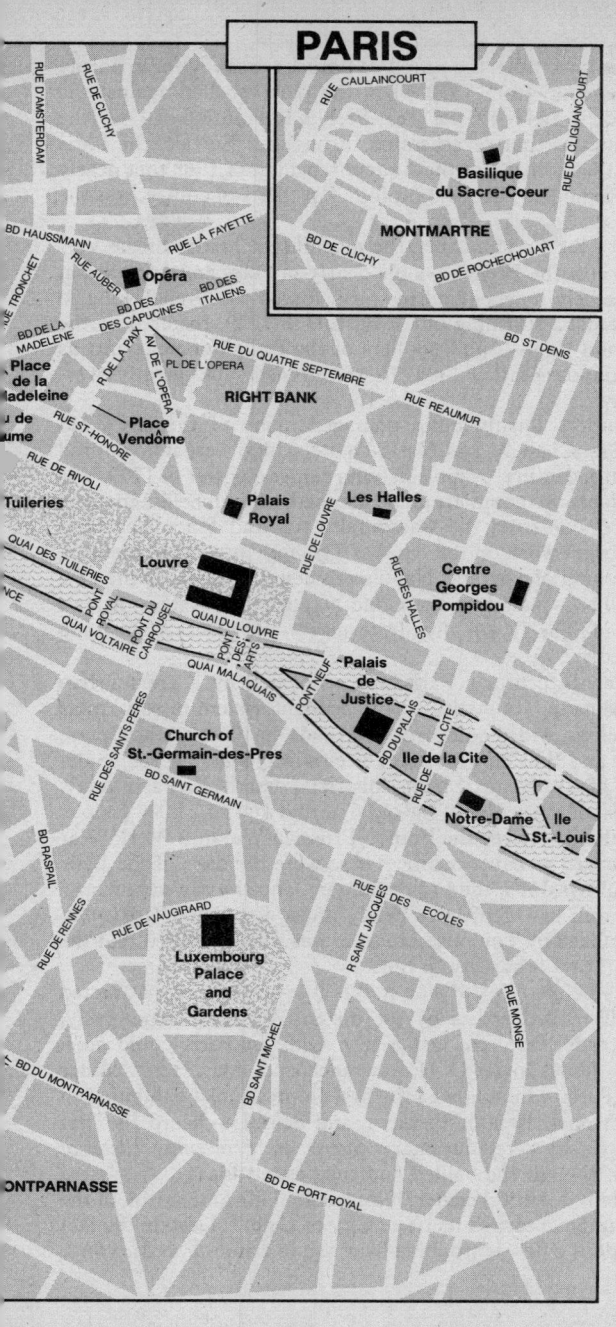

PARIS

RUE D'AMSTERDAM

RUE DE CLICHY

RUE CAULAINCOURT

RUE DE CLIGNANCOURT

Basilique du Sacre-Coeur

BD DE CLICHY

MONTMARTRE

BD DE ROCHECHOUART

BD HAUSSMANN

RUE LA FAYETTE

RUE TRONCHET

RUE AUBER

Opéra

BD ST DENIS

BD DE LA MADELENE

BD DES DES CAPUCINES

BD DES ITALIENS

Place de la Madeleine

R DE LA PAIX

AV. DE L'OPERA

PL DE L'OPERA

RUE DU QUATRE SEPTEMBRE

RUE ST-HONORE

Place Vendôme

RIGHT BANK

RUE REAUMUR

u de ume

RUE DE RIVOLI

Tuileries

Palais Royal

Les Halles

QUAI DES TUILERIES

Louvre

RUE DE LOUVRE

RUE DES HALLES

Centre Georges Pompidou

PONT ROYAL

NCE

PONT DU CARROUSEL

QUAI DU LOUVRE

QUAI VOLTAIRE

PONT DES ARTS

QUAI MALAQUAIS

PONT NEUF

Palais de Justice

RUE DE LA CITE

RUE DES SAINTS-PERES

Church of St.-Germain-des-Pres

BD SAINT GERMAIN

BD DU PALAIS

Ile de la Cite

RUE DE LA CITE

BD RASPAIL

Notre-Dame

Ile St.-Louis

BD DE RENNES

RUE DE VAUGIRARD

RUE SAINT JACQUES DES ECOLES

Luxembourg Palace and Gardens

RUE MONGE

BD DU MONTPARNASSE

BD SAINT MICHEL

ONTPARNASSE

BD DE PORT ROYAL

formal gardens. At the same time, the people of Paris have always been noisily rebellious and independent: from 1358 when the mob rebelled against the dauphin, to the Fronde in 1648–49, the great French Revolution of 1789, the 1830 and 1848 revolutions that reverberated throughout Europe, the Paris Commune of 1870–71, and finally to the student rebellion of 1968 that nearly overthrew the Fifth Republic. The most profound of these, of course, was the French Revolution.

The very excesses of the French court, the magnificent luxury of the Versailles of Louis XIV, cost the French people dearly in taxes and oppression. And the Parisians, fiercely independent in spirit, forced the French king to his knees by their dramatic storming of the Bastille in 1789. Inspired by the ideas of the French and English philosophers of the Enlightenment, just as were the American founding fathers in 1776, the French subsequently overthrew their monarchy.

During the Revolution, unruly mobs damaged many of the city's old buildings, including Ste.-Chapelle and Notre-Dame, which were not restored until the mid-nineteenth century. Napoleon, who came to power in 1799, was too busy being a conqueror to complete all he planned, though he did manage to restore the Louvre, construct the Carrousel Arch and Place Vendôme victory column, and begin work on the Arch of Triumph and the Madeleine. Though he was something of a tyrant, Napoleon's conquests spread the new ideas of the Revolution — including the Code Napoléon, a system of laws embodying the ideals of "liberty, equality, fraternity" — to places as far-flung as Canada and Moscow.

Later in the nineteenth century, Paris was renovated by a great urban planner, Baron Haussmann. He instituted the brilliant system of squares as focal points for marvelous, wide boulevards and roads; he planned the Opéra, the Bois de Boulogne and Bois de Vincennes, the railway stations, the boulevards, and the system of 20 *arrondissements* (districts) that divide Paris today. He also destroyed most of the center of the old Cité and moved 25,000 people.

During the peaceful lull between the Franco-Prussian War and World War I, the city of Paris thrived as never before. These were the days of the Belle Époque, the heyday of Maxim's, the Folies-Bergère, and the can-can, whose spirit is captured so well in Offenbach's heady music for *Gaité Parisienne*. Montmartre, immortalized by Toulouse-Lautrec, was so uninhibited that the foreign press dubbed Paris "the City of Sin."

In the two decades before World War I, this free-spirited city attracted politically and socially exiled artists by the dozens: Picasso, Hemingway, Fitzgerald, and Gertrude Stein are just a few. Only in Paris could such avant-garde writers as James Joyce, D. H. Lawrence, and, later, Henry Miller find publishers. And Paris, which hosted the first Impressionist exhibition in 1874 — introducing Monet, Renoir, Pissarro, and Seurat — heard the first performance of Stravinsky's revolutionary *Sacre du Printemps (Rite of Spring)* in 1913, even though the baffled audience jeered loudly.

As the quintessentially beautiful center of intellectual life and patron of the arts, Paris can claim to have earned its title "City of Light." Despite the fact that it, like other modern cities, is troubled by a rise in crime — at *Maxim's,* for instance, a precautionary bulletproof window has been installed — its beauty and its libertarian atmosphere remain. Its supreme talent for civilized living has made Paris beloved by Frenchmen and foreigners alike. After all, these are the people who made the careful preparation of food into fine art, and despite the presence of fast-food establishments on the Champs-Élysées, the French passion for haute cuisine is unrivaled. And as the undisputed capital of fashion, male and female, Paris continues to be the best-dressed city in the world, and the rue du Faubourg-St.-Honoré remains the standard by which all other shopping streets are measured.

However avant-garde in dress, Parisians are a conservative lot when it comes to any changes in the appearance of their beloved city. When the Eiffel Tower was built in 1889, Guy de Maupassant commented, "I spend all my afternoons on the Eiffel Tower; it's the only place in Paris from which you can't see it." So today's Parisians grumble about the ultramodern Centre Georges Pompidou, a center for every type of modern art: theater, music, dance, circus, paintings, sculpture, photography, and film, or about Le Forum, a sunken glass structure filled with boutiques in what was the Les Halles market.

Parisians accept innovations reluctantly because they want their city to remain as it has always been. They love Paris inordinately, and perhaps it is this love by its citizens, together with the irrepressible sense of good living, that has made Paris so eternally attractive to others.

PARIS AT-A-GLANCE

SEEING THE CITY: It's impossible to single out just one perfect Paris panorama; they exist in profusion. The most popular is the bird's-eye view from the top of the Eiffel Tower on the Left Bank; there are three places to have snacks and drinks and enjoy a view of over 50 miles on a clear day. Champ-de-Mars (phone: 705-4413). From the top of the towers of Notre-Dame you can see the cathedral's Gothic spires and flying buttresses along with a magnificent view of the Cité and of Paris. Start climbing the steps at the foot of the north tower on rue du Cloître Notre-Dame; it's open daily, except Tuesdays, for an admission fee. On the Right Bank there's a stunning view from the terrace of the Sacré-Coeur. The observatory atop Tour Montparnasse also offers a striking panorama.

The most satisfying view, if not the highest, can be seen from the top of the Arc de Triomphe for a small fee, daily except Tuesdays. The arch is the center of the place Charles-de-Gaulle, once place de l'Étoile (Square of the Star), so called because it is the center of a star whose radii are the 12 broad avenues, including the Champs-Élysées, planned by Baron Haussmann in the mid-nineteenth century (phone: 380-3131).

For the truly extravagant, there are helicopter tours that start at $25 from the Heliport de Paris at the foot of the *Hôtel Sofitel* (phone: 544-9500). Heli-France (phone: 557-5367) and Helicap (phone: 557-7551) also have tours.

SPECIAL PLACES: Getting around this sprawling metropolis isn't difficult once you understand the layout of the 20 *arrondissements* (wards or districts), but at first it can be rather hectic and confusing. We suggest that first-time visitors get themselves oriented by taking one of the many excellent sight-seeing tours offered by *Cityrama,* 4 pl. des Pyramides (phone: 260-3014), or *Paris Vision,* 214 rue de Rivoli (phone: 260-3125). Their bubble-topped double-decker buses are equipped with earphones for simultaneous commentary in English and several other languages. Reserve through any travel agent or your hotel's concierge.

Once you have a better idea of the city, the next step is to buy a copy of *Paris Indispensable* or *Plan de Paris par Arrondissement* at any bookshop or newsstand. These little lifesavers list streets alphabetically and indicate the nearest Métro station on individual maps and an overall plan. Now you're ready to set out by foot (the most rewarding) or by Métro (the fastest and surest) to discover Paris for yourself.

RIGHT BANK (RIVE DROITE)

Arc de Triomphe and place de l'Étoile – This monumental arch (165 feet high, 148 feet wide) was built between 1806 and 1836 to commemorate Napoleon's victories. Note the frieze and its 6-foot-high figures, the ten impressive sculptures (especially Rude's *La Marseillaise* on the right as you face the Champs-Élysées), and the arches inscribed with the names of Bonaparte's victories as well as those of Empire heroes. Underneath the arch is the French Tomb of the Unknown Soldier and its Eternal Flame, which is rekindled each day at 6:30 PM. An elevator or 284 steps take you to the top for a magnificent view of the city and the 12 avenues radiating from l'Étoile. Open daily, except Tuesdays, for a small fee. Pl. Charles-de-Gaulle (phone: 380-3131).

Champs-Élysées – Though the name of Paris's legendary promenade means "Elysian fields," it was swampland until 1616 and came to be synonymous with everything glamorous only in the nineteenth century. It stretches for over 2 miles between the place de la Concorde and the place Charles-de-Gaulle (l'Étoile). The lovely, very broad avenue, lined with rows of plane and horse chestnut trees, shops, cafés, and cinemas, is perfect for a stroll, window shopping, and just plain people watching.

The area from the place de la Concorde to the Rond-Point is a charming park, to which Parisians often bring their children. On the north side of the gardens is the Palais de l'Élysée (Élysée Palace), home of the president of the French Republic. Ceremonial events, such as the Bastille Day Parade (French Independence Day: July 14) and the funeral parade in honor of Charles de Gaulle in 1970, frequently take place on the Champs-Élysées.

Grand Palais – Off the Champs-Élysées on opposite sides of the avenue Winston-Churchill are the elaborate turn-of-the-century Grand Palais and Petit Palais (Large Palace and Small Palace), built of glass and stone for the 1900 World Exposition. With its stone columns, mosaic frieze, and flat glass dome, the Grand Palais contains a large exhibition area and the Palais de la Découverte, the Paris Science Museum, and the Planetarium. Av. Franklin-Roosevelt (phone: 261-5410).

Petit Palais – Built contemporaneously with the Grand Palais, this is now the Paris Musée des Beaux-Arts (Museum of Fine Arts), containing exhibits of the city's history as well as a variety of fine and applied arts. Open daily except Mondays and Tuesdays for a fee. Av. Winston-Churchill (phone: 265-1273).

Place de la Concorde – This square, surely one of the most magnificent in the world, is grandly situated in the midst of grand landmarks: the Louvre and the Tuileries on one side, the Champs-Élysées and the Arc de Triomphe on another, the Seine and the Napoleonic Palais Bourbon on a third, and the pillared facade of the Madeleine on the fourth. Designed by Gabriel for Louis XV, the elegant square was where his unfortunate successor, Louis XVI, lost his head to the guillotine, as did Marie Antoinette, Robespierre, Charlotte Corday, and others. It was first named for Louis XV, then called place de la Révolution by the triumphant revolutionaries. The 3,300-year-old 75-foot-high obelisk was a gift from Egypt in 1829.

Tuileries – Carefully laid out in patterned geometric shapes with clipped shrubbery and formal flower beds, statues, and fountains, this is one of the finest examples of a

French-style garden (in contrast with an English garden, exemplified by the Bois de Boulogne, which is informal, characterized by more natural, luxuriant growth, and made to be in rather than to be looked at). The Tuileries are between the place de la Concorde and the Louvre.

Rue de Rivoli – This charming old street houses perfume shops, tourist shops, cafés, and such hotels as the *Meurice* and the *Brighton* under its nineteenth-century arcades. The section facing the Tuileries from the place de la Concorde to the Louvre is an especially good place to explore on rainy days.

Jeu de Paume Museum – On the edge of the Tuileries nearest the place de la Concorde is one of Paris's major museums, housing an outstanding collection of Impressionist paintings (these are scheduled to move in 1986 to the Musée d'Orsay, in the Gare d'Orsay, across the Seine). In the Orangerie, a museum across the gardens, is a series of large Monet paintings of water lilies called the *Nymphéas* and the collections of Jean Walter and Paul Guillaume, with works by Cézanne, Renoir, Matisse, Picasso, and others. Closed Tuesdays. Jeu de Paume, pl. de la Concorde and rue de Rivoli (phone: 260-1207); Orangerie, pl. de la Concorde and quai des Tuileries (phone: 265-9948).

The Louvre – This palace was built on the site of a medieval fortress on the banks of the Seine, and French kings lived here in the sixteenth and seventeenth centuries, until Louix XIV moved the court to Versailles in 1682. In 1793 the museum, now one of the world's greatest art museums, was opened. You can easily spend at least a couple of days here, savoring treasures like the *Venus de Milo,* the *Winged Victory,* the Mona Lisa, and the French crown jewels, just a few' of the 200,000 pieces in six different collections.

Nor is the outside of this huge edifice to be overlooked, especially the classical colonnade along its eastern facade, the beautifully designed Cour Carrée (courtyard of the old Louvre), and the palace gardens, with their central Arc de Triomphe du Carrousel, erected by Napoleon. From here, the vista across place de la Concorde and on up the Champs-Élysées to the Arc de Triomphe is one of the most beautiful in Paris — which says a lot.

Good guided tours in English, covering the highlights of the Louvre, are available daily. Open evenings until 5 PM or 6:30 PM, depending on the section, and closed Tuesdays. The museum charges a fee but is free on Sundays. Pl. du Louvre (phone: 260-3926).

Place Vendôme – Just north of the Tuileries is an aristocrat of a square, one of the loveliest in Paris. Octagonal in shape, place Vendôme was designed by Mansart in the seventeenth century. Its arcades contain world-famous jewelers, perfumers, and banks, the *Ritz Hotel,* and the Ministry of Justice. The 144-foot column in the center is covered with bronze from the 1,200 cannons captured at Austerlitz by Napoleon in 1805. Just off the place Vendôme is the famous rue du Faubourg-St.-Honoré, one of the oldest streets in Paris, which now holds elegant shops selling the world's most expensive made-to-order items. To the north is the rue de la Paix, noted for its jewelers.

Opéra – In its own busy square stands an imposing rococo edifice, its facade decorated with sculpture, including Carpeaux's *The Dance.* The ornate interior has an impressive grand staircase, a beautiful foyer, lavish marble from every quarry in France, and Chagall's controversially decorated dome. Until recently, the opera house could only be seen by attending a performance; now, however, visitors may explore its magnificent interior from 11 AM to 4 PM, solo or on guided tours. Closed Saturdays and during August. Pl. de l'Opéra (phone: 266-5022).

La Madeleine – Begun in 1764, razed and rebuilt twice, the present Church of St. Mary Magdelene was finally commissioned by Napoleon to honor his armies. Based on a Greek temple design, its 65-foot-high Corinthian columns support the sculptured frieze. From its portals, the view extends down rue Royale to place de la Concorde and over to the dome of Les Invalides. Nearby are some of Paris's most tantalizing gourmet shops. Open from 7 AM to 7 PM and during frequent concerts. Pl. de la Madeleine (phone: 265-5217).

Sacré-Coeur and Montmartre – Built on the highest of Paris's seven hills, the white-domed Basilica of Sacré-Coeur provides an extraordinary view from its steps, especially at dawn or at sunset. The area around the church was the artists' quarter of late-nineteenth- and early-twentieth-century Paris. The more garish aspects of Montmartre's notoriously frivolous nineties nightlife, particularly the dancers and personalities at the Moulin Rouge, were immortalized by the paintings of Henri de Toulouse-Lautrec. And if the streets look familiar, chances are you've seen them in Utrillo's paintings; they still look the same. The place du Tertre is still charming, though filled with tourists and overly eager, mostly undertalented artists. You have to go early in the day to see it as it was when Braque, Dufy, Modigliani, Picasso, Rousseau, and Utrillo lived here. Montmartre has the last of Paris's vineyards — and still contains old houses, narrow alleys, steep stairways, and carefree cafés enough to provide a full day's entertainment; at night this is one of the centers of Paris life. Butte Montmartre.

Les Halles – Just northeast of the Louvre, this 80-acre area, formerly the Central Market, "the Belly of Paris," has been completely razed and is in the process of being rebuilt. Gone are the picturesque early morning fruit and vegetable vendors, butchers in blood-spattered aprons, truckers transporting the freshest of produce from all over France. Their places are beginning to be taken by shops and galleries of youthful entrepreneurs and artisans, small restaurants with lots of charm, the world's largest subway station, and Le Forum, a vast complex of boutiques, ranging from the super-chic designer ready-to-wear to more ordinary shops, and including concert space and movie theaters. A few echoes of the past remain, however, and you still can dine at *Au Pied de Cochon, Pharamond,* and *L'Escargot Montorgueil* or have a drink with the workmen before noon at one of the old brasseries.

Le Centre National d'Art et de Culture Georges Pompidou – Better known as Beaubourg, after the plateau on which it is built, this stark, six-level creation of steel and glass, with its exterior escalators and blue-white-red pipes, created a stir the moment its construction began. This wildly popular museum brings together all the contemporary art forms — painting, sculpture, plastic arts, industrial design, music, literature, cinema, and theater — under one roof, and that roof offers one of the most exciting views of Paris. The old houses and cobbled, tree-shaded streets and squares vie for attention with galleries, boutiques, and the spectacle provided by jugglers, mimes, acrobats, and magicians in the plaza out front. Open weekdays from noon to 10 PM; 10 AM to 10 PM weekends. Closed Tuesdays. Admission fee for some exhibitions; free Sundays. Rue Rambuteau, at the corner of rue St.-Martin (phone: 277-1233).

The Marais – Northeast of the Louvre, a marshland until the sixteenth century, this district became the height of fashion in the seventeenth century. As the aristocracy moved on, it fell into disrepair, but after long neglect, the Marais has recently had a complete face-lifting. Over 100 of the magnificent old mansions have been lovingly restored to their former grandeur and are now museums of exquisite beauty with muraled walls and ceilings. Their courtyards are the scene of drama and music presentations during the summer Festival du Marais. Among the houses to note are the Palais de Soubise, now the National Archives, and the Hôtels (*hôtel* in this sense means private residence or town house) d'Aumont, de Clisson, de Rohan, de Sens, and de Sully. The Caisse Nationale des Monuments, housed in the latter, can provide maps of the area and also fascinating and detailed lecture tours with English-speaking guides (phone: 274-2222).

Place des Vosges – In the Marais, the oldest square in Paris — and also one of the most beautiful — was completed in 1612 by order of Henri IV, with its houses elegantly "built to a like symmetry." Though the houses have been rebuilt, their original design remains. Corneille, Racine, and Madame de Sévigné lived here.

At number 6 is the Victor Hugo House, once the poet's home and now a museum, open every day except Mondays for a small fee (phone: 272-1665).

Carnavalet Museum – Also in the Marais, this was once the home of Madame de Sévigné, noted letter writer of her time, and now its beautifully arranged exhibits cover the history of Paris from the days of Henri IV to the present. Open daily for a small admission charge; closed Mondays. 23 rue de Sévigné (phone: 272-2113).

Père Lachaise Cemetery – For those who like cemeteries, this one is a beauty. Set in a wooded park, it's the final resting place of many illustrious personalities. A map is available at the gate to help you find the tombs of Balzac, Sarah Bernhardt, Chopin, Colette, Corot, Delacroix, Héloise and Abelard, La Fontaine, Modigliani, Musset, Edith Piaf, Rossini, and Oscar Wilde, among others. Blvd. de Ménilmontant (phone: 370-7033).

Bois de Vincennes – A park, a castle, and a zoological garden were laid out on 2,300 acres as a counterpart to the Bois de Boulogne during Napoleon III's time. Visit the fourteenth-century château and its lovely chapel; the large and lovely floral garden; and the zoo, with animals in their natural habitats. It's at the southeast edge of Paris (Métro: Château de Vincennes).

Bois de Boulogne – Originally part of the Forest of Rouvre, this 2,500-acre park on the western edge of Paris was planned along English lines by Napoleon. Ride a horse or a bike, row a boat, shoot skeet, go bowling, smell roses, picnic on the grass, see horseraces at Auteuil and Longchamp, visit a zoo, see a play, walk to a waterfall — and there's lots more.

Palais de Chaillot – Built for the Paris Exposition of 1937 — on the site of the old Trocadéro left over from the Exposition of 1878 — its terraces have excellent views across gardens and fountains to the Eiffel Tower on the Left Bank. Two wings house a theater, an aquarium, and four museums — du Cinéma (phone: 704-2424), de l'Homme (Anthropology; phone: 553-7060), de la Marine (maritime; phone: 553-3170), des Monuments Français (monument reproductions; phone: 727-3574). Pl. du Trocadéro.

LEFT BANK (RIVE GAUCHE)

Tour Eiffel – It is impossible to imagine the Paris skyline without this mighty symbol, yet what has been called Gustav Eiffel's folly was never meant to be permanent. Originally built for the Universal Exposition of 1889, it was due to be torn down in 1909 but it was saved because of the development of the wireless — the first transatlantic wireless telephones were operated from the tower in 1916. Extensive renovations have taken place, and a post office, three restaurants (*Jules Verne* is the best), and a few boutiques have opened up on the first-floor landing. On a really clear day, it's possible to see for 50 miles. Open daily. Champ-de-Mars (phone: 550-3456).

Chaillot to UNESCO – While you're at the Eiffel Tower, you may want to look over a group of Paris's early-twentieth-century buildings and gardens — on both sides of the Seine — including the Palais de Chaillot, the Trocadéro and Champs-de-Mars gardens, and the UNESCO buildings. Also part of the area but not of the same century is the huge École Militaire, an impressive example of eighteenth-century French architecture on avenue de la Motte-Picquet. The Y-shaped building just beyond it, facing place de Fontenoy, is the main UNESCO building, dating from 1958. It has frescoes by Picasso, Henry Moore's *Reclining Silhouette,* a mobile by Calder, murals by Miró, and Japanese gardens by Noguchi.

Les Invalides – Built by Louis XIV as a refuge for disabled soldiers, this vast classical building has over 10 miles of corridors and a golden dome by Mansart. For yet another splendid Parsian view approach the building from the Alexandre III

Bridge. Besides being a masterpiece of the age of Louis XIV (seventeenth century), the Church of St. Louis, part of the complex, contains the impressive red and green granite Tomb of Napoleon (admission fee). Also at Les Invalides is the Army Museum, one of the world's richest, displaying arms and armor, together with mementos of French military history. Esplanade des Invalides, pl. Vauban (phone: 555-9230).

Rodin Museum – The famous statue *The Thinker* is in the garden of this splendid eighteenth-century residence. The chapel and the mansion also contain Rodin sculpture. Open daily for a fee; closed Tuesdays. 77 rue de Varenne (phone: 705-0134).

Montparnasse – Just south of the Luxembourg Gardens, in the early twentieth century there arose an artist's colony of avant-garde painters, writers, and Russian political exiles. Here Hemingway, Sartre, and Simone de Beauvoir sipped and supped in places like *La Closerie des Lilas, La Coupole, Le Dôme, Le Select,* and *La Rotonde.* The cafés, small restaurants, and winding streets are still there in the shadow of a new shopping center.

Tour Montparnasse – This giant new complex now dominates Montparnasse. The fastest elevator in Europe whisks Parisians and tourists alike up 59 stories for a view *down* over the Eiffel Tower, daily 10 AM to 9:30 PM for a fee. The shopping center here boasts all the famous names, and the surrounding office buildings are the headquarters of some of France's largest companies. Av. du Maine and blvd. de Vaugirard.

The Luxembourg Palace and Gardens (Palais et Jardins du Luxembourg) – In what were once the southern suburbs, the palace and gardens were built for Marie de Médicis in 1612. A prison during the revolution, the Renaissance palace now houses the French Senate. The classic, formal gardens, with lovely statues and the famous Médicis fountain, are popular with students meeting under the chestnut trees and with neighborhood children at play around the artificial lake. 15 rue de Vaugirard.

The Paris Mosque – One of the most beautiful structures of its kind in the non-Moslem — or even in the Moslem — world, it is dominated by a 130-foot-high minaret in gleaming white marble. Shoes are taken off before entering the pebble-lined gardens full of flowers and dwarf trees. Inside, the Hall of Prayer, with its lush Oriental carpets, may be visited any day except Friday. There is also a restaurant and a patio for sipping Turkish coffee and tasting Oriental sweets. Pl. du Puits-de-l'Ermite.

The Panthéon – This eighteenth-century "non-religious Temple of Fame dedicated to all the gods," has an impressive interior with murals depicting the life of St. Geneviève, patron saint of Paris. It contains the tombs of Victor Hugo, Resistance leader Jean Moulin, Rousseau, Voltaire, and Émile Zola. Open Daily. Admission fee. Pl. du Panthéon (phone: 354-3451).

Latin Quarter (Quartier Latin) – Extending from the Luxembourg Gardens and the Panthéon to the Seine, this famous neighborhood still maintains its unique atmosphere. A focal point for Sorbonne students since the Middle Ages, it's a mad jumble of narrow streets, old churches, and academic buildings. Boulevard St.-Michel and boulevard St.-Germain are its main arteries, both lined with cafés, bookstores, and boutiques of every imaginable kind.

In addition to the boulevards, there are some charming old side streets, such as the rue de la Huchette, near place St.-Michel. And don't miss the famous *bouquinistes* (book stalls) along the Seine around the place St.-Michel on the quai des Grands-Augustins and the quai St.-Michel.

Church of St.-Germain-des-Prés – Probably the oldest church in Paris, it once belonged to an abbey of the same name. The original basilica, constructed in 558, was destroyed and rebuilt many times. The Romanesque steeple and its massive tower date from 1014. Inside, the choir and sanctuary are as they were in the twelfth century, and the marble shafts used in the slender columns are fourteen centuries old. Pl. St.-Germain-des-Prés (phone: 325-4171).

Surrounding the church is the *quartier* of Paris's "fashionable" intellectuals and artists, with art galleries, boutiques, and renowned people-watchers' cafés such as the *Flore* and *Aux Deux Magots.*

Cluny Museum – This is one of the last remaining examples of medieval domestic architecture in Paris. The fifteenth-century residence of the abbots of Cluny later became the home of Mary Tudor and is now a museum of medieval arts and crafts, including the celebrated *Lady and the Unicorn* tapestry. Closed Tuesdays. Admission fee. 6 pl. Paul-Painlevé (phone: 325-6200).

St.-Séverin – This church still retains its beautiful "Flamboyant Gothic" (late Gothic with ornate tracery, the shape of which suggests flames) ambulatory, considered a masterpiece of its kind, and lovely old stained-glass windows dating from the fifteenth and sixteenth centuries. The small garden and the restored charnel house are also of interest. 1 rue des Prêtres (phone: 325-9663).

St.-Julien-le-Pauvre – One of the smallest and oldest churches (twelfth to thirteenth century) in Paris offers a superb view of Notre-Dame from its charming place René-Viviani. 1 rue St.-Julien-le-Pauvre (phone: 354-2041).

THE ISLANDS

Île de la Cité – The birthplace of Paris, settled by Gallic fishermen about 250 BC, this island in the Seine is so rich in historical monuments that an entire day could be spent here and on the neighboring Île St.-Louis. A walk all around the islands, along the lovely, tree-shaded quais on both banks of the Seine, opens up one breathtaking view of Notre-Dame after another.

Cathedral of Notre-Dame – It is said that the Druids once worshiped on this consecrated ground. The Romans built their temple, and many Christian churches followed. In 1163, the foundations were laid for the present cathedral, one of the world's finest examples of Gothic art, grand in size and proportion. Henry VI and Napoleon were crowned here. Take a guided tour or quietly explore on your own, but be sure to climb the 225-foot towers for a marvelous view of the city, and try to see the splendid stained-glass rose windows at sunset. Pl. du Parvis (phone: 326-0739).

Palais de Justice and Sainte-Chapelle – This complex recalls centuries of history as the first seat of the Roman military government, then the headquarters of the early kings, and finally the law courts. In the thirteenth century, St. Louis (Louis IX) built a new palace and added Sainte-Chapelle to house the Sacred Crown of Thorns and other holy relics. Built in less than 3 years, the chapel, with its 15 splendid stained-glass windows and 247-foot spire, is "one of the jewels of Paris." Closed Tuesdays. Admission fee. Blvd. du Palais.

The Conciergerie – This remnant of the Old Royal Palace was used as a prison during the revolution. Here Marie Antoinette, the duke of Orléans, Madame DuBarry and many others of lesser fame awaited the guillotine. Open daily except Tuesdays. Admission charge. Blvd. du Palais.

Île St.-Louis – Walk across the footbridge at the back of Notre-Dame and you're in a charming, tranquil village. This "enchanted isle" has managed to keep its provincial charm despite its location. Follow the main street, rue St.-Louis-en-l'Île, down the middle of the island, past courtyards, balconies, old doors, curious stairways, the Church of St.-Louis, and discreet plaques bearing the names of illustrious former residents (Madame Curie, Voltaire, Baudelaire, Gautier, and Daumier, for example); then take the quai back along the edge.

■**EXTRA SPECIAL:** Versailles, by far the most magnificent of all the French châteaux, is 13 miles (21 km) southwest of Paris, accessible by train or bus. Louis XIV, called the Sun King because of the splendor of his court, took a small château used by Louis III, enlarged it, and really outdid himself here. The vast, intricate formal gardens, designed by the great Le Nôtre, cover 250 acres and include 600 fountains

— for which a river had to be diverted. At one time, the palace itself housed 6,000 people, and the court numbered 20,000. Louis kept his nobles in constant competition over his favors, hoping to distract them from any opposition.

It's impossible to see all of Versailles in one day, but don't miss the Hall of Mirrors, the Royal Apartments, and the Chapel. Also on the grounds are the Grand Trianon, a smaller palace often visited by Louis XIV, and the Petit Trianon, a favorite place of Marie Antoinette, who also liked Le Hameau (the hamlet), a model farm where she and her companions played at being peasants. Gardens open daily; château and Trianons closed Mondays (phone: 950-5832).

A spectacular illumination and display of the great fountains takes place on Sunday evenings during the summer. For more information, contact the Versailles Tourist Office, 7 rue des Reservoirs (phone: 950-3622).

SOURCES AND RESOURCES

For information in the US, contact the French Government Tourist Office, 610 Fifth Ave., New York, NY 10020 (212–757–1125). In Paris, the Office de Tourisme de Paris, 127 Champs-Élysées (phone: 723-6172), open daily from 9 AM to 10 PM April through October (shorter hours in winter), is the place to go for information, brochures, maps, or hotel reservations. Other offices include those at major train stations such as Gare du Nord (phone: 526-9482) and Gare de Lyon (phone: 343-3324).

For Local Coverage – *Paris Selection* is the official Tourist Office magazine in French and English. It lists events, sights, "Paris by night," jazz, some hotels, restaurants, shopping, and other information. Far more complete are two weekly guides, *L'Officiel des Spectacles* and *Une Semaine à Paris — Pariscope,* both in French but very easy to understand. Both are available at newsstands.

Most major newsstands carry *Passion,* an English-language tabloid that comes out ten times a year listing cultural events and giving a youthful, lively, American perspective on Paris. And the *International Herald Tribune* is available daily except Sundays, all over town. For those planning a trip and wanting to get a jump on things, there's *La Belle France,* a monthly newsletter with hotel and restaurant reviews and shopping information for Paris and other cities. Subscriptions ($39) are available from Travel Guide, Inc., 1835 University Circle, Charlottesville, VA 22903.

For Food – *Gourmet's France,* published by *Gourmet* magazine ($30), is a comprehensive guide to French cooking, arranged by regions, with color photographs and descriptions of specific restaurants. In addition, there are two handy and excellent guides to restaurants (and hotels) in France which, although written in French, use symbols that are easily understood even if you don't speak the language: the red *Michelin,* and the Gault Millau *Guide de la France.* Both are available in France; the *Michelin* can be bought in many bookstores in the US, and an English translation of the Gault Millau guide, *The Best of France,* is now also widely sold in the US.

For a good paperback on French food, see Waverley Root's *Food of France,* and for a guide to French wines, Alexis Lichine's *Guide to the Wines and Vineyards of France.* Patricia Wells's *Food Lovers Guide to Paris* covers eating places, markets, kitchenware stores, and other food-related shops.

Note: By 1986, the French expect to have completed an overhaul of their telephone system, giving each subscriber a basic number of eight figures. In the case of phone numbers for the city of Paris given in this chapter, this means adding the number 4 to the existing number: thus 222-0125 (old number) becomes 4222-0125. In the area surrounding Paris, either 3 or 6 is added to the existing seven-figure number: so 951-9536 (old number) becomes 3951-9536. Numbers in the provinces will be preceded by their existing prefix (area code).

CLIMATE AND CLOTHES: Paris has about the same weather as our Middle Atlantic states, though it's usually not warmer than 75°F (24°C) or colder than 30°F (−1°C). It rains frequently year-round, so a raincoat and folding umbrella are absolute musts. Air-conditioning is still rather rare and thermostats are usually set low in winter. On the Left Bank, anything goes; on the Right Bank wear what you would in any cosmopolitan American city. A blazer or sport jacket, trousers, and tie will get a man into the finest restaurants in Paris; for women, a pretty dress or a suit will do in the same situations. Attire more formal than a cocktail dress for women or as formal as black tie for men is necessary only for Friday dinner at *Maxim's,* a ball, or an Opéra opening night. A sweater for inside chilly historic stone walls is a good idea for the ladies; men will be comfortable with a blazer or sports jacket.

 GETTING AROUND: Métro – Operates 5:30 AM to 1:15 AM. It is safe, clean, quiet, and easy to use. The different lines are identified by the names of their terminals at either end. Every station is equipped with clear directional maps, some with push-button devices that light up the proper route after pushing a destination button. Keep your ticket (you may need it to exit) and don't cheat; there are spot checks. Those caught in first class with a second-class ticket are subject to an immediate fine except from 6 PM until 9 AM, when anyone is allowed in a first-class car.

A 10-ticket book *(carnet)* is available at a reduced rate. A tourist ticket *(billet de tourisme)* may be purchased upon presentation of your passport at 44 subway stations and four regional express stations or at any of the six French National Railroads stations. This entitles the bearer to 4 or 7 consecutive days of first-class travel on the Métro or on city-run buses.

Roissy-Charles de Gaulle Airport is now linked by rail with the Gare du Nord, which is also a Métro stop. If you don't have too much luggage, this is the cheapest and fastest route to the center of Paris.

Bus – Generally operates 6:30 AM to 9:30 PM. Slow but good for seeing. Métro tickets are valid on all city-run buses. Lines are numbered, and both stops and coaches have signs indicating routes. One or two tickets may be required, depending on the distance traveled. The RATP, which operates the Métro and bus system, has also designated certain lines as being of particular interest to tourists. A panel on the front of the bus indicates in English and German "This bus is good for sightseeing." RATP has a tourist office at pl. de la Madeleine, next to the flower market (phone: 265-3118), which organizes bus trips in Paris and the region.

Taxi – Taxis can be found at taxi stands at main intersections, outside railway stations and official buildings, and in the streets. You can also call *Allo Taxi* (phone: 203-9999 or 200-6789) or *Radio Taxi* (phone: 739-3333). The meter starts running from the time the cab is dispatched. Fares increase at night. A 10% tip is considered adequate.

Car Rental – Book when making your plane reservation or contact *Avis* (phone: 550-3231), *Europcar* (phone: 500-0806); *Mattei* (phone: 346-1150); or *Hertz* (phone: 788-5151). Rented cars are not recommended in the city.

Boat – See Paris from the Seine by day and by night for about $4. Modern, glass-enclosed river ramblers provide a constantly changing picture of the city. Contact *Bateaux Mouches,* Pont d'Alma (phone: 225-9610), *Vedettes Paris–Tour Eiffel,* Pont d'Iéna (phone: 551-3308), *Vedettes Pont-Neuf,* Square Vert-Galant (phone: 633-9838).

Train – Paris has six main train stations, each one serving a different area of the country. The general information number is 261-5050; for information in English, call 380-5050. North: Gare du Nord, 18 rue de Dunkerque (phone: 208-0303); East: Gare de l'Est, pl. du 11-Novembre (phone: 208-4990); Southeast: Gare de Lyon, 20 blvd. Diderot (phone: 345-9222); Southwest: Gare d'Austerlitz, 51 quai d'Austerlitz (phone: 584-1616); West: Gare Montparnasse, 17 blvd. de Vaugirard (phone: 538-5229); West and Northwest: Gare St.-Lazare, 20 rue de Rome (phone: 261-5050). The TGV (train à grande vitesse), the world's fastest train, has cut 2 hours off the usual 4-hour ride between Paris and Lyon and shortens traveling time to the Côte d'Azur and Switzerland. It leaves from the Gare de Lyon; reservations are necessary.

 MUSEUMS: The long-awaited Picasso Museum, which contains the artist's private collection, is finally open at the Hôtel Salé, Rue de Thorigny, and the new home for the Louvre's nineteenth-century French art will be at the gigantic Belle Époque Gare d'Orsay. Other museums of interest not described in *Special Places* include:

Musée de l'Affiche et de la Publicité – Three centuries of French posters and exhibits on advertising history. 18 rue de Paradis (phone: 246-1309).

Musée des Arts Décoratifs – Furniture and applied arts from the Middle Ages to the present day, Oriental carpets, and Dubuffet paintings and drawings. 107 rue de Rivoli (phone: 260-3214).

Musée des Arts Africains et Océaniens – One of the world's finest collections of African and Oceanic art. 293 av. Daumesnil (phone: 343-1454).

Maison de Balzac – Old house where he lived, with a garden leading to one of the prettiest little alleys in Paris. 47 rue Raynouard (phone: 224-5638).

Musée Cernuschi – Art of China. 7 av. Velasquez (phone: 563-5075).

Musée Cognacq-Jay – Seventeenth- and eighteenth-century art, snuff boxes, and watches. 25 blvd. des Capucines (phone: 261-9454).

Musée Eugène-Delacroix – Studio and garden of the great painter; exhibits change yearly. 6 rue de Fürstenberg (phone: 354-0487).

Musée Grévin – Waxworks of French history from Charlemagne to the present day. 10 blvd. Montmartre (phone: 770-8505). A branch devoted to La Belle Époque is in the Forum des Halles shopping complex (phone: 261-2850).

Musée Guimet – Louvre Far East collection. 6 pl. d'Iéna (phone: 723-6165).

Manufacture des Gobelins – The famous tapestry factory, in operation since the fifteenth century. Guided tours of the workshops take place Tuesday, Wednesday, and Thursday afternoons. 42 av. des Gobelins (phone: 570-1260).

Musée Jacquemart-André – Eighteenth-century French decorative art and European Renaissance treasures. 158 blvd. Haussmann (phone: 562-3994).

Musée Marmottan – Superb Monets. 2 rue Louis-Boilly (phone: 224-0702).

Musée de Sèvres – Next door to the Sèvres factory, one of the world's finest collections of porcelain. 4 Grande-Rue, Sèvres (phone: 534-9905).

Catacombs – Dating from the Gallo-Roman era and containing the remains of Danton, Robespierre, and many others. 2 pl. Denfert-Rochereau (phone: 322-4763).

Les Égouts (The Sewers of Paris) – Underground city of tunnels, a very popular afternoon tour on Mondays, Wednesdays, and the last Saturday of the month. 93 quai d'Orsay (phone: 705-1029).

Archaeological Crypt of Notre Dame – Under the square in front of the cathedral. There are foundations of third-century Roman structures and remains of walls and floor plans from later periods (phone: 274-2222).

 SHOPPING: Prices are generally high, but many people are willing to pay for the cachet of a Paris label and the style and quality of the products. For Paris sets the styles and trends that the world copies — from the elegant salons of the couturiers to the chic boutiques, antique shops, and galleries.

Paris is particularly famous for clothing, perfumes, and other beauty products, jewelry, leathergoods and accessories, wine and liqueurs, porcelain, and art. The big department stores are excellent places to get an idea of what's available. They include *Galeries Lafayette,* 40 blvd. Haussmann (phone: 282-3456); *Au Printemps,* 64 blvd.

Haussmann (phone: 282-5000); *Aux Trois-Quartiers,* 17 blvd. de la Madeleine (phone: 260-3930); and *Au Bon Marché,* 22 rue de Sèvres (phone: 260-3345). Two major shopping centers — Porte Maillot, pl. de la Porte Maillot, and Maine Montparnasse, at the intersection of blvd. Montparnasse and rue de Rennes — should also be visited.

There are several shopping neighborhoods, and they tend to be specialized. Haute couture can be found in the streets around the Champs-Élysées: av. George V, av. Montaigne, rue François I, and rue du Faubourg-St.-Honoré; famous designers are also represented in department stores. Boutiques are especially numerous on the av. Victor-Hugo, rue de Passy, the blvd. des Capucines, in the St.-Germain-des-Prés area, in the neighborhood of the Opéra and in the Forum des Halles shopping center.

The rue de Paradis is lined with crystal and china shops, and St.-Germain-des-Près has art galleries. The best and most expensive antique dealers are along the Faubourg-St.-Honoré on the Right Bank. On the Left Bank there's Le Carré Rive Gauche, an association of more than 100 antiques shops in the area bordered by quai Voltaire, rue de l'Université, rue des Sts.-Pères, and rue du Bac. Antiques and curio collectors should explore Paris's several flea markets: Marché d'Aligre, at the Place d'Aligre; Montreuil, near the Porte de Montreuil; Vanves, near the Porte de Vanves; and Puces de Saint-Ouen, near the Porte de Clignancourt.

A few more tips: Sales take place the first weeks in January and the last weeks in June. Any shop labeled *dégriffé* offers discounts on brand-name clothing — rue de Rennes and rue St.-Placide on the Left Bank have several. The French value-added tax (VAT; typically 18.6% and as high as 33.33% on luxury articles) can be refunded on most purchases made by foreigners provided a minimum of 800F is spent in one store. Forms must be filled out and the refund is usually mailed to your home. Large department stores and the so-called duty-free shops have facilitated the procedure, but refunds can be obtained from any store willing to cooperate. If the refund is not exactly equal to the tax — 15% to 25% refunds are common — it's because stores may retain some of it as reimbursement for their expense in handling the paperwork.

Here is a small sampling of a wealth of shops in Paris, many of which have more than one location in the city:

Agnès B – A very popular boutique. 3 rue du Jour, 13 rue Michelet, 17 av. Pierre-I-de-Serbie, and 81 rue d'Assas.

Baccarat – For high-quality porcelain and crystal. 30 rue du Paradis.

La Bagagerie – One of the finest bag and belt boutiques in the world. 74 rue de Passy and 41 rue du Four.

Pierre Cardin – A famous designer with his own boutique. 83 rue du Faubourg-St.-Honoré, 27 av. de Marigny, and other locations.

Carel – For beautiful shoes. 12 Rond-Point des Champs-Élysées and other locations.

Cartier – For fabulous jewelry in every sense of the word. 7 pl. Vendôme and other locations.

Catherine – Good duty-free prices on perfume, makeup, accessories. 6 rue Castiglione.

Céline – A popular boutique. 24 rue François I; for shoes it's 3 av. Victor-Hugo.

Cerruti – For women's clothing, 15 pl. de la Madeleine; for men's, 27 rue Royale.

Chanel – Needs no introduction. 31 rue Cambon.

Courrèges – Another bastion of haute couture with its own boutique. 40 rue François I and 46 rue du Faubourg-St.-Honoré.

E. Dehillerin – An enormous selection of professional cookware. 18-20 rue Coquillière.

Christian Dior – The most famous couture house in the world. 30 av. Montaigne; *Miss Dior* and *Baby Dior* for children are also at this location.

Dorothée Bis – One of the oldest and most successful Paris boutiques, definitely a trend setter. 33 rue de Sévres.

Hotel Drouot – Paris's huge auction house operates Monday through Friday afternoons. Good buys. 9 rue Drouot.

Le Drugstore – A uniquely French version of the American drugstore, with an amazing variety of goods — perfume, books, records, newspapers, magazines, film, food. 149 blvd. St.-Germain, 133 Champs-Élysées, and 1 av. Matignon.

Erès – Avant-garde sportswear for men and women. 2 rue Tronchet.

Fabrice – For trendy, fine-quality costume jewelry. 33 and 54 rue Bonaparte.

Fauchon – This is *the* place to buy fine food and wine of every variety, from *oeufs en gêlée* to quiches Lorraine. 28 pl. de la Madeleine.

Freddy – A popular shop for gifts, offering perfumes, gloves, ties, scarves, and other items at good prices. 10 rue Auber.

Maud Frizon – For shoes. 81 rue des Sts.-Peres.

La Gaminerie – Reasonably priced, good sportswear and outstanding window displays. 137 blvd. St.-Germain.

Givenchy – One of the legendary designers. 3 av. George V; *Nouvelle Boutique,* 66 av. Victor-Hugo; and *Givenchy Gentleman,* 8 av. George V.

Guerlain – For perfume, of course. 2 pl. Vendôme, 68 Champs-Élysées, 29 rue de Sevres, and 93 rue de Passy.

Hermès – For the very best ties, shoes, saddles, and accessories; the prices will put you into cardiac arrest. 24 rue du Faubourg-St.-Honoré.

IGN (French National Geographic Institute) – All manner of maps — ancient and modern, foreign and domestic. 107 rue La Boétie.

Charles Jourdan – These high-fashion shoes are very popular everywhere. 5 blvd. de la Madeleine is one of many outlets.

Lancôme – For perfumes. 29 rue du Faubourg-St.-Honoré.

Lanvin – Another fabulous designer, with several spacious, colorful boutiques under one roof. 15, 17, and 22 rue du Faubourg-St.-Honoré.

Lanvin Solde Trois – A source of inexpensive Lanvin fashions. 3 rue de Vienne.

Ted Lapidus – A compromise between haute couture and excellent ready-to-wear. 23 rue du Faubourg-St-Honoré, 35 av. Pierre-I-de-Serbie, and other locations.

Liz – A popular gift shop with a large variety of merchandise. 194 rue de Rivoli.

Madd – A ready-to-wear boutique for men and women. 20 rue Tronchet.

Marché aux Puces – Paris's famous Flea Market, with 3,000 dealers in antiques and secondhand items. Open Saturdays, Sundays, and Mondays. Bargaining is a must. Porte de Clignancourt.

Mendés – Less than wholesale prices on haute couture items, especially St. Laurent and Chanel. 65 rue Montmartre.

Le Must de Cartier – These two boutiques, on either side of the *Ritz Hotel,* offer such Cartier items as the lighter and the watches at prices that, though not low, are almost reasonable when you deduct the VAT tax. 23 pl. Vendôme.

Per Spook – One of Paris's young designers. 18 av. George V and other locations.

Le Petit Faune – A marvelous place to buy children's things. 33 rue Jacob and other locations.

Sonia Rykiel – Stunning sportswear and knits. 6 rue de Grenelle.

St.-Laurent – The world-famous designer who made slacks for women fashionable. 38 rue du Faubourg-St.-Honoré, 5 av. Marceau, and other locations.

Shakespeare and Company – This legendary English-language bookstore opposite Notre-Dame is something of a tourist attraction in itself. 37 rue de la Bûcherie.

W. H. Smith and Sons – This is the largest and best English-language bookstore in Paris, where you can buy the Sunday *New York Times* and many magazines and books. 248 rue de Rivoli.

Vuitton – High-quality luggage and handbags. 78 *bis* av. Marceau.

SPECIAL EVENTS: March is the month of the first *Foire à la Ferraille et aux Jambons* of the year. This fair of regional foods held with an antiques flea market (not best quality, but not junk) comes back in September. The running of the *Prix du Président de la République*, the first big horse race of the year, takes place the last Sunday of the month. From late April to early May is the *Foire de Paris*, the capital's big trade fair. In mid-May, there's the *Paris Marathon;* in late May (through early June), the *French Open Tennis Championships;* and in early June, odd years only, the *Paris International Air Show.* June is also the month of the nine horse races of the *Grande Semaine (Big Week)*, and in the middle of June begins the *Festival du Marais*, a month of music and dance performances. *Bastille Day*, July 14, is celebrated with music, fireworks, and parades. Later in July, the cyclists of the *Tour de France* arrive in Paris for the finish of the 3-week race. August is vacation time for Parisians, and the classical concerts of the *Festival Estival* (mid-July to mid-September) are among the few distractions. When they finish, the *Festival d'Automne*, a celebration of contemporary music, dance, and theater, takes over (it goes until December). In even years, the *Biennale des Antiquaires* is a major antiques event from late September to early October. Also in even years in early October is the *Paris Motor Show.* Every year on the first Sunday of October the last big horse race of the season, the *Prix de l'Arc de Triomphe*, is run, and every year in early October the *Fête des Vendanges à Montmartre* celebrates the harvest of the city's last remaining vineyard. On November 11, ceremonies at the Arc de Triomphe and a parade mark *Armistice Day.* A moving Christmas Eve midnight mass at Notre-Dame is part of the Christmas season, and at midnight one week later, the New Year bows in to spontaneous street revelry in the Latin Quarter and along the Champs-Élysées.

SPORTS: Biking – Rentals are available in the Bois de Boulogne and the Bois de Vincennes, or contact the *Fédération Française de Cyclo-tourisme*, 8 rue Jean-Marie-Jégo (phone: 580-3021), or *Paris-Vélo*, 2 rue du Fer à Moulin (phone: 337-5922).

Golf – For general information contact the *Fédération Française du Golf*, 69 av. Victor-Hugo (phone: 500-6220). It is usually possible to play on any course during the week for a simple greens fee. Weekends may be more difficult and require an invitation from a member. Nearby clubs that welcome Americans are the *Racing Club de France*, La Boulie-Pont-Colbert, Versailles (phone: 950-5941); *Ozoir-la-Ferrière*, Château des Agneaux, 15 miles (25 km) away (phone: 028-2079); *St.-Cloud*, Parc de Buzenval (phone: 701-0185); *St.-Germain-en-Laye*, 12.5 miles (20 km) away (phone: 451-7590); and *St.-Nom-la-Bretèche*, 19 miles (30 km) away (phone: 462-5400). It's best to call at least 2 days in advance to set up a time.

Horse Racing – Of the eight tracks in and around Paris, two major ones are in the Bois de Boulogne: *Longchamp* (phone: 772-5733) for flat races and *Auteuil* (phone: 723-5412) for steeplechase. *St.-Cloud* (phone: 771-6926), a few miles west of Paris, and *Chantilly* (phone: 4-457-2135), about 25 miles (40 km) north, are both for flat racing. *Vincennes*, Bois de Vincennes (phone: 742-0770), is the trotting track.

Soccer – There are matches from early August to mid-June at Parc des Princes, av. du Parc-des-Princes (phone: 288-0276).

Tennis – For general information, call *Ligue Régionale de Paris*, 74 rue de Rome (phone: 522-2208), or the Fédération Française de Tennis, Roland Garros Stadium (phone: 743-9681).

THEATER: The most complete listings of theaters, operas, concerts, and movies are found in the *Officiel des Spectacles* and *Une Semaine à Paris-Pariscope* (see above). The season is generally from September to June. Tickets are less expensive than in New York and are obtained at each box office, through brokers (American Express and Thomas Cook are good), or your hotel's trusty concierge. The curtain usually goes up at 8:30 PM.

For those who speak French: Performances of classical plays by Molière, Racine, and Corneille take place at the *Comédie Française,* pl. du Théâtre (phone: 296-1020). Two other national theaters are *Théâtre de France* (Odéon), 1 pl. Paul-Claudel (phone: 325-7032), and *TNP Palais de Chaillot,* Pl. du Trocadéro (phone: 727-8115).

It's not really necessary to speak the language to enjoy the opera, dance, or musical comedy at *L'Opéra,* pl. de l'Opéra (phone: 742-5750); *Salle Favart-Opéra Comique,* 5 rue Favart (phone: 296-0611); *Théâtre Musical de Paris,* pl. du Châtelet (phone: 261-1983). Theater tickets can be reserved through SOS-Theatre (225-6707).

For those who consider French their second language, Paris's many café-theaters offer amusing songs, sketches, satires, and take-offs on topical trends and events. Among them are *Café de la Gare,* 41 rue du Temple (phone: 278-5251), and *Café d'Edgar,* 58 blvd. Edgar-Quinet (phone: 320-8511).

US films with original sound tracks (always marked "VO" — *version originale*) may be found along the Champs-Élysées and in the Latin Quarter and Montparnasse.

MUSIC: The *Orchestre de Paris,* under the direction of Daniel Barenboim, is based at the *Salle Pleyel* — the Carnegie Hall of Paris, 252 rue du Faubourg-St.-Honoré (phone: 563-8873). Other classical recitals are held at the *Salle Gaveau,* 45 rue La Boétie (phone: 563-2030), at the *Théâtre des Champs-Élysées,* 15 av. Montaigne (phone: 723-4777), and at the *Palais des Congrès,* Porte Maillot (phone: 758-1373). The *Orchestre National de France* performs at a variety of places, including the Grand Auditorium at *Maison de la Radio,* 116 av. du Président-Kennedy (phone: 524-1516). Innovative contemporary music — much of it created by computer — is the province of the *Institut de Recherche et de Coopération Acoustique Musique* (IRCAM), whose musicians can be heard in various auditoriums of the Centre Georges-Pompidou, 19 rue Beaubourg (phone: 278-7995). Special concerts are frequently held in Paris's many places of worship, with moving music at High Mass on Sundays. The *Palais des Congrès* and the *Olympia,* 28 blvd. des Capucines (phone: 742-5286), are the places to see well-known international pop and rock artists.

NIGHTCLUBS AND NIGHTLIFE: Organized *Paris by Night* group tours (Cityrama, Paris Vision, and other operators) include at least one "Spectacle" — beautiful girls in minimal yet elaborate costumes, with lavish sets and effects and sophisticated striptease. Most music halls offer a package (running as high as $60 per person), with dinner, dancing, and a half-bottle of champagne. It is possible to go to these places on your own, save money by skipping dinner and champagne (both usually way below par), and take a seat at the bar to see the show. The most famous extravaganzas occur nightly at *Alcazar,* 62 rue Mazarine (phone: 329-0220); *Crazy Horse Saloon,* 12 av. George V (phone: 723-3232); *Folies-Bergère,* 32 rue Richer (phone: 246-7711); *Lido (Cabaret Normandie),* 116 *bis* Champs-Élysées (phone: 563-1161); *Moulin Rouge,* Pl. Blanche (phone: 606-0019); and *Paradis Latin,* 28 rue du Cardinal-Lemoine (phone: 325-2828). An amusing evening can also be spent at smaller cabaret shows like *René Cousinier (La Branlette),* 4 impasse Marie-Blanche (phone: 606-4946); *Au Lapin Agile,* 22 rue des Saules (phone: 606-8587); and *Michou,* 80 rue des Martyrs (phone: 606-1604). Reserve all a few days in advance.

Discotheque or private club, there's one big difference. Fashionable "in" spots like *Le Palace,* 8 rue Faubourg Montmartre (phone: 246-1087); *Régine's,* 49 rue de Ponthieu (phone: 359-2113); *Chez Castel,* 15 rue Princesse (phone: 326-9022); *Club Sept,* 7 rue Ste.-Anne (phone: 296-4705); and *Élysées Matignon,* 2 av. Matignon (phone: 225-7313), superscreen potential guests. No reason is given for accepting some and turning others away; go here with a regular or look like you'd fit in with the crowd; go early and on a weeknight and your chances of getting past the gatekeeper are 50–50. Don't despair if you're refused; the following places are just as much fun and usually more hospitable: *Les Bains-Douches,* 7 rue du Bourg-l'Abbé (phone: 887-0180); *Le Bilboquet,* 13 rue St.-Benoit (phone: 222-5109); *Whisky à Gogo,* 57 rue de Seine (phone: 633-7499); *Le Privé,* 12 rue de Ponthieu (phone: 225-5170); *l'Aventure,* 4 av. Victor-Hugo (phone: 501-6679); and *L'Écume des Nuits,* Hotel Meridien, 8 blvd. Gouvion-St.-Cyr (phone: 758-1230).

Some pleasant, popular bars for a nightcap include: *Bar de la Closerie des Lilas,* 171 blvd. Montparnasse (phone: 326-7050); *Harry's New York Bar,* 5 rue Daunou (phone: 261-7114); *Fouquet's,* 99 Champs-Élysées (phone: 723-7060); *Ascot Bar,* 66 rue Pierre-Charron (phone: 359-2815); *Bar Anglais,* Plaza-Athénée Hotel, 25 av. Montaigne (phone: 723-7833); *Pub Winston Churchill,* 5 rue de Presbourg (phone: 500-7535); and *Le Bistro,* Hotel Inter-Continental, 3 rue de Castiglione (phone: 260-3780).

Jazz buffs have a large choice with *Caveau de la Huchette,* 5 rue de la Huchette (phone: 326-6505); *New Morning,* 7-9 rue des Petites Ecuries (phone: 523-5141); *Slow Club,* 130 rue de Rivoli (phone: 233-8430); and *Le Petit Journal,* 71 blvd. St. Michel (phone: 326-2859).

Enghien-les-Bains, 8 miles (13 km) away, is the only casino in the Paris vicinity (phone: 412-9000). Open 3 PM to 3 AM, it can easily be reached by train from the Gare du Nord (phone: 280-0303).

 SINS: The first one that comes to mind is *gluttony.* You've overindulged in all that fine food and wine? You now have a *crise de foie* (liver crisis); relax, feel French (they have this all the time!), and buy a bottle of Fernet Branca or a tealike infusion called Boldoflorine. Both settle tummy and liver butterflies. More serious cases can contact the American Hospital at Neuilly (phone: 747-5300) or call SOS Médécin (phone: 337-7777), a 24-hour medical service whose doctors make house calls.

Les Halles is filled with very international sex shops, in Pigalle you can satisfy your *lust* for just about anything for a price, and the erotic theaters in the rue St.-Denis area give billings like "Supra Erotique, du Jamais Vu, Le Plus Sexuel, and Les Plus Sensuels" to their presentations. Ladies of the evening roam the streets in full force (it's estimated there are about 40,000 professionals in Paris) and the elegant avenue Foch is very popular. Some girls even operate from Cadillacs and Mercedes along the Champs-Élysées, certain parts of the Bois de Boulogne, and in the ritzier arrondissements. You're on your own here!

BEST IN TOWN

 CHECKING IN: Paris offers a broad choice of accommodations, from luxurious palaces with every service to more humble budget hotels. They are strictly controlled by the government and must post their rates, so that you can be sure that the price you are being charged is correct. Below is a selection from all categories; in general, expect to spend up to $200 a night for a double room in the "palace" hotels, which we've listed as very expensive; from $70 to $110 in expensive; $40 to $75 in moderate; and $35 and less in inexpensive.

Except for July, August, and December, the least crowded months, rooms are usually at a premium in Paris. To reserve your first choice, we advise making reservations at least 1 month in advance, even further ahead for the smaller, less expensive places listed. Watch for the dates of special events in Paris, when hotels are even more than normally crowded. You can call the hot line daily, except Sundays and holidays, from 9 AM to 10 PM, at 359-1212, for an immediate reservation in Paris and vicinity.

Nova-Park Élysées – Opened in 1981, this is the city's newest "palace" and one of the most expensive hotels in the world. A minimum of $180 per night is charged for any of the 12 rooms, and prices climb from there for the 15 duplex apartments and 36 other suites. The Royale suite is the largest in Europe and the Thousand and One Nights triplex has a private garden and swimming pool for a mere $1,500 a night. Several restaurants and bars, a disco, jazz club, dinner dancing club, conference rooms, and other amenities are also offered. Near the Champs-Élysées. 51 rue François ler (phone: 562-6364). Very expensive.

The Ritz – Optimum comfort, privacy, and personalized service are offered here, in one of the world's most gracious and distinguished hotels. The 162 recently redecorated rooms still preserve their antique treasures. This turn-of-the-century monument is *the* place to splurge, and even its sale to "English" (read Arab) interests has not diminished the glow. The bars are fashionable meeting places, and the two-star *Ritz-Espadon* restaurant carries on the tradition of the legendary Escoffier. 15 pl. Vendôme (phone: 260-3830). Very expensive.

The Bristol – A palace with a special, almost intimate cachet. Service is impeccable, as are the 212 spacious, quiet rooms and huge, marble baths. The beautiful little restaurant and comfortable lobby cocktail lounge are additional pleasures. A new wing includes a heated pool on the seventh-floor terrace. 112 rue du Faubourg-St.-Honoré (phone 266–9145). Very expensive.

Plaza-Athénée – One of the legendary hotels, this is a favorite of the sophisticated seeking serene surroundings and superior service, with 218 elegantly appointed rooms. The *Relais* tables are much in demand at lunch and late supper, and the two-star *Régence,* summer patio, tea tables, and downstairs English bar are places to see and be seen. 25 av. Montaigne (phone: 723-7833). Very expensive.

George V – The nonpareil pick of movie moguls and international tycoons, with 315 elegantly traditional or handsome contemporary rooms; some, facing the lovely courtyard, have their own balconies; those on the upper floors, a nice view. One of the liveliest and most chic bars in the city is here, with a bartender who mixes a mean martini. The patio is a summer delight. 31 av. George V (phone: 723-5400). Very expensive.

Hôtel de Crillon – No sign out front, just discreet gold "C's" on the doors. The *Crillon* was recently renovated, and is currently the only "palace" hotel in Paris owned by French. Rooms on the place de la Concorde side, albeit rather noisy, have the view of views; rooms facing the courtyards are just as nice and much more tranquil. The popular bar and the elegant restaurant, *Les Ambassadeurs,* are frequented by newsmen and US and British embassy personnel. 10 pl. de la Concorde (phone: 265-2424). Very expensive.

Lancaster – This small, smart, 67-room townhouse has quiet, beautifully furnished accommodations. There are flowers everywhere, a cozy bar, and a top-notch restaurant (closed weekends), with courtyard service in summer. 7 rue de Berri (phone: 359-9043). Very expensive to expensive.

Meurice – Refined Louis XV and XVI elegance and a wide range of services are offered at prices slightly below those of the other deluxe palaces. The *Meurice* has 192 rooms and especially nice suites, a popular bar, a restaurant, *Le Meurice*, and the chandeliered tearoom *Pompadour.* 228 rue de Rivoli (phone: 260-3860). Very expensive to expensive.

Inter-Continental – The 500 rooms and suites have been meticulously restored to recreate turn-of-the-century elegance with modern conveniences. The top-floor Louis XVI "garret rooms" are cozy and look out over the Tuileries. There's a US-style coffee shop, a grill, popular bar, and nightclub. 3 rue de Castiglione (phone: 260-3780). Expensive.

Paris Hilton – Its 480 balconied, modern rooms are a few steps from the Eiffel Tower. Those facing the river have the best view. The glass-walled rendezvous *Le Toit de Paris* has dancing and a glittering nighttime view; *Le Western* serves Texas T-bones, apple pie à la mode, and brownies (mostly to French diners). 18 av. de Suffren (phone: 273-9200). Expensive.

Montparnasse Park – With 952 rooms, this ultramodern giant is in the heart of Montparnasse. It has a futuristic lobby, efficient service, a coffee shop, bars, and the *Montparnasse 25 Restaurant*, with a view. 19 rue du Commandant-René-Mouchotte (phone: 320-1551). Expensive.

Le Méridien – Air France's well-run, 1,027-room, modern American-style hotel has a French flair. Rooms are on the smallish side but tastefully decorated, quiet, and with good views. There are several attractive restaurants, a shopping arcade, lively bars, and a chic nightclub — *L'Écume des Nuits*. 81 blvd. Gouvion-St.-Cyr (phone: 758-1230). Expensive.

Le Grand Hôtel – This has long been a favorite of Americans abroad, with its "meeting place of the world," the *Café de la Paix*. It has 600 completely modernized rooms, cheerful bars, and restaurants — and what a location (next to the Opéra). 2 rue Scribe (phone: 268-1213). Expensive.

Lotti – Once very fashionable, always fashionably located right near the *Ritz,* this smaller, more intimate hotel is popular with Italians. The atmosphere is congenial, the restaurant is pleasant, and the rooms are comfortable but not outstandingly attractive. 7–9 rue de Castiglione (phone: 260-3734). Expensive.

Résidence du Bois – Formerly a nineteenth-century home, this small hotel has elegant rooms, individually decorated with period furnishings. It's private, sophisticated, and frequented by French people; it has a garden and a charming bar. 16 rue Chalgrin (phone: 500-5059). Expensive.

L'Hotel – This is the very chic, small Left Bank hotel favored by experienced international travelers. The rooms are tiny, but beautifully appointed, and the location can't be beat. 13 rue des Beaux-Arts (phone: 325-2722). Expensive.

Westminster – Between the Opéra and the *Ritz* and once prestigious, it declined somewhat but has been recently renovated. The paneling, marble fireplaces, and parquet floors remain; air-conditioning has been installed; and a new restaurant and cocktail lounge replace the old grill and bar. Some of the 102 rooms overlook the street, some an inner courtyard. 13 rue de la Paix (phone: 261-5746). Expensive.

Raphael – A very spacious, stately place with a Turner in the lobby and paneling painted with sphinxes in the generous rooms. Less well known among the top Paris hotels, but favored by film directors and the like. 17 av. Kléber (phone: 502-1600). Expensive.

Relais Christine – A thorough renovation turned this sixteenth-century cloister into a lovely small hotel with modern fixtures and old-fashioned charm. 3 rue Christine (phone: 326-7180). Expensive.

PLM St.-Jacques – This four-star hotel has 800 up-to-date rooms, a nice shopping arcade, a cinema, four restaurants, and the lively *Bar Tahonga*. A bit out of the way, but the Métro is close by. 17 blvd. St.-Jacques (phone: 589-8980). Expensive.

Vendôme – This older house has 45 immaculate high-ceilinged rooms, with brass beds; the location couldn't be better. 1 pl. Vendôme (phone: 260-3284). Moderate.

Odéon – A small, modernized, charming hotel in the heart of the St.-Germain area on the Left Bank. 3 rue de l'Odéon (phone: 325-9067). Moderate.

Lenox – Well located between the busy St.-Germain area and the boutiques nearby, it's small and very tastefully done. Popular with the fashion crowd. 9 rue de l'Université (phone: 296-1095). Moderate.

L'Université – Its 28 charmingly renovated rooms of all shapes and sizes are in a former eighteenth-century mansion. 22 rue de l'Université (phone: 261-0939). Moderate.

De Lutèce – Offers 23 luxurious rooms (one split-level) on the charming Île St.-Louis. Positively ravishing, with exquisite toile fabrics and wallpaper and raw wood beams. 65 rue St.-Louis-en-l'Île (phone: 326-2352). Moderate.

Abbaye St.-Germain – On a quiet street, this small, delightful hotel was once a convent. The lobby has exposed stone arches, and the elegant public and private rooms are furnished with antiques and tastefully selected fabrics. There's a lovely garden and a bar, but recently there have been complaints about the service. 10 rue Cassette (phone: 544-3811). Moderate.

Deux Îles – This beautifully redecorated seventeenth-century house is on the historic Île St.-Louis. It has a tropical garden and the decor is in bamboo, rattan, and braided rope. The rooms have French provincial fabrics and Louis XIV ceramic tiles in the bathrooms. 59 rue St.-Louis-en-l'Île (phone: 326-1335). Moderate.

Colbert – It's small but right around the corner from Notre Dame. Some rooms have views. 7 rue de l'Hotel Colbert (phone: 325-8565). Moderate.

Grand Hotel de l'Univers – This modern hotel is tucked away on a quiet street, but only two steps away is all the activity of St.-Germain-des-Pres and the Latin Quarter. 6 rue Gregoire de Tours (phone: 329-3700). Moderate.

Regent's Garden – Country atmosphere on a quiet street near the Étoile. The 41 rooms are now run by young hoteliers who make you feel you are in your own home. 6 rue Pierre-Demours (phone: 574-0730). Moderate.

Angleterre – Its 31 classic, clean, unpretentious rooms are in what was once the British Embassy, now a national monument. 44 rue Jacob (phone: 260-3472). Moderate.

Madison – Offers 57 large, bright rooms, some with balconies. 143 blvd. St.-Germain (phone: 329-7250). Inexpensive.

Isly – A gracious old Left Bank house, it has 36 attractive, quiet rooms and new baths. 29 rue Jacob (phone: 326-3239). Inexpensive.

Welcome Hotel – Overlooking the blvd. St.-Germain, it's simple but comfortable. 66 rue de Seine (phone: 634-2480). Inexpensive.

Du Globe – A tiny, charming hotel on a quiet street in the heart of the St.-Germain area. 15 rue des Quatre Vents (phone: 326-3550). Inexpensive.

Scandinavie – There are 22 rooms (each uniquely decorated) with lots of character in this 300-year-old inn. Plants are everywhere. 27 rue de Tournon (phone: 329-6720). Inexpensive.

Family Hotel – A long-time favorite with Americans — you're treated just like part of the family. It has 25 small but comfortable rooms. 35 rue Cambon (phone: 261-5484). Inexpensive.

Marronniers – In a courtyard and garden in the heart of the Left Bank, this hotel, recently given a complete overhaul, has kept a faithful clientele. 21 rue Jacob (phone: 325-3060). Inexpensive.

Sevigné – This hotel recently moved up a notch in the government's classification system, and an elevator and new bathrooms have been installed. If it's a little noisy (right on the rue de Rivoli), the warm welcome and handy location make up for it. 2 rue Malher (phone: 272-7617). Inexpensive.

Solférino – A cozy place with Oriental rugs scattered about. The 34 tiny rooms have floral wallpaper, and there's a plant-filled breakfast and sitting room. 91 rue de Lille (phone: 705-8554). Inexpensive.

St.-Louis – On the Île St.-Louis, it's small, tastefully furnished in Louis XIII style, flawlessly elegant, and very quiet. Some rooms on the sixth floor have fine views. 75 rue St.-Louis-en-l'Île (phone: 634-0480). Inexpensive.

EATING OUT: Paris considers itself the culinary capital of the world, and you will never forget food for long here. Whether you grab just a crisp croissant and café-au-lait for breakfast or splurge on an epicurean fantasy for dinner, this is the city in which to indulge all your gastronomic fantasies.

There are basically two types of French cooking, *haute cuisine* and *cuisine bourgeoise*. *Haute cuisine* is a fine art with a long history — and its presentation in restaurants is almost always elaborate and expensive. This classic French cooking *(cuisine classique)* has recently been expanded to include *nouvelle cuisine* — a slightly simpler, less heavy incarnation with fewer rich and fattening sauces, which was designed to allow the basic ingredients to speak better for themselves. *Cuisine bourgeoise,* or French family-style cooking, is much less expensive and usually uses regional ingredients. At these smaller, more intimate restaurants you can either order à la carte or save money with the *menu* or prix fixe — offering a choice of complete dinners including an appetizer, entrée, vegetables, salad, cheese, and/or dessert. If the proprietor is very much on the premises, it might be a good idea to let him order for you.

French breakfast is Continental, typically coffee and croissants or brioches (both are delicious, buttery rolls), and lunch rather than dinner is the main meal here. The French dine late, no earlier than 8 PM.

French wines are an adventure for which we lack space to deal with in depth (see *Sources and Resources*), but you can either order the famed château-bottled wines or save money by ordering *vin maison* (house wine), which comes by the carafe and is generally quite palatable.

Don't miss the adventure of the sidewalk cafés, truly a way of life in Paris. Order coffee, wine, an apéritif (cocktail), or a snack, and sit and watch Paris go by, just as the Parisians do. And for simpler fare, a *brasserie* specializes in beer, wine, and hearty food from Alsace like *choucroute* (pork chops, sausage, and sauerkraut).

And the ultimate economy is also one of the tastiest: a true Parisian *pique-nique* — remember, they invented the idea here. The recipe requires stopping at a local *boulangerie* (bakery) for a fresh (baked at least twice daily) *baguette* (bread), some *fromage* (cheese), and perhaps a little Bayonne ham at a *charcuterie,* and add some *vin ordinaire* or mineral water to taste. It's how the French often do it.

Restaurants classed as very expensive charge $80 and way up for two; expensive is $60 to 80; moderate, $40 to 60; inexpensive, under $40; and very inexpensive, $20 or less. A service charge of 12% to 15% is usually added to the bill, but most people leave a small additional tip of about 5% to 7%.

Note: Most Paris restaurants are closed for part or all of July and August, so it's best to check ahead in order to avoid disappointment at the restaurant of your choice. Here is a small sampling of the best restaurants that Paris has to offer:

Le Taillevent – Full of tradition, Louis XVI furnishings, eighteenth-century porcelain dinner service — all in a nineteenth-century mansion — *Taillevent* offers nononsense *cuisine classique* that is currently the best in Paris. Try terrine of truffled sweetbreads, duck in cider, and especially chef Claude Deligne's soufflés in original flavors like Alsatian pear and cinnamon chocolate. Three stars in the *Guide Michelin*. Closed Saturdays, Sundays and the month of August. Reserve more than 60 days ahead. 15 rue Lamennais (phone: 563-3994). Very expensive.

La Tour d'Argent – Another of the four Parisian restaurants to be awarded three Michelin stars and probably the best-known Paris eating place, though recent visits have not been up to the standards of years past. The spectacular view of Notre-Dame and the Île St.-Louis competes with the food for the attention of a very touristy clientele. Pressed duck — prepared before you — is the specialty, but the 15 other varieties of duck are equally good. Closed Mondays. 15 quai de la Tournelle (phone: 354-2331). Very expensive.

Alain Senderens–Lucas Carton – Once proprietor of the three-Michelin-star restaurant called *L'Archestrate,* owner-chef Alain Senderens dropped that name when he recently moved. His larger, more convenient quarters are in a historic building that boasts a stupendous Belle Époque interior that used to house the legendary *Lucas Carton* restaurant. Senderens enjoys a reputation as one of France's most innovative culinary talents, combining many tenets of nouvelle cuisine with Oriental and African influences. This is not a place for timid diners. In the past, Senderens also earned a reputation for arrogant service. 9 pl. de la Madeleine (phone: 265-2290). Very expensive.

Lasserre – The ultimate in sumptuous, romantic luxury, with a magical ceiling that opens periodically during dinner to reveal the nighttime sky. The food is equally sublime — served in the *style Lasserre* — that is, vermeil dessert settings, plates rimmed in gold, and extravagant garnishes to accompany each dish. The recent loss of its third Michelin star in no way diminishes its appeal. Closed Sundays, Mondays, and all of August. 17 av. Franklin-Roosevelt (phone: 359-5343). Very expensive.

Le Grand Véfour – Founded in 1760, this sedately elegant Empire-style establishment — with paintings on the mirrors — is known for light, refined menus and perfect service. It's famous for toast Rothschild (shrimp in crayfish sauce set in a brioche) and pigeon Aristide Briand (boned roast pigeon stuffed with foie gras and truffles). Closed Saturdays, Sundays, and during August. 17 rue Beaujolais (phone: 296-5627). Very expensive.

Maxim's – This place is a legend for its Belle Époque decor and atmosphere. It's good for celebrations, but it's hard to feel comfortable if you aren't known here. Now owned by fashion designer Pierre Cardin, *Maxim's* has been entirely refurbished and moderately priced menus have been introduced in the first-floor salons. This is one of the few places in Paris where you can dress formally — on Fridays. There's an orchestra for dancing from 9:30 PM until 2 AM. Saddle of lamb with cream of basil is delicious. Closed Sundays. 3 rue Royale (phone: 265-2794). Very expensive.

Restaurant d'Olympe – Owner and chef Dominique Nahmias is the first female chef to be awarded three toques — very high honors — by Gault and Millau. Her *nouvelle cuisine* is painstakingly prepared and simply glorious; an excellent wine list adds to the meal's enjoyment. Closed Mondays and August. 8 rue Nicolas Charlet (phone: 734-8608). Very expensive.

Jamin – Due to the culinary talents of owner-chef Joel Robuchon, *Jamin* is now one of the city's finest restaurants and has recently been promoted to three stars by Michelin. Robuchon calls his cuisine "moderne," similar to but not always as light as *la nouvelle.* Closed Saturdays, Sundays, and July. 32 rue de Longchamp (phone: 727-1227). Expensive.

Lamazère – This is truffle heaven, the menu a triumph of rich products from the southwest of France. The owner is a magician in the real sense of the word as well as with food. The elegant bar and salons are open late. Closed Sundays and the month of August. 23 rue de Ponthieu (phone: 359-6666). Expensive.

Le Divellec – This bright and airy place serves some exquisitely fresh seafood. Try the sea bass, the rouget, and the sautéed turbot. The latter is served with "black pasta" — thick strips of pasta flavored with squid ink — an unusual and delicious concoction. Closed Sundays and Mondays. 107 rue de l'Universite (phone: 551-9196). Expensive.

Ledoyen – The setting is extravagant, the refinement supreme, in food, service, and decor; *Ledoyen* is a favorite of ministers and diplomats. Though the food is superb, the atmosphere is oppressively stuffy. Closed Sundays and the month of August. Carré des Champs-Élysées (phone: 266-5477). Expensive.

Vivarois – Claude Peyrot is one of France's finest chefs. Specialties here include curried oysters au gratin, turbot, and assortments of desserts. Closed Saturdays, Sundays, and August. 192 av. Victor-Hugo (phone: 504-0431). Expensive.

Prunier Traktir – Offers the best of everything that comes from the sea; the *marmite Dieppoise* alone is worth the trip. Closed Mondays, Tuesdays, and July. 16 av. Victor-Hugo (phone: 500-8912). Expensive.

Relais Louis XIII – Old-style decor and new cuisine in one of Paris's prettiest houses. Closed Sundays and at lunch on Mondays. 8 rue des Grands-Augustins (phone: 326-7596). Expensive.

Les Semailles – Jean-Jacques Jouteux has gained renown for his inspired renderings of *nouvelle cuisine*. He recently moved *Les Semailles* from its small quarters into a more spacious building that once housed *Le Boeuf sur le Toit* restaurant, a haunt of Jean Cocteau and other Paris artists in the 1940s. Closed Sundays, Mondays, and during July. 34 rue du Colisée (phone: 256-1682). Expensive.

Castel – You might be able to get a reservation at this, one of the few private clubs in Paris, if you ask the concierge at one of the grand hotels. The Belle Époque interior is breathtaking, the cooking fine, and there's a disco in the basement. Specialties include lobster and chicken with cucumbers. Closed Sundays. 15 rue Princesse (phone: 326-9022). Expensive.

Régine's – The food is actually good in this beautifully decorated nightclub, which is frequented by Parisians as well as the chic international set. Ask your hotel manager to get you in because it's a private club. Try the foie gras (made on the premises) and the goose. Closed Sundays. 49 rue de Ponthieu (phone: 359-2113). Expensive.

Le Pré Catelan – It's the large restaurant right in the middle of the Bois de Boulogne, and believe it or not, the food here is good. Ingredients are fresh and sauces are light. Specialties include four or five new dishes daily along with fresh smoked salmon. Closed Sunday evenings and Mondays. Rte. de Suresnes, Bois de Boulogne (phone: 524-5558). Expensive.

Jacques Cagna – This rising young chef always provides an interesting menu. Closed August, Christmas week, two Saturdays a month, and Sundays. 14 rue des Grands-Augustins (phone: 326-4939). Expensive.

Chiberta – Elegant and modern, the recently acclaimed cooking of Jean Michel Bédier is basically *nouvelle cuisine*. Try the *bavarois de saumon au coulis de tomates frais* (salmon mousse with fresh tomato sauce) and *marbré de rouget au fenouil* (red mullet with fennel). Closed Saturdays, Sundays, and August. 3 rue Arsène-Houssaye (phone: 563-7790). Expensive.

Le Petit Montmorency – In his new restaurant near the Champs-Elysées, chef Daniel Bouché still presents one of the most exciting and unusual menus in Paris. Very, very popular. Closed Saturdays, Sundays, and all of August. 5 rue Rabelais (phone: 225-1119). Expensive.

La Bourgogne – Rich, Burgundian specialties are offered with fine wines. *La Bourgogne* is beautiful outside and inside, small, and popular; it has a country feeling. Closed Saturdays at noon, Sundays, and all of August. 6 av. Bosquet (phone: 705-9678). Expensive.

Dodin Bouffant – Popular because it was set up by the gifted and imaginative Jacques Manière, one of France's premier chefs. Excellent seafood and inventive cuisine, open late. Closed Saturdays, Sundays, for 2 weeks around Christmastime, and all of August. 25 rue Frédéric-Sauton (phone: 325-2514). Expensive.

Faugeron – Among the finest restaurants of the *nouvelle* discipline. Superb cuisine, lovely service, and one of Paris's prettiest table settings in what was once an old school. Closed Saturdays, Sundays, and all of August. 52 rue de Longchamp (phone: 704-2453). Expensive.

Bistrot d'Hubert – Inventive cuisine is served in this old-time bistro, which is open late. Closed Sundays and Mondays. 36 pl. Marché-St.-Honoré (phone: 260-0300). Expensive.

Au Quai des Ormes – Elegant dining on the Seine, with an English-speaking staff. In summer, sit on the terrace overlooking Notre-Dame. Closed Saturdays, Sundays, and holidays. 72 quai de l'Hôtel de Ville (phone: 274-7222). Expensive.

L'Escargot Montorgueil – Kouiquette Terrail has given new life to this ornamental old monument from the 1800s. Snails, of course, five different ways, but also delicious fish, pheasant, beef, soufflés, and excellent wine values. Closed Mondays and Tuesdays. 38 rue Montorgueil (phone: 236-8351). Expensive.

L'Ami Louis – The archetypical Parisian bistro, rather unattractive looking, but with huge portions of marvelous food. Specialties include foie gras, spring lamb, ham, and Burgundy wines. Closed Mondays, Tuesdays, and all of July and August. 32 rue du Vertbois (phone: 887-7748). Expensive to moderate.

Le Bernardin – Here you can sample the original seafood preparations of Breton (from Brittany) Gilbert Le Coze, a real fish perfectionist. There's a spectacular seafood platter with 15 different kinds of shellfish. Closed Sundays, Mondays, and all of August. 18 rue Troyan (phone: 380-4061). Moderate.

Le Trou Gascon – Alain Dutournier creates inspired and unusual cuisine with southwestern specialties and a vast choice of local wines and Armagnacs. Closed Saturdays and Sundays. 40 rue Taine (phone: 344-3426). Moderate.

Chez Allard – A very popular, high-class bistro with hearty country cooking by Madame Allard and excellent Burgundy wines. Spring, when the new turnips arrive, is a special time here. Closed Saturdays, Sundays, and during August. 41 rue St.-André-des-Arts (phone: 326-4823). Moderate.

Bistro 121 – The hearty menu and excellent wines are offered in a modern setting that's always chic and crowded. Try *poisson crue mariné au citron vert* (seafood marinated in lime juice) and pear charlotte for dessert. Closed Sunday evenings and Mondays. 121 rue de la Convention (phone: 557-5290). Moderate.

Auberge des Deux Signes – This place was once the cellars of the priory of St. Julien-le-Pauvre; try to get an upstairs table overlooking the gardens. Auvergnat cooking *à la nouvelle cuisine.* Closed Sundays. 46 rue Galande (phone: 325-4656). Moderate.

L'Épicurien – There are just 55 seats here, in three little rooms around a garden. Closed Sundays and at lunch on Mondays. 11 rue Nesle (phone: 329-5578). Moderate.

Drouant – The place was founded in 1880, and the recipes have passed down virtually unchanged; they are classic and consistently good. Open daily. 18 rue Gaillon (phone: 742-5661). Moderate.

Le Duc – The atmosphere is warm and comfortable, and Paul Minchelli is incomparably inventive with fish and shellfish (cooked and raw). Quality and variety are the rule here, with such specialties as curried oysters, tuna tartar, coquilles St.-Jacques cru, and an extraordinary seafood platter. Closed Saturdays, Sundays, and Mondays. 243 blvd. Raspail (phone: 320-9630). Moderate.

Chez Josephine and La Rotisserie chez Dumonet – Two restaurants share the same building and the same management. *Josephine* is an old-time bistro with traditional cuisine and an excellent wine cellar; the *Rotisserie* is lively and more modern, with steaks and grills over an open fire. *Josephine* is closed Saturdays, Sundays, and all of July; the *Rotisserie,* Mondays, Tuesdays, and all of August. 117 rue du Cherche Midi (phone: 548-5240). Moderate.

Le Bistrot de Paris – Michel Oliver offers informality, original and classic bistro fare, and a good wine list, which attract a crowd. Closed Saturdays and Sundays. 33 rue de Lille (phone: 261-1683). Moderate.

La Marée – Unobtrusive on the outside, there is great comfort within — also the freshest of fish, the best restaurant wine values in Paris, and fabulous desserts. Closed Saturdays, Sundays, and August. 1 rue Daru (phone: 227-5932). Moderate.

Le Muniche – St. Germain's best brasserie is a bustling place with a rather extensive menu, and it's popular until 3 AM. 27 rue de Buci (phone: 633-6209). Moderate.

Ty-Coz – Breton cuisine featuring fish, cider, and crêpes; no meat, no cheese. Closed Sundays and Mondays. 35 rue St.-Georges (phone: 878-4295). Moderate.

Restaurant du Marché – Cuisine Landaise, which means solid, country-style cooking — foie gras, *confits d'oie*, and fine wines from the Landes region in the southwest of France, near Bordeaux. An amazing choice of herb teas and a pretty terrace for summer dining. 59 rue Dantzig (phone: 828-3155). Moderate.

L'Aquitaine – This is the seafood branch of the establishment above. Unusual dishes are prepared by Christiane Massia, and there's a delightful summer terrace. Closed Sundays and Mondays. 54 rue Dantzig (phone: 828-6738). Moderate.

Au Quai d'Orsay – Fashionable, sophisticated, very French, and very intimate. Traditional copious bourgeois cooking and good Beaujolais. Closed Sundays and August. 49 quai d'Orsay (phone: 551-5858). Moderate.

Chez Benoît – An unpretentious bistro with good old-fashioned Lyonnaise cooking and exquisite wines. Closed Saturdays, Sundays, and August. 20 rue St.-Martin (phone: 272-2576). Moderate.

Cartet – A tiny 14-seat place for old-fashioned cooking that's terrific for the price. Closed Saturdays, Sundays, and all of August. 62 rue de Malte (phone: 805-1765). Moderate.

Le Train Bleu – Fine food, good wine, and baroque decor so gorgeous it's been made a national monument. Gare de Lyon (phone: 343-0906). Moderate.

Ambassade d'Auvergne – This young chef creates delicious, unusual, classic Auvergnat dishes with a modern touch. Seasonal specialties and wonderful cakes. Closed Sundays. 22 rue Grenier-St.-Lazare (phone: 272-3122). Moderate.

Pierre Traiteur – This is a delightful place with admirable bourgeois cooking and lovely Chinon and Saumur wines. Closed Saturdays, Sundays, and all of August. 10 rue de Richelieu (phone: 296-0917). Moderate.

Bofinger – For magnificent Belle Époque decor, this is the place; it's one of Paris's oldest brasseries and it is beautiful. Open daily. 5 rue de la Bastille (phone: 272-8782). Moderate.

Chez Pierre Vedel – Truly original cuisine. Closed Saturdays, Sundays, from mid-July to mid-August, and at Christmastime. 19 rue Duranton (phone: 558-4317). Moderate.

Brasserie Lipp – This famous café is fashionable for a late supper of choucroute and Alsatian beer and for people-watching inside and out, but be aware that you are likely to be dispatched to second-floor "Siberia." The food's just as good there, however. Closed Mondays, July, and 15 days at Easter and Christmas. 151 blvd. St.-Germain (phone: 548-5391). Moderate.

Le Bourdonnais – The talented young chef trained with Jacques Maximin at the *Hôtel Négresco* in Nice and specializes in light, inventive creations of high quality. Closed Sundays and Mondays. 113 av. Bourdonnais (phone: 705-4796). Moderate.

La Barrière Poquelin – The excellent bistro cooking *à la nouvelle cuisine* includes a splendid foie gras salad. Closed Saturday noon and Sundays. 17 rue Molière (phone: 296-2219). Moderate.

Le Moi – A French owner and his Vietnamese wife serve the best Vietnamese food in Paris. Try pork with caramel, chicken with Chinese cabbage, ravioli with coriander, or crisp noodles with pork or crab. Open daily; closed August. 7 rue Gustave-Courbet (phone: 704-9510). Moderate.

Le Récamier – Come here for a taste of truly fine French cooking. Prices are slightly expensive, but if you stick to the delicious *boeuf bourguignon* and house wine, your tab will be reasonably low. All ingredients are fresh from the owner's farm and the atmosphere is charming. Closed Sundays. 4 rue Récamier (phone: 548-8658). Moderate.

Léo le Lion (Barbecue de la Tour) – A warm, cozy, and friendly place for grilled and skewered meats. Closed Saturdays, Sundays, and early August to early September. 23 rue Duvivier (phone: 551-4177). Moderate to inexpensive.

Pharamond – Serves only the best Norman food in a beautiful Belle Époque, timbered townhouse. Famous for *tripes à la mode de Caen* and *pommes soufflés*, since 1862. Closed Sundays, Monday noon, and July. 24 rue de la Grande Truanderie (phone: 233-0672). Moderate to inexpensive.

Androuët – There's a great cheese emporium on the main floor and, upstairs, a unique restaurant where cheese is the base of every dish. Closed Sundays. 41 rue Amsterdam (phone: 874-2693). Moderate to inexpensive.

Au Petit Riche – Genuine 1900s decor, subtle Touraine cooking, and inexpensive Vouvray, Chinon, and Bourgeuil wines. Closed Sundays and August. 25 rue le Peletier (phone: 770-6868). Moderate to inexpensive.

Au Pied de Cochon – Crowded and colorful 24 hours a day, its customers enjoy shellfish, pigs feet, and onion soup, in Les Halles area. 6 rue Coquillière (phone: 236-1175). Moderate to inexpensive.

La Coupole – This big, brassy brasserie, once the haunt of Hemingway, Josephine Baker, and Picasso, still clings to its *cuisine classique* heritage. Open until 2 AM. Closed August. 102 blvd. Montparnasse (phone: 320-1420). Moderate to inexpensive.

Clos de la Tour – This is a popular new restaurant with "bistro moderne" decor. Closed Sundays, Saturday noon, and August. 22 rue Falguière (phone: 322-3473). Moderate to inexpensive.

Au Charbon de Bois – This is one of the best, on a street with many small restaurants. Steaks and skewered brochettes are charcoal broiled and served with a delicious thyme sauce, plus a baked potato, onion rings, and salad. Closed Sundays and Monday noon. 16 rue Dragon (phone: 548-5704). Moderate to inexpensive.

Joe Allen's – Just like Joe Allen's on W 46th street in New York, it has good steaks, hamburgers, chili, and apple pie. Open till 1 AM. Reserve after 8 PM. 30 rue Pierre-Lescot (phone: 236-7013). Moderate to inexpensive.

Chez Toutoune – This modest place, specializing in Provençal dishes, has become very popular for two good reasons: The food is tasty and the prices are reasonable. The five-course, prix fixe menu features a rather short but very interesting selection of appetizers, entrées, and desserts. Closed Sundays, Mondays, and from mid-August to mid-September. 5 rue de Pontoise (phone: 326-5681). Inexpensive.

Chez La Vieille – Adrienne's cooking is simple, savory, and very popular. Lunch only. Closed Saturdays and Sundays. 37 rue Arbre-Sec (phone: 260-1578). Inexpensive.

Moissonnier – Solid Lyonnaise specialties and excellent wines are served in a homey bistro. Closed Sunday evenings, Mondays, and all of August. 28 rue des Fossés-St.-Bernard (phone: 329-8765). Inexpensive.

Atelier Maître Albert – Unlike most other restaurants on the Left Bank, this one is pleasantly roomy, with a log fire in winter and an honest prix fixe menu year-round. Notre-Dame looms in front of you as you walk out the door and onto the quai. Closed Sundays. 1 rue Maître Albert (phone: 633-1378). Inexpensive.

Chez Maître Paul – This place offers quality Franc Comtoise cooking (that means excellent chicken) and good Bourgueil and Jura wines. Closed Sundays, Mondays, and all of August. 12 rue Monsieur-le-Prince (phone: 354-7459). Inexpensive.

Brasserie Flo – One of the last of the brasseries of the 1900s. Hidden in a hard-to-find courtyard, it's excellent for oysters, foie gras, wild boar, and Alsatian specialties. Open late. Closed August. 7 cour de Petites-Écuries (phone: 770-1359). Inexpensive.

Le Monde des Chimères – Excellent well-tested *nouvelle cuisine* and fabulous desserts. This place is charming as well as popular. Closed Sundays and all of September. 69 rue St.-Louis-en-l'Île (phone: 354-4527). Inexpensive.

Petit Zinc – This is a popular late (3 AM) spot for fish, oysters, foie gras, and an ample, reasonably priced wine list. 25 rue Buci (phone: 354-7934). Inexpensive.

Le Mange Tout – A modern (but cozy) setting for some very good traditional country cooking, The ingredients are the freshest of produce from the restaurant's own farms. Closed a week at Easter, mid-August to mid-September, Sundays, and Monday noon. 30 rue Lacépède (phone: 535-5393). Inexpensive.

Chez Paul – Once a secret bistro, it is now known by the whole world. There's good solid fare here, and the premises are packed every day. Closed Mondays, Tuesdays, and all of August. 15 pl. Dauphine (phone: 354-2148). Inexpensive.

Au Gourmet-de-l'Isle – Remarkable for its location, ambience, quality, and prices. Closed on Mondays, Thursdays, and during August. 42 rue St.-Louis-en-l'Île (phone: 326-7927). Inexpensive.

Vellu – Norman cuisine is served in this cozy family-run restaurant near the rue Mouffetard market. Closed Sundays, Thursdays, and August. 12 rue Mirbel (phone: 331-6489). Inexpensive.

Monsieur Boeuf – Established in 1972, all of Paris has been flocking here ever since. Excellent beef, good little wines. Closed Sundays at lunch. 31 rue St.-Denis (phone: 508-5835). Inexpensive.

Chez Yvette – This excellent, small, bourgeois restaurant has good home cooking, lots of choice, and great desserts. Closed Saturdays, Sundays, and August. 1 rue d'Alençon (phone: 222-4554). Inexpensive.

Le Soufflé – Located on the street just behind rue Rivoli, not far from place Vendôme, this is the place to enjoy an orgy of soufflés. We suggest crayfish soufflé for an appetizer, cheese soufflé for the main course, and chocolate soufflé for dessert. Closed Sundays. 36 rue du Mont-Thabor (phone: 260-2719). Inexpensive.

Le Procope – One of Paris's oldest restaurants, where the food is reasonably good and the atmosphere couldn't be more Parisian. 13 rue de l'Ancienne-Comédie (phone: 326-9920). Inexpensive.

Aux Bigorneaux – A souvenir of the old Les Halles, this place is frequented by arty types and journalists. Especially recommended are the *foie gras frais maison,* the dandelion salad *(pissenlit),* the blood sausage, the steak au poivre, the Reserve Maison wine, and the sumptuous desserts. Reservations recommended. 12 rue Mondetour (phone: 508-4933). Inexpensive.

Robert et Louise – A family bistro, with warm wood-paneled decor and a very high standard for ingredients and cooking. Try the *soupe de poisson, boeuf bourguignon,* or the *côte de boeuf* grilled on an open fire. Also good are the *fromage blanc* and the wine *en pichet.* Closed Saturdays in summer, Sundays, holidays, and August. 64 rue Vieille du Temple (phone: 278-5589). Inexpensive.

La Route de Beaujolais – It's a barnlike workers' bistro on the Left Bank, serving Lyonnaise specialties and Beaujolais wines. Don't miss the *charcuterie* and the fresh bread here, and try the *tarte tatin* (caramelized apple tart) for dessert. Closed Sundays. 17 rue de Lourmel (phone: 579-3163). Inexpensive.

Vagenende – An art nouveau spot with fantasy decor that has changed little since it opened in 1898. It features adequate, filling meals at low prices. Open until 2 AM. 142 blvd. St.-Germain (phone: 326-6818). Inexpensive.

Au Pied de Fouet – This former coach house has had its habitués, including celebrities as diverse as Graham Greene, Le Corbusier, and Georges Pompidou. Service is fast and friendly, and it's a place to order the daily special. Desserts, such as *charlotte au chocolat,* are marvelous. Arrive early — it closes at 9 PM. Closed Saturday evenings, Sundays, two weeks at Christmas, and the month of August. 45 rue de Babylone (phone: 705-1227). Very expensive.

Le Tourtour – Enter through the 1920s gallery boutique and you're in a cozy room serving a full menu until 2 AM. Specialties include beef with mustard sauce and Berthillon sherberts. 20 rue Quincampoix (phone: 887-8248). Very inexpensive.

Les Noces de Jeannette – Good, simple, hearty four-course meals here include red and white wine. Open daily. 14 rue Favart (phone: 296-3689). Very inexpensive.

La Chaumière – The prices here draw a crowd of regulars, especially at lunch. They keep coming back, so you know it has to be good. Closed Saturday noon and Sundays. 38 rue du Mont-Thabor (phone: 260-7979). Very inexpensive.

Chartier – A huge, turn-of-the-century place with lots of down-to-earth food for the money. 7 rue du Faubourg-Montmartre (phone: 770-8629). Very inexpensive.

Le Jardin de la Mouffe – There's a choice of hors d'oeuvres, entrées, and desserts, plus a cheese course and half a carafe of wine and a pretty garden view. 75 rue Mouffetard (phone: 707-1929). Very inexpensive.

Bistro de la Gare – Michel Oliver offers a choice of three appetizers and three main courses with pommes frites. Excellent for a quick lunch. Open daily. No reservations. 73 Champs-Élysées (phone: 359-6783); 59 blvd. Montparnasse (phone: 548-3801); 30 rue St. Denis (phone: 260-8492); 38 blvd. des Italiens (phone: 246-1574). Very inexpensive.

Assiette au Boeuf – Again Michel Oliver, but this time it's steak, salad, and pommes frites with music in the evening. Open daily. No reservations. 123 Champs-Élysées (phone 720–0113); pl. St.-Germain-des-Près (phone: 260-8844); 103 blvd. Montparnasse (phone: 325-2525); and 22 rue Guillaume-Apollinaire (phone: 260-8844). Very inexpensive.

■**EXTRA SPECIAL:** Although we've noted the existence of *Fauchon* in *Shopping,* we would be remiss in omitting it from the restaurant listings. Actually two spectacular stores stocking elegant edibles, *Fauchon* is considered so much a bastion of the privileged that one of its stores was bombed by radicals in 1978. But both shops are now thankfully back in full working order, which is a blessing for every abdomen in town.

One *Fauchon* shop specializes in the most beautiful fruits and vegetables available anywhere, plus pâtés, terrines, and as many other incomparable carry-out items as even the most jaded gourmet's palate could conceive. If you're planning any sort of picnic, this is the place to pack your hamper.

But it's across the narrow street in the far corner of the place de la Madeleine that all of Paris congregates for nonpareil pastries, coffee, and an occasional snack or drink. Chocolate *opéra* cakes and macaroons in many hues, plus *mille feuilles* and other custardy concoctions, are sold by the slice and can be eaten standing at one of the narrow ledges right in the store. If you need a sugar surge during the course of your Paris meanderings, this is the place to take your high-caloric break.

For chocoholics: The very best hot chocolate in Paris (if not the universe) is served at *Angelina's* on the rue Rivoli. The best chocolate ice cream in the City of Light is at *Berthillon's* on the Île St.-Louis.

PRAGUE

Goethe once called Prague "the most precious stone in the stone crown of the world." The beauty of Prague has remained legendary ever since the Middle Ages. If you want to step back into the twelfth century and experience life in medieval times, you can choose no better country than Czechoslovakia and no better city than its 1,000-year-old capital, Prague.

The historical center of this city is the largest protected area in the world for two reasons. First, Czechoslovakia escaped the heavy bombings of World War II, emerging almost unscathed. Second, Czechoslovaks have a passion for preserving their past, spending more than $30 million annually on the upkeep of the country's 40,000 monuments, its 2,500 castles (500 of which are open to the public), and its 40 preserved towns, of which Prague is the most important.

Located in the western part of Bohemia, Czechoslovakia's westernmost province, Prague is a sumptuous blend of nature and architecture. Like Rome, it is built on seven hills and is divided by a river, the powerful Vltava (called the Moldau in German), which is spanned by 13 bridges. The city, everywhere dotted with parks, waterways, and gardens, overwhelms the first-time visitor with its architecture. As in many European cities and towns, you can see layers of architectural periods and styles — romanesque, Gothic, baroque, classical, and even art nouveau and modern. The Old Town is itself a course in the architecture of the last 500 years.

But Prague is best known for its distinguished examples of the Gothic and baroque styles. Gothic spires are literally everywhere in Prague, particularly in the Old Town, which boasts the Týn Church, 1365, with its Gothic exterior, complete with twin towers and flying buttresses — and typically, a baroque interior — and the inspiring early Gothic Old-New Synagogue — majestically tall, with fluted pillars, pointed arches, and delicate stone embellishments.

If Prague's skyline is dominated by its 500 Gothic towers and spires, some of its most glorious palaces are baroque. The Wallenstein Palace, for example, was built by the Italian architect Andrea Spezza in 1622 — its harmony of art including sculptures, paintings, fountains, gardens, and lighting effects. In an exuberant mood, Bohemia's rich seventeenth-century merchants and nobles invited Italian and German architects — notably the great Kryštof Dienzenhofer — to decorate the capital in magnificent baroque style. The Church of St. Nicholas is only one of his masterpieces, complete with typically baroque features such as great curving forms, painted ceilings, and elaborate decorative effects.

Prague's history can be read not only in its buildings but also on the map of the city. The earliest settlements first recorded in the ninth century were

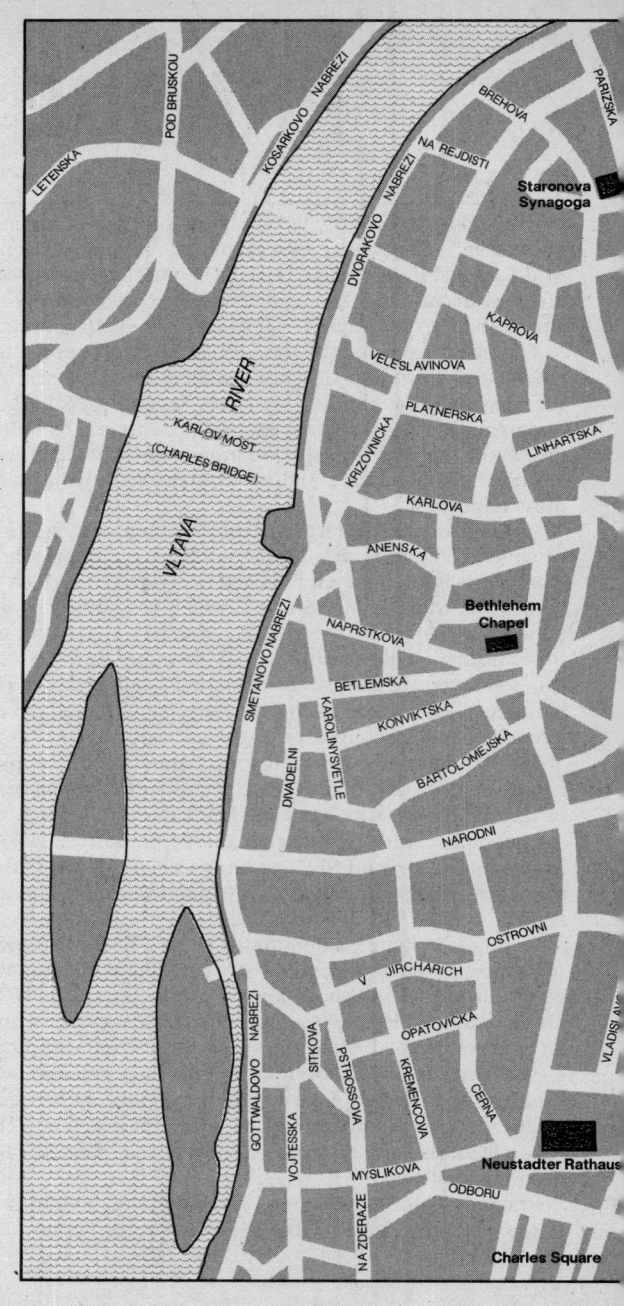

PRAGUE

U MILOSRDNYCH

DUSNI

BILKOVA

KOZ

RASNOVKA

HRADEBNI

KLIMENTSKA

SOUKENICKA

VEZENSKA

OKA

DLOUHA

MASNA

BENEDIKTSKA

REVOLUCNI

TRUHLARSKA

RYBNA

Old Town Square

STUPARTSKA

Altstadter Rathaus

CELETNA

ZELEZNA

Prasna Brana

HYBERNSKA

IAVELSKA

rTIRSKA

NA PRIKOPE

PANSKA

NEKAZANKA

SENOVAZNA

JERUZALEMSKA

RUZOVA

POLITICKYCH

VACLAVSKE NAMESTI (WENCESLAS SQUARE)

JUNGMANNOVA

PALACKEHO

VODICKOVA

V JAME

SKOLSKA

STEPANSKA

VE SMECKACH

KRAKOVSKA

National Museum

VRATILOVA

PHICNA

REZNICKA

ZITNA

at the foot of two ancient castles perched high on the tops of hills — Vysehrad on the right bank of the Vltava and Hradčany on the left; these strongholds later became residences of the Bohemian kings. On the right bank a small settlement then formed a market center, which developed into the Old Town, and on the opposite bank, the Lesser Quarter grew up. Finally, Charles IV founded the New Town near the Old Town during the fourteenth century. The five towns of the city, each retaining its distinct personality, officially became one in 1784.

Prague, first the seat of the Holy Roman Empire, then of the Hapsburgs, was the capital of the kingdom of Bohemia for centuries. Prague came into full glory during the reign of Charles IV (1346–78). Charles, a man of culture and vision, founded New Town, built Charles University, reconstructed Prague Castle in Gothic style, and initiated the construction of St. Vitus Cathedral.

Beginning in 1402, John Huss preached his "fighting words" — advocating the reform of church abuses and the supremacy of Czech national aspirations in the face of German influences — from Prague's Bethlehem Chapel until he was burned at the stake in 1415; his martyrdom triggered the religious Hussite wars. In 1526, when Ferdinand I of Hapsburg became king, the 300-year-long oppression of the Czechs by the Hapsburgs followed. The Hapsburgs tried to reintroduce Catholicism and Germanization by force, an effort that inspired the Czechs to passionate resistance — climaxed by the famous "defenestration" of two Czech Catholic officials: They were literally thrown out of the windows of Hradčany Palace on May 23, 1620.

After 1621, however, Prague declined. Foreign nobles confiscated Czech lands, and Germanization reached its height under Empress Maria Theresa in 1749, when German was made the official language. The Czech national spirit, however oppressed, was never vanquished; by 1918 the Republic of Czechoslovakia was born. Independence was tragically short-lived: Hitler occupied Czechoslovakia from 1939 until 1945, when the Czechs rose up against him and held out bravely until the Russians arrived 4 days later.

Prague is a subtle and complex city, unfolding itself leaf by leaf, and then only to the most observant and curious visitors. To know Prague is to amble through its five sections one at a time, slowly to discover a palace here, a tower there, a decorative touch somewhere else, and now and then to linger at one of its numerous wine cellers and beer halls for refreshment.

Don't look here for the glitter of Paris nightlife or the hurlyburly of London's Piccadilly Circus. Instead, stop, look, and listen to Prague, because the city has much to tell, primarily through the rich blend of its architecture and its lovely natural setting.

This is a city for wanderers, and those who choose to stroll through its cobblestoned streets, gaslit at night, will follow in the footsteps of Mozart, Rilke, and Apollinaire, who lived here, to say nothing of Franz Kafka, who was born here and who resided for a while in Golden Land, the crooked little street where alchemists once practiced their mysterious art. In the words of another lover of Prague, the French poet Paul Valéry, "There is no city in the world in which magnificent wholes and valuable details and corners would be better combined, more happily situated."

PRAGUE AT-A-GLANCE

SEEING THE CITY: To catch the drama of Prague, visit the *Golden Prague Restaurant,* on the eighth floor of the *Prague Inter-Continental Hotel,* for a spectacular view of Prague Castle, particularly beautiful at sunset when the castle is silhouetted in black and the last rays of the sun splash red and gold into the Vltava River. You'll know at once why this city is called Golden Prague.

The restaurant is noted for its international cuisine, which should be accompanied by a glass of Czech wine. The hotel is located at Náměstí Curieových, on the banks of the Vltava.

SPECIAL PLACES: Any exploration should begin with a half-day tour of the city by motorcoach, with bilingual guide, offered by Čedok Overseas (phone: 22-42-59). From then on, put on your walking shoes, and, as we said, take the city, one part at a time.

Historical Prague was originally five independent towns. Each of these five districts — New Town, Old Town, Lesser Town, Hradčany, and Vyšehrad — retains its individual character, virtually undisturbed since the Middle Ages.

NEW TOWN (NOVÉ MĚSTO)

Prague's New Town dates back to 1348, when it was established by King Charles IV. Wenceslas Square, with its profusion of shops, hotels, and restaurants, is the center of the modern city of Prague and a logical starting point for seeing the city.

Wenceslas Square (Václavské náměstí) – Vaclav I ("Good King Wenceslas"), seated on his horse, guards this square, which is more like a boulevard. Dominated by the National Museum, Wenceslas Square is the central thoroughfare of the city, lined with hotels, restaurants, outdoor cafés, and a remarkable array of shops, including the *House of Food* (*Dum Potravin*) and the *House of Fashion* (*Dum Mody*). Two excellent shops for craft items are *Slovenska Izba,* at 40 Wenceslas Square, and *Krasna Jizba,* at Národní Trida 36 (right off the square).

National Museum (Národní muzeum) – The imposing neo-Renaissance facade and the interior decorations of this building express the spirit of late-nineteenth-century Czech nationalism in which it was built. Inside are paintings on Czech historical themes, fossils, stamps, and archaeological items; there is also an extensive musical section containing a great many old instruments. Václavské náměstí 68.

Flek's Inn (U Fleku) – Stop in and see one of Prague's most famous old pubs. No one knows quite how old it is, but it was in existence in 1499. Huge, with music and singing guests, *U Fleku* specializes in dark beer; Flek's 14 is the strongest in Prague. Křemencova 11 (phone: 29-24-36).

U Kalicha – Another famous beer hall, which is disappointingly modern in character, is where the Good Soldier Svejk consumed his Pilsner. Na Bojisti 12 (phone: 29-60-17).

Charles Square (Karlovo náměstí) – Now a park surrounded by old buildings, the New Town's oldest square was the center around which the town was proudly planned by Charles IV in 1348. Charles Square remains Prague's largest square. On the north side is the oldest building in the New Town, the New Town Hall (Novoměstska Radnice), site of its government from 1398 to 1784. On the south side of Charles Square, at number 502/30, is an eighteenth-century baroque building known as Faust's House. Ever since the fourteenth century, houses on this site have been associated with alchemy and other occult practices. (The origin of the Faust legend is uncertain; it is sometimes said to have arisen from the strange adventures of a sixteenth-century English alchemist named Edward Kelley.)

Dvořák Museum – Once a summer residence called Villa Amerika (in the early eighteenth century), this lovely baroque building was designed by the noted architect K. I. Diezenhofer. Fittingly, the building now houses mementos of the Czech composer of the great *New World Symphony* (which uses American folk tunes), Antonín Dvořák. In the sculpture garden in back of the house, Dvořák's music is performed during the summer. Closed Mondays. Ke Karlovu 20, not far from Charles Square.

OLD TOWN (STARÉ MĚSTO)

Walk here just before dusk when gaslamps light the winding, narrow, cobblestoned streets. The Old Town, which contains most of the oldest buildings in Prague, dates back to 1120. A great many medieval exteriors have been preserved in this area.

Powder Tower (Prasna Brana) – This gate to the Old Town, once used to store gunpowder, was first built in 1475, then rebuilt in the late nineteenth century. Here the Czech kings departed for the coronation route long ago. If you climb its 185 steps, the view is delightful. Na Příkopě.

Celetna Street (Celetná ulice) – If you follow this short street from the Powder Tower to Old Town Square, you will pass two historical landmarks. In the Carolinum, a fourteenth-century building that was part of the original university founded by King Charles IV, examinations are still held (Celetna 9). Nearby, at number 11, is the Tyl Theater, where Mozart's *Don Giovanni* had its world première in 1787.

Old Town Square (Staroměstské náměstí) – The center of Prague's Old Town. The statue of John Huss stands in the middle, built in 1915 by Ladislav Saloun. You will not want to miss Prague's great landmark, the astronomical clock built in 1490 on the Old Town Hall, where every hour on the hour crowds gather to see the solemn march of Christ, the 12 apostles, Death, and other allegorical figures. The Town Hall itself was founded in 1338 and rebuilt many times; the many treasures within include a dungeon and a well in the cellar and a fifteenth-century council chamber still used by Prague's city government, decorated by 60 imaginative coats of arms belonging to the guilds of Prague.

On the east side of the square is the Týn Church, dating from 1365, with its twin Gothic spires. Once the property of the Hussites and later of the Jesuits, this beautiful church combines a Gothic exterior with a baroque interior. Tycho Brahe, the Danish astronomer, was buried here in 1601.

Off the square is Na příkopě, a shopping street with dozens of little shops selling glassware and antiques; at *Panorama,* opposite the clock tower, you can find posters and prints — a Czech specialty. And do stop for a Pilsner beer at *U Bindru* next door.

The Jewish Quarter – If you walk north from the Old Town Hall on Pařížská street and turn left on Červená, you will see the Old-New Synagogue (Staronova Synagoga), which is the oldest synagogue in Europe, built in 1270. This building, one of Prague's most beautiful examples of early Gothic, is truly inspiring, with its fluted pillars and sculptural decorations.

Jewish traders founded the Prague ghetto as early as the ninth century, and it became a center of Jewish culture by the seventeenth century. Visit the Old Jewish Cemetery (fifteenth century), with its 12,000 tombstones, several layers deep. In the nearby Klaus Synagogue, U Starého hřbitova 5, is a museum that tells the tragic story of the extinction of most of Czechoslovakia's 90,000 Jews. And in the Pinkas Synagogue, Široká 3, the 77,289 names of Jewish men, women, and children murdered by the Nazis are painted on the interior walls.

Bethlehem Chapel (Betlémská kaple) – At this Gothic chapel on the southern edge of the Old Town near the New Town, John Huss preached his revolutionary ideas from 1402 until his martyrdom in 1415. To the Czechs, Huss has become a symbol of freedom from oppression and is revered as a national hero. Although the old church was reconstructed in this century, it has an air of antiquity about it. The wooden threshold of the pulpit, once trod by Huss himself, is now protected under glass. Betlémské náměstí.

Charles Bridge – One of the oldest and most beautiful bridges in Europe was built of stone in 1357 by Charles IV, between the Old Town and the Lesser Town. It is lined on both sides by fine statues of the baroque period (1683–1714), including one of Charles himself. The Lesser Town end has two towers. The bridge is a favorite strolling place day or night, and it offers views of the castle, the Vltava River, and the lovely island of Kampa with its chestnut trees.

LESSER TOWN (MALÁ STRANA)

Sometimes called Little Town, this is Prague's baroque soul, founded by Charles IV and embellished during the seventeenth and eighteenth centuries by rich foreign (German, Spanish, Italian) merchants and noblemen who engaged some outstanding architects and artists for the purpose. The Lesser Town is the city's most picturesque quarter, full of old palaces — including the magnificent Wallenstein Palace, where concerts are held during the summer. Lesser Town is a maze of little, crooked, cobblestoned lanes full of old churches, museums, inns, wine cellars, and charming little parks. It is best just to wander around the town and discover its nooks and crannies for yourself.

Lesser Town Square (Malostranské náměstí) – Surrounded by sixteenth-century houses with arcades, the square — and the entire Lesser Town — is dominated by the imposing baroque Church of St. Nicholas; another impressive building is the Lichtenstein Palace on the north side.

St. Nicholas's Church (Kostel sv. Mikuláše) – Designed by two famous earlyeighteenth-century architects, Kryštof Dienzenhofer and Anselm Lurago, this is the finest baroque building in Prague. Particularly noteworthy are the dome, the nave, the belfry, and the ceiling frescoes. You can't miss it, right in Lesser Town Square (Malostranské náměstí).

Wallenstein Palace (Valdstejnský palác) – North of St. Nicholas's Church is the magnificent baroque palace built in 1623 by Italian architects for the great Hapsburg general Albrecht Wallenstein. With several buildings, five courtyards, two gardens, and a lake, the palace serves many purposes today: It houses the Ministry of Culture, an exhibition hall for nineteenth-century Czech paintings — and best of all, holds outdoor concerts in gorgeous surroundings, an experience that should not be missed. Valdštenjské náměstí.

Neruda Street (Nerudova ulice) – Leading from the Lesser Town to the castle and lined on both sides by Renaissance and baroque houses is one of the most beautiful streets in the Lesser Town. The Morzini Palace at number 5 houses the Romanian Embassy; the Thun-Hohenstein at number 20 is the Italian Embassy. Many townhouses on this street have preserved the old signs used before numbers were introduced: red eagle, three violins, golden goblet, and other quaint names.

HRADČANY

Near the castle of the same name, which was probably begun in the ninth century, there grew up the Prague town of Hradčany, officially founded in 1320.

Prague Castle (Hradčany) – Today the seat of the government, this castle has been a Slav stronghold, residence of the kings of Bohemia, and the seat of the presidents of the 1918 republic; it is the history of the Czech nation in stone. With three walled and dizzyingly complex courtyards, the castle is best grasped with the help of a Čedok tour (see *Sources and Resources*). Oblong in shape, the three courtyards progress from the medieval to the more modern, each generation adding to the existing structures.

St. Vitus's Cathedral (Katedrala sv. Vita) – Set in the third courtyard of the castle is this mausoleum of the Czech kings and the repository for the Czech crown jewels. (The jewels, however, are rarely shown to the public.)

Golden Lane (Zlatá Ulicka) – Just south of the castle, one of Prague's most charming cobblestoned streets with little houses and shops is famous as the street of alchemists who tried to turn lead into gold. Franz Kafka lived at number 22 in 1917; it is now a bookstore.

Sternberk Palace (Sternberský palác) – Also in the Castle Square is the palace built by Italian architects in the early eighteenth century, which also happens to be the National Gallery. This is one of Europe's leading museums, especially noted for the number and quality of its Gothic paintings (1350–1450). Hradčanské náměstí 15.

Loretto Church – So named because it was built in 1626 on the model of a church in Loretto, Italy, its facade was reconstructed in 1720 by the great K. I. Dienzenhofer. It is famous for the 1694 carillon in its clock tower and for the "Loretto treasure," which is a collection of extremely valuable sixteenth- to eighteenth-century artifacts. Loretánské náměstí.

Strahov Monastery (Strahovský Klášter) – West of the castle, high above the green slopes of Petrin Hill, is a gigantic monastery, which once rivaled the castle itself in magnificence and whose gardens provide a lovely view of Prague. Today it is the Museum of Czech Literature, with a library of more than a million volumes. In the basement is the *Living Wood Wine Cellar (Ozivle Drevo)*, one of Prague's best (see *Eating Out*). Pohorelec.

VYŠEHRAD

High up on cliffs that rise above the Vltava on the side opposite Hradčany, this fortress and the town around it were probably founded in the ninth century. However, no one knows how old Vyšehrad really is; it may be much older.

Vyšehrad Fortress – Walk around the grounds, which include a park, the eleventh-century Rotunda of St. Martin, and the Church of St. Peter and St. Paul.

Vyšehrad Cemetery – When you are in Vysehrad, don't miss the burial place of the country's greats: Antonín Dvorák, Karel Capek, Jan Kubelik, Jan Neruda, and Bedřich Smetana are just a few.

■**EXTRA SPECIAL:** Kutná Hora, 42 miles (67 km) southeast of Prague, is a former silver mining town, which boomed in the thirteenth century when its rich deposits were used to help create the splendor of the Bohemian court. Here coins — including the thaler — were minted by craftsmen imported from Florence. You can see the Vlasky Dvur, a thirteenth-century palace where the craftsmen worked, a fine coin museum, and a church whose vault is lined entirely with human skulls.

If you take Čedok's guided 1-day bus excursion, you can also see Cesky Sternberk, a thirteenth-century castle set on a rocky mountain — and then return to Prague by way of the wooded and hilly Bohemian terrain.

SOURCES AND RESOURCES

For general information, brochures, maps, and tour bookings, contact Čedok Overseas, Na příkopě 18, Prague 1 (phone: 22-42-59). In New York, contact Čedok, Czechoslovak Travel Bureau, 10 E 40th St., New York, NY 10016 (phone: 212-689-9720).

CLIMATE AND CLOTHES: Prague has mild winters and warm summers, with clearly defined spring and autumn seasons. The average winter temperature is 30°F (−1°C); the average summer temperature, 70°F (21°C). Wear comfortable clothes, not too dressy, and good walking shoes.

GETTING AROUND: Bus and Tram – Public transportation is inexpensive and good; for one crown (10 cents) you can buy a ticket at any newsstand or tobacco shop — not on the bus or tram. The ticket is punched once you are aboard. Čedok's half-day motorcoach tour is a good introduction to the city and costs $8.

Metro – Built in the last 3 years in cooperation with the Russians, this is one of the most beautiful subways in the world. There is an entrance at Wenceslas Square.

Taxi – Reasonably priced taxis can be called at major hotels.

Car Rental – At *Pragocar,* Nové Město, Štěpánská 42 (phone: 24-84-85).

 MUSEUMS: In addition to the museums mentioned in *Special Places* are the *Centrum Gallery,* 28 Rijna 6, for Czech applied arts; the *Bedřich Smetana Museum,* Novotneho lavka 1, Staré Město; and the *Bertramka,* Mozartova 169, a seventeenth-century mansion where Mozart stayed, now the Mozart museum.

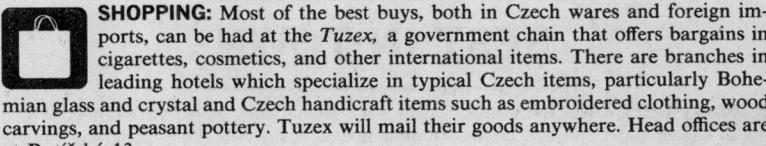 **SHOPPING:** Most of the best buys, both in Czech wares and foreign imports, can be had at the *Tuzex,* a government chain that offers bargains in cigarettes, cosmetics, and other international items. There are branches in leading hotels which specialize in typical Czech items, particularly Bohemian glass and crystal and Czech handicraft items such as embroidered clothing, wood carvings, and peasant pottery. Tuzex will mail their goods anywhere. Head offices are at Rytířská 13.

Bohemian glass and crystal are world famous. Especially recommended is *Moser,* Na příkopě 12. Na příkopě in the Old Town is Prague's shopping street for glassware as well as antiques. Also on Na příkopě opposite the clock tower is *Panorama,* where you can find posters and prints — another Czech specialty.

Czech craft items can be bought in the Wenceslas Square area at *Slovenska Izba,* 40 Wenceslas Square, and *Krasna Jizba,* Národní Trida 36, right off Wenceslas Square. *Note:* In Prague there are a number of black market currency "converters" who offer roughly twice the official exchange rate. However attractive, stay away — if you are caught, the penalty is prison.

 SPECIAL EVENTS: *Prague Spring (Pražské Jaro),* held every May 12 to June 4 since 1946, offers visitors concerts, including internationally known soloists, orchestras, chamber ensembles, and operas. Tickets are about $5. Inquire at Čedok for further information (see above).

 **SPORTS: Mini-Golf** – At the *Hotel International,* Prague 6, Dejvice nam, Druzby 1 (phone: 32-10-51).

    Soccer – You can see games at *Strahov Stadium,* which seats 250,000. Brevnov 100 (phone: 35-55-41).

  Tennis – There are indoor and outdoor courts at Klamovka, Prague 5, Košíře (phone: 52-13-33).

 **THEATER:** Don't miss going to *Laterna Magika,* which is a unique theater experience invented by the Czechs. You don't have to know Czech to enjoy this review, which includes dance, music, and film. The cost is about $3. Národní 40 (phone: 26-00-33). Other theaters include *Smetana Theater,* Vitezneho unora (phone: 26-97-46), and the *Tyl Theater,* Zelezna 11 (phone: 22-32-95).

 MUSIC: Prague is a city that Mozart loved, where *Don Giovanni* had its world première; here Dvořák and Smetana lived and composed their music. Prague is still a very musical city. Concerts can be heard at House of Artists, *Dvořák Hall,* náměstí Krasnoarmejcu (phone: 231-9164); Municipal House,

Smetana Hall, náměstí Republiky 5 (phone: 231-8015); Composers' Club, *Janacek Hall,* Besedni 3 (phone: 53-05-46); and *Theater of Music,* Opletalova 5 (phone: 22-45-37).

During Prague Spring, concerts take place at St. Vitus's Cathedral, Prague Castle; St. James's Cathedral, Mala Stupartska; St. Nicholas's Cathedral, Malostranska n áměstí; and at other historical buildings. For specific information inquire at Čedok (see above).

NIGHTCLUBS AND NIGHTLIFE: Prague is not a big nightclub town, but there are a few interesting after-dark places with live music and dancing. For dancing try *Alfa,* Václavské náměstí 28 (phone: 22-32-20), or *Jalta,* Václavské náměstí 45 (phone: 26-46-79); *Est-Bar,* Washingtonova 19 (phone: 22-25-52) has dancing and entertainment; *International Club,* Náměstí Druzby 1 (phone: 32-10-51), dancing; and *Lucerna,* Vodičkova 36 (phone: 24-61-53), entertainment.

BEST IN TOWN

CHECKING IN: Čedok operates a vast network called Interhotels, which includes most of the best hotels in Czechoslovakia. One intriguing Prague option is called a "boatel" *(boat* plus *hotel),* several of which are anchored in the Vltava River. For all hotels, advanced bookings are highly rely recommended, as there remains a shortage of space in Prague. Interhotels are rated Deluxe, First Class (A), and Second Class (B); our categories of expensive, moderate, and inexpensive are roughly parallel. Expect to pay from $60 to $70 for a double room in an expensive hotel; $40 to $60 for moderate; and $20 to $40 for inexpensive.

Prague Inter-Continental – Built in 1974 in the Old Town, this 11-story modern hotel with 398 rooms is within walking distance of shops and theaters. It offers a superb view of the castle and the Old Town and superb dining at the *Golden Prague* or the *Brasserie.* Náměstí Curievych (phone: 2899). Expensive.

Hotel Alcron – A long-time favorite with journalists and diplomats, the hotel, with 140 rooms and plenty of old-world charm, has a restaurant offering French and Czech specialties and is decorated with crystal chandeliers and rose carpeting. There are two other restaurants, a beer restaurant and a lounge café. Off Wenceslas Square at Stepanska 40 (phone: 24-57-41). Expensive.

Hotel Jalta – On Wenceslas is another favorite place with Americans. Built in 1958, the *Jalta* has 88 rooms, all with their own bath. The food in its French restaurant is excellent, and the *Jalta Club* has live music for dancing. Václavské náměstí 45 (phone: 26-55-41). Expensive.

Interhotel International – Built in 1956, this is a comfortable modern hotel with 13 floors; it is 30 minutes by tram from the center of Prague. Czech murals decorate the lounges and halls. There is a French restaurant, a café, and a night bar. Náměstí Družby 1 (phone: 321-051). Moderate.

Hotel Ambassador – On Wenceslas Square, the *Ambassador* has 115 rooms and a French restaurant, the *Pasaz Café,* and the *Embassy Bar.* This hotel exudes old-world charm, with many of its rooms furnished in Louis XIV style and beautiful Czech crystal chandeliers. Václavské náměstí 5 (phone: 22-13-51). Moderate.

Park Hotel – Modern and a favorite with businesspeople, this hotel has 235 rooms. Built in 1967, its main restaurant seats 140. There is also a café, seating 50, a grill, and an open terrace in summer for dinner. It is about 3 miles from the center of town. Veletržní 20 (phone: 380-7111). Moderate.

Flora Hotel – A good example of a second-class hotel that is clean and a good value. The rooms have toilets and baths. This 209-room hotel, with an attractive lobby and a very pleasant wine restaurant, is 15 minutes from downtown by tram. Vinohradská 121 (phone: 27-42-50). Inexpensive.

Hotel Palace – Situated in the center of town, it has 136 rooms, its own money-exchange office, and a shop for souvenirs. Its French restaurant and café are moderately priced and the *Poultry Grill* is inexpensive. Panská 12 (phone: 26-83-41). Inexpensive.

Note: Three boatels (built as hotels) are anchored in the Vltava River, with staterooms and bars — all are shipshape, lots of fun, and inexpensive. Each of them has about 80 rooms that are charming, though understandably somewhat cramped. They are: *Admiral,* Hořejší nábřeží (phone: 54-86-85); *Albatross,* Nábřeží L. Svobody (phone: 231-3634); and *Racek,* Dvorecká louka (phone: 42-60-51). All are inexpensive.

EATING OUT: Prague has thousands of eating places — outdoor cafés, wine cellars, pubs, and international restaurants. Most require advance reservations; most are reasonable in price and accept major credit cards. Czech cuisine — influenced by German, Hungarian, and Slav styles — is hearty but good. Specialties include *knedliky* (dumplings), both plain and filled with fruit or meat; baked pork with sauerkraut; *svickova,* a beef marinated in spicy cream sauce; *uzene,* or smoked pork with potato dumplings and spinach; and *placky,* or potato pancakes.

Wines from southern Moravia are the best; sample Tri Gracie in red, rosé, or white. For moderate to inexpensive eating, try the beer halls *(pivnice)* and wine cellars *(vinárny)* all over town.

The following is a small selection of restaurants. Prices are quite reasonable; we have rated a dinner for two at $30 and up as expensive; $20 to $30 as moderate; and $10 to $20 as inexpensive.

Opera Grill – All agree that this is Prague's finest restaurant — a small, intimate, parlor-style place with comfortable stuffed chairs, round tables, candelight, and a pianist. The food is excellent, and so is the wine cellar. After dinner, a specialty is brandy served in giant crystal snifters. Reservations are a must, since there are only 25 seats. Divadelní 24, in the Old Town (phone: 26-55-08). Expensive.

Golden Prague (Zlatá Praha) – The eighth-floor restaurant in the *Prague Inter-Continental* has international cuisine as well as Czech specialties, including one of the best roast duck, sauerkraut, and dumplings dinners in town (a national favorite). There is a marvelous view of the castle. Náměstí Curieových (phone: 2899). Expensive.

Ozivle Drevo (The Living Wood) – Romantically situated in the basement of the Strahov Monastery, this wine restaurant serves international cuisine. See the fantastic view from the garden in front. Reservations necessary. Strahovske Nadvori (phone: 53-18-79). Expensive.

Chinese Restaurant (Cínská Restaurace) – Run by a Czech, this place has some of the best Chinese food anywhere and a decor that is authentically Oriental. There are intimate booths for quiet dining. Vodičkova 19 (phone: 26-26-97). Expensive.

The Swan (U Labuti) – This wine restaurant offers Czech specialties and atmosphere, with its old-fashioned nooks, vaulted ceilings, and window casings dating to the fourteenth century. Hradčanské náměstí (phone: 53-94-76). Expensive.

Brussels/Praha Restaurant – Winner of the 1958 Brussels World's Fair medal, this restaurant, in Lesser Town on the other side of the Charles Bridge, offers diners a splendid view of the Vltava River and of the city. The food is excellent, particularly the pastries, which are a house specialty. Letenské sady (phone: 37-45-46). Moderate.

The Green Frog (U Zelene zaby) – A favorite wine cellar with Americans, this place, more than eight centuries old, was reconstructed in 1965 to preserve the Gothic, Renaissance, and baroque styles. The house specialty is grilled meat with sauerkraut. U Radnice 8 (phone: 26-28-15). Moderate.

The Golden Deer (U Zlateho Jelena) – This is a small, intimate wine cellar with vaulted ceilings, tile floors, and wooden tables. Celetná 11 (phone: 26-85-95). Moderate.

Restaurant Vikarka – In the shadow of St. Vitus's Cathedral at Prague Castle, this small pub originally prepared meals only for church dignitaries. Now it is a favorite with Czechs and visitors. The restaurant specialty is called Bishop's Hat, a veal and cheese dish. Vikarska 6 (phone: 53-51-50). Moderate.

Golden Snake (Zlaty Had) – Near the Charles Bridge in the Old Town, the *Golden Snake*, Prague's oldest café, serves good meals and wine. Coffee was made here in the seventeenth century by a Turk, and it's still a good place to have coffee, Turkish, Viennese, or Irish, along with little Prague cakes. Karlova 18. Moderate.

U Fleku – Prague's most famous pub, the one to visit if you can only see one. It is huge, with sawdust on the floors and waiters balancing huge silver trays loaded with dark beer. There is also a Czech band and group singing. In summer, guests can eat in an outdoor garden. Křemencova 11 (phone: 29-24-36). Inexpensive.

U Sv. Tomase – Prague's oldest beer hall is huge, with vaulted ceilings. Populated by young students, the place offers plain wooden tables and huge steins of beer. The best dish is pork, sauerkraut, and dumplings. Letenská 12 (phone: 53-00-64). Inexpensive.

At the Town Hall (U Radnice) – Under the arcades of the southeast side of the square, this typical beer cellar caters to businesspeople who meet here at lunch and dinner. It serves one of the best duck dinners in town. Malé náměstí 2 (phone: 26-28-22). Inexpensive.

The Chalice (U Kalicha) – Here the Good Soldier Svejk consumed his Pilsners. Not too much atmosphere, but there are paintings of the Good Soldier on the walls. Na bojišti 12 (phone: 29-60-17). Inexpensive.

ROME

If you're traveling from the north, you'll quickly understand why *Italia meridionale,* or southern Italy, begins in Rome: ancient stone ruins basking in the southern sun, baroque swirls teasing the senses at every turn, religious art exploding with color and Catholic sensuality — celebrating life with the conspicuous joie de vivre of southern Europe. Rome reaches out to your senses, blinding you with colors, beckoning you to stay. Rome's appeal is gripping and obviously romantic, inspiring throughout history many an illustrious northern visitor — such as Goethe, Keats, Byron, and Shelley — though today these romantic souls might be repelled by the insufferable noise, the screaming traffic, the exasperating strikes, political demonstrations, and general chaos of modern Rome. Yet despite the familiar symptoms of contemporary blight, Rome remains the Eternal City, ancient capital of the Western World, and center of Christianity for nearly 2,000 years.

Rome lies roughly in the center of the region of Latium, just below the knee of boot-shaped Italy, between the Tyrrhenian Sea to the west and the Apennine Mountains to the east. The Tiber River gently curves through the city, with ancient Rome on its left bank, the Vatican City and Trastevere (*tras* means across; *tevere,* Tiber) on its right. The original seven hills of Rome are all on the left bank, as is its modern center — the shopping areas that surround the piazza di Spagna (the so-called Spanish Steps), piazza del Popolo, via del Corso, via del Tritone, and the legendary via Veneto zone, celebrated in Fellini's film *La Dolce Vita.*

The ancient Aurelian Wall, dating from the third century, still surrounds ancient Rome as well as most of papal and modern Rome. The city is unique because its fine buildings span so many centuries of history. There are ancient Roman remains, the most famous of which are the Colosseum and the Forum; the buildings from the early Christian period such as the Castel Sant'Angelo; and a wealth of dazzling Renaissance and baroque architecture — from St. Peter's itself to the piazza del Campidoglio designed by Michelangelo. The city abounds in churches, palaces, parks, squares, statues, and fountains — all of which sparkle in the golden light and clear blue sky of the region.

Even Rome's beginnings are shrouded in a romantic legend that attributes the city's birth to Romulus and Remus, twin sons of the war god Mars and Rhea, a Vestal Virgin, who encountered Mars in a forest one day. The babies, left to die on the shore of the Tiber River at the foot of the Palatine Hill, were rescued and suckled through infancy by an old she-wolf and grew up to lead a band of adventurers and outlaws. Romulus, the stronger leader of the two, is said to have founded Rome in 753 BC, killing his brother to become its first king.

The traditional founding date of 753 BC more likely refers not to the first

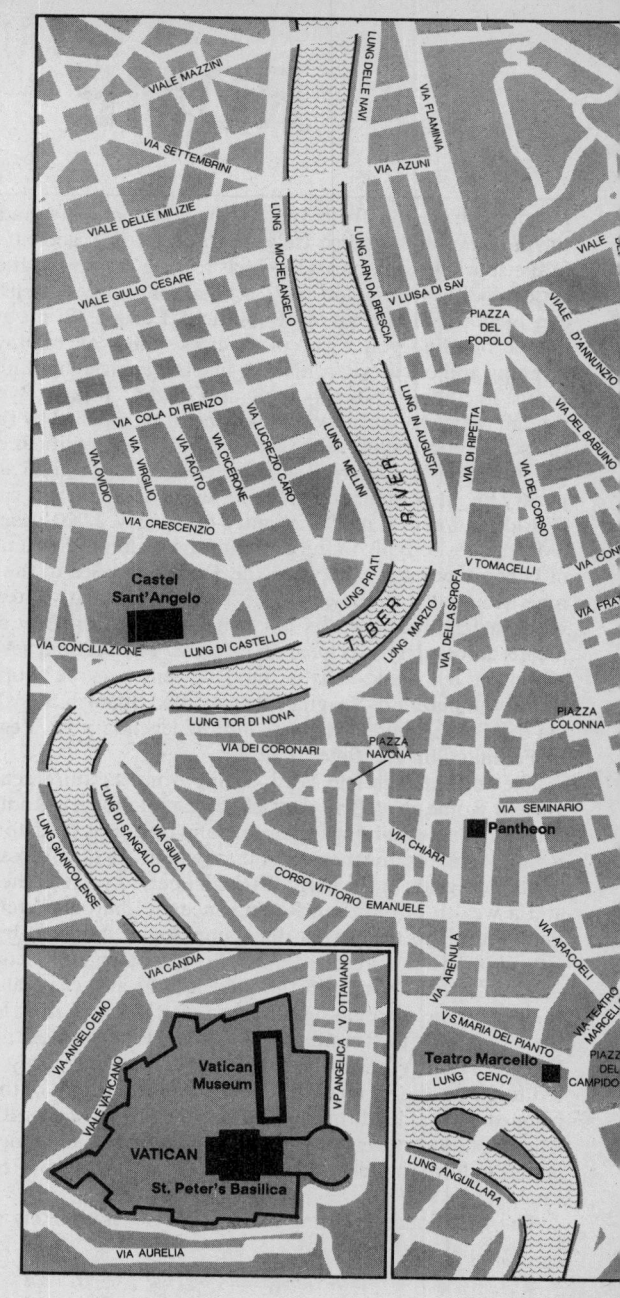

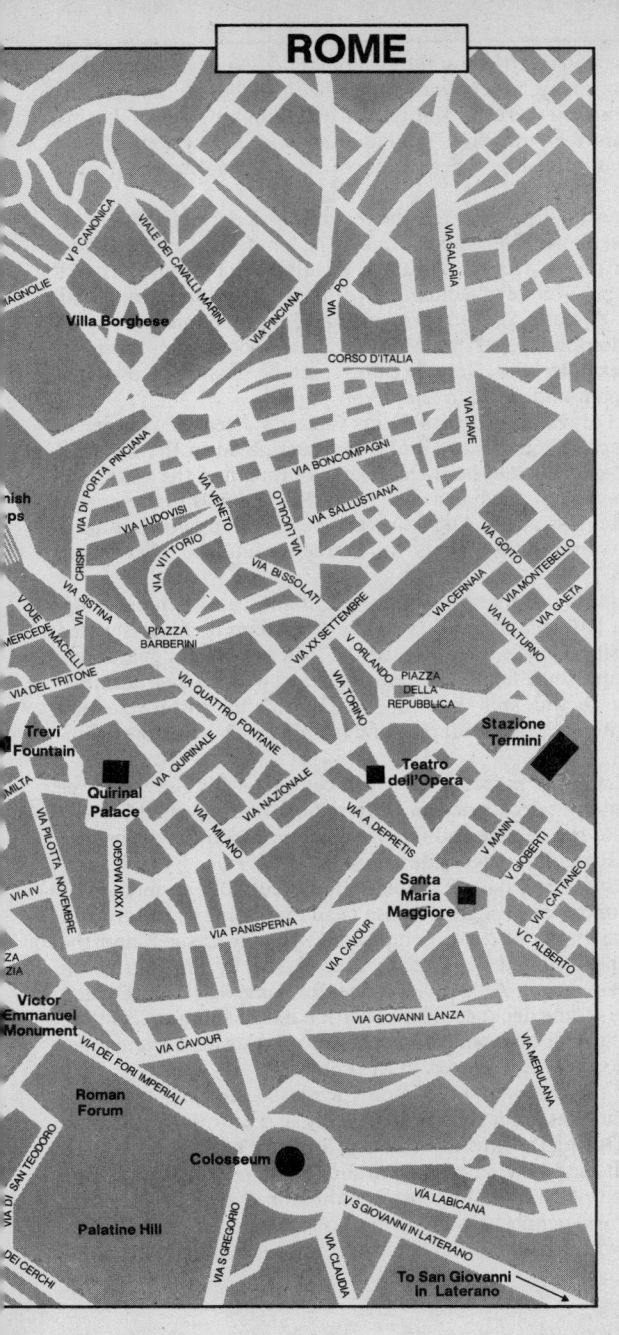

ROME

shepherds and farmers who settled on the Palatine Hill — one of the original seven hills, which are today largely undistinguishable — but to the first city aspects that were formed there by the fusion of various nuclei of Latins, Sabines, and Etruscans who inhabited the Palatine under one system of laws. The name *Roma* was probably a derivation of *Ruma,* an Etruscan noble name.

Following a succession of seven kings, the republic was declared in 509 BC, thus beginning the expansion of Rome. By 270 BC or so, the entire Italian peninsula was under the protection of Rome, resulting in a cultural as well as political unification — a new Roman style in art and literature. With Hannibal's defeat at Zama in 201 BC, bringing the Second Punic War to an end, Rome gained dominion over the Mediterranean, soon establishing its supremacy over Alexander the Great's empire in the East and over the semibarbarians of Spain and Gaul in the West.

A long period of civil war ended with Julius Caesar's defeat of Pompey in 48 BC, but the brilliant conqueror of Gaul was assassinated in the Senate 4 years later. His great-nephew and heir, Octavian, continued in the victorious vein, becoming, with the honorific name of Augustus, Rome's first emperor and one of its best administrators. Augustus constructed many fine buildings that survive today, including the Theater of Marcellus and the Mausoleum of Augustus.

Wherever they went, the Romans introduced brilliant feats of engineering, architecture, culture, government, and law. The Christians were persecuted until 313, when Constantine the Great issued the Edict of Milan, guaranteeing freedom of worship. Rome finally became top heavy with its own administration, and the empire was split in two in 395, with an eastern section established in Byzantium (Constantinople, now Istanbul). This was the beginning of the end.

Rome's grandeur had long passed by the fifth century, which saw a series of economic crises, internal decadence and corruption, and repeated barbarian invasions leading to the decline and fall of the empire with the deposition of her last emperor, Romulus Augustulus, in 476.

Thus began the Dark Ages, out of which Rome eventually reemerged as a papal state, united under one religion whose head and home today are still the pope and Rome. Struggles between empire and papacy ensued, and the Holy See, under Pope Clement V, actually fled Rome in the fourteenth century, taking up residence in Avignon, France, for some 70 years. During that period, the city of Rome declined, its population diminishing to less than 50,000. The Capitoline Hill and once-bustling Roman Forum became pastures for goats and cows. Sheep grazed in St. Peter's.

With the return of the popes in 1377, Rome again became the capital of the Catholic world and was soon reborn artistically and culturally with the Italian Renaissance. During the fifteenth century, St. Peter's was restored, the Vatican complex built, and new palaces, churches, and well-laid-out streets changed the face of the city. Powerful popes commissioned artists to beautify Rome, their architectural genius creating sumptuous palaces, splendid villas, and squares adorned with fountains and obelisks, until a second city grew out of the ruins of ancient Rome, matching its former splendor. The seventeenth century brought the birth of baroque Rome, with its dominating figure, architect, sculptor, and painter Gian Lorenzo Bernini, whose masterpieces perhaps still best symbolize the spirit of this magnificent and undeniably theatrical city.

The comfortable security of the popes was shaken by the arrival of Napoleon Bonaparte in 1798. He soon set up a republic of Rome, deporting Pope Pius VI briefly to France, and in 1805 he was crowned king of Italy, proclaiming Rome a sort of second capital of the French Empire. The French were subsequently excommunicated by Pope Pius VII, who was deported to Fontainebleau until the papal kingdom was later reconciled with France. The Napoleonic regime staggered and finally collapsed, but the sparks of nationalistic passion had already been ignited in Italian hearts.

Friction between papal neutralism and patriotic fervor drove the pope out of Rome to Gaeta in 1848. In 1849, Rome was again proclaimed a republic under patriot Giuseppe Mazzini. Twice the French tried to restore the temporal power of the pope in Rome, meeting strong resistance from the Republicans, led by Garibaldi. Finally, in 1870, the Italians entered Rome through the breach in the Porta Pia and incorporated the city into the kingdom of Italy, dissolving the pontifical state and making Italian unity complete. Rome again became the capital of the kingdom.

Mussolini's march on Rome in 1922 began the infamous Fascist regime that lasted until his downfall some 20 years later. The city was then occupied by the Germans until its liberation in 1944 by the Allies. In 1946, a referendum was held, and Italy was declared a republic again — just as it had been nearly 2½ millennia earlier!

Today Rome is still the capital of Italy and of the Catholic Church as well as home to about four million people (up from 260,000 inhabitants in 1870). Many Romans are employed in tourism and in government offices — in a city often strangled by bureaucratic problems. Aside from film making (in its cinematographic heyday, Rome was called "Hollywood on the Tiber") and a certain amount of printing as well as a small production of foodstuffs, pharmaceutical products, and handmade goods, there is no real industry to speak of in Rome.

Yet, for a society with significant problems — double-digit inflation, insufficient housing, impossible traffic — the Romans of today still enjoy a relaxed way of life, as they have done for centuries. Perhaps nowhere north of Naples is the *arte di arrangiarsi* — the art of making do or surviving with style — learned with such skill and practiced with such a timeless sense of resignation.

La dolce vita nightlife, more a figment of Fellini's imagination than a reality for any more than a handful of rich and/or famous Romans, has become somewhat subdued, but the average Roman today enjoys the same sweet life he always has. Despite the country's pressing problems, an air of conviviality pervades.

Three-hour lunches are still an essential part of life, and a sunny day at any time of the year fills the cobblestoned squares with diners at open-air *trattorie*.

You'll see them involved in animated conversation over their robust Roman food and inexpensive carafe wine from the *castelli* (the surrounding hill towns such as Frascati). Most visitors to this city are pleased to "do as the Romans do." No sense worrying about the city's crushing debts if her inhabitants don't. And even with many of its museums and ruins half shut because of lack of custodians, there is still more than enough to satisfy the most enthusiastic tourist.

Roma, Non Basta Una Vita (Rome, A Lifetime Is Not Enough) is the title of a book by Silvio Negro, the late Italian author and journalist, which hints, with justification, at the impossibility of ever knowing everything about this city. For visitors who harbor the illusion of having seen all the ruins, churches, and monuments of Rome's glorious past, it may be time to begin discovering her countless hidden treasures, best done by walking the back streets and alleyways of the historical center (which is now, for the most part, a "pedestrian island").

If you feel suffocated by city life, try a day or two in the neighboring countryside. The surrounding Latium (Lazio) region, sandwiched between the Tyrrhenian Sea and the Apennine Mountains, offers seaside resorts, rolling hills topped by medieval towns, picturesque lakes, rivers and green meadows studded with umbrella pines, cypress trees, and wild flowers. Organized excursions are available to Tivoli's Villa d'Este and Hadrian's Villa; to the Castelli Romani, or Roman hill towns, where the pope has his summer home; and to the excavations of Ostia Antica, the ancient port of Rome.

But take time to sit back and enjoy Rome. Visit the Forum and the Colosseum by day, and return at night to meditate over the rise and fall of ancient Rome when the ruins are bathed in gentler light. Watch the playing of the Trevi or any of Rome's 300 fountains of every size and shape. See the ancient Roman Theater of Marcellus, which has been a Roman amphitheater, a medieval fort, a Renaissance palace, and which now contains apartments. Enjoy the superb cooking of the Latium region. Ride a bicycle or jog in the Borghese Gardens. Sip an *aperitivo* on the famed via Veneto.

Locally it is believed that on the last day of the world, while all mankind broods and repents, the Romans will throw a great farewell party, a gastronomic feast to end all, with wine flowing from the city's many fountains. With the apocalypse not yet at hand, and despite the agonies besetting the country at large, the Eternal City remains eternally inviting.

ROME AT-A-GLANCE

SEEING THE CITY: You can enjoy a magnificent view of all of Rome and the surrounding hill towns from piazzale Garibaldi at the top of Janiculum hill. It's best at sunset. From a terrace on the Pincio Hill in the Borghese Gardens, above the piazza del Popolo, there's a panoramic view of Rome dominated by St. Peter's. And the most unusual view is of the dome of St. Peter's, seen in miniature through the keyhole of the gate to the priory of the Knights of Malta on the Piazza dei Cavalieri di Malta at the end of via S. Sabina, on the Aventine hill. The picturesque piazza was designed by engraver Piranesi, a surrealist in spirit though he lived in the eighteenth century.

 SPECIAL PLACES: Rome cannot be seen in a day, 3 days, a week, or even a year. If your time is limited to a few days, you'd best get a general idea of the city by taking an organized bus tour or two, get a feel of where your interests mostly lie, then grab your most comfortable walking shoes, adventurous spirit, and map of the city. Most of historical Rome, which is also the city's center today, is within the third-century Aurelian Walls and is delightfully walkable.

For practical purposes, we have divided our "must sees" into ancient, papal, and modern Rome, but elements of two or all three categories are often found in one site — such as a sleek modern furniture shop in a Renaissance palace built with stones from the Colosseum.

Opening and closing hours of archaeological sites and museums change often (some closing indefinitely because of personnel strikes or restorations), so check with your hotel before starting out. Where possible, we have listed hours that seem relatively reliable.

Warning: Although the terrible crime wave of a few years ago has subsided, one must still be aware of pickpockets all around the city of Rome; they are especially numerous at tourist spots.

ANCIENT ROME

The ancient center of the city is very close to the piazza Venezia, the heart of the modern city. Most of the sights of ancient Rome are around the Capitoline, Palatine, and Aventine hills and can be seen on foot — though of course they were not built — in one day. You might choose to linger a bit and soak it all in.

Colosseum – It's said that when the Colosseum falls, Rome will fall — and the world will follow. This symbol of the eternity of Rome, the grandest and most celebrated of all its monuments, is a logical starting point for a visitor to ancient Rome. See it in daylight, and return to see it by moonlight. The enormous arena, a third of a mile in circumference and 137 feet high, once accommodated some 55,000 spectators. In order to provide shade in the summer, a special detachment of sailors manipulated a great silk awning stretched over the top. There were 76 numbered entrances, marble seats, and subterranean passages to the Caelian, where animals and other apparatus were hidden from view. Here Christians were thrown to lions, wild beasts destroyed one another, and gladiators fought to the death. Gladiatorial combats lasted until 404, when Onorius put an end to them (perhaps after the monk Telemaco threw himself into the arena in protest and was killed by the angry crowd); animal combats were stopped toward the middle of the sixth century.

The Colosseum was abused by later generations. It was a fort in the Middle Ages; its marble and travertine were used to build St. Peter's and other buildings during the Renaissance; and in the eighteenth century it even became a manure depot for the production of saltpeter. Yet the Colosseum remains a symbol of the grandeur of Rome. Piazzale del Colosseo.

Palatine Hill – A twelfth-century author called this spot the "palace of the Monarchy of the Earth, wherein is the capital seat of the whole world." Its Latin name is the source of the word *palace,* and on this regal hill lived great rulers and great men: Cicero, Mark Anthony, Augustus, Crassus, Nero. In ruins during the Middle Ages, the ancient structures were incorporated into the sumptuous Villa Farnese in the sixteenth century. The Farnese Gardens were the first botanical gardens in the world.

Adjacent to the Colosseum and the Forum, the Palatine is a lovely spot for a walk or a picnic. See especially the House of Livia (actually of her husband, Augustus), with its remarkable frescoes; Domitian's Palace of the Flavians, built by his favorite architect Rabirius; the impressive stadium; the view from the terrace of the Palace of Septimius Severus; and the remains of the Farnese Gardens at the top with another superb panorama of the nearby Forums. Enter at the Via di S. Gregoria or by way of the Forum on the Via dei Fori Imperiali.

Forum (Foro Romano) – Adjoining the Palatine Hill is the Roman Forum, a mass of ruins overgrown with weeds and trees. Here stood several large ceremonial buildings, including three triumphal arches, two public halls, half a dozen temples, the house of the Vestal Virgins, and numerous monuments and statues. This was the commercial, civil, and religious center of ancient Rome. Set in what was once a marshy valley at the foot of the Capitoline Hill, the Forum was abandoned after the barbarian invasions and had become a cattle pasture by the Renaissance. When excavations began during the last century, it was under 20 feet of dirt.

As this is one of the most bewildering of archaeological sites, a guide is extremely useful, especially for short-term visitors. A detailed plan and portable sound guide are available at the entrance.

Highlights of the Forum include the triumphal Arch of Septimus Severus, built by that emperor in AD 203; the Arch of Titus (AD 81), adorned with scenes depicting the victories of Titus, especially his conquest of Jerusalem and the spoils of Solomon's Temple; the ten magnificent marble columns — with a sixteenth-century baroque facade — of the Temple of Antoninus and Faustina; the eight columns of the Temple of Saturn (497 BC), site of the Saturnalia, the precursor of our Mardi Gras; three splendid Corinthian columns from the Temple of Castor and Pollux (484 BC); the Temple of the Vestal Virgins, in which highly esteemed virgins guarded the sacred flame of Vesta, and their virginity — under the threat of being buried alive if they lost their virginity.

Enter the Forum at the via dei Fori Imperiali, opposite the via Cavour. Closed Tuesdays.

Imperial Forums (Fori Imperiali) – Opposite the Forum on the via dei Fori Imperiali is the civic center started by Caesar to meet the demands of the expanding city when the Roman Forum became too congested. It was completed by Augustus, with further additions by later emperors. Abandoned in the Middle Ages, the Imperial Forums were revived by Mussolini, who constructed the via dei Fori Imperiali in 1932.

Two of the major sights here are Trajan's Forum and Markets and the Basilica of St. Maxentius. Trajan's Forum is memorable for its formidable 138-foot-high Trajan's Column, composed of 19 blocks of marble; reliefs on the column show the Roman army under Trajan during the campaigns in Dacia, with some 2,500 figures climbing up the column, which was topped in 1588 by a statue of St. Peter. The Markets are a three-story construction with about 150 shops and commercial exchanges. The once-imposing Basilica of St. Maxentius still has imposing proportions: 328 feet by 249 feet. Only the north aisle and three huge arches remain, but this site, once a law court and exchange, is now used for open-air concerts during the summer. Closed Mondays. Via dei Fori Imperiali.

Mamertine Prison – Just off the via dei Fori Imperiali between the Forum and the Capitol is the prison where St. Peter was imprisoned by Nero; here he used a miraculous spring to baptize his fellow inmates. The prison is now a chapel consecrated to St. Peter (it's called San Pietro in Carcere), but the gloomy dungeons below, made of enormous blocks of stone, may be the oldest structures in Rome. It was a prison from 509 to 27 BC. Charles Dickens described it as a "ponderous, obdurate old prison . . . hideous and fearsome to behold." Many were tortured and slaughtered here. Via San Pietro in Carcere off the via dei Fori Imperiali.

Pantheon – This is the best-preserved Roman building, with balanced proportions (the height and the diameter of the interior are the same) and a stately dome. Its rectangular porch has 16 Corinthian columns, 3 of which were replaced during the

Renaissance. Seven niches inside — now altars — were probably once dedicated to the seven planetary divinities. Founded by Agrippa in 27 BC and rebuilt in AD 125, it became a Christian church in 606 and contains the tombs of Raphael and the kings of Italy. Piazza della Rotonda.

Appian Way (Via Appia Antica) – Portions of this famous 2,300-year-old road leading to ancient Rome are still paved with the well-laid stones of the Romans. By 190 BC the Appian Way extended to Brindisi, on Italy's southeastern coast. The first 10 miles were lined with graves of patrician Roman families, because Roman law did not allow them to be buried in the city. Though many interesting ruins are scattered along the Appian Way, the road is difficult to navigate on foot because of heavy modern traffic. Its most famous sights are the Baths of Caracalla and the Catacombs (see below). Also on the via Appia are the Tomb of Cecilia Metella, daughter of a Roman general; a fourth-century stadium called the Circus of Maxentius; and the Domine Quo Vadis chapel, built in the mid-ninth century on the site where St. Peter, fleeing from Nero, had a vision of Christ. St. Peter said "Domine quo vadis?" ("Lord, whither goest thou?") Christ replied that he was heading back to Rome to be crucified again because Peter had abandoned the Christians in a moment of danger. Peter then returned to Rome to face his own martyrdom.

Catacombs of St. Calixtus – Although these most famous of the catacombs belong to Christian Rome, they date back to the days of ancient Rome. Catacombs are underground burial places, often arranged in up to five tiers. Marble or terracotta slabs mark the openings where bodies of early Christians — many of whom were martyrs — were laid to rest. Here are buried St. Cecilia, St. Eusebius, and many martyred popes. Early Christians prayed and hid underground in the catacombs. On the via Appia, the catacombs are closed Wednesdays. Take a public bus or guided bus tour. At the catacombs, guides, who are often priests, conduct regular tours in several languages and expect a nominal "offering" at the end. 110 via Appia Antica.

Baths of Caracalla (Terme di Caracalla) – In the southern part of the city, near where the Appian Way begins, are the Baths of Caracalla. The vast scale of these baths built in the third century is impressive; they make a picturesque ruin. The baths accommodated 1,600 bathers, and all that's left are sun-baked walls and some wall paintings. Here Shelley composed his famous *Prometheus Unbound*. In the summer, operas are performed here. The baths are closed Mondays. Enter on the via delle Terme di Caracalla, just short of the piazzale Numa Pompilio.

Baths of Diocletian – West of the center of Rome are the largest baths in the empire, made for 3,000 people in AD 305. The site now houses the Church of Santa Maria degli Angeli, designed by Michelangelo, and the National Museum of Rome. But first visit the baths themselves — eleven rooms full of sarcophagi and other relics. Closed Mondays. Enter from via delle Terme di Diocleziano.

National Museum of Rome (Museo Nazionale Romano) – At the Baths of Diocletian is one of the great archaeological museums of the world, containing numerous objects from ancient Rome — paintings, statuary, stucco work, bronzes, objects of art, and even a recently discovered mummy of a young girl. The museum itself was designed by Michelangelo. Closed Mondays. Via delle Terme di Diocleziano.

Castel Sant'Angelo – Dramatically facing the second-century Ponte Sant'Angelo (St. Angelo Bridge — lined with statues of angels by Bernini), this imposing fortress was built by Hadrian in AD 139 as a burial place for himself and his family. It was later converted into a fortress by popes who took refuge there from antipapal forces. The circular Castel Sant'Angelo is surrounded by a square wall with bastions at each corner named after the four evangelists. It is now a museum containing historical relics, works of art, ancient weapons, and a prison. Closed Mondays. Lungotevere Castello.

Theater of Marcellus (13 BC) – Begun by Caesar, completed by Augustus, and named after the latter's nephew, this was the first stone theater in Rome and was said to be the model for the Colosseum. It seated from 10,000 to 14,000 spectators and was in use for over 300 years. During the Middle Ages the edifice became a private fortress of the powerful Orsini family who, in the early sixteenth century, built the present palace over the stage area and part of the audience section. The sumptuous apartments at the top are still inhabited by the Orsinis. Their device of a bear (*orso*) appears on the gateway in the via di Monte Savello, where the theater's stage formerly stood. Via del Teatro di Marcello. The palace can be visited only with a permit from the City Hall: Comune di Roma, Ripartizione X, Via del Portico d'Ottavia, 29.

Pyramid of Caius Cestius – At the piazza San Paolo in the southern section of the city, near the Protestant Cemetery, is Rome's only pyramid. Completely covered with white marble, 121 feet high, it has a burial chamber inside which is decorated with frescoes and inscriptions. Piazza San Paolo.

Largo Argentina – Just west of the piazza di Venezia are the remains of four Roman temples, which, still unidentified, may be the oldest relics in Rome. The area is also home to Rome's largest stray cat colony. Corso Vittorio Emanuele.

PAPAL ROME

Much of papal Rome is centered in the Vatican, but all of Rome is a religious center; it's a city of many fascinating and beautiful churches, a few of which are listed below. (For other churches see Museums, *Sources and Resources.*)

Vatican City – The Vatican City State, the world's second smallest country (the smallest is also in Rome, on via Condotti), is contained in a land area of less than one square mile within the city of Rome. Headquarters of the Roman Catholic Church, the Vatican has been an independent state under the sovereignty of the pope since the Lateran Treaties were concluded in 1929. The Vatican has its own post office and postage stamps (thriving right now with the surrounding Italian post offices functioning so badly — do all your mailing from here!), its own printing press and newspaper *(Osservatore Romano),* its own currency, railway, and radio station. Its extraterritorial rights cover the other major basilicas, the pope's summer home at Castel Gandolfo, and a few other buildings. The Vatican is governed politically by the pope and protected by an army of Swiss Guards whose uniforms were designed by Michelangelo.

General audiences are held by the pope every Wednesday at 11 AM year-round on St. Peter's Square; special audiences can be arranged for groups of 25 to 50 persons.

St. Peter's Square (Piazza San Pietro) – This seventeenth-century architectural masterpiece was created by Bernini, the originator of the baroque style. The vast, open area is elliptical in shape, with two semicircles of Doric columns framing the facade of St. Peter's Basilica. The colonnades are lined with statues of saints. An 83.5-foot obelisk, which was brought to Rome by Caligula, marks the center of the square. It is flanked by two fountains by Maderno and Bernini.

St. Peter's Basilica – Constructed over the first church, which was built by Constantine on the site of Nero's circus, where St. Peter was martyred and later buried, the present seventeenth-century basilica is the jewel of artists such as Bramante, Raphael, Michelangelo, Della Porta, and Maderno. Michelangelo's vast dome is visible from everywhere in the city, just as the entire city is visible from the summit of the dome. You can go up into the dome by an elevator for a fee — then take a staircase to the top for a panoramic view of the Vatican City and of Rome.

Among the treasures and masterpieces the basilica contains are the famous *Pietà* by Michelangelo (now encased in bullet proof glass since its mutilation and restoration several years ago) and the *Baldacchino* by Bernini, weighing over 46 tons (a colossal baroque amalgam of architecture and decorative sculpture), as well as the thirteenth-century statue of St. Peter by Di Cambio, his toes kissed smooth by the faithful. The interior of St. Peter's is gigantic, but so overloaded with decoration that it takes some time to get a sense of the whole. Piazza San Pietro, Vatican City.

Vatican Museums – One of the most impressive collections in the world, the Vatican contains works of art of every epoch. It includes the extraordinary Sistine Chapel, with Michelangelo's ceiling representing the Creation and his wall painting of the Last Judgment (currently undergoing an extensive restoration that will last about 12 years); the magnificent Raphael Rooms commissioned by Pope Julius II when the artist was only 25 years old; the Pio-Clementino Museum of Greco-Roman antiquities, housing such marvelous statues as *Laocöon and his Sons* and the *Apollo Belvedere;* the Pinacoteca or Picture Gallery; the Library; and the new Gregoriano, Pio Cristiano, and Missionary-Ethnological sectors. There's an admission fee. The museum is closed Sundays. North of St. Peter's on viale Vaticano.

Church of St. John Lateran and the Holy Stairs (San Giovanni in Laterano and Scala Santa) – Founded by Pope Melchiades in the fourth century, this was the church of the popes until 1307. It stands on a large esplanade near the Scala Santa (the Holy Steps), the principal ceremonial staircase of the old papacy, traditionally believed to have come from the palace of Pontius Pilate in Jerusalem. Christ is believed to have ascended these stairs at the time of the Passion. The 28 marble steps may be climbed only by worshipers on their knees. The church itself is known as the "Cathedral of Rome and of the world" and contains an interesting baptistry and thirteenth-century cloisters. Southeast of the Colosseum at the piazza San Giovanni in Laterano 4.

Church of St. Mary Major (Santa Maria Maggiore) – Originally a fourth-century church, rebuilt in the thirteenth, with an eighteenth-century facade and the tallest campanile in Rome. It has particularly interesting fifth-century mosiacs. Via Liberiana 27.

PIAZZAS, PALACES, AND OTHER SIGHTS

Rome is not only a city of ruins and holy places, but of Renaissance palaces, splendid piazzas, lovely fountains, museums, and streets.

Piazza del Campidoglio – This harmonious square was beautifully designed by Michelangelo, with its delicate, elliptical, star-patterned pavement centered around a magnificent second-century bronze statue of Marcus Aurelius (removed for restoration). Flanked by palaces on three sides, the piazza is traditionally the political center of Rome. The Senatorial Palace houses government officials; the other two palaces are museums, the Capitolino and the Conservatori.

Capitoline Museum (Museo Capitolino) – This seventeenth-century palace contains an especially valuable collection of antique sculptures, including the *Capitoline Venus* and the *Dying Gaul.* Piazza del Campidoglio 7.

Piazza Navona – This harmonious ensemble of Roman baroque is today a favorite haunt of Romans and tourists alike. It is also one of Rome's most historical squares, designed by Bernini for Pope Innocent X and built on the site of Domitian's stadium. In the center of the square is Bernini's fine *Fountain of the Four Rivers,* the huge figures representing the Nile, Ganges, Danube, and Plata. On the west side of the square is an ancient little church, Sant'Agnese in Agone, built on the ruins of the stadium. South of the church is the Palazzo Doria Pamphili, now the Brazilian Embassy, harboring a gallery by Borromini with a ceiling painted by Pietro da Cortona. During the Christmas season and until Epiphany, the piazza is lined with booths selling sweets, toys, and Christmas crib figures.

Piazza di Spagna (Spanish Steps) – One of the most picturesque settings of eighteenth-century Rome was named after a palace that housed the Spanish Embassy to the Holy See. The steps were actually built by the French to connect the French quarter at the top with the Spanish area below. One of Rome's fine French churches, Trinità dei Monti, hovers over the 137 steps, as does the Sallustian obelisk, which was brought to Rome in the third century. At the bottom of the steps — which in the spring are covered with hundreds of pots of azaleas — is the Barcaccia Fountain, depicting a sinking barge inspired by the Tiber's flooding in 1589. Modern art historians disagree on whether this fountain, the oldest architectural feature of the square, was designed by Pietro Bernini or his son, the famous Giovanni Lorenzo Bernini, in the seventeenth century.

Keats-Shelley Memorial – Next to the steps at number 26 is the house where Keats lived and died, now a Keats and Shelley museum. Open weekdays only, for a fee.

Piazza del Popolo – At the foot of the Pincio, this semicircular square was designed in neoclassical style by Valadier between 1816 and 1820. It was built around treasures covering a span of three centuries and has the second oldest obelisk in Rome — dating from the thirteenth century BC — in its center. (Because it was struck by lightning in 1983, the obelisk is now surrounded by a maze of scaffolding.) Twin-domed churches face a ceremonial gate where the via Flaminia enters Rome. The piazza's two open-air cafés, *Rosati* and *Canova,* are favorite meeting places.

Piazza Farnese – This square is dominated by the most beautiful sixteenth-century palace in Rome. Palazzo Farnese was begun in 1514 by Sangallo the Younger, continued by Michelangelo, and completed by Della Porta in 1589. Today it is occupied by the French Embassy and can be visited only by special permission. The two fountains on the piazza are bathtubs of Egyptian granite from Caracalla. On the right of the square stands the little modern church built on the site where St. Bridget died in 1373.

Piazza del Quirinale – The Quirinal Palace, built by the popes at the end of the sixteenth century, is now the official residence of the president of Italy (although the current president, Pertini, prefers to live in his own home). The so-called Monte Cavallo (Horse Tamers') Fountain is composed of two groups of statues depicting Castor and Pollux with their horses and a granite basin from the Forum once used as a cattle trough. The obelisk in the center is from the Mausoleum of Augustus. The square affords a marvelous view of Rome and St. Peter's.

Trevi Fountain – Designed by Nicola Salvi and completed in 1762, the Trevi Fountain took 30 years to build and is the last important monumental work in the baroque style in Rome. This magnificent fountain is incongruously situated in a tiny square surrounded by narrow, cobblestoned streets. A colossal Oceanus in stone rides a chariot drawn by seahorses and surrounded by a baroque fantasy of gods, tritons, and horses. A Roman legend assures you of returning to Rome if you throw a coin over your left shoulder into the fountain. Young Roman men like to congregate in the small square on summer evenings, trying to pick up foreign girls. Some prefer to pick your pocket — so be careful here. Piazza di Trevi.

Piazza Barberini – At the foot of via Veneto, this square in northern Rome has two of Bernini's famous fountains: the Triton Fountain in travertine, representing a triton sitting upon a scallop shell supported by four dolphins and blowing a conch; and the Fountain of the Bees on the corner of via Veneto, with three Barberini bees (of that family's crest) on the edge of a pool spurting thin jets of water into the basin below.

Piazza Campo dei Fiori – One of Rome's most colorful squares is the scene of a general market every morning. In the center, surrounded by delicious cheeses, salamis, ripe fruit and vegetables, and flowers (*fiori*) of every kind, is a statue of philosopher Giordano Bruno, who was burned at the stake here for heresy in 1600. Again, watch your wallet — this is a hangout for thieves.

Piazza Mattei – A delightful clearing on the edge of the ancient Jewish ghetto, this small square's famous Fountain of the Tortoises, sculpted in 1585 by Taddeo Landini, is one of Rome's most delightful: Four naked boys lean against the base and toss life-size bronze tortoises into a marble bowl above. The water moves in several directions, creating a magical effect in the tiny square.

Via Condotti – A sort of Fifth Avenue of Rome, this street is lined with the city's most exclusive shops, including *Gucci, Bulgari,* and *Ferragamo.* Only a few blocks long, via Condotti begins at the foot of the Spanish Steps, ends at via del Corso, and is a favorite street for window shopping and the ritual evening *passeggiata,* or promenade, as it is — like much of the area — closed to traffic. Via Condotti's name derives from the conduits built under it by Gregory XIII in the sixteenth century to carry water.

One of via Condotti's landmarks is the famous *Caffè Greco* at number 86, long a hangout for Romans and foreigners. Among its habitués were Goethe, Byron, Liszt, Buffalo Bill, Mark Twain, Oscar Wilde, and the late Giorgio de Chirico, a contemporary Italian painter. Tennyson and Thackeray both lived in a house across the street. The place is full of busts, statues, and varied mementos of its clientele, and the somber waiters still dress in tails. Great for a quick sandwich or *aperitivo* (cocktail).

At number 68 on via Condotti is the smallest sovereign state in the world, consisting of one historic palazzo. If you peek into its charming courtyard, you'll see cars parked there with number plates bearing the letters SMOM, the initials of the Sovereign Military Order of Malta. Besides its own licenses, the order also issues just a few passports and has its own diplomatic service and small merchant fleet.

Protestant Cemetery – In the southern part of the city, behind the pyramid of Caius Cestius, the Protestant Cemetery is principally a foreign enclave which harbors the remains of many an adopted non-Catholic son who chose to live and to die in Rome: Keats; Shelley; Severn; Coleman, Goethe's bastard son; and the Italian Communist leader Gramsci. There is nothing sad here — no pathos, no morbid sense of death — and few gardens are so delightful on a spring morning. Via Caio Cestio.

Villa Borghese – In the northern section of the city, this is the most magnificent park in Rome, with hills, lakes, villas, and vistas. The villa was designed for Cardinal Borghese in the seventeenth century. Today its former estate includes two museums — the Galleria Borghese, and Galleria d' Arte Moderna — as well as Rome's zoo. The main entrance is on the west, at the piazzale Flaminio, just outside the Porta del Popolo, with another at Porta Pinciana at the top end of Via Veneto.

Borghese Museum (Galleria Borghese) – Housed in the seventeenth-century Casino Borghese, this is one of Rome's most outstanding collections of painting and sculpture. Its many famous pieces include those of the Caravaggio Room and works of Titian, Raphael, Bernini, and others. Piazza del Museo Borghese, near via Pinciana, Via del Museo 3.

MODERN ROME

Modern Rome had its beginnings in 1870, when it became the capital of a unified Italy and the pope retired to the Vatican.

Monument to Victor Emmanuel II – In the piazza Venezia, this most conspicuous landmark of questionable taste was completed in 1911 to celebrate the unification of Italy. Built in white Brescian marble and overshadowing the surrounding mellow tones of old Rome in size as well, it is often derided by Romans as the "wedding cake" or the "typewriter." It contains Italy's Tomb of the Unknown Soldier from World War I and it was on this square that Mussolini made his speeches — from a small balcony of the fifteenth-century Palazzo Venezia, his official residence. From the top of the *"Vittoriano"* you can see the network of modern boulevards built by Mussolini to open out the site of ancient Rome: via dei Fori Imperiali, via di S. Gregorio, via del Teatro di Marcello, and via Nazionale — a busy and somewhat chaotic shopping street leading to the central railway station.

Via Vittorio Veneto (popularly called Via Veneto) – This wide, tree-lined street extends from Porta Pinciana at its top and winds down past the American Embassy to the piazza Barberini. The portion around the via Boncompagni is lined with outdoor cafés; however, the once elegant street now attracts a mixed bunch — from down-and-out actors and decadent Roman nobility to seedy gigolos and well-to-do American tourists and businesspeople staying in the fine hotels nearby.

Porta Portese – Rome's flea market takes place on the edge of Trastevere in Rome's southwest corner on Sunday mornings from dawn to about 1 PM. It's a colorful, chaotic happening. Genuine antiques are few and far between, quickly scooped up before most people are out of bed. Still, you'll find some interesting junk, secondhand clothes, pop records, used tires and car parts, black market cigarettes — everything from Sicilian puppets to old post cards, sheet music, and broken bidets.

OUT OF TOWN

Rome's surroundings are remarkably scenic and offer the visitor a considerable variety of attractions.

EUR (Esposizione Universale Roma) – Mussolini's ultramodern quarter was designed southwest of Rome in 1942 for an international exhibition that never took place. It's now a fashionable garden suburb and the site of international congresses and trade delegations as well as some remarkable sports installations that were built for the Olympic Games of 1960. EUR also houses some interesting museums, such as the museum of Civiltà Romana (Roman Civilization), worth seeing for its thorough reconstruction of ancient Rome at the time of Constantine. Piazza G. Agnelli, EUR.

Ostia Antica – This immense excavation site lies only 15 miles (24 km) southwest of Rome. At the mouth of the Tiber, Ostia was once the great trading port of ancient Rome. Fairly recently uncovered, the ruins of Ostia have not had much chance to crumble and they reveal a great deal about the building methods of the Romans.

It takes about half a day to walk through the ruins, picturesquely surrounded with pines and cypresses. The chief sites are the Corporations' Square (piazzale delle Corporazioni), once 70 commercial offices, with mottoes and emblems in mosaics that reveal that the merchants here were caulkers, ropemakers, furriers, and shipowners from all over the ancient world. A local museum traces the development of the town and exhibits some outstanding statues, busts, and frescoes. There are also firemen's barracks, a forum, and several other interesting sights.

The Lido di Ostia or Lido di Roma is 2.5 miles (4 km) southwest of Ostia. It's the most popular, most polluted, and most crowded seaside resort near Rome. There are more pleasant beaches both north and south of Rome.

Castelli Romani – Southeast of Rome is the lovely region of the Alban hills called the Castelli Romani, or Roman hilltowns. You can visit all or a few of the thirteen interesting villages here and enjoy the delightful scenery — mountains, the volcanic lakes of Nemi and Albano, chestnut groves, olive trees, and vines that produce the renowned Castelli wine. Particularly charming are Frascati, known for its villas and its wines; Grottaferrata, famous for its fortified monastery; beautiful Lake Nemi, with its vivid blue waters and wooded surroundings, where Diana was worshiped; and Monte Cavo, a mountain whose summit can be reached by a toll road and which offers a panorama of the Castelli Romani from a height of 3,124 feet. The Castelli Romani are best seen on an organized tour or by car.

■ **EXTRA SPECIAL:** Tivoli, 19 miles (31 km) east of Rome, is a charming river town perched on a hilltop and should not be missed. It's famous for magnificent gardens, villas, and cascading waters — all immortalized by Fragonard's landscapes in the eighteenth century. Tivoli, called Tibur by the ancient Romans, was a resort for wealthy citizens, who bathed in its thermal waters that remain therapeutic to this day.

The Villa d'Este, a sixteenth-century cardinal's palace, is famous for its fabulous gardens and fountains — among them the Avenue of the Hundred Fountains, lined with jets of water, and the huge Organ Fountain, so named because it once worked a hydraulic organ. The villa and gardens are open to the public for a fee.

On summer nights the fountains are beautifully illuminated, and there's a sound and light show daily except Mondays.

Nearby, the Villa Gregoriana, built by Pope Gregory XVI in the nineteenth century, has sloping gardens and magnificent cascades — which can best be seen on Sundays, since most of the water is used for industrial purposes on other days. The gardens and waterfalls are open to the public for a fee.

And only 4 miles (6 km) southwest of Tivoli is Hadrian's Villa, the most sumptuous of the ancient Roman villas, built for the Emperor Hadrian in about AD 120. Extensively excavated, the ruins of the villa, surrounded by greenery, include the Maritime Theater, built on an island and surrounded by a canal, the Golden Square in front of the remains of the palace, and the Terrace of Tempe, with a view of the valley of the same name. There are statues, fountains, cypress-lined avenues, pools, lakes, and canals. It's open daily for a fee.

You can see Tivoli with a guided tour or take a bus or a train from Rome.

SOURCES AND RESOURCES

For general information, brochures, and maps of Rome and Latium, contact the EPT offices (Ente Provinciale per il Turismo) at the central railway station or at its headquarters at via Parigi 5 (phone: 46-37-48). There is also an EPT office at the airport. The Regional Tourism Board for Latium is at Via della Pisana 1301 (phone: 6708).

For some good background material about Rome, see the excellent pictorial essay written for Time-Life Books by E. R. Chamberlin entitled *Rome.* Georgina Masson's *Companion Guide to Rome* and Eleanor Clark's *Rome and a Villa* are delightfully amusing. A locally published book on the city's hidden treasures, *In Rome They Say,* by Margherita Naval, is also good reading. There are several English-language bookstores in the Spanish Steps area: the *Lion Bookshop,* Via del Babuino 181, *Anglo-American Book Company,* Via della Vite 57, the *Economy Book Center,* Piazza di Spagna 29, and the *Bookshelf,* Via Due Macelli 23 (in the Tritone Gallery).

For Local Coverage – The *Daily American* is an English-language daily newspaper published in Rome and available at most newsstands. Consult *This Week in Rome* or *A Guest in Rome* for varied information such as theater, galleries, and special exhibitions.

For Food – There are over 3,500 restaurants in Rome. The red *Michelin* for Italy provides a useful listing of restaurants, but it has been severely criticized by Italian food experts for its lack of awareness of regional specialties. Much better is the book by food critics Henri Gault and Christian Millau called *The Best of Italy.* If you want to read about Italian cuisine, try *The Food of Italy,* by Waverly Root, available in paperback.

CLIMATE AND CLOTHES: Generally, it should be hot from mid-June through September, and only very light clothing is needed. Average temperatures in July and August hover around 82°F (27°C), but a heavy sirocco wind from the African deserts often brings the maximum above 100°F (38°C). Fortunately, Romans are quite informal except for very special occasions, and men rarely wear ties or jackets in the summer. Women should be careful when visiting churches, where immodest dress (bare shoulders included) is frowned upon if not downright forbidden. A refreshing breeze often offers relief on summer evenings, making a light wrap advisable. Winters are moderate, with temperatures averaging 47°F (8°C) December through February. Although snow is very rare, and it seldom drops below freezing, the *tramontana* wind from the north can be very chilly (definitely overcoat weather) and winter rains are heavy.

GETTING AROUND: Bus – ATAC, the city bus company, is the backbone of Rome's public transportation system. Buses run frequently throughout the city, particularly through the center, and fares are still among the cheapest in Europe. But beware — most central routes are extremely crowded, getting off where you'd like sometimes impossible, and pickpockets are rampant. Depending on the bus route, you'll need either 400 lire or a pre-purchased ticket available at certain newsstands, tobacco shops, and bars. A few trams still operate, including the *circolare,* which rings the city center passing several interesting monuments. Maps of bus and tram lines are sold at the ATAC Information Office on piazza del Cinquecento (facing the railway station on the left). The Rome telephone directory's Tutto Citta lists every street in the city on detailed maps of each zone as well as zip codes, bus routes, and local taxi stands.

Subway – The *Metropolitana,* Rome's subway, finally opened its new network in 1980. The line covers a 9-mile route through the heart of Rome, from an area close to the Vatican, across the Tiber River, through the historic center, and over to the eastern edge of Rome just past Cinecittà. The fare is 400 lire; subway entrances are marked by a large red M.

Taxi – Cabs can be hailed or found at numerous stands throughout the city, which are listed in the Yellow Pages with their phone numbers. The Radio Taxi telephone numbers are 3570, 3875, 4994, and 8433. Taxi rates are increasing regularly, and drivers are obliged to show you, if asked, the current list of added charges. After 10 PM, an approximate $1 night fare is added. The fare from the Leonardo da Vinci airport at Fiumicino (about 21 mi/34 km) to Rome is double the fare on the meter; from Rome to Fiumicino, pay the meter amount plus about 11,000 lire. (Airport buses leave every 15 minutes from the air terminal at the central railway station and cost about 4,000 lire.)

Car Rental – Major car rental firms such as *Avis,* Via Sardegna 38/a (phone: 4701), *Hertz,* Via Sallustiana 28 (phone: 51712), and *Europcar,* Via Lombardia 7 (phone: 547811), as well as several reliable Italian companies such as *Maggiore,* Via Po 8A (phone: 851620), have offices in the city and at the airport and railway stations.

Boat – There are boat excursions on the Tiber River on Saturdays and Sundays during the summer from Lungotevere Dante 271 (phone: 637-0268). They stop at Ostia Antica — the ancient port of Rome — on the way to Fiumicino. The return trip is by bus. The price is reasonable, and reservations are necessary.

MUSEUMS: Many museums are described in *Special Places.* Because of their artistic value, we have included some churches in the following list of additional museums of special interest:

Villa Giulia. A remarkable Etruscan collection housed in a sixteenth-century villa by Vignola. P. le Villa Giulia 9.

Modern Art Gallery (Galleria d'Arte Moderna). Nineteenth- and twentieth-century Italian art. (At press time, the permanent collection was closed for restoration.) Viale delle Belle Arti 131.

National Gallery of Palazzo Barberini. Paintings by artists from the thirteenth to the eighteenth century. Via IV Fontane 13.

National Gallery of Ancient Art (Galleria Nazionale d'Arte Antica). Seventeenth- and eighteenth-century art, plus some Dutch and Flemish works. Palazzo Corsini, via della Lungara 10.

Galleria Spada. Renaissance art and Roman marble work from the second and third centuries. Palazzo Spada, Piazza Capo di Ferro 13.

Galleria Doria Pamphilj. Italian and foreign paintings from the fifteenth to seventeenth century. Piazza del Collegio Romano 1/a.

National Museum of Oriental Art (Museo Nazionale d'Arte Orientale). Pottery, bronzes, stone, and wooden sculpture in the Iranian, Chinese, and Indian sections. Via Merulana 248.

Roman Museum (Museo Romano). Paintings, sculptures, and other objects illustrating the history of Rome from the Middle Ages to today. Piazza S. Pantaleo 10.

Palazzo Venezia Museum. Paintings, sculpture, and varied objects. Via del Plebiscito.

Galleria Colonna, Palazzo Colonna. The Colonna family collection of mainly seventeenth-century Italian paintings. Via della Pilotta 17.

St. Peter in Chains (S. Pietro in Vincoli). Erected in the fifth century to preserve St. Peter's chains, this church contains Michelangelo's magnificent statue of Moses. Piazza S. Francesco di Paola 4A.

St. Mary of the People (S. Maria del Popolo). Early Renaissance architecture and Baroque interior. Piazza del Popolo 12.

S. Clemente. An early Christian basilica with frescoes and a remarkable mosaic. Piazza di San Clemente.

St. Augustine (S. Agostino). *Madonna of the Pilgrims* by Caravaggio and the *Prophet Isaiah* by Raphael. Via S. Agostino.

St. Mary over Minerva (S. Maria sopra Minerva). Built over a Roman temple and containing frescoes of Filippino Lippi. Piazza della Minerva, via del Beato Angelico 35.

 SHOPPING: Although most important Italian firms have branches here, Rome is not the best place to shop for Italian goods. The best handicrafts are in Florence; Milan is the center for manufactured products. You'll find the great couturiers here, many of whom have boutiques. The best buys are in leathergoods, jewelry, fabrics, shoes, and sweaters.

The smartest shopping center is around the bottom of the Spanish Steps, starting with the elegant via Condotti, which runs east to west and is lined with Rome's most exclusive shops, such as *Gucci, Bulgari,* and *Ferragamo.* Running parallel to via Condotti are several fashionable streets for boutiques, such as via Borgognona, via delle Carrozze, via Frattina (for costume jewelry, lingerie, and some ceramics), via Vittoria, and via della Croce (known particularly for its delicious delicatessens) — most closed to traffic.

These streets end in the via del Corso, the main street of Rome, which runs north to south and is lined with shops carrying the latest fashions in shoes, handbags, and sportswear, particularly in the section between the piazza del Popolo and Largo Chigi where the via del Tritone begins. There are some fine shops along the via del Tritone, the via Sistina, and in the via Veneto area.

On the other side of the river toward the Vatican are two popular shopping streets that are slightly less expensive, the via Cola di Rienzo and via Ottaviano; another one is via Nazionale near the railway station. For inexpensive new and secondhand clothes, visit the market open daily on via Sannio, near S. Giovanni, and of course, the flea market on Sunday mornings at Porta Portese. For old prints and odds and ends, try the daily market on piazza Fontanella Borghese; antiques can be found along via del Babuino, via dei Coronari, via Margutta, and via Giulia.

The following are but a few recommended shops in Rome:

Alexander – An outstanding boutique for women at Piazza di Spagna 49–50 (corner of via Frattina).

Anticoli – A good place for sweaters. Via del Corso 333 and via del Tritone 133.

Giorgio Armani – High fashion for men and women. Via del Babuino 102.

Bilgoraj – Eyeglasses and contact lenses fitted by one of Rome's best and most scrupulous optometrists; camera supplies also. Via delle Convertite 19 (near Piazza San Silvestro).

Bises – A place for fine fabrics. Via del Gesù 93 (Corso Vittorio Emanuele) in Palazzo Alfieri.

Borsalino – World-renowned hats. Via IV Novembre.

Buccellati – An expensive jeweler specializing in Florentine silver, gold jewelry, and antiques. Via Condotti 31.

Bulgari – One of the world's most famous high-style jewelers, offering fabulous creations in gold, silver, platinum, and stones. Via Condotti 10.

Capodarte – The latest styles in shoes and boots, many with matching bags. Via Sistina 14a.

Coin – Newest and most fashionable of Rome's comparatively small department stores. Good boutique wear, leathergoods, knits, gifts. Piazzale Appio (near San Giovanni metro station). *Coin Lei,* at Viale Libia, is for women only.

Di Cori – A good place for gloves. Piazza di Spagna 53; Via del Tritone 52.

Fendi – Canvas and leather bags, baggage and clothing. Via Borgognona 39.

Ferragamo – For high-style women's shoes. Via Condotti 66.

Gianfranco Ferré – High fashion for women. Via Borgognona 42B.

Filippo – An avant-garde "in" boutique with fairly reasonable prices. Via Borgognona 7/bis; Via Condotti 6.

Fiorucci – Famed, funky sportswear and shoes. Via Genova 12; Via Farnesina 19; Via Nazionale 236; via della Maddallena 27.

Fornari – Fine silver and other gifts. Via Frattina 71-72.

Maud Frizon – Really original shoes for women, with corresponding prices. Via Borgognona 38.

Nazareno Gabrielli – Leathergoods. Via S. Andrea delle Fratte; Via Borgognona 29.

Galtrucco – A place for all kinds of fabrics, especially silks. Via del Tritone 23.

Gucci – Famous for men's and women's shoes, luggage, handbags, and other leathergoods. Via Condotti 8; Via Borgognona 25 (the latter belongs to Gucci's son and is rather younger in style).

Krizia – Elegant women's boutique. Piazza di Spagna 11B.

Laurent – Good buys on leatherwear. Via Frattina 3.

Maccalé – Yet another fine boutique for women. Via della Croce 69.

Bruno Magli – Top-quality shoes and boots of classical elegance. Via Veneto 70; Via Gambero 1; Via Cola di Rienzo 237.

Miranda – Colorful women's woven shawls and jackets. Via delle Carrozze 220.

Missoni – High-fashion knitwear. Via Borgognona 38/B.

Nia – A fine boutique for women's clothes. Via Vittoria.

Carlo Palazzi – Creative, high-quality fashions for men. Via Borgognona 7/C.

Pineider – Italy's famed stationer (with a branch in New York City's chic Trump Tower). Via Due Macelli 68/69 and Piazza Cardelli.

Ramirez – Latest shoe fashions at reasonable prices. Via del Corso 73; Via Frattina 85/A.

Salato – For famous maker Italian men's and women's shoes, at reasonable prices. Via Veneto and Piazza di Spagna.

Rinascente – One of the few department stores, sometimes offering good buys. Piazza Colonna; Piazza Fiume.

Roberta di Camerino – Women's wear, handbags, umbrellas, and other items. Piazza di Spagna 30.

Sabatini – Best buys on film and camera equipment, catering to the professional photographer. Via Germanico 166/A (downstairs).

Sansone – Italy's largest selection of Italian and imported luggage, trunks, and travel bags. Repairs and custom designs. Via XX Settembre 4.

Spazio Sette – Elegant design products from Italy, Scandinavia, and other places;

gifts·for those who have everything. Via Santa Maria dei Anima 55 (behind Piazza Navona).

Testa – For offbeat, resort, and casual clothes for men. Via Borgognona 13; Via Frattina 104–106.

Trimani – Rome's oldest wine shop. Via Goito 20.

Valentino – Bold, high-fashion clothes for men and women. Via Condotti (corner Mario dei Fiore) for men; Via Bocca di Leone, 15/18, for women; haute couture salon at Via Gregoriana 24.

Gianni Versace – Another name in high fashion. Via Borgognona 39; Via Bocca di Leone 29.

 SPECIAL EVENTS: The events of the church calendar — too numerous to mention here — are extra special in Rome. The center of Rome is lavishly decorated for *Christmas*. On the *Epiphany* (January 6) and all night the night before, parents swarm into the piazza Navona to buy sweets and toys for their children, concluding the colorful fair begun before Christmas. During *Holy Week* in April, the city swarms with visitors. Religious ceremonies abound, particularly on Good Friday, when the pope conducts the famous *Via Crucis (Way of the Cross)* procession between the Colosseum and the Palatine Hill. The arrival of spring in April is celebrated with a colorful display of potted azaleas covering the Spanish Steps, and the nearby picturesque street, the via Margutta, is filled with an exhibition of paintings by artists of varied talents. (The via Margutta art fair is repeated in the fall.) Toward the end of April, Villa Borghese's lush piazza di Siena becomes the site of the *International Horse Show,* and soon after that is the *International Tennis Championship* at Foro Italico. The Tourist Office also sponsors an antique show along the charming via dei Coronari (near piazza Navona), and there's an *International Rose Show* at the delightful Roseto di Valle Murcia on the Aventine Hill. In late May or June, the vast *Fair of Rome,* a national industrial exhibition, takes place along the via Cristoforo Colombo. In mid-July the *Festa di Noiantri* is celebrated in one of Rome's oldest quarters, Trastevere. This is a great pagan feast, involving plenty of eating, music, and fireworks — as filmed by Fellini in his surrealistic/realistic *Roma.*

There are also innumerable characteristic *feste* or *sagre* (the latter meaning "consecrations," usually of some local food or beverage at the height of its season) in the many hill towns surrounding Rome. Two are especially worth seeing: the *Infiorata* in May at Genzano, when a brightly colored carpet of beautifully arranged flowers is laid along the entire via Livia, and the *Sagra dell'Uva* (consecration of the grape) in October at Marino, which celebrates the new vintage with grapes sold from stalls set up in the quaint old streets and wine instead of water gushing out of the fountain in the main square! Both towns are about 15 miles (24 km) south of Rome in the Castelli Romani district.

 SPORTS: Auto Racing – *Autodromo di Roma* (Valle Lunga), Campagnano di Roma, Via Cassia (phone: 904-1027). Take a bus from Castel Pretorio.

Golf – *Circolo del Golf Roma,* Via dell'Acqua Santa — 2 miles (3 km) from Rome's center (phone: 78-34-07); and *Olgiata Golf Club* near Rome on the Via Cassia (phone: 378-8004).

Horseback Riding – *Circolo Ippico Appia Antica,* Via Appia Nuova (phone: 60-01-97); *Società Ippica Romana,* Via M. della Farnesina 18 (phone: 396-6386); *Circolo Ippico del Tebro,* Via Tiberina 198 (phone: 691-2974), and *Circolo Buttero Fontana Nuova* near Sacrofano, outside Rome (phone: 903-6040).

Soccer – Rome boasts two highly competitive teams, *Roma* and *Lazio,* which play regularly (Sundays) at the Olympic Stadium, Foro Italico.

Swimming – The pools at the *Cavalieri Hilton,* Via Cadlolo, 101 (phone: 3151) and the *Sheraton Roma,* Viale del Pattinaggio (phone: 5453), are open to nonguests for a fee. Public pools: *Piscina Olympica* at Foro Italico (phone: 360-8591 or 360-1498) and *Piscina delle Rose* at EUR (phone: 592-6717). The beach nearest Rome and most accessible (by Metropolitana) is at Ostia, and it's polluted and very crowded; Fregene, farther north, is very "in" with fashionable (and mostly topless) Romans. Windsurf boards are available for rent at both beaches as well as at Lake Bracciano, about 20 miles (32 km) north of Rome.

Tennis – Most courts belong to private clubs. Courts at the *Cavalieri Hilton,* Via Cadlolo 101 (phone: 3151), and at the *Sheraton Roma,* Viale del Pattinaggio (phone: 5453), are open to nonguests for a fee. There are public courts at the *Foro Italico* (phone: 361-9012).

THEATER: Check *This Week in Rome.* Most Italian theater consists of revivals of the classics and a few avant-garde groups. In English, check the *Workshop Theater* at St. Paul's American Church (Anglican-Episcopal), Via Napoli 58, the *Teatro Goldoni,* Vicolo de'Soldati 4 (phone: 656-1156), and *Alla Ringhiera,* Via dei Riari 71. A season of classical drama (in Italian, and sometimes in Greek) is held in July each year in the open-air Roman theater at Ostia Antica. The *Teatro Sistina,* Via Sistina 129 (phone: 475-6841), is Rome's best music hall, offering top-class, often imported, musical entertainment Monday nights, when the regular rep is resting (in the fall, they usually run top-name Brazilian entertainment Monday nights). For films in English, check the newspapers for *Cinema Pasquino* at Vicolo del Piede (phone: 580-3622) in Trastevere.

MUSIC: Again, for current schedules, check the local publications listed above. Opera season is from December to June at the *Teatro dell'Opera* (phone: 474-2595) and outdoors at the Baths of Caracalla during July and August. The Rome Ballet Company also performs at the *Teatro dell'Opera.* From October to May there are first-class concerts with international guest artists at the *Auditorium of the National Academy of Santa Cecilia* on via della Conciliazione and at their *Sala dei Concerti* (Concert Hall) on via dei Greci (phone: 679-0389), as well as an outdoors season during July and August at the Basilica di Massenzio. Also between October and May, concerts are held at the University Auditorium of S. Leone Magno (phone: 396-4777), at the Roman Philharmonic Academy on via Flaminia 118 (phone: 360-1752), and at the Teatro Olimpico. From November to April, there are concerts at the Gonfalone Auditorium and around Rome by the Coro Polifonico Romano (phone: 65-59-52), and many churches hold concerts throughout the year. There are also occasional jazz, pop, and folk festivals, some held outdoors in the parks, and a jazz club at *Centro Jazz St. Louis,* Via del Cardello 13a (phone: 48-34-24); others are the *Music-Inn,* Largo di Fiorentini 3 (phone: 654-4934); *La Clef,* Via Marche 13 (phone: 475-6049); *Dei Satiri,* Via di Grotta Pinta 19 (phone: 656-1311); *Dei Servi,* Via del Mortaro 22 (phone: 676-5130); *Casablanca* at Lungotevere Arnaldo da Brescia; and *Mississippi Jazz Club,* Borgo Angelico 16 (phone: 654-0348).

NIGHTCLUBS AND NIGHTLIFE: Currently popular are the *Open Gate,* Via San Nicola Tolentino 4 (phone: 475-0464), *Jackie O',* Via Boncompagni 11 (phone: 461401). *Much More,* Via Luciani 52 (phone: 87-05-04), and *Super Sonic,* Via Ovido 17 (phone: 654-8435), are preferred by punkers. *Bella Blu* at Via Luciani 21 (phone: 360-8840), also serves expensive late-night dinners. *La Makumba,* Via degli Olimpionici 19 (phone: 396-4392), jumps with African, Caribbean, and Latin rhythms, while *Gil's,* Via Romagnosi 11a (phone: 361-1348), is also rather exotic but somewhat more elegant. *Easy Going,* Via della Purificazione (phone: 474-5578), is for gays as are *Angelo Azzurro,* Via Cardinale Merry del Val (phone:

580-0472), and *L'Alibi*, Via Di Monte Testaccio 44 (phone: 578-2343). *Piper '80*, Via Tagliamento 9 (phone: 85-44-59), has roller disco on Wednesdays, live rock or new wave concerts on Thursdays and Saturdays, and disco music on Fridays. Other clubs include *Il Veleno*, Via Sardegna 27 (phone: 493-583), decorated in mock-ancient-Roman-style with marble-like columns; *La Cage aux Folles*, Via Gregoriana 9 (phone: 679-0490); *Club 84*, Via Emilia (phone: 474-2205); *L'Incontro*, disco and piano bar at Via della Penna 25 (phone: 361-0934); the Cavalieri Hilton Hotel's roof garden *La Pergola*, Via Cadlolo 101 (phone: 3151) The *Sheraton's* piano bar *Tuttaroma*, Viale del Pattinaggio (phone: 5453); and the *Aldrovandi's* piano bar in Parioli at Via Aldrovandi 15 (phone: 841091). The *Hostaria dell'Orso* has a disco upstairs (*La Cabala*), and a quiet comfy piano bar *(Blue Bar)* with guitarists on the main floor. *L'Arciliuto* on piazza Montevecchio, an intimate musical salon and bar reputed to be Raphael's old studio. A pianist accompanies the owner–guitarist–lutist–music historian, whose repertoire includes ancient madrigals, classic Neapolitan love songs, and current Broadway hits! There are several other bars with music but no dancing, such as the *Tartarughino* on the via della Scrofa; *Cappello a Cilindro*, Via del Vantaggio 47; and several hotels and cafés in the via Veneto area, such as the *Eden Hotel's Roof Garden Bar*, the *White Elephant* and *George's*. *Manuia* in Trastevere is a restaurant as well as piano bar that usually has live Brazilian music. Several bars around the piazza del Popolo are hangouts for local artists and film makers, such as *La Privé* on via della Penna and *Dita al Naso* on Via Fiume. *L'aperitivo* or predinner drink is most fashionable on via Condotti, at *Caffè Greco* or the *Baretto*, on piazza del Popolo at *Rosati* or *Canova*, or at *Harry's Bar, Carpano, Café de Paris, Doney's*, and others on via Veneto. Have a nightcap at the piazza Navona bars in fine weather, or on the square facing the Pantheon, along via Veneto, the *Bar Zodiaco* on Monte Mario (with a view), or at the tiny unpretentious *Bar Eustacchio* on the square of the same name, reputed to serve the best espresso in town. Folk music and jazz are at *Folkstudio*, Via Gaetano Sacchi 3, Trastevere (phone: 679-8269), and the *Mississippi Jazz Club*, Borgo Angelico 16 (phone: 654-0348); cabaret in Italian at *Il Bagaglino (Salone Margherita)*, Via Due Macelli 75 (phone: 679-1439); and *Il Puff*, Via Gigi Zanazzo 14 (phone: 581-0721). Roman music can be heard at the supper clubs *Fantasie di Trastevere*, Via S. Dorotea 6 (phone: 589-2986), *Da Meo Patacca*, Piazza dei Mercanti 30 (phone: 581-6198), and *Da Ciceruacchio*, Via del Porto 1 (phone: 580-6046), all in the heart of Trastevere. The city's English-speaking community frequents the *Fiddler's Elbow* near Santa Maria Maggiore, the *Falcon* near Piazza Barberini, and the *Little Bar*, at Via Gregoriana 54a.

 SINS: Although prostitution was declared illegal in 1958, like most laws in Italy, it has been blatantly ignored. The *bordelli* closed down, sending most *prostitutes* (more vulgarly called *puttane*) out on the streets with less medical control — so be careful. *Ragazze squillo* or call girls can often be arranged with the help of your friendly hotel *portiere*, or those free-lance, multilingual tour guides who hang around the better hotels soliciting customers. Some can be found sitting alone at the tables of the more popular cafés near the top of via Veneto. (An Italian lady would never sit alone, so don't worry about making a great gaffe.) Sit next to her, or tactfully solicit assistance from a smiling waiter. The best streetwalkers' beat is the lower part of via Veneto, less expensive along via Sistina and via Francesco Crispi. Pretty prohibitive (though not in price) are the girls (some as ancient as their surroundings) along the road circling the Baths of Caracalla, along the Appia Antica, and on the truck routes leading into the city. They often attract potential customers and keep warm by building themselves bonfires along the road.

Unlike prostitution, *gluttony* is not illegal; it can be enjoyed outdoors, and it is probably Rome's most popular sin. So by all means, do as the Romans do, and gorge yourself on the Italian ice cream in the piazza Navona, comparing the *gelati* at *Tre*

Scalini with that of *Giolitti* near the Pantheon. And whatever you do, don't miss out
on *fettucine Alfredo,* which is hard to beat for calories — pasta plus cream plus butter
plus cheese. Enjoy it now; you can diet later.

When you are sated with wonderful Roman food, sit back and be *slothful* at your
favorite Roman site, whether it be the Villa Borghese, the Trevi Fountain, or even the
Colosseum.

BEST IN TOWN

 CHECKING IN: There are more than 500 hotels and pensions in Rome, all
of which are listed annually by the Italian State Tourist Office in a catalogue
that may be consulted in any of their offices. The following are recommended
either for some special charm, location, or bargain price in their category.
Those without restaurants are noted as such, although all serve breakfast if desired, and
all have heating and telephones in the rooms unless otherwise stated. You'll pay
between $120 and $300 for a double room with bath in the hotels listed as expensive;
between $60 and $120 in the moderate category; and under $60 (as low as $30) in the
inexpensive.

Le Grand Hotel et de Rome – The pride of the CIGA chain in Rome and traditionally the capital's most dignified hotel, the *Grand* is truly grand — formal, well run,
and dignified — in style and service. 175 rooms. Major credit cards accepted. Via
Vittorio Emanuele Orlando 3, between the railway station and via Veneto areas
(phone: 4709). Expensive.

Hassler — Villa Medici – Perched at the top of the Spanish Steps and at the bottom
of the elegant via Sistina, the *Hassler* is ideally located and is favored by an elite
clientele. Each room has a charm of its own, and the roof garden restaurant has
one of the city's most splendid views (but less splendid food). 101 rooms. Piazza
Trinità dei Monti 6 (phone: 679-2651). Expensive.

Cavalieri Hilton – Inconveniently located at the top of a lovely hill (Monte Mario)
overlooking much of the city (shuttle buses run every hour between 9:30 AM and
7:30 PM to the via Veneto and the piazza di Spagna). This is a resort hotel with
year-round swimming, tennis, jogging, and other diversions. The *Hilton* swimming
pool is especially desirable in summer, and its restaurant, *La Pergola,* has been
gathering high praise from food critics. 400 rooms. Major credit cards. Via Cadlolo
101 (phone: 3151). Expensive.

Excelsior – A favorite with Americans, the big, bustling, but efficient *Excelsior*
dominates the via Veneto, next to the US Embassy. The bar is a popular meeting
place. 394 rooms. Major credit cards. Via Vittorio Veneto 125 (phone: 4708).
Expensive.

Sheraton Roma – Opened in 1983, the *Sheraton* is Rome's largest hotel (700 rooms)
sprawling over the modern suburb of EUR, an area originally developed by
Mussolini for a world's fair and connected to the center of town by bus and
subway. Full 24-hour room service (rare in Italy), piano bar, swimming pool,
tennis courts, sauna. Major credit cards. Viale del Pattinaggio (phone: 5453).
Expensive.

Eden – Among the most elegant in Rome, this hotel has excellent service, an intimate
roof garden restaurant, and panoramic bar. 116 air-conditioned rooms with TV.
No credit cards. Via Ludovisi 49 (phone: 474-3551). Expensive.

Parco dei Principi – This modern hotel is on the edge of the Borghese Gardens in
the fashionable residential quarter of Parioli, not far from the via Veneto. There's
a small swimming pool in a lovely garden. 203 rooms. American Express, Visa,
Diners Club. Via G. Frescobaldi 5 (phone: 84-10-71). Moderate.

Flora – At the top of the via Veneto overlooking the Borghese Gardens, the *Flora* is traditional, reliable, and not without charm. 177 rooms. American Express, Visa, Diners Club. Via Vittorio Veneto 191 (phone: 49-78-21). Moderate.

Forum – Built around a medieval tower in the middle of the Imperial Forum, this charming hotel is a bit out of the way but worth any inconvenience for the spectacular view of ancient Rome from its roof garden. 82 rooms. Major credit cards. Via Tor de' Conti 25 (phone: 679-2446). Moderate.

Cicerone – Conveniently located in the residential and commercial area of Prati on the Vatican side of the river, just across from Piazza del Popolo and the Spanish Steps, it has modern and spacious public areas, well-appointed guest rooms, and friendly, attentive service. Large garage. Major credit cards. Via Cicerone 55/c (phone: 3576). Moderate.

Lord Byron – A small first-class hotel in fashionable Parioli with a private club atmosphere and a good restaurant, *Le Jardin.* 47 rooms. Diners Club, Visa, and American Express. Via G. de Notaris 5 (phone: 360-9541). Moderate.

Aldrovandi Palace – This quiet hotel in a fashionable residential area next to the Borghese Gardens not far from Via Veneto has a delightful park with swimming pool and a full-facility health club. Major credit cards. Via Aldrovandi 15 (phone: 84-10-91). Moderate.

Cardinal – On Renaissance Rome's most stately street, this restored palace (attributed to Bramante) is convenient for exploring the city's hidden treasures (but not for shopping in the city center). 66 rooms. Major credit cards. Via Giulia 62 (phone: 654-2719). No restaurant. Moderate.

Raphael – Conveniently located behind the piazza Navona, the *Raphael* is a favorite of Italian politicians (it's near the Senate and the Chamber of Deputies), but it has been slipping lately. It also has lost its roof garden to Prime Minister Craxi, owner and now permanent resident. 85 rooms. American Express. Largo Febo 2 (phone: 656-9051). Moderate.

D'Inghilterra – Extremely popular with knowledgeable travelers, the *Inghilterra* has numbered Anatole France and Ernest Hemingway among its many illustrious guests. Conveniently near the Spanish Steps–central shopping area, it has undergone radical redecoration and lost some of its old-fashioned charm as well as its old-fashioned prices. 102 rooms. No restaurant. Major credit cards. Via Bocca di Leone 14 (phone: 67-21-61). Moderate.

Sitea – Gianni de Luca and his Scottish wife, Shirley, have bestowed on their 40-room, 5-floor hotel the coziness of a private home. Rooms have high ceilings, crystal chandeliers, and hand-painted Florentine dressers. Other amenities: sitting rooms, a sun-drenched penthouse bar, and a rustic dining room with a rooftop view. Via Vittorio Emanuele Orlando 90, opposite the Grand Hotel. (phone: 474-3647). Moderate.

Nazionale – Another centrally located old favorite (of Sartre and de Beauvoir, among others), the *Nazionale* lies next to the Chamber of Deputies between the Corso and the Pantheon. 78 rooms. Major credit cards. Piazza Montecitorio 131 (phone: 678-9251). Moderate.

La Residenza – An exceptional bargain on a quiet street just behind Via Veneto. With only 27 luxurious rooms, it feels much more like a private villa than a hotel. Book well in advance. No restaurant. Via Emilia 22 (phone: 679-9592). Moderate.

Gregoriana – On the street of the same name — high fashion's headquarters in Rome — this tiny gem attracts the fashionable. Its decor is reminiscent of art deco, with room letters (rather than numbers) by 1930s fashion illustrator Erte. No restaurant. 19 rooms. Via Gregoriana 18 (phone: 679-4269 or 679-7988). Moderate to inexpensive.

Anglo-Americano – Conveniently off the piazza Barberini, its back rooms look out on the garden of Palazzo Barberini. 115 rooms. Diners Club, Visa, American Express. Via 4 Fontana 12 (phone: 47-29-41). Moderate to inexpensive.

Columbus – This second-class hotel in a restored historic palace near St. Peter's has a garden and antique furniture. 107 rooms. American Express, Visa, and Diners Club. Via della Conciliazione 33 (phone: 656-5435). Inexpensive.

Carriage – Another small inn without a restaurant, this one is on the picturesque street where the grand touring carriages *(carrozze)* of the eighteenth century were cleaned and repaired. It's a mere hop from the Spanish Steps, but is starting to get a little tacky. 24 rooms. Major credit cards. Via delle Carrozze 36 (phone: 679-5166). Inexpensive.

Dinesen – Conveniently situated behind the via Veneto and next to the Borghese Gardens, the rooms in this charming hotel are a real bargain. No restaurant. Via di Porta Pinciana 16/18 (phone: 475-4501 or 46-09-32). Inexpensive.

Margutta – Try for the two rooms on the roof complete with fireplaces and surrounded by a terrace. This hotel is near the piazza del Popolo. No restaurant. 21 rooms. Major credit cards. Via Laurina 34 (phone: 679-8440). Inexpensive.

Pensione Scalinata di Spagna – Spectacularly located overlooking the Spanish Steps, it's opposite the deluxe *Hassler*. No restaurant and no phones in rooms. 14 rooms. Piazza Trinità dei Monti 17 (phone: 679-3006). Inexpensive.

Fontana – A recently restored thirteenth-century monastery next to the Trevi Fountain, with cell-like rooms, some facing the fabulous fountain, and a lovely rooftop bar. American Express, Visa, Diners Club. Piazza di Trevi 96 (phone: 678-6113). Inexpensive.

Santa Elisabetta – This charming pension at the top of via Veneto has only 10 rooms. No restaurant. Via Vittorio Veneto 146 (phone: 475-8837). Inexpensive.

EATING OUT: Most Romans spend a great deal of their nonworking time eating, and they eat out more often than other Italians.

Italian food is generally marvelous, and it's good to remember that the much-heralded haute cuisine of France had its origins in Italy. Furthermore, any idea that Italian fare is limited to pasta and pizza is nonsense, and it is the enormous variety of Italian regional cooking that makes many gastronomes consider Italian food the premier national cuisine on this planet.

A visit to Rome can, therefore, be limited to merely experimenting with various Italian dishes and still be sublime. From the tomato-laced specialties of Naples and the garlic-filled dishes of Sicily to the exquisite concoctions served *Veneziana* (in the style of the kitchens of Venice) or *Bolognese* (from Bologna), there's plenty to try.

A few Roman specialties to be sure to sample are *saltimbocca* (which means "jump in the mouth"), veal scallopine covered with sage and ham and simmered in Marsala wine; *abbacchio al forno,* roast baby lamb; or *scottadito* ("finger-burning"), tiny grilled chops. Local pastas include *fettucine,* strips of egg pasta made by hand, often eaten *al'Alfredo,* in a butter, cream, and Parmesan cheese sauce; *gnocchi alla Romana,* semolina-based dumplings; and *spaghetti alla carbonara,* in a delicious egg sauce with unsmoked bacon. Artichokes are a favorite vegetable, often cooked with garlic and oil *(carciofi alla Romana),* or opened out like a flower and fried *(alla Giudia),* and so are very tasty mushrooms called *porcini,* also cooked in oil and garlic or simply grilled.

Italian wines are finally receiving the recognition they've long deserved and you can drink well ordering bottled wines with a DOC label (Denominazione di Origine Controllata), a government quality-control stamp of approval.

Finally, Italian ice cream is merely the best in the world, and only one taste will make you a believer. There are still people who come to the piazza Navona for the statues and baroque facades, but frequent visitors to Rome are really there for the *tartufo* (a truly scrumptious chocolate ice cream dish) at *Tre Scalini.* The ice cream at *Giolitti's,* just around the corner from the piazza Colonna at via Offici del Vicaro 40, is even better, and they have fresh fruit flavors that will bring tears of joy to your eyes.

It is possible to have a full meal, including house wine, for as little as $6 in a modest restaurant, while the same fare may cost twice that amount if the restaurant is even marginally fashionable. Most dining is à la carte; a *menu turistico* is offered at some unpretentious *trattorie* for very reasonable prices, and less expensive still are the quick service, often cafeteria-style, *rosticcerie* and *tavole calde* (literally "hot tables"). Most café-bars serve sandwiches as well as that delicious and filling health snack, *frullato di frutta* (a mixture of frothy liquidized fruit and milk), which is as inviting as a swim on a hot summer day. Be careful when ordering fresh fish or Florentine steaks *al kilo* — by weight — as this may swell a bill way out of proportion, even at average-priced restaurants.

Dinner for two (with wine) costs from $45 to as much as $90 in restaurants below classed as expensive; $25 to $45 is moderate; and $12 to $25 is inexpensive. The following is our current list of preferences:

El Toulà – Possibly the best restaurant in Rome today as well as one of the most expensive (starting at about $30 per person). The decor is elegant: softly lit warm browns and beiges, antique paintings, fresh flowers, and deep chairs. The cuisine is international, but their regional (Venetian) dishes outshine all others — and the simpler the better. Try the *risotto nero di seppie* (rice dish black with cuttlefish ink), *radicchio di Treviso ai ferri* (a sort of red lettuce grilled), and *gigot alla menta* (roast lamb with mint sauce). There's an impressive wine list. Closed Sundays and August. Reservations necessary. Major credit cards accepted. Via della Lupa 29B (phone: 678-1196). Expensive.

Papà Giovanni – Giovanni's son Renato now runs the show with great aplomb, though the service is sometimes slow. It's small and intimate, with paintings and wine bottles lining the walls, and the bar is very well stocked — sip a Kir as an *aperitivo* while choosing from over 700 wines. The cuisine is basically refined Roman, with truffles a seasonal specialty. Try *panzerotti al tartufo* (small ravioli with truffles) and *stufatino alla romana* (colorful Roman beef stew served on a hot king-size plate). Closed Sundays and the month of August. Reservations necessary. Via dei Sediari 4 (phone: 656-5308). Expensive.

Taverna Giulia – Authentic Genoese cuisine, with the addition of a few French dishes, is featured here, in the heart of Renaissance Rome (at the Florentine end of via Giulia). There are a few outdoor tables during the summer. *Crostini al salmone* (smoked salmon canapés) make a good starter, followed by *trenette al pesto* (thin noodles in a sauce of fresh basil, garlic, pine nuts, and olive oil) and *stinco al forno* (roast shoulder of veal in a flaky pastry shell). Closed Sundays and the month of August. Reservations advisable. American Express, Diners Club. Vicolo dell'Oro 23 (phone: 656-9768, 656-4089). Expensive.

Carmelo alla Rosetta – Carmelo is as Sicilian as the fish he flies in daily from Mazara del Vallo, Sicily, and his small *trattoria,* disguised as a fishing boat, smells of salt water and sun with just a hint of garlic. Not only does he manage to find the best oysters we've ever had in Italy, but his chef grills, fries, boils, or bakes to perfection any or a mixture of all the fish and seafood available. He also whips up a mean *pappardelle alla pescatore* (wide noodles in a garlicky, piquant tomato sauce with mussels, clams, and crispy parsley). Closed Sundays and Monday lunch. Reservations advisable. Via della Rosetta 9 (Pantheon) (phone: 656-1002). Expensive.

Cucurucu – Delightful gardens overlooking the Tiber provide one of Rome's most pleasant summer settings for dining al fresco, while inside it's cozy and rustic. Good *antipasti,* and meats grilled on an open fire. Ask for *bruschetta con pomodori* (toasted country bread smothered in fresh tomatoes and oregano) and *insalata di rughetta* (a salad of Rome's deliciously bitter rucola — summer only). Closed Mondays. Via Capoprati 10 (phone: 35-44-34 and 38-25-92). Expensive.

Bacaro – A new, tiny, exclusive gastronomic refuge with a total seating capacity of 20. Innovative cuisine is accompanied by an intelligent selection of wines (let them choose the wines for each course). *Bacaro*'s unwritten menu changes daily, but usually includes *originalissimi* homemade pasta dishes such as *tortelli di magro ai peperoni* (pasta stuffed with greens and ricotta cheese and served in an amazingly delicate sauce of sweet peppers). Closed Sundays. Reservations a must. Via degli Spagnoli 27 (phone: 656-4110). Expensive.

Il Cardinale – In a restored bicycle shop off the stately via Giulia, decorated in a cozy turn-of-the-century style, this eatery produces such fine dishes as *timballo di maccheroni in crosta dolce* (baked pasta in a pastry shell) and *aliciotti con l'indivia* (an anchovy and endive dish) as well as good *soufflé alla francese.* Closed Sundays and the month of August. Reservations necessary. Via delle Carceri 6 (phone: 656-9336). Expensive.

Le Cabanon – French and Tunisian food are served in an intimate ambience accompanied by Mediterranean melodies sung by the well-traveled Italian-Tunisian owner. South American, currently Venezuelan, singers ably fill in the gaps. The usual onion soup and *escargots,* as well as a delicious Tunisian *brik à l'oeuf* (a pastry concealing a challengingly dripping egg within), *couscous,* and *merguez* sausages. Open evenings only, and until late. Closed Sundays and the month of August. Reservations. Vicolo della Luce 4 (phone: 581-8106). Expensive.

Girarrosto Toscano – Brightly lit and bustling, a perfect place for hungry indecisive nonlinguists, as there's little opportunity to choose from the Tuscan menu or to speak at all. If you don't say no, you'll be brought various salamis, prosciutto, and fresh ricotta cheese, followed by some *fettuccine al prosciutto,* at which point you'll be asked about a main course. Simply nod positively and you'll probably be served a sizzling Florentine steak grilled to perfection. The rest is perfect too, but this is not a restful place. Closed Wednesdays and 2 weeks between late July and early August. Reservations necessary. American Express, Visa, Diners Club. Via Campania 29, behind via Veneto (phone: 49-37-59). Expensive.

Pino e Dino – A southerner and a northerner have created a menu of exciting regional dishes from the robust *pasta e broccoli alla calabrese* (for women it's served with a delicate rose) to *capretto abruzzese arrosto* (roast Abruzzi kid). It's located on one of Rome's more picturesque squares. A summer meal *en plein air* is only slightly more enticing here than a cozy winter meal indoors surrounded by wine bottles and artisan products from all over Italy. The two boys can be terribly touchy, so don't arrive late for your reservation. Closed Mondays and most of August. Piazza di Montevecchio 22 (phone: 656-1319). Expensive.

La Majella – On a delightful square colorfully illuminated in the summer for outdoor dining, this efficient organization with delicious food owes its fame and popularity to owner/manager Signor Antonio. The pope (while still a cardinal) numbered among its clientele, and the menu is nearly as long as the Bible. Fresh seafood is the major attraction. Closed Sundays and a week in August. Reservations advised. Major credit cards. Piazza S. Apollinare 45 (phone: 656-4174). Expensive to moderate.

Da Zorzetto – Distinguished northern (Veneto) cuisine with a few international additions, in a quiet ambience with friendly service. Start with an antipasto of *bresaola* or *soppressa veneta* or with the exceptional rice dish *risotto alla Zorzetto.* Fish or frogs' legs if available, game in season, and pepper steak or thinly sliced *carpaccio* (raw beef) are other good bets. Try a house wine from Venice's low-lying region, Tocai white or Raboso red. Closed Sundays. American Express, Diners Club. Reservations recommended. Via Flavia 63-65 (phone: 48-64-87). Expensive to moderate.

Taverna Flavia – It's been fashionable with the film world, journalists, and politicians for over 30 years. Owner Mimmo keeps their autographed pictures hanging on the walls, and the Sardi's style survives, despite the crash of the "Hollywood-on-the-Tiber" a decade ago. Fun for the trendy people. Open until quite late. Closed Sundays and August. Reservations necessary. Via Flavia 9/11 (phone: 474-5214). Expensive to moderate.

Piperno – A summer dinner outdoors on this quiet Renaissance piazzetta, next to the Palazzo Cenci — which still reeks "of ancient evil and nameless crimes" — is sheer magic. The indoors is modern and less magical, and the classical Roman-Jewish cooking can be a bit heavy. *Pasta e ceci* (pasta and chick pea soup) is always good, and the great specialty is *fritto vegetariano* (zucchini flowers, mozzarella cheese, salt cod, rice and potato balls, and artichokes — the latter "alla giudia" or "Jewish style" — all individually deep fried, the artichokes golden brown, crisp and crackling). Closed Mondays and the month of August. Reservations necessary. Monte de' Cenci 9 (phone: 654-0629). Expensive to moderate.

Alvaro al Circo Massimo – Let Alvaro suggest what's best that day and you'll not go wrong, whether it's fresh fish, game such as *fagiano* (pheasant) or *faraona* (guinea hen), or mushrooms (try grilled *porcini*). Its ambience is rustic indoors, and there are tables outdoors during the summer. Reservations are generally not necessary. Closed Mondays. Via dei Cerchi 53, on the corner of S. Teodoro (phone: 678-6112). Expensive to moderate.

Nino – A reliable place, frequented by artists, actors, and aristocrats, and centrally located near the Spanish Steps, *Nino's* is truly Tuscan, the cuisine composed of best-quality ingredients, ably yet simply prepared, and the service serious if not exactly heart-warming. Specialties: *zuppa di fagioli alla Francovich* (thick Tuscan white bean soup with garlic), *bistecca alla Fiorentina* (thick succulent T-bone steak), and for dessert *castagnaccio* (semisweet chestnut cake). Closed Sundays. Reservations advised. American Express. Via Borgognona 11 (phone: 679-5676). Moderate.

Dal Bolognese – Conveniently located next to the popular *Caffè Rosati* on the piazza del Popolo and with a menu nearly as long as the list of celebrities who frequent this fashionable eatery, the *Bolognese* is run by two brothers from Bologna. Although the food quality has been slipping lately, star-gazers will still enjoy their specialties such as homemade *tortelloni* (pasta twists stuffed with ricotta cheese) and the *bollito misto* (boiled beef, tongue, chicken, pig's trotter). There are tables outdoors in fine weather. Closed Mondays and most of August. Reservations necessary. Piazza del Popolo 1 (phone: 361-1426). Moderate.

Vecchia Roma – The setting is truly out of a midsummer's night dream on magical Piazza Campitelli on the fringe of Rome's Jewish "ghetto." The menu is varied, the ingredients fresh, the salads many and unusual. Closed Wednesdays and two weeks in August. Reservations recommended. Piazza Campitelli 18 (phone: 656-4604). Moderate.

Piccolo Mondo – Not exactly a "find," this cheerful and busy restaurant behind the via Veneto has been popular with Italians and foreigners alike for years. Among the many varied *antipasti* displayed at the entrance are exquisite *mozzarellini alla panna* (small balls of fresh buffalo's milk cheese swimming in cream), as well as eggplant and peppers prepared in several tempting ways. The good-natured waiters ply you with far too many tastes of different pasta dishes, leaving little hope of arriving at a main course. There are tables on the sidewalk in good weather. Closed Sundays and most of August. Reservations recommended. Major credit cards. Via Aurora 39 (phone: 475-4595). Moderate.

Il Drappo – Drapes softly frame the two small rooms of this romantic *ristorantino* run by the brother-sister team of Paolo and Valentina Tolu from Sardinia. The Tolus offer a delicate cuisine based on the robust island fare, but add fragrance

636 ROME / Best in Town

with wild fennel, myrtle, and herbs. The short but innovative menu, recited by
Paolo and artfully prepared by Valentina, always begins with mixed *antipasti*
including *carta di musica* (hors d'oeuvres on Sardinian crispy wafers). Closed
Sundays and 2 weeks in August. Reservations required. American Express. Vicolo
del Malpasso 9 (phone: 65-73-65). Moderate.

Ristorante della Campana – This unprepossessing place is favored by everyone
from neighborhood folk to the stars and staff of RAI, Italian radio-television.
Waiters help decipher the menu, which tempts most with perfect *carciofi alla
Romana* (fresh artichokes in garlic and oil), *tonnarelli alla chitarra* (homemade
pasta in an egg and cheese sauce) and ricotta-filled ravioli with butter and fresh
sage. Closed Mondays and August. Vicolo della Campana 18 (phone: 65-52-73,
656-7820). Moderate.

Osteria La Carbonara – Be it at one of the tables on the tables on the piazza or
inside amid exuberant peasant decor, this is the spot to sample the earthiest Roman
delights, from tripe to oxtail stew. The carafe wine is chancey, the bottled wines
good. Closed Tuesdays. Piazza Campo de' Fiori 23 (phone: 656-4783). Moderate
to inexpensive.

Mario – A Tuscan favorite, with the usual Tuscan specialties such as Francovich
soup, Florentine steaks, and delicious game in season, all prepared with admirable
care and dedication by Mario himself, but served by only three overworked waiters. Closed Sundays and August. Major credit cards. Via della Vite 55 (phone:
678-3818). Moderate to inexpensive.

Il Falchetto – Conveniently located off the Corso and with a few tables outdoors in
fine weather, this might seem a tourists's haven, but knowledgeable Romans fill
the small rooms even in the gray days of winter. One of the pasta specialties to
try is *paglia e fieno al salmone* (green and yellow noodles with a creamy smoked
salmon sauce). The imaginative game, veal, and fish dishes are also delicious.
Closed Fridays. American Express. Via Montecatini 12/14 (phone: 679-1160).
Moderate to inexpensive.

Arnaldo – A charming grotto of sorts decorated with curiosities that reveal Arnaldo's passion for the ballet. Not surprisingly, dancers number among his clientele. The cuisine features unusual combinations of pasta and vegetables and pork
with various fruit sauces as well as traditional fondue bourguignon or steak tartare
with caviar. Closed Tuesdays and a week in August. Via di Grotta Pinta 8 (phone:
656-1915). Moderate to expensive.

Osteria Ar Galletto – A beautiful warm-weather spot, it's set on Piazza Farnese
opposite the finest Renaissance palace in Rome. By all means, dine outside (inside
is dreary). Try Rome's favorite *bucatini all'amatriciana* (thick spaghetti with
tomato, bacon, and onion sauce) or *galletto alla diavola* (spring chicken heavily
peppered and grilled to a crunch). Closed Sundays. Piazza Farnese 102, corner
Vicolo del Gallo (phone: 656-1714). Inexpensive.

Carmelo – It's a trattoria, Sicilian style, with strolling minstrels and such typical
specialties as *maccheroni con melanzane, pasta con i broccoli* (pasta with broccoli),
and *pescespada alla messinese* (fresh swordfish in season, Messina style). Closed
Sundays. Via Roma Libera 5/7 (phone: 581-8088). Inexpensive.

Da Ciccio – Similar to *Carmelo,* but Calabrian. Busy, noisy, musical, and good fun.
Antipasti alla calabrese, spaghetti with broccoli or eggplant, and other southern
specialties. Several times a week, the owner's friend Maria dances — bordello style
— between the crowded tables. Closed Sundays. Reservations recommended. Via
dei Genovesi 37 in Trastevere (phone: 581-6017). Inexpensive.

Otello alla Concordia – A delightful trattoria in the middle of the shopping center,
with certain tables reserved for habitués and a colorful courtyard for fine weather
dining. The menu is Roman, and it changes daily, depending a great deal on the

season. A regular reliable is *cannelloni alla concordia.* Closed Sundays, Christmas week, and the first week in January. Reservations not accepted. Via della Croce 81 (phone: 679-1178). Inexpensive.

Da Giulio – Another bargain for budget-minded travelers, *Giulio's* is on a tiny street off via Giulia in a historic building. A few tables line the sunless street in the summer, and inside is most pleasant — if a bit noisy — with an original vaulted ceiling and paintings by local artists. Roman family-style cooking. Closed Sundays. No reservations. Via della Barchetta 19. Inexpensive.

Ettore Lo Sgobbone – A trattoria popular with newspaper and TV journalists. Noted for its unpretentious Northern home-style cooking. Pasta and rice *(risotto)* courses are excellent: try the simple *tonnarelli al pomodoro e basilico* (pasta with fresh tomato and basil sauce) or *risotto nero* (rice cooked with cuttlefish — and its ink!). Closed Tuesdays. Reservations recommended for the few tables outdoors. Via dei Podesti 8/10 (phone: 39-07-98). Inexpensive.

Palmerie – A trendy restaurant with fifties' fashions and ambience, and marble-topped tables with paper mats. The fixed-price menus appeal to the young. Dinner only. Closed Mondays. Reservations recommended on Fridays and Saturdays. Via Cimarra 4/5 (phone: 474-4110). Inexpensive.

La Fraschetta – A crowded restaurant/pizzeria with good Roman pasta dishes *(alla carbonara, matriciana)* and pizzas. Closed Mondays. Via San Francesco a Ripa 134 in Trastevere (phone: 581-6012). Inexpensive.

La Tana de Noiantri – Possibly more popular than the good wood-fired pizza here is the *focaccia,* crunchy flat bread. It's not on the menu, so ask the waiter for it. Closed Tuesdays. Via della Paglia I (phone: 580-6404, 580-6575). Inexpensive.

Ristorante La Capricciosa – This vast, comfortably shabby establishment makes some of the best pizza in Rome, but only in the evening. Its pizza and pasta menu must be the longest anywhere; mercifully, it is typewritten. Largo dei Lombardi 8. Inexpensive.

SALZBURG

For music lovers, Salzburg is mostly Mozart. But even those unenthralled by classical music are captivated by the charm of this almost picture-perfect small city in the mountains of west central Austria.

Salzburg is a city of four distinct seasons and moods. Spring brings blossoms to the orchards, music to the theaters and churches, and wild flowers to the meadows within sight of the heart of the city. Summer is the exuberance of the renowned Salzburg Music Festival, lazy days sailing on lakes, hours spent nursing a glass of wine or iced chocolate in a terrace café. In fall, the foliage show can rival New England's, and the city seems to return to its birthright as the masses of tourists evaporate. Winter is, for some, the best season — almost romantically silent and personal as the snowflakes waft through wrought-iron shop signs onto twisting, cobbled streets.

The visitor is blessed with an astonishingly small area to get to know. Familiarity of place comes rapidly. The Old City — a maze of unsquared corners, labyrinthine lanes, curious steeples, and surprisingly spacious squares — is nestled between Monk's Mountain (Mönchsberg) and the Salzach River, which divides the city. On the right bank, modern Salzburg spreads east. The city's environs are breathtaking: Azure glacial lakes, stunning châteaux, charming, timeless villages, and, always, the Alps.

The economy here was long based on the salt from the mines of the region, hence the name of the city and province. Today, industry, farming, and the development of resorts and spas, as well as tourism, contribute to a comfortable standard of living for the more than 400,000 people of the province.

Although Wolfgang Amadeus Mozart was born here and it was here that his remarkable prodigy was first acknowledged, he was not really appreciated in Salzburg during his brief lifetime. Today, however, the apartment in which he was born (in 1756) and the house in which he and his family later lived are landmarks. There is a square bearing his name with a statue of the composer at its center. A music academy, the Mozarteum, honors him, and in its garden is a wooden pavilion in which Mozart is said to have worked on his last opera, *The Magic Flute*. The garden pavilion was brought here from Mozart's Vienna home a century ago.

The Salzburg Festival, which draws thousands of visitors to the area in late July and August each year, is often dominated by his music. And there is a special Mozart Week music festival during the last week in January. Also of note are the Easter festival, the Whitsun concerts later in the spring, and the Salzburg Cultural Days in October.

Mozart left Salzburg for good at the age of 25, after breaking with Archbishop Hieronymus Colloredo, one of the last of the long line of autocratic archbishops who ruled Salzburg for nearly 1,000 years. An ancient Celtic settlement and then a Roman trading center, Salzburg was by AD 798 the seat of an archbishopric. The Salzburg archbishops also held the title of princes of the Holy Roman Empire and were the leading ecclesiastics of the German-speaking world. They built a beautiful city, but some ruled with extreme intolerance, expelling Jews and persecuting Protestants. After Salzburg was secularized in 1803, it became part of Bavaria for a time, but was returned to Austria in 1818.

Salzburg escaped serious damage during World War II while Austria was annexed to Germany. However, the Salzburg Festival — though it continued through 1943 — declined in significance because many musicians could not or would not participate. Following the Allied victory in Europe, the festival was revived and continues to be one of the most important musical events in Europe.

SALZBURG AT-A-GLANCE

SEEING THE CITY: The almost fairy-tale quality of Salzburg envelops you immediately as you approach the city from the east: the copper domes and belfries of the Old City outlined against a backdrop of mountains, the mighty fortress-castle (Festung Hohensalzburg) silhouetted against the sky. The terraces and the watch tower of the fort afford fine panoramas of the city and the Salzburg Alps to the south. It is reached by funicular (for a small charge) from Festungsgasse, near St. Peter's Churchyard at the foot of the mountain.

SPECIAL PLACES: The Old City lies on the left bank of the Salzach River, girded by Hohensalzburg and the orchard-laden Monk's Mountain (Mönchsberg). The modern city, on the right bank, is bordered on the south by a third mountain, Kapuzinerberg.

Hohensalzburg – The castle and fortress 400 feet above the city, atop a block of Dolomite rock, was begun in 1077 and completed in 1681. It was the stronghold, and sometime residence, of the archbishops of Salzburg. The castle's staterooms retain original decorations of Gothic wood carving, coffered ceilings, and intricate ironwork. Of particular interest are the huge porcelain stove (circa 1501) in the Gilded Room and the hand-operated barrel organ dating from 1502. Guided tours. Open daily. Small admission charge. From March through October and Christmas to mid-January it can be reached by funicular from Festungsgasse near St. Peter's Churchyard.

The Old City – Beneath Hohensalzburg, crowded between the mountains and the river, are the colorful, narrow streets of the Old City. The main thoroughfare, Getreidegasse, is lined with quaint shops and charming five- and six-story houses. In the typical old patrician house at number 9 is the third-floor apartment in which Mozart was born (Mozarts-Geburtshaus) and where he composed nearly all his early works. It is now a museum. (Open daily; small admission fee.) Getreidegasse leads into Judengasse, in the middle of what once was the Jewish ghetto. It, too, has shops adorned with medieval wrought-iron signs and picturesque buildings. The two streets meet near the Old Market Square (Alter Markt), with its colorful flower stalls, sixteenth-century fountain, and eighteenth-century pharmacy.

The Cathedral (Dom) – This fine early baroque cathedral with its two symmetrical towers, fine marble facade, and massive bronze doors was consecrated in 1628. When fire destroyed the previous late Romanesque cathedral in 1598, Archbishop Wolf

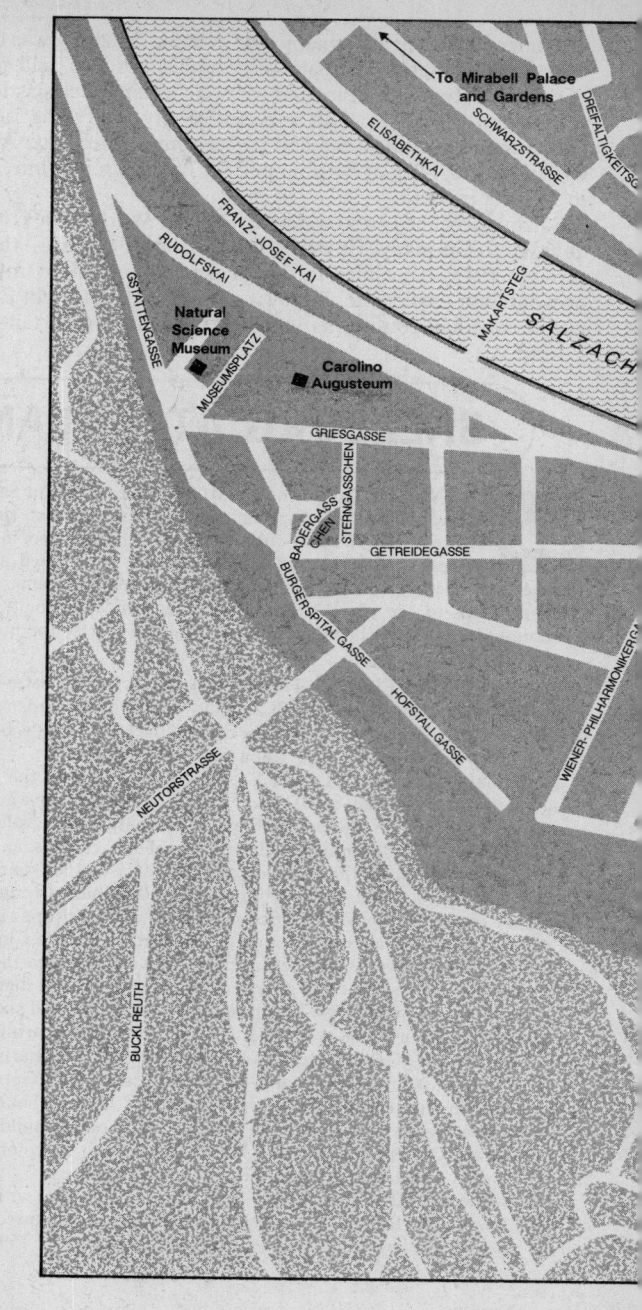

To Mirabell Palace
and Gardens

ELISABETHKAI

SCHWARZSTRASSE

DREIFALTIGKEITSC

FRANZ - JOSEF - KAI

RUDOLFSKAI

MAKARTSTEG

SALZACH

GSTÄTTENGASSE

Natural
Science
Museum

MUSEUMSPLATZ

Carolino
Augusteum

GRIESGASSE

BADERGASS
CHEN

STERNGASSSCHEN

GETREIDEGASSE

BÜRGERSPITAL GASSE

HOFSTALLGASSE

WIENER- PHILHARMONIKER G.

NEUTORSTRASSE

BÜCKLREUTH

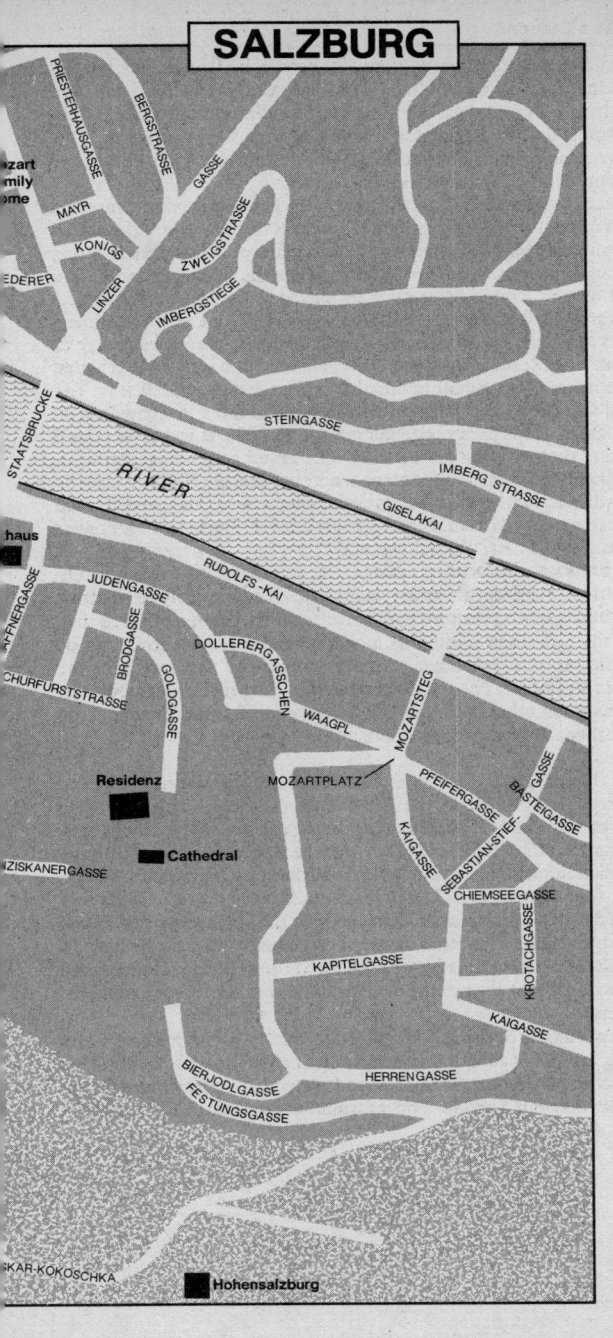

SALZBURG

Mozart family home

PRIESTERHAUSGASSE

BERGSTRASSE

GASSE

MAYR

KONIGS

ZWEIGSTRASSE

EDERER

LINZER

IMBERGSTIEGE

STAATSBRUCKE

STEINGASSE

RIVER

IMBERG STRASSE

GISELAKAI

haus

RUDOLFS-KAI

JUDENGASSE

KFNERGASSE

BROGASSE

DOLLERERGASSCHEN

CHURFURSTSTRASSE

GOLDGASSE

WAAGPL

MOZARTSTIEG

Residenz

MOZARTPLATZ

PFEIFERGASSE

GASSE

BASTEIGASSE

ZISKANERGASSE

Cathedral

KAIGASSE

SEBASTIAN-STIEF-

CHIEMSEEGASSE

KROTACHGASSE

KAPITELGASSE

KAIGASSE

BIERJODLGASSE

HERRENGASSE

FESTUNGSGASSE

KAR-KOKOSCHKA

Hohensalzburg

Dietrich wanted to build a new one larger than St. Peter's in Rome. But he was condemned for misconduct (he had 12 children by Salome Alt, his mistress) and died imprisoned in Hohensalzburg. His successors built a more modest, though quite beautiful, version. Note the Romanesque baptismal font where Mozart was baptized in 1756. The cathedral's treasure is on view in the museum, which is open daily from May to October. Small admission charge for the Museum. Dompl.

Residenz – The series of buildings on the north side of the Domplatz once comprised the ecclesiastical palace of the prince-archbishops. There are 15 staterooms, decorated with fine frescoes and paintings, on the second floor, and a gallery of European painting from the sixteenth through nineteenth century that includes the work of Rembrandt, Rubens, Breughel, and others. Young Mozart often played for guests of the prince-archbishop in the Conference Hall. Across the large square in front of the Residenz is an eighteenth-century carillon, or *Glockenspiel,* with 35 bells, played each day at 6 AM, 11 AM, and 7 PM. The Residenz is open daily; closed Sundays. Guided tours, except when events are in progress. Small admission charge. Residenzpl. 1.

Mirabell Palace and Gardens – Archbishop Wolf Dietrich built a lovely palace on the right bank of the Salzach for his paramour, Salome Alt, in 1606. It was later rebuilt and remodeled after being destroyed by fire in 1818. The grand ceremonial staircase, decorated with marble angels, is of particular interest, and the Marble Hall is a favorite place for weddings. Candlelit chamber music concerts are held here. The gardens, laid out in the early eighteenth century, are adorned with statues and marble vases, flowers of great variety, and small pools. East of Schwarzstr.

Hellbrunn Palace (Schloss Hellbrunn) – Once the summer residence of Archbishop Marcus Sitticus, this seventeenth-century castle is known primarily for its trick fountains, which spray unsuspecting visitors with water, and its theater of more than 100 mechanical figures that are set in motion by a clockwork movement to the music of an organ. Also on the grounds are a zoo (Alpenzoo) and the Salzburg Folklore Museum in the Monatsschlösschen. The palace is open daily, April through October; the zoo is open all year. Small admission charge. At the end of Hellbrunnerstr., off Alpenstr., 3 miles (5 km) south of downtown Salzburg.

■**EXTRA SPECIAL:** The fantastic ice formations that have developed at the entrance to the caves of the World of the Ice Giants (Eisriesenwelt) are world renowned. The caves open at 5,459 feet on the western cliffs of the Hochkogel, some 30 miles (48 km) south of Salzburg. They may be visited from May through early October; detailed information is available from the state tourist information office in Mozartpl. (see *Sources and Resources*). You'll need warm clothes and sturdy shoes. If you drive there, stop at Hallein and visit the Dürnnberg salt mines, which have been worked since Neolithic times, and the lovely Golling Waterfalls near the village of Golling. Leave Salzburg on Route 311 for Hallein, Golling, and the village of Werfen. It is best to take the Werfen taxibus service to the cable car station for the caves.

American Express runs a *Sound of Music Tour* of the film's locations and settings: a rewarding excursion covering some 65 miles in 3 hours with the Rodgers and Hammerstein score playing on the bus's sound system. It's corny but still fun. Tours are given every day but Sunday. For information: American Express, Mozartplatz 5 (phone: 4-2501).

SOURCES AND RESOURCES

The City of Salzburg Visitors' Bureau (Stadtverkehrsbüro), which can provide you with maps, brochures, and various information, has its main office at Auerspergstr. 7 (phone: 7-3866, 7-1511 or 7-4620). There are several other branches, including one at Mozartpl. 5, in the Old City, and another in the main railway station. The tourist office for the state of Salzburg (Landesverkehrsamt) is at Mozartpl. 1 (phone: 4-1561 or 4-3202).

 **CLIMATE AND CLOTHES:** Salzburg has moderate weather. Even in the coldest month, January, temperatures don't go much below 25°F (−4°C). July is the warmest month; temperatures reach about 85°F (29°C). September is the most consistently pleasant month. Tweeds, knits, and woolens are apropos for the cooler months, and many visitors buy locally made loden coats and folkwear. For important events during the Salzburg Festival, dress is quite formal.

 GETTING AROUND: Just about everything of interest to the visitor is within easy walking distance of the Residenzplatz. The entire Old City and the Getreidegasse are pedestrian zones.

Bicycle – *Willy Krois,* Ignaz Harrerstr. 88 (phone: 3-2263), rents bicycles all year round.

Bus – There is quick, comfortable bus service. Buses stop running at 11 PM.

Taxi – There are taxi stands at key spots throughout the city, and you may book one in advance by calling 7–6111. Fares, even though cabs are metered, are high.

Car Rental – Major international firms are represented.

 MUSEUMS: In addition to those already mentioned in *Special Places,* Salzburg has several museums of interest:

Mozart Family Home (Mozarts Wohnhaus), Makartpl. 8 (phone: 74-89-73).

Natural Science Museum (Haus der Natur), Museumspl. 5 (phone: 4-2653).

Carolino Augusteum, Museumspl. 6 (phone: 4-3145).

Baroque Museum (Salzburger Barockmuseum), Mirabell Gardens Orangerie (phone: 7-7432).

Burg Museum (exhibits about the city's development), Hohensalzburg.

Toy Museum, Bürgerspital.

 SHOPPING: Loden coats and Lederhosen, antiques, and handmade sweaters are good buys in Salzburg.

M. H. Grotjan – Antique small furnishings. Goldgasse 13.

Jahn-Markl – Lederhosen and leather garments. Residenzpl. 3.

Lanz – Home of the internationally known line of cotton prints, flannel nightwear, and other sporty women's clothes. Schwarzstr. 4.

Salzburger Heimatwerk – Handmade peasant crafts of the region. Residenzpl. 9.

Slezak – High-quality leather handbags and briefcases, gloves, sweaters, and souvenirs. Makartpl. 8.

Street Markets – Fruits and vegetables are on sale at the *Grünmarkt* at Universitätsplatz and Wiener Philharmonikergasse every morning but Sunday (Saturday is liveliest) and on weekday afternoons. On Thursday mornings, flowers and crafts, as well as a wide variety of edibles, are sold at the *Schrannenmarkt* near St. Andrew's Church.

SPECIAL EVENTS: Programs for the *Salzburg Festival* are announced at the beginning of the year. Information about advance tickets is available from Austrian National Music Festivals, 20th floor, 500 Fifth Ave., New York, NY 10110 (phone: 212-944-6880). The advance sale of tickets in the US usually ends about mid-May. After that, ticket requests must be addressed to: Ticket Office of the *Salzburg Festival,* Festspielhaus, A-5010 Salzburg, Austria. It is often impossible to secure tickets to major events once the festival has begun. However, tickets may be available for chamber music concerts and outdoor performances.

Information about programs and tickets for the *Mozart Week* music festival, during the last week in January, and the *Easter Festival* and Whitsun concerts, both under the direction of Herbert von Karajan also is available from the New York office of the Austrian National Tourist Office.

 SPORTS: Golf – A 9-hole course is available at the *Klesheim Golf Country Club,* Klesheim, on the western outskirts of the city (phone: 3-1414).

Running – There are fitness runs, ranging from a mile at *Naturpark Aigen* to the slightly more than 3-mile (5-km) *Gaisberg Circular Run.*

Swimming – An indoor pool is at the *Kurhaus* in the Mirabell Gardens and there are outdoor pools in several parks. Bathing caps are a must for everyone.

Tennis – Courts are available at *Tennisklub Salzburg,* Ignaz Rieder Kai 3 (phone: 2-2403), or the *Tenniscentrum,* Kasern, in the suburb of Lengfelden (phone: 7-6550).

 THEATER: The performance of *Everyman (Jedermann),* the morality play by Hugo von Hofmannsthal, each year in the forecourt of the cathedral is one of the few non-Mozart traditions connected with the *Salzburg Festival.* The famous *Salzburg Marionette Theater (Salzburger Marionetten Theater),* Schwarzstr. 24 (phone: 7-2406), gives performances of operas and operettas. The season runs from Easter through September; events also take place at Christmastime. Schedules and advance tickets are available from Austrian National Festivals, 20th floor, 500 Fifth Ave., New York, NY 10110 (phone: 212-944-6880).

 MUSIC: Salzburg is a city of music even in nonfestival months. The *Landestheater,* Schwarzstr. 22 (phone: 7-4086), schedules operettas and operas as well as its regular diet of classical and contemporary drama from September through mid-June. There are organ concerts and other music at the *Mozarteum,* Schwarzstr. 26 (phone: 7-3154), chamber music in the Residenz and Mirabell palaces, and more music in churches and parks throughout the year.

 NIGHTCLUBS AND NIGHTLIFE: Evenings in Salzburg tend more toward quiet dinners and concerts than toward floor shows and discotheques. But if you must boogey, try *Friesacher Stadl,* Anif 57 (phone: 06246-2411), in the suburb of Anif. And there is folk dancing at the *Sternbräu* beer garden, Getreidegasse 23 (phone: 4-2140), every Friday night. If you see posters advertising that the Salzburger Stierwascher folkloric group is playing in town, be sure to go.

 SINS: You could *gamble* the night away at the elegant *Salzburg Casino* on Mönchsberg (phone: 4-5656) or make *gluttony* your most serious vice by indulging in fanciful pastries and ice cream creations at one of Salzburg's delightful *Konditoreien,* such as *Schatz,* Getreidegasse 3 (phone: 4-2792); *Bazar,* Schwarzstr. 3 (phone: 7-4278); and *Tomaselli* (phone: 4-4488 or 4-5070) and *Fuerst* (phone: 4-3759) in the Alter Markt.

BEST IN TOWN

 CHECKING IN: Salzburg has a rich range of accommodations, but it must be stressed that reservations should be made months in advance for the festival season. There is a hotel "finding service" at the railway station and at Mozartplatz 5. The price of a double room with breakfast in an expensive hotel will range from $70 to $120 a night; in a moderately priced hotel, from $45 to $70; and in an inexpensive one, from $30 to $45. The highest rates apply during the Salzburg Festival.

Goldener Hirsch – A group of 800-year-old patrician houses have been joined to create a country-inn ambience in the heart of the Old City. Rooms vary in size; many have antique furnishings or native folk art hangings. The dining room serves just about the best food in the city (see *Eating Out*). Major credit cards. Getreidegasse 37 (phone: 4-1511). Expensive.

Sheraton – Opened in 1984, this hotel chain's Viennese base is perfectly situated downtown beside the Paracelsus Kurhaus spa, the Mirabell Gardens, and the Salzburg Conference Center. Major credit cards. Auerspergstrasse 4 (phone: 79-32-10 or 79-33-10). Expensive.

Österreichischer Hof – Across the Salzach River from the Old City near the Mozarteum, this traditional hotel has an impressive skylighted central court. Rooms vary, but many are high-ceilinged, and all are large, comfortable, and cheerful. Try to reserve a room overlooking the river. Excellent food (see *Eating Out*). Major credit cards. Schwarzstr. 5–7 (phone: 7-2541). Expensive to moderate.

Weisse Taube – In the center of the city, this is a small hotel with rafters, wrought iron, and all amenities. Kaigasse 9 (phone: 4-2404 or 4-1783). Moderate to inexpensive.

Pitter – A rambling, cozy, family-run downtown hotel with five restaurants, of which the *Rainer Stube* is favored by natives in the know. Major credit cards. Rainerstrasse 6-8 (phone: 7-5871). Moderate to inexpensive.

Steinlechner – The only drawback — for some people — to this charming little hotel in an old, converted mansion is its location: a 15-minute ride from the center. But the *Steinlechner,* on the southern edge of the city, is on a good bus line. It has lovely, though small, rooms and is set in beautiful gardens. Aignerstr. 4 (phone: 2-0061). Moderate to inexpensive.

Elefant – This ancient inn in the heart of the Old City is well kept and friendly. Folk art embellishes a basic simplicity. Major credit cards. Sigmund-Haffnergasse 4 (phone: 4-3397 or 4-3409). Inexpensive.

 EATING OUT: Besides the breaded veal cutlet, called *Wiener Schnitzel,* typical Austrian fare includes dumplings, *Knödel* and *Nockerl;* spicy stew, *Gulasch;* and, of course, pastries. But the city's most famous dessert is the soufflé, *Salzburger Nockerln,* an extravagant meringue that's usually served with a dollop of raspberry or other fruit jam. Dinner for two with beer or house wine at an expensive restaurant will cost between $35 and $70; from $20 to $35 at a moderately priced restaurant; and from $10 to $20 at an inexpensive one. Although a 10% tip is included in most menu prices, an extra 5% gratuity is expected if service has been adequate.

Goldener Hirsch – The most discriminating palate will find satisfaction at this fine restaurant in one of Salzburg's most attractive hotels. Its exciting and inventive kitchen prepares both Continental dishes and Austrian specialties. As for dessert, the *Goldener Hirsch* is noted for its excellent *Salzburger Nockerln.* Getreidegasse 37 (phone: 4-1511). Expensive.

Café-Restaurant Winkler – For the price, the food is tolerable, but the view from Mönchsberg makes it all worthwhile. Reached by lift from the foot of the mountain at Gstättengasse. Mönchsberg 32 (phone: 4-1215). Expensive.

Österreichischer Hof – Some of the best dishes in Salzburg are prepared in the kitchen of this fine hotel restaurant (see *Checking In*). Specialties include pike in crayfish sauce, *Hechtspatzen in Krebsensauce,* and venison pie, *Wildpastete.* Schwarzstr. 5–7 (phone: 7-2541). Expensive to moderate.

Das Beisl – This small inn, just the other side of the Neutor tunnel from the Old City, is furnished in Jugendstil (turn-of-the-century Austrian art nouveau). The house pâté *(Hauspastete)* is a stunning overture to a fine selection of dishes from an imaginative menu. Neutorstr. 28 (phone: 4-5659). Moderate.

Stiftskellerei St. Peter – A wine cellar in the sixteenth century, this popular spot serves local peasant dishes, such as *Bauernschmaus:* smoked pork, sausage, sauerkraut, and dumplings. The wine is from the abbey's own vineyards. Adjacent to St. Peter's Church (phone: 4-1268). Moderate to inexpensive.

Festungsrestaurant – Good food and a view from the fortress-castle can be had here. Festung Hohensalzburg (phone: 4-1780). Moderate to inexpensive.

Stieglkeller – This beer garden, seat of the Stiegl brewery, is a beloved institution for natives as well as tourists, and folklore shows are presented between June and September. Closed October through April. Festungsgasse 10 (phone: 4-2681). Inexpensive.

STOCKHOLM

When Stockholm officials announced a few years ago that the city's waterway had been restored to a level of cleanliness that permitted swimming, the news was received with due pride but little surprise by local residents. It merely confirmed their conviction that Stockholm was that rare phenomenon: a city that improves with age.

Sweden's 700-year-old capital is quite simply one of the most beautiful cities in the world. From the winding, cobbled streets of its medieval district to the granite, marble, and glass of its modern downtown commercial and shopping complexes, it exudes a serene majesty. While Venice crumbles and city administrations around the world struggle with the ubiquitous demons of traffic, pollution, and crime, Stockholm grows stronger in its quiet way.

Stockholm was founded in the thirteenth century on a small, strategically located island on Sweden's east coast where the waters of Lake Mälaren join the Baltic Sea. As Stockholm grew, the original Old Town (Gamla Stan) became known as the City between the Bridges. Through the centuries, the number of bridges it was between proliferated as the city spread across wide bays, broad channels, and narrow waterways until today its population of 463,000 is spread over 14 islands. Stockholm's harbor opens into an archipelago of 24,000 islands, skerries, and islets. It is the Baltic's largest port, and yet it has no bawdy, tawdry waterfront quarter to act as a breeding ground of poverty and vice. And its encircling bracelets of water have freed Stockholm from the ugly collar of drab suburbs that blight so many of Europe's cities.

Not so many years ago, Stockholm was looked upon as a beautiful, romantic city, but sadly provincial by Continental standards. Today Stockholm stands as the showpiece of Sweden's democratic socialism: a clean, well-planned metropolis as sophisticated, subtle, and savvy as any, whose people enjoy a high standard of living. Remote from the power blocks and conurbations of central Europe, Stockholm has been content to pursue a slow, steady plan of development. Sweden's geographic and political isolation helped spare it the ravages of World War II, and public officials with a sense of aesthetics guided the city's growth to ensure a pleasing harmony of line and tone. The result has been a comfortable marriage of modern — and super modern — architecture and restored historic facades. Once one of Europe's poor countries, its economy dominated by agriculture, Sweden has been transformed over the past 100 years into a modern welfare state. It is a constitutional monarchy with a parliamentary government system. Yet despite the obvious social equality of its citizens, the sober elegance of some of Stockholm's older districts still manages to convey an overall impression of bourgeois complacency.

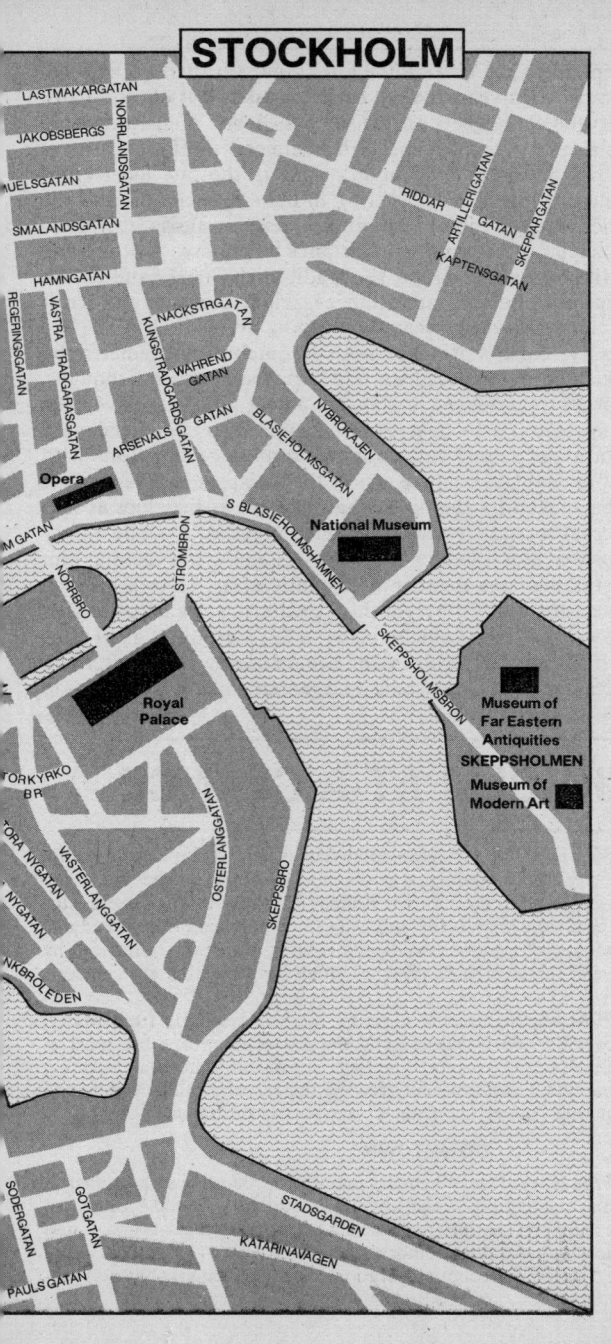

STOCKHOLM

LASTMAKARGATAN

JAKOBSBERGS

NORRLANDSGATAN

MUELSGATAN

SMALANDSGATAN

HAMNGATAN

REGERINGSGATAN

VASTRA TRADGARASGATAN

KUNGSTRADGARDSGATAN

NACKSTRGATAN

WAHREND GATAN

ARSENALS GATAN

BLASIEHOLMSGATAN

NYBROKAJEN

RIDDAR GATAN

ARTILLERIGATAN

SKEPPARGATAN

KAPTENSGATAN

Opera

M GATAN

NORRBRO

S BLASIEHOLMSHAMNEN

STROMBRON

National Museum

SKEPPSHOLMSBRON

Museum of Far Eastern Antiquities

SKEPPSHOLMEN

Museum of Modern Art

Royal Palace

TORKYRKO BR

TORA NYGATAN

VASTERLANGGATAN

NYGATAN

OSTERLANGGATAN

SKEPPSBRO

NKBROLEDEN

SODERGATAN

GOTGATAN

STADSGARDEN

KATARINAVAGEN

PAULS GATAN

There is one exception to the city's ultra-low profile on the international scene. In mid-December each year, the red carpet is taken out of mothballs, the silverware and crystal chandeliers are given a polish, and preparations are made to receive the annual crop of Nobel Prize winners (the Peace Prize is presented in Oslo; the others in Stockholm). This is the one local event guaranteed to set teletype machines chattering in news agencies around the world. With its ancient streets and contemporary consciousness, Stockholm is a fitting place for such a pomp-and-circumstance ceremony. Visitors who wonder how strict the formalities are at the traditional Nobel banquet are merely informed that all who seek admittance — right down to the hard-bitten press photographers — must wear full evening dress.

Yet the city's stuffy, elder statesman pose is quickly contradicted by manifestations of bustling commercialism and progressive liberal thought. Turning the next corner may delight or shock. Cabinet ministers have been known to ride the subway to Parliament. Palace guards wear shoulder-length hair. And the city ordinance most strictly imposed on sex clubs deals with precautions against fire. One has come to expect the unexpected. Even so, the mood of calm can be shaken by the occasional incident as puzzling as it is bizarre. Zealous internal revenue investigators once triggered a public outcry by seizing distinguished film director Ingmar Bergman and taking him "downtown for questioning" in a manner as dramatic as the plots of his own films. On another occasion a sit-in by youthful demonstrators actually succeeded in thwarting well-advanced official plans to fell a group of giant elms in a city park. Even if nothing half as dramatic occurs during your visit, there is a wealth of historical buildings, museums, and monuments, not to mention uninhibited nightlife, to occupy your time.

STOCKHOLM AT-A-GLANCE

SEEING THE CITY: The very best aerial view of Stockholm is from planes circling the city before landing; if you can't have that, ascend to the the observation gallery atop the 500-foot Kaknäs TV tower on the eastern edge of town. A bird's-eye view is the only way to comprehend fully the idyllic setting of the city. A mosaic of wooded islands and winding waterways enhanced by twisting copper spires and turreted roofs stretches almost as far as the eye can see.

SPECIAL PLACES: Sightseeing tours by bus run regularly from March through November (on weekends only the rest of the year), but most of central Stockholm can be explored on foot. The narrow lanes and charming squares of the Old Town especially reward the casual stroller. Sightseeing barges provide a fascinating "under the bridges" perspective on the city.

DOWNTOWN

Wasa Dockyard (Wasavarvet) – When the man-of-war *Wasa* was launched in 1628, she was intended as the flagship of the Royal Swedish Navy. But she foundered on the way out of Stockholm's harbor on her maiden voyage. This tragic — and embarrassing — mishap was but a dim memory when the wreck was rediscovered in 1956. During the next 5 years, a salvaging operation raised the remarkably well preserved warship and some 24,000 historic items aboard her from the harbor bottom. The *Wasa* and her fittings are now housed in a special museum complex. A short film detailing the salvage operation precedes regular guided tours in English. Open daily. Small admission charge. Djurgården (phone: 22-39-80).

Skansen – This folklore center and summer meeting place for people of all ages is a short walk from the Wasa Museum. Opened in 1891, Skansen was the prototype for outdoor museums now found throughout the world. More than 150 buildings of historic interest, brought here from various regions of Sweden, reflect the daily lives of rural and urban Swedes through the ages. In summer, craftsmen demonstrate glass blowing, weaving, and other traditional skills. Skansen's hilltop setting also houses a zoo; and concerts, open-air dancing, and shows here enliven the Stockholm summer scene. The grounds are not fully open during the winter, but a traditional Christmas market is held at Skansen on several Sundays during Yuletide. Grounds open daily in summer until 11:30 PM, buildings close earlier. Small admission charge. Djurgården (phone: 63-05-00).

The Old Town (Gamla Stan) – Birger Jarl founded the city of Stockholm on the central island of Gamla Stan in 1252. This Old Town district, a warren of small buildings jumbled together in crooked rows, is unmistakably medieval in character. Narrow lanes open onto market squares where merchants have traded since the thirteenth century. Even today, this remains one of the liveliest districts of the city. Careful and continuous renovation has preserved the buildings that now house about 300 small shops, restaurants, nightclubs, artists' studios, and boutiques. South of Stockholm's modern center; reachable by several short bridges.

The Royal Palace (Stockholms Slott) – The Royal Family has now taken up residence at Drottningholm Palace (see below) to provide a greener environment for the children. Parts of the Royal Palace and the Royal Treasury with the crown jewels are open to the public, official engagements permitting. The palace, with its baroque and rococo furnishings and exquisite collections of tapestry and chinaware, was built in the late seventeenth and early eighteenth centuries. A colorful changing-of-the-guard ceremony takes place each midday in summer; 1 PM Sundays. Open until mid-afternoon daily; closed Mondays. Small admission charge. At the foot of Norrbro Bridge, on Gamla Stan (phone: 11-85-51).

Stockholm Cathedral (Storkyran) – A short walk from the Royal Palace, through the Old Town, takes you to Stockholm Cathedral, built in the thirteenth century and rebuilt between 1736 and 1742. Its ornate interior includes a masterful wood sculpture, *Saint George and the Dragon* by Bernt Nötke, dating from 1479. Behind the Royal Palace on Trångsund.

City Hall (Stadshuset) – The colonnaded red brick facade of this seat of Stockholm government is a masterpiece of architectural understatement. The building, inaugurated in 1923, contains a spectacular Gilded Hall. Guided tours are offered daily at 10 AM and there is sometimes an additional tour at noon on Sundays. The 320-foot City Hall tower offers an impressive panorama of the city. Small admission charge. Hantverkargatan 1 (phone: 785-9060).

Postal Museum (Postmuseum) – A large and outstanding collection of postage stamps is housed in this lovely old building in Gamla Stan which has an interesting history connected with the postal services. There is an authentic nineteenth-century mail coach. If you ask nicely, they will open the safelike display case to reveal the pride of the collection — two rare 1847 Mauritius stamps and a quarter-sheet of 4-Skilling banco. Don't bother making an offer, they're priceless. Open daily. Free. Lilla Nygatan 6 (phone: 781-1755).

Museum of Far Eastern Antiquities (Östasiatiska Museet) – Surprisingly, Sweden has a long tradition in Sinological studies. The Chinese exhibit here includes Stone Age ceramics from 2000 BC; a rich collection of jade pieces; carvings in wood, ivory, and horn; Chinese lacquer; and interesting everyday paraphernalia such as mirrors and dress hooks. The museum also has collections of fine arts and handicrafts from Japan, Korea, and India. Open daily; closed Mondays. Small admission charge. Skeppsholmen (phone: 24-42-00).

Östermalms Saluhall – This large old covered market is where Stockholm's gourmets buy fresh meat, fish, and delicatessen goods. Steeped in atmosphere and rich in lively characters, the market offers visitors a taste of typical Swedish market trading from the past. A few blocks east of the city center on Östermalmstorg.

Kungsträdgården – This broad, tree-lined avenue-cum-park with its dancing fountains in summer and ice skating during the winter months is an ideal place to engage in the pleasures of people-watching. Kungsträdgardsgatan.

Stockholm's Steamers – By the City Hall and opposite the *Grand Hotel* one can catch sight of smart white steamships bobbing at their moorings. These genuine turn-of-the-century steam vessels are lovingly preserved and still contribute to the heavy summer traffic out to the archipelago. There is a powerful, romantic attachment to the islands they serve that stretch from Stockholm's doorstep right out to sea. You will not have touched the heart of the city until you have made the steamer trip out to an island paradise, such as the yachting center, Sandhamn. Several steamer operators offer frequent trips of varying lengths to the islands. Throughout the summer, daily ferry service to Sandhamn is operated by *Strommakanal AB*, Nybrogatan 76 (phone: 24-11-00). Local tourist offices have information on other schedules.

Waldemarsudde – This beautiful retreat in an exquisite setting was the home of the late Prince Eugen, an accomplished artist. His fine collection of paintings and sculpture is on exhibit here. Open daily; closed Mondays. Small admission charge. Djurgården (phone: 62-18-33).

House of Culture (Kulturhuset) – A modern center where exhibitions of art, handicraft, and design are featured and information is available on urban planning, history, culture, and Swedish social policies. Creative activities for children and adults are scheduled regularly. Tourists may find its library and foreign newspapers particularly useful. Open daily except Mondays. Sergelstorg 3 (phone: 14-11-20).

Museum of Modern Art (Moderna Museet) – Interesting special exhibitions of the work of contemporary artists complement the museum's permanent collection of twentieth-century art. Open daily until 9 PM; weekends until 5 PM; closed Mondays. Small admission charge. Skeppsholmen (phone: 24-42-00).

SUBURBS

Millesgården – Many of the finest works of sculptor Carl Milles are displayed in the terraced garden of his former home on fashionable Lidingö Island overlooking central Stockholm. The waterside residence also contains the sculptor's rich art collection, including some of the classical Greek and Roman statues that influenced his own work. Open daily, May through October 15, with evening hours on Tuesdays and Thursdays in June and July. Small admission charge. Reached by subway to Ropsten, where buses leave frequently for Millesgården. Carl Milles väg 2, on Lidingö (phone: 765-0553).

Drottningholm Palace – This seventeenth-century palace was built for dowager Queen Hedvig Eleonora in extensive parkland on the island of Lovön just 5 miles west of Stockholm. The French-style palace and its beautiful gardens suffer from the inevitable comparison with Versailles but deserve recognition in their own right. The Chinese Pavilion, a small, rococo summer house in the park, also is open to visitors from April through mid-October. The palace and grounds are reached by road or by steamer that departs from Klara Mälarstrand near City Hall. Visitors also can take the subway to Brommaplan and then change to Mälaröbuses, which stop here. Open daily May through September. Small admission charge. Lovön (phone: 759-0310).

Drottningholm Court Theater (Drottningholms Slottstheater) – On the palace grounds, this superb rococo building is fully deserving of separate mention as one of the most perfectly preserved eighteenth-century theaters anywhere. During summer months, the theater's original stage sets and machinery are used for performances of period operas and ballets. But the 350-seat auditorium and theater museum are worthy of a visit at any time. Guided tours are available. Open May through September. Small admission charge. Lovön Island (phone: 759-0406).

■ **EXTRA SPECIAL:** The university and cathedral city of Uppsala lies less than 40 miles (64 km) north of Stockholm and offers much of historic interest to make the trip worthwhile. In addition to the medieval cathedral and fine seventeenth-century castle, the famous silver Bible *Codex Argenteus* is housed in the university library; Swedish botanist Carolus Linnaeus is honored with a museum at his former home; and there are burial mounds that represent the only Viking remains in this part of Sweden. Soak up the atmosphere as you down Viking mead, brewed from hops and honey and served in traditional ornamental horns at pubs.

On the way to Uppsala, a short detour will take you to the oldest town in Sweden, Sigtuna. This small community was once immensely important, serving as the capital of the nation for over a century.

SOURCES AND RESOURCES

For general tourist information, call at Sweden House, Kungsträdgården (phone: 789-2000), where the Swedish Tourist Board and the Stockholm Information Service provide maps and literature. The $7-a-day Key to Stockholm tourist card — good for a free sightseeing tour, unlimited use of public transportation, and admission to most museums — is also available from the Information Service. Call *Miss Tourist* (phone: 22-18-40) for a summary of the day's events in English. Most hotels supply copies of *This Week in Stockholm,* a free review of current goings-on in the city.

A useful address for businesspeople is Industrihuset, Storgatan 19 (phone: 783-8000), headquarters for numerous Swedish industrial organizations and export bodies.

CLIMATE AND CLOTHES: Bear in mind that Stockholm shares the same latitude as lower Alaska, and the climate will seem surprisingly mild. June, July, and August usually are the warmest months, with a good chance of sunshine and temperatures averaging about 70°F (21°C) during the daytime. You'll need cardigans for cool summer evenings from May through September. During May and June, there is only a short period of darkness each night at this latitude, resulting in long, gloriously romantic evenings. Winter usually sets in sometime during November. Thereafter, temperatures fall well below zero and heavy snowfall can be expected on and off until March or April. The good news is the low humidity, which makes for a dry, crisp, and, in some ways, pleasant cold. Woolen underwear, a heavy topcoat, warm gloves, and sensible footwear are recommended. Rubber overshoes are useful and can be purchased locally.

GETTING AROUND: Subway and Bus – The Stockholm subway is clean, efficient, extensive, and by far the quickest means of intracity transportation. The newer stations have been designed by leading artists. The Kungsträdgården station downtown, for instance, has stone statues and miniature waterfalls. Some locals avoid the subway at night because of intermittent disturbances by homeward-bound revelers (harsh drinking-and-driving laws keep them off the roads).

All parts of the city are linked by bus routes, but during morning and evening rush hours progress can be slow despite special bus-only traffic lanes. Special tourist discount passes for subways, buses, and streetcars can be purchased at major bus and subway stations as well as at newspaper stands called *Pressbyra*.

Taxi – Taxis are plentiful except during rush hours and inclement weather. They can be hailed in the street — an illuminated roof sign indicates they are available for hire — but the surest way is to call 15-00-00 or book in advance by calling *Tourist-Taxis*, which has bilingual drivers (phone: 15-04-00).

Car Rental – Major firms are represented at the domestic and international airports and at downtown locations.

Ferry Service – Small ferryboats operate regular services between Räntmästartrappan by the Old Town and Allmänna Gränd on Djurgården, and in summer between Nybroplan downtown and Allmänna Gränd. Cheap and great fun.

MUSEUMS: Stockholm has over 50 museums, art galleries, and historic buildings. Those of note not listed in *Special Places* are:
  Museum of National Antiquities and the Royal Coin Cabinet, Narvavägen 13–17 (phone: 783-9400).
Royal Army Museum, Riddargatan 13 (phone: 60-38-53).
House of Nobility, Riddarhustorget (phone: 10-08-57).
National Museum of Fine Arts, Södra Blasieholmshamnen (phone: 24-42-00).
Nordiska Museet, Djurgården (phone: 22-41-20).
Riddarholm Church, Riddarholmen across the bridge from the Old Town (phone: 11-85-61).
Strindberg Museum, Drottninggatan 85 (phone: 11-37-89).
Thiel Gallery, on Djurgården (phone: 62-58-84).
National Museum of Science and Technology, Museivägen 7 (phone: 63-10-85).
Swedish Museum of Natural History, Frescati (phone: 15-02-40).
The Hallwyl Museum, Hamngatan 4 (phone: 10-21-66).
National Maritime Museum, Djurgårdsbrunnsvägen (phone: 22-39-80).

SHOPPING: Shopping is a major pastime of the affluent Swedes, a fact reflected in the heavy concentration of richly stocked department stores, trendy boutiques, and exclusive shops. Stockholm's main shopping district is the area around Sergelstorg Square, Hamngatan, Kungsgatan, and the market square, Hötorget, and adjoining streets. Adjoining Hötorget is the department store *PUB*, where you can buy anything from souvenirs to mink coats. *Nordiska Kompaniet* (just called *NK* in Sweden), Hamngatan 18–20, is the largest department store in Scandinavia and offers a good selection of knitwear. The department stores usually have a shopping service with English-speaking clerks. The newest indoor shopping arcade, *Gallerian*, accessible from Hamngatan and Regeringsgatan, saves you from getting a blue nose from window-shopping outdoors in the depth of winter. Best buys are Swedish glass, textiles, ceramics, stainless steel houseware, furs, and Swedish crafts. Devaluation of the Swedish krona has made price levels more attractive, but the high standard (and, therefore, high cost) of living locally precludes absolute bargains. Try the Old Town for antiques. Shopping hours are 9 AM to 6 PM weekdays and to 3 PM Saturdays. Some shops stay open an hour later during winter months.

Carl Malmsten – The largest exponent of Swedish modern furniture. Strandvägen 5B.
Duka Aveny – Stock of over 1,700 different glasses. Kungsgatan 41.
Georg Jensen Silver AB – Specializes in green-glazed Argenta ware. Birger Jarlsgatan 13.
Hasselblads Foto – Home of the Swedish-made camera that American astronauts

used in their space explorations. Hamngatan 16, Drottninggatan 35, and Sveavä-gen 71.

Hemslöjden – Center for Swedish handicrafts and souvenirs. Drottninggatan 18–20.
Nordkalottshoppen – Genuine handicrafts from Lappland. Birger Jarlsgatan 35.
Svenskt Tenn – Outstanding pewter designs. Strandvägen 5A.

SPECIAL EVENTS: *Labor Day,* May 1, is an occasion for parades and political speeches. *Walpurgis Night,* April 30, heralds the arrival of spring and is celebrated with bonfires in public places. *Midsummer* is a charming festival (originally pagan and very ancient) occurring in the third or fourth week of June, when pagan rites are celebrated with folk dances, raising the Maypole, and general merrymaking. The month of July sees *Summer Stockholm,* a festival of athletic contests, music, and drama. The Nobel festivities take place annually in De-cember, but access is difficult to everything but the public lectures of the prizewinners. On *St. Lucia's* feast day, December 13, Swedish children traditionally wake their parents in the early morning hours to serve them saffron buns and coffee. Some of Stockholm's major hotels celebrate the *St. Lucia Festival of Light* by sending blonde *Lucia* maidens, wearing wreaths of candles on their heads, to serve the traditional breakfast to guests in their rooms. There are also special evening festivities at Skansen (see *Special Places*).

SPORTS: Stockholm has several soccer and ice hockey teams in the premier division of the league, and these are the major spectator sports. Schedules and ticket information are available from the tourist offices (see *Sources and Resources.*)

Basketball – Swedish basketball has had quite a lift from imported American players in recent years. Stockholm's top teams are *Solna* and *Alvik.* Games are played at various stadiums.

Golf – There are some fine 18-hole courses in the Stockholm region, *Drottningholm, Lidingö,* and *Djursholm* being among the finest. During the Swedish vacation month, July, it may well be possible for foreign visitors to play these courses as guests.

Ice Hockey – Swedish teams are very competitive internationally and players are known for their good skating ability. Stockholm's top teams *AIK* and *Djurgården* play at the Johanneshov Ice Stadium, on Johanneshov, during the winter season, November through March.

Soccer – The season is split into spring and autumn. *AIK* plays at Råsunda Football Stadium, Solna; *Djurgården* at the Stockholm Stadium; and *Hammarby* at Söder Stadium.

Tennis – Future Bjorn Borgs and lesser mortals can keep up their game at the *Royal Tennis Hall,* Lidingovagen 75 (phone: 67-03-50). The tennis hall also has squash courts.

Trotting – A popular spectator sport with gambling permitted. *Solvalla Stadium* has regular meetings during most of the year.

THEATER: Few visitors from abroad would wish to sit through Strindberg in the original or hear *West Side Story* sung in Swedish, but those who do will find the current program at the *Royal Dramatic Theatre,* Nybroplan, and other theaters in *This Week in Stockholm.* The regular theater and opera season runs from the end of August to the middle of June.

MUSIC: The *Royal Opera House,* just off Gustav Adolphs torg, offers fine performances during the season, with local talent and prominent interna-tional singers, at Operan (phone: 24-82-40 for reservations and 20-35-15 for other information). In summer there are performances at *Drottningholm*

Court Theater (see *At-a-Glance*). During the season there are also frequent concerts at: *The Concert Hall* (phone: 10-21-10), *Berwaldhallen, Old Academy of Music, Stockholm Exchange,* and *House of Culture.* In summer, there are outdoor concerts in several city parks and at Skansen. Church recitals take place at the cathedral, Engelbrekts Church, Adolf Fredriks Church, Gustav Vasa Church, and St. Jacobs.

NIGHTCLUBS AND NIGHTLIFE: Top discos: *Atlantic,* Teatergatan 3 (phone: 21-89-07), *Café Opera*, Operahuset (phone: 11-00-26), and *Alexandra's,* Birger Jarlsgatan 29 (phone: 10-42-02), are the places to be seen; known habitués include royalty, pop stars, and international tennis aces. Otherwise the plethora of disco night spots is a fast-changing scene. *Bacchi Wapen,* Järntorgsgatan 5 in the Old Town (phone: 11-66-71), is a nightclub with a cabaret featuring more Swedish than international entertainment. *Hamburger Börs,* Jakobsgatan 6 (phone: 24-92-10), is the exclusive nightclub that once tried to book Sammy Davis, Jr., and got the reply: "Mr. Davis doesn't play hamburger joints." The misleading name was explained and Davis finally joined the many top-line artists who have performed there.

SINS: For better or worse, Sweden and sin have almost become synonymous. Although Stockholm's sex clubs used to uphold this reputation with racy, erotic spectaculars, you won't find many spicy revues nowadays. A recent clean-up campaign has curbed the more daring shows, and what's left can hardly be considered the ultimate in sinning.

BEST IN TOWN

CHECKING IN: Stockholm hotels have a high rate of occupancy all year round, so it's wise to arrange reservations well in advance of arrival. If you do arrive without a hotel reservation, *Hotellcentralen,* located on the lower floor at the central railway station, is the official accommodation agency (phone: 24-08-80). Those visiting from mid-June through August should find out about the discount accommodations coupons called Swed-Cheques. Accepted at some 200 Swedish hotels, each voucher includes bed, breakfast, and — for a few extra dollars — a private bath. For details, contact the Swedish Tourist Board. A double at one of the hotels listed as expensive can cost you $100 and upward; at those classed as moderate, up to $95; and inexpensive hotels still expect around $30 to $50.

The Grand Hotel – Steeped in European tradition and good old-fashioned luxury. Lying opposite the Royal Palace, it is the most exclusive hotel in town. If the purpose of your visit is to collect a Nobel Prize, you won't want to settle for anything less; 352 rooms, two restaurants, a winter garden, and bar. Every room has a telephone. Södra Blasieholmen 8 (phone: 22-10-20). Expensive.

Sheraton-Stockholm – Large, modern, very much an American-owned, international-style hotel with an excellent location on the waterfront overlooking the Old Town. The *Sheraton*'s big, impressive lobby is always busy. The main restaurant, *Royal Blue,* has an extraordinarily rich ambience for such a newcomer. The hotel has 476 rooms, all with telephones. Tegelbacken 6 (phone: 14-26-00). Expensive.

Park Hotel – In a quiet location but still close to the center of things. The *Park* is modern, exclusive, and not too large to fail to offer attentive service. It has 205 rooms, all with telephone and a cocktail bar and restaurant. Karlavägen 43 (phone: 22-96-20). Expensive.

Hotel Diplomat – Small, sophisticated, tastefully furnished in period style. The hotel is centrally located at the edge of the fashionable diplomatic quarter in a building of historic significance and great character. It has 132 rooms with telephones, a cocktail bar, and an elegant *Tea House.* Strandvägen 7C (phone: 63-58-00). Expensive.

Royal Viking Hotel – The special features of this modern, 400-room hotel include three duplex suites with whirlpool and sauna, a glass-roofed winter garden with arcades and restaurants, and a dining room on the top floor with a lovely view. Near the Central Station. Vasagatan 1 (phone: 14-10-00). Expensive.

Hotel Reisen – An interesting old building in the Old Town, with modern facilities and a fine view of the harbor. The hotel has 125 rooms with telephones, a grill room, piano bar, sauna, and pool in its medieval vaults. Skeppsbron 12–14 (phone: 22-32-60). Moderate.

Continental – Excellent central location. The *Continental*'s modern apartments were recently spruced up. There are 250 rooms with telephone, a cafeteria, restaurant, bars, and bistro. Klara Vattugränd 4 (phone: 24-40-20). Moderate.

Adlon Hotel – Centrally located but small and unpretentious. The less expensive rooms have no private shower or toilet facilities. Only 58 rooms, all with telephone; breakfast only is served in the dining room. Vasagatan 42 (phone: 24-54-00). Moderate.

Hotel Frescati – Not really a hotel at all but a student accommodation that doubles as a tourist accommodation during the summer: Open from June 1 to August 31. Rooms are pleasant but far from luxurious. There is a restaurant, but little traditional hotel service, and it is recommended strictly as a means of stretching a tight travel budget. Professorsslingan 13–15 (phone: 15-79-96). Inexpensive.

EATING OUT: Swedish food was made famous by the smorgasbord, a seemingly endless array of delicacies from smoked salmon and dozens of varieties of herring to smoked reindeer meat and lingonberry jam and honey. If it's on the menu, you might want to try another Swedish specialty: elk steak accompanied by red currant or rowanberry jelly. *Surstromming,* fermented Baltic herring, has as many detractors as fans. If you'd like to sample some in the traditional way, eat it on a slice of *norrland* bread with Swedish *mandel* potatoes and, perhaps, a glass of *snaps* to wash it down. Recent years have seen a great expansion of inexpensive, mass-production pizzerias, hamburger restaurants, and self-service cafeterias in Stockholm. But this new food culture has done little to harm the more established (and expensive) restaurants. A three-course dinner for two, with wine and service, can run $60 and upward at an expensive restaurant; $30 to $55 at moderate-priced restaurants; $25 or less is inexpensive. One tip to help cut costs: Look for the words *Dagens ratt* on the menu. That means "today's special."

Operakällaren – An institution in Sweden and a restaurant with a truly international reputation. Prepares the state banquets at the Royal Palace. Its kitchen sets the standard by which other restaurants all over the country are judged. Palatial apartments with high ceilings and carved oak paneling hung with fine art. Baroque grill room. Magnificent smørgasbord. *Operabaren* and *Café Opera,* in the same building, are meeting places for Stockholm intellectuals. Open daily. Reservations necessary. Operahuset. Main dining room (phone: 24-27-00, 11-11-25), *Café Opera* (phone: 24-27-07, 11-00-26), *Operabaren* (phone: 10-79-35). Expensive.

Grappe d'Or – This relative newcomer has quickly established itself as one of the best restaurants in Stockholm, with a cuisine based on the finest and freshest ingredients. The immaculate dining rooms are imposing yet light and airy; the Jugend-inspired furnishings make it warmly inviting. Closed weekends. Reservations necessary. Tyska Brinken 36 (phone: 20-42-50). Expensive.

Eriks's – The fish and seafood dishes are well prepared at this restaurant, fittingly located on a converted barge. Closed Sundays. Reservations advised. Kajplats 17, Strandvägen (phone: 60-60-60). Expensive.

Stortorgskällaren – Near the Royal Palace. Veranda dining in summertime. Open daily. Reservations recommended. Stortorget 7 (phone: 10-55-33). Expensive to moderate.

Aurora – Intimate hideaway. Closed Sundays. Reservations. Munkbron 11 (phone: 21-93-59). Expensive to moderate.

Latona – Swedish specialties in a medieval setting. Closed Mondays. Reservations. Västerlånggatan 79 (phone: 11-32-60). Expensive to moderate.

Wärdshuset Godthem – Hundred-year-old inn in the Djurgården park. Good, varied menu, pleasant view across the bay, intoxicating atmosphere, and welcoming staff make this more a journey into nineteenth-century hospitality than just dining out. Open daily. Rosendalsvägen 9 (phone: 61-07-22). Expensive to moderate.

La Brochette – Delightfully and authentically French. The proprietor and all eight chefs are French. The traditional but varied menu offers well-prepared food served in an inviting but constantly crowded dining room. *La Brochette* offers a good selection of wines. Closed weekends. Reservations. Storgatan 27 (phone: 62-20-00). Expensive to moderate.

Östergök Fish – Flanked by a steakhouse and pizzeria with which it shares name and management. The fish restaurant is the undoubted flagship of the three. Sterile white-tiled walls and marble tabletops as befitting a serious seafood restaurant. Nobody comes to soak up the atmosphere, just savor the food. Open daily. Kommendörsgatan 46 (phone: 61-15-07). Expensive to moderate.

Capri – One of the best of the wave of pizzerias that has swept to popularity in Stockholm over recent years. Mock grotto interior contrasts with the genuine Italian cooking. Friendly and informal. Reservations desirable. Open daily. Nybrogatan 15 (phone: 62-31-32). Moderate.

Finsmakaren – A modest little restaurant a way out from downtown. The fine food and friendly service draw praise from all quarters. Closed weekends. Reservations. Råsundavägen 9, Solna (phone: 27-67-71). Moderate.

Ceasar – A small unpretentious neighborhood restaurant that somehow manages to put its bigger rivals to shame through a combination of inspired cuisine, personalized service, and good prices. Wonderfully relaxed atmosphere despite sober interior. Closed Sundays. Reservations optional. Fredrikshovsgatan 4 (phone: 60-15-99). Moderate to inexpensive.

Gässlingen – This small restaurant is somewhat off the main tourist beat, but worth the detour if you want to eat well and mingle with the locals without denting a modest travel budget. Homely interior. No reservations. Closed weekends. Brännkyrkagatan 93 (phone: 69-54-95). Inexpensive.

Coco and Carmen – This lunch restaurant opened on the former premises of a bakery whose original ovens are preserved as a curiosity. The very tasteful interior has authentic 1930s furnishings. Serves reasonably priced light dishes such as cheese pie, toast *skagen*, soups, salads, and herring. Caters to a very genteel public but leans more toward friendliness than stuffiness. Closed weekends. Reservations. Banergatan 7 (phone: 60-99-54). Inexpensive.

The Restaurants of the Old Town – There are several cellar restaurants located in the narrow lanes of the Old Town. They are housed in centuries-old vaults where every nook and cranny seem to have a story of their own. The proprietors are for the most part lively individualists whose feeling for haute cuisine is equaled only by their love of the Old Town and its medieval history. The food is excellent and the menus normally include delicacies from the traditional Swedish kitchen, perhaps chilled roast reindeer, raw spiced salmon, or snow grouse.

Which restaurant is best? Everyone has a favorite, but here are our two:

Diana – Unconventional, mixed clientele. Closed Sundays. Reservations. Brunnsgränd 2 (phone: 10-73-10). Moderate.

Fem Små Hus – Five interconnected buildings comprising a honeycomb of vaults, arches, and alcoves. Ideal setting for intimate dining. Open daily. Reservations. Nygränd 10 (phone: 10-87-75). Moderate.

VENICE

As the sun sets in this most poetic of all the world's cities, the old red brick buildings are burnished by a splendid, rosy glow that is reflected, then refracted, in the waters of the canals. There is a special light in Venice that transforms almost every building into a palace. This is a city that is equally beautiful in radiant, peak-season August and in bleak, wet November. And it is painfully beautiful when suddenly, on some late winter morning, the rain trickles to a halt, the curtains of cloud part, and trapezoids of sunlight reheat the ancient stones. Then there is an inexplicable sense of renewal as the café tables are set up again in St. Mark's Square and pigeons and waiters swoop out from the dark arcades while an orchestra begins another syrupy melody.

Venice is 117 islets, separated by 150 canals and joined by 400 bridges on Italy's northeastern Adriatic coast. A 3-mile bridge reaches across the Venetian Lagoon (Laguna Vèneta), connecting it to the mainland near the small town of Mestre. The city is protected from the force of the Adriatic Sea by the natural breakwater of the Lido, a long, narrow sandbar that is one of the most fashionable resorts on the Adriatic.

The city had its origins as a place of refuge from the violent barbarian invasions of the fifth century, as mainland inhabitants fled out to the deserted islands in the lagoon. As communities grew up, the islands became connected to one another, and Venice developed into a powerful, flourishing city-state. During the Crusades, this little maritime republic came to dominate the entire Mediterranean, and the winged Venetian lion, symbol of the city's protector, St. Mark, stood guard on a network of palaces from the Strait of Gibraltar to the Bosphorus. This was the city of Marco Polo.

Renaissance Venice was the focal point for the great trade routes from the Middle East, and the markets on the city's Rialto Bridge (Ponte di Rialto) were a pulse of European commerce. The doges — the city's rulers — celebrated their mastery of the Mediterranean with an annual ceremony of marriage to the sea, and the golden ducats that overflowed the city's coffers financed some of the world's most spectacular art and architecture. The Venetian School of painting, which produced magnificent colorists, began with Giorgione and achieved its apogee with Titian Vecellio, Paolo Veronese, and Tintoretto in the sixteenth century. The proud, thousand-year Venetian independence ended with the Treaty of Campoformio in 1797, when Napoleon handed over the territory to Austria. In 1866, the city was joined to newly unified Italy.

The city today has a population of nearly 400,000, including some who live in the industrialized areas on the mainland side of the lagoon. The millions of tourists who swarm through its narrow streets and tiny squares make up Venice's chief industry — and they leave behind well over $100 million a year.

There is a gaudy carnival atmosphere from Easter to October, with a midsummer explosion sometimes as crass as it is colorful: The landing stages jammed and listing with tour groups, long lines for frozen custard by the Doges' Palace, the big Lido ferries packed with sun-scorched day trippers to the beach, and hawkers and hustlers on every corner — in its way as vibrant, insistent, chaotic, and vulgar a commercial outpouring as anything from the days of the international market on Rialto Bridge.

And yet, even on *Ferragosto* weekend, Italy's state holiday in August, if you turn deliberately from the main thoroughfare and string together a few random rights and lefts, you can find yourself in a haven of quiet back alleys, on a tiny bridge across a deserted canal, in the middle of a silent, sun-baked bit of space called a *piazzetta,* with a fruit stall, a splashing fountain — and not a tourist in sight.

Venice in winter is a totally different experience: placid, gray, a trifle melancholy, and startlingly, strikingly visible. Suddenly, there is no one between you and the noble palaces, the soaring churches, the dark canals.

D. H. Lawrence once called Venice "an abhorrent, green, slippery city," and there is undeniably a dark and decadent quality about the city. But as the inscription on a sundial in Venice says, "I count only the happy hours."

VENICE AT-A-GLANCE

SEEING THE CITY: The traditional vantage point from which to admire Venice is the summit of the 324-foot-high, red *campanile,* bell tower, in St. Mark's Square. The view on all sides is breathtaking — from the red-shingled rooftops and countless domes of the city to the distant islands that dot the wide lagoon. There's an elevator to the top or, for the heartier, a sloping ramp. Open daily. Small admission charge.

SPECIAL PLACES: St. Mark's Square is the center of life in Venice; from here you can get steamers to the Lido and other islands as well as to the various quarters of the city. The *Corso della Gente* is not a street, but a phrase Venetians use to describe "the flow of people" that roughly parallels the Grand Canal, snaking through the heart of the city from the bridge (Ponte degli Scalzi) near the Santa Lucia Railway Station to St. Mark's Square. You can follow it instinctively without once asking for directions.

DOWNTOWN

St. Mark's Square (Piazza San Marco) – Napoleon called this huge marble square the finest drawing room in Europe. Bells chime, flocks of pigeons crisscross against the sky, violins play, couples embrace in the sunset — while you take it all in from a congenial café. A mere turn of your head allows you to admire St. Mark's Basilica, the Doges' Palace, the ninth-century bell tower, the clock tower where giant bronze Moors have struck the hours for five centuries, the old law courts, and the old library, which now houses the archaeological museum. In the *piazzetta,* through which the square opens onto the Grand Canal, there are two granite columns — one topped by the Lion of St. Mark and the other, by a statue of St. Theodore. St. Mark's Square.

St. Mark's Basilica (Basilica di San Marco) – This masterpiece of Venetian-

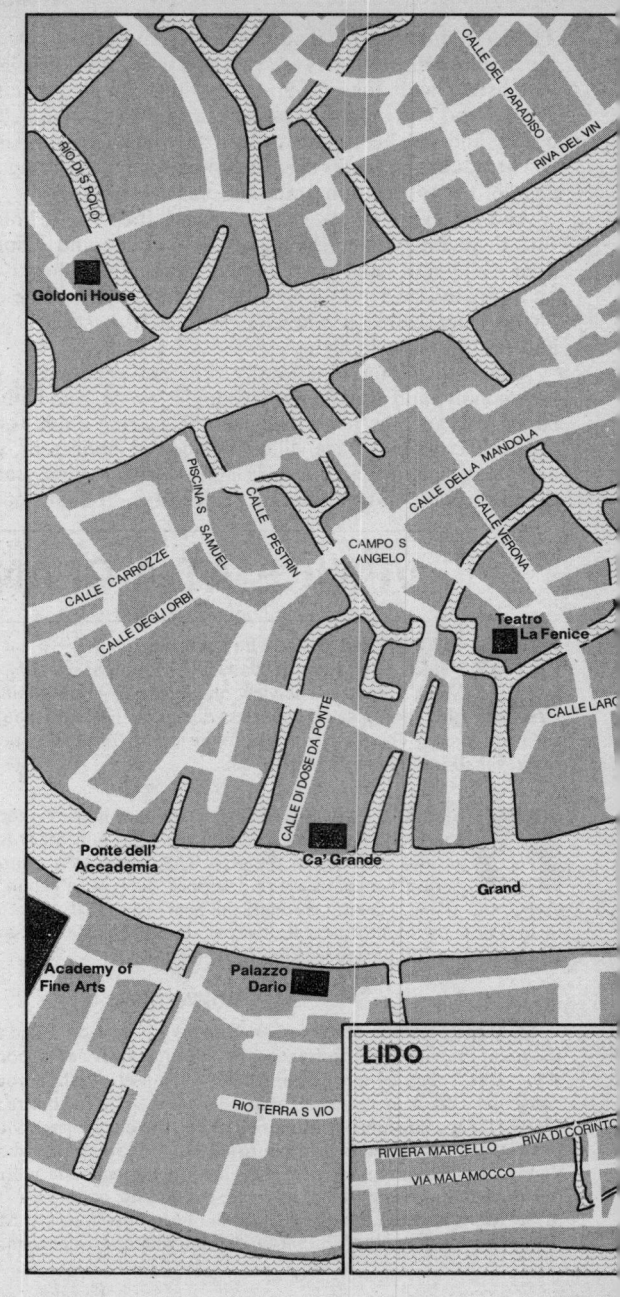

Goldoni House

RIO DI S POLO

CALLE DEL PARADISO

RIVA DEL VIN

CALLE DELLA MANDOLA

PISCINA S SAMUEL

CALLE PESTRIN

CALLE VERONA

CAMPO S ANGELO

CALLE CARROZZE

CALLE DEGLI ORBI

Teatro La Fenice

CALLE DI DOSE DA PONTE

CALLE LARG

Ponte dell' Accademia

Ca' Grande

Grand

Academy of Fine Arts

Palazzo Dario

LIDO

RIO TERRA S VIO

RIVIERA MARCELLO

RIVA DI CORINTO

VIA MALAMOCCO

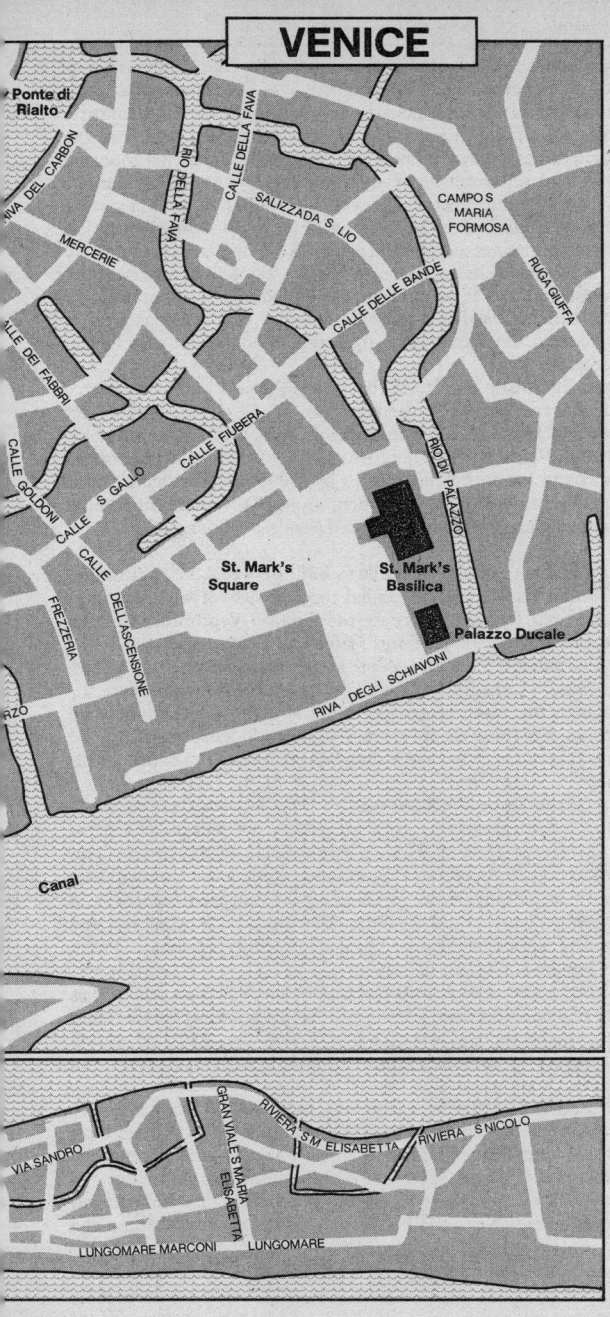

VENICE

Ponte di Rialto

RIVA DEL CARBON

MERCERIE

CALLE DELLA FAVA

RIO DELLA FAVA

SALIZZADA S LIO

CALLE DELLE BANDE

CAMPO S MARIA FORMOSA

RUGA GIUFFA

CALLE DEI FABBRI

CALLE RIUBERA

CALLE S GALLO

CALLE GOLDONI

CALLE DELL'ASCENSIONE

FREZZERIA

RIO DI PALAZZO

St. Mark's Square

St. Mark's Basilica

Palazzo Ducale

RIVA DEGLI SCHIAVONI

Canal

RZO

VIA SANDRO

GRAN VIALE S MARIA ELISABETTA

RIVIERA S M ELISABETTA

RIVIERA S NICOLO

LUNGOMARE MARCONI

LUNGOMARE

Byzantine architecture was built in 830 to shelter the tomb of St. Mark, whose bones had been smuggled out of Alexandria. When first built, it was not a cathedral but a chapel for the doges. The present basilica was constructed during the eleventh century, but the phenomenal decoration of the interior and exterior continued well into the sixteenth century. The basilica has a large dome and four smaller ones; its imposing facade of variegated marble and sculpture has five large doorways. The four famous bronze horses that have adorned the central doorway since 1207, when they were brought here after the sack of Constantinople, were removed in 1980 for restoration work. Plaster replicas have taken their place, and the originals are on permanent display in the basilica's museum. Inside, the walls are encrusted with precious art, rare marbles, and magnificent mosaics. Behind the high altar in the chancel is the famous gold altarpiece, the Pala d'Oro, and the basilica's treasury includes rare relics as well as Byzantine goldwork and enamels. Open daily. Small admission charge for the chancel and treasury. St. Mark's Square.

Doges' Palace (Palazzo Ducale) – Next to the basilica is the pink and white palace with an unusual double loggia that served as the residence of the doges and the seat of government. The finest room in the palace is the Grand Council Chamber, containing paintings by Tintoretto and Veronese. You may also visit the doges' apartments and the armory. The palace is connected to the old prisons by the famous Bridge of Sighs (Ponte dei Sospiri), which takes its name from the lamentations of prisoners supposedly taken across the bridge to be executed. Open daily. Small admission charge. St. Mark's Square (phone: 3-6830).

Grand Canal – Lined with some 200 marble palaces built between the twelfth and eighteenth centuries, the Grand Canal has been called the finest street with the finest houses in the world. On the right (or east bank) are the Palazzo Vendramin-Calergi, where Wagner died, now the winter home of the *Municipal Casino* (see *Sins*); the Golden House (Ca' d'Oro), so called because its ornate facade once was entirely gilded; and the Palazzo Mocenigo, where Lord Byron lived. On the left (or west bank) are the Palazzo Pesaro, which houses the modern art gallery, and Palazzo Rezzonico, an architectural jewel that now houses the civic museum of eighteenth-century art. A good way to see all of these beautiful *palazzi* is to take a slow boat ride over the entire 2-mile length of the Grand Canal.

Academy of Fine Arts (Galleria dell'Accademia) – Brief but frequent visits are the best way to savor the rich contents of this great art gallery. Of particular interest are Veronese's *Supper in the House of Levi;* Titian's *Presentation of the Virgin;* Tintoretto's *Transport of the Body of St. Mark;* and Giorgione's *Tempesta.* You will also want to see the paintings of Venice by Antonio Canaletto, Francesco Guardi, and Gentile Bellini. These are the academy's most Venetian selections, both by subject and artist, and will meld your impressions of the city. Open daily; closed Mondays. Small admission charge; free on Sundays. Campo della Carità.

Great School of San Rocco (Scuola di San Rocco) – The Venetion *scuola* was not a school, but something of a cross between a trade guild and a religious brotherhood that furnished wealthy patronage for the arts. At San Rocco you will find a rich collection of Tintorettos — some 56 canvases representing stories from the Old and New Testaments. Open daily. Small admission charge. Campo San Rocco.

St. Mary's Church (Chiesa di Santa Maria Gloriosa dei Frari) – Known simply as Frari, this church is considered by many to be the most splendid in Venice after St. Mark's. It contains three unquestioned masterpieces: The *Assumption* and the *Madonna of Ca' Pesaro,* both by Titian, and Giovanni Bellini's tryptych on the sacristy altar. An excellent way to appreciate its beauty is to attend an early morning mass before the tourists come. Next to the Scuola di San Rocco. Campo dei Frari.

School of St. George (Scuola San Giorgio degli Schiavoni) – This small building, beyond St. Mark's Square in a part of the city most visitors never get around to, contains one of the city's most overlooked treasures: the frieze of paintings by Vittore Carpaccio depicting stories of St. George, St. Jerome, and St. Tryphon. Closed Mondays. Small admission charge. Castello, Calle dei Furlani.

ENVIRONS

The Lido – For most of this century, this shoestring island across the lagoon from Venice proper has been one of the world's most extravagant resorts. Indeed, the word *lido* has come to mean, in much of the world's lexicon, any fashionable, luxuriously equipped beach resort. There has always been a touch of decadence to the Venetian Lido and its elegant, rambling, old hotels, sumptuous villas, swank casino, and its world-weary, wealthy clientele. Thomas Mann used the Lido's posh *Grand Hotel des Bains* (see *Checking In*) as a background for his haunting novella, *Death in Venice.* These days, thousands of cabins and cabanas line the Lido's fine sandy beaches, and purists will tell you the old resort has fallen to seed. But the tourists still come by the thousands — some drawn by the tinsel of an international cinema festival, others by the trendiness of a pop music celebration, but most lured by the legendary Lido ambience. There is bus service on the island, which can be reached by frequent boat service from Riva degli Schiavoni. There is also a car ferry from piazzale Roma.

Murano – This island has been the home of Venetian glassmaking since the thirteenth century. You can watch the glass blowing and molding processes at any one of the island factories, but gird yourself for the high-pressure tactics used to get you to buy some glass. The island's Glassworks Museum (Museo Vetrario), Fondamenta Giustinian 8, has one of the world's best collections of Venetian glass. Closed Tuesdays. Small admission fee; free on Sunday. Murano is 15 minutes by steamer from Fondamenta Nuove.

Burano – The colorful homes, small boats, and nets and tackle of the fishermen who live here add charm to this little island, best known as a center of lacemaking, still practiced by some island women. Burano is 30 minutes by steamer from Fondamenta Nuove.

Torcello – This was one of the most prosperous colonies on the lagoon in the fifth and sixth centuries, but as Venice grew, Torcello declined. The main square is now overgrown with grass. Most of the cathedral, as it appears today, dates from the early eleventh century. It has several fine Byzantine mosaics and an interesting iconostasis. The island is 45 minutes by steamer from Fondamenta Nuove.

■**EXTRA SPECIAL:** The so-called Brenta Riviera was where all Venetians who could afford to built summer residences in the sixteenth century. So many Venetian villas were built along the Brenta Canal, it seemed to be an extension of the Grand Canal. During the seventeenth and eighteenth centuries a luxurious barge, the *Burchiello,* made a daily trip along the Brenta Canal, which links Venice and Padua. Today's tourist can enjoy the same cruise, in summer months, by motorized boat from Pontile Giardinetto near St. Mark's Square. The excursion, which includes lunch in Oriago and a bus return from Padua, takes a full day. Apply to Compagnia Italiana Turismo (CIT) in St. Mark's Square (phone: 8-5480) for information.

SOURCES AND RESOURCES

A free pocket-sized map of Venice, listing the various boat routes around the city, is available from the Azienda Autonoma di Soggiorno e Turismo, 4089 Rialto, Palazzo Martinengo (phone: 3-0313, 3-0399), and from the Ente Provinciale per il Turismo in the Santa Lucia railroad station (phone: 71-50-16).

For Local Coverage – *Venezia Per Conoslere La Citta* is a useful multilingual booklet published weekly, which lists up-to-date museum schedules, special events, entertainment programs, and other activities. *The Companion Guide to Venice,* by Hugh Honour (Collins, London; $6.95), is a sensitive, well-written guide to the city; available in many bookstores.

CLIMATE AND CLOTHES: The lightest, coolest clothes you have will be appropriate for Venice in summer. Temperatures in July can reach 90°F (32°C). Although there is rarely extreme cold in winter — 40°F (4°C) is considered a very chilly January — precipitation ranges from fine mist to torrential downpour and the winds off the lagoon can be more chilling than Alpine snow. You'll need woolens and sweaters to wear under wind- and raingear, and, if the high water, *acqua alta,* comes up over the canal banks, you'll want high rubber boots for slogging around.

GETTING AROUND: There are no cars in Venice. If you arrive in one, you'll have to park it in one of the lots or garages at piazzale Roma until you're ready to leave. People walk, and traffic moves on water.

Gondola – An hour's tour of the city in one of these sleek, black boats can cost you as much as $30, but for 15¢ you can get a short sample by taking a canal ferry, called a *traghetto,* across the Grand Canal at various points some distance from the bridges. If it's the gondoliers' barcaroles you've been waiting to hear, you can enjoy them for free by leaning over one of the bridges as they pass by in the evening.

Motoscafi and Vaporetti – The little steamers that make up the municipal transit system are cheap and fun. The *motoscafi* are express boats, making only a few key stops. The *vaporetti* are much slower. Number 1 chugs leisurely along the whole length of the Grand Canal and number 5's route meanders for over an hour through various interesting parts of the city. Tickets cost between 60¢ and 80¢.

MUSEUMS: Besides those mentioned in *Special Places,* Venice has a number of museums of special interest:

Galleria G. Franchetti, Alla Ca' D'Oro, Cannareggio 3932 (phone: 2-2349).

International Gallery of Modern Art (Museo d'Arte Moderna), Ca' Pesaro, S Croce (phone: 2-4127).

Guggenheim Collection, Palazzo Venier del Leoni, San Giorgio 701. Closed November through April (phone: 2-9347).

Correr Civic Museum, Piazza San Marco (phone: 2-5625).

Archaeological Museum, Piazza San Marco (phone: 2-5978).

Museum of Eighteenth-Century Venice (Museo del '700 Veneziano), in the Palazzo Rezzonico where the poet Robert Browning lived and died, Dorsoduro Ca' Rezzonico (phone: 2-4543).

SHOPPING: Venetian glass is the most seductive item here, but not all of it is high quality. Do a bit of comparison pricing first, and if you can, visit the museum and factories on Murano (see *Special Places*). Also consider the inexpensive necklaces of colorful Venetian glass beads. Other items worth purchasing are the traditional, handmade Carnival masks, which are currently enjoying a renaissance. Two of the best mask workshops are in Piazza San Paolo 2008/A and at 1077/A Calle de l'Ogio o de la Rughetta (midway between the Rialto and St. Mark's Square). In addition, there are many fine jewelry stores on the Rialto Bridge, and the Mercato di Rialto is one of the city's most colorful outdoor food markets.

Fendi – Elegant clothes and leather. Salizada S. Moisé, St. Mark's Square.

Jesurum & Co. – Lace and other needlework. Shops on Ponte Canonica and in St. Mark's Square.

Nardi – Beautiful jewelry in the Venetian tradition. St. Mark's Square 69.

Salviati – A 100-year-old firm with the highest traditions of craftsmanship in Venetian glass. Shops at San Gregorio 195, in St. Mark's Square, and on Murano.

Piazzesi – Beautiful notebooks, boxes, albums, and other gift articles superbly crafted from handmade marbled papers in antique Venetian style. San Marco 2511 (phone: 2-12-02).

 SPECIAL EVENTS: Illuminated gondolas glide along the canals, while musicians play from barges on the lagoon and fireworks paint the sky on the night between the third Saturday and Sunday in July. This is the *Feast of the Redeemer (Festa del Redentore),* one of the most special celebrations of the year in Venice. No one goes to bed before dawn. On the first Sunday in September, gondola races and a procession of decorated barges manned by Venetians in Renaissance dress highlight the *Historic Regatta (Regata Storica),* on the Grand Canal. An *International Film Festival* is held on the Lido in late August and early September, and in even-numbered years, the important *International Biennale of Modern Art (Esposizione Internazionale d'Arte Moderna)* takes place in a small park beyond the Riva dei 7 Martiri from June through October. In late February, Venetians celebrate *Carnival (Carnevale),* a 10-day pre-Easter fete that includes outdoor masked balls, 24-hour street theater, and pop music.

 SPORTS: The visitor to Venice gets plenty of exercise climbing up and down its hundreds of bridges. For more organized sports, you have to transfer to the open spaces of the Lido.

Golf – The *Alberoni* is a beautiful 18-hole course at the far western end of the Lido (phone: 73-10-15). It's reached by the number 11 boat line from Riva degli Schiavoni or by the C bus from Santa Maria Elisabetta, the main Lido dock.

Swimming – The northern end of the Lido has municipal beaches, all of which charge admission. The beaches farther along are the domain of the great luxury hotels of the Lido, but an entrance fee will get you a cabana.

Tennis – *The Tennis Club,* Lungomare Marconi 41D (phone: 60-385), has seven courts (two covered; two illuminated). You can also play at the *Tennis Club Lido,* Via Sandro Gallo 163 (phone: 76-05-94), or the *Henkell Club,* Via Malamocco (phone: 76-01-22).

 THEATER: Music, rather than drama, is the performing art of Venice. However, the *Teatro Verde,* on the little island of San Giorgio Maggiore just across from St. Mark's Square, is a lovely outdoor amphitheater that looks out over the lagoon. It's a marvelous place to spend a summer evening, even if you're watching a classic theater piece done in incomprehensible Venetian dialect. Another pleasant theater for traditional and contemporary productions is *Teatro Goldoni*, Calle Goldoni 4650/B, San Marco (phone: 70-75-83).

MUSIC: Venice is a city with a rich musical tradition and a full calendar of musical events — as you will see from the wall posters that announce forthcoming concerts. *Teatro La Fenice,* Campo San Fantin 1977 (phone: 2-3954), which dates from the end of the seventeenth century, is the city's main auditorium. Its gold and pink plush interior is pure Venetian, and a first night at the *Fenice,* site of world premières of opera classics by Verdi and Rossini, is a highlight of the social season. Admission to see the theater's charming interior is permitted when rehearsals are not in progress. In summer, open-air concerts are held in the courtyard of the Doges' Palace, and there are concerts in various churches. If possible, attend a performance by either of the city's stellar chamber music groups: the *Solisti Veneti* or the *Venice Wind Sextet (Sestetto a Fiati di Venezia)*.

NIGHTCLUBS AND NIGHTLIFE: *Antico Martini,* 1983 S Marco (phone: 3-7027), is Venice's chicest nightspot. Next to the *Teatro La Fenice,* which supplies it with a glossy, after-theater crowd, it has a floor show, dancing, a pleasant outdoor terrace, and good food (see *Eating Out*). As long as the weather holds, the city's best nightlife is the nonstop show in St. Mark's Square. Take up residence in one of the cafés, listen to the schmaltzy orchestra, and watch the world go by. Popular places for rock and disco are the *Piper Club,* on the Lido at 125 Lista di Spagna (phone: 71-66-43), and *El Souk Disco,* 1056/A Accademia (phone: 70-03-71).

SINS: Venice encourages *dolce far niente* — sweet *idleness* — so enjoy it. The *Municipal Casino* is out at the Lido (phone: 76-06-26) from April through September and at the elegant Palazzo Vendramin-Calergi (phone: 71-02-11) on the Grand Canal from October through March. Just past the narrow end of St. Mark's Square is the *Frezzeria,* where there is lively late-night traffic.

BEST IN TOWN

CHECKING IN: Your first decision is whether to stay out at the Lido or in town. But even if you do stay in the center, you can use the frequent ferry service from Riva degli Schiavoni any time you want to swim or play a game of tennis. Expensive hotels here will charge from $150 to $300 per night for a double; moderately priced hotels, $70 to $150; and inexpensive ones, $30 to $70.

Gritti Palace – There are those — Ernest Hemingway was one — who would rather stay in this small crown jewel than anywhere else in Europe. Once the Renaissance residence of Venetian nobility, this hotel is famous for its excellent service, classic dining room, and its beautiful dining terrace on the canal. Campo Santa Maria del Giglio 2467 (phone: 2-6044). Expensive.

Bauer Grünwald – Visiting royalty often stay in the poshest of this Grand Canal hotel's suites. This luxury hotel near St. Mark's Square has a roof garden that offers one of the loveliest vantage points from which to admire the city. Campo San Moisè 1459 (phone: 70-70-22). Expensive.

Danieli – Venice's largest hotel, part of Italy's CIGA chain, occupies three connected buildings on the quay east of St. Mark's Square. It is more modern in feeling, if slightly less romantic, than the hotels that hug the smaller canals. Riva degli Schiavoni 4196 (phone: 2-6480). Expensive.

Cipriani – On the serene Giudecca island, the *Cipriani* is a charming hotel with a peaceful, luxuriant garden, a swimming pool, and stunning views of the lagoon. Frequent shuttle service takes you to St. Mark's Square in 5 minutes. Open April through November. Giudecca 10 (phone: 70-77-44). Expensive.

Grand Hotel des Bains – On the Lido, this luxurious and gracefully old-fashioned hotel is where Visconti filmed much of *Death in Venice.* It has spacious rooms and new tiled bathrooms. The stately porticoed hotel is across the road from the private beach. Open April through October. Lungomare Marconi 17, on the Lido (phone: 76-59-21). Expensive.

Hotel Excelsior Palace – This luxurious modern hotel has its own fine restaurant, beach, tennis courts, and golf course. Open April to October. Lungomare Marconi 40, Lido (phone: 76-02-01). Expensive.

Londra Palace – This charming hotel on a popular promenade offers wonderful views of St. Mark's Lagoon and the Byzantine San Zaccaria Church. All 69 rooms have modern bathrooms, and many have private balconies. Other pluses include an elegant bar and a very good restaurant. Riva degli Schiavoni 4171 (phone: 70-05-33). Expensive.

La Fenice et des Artistes – Just alongside the *Teatro Fenice* (see *Theater*), this hotel is popular with performers and musicians. It's in four buildings around a pretty garden, and has comfortable, well-appointed rooms. One of the city's fine restaurants, *Taverna La Fenice* (see *Eating Out*), is right downstairs. Campo San Fantin 1937a (phone: 3-2333). Expensive.

Ala – Across a small square from the *Gritti*, this hotel has many of the more expensive hotel's advantages at about a third the cost. The atmosphere is gracious and intimate, and you're about equidistant from St. Mark's Square and the Academy of Fine Arts (see *Special Places*). Campo Santa Maria de Giglio 2494 (phone: 2-3111). Moderate.

Flora – This small jewel of a hotel has a lovely patio and garden. The atmosphere is tranquil and gracious, and you're just around the corner from St. Mark's Square. Closed November through January. Calle Larga 22 Marzo 2283/a (phone: 70-58-44). Moderate.

Do Pozzi – A small, attractive hotel just a block away from St. Mark's Square, it has a pleasant atmosphere and a lively canalside restaurant, *Da Raffaele* (see *Eating Out*). 2373 Calle Larga 22 Marzo (phone: 70-78-55). Moderate.

Hotel Bonvecchiati – This comfortable, 86-room hotel near St. Mark's Square is tastefully decorated and boasts an impressive collection of contemporary art. 4488 Calle Goldoni (phone: 8-5017). Moderate.

Etap-Park Hotel – This modern, luxurious hotel is a short walk from Piazzale Roma, the first stop for everyone en route from the airport by bus or car. It also has easy access to the main vaporetto lines connecting to all parts of Venice. Santa Croce 245/246 (phone: 8-5394). Moderate.

Santa Chiara Hotel – This charming, small hotel on the Grand Canal has beamed ceilings and antique furniture and is particularly convenient for guests arriving by car (the Piazzale Roma is around the corner). Private garage space, and easy access to the main vaporetto stops. Santa Croce 548 (phone: 70-69-55). Moderate.

Pensione Accademia – Also known as *Villa Maravegie,* this tranquil, rather stately establishment is near the Academy of Fine Arts. It has a lovely garden with a view down a small canal to the Grand Canal as well as wide vestibules, high ceilings, and the ambience of a private home from another era. Dorsoduro 1058,60 (phone: 71-01-88). Inexpensive.

 EATING OUT: One of life's great pleasures is dining out in Venice in good weather — alongside a canal, on one of the wide, sunny squares, or in little arbored gardens shaded by vine leaves. But in winter you'll welcome the crowded tables and warm interiors that offer refuge from the misty, melancholy streets. Prices for dinner for two with wine range from $70 to $85 at an expensive restaurant; $50 to $65 at a moderate one; and $30 to $45 at an inexpensive one.

Club del Doge – Part of the Gritti Palace Hotel on the Grand Canal, this is the place for fine food in deluxe surroundings. In good weather, diners are served on a canalside terrace. Reservations advised. S Maria del Giglio 2467 (phone: 2-6044). Very expensive.

Antico Martini – Venice's classiest restaurant, across the square from the *Teatro Fenice* (see *Theater*), is open for dinner only. The seafood cocktail, *cocktail di crostacei,* and the filet of sole, *filetto di sogliola,* are dishes of national repute. Open

March 15 through November 30; closed Tuesdays. Reservations required. Campo San Fantin 1938 (phone: 2-4121). Expensive.

Harry's Bar – Long a Venetian landmark, and the city's only restaurant with two Michelin stars, this popular spot is crowded with tourists in summer, but it makes an elegant, international rendezvous in the off-season. The food is splendid 12 months a year, but many feel it is overpriced. Closed Mondays and January. Reservations advised. Near the San Marco motorboat station. Calle Vallaresso 1323 (phone: 8-577). Expensive.

Locanda Cipriani – The almost pastoral tranquillity of the garden makes this a perfect place for a leisurely lunch. The restaurant, under the same management as *Harry's Bar,* sits on an ancient piazza on the sleepy island of Torcello (see *Special Places*). You can get lunch and transportation in one inclusive fare by taking the motor launch that leaves from *Harry's Bar* at noon and brings you back after lunch. Open March 15 through October; closed Mondays. Reservations advised in summer. Piazza Torcello on Torcello (phone: 73-01-50). Expensive.

La Colomba – Sooner or later, everyone drops in at this favorite Venetian hangout. Large and crowded, the restaurant has a lovely outside terrace, a creative array of seafood specialties, and modern art on the walls. Try Adriatic fish baked in a paper bag, called *cartoccio Colomba.* Closed Tuesdays and all of January. San Marco 1665 (phone: 2-3817). Expensive.

Al Giglio – Set in a charming piazza, this intimate restaurant offers very good fish and meat dishes in an atmosphere of calm and elegance. Closed Wednesdays and all of December and January. Reservations advised. Near Piazza San Marco on Campo Santa Maria del Giglio (phone: 3-2368). Expensive to moderate.

La Caravella – It has a typically Venetian atmosphere, and the chef's specialties include scampi in champagne and filet mignon. Reservations advised. Closed Wednesdays. Largo XXII Marzo 2399 (phone: 7-08-901). Expensive to moderate.

Al Graspo De Uva – This colorful, popular restaurant in an old blacksmith's shop offers great Venetian food and a good selection of wines. Closed Mondays and Tuesdays. San Marco 5094, on Calle Bombaseri (phone: 2-3647). Expensive to moderate.

Noemi – Salmon mousse and shrimp pâté are the specialties at this lesser-known (but still one-star) cozy, family-run restaurant. Closed Sunday evenings and Mondays, and from January 5 to February 15. Calle dei Fabbri 909-912 (phone: 2-52-38). Expensive to moderate.

Taverna La Fenice – This elegant restaurant, popular with performers, musicians, and theatergoers, is part of the hotel *La Fenice et des Artistes* (see *Checking In*). Its food and decor are characteristically Venetian. Closed Sundays and all of January. Reservations suggested. Campiello Marinonio 1938 (phone: 2-3856). Moderate.

Al La Madonna – This is a brightly lit, lively restaurant on a little side street near the Rialto bridge. It has a fixed menu daily featuring Venetian specialties. Closed Wednesdays, the first week in August, and January. Calle della Madonna 594 (phone: 2-3824). Moderate.

Tratoria Do Forni – Open all year in the *Montecarlo Hotel,* fish of various sorts are a specialty here, on a menu that's extensive and varied. A favorite dining spot for Venetians. Closed Thursdays. Calle dei Specchieri 468 (phone: 3-2148). Moderate.

(Antica Locanda) Montin – You'll find simple decor, simple food, and some of the city's most interesting people in this out-of-the-way restaurant, usually referred to simply by its last name. It's popular with artists and journalists and has a cool, attractive arbor. Closed Wednesdays. Near Campo San Barnabà. Fondamenta Eremite 1147 (phone: 2-3367). Inexpensive.

Da Ivo – Good, solid food is found at this Venice trattoria frequented by more locals than tourists. Try the *pappardelle alla marinara* for your pasta course. Closed Sundays and January. San Marco 1809 (phone: 8-5004). Inexpensive.

Al Teatro – An after-show meeting place for performers, musicians, and hungry roulette players, this popular *rosticcería* serves everything from a late-night pizza to a five-course meal. Right next to *Teatro La Fenice*. Closed Mondays. Campo San Fantin (phone: 2-1052 or 3-7214). Inexpensive.

Florian – This beautiful, slightly frayed café looks out on the entire St. Mark's scene. It's the perfect site from which to watch the world go by as you sip coffee and nibble on a sweet confection. 57 San Marco. Inexpensive.

Lavena – The most intrepid of the St. Mark's cafés. Watching drinks and coffee being served to patrons (occasionally in hip boots) while the rain pelts down and the whole square floods, demonstrates the determination of server and guest alike. 133 San Marco. Inexpensive.

VIENNA

For more than 600 years, Vienna was the glittering capital of the Hapsburg
Empire. Its magnificent palaces and ballrooms are now active with tourists
and special events when not housing ministries and other organizations, but
the city lives on in a mood of genteel nostalgia. Although a quarter of its 1.5
million people are over 60, Vienna is experiencing a rejuvenation and is
gaining an international character as it emerges as an East-West crossroads.
Even with an influx of foreigners, however, the Viennese traditions of formality and hand-kissing live on within an active social life that centers around
the ubiquitous coffee houses and a flourishing musical scene.

Vienna does not let you forget that it is the city of Mozart, Beethoven,
Schubert, Haydn, Brahms, Johann Strauss, and so many other musical giants.
Its major opera house, operetta theater, Philharmonic and Symphony orchestras, and Vienna Boys' Choir are as remarkable in quality as in popularity.
And the richness of its cultural life is matched only by the richness of its
divine pastries, strudel, and the legendary Sachertorte. Most endearing of all,
perhaps, is the civilized indolence that is cultivated in the coffee houses, where
people read, converse, receive mail and telephone calls, or merely relax and
slowly sip coffee.

Situated in the northeast corner of Austria, only 33 miles west of Bratislava,
Czechoslovakia, and a few hours' drive from Budapest, Vienna has a distinctly middle European flavor that sets it apart from such Western cities as
Paris, Brussels, and Geneva. It's even a bit provincial. Women still wear the
traditional gray and green hunting hat with a long, imperious feather, while
men will occasionally sport capes, knickers, and green-trimmed Sunday-best
uniforms. The mountains and the countryside never seem very far away. They
aren't; the Vienna Woods begin at the city's western edge and are very much
a part of the city life.

Downtown Vienna is not on the Danube; that river runs through its northeastern quarter, though the Danube Canal, diverted from the river, does
touch the inner city. Vienna is easy to grasp geographically if you think of
it from the inside out. Begin with the Stephansdom, the great cathedral that
towers over the heart of the inner city. Its square, the Stephansplatz, is at the
intersection of Graben and Kärntnerstrasse, and if you stand there, all Vienna
will eventually pass by. Surrounding the cathedral, the Innere Stadt (Inner
City) is a wobbly circle bounded on three sides by the Ringstrasse and on a
fourth by the Danube Canal. The Ringstrasse changes names nine times, but
all the versions end with the syllable "ring," which accurately describes its
shape; it follows the outline of the old city walls. Inside the Ring, the narrow
winding streets seem in perfect harmony with the old-world charm and
Gemütlichkeit (companionable coziness) for which Vienna is famous. The

Hofburg, the old imperial winter palace, still sprawls impressively in the heart of the city. To the northwest is the little suburb of Grinzing, with its many wine taverns, and the vast expanse of the Wienerwald, the Vienna Woods. And to the east, across the Danube Canal, is the park of the Prater, where the giant Ferris wheel turns.

Vienna — like so many of the cities of Europe — started as a Roman legionnaires' camp in the early years of the Roman Empire. It had a turbulent and violent history until the powerful and commercially oriented dukes of Babenberg arrived in the tenth century. The city's modern history begins with the accession of the great Hapsburg dynasty in 1278, and the Hapsburgs dominated Vienna until the end of World War I. As the nucleus of the flourishing Austro-Hungarian Empire, Vienna was one of the cornerstones of Europe.

In 1814, in the ballrooms and dining halls of the Schönbrunn Palace, the Congress of Vienna, composed of the most powerful rulers of Europe and dominated by the shrewd negotiations of Austrian Prince Metternich, redesigned the map of Europe in the wake of Napoleon's downfall. Meetings were held in leisurely Viennese style, accompanied by receptions and balls, so that it was said that "the Congress doesn't advance, it dances." Beethoven himself conducted a gala concert for the dignitaries.

A few years later, in 1820, a new dance, the waltz, was introduced by Josef Lanner and Johann Strauss senior. The waltz reached the height of its popularity during the days of Strauss's son, Johann Strauss junior, "the king of the waltz," who composed "The Blue Danube," "Tales from the Vienna Woods," and numerous other pieces, and who shuttled the 300 musicians in his employ from one ballroom to another.

Vienna's golden era coincided with that of the waltz and spanned the 68-year reign of the beloved Franz Joseph I (1848–1916). The emperor undertook to transform Vienna much as Baron Haussmann redesigned Paris during the same period. The medieval city walls were removed and the Ring boulevards constructed, together with trees, parks, gardens, buildings, and monuments. The Opera, the Fine Arts Museum, the Burgtheater, the Town Hall, and the Parliament were part of Franz Joseph's plan. And while the emperor was transforming the city, Sigmund Freud, an outwardly conventional Viennese doctor, was patiently transforming our ideas about the human mind.

Vienna began a period of decline with the end of World War I, the dissolution of the empire, and the ruinous depression. World War II brought Nazi occupation, drastic damage by Allied bombings, and a decade-long four-way division of the city by the Allied powers — a division that ended with the State Treaty of 1955.

Modern Vienna, the capital of a democratic republic, has recovered sufficiently to experience a renaissance of its nineteenth-century role as Europe's boardroom. Officially the world's "Third United Nations City," Vienna is headquarters for a number of UN agencies, like the Industrial Development Organization and the Atomic Energy Agency; the home of the Organization of Petroleum Exporting Countries; and — because of its East-West straddle — a natural point of contact between the NATO countries and those of the

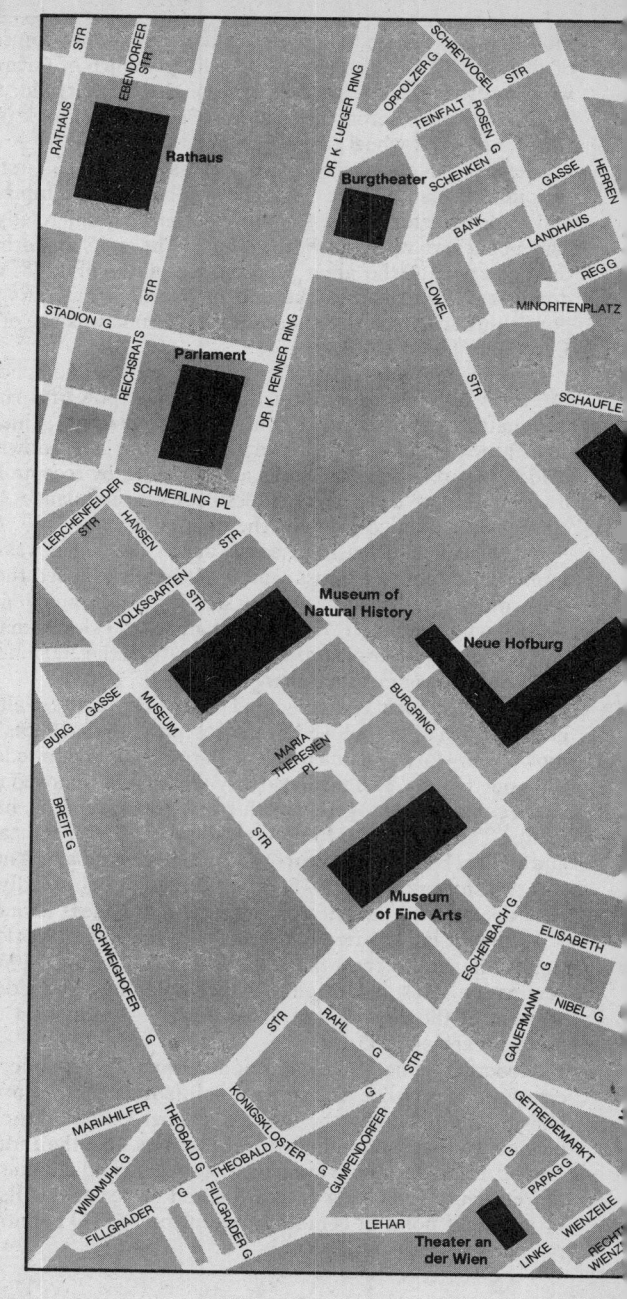

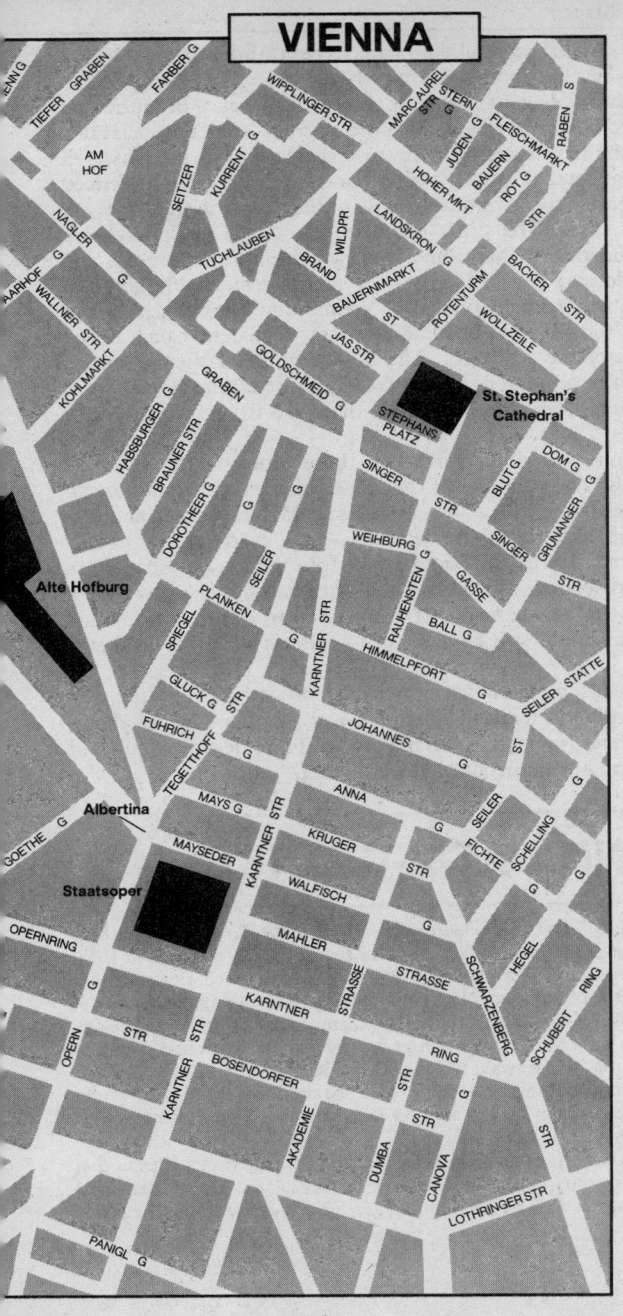

VIENNA

TIEFER GRABEN

FARBER G

WIPPLINGER STR

MARC AUREL STR

STERN G

JUDEN G

FLEISCHMARKT

RABEN S

AM HOF

SEITZER

KURRENT G

HOHER MKT

BAUERN

ROT G

STR

NAGLER G

LANDSKRON G

WILDPR

BACKER STR

AARHOF

WALLNER STR

TUCHLAUBEN

BRAND

BAUERMARKT

ST

ROTENTURM

WOLLZEILE

KOHLMARKT

GOLDSCHMEID G

JAS STR

STEPHANS PLATZ

St. Stephan's Cathedral

GRABEN

HABSBURGER G

BRAUNER STR

SINGER

BLUT G

DOM G

DOROTHEER G

G

WEIHBURG

SINGER STR

GRUNANGER

Alte Hofburg

SPIEGEL

SEILER

PLANKEN

KARNTNER STR

RAUHENSTEIN G

GASSE

BALL G

STR

HIMMELPFORT

GLUCK G

STR

SEILER STATTE

FUHRICH

JOHANNES

G

ST

SEILER

SCHELLING

TEGETTHOFF G

ANNA

G

Albertina

MAYS G

KARNTNER STR

KRUGER

FICHTE

GOETHE G

MAYSEDER

WALFISCH

STR

HEGEL

Staatsoper

MAHLER

STRASSE

SCHWARZENBERG

OPERNRING

G

KARNTNER

STRASSE

RING

SCHUBERT RING

OPERN

STR

KARNTNER STR

BOSENDORFER

RING

STR

AKADEMIE

STR

DUMBA

CANOVA

STR

LOTHRINGER STR

PANIGL G

Warsaw Pact. Today, Austria carefully protects its neutrality by law, allowing no military alliances and no foreign military bases.

The period of postwar peace has brought about a resurgence of music and coffee houses, the two basic ingredients of contemporary Viennese social life. The musical life of the city seems to involve everyone: Kiosks are plastered with notices of a cornucopia of concerts; the sounds of music being practiced seem to float from nearby open windows; many of the people in the street are carrying instrument cases. The great events of the social season revolve around the Opera and the Philharmonic, and people in dinner jackets and long gowns who glide past you in the early evening are inevitably going to *hear* something. But it is perhaps typical of Vienna that the finest places in the Opera House are the ten rows of standing room, dead center on a raised platform at the back of the orchestra. The houses of all of Vienna's great composers are carefully preserved and reverently visited. And a visit from Leonard Bernstein arouses far more passion than one from the American president.

Pastry eating is a national ritual that seems to be almost as important as Sunday morning mass. The windows of the city's bakeries and *Konditoreien* overflow with strudel, Sachertorte, cheesecakes, and nut horns, and the whipped cream flows like water. At teatime — and every other time — Viennese families stand with high seriousness before the glass pastry altars choosing, after long reflection, the afternoon's two thousand calories. When in Vienna, gorge as the Viennese do: If you start early and fit your last pastry in by five, you should still have room for dinner — and a little evening pastry.

Or if you are sated with pastries, just sit in a café, order coffee or wine, and drink in the spectacle of old Vienna. Though it is a city haunted by the ghosts of the vanished Hapsburg rulers, it is also blessed with their legacy of cultural brilliance, architectural splendor, and leisured living.

VIENNA AT-A-GLANCE

SEEING THE CITY: The Donauturm — the Danube Tower — is an 846-foot-high column that was, in fact, built for seeing the city. Opened in 1964, across the river from the main city, it has two high-speed elevators that whisk you to the observation platform and the two revolving restaurants at the summit. From the tower you look over the green expanse of the Danube Park below, and the adjacent United Nations City, and across the river to the spires and domes of the Innere Stadt, and to the Wienerwald beyond. On a clear day, the horizon sweeps from the Alps to the plains of Hungary. Open from 9 AM until midnight, with winter times an hour shorter at each end. The last elevator leaves an hour before closing. Wien XXII, Donaupark (phone: 23-53-68).

For a more accessible view from an enchanting public garden across a Vienna that still resembles a Canaletto cityscape, stand on the terrace of the Upper Belvedere Palace. The entrance is from Prinz-Eugen-Strasse 27, near the Südbahnhof railway station.

SPECIAL PLACES: The Inner City (Innere Stadt), encircled by the Danube Canal and the Ring boulevards, spans about one square mile and is best explored on foot. Its main street is the Kärntnerstrasse-Rotenturmstrasse, and its heart is the Stephansplatz, the cathedral square.

DOWNTOWN

St. Stephen's Cathedral (Stephansdom) – The most important Gothic structure in Austria, its soaring, ornate spire is a trademark of Vienna. Though called the Dom, its roof is actually a dramatically sloped wedge whose intricately patterned inlay gleams in the sun. The scene of some great events in Austrian history, the Stephansdom was the site of the famous double marriage of 1515 between the Hapsburgs and the Bohemian and Hungarian dynasties, a union that laid the foundations of the Austrian Empire. You can climb the staircase to the south tower or go down to the catacombs for a fee. An elevator will take you up the north tower to the cathedral's giant bell, the Pummerin, and another good view of Vienna. Noteworthy are the Romanesque west door, called the Giants' Doorway, the carved wood altarpiece in the left apsidal chapel, and the fifteenth-century red marble tomb of Friedrich III. Stephanspl. 1.

The Spanish Riding School – The history of this most unique of Viennese institutions goes back some four hundred years, when the first Spanish horses were brought to Austria under the aegis of Emperor Maximilian II. The imperial stud originated at Lipizza near Trieste; today its stunning white thoroughbred Lipizzaners are raised at Piber in southeastern Austria. The Riding School holds about fifty performances a year in Vienna on most Sunday mornings at 10:45 and Wednesday nights at 7 from March to June and September to December. Tickets are in fierce demand for the 600 seats and 275 standing places, and the rule of thumb for Sunday performances is to write *six months ahead* to Spanische Reitschule, Hofburg, A-1010 Wien, Austria (don't send any money; you pay when you pick them up). Or buy a ticket from a local travel agent for a 21.6% fee; try *Wagons-Lits Cook,* Kärntner Ring 2A, A–1010 Wien (phone: 65-76-31), or *Austrian Travel Agency, Inc.,* Opernring 3–5, A–1010 Wien (phone: 5600-0). Tickets for Wednesday night performances and for the shorter program on Saturday mornings are available only through agencies.

Second best are the training sessions, usually held every morning from 10 AM to noon for a fee. No advance reservations are taken — you stand in line in the Josefsplatz. Closed Sundays and Mondays. The traditionally uniformed riders lead the majestic white stallions through their paces to the strains of classic Viennese music in a great baroque hall that is like an equestrian ballroom. The all-white building was designed in 1735 by the master Viennese architect Josef Fischer von Erlach. Michaelerpl. 1 (phone: 52-18-36).

Imperial Stables (Stallburg) – A glassed-in passageway separates the riding school from the stables, which are open on a very limited basis for a small fee. The adjacent New Stallburg painting gallery houses some fine French impressionists.

The Hofburg – This was the winter residence of the Hapsburgs, and, in fact, you will be inside it while you visit the Riding School and the Imperial Stables. It is an extensive architectural complex whose buildings range from early Gothic to turn of the century. The oldest part is the thirteenth-century Swiss Court (the Schweizerhof), with the Imperial Chapel (the Burgkapelle), where Schubert was a choirboy and Mozart a young music master. Today, the chapel is the site of the Sunday morning masses sung by the Vienna Boys' Choir. You should also visit the sumptuous Imperial Apartments and the Treasury, which contains the fabulous crown jewels. (However, because of renovations they might be temporarily in a special room at the Museum of Fine Arts.) Michaelerpl. 1 (phone: Apartments 57-55-54-515; Treasury 52-63-99).

The Albertina – Near the Hofburg, the Albertina — whose name derives from its founder Duke Albert of Sachsen-Teschen — houses the world's greatest collection of graphic arts: etchings, engravings, color prints, sketches, woodcuts. The highlight is a complete collection of Albrecht Dürer's etchings, which are only a fraction, however, of the more than one million items in the Albertina. Whatever is not on display can be studied in portfolios in the Albertina's library. The Albertina is open daily; closed Sundays in July and August. Augustinerstr. 1 (phone: 52-42-32).

Museum of Fine Arts (Kunsthistorisches Museum) – One of the most dramatic experiences of painting in Europe is the roomful of Pieter Breughels (the Elder), which represents more than half the known production of this strange genius. *Children's Games, The Ascent to Calvary, Hunters in the Snow, Peasant Wedding, The Country Dance, Battle Between Carnival and Lent* — they're all here. Unlike the usual quick peek at an isolated world-famed canvas, this room provides a unified perception of the vision of a great creative mind; it's like reading Joyce's *Ulysses* or listening to Beethoven's *Ninth*. The vision is dark, ironic, disturbing, almost satanic; the paintings are simply superb. Here too are some of Rubens's finest works — including the great Ildefonso Altar painting, the portrait of his second wife, Helène Fourment, and a splendid self-portrait which is one of his last paintings. The museum also has works of Velázquez, Titian, Rembrandt, Holbein, Van Dyck, Giorgione, Cranach, and Raphael, as well as a Cellini salt cellar that is a Renaissance gold masterpiece. Open daily; closed Mondays. Certain collections are open Tuesday and Friday evenings from 7 until 9. Maria-Theresienpl. 1 (phone: 93-45-41).

The Viennese Cafés – If you only had an hour to see all of Vienna, you might get the best cross section of the city in one of its traditional cafés, sipping one of the ten-odd varieties of coffee you can order, munching a piece of *Apfelstrudel*, leafing through one of the newspapers the house provides, clipped onto a kind of short browsing pole. The Viennese café is a cross between living room, office, club, and enclosed street corner — where habitués lounge by the hour. *Jause* — the Viennese version of five o'clock tea — is generally the liveliest café hour.

Some of the city's most pleasant traditional cafés include: *Tirolerhof*, corner of Führichgasse and Tegetthoffstr.; *Landtmann*, Dr.-Karl-Lueger-Ring 4; *Ritter*, Mariahilferstr. 73; *Hummel*, Josefstädterstr. 66; and *Hawelka*, Dorotheergasse 6.

More pastry-oriented cafés or *Konditoreien* include: *Demel*, Kohlmarkt 14; *Lehmann*, Graben 12; *Heiner*, Kärntnerstr. 21 and Wollzeile 9; *Sluka*, Rathausplatz 8; and *Bürgerhof*, Gentzgasse 127.

Some of the most enjoyable coffeehouses include: *The Blue Bottle* (dating from the late 1600s, this was history's first Viennese coffeehouse), Singerstrasse 11; *Café Rathaus*, Landesgerichtsstrasse 5; *Sperl*, Gumpendorfer Strasse 11; *Café Grünwald*, Bauernmarkt 10; *Café Central*, Herrengasse 14; *Café Museum*, Friedrichstrasse 6; and *Alte Backstube*, Lange Gasse 34.

Cafés that regularly offer music to munch pastries by include: *Café Schwarzenberg*, Kärntner Ring 17; *Hotel Imperial* café, Kämtner Ring 16; and *Café Prückel*, Stubenring 24.

BEYOND THE CENTER

Schönbrunn – West of the center of town, Schönbrunn, the summer residence of the Hapsburgs, is inevitably compared with the Bourbons' little country place in Versailles, which was built at almost exactly the same time. The palace itself has 1,441 rooms; the grounds are vast, and the sights various. There are the royal apartments and gala rooms, the delightful rococo palace theater (which was the stage for Max Reinhardt's world-famed acting school), the dazzling collection of imperial carriages, the beautifully groomed baroque park and gardens, the Pheasant Walk, the Tyrolean Garden, the Imperial Chapel, and the Gloriette — a colonnaded structure on the panoramic hill where the palace was originally meant to stand.

At Schönbrunn too is the oldest zoo in Europe, once the imperial menagerie, with several thousand exotic animals centered around the graceful pavilion where the Empress Maria Theresa used to take her morning coffee. The palace itself is open daily and on summer evenings. During the summer, evening tours are frequently combined with concerts. The park and the zoo are open throughout the year; the Gloriette only from May through October. Schönbrunner-Schloss-Str. (phone: 83-36-46).

The Prater and the Riesenrad – For a change of pace, visit this immense green space, northeast of the center of town. The Prater was once the private game preserve of the Hapsburg princes, but as early as 1766 the Emperor Joseph II opened the gardens to the public. Ideal for strolling or bicycling, the Prater's Hauptallée is a 3-mile-long boulevard, flanked by lovely chestnut trees and leading to the Lusthaus, once the imperial hunting lodge. In summer, veer left at the Lusthaus onto Aspernallee or Schwarzenstockallee and wend your way to *Gustav Lindmayer's Fischrestaurant* (phone: 74-21-83; closed Mondays), where you can sit on the banks of the Danube and enjoy a bowl of *Fischbeuschl* soup or a Pilsener while barges and hydrofoils pass by.

At the entrance to the Prater amusement park stands the Riesenrad, the giant Ferris wheel, almost as much a symbol of Vienna as the Stephansdom spire. A landmark since the end of the nineteenth century, its great iron superstructure survived World War II, despite the bombs and fire that consumed most of the Prater. Only half as many of the bright red cars were replaced after the war, but the Riesenrad turns as ever. The panorama of Vienna is stunning as you swing to the top of the wheel's orbit — and *Third Man* devotees will remember Joseph Cotten and a menacing Orson Welles standing precariously by the open car door. Open April to November.

Grinzing – The place is a charming little suburb not even half an hour to the north of Vienna, but the name really stands for a whole aspect of Viennese life. Grinzing is where the Viennese go in the evening, in the summer, on Sunday afternoon — for food, wine, and merriment, and perhaps to remind themselves of the simple, hearty country pleasures that are at the root of so much of Austrian life. The food is the traditional *Brathendl* and *Backhendl* — tender young grilled and fried chicken; the wine is the *Heurigen*, which really means "from this year." In fact, *Heurigen* is the general name for the rustic taverns that dot Vienna's outskirts and specialize in the new wine, with old wooden tables and middle-aged musicians. In the warm season, there is a place to sit out under an arbor; in the winter there may be a crackling fire. Many of the Viennese arrive with elaborate box lunches from home or from richly stocked delicatessens. It is wise to take the No. 38 tram to and from Grinzing instead of driving.

■**EXTRA SPECIAL:** The Wienerwald, the Vienna Woods of the Johann Strauss waltzes, is a vast, unspoiled forest to the west and south of the city. The nearer edges are popular for Sunday outings, the deeper recesses fine for serious hiking or bike riding. (Bikes can be rented.) There are numerous well-marked trails.

At Mayerling in the middle of the Vienna Woods, on a snowy night in 1889, Crown Prince Rudolf — the only son of the Emperor Franz Joseph — and his lover, the Baroness Mary Vetsera, committed double suicide in a hunting lodge. The emperor, who had refused to allow the dissolution of his son's unhappy marriage, had the fatal bedroom torn down and a chapel built in its place.

A day's excursion can also take you to the ancient Cistercian monastery at Heiligenkreuz, through the lovely wooded Helenental and Europe's largest underground lake, the Seegrotte, to the vineyards of Perchtoldsdorf and Gumpoldskirchen and past one of the Prince of Liechtenstein's Austrian castles. Rent a car, take a sight-seeing tour offered by *Vienna Sightseeing Tours (Wiener Rundfahrten)* Stelzhamergasse 4/11, A–1030 Wien (phone: 72-46-83), or take trolley 38 to Grinzing and continue by bus 38A to Kahlenberg and explore the many hiking trails in the woods.

Or take the No. 2 tram from downtown to Neuwaldegg and a 1½-hour hike (one-third of it uphill) to the *Sofienalpe Hotel,* Sofienalpenstr. 13 (phone: 46-24-32), where you can stay the night or just have wild boar and *Millirahmstrudel,* a cottage cheese pastry served hot with vanilla sauce.

SOURCES AND RESOURCES

The Vienna City Tourist Office, in the underground passage by the opera (Opernpassage), is open daily (phone: 43-16-08) and issues a free monthly program of all events of note in the city. A calendar of events is posted in every hotel and in other places throughout the city. Be sure to pick up a list of museum hours, as these are often subject to change. Freytag and Berndt publishes a good map of Vienna, which includes a brief guide to the city in English. The *Falk Plan* is a gorgeous, intricate, fold-out map that comes in two sizes. These maps are available at many of the city's bookstores.

For Local Coverage – *Vienna Life, Falter,* and *Wiener,* which list everything going on, are available at the *Shakespeare & Co.* bookstore (Sterngasse 2) and other outlets. Or tune in to Blue Danube Radio — in English, with news, pop music, and a list of events — at 102.2 on the dial between 7 and 9 AM, noon and 2 PM, 6 and 8 PM.

 CLIMATE AND CLOTHES: Perched 561 feet above sea level, Vienna is warm and sunny in summer. Temperatures average about 77°F (25°C). Winters are rainy, raw, gusty, and snowy, but temperatures average above freezing, 34°–37°F (1°–3°C). If you go to Vienna in the winter, be sure to take appropriate footwear against the cold and wet. As for dress, Vienna is a surprisingly formal city, with classic dressiness still pretty much the rule at theaters, concerts, or restaurants. Take something reasonably elegant along, or you may feel uncomfortable.

 GETTING AROUND: Public Transport – Three efficient subway lines penetrate the heart of the Innere Stadt. Pleasant and quaintly Viennese are the lumbering red and white streetcars that weave through the city. For a few cents, the public transport office, in the underground passage by the Opera, will sell you a beautiful multilingual transport map that marks all the routes of the U-Bahn, Stadtbahn, Schnellbahn, tram, and bus, and explains the mysteries of tickets, passes, stamping machines, and the like. Buy tickets at any tobacconist's (Tabak Trafik) at reduced prices or from the conductor or machine. Tourists can buy a discount "3-day Vienna" ticket, good for unlimited riding on all public transport, at tourist counters in the airport and rail stations.

Taxi – You can call radio taxis by phoning any of these numbers: 3130; 4369; 6282; 9101 — or look in the phone book under *Taxi* for the number of the nearest stand.

Shuttle Service – *Mazur Shuttle* is a minibus service that will drop you or pick you up at your hotel. Make arrangements through the airline, the desk at the airport, or at your hotel (phone: 64-91-91, 64-22-33).

Fiaker – A horse-drawn carriage, as Viennese as the Hapsburgs, is a favorite mode of transportation to weddings and carnival balls or just for trundling about the old city. The public transport map marks Fiaker stands, and three reliable coachmen are Martin Stelzel, Gumpendorferstr. 32 (phone: 57-09-455); Rudi Glück, Gestettengasse 16/VII (phone: 72-29-804); and Johann Paukner, Mohsgasse 13/8 (phone: 73-88-385).

Car Rental – *Hertz* is at Kärntner Ring 17 (phone: 52-86-77); *Avis* at Weyringergasse 33 (phone: 65-58-390); and *Inter-Rent Austria* at Seiftgasse 3-9 (phone: 93-95-88). *Foremost Euro-car* runs *Rent-A-Car-Union* at Wiedner Hauptstr. 51 (phone: 65-01-96).

Boat – Between April and October, the *Danube Steamship Company* (DDSG) provides sight-seeing boat trips along the canal. Boats depart frequently for 1- to 2½-hour excursions from Schwedenbrücke on the canal. They also offer Hungarian-operated hydrofoil trips to Budapest (a 4½-hour trip; it's as fast as the train and much more scenic) as well as 10-hour excursions on a pleasure boat called the *Tancsics,* around the Danube Bend and past (but not into) Bratislava, Czechoslovakia, and Rajka, Hungary. For information, call 26-65-35.

MUSEUMS: Besides those mentioned in *Special Places,* the following museums are also interesting:

Clock Museum of the City of Vienna (Uhrenmuseum der Stadt Wien), Schulhof 2 (phone: 63-22-65).

Sigmund Freud Museum, Berggasse 19 (phone: 31-15-96).

New Hofburg Collections of Weapons and Ancient Musical Instruments and Ephesus Museum of Archeology, all at Heldenpl. (phone: 93-45-41).

Schubert Museum, Nussdorfer Str. 54 (phone: 34-59-924).

Picture Gallery of the Academy of Fine Arts, Schillerpl. 3 (phone: 57-95-16).

Johann Strauss Museum, Praterstr. 54 (phone: 24-01-21).

Mozart Memorial, Domgasse 5 (phone: 52-40-722).

Austrian Gallery of Nineteenth- and Twentieth-Century Art, Upper Belvedere, Prinz-Eugen-Str. 27 (phone: 78-41-580).

Museum of Baroque Art and the Museum of Austrian Medieval Art, Lower Belvedere, Rennweg 6a (phone: 78-41-580).

Historical Museum of the City of Vienna, Karlspl. 4 (phone: 42-804).

SHOPPING: The center for shopping is the area around Kärntnerstrasse, Graben, and Kohlmarkt; most department stores are on Mariahilferstrasse. Some good buys are antiques, knitwear, glassware, crystal, porcelain, petit-point, musical instruments and scores, fur hats, riding gear, and, of course, léderhosen (leather pants), loden-cloth coats, and *Sachertorte* (chocolate cake).

The *Dorotheum* is the oldest auction house in Europe. Founded in 1707 by the Emperor Joseph I as a pawnshop for the poor, the *Dorotheum* is a city landmark and part of Viennese social life, even if you aren't interested in antiques. (You can pay a *Sensal,* a licensed bidder — who is absolutely honest — to bid for you at a small fee.) The Dorotheergasse, along with its surrounding streets, is one of Europe's finest streets for antiques. Dorotheergasse 11 (phone: 52-31-29).

The *Naschmarkt,* an outdoor fruit and vegetable market, is not to be missed. It's held daily except Sundays south of the Opera Quarter, between Linke and Rechte Wienzeile. The *Flohmarkt,* a flea market, is held every Saturday near the Naschmarkt.

Note: You can avoid most of the 8% to 30% VAT if you are not going to use your purchases in Austria. Fill out a tax refund slip in the shop. The slip has to be stamped by the customs inspector when you leave Austria. You can bring it to the Austrian Automobile-Motorcycle & Touring Club (ÖAMTC) border stations or the Austrian Credit Institute (ÖCI) counters at airports or mail the slip and sales receipt, along with the address of your bank and your account number, either to the shop or to ÖAMTC Mehrwertsteuerverrechnung, Schubertring 1-3, 1010 Vienna. Eventually you should receive a refund.

Here are just a few recommended shops:

W.F. Adlmüller – The highest fashion (and the most imaginative) in Vienna, for women and men. Kärntnerstr. 41 (phone: 52-66-50).

Lobmeyr – For crystal. Kärntnerstrasse 26 (phone: 52-21-89).

Loden Plankl – A very reputable but expensive place for dirndls, lederhosen, and other regional wear. Michaelerpl. 6.

Österreichische Werkstätten – Austrian handicrafts. Karntnerstr. 6 (phone: 52-24-18).

Polak – Riding gear. Arnsteing 17 (phone: 83-12-38).

Resi Hammerer – This is *the* place for haute couture loden and sports apparel for ladies. Kärntnerstr. 29–31.

Rosenthal-Studio – China and silver — and a beautiful wall mosaic outside. Kärntnerstr. 16.

Hotel Sacher – This has been the official chocolate cake *(Sachertorte)* outlet since 1832. You can eat one or have one shipped in six different sizes. Kärntnerstr., around the corner from the main entrance of the hotel.

Smejkal – This is one of the best of many places in Vienna that specialize in petit-point embroidery. In the underground Opernpassage and at Kohlmarkt 9.

Susi – Traditional Austrian clothing, including capes and hand-embroidered sweaters. Währingerstr. 58 (phone: 34-40-992).

F. and J. Votruba – A century-old dynasty which deals in musical items, including instruments, scores, records, and anything you can think of. Lerchenfelder Gürtel 4 (phone: 93-68-675).

 SPECIAL EVENTS: The Viennese special event par excellence is *Fasching,* which loosely describes the carnival period from the New Year until Ash Wednesday — the beginning of Lent. For some 2 months, the city bursts into organized merriment with a series of *Fasching* balls ranging from white-tie-and-champagne affairs like the *New Year's Eve Emperor's Ball* in the Hofburg to the *Vienna Plumbers Guild Ball* at a large hotel. The season's highlight is always the *Opera Ball,* which is held in the Opera House in February or March with the Austrian president on hand. Other old favorites: the *Wiener Philharmoniker Ball,* held in the Musikverein concert hall; the *Vienna Physicians Ball; Huntsmen's Ball of the Green Cross;* and the *Fool's Night of the Vienna Men's Choir.* The names are those of the sponsoring society, but they are all open to the general public. A complete schedule and ticket information are available from the Vienna Tourist Board, Kinderspitalgasse 5 (phone: 43-16-08).

The Wiener Festwochen is an orgy of music and theater, five festival weeks that generally run from mid-May to late June and attract internationally known musicians and theater groups. There is a garnish of side events: exhibitions, conferences, song festivals, and the like. For information and tickets: Büro der Wiener Festwochen, Friedrich Schmidtpl. 4 (phone: 42-800, then dial 4257 or 4255).

■**EXTRA SPECIAL:** The Ultimate New Year's Eve. If you've spent all your life hating New Year's Eve, there's a spectacular way to get over the grudge — that's to spend it in Vienna. It requires substantial planning (and even more money — to motivate the concierge at your hotel to produce hard-to-get tickets to otherwise sold out performances), but it's an event you will not soon forget.

Your New Year's celebration should begin with the annual exuberant performance of *Die Fledermaus* at the *Staatsoper* or *Volksoper* (see *Theater*). From there, you move on to the Imperial Ball at the Hofburg Winter Palace, where the New Year's Eve party is held in the old Imperial Ballroom. After seeing how the Hapsburgs lived (and partied), move on. The best New Year's ball in town is held at the *Hotel-Palais Schwarzenberg,* where 150 guests are entertained royally in the old palace ballroom and drinks are served in a small room notable for the two immense Renoirs on the walls. The Gobelin tapestries aren't exactly shabby, either. At midnight, the fireworks display rivals a Fourth of July extravaganza, and there's something special about dancing in the New Year to the strains of the *Blue*

Danube Waltz rather than *Auld Lang Syne.* At about 2 AM, a Tyrolean oompah band marches through the palace trumpeting away and all the guests march after. Not bad.

Don't stay up too late, however, because festivities begin again early on New Year's Day. At 11 AM in the Musikverein, the Vienna Philharmonic rouses you from any morning lethargy with a program of Strauss (father and son) waltzes and polkas that just about takes the roof off the hall. The flowers come from Holland, but the music is pure Vienna. If you can't get tickets for the performance, the next best thing is to buy a ticket for the sumptuous buffet brunch in the Johann Strauss Ballroom of the *Hotel Inter-Continental* (Johannesgasse 28). Fill up your plate with food and your glass with champagne, then take them into the adjoining room where the Philharmonic concert is televised on a larger-than-life screen.

Otherwise, New Year's lunch is at *Demel's* (for those who can get in), though any other coffee house will do. The late afternoon is for napping, and the New Year's climax is that evening, when the Vienna Symphony performs Beethoven's *Ninth Symphony* in the *Konzerthaus* (see *Music*). Hearing the hundreds of voices sing the "Ode to Joy" last movement is quite an experience.

 SPORTS: Bicycling – Both the Prater and large tracts of the Vienna Woods are delightful for riding. Bicycles can be rented from *Radfahrverein Prater,* 1020, Böcklinstr. 2 (phone: 24-85-38).

Golf – *Vienna Golfclub,* Freudenau 65a (phone: 74-17-86).

Horse Racing – Year-round at the beautiful *Freudenau* (for flat racing and steeplechase racing) or *Krieau* (harness racing) tracks, both in the Prater.

Horseback Riding – If you want to be a participant rather than a spectator, this is the city in which to do it. Three good riding centers are the *TSA Reitclub,* good for first-timers and tournament jumpers alike, at Oberlaaerstr. 225 (phone: 68-17-654); *Wiener Reitinstitut,* 1030, Barmherzigengasse 17 (phone: 73-16-52); and *Reiter Zentrum Kreuttal,* 9 miles (15 km) north of the city, with a nice restaurant and guest rooms. A-2112 Ritzendorf 1 (phone: 02263-300).

Tennis – The *Floridsdorfer Tennis Club* has fifteen courts, an indoor hall, and no fee. Lorettopl. 5 (phone: 38-12-83); there's *Vereinigte Tennisanlagen,* pleasantly situated in the Prater, with its own restaurant at Prater Hauptallée (phone: 24-63-84); and *Reifen Tree,* Wien-Liesing, Breitenfurterstr. 370 (phone: 86-95-74).

Walking – Virtually the Austrian national sport; there is a several-hundred-kilometer circuit of walking and hiking trails in the Vienna Woods, excellently marked and serviced by numerous inexpensive inns.

 THEATER: The *Staatsoper* is one of the three or four most important opera houses in the world. During the course of a long season (September through June), most of the great names in today's opera world make an appearance. Opernring 2. In addition to the opera, there are three other state theaters: the *Burgtheater,* Dr. Karl Lueger-Ring 2, which specializes in classical repertory; the *Volksoper,* Währingerstr. 78, which specializes in light opera, Viennese operetta, and musicals; and the *Akademietheater,* Lisztstr. 1, which specializes in modern plays, using the *Burgtheater* company. Tickets for all four state theaters are available from 15 days to 2 months ahead by writing to Bundestheaterverband, Goethegasse 1, A-1010 Wien. Starting the week preceding a performance, you can buy tickets at the central state-theater box office: Bundestheaterkasse, Hanuschgasse 3 — in a courtyard just behind the opera house (phone for all state theaters: 5324-0).

Two other famous old theaters are worth a visit, even if you have only a rudimen-

684   VIENNA / Sources and Resources

tary knowledge of German: the beautiful *Theater in der Josefstadt,* Josefstädterstr. 26 (phone: 42-51-27); and the musical house *Theater an der Wien,* which played host to the world premières of classics like Beethoven's *Fidelio* and Lehar's *The Merry Widow,* Linke Wienzeile 6 (phone: 57-71-51). Tickets for all Vienna productions are also available from the many agencies around town, but you will pay a 21.6% markup.

Vienna also has an English theater, which has been going strong since 1963 and is now housed in a lovely neo-baroque building at Josefsgasse 12 (phone: 42-12-60 or 42-82-84). Its perennial attraction, Ruth Brinkmann as Ruth Draper, is a must.

 **MUSIC:** The great Viennese musical experience is a concert by the *Wiener Philharmoniker,* whose headquarters are at the *Musikverein,* Dumbastr. 3 (phone: 65-81-90). Daytime box office at Karlspl. 6. The other major concert hall, with three separate auditoriums, is the *Konzerthaus,* Lothringerstr. 20 (phone: 72-12-11). Also on any "must" list of Vienna musical experiences is the *Vienna Boys' Choir (Wiener Sängerknaben).* There is singing at mass in the Burgkapelle of the Hofburg most Sunday and religious holiday mornings at 9:15, though not in July or August. Tickets can be obtained by writing in advance to Verwaltung der Hofmusik-kapelle, Hofburg, Schweizerhof, A–1010 Wien; what's left is sold every Friday after-noon from 5 PM on (get there at least an hour before) at the Burgkapelle for the following Sunday morning.

Devoted music lovers might enjoy a visit to the old Bösendorfer Piano building, at Canovagasse 4, back to back with the *Musikverein;* and, in summer, a tour of the homes of the great composers — Beethoven, Schubert, Mozart, Haydn, Strauss — who lived and worked in Vienna, organized by *Cityrama,* Börsegasse 1 (phone: 63-66-190), or by other major travel agencies.

 NIGHTCLUBS AND NIGHTLIFE: The most traditional Viennese night on the town is at one of the *Heurigen* in Grinzing: lots of new wine to wash down dinner and a good dose of *Schrammelmusik* — Viennese folk music. Cobenzlgasse is the main street of Heurigen-dom: try the *Altes Presshaus* at number 15, *Gertrude Marchart* at number 17, the *Grinzinger Hauermandl* at number 20, the *Grinzinger Weinbottich* at number 28, or *Bach-Hengl,* a block away, at Sand-gasse 9. The two most "in" bars with music and a lively, classy crowd are the *Eden-Bar,* Liliengasse 2 (phone: 52-74-50), and the *New Splendid Bar,* Jasomirgottstr. 3 (phone: 63-15-15) — both open until 4 AM. The reigning discos are the *Queen Anne,* Johannes-gasse 12 (phone: 52-02-03), and the *Take Five,* Annagasse 3a (phone: 52-32-76). For floor shows, try *Renz,* Zirkusgasse 50 (phone: 24-31-35), near the Prater, or the *Casa-nova Erotic Revue Bar Theater,* Dorotheerg. 6–8 (phone: 52-98-45 or 52-98-69).

 SINS: Vienna is one of the few major European cities with gambling. The *Casino Cercle Wien* is in the Palais Esterhazy, Kärntnerstr. 41 (phone: 52-48-36). In nearby Baden-bei-Wien, the casino is bigger, flashier, and cash-ier.

If you're interested in Viennese dishes (other than those of the Wiener schnitzel sort), there are opportunities for both spectators and participants at *Madame Bar,* Hofene-dergasse 4 (phone: 24-54-54); *Club Emanuela-Erotikgarten,* Nussdorferstr. 75 (phone: 34-14-99); the *Renz,* Zirkusgasse 50 (phone: 24-31-35); and the *Casbah,* Naglergasse 23 (phone: 63-21-50). Or, at no charge, just take a stroll on a warm evening around the Tuchlauben downtown.

But in Vienna, there is really no sin that can match an *Indianer mit Schlag* and an *Einspänner* at *Demel's,* Kohlmarkt 14 — 10,000 calories of coffee, chocolate, and whipped cream in a fine old-world setting.

$$\boxed{\textbf{BEST IN TOWN}}$$

CHECKING IN: The nicest place to stay in Vienna is in the Innere Stadt — or just on the edge of it. Don't be put off by appearances; many of the quaint hotels look older than they do quaint — but they do have a particular Viennese charm. A double room with bath and breakfast costs from about $70 to $140 in hotels listed as expensive; $50 to $70 is moderate; and below $50 is inexpensive.

The Bristol – It's just across the street from the Opera, overlooking the Ring, and the rooms are large and beautifully furnished. Lots of polished wood, black-tiled bathrooms with twin sinks, instant room service — and one of the great hotel bars of Europe. 128 rooms. Major credit cards. Kärntner Ring 1 (phone: 52-95-52). Expensive.

Hotel Sacher – Over 100 years old, the *Sacher* is really a symbol of Vienna and a favorite of the music lovers, listeners, and performers. Elegance, tradition, and the past are all in the air, in the ornate rococo decor, and in the faithful and distinguished clientele. The rooms are modest but comfortable, and the service is impeccable. The concierge here is legendary for his ability to produce tickets (albeit sometimes at staggering prices) to Vienna's most noteworthy musical events. The hotel's restaurant is a center of Viennese social life, and the elegant coffee house made the *Sachertorte* legendary. The opera house is a 10-second walk away. 121 rooms. No credit cards. Philharmonikerstr. 2 (phone: 52-55-75). Expensive.

The Imperial – This regal building, built in 1869 as a private palace for the duke of Württemberg, served as the Russian headquarters after World War II. It's more palatial in feeling and style than the *Bristol* and *Sacher;* its rooms are superb and its service sublime. Wagner lived here for months during the productions of his operas around the corner. The quality of the hotel's restaurant was deteriorating, but finally seems to be making a comeback. 160 rooms. Major credit cards. Kärntner Ring 16 (phone: 65-17-65). Expensive.

Hotel Ambassador – Beautifully situated between the pedestrian shopping zone and a market square crowned by a baroque Raphael Donner fountain, this 106-room elegant luxury hotel has a tradition of treating every guest like a diplomat. Major credit cards. Neuer Markt 6 and Kärntnerstr. 24 (phone: 52-75-11). Expensive.

Hotel-Palais Schwarzenberg – Incomparably situated in its own manicured garden park in the center of Vienna, the hotel rooms are set in a section of the old castle and exude an incomparable aura of dignity and old-world character. The only hotel in Vienna that's a member of the Relais de Campagne. The kitchen is one of the most elegant in the city and the service is first rate. Schwarzenbergpl. 9 (phone: 78-45-15). Expensive.

Hotel König von Ungarn – In one form or another, this fine old house has been in the hotel business since 1764. After its most recent renovation in 1977, it blossomed forth with a glass-roofed atrium and a three-story, century-old, indoor tree around which coffee and cocktails are served. The hotel's *King of Hungary* restaurant serves international cuisine. 32 rooms. Schulerstr. 10 (phone: 52-65-20). Expensive.

Vienna Inter-Continental – Built in 1964 at one end of the elegant Stadtpark, this glittering gem in a worldwide chain has become a landmark where the Viennese love to eat, meet, dance, and gossip. Among its many virtues are imaginative and excellent Austrian and international cuisine in its *Rôtisserie* and a special floor for nonsmokers. 498 rooms. Major credit cards. Johannesgasse 28 (phone: 7505). Expensive.

Wien Hilton – Built directly across the Stadtpark slightly more than a decade after its arch-rival, this high-rise slab quickly earned a loyal following for its turn-of-the-century-style *Klimt Bar;* folksy, traditional *Vindobona Cellar; Park Café,* good food and drink with a view; and *Rôtisserie Prinz-Eugen,* a fine restaurant that was the first in Vienna to win a Michelin star. 620 rooms. Major credit cards. Am Stadtpark (phone: 75-26-52). Expensive.

The Mailbergerhof – Tucked quietly into a courtyard in the Annagasse with an unimposing entrance and a first-floor reception room, this is nevertheless a favorite of music and theater people, particularly for longer stays in one of its six lovely apartment suites. 46 rooms. American Express. Annagasse 7 (phone: 52-06-41). Expensive to moderate.

Hotel Am Stephansplatz – Just five paces across the new pedestrian mall to the main portal of the Stephanskirche, this may be the best location in town. It's also perched above a subway station that has a medieval chapel within; though the hotel's architecture is modern and without character, you are in the heart of Vienna, and the first-floor café is the heart of the heart. 72 rooms. Major credit cards. Stephanspl. 9 (phone: 63-56-05). Moderate.

The Kaiserin Elisabeth – In a building that dates from the fourteenth century, just off the Kärntnerstrasse, this hotel on the same street as several of Vienna's better restaurants, so you're always sure of a good dinner — come snow or high water. 77 rooms. Major credit cards. Weihburggasse 3 (phone: 52-26-26). Moderate.

The Astoria – The hotel lies in the pedestrian haven behind the Vienna State Opera. There's a lively international atmosphere in the lobby, but the upstairs restaurant attracts a local crowd that enjoys the four-course Opera Menu (which can be taken in installments before and after performances). 110 rooms. Major credit cards. Kärntnerstr. 32–34 (phone: 52-65-85). Moderate.

Römischer Kaiser – This handsome, baroque, national trust building was erected in 1684 as the private palace of the imperial chancellor, then served as a military academy. It has been a hotel since the turn of the century. There is a charming little café on the front doorstep. 26 rooms. Major credit cards. Annagasse 16 (phone: 52-77-51). Moderate.

Graben Hotel – It's in a little dark street just off the Graben, but right in the middle of artistic and antiquarian Vienna. The building is a little drab, but just across the street is the city's liveliest hangout, the *Café Hawelka,* and the best sandwiches in Vienna are next door at *Tržesniewski.* 46 rooms. Major credit cards. Dorotheergasse 3 (phone: 52-15-31). Moderate to inexpensive.

Pension Wiener – When Sam and Helen Thau retired, they sold their posh *Hotel de France* on the Ring and opened this small hostelry atop a well-located but quiet downtown office building. If you like to take your Viennese *Gemütlichkeit* with a little Jewish-mothering and all modern conveniences, this is the place for you. No credit cards. Seilergasse 16 (phone: 52-33-310). Moderate.

Ring Hotel – This reasonably priced, well-maintained hotel is surrounded by a lovely stone staircase leading up to the most surprising church in Vienna: a Gothic gem with a narrow, slightly crooked nave. Service is personal; rooms, small but very comfortable, all with baths. There's a restaurant that serves Viennese cuisine and a wine cellar. 45 rooms. Maria am Gestade 1 (phone: 63-77-01). Moderate to inexpensive.

The Schweizerhof – Just behind a marvelous clock on which statues of Vienna's greats — from Marcus Aurelius to Josef Haydn — march at midday, this 57-room hotel is very much a slice of old Wien, with something rather pleasantly faded about its stylishness. Major credit cards. Bauernmarkt 22 (phone: 63-19-31). Inexpensive.

 EATING OUT: Viennese cooking ranks with the best. Don't eat for a week before; you won't be able to for a week after. Make sure, at some point, to have a stand-up sausage in the street (the safest and best *Würstelstand* is outside the main Creditanstalt-Bankverein, Schotteng. 6) and to fit in at least one *Beisel,* one *Heurigen,* and one coffeehouse. A *Beisel* is like a bistro, a cozy inexpensive neighborhood restaurant, open all hours. A *Heurigen* is a tavern that specializes in wine of new vintage, sometimes has entertainment, and often offers food. It can be recognized by a tuft of greenery hanging over the door. And coffeehouses are a way of life in Vienna, a place to sit, read newspapers, converse, receive guests and mail, and make phone calls.

The highlights of Viennese cuisine include, of course, Wiener schnitzel, ideally a lightly breaded veal cutlet. Hungarian goulash *(Rindsgulasch)* is also popular, as is *Tafelspitz,* or boiled beef with vegetables or horseradish sauce. Desserts in Vienna are positively sinful, especially baked ones such as *Strudel, Sachertorte,* and *Linzertorte,* a tart of apricot jam and almonds. And of course there are always mounds of *Schlag* (whipped cream). Coffee is special in Vienna and it comes in many varieties, especially *Mokka,* which is black; *Brauner,* coffee with milk; *Melange* or *Milchkaffee,* frothing with hot milk; and *Einspänner,* with whipped cream in a glass.

A meal for two with wine will cost between $40 and $90 in restaurants classed as expensive; $20 to $40 is moderate; and below $20 is inexpensive. Although a 10% tip is included in most menu prices, an extra 5% gratuity is expected if service has been adequate.

Sacher – There are those who would rather dine here than at any other place in Europe. It's superbly elegant, and it reeks of tradition. Dinner here before or after the Opera is the quintessence of Vienna. Ordering *Tafelspitz* and wearing a tie are mandatory, and will put the waiter on your side from the start. Reserve well in advance. Philharmonikerstr. 4 (phone: 52-55-75). Expensive.

Zu Den Drei Husaren – *The Three Hussars* has beautiful, typically Viennese decor in the old style, an abundance of plush velour and drapery. It's famous for the incredibly huge procession of hors d'oeuvres that is wheeled by your table. But leave room for the special dessert, *Husaren Pfannkuchen.* Open only for dinner; closed Sundays and often from mid-July to mid-August. Reservations are always necessary. Weihburggasse 4 (phone: 52-11-92). Expensive.

Palais Schwarzenberg – In the domed cellar of the palace/hotel of the same name, this elegant restaurant is a reflection of the establishment's status as Vienna's only member of the Relais de Campagne. The menu is French-flavored more than typically Viennese, and the service is merely perfect. A fine respite from an excess of schnitzels and schlag. At Schwarzenbergpl. 9 (phone: 78-45-15). Expensive.

Gasthof Wegenstein–Weisser Schwan – One of the great preparers of game in the world: 250 years old and handy to the Volksoper. Order whatever the waiter or owner recommends as being in season and wash it down with Pilsener beer from the barrel. When weather permits, reserve a table outdoors in the cozy historic courtyard. Closed Saturdays and Sundays. Nussdorfer Str. 59 (phone: 34-16-50). Expensive to moderate.

Passauerhof – This is one of Grinzing's best *Heurigers* for dining. In a venerable house dating back to 1150 and beautifully restored, it has some of the latest cuisine (kiwi and mango sauces, for instance) as well as the traditional dishes that go well with new wine. There's also good music, a lovely garden, and an ancient wine press in the cellar. Cobenzlgasse 9 (phone: 32-63-45). Moderate.

Zum Weissen Rauchfangkehrer – A homey place — rustic furnishings, wooden benches, lovely hanging iron lamps, painted glass — on a street of elegant restaurants. The food is good, and for dessert take a deep breath and ask the waiter for *Brandteigschokoladecremekrapfen.* Your reward for saying that 31-letter mouthful will be one of the best chocolate creampuffs ever. Reservations required. Weihburggasse 4 (phone: 52-34-71). Moderate.

Wiener Rathauskeller – A popular place with the tourist trade, it's a vast dining center below the City Hall. Music and bustle as well as food. Closed Sundays. Rathauspl. 1 (phone: 42-12-19). Moderate to inexpensive.

Hermann Adam's Restaurant Neues Rathaus – If the *Wiener Rathauskeller* is too touristy for you, try this place nearby. The food is very authentic, imaginative, and delicious. Closed Saturdays and Sundays. Florianigasse 2 (phone: 43-44-66). Inexpensive.

Tržesniewski – A must of musts. This isn't a proper restaurant, but an ever-thronged sandwich bar, offering endless varieties of miniature open sandwiches from great bins of assorted Viennese goodies. Dark bread, draft beer, and *Apfelsaft,* apple cider. Open weekdays until 7:30 PM; closed Saturday afternoons and Sundays. No reservations. Dorotheergasse 1 (phone: 52-32-91). Inexpensive.

Toni Wagner's Glacisbeisel – Inside the walls of the former imperial stables (now a trade fairgrounds), this *Beisel* near the English Theater happens to have the very best Wiener Schnitzel in town. During summer, you can eat in a garden built into the ramparts. Open for lunch sometimes, and dinner except weekends. Messepl. 1 (phone: 93-07-374). Inexpensive.

S'Weinfassl – This two-level, wood-beamed restaurant offers intimate dining, very good food, beer and wine, and a congenial atmosphere. It's west of the center of town, very near the *Stadthalle,* Vienna's big indoor sports arena and entertainment hall. Closed Mondays. Gablenzgasse 15 (phone: 92-37-362). Inexpensive.

WARSAW

Warsaw, like its people, is a pleasant surprise. It takes a little effort to get to know both. On first impression, the capital seems as gray and forbidding as the poured concrete buildings with which the Poles quickly rebuilt their city after it was reduced to smoking rubble during World War II. The skyline, dominated by the Stalinesque Palace of Culture and Science, seems as no-nonsense and functional as the 1.5 million inhabitants who go about their business each day in the Polish capital.

But, on closer look, you discover the statuary of nymphs and satyrs in the eighteenth-century Saxon Gardens, where cavalrymen once exercised their horses. You admire the elegance of the neoclassic Lazienki Palace and baths where Polish kings entertained their guests. You begin to share the pleasure of strolling couples and the glee of children feeding ducks. Everywhere, you see little kiosks selling flowers. Varsovians — as the residents of Warsaw are called — take the time to beautify their lives in small ways.

Go a little farther, and you will find the true heart of the city, the Old Town. Dating from the fourteenth century, it is a mixture of Renaissance and baroque buildings around a central marketplace. Every detail, from the wrought-iron shop signs to the widening medieval streets, was lovingly restored after the Nazi destruction of World War II. To some the obvious newness of the buildings gives too much of a feeling of a Hollywood set. But to the Poles, the new Old Town is a symbol of their determination to keep their heritage.

The Poles have had to work hard to preserve their past and their identity as a people. Three times in Warsaw's 900-year history there have been attempts to annihilate the city. Throughout the seventeenth and eighteenth centuries, the city was occupied repeatedly by Swedes and Russians. The Swedes razed the city in the seventeenth century, and it was sacked in the eighteenth century during the suppression of an insurrection. Poland ceased to exist as a nation when it was partitioned in 1795 and Warsaw was given to Prussia. Napoleon captured the city in 1806 and formed the Duchy of Warsaw, but in 1813 it was taken again by the Russians. Poland was not restored as a nation until after World War I.

Then came the Nazi occupation of World War II, and Hitler's order that not one stone of the city be left standing. The Jews of the Warsaw ghetto had inspired the world in 1943 by rising up in a fierce, if losing, battle against the Nazis. The following year, all the underground groups united in a 63-day battle against the Nazis, which is remembered as the Warsaw Uprising. When it failed, the Nazis began the systematic destruction of the city. More than 200,000 people were killed here; most of those who survived were deported.

Warsaw and its people were devastated by the war. And the city remem-

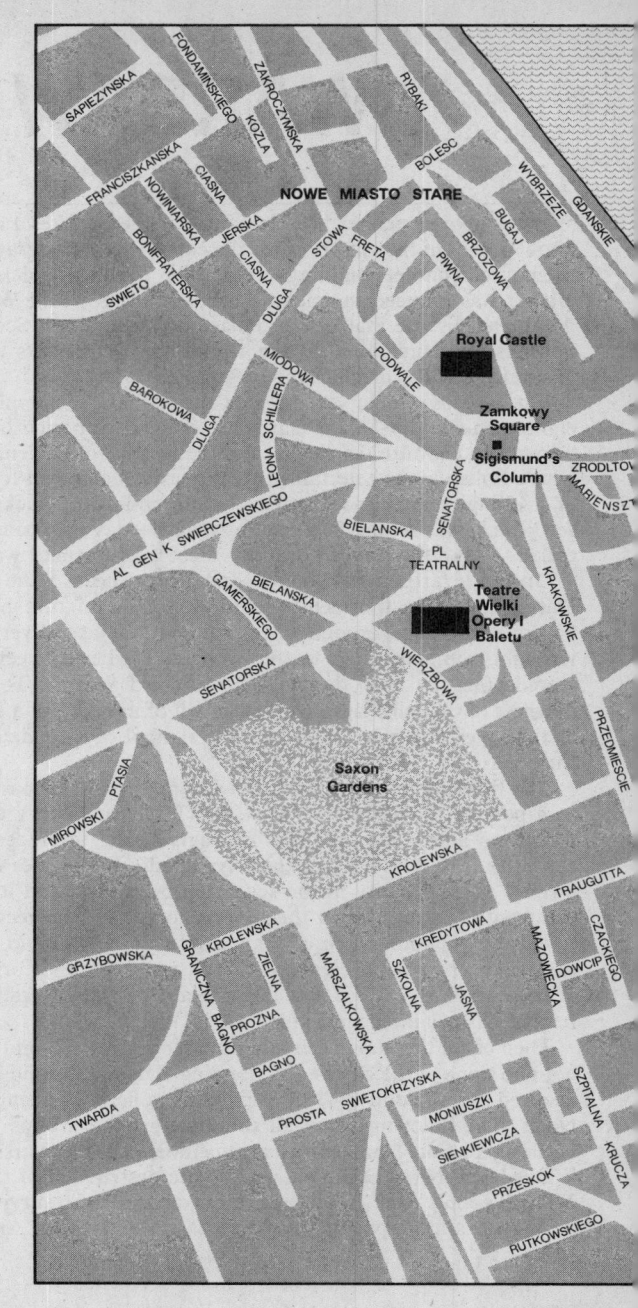

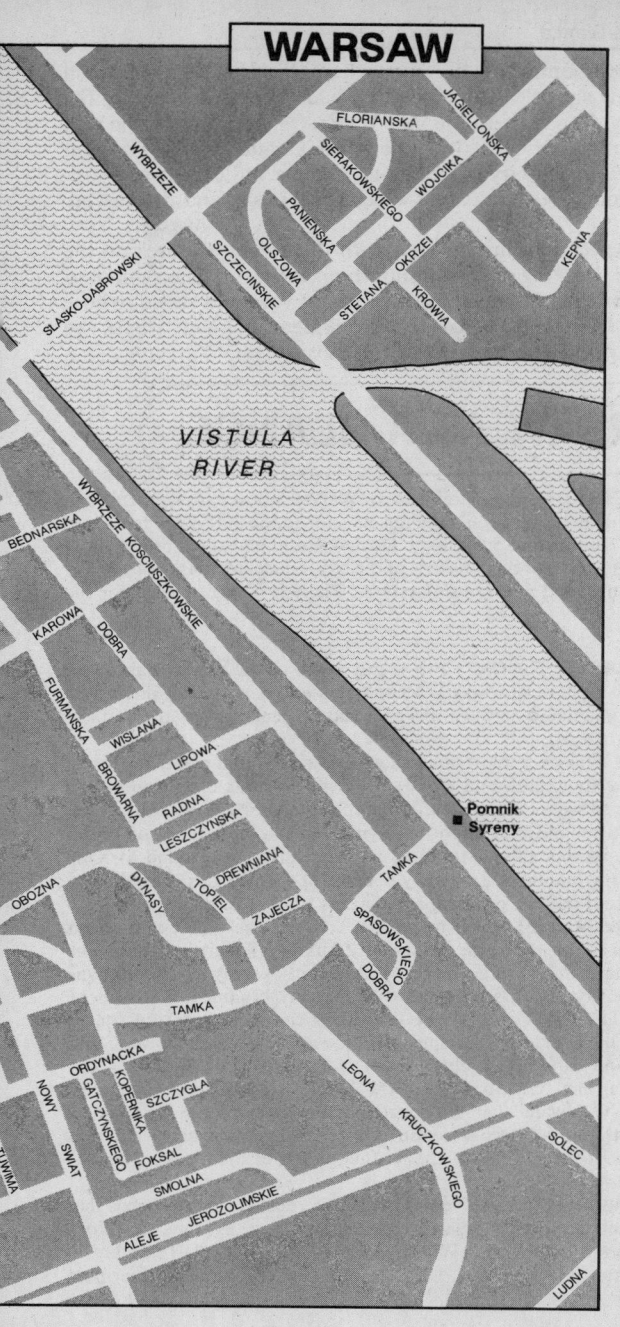

bers. War plaques and monuments are everywhere; the Historical Museum of the City of Warsaw shows visitors captured Nazi film, documenting the destruction of the city. Today there is a new Warsaw, incorporating the past and celebrating the future. After the war, the Polish Communist government took advantage of the opportunity in rebuilding to move industrial and warehouse facilities to the outskirts. Park areas were tripled in size and streets were widened.

The Vistula (Wisła) River splits the city, with the downtown area on the left, higher bank, and the Praga housing suburb on the right. The symbol of Warsaw is Syrena, a winged mermaid armed with a sword and shield, whose statue guards the city from the Kościuszko embankment. For Varsovians, she personifies the city's proud motto: "Defies the Storm."

WARSAW AT-A-GLANCE

SEEING THE CITY: For a general sense of Warsaw's postwar reconstruction and continuing modernization, take the elevator to the 30th-floor terrace of the Palace of Culture and Science, pl. Defilad. From here, on a bright, clear day, you can see beyond the outskirts of the city, which are marked by heavy industry, modern buildings, and new housing estates. There is a small charge for the elevator.

SPECIAL PLACES: The Old Town is just north of the Slasko-Dabrowski Bridge (Most Śląsko-Dąbrowski). Most sights and activities of interest to tourists are to be found between this area and Łazienkowska Park south of pl. Na Rozdroźu.

The Royal Castle – Warsaw's most important historical monument, its Royal Castle, built between the fourteenth and eighteenth centuries, was blown up by the Nazis in their campaign to wipe Poland off the face of the map. Now, after 35 years, the painstaking effort to rebuild this important symbol of the continuity of Polish history is finished. Its imposing silhouette forms an impressive background to King Sigismund's Column in the middle of Zamkowy Square. The Royal Castle rejoins the ranks of the most beautiful palaces in Europe. Adjacent to pl. Zamkowy.

The Old Town (Stare Miasto) – Sigismund III Column, the oldest monument in Warsaw (erected 1644), stands in the center of Zamkowy Square adjoining the Royal Castle grounds and at the edge of the Old Town. Nearby is the baroque Tin-roofed Palace, noted for its attic crowned with a richly ornamented cartouche bearing coats-of-arms. The Old Town Market Square is the most beautiful square in Warsaw — enclosed by re-created baroque-style houses, filled with flowers, and alive with little shops and café life. A block south of this square is St. John's Cathedral, where Jozef Cardinal Glemp delivers the homily to the deeply religious, Roman Catholic Poles. Old walls that once fortified the city and the Barbican, a sort of tower house of the mid-sixteenth century, have been reconstructed and add to the atmosphere of the district. West of the Vistula, north of the Śląsko Dąbrowski Bridge.

World War II Monuments – So extensive was the heroic resistance to the Nazis that even the churches and cemeteries of Warsaw were scenes of fierce fighting. The city's Monument to the Heroes of Warsaw — Warsaw Nike — stands in pl. Teatralny in front of the Wielki Theater (see *Theaters*). It is sort of a new version of the mermaid

Syrena, a fighting goddess with sword raised. The Pawiak Prison, ul. Dzielna 24/26, where 35,000 Poles were executed and another 65,000 were detained, is now a museum. The ghetto where the Jewish population was walled up in 1940 was not rebuilt. It is remembered by a Monument to the Heroes of the Ghetto on a small grassy square at Zamenhofa and Anielewicza streets and exhibits connected with the Ghetto Uprising at the Jewish Historical Institute, al. Świerczewskiego 79 (phone: 27-18-43). The former Gestapo headquarters and prison on Armii Wojska Polskiego Street near pl. Na Rozdroźu is now a Mausoleum to Struggle and Martyrdom. Across the river in Praga is a Monument to Brotherhood-in-Arms, celebrating Polish friendship toward the Soviet Union, whose soldiers liberated Warsaw. The monument is near the crossing of Targowa and Świerczewskiego streets.

Łazienki Palace and Park – The splendid Island Palace in Warsaw's loveliest park was built in the eighteenth century for Stanisław August Poniatowski, last of the Polish kings. The Nazis plundered its collections and set the palace afire, but the interiors have been carefully copied and restored. There are some 18 other buildings and monuments in the spacious park, including the White House, once the residence in exile of the future King Louis XVIII of France. The monument to Chopin at the southern end of the park is the scene of Sunday afternoon Chopin concerts. The Belweder Palace, official residence of the President of the State Council, is in Belweder Park, adjacent to Łazienki Park. Southeast of pl. Na Rozdroźu, along al. Ujazdowskie.

Wilanów Palace and Park – This Polish version of Versailles was built in the late seventeenth century as a summer residence for King Jan Sobieski III and is now a branch of the National Museum. Baroque terraces lead to a small lake. The baroque palace was restored after World War II and contains furniture, china, portraits, and other mementoes of the Sobieski family. The Museum of the Polish Poster (Museum Plakatu) is in a new building on the palace grounds. The palace is open daily, except Tuesdays; the poster museum closes Mondays. Small admission charge. Just south of the city, less than 6 miles from the city center. Reached by express bus B from ul. Marszałkowska.

■**EXTRA SPECIAL:** The manor house where Chopin was born in 1810 is now a museum. It is set in a lovely park in Żelazowa Wola, some 33 miles (53 km) west of the city. Chopin concerts are held on Sundays during the summer at the Chopin home. Six miles (10 km) to the north of Żelazowa Wola, in the village of Brochów, there is a mid-sixteenth-century Renaissance fortified church where Chopin was baptized. The Chopin family birth certificates are in the parish church. Leave Warsaw by Route 1.

SOURCES AND RESOURCES

Maps and information are available at Tourist Information Centers, which can be recognized by their "IT" signs. The main Tourist Information Center in Warsaw, at ul. Krucza 16, is open around the clock (phone: 27-00-00).

This Is Warsaw, text by Olgierd Budrewicz and photos by Jan Styczyński, is an excellent, often witty, pocket-size guide in English (Wag Art Publishers; about $1.50).

 CLIMATE AND CLOTHES: Warsaw winters can be bitter. Snowfall was so heavy during the winter of 1978–79 that the city was immobilized for several weeks. Temperatures are usually below freezing during January and February, and even in summer, they normally don't go much above 75°F (24°C). Rainwear is essential for most of the year.

GETTING AROUND: The Old Town, the Vistula embankment, and the whole route of Krakowskie Przedmieście, Nowy Świat, and Ujazdowskie streets are best seen on foot. But Poland's capital is a very big city, so at some point you will probably want to use municipal transportation.

Bus and Tram – Avoid them if possible during rush hours, but they are the cheapest way to get around. Route signs are at each stop. Buy your ticket before boarding at a nearby tobacco or newspaper kiosk, called a *Ruch,* then cancel it in a special machine on the coach.

Taxi – Rates are quite inexpensive, and they may be hailed on the street.

Car Rentals – The government-run Orbis Travel Bureau, ul. Marszałkowska 142 (phone: 27-36-73), arranges for self-drive or chauffeur-driven car rentals. Arrangements also can be made at major hotels and the airport.

MUSEUMS: In addition to those described in *Special Places,* Warsaw has a number of other interesting museums:

National Museum, Poland's greatest art collection, ul. Jerozolimskie 3 (phone: 21-10-31).

Archaeological Museum, ul. Długa 5 (phone: 31-32-21).

Ethnographic Museum, folk art and costumes, ul. Kredytowa 1 (phone: 27-76-41).

Chopin's Drawing Room, in the former Raczyński Palace (now the Academy of Fine Arts), ul. Krakowskie Przedmieście 5.

Maria Skłodowska-Curie Museum and House, ul. Freta 16.

Historical Museum of the City of Warsaw, Old Town Market Square 48 (phone: 31-02-51).

SHOPPING: Shops in Warsaw generally are open from 11 AM to 7 PM, but department stores open earlier and close later. Avoid the crowds by shopping before 3 PM. Leather, linen, and folk art ranging from wonderful wood carvings to handsome handwoven rugs are good buys here. (There are restrictions on the quantity and types of items you can take out of Poland; check with authorities before your trip.)

Art – Stylized folk art and works of modern art. ul. Krakowskie Przedmieście 17.

Cepelia – Government shops that sell souvenirs and folk art. pl. Konstytucji 2 and 5; Old Town Market Square 8/10; ul. Krucza 23/31; and ul. Marszałkowska 99/101.

Desa – Government-owned shops specializing in old and contemporary Polish art. For posters, etchings, and woodcuts, the shop is at ul. Rutkowskiego 30; for coins and medals, ul. Nowotki 17; and for antique jewelry, ul. Nowy Świat 48.

Orno – Handmade artistic silverwork. Ul. Marszałkowska 83; ul. Nowy Świat 52; and ul. Świętojańska 13.

Persian Market (Perski Rynek) – Capitalism runs rampant each Sunday between 9 AM and 3 PM at the flea market, where you can buy anything from antiques and homemade tripe soup to German war medals and pornographic books. Take bus A to the end of the line, then follow the crowd. Ul. Jana Kasprowicza at ul. Przytyk.

Supersam – A huge supermarket where shortages are often apparent. Near pl. Unii Lubelskiej and ul. Warynskiego.

SPECIAL EVENTS: The holidays most important to the predominantly Catholic Poles tend to be religious, such as Christmas, Easter, and the Feast of Corpus Christi. In addition, an *International Book Fair* is held here each May, and there is an *International Poster Biennale* in June of even-numbered years. The *"Warsaw Autumn" International Festival of Modern Music* is an important

September event, and the *Jazz Jamboree* held in late October is the oldest jazz festival in central and Eastern Europe.

 SPORTS: Horse Racing – *The Suzeweicz Race Course,* on the southern extremity of the city, is one of the largest in Europe. Races are held on Wednesdays, Saturdays and Sundays.

Ice Hockey – Matches are played at the *Torwar Artificial Rink,* ul. Lazienkowska.

Soccer – *Legia,* the best and most popular Warsaw team, plays its matches at various stadiums around the city.

Swimming – In summer you can swim at the *Legia* pool on ul. Lazienkowska or at public beaches in the Zoological Garden, near Hel Pier, and along the Vistula River. There's an indoor pool at the Palace of Culture and Science, pl. Defilad 6.

 THEATER: Advance booking for theater or cinema tickets can be made through the Tourist Information Center, ul. Krucza 16 (phone: 25-70-01, extensions 10, 15, and 21), or the SPATIF ticket office, Al. Jerozolimskie 25 (phone: 21-93-83). The city's foremost drama theaters include *Polski,* ul. Karasia 2 (phone: 26-79-92); *Dramatyczny,* in the Palace of Culture and Science, Pl. Defilad (phone: 20-02-11); and *Ateneum,* ul. St. Jaracza 2 (phone: 26-73-30 or 26-24-21). There are several children's theaters in Warsaw, including the *Lalka* puppet theater in the Palace of Culture and Science (phone: 20-02-11).

 MUSIC: Opera and ballet are performed at *Warsaw's Grand Theater of Opera and Ballet (Teatr Wielki Opery I Baletu),* pl. Teatralny (phone: 26-50-19). The prestigious international *Chopin Piano Competitions* are held every 5 years at the *Filharmonia,* ul. Sienkiewicza 12 (phone: 26-57-12), and there are operettas staged at the *Operetka,* ul. Nowogrodzka 49 (phone: 28-03-60).

 NIGHTCLUBS AND NIGHTLIFE: You'll need a fairly sophisticated knowledge of Polish to appreciate the humor at one of Warsaw's popular satirical cafés, but you might try one for the atmosphere.

Pod Egida, in the basement of ul. Rutkowskiego 3, is very popular. For jazz, try *Akwarium,* a modern glass night spot on Emilii; *Plater,* near the Palace of Culture and Science. One of the city's best discotheques is SARP, Foksal 13, which is run by the association of Polish architects.

 SINS: Polish vodka is so good — some say it's better than the Russian variety — that it's easy to overindulge. Some restaurants serve half-bottles with dinner and *drunkenness* is a not infrequent occurrence. There is also surprisingly open prostitution solicitation at Warsaw hotels.

BEST IN TOWN

CHECKING IN: Expect to pay from $65 to $90 a night for a double in one of Warsaw's expensive hotels; from $35 to $60 in the moderate range; inexpensive hotels will charge $25 to $35 per night. Prices include breakfast.

Victoria Inter-Continental – Warsaw's best hotel is located close to the Wielki Theater and Saxon Gardens. Its 410 rooms are pleasantly decorated and the *Canaletto Restaurant* specializes in Polish dishes. Swimming pool. Major credit cards. Ul. Królewska 11 (phone: 27-80-11 or 27-92-71). Expensive.

Orbis Forum – The Inter-Continental chain's second hotel in Warsaw is bigger, but not as nice. Its 750 rooms are modest-sized and sparsely decorated. It has a central location, however, near the Palace of Culture and Science. Major credit cards. Ul. Nowogrodzka 24/26 (phone: 21-02-71). Expensive to moderate.

Orbis-Europejski – Rooms are functionally modern in this grand old four-story hotel building, over a hundred years old. The hotel's café looks out on the Saxon Gardens and the Monument to the Unknown Soldier. Major credit cards. Ul. Krakowskie Przedmieście 13 (phone: 26-50-51). Expensive to moderate.

Orbis–Grand Hotel – The more than 430 rooms here are rather plain, but the hotel's midtown location is a plus. It has a rooftop café with glass-enclosed terrace and a swimming pool. Ul. Krucza 28 (phone: 29-40-51). Moderate.

Orbis-Solec – Somewhat away from the center, but nicely situated on the bank of the Vistula, this hotel has 145 rooms with showers and toilets. The décor is minimal motel-modern. Ul. Zagórna 1 (phone: 25-92-41). Moderate.

 EATING OUT: Food shortages are a fact of life in Poland. The best victuals usually go to the first-class hotels, so local restaurants with character may not always have the ingredients they need. In any event, dinner for two with wine at an expensive restaurant will be relatively inexpensive — $25 to $35; A moderately priced restaurant will charge $15 to $25; and an inexpensive restaurant will serve meals from a dollar or two per person.

Bazyliszek – Easily Warsaw's premier restaurant, the *Bazyliszek* is best known for its wild game. It's on the second floor over a snack bar and has an Old Warsaw ambience. The decor features hussars' armor and wooden beams. A horse and carriage is usually outside to take you for a romantic ride through the city after dinner. Old Town Market Square 7/9. Expensive.

Cristal-Budapest – *Cristal* and *Budapest* are the names of two separate rooms in this popular Hungarian restaurant. The *Budapest Room* has a folk motif and gypsy orchestra; the *Cristal* has a modern Polish discotheque atmosphere. In either room, start with *zupa gulaszowa:* meat and vegetables in a delicious paprika-seasoned broth, served in steaming cauldrons. Marszałkowska 21/25 (phone: 25-34-33). Moderate.

Karczma Słupska – Traditional Kashubian — northern Polish — cuisine is served in a quaint regional restaurant decorated with embroidered curtains and an unusual bar. The seats at the bar are carousel horses that move up and down, controlled from behind the bar. Among the specialties are the nut soup and boar pâté. Czerniakowska 125. Moderate to inexpensive.

Staropolska – Near the university, this restaurant is a mainstay among academic types. Although the menu is limited, it has one of the best cold buffets in Warsaw, with veal in aspic and steak tartare. Also sample the broth with hard-boiled egg and sausage, called *zurek staropolski.* Old Beatles tapes or European disco music play continuously. Krakowskie Przedmieście 8 (phone: 26-90-70). Inexpensive.

Dzik – You'll recognize this restaurant by the mounted head of a wild boar, or *dzik,* outside over the front door. The specialty here, naturally enough, is wild game. There are a number of rather threadbare stuffed animal heads mounted on the wall. Customers here tend to get a bit rowdy as the evening progresses. Nowogrodzka 42 (phone: 21-97-28). Inexpensive.

Rycerska – In the shadow of the walls of the Old Town, this budget restaurant serves typical hearty Polish fare: potatoes, cabbage, pork, and borscht — called *Barszcz.* Szeroki Dunaj 11 (phone: 31-36-68). Inexpensive.

ZÜRICH

Zürich is Switzerland's largest city, and the country's hundreds of years of peace and democracy have enabled it to develop into a great industrial and financial center, city of the fabled "gnomes" of the international money market. Indeed, banks dominate the Bahnhofstrasse, the famous shopping street, almost as much as the elegant shops do — and vaults of gold are literally buried beneath its pavement. C. G. Jung, one of Zürich's most celebrated residents, once said, "The relation of Zürich to the world is not spiritual but commercial."

You should not go to Zürich if you are on a tight budget; this is one of Europe's most expensive cities. With about 380,000 residents, Zürich is Switzerland's richest city, where land prices are so high that the number of citizens who can afford to live in town declines steadily, and a constant migration to the suburbs decreases the population each year.

Situated at the foot of Lake Zürich and offering a panoramic view of the Alps on clear days, Zürich is also one of the most beautiful cities in Europe. It is in northern Switzerland, not far from the West German border, on the spot where the Limmat River flows *out* of (not into) Lake Zürich. Its modern social center is concentrated on both banks of the river, its broad shopping street running parallel to the river from the main railroad station to the lake. Old Zürich is close by; the picturesque quay on the right side of the river is lined with sixteenth- and seventeenth-century guild houses, now converted into homes, shops, and restaurants. And the town's oldest quarter surrounds its two medieval churches, the Grossmünster on the right bank and the Framünster on the left, with narrow, winding streets, old houses with typical "oriel" windows, and interesting wrought-iron signs.

Zürich derives its name from the Latin *Turicum,* which is derived from the Celtic *dur,* meaning "water." The first signs of habitation (4000–1800 BC) were found near the "island" of Bauschänzli, now a summer restaurant offering a lovely view of the old town; the later Celtic settlement was colonized by the Romans in the first century BC, becoming a customs outpost; after the fall of the Roman Empire, the barbarian tribe of the Allemans settled here, giving many of the people their Germanic physical and psychological traits that are still recognizable today. At the crossing of two important trade routes, one from France to Eastern Europe and the other from Germany to Italy, Zürich was a busy commercial town from its earliest days. The city expanded continuously, becoming a powerful city-state; always fiercely independent in spirit, it joined the Swiss Confederation in the fourteenth century. During the Protestant Reformation in the sixteenth century, the Grossmünster Cathedral became the pulpit of the zealous and controversial Protestant reformer Ulrich Zwingli.

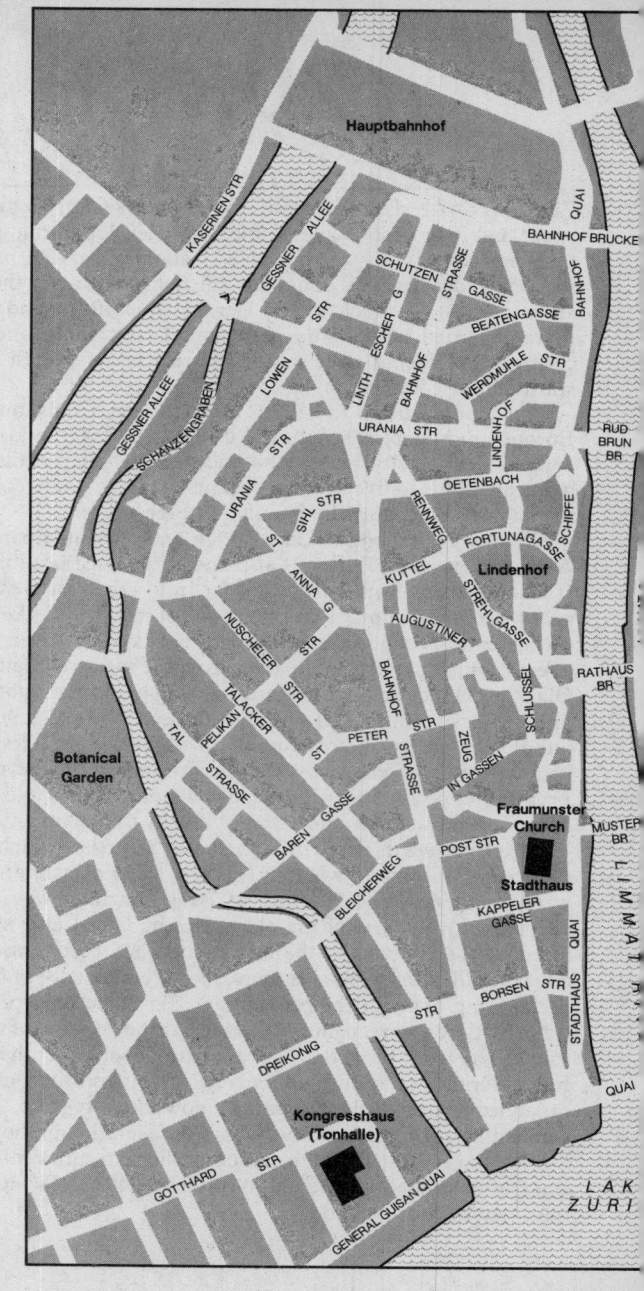

The majority of Zürich's people speak the Schwyzerdütsch dialect that you won't understand even if you speak German. Yet many will speak English, and tiny Switzerland has always been a country of many languages and many cultures; 70% speak Swiss German, 20% speak French, 9% Italian, and 1% Romansh. The social spirit of the Swiss has been one of wise tolerance and cooperation, and the justly celebrated Swiss political neutrality has made the city of Zürich a haven for such twentieth-century greats as James Joyce, Lenin, and Thomas Mann.

Paradoxically, it was in Zürich, the most bourgeois of cities, that several revolutionary modern movements were nurtured: Here Lenin pored over Marx and Engels, wrote his famous essay, "Imperialism, The Highest State of Capitalism," and left in 1917 to organize the Bolshevik Revolution; here James Joyce — when he wasn't romping through the streets and cafés — wrote that ultimate modern novel *Ulysses;* and in the noisy *Cabaret Voltaire,* Tristan Tzara and Hans Arp formulated the ideas of the outrageous Dada movement, a vanguard of modern art. Harry Lime notwithstanding, the peaceful comfort of Zürich has harbored creations far more significant than the cuckoo clock.

ZÜRICH AT-A-GLANCE

 SEEING THE CITY: No question, the most enchanting view of the city and lake is from Quai Bridge, where river and lake join. From here you can see both sides of the Old Town, with church towers, bridges, and medieval facades: this is a beautiful sight in daylight or at night. If you turn around, you can see the lake, dotted with sailboats — and on a Föhn (warm Alpine wind) day a picture-book view of the Alps.

To see the general layout of the city, try the *Sonnenbergterasse,* in front of the *Hotel Sonnenberg* on Zürichberg, on the eastern edge of town, or have a drink or a meal at the *Restaurant Sonnenberg,* at Autorastr. 98 (phone: 47-00-47).

 SPECIAL PLACES: Located on both sides of the Limmat, the old town has cobblestone streets, narrow lanes, corners decorated by fountains, small antique shops, high fashion boutiques, and art galleries. Watch for the dates of the buildings, which are hewn into the stone doorways.

A good starting point is Münsterhof, a former pig market where recent excavations uncovered several layers of housing and burial, dating back to the twelfth century.

DOWNTOWN

Framünster Church – This twelfth-century church at Münsterhof is noted for its chapel, with marvelous stained-glass windows created in 1970 and 1978 by Marc Chagall. Try to see them in the morning light. The organ here is also justly famous.

Guildhouse "Zur Meisen" – This splendid rococo building with a wrought-iron gate houses the excellent ceramic collection of the Historical Museum, which is worth visiting if only for the marvelous view its stuccoed rooms afford. Admission is free. Closed Mondays mornings.

Lindenhof – This romantic, tree-covered lookout point, a few climbing crooked alleys away from the Framünster, was a fort in Celtic and Roman times; a Freemason lodge stands there now. Lindenhof offers a lovely view of the old town and is a favorite spot for lovers after dark.

Peterhofstatt – This is another small, charming square surrounded by old buildings.

Grossmünster (Cathedral) – According to legend, this church was founded by Charlemagne, whose horse bowed down on the spot where the city's patron saints, martyrs Felix and Regula, died after walking from the river carrying their cut-off heads. This was the parish church of Ulrich Zwingli, one of the Reformation's most revered leaders, who converted Zürich to Protestantism in the mid-sixteenth century. Its towers became a landmark of Zürich; the inside is rather cold and austere.

Nägelihof – A delightful, small enclave, off Limmatquai 42, which is still unknown to many natives, is this recently reconstructed square with cafés, amusing shops, two movies, and a most unusual view of the Grossmünster towers.

Bahnhofstrasse – "The most beautiful shopping street in the world," and certainly one of the most expensive, Bahnhofstrasse was built on the site of an ancient moat about 100 years ago. Running from the lake to the main railway station, it's a shopper's and stroller's paradise — with rows of banks, shops, cafés for people-watching — graced in summer with the intoxicating scent of linden trees and around Christmas with magnificent illuminations. There is a colorful flower and vegetable market at its lake end every Tuesday and Friday morning and a flea market every Saturday in summer.

Swiss National Museum (Schweizerisches Landesmuseum) – This is the largest and most complete collection of Swiss history, located in a pseudo-castle behind the railroad station. Especially interesting are the prehistoric finds, the reconstructed Celtic tomb, Carolingian frescoes, and the treasury and some old paintings of Zürich. A brochure is available in English. Closed at lunch hour in winter and on Monday mornings. Admission is free. Museumstr. 2 (phone: 221-1010).

Museum Rietberg – One of the most important collections of non-European art in Europe is set in the enchanting Wesendonck Villa, outside of the city center. Here Richard Wagner was often a guest, and his love affair with the hostess inspired *Tristan and Isolde.* The villa is surrounded by a magnificent private park, so bring a sandwich and you can spend a delightful day wandering in and out of the museum. The backbone of this collection is the donation of Baron von der Heydt, who had his world-famous treasures in 24 different museums before the Rietberg opened in 1952. Art items are mainly Indian, Southeast Asian, Chinese, Japanese, and African. The guidebook in English is recommended. Admission is free; the museum is closed Mondays. Gablerstr. 15 (phone: 202-4528).

Fine Arts Museum (Kunsthaus) – In 1976, the building was rebuilt in "open museum" style, without rigidly dividing floors, walls, and stairs. The permanent exhibit includes an excellent collection of art from the Middle Ages until today, with emphasis on nineteenth- and twentieth-century European works by Monet, Munch, Giacometti, Rodin, Chagall, and others. Closed Monday mornings. There is an admission fee every day except Sundays and Wednesday afternoons. Heimpl. 1 (phone: 251-6765).

Boat Trip on the Lake – You should not miss this on a beautiful day. There are daily cruises that vary in length from 1½ to 4 hours; the long one that includes Rapperswil is best. Boats depart from Bürkliplatz, at the lake end of Bahnhofstrasse. In summer there are special lunch cruises. For information call Zürichsee Schiffahrtsgesellschaft (phone: 482-1033) or the Zürich Tourist Office (phone: 211-4000).

Wohnmuseum – Two charming private houses from the seventeenth and eighteenth centuries display period interiors with interesting furniture; in the basement there is a collection of dolls made by the famous Swiss artist Sacha Morgenthaler. Closed at lunch hour in winter and Monday mornings. Free. Bärengasse 22 (phone: 211-1716).

E. G. Bührle Collection – This is an extremely important private art collection, mainly from the nineteenth century, which includes French Impressionist paintings, medieval sculptures, and other items. The collection is housed in the private villa of the industrialist Emil Bührle, who died in 1956. It is open on Tuesday and Friday afternoons only. Admission charge. Zollikerstr. 172 (phone: 55-00-86).

Beyer's Watch & Clock Museum – This is the oldest watch shop in Switzerland. Inside is the private collection of the Beyer family — rare and interesting items dating from 1400 BC to the present. Closed weekends. Free. Bahnhofstrasse 31 (221-1080).

Botanical Garden – Rare plants from all over the world, plastic domes with tropical and desert plants, and a good cafeteria with a large terrace. The gardens could be combined with a visit to the nearby Bührle villa. Open daily. Free. Zollikerstr. 107 (phone: 251-3670).

Zürich Toy Museum – The exhibits here are from the antique collection of the same Franz Carl Weber who owns the famous toy shop (see *Shopping*). Closed mornings and weekends. Free. Fortunagasse 15 (phone: 211-9305).

OUT OF TOWN

Schaffhausen-Rhinefall and Stein am Rhein – Schaffhausen, 35 miles (56 kilometers) north, is a wonderfully preserved medieval town, with a most photogenic fortress and the Rhinefall, Europe's largest waterfall (no match for Niagara); the best view is from Neuhausen, on the terrace of the *Hotel Bellevue.* (Try their wine and fish while admiring the view.) Open daily (phone: 2-2121). Stein am Rhein, 13 miles (21 kilometers) further east, is a delight with its intricately painted housefronts and a museum in a former monastery. (You have to share it with loads of other tourists, though.) If possible, return through the gentle wine country around Stammheim, with villages of half-timbered houses, vineyards, and orchards.

St. Gallen and Appenzell – About 70 miles (112 kilometers) northeast is St. Gallen, a Swiss textile center, with a spectacular abbey-library in its cathedral (100,000 volumes of rare books and manuscripts). From here it is only a short drive into the country's most genuinely rural region, the Appenzell. (Its capital has the same name.) The region has farms, pastures, folk art (embroidery and wood carving), and lovely painted houses; around the Säntis (mountain) there is some high Alpine scenery, including a cable car that climbs to a 7,500-foot peak. Return via the picturesque road to Wattwil, with a stop in Rapperswil on the lake; then follow the shore to Zürich. This trip offers a good cross-section of the "real" but not so well known Switzerland.

■ **EXTRA SPECIAL:** Zürich is a perfect base for dozens of short and long excursions, easily accessible also by public transportation (or organized tours).

An excellent half-day trip would be to Einsiedeln about 25 miles (40 km) southeast of Zürich, which offers Alpine scenery (splendid walks in summer, skiing in winter), and a world-famous baroque abbey, which is magnificent.

A cable car in Weglosen, only 10 minutes farther by car, takes you into the "real" mountains.

SOURCES AND RESOURCES

For general information, brochures, and maps, contact Verkehrsverein Zürich, Hauptbahnhof (phone: 211-4000). In the US, contact the Swiss National Tourist Office, 608 Fifth Ave., New York NY 10020 (phone: 212-757-5944).

The best pocket guidebook in English is *Travel Guide Zürich,* published by Polyglot, available at any local bookstore. (You can order it in the US, but be sure to get the latest edition.)

For Local Coverage – The tourist office distributes *Spotlights on Zürich,* a bilingual bimonthly publication covering local events. The *Zürich Weekly Official,* which comes out every Friday with detailed events of the coming week and a list of restaurants and shops, is available at all hotels and at the Tourist Office.

There is no English-language newspaper, but for world news the best is the daily (Paris) *International Herald Tribune.*

For business travelers, a good address to know is that of the Swiss-American Chamber of Commerce, Talacker 41 (phone: 211-2454).

CLIMATE AND CLOTHES: Good weather cannot be taken for granted, but if it is good, it's intoxicatingly so. Zürich weather is Atlantic influenced, with the moderating effect of the Alps; long rainy periods are possible, mainly in spring and summer — weather is best generally in the fall. Föhn wind brings magnificent days with deep blue skies and high temperatures in winter; it can bring rain in summer. Winter is quite mild, around freezing; summer temperature is seldom over 80°F (26.6°C).

A warm sweater and a raincoat are necessary in any season. Dress styles are similar to those in New York; people dress fashionably, although the Swiss tend to be more conservative and more careful about color coordination. Jackets and ties are right for some restaurants.

GETTING AROUND: Bus – The supermodern blue streetcars (VBZ) are best. Automatic machines at every stop issue tickets for exact change. (You cannot pay on the tram and you are fined if found without a ticket.) The same applies to buses. If you intend to use them a lot, it is best to get a 1-day or a season ticket. An informative multilingual brochure, giving all the details, including rates and routes, is available at information booths marked "VBZ" in the underground Shopville at the main railroad station, at Paradeplatz and Bellevueplatz, or at the Zürich Tourist Office.

The in-season city tours by a golden tram, "Goldtimer," on Wednesdays, Fridays, and Sundays are lots of fun.

Taxi – Among the most expensive in the world (tip already included).

Car Rental – All major firms are represented at the airport and in the city. *Avis* has offices at Gartenhofstr. 17 (phone: 242-2040); *Budget* at Tödistr. 9 (phone: 201-2670); and *Avag,* a local firm whose rates are sometimes lower, at Sihlfeldstr. 123 (phone: 242-8866).

Bikes – Available for rent at most railroad stations, bikes provide a somewhat cheaper (and certainly delightful) means of getting where you're going. They can be taken onto passenger trains for a small fee and returned at any station.

MUSEUMS: Most Zürich museums are described in *Special Places.* Also noteworthy is the *Museum Bellerive,* at Höschgasse 3 (phone: 251-4377), annexed to the *Museum of Applied Arts,* in a charming villa on a lake with excellent temporary exhibitions. The university has several interesting collections, among them the *Ethnological Museum* (non-European), Pelikanstr. 40 (phone: 221-3191), and the *Medicinhistorical Collection,* including items ranging from primitive instruments and techniques to present-day ones, Rämistr. 71 (phone: 257-1111). The *Museum of Applied Arts,* Austellungstr. 60 (phone: 42-67-00), and *Helmhaus,* Limmatquai 31 (phone: 251-6177), have interesting temporary exhibitions.

SHOPPING: It is hard to know where to begin in this shopper's paradise, with some of the best and most expensive buys in the world. The major hunting ground for shoppers is, of course, the ultra-elegant Bahnhofstrasse and its side streets.

The best buys in Switzerland are watches, which can be purchased here even though most are made in Geneva. Other interesting items are Swiss chocolates, embroidery and linens, optical instruments, and, of course, the wonderful Swiss Army knives. *Jelmoli,* at Bahnhofstrasse and Seidengasse, and *Globus,* at Bahnhofstrasse and Schweizergasse, are the two best-known department stores (the former with more solid quality and larger choice, the latter more "with it" and with lower prices); you can sample all Swiss wares here.

The old town is full of fashion boutiques, art galleries, and antique shops, and there is more casual shopping along Limmatquai. In rainy weather you might want to try Shopville under the main railroad station.

Here are just a few recommendations:

Albrecht-Schlapfer – Lovely eiderdowns and linens. Lintheschergasse 10.

Arts et Décor – One of many antique shops in the old town. Kirchgasse 22.

Bally – Famous for shoes. Bahnhofstr. 66.

Bucherer – Fine watches and jewelry. Bahnhofstr. 50.

Grieder – For fashion, the Bonwit Teller of Zürich. Bahnhofstr. 30.

Gübelin – Watches and jewelry. Bahnhofstr. 36.

Heimatwerk – Top-quality Swiss handicrafts. Bahnhofstr. 2.

Hermès – Fine and expensive fashions and leathergoods. Bahnhofstrasse 31.

Koch – Optical instruments. Bahnhofstr. 11.

Payot – Books in English. Bahnhofstr. 9.

Rosenfeld – Discounted watches, music boxes, and Swiss army knives. Strehlgasse 33.

Spitzenhaus – Handmade lace and embroidered organdy. Börsenstr. 14.

Sprüngli – This place is 100 years old, and famous for chocolates. There is also a café here (see *Eating Out*). Bahnhofstr. at Paradepl.

Sturzenegger – Fine Swiss embroidery and linen. Bahnhofstr. 48.

Teuscher – For great chocolates. Storchengasse 9. The company also has its own tea and coffee shop called *Schober,* on Napfgasse 4 (phone: 32-80-60).

Travel Book Shop – Books about all aspects of travel — mostly in English and unavailable elsewhere. Informed staff. Seilergraben 11.

Vogt – An antique store in the old town that specializes in folk art. Neumarkt 13.

F. C. Weber – Toys and (yes) cuckoo clocks. Bahnhofstr. 62.

SPECIAL EVENTS: The most typical and colorful event of all, the *Sechseläuten,* generally on the third Monday in April, celebrates the burning of winter on Bellevueplatz (a giant snowman is stuffed with firecrackers) as the six o'clock bells ring. This ceremony is preceded by a picturesque procession of medieval guilds in traditional costumes and carriages. These are members of fraternities, whose membership is inherited by the males in the best Zürich families.

There is also the yearly *June Festival,* with top musical and theatrical events. The first of August is a national holiday, commemorating the founding of the Swiss Confederation; it is celebrated with fireworks and bonfires. The *Zürich Carnival (Fastnacht)* is celebrated with masked processions and costume balls at the end of February or early March.

SPORTS: Golf – There are no public courses; the *Dolder Golf Club* accepts visitors. Kurhausstr. 66 (phone: 47-50-45).

    Hiking – There are dozens of marked trails on the outskirts of town.

    Sailing and Rowing – Boat rental is along Utoquai.

Skating – The ice rink at Dolder is open only in winter.

Skiing – From December to March skiing is good; there are accessible runs within an hour from Zürich; equipment rental is possible.

Swimming – There are two good beaches on the lake (best is Tiefenbrunnen, popular with topless bathers) and an attractive pool at Dolder in the Zürichberg forest. In winter there are very limited possibilities.

Soccer – Several national and international matches are played at Hardturm and Letzigrund stadiums.

THEATER: There are two main theaters: *Schauspielhaus,* at Rämistr. 34, produces plays in classical German and *Theater am Neumarkt,* Neumarkt 5, performs avant-garde works. There are twice yearly productions of the *British Comedy Club* and also of guest companies — mainly during June Festival. (See listings in local publications.) Movies are all in the original language with subtitles.

MUSIC: There is a variety to choose from. Top-quality operas, ballets, and operettas are presented at the Opernhaus, Schillerstr. 1 (phone: 251-6922). Regular classical concerts of the *Tonhalle Orchester* and visiting orchestras are given at the Tonhalle, Claridenstr. 7 (phone: 201-1580). There are also frequent concerts and recitals in several churches, mainly Fraumünster, Grossmünster, and St. Peter. Much less choice is available in jazz, rock, pop, and folk. The central ticket office for most cultural events is at Kulturpavillion, Werdmühleplatz (phone: 221-2283). Closed Saturdays and Sundays.

NIGHTCLUBS AND NIGHTLIFE: The latest any public establishment can stay open is 2 AM (a few private clubs excepted, but outsiders cannot get in). *Diagonal* discotheque is the best, and if you are the guest of the *Hotel Baur au Lac,* you can get a temporary membership. The *Joker-Club,* Gotthardstr. 5 (phone: 202-22-62), is the best place for live music and dancing; it often offers top shows as well. The *Queen Anne Club,* at Kreuzstr. and Dufourstr. (phone: 251-9422), is a chic, intimate discotheque. *Kindli,* at Pfalzgasse 1 (phone: 211-59-17), is *the* folklore show in town — very touristy, but fun. The *Birdwatcher's Club,* Schutzengasse 16 (phone: 211-5058), is a smart, semiprivate club that opens at 5 PM and becomes a lively disco by 9. *Bazillus,* the restaurant in the *Hotel Hirschen,* Niederdorfstr. 13 (phone: 251-4252), features jazz Thursdays through Sundays, disco other nights, and imaginative, inexpensive food every night. For striptease with live music, try *The Red House,* at Marktgasse 17 (phone: 252-1530).

SINS: Dozens of peep shows, massage salons, and sex shops are the background for the numerous streetwalkers, "on duty" from morning on, with real Swiss diligence. Around Niederdorfstr., near Central (Square).

BEST IN TOWN

CHECKING IN: The following is a small selection from over 90 hotels. During the week, reservations are necessary. Continental breakfast is included everywhere, whether it is taken or not (but juice is generally extra). All hotels listed have telephones in rooms; most also have radios.

Be warned that prices in Swiss cities are *very* expensive, even higher than in Germany or the US. The range for a double room with a shower or bath in the expensive category is $115 to $165; in the moderate category, $60 to $115; in the inexpensive category $40 to $60 (slightly less without a private bath). Several smaller hotels offer winter reductions.

Baur au Lac – The most prestigious hotel in the city center, with understated old-world luxury, a garden, and a celebrity-dotted guest list; its 170 rooms are always full. The *Grill Room* is among the best restaurants in town. American Express only. Talstr. 1 (phone: 221-1650). Expensive.

Dolder Grand – The justifiably famous and luxurious hotel located in the Zürichberg forest and built in fairy-tale-castle style, with a fabulous view, 200 antique and modern rooms, and a first-class restaurant. Credit cards accepted. Kurhausstr. 65 (phone: 251-6231). Expensive.

St. Gotthard – This first-class hotel has a terrific location on the upper end of the elegant Bahnhofstrasse (and near the railway station) as well as 140 modern rooms, a very good seafood restaurant, and a restored art nouveau café that serves snacks. Bahnhofstrasse 87 (phone: 211-5500). Expensive to moderate.

Helmhaus – An excellent value — superbly run, central location in a historic building, with 24 modern, cheerful rooms. No restaurant. Schiffländepl. 30 (phone: 251-8810). Moderate.

Opera – Possessed of 67 modern rooms next to the opera house (best rooms are on the top floor). With a pleasant, large lobby/sitting room. No restaurant. Major credit cards. Dufourstr. 5 (phone: 251-9090). Moderate (especially in winter).

Kindli – Although its exterior is 500 years old, inside is a modern, tastefully furnished hotel with but 22 rooms (each with TV). Its restaurant is where the well-known folklore show is presented (see *Nightclubs and Nightlife*). Pfalzgasse 1 (phone: 211-59-17). Moderate.

Florhof – A lovely old patrician building — renovation, unfortunately, destroyed the atmosphere-filled coziness. Good restaurant. Florhofgasse 4 (phone: 47-44-70). Moderate.

Tiefenau – Private atmosphere is special in this quiet, 150-year-old town house with garden; all recently restored 27 rooms are bed/sittingrooms, most antique furnished, some very large; lovely sitting and dining rooms. Near Fine Arts Museum. Steinwiesstr. 8/10 (phone: 251-2409). Moderate.

Limmathof – This perfectly located, rather modest hotel is near the railroad station, with 55 no-frills but pleasant modern rooms. No credit cards. Limmatquai 142 (phone: 47-42-20). Inexpensive.

Zelthof – Run by the Methodist Church, *Zelthof* offers a homey atmosphere; rooms are without private bath but with running water. There are 25 nicely furnished rooms. No restaurant. No credit cards. Zeltweg 18 (phone: 251-0647). Inexpensive.

 EATING OUT: More than 1,000 restaurant choices flourish here in all varieties and price ranges. A service charge is included in all bills, but it is customary to leave a small tip anyway. It is rare to see plain water on the table, and as the only beverage ordered, it is certainly frowned on. One American woman reports being threatened by a Swiss waiter who warned that if she drank only water with her fondue, all manner of ills would strike her digestion. (Incidentally, most restaurants serve wine by the glass at reasonable prices.)

Switzerland, of course, is a country where the culinary traditions of Germany, Italy, and France meet, but there are specialties that are particularly Swiss. The people of Zürich — known for their interest in good food — like minced veal or calf liver with cream *(geschnetzeltes Kalbsfleisch)* or roasted calf liver with bacon *(Leberspiessli)*. Also local in Zürich is *Kalbsbratwurst,* a delicious veal sausage.

If you like cheese, you shouldn't miss fondue, the national dish made with a combination of several Swiss cheeses and wine. Also try the fluffy hash brown potatoes called *Rösti.* Desserts feature fresh cream and delicious Swiss chocolate; try *Zuger Kirschtorte,* a cake soaked in Kirsch, a cherry brandy. You should visit at least one of the many tearooms for which Zürich is famous; they serve tea or coffee with a choice of pastries. Try the *Sprüngli* on Bahnhofstr.

Like hotel prices, restaurant costs can also be stiff. Many places have cheaper lunch menus. Our price range is for a three-course dinner for two without drinks, wine, or coffee. Count $70 and up as expensive; $35 to $55 as moderate; about $35 and under as inexpensive.

Chez Max – In the suburb of Zollikon, this is one of the best restaurants in Switzerland; Max Kehl, its owner-chef, creates culinary masterpieces worth a sin and never heavy on the stomach (only on the memory and the pocketbook). Closed Sunday and Monday lunch. Reservations for dinner are imperative. Major credit cards. Seestr. 53, Zollikon (phone: 391-8877). Very expensive.

Kronenhalle – This place is the best known in Zürich, where "everybody" goes, from local artists to visiting celebrities; walls are covered with original Picassos, Miros, and other works from the private collection of the owner. International food with Swiss specialties. Try the chocolate mousse. Open daily. Reservations necessary. Major credit cards. Rämistr. 4 (phone: 251-0256). Expensive.

Zum Rüden – One of the most spectacular medieval guild houses with a Gothic interior and a fabulous view on the Limmat offers delicious food. Reservations are recommended. Major credit cards. Limmatquai 42 (phone: 47-95-90). Expensive to moderate.

Oepfelchammer – This place has the *most* enchanting, cozy atmosphere. In this historic house, a special student fraternity room accepts anybody for a glass of wine at one long wooden table. The small restaurant has excellent "Old Zürich" specialties and other dishes; good open wines. Closed Sunday. Reservations necessary. Diners Card. Rindermarkt 12 (phone: 251-2336). Moderate.

Mövenpick – Whether you want a good hamburger, some homemade cakes, or a full meal, the smart snack shop/restaurants in this chain are almost always open. Paradepl. 4 (phone: 221-3252) and Zeltweg 1 (phone: 69-04-44). Moderate.

Pinte Vaudoise – Swiss cheese specialties, like fondue and raclette, are offered in a cozy, wood-paneled tavern. Closed Sundays. No credit cards. Kruggasse 4 (phone: 252-6009). Moderate to inexpensive.

Pomodoro – This very popular Italian restaurant with pizza and other specialties is near the Fine Arts Museum, and it serves a smart, youngish crowd. Open daily. It is advisable to reserve, even for lunch. No credit cards. Zeltweg 4 (phone: 47-57-81). Inexpensive.

California – This offbeat restaurant has menus in English, California wines, and American food with an international touch. Informal, friendly atmosphere, and small garden. Open daily; Saturdays and Sundays from 6 PM only. Major credit cards. Asylstr. 125 (phone: 53-56-80). Inexpensive.

Kropf – Art nouveau beer hall, almost an institution, with good-and-plenty Swiss/German/Austrian food, frequented by all classes. Pleasant terrace in summer. Closed Sundays. American Express. In Gassen (near Paradelpl.) (phone: 221-1805). Inexpensive.

Gleich – A vegetarian's delight, with dishes of great fantasy and quality, *Gleich* is famous for homemade fruit tarts. No alcohol. Closed Saturday afternoons and Sundays. No credit cards. Seefeldstr. 2 (phone: 251-3203). Inexpensive.

Select – This is the most popular meeting place of artists, students, and chess players; serves good food and snacks (outstanding ice cream). No alcohol. Sidewalk tables. Open daily. No credit cards. Limmatquai 16 (phone: 252-4372). Inexpensive.

Sprüngli – For a snack lunch or afternoon hot chocolate, this is a most famous and elegant café and candy shop. Closed for dinner and Sundays. No credit cards in the café (accepted in shop). Paradepl. (phone: 211-0795). Moderate.

Schober – A delight of gilded, picture-post-card charm, this is the oldest confectionery in town. Cold snacks and marvelous sweets are available to eat there or to take with you. Open daily, closed evenings. No credit cards. Napfgasse 4 (phone: 251-8060). Inexpensive.

DIRECTIONS

Introduction

Fussy as they were, the Victorians were magnificent travelers: extremely thorough, compulsively curious, and driven with intense energy. Their Grand Tour of the Continent took months and led from Europe's major cities to the farthest outposts of civilization, wherever interest or curiosity directed.

Rare is the traveler today who can spend more than 2 or 3 weeks at a time exploring Europe. As deplorable as this limit would seem to our Victorian predecessors, their alarm would be misplaced, for though trips are shorter, they are more frequent than ever. The days when transatlantic visitors felt they had only one chance to "do" Europe are long over. Two weeks this year, 2 weeks next year, a hard-won month the year after — the North Americans' love affair with Europe intensifies with the frequency of acquaintanceship, not its duration.

Our indefatigable Victorian would be wrong to raise a skeptical eyebrow for another reason. Europe is especially suited to a series of short visits precisely because of the cultural and historical density that makes it such a daunting prospect taken as a whole. Spend 2 days touring a tiny area in depth or hopscotching the length of the Continent — the time will be equally well spent and the experiences, though very different, equally enlightening.

In the following pages are touring routes through 32 European countries. Organized to cover 3 to 5 days of traveling, they are designed to take you to Europe's areas of greatest scenic and historic interest. From the tiny villages of England's Cotswolds and its great cathedral cities, through France's wine country and the corniches of the Côte d'Azur, across the ancient Roman via Emilia — used by Roman legions to conquer a continent, through fjords, moors, tors, and lava pours — this is Europe at its most intimate, historic, and dramatic.

Where possible, tours begin at major cities, and though they are most easily negotiated by car, in most cases local buses and tour operators cover the same territory, freeing you from the necessity of driving. Entries are not exhaustive or comprehensive; they discuss the highlights of each route and are, in some sense, starting points for longer journeys.

Entries are organized by country; an introduction gives some background and explains the routes that follow. The *Best en Route* section of each route gives hotel and restaurant recommendations along the way (under each city, hotels will come first, in order of expense, followed by restaurants). There is no effort to be comprehensive in these selections; our choices are made on the basis of places that offer memorable experiences. Since most countries are divided into several routes, it is often possible to string these together into longer itineraries. But if you are pressed for time, you will find that by following any single itinerary you will see the most notable spots (and attractive accommodations) in the area.

Exploring Andorra

A visit to the tiny principality of Andorra, 175 square miles nestled in the Pyrenees, is an enchanting adventure back in time to feudal Europe. Isolated by dramatic mountains, Andorra presents a picturesque setting that seems far removed from the pace of this century. Yet, entering Andorra by car from France or Spain (no plane or train service is available), the visitor soon realizes that the quaint mountain villages and scenic landscapes are anachronistically populated by customs agents, real estate speculators, and aggressive merchants. As a free port and bargain haven, this charming medieval country is also a favorite destination for the weekend traveler from Spain or France with an eye for leisure, outdoor sports, and unbeatable shopping. Whether visiting Andorra for the fine fishing, game hunting, or camping facilities; for the duty-free prices on European goods; or for the curiosity of the ministate itself, you will be sure to be charmed by the contrasts and intrigued by all that little Andorra has to offer.

The most direct route to Madrid from Andorra, passing through the provinces of Lérida, Zaragoza, and Guadalajara, takes you through 325 miles of diverse topographical landscape. The dramatic verticality of the Catalonian Pyrenees is softened by the rolling hills of agricultural Aragón and, finally, flattened by the dry, Central Meseta of Castile. Each region has a distinctive note of architecture, gastronomy, and language, and stops at such towns and villages as Lérida, Zaragoza, Calatayud, the Monasterio de Piedra, and Alcalá de Henares provide a varied itinerary to the capital of Spain from the remote land of Andorra.

The Catalonian region that includes Andorra was reconquered from invading Moors in the year 801 by the son of heroic Charlemagne, Louis I. This prince granted a small tract of his realm to the Spanish bishop of Seo de Urgel. Successors to the bishop eventually felt their rule challenged by French noblemen and agreed to joint control over the area. Valls d'Andorra (Valleys of Andorra, as it is officially named) was created as a principality under the tandem rule of the Count of Foix of France and the Spanish bishop of Seo de Urgel. Andorrans first waved the country's blue, red, and yellow flag in 1298 and accepted an agreement whereby, in even-numbered years, the Spanish bishop would receive as tribute the equivalent of $12 in addition to six hams, six chickens, and six cheeses. In odd-numbered years, the French prince would be presented with a cash tribute of the equivalent of $460.

Celebrating the 700th birthday of the nation in October 1978, Andorrans gathered to pay homage to their two liege lords, France's President Valéry Giscard d'Estaing and Spanish Bishop Joan Martí Alanis. It was the first time that both sovereigns ever met on Andorran soil, and every indication was given that the feudal state would enjoy an updating of tradition in the future.

At present, French and Spanish authorities oversee the justice and postal systems (all mail is delivered free within Andorra, and peseta or franc denominations of stamps are issued for mail outside the country). But since 1419 Andorrans have enjoyed free elections of their 24-member Council General and legislative head, the Sindic General, and are therefore proud to have one of the oldest parliaments in Europe. The total independence of the principality is not generally sought by the populace, whose national anthem underscores their present political feelings: "Faithful and free I wish to live, with my Princes as my protectors." Certainly only the unique political arrangement of joint rule provides Andorra with its privileged economic situation today. Originally dominated by a strictly agricultural economy, Andorra is now a model of modernization and growth.

Due to the influx of foreigners eager to establish residency in Andorra and enjoy its tax shelter, the country is attempting to restrict immigration and discourage speculators. In accordance with Andorran tradition, citizenship is only acquired after three generations of permanent residence or by the more expedient method of marriage to an *andorrano,* which is becoming the Catch-22 of the census bureau. At present, therefore, Catalán-speaking mountaineers, shepherds, and farmers share their nationality with savvy French- and Spanish-speaking hoteliers, real estate agents, and department store owners. Andorra is at the crossroads of time, perched in the Pyrenees, isolated from and dependent on the modern commercial world.

One's first impression upon crossing the border into Andorra (a valid passport and the international insurance "green card" for drivers is required) is the monumental traffic jam of cars lined up to leave the country. This situation is evident in the French border town of Pas de la Casa in northeast Andorra (Route 20 from Toulouse), but much more so at the southwestern Spanish border town of Farga de Moles (Route 145 from Lérida). This tie-up is created by the conscientious customs agents of each of the neighboring countries assessing the real value of duty-free purchases made in Andorra. This process is time-consuming since so many ingenious French and Spanish fill every imaginable cranny of their car, luggage, and personal attire with bargain-priced cameras, cosmetics, radios, watches, Scotch, pâté, skis, crystal, jewelry, perfume, and the like, that have not been listed on their customs declaration. In addition, the service stations just within the Andorran border are a mandatory last stop for motorists, since gasoline prices are often one-third less than those of Spain or France.

Once past the entry ordeal, the visitor to Andorra will be impressed by the dramatic landscape, racing rivers, and verdant meadows. The one major highway that crosses the country is excellent, and secondary roads to scenic lakes or hamlets are adequate. It is with a certain nostalgia that the visitor views the peaceful mountain villages and hears distant cowbells. Time should definitely be set aside for serenely experiencing the majesty of the mountains. Agencies in Andorra's capital, such as Andotour (47 av. Meritxell) and Evisa (11 pl. Rebes), offer half-day excursions to the most remote forests and peaks of the country. Day trips by private car or reasonably fared minibuses to the ski slopes of Evalira and Pas de la Casa provide exhilarating encounters with nature at its most beautiful. A pleasant afternoon can be enjoyed riding the cable car to Engolasters Lake from the village of Encamp or relaxing in a thermal bath at a hotel spa of Les Escaldas.

ANDORRA LA VIEJA: Such therapeutic renewal of body and soul is needed after facing the bustle of Andorra la Vieja, the capital of the nation and the highest capital in Europe (3,000 feet). The modern, high-rise buildings almost block out the view of the surrounding peaks, and only the crisp mountain air suggests the splendor beyond the cement constructions. Spending money is the number one pastime, so the visitor should come prepared with American dollars or Spanish or French currencies (almost anything is accepted), comfortable shoes, and a shopping list. All purchases on international name-brand items are bargains (up to 40% off), and many happy hours will be spent window shopping in the throngs of shops lining Andorra la Vieja's streets. To recommend one store or another is futile, since most shops have standard prices and stock only the most marketable merchandise. This may prove less fun to the shopping enthusiast who loves to compare and haggle down the price, but it is infinitely more pleasurable to the buyer who knows the cost of the item at home and recognizes a bargain. Shopping hours are amenable even to late sleepers: 9 AM to 10 PM; most stores are open on Sundays.

A visit to the Casa de le Vall, the Renaissance meeting house and seat of the Council General, is a cultural parenthesis in this shopping tour. Other adventures of a primarily cultural nature involve contact with the regional cuisine — a marvelous mixture of Spanish and French specialties, seasoned with that special Catalonian flavor. Fine restaurants include *Els Fanals* (20 av. Meritxell), expensive and specializing in French cuisine, and *La Nica,* more informal and reasonably priced, famed for its grilled trout. For those ready for a big splurge, fine eating and spectacular dining facilities are primarily found in hotels such as the *Andorra Palace* (Prat de la Creu), the *Andorra Park* (Plana Guillemo), or the *Eden Roc* (av. Dr. Mitjanvila). More modest eateries are abundant throughout the city as well, but most hotels will require that guests take full pension during tourist season; travelers should keep this in mind when checking in. After-dinner drinks can be cozily sipped at the bodega of the Hotel Eden Roc, which combines rustic decor with top disco dancing.

En Route from Andorra – Directly after leaving Andorra — calculating ample time to get through customs and replenish the gas tank — and heading south down Route 145 to Seo de Urgel, the traveler immediately senses the entry into Spain. The terrain becomes coarser, drier, and the towns less quaint. After passing Seo de Urgel, noted for the bishop and co-prince of Andorra, follow Route 1313 along the Segre River past 77 miles (128 km) of farmland to Lérida. Route 1313 is a poor road, so this drive will take the better part of the morning. The villages passed along the way, however, are interesting and typical of the fertile Valley of Aran in western Catalonia. The medieval parador *Jaime de Urgel* in the town of Balaguer, 5 miles (8 km) west of Route 148, 62 miles (100 km) south of Andorra, is a pleasant place for refreshment before continuing the remaining 16 miles (27 km) along Route 145 through the plains to Lérida.

LÉRIDA: The capital of the province, with a population of 95,000, Lérida is built on a hill overlooking the Segre River. At the highest point of the city, the Gothic cathedral of Antigua Seo can be admired and the remains of the ancient Arab fortress of La Zuda explored. The panoramic view of Lérida and the surrounding orchards is spectacular and deserves the drive up the hill. From this vantage point, the strategic importance of Lérida can be appreciated. Indeed the city's name derives from the Latin word *ilerda,* or "stronghold," so named when the Roman troops of Caesar conquered the original Iberian fortress and, later, the rival army of Pompeii. The invading Moors made

"Lareda" the capital of the *taifa,* or feudal realm, until the Christian armies came from the north to reconquer the region. Besieged by invading French troops at various times in its history, Lérida still presents itself as a well-fortressed city.

Due to its strong Catalonian ties, Lérida offers a cultural shock to visitors who think they can speak Spanish. The Catalán accent is more pronounced here than in Barcelona, but the warmth of the people compensates for the language barrier. Enjoy the Catalonian accent in the regional cuisine: the *ensalada catalana, la cazuela,* and game dishes. The confection of turron and holiday pastries are famous. Recommended is the regional wine, Castelle de Remy. Fine restaurants include *La Rada* (39 Mayor), *Florida* (27 José Antonio), and *El Meson* (Calle San Martín). Outside the city, on Route NII, the *Hotel Condes de Urgel* has fine dining facilities in a picturesque setting.

For further information regarding sights in Lérida, a map of the city and a brochure in English are available at the Office of Tourism (Plaza de la Catedral).

En Route from Lérida – Drive west on Route NII to Zaragoza, 86 miles (143 km) away. This is a better road, so the trip should not be very tiring. Additionally, the new six-lane highway from Barcelona can be picked up shortly outside Lérida, further speeding the mainly uneventful journey past fertile valleys to Zaragoza, a city at the geographic crossroads between the Cantabric and Mediterranean seas and between the Pyrenees and the Central Meseta.

ZARAGOZA: The provincial capital and the largest city of the region of Aragón, with a population of half a million, Zaragoza has been called the Lady of Four Cultures. The original Iberian city on the banks of the majestic Ebro River was conquered in AD 24 by Roman troops. The plan was to make it a city of peace for legion veterans. The name of the city derives from the Latin name Caesar Augustus, which, when pronounced rapidly, transforms to Zaragoza. The invading Arabs made the city, called Sarakosta by them, a cultural center and the seat of the regional king of Taifa until 1118, when the Christians reconquered Zaragoza for the crown of Aragón. These four cultures blend harmoniously to form the personality of Zaragoza, where Iberian and Roman ruins, Arab palaces, and Christian temples can be seen.

Zaragoza is a modern city today, important for its university and commercial vitality. Still, its main importance is for many visitors spiritual, since it was on a column of a Roman temple in Zaragoza that the Virgin Mary is said to have miraculously appeared to St. James with promises of salvation. The religious devotion to Nuestra Senora del Pilar is most profound in Spain and in Spanish America, since the feast day coincides with October 12 celebrations of Hispanic culture. The monumental neoclassic Basilica del Pilar dominates the skyline from the Ebro River and is noted for its sculptured facade and interior frescoes by Goya, a native son. Most of the cultural sights of Zaragoza are within walking distance of the basilica, so it is a very good place to start a city tour.

Remains of Roman walls can be found west of the basilica. Farther west, the church of San Pablo can be seen, noted for its octagonal tower of the Mudéjar style, reflecting the design of Arab architects for Christian temples. A 10-minute walk farther, and not to be missed, is the Aljaferia, the spectacular Arab palace of the eleventh century constructed by the Taifa King Abu Chafar Ahmed Almoctadir-bilah. This pleasure retreat is the only example of Taifa architecture still standing and therefore has special artistic interest for those intrigued by Granada's Alhambra and Córdoba's mosque. Under restoration today, the Aljaferia is an unexpected treat for the visitor to Zaragoza. Other sights in Zaragoza are found east of the basilica and include the sixteenth-century Ayuntamiento, or government house; La Lonja, or market center; and the fourteenth-century Cathedral of La Seo, with its elaborate Plateresque altar and baroque interior. The Office of Tourism, near the old Roman walls, can provide brochures and maps that facilitate sightseeing.

Eating is excellent in Zaragoza, as in all of Aragón, and is characterized by simple but delicious preparation. The abundance of locally grown fruits and vegetables allows for great variety and selection in cooking. Such dishes as eggs *al salmorejo,* chicken *a la chilindron,* lamb *a la pastora,* or the *ternasco asado* are famed local delicacies, as are the sweets and candied fruits covered with chocolate. The robust table wines of Cariñena are outstanding.

When looking for a place to eat, do not be timid and miss out on the experience of seeing El Tubo, a winding labyrinth of streets in the area directly in front of the basilica. Row upon row of taverns and restaurants serve hearty regional fare in a rustic atmosphere. Since Zaragoza is a university town, there is always singing and guitar music in the air as students converge on their favorite haunt in El Tubo. Recommended restaurants include *El Tubo,* one of the taverns in this maze of streets. Elsewhere in the city, good cooking can be found at the *Savoy* (42 Coso), *Maravilla* (1 Independencia), and the *Mesón del Carmen* (4 Hernán Cortés). *El Cachirulo,* a little over 2 miles (3 km) outside town on Route 232, offers fine dining. The restaurant and *parilla,* or grill room, of the *Hotel Corona de Aragón,* offer luxury dining at expensive prices.

Taking Route NII south out of the city, you drive past 50 miles (80 km) of orchards and vineyards before reaching Calatayud, the second largest city of the province.

CALATAYUD: The ancient Roman city of Bilbilis sat here, at the confluence of the Jalon and Jiloca rivers. Bilbilis flourished in pre-Christian times and is famous for being the home of the philosopher and writer Marcial. The city was renamed Zalat-Ayud by the Arabs, and ruins of the Moorish *ayud,* or castle, can be seen on the hilltop above the city. The many Mudéjar buildings such as the Colegiata de Santa Maria and the churches of San Andrés and San Pedro de los Francos are of artistic interest. Our itinerary takes us just past Calatayud, however, 12 miles (20 km) down Road 202 to the Monasterio de Piedra, founded in the twelfth century by monks of the Order of Cister.

MONASTERIO DE PIEDRA: The medieval monastery, today converted into a four-star hotel, is an ideal place to stop and eat or spend the night. In accordance with the purpose of the monastery, the monks sought solitude and self-sufficiency, and the surroundings of the Monasterio de Piedra lend themselves to this need for quiet contemplation. Of absolutely breathtaking beauty is the surrounding national park. It seems a wonder, in such an arid region, that the River Piedra could sculpt such spectacular caverns and create such dramatic cascades. The highlights of the park are conveniently indicated by arrows along a mile-long path. The natural beauty at every turn makes this 2-hour walk a delightful afternoon stroll. For those spending the night at the monastery, the evening in itself will provide a memorable experience.

En Route from the Monasterio de Piedra – After winding your way back to Route NII, the remaining drive to Madrid includes a varied panorama of rural landscape and the opportunity for several brief stops in interesting towns. Fifty miles (80 km) from Calatayud is the ancient city of Medinaceli, the "city in the sky."

MEDINACELI: A drive to the top of the steep hill upon which the town was founded affords a magnificent view of the area and a chance to get close enough to admire the unique Roman arch that is unexpectedly perched on the edge of a plunging cliff. This second-century construction is one of only two triple-tiered arches still in existence (the other one is in Rome) and seems to usher the traveler on toward the heavens — or at least on to the Central Meseta of Castile.

Returning to Route NII for 10 miles (16 km), one can take a short side trip down road C114 for 13 miles (21 km) to medieval Sigüenza.

SIGÜENZA: Built by the Romans on the banks of the Henares River in the fifth century, this picturesque town is best known today for its twelfth-century Gothic cathedral. Here is the famous sculpture *El Doncel,* marking the tomb of the poetic and heroic nobleman slain in Granada in 1486, D. Martín Vázquez de Arce.

The remaining 80 miles (128 km) to Madrid, backtracking again to Route NII, bring you past Castilian towns large and small. Thirty-five miles (56 km) from Madrid you'll come to the city of Guadalajara.

GUADALAJARA: Today an industrial center, Guadalajara was at one time a Moorish stronghold, as its name, Valley of Stones, suggests. Later the feudal seat of the powerful Mendoza and Santillana families, it was an important center of Renaissance culture. The only vestige of this noble past, however, is the facade of the Infantado Palace, whose interior was totally destroyed during the Spanish Civil War.

Continuing the journey down Route NII for 14 miles (23 km) to Alcalá de Henares, one last stop can be made before reaching Madrid.

ALCALÁ DE HENARES: The highlights of a visit to Alcalá are: the original Universidad Complutense, founded in 1499 by the humanist Cardinal Francisco Jiménez de Cisneros; the house where Cervantes was born; and the Municipal Hall, where an edition of the rare Polyglot Bible is displayed. You can have a medieval meal at the *Hostería del Estudiante,* adjacent to the university, or homemade candied almonds bought through a turntable from the cloistered nuns of the Franciscan Convent of Beaterio de San Diego.

En Route from Alcalá – Back on Route NII, the 21-mile (35-km) drive to Madrid, passing the American Air Force base at Torrejon de Ardoz and the international airport of Barajas, will take approximately half an hour.

BEST EN ROUTE

Hotels in Andorra and the southwestern provinces of Spain are moderately priced, running from as high as $15 to $20 a night, double occupancy, with private baths, to as low as $10 to $12 and under (inexpensive). Restaurants are also inexpensive, costing between $5 and $8 per person for a full-course meal. Most hotels, however, prefer their guests to take full-pension plans. Be sure to make reservations, particularly during the summer, at whichever hotel you intend to stay.

ANDORRA LA VIEJA

Andorra Palace – 140-room hotel offers private baths, swimming pool, dining room, and cafeteria service. Prat de la Creu (phone: 2-1072). Moderate.

Andorra Park – 78-room hotel offers a view of the mountains, balconies, private baths, dining services, and a swimming pool. Plana Guillema (phone: 2-0970). Moderate.

Hotel Eden Roc – 60-room hotel has private baths and dining room. Centrally located at 1 av. Mitjanvila (phone: 2-1000). Moderate.

Hotel de l'Isard – 51-room hotel has a dining room. 36 av. Meritxell (phone: 2-0092). Inexpensive.

Hotel Flora – 44-room hotel offers a bar and breakfast only. 23 Antic Carrer Jajor (phone: 2-1508). Inexpensive.

Els Fanals – Restaurant in center of the city serves local dishes of lamb and trout. 20 av. Meritxell. Inexpensive.

La Nica – This restaurant is famous for its grilled trout. Centrally located. Inexpensive.

LÉRIDA

Hostal Condes de Urgel – 105-room hotel features private baths, swimming pool, and dining. Rte. NII (phone: 20-23-00). Moderate.

Hotel Ilerda – Small hotel offers dining facilities. Barcelona Hwy. at Km. 467 (phone: 21-42-76). Inexpensive.

El Mesón – Restaurant offers regional lamb dishes. Calle San Martín. Inexpensive.

Florida – This restaurant also offers lamb specialties; also try the turron candies and local wine. Castelle de Remy. 27 José Antonio. Inexpensive.

La Rada – This restaurant serves various regional dishes. 39 Mayor. Inexpensive.

ZARAGOZA

Goya – 141-room hotel provides private baths, dining room. 5 Pyquete Aragónes (phone: 22-93-31). Moderate.

Gran – 169-room hotel provides dining service. 5 Costa (phone: 22-19-01). Moderate.

Hotel Corona de Aragón – 232-room hotel has a rooftop swimming pool and dining room. Via Imperial (phone: 22-49-45). Moderate.

Ramiro – 64-room hotel has a bar, no dining room. 123 Corso (phone: 29-82-00). Inexpensive.

El Tubo – This tavern is in the famous El Tubo district, a winding labyrinth of streets in front of the basilica. Inexpensive.

Maravilla – Egg, chicken, and lamb dishes and hearty table wines are served. 42 Coso. Inexpensive.

Mesón del Carmen – Offers the same specialties as the above. 4 Hernán Cortés. Inexpensive.

CALATAYUD

Hotel Rogelio – 62-room hotel provides private baths and dining services. Rte. NII, Km. 237 (phone: 88-13-23). Inexpensive.

MONASTERIO DE PIEDRA

Monasterio de Piedra – 47-room hotel with swimming pool, bar, and dining room was a twelfth-century monastery for Cistercian monks. Rte. 202, 12 miles (20 km) outside Calatayud (phone: 2). Inexpensive.

GUADALAJARA

Pax – 64-room hotel offers a swimming pool and dining room. Rte. NII, Km. 57 (phone: 21-29-40). Inexpensive.

Exploring Austria

Surrounded by West Germany and Czechoslovakia to the north, Hungary to the east, Yugoslavia and Italy to the south, and Switzerland and Liechtenstein to the west, landlocked Austria (covering an area of about 32,375 square miles) is smaller than the State of Maine. Nevertheless, Austria offers more variety than almost any country in Europe. Moody plains with rocky outcroppings are crowned by castles and dense green forests evocative of medieval legends and fairy tales. The beautiful Danube flows for miles through the country's heartland, where robber baron battlements still look down on waters that are no longer blue. In the Salzkammergut Lake Region, ancient glacial waters lap calmly against the shores of little spa towns. There are acres of vineyards in settings more romantic than those in Burgundy or Bordeaux, and of course there are the Alps — some of the most breathtaking and dramatic peaks in the world.

Austria's 7.5 million people are spread out comfortably among city, town, spa, and farm, but the population swells annually by at least a million as tourists flock here to ski, sample the pastries, take the waters, listen to the music, or just generally absorb the splendor of this cultural jewel at the crossroads of Europe. If Vienna, Austria's capital, is the most distinguished city in the German-speaking world, Salzburg is certainly the most elegant; Innsbruck, high in the mountains, combines the best qualities of both and adds its own Alpine flavor; while Graz, to the south, is a medieval gem of an imperial city.

The history of Austria is an incredible mosaic of peoples and religions. Indeed, some of the earliest human relics (dating from the Iron Age) are still being unearthed and studied in the Hallstatt area. Austria (Österreich) means "Eastern Empire" and in AD 788 referred to the eastern reaches of Charlemagne's conquests. The first indigenous monarchy was established by the Babenbergs in 976 at the town of Melk. Much of the country was still independently ruled (Salzburg was in the hands of the prince-archbishops long after this), and it wasn't until the thirteenth century, after the throne was moved to Vienna, that the Hapsburgs came to power and the empire unified and expanded. It grew not only through conflict but through cagey political alliance, and it was during this period that Austria gained its reputation for being more successful in marriage than in war. After repelling the Turks in 1683 (who in retreat left their sacks of coffee outside the walls of Vienna and are therefore credited with the rise of the Viennese coffee house), the Empire became, by 1700, the great power of Europe. But though the Hapsburgs reigned on, Austria's power was diluted in the nineteenth century, first by Napoleon and then by the revolution of 1848. The empire never regained its former prominence and was reduced to its present dimensions after World

War I. Annexed by Hitler before World War II, Austria was occupied by the Americans, British, French, and Russians after Germany's defeat until 1955, when it once again became an independent state.

Though the political names associated with Austria are notorious — Charlemagne, Richard the Lion-Hearted, Napoleon, Metternich, and Hitler — the musical names are the ones that more happily spring to mind — Beethoven, Bruckner, Haydn, Mahler, Mozart, Schubert, and the Strausses — and almost every Austrian city boasts a festival in their honor.

Three Austrian routes are outlined below; two start from Vienna and one begins at Salzburg.

The Burgenland route is a 1- or 2-day drive south from Vienna through the quiet towns along the Hungarian border where the food — especially the wild game — is excellent and the wine is fresh. You follow the coast of the Neusiedler See down to the castle of Bernstein and come back north across the face of the Schneeberg, Vienna's Alp, to Baden and then back to the capital.

The trip from Vienna to Salzburg is one of the most picturesque in Europe, taking you through the famous Wachau wine-growing district, along the meandering Danube through Dürnstein (where King Richard Lion-Hearted was imprisoned), to the historic golden abbey at Melk and on to the city of Linz. Then you head south through the beautiful lakes of the Salzkammergut, skirting the northern Alpine slopes and crisscrossing west to the elegant, three-hilled town of Salzburg.

The route south from Salzburg takes you first to the spa town of Badgastein with its thundering waterfalls and then south to the Grossglockner highway — the famous hairpin-turn road around one of the highest peaks in the Alps. From Lienz you head back north to Kitzbühel in the Tyrol and drive west along the Inn River, with mountains rising on both sides all the way up to Innsbruck, an urbane, medieval city where snow-capped peaks are visible from every corner. Through the Arlberg Pass to the Swiss border the Alpine landscape becomes more majestic, and the hillsides are clustered with white, spacious chalets. You gradually come down out of the mountains and finally arrive at Bregenz, a neat resort town on Lake Constance at the western tip of the country.

Burgenland

This trip from Vienna into the province of Burgenland and back covers about 230 miles (375 km) and affords a look into the small towns that ring Vienna to the south and hug the Hungarian border to the east. It's a relaxing trip with good food, comfortable lodgings, and an uncrowded itinerary.

Burgenland itself was actually Hungarian until a vote of the citizens after World War I opted for joining with the new Austrian republic. The area boasts superb castles and estates, one of Europe's larger lakes, thousands of acres of prime vineyards, and probably the nation's finest regional cooking. It is difficult to find a really bad restaurant in Burgenland proper. Wild game, duck, and goose dishes, spicy homemade sausages, rich goulashes, and strudels of poppy seed and jam-filled crêpes highlight a cuisine that is at once hearty and still sophisticated enough for the most selective palate. The entire area was under Soviet occupation until Austria was granted her freedom in 1955. For many years people in the region hesitated to make improvements, but this has changed dramatically. Still, the region is not extensively toured, and the farther south from Vienna you get the more of a novelty a North American becomes.

In this section of Austria it is much wiser to follow "town to town" signs rather than highway signs. Many of the towns are so small that a quick stop is enough to absorb their flavor. Some of the highlights of these smaller towns have been lumped together, so, depending on how much time you want to spend, pick your stops in advance. From Vienna you drive east to the plains area of Marchfeld, then south to Rohrau, Haydn's birthplace, and on to the marshy lake country and bird sanctuary surrounding the Neusiedler See. From the lake town of Rust, you abruptly climb westward through low hills to Eisenstadt, the capital of Burgenland, and then south to Bernstein, the southern fulcrum of the trip and suggested evening stopover. Leaving this wooded plains area you reenter Lower Austria and, driving north, encounter the Bucklige Welt ("bumpy world"), a gentle pre-Alpine region of round hills covered with deep forests and orchards. At Puchberg you can climb the Schneeberg — called "our Alp" by the Viennese. Continuing north, the land flattens out as you reach the decorative spa town of Baden, the largest city on the trip and a stone's throw from the Vienna Woods.

VIENNA: For a detailed report on the city and its hotels and restaurants, see *Vienna,* THE EUROPEAN CITIES.

En Route from Vienna – You leave Vienna by crossing the main channel of the Danube, noting the signs pointing right, to Grossenzersdorf, where you pick up Route 33 east. You have entered the plains of Marchfeld, an area fought over by the Romans, the Turks (they besieged Vienna from here in 1529), Napoleon (he suffered his first defeat near the village of Aspern), and the Red Army, who sliced through the retreating Nazis here during World War II on their way to liberate Vienna. You go through Orth, 17 miles (28 km) from Vienna, where you can stop at the huge, forbidding, twelfth-century castle that is now the Austrian Museum of Fishery and Water Conservation and have fish soup and carp (daily, except Wednesday) at the nearby Uferhaus. Another 5 watchful miles (8 km) brings you to the tiny hamlet of Eckartsau.

ECKARTSAU: Here is the half-ruined château of Karl I, the last Austrian emperor, to which he fled in 1918 as his empire crumbled around Vienna. For a long time the Austrian government seemed satisfied to let this property crumble, too, but now you can walk through the overgrown baroque gardens and the display rooms of the Imperial Hunting Lodge (1722) and think about the frightened and abandoned royal family holing up here.

En Route from Eckartsau – Make a 19-mile (30-km) deviation northeast on back roads to the little market town of Marchegg, which sits directly on the March (Morava) River, the Czechoslovakian border. There's a castle here from the thirteenth century (it's since been more comfortably renovated to the spacious Renaissance proportions of the seventeenth century) that's now a hunting museum. This area offers fine bird hunting (if you've brought your gun this far, you must already know this), and the museum has scenes of various royal hunts, where the harsh outdoor life was softened for the nobles by the chamber orchestras that accompanied them and played as they beat the bushes. Head directly south on Route 49 to the new Danube Bridge in 12.5 miles (20 km).

ROHRAU: On the south side of the river is the village of Bad Deutsch-Altenburg, where there are some Roman ruins (an 8,000-seat amphitheater and a museum); 6.2 miles (10 km) farther south on Route 211 — you have to pick your way carefully — you'll find Joseph Haydn's birthplace, the village of Rohrau, on the Burgenland state line. The house where Haydn was born has been restored, showing off not only the musician's souvenirs but also the simplicity with which the people lived. The thatched houses in the white-walled compounds of Burgenland are a counterpoint to the splendor of Vienna and quite simply different from the rest of the country. Rohrau also has a fine château of the Harrach family. When the occupation ended in 1955, the family's painting collection, one of the outstanding private collections in the world, was moved here from Vienna. The Harrach Collection is open to the public from April through October, daily except Mondays; its Spanish and Dutch works are particularly fine. Also in the château is a good and surprisingly inexpensive restaurant.

THE NEUSIEDLER SEE: From Rohrau drive southwest on 211 and southeast on 10 to reach the reedy edges of the great Lake of Neusiedl at the village of Winden. This enormous lake, about half the size of Lake Geneva, is a geological freak of nature — it is so shallow that a tall person can literally walk across it. (Every year on the first or second weekend in August an organized walk takes place.) The lake dried up completely in the mid-nineteenth century, filled again, and now has receded a bit. The lake's banks are covered with millions of reeds that give nesting and migratory protection to over 200 species of birds. Symbolic of the region are the cumbersome stork's nests found on top of many cottage chimneys. Used by the Viennese as a prime summer weekend retreat, the Neusiedler See is often filled with hundreds of sailboats.

RUST: As you travel south to the unofficial lake capital of Rust (25 mi/40 km from Rohrau), you cross very old vineyards that grow westward in the low hills surrounding the shore. The wine of the region, notably the unique Blaufränkisch red (with the taste of a particularly robust Burgundy), is highly prized, but little of it is exported, as the demand in Vienna often exceeds the supply. Many of the farmhouses in the region will display green boughs on their doors, indicating that you may stop to taste and possibly purchase the vintages. You can also visit a village market and purchase a picnic lunch to take along to these al fresco taverns. Two of the most hospitable winemakers are *Just of Rust,* Weinberggasse 10 (phone: 02685-251), makers of white wines, and the *Klosterkeller,* Rathausplatz 4, in nearby Siegendorf (phone: 02687-8252 or 8575), for red wines. Both are closed Sundays. You won't have to carry your Siegendorf wines home with you because they're distributed in the US by H&S, 30 Somerset St., Belmont, MA 02178 (phone: 617-484-5432) and featured at Boston Pops concerts.

Rust is a small, quiet town where German is spoken, but Hungarian lurks between the lines. If you're lucky, you'll get to hear gypsy music in the taverns on summer nights and watch costumed, high-booted residents dance to it.

En Route from Rust – Less than 4 miles (6 km) south is the small village of Mörbisch on the Hungarian frontier. There's good swimming and a midsummer music festival on a lakeside stage, where traditional Viennese operettas are performed outdoors (however, bring along some insect repellent).

EISENSTADT: Some 12.5 miles (20 km) west of Rust is Eisenstadt. The road here rises sharply, so you'll see some nice vistas as you arrive. The largest building in town is the hulking Esterhazy Palace, noted not so much for its architecture as for its history. Haydn was a member of Prince Esterhazy's court and, in 1766, was made musical director of the prince's orchestra and chorale. In return, the royal family named a room after Haydn. There are tours of this great hall, where the master nightly conducted his own compositions for the entertainment of his patrons. The rest of the château serves as administrative offices for the provincial government. (You can also see Haydn's house at Haydngasse 21 or his tomb at the Church of the Calvary.)

En Route from Eisenstadt – Drive south for 9.3 miles (15 km) to the large market town of Mattersburg. Turn west for a few miles at Mattersburg and follow signs to the imposing Forchtenstein Castle. This castle, sitting on a towering dolomitic rock, dates from the thirteenth century, and its vast rooms house good collections of medieval armor, weaponry, and hunting memorabilia. There's also a well almost 500 feet deep, dug by hand by Turkish prisoners of war in the seventeenth century.

BERNSTEIN: From Mattersburg drive south on Route 331 for 10.5 miles (17 km) through Stoob. Continue south through Oberpullendorf and Lockenhaus, and 12 miles (19 km) from Stoob you'll find Bernstein, the southernmost point on the trip. There's a thriving serpentine jade business here and also the *Almassy* castle hotel. The hill castle in Lockenhaus was built around 1200 by an itinerant Roman archbishop who liked the terrain. This castle is also a museum with a knights hall and a torture chamber. Indeed, one medieval lord of the manor, Graf Uilaky, is rumored to have come home from a 2-week plunder to find his wife's servant at her bedside. He knifed the servant immediately, but chose to brick up his beloved alive behind a handy castle wall. It is said that her ghost occasionally wanders the halls. In July, the castle is one of the sites for the International Chamber Music Festival, founded by violinist Gidon Kremer.

THE SCHNEEBERG TOWNS: The next morning head north 7.5 miles (12 km) to Kirchschlag, pick up Route 55 north, and watch for signs pointing northwest to Neunkirchen. There take Route 26 northwest, a road that runs through one of the finest wooded canyons in all of Europe, to Puchberg (29 mi/47 km from Kirchschlag). At Puchberg you suddenly find yourself in the Alps. The Schneeberg is one of the easternmost mountains, and you can catch a steam-driven, cog-wheel train here to its peak.

Four miles (6 km) east, at Grünbach, you can take a chair lift up to the Hohe Wand, a high plateau nature reserve. From Grünbach continue east another 4 miles (6 km) to Urschendorf and then follow back lanes for about 5.5 miles (9 km) to the famous brewery town of Markt Piesting, where you have a chance to drink as many steins of Piestingerbräu as you can (or want). This famous brew is dark and a little bitter, like stout, and almost impossible to buy elsewhere.

BADEN: From Markt Piesting drive north 21 miles (34 km) through Bad Vöslau and 2.5 miles (4 km) farther to Baden (*Bad* is German for "spa"), the grandfather of all health resorts. The Romans called the town Aquae and used the sulfur thermal springs. Even the city's coat of arms depicts two people in a bathtub. Baden was Soviet occupation headquarters for Austria until 1955, and during this period the city's reputation as a resort suffered. Since the return of capitalism, however, the waters are bubbling again. There are a few historic highlights (Beethoven's house at Rathausgasse 10; the famous death mask collection at the Städtisches Rollett-Museum at Weikersdorfer Platz 1; and the formal, triangular Hauptplatz with its ornate Trinity column commemorating the plague), but for the most part this is a place for vacationers. For those who can't wait for the waters to cure them there is more instant gratification (or demoralization) available at the Baden Casino in the Spa Center, where you can play roulette, baccarat, blackjack, or slot machines. There are also facilities for swimming, riding and cycling, saunas, and whatever else you can think of that's healthy. From here it's only 15.5 miles (25 km) back to Vienna; the two cities are connected by a showy old streetcar service, by railroad, and frequent buses.

BEST EN ROUTE

Expect to pay from $60 to $120 for a double room with breakfast per night in hotels listed as expensive; $35 to $60 in those listed as moderate; and $15 to $35 in the inexpensive places. Restaurant prices range from $35 to $60 for dinner for two in the expensive category; $15 to $35 in the moderate; and $8 to $15 in the inexpensive category. Prices include wine. Although a 10% tip is included in most menu prices, an extra 5% gratuity is expected if service has been adequate.

GROSSENZERSDORF

Taverne am Sachsengang – This is one of the most remarkable and romantic restaurants in all of Austria. Grossenzersdorf is right outside Vienna, so you might want to plan your trip so you can stop here for lunch — outdoors, over a canal, when weather permits. The wild game is beautifully prepared, and trout or *Fogosch* (a sweet Hungarian fish resembling pike) in *Blätterteig* (pastry dough) are unique specialties. On the main road (phone: 02249-2297). Expensive.

RUST

Storchenmühle – The name means "stork's mill," and though it's in the minuscule village of Oslip, just outside Rust, it's one of the most famous places to eat in the Burgenland. You'd better book a table in advance (phone: 02684-2127). Moderate.

Am Spitz – Actually in Purbach, on the route from Winden to Rust, this country inn serves the biggest and best *Backhuhn* (Austrian fried chicken) in Burgenland (phone: 02683-5519). Inexpensive.

FORCHTENSTEIN

Reisner – In the village just below the castle sits an unpretentious little inn that might be the best in all of Burgen. French food critics Henri Gault and Christian Millau found *Reisner's* a few months before we did and gave it a toque, but we're glad to share the discovery. Be sure to reserve ahead and, when you do, someone who speaks German should tell Johann Reisner your likes and dislikes in ingredients. He'll do the rest. Closed Wednesdays and half of January. Hauptstrasse 141 (phone: 02626-3139). Moderate to inexpensive.

BERNSTEIN

Hotel Burg Bernstein – A famous old castle on top of a hill, it has only 11 rooms in a quiet setting. All the furniture is antique and the kitchen is excellent. It's closed in winter and still undiscovered (phone: 03354-220). Moderate.

LOCKENHAUS

Burg Lockenhaus – Gidon Kremer's music festival, which runs for 2 weeks every July, has given the castle restaurant in this medieval ruin a new lease on life, and it stays open daily all year. On Saturday nights, there is a six-course Robber Baron's Feast *(Raubrittermahl)* that also includes wine, schnapps, live music, and a guided tour. Make reservations (phone: 02616-2321). Inexpensive.

PUCHBERG

Hotel Puchbergerhof – This country hotel is filled with folk art and hunting trophies. It's got 40 beds and a good kitchen. Just east of the town center (phone: 02636-2278). Moderate.

Forellenhof – This 145-bed hotel is a little higher up than Puchberg in the Alpine meadows near Losenheim. At the restaurant you can get marvelous mountain trout (phone: 02636-22-05-11). Inexpensive.

BADEN

Hotel Gutenbrunn – Housed in a château, this hotel is one of the city's best. Pelzgasse 22 (phone: 02252-48171). Expensive.

Cholerakapelle – Just west of town, this restaurant set in a striking gorge, has good Schnitzel and game. Helenental 40 (phone: 02252-44315). Moderate.

Vienna to Salzburg

A traveler may speed along the Autobahn between Vienna and Salzburg in 3 or 4 easy hours, yet this would be a mistake. The lands between the great Austrian cities offer some of the richest rewards in Europe. Spending 2 days on the route will give you time to experience some of the most beautiful countryside in the world; if you have even more time to spend, it wouldn't be wasted.

Our suggested route meanders north, south, and west, but, including side trips, it is still only about 310 miles (500 km) long. You'll drive through four Austrian Bundsländer (provinces): Wien (Vienna) is the capital province; Niederösterreich (Lower Austria) is the stable core of a nation whose boundaries and politics have played musical chairs for ten centuries; Oberösterreich (Upper Austria) is where the Alps start to rise and the landscape becomes more severe and breathtaking with every kilometer; and Salzburg is another Alpine province bordering Germany on one side and the spa-studded Salz-kammergut (Lake Region) on the other. A word here about Upper and Lower Austria: The names are confusing, for Lower Austria is actually northeast of Upper Austria. The logic behind this is the course of the Danube River: From Germany it enters Upper Austria, continues into Lower Austria, and exits into Czechoslovakia and Hungary. (If you're still confused, just accept it and take solace in the fact that if you want to go from Virginia to West Virginia you probably travel north.)

This route offers a mix of history, culture, and physical beauty that is a great source of pride and enjoyment to the Austrian people. It's hard to turn down this opportunity to share it.

VIENNA: For a detailed report on the city and its hotels and restaurants, see *Vienna,* THE EUROPEAN CITIES.

    En Route from Vienna – Heading northwest from downtown Vienna, you cross the Danube and find yourself climbing into the quietly rolling hills of the Wine Quarter. Austrians like to drink their wine new, and the word for the current year's beverage is Heuriger. It's generally white, not too dry, strong, inexpensive, and good. Once you get over any "fresh wine" prejudice you may harbor, you'll find yourself stopping at the many Heurigen (wine taverns) along the route.

    Take S3 northeast from Vienna to Stockerau, then pick up Route 4 and take it as far as Maissau. There, turn north on Route 35, and in about 5 miles (8 km) you'll be in Eggenburg.

EGGENBURG: Like many of the other Lower Austrian towns, this small medieval center used to be a walled fortress. Several of the fourteenth-century walls are still intact, and so are some of the towers that intersect them. In the Hauptplatz (town square) beside a Trinity column is a late medieval pillory, a squat, primitive reminder of the absolute power of the feudal lords and the circus-like quality of brutal, Gothic justice. Most of the houses are gabled, distorting their actual size and shape; for the church seekers there is Gothic St. Stephan's, with two Romanesque towers. The violence of the Middle Ages and the religious desire to continually redecorate created many churches like this, with different sections from different periods. The Romanesque style predates the Gothic and is usually simpler. (To distinguish between the two, the schoolboy maxim is: "Round arch, Romanesque; pointed arch, Gothic." Don't apply this rule to any later buildings because the romantic styles of the Renaissance took plans and details from every earlier movement and elaborated on them.)

Head west from Eggenburg on Route 303 for 9 miles (14 km) to Horn, the chief town and resort of the Forest District. Continue southwest another 4 miles (6 km) to the great abbey of Altenburg.

ALTENBURG: You've only driven 13 miles (20 km), but you've jumped a century or two into a new architectural style. The Benedictine abbey here was entirely rebuilt between 1650 and 1742, when baroque was the rage and the straight lines of Gothic discipline were softened by a multitude of curves (the vault gave way to the dome). Decoration was not only allowed but encouraged. The architects studied in Italy, but the abundance of bulbous church domes and tower topknots (there's a bulbous belfry here) were taken from more Eastern traditions like the Russian and the Greek. One look at the intricate, hand-carved, gilded woodwork on the church organ is proof that the craftsmen were encouraged to indulge themselves. The abbey library, ornamental staircase, and colorful grotesque baroque frescoes in the crypt are also interesting. It lost some of its collection during the Thirty Years War in the early 1600s and even more when the Red Army used it for a barracks during World War II, but the structure itself has been artfully restored.

If you pick up Route 34 south out of Altenburg, you soon meet up with the beautiful Kamp River.

THE KAMP RIVER VALLEY: The trip south through the Kamp River valley is reason enough to travel north from Vienna. In a 30-mile (48-km) stretch you'll see castles and fortresses on either side of a quiet river that flows between flat and wooded banks, neatly planned towns, and occasional low, flat hills. The three towns you shouldn't miss are Rosenburg, Gars, and Langenlois, but travel at your own pace and stop whenever something catches your eye. As you go south you reenter the Wine Quarter, so Heurigen will be popping up frequently.

Rosenburg is a good first stop because its castle is both magnificent and well preserved. It's open every day except Friday, and many of its rooms are fully furnished with sculpture, paintings, and weaponry. There is a fine jousting yard.

The next stop on the way south is the pretty market town of Gars, with clean white buildings, small flowered plazas, and a neoclassic archway. We suggest stopping here on the first night out of Vienna because the town has especially good accommodations. Our choice is the *Kamptalhof;* the town is small and the hotel is big, so you won't have any trouble finding it.

Langenlois, 13 miles (20 km) south of Gars, is a larger town, with the most wine growers in Austria. (The best local wine is the dry white called Grüner Veltliner.) The houses are Renaissance, but the Heimat Museum deals mostly with earlier subjects, such as prehistory, regional folklore, and, of course, wine making. From Langenlois it's about 6 miles (10 km) to Krems, at the eastern end of the well-known Wachau.

THE WACHAU: You can practice your German pronunciation on this word — the *w* is a soft *v* and the *ch* is hard and guttural. However you pronounce Wachau, though, you'll still find it to be a series of river towns strung together on either side of the Danube. The area is steep and rocky but still manages to produce an abundance of wine, apricots, plums, and peaches. All this farming has kept the land rural and the towns thriving. The vineyard terracing neatly climbs the hillsides, and the hills themselves are topped by ruins of fortified castles. The Wachau has a rich folklore, with every town, castle, or church spinning its own heroic legend like that of the Kuenringer (tenth-century lords), who blocked the Danube at its narrowest bend and extracted heavy tolls from all the unsuspecting merchantmen on the river. The aristocratic pirates are gone, but a sense of adventure and the beauty of the river landscape remain. Wander west along the river, stopping at Krems, Dürnstein, and Melk.

The city of Krems started doing business 1,000 years ago. Its business is wine, and a stop at the Weinbaumuseum (Dominikanerplatz) is a good idea. Wine is so important to Krems that during the German occupation of World War II the residents complained that besides being Nazis, their captors were beer drinkers to boot.

There are some striking Renaissance houses in Krems: One good example is the building at Steiner Landstrasse 84. The facade is at once Byzantine, Venetian, and German, with golden domed windows, layers of colored friezes, and an ornamentally columned stoa in front of the entrance.

On Route 3, about 4.5 miles (7 km) west of Krems on the north side of the river, is Dürnstein, considered the most beautiful town on the Danube. If time permits you only one stop in the Wachau, this should be it. (The modern road bypasses this small town by tunneling under it, so be on the lookout.) Dürnstein's legend is that Richard the Lion-Hearted was imprisoned here in 1193.

The city is walled and filled with winepresses, ancient houses, and cafés. If Richard didn't enjoy his captivity, it was probably because he never got to sit in one of the cafés and watch the river flow by while sipping some of the strong regional specialty, apricot schnapps. (There is also, of course, gallons of Heurige to be had.) There are tours of the parish church and a former Augustine monastery during the summer, both primarily baroque, but the more secular will appreciate the old wrought-iron signs hanging from the inns along the Hauptstrasse (main street).

Drive west on Route 3 another 19 miles (30 km), cross over to the south side of the Danube, and you'll be in Melk, a historian's paradise. Besides hosting Napoleon between 1805 and 1809 during one of his more successful jaunts, it was also the home of the first Austrian monarchy after 976. At the end of the eleventh century, when Leopold III von Babenberg decided to move to Vienna, he presented his castle to the Benedictines, who converted it, after several renovations, into the finest baroque abbey north of Italy. The renovations were a result of various disasters that are recounted during the hour-long tours given in English. As it stands today, this huge, yellow abbey was designed by Jakob Prandtauer and completed by his son-in-law, Franz Munggenast (whose work you have probably already admired in Dürnstein and Altenburg). The interior of the church at Melk seems even grander and more spacious than it is because of its great dome, many windows, colorful frescoes, and statuary. The terrace of Melk's splendid baroque library affords a wondrous view of the Danube.

The town of Melk, though one of the largest in the Wachau, has resisted industrialization and kept its ancient plan intact and functioning. From Melk you can either continue west along the Danube or take E5 (the Autobahn) into Linz.

En Route from Melk – About 55 miles (88 km) west is the ancient town of Enns, believed to be the oldest Roman settlement in Austria. More recently, it marked the dividing points of the American and Soviet zones of post–World War II occupation in Austria. If you get off the Autobahn here and follow Route 337 and the Enns River north, you'll soon hit its confluence with the Danube, where you'll find a far more dramatic wartime reminder — the small quarry town of Mauthausen.

Until World War II, this town was on few travelers' itineraries. During the war the Nazis built a concentration camp here; the postwar Austrian government declared the campsite a national monument in 1949. Since then, Mauthausen has had many visitors. Outside the camp, memorials have been erected by the various countries of the 200,000 victims exterminated by the Nazis. There's a tour of the camp that takes you through the memorials, the prisoners' huts, the gas chamber, and the notorious Steps of Death that lead into the quarry. This isn't average tourist fare, but most visitors find the trip very moving.

From Mauthausen it's a short jump on Route 3 west to Linz.

LINZ: Linz, a big city that straddles the Danube, is the capital of Upper Austria and a good place to stop. In the Hauptplatz there's a Trinity column that's as much a symbol of this city as the Statue of Liberty is of New York. The column is a baroque totem pole of white marble with cherubs adorning a twisting trunk and a Trinity capped by a golden sun on the top. Linz is also the home of St. Martin's, the oldest church in Austria. It is a simple church of stone with its original beams intact (there's not much in the way of vaulting) and some rare stained glass windows in the apse. The windows here were probably French inspired, for the church was built on Roman foundations by Charlemagne in the eighth century.

Besides preserving St. Martin's, the city has given its name to the Linzer torte, the crown prince of Austrian pastries (the Sacher torte is the reigning king). The Linzer torte is a far more complex affair, involving varying configurations of almond cake and raspberry jam, with or without Schlag — whipped cream.

Linz is the modern art center of Austria, and the Neue Galerie der Stadt Linz (Hauptplatz 8) exhibits works by Corinth, Klimt, Kokoschka, Kubin, Liebermann, and Schiele. There's also the Oberösterreichische Landesmuseum (Museum of Upper Austria; Tummelplatz 10). This fortress museum houses a large collection of weaponry as well as folk art and musical instruments.

Every September, Linz holds a Bruckner Festival to commemorate the symphonies and choral work of Anton Bruckner, a notable native son. Bruckner was actually from nearby St. Florian, a small town 11 miles (18 km) southeast of Linz on Route 1, where he was the organist at the famous St. Florian's Abbey during the 1840s and 50s. He composed his greatest work there and actually wished to be buried under the organ. The pipe housing of the organ is another baroque masterpiece, with gilded angels and cherubs on neoclassic pilasters that run up to a red and gold cross and a ceiling painted with more angels over a fiery orange background. (St. Florian himself was drowned, but is the saint to be invoked in firefighting situations.) The organ appears in many art texts as the prime example of the baroque in Austria. There are tours of the abbey that also take you through the library, the imperial apartments, and the Altdorfer Gallery, with paintings by the Danubian master Albrecht Altdorfer (1480–1538).

If you continue east on Route 1 back to Enns, you can pick up Route 337 south and drive 13 miles (21 km) to Steyr.

STEYR: At the confluence of the Enns and the Steyr rivers, this 1,000-year-old industrial center has a lovely Old Quarter that is a preserved wrought-iron wonder of enduring Baroque, largely closed to cars. Besides exploring the Stadtplatz (main square), walk down Grünmarkt to the Neutor (town gate), which looks out at the Enns River.

Just next door to Steyr is the tiny village of Christkindl (Christ Child), where on some Christmas Eves the midnight mass is televised to all of Europe. If you're here in December, a special post office with a special postmark will endorse and endear your mail to all your stamp collecting friends.

Head west out of Steyr on Route 122 through Bad Hall and pick up the Autobahn west at Sattledt. Get off at Steyrermühl and drive south to Gmunden on the Traunsee, 45 miles (72 km) from Steyr and the easternmost lake of the Salzkammergut (Lake Region).

THE SALZKAMMERGUT: Every lake town here is a resort offering swimming, hiking, sailing, and fishing. Though the scenery is beautiful and there are landmarks and architecture to be seen, the accent here is more on vacationing than touring. These are the hills that Julie Andrews sang about, and though the Alpine vistas are special, the lakeside towns are fairly similar, so if you have time pick one and vacation a little. If you don't, drive through them with the windows open to smell the wild flowers and absorb the good health (Salzkammergut means "district of salt mines," and the area is rich in minerals, with mines and health spas).

Gmunden has a mile-long esplanade with picturesque views of Lake Traun and the surrounding mountains. The town has always prospered (both from the salt trade and the upper-class vacationers), and the lakeside is cluttered with expansive villas.

There is no lakeside at Bad Ischl, 20 miles (33 km) farther on Route 145, but there are two small rivers, the Traun and the Ischl. Between 1848 and 1914, Emperor Franz Joseph summered here with his entourage, so the town has a formal and imperialistic bearing. Franz Lehár also lived here, and there is operetta in summer. There are tours of the Kaiservilla or you can roam the park on your own and see the garden–chess ground on foot or from a horse-drawn carriage.

En Route from Bad Ischl – A short detour south on Route 145 brings you to the old mining town of Bad Aussee, now another fashionable resort. Turn west on Route 166 for Obertraun, on Lake Hallstatt. There's a funicular ascent here to the ice caves of Dachstein (the local Alp) that's one of the best in Europe. Follow 166 around the lake to the town of Hallstatt, one of the most ancient places south of Stonehenge. It gives its name to the Hallstatt period (1000–500 BC). The diggings in the area show that it was an Iron Age metropolis. You can go down into a salt mine or up another cable railway to a mountaintop inn. The town itself looks Swiss, with lakeside buildings of yellow stucco, vertical timber siding, and a solitary stone steeple. The return trip north to Bad Ischl makes a loop drive of about 40 miles (65 km).

Route 158 west from Bad Ischl takes you to the base of the Wolfgangsee, where you turn right through Strobl and follow the road until it ends at the village of St. Wolfgang, on the north shore of the lake. Since the road ends so abruptly and the town is such a popular tourist attraction, parking is a major problem, so put your car in one of the two lots at the town entrance and walk. Besides the lake views, hiking paths, and brass band concerts, there's also a Gothic masterpiece in the town church and a long rack-railway ride up the side of the Schafberg (another Alp), from which you can see 13 lakes. The altar in the church is by Michael Pacher and was carved and painted on gilded backgrounds 500 years ago. A paddle-wheel boat ride on this loveliest of lakes and a visit to St. Wolfgang's legendary *White Horse Inn* are highly recommended.

You follow the same road you entered on to Route 158, which you take west through St. Gilgen and on to the Fuschlsee, the smallest lake of the region and the last before you reach Salzburg, 35 miles (56 km) from Bad Ischl.

SALZBURG: For a detailed report on the city and its hotels and restaurants, see *Salzburg,* THE EUROPEAN CITIES.

BEST EN ROUTE

Expect to pay $60 to $120 per night for a double room with breakfast in hotels listed as expensive; $35 to $60 in those listed as moderate; and $15 to $35 in the inexpensive places. Restaurant prices range from $35 to $60 for dinner for two in the expensive category; $15 to $35 in the moderate; and $8 to $15 in the inexpensive category. Prices include wine. Although a 10% tip is included in most menu prices, an extra 5% gratuity is expected if service has been adequate.

GARS

Hotel Kamptalhof – An ideal stopover in this pretty river valley town, this hotel is in a large country house and has 90 beds, splendid grounds, and a fine kitchen.

It's open all year and has facilities for swimming, riding, and tennis (phone: 02985-2316). Expensive.

DÜRNSTEIN

Hotel Schloss Dürnstein – This 65-room hotel is a fine Baroque castle overlooking the Danube. There are swimming and sauna facilities, and the management is especially welcoming. Dürnstein 2 (phone: 02711-212 or 240). Expensive.

Hotel Richard Löwenherz – This cozy inn in a former convent houses a swimming pool, a dreamlike garden, a terrace restaurant on the Danube, and, in every hallway, rustic furnishings worthy of a folkloric museum. Open mid-March to November (phone: 02711-222). Expensive to moderate.

STEYR

Hotel Minichmayr – This newly renovated hotel has 105 beds and a very good restaurant. Steyr is a small ancient town and the hotel is right in the middle (phone: 07252-23410). Moderate.

BAD ISCHL

Hotel Post – A fine hotel in the center of town, the *Post* has 95 beds, a dining room decorated with hunting trophies, and extensive grounds. Its large rooms evoke the old empire days, and consequently it charges empire prices (phone: 06132-3441). Expensive.

HALLSTATT

Seehotel Grüner Baum – This is a family operation, and guests often stay for an entire vacation. It has 36 rooms (ask for one facing the lake) and an excellent kitchen. Marktplatz 104 (phone: 06134-263). Moderate.

SAINT WOLFGANG

Romantikhotel im Weissen Rössl (The White Horse Inn) – The setting of a famous operetta is alive and well and thriving as a charming 100-bed resort hotel with lakeside eating facilities. Swimming in lake or indoor pool; sauna, gym, boating (phone: 06138-2306). Expensive to moderate.

Gasthof Fürberg – Reached by boat from St. Wolfgang or St. Gilgen, and also by car from the latter, this rambling flower-lined inn has a sculpture of a fish over its door and features *Reinanke* and *Saibling,* the fish (distantly related to salmon) of the Wolfgangsee. Closed in winter (phone: 06227-385). Inexpensive.

Salzburg to Innsbruck to the Swiss Border

The trip from Salzburg through Innsbruck to the town of Bregenz on Lake Constance at the Swiss border runs in a relatively straight east-west line, but as routed here with north-south deviations it covers about 415 miles (670 km). You can drive the distance easily in about 2 days, but to enjoy the Alpine scenery and stave off fatigue, take at least 3 or 4. One of the joys of this trip is the combination of fairly short driving distances between stops, un-retouched medieval towns, and the natural beauty of the Alps themselves.

This is primarily a trip through the Alps, and the views of craggy, snow-capped peaks rising dramatically around small, chalet-filled villages neatly set in mountain valleys are quite striking and unending. As you drive through the mountains you'll find each new vista more exciting than the last — the Alps are something you don't get used to. It's best to make this drive between June and October; the Alpine winters force road closings and the snows will abridge the route, cutting off some of the more breathtaking, twisting mileage. It's also best to start driving early in the day; as the valleys and lowlands heat up in the morning, the warm air rises and, meeting the cooler air around the mountaintops, shrouds the peaks in clouds by afternoon.

Before leaving the province of Salzburg you leave the city of Salzburg and drive south to Badgastein, Austria's premier spa, with health-giving, naturally hot water, an invigorating atmosphere, and cascading waterfalls in the center of town. From there you come back north a bit and dogleg west to the lakeside resort of Zell am See, the jumping-off point for the spectacular southern loop drive down the winding mountain highway around the Grossglockner, the highest Austrian Alp. This road links the provinces of Salzburg and Carinthia and ends at Lienz, the capital of the East Tyrol. From here you take the new Felbertauern route back north, burrowing through the mountains this time instead of going over them. There are no mountain routes in the world that compare with these, and the sharp peaks and blazing glaciers both elate and chill the viewer with a majestic sense of natural history.

Your northern progress stops at Kitzbühel, a medieval town swollen with the ski boom but still picturesque, with tree-lined streets and large old houses. You're in the Tyrol now, and driving west you meet up with the Inn River and follow it, locked between high, green plateaus all the way to Innsbruck. No matter where you're from, Innsbruck is a town you won't want to leave. It combines rangy, Alpine scenery with formal, urban splendor and history — a resort city that hasn't lost its cultured, civilized charm.

From Innsbruck you continue west to the Arlberg region, your second twisting, heady mountain drive that's topped in altitude only by the Grossglockner. During the summer you can deviate south, around and over the peaks via the Silvretta road, and stop for a breather at the flat, man-made Vermunt Lake and Silvretta Dam. At other times of year you travel directly west over the Arlberg Pass or, when driving conditions are very poor, through the new highway tunnel (toll) underneath the Arlberg between St. Anton and Langen. Both routes take you to Bludenz in the prosperous Vorarlberg, Austria's westernmost province, where the towns adopt a precise, Swiss mien. You drive on to Feldkirch with its rectangular towers and round turrets and turn north, following the Swiss border to the provincial capital of Bregenz. Here the route ends at the shore of the Bodensee (Lake Constance).

The provinces along this route blend a fierce, local patriotism with a sophisticated European worldliness that articulates itself through expressive folkways (the chalets here aren't just old houses but works of art, with painted and sculpted elevations) and proud, outgoing natives. If you like to ski, you've probably heard of almost every town along this route, but even if you think speeding down mountains is better left to goats, you'll find you won't have a dull moment from start to finish.

SALZBURG: For a detailed report on the city and its hotels and restaurants, see *Salzburg,* THE EUROPEAN CITIES.

BADGASTEIN: From Salzburg drive south through Bischofshofen and Lend for 62 miles (101 km) to the elegant spa town of Badgastein. This is more of a spender's park than a town, with a curved strip of imperious shops and hotels that compete with each other over who can use the most space. Badgastein is built into the north slope of the Tauern Range, and the Gasteiner Ache roars down this slope, creating an enormous waterfall in the middle of town. You can park your car and stroll up and down the Kaiser Wilhelm Promenade to see both mountains and town.

The Badgastein waters are world famous, and their therapeutic properties keep the money flowing through this town. The springs supply water that is naturally in the amazing range of 115° to 120°F (about 47°C). This thermal water is rich in radon, an element that the faithful claim eases (among other things) rheumatic complaints, circulatory problems, gout, and asthma. You can pay for a full cure with a lucky visit to the Badgastein casino; or, just to get your feet wet, there's a large open-air swimming pool fed by the thermal springs opposite the railway station.

THE GROSSGLOCKNER: From Badgastein, return to Lend and head west for 16 miles (26 km) on Route 311 to Zell am See, a resort town built on a flat tongue that extends off a wooded slope onto the Zeller See, a deep glacial ditch filled with blue Alpine water. There's a short cable car ride up the Schmittenhöhe that gives you a foretaste of the Grossglockner highway. This is a good place to stop if you want to get an early morning start for the highway climb south. (In the winter, you skip this loop drive and just head 16 mi/26 km west on 168 to Mittersill, the return point of this southern deviation.)

The Grossglockner highway begins south of Zell am See at Bruck-an-der-Grossglocknerstrasse. This amazing tollway, completed in 1935, is the prototype for almost all mountain engineering, and if you could only drive a car for one day, this is the road you should take. You start out by going down into the dark Fusch Valley, but little by little you start ascending through a series of Grand Prix bends and hairpin turns that force you to take your time and pay homage to the immortal ledges and crags around you. There are car parks and overlooks for patient studiers, but even fanatical nonstoppers won't escape the hundreds of breathtaking panoramas.

You can stop at Edelweiss-Spitze and climb an observation tower to 8,453 feet or just keep driving to the Hochtor Tunnel, the high point of the roadbed at 8,216 feet. There's a cul-du-sac detour west on the Glacier road up to the Franz-Joseph-Höhe that ends in a terrace cut out of stone. Emperor Franz Joseph built a mansion here at the beginning of the Pasterze Glacier, Europe's largest. (In summer, you can walk on the glacier at your own risk.)

Back on the main road, you wind down and bear right for Lienz, the southern turnaround of the loop 56 miles (90 km) from Zell am See.

LIENZ: Lienz is an East Tyrolean town that has begun to crowd up in the summer since 1967, when the Felbertauern Tunnel was finished, opening a western route through the mountains. Now motorists can come through this hub from east and west, entering the Grossglockner road and leaving on the Felbertauern road or vice versa. This newer road has spawned speedy modernization in areas previously cut off from the rest of Austria by the imposing Alpine barrier. This toll road is open all year, and, though no match for its older brother to the east, the sights here are splendid.

En Route from Lienz – Start north from Lienz, again going down into a wooded valley; and then you rise to the resort of Matrei, a thriving ski spot since the road came through. Matrei is also the gateway to the Hohe Tauern National Park, comparable in size and beauty to Yosemite. Beyond Matrei, until very recently, no road at all existed, so that the last stretch of the highway toward

Kitzbühel offers a particularly fresh view of virginal forests and once isolated folk life. From here you rise farther, passing deep gorges and hanging glaciers. The new tunnel moles its way under a ridge of peaks to emerge on the north mountain slopes; you head downhill into Mittersill, 42 miles (67 km) from Lienz. Cruise through town and push on to Kitzbühel, 17 miles (29 km) up Route 161. You're officially in the Tyrol.

KITZBÜHEL: Kitzbühel's old streets are lined with cafés and pastel-colored houses whose gables extend over the street with arrogant disregard for one-dimensional vertical planes. There are two churches here that are a nice man-made counterpoint to the mountains you just came from (the parish church is Gothic, but its shingled overhanging roof disguises it as yet another chalet).

En Route to Innsbruck – Leave Kitzbühel, driving west on 170 until you hit the Inn River; turn left on the southern bank, taking the local road if you're meandering or the Autobahn if you're in more of a hurry.

Rattenberg is the kind of tiny village you can tell your friends you "discovered" when you get home. The riverside buildings have high, flat, stucco faces that at first glance are reminiscent of the false fronts on movie sets. If you climb up to the fortified stone castle, you can look down and see the sloped roofs that the higher walls conceal. Just above Rattenberg is Alpbach, one of the loveliest resorts in the Tyrol. If you spend a night here, you'll be tempted to stay a week.

INNSBRUCK: Innsbruck is one of Europe's most delightful smaller cities. Particularly vital, it combines light industry, commerce (the main junction since almost prehistory for trade between Germany and Italy, France and Eastern Europe), learning (the university is over 300 years old), and tourism. Perhaps no city has a more dramatic setting, with towering, snow-capped Alps on display from almost every street corner. Stroll down the main shopping street, the Maria-Theresien-Strasse, walking from the Triumphal Arch (to celebrate a successful Hapsburg marriage). You'll pass impressive patrician houses, then find yourself in the heart of an arcaded Gothic town with colorful detailing, various bulbous belfries, and intricate wrought-iron signs. The symbol of Innsbruck is the Goldenes Dachl (Little Golden Roof), an ornate Gothic balcony built in 1500 by Maximilian I, who used it to watch parades and concerts. The sculpted crests on the balcony and lower frieze and the heroic wall paintings give the facade an especially regal bearing. The golden roof that covers the balcony consists of over 3,000 gilded copper tiles. In the Hofkirche (Royal Church), which is known as the "Tyrolean Westminster Abbey," 28 bigger-than-life statues of ancestors line the tomb of Maximilian, who, alas, isn't buried there.

If you momentarily forget you're in the mountains, hop on a No. 6 streetcar, and in a little while you'll feel a jerk as the city starts to fall away below you. The trolley has become a cog-wheel train and the conductor has become a tour guide, pointing out peaks and glaciers. The train will take you to the ski spa suburb of Igls (pronounced "eagles"), but the destination isn't as important as the trip. You won't find a better vantage point from which to look at Innsbruck, an Alpine jewel. If you're tired of rides at this point, stay in town and sit in the Hofgarten under the weeping willows where you can listen to concerts on summer evenings.

From Innsbruck you continue west on Route 171 through Landeck into the Arlberg mountain region.

THE ARLBERG: At Landeck you have another seasonal choice: If it's summer, you can take another southern loop up and over the peaks on the Silvretta road; during the winter you must go directly west over the Arlberg Pass or through the Arlberg Tunnel, where you cross an interior border into the last Austrian province of Vorarlberg.

The northern route through the pass takes you by the austere Castle of Wiesberg, past the shimmering, reedlike span of the Trisanna bridge, and up to the posh, treeless slopes of St. Anton, where the Arlberg method of skiing (the art of snowplowing and parallel turning) was developed. As you continue the ascent, you reach the pass at 5,910 feet, just beyond St. Christoph. As your descent begins, the road over the Flexen Pass branches off to the right. Several scenic hairpin turns drop you into Stuben, and a few minutes later you reach Langen. This is also where you emerge if you decide to take the tunnel. From the western end of the tunnel, the route down to Bludenz becomes bleak, passing through a sparsely populated area that's punctuated only by an occasional power station.

The Silvretta route (not much longer than the Arlberg Pass road) is a tollway much more like the Grossglockner and affords the viewer another round of heart-stopping vistas. As you start the climb driving south (you take the left fork at Pians, under the Trisanna bridge), you pass through several neat ski villages with large farmhouse chalets characterized by long balconies, ornate window detailing, and little belfries on the roof peaks. The Silvretta and Vermunt lakes were created by modern dams, and either makes a good rest stop. The Silvretta is at the highest point on this winding road; you can walk across the dam either mulling over man's relationship with his environment or deciding what to have for lunch. On the downhill trip toward Bludenz you pass the ski and cattle town of Schruns, which Hemingway wrote about affectionately in *A Moveable Feast.*

THE VORARLBERG: The Arlberg and Silvretta routes converge at Bludenz, a busy valley town with ancient gates, cobbled plazas, and flowered, marble fountains. Depending on how long you've been driving, you might consider a night's rest here.

From Bludenz it's only 13 miles (21 km) to Feldkirch, a Gothic marketplace equidistant from Paris and Vienna. The Marktplatz is a square in which large houses with high, round-arched entries open onto the street, occasional bulbous belfries break up the roof lines, and wrought-iron signs with almost art nouveau spiraling hang from the fronts of the inns. The primitive, stone, thirteenth-century Schattenburg Castle is here, as are many old town walls, and it doesn't take much imagination to picture Feldkirch as a medieval armed camp. The castle is a museum now, with folk art from the Vorarlberg and the Tyrol well represented. It has an elegantly rustic cellar restaurant.

Leaving town head north about 22 miles (36 km) through Dornbirn to Bregenz, the last leg of the journey, along the meadowlands of the Rhine Valley and the Swiss border.

BREGENZ: The Vorarlberg capital is a slick and classy lake resort that is unfortunately bisected by a railroad line separating the preserved upper town from the graceful shorefronts of Lake Constance. On the harbor side of the railway are relaxing walks, manicured gardens, and a lakeside stage, where the Bregenz Festival is held every summer. A splendid new indoor festival hall has recently opened. On the inland side of the tracks in the upper town is the domed St. Martin's tower, quiet squares, and twisting streets that offer sanctuary when the beachfronts crowd up during the season. There's also a last-chance cable railway ride up the richly forested mountain slope of the Pfänder just outside the town. When you reach the peak, you'll find this last aerial view of the lake and the town is another beauty and one that brings back so many of the previous unforgettable vistas this journey offers.

BEST EN ROUTE

Expect to pay $60 to $120 per night for a double room with breakfast in hotels listed as expensive; $35 to $60 in those listed as moderate; and $15 to $35 in the inexpensive places. Restaurant prices range from $35 to $60 for dinner for two in the expensive category; $15 to $35 in the moderate; and $8 to $15 in the inexpensive category. Prices include wine. Although a 10% tip is included in most menu prices, an extra 5% gratuity is expected if service has been adequate.

ZELL AM SEE

The Grand Hotel – This place is not only on the lake, it's also really grand, with a convivial café, a good restaurant, and large bedrooms. You'll feel as if you just stepped off the first-class carriage of the Orient Express (phone: 06542-2387 or 2388). Expensive.

Berghotel Schmittenhöhe – Here's a place for the adventurous — the no sheet–woolen blanket set. It's at the top of the aerial tram with no-frill bedrooms, nourishing hot meals, and vertigo-inducing views (phone: 06542-2489). Inexpensive.

LIENZ

Hotel Traube – The bedrooms are comfortable and pretty, but the main attraction here is the restaurant in the cellar, the social center of the entire Eastern Tyrol (phone: 04852-2551 or 2552). Expensive.

MATREI-IN-OSTTIROL

Hotel Rauter – This resort hotel is a longtime favorite of fishermen as well as skiers and other sports-minded people. It was recently modernized in a manner that makes it one of the architectural wonders of Austria: Many of the rooms are spacious A-frame chalets *within* the main building. All offer splendid mountain and meadow views. The room rate includes a four-course dinner and a breakfast buffet (phone: 04875-6611). Moderate.

ALPBACH

Hotel Böglerhof – Thomas Wolfe discovered this inn in 1936 when it was just a farmhouse that took in guests. He wrote home to mother that the Alpbach Valley had "some of the most beautiful mountains and villages" he'd ever seen. Today the *Böglerhof* is a thriving 110-bed hotel ablaze with geraniums and petunias. The surprisingly good room rate includes a breakfast buffet with a medley of freshly baked breads that are a feast in themselves (phone: 05336-5227 or 5228). Moderate.

INNSBRUCK

The Hotel Goldener Adler – This inn has actually been in business in the same building for over 600 years. During the 1976 Winter Olympics, television coverage originated from this hotel's romantic Stube. It's in the heart of the old town, and if you really want to get into the spirit, request a room with traditional trappings and pretend you're Friar Tuck. Herzog-Friedrichstrasse 6 (phone: 05222-26334). Expensive.

The Hotel Goldene Rose – This budget find is a simple yet well kept and ambient Tyrolean country hotel in the city. Herzog-Friedrichstrasse 39 (phone: 05222-22041). Inexpensive.

LECH

Hotel Post – Lech, just outside St. Anton, is one of the great ski resorts of Europe. The *Post* is an easy pick because of its rich Vorarlberg folk decorations and chic international clientele. There's no pretense here, though, and the management is especially welcoming. Off season the rates are reasonable, but when the skiers hit town the prices go up (phone: 05583-22060). Moderate.

FELDKIRCH

Hotel Weisses Kreuz – This solid, well-run, country town hotel has an efficient management in the best Swiss tradition. The kitchen here is excellent. In the Königshofstrasse in the old quarter (phone: 05522-22209). Moderate.

BREGENZ

Hotel Weisses Kreuz – This, the best hotel in town, is an ancient, expertly run place that also serves as the town's prime social center. Römerstrasse 5 (phone: 05574-22488 or 22489). Moderate.

Berghaus Pfänder – Open only from May until late September, this is a mountain restaurant with food as wonderful as the view. Try the *Hasenrücken Pfänder*, saddle of hare served with *Spätzle* (Swabian noodles), potato croquettes, red cabbage, cranberries, and *Pfifferlinge* mushrooms. Adjacent to the Pfänder cable-car station and a charming alpine game preserve (phone: 05574-22184). Moderate.

Exploring Belgium

The kingdom of Belgium is a tiny, industrious, and economically mighty nation about the size of Maryland jammed into the North Sea coast between France and the Netherlands. Belgium's 10 million people live on only 11,781 square miles — it's the second most densely populated country in the world — and they make every square meter count, from their ferociously productive factories, to their meticulously cultivated farmlands, to the tight and efficient network of roads, railroads, and inland waterways connecting it all. On a smaller scale, you can see how they make the most of space in the burgeoning flower gardens behind nearly every house. Close as things are, Belgium has forests that support a great variety of wild birds, such as avocets, shrikes, godwits, and grouse, and four-footed animals ranging from wild hamsters to wild boar.

Belgium is a constitutional monarchy, with power distributed among the king, his appointed cabinet, and the bicameral Parliament, consisting of a Senate and House of Representatives. The present king is Baudouin, a direct descendant of Belgium's first king, Leopold I, who took the throne in 1831.

Brussels is the capital, the center of business, industry, and culture; Antwerp is the most cosmopolitan city, one of Europe's greatest ports, a center of the world diamond market, and the birthplace of Peter Paul Rubens; Liège is an important university and factory town and a world-class maker of firearms; Bruges is famous for its handmade lace and the spectacle of its perfectly preserved medieval Flemish architecture; Ghent is another medieval city — larger, more gracious, and more commercial than Bruges; Ostend is a summer resort on the North Sea.

Julius Caesar found Celts in Belgium when he conquered Gaul in the first century BC. The Franks pushed in from Germany in the third century; Belgium's northern people, the Flemish, are descended from the Franks, and the Walloons of the south from the Romanized Celts. The two groups have been squabbling ever since the Frankish invasion. Clovis and Charlemagne put Belgium under the Holy Roman Empire and Christianized it. The empire fell apart after Charlemagne's death in 814, and from the ninth century to World War II, the strategic land that is now Belgium was overrun almost continuously by the Vikings, French, Spanish, English, Austrians, Dutch, and finally the Nazis. National instability strengthened the economic self-reliance and chauvinism of the Belgian cities, which had to fortify themselves as best they could against invaders and to make protective pacts with one ruler to avoid being absorbed by another. In medieval and Renaissance times, Ghent, Bruges, Antwerp, and Ypres grew fat and powerful from the commerce passing through their ports, becoming great centers of art, architecture, and scholarship. The varying condition of Belgium's inland waterways has made their fortunes fluctuate wildly since the Renaissance.

In this century, Belgium was a trampling ground in both world wars and was occupied by Germany both times. During World War II, the Nazis bombed Belgium mercilessly, pilfered machinery, abducted laborers to work in Germany, and imposed general tyranny; the Battle of the Bulge, the German army's last stand before being decimated, took place in Luxembourg province, near the German border. Damage from both wars was so catastrophic that much of the country had to be rebuilt from scratch. Nevertheless, Belgium has recovered better than most countries in Europe, enjoying worldwide trade and the success of her chemical, metalwork, and food-processing industries.

Belgium is bilingual. Among the 10 million inhabitants, about 56% speaks Dutch, and about 33% speaks French. Dutch is the official language in the northern four provinces, French in the southern four; the central province of Brabant, containing Brussels, is officially bilingual. For centuries, French was the official language of all Belgium, spoken by the wealthy and powerful throughout. However, as Flanders became richer and more industrialized and Flemish nationalism acquired more political clout, the Dutch language was accorded more and more official respect; in 1962, Brussels was made officially bilingual as a concession to the northerners. Although political division in Belgium still tends to be along the language barrier, the matter of Flemish equality is largely settled.

The country is almost unanimously Roman Catholic, and over half the population attends mass regularly. Religious tolerance is written into the constitution, and there are some Jewish and Protestant enclaves. Among the Walloons, there is a strong anti-Church movement; pro- and anticlerical feelings probably rank second, after the language question, as a source of political turmoil.

Belgians are contemptuous of authority, no doubt from centuries of foreign rule. The rights of the individual are considered more important than obligations to society; tax evasion, for example, has been developed to the level of an art. The Flemish in particular are highly independent, living mostly as small farmers and shopkeepers. They have the Teutonic bent for work, order, cleanliness, and conservative rectitude and tend to have large families. Walloons are more urbane and Gallic in their outlook, tending more toward radicalism, socialism, big government, and small families — although, like the Flemish, they are very industrious. Family life is a high priority with both groups; parents and grown children often live near each other. Belgians make no major decisions without consulting their families, and they spend most of their social lives with relations and the friends with whom they grew up. Households often do things as a group: Even a shopping trip is a family outing, with the father leading the brood.

In sports, Belgians love cycling best: Bicycles are used not only in races but also for commuting and recreation. Soccer is the most popular organized sport; pigeon racing is also important; and cockfighting, though illegal, still has a following.

Belgians are perhaps most passionate about good food, both at home and in restaurants. Belgian food, even in a cheap bistro, is plentiful, substantial, and good. Butter and rich sauces are used prolifically in pastries, vegetables, and meat dishes; the most popular meat is beef, and dessert is often made with chocolate or whipped cream. (It's not surprising that the nation has a high incidence of obesity, gout, and stomach and intestinal troubles.) Brussels is considered one of the two or three culinary capitals of the world, so prices for a meal in a top restaurant tend to be high. In addition to food, Belgians also take great pride in brewing beer; some brands to try are Orval, Gueuze, Kriek, Trappiste, and Rodenbach.

We've laid out two routes for you to follow through Belgium; they both begin in Brussels, which should be a major stop in its own right (see the city report in THE EUROPEAN CITIES). The first route takes you through the Flemish-speaking North, to Antwerp, Ghent, Bruges, and Ypres, hotbeds of the great northern Renaissance in painting and architecture. Evidence of it will loom at you as soon as you enter Antwerp — the churches, cathedrals, and guildhouses from the twelfth to the seventeenth century still tower over the narrow streets in many sections; inside are the huge, opulent paintings of Antwerp's most famous son, Peter Paul Rubens. You drive west across the poppy-covered plains of Flanders to sights like the dank and massive forts of 's Gravensteen, in Ghent; Ghent itself has more historic buildings than anyplace else in Belgium; you'll visit the idyllic Princely Béguinage in Bruges; you'll pass on to the white, sandy beaches of Ostend to swim or play tennis, where dikes, fences, dunes, and waterpumps have conspired to hold back the North Sea for 700 years. At Ypres, farther south, is the reconstruction of the great Cloth Hall (a monument to medieval commerce) and the improbable Festival of the Cat, a vestige of a prehistoric culture.

The second route, for the nature lover as well as the history buff, goes through the pastoral, French-speaking area of southern Belgium known as the Ardennes. The countryside here is hilly and forested, less populous than the north, and the country's most scenic region. The trek is a long loop through the provinces of Liège, Luxembourg, Namur, and Hainaut, a green country of bluffs, valleys, and ancient armed citadels. The Ardennes is a hunter's paradise: Wild boar abound all year, and deer, pheasant, water birds, and wild sheep all have their season. If you like camping or hiking, allow several days for the wilderness of the Ardennes and the mysterious Belgian Lorraine, with its steep cliffs, dense woods, and lavish wild flowers. As you swing back north, you can witness dramatic folk pageants and idyllic country castles such as Annevoie and Beloeil.

Antwerp and Flanders

The western Flemish provinces of Antwerp, West Flanders, and East Flanders were one of the most important medieval and Renaissance art centers in the world. In Antwerp city, Ghent, and Bruges, much of the past is still standing and very much a part of daily life. It is to be expected that 1,000-year-old churches are still in use; it's more surprising that many other ancient monuments still function as private houses and government buildings. Northern Belgium makes way for its teeming industries while it holds on to a rare respect for the past and local identity.

Antwerp is a center of publishing, the performing arts, and several industries — notably the diamond trade — and one of the major ports of Europe. Ghent is another industrial and cultural power, with its own port and more than its share of great Flemish art and architecture. Bruges is the preserved and polished medieval jewel of Belgium, having survived 400 years and two world wars with its ancient atmosphere intact. Ypres survived World War I with not much of anything intact and had to be completely rebuilt — it's now a modern city. The seacoast has been vital to Belgium's fortunes throughout history.

The rivers and canals connecting the interior with the ocean at one time made seaports of all the major Flemish cities. The Flanders terrain is so level you can smell the ocean 40 miles inland. The 41-mile shore, which actually sits below sea level, is mostly land reclaimed from the sea over the centuries for farming; the townspeople built dikes and windmills to keep the sea from taking it back. Although resorts and restaurants dot the white sand beaches, the ancient tradition of paying ceremonial homage to the power of the waters in a solemn Blessing of the Sea survives in many of the fishing villages from Knokke-Het-Zoute to the French border.

BRUSSELS: For a detailed report on the city and its hotels and restaurants, see *Brussels,* THE EUROPEAN CITIES.

En Route from Brussels – Head north from Brussels, out of Brabant and into the province of Antwerp. Your first stop is the city of Mechelen, the religious capital of Belgium and the seat of the primate. Not only does Mechelen have a grand 49-bell carillon — which peals out concerts regularly — but also a school for *carilloneurs* (bell ringers) to perpetuate the art. Both school and carillon are in the Gothic cathedral of St. Rombout, begun in the thirteenth century and still not finished: Its great tower was supposed to be 551 feet high but never topped the mere 318 it is now — it's unlikely that anyone will suggest going ahead with those last 233 feet at this point. Inside, the cathedral is sumptuously baroque, with black and white marble and paintings by Van Dyck and other Flemish masters. For Rubens lovers, the church of St. John in Mechelen has his famous *Adoration of the Magi.* Near Mechelen, in Muizen, is a "suburb" of the Antwerp Zoo called Plankendaal Park; it's a special breeding farm and resort for endangered animal species and a beautiful setting in which to see them (open in the warm weather).

ANTWERP: Continue north to Antwerp. Founded in the seventh century by missionaries, it is now Belgium's second largest city (pop. 929,000), the third largest seaport in Europe, and a major producer of cars, petrochemicals, and cut diamonds. The diamond trade goes back to the days of Charles the Bold, duke of Burgundy, who reigned from 1467 to 1477. According to an old story, a young student invented a method of cutting and polishing stones; Charles entrusted him with three diamonds and was so pleased with the results that he presented one of the stones to the pope, another to King Louis XI of France, and kept the third for himself. Presumably, the student took the hint and went into business.

The center of the diamond trade today is around Pelikaanstraat. Be sure to visit the diamond museum at Jezusstraat 28–30, where you can watch the diamond cutters at work (closed Mondays and Tuesdays).

Antwerp was the birthplace of the painter Peter Paul Rubens; the city celebrated the 400th anniversary of his birth in 1977. In a way, Rubens personified all that makes Antwerp what it is: art, international affairs, and wealth. He studied in Italy, became a diplomat, traveled widely, and brought an Italian touch to the Flemish painting tradition. His house (Wapper 9–11), open to the public, contains his own art and that of his contemporaries — as well as his furniture. Some of the pupils who studied there included Van Dyck, Jordaens, Snyder, and Jean Breughel. Besides painting prolifically, Rubens was a prominent politician, and his house gives you some idea of the private world of a public man in seventeenth-century Antwerp.

Near the Rubens house is the Plantin-Moretus Museum (Vrijdagmarkt 22), site of the Plantin printing shop, famous all over Europe in the sixteenth century. In the richly furnished interior are Plantin's office and printing room, containing many first editions and engravings. Tapestries, gold-embossed leather bindings, the Biblia Regia, and 13 examples of the Gutenberg Bible are among its treasures.

The Cathedral of Our Lady is the largest church in Belgium and Antwerp's major landmark, containing some of the world's greatest paintings — including Ruben's *Elevation of the Cross, The Descent from the Cross,* and *The Assumption.* The cathedral is open weekday afternoons until 5 PM.

The Stadhuis (City Hall) built in a grand, far-flung style in 1564, fronts on the main square near the cathedral (closed Fridays and Tuesday and Saturday mornings). Around it are the headquarters of Antwerp's rich tradesmen's guilds from the same period, furnished with sculpture, paintings, and tapestries.

Rubens is buried in the church of St. James (St. Jacob), a flamboyant Gothic church with a baroque interior. Built in 1491, St. James has an amazing inventory of art by Flemish masters: The marble Communion table is by Verbruggen and Kerricx (late seventeenth century); the carving in the choir stalls is the work of Artus Quellin; there is a *Temptation of Saint Anthony* by Martin de Vos; and one of Rubens's own last works, *The Holy Family,* hangs in the chapel where he is buried.

Antwerp's Royal Museum of Fine Arts (L de Waelplaats; closed Mondays) is often called the richest museum in Belgium, a land of museums. There are about 2,500 paintings here, including a staggering collection of Rubens, Frans Hals, Van Dyck, Memling, and Rogier Van der Weyden. Even if you are not a student of art, you will be fascinated at the 800-year history of northern painting displayed here.

As in any seafaring country, Belgium's Marine Museum (Steenplein 1), with ancient maps, ships, relics, and instruments, is worth a visit. The museum is housed in the Steen, a tenth-century fortress and the city's oldest building.

The world-famous Antwerp Zoo is a must. Check out the new Reptile House and the Nocturama, a special darkened habitat for nocturnal animals.

If you are in Antwerp during Lent, make your way to a Goose Race, held on Sundays in several of the surrounding villages; it's just one of the many bizarre and dramatic traditions still thriving in this proudly parochial country. In a Goose Race, competing horsemen thunder along a track trying to snag the head of a dead goose suspended above them. The winner is proclaimed king, and festivities ensue in his honor.

En Route from Antwerp – Go west from Antwerp province into East Flanders (Oost-Vlaanderen), on the road to Ghent. You are entering the historic region of Flanders proper, which starts in the Netherlands and stretches down the North Sea coast into northern France. The poppies grow here, the sheep graze, and everything looks like a familiar landscape — which it is, because it's been painted hundreds of times by the Flemish masters whose works hang in museums all over the world; and centuries of armies have passed this way, leaving memories of the fields of Flanders in our collective consciousness.

If you are here in early September, try to arrive in time to watch the surreal, elephantine grace of the hot-air balloons in the international balloon race held every year in Sint-Niklaas, just west of the Antwerp border.

GHENT: Continue southwest to Ghent (pop. 250,000), the gracious and prosperous capital of East Flanders. Ghent has a long history of civic feistiness that put it in combat with a variety of governments and overlords from Burgundy, Flanders, Spain, and Holland. The city itself spawned an overlord in Charles Quint, the Holy Roman Emperor; King Edward III of England was living in Ghent when his son John was born, best known as John of Gaunt in Shakespeare's *Richard II,* who fathered a long line of English kings.

The center of Ghent is its medieval port, with more historic buildings than any other Belgian city. Surrounding the old quarter are the modern commercial and industrial sections.

The most dramatic introduction to Ghent is by way of 'sGravensteen, the formidable castle of the counts of Flanders. Built in the twelfth century over a ninth-century dungeon, it is a no-nonsense fortress, with walls 6 feet thick. Inside, the cold and damp of centuries hang in the air even in the summer. It has a small museum displaying instruments of torture.

The most important medieval building in town is the cathedral of St. Bavo, a hybrid of Gothic, Romanesque, and baroque styles. The elaborately carved wood pulpit inside warrants a visit on its own. The four massive bronze candlesticks were ordered by Henry VIII of England for his tomb, but Cromwell got his hands on them after Henry's death and sold them to the Ghent clergy for the cash. In one of the chapels is the Van Eyck *Mystic Lamb,* one of the world's most famous paintings. The history of this painting is a detective thriller in progress, for its origin is still vague. No one knows whether it was painted by both Van Eyck brothers or by only one. Its panels have been cut off, buried, and returned several times. During the religious riots of the sixteenth century, the panels were hidden in the cathedral tower. They reemerged and were being sent to England as a gift to Queen Elizabeth I when they were intercepted by the family who had originally commissioned them. Two panels were stolen in 1934, and only one returned. Some believe the missing panel, *The Just Judge,* is hidden in the cathedral.

Next door is the belfry, the rallying point for the people of Ghent in their many rebellions against their rulers. There is a fine view of the countryside from the tower. The sound and light show here (in English) is a must, as is the unique Folklore Museum.

The Museum of Archaeology, in the ancient Cistercian Abbey of Byloke, contains a rich assortment of art, glass, porcelain, weapons, and clothing. The Museum of Fine Arts has a splendid collection of Flemish primitives as well as Dutch, German, French, English, Italian, and Spanish masters.

Ghent has been noted for its horticulture industry for the last 200 years: It has historically been the center for the growing, breeding, and distribution of new varieties of flowers to all points of the globe. The flowering azalea, native to Korea, was developed in Ghent, and the city's nurseries now supply 40% of the world market — 200 million plants worth 1 billion Belgian francs. Coming in second, at 260 million Belgian francs, is the begonia, developed in Ghent into its present form from a South American flower. Hothouses dot the outskirts of the city. The town of Lochristi, 6 miles (10 km) outside Ghent, holds a begonia festival every August, when nurserymen put together floats and pictures using different-colored begonias.

A major event in Ghent is a mammoth flower festival held in the city every 5 years. It will take place in 1985 for a week beginning on April 20. Over 450 horticulturists from all over the world will show their best plants in a 9-acre indoor expanse, with a total of 2 million Belgian francs offered in prize money. The first Floralies, in 1809 in the *Frascati Inn,* consisted of 50 potted plants arranged in front of a field of French tricolor flags around a bust of Napoleon.

In the twentieth century the crowds get thick — 700,000 strong over the week-long run — peering at the likes of sweet peas and conifer arrangements to be judged by the Belgian Flower Arranging Society, blooming roses and daffodils, and every other conceivable plant presented to the Royal Society of Agriculture and Botany.

En Route from Ghent – Leaving Ghent, make a slight detour southeast to the thirteenth-century castle of Ooidonck on the River Lys. Ooidonck is decorated with seventeenth- and eighteenth-century furniture, china, silver, and crystal (open only afternoons on some religious holidays and Sundays in July, August, and early September). The Lys borders the grounds on two sides, and a long avenue of linden trees links the castle with the Ghent road.

BRUGES: The main road leads directly to Bruges, the capital of West Flanders and the long-time rival of Ghent. Bruges is smaller (pop. 120,000), with a totally different appearance and atmosphere.

The city is virtually a moated museum of the Middle Ages, with stiff-gabled houses perched over cobbled streets and long-necked swans gliding along misty canals. For 200 years, Bruges was the most important commercial center in Western Europe, linking the Baltic and the Mediterranean seas. The riches of the world were piled high on its docks, and no king could equal the splendor of its court. The counts of Flanders and their merchant princes brought artists and artisans from all over Europe to decorate their palaces, churches, and guildhalls. Their wives were so magnificently gowned that a visiting queen of France once complained, "I thought that I alone was queen, but here I see hundreds of them around me."

But year after opulent year, the silt rose in the estuary linking Bruges with the North Sea until ships could no longer navigate the narrow, sand-choked waterway, and Bruges became landlocked. This put an end to the city's commercial importance, and Bruges was frozen in time, retaining its medieval atmosphere to this day. The nineteenth-century English poet Ernest Dowson called Bruges "this autumnal old city — the most medieval town in Europe."

Bruges must be visited on foot. The streets are narrow and twisting; some, like Stoofstraat, are only 3 or 4 feet wide. No skyscraper or high-rise blots the sky; for 7 centuries the highest point has been the 365-foot spire of the church of Notre Dame. The canals that weave in and around the city give it a melancholy charm; lime trees and willows grow from the banks, and centuries-old buildings of faded brick are reflected in the silent waters. A few places in town offer canal boat tours.

Probably the greatest event in the city's long history took place in 1150, when Thierry d'Alsace, count of Flanders, rode home from the Second Crusade. According to tradition, he brought with him some drops of Christ's blood, collected on Golgotha by Joseph of Arimathea and given to him by the king of Jerusalem. They are kept in a reliquary in the Basilica of the Holy Blood (around the corner from the town belfry) and once a year are carried through the city in procession on Ascension Thursday, a religious holiday in May.

The churches of Bruges are as rich in history as they are in art, some with foundations going back to the eighth and ninth centuries. The dim, dusty-aisled crypt of the basilica, a twelfth-century Romanesque chapel, is the oldest unaltered building still standing in Bruges.

The cathedral of St. Salvator was begun more than a thousand years ago. It's hung with Gobelin tapestries, and some of its choir stalls are carved with the crest of one of Europe's oldest orders of chivalry, the Golden Fleece, founded in Bruges by Philip of Burgundy in 1429. It was in this cathedral that his knights assembled to worship.

Only a block away is the church of Notre Dame, where you'll find Michelangelo's marble *Madonna and Child,* the 500-year-old Paradise Porch, and the magnificent mausoleum of Charles the Bold.

Even the former hospital is a museum, for St. John's goes back to the twelfth century. One of its thirteenth-century wards contains six paintings by Hans Memling; other wards have twelfth-century frescoes of the Virgin Mary (closed Wednesdays).

Scattered throughout Bruges (and other old cities in Flanders) are "God's houses," a series of compounds built by wealthy families or guilds for the poor and the old. The only requirements for residence are "honesty, good character, and a peaceable nature." There is one in Bruges built by the Meulenaere family in 1613 that has 24 one-story houses, each with its own garden. The community begins and ends each day with prayers for the generations that have lived and died there before them.

At the other extreme is the Gruuthuse Museum, the former home of one of the lords of Bruges. Its great hall, reception rooms, and collections of armor, porcelains, lace, coins, and furniture hint at the magnificence of private houses in the city's prime (closed Tuesdays).

Next to it is the Groeninge Museum, housing some of the great masterpieces of Flemish art, including paintings by Jan Van Eyck, Hans Memling, Hieronymus Bosch, and Pieter Breughel the Younger (closed Tuesdays).

In all of Bruges there is probably no lovelier place than the Princely Béguinage, one of the convents of the peasant Béguines, who wore a *béguin,* or headdress, tied under the chin. There are *béguinages* throughout Belgium, famous for their manicured gardens. Today they are either maintained as museums or occupied, as in Bruges, by Benedictine nuns who still dress in the fifteenth-century style of their predecessors. You reach the Princely Béguinage by crossing the Bridge of the Vine, which spans the Lake of Love, between the cloister and the main city. Across the lake, sunlight filters through the trees, and the only thing to break the peace is the song of a bird.

The miracle of Bruges is that it still stands, considering all the wars that have raged around it. The port of Zeebrugge, 8 miles (13 km) away, was seized by Germany during World War I and made into a U-boat base. When the British stormed the port, the Germans blew it up. It was rebuilt, destroyed again in World War II, and rebuilt once more.

When the eighth-century chapel of the ironmongers' guild was torn down to make way for a garage a few years ago, a preservation society was created to prevent further desecration. They named it the Marcus Gerards Foundation after a sixteenth-century Bruges mapmaker who drew to scale every house and street in town. The foundation researches the history of the old buildings in this monumental city and keeps an eye on how they are maintained.

En Route from Bruges – Ostend and the 41-mile (66-km) stretch of Belgian coast are a short drive west of Bruges. There are resorts, casinos, and nightclubs from nearly one end to the other of this unbroken stretch of fine white sand. July and August are good for swimming, but beaches get very crowded with vacationing Belgians. If you avoid these peak months, you can still have a fine time playing tennis, breathing the sea air, and gambling away your money. At Ostend there is a long boardwalk along the North Sea, and the area is dotted with restaurants specializing in fresh fish, for this is Belgium's main fishing port.

The best areas in which to enjoy the sea away from honky-tonk civilization are in the extreme north and south of the coast. At the Zwin bird sanctuary up by the Dutch border, the sea lavender blooms on the marshes in July and August, and over 100 bird species live there.

If you are in Ostend just before Lent, you will find yourself caught up in the Masked Ball of the Dead Rat, a stupendous carnival that occupies the entire town. Candies in the shape of clogs are scattered to the throng at the festival's close.

North of Ostend, at Knokke, an international fireworks festival is held every August on five nights spread out over the month.

On the final Sunday in May, a solemn procession in the town of Blankenberge culminates in the Blessing of the Sea, when seafaring people make a special peace with their ancient friend and enemy, a ritual that takes place at different times of the year along the coast.

Note: Jetfoil service is now available daily from Ostend to Dover (it's a 1½-hour crossing), where trains to London are available. Ferries also operate from here daily.

YPRES: Head south to Ypres when you have had your fill of the coast. One of the three great cities of Flanders in the Middle Ages, Ypres was razed to the ground in World War I. A modern city, which naturally lacks the medieval beauty of Ghent and Bruges, has been built in its place. The seventeenth-century facades along many streets have been reconstructed, as have the city's two greatest buildings, St. Martin's Cathedral and the towering Cloth Hall — a monument to Ypres's textile industry built in 1214. Unfortunately, no original buildings survived the bombardment of 1914–18.

Ypres never fell in World War I, despite the bombardment, but the battles around the town took over a quarter-million Allied lives. At the Menin Gate, a memorial to the soldiers of the British Commonwealth who died defending Ypres, traffic is stopped every evening for a few minutes while buglers blow a salute on silver bugles.

On the second Sunday in May, Ypres holds what is possibly the strangest rite in all of Belgium, Kattenwoensdag, or Festival of the Cats. Some 2,000 revelers dress up in gaudy costumes portraying cats, witches, and giants and march in procession accompanied by bagpipes. The parade has giant floats dedicated to feline folklore heroes, including Puss in Boots and Cieper, the king of the cats — Cieper has a wife, Minneke Poes, and a kitten-child, Piepertje. The culmination of the festival is when the town jester hurls little wooden cats to the crowd from the top of the town belfry (until 1817, he threw live cats). It is said that the holiday is a vestige of an ancient witch cult.

BEST EN ROUTE

All the major cities and towns you visit in Belgium have comfortable hotels and first-rate restaurants. There are also several good *relais* (inns) in the countryside where you can spend the night or have a splendid lunch or dinner. It's wise to book ahead for a room in a hotel and essential to make a reservation for a meal or a room at a *relais*.

Accommodations at an expensive inn will cost about $60 per night in a double for two; moderate, about $50; and inexpensive, about $30. A meal at an expensive restaurant will run about $40 or more per person for dinner, including tip, without wine; moderate, about $25; and inexpensive, about $12.

GHENT

St. Jorishof – Built in 1228, this is believed to be the oldest hotel in Northern Europe. It has a Gothic hall with a huge chimney. The interior is hung with the pennants of various clubs and organizations ranging from the medieval guilds to the Rotary Club. Charles Quint and Napoleon Bonaparte have stayed here. Botermarkt 2 (phone: 23-67-91). Moderate.

BRUGES

Duc de Bourgogne – There are only 9 small rooms in this hotel, but the restaurant is the best in Bruges. Both rooms and restaurant are nearly always booked full.

The dining room extends over a canal, and the area is most impressive at night, when it's floodlit. Near the entrance hall is the medieval version of a small cocktail lounge, where you wait for your table; its walls are hung with tapestries of saints and knights, the chairs and tables are heavy mahogany, and there is a huge fireplace. In the restaurant, order the North Sea fish and, if it's spring or summer, the asparagus. Huidenvettersplaats 12 (phone: 33-20-38). Expensive.

ANTWERP

Sir Anthony Van Dijck – You walk through a cobblestone passage to reach the ancient building that houses the restaurant. The combination of fine food and a dramatic setting make this worth a stopover, especially for lunch. Closed Saturday afternoons and Sundays. 16 Oude Koornmarkt Vlaaikensgang (phone: 231-61-70). Expensive.

The Ardennes

South of Brussels is a world so different from Flanders that it's hard to believe they are part of the same country. This is the Ardennes — Shakespeare's Forest of Arden in *As You Like It* — stretching across the south of Belgium. The Ardennes extend into the three provinces of Namur, Liège, and Luxembourg (not to be confused with the Grand Duchy of Luxembourg, a separate country). It is gentle, green, and somehow a bit mysterious compared with the North, a countryside of legends and spirits, abbeys and castles. It is also the place to go if you want to spend your vacation skiing, hunting, hiking, or camping.

You can make a loop through the region by driving southeast of Brussels through Liège, Spa, and Malmédy, south to Bastogne and Arlon, west to Bouillon, north to Namur, west to Mons, and finally north back to Brussels.

BRUSSELS: For a detailed report on the city and its hotels and restaurants, see *Brussels,* THE EUROPEAN CITIES.

    En Route from Brussels – Heading southeast to Liège, on the left you will pass Catholic University in Louvain, Belgium's oldest university, founded in 1425. Erasmus is one of its distinguished alumni. Architecturally, it ranges from the fifteenth to the twentieth century. The town was badly damaged during the two world wars, but the fifteenth-century Town Hall and St. Peter's Church are worth visiting. Like Oxford, Louvain has become somewhat commercial and industrial but basically preserves its clerical-academic serenity.

LIÈGE: Seventy miles (112 km) east of Brussels is Liège, Belgium's third largest city and a gateway to the Ardennes. Liège has been a prosperous industrial town since coal was discovered here in 1198. Most of the citizens are shopkeepers, artisans, miners, or steelworkers. The nickname for a Liègeois is "coalhead" (not an insult) — a stubborn, hotheaded, goodhearted fellow. Coal is much appreciated as a source of butter and eggs in Liège: The grisly looking opening of a mine shaft is called, with a note of irony, a *jolie fleur* ("pretty flower"); all coal mines, however, are closed.

The streets of Liège are laid out as fitfully and capriciously as the local temperament, so don't plan your time here too closely. You should enjoy what you find, however. The skyline shows over 100 church spires, and the River Meuse winds its way through every quarter, which means you will often find yourself going over one nice little bridge or another. Liège has one of Belgium's most important universities, the University of Liège, so the café life is well catered to.

On Mont St. Martin are some particularly fine houses, with winding outdoor stairways and hidden gardens. The place du Marché and the place St.-Lambert are the heart of the city. The eleventh-century Palace of the Prince Bishops (who ruled Liège until the eighteenth century) has two great courtyards. Each of the capitals atop the 60 columns of the portico is different from the others. Since the nineteenth century, the building has been used as the Palace of Justice.

One of Belgium's greatest art treasures is the baptismal font by Reinier van Hoei in the church of St. Barthélemy, made of tin-coated brass sometime between 1107 and 1118. The church of St. James is an old abbey with five Renaissance stained-glass windows and an exquisite north portal. At the church of the Holy Cross are a twelfth-century enamel reliquary and an eighth-century key of St. Hubert. St. Hubert, the patron saint of hunters, established his bishopric at Liège in the eighth century; he is a very important saint in the Ardennes.

The city has a wide assortment of museums, but make sure to see the Museum of Walloon Life; in a seventeenth-century convent, it has, among other things, an amazing puppet collection; closed Mondays. There's also the Curtius Museum, with its unique glass and crystal collection, which displays the history of glassmaking; closed Tuesdays. At the theater on the rue Féronstrée, marionettes (large, intricate puppets) perform in Liège folklore pageants, religious plays, and sketches based on contemporary gossip. The characters include Tschantches (a Liègeois Punch), biblical characters, and historical figures like Charlemagne and Napoleon. If you understand enough French to try to decipher Liègeois, the local dialect, you will appreciate a real folk art that is still very much alive. Liège is famous for its manufacture of guns, and the Museum of Weapons, with 8,000 pieces, is considered the best firearms collection in the world; closed Mondays.

Before leaving, be sure to visit the Citadel; you can climb the 407 steps to the top or drive there. You will get a splendid view of the city and the surrounding countryside.

On the Sunday following St. George's Day in the neighboring town of Visé, the guild of crossbowmen, the Ancient Arquebusiers, wearing starched shirtfronts and stovepipe hats, celebrate St. George (the patron of archers) with a mass, procession, and an archery contest.

In the village of Rutten on May 1, the sanguine *Play of St. Evermeire* is performed in an orchard by the townspeople, just as it has for over 1,000 years; it portrays the story of St. Evermeire and his fellow pilgrims, who were massacred by highwaymen in 699.

And you surely won't want to miss the Pageant of the Flying Cat in the town of Verviers on the third Sunday in June. An annual publicity stunt for the town, it commemorates the grand experiment of a chemist named Saroléa in 1641. Saroléa wanted to see if he could get his cat to fly, so he attached pig bladders filled with air to the luckless beast and dropped it off the tower of St. Remacle's Cathedral. Naturally, it plummeted like a stone — although it landed in good enough condition to scamper away and, being a wise cat, never returned. Every year the experiment is repeated (with a toy cat) at the place du Martyr at 5:30 PM, accompanied by a triumphal procession with giant, confetti-belching cat floats. In this technological era the cat does fly successfully, since the bladders are now filled with helium.

En Route from Liège – Drive 24 miles (38 km) southeast to Spa, the site of the thermal spring from which all the spas in the world take their name. During the eighteenth and early nineteenth centuries, Spa was a favorite resort for the European nobility and royalty. The oldest spring is named for Peter the Great, who used to make his way from Russia to take the waters. Nowadays Spa is visited more for its grand hotels and wooded environs rather than the curative power of its waters.

Drive southeast to Malmédy, where the countryside is covered with alpine flowers in the summer and meadows and dense pine forests line the road. During the winter, this is a popular ski area. Malmédy, a monastery city founded in the seventh century, is best known today for its pre-Lenten carnival, which includes mass folk dancing and satirical plays in the local dialect. Nearby is the château of Reinhardstein, the ancestral home of the Metternichs and a completely furnished feudal stronghold.

BASTOGNE: Drive southwest, pick up the Liège road, and go directly south to Bastogne, 100 miles (160 km) from Brussels.

This is the site of the Battle of the Bulge, where the Nazis made their last stand as the Allies pushed toward Germany. The Germans launched their counteroffensive on December 16, 1944; the Americans holding Bastogne were hampered by snow and fog, which prevented any air support. On December 22 the Germans demanded an American surrender. The American General Anthony McAuliffe spurned their ultimatum with a single word: "Nuts." The next day the skies cleared, and Allied planes again took to the air; the Third Army, under General George Patton, counterattacked and reached Bastogne on December 26. Early in January, the First Army arrived from the north. By the end of the month, the Germans had been pushed back behind their own frontier, losing 120,000 men.

McAuliffe and his curt reply became part of Belgian folklore. There is a bust of him in town as well as a few derelict tanks scattered around the outskirts, mostly bearing the word "Nuts"; there is a "Nuts" Museum in town. The Mardasson American war memorial is laid out in the shape of a five-pointed star and inscribed with the names of the home states of the fallen GIs. Across from the Mardasson, also in the shape of a five-pointed star, is the Bastogne Historical Center, with the largest collection of Bastogne battle relics in the world, as well as a film of the battle in four languages.

ARLON: Continue south to Arlon, the capital of the province of Luxembourg, where the great Roman road from Rheims intersected the road from the north. While the site of Arlon is the oldest settlement in Belgium, most of the buildings are new. The Archaeology Museum has a wealth of Gallo-Roman artifacts; the Church of St. Donat is built on the site of the castle of the counts of Arlon, where Richard Lion-Hearted set out for the Crusades. The church's terrace commands a sweeping view of the valley of the River Semois and Luxembourg, Germany, and France.

BOUILLON: Swing west to Bouillon, the home of Godfrey of Bouillon, a hero of the First Crusade and first king of Jerusalem. Looking out from his castle, it is easy to understand why whoever held this spot ruled the surrounding countryside: You can see a single figure approaching for miles in every direction. Be sure to see the Hall of Justice inside, with its gallows, and take a walk along the battlements (open daily, March through November).

En Route from Bouillon – Leave some time for hiking in the Ardennes and the Belgian Lorraine as you travel in this entire southeastern region. You can explore the densely wooded plateau country north of the River Semois all the way to Liège and the steep gorges and lush wild flowers of the Belgian Lorraine south of Arlon. Bring some sturdy shoes or boots, a compass, a light jacket or heavy sweater, and perhaps a camera. It's easy to get lost in this rolling landscape, so either stick to the trail markings or know where you are at all times — and beware of marshes after dark. The mountain peaks go to two thousand feet, and the views are spectacular.

As you drive north, you'll be in the grotto district, where stalagtites and stalagmites stretch from floor to ceiling in underground caverns. The most spectacular is the grotto of Han-sur-Lesse, which was sacred to a local prehistoric civilization.

North of Han-sur-Lesse, in the valley of the River Meuse, is the town of Annevoie, the site of one of Belgium's most beautiful castles. The Castle of Annevoie is relatively small and cozy, more like an eighteenth-century manor house than a fortress. Its gardens are often compared with those of Versailles, but in fact the gardens of Annevoie are prettier and more human. There are fountains, pools, cascades, and canals, one after another, between avenues of trees and flowers. The castle is closed from September until Easter; the gardens are closed from November until April.

Namur is 20 miles (32 km) north, at the junction of the Sambre and Meuse rivers, a neat little city of seventeenth-century brick homes. Since the days of Julius Caesar, it has been blasted by one army after another. Louis XIV and William III of Orange fought for it; in both world wars the Germans sacked it and set fire to it. Yet many of its historic treasures have survived. Be sure to visit the House of the Sisters of Notre-Dame (closed Tuesdays), with its magnificent treasury of art and relics. In particular, note the work of Hugo d'Oignies, who embellished his crosses and icons with figures of animals of the region.

Namur also has its own casino.

THE MONS AREA: Mons lies west of Namur along the River Sambre; this region is an essential stop before you make your way back to Brussels.

Shrove Tuesday (before Lent) is celebrated in Belgium's usual splashy and improbable style in the town of Binche, near Mons. In a noisy carnival procession, the revelers, called Gilles, wearing bells, green glasses, and ostrich-plumed hats, perform rhythmic dances while marching and pelt the surging crowd with oranges. The onlookers then join in an increasingly frenzied circle dance with the Gilles. It is said that this pageant somehow portrays the Spanish conquest of the Aztecs in the New World, with the Gilles playing the Indians, hurling gold (oranges) at the Spaniards. However, while the fruit is flying, the anthropology of it probably makes very little difference to the Binchois.

In Jumet, around July 21, an observance honors St. Mary Magdalene and celebrates the town's deliverance from the plague, dating from the epidemic of the 1380s. The procession begins solemnly until the chosen moment, when a messenger announces that the plague has ended because of their prayers to St. Mary; at this point, the entire parade, including the decorous clergy, break into a jubilant dance. In Belgian folk rites, the popular conscience exorcises the terrors and deliverances of the last 1,000 years to show the proper respect for fate so disaster will not strike again.

BELOEIL: It is a short drive from Mons to the castle of Beloeil, the proper culmination of this tour. For at least 10 centuries it has belonged to the same family of the prince of Ligne. The castle is virtually a museum of furniture, tapestry, paintings, sculpture, and porcelain. The family can trace its ancestry to the seventh century; the portraits in the castle are a history of Europe. The treasures of the house include memorabilia from Peter the Great and Catherine II of Russia and a lock of Marie Antoinette's hair. The formal gardens, laid out in the seventeenth century, include a lake and tree-lined avenues and cover nearly 300 acres. There, among the flowers of the centuries, you may hope to lose yourself before finding your way home. Closed from October until April.

BEST EN ROUTE

All the major cities and towns you visit in Belgium have comfortable hotels and first-rate restaurants. There are also several good *relais* (inns) in the countryside where you can spend the night or have a splendid lunch or dinner. It's wise to book ahead for a room in a hotel and essential to make a reservation for a meal or a room at a *relai.*

Expensive accommodations will cost about $60 per night in a double for two; moderate, about $50; and inexpensive, about $30. A good meal in an expensive place will run $40 or more per person for dinner, including tip, without wine; moderate, $25; and inexpensive, $12.

LIÈGE

La Commanderie – A command post of the Knights Templar during the Middle Ages, this is now a small inn (12 rooms) with an excellent restaurant. The old stone buildings are in a private park a short drive southwest of Liège. Closed Wednesdays except in summer, and most of January. 28 rue Joseph Pierco, Villers-le-Temple (phone: 51-17-01). Expensive.

MALMÉDY

Trôs Marets – Once a private house, this 11-room inn is surrounded by pine forests and has food that lives up to the lush setting. 1 rue de Mont (phone: 77-79-17). Expensive.

EREZÉE

Auberge du Val d'Aisne – Near Erezée, some 6 miles (10 km) west of the Liége road. Though the rooms are rustic, the nouvelle cuisine served at this 300-year-old inn is very fine; try the wild mushroom salad and the trout. From the cozy dining room, guests can gaze out over farmlands and a stream. It's worth a stop for the food alone. 15 rue Moulin, Fanzel (phone: 49-92-08). Moderate.

BASTOGNE

Hostellerie du Prieuré de Conques – Between Bastogne and Bouillon on the banks of the Semois, this magnificent eighteenth-century priory is now a small hotel. Route de Florenville 176, Herbeumont (phone: 41-14-17). Expensive.

Auberge du Moulin Hideux – This inn, an old mill that serves some of the best food in Belgium, can be your base for Bastogne, Bouillon, and Annevoie (if you can afford it). There is a little pool by the mill where you can select the trout that will be on your plate for lunch. Even if you don't book one of its cozy bedrooms, try to have a meal; it is worth any inconvenience you may encounter getting here. 1 Route de Dohan, Noirefontaine (phone: 46-70-15). Expensive.

NAMUR

L'Air Pur – This hotel, off the road to Namur, has comfortable rooms but no atmosphere inside. Outside, the view of the valley of the Ourthe is dazzling, and the food is excellent. 1½ miles (2 km) from Houffalize. Route de Houffalize 11, La Roche-en-Ardenne (phone: 41-10-97). Expensive.

Exploring Bulgaria

Bordered by Romania, Yugoslavia, Greece, Turkey, and the Black Sea, Bulgaria is 325 miles wide and 250 miles long — about the size of Maine and New Hampshire put together — and one of the countries sharing the Danube River. Though it has a population of about 9 million, Bulgaria is the smallest Eastern European country, with an ancient history that predates even that of Crete.

Bulgaria is the rose capital of the world, exporting more than 95% of the world's supply of rose attar. It is credited with the discovery of yogurt, and its people are among the most long-lived anywhere in the world. Two Bulgarian monks, St. Cyril and St. Methodius, evolved the Cyrillic alphabet, now used by the Bulgarians, the Russians, and the Ukrainians. In antiquity, the legendary Orpheus sang of Bulgaria's flower-covered meadows, the imposing Balkan and Rhodope massifs, and the deep forests of pine and walnut.

Bulgaria was once a part of ancient Thrace and Moesia, and its history, which spans some fifty centuries, is very much in evidence at the various Thracian burial mounds. In 1977 an exhibit of Thracian gold, collected from 90 Bulgarian museums, toured the world, dazzling millions. Of the pieces displayed, 60% had been dug up in the last 10 years, indicating that the study of history and an awareness of national heritage are alive and well here.

In the ninth century, Bulgaria was the cradle of Slav literature; in the fourteenth century, when its arts and world trading flourished, it became the most powerful country in southeastern Europe largely because of its borders on the Black, Aegean, and Adriatic seas. Bulgaria was the envy of its neighbors, which led to its invasion and conquest by the Ottomans in 1396. Through the next 500 years, the Bulgarians tenaciously managed to hold on to their culture through an underground network of monasteries — sacrosanct even to the Turks — where artists and writers were sheltered, producing paintings, books, frescoes, icons, carvings, and musical scores. Today, 150 of these monasteries remain, the most famous of which is Rila.

In 1876 the Great People Uprising occurred, and although it was cruelly crushed, it provoked a larger conflict — the Russo-Turkish War of 1877, known in Bulgarian history as the War of Liberation. An independent state was established with strong bonds to Russia; in 1978 Bulgaria celebrated 100 years of independence. An interesting footnote is that the Bulgarian-Russian connection was well established long before the Russian Revolution, so the ties of the two countries are based not so much on ideology (although Bulgaria is a Soviet satellite) as on traditional friendship.

The first Bulgarian route starts with the capital, Sofia, on the western plain and climbs through the surrounding pine-forested mountains (with the beautiful Rila monastery), then runs south and east to Plovdiv and Bachkovo, the historic center of the country. The second route starts in Varna, Bulgaria's main port on the Black Sea, and discusses the new luxury resorts that dot the coastline.

Sofia and the Mountains

This route skirts the country's major ski resorts and takes you into the Rila Mountains, the highest range on the Balkan Peninsula and the fourth highest in Europe. The route ends in the Thracian plains. This 200-mile (322-km) stretch plunges you into the heart of the country's dramatic and cultural past. While the asphalt roads are good (as they are throughout Bulgaria), go slowly to catch the elusive and mysterious notes of ancient history.

SOFIA: In the middle of the Balkan Peninsula, Sofia is the 5,000-year-old capital of Bulgaria and one of the most interesting cities in Eastern Europe. Nestled in a valley and circled by the granite slopes of Mt. Vitoša (where skiing is less than a half-hour away), it is known as the Greenest City in Europe because of its 80 beautifully spaced parks. This ancient capital, with a population over a million, clusters most of its hotels, department stores, outdoor markets, memorials, churches, theaters, and opera houses in a downtown area that can be seen on foot, making it an easy and pleasant city to explore on your own. "Ever Growing, Never Old" is the motto of Sofia, inscribed on its coat of arms. The city traces its beginnings to the fourth century BC, when it was settled by the Thracians, who left the country its beautiful gold treasures.

Sofia has gone through several name changes. Under the Thracians it was called Serdi. The Romans, who conquered the city in AD 809, called it Sredets, meaning "middle" or "center." The Greeks who ruled for a time renamed it Serdica, and in the fourteenth century it became known as Sofia. These various settlers left their imprint on the city, creating a strange and exciting mix of Byzantine, Roman, Greek, and Turkish architecture, all of which blends harmoniously with more modern hotels, department stores, and government offices. Sofia is a cosmopolitan city; besides many colleges and libraries, it has theaters, museums, and major art galleries, displaying the fine art of contemporary Bulgarian masters. Bulgaria is also known for opera, and there are two fine opera houses here. Dancing is very close to the Bulgarian heart, and no visit could be complete without a stop at one of the folklore restaurants where you'll find young men and women in their blue and red sequined costumes kicking up their heels.

While English is spoken in the major hotels and restaurants, visitors are confronted with the Cyrillic alphabet, making it a little difficult to know where you are at all times. A good map of the city will solve any problems. Your first stop should be at Balkantourist, 1 Vitoša Blvd. (phone: 84-131, ext. 284); the staff can provide you with maps of the city and country as well as brochures, guides, tours, and even a translation of the Cyrillic alphabet into English, which you will find useful. You can also take a Balkantourist half-day motorcoach tour with a bilingual guide or hire a guide for a walking tour. From then on you'll be completely oriented and able to explore the city on your own. Use the Old World *Balkan Hotel* as a focal point, even if you don't stay there, because it's the dead center of town.

The heart of Sofia is Lenin Square, where Vitoša Boulevard meets Georgi Dimitrov Boulevard as they cross the end of Largo Square. The *Balkan Hotel* faces the TZOUM department store across the flower beds, ablaze with color. Between the hotel and the

TZOUM is an underground passage, open in the middle, with a mini–shopping center and a coffee shop decorated with bright umbrellas. While digging this underpass, the excavators unearthed Roman ruins that are now an integral part of the new passage, encased in glass.

Immediately behind the hotel (indeed, partly surrounded by it) is Sofia's most ancient building, the Church of St. George, built by the Romans in the third century, restored much later, and containing three layers of eleventh- to fifteenth-century frescoes.

As you go toward Russki Boulevard, notice the ocher road tiles that make this street distinctive as well as the animated traffic police controlling pedestrian and vehicle flow with ballet-like performances.

The Ninth of September Square (on your way) is dominated by the block-long marble mausoleum of Georgi Dimitrov, Bulgaria's well-loved prime minister. Watched over by two uniformed soldiers, there is a changing of the guards on the hour here rivaling that of London's Buckingham Palace. Behind the mausoleum are the city gardens, a perfect place to sit and watch the people. On the other side of Russki Boulevard is the former Royal Palace of the King, now the National Gallery of Painting and Sculpture and the Ethnographical Museum, both worth seeing.

Continuing down Russki Boulevard, you'll notice the first of many onion-domed Orthodox churches on your left. Along this street you can buy some of Bulgaria's best leathergoods, baskets, and jewelry. Two shops of note are the *Bulgarian Committee of Artists* at No. 6 and the *Souvenir Shop* at No. 4.

Russki Boulevard leads to the modern six-story *Sofia Grand Hotel,* which forms a crescent on the Square of the National Assembly and faces a huge statue of Alexander II (called the Czar Liberator because he was czar when Bulgaria gained its independence). Opposite the statue is the Parliament Building. Have a glass of Bulgarian wine or a cup of coffee on the terrace of the *Sofia Grand* and be sure you are well rested before taking in the next — and most glorious — sight in the city: the magnificent Alexander Nevsky Cathedral. Built in 1912 as a memorial to the Russians, the cathedral, with its gold-leafed dome visible from high in the air, has a crypt open to the public every day but Tuesday. It contains a beautifully displayed, remarkable collection of icons and church regalia.

If you keep walking along Ruski Boulevard, on your right you come to the great Park of Freedom, with a zoo and a number of stadiums. Opposite are the college buildings of Sofia University. As you stroll around, look up often to catch glimpses of Mt. Vitosha's snow-tipped peaks looming over the city.

Sofia is most crowded during its Music Weeks (May 24–June 15), when it is filled with music competitions, concerts, chamber music, and opera. Also, on the first day of Lent is the Koukeri Festival, somewhat similar to Rio's Carnival and definitely worth seeing. For something a little different, try to see a performance at the *Central Puppet Theater* (14 Gurko St.; phone: 88-54-16).

Boyana and its church make a pleasant half-day excursion from Sofia. Leave on the road to Athens and turn left over the tramlines up a road marked "To Boyana and Kopitoto." The road climbs steadily but easily through Boyana village, where you turn left to visit the famous Boyana Church, hidden in the trees and only about 10 minutes from the center of Sofia. The church, open daily, may only be entered by six people at a time because the temperature and humidity have to be strictly controlled to preserve the murals that completely cover the walls and ceiling. Painted by an unknown Boyana master in the 1200s, they are among the oldest murals in Bulgaria, depicting real people like King Constantine and Queen Irene. Back in the village, you go up the hill again to a fork in the road, where you turn right to get to the *Kopitoto Hotel* and restaurant, with wonderful views of Sofia. You can also continue farther to the *Golden Bridge Restaurant,* just above a dramatic formation of huge boulders.

En Route from Sofia – Heading southwest, you'll find the Rila Monastery 75 miles (121 km) from Sofia. Leave early in the day so you can enjoy Rila before proceeding to Plovdiv, which has better accommodations. Leave Sofia on the road for the Greek frontier and Thessaloniki. It's an easy route mostly through open rolling country, with the Rila Mountains beginning to appear on your left. In about 40 miles (65 km) you'll come to Stanke Dimitrov, where you turn left. On your way, you can visit the thermal hot springs of Sapareva Banja before continuing another 16 miles (25 km) and turning left for the monastery.

Here the road starts to wind and climb. The hills are thickly wooded, and the valley falls away below. Driving through these dark pine forests, you cross a bubbling brook, turn a bend, and high up, on the side of the mountain, you see an imposing stone wall over 80 feet high — your first sight of the Rila Monastery.

RILA: Founded in the ninth century by John of Rila, who fled the excesses of court life to found a hermitage, the monastery has always been the cultural shrine of Bulgaria, the defense of its cultural values against the pressures of the Ottomans. Destroyed several times, it was rebuilt in its present form after a devastating fire in 1833. Only Hrelyu's stone tower, built in 1335, remains of the ancient monastery; it dominates the huge inner courtyard of the four-story, eccentrically shaped building.

Behind the imposing gates, the inside courtyard is an amazing scenario of delicate architecture, brightly painted porches, winding staircases, beautiful arches, frescoed walls, and a rectangular courtyard paved with slate. Look for the Chapel of Transfiguration, with fourteenth-century mural paintings, on the top floor and the Monastery Church in the courtyard, with its lovely wood carvings and murals. The monastery houses a museum containing hundreds of manuals, Bibles written on sheepskin, icons, old weapons, coins, and a crucifix on which are carved 140 scenes with 1,500 figures — each no larger than a grain of rice — representing the life work of one monk. For the practical-minded, there's a vast ancient kitchen (with a flue 62 feet high) that once catered to the brisk pilgrim trade.

To get to Plovdiv, you have to return to Stanke Dimitrov and take a crossroad via Samekov-Borovett to get to the main road to Plovdiv, International Highway 5.

PLOVDIV: Bulgaria's second largest city, Plovdiv (pop. 261,732) was founded in 342 BC. It is the capital of the Thracian Plain and a gateway to the Rhodope Mountains.

By day, Plovdiv is a bustling, modern city; at night, it turns into a stroller's paradise — quiet and tranquil. Divided by the Maritsa River, Plovdiv (which used to be called Trimontium because it's built on three hills — Nebet Tepe, Djambaz, and Taxim Tepe) boasts an old section reached by climbing hundreds of stone steps. At the top you first see the remains of a Roman amphitheater, where chariot races were held. (You'd be well advised to wear "sensible shoes" up here; after the climb up, you've still got to negotiate the ancient cobblestone streets. Going through the Hissar Kapiya gate of Pavel Kourtovich and Strumma streets, you enter a world of exquisite Renaissance and baroque houses. Built during the seventeenth century, their facades are decorated with eaves in the form of waves and bay windows overhanging far into the streets, making the houses look top-heavy. The overhanging bays were a method of extending the house without impinging on pedestrian space in busy thoroughfares.

At the *Crafts Carshiya* (Bazaar) on Strumma Street is a group of five restored houses in which ten workshops sell handmade tufted rugs, embroideries, copper vessels, and carvings. You can also visit the Kouyoumdjioglou House (2 Dr. Chomakov St.), now an ethnographic museum with extensive displays of rare Thracian gold treasures. More gold artifacts are exhibited at the Archaeological Museum (Suedíneniyé Sq.). A nice ending to the tour is a stop at the open-air market for some peaches and cherries, typical native fruits. You can eat these comfortably ensconced on one of the terraces overlooking the city.

BACHKOVO: The Bachkovo Monastery is 18 miles (28 km) from Plovdiv on the old Roman road connecting it to the Aegean coast. This is Bulgarian wine country; you'll find both red and white wines, the best this side of France. The monastery complex is on the right bank of the Chaya River. Seen from the road, the monastery looks like an ancient fortress with two courtyards; in the center of each is a cruciform church. Founded in the eleventh century, the walls of this massive building are decorated with frescoes of exceptional quality. The main Church of the Holy Virgin has rare, silver-clad icons and a wooden iconostasis of the finest workmanship.

BEST EN ROUTE

Bulgaria is one of the most inexpensive places to vacation in Europe. Double rooms are around $60 per night in the expensive places (a little more expensive during festivals), and meals are almost always reasonable. (In the country you'll get more food and wine than you can handle for $10 to $15.) Make hotel reservations in advance.

SOFIA

The Balkan Hotel – A city hotel with Old World ways, in its dining room every table has a small vase of fresh roses. The Turkish coffee is good, but the Bulgarian pastry is better. In the middle of town. 3 Lenin Sq. (phone: 87-65-41). Expensive.

Novotel Europe – This French-built hotel is close to the main railway station. 131-G Dimitrov Blvd. (phone: 31261). Expensive.

Sofia Grand Hotel – This modern hotel has a complex of shops and restaurants and a nightclub. 3 Narodno Sobranie Sq. (phone: 87-88-21). Expensive.

Vitosha New Otani Sophia – This Japanese-built hotel is the most luxurious in Sofia. 100 Anton Ivanov Blvd. (phone: 624-151). Expensive.

Astoria – The best-known discotheque in Sofia. Open from noon to midnight. 3 Stambolijski Blvd. (phone: 88-01-26). Moderate.

Strandja Tavern – This charming restaurant features the rich local cuisine. 19 Lenin Sq. (phone: 88-40-24). Moderate.

BOYANA

Boyansko Hanche Tavern – Near the historic church, this restaurant has delicious specialties and Bulgarian wines. There's also a folk orchestra and a floor show. In town (phone: 56-30-16). Moderate.

RILA

The Rila Restaurant – It's plain and clean and serves excellent Bulgarian food. Try Shopska salad with roasted sweet red peppers, cucumbers, small tomatoes, onions, olive oil and vinegar, topped with mounds of feta cheese. Then have some Tarator soup, made of yogurt, walnuts, garlic, dill, and cucumbers. For the main course, try the grilled or roasted beef, lamb, or pork.

PLOVDIV

Novotel Plovdiv – Another member of the French chain with pleasant accommodations. 2 Zlatyu Boyadjiev St. (phone: 55171). Expensive.

Trimontium – A fine hotel with an Old World atmosphere, first-class accommodations, and a garden. 2 Kapitan Raicho St. (phone: 2-55-61). Moderate.

Bounara – A folk tavern with good food and Bulgarian dancers. 13 Patriarch Eftimi St. (phone: 6066). Moderate.

BACHKOVO

The Bachkovo Monastery Hotel – This is a nice place for an atmospheric, monastic evening. There are campsites here as well as bungalows. Inquire at the monastery or call them for reservations. Inexpensive.

The Bulgarian Black Sea Coast

The Romans called it Pontus Euxinus — the Hospital Sea — but the Turks, who feared its storms, renamed it the Black Sea. Whatever its name, the Black Sea coast of Bulgaria — a 235-mile stretch of sandy beach now boasting numerous hotel colonies — is fast becoming known as the Riviera of Eastern Europe. These modern resorts have sprung up relatively recently (most were built in the last 30 years) and today are visited by tourists from the US, Western Europe, Eastern Europe, and the USSR.

The major coastal town, however, is anything but recent. Varna, now an industrial center, is an ancient port and Bulgaria's main commercial outlet to the sea. Some 290 miles (469 km) from Sofia, Varna is also known as Bulgaria's summer capital and is only a little more than an hour's drive south from the Romanian border. Varna is a perfect starting point for trips up and down the coast as well as for longer excursions across the sea to Istanbul or inland to the eastern monastery towns of Bulgaria.

Varna's original name was Odessos, and remnants of various past cultures are everywhere. Just outside the town are the remains of the Byzantine basilica, but predating this church is a large thermae built by the Romans that still stands in the middle of the city. Before the Romans, the Greeks were the masters here. And before the Greeks, the Thracians, who founded the city in the sixth century BC, left their imprint on the area. Also outside of town is the Aladja Rock Monastery, built in the Middle Ages. Varna's town square evokes yet another period with its cobbled, landscaped, Renaissance flavor.

Tours to the modern resort towns north and south of Varna should be booked through Balkantourist in Sofia (phone: 84-131). For the most part, the hotels are quite similar — modern buildings facing the sea — but the amazing thing about this resort is that in-season hotel accommodations right on the sea, including 3 meals a day, cost from $12 to $28 per person per day. The beach towns are small and generally have uncomplicated layouts. (Unless otherwise noted, the address of a hotel or restaurant is nothing more than the establishment's name.) From Albena, north of Varna, to Nessebur, to the south, the beach towns are all connected by International Highway E95.

ALBENA: The newest of the Black Sea resorts, Albena was named after one of the most attractive female characters in Bulgarian literature. The town caters to a predominantly younger set, who yearly crowds the many hotels, bars, folk taverns, and 4-mile-long beach. You can play tennis or golf or even brush up on your equestrian skills at the riding school. The town hot spot is the *Starobulgarski Stan* nightclub, with an architectural style that recalls old Bulgarian gypsy tents. On the beach, it offers music and floor shows until 2 AM.

ZLATNI PYASSUTSI: Also known as Golden Sands, Zlatni Pyassutsi is about 8 miles (14 km) from Albena and probably the resort most popular with Americans, having often been compared to Long Beach, California. Again, you'll find an abundance of hotels and bars. The favorite here is a nightclub called the *Koukeri*, which has a wonderful view of the ocean and entertainment by the Koukeri Dancers — masked men performing stylized tribal routines.

DROUZHBA: Drouzhba, whose name means "friendship," is only 6 miles (10 km) from Varna. It's one of the older resorts, better suited to low-key revelers, and is the home of the *Grand Hotel Varna,* the most famous of all the Black Sea hotels. Completed in 1977 with a complex of restaurants and nightclubs, it also has two subfloors of spa facilities for exercise, massages, and pearl and mud baths (Cervenoarmeiski Blvd. 4; phone: 61491). If the *Grand Hotel Varna* is too expensive, consider stopping at the *Monastery Cellar,* a nightclub that serves a memorable wine called Monastery Whispers.

SLUNCHEV BRYAG: About 60 miles (96 km) down the coast from Drouzhba, Slunchev Bryag (Sunny Beach) is a 4-mile stretch of sandy shores surrounded by a deciduous forest on three sides. This family resort has day-care facilities and supervised children's activities, which leave parents free to roam into places like *Khan's Tent Tavern,* another tent nightclub on the beach, or the *Pirate Ship,* a restaurant built like a ship and offering Bulgarian specialties and folk entertainment. Between June 15 and 20, you can also visit the nearby town of Bourgas and its international music and folklore festival.

NESSEBUR: The southernmost resort, Nessebur is a vintage seventh-century BC fishing village on a peninsula where ancient Greek churches and wooden fishermen's houses along narrow cobblestone streets take you back in time. Nessebur is an architectural gem and should be included on any Black Sea tour — but just for a visit, not an overnight stay.

Exploring Czechoslovakia

At the geographical center of Europe, Czechoslovakia has been the crossroads over which many different peoples have traveled and the sometimes unwilling recipient of their religious, cultural, and political domination. Much that remains of this involved past has been carefully preserved. Indeed, although Czechoslovakia is quite a small country — a little larger than New York State — it contains some 40,000 monuments, 4,000 castles, and 40 villages where the Gothic, Renaissance, and baroque architecture has been painstakingly protected, down to the cobblestone streets, many of which are still lit by gas.

The country is composed of three areas: the Bohemian plateau in the west, the Moravian lowlands in the center, and mountainous Slovakia in the east. Each region has many historic sights. The territory of Bohemia and Moravia was the center of European culture in the fourteenth century. Renaissance buildings in Prague and the baroque town hall in Plzeň are among the reminders of this age of achievement in art and architecture. In Slovakia, historical monuments date back further, recalling the former presence of Roman legions.

Despite its attention to the past, Czechoslovakia is an advanced country, with some 90% of the population of 15 million involved in commerce and industry and only 10% in agriculture. Czechoslovakian companies produce everything from heavy machinery and Skoda cars to bentwood chairs and famous Bohemian glass. Some 95% of the population is Czech and Slovak, the remainder a mix of Germans, Poles, Hungarians, and Ukrainians. Only 15% of the population lives in cities of more than 100,000 — Prague, the capital and largest city (pop. 1,078,026); Brno, the second largest city (pop. 335,918) and the capital of Moravia; and Bratislava, the third largest city (pop. 335,000) and the capital of Slovakia. The rest of the population inhabits some 10,000 small towns.

This predominantly small-town culture opens up some appealing possibilities for those interested in folk traditions. If you visit in the spring and the summer, you will encounter (indeed, become part of) the numerous folk festivals in the small towns, some of them extravagant events attracting folk enthusiasts from all over the world. Men and women, young and old, dig into their trunks and don hand-embroidered, brightly colored, native costumes, trimmed with lace and ruffles, to perform the rituals of spring and summer. The festivals are a joyous blend of dance and music competitions, maypole dancing, parades of the king, wine tastings, and open-air markets displaying handsome homemade crafts.

Spring and summer are also the most pleasant times for sight-seeing and most sports. Being in the temperate zone, Czechoslovakian springs and summers are warm and sunny, with average May temperatures in the high 50°s F (15° C) and summer temperatures in the high 60s and low 70s F (21° C). Though Czechoslovakia is landlocked, it has thousands of ponds and lakes, many developed for swimming, boating, and fishing. A preponderance of these lakes are in southern Bohemia. In northeastern Bohemia stand the Giant Mountains, while the High Tatras — the highest mountains in the Carpathian chain — rise in Slovakia. This eastern region is a winter resort center popular for its downhill and cross-country skiing, tobogganing, and sleighriding.

Czechoslovakia is an easy country to explore and is well organized to accommodate its many visitors. English is required as a second language in secondary schools, so you will have little difficulty being understood in the better shops, restaurants, and hotels. However, advance hotel reservations are necessary even in the off-season (particularly for stays in smaller towns) because the tourist traffic exceeds the population. Make arrangements through your travel agent or through the Czechoslovakian government office of tourism, Čedok, Prikopy 18, Prague 1 (phone: 22-42-59), or in the US at 10 E 40th St., New York, NY 10017 (phone: 212-689-9720).

The longest of the following three routes links Prague, the national capital, with Bratislava, the capital of Slovakia, passing through Bohemia, Moravia, and Slovakia, seeing the most famous spas, castles, and medieval towns. The remaining routes both start from Poprad, a town in eastern Slovakia. One route heads northwest into the High Tatras mountain resorts. The second runs east of Poprad, taking in the small towns in the Spiš-Gemer Ore Mountains, where the townsfolk carry on the traditions of their ancestors in settings that have changed little over the generations.

Prague to Bratislava

This 227-mile (365-km) route links Bohemia, Moravia, and Slovakia — Czechoslovakia's three major regions — and takes in the country's capitals as well as its most famous spas, castles, and medieval towns. To follow the route, head northwest out of Prague, circle through Plzeň, south to Tábor, east to Brno, and farther south to Bratislava. You can spend several days touring, for all of the places along the route have reasonable overnight accommodations.

Since you will be passing through the three distinct areas of this country, be alert to subtle changes in traditions and customs. These regional differences will be most obvious at the folk festivals, held during the spring and summer in the small towns. You'll find that the cuisine also differs: In Bohemia, try the homemade dumpling soups accompanied by Pilsner beer. In the lake country of southern Bohemia, keep an eye out for menus offering fresh trout and carp. In Moravia, be sure to sample the local wines.

The highlights of the route include the renowned spa of Karlovy Vary; the

Burgher's Brewery in Plzeň, where Pilsner beer has been produced since the Middle Ages; the preserved historic town of Tábor; the formidable Spilberk Castle in Brno; and the capital of Slovakia, Bratislava.

PRAGUE: For a complete description of the city and its restaurants and hotels, see *Prague,* THE EUROPEAN CITIES.

    En Route from Prague – Heading northwest for 2 hours along Route 6, you pass through some of Bohemia's loveliest countryside — deep forests and rich farmlands, where hops are grown. Hillside castles dot the landscape.

KARLOVY VARY: In the narrow valley at the juncture of the Teplá and Ohře rivers lies Karlovy Vary, the most famous of Czechoslovakia's spas. It has 12 developed hot springs, and more than 100 springs in all. Legend has it that Karlovy Vary (Carlsbad in German) was discovered in 1358 by Charles IV — actually by the dog of Charles IV, who stumbled into a hot spring while chasing a stag. Today, the stag is still the symbol of the spa.

The huge baroque spa building is reserved for guests taking the waters, but visitors can stroll along the ornate Colonnade, built in 1871, following in the footsteps of kings and queens and such notables as Beethoven, Goethe, and Mozart. The area still retains an elegant atmosphere.

The most luxurious hotel here is the *Grandhotel Moskva Pupp,* built in 1898, whose French restaurant is first rate. A stay at the new *Thermal Hotel* can also be memorable: It has restaurants, a movie theater, and a huge swimming pool open to the public. Concerts, theater, film festivals, tennis, and golf are also available.

While you're visiting the spa, indulge in a few Karlovy Vary rites: Taste the hot bitter waters from a special mug with a long clay straw. Buy a box of *karlovarske oplatky* — delicious large round chocolate and vanilla wafers. Order Becherovka, a liqueur also known jokingly as "the thirteenth spring." Visit the world-famous *Moser Glassworks* and the *Horní Slavkov* and *Stará Role* chinaworks, where you can buy some of the fine Czechoslovakian wares.

    En Route from Karlovy Vary – Stop at the regal Kynžvart, the former summer residence of Count Metternich, the nineteenth-century Austrian statesman. Constructed in baroque and Empire styles, the château contains valuable collections of furniture, art, china, glassware, and arms.

MARIÁNSKÉ LÁZNĚ: Established in 1808, this spa (previously called Marienbad) was a favorite with such notables as Richard Wagner and King Edward VII. It is nicely designed, with parks and colorful facades lining Gottwald Square. Spa yellow, the soft yellow of the exteriors of the major buildings and hotels, can be seen here and at spas throughout the country. Of the 40 springs here, the most well known are Křížový, Lesni, and Rudolph. When you're not soaking, you can take advantage of the spa's many other recreational facilities: movies, concerts, a golf course, tennis courts, a pool, cafés, restaurants, and nightclubs. Take a side trip of 10 miles (16 km) east to Teplá to see the monastery where the spa began. The monastery, founded in 1193, houses an impressive collection of rare books, manuscripts, and prints.

PLZEŇ: With large factories and a smoky skyline, this city of 150,000 contrasts sharply with the other small Bohemian towns en route. But it is worth a visit to see the Burgher's Brewery, which has produced Pilsner Urquell beer since the Middle Ages. Begin the tour at the Brewing Museum, in an old brewing house on Roosevelt Street. The museum has a fine collection of beer mugs, jugs, pewter tankards, and glasses produced during the last six centuries. Also on display is an iron collar — the collar of dishonor — worn by brewers whose beer didn't make the grade. The town's beer stewards will tell you that Pilsner should be drunk from a sparkling clean glass accompanied by sharp cheese, smoked meats, and dark bread. And they're right.

Náměstí Republiky, the square in the center of town, is lined with houses that have Renaissance, baroque, Empire, and neo-Gothic facades. Two particularly lovely Gothic buildings are St. Bartholomew's Church, with its 340-foot tower, and the Abbey Church of the Virgin Mary.

TÁBOR: Set on the River Lužnice amid the forests and lakes of the South Bohemia valley, this Romanesque town is one of the six historical reservations in Czechoslovakia. Tábor was the site of the peasants' revolt led by John Huss in 1415 against crushing taxes and a corrupt Roman Catholic Church. Huss was tried as a heretic and burned at the stake, but the Hussite struggle continued for the next 20 years. Today the modern Czechoslovakian Church claims to continue in his tradition.

Tábor is now a modern, growing town of 20,000, whose historic area is of greatest interest. An equestrian statue of military leader Jan Zizka, who commanded the Hussite forces, stands in the middle of Zizka Square. The most notable building is Town Hall, which houses a museum documenting the Hussite movement. Underneath the museum are catacombs of tunnels and cellars, built as living quarters and later used to store beer and wine. The narrow, winding streets off Zizka Square, so laid out to confuse attackers, lead to the Old Town. Originally surrounded by ramparts and bulwarks, the Old Town now has only one bulwark remaining. Also standing is Bechyne Gate, with its Kotnov Tower, which was used as a brewery in the seventeenth century.

If you want to spend some time here, stay at the *Jordan Hotel,* named for nearby Lake Jordan where you can swim or fish.

BRNO: The capital of Moravia and the second largest city in Czechoslovakia, Brno combines historic and contemporary Czechoslovakia. Here you'll find castles, museums, a baroque outdoor market, fairgrounds, a racetrack, and some of the hottest night spots around.

The Spilberk Castle, which dates to 1287, was built as a fortress to resist invaders and later made a prison; it is deeply engraved on the collective conscience of the country. Here, political dissenters were detained and tortured by the ruling Hapsburgs. During World War II, Nazi forces reopened the prison, and Spilberk became once again a dungeon and death knell for the hapless. Instruments of torture are on display.

The castle restaurant offers a game menu, Moravian wines, and a view of the city. The park outside the castle has covered benches — a pleasant spot to rest.

The main streets in Brno all converge on Freedom Square, which is flanked by splendid baroque and Renaissance homes. From the square you can see Petrov Hill, the site of the Cathedral of Saints Peter and Paul, whose original Romanesque basilica dates from the eleventh century and withstood the siege of the Swedes during the Thirty Years' War.

From the cathedral, descend the steps to the outdoor Cabbage Market, sprawled over a steep cobblestone hill; you'll find hundreds of tables attended to by peasant men and women selling fruits, vegetables, and a wide variety of handicrafts and kitchen utensils. The market is centered around Parnassas Fountain, which features a baroque sculpture depicting Cerberus, the Watchdog of Hell, and the four continents (its designer, Johann Fisher, was unaware of Australia). Among the other notable buildings are Town Hall and the Gothic Church of St. Jacob, both in Old Town.

Brno's fairground, down the hill and past the railway station, is the site of events all year, highlighted by the Consumers' Fair in April. While here, have lunch at the *Myslivna,* or *Forest House,* reached by crossing a woods on the south side of Svratka River. Try the broiled trout à la Brno.

The city has many first-class hotels, the newest and most convenient of which is the *International.* Its bar, *Interclub,* is one of the most popular night spots in the city.

BRATISLAVA: Rising from the banks of the Danube, this capital of Slovakia was the capital of Hungary from 1541 to 1784, and 17 monarchs were crowned here over the centuries. The renowned French architect Le Corbusier called Bratislava "the crossroads of importance for all Europe." Tracing its history back 4,500 years, Bratislava was a Roman outpost called Posonium; it was later known as Pressburg, its German name, until 1918, when Slovakia was incorporated into the new nation of Czechoslovakia.

Bratislava is a modern city that also boasts some 400 historic buildings, museums, monuments, and castles. Most noteworthy of all is the Bratislava Castle, the thirteenth-century fortress that long guarded the city. Other sites in the Old Town that you shouldn't miss are the Gothic-baroque Old Town Hall; the Primatial Palace with its famous Hall of Mirrors, where Napoleon and Emperor Franz II signed the Peace Treaty of Bratislava in 1805; St. Martin's Cathedral, the scene of many coronations; and the Red Crayfish, a pharmacy museum with a nice collection of apothecary jars. The Slovak National Museum (Vajanského 2) has a special exhibition, "The Development of Man," which traces evolution from primitive times to the present.

If you've been eating the Bohemian and Moravian favorites of pork or roast duck with dumplings and sauerkraut, you'll find a marked difference in Slovakian food. Its generous use of sour cream, paprika, and barbecued meats echo the cuisine of neighboring Hungary. A few places in town that serve regional specialties are the restaurants in Bratislava Castle; the *Cloister Wine Shop*, Klastorna Pivnica (especially its Detva stuffed steak); and the *Bystrica Café*, a revolving glass disk set on a 270-foot tower over the Slovak National Uprising Bridge, which spans the Danube. The *Koliba*, on Kamzik Hill, is one of the many shepherd's huts scattered throughout Slovakia that serve barbecued meat cooked over open pits, mulled wines, and Tatra tea. Gypsy violinists provide entertainment.

If you are visiting during the late spring or summer, you can take a one-day trip by hydrofoil to Vienna or Budapest.

BEST EN ROUTE

Expect to pay $60 and up per night for a double room in hotels in the expensive range; $40 to $50 in the moderate; and around $30, inexpensive. A dinner for two will cost $30 and up in the expensive range; between $20 and $30 in the moderate; and $10 and under, inexpensive.

KARLOVY VARY

Grandhotel Moskva Pupp – Favored by Europe's "elite," this luxurious, 171-room hotel is in the spa center. Among the facilities are golf, tennis, several restaurants including a fine French one, a bar, nightclub, café, and a terrace during the summer. Mirove náměstí 2 (phone: 22-12-15). Expensive.

Parkhotel Moskva – Right next to the *Grand Moskva*, this old hotel (opened in 1885) has 117 rooms, a French restaurant, and a subdued atmosphere. Mirove náměstí 6 (phone: 22-12-15). Expensive to moderate.

Central – Built in 1910, this hotel has 70 rooms, all with balconies. Restaurant and wine bar. Leninovo náměstí 17 (phone: 25-10-12). Moderate.

MARIÁNSKÉ LÁZNĚ

Esplanade – This first-class 63-room hotel opened in 1916 is near the spa center. The restaurant and café are good, and guests have golf privileges nearby. Karlovarska 434 (phone: 2-1624). Moderate.

Campanella – This small hotel is convenient to the spa center. Karlovarska 434 (phone: 2-1624). Inexpensive.

PLZEŇ

Continental – This first-class hotel in the center of town was built in 1895 and renovated in 1965. It has 52 rooms and a restaurant and wine bar. Zbojnicka 8 (phone: 3-0473). Expensive to moderate.

BRNO

International – This deluxe modern hotel, with 294 rooms, has a good view of Spilberk Castle and the Old Town. Among the facilities are two restaurants serving international and regional specialties, a bar, café, and a lively nightclub. Husova 16 (phone: 2-6411). Expensive to moderate.

Grandhotel – In the center of town, this first-class, 118-room hotel has an excellent restaurant serving Moravian specialties and wines. Tř. 1 Máje (phone: 2-3526). Expensive to moderate.

Slavia – Renovated in 1973, this hotel in the center of town has a garden restaurant. Solniční 15–17 (phone: 2-3711). Moderate.

BRATISLAVA

Devín – In the center of the Old Town, this deluxe modern hotel has 103 rooms and a restaurant, café, wine bar, and terrace. Riečná 4 (phone: 33-08-51). Expensive.

Hotel Kyjev – This fairly new first-class hotel, with 217 rooms, offers all the amenities — a restaurant, café, wine bar, nightclub, sauna, air-conditioned recreation rooms, and shops. Rajská 2 (phone: 5-6341). Expensive.

The High Tatras

Starting in Poprad, this route takes in the nearby resorts of the High Tatras, the highest mountains of the Carpathian range. In fact, the Tatras are not really that high (Mt. Gerlach, the highest, rises only 8,500 feet), but their peaks etch themselves sharply against the skyline. The mountains are popular year round — in the winter for skiing, tobogganing, and sleighing, and in the summer for hiking, boating, fishing, and swimming. The highlights of the route include the large resort center of Starý Smokovec, the beautiful mountain lake Štrbské Pleso, and the best skiing in the area at Tatranská Lomnica.

POPRAD: The route begins here because the airport accommodates flights from Prague, Brno, and Bratislava. Poprad has some interesting sights; among them are the thirteenth-century Gothic Church of St. Egidius, which contains a fresco of a biblical scene with the Tatras Mountains in the background, and the medieval streets of the Old Town, which are lined with shingle-roofed Renaissance buildings.

STARÝ SMOKOVEC: At 3,280 feet, this largest of the resort centers is a complex of chalets, restaurants, and hotels with all facilities for downhill and cross-country skiing. In the summer, mountaineers can climb Mt. Gerlach or take a side trip to the Studenovodske (Cold Water) Falls. A railway leads up to Mt. Hrebienok, a small village with a toboggan run and a beginner's slope with night lighting.

The most luxurious hotel in Starý Smokovec is *Hotel Grand,* which opened in 1898. Starting from the *Grand,* you can hike for 1 mile into the forest to the *Koliba,* or *Shepherd's Hut,* a type of restaurant unique to Slovakia. In this huge A-frame cabin you can dine on meat barbecued over an open pit, mulled wine, and Tatra tea while being serenaded by the violins of Gypsy musicians.

ŠTRBSKÉ PLESO: The scene of the World Championship of Nordic Events in 1970, this year-round resort town is perched over 4,000 feet high in the Tatras. The spectacular mountain lake of Štrbské covers more than 40 acres. On its shore stands the newest and finest of the hotels, *Hotel Patria;* the rooms naturally offer views of the lake or the mountains.

TATRANSKÁ LOMNICA: The most elegant of the resort centers, this village is set in the second highest park in the Tatras. Restaurants and hotels here are open all year; the favorite is *Grandhotel Praha,* which opened in 1905. It offers sleigh rides in the winter and an excursion on the overhead cable railway to Skalnate Pleso (Rocky Lake), 5,255 feet high. The downhill skiing on Lomnica Mountain is the best in the Tatras. The museum of Tatra National Park has excellent exhibits documenting the area's past and its natural history.

BEST EN ROUTE

Expect to pay $60 and up per night for a double room in hotels in the expensive range; $40 to $50 in the moderate; and around $30, inexpensive. A dinner for two will cost $30 and up in the expensive range; between $20 and $30 in the moderate; and $10 and under, inexpensive.

STARÝ SMOKOVEC

Hotel Grand – With a spa yellow exterior, this large alpine chalet is the place to stay. The 103 rooms are first class and the atmosphere is old-fashioned. There's a restaurant and wine bar (phone: 2154). Expensive.

ŠTRBSKÉ PLESO

Hotel Patria – Opened in 1976, this 11-story A-frame hotel has 151 rooms and 6 suites, all with private baths and either mountain or lake views. Among the facilities are restaurants, a café, bar, snack bar, and nightclub (phone: 9-2591). Expensive.

Hotel Panorama – Near Štrbské Lake, this modern, 106-room hotel has a restaurant, café, and game rooms (phone: 9-2111). Moderate.

TATRANSKÁ LOMNICA

Grandhotel Praha – Opened in 1905 and remodeled in 1973, this first-class hotel is the favorite in the area. Its 45 rooms are convenient to ski lifts. There's a restaurant, a wine bar, and a parking lot. A unique *Koliba* — a shepherd's hut restaurant where you can have barbecued meat, mulled wine, and tea — is nearby (phone: 96-76-07). Expensive.

The Spiš

This route links several small towns clustered around the Spiš-Germer Ore Mountains. In these towns you get a glimpse of life as it was centuries ago: People farm, weave, and make pottery using the methods of their ancestors. The Czechoslovakian government supports a cottage industry to keep its arts and crafts alive, and many of the cottages are here in Eastern Slovakia. The highlights of the route include the lovely Gothic town of Levoča, the medieval town of Bardejov, and Hervartov, which has the oldest wooden church in the Carpathians as well as many cottages producing crafts.

POPRAD: This town is the starting point for trips to the Spiš towns. For details on the town, see the Poprad section in the *The High Tatras* route.

LEVOČA: Established in the thirteenth century, this small Spiš town has been classified by an international architectural commission as one of the loveliest Gothic towns in Europe. The town is surrounded by ramparts, and the older section has well-preserved buildings dating from the Middle Ages through the sixteenth and seventeenth centuries.

Laid out around a central square, the town plan still follows the chessboard pattern of its original design. Town Hall (1615) is outstanding, as are the old burghers' houses with arched Gothic entries. The Thurzo House, No. 7, epitomizes the Slovak Renaissance style, with elaborate balconies and loggias characteristic of the Spiš region. The interior of St. James's Church on the main square has magnificent wooden altars. The main altar, carved in limewood by Master Paul of Levoča in 1508, depicts the Last Supper.

BARDEJOV: Tracing its history to the twelfth century, this spa town was declared an urban monument reservation by the government in 1952 because of its notable Gothic and Renaissance architecture.

Bardejov looks medieval, with cobblestone streets, a checkerboard housing pattern, and ramparts built in 1351. The main architectural monuments line the town square: The Gothic church of St. Egidius, built in the fourteenth, fifteenth, and sixteenth centuries, has 11 winged altars, intricately hand-carved pews, and shimmering rose windows. Constructed in 1506 at the dawn of the Renaissance in Slovakia, Town Hall has an interesting blend of Renaissance and Gothic features. Also notable is the Humanistic Gymnasium (1435).

HERVARTOV: Five miles (8 km) southwest of Bardejov, this little Spiš town has the oldest wooden church in the Carpathians, dating to the sixteenth century. Thatch- and shingle-roofed wooden cottages offer displays of native folk art on the walls and lawns.

BEST EN ROUTE

If you plan to visit the Spiš region, check with Čedok in advance for listings of accommodations. The place we have listed below as moderate costs between $40 and $50 per night for a double room, MAP.

POPRAD

Europa – This modest 73-room hotel has two restaurants, a café, wine bar, and a nightclub. Vysoke Tatry Wolkerova (phone: 2-3753). Moderate.

Exploring Denmark

With low, rolling meadows, a countryside virtually littered with stately cas-tles, charming provincial towns, and remnants of a Viking past, this smallest of the Scandinavian countries has all the enchantment of a Hans Christian Andersen fairy tale and the drama of a Shakespeare play. Once you have seen Denmark, it is not difficult to understand how Andersen, the nineteenth-century Danish poet, novelist, and author of children's stories, found his inspiration. But it is also here, at Kronborg Castle in Helsingør, that William Shakespeare installed his brooding Hamlet.

Denmark's 16,600 square miles include the large Jutland Peninsula north of West Germany and some 500 islands, about 100 of which are inhabited. Several of the larger islands form steppingstones across the Baltic Sea from Jutland to Sweden; the easternmost of these is Zealand, where the Danish capital, Copenhagen (København in Danish) is situated. Some of the smaller islands, such as Bornholm and Aerø, have picture-perfect provincial villages with quaint cottages and cobblestone streets. With all its islands, Denmark has 4,600 miles of coastline, although in total size the country is only one-third as large as New York State.

Traditionally an agricultural country, Denmark became more industrial-ized after World War II — accomplishing this in a more tasteful fashion than almost any other country in Europe. The country is also know for its ad-vanced social planning. Social reforms were carried out in Denmark in the eighteenth century (serfdom was abolished in 1788), and a system of folk high schools were set up to reeducate Danish farmers. By the latter half of the nineteenth century, poor peasants were becoming prosperous small farmers. In 1914 and 1915, suffrage was extended to members of the lower classes and to women, and the cooperative movement flourished. During this century, further social welfare legislation has provided a wide variety of government services from day-care centers to housing and care for the elderly.

Denmark's royal family (House of Glücksborg) represents the oldest con-tinuous monarchy in the world. It is descended from the House of Oldenburg, which was established on the Danish throne in 1448, when Christian I became king. However, Denmark became a constitutional monarchy governed by a bicameral parliament (the Rigsdag) in 1849.

Denmark was first occupied 10,000 years ago by people who followed the receding glaciers north. These inhabitants left numerous dolmens, barrows, and other prehistoric monuments that still fascinate us, and archaeological finds from the Old and New Stone Ages and the Bronze Age are displayed in Danish museums. The country's recorded history dates from the time of the Vikings, about AD 800. These seagoing warriors conquered parts of En-gland and Normandy, invaded the Mediterranean, and visited the coast of

North America. From the eighth to the eleventh century, they forged Denmark into the most powerful European empire of the era. The dramatic events and heroic figures of the Viking Age were often inscribed on runic stones, some of which may be seen today in forest clearings and along rural roadways.

The Middle Ages was a period of prosperity for Denmark. Beautiful castles with moats were built during this period. (The later Renaissance castles and manors are frequently noted for their beautifully landscaped gardens and grounds.) In 1397, Queen Margrethe I thought the time propitious to unite Sweden and Norway under the Danish crown. The union with Sweden dissolved in 1523, but Norway and Denmark remained united until 1814, a year after the state went bankrupt.

Nonetheless, the nineteenth century was a golden age for Denmark culturally; there was a flowering of literature and philosophy led by Andersen and Søren Kierkegaard, respectively, and August Bournonville's choreography brought renown to the Royal Danish Ballet. Copenhagen developed into a handsome, sophisticated capital.

Denmark was neutral in World War I, but although it had signed a nonaggression pact with Hitler, it was occupied by German troops from 1940 to 1945. Most of the Jewish population, as well as Jews fleeing from other countries, were helped to escape from the Nazis by the Danes, who also mounted a strong resistance movement.

In the postwar years, Denmark's beer and cheeses, modern furniture, architecture, porcelain, and pottery have won acclaim throughout the world. The Danes, proud of their noble history and their country's well-groomed appearance, have also made tourism an important part of the country's modern economy.

Our first Danish route explores Fyn, the island between the mainland of Jutland and the island of Zealand, with stops at Odense, where Hans Christian Andersen was born, Aerø, a small island with cozy old villages, and Langeland, with its Viking burial grounds and small farming villages. Next visit the flat Jutland Peninsula, the country's heartland — an area of crystal fjords, stark moors, dense forests, sandy beaches, and small, medieval towns. The Zealand route from Copenhagen heads north around the large outer island past churches and castles that recall the warrior days of Viking rule.

Fyn (Fünen)

This route follows small, well-maintained highways with bridge and ferry connections to various islands in the archipelago, taking you through a land of fairy tales and a charming countryside known as Denmark's Garden. A tour of Fyn is an easy 2- or 3-day swing, whether you're circling around from Copenhagen or on your way there from the Jutland Peninsula.

Hans Christian Andersen wrote about his birthplace: "Perhaps Odense will one day become famous and people from many countries will travel to Odense because of me." This was a daring prediction to make in the mid nineteenth century, but in fact, the Hans Christian Andersen museums and settings have prompted many people to make a special trip to Odense and the isle of Fyn.

Along with literary and historical attractions, Fyn and the islands are noted for their unhurried charm and subtle, disarming beauty. Centuries-old inns and museums are scattered throughout a landscape that alternates between gentle, rolling farmland and picturesque harbors, coastline, and beaches. While the Danes here are slightly less sophisticated than their compatriots in Copenhagen, they are more open to visitors and quite proud of their region.

To reach Odense from Copenhagen, you will have about 1½-hour drive to the Korsør-Nyborg ferry, a 50-minute ferry ride, and another half-hour's drive from Nyborg to Odense. In peak tourist season, it's advisable to book the ferry in advance. Driving east from Jutland, take E66 or A1 across the island to Odense.

ODENSE: Denmark's third largest city, tracing its origins back to 988, has for centuries been the trade and transportation hub of Fyn. Its university, theater, and orchestra also provide a solid cultural base, important for an area far from the nation's capital.

In addition, the white swan and little brown "ugly" duckling embossing most Odense posters and information brochures signify that Hans Christian Andersen still plays a major role in the life of the city. You can visit the storyteller's birthplace at Hans Jensenstræde 39–45; the museum here has been open since 1908 and contains letters, manuscripts, published editions, and drawings that have illustrated his works. Next door is a delightful, intimate restaurant called, appropriately enough, *Under Linde Trt (Under the Linden Tree)*. Andersen buffs will also treasure his childhood home at Munkemøllestræde 3–4, which no doubt inspired many of his children's stories.

To see one of the largest and most complete open-air museums in Denmark, head south from downtown (bus 2) on Sejerskovvej to Fyn Village. In a peaceful, wooded setting, a cluster of farms, houses, mills, and brickworks recreate a Fyn village typical of the eighteenth and nineteenth centuries.

En Route from Odense – The perfect setting for a Danish *Alice in Wonderland*, Egeskov is a sixteenth-century island fort 1 hour south of Odense, just off A9 on the way to Fåborg or Svendborg. The castle, encircled by a moat edged by gardens in various styles, boasts a maze of hedges from which little Alice would have had trouble escaping (taller visitors can see over the hedges). You can also visit the collection of vintage cars, carriages, and other antique conveyances on the grounds. The castle itself is open only on special occasions.

The *Falsled Inn*, outside Fåborg, is more than a hotel; it is a trip back into nineteenth-century style and splendor. (It is also expensive, but worth an overnight stay.) Fåborg itself is a quiet town with many eighteenth- and nineteenth-century homes.

Depending on the direction of your travels, Svendborg can serve as the gateway either to the gardens of Fyn or to the southern Danish archipelago. A market town since 1253, Svendborg and its port are still a center of trade. The town makes a good dining spot or resting place for 1 day of the journey. Drive across the bridge to the island of Tåsinge and climb the Bregninge Church tower for a remarkable view of Svendborg, Tåsinge, and the nearby islands.

ÆRØ: Still relatively well protected from modernization, Ærø has, among other things, several fine beaches and the old-fashioned port town of Marstal. Car ferries link "the jewel of the archipelago" to other islands, but the best way to visit is to leave your car in Svendborg and board the ferry as a foot passenger to explore the fairy-tale village of Ærøskøbing. As soon as you get off the ferry, the charm of cobblestone streets, narrow lanes, and half-timbered gingerbread houses tells you this Lilliputian town is something special. It is delightfully cozy and compact, and if the store you'd like to visit doesn't seem to be open, you probably just have to fetch the shopkeeper from down the block.

One special museum in the village is the home of "Bottle" Peter Jacobsen, the man who reputedly invented the art of building ships in bottles. Before his death in 1960, "Bottle" Peter crafted over 1,700 different bottled ships and 150 scale-model sailing ships. Also in Ærøskøbing are the Ærø Museum, in the 1780 Bailiff's House, and the furniture and tile display in Hammerich's House.

TÅSINGE: Elvira Madigan lived and died on this island, also known as Fyn's Garden. Although A9 bisects Tåsinge, heading toward Langeland, your best bet is to crisscross it, making frequent stops. Almost in the shadow of the Bregninge Church is the tiny village of Landet and the churchyard where Elvira Madigan and her lover, Count Sixten Sparre, were both buried in 1889, when death ended the ill-starred romance of the Swedish officer and the beautiful performer.

Back across A9 the road leads to Troense, with its small seaman's museum and nearby Valdemar's Castle, which was built in 1644, then remodeled in the baroque style in 1754. The manor house is open to visitors, and the compound also includes a naval museum featuring royal barges and other vessels.

After Troense, just continue crisscrossing A9 through the farmland and small towns of Tåsinge at your leisure, stopping whenever the urge hits at a roadside *bageri* (bakery) for one of its fabled pastries.

LANGELAND: This "long island" (54 miles long and 5 miles wide), reached by one bridge and five ferries, offers both historical sites and places for relaxation. Coming from Tåsinge across Langelands Bridge you reach Rudkøbing, the island capital. A town of half-timbered buildings, winding streets, and carved house doors, it was the birthplace of Denmark's famous physicist H. C. Ørsted.

But in this region of manor houses and castles, it's best to stay outside the city in a place like the *Tranekr Gstgivergaard,* where a typical dinner might be leek soup, roast pheasant, fresh vegetables, good Danish beer, and of course pastries and coffee. Less than a mile from the inn is Tranekær Castle, which according to some records is the oldest inhabited building in Denmark.

Other attractions on Langeland include small farm villages, beaches, and pleasant rolling countryside. For the return trip to Copenhagen, a ferry goes from the fishing village of Spodsbjerg to Tårs, near Nakskov. (On the road back to Copenhagen, a detour at Vordingborg out to the majestic cliffs of Møn is well worth the time.)

BEST EN ROUTE

Expect to pay $55 and up per night for a double room in the places listed as expensive and $30 to $55 in those listed as moderate. Restaurant prices range from $40 and up for a meal for two in places listed as expensive and from $30 to $40 in those listed as moderate. Prices do not include drinks, wine, or tip.

ODENSE

Hotel Windsor – Simple Scandinavian rooms, with Victorian lobby and restaurant. Vindegade 45 (phone: 09-12-06-52). Expensive to moderate.

H. C. Andersens Hotel – This is a fine example of modern Danish architecture as well as a first-class hotel. Claus Bergsgade 7 (phone: 09-14-78-00). Expensive to moderate.

Grand Hotel – Traditional old-style hotel, with furnishings representative of the eighteenth and nineteenth centuries. Jernbanegade 18. (phone: 09-11-71-71). Moderate.

FALSLED

Falsled Inn – Former Royal Charter House with an exquisite garden, totally romantic setting. Many rooms have private entrances and courtyards. Superb international cuisine with French accent (phone: 09-61-94-90). Expensive.

SVENDBORG

Hotel Ærø – Good service, warm hospitality; the delicately sautéed fish could hardly be beat in a restaurant costing twice as much (phone: 09-21-07-60). Moderate.

LANGELAND

Tranekær Gæstgivergaard – Intimate and homelike; most of the pheasant, wild duck, and other game served at dinner has been shot by a member of the innkeeper's family. Just around the bend from Tranekær Castle (phone: 09-59-12-04). Moderate.

Jutland

The most direct road from southern Denmark to Skagen, the idyllic resort town on the North Sea, is Highway E3. Following this route, you can reach Skagen in a day or so, but you will be missing most of the special sights of Jutland, the ancient heart of Denmark, the world's oldest kingdom.

A long peninsula separating the North Sea from the Baltic, Jutland (or Jylland, as it is known in Danish) features a topography laced with charming fjords and trimmed with wind-swept moors, beaches, and forests. The only part of Denmark linked to the European continent, it is considerably larger than the 500 or so islands that make up the rest of the country. Thanks to its countryside, its undisturbed medieval hamlets, and its magnificent, sandy coast, Jutland has been the major vacation spot for the Danes since the days of Hans Christian Andersen.

Andersen himself spent many summers there; and he wrote: "It was so beautiful out in the country. It was summer — the wheat fields were golden, the oats were green, and down among the green meadows, the hay was stacked. There the stork minced about on his red legs, clacking away in Egyptian, which was the language his mother taught him."

In addition to their passionate love for the countryside, the Danes have close ties with their historical tradition, one that has its roots in Jutland. By present dating methods, Jutland was settled about 12,000 years ago by nomadic hunters and fishermen who were following the receding Ice Age. Remains of this culture are scattered in peat bogs and burial mounds all over Jutland and include a wide variety of weapons, tools, and even several well-mummified corpses a few thousand years old, now displayed at local museums.

For the Danes, however, history really begins around the ninth century, when the Danish Vikings, operating from bases in North Jutland, laid waste to England and Scotland, besieged Paris, and plundered towns as far south as Lisbon. King Gorm the Old and Queen Thyra built the Danevirke in this era, establishing Denmark's southern border, and their son, Harald Bluetooth, introduced Christianity to the region in about 960. Harald's heirs, Swein Forkbeard and Canute the Great, ruled over an empire consisting of Denmark, England, Norway, and southern Sweden.

With the construction of Roskilde Cathedral and Copenhagen in the twelfth century, the focus of Danish culture shifted to Zealand, the large island east of Jutland. Since then, aside from a few bloody Swedish invasions and a fierce border war with the Prussians in 1864, Jutland has been a tranquil repository of agriculture and traditional Danish mores.

The Jutland trip is a winding, 9-day excursion with many stops; it is divided into three sections. Should you need to curtail your vacation, you will invariably be within a short distance of E3 or a ferry to England, Sweden, or Norway.

En Route from Germany – If you are coming from Germany on the Autobahn, you will probably need a break by the time you reach the Danish border town of Frøslev. If so, head east on A8, where, after a 12.5-mile (20-km) ride on the northern shores of Flensburger Förde, you will reach Gråsten, the site of Gråsten Castle, dowager Queen Ingrid's summer home. The present baroque palace dates from 1759 and the castle church is open to visitors from April to September — provided, of course, that Queen Ingrid isn't vacationing with her grandchildren.

If old battlefields are your cup of tea, 3 miles (5 km) east is Dybbøl, where the major battle of the 1864 war with the Prussians was fought. The Prussians took over Schleswig-Holstein, but the Danes' heroic resistance has been memorialized at the Dybbøl Heights, overlooking the old fortifications.

Next to Dybbøl is Sønderborg and the huge Sønderborg Castle, which dates back to the thirteenth century. It was the prison of Danish King Christian II in the sixteenth century and was burned and looted by the Swedes in the seventeenth century.

The road north to Åbenrå runs from Augustenborg Fjord to Åbenrå Fjord, and it should give you a feeling for Jutland's symbiotic relationship with the sea. Åbenrå itself has a museum with an intriguing collection of maritime miscellany (H. P. Hanssensgade 33).

Ribe, a fairy-tale village of straw chimneys and non-Egyptian-speaking storks, is the next destination, about 50 miles (80 km) northwest on A12. If you are interested in Viking lore, make a detour on Hærvejen, an old Viking road, and see the runic stone at Horslund.

RIBE: First mentioned in 850, Ribe was the site of a church built by St. Ansgar, the man who brought Christianity to Scandinavia. The dominant feature is the cathedral, Vor Frue Domkirke, built on the site of Ansgar's church and the first thing you see as you approach the town. Built in the first half of the twelfth century, it is a striking mixture of Romanesque and Gothic elements and is full of legend and interesting architectural detail. The Ribe Museum of Antiquities is also worth a visit, and the town boasts over 100 protected old houses from the sixteenth and seventeenth centuries.

The North Sea is just a few minutes away, and its tides are so strong that you may have to resist the temptation to drive across the mud flats of Vadehavet to the island of Mandø. Take the bus instead.

En Route from Ribe – About 15 miles (25 km) north of Ribe on A12 is the city of Esbjerg, the base for Denmark's fishing industry as well as the country's oil capital. Fishmeal plants, a busy ferry terminal, and waterfront grain silos give Esbjerg a prosaic look, with none of the atmosphere of older Danish towns. Do drive down to the docks, however, and take the 20-minute ferry ride to the remarkable little island of Fanø.

FANØ: The ancestors of the 3,000 inhabitants of Fanø bought this island from the Danish Crown in 1741, which explains the preservation of a unique culture on the island. Its lengthy beaches and grassy dunes make it a popular bathing resort, and on the southern spit of the island is the restored old fishing village of Sønderho. The villagers dress in traditional costumes on special days and live in low houses characteristic of the area's architecture.

En Route from Fanø – Leave the west coast and get acquainted with another kind of scenery by cutting back across Jutland on 337, a straight, speedy road leading northeast to Grindsted. The land changes noticeably as you leave the coast, and you will see some of the rolling farmland for which Denmark is famous.

If you are traveling with children, you might want to take the Vejle road 6 miles (10 km) to Billund and turn them loose on Legoland, a miniature world made from 15 million Lego toy bricks. There is a 40-foot replica of Mt. Rushmore, another of Cape Kennedy, and a plethora of activities for youngsters.

Another 19 miles (30 km) takes you to Vejle and the nearby village of Jelling, the ancient Viking capital, where you can see some of Denmark's most famous runic stones and the burial mounds of old King Gorm and Queen Thyra. The *Jelling Kro* is a fine place to sup with the ghosts of the Vikings.

The road north to Horsens via Juelsminde has a spectacular view of the coast and Palsgård Manor House, which is open to tourists.

HORSENS: Founded in the twelfth century, this was a Franciscan abbey town during the Middle Ages before becoming a prosperous trading center in the eighteenth century. The old abbey church still exists, and many of the original decorations and carvings are still intact. The town itself is on a fjord and has many picturesque lanes and lovely eighteenth-century houses.

Horsens is the end of the first 3-day leg of the tour; you are now entering central Jutland, the second leg. Continuing north on A10, you leave the coast and approach Århus. Here the landscape becomes more wooded, and you may even notice a slight elevation as you pass Yding Skovhøj Hills, the highest point in Denmark at 567 feet.

ÅRHUS: Denmark's second largest city (pop. 250,000), Århus is a major industrial and cultural center, thanks to its harbor and the University of Århus. Among the city's many sights are the twelfth-century Århus Cathedral, which contains, among other things, Denmark's biggest church organ; the Old Town, a reconstructed sixteenth-century village; the Viking Museum; and the Museum of Prehistory, with an Iron Age collection highlighted by the red-haired mummy of the Grauballe man, at the Moesgård Manor House. If you visit in early September, be sure to catch the Århus Festival, the biggest celebration of theater, dance, and music in Scandinavia.

SILKEBORG: Heading due west on A15, you reach the beautiful Lake District and, in its center, the town of Silkeborg. Its museum, at Silkeborg Hovedgård, is worth a stop, particularly if you want to see another early Dane, the 2,200-year-old Tollund man. Take a boat trip on the lakes, where you can relax and gaze at slender herons and other waterfowl. One of Denmark's great Resistance heroes, the poet and pastor Kaj Munk, was killed in 1944 by the Nazis at Hørbylund Bakke, 5 miles (8 km) west of Silkeborg.

En Route from Silkeborg – Drive west on A15 to Herning, the center of the Danish textile industry. Here you can get a good buy on a sweater or fabric design, and you can observe nineteenth-century peasant life and weaving techniques at the Herning Museum (Museumsgade). The town has fine modern art collections.

From Herning, A15 winds through the moors and lowlands of the west coast to Ringkøbing, a town economically ruined in the eighteenth century when accumulated silt deposits on Holmsland Klit cut off Ringkøbing Fjord from the

North Sea. To prevent flooding, the Danes have built dikes similar to those in Holland. The area is thus undeveloped. Driving south on Holmsland Klit, you come to Tipperne Bird Sanctuary, the largest in Denmark.

HOLSTEBRO: North of Ringkøbing on A16, Holstebro is Jutland's center for theater and music. A depressed town some 20 years ago, it came into a windfall and spent the money on encouraging the arts. Today it has one of the leading experimental theaters in the world, the Odin Theater, at Sækergaard and a lovely new art museum. Holstebro is a great example of creative city planning.

VIBORG: One of Denmark's oldest towns, Viborg dates back to the sixth century, when it was the site of the Viking *ting* and various sacrificial rites, thanks to its placement at a critical crossroads. The Christians who later occupied the area decided to keep it as a religious center, and in 1130 built a large cathedral; it was largely destroyed by fire but was restored in the nineteenth century. Today it is still the largest granite cathedral in all of Europe. It is decorated with a series of lavish frescoes, executed around the turn of the twentieth century by the painter Joakim Skovgaard.

En Route from Viborg – The final leg of the Jutland trip covers the rugged scenery of North Jutland, which is virtually cut off from the rest of the peninsula by the Limfjord, a large body of water that was an important navigation route in Viking times. Here again, deposits of silt have wreaked havoc with maritime commerce, making the passage quite treacherous. Heading northwest toward Nykøbing and Thisted, you will first see the Limfjord at Skive, a small town with an interesting museum collection of Eskimo and prehistoric relics.

About 15 miles (25 km) northwest of Skive, connected by the Sallingsund Bridge, is the Limfjord island of Mors. Its largest town is Nykøbing Mors, the home of the Limfjord oyster industry and Dueholm Abbey, founded in 1377 by the Knights of St. John.

The best view on Mors is from the cliffs of Hanklit and Salgerhøj, near the Thisted bridge across Vilsund. Thisted itself is the principal town in northwest Jutland, located in the Thy area. Nearby, at Hørdum, is a fantastic runic stone depicting Thor's epic struggle with the Midgård serpent.

Following A11 northwest along the northern banks of the Limfjord, you pass the promontory of Feggeklit on the island of Mors. According to the Danish medieval historian Saxo, this was where Hamlet avenged his father's death by killing his treacherous Uncle Fegge. From here, take the north road to Fjerritslev; stop for a swim and a look at the North Sea at Torup Strand.

From Fjerritslev, one can choose either A11 to Ålborg, the next destination, or the southern route via Løgstør. The latter is slower but much more interesting; it passes the Viking town of Aggersborg as well as Løgstør, a fishing hamlet with a good museum on the history and culture of the Limfjord.

ÅLBORG: Denmark's fourth largest city and Jutland's most important town, Ålborg is the center of the tobacco, cement, and — as every good Dane knows — aquavit industries. Like many Danish cities, it has a well-preserved Old Town that must be explored on foot. Be sure to see the Jens Bang's Stenhus, one of the finest Renaissance houses in Denmark. The Ålborg Historical Museum contains interiors from bourgeois homes of the seventeenth century (Algade 48), and the new North Jutland Museum of Art houses a very modern collection in a marble structure designed by the architect Alvar Aalto. Also of interest are the Ålborg Zoological Garden, Mølleparken, and a smaller replica of Copenhagen's Tivoli called Tivoliland.

En Route from Ålborg – Nørresundby, a suburb of Ålborg on the northern side of the Limfjord, has the most important Viking burial ground in Scandinavia (Lindholm Høje). There are 682 graves as well as the ruins of a nearby settlement. From here, A17 runs northwest to Åbybro, where it joins A11 running due north to Løkken and the coast. En route you may want to stop and see the famed church in Jetsmark or detour to swim at the small seaside town of Blokhus. Løkken itself is a popular summer resort, and you can drive the 10 miles (16 km) to Blokhus on the beach. Not far from Løkken is the twelfth-century monastery and manor house at Børglum Kloster.

Your route leads next to the commercial center of Hjørring, a thirteenth-century town, which has a quaint historical museum, Vendsyssels, and St. Catherine's, a fine medieval church.

On the road north to Skagen, you'll see one of the most exotic sights in Denmark. Huge, shifting dunes up to 35 feet high that migrate 25 to 30 feet every year, the Råbjerg Mile is on the northern peninsula of Skagen, the juncture of the Baltic and the North seas.

SKAGEN: This charming little town became an artists' colony in the 1880s and has been a popular resort ever since. The artists' inspiration can be seen in the low, yellow-washed houses and in the town's various museums — the Skagen Museum, the Museum of Old Skagen, and Drachmann's House. Just west of town is the "church of the dunes," a thirteenth-century church that was abandoned to the sands in 1795. The history of Skagen's relationship with the sea is reflected in its five lighthouses, only one of which, Grenen, is still in use today. Skagen is the ideal place to end a tour of Jutland, and you may want to stay in one of its quiet little cottages for a while to digest your travels.

BEST EN ROUTE

Expect to pay $55 to $60 and up per night for a double room in the places listed as expensive; $35 to $55 in those listed as moderate; and under $35, inexpensive. Restaurant prices range from $40 and up for a dinner for two in the expensive category; $25 to $40 in the moderate category; and $25 and under, inexpensive. Prices do not include drinks, wine, and tip.

RIBE

Hotel Dagmar – On the main square of this beautiful little village, this is the best hotel in town. 80 beds and full accommodations. Torvet 1 (phone: 05-42-00-33). Moderate.

FANØ

Sønderho Kro – A tiny, elegant, 14-bed inn on the southern tip of the island. Full accommodations. Sønderho (phone: 05-16-40-09). Moderate.

HORSENS

Snaptun Færgegård – Following the principle of sleeping near the sea, this inn gives you the chance to be lulled into slumber by the Baltic. 54 beds, full accommodations. Snaptun (phone: 05-68-30-03 or 05-68-35-11). Moderate.

SILKEBORG

Hotel Dania – A nice, respectable, businessman's hotel on the main square of town. 80 beds, full accommodations. Torvet 5 (phone: 06-82-01-11). Moderate.

RINGKØBING

Hotel Klitten – A fine hotel right on the beach. Open from June 1 to September 1. Søndervig (phone: 07-33-91-00). Moderate.

Strandkroen – Planning an off-season trip? This cozy little inn might be just the thing. 32 beds, full accommodations (phone: 07-33-90-02). Inexpensive.

VIBORG

Missionshotellet – Somehow in this spiritual center it seems appropriate to stay in the inn with an ecclesiastical ring. Also, it's the best in town, with 70 beds, 4 apartments with bath and kitchen, and full accommodations. Sankt Mathias Gade 5 (phone 06-62-37-00). Moderate.

THISTED

Strandhotellet – Good view of the Limfjord; 38 beds and full accommodations. Oddesundvej 39 (phone: 07-92-40-11). Moderate.

ÅLBORG

Hotel Hvide Hus – A big-city hotel with all the trimmings, including a swimming pool, 400 beds, and full accommodations. Vesterbro 2 (phone: 08-13-84-00). Expensive.

SKAGEN

Hotel Skagen – The biggest place in this tiny town, with 82 rooms. Gammel Landevej (phone: 08-44-22-33). Expensive.
Kandehus Kro – On the Skagerrak side of Skagen in the middle of the Råbjerg Mile. Watch out for the creeping dunes. Open from January 15 to December 1. Kandestederne (phone: 08-48-81-19). Inexpensive.

Important: Skagen and Fanø are very popular in the summer, so be sure to make bookings in advance if you want to stay here.

Zealand

Tours from Copenhagen can be either 1-day loops or extended 2- to 3-day excursions that allow you to take greater advantage of the Zealand countryside and perhaps stay in a charming Danish manor house or traditional hotel.

While Copenhagen is considered one of the most modern and sophisticated cities in Europe, a half-hour's drive transports you to an area of farmland and woods dotted with towns dating back more than 500 years.

Some of the high points of such tours are castles and churches that vividly recreate the time when kings ruled the realm we now call Scandinavia. You can visit a palace still used by the reigning monarch, a church with the tombs of almost all the royalty from the last several hundred years, and the ramparts of Kronborg Castle in Helsingør, the scene of Shakespeare's Hamlet.

There is more to enjoy here, however, than colorful history. You can also stop at Louisiana, the modern art museum overlooking the sound, drive through an area of posh homes known as the Danish Riviera, and relax on sandy beaches or in old fishing villages.

The most frequently traveled tour bus route is a 1-day loop that heads north from Copenhagen to Louisiana and Helsingør, turns west to castles in Fredensborg and Hillerød, and then returns to Copenhagen. To get the most out of each stop, however, 1½ to 2 full days is recommended.

KLAMPENBORG: Heading north from Copenhagen off the coast road, the first stop is Klampenborg, which, in addition to a bathing beach, has Jaegersborg Dyrehave, the royal hunting ground since the end of the seventeenth century. This is a favorite retreat for Copenhagen residents, where they can stroll among the old oak trees and watch the nearly tame deer. The highlight of the park between mid-April and the end of August is Dyrehavsbakken — or Bakken, as it's commonly known. Denmark's oldest amusement park, it is a kind of people's Tivoli set in the woods. You won't find too many tourists, yet the park has enough attractions to merit a full day's visit.

En Route from Dyrehave – While A3 is the fastest route to Helsingør, the 27-mile (43-km) road that winds along the Øresund coast really doesn't take much more time. Along the way are many elegant homes, fine examples of modern Danish architecture, that make it easy to understand why this stretch is known as the Danish Riviera.

HUMLEBÆK: About 20 miles (32 km) north of Copenhagen, this town is noted for Louisiana, a center for modern art. Established in 1958, Louisiana stands majestically on the Øresund coast, looking out toward Sweden. Not only does it have an outstanding collection of Danish and foreign art and sculpture, but the museum and gardens themselves comprise a work of art.

HELSINGØR: Less than a half-hour north of Louisiana, the coast road winds into Helsingør. According to the history books, people were living in the area before AD 1000, and Helsingør had already been named by 1231. But it wasn't until 1574, when Frederik II began the reconstruction of Kronborg Castle, that Helsingør took on strategic and historical importance.

Dating from around 1426, the castle had been completely rebuilt in its present Renaissance style by 1585. Open to visitors every day, it houses collections of armor and Renaissance clothing and art. There is a memorial to Shakespeare in the surrounding wall, and the castle itself is well preserved. Also on the Kronborg grounds is the Mercantile and Maritime Museum, founded in 1915.

At Helsingør, Denmark and Sweden are less than 2 miles apart. If you haven't taken the Copenhagen hydrofoil to Malmö, it's worth making the 40-minute round trip to Hälsingborg and back — if only to say you've been in Sweden.

To see the technological history of Denmark, visit the Technical Museum, with its collection of over 2,000 pieces, most of which are displayed at Ndr. Strandvej 23.

HORNBÆK/GILLELEJE: From Helsingør, the longer tour of North Zealand continues up the coast to the resort towns of Hornbæk and Gilleleje. Both have picturesque fishing harbors and adequate bathing beaches. Don't be surprised at the amount of nudity on the beaches, or at the Danes' attendant nonchalance. The *Strand* in Gilleleje and the *Trouville* in Hornbæk are both well-known hotels that tend to fill up in summer months. Both towns also have campgrounds.

FREDENSBORG: Here is the Fredensborg Palace, the spring and fall home of the reigning monarch. The gardens were designed by the French landscape architect Jardin, who patterned them after those of Versailles. The castle is open only in July (1–5 PM), but the magnificent grounds are open year round.

If you opt for the shorter circle route, a good place to stop for a late lunch is the *Store Kro,* next to the palace. The inn has been around for centuries and serves typical Danish fare in traditional settings.

HILLERØD: Continuing west on A6, you come to Hillerød, one of the largest towns in North Zealand. Dominating the town is Frederiksborg Castle, which many people consider the most beautiful Renaissance castle in Europe. Built between 1600 and 1620 by Christian IV, it was reconstructed from the original drawings after fire gutted most of the structure in 1859. Since 1878 the castle has been the National Historical Museum; it contains collections of Danish artifacts, costumes, armor, and artwork. Particularly impressive is the chapel, which was untouched by the fire. Adjacent to the edifice is the baroque Castle Park and the Badstuen, a country hunting house for royalty.

ROSKILDE: The focal point of Zealand tours west of Copenhagen is Roskilde, reached via A1. In the center of town is the Roskilde Cathedral, built in the 1170s, the final resting place of nearly all Danish royalty since Margrethe I (1353–1412). The church is a mélange of Romanesque and Gothic architecture, and its interior is rich in frescoes, monuments, sarcophagi, and art.

By the harbor in Roskilde Fjord is the Viking Ship Museum. Inside are five Viking ships, dating from around 1000, which were found in the fjord in 1962. In addition to the well-restored vessels, the museum offers an illuminating film describing the delicate, painstaking procedures used to excavate the Norse relics.

LEJRE: About 10 miles (16 km) southwest of Roskilde is the Historical-Archaeological Research Center at Lejre. The center is a working village, built to simulate conditions in the Iron Age, 3,000 years ago. The project, supported by the Carlsberg (beer) Foundation, as well as by the Danish government, is a favorite with youngsters.

BEST EN ROUTE

Expect to pay $60 and up per night for a double room in the places listed as expensive; $40 to $60 in those listed as moderate; and under $40 in the inexpensive. Restaurant prices range from $35 and up for a dinner for two in the expensive category; $30 to $40 in the moderate category; and $30 and under, inexpensive. Prices do not include drinks, wine, and tip.

HELSINGØR

Marienlyst – Along the coast road just outside Helsingør, the *Marienlyst* is the premier hotel in North Zealand. Sitting by the pool, you can see Kronborg Castle in the distance. Superb international cuisine; 150 rooms (phone: 02-21-18-01). Expensive.

FREDENSBORG

Store Kro – This is perfectly situated — on the road between Helsingør and Hillerød and a short walk from Fredensborg Palace. One building dates from 1723, and over the years the hotel has been the scene of receptions and royal weddings. The atmosphere is one of old-fashioned elegance. Slotsgade 6 (phone: 02-28-00-47). Expensive.

SØLLERØD

Søllerød Kro – Only 10.5 miles (17 km) north of Copenhagen but surrounded by woods, this is one of the most popular spots for the Danes' Sunday outings. After a meal, a walk in the woods is recommended. No overnight accommodations. Søllerødvej 35 (phone: 02-80-25-05). Expensive.

Exploring Finland

Finland, a country of about five million people, is the easternmost Scandinavian landmass. Its southern end juts into the Baltic Sea to create two smaller bodies of water: the Gulf of Bothnia to the west, which forms a natural barrier with Sweden, and the Gulf of Finland to the south, which separates Finland from the Baltic state of Estonia. Finland shares its borders with Norway and Sweden to the west and north and with the USSR to the east.

Finland's neighbors have dominated its history. First part of the Swedish Kingdom, then of the Russian Empire, Finland wasn't officially independent until 1917. This is important because anthropologically Finland is neither Scandinavian nor Russian. The language is called Finno-Ugric, and the people are Magyar-Estonian hybrids who migrated from the southeast.

Finland covers 130,120 square miles (about the size of New England plus New York and New Jersey), one-third of which is above the Arctic Circle. The southern two-thirds of the country is marbled with over 60,000 lakes dotted with more than 30,000 islands.

Wood-related and metal industries are the main Finnish occupations, but the national pastime is the sauna, and you'll miss something special if you leave Finland without trying one.

Helsinki, the capital, with a half-million people, is on the southern coast. It's a good starting point for any visit to the country. Finland's roads are good and so are the railway and airline connections, with special holiday tickets for unlimited travel within the country. Car rental is easy and uncomplicated as well. The first route takes you in and out of the beautiful southern lakeland. The waters are cold, clear, and shallow; the land is green and forested. There are also 2- to 5-day guided tours to the Lakelands by bus-boat-plane. The lake networks are vast and trafficked by romantic steamers, modern ferries, and hydrofoils.

The second route takes you into the Arctic wilderness of Lapland, where the people are as much an attraction as the landscape. The fells (mountains raised from early glacial movement) make the land strangely beautiful, even where fir and birch forests end and the tundra begins.

The Lakelands

This long route (703 mi/1,132 km) takes you from Helsinki up, around, and through the beautiful Finnish lakeland. There are ten major towns along the way and many interesting stops that could take a week's meandering, but if you don't have time, you can get a good map and reroute, cutting across some of the larger lakes by ferry.

HELSINKI: For a detailed report on the city and its hotels and restaurants, see *Helsinki*, THE EUROPEAN CITIES.

En Route from Helsinki – Leaving the capital for the lakeland, take Route 3 for 65 miles (104 km) to Hämeenlinna. The landscape is luxuriant farmland enriched by clear, blue waters. Before you reach Hämeenlinna, you pass through Riihimäki, where there is the famous Glass Museum (Koulukatu 14) and two glass works, where you can purchase samples of beautiful Finnish glassware.

HÄMEENLINNA: Having received its royal charter in 1639, this is the oldest inland town in Finland. The city, which grew around the medieval Häme Castle in the northern part of town on Lake Vanajavesi, is a garrison town. At Hallituskatu 11 you can visit Sibelius House, where the Finnish composer was born. Hämeenlinna is also a terminal for the Finnish Silverline lake route; you can take a waterbus to Tampere or Kangasala.

About 48 miles (77 km) along Route 3 and E79 is the town of Tampere. On the way you might stop for lunch at the Sääksmäki Bridge and eat on the picturesque lakeshore.

TAMPERE: The second largest city in Finland, Tampere was founded 200 years ago on the banks of the Tammer River rapids on the isthmus between two big lakes, Näsijärvi and Pyhäjärvi. There are also some 180 lakes inside the city limits. Tampere is an industrial center known especially for metal, textiles, and footwear, but it is also famous for its theaters.

Just before the center city, you cross a bridge; down to your right you'll see the charming Koskipuisto (Rapids Park), where you can sit and watch the river flow. Here as well as in Hämeenpuisto (Häme Park), a little farther on, there are summertime folk dances and open-air concerts. There are two impressive churches: The Kaleva is Finnish modern, and the Eastern Orthodox church of Tampere, with its bulbous towers, is the only neo-Byzantine church in Scandinavia. From Näsinneula, the highest observation tower in Finland, which also boasts a revolving restaurant, you can drink in wide views of both the city and the lakes. Besides an aquarium and a planetarium, Tampere also has one of Finland's best collections of twentieth-century art at the Sara Hildén-Museum.

On a northern lake isthmus is Pyynikki National Park, with a beautiful ridge of pine trees, calm lake views, and a revolving summer theater.

JYVÄSKYLÄ: The trip from Tampere is 93 miles (150 km), but you can stop outside town at the industrial island commune of Säynätsalo on Lake Päijänne, where you find one of Alvar Aalto's famous buildings, the Säynätsalo Civic Center. If you're in a hurry, however, don't worry about missing it; the Aalto Museum, where you can get a look at most of the Finnish master's buildings, is in Jyväskylä (Seminaarinkatu 7).

Jyväskylä, one of the most popular tourist cities in the country and the capital of Central Finland, was founded in 1837 at the northern end of Lake Päijänne on the site of an ancient marketplace. Its importance as a cultural center is especially obvious in summertime, when various seminars, theater performances, concerts, and exhibitions are staged and well attended. More than anything else, though, this is a city of fine modern architecture, with a university designed by Alvar Aalto and the Laajavuori Hotel with its Sports Center just north of the center city.

For information about lake cruises, sight-seeing tours, or other activities, stop at the City Tourist Office (Vapaudenkatu 38; phone: 29-40-83).

En Route to Kuopio – If it's July and you can't resist strawberries, stop at Suonenjoki, a small town that holds an annual Strawberry Carnival. If you've got lots of time, you can continue this detour through the towns of Iisvesi, Tervo, and Karttula, where the lake scenery is unmatched.

KUOPIO: This provincial capital is a center of the Savo (province) way of life, humor, and folklore. The city was founded about 200 years ago, and the old traditions are kept alive at the marketplace, where the high-tempered townsfolk meet to barter. You can buy a *kalakukko* (a tasty fish and pork pie), all sorts of vegetables, berries, and regional clothing and souvenirs. If you're not too full to keep exploring, try the Orthodox Church Museum (Karjalankatu 1), which has a unique collection of religious icons.

En Route from Kuopio – To get to Joensuu the shortest way, take Route 17, which connects the two provinces and tourist regions of Savo and North Karelia. An alternate route goes south to the city of Varkaus, then northeast along Route 70 to Joensuu.

If you take the longer alternative you can stop at Varkaus, an industrial town at the junction of two extensive lake networks: Kallavesi to the north and Haukivesi to the southeast. The town's business is wood pulp and, except for a large Scandinavian altar fresco in the church, it is best explored by boat. Two-hour sight-seeing cruises take you through many idyllic channels and canals, the oldest of which, Taipaleen Kanava, was built in 1830.

Farther along this route is the village of Heinävesi, with the only cloisters in Finland, the Valamo Monastery, with typically Russian cupolas built, oddly enough, out of copper, and the Lintula convent of nuns.

JOENSUU: The main town of North Karelia, Joensuu was founded in 1848 at the mouth of the Pielisjoki River. Its culture is documented at the Karelia House Museum (Karjalan Talo) in Ilosaari, where you'll also find a summer theater and restaurant serving regional fish and some of the best pastries in Finland. Again, there's an opportunity to take a lake cruise. Even the most inveterate landlubber shouldn't take the lakeland route without at least one boat trip.

A northern loop trip of about 185 miles (300 km) from Joensuu goes up and around Lake Pielinen. It takes you past the mountains of Koli, the old wooden houses and reconstructed log Bomba Castle at Nurmes, and the Ruunaankoski Rapids near Lieksa. Throughout the trip you might happen upon local bards, founts of indigenous lore who will be glad to sell you the best in regional handicrafts, from unique leathergoods to fine linen tablecloths. There's also a variety of wooden souvenirs fashioned from the knot and splint pieces that go unused in the forest industries. There are also many *prazniks,* religious Russian Orthodox festivals.

SAVONLINNA: From Joensuu, head southeast toward the Russian frontier on Route 6. You can follow this road all the way to the border, but to get to Savonlinna you cut back west into the lakeland and eastern Savo region. Just outside Savonlinna is the small town of Kerimäki, with the world's largest wooden church. It holds 3,300 people, and during the summer the Savonlinna Opera Festival holds concerts here.

Savonlinna itself dates back to 1475, when the Olavinlinna Castle was built. The castle was then a border fort manned by united Swedes and Finns on the lookout for czarist armies. The city that surrounds the castle wasn't founded until 1639, and today it is a beautiful lake and spa town. Again, you can take steamer cruises on the lakes from here. The boats leave from slips beside the marketplace and zigzag through the surrounding archipelagos. There are direct boats to and from Kuopio, Joensuu, and Mikkeli. The castle, worth a visit, is the main site of the opera festival, which is always popular. If you're interested, you should book tickets well in advance.

MIKKELI: Mikkeli, 64 miles (104 km) southwest of Savonlinna, is the main city of Savo province and is on the banks of the huge Lake Saimaa. It was the popular headquarters of the national hero Marshal Mannerheim. You can visit his headquarters, now a museum (Päämajankatu 1–3). Then walk north on Porrassalmenkatu to the church museum, where there's a stone sacristy dating from the 1320s. If you crave more lake views, climb the Naisvuori observation tower and admire the various shades of green, blue, and white of the lakes and countryside.

En Route from Mikkeli – There's a choice of two picturesque routes to the town of Imatra, both of which return east toward the Russian border. The first is along Route 434, also called "the panoramic road of Savo," which passes over islands and straits on the shores of Lake Saimaa. The road wanders around hills and meadows with open lake vistas and at one point is punctuated by a short ferry ride.

The second, longer route goes back to Savonlinna (this is the route to take if you've skipped Mikkeli entirely) and takes you through the Punkaharju Ridge, a narrow Ice Age spit that separates Lakes Puruvesi and Pihlajavesi.

IMATRA: Imatra is known mainly for the Vuoksi River rapids that roar through the center of town. On selected summer Sundays you can also see the release of the controlled Great Falls. Imatra is another good place to study Alvar Aalto's bold architectural creations, such as the Church of the Three Crosses. The town line is also the national border. As in most of the other lake towns, you can arrive or leave by boat, for Imatra is on the easternmost edge of Lake Saimaa.

LAPPEENRANTA: This city, only 23 miles (37 km) southwest of Imatra, is at the southernmost point of the Saimaa Lake network. There's an involved channel and canal system from here to the Gulf of Finland that gives almost all the lakeland towns access to salt water. The channels, however, flow east through Russian territory before they reach the sea at Viborg. In 1968, Finland worked out a complicated leasing agreement with the USSR that covers boat traffic along the system.

Lappeenranta was founded in 1649, and you can visit the Old Park, surrounded by an eighteenth-century rampart that encloses a fortress, various museums, and the oldest Orthodox church in Finland, dating from 1785.

En Route from Lappeenranta – About 56 miles (90 km) southwest on the Gulf of Finland is the small military town of Hamina. The entire town was planned and executed as a Renaissance fortress. Much of the 250-year-old wall still stands, enclosing the circular interior where you can see the old Finnish military traditions carried out at the Reserve Officers' Academy. There's also a bulbous Orthodox church dating from 1837.

KOTKA: Only 6 miles (10 km) from Hamina, Kotka lies on the peninsula between the two eastern tributaries of the Kymi River and stretches farther over Kotka Island. The Russians built naval fortifications here that were destroyed when the Russian fleet was overwhelmed by English seapower during the Crimean War. The only building left after the battle was the Orthodox Church of St. Nicolaus, which still stands and houses a collection of valuable icons.

The Finnish town was built in 1878 without Russian aid and is now an industrial center and a major port. You can still get a taste of Imperial Russia if you visit the czar's fishing lodge at the Langinkoski Rapids. If you want more naval history, there's a motorboat to Varissaari Island, where you can review the Battle of Ruotsinsalmi (between the Russians and the Swedes) of 1790. You can examine the cannons and the salvaged ships and plot how you might have guided one fleet or the other more strategically than their admirals did.

PORVOO: Still farther west on the gulf and only 31 miles (50 km) east of Helsinki is Porvoo, the only Finnish city that still has an intact town plan from the 1700s. Porvoo's mercantile heritage goes back to the Middle Ages, when it was established as a trade center in 1346 by King Magnus Eriksson. It's got narrow winding streets, a town hall from 1764 in the middle of a quiet cobbled square, and an A-roofed cathedral built in 1418. The town's layout gives it a more southern European flavor, but the old pastel-colored wooden houses and the brown and white wood detailing of the cathedral facade make it distinctly Scandinavian. Because of its style, Porvoo has always lured the more artistic and poetic Finns. You can visit the house (Aleksanterin-katu) where Finland's national poet, Johan Ludvig Runeberg, lived and worked. There's also an honorary residence for Swedish and Finnish poets called the Poet's House; it is easily confused with Runeberg's home but is actually an entirely different building near the cathedral. From this calm town, it's only a little more than a half-hour drive back to Helsinki.

BEST EN ROUTE

A double room in a good hotel in Finland costs 500 marks. This is $85 plus per night, and we call it expensive. There are fancy places for less in the country, but not that much less — even in Lapland (tourism is one of its major industries). A first-class meal in Helsinki, especially during the crayfish season, is at least $40 to $55, depending on drinks; again, we consider this expensive. Specialties in the smaller towns are cheaper; reindeer dishes are good but usually expensive.

HÄMEENLINNA

Aulanko – This fancy hotel is next to a lake in a beautiful national park. There's a restaurant, a nightclub, a pool, and a beach, plus horses, golf, tennis, boats, bicycles, and whatever else you need for outdoor activities. Rantasipi Aulanko (phone: 2-9521). Expensive.

TAMPERE

Rosendahl – On the stately and beautiful Pyynikki Ridge, this is the poshest place in town. Pyynikintie 13 (phone: 11-22-33). Expensive.

Kaupunginhotelli – It has unpretentious but comfortable rooms. Centrally located. Hämeenkatu 11 (phone: 2-1380). Moderate.

JOENSUU

Hotel Kimmel – This large but good hotel has a nightclub and an excellent restaurant. Itäranta 1 (phone: 3-4521). Expensive.

NURMES

Bomba – This huge, reconstructed Karelian "log castle" has a good restaurant serving Karelian food. Suojärvenkatu 1. Moderate.

SAVONLINNA

Casino – This pleasant lake resort hotel has a private beach, tennis, boating, and other outdoor sports facilities. 79 rooms. Kasinosaari (phone: 2-2864). Expensive.

MIKKELI

Varsavuori – This modern and comfortable hotel has a sauna, pool, and disco, as well as facilities for tennis, boating, skiing, and fishing. Kirkonvarkaus (phone: 36-71-11). Moderate.

IMATRA

Hotel Valtionhotelli – Here's an island hotel almost in the midst of the Imatra Rapids. It's actually a stone castle with big rooms and first-class cuisine. Torkkelinkatu 1. (phone: 6-3244). Expensive.

LAPPEENRANTA

Hotel Lappeenranta – It has 40 rooms, a beach, and facilities for boating and fishing. Helsingintie 1 (phone: 1-4940). Moderate.

PORVOO
Haikko Manor and Health Spa – This luxurious place has complete spa facilities and a restaurant serving good Continental food. About 4 miles (6 km) from the middle of town (phone: 15-31-32). Expensive.

Lapland

Lapland is the great remaining wilderness of Finland. Covering the northern third of the country, almost all of it is above the Arctic Circle. This is truly the Land of the Midnight Sun, and in the northernmost town of Utsjoki, at the Norwegian border, there are 70 straight days of uninterrupted daylight that begin in mid-May. After a 50-day sunset the sky gets dark at the end of November, and the eerie and beautiful Northern Lights blaze in shafts of color across the nighttime Arctic landscape.

The roads across this wilderness run mainly north and south, with rather few connecting east-west arteries. The major routes have hard surfaces (blacktop or concrete) and are plowed regularly through the winter. You'll notice many warning signs for reindeer crossings — pay attention to them. In the dark, surprised reindeer, like deer in America, will often bolt directly into oncoming headlights. If you inadvertently hit a reindeer, you must inform the nearest police unit.

With the exception of its few urban centers, Lapland is a very sparsely populated area, with a density of only about 2 people per square kilometer. That leaves a lot of space for herds of roaming reindeer. You'll find fewer lakes here than in southern and central Finland, but there are many rivers, and between them are vast uninhabited areas. The topography varies greatly: low-lying swamps, river valleys with stands of pine and spruce, and regions of treeless tundra with an occasional scrub of birch on a low fell. (Fells are elevated plains that were left as high ground around gorges formed by retreating glaciers. The Lapp landscape is covered with these gently rounded, bare-topped hills.)

Along the northern highways of Finland, many roadside stalls sell authentic Lapp souvenirs. There are about 4,000 Lapps here and their population is diminishing. Much like the American Indian, they were shunted off to less civilized terrain as the more industrialized Scandinavians, Russians, and Finns came to Finland. The Lapps live off the reindeer, and they use almost every part of the beast for clothing and food. They prize the antlers and make them into sculpture, as whalers do with whalebone. The reindeer wander freely but are owned by some 800 Lapp families, who depend on them entirely for their living. Reindeer roundups take place from September to January and are colorful events. The Lapps dress in their traditional blue, red, and yellow outfits and their embroidered "caps of the four winds."

The shortest way from Helsinki to Rovaniemi, the capital of Lapland, is Route E4 through Lahti, Jyväskylä, Oulu, and Kemi — almost 520 miles (837 km). And this is before the main Lapland route through Rovaniemi,

Sodankylä, Inari, and Utsjoki — another 284 miles (458 km). The thing to do is to take one of the car-sleeper trains. From Helsinki they take 12 hours, but they let you and your car off perfectly rested at the beginning of the route. There are several daily flights, which take about 1½ hours..

ROVANIEMI: Though people have lived at the confluence of the Kemi and Ounas rivers just south of the Arctic Circle since the Stone Age, the Nazis, on leaving, torched the city and left it looking like a cigarette stub in the Arctic snow. As a result, the "Gateway to Lapland" is an almost entirely new city, planned with meticulous and functional beauty by the Finnish architect Alvar Aalto. Since World War II, the population here has more than tripled. There are two tourist lodges worth visiting, one a few miles north at the actual line of the Arctic Circle, where you can get a Crossing the Line certificate, and another on top of Ounasvaara, an Arctic hill overlooking the town from which there is a wonderful urban/Arctic panorama. In town you can visit the Lapland Provincial Museum at the Lappia House and see the theater-congress building (Hallituskatu 11), designed by Aalto himself.

Rovaniemi is the most cosmopolitan city in Lapland; consequently, it's the best place to sample a variety of Lapp delicacies. The dishes are usually based on local fish or game birds such as salmon, whitefish, ptarmigan, grouse, and capercaillie. There's also a wide variety of reindeer concoctions, such as reindeer stew, smoked reindeer, reindeer tongue, cutlets, steaks, and roasts. For dessert, try any of the cloudberry variations; afterward, a liqueur distilled from one of the native berries — bramble- or cranberry — is appropriate.

SODANKYLÄ: After an 80-mile (130-km) drive north through typical Lapland fell scenery (the roadbed curves between 1,640-foot hills) you reach the lively village of Sodankylä. Here is the oldest church in Lapland, an unpainted timber church in the middle of town.

Outside of town you can stop at smaller villages, all of which are interesting. If it's July, hop south to Porttikoski, where you can see the annual lumberjacks' championships. Heading north, you pass between the two big artificial lakes of Lokka and Porttipahta on your way to Tankavaara, where you can actually pan for gold. If you don't want to get your feet wet, go to the Gold Museum and research the history of the Finnish gold rush.

The scenery grows intensely beautiful as you pass wide fells and long vistas.

INARI: Not as much a town as a borough, Inari is classified as the Finnish city with the largest area. Of its 6,800 people, there are about 1,500 Lapps — or Sami, as they call themselves. Stretching to the northeast is the huge 50-mile-long Lake Inarinjärvi, with cold, exceptionally clear water and 3,000 islands.

At Inari village is the outdoor Sami museum (actually more preserve than museum, it covers almost 2,500 acres), with exhibits of Sami history and examples of Sami dwellings and towns. In March there's a Lapland "rodeo," with reindeer races, lassoing, and relay skiing races. You can also take several different boat excursions on the lake.

UTSJOKI: As you continue driving north, you suddenly descend from the high fell plateau into the Teno River valley. This area used to be crowded with birch trees, but maggots feasted on them for years before anyone thought about conservation. The experts say it's too late to reforest, and the region is fast giving in to encroaching tundra.

Utsjoki is the only city in Finland where the Lapps outnumber the Finns. It's an outdoorsman's town, so don't expect too much in the way of creature comforts. Also, don't assume that just because it's above the Arctic Circle it's always freezing. During the summer, Utsjoki can be one of the hottest places in Europe. The fishing here is great but if it's not one of your first loves, Utsjoki won't be either.

BEST EN ROUTE

Lapland is a tourist area and therefore commands surprisingly high rates. An expensive room for two runs $50 or more per night, and an expensive meal, between $30 and $40.

ROVANIEMI

Hotel Pohjanhovi – This is the city's most famous and traditional hotel. The restaurant is known all over the province and is generally crowded. It probably serves some of the best reindeer dishes in the world. Pohjanpuisto 2 (phone: 1-3731). Expensive.

SODANKYLÄ

Kantakievari – This 53-room hotel has a restaurant with fine food, a bar, sauna, and pool. There are also very good outdoor sports facilities (phone: 1-1926). Moderate.

IVALO

Hotel Ivalo – A new hotel with modern comforts, an indoor pool, and gastronomic delights in the midst of the wilderness. Some 30 miles (50 km) before arriving at Inari. Ivalontie 24 (phone 11-911). Moderate.

UTSJOKI

Utsjoki Tourist Hotel – By the shores of a famous salmon river, this place offers everything you came this far north to see. The restaurant has fresh salmon and reindeer dishes (phone: 7-1121). Moderate.

Exploring France

Thomas Jefferson once said, "Every man has two countries — his own and France." The ideals of the French eighteenth-century Age of Enlightenment were embraced by the American founding fathers; in fact, Rousseau's theory of government by "social contract" formed the basis for the new kind of government boldly proposed in Jefferson's Declaration of Independence. The French inherited their love of reason from the Greeks and the Romans, and for many people, France represents an epitome of human achievement in 2,000 years of Western civilization. Paris is universally beloved as the City of Light, a leader in artistic and intellectual endeavors, and possibly the world's most beautiful city. Most significant, perhaps, has been the French talent for making art out of life. French food, wine, and fashion represent the ultimate in elegance, the perfection of civilized virtues.

To many, Paris is France. Almost 2.5 million of the nation's 53 million people live in the capital; Marseille, which ranks second, has less than a million people; but neither Marseille nor any other city can begin to compare with Paris's influence in French politics and culture. France is star-shaped, with Paris at its heart. All roads and railroads lead there, and anywhere outside Paris is regarded as provincial. Like the roads, the French Revolution radiated from Paris, and it is said that when Louis XIV made the mistake of building his palace at Versailles (only 12 miles outside Paris), he began to lose control over the entire country.

But visitors can hardly be expected to accept such a parochial view of national life. France, of course, is much more than Paris. It is the largest nation in Western Europe and a third larger than California, with an area of 211,208 square miles. To the delight of the French aesthetic sense of symmetry and balance, the country is shaped roughly like a hexagon, three sides bordering on land and three on water. It is a land blessed with great natural beauty and variety: southern sea and northern coast, high mountains and fertile valleys laced with rivers. The jagged Atlantic coastline of Normandy and Brittany forms its western border, and the sun-drenched bays and inlets of the Mediterranean lie to the southeast. The snow-covered Alps, which rise to the dramatic 15,771-foot peak of Mont-Blanc, form the Swiss and Italian borders to the east, and in the south, the high, rugged, olive-treed Pyrenees form a natural border with Spain. The gentle, pine-clad slopes of the Vosges are a continuation of Germany's Black Forest region to the northeast, and the fertile hills and valleys of Champagne and Burgundy are covered with priceless vineyards whose harvest is the source of the world's finest wines.

The French countryside is noted for its long stretches of straight, tree-lined roads, many of which date from Roman times. And although it is an industrial country, France is also a nation of many small privately owned farms.

Its rural population comprises 25% of its total population. A visitor can often catch a glimpse of a plow being drawn by horses or oxen. Thus it is not difficult to understand why the French people regard the soil of their country with an attachment that amounts to reverence.

Not only is their land remarkably beautiful, it has been inhabited since prehistoric times. Wall paintings at Lascaux and in other caves in the Dordogne are probably 20,000 to 30,000 years old. When the Celts migrated to the land they called Gaul sometime before the seventh century BC, it was inhabited by Iberians and Ligurians. Greeks colonized the area around Marseille — which they called Massilia, founding the oldest city in France — and Julius Caesar conquered Gaul for Rome in 57–52 BC. During the fifth century AD, Germanic tribes invaded, especially the Franks, who converted to Christianity under Clovis I and established the kingdom that became known as France.

A unified national spirit was born in France on Christmas Day, 800, when Charlemagne, king of the Franks, was crowned by the pope in Rome as Holy Roman Emperor. Although Charlemagne's empire was short-lived, it left a lasting impression upon the French consciousness, even though the weakness of successive rulers allowed territorial princes, such as the dukes of Burgundy and Normandy, to gain great power. In 987, however, the French nobility elected Hugh Capet king of France, and from this point, French national history is generally agreed to begin. Capet helped to centralize the monarchy, led in the Crusades and wars with England, and founded the Capetian dynasty. During the twelfth and thirteenth centuries, trade flourished, craft guilds were established, and towns sprang up. Paris grew in importance as the royal city and as the intellectual center of Europe; the newly founded Sorbonne drew such teachers and philosophers as Abelard, Albertus Magnus, and Thomas Aquinas.

This time of peace was followed by the devastation and bloodshed of the Hundred Years War of 1337–1453 (the period covered by Barbara Tuchman's brilliant history, *A Distant Mirror*). Essentially a dynastic struggle with England, whose Norman kings held vast fiefs in France, this series of wars ended well for France, driving out the English and strengthening the power of the French monarchy. As in the days of Charlemagne, the French throne was once again endowed with a mystic aura, this time with the help of Joan of Arc, whose divine voices encouraged her to lead the French to victory at Orléans in 1429 and to champion Charles VII as king of France.

During the sixteenth and seventeenth centuries the Valois and Bourbon kings further increased the royal authority, moving the country toward absolute monarchy. The strong-armed rule of Cardinals Richelieu and Mazarin (1624–61) set the stage for their splendid successor, Louis XIV, whose reign was probably unequaled in the history of Europe for its elaborate and magnificent style. His attitude can be summarized in his famous remark, "L'État c'est moi" ("I am the state"). His was an age of brilliant achievements in art and literature, making France indisputably the intellectual capital of Europe. French became the international language for more than a century afterward. Frederick the Great of Prussia, who lived during the mid-eighteenth century, spoke French, employed the French philosopher Voltaire as a tutor, and was rumored to have said that German was a language fit to be spoken only to horses and dogs.

The very magnificence of the French monarchy helped precipitate its downfall, for it was expensive to maintain and someone had to pay. The major cause of the French Revolution was the system of special privileges that exempted nobles and clergy from the taxes paid by the peasants and the middle class. In 1789, these latter groups rebelled against the monarchy in the person of Louis XVI, guillotined both the king and his queen, Marie Antoinette, and established the short-lived First Republic.

The chaos that followed the revolution resulted in the rise of Napoleon, who proclaimed himself emperor in 1804 and, though a dictator, undertook to spread the ideal of liberty to the world through his conquests. After his fall in 1814, the monarchy was restored. Nineteenth-century France alternated between democracy and dictatorship and was characterized by the steady growth of a new French Empire (which disintegrated in the twentieth century). A revolution in 1848 established a Second Republic, which was superseded by the dictatorship of Napoleon III, nephew of the emperor. Finally, a Third Republic emerged in 1870 that lasted until 1940, that saddest time in all French history when France capitulated to Nazi Germany. Between 1940 and 1945, the government was led by World War I hero Marshal Philippe Pétain, who, in collaboration with the Nazis, established a puppet government in Vichy in the South of France.

After World War II, the Fourth Republic was created; it collapsed in 1958 under the pressure of a revolution in Algeria. Although the Fifth Republic, engineered by Charles de Gaulle, has been threatened by the great number of political parties in France, it has managed to stand up in the face of such serious threats as the student revolt and general strike of May 1968.

The France of the past can, for the most part, still be seen today. The French preserve their old buildings well, be they the royal châteaux of Blois and Chambord in the Loire Valley or the magnificent cathedrals of Chartres and Reims. The landscapes of France are exciting, from the Pyrenees, the rugged mountains of southern France, and the snow-covered Alps farther north, to the luxuriant vegetation and posh villas of the sun-drenched Riviera on the Mediterranean coast, to the stark, chalk cliffs of Normandy's beaches. If you enjoy wine, you can tour the vineyards of Burgundy, Bordeaux, and Dordogne, and for food, every region of France has a different and highly developed style.

Our ten routes include Paris's weekend vacation land, a 50-mile radius called the Île-de-France, extending north of the capital to Chantilly, west to Beauvais, and south to Chartres; it contains peaceful forests and valleys, châteaux and cathedrals. Paris itself is treated in detail in *Paris*, THE EUROPEAN CITIES. From Paris you can also zigzag west into Normandy in the direction of Cherbourg, passing through green pastures and exploring the cheese industry, fashionable beaches, and busy harbors. Jutting out between the English Channel and the Bay of Biscay, Brittany's peninsula can be toured in a semicircular route from the magnificent shrine at Mont-St.-Michel west to Quimper and back east to the port of Nantes and its château. The Loire

Valley, France's most splendid château country, extends east from Angers to Blois and includes some wine country as well. Two celebrated wine routes begin in the city of Bordeaux: The Dordogne lies east toward Rocamadour and Les Eyzies-de-Tayac, including fertile farmlands and prehistoric cave paintings, while Bordeaux runs north toward Pauillac and the fabled wine cellars of Lafite-Rothschild and Mouton-Rothschild.

Two of the most glorious areas in France, Provence and the Riviera, are adjacent to one another and can be seen together. Sunny Provence includes towns unmatched anywhere for their charm and beauty; they are set in the craggy mountains from Avignon southeast to Aix-en-Provence. Just south and west is the Riviera, stretching along the coast from Menton to St.-Tropez, a country beloved by modern painters like Picasso and Matisse for its dramatic cliffs overlooking the clear blue Mediterranean waters, its charming bays and fishing villages, its splendid villas and fashionable beaches.

Burgundy, yet another wine district, opens southward from Auxerre to Bourg-en-Bresse, passing through peaceful hills and valleys and ancient towns. Finally, there are the provinces of Alsace and Lorraine, with their strongly Germanic atmosphere and their beer as well as wine; when you travel east from Nancy to Strasbourg, it often seems that you're in Germany.

The Île-de-France

The first thing you should know about the "island of France" (Île-de-France) is that it is not an island. It is, in fact, the region surrounding Paris, and the name "Île" comes from the rivers that form its boundaries: the Epte, the Aisne, the Marne, the Yonne, and the Eure, with the Seine and the Oise also running through the territory. Don't look for it on a map, though: legally, the region doesn't exist. Its population can't be counted, and neither train nor bus schedule knows it by name.

The Île-de-France, extending around the city to a radius of roughly 50 miles (80 km), offers something for every visitor. Through this area traveled Charlemagne, St. Louis, Joan of Arc, Louis XIV and all the kings of France, not to mention Emperor Napoleon, leaving memorials of their passing. The art lover is drawn to the magnificent cathedrals, beautifully preserved medieval abbeys, and sumptuous châteaux — architecture and design unparalleled anywhere else in France. For the nature enthusiast or the weary city dweller, the Île-de-France has peaceful valleys, forests, and wildlife.

We suggest you make Paris your base for forays into the region. Every site on the route makes a comfortable day trip or can be combined with other stops to fill out a weekend jaunt. To strangers, Paris — the City of Light — can seem rather dark on Sundays and Mondays when the shops and many restaurants are closed. These are ideal days to visit this nearby countryside.

CHANTILLY: Only 25 miles (40 km) from Paris via N16, Chantilly is famous for its château, its parks, and, of course, the racetrack. Five different châteaux have existed on this site in the last 2,000 years, but the present one was built only between 1875 and

1881 at the direction of the duke of Aumale, a son of King Louis-Philippe. The château is small by French standards but exceptionally elegant. Inside is an excellent museum with over 2,000 artworks, including more than 600 oils by French, Flemish, and Italian masters of the sixteenth to eighteenth centuries. Also visit the library, with its prodigious collection of rare books; the eighteenth-century stables; and the chapel, where, to this day, the descendants of the last owner gather for Sunday services. Take time as well to wander through the gardens and the extensive forest which was a favorite hunting ground of the kings and nobles of France for five centuries.

En Route from Chantilly – A few miles southwest, taking D118 to D909, you'll come to Royaumont, one of the best-preserved medieval abbeys in France. Royaumont was founded by St. Louis in 1228, and the wealth and beauty that are still apparent attest to the protection lavished on it by successive kings of France.

St.-Leu-d'Esserent lies 3 miles (4.8 km) northwest of Chantilly via N16 to D44. Its mellow and beautiful twelfth-century stone church is renowned for its architectural excellence on a commanding site overlooking the Oise.

Route N924 east leads to the charming town of Senlis, dominated by the Ancienne Cathédrale de Notre-Dame (pl. Notre Dame), begun in 1153. Of particular interest is the portico, dedicated to the Virgin and the prototype for the porticoes of Chartres, Notre-Dame-de-Paris, and Reims. Also well worth a visit are the ancient church of St.-Pierre (pl. St.-Pierre), the Château Royal (for its Gallo-Roman walkway), and the hunting museum (Musée de la Vénerie) in front of the château. The Gallo-Roman walkway, a defense wall around the chateau's perimeter, provides a good vantage point from which to view the principal monuments.

At Chaalis (7 mi/11.3 km south via N330) are the picturesque ruins of a thirteenth-century abbey and, in the park, yet another château in addition to a museum that has three rooms devoted to the works of Jean-Jacques Rousseau, who died in nearby Ermenonville in 1778. You can also enjoy the countryside: There are numerous ponds, the famous Mer de Sable (Sea of Sand), and a small zoo at Ermenonville, 2 miles (3.2 km) south on N330.

COMPIÈGNE: On the banks of the Oise, 49 miles (78.4 km) north of Paris via N17, is this village, justly famous for its palace (pl. du Palais). The palace's exterior is somewhat austere, but the exquisite interior decoration is beautifully preserved.

Compiègne has played a significant role in French history: Most of the kings of France visited the town at one time or another, and Joan of Arc was taken prisoner here in 1430. In more recent conflicts, the armistices of November 11, 1918, and June 22, 1940, were signed here (the exact site is marked in a clearing — Clairière de l'Armistice — in the woods surrounding the palace). In a sad footnote, from 1941 to 1944, Compiègne served as a deportation center for France's Jewish community en route to concentration camps.

The forest of Compiègne, with nearly 35,000 acres, has majestic avenues, pools (étangs de St.-Pierre), and picturesque villages, such as Vieux-Moulin and St.-Jean-aux-Bois. Just beyond the forest, via D85, is the splendid twelfth-century château-fortress of Pierrefonds, once the property of Napoleon.

BEAUVAIS: About 45 miles (72 km) from Paris via A15 and D927 lies Beauvais. Although the city is in one of the less attractive parts of the Île-de-France, a visit to the imposing Cathédrale St.-Pierre makes the trip worthwhile.

The cathedral, whose Gothic style is in rather jarring contrast to that of the rest of the city, has had an erratic history, plagued by overambition and underfinancing. The soaring choir section, begun in 1247, was a challenge to architects throughout Europe. Unfortunately, they proved unequal to the challenge, and in 1284 the choir collapsed. In 1500, another generation of bishops decided to continue the work and undertook to finance it by the expedient sale of indulgences. But again the architects literally let

Beauvais down: An experimental cross tower was constructed, but the supporting pillars gave way in 1573. Since then, the cathedral of Beauvais has remained a magnificent — but unfinished — monument.

The vaulted interior of the cathedral appears to rise to dizzying heights. The well-preserved stained glass windows give a luminous light that serves to illuminate the church's magnificent tapestries, attesting to the city's renown as a center of weaving. Before leaving the city, look also at the Église St.-Étienne (rue de l'Étamine and rue de l'Infanterie). The stained glass of the choir section is among the most beautiful of the Renaissance.

En Route from Beauvais – Heading south toward Paris, take a detour west on D981 and D181 until you reach the town of Vernon. Nearby you'll find Giverny, the home of impressionist painter Claude Monet from 1883 until his death in 1926. Forty years after Monet died, his home and its gardens were given to the Academy of Beaux-Arts by his son, but they did not open to the public until 1980, after painstaking restoration of the grounds and structures according to Monet's many canvases of the place. Visitors can stroll through the exquisite flower-strewn French gardens and, across the road, the Oriental garden with its familiar Japanese bridge and lily pond, so often painted by Monet. The pink farmhouse and Monet's studio can also be visited. Open daily except Mondays from April to November 1.

From Giverny, take N15 and N13 to St. Germaine-en-Laye (from Paris it's 13 miles/21 km west on N13). This former home of kings is today a favorite weekend retreat for Parisians. Its château was originally begun in the twelfth century, but completely rebuilt in the sixteenth to bring it up to Renaissance standards. Two floors are occupied by the Musée des Antiquités Nationales, with displays of ceramics, glass, and jewelry through the time of Charlemagne. The gardens and terraces are splendid, and the extensive forest surrounding the town offers all manner of recreational activities. The restaurants here include the well-regarded *Cazaudehore,* in the inn *La Forestière* (see *Best En Route*).

Continue west on N13 until you reach the château of Malmaison, bought by Napoleon as a gift to Josephine in 1799 and the place where she settled after her divorce in 1809. It's now a museum with many impressive artworks of the Napoleonic period, some of the house's original furnishings, and documents and mementos of battle tracing the era's history.

Return east on the N13 to N186. Following it south, you pass the most famous palace in all of France: Versailles, the crowning glory of Louis XIV. You will certainly want to stop here — and allow plenty of time; the palace and gardens are immense!

VERSAILLES: The building of this incredibly lavish palace nearly bankrupted the French monarchy. About 6,000 people once lived in the palace, and its vast gardens, designed by the famous royal gardener Le Nôtre in the formal French style, are spread out over 250 acres. A river was diverted to keep the 600 fountains flowing.

There is so much to see in Versailles that you might even want to spend more than 1 day here. On Sunday evenings in the summer, you can see the fountains illuminated in a splendid *son-et-lumière* show (phone: 950-5832).

The highlights include the Royal Apartments, the Chapel, and the Hall of Mirrors. Don't miss the gardens and some of the smaller buildings on the grounds, including the Grand Trianon and the Petit Trianon, smaller retreats for kings, queens, and royal mistresses; and Le Hameau, Marie Antoinette's model farm, where she and her companions pretended to be shepherds. Information about Versailles is available from the Versailles Tourist Office, 7 rue des Reservoirs (phone: 950-3622 and 950-5390).

En Route from Versailles – Just south of Versailles via D91, you enter an area that many Frenchmen consider the prettiest countryside in the Île-de-France

— the Vallée de Chevreuse. Picturesque villages abound: Châteaufort, with its twelfth-century fortress; St.-Rémy-lès-Chevreuse; St.-Lambert; Dampierre, the site of a sixteenth-century château; and Les Vaux de Cernay, one of the loveliest valleys in France. Just south of Les Vaux de Cernay on N306 is Rambouillet, the château that served as a rural retreat for Louis XVI and Napoleon, and is still used today by President François Mitterrand. Originally a medieval fortress, it retains its impressive fourteenth-century tower. You can tour the château whenever President Mitterrand is away (which is often). From here, take N306 and then N10 straight to Chartres.

CHARTRES: Even though you may think you've seen enough cathedrals for a lifetime, Chartres remains a must. About 50 miles (80 km) southwest of Paris via D988 and N10, Chartres is without doubt the jewel of medieval cathedrals. The Portail Royal, portraying Christ in triumph, is one of the finest examples of French religious art. And Chartres is known above all for its stained-glass windows. Dating mostly from the twelfth and thirteenth centuries, with later replacements made from the original designs, they are considered the most beautiful in France, a country where exquisite stained glass has been preserved in remarkable quantity.

The city of Chartres, dotted with ancient gabled houses and charming corners, lives up to the beauty of the cathedral. Walk along the path from the cathedral to the St.-André church, for example, or, behind the bishopric, take the Tertre-St.-Nicholas down to the River Eure with its series of bridges. As you head back toward the cathedral, wander along rue Chantault, rue aux Herbes, rue de la Petite Cordonnerie, and the place de la Poissonnerie, where curious old houses give one a sense of the medieval city come alive. The museum of Chartres (right behind the cathedral) houses some paintings and sculptures by the Fauvist artist Maurice Vlaminck.

En Route from Chartres – If you reached Chartres via Versailles and have already seen the sights there, you'll find little of interest on the road directly back to Paris. But if you've time for a detour east, you'll enter into the region of Fontainebleau, where there's plenty to see and do (from Chartres take D24 to N837; from Paris take N7 south).

FONTAINEBLEAU: Surrounding the fabulous Renaissance palace is a forest of 50,000 acres, the ancient hunting preserve of the kings of France. Today, the grounds are open to the public, and picnicking, hiking, or horseback riding among the trees, ravines, and ponds makes a perfect counterpoint to a day of city sight-seeing.

The palace itself was transformed from a twelfth-century medieval château to a Renaissance palace by Francis I during the early sixteenth century. Later kings added further alterations and wings, including Napoleon, who lived here during most of his reign. Many people find Fontainebleau more beautiful than Versailles. It's open daily except Tuesdays for a fee, and there's a guided tour through the Throne Room, the Queen's bedroom, which was redone for Marie-Antoinette, the splendid Royal Apartments with their Gobelin tapestries, the Council Room, and the Red Room, where Napoleon abdicated in 1814.

En Route from Fontainebleau – Just on the edge of the forest lies Barbizon, made famous as an artist's colony in the nineteenth century by the likes of Daumier, Troyon, Musset, and George Sand. You can visit Rousseau's house on the Grand Rue, just behind the Monument aux Morts, and you can stop for a drink at the celebrated *Bas-Bréau,* an elegant second home to many Parisians.

Taking N5 out of Fontainebleau, you'll pass by the ruins of the ancient Abbaye-du-Lys. The next important landmark is Vaux-le-Vicomte, whose seventeenth-century château and gardens are among the most beautiful in Europe. The château was commissioned by Fouquet, an important government official under Louis XIV. Unfortunately, Fouquet's exquisite taste required greater resources than his personal fortune could accommodate, and access to state funds was all too simple.

To build Vaux-le-Vicomte, Fouquet hired the greatest talents of the day: Le Vau as architect, Le Brun as decorator, Le Nôtre as landscape architect. Employing a total of 18,000 laborers, the work was finished 5 years and the equivalent of $10 million later. But Fouquet had committed the fatal error of being grander than his sovereign. In August 1661, he gave a fabulous dinner for Louis XIV. The decoration, the food, and the entertainment were so dazzlingly elegant that they provoked the king's jealous curiosity, and in no time Fouquet's embezzlement was exposed. A few days later, Fouquet was in prison and his property confiscated. But the château had lit a spark in the king's imagination, and Louis XIV employed the same team to build his own dream palace at Versailles, the site of his father's hunting lodge. Many of the splendidly decorated rooms of Vaux-le-Vicomte are open to the public from late March through October.

A 30-mile (48-km) drive along the valley of the Seine (N5) returns you to Paris.

BEST EN ROUTE

Because of their close proximity to Paris, country inns in the Île-de-France tend to have city prices. Reservations are almost always required. Expect to pay $70 and up per night for a double room in hotels listed as expensive; $30 to $45 in those listed as moderate; and $20 to $30, inexpensive. The restaurants range in price from $50 and up for a dinner for two in the expensive range; $30 to $50 in the moderate range; and $15 to $30 and under, inexpensive.

CHANTILLY

Le Relais Condé – Small and bright, with a beamed ceiling and huge stone fireplace, this restaurant serves classic cuisine. 42 av. du Maréchal-Joffre (phone: 457-0575). Expensive.

Hôtel d'Angleterre – A pleasant inn, simply furnished. 9 pl. Omer-Vallon (phone: 457-0059). Moderate to inexpensive.

LYS-CHANTILLY

Hostel du Lys – A modest hotel in a calm, beautiful park. 63 av. Septième (phone: 421-2619). Moderate.

TOUTEVOIE

Pavillon St.-Hubert – A small hotel in a relaxing setting overlooking a placid pond. (phone: 457-0704). Inexpensive.

COMPIÈGNE

Résidence de la Forêt – A small, comfortable hotel. 112 rue St.-Lazare (phone: 420-2286). Inexpensive.

ST.-JEAN-AUX-BOIS

La Bonne Idée – A fine restaurant in a peaceful setting; 12 rooms available. Royer. (phone: 442-8409). Moderate.

BEAUVAIS

Mercure – A comfortable hotel with modern facilities and swimming. Quartier St.-Lazare (phone: 402-0336). Moderate.

WARLUIS

Alpes Franco-Suisse – A modest hotel in a wonderful country setting, with modern facilities and swimming. Rt. National 1 (phone: 402-0121). Moderate.

ST.-GERMAIN-EN-LAYE

Le Forestière – This charming country inn with lovely gardens is a comfortable place for an overnight stay, but many visit simply for its *Cazaudehore* restaurant. The kitchen turns out wonderful Basque specialties and classic French dishes. 1 av. Président-Kennedy (phone: 451-9380). Expensive.

Pavillon Henri IV – An old-fashioned hotel with plush accommodations and a pleasant restaurant (where sauce Béarnaise was invented) overlooking the gardens of the château. 21 rue Thiers (phone: 451-6262). Expensive.

VERSAILLES

Trois Marches – Warm, intimate decor, charming service, and highly original cooking mark this celebrated restaurant. Chef Gérard Vié invents new recipes daily, but his foie gras is famous, as are his oysters and his wild goose. The wines here, especially the Burgundies, are excellent, too. Closed Sunday and Monday. 3 rue Colbert (phone: 950-1321). Expensive.

VÉSINET

Les Ibis – Set in a large park in an attractive residential area, the restaurant offers good food and a warm atmosphere. The rooms are simple but comfortable. Île du Grand Lac (phone: 952-1741). Moderate.

ORGEVAL

Auberge Provençale – A very attractive country inn and restaurant set in private gardens. Take N13 and D198 from St. Germaine-en-Laye (phone: 975-8757). Moderate.

BOUGIVAL

Coq Hardy – A superb restaurant, with elegant country decor and a reputation as host to many of France's VIPs. Closed Wednesdays. 16 quai Rennequin-Sualem (Rte. N13) (phone: 969-0163). Expensive.

La Caméllia – One of France's highest-rated restaurants. The country decor is charming and the food exquisite. Specialties include sole and baby pigeon. Closed Sundays and Mondays. 7 quai G.-Clemenceau (phone: 969-0302). Expensive.

CHARTRES

Grand Monarque – The town's fanciest hotel with a good (expensive) restaurant serving nouvelle cuisine. Rooms are individually decorated, some with both bath and shower. 22 pl. des Épars (phone: 21-00-72). Moderate.

Boeuf Couronne – Half of the 26 spotless rooms here look over at the cathedral. There are a bar and outside terraces and a restaurant that serves local specialties. 15 pl. du Châtelet (phone: 21-11-26). Inexpensive.

La Vieille Maison – Elegant dining in an old house near the cathedral. Meals feature the freshest local produce. 5 rue au Lait (phone: 34-10-67). Expensive.

Café Serpente – In the former post office building facing the cathedral, this bistro offers a fixed menu along with good desserts and some fast-food items for tourists in a hurry. 2 Cloître Nôtre Dame (phone: 21-68-81). Moderate to inexpensive.

BARBIZON

Hôtellerie du Bas-Bréau – An elegant hotel that has hosted well-heeled Parisians and celebrities since 1867. Modern bathrooms, an intimate bar, and a fine restaurant. 22 Grande Rue (phone: 066-4005). Very expensive.

Normandy

Settled by successive waves of Celts, Gauls, and Britons, Normandy was the target of the Roman invasion in 56 BC. In the ninth century AD, the Vikings (north men, hence Normans) sailed from Scandinavia in their longboats — massacring, looting, burning, and taking possession of the land. Finally, in 911, the astute King Charles the Simple (whose name means "honest and straightforward" rather than "feeble-minded") and the Viking leader Rollo agreed to a truce, the terms of which granted to the "Normans on the Seine" the lands they already occupied in exchange for a permanent peace. Thus the duchy of Normandy was founded, and Rollo — later baptized Robert — was its first duke.

The erstwhile pirates proved to be adept both as farmers and as administrators in the rich and fertile valley of the Seine, and a prosperous, civilized state began to flourish within a century. The turbulent Norse blood rose one more time, however, when in 1066 William the Bastard, a direct — if left-handed — descendant of Rollo/Robert was thwarted by the Englishman Harold Godwinson in his claim to the throne of England on the death of Edward the Confessor. William enlisted the pope to his cause and, by September, was able to set sail for England with 12,000 men in almost 3,000 vessels. The English resistance was fierce, but on October 14, Harold lay dead on the battlefield near Hastings "with an arrow in his eye," and William — now no longer the Bastard but the Conqueror — was crowned king of England in Westminster Abbey on Christmas Day. A remarkable, graphic record of the conquest is preserved in the Bayeux tapestry across from the Bayeux cathedral. Nine hundred years later, an invasion in the opposite direction was accomplished with equal success at the beaches on the coast of Calvados.

The landscape of Normandy is graced by a wealth of historic buildings that reflect the affluence and expansive generosity of the Norman people. Churches, abbeys, castles, and manor houses abound in styles that exemplify the finest of the last ten centuries of European architecture. The materials for these buildings were delved from the land that supports them: soft, chalky stone in Rouen and the towns bordering the Seine; harder, fine-grained limestone around Caen. The simpler, half-timbered farmhouses and cottages of lower Normandy are typically constructed of whitewashed clay rammed between dark-stained lathes and topped with intricately woven thatch. In the Suisse Normande, an Alpine character is suggested by shale-covered cottages clustered against the hillsides. Sandstone and granite lend an austere effect to the time-weathered buildings of the Bocage and the Cotentin.

The seaside diversions of the Normandy coast range from the sophisticated glamour of the international resort of Deauville to the long, sandy stretches of Arromanches and Omaha (a name used only since the Allied landing of D-day, June 6, 1944; the three beaches comprising Omaha were formerly called St.-Laurent, Colleville, and Vierville-sur-Mer). The hinterland offers grassy plateaus and undulating valleys threaded with freshwater streams.

The rolling green pastures of Normandy sustain horses ranging in size and temperament from spirited thoroughbreds to the massive Percheron draft-horses. Thousands of acres are given over to raising apples and flax. Most important, goats and sheep are raised for the cheese-making industry, for Normandy is the dairy of France. Norman cheeses such as Camembert and Pont l'Évêque are renowned the world over.

The cream of Normandy — like liquid ivory — complements the fine fish, vegetables, fruit, and game of the region, and for true Normans, of course, cider — *bon bère* — accompanies hearty dinners of regional specialties such as *tripes à la mode de Caen, présalé* lamb from the salt marshes, or duck from Rouen. A pause is customarily taken in the middle of the Norman meal for the *trou Normand* — a quick gulp of the fiery Calvados, applejack distilled from cider and aged for as long as 12 years to achieve a perfect fullness of flavor. An apple tart with cream is a memorable finish to any meal in Normandy.

Since the end of World War II, the Seine Valley and the Caen area have undergone dramatic industrial development. New industries such as motor vehicle assembly and oil refining have drawn workers away from the traditional Norman crafts of tanning and coppersmithing. The old *métiers* still survive on a reduced scale, however, and latter-day planners and developers have preserved — and often restored — the historic monuments and natural features of the landscape.

The arts have enjoyed a long and distinguished tradition in Normandy. The agonies suffered by France during the Hundred Years War inspired Olivier Basselin, a weaver from Les-Vaux-de-Vire, to write songs so spirited and timely that, although the songs themselves eventually passed from common currency, the name by which they were collectively known evolved from its original form to "vaudeville," passing out of the French language into English. Corneille, Flaubert, and Maupassant, among others, were natives of Normandy; Victor Hugo, although not a Norman, is inextricably bound to the province through his moving *Les Contemplations,* in which he mourns the tragic deaths by drowning of his daughter Léopoldine and her husband in the Norman village of Villequier in 1843. The village today is marked by a statue and a museum honoring the author. The luminous skies and delicate tints of the Norman countryside attracted the group of mid-nineteenth-century painters who, in prefiguring the Impressionists, became known as the Barbizon School, after the village in the forest of Fontainebleau. A few years later, the Impressionists — Monet, Renoir, the Englishman Sisley, and others — in turn took their inspiration from the light of Normandy. In the early twentieth century, the province was a magnet for some of the finest painters of the period — Valloton, Van Dongen, and Dufy.

Only a half-day's drive from Paris, Normandy has beckoned tourists for generations, and its innkeepers and restaurateurs have maintained a tradition of comfort and hospitality at reasonable prices. The chic terrace cafés of Deauville and other coastal towns are full of Parisian weekenders and vacationers from May to September. Well-organized Syndicats d'Initiative (tourist information offices) in the smaller towns will supply all the information you need to enjoy the countryside and its seasonal specialties.

You can drive to Normandy from any point in France, but since most visitors come from Paris, we'll give the quickest route from that direction: Take Autoroute A13 (Autoroute de Normandie) as far as the Chaufour exit, about 48 miles (77 km) from Paris. Then join route N13 for about 6 miles (10 km) to Pacy-sur-Eure; you're in Normandy.

PACY-SUR-EURE: Pacy is the commercial and service center both for residents and for Parisians with country homes in the area. The Gothic church of St.-Aubin, remodeled in the sixteenth century, is worth a quick visit, and don't miss the well-known restaurant *Mère Corbeau*.

En Route from Pacy-sur-Eure – Autoroute N13 toward Évreux takes you 22 miles (35.2 km) across the flat plateau of St.-André-de-l'Eure, which is strongly reminiscent of the plain of Beauce surrounding Chartres. Wheat and corn are the principal crops in this area of comfortable, conservative farmers.

About 4 miles (6 km) on the right before Évreux you'll see an air force base, built by the US after World War II and turned over to France in 1965. Signs reading "Centreville" lead you off N13 and into Évreux along the rue F. D. Roosevelt.

ÉVREUX: The religious and commercial capital of the Eure is a charming, typically Norman town too often neglected by travelers. The town has existed since Gallic times and has survived sacking and pillage by Vandals, Normans, English, and even fellow French. Évreux suffered heavy damage in the 1944 bombings, with the result that today its architecture is a medley of the very new cheek by jowl with ancient Norman half-timbered houses. Rue Chartraine, the main shopping street, is lined with elegant shops offering the products of local craftspeople. The many cafés are an important focus for business discussions and general "catching up" on market days.

If you park in the Cathedral of Notre Dame parking lot, you're in an excellent position to begin a walk at the foot of the Gallo-Roman ramparts along the Iton River, past the elegant fifteenth-century clock tower. The cathedral itself is a superb example of Gothic construction, with the earliest parts dating from the twelfth century. English-language guides are available. In the former Bishop's House not far from the cathedral is a museum with displays of prehistoric and Gallo-Roman archaeology and artifacts of medieval Normandy.

En Route from Évreux – Taking N13 toward Lisieux leads you through the richest cultivated land south of the Seine, dotted here and there with picturesque country churches. At the intersection of N13 and D840, turn right for Neubourg, a pleasant rural town with a lively marketplace. At the market, turn left to enter D137. After about 6 miles (10 km) you come to Champ de Bataille, an imposing seventeenth-century mansion. A guided tour is well worth the 45 minutes, especially for art lovers, who will admire the fine paintings by Drouais, Van Loo, and Fragonard, among others, as well as sculpture by Canova, Lemoyne, and Pigalle.

Now you are in the heart of the region, the Normandy of legend. Drive carefully, keeping an eye out for the farmers who lead their herds back to the barns for milking in the late afternoon. Continue on D137 toward Brionne, once a medieval stronghold and now a living museum. From Brionne, N138 will take you on one of the most beautiful routes in France to the city of Rouen. Allow time to stop on the way, for every village is a gem. You should be prepared to spend at least a night and half a day in the picturesque and historic city of Rouen.

ROUEN: Though famous as the scene of the disgraceful trial and execution of Joan of Arc, quite independently of "the Maid," Rouen is renowned as a treasury of medieval architecture — the City of 100 Steeples. The capital of upper Normandy, Rouen has kept its ancient character, with houses dating from the fifteenth century still inhabited on narrow streets. The Syndicat d'Initiative (25 pl. Cathédrale) can provide detailed tourist information in English. Be sure to see Rouen Cathedral, a fine Gothic structure built in the eleventh and twelfth centuries. Walk along the renowned rue du Gros-Horloge (Street of the Great Clock), whose enormous clock is the best-known monument in the city. Two blocks away is the place du Vieux-Marché (Old Marketplace), where Joan of Arc was burned at the stake in 1431. She is publicly commemorated at the site on the last Sunday of every May.

Small shops in Rouen sell original drawings and paintings and the distinctive blue and white Rouen ceramics.

To reach the coast at Dieppe, take N27 north for 36 miles (58 km) through the Caux Plateau, a rich agricultural region.

DIEPPE: This ancient port has lost only a little of its character to the efficient modern harbor that has turned Dieppe into the largest passenger port in France. Today the traffic through the harbor is likely to consist of fishing vessels or private boats, but in the sixteenth century the city was a major point of embarkation for explorers, privateers, and merchant ships.

A stroll through old Dieppe is a little like opening a history book tracing ten centuries of development. In the middle of the Fish Market is the ancient place du Puits Sale (Square of the Salty Well), a major crossroads. The Church of St. James was begun in the thirteenth century and has portions from the succeeding three centuries, and Dieppe Castle, built for the most part in the fifteenth century, was constructed around a much earlier tower fortification.

The beach along Maréchal Foch, at the foot of the castle, is extremely popular.

En Route from Dieppe – Travel along D75 and D79 via Fécamp toward Étretat. The road offers breathtaking views of the cliffs of the Côte d'Albâtre (Alabaster Coast). Fécamp is worth a stop for its typical Norman architecture and equally traditional ivory handicrafts. From Fécamp to Étretat, take D11, a pretty drive through the countryside, which alternates between dairy land and high cliffs.

ÉTRETAT: Étretat is famous for its high cliffs, which inspired many Impressionist painters, including Monet and Boudin. An eleventh-and twelfth-century church and a reconstructed market add charm and character to the town.

A drive via D910, N810, the Tancaxuitte Bridge, and Autoroute A1 takes you to the famous seaside resort of Deauville.

DEAUVILLE: This beautiful and elegant northern counterpart to St.-Tropez on the Riviera has all the accoutrements of a fashionable resort, complete with casino, lovely sailing harbor, and horse racing. Deauville life is marked by the activity on the boardwalk that runs the length of the beach. (Avoid the restaurants on the promenade, which are overpriced for the quality.) Hotels and restaurants here are very expensive, so we recommend that you spend the night at Honfleur, only 20 minutes away. Trouville is Deauville's twin city and a fishing town, where at sunset you can watch the fishermen bringing in the day's catch. An evening stroll along the harbor is lovely.

En Route from Deauville – The drive from Deauville-Trouville to Honfleur takes you along the Normandy Corniche, with breathtaking views of the sea. Take N834 through Trouville, past Touques, and into D288. At the David crossroads, bear left onto D279 for Honfleur.

HONFLEUR: Honfleur is a tiny, perfectly preserved old fishing harbor, with many monuments dating as far back as the thirteenth century. Honfleur was the base for the seventeenth-century voyages of discovery that led to the settlement of the most important French colonies, including Canada and Louisiana.

A 45-minute drive along A13 takes you to Caen.

CAEN: As the capital of lower Normandy, Caen is the region's agricultural and industrial center. Extensively damaged by World War II, Caen has been rebuilt with the traditional limestone to modern, urban plans.

Few monuments survived the 1944 shellings, but among those undamaged were the twin Abbaye aux Hommes and Abbaye aux Dames — reparation offerings of William the Conqueror and his wife, Queen Matilda. Restorations were carried out in the seventeenth century to replace areas damaged in the Wars of Religion.

A "must" for gourmands is the local specialty: *tripes à la mode de Caen.*

Less than 20 minutes away on N13 lies Bayeux, another town intimately connected with William and his consort.

BAYEUX: This was the first town liberated after D-day. The Gothic cathedral, built in the eleventh century, is well worth a visit to see the extraordinary Bayeux tapestry, which presents a blow-by-blow account of the decisive Battle of Hastings. (Recorded English-language tours are available daily except Christmas.)

To reach the historic D-day shore of Arromanches, take a 15-minute drive on D156.

ARROMANCHES: "If we want to land, we must take our harbors with us." With these words, the historic decision was taken to build artificial harbors for the D-day landing. Some parts of the harbor foundation built by the Allies can still be seen. The invasion museum provides an English-language commentary on the events of 1944.

En Route from Arromanches – The American Military Cemetery is about 1.5 miles (3 km) beyond Colleville-sur-Mer (Omaha). A memorial fountain stands in front of the monument, surrounded by trees. The site commands an impressive view of the sea.

From the cemetery, take N13 to Cherbourg for the night.

CHERBOURG: When still a naval base, Cherbourg was an important harbor during World War II. The War and Liberation Museum illustrates the progress of the war from the Allied landing on D-day right up to the German capitulation in May 1945. Technically speaking, Normandy ends with Cherbourg, although your visit is not complete without seeing the monastery of Mont-St.-Michel, the romantic and beautiful peak that has been a source of dispute between Normandy and Brittany for centuries.

The drive from Cherbourg to Mont-St.-Michel — via D900, D971, and D973 — takes 2½ hours.

MONT-ST.-MICHEL: Atop soaring cliffs that rise from a flat, sandy marsh, the abbey of Mont-St.-Michel dates back to the eighth century, when it is said that the Archangel Michael appeared and commanded that a church be built on the spot. The archangel's footprint — admittedly vague in outline — is still shown to visitors. To tour the abbey, leave your car in one of the official parking lots and enter on foot through the outer gate of the ramparts. Don't miss the Lacework Staircase (Escalier de Dentelle), the superb Gothic buildings (Merveille), and the cloister, which seems suspended between sky and sea. The view from the North Tower is especially dramatic.

BEST EN ROUTE

Expect to pay $50 and up per night for a double room listed as expensive; $30 to $50 in those listed as moderate; and $20 to $30, inexpensive. The restaurants range in price from $40 and up for a dinner for two in the expensive range $30 to $40 in the moderate range; and $30 and under, inexpensive.

ÉVREUX

Normandy – Just off the main street and recently restored as a fine example of the best of Norman hospitality. Good restaurant features local specialties. 37 rue E. Féray (phone: 33-14-40). Moderate.

ROUEN

La Couronne – With a lovely old Norman decor, this is Rouen's most famous restaurant. It's known mostly for duck, but other local classics are just as fine. Closed Sunday nights and Mondays. 31 pl. Vieux-Marché (phone: 71-40-90). Expensive.

Frantel – Part of the modern chain, but it fits astoundingly well into the old quarter. There are 125 rooms and all comforts. Rue Croix de Fer (phone: 98-06-98). Expensive.

Grand Hotel Nord – Old but charming; in the center of vibrant Rouen. 91 rue Gros-Horloge (phone: 70-41-41). Moderate.

DIEPPE

Horizon – The view over the sea is amazing, and the menu is superb. Try their famous *sole Normande*. There is a casino on the second floor. Closed Wednesdays. Blvd. Verdun (phone: 82-33-60). Expensive to moderate.

Univers – Beautiful antique furnishings. Make sure to reserve ahead for this small, popular hotel. 10 blvd. Verdun (phone: 84-12-55). Moderate.

DEAUVILLE

PLM Port de Deauville – Overlooking the picturesque harbor; reservations essential, especially in summer (phone: 88-62-62). Moderate.

HONFLEUR

Hostellerie Lechat – This comfortable hotel is in the heart of the old harbor district. 15 pl. Ste.-Catherine (phone: 89-23-85). Expensive to moderate.

Ferme de la Grande Cour – In the middle of a beautiful orchard, offering the best cider in the area along with a wide selection of local specialties. Côte de Grâce (phone: 89-04-69). Moderate.

BÉNOUVILLE

Manoir d'Hastings – Six miles (10 km) north of Caen, this restaurant is in an ivy-covered seventeenth-century priory with a garden. M. and Mme. Scaviner serve memorable lobsters with herbs, truffles, and foie gras in puff pastry. (phone: 93-30-89). Expensive.

BAYEUX

Lion d'Or – Particularly pleasant old Norman decor; the cuisine is among the finest in the province. 71 rue St.-Jean (phone: 92-06-90). Expensive to moderate.

CHERBOURG

Sofitel – Member of the reliable, comfortable chain. Gare Maritime (phone: 44-01-11). Expensive to moderate.

Café du Théâtre – Excellent food in attractive surroundings. Pl. du Géneral-de-Gaulle (phone: 53-01-14). Moderate to inexpensive.

MONT-ST.-MICHEL

Mère Poulard – This serene hotel is a local tradition, as are the omelettes served in its fine restaurant (phone: 60-14-01). Moderate.

The Brittany Coast

The natives of France's northwestern peninsula consider their region a country apart, and with good reason. The vast, jagged coastline of Brittany resembles no other in France, and the tranquil interior, still primarily agricultural, seems to be part of another century. First inhabited by a mysterious race whose large, prehistoric megaliths can still be seen, the region was later invaded by the Gauls, the Celts, and finally the Romans. Brittany did not come under French rule until 1532, and even today, the Breton language and folklore are closer to the Celtic-based Welsh and Gaelic than to the French.

Brittany is a land of superstition sometimes verging on the mystical. It is the land that gave birth to the legend of Tristan and Iseult, to the tragic history of Peter Abelard and to the fabulous tales of Chateaubriand. But its traditions are living, as on feast days, when women still wear picturesque, lacy Breton costumes.

The Breton peninsula reaches inland from a rocky, bay-lined coast with numerous excellent natural harbors and several stretches of treacherous rocks. The A11, a new superhighway, has cut the travel time from Paris to Brittany. The route described below begins at St.-Malo and roughly follows the coast.

ST.-MALO AND DINARD: The beaches of the Emerald Coast and St.-Malo, a fortified island, city, and port dating from the twelfth century begin this route. The site is remarkable, and you'll appreciate it most from the ramparts (take the St.-Vincent gateway and then the stairway to the right). From inside the walls you can see the castle and the St.-Malo Museum, part of the castle structure. The tomb of the storyteller Chateaubriand lies on nearby Grand Bé Island, which can be reached only at low tide (take the Champs-Vauverts Gate out of town and cross the beach diagonally to the highway).

Across the estuary from St.-Malo is the elegant resort of Dinard, with an atmosphere of opulence topped off by the sparkling white Casino (Plage de l'Écluse). At Moulinet Point you'll have splendid panoramas of the coast. The Grande Plage is a popular beach for swimming and sunbathing.

En Route from St.-Malo and Dinard – From Dinard you can take a boat (or go by car via D766 inland for 18 mi/30 km) to the lovely old town of Dinan, boasting an impressive fourteenth-century castle overlooking the Rance. To see the old part of town, go along the rue Ste.-Claire to the rue de l'Horloge and rue du Jerzual. (A good place for classic Breton crêpes: *Le Connétable,* 1 rue Apport.)

The coastal road west (N786) goes to the resorts of St.-Lunaire and St.-Cast, both of which offer fine beaches and seascapes. Taking D13 to N786 and then following the coast on D16 takes you to Fort-la-Latte, a feudal castle begun in the thirteenth century and finished in the fourteenth and perched atop the cliffs like some pirate stronghold.

CAP FRÉHEL, LE VAL-ANDRÉ, ST.-BRIEUC: Just a few miles down the coast is Cap Fréhel, its spectacular red, gray, and black cliffs rising to a height of 229 feet above the sea. You can enjoy breathtaking views from the top of the lighthouse.

One of the finest sand beaches in Brittany is just along N786 at Le Val-André, and if you follow N786 to N12 you come to St.-Brieuc, the town that many Bretons consider the beginning of authentic Brittany. A short drive northwest on D6 brings you to Notre-Dame-de-la-Coeur, a lovely village noted for a serenely beautiful fifteenth-century chapel.

En Route from St.-Brieuc – Follow N786 along the coast for about 45 miles (72 km) to the busy resort of Perros-Guirec. Nearby are the lovely resorts of Ploumanach and Trégastel and the picturesque village of St.-Jean-du-Doigt, whose quaint name is derived from a prized relic — supposedly the finger of St. John the Baptist — which has been kept in the town church since the fifteenth century.

Along the coast at Carantec and St.-Pol-de-Léon (D786 to D73) and into the northwestern corner, the Coast of Legends, you'll travel windswept shores and be captivated by the typical Breton seascapes. If you find yourself in the area on the Sunday before September 8, drive inland to Le Folgoët (D788 from St.-Pol) for the annual public *pardon* ceremony. These *pardons* are the most characteristic expression of Breton religious fervor, when groups and individuals gather to do public penance, to fulfill a vow, or to seek divine favor. A colorful procession to and from the church is highlighted by the wearing of traditional Breton costumes — for women, a high lace cap of exceptional delicacy — afterward, the whole town takes part in a festival of dancing, feasting, and country games and competitions.

N788 south will also take you to modern Brest (or follow the coast via D27 to D28 and N789). This naval base is also a major urban center. There are numerous historical relics to be seen, and the arsenal and dockyards are worth a visit. A stroll along the eighteenth-century ramparts is especially interesting. However, it doesn't hold a candle to the smaller towns that lie farther south around the coast — in particular, delightful Locronan, once a center for the manufacture of sailcloth, now noted for well-preserved Renaissance houses built of granite and a marvelous central square (N170 to D7). If you see only one small Breton town, it should be this one. From here, D7 leads to D9 and the road to Raz Point, where deep, rocky chasms plunge down into the sea. It's a busy place, but the view is nothing short of spectacular.

A brief alternate route: If time prevents your going along the entire northwestern coast, we suggest turning inland at St.-Brieuc. Take N778 south and then follow D778 for a sample of the incredibly peaceful and generally unexplored countryside and a visit to the huge, magnificent castle at Josselin. From there you can reach the southern coast directly via N166 into Vannes. Or take D790 out of St.-Brieuc, then D3 and D15 through the Black Mountains for 84 miles (135 km) into Quimper.

QUIMPER: Thirty miles (48 km) from Raz Point via D784, 42 miles (67 km) south of Brest on N170, and 69 miles (110 km) east of Vannes (N165) is the prosperous old trading city of Quimper. In the fish market, the Breton costume is still often worn; there's a fine Gothic cathedral (pl. St.-Corentin) with a superb organ, which can be heard on weekends, and a charming old quarter with streets such as the rue Kéréon, the rue du Guéodet, and the rue du Sallé (stop for tea at no. 10, *Le Minuellou*). Quimper is also a center of the manufacture of a distinctive style of blue or yellow pottery. On the fourth Sunday in July, the city hosts the colorful Great Festival of Cornouaille.

En Route from Quimper – Following the coast via D783 brings you to Pont-Aven, a flower-filled town with a small museum dedicated to the works of Paul Gauguin, who lived here and founded the Pont-Aven School of Painting. A few miles east along D765 there's a wonderful secluded beach at Kerfany-les-Pins. A short detour north on D16 brings you to Quimperlé, on the Ellé and Isole rivers. The "upper" town is centered around Notre-Dame-de-l'Assomption church (pl.

St.-Michel), and the "lower" town is grouped around the old Abbey of Ste.-Croix (pl. Hervo). The apse is an excellent example of Romanesque architecture, and the spooky crypt is well worth a visit.

QUIBERON PENINSULA AND BELLE-ÎLE: Still farther south and east along the coast, turn into D768 to reach the Quiberon Peninsula, whose myriad rocks, caves, and reefs make its stretch of surf-pounded coast one of the most exciting in the province. We suggest walking the Wild Coast (Côte Sauvage) from end to end and stopping at the Bull's Cave (Grottes du Taureau), the Window (Fenêtre), and the Old Woman (Vieille) — all well-marked sights. East and south of the coast are wide beaches and lively fishing ports, and there's a boat to take you to one of the major attractions of the southern coast: Belle-Île.

The largest of the Breton islands, Belle-Île is a landscape filled with picturesque whitewashed villages surrounded by farmland. You'll want to see the Apothicairerie Grotto, the Grand Lighthouse, and the boiling surf at Port-Coton. Leaving your car at the port, turn right and you'll come upon stone "needles" (Aiguilles), some of them like pyramids pierced by grottoes. At Port Donnant there's a fine sand beach between soaring cliffs; the setting is splendid but the swimming treacherous.

En Route from Belle-Île – Regaining D768 north, turn onto D781 east into Carnac, a center for the curious prehistoric megaliths that dot Brittany, presumed to be Druidic, though possibly much older. Of special interest are the Ménec Lines (Alignements de Ménec) 2 miles (3.2 km) outside town along D196. The Lines include more than 1,000 menhirs, as these prehistoric, upright monoliths are known. The spectacle of these stones, set in miles-long rows as straight as a single file of soldiers, is positively eerie.

Taking N781 and D28 north for 8 miles (13 km) brings you into Auray, one of the most enchanting towns in the region. There are wonderful views from Loc Promenade, and the St.-Goustan quarter is charming (access is through the fifteenth-century place St.-Sauveur). From Auray, take N165 east for 10 miles (16 km) to Vannes.

VANNES AND THE GULF OF MORBIHAN: The Gulf of Morbihan is the tourist center of southern Brittany. An inland sea dotted with islands — many still privately owned — it is a place of extraordinary sunsets and the almost hallucinatory play of light on water. The best way to see this area is by boat, with excursions leaving from Vannes, Port Navalo, and Auray.

At the head of the gulf, Vannes has a picturesque old quarter enclosed by ramparts and centered around the Cathédrale St.-Pierre (pl. Henri-IV). From the lower alley of the Promenade de la Garenne you see the most alluring corner of the city, where a stream flows at the foot of city walls built in the thirteenth century. Vannes makes an agreeable base for your tour of the area. Local cafés and stores can supply all your practical needs, and boat excursions start here for all other points on the gulf.

En Route from Vannes – The short boat trip to Monks' Island (Ile aux Moines) is highly recommended. You can cover the island on foot, exploring the old village where houses are nestled into winding hills overlooking the gulf.

Another stop on the boat tour is Locmariaquer, a village with some of the most important megaliths in Brittany (by car, take N165 west from Vannes and D28 and D781 south). The Great Menhir and the Merchants Table dolmen can be seen if you turn left before the cemetery as you leave town via D781. The island of Gavrinis also has an impressive collection of megaliths and is only a 15-minute boat ride from the colorful fishing village of Larmor-Baden (from Vannes, take D101 and D316).

NANTES: Leaving Vannes by N165 east, turn south at D774 for the chic, bustling resort of La Baule and the busy but unpicturesque seaport of St.-Nazaire. From there, N771 rejoins N165 to lead you into Nantes, once the capital of Brittany and today the major city on the River Loire. At place de la Duchesse-Anne you can see the fifteenth-century château, with its low moat and wrought-iron cupola. The beautiful Gothic Cathédrale St.-Pierre et St.-Paul was badly burned in 1972, but it is still very much worth seeing (pl. du Maréchal Foch). At place Graslin, in the eighteenth-century section of the city, you can stop for a drink at *La Cigale,* a famous café decked out with art nouveau murals and gilt woodwork. Rue Crébillon, toward place Royale, leads you to the Passage Pommeraye, an interesting mid-nineteenth-century shopping arcade with cast-iron railings and footbridges. And the Fine Arts Museum (rue Clemenceau) is one of the best in France. Don't forget to try some of the food specialties in Nantes — the city is known for its crêpes and the Muscadet wine that is bottled here. From Nantes, Paris is 237 miles (383 km) northeast via N23 and A-11.

A final suggestion: Wherever possible, you should fill out the coastal routes by venturing into the interior of Brittany: towns such as Fougères, a favorite of Victor Hugo and Balzac; Vitré, 18 miles (29 km) south along N178, an enchanting Old World city; Les Rochers, Madame de Sévigné's château, 4 miles (6.4 km) southeast of Vitré; Lampaul-Guimiliau and St.-Thégonnec, the site of elaborately decorated Breton chapels; Tocky Questembert; Kernascléden; Le Faouet; Huelgoat; and hundreds of other towns and villages that make the Breton interior just as entrancing as the fabled coast.

BEST EN ROUTE

Expect to pay $70 and up per night for a double room in hotels listed as expensive; $30 to $40 in those listed as moderate; and $20 to $30, inexpensive. The restaurants range from $45 and up for a dinner for two in the expensive range; $25 to $35 in the moderate range; and $10 and under, inexpensive. Prices do not include drinks, wine, and tip.

ST.-MALO AND DINARD

Hotel Central – The most luxurious hotel in St.-Malo. Grande-Rue 6 (phone: 40-87-70). Expensive to moderate.

Duchesse Anne – This polished and gleaming turn-of-the-century restaurant specializes in seafood. 5 pl. Guy la Chambre (phone: 40-85-33). Expensive to moderate.

Elizabeth – A true gem in a town where sparkling exteriors usually conceal run-down guest quarters. 2 rue des Cordiers (phone: 562498). Expensive.

Printania – A modest hotel in Dinard with a good view over St.-Malo and the Rance. 5 av. Georges-V (phone: 46-13-07). Moderate to inexpensive.

DINAN

D'Avaugour – A lovely hotel with an exceedingly good restaurant. 1 pl. Champs-Clos (phone: 39-07-49). Expensive to moderate.

PLEVEN (NEAR PLANCOET)

Manoir du Vaumadeuc – Sumptuous granite manor house-turned-auberge is one of Brittany's most luxurious hostelries (phone: 844615). Expensive.

VAL-ANDRÉ

La Cotriade – Excellent restaurant specializing in the local seafood. Port de Piégu (phone: 72-20-26). Expensive.

PONTS-NEUFS

Lorand-Barre – Charmingly decorated in rustic Breton style is one of the better-known restaurants in France, 8 miles (13 km) east of St.-Brieuc. Order grilled lobster, sweetbreads in port wine, or delicious crêpes. Damour (phone: 32-78-71). Expensive.

TREBEURDEN

Ti Al Lannec – A handsome mansion that's now an inn with capacious bathrooms, friendly management, very good nouvelle cuisine, and charm to spare. Allée de Mézo-guen (phone: 235726). Expensive to moderate.

QUIMPER

Tour d'Auvergne – A modest hotel with modern facilities. 13 rue Réguaires (phone: 95-08-70). Moderate.

PONT-AVEN

Moulin de Rosmadec – An excellent Breton restaurant set in a fifteenth-century stonemill amid beautiful gardens (phone: 060022). Expensive to moderate.

RIEC-SUR-BELON

Chez Mélanie – Charming old-fashioned auberge with original nineteenth-century art everywhere and much-polished antique mahogany and brass. 2 pl. de l'Église (phone: 060105). Expensive to moderate.

MOËLAN-SUR-MER

Les Moulins du Duc – Relais et Châteaux establishment with a lake, swans, doves, comfortable cottage quarters, a woodsy setting, and an inventive menu (phone: 966073). Expensive to moderate.

HENNEBONT

Château de Locguénolé – Elegant rooms, sumptuous food, and manicured, river-view grounds make this stately former castle one of the region's loveliest places to stay. Off the D781 (phone: 762904). Expensive.

QUIBERON

Diététique – Posh and modern, well-kept with a good view (phone: 50-08-68) Expensive.
Sofitel – One of a modern chain, in a pleasant setting. The hotel boasts a very good restaurant (phone: 50-20-00). Expensive to moderate.
Ker Noyal – A lovely and well-kept although modest hotel (phone: 50-08-41). Moderate.

VANNES AND THE GULF OF MORBIHAN

La Marébaudière – Together with the *Richemont,* the most pleasant hotel in Vannes. 4 rue A.-Briand (phone: 47-34-29). Moderate.
Richemont – As above. 28 av. Favrel-et-Lincy (phone: 47-12-95). Moderate.

PEN-LAN POINT (MUZILLAC)

Hôtel de Rochevilaine – A beautiful old structure spectacularly set overlooking the sea. Closed January and February (phone: 41-69-27). Expensive to moderate.

QUESTEMBERT

Bretagne – This old stone house wrapped in vines is a Relais et Châteaux establishment with an innovative young chef. 13 rue St.-Michel (phone: 261112). Expensive.

NANTES

Sofitel – Another in the modern chain dotting France. Île Beaulieu (phone: 47-61-03). Expensive to moderate.

La Rôtisserie – An excellent restaurant specializing in seafood and duck. Closed Sundays. Pl. A.-Briand (phone: 48-69-28). Expensive to moderate.

Central Hotel – A comfortable hotel. 4 rue Couëdic (phone: 20-09-35). Moderate.

Chez Biret – A decidedly "unfancy" restaurant, but with superb food. 161 rue Hauts-Pavés (phone: 76-59-54). Moderate to inexpensive.

The Loire Valley

Early in the history of France, the mild climate and natural beauty of the provinces of Orléanais, Touraine, Maine, and Anjou — just southwest of Paris, slightly east of Brittany — attracted the pleasure-loving nobility. First they built feudal fortresses to protect themselves in an age of constant warfare; in more peaceful times — and as the Renaissance flowered in the valley of the Loire — watchtowers were softened with graceful Italianate spires, and windows were pierced in solid walls, the better to enjoy the terrain. Royalty raised pleasure palaces along the banks of the languorous river and its tranquil tributaries. Luxurious mansions and hunting lodges sprang up in the game-filled forests.

More than seven centuries of architectural splendor are unfolded here, and six castles bring the past to life with *son-et-lumière* spectacles nightly in the summer. As spotlights play across facades, towers, and courtyards, voices recreate the bygone pageantry and intrigue of courtiers and their ladies.

All along the way, travelers will find pleasant wayside inns, frequently in historic residences. It's possible not only to see châteaux, but to sleep and dine in them as well. Don't try to see too many castles in one day: There are 120, plus 20 abbeys and 100 churches — all suffused with the royal "sweetness of life" of which court poets sang. Late spring or fall is the best time to visit, but if you must go in high (summer) season, stay off the main roads and go early everywhere to avoid buses crammed with tourists, for this is one of Europe's classic tourist circuits. The castles for the most part are closed every day between noon and 2 PM.

In the Loire, it is said, the purest French is spoken. The food of the region is superb and is perfectly complemented by the fresh and lively wines. The river and its tributaries are teeming with delicious freshwater fish, most of them familiar to Americans but masquerading on the menu under their French names. It may be useful to know that *alose* is shad; *brême*, bream; *brochet*, pike; *anguille*, eel; *truite*, trout; and *saumon* — well, you can guess that one. A *matelote* is a fish stew; a *friture de la Loire*, a plate of fried river fish; and a *quenelle*, a fish dumpling — usually of pike. Local chefs are fond of serving fish with a white sauce of butter whipped to a froth with a hint of shallots and vinegar *(beurre blanc)*. Game is also plentiful: quail, pheasant, and partridge *(caille, faisan, perdix)* and, of course, venison, called *chevreuil*. The lowly prune is an ingredient favored by Loire cooks. *Pruneaux* (prunes) come from *prunes* (plums), and the orchards are celebrated in the plum tarts of Anjou. The *charcuterie* of Anjou and Touraine is known for *rillons* and *rillettes* (minced and potted pork) as well as for the tripe sausages called *andouilles.*

The wide variety of local white, red, and rosé wines ideally accompany the regional cuisine. The celebrated whites of Vouvray (both still and sparkling), Sancerre, Muscadet, and Pouilly-Fumé are perfect with fish. The fragrant red wines of Bourgueil and Chinon should be sampled here, for they don't travel well. The white dessert wines of Anjou almost rival the more famous Sauternes, and the Champigny of Saumur is a red wine of rare quality. Don't forget the rosés of Anjou — light, dry, delicately perfumed, and wonderfully refreshing on a summer day.

ANGERS: Straddling the Maine River, this pleasant city is famous for fruit and wine and for having given rise to the Plantagenets, who became kings of England.

High up on a hill, the moated, 17-tower Angers château gives a powerful impression of impregnable strength even in its current half-ruined state. A set of tapestries depicting the Apocalypse is the castle's main attraction. Woven in medieval Paris, the 70 pieces are over 550 feet long and more than 16 feet wide. They are magnificently displayed in a modern gallery in the former Courtyard of the King.

Other things to see in Angers include: the Logis-Barrault Fine Arts Museum; the Hôtel Pincé and the Turpin de Crissé museum; the former Hôpital St.-Jean, housing ten contemporary tapestries and a small wine museum; the "Doutre" on the right bank, with lovely old houses dating from the fifteenth to the eighteenth century; Trinity Church; and the impressive cathedral of St. Maurice, which has three towers and fine stained glass. Each January the city hosts a wine fair lasting 2 weeks and, in June, an arts festival. Summer *son-et-lumière* performances are given at the château.

En Route from Angers – The 66 miles (106 km) between Angers and Tours offer many points of historical and scenic interest as well as several good inns for lunch, dinner, or overnight stays. To reach Saumur, follow D751 through Gennes and Cunault, with its fine church. Along the way you pass scattered dolmens and menhirs, relics of the Celts who lived here in early times.

SAUMUR: This charming town is famous for wine and for its world-renowned cavalry troupe, the Cadre Noir (exhibitions are given the last 2 weeks in July). The château, on a steep promontory, was once splendidly adorned with spires, pinnacles, gilded weathervanes, pointed dormers, and tall chimneys. It is still a majestic structure, with a particularly fascinating museum devoted to the history of the horse. From the watchtower, the view over the blue slate roofs and the church of Notre-Dame-de-Nantilly extends to the vineyard-covered valleys of the Loire and the Thouet. This is rewarding country for antique hunting. You should not miss a sunset over the Loire viewed from the superb restaurant of *Le Prieuré* at nearby Chênehutte-les-Tuffeaux.

En Route from Saumur – Follow D947 along the Loire to Montsoreau, then turn south on D147 to Fontevrauld and its domed abbey. Here are the tombs of the Plantagenets (Henry II, Eleanor of Aquitaine, Richard the Lion-Hearted, Isabelle of Angoulême) and an extraordinary Romanesque kitchen with 5 immense fireplaces and 20 chimneys, unique in France. Continue east on Routes VO4, D117, D24, and N759 to Chinon, with a stop at La Devinière, the country house where Rabelais spent his childhood.

CHINON: Historic Chinon, overlooking the Vienne River, hasn't changed much since the Middle Ages. Above the town frowns the huge château, dramatically set on a high ridge. The ruins of three fortresses guarded by deep moats jut from the terrain, .

but only a hearth, now overgrown with ivy, recalls the great hall in which Joan of Arc recognized Charles VII. A steam train transports tourists back and forth to Richelieu, a model of classic seventeenth-century building.

En Route from Chinon – North on D7 about 9 miles (14 km) is the Château d'Ussé, said to have inspired Charles Perrault's fairy tale *Sleeping Beauty*. Bell turrets and towers rise delicately from flowering terraces against the rather somber background of the forest of Chinon. The chapel displays Aubusson tapestries depicting the life of Joan of Arc. Your next stop is Azay-le-Rideau; take Routes D7, then D17.

AZAY-LE-RIDEAU: The château here was constructed between 1518 and 1527 by Gilles Berthelot, treasurer under François I, and its fully furnished interior is a fascinating Renaissance museum. Bright white walls, four graceful corner turrets, and a slate roof of blue mirrored in the quiet River Indre form an enchanting backdrop for this fairy-tale castle's *son-et-lumière* performance.

Of interest in Azay are the church of St. Symphorien, with its unusual facade, and the nearby Château Saché, which houses the Balzac Museum.

VILLANDRY: North of Azay by about 6 miles (10 km) on Route D7, past poppy fields and rose-covered stone walls, is Villandry, "garden château of the garden of France." The famous triple-tiered gardens cover several acres and are best seen from a balustrade that runs along one side. The handsome Renaissance residence, constructed around the massive square tower of a medieval keep, was built by Jean le Breton, secretary of state to François I.

En Route from Villandry – Return to D57 and cross the Loire to Langeais, an impressive medieval fortress standing exactly as it was built. This château, where Charles VII married Anne of Brittany, was owned and occupied for many years by a millionaire who furnished it in exact detail to reflect fifteenth-century life. Continue along the Loire on N152 to Tours.

TOURS: The capital of Touraine, in the heart of château country, is a major tourist center, with a charming old quarter, flowering parks and gardens, elegant shops, tree-shaded streets, and lively sidewalk cafés. No less appealing is the city's characteristically superb, refined cooking. In short, Tours offers everything the visitor needs for a taste of the good life typical of the area.

Among the special attractions of Tours are: St. Gatien Cathedral, as beautiful by night, when fully floodlit, as it is by day; the Basilica of St. Martin; St. Julien Church; and Charlemagne's tower. For a look at the balconies, stairways, and charming little courtyards of the old town, start with place Plumereau's fifteenth-century wooden houses, then continue to the Maison de Tristan on rue Briçonnet, then to place des Carnes, rue Paul-Louis Courier, rue du Change, and the Hôtel Gouin's Renaissance Museum. Also of note are the Musée des Beaux-Arts and the Gemmail Museum on the terraces facing Pont Wilson.

LOCHES: About 25 miles (41 km) south of Tours, via N10 and N143 through the forest of Larçay, is the town of Loches. The château, once notorious as a top-security prison for the enemies of the king, is a fortified acropolis combining several buildings that are totally dissimilar in style and date from several centuries. Four thick walls supported by semicircular buttresses make up the enormous Romanesque keep — really three levels of dungeons — known as the Martelet. In these sinister premises, Louis XI and Louis XII kept such distinguished prisoners as Ludovico il Moro, duke of Milan, whose paintings and inscriptions can still be seen on the walls. Evoking more pleasant memories are the recumbent statue of Charles VII's beautiful mistress, Agnès Sorel; Anne of Brittany's peaceful oratory; the folklore museum in the gatehouse; and the eleventh-century collegiate church of St. Ours, with two curious hollow pyramids roofing the nave. In mid-July, the town stages an old-fashioned "peasants' market," with costumes, artisans selling their wares, and singing and dancing in the streets.

VALENÇAY: Peacocks strut through the gardens of this romantic château, 30 miles (48 km) from Loches via D760 and D960. The castle still remains in the family of Talleyrand, who acquired it in 1803. Luxuriously furnished in Louis XVI, Regency, and First Empire styles, it has the charm of a much-lived-in home. The museum facing the château is devoted to souvenirs of Talleyrand's career and includes a reconstruction of his bedroom. In the surrounding park, deer, flamingoes and llamas roam at liberty.

CHENONCEAUX: The château that many consider the most beautiful in the Loire lies about 34 miles (54 km) from Valençay via D956, then N76. Chenonceaux is certainly the most feminine and graceful of the castles of the Loire, and it is especially interesting because it was fashioned by and associated with some of the most fascinating and accomplished women in France. Thomas Bohier, controller of the Royal Treasury under François I, and his wife, Catherine Briçonnet, built the earlier part between 1513 and 1521. Bohier's official duties kept him away from home for long periods, and the responsibility for the design and construction fell to the capable Catherine. At Bohier's death, the château passed to the Crown in settlement of his debts. To mark the joyful occasion of his accession to the throne in 1547, Henri II presented Chenonceaux as a love token to his mistress, Diane de Poitiers, who commissioned a five-arch bridge to be built to the far bank of the Cher and planted fine gardens. When Henri died in 1559, his widow, the patient Catherine de' Medici, saw her chance for revenge. Catherine forced Diane to vacate Chenonceaux in exchange for the much lesser château of Chaumont. Catherine then added her own touches, which included a magical two-story, 197-foot gallery. Louise of Lorraine, Catherine's daughter-in-law, inherited the castle, which stood empty after her death until Madame Dupin arrived to enliven it with her famous salons. Madame Dupin's greatest fame, however, is derived from her position as grandmother of George Sand, née Aurore Dupin. The sixth mistress of Chenonceaux was the wealthy Madame Pelouze, who purchased the castle in 1864, then spent her life restoring it to its original grandeur. The property now belongs to the Menier family, chocolate manufacturers.

The château is approached by a long alley of towering trees. Two sphinxes guard the entrance, with Diane's gardens on the left, Catherine de' Medici's on the right. The interior is richly furnished with tapestries, marble statues, and portraits. Allow time for a walk in the gardens and along the river for a splendid view of the castle reflected in the water below its arches in the late afternoon sun.

Within walking distance, in the village, are two good restaurants — *Hôtel du Bon Laboureur* and *Le Gâteau Breton* — where you can enjoy dinner before the spectacular *son-et-lumière* performance, which dramatically unfolds the triumphs and defeats of the six chatelaines of Chenonceaux. Return to Tours via N76.

AMBOISE: On the left bank of the Loire, 18 miles (25 km) from Tours via N751, is Amboise. Charles VII was born here, and he died here of injuries sustained when he walked into the stone lintel of a low doorway. Charles was responsible for beautifying Amboise, importing Italian architects, sculptors, decorators, and gardeners to embellish the château. François I came to Amboise as a child and later gathered about him a court of artists and scholars. He was a patron of Leonardo da Vinci, who spent his last years here and was buried in the Gothic chapel of St. Hubert. Clos-Lucé, the brick manor house where he lived, has an interesting exhibit of the models of his inventions. Nightly *son-et-lumière* performances at the château recount one of the more violent episodes in French religious history, the hanging of the Protestant conspirators of Amboise in the castle's courtyard.

The Town Hall Museum should be seen for its fourteenth-century sculpture, Aubusson tapestries, and royal autographs. The *Auberge du Mail* sets an excellent table.

Cross the river, take a last and best look at the château, and return via the Loire's right bank and Route N152. About 6 miles (10 km) from Tours, turn off on the Route du Vouvray through 3,000 acres of vineyards and stop for a sip of still or sparkling white wine at one of the tasting cellars along the way.

Take the quick A10 (Autoroute Aquitaine) 36 miles (58 km) east to Blois.

BLOIS: On the heights above the right bank of the Loire, the city of Blois clusters around the castle. The residence of kings, Blois is steeped in four centuries of history, and the castle provides a nutshell review of French architecture — a composite of the styles of several periods, from the massive simplicity of the Middle Ages to the classicism of the seventeenth century. The highlights are Louis XII's original brick and stone edifice; the François I wing, with its ornate, winding, exterior staircase; and the majestic western wing, a superb example of seventeenth-century refinement, built by Mansart for Gaston d'Orléans, the scheming brother of Louis XIII. The assassination of the Duc de Guise took place in Henri III's bedroom on the second floor, and the intrigues of Catherine de' Medici are revealed by the 237 secret panels and hidden closets in her room. The Louis XII wing has a museum with sixteenth-century frescoes, furniture, paintings, and sculpture. Explore the castle's outer façades from the place du Château; visit St. Louis Cathedral and the Old Quarter, St. Nicholas Church, and the basilica of Notre-Dame. The former Bishop's Palace, now the Town Hall, has gardens and a terrace overlooking the hump-backed bridge across the Loire. On the terrace is a statue of Joan of Arc that is the work of the American sculptor Anna Hyatt Huntington. Stay at either the modern *Novotel* or the simple but comfortable *La Loire* in town or at one of the country inns at nearby Onzain or Ouchamps.

CHAMBORD: Cross the river by N765, then drive upstream on D951 for 11 miles (18 km) to the largest of all the Loire châteaux. Built by François I as a pleasure palace, Chambord is set in a game reserve extending over 13,600 acres enclosed by the longest wall in France — 20 miles around. A striking feature of this extravagant 440-room hunting lodge is the roof — a bristling forest of spires, pinnacles, gables, turrets, and towers, including 365 chimneys. Behind the handsome Renaissance facade are well-maintained royal apartments. The palace has 74 stairways, including the ingenious double staircase, twin spirals constructed so that one person can ascend and another descend without meeting. Don't miss a promenade on the roof terraces, where the king's guests enjoyed a grandstand view of the progress of the royal hunts from a height of 80 feet. Take lunch or tea at the *Hôtel St. Michel,* next to the château. The first *son-et-lumière* performance was presented here in the spring of 1952, and the spectacle still brings the past to life with stunning effect twice nightly.

CHEVERNY: Continue via D112 and D102 to Cour-Cheverny. Built in 1634 for the counts of Cheverny, the castle is now occupied by a descendant of the original owner. Unlike the royal palaces, this less flamboyant yet handsome house has changed little over the centuries and still retains most of its original furnishings. A long avenue leads to the vast building, Louis XIII in style but already neoclassical. The splendor of the interior decoration and furniture make Cheverny a miniature Versailles, complete to a magnificently ornate king's bedroom. No monarch ever stayed at Cheverny, although the bedroom was kept in readiness in case the king should choose to exercise his right to stay. An outbuilding houses a hunting museum with 2,000 sets of antlers mounted on the walls, and the kennels are home to a pack of 70 hounds. Over 5,000 acres of forest belong to Cheverny; formal hunts are held twice a week from November to April. Nonmembers may join, but only the master of the hunt has the right to dispatch the quarry with a sword. *Hôtel des Trois Marchands* and *Restaurant St.-Hubert,* close to the château, are fine for lunch. Return to Blois, about 8 miles (13 km) via N765.

CHAUMONT: This final castle to be visited is just over 10 miles (16 km) southwest of Blois on D751. A 10-minute walk up from the village along an avenue lined with venerable old cedars brings you to the château. Chaumont has much of the fortress about it — four wide towers, sentry walls, and a stern drawbridge — but ornamented windows lighten the facades, and the stonework is delicately carved. In the inner courtyard, the three facades opening onto the valley are ornamented by turreted staircases, dormers, and picturesque little bell towers. Catherine de' Medici built an observatory at Chaumont, where, with her resident astrologer, she attempted to divine the future. Here, it is said, she foresaw the violent deaths of all three of her sons. At the beginning of the nineteenth century, Chaumont provided a haven, if not a home, for Madame de Staël when she was exiled from Paris by Napoleon.

En Route from Blois – Follow N152 east with short stops at Beaugency, known for its wine; Meung, with its tree-lined mall and pleasant riverside rambles; and historic Orléans. Each year this ancient city celebrates the victory of Joan of Arc with processions, bell ringing, and the illumination of the restored Cathédrale de St.-Croix. Few reminders of the Maid of Orléans survived World War II, but there are statues of Joan in place du Martroi and on the porch of the Hôtel de Ville. Return to Paris, about 72 miles (116 km) via superhighway A10.

BEST EN ROUTE

Expect to pay $70 to $85 and up per night for a double room in hotels listed as expensive; $50 to $70 in those listed as moderate; and under $40 in the inexpensive ones. The restaurants range in price from $50 and up for a dinner for two in the expensive range; $30 to $50 in the moderate range; and $15 to $30, inexpensive.

ANGERS

Hotel Concorde – Modern convenience in the center of town, with 73 deluxe rooms, a pleasant restaurant, and a brasserie open until 1 AM. 18 blvd. Foch (phone: 87-37-20). Moderate.

Le Vert d'Eau – Well-known restaurant with original dishes. Specialties include *poissons de Loire beurre blanc, fricassée de poulet à l'angevine, fraises Marguerite d'Anjou* in season. Closed in August, Sunday evenings, and Mondays. 9 blvd. G.-Dumesnil (phone: 48-52-86). Moderate.

Toussaint – This comfortable restaurant features simple and creative cooking — vegetable cake, *aiguillettes de caneton aux noix vertes* (sliced duckling with green walnuts), fresh fruit sherbets. Closed Sundays and Mondays, 2 weeks in August and late February. 7 rue Toussaint (phone: 87-46-20). Moderate.

Le Logis – Endowed with a Michelin star, it's known for seafood. 17 rue St.-Laud (phone: 87-44-15). Moderate to inexpensive.

L'Entr'acte – Popular rustic restaurant near the post office. Specialties: *coquilles St.-Jacques au champagne, saumon du Bourgueil.* Closed Saturdays, Sunday nights, and mid-July to mid-August. 9 rue Louis-de-Romain (phone: 87-71-82). Moderate to inexpensive.

Hôtel de France – Opposite the train station and tourist office, with 61 attractive rooms. Its restaurant, *Plantagenets,* offers fine food and service. Restaurant closed Saturdays and Sunday midday. 8 pl. de la Gare (phone: 88-49-42). Inexpensive.

Croix de Guerre – Some 28 pleasantly decorated rooms in a flower-bedecked inn on a quiet street. 23 rue Châteaugontier (phone: 88-66-59). Inexpensive.

SAUMUR

Le Prieuré – Gracious living and dining in an elegant Renaissance manor house in a 60-acre park. Member of Relais et Châteaux hotel group. Its 36 rooms have period furnishings; there's a pool, riding, and golf nearby. Closed January and February. Reserve several months in advance for summer; at least 2 weeks other times of the year. Five miles (8 km) west of Saumur via D751 in Chênehutte-les-Tuffeaux (phone: 50-15-31). Expensive.

FONTEVRAUD-L'ABBAYE

La Licorne – This small, elegant restaurant with a young, hospitable owner features Loire Valley fish with sorrel sauce, beef with tarragon sauce and homemade carrot-tinted noodles, and a scrumptious chocolate cake. In good weather, ask for a table outside. Closed Sunday nights and Mondays; Tuesdays off-season; mid-November to mid-December; and the first half of January. Rue Robert d'Arbrissel (phone: 517249). Moderate.

CHINON

Hostellerie Gargantua – Brick and timbered fifteenth-century mansion with 17 simple but pleasant rooms and an excellent restaurant. Specialties: *poussin braisé en soupière aux écrevisses; omelette gargamelle.* Open March 1 to November 5. 73 rue Haute St. Maurice (phone: 93-04-71). Moderate.

Château de Marçay – Beautifully restored fifteenth-century château with 23 charming rooms, 3 suites, and a good restaurant, set in a park with terrace, pool, and tennis. Member of Relais et Châteaux hotel group. Closed January and mid-March. About 4 miles (7 km) south of Chinon on Route D116 (phone: 93-03-47). Expensive.

La Giraudiere – This picturesque manor house offers simple charm and 25 rooms, some with kitchenettes. No restaurant, but breakfast is served. Closed November to mid-March. Three miles west of Chinon via the road to Bourgueil and the Savigny turnoff (phone: 584036). Inexpensive.

AZAY-LE-RIDEAU

L'Auberge du XII Siècle – Gothic house serving beautifully prepared dishes. Closed Tuesdays and late January through February. About 4 miles (6 km) from Azay in Saché (phone: 26-86-58). Expensive to moderate.

Hôtel du Grand Monarque – Peaceful little 30-room inn with a restaurant serving good local specialties and wines. The restaurant is closed mid-November to mid-March. Pl. République (phone: 43-30-08). Moderate to inexpensive.

VILLANDRY

Le Cheval Rouge – A short stroll from the château gardens, this pleasant provincial restaurant has home-prepared foie gras and smoked salmon, Loire fish including *sandre* (perch-pike), and good regional wines. Closed Mondays and January and February (phone: 500207). Moderate.

LANGEAIS

Hosten – Charming 14-room hostelry with an excellent restaurant. Specialties: *homard cardinal, escalope de saumon à l'oseille, écrevisses au Vouvray, filet à la moëlle.* Reserve in advance. Closed December, January, and Tuesdays. 2 rue Gambetta (phone: 96-82-12). Expensive to moderate.

TOURS

Barrier – This charming restaurant with a flowering courtyard is known as one of the best in France. Specialties: *terrine aux trois poissons de Loire, cassolette de queues d'écrevisses à la crème; pigeonneau à la fleur de thym.* Closed Sunday evenings, Wednesdays, and February. Reserve in advance. 101 av. Tranchée (phone: 54-20-39). Expensive.

Hotel Chantepie – Intimate and comfortable hostelry with 20 rooms. No restaurant. Joué les Tours, 6 km from Tours (phone: 53-06-09). Expensive.

Le Lyonnais – This restaurant offers food of consistently high quality. Specialties: *terrine d'anguille, aiguillette de canard, ris de veau belle époque, noisette de porc aux pruneaux.* Closed Sunday evenings and Mondays. 48 rue Nationale (phone: 05-66-84). Moderate.

L'Univers – The 92 comfortable rooms have all modern conveniences and a more-than-acceptable restaurant. Closed Sundays and February. 5 blvd. Heurteloup (phone: 05-37-12). Moderate to inexpensive.

Hôtel Bordeaux – Old, completely renovated 54-room hotel in the center of town serves classic Touraine cuisine in the good, reasonably priced restaurant. Specialties: *sandre au beurre blanc, coquelet au vin de Chinon.* 3 pl. Maréchal-Leclerc (phone: 05-40-32). Moderate.

Les Tuffeaux – New and already highly regarded, it boasts a special location in Tours' old quarter, near the cathedral. Loire Valley fish are especially good here, as are puff pastry desserts. Closed Sundays, Mondays, and most of January and August. 19 rue Lavoisier (phone: 471989). Moderate.

Le Royal – Pleasant 32-room hotel with modern conveniences and antique furnishings. Bar, but no restaurant. 65 av. Grammont (phone: 64-71-78). Moderate to inexpensive.

La Petite Marmite – Next door to and under the same ownership and management as *Barrier.* A rustic, simple restaurant with perhaps less spectacular but nonetheless excellent cuisine. Same closing dates as *Barrier.* 103 av. Tranchée (phone: 54-03-85). Moderate to inexpensive.

Rôtisserie Tourangelle – Good little restaurant facing St. Julien Church. Closed Sunday evenings, Mondays, and mid-July to mid-August. 23 rue Commerce (phone: 05-71-21). Inexpensive.

CHÂTEAUX-HOTELS NEAR TOURS

Domaine de Beauvois – With 39 spacious rooms, pool, tennis, riding, fishing, and a popular dining room. Specialties: *gâteau de légumes, mousseline de brochet de queues d'écrevisses, tarte aux pommes chaude;* Bourgueil and Vouvray wines. Restaurant closed January 15 to March 15. Luynes, Route D49, about 7 miles (12 km) from Tours (phone: 55-50-11). Expensive.

Château d'Artigny – A stately château on a plateau above the Indre; it's the most luxurious hotel in the valley, in a 50-acre park with formal gardens, pool, tennis, riding, fishing, and golf nearby. The superb Touraine cuisine in the elegant restaurant is well known, and there's a 40,000-bottle cellar to choose from. Closed December 1 to January 10. Reserve well ahead. About 1 mile (2 km) southwest by D17 from Montbazon; 7 miles (12 km) from Tours (phone: 26-24-24). Expensive.

Domaine de la Tortinière – Beautiful rooms and suites in the Belle Époque manor house, two-story stable, or cozy stone cottage. Peaceful, beautiful grounds, superb service, and perfect cooking in the restaurant. Specialties: *saumon fumé, meurettes d'anguilles au Bourgueil, filet aux truffes;* Oisly and Montlouis wines. Open February 15 to November 15. Reserve well in advance. One mile (1.5 km) north of Montbazon via N10 and D287 (phone: 26-00-19). Expensive.

VALENÇAY

Hôtel d'Espagne – A former coaching inn with 10 lovely rooms and 9 suites. The restaurant features classic, regional specialties, including *terrine de foies de volailles aux truffes, noisettes d'agneau à l'estragon, delicieuse au chocolat;* Valençay and Chinon wines. Closed mid-November to mid-March. 8 rue du Château (phone: 00-00-02). Moderate.

CHENONCEAUX

Hôtel du Bon Laboureur et Château – Pretty house covered with ivy and surrounded by a garden where meals are served in summer. Specialties of the restaurant include: *sandre beurre blanc, mousseline de brochet au coulis d'écrevisses, tournedos mariné Vendôme;* Montlouis and Oisly wines. Closed November to mid-March. 6 rue Dr.-Bretonneau (phone: 29-90-02). Moderate to inexpensive.

Le Gâteau Breton – Rustic Breton bistro in the heart of the village. The simple home cooking and tasty pastries are more than just good for the price. Closed Tuesdays and mid-November to mid-February. Rue National (phone: 29-94-45). Inexpensive.

AMBOISE

Auberge du Mail – The best restaurant in Amboise. Specialties: *confit d'oie au Vouvray, saumon poché, célestine de fruits de mer, filet en chevreuil;* Montlouis and Chinon wines. Closed Tuesdays and January. 32 quai de Gaulle (phone: 57-60-39). Moderate to inexpensive.

Château de Pray – This lovely old château has 16 guest rooms, a dining room, and a terrace for pleasant summer lunches. Linger over the salmon in sorrel sauce. Closed January to mid-February. About 2 miles northeast of Amboise via D751 (phone: 572367). Moderate to inexpensive.

BLOIS

Novotel – Modern, air-conditioned rooms, with restaurant, snack bar, and pool. About 2.5 miles (4 km) east of Blois by N152 at La Chaussée St.-Victor (phone: 78-33-57). Moderate.

Relais des Landes – A country inn with 18 pretty rooms and good food. Closed January 10 to February 1. Ouchamps, about 10 miles (16 km) south of Blois by D751 and D7 (phone: 44-03-33). Moderate.

La Loire – A small hotel on the river with lots of atmosphere. Simple but comfortable rooms and one of the best restaurants in town. Hotel closed January 15 to February 15; restaurant closed Sundays. 8 rue Maréchal-de-Lattre-de-Tassigny (phone: 74-26-60). Moderate to inexpensive.

CHAMBORD

Hôtel St.-Michel – This rambling place with 38 rooms provides a mesmerizing view of Chambord castle across the road. The dining room specializes in game in hunting season, but also has tasty *rilletes* (spiced, cubed pork) and poached salmon and trout. The restaurant is closed Monday nights and Tuesdays mid-October to March; the entire place shuts down mid-November until Christmas (phone: 463131). Moderate to inexpensive.

COUR-CHEVERNY

Restaurant Hôtel St.-Hubert – Pleasant provincial inn close to the château known especially for its fine game (the specialty is *côtelette de chevreuil St.-Hubert).* Closed December 5 to January 15, and Tuesdays, October to Easter. Rue National (phone: 79-96-60). Moderate to inexpensive.

Hôtel des Trois Marchands – Former coaching inn: sidewalk tables, a courtyard, and good fresh food. Closed mid-January to March and Tuesdays from October to Easter. Pl. de l'Église (phone: 79-96-44). Moderate to inexpensive.

Bordeaux

The region of Bordeaux is known to America and most of the world by a litany of wine labels of renowned châteaux — Margaux, Mouton-Rothschild, Haut-Brion — and by famous place names such as Haut-Médoc, St.-Émilion, and Sauternes. To the French, however, Bordeaux simply means the riverport itself, known for some of the finest eighteenth-century architecture outside of Paris as well as for a measured, contented style of living. As for the Bordelais, as they are called, they have been blessed beyond the measure of most people.

Until the middle of the fifteenth century, Bordeaux — and much of the southwest of France — was a privileged colony of the English, who for the most part let the local burghers have their way. Although the English influence waned after France's victory in the Hundred Years War, the long arm of the Parisian government did not make itself felt in any consistent way until the eighteenth century, when Louis XV ascended the throne. In the opinion of the king, Bordeaux's commercial and strategic importance made it necessary to assign special governors, called *intendants,* to manage affairs on the spot. It is to this era of the king's *intendants* that Bordeaux owes the soberly elegant facades of its municipal buildings (the Bourse), monuments, and public buildings (the Grand Théâtre) as well as of the *hôtels-particuliers,* or townhouses (along allées Tourny).

The king often used these appointments to rid himself of overly ambitious men in his court. Such was the case of the duc de Richelieu (1692–1788). A sometime general (he made a poor showing against Frederick II of Prussia in the Seven Years' War), professional charmer, and jaded cosmopolite, Richelieu found the city of Bordeaux a maze of narrow alleyways and decrepit provincial buildings. He set out at once to change it, broadening streets into boulevards and commissioning a number of buildings, among them Bordeaux's Grand Théâtre. Successive *intendants* continued to reshape and refine the city's image, each trying to outdo his predecessors.

The sum of their legacy in design — beyond the monuments, the allées Tourny, the Bourse, the Hôtel de Ville, and the numerous fine *hôtels-particuliers* — is greater than the whole of its elegant parts, for the overriding feeling in Bordeaux is one of order, calm, and refined well-being.

Though not exactly at the gate of the city, vineyards — the world's greatest for their variety and overall excellence — surround Bordeaux on all sides. A half-hour drive northwest puts you in the heart of the Médoc, with its aristocratic red wines. A forty-five-minute drive east is the medieval village of St.-Émilion, whose fine red wines tend to overshadow the charms and attractions of the town itself. To the south of Bordeaux (actually in its southern suburbs) are found the reds and dry whites of Graves, while still farther south are the fine sweet wines of Sauternes and Barsac. Just a couple of miles southwest of downtown Bordeaux, in Pessac, is Château Haut-Brion, owned by a former US ambassador to France, Douglas Dillon. This famous red wine was the only wine produced outside the Médoc to be classified in 1855.

The bounty to accompany all this drink comes from the farms, forests, and waters surrounding Bordeaux. Between the city and the Atlantic are the Landes, sandy plains, and pine barrens that stretch inland 90 miles or so, the source of excellent duck as well as of foie gras, the liver of fatted duck or goose. The ocean and the rivers provide oysters, mussels, fish, and lampreys — eels that are a local delicacy.

The well-fed Bordelais have any number of beaches at their disposal — from Biarritz, 110 miles (185 km) south, to the tip of the Médoc peninsula — along what they've rather fancifully called the Côte d'Argent. The favorite beaches are Cap Ferrat, Le Porge, Carcans, and Montelivet. The last three, on the ocean side of the Médoc, are national parkland and still have many wild, undeveloped stretches.

The best road maps for the region are the Cartes Touristiques of the Institut Géographique National (IGN), scaled 1/100,000. For the Médoc, buy map 46; for St.-Émilion, 47; and for Graves and Sauternes, 55. Less detailed but also very good are the IGN maps scaled 1/250,000. The regional map Bordeaux-Périgord (110) is also good, as are the Michelin maps.

For a thorough tour of the vineyards, we recommend Alexis Lichine's *Guide to the Wines and Vineyards of France,* a comprehensive review of wine-making throughout the country.

BORDEAUX: This city can be explored by foot, and the best place to start is at the place de Comédie by the Grand Théâtre, whose location and grand scale make it the most impressive monument in the city. On the exterior balcony, twelve columns are surmounted by twelve goddesses and muses of the arts. The view from the theater along the allées Tourny, with its broad promenade lined on either side by elegant shops and townhouses, gives a measure of the scale on which the Bordeaux *intendants* worked.

Walk along the allées Tourny to the place Tourny; a turn to the left will take you up boulevard Clemenceau, where the smarter citizens of Bordeaux do much of their shopping for elegant clothes. At place Gambetta is a small square park surrounded by cafés and pastry shops. Pause here for a cup of coffee at *Le Regent* or for tea and a pastry at the fine *salon de thé* called *Darricau;* or continue through the square to Porte Dijeaux and rue Bouffard, which leads to the Cathédrale St.-André (built from the eleventh to the fifteenth century) and is a tiny street lined with shops selling antique porcelains, engravings, and prints, silver, furniture, and bibelots.

Rue Ste.-Catherine is a crowded pedestrian walkway and shopping artery that is impossible to avoid; it has a fine bookstore, *Librarie Mallat,* but lacks the delights found elsewhere. More interesting are the small streets that branch off it toward the river leading to old Bordeaux, with its tangle of shops, bistros, and galleries and an open-air market. The recent revitalization here makes this the most exciting area of the city.

The best-known (and purportedly the best) wine stores in Bordeaux are the small, discreet *Badie,* at pl. de Tourny, and *La Vinotheque,* on Cours du XXX Juillet; also of note is *Vignes et Vins de France,* a tiny shop in old Bordeaux at 4 rue des Bahutiers. The Maison du Vin is Bordeaux's center for wine promotion. The bureau offers adequate maps for the wine regions of Médoc, Graves, Sauternes, St.-Émilion, and Pomerol and has lists of which châteaux receive visitors and when.

Follow the cour Intendance on the right side of the Grand Théâtre down to the quai and turn right, where you'll find the place de la Bourse on your right. The building now houses the chamber of commerce of Bordeaux and is a magnificent example of eighteenth-century municipal architecture. The buildings that edge the quays from place de la Bourse to St. Michael's Church are notable for the faces, called *mascarons,* carved over doorways and in walls, perhaps 200 in all and no two alike.

THE MÉDOC

You don't need to be a wine connoisseur to enjoy a tour of the Bordeaux wine country, especially of the Médoc. Of the hundreds of so-called châteaux in the Médoc, 65 were classified according to excellence in 1855, and these *grands crus classes* continue to demand top dollar today.

The special attraction of the Médoc — apart from its eminence as the source of exquisite, often expensive wine — is the incongruity of the flat, slightly undulating terrain carpeted with green vines. The landscape is dominated by the sky, and the whole vista is seen against the fantastic architecture and gentrified air of the wine châteaux. Some of these estates amount to no more than a good-sized house with a surface cellar (here called a *chai*) where wine is made and stored. Others are grandiose affairs indeed, either built in a style consonant with their times, like Château Margaux (generally Empire) or Château d'Issan (seventeenth century), or built only to express a nineteenth-century bourgeois conception of a château (Palmer, Lascombes, Cos d'Estournel). (Note that most châteaux are closed at lunchtime; it's always best to call ahead to arrange a visit).

In spite of its fame, the Médoc is not well marked from Bordeaux. From the center of town, follow the signs for Soulac or ask directions to the Barrière du Médoc. This will get you out of town in the right direction. About 2 miles (3.2 km) beyond the turnoff for the Paris Autoroute, the road branches to the right toward Pauillac. This is D2e, the vineyard road, which leads past the greatest of the Médoc châteaux.

CANTENAC: About 9 miles (15 km) from the turnoff, just beyond a church on the left, is the entrance to Château Prieuré-Lichine. Park on the right side of the road opposite the archway and walk into the inner court. Once inside, on your left is a cloister decorated with antique firebacks; follow the gravel walk to the office, where you'll find an English-speaking guide to take you through the *chai.* This sixteenth-century *chai* is one of the oldest in the Médoc, but it has some of the newest winemaking equipment. Tasting may be enjoyed with the permission of the cellar master, and wines may be purchased. Open daily and during lunch (phone: 883628).

Across the road from Prieuré-Lichine is the stone wall and gateway to Château d'Issan. Take a peaceful walk down a long alley of plane trees to the moated, turreted sixteenth-century château, which is privately owned. Visits to the *chai* can be arranged.

MARGAUX: Another .75 mile (1.5 km) up D2 from Cantenac will bring you to the turnoff on the right to the renowned Château Margaux. On the way you'll see signs for other prestigious châteaux including Palmer and Lascombes. Château Margaux was rated a first growth (*cru*) in 1855 with only three others, and this privileged position is evident from the building and the grounds. The Empire château (built around 1802) has sober, classical lines and an imperial-looking stairway. The carefully laid out gardens include ponds where languid swans swim about — a present from Queen Elizabeth II. Although the château is privately owned and not generally open to visitors, a guide is available to take you through the *chai* if you make an appointment (phone: 887028).

ST.-JULIEN: About 10 miles (16 km) beyond Margaux is St.-Julien. Here, Château Beychevelle is the main attraction; take a tour of the *chai* and of the impressive gardens in the rear. Appointments may be made to the château (phone: 592300).

The grounds of the stately Château Ducru-Beaucaillou adjoin those of Beychevelle (phone: 590520). Not far away is the fabled first growth, Château Latour, which actually straddles the boundary between St.-Julien and the commune of Pauillac. Today all that remains of the ancient fortress that once stood here is the tower (phone: 590051).

PAUILLAC: Pauillac as a wine district takes in more than just the town and includes two of the four first growths: Lafite-Rothschild and Mouton-Rothschild (elevated to first growth in 1973). Mouton "tried harder" during all its years as a second growth, but now, through the efforts of Baron Philippe de Rothschild and his late American wife Pauline, it has become the premier attraction of the Médoc and the second most popular tourist site in the southwest of France (after the shrine of Lourdes). An appointment is necessary, but worth making, to see the Mouton wine museum, the *chai,* and the cellars. The wine museum contains the Rothschilds' collection of paintings, tapestries, and art objects celebrating the cult of wine and the cultivation of the vine. This *chai* is the most impressive in the Médoc, with ten long neat rows of barrels stretching out for nearly 100 yards. On the far wall, perfectly centered and lit from behind, is the seal of Mouton carved in wood. The château is closed in August and on weekends. Call 592222 for tour times.

Continuing up D2, you pass Lafite-Rothschild on your left. Its wine is said to have been the favorite of two royal mistresses, Mme. de Pompadour and Mme. du Barry. To visit the exquisite vaulted *chai,* call 590174.

ST.-ESTEPHE: No visit here is complete without a stop at the nineteenth-century Château Cos d'Estournal, the most exotic of all the Médoc châteaux, with its pagoda towers and massive carved wood doors (phone: 441137). Also in St.-Estephe is Château Montrose run by a mother-and-son team (phone: 593012).

Continuing north, the flatness of the vineyards gives way to wooded slopes and fields of more conventional farm crops. A salty breeze is a reminder that this last stretch of the Gironde River is the estuary where fresh water meets the Atlantic.

ST.-ÉMILION AND POMEROL

The wine châteaux of St.-Émilion and Pomerol are more modest than those of the Médoc: The properties are smaller and the châteaux usually no more than houses, so there are few formalities when it comes to visiting.

The two regions border each other on the right bank of the Dordogne. To get there from the center of Bordeaux (a 45-minute drive), follow signs for Périgueux. This will put you on N89 to Libourne. At Libourne take D21e toward Montagne. Two interesting châteaux to visit in Pomerol are Vieux-Château-Certan (follow D21e past Catusseau and take the left-hand fork toward Néac) and Château l'Évangile (take the right-hand fork after Catusseau). To reach St.-Émilion from Pomerol or Libourne, take D17e or D670.

ST.-ÉMILION: One of the most picturesque wine villages in France, this is a medieval treasure perched on a small limestone plateau overlooking the valley of the Dordogne. In the twelfth century, St.-Émilion was a stopping place for the pilgrims who wound their way on foot to the shrine of Santiago da Compostela in Spain. Pilgrims of one sort or another — for wine or for the love of old stones — have been passing through ever since.

Park your car at the place des Créneaux and walk to the edge of the square for a view over the Dordogne Valley and the houses of the village below. At the nearby Syndicat d'Initiative (pl. des Créneaux) you can pick up a map of the town with a list of tourist sites and wine châteaux, including visiting times.

St.-Émilion's charm is best appreciated in a leisurely amble through the town, which permits you to take in the sites as well as the peaceful, Old World feeling imparted by the narrow streets and small ocher stone houses with red tile roofs.

L'Église Monolithe is a ninth- to twelfth-century church hewn into the side of the limestone cliff, the most important monolithic church in France. The Chapelle de la Trinité and the alleged Hermitage de St.-Émilion are part of the church.

Of less historical importance than L'Église Monolithe and the Chapelle, but no less compelling for their half-natural, half-man-made strangeness, are the remains of the Couvent des Cordeliers, a fourteenth- to fifteenth-century convent and cloister, now an overgrown shell of stone walls and stairways. In an interior court you can buy the locally made sparkling wine by the glass or bottle.

On the northern edge of town is Château Villemaurine. If you have time to visit only one of the almost countless châteaux in St.-Émilion, let this be it. The system of labyrinthine cellars scooped deep into the limestone is among St.-Émilion's (and even Bordeaux's) most dramatic. Philippe Giraud, the owner's son, speaks excellent English and can arrange visits for you (phone: 43-01-44).

BEST EN ROUTE

The city of Bordeaux offers a number of first-class restaurants and hotels. However, although the Médoc produces some of the greatest wines in the world, it is very poorly served in the matter of food and lodging. There are no hotels to speak of and only one or two restaurants worth the name. With this caution in mind, visitors should visit the Médoc restaurants cited below only for light lunches or suppers. The hotels we have listed as expensive will cost $50 and up for a double room per night; moderate, $30 to $50; and inexpensive, $15 to $30. In the restaurants we've mentioned, a meal will cost $45 and above at an expensive place and $25 to $45 at a moderate one, and $25 or less at an inexpensive one.

BORDEAUX

La Réserve – In the suburb of Alouette, this is the most pleasant of the Bordeaux hotels and is also blessed with an excellent restaurant, surrounded with gardens and trees. The restaurant alone is worth the trip. 74 Av. Bourgailh, L'Alouette Pessac, about 2 miles (3.2 km) southeast of the airport (phone: 45-13-28). Expensive.

Le Grand Hotel – A hotel since 1850 with a lovely façade. Rooms have been modernized and are quiet and comfortable. There's also a good restaurant and a golf course nearby. Pl. de la Comédie (phone: 909344). Moderate.

Royal Médoc – A charming hotel with 45 modern, tastefully decorated rooms and a bar. 3–5 rue de Sèze (phone: 817242). Inexpensive.

Vieux Bordeaux – A renovated eighteenth-century gem with a spiral stone stairway leading up to 11 rooms, each with a lovely brass bed. 22 rue du Cancera (phone: 480727). Inexpensive.

Dubern – Long Bordeaux's best restaurant, *Dubern* offers excellent service and fine cuisine in extremely comfortable and tasteful surroundings. 42 allées Tourny (phone: 48-03-44). Expensive.

Christian Clément – A small, pretty place with inventive food and a fine wine list drawn from the lesser-known vineyards of the Médoc. 58 rue du Pas-St.-Georges (phone: 810139). Expensive.

Clavel – Tasty variations on regional specialties served in elegant surroundings. 44 rue Charles-Domercq (phone: 929152). Expensive.

Le Chapon Fin – A 160-year-old restaurant that looks like a summer garden year-round and offers regional dishes and wines by the glass, bottle, or carton (there's a wine boutique). 5 rue Montesquieu (phone: 447001). Moderate.

Le Bistrot de Bordeaux – Tiny, attractive, and busy, this place has good bistro fare, such as skate salad and stuffed chicken, along with local wines. 10 rue des Piliers de Tutelle (phone: 529232). Moderate to inexpensive.

La Tenareze – An intimate little place on one of Bordeaux's loveliest public squares. Flavorful dishes of southwest France are served at both indoor and outdoor tables. 18 pl. du Parlement (phone: 444329). Inexpensive.

MARGAUX

Auberge de Savoie – A pleasant enough café with a restaurant that serves straight-forward French cooking. Closed Sunday nights and February (phone: 58-31-76). Moderate.

LAMARQUE

Relais du Médoc – A simple family-run restaurant, perhaps the best in the Médoc, open only for lunch; hearty, satisfying fare. Just off D2 between Margaux and St.-Julien (phone: 589227). Moderate.

PAUILLAC

Le Relais du Manoir – Modest as it is, this small *relais* (a former *bordelle*) is making an honest attempt at refined and imaginative cooking. Good seafood. Less than ½ mile along the quay north of the center of Pauillac (phone: 59-05-47). Expensive to moderate.

LESPARRE

La Mare aux Grenouilles – If the good food here were as charming as the setting, the proprietor M. De Wilde would have the Médoc's finest restaurant. Fair value in homey surroundings; fair wine list (phone: 41-03-46). Expensive to moderate.

ST.-ÉMILION

Auberge de la Commanderie – Perched on a hill above place du Marché, it has the look and feel of a French country house. There are 14 rooms (be sure to reserve in advance) and a very charming restaurant. Rue des Cordeliers (phone: 247019). Moderate.

Les Petunias – For a unique, down-home stay, accept the warm hospitality of Mme. Margouty, a delightful resident in her seventies who has five rooms to let. Rue Petite Fontaine (phone: 246126). Inexpensive.

Auberge Saint-Jean – Well worth the 5 mile (8 km) drive south from St.-Émilion, this place is easily one of the best in the entire Bordeaux area. Excellent food prepared with great finesse in a pleasant riverside setting. Closed Sunday nights and Mondays and the last 2 weeks of September. On D670; follow signs for Marmande until you cross the Dordogne at St.-Jean-de-Blaignac; the restaurant is on your left just after the bridge (phone: 84-51-06). Expensive.

La Jadouine – Our top choice in town for its menu and its prices. Modern and intimate with only 12 tables and a wine list that changes frequently. Dinner only. Closed Mondays. Halfway up the street behind pl. du Marché. Moderate.

Logis de la Cadène – Upstairs, and uphill, from *La Jadouine,* this rustic place has ten tables inside and another six outside under arbor. Basic fare including *entrecôte* and omelets. Lunch only. Moderate to inexpensive.

The Dordogne

The appeal of the Dordogne is the attraction of extremes: This country of foie gras and truffles prepared with all the country cook's art is the same country whose long-hidden grottoes and secret caves have offered spectacular evidence of man's earliest organized societies — cave drawings, tools, and weapons thousands upon thousands of years old, a glimpse into the prehistory of humankind.

In southwestern France between the Massif Central and the Atlantic seaboard, Dordogne includes the old and historic province of Périgord as well as parts of Limousin, Angoumois, and Saintonge. The entire region is endowed with luxuriant valleys, riverbanks lined with poplars and willows, vineyards, hillsides covered with walnut and fruit orchards, steep peaks crowned with medieval castles, and red-roofed fortified towns *(bastides)* perched above the half-dozen rivers that lace the terrain. Rugged granite and limestone plateaux and rocky outcroppings contrast with the fertile farmland to provide a profusion of natural beauty. The area includes the Périgord Blanc, named for the chalky limestone that imparts a whiteness to the countryside, and the Périgord Noir, which takes its name from the forests of dark oak.

To reap the fullest enjoyment from the Dordogne, equip yourself with a detailed map (Michelin 75 or IGN 47/48) and take your time. Just about every bend in the road (and there are plenty) offers a surprise to delight the eye and the imagination — a fisherman reeling in a trout; a perfect picnic spot; panoramas to photograph or paint; or cool forests inviting you to stroll where prehistoric man once hunted mammoth, bison, and deer.

Lingering over meals will certainly be a highlight of any itinerary. The Périgord's gastronomic glories are world renowned. In addition to the justly famed foie gras confit d'oie, and truffle, the chefs of the Dordogne have almost infinitely subtle ways of preparing game, crayfish, trout, and other lake and river fish. Try *morilles* (morels) and *cèpes* (flap mushrooms); strawberries in season; jams and preserves from the native plums and walnuts. Among the wines to note are robust Cahors; full-bodied white or red Bergerac; Pécharmant, a fruity red wine that goes well with game and poultry; and Monbazillac, the fragrant sweet wine served as an apéritif with foie gras or with desserts.

The logical gateway to the Dordogne is Bordeaux, accessible by a 1-hour flight from Paris or by an enjoyable 4-hour ride on one of Europe's fastest trains, which average speeds of 95 mph. Then it's just 145 miles (about 230 km) by car from Bordeaux to Rocamadour, the easternmost point on our itinerary. In between, however, is a good week's worth of wandering on well-maintained country roads with relatively little traffic, except in high season (July and August).

   En Route from Bordeaux – For a description of Bordeaux, see the *Bordeaux* route. Leave Bordeaux by Route N89 via Libourne, an ancient stronghold founded by — and named for — Roger de Leybourne, an agent of the thirteenth-century king of England to whom the region belonged. Proceed along the course of the Isle River to Périgueux (about 75 mi/120 km), the capital of the Dordogne and a good place to make your headquarters for one or two nights.
PÉRIGUEUX: Once two towns separated by a wall, the lower section of Périgueux dates from the Roman era, with the remains of a third-century Gallo-Roman amphi-

theater and the cylindrical shell of a pagan temple, the Tour de Vésone. The town was devastated in the Vandal invasion of the fourth century, and a new defensive wall was built with stones taken from the ruins. Portions of this fortification may still be seen near the Château Barrière and the Arena.

Two excellent examples of Périgord-Romanesque architecture remain from the Middle Ages: the Church of St.-Étienne-de-la-Cité and the Cathédrale St.-Front. The latter, one of the largest churches in the area, is also one of the most unusual in all of France. The structure is built in the shape of a Greek cross; and the domes and cupolas show Byzantine influence. The bell tower, topped by a lantern-like structure supported by slender columns, is one of the finest Romanesque towers still standing. From the Barris bridge, St.-Front looms huge and white above the upper town, but its impressive interior is well worth a close inspection, and the rooftop gives you a panoramic view of the town.

Browse for souvenirs and food specialties in the shops that line the square near the cathedral, then walk up rue de la Clarté and rue Limogeanne to the old quarter, with its fascinating late medieval and Renaissance houses, many with remarkable stairways, gates, and ornate facades. Continue to Cours Tourny and the Musée du Périgord, which has a rich collection of more than 14,000 prehistoric artifacts as well as Gallo-Roman mosaics, ceramics, and bronzes. Cours Tourny also has the town's best restaurant, *Léon.* Nearby *La Flambée* and, on the outskirts of town, *Marcel* provide a seductive introduction to the gastronomic specialties of the region. Pick up additional tourist information at the Syndicat d'Initiative (1 av. d'Aquitaine; phone: 53-10-63) and the Office Départemental du Tourisme (16 rue du Président Wilson; phone: 53-44-35).

A pleasant half-day excursion (via D710 and D78) can be made of a drive north through the valley of the Dronne River, taking in a visit to the Château de Bourdeilles and the town of Brantôme.

BOURDEILLES: The medieval ramparts of Bourdeilles enclose a double château built on a promontory: The first house is an imposing feudal fortress with a superb octagonal keep; the other is a sixteenth-century Renaissance palace with sumptuously decorated salons and a comprehensive collection of ancient furniture and tapestries.

BRANTÔME: Brantôme is a delightful little town between two arms of the Dronne. Its fine eighteenth-century Benedictine abbey is now the Town Hall and houses the Musée Desmoulin, with an absorbing vignette of the town's history. A stroll from the Renaissance Pavillion through the Monks' Garden and along the canalside quays past old houses with flowered balconies and terraces is a peaceful and reflective way to pass an hour or two. Lunch or dinner at the *Restaurant Chabrol* is highly recommended before the return to Périgueux via D939.

En Route from Périgueux – Start early in the morning heading east on N89 for Brive-la-Gaillarde. En route you will pass the partly restored, late Greek revival Château de Rastignac. There's a striking similarity between its eighteenth-century semicircular Ionic peristyle and the southern portico of the White House.

South via Routes D65, 67, and 704 is Montignac and the celebrated caves of Lascaux, unfortunately closed to the public since 1963, when it was found that microorganisms were damaging the beautiful prehistoric frescoes. At nearby Le Thot, a modern prehistoric art center that shows photographic blowups of the most typical paintings, film projections, and models is open year-round. The terrace provides a good view of the Vézère Valley and the hill of Lascaux.

Head back through Montignac to pick up D704 north and return to N89, following the course of the Vézère River to Terrasson, an active little city at the crossroads of three provinces and the scene of an important truffle and walnut market. From the ramparts of the fifteenth-century abbey, there's an excellent view over the slate-roofed houses down to the Vézère and the enchanting countryside dotted with poplars beyond. Continue on N89 through the Brive basin's rich plum orchards and vegetable gardens, and try to take time out at the *Château de Castel Novel,* an old mansion in its own park with an excellent restaurant, just north of Brive at Varetz.

At Brive, turn south on N20 to Cressesac, then left on N140 for Martel and Rocamadour. At Réveillon, take D673 through the woods to the hamlet of l'Hospitalet. There's a spectacular vista over the narrow gorge of the Alzou, its rocky wall scaled by the extraordinary little fortified town of Rocamadour, the next stop. But be careful of roaming gaggles of geese along the winding country roads.

ROCAMADOUR: Rocamadour is built in superimposed tiers that are literally hewn out of the steep cliff face. Enter the town by the thirteenth-century Porte du Figuier near the Gendarmerie and you're on the principal thoroughfare, a narrow cobblestone street lined with souvenir shops. Continue down to the Porte Basse through a picturesque quarter of tiny houses clinging to the cliff, then return to place de la Caretta and the Great Staircase, which pilgrims have been climbing on their knees each September since the Middle Ages. Some 141 steps up is place Senhals, with the former clerics' quarters now converted into hotels such as the charming *Ste.-Marie,* with an attractive dining terrace. Higher still by 75 steps is place St.-Amadour and the Basilica of St.-Sauveur with its crypt and chapels; Notre-Dame, with a shrine honoring an ancient miraculous Virgin and child carved out of walnut; and St.-Michel, with two fine exterior frescoes.

Less energetic travelers should take the elevator near the Porte Salmon to the château on the third level and work their way down. From the turrets of the château, built on a promontory and now the home of the caretakers of the shrines, you have an unforgettable view of the sheer drop over the gorge and the town.

From Easter to October, there's a spectacular *son-et-lumière* from the terrace of the Musée Roland-le-Preux each evening at 9 PM and 9:45 PM.

From Rocamadour it's just 9 miles (15 km) to the Gouffre de Padirac, a 310-foot-deep gallery and caverns carved out of the limestone by a subterranean river. In an excursion lasting about 1½ hours, you can follow the course of the river for about ½ mile by a succession of narrow footpaths, switching to a boat that glides in and out of vast lakes and chambers and around bizarre rock formations.

En Route from Rocamadour – Route N673 twists and turns for about 13 miles (21 km) to Payrac. Turn left on N20 and head south for 2 miles (3.2 km), then pick up N673 again. At Gourdon turn north on D704 for Sarlat, stopping at the Grottoes of Cougnac. These clearly illuminated, accessible caves have prehistoric wall paintings of red ocher and black pigments that have been remarkably preserved.

SARLAT: Sarlat is a gem of a small, country town — a living museum with narrow, winding streets and ancient houses of gold-colored stone that painstaking restoration has returned to its original beauty. Don't be put off by the rather commercial, modern main street, rue de la République. Get settled in one of the many pleasant hotels and head straight for the Syndicat d'Initiative (pl. de la Liberté) for a walking-tour map. If you happen to be there on Saturday morning, stop by the colorful street market in the same square.

The cathedral (pl. du Peyrou) is a good central point for your explorations. Just across the way is one of Sarlat's most handsome Renaissance houses, the Maison de La Boétie, birthplace of the brilliant magistrate, author, and poet Étienne de La Boétie. Continue your visit to the Lanterne des Morts (Lantern of the Dead), the town's oldest and most curious structure; the rue Montaigne, with a stop at the former coaching inn, now the Galerie Montaigne, displaying the works of local artists and craftsmen; the Présidial, with its splendid gardens, slate roof, and unusual lantern tower; rue de la Salamandre and its rustic houses; and the Hôtel Plamon, a fascinating private home with three cathedral-like Gothic windows on the second floor. In the western part of town are steep, twisting streets such as rue des Trois Conils, rue du Siège, and rue J.-J. Rousseau.

Sarlat is also the gastronomic capital of Périgord Noir, so stop by one of the inviting food shops for picnic makings or head for a restaurant such as *La Madeleine* to sample the foie gras that is a specialty of the town.

During the tourist season, guided tours of Sarlat are available. In August the town is host to a famous open-air drama festival, an antiques exhibition, numerous concerts at the cathedral, and important regional fairs.

En Route from Sarlat – The day-long excursion through the Dordogne Valley between Sarlat and St.-Cyprien takes you along 40 miles (64 km) of meandering river, with great rocks towering high above and cliffs crowned with ancient castles and villages in the most romantic settings imaginable.

Take D704 to Carsac; then follow D703 along the right bank of the Dordogne. The highlights include the Château de Montfort, destroyed and rebuilt four times, dominating a narrow loop of the river from its promontory; Dronne, a charming fortified town on the opposite bank with one of the more spectacular views of the valley from its ramparts and precipitous cliffside promenades; La Roque-Gageac, often called France's most beautiful village, especially when the stone houses are reflected by the late afternoon sun in the stream far below; and Beynac, clinging to another bend in the river with a château like an eagle's nest perched 800 feet above. This matchless setting overlooks another loop in the river as well as four more castles: the ruins of Beynac's great rival, feudal Castelnaud; Marqueyssac, with its lofty terraced gardens; Fayrac, the well-restored sentinel castle; and Les Milandes, once owned by the American singer and cabaret star Josephine Baker. Each, of course, has its own dramatic views and is of enough historical interest to merit a brief visit. A late lunch, dinner, or even an overnight stay at Beynac's *Hôtel Bonnet* or St.-Cyprien's *L'Abbaye* is recommended. Or you can continue to D49, then D706, and Les Eyzies-de-Tayac.

LES EYZIES-DE-TAYAC: This tiny village, hovering under a 600-foot overhanging cliff, is a prehistoric time capsule. Here, in 1868, skeletons dating from more than 30,000 years before were found in the Cro-Magnon Cave by railway workmen. Shortly thereafter, explorations of the nearby caves at Le Moustier and Madeleine uncovered other relics that are landmarks in the chronology of man. Organized tours with commentaries in French, English, and German depart from the Syndicat d'Initiative to the museum and the grottoes of Les Eyzies as well as to other important historical sites Mondays through Saturdays, June to September.

Halfway up the cliff in the center of town is the National Museum of Prehistory, housed in the former castle of the lords of Beynac. There is a good view from the terrace with Dardé's larger-than-life 1930 sculpture of Cro-Magnon man. Inside are eight exhibition rooms with a fascinating collection of artifacts, art, skeletons, tools, weapons, and engravings from local excavations.

Within walking distance is the Font de Gaume cave, with over 200 red ocher paintings of animals. This art appears extraordinarily sophisticated to twentieth-century eyes. Other nearby sites of interest include the troglodyte Madeleine deposit; Le Moustier; Grand Roc, with a garden of crystalline deposits; Les Combarelles, with more than 300 paintings of animals, including running mammoths; Laugerie; La Mouthe; and the Fish Cave, with a superb salmon figure.

En Route from Les Eyzies – As you head west on D706 and D703, the Vézère curves to Le Bugue, another lovely village with the excellent *Royal Vézère* hotel right on the river; Limeuil, which clings to a hillside above the junction of the Dordogne and the Vézère, each river crossed by an arched stone bridge; and Trémolat, little changed from the Middle Ages, with a view of the sunlit valley and the loop of the river spread out below. From Trémolat to Lalinde, follow D31 along the river, then detour south on N660 for Monpazier, probably the best-preserved fortified town of the region. The great square is surrounded by covered arcades, ancient houses, and arched gateways.

Return to Beaumont and Lalinde, then proceed west on N660 to Bergerac, at the western edge of the Dordogne. This is an active, pleasant little town brimming with flowers. Its old quarter is a maze of twisting streets and Renaissance porches and facades. The elegant silhouette of the Château de Monbazillac dominates a nearby hill, and a tour of its massive round towers and battlements can also include a tasting of the products of the local wine cooperative, which now owns the château. From Bergerac, it's only about 57 miles (92 km) back to Bordeaux along Route 936, past tobacco fields and vineyards on the rich alluvial plain.

BEST EN ROUTE

Expect to pay $50 and up per night for a double room in hotels listed as expensive; $30 to $50 in those listed as moderate; and $20 to $30, inexpensive. The restaurants range in price from $50 and up for a dinner for two in the expensive range; $30 to $45 in the moderate range; and $25 and under, inexpensive. Prices do not include drinks, wine, and tip.

PÉRIGUEUX

Hôtel Domino – First class, with 37 rooms and all conveniences. Bar, summer garden, and restaurant. 21 pl. Francheville (phone: 08-25-80). Moderate.

Hôtel Lion D'Or – Near the center of town, it has 15 rooms and a lively restaurant. 17 Cours Fenelon (phone: 534903). Inexpensive.

Léon – Périgueux's best restaurant, serving light nouvelle dishes as well as local specialties. 18 Cours Tourny (phone: 53-41-93). Moderate.

BRANTÔME

Hostellerie le Moulin de L'Abbaye – An old mill-turned-inn on a gentle bend in the Dronne River, this is one of the most delightful spots in the region. Eight elegantly furnished rooms, a wonderful dining room, and a lovely riverside terrace. Rt. de Bourdeilles (phone: 058022). Expensive.

Hostellerie du Moulin du Roc – Another old mill that's been transformed into a friendly inn with five rooms. Its fine restaurant makes it worth a stop just for a meal. Four miles (6 km) northeast of Brantome via D78, in Champagnac-de-Belair (phone: 548036). Expensive.

Grand Hôtel Moderne et Chabrol – Refined and comfortable and overlooking the Dronne. The 21 rooms are small but charmingly decorated, and the restaurant serves good regional dishes. Rue Gambetta (phone: 057015). Inexpensive.

VARETZ

Château de Castel Novel – Old mansion in its own park with pool and tennis. Member of the Relais et Châteaux group. Twenty-eight rooms and an exceptionally fine restaurant serving inventive regional dishes and Cahors and Bergerac wines. Open early May to late October. Reserve in tourist season. Near Varetz, about 7 miles (11 km) northwest of Brive-la-Gaillarde on N901 (phone: 85-00-01). Expensive.

ROCAMADOUR

Château de Roumégouse – Ten rooms in a wooded park with terraces overlooking Le Causse. Member of the Relais et Châteaux group. Riding and tennis nearby; pleasant restaurant. Between Rocamadour and Gramat off D677 (phone: 33-63-81). Expensive.

Beau Site et Notre-Dame – In a restored fifteenth-century house with all modern comforts, 54 rooms and a good restaurant. Rue Roland-le-Preux (phone: 33-63-08). Moderate.

Hôtel Ste.-Marie – Small hotel with 23 comfortable rooms and a lovely, flower-lined terrace restaurant overlooking the Alzou Canyon. Pl. des Senhals (phone: 336222). Inexpensive.

SARLAT

Hôtel de la Madeleine – Comfortable, pleasant, and Sarlat's best; 19 well-kept rooms and an excellent restaurant with hearty regional food. 1 pl. Petite-Rigaudie (phone: 59-12-40). Moderate.

Hôtel de la Hoirie – Cozy 13-room inn with lots of local atmosphere just outside of town. No restaurant. A mile and a half south of town at la Canéda (phone: 59-05-62). Moderate.

Hostellerie de Meysset – Charming, ivy-covered manor house with 27 rooms and a very agreeable restaurant. One mile northwest from town on Rte. de Eyzies (phone: 59-08-29). Expensive.

Couleuvrine – A new and noteworthy addition to Sarlat's hotels, this is actually a restored thirteenth-century structure. It has 20 rooms with antique furnishings but all the modern amenities. 1 pl. de la Bouquerie (phone: 592780). Moderate.

Auberge de la Lantern – The aroma emanating from this corner restaurant draws diners like a magnet. A variety of menus are offered. 1 pl. de la Bouquerie. Moderate.

BEYNAC

Hôtel Bonnet – Delightful small inn nestled in a grove of walnut trees on the banks of the Dordogne, with a wonderful view up to the castle of Beynac. There are 24 rooms, a pleasant staff, and a very popular restaurant. Closed mid-October to mid-April (phone: 29-50-01). Moderate.

ST.-CYPRIEN

L'Abbaye – Small hostelry of 20 rooms, most with views down to the Dordogne and an excellent restaurant. Open mid-March to mid-October; closed Wednesdays in September. Rue Entrepot (phone: 29-20-48). Moderate.

LES EYZIES-DE-TAYAC

Cro-Magnon – Said to be where Cro-Magnon skeletons were found over 115 years ago, this delightful, vine-covered inn provides modern luxury and efficiency without forfeiting charm. There are 27 rooms, a swimming pool, extensive grounds, and a very good restaurant for classic traditional fare as well as a few specials. Rte. de Périgueux (phone: 069706). Expensive.

Hôtel du Centenaire – A sparkling 29-room hotel — more modern than the *Cro-Magnon* but equally worthy of praise. Chef Roland Mazere, who apprenticed with a few of the country's best, takes an up-to-date approach to cooking that's been successful enough to win him two Michelin stars (phone: 069718). Expensive.

LE BUGUE

Royal Vézère – Comfortable, modern, 48-room hotel on the bank of the Vézère with rooftop pool, sunny terrace, and a nightclub. Small, exclusive restaurant with well-prepared regional specialties. Open late April to early October. Pl. Hôtel-de-Ville (phone: 06-20-01). Expensive.

TRÉMOLAT

Le Vieux Logis – The epitome of rustic charm in an old house with antique furniture and lovely gardens. With 20 rooms and a good restaurant. Closed in January.

Nearby tennis, sailing, fishing, hunting, and riding. Member of the Relais et Châteaux group (phone: 228006). Expensive.

BERGERAC

Château Mounet-Sully – This comfortable little place is housed in a former cloister set in a lovely park and has its own restaurant. Route de Mussidan (phone: 57-04-21). Expensive to moderate.

Le Cyrano – This unpretentious little restaurant has a star from Michelin. The owner's son directs the kitchen, and generally sticks to the classics of the region — try quail galantine with prunes or grilled lamb with crème d'ail. 2 blvd. Montaigne (phone: 57-02-76). Moderate.

Provence

As the French who flock here every summer know, one of the most charming regions in the country is Provence, the area along the southern banks of the Rhône River, just north and west of the Riviera. Like the Riviera, Provence is known for its cloudless skies and brilliant southern sunshine. It is also known for its pretty little villages perched high up in the hills or nestled down in the valleys, with their typical red roofs and, in many cases, medieval stone walls intact. Small farms are plentiful here; typical crops are fruits and vegetables. Grapes are cultivated, and thyme, marjoram, and lavender grow wild. Olive groves are everywhere, and rows of tall cypress trees are planted to protect crops from the mistral, the powerful north wind of southern France.

The name "Provence" is derived from the historic fact that the region was once a Roman province; yet its history begins earlier, with the founding of Marseille by the Greeks in 600 BC. The Romans invaded in about 125 BC and scattered traces of their stay everywhere. As a result, Provence is the section of France most renowned for its magnificently preserved Roman temples, arches, and amphitheaters. Its star attraction is the amazing 2,000-year-old, three-tier Pont du Gard, between Nîmes and Arles, a Roman aqueduct that stands virtually intact.

In addition to Roman remains, Provence is dominated by Avignon, once the papal residence, with its impressive fourteenth-century Papal Palace (Palais des Papes), a vast stone fortress built during the schism within the papacy known to history as the Babylonian Captivity. The Pont d'Avignon, a bridge made famous in a French children's song, is actually called the Pont St.-Bénézet, and though partly destroyed, it still stretches picturesquely halfway across the Rhône. There's a fascinating side trip from Arles to the strange, marshy land of the Camargue, where bulls are raised for bullfights and wild horses, ducks, and flamingos roam free. At the eastern extreme of the route is Aix-en-Provence, which, except for its festival in July and August, is a quiet old university town adorned with boulevards, fountains, and cafés. Paul Cézanne lived here, and it's one of the loveliest towns in all of France.

Provençal cooking shows the Italian influence in its typical ingredients of garlic, tomatoes, and olive oil. The region produces the outstanding Côtes du Rhône wines such as Châteauneuf-du-Pape, Tavel, and Rasteau.

Avignon, the starting point of the route described below, is a 7-hour drive from Paris along Routes A6 or N7; if you prefer, you can choose the more scenic itinerary along the Loire Valley and through Burgundy. The best maps of the region are the Institut Géographique National's IGN 115 or Michelin nos. 83, 80, 81.

Note: Both Aix-en-Provence and Avignon host 3-week arts festivals in mid-July; both, but especially the one in Aix, are very popular, so you'd best make hotel reservations well in advance if you plan to visit then.

AVIGNON: The walled city of Avignon was the ancient seat of the papacy during the Church's period of schism in the fourteenth century. Park near the train station (blvd. St.-Roch) and enter the city through the Porte de la République. As you walk straight along the tree-lined rue de la République, you'll come to the place de l'Horloge, a good spot to pause at an outdoor café and take in some of the local color. From here it's only a few steps to the place du Palais, which is dominated by the immense, fortress-like stone walls of the medieval papal residence. Informative English-language tours are given through the vast interior halls of this historic palace.

Coming back out onto the place du Palais, you'll see a toylike train. Take it. It will carry you up to the Rocher des Doms, a lovely park with a superb view of the Rhône River and its twelfth-century bridge, Pont St.-Bénézet. For a better feeling of daily life in Avignon, wander into the pedestrian zone off place de l'Horloge, browsing, for example, in rue des Marchands and rue des Fourbisseurs, then following rue du Roi-René to the picturesque rue des Teinturiers, beside a canal and old water wheels. Avignon boasts elegant shopping, particularly for fine (but not cheap) regional antiques. Turn left anywhere off rue de la République and you'll find many shops. Finally, cross the river to Villeneuve-les-Avignon. It is from this ancient city of cardinals, with Philippe le Bel's tower and the St.-André fort, that you'll get a spectacular view of Avignon at sunset.

En Route from Avignon – Take Route N100 directly west for 15 miles (24 km) to the Pont-du-Gard. This superb Roman aqueduct, some 2,000 years old, is almost completely intact. Standing three tiers high, it is a startling example of Roman engineering.

Doubling back a bit, you can follow N86 for 14 miles (about 22 km) directly into Nîmes, one of the major Roman cities of Provence, dating from the time of Emperor Augustus. Of principal interest are the Roman amphitheater (pl. des Arènes — still used for bullfights) and Roman temple, the Maison Carrée (blvd. A.-Daudet just beyond Antonin Sq.). For a change of atmosphere, follow the quai de la Fontaine along the canal to the eighteenth-century Jardins de la Fontaine. Here are the Temple de Diane and the Tour Magne, a Roman monument built about the end of the first century. The gardens offer a good look at the surrounding countryside and in summer are the setting for open-air art exhibitions.

Eleven miles (about 17 km) from Nîmes, via D42, is St.-Gilles, a good coffee stop. This typical Provençal town is known for the superb facade of its church (pl. de la République), sculpted between 1180 and 1240.

Taking N572 east and N570 north brings you to Tarascon. The medieval château here is exceptionally well preserved, and its terraces, with a splendid view over the Rhône, make it one of the most beautiful feudal structures in France.

From here, taking N99 east, you are only 9 miles (about 14 km) from St.-Rémy-de-Provence, a lovely town with an active weekend open-air market and plenty of tree-shaded streets.

LES ANTIQUES and LES BAUX: Only ½ mile from St.-Rémy, south along Route D5, is Les Antiques, yet another admirably preserved Roman site with a mausoleum

— one of the finest Roman structures of its kind to be found today — a municipal arch, and the ruins of Glanum, a thriving city founded six centuries before Christ.

Five miles (8 km) farther down D5 is Les-Baux-de-Provence. In the Alpilles Mountains, this village presents an austere and almost lunar landscape of limestone hills. The view from the ancient fortress is breathtaking during the day and quite eerie at night. Understandably, Les Baux's unique beauty is no secret, and nestled into its haunting hills are some of the most fashionable and expensive restaurants and hotels in France. (One such is the three-star *Oustaù de Baumanière,* where you should try the red mullet mousse or the sweetbreads.)

Taking D17 west for 11 miles (17.7 km) brings you to Arles, the next stop.

ARLES: Founded by the Greeks who settled Marseille, Arles was a major capital during the Roman period, an important religious center during the Middle Ages, and today preserves its past in magnificent architectural ruins and relics. Of special interest are the amphitheater (Rond-Point des Arènes), the "sister" of the one at Nîmes, and the remains of a Roman theater, erected toward the end of the first century BC (leaving the amphitheater, take the tiny street right before rue Porte-de-Laure to reach the theater). At the place de la République is the city hall (Hôtel de Ville); the Musée d'Art Paien, containing antique statues, sarcophagi, and mosaics; and the church of St. Trophime, founded in the reign of Charlemagne, with a magnificent portal and cloisters. Just to the right of the intersection of rue du Président-Wilson and rue de la République is the splendid Museum of Christian Art (Musée d'Art Chrétien). From its interior, you can descend into a subterranean gallery dating from the first century BC. Finally, visit Les Alyscamps (av. des Alyscamps and Craponne Canal), which was used as a cemetery from Roman times to the end of the Middle Ages.

En Route from Arles — In this case it's more precisely "off the route" — an 82-mile (131-km) detour into the Camargue, a region whose landscape is unique in France: a vast, marshy delta of the two arms of the Rhône, where herds of wild bulls and horses run free and the terrain is dotted with the slender figures of heron stalking fish. In Stes.-Maries-de-la-Mer, the capital of the Camargue, Gypsies from all over Europe gather each May and October to honor their patron saint. From Arles, take N570 south. Come with the Gypsies; May and October are the recommended seasons.

Back in Arles, take N113 to N538 and the turnpike (A7, later becoming A8) for the 45-mile (72-km) trip into Aix-en-Provence.

AIX-EN-PROVENCE: Founded as Aquae Sextius (the Waters of Sextius) by the Roman consul Sextius in 122 BC, this ancient capital of Provence today offers a largely seventeenth- and eighteenth-century facade, with elegant private mansions, graceful squares, majestic avenues, and numerous fountains. It is also an intellectual center, having had a famous university since 1409.

The main boulevard — Cours Mirabeau — is bordered by towering, shady plane trees and lined with cafés, shops, and fine, aristocratic-looking townhouses. At each end of the Cours are the fountains that recall Aix's origin as a watering place for the Roman legions. This avenue is one of the most pleasant in Provence for strolling, café hopping, and window shopping.

At the place de l'Hôtel-de-Ville there's a flower market and the remains of the old grain market. Enter the Hôtel de Ville to visit the remarkable 300,000-volume library founded in the eighteenth century by the Marquis de Méjanes, for whom it is named. Other points of interest can be found at the place des Martyrs-de-la-Résistance: the Musée des Tapisseries, the Cloître St.-Sauveur, and the Cathédrale St.-Sauveur, whose architecture runs the gamut of styles from the fifth to the sixteenth century. At 34 rue Célony, the facade of the seventeenth-century Pavillon de Vendôme offers a fine example of Provençal decorative art. At the place des Prêcheurs, there's the Église Ste.-Marie-Madeleine, containing important paintings, including a large work attributed to

Rubens. You'll also want to see Paul Cézanne's studio (atelier) on avenue Paul-Cézanne. The painter was born in Aix in 1839, and his studio has been reconstructed as it was found at his death in 1906.

In July and August, Aix holds an international music festival. This is the high season, action-packed and crowded: Last-minute reservations are risky. Open-air concerts are held in the archbishop's court as well as in the surrounding countryside.

En Route from Aix – Only a few miles outside Aix are several charming restaurants and hotels.

From Aix the route to Marseille is simple: Just take N8 straight south for 19 miles (30.4 km). For a complete report on Marseille, see *Marseille*, THE EUROPEAN CITIES.

BEST EN ROUTE

Expect to pay $60 and up per night for a double room in hotels listed as expensive; $40 to $50 in those listed as moderate; and $25 in the inexpensive. The restaurants range in price from $60 and up for a dinner for two in the expensive range and $30 to $40 in the moderate range. Prices do not include drinks, wine, and tip.

AVIGNON

Le Prieuré – The luxury hotel of the area, set in shady grounds with a pool and tennis courts and boasting a celebrated restaurant that specializes in grilled duck or tournedos with truffles. Closed November through February. Pl. du Chapitre at Villeneuve-Les-Avignon (phone: 25-18-20). Expensive.

Hiely-Lucullus – This large, comfortable restaurant is the best in town. The menu is only prix-fixe, but the choices are considerable and the value extraordinary. There are fine local wines from the Côtes-du-Rhone. Reservations are essential. Closed Mondays, except in summer, Tuesdays, and mid-June through early July, and 2 weeks at Christmas. 5 rue de la République (phone: 86-17-07). Expensive.

Europe – A palace in the sixteenth century, it is now the best hotel in the city. Aubusson tapestries decorate the high walls in the antique-furnished public rooms, the 65 bedrooms are richly appointed, and it has a pleasant restaurant. 12 pl. Crillon (phone: 826696). Moderate.

ST.-RÉMY-DE-PROVENCE

Hostellerie du Vallon de Valrugues – A beautiful setting, with 24 rooms, tennis, and swimming. Chemin Canto Cigalo (phone: 92-04-40). Expensive to moderate.

Les Antiques – Very attractive reception rooms, 27 guest rooms, a park, riding, and swimming. 15 av. Pasteur (phone: 92-03-02). Moderate.

Château de Roussan – A delightful hotel in an eighteenth-century mansion surrounded by a park. No restaurant. Rte. Tarascon (phone: 92-11-63). Moderate.

Canto Cigalo – A modest hotel in quiet surroundings. No restaurant. Closed November through February. Chemin Canto Cigalo (phone: 92-14-28). Inexpensive.

LES BAUX

Oustaù de Baumanière – The jewel of Les Baux, this hotel is elegantly furnished and offers flowered terraces, tennis, swimming, riding, and one of France's top restaurants. The building looks like a medieval castle and is decorated with antiques. Restaurant specialties include stuffed pigeon, duckling with lime, and *marrons glacés* (glazed chestnuts). Thuilier (phone: 97-33-07). Expensive.

La Cabro d'Or – A small hotel with a pleasant setting, tennis, swimming, good views, and a fine restaurant. Closed mid-November through mid-December, Tuesdays at lunch, and Mondays mid-October through March. (phone: 97-33-21). Moderate.

Mas d'Aigret – A very appealing, modest hotel, with 17 rooms, swimming, a restful setting, and good views. Closed mid-November through mid-December. D27 east (phone: 97-33-54). Moderate.

ARLES

Jules César – This hotel was formerly a convent and still features cloisters and interior gardens. Its restaurant, *Lou Marqués,* serves very good regional cuisine. Blvd. Lices (phone: 96-49-76). Expensive to moderate.
Hotel d'Arlatan – A small hotel with fine antique furnishings, a patio, and a garden. 26 rue du Sauvage (phone: 96-36-75). Moderate to inexpensive.

AIX-EN-PROVENCE

Roy Ren – Aix's old-style grand hotel has served Winston Churchill, among others, and still provides excellent service. It offers 65 elegant rooms, a restaurant, and a heated pool. 14 bd. du Roi (phone: 260301). Expensive.
Charvet – Widely considered the best in Aix, this restaurant is elegant and traditional, with a deliciously light, inventive cuisine. Closed Sunday nights, Mondays, and 2 weeks in August. Reservations recommended. 9 rue Lacépede (phone: 384382). Expensive.
Paul Cézanne – A very comfortable hotel with a beautiful interior. 40 av. Victor-Hugo (phone: 26-34-73). Expensive to moderate.
Mas d'Entremont – A tiny hotel in a typical Provençal setting with terraces, a park, a fine restaurant, and swimming. Célony, 2 miles (3.2 km) north via N7 (phone: 23-45-32). Moderate (bungalows more expensive).
Château de Meyrargues – Hotel in a restored eleventh-century fortress; good restaurant. The rooms range from the simple to the "master bedroom," where you'll truly feel like a feudal lord. Closed December and January. Meyrargues, 10 miles (16 km) via N96 (phone: 57-50-32). Moderate to inexpensive.

The Riviera

The French Riviera, known in France as the Côte d'Azur, is the privileged Mediterranean coastline stretching from Menton in the east to St.-Tropez in the west and including such world-renowned resorts as Nice, Cannes, and Antibes. It is an area of spectacular beauty, with dazzling white cliffs rising from the sea, gracefully curved bays, and some of the most luxurious and palatial hotels and private villas anywhere in the world. The Riviera includes discreet corners and jet-set haunts, picturesque villages and major cities, but it all is a playground. This is the place for sunning, swimming, gambling, eating, nightclubbing, and, on the cultural side, for seeing some of the finest collections of paintings by modern masters in France (many of the most prominent figures in twentieth-century art lived here at one time or another, drawn by the beauty of the terrain and the extraordinary clarity of the light).

Although the Riviera has the reputation of being the playground of the rich and famous (which indeed it is), you'll find a remarkably wide spread of prices. After all this is the vacation paradise of the French themselves (the most demanding of peoples) who ritually crowd down here during the months of July and August. And you can be sure that they have contrived to keep standards high across all price ranges, from simple bistros and camping sites to the renowned gourmet restaurants and luxury hotels. Mind you, "expensive" can really mean just that — up to $140 for a single night. Although even at the ultra chic *Hotel de Paris* in Monte Carlo, the rococo *Négresco* in Nice, and the *Byblos* in St.-Tropez, it is possible to get a room for $70. And don't forget that in France it is usual to pay for the room not the number of persons. So couples often get a better deal than singles.

Many beaches are rocky or pebbly, but there are plenty of sandy beaches especially between Antibes and St.-Tropez. Some beaches are public and free of charge; others are "private," which usually means they belong to a restaurant or a hotel. But it's worth renting an air mattress and a beach umbrella at one of these for around $5 a day. Topless sunbathing (said to have originated at Tahiti Plage near St.-Tropez) is ubiquitous but hardly the rule. One of the great delights about the Riviera is that everyone does his or her own thing — the French are consummate individualists. So relax. High season is July and August when the inundation of tourists can make it a bit tacky. It's best to visit in May and June or even September and October. The temperatures will be cooler, of course, but still mild, and you'll be able to see something more than wall-to-wall people.

Nice–Côte d'Azur Airport is the busiest in France after Charles de Gaulle and Orly in Paris. It is certainly the most attractive. You come in over the sea to touch down on the edge of a bright white runway and step off the plane to palm trees and a fragrant breeze (called the *mistral* when it really blows). There's a fine restaurant *(Le Ciel d'Azur)* on the second floor of the airport. There are buses to Nice and many towns along the Riviera including Monte Carlo. A taxi to downtown Nice will cost you about $6. There's also helicopter service to Monte Carlo.

You'll have no trouble finding your way around if you take along the IGN map no. 115 (Provence–Côte d'Azur) or Michelin map no. 195 (Côte d'Azur–Alpes Maritimes). There is sun and sea and scenery wherever you turn, so stop anywhere and enjoy it. That's what the Riviera's all about.

LES CORNICHES: Nice is the usual starting point for the Côte d'Azur. (For a complete report on the city and its hotels and restaurants, see *Nice,* THE EUROPEAN CITIES.) But the "real" Riviera begins once you leave the city. You don't have to go far. Between Nice and Menton, a 19-mile (30-km) trip, you'll travel by mountain passes, or *corniches,* that compel you to marvel at dramatic views of both sea and shoreline. From Nice you take N7 to the Grande Corniche. The ascent is quick, and especially magical views can be enjoyed as you pause briefly at Belvédère d'Eze, at La Turbie, at Vistaëro and its medieval château, and at Roquebrune-Cap-Martin. The old towns are enchanting and the landscape, superb. This road also leads to Monaco — where you'll certainly want to spend some time (see *Exploring Monaco,* DIRECTIONS) — and terminates in Menton, a city known for its excellent climate, tropical vegetation, and the international chamber music festival held each year in August.

On the return trip, take the lower pass (Corniche Inférieure) to enjoy panoramas that include bird's-eye views of some of the loveliest resorts in the world. At Beaulieu-sur-Mer, as you drive past *La Réserve,* the prestigious hotel and restaurant, you begin to enter the "gold coast" ambience of the Riviera. Stop next at St.-Jean-Cap-Ferrat and visit the Fondation Ephrussi de Rothschild, set among exquisite gardens overlooking the sea. The splendid artworks and furniture date from the fourteenth to the nineteenth century. Just a few miles down the coast, the picturesque town of Villefranche is the classic model of a Mediterranean fishing port, with high cliffs that seem to fall into the sea. From here, return to Nice via N559.

En Route from Nice – Between Nice and Cannes, half the fun is definitely getting there. Cagnes-sur-Mer, with its Renoir museum, is 8 miles (about 12 km) west via N7. St.-Paul-de-Vence, while not actually on the coast, is only a few miles inland and well worth the detour (take N7 west and N85 to D2). For lovers of the good life, there's the *Hôtel Mas d'Artigny* and *La Colombe d'Or,* a second home to some of France's best-known personalities. For art lovers, this one-time home of Georges Braque boasts the Maeght Foundation, which houses one of the finest collections of contemporary art in France. Nearby, St. Paul de Vence (3 mi/4.8 km inland via D2) is Chagall's adopted city; it, too, has an impressive art collection at the Galerie les Arts. The jewel-like Chapelle du Rosaire at Vence was designed entirely by Matisse, from the stained glass to the white ceramic walls.

A few miles west back along the coast brings you to Biot, a medieval village perched on a hilltop. Visit the glassworks, where you can buy hand-blown glass and watch it being made. The Fernand Leger Museum is also worth a look. From Biot, the RN7 will take you to Antibes, where the Château-Musée Grimaldi houses a fine collection of the works of Picasso. Antibes, once the home of Monet, is a beautiful port with fortress walls and tiny, winding streets. Just beyond Antibes, you pass through Juan-les-Pins, somewhat gaudy, but a famous resort with good sand beaches.

This is really the heart of luxury sun worship, and elegant private villas line the approach to Cap d'Antibes, one of the most exclusive spots on the Riviera. Take time just to walk around the *Hôtel du Cap d'Antibes* and enjoy a drink on the terrace or a swim at the leafy pool of the *Hotel Residence du Cap.* It's every glamorous story come to life and epitomizes the Riviera's status as a haven for the rich and famous. Napoleon's Naval Museum at Cap d'Antibes is well worth a visit. Follow the coast right around for 6 miles (10 km) to reach Cannes.

CANNES: Unlike some of the earlier stops, Cannes is not quiet and discreet, but it too is the Riviera. The elegant (if sometimes noisy) boulevard de la Croisette, with riotously colorful gardens tracing the line of the Gulf of Napoule, is the key to Cannes. Here are smart boutiques, myriad outdoor cafés, and the *Majestic* and *Carlton* hotels — the headquarters for international stars during the city's annual film festival in the spring. As you follow the boulevard to pointe de la Croisette you come to the famed (and original) Palm Beach, with your walk enhanced by constant views of the water. Take the boulevard in the opposite direction to get to the port, a harbor for the most extravagant yachts you could hope to see.

Cannes is a chic city, with its café society, nightclubs, and two casinos. But it has more quaint charms as well — for example, the flower market in the Allée de la Liberté or the old city, centered around place de la Castre. End your visit with a trip to the observatory of Super-Cannes, 3 miles (5 km) outside the city, north on avenue Isola-Bella. It goes without saying that the panoramas are really sublime from here.

En Route from Cannes – Excursions from Cannes offer some interesting stops for a change of pace. Take D803 to Vallauris, an important center for ceramic art; regular exhibitions are held in the summer. Via N567 and the Esterel–Côte d'Azur Autoroute you arrive at Mougins. This ancient fortified town, once Picasso's home, today houses one of France's finest restaurants, the *Moulin de Mougins.* Seven miles (11.2 km) farther inland is Grasse, the perfume production center of France and a sought-after residential area as well. The perfume factories Molinard (52 blvd. Victor-Hugo) and Fragonard (blvd. Fragonard) are open to the public.

Returning to Cannes, you can take a boat from the port to the nearby islands

(Îles de Lérins). The excursion takes half a day, including stops at Île Ste.-Marguerite, fragrant with eucalyptus and pine forests, and at Île St.-Honorat, the site of an ancient fortified monastery.

As you wind along the coast westward from Cannes (N559 to N98), the seascapes become vast leading into St.-Tropez, a distance of 45 miles (72 km).

ST.-TROPEZ: Rivaling Cannes as a jet-set favorite, St.-Tropez first became famous when Brigitte Bardot made it her home. Everything you've ever heard about this city is found at the port. You'll see starlets, swingers, spectators, and a whole coterie who'd give anything to be part of the action. The scene is hypnotizing, so settle back to watch with an early-evening Pernod or Blanc Cassis at *Senequier's* in the port. Next day, take a trip out to Môle Jean Réveille or to the Citadelle, built in the sixteenth and seventeenth centuries, which offers imposing views. Don't miss the Musée de l'Annonciade (quai G.-Péri), which has an outstanding collection of twentieth-century art.

The best beaches at St.-Tropez are a few miles out on the Caps de St.-Tropez, du Pinet, and Camarat. Pampelonne beach is also good, but the most chic is Tahiti Plage (strictly speaking, at Ramatuelle), where you can have a delicious and moderately priced lunch on the terrace overlooking the beach.

A warning: St.-Tropez has experienced a surge of construction — both residential and commercial — in the last several years. It is, of course, one of the "in" fun spots of the Riviera, but in the summer the congestion — both human and automotive — may be more than you care for. If frenzy is not your idea of vacation, you might prefer St.-Tropez in the off-season.

En Route from St.-Tropez – The heart of the Riviera ends at St.-Tropez, and although the region to the west offers fewer restaurants and hotels, the scenery is still dazzling. If you follow N98 to N559, you find high cliffs and expansive seascapes around Cavalaire-sur-Mer; at Lavandou, a long-time favorite of artists, good sand beaches and one of the loveliest fishing ports on the coast await you. From here, it's only 23 miles (37 km) back to St.-Tropez along the coast; but if you have time, take the mountain route (Rte. du Littoral) via the Corniche des Maures. It's twice as long, but the scenery is spectacular. The route ends in St.-Raphaël; from there just follow the coast 45 miles (72 km) east back to Nice.

BEST EN ROUTE

Expect to pay $70 to $80 and all the way up per night for a double room in hotels listed as expensive; $50 to $70 in those listed as moderate; and under $50, inexpensive. The restaurants range in price from $60 to $80 and up for a dinner for two in the expensive range and around $50 in the moderate range. Prices do not include drinks, wine, and tip. Service charge and tax are invariably included in the check. In high season you may need to buy dinner or lunch in order to get a room.

Note: For the entire Riviera, reservations are a must in high season.

ROQUEBRUNE-CAP-MARTIN

Vistaëro – A luxury hotel with swimming and a beautiful setting. The views are exceptional. About 2 miles from downtown on the Grande Corniche (phone: 35-01-50). Expensive to moderate.

BEAULIEU-SUR-MER

La Réserve – One of France's top luxury hotels with an internationally known restaurant; heated swimming pool. Right on the sea. Closed December through mid-January. 5 Blvd. du Gén-Leclerc (phone: 01-00-01). Expensive.

Comté de Nice – A nice hotel with reasonable prices; no restaurant. Closed November through mid-December. 25 blvd. Marinoni (phone: 01-19-70). Moderate.

ST.-JEAN-CAP-FERRAT

Voile d'Or – An elegant hotel with a fine restaurant, pool, and superb views of the port. Closed November through January. (phone: 01-13-13). Expensive.

Grand Hôtel du Cap-Ferrat – A fine luxury hotel right on the water, with lovely grounds, a beach, and tennis. Closed November through March. Blvd. Gén.-de-Gaulle (phone: 01-04-54). Expensive.

Cappa – A top-rate yet reasonably priced seafood restaurant overlooking the port. Closed November through January. Av. J.-Mermoz (phone: 01-30-07). Moderate to inexpensive.

ST.-PAUL-DE-VENCE

La Colombe d'Or – Luxury combining Provençal atmosphere and lush, beautiful gardens. This sumptuous, small hotel is famous for its art collection of works by Miró, Calder, Picasso, and Chagall (phone: 32-80-02). Expensive.

Mas d'Artigny – A stunning luxury hotel; all 25 suites come with private swimming pools. Dining room serves fine seafood. Rte. de la Colle and des Hauts de St.-Paul (phone: 32-84-54). Expensive.

Les Orangers – This pleasant hotel has 10 rooms but no restaurant. Closed mid-November to mid-December. Rte. de la Colle, D7 (phone: 328024). Moderate.

Les Oliviers – Tasty regional food in a pretty garden setting. Rte. D7 (phone: 32-80-13). Moderate.

Aubergo Duo Souleü – Diners can enjoy excellent food along with a beautiful view over St.-Paul (phone: 32-80-60). Moderate.

CAP D'ANTIBES

Hôtel du Cap d'Antibes – A truly grand and exclusive luxury hotel with gorgeous grounds and views, swimming, and tennis. Its restaurant, *Pavillon Eden Roc,* serves delicious food. Blvd. Kennedy (phone: 61-39-01). Expensive.

La Gardiole – A simple, quiet hotel set among the pines; some rooms overlook the sea. Chemin la Garoupe (phone: 61-35-03). Moderate.

Restaurant de Bacon – From a terrace overlooking the sea, diners can enjoy very good bouillabaisse or fresh fish. Closed Sunday nights, Mondays, and mid-November through January. Blvd. de Bacon (phone: 615002). Expensive.

ANTIBES

La Bonne Auberge – This three-star restaurant specializes in Provençal cuisine. On the right-hand side of N7 coming from Nice (phone: 33-36-65). Very expensive.

Hotel Mas Djoliba – This quiet hotel has a beautiful garden setting. 27 ave. de Provence (phone: 34-02-48). Moderate to inexpensive.

L'Oursin – This popular but plain little restaurant has the best seafood in the downtown area. Closed Monday nights, Wednesdays, and August. Reservations necessary. 16 rue République (phone: 34-13-46). Inexpensive.

Le Yacht – A charming pub-restaurant, which caters to yacht crews who've put into Port Vauban Harbor, with a grand view of the boats; a few rooms are available. 15 av. de la Libération (phone: 742400). Moderate.

CANNES

Majestic – With the *Carlton,* one of the classic, glamorous hotels of Cannes. Closed November. Blvd. de la Croisette (phone: 68-91-00). Expensive.

Carlton – Like the *Majestic* and more — there's a beach for swimming. 58 blvd. de la Croisette (phone: 68-91-68). Expensive.

Gray d'Albion – This is a modern and comfortable hotel with a restaurant that's quite good. 38 rue des Serbes (phone: 48-54-54). Expensive.

Fredante – Superb seafood dishes from Corsica are the specialties here. Just off the Croisette, it's bright and sophisticated. 14 rue Bateguier (phone: 683030). Expensive to moderate.

Saint-Yves – A quaint, cozy old-fashioned villa in a delightful garden of palm trees, it has 21 rooms. 49 blvd. d'Alsace (phone: 386529). Moderate.

MOUGINS

Le Moulin de Mougins – Set in a sixteenth-century mill with exotic plants outside the windows and original paintings on the walls, this is one of the most famous restaurants in France. Chef Roger Vergé's specialties include: lobster fricassée, pâté of sole, escalope of fresh salmon, and salade Mikado (with mushrooms, avocado, tomatoes, and truffles). The Réserve wine, a very fine rosé, comes from nearby vineyards, and cold wild strawberry soufflé is delicious. (There are also three hotel rooms here that should be booked well in advance.) Closed mid-October through mid-December. Notre-Dame-de-Vie southeast; 1 mile via D3 (phone: 75-78-24). Very expensive.

L'Amandier de Mougins – Roger Vergé's other restaurant, it serves simpler and less expensive food. Closed Wednesdays and January. Pl. du Commandant-Lamy (phone: 900347). Expensive.

Hotel de France – Very good, if not as famous as its neighbor. Broiled rabbit is a specialty. Eight guest rooms are also available. Pl. du Commandant-Lamy (phone: 90-00-01). Moderate.

LA NAPOULE

L'Oasis – Only 5 miles (8 km) south of Cannes, this extraordinary three-star restaurant near the harbor is well worth a detour. It has a lovely shaded patio with white tables, a palm tree, and many flowers (phone: 49-95-52). Expensive.

ST.-TROPEZ

Byblos – A grand luxury hotel, decorated in Provençal style with some of the best food in town. Good views are matched by excellent swimming. Closed November through mid-December. Av. Paul-Signac (phone: 97-00-04). Expensive.

Levant – On the road where Colette used to live, this hotel by the sea has 28 rooms, a pool, and a restaurant. Closed mid-October through March. Rte. des Salins (phone: 973333). Moderate.

Sube – The most famous of the town's cheaper hotels is set right on the harbor. It has 28 unpretentious rooms. Closed November through February. 15 quai Suffern (phone: 973004). Inexpensive.

Burgundy

Burgundy begins 100 miles (160 km) south of Paris and stretches almost to Lyon. The region has always been a place of passage, a transit zone between northern France and the Mediterranean south and between France and Switzerland. But Burgundy is also important in its own right because of its history, its produce, its art, and its architecture.

The region was conquered by the Romans in 52 BC, when Julius Caesar forced Vercingetorix, the Gallic ruler of the Arverni, to surrender at Alesia.

A fifth-century invasion by the Burgundians, who came from the region of the Baltic Sea, gave Burgundy its modern name.

In 534, the Franks conquered the kingdom of Burgundy. The death of the great Frankish king Charlemagne in 814 heralded a 200-year period of chaos and turbulence. The long strife ended when the kingdom, by then reduced to a duchy, passed into the hands of King Robert II of France (known as Robert the Pious), who made his son Robert the first Capetian duke of Burgundy.

Under the Capets, Burgundy became a bastion of Christianity. Monasteries were founded and magnificent churches built. But Burgundy's true golden age came when the Capets were succeeded in 1364 by the Valois — the grand dukes of Burgundy. During their reign, Burgundy spread well beyond its present borders and even beyond those of France to include most of Belgium and Luxembourg and part of Holland. It became a center of art and culture because of the many French and Flemish artists the dukes brought to Dijon, the capital. The dukes of Valois ruled until 1477. After the death of the last duke, Charles the Bold, the duchy was taken by Louis XI of France as part of his kingdom.

Topographically, Burgundy is a land of hills and valleys laced with many streams. One-third of it is forested; in the rest, agriculture is the most important activity. Burgundy's agricultural products are world-famous — the mustard of Dijon, the beef of Charolais cattle, and, of course, the wine. Burgundy also has some industry — steel mills and glass and ceramic manufacturers — concentrated south of Dijon.

The wine country of Burgundy stretches from Dijon to the outskirts of Lyon, a treasure trove of beautiful medieval buildings. Because Burgundy was a center of monastic activity, most of these medieval remains are religious — either churches or abbeys. The predominant architectural style is Romanesque with a Burgundian accent, but there are Gothic structures and some Roman ruins as well.

Burgundy is crossed from north to south by Route A6, a major toll freeway. Most of the other roads have only two lanes but are well paved and maintained. From Paris, take A6 due south to the exit of Auxerre-Nord to enter Burgundy at Auxerre. It's a distance of 104 miles (167 km).

AUXERRE: The gateway to Burgundy was first a Celtic settlement, then a Roman town, and later a religious center in the Middle Ages. The most impressive feature as you approach the town is the view of the Roman ramparts and the silhouettes of church spires above the River Yonne. Inside you get a closer look at the Gothic cathedral and Gaillarde clock tower.

Take N6, then D100 south about 30 miles (48 km) to Vézelay.

VÉZELAY: Once a pilgrimage center and now a Christian shrine, Vézelay began as an abbey in the ninth century. Its church became famous in the eleventh century, when a monk associated with the abbey obtained relics reputed to be those of St. Mary Magdalene. Pilgrims flocked to Vézelay, and the town became prosperous. At the beginning of the twelfth century, a modest Carolingian church was replaced by the present Romanesque basilica.

At the end of the thirteenth century, Vézelay declined. When other "relics" of St. Mary Magdalene were found in Provence, the pilgrims dwindled. Huguenots looted Vézelay in 1569, and part of the town was destroyed in the revolution. Not until 1859, after restorations by Viollet-le-Duc (who had achieved fame with his restoration of Notre-Dame de Paris) did Vézelay again become a pilgrimage site — for tourists.

Leave your car at the foot of the village and walk to the basilica, with a superb carving over its main door that represents the apostles' mission after the resurrection of Christ. Once inside, your first impression is one of light and airiness. Next, you notice details, such as the carved capitals on the columns. These figures, representing biblical characters, are very moving for their familiar, human facial expressions. If you want to know who's who, buy an English-language guidebook, on sale in the church.

The village of Vézelay has many shops selling the wares of local artisans. Unusual items include pewter jewelry in religious or zodiac designs and the blue, white, and gilt earthenware from nearby Clamecy.

Vézelay is also a good starting point for the rugged Morvan region just to the south, an area with many fine trout streams. You can get details on the fishing at any of the several charming country inns in the Vézelay region, the *Hôtel Poste et Lion d'Or* in Vézelay, the *Hostellerie du Moulin des Ruats* between Vézelay and Avallon, or the *Hostellerie de la Poste* in Avallon (see *Best en Route*).

En Route from Vézelay – The 52-mile (83-km) drive east to the Abbey of Fontenay is one of the most interesting on the whole Burgundy route. Take D457 to Avallon, a former walled town. Then follow D954 through the cheese-making town of Epoisses — where you pass a castle with a water-filled moat — to Semur-en-Auxois.

Just before Semur you come to D980, a fork that takes you to Montbard and the Abbey of Fontenay. Pass the abbey for the moment and drive into Semur itself, once a feudal fortified town. It's worth a drive around to see the walls and towers where the townsfolk defied Louis XI's troops in 1478.

Return to D980 and, after driving through the industrial town of Montbard, take D905 and D32 to Fontenay.

FONTENAY: If you want an unspoiled picture of monastic simplicity not crowded by tourists, don't miss Fontenay. At first sight, the abbey looks like a large farm — which is just what a self-contained, self-supporting, twelfth-century Cistercian monastery was supposed to be.

Fontenay was founded by Bernard de Clairvaux in 1118. The abbey prospered until the sixteenth century, at times with as many as 300 monks in residence. With the Wars of Religion, the institution declined and, by the time of the revolution, only three monks remained. They were driven out, and the buildings were sold and turned into a paper mill. In 1906, Fontenay was sold again, and the new owner set out to restore the buildings.

There are guided tours of Fontenay in French; even if you don't understand French, you will understand more of medieval monastic life when you visit, in order, the church with its plain windows and dirt floor; the monks' dormitory; the arched cloister; the chapter house, or meeting hall; the scriptorium, where the monks wrote and illuminated manuscripts; the adjoining *caldarium* — the only heated room other than the kitchen — where the writing monks warmed their fingers to prevent frostbite; the prison, used for minor violators; and the forge.

If you visit Fontenay in the winter, don't go late in the day. There are no lights in the buildings, and late afternoon tours may be canceled because of darkness. There is an admission charge.

Take Route D905 and freeway A8 to Dijon, 52 miles (83.2 km) away.

DIJON: The capital of Burgundy reached the height of its glory under the four Valois dukes of Burgundy — Philip the Brave, John the Fearless, Philip the Good, and Charles the Bold — who gave it its fine buildings. After Burgundy was annexed by France, Dijon declined for a time, but it revived after 1850 with the coming of the railroad. Today the city is an important industrial and commercial center. It is known especially for its gastronomic specialties: mustard, spice bread, black currant liqueur *(cassis),* and snails. An annual gastronomic fair is held in Dijon during the first 2 weeks in November.

Dijon's main tourist attractions are the former ducal palace and the streets around it. The palace now houses an art museum, with paintings and Burgundian sculptures. The most interesting parts of the palace, however, are the kitchen, with six fireplaces so large you can walk into them, and the guard room, housing the marble and alabaster tombs of Philip the Brave and John the Fearless. The museum charges a small admission fee.

En Route from Dijon – Route N74 leads 23.5 miles (38 km) south to Beaune through famous wine villages: Gevrey-Chambertin, Vougeot, Nuits-St.-Georges. Wherever you see a sign announcing *Dégustation,* you can stop and taste the wines of the region.

BEAUNE: This town is the wine capital of Burgundy, and each year a famous wine auction is held on the third Sunday in November. All proceeds go to the hospital, the Hôtel-Dieu, a marvel of Flemish-Burgundian wooden architecture, founded in 1443 as a general hospital. It remained so until 1971 and is used as a geriatric institution. Parts of the building have been set aside as a museum. Most striking are the main ward — a perfect preservation of a medieval hospital — and an art masterpiece, Rogier van der Weyden's multipaneled painting of the Last Judgment. In medieval times, this vivid depiction of heaven and hell stood in the main ward. There are guided tours for an admission charge.

Wine lovers will want to visit the wine museum and the many cellars around the town's main square. Here you can taste and buy wine and wine accessories, including glasses, corkscrews, serving baskets, and tasting cups.

En Route from Beaune – You have several choices. Wine lovers can continue down N74 through Pommard, Volnay, Meursault, Puligny-Montrachet, and Mercurey, south toward Mâcon. Or you can make a 32-mile (50-km) side trip via D973 to Autun, a former Roman town now best known for its cathedral. However, this cathedral, with a Last Judgment panel over the main door and carved capitals inside, is much like the basilica at Vézelay, so you may just wish to continue down freeway A6 to Mâcon, via Tournus.

TOURNUS: An industrial town, it is worth a stop for its eleventh-century Romanesque church. The austere arches and columns and the circular stairway to the bell loft give a special flavor of medieval piety.

You can also get an excellent meal here at *Greuze* (4 rue A.-Thibaudet) before heading down A6 to Mâcon.

MÂCON: Though this is not a true tourist town, wine lovers may want to visit the *Maison Mâconnaise des Vins,* on N6 at the north end of town, which sells Burgundies at lower cost than in Beaune and offers a good inexpensive meal. Mâcon is a good base for side trips, west via N79 to Cluny and Paray-le-Monial or east on N79 to Bourg-en-Bresse and the church of Brou.

CLUNY: One of the most famous abbeys in France, Cluny was founded in 910 by Duke William the Pious of Aquitaine. In its heyday, from the eleventh to the fourteenth century, the abbey exercised a widespread influence on religious, intellectual, artistic, and political life. Burgundian Romanesque architecture started at Cluny, and its abbey gave the Church three popes. The city enjoyed enormous power and wealth. "Wherever the wind blows, there Cluny's wealth grows," the saying went.

And that, eventually, proved its downfall. The abbots became corrupt, and in 1790, during the Revolution, the abbey was closed. In 1798, the building was sold to a Mâcon dealer, who tore down parts of it for the stone. Fewer than half of the original abbey buildings remain today.

Because of the massive destruction that has taken place, a visit to Cluny may be disappointing. If you take the guided tour, buy a pamphlet in English and study Cluny's history before you begin. Then look for the two buildings that tell the whole story of Cluny's rise and fall: the south transept with its simple lines, all that remains of the great abbey church; and the Gothic chapel of Jean de Bourbon, with its heated side room where the privileged could worship in comfort while the ordinary monks braved the Burgundian winter chill.

PARAY-LE-MONIAL: This town, 43 miles (69 km) west of Mâcon, is dominated by its Romanesque basilica of the Sacred Heart. Founded in 1109 by St. Hugues, founder of the great Cluny church, it is a smaller version of the Cluny building.

Because of the golden limestone used to build it, the basilica appears most impressive on sunny days at sunset. If the weather is poor, you may prefer not to journey out to Paray-le-Monial but turn east to Bourg-en-Bresse.

Go east on N79 from Mâcon for 21 miles (34 km) to D975 and Bourg-en-Bresse.

BOURG-EN-BRESSE: A chicken-raising and furniture-making center, it is noted for its *appellation contrôlée* chickens. Ignore the town itself and go straight to the suburb of Brou and its church, the most beautiful in Burgundy.

Flamboyantly Gothic with a Renaissance cast, the church was completed in 1532. It was a work of love. In 1480, Count Philippe of Bresse was gravely injured in a hunting accident. His wife, Marguerite de Bourbon, vowed that if he recovered, she would turn the priory of Brou into a monastery. The count did recover, but Marguerite died before she could carry out her vow. The count and his son Philibert promised to fulfill it for her, but time passed and they forgot. Then Philibert, married to Marguerite of Austria, died unexpectedly of a chill. Marguerite saw his death as divine punishment and hastened to carry out the lapsed vow as a memorial to her beloved husband. For 400 years the church has stood as a symbol of married love.

Every part of this church — its golden light, its rich ornamentation — delights the eye. Most outstanding are the choir and the chapels. Note the realistic figures in the carved oak choir stalls (one even shows a naughty youth being spanked), the tombs of the two Marguerites and Philibert carved in Italian marble, the sumptuous stained-glass windows, the white marble rood screen showing the seven joys of the Virgin.

There are guided tours of the church; the hours vary according to the seasons. The small charge also admits you to an art museum in the former monastery buildings.

Leave Burgundy via N83 for Lyon.

BEST EN ROUTE

Expect to pay $50 and up per night for a double room in hotels listed as expensive; $30 to $50 in those listed as moderate; and $20 to $30 and under, inexpensive. The restaurants range in price from $45 and up for a dinner for two in the expensive range; $25 to $40 in the moderate range; and $25 and under, inexpensive. Prices do not include drinks, wine, and tip.

JOIGNY

À la Côte St.-Jacques – In a charming little cobblestone town 17 miles (27 km) north of Auxerre, this is an elegantly decorated restaurant known for its imaginative Burgundian food. Their selection of Burgundy wines is one of the finest anywhere. Closed January to mid-February. 14 faubourg Paris (phone: 62-09-70). Expensive.

VÉZELAY-AVALLON

Hôtel Poste et Lion d'Or – At the foot of Vézelay village, with a view of rolling hills, 42 rooms, and a good restaurant featuring classic cuisine. Open mid-April to early November (phone: 33-21-23). Expensive to moderate.

Hostellerie de la Poste – An atmospheric inn with 24 rooms and a very fine restaurant. Closed in December. 13 pl. Vauban, Avallon (phone: 340612). Expensive.

Hostellerie du Moulin des Ruats – A charming former mill with a garden on the bank of a stream, where you can eat in pleasant weather. There are 21 rooms and a restaurant. Closed November through February; 2 miles (3.2 km) southwest of Avallon in Vallée du Cousin (phone: 340714). Moderate.

L'Espérance – This 19-room hotel provides lovely accommodations, but it's most notable for its restaurant, which has won high praise from many critics including three stars from Michelin. Closed early January to early February. St.-Père-sous-Vézelay (phone: 332045). Expensive to moderate.

DIJON

Chapeau Rouge – Tastefully decorated, comfortable, and centrally located hotel with a good restaurant serving both regional and nouvelle cuisines; excellent wines. 5 rue Michelet (phone: 30-28-10). Expensive.

BEAUNE

La Poste – Charming older hotel with a garden courtyard; the best restaurant in Beaune. 3 blvd. Clemenceau (phone: 22-08-11). Moderate.

CHAGNY

Lameloise – Nine miles (14 km) south of Beaune, this restaurant is worthy of a detour. At this atmospheric, fifteenth-century country mansion, which has been rated three Michelin stars, Burgundian cooking is raised to a high art. Prices are pretty high, too, but the gustatory experience is worth it. Closed Wednesdays and Thursday at lunchtime. 36 pl. d'Armes (phone: 870885). Expensive.

TOURNUS

Greuze – Fine Burgundian food and Beaujolais wines are offered at this charming country inn named for Jean-Baptiste Greuze, an eighteenth-century artist born in Tournus. Chef Jean Ducloux's efforts have earned him two Michelin stars. Closed Thursdays. 1 rue Thibaudet (phone: 511352). Expensive.

MÂCON

Château d'Igé – A remodeled thirteenth-century fortified castle in a village surrounded by vineyards not far from Cluny; 6 rooms and 6 suites. Closed early November to mid-December. Igé, 8 miles (14 km) northwest of Mâcon via N79 and D85 (phone: 33-33-99). Expensive to moderate.

Frantel – Modern motel with 63 rooms and a good restaurant. 26 rue Coubertin, less than 1 mile south via N6 (phone: 38-28-06). Moderate.

BOURG-EN-BRESSE

Auberge Bressane – Rustic inn specializing in local products, especially Bresse chicken. Closed Monday evenings and Tuesdays; and mid-November to mid-December, and 2 weeks in June. 166 blvd. de Brou (phone: 22-22-68). Expensive.

Le Logis de Brou – Comfortable, old-style hotel with a view of the park; 30 rooms. (Although the hotel has no restaurant, an excellent one, the *Auberge Bressane*, is nearby.) 132 blvd. Brou (phone: 22-11-55). Moderate to inexpensive.

Alsace-Lorraine

Since 1870, Alsace and part of Lorraine have spent almost equal time under the German flag and the tricolor. The two provinces are profoundly different from each other, yet their common destiny as "puzzle pieces" on France's northeastern border has caused them to be inextricably linked in people's minds. In Alsace particularly, there is much to make you think you are in Germany. Virtually all Alsatians speak French, but many of them also speak the local German dialect; folk dress appears at festivals celebrating the new wine; houses are frequently decorated with heavy timbered furniture and may even be heated by a ceramic stove in the main room. Indeed, if you had been traveling in Alsace or the Moselle area of Lorraine between 1870 and the end of World War I, you would have been in Germany.

Today, however, the provinces belong wholeheartedly to France even if there is some inevitable ambivalence in culture, language, customs, and accents. Its specialties — *choucroute garnie, kouglof (kugelhopf),* quiche Lorraine, Strasbourg sausages, and foie gras — are part of French gastronomic life, as are the magnificent white wines of Alsace and the *vin gris* of Lorraine. The place Stanislas and the cathedral of Strasbourg are works of French architecture, and who would deny Joan of Arc — the Maid of Lorraine — her French nationality?

With their turbulent history and strategic border position, Lorraine and Alsace offer a side of France that is very different from the sunny face of Nice or the craggy coast of St.-Malo. Here is a France whose citizens drink beer as often as they drink wine, that celebrates Christmas with decidedly Germanic *gemütlichkeit,* and that enjoys life with a heartiness which, on first acquaintance at least, bears little resemblance to the legendary refinement of French joie de vivre. An evening stroll around the place Stanislas in Nancy or a stop in *La Petite France* in Strasbourg for a glass of framboise, the fragrant raspberry brandy customarily savored in large balloon glasses, testifies more to the particular charm of Lorraine and Alsace than any words. It is impossible not to be captivated.

Nancy, the starting point of our tour of Alsace-Lorraine, is 190 miles (360 km) east of Paris. For the fastest route from Paris, take A4 east to Metz; then take E12 south to Nancy.

NANCY: An old proverb says: "In Europe there are three magnificent ceremonies: the coronation of an emperor at Frankfurt, the investiture of a king at Reims, and the burial of a duke at Nancy." Founded in the eleventh century, Nancy is the capital of Lorraine and was a seat of power during the seventeenth and eighteenth centuries. The dukes of Lorraine wielded international power until François III exchanged his duchy for that of Tuscany. In his place Louis XV installed Stanislas Leczynski, his father-in-law and the dethroned king of Poland, on the throne of Nancy in 1737. This was an astute political move, for on Stanislas's death, Nancy reverted to France.

Stanislas Leczynski is the man responsible for the glory of Nancy. He summoned artists and architects from all over France to celebrate his reign. The result is the place Stanislas, a magnificent eighteenth-century square surrounded by seven pavilions decorated with wrought-iron grills and balconies, all in a harmonious eighteenth-century style. This square is the center and soul of Nancy. The area around the place Stanislas is also a part of Stanislas's urban plan. The place de la Carrière, the Arc de Triomphe, and the Palais de Gouvernement all attest to the duke's refined architectural taste. Behind the place de la Carrière, La Pépinière is an English garden and zoo. It's also a pleasant spot to while away an hour or two watching the Nancéiens at play.

Other spots of interest are the Musée Historique Lorraine (64 Grande-Rue), which has a wonderfully rich collection relating to the history of Nancy. An archaeological garden displays Celtic, Gallo-Roman, and Frankish artifacts, and there's an almost complete collection of the engravings of Jacques Callot, numerous paintings of Georges de la Tour, a collection of furniture and folk art of the area, Judaica, and a museum of pharmacology.

The Musée des Beaux-Arts, in one of the pavilions of the place Stanislas, is devoted to European painting from the fourteenth century to modern times. The museum displays works of Delacroix, Manet, Utrillo, Poussin, and Rubens, among others.

Nancy has numerous churches; two are well worth a visit: Église des Cordeliers, burial place of the dukes of Lorraine, and Église Notre-Dame-de-Bon-Secours (av. Strasbourg), where Stanislas Leczynski and his wife, Catherine Opalinska, are buried.

For lovers of art nouveau, Nancy offers the Musée de l'École de Nancy (rue du Sergent Blandan), with objects from the workshop of Emile Gallé. The fluid lines of nature are captured in ceramic, glass, furniture, and other media.

LUNÉVILLE: Leaving Nancy by the southeast route, within 18 miles (30 km) you come to Lunéville — "little Versailles." Built by Léopold, duke of Lorraine and an admirer of Louis XIV, the palace is a modest replica of the great palace of Versailles. Later, Lunéville became the favorite residence of Stanislas Leczynski, and its corridors resounded with the voices of such notables as Voltaire, Helvetius, and Diderot. There is a museum of documents relating to Lunéville's history. The local museum contains military memorabilia and documents relating to Lunéville's history, but is better known for its collection of Lunéville porcelains.

BACCARAT: Southeast from Lunéville, it's 15 miles (25 km) to Baccarat, a name that has spelled fine crystal to lovers of the very best for more than two centuries. A museum displays antique and contemporary crystal works, some dating from the founding of the factory in 1764. Although the factory itself is not open to the public, several shops in town display and sell Baccarat items.

ST. DIÉ: Continuing southwest from Baccarat, you come to St. Dié. It was in the *Cosmographiae Introductio,* printed and published in St. Dié in 1507, that the continent of America was so named for the first time. The town owes its origin and its name to a Benedictine monastery founded in the seventh century by St. Déodat. The Romanesque Église Notre-Dame-de-Galilée and the eighteenth-century Cathédrale St.-Dié, which are united by a fifteenth-century cloister, are the major points of interest.

En Route from St. Dié – From St. Dié, at the foot of the Vosges, head through the crest of the Vosges at Col Ste.-Marie and continue through Ste.-Marie-aux-Mines, then east through Fertrupt, winding to the Col du Haut Ribeauvillé and down to Ribeauvillé.

Ribeauvillé, at the foot of the Vosges, is one of the many wine-growing towns in this area of Alsace. The town is noted for its gewürztraminer and its Riesling. It is also noted for the Pfifferdag (Day of the Fifes) festival, held on the last Sunday in August. If you're lucky enough to be in town, you'll see an historic parade, townspeople in regional costume, and folk dances. And you'll be able to drink wine from the "wine fountain" in front of the town hall. *John,* a pastry shop at 58 Grande Rue, sells *kugelhopf* by the slice.

From Ribeauvillé it's south to Riquewihr, a town that escaped war damage and remains today almost exactly as it was in the sixteenth century. There are no grand monuments to see in Riquewihr; you see, rather, a lifestyle, an era that has long since passed into history. The half-timbered houses, the old courtyards, the carved stone wells, and the fountains — all join to bring the past to life. If you are in town for the grape harvest in the autumn (usually October, occasionally September), you have the feeling of having stepped into a picture book.

From Riquewihr, continue south, then west, to Kayserberg. Known mainly as where Albert Schweitzer was born (in 1875), this farm town is also a delightful wine village filled with medieval houses. Sites include the ruins of an ancient castle, elegant sixteenth-century buildings, the Romanesque Église de la Ste.-Croix, and the Schweitzer birthplace (124 rue du General-de-Gaulle), now a museum. A grape harvest festival is held here every 5 years (the next is in 1985).

COLMAR: From Kayserberg head east to Colmar. Unquestionably Alsace's most beautiful city, it is noted for its typically Alsatian character, for the Petite Venise section interlaced by a canal, for the old town with its sixteenth- and seventeenth-century houses, for the Église St.-Martin with its Gothic choir, and, most of all, for the Musée d'Unterlinden, in an old convent that was founded by two widows from a noble family. The thirteenth-century structure is entered through the cloister. In the chapel is the magnificent Issenheim altarpiece painted in the sixteenth century by Mathias Grünewald. This masterwork alone is certainly worth a trip to Colmar, as it symbolizes the mysticism, the passion, and the fervor of the turbulent age from which it sprang. The chapel also has a 24-panel series of the Passion conceived by Martin Schongauer in the late fifteenth century. The rest of the museum contains diverse displays, including works by Picasso and Léger.

STRASBOURG: The sights are many and varied, but the number one spot for the visitor with only hours to spare is the cathedral, one of the glories of European medieval art and architecture. The original cathedral was begun in 1015 in the Romanesque style, but it burned several times; work on the present cathedral began in the twelfth century, this time in pure Gothic. When complete in 1439, the lacy open-work spire made it the tallest building in Christendom. The cathedral has witnessed much of Alsace's turbulent history and has even served the Protestant faith, during the Reformation. Louis XIV and Louis XV worshiped here, and in 1770 Marie-Antoinette was formally greeted here on the way to her wedding to Louis XVI. During the revolution, the spire was saved by being crowned by a huge, red Phrygian cap. The wars of the nineteenth and twentieth centuries damaged the structure, but it survived to present the splendid sight we see today.

Before going inside, note the richly sculptured façade; its complex iconography alone almost sums up medieval religious belief. Stained glass is the marvel of the interior, whether richly colored as in the large rose window or in gray-green *grisaille,* as in St. Catherine's Chapel. Be sure not to miss the Pillar of Angels (Pilier des Anges) and the wonderful sixteenth-century astronomer's clock, both in the south transept. The latter is an ingenious device that goes into action at 12:31 PM each day — be on hand by 12:15 to catch the taped presentation. Afterward, take a close look at the wood carving of the Maison Kammerzell, the striking half-timbered house on the cathedral square. Now a restaurant, it was built in the sixteenth century by a rich merchant.

The Musée de l'Oeuvre Notre-Dame, to the side of the cathedral, has on display original working drawings of the raising of the cathedral as well as originals of many of its statues that have been replaced by copies. The Château des Rohan, next door, built by a great French family that produced many statesmen and churchmen, is an eighteenth-century palace where private apartments can be seen, plus a decorative arts museum notable for its collection of ceramics, a fine arts museum, and an archaeological museum. Don't linger, however, because the city also has a historical museum, a museum of modern art, and the thoroughly charming Musée Alsacien of the folk art and traditions in rural Alsace.

The Petite France area is noted for its picturesque views of half-timbered houses reflected in the waters of small canals — this is a must. In the summer, you can take guided tours of old Strasbourg by miniature train; boat trips are also available. Information can be obtained at the Tourist Office (pl. Gutenberg; phone: 325705). But remember that the best way to absorb the feel of a town is by sitting and watching. Find a suitable café, order a cold Alsatian beer, and relax as you savor the other side of France.

BEST EN ROUTE

Expect to pay $60 and up per night for a double room in expensive hotels; $30 to $40 is moderate; and $20 to $30, inexpensive. The restaurants range in price from about $70 for a dinner for two in the expensive range; $30 to $40 in the moderate range; and $15 to $20 and under, inexpensive.

NANCY

Frantel – Its 192 rooms are comfortable and nicely decorated, and it has a fine restaurant and bar. 11 rue Raymond Poincaré (phone: 3556101). Expensive.

Grand Hôtel Concorde – In a landmark eighteenth-century building on place Stanislas, this lovely hotel also has a restaurant. 2 pl. Stanislas (phone: 3350301). Expensive.

Albert 1er et Astoria – Quiet and comfortable with 140 rooms, but no restaurant. Close to the train station. 3 rue de l'Armée-Patton (phone: 3403124). Moderate.

Capucin Gourmand – The city's finest restaurant with some outstanding traditional dishes and some varied light specials. A relatively inexpensive fixed-price menu is also available. Closed Sundays, Mondays, and August. Reservations advised. 31 rue Gambetta (phone: 3352698). Expensive.

Le Gastrolatre – Nouvelle cuisine at its best plus some nice regional dishes. Closed Sundays, Mondays, Easter and Christmas weeks, and the last 2 weeks in July. 39 rue des Maréchaux (phone: 3350797). Moderate.

La Gentilhommière – A charming provincial restaurant with very good meat dishes (veal, squab, duck). Closed Saturdays, Sundays, and August. 29 rue des Maréchaux (phone: 3322644). Moderate.

LIVERDUN

Des Restaurant des Vannes et sa Résidence – Some 10 miles (16 km) northwest of Nancy, this distinguished restaurant is well worth a detour. The preparation of fish is special, as is the lamb. Good desserts, too. Also, five attractive rooms are available for overnight guests. Closed Mondays, Tuesdays at lunchtime, and February. 6 rue Porte-Haute (phone: 3494601). Expensive.

RIBEAUVILLÉ

Hotel des Vosges – This clean, modern hotel has 12 rooms and a good restaurant with an extensive menu that includes a three-course prix fixe meal for under $10. 2 Grande Rue (phone: 736139). Moderate.

Hotel La Tour – A picturesque, renovated old winery with 32 pleasant rooms. 1 rue de la Mairie (phone: 737273). Moderate.

Pfifferhuss – An appealing *winstub* in a landmark building with very tasty *choucroute*. Grande Rue. Inexpensive.

RIQUEWIHR

Auberge de Schoenenbourg – Enjoy Alsatian food with flourishes of nouvelle cuisine while gazing at the vineyard behind the restaurant. The wines served are made from grapes grown here. Rue de la Piscine (phone: 479228). Expensive.

KAYSERSBERG

Chambard – One of the best classic restaurants in Alsace with a gracious dining room and specialties like foie gras in cabbage leaves. (A comfortable hotel with 18 rooms is in the annex behind the restaurant.) 9 rue du Général-de-Gaulle (phone: 471017). Expensive.

COLMAR

Terminus Bristol – Pleasant, reliable hotel near the train station. 7 pl. de la Gare (phone: 23-59-59). Moderate.

Champ de Mars – Comfortable accommodations and pleasant service. 2 av. Marne (phone: 41-54-54). Moderate.

Maison des Têtes – This restaurant is set in a beautiful seventeenth-century house replete with local atmosphere. Closed Wednesdays. 19 rue de Têtes (phone: 41-21-10). Expensive.

STRASBOURG

Sofitel – A modern hotel with an excellent location, all the comforts of any first-class establishment, and a good restaurant. Pl. St.-Pierre-le-Jeune (phone: 329930). Expensive.

Bristol – Near the train station with an above-average restaurant and 40 rooms, most with private bath. 4 pl. de la Gare (phone: 320083). Moderate.

Des Rohan – Completely modernized, though it looks like a historic landmark. The 36 rooms have private baths and are done in seventeenth- and eighteenth-century styles. 17-19 rue du Maroquin (phone: 328511 or 328943). Moderate.

Gutenberg – A small, simple, clean hotel in an old château. Some rooms have private bath. 31 rue des Serruriers (phone: 321715). Inexpensive.

Buerehiesal – A beautiful dining room, very attentive service, wonderful fish and game dishes (in season), and a large list of fine wines. Closed Tuesday nights, Wednesdays in mid-August, and for periods during the winter. 4 parc de l'Orangerie (phone: 616224). Expensive.

Au Crocodile – Unquestionably one of the city's best (two Michelin stars), featuring French cuisine with an Alsatian touch; fish and game specialties are outstanding. Closed Sundays, Mondays, mid-July to early August, and a week at Christmas. 10 rue de l'Outre (phone: 321302). Expensive.

Maison des Tanneurs – Bedecked with balconies and flowers at the edge of a canal, this is the place to try *choucroute* (share it). Closed Sundays, Mondays, the first half of July, and late December to mid-January. 42 rue du Bain-aux-Plantes (phone: 327970). Moderate.

Strissel – Good Alsatian food, wines, and atmosphere make it a local favorite. Convenient to the museums and the cathedral. Closed Sunday nights, Mondays, a week in February, and most of July. 5 pl. de la Grande Boucherie (phone: 321473). Inexpensive.

Chez Tante Liesel – It's friendly and cheerful with only nine tables and popular with diners for its family recipes and unexpected treats. Closed Tuesdays, Christmas, and New Year's Day. 4 rue des Dentelles (phone: 230216). Inexpensive.

Exploring
East Germany

For the Western tourist, East Germany, or the German Democratic Republic (GDR, or in German, DDR for Deutsche Demokratische Republik), is one of Europe's undiscovered travel lands. Diplomatically isolated from the West until the early 1970s, it became a "concentration camp" country in the popular Western imagination, gray and forbidding behind the barbed wire and mines of its border. The truth, as tourists who are now flocking to the country are finding out, is very different. The barbed wire and the minefields still exist, but the border guards are generally as friendly and helpful as most of their countrymen. Theirs is a land of beautiful, quiet plains, thickly forested mountains, and lingering rural traditions. East Germany also offers Westerners a peek into a Communist state right in the center of Europe. Besides being inquisitive and eager to strike up conversations, its people are now prosperous by Eastern European standards and justly proud of their economic achievements. Most of them are quite content to live in a socialist country.

The modern state of East Germany was created by the cold war aftermath of World War II. In 1945, right in Potsdam, an East German city near Berlin, the victorious Allies divided a bombed and defeated Germany into four zones: American, French, British, and Soviet. As the political split with the USSR grew, the Soviet zone became increasingly isolated from the others. Finally, the unsuccessful Soviet blockade of West Berlin in 1948–49 precipitated the present division of Germany into its two separate states.

Some three million of the country's best qualified engineers, doctors, and craftsmen left East Germany during the 12 years after 1949. The GDR has stemmed the debilitating flow of refugees to the West with the building of the much-reviled Berlin Wall in 1961 and has undergone its own "economic miracle." East Germany is now among the top ten industrial countries in the world, and the East Germans enjoy the highest standard of living in Eastern Europe, without the American aid that West Germany received after the war. This is a country that 40 years ago was utterly devastated by a war, in which Dresden — second only to Hiroshima — lost 80% of its old town center and about 35,000 people on February 13 and 14, 1945.

The GDR is roughly the size of Ohio, covering 41,610 square miles. Its area is half the size, and its population of 17 million people only one-third that of West Germany. East Berlin is the nation's largest city, with a population of 1.1 million people; Leipzig is second with 577,000; and Dresden third with 505,000. Most of the country — bounded by West Germany to the south and west, Czechoslovakia to the south, the Baltic Sea to the north, and Poland to the east — lies in what was once the north German plain, the agricultural section of Germany in former years.

Although East Germany has been transformed into an industrial power, many of its rural attractions still remain. There are the Harz Mountains in the west, the Thuringian Forest in the southwest, and the Erzgebirge (mountains) in the south. The Elbe, one of Europe's major rivers, flows northwest from Czechoslovakia, cutting right across the whole country, past Dresden, Wittenberg, and Magdeburg, and into West Germany; and the Oder River flows along the eastern boundary of the country.

To see the GDR, you can choose one or both of our proposed routes, either singly or in combination. Each one lasts about 3 to 5 days and both originate in Berlin. The first, about 470 miles (752 km) long, follows the western edge of the country from Potsdam, across gently rolling hills to Magdeburg, over the Harz Mountains southward to the foothills of the Thuringian Forest, and then back north to Naumburg. From here you can return to Berlin or branch eastward to Leipzig and the second route (340 mi/544 km) — the better known of the two — which includes the old cultural center of Dresden; Meissen, the town that has manufactured Dresden china since 1705; and the country of the Sorbs, East Germany's largest minority.

Roads in the GDR are adequate to good on the whole, and, to a Western motorist, delightfully empty. Tractors, recklessly piloted Soviet military vehicles, and slippery cobblestones even on the main routes are the chief dangers, but signposting is thoughtful. Gas stations are, however, few and far between, so it is advisable to take a canister for a reserve supply of gas. A pack of spare parts (light bulbs, fan belt, oil, spark plugs) could be your salvation, and don't forget to fill up wherever you can.

The Harz Mountains and the Thuringian Forest

Shaped like a large slanted block, the rugged Harz Mountains in the southwest corner of the GDR are silent witnesses to much of German history. The region, pocked by limestone caves and pierced by tall mountain peaks, is dotted with numerous castles, churches, and fortresses built during the Middle Ages. Our route runs through several cities of import: Potsdam, a residence of Frederick the Great during the eighteenth century, as well as the site of the conference in which Churchill, Stalin, and Truman decided the fate of postwar Germany; Eisenach, birthplace of Johann Sebastian Bach; and Weimar, where Goethe and Schiller lived, and center of the short-lived republic that fell with the rise of Hitler. Near Weimar is a memorial to Buchenwald, not long ago a notorious concentration camp.

The route begins in Berlin, then goes to Potsdam, Magdeburg, and the Harz Mountain towns of Quedlinburg and Wernigerode. From Wernigerode it continues southwest to Eisenach, after which it swings westward to Erfurt and Weimar; this is the area known as the Thuringian Forest, its gentle wooded slopes rounded rather than jagged, peaceful rather than dramatic. After turning northward to Naumburg, you can go on to Leipzig and our second route, or you can return to Berlin.

Maps, brochures, organized tours, and other information are available from the tourist offices in each of the cities and some of the towns. Their headquarters are in Berlin at the Reisebüro der DDR, Alexanderpl. 5 (phone: 215-4402).

POTSDAM: Most people know Potsdam as the place where the four victorious powers of World War II — Russia, Britain, the US, and France — signed the 1945 agreements that split Germany and Berlin into four zones of occupation. But Potsdam has been known since 1660, when the princes of Hohenzollern chose it as their country residence and began a palatial building program that ended only in the late nineteenth century. The eighteenth century saw the city develop as the military center of Old Prussia, boasting at one time a ratio of 8,000 soldiers to just 17,000 inhabitants. Since World War II, shapeless modern architecture and now-regretted demolition programs have destroyed some of Potsdam's old charm, but the palaces and the parks are still as delightful as ever. Potsdam is also East Germany's Hollywood, producing feature films at its DEFA studios.

The road from Berlin brings you southeast of the town, near the *Interhotel Potsdam*. You might start with a walk round the old town, centering on Klement-Gottwald-Strasse, recently designated a pedestrian precinct with small cafés, shops, and an information bureau at number 24. From here it's an easy walk along the Allee nach Sans Souci to Potsdam's main attraction, the Sans Souci Park and Sans Souci Palace (built on Frederick the Great's orders in 1745–47); a picture gallery next door with works by Rubens, Van Dyck, Tintoretto, and others; the ornate Chinese teahouse; statues; shrubberies; and at the end, the New Palace (1769), another creation of Frederick's 46-year reign. Never actually lived in, it was intended to demonstrate the Prussian state's unbroken might after the Seven Years' war.

In the northeastern part of town, the Cecilienhof, at Neuer Garten, built during World War I in the style of an English country mansion, is where the 1945 conference took place. The Cecilienhof houses an interesting museum devoted to the conference, which includes the original furniture. Ironically, as if to remind visitors of the consequences of that conference, a stretch of the Berlin Wall, sealing West Berlin from surrounding East Germany, stands just 200 yards away in full view at the bottom of the garden.

Cecilienhof is, by the way, also an excellent hotel with a mediocre restaurant.

En Route from Potsdam – Route F1, part of the main trans-European artery intended by Hitler to link occupied Paris with Berlin in the 1930s, takes you out of town into the farmland along the Havel River. If you are here in spring, the cherry blossoms on either side of the two-lane highway are breathtaking. Brandenburg, 25 miles (40 km) along the route, was the capital of the Prussian state for centuries, but it declined as Berlin took over the role of administrative center. A further hour's drive along the tree-lined F1 brings you via sleepy villages to Magdeburg, on the Elbe. You are now entering the Harz ("woodland") Mountains, a region of rugged, weather-beaten rocks, medieval churches and castles, rich woodlands, and fertile farm country.

MAGDEBURG: The country's main heavy machineworks, the Ernst Thälmann Engineering Combine (SKET), has its headquarters here, a fitting location since this is where Magdeburg's most famous citizen, former mayor Otto von Guericke (1602–86), proved the power of vacuum and invented the "Magdeburg Hemispheres." Sadly, Magdeburg has had a history of destruction. It burned down almost totally during an attack in 1631, and more than 90% of the rebuilt city was razed by Allied bombing in January 1945. Only parts of the city center have been reconstructed as they once were. If you begin with the Old Town Hall (the *Rathaus*), you'll notice the famous thirteenth-century statue of the *Magdeburg Rider* on his horse facing the building from the square. He's only a copy of the original statue, sculpted in 1240 but now shown in the city museum on Otto von Guericke Str. A 10-minute walk through what's left of the old town brings you to the mainly twelfth-century Cloister of Our Dear Lady, possibly one of the best-restored architectural ensembles in the whole of Germany. Next door is the cathedral, with quaint cloisters around the side entrance; it was first recorded as a place of worship in 955. In the northern transept a group of six wooden figures by Germany's greatest twentieth-century sculptor, Ernst Barlach, memorializes starkly and impressively the dead of World War I. The Nazis had it removed from the cathedral, but the ensemble was reinstalled in 1957.

En Route from Magdeburg – You can take Route F81 out of Magdeburg, through Egeln and Halberstadt, but for a taste of the small country roads almost completely free of traffic, bear right on the outskirts of the town to head for Wanzleben. You'll pass through typical East German provincial towns, hardly changed in 40 years. From Kroppenstedt you go over the top of a small range of hills, a foretaste of things to come. At Halberstadt, drive farther on F79.

QUEDLINBURG: This is East Germany's tourist pride. Hardly hit by the war, it still boasts hundreds of picturesque half-timbered houses, many with the old signs of their former owners. Head for the marketplace, where restorers have done an impressive job on the Renaissance Town Hall and on the colorful wood carvings on the facades of the surrounding sixteenth-century houses. Looking away from the Town Hall, you'll see the Schlossberg, crowned by a cathedral with its nineteenth-century towers resting on a medieval body. (Guided tours are given on the half hour until 3:30.) From the balustrade of the castle (Schloss) there's a stunning view of old Quedlinburg with its tiled roofs tilting at all angles. The restaurant in the castle complex serves a respectable lunch, outside if the weather's good, and fine afternoon coffee. It's worth a stop before continuing to drive along the northern base of the Harz Mountains, taking the minor road to Weddersleben and Thale.

En Route from Quedlinburg – After Thale you pass through Blankenburg. Stop briefly at the Regenstein Castle just out of town to the right. It was chiseled out of sandstone, and was first used as a fortress in the fifth century.

WERNIGERODE: Nine miles (15 km) farther on is the center of the Harz vacation area. Its colorful and half-timbered sixteenth-century Town Hall at the crossing of Marktstrasse and Breite Strasse looks like something out of a fairy tale by the Brothers Grimm. There is an unusual feudal museum here, in the medieval castle that overlooks the town; its exhibits include medieval furniture and objects illustrating daily life in the Middle Ages and the history of the Harz region. Wernigerode is also the northern terminal for a narrow-gauge steam railway that links the northern and southern Harz. If you have time, leave the car here and take a trip (it costs only a few pfennigs) up through Drei-Annen-Hohne, and past the Brocken, which at 3,747 feet is the highest peak in the Harz, although inaccessible from the west. It was chosen by Johann Wolfgang von Goethe for the "Walpurgisnacht" scenes in *Faust*.

En Route from Wernigerode – Take Route F244 toward Elbingerode. On the left toward Rübeland there are some impressive limestone caves worth seeing — if you have the patience to join the long lines. Then head along F81 to Hasselfelde and down through deep leafy gorges along F4 to Nordhausen, southern terminal of the railway from Wernigerode. Nordhausen is the town that produces East Germany's most famous schnapps, Nordhauser Doppel korn. Most goes for export, so you'll probably find there's none to buy here. Get it at an Intershop for Western currency instead.

The Kyffhäuser Mountain 15 miles (24 km) southeast of Nordhausen rises 1,565 feet out of the north Thuringian plain, and is shrouded in legend. One was that Emperor Redbeard, or Barbarossa, would sleep in his underground cave here until the time came to unite the German people. With the proclamation of the united German Reich in 1871, formed by joining the 24 previously independent German states, Kaiser Wilhelm I had a monument erected on the Kyffhäuser mountain peak, representing himself as a glowering and mighty Barbarossa in red sandstone. In good weather, the view from the top of the mountain is breathtaking, extending northward to the Harz and westward into West Germany. The GDR has now formally renounced the goal of reunification with West Germany, and making the best of an awkward memorial to an abandoned aim, publications now describe it as evidence of the "aggressive and military nature" of Germany's imperialist past.

Now, you have a choice. You can either go to Eisenach, Erfurt, and Weimar by way of Bad Frankenhausen, Route F85 to Sachsenburg, and Route F86 to Strassfurt — it's 54 miles (87 km) to Eisenach — or, if you wish, you can skip this section and head for Leipzig and the second route.

EISENACH: Now famous as an automobile manufacturing center, Eisenach (pop. 50,000) is better known as the site of the Wartburg, a castle dating back to 1067, now a museum. It was the home of the medieval Minnesänger poets immortalized by Richard Wagner in his opera *Tannhäuser.* It it also served as Martin Luther's retreat in the sixteenth century, when he translated the Bible into German, laying the foundations for today's spoken language. The composer Johann Sebastian Bach was also born in Eisenach, and the family home at Am Frauenplan 21 houses a fascinating collection of musical instruments and Bach family memorabilia.

En Route from Eisenach – Route F7 — with views of the hills on the right — takes you 34 miles (54 km) east to Erfurt. On the way, a half-hour excursion southeast to Arnstadt is very rewarding: This is one of the oldest towns in the GDR (first mentioned in 704). Bach was an organist here from 1703–1709. Besides a beautifully restored marketplace, Arnstadt also has a two-centuries-old doll collection in the Neue Schloss (New Castle). From here, Erfurt is a 20-minute drive north.

ERFURT: Provincial capital and major industrial center, Erfurt with its 200,000 inhabitants is the only sizable town in the GDR that was not largely destroyed in World War II. It was liberated by the Americans in April 1945, but was handed over to the Russians under the agreements that divided Germany into occupied zones. Dominating Erfurt are two Catholic churches side by side on the Domberg. The walls of the cathedral and those of St. Severi (both finished by the fifteenth century) lie just a few feet apart at their closest point. In town, a walk down the Markstrasse brings you to the Krämerbrücke, a fourteenth-century ensemble of houses on a bridge over the Gera River. Formerly houses of petty traders, they were restored in the 1960s as delightful little antique shops, book stalls, and cafés. This is a good place to find that unusual souvenir.

WEIMAR: Thirteen miles (21 km) east of Erfurt on Route F7 lies Weimar, today a town of just 65,000 people but one of the most important centers of German history and culture. Goethe and Schiller both wrote their greatest works here in the eighteenth and early nineteenth centuries. In 1919, the first German Republic, also known as the Weimar Republic, proclaimed its constitution in the town's now reconstructed National Theater; the Weimar Republic fell during the world economic crisis in the early 1930s, when the extremely nationalistic Nazi party rose to power. The homes of Goethe and Schiller (the former on the Frauenplan and the latter on the Schillerstrasse) are now open as museums. A short walk from Goethe's house past the *Interhotel Elephant* brings you to a park now named after the poet, a place where he used to walk. Across the river is the garden house he used in the summer, now an extension of the main museum.

BUCHENWALD: Before leaving the area, take a detour to Buchenwald, 4 miles (6 km) northwest. Now run as a national memorial, it's the site of one of Hitler's most notorious concentration camps, opened in 1937. Here 56,000 people, including Jews, Communists, and prisoners of war, died before the surviving inmates were freed by the Americans in April 1945. The contrast between the barbarities once perpetrated here and the humanistic ideals of nearby Weimar is chilling.

En Route from Weimar – Route F7 (we have purposely kept off the Autobahns, as these show you so much less of the countryside than the quieter country roads) takes you toward Jena, but turn left at F87 and head past Apolda to Naumburg.

NAUMBURG: If, after Magdeburg and Erfurt, you can still take some more medieval architecture, the cathedral has to be seen. The town was a major trading and religious center in the Middle Ages. The Cathedral of St. Peter and St. Paul has been beautifully preserved, and its earliest parts date back to 1210. Inside are realistic and humorous carved figures of ordinary folk of the time, installed in the late thirteenth century. Before you leave Naumburg, visit the *Ratskeller* in the town hall (Wilhelm Pieck Pl.), where with any luck you'll find a bottle of excellent and very dry local wine. Try it, as it's little known outside the GDR.

En Route from Naumburg – Taking Route F87 again out to the east, you pass through Weissenfels 11 miles (18 km) away, before reaching the main north-south highway. That's the end of this route, and you can return to Berlin, or leave the GDR from the south. But if you've developed a taste for more, take the slightly shorter tour through Leipzig and Dresden, with many attractive tidbits along the way.

BEST EN ROUTE

In East Germany, hotel reservations must be made in advance and prices are generally high; in fact, they are double the rates charged to visitors from Communist countries. Contact Reiseburo der DDR, Alexanderpl. 5, East Berlin (phone: 215-4402), or Koch Overseas Company, Inc., 206–208 E 86th St., New York, NY 10028 (phone: 212-535-8600).

For a double room in expensive hotels, expect to pay $80 and up; $50 to $80 in the moderate category; under $50 in the inexpensive class. Payment must be made in Western currency or by credit card.

Dinner for two, with drinks and wine, costs about $25 or more at expensive restaurants; between $20 and $25 in the moderate range; and under $20 in inexpensive places. Tips are included in the bill.

POTSDAM

Interhotel Potsdam – This large high-rise hotel, at the entrance to town nearest Berlin, is one of the GDR's most prestigious, with prices to match. It has a sauna, an Intershop, dancing, entertainment, a restaurant, and a bar. Lange Brücke (phone: 4631). Expensive.

Hotel Cecilienhof – Set in a twentieth-century version of an English country house, this historic building was the site of the Potsdam conference in 1945. As a hotel it's smaller and less luxurious than the *Potsdam,* but it has a restaurant, a café, an Intershop, and some rooms with baths. Neuer Garten (phone: 2-3141). Moderate.

Klosterkeller – This is a comfortable restaurant with decent food. Gutenbergstr. and Friedrich Ebert Str. Inexpensive.

MAGDEBURG

Interhotel International – This is a big hotel — 358 rooms — with baths in all rooms, a restaurant, a café, dancing, and an Intershop. Some might consider it modern and characterless, as are most of East Germany's better hotels. Otto von Guericke Str. 87 (phone: 3840). Moderate.

QUEDLINBURG

Schlosskrug – The restaurant is in the castle forecourt, and it serves up good lunches and afternoon coffee. Müllerstr. (phone: 2836). Expensive to moderate.

EISENACH

Stadt Eisenach – This 85-bed hotel has a restaurant and parking. Luisenstr. 11–13 (phone: 3682). Moderate.

Auf der Wartburg – Set within the walls of Wartburg castle. The 30 guest rooms are in the usual German-modern style, and there is a restaurant on the premises. Wartburg (phone: 5111). Moderate.

Hohe Sonne – This restaurant is just outside the city, in a lovely rustic area with a view of the Wartburg. Regional Thuringian dishes are its specialty. Open daily. Am Rennsteig (phone: 2903). Inexpensive.

ERFURT

Erfurter Hof – Opposite the railroad station is one of East Germany's best kept and most distinguished hotels, which hosted West Germany's Chancellor Willy Brandt in 1970 on his journey of reconciliation to the GDR. It has all conveniences and an excellent restaurant serving interesting culinary inventions. The rooms in the back are much less noisy than those facing the train station. Bahnhofsvorpl. ½ (phone: 5-1151). Expensive.

Tourist – This is a much less pretentious hotel, but it's modern and characterless. Yuri Gargarin Ring 158 (phone: 5-1076). Inexpensive.

Hohe Lilie – An interesting restaurant, it occupies the first two floors of a building that dates back to 1540. Spicy Balkan dishes are the house specialty. Closed Mondays. Turmpl. 31 (phone: 2-25-78). Inexpensive.

WEIMAR

Elephant – This centrally located, extensively remodeled hotel dates from 1696 but has most of the facilities you could want and some extras such as horseback riding and dancing. There's a fine restaurant in the basement. Am Markt (phone: 6-471). Moderate.

Leipzig, Dresden, and Sorb Country

This short but quite interesting route connects Leipzig and Dresden, East Germany's two major cities after Berlin, which were both heavily damaged during the war and have since been restored. Leipzig, long known for its medieval trade fairs, still hosts two important international fairs in November and March. And amazingly enough, you can still eat and drink here in *Auerbachs Keller,* the restaurant and tavern where Goethe set his debate between Faust and the Devil in *Faust.* Dresden is the place for great art treasures, both in the Zwinger fortress and in the Albertinum, and its restaurants are among the best in East Germany.

You can begin your drive in Berlin, or in Naumburg, where the first route ended. For maps, brochures, and further information, contact the local tourist office. In Berlin it's Reisebüro der DDR, Alexanderpl. 5 (phone: 215-4402); in Dresden it's Ernst Thälmann Str. 22 (phone: 4-8650); in Liepzig, Katharinenstr. 1/3, Alte Wagge (phone: 7-9210).

LEIPZIG: East Germans call this city of 575,000 people the secret capital of the GDR. It is the country's second most important industrial and commercial center, hosting a week-long trade fair twice a year that attracts exhibitors from up to 60 countries at a time. Leipzig, its name derived from the Slavonic *Lipsk,* "place of the lime tree," is also home of the East German printing industry, of the second largest GDR university, and of the main sports institute. Bach spent his most creative years, from 1723 to 1750, as choirmaster at the St. Thomas Church here, and Goethe staged the encounter between Faust and the Devil in *Auerbachs Keller* just off the market square. Leipzig was badly damaged by World War II bombing, but architects have succeeded here better than elsewhere in restoring its former character. The Old Town Hall (sixteenth century) and the Thomaskirche (1482) have been completely restored; the newer Rathaus (nineteenth century), on the edge of the neatly circumscribed old town, was hardly touched. (It has an excellent restaurant in its basement.) In *Auerbachs Keller,* in Mädlerpassage, which provides beers and quality wines accompanied by excellent food, don't miss the murals depicting scenes from *Faust.* Grimmaische Strasse leads to Karl-Marx-Platz, the new university, and the opera, and it's lined with souvenir and book shops. The Gewandhaus concert hall has recently been rebuilt.

A short walk back across the market square brings you to the Thomas Church, where the boys' choir, which Bach used to conduct, still gives free concerts of motets every Friday evening and Sunday morning when they are not on tour. Bach lies buried at the eastern end of the church. More than any other East German town, Leipzig abounds in good eating and drinking places. Apart from the main hotels, the *Kaffeebaum* (coffee tree) on the corner of Kleine Fleischberg and Barfussgässchen has been serving beer and food for centuries.

Before leaving Leipzig, follow the Strasse des 18 Oktober to the memorial to the Battle of the People (Völkerschlachtdenkmal). You will pass the fairground and a fine Russian Orthodox church erected in 1913. The memorial to the 1813 victory of Russian and German troops over Napoleon's *Grande Armée* is a monstrous, 300-foot-high edifice completed the same year as the church. The view of Leipzig, and the remarkable acoustics inside, are worth the climb to the top of the monument.

En Route from Leipzig – Route F6 leads to the cathedral, wine, and porcelain town of Meissen, 53 miles (85 km) east, through rolling farming landscapes; later it joins up with the Elbe, one of Europe's greatest rivers, and the GDR's main water artery. Where the Elbe winds between the cliffs of Saxonian Switzerland, between Dresden and the Czech border, visitors might think they are on the Rhine.

MEISSEN: This is the town that gave the world Dresden china, and it is a must on any tourist's itinerary in East Germany. The first porcelain was produced here in 1710, in the fifteenth-century Albrechtsburg castle that dominates the town. Dresden china was ideally suited to the extravagant rococo style in eighteenth-century art, and for the first few years the Meissen princes kept their craftsmen virtual prisoners here, lest rivals learn the secret of the "white gold." But it got out, needless to say. Today the factory in the Triebischtal produces china mainly for export, and can be visited during the week.

The town itself, founded in 929 and once the seat of the Saxonian bishops, is one of the best preserved in East Germany. Visit the Albrechtsburg castle, now a museum, and the delightful and still privately owned wine house of Vincenz Richter, just off the market square at An der Frauenkirche 12. A good lunch can also be had in the cafés in the courtyard of the Albrechtsburg. Sample the local wines, especially the rare Meissner Domherr.

En Route from Meissen – Rather than go straight along Route F6 to Dresden, take the road north across the river in Meissen and follow the signs to Weinböhla along a small country road. Continue through Auer and in 10 miles (16 km) you come to one of the most beautiful of the country residences built around Dresden by Saxon prince Frederick Augustus (the Strong) in the eighteenth century. The Schloss Moritzburg is now a museum of baroque porcelain, furniture, and hunting weapons.

Another way to reach Moritzburg is to leave the car in nearby Radebeul and take a narrow-gauge steam railway for five stops.

DRESDEN: One of the high points of any visit to East Germany, this city is alive with cultural tradition and political history. Its many art collections rank among the most valuable in the world, and Dresden is today the GDR's third largest city, with a population of over half a million. To visitors from Britain and America, its name, like that of Hiroshima, is synonymous with the horrors of modern warfare. Up to 35,000 people are believed to have died in the Anglo-American bomber raids on February 13 and 14, 1945, and some 80% of the town center, with its narrow old streets and passageways, was razed to the ground. The Schlosskirche, the Semper opera house, and the galleries along the Brühlsche Terrasse have been rebuilt to restore to Dresden the silhouette made famous by the eighteenth-century painter Canaletto. But behind that waterfront, the rest of the city center has been rebuilt in characterless concrete and glass.

The city was founded in about 1200, and it remained a trading city until it was chosen by the lavishly spending Saxon princes for their court in the seventeenth century.

Pragerstrasse, once Dresden's most fashionable street, is now flanked by blocks of flats and shops, but it's pleasantly landscaped with fountains and benches. Past a new cinema and department store, you reach the Old Market (Altmarkt) with the restored Kreuzkirche (Church of the Cross), home of the world-renowned Kreuzchor (a boys' choir) on the right. Ahead of you is the new Palace of Culture (1969), and behind that the memorial ruins of the Frauenkirche that once bore one of Europe's most famous cupolas. You are now in the heart of old Dresden, surrounded by car parks and bomb sites that drive home the devastation of that terrible time in 1945. Follow on toward the river and up the steps, and you come to the Albertinum (1559) with its glass dome and exhibitions of state art collections within (closed on Thursdays). There are nineteenth- and twentieth-century German paintings, French Impressionist works, and the famous Green Vault (Grünes Gewölbe) with works of goldsmiths and jewelers from the fifteenth to the eighteenth centuries. The Zwinger, a fortress built between 1711 and 1722 at the height of Augustus's reign, was lovingly restored in the postwar years. In magnificent baroque style, with lovely sculptures and chimes of Dresden porcelain, it houses one of the world's most stunning art collections, the Picture Gallery of Old Masters, which includes Raphael's *Sistine Madonna* (1513). Also visit its unparalleled collections of china, coins, and hunting weapons.

En Route from Dresden – You can return directly to Berlin via the Autobahn, a distance of about 122 miles (196 km). Or you can spend some time in the Spreewald, a 93-square-mile network of canals, woods, and pastures along the Spree River southeast of the capital. Get off the Autobahn at Lübbenau. Carved wooden road signs tell you the way to the port *(Hafen)* where you can either take a leisurely 3-hour ride in a punt along the slowly flowing canals, or hire a canoe if you're feeling energetic. That's the best way to do it, and try the private boat-hiring establishment of Herr Franke (Maxim Gorky Str. 72) down a small unpaved road before you reach the main harbor. The prices are staggeringly low.

During your excursion, possibly poled along by a Sorb woman in national dress (all the punt owners are private, incidentally, and pool only their passengers in a punting collective), don't miss the waterside cafés along the route. They generally serve good coffee and cakes in the afternoon.

BEST EN ROUTE

In East Germany, hotel reservations must be made in advance and prices are generally high; in fact, they are double the rates charged to visitors from Communist countries. Contact Reisebüro der DDR, Alexanderpl. 5, East Berlin (phone: 215-4402), or Koch Overseas Company, Inc., 206–208 E 86th St., New York, NY 10028 (phone: 212-535-8600).

For a double room in expensive hotels, expect to pay $80 and up; $50–$80 in the moderate category; under $50 in the inexpensive class. Payment must be made in Western currency or by credit card.

Dinner for two, with drinks and wine, costs about $30 or more at expensive restaurants; between $20 and $30 in the moderate range; and under $20 in inexpensive places. Tips are included in the bill.

LEIPZIG

Merkur – The best hotel in town, it has four restaurants, a swimming pool, a sauna, and a nightclub on the 27th floor that offers a breathtaking panorama of the city. And it's away from the downtown area, so it's quiet. Gerberstrasse (phone: 7990). Expensive.

Astoria – An excellent quality hotel, elegantly furnished in traditional late-nineteenth-century style, with all the modern conveniences. It has a good restaurant, a pleasant terrace, a café, and dancing. (Like the other big hotels here, it's much used by visiting businesspeople for the local trade fairs in March and September.) Platz der Republik (phone: 7-1710). Expensive to moderate.

Auerbachs Keller – Goethe made this tavern famous in *Faust*, and the place is decorated with sculptures and paintings inspired by that drama. It's a beautiful restaurant, which serves excellent food, beers, and wines. No reservations. Mädlerpassage (phone: 20-91-31). Expensive to moderate.

Stadt Leipzig – Conveniently situated opposite the main railway station, this is a high-class hotel by GDR standards. All amenities are available here, including a barber shop and a sauna. The front rooms do tend to be noisy. Richard Wagner Str. (phone: 7-1131). Moderate.

Kaffebaum – The oldest coffee house in Leipzig dates from 1694 and was frequented by many famous people: Goethe, Lessing, Wagner, Liszt, and others. Its original décor includes lovely old wooden tables. The food is basic but good; the beer is good, and the place is very popular. Fleischberg (phone: 2-0452). Moderate.

Stadtpfeiffer – Excellent food in the new Gewandhaus concert hall complex. Lunch only in July and August. Karl-Marx-Platz (phone: 713-23-89).

Ratskeller – This is a wonderful student haunt in the basement of the new town hall. Its specialty is a fine potato omelette (Bauernfrühstück).

DRESDEN

Bellevue – The city's newest and largest (330 rooms) hotel. Guest rooms have a magnificent view, across the Elbe, of the historic city center. Quiet, pleasant atmosphere. Neustädter Markt (phone: 566-20). Expensive.

Königstein – Opposite the *Newa*, this large place is less pretentious, less luxurious, and more popular with local and East European tourists. Pragerstr. (phone: 4-8560). Moderate.

Secundogenitur – Though the place offers only one dish a day, the quality is excellent. Brühlsche Terrasse (phone: 49-61-47). Moderate.

Gewandhaus – The hotel is not open to foreigners, but the fine restaurant is, and it's one of the most pleasant and popular eating places in Dresden. Ringstr. 1 (phone: 49-62-86). Moderate.

Ratskeller – As in most German towns, the Rathaus (town hall) here has its own restaurant, and like most Ratskellers, it's a good value, unpretentious and noisy. It's great for meeting townsfolk and sampling the atmosphere (phone: 49-32-12). Moderate to inexpensive.

Kügelgen-Haus – Behind the baroque facade is a gastronomic complex consisting of several restaurants and a beer cellar where good food and drink can be found at good prices. The nearby Meissener Weinkeller features some very rare East German wines. Str. der Befreiung (phone: 5-56-05). Inexpensive.

Exploring
West Germany

Germany has been the cradle of heroes and monsters — a land of giants such as Bach, Brahms, Beethoven, and Wagner in music; Hegel, Kant, and Heidegger in philosophy; and Goethe, Schiller, and Thomas Mann in literature. Karl Marx and Friedrich Engels were the originators of modern Communist ideology, just as Albert Einstein was the pioneer of modern physics. Paradoxically, it was in Germany that Hitler came to power, and, not long ago, this great people nurtured the cancerous growth of Nazi government by terror, violence, and crime.

Many people fear a recurrence of the Nazi nightmare in Germany; yet with each year, the possibility seems more remote. In 1977, leftist terrorists committed several acts of random violence, among them the kidnapping and murder of German industrialist Hanns-Martin Schleyer and the hijacking of a Lufthansa Boeing 707. Such outbreaks of leftist terrorism and an occasional rumble of neo-Nazism have nourished the fantasies of prophets of doom around the world. Nevertheless, West Germany, its very existence a result of World War II, continues to live in peace and prosperity, with its government remaining steadfastly democratic.

Since the end of World War II, West Germany has accomplished two miracles, one economic and one political. From a country forced into unconditional surrender, devastated by bombings, and suffering from severe food shortages, West Germany has transformed itself — thanks to the Marshall Plan (more than $5 billion worth of US aid) and to the laborious efforts of the German people — into one of the world's wealthiest industrial powers, ranking fourth in the world in steel manufacture and third in the automotive industry. Once characterized by political divisiveness, instability, and a strong tendency toward totalitarianism, West Germany is now firmly committed to the Western European tradition of democracy. In fact, its stability is remarkable, especially when it is compared with France or Italy; between 1949 and 1983 West Germany has had only six chancellors.

Though its recently devastated cities and towns have been rebuilt, for the most part, in modern style, much of the old Germany is still there for the visitor to see. Many historical buildings were spared the devastation of the bombs; others have been carefully restored. You can still see Neuschwanstein, the unbelievably elaborate castle on Bavaria's Romantic Road, which was created according to the fantasies of King Ludwig II. Cologne Cathedral is one of the world's finest Gothic structures, and the Dahlem Museum in Berlin contains some of the world's greatest art treasures. Everywhere in Germany there are sleepy little villages with their characteristic half-timbered houses, places where it is still common for peasants to wear traditional costumes to local markets and festivals.

Bavaria still looks like the setting of a fairy tale by the Brothers Grimm; one medieval walled town after another — Rothenburg, Dinkelsbühl, and Nördlingen — has remained remarkably intact. Germany has always been known for its legends and folktales: the Pied Piper of Hamelin, Snow White and the Seven Dwarfs, Till Eulenspiegel's pranks, and Baron Münchhausen's adventures. Heroic tales of Siegfried and the Nibelungen haunt the eternally beautiful Rhineland, known for its castles and its magnificent clusters of rock such as the Lorelei and the Drachenfels.

The Rhine is celebrated, not only for its great beauty, but as the most important commercial waterway in Europe, highway for the industrial Ruhr; the river passes by such great cities as Düsseldorf, Cologne, and Mainz. It flows in a northwest direction through the western half of West Germany from Switzerland to the Netherlands. On both sides of the Rhine, a truncated West German nation is one of the most densely populated areas in Western Europe. With an area of 95,976 square miles, it is approximately the same size as the United Kingdom. But while Britain has only 56 million people, West Germany has 62 million. Its largest city, West Berlin (pop. 1.9 million), sits 110 miles inside Communist East Germany. Bonn, the capital, is relatively small and uninteresting, with a population of 283,260 and nothing much to recommend it except for the fact that Beethoven was born there. Much larger and more alive are the busy port city of Hamburg (pop. 1.7 million) and Munich, the gay and charming capital of Bavaria (pop. 1.3 million).

In the 500-mile (800-km) stretch from north to south, the terrain of West Germany varies greatly, with coastal lowlands in the north, low mountains in the center, and the higher Bavarian Alps in the south. The center and the south contain vast forests such as the Schwarzwald (Black Forest), with its predominance of fir trees, the Harz with its beeches, and the Spessart with its giant oaks.

A bewildering number of countries, nine in all, border on West Germany. To the west are France, Luxembourg, Belgium, and the Netherlands; East Germany and Czechoslovakia lie to the east; Austria and Switzerland to the south; and the North Sea, the Baltic, and Denmark to the north. Its dearth of natural boundaries has been a source of trouble throughout German history, creating a perpetual state of uncertainty, disunity, and divisiveness. To begin with, the land was inhabited as early as the seventh century BC by numerous and distinctly differentiated Germanic tribes such as the Franks, Frisians, Saxons, Thuringians, Franconians, Swabians, and Bavarians — most of whose names survive as regional place names. During the first century BC, the Germans expanded at the expense of the Celts, while they were invaded and threatened by the Romans. Eventually, the Franks migrated to France, the Angles and Saxons to Britain, but most of the tribes settled in the area later known as Germany.

The German tribes were gradually converted to Christianity during the fifth through the ninth century. However, with the exception of Charlemagne, emperor of the Franks, who united a great deal of territory under his sovereignty, localization and feudalism were the rule. The Holy Roman Empire, established by Otto I in 962 and lasting until 1806, was an empire in name only. Claiming descent from ancient Rome and supremacy over Christendom, it was threatened continually both by popes and by local powers, which were often much more powerful. A medieval rival was the Hanseatic League of wealthy trading towns including Hamburg, Lübeck, Bremen, and Brunswick — formally organized in 1348.

While the rest of Europe tended to consolidate into nation-states, Germany remained divided for centuries, both in politics and in religion. The most significant separative force was that of the Reformation, which was begun by Martin Luther (1483–1546), priest and professor of theology at the University of Wittenberg. Luther, a devout ascetic, opposed such excesses of Catholicism as the sale of indulgences (pardons for sins). After studying the Bible, he originated the doctrine of salvation by faith, advocated German control of German religious matters, and was finally excommunicated by the pope in 1521. His forceful writing and preaching converted many to the Protestant faith, and his uncompromising attitude in matters of doctrine pressed the Lutherans to break with Calvin and Zwingli and resulted in the subdivision of Protestants into sects.

Luther's enormous influence was not confined to matters of religion. His 1534 translation of the Bible was the first major literary work in the German language. Most important, his increasing opposition to the power of the Church spurred all kinds of political conflicts, and resulted in a confusion of religious and political issues. Resistance to the church included resistance to the power of the Holy Roman Empire. Ambitious nobles were eager to join the Reformation in order to seize the church lands. The general dissension reached a climax in the Thirty Years' War of 1618–48 between the Protestant Union and the Catholic League. Though the war spread to the rest of Europe and had less and less to do with religion, it was fought, for the most part, on German soil. German cities, towns, and countryside were destroyed in its wake.

The seventeenth and eighteenth centuries marked the emergence of Prussia and its rivalry with Austria. Power seesawed between the two, with Frederick the Great challenging Austria in the eighteenth century; the German Confederation emerging under the Austrian leadership of Metternich in 1815; and, at long last, the unification of a Germany dominated by Bismarck's Prussia in 1871. Bismarck's German Empire excluded Austria, and its autocratic government delegated little power to its parliament. A policy of colonial expansion, especially during the reign of Wilhelm II (1888–1918), led to growing conflicts with Britain and France which culminated in World War I.

After that war, the Kaiser was exiled; unfortunately, however, the Weimar Republic was to be weak and short-lived, split by many small political parties. This disunity, together with the worldwide depression of 1929, allowed Adolf Hitler to rise rapidly. His totalitarian Third Reich, which lasted from 1933–45, brought havoc and bloodshed to Germany and to the world. After World

War II, in 1945, the victorious Allies met at Yalta and at Potsdam to divide Germany into four zones: British, French, American, and Russian. The tension between East and West, aggravated by the Russian blockade of Berlin in 1948–49, resulted in the present division of Germany into East (German Democratic Republic) and West (Federal Republic of Germany) in 1949.

Dividedness, the theme of German history, continues to be that nation's destiny. Oddly enough, the erection of the Berlin Wall in 1961 — concrete monstrosity though it is — has brought about a condition of peace and stability for both Germanys. Relations between the two countries have warmed considerably since Chancellor Willy Brandt, pursuing his open-door policy toward the Eastern powers, signed a treaty with the USSR in 1970 and with East Germany in 1972. West Germans can now visit relatives in East Germany as a matter of course, and foreign visitors to West Berlin can easily obtain day passes to East Berlin upon request.

A visit to West Germany offers many delights, not the least of which are Rhine wines and Munich beer halls; carnivals such as Fasching and Oktoberfest, both in Munich; and the world-famous ballet in Stuttgart. We have split the extraordinary variety of West German landscapes, cities, and towns into seven routes. There's northern Germany, which extends from Bremen to Schleswig, where a visitor can explore the Hanseatic cities of Hamburg and Lübeck and relax in the lake country of "little Switzerland" or on an ocean beach such as Travemünde on the Baltic Sea. The short, pleasant route from Frankfurt to Heidelberg follows the charming Main River valley through the gentle wooded hills of the historic Odenwald and Spessart areas. Westphalia, land of ham and pumpernickel, castle hotels and wayside inns, can best be seen in a circular route that begins in Dortmund. Castles, vineyards, and dramatic vistas mark the fabled Rhineland, which includes the area from Mainz to Koblenz, but can be extended to Cologne and Düsseldorf. Germany's Castle Road meanders along the Neckar River valley, passing more than a dozen castles on the way from Heidelberg to Heilbronn. Rolling hills and thick forests characterize the Black Forest region, which extends from Basel, Switzerland, to the exclusive German spa of Baden-Baden. Last is the Romantic Road from Würzburg on the Main River to Füssen in the Alpine foothills, passing through Bavaria's fabulous walled medieval towns.

Northern Germany

Northern Germany, the area bounded roughly by Bremen, Hamburg, Lübeck, Kiel, and Schleswig, has been virtually undiscovered by modern American tourists. Yet it offers the only ocean beaches in all of the Federal Republic and some of its most historical cities. Relatively flat, the terrain of northern Germany is a pleasant blend of gently rolling hills, sunlit lake country, and fine sandy beaches.

Hamburg, a highly sophisticated city that is rarely visited on the usual tourist itinerary, is Germany's second largest, with a population of 1.7 million people. Bremen, with over half a million inhabitants, is the oldest German maritime city, having been a market since 965; its 500-year-old medieval section still remains. You can vary your trip to northern Germany by visiting its important port cities; exploring its tiny undiscovered towns such as Stade and Ratzeburg; and enjoying its ocean resorts such as Travemünde. For information and maps about the area, contact the regional tourist office in Oldenburg, just northwest of Bremen: Fremdenverkehrsverband, Nordsee-Niedersachsen-Bremen, Gottorpstr. 18, 2900 Oldenburg (phone: 6-4011).

The dominant force in northern German history was the Hanseatic League, a free association of medieval towns which concentrated on trade. Foremost in the league were the city-states of Bremen, Hamburg, and Lübeck. Since they paid taxes to no larger power, these cities became a powerful force in both domestic and foreign trade. Even today, people from the Hanseatic cities take immense pride in their localities, often identifying themselves as Lübeck-ers or Hamburgers before saying they are Germans.

Today the Hanseatic League is mere history, although Germans still refer to the direct train line running from Bremen to Hamburg to Lübeck as the Hanseatic Line. This route is convenient not only for travelers who choose to ride the modern, efficient railways of Germany, but for people who wish to tour northern Germany by car. The tour covers roughly 225 miles (360 km), so you will need at least 3 days.

BREMEN: The natural starting point for any tour of northern Germany, Bremen, along with its sister city of Bremerhaven, is the oldest seaport in Germany. Interestingly enough, it is because of Bremen that Bremerhaven exists at all. In the early seventeenth century, the merchants of Bremen noticed that their precious port was becoming clogged with mud from the Weser River that flows into it. Dredging operations were not then what they are now, so they simply moved the port downstream to Vegesack. Two hundred years later, Vegesack too became clogged with mud, so the merchants moved on to Bremerhaven, which now ranks as one of Germany's greatest seaports.

The tourist information service in Bremen, right in front of the main train station, offers maps, brochures, tourist information, and information about hotels and pensions (phone: 3-6361).

Like most European cities, Bremen is best seen on foot. The heart of the city is the old medieval section surrounding the Marktplatz and most of the modern city has grown up around this area. The city used to be encircled by a great wall, but the land where the wall used to stand is now a ring road that completely encircles the older part of the city.

Bremen's huge market square is worth a visit, if for nothing more than the delicious smell of roasting coffee from the surrounding coffee houses, or the lovely colors and shapes of fruits and vegetables grown by local farmers. The old Rathaus, which is right on the market square, is well worth seeing; it houses an excellent restaurant, the *Ratskeller,* with the largest wine list in Germany, featuring more than 600 wines, all of them German.

Other sights worth seeing in Bremen are the Focke Museum (Schwachhauser Heerstr. 240), renowned for its fine collection of historical artifacts from the north, and St. Peter's Cathedral, directly on the market square. The eleventh-century cathedral has an unusual cellar called the *Bleikeller* (lead cellar), where the lead slates for the roof were originally kept. A roofer who fell to his death was once put in the cellar for safekeeping, along with the roofing tiles. Everyone forgot about his body and it was some time before he was discovered, perfectly preserved. Apparently the air in the cellar is so dry that it mummifies anything that is put down there. Several mummified corpses are included in the collection, which is open on weekdays only.

While in Bremen, don't miss the old section of town referred to as the Schnoor, with its narrow 400- and 500-year-old streets, half-timbered houses, and quaint gabled roofs. Many art galleries and crafts shops are located here and they offer some excellent buys on handicraft items. Walk on the Rampart Walk (Wallanlagen), with its windmill and lovely green spaces. Here is the *Café Knigge,* a lovely outdoor café with a terrace, on an old pedestrian street (Sögestr. 42).

For people who have an undeniable urge to set out to sea, there are daily tours of the harbor area by boat, leaving the Martini jetty three times a day.

En Route from Bremen – It is only 75 miles (120 km) to Hamburg, little more than an hour's drive along the speedy German autobahns. If you have the time, the drive to Hamburg along the secondary highway that more or less parallels the Autobahn (Rte. 75) is well worth the effort, as it weaves through open moors and forests that are so common to this section of Germany. A good overnight stopping place is the little town of Rotenburg; it's just the place for a quiet rest.

STADE: About 25 miles (40 km) north of the Autobahn, on Route 73, lies the town of Stade, which is starting to make a name for itself as a medieval city. Virtually unknown to most tourists, the quiet little town has some beautifully restored buildings, and restoration continues all the time. Be sure to see the Rathaus, the fish market, and the Burgomeister Hintze House. At one end of the fish market is the restored Swedish warehouse that was built between 1692 and 1705 to serve as a supply depot for the Swedish troops that occupied the region at that time. Today, the warehouse serves as a regional museum for Lower Saxony.

HAMBURG: Hamburg is less than an hour's drive from Stade. Germany's largest seaport and second largest city after Berlin, Hamburg was an independent city-state in the Middle Ages, and even today, the city is a state of Germany. Hamburgers have always been extremely proud of their independence, a pride that never showed more clearly than in 1871, when the Kaiser was going to raise a Hamburg merchant to the nobility. The mayor of Hamburg informed the startled Kaiser: "It is impossible to raise a Hamburg citizen." That feeling still lingers today, and the citizens of this great harbor city are never so proud as when they can show off their city to visitors.

Hamburgers are quick to point out that the area the city now occupies has been inhabited continuously over the past 15,000 years, although permanent settlements can be traced back only 6,000 years. The first fortifications were built in 811, and although they were repeatedly pounded by the fierce Viking raiders of the north, the town continued to grow. In 1189, Frederick Barbarossa granted the city a charter as a free city and port, thereby exempting its ships from paying duty. After that, the merchants of the city prospered greatly. During the years of the Hanseatic League, no trading power on earth was the equal of Hamburg.

Despite the heavy bombing raids of World War II that all but flattened the city, it has recovered very well. Its port on the Elbe River is one of Europe's largest and it continues to grow, with a record of 60 million tons traded during 1980. Though less popular with tourists than Munich or Berlin, today's Hamburg is an elegant and sophisticated modern city, with a 300-year-old opera and a renowned vaudeville theater (the *Hansa Theater*).

The tourist office at Bieberhaus near the Central Station at Hachmannpl. (phone: 24-87-00) can provide you with maps: the *Hamburg Guide,* a brochure containing a wealth of tourist information; and a fortnightly program guide to local events called *Where to Go in Hamburg.* For hotel reservations and information, contact the Information Office (Hotelnachweis), also at Central Station, Hachmannpl. exit (phone: 32-69-17). They charge a small fee for their services.

You might want to get an idea of the layout of this large and sprawling city by means of its excellent 2-hour bus tour, which begins at the train station daily.

Some of the sights that should not be missed are Europe's only privately owned zoo and the harbor, an incredible mélange of pleasure boats, oceangoing freighters, coal barges, tugs, and fishing boats. Harbor tours are offered from entrance 2 to the St. Pauli landing, by Hadag Ships (phone: 319-6280). The Aussenalster, a particularly wide and lovely branch of the Elbe that looks like a lake, is bordered by long, shaded avenues and green spots, and makes a particularly fine place for strolling or boating. During the summer months, a very pleasant 50-minute Alster cruise departs from Jungfernstieg at frequent intervals and affords a lovely view of the city's towers and spires (phone: 34-11-41). Also interesting is St. Michael's Cathedral, a fine baroque church built in 1646, with a famous tower from which you can see a panorama of the city.

For those who enjoy museums, Hamburg is just the place. There's an excellent art museum, the Hamburg Art Gallery (Glockengiesserwall 1). It has a fine collection of paintings ranging from medieval to modern; the modern section is best, with works by Klee, Munch, and others. There's the Historical Museum (Museum für Hamburgische Geschichte, Holstenwall 24; phone: 34912-2360), with an interesting collection relating to the ports and navigation; and the Decorative Arts and Crafts Museum (Museum für Kunst und Gewerbe, Steintorpl. 1; phone: 24825-2630), specializing in medieval gold and silver statuary, Renaissance furniture, clocks of northern Germany, and Jugendstil (art nouveau) items. The Helms Museum (Museumsplatz 2) specializes in prehistory and early history of the Hamburg region. For a more up-to-date impression of this North German countryside and its residents, visit the Altonaer Museum (Museumstr. 23).

Naturally it is impossible to overlook one of the most famous areas of Hamburg, the Reeperbahn. After dark, this area comes alive with neon lights, loud music, thick crowds, and barkers trying to attract those crowds to their establishments. Here sex shows, porno movies, strip clubs, and bars are the order of the day — or night, as the case may be. Many of these places are clip joints, pure and simple, but some of the better sexy stage shows are pretty safe bets. Among these are those at the *Regina Club,* the *Safari Club,* the *Colibri,* and the *Salambo Cabaret.*

One of the best things about Hamburg is its restaurants. Everything is available from haute cuisine to pickled rollmops, in settings that vary from the crystal and china atmosphere of the top restaurants, to the beer and herring atmosphere of the waterfront snack bars *(Imbiss).* Because it's a port city, there are many fine foreign restaurants, the best of which is *Le Canard,* Martinistr. 11. But Hamburg's specialty is fish, and its most famous specialties are *Aalsuppe* (eel soup) and oysters, raw or baked with Cheshire cheese. You can sample these and many other fine dishes right in the St. Pauli fish market at the Fischerhaus.

RATZEBURG: The distance from Hamburg to Lübeck is only 41 miles (66 km). Still, for the adventurous, the lovely island town of Ratzeburg on Route 208, located in the middle of a lake to the south of the E4 Autobahn, makes a lovely place to stay for a weekend, with plenty of swimming, boating, and fishing. Surprisingly enough, the town is only a couple of kilometers from the East German border, yet the easygoing way of life is so pleasant that it is hard to imagine the border, with its ghastly fences, mine fields, and machine guns less than 2.5 miles (4 km) away. By all means see the local church, which has an interesting carved altar and is one of the largest brick churches in northern Germany.

LÜBECK: The capital of the Hanseatic cities during the Middle Ages, Lübeck retains the flavor of a medieval town, complete with towers, and old houses. The huge twin-towered gates at the entrance to the city — the Holstentor — can hardly fail to impress a visitor. These gates were built in 1477 as part of the fortifications, and today the massive towers serve as the symbol of Lübeck; they also house the Municipal Museum.

While you're there, take a look at the old salt warehouses along one side of the Holstentor.

Like most other German cities, Lübeck has an excellent tourist office, which can provide information and maps, and will help arrange for a room for the night in almost any price range for a small fee. It's on the old market square at Rathaushof 14 (phone: 121).

There are four museums in Lübeck, each of them a minor gem. Besides the Holstentor, there is St. Anne's Museum (St. Annenstr. 13), an old monastery that now houses local art and handicrafts; the Behnhaus (Königstr. at Glockenstr.), a perfectly preserved residence from 1780, gives an excellent impression of how people lived in those times; and a museum in the cathedral contains all the natural history discoveries from the area.

The Rathaus is an unusual brick medieval building in the northern German style, on two sides of the Marktplatz. St. Mary's Church, a French Gothic structure that was built between 1251 and 1350, is known for its famed seventeenth-century organist, the composer Buxtehude.

The Haus der Schiffergesellschaft (Breite Str. 2), an old sailors' guild house dating from 1535, has an excellent restaurant inside, decorated with marine furniture and artifacts.

One of the products for which Lübeck is most famous is the luscious marzipan candy, made from sugar and crushed almonds. It comes in virtually any shape, so that you often see Lübeckers strolling along the streets, happily munching on a marzipan pig, pear, or apple. The best place in Lübeck, probably the best place in the world, to buy marzipan is the *I. G. Niederegger Konditorei and Café*, next to St. Mary's Church. Not only can you have a sinfully sweet piece of marzipan, but a delicious cup of coffee to go with it. You can take some marzipan with you, or mail it to friends as the perfect gift from Lübeck.

En Route from Lübeck – The drive from Lübeck to Kiel goes through what the Germans call the Holsteiner Schweiz, or little Switzerland because of its numerous lakes and forests. It is best to take Route 76, which runs north through Plön and Preetz, rather than the faster, but more boring, Route 404 that runs through Bad Segeberg. If you are in the mood for an ocean beach, you might want to detour to Travemünde, just a few miles northeast of Lübeck, on the Baltic Sea; it's a fashionable resort with a casino. If not, your next stop might be either Plön, which is on the Plönersee, a large, scenic lake, or a bit farther north, Preetz, in the heart of the lovely and peaceful lake country.

KIEL: Kiel attracted a lot of attention when it hosted the sailing event of the 1972 Olympics, but as a center for tourism it leaves a lot to be desired. Most of Kiel was destroyed by the bombing during World War II, and the city has been rebuilt in modern style. It is a clean city, almost spotlessly so, but it has little to offer tourists, except perhaps for its bustling fish market, with an astonishing variety of fish. Besides the market, you will enjoy seeing the Kiel Canal, an outstanding engineering achievement that connects the North Sea and the Baltic and is the busiest canal in the world. Nearby, the Hindenburg Quay (Hindenburgufer), a 2-mile, tree-shaded promenade along the Kiel Ford, offers pleasant views of the harbor.

SCHLESWIG: About 31 miles (50 km) northwest of Kiel is Schleswig, the oldest town in the northern state of Schleswig-Holstein. It was founded by the Vikings and for many years it was a Viking stronghold; from here they plundered and looted the towns to the south, such as Hamburg and Bremen. Schleswig is well worth a visit, as it contains some of the richest Viking artifacts in northern Germany. By all means see the cathedral, built in 1100, with its incredible altarpiece carved elaborately in wood by Bruggeman in 1521.

Schleswig's other big attraction is the Nydam boat, an Anglo-Saxon boat dating from the fourth century, one of the few of its type in the world. The boat is housed in a building near Gottorf Castle, a huge castle that was built in the twelfth century. The castle is the oldest in Schleswig-Holstein and is well worth a trip all by itself, since it houses the Schleswig-Holstein Museum, containing fine exhibits of folklore and handicrafts.

Germans and Scandinavians have enjoyed the beaches, forests, lakes, cities, and towns of northern Germany for many years. Since Americans and other tourists have not yet discovered this area, it is still a place for the more adventurous souls to explore.

BEST EN ROUTE

Hotel prices vary a great deal along this route; costs are generally higher in the larger cities, especially in Hamburg, which is the site of the *Vier Jahreszeiten,* known as one of the world's most outstanding — and expensive — hotels. A double room with breakfast costs about $50 to $100 in the hotels listed as expensive; moderate is $35 to $50; and inexpensive is below $35. In an expensive restaurant, dinner for two without wine will cost $30 to $60; moderate is $20 to $30; and inexpensive is $10 to $20.

BREMEN

Park Hotel – Bremen's leading hotel is in an out-of-the-way spot, the lovely Bürgerpark. It has spacious, cheerful public rooms, a heated garden terrace, a fine restaurant, and many rooms with balconies overlooking the pond. Bürgerpark (phone: 340-8555). Expensive.

Hotel Zur Post – Opposite the main railroad station, this newly redecorated modern hotel includes a health club, a swimming pool, and a sauna. The rooms are comfortable as are the wine tavern and dining room. Bahnhofspl. 11 (phone: 3-0590). Moderate.

Le Bistro – Don't be misled by the plain (but comfortable) surroundings; the kitchen here is very accomplished. Try the fish dishes, such as crab soup, haddock in mustard sauce, or turbot in baked pike mousse. Centrally located; closed Sundays. Reservations recommended. Contrescarpe 80 (phone: 31-47-49). Expensive.

Ratskeller – Right in the 500-year-old city hall, this place has lots of atmosphere and also serves good food. It's popular with the local people who meet here to sample its 600 German wines. Closed Mondays. Am Markt (phone: 32-09-36). Moderate.

Landhaus Louisenthal – A few miles northeast of the city center, in the suburb of Horn, this charming 1835 house is noteworthy for its quiet, Old World atmosphere. Leher Heerstr. 105 (phone: 23-20-76). Inexpensive.

HAMBURG

Vier Jahreszeiten – One of the world's ten best hotels, this elegant and prestigious place is on Alster Lake in downtown Hamburg. It features conservative patrician furniture, streamlined modern facilities, and the atmosphere of a private home. There's an excellent restaurant, named *Haerlin* after the family that runs the hotel, two bars, and a nightclub featuring international bands. Neuer Jungfernstieg 9 (phone: 3-4941). Very expensive.

Europäischer Hof – Facing the railroad station, this is Hamburg's second largest hotel and a pleasant, traditional establishment. There is a good restaurant (in the breakfast room, you can serve yourself from a marble fountain that spouts six different kinds of juices — and occasionally champagne). Kirchenallee 45 (phone: 24-81-71). Expensive.

Graf Moltke Hotel – Opposite the South Station, this old-world hotel has high, ornate ceilings, a skylighted central stairway, and comfortable traditional furniture. Front rooms can be noisy. Steindamm 1 (phone: 280-1154). Moderate.

Schümanns Austernkeller – Founded in 1884, this elegant Belle Époque restaurant is one of the most expensive in town. Situated in a commercial building, the restaurant is sumptuously decorated and has excellent service; it's been in the same family for years. The seafood platter *(Seezungenplatte)* is excellent, as are the oysters and the crab soup. Closed Sundays. Jungfernstieg 34 (phone: 34-62-65). Expensive.

Landhaus Scherrer – Its delicious North German regional cuisine and its lovely view of the Elbe make this one of Hamburg's finest restaurants. Closed Sundays. Reservations necessary. Elbchaussee 130 (phone: 880-1325). Expensive.

Old Commercial Room – This highly traditional Hamburg restaurant, in the old town across the street from St. Michael's Church, offers a wide choice of North German dishes at reasonable prices. Try the eel soup. Englische Planke 10 (phone: 36-63-19). Moderate.

Fischerhaus – This place specializes in absolutely perfect fish served in a very plain and unadorned atmosphere. St. Pauli Fischmarkt 14 (phone: 31-40-53). Moderate.

Mellingburger Schleuse – An idyllic forest setting enhances this rustic-looking 28-room hotel. A small restaurant is on the premises. Mellingburgredder 1 (phone: 602-40-01). Moderate.

RATZEBURG

Seehof Gästehaus Hubertus – This quiet, charming hotel is directly on the lake, and it would be hard to find a more charming place to spend a weekend. Even the restaurant is a bargain. Lüneburger Damm 3 (phone: 4161). Expensive to moderate.

LÜBECK

Lysia Hotel – The finest hotel in Lübeck is on a canal at the edge of the old town. It has a sauna and an exercise room, a popular dance bar, a restaurant, and two conference rooms. Auf der Wallhalbinsel, corner of Holstentorpl. (phone: 1-5040). Expensive.

Hotel Wakenitzblick – This quiet and comfortable hotel, which faces the canal, is reasonably priced. It has parking, a restaurant, and bath and telephone in the rooms. Augustenstr. 30 (phone: 79-12-96). Moderate.

Restaurant Schabbelhaus – Reservations are always necessary at this rustic restaurant, decorated with antiques. The food is as good as the décor. Try any of their fish dishes. Closed Sundays after 3 PM. Reservations recommended. Mengstr. 48 (phone: 7-2011). Expensive.

Haus der Schiffergesellschaft – This historic sailors' guild house dates back to 1535 and features nautical décor. Closed Mondays. Reservations recommended. Breite Str. 2 (phone: 7-6776). Moderate.

PREETZ

Drillers Hotel – This excellent hotel, beautifully set on a lake, offers an especially good breakfast. Bismarckpl. 2 (phone: 8-1241). Moderate to inexpensive.

SCHLESWIG

Waldhotel – This hotel is part of the Gottorf Castle. It is quiet, very well maintained, and reasonably priced. The restaurant has a good and fairly inexpensive menu. If peace and quiet are what you seek, then look no farther. Stampfmühle 1 (phone: 2-3288). Moderate.

Frankfurt to Heidelberg

If you drive the 59 miles (94 km) from Frankfurt am Main to Heidelberg on the Autobahn, the trip will take about an hour, but you won't see much more than the backs and sides of huge high-speed trailer trucks. There's a lovely alternate route, however, that wriggles its way south along the Main River valley, through charming old river towns with half-timbered houses, historic churches and abbeys, romantic castles, gentle wooded hills, and fertile green valleys.

Without any side trips, the Main River valley route from Frankfurt to Heidelberg covers about 107 miles (171 km); pleasant detours can add 50% to that distance. You can drive the whole route easily in a single day, but it's far more pleasant to give yourself at least a day and a half.

The areas you'll be driving through are known as the Odenwald and the Spessart. Prehistoric peoples lived along the banks of the Main, but there was no real development until about AD 800, when many monasteries, like the one you can still see in Seligenstadt, were established, and the monks began the region's agricultural development.

Through the centuries, the Odenwald and the Spessart were the territories of various bishoprics. They were shuttled more or less peacefully from one owner to another. During the Thirty Years' War (1618–48), these areas, like most of Germany, were the scene of many bloody battles.

Although the Main River may eventually become part of an overall Rhine-Danube international waterway system, its banks are still relatively quiet and peaceful, even in Frankfurt and in the other highly populated industrial areas. The area is not touristy in any way. Tourists in the Main Valley are usually vacationers from Frankfurt and other German cities who are not partial to discos and pizza stands.

Its small towns are unspoiled — like Michelstadt, with its lovely old Marktplatz, or Wertheim, with its red sandstone castle. And Heidelberg may well be the most beautiful city in Germany.

For maps, pamphlets, and information about the Frankfurt area, contact the tourist office in Wiesbaden (Hessische Landeszentrale für Fremdenverkehr, Bahnhofstr. 55–57, 6200 Wiesbaden; phone: 34-12-84); for the Heidelberg vicinity it's Fremdenverkehrsverband Neckarland-Schwaben e.V. (Theaterstr. 9, 6900 Heidelberg 1; phone: 5-8438).

En Route from Frankfurt – Take Route 43 east toward Mühlheim and Hanau. You might want to stop at Offenbach to see the German Leather Museum, containing leather objects from all over the world, or at Hanau, birthplace of the Brothers Grimm and site of an interesting museum of local jewelry called Goldsmith's House, a baroque castle, Schloss Philippsruhe, and a monument to the celebrated brothers.

At the intersection of Routes 43 and 45, continue on the unnumbered road toward Hainstadt and Seligenstadt. Park before you reach the center of Seligenstadt, since parking usually is not permitted in the center of small villages in Germany.

SELIGENSTADT: Its principal attraction is a magnificently maintained, former Benedictine abbey founded in AD 825 by Einhard, biographer of Charlemagne. However, the town itself is much older. It was a fortified castle on the *limes* — the wall built by the Romans through most of central Germany until the Romans were ejected from their fort by the Alemanni in AD 260.

Guided tours (in German) of the abbey are conducted year round every day except Mondays. Don't let a German-only tour put you off; you'll understand more than you think you will.

Seligenstadt is a place where you can see the various architectural styles and periods of German history. The abbey itself has undergone many remodelings in a thousand years, and each remodeling has left traces of the style characteristic of the period.

From the abbey, walk toward the Main River. Then turn left and walk toward the ruins of the Kaiserpfalz, known also as the Palatium or the hunting lodge *(Jagdsitz),* built about 1235 for Frederick II, Holy Roman Emperor, who led a fascinating life that included no fewer than three excommunications.

Walk to the Marktplatz along the narrow Palatiumstrasse. All along the way and around the Marktplatz itself you will see some outstanding examples of the famous German *Fachwerkhäuser,* or half-timbered houses.

En Route from Seligenstadt – Leave Seligenstadt on the same road from which you entered, but this time head south toward Stockstadt. You may make a short detour to Aschaffenburg or continue on under the Mainhausen cloverleaf, pick up Route 469 at the Stockstadt Autobahn exchange, and head for Miltenberg.

ASCHAFFENBURG: Chosen by the electors of Mainz as one of their residences, Aschaffenburg has beautiful parks, a large Renaissance castle, and an interesting church. St. Johannisberg Castle, built in 1605–14 for the powerful bishops of Mainz, is most impressive, shaped like a hollow square. See the palace and walk through its gardens to the Pompeianum, a reproduction of the Castor-and-Pollux house at Pompeii, built for the capricious Ludwig I of Bavaria. Then walk along the Landingstrasse behind the palace to the Stiftskirche, a tenth-century church that is an interesting mixture of baroque, Gothic, and Romanesque styles of architecture, but its real attraction is the exceptional church art. There is a Grünewald altarpiece and a Resurrection scene by Lucas Cranach the Elder (1520). To visit the lovely chapel, the altarpiece, and other treasures, look for the sexton. If he's not in the church, try at Stiftgasse 1.

En Route from Aschaffenburg – Leave Aschaffenburg via Löherstrasse, the street directly behind the church, and watch for signs directing you to Schönbusch. This eighteenth-century park is one of Germany's most charming, with pools, islands, and a country house built for the archbishops in 1780.

Leave Schönbusch Park area on the south side (the one closest to the river) and follow the unnumbered road to its intersection with Route 469. Stay on 469 south for 22 miles (35 km) until you reach Miltenberg.

MILTENBERG: Again, park your car in the first convenient parking lot. Don't try to drive in or through the town center. You can walk from one end of Miltenberg to the other in 15 minutes.

The town showplace is its Marktplatz. It's triangular, relatively small, and surrounded by exceptional half-timbered houses; from the marketplace walk along the main street, the Hauptstrasse, which is also lined with fascinating houses.

The *Riesen Hotel* is not as old as Miltenberg, which was little more than a wide spot in the Roman wall until the Thirteenth Legion was ousted by the Germanic tribes in 260 AD. The Germans are avid record keepers, and there are files in Mainz, Munich, and Würzburg to prove that the *Riesen* was open and operating in the twelfth century. A whole string of Holy Roman Emperors stayed at the *Riesen,* beginning with Frederick Barbarossa who took shelter here in 1158 and 1168, and during the Thirty Years' War it housed VIPs from both sides — depending on who was in control at the moment. It's still an ideal overnight stopping place.

The tourist office (Städtisches Verkehrsbüro) in the city hall (Rathaus) has an excellent walking guide to Miltenberg (phone: 6-7272). It's in German only, but so clearly arranged that you can walk in sequence from one spot of interest to the next with no trouble.

En Route from Miltenberg – A worthwhile side trip from Miltenberg is the 18-mile (29-km) jaunt to Wertheim. The road parallels the Main River all the way, or if you want to take a rest from driving, leave your car in Miltenberg and go by boat.

The Main and Tauber rivers meet at Wertheim, and the town is dominated by a castle constructed of red sandstone, which is peculiar to the Odenwald and Spessart areas. A guide is available from the Wertheim tourist office (Verkehrsamt) in the city hall (phone: 30-12-30): The Marktplatz is worth seeing, with a Renaissance monument known as the *Engelsbrunnen* ("Angel's Well") at one end. The church has a number of unusually beautiful, well-preserved tombstones and memorials from the sixteenth century. You'll have to climb around to see the old castle, but the view of Wertheim and the rivers is worth a little puffing.

Pick up Route 469 in Miltenberg again for 5 miles (8 km) to Amorbach.

AMORBACH: You'll notice the red sandstone towers of an abbey church that dominates Amorbach. It was built between 1742 and 1747 on the site of an earlier Romanesque church. The interior of this now-Baroque abbey is worth seeing. Its chancel screen is one of the finest in Germany, and it has a justifiably well-known organ; concerts are given here in the high tourist season.

MICHELSTADT: Pick up Route 47, the Nibelungenstrasse, for 15 miles (24 km) to Michelstadt, the heart of Wagner country; this is where all the mythical action of the great operas was set. This is where the Nibelungen, evil guardians of a magic hoard of gold, are supposed to have done their hunting, and somewhat farther south, the great hero Siegfried went on the royal hunt during which Hagen killed him. Whether you are a true believer or not, the gently sloping countryside is lovely.

Michelstadt has what may be the most enchanting Marktplatz in the Oldenwald, with a sixteenth-century fountain, a charming town hall, and many remarkable half-timbered houses. Notice especially the unusual design of the two bay windows in the town hall.

From Michelstadt it's about 42 miles (68 km) to Worms or 38 miles (61 km) to Heidelberg.

WORMS: This city is so packed with history and interest, you will want to take time to see as much as possible. It was destroyed in 436 by Attila the Hun, and in 1521 it was the scene of the famous Imperial Diet that passed judgment on Martin Luther. Worms became a Protestant city in 1525 and, as a result, was subject to heavy reprisals during the Thirty Years' War. It was almost totally destroyed by the French in 1689, deprived of its free city status, annexed by France in 1801, and finally awarded to Germany by the Congress of Vienna in 1815. All of this major European history is written on its streets, its buildings, and on every street corner.

The tourist office (Verkehrsverein, Neumarkt 14; phone: 2-5045) has a great deal of helpful material and information in English. Look for it just opposite St. Peter's Cathedral, which is itself one of Germany's finest examples of thirteenth-century Romanesque architecture. The high altar is by Balthasar Neumann, a famous eighteenth-century master of German baroque architecture.

Worms is one of the oldest centers of Jewish culture in Germany and has the oldest synagogue in the country, founded in the eleventh century. The ancient Jewish cemetery, just behind the cathedral, has been in use since the eleventh century and is worth a visit. Worms is also the home area of Liebfraumilch wine. Its name came from the Church of Our Lady (Liebfrauenkirche) at the city's northern end.

HEIDELBERG: Beautiful old Heidelberg is surrounded by thickly wooded hills, which rise above its massive ruined castle. Beneath the castle, its old buildings with their red roofs and romantic towers face the peaceful Neckar River and its Old Bridge (Alte Brücke). The oldest university town in Germany, Heidelberg is still best known as an intellectual and cultural center. During the Middle Ages, the city was the political center of the Rhineland Palatinate. Heidelberg and its castle were destroyed by Louis XIV of France in 1689, and to make matters worse, the city was completely demolished by fire in 1693. After these disasters the electors turned their backs on Heidelberg and the town was rebuilt in baroque style.

Stop in at the local tourist office for maps, brochures, and all sorts of useful information (Pavillon am Hauptbahnhof, the central railroad station; phone: 2-1341).

Both banks of the river afford excellent views of the town. Walk along the right bank, taking Neuenheimer Landstrasse, which runs west from the Old Bridge, and Ziegel-häuser Landstrasse, which runs east; then try the more ambitious Philosophers' Way (Philosophenweg) farther from the river, starting from Bergstrasse in the suburb of Neuenheim and ascending the slopes of the Heiligenberg.

Don't miss the castle, which can be reached on foot, by car, by escalator, or by cable car. See its seventeenth-century gardens, with their remarkable view from the Scheffel Terrace (named for a Heidelberg poet). You may want to take the guided tour, offered daily at frequent intervals. Be sure to see the Great Vat (Grosses Fass) here, made in the eighteenth century, with a capacity of 49,000 gallons and a stairway to the top. According to local lore, a dwarf named Perkeo once emptied the whole thing.

Other sights in Heidelberg include the curious Students' Jail (Augustinergasse 2), where unruly students were incarcerated during the eighteenth and nineteenth centuries; the Electoral Palatinate Museum (Kurpfälzisches Museum; Hauptstr. 97), housed in a baroque palace, containing a cast of the jaw of Heidelberg man (50,000 BC) and the great Altarpiece of the Twelve Apostles (Windsheimer Zwölfbotenaltar) by Riemenschneider (1509), among its treasures.

Heidelberg is a small city, well suited to walking and lingering about, especially in the streets of the old quarter and the quays along the river. Fortunately, it came through the Second World War unscathed. From here you can explore the scenic Neckar Valley to the east, its gorge surrounded by high, thickly forested hills.

BEST EN ROUTE

Prices along this route vary; they're significantly higher in the larger cities, so that you'll have to pay more for everything in Frankfurt and Heidelberg. Plan to spend $55 to $90 (higher in Heidelberg) for hotels we have classified as expensive; $35 to $55 is moderate; and below $35 is inexpensive. A dinner for two without wine will cost $45 to $100 in restaurants listed as expensive; $25 to $45 is moderate; and $10 to $25 is inexpensive.

SELIGENSTADT

Klosterstuben Restaurant – Next to the church and the convent garden, the *Klosterstuben* features excellent German-style cooking. It also serves a locally brewed beer (becoming increasingly rare in Germany as big breweries take over). Freihofpl. 7 (phone: 3571). Moderate.

AMORBACH

Schafhof – A romantic 16-room hotel in a former Benedictine monastery. It has an excellent restaurant, noteworthy for its lamb dishes. Der Schafhof (phone: 8088). Moderate.

ASCHAFFENBURG

Romantik-Hotel Post – Not far from the Schloss Johannisberg, this hotel is beautifully decorated in the traditional sense of comfort and friendliness. The restaurant offers good Continental food with a broad range of choices. Goldbacherstr. 19 (phone: 2-1333). Moderate.

MILTENBERG

Gasthaus zum Riesen – In operation since the twelfth century, this place claims to be Germany's oldest hostel. Based on authenticated guest lists, the owner and restorer, W. Jöst, has furnished a series of bedrooms after the period of some famous visitors — Queen Christina of Sweden, for example. All furnishings are genuine antiques. This is a relatively expensive but a fascinating experience. Reservations are a necessity for the "name" rooms and a good idea at any time. Hauptstr. 97 (phone: 3644). Moderate.

WERTHEIM

Schweizer Stuben – Follow the signs to this truly excellent restaurant, featuring fine Swiss-French-German cuisine in comfortable surroundings. There are also nine rooms here. Reservations necessary. Closed Sundays, Monday evenings, and the month of January. Geiselbrunnweg 11 (phone: 43-51). Expensive.

HEIDELBERG

Der Europäische Hof – The leading hotel in Heidelberg consists of three wings, each from a different period. Centrally located facing a park, it's known for its service and for the fine French-style food in its *Kurfürstenstube* restaurant, which many agree is Heidelberg's finest. There's a terrace for summer dining, a bar with dancing, conference rooms, and public rooms nicely furnished with antiques. Rooms are large and comfortable, and most have refrigerators and TV. Friedrich-Ebert-Anlage 1 (phone: 2-71-01). Very expensive.

Hotel Hirschgasse – This moderately priced, family-run hotel is in a building that dates from 1472. Tastefully restored, its rooms are modern and comfortable. The hotel has a very good restaurant and a lovely, tree-shaded terrace where you can eat breakfast (closed Sundays). Hirschgasse 3 (phone: 4-9921). Expensive.

Weinstube Schloss Heidelberg – This restaurant, with a terrace right in the castle courtyard, offers a marvelous view of the castle and good food. The tasteful décor is that of a wine tavern, with an ornately paneled ceiling, natural wood tables, and framed engravings. Closed Tuesdays. Schlosshof (phone: 2-0081). Moderate.

Roter Ochsen – A very famous student hangout dating from 1703, this place has students' initials on the walls, oak tables, and mementos of all sorts. There's piano music in the evening, lots of beer, and typical German cooking. Hauptstr. 217 (phone: 2-0977). Inexpensive.

Westphalia

Though well liked by Germans and other Europeans, Westphalia, a dreamy area of castles, country inns, half-timbered houses, windmills, forests, hills, and mineral spas, has been little explored by Americans. (The proprietor of the noted *Hotel-Restaurant Schütte* in Oberkirchen tells us he has never had an American guest.) Perhaps Americans have shunned Westphalia because it contains the great industrial Ruhr Valley; in fact, Dortmund, Westphalia's principal city, is one of the major cities of the Ruhr. However, the well-heeled Ruhr residents like to have a peaceful, picturesque country area to which they can slip away for a weekend or a business conference.

Westphalia is a region of small hedged-in farms that form a checkerboard pattern. Strict laws keep the villages small, the forests intact, and the air unpolluted. The castle hotels and wayside inns have turrets and half-timbered exteriors, with baronial interiors and open fireplaces. Yet they also have indoor plumbing, central heating, and twentieth-century mattresses. There is none of that rundown look you will find in Europe's more remote and poorer country areas.

In the northern part of Germany, Westphalia extends from the Rhine to the Weser River. For maps and information about the region, contact the tourist office, Landesverkehrsverband, Westfalen e.V., Balkenstr. 4, 4600 Dortmund (phone: 57-17-15).

The name Westphalia first appears in connection with a section of the duchy of Saxony in the tenth century. In the later Middle Ages, its major towns of Münster, Paderborn, Bielefeld, and others, were prosperous members of the Hanseatic League (an association of mercantile city-states). The Peace of Westphalia, which was signed in Münster in 1648 to end the Thirty Years' War, gave Prussia a foothold in the area, which it maintained — except for the brief Napoleonic reign in 1808–13 — until 1945.

Westphalia is noted for its cuisine, which is the most distinctive in Germany. Lufthansa gets its first-class passengers "in the mood for Germany" by serving them a Westphalian snack en route. It starts with an ice-cold *Steinhäger*, a ginlike schnapps drink from the town of Steinhagen near Bielefeld; the drink is poured from a stoneware bottle into one of the deep pewter spoons Westphalians use as shot glasses. Then comes a chaser of cool Westphalian beer from Dortmund, which is second only to Munich as a German brewing city. Finally, there's pumpernickel — also Westphalian in origin — with butter, and justly famous Westphalian ham, eaten on a wooden board just as they do in Westphalia.

You can enjoy the culinary and visual riches of Westphalia by touring the area in a circular route that begins and ends in Dortmund. The round trip is about 400 miles (640 km).

DORTMUND: Like all the cities in the Ruhr, Dortmund was leveled in World War II and rebuilt along coldly modern lines that are rather devoid of character. It is not dirty, however; the whole Ruhr has strict air pollution laws. Have a look at the Westfalenpark, with its German Rosarium (1500 varieties of roses, half a million plants) and its TV tower topped by a revolving restaurant. Dortmund is best known as a beer-producing center; if you want to visit a brewery, contact the Verband Dortmunder Bierbrauer (Karl Marx Str. 56; phone: 52-89-73).

Now head east into Westphalia proper, toward the Sauerland, an unspoiled region of woods and lakes to the east and south. The Autobahn gets you out there quickly. Take the Sauerland Line (A 45), following the signs to Siegen and Frankfurt, but exit at Olpe and follow the very scenic Route 55 north.

En Route from Dortmund – At this point you may wish to take a short detour to Attendorn, a place of lakes, a huge stalactite cave, and remarkable rock formations. The cave, called Attahöhle (follow the signs to Tropfsteinhöhle), is open daily for a small fee. Or continue on Route 55 to Lennestadt and then take the scenic Route 236 via the beautiful little village of Oberkirchen to Winterberg (one of the biggest German winter sports areas outside the Alps), and then drive north on Route 480.

OLSBERG: If they are so inclined, summer visitors can get a look at the Old West here at Fort Fun City, an "authentic" Western town, replete with saloon, jail, gambling hall, and a print shop where you can get a wanted poster with your own name on it.

Gevelingen Palace here is the starting point for Gypsy wagons, which you can rent for a tour of the Sauerland on "two horsepower." The wagons come complete with sleeping facilities for seven, blankets, linen, stove, dishes, pots and pans, gas lanterns, and gas heater. You follow a prescribed route and stop each night at a farm where they stable the horses. Continue on Route 480 via Brilon ("the most forested town in Westphalia") to Paderborn. Then take Routes 1 and 239.

DETMOLD: You now are in the middle of the Teutoburg Forest, another popular Westphalian district, which is famous to Germans as the place where the Romans were stopped in their northward march, in an epic battle in AD 9. Germanic tribesmen dealt them a stunning defeat, and the Roman Empire never extended any farther north in continental Europe. A giant statue to the tribal chief Hermann, who led the battle, commands a hill just 4 miles (6 km) outside the city at the village of Heiligenkirchen. It is 82 feet from Hermann's feet to the tip of his upraised sword. Also not to be missed while you are in Detmold is the bird of prey sanctuary at nearby Bad Berlebeck. The eagles, vultures, and other big birds fly freely at 11 AM and 3 PM each day. Detmold also is the site of an open-air museum, the Lippisches Landsmuseum, with typically Westphalian farmhouses, which usually combine red brick and half timbering. Continue on Routes 239 and 66.

BIELEFELD: One of Westphalia's larger cities, Bielefeld is coldly modern for the most part, but some fine patrician houses remain and there's also the Sparrenburg Castle (Am Sparrenberg 1), with a network of underground passages below. On the ground level there's a museum devoted to playing cards and a good view of the Teutoburg Forest from the tower.

En Route from Bielefeld – From Bielefeld take Route 61 via Herford. On the way to Minden you pass the Porta Westfalica, where the Weser River suddenly emerges spectacularly from between two hills, out of the mountains, and on to the broad north German plain. One of the hills that has a fine view is topped with a monument to Kaiser Wilhelm.

MINDEN is a good place to board one of the old paddle boats that ply the Weser. See the outstanding Romanesque cathedral with its eleventh-century crucifix and a 1480 painting of the Crucifixion by a Westphalian master. There's a bridge where the Mittelland Canal passes over the Weser. Also interesting is the Great Lock (Schachtschleuse), which is just north of town; it's 276 by 33 feet long and it links the Mittelland Canal with the Weser.

En Route from Minden – Proceed along Route 65 to Lübbecke. (Once a year, during a festival in August, a fountain here bubbles with beer instead of water. You can help yourself if you can get near it.) Then take Route 239 to Löhne, and take a short drive west on the Autobahn.

BÜNDE: What is alleged to be the world's only tobacco museum is located in this cigar-making town. When you pay your money you get, instead of a ticket, a cigar or a cheap clay pipe, which you can fill at a handy humidor. Exhibits include the world's largest cigar (5½ feet long, 20 pounds) and a pipe that was obviously highly prized by the Sea Devil, Count Luckner. He lost it out of a train window and pulled the emergency brake so he could recover it. Continue on the Autobahn to Osnabrück and head south on Routes 51 and 475.

WARENDORF: This is the horse capital of Germany, site of a state-operated stud farm, an important riding school, and the headquarters of the German Olympic Equestrian Committee. There are plenty of rental horses here, and lots of riding paths; it is a good place to book a vacation in the saddle if you're so inclined. There are big parades here on the last Saturday in September and the first Saturday in October, when horses are led by saddle masters in elegant uniforms. Drive from Warendorf along Routes 64 and 51.

MÜNSTER: Westphalia's historic capital is the site of one of Germany's biggest universities. Every year, on May 15, Münster holds a festival to mark the Peace of Westphalia, negotiated here in 1648 to end the Thirty Years' War. See the Prinzipalmarkt, the oldest and busiest street in town, with its elegant Renaissance houses. If you continue along Bogenstrasse, you'll see the Kiepenkerl, a statue of a peddler with his basket. The low-lying Romanesque cathedral is typically Westphalian, with its astronomic clock in the ambulatory and a Glockenspiel that plays at noon.

The area surrounding Münster is known for its moated medieval castles, particularly the Castle of Vischering, set on an island, with an interesting interior and a prison beneath. It's open daily except Tuesdays. Also noteworthy are the castles of Hülshoff and Nordkirchen (the latter is now the university's School of Finance). Farther west is the medieval walled city of Coesfeld.

En Route from Münster – Continue along Route 51 through Dülmen; the estate of the duke of Croy here is the only wild horse sanctuary (with 200 horses) in Europe. The event of the year here is the annual roundup on the last Saturday in May.

Take Route 51 to Recklinghausen and visit the Icon Museum (Kirchplatz 2a), where icons are exhibited thematically (closed Mondays). In May and June, Recklinghausen is the site of the annual Ruhr Festival of music, theater, opera, and art exhibitions.

Next take the Autobahn (Route A43) south to Bochum.

BOCHUM: This is the site of another unique museum, the Museum of Mining (Bergbau Museum; Wielandstr.). The big attraction is an actual coal mine below the building, with nearly a mile of shafts that the visitor can explore. Bochum also has Germany's best-known public observatory and planetarium (corner of Castroper Str. and Hagenstr.), run by Professor Heinz Kaminski, a well-liked television personality. Take Route 1 back to Dortmund.

BEST EN ROUTE

The visitor to Westphalia will delight in the many charming hotels and inns to be found in the smaller towns. Prices here also tend to be lower than they are in the larger, more frequented city areas. A double room with breakfast in an expensive hotel will cost about $55 to $80; moderate is $30 to $55; and inexpensive is below $30. In the expensive restaurants, a dinner for two without wine will cost about $25 to $50; in moderate places it will be $15 to $25; inexpensive meals are $10 to $15.

ATTENDORN

Burghotel Schnellenberg – This is a thirteenth-century castle in the middle of the woods with a commanding view of the town below. Many of the rooms are in the towers. You can dine in the rustic *Rittersaal Salon* where game and fish dishes are especially recommended. Recreational opportunities here include tennis, hikes in the woods, and swimming in the Biggesee 2 miles away (phone: 6940). Expensive to moderate.

OBERKIRCHEN

Hotel-Restaurant Schütte – This former eighteenth-century coach house is in the middle of a Sauerland village of 800 inhabitants. It offers many miles of hiking paths in the surrounding woods, its own swimming pool, and its own stable, where visitors either rent horses or stable their own. Its Westphalian food specialties include ham and *Pfefferpothast,* a very spicy stew. The game dishes are excellent: Try venison with red wine. The typically Westphalian interior is rustic and has an open fireplace. Eggeweg 2 (phone: 423). Moderate.

PETERSHAGEN

Schloss Petershagen – This moated castle is situated on the Weser River, and is surrounded by meadows and parks. It has a small hotel (11 rooms) and an elegant restaurant with international cuisine. The restaurant has deep carpets, rich cloth on the walls, oil paintings, and linen tablecloths. It's not the place for Westphalian specialties, although it does feature fish from the Weser — smoked eel and trout soup. The Palace also offers a "knightly banquet" for groups only, with service personnel in medieval costumes and menus offering old recipes. There's a bar in the cellar, and the surrounding park has tennis courts and a heated swimming pool. Originally built in 1306, it doesn't have the usual castle appearance; the tower with the spiral staircase is of recent construction. Schlosstr. 5 (phone: 346). Expensive to moderate.

WARENDORF

Hotel im Engel – Established in 1557, the hotel has been in the hands of the Leve family, the present proprietors, since 1692. It is right in the center of the old city, and has the usual rustic interior, with oak furniture, carved beams, pewter, old pictures, and the standard open fireplace. Westphalian specialties include mussel soup; steak garnished with scrambled eggs; turbot served in white Burgundy sauce; and *Schlachtplatte,* literally, "slaughter platter," consisting of Westphalian ham, sausages, and other smoked meats, heaped on a mound of sauerkraut. Facilities include a swimming pool, sauna, and solarium. Brünebrede 37 (phone: 7064). Expensive to moderate.

MÜNSTER

Waldhotel Krautkrämer – About 4 miles from the center of town, this 70-room hotel has its own lake. It provides a rare combination of comfort, hospitality, sublime surroundings, and one of West Germany's best restaurants. Am Hiltruper See 173 (phone: 8050). Expensive.

Gasthof Stuhlmacher – This seventeenth-century restaurant has typical Westphalian decor and cuisine, with ten famous beers on tap. The gabled exterior, right next to the city hall, displays a century-old metal figure of a professor and a worker sitting at a beer barrel, which means that the restaurant catered to all social classes. The interior is elaborately carved in wood and has stained-glass windows, leather-covered seats, and old pictures. Specialties include calf's head stew, homemade *Sülze* (pickled meat in aspic), homemade cheese, and Westphalian ham. Reservations are recommended. Prinzipalmarkt 6 (phone: 44877). Moderate.

Pinkus Müller – At this 160-year-old student hangout, tourists, professors, and students sit side by side at long wooden tables on which every inch of surface has been carved with the initials of generations. Each regular customer has his own mug, with his name on it, which hangs from a peg on the wall. The decor is German "schmaltz," with stained-glass windows, overhead beams with painted mottoes in Low German, an open fireplace, a cannon, and a wooden board (no longer used) on which the names of those delinquent in their accounts were revealed to the public. The customary drink is *Altbier*, a heavy, somewhat sweet beer. You may want to start things off with a schnapps served from a deep spoon. Full meals can be had, but food specialties tend to be snacks that go well with beer, such as *Töttschen*, a small dish of veal and mustard, or a Westphalian stew of various smoked meats and sausages. Closed Sundays. Reservations suggested. Kreuzstr. 4–10 (phone: 5-7027). Moderate to inexpensive.

The Rhineland

Long before the Autobahn and jetport, before the rail lines stitched the continent into a whole, the Rhine River was Europe's main street and commercial thoroughfare. Fed by melting Alpine snows in Switzerland, and sharing frontage with France and the Netherlands, the Rhine is 820 miles long; it is nevertheless the section that flows through Germany that captures the imagination with its castles, vineyards, dangerous whirlpools, and legends of heroes, Rhine maidens, and Lorelei. The river flows steadily northward, broad, even-tempered, and unimpeded, in contrast with the tempestuous history of Germany, past and present.

Today as ever, the Rhine is a busy and important shipping route linking dozens of inland ports such as Ludwigshafen and Duisburg to the North Sea and the oceans beyond. However, this majestic river is also part playground, part historical monument, and part natural wonder. Despite the Rhine's more than 800-mile length, *The Rhineland* is a much narrower term, encompassing by common consensus only the 50-mile Rhine gorge between Mainz and Koblenz where the steep banks, striated by vineyards and crowned with castles, create the romantic picture most people associate with this famous river.

History, legend, and magnificent scenery have their attractions, but one cannot forget that the Rhineland is wine land. By most accounts, Germany's top-rated wine district is the Rheingau, extending roughly from Wiesbaden to the mouth of the Lahn River near Kamp, only a few dozen miles downstream. Along this short stretch, a southern exposure ripens noble Riesling grapes to perfection. For the confirmed wine connoisseur, a trip down the Rhine gorge is something of a pilgrimage. For the neophyte sipper, a few well-chosen stopovers here will provide a succinct introduction to the white wines many experts claim are the best in the world. For information about German wine, write to one of these addresses: The German Wine Information Bureau (Alan Olson), 99 Park Ave., New York, NY 10016 (phone: 212-599-6900); or the German Wine Academy, Postfach 1705, D-6500 Mainz, West Germany. And the wine seems to impart an easygoing and fun-loving nature to the people in the surrounding countryside. The traveler can only agree that a relaxed and joyous outlook on life is an excellent one for hoteliers and restaurateurs. In fact, one often finds that Rhinelanders cultivate their guests as attentively as they do their vines.

The Rhine can be explored by car, by rail, or by excursion boat. Multilingual bus tours are also available, and for these, contact the German National Tourist Office (Deutsche Zentrale für Tourismus), Beethoven Str. 69, 6 Frankfurt am Main (phone: 0611-75721); or stop in at one of the city tourist offices — labeled Verkehrsamt or Verkehrsverein — along the Rhine route. These offices also provide maps and tourist information. The central tourist office for the region has two branches, one in Bad Godesberg, a suburb of Bonn, and the other in Koblenz. Their addresses are Landesverkehrsverband, Rheinland e.V., Rheinallee 69, 5300 Bonn–Bad Godesberg 1 (phone: 36-2921); and Fremdenverkehrsverband Rheinland-Pfalz e.V., Hochhaus, 5400 Koblenz (phone: 3-5025).

The above modes of travel can be combined, of course, and the bearer of a Eurailpass can make as many stops as desired along the way to, say, Koblenz, and then use the pass at no extra charge on one of the many Köln-Düsseldorfer (K-D) or Rüdesheim-Bingen river steamers that ply this route, for a pleasant return trip. For information about boat trips contact K-D Schiffsagentur in Köln (Cologne), Frankenwerft 15 (phone: 21-18-64); or in Mainz, Am Rathaus (phone: 2-4511). Rail lines parallel the river on both sides, but the west bank affords the best scenery and most interesting stops. Travelers touring by car have the opportunity to stop and take pictures anywhere or to picnic at rest stops; the auto traveler can easily cross the Rhine at one of several bridges at Koblenz and made a round trip by returning along Route 42 on the east bank. Campgrounds are plentiful along both sides, and at several points car ferries, called *Autofähre,* will transfer you across the river for a nominal fee. The entire route covers about 143 miles (229 km) one way, but you'll want to spend at least 2 or 3 days in this glorious region.

MAINZ: This 2,000-year-old city founded by the Romans is most notable for its favorite son, Johannes Gutenberg, who invented moveable type here in 1440. In the Gutenberg Museum (Liebfrauenpl. 5), you can see an original Gutenberg Bible and a replica of the famed printer's press, as well as an exhibit depicting printing through the centuries. Mainz is also the scene of a boisterous carnival, climaxing in the Rosenmontag parade on the last Monday before Ash Wednesday. Mainz Cathedral, though not architecturally impressive, is worth visiting for its art treasures, particularly the medieval sculpture by the Master of Naumburg in its Diocesan Museum.

RÜDESHEIM: It's downright touristy — and for good reason. Head straight for the Drosselgasse, a narrow, cobblestone alley lined with restaurants, wine taverns, and souvenir shops. Pick a pub where the oompah band isn't too loud, order yourself a *Römer* (wine goblet with a bottle-green pedestal) of the local product, and get a taste of what the Rhineland is all about. This small city boasts rousing wine festivals in May and August and also has one of Germany's best wine museums, located in Brömser Castle along Route 42 at the west end of town. For a small fee you can browse through 28 display rooms containing wine presses and various viticultural artifacts showing man's 6,000-year wine-making tradition. A free, three-page brochure is available upon request. If you make this recommended stop, carry a jacket or sweater with you, for the cellarlike rooms are cool even in summer. To find a room or to collect a handful of brochures describing the sights ahead, contact Rüdesheim's city tourist office, Rheinstr. 16 (phone: 2962), where English-speaking personnel will answer all your questions. Another Rüdesheimer attraction is the curious Siegfried's Mechanical Music Cabinet, a collection of self-playing musical contraptions of the past, housed just off Drosselgasse.

Rüdesheim is a good place to catch a K-D river steamer. The trip to St. Goarshausen and back makes a nice afternoon jaunt, allowing plenty of time for wine sipping and a leisurely meal in the ship's surprisingly good restaurant.

En Route from Rüdesheim – Before you cross the river to Bingen and the more scenic west side of the river, you might want to take a 9-mile (14-km) side trip north to Assmannshausen by way of Niederwald Hill. Just north of Rüdesheim along Route 42, you will pass the grim-visaged Amazon that is the Germanic Monument, built on Niederwald Hill by Bismarck in the 1870s to commemorate the unification of Germany. You can get there from Rüdesheim by bus or by a chair lift, which carries you up the steep, vine-bearing slopes for spectacular views and picture taking.

On an island in the middle of the river is the Mouse Tower (Mäuseturm) — not to be confused with the Mouse Castle, encountered later — built centuries ago by the wicked archbishop of Mainz as a stronghold for extracting tolls from passing ships. According to legend, the nasty archbishop ordered his henchmen to wipe out a band of beggars who came pleading for handouts. An army of mice rose up to avenge the slain beggars, chased the archbishop into the tower, and gobbled him up alive. One can readily see how the Brothers Grimm found plenty of fairy-tale material in Germany! There are short daily boat excursions from Rüdesheim to the village of Assmannshausen via the Mouse Tower.

Assmannshausen is an oddity because it produces only red wine, which comes from the Burgundy-type (Pinot Noir) grape; however, only a local vintner with an exaggerated view of his own product would rank Assmannshausen red anywhere near the noble white Rieslings from the surrounding area.

BINGEN: For the motorist, the left bank of the river affords the best view, so return to Rüdesheim and take the car ferry to Bingen, picking up Route 9 on the other side. In itself, Bingen is not especially interesting. But in common with its sister villages, Bingen shares the typically relaxed Rhineland ambience. After a fine meal with wine, there's no better place in Germany for an evening stroll than through Bingen's narrow brick and cobblestone streets or along the riverfront of one of these delightful Rhineside towns.

En Route from Bingen – The stretch from Bingen to Koblenz is justly celebrated for its dramatic scenery, romantic castles, and legendary landmarks. The last section on the west bank, between Bacharach and St. Goar, is the narrow, steep road known as the Rheingoldstrasse. Just north of Bingen, several castles on the hills to the left invite you to do a little historical poking around. Especially worthy are Burg Rheinfels, perched on a rock, and Burg Reichenstein, set in a valley — both open to the public. It's useful to know the difference between the German words *Burg* and *Schloss,* both translated as "castle" by most German-English dictionaries. A *Burg* is a fortified medieval structure, today often in ruins. Its military aspect is obvious. A *Schloss,* on the other hand, is more of a palace, and is usually lavishly decorated and furnished. Many even offer guest accommodations.

The towns of Bacharach and Oberwesel bid the traveler to stop and explore. There are more castles in the area than one could comfortably see in a week, so don't feel bad about passing up most of them. The Jost family in Bacharach runs a justly famous antique porcelain and glassware shop called *Trödel's* (7 Oberstr.).

On the right, between Bacharach and St. Goar, are the Rhine gorge's two most distinctive landmarks — one might even say trademarks. Die Pfalz is a squat, dome-roofed medieval toll station in the middle of the current between Bacharach and Oberwesel. In the romantic past, Die Pfalz had chains stretched across the river to stop passing ships, and cannons were leveled at stubborn river captains. This fortified structure did a brisk business until an international agreement in

1868 eliminated all such extortion on the Rhine. Try to get a photo of Die Pfalz when an especially colorful river barge is passing in the foreground or background. Seven miles downstream from Die Pfalz is the legend-haunted Lorelei, a sheer outcropping of rock forever immortalized by the music of Robert Schumann. According to the sagas, a blond maiden — a Germanic version of the Sirens — lured sailors from this rock to their deaths with song. As K-D excursion boats pass this point, Schumann strains are played on a sound system, and the German tourists on board suddenly look very reverent indeed — understandably so, because the Lorelei is as characteristically German as Old Faithful is American. It's a "must" stop, and today an auto road runs to the top.

ST. GOAR and ST. GOARSHAUSEN: These twin towns face one another across a broad, lakelike expanse of the Rhine. St. Goar's castle, Burg Rheinfels, is worth a stop.

A few steps beyond St. Goar's tourist office (Heer Str. 120; phone: 383) is the shop of *Doris Mühl,* which offers an incredible array of cuckoo clocks, beer steins, quality glassware, and famous Hummel figurines. Three decades of American GIs have helped this shop to thrive, and its English-speaking proprietors gladly welcome Americans.

You can take the car ferry across to St. Goarshausen, which is as delightful as its sister village on the left bank. Travelers with children may find the carnival rides set up near the K-D steamer dock a welcome distraction. St. Goarshausen is the scene of the majestic Rhine in Flames fireworks and spotlight extravaganza on the third Saturday in September. But alas! (for St. Goarshausen-ites): The spectacle is best seen from St. Goar across the river. Just south of St. Goarshausen is the Lorelei.

The steep-sided Rhine gorge ends beyond the village of Boppard, a residential valley town with a particularly pleasant promenade aptly, but not too imaginatively, named Rhine Promenade (Rheinallee). At Koblenz the Rhine is joined by the Moselle river, a famous wine river well worth a side trip.

En Route from Koblenz – Though less dramatic than the stretch between Bingen and Koblenz, the area north of Koblenz has many intriguing features. Continuing up the west bank, you may wish to take a look at the abbey of Maria Laach, a Benedictine monastery, with its Romanesque basilica. It's a short detour of 9 miles (14.4 km) west of the river at Andernach. The abbey is most interesting for its location on the Laacher See, the largest of the volcanic lakes in the Eifel plateau, a peaceful, wooded area.

Farther north along the Rhine is the Rheineck, a Burg with a view of the surrounding valley. Still farther, on the slope of a former volcano, is the Rolandsbogen (Roland's arch), the ruins of the castle of the knight Roland, hero of the *Chanson de Roland.*

Southeast of Bonn, on the right bank (there's a car ferry from Bad Godesberg to Königswinter), is the Drachenfels, a romantic, rocky summit with a ruined tower and a panoramic view that includes the Eifel plateau, Bonn, and Cologne. It's in the Seven Mountains (Siebengebirge) range, whose low summits, once crowned with castles, are now crowned with forests; the whole area is a national park. The Drachenfels was named for the legendary dragon slain by Siegfried, the hero who became invincible by bathing in its blood. The area is also known for its wines, the best of which is called Drachenblut ("dragon's blood"). Excursions for Drachenfels (15 minutes by cog railway) leave from Königswinter at frequent intervals.

BONN: The postwar Germans must have wanted the capital of the new Germany in a place where nothing exciting ever happens, for after its spirited street carnival on Weiberfastnacht and Rose Monday (the dates vary with the calendar), the city goes back into hibernation. Besides the seat of government Bonn has another claim to fame: The composer Ludwig van Beethoven was born and spent his early years in this Rhineside city. The excellently restored Beethoven House (Bonngasse 20) deserves a stop. See also the Alter Zoll, a bastion with a view of the Rhine, and stroll along the promenade on the banks of the river, past the Bundestag, the West German parliament.

COLOGNE (KÖLN): The silhouette of Cologne's great Gothic cathedral dominates the city's skyline. You can't miss it — nor would anyone want to, since it's one of the world's finest. Begun in 1248, the cathedral was an on-again, off-again project not completed until 1880. Although 90% of the city was leveled in World War II bombing, the cathedral escaped virtually intact. See the fourteenth-century stained-glass windows, the altarpiece, and the Magi's Shrine. The Cologne tourist office, off the cathedral square (phone: 221-3340), has a good selection of tourist brochures covering the cathedral and other city sights. Cologne's Roman beginnings are on display at the Roman-Germanic Museum opposite the cathedral, where one may see the striking one-million-piece Dionysus Mosaic, dating from AD 200. Other museums include the Wallraf-Richartz and Ludwig Museum, at An der Rechtschule, near the cathedral, with an excellent collection of old Dutch and Flemish paintings, as well as old German and modern German works; the modern and contemporary section is outstanding with a large collection of pop art.

After a round of sight-seeing, you might want to take a cable car (near the zoo) over the Rhine, enjoy an excellent view of the cathedral, and relax in the Rheinpark. Nearby is the city exposition center, site of Photokina, the world's fair of the photographic industry, held during September in even-numbered years. There's shopping galore along Hohe Strasse and Schildergasse, where every major German department-store chain seems to be represented. In the evening, this shopping district blossoms with street vendors and musicians. Other evening entertainment is offered by the pubs of Cologne's modest *Altstadt* (old town), which is nevertheless lively with music. Finally, the carnival here is reputed to be the best in Germany, with events reaching their highest pitch during the weekend before Ash Wednesday.

DÜSSELDORF: The locals have a saying: Düsseldorf is not on the Rhine, it's on the Kö. Certainly, Düsseldorf turns its back on the river and faces instead Königsallee — Kö for short — an elegant, kilometer-long promenade whose fashionable shops are a major center of German haute couture. The Kö is jewelry, furs, fine silverware, art, rare books. But the Kö is also restaurants and friendly open-air cafés where you can sip a drink and see and be seen.

At night the spotlight shifts to Düsseldorf's other center, the lively *Altstadt*, where some 200 pubs and inns jump to the sounds of live music. Nightlife here is rollicking, rather than vulgar. But proof that the mellow Rhineland wine villages are far away may be seen in what Düsseldorfers are drinking, for this is beer country, and the local specialty is Altbier or Düsseldorfer Alt, a dark lager brew. The many Yugoslavian, Japanese, Italian, Argentinian, and other ethnic restaurants indicate that this is a city of international business, and the business center for the Ruhr region.

Though a very modern city, Düsseldorf has a distinguished history that dates back to the thirteenth century. The city was known for its prominence in the arts, especially during the nineteenth century, when Napoleon made it the capital of the grand duchy of Berg; among those who lived here were Heinrich Heine, Robert Schumann, and Felix Mendelssohn. The Hetjens Museum (Palais Nesselrode, Schulstr. 4) has a large collection of ceramics; Kunstsammlung Nordrhein-Westfalen (Schloss Jägerhof, Jacobistr. 2) has some fine works of modern art, especially those by Paul Klee; and the Goethe Museum (Jägerhofstr. 1) has an extensive collection of the great writer's manuscripts and memorabilia. The opera house (Heinrich-Heine-Allee) is also an interesting place.

For maps and for further information about Düsseldorf, contact the tourist office (Konrad Adenauer Pl. 12; phone: 35-05-05).

BEST EN ROUTE

The Rhineland is prime tourist country, and has been for over a century. Good hotels abound (little Rüdesheim alone has over 60), though in the wine villages the best were built in an age when guests arrived with servants and steamer trunks. Today they are like faded aristocrats, and seem somewhat overpriced by American standards. Hotel restaurants can be excellent, however, and a Continental breakfast — often augmented by eggs or sausage — is invariably included in the overnight price. Good double rooms may be found all along the river at prices ranging from $20 to $35 and up. Even at those prices, private bathrooms may not be included, so make sure you get what you want before booking. Our advice is to arrive early and head for the city tourist office, whose personnel can locate a room without language problems. In the Rhenish cities, the top hotels meet the highest international standards and command prices to match; here, English is the second language. Below are just a few of the top hotels to choose from. Modest *Gasthäuser* and pensions are plentiful everywhere.

We have classified hotels that charge $55 to $100 for a double room with breakfast as expensive; moderate is $35 to $55; and inexpensive, below $35. A dinner for two without wine will cost $35 to $70 in an expensive restaurant; $25 to $35 is moderate; and $10 to $25, inexpensive.

RÜDESHEIM

Waldhotel Jagdschloss Niederwald – Here's a true *Schloss* hotel high on the Rhine hills, 3 miles (5 km) northwest of Rüdesheim, with an imperial view of the river. The restaurant features wine tasting and game in season — as well it should, for this was the former hunting lodge of the Archbishop of Mainz. Closed in the winter (phone: 1004). Expensive to moderate.

ASSMANNSHAUSEN

Hotel Krone – Overlooking the Rhine, this 400-year-old inn has a museum in the second-floor lounge, with letters and manuscripts by famous people who have stayed here. The spacious bedrooms have traditional furniture and the public rooms are oak-paneled and full of antiques. The food in the restaurant is outstanding; try especially the turtle soup, fresh salmon, or eels. Closed in the winter. Rheinuferstr. 10 (phone: 2036). Expensive to moderate.

BINGEN

Rheinterrassen – At the end of a parklike promenade directly on the Rhine, this small hotel has comfortable rooms, a few suites, and a fine restaurant (closed Mondays). Museumstr. 2 (phone: 1-2021). Moderate.

ST. GOAR

Schlosshotel auf Burg Rheinfels – Tucked in the picturesque ruins of a medieval castle, this hotel looks out over St. Goar, the Lorelei rock, and the Cat and Mouse castles. It has an open-air terrace with a spectacular view, an indoor pool, a sauna, a museum, a conference room, and a restaurant specializing in venison. Schlossberg 47 (phone: 7455). Expensive to moderate.

Hotel Zum Goldenen Löwen – Overlooking the Rhine, this small, moderately priced hotel has a restaurant with an outdoor terrace where the view is excellent. Heerstr. 82 (phone: 1674). Expensive to moderate.

Hotel Hauser – With a lovely view of St. Goarshausen across the river, this small, modest hotel has a café and a terrace. Heerstr. 77 (phone: 333). Inexpensive.

BONN

Steigenberger Hotel Bonn – This modern high-rise hotel is frequented by diplomats. The interior is tastefully furnished, using bright colors and natural woods. The spectacular indoor rooftop pool has walls of glass and looks out onto the Rhine. There's a sauna too, a disco, and an eighteenth-floor restaurant with very good food and a panoramic view. Bundeskanzlerpl. (phone: 2-0191). Expensive.

COLOGNE (KÖLN)

Excelsior Hotel Ernst – Opposite the cathedral and near the train station, this establishment is everything you would expect from an old-world hotel. Its rooms radiate an aura of luxury, comfort, and charm; the service is very efficient, although not ostentatious. On the premises is *Hansa-Stube*, a very well regarded restaurant. Trankgasse 1 (phone: 2701). Expensive.

Goldener Pflug – This fine restaurant serves exquisite house specialties and has a pleasant setting. Service is first rate. Reservations advised. Closed Sundays and in July. Olpener Str. 421 (phone: 89-55-09). Expensive.

Weinhaus im Walfisch – Seafood dishes and some of the best German wines are the specialty here. The building, a rarity in hard-hit Cologne, predates the last war by more than 300 years. Reservations recommended. Closed Sundays and in July. Salzgasse 13 (phone: 21-95-75). Moderate.

Altstadt Hotel – This small hotel is in the old city near the landing dock for Rhine boats. The owner, Herr Olbrich, once was a steward for the German-American Line. His tastefully decorated rooms are impeccable, and the personalized service is outstanding. Rooms have bars and refrigerators. Reserve in advance. Closed most of July. Salzgasse 7 (phone: 23-41-87). Moderate.

DÜSSELDORF

Breidenbacher Hof – Convenient to both the activities of the downtown area and the Old World charms of the *Altstadt,* this is one of Germany's best addresses. Tradition, luxury, and elegance combine well with very efficient service. Its restaurant, *Grill Royal,* ought not to be missed. Heinrich-Heine-Allee 36 (phone: 86-01). Expensive.

Zum Schiffchen – Don't miss the jovial atmosphere and hearty food of this beer garden that's a favorite town haunt. Napoleon is said to have dined here, as well as Heinrich Heine, Curd Jürgens, and Arthur Miller. Closed Sundays. Hafenstr. 5 (phone: 13-24-22). Inexpensive.

The Neckar River Valley

This route along the meandering Neckar River follows Germany's Castle Road (Die Burgenstrasse) from Heidelberg to Heilbronn. More than a dozen castles and strongholds are located along this road, some of which housed aristocratic families during the Middle Ages. Many of the princely feudal dwellings are in ruins; others are intact and have been restored as museums, hotels, inns, and wine taverns. Zwingenberg Castle, for example, is still inhabited by royalty — by relatives of Britain's Prince Philip — but Hirschhorn and Hornberg castles are now hotels.

One of Germany's wine districts, producing mainly red wines, the scenic

Neckar River valley is surrounded by high, forested hills crowned with castles, fortresses, and quaint old towns. Beginning in Heidelberg (see *Frankfurt to Heidelberg*), this 1- or 2-day drive runs 50 miles (80 km) south to the wine-producing town of Heilbronn, where the Castle Road ends. From here it's an additional 32 miles (52 km) through the Swabian Hills to the major industrial and cultural center of Stuttgart, home of the Stuttgart Ballet and Mercedes-Benz. Finally, you can drive yet another 27 miles (43 km) south to see Tübingen, a charming old university town.

Well-marked hiking trails connect towns and castles, and the forested castle areas are generally honeycombed with quiet, scenic trails. Boat trips leave from many locations on the Neckar; passenger and car ferries transport you to interesting sites on the opposite bank. A bicycle lane runs along most of the route. The valley also has health spas and resorts for the recreation-minded. For maps and further information about the region, contact the tourist office in Stuttgart, Landesfremdenverkehrsverband, Bussenstr. 23, 7000 Stuttgart (phone: 48-1045).

En Route from Heidelberg – Neckargemünd, a 1,000-year-old town by the winding Neckar, features old inns such as *Zum Ritter* (Neckarstr. 40), with open-air terraces overlooking the valley. A church steeple rises over half-timbered houses and the old town hall. Neckargemünd also has the only parachute museum in Western Europe. From here Dilsberg is a short detour of 1.2 miles (2 km).

Dilsberg, a fortified hamlet high above the Neckar River, resisted Imperial General Tilly and his Bavarian men during the Thirty Years' War. The stout ramparts and lookout towers of this walled city are visible from both banks. If you park your car outside the town walls and enter the town on foot, you can explore the fortress, a mysterious subterranean tunnel, and the castle ruins (Burgruine). The tower (with almost 100 stairs) offers a panoramic view of the river. Return by the same route to Neckargemünd, take Route 37 to the north bank, and drive toward Neckarsteinach. You'll spot castle ruins on the ridge as you approach the town, which is 3 miles (5 km) from Neckargemünd.

NECKARSTEINACH: Also known as the Four Castles Corner (Vierburgeneck), this town boasts four medieval citadels built in the twelfth and thirteenth centuries. On the left side of Route 37, shortly before you reach the town, a parking area marks the start of a wooded trail that connects Vorderburg, Mittelburg, Hinterburg, and Shadeck castles. The walk takes about 45 minutes and ends in the town itself, not far from the parking area. On many summer evenings, the town holds the Four Castles Festival, in which the castles are illuminated and fireworks are exploded. Neckarsteinach's center is carefully preserved, so you may also want to stroll around the town. From here follow Route 37 to Hirschhorn, approximately 6 miles (10 km) away.

HIRSCHHORN: This town is dominated by its impressive castle fortress, *Hirschhorn Castle*, which is now a hotel and restaurant. The towered defenses were built in the twelfth century but the castle itself dates from the eighteenth century. For a small fee you can climb the 120 steps of the tower, which lead to a magnificent view of the sharp Hirschhorn bend in the river. Below the castle, the walled village still holds the remains of a deep moat. Historic Ersheimer Chapel is across the river; from there you can have a good view of the castle. From Hirschhorn continue up the north bank for about 7 miles (11 km) to Eberbach.

EBERBACH: This ancient imperial city has fortress ruins that date from the eleventh century. Four powerful towers attest to its medieval beginnings. The old Deutscher Hof, the medieval center of town, is alive with colorful inns, half-timbered houses, and cobbled streets. In the old market square, the town's eventful history is recorded in 14 scenes painted on a front wall of the *Karpfen Hotel.* You can see other engraved murals on the oldest inn in the city, the *Gasthaus zum Krabbenstein,* and at the Hay Market (Heumarkt).

After a walk in the old city, stop at the large red and white *Victoria Café* and choose from an immense assortment of confections, candies, and desserts. The town also has a health resort park, large forested reserves, indoor and outdoor swimming pools, and ring-tennis courts.

ZWINGENBERG: Continue on Route 37 for 7 miles (11 km) to Zwingenberg. Follow signs to the train station (Bahnhof) and park your car. A short distance up the road, a paved path leads to the Zwingenberg Castle, one of the most magnificent of the castles on the Castle Road. The interior of the residence of the Battenbergs, relatives of Britain's Prince Philip, is only open to the public from May 1 to September 30, Tuesdays, Fridays, and Sundays from 2 to 4:30 PM. The fortress has been undamaged by war and almost untouched by renovation. The lords of Zwingenberg, its first owners in the thirteenth century, supplemented their income by imposing customs fees on shipping on the Neckar River. Two more castle ruins — Stolzeneck and Minneburg — are on the opposite bank of the river.

NECKARZIMMERN: From Zwingenberg, drive on Route 37 to its junction with Route 27 at Neckarelz, a distance of about 10 miles (16 km). Then follow Route 27 a few miles to Neckarzimmern. Look for the sign for Burg Hornberg and follow the paved road to the left to the *Burg Hotel Hornberg* (*Hornberg Castle,* now a hotel).

Overlooking vineyards sloping to the river's bank, this castle was once the home of the Knight of the Iron Fist, Götz von Berlichingen, who wore an artificial hand after losing his right hand in the Bavarian War of 1504. For a small fee, you can explore the castle ruins, visit the museum with its medieval armor and implements, and climb the watchtower (almost 140 wooden steps) for a commanding view of the Neckar Valley. This castle was first mentioned in a document in 1184. Since that time it has changed hands several times; it has been sold, given away, and even pawned during its colorful history.

You may want to pause for a meal or a drink in the castle's former stable, now converted into a restaurant and bar. The windows of the restaurant look out over the valley, and you can sample wines that come from the slopes below.

NECKARMÜHLBACH: From Hornberg drive on Route 27 to Gundelsheim (an interesting historical town with its Castle of Horneck). At Gundelsheim, drive over the bridge across the Neckar and follow the marked road near Neckarmühlbach to Burg Guttenberg (Guttenberg Castle).

Dating from the twelfth century, this castle offers more than just historical and architectural interest. It also houses an extensive collection of live birds of prey, many uncaged, from throughout the world. Here, amidst the stately castle fortifications, stand eagles, vultures, and other predators. The birds entertain visitors during a show in which vultures swoop down over the heads of the audience.

The museum also displays historical remnants, such as a skillfully crafted Madonna, medieval books and documents, instruments of torture, woodcuts, engravings, copper etchings, jewelry, kitchenware, porcelain, and glass. An old spiral stairway takes you to the different floors of the museum and leads to a door marked "zum Turm" (to the tower). If you decide to climb the more than 100 steps to the open tower, you'll be rewarded with a sweeping view of the countryside.

From here, continue on the south side of the river to Bad Wimpfen.

BAD WIMPFEN: This royal city of the Castle Road was the imperial residence of the Hohenstaufens in the thirteenth century. The Upper Town (Bad Wimpfen am Berg), as the old part of Bad Wimpfen is called, is marked by the towers, spires, and red-tiled roofs that crown its half-timbered structures.

A short walking tour of the old section takes about an hour and is well worth it. You can see the town hall, market square, the Blue Tower, the picturesque house of Mayor

Elsesser, the Steinhaus (Romanesque, from about 1200), the imperial chapel, and the Red Tower, the emperor's refuge in times of danger. A walk down Klostergasse passes half-timbered houses with gardens, the Mansion of the Knights, and the former bath houses dating from 1543.

En Route from Bad Wimpfen – You can continue on the south bank of the Neckar to Heilbronn or cross the river to Route 27 and drive a short distance to Bad Friedrichshall, a spa town with salt mines. Here you can arrange a tour of the saltworks or visit the local castle-hotel, *Schloss Lehen* (Hauptstr. 2). Then drive along the north bank to Neckarsulm, a town that will interest automobile and motorcycle buffs. You can tour the NSU Automobile Factory weekdays at 10 AM and 2 PM or visit the Zweiradmuseum, housed in the former castle of the Teutonic Order. This exhibit shows the development of original models of bicycles and motorcycles. Follow either the north or south bank and you'll reach Heilbronn.

HEILBRONN: Set in the midst of forests and vineyards, this is one of Germany's major wine-producing towns. You can sample the fine wines at the Heilbronn Harvest, a traditional wine festival in early September; Wine Village, a festival centered around the city hall, also held in September; or at any time in any of Heilbronn's inns such as the *Insel* at Friedrich Ebert Brücke, on an island in the river.

Formerly a free imperial city, Heilbronn has many interesting buildings. The 1315 Tower of the Church of St. Kilian was Germany's first Renaissance structure. Also in the city's center, you can see the fifteenth-century city hall with its ornamental clock, made in 1580, and the fourteenth-century Gothic Käthchenhaus, a patrician dwelling in the market square.

En Route from Heilbronn – If you have additional time, you may want to continue along the Neckar, taking Route 27 on the north bank, for 32 miles (52 km) to Stuttgart, passing through gently rolling vineyards and small, picturesque medieval towns such as Lauffen, Kirchheim, and Besigheim. You may want to stroll along some of the streets in these old towns.

STUTTGART: A city of more than half a million people, Stuttgart is more than an industrial center. Besides Mercedes, Stuttgart is home of the highly acclaimed Stuttgart Ballet, as well as the State Opera and a Philharmonic Orchestra. Surrounded by the wooded Swabian Hills, Stuttgart has devoted two thirds of its land to green spots, including vineyards that are right in the vicinity of the business district and the main railroad station. It is also the capital of the federal state of Baden-Württemberg.

Enjoy the view of Stuttgart and the Swabian Jura from the Television Tower (Fernsehturm) south of the city on Bopser Hill. Built in 1956 from a unique design by Dr. Fritz Leonhardt, the tower has an observation platform and a good restaurant, the *Fernsehturm*. Then visit the old town where, on the Schillerplatz, you can see Stuttgart's castle, built in sixteenth-century Renaissance style with a courtyard surrounded by galleries. The castle now houses the Württemberg Regional Museum, which is devoted to regional history. Schillerplatz is also the site of a vegetable and flower market on Tuesdays, Thursdays, and Saturdays. Nearby, the ultramodern Rathaus is also of interest, with its Glockenspiel that plays folk songs.

The Stuttgart State Gallery (Neue Staatsgalerie), Konrad-Adenauer-Str. 30-32, houses a fine collection of paintings from the Middle Ages on; see especially the French paintings and the modern German Expressionist and Bauhaus works. The most popular museum here, however, is the Daimler-Benz Museum in the Mercedes-Benz plant in the suburb of Untertürkheim. Accessible by bus D from the bus station, it contains exhibits of cars, car engines, and other motors — racing car, boat, airplane, motorcycle — in addition to the history of the venerable old firm that dates from 1900.

Stuttgart is graced by parks, the most beautiful of which is Killesberg Park, set on a hill in the northern part of town. It's also known for its modern buildings, particularly the asymmetrical Liederhalle near the town center, designed in 1956 by Adolf Abel and

Rolf Gutbrod. The concrete exterior of the Liederhalle, containing three concert halls with excellent acoustics, is enlivened with mosaics, glazed brick, and quartz.

Stuttgart's tourist office is below the main railroad station at Arnulf Klett Passage (phone: 222-82-40). On Saturdays at 9:30 AM, free sightseeing tours leave from Schiller-platz.

TÜBINGEN: From Stuttgart it's 27 miles (43 km) to this lovely old university town. The University of Tübingen, founded in 1477, still uses the town's Renaissance castle, whose terraces, bastions, and gardens offer a fine view of the Neckar and the old town. Nearby is the Marktplatz, which is especially colorful on market days — Mondays, Wednesdays, and Fridays — when you can see local peasants in regional dress selling produce.

Don't miss the famous Platanenallee, an avenue of plane trees on a man-made island in the Neckar, a pleasant place both day and night. The Platanenallee may be reached by the Eberhard Bridge. Both the bridge and the island offer excellent views of the town, with its river, its old houses, and its willow trees.

BEST EN ROUTE

On this, Germany's Castle Road, hotels and inns — even those in the castles — are surprisingly reasonable. The most expensive places are in the larger cities such as Stuttgart. A double room with private bath, breakfast, tax, and service included in the price will cost $45 to $90 in hotels listed as expensive; $25 to $45 is moderate; and under $25 is inexpensive. Many of the restaurants along this route are in the hotels and inns; a dinner for two will cost $30 to $70 in an expensive restaurant, $20 to $30 is moderate, and below $20 is inexpensive.

NECKARGEMÜND

Zum Ritter – This charming inn has 41 rooms, a terrace with an extraordinary view, and a good restaurant. Neckarstr. 40 (phone: 70-35). Moderate.

HIRSCHHORN

Schloss-Hotel – A hilltop castle hotel with 8 rooms, it overlooks the Neckar River valley and the small town below. Dining facilities include indoor restaurants and an outdoor terrace with an excellent view. Accommodations in the guesthouse annex are less expensive than those in the castle. Auf Burg Hirschhorn (phone: 1373). Moderate.

NECKARZIMMERN

Burg Hornberg – Another, equally interesting, castle hotel high above the river, this place has 27 rooms and a terrace with a view of the river valley. The restaurant serves regional specialties (don't miss their mushrooms) and wines from the castle vineyards below. The atmosphere is informal (phone: 4064). Moderate.

NECKARMÜHLBACH

Burgschenke Terrace – This fine restaurant offers game dishes such as venison, good desserts, and local wines. The view of the valley is memorable. Burg Gutten-berg (phone: 06266-228). Moderate.

HEINSHEIM

Schloss Heinsheim – This baroque manor and guesthouse has its own palace chapel, swimming pool, estate gardens, and vineyard. Indoor and outdoor dining and a classic drawing room provide the final touches. It has excellent service, friendly atmosphere, and good food. In Heinsheim on the south bank, near Bad Wimpfen (phone: 1045). Moderate.

BAD FRIEDRICHSHALL

Schloss Lehen – A quiet, elegant house set back from the road, this hotel is surrounded by greenery and gardens. Built in the 1400s, it offers a homelike atmosphere and a good restaurant. Hauptstr. 2, on the edge of town on the north bank (phone: 7441). Moderate.

HEILBRONN

Insel – In the heart of the city, this 120-room hotel with its own park is actually on a small island in the middle of the Neckar. The modern hotel has a café terrace, a restaurant offering Swabian specialties, and a French restaurant. Most of its rooms have balconies. Friedrich Ebert Brücke (phone: 8-89-31). Expensive.

Wirtshaus zum Götzenturm – The idols' tower *(Götzenturm)* in the medieval city wall gave this restaurant its name. Try the fish and the local Württemberg wines. The owner also runs the *Beichtstuhl* wine cellar around the corner. Closed Sundays, Mondays after lunch, and in August. Allerheiligenstr. 1 (phone: 8-05-34). Expensive to moderate.

STUTTGART

Graf Zeppelin Hotel – Near the main railroad station, this hotel is the city's largest. It has an indoor swimming pool, sauna, health club, disco, and a pleasant dining room. Arnulf Klett Pl. 7 (phone: 29-98-81). Very expensive.

Schlosshotel Solitude – This 32-room hostelry is in what used to be a princely eighteenth-century rococo residence, opposite the Solitude Palace. Its old-world charm is further enhanced by a very good restaurant. Schloss Solitude (phone: 69-10-91). Expensive.

Alte Post – In a comfortable old tavern, this inn provides regional cuisine and seafood. Among the specialties are medallions of veal, filet of sole in lobster sauce, shrimp cocktail, and fresh oysters when in season. The service matches the high standards of the kitchen. Reservations suggested. Closed Sundays and early August. Friedrichstr. 43 (phone: 29-30-79). Expensive.

Goldener Adler – Regional Swabian dishes — maultaschen, spätzle, and fresh mussels — are the specialties of this downtown restaurant. Also, try a bottle of their Württemberg red wine. Böheinstr. 38 (phone: 64-17-62). Moderate.

TÜBINGEN

Krone – With tasteful traditional furnishings, modern facilities, and an international menu, this 55-room hotel fits well into the atmosphere of the old university town. Uhlandstr. 1 (phone: 3-1036). Expensive.

The Black Forest

The Black Forest (*Schwarzwald,* in German) lies in southern Germany, bounded roughly by a rectangle made from the cities of Rastatt, Basel, Schaffhausen, and Pforzheim. It is inappropriately named, as the forests are no darker or blacker here than any other forests in Germany; in fact, the whole area receives considerably more sunshine than the overall average for the rest of the country. It is a bright, open land of tree-covered mountains, rolling hills, and intermittent pine and birch forests. There are ski resorts and spas. The ordinary mountain towns are small, rustic, and colorful, often tucked away in valleys of stunning serenity and beauty. Some of the larger cities, such as Baden-Baden and Freiburg, are renowned as cultural centers, but many of the small towns are quaintly provincial in their outlook — in fact, some of the people still wear their regional costumes.

Throughout its history, the Black Forest region has clung tenaciously to its own identity. During the Thirty Years' War, the area passed from the hands of the Austrians to the French and then to the Bavarians. The French got it back again for a short time in 1679, then the Austrians returned in 1697, after which the area remained in the Austrian sphere of influence. It became part of the German duchy of Baden and the Kingdom of Württemberg in 1815. Now it's part of the state known as Baden-Württemberg. All of this turbulent history has given the Schwarzwalders a strong sense of their own identity; indeed, they revel in their own customs and manners.

There's hardly a section of the Black Forest that is lacking in beauty and charm. If you take the Autobahn from Basel to Baden-Baden, the distance is 102 miles (163 km); our incomparably more scenic byway climbs over the 4,898-foot Feldberg mountain peak and runs along the renowned Schwarzwälder Tälerstrasse (Rte. 294), just to name two of its highlights. The tour could be made in as little as one day, but you'll probably prefer to spend two or three.

To hurry through an area like the Schwarzwald is to miss such delights as staying in half-timbered little *Gasthäuser* (hotels) with warm smoky dining rooms where the locals drink their nightly beer and *Kirschwasser,* a fiery local distillation made from cherries. The speedy traveler would also miss such regional specialties as *Schwarzwälder Schinken,* a smoked ham sliced so thin it is transparent; or the luscious taste of fresh mountain trout, cooked in almonds, with heaps of boiled salted potatoes as the perfect side dish. Brochures, maps, and information about the region are available from the tourist office, Verkehrsgemeinschaft Hochschwarzwald, Goethestr. 7, D-7820 Titisee-Neustadt (phone: 5041).

En Route from Basel – Starting from the southwest corner of the Black Forest, near the Swiss border town of Basel, it is only a quick 5-minute drive north to Lörrach on Route 317. There are some interesting ruins above Lörrach called Burg Rötteln, and a new town museum has recently been opened, containing many fine examples of local Black Forest handiwork, such as woodcarving, clockmaking, and religious figurines.

Continuing on Route 317, it is a 25-mile (40-km) drive to the village of Todtnau, which is situated at an altitude of 1,968 feet. The air here is so clean and pure that Todtnau has been recommended as a resort for people with breathing afflictions. There are not many man-made attractions in the area, but there is still plenty to do. In the winter, the area is renowned for its skiing (both downhill and cross-country) and in the summer, the hikers come out in droves to tramp through the woods and valleys that make up the region surrounding the town. For summer visitors, there is also swimming (both indoor and outdoor pools available), miniature golf, and open-air concerts.

At Todtnau, the road splits, with Route 317 continuing east to Titisee via the route over the Feldberg, the highest mountain peak in the Black Forest (4,898 feet). This is a very scenic drive, well worth the time. The Feldberg offers the best skiing in the Black Forest, and during the summer the views from this mountain area are unequaled in the entire region.

As magnificent as the drive over the Feldberg may be, there is an equally attractive way to the city of Freiburg from the turnoff at Todtnau. The road is smaller and narrower, and closed in the winter, but the mountain scenery is superb. This is the Schauinsland Strasse, over the Schauinsland peak, which at 4,212 feet is one of the taller mountains in the Schwarzwald.

FREIBURG: Freiburg is a modern, bustling city of more than 170,000 people, yet it maintains its sense of old-world charm as surely as an aged *Schwarzwälderin* with her round *Bollenhut* on her head. Where else can you find a modern city that has the cleanest and most sparkling gutters in Europe, with fresh mountain water running through them continuously?

Freiburg was badly damaged during bombing raids in World War II, yet today all of the damage has been repaired and the famed cathedral, with its 386-foot-tall Gothic tower and spectacular stained-glass windows, is the equal of any European church. This is the only Gothic cathedral in Germany that was totally completed during the Middle Ages. (The cathedrals in both Cologne and Ulm were not finished until the nineteenth century.) Opposite the south side of the cathedral stands the sixteenth-century *Kaufhaus,* originally erected as a merchants' hall, but now used as a festival hall on special occasions. Its shocking color — a cross between blood red and gall-bladder yellow — only makes it stand out from the rest of the buildings in the Münsterplatz. Nearby is the Rathausplatz, which contains an unusual Rathaus (town hall), formed by joining two old patrician houses that stood beside each other. Other important sights in the city are the Haus zum Walfisch (Whalehouse) near the Rathaus and the Augustiner Museum (Augustinerpl.), which contains medieval and baroque art of the Upper Rhine region.

Freiburg is also known for its cozy little wine taverns, with many of them dispensing wine that has been grown and cultivated within the city limits. For a good local wine, try a Freiburger Schlossberg (though perhaps the best wine in the entire Baden region is made a few miles to the west in the village of Ihringen, where the Doktorgarten and Winklerberg are both considered excellent vineyards).

FURTWANGEN: From Freiburg it is a short drive along Route 31 to the turnoff for Route 500 (north). There are several scenic overlooks along this road, each one of them worth a stop. During the summer, the mountain valleys will be alive with little white and blue flowers, and the tiny villages, many of them nothing more than a handful of houses with barns attached, all seem too perfect to be real.

Furtwangen is worth a stop because of its excellent clock museum (Uhrensammlung), which is open daily from the beginning of April to the end of October. Here, virtually anything that can be made to tell time has been garnered into the museum and displayed. There are cuckoo clocks of every shape, size, and description, from a tiny clock that would fit into the palm of the hand and gives off a cuckoo like a canary with laryngitis to a monstrous old wall-hanger that has a cuckoo that still sounds like a canary with laryngitis. There are grandfather clocks, grandmother clocks, and clocks that are simply grand.

TRIBERG: Just before Route 500 winds its way down into Triberg, there is a turnoff with a magnificent view of the valley in which Triberg is set. This is also the entrance to the Triberger Waterfall, the highest waterfall in all of Germany at more than 500 feet. An interesting walk begins at the top of the waterfall and continues down the path beside it to the town of Triberg, a distance of about 3 miles (4.8 km), all on carefully manicured trails with handrails. Sections of the waterfall are beautiful, but don't expect anything on the scale of Niagara or Victoria falls: It simply is not that kind of waterfall.

Triberg itself is both pretty and interesting. No visitor should miss the Heimat-museum, a collection of local handicrafts and wood carvings. There is also a fine collection of clocks in the museum, and a room completely decorated with wood carving — walls, ceiling, benches, everything. Among the other sights in the museum is a collection of old mechanical musical instruments, including player pianos and an old pipe organ that still plays with the loudest racket imaginable. Children of all ages will be entranced by the moving characters in the mechanical band.

NIEDERWASSER: Just outside Triberg, Route 500 intersects Route 33 and continues north. There is an excellent restaurant in the tiny village of Niederwasser, the *Gasthaus Rössle.* Directly across the road from the restaurant is a gift shop selling everything from cuckoo clocks to hand-carved wooden plates, all at prices much lower than at the main tourist centers in Germany. The gift shop accepts major credit cards, a rarity in this part of Germany. Both the restaurant and the gift shop can hardly be missed, as they are the *only* things on the road near Niederwasser.

ALPIRSBACH: At Hausach, Route 500 intersects Route 294, the famous Schwarz-wälder Tälerstrasse, which continues on up to Freudenstadt. Along the way, it passes through the charming village of Alpirsbach, with its Benedictine monastery, built in the year 1095.

FREUDENSTADT: Freudenstadt has one of the most elegant new market squares in all of Germany. The original market square was destroyed during the war, but the reconstruction has been well done. Aside from the Marktplatz, there is little to see in Freudenstadt, but it is an excellent town for shopping for such things as clocks and wood carvings. There are also more than 560 miles of hiking trails leading through the woods and valleys around the town.

En Route from Freudenstadt – From Freudenstadt, there are two roads to Baden-Baden. One is called the Schwarzwälder Hochstrasse, or the High Road, and the other is the continuation of the Schwarzwälder Tälerstrasse, or the Low Road. Both are beautiful at any time of year, but the Hochstrasse probably has a slight edge in natural scenery; the Tälerstrasse is easier and smoother driving, with fewer curves and hills.

BADEN-BADEN: Baden-Baden is internationally famous for its casino and its baths, which have been in operation since Roman times. During the nineteenth century, this was the most famous spa in Europe and kings and emperors from the world over came here to gamble away their fortunes by night and nurse their hangovers the next day. Though royalty is no more, Baden-Baden remains one of the most exclusive resort towns in all of Europe.

The casino at Baden-Baden is one of the most formal and elegant in all of Europe. By all means visit the casino, with its crystal chandeliers and oh-so-deep carpets. James Bond would feel right at home here. Besides the casino, the castle, called the Neues Schloss, is worth a visit. Be sure to see Lichtentaler Allee, Baden-Baden's lovely and fashionable promenade along the Oos.

Baden-Baden is located directly beside the main A5 Autobahn, one of the major north-south arteries in Germany and from this point, the rest of the country can easily be reached in a few hours' time.

BEST EN ROUTE

Because it is an area of small towns, the Black Forest (except for Baden-Baden) is generally less expensive than many other parts of Germany. A double room with breakfast will cost $55 to $90 in expensive hotels; $30 to $55, moderate; and below $30, inexpensive. A dinner for two without wine runs $30 to $60 in expensive restaurants; $20 to $30, moderate; and $10 to $20, inexpensive.

FREIBURG

Colombi Hotel – Near the old city, opposite a park is Freiburg's top hotel, with fine service, a comfortable and inviting lobby, a good restaurant, and a popular wine tavern. Many rooms have balconies. Rotteckring 16 (phone: 3-1415). Expensive.

Kühler Krug – Don't miss this small gem whose menu features both French and regional specialties. Chef/owner Wolfgang Stolz offers pleasantly personal attention to his guests. Closed Thursdays. Reservations recommended. Torpl. 1 (phone: 2-91-03). Expensive to moderate.

Oberkirch's Weinstuben – This is the place for regional cooking (and comfortable guest rooms in the hotel as well). It's on a little square adjoining the lovely old *Kaufhaus*. The restaurant is an old, dark-paneled place with rustic wooden chairs. Try game dishes here: pheasant, wild boar, deer, and rabbit — all deliciously prepared. Closed Sundays. Münsterpl. 22 (phone: 3-1011). Moderate.

Zum Roten Bären – Directly on the Schwabentor, the old gate that still guards the entrance to the city, this is one of the oldest Gasthäuser in Germany, founded in 1120. Its charming old-world rooms and its excellent food at moderate prices are hard to beat. Closed Sundays. Oberlinden 12 (phone: 3-6913). Moderate.

FURTWANGEN

Hotel Ochsen – This is a quiet place to spend the night, with good simple rooms, inexpensive food, and truly gargantuan portions. Marktpl. 7 (phone: 7813). Moderate.

TRIBERG

Park Hotel Wehrle – In a lovely park, the *Wehrle*, one of the finest hotels in the Black Forest, offers fine service, a swimming pool, sauna, solarium, and an excellent restaurant known for its trout dishes (20 different ones are listed on the menu). It has comfortable period furniture and lots of atmosphere. Major credit cards. Marktpl. (phone: 4081). Expensive to moderate.

NIEDERWASSER

Gasthaus Rössle – In a tiny village, this excellent and reasonably priced restaurant specializes in *Rinderroulade* (small rolls of beef in a tasty brown sauce) and tender veal steaks served with fresh peas and carrots. Closed Wednesdays (phone: 392). Inexpensive.

ALPIRSBACH

Hotel Löwen Post – In the marketplace of a charming village, this is a comfortable and pleasant hotel for overnight guests. Good restaurant. Marktpl. 12 (phone: 2393). Inexpensive.

FREUDENSTADT

Kurhotel Sonne am Kurpark – This small hotel, set in a park opposite the spa center, not only has comfortable accommodations but also boasts one of the Black Forest's best restaurants, featuring regional dishes. Turnhallestr. 63 (phone: 6044). Expensive to moderate.

BADEN-BADEN

Brenners Parkhotel – One of Germany's most luxurious hotels, it's very expensive but worth it. Here kings, celebrities, and Arab sheiks stay. It has everything — indoor and outdoor pools, a fine restaurant, gracious service, public areas with river views, music, dancing, miniature golf, and riding. Solidly booked in season. Schiller Str. 6 (phone: 3530). Very expensive.

The Romantic Road

The so-called Romantic Road (Romantische Strasse) runs south through Bavaria, from the imperial city of Würzburg on the Main River to the mountain frontier town of Füssen in the foothills of the snow-clad Bavarian Alps. It is romantic, not for any dramatic scenery on the road itself, which traverses gentle, wooded hills and quiet valleys, but for its glorious medieval towns, some of which are 2,000 years old, and many of which have survived much as they appeared in the Middle Ages.

The wealth of sights along this route almost defies belief. In Würzburg and some of the other towns a visitor can see the incomparable works of Tilman Riemenschneider, Master of Würzburg, a sixteenth-century Gothic wood-carver and sculptor with a very distinctive style. There's Rothenburg ob der Tauber, Germany's best preserved medieval city, with its walls, fountains, and gabled patrician houses, and Augsburg, once the richest city in Europe, with elegant avenues, lovely fountains, and mansions of the rich, as well as what is probably the world's oldest extant housing project for the poor, dating from 1519. Also not to be missed are the Wies Church, the rococo masterpiece of Dominikus Zimmermann, set in the midst of meadows, and Germany's two most magnificent castles, called the Royal Castles. During the summer, the area hosts folk festivals, open-air operas, concerts in royal palaces, and traditional centuries-old plays.

This 215-mile (344-km) route begins in Würzburg, taking Route 27 south to Tauberbischofsheim, Route 290 to Bad Mergentheim, and Route 19 to Igersheim. It follows the Tauber River through Weikersheim and Creglingen to Rothenburg, then takes Route 25 through central Bavaria, shifts to Route 2 to Augsburg and Route 17 to Füssen in the Alpine foothills.

Although much of the route follows principal highways, some portions are on small, winding, two-way roads that pass through tiny villages. Look out for signs, because the route is not always clearly marked. In the towns, narrow, cobblestoned streets make driving difficult, so you may want to look for a parking area (marked with a large, white *P* on a blue background), and then walk into the old city areas. Since there aren't many gas stations along this route, don't let your gas get too low.

For information and maps of the region, contact the tourist office in Nürnberg: Fremdenverkehrsverband, Franken, Postfach 269, 8500 Nürnberg 81 (phone: 26-42-02).

WÜRZBURG: Set amid the vine-clad hills of the Franconian wine country, this is Germany's outstanding baroque city. Though bombed heavily during World War II, it has been completely restored. Würzburg, which remained staunchly Catholic throughout the Reformation, is known as the "city of the Madonnas," for more than

300 statues of the Virgin stand in front of its houses. The early history of the town was dominated by the prince-bishops who lived there, first in the Marienberg Fortress and later in the Residenz, both of which are still standing. Würzburg is also famous for its art treasures, most of which are the creations of two men: the sixteenth-century Gothic sculptor, Tilman Riemenschneider, known as the Master of Würzburg, and the eighteenth-century German baroque architect, Balthasar Neumann, court architect to the prince-bishops.

The fortress and the palace, on opposite banks of the Main River, are still the major sights in the city. High above the town is the Marienberg Fortress, which now houses the fine Franconian Museum of the Main (Mainfränkisches Museum), with its extraordinary sculptures by the Master of Würzburg. Near the fortress is the Käppele, a baroque chapel with rococo decorations and a lovely view of the town, the river, and the fortress. Cross the old bridge (Mainbrücke), dating from the fifteenth century and decorated with statues of 11 saints, to the Residenz, where you can see the court gardens, the imperial hall (Kaisersaal), the church (Hofkirche), and the grand staircase (Treppenhaus). You might also want to see the Cathedral of St. Kilian, a Romanesque church with sculptures by Riemenschneider, and such secular baroque buildings as Zum Falken House; both are near the Marktplatz on the palace side of the river.

While in this city, stop in one of the restaurants or wine taverns offering Franconian wine and *Mainfischli* (little fish from the Main River).

TAUBERBISCHOFSHEIM: This lovely little town with a 1,200-year history has several focal points: the Palace of the Prince Electors of Mainz, the Manor House and watchman's tower, the double Gothic Chapel of St. Sebastian, and the baroque Church of St. Lioba. Half-timbered buildings and baroque courtyards lend this valley township the tranquil atmosphere of the past. From here drive 11 miles (18 km) on Route 290 to Bad Mergentheim.

BAD MERGENTHEIM: This small town is both a spa resort community and a historical center. The Order of Teutonic Knights was headquartered in the magnificent Renaissance Mergentheim Palace from 1525 until they were dispossessed by Napoleon in 1809. Founded in 1128, during the Crusades, this religious and military order wielded considerable political power in the surrounding area. You might want to take a look at the palace with its noteworthy baroque church that was redesigned by Balthasar Neumann during the eighteenth century.

En Route from Bad Mergentheim – Continue for 9 miles (14 km) to Weikersheim, where the Renaissance castle of the Princes of Hohenlohe is worth a stop for its remarkable sixteenth- to eighteenth-century furniture, tapestries, porcelain, and sculptures of emperors and empresses. Continue from Weikersheim about another 9 miles (14 km) to Creglingen and its Church of Our Lord (Herrgottskirche), about a half-mile outside the town on the Blaufelden Road. This little church in the countryside, completed in 1389, contains many art treasures, among them the masterpiece of woodcarver Tilman Riemenschneider (the sixteenth-century Gothic Master of Würzburg), the altar of the Virgin Mary. It's 14 miles (23 km) from here to Rothenburg. To get in the right mood for this medieval walled town, park outside the walls and walk through a gate into the medieval fortress.

ROTHENBURG: Overlooking the steep, beautiful Tauber River valley, Rothenburg ob der Tauber is the best preserved example of a medieval town in Germany. This one-time imperial residence has remained intact largely because it failed to recover from the Thirty Years' War, so it is still a typical sixteenth-century town, its old gabled houses retaining their steep Gothic roofs and oriel windows. Its huge encircling fortress walls and watchtowers are straight out of a fairy tale, and the town inside the walls is intriguingly medieval as well, with its narrow, cobbled streets and graceful, flowing fountains. Historical inns here display skillfully crafted wrought-iron signs, and horse-drawn carriages still carry visitors through the central area of the city.

According to legend, Rothenburg was saved from destruction during the Thirty Years' War by the drinking prowess of its leading citizen. When Tilly, commander of the Imperial Army, threatened to destroy the town, the burgomaster, Nusch, offered him a cup of the best local wine, after which Tilly agreed to spare the town if someone could quaff 6 pints all at once. Nusch obliged, and this tale is re-enacted seven times a day when the clock ȯn the *City Councillors' Tavern (Ratstrinkstube)* strikes 11 AM, noon, and 1, 2, 3, 9, and 10 PM. The doors on each side of the clock open to reveal two figures — a disbelieving General Tilly watching the town mayor empty a more than 3-liter bumper of wine in one draught.

The town hall, also in the market square, has two sections, one of which is fourteenth-century Gothic and the other seventeenth-century Renaissance. You can climb its tower for a spectacular view of the city fortifications, which are shaped like a wine goblet. From the town hall you can walk to the Herrngasse, the widest street in the city, which begins at the market square. The Herrngasse is lined with stately patrician houses, which are decorated with a variety of gables. It's a short walk to the city's oldest and mightiest gate tower, the Burgtor, which leads into the Burggarten, a lovely public garden with a view of the Tauber bend, the curious medieval two-tier bridge called the Topplerschlösschen, and the village of Detwang.

Within the city's walls, countless streets and alleyways beckon you to explore shops, galleries, restaurants, taverns, and museums.

There's a festival here at Whitsuntide (seven Sundays after Easter) and in September, but throughout the year the local community sponsors cultural events, concerts, and historical plays. Information about such events is usually posted in the market square. There is much to see and do in Rothenburg, so that this is a good place to spend at least one night.

En Route from Rothenburg – Drive 19 miles (31 km) on Route 25 to Feuchtwangen, where you might want to see the excellent Heimatmuseum, with its fine folklore collection including Franconian costumes, crafts, and furniture. From here it's 8 miles (13 km) to Dinkelsbühl.

DINKELSBÜHL: Here we have yet another beautifully preserved medieval city, complete with walls, towers, and gateways — all mirrored dreamily in the green waters of the town moat.

This is a sleepy sixteenth-century town, except during a week-long festival in mid-July known as Children's Treat (Kinderzeche). The festival celebrates the children of the town, who during the Thirty Years' War induced the Swedish invaders to let Dinkelsbühl be. During the summer months there is also an outdoor theater, performances by the Dinkelsbühl Boys' Band, and a night watchman who makes his rounds.

You might want to wander around the old town, with its unpaved medieval streets lined with fifteenth- and sixteenth-century houses, which are decorated with hand-carved signs and with flowers hanging from their balconies. Segringer Strasse and Nördlinger Strasse are particularly interesting, as is the Deutsches Haus on Martin Luther Strasse with its elaborate Renaissance decorations. St. George's Cathedral, in the center of town, is a fifteenth-century Gothic structure with remarkable carvings and a Romanesque tower. It's about 19 miles (31 km) from here to Nördlingen on Route 25.

NÖRDLINGEN: Known as the living medieval city, this fortified town has retained not only its ancient buildings and city walls, but medieval customs and costumes as well. In the Rübenmarkt in the center of this circle-shaped town, local peasants still wear traditional dress on market days. The town is completely encircled by roofed parapet walks which pass the wall's many towers and gates. A watchman still surveys the town, calling out at night from the top of the tower of the late-Gothic Church of St. George. The fifteenth-century church, with its tower of volcanic rock and its lavishly decorated interior, is worth seeing; its lovely painted altarpiece by Friedrich Herlin, however, is in the local museum.

En Route from Nördlingen – It's 11 miles (18 km) to Harburg, where a castle stands guard over a lovely hamlet on the Wörnitz River. The Harburg Castle is worth a stop for the art treasures in its museum — illuminated manuscripts, engravings, Gothic tapestries, and wood carvings by the incomparable Riemenschneider.

At Donauwörth, yet another medieval town 6 miles (10 km) farther, the Wörnitz River meets the Danube; here our route continues along the Lech River on Route 2 for the 27 miles (43 km) to Augsburg.

AUGSBURG: Historical buildings of every style and epoch grace this, Bavaria's third largest city, the oldest on the Romantic Road. Founded in 15 BC, Augsburg was a Roman provincial capital for 450 years and a free imperial city for 500 years. Two fabulously wealthy families dominated Augsburg during the fifteenth and sixteenth centuries, making it a major trading and banking center. The Fuggers, financiers of the Hapsburg dynasty, wielded enormous power and influence; the Welsers once owned most of Venezuela.

During and after its Renaissance heyday, Augsburg attracted artists and humanists. Both Holbeins were born here as was the architect Elias Holl, who created the town hall (1620) and other Renaissance-style buildings. Later, Leopold Mozart, father of the great composer, was born here, and his house still stands as a museum (Frauentorstr. 30; phone: 324-2898).

Start at the huge town hall; in front is the impressive Fountain of Augustus, created in 1594. Walk south on the beautiful, wide Maximilianstrasse, the town's main street, decorated with fountains and lined with mansions built by the wealthy Renaissance burghers. Behind the lovely Hercules Fountain is the very attractive Church of St. Ulrich and St. Afra, built in 1500. Since the 1555 Peace of Augsburg between German Catholics and Protestants, it has contained a Catholic and a Protestant church.

Also worth seeing is the town cathedral, north of the town hall, which has eleventh-century bronze doors, the oldest stained-glass windows in Germany (twelfth century), and paintings by Holbein the Elder. The Schaezler Palace (Maximilianstr. 46) contains a magnificently decorated rococo banqueting hall and displays works by such German masters as Hans Holbein the Elder and Dürer, and by non-Germans such as Rembrandt, Rubens, and Veronese. Take a look at the Fuggerei, east of the town center, a housing project for the poor, built by the Fugger family in 1519, and still in operation today; it includes 4 gates, a church, 8 streets, and 66 gabled houses.

For further information about Augsburg, whose attractions we have only begun to enumerate, contact the tourist office, Verkehrsverein (Bahnhofstr. 7; phone: 3-6024).

En Route from Augsburg – Continue on Route 17 to Landsberg, a distance of about 24 miles (39 km), where there are many works of the rococo (eighteenth-century) master architect Dominikus Zimmermann, including the Rathaus, the Johanniskirche, and the Ursulinenkirche. See the lovely Hauptplatz (main square) with its fountain and the 1425 Bavarian Gate (Bayertor) with its turrets and sculptures.

Continuing toward Füssen on Route 17, don't miss the short detour at Wies to see the marvelous Wies Church, acknowledged as the greatest achievement of rococo art in Germany, the work of Dominikus Zimmermann. Set in the meadows, surrounded by woods, this magnificently ornamented structure was so lovingly built between 1746 and 1754, that Zimmermann spent the last 10 years of his life nearby, unwilling to leave his finest creation. The simple exterior stands in marked contrast to the rich interior with its oval cupola, elaborate wood carvings, paintings, frescoes, and gilt work — all beautifully lit by many well-situated windows. Time has taken its toll, however, and for the next two years, the church will be closed for renovation.

SCHWANGAU: Near this small town just 2 miles (3 km) east of Füssen are the two most impressive castles in all Germany, Hohenschwangau and Neuschwanstein, called the Royal Castles (Königsschlösser). Originally a twelfth-century castle, Hohenschwangau was restored in 1832–36 by Maximilian II of Bavaria, father of King Ludwig II, "mad king Ludwig," who grew up here, befriended Richard Wagner, and later created the far more extravagant Neuschwanstein in 1886.

Hohenschwangau is in neo-Gothic style, furnished with cherry and maple Biedermeier furniture and decorated with many heavy royal art objects, including a piano on which Wagner played. Neuschwanstein was designed to look like a fairy tale, with its gables, turrets, and pinnacles, perched on a hill overlooking the forests and lakes of the Füssen region. Many of its interiors are made to recall Wagner operas, including an artificial stalactite grotto straight out of *Tannhäuser*. Furnishings are so fabulous as to appear unreal, with tapestries, carvings, chandeliers, gilt, and marble — all on a grand scale. Unfortunately King Ludwig lived here only 102 days before he committed suicide.

FÜSSEN: This mountain frontier town, once the summer residence of the Augsburg bishops, includes a palace and church situated high above the River Lech. The majestic wall of Alps behind the town provides a fitting setting for this spa and winter-sports resort. The medieval stone buildings of the town lend a picturesque quality to this, the final stop on the Romantic Road. From here, if you wish, you can cross through mountain passes into the Austrian portion of the Alps.

BEST EN ROUTE

Even though the Romantic Road is very popular with tourists, its hotel and restaurant prices are rather reasonable by West German standards. Rooms with baths are often much more costly then those without. Prices quoted here are for a double room, with bath, breakfast, VAT, and service included. On this route, expensive hotels will charge $45 to $85; moderate prices are $25 to $45; and inexpensive is $15 to $25.

A dinner for two will cost $30 to $60 in an expensive restaurant; $20 to $30 in a moderate one; and below $20 in an inexpensive place. Note that many of the restaurants on this route are in the hotels and inns and are described in the hotel listing.

WÜRZBURG

Rebstock – Once a palace, now a modern hotel with more than 80 rooms, the *Rebstock* has a neoclassic facade and is furnished with a harmonious mixture of traditional and modern pieces. It has an attractive terrace, two restaurants, and comfortably furnished rooms. Neubaustr. 7 (phone: (5-0075). Expensive.

Wein und Fischhaus Schiffbäuerin – This fine fish and wine restaurant is on a narrow side street. Fish specialties include eel, perch, pike, and blue carp — all priced by weight. Katzengasse 7 (phone: 4-2487). Moderate to inexpensive.

ROTHENBURG OB DER TAUBER

Eisenhut – A colorful, historical inn, this luxurious 86-room hotel is actually made up of medieval patrician houses joined together. This is also Rothenburg's top restaurant with prices to match. Excellent international cuisine and wine can be enjoyed in the richly paneled, galleried dining hall or on the garden terrace overlooking the Tauber River. Try the trout specialties in season. Closed in January and February. Herrngasse 3–5 (phone: 2041). Expensive.

Goldener Hirsch – In a quaint section of the city, this 80-room hotel is a remake of a seventeenth-century inn. A comfortable hotel with traditional taste and good service, it features the *Blue Terrace (Blaue Terrasse)* restaurant with a panoramic view of the river valley. Untere Schmiedgasse 16 (phone: 2051). Expensive.

Burg Hotel – A large half-timbered house on the old city wall, this hotel also offers a good view, though at less expensive prices than the hotels listed above. It's charmingly set in a small garden with a pool, is attractively decorated, and offers friendly service. Klostergasse 1 (phone: 5037). Expensive to moderate.

Baumeisterhaus – Right off the marketplace in a patrician residence built in 1596, this restaurant has a beautiful courtyard, good German food, and reasonable prices. Obere Schmiedgasse 3 (phone: 3404). Moderate.

Ratsstube – Also on the marketplace and very popular, this tavern-style restaurant features such regional dishes as blood sausages with sauerkraut and Bavarian mixed grill. Don't miss the white asparagus dishes in season (May–June). Marktpl. 6 (phone: 3404). Inexpensive.

BAD MERGENTHEIM

Kurhotel Victoria – This spa hotel with 100 rooms has bath, massage, and swimming facilities, and a restaurant specializing in diet meals for the overweight. You can dine on the attractive garden terrace on the roof, where there is a heated, glassed-in swimming pool. Rooms have baths and glassed-in balconies. Poststr. 2 (phone: 5930). Moderate.

DINKELSBÜHL

Deutsches Haus – A half-timbered house dating from 1440, this 13-room historical inn, decorated with richly painted designs and wood carvings, is elegantly furnished. Its restaurant serves local specialties. Closed in January and February. Weinmarkt 3 (phone: 2346). Moderate.

Goldene Rose – In the heart of town, this pretty, six-story inn dates from 1450. The 20 rooms are modernized though furnished with antiques, and the hotel offers a homey atmosphere at a reasonable rate. It also has a good restaurant. Closed January 1 to mid-March. Marktpl. 4 (phone: 2276). Moderate. ·

NÖRDLINGEN

Sonne – Next to the town hall and the cathedral, this old-world inn, which has been in existence since 1477, has been modernized. It offers 40 comfortable rooms, good service, and a choice of dining rooms. Restaurant closed Fridays. Marktpl. 3 (phone: 5067). Moderate.

AUGSBURG

Drei Mohren Hotel – Combining contemporary with traditional décor, this rebuilt 110-room hotel, famous since 1723, was destroyed in an air raid in 1945. It still offers first-class accommodations. Its formal dining room serves international cuisine and features such specialties as venison and filet of sole with white wine sauce. It also has an attractive garden terrace. Maximilianstr. 40 (phone: 51-00-31). Expensive.

Zum Alten Fischertor – This new restaurant is one of Augsburg's finest. Nouvelle cuisine reigns supreme here. Try the duck with shrimp and avocado cream or the calf's liver with mushrooms. The wines and the service are equally topnotch. Reservations suggested. Closed most of July. Pfärrle 14 (phone: 51-86-62). Expensive.

Gunzenlee – Six miles (10 km) southeast of town, this restaurant has an extensive international menu. The charcoal-grill meats are one of the best bets. In warm weather you can dine on a pleasant garden terrace. Kissing, Münchner Str. 14 (phone: 6139). Moderate.

Ratskeller – This town hall restaurant has particularly good, solid German food at reasonable prices. Closed Mondays, Sunday evenings, and in June. Rathauspl. 2 (phone: 51-78-48). Inexpensive.

Fuggerkeller – Noted not only for its setting — vaulted, cavelike rooms below street level in the former Fugger residence — but also for its fine food and drink. The strong, dark Fugger beer is an experience. Closed Sundays after lunch and in August. Maximilianstr. 38 (phone: 51-62-60). Moderate to inexpensive.

HOHENSCHWANGAU

Schlosshotel Lisl and Jägerhaus – Near the two royal castles, this 50-room hotel is comfortable and offers a spectacular view. The graciously styled hotel has a terrace and is surrounded by its own gardens. Its dining rooms serve local and international foods. Closed January and February. Neuschwansteinstr. 1 (phone: 8-1006). Moderate.

FÜSSEN

Hirsch – This 48-bed hotel, centrally located, has a large restaurant. Closed from December to mid-February. Schulhausstr. 4 (phone: 6055). Moderate.

Sonne – Also in the center of Füssen, this hotel has 32 comfortable, rustic rooms and a café. Reichenstr. 37 (phone: 6061). Moderate.

Kurhaus Pulverturm – Located in the idyllic spa center, it serves both Continental and regional dishes. You can also dine on the pleasant terrace. Closed in November. Schwedenweg 1 (phone: 6078). Moderate to inexpensive.

Exploring Gibraltar

The expression "steady as the Rock of Gibraltar" hardly holds true for most visitors to "Gib," as this British Crown Colony is affectionately called by its 29,000 inhabitants. After disembarking from the boat ride to the Rock, your knees are still likely to shake from the vessel's vibration, giving the impression that Gib is none too steady. Most Spaniards would be quick to agree — not because it's true, but because Gib is a thorn in their national pride. The reasons for this go back 265 years to the Treaty of Utrecht, which ended the War of Succession between rival French and Anglo-Dutch pretenders to the Spanish throne. At that time, Bourbon King Philip V gained the crown of Spain but was forced to cede Gibraltar to England. To this day, Spaniards will find every fault with the present British rule of the Rock and insist that Gibraltar will not be steady again until returned to its rightful owners. The issue over tiny Gibraltar became so bitter that the one point of entry, over an isthmus between La Linea on the Spanish mainland and the Rock itself, was closed for a number of years to all vehicular and pedestrian traffic. And that's quite a controversy when you consider the size of the place — 3 miles long and ¾ mile wide.

On February 4, 1985, Spain reopened its border with Gibraltar, making it vastly easier on travelers who, until then, had to take a ferry or hydrofoil from Málaga or Algeciras to Tangiers, then ferry from the North African port across the Strait of Gibraltar. The crossing took 1½ hours.

Regardless of the complications, however, Gibraltar attracts plenty of foreign visitors. All purchases are duty and tax free, so many people come here just to shop. Others come to bask in the sun: Gibraltar has a mild climate throughout the year, as does the southern Spanish coast. There are yachting marinas, other water facilities, and deep-sea fishing. And, in addition to the historic interest, Gibraltar's very British atmosphere exists in striking contrast to the neighboring Spanish communities and the Moroccan cities across the Strait. Bobbies direct traffic down narrow streets to the right, as in England. The Union Jack flies over photographs of the queen that are emblazoned with the slogan: "Keep the Rock British." Gib is very much a part of the British Empire.

Conflict over who owns the Rock goes back many centuries. In the year 711, the Moorish King Tarik ibn Ziyad landed on the Rock and gave his name to the promontory that was to be the stepping-off point of his invasion of Spain. The pronunciation of Jabal al Tariq (Tarik's Mountain) was modified over the six centuries of Moorish rule to become "Gibraltar." Queen Isabel herself personally led Christian troops to capture Gibraltar in 1462 as part of her strategy to weaken the Moors' supply route from nearby Morocco and definitively reconquer all of Spain. The Peñón de Gibraltar, or Rock of

Gibraltar, was an integral part of peninsular Spain until the early eighteenth century when the Rock was ceded to England following the War of Succession. During the Great Siege of 1779–82, the Strait of Gibraltar was the battleground of rival European navies. As proved by the Battle of Trafalgar, the British fleet led by Admiral Nelson was far superior to the Hispano-French armadas, and Gibraltar was retained by the victorious British.

The border was finally closed in 1969 by Francisco Franco after a last attempt to seize the Rock. And each year since then the Spanish Ambassador to the United Nations issues a strong protest against the British colonial "occupation" of a territorial possession of Spain. Each year, the matter reaches a diplomatic stalemate that seems to bemuse everybody involved except the Spaniards. The countries of the NATO Pact repeatedly veto the annual attempt to challenge British control over the vitally strategic air and naval bases that are located on the Rock of Gibraltar. However, with the reopening of the border in 1985, British and Spanish diplomats began talks to determine Gibralter's future — whether it will remain a colony of Britain, reunite with Spain, or even achieve independence. In any event, the major attraction in Gibraltar is unquestionably the Rock itself, followed by Gibraltar Town, the capital and only city of the Crown Colony.

THE ROCK OF GIBRALTAR: Surging from the sea to a height of 1,400 feet, the Rock looms up like some familiar life insurance company's advertisement. Originally, the Romans believed the Rock to be one of the two Pillars of Hercules, the entryway to the Mare Nostrum (literally, "Our Sea," or the Mediterranean) and gateway to Western civilization. Beyond the pillars to the west was the Unknown, the end of the world. What was unknown has long since passed into the domain of knowledge, and you can gaze upon it by taking a cable car to the summit of the Rock. The view on a clear day extends north to Granada's Sierra Nevada, south to the glimmering Strait of Gibraltar, and beyond to the Atlas and Rif mountains of Morocco.

Halfway up the hill, the Barbary Apes' Den is the home of the only wild simians of Europe. The mystery surrounding the presence of these tailless monkeys on the Rock has given rise to several theories. The one most generally accepted is that the monkeys found subterranean caves in Morocco and followed the passageways 10 miles under the Strait to emerge on Gibraltar. Recent legend has it that as long as the monkeys stay, the Rock will remain British. In any event, by order of Sir Winston Churchill some years ago, the apes were declared a protected species. A word of warning for your own protection: Do not feed the apes — they are fond of human fingers.

At another ridge of the Rock, the ruins of the fourteenth-century Tower of Homage are a reminder of the original Moorish castle overlooking this strategic strait. The Tower can be reached via winding Willis' Road; inexpensive minibus tours of the Rock leave from Gibraltar Town or cars can be rented. When hiring a car, be advised that traffic stays to the left. Since horn blowing is forbidden, it is customary to pound on the side of the car to warn other drivers of your approach or to signal danger.

GIBRALTAR TOWN: The capital has three movie houses, one museum containing intact Moorish baths, several nightclubs, and a casino. The township attempts to maintain constant contact with distant Britain.

The Week of the Sea sailing competitions lure plane loads of English visitors every summer, as do the July concert festivals. Shoppers always crowd Gibraltar Town's Main Street to take advantage of duty-free prices on brand-name and luxury items or to barter for Moroccan handicrafts at the Oriental bazaars.

THE GALLERIES: Northeast of town, farther up Queen's Road, are the galleries. Carved out of the Rock by the British during the Great Siege and expanded by Allied engineers during World War II, some sections of the 30 miles of tunnels can be visited today. Labyrinths winding 370 feet deep remain off-limits to civilians.

THE CAVES OF ST. MICHAEL: First explored in 1936, these caves are testimony to the extraordinary geological formation of Gibraltar. Located 1,000 feet above sea level, they feature an underground lake, an amphitheater bedecked with wonderfully illuminated stalactites, and an eerie subterranean breeze that could well come from Africa. The Sound and Light spectacle is thrilling, as is the drive to the caves, up steep Queen's Road, to the southwest of Gibraltar Town.

BEACHES: The best swimming and fishing spots are at Catalán Bay, a village first founded by Italian immigrants on the Mediterranean side of the Rock. Other Mediterranean swimming sites are Eastern Beach and Sandy Bay. On the Atlantic side, the best beaches are Camp Bay and the Montague Bathing Pavilion.

EUROPA POINT: Marking the very tip of continental Europe, this is a good spot to view Africa, to the south. The lighthouse of Our Lady of Europe, dating to 1838, guides mariners to safe port. Driving back to Gibraltar Town along Europa Road, stop off at the Alameda Gardens, which has an open-air theater and miniature golf course.

BEST EN ROUTE

Expect to pay about $45 for a double room at either hotel and between $30 and $40 for a meal for two at the *Rock Hotel*. The pubs are inexpensive, about $10 for two.

Holiday Inn – All of the well-equipped rooms command a view of the sea. Other facilities include a rooftop pool, sauna, dining room, and coffee shop. Airport transportation is provided and pets are welcome. Major US credit cards accepted. St. Governor's Parade (phone: 7050). Expensive.

Rock Hotel – A 3-day minimum stay is required at this older hotel. Some of the comfortable rooms have balconies overlooking the Mediterranean. There is a saltwater pool and a playground on the premises. The dining room is quite modern and features international, predominantly European cuisine. Roast beef with Yorkshire pudding is on the menu. 3 Europa Rd. (phone: 3456). Expensive.

Main Street pubs – Too numerous to list individually, these most British of establishments are the best places to eat in Gibraltar. They have English beers, such as Watney's Red and Guinness, plus a full complement of munchies — Scotch eggs, sausages, and cheese. Main St. 9 (no phones). Inexpensive.

Exploring Great Britain

The term "Great Britain" properly refers to an island rather than to the nation that is officially named the United Kingdom of Great Britain and Northern Ireland. Included in the United Kingdom is the entire island of Great Britain — which comprises England, Scotland, and Wales — as well as the northeastern tip of the island of Ireland, which lies to the west of Great Britain across the Irish Sea. Although the Scots, the Welsh, and the Irish continue to maintain very distinct national characters, the English, whose land is the largest of the four, have dominated and controlled the others for many centuries. Wales and Ireland were joined to England by the end of the thirteenth century, and the English and Scottish thrones were united in 1603 in the person of James I of England, who was also James VI of Scotland. To a great extent, the history of Great Britain is the history of England, which was the world's greatest power from the mid-eighteenth century until the end of World War II.

It is now clear that Britannia no longer rules the waves, and the English have been adjusting to that hard fact for the last 30 years. Like the Romans, who also once dominated most of the world, the English possess a genius for government. Since 1215, when the nobles forced King John to sign the Magna Carta, English rulers have wisely recognized the rights of their subjects. With no written constitution, the complicated British system of Common Law has also long contained safeguards for individual liberties. Above all, the English system is stable, and its revered institutions and traditions have survived the vicissitudes of history with a single brief civil war. Since revolution just isn't the English way, the people have incorporated changes into their existing institutions by yielding certain rights to the nobles in 1215, to Parliament in 1660, to the middle class in 1832, and to the working class in 1867. Characteristically, the English never abandoned their aristocracy as the French and others did; instead, they kept augmenting its ranks by admitting new wealthy or accomplished men to the peerage.

English people are known for their reserve. Foreigners have viewed them as silent, cold, morose, melancholy, or just plain snobbish. Many writers, English and foreign, have wondered about the British character. Some have claimed that the British silence stems from a need, as inhabitants of a crowded island, for solitude and peace. Others have claimed they are merely shy. George Santayana, the Spanish-born philosopher, suggested that the Englishman is governed by an "inner atmosphere, the weather in his soul"; similarly, J. B. Priestley, the English novelist and critic, asserted that the English are suspicious of the purely rational and rely upon instinct and intuition more than other Western Europeans do. Their reliance upon intuition might be one clue to the extraordinary wealth and beauty of English literature, which

— unlike the stereotypical and probably mythic Englishman — tends to be exuberant and romantic, as the plays of Shakespeare amply testify. The more one examines the English character, however, the more elusive and contradictory it appears; for if the English are traditional and conservative, they are also a nation of eccentrics. If they're gloomy, they are also well known for their marvelous sense of humor, as evidenced by the fact that English comedies continue to delight audiences of stage and screen.

The British inhabit, in the words of poet William Blake, a "green and pleasant land." Their plentiful rainfall makes for grass that is greener than that of most other countries. Because of the warming effects of the Gulf Stream, roses often bloom until Christmas. Moderation, a keynote of the British character and climate, extends also to the islands' geography. Both are moderate in size, with Great Britain the eighth largest and Ireland the twentieth largest island on earth. Compared with other places, Britain has no dramatic geographical features; its mountains and lakes, though lovely, are not unusual in magnitude.

With Northern Ireland, Britain occupies a total of 94,196 square miles a few miles off the northwestern coast of Europe. The island of Great Britain is not much larger than the state of Arkansas. Roughly speaking, Great Britain is divided into two areas, the lowlands in the west and south and the uplands in the east and north. Most of southern England except Devon and Cornwall is lowlands, while the Lake District, Scotland, and Wales are chiefly mountainous. Much of northern England consists of rolling uplands scenery. England is divided from Scotland to the north by the Tweed and Liddel rivers and the Cheviot Hills; Wales is a landmass on England's west coast.

The British are a nation of city dwellers; 78% of Britain's 56,186,071 people live in urban areas. London, the capital of England (Edinburgh is the capital of Scotland; Cardiff, of Wales; and Belfast, of Northern Ireland), is by far Britain's largest city, with a population of 7,281,080. Manchester and Birmingham, English industrial cities farther north, rank second and third, with more than 2 million each.

If you have come in search of the "merrie England" of villages and farms, you will be disappointed, because little of that has remained; nevertheless, mementos of earlier days are everywhere, for the British love history and tradition. Stonehenge and Avebury stand as awesome reminders of a prehistoric Britain, occupied by Bronze Age people even before the Celts arrived in the fifth century BC. Later invaders included the Romans in 55 BC, the Germanic tribes of the Angles, Saxons, and Jutes in the fifth century, and finally the Normans in 1066.

When the Angles and Saxons invaded, the Celts retreated to Wales, Cornwall, Scotland, and Brittany (France), where they remain to this day. Both Welsh and Gaelic are linguistic outgrowths of a Celtic tongue; English, however, is based upon the Germanic Anglo-Saxon, with the addition of a heavy sprinkling of Norman French. Besides French vocabulary and manners, William the Conqueror brought feudalism to England. Nearly 2 centuries later, in 1215, powerful nobles forced King John to sign the Magna Carta in recognition of their feudal rights.

The next important event in English history was the Hundred Years War, a dynastic struggle with France from 1337 to 1428 punctuated by outbreaks of the Black Death. As England recovered from these disasters, its wool trade prospered and towns grew, along with their new merchant and artisan classes.

The central government expanded under the great Tudor monarchs, particularly Henry VIII and Elizabeth I, who ruled an increasingly strong and prosperous nation from 1485 to 1603. In 1529, Henry VIII broke with the Pope, who refused to grant him a divorce, and established the Church of England. Elizabeth was queen during England's golden age, when Sir Francis Drake and Sir John Hawkins (and the weather) defeated the Spanish Armada and when Christopher Marlowe, William Shakespeare, Ben Jonson, John Donne, and many other great poets and playwrights illumined the English scene.

Although James I united England and Scotland with his ascent to both thrones in 1603, the seventeenth century brought England to civil war, with the parliamentarians defeating the royalists in 1649, beheading Charles I, and creating the Commonwealth that lasted for 11 years under Oliver Cromwell. The monarchy that was restored in 1660 was different from the earlier one, for this time Parliament had summoned the king; from then on, kings were forced to cooperate with Parliament.

During the eighteenth century, the British Empire expanded to places as remote as India and North America. Britain became the world's greatest power for 200 years — this despite the loss of the 13 American colonies in 1776.

The Industrial Revolution transformed England in the late eighteenth century; as a result, the landed aristocracy was joined by a newly powerful middle class that was enfranchised by the Reform Bill of 1832. During the long era of Queen Victoria (1837–1901), Britain led the world in commercial, industrial, and political power. Military and economic rivalry with Germany resulted in World War I. Hitler's rise plunged Britain into World War II, when Britain had to fight Germany alone for an entire year after France fell in 1940 (Russia joined the war effort in 1941). During the heavy night bombings of its cities and the long and lonely Battle of Britain, the nation marshaled truly remarkable courage and strength. The war destroyed large urban areas, including vast chunks of London.

Like the Green Knight in the medieval tale *Sir Gawain and the Green Knight,* who walked off after a duel bearing his chopped-off head under his arm, the British nation has survived and renewed itself. It has transformed its colonial empire into an extensive commercial network, the British Commonwealth of Nations, and it has joined the European Common Market. Since the war it has also nationalized the Bank of England, coal, steel, and communications, and in 1948 it established a system of socialized medicine.

Although Britain today is struggling with the same economic pressures as the rest of the world, it is a good place to visit because, among other things, the Britons speak our language — rather, we speak theirs. You will probably notice, by the way, that they speak English better than we do. (They should, having had centuries of practice.) Whether you dream of seeing the changing of the guard at Buckingham Palace, touring the still-rural Shakespeare country, walking through the mountainous Lake District as Wordsworth and Coleridge did, surveying the English moors or the Scottish highlands, drinking Scotch at the source, watching the sun set in a sleepy Welsh fishing village, or making idle conversation in a genuine Irish pub — these joys and many other surprises await you in Britain.

Any trip to Great Britain should begin in London, one of the great cities of the world. From here you can explore Britain, using any or all of our suggested tour routes. You can see Southeast England by starting near London in Canterbury, proceeding to the coast at Dover, and from there southwest to the resort of Brighton. Traveling farther west our tour of Southwest England begins at the ancient religious site of Stonehenge and continues west to the rocky peninsula of Devon and Cornwall, past Exeter, the wild and forbidding plain of Dartmoor, and the castle at Tintagel, where the legendary King Arthur is said to have been born. Also to the west is Wales, with its moorland of Brecon Beacons and its jagged coast sprinkled with charming fishing villages.

Southeast of Wales, the Cotswolds, Shakespeare's country, is one of the prettiest rural districts in England; our circular route, which begins at Bath and ends in Oxford, includes the lovely Cotswolds and Stratford-upon-Avon, Shakespeare's birthplace. Farther north, the Lake District, where the nineteenth-century Lake Poets — William Wordsworth and Samuel Taylor Coleridge among them — loved to roam, has been preserved as a national park with its mountains, lakes, and fields bounded by dry stone walls.

Crossing England's narrow waist to the opposite coast, our tour of Northeast England begins north of London at York, circling through the Yorkshire moors before heading north along the coast branching inland through Durham and Newcastle upon Tyne to Berwick-on-Tweed at the Scottish border. It's easy to explore Scotland in three parts: the Lowlands, or flat southern section, from Edinburgh to Glasgow and Abbotsford, with their battlefields and sites made famous by Sir Walter Scott; the Highlands, the eastern and central region of magnificent mountains and moors; and finally, Western Scotland, Robert Burns country — a coastal route, a place of resorts, and an ideal departure point for the Hebrides, the lovely islands off Scotland's western coast. The last route goes through Northern Ireland, the ancient province of Ulster, with its uncrowded beaches, bays, cliffs, and castles and its two highest ranges, the Mountains of Mourne in the southeast and the Sperrin Mountains in the north. If recent headlines about Northern Ireland don't scare you (they shouldn't; violence has erupted mostly in the cities of Belfast and Londonderry), they have scared others, so no crowds of tourists will interfere with your pleasure.

Southeast England: Kent, Canterbury, and the Coast

For better or worse, geography conspired to make Kent and East Sussex — the broad foot of land that spills out below London to form the bluff-lined and beach-speckled coast of southeast England — the only welcoming mat England has ever extended to the Continent. It is country suited to landing parties, Kent's rich orchards, hop fields, thatched barns, and high-hedged roads giving way to Sussex's high South Downs, from which one can see for miles in all directions. To the north is the wide estuary of the Thames; to the south, the English Channel; and to the east, where England and France are only some 20 miles apart, the Straits of Dover.

Such an invitation has been hard for European warlords to resist, and for 2,000 years attempts have been made to enter England through the southeast. Some have been successful. The Romans established an administrative center in London, and the Normans conquered all of England after their decisive victory at Battle, near Hastings, in 1066, when William the Conqueror killed King Harold. Others attempts have failed. From August to October 1940, Britain stood virtually alone against the full weight of the Nazi war machine as the Battle of Britain raged over the Weald of Kent. But each of these efforts has left some mark on this extraordinarily rich part of England. Kent, the Garden of England, nurtures as much history as fruit and hops in its fertile countryside.

The major sites along England's southeast coast — as well as Canterbury, Dover, Hastings and Battle, and Brighton — can be visited on day trips from London. Travelers with little time should certainly choose the most appealing destination and make the journey (by car or, even more simply, by train). But more rewarding is a perambulation through the countryside, following the coast as a rough guide, and seeing sites great and small along the way. From Canterbury clockwise to Brighton is the route outlined below.

This route begins south of London at Westerham, near the late Sir Winston Churchill's home, Chartwell, and tours some of the estates and castles in the area as it moves east to the cathedral city of Canterbury. Here, within the city's ancient walls, are the cathedral and shrine associated with St. Thomas à Becket, who was murdered here in 1170 by four knights after he defied his old friend and former lord, King Henry II.

The historic ports of Sandwich and Deal are a short drive east of Canterbury, and the famed white cliffs of Dover are just to the south. This scalloped shore, across the narrow Straits of Dover from the French coast, has been the target of invading armies from Caesar to Hitler. Along the coast are layers of fortifications, rebuilt and enlarged by successive generations, and castles and seawalls that seem ageless. The narrow channel invited smuggling during more peaceful days, and coastal marshes bred stories of betrayal and death.

Read a gentle primer of gothic horror tales before you journey forth — the legends of pre-Roman and Roman blood sacrifices will come alive for you. Perhaps a little inquisitive exploration will lead you to solve the mystery of the skulls in Hythe's church.

Farther south and west, Pevensey Bay was the site of William the Conqueror's landing, and nearby is the town of Battle, where he fought Harold's army. His defeat of King Harold at the Battle of Hastings (October 14, 1066) marked the beginning of a new era for England; it is a date no English schoolchild ever forgets. Farther along the coast is the Royal Pavilion at Brighton, and the trip ends with a visit to the springs at Royal Tunbridge Wells. Its medicinal waters prompted Edward VII to elevate the town to royal status, and its charming atmosphere makes it still popular today. It is just a short drive north from here to London. For more information, write South East England Tourist Board, 1 Warwick Park, Tunbridge Wells, Kent TN2 5TA.

LONDON: For a complete description of the city and its hotels and restaurants, see *London,* THE EUROPEAN CITIES.

En Route from London – Take Route A21 south through Bromley, continuing as far as the A233 cutoff. Follow A233 south to its junction with A25 near Westerham.

WESTERHAM: *Pitt's Cottage,* a timbered house used as a summer cottage during the late 1700s by William Pitt the Younger, stands on the outskirts of town. Pitt was well regarded as a wartime prime minister and was a motivating force behind two anti-Napoleonic coalitions involving several European nations as well as Russia and England. The cottage has since been converted into a restaurant.

Westerham is the birthplace of General James Wolfe, whose victory over the French troops under the Marquis de Montcalm at Québec on September 13, 1759, gave England control of Canada. A statue of Wolfe, who was mortally wounded during the decisive battle, stands in the village green not far from his childhood home, now called Québec House. The statue of a more recent war hero, Prime Minister Winston Churchill, shares the town center with General Wolfe. Churchill's country home, Chartwell, is about 2 miles (3.2 km) south of town (via Route B2026) on a wooded hillside terraced with a series of gardens. The study where Churchill worked remains as he left it.

En Route from Westerham – Take Route A25 east about 6 miles (10 km) to the village of Sevenoaks. Knole, one of the largest and most magnificent baronial mansions in England, lies just off A25 on A225. The building, referred to by Virginia Woolf as "a town rather than a house" in her novel *Orlando,* sprawls over 3 acres and includes (according to legend) 7 courtyards corresponding to the days of the week, 52 staircases for the weeks, and 365 rooms — one for each day in the year. The house was begun in 1456 by Archbishop Thomas Bourchier and was held by the archbishops of Canterbury until turned over to Henry VIII. The estate, named for the grassy knoll on which it stands, was given to the Sackville-West family by Queen Elizabeth I in 1603, the year she died. The house was enlarged, and over the years the estate acquired an incredible art collection, including canvases by Gainsborough, Van Dyck, Reynolds, and others. Today the interior is furnished entirely in the Elizabethan mode, with furnishings virtually untouched since the family was first given the house (open Wednesdays through Sundays and holidays; March through December).

Return to Route A25, traveling east about 2 miles (3.2 km) to the cutoff to

Ightham. On Friday afternoons Ightham Mote is open. This stately fourteenth-century manor house, encircled by a moat, contains a beautiful Tudor chapel. If you find yourself working up a thirst, travel a bit farther to the *Crown Point Inn,* a comfortable wood-paneled pub with its own garden in the tiny village of Seal Chart, outside Plaxtol.

Route A25 becomes M20 and leads directly into Maidstone.

MAIDSTONE: Many historic buildings line the streets of Maidstone, the bustling capital and agricultural center of Kent. Several streets in the High Street area have been closed to vehicular traffic in an effort to preserve these fine examples of early architecture. Near the town's fourteenth-century Church of All Saints is a tithe barn of the same period, part of the palace of the archbishop of Canterbury, when it was used as a stable. It's now the home of the Tyrwhitt Drake Museum, a fine collection of ornate horse-drawn carriages (open weekdays). The palace itself, which still exists, is only open by special arrangement.

Chillington Manor, an Elizabethan mansion on St. Faith's Street, is now the home of the Museum and Art Gallery containing the memorabilia of essayist William Hazlitt, a native of Maidstone. North of town, on A229, are Allington Castle, an imposing, moated, thirteenth-century castle, and the Carmelite retreat, Aylesford Priory. The Order controls both structures and conducts afternoon tours daily.

En Route from Maidstone – Readers of Charles Dickens will enjoy a short (8 mi/12.8 km) side trip north to Rochester, which appears so often in his work and, thinly-disguised, is the city of Cloisterham in his last story, *The Mystery of Edwin Drood.* Dickens's Rochester home at Gad's Hill is not open, but the food, drinks, and atmosphere at the author's favorite inn, *The Leather Bottle* (in Cobham), are ample recompense. Other buildings that figure in his work — Eastgate House, which is home to the newly opened Dickens Center; the Six Poor Travellers' House; the Cathedral; and Guildhall — can be visited in Rochester.

Rochester Castle, a massive Norman fortress, was erected late in the eleventh century and partially rebuilt during the fourteenth century. The castle is 120 feet high and has walls 12 feet thick. Rochester Cathedral incorporates architectural styles from several periods, from the crypt and tower built in 1082 and the decorative mid-fourteenth-century doorway to the Chapter Room.

Route A20 continues east-southeast from Maidstone toward Ashford, passing Leeds Castle. This fairy-tale fortress stands in the middle of a lake — no mean task in the 1200s, when it was built. It was the home of Lord Culpepper (governor of Virginia, 1680–83) and later his grandson, Lord Fairfax, and is open daily from April to October (except on Mondays in April and May); open weekends only November through March.

The remains of a palace of the archbishops of Canterbury lie within the ancient village of Charing, about 13 miles (21 km) from Maidstone. Stop at the *Swan Hotel* for an ample lunch and a tasty brew before continuing south on A20 to Ashford. Pick up A28 eastbound from here to Canterbury, a distance of about 14 miles (22 km) across the meadowy downs that extend through Kent from the outskirts of London to the coast at Dover.

The main road neatly bypasses the delightful village of Chilham, so keep an eye open for the turnoff. The gardens and grounds of Chilham Castle, complete with aviaries and a "pets' corner," are open daily from May to October. Bird-handling demonstrations, with falcons and eagles, are held each afternoon. The castle is the Center of the British Jousting Association (jousts are held on most public holidays). The atmosphere of the *White Horse Inn* will confirm the feeling of earlier times; it has often been used in movies because of its virtually unchanged fifteenth-century appearance inside and out. The food is as enjoyable as the fireplace on a chilly evening, so reservations are advised.

Continuing east on Route A28, a glimpse of the three pinnacled towers of Canterbury Cathedral heralds the ancient city.

CANTERBURY: This approach leads into the heart of Canterbury through the massive West Gate used by countless pilgrims traveling to the shrine of St. Thomas à Becket. It was the murder of Archbishop Thomas à Becket in 1170 and his canonization 2 years later that elevated the cathedral to its status as a shrine. Following nine centuries of pilgrims, make your way along the main street and then turn left into the narrow course called Mercery Lane. Straight ahead is Christ Church Gate, leading to the cathedral precincts (or close). Give yourself plenty of time to explore the cathedral treasures — the glowing medieval stained-glass windows, the ancient paintings in the crypt, and the elaborate vaulted cloisters; but there is much more to see here.

The Romans built the fortress of Durovernum on this site in AD 43. The remains of the city walls are visible near the Dane John Gardens, and the characteristic mosaic Roman roadway can still be seen at Butchery Lane.

St. Martin's Church, one of the ancient landmarks mentioned in the rhyme in George Orwell's *1984*, is one of the oldest functioning churches in England. Christian services were held here as early as AD 500, and the present building may have evolved from fourth-century Roman villas on the same site. The ruins of St. Augustine's Abbey, established by St. Augustine in AD 602 with the support of King Ethelbert, lie outside the city's East Wall, near the foot of St. Martin's Hill along Longport Street.

There are several inviting inns for food and drink, such as *The Beehive* at 52 Dover St., *The House of Agnes*, referred to in Dickens's *David Copperfield*, at 71 St. Dunstan's St., and the bow-windowed *Olive Branch* in Burgate.

En Route from Canterbury – Route A257 leads due east from Canterbury to the medieval port of Sandwich, one of the original five Cinque Ports (see *En Route from Deal*). As Sandwich's harbor became clogged with silt in the sixteenth century, the city lost importance. It gained lasting fame, however, when the fourth earl of Sandwich invented the world's most popular and enduring meal — the sandwich. According to legend, the earl was loath to leave the gaming tables to eat and asked that a concoction of bread and meat be made for him. The earl — who was infamous for being in charge of the admiralty when Britain lost its North American colony — was a dissolute man, and the story has something of the ring of truth about it. Two inns, the *Bell* and the *King's Arms*, will be glad to provide a sample of this handy bar snack and something with which to wash it down. Richborough Castle, just off Route A257 1.5 miles (2.5 km) outside of Sandwich, was established by the Romans around AD 43 and added to by the Saxons during the third century. Route A258 leads to Deal, about 6 miles (10 km) south along the coast.

DEAL: Deal was an important shipping center through the early nineteenth century. Under Henry VIII, three castles were erected here: Deal Castle (open daily), Walmer Castle, open daily (a mile/1.6 km south on A258), and Sandown Castle (since washed away). There is a good possibility that Caesar's forces landed along this shore when the Romans invaded Britain, and here Henry VIII feared the pope would launch a Holy War against him as the self-proclaimed head of the Church of England. The coast off Deal, called Goodwin Sands, is a complicated series of sandbanks that are exposed at low tide. Lighthouses and lightships illuminate the area after dark, but maritime accidents persist. The narrow roadstead formed between Goodwin Sands and the coast, not the safest anchorage for shipping, is popularly known as the downs.

En Route from Deal – Traveling south on A258 toward the busy port of Dover, Walmer Castle is only 1 mile (1.6 km) from Deal. The castle has been the residence of the Lord Warden of the Cinque Ports since the mid-1700s. This association of seaports began in the eleventh century, when five principal ports (Hastings, Romney — now New Romney — Hythe, Dover, and Sandwich) banded together to provide England with a makeshift navy. Later this was formalized by a charter that granted certain privileges in exchange for the pledge of supplying ships and men for the country's defense. Other ports along this southeast foot of England, the part closest to France, became involved in this arrangement during the dangerous period from the thirteenth to the sixteenth century. Following the establishment of the Royal Navy, the importance of the association and the post of Lord Warden declined drastically. Dover is only 7 miles (11 km) farther south on A258.

DOVER: The chalky white cliffs of Dover have been a strategic landmark ever since the early Iron Age, when a settlement was established here. Roman invaders quickly erected a fortress and an octagonal lighthouse, or pharos, that still stands beside a more recent Norman castle. The castle keep surrounds a 240-foot-deep well, and there are rumors that some of the underground passages inside the castle connect with the caves beneath the cliffs once used by smugglers. The ancient Roman roadway called Watling Street begins here and leads to London via Canterbury. On clear days, France is easily visible across the Straits of Dover, 20 miles (32 km) away, and the view from the battlements of Dover Castle atop the 400-foot bluff overlooking the city and sea is magnificent. Dover is one of the main embarkation points for ferries to France (Calais, Dunkirk, and Boulogne) and Belgium (Ostende and Zeebrugge).

During both world wars, Dover again rose to prominence as a point of departure for troops bound for the Continent and as the goal of planes straggling back from the fighting. The city was pounded by long-range artillery during World War II, and the thick castle walls sheltered the population through the 4-year bombardment.

En Route from Dover – The famous cliffs extend southwest toward Folkestone, neatly trimming the coastline with a tall white chalk seawall for almost 7 miles (11 km). Beyond this point the cliffs fall away, exposing the shore. Stretching westward is a double line of defenses constructed in the early nineteenth century against the threat of an invasion by Napoleon: a series of 74 small coastal fortresses — circular Martello towers — reinforced by a Royal Military Canal a short distance inland. Additional defenses were erected in 1940 when Hitler massed his forces along the French coast. Take Route A20 southwest along the coast from Dover to Folkestone before picking up Route A259 for the additional 4 miles (6.4 km) to Hythe.

If you're favored with good weather in Folkestone, take a stroll on the Leas — a broad, mile-long, grassy walkway on the crest of the cliffs just west of the harbor. From here the coast of France unfolds in a beautiful panorama 22 miles (35 km) distant. On the east side of the harbor is the Warren, where a section of the chalk cliff has crumbled and fallen on the beach — a great hunting ground for fossils.

HYTHE: Three Martello towers still guard the one-time Cinque Port of Hythe, although the harbor has long since silted up and the sea receded. There are also fortifications from other periods, including the ruins of a Roman castrum, Stutfall Castle, near the Royal Military Canal that bisects the city. Lympne Castle, a residence of the archdeacons of Canterbury until the mid-1800s, incorporates a square twelfth-century Norman tower into its otherwise fourteenth- and fifteenth-century construction (open on bank holidays only from June to September). The castle overlooks Romney Marsh, a sparsely populated, low-lying pasture full of memories of the old smuggling days, when untaxed (and often illegal) cargoes were unloaded here. The fields and marsh grass support a large number of Romney Marsh sheep. A miniature steam railway (open daily Easter to September, and weekends in March and October) runs a 13-mile (21-km) course from Hythe to New Romney along the fringe of the marsh. The presence of over 1,500 human skulls in the town church has never been explained.

En Route from Hythe – Route A259 parallels both the coast and the railway, passing through Romney Marsh as it travels to New Romney. Dymchurch, halfway between the two closed ports (New Romney lost the use of its harbor in the thirteenth century), is a popular weekend resort with a 5-mile beach. The small village itself lies in the shelter of a 3-mile fortified seawall built by the Romans to prevent the marshes from flooding. The wall has been continuously improved, and the fortifications were added in 1940. At New Romney the road bears inland, crossing the border of Kent and heading toward the ancient towns of Rye and Winchelsea (21 mi/33.5 km and 24 mi/38.5 km from Hythe, respectively) in neighboring East Sussex.

RYE: The receding sea and centuries of silt buildup have obstructed the port of Rye, limiting traffic to small coastal vessels and fishing boats. The town was razed by the French in 1377 and again in 1448, destroying the most historic buildings, but many of the houses erected during the late fifteenth century still grace Rye's cobblestone streets. The town retains the atmosphere of that medieval time and a measure of its former bustling activity within its crumbling fourteenth-century walls.

Both the *Mermaid Inn,* rebuilt during the fifteenth century and rumored to have been a smugglers' rendezvous, and the timbered *Flushing Inn* (fifteenth century) are excellent haunts for travelers. The works of the great clock (c. 1560) in the twelfth-century Church of St. Mary are thought to be among the oldest still functioning in England. Lamb House (West St.) was the residence of novelist Henry James from 1898 until his death in 1916 (open Wednesday and Saturday afternoons April to October). The sixteenth-century dramatist John Fletcher's birthplace, a vicarage near Lion and Market streets, is now a tea shop. The de Ypres family purchased the thirteenth-century tower that bears its name in the early fourteenth century; it is now a museum (open daily; April to October).

Winchelsea, also added to the Cinque Ports alliance before the changing coastline ruined its harbor, was completely relocated to its present site in 1283 by Edward I. The church, begun soon afterward, is dedicated to St. Thomas à Becket. Parts of William Thackeray's *Denis Duval* are set in the two towns.

En Route from Rye – South of Winchelsea, Route A259 descends toward the shore. At Hastings, 9 miles (14.4 km) from Rye, the road regains the coast. The strategic and psychological importance of this area to England becomes clear when viewed against the historic background of this section of coastline.

Following Edward the Confessor's death in January 1066, Harold ascended to the throne of England, but his claim to the monarchy (through his mother's bloodline) was weak. Duke William of Normandy felt his kinship to Edward (his father had been Edward's cousin), coupled with the oath Harold had sworn in support, justified his claim to the throne.

It was just a few miles west of Hastings, at Pevensey Bay, that William landed his forces on September 28, 1066.

King Harold and his men were busy fighting Tostig in the north and had to march southward from the Battle of Stamford Bridge. He gathered additional support as he traveled but it was not until the morning of October 14 that Harold's army, perhaps 10,000 ax-and spear-carrying foot soldiers, formed a shield wall along a ridge just north of Hastings. William's force was composed of a few thousand archers and several thousand mounted knights and armed men. Norman arrows rained on the defenders, and cavalry charges broke on the wall of spears and shields. In the late afternoon William faked a retreat, drawing many of the inexperienced English militiamen from their positions, and decimated them with his cavalry. King Harold and the remainder of his army were soon slaughtered. On the spot where Harold planted the Royal Standard, where he and his closest followers actually died, William the Conqueror erected Battle Abbey. By Christmas, William was crowned king of England in Westminster Abbey.

HASTINGS (ST. LEONARDS and BATTLE): Although Hastings and adjoining St.

Leonards now form a popular resort area, the original Cinque Port city stagnated after the harbor became clogged with silt during the late twelfth century. This 600-year sleep kept the Old Town beautifully intact. Narrow streets and age-old houses characterize the east end of town, where Hastings began as a fishing village. Even the tall, skinny sheds used to store the fish nets, built during the sixteenth century, have survived, as did the fourteenth-century St. Clement's and the fifteenth-century All Saints' churches. The Fisherman's Church is now a museum.

The ruins of Hastings Castle, erected around the time of William's invasion, overlook the 3-mile beach area. The magnificent homes in this section of town reflect the resurgence of Hastings as a resort during the late eighteenth and early nineteenth centuries. An amusement pier adds to the gaiety of the promenade along the beach, but the most beautiful aspect of the town is natural — the cliffwalks to the east of Hastings and St. Clement's Caves (below the castle), once used by smugglers.

The nearby small town of Battle, which derives its name from the famous Battle of Hastings, includes the abbey founded by William the Conqueror. The battle site, from the ridge where Harold formed his lines to the heights of Senlac and Telham on the far side of the valley, where William's forces gathered, is just southwest of the town. The abbey gatehouse fronts on Market Square, and the ruins of the abbey church (destroyed around 1540) center on the spot where Harold fell. Those sections of the abbey that survived intact and those added in later years are now used as a school. (The Abbey ruins are open throughout the year excluding Sunday mornings from October to March.)

En Route from Hastings – Continue southwest along the coast on Route A259 toward the popular seaside resort of Brighton, a distance of about 45 miles (72 km). Since this coastal road may be clogged with traffic during the summer months, it might be a good idea to take the inland route, A27, which veers off from A259 at Pevensey.

BRIGHTON: The flow of travelers and bathers to the shore at Brighton started in the mid-eighteenth century, when a local doctor began recommending the salt water and sea air to several members of England's fashionable elite. It hasn't stopped. By 1783, the Prince of Wales (later George IV) made his home here and ordered the construction of the Royal Pavilion. In 1817, he had the building altered to a more Oriental style; by that time the carnival atmosphere of the resort was well established. Even a partial listing of those who frequented Brighton would sound like a *Who's Who* of English history and literature: Lewis Carroll, Sir Winston Churchill, Conan Doyle, Gladstone, and Herbert Spencer. Aubrey Beardsley was born here, and George Holyoake died here. By 1929, Brighton had tripled in size, sprawling from Hove to Rottingdean (a 7-mile seafront) and several miles inland.

An esplanade stretches the length of the beach, and two amusement piers extend from it at either end. West Pier, partially damaged, has been closed; Palace Pier, almost directly in front of the pavilion, is still operating. On the east end of the walk are splendid nineteenth-century terraces. Maderia Drive leads on to Black Rock, where the Brighton Marina, the largest yachting marina in Europe, opened in 1979. The older section of Brighton forms a permanent bazaar in the area bounded by Old Steine Street (near the pavilion) and West Street. The Royal Pavilion and the Royal Stables, now the Dome Theater, mark the inland border of this shopping haven. The Museum and Art Gallery are on the next corner. The Sussex Room at the museum contains a thorough history of the area and a fabulous collection of English ceramics (the Willet Collection; both museum and gallery are open daily). And of course the Royal Pavilion is itself a living museum of one of the most vivid periods in English taste.

Brighton is not, however, the place for spending your days indoors or even out shopping. Virtually every holiday sport is available here, and if none of the active amusements (sailing, golf, tennis, and such) are to your taste, there are the shows at the Dome, the greyhound racing, cricket, and football at Hove, or the horse racing at the Racecourse. Then there's the Sports Arena and the Volk's Electric Railroad from Palace Pier to Black Rock. Many theater productions open here before going to London's West End, and there are some 8 movie houses in the area.

   En Route from Brighton – Route A23, aided by the M23 motorway, makes a beeline for London, 60 miles (96 km) due north of the beaches. A more entertaining route is A27 northeast from Brighton to Lewes and A26 from there to Royal Tunbridge Wells, the health resort that has been extremely popular since the discovery of the "healing powers" of its mineral waters in 1606. It's about 30 miles (48 km) from Brighton at the junction of A26 and A21. A promenade called the Pantiles, designed as a shopping and visitor area in 1638, is just as popular today. The mineral waters can be sampled from the springs at the far end of the walkway, and the *Duke of York* pub serves those looking for something a little stronger at the tables outside its Victorian building on the promenade. Route A21 leads north toward Westerham and Sevenoaks, about 10 miles (16 km) away.

BEST EN ROUTE

The roads from the coast to London have been lined with inns and guesthouses for centuries, and many of those available to modern travelers are the same ones patronized by kings' messengers (and murderers) six centuries ago. The degree of comfort has increased a good deal in the intervening years, however, and you should have no complaints about the quality or range of accommodations available. Expect to pay $60 or more for a double in those places categorized as expensive; between $40 and $60 in the moderate range; and under $40 in any hotel or guesthouse listed as inexpensive. Full English breakfast is usually included in the overnight charge. A meal for two, excluding drinks, wine, or tips, will run about $35 to $50 in places listed as expensive; $25 to $35 in moderate; and under $20 in inexpensive.

WYE

Wife of Bath – Five miles (8 km) south of the tiny town of Chilham is Wye, a village that would escape notice altogether if it weren't for this very fine restaurant with English and French cuisine. Weekly menus change with the season to ensure absolutely fresh food. Make reservations. Closed Sundays and Mondays and a week at Christmas. 4 Upper Bridge St. (phone: 812540). Moderate.
New Flying Horse Inn – It's a seventeenth-century coaching inn with oak beams, gleaming brasses, and good food. 10 rooms. Upper Bridge St. (phone: 812297). Moderate to inexpensive.

CANTERBURY

County Hotel – Although this sixteenth-century hotel has been refurbished in the name of creature comforts, it retains the feel of its older rooms. The original timbers and exposed beams are still there, but certain modern niceties (like private baths in all rooms) have been added. High St. (phone: 66266). Expensive.

DOVER

Holiday Inn – A large, modern hotel that's conveniently close to the ferry terminals. Amenities include a restaurant and a heated indoor pool. 83 rooms. Townwall St. (phone: 203270). Expensive.

RYE

The Mermaid Inn – This beautifully preserved fifteenth-century inn is one of the most charming old hotels in England. Its walls still conceal the priest holes and secret staircase used to avoid arrest in the old days of pirates and smugglers. Mermaid St. (phone: 223065). Moderate to inexpensive.

HASTINGS

Beauport Park Hotel – Set off in a beautiful park area, the stately Georgian hotel has a formal garden to add to the timeless atmosphere. The service is in keeping with that feeling of another age, and the heated outdoor pool is a bonus during the summer. Battle Rd. (phone: 51222). Expensive to moderate.

BRIGHTON

The Grand – Right in the center of the seafront, this is an old and very attractive hotel with Victorian architecture at its best in the lobby and landings. The rooms are modern and comfortable. King's Rd. (phone: 2-6301). Expensive.

Old Ship – On the seafront close to the Lanes, much of its original style and charm remains, especially in the 200-year-old banqueting room used by the Prince Regent. The rooms vary from simple singles to lavish antique-four-poster-bedded delights. King's Rd. (phone: 29001). Moderate.

ROYAL TUNBRIDGE WELLS

Calverley Hotel – An elegant eighteenth-century stone mansion set in a delightful garden, the *Calverley* overlooks the lower town. There are antiques throughout the hotel, but the chintz coverings detract more from the style than they add to the countrified atmosphere. Crescent Rd. (phone: 26455). Moderate.

Southwest England: Devon and Cornwall

Its atypically warm climate is not all that distinguishes southwest England from the rest of Great Britain, although it is the feature of this thumb of land stuck into the Atlantic that most attracts other Britons. With coasts on the English Channel and the Atlantic Ocean and weather that at its most extreme approaches the subtropical (indefatigable Cornish gardeners have been known to grow palms, much to the consternation of unsuspecting passersby, who find palm trees in England a touch surreal), popular resorts like Torquay and Newquay are full all summer long.

But there is a mysterious quality to Devon and Cornwall born of centuries of relative isolation that is both fascinating and a little frightening. It is this quality — not its reputation for warm weather or seaside frolics — that draws most foreign visitors. For the distinction between rural Somerset and Dorset and Devon's famous moors couldn't be more pronounced. Dartmoor — now a protected national park — is a vast sparse expanse of exposed rock and chalk, eerie and mystical at night, yet beautifully trimmed in a verdant layer of wild grasses and purple heather that glow in the sunlight in the day. Across them sweep sudden storms and lashing gales of wind and rain, and from them have come stories of the hounds of hell, dark demons, and druids. The coasts of Cornwall, isolated for centuries, bred generations of sea scavengers as well as culture, language, and customs unlike any others in England.

In Plymouth, Sir Francis Drake busied himself with a game of bowls as the Spanish Armada gathered offshore; from this same port the Pilgrims departed for the New World. Pirates and scavengers alike took delight in hiding among the coves and inlets that line both the north and south coasts of the region, preying on shipping by force and luring their victims to destruction on unmarked rocks and shoals.

From London to the ancient religious site of Stonehenge, the route we offer below bears south into Salisbury and then Dorchester before heading west to Exeter. The district is scattered with Roman ruins, and some of this ancient architecture can still be seen. Farther west, across the wilds of Dartmoor, lies Plymouth, a major port of the British navy since the days of wooden ships. Cornwall's twin peninsulas of Land's End and the Lizard form the southwestern tip of England, and in the bay between these outstretched arms of land is Penzance, a resort and a point of departure for the offshore Isles of Scilly. Nearby is one of England's most spectacular castles, St. Michael's Mount, on a mountain rising 200 feet from the sea.

Returning east along the north coast of Cornwall and then Devon, the route passes the island-fortress of Tintagel, claimed to be the birthplace of King Arthur, and the surfing resort of Bude before ending in the forests and valleys of Exmoor National Park. For more information write to the West Country Tourist Board, Trinity Court, 37 Southernhay East, Exeter EX1 1QS, Devon (phone: 0392-76351).

LONDON: For a detailed report on the city and its hotels and restaurants, see *London,* THE EUROPEAN CITIES.

En Route from London – It's about a 2½- to 3-hour journey to Stonehenge via either the M3 motorway or Route A30, but switch over to A30 at exit 8 of the motorway and follow it until the point where A303 originates and A30 bears south. Take A303 into Amesbury, which marks the eastern entrance to the Salisbury Plain, about 120 miles west of London. This windblown 200-square-mile table of chalk and rock is the bedrock of English history.

STONEHENGE: The best known of almost 80 ancient religious sites in the area, Stonehenge lies 2 miles (3 km) west of town just off Route A303. An earthwork 300 feet in diameter raises the crude formation above the plain and sets it apart from its surroundings. Although the site was used by the Druids for their sun-based festivals beginning around 250 BC, computer evidence supports the theory that these circles served as an astronomical calendar for timing the movements of the moon and stars — and predicting eclipses — around 1500 BC. That anyone could have moved and placed these massive chunks of stone at any time, let alone in 1500 BC, is an incredible act of faith in itself.

The stone monoliths, mined, shaped, and moved to this spot, are arranged in two concentric outer circles with two interior horseshoes. The uprights in the outer circle are 13½ feet tall and linked by fitted capstones; the inner circle is slightly smaller. Many segments of both circles remain intact. The two horseshoes are formed of unconnected trilithons (two uprights supporting a single capstone) in a concentric pattern. The largest of the five still standing is over 20 feet tall and extends 8 feet below ground.

En Route from Stonehenge – Backtrack into Amesbury and stop at the *Antrobus Arms Hotel* to discuss the Druids. The present hotel, which evolved from a coaching inn for passengers on the London-to-Exeter coach, carries its age well. On a cold night its roaring fireplaces (and a whiskey) will chase the chill as well as ever. The abbey at Amesbury was founded by the widow of King Edgar the Peaceful after his death in 975, although parts of the structure date from the seventh century. It was here, according to the tales of King Arthur, that Queen Guinevere took final refuge after the death of Arthur. Route A345 leads directly south to Salisbury, just a few miles away, but there is a much nicer, smaller road running through the Avon Valley, slightly west of the main route.

SALISBURY: The 400-foot spire of Salisbury Cathedral, the tallest in England, dominates the entire plain on which the city is located. Salisbury was established and construction of the cathedral began in 1220, when religious jurisdiction over the area was transferred here from the ancient city of Old Sarum. The remains of Old Sarum — which began as a crude earthwork, grew to a Saxon town, and later became a Norman fortress — lie on a hill north of Salisbury. On the banks of the Avon, the *Rose and Crown Hotel* provides comfortable accommodations; and you're bound to feel welcome at one of the three bars at the *Haunch of Venison*.

Take Route A354 southwest from Salisbury to Dorchester, about 40 miles (64 km) distant, across the hills of Dorset Downs. South of Puddletown lies the countryside Thomas Hardy called Egdon Heath in his novels; Salisbury appeared as Melchester.

DORCHESTER: Thomas Hardy transformed this quiet agricultural center where he was born into the city of Casterbridge for his Wessex novels, but Dorchester has withstood much greater alterations throughout its existence. Maiden Castle, a pre-Roman earthwork, is a magnificent ruin left by the native Neolithic Britons. Later, under the Romans, this was a crossroads called Durnovaria, and the nearby Maumbury Rings was the site of an amphitheater. King John later used the town as a hunting center. Today it has an interesting county museum that displays finds from the nearby Iron Age fort, Maiden Castle, and a reconstruction of Hardy's study taken from his house at Max Gate; there are also some of his original manuscripts, notebooks, and drawings. The museum is open daily except Sundays. In the seventeenth century, Judge Jeffreys held his Bloody Assizes in Dorchester, consigning some 200 men to the gallows in the wake of the duke of Monmouth's failed rebellion in 1685. Jeffreys was a notoriously cruel man, and the High West Street building where he roomed is said to be haunted; if you spot the judge, don't speak. The *Royal Oak Pub* right up the street should be your next port of call. Hardy's cottage and the fringes of Egdon Heath are accessible from Route A35 about 3 miles (5 km) east of town. The current tenant will open the cottage by appointment, but the gardens are open to the public daily from April to October.

En Route from Dorchester – Route A35 leads west, cutting across the hills and farms of beautiful Dorset Downs. Bridport, about 16 miles (26 km) from Dorchester, was Hardy's Port Bredy; it has a good beach on West Bay. The town achieved some notoriety as a major producer of rope and netting, leading to the designation of a hangman's noose as a Bridport dagger. West of Bridport the road divides, and A3052 leads southwest to the resort town of Lyme Regis, on the coast.

LYME REGIS: The steep streets of Lyme Regis lead downhill from the coastal farmlands to the old stone pier known as the Cobb, famously portrayed in *The French Lieutenant's Woman*. It was here that the duke of Monmouth landed to raise an army among the men of southwest England in his attempt to wrest the crown from James II in 1685. Jane Austen kept a cottage called Wings atop the promenade overlooking the area; she used the setting for Louisa Musgrove's accident in the novel *Persuasion*. The worn chalk cliffs are studded with fossil formations, and an ichthyosaurus was recovered here in 1811 by Mary Anning. The town church contains a magnificent tapestry celebrating the union of Catherine and Henry III in 1509.

Route A3052 continues west through Colyford to the resort area of Sidmouth and goes on to Exeter, a total distance of 32 miles (52 km).

EXETER: The strategic and historic city of Exeter, dominated by beautiful Exeter

Cathedral, stands on the banks of the Exe River, guarding the neck of the southwest peninsula containing Devon and Cornwall. It is the county town of Devon. The Romans created a fortified city here, Isca Dumnoniorum, and the crumbling walls that once marked its boundaries can still be seen. Over the years, this site has been besieged, stormed, taken, and sometimes held by and against a long series of attackers. The Saxons called the town Escanestre and founded a monastery in 680. The ruins of Rougemont Castle, erected by William the Conqueror after he seized the town in 1068, testify to the area's military importance.

Exeter Cathedral (High St. near South St.), which evolved from a Norman structure begun in 1112, includes only the massive towers from that period, having been continually rebuilt and altered for almost a century from 1270 until the late fourteenth century. Intricate construction details, like the vaulted roof and elaborately carved figures on the west facade, contribute to its appeal. The fourteenth-century Guildhall, decorated inside and out with coats of arms and the insignia of various trade guilds and individuals, may be the oldest municipal building in England.

In its younger days Exeter was a port city, accessible from the English Channel via the navigable Exe River. Several of Queen Elizabeth's favorite sea captains, Sir Francis Drake and Sir Walter Raleigh among them, docked at Exeter and often stepped into Mol's Coffee House (now a silver- and goldsmith's shop) in the Cathedral Close. Drake is also thought to have had a few at the *Ship Inn*, which still serves thirsty travelers.

En Route from Exeter – Pick up Route B3212 on the western outskirts of the city, leading into the heart of Dartmoor National Park. The magic of the wild and rugged moors has fascinated English authors, their readers, and travelers for centuries. The bleak windswept hills, capped by high outcroppings of granite called tors, and coarse wild grasses are the home of wild ponies, grazing sheep, literary pilgrims, and even tales of the "hounds of hell," adapted from older legends of the "beast from below" left over from pre-Roman Druidic cults. Ruins of ancient religious sites and bits of Roman construction are scattered about the 300-square-mile area punctuated by tors that reach as high as 2,000 feet. The peaceful air and quietude of the moors make them ideal for an afternoon's tramp or horseback ride, but remember Sherlock Holmes's admonition to Sir Henry Baskerville, "Don't go out upon the moors at night!" Even if the hounds of hell don't get you, the moors are interspersed with spots of soggy marsh and dotted with tiny lakes, and more than one wanderer has been lost here. Also, be wary when setting off on daytime hikes; take along a compass, map, some food, and extra clothing, since Dartmoor can quickly become enshrouded in mist and cold even in summer.

The *Warren House Inn,* about 18 miles (29 km) from Exeter, once quenched the thirsts of tin miners walking home across the moor. The structure dates from the early eighteenth century but has since been rebuilt. Pause for a bracing Scottish & Newcastle ale before continuing to the intriguing early granite bridge that leads toward Dartmoor Prison. Princetown, the highest town in England and administrative headquarters for the dark-walled prison, is only 6 miles (10 km) beyond the bridge. The prison was established for captured French soldiers in 1809 and was used for American prisoners during the War of 1812. The facility began over a century of service as the Dartmoor Convict Prison in 1850, although sections were destroyed by fire during an insurrection in 1932.

Continue southwest on Route B3212 about 5 miles (8 km) to Yelverton, and take A386 the remaining 8 miles (13 km) into Plymouth.

PLYMOUTH: A principal English seaport for over 500 years, Plymouth dominates the mouths of the Plym and Tamar rivers at Plymouth Sound. This natural harbor, protected by rocky headlands on either side, has been an important military installation since it was fortified during the early 1400s, and many of the famous English privateers used Plymouth as their base for shipping raids. It was here that the outnumbered English fleet awaited the Spanish Armada in 1588.

English naval legends say that Sir Francis Drake was in the middle of a game of bowls on Plymouth Hoe when the Armada was sighted — and calmly finished his game before the battle. A statue of Drake and several other memorials stand on the Hoe's green lawns today, on the southeastern point of the waterfront near the Citadel. The Citadel, part of the fortifications erected under Charles II in the 1660s, is currently in use by the British military, although certain sections may sometimes be toured by arrangement with the commanding officer.

The *Mayflower* colonists set sail from Plymouth's pier at the Mayflower Steps, on the west side of the point near Sutton Pool. Near Barbican Quay, at the foot of Lambhay Street, is the ruin of a gatehouse, part of a fourteenth-century castle. Large sections of this historic city were damaged by bombs in World War II, but the Barbican area survived in its Elizabethan purity. It is now a lively area full of antique shops, art galleries, restaurants, and pubs, and the narrow cobbled streets are overhung by the timber frames of merchant homes. Note the particularly fine Elizabethan house on New Street (open weekdays), beautifully furnished with sixteenth-century pieces. Other parts of Plymouth have been extensively rebuilt, and, together with the adjoining communities, have grown into a single maritime center. The Royal Dockyards, established by William of Orange at Devonport, a mile west of Plymouth, contributed heavily to this effect. Entrance to the dockyards is restricted.

En Route from Plymouth – The River Tamar marks the boundary between Devon and Cornwall, and Route A38 crosses Plymouth Harbour on the Tamar Suspension Bridge, traveling 30 miles (48 km) west toward the town of Bodmin. Much of the china and raw china clay shipped through the port of Plymouth comes from this area, evidenced by the chalky white piles of mining waste lining the roadways. The route bears north to Liskeard, and then turns west again to Bodmin, skirting the southern fringe of Bodmin Moor. There are some interesting stone formations on this edge of the moor: three odd stone circles known as the Hurlers and a 30-foot mound of granite blocks dubbed "the Cheesewring." If you have some extra time, detour south from Liskeard on B3254 to visit the picturesque fishing ports of Looe, Polperro, and Fowey; then take B3269 into Bodmin.

BODMIN: On the steep western slopes of the rocky tablelands of Bodmin Moor, this agricultural center is a natural touring base for the entire moors area. St. Petroc's Church, rebuilt during the fifteenth century, is the largest medieval church in Cornwall, and the nearby waters of St. Guron's Well are reputed to have brought about miraculous cures for eye troubles and blindness. If you'd like the mud in your eye to be a little stronger, make your way to the *Hole in the Wall Pub* — through a hole in the wall! The building may have been a debtors' prison during the eighteenth century. In addition to the stoneworks found in the southern area on the approach to Bodmin and the Roman ruins scattered about, Dozmary Pool (off A30 in the northeast sector) is deep with legends. In the legend of King Arthur, the sword Excalibur was cast into the lake, where it was caught by a single arm extended from beneath the surface. Cornish legends also tell of Jan Tregeagle, who was condemned for his sins to the task of emptying the pool with a leaky shell. Perhaps Tregeagle has escaped his doom, because these days the waters are not deep, and periods of drought dry the lake. The grouping of houses that surround the turnoff to Dozmary Pool comprises the village of Bolventor, the site portrayed by Daphne du Maurier as the pirate rendezvous in *Jamaica Inn.*

Arrange to have tea in *Lanhydrock House,* an impressive estate of woods and gardens covering over 400 acres, about 2.5 miles (4 km) south of Bodmin on Route B3268. Both the gatehouse and the portrait gallery in the north wing are remnants of the original seventeenth-century construction; other sections of the house were rebuilt in 1881. The elaborate plaster ceiling of the gallery depicts scenes from the Old Testament (open April to October).

En Route from Bodmin – Take Route A30, then A391 south 12 miles (19 km) through Cornwall to St. Austell, an attractive industrial center bounded by both stark moorlands and sandy beaches. Just outside town are the Medacuddle Holy Well and an ancient stone formation called the Stone Chair.

It is 14 miles (22 km) farther on A390 to the market town of Truro, the administrative center of Cornwall, officially established in 1877. The Georgian edifices along Truro's Lemon and Prince's streets and Trafalgar Row attest to the town's earlier prosperity. Small wonder that when the See of Cornwall was reestablished in 1876, the city was chosen for the first cathedral to be erected since the Reformation. Its bold early Gothic design, added to the site of a sixteenth-century church, was completed shortly before World War I.

Route A39 leads southwest about 11 miles (18 km) from town to the intersection with A394. A short side trip from here along A39 descends to the port of Falmouth and Pendennis Castle. It's only 13 miles (21 km) west, from the intersection to Helston, at the base of the broad promontory called the Lizard, via A394. Every year in early May, Helston's residents dance through the town's streets in their traditional Flora or Furry celebration. Popular legends say that this is related to the death of a dragon that dropped a huge rock on the town, but a more likely hypothesis is that it is the remnant of Druidic spring fertility rites.

THE LIZARD: This broad peninsula, varying from 200 to 400 feet above sea level, is the place to go for dramatic views of England's rugged southernmost shore. On the west side of the Lizard is Mullion Cove, where many caves cut into the cliffsides are exposed during low tide — a find for spelunkers and treasure seekers. The colorful cliffs of Kynance Cove lie farther south along the western shore. Lizardtown itself is less than a mile from the lighthouse that marks the southernmost spot in England, Lizard Point. On the eastern shore (off B3293) is the port of Coverack, once a base for smugglers. It is partially protected by the Manacles Rocks, an offshore hazard that wrecked many a ship.

Penzance, the principal town of the western peninsula known as Land's End, is 13 miles (21 km) west of Helston on A394.

PENZANCE: The fishing and seaport center of England's southwestern extremity, Penzance is well sheltered within Mount's Bay, which splits the tip of Cornwall into the Lizard and Land's End peninsulas. The mild climate here has attracted travelers for centuries, and the city has become a popular resort and shopping center. In bygone days, the town was often sacked by pirates, and it was virtually destroyed by Spanish raiders in 1595. The 1836 Market House (Market Jew St.) is worth seeing, but a far greater rarity in England are the subtropical plants and flowers in Morrab Gardens; only the exceptionally warm climate of this distant area allows these plants to survive in Britain.

Frequent departures from the port by both boat and helicopter shuttle visitors to the Isles of Scilly (pronounced "silly"), an archipelago of over 150 islands and rocky outcroppings about 30 miles southwest of Land's End, near where the Atlantic meets the English Channel. Only five islands are large enough to support populations, but there are several interesting forts and religious sites spread throughout the chain. Star Castle, on St. Mary's, was erected in 1593; Tresco Abbey on Tresco Island has lovely gardens, with between 3,000 and 4,000 varieties of plants, and the Valhalla Maritime Museum has some fascinating exhibits; St. Helen's has two ancient ruins: a church and a monastery; and there are numerous other structures on the islands. Legends are the only firm evidence that these islands are the mountaintops of the lands of King Arthur, Lyonnesse, although some of the earlier fortifications could be from that semimythical period.

One of the most spectacular visions in all of England is St. Michael's Mount, standing majestically about ¼ mile off the sandy shore of Marazion, a tiny market town 3 miles (5 km) east of Penzance. In 495, fishermen claimed to have seen a vision of St. Michael appear on the 200-foot mountain that rises from the calm waters of Mount's Bay. In the eleventh century the grounds were used for a priory. The castle, open to visitors, can be reached by a causeway during low tide or by ferry from either Penzance or Marazion at highwater periods.

En Route from Penzance – A generous coastal esplanade leads south to the picturesque fishing villages of Newlyn (1 mi/1.6 km) and Mousehole (pronounced "mowzal"; 3 mi/5 km), sheltered in the lee of Mount's Bay — perfect material for a beautiful morning's walk. Be sure to stop at the *Ship Inn* for a taste of a local beer, St. Austell, and prevail upon the publican to tell you the story of fisherman Tom Bowcock. Save your evenings for viewing the sunsets from the western tip of Land's End — they're incredible!

About 10 miles (16 km) southwest of Penzance (via either B3315 or an extension of the esplanade, the cliff path) are the sandy beaches of Porthcurno, the cultural hub of Land's End. Here, on a cliff west of the village, is the open-air Minack Theatre, which uses its vast panorama of the Atlantic for a backdrop. On the village's east boundary is Logan's Rock, a delicately balanced 65-ton granite boulder that can easily be rocked in place — however, local custom insists that if it falls over, you've got to replace it.

LAND'S END: This immense granite ridge extending into the sea is the westernmost point of England. Once called Penwith in Cornish, the area is now privately owned and open to the public only from March to October. Avoid the souvenir shops and crowds; slip out onto the point just before dawn or, even better, at dusk for fantastic views of the sun. The Isles of Scilly are easily visible on a clear day, and lighthouses illuminate the most treacherous rocks after dark. Afterward, stop at the *Old Success Inn* overlooking Sennen Cove and relax before heading on.

Inland (toward Zennor, Morvah, and St. Just) are several Stone Age quoits, or dolmens — burial chambers formed by laying a top, or capstone, across stone uprights. Chysauter is the site of an Iron Age village of huts used by Roman and British miners until about AD 100.

The resort of St. Ives, on the north coast of the peninsula, is only 7 miles (11 km) northeast of Penzance. Here the narrow cobbled streets are lined with the cottages of fishermen and their families. The town, long popular with artists, swells with summer-time painters each year. You'll find St. Austell in pubs throughout town as well as national brews.

En Route from Land's End – Traveling northeast from Penzance, Route A30 runs parallel to the coast, gradually bearing inland toward the village of Fraddon, 35 miles (56 km) away. All of the small roads to the left (north) of the highway lead to the coast, and many run along the shoreline before returning to A30. The region is edged with tiny coves and long strands of beach, which can stretch to 4 or 5 miles (6 or 8 km) during low tide. At Fraddon, the *Blue Anchor* deserves a pause for a beer before taking A39 through the attractive countryside of the Vale of Mawgan to Camelford, a trek of some 23 miles (37 km). Then follow B3266 a mile north to B3263, which brings you into Tintagel.

TINTAGEL: Along the craggy slate cliffs of the western Cornish coastline are the ruins of one of the most famous castles in England, Tintagel Castle, reputed to be the birthplace of King Arthur, born to Uther Pendragon and his queen, Igerne. The castle sits on a headland of slate, called Tintagel Head, high above the Atlantic cove. The ancient village of Tintagel, at one time known as Trevena, is on the mainland less than a mile away. The cave in which Merlin is said to have weaved his spells (and perhaps to have been sealed in) is at the foot of the castle's steep cliffs, accessible only at low tide. The castle was built in the twelfth century on the ruins of an earlier Celtic monastery. The mainland fortifications were added during the following century to protect the natural rock bridge that once served as the castle entranceway; it has since collapsed and a man-made bridge has been built.

En Route from Tintagel – Continuing east on Route B3263 returns you to A39 headed north and east to Bude, an attractive resort about 14 miles (23 km) up the coast. Bude's sandy beaches, though lightly laced with rocky headlands, are famous for both swimming and surfing, and the festive atmosphere of this summer resort has also spawned a golf course and tennis courts.

Route A39 makes it way north about 30 miles (48 km) from Bude to the huge bay (known both as Bideford and Barnstaple Bay) formed at the mouth of the River Taw. The beautiful fishing village of Clovelly, deeply set in a cleft face of the cliffs that line the western curve of the bay, has been fairly inundated by artists and travelers. At one time Bideford, perched on the hills that overlook the mouth of the Torridge River on the west side of the bay, was one of England's busiest seaports, frequented by Sir Walter Raleigh, Sir Francis Drake, and Martin Frobisher. Many fine homes, built by wealthy merchants in the seventeenth century, still line the town's old main street, Bridgeland Street. The town Westward Ho! was named for Charles Kingsley's 1855 novel (3 mi/5 km northwest of Bideford, or take an excursion boat); but, in fact, parts of the book were actually written in Bideford (it's the "little white town" in the book) at the *Royal Hotel.* Take a moment to examine the 24-arch bridge in the center of town — it was built in 1460 (and altered slightly in the 1920s). Barnstaple, although no longer the bustling seaport that thrived for 1,000 years, is still a busy market town for the surrounding area. Relieved of the pressures of constant growth, Barnstaple has become a delightful town to visit and a pleasant base for touring the north coast and Exmoor. The *Three Tuns Pub,* over 500 years old, is an excellent place for meeting people. The downstairs attracts younger drinkers; the upstairs bar tends to be a bit quieter and conservative.

EXMOOR: The twin resorts of Lynton and Lynmouth, both within the boundary of Exmoor National Park, lie another 20 miles (32 km) northeast along A39. Approaching from the lower coastal area of Barnstaple, the rising granite and slate hills of Exmoor are a grand sight. Lynton is the higher of the two resorts, on a cliff almost 500 feet above the sea; Lynmouth lies at the water's edge, where the East and West Lyn rivers join the sea. Coastal walking paths lead both east and west through beautifully wooded rocky high ridges and combes. Inland, the moor's gentle ridges create a maze of valleys and vales.

The Doone Valley, setting for Richard Blackmore's novel *Lorna Doone,* is about 4 miles (6 km) south (inland) from the resort areas. The Lorna Doone tale is in part an amalgamation of stories about the outlaw band that terrorized the moor for several decades during the seventeenth century, and Blackmore drew heavily upon both factual events and local legends as well as places in his work.

Route B3223 leads inland from the resorts, through the very heart of Exmoor. Simonbath (9 mi/14 km southeast of Lynmouth) lies just a few miles from the head of the Doone Valley. Time has almost obliterated the ruins at this end of the valley, which are thought to have been occupied by the outlaw band. Route B3223 joins B3224 east of Simonbath and continues to the hunting and fishing center of Exford. Here the staghounds that track Exmoor's famed wild red deer are kenneled, and anglers by the score test their skills against elusive trout. Check with the proprietor of the *Crown Hotel* about obtaining a horse for an afternoon ride through the moors, then head off about 4 miles (6 km) northeast to Dunkery Beacon. The beacon is the highest point on the moor, 1,705 feet, and the view extends almost 100 miles in good weather. A healthy trek of about 4 miles (6 km) north across the moors returns you to near the coast at Porlock. This village lies right on A39, about 6 miles (10 km) east of Lynmouth, and somewhere in the intervening stretch may well be the cottage "twixt Porlock and Lynton" where Samuel Taylor Coleridge had the opium vision that resulted in *Kubla Khan*. Some sources claim, however, that the vision occurred in his home at Nether Stowey, about 35 miles (56 km) east of Lynton on A39.

BEST EN ROUTE

Southwest England is amply provided with small inns and historic accommodations, and the traveler so inclined can spend just about every night holed up with the ghosts of his or her choice, though in most cases the accommodations are not going to be modern or splashy. On the other hand, in the major resort areas, every kind of guesthouse, hotel, motel, and rental is available. Expect to pay up to $80 (or more) a night for a double in the hotels listed as expensive; from $30 to $60 in the moderate range; and under $30 in the inexpensive category.

Remember that the value of the dollar does fluctuate, and prices will always vary slightly. The hostelries listed below are merely a selection of our choices for the district; there are any number of acceptable inns lining the roads you will travel.

AMESBURY

Antrobus Arms Hotel – This former vicarage has combined modern comfort with its antique style quite nicely. Features include both log fires and central heating, plus walled garden with a fountain and Cedar of Lebanon tree. Church St. (phone: 23163). Expensive to moderate.

SALISBURY

The White Hart Hotel – A blend of Georgian and modern styles heightens the delightful atmosphere of this well-aged establishment. Three bars to fit your moods, traditional English fare, and a warming fire on chilly days complete this comfortable nest. St. John St. (phone: 27476). Expensive to moderate.

Rose and Crown Hotel – On the banks of the Avon, this hotel is a happy amalgam of ancient inn and contemporary hotel. There are four-poster beds in the half-timbered old inn and comfortable modern rooms in the new annex. Harnham Rd. (phone: 27908). Moderate.

EXETER

Buckerell Lodge Crest Hotel – When built in the thirteenth century, this building served as a hunting lodge. Now it has 54 guest rooms and wonderful views. Topsham Rd. (phone: 52451). Expensive to moderate.

Royal Clarence Hotel – This historic building with 63 rooms overlooks the cathedral in the city center. Cathedral Yard (phone: 58464). Expensive.

PENZANCE AND ILES OF SCILLY

Island Hotel – On a wonderfully quiet island (no cars!), this hotel combines old and new architectural styles into a beautiful beach resort. The hotel also has a good restaurant, and arranges fishing charters; sailboats are available too. Closed mid-October to mid-March. Tresco (phone: 0720-22883). Expensive.

Lesceave Cliff Hotel – White walls and Mediterranean arches, combined with beach views, belie this hotel's location in England. The staff is exceptionally helpful, can arrange fishing trips. Praa Sands (phone: 073676-2325). Moderate.

Lamorna Cove Hotel – Although the modern additions can't compare with the original granite house or its lovely setting above a tranquil wooded cove, the hotel is a delight. Lots of tasty seafood is served in its restaurant. Lamorna (phone: 0736-731411). Moderate.

ST. IVES

Tregenna Castle Hotel – Perched above the old fishing village, this eighteenth-century home certainly offers the grandest view of the bay available. It is something of a resort, with tennis, golf (18 holes), squash courts, a pool outside, and more. St. Ives (phone: 795254). Expensive to moderate.

Trecarrell Hotel – Less grand, but homey, in a rambling Victorian house that has been nicely refurbished. Carthew Terrace (phone: 795707). Moderate to inexpensive.

BARNSTAPLE

The Imperial Hotel – In the center of Barnstaple's charming waterfront, the older parts of this hotel are quite beautiful. Taw Vale Parade (phone: 45861). Expensive to moderate.

Wales

Like all mountainous countries, Wales has been slow to react to outside change. In part this has been due to poor communications; the roads here rise and fall sharply, twisting and turning around the mountainsides, making contact with the outside world rather difficult. In part, however, it has been due to the character of the Welsh people, who, throughout five centuries of Roman occupation, brutal conquest by the Normans, and 700 years of uninterrupted English rule, have managed to hold on to a unique culture, age-old customs, and their own ancient, sonorous language (it is estimated that about one-quarter of the population still speaks Welsh). Although technically and for all practical purposes a British principality whose 2.5 million people are governed from Westminster, Wales has retained a distinct identity and an aura of legend and mystery even in the eyes of its English neighbors.

While the scenery here is always marked by its grandeur, it is more diverse than one might imagine. Occupying an 8,000-square-mile landmass that juts west from England into the Irish Sea, Wales is divided informally into three areas — South, Mid, and North Wales — each possessing distinctive topography and points of interest. The route described below covers all three, beginning in the South, at the bustling seaport of Cardiff, and threading its way some 275 miles (440 km) north, first through the grassy mountains and wild moorlands of Brecon Beacons National Park, then west toward the coast. After visiting some of the loveliest seaside resorts and coastal villages of Mid Wales, the route enters the rugged mountain country of the North, passing through the towering beauty of Snowdonia National Park, in the northwest corner of the country. Snowdonia's range is capped by the 3,560-foot peak of Snowdon itself, the highest point in Wales, the summit of which can be reached on the Snowdon Mountain Railway. This rack-and-pinion line is one of many still powered by steam engines, all of which operate on extremely narrow-gauge track using small locomotives and carriages, known locally as "the great little trains of Wales."

Wales is renowned for its castles, huge, warlike bastions, many of which were built by Edward I in the thirteenth century to demonstrate the supremacy of the English Crown over the Welsh. Some of the greatest of these fortresses are along your route in North and South Wales, where they stand, often overlooking the sea, as impressive reminders of the country's turbulent past.

The Wales Tourist Board puts out three excellent publications covering North, South, and Mid Wales. In addition to extensive gazetteers and a regional map, each gives details on activities, nature trails, good beaches, and so forth. For more information, write to the tourist board at Brunel House, 2 Fitzalan Rd., Cardiff CF2 1UY (phone: 0222-499909).

CARDIFF: Connected to London and the rest of the outside world by the M4 motorway, high-speed train service, and its own small airport, Cardiff is an ideal starting point for a tour of Wales. With a population of 277,000, it is the capital and largest city in Wales and one of Britain's most important seaports. Spacious and dignified, the city is also thoroughly cosmopolitan, with large, covered shopping arcades and excellent sports facilities, including that holiest of places for rugby fans, the National Rugby Stadium.

Among the city's chief attractions for visitors are its castle and the National Museum of Wales, both near the center of town. Cardiff Castle was begun by the Normans in the eleventh century on the site of an old Roman camp. A thin layer of brown stone can still be seen running through the castle's surrounding wall, marking the spot where the Roman defenses left off and, centuries later, the Norman work began. The original castle keep stands on a small, moated mound, an example of the Norman motte and bailey. Expanded over the years, the castle was reconstructed in 1865 by the third marquis of Bute, a young man with a passion for architectural fantasy. Although the ornate Victorian exterior is not to everyone's liking, the castle's interior, with its lavish decorations and rich historical murals, is fascinating. The National Museum of Wales (Museum Ave.) displays interesting Welsh archaeological finds, handicrafts, and folk art and is especially noted for its collection of French Impressionist paintings, the centerpiece of which is Renoir's *La Parisienne.*

Two miles (3 km) from the city center, on the banks of the River Taff, is the village-like suburb of Llandaff, home of the twelfth-century Llandaff Cathedral, with its striking modern sculpture, *Christ in Majesty,* by Jacob Epstein.

Five miles (8 km) west of Cardiff at the village of St. Fagans is the Welsh Folk Museum. This open-air museum is in a woods and garden. Many old houses, mills, chapels, and farms have been moved from all over Wales and rebuilt on the site to illustrate early Welsh life. Caerphilly, with its thirteenth-century castle, is 6 miles (10 km) north on A469. A fine white cheese is named after the town (where it was once made).

En Route from Cardiff – Route A470 takes you through Tongwynais, home of the Victorian extravaganza Castell Coch, another fairy-tale edifice built by the young marquis of Bute. From the outside this castle looks like an ornate French château, and its interior is lavishly fitted.

BRECON: The major center for touring the 519 square miles of Brecon Beacons National Park, Brecon sits at the junction of the rivers Usk and Afon Honddu. It has a massive thirteenth- and fourteenth-century fortified priory that stands high above the Afon Honddu on Priory Hill. The town's castle, in the garden of the *Castle of Brecon Hotel,* was dismantled by the townsfolk during the seventeenth-century civil war in an attempt to avoid the bloodshed necessary to defend it.

The Brecknock Museum, in the old County Hall in Glamorgan Street (closed Sundays), displays interesting examples of Welsh folk art and local crafts, such as the hand-carved wooden "love spoons" young Welshmen used in bygone days to plight their troth. Just west of the town is the Mountain Center, which has advice and literature for hikers.

En Route from Brecon – Route A40 follows the girth of the Brecon Beacons, three red sandstone peaks, the highest of which looms nearly 3,000 feet high through scenery that is inspiring at any time of year. Often mist rolls downward from the Beacons and the nearby Black Mountains, creating an atmosphere of eerie solitude.

Anglers may want to stop at Llandovery, an important market town well known in the area for its excellent salmon fishing.

CARMARTHEN: Carmarthen is the administrative hub of the southwestern corner of Wales. Its large covered market draws crowds every Wednesday and Saturday, and behind it the cattle market holds sales each Monday, Wednesday, and Thursday.

In Nott Square stands a monument to Dr. Robert Ferrar, bishop of St. David's, who was burned at the stake on this site in 1555. Also of interest are the Dyfed County Museum, housed in the former Bishop's Palace at Abergwili on the outskirts of the town, and Merlin's Oak, also on the museum grounds. Legend says that when the oak falls, so will the town; to make sure it does not topple, the townspeople have propped it up with concrete.

En Route from Carmarthen – Fans of the poet Dylan Thomas may want to divert onto A4066 at the village of St. Clears for a side trip to Laugharne, where Thomas lived and wrote and where he lies buried in a simple grave in the village churchyard. The Boathouse, open to the public, was the poet's residence. Otherwise, take the A477 to Tenby.

TENBY: This ancient walled town stands on a rocky peninsula at the western edge of Carmarthen Bay. With two sandy beaches and a pretty harbor, it makes a delightful base for touring the Pembrokeshire coast. Some 2.5 miles offshore is Caldey Island, the home of an ancient but still functioning monastery where Cistercian monks make perfume from the island's flowers.

There are many good hotels within the town's fourteenth-century walls, including the *Imperial,* which actually incorporates parts of the walls in its structure. Local events include golf tournaments (Tenby Golf Club's 18-hole course is at South Beach), St. Margaret's Fair, and a lively regatta and carnival, all of which occur in August. Local pottery and paintings are for sale in the many art shops of Upper Frog Street.

CARDIGAN: Another market town also popular with visitors, Cardigan has a number of cafés and restaurants and a good number of accommodations, mainly in small guesthouses. Its chief attraction is salmon fishing. There are good catches to be had on the Afon Teifi, which flows from here into Cardigan Bay. Some fishermen still use *coracles* — homemade boats of intertwined willow and hazel that look rather like wicker shopping baskets; they have been used for salmon fishing for over a thousand years. Coracle races are held at the Teifiside village of Cilgerran in August.

Three-quarters of a mile away, across Cardigan Bridge, is St. Dogmael's, an old Welsh house that was sacked by the Norse and later claimed by the Normans, who turned it into an annex of the Abbey of Tiron in France. The church contains the ancient Sagranus Stone, whose inscriptions in Latin and old Gaelic served as a key to the language of the tribes of the Dark Ages.

En Route from Cardigan – Head north on Route A487 for the 39-mile (63-km) drive along the coastline to Aberystwyth (pronounced "aber-ist-with").

From this road you can reach many of the small coastal villages, including New Quay, which some say is the setting of Dylan Thomas's play *Under Milk Wood* (others claim it's Fishguard). You pass through the popular yachting center of

Aberaeron, a nineteenth-century Georgian town, many of whose buildings are of special architectural or historic interest.

ABERYSTWYTH: A popular seaside resort with both sand and pebble bathing beaches, Aberystwyth is also the seat of the University of Wales and the administrative center for Cardigan Bay. Its lively seafront promenade is lined with hotels and has a pier, bandstand, and the ruins of a castle, which stand sentinel on the headland.

History is carefully preserved at the National Library of Wales (Penglais Rd.), which houses some of the earliest Welsh manuscripts; and the past is still very much alive at Alexandra Station, where British Railways' last steam-powered service departs for the spectacular falls at Devil's Bridge, high in the Vale of Rheidol, which according to legend was built by the devil himself. Closer to home, the town's cliff railway carries visitors to the peak of Constitution Hill, where they have a splendid view of the bay and the town.

Concerts and evening shows are regular features along the promenade, and at the Arts Centre on the university campus. The Arts Centre also holds frequent exhibitions and the University Theatre presents a summer season of plays. Nearby is the Nanteos Stately Home, a Georgian mansion with an imposing oak staircase, some fine plasterwork, and Italian marble.

En Route from Aberystwyth – Route A487 skirts the base of the mountains, heading up into the Doyey Valley to Machynlleth, a market town that was made capital of Wales by Owain Glyndwr in the fourteenth century, during the great Welsh hero's drive to rid the country of English rule. As you drive through town, you pass an immense clock tower, standing like a rocket ready for launching, a gift from the marquess of Londonderry in 1873. Plas Machynlleth, also in the town, was formerly the Londonderry residence and now houses the local Council.

DOLGELLAU: At the head of the lovely Mawddach Estuary and almost at the foot of the famous Cader Idris Mountain, scenic Dolgellau is an important market town for the many small mountain villages in the vicinity. It makes an ideal base for walks and excursions into the lake and mountain country to the east.

The customs and speech here remain distinctly Welsh, but thanks to its large number of visitors, you should have no trouble being understood. The town itself is quite old and is built largely of the native gray stone. Its bridge, crossing the Afon Wnion, was built in 1638 and is now an officially protected structure. Close to the primary school is an old tollhouse left from the days of turnpikes.

In the Mawddach Valley close to the town you can try your luck panning for gold; gold has been excavated in the surrounding mountains since Roman times, and it is this Welsh gold that was used in some royal family wedding rings.

HARLECH: Still a small village, Harlech is dominated by its immense gray stone castle, another of the chain of fortifications ordered by Edward I. It was this massive stronghold, the last to yield to the Yorkists in 1468, that provided the inspiration for *Men of Harlech*, one of the best-known traditional Welsh songs. Standing high on a rocky promontory, Harlech Castle offers extensive views of land, sea, and mountains. Those with no fear of heights can walk all around the castle on its unfenced, 10-foot-thick walls and climb the 143 steps to the top of its gatehouse. Look toward the sea, half a mile away, and recall that when the castle was built in 1283 it actually stood on the shore. Since that time, however, the sea has receded.

En Route from Harlech – The private village of Portmeirion, near Penrhyndeudraeth, was built by architect Sir Clough Williams-Ellis, who died in 1978. Portmeirion, a strange, pastel-colored dream world built in an Italianate style, became known as the setting for the television series *The Prisoner*.

CAERNARFON: Still mostly enclosed in its thirteenth-century town walls, Caernarfon is perhaps the best-known Welsh town since the 1969 investiture of Prince Charles as Prince of Wales in its beautiful castle. The castle stands defiantly at the junction of the River Seiont and the Menai Strait, overlooking the Isle of Anglesey. Begun, like Harlech Castle, in 1283, it took 37 years to build, and today it is regarded as a masterpiece of medieval architecture. Inside is the museum of the Royal Welsh Fusiliers.

In addition to being a market center (on Saturdays in Castle Square), Caernarfon also boasts two yacht clubs, tennis, golf, and bowls facilities, and good river and sea fishing. In Castle Square is a statue of Prime Minister David Lloyd George, who was instrumental in securing a future for Caernarfon Castle. He spent his boyhood in the village of Llanystumdwy, near Criccieth.

Near the town is the Roman fort of Segontium, a military center founded in AD 78. A museum here exhibits the area's archaeological finds. The town of Llanberis, 8 miles (13 km) southeast of Caernarfon is the base station for the Snowdon Mountain Railway (April–September). Or follow the spectacular Llanberis Pass, a winding road flanked by steeply rising mountains and the debris of rock slides, to the village of Beddgelert. From the top of the pass, know locally as Pen-y-Pass, you can walk up to the summit of Snowdon.

BEST EN ROUTE

During the peak summer months, the famous Eisteddfodau — festivals of music and poetry — are held in towns and villages throughout Wales. If your trip will coincide with any of these, make sure you book hotel reservations well in advance. Note, too, that drinking laws are rather idiosyncratic in parts of Wales; in certain districts you cannot drink alcoholic beverages on Sundays except as a guest in a hotel. Under the Taste of Wales scheme inaugurated by the Wales Tourist Board, hotels and restaurants are being encouraged to serve traditional Welsh fare. Look for the round Taste of Wales sign, indicating a participating establishment. In the listing below, any establishment charging under $40 per night for a room for two persons is considered inexpensive; $40 to $60, moderate; and more than $60, expensive; prices are slightly higher in Cardiff.

CARDIFF

The Park – Beautifully appointed hotel combining the traditional air of a country house with the luxury and comfort of a modern hotel. Two good restaurants. 108 rooms. Park Pl., in the center of town. (phone: 383299). Expensive.

Royal Hotel – Centrally located, this is one of Cardiff's most dependable hotels, and offers good service, all modern conveniences, a fine restaurant, and an extensive wine list. St. Mary St. (phone: 23321). Moderate.

BRECON

Mountains Hotel – On the A470, in the heart of the Brecon Beacons National Park. Its 26 rooms have private baths (phone: 2939 or 4242). Moderate.

Lansdowne Hotel – Simple but comfortable Georgian hotel has 12 bedrooms, 4 with bath. Restaurant. The Watton, Brecon (phone: 3321). Inexpensive.

CARMARTHEN

Ivy Bush Royal Hotel – Historic hotel has been thoroughly streamlined, offering saunas, grill room, and a choice of cocktail lounges. Good restaurant with Welsh cuisine. Spilman St. (phone: 235111). Moderate.

TENBY

Imperial Hotel – Immediately above the beach, with fabulous views of St. Catherine's and Caldey islands from most of the rooms. The terrace incorporates part of the medieval town walls. Two restaurants with Welsh cuisine, dinner dances, private tennis court. The Paragon (phone: 3737). Moderate to inexpensive.

Royal Lion – Overlooking Tenby Harbour, this old establishment has been recently modernized. Basically a family hotel, open February until Christmas with a resident's dining room and a seafood restaurant; 36 rooms, 15 with private baths. High St. (phone: 2127). Moderate.

CARDIGAN

Castell Malgwyn – This country house hotel has 24 rooms and is set in 80 acres of parkland and woods alongside the River Teifi. Salmon fishing, putting green, outdoor heated swimming pool, 2 dining rooms, 3 well-stocked bars, and cellars (phone: 023987-382). Moderate.

ABERYSTWYTH

Belle Vue Royal Hotel – Comfortable hotel overlooking Cardigan Bay has a restaurant and 42 rooms; an 18-hole golf course is nearby. Marine Terrace (phone: 617558). Moderate.

DOLGELLAU

George III Hotel – This 300-year-old hotel with restaurant is delightfully situated at the head of the Mawddach estuary. Freshly caught fish is the restaurant's specialty in summer, and in winter, the menu turns to local game. All 12 rooms have views of the Mawddach estuary and the mountains. Just out of town on the A493 in Penmaenpool (phone: 422525). Moderate.

Golden Lion Royal Hotel – The decor here ranges from casual to formal, with 28 comfortable, antique-furnished rooms. Lion St. (phone: 422579). Moderate.

CRICCIETH

Bron Eifion – A country house hotel, conveniently close to Portmeirion and within sight of Cardigan Bay. Lots of Oregon pine paneling distinguishes the interior, as does the caring approach of the Robertson family, who own it (phone: 2385). Moderate.

CAERNARFON

Royal Hotel – A historic coaching inn that's been updated and made very comfortable. Its good dining room specializes in local produce. North Rd. (phone: 3184). Moderate.

Black Boy Inn – Within the town's medieval walls this inn dates back to the fourteenth century. Oak beams and inglenooks abound, and the cuisine of its restaurant is simple but good. North Gate St. (phone: 3604). Inexpensive.

The Cotswolds

Less than 100 miles west of London is the region known as the Cotswolds. It encompasses about 450 square miles of rolling limestone upland of the Cotswold Hills, punctuated by charming, carefully preserved medieval towns and villages built from the hills' honey-colored stone, which gives the region its character. The Cotswolds themselves stretch northeast in a curving 60-mile arc from Bath to the vicinity of Stratford-upon-Avon. Along their western edge they form a steep ridge of solid limestone, and their crest is the

Thames-Severn watershed. But the overall character of the countryside is tranquil and picturesque, like a rich tapestry. Much of this land is a great, sweeping pasture for the famous Cotswold sheep, with their heavy ringlets of fleece that once upon a time brought wealth to the area.

This is the England of the imagination: rolling hills covered by copses of ancient oaks, a landscape scaled to size for country walks and bird-watching. Towns are tied to one another by twisting country lanes that carry a constant commerce of farmers and sheepers, postmen, parsons, and pubgoers. The vista from any hill is as likely to include the square tower of a Norman church as a far field of cropping sheep, and any church is likely to be surrounded by the stone-tiled roofs of a tiny village, now no longer populated by farm workers but by retired folk, weekenders, and commuters to the larger towns. Relatively few ancient customs have survived. Village cemeteries are shaded by yews and village streams guarded by weeping willows. Nothing is very far from anything else, but privacy and protective isolation are accentuated by the quiet and country peace that settles over all. Village names are remnants of an earlier language and a younger England: Wyck Rissington, Upper and Lower Slaughter, Oddington, Guiting Power, Clapton-on-Hill, Bourton-on-the-Water.

The Cotswolds provided a rich agricultural center for the Romans until the fifth century, and the Roman presence is still visible in many places, such as the roads in Cirencester and the baths in Bath. The Romans left, the Danes took over, the Saxons routed the Danes, and the Normans routed the Saxons; and they all left their mark. But when the Cotswold sheep began to pay off, it was the wool merchants of the Middle Ages who built the symbols of the area that have endured — magnificent churches like the fifteenth-century one at Northleach and the fourteenth-century one at Cirencester.

The route described below begins in Bath, 115 miles (184 km) west of London, goes north through the heart of the Cotswolds to Stratford, and returns to London by way of Oxford. Starting from London, take the south-westerly Route M3 and the A303 past Stonehenge and swing northwest on A36 to Bath.

An eminently English way to see the Cotswolds is to take to shanks' mare and walk all or part of the 100-mile Cotswold Way, a series of well-marked and easily negotiated paths that follow the crests of the Cotswold hills from Bath to Chipping Campden in the north. Parts of the Way were first used by travelers 3,000 years ago, and later by medieval traders moving from village to village, the same villages that dot its course today. One need not be an accomplished hiker to follow the Way for a distance, and the weak of spirit can take heart in the thought that village and pub are never far apart. The benefits are multiple: Immersed in the countryside, you have a walking-pace view of the villages, buildings, cottages, churches, Roman ruins, Iron Age hillforts, and barrows — Stone Age burial mounds — that dot the region (the barrow at Belas Knap, between Cheltenham and Winchcombe, is one of the most impressive specimens in England). The Way is maintained by the Gloucestershire County Council, which marks its course with large yellow arrows to make hiking easier. Thornhill Press publishes an excellent guide, *The Cotswold Way,* by Mark Richards, available throughout the area.

A detailed guidebook, *The Cotswolds,* is available from the Heart of England Tourist Board, PO Box 15, Worcester WR1 2JT (phone: 0905-29511).

BATH: In the southwest corner of the Cotswolds region, Bath is Britain's oldest and most famous spa, where each day over 250,000 gallons of water from the mineral springs gush to the surface at a temperature of 120°F (49°C). The city's popularity through the ages is reflected in its architectural styles. Many quarters were built and rebuilt to suit the tastes of successive generations who came to "take the waters." But in a tremendous urban planning effort in the eighteenth century the whole was unified, laid out along classical lines in tier upon tier of Georgian crescents, terraces, and squares up the steep sides of the wooded hills along the winding Somerset Avon. Today it is an elegant Georgian spa that proudly calls itself the best-planned town in England.

According to legend, Bath was founded by the father of Shakespeare's King Lear, who was expelled from court as a leper, became a swineherd, and regained his health by imitating his swine and rolling in the warm mud of the mineral waters. In reality, it was probably the Romans who founded the town when they established an elaborate system of baths here in AD 54 and named the place Aquae Sulis, after a local god.

In the fifth century, after the Romans departed, the town fell into ruin. It was not until the tenth century that the region regained some prominence, when a newly built abbey was chosen for the coronation in 973 of King Edgar as the first king of England. Its fame was short-lived, and it didn't regain its reputation as a spa until the early seventeenth century, when the ailing Anne of Denmark, the wife of King James I, visited the baths. Kings and queens and their entourages, members of court, country gentry, and notables from all walks of life followed her lead to take the cure or just luxuriate. The baths became so popular that diarist Samuel Pepys wondered how the water could be sanitary with so many bodies jammed in it.

Today's city of elegant squares and exquisite crescent streets is the labor of love of two eighteenth-century architects, father and son, both named John Wood. They oversaw the rebuilding of the fashionable resort town, built the now-famous *Pump Room,* with its terrace restaurant, and the Assembly Rooms that today house one of the largest costume collections in the world. (The entire complex, including the Roman baths — which took archaeology 250 years to uncover — the Pump Room, and the Assembly Rooms, are open daily to the public.) Near the baths is the fifteenth-century Abbey Church.

But the Royal Crescent is the ultimate expression of Bath, a beautiful scimitar of street with 30 pale amber Georgian stone houses whose 114 Ionic columns, like soldiers on parade, support a continuous cornice the length of the street. It is considered the handsomest street in England. Visitors can see the interior of 1 Royal Crescent, perfectly restored in its Georgian splendor. Landsdown Crescent is another testament to the elegance of the Regency period. At Great Pulteney Street is the Holburne of Menstrie Museum (closed Mondays and January and February), with a superb collection of silver, glass, porcelain, miniatures, and paintings by English masters.

A $15 million development plan has restored three of the city's eighteenth-century baths and erected a new shopping arcade behind an original façade. The Royal Bath is now a luxury health club, while the Cross Bath is being used for teaching children to swim.

To see Bath as the Georgian era left it, it is best to go by foot, and because Bath is a small city, this is no hardship. Start with a map at the Abbey Church Yard, opposite the Pump Room, site of the tourist office (open daily; phone: 6-2831). Here you can also get complete information on the city and its environs, including a detailed plan of the baths. Guided tours are available.

About 2 miles (3.2 km) east of the city, on A36, is Claverton Manor, home of the American Museum in Britain, which has 18 rooms with period furnishings from the seventeenth to the nineteenth century. Open from March to October; closed Mondays.

En Route from Bath – Route A46 north takes you immediately into the hills, lifted by an enormous underpinning arm of limestone tilting south and east, where the road winds left and right with the contours of the terrain. It is a particularly beautiful road, lined with hedgerows and trees and many wild flowers in early spring. After about 11 miles (18 km) turn right onto B4040, marked Malmesbury. This narrow road passes close to the village of Badminton, the site of the duke of Beaufort's stately mansion and the birthplace of the game that bears its name. The 15,000-acre estate of Badminton House is the scene of the renowned horse trials every April. The house is open on Wednesday afternoons between June and September. To get to Badminton village, turn left at Acton Turville for about a mile (1.6 km). Ten miles (16 km) farther is Malmesbury.

MALMESBURY: This pleasant little town high above the Wiltshire Avon is the site of a magnificent Norman abbey with a most unusual history: During the dissolution under King Henry VIII in the sixteenth century, the building was sold to a clothier for £1,500. The man promptly brought in his weaving machinery and converted it into a factory. It was not until 1823 that a restoration effort was begun. Despite the many years of decay, the restoration was eminently successful, and today the abbey represents the finest example of Norman building remaining in Britain. The richly carved south porch and the musicians' gallery are especially impressive.

The town has two special connections with aviation. The first was at Malmesbury Abbey in the eleventh century, when Elmer, a monk, attempted to defy gravity by leaping from the tower wearing a pair of homemade wings. He survived the leap but was lame ever after. And at Kemble, 6 miles (10 km) north of Malmesbury, the Royal Air Force aerobatic team, the Red Arrows, practice their aerial formations.

Malmesbury is one of the oldest boroughs in England and a very well planned medieval city; it was already an important town before the Norman invasion. Some medieval remains are still extant, including fragments of walls and ruins of a twelfth-century castle that can be seen today at the *Old Bell Hotel*. Six bridges lead to the Market Square, at whose center is an impressive octagonal Tudor market cross. There are several lovely seventeenth- and eighteenth-century houses built by rich weavers on the adjoining streets. George Washington's ancestors appear to have come from this region, since at least five Washington predecessors are buried in a churchyard in Garsdon, 2 miles (3.2 km) east of Malmesbury.

At Kemble, 8 miles (13 km) after leaving town on A429, the road crosses a frail stream that rises to the surface only a few hundred yards away. This trickle is the mighty River Thames, just starting on its epic journey to London and the sea. Just after Kemble is the Smerrill Farm Museum with its interesting collection of agricultural bygones. Four miles (6 km) farther is the ancient Roman town of Cirencester.

CIRENCESTER: A bustling market town (there is a market on Fridays in Market Place), Cirencester was called Corinium when it was the capital of the Romans' first province in Britain and second in size only to London. Three Roman roads — Akeman Street, Fosse Way, and Ermine Street — radiated from the town, and are still used by traffic today. Mosaic floors, sculpture, and pottery recovered from the digs now form the extensive collection of Roman relics in the Corinium Museum on Park Street (open daily from May to September; closed Mondays from October to April). Just outside town, on Quern Hill, are the remains of a Roman amphitheater, just as one would expect in a major provincial capital. Don't miss the magnificent array of medieval stained glass in the fifteenth-century parish church. A number of events are staged in Cirencester each year, including horse trials, hot-air balloon meetings, polo competitions in May, June, and August, the ancient Sheep Fair in September, and a cattle market every Tuesday.

En Route from Cirencester – Take Route A429 out of town. If you have time, travel the more circuitous route to Fossebridge via Barnsley and Bibury. The latter is a most attractive Cotswold village with a trout farm and an interesting folk museum in an old watermill whose moving parts still work. At Fossebridge, 7 miles (11.2 km) north, there is excellent trout fishing. This is also the turnoff for Chedworth Roman Villa which has some of the best preserved remains of a Roman house in England. The villa displays mosaic pavements and the hypocaust, or central heating system — an underground fire chamber and a series of tile flues for distributing heat. In season, there is a display of lilies of the valley in the garden, thought to have been originally planted by the Romans (closed Mondays in summer, Wednesdays through Sundays in winter, and for the month of January).

Continuing north on A429 for 5 miles (8 km), you come to the junction with A40 and the town of Northleach. You can stop at this picturesque old coaching town before going 9 miles (14.4 km) farther to Bourton-on-the-Water.

NORTHLEACH: Important in the wool trade in the fifteenth century, this village of winding streets has changed little. Its proud church with its richly carved south porch is one of the finest built by the medieval wool merchants. Unlike many others in the region, this church miraculously escaped defacement by the Puritans. Also worth visiting are some lovely Tudor almshouses in the village and the Blind House, the windowless eighteenth-century jail.

BOURTON-ON-THE-WATER: With the River Windrush flowing gently beside the main street, this village is sometimes called the Venice of the Cotswolds. It has a picture-postcard quality: The stream is so clear, the banks are so green, and the tiny eighteenth-century stone bridges are so picturesque — it all seems like a tableau. A good starting point for a walking tour is the New Inn, which has a scale model of the village at one-ninth the original size. Don't miss the quaint old house on Sherborn Street, built in 1650 with dovecotes set right into the wall. Dial House is another old cottage (1698). Most other houses in town date from the eighteenth century.

Another attraction is Birdland, a bird garden, which contains more than 600 exotic species from all over the world (open daily). Much of the Cotswolds is a bird-watcher's paradise, and the English pursue this favorite pastime with single-minded vigor. A midsummer walk down any wooded lane or along the Cotswold Way is likely to turn up magpies, rooks, or ravens; larks, thrushes, or blue tits; blackbirds, wood pigeons, and the English robin. You might want to take a pair of binoculars and a field guide.

En Route from Bourton-on-the-Water – This is the heart of the Cotswolds, a series of tiny villages signposted along unclassified roads that lead to an England long gone elsewhere. The Rissingtons — Wyck, Little, and Great — are three quiet villages on the western slope of the Windrush Valley. All have the Norman churches so commonly found in Cotswold towns, though Wyck Rissington's is perhaps the oldest, with remnants of an earlier Saxon church incorporated in the structure of its Norman edifice. More imposing — and more than slightly daft — is the tall, straight, comely redwood that rises over the village; visible for miles, the tree was planted by an early visitor to the US.

More famous than the Rissingtons are the Slaughters — Upper and Lower — if fame is the correct word to use for a village of 165 people (in the case of Upper Slaughter), a crystal-clear stream full of watercress and crossed by a ford and a tiny stone bridge alongside. The village center lies behind an old castle mound, and from the byroad to Lower Slaughter, down an avenue of evergreens, you can see the magnificent Upper Slaughter Manor House, with Elizabethan front intact. Opposite the church is the entrance to the *Lords of the Manor Hotel.* Lower

Slaughter is one of the most renowned villages in England. The footbridge over the gently curving stream has provided a subject for countless artists and photographers. Pick up A436 to Stow-on-the-Wold, now a quiet hill town but once the bustling, prosperous center of the Cotswold wool trade because of its location at the junction of several main roads. The market square is a jumble of old inns and houses, among them the fine St. Edward's Hall, which contains a collection of armor. Continue to Moreton-in-Marsh.

MORETON-IN-MARSH: The town astride the Roman Fosse Way has a medieval stone tower on its main street that was used as a jail; a bell in the tiny tower once sounded curfew. One of the town's most interesting houses is seventeenth-century Creswyke House; the mulberry tree in its garden is said to have been grown from a cutting of Shakespeare's tree in Stratford. Take A44 out of town and go 16 miles (25.6 km) to Broadway.

BROADWAY: Here the diverse elements of Cotswold life come together in perfect harmony. The uniform honey-colored stone buildings lead to the inevitable cricket green; on any afternoon of a match you will hear the distinct Cotswold accent rollicking back and forth from players to spectators in support or friendly raillery. Behind a yew hedge is Abbot's Grange, a fourteenth-century house with its own chapel. Lording over all is the splendid *Lygon Arms Hotel,* today one of England's finest hostelries and kitchens, a former coaching inn visited by Charles I and Cromwell. The famous hotel has even brought some industry to Broadway. The workshop set up in 1904 to repair the inn's antique furniture today exports its products worldwide to collectors (the Russell showroom is open Tuesdays and Fridays). The village has many lovely old buildings, among them the three-gabled Tudor House, the Prior's Manse, and Court Farm, with its garden of rare shrubs, an English passion. If Broadway is an attractive base for Cotswolds' exploration, the *Lygon Arms* is only half the attraction. The other half is Stratford-upon-Avon, only 15 miles (24 km) away.

STRATFORD-UPON-AVON: This illustrious town, forever synonymous with William Shakespeare, is the place of his birth and burial. England carefully guards this image, and the whole town is something of a shrine to Shakespeare's memory, an international center of pilgrimage administered by an official body called the Shakespeare Birthplace Trust. And yet around and beside the thousands of visitors that come to see plays at the Royal Shakespeare Theatre and to make the rounds of the Shakespeare sites, Stratford's ancient existence as a very lively market town continues unabated. The town received its first market charter in 1196 — fully 368 years before Shakespeare's birth — and still holds three central markets and one important cattle market a week. As has happened for centuries, once a week Cotswold farmers bring their produce into this charming town filled with half-timbered early-sixteenth-century buildings, set in peaceful countryside of green fields, the gentle Avon, and lovely old halls, castles, and churches.

Stratford is best explored on foot, with a walking map available at the tourist office, Judith Shakespeare House (1 High St; phone: 29-31-27). Inevitably, most of the sites you will want to visit are related to the playwright. So perhaps the best place to start is at his birthplace (Henley St.; open daily), a half-timbered sixteenth-century building with a lovely garden in back. The house has been furnished in the style of the period and contains memorabilia, including books and manuscripts. Going along Bridge Street, you come to the River Avon and to the lovely 14-arch Clopton Bridge, dating from the fifteenth century. Spacious riverside gardens lead to the Royal Shakespeare Theatre, which in itself draws many visitors. The modern building, beside the theater, opened in 1932. The season runs from April through January, and tickets should be bought as far in advance as possible from the box office (Royal Shakespeare Theatre, Stratford-upon-Avon, Warwickshire CV37 6BB). Adjoining the theater is the picture gallery and exhibition of portraits and relics of famous Shakespearean players (open daily). A pleasant riverside path leads to Holy Trinity Church, where Shakespeare and his family are buried. Nearby is Hall's Croft, once the home of Shakespeare's daughter Susanna and one of Stratford's finest Tudor townhouses. In the center of town and dating from 1596 is Harvard House (High St.), the home of the mother of John Harvard, benefactor of Harvard University. The half-timbered house is now owned by the university. A few yards away is New Place on Chapel Street, all that remains of Shakespeare's last home — the foundation — and in the fine Elizabethan garden is the venerated mulberry tree said to have been grown from a cutting planted by Shakespeare himself. Nash's house next door, which once belonged to the husband of Shakespeare's granddaughter, is now a museum of local history.

Close to Stratford are several other Shakespearean landmarks. Anne Hathaway's Cottage in Shottery, 1 mile (1.6 km) west, is a well-preserved English thatched farmhouse that was the early home of Shakespeare's wife (open daily except Sunday mornings in winter). Mary Arden's House in Wilmcote, north of Shottery, was Shakespeare's mother's home before her marriage. It is one of the outstanding farmsteads in Warwickshire. Most of the sixteenth-century buildings are made of close-timbered oak beams and native stone, an ideal setting for the museum of rural life they now house. Within the pleasant countryside north of Stratford via A46 is Charlecote Park, where young Will was allegedly caught poaching. The massive Elizabethan mansion, fronted by an avenue of lime trees, is now a museum of historic carriages (closed Mondays and Tuesdays May to September, and open weekends only October to April). Farm buildings near the picturesque gatehouse have been converted into an attractive restaurant with a walled garden.

From Stratford, take Route A34 to Oxford, 40 miles (64 km) away through rich farmland.

OXFORD: A much-quoted description of Oxford by the nineteenth-century poet Matthew Arnold — "that sweet city with her dreaming spires" — is still apt today, at least from afar when one first sees the university's towers, domes, and pinnacles rising impressively above the skyline. But it soon becomes clear that today a busy industrial city surrounds the ancient university community. In fact, town preceded gown. Oxford the city was established about 912, the university 250 years later. Relations between the two were hostile, and after a series of riots the university took virtual control of the town — for 600 years. But peace was eventually made, and now town and gown work closely together to guard the character of the city and keep the historic core of Oxford intact. This core — one of the great living architectural treasures of the world — contains examples of every style of building from Saxon times in less than a square mile.

To do Oxford justice, spend at least one full day, during most of which you will be on foot. The city's charm is in its streets: High Street, with its sweeping curve and magnificent skyline; lovely seventeenth-century Hollywell Street; and ancient, cobblestone Merton. Peace and quiet here collect in out-of-the-way places: alleyways such as Magpie Lane and Logic Lane off busy High Street; the well-kept college gardens and quadrangles along the banks of the city's two rivers — Thames and Cherwell; the green open spaces in the heart of the city, including Christ Church Meadow, only a few hundred yards from High Street and St. Aldate's. The latter is a good starting point for a walking tour of the historic buildings. A first stop should be the information center in St. Aldate's, opposite Town Hall (phone: 726871), which arranges sight-seeing tours and provides maps.

More than 600 buildings in the city are considered of outstanding architectural or historic merit. Most belong to the university, and among those you should not miss are Christ Church, established by Henry VIII in 1546, with Tom Tower, which dominates St. Aldate's; Tom Quad, the largest quadrangle in Oxford, and the college chapel, which is Oxford Cathedral; Magdalen College, dating from 1458; Merton, the oldest college, built in 1264, which also has the oldest library and Mob Quad, the oldest complete quadrangle; New College, founded in 1379, which contains parts of the ancient city wall; twin-towered All Souls College, which has a sun dial by Christopher Wren; St. John's College with the Canterbury Quadrangle, a masterpiece of seventeenth-century architecture; the circular Sheldonian Theatre, designed by Wren and completed in 1669, used for university ceremonies; St. Mary the Virgin, the university church dating from the thirteenth and fourteenth centuries; and the Ashmolean Museum, the first public museum in Britain (closed Mondays).

From Oxford, London is distance of 57 miles (91 km) away.

BEST EN ROUTE

The Cotswolds are inn country. There is a plethora of coaching or posting inns, converted manor houses, and small historic hostelries. Someone famous has invariably slept in every one of them, and it's often a matter of deciding whether you would rather put your head on a pillow where Cromwell slept before a great battle or rest in a one-time royal stopover.

The places listed here have a common denominator best described by the word "outstanding," but the outstanding feature may range from the architecture, history, or location of a building to the quality of service, degree of comfort, or price of the establishment. It was especially difficult to set a price range due to inflation and the fluctuations of the pound and the dollar. Generally, expect to pay at least $60 per night for a double in those hotels we've listed as expensive; from $40 to 60 in the moderate category; and under $40 in the inexpensive range. The Cotswolds are chockablock with small bed-and-breakfast houses in which a bed and a meal can cost $30 to $40 for two, and though we've restricted the listings below to the more historic and intriguing hostelries, don't overlook these homey, comfortable places while you travel. Expect to pay as much as $50 or more for two for a meal in the expensive restaurants; $25 to $40 in the moderate; under $20, inexpensive.

BATH

Hole in the Wall – This restaurant sounds like a cellar but in fact is a beamed and flagstoned room, an altogether delightfully civilized place to have dinner. Although the restaurant seats 40 people, reservations are required, especially for Saturday night. Dishes are enticing and there is great variety; the cuisine is mostly French and usually superb. Closed Sundays and 2 weeks at Christmas. 16 George St. (phone: 25242). Expensive.

Royal Crescent Hotel – Forming the impressive center of the famous Royal Crescent, this elegant Georgian hotel occupies an unrivaled location. With commanding views, it is within walking distance of the Assembly Rooms, the Roman baths, the Pump Room, and the abbey. It has 36 super-deluxe rooms and some extra-special apartments. There are magnificent Georgian public rooms, a good restaurant, and attractive gardens. 15-16 Royal Crescent (phone: 319090). Expensive.

Pratt's Hotel – Equally historic, this hotel is in a quiet cul-de-sac of the South Parade near the River Avon and the city center. It has 48 modern, comfortable rooms, all with a private bath. The restaurant serves traditional meals. South Parade (phone: 60441). Moderate.

MALMESBURY

Old Bell Hotel – This is a fabulous old inn, a wisteria-clad gabled building, originally the guesthouse of a famous Norman abbey. It still retains a medieval spiral staircase and part of the castle wall. There are 18 rooms, all with central heating. The inn has pretty gardens, a good restaurant, and the charming *Castle Bar*. Abbey Row (phone: 2344). Expensive.

CIRENCESTER

Fleece Hotel – Dating from the time of Henry VIII, this hotel has an attractive black and white timbered frontage. Inside the downstairs rooms, lounge, and bar have Cotswold stone walls, fine open fireplaces, and low beamed ceilings. A Jacobean staircase leads upstairs to 23 well-furnished rooms (6 with bath), some with teak furniture. The restaurant specializes in nouvelle cuisine. Real ales (try the Cotswolds' local brew, the Three B's Ale) and hot punches are served. The staff is helpful and pleasant. Market Pl. (phone: 2680). Moderate.

The King's Head – Opposite the famous parish church in the attractive marketplace is this fifteenth-century coaching inn, completely modernized without destroying its charm. The hotel has 70 well-appointed rooms. The elegant restaurant offers high-quality extensive à la carte or table d'hôte menus. Market Pl. (phone: 3322). Moderate.

UPPER SLAUGHTER

Lords of the Manor Hotel – If Upper Slaughter didn't have a beautifully preserved seventeenth-century manor house and surrounding grounds as a hostelry for visitors, it would be necessary to invent one. Luckily it was done some 300 years ago, and we need only call for reservations. Just outside town (phone: 20243). Expensive.

STOW-ON-THE-WOLD

Fosse Manor – An ivy-covered manor house with 23 spacious rooms and a restaurant. Fosse Way (phone: 30354). Moderate.

King's Arms – So named because King Charles spent a night here in 1645, this 500-year-old inn offers simple lodgings. Market Sq. (phone: 30364). Moderate to inexpensive.

MORETON-IN-MARSH

White Hart Royal Hotel – If you stay here, you will have shared a place with royalty — Charles I spent the night in this half-timbered posting inn in 1644. The hotel has 27 rooms and a small timbered dining room. High St. (phone: 50731). Moderate.

BROADWAY

The Lygon Arms – This is one of England's fine old inns. The main building dates from 1530, though parts of it are more like 600 years old. It was frequented by Charles I and Oliver Cromwell, and rooms named after each have been carefully preserved or restored. There is also a well-designed modern extension, and the harmonious relationship of old and new gives the inn a vivid and lively air. There are 64 beautifully appointed rooms (all with bath) with classic antique furnishings. The magnificent Tudor dining room serves expensive meals, but they're worth it. The cuisine has won awards. High St. (phone: 852255). Expensive.

STRATFORD-UPON-AVON

Stratford Moat House International – Behind the somewhat pedestrian facade are all the comforts expected of a major hotel chain. The hotel has 250 rooms, all elegant, many with marvelous views. Bridgefoot (phone: 67511). Expensive.

Grosvenor House – On the main Warwick Road, this hostelry is actually several large houses imaginatively linked into one comfortable hotel. Close to the center of town. 12 Warwick Rd. (phone: 69213). Moderate.

Payton – A well-maintained little hotel with a homelike atmosphere in a quiet part of town, though only a short walk from the back gate of Shakespeare's Birthplace. 6 John St. (phone: 66442). Inexpensive.

OXFORD

The Randolph – The best in town, with Victorian-Gothic charm, an efficient staff, and a very good location directly opposite the Ashmolean Museum. There are 110 rooms, a restaurant with Continental cuisine, a snack shop, and a bar. Beaumont St. (phone: 247481). Expensive.

Studley Priory Hotel – A marvelous alternative to an indifferent overnight stay in town is this excellent hotel that was once a twelfth-century Benedictine priory, later an Elizabethan manor house. On 13 acres amid rural peace and quiet, it is only 7 miles from Oxford. Filmgoers will recognize it as Thomas More's Tudor manor in *A Man for All Seasons*. The 19 rooms provide modern comfort in harmony with period furnishings. There are log fires in the public rooms and good food in the lovely dining room. The easiest approach is from the Headington roundabout on the A40 bypass east of Oxford. Horton-cum-Studley (phone: 086735-203). Expensive.

The Lake District

The drive from London to Scotland can hit some heavy weather in the western Midlands, where the concentration of heavy-duty industrial cities is particularly high. Stoke-on-Trent, Sheffield, Manchester, Liverpool — these names reverberate with the crash of the steel mill and the roar of the factory. A well-meaning Londoner might urge you to stay steadfastly to the east, ensuring that you encounter the more bucolic pleasures of Cambridge, Lincoln, York, and Northumberland (see the *Northeast England* route). And indeed, so splendid are those towns and the country around them that it would be hard to argue with such advice.

Unless it meant forgoing forever that crumpled, rumpled, well-watered mountain country known as the Lake District, squeezed tarn, mere, beck, and fell into the small county of Cumbria, just an hour or so north of Manchester. Only 30 miles across in any direction, there is a special intensity in the beauty of the Lake District, as if nature were offering a unique reward for the sprawling rigors of the industrial belt. No part of England is so universally loved by Britons — for the purity of its meres, clearwater mountain lakes; its almost vertical fields filled with grazing sheep, each field carefully delineated by painstakingly maintained stone walls; its sharp rocky peaks; and the thousands of tiny lakes (tarns) fed year in and year out by innumerable waterfalls and streams — the becks. What is earth-loving and ancient in the English spirit is drawn irresistibly to the uncompromising beauty of the Lake District.

Small wonder that the Lake District is primarily associated with a group of poets of the late eighteenth and early nineteenth centuries who not only celebrated the beauty of the region, but discovered here values to stand against the encroaching horrors of the Industrial Revolution. Chief among these poets was William Wordsworth, who lived here for most of his life, but others are equally well known: Robert Southey, Samuel Taylor Coleridge, and writers John Ruskin and Thomas De Quincey. Much of what you see and do in the region is associated with the Lake Poets.

One of the most surprising things about the Lake District is how small this famous area really is. You can drive right through it in less than an hour and yet spend a month without ever seeing half of what time and nature have created here. Looking at a map, you see that the principal lakes — Derwentwater, Ullswater, Windermere, wild Wastwater, Buttermere, Crummock Water, Tarn Hows, Grasmere, and Rydal Water — radiate from a central mountain mass like the spokes of a wheel. The distances between these postcard-perfect lakes are short, but each of the larger lakes provides a good base for exploring the nearby area. You could easily spend two days around each major lake — Derwentwater, Windermere, and Ullswater especially — before moving on, allowing time for some hiking as well as exploring the towns and villages of the district.

The route described below actually begins in the northeastern corner of the Lake District, at the town of Penrith near Ullswater, and cuts a deep V into the heart of the area. From Windermere, in the south-central section of the lakes, there is easy access to the challenging mountain peak of Helvellyn (3,113 feet). The next leg of the trip, north from Windermere to Derwentwater, crosses the paths of the Lake Poets. For the last 37 years of his life Wordsworth lived at Rydal Mount, just a few miles from Ambleside. The home he had occupied previously, Dove Cottage, is a few miles farther north, at Grasmere. Thomas De Quincey, author of *Confessions of an English Opium Eater,* took over the cottage after Wordsworth moved on to Rydal Mount. At the north end of this leg is Derwentwater — perhaps the most beautiful of all the lakes. Robert Southey made his home here, in the town of Keswick, where he frequently was joined by Percy Bysshe Shelley and Coleridge. The twins, Buttermere and Crummock Water, are just a short drive southwest of Keswick, and beyond them, in the northwest corner of the Lake District, is Cockermouth. Wordsworth and his sister Dorothy were both born and raised in Cockermouth, and the family home and nearby fields became part of the joyous imagery of the poetry that introduced this area to readers everywhere. From Cockermouth, the route follows the western boundary of the Lake District, heading south, from where numerous small roads lead into the heart of the mountains and the area's best climbing. The route cuts across the base of the Lake District to return you to the main highway and London, or north to Scotland or east to Yorkshire.

LONDON: For a complete description of the city and its hotels and restaurants, see *London,* THE EUROPEAN CITIES.

En Route from London – Leave London on either the M4 west (through the Cotswolds) to the M5 and north into the M6, or by taking the M1 north to Rugby and picking up the M6 westbound, later bearing north at Birmingham. Beyond Manchester and Liverpool lies the beautiful Forest of Bowland, and just beyond, the fringes of the Lake District. Drive along the edge of this mountainous area to Penrith (exit 40), at the northern end of the district.

PENRITH: The charming town of Penrith has withstood time and the onslaught of travelers comfortably. The oldest section of town has grown up around the thirteenth-century Church of St. Andrew (rebuilt in the early 1700s) and the nearby sixteenth-century schoolhouse. Several conflicting legends surround the presence of the two stone formations on the church grounds, known as Giant's Grave and Giant's Thumb: One version holds that this is the burial place of an ancient king. The ruins of Penrith Castle are now a town park, but two excellent sixteenth-century inns are still thriving, the *Gloucester Arms* and the *Two Lions*.

En Route from Penrith – Just outside Penrith on B5320 is the village of Tirril. A few minutes' drive beyond is Pooley Bridge, at the northern end of Ullswater, the second largest of the region's lakes. It is possible to arrange a day's boating or fishing at Pooley Bridge, a fine way to explore this beautiful lake. And keep an eye out for the elusive wild red deer that frequent the southeastern shore of Ullswater. A worthwhile diversion from Pooley Bridge is the secondary road along the southern shore of the lake past the *Sharrow Bay Hotel*, which surveys the most scenic views in the district; the road leads ultimately to the peaceful valley of Martindale. Route A592 continues to skirt the northwestern bank of Ullswater, bypassing Gowbarrow Park. This grassy fell comes alive with daffodils each year, and traveling poets can, as Wordsworth did, pause to write about the yellow blooms.

The village of Glenridding, at the head of Ullswater Lake, has a pier to match that of Pooley Bridge 13 miles (21 km) away by road. (By water, the lake is only 7½ miles long.) Patterdale, which shares the head of the lake, is only a mile farther.

From here the roadway crosses over the Helvellyn mountain range through Kirkstone Pass. There are several good climbing trails through these hills, and some of the most challenging paths lead to the peak of Helvellyn Mount (3,113 feet). But the ascent of Kirkstone Pass (1,489 feet), though fairly steep in some places, certainly holds no difficulties for drivers. At the summit is *Kirkstone Pass Inn*, which has the distinction of being one of the highest taverns in England. On the far side of the pass the road leads down to Troutbeck Valley and the small town of Troutbeck. At the southern end of Troutbeck is the seventeenth-century Townend House, used as a residence by the family of Yeoman Browne. The interior and furnishings remain intact, as does the timbered barn (open daily except Mondays and Saturdays, April to October).

WINDERMERE AND BOWNESS: The adjoining resort areas of Windermere and Bowness mark the middle of Lake Windermere's east bank. The view of the lake from the town is unimpressive, but if you climb to the peak of Orrest Head (just north of the railroad station) you'll get a far better perspective of the lake and its surrounding mountains. Virtually every recreational activity imaginable — fishing, boating, sailing, golf, tennis, scuba, and even pony-trekking — is available in this busy visitor center.

Charles Dickens is known to have spent many hours in the *New Hall Inn* in Bowness, although in his time the inn, founded in 1612, was called the Hole in the Wall. When Dickens visited, the proprietor was Thomas Longmire, a well-known wrestling champion (which may account for the lack of damage inflicted upon the pub over the years).

Lake Windermere, the largest of the lakes (10½ miles long), has a much softer aspect than most of the lakes in the region, the happy product of its luxuriantly wooded banks, filled with rhododendrons that burst into flaming color each June. The best way to see it is to take one of the regular cruises that operate between Lake Side in the south and Bowness and Waterhead at the lake's northern end (May through September). There are several small islands in Windermere, on one of which, Belle Isle, stands a magnificent eighteenth-century mansion (open May through September; ferry from Bowness). Seen from Bowness and other points along the more civilized side of Windermere, the western shore has all the lure of undiscovered territory. Fortunately for intrepid explorers, there is a ferry from Bowness to the far side that deposits travelers on a secondary road leading to the village of Near Sawrey, the site of Hilltop Cottage. This quaint seventeenth-century house was the home of Beatrix Potter, the author and illustrator whose Peter Rabbit, Squirrel Nutkin, and other characters have been loved by generations of children. A collection of her drawings is on display, and children will be pleased to find the setting of most of her tales right around the house and grounds (open daily, except Mondays, April through October). The road passes a small lake, Esthwaite Water, and continues into Hawkshead, just under 6 miles (9.6 km) from the ferry.

HAWKSHEAD: Far from the resort mood of Windermere, this quiet little village beyond Esthwaite Water offers an introductory course in Lake District life that begins at the seventeenth-century *Queen's Head Inn,* where you can get a pint of ale to fortify you for a stroll through the stone cottages of the town. Start at the schoolhouse, founded in 1585 by native son Edwin Sandys, archbishop of York, and attended by Wordsworth between 1778 and 1783. You'll find his name scratched in one of the desks. Wordsworth may have lodged at Ann Tyson's cottage, on a lane off Red Lion Square. Northwest of Hawkshead, a steep byroad leads to Tarn Hows, a small fir-fringed lake high in the hills that has the best views of the surrounding countryside, especially of Coniston Water to the south and the mountain called the Old Man of Coniston, which lords it over the lake. John Ruskin is buried at Coniston Church; his home at Brantwood is open to the public. Take the northbound secondary road out of Hawkshead to nearby Ambleside.

AMBLESIDE: Just less than a mile from the north end of Lake Windermere, Ambleside is an excellent touring base for climbers eager to explore the lakeland's hills and forests. Wordsworth's famed Scafell Pike (3,210 feet) is a considerable hike from Ambleside, but other peaks are more accessible. It is best to obtain detailed maps of trails and to make proper arrangements before starting any trek. The local information center is in Ambleside's old Court House in the Market Square. A short distance away, up the lane past *The Royal Yachtsman,* is Stockghyll Force, a beautiful waterfall cascading 70 feet to rocks below. St. Mary's Church, erected in 1854 by Sir Gilbert Scott, has a memorial to Wordsworth and a mural of the village's rush-bearing festival, still held yearly on the last Saturday in July. The festival is thought to descend from a Roman harvest ceremony. Just 2 miles (3.2 km) north of Ambleside on A591 is Rydal.

RYDAL: William Wordsworth, with his wife, three children, sister, and sister-in-law, moved to this village in 1813 and lived here until his death 37 years later. His home, Rydal Mount, contains a large collection of memorabilia, including several portraits of his family and friends, and his personal library. Wordsworth drew heavily on the surrounding countryside for inspiration and poetic images, and the mute crags and flowered hillsides around his home appear repeatedly in his work. His love of nature is reflected in the 4.5-acre garden he grew around Rydal Mount, as attentively cared for today as by Wordsworth.

Just a short distance up the road is Nab Cottage, occupied briefly by Thomas De Quincey (1806) and later by Samuel Taylor Coleridge's eldest son, Hartley. Skirting the north bank of Rydal Water (which, together with the Rothay, links Grasmere and Windermere lakes), the roadway continues to the village of Grasmere.

GRASMERE: Grasmere Lake, just a mile long and half as wide, is almost too perfect for words, complete with an emerald green island in its center. Wordsworth and his sister Dorothy lived on the lake at Dove Cottage from 1799 until 1808. After William married (and fathered three children), he and his family moved to Rydal Mount, turning the cottage over to their friends Thomas De Quincey and his wife, who had been living at Nab Cottage. The Wordsworth Museum, across the way from Dove Cottage, is really a tribute to Wordsworth and his circle. Pages and materials from many area writers, famous and obscure, are displayed along with some interesting relics.

Although August is the most crowded month in which to visit the Lake District, it is also the month of the Grasmere Sports, usually held on the third Thursday of the month. The games feature traditional Lakeland sports, such as fell racing, an all-out dash to the top of the nearest mountain and back, and Cumberland wrestling. Until Cumberland and Westmorland were combined into Cumbria County, competition between these rivals was intense, and the administrative alteration hasn't changed anything; these games have been held every year since 1852. While you're in town, stop in at the Church of St. Oswald (parts of which may be thirteenth century) and, in the yard, at the graves of William Wordsworth, his wife and sister, and Hartley Coleridge. Then go over to the *Old Gingerbread Shop* and sample its tasty wares; they will put some pleasant thoughts in your head, and the gingerbread makes a great snack while driving.

En Route from Grasmere – Continuing north along the Rothay on A591 toward the wooded shores of Thirlmere, Helvellyn Mount rises to the right. The tiny seventeenth-century chapel at Wythburn is worth a visit. Its parking lot is the starting point of a climbing trail to the peak of Helvellyn (the parking lot at the north end of Thirlmere is the start of a gentler forest trail). Keswick, 13 miles (21 km) from Grasmere, is just a few miles beyond the north end of the lake. You'll get an excellent view of the area from the crest of Castlerigg, and a road on the right leads to the Castlerigg Stone Circle.

KESWICK: Sheltered by the towering Skiddaw (3,053 feet), this ancient market town sits near the shore of beautiful Derwentwater, 3 miles long and a mile wide, surrounded by a delightful mixture of bare rock, grassy banks, and forested glens and crowned by a wreath of tiny islands. One of these, Floating Island, is no more than a tangled mass of lake weeds riding on a bubble of swamp gas. The other islands, however, are more substantial, and several support beautiful homes; the remains of a seventh-century retreat are on the island of St. Herbert.

Many poets, including Shelley, Southey, Wordsworth, and Coleridge, were drawn here, and Keswick's Fitz Park Museum displays some of their manuscripts, letters, and personal effects (open daily; Easter to October). Southey's home, Greta Hall, has become Keswick School, and his body lies at the Crosthwaite Churchyard. Southey, Wordsworth, and Coleridge all patronized the bar at the *George Hotel,* which claims to be the oldest structure in town. Judging by the crude stone masonry and faded walls, it may well be.

Two of the best points for viewing Derwentwater and its environs are at Castle Head (529 feet), just south of Keswick, and at Friar's Crag, a rocky headland on the lake. John Ruskin was particularly enamored of this spot, and there is a memorial to him here. Southey favored the view from the hill near Greta Bridge.

En Route from Keswick – Drive south along the eastern shore of Derwentwater on B5289 to the incredibly beautiful Borrowdale Valley. Here the Bowder Stone, a huge boulder that tumbled from some nearby height, stands precariously on edge near Castle Crag, a 900-foot-tall rock cone that can be climbed without too much effort in under half an hour. Great Gable, a little farther along the route, is a more challenging target — 2,949 feet of tough climbing. It takes about 3 hours to ascend this monster, but the view is well worth the effort: The entire area from Skiddaw to Windermere, and even the Isle of Man are visible from the crest.

Continue on B5289, crossing over Honister Pass, then dropping through some rough territory until you reach the farm of Gatesgarth. The placid waters of Buttermere come into view as the roadway curves in a giant U, first west and then north. Buttermere's nearby twin, Crummock Water, lies just beyond to the north-west. Scale Force, a lively waterfall with a drop of over 120 feet, is not far from the pretty village of Buttermere. The easiest access is by crossing the stream between the two lakes and following the path on the far side. It will be muddy, so wear boots or hiking shoes. A few miles farther north, B5289 intersects B5292; you can either take B5292 east toward A66, Keswick and Penrith, or extend your trip by heading west toward Cockermouth.

There is no direct road across the mountain barrier in the western half of the Lake District, making it a particularly appealing area for experienced and properly equipped backpackers and hill walkers.

COCKERMOUTH: Strategically placed at the junction of the Cocker and Derwent rivers, Cockermouth is a pre-Roman community, though little remains from its earliest period. Even its twelfth-century castle was destroyed during the violence of the mid-1600s. Wordsworth House (open daily except Sundays and Thursday afternoons from April to October), was built in 1745. This house, in which Dorothy and William grew up, is a fairly simple, countrified example of Georgian architecture that has survived intact. The furnishings used by the Wordsworth family, however, are long gone. William's father is buried in the churchyard. Fletcher Christian of *Mutiny on the Bounty* was born at nearby Moorland Close (1764).

En Route from Cockermouth – Take A5086 south from Cockermouth along the western fringe of the Lake District. Ennerdale Water, perhaps the least visited of the larger lakes, lies about 10 miles (16 km) away, on a secondary roadway to the east. A similar turnoff about 10 miles (16 km) beyond leads to Wastwater, the deepest of the lakes, set among a group of stern and savage-faced mountains. The contrast to gentle Windermere is marked. The village of Wasdale Head, a mile beyond the lake, is an excellent climbing center, but strictly for experts.

Returning to the main road (A5086 becomes A595 near Ennerdale Water), you arrive at Ravenglass, a port at the mouth of the Esk River about 25 miles (40 km) from Cockermouth. The Eskdale Valley can be explored either by road or on the narrow-gauge, steam-powered Ravenglass and Eskdale Railway (narrow is an understatement — 15 inches make it positively skinny), which runs from Easter to October.

Overlooking the River Esk, just beyond the town, is Muncaster Castle, the seat of the Pennington family for 700 years (open Easter till early October except on Mondays, Fridays, and Saturdays). Farther on, at Broughton, another secondary road (A593) leads up the Duddon Valley toward Coniston Water and Hawkshead. Just east of Broughton, A595 bears south along the coast, and A590 continues east toward A6, the city of Kendal, and the M4 motorway.

BEST EN ROUTE

Travelers to the Lake District have a wide choice of excellent accommodations, varying from some of the best hotels in the country to small (but comfortable) inns and bed and breakfast (B&B) spots. Any number of inns and homes that provide the basics — a warm room and breakfast for a modest price — are hidden among these wooded hills. Expect B&B charges for two, inclusive of the 15% VAT (sales tax), to run about $25 to $40. Expect to pay $60 and up per night for a double room in inns listed as expensive; between $40 and $60 for those in the moderate range; and $25 to $35 for those considered inexpensive. Remember that the value of the dollar does fluctuate in relation to these prices, but these ranges should not vary much. The hostelries listed below are a selection of our choices for the area; there are many other inns along the roads you'll be traveling, and the experience of exploring an unknown inn should be all your own. Dinners at the two best establishments in the area are about $40 to $60 for two people (moderate).

ULLSWATER

Sharrow Bay Country House Hotel – Partners Francis Coulson and Brian Sack have spent 30 years making the Sharrow Bay one of the most respected and attractive hotels in the area. The dinners at the restaurant are a pleasure. Closed December to early March (phone: 08536-301). Expensive.

Leeming House Hotel – Commanding fine views over the lake, it's a gracious country house and restaurant. Closed December to early March. Watermillock (phone: 08536-444). Expensive.

The Old Church Hotel – With the Ullswater lapping on their front lawn, owners Kevin and Maureen Whitemore offer an enormous range of sporting activities in the surrounding area along with good food and comfortable accommodations. Watermillock (phone: 08536-204). Moderate.

WINDERMERE

Rothay Manor – It's an elegant hotel near Ambleside with its own croquet lawn. Excellent cuisine. Closed mid-January to early February. Rothay Bridge (phone: 0966-33605). Expensive.

Miller Howe Hotel – Is it the beautiful view of placid, tree-lined Lake Windermere that makes this hotel seem such a bastion of calm or rather the impeccable service? In either case, there is hardly a better headquarters for touring the area. Excellent restaurant. Closed mid-December to mid-March. Rayrigg Rd. (phone: 09662-2536). Expensive.

Belsfield Hotel – A magnificent Georgian mansion overlooking Lake Windermere with an interesting blend of period pieces and modern furnishings. A newer wing (in the garden) has been added making a total of 67 rooms. Bowness on Windermere (phone: 09662-2448). Expensive.

Quarry Garth – A solid, no-nonsense mansion, typical of scores of private retreats built in the lakes by wealthy industrialists, with just seven bedrooms, a cozy paneled lounge, and an elegant dining room. Troutbeck (phone: 09662-3761). Moderate to inexpensive.

GRASMERE

Michaels Nook – A charming Victorian country home furnished by the proprietor, Reginald Gifford, with many beautiful antiques. Some of the bathrooms have been "modernized," but the older ones are more fun (phone: 496). Expensive.

The Swan – Immortalized by Wordsworth, this very friendly 31-room hotel is admirably managed and has a good restaurant featuring a number of vegetarian dishes (phone: 09665-551). Moderate.

KESWICK

Lodore Swiss Hotel – Also on the edge of Derwentwater, with glorious views of the lake and Lodore Falls. Though the building is fairly large and very grand in appearance, it is run by a family (the Englands), and their high standards are readily apparent. Closed November through March (phone: Borrowdale 285). Expensive.

Mary Mount Country House Hotel – On the shores of Lake Derwentwater, 3 miles south of Keswick, this comfortable and cozy hotel is set in beautiful woodlands. Closed in December (phone: 059684-223). Expensive to moderate.

The Pheasant Inn – This old coaching inn that still retains its traditional atmosphere is on Bassenthwaite Lake near Thornthwaite Forest (phone: 059681-234). Moderate.

Northeast England

Between the Midlands and the border of the Scottish Lowlands, where England narrows to a tight, trim waist of land, lies a section of exceptionally rugged and beautiful geography. The Pennine Chain — a group of hills that reach only 3,000 feet above sea level at their highest — runs straight down the center of this neck of land, dividing east and west as neatly as a surgeon's blade. To the west falls the Lake District and Cumbria (see *The Lake District* route); to the east, stretching across chasms and caves, are the dales and moors of Yorkshire and a long coast on the North Sea.

At England's narrowest point, Roman legions were once posted in an uneasy vigilance against the raids of marauding Pict warriors from the north. In AD 122, goaded past endurance, Emperor Hadrian ordered the construction of an immense wall, to reach from the North Sea at the River Tyne to Solway Firth on the Irish Sea coast, to discourage the savage northerners. The high, parapeted wall, 6 feet high and 8 feet thick, stretched for 73.5 miles and was punctuated at every mile by a guard station filled with Roman soldiers — still uneasy. What remains of this magnificent effort are various ruins across Northumberland and many mile stations still standing.

Later, with the coming of the Normans, a network of castles was built across this area. Many of these medieval fortresses are also extant, as obdurate and impregnable as ever, firm against age. Others have crumbled, leaving the history of their passing in broken walls and weary battlements.

It is rather apt that the gateway to this country of rocky moors, forested dales, and sandy resort beaches on the North Sea coast is the ancient city of York, home of York Minster, one of Great Britain's most beautiful cathedrals. As wild as the country is, it has always been a center of British religious experience, and Christianity actually came to Britain through the coastal island of Lindisfarne (Holy Island).

The route described below is circular, leaving York for the journey north through the North York moors to Durham, dominated by Britain's finest Norman cathedral, and then on to Newcastle upon Tyne and along the coastline to Berwick-upon-Tweed on the Scottish border. Here the route turns south again to wander through the central highlands of the Pennines, the moor, and Yorkshire dales on its way back to York. For more information write to the Northumbria Tourist Board, 9 Osborne Terrace, Jesmond, Newcastle upon Tyne NE2 1NT (phone: 0632-817744), and the Yorkshire and Humberside Tourist Board, 312 Tadcaster Rd., York Y02 2HF (phone: 0904-707961).

LONDON: For a complete description of the city and its hotels and restaurants, see *London,* THE EUROPEAN CITIES.

En Route from London – You can take the M1 motorway directly north from London to Leeds and pick up A64 going northeast to York. It's a fairly long journey, about 225 miles (360 km) all told, and will take about four hours.

YORK: Its very name has the ring of ancient authority about it, and well it should. The Romans established York — then called Eboracum — in AD 71 as a garrison town and the seat of the province. A succession of Roman emperors visited, and it was here, in 306, that Constantine the Great was proclaimed ruler of the known world. Such is the fleeting nature of glory that the Romans abandoned the town only 75 years later, and it slipped quietly from history until the Anglo-Saxons moved three centuries later. It was a walled city when King Harold II was in the area in 1066, fighting the Scandinavians, only to be called back to the south of England on the double to meet the forces of William the Conqueror.

The section of the city within the ancient walls is perhaps the best-preserved medieval city in Great Britain, and from its heart rises the largest Gothic cathedral in the country, York Minster. Begun in 1081 on the site of a series of earlier churches, it was not completed until the fifteenth century. More stunning than its awesome proportions are its stained-glass windows, the largest concentration of stained glass in Great Britain. The giant Great East Window is the size of a tennis court.

The medieval heart of the city is girdled by 3 miles of defensive wall, and the most interesting parts of the city are within them. Just as in the Middle Ages, the quirky, timbered, slightly akimbo buildings in the Shambles — once the butchers' quarter — are devoted to shops, though the butchers have given way to boutiques, galleries, and craft shops, most with original butcher's block and meat hooks intact. Goodramgate is another medieval shopping area, and Micklegate, the central highway of yore, is lined with much later but very beautiful Georgian homes and buildings. Other required stops are the pillared Assembly Rooms, evoking the elegance of the eighteenth century, and the medieval timberwork of the Merchant Adventurers' Hall. Then relax at the *Black Swan* in Peasholme Green; in 1417, the Lord Mayor of York lived in the house. You should definitely see the reconstructed period scenes at the Castle Museum (open daily, late March to mid-October) and National Railway Museum (open daily), which houses a history of the railroad.

En Route from York – Take A64 northeast toward the North York Moors National Park, about 40 miles (64 km) away. A roadway about 9 miles (14 km) outside York leads to Castle Howard, a palatial mansion topped by a gilded dome that was used as the setting for the television production of Evelyn Waugh's *Brideshead Revisited* (open daily from Easter through October). Sir John Vanbrugh designed the central structure, erected early in the eighteenth century. A wing was added in the 1750s. A collection of period clothing is on display; the house is magnificently decorated and furnished. The grounds, including a lake, complete the image of luxuriant living.

Rejoin A64 and continue to the small market town of Malton. Then go north on A169 through Old Malton to Pickering.

PICKERING: This little town is on the fringe of the national park, a vast expanse of rolling hills and valleys that becomes a purple sea abloom with heather during the late summer. Pickering is well suited to the quiet atmosphere of the moor — time has not altered either appreciably. Relax at the *Black Bull Inn,* an ancient stone tollhouse, before exploring the moors. An easy way to view these beautiful valleys and ridges of exposed rock is aboard the Moorsrail, a steam-powered line built in 1836 by George Stephenson that runs between Pickering and Goathland in summer.

En Route from Pickering – Route A169 cuts right through the moorlands to the coast, passing the *Saltersgate Inn* (where peat fires have welcomed travelers for uncounted years) along the road to Whitby. This delightful old port is overlooked from a cliff by the impressive ruins of Whitby Abbey, established in 657 and extensively rebuilt around the twelfth century (open daily). Long associated with the sea and sailing ships, the older parts of Whitby still consist of cobbled streets and the red-tiled cottages used by fishermen and shipwrights. A resort area has grown on the town's West Cliff.

Just a few miles south of Whitby along the coast (off A171), clinging to the cliffs, is the village of Robin Hood's Bay. Here the tall cliffs drop to their lowest point, creating a beautiful setting for the picturesque fishing settlement. Those jumbo globes visible from the road are part of the Ballistic Missile Early Warning Station in the Fylingdale Moor area.

The leading resort town on the Yorkshire coast, Scarborough, lies about 15 miles (24 km) farther south. The clifftop ruins of a twelfth-century castle and the Church of St. Mary (also twelfth century) separate the two sandy bays that are Scarborough's principal attractions. The shrinking old sector, near the harbor, still preserves its craft and fish markets and several early homes. The bluff, now the site of a castle ruins, once held an Iron Age lookout-earthwork, a Roman firebeacon, and later a chapel. Beyond is South Bay and a spa with beautiful gardens. This is a residential area, reflected in stately homes and abundant gardens.

Return to Pickering on A170 westbound, skirting the southern fringe of the moors. Having traced a circle northeast of Pickering, continue west on A170 past the town toward Kirkbymoorside and Helmsley.

HELMSLEY: The ruins of a twelfth-century castle dominate this small town at the foot of the ridges where the valleys of Pickering and Rye meet. Just 2 miles (3.2 km) away, in the Ryedale Valley, are the magnificent ruins of Rievaulx Abbey, built over a period of almost 200 years in the twelfth and thirteenth centuries. The terrace above the abbey overlooks the ruins themselves and offers a fine view of the pastoral vale. If staying overnight, try the *Black Swan Hotel,* a 400-year-old Georgian and Tudor building with a modern wing.

En Route from Helmsley – Route A170 goes west, descending to Thirsk in the southwest corner of the moors. From Thirsk, take A19 north toward Middlesbrough and look for signs for A177, which leads northwest to Durham. The whole drive from Helmsley to Durham is about 50 miles (80 km).

DURHAM: Whether it was worship of God or defense against the Scots that was uppermost in the minds of the builders of Durham's magnificent cathedral and equally dramatic castle, the two buildings, facing each other across the Palace Green on a wooded gorge literally hanging over the River Wear, make Durham one of the most dramatically situated cities in Great Britain. When the cathedral was built in the eleventh century, the bishop was responsible for the physical as well as the spiritual well-being of his flock, and defense was certainly part of his purpose. The original castle, built about 100 years later at the insistence of William the Conqueror, was replaced by the current keep in the fourteenth century and the Great Hall added at the same time (the castle is part of Durham University today). The two buildings are literally breathtaking, with the triple towers of the cathedral visible. Altogether, Durham Cathedral is one of the finest Romanesque churches in Europe. Not to be missed in Durham is the Gulbénkian Museum of Oriental Art, on Elvet Hill, with an incredible collection of Eastern art forms spanning many centuries. After a culturally enhancing day of touring, have a beer at the old *Market Tavern.*

En Route from Durham – Route A167 leaves Durham at a leisurely pace, going north about 15 miles (24 km) toward Newcastle upon Tyne. A few miles before Newcastle lies Washington, once a small mining town. The town's Old Hall, erected early in the seventeenth century, incorporates parts of an older structure — the twelfth-century home of the family of George Washington.

NEWCASTLE UPON TYNE: This lively industrial center of the northeast first became famous as an exporter of coal during the thirteenth century. Today, Newcastle's steel, petroleum, and shipbuilding industries lead the city's current redevelopment phase. Originally this site was called Pons Aelius, one of the guard stations of Hadrian's

Wall. This massive line of fortifications defined the limit of Roman-dominated Britain when it was built. To the north was the land of the blue-painted Pict warriors, who the Romans could not subdue. Outbreaks of violence between these fierce warriors, later called the Scots, and the area residents continued until the seventeenth century.

Robert Curthose, son of William the Conqueror, erected a castle here late in the eleventh century. The "new" castle was constructed over a century later, between 1170 and 1250. The Black Gate (1247) contains a library and museum, including a collection of Northumbrian musical instruments (open Wednesdays through Saturdays). The towering spire of St. Nicholas's Cathedral is 194 feet tall and reinforced by flying buttresses. Plan to visit the Beamish open-air "living museum" of the region's past ways of life near Stanley, a short bus ride from the city center.

En Route from Newcastle upon Tyne – Take A1 north, traveling between the coast and the forested hills of Northumberland National Park, one of the wildest and least traveled areas in England — a good spot for experienced hikers to get a taste of the country through which Romans and Picts warred. Nearer the roads are fine spots for the more civilized pleasures of a quiet picnic. Some 35 miles (56 km) away is Alnwick, an attractive old town outside the gates of the duke of Northumberland's Alnwick Castle. These stern walls, reinforced between 1310 and 1312, when its towers were erected, mask an interior of truly ducal magnificence (open daily, except Saturdays, May through September). A secondary roadway leads northeast from B1340 to the tiny fishing village of Craster, about 6 miles (10 km) from Alnwick. Treat yourself to a breath of sea air: Park the car and walk 1.5 miles (2.5 km) along the coast path to the ruins of Dunstanburgh Castle. This dramatic fourteenth-century structure, perched on a cliff 100 feet above the sea, was hotly contested during the Wars of the Roses (open daily).

The popular resort of Seahouses, with an excellent beach area, is only a few miles farther along the coast. Take a boat ride to Inner Farne, a sanctuary for birds (puffins, terns, guillemots, kittiwakes, and others) and gray seals (open May to September).

Bamburgh Castle, one of the largest and most imposing medieval castles in Britain, still stands on a craggy headland overlooking the beach. Built in the early twelfth century, the fortress was extensively restored at the beginning of the twentieth century (open afternoons, Easter through October).

Continue north along the coast to Beal, where a 3-mile causeway (usable only at low tide) connects the mainland to Holy Island.

LINDISFARNE, or HOLY ISLAND: Here, in the seventh century, St. Aidan established the missionary center from which Christianity spread to the mainland. The ruins of the eleventh-century Benedictine priory, including a red sandstone church, and a small castle stand among the picturesque fishermen's cottages on the island today. Lindisfarne is known for the brewing of mead, a potent honey-based liquor. Pick up an extra bottle for yourself before returning to the mainland and the northbound coast · road.

BERWICK-UPON-TWEED: The heavily fortified city of Berwick-upon-Tweed shifted between Scotland and England thirteen times before being settled in England in 1482. The sixteenth-century ramparts ringing the old city are in excellent condition and create a massive circular 2-mile promenade. Several well-preserved eighteenth-century buildings, including the Town Hall and Barracks, are open for inspection. Charles Dickens is said to have read poetry in the eighteenth-century *King's Arms Hotel,* on a rise above the dockyards.

En Route from Berwick-upon-Tweed – Edinburgh is about 60 miles (96 km) northwest along the coast road. If, however, you're returning south, follow the bank of the River Tweed on A698. The ruins of Norham Castle, on the riverbank, are just off the main road 7 miles (11 km) from Berwick (open daily). Continue south on A698 to Cornhill on Tweed, and there pick up A697 southeast to Wooler, at the foot of the Cheviot Hills on the fringe of Northumberland National Park. There you can call for refreshments at the creeper-clad *Tankerville Arms*. The earl of Tankerville's fourteenth century Chillingham Castle is about 5 miles (8 km) east of the village. A unique herd of pure white wild cattle have grazed the castle grounds for 700 years (open April through October; closed Tuesdays).

Return to A697, veering southeast away from the border of the Northumberland Park to the junction with B6341. Take B6341 southwest to Rothbury, deep in the wooded valley of the River Coquet, then continue south until B6342 becomes A6079 leading into Hexham.

HEXHAM: The beautiful priory church typifies the town of Hexham. Little remains of the original structure, but some interesting twelfth-century sections are in good shape. There is a thirteenth-century stone chair used as a frithstool: a sanctuary for whoever sat in it. The present Manor Office is a fourteenth-century prison, and the fifteenth-century Moot Hall was used by the court bailiff. The town is well situated for a detailed look at the Roman wall, being just about halfway along its length.

En Route from Hexham – Richmond lies about 70 miles (112 km) southeast of Hexham. From Hexham, forsaking the main highways for a spell, take the hill road (B6306) that climbs up from the Tyne Valley to the village of Blanchland, built around the site of a twelfth-century abbey; part of the original church now serves the parish. In the heart of the Pennine Hills, the road makes a switchback to Barnard Castle, an agreeable little town named for its ruined twelfth-century castle, from which there is a great view over the River Tees. The town's Bowes Museum is a bit of a surprise, since it looks exactly like a French château. John Bowes built it in 1869 in honor of his French wife. Another surprise is its fine collection of paintings, furniture, and porcelain, hardly to be expected on the outskirts of a such small country town. The art collection at Lord Barnard's splendid fourteenth-century Raby Castle is also quite notable and worth the 6-mile (10-km) drive from the main road. Take B6277, then A66 east to B6274, which leads into Richmond.

RICHMOND: Here the great ruins of Richmond Castle stand precariously above the River Swale, guarding Swaledale and the eastern access to the Yorkshire dales. The original fortress was erected in 1071, and the keep added about 100 years later. The Georgian Theatre Royal (1788) has opened to the public after a century of gathering dust; it is one of the oldest theaters in England.

Explorers will find a tour of the dales, a series of beautiful valleys in the Pennine Hills, a delightful activity. They are filled with small villages and warm Yorkshire stone houses. Swaledale, deeper and wilder than most other valleys, is worth following for the village Thwaite at the far end. Here the steep Buttertubs Pass (the buttertubs are circular holes in the limestone) leads over the hills to Hawes, a noted cheese center in pastoral Wensleydale.

En Route from Richmond – Take A6108, then B6270 and a secondary road to Hawes. Stay on the secondary road leading southeast from Hawes toward the villages of Grassington and Burnsall. Visit the ruins of Bolton Abbey just a few miles farther south (open daily).

From here a bona fide main road (A59) goes east to the resort town of Harrogate.

HARROGATE: Now a thriving convention center due to its hotels, parks, and shops, Harrogate had been noted for its mineral waters and clean mountain air (atop a plateau 500 feet above sea level). The 200-acre common, called the Stray, is still the town center. The Royal Pump Room, where the public baths were located, is now a museum.

En Route from Harrogate – York is only 23 miles (37 km) east of Harrogate on A59, but be prepared to stop at the old town of Knaresborough. Chief among the local sights is the celebrated Dropping Well, which has petrifying properties — you can leave something here and come back in a few years to find it turned to stone.

BEST EN ROUTE

Some of the nicest places to stay in northeast England are not the larger hotels but the small inns and private homes that offer bed and breakfast. In general, they are undistinguished places — roomy, warm, and comfortable — and they provide a basic level of service at a moderate price. Expect to pay $60 and up for bed and breakfast for two in establishments classified below as expensive; $45 to $60 in those listed as moderate; and $45 and under at places in the inexpensive category. (Prices in York are slightly higher.)

Please bear in mind that these ranges are expressed in American dollars and that the currency exchange market is far from stable. You will find good food at reasonable prices in most places, but for a really excellent dinner for two with wine, expect to pay about $25 to $30.

YORK

Viking Hotel – A large, centrally located modern hotel, the *Viking* stands out because of its excellent service. The interior is quite pleasant, and if you can get a room overlooking the river, it will add immeasurably to your stay. North St. (phone: 59822). Expensive.

Royal York Hotel – A magnificent Victorian structure, this railway hotel has been operating for just over 100 years. Although certain necessary steps toward modernization have been taken, the traditional air remains, especially at teatime in the high-ceilinged lounge. Station Rd. (phone: 53681). Expensive.

Hill Hotel – This Georgian establishment is family run, and since it has only 10 rooms, staying here is like staying in a private home — with your own bath or shower, use of a delightful garden, and traditional cuisine. About 2 miles from the city center. 60 York Rd., Acomb (phone: 790777). Moderate.

PICKERING

Forest and Vale Hotel – In summer the walled garden is a joy, and in winter curling up by the fireplace in this comfortable Georgian inn is the ultimate expression of quiet and cozy. Malton Rd. (phone: 72722). Moderate.

SCARBOROUGH

Royal Hotel – Truly a luxury liner among the resort hotels dotting this small town, the *Royal* is a picture-perfect example of how the good life should be led. In this aged structure, the idea of ornate decoration comes back to life and blends well with the artwork on display. St. Nicholas St. (phone: 64333). Moderate.

HELMSLEY

Black Swan Hotel – As traditional a northern inn as it is possible to find, this hotel was built in the sixteenth century of local stone, with public rooms of old wood and large fireplaces. Market Pl. (phone: 70466). Expensive.

Feversham Arms – Built of Yorkshire stone with 15 pretty bedrooms, the hotel also has an enjoyable restaurant with some good Spanish dishes. 1 High St. (phone: 70766). Moderate.

DURHAM

Royal County Hotel – The aviary in the public area must have been added since this inn's days of catering to the horse and carriage set, and it's only one of the many tasteful improvements made over the years. A newer wing of rooms and a sauna have been added. Old Elvet (phone: 66821). Expensive.

NEWCASTLE UPON TYNE

Gosforth Park Hotel – One of the very modern, very luxurious establishments in the area, the *Gosforth* is set in a wooded sector close to the racetrack about 4 miles north of the city. There is no shortage of facilities, and the service is excellent. High Gosforth Park (phone: 364111). Expensive.

Royal Station Hotel – An airy Victorian railway hotel, with just enough modernization to make you comfortable, but not so much that the hotel's own personality doesn't show through . . . and the grand central staircase says it all. Neville St. (phone: 320781). Expensive to moderate.

BERWICK-UPON-TWEED

King's Arms Hotel – This is a lovely Georgian coaching inn with a walled garden; two restaurants, including a coffee shop modeled on an eighteenth-century stage coach; and two bars, one housed in the converted stable block. Hide Hill (phone: 307454). Moderate.

BLANCHLAND

Lord Crewe Arms Hotel – The medieval atmosphere isn't surprising, since the building includes parts of an eleventh-century monastery that once occupied the site of the village. It's haunted, not by a monk, but by the ghost of a pretty girl, one Dorothy Foster, who has apparently been trying to deliver a message for the past 250 years. Near Consett (phone: 251). Moderate.

HARROGATE

The Old Swan Hotel – A charming building dating from 1700, the *Old Swan* appeals to an old-fashioned sense of comfort and service. The rooms are large, and the manners of the staff belong to an earlier time, when graciousness was a way of life rather than a business. Swan Rd. (phone: 504051). Moderate.

Oliver Restaurant – The cooking expertise of Peter Jones has made this one of the most respected restaurants in England. The menu, which consists of four courses, is changed to take advantage of the best fresh produce. The setting is definitely Edwardian, with no detail overlooked, and the service is attended to equally well. Dinner only. 24 King's Rd. (phone: 68600). Expensive.

The Scottish Lowlands:
Sir Walter Scott Country

The Scottish Lowlands — the central and southern parts of the country — are, in the international popular imagination, at variance with the Highlands in almost every way. Whereas Highlanders are thought to be romantic, Catholic, Celtic, and volatile, Lowlanders are thought to be practical, Presbyterian, steady, and narrow. There is a grain of truth in this, but only a grain.

The Lowlands are nothing if not romantic. They include Scotland's two best-known battle sites, for instance, each of them a mile from Stirling Castle: Stirling Bridge, where William Wallace drove back the English forces in 1297, and Bannockburn, where Robert the Bruce was victorious in the same cause in 1314.

The Scottish Borders, where Sir Walter Scott lived for most of his adult life, are noted for their peaceful rivers and famous ruined abbeys, to say nothing of numerous literary landmarks, including Scott's baronial country house at Abbotsford. The Trossachs, where so much of Scott's writing is set, are known as the Gateway to the Highlands (a title also claimed by Stirling) and are very lovely. Loch Lomond is there. And Glasgow, though inferior to Edinburgh in glamorous topography, is superior in theater and the arts.

An important tip for the unsuspecting motorist: Don't wait for good weather before setting off in your car in the morning — you might be a grandparent by the time it arrives. Pack snacks, bought from your hotel or a local bakery, for everybody (there are tearooms in the palatial *Gleneagles Hotel* in Perthshire, but precious few anywhere else). Scottish bakeries sell milk, sandwiches, and stuffed rolls as well as cakes and buttered scones. Try to tour Scotland in April and May or September and October, when crowds are thinner, the air crisper, and colors brighter. If you go in midsummer you will miss the beauteous yellow gorse (spring) and purple heather (autumn).

Your best bet in maps comes in a Scottish Tourist Board kit called *Enjoy Scotland,* which includes a small book listing 1001 Scottish sights. All are marked on the map, along with golf courses, picnic tables, information centers — everything that legibly fits. The kit costs about $5 from the Scottish Tourist Board, 23 Ravelston Terr., Edinburgh EH4 3EU. It is available in person from the tourist office at 5 Waverley Bridge in Edinburgh.

EDINBURGH: For a detailed report on Edinburgh and its hotels and restaurants, see *Edinburgh,* THE EUROPEAN CITIES.

En Route from Edinburgh – Seventeen miles west of Edinburgh on the M9 is Linlithgow Palace, on the south shore of Loch Linlithgow (27 km). This breathtaking piece of fairy-tale architecture was the birthplace of Mary, Queen of Scots in 1542 and is one of Scotland's four royal palaces (the others — Falkland Palace in the Kingdom of Fife, Stirling Castle, and Edinburgh's Holyrood House). James I of Scotland built it in the fifteenth century; later rulers extended it. Adjoining the palace is St. Michael's, one of the finest medieval parish churches in Scotland.

STIRLING: If you want to see into Scotland's soul, stand on the heights of Stirling Castle Rock behind any of the castle cannonades and gaze northeast to the Grampian Mountains, northwest to Stirling Bridge, or south to Bannockburn. Here, for centuries, was Scotland's sole defense against any English invasion of northern cities like Perth (an important medieval Scots town) and the Highlands. Whoever controlled Stirling Castle controlled the only route north across the River Forth. Scots' patriot Sir William Wallace (1272–1305) and King Robert Bruce — known to history simply as the Bruce — had to hold the castle against the English to hold Scotland. They succeeded, though after years of intermittent battle, brave Wallace was betrayed to the English and hung, drawn, and quartered in London. Since that time, all kinds of psychological and historical defense mechanisms against the English have become deeply rooted in Scottish hearts.

Once a residence for Stuart kings, the palace section of the castle is intriguing. Mary of Guise, the wife of James V, employed stonemasons from her native France to decorate its facade with Bacchanalian figurines, providing a touch of Renaissance French fancy that is amusingly out of place in such a stern Scottish context. Both Mary, Queen of Scots and King James VI were crowned at Stirling Castle. Surrounding the castle are many impressive buildings from the sixteenth and seventeenth centuries as well as the Visitor Centre with a multiscreen show and an imaginative picture gallery (there's a bookshop, crafts shop, and tea garden); open year-round.

A mile away, at Bannockburn, is another exhibition on Robert the Bruce, organized by the National Trust for Scotland (open March through October; off the A9, south of Stirling).

DOUNE: The fourteenth-century castle here is pure picturebook stuff. Owned since the sixteenth century by the earls of Moray, one of whom was a half-brother to Mary, Queen of Scots, this stark, towering edifice in a woodland between two streams has survived more or less in its original form, a rarity in Scotland. And it is so medieval that no one lives in it today. Also at Doune, 2 miles (3.2 km) past the castle on A84, is the present earl's collection of vintage, veteran, and modern cars, the Doune Motor Museum, next to Doune Park Gardens, an idyllic 60 acres of woodland walks and flowering shrubs. The castle, museum, and gardens are open from April through October.

TROSSACHS: Scott made this part of Scotland famous with his narrative poem *The Lady of the Lake,* set at Loch Katrine, and with his novel *Rob Roy.* He encouraged his London acquaintances to visit the area until so many came that he complained, "Every London citizen makes Loch Lomond his washpot and throws his shoe over Ben Nevis." Yet today the Trossachs are curiously underdeveloped, which adds to their beauty but makes it difficult to find adequate hotels and restaurants. You will want to drive north on A84 from Callander past Loch Lubnaig to Rob Roy's grave at Balquhidder, a route almost smothered in wild primroses. Turn left onto A821 just north of Callander to tour Lochs Katrine, Achray, and Venachar. Then follow A811 southwest through Killearn to the famous loch itself.

LOCH LOMOND: Loll on the beach on the eastern shore, gazing at purple mountains studded with rivulets and waterfalls. Visit Rossdhu on the western shore, the historic home of the Clan Colquhoun, whose kitchen still turns out home baking (on sale April through September). A tourist center at Balloch on the southern tip of Loch Lomond, will provide lots of information to inspire you (open May through September).

GLASGOW: This preeminently industrial city has fallen on hard times since the great days of the "tobacco lords" (merchants involved in trade with America) in the eighteenth century and the Clydeside shipbuilders in the nineteenth. Yet nowhere in Scotland is the spirit more indomitable or the humor more pungent, as you'll quickly learn when you talk to Glaswegians. The city is medieval — like so many medieval cities, growing up around a thirteenth-century cathedral — but little is left of its earliest period. Its most imposing architecture is Victorian, and the buildings around George Square could provide a primer in Victorian excess and excellence. After a stroll through George Square, make for the Glasgow University area in Kelvingrove. The art gallery here is studded with the work of French Impressionists and of talented Scots Impressionists who were influenced by them. Treat yourself to a stroll through Kelvingrove Park along the River Kelvin.

At night the excellent Scottish Opera Company performs at the Theatre Royal (Hope St.; phone: 331-1234). The Glasgow Citizens' Theatre Company (119 Gorbals St.; phone: 429-0022) stages avant-garde productions of traditional plays that make off-Broadway look like a vicar's tea party.

NEW LANARK: The old mills here and the town that is an integral part of them are one of the earliest experiments in progressive labor management. In 1799 the Welsh socialist Robert Owen bought the mills at New Lanark and went about creating a humane work situation. He stopped child labor, instituted a program of health insurance for workers, built clean, livable housing, and opened schools and recreation facilities. In 1829, after disagreements with his partners (one of whom was Jeremy Bentham), he withdrew, but in the meantime he financed a new utopian experiment in New Harmony, Indiana, that was far less successful (in part, because it was a community of intellectuals committed more to ideology than cooperation).

PEEBLES: This pleasant old wool manufacturing town by the River Tweed is an excellent base for exploring the borders. Adjoining Peebles on the west is Neidpath Castle, a striking, thirteenth-century stronghold with walls 11 feet thick.

En Route from Peebles – Seven miles (11 km) east of Peebles on A72 is Traquair House, dating from the tenth century, the oldest continuously inhabited dwelling in Scotland. Twenty-seven Scottish and English monarchs have visited it. Ale is still produced at its eighteenth-century brewhouse. However, the schedule of opening hours is erratic, so phone 830323 before you visit.

ABBOTSFORD: No visit to Scott country would be complete without a stop at Scotts' home. It's on A72, 12 miles (19 km) east of Traquair House. Scott built this ornate mansion between 1817 and 1822, using the most romantic materials he could find: He made a special trip to attend the razing of Edinburgh's fourteenth-century tollbooth, for instance, known as "the Heart of Midlothian" (also the title of a Scott novel), in order to make off with its front door, which he then had incorporated into the design of his new abode. A guide will take you through (open from April through October).

Nearby are Melrose and Dryburgh abbeys, two famous border abbeys dear to Scott's heart. Melrose Abbey, founded in 1136, is renowned for its traceried stonework; Dryburgh Abbey, which also dates from the twelfth century, houses Scott's tomb. Both are below Abbotsford, on A6091.

BEST EN ROUTE

From May through September it is advisable to book your bed in advance of your trip, as accommodations are often hard to find on the spot. Lunches in Scottish hotels are served approximately between 12 and 2, dinners approximately between 7 and 9 unless otherwise noted. Establishments charging under $60 per night for two occupants are listed as inexpensive; those with rates from $60 to $80 are considered moderate; and those charging $80 and up are listed as expensive.

STIRLING

Golden Lion – Though now clinging for dear life to its immaculate historic pedigree, this 75-room hotel is nonetheless the best of Stirling's lately rather dubious center-city bets. Robert Burns, the royal family, and a host of film stars have all stayed here. 8 King St. (phone: 75351). Moderate to inexpensive.

CALLANDER

Roman Camp Hotel – There are 11 bedrooms and a few very decorative and very alive peacocks trailing across the lawn of this seventeenth-century hunting lodge. English, Scottish, and Swiss dishes are served in its restaurant. Closed in January. Reservations necessary. Off Main St. (phone: 30003). Moderate.

KILLEARN

Black Bull Hotel – Famed for its food as far afield as Glasgow, the cuisine is traditional English and Scottish and perfectly wonderful. Evening meals from 5 on (lunches, usual hours). Reservations necessary May through September. Off Main St. (phone: 50215). Moderate.

GLASGOW

Albany Hotel – Glasgow's finest business-center-cum-hotel where the visiting pop stars stay in the uneasy company of executives. This is a slick 251-room flat-topped box with a big-city image. Inside, it's soft lights, carpets, and chrome. One of the two dining rooms is a popular carvery with Scottish traditional cooking. Bothwell St. (phone: 248-2656). Expensive.

Central Hotel – It's comfortable in old-fashioned style. There are 211 sumptuous bedrooms, a hairdresser, and three dining rooms, including *The Malmaison,* a French restaurant that's just about the best in town (closed Sundays). Gordon St. (phone: 221-9680). Moderate.

PEEBLES

Peebles Hotel Hydro – This palatial estate stands by a lovely waterfall in one of Scotland's most historic areas. English and Scottish traditional cooking. Off A702, on Innerleithen Rd. (phone: 2-0602). Expensive to moderate.

Park Hotel – Ideally situated for fishing, riding, golf, and tennis, and its paneled dining room, bar, and lounge look out over landscaped gardens. Innerleithen Rd. (phone: 20451). Moderate.

Scotland's Fabled Golf Courses

If you're a golfer and haven't played in Scotland, you haven't seen where it all began and where it's still mostly at. Assuming your plane lands at Prestwick, just above the old market town of Ayr, you are already in the heart of Scottish golf country. There are seven championship courses in the Prestwick area, including the course at Prestwick itself, the site of the first-ever Open in 1860. All the courses on the tour outlined below (except Gleneagles and Rosemount) are links courses, which means they consist of tough seaside dunes riddled with furzy clumps and covered by the merest modicum of grass (except, of course, for the bunkers). Americans aren't used to playing on links courses; for a few tips see the *Useful Hints* insert at the end of this route.

TURNBERRY HOTEL GOLF COURSE: This massive vacationers' paradise, which looks like a landlocked ocean liner, has as its front lawn the world-famous Ailsa Course. If you can afford it, stay here for 2 or 3 days and use it as a base to make the rounds of the six neighboring championship links (the desk clerk will give you directions).

The 9th hole of the Ailsa, Bruce's Castle, has a tee isolated on a promontory, complete with a picturesque lighthouse, that juts into the Firth of Clyde. You'll need a crack shot over the water to get your ball back on the mainland. *Turnberry Hotel* caters to golfing needs, at a reduced rate for residents. Turnberry Hotel Golf Course, Turnberry, Strathclyde KA26 9LT, Scotland (phone: 202).

ROYAL TROON: Laid out along the beach, with the outgoing nine heading virtually straight down the strand and the closing nine paralleling it only a few yards inland, the only distraction is that the course lies directly below the flight path into Prestwick Airport. Another classic British Open layout, it is one of the few important private clubs in Scotland, though playing privileges are usually made available to visitors who are members of clubs in the US. Women are admitted only to certain areas on certain days. Royal Troon Golf Club, Craigend Rd., Troon, Strathclyde, Scotland (phone: 31-15-55).

PRESTWICK GOLF COURSE: Now considered too old-fashioned for the British Open rota because of its small, whimsical fairways and limited facilities for handling crowds, this tough, historic course, the scene of 24 Opens, is nonetheless full of hidden surprises and is worth playing at least once. This course also gets its share of racket from Prestwick Airport. Prestwick Golf Club, Links Rd., Prestwick KA9 1QG, Ayrshire, Scotland (phone: 7-7404).

THE OLD COURSE, ST. ANDREWS: St. Andrews is Scotland's "home of golf," a shrine to which all serious golfers should eventually make a pilgrimage. The Old Course, famous since golf was played with knives and forks, is on the West Sands at the junction of Golf Place and the Links. It is shaped as God made it, bunkers and all, even where, as on Heathery Hole (the 12th), the bunkers are in the middle of the fairway and not seen from the tee. The Old Course is full of bad kicks and subject to capricious changes in the direction of its high winds. It never plays the same way twice and can damage your ego, yet such is its magic that golfers who begin by hating it invariably end loving it.

Just behind the first tee is the stately, sacrosanct clubhouse headquarters of the Royal and Ancient Golf Club (known as the R & A). Its members, a kind of board of directors of world golf, gaze at you sardonically from the "Big Room" through a bay window as you tee off. Pay no attention to them. For a real slice of local color, try to get a caddie from the Caddie Master opposite the R & A clubhouse. The true Scottish caddie, now a dying breed, is a dwarf with bandy legs and a 10-day growth of beard who is too old to lift a club but too young to forget when he could. He knows each blade of grass on the course by heart and has seen 22 Opens. His accent sounds like a pneumatic drill. He'll advise what club you need for every shot, then stand aside implacably while you blow it. Clubs and carts are also for hire.

It's a good idea to contact the Links Management Committee of St. Andrews 8 weeks before your visit to apply to play on the Old Course. Otherwise you may find you can't get near it. Forms are not issued for July, August, Saturdays, or Thursday afternoons. Greens are closed Sundays. Write to Links Management Committee of St. Andrews, Golf Pl., St. Andrews, Fife, KY16 9JA Scotland (phone: 7-5757).

En Route from St. Andrews – Take A91 west across Fife, past peaceful Loch Leven, to the Yetts of Muckart (about 37 mi/59.2 km), where you'll join A823. Follow it north 9 miles (14.4 km) into Perthshire to *Gleneagles Hotel*. About 5 miles (8 km) beyond the Yetts of Muckart you'll be high above Glen Devon, with a panoramic view southwest across Stirling Plain. Go slowly and enjoy it.

GLENEAGLES HOTEL: This is Scottish heaven for American golfers, not only because Open championships are played there, but also because the moist, thick turf on its greens is comfortably like the turf at home. *Gleneagles* is the only five-star hotel in Scotland; it's even more grandiose than *Turnberry* and has almost as many ballrooms as tearooms. It has a system of decreased equipment-hire and greens fees for hotel residents. Gleneagles Hotel Golf Course, Auchterarder, Perthshire PH3 1NF, Scotland (phone: 3543).

Useful Hints: To play on links courses you need a wedge, a brush-up on your pitch-and-run technique, and a canny way of sizing up the wind, which can change a par here and there during the game. Bring a nylon rainsuit that fits over your clothes, wear dark colors if you don't want to be stared at, and take note that women are not allowed in many clubhouse bars. Cut down the number of clubs you carry to eight or less. Most important of all, speed up your game. Only at Turnberry and Gleneagles dare you pause to make bets, drink beer, or tell jokes. No four-ball games are allowed at private clubs on weekends. A letter of introduction from your home club secretary must be handed to the secretary of any private club whose greens you want to play a day in advance. Order lunch in advance in clubhouse dining rooms and wear a shirt and tie.

Listed below, area by area, are suggestions for family outings while the golfers are slamming balls down the fairways.

At St. Andrews:
The West Sands, the town's lovely, long, clean beach.
The Woollen Mill and Mill Shop, just by the Old Course on the street called the Links. Gorgeous Fair Isle and Shetland knitwear is sold at factory prices. Open Mondays through Saturdays.
St. Andrews University, the oldest in Scotland, founded in 1412. Its buildings dot the town's central shopping area (South St. and district).
Falkland Palace, one of the homes of the Stuart kings, built 1530–40, 15 miles (24 km) west of St. Andrews on A91, then 2 miles (3.2 km) south on A912. Open April to October.

At Gleneagles:
The town of Auchterarder, a mile away, famed for its antique shops (the hotel desk clerk will give you directions).

In Ayrshire:
See the *Western Scotland* route, Ayrshire section.

BEST EN ROUTE

Expect to pay $80 and up per night for a double room in hotels classified as expensive; $60 to $80 in the moderate category; and under $60 in the inexpensive category. For restaurants, the ranges are $45 and up for a dinner for two in the expensive category; $25 to $45 in the moderate; and $25 and under in the inexpensive category. Prices do not include wine, drinks, and tip.

PRESTWICK

Adamton Hotel – A charming, small eighteenth-century mansion renowned for its medieval banquets with mead (Fridays and Saturdays). Otherwise, cooking is English, Scottish, and French. Reservations necessary, May through September. Off Monkton Rd. (phone: 70678). Expensive to moderate.

TURNBERRY

Turnberry Hotel – Its restaurant features English and Scottish traditional cooking served in a lavish Edwardian atmosphere, and the hotel has a lovely setting overlooking the sea. Off A719, by Turnberry Lighthouse (phone: 202). Expensive.

TROON

Marine Hotel – Troon's finest hotel has, in addition to its main dining room, a grill room that's open daily; and a French restaurant (closed Sundays and Mondays). Reservations necessary May through September. Crosbie Rd. (phone: 314444). Expensive to moderate.

ST. ANDREWS

St. Andrews Golf Hotel – The view here, through bay windows with flower boxes out to sea, is completely delightful. So are the resident owners. English and Scottish traditional cooking. The Scores (phone: 72611). Moderate.

Rusacks Marine – On the 18th hole of the Old Course, this hotel, established in 1887, offers 50 comfortable rooms, off-season golf packages, and full clubhouse facilities. St. Andrews (phone: 74321). Moderate.

Old Course Golf & Country Club – Formerly the *Old Course Hotel,* it's been completely converted into a very exclusive golf club with full facilities and newly stylish rooms available to members on a time-sharing plan. Rooms are occasionally available to nonmembers. St. Andrews (phone: 74371). Moderate.

AUCHTERARDER

Gleneagles Hotel – Almost indescribably palatial, with incomparable service and decor and a menu that is a magnum opus. It's a haven for golfers, with four of the best courses in Scotland; it recently added shooting to the roster of activities as well. There's also a new domed leisure center with a pool, squash court, sauna, and more. Off A823, by Auchterarder (phone: 07646-2231). Expensive.

The Scottish Highlands: Edinburgh to Inverness

The Scottish Highlands, scene of some of the most barbaric events in the history of Britain, are also full of some of the most breathtaking scenery in the world. Highlanders, many of whom are pure Gaels, have the lilting voices and mercurial natures associated with their Irish cousins. As with the peasant Irish, the ancestors of these people were victimized and exploited by an ascendancy class. During the so-called Highland Clearances, which began in the late eighteenth century, crofters were driven from their homes so that landowners could replace them with sheep, at that time a more lucrative proposition. Those who refused to go had their houses and worldly goods burned. Hundreds of families fled south, jobless and possessionless, at the mercy of fortune, speaking only their native Celtic tongue.

Today 7% of the Scottish population owns 84% of the land, which shows how little things have changed since the eighteenth century. Great regions of lonely moors and mountains are in the grip of a handful of aristocrats who live in London and come north to hunt, shoot, and fish. You can see them in droves in the spring at 9 AM in the *Station Hotel* dining room in Inverness, just off the London train, madly excited by the chill Highland air, dripping with tweeds, and all barking at once for kippers and cream at shy native waitresses.

The Edinburgh-to-Inverness route described here takes you through the eastern and central Highland regions, which are lusher, more prosperous, more forested, and less Gaelic than the western regions. Some west Highland areas (not Gaelic ones) are included in the *Western Scotland* route.

EDINBURGH: For a complete description of the city and its hotels and restaurants, see *Edinburgh,* THE EUROPEAN CITIES.

    En route from Edinburgh – From the west end of Princes Street, follow Queensferry Road north across the Forth Road Bridge to the two-lane M90 (about

13 mi/22 km). Three miles (5 km) farther is Dunfermline, the capital of Scotland in the early Middle Ages, when Edinburgh was a mere castle.

DUNFERMLINE: Dunfermline Abbey is a royal imperative for tourists. King Robert the Bruce was buried in the abbey choir in 1329 and King Charles I, born in the abbey guesthouse in 1600. An attractive modern brass marks Bruce's grave, now under the roof of the parish church, the Norman nave of which is built over the abbey ruins. Parts of the original eleventh-century monastic buildings can still be seen here (Monastery St.; open daily).

Steel king Andrew Carnegie (1835–1919), the American millionaire, is a third royal personage associated with Dunfermline. He was born here in a damask weaver's cottage now escalated into a museum (Moodie St.; open daily).

En Route from Dunfermline – Twelve miles (20 km) beyond Dunfermline you might stop for a *coup d'oeil* at the Moors of Kinross and peaceful Loch Leven, on your right. Mary, Queen of Scots was imprisoned in Loch Leven Castle — on the island in the center of the lake — for 11 months in 1567. You can visit the castle by getting off the M90 at the Kinross interchange and taking a ferry from Kinross pier (daily; April through September).

DUNKELD: Want a taste of paradise? Have a picnic on the Dunkeld Cathedral grounds by the bonnie banks of the River Tay (you can get sandwiches at *Country Bakery*, Atholl St.). This idyllic spot was the ancient capital of the Picts and Scots from AD 850, and the bones of the great St. Columba of Iona, founder of the Celtic Christian church, were lodged at Dunkeld Cathedral for a time after the Vikings raided Iona in 597. Along with the charming cathedral, you'll love the 40-odd seventeenth-century row houses, restored by the National Trust for Scotland, that comprise the main part of the village.

PITLOCHRY: It seems a veritable Brigadoon with its storybook array of gabled houses and country churches rising sharply up the Tummel River valley brae only to be locked in by giant heather-covered mountains. The town is beautifully situated and consequently a famous resort with many activities, including the Pitlochry Festival Theatre, bagpipe and drum pageants, Highland games (mid-September), mountain climbing, pony trekking, organized nature-trail hiking (with Scottish National Forest brochures on plants, birds, and animals), golfing, and salmon fishing.

Use Pitlochry as a base for a couple of side trips. A couple of miles north of Pitlochry on B8019 is the entrance to the famed Queen's View above Loch Tummel, where Queen Victoria used to picnic. As you leave Loch Tummel, look to your left for Mt. Schiehallion, the conical peak so perfect in shape that scientists used it to compute the earth's mass. At the village called Kinloch Rannoch, follow the small, unnumbered road around Loch Rannoch's south shore. Here is the beautiful Black Wood of Rannoch, the last piece of medieval forest in Scotland.

South of Pitlochry, cross the River Tay and follow the A846 to the turnoff for Glen Lyon (follow the signs for Fortingall). Glen Lyon is the longest glen in Scotland, beloved for its sun-speckled, wooded glades and the plethora of legends associated with it.

En Route from Glen Lyon – At the Bridge of Balgie, over the River Lyon, an unnumbered road runs south to join A827 beside Loch Tay. Take this and turn right at the junction. In 6 miles (10 km) you'll be at Killin, famous for its lake view and dazzling waterfall, a typical example of Highland scenery at its finest.

PASS OF KILLIECRANKIE: At this luscious wooded gorge, especially beautiful in autumn, Viscount Claverhouse ("Bonnie Dundee") and his Jacobite army routed the English troops of William III in 1689. The National Trust for Scotland has a Visitor Centre and Battle Display here (open Easter to mid-October).

BLAIR ATHOLL: Nearby is Blair Castle, the family seat of the dukes of Atholl, head of the Clan Murray. The present duke lives in Blair Castle, where he keeps the last and only legal private army in Britain (about 65 men). Thirty-two rooms of his 700-year-old abode are awash in Chippendales, Limoges, Zoffanys, and Jacobite relics (open, including the attractive tearoom, from the first Sunday in May to second Sunday in October).

En Route from Blair Atholl – The A9 runs near Newtonmore, known throughout the Highlands for its shinty team (shinty is a faster, fiercer form of hockey). You pass the usually bustling shinty field as you enter town.

KINGUSSIE: The ruins of rocky Ruthven Barracks are visible from the main road. These were maintained by English forces as a defense against Jacobite uprisings between the rebellions of 1715 and 1745. (The fact that there *was* a Jacobite Rebellion in 1745 may say something about their effectiveness.) Visit Am Fasgadh (the Shelter, in Gaelic), the Highland folk museum by the river. It has a furnished thatched cottage that illustrates how bleak life in northern Scotland once was (open weekdays year-round).

AVIEMORE: Several top-class if rather drearily formal new hotels overlook this popular ski resort's snow-studded Cairngorm Mountains. Slalom into the sunset above an incredible view at 11 o'clock at night! The slopes are rough but cheap (information about prices, opening times, equipment rental, and so forth is available at the Spey Valley Tourist Organization, Aviemore, phone: 810363).

En Route from Aviemore – Detour off A9 to the town of Carrbridge, nip into the Landmark Visitor Centre, the first exhibition of its kind in Europe. Ten thousand years of Highland history are surveyed entertainingly in a triple-screen audio visual theater (open daily all year).

INVERNESS: Despite its glamorous site on the Moray Firth, Inverness is the Plain Jane of Scottish cities. It won't make you wish you were a painter, but it *will* give you a center from which to strike out in all directions for Scotland's most ethereal parts. Ideas for day trips are legion at the Inverness, Loch Ness, and Nairn Tourist Board, 23 Church St. (phone: 234353). Musts are Culloden Moor, where Bonnie Prince Charlie's army was decimated in the famous Jacobite uprising of 1745, and Loch Ness, the 22-mile (35-km) length of which you can scout for the monster by driving south on A82. The first recorded sighting of the monster was by St. Columba nearly 1,500 years ago; it continues to be at home to visitors, but with no formal hours.

BEST EN ROUTE

Expect to pay $60 and up per night for a double room in hotels classified as expensive; $45 to $60 in the moderate category; and under $45 in the inexpensive category. For restaurants, the ranges are $45 and up for a dinner for two in the expensive category; $25 to $45 in the moderate; and $25 and under in the inexpensive category. Prices do not include wine, drinks, and tip.

DUNFERMLINE

King Malcolm Thistle Hotel – Dunfermline's finest is named for the Malcolm who overthrew Macbeth (his wife, Queen Margaret, founded Dunfermline Abbey). Modern by design, but with English and Scottish traditional cooking. Queensferry Rd., Wester Pitcorthie, just south of the Dunfermline at A823 (phone: 722611). Expensive.

PITLOCHRY

Atholl Palace Hotel – This turreted Victorian monster with a glowingly comfortable interior and sweepingly glorious view was built in 1880 as a health resort alongside some healing spas. More soothing today is its fine Scottish cooking, including grouse and other game. It's on its own secluded grounds on Atholl Rd.; look for the sign at the turnoff south of Pitlochry on A9 (phone: 2400). Expensive to moderate.

Green Park Hotel – It has a very beautiful setting — on Loch Faskally overlooking the mountains — much admired by the outdoorsy people who visit this area to fish, hike, or ski. Dinner as well as breakfast comes with the price of the room, which is an advantage only to those who don't mind mediocre food. Clunie Bridge Rd. (phone: 2537). Moderate.

AVIEMORE

Stakis Coylumbridge Hotel – Very modern and plush, *Coylumbridge* has its own ice/roller rink. English and Scottish traditional cooking in the dining room at the usual hours and snacks in the coffee shop from 10 AM to 2 PM. At Coylumbridge, on A951 en route to the Cairngorms from A9 (phone: 810661). Moderate.

Post House Hotel – Every morning the chef decides what will be on the evening's menu; try requesting your favorite dinner dish at breakfast by getting your waitress to carry a message on a paper napkin. In addition to the main dining room, the hotel has another eatery that's open form 10 AM to 10 PM. On the road to the Cairngorms just past Aviemore Centre; follow the signs from A9 (phone: 810771). Expensive to moderate.

INVERNESS

Culloden House – *The* place to stay at Inverness, in rural splendor below Culloden Moor. The light, spacious rooms of this beautiful eighteenth-century palace are full of ornate plasterwork and priceless antique furniture. On Culloden Moor (phone: 790461). Expensive.

Station Hotel – The comfortably plush Victorian decor of this 65-room relic contradicts its scruffy exterior. Its restaurant serves good traditional English and Scottish fare. Academy St. (phone: 231926). Expensive to moderate.

Kingsmills Hotel – Ten minutes' walk from downtown, this striking white 200-year-old time capsule with its front door in an architraved turret has 54 bedrooms and 6 apartments, private squash courts, and 2 acres of gardens. Damfield Rd. (phone: 237166). Expensive to moderate.

Cummings Hotel – The complete ordinariness of this 38-bedroom rectangle somehow manages to be endearing. Nightly Scottish cabarets here have been wowing audiences from June to September. Church St. (phone: 232531). Moderate to inexpensive.

Western Scotland

Ayrshire is famous for its golf courses, its cattle, its golden beaches and quaint Victorian resort towns, its comparatively dry climate, and its view of the Isle of Arran. It is even more famous, however, as the home of Robert Burns, the eighteenth-century rustic bard who heralded poetry's Romantic Age. Scotland may be the only country in the world to celebrate its national identity by paying homage to a poet. On February 22, when Americans are sedately eating cherry pie in memory of George Washington, the Scots are just beginning to surface after the revels of Burns Night (January 25). The festivities include elaborate banquets of *haggis, tatties* and *neeps* (potatoes and turnips), innumerable toasts, poetry recitals, and piping, singing, and dancing till dawn. This night (together with New Year's Eve) is traditionally sanctioned as a time for the wild side of the Scot, seemingly shrouded the rest of the year in rock-ribbed Presbyterianism, to come out, as it were, for Ayr.

North of Ayrshire is world-famous Inveraray Castle, the seat of the dukes of Argyll. About 40 miles (64 km) farther up the coast is lovely Oban, a starting place for the Western Isles and a good point of departure for touring the western Highlands.

Assuming you have arrived at Prestwick Airport, take the coast road, A719, 5 miles (8 km) south to Ayr past a succession of Victorian villas that are now small hotels specializing in malt Scotch whiskies.

AYR: This cozy harbor and market town was chartered in the thirteenth century and is now a popular resort, with a marvelous beach and a nationally famous racecourse. The only architectural relics left in the town are the Tower of St. John, which is believed to date from the thirteenth century (Citadel Pl. and Eglinton Terr.); the Auld Brig, which Burns praised in his poem *The Twa Brigs* (High St.); sixteenth-century Loudun Hall, townhouse of the hereditary sheriffs of Ayrshire (Boat Vennel); and the Auld Kirk, built by Oliver Cromwell in 1654, in which Burns was baptized (off High St., diagonally opposite Newmarket St.). Also on High Street is the famous *Tam O'Shanter Inn,* the traditional starting point of Tam's legendary ride, which now displays Burns relics and memorabilia.

South of the town, off B7024, you might want to spend a happy hour or two at Belleisle Park, which has a zoo, nature trail, gardens, and a championship golf course.

ALLOWAY: Burns's birthplace is a tiny, pastoral village on the River Doon, a leafy haven dominated by the rather incongruous Corinthian columns of the Burns Monument, which makes you feel as though you'd wandered into a painting by Fragonard. The only evidence of time's incursion into Alloway is the Land O'Burns Centre, featuring a visual display, crafts shop, bookstall, cafeteria, and landscaped gardens with picnic tables. Across the street, the humble, whitewashed cottage in which the poet was born in 1759 has been preserved intact. Nearby is the Burns Museum. A little farther up the road are the 700-year-old Brig O'Doon, the arched bridge where the witch in Burns's poem *Tam O'Shanter* caught hold of Tam's mare's tail, and Auld Alloway Kirk, the scene of the witches' revels in the poem. If you have a day to spare, you can follow the Burns Heritage Trail, visiting every place Burns ever went, from Ayr to Dumfries in the next county.

En Route from Alloway – On A719, heading south toward Culzean Castle, there's a sign marking the Croy Brae, also known as Electric Brae. As you climb it, switch off your motor: you will then coast *uphill!* Coming down the other side, switch off your motor again: Now you are coasting uphill backward! Natives swear it is an optical illusion.

CULZEAN CASTLE: Standing on a cliff overlooking the Firth of Clyde, this breathtaking edifice is Scotland's most-visited castle. Culzean Castle (the name, pronounced "culane," refers to the caves over which the castle is built) was for centuries the seat of the Kennedy family, later the Kennedys of Cassilis. Most of the present structure was designed for the tenth earl of Cassilis in the late eighteenth century by the famous Scottish architect Robert Adam. Adam's achievements here include the much-admired oval staircase and his remarkable drum-shaped drawing rooms (with curved fireplaces) giving onto the sea. The uppermost apartments were given to President Eisenhower to use as his Scottish residence as a token of appreciation after World War II. The castle's portrait of Napoleon was a gift from Josephine, a relation of the Kennedys. Go in the morning to avoid the tourist buses that swamp the place after lunch and ask for the head guide, Isabelle Mullin; there's nothing she doesn't know about Culzean Castle or the earls of Cassilis.

En Route from Culzean Castle – Return to Ayr by A77, past the ruins of Crossraguel Abbey, founded in 1244, whose last abbot was roasted by the Kennedys in the sixteenth century until he signed away his lands.

Beyond Ayr, traveling north on A78, you come to the sailing towns of Irvine, Saltcoats, and Largs. You can rent boats at the latter (contact the Ayrshire Valleys Tourist Board, Civic Centre, Kilmarnock; phone: 21140). At Gourock, also a seaside holiday center, hop a ferry for Dunoon, the main town across the firth on the Cowal Peninsula. Ferries run every 20 minutes, but play it safe by booking in advance (phone: 3-3755).

DUNOON: This burgeoning vacationland has a 4-mile (6-km) waterside promenade running alongside piers, gardens, amusement arcades, amazing views, and fancy hotels. On summer nights in the gardens there are band concerts, model boat displays, variety shows, flower shows, dances, tournaments, and Highland games. It's a good place to spend a night if you like crowds and gaiety. Holy Loch, with its US submarine base, is just beside it.

INVERARAY: Far more peaceful than Dunoon and more beautiful as well, the hereditary seat of the dukes of Argyll, chiefs of the powerful Clan Campbell, is ethereal in its isolation by the quiet waters of Loch Fyne. The original village was destroyed in 1644 by the royalist marquess of Montrose, then rebuilt by the third duke of Argyll; successive dukes of Argyll have lavished a great deal of money on preserving its seventeenth- and eighteenth-century architecture. The 140-foot bell tower, part of the Episcopal Church of All Saints (the Avenue), houses the world's second heaviest ring of ten bells, which are chimed daily. The view from the top of the tower is glorious.

For centuries, the dukes of Argyll lived in the famous Inveraray Castle nearby. The present castle, which dates from the early sixteenth century, was replanned and rebuilt from 1743 to 1770. Its unusual mixture of neo-Gothic and Scottish baronial styles and its strange colors and conical towers make it look for all the world like a Disneyland castle. Unfortunately, the castle's roof caught fire in 1975 and is now fully restored. The interior, however, is worth a visit by itself. It contains a wealth of eighteenth-century ornamentation and architectural curiosities, portraits by Gainsborough and other great artists, and a collection of historical relics that virtually provide a crash course in Highland history. A guided tour is available; open April to mid-October.

En Route from Inveraray – Following A819 north, you'll pass through Glen Aray and along the northeastern shore of Loch Awe. The islands in the loch are the traditional Clan Campbell burying ground. It's romantic to imagine those stark, ancient funerals, in which only the father, brothers, and a lone piper accompanied the dead in a small boat across the waves.

Visible on your left as you skirt the north tip of Loch Awe is the impressive ruin of Kilchurn Castle, a Campbell stronghold since 1440. Six miles (10 km) farther on, on the right, at Cruachan Waterfall, is the Cruachan Underground Visitor Centre. This is a 4-million-kilowatt power station in a vast cavern inside Ben Cruachan, run by the North of Scotland Hydro-Electric Board using water pumped from Loch Awe to a reservoir 1,200 feet up the mountain. Guides and a minibus tour are on hand.

West of Ben Cruachan is the Pass of Brander, where the Clan MacDougall tried unsuccessfully to ambush Robert the Bruce in 1308.

OBAN: Oban was set up as a fish market by a government agency in 1786. Today it is a bustling holiday spot with a picturesque circular harbor, quaint wedding-cake hotels, and a distinctly Highland flavor. Fish auctions are still held on the docks every morning.

As you waft down the town's mile-long esplanade with a couple of glasses of the local whiskies inside you, gaze across the firth to the sun-studded Hebridean islands for a true glimpse of heaven.

There's a variety of good boat trips, including day cruises to the island of Iona, the first Christian settlement in Scotland, famous for its association with St. Columba, who founded a monastery here in 563. Forty-eight Scottish kings lie buried on the island, including Macbeth. Wear a sweater for the boat ride; it's an open boat. For details, contact the Oban, Mull, and District Tourist Board (Argyll Square; phone: 63122/63551).

GLENCOE: This ominous, mist-enshrouded glen was the scene of a famous massacre in 1692, when a government force of Campbells wiped out an entire branch of the Clan Macdonald — who had received them as guests — by stabbing them in their beds at daybreak. To learn more details, visit the Glencoe and North Lorn Folk Museum off A82 just past Ballachulish, Glencoe's only village.

En Route from Glencoe – The small resort town of Fort William is popular and bursting with hotels, but its setting is drab and moorish. The shopping here is quite good, however, and about 5 miles (8 km) beyond the town, on the right, is Ben Nevis, which at 4,406 feet is Britain's highest mountain.

At Loch Oich you can either take A87 west for 50 miles (80 km) to Kyle of Lochalsh or continue up A82 along Loch Ness to Inverness. From Inverness you can follow the Highlands tour route backward to Edinburgh.

If you head west, as you approach Kyle of Lochalsh you pass Loch Duich and, just offshore, Eilean Donan, Scotland's most-photographed castle. Try to be there at sunset, when all is bathed in unearthly light. Then suddenly you come upon the sea and, opposite you, the fabled Isle of Skye, the largest and most famous of the Hebrides, with its dark, jagged Cuillin hills. You may never want to go home.

BEST EN ROUTE

Expect to pay $80 and up per night for a double room in hotels classified as expensive; $60 to $80 in the moderate category; and $45 to $60 in the inexpensive category. For restaurants, the ranges are $50 and up for a dinner for two in the expensive category; $30 to $50 in the moderate; and $30 and under in the inexpensive category. Prices do not include wine, drinks, and tip.

AYR

Belleisle House – An aristocrat's home before it became a hotel, this delightful place with 15 bedrooms retains such personal embellishments as engraved fireplaces. Elegant dining is also available. Inside Belleisle Park grounds, just south of Ayr, off the B7024, on Doonfoot Rd. (phone: 42331). Inexpensive.

The Pickwick Hotel – This is one of the best of a seafront string of Victorian villas specializing in pure malt whiskies and Taste of Scotland foods. It has 15 bedrooms, each with a bath. 19 Racecourse Rd. (phone: 60111). Inexpensive.

OBAN

Great Western Hotel – This lavishly decorated hotel has two dining rooms serving English, Scottish, and Continental dishes. Reservations necessary from May through September. The Esplanade (phone: 63101). Moderate.

Alexander Hotel – A modernized, well-furnished hotel with 56 rooms and magnificent views over the harbor, Oban Bay, and the Firth. Scottish and English cuisine. The Esplanade (phone: 62381). Moderate to inexpensive.

GLENCOE

Kings House Hotel – Scotland's oldest licensed inn, this 22-room hotel on Rannoch Moor stands on an old drovers road, along which cattle were once herded to market. A great base for climbers, fishermen, skiers, and hikers. Closed November to January (phone: 259). Inexpensive.

KYLE OF LOCHALSH

Lochalsh Hotel – A comfortable resort hotel just beside the ferry to the Isle of Skye, with glorious views from most of the 45 rooms. English, Scottish, and French cuisine are served here. Ferry Rd. (phone: 4202). Expensive to moderate.

Northern Ireland

Northern Ireland's troubles have given it bad press. This has had two effects: People have become aware of Northern Ireland as a part of the United Kingdom (it has been part of Great Britain since 1920), and the violence has scared away tourists and isolated the country. The visitors who did come, however, found hostility sporadic, confined mostly to the two large urban centers of Belfast and Londonderry. They also found unspoiled coastline and countryside, empty beaches, uncrowded roads, inexpensive accommodations, and friendly people. Even the British army's presence was said to be nearly invisible.

Northern Ireland — virtually synonymous with the ancient province of Ulster and still often so referred to — covers only about one-sixth the total area of Ireland. The province is so compact — about 70 miles at its widest by about 100 miles long — that in a short tour of 3 to 4 days you can crisscross its six counties and take in most of their highlights. Among these are several hundred miles of bay-indented coast, with coves and cliffs and castles and beaches; scores of beautiful inland lakes and hundreds of rivers and streams; two great mountain chains — the fabled Mountains of Mourne, sweeping down to the sea in the southeast, and the Sperrin Mountains in the northwest.

The tour described below begins in Belfast, the capital of Northern Ireland, and makes a clockwise circle around the province, following the southern part of Ulster's long coastline that encircles County Down. County Down has its share of fine resorts along the winding shore, but it is overshadowed by the Mourne Mountains in the south, where Slieve Donard rises from the sea to 2,796 feet.

County Down is bordered by Armagh to the west, the county whose rich northern fruit-growing area has earned its title as "the garden of Ulster."

County Fermanagh, the farthest west, is "the lakeland of Ulster." The River Erne winds through its center, expanding into two large lakes, Upper and Lower Erne, both with many islands.

The inland county of Tyrone has a fine variety of scenery — gentle hills, glens, river valleys, moors, and small towns. But the bulk of the land piles up to the 2,000-foot peaks of the Sperrin Mountains.

Derry, the northwestern corner, is an interesting mix: To the south are the Sperrin Mountains (shared with County Tyrone); to the north is the Atlantic coast, fringed with magnificent beaches of surf-washed sands. The county's boundary with County Antrim in the east is the River Bann; in the west the River Foyle borders the Irish Republic.

Antrim is the northeastern corner, its southeastern end buttressed by Belfast. Its magnificent east coast curves around the base of steep headlands, between which the beautiful nine glens of Antrim open to the sea. Almost every bay along the coast is a link in a chain of fine holiday resorts. Near the northernmost point, Torr Head is only 13 miles (21 km) from Scotland. On the northwestern end of Antrim's coast is the Giant's Causeway, a curious rock formation that's a celebrated natural wonder. The River Bann and Lough Neagh, the largest lake in Ireland and Britain, form the western boundary.

BELFAST: This is a fairly new city that grew rapidly during the nineteenth-century shipbuilding and linen production boom. Belfast was dubbed "the Athens of the North" during a great cultural blooming in the late eighteenth and early nineteenth centuries, when prominent citizens became patrons of learning and art. In the same period the shipbuilding industry grew by leaps and bounds, and new machinery and processes helped Belfast gain a position of supremacy in the linen industry. When the six Ulster counties were separated from the rest of Ireland by an act of the British Parliament in 1920, Belfast became the capital of the province of Northern Ireland.

The port city is on the River Lagan where it joins the sea. Its center is Donegall Square, dominated by the large city hall, a Renaissance building with a tower at each corner and a graceful dome in the center. On the east side stands a sculpture commemorating the 1912 *Titanic* disaster — the largest ship of its time was built here.

Other impressive buildings are St. Anne's Cathedral, the Ulster Museum and Art Gallery, and, on a hill in the suburb of Stormont, Parliament House. One important building damaged during the violence of the 1970s, the ornate Edwardian grand opera house has been restored and stages all kinds of entertainment. Belfast has 1,400 acres of parkland, three theaters, a fine university, more than 300 churches, and excellent shops in the center of town. The port has 7 miles (11 km) of quays. The shipyards of Harland and Wolff include the largest shipbuilding dock in the world.

Six miles (10 km) east of Belfast on Route A2 is the small residential town of Holywood beside Belfast Lough.

HOLYWOOD: Although the town has a good promenade, a golf course, and tennis and yachting facilities, the main reason to stop here is the Ulster Folk and Transport Museum, which spreads over 166 acres and faithfully recreates nineteenth-century life — from a blacksmith's forge to a weaver's house. There are farms and craftsmen working at their craft. You can buy their products (open daily; Cultra Manor).

BANGOR: Ulster's chief yachting center, Bangor is well laid out, with fine promenades, gardens, and recreation grounds. Yacht races go on all the time, setting out from the Royal Ulster or the Ballyholme clubhouse.

En Route from Bangor – Take A21 south to Newtownards, at the northern end of Strangford Lough, a busy marketing and industrial town. Continue to Comber, where flax yarn for linen is spun. Go south on A22 along Strangford Lough passing Killyleagh, with Ulster's finest residential castle, en route to Downpatrick. Halfway between this quiet hilly town and the pretty village of Strangford, 9 miles (14 km) east, lies Saul (signposted), a place with a special meaning for Irish everywhere, for it was here that St. Patrick landed in 432 to begin his Irish mission and build his church. Although the church was destroyed several times, fragments of earlier buildings remain. On the height above the village is the little memorial church of St. Patrick (Church of Ireland). The Shrine of St. Patrick, a mile farther west of the prominent hill of Sliabh Padraig, is a place of pilgrimage. A granite figure of the saint stands on the summit.

Continue to Strangford, on the western shore of the strait connecting Strangford Lough with the sea. There is a car ferry to the village of Portaferry on the opposite shore. This area is noteworthy for the many castle and monastic ruins around the Lough's indented shore, including Portaferry and Strangford castles, large rectangular structures built by the Anglo-Normans to guard the strait entrance. Portaferry also has the Queen's University Marine Biology Station, which is worth a visit for its ecological interest.

From Strangford, take A2 around Dundrum Bay all the way to Newcastle, driving toward the impressive Mourne Mountains looming to the southwest.

NEWCASTLE: This seaside resort is beautifully situated along the sandy beach that fringes Dundrum Bay, with the great bulk of Slieve Donard filling the skyline behind the town.

Two miles (3 km) west, at Bryansford, is scenic Tollymore Forest Park. There are many planned walks here along the Shimna River and on the mountainside. Three (5 km) miles north of Tollymore is another forest park — Castlewellan — with an outstanding arboretum.

Extending southwest for nearly 15 miles (24 km) are the Mourne Mountains.

En Route from Newcastle – The scenery along the Mourne coastline, Route A2, is superb. About 13 miles (21 km) from Newcastle is Kilkeel, the headquarters for a large fishing fleet. The town is a good center for exploring the Mournes and the coast of south Down.

The coast road continues through the charming little resort towns of Rostrevor and Warrenpoint on the edge of Carlingford Lough, where you look across the water to the shores of the Irish Republic and on to the "frontier" town of Newry. This industrial center and port, in a hollow among hills at the head of the Newry River estuary, has been important from ancient times because of its strategic position at the "gap of the north" — the main crossing into Ulster from Dublin and the south. Take A28 into County Armagh and to the town of Armagh, about 20 miles (32 km) northwest.

ARMAGH: This ancient city — once the seat of Ulster kings — has been the ecclesiastical capital of Ireland for over 1,500 years. It was here in 443 that St. Patrick established a cathedral and monastic school, which have been destroyed and rebuilt many times. The Church of Ireland cathedral now occupies the site. The Catholic cathedral stands imposingly on an adjoining hilltop, approached by a long series of steps with terraces. Its inside walls are covered with mosaics, including medallions of the saints of Ireland. Marble is used for everything from altars to pulpit.

The city has an air of quiet dignity. Its well-laid-out streets are dominated by the two cathedrals. At the center of town is the Mall, a pleasant green lined by fine Georgian houses, the excellent County Museum (whose curator is a font of local knowledge), the courthouse, the seventeenth-century Royal School, and the eighteenth-century observatory and modern planetarium.

Take Route A28 to Augher and join A4 to Fivemiletown, where you cross into County Fermanagh. Continue to Enniskillen.

ENNISKILLEN: Between the Upper and Lower Lough Erne, the town is a convenient base for exploring this peaceful countryside on roads along the wooded lakeshores or by boat on the lakes. Abundant fishing and the availability of modern boats for rent have made these lakes very popular.

En Route from Enniskillen – Take Route A46 to Belleek, the westernmost point of Ulster. This border town, where Northern Ireland meets the Republic, is known for its lovely handmade eggshell-thin pottery. Souvenirs can be bought at the pottery (open weekdays).

From Belleek take A47 to Kesh, and A84 into County Tyrone until it joins A32 to Omagh. The Ulster-American Folk Park, 4 miles (6 km) north of Omagh, illustrates Northern Ireland's notable contributions to US history, including the ancestors of US presidents. Open weekdays throughout the year. The Folk Park is also the ideal starting point for the Ulster American Heritage Trail through the Northern Ireland. Special signposts along the trail indicate the various sites.

LONDONDERRY: This ancient seaport, which stands on a commanding hill overlooking a broad tidal curve of the River Foyle, was founded as a monastic settlement in 546. Although it was never occupied by the Anglo-Normans, it was the scene of many struggles between Irish forces and a succession of invaders. In 1608, with the English in control, the land was granted to the citizens of London (thus, Londonderry). A large colony of Protestants was imported and the walls were fortified. These walls withstood several sieges; the most famous, in 1689, lasted 105 days.

The Old Walls, the city's most prominent feature, are in excellent condition. They are now laid out as a promenade, with many of the old cannons still standing where they once stood, by the four old city gates. Guided tours of the city walls leave from the Tourist Information Centre (Foyle St.) on weekdays.

In Shipquay Place is the Guildhall, an impressive modern Gothic structure with a fine series of stained-glass windows illustrating events in the city's history. It was partly destroyed in the disturbances of 1972 but is now mostly restored. Shipquay Street leads to the seventeenth-century Protestant cathedral.

Outside the walls is Bogside, the Catholic area, with the nineteenth-century Catholic cathedral on Great James Street.

En Route from Londonderry – Take Route A2 out of the city; you are in for a 74-mile (119-km) treat of the most scenic coast road in Northern Ireland, which leads all the way into Belfast. The road goes east to Limavady, then curves northeast to hug the shore and pass through two noted County Derry resorts: Castlerock and Portstewart. They offer what all resorts on the north coast have in common: excellent beaches, good sea and river fishing, and several fine golf courses. Continue 4 miles (6 km) to Portrush in County Antrim.

PORTRUSH: This resort has an outstanding golf course — the Royal Portrush, site of the British Open in the past. There is bus service to the Giant's Causeway, the absolute must-see on this route.

Often called the eighth wonder of the world, the causeway is an intriguing rock formation on the coast near Bushmills. It was formed by cooling lava that burst through the earth's crust in the Cenozoic period as long as 70 million years ago. Here the basaltic lava split into prismatic columns as it cooled. And there they stand, about 40,000 basalt columns packed together in a shape so regular they seem cut by hand.

En Route from Portrush – Continue east to Portballintrae and Bushmills, home of the world's oldest whiskey. (The distillery is open to visitors who give advance notice; phone: 31521.) From both places there is bus service to the Giant's Causeway, just north.

Continue past resorts with wide beaches separated by cliffs — white, black, and red — fretted by the sea into strange shapes. Ballycastle is the point of departure for white-cliffed Rathlin Island, the haunt of millions of sea birds. Special trips are available from Easter to September, although visitors can also catch the regular mailboat that leaves from Ballycastle at about 11:30 AM on Mondays, Wednesdays, and Fridays. Six miles (10 km) ahead is Ballyvoy. From here a signposted road goes to Fair Head, the northeastern extremity of Ireland, which rises to 636 feet of sheer cliffs of columnar basalt and offers a fabulous view of Rathlin Island and Scotland. The road goes on to Torr Head, the closest point to the Scottish coast. Rejoin Route A2 near Cushendun and enter the area of the nine glens of Antrim. Continue to Glenariff.

GLENARIFF: Here is the most famous of the Antrim glens. Formed by the Glenariff River at Red Bay, the glen stretches inland for about 5 miles (8 km) between steep mountains. It has a nature information center.

En Route from Glenariff – The coast road takes you past more glens and beautiful sea views to Larne, the crossing point for car-ferry service from Stranraer and Cairaryan in Scotland, the shortest cross-channel passages between Ireland and Britain. Continue south for 21 miles (34 km) to Belfast.

BEST EN ROUTE

Northern Ireland has an adequate supply of hotels and restaurants. Hotels and guest-houses are generally clean and fairly inexpensive. The more expensive ones may have a special feature, such as a great view or an unbeatable location. The prices listed here range from expensive — more than $60 per night for a double; to moderate — $30 to $60; to inexpensive — under $30. The range for dinner per person is: more than $15, expensive; $10 to $15, moderate; under $10, inexpensive.

BELFAST

Forum Hotel – In the center of town, this is a modern, elegant place with pleasant, well-equipped rooms. There is a coffee shop on the granite and marble ground floor; also a pub bar. Another cocktail bar is upstairs, and there's a nightclub on the top floor. Great Victoria St. (phone: 245161). Expensive.

Stormont Hotel – This hotel is about 4 miles out of town and just across the road from the Parliament Houses and Stormont Castle. It has 50 modern bedrooms and ample parking facilities. The dining room features Irish specialties, and dancing on Saturday nights. 587 Upper Newtownards Rd. (phone: 658621). Expensive.

Wellington Park Hotel – One of the city's newest hotels, the Wellington is in south Belfast, close to Queen's University, the Botanic Gardens, and the Ulster Museum. The decor here includes a permanent display of contemporary Irish painting and sculpture. 21 Malone Rd. (phone: 661232). Expensive.

HOLYWOOD

Culloden Hotel – This sumptuous baronial Victorian mansion is set amid gardens and woodlands 6 miles (10 km) east of Belfast. It was once the palace of the Bishops of Down, who must have approved of the Gothic arches and stained glass. There are 76 comfortable rooms, many furnished with antiques. The elegant restaurant has traditional international cuisine. Craigavad (phone: 5223). Expensive.

CRAWFORDSBURN

Old Inn – This attractive village inn, partly thatched, dates from 1614. Its 28 pretty bedrooms have many charming old-world features. There is a lovely garden, and they serve very good food. 15 Main St. (phone: 853255). Expensive to moderate.

SAINTFIELD

The Barn – A cozy farmhouse restaurant with high-quality food and pleasant surroundings. 120 Monlough Rd. (phone: 510396). Expensive to moderate.

KILKEEL

Kilmorey Arms Hotel – Small and friendly, this place is set in a garden in the equally friendly fishing village on the Mourne coast. There are 12 pretty rooms. Greencastle St. (phone: 62220). Moderate.

ENNISKILLEN

Killyhevlin Hotel – This stately mansion overlooking Lower Lough Erne, with lawns sloping down to the waterside, provides a very special overnight stay. There are fine views from the 26 spacious rooms; some have balconies. Dublin Rd. (phone: 3481). Moderate.

LONDONDERRY

Everglades Hotel – Just outside town with 38 rooms and a sauna. Prehen Rd. (phone: 46722). Moderate.

BALLYGALLY

Ballygally Castle Hotel – This is one of the most romantic places in Northern Ireland. Built in 1625, with modern extensions, the 30-room hotel faces the sea. Antrim Coast Rd. (phone: 83212). Moderate.

CARNLOUGH

Londonderry Arms Hotel – Once the property of Sir Winston Churchill, the great-grandson of the original owner, this nineteenth-century building is in a seaside village at the mouth of Glencloy, one of the nine glens of Antrim. There are only 12 rooms, so make reservations. Harbour Rd. (phone: 85255). Expensive to moderate.

Exploring Greece

At the southern tip of the Balkan Peninsula, Greece occupies a prominent position on the continent and in European history. Greece covers some 50,960 square miles; the mainland spreads between the Ionian Sea on the west, the Aegean on the east, and the Sea of Crete to the south; more than 1,400 islands lie in the surrounding seas. Because of its island territory (170 of the islands are inhabited), Greece is actually larger than it appears, exceeding neighboring Bulgaria in size.

The sea is a major influence on life in Greece. The Greeks have been seafarers throughout their history, and today their shipping industry is one of the largest in the world. The 9,300-mile-long coastline is exceeded by few countries, and Greece is known for the beauty of its many beaches.

Greece's terrain is quite rugged; some 80% of the land is mountainous. Mt. Olympus, the legendary home of the gods, rises 9,570 feet and is one of the highest peaks in the country. Only 30% of the land is arable. The fertile plains of Thessaly support the country's major crops, wheat and tobacco, though olive groves, fruits, and vegetables are grown in other areas.

Greece has a population of nearly 10 million, 53% of which is urban. Athens is the capital and largest city (pop. 3.26 million in Greater Athens), the other major cities are Thessaloniki (pop. 816,063) and Patras on the Peloponnese (pop. 209,387). Most of the people are Greeks, with Turks and Vlachs comprising the largest ethnic minorities and Slavs, Albanians, and Jews forming smaller groups.

The very cradle of Western civilization, Greece has an extremely rich history. Traces of a Neolithic population in Greece date back to 6000 BC, but sometime around 3000 BC a more advanced civilization lived on Crete, which was followed by the development of tribes on the mainland. Some of these tribes banded together to form city-states and eventually developed the more sophisticated social structure of democracy, Greece's greatest contribution to the civilized world. Hellenistic culture reached its apex in the fourth century BC in Athens, where democracy nurtured the works of Plato and Aristotle. Later, in the third century BC, Alexander the Great confederated numerous city-states and conquered new territories, creating a world empire. Greece subsequently (AD 395) became part of the Byzantine Empire and still later (in the fifteenth century) was conquered by the Ottomans. Not until the early nineteenth century did Greece again regain its independence.

The heritage of ancient Greece is the legacy of all contemporary Western nations, but it is a special source of pride to present-day Greeks. Numerous reminders of it remain — Greek, Roman, and Byzantine ruins from the majestic Acropolis in Athens to the extremely well preserved Theater of Epidaurus on the Peloponnese, where visitors can still see ancient Greek drama as it was performed millennia ago.

In addition to sites of great historical significance, Greece has an extraordinarily beautiful countryside. The Mediterranean landscape dominates the southern mainland, much of the Peloponnese Peninsula, and many of the islands. Here, rocky hills drop down to long stretches of coast and seas of deep blue and aquamarine. In the north, the vegetation is more dense and similar to that found elsewhere on the continent. The summers are hot, sunny, and dry; winters, damp and cold. Spring is warm and pleasant, when the hills come to life with colorful wild flowers, though Greece in summer reaches its most basic state — sun, rock, and sea.

The following routes originate in Athens except for the tours of the islands, which are accessible by sea and air from Athens or major island ports. The route through northern Greece heads to Thessaloniki by way of Mt. Olympus and Meteora, then branches off, east to the Turkish border and west to the Yugoslavian border. A short route leads through the Parnassus mountain region to Delphi, the most celebrated oracle of all time. Island routes focus on Crete, Greece's largest island; the Dodecanese Islands, of which Rhodes is the largest and most popular; the Cyclades, including Mykonos and Delos, which offer everything from varied night life to archaeological splendor; the Eastern Aegean islands, of which Lesbos is the most prominent; and Corfu to the west, considered by many to be the most beautiful of all. Another route loops around the Peloponnese Peninsula, taking in 4,000 years of history scattered over 8,000 square miles.

Northern Greece

Northern Greece is markedly different from the rest of the country in both geography and history. Nature seems to have acted more intensely here; the climate is continental rather than Mediterranean, as is the vegetation. The region's history has been turbulent from ancient times through World War II and the civil war. Perhaps as a result of this, the people are less outgoing than other Greeks, though they are still warm and hospitable.

You need time to explore this area. The two suggested routes, from Athens to Thessaloníki, and then either west to the Yugoslavian border or east to the Turkish border, take from 3 to 5 days each. To cut the trip shorter, you can fly to Thessaloníki from Athens and rent a car for the rest of your touring. So as not to miss a visit to Meteora, a fascinating monastic community, and the climb up Mt. Olympus, you can also take an airplane to Ioannina, then a bus to Meteora. You can get another plane at Ioannina or rent a car there for the trip to Thessaloniki. To follow the route outlined below, get an early start driving from Athens.

ATHENS: For a complete description of the capital and its hotels and restaurants, see *Athens* in THE EUROPEAN CITIES.

En Route from Athens – Take a break at Kamena Vourla, about 100 miles (160 km) from Athens. You can go for a swim in this attractive resort town or have some refreshments. Between here and Larissa, the route crosses one of the most fertile plains in Greece. Stop at one of the restaurants just before Larissa for lunch. Heading for Meteora, turn west on the road for Trikala for 36 miles (58 km), where a 12-mile (20-km) drive leads to Kalambaka.

METEORA: Rising 1,820 feet high, the 24 formidable rock pillars stand isolated in space. On these precipitous cliffs, fourteenth-century Byzantine monks built a monastic community that became a sanctuary for the persecuted and the devout. Some centuries later, the community started to deteriorate, and today only 4 of the original 24 monasteries are inhabited. You can spend the night in Kalambaka. The hotels are small, however, so book ahead during the summer.

En Route from Meteora – Back on the National Road, you can break for an excellent seafood meal at Platamon. Turn off the road 12 miles (20 km) farther at the village of Plaka to start the ascent to Mt. Olympus, Greece's tallest mountain (9,620 feet) and home of the Olympian gods. A paved road leads to Litohoron, 1,150 feet up the mountain, and on to the chalet at 4,290 feet. From here you can hike to the highest refuge at 6,930 feet. The climb is a rewarding one, especially in spring, when there is still snow but the weather is mild.

THESSALONÍKI: Established in 316 BC and named after the sister of Alexander the Great, Thessaloníki provides all the amenities of a modern coastal city while preserving its notable past. Touring Greece's second largest city, you'll see numerous Roman remains and interesting Byzantine churches. The Archaeological Museum (YMCA Sq.) contains magnificent golden treasures from the tomb of Philip II, father of Alexander the Great. Discovered in 1977, the tomb was the first unlooted one found in Macedonia and confirms the theory that Vergina, where it was found (48 mi/77 km from Thessaloníki), was the burial ground of Macedonian kings.

For a break in sight-seeing, have an ouzo and some seafood at the appealing ouzo bar right behind the *Mediterranean Hotel.* Among the most popular restaurants in town are *Olympos-Naoussa,* where you can have excellent meals in a simple setting, and *Krikelas,* where the parade of appetizers leaves little room for the main course. You can have a pleasant lunch at one of the seaside tavernas in the suburb of Panorama. For drinks, try the *White Tower,* and cap it off with music and dancing into the morning hours at a bouzouki club outside the city.

From Thessaloniki, men can make a fascinating side trip.

MT. ATHOS: The grounds of the 1,000-year-old monastic republic are forbidden "to any woman, any female, to any eunuch, to any smooth visage," according to an edict issued by Emperor Constantine IX in 1060. There aren't many eunuchs around these days, and it's no longer necessary to grow a beard, but females are still excluded.

Mt. Athos, or Aghion Oros (Holy Mountain), the easternmost of the three peninsulas of the Chalkidiki, is reached from Thessaloníki by the road to Poligiros, the local capital. At Paleocastron, 35 miles (58 km) from Thessaloníki, the road branches right and left; head left via Arnea, a small village that produces excellent wine and hand-woven textiles, and Stagyra, the birthplace of Aristotle. The road leads down the coast along the Bay of Ierissos and on to Ouranoupolis, a lovely seaside town. This is as far as women and cars go, but there are several good hotels on the beach.

From Ouranoupolis, a short boat ride leads to the port of Daphne; from here a cobbled path ascends through thickets of oleanders to Karies, capital of the autonomous Mt. Athos community. The imposing monasteries are scattered — sometimes 5 hours' walking distance from one another — among the lush vegetation of the valley. In the sixteenth century, Athos accommodated about 40,000 monks in 40 monasteries; today the number has dwindled to 1,500 monks in 20 large monasteries and monastic hermitages. In recent years, however, there's been a reviving interest in monastic life, and those numbers are increasing slightly now. Athos is a living Byzantine museum, and its treasures are priceless.

Visit as many of the monasteries as you care to; hospitality is always extended to the visitor, though it is customary to leave a contribution. A permit from the Foreign Ministry in Athens (phone: 362-6894) or the Ministry of Northern Greece in Thessaloníki (phone: 27-00-92) is needed to enter Mt. Athos; Americans must first obtain clearance from the US Embassy in Athens (phone: 721-2951).

En Route from Mt. Athos – On the way back to Thessaloníki, you can stop off and relax for a few days at one of the lovely beach resorts of Kassandra, the westernmost of the Halkidiki peninsulas. Back in Thessaloníki, there are two alternative routes: west to the Yugoslavian border or east to the Turkish border.

THESSALONÍKI TO THE YUGOSLAVIAN BORDER: About 25 miles (40 km) from Thessaloníki en route to Edessa, make a slight detour to see the remarkable ruins of ancient Pella, the birthplace of Alexander the Great. The remains cover an extensive area, including entire streets with buildings that had courtyards surrounded by peristyles. Well-preserved pebble mosaics on the floors depict mythological scenes. The small museum houses many of the finds.

At Edessa, the capital of ancient Macedonia, stop and buy the enormous juicy peaches known as *yarmades.* Some 42 miles (72 km) farther you'll reach Florina, which is only 10 miles (16 km) from Yugoslavia. Vendors in the open-air market speak Yugoslavian as a second language. While dining in Florina, try the local specialties made of sweet red peppers.

Take a side trip to Prespes Lake, a resort and wildlife preserve whose shores are skirted by Greece, Yugoslavia, and Albania. You can spend some time on a nicely laid-out beach, have some refreshments at the tourist pavilion, and get a glimpse of the off-limits coast of Albania.

The road to Kastoria passes through spectacular mountain scenery (note: the route can be hazardous in the winter). Once in this lakeside town — the fur center of Greece — you can watch furriers turn scraps into luxurious coats, available at low prices. Take a boat ride around the lake and stop at the Monastery of Mavrotissa, with its interesting frescoes.

THESSALONÍKI TO THE TURKISH BORDER: If you're traveling through the area from May 20 to 23, take a side trip to the village of Langada, about 12 miles (20 km) from Thessaloníki. Here you can see the *anastenarides* (firewalkers), who dance on burning embers, apparently transported and oblivious to the pain. The tradition originates from a pagan rite but is now a Christian ritual, performed in honor of St. Constantine.

Some 45 miles (75 km) farther, the road climbs high before zigzagging down to Kavalla, opening up a sweeping view of the harbor town and the nearby island of Thassos. Kavalla is a large, picturesque town, built around the harbor. Among its highlights are the Roman aqueduct that curves through the center of town and the Byzantine fortifications above the decidedly Oriental eastern section. Mohammed Ali, founder of the Egyptian royal line, was born in an old Turkish building in this area in 1769.

Several waterfront tavernas specialize in fresh fish. If you have time, take a boat to Thassos, a lush green island whose serene beauty is in counterpoint to the sight of oil derricks drilling offshore at Prinos, Greece's only commercially exploited oil field.

You can take a side trip to Philippi, built by Philip II in 356 BC. The extensive remains of the town lie on both sides of the road.

A good road leads to Xanthi and Komotini. Both towns have a strongly Oriental flavor: Mosques with minarets and black-veiled women wearing Turkish pants attest to the Moslem minority living here since the exchange of citizens between Greece and Turkey in 1923. In Xanthi, stop at the lovely Porto Lagos beach for a swim and some lunch.

En route to Alexandroupolis, you'll probably encounter some ox carts. The town is pretty but not particularly interesting. A short drive farther leads to the west bank of the Evros River, which separates Greece from Turkey. Soldiers of both nationalities guard the bridge.

BEST EN ROUTE

Expect to pay $50 and up per night for a double room in hotels listed as expensive and around $30 in the moderate category.

LARISSA

Divani Palace – Each of the 77 rooms is air-conditioned and contains telephone and radio. 19 Vassilissis Sophias (phone: 25-27-91). Expensive.

KALAMBAKA

Motel Divani – This modern hotel has gardens, a large pool, a restaurant, bar, and 111 air-conditioned rooms with telephone and radio. Below the Meteora (phone: 2-3330). Expensive.

THESSALONÍKI

Macedonia Palace – The large hotel on the quay provides luxurious modern accommodations. Alexander the Great Ave. (phone: 83-75-21; 83-76-21). Expensive.

Electra Palace – This stylish hotel has plenty of atmosphere, very good views of the city's Aristotelous Square and the well-kept waterfront, and 131 air-conditioned rooms. 5a Aristotelous Sq. (phone: 23-22-21). Moderate.

Capsis – This 428-room hotel in the commercial section of town has a friendly atmosphere. 28 Monastiriou (phone: 52-14-21; 52-13-21). Moderate.

IERISSOS

Mt. Athos – This nicely situated 42-room hotel is a good place to stay before or after heading to Mt. Athos. In town (phone: 2-2285). Moderate.

OURANOUPOLIS

Xenia – This is a pleasant place to spend the night before taking off for Mt. Athos. Accommodations are in a hotel or bungalow. In town (phone: 7-1202). Moderate.

FLORINA

Lyngos – The 40 rooms here are simple and comfortable. In town (phone: 2-8322). Moderate.

KAVALLA

Galaxy – This centrally located hotel has 149 rooms. In town (phone: 22-45-21; 22-48-11). Moderate.

ALEXANDROUPOLIS

Astir – This 27-room motel is cozy and comfortable. On the beach (phone: 2-6448). Moderate.

Delphi and the Parnassus Region

Even if you're spending only a few days in Greece, the trip to Delphi is a must. Rising from the heart of the mountainous Parnassus region, Delphi is the home of the most celebrated oracle of all times — awe-inspiring in its beauty and austerity. The best time to visit is in the spring or fall, when the wild flowers bloom in colorful variety on the hills and the tourist flow is limited. In the summer, avoid the climb in the early afternoon; the heat and intense sunlight can be exhausting. At all times, Delphi leaves a profound impression on the visitor.

ATHENS: For a complete description of the capital and its hotels and restaurants, see *Athens*, THE EUROPEAN CITIES.
    En Route from Athens – For a cold drink, stop at the tourist pavilion in Levadia, 70 miles (113 km) from Athens, and sit by the waterfall.
ARAKHOVA: Perched over 3,000 feet high on a winding mountain road, this town has cobblestone streets and neat stone houses with pots of aromatic basil and lavender out front. For lunch, have lamb roasted on the spit and the potent local wine, then browse in the shops featuring the splendid multicolored fabrics woven by the towns-women.
    You can climb up to the nearby Corycian grotto, dedicated in ancient times to Pan, the god of shepherds, and to the forest nymphs. In ancient times, women from Athens, Boeotia, and Delphi gathered here every 5 years, dressed in animal skins and carrying torches, to dance all night in celebration of the Bacchanalia.
    To reach the highest peak of Mt. Parnassus, get set for 3 more hours of climbing. Mountain refuges are available at Kontokedro and Yerondovrahos.
DELPHI: The road, winding through olive groves and vineyards, suddenly opens up on the awesome site of the ancient oracle. In this setting, you can understand why the ancient Greeks regarded Delphi as the "navel of the earth." Such is the magnificent isolation of the oracle, with golden-red cliffs looming around it, the serenity of the sacred valley below, and, in the distance, the Gulf of Itea sparkling in the sunlight. At the center of Delphi stands the sanctuary of Apollo; from here the narrow Sacred Way zigzags up to the ruins of the Doric Temple of Apollo. After being purified with water from the nearby Castalian spring, the priestess, dressed in full ceremonial robes, would utter her prophecies.
    Above the temple rises the fourth-century BC theater; the high tiers command a panoramic view of the sanctuary and the profoundly secluded landscape. At sunset, when a soft blue light spreads over the glowing pinkish mountains, the feeling that you're alone in the world can be complete — unless a busload of tourists has joined you.
    The ruins of the Marmaria (the Marbles), dedicated to the goddess Athena, lie below the main road. Midway between the Marmaria and the sanctuary is the Castalian spring, where you can stop for a drink under the huge plane trees.
    The Museum on the main road between the village and the sanctuary contains numerous pieces found in the sanctuary and the Marmaria or nearby. The highlight of the collection is the bronze statue of the Charioteer, dating from 478 BC. Among the other displays are the pediments from the Temple of Apollo, several exquisite archaic statues, and the recently discovered statuettes of gold and ivory.

BEST EN ROUTE

Prices for double rooms per night in the hotels listed below start at around $25.

DELPHI

Amalias – This large hotel has 185 elegant rooms with air-conditioning and good views. In town (phone: 8-2-101).

Vouzas – Closer to the ruins, this 58-room hotel has good service and nice views. (phone: 8-2232).

Crete

Equidistant from Europe, Asia Minor, and North Africa, Crete has a unique location, history, and heritage. Legend has it that Zeus, supreme god of heaven and earth, was born and raised here. The myths of the labyrinth, the minotaur, and the wings of Icarus originated here. And from 3000 to 1400 BC the Minoans flourished here, leaving behind remnants of the first great civilization in Europe. Crete was ruled by Romans, Arabs, Venetians, and Turks at different times until it was finally united with Greece in 1913.

The natural setting of Crete, Greece's largest island and the fourth largest in the Mediterranean, is truly magnificent. Rugged mountains rise in the center, east, and west. Between them stretch fertile plains and valleys. At the coasts, the mountains drop down to the sea, forming stretches of sandy beaches and secluded coves.

The best way to see Crete is to rent a car, although regular bus service connects the various towns on the island. Daily air and sea connections link the mainland and other islands with Heraklion and Hania. You can begin your tour in either city; the route outlined here starts in Hania.

To get a full taste of Crete, try the local specialties: cheeses, ranging from the mild manouri to the stronger graviera, a Gruyère-type cheese mellowed in caves; honey from Sfakia usually served over thick yogurt; and figs and pomegranates. Sample *raki,* the local moonshine, or *tsikoudia,* the gin-based aperitif served in tiny glasses. Cretans down these drinks in one gulp. They're strong stuff, so don't get carried away when they start offering rounds in honor of the foreigner enjoying their favorite drinks.

HANIA: The capital of Crete, Hania is an interesting mixture of Venetian and Oriental influences. A fruit and vegetable market dominates the center of town, with open stalls and lively scents and colors. Buy *diktamo* here, a rare herb that can be used to brew a delicious tea, considered a panacea by the islanders. After browsing around, have a cold drink at the town square before going down to the harbor, with its arched buildings, cobblestone streets, and Venetian lighthouse. After lunch, spend the afternoon at the beach and return to the harbor in the evening for a leisurely dinner at a taverna on the quay. Get a good night's rest before starting out the next day for an adventurous all-day hike through the Samarian Gorge.

SAMARIAN GORGE: Reputed to be the longest in Europe, this gorge can take anywhere from 5 to 8 hours to cross. Pack a picnic lunch. Take a bus or drive the 25 miles (40 km) to Omalos. From here you start the descent on a path that zigzags down into the gorge. At this point the hike may seem awesome, but it's actually quite manageable if you're wearing comfortable shoes. The next 11 miles (18 km) are filled with fascinating scenery — mysterious shadows; unusually shaped rocks; and pine, cypress, and fig trees scattered among a myriad of wild flowers. The hike ends at the fishing village of Aghia Roumeli, where you can take a boat across to Chora Sfakion, which claims to produce the tallest and longest-living Greeks. Spend the night here or take a bus back to Hania.

RETHYMNON: Attractive Venetian and Turkish architectural styles predominate in Crete's third largest city. The fortress (1574) is the best-preserved Venetian building on the island. There is a beach in town. If you are visiting Rethymnon on St. George's Day (usually April 23, sometimes later), don't miss the celebration at the mountain village of Asi Ghonia, about an hour's drive away, where flocks of sheep are brought to the churchyard to be blessed; then they're milked and the milk is distributed to visitors. A traditional Cretan *glenti* with songs and dances follows. While here, buy the pungent graviera cheese that is allowed to mellow in the many nearby caves.

　　En Route from Rethymnon – Before the next few days of sight-seeing, you can relax for a day or two in the beach resort of Aghia Pelagia, 12 miles (20 km) before Heraklion.

HERAKLION: Begin your tour of Crete's largest, but certainly not most attractive, city at the Venetian port, where you can walk beside the fortified walls to the sixteenth-century Venetian castle. Stroll around the marketplace and have a typical Cretan lunch in one of the many tavernas in the area. The Archaeological Museum has the world's greatest collection of Minoan treasures, including the famous Disc of Phaistos. Also of interest is the Historical Museum, with exhibits covering the early Christian, Byzantine, Venetian, and Turkish periods.

You can take several interesting side trips from Heraklion. The recreated Palace of Knossos, home of the legendary King Minos, is a few miles southwest. Plan to spend a few hours here (you can buy a guidebook to the site at the entrance).

For a glimpse of village life, drive up to Anoghia in Mt. Idi, 21 miles (35 km) from Heraklion. From here, ardent climbers can attempt to reach the Idian Cave, where legend says Zeus grew up. Farther up from Anoghia is the village of Axos. You can buy stunning handmade crafts in both villages.

Another must in the area is a visit to the Minoan site of Phaistos, 37 miles (62 km) from Heraklion (a guidebook available on the site is recommended). For a relaxing break, drive 6 miles (10 km) to Matala, where you can swim in the warm waters of the Libyan Sea and lie on the sandy white beach surrounded by caves — once inhabited by early Christians, since the 1960s by hippies from all over the world.

　　En Route from Heraklion – On the way to Aghios Nikolaos, stop at Malia with its Minoan palace, narrow winding alleys, and lovely beach. Break for lunch near Malia beach at *Taverna Kalypso*.

AGHIOS NIKOLAOS: This chic resort town is a place to sit back, relax, and enjoy the sun and sea. The area has luxury accommodations, and the harbor is packed with tavernas, discos, and souvenir shops.

For a change of pace, visit the village of Critsa, 7 miles (12 km) away, with a superb view of the bay below. Every year, on the last Sunday in August, an old Cretan wedding is performed here, with festivities lasting well into the night.

You can make another side trip to the Diktian Cave, the legendary birthplace of Zeus. The hike entails a drive to the Lasithi Plains and a climb to the cave, starting from the village of Psychro. With stalactites and stalagmites over 200 feet long, the cave's interior is fascinating. If you're up to the arduous 6-hour climb to the summit, start out in the village of Aghios Georgios, 2.5 miles (4 km) before Psychro, and hire a guide in the village. The hardships of the climb are rewarded by a spectacular view of the entire island.

     En Route from Aghios Nikolaos – The 44-mile (73-km) drive to Sitia passes through whitewashed villages set among orchards and olive groves. Next to the road there's a frightfully sharp drop to the sea. Don't attempt the drive if you've been drinking.

    SITIA: This lovely town has many beautiful beaches, the best known of which is Vai (a few miles out of town), a long sandy beach with a dense growth of palm trees. It's a romantic spot to camp out; you can also stay at one of the hotels in town.

    IERAPETRA: The largest town in southern Crete, Ierapetra retains an Oriental flavor with Venetian touches here and there. The coast is lined with tavernas, discos, and a few hotels where you can spend the night before crossing Crete at its narrowest point to return to Heraklion or Hania.

BEST EN ROUTE

Expect to pay $42 and up per night for a double room in hotels listed as expensive; $25 and up for those in the moderate category; and under $20 for those in the inexpensive range.

HANIA

Kydon – Centrally located, this 117-room hotel has an old-fashioned atmosphere. S Venizelou Sq. (phone: 26-190). Expensive.

Porto Veneziano – This charming, family-run establishment on the Venetian harbor has 63 rooms (phone: 2-9311). Expensive to moderate.

RETHYMNON

El Greco – Right on the beach, this resort has a pool, tennis, mini-golf, Ping-Pong, a playground for the children, and all water sports. The 310 rooms are in hotel accommodations or bungalows (phone: 7-1102). Moderate.

AGHIA PELAGIA

Capsis Beach – On a lovely stretch of beach, this hotel provides all amenities. There are 191 hotel rooms and 354 bungalows (phone: 26-22-04). Moderate.

HERAKLION

Knossos Beach – Near town, this hotel has 125 pleasant rooms and bungalows (phone: 28-84-50). Moderate.

Anna-Bella – This pension offers 9 comfortable rooms. In town (28–97–28). Moderate.

AGHIOS NIKOLAOS

Minos Beach – This luxurious resort on the beach has 118 bungalows facing the sea, an outdoor pool, and good recreational facilities (phone: 2-2345). Expensive.

Elounda Beach – Overlooking the sea, this deluxe resort has a pool, tennis, putting green, water sports facilities, an art gallery, a taverna, snack bar, and nightclub. The 301 rooms are in the hotel building or bungalows set in an attractive wooded area (phone: 4-1412). Expensive.

IERAPETRA

Atlantis – This comfortable 69-room hotel is a good place to spend the night before heading back to Hania or Heraklion. Aghios Andreas (phone: 2-8555). Inexpensive.

The Dodecanese Islands: Rhodes, Kos, Patmos, and Karpathos

Southeast of the Greek mainland, off the coast of Asia Minor, the 12 islands of the Dodecanese group offer a wide variety of natural attractions and historical ruins. Lying relatively close to one another, the islands have similar histories but diverse personalities. Rhodes is the largest and most popular of the group, with Kos running second in tourist flow and amenities. Two of the less frequented islands — Patmos and Karpathos — are included here for those who want a taste of simple island life. The most rewarding aspect of spending some time on the smaller islands is the genuine warmth and hospitality extended by the islanders.

RHODES: Rhodes has something for everyone: sites of great historic interest, a wealth of natural beauty, accommodations ranging from luxury hotels to simple rooms in village houses, a variety of sports facilities, and one of the three casinos in Greece.

According to Greek mythology, the island sprang out of the sea and was offered as a gift by Zeus to Apollo, the sun god, who named it after his current fling, Rhodos, daughter of Venus. Archaeological evidence indicates that Rhodes was originally settled by the Minoans and Myceneans. The island prospered in the eleventh century BC under the Dorians, who founded Ialysos, Kameiros, and Lindos; in 408 BC these three cities united to form the city of Rhodes.

Incorporated into the Byzantine Empire in AD 395, Rhodes was sold by its Genoese masters to the crusading Knights of St. John in 1306. During their 200-year rule, they converted the island into a Christian stronghold; they were finally forced out by the Ottomans, who controlled Rhodes until 1912, when the Italians seized the island. Rhodes was finally reunited with Greece and the other Dodecanese islands in 1947.

The most striking reminders of this diverse history can be found in Rhodes, the capital of the island. The Old City has remnants of the Crusaders and the Middle Ages — narrow streets; thirteenth-, fourteenth-, and fifteenth-century buildings adorned with coats of arms; and powerful walls built by the Knights of St. John. Visit the Archaeological Museum, housed in the fifteenth-century Hospital of the Knights, and the massive Palace of the Grand Masters, a fourteenth-century fortress with underground passages and chambers. The Turkish quarters are nearby, marked by mosques and old Ottoman homes.

Surrounding the Old City is the modern section, a cosmopolitan Greek island capital with fine hotels, a myriad of duty-free shops, and the *Grand Hotel* casino. The entrance of Mandraki, the harbor, was once dominated by the immense Colossus of Rhodes, one of the Seven Wonders of the World, which towered 126 feet and weighed 300 tons.

You can take side trips to the three Dorian cities from the capital. Little remains of ancient Ialysos, 5 miles (8 km) from Rhodes, but there's a good view from the Acropolis. Kameiros, 20 miles (32 km) from Rhodes, has more of interest, including a third-century BC temple and colonnade, a fifth-century cistern, and the agora, or ancient marketplace. Lindos, 21 miles (34 km) from Rhodes, is an attractive old village. The Acropolis (which can be reached on foot or by hired donkey) dominates the ancient city, which was once the center of the cult of the goddess Athena. A fourth-century temple dedicated to her still stands. Many fifteenth-century houses, built when the Knights of St. John converted Lindos to a fortress, line the narrow streets of the town.

Petaloudes (Valley of the Butterflies), 16 miles (26 km) south of Rhodes, is one of the island's most stunning highlights. Each spring, thousands of butterflies nestle in the trees of this narrow, thickly wooded valley. If you stir the branches, butterflies fill the air in a bursting reddish-gold cloud.

In Rodini, 2 miles (3 km) south of Rhodes, an annual wine festival is held from mid-July to the end of September. Visitors can sample the local wines to their hearts' content and watch musicians and dancers perform late into the night.

Fine beaches line the shores of the island. Good fishing grounds are found near the villages of Kameiros, Lindos, Kallithea, and Gennadi.

KOS: The birthplace of Hippocrates, the father of medicine, this island has a history similar to that of Rhodes, but it has a quieter atmosphere. The town of Kos is quite attractive, with white, arched houses set in lovely gardens. The coastal road to the port of Mandraki is particularly pleasant for a walk or a bicycle ride. Beaches are excellent all over the island, as are the accommodations.

Historical highlights include the Castle of the Knights of St. John, the ancient agora, the Temple of Dionysus, the Roman baths, the gymnasium, and the town museum, with a statue of Hippocrates.

PATMOS: The northernmost of the Dodecanese, Patmos is known primarily in connection with St. John the Divine, who received the Revelations and dictated them to a disciple in the Sacred Grotto, which lies between the harbor and the capital. The massive, elaborately decorated Monastery of St. John, which has also served as a fortress, is the principal historic site.

Patmos has fine sandy beaches and the white architecture characteristic of many Greek islands. You can do some challenging hiking here, too. Every year on August 15 (feast of the Assumption) there's an all-out celebration with food, music, and dancing.

To really get away from it all, take a caique to the small nearby island of Lipsi, with isolated beaches, good tavernas lining the harbor, and hardly any tourists.

KARPATHOS: Midway between Rhodes and Crete (and accessible from both), Karpathos offers a folklore lover's paradise. In the densely forested north, people maintain centuries-old traditions. In the village of Olympos (reached by a poor road from the little harbor of Diafani), the women till the fields and do most of the heavy chores. They work in long, dark blue coats worn over bright tops and white breeches, with brightly patterned scarves covering their heads. Bear in mind that this is not a tourist attraction but a way of life.

If you are in Olympos after Easter or in late summer (August 15 and 29 or September 8), you can watch and perhaps participate in a traditional celebration, with plenty of wine, songs, and dances. If a wedding is to take place, too, the villagers hold an extravagant *glenti,* or feast — 3 days of music, dance, food, wine, and strictly adhered to customs.

There are several good beaches on the island near the capital, Pigadia. You can take interesting side trips by motorboat to the nearby uninhabited islets of Saris and Armathia.

BEST EN ROUTE

Expect to pay $42 and up per night for a double room in hotels listed as expensive; $25 and up for those in the moderate category; and under $20 for those in the inexpensive range. Homeowners on the smaller islands rent clean, comfortable rooms at modest prices.

RHODES

Rodos Palace – The tallest building on the island, this luxury resort has all the amenities and then some — outdoor and indoor pools, tennis, mini-golf, a sauna, restaurants, a disco, shops, a nightclub, and a bowling alley. The 610 rooms are fashionably decorated and comfortable; some have gardens or sea views. Fanoromeni, 2.5 miles (4 km) from town (phone: 2-5222). Expensive.

Rodos Bay – Set on a hillside, this modern resort has all recreational facilities. Most of the 330 rooms and bungalows are in the main building — best of all are the maisonettes, split-level bungalows facing the sea with spectacular views. Ixia Tiranta (phone: 2-3661). Moderate.

KOS

Dimitra Beach – Right on the beach, this resort has 134 rooms and some bungalows, restaurants, bars, a lounge with dancing, and a snack bar. Aghios Fokas (phone: 2-8581). Moderate.

PATMOS

Xenia – This 35-room hotel provides simple and comfortable accommodations. In town (phone: 3-1219). Inexpensive.

KARPATHOS

Porfyris – This 21-room comfortable hotel is one of the few around. In town (phone: 2-2294). Inexpensive.

The Cyclades:
Mykonos and Delos

In Greece, this group of islands is called Kiklades because they form a rough circle around the sacred island of Delos, a religious, cultural, and commercial center of the ancient world. Apart from their archaeological interest, each of the 39 islands comprising the group (24 are inhabited) has much to offer the visitor, from the intense nightlife of Mykonos to the isolated beaches of Kimolos, where there are no hotels but plenty of hospitality. The best-known Cycladic islands are described below.

MYKONOS: "Is Greece near Mykonos?" the American tourist is said to have asked his travel agent; though it's probably apocryphal, the question is indicative of the island's fame — and perhaps notoriety.

You name it, and Mykonos is bound to have it: a harbor teeming with luxury yachts and fishing boats; more discotheques, bars, and restaurants than all the other Greek islands put together; narrow cobblestone streets lined with art galleries and chic boutiques; officially designated nude beaches; many windmills; and over 300 churches.

The most outstanding feature of this island is its dazzling brightness; blazing sunlight reflects off the always freshly whitewashed houses and churches. Practically everything is white — even the trunks of the few trees in town are painted white. This brightness makes getting up in the morning a pleasure; it seems a shame to sleep at night. Actually, hardly anyone turns in before the early morning hours, so the popular beaches don't get crowded before noon. These are to the south and are accessible by bus, taxi, or boat. For nude swimming, try Paradise, Super Paradise (preferred by homosexuals), or Helia.

When night falls, Mykonos comes alive with activity to suit every taste. You can watch the colorful international set that frequents the island, have a drink at a bar, take your time over dinner, then head to one of the current hot spots.

If possible, avoid Mykonos in August; the *meltemi,* or north wind, can be annoying, and the island is most crowded then.

DELOS: No one should leave Mykonos without taking the half-hour boat trip to Delos. First settled some 5,000 years ago, Delos became the religious, cultural, and financial center of the Aegean around 1000 BC. It remained prominent until 454 BC, when the island treasury was moved to the Parthenon for safekeeping. In Hellenistic times, Delos revived as a commercial center.

Many of the island's temples and shrines are extremely well preserved. Highlights include the Terrace of the Lions, the Temple of Apollo (according to mythology, the sun god was born here), the agora, the sanctuaries, and the museum. Spend the night in the small hostel and take an evening walk in the moonlight. Delos is virtually uninhabited, and the solitude can be deeply moving.

THIRA: Also known as Santorini, this striking island is of volcanic origin. Some believe that a massive volcanic eruption here in the sixteenth century BC caused the decline of the Minoan civilization, centered on Crete, to the south.

Thira is a crescent-shaped mass of rock with precipitous cliffs up to 1,000 feet high. Donkeys lead up from the harbor, where the ships dock, to the island capital of Fira, with its narrow, cobbled streets and medieval quarter. Ancient Thira was inhabited at various times by Phoenicians, Dorians, Romans, and Byzantines, and some impressive ruins remain. You can swim at one of the black (lava) sand beaches or take a motorboat excursion to the volcano, on an adjacent islet.

BEST EN ROUTE

Expect to pay $42 and up per night for a double room in hotels listed as expensive; $25 and up for those in the moderate category; and under $20 for those in the inexpensive range.

MYKONOS

Petinos – This small 28-room hotel on the beach has a taverna. Platia Yalos (phone: 2-2127). Inexpensive.

DELOS

Tourist Pavilion – Since this is the only place on the island to spend the night, you have to be lucky to get one of the few beds available. It's worth a try to experience the solitude after dark. Some camping is also permitted, and there's a restaurant. (phone: 498). Inexpensive.

THIRA

Atlantis – On a cliff overlooking the sea, this simple 2-story whitewashed house has 25 spacious, high-ceilinged rooms. The bar and breakfast terrace have excellent views. In town (phone: 2-2232). Expensive.

The Islands of the Eastern Aegean: Lesbos, Samos, and Chios

Lush green vegetation in parts, crystal-clear waters in every shade of blue, and small villages clinging to tradition characterize the islands of the northeastern

Aegean Sea. The three described here can be reached by air from Athens or by boat from Piraeus, northern Greece, and Rhodes.

LESBOS: In the time of Sappho (600 BC), Lesbos was probably the most advanced city in the world, with its intellectual life at a remarkably high level. It was here that the world's first great woman poet sang her poems to the young girls she loved; the passion of her descriptions was such that the term "lesbian" has been used to denote female-female love ever since. Lesbos was also the birthplace of Aesop, one of the most famous storytellers of all time.

Today Lesbos (sometimes known as Mytilene) preserves little of its ancient glory, but it's a marvelous place for sunning, swimming, hiking, and exploring ancient and Byzantine ruins.

From the island's capital, Mytilene, good roads lead to practically all parts of the island. On the northern tip is Molivos, or Mithimna, reached by a lovely coast road. En route, stop at Thermi to see a recently excavated prehistoric settlement. Swim at the excellent beach in Aghios Stephanos, and have lunch at one of the numerous tavernas. The road passes through extensive olive groves — the island is famous for its olives and olive oil — until reaching Molivos. Set over the beach and fishing harbor, this attractive town seems to grow right out of the surrounding hills. A Genoese castle dominates the town and offers a fine view of the Turkish coast.

SAMOS: Inhabited since 3000 BC, Samos was the birthplace of the great mathematician Pythagoras (sixth century BC) and also, according to mythology, of the goddess Hera, sister and wife of Zeus. The landscape is quite striking — golden beaches, blue sea, and mountains in the east and west. About 10% of the island is cultivated with vineyards that produce a sweet white wine.

Vathi is the capital and tourist center of the island. The Archaeological Museum and Museum of Byzantine Art both have interesting exhibits. You can hike up to the monastery of Zoodohos Pighi for a sweeping view of the Turkish coast, only a few miles away.

Samos is a great place for hikes and excursions. Buses link different towns on the island and travel on good roads. You can take a break at any of the beaches or fishing villages along the way, and, in most, you can spend the night in comfortable hotels or in rooms in private houses.

Visit Pithagorio, once the island's capital and now an enchanting fishing village, 10 miles (16 km) south of Vathi. Natives call the town Tigani ("frying pan") because of its shape. Here you can see the remains of an ancient wall, a theater, and an aqueduct that was built through the mountain in the sixth century BC. The view of nearby Asia Minor is superb. Less than a mile away is a monastery constructed deep inside a cave surrounded by a natural cistern. The Heraion, 3 miles (5 km) from Pithagorio, is the site of a temple dedicated to Hera that was considered one of the Seven Wonders of Antiquity.

CHIOS: Chios is beautiful, but mainly, Chios is rich: Many of the Golden Greek shipowners come from the island that Homer referred to as "the rocky realm."

Chios is the original chewing gum producer. For centuries the island's prosperity was based on the cultivation and sale of mastic gum, popular with the courtesans of antiquity for the pleasant aroma it gave their breath. Today, you can buy it wrapped in cellophane or drink it in the form of mastiha — but go easy, it's very potent.

You can take a pleasant walk through the pine trees to Nea Moni (New Monastery), a fine example of Byzantine architecture. The mastic gum tree area spreads south from the monastery of Aghios Minas. Villages in the area retain a medieval character, with stone houses, narrow arcaded streets, and interesting churches.

While in Chios, take a boat to the five small Oinoussai islands off the northeastern coast. They have good fishing and hunting grounds and sandy beaches. Many of the richest Greek shipowners were born here, and they return every summer with their families, filling the harbor with luxury yachts.

BEST EN ROUTE

Expect to pay $42 and up per night for a double room in hotels listed as expensive; $25 and up in the moderate category; and under $20 in the inexpensive range.

LESBOS

Lesbos Beach – Outside town, the accommodations are 39 furnished apartments. Neapolis (phone: 6-1531). Moderate.

Lesbion – On the harbor of Mytilene, this hotel has 38 comfortable rooms. In town (phone: 2-2038). Moderate.

Sappho – Also on the harbor, this hotel offers standard rooms for modest prices. In town (phone: 2-8415). Inexpensive.

SAMOS

Doryssa Bay – This attractive hotel has 176 rooms. Pithagorio (phone: 6-1360). Moderate.

Xenia – This is the most comfortable of the in-town accommodations with 31 rooms (phone: 2-7463). Moderate.

Merope – The attraction here is the lovely view; 80 rooms. In Karlovassi (phone: 3-2650). Moderate.

CHIOS

Chandris – On the port, this branch of the quality hotel chain is well run. The 156 rooms are nicely appointed. In town (phone: 2-5761/6). Moderate.

Corfu

Considered by many to be the most beautiful of the Greek islands, Corfu has been praised by Homer in the *Odyssey,* chosen by Shakespeare as the setting for the *Tempest,* and extolled by Henry Miller in the *Colossus of Maroussi.* Many prominent Greeks frequent Corfu, known locally as Kerkyra.

In the North Ionian Sea, Corfu marks Greece's westernmost point. The semimountainous terrain supports more lush vegetation than any other Greek island. Millions of olive trees grow on the gentle slopes. Orange, lemon, cypress, acacia, and plane trees take root here, and the fragrance of a wide variety of flowers fills the air.

Good roads leading to all parts of the island start from the capital, the town of Corfu on the east coast. You can tour by car, bus, or taxi, or, if you're taken with the island's romantic atmosphere, horse and carriage. For sunning and swimming, you can head to the beaches of the luxury resorts or find isolated beaches and coves all over the island.

Corfu is an entry point into Greece from other places in Europe. The island is accessible by ferry from Brindisi, Ancona, and Otronto, Italy, and from

Dubrovnik, Yugoslavia, or by air from most European capitals. Daily flights link Corfu and Athens, and the island can also be reached by ferry from Igoumenitsa in western Greece or Patras on the Peloponnese.

CORFU: This town is a cosmopolitan island capital with an interesting architectural style incorporating Byzantine, Venetian, French, Russian, English, and Italian elements. One of the best introductions to the spirit of the Corfiots is to spend an evening at a taverna or cafenion on the Splanada (Esplanada), Greece's largest public square. On summer evenings you can enjoy open-air concerts given by earnest local bands.

Corfu is an old town, and you can see the remnants of the civilizations that have played a role in its history. At the tip of Aghios Nikolaos, the northern section of town, there is a Venetian fortress, which many historians identify with the Heraion Acropolis, mentioned by Thucydides. Corfu's Town Hall (1663) is a splendid example of Venetian architecture. Mon Repos, the former royal palace, is a neoclassical structure with a Doric portico. Britain's Prince Philip was born here. Other highlights include the Archaeological Museum (5 Vraila), which houses finds from excavations; the Museum of Asiatic Art (Kato Platia), with its rich collection of Chinese, Japanese, and Indian art; and Kanoni, 2½ miles (4 km) south of town, a semicircular terrace that commands an excellent view of the harbor and provides access to two little islets with monasteries.

The town has excellent facilities for sports and recreational activities. The major resorts have mini-golf, tennis, water skiing, and swimming at their own beaches. There's a public beach at the Mon Repos palace; the most popular beaches on the island are Roda, 22 miles (35 km) north of town; Glyfada, 10 miles (16 km) west of town; and Benitses, 7 miles (11 km) to the south. Tennis is available at the Tennis Club (Vraila and Romanou) and golf, at the 18-hole course near the village of Vatos. Corfu is also good for other activities — fishing, hiking, and even cricket, an odd relic of British rule, at the Corfu Cricket Green. You can go horseback riding at the stables in Gouvia, 5 miles (8 km) from town, or in Alikes, 3 miles (5 km) from town.

In the evenings there is ample entertainment at the hotel clubs and the discos around town. In 1891, Empress Elizabeth of Austria had her summer palace built in Gastouri, 5 miles (8 km) south of town. Named the Achilleon after her favorite hero with the famous heel, today the palace is one of three casinos in Greece. The structure itself is considered amusing by some and an atrocity by others, but the lovely gardens stretching down to the sea are appreciated by most everyone for evening strolls.

MT. PANTOCRATOR: Rising 3,000 feet in the northern section of the island, Corfu's highest summit commands an excellent view of the surroundings. To the south spreads the city of Corfu and the rest of the island. To the east lies Albania (only a mile away at the closest point). On a clear day, the coast of Italy is visible to the northwest. The monastery on the mountain dates back to 1347.

PALEOCASTRITSA: On a small bay surrounded by hills, this popular resort, 16 miles (26 km) west of Corfu, is popular for its clear water, good fishing, and excellent seafood. Local tavernas specialize in lobster.

PAKI: Less than 8 square miles in area, this islet, 2.5 hours by motorboat from Corfu Harbor (boats leave twice daily except on Sundays), is a great place to spend a serene day or two. Covered with dense vegetation, including olive trees and vine plants, the island is unique in its underwater caves and excellent lobsters. You can stay in bungalows on the beach or rent rooms in islanders' houses.

BEST EN ROUTE

Prices for double rooms per night in the hotels listed below start around $30 (moderate) and go up to about $70 (expensive).

Hilton – This attractive resort has fine facilities — indoor and outdoor pools, tennis, a disco, bowling, several restaurants, bars, and 274 rooms. The landscaped beach-front gardens are very pleasant. The hotel provides shuttle service to town and the golf course. Kanoni (phone: 3-6540). Expensive.

Hermones Beach – Sloping down to a private beach, this first-class facility has 272 hotel rooms and bungalows. Among the facilities are a pool, restaurants, bars, and a lounge with music. 8.5 miles (14 km) from Corfu just before Paleocastritsa (phone: 9-4241). Expensive.

The Peloponnese

Separated from mainland Greece by the Gulf of Corinth, the Peloponnese Peninsula encompasses some 8,000 square miles of varied and impressive scenery. Much of the peninsula is mountainous, though the different ranges are separated by sweeping, fertile plains, and the low-lying coastal regions give way to some fine beaches. The area is rich in archaeological ruins. Its history has been traced back some 4,000 years through excavations at Mycenae, a great capital of Hellenic civilization.

The route spans large distances, historically and geographically, and requires about 5 days, though you could easily spend more time. Starting in Athens and heading west to Corinth, the route loops around the peninsula. Among the highlights are Olympia, the site of the first Olympic games; Vassai, with the fifth-century BC Temple of Apollo Epicurus; Mistra, a wonderfully preserved former Byzantine settlement on a mountainside; Mycenae; and Epidaurus, where you can watch a performance of an ancient drama in a huge open-air amphitheater.

ATHENS: For complete details on the capital and its hotels and restaurants, see *Athens,* THE EUROPEAN CITIES.

En Route from Athens – It's best to start out in the morning on the Athens-Patras National Road. Stop at the Corinth Canal, about an hour's drive away, and look at the isthmus that connects the Peloponnese with mainland Greece.

CORINTH: Once the largest city of Greece, Corinth was prosperous to the point of decadence when it was destroyed by the Romans in 146 BC. The area remained uninhabited for the next 100 years until a Roman colony was founded by order of Julius Caesar. Corinth regained its former prominence, though earthquakes and a series of barbarian invasions brought about its decline. The modern town has little of interest. The sixth-century Temple of Apollo, in the old town, is the only Greek ruin in ancient Corinth. The museum opposite the temple contains primarily Roman exhibits. Beyond the old town, the mountain Acrocorinth rises 1,885 feet. Easily reached by car, the summit is topped by an ancient fortress, commanding a spectacular view of the Saronic and Corinthian gulfs.

En Route from Corinth – Head to Patras along either the National Road or the narrower but infinitely more attractive coastal road, which winds its way between a plain of olive trees and the blue waters of the Corinthian Gulf. The largest town along the way is Aegion, designed attractively on three layers above the sea. Stop for a fresh fish lunch here or at one of the smaller villages on the road.

PATRAS: Greece's main western port is a well-laid-out town with arcaded streets and large squares at the harbor. Ancient ruins are scarce, though the history dates back to Mycenaean times. The main sights are the Odeion, built in Roman times; the Archaeological Museum; and the Church of St. Andrew, the largest church in the country. From Patras, you can make connections to the Ionian islands (see the *Corfu* route) or Italy. You can spend the night at a hotel in town or, better yet, at Loutra Killini, 50 miles (85 km) southwest, where there are excellent accommodations right on a lovely beach.

OLYMPIA: This fertile valley is the home of the Olympic Games, held in honor of Zeus, their legendary founder. In the first games in 776 BC the gods were pitted against human heroes. Two hundred years later, the games were instituted on a regular, 4-year basis. Events included competitions in wrestling, foot racing, chariot racing, horse racing, the pentathalon, and various artistic contests. The games were discontinued when the Romans conquered Greece. In 1896, they were reinstituted in Athens and since then have been held at 4-year intervals in cities around the world.

The Olympic ideal, combining strong physical development with high intellectual achievement, has been universally adopted. The sacred flame burning at the Altis, symbol of this ideal, has never been extinguished and is still carried to wherever the games are being held.

Some of the best-known Greek myths originated in Olympia. According to legend, Apollo and Hercules were among the first winners. After a questionable victory in a chariot race, Nero introduced a singing contest to display his artistic talents. Statues of the victors were erected in the Altis sanctuary, which contains the ruins of many buildings, including the fifth-century Temple of Zeus. The gold and ivory statue of Zeus was destroyed in a fire, but the pediments of the temple are displayed in the Museum of Olympia. The ruins of the stadium, which could seat 20,000 spectators, are also here.

    En Route from Olympia – If you want to do some alpine exploring or just relax amid mountain scenery, take a side trip to Vytina, 60 miles (96 km) west of Olympia. You can stay at a hotel built right on the cliff, with spectacular views of the surrounding area. The food and wine are excellent, and there are good buys in wood carvings made by local craftsmen.

VASSAI: The road ascends to a plateau on which the splendid Temple of Apollo Epicurus sits in awesome solitude. Built in 420 BC by Ictinus, the architect of the Parthenon in Athens, the temple was erected as a token of gratitude after the population was spared decimation by a cholera epidemic. The temple is constructed of gray stone indigenous to the area and is unusually designed with elements of three architectural styles — Doric, Ionic, and Corinthian. Before or after the ascent to Vassai, stop at the village of Andritsaina below for a cool drink.

    En Route from Vassai – Stop in the seaside village of Kalamata for a meal of fresh fish. At the monastery in town, you can buy lovely silk kerchiefs.

PYLOS: This attractive little town rises from the Bay of Navarino, where, in 1827, the allied fleets of Great Britain, France, and Russia destroyed the Turkish and Egyptian forces to ensure Greek independence. Remains of the sea battle can still be seen from the harbor on a clear day. A memorial to the British sailors stands on the low rock in the center of the harbor.

King Nestor of Pylos, who aided the Achaians in their campaign against Agamemnon's Trojans, dwelt in a palace above the road south of town. The remains of the palace are quite impressive, particularly the throne room and the monumental entrance on the southeastern side. On a hill, the palace also commands a superb view of the area.

METHONI: Seven miles (11 km) south of Pylos, this small town on the west of the peninsula, along with Coroni on the east of the peninsula (linked by a dirt road), were known as the Eyes of Venice. The towns were the first Venetian foothold on the Greek mainland; the Venetian fortress still stands in Coroni. Nice beaches line the shores, and fishing is good in the area.

SPARTA: The drive to Sparta is delightful, particularly in spring when the wild flowers on the Taygetus mountain are in full bloom. The contemporary town of Sparta is an agricultural center of the Eurotas Valley and a convenient place to spend the night. Little remains of the ancient town, situated north of the modern town, except for the scant ruins of an acropolis and theater. However, ancient Sparta became the greatest military power in Greece after the Spartans defeated the Athenians in the Peloponnesian War. The term "spartan" is still used to denote fierce discipline and endurance.

MISTRA: This medieval town has some of the best-preserved examples of Byzantine architecture in Greece. The narrow winding streets are lined with fourteenth- and fifteenth-century churches and houses.

For dinner, go to the *Kotopouladiko* in the village of Mistra, below the ruins. Here you can get delicious fried chicken served with salads and bread. There's no street address, but everyone in town knows where it is.

THE MANI: This highland region is the most austere and isolated in the country. The inhabitants live in small villages, of which they are very proud. They have always resisted outside rule by both foreign powers and union with Greece, and the many fortified towers seen in the area attest to their independent spirit.

At Diros, you can explore caves with impressive stalactites and stalagmites. Have lunch at a taverna on the quay at Gythion, the port of the Mani.

MONEMVASIA: On a great rock, this Byzantine town repulsed numerous attacks because of its strategic location and almost impregnable Byzantine and Venetian fortifications. Now the town is a chic summer retreat with beautifully restored old houses.

MYCENAE: This ancient city was the capital of a great Hellenic civilization. Archaeologists maintain that Mycenae was inhabited around 3000 BC, but its great significance was undiscovered until 1882, when Heinrich Schliemann excavated six shaft graves rich with golden treasures, now on exhibit at the Archaeological Museum in Athens. According to some legends, Mycenae was the capital city of Agamemnon. The principal points of interest are the six shaft graves, the Hellenistic walls, a theater, and a cemetery.

En Route from Mycenae – Take a short detour to Tyrins, the birthplace of Hercules. The palace and cyclopean walls made of huge blocks of stone date back to Mycenean times.

NAUPLIA: According to legend, this town was created by Palamidi, son of the sea god Poseidon. Set amid orchards on the Bay of Nauplia, Nauplia was the first capital of Greece after the War of Independence. Visit the restored castle of Palamidi (reached by road or 1,000-step footpath), and the Bourtzi fort, built by the Venetians on an islet in the bay. The nearby beaches of Assini and Tolo are very pleasant, as is a lunch of freshly caught fish at one of the waterfront tavernas.

EPIDAURUS: Once the sanctuary of Asklepios, the god of medicine, this ancient site includes the Doric Temple of Asklepios, the Tholos with its Corinthian columns, and notable Greek and Roman baths.

Spend the evening at the open-air theater, where you can experience a memorable performance of ancient drama. In stunning natural surroundings, the theater, designed by Polycleitus the Younger, is one of the best-preserved structures of ancient Greece. Its seating capacity is 14,000; despite its size, the theater's acoustics are remarkable — even on the last of its 55 tiers you can hear every word uttered onstage. The annual festival of ancient drama lasts from early July to late August. Performances finish at about 11 PM, so you can either spend the night or make the 2-hour drive back to Athens.

BEST EN ROUTE

Expect to pay $42 and up per night for a double room in hotels listed as expensive; $25 and up for those in the moderate category; and under $20 for those in the inexpensive range.

PATRAS

Astir – This comfortable 120-room hotel is in the center of town. 16 Aghiou Andreou (phone: 27-98-09). Moderate.

Galaxy – Also convenient, this 53-room hotel offers standard accommodations. 9 Aghiou Nikolaou (phone: 27-88-15). Moderate.

OLYMPIA

Spap – Just outside of town; most of the 51 rooms have lovely views of the ancient site and the surrounding area. Above the site (phone: 2-2514). Moderate.

Hermes – For a pleasant alternative, try this cozy 7-room pension. In town (phone: 2-2577). Moderate.

VYTINA

Xenia Motel – Right on the cliff, this 20-room hotel offers a fantastic panorama of mountain scenery. Good food and wine are also available. In town (phone: 2-1218). Moderate.

KILLINI

Golden Beach – This 350-room resort hotel is on a lovely beach (phone: 9-5205). Expensive.

SPARTA

Xenia – This comfortable 33-room hotel is conveniently located. In town (phone: 2-6524). Moderate.

Menelaion – These 48 high-ceilinged rooms are decorated with antique furniture. In town (phone: 2-2161). Moderate.

GYTHION

Belle Helene – Right on the port of the Mani, this 90-bed hotel is comfortable, and has a cozy bar, swimming pool, and tennis court (phone: 2-2249, 2-2408). Moderate.

KALAMATA

Filoxenia – On a secluded beach, this attractive hotel has 118 rooms and reasonable prices (phone: 2-3166). Moderate.

Alex – This small pension has 8 comfortable rooms. In town (phone: 2-2470). Inexpensive.

MYCENAE

Agamemnon – About a mile from the ruins, this 8-room pension has modest prices. In the village (phone: 6-6222). Inexpensive.

NAUPLIA

Xenia's Palace – Overlooking the Bourtzi fortress, this luxury 51-room hotel offers pleasant accommodations in comfortably furnished, air-conditioned suites and bungalows. The dining area and pool are built on the hillside a quarter mile above the beach; accessible by elevator (phone: 2-8981). Expensive.

Xenia – Many of the rooms in this 58-room hotel have balconies overlooking the bay. The food and service are good. Above town (phone: 2-8991). Moderate.

EPIDAURUS

Xenia – This hotel has 24 comfortable cottages near the ancient site (phone: 2-2003). Moderate.

Exploring Hungary

This small, landlocked country near the geographic center of Europe, with a blend of Eastern and Western traditions, has long appealed to travelers. It is a land of beautiful landscapes, romantic music, decorative folk art, historic monuments, and excellent cuisine.

Despite its size — it is not quite as big as Indiana — and its relative flatness, the country has an extremely colorful and varied landscape. Hungary is bisected by the Danube River (called Duna in Hungary), which rushes south after carving a sharply angled route through mountains along the country's northwestern border.

To the west of the Danube is Transdanubia, a picturesque area of rolling hills, cultivated vineyards, old towns, and Balaton, Europe's largest warmwater lake. Within the Great Hungarian Plain, east of the Danube, are abundant fruit orchards, fields of waving wheat, sunflowers, and corn, and the desertlike *puszta*. This vast granary is the historic home of Hungary's famous whip-cracking herdsmen on horseback. In addition to the scenic mountains of the Danube Bend in the northwest, there are low, forested mountains along the northeastern frontier, which is also famous for its wine-growing regions. Deer, wild boar, and spiral-horned moufflon roam freely in state game reserves.

Hungary is bordered on the west by Austria, on the north by Czechoslovakia, on the east by the USSR and Romania, and on the south by Yugoslavia. Winters can be quite cold; summers are hot and dry.

The fact that Hungary has an extremely homogeneous population today — nearly 96% of its 10.7 million people are Hungarian — is the result of this century's two European wars. On the losing side in World War I, Hungary was forced to give up various non-Hungarian territories that had been part of its kingdom. Then, some 500,000 Jews, nearly two-thirds of the country's Jewish population, were slaughtered during World War II.

Adding to Hungary's singularity is its language, which is unlike any other in Europe although distantly related to Finnish. Modern Hungarian developed from the Magyar tongue, which was part of the Finno-Urgic language group. The Magyars were fierce hordes of mounted tribesmen from the Ural Mountains who staged forays deep into Western Europe. When they were checked by the forces of the Holy Roman Empire in the ninth century, they settled in the general area of what is now Hungary.

Stephen (or István), a descendant of the semilegendary Magyar leader Árpád, became the first king of Hungary in AD 1000 and worked strenuously to convert his people from paganism to Catholicism. For his efforts, he received a crown from the pope and later was canonized a saint. St. Stephen's crown has been a symbol of Hungarian nationhood ever since. (The crown was taken to the US for safekeeping during World War II but was only returned in 1978, some time after tensions between the Church and the Communist government were eased.) About two-thirds of Hungary's population is at least nominally Roman Catholic.

After the Árpád line died out in 1301, various royal houses of Europe struggled for control of Hungary. During this time, Hungary developed on the feudal model of other European monarchies.

The election of Mátyás Hunyadi (known as Matthias Corvinus) as king in 1458 brought prosperity and national glory to Hungary. This Renaissance king, famous for his dazzling court at Visegrád, restored public finances and reduced the power of masters over serfs. But after his death, central Hungary fell under the yoke of the Turks for some 150 years, while the northern and western sections were drawn into the Austrian Hapsburg domain. When the Turks were finally forced to withdraw in 1686, the Hungarians were compelled to accept Austrian succession to the Hungarian throne. The Hungarians rose up against Austrian absolutism several times, finally winning the establishment, in 1867, of a dual monarchy in which Austria and Hungary were partners.

After the fall of the Austro-Hungarian Empire in World War I, Hungary remained under a regent from 1919 to 1946. In 1949, its government was taken over by the Hungarian Socialist Workers party (Magyar Szocialista Munkáspárt — MSZMP, the Communist party in Hungary), and Hungary has been politically, economically, and militarily aligned with the Soviet Union ever since. In 1956, Soviet forces were called in to help crush an uprising, and 200,000 Hungarians fled in exile. However, during the past 20 years the government has enacted a number of reforms that have earned it some measure of popular support.

The regime has been particularly supportive of Hungarian folk culture, promoting and subsidizing both the decorative and performing arts. Cooperatives have been set up to ensure the continuation of the art of fine Halas lacemaking; folk dancing is encouraged as a form of mass culture; and folk artists are singled out for recognition.

The Magyar musical heritage is conveyed by classical as well as folk music. It was dramatically expressed in the romantic rhapsodies of Ferenc (Franz) Liszt in the nineteenth century and in the modern music of the twentieth-century masters Béla Bartók and Zoltán Kodály, both of whom devoted years of intensive study to Hungarian folk songs.

The special Hungarian harmony of flavors has made the country's cuisine, based on a superb marriage of meats, spices, and fresh vegetables, internationally appreciated. The special sweet Hungarian paprika is one of the world's most versatile condiments.

This wealth of historical, cultural, and culinary interest, coupled with the fact that Budapest is the brightest and most romantic capital of any Communist country in Europe — indeed, one of the loveliest cities in Europe — has increased tourism to the point where the number of visitors to Hungary each year exceeds the country's population.

For those who would like to see more of the country than its wonderful capital, we have provided three tour routes. If you have only a short time to spend outside Budapest, a visit to nearby Danube Bend offers the opportunity to enjoy some of the country's most breathtaking scenery while encountering its royal and ecclesiastical past. Our second route, into Transdanubia, is through a softer landscape, also rich in history, to Hungary's busiest center of recreation and relaxation, Lake Balaton. The final route, through the Great Hungarian Plain, allows you to explore the Hungary of peasant folk legend and to see some of Europe's most desirable farmland.

The Danube Bend

As it heads east from its route along the Czechoslovakian border, the Danube River makes an elbow bend through the wooded hills of the Pilis and Börzsöny mountains, divides into two channels that will unite again at Budapest, and gracefully curves south on its long journey to the Black Sea.

This scenic, history-rich area about 31 miles (50 km) north of Budapest is called Danube Bend and is a favorite place for excursions for residents as well as visitors. Its picturesque environs can be explored leisurely, and most pleasantly, by steamer on the river or by car. The main towns along the route also can be reached by train.

If you drive, Route 11 follows the general contour of the right bank of the river between Budapest and Esztergom, an early seat of Hungarian kings and an ancient ecclesiastical center. To the west, all along the route, is the Pilis Park Forest, which harbors wild boar and deer. You can make the trip upriver along one bank and downriver along the other, or you may prefer to crisscross the river, visiting key cities on either bank as they appear on the route. For the purposes of description, this route will take the latter course, beginning at Budapest and ending at Esztergom, 40 miles (65 km) away.

BUDAPEST: For a detailed report of the city and its hotels and restaurants, see *Budapest,* THE EUROPEAN CITIES.

En Route from Budapest – The highway leaves the capital on the Buda side of the Danube, which divides into two channels around the huge Szentendre Island just north of the city. The route upriver along the Szentendre channel, to the west of the island, offers the most rewards for tourists and is one of the busiest roads in Hungary on weekends.

SZENTENDRE: This old Serbian market town, where the great Hungarian painter Károly Ferenczy worked for the greater part of his life, is filled with interesting churches and art museums. Many artists have settled here in the old merchant houses of the original Serbian-Dalmatian settlers.

The small main square, Karl Marx tér, is lined with lovingly restored, eighteenth-century baroque houses. Each summer the Theatrum of Szentendre, a festival of comedies and dramas, is held in the square. The Károly Ferenczy Museum (Karl Marx tér 6) contains historical, archaeological, and ethnographical exhibits as well as paintings by artists who worked at the art colony established here by Ferenczy.

An open-air park-museum, near Angyal street in the north of town, contains original buildings and homes brought here from Hungary's 23 regions. There is also a very good restaurant, *Új Étterem,* in the park.

The Serbian Museum for Ecclesiastical History (Engels út. 6) contains ecclesiastical art from the fourteenth through the eighteenth century, and you can see one of the finest iconostases in Hungary in the Greek Orthodox Episcopal church on Alkotmány Street. There is an interesting medieval Roman Catholic parish church on Templom Domb, a hill near the main square. This church was rebuilt in 1710, but parts of it date from the twelfth century.

Traces of Stone Age men have been found in caves in the vicinity, and the largest Bronze Age cemetery in Central Europe was excavated in nearby Budakalász.

En Route from Szentendre – At Pomáz, an unnumbered road toward Csobánka takes you to the popular mountain resort of Dobogókö in the Pilis forest. At Leányfalu, you can stop and hike to the 1,500-foot Red Stone Cliff (Vöröskö Szikla) for a wonderful panoramic view of the plain and the Danube Bend.

The town of Tahitótfalu spreads along both sides of the channel, and the bridge here is a good place to cross over to the island if you want to stop for some swimming, canoeing, or rowing. The river is quite shallow near the village of Kisoroszi, at the northern tip of the island. It has a good beach and and a ferry can take you back across the channel.

You are now leaving the plain and entering the mountain area, and the two channels of the Danube reunite as the river is forced into a more constricted course.

VISEGRÁD: The setting of this small village among the mountains at the center of the Danube Bend, and the relics of its illustrious past as a royal stronghold during the Middle Ages, make Visegrád an immensely popular tourist center.

During the past few decades, a magnificent summer palace that flowered during the reign of King Matthias (1458–90) has been excavated and reconstructed on a hillside on the main street (Fö utca). A fine Renaissance fountain of red marble in the ceremonial courtyard bears the king's coat of arms.

You can also see the remains of the citadel (Fellegvár) on Castle Hill and the hexagonal Solomon's Tower, a typical thirteenth-century fortified dwelling with walls 9 feet thick to resist prolonged attacks. On another hill (Sibrik) are the remains of a Roman camp from about the fourth century.

Some of the discoveries of modern excavations and exhibits of Visegrád's royal past can be seen at the King Matthias Museum (Mátyás Király Muzeum; Fö út. 41). The museum is in an eighteenth-century baroque mansion once used as a royal hunting lodge.

En Route from Visegrád – Dömös is at the southernmost point of the bend the Danube makes around the southern foothills of the Börzsöny Mountains. From the slopes of the little town's hills, you get an impressive view of the V-like path of the river. This popular resort is frequently used as a starting point for hiking into the Pilis Mountains.

Pilismarót, near the start of the Danube Bend, has a wonderful 2-mile beach and numerous small bays. The picturesque town across the river, Zebegény, is an artists' colony and popular summer resort that can be reached by ferry.

Up stream from Zebegény is the frontier station of Szob, on the Czechoslovakian border. You can visit two baroque castles or enjoy the town's pleasant beach before taking the ferry back to the right bank of the Danube and the last few miles to Esztergom.

ESZTERGOM: The philosopher-emperor Marcus Aurelius is said to have written some of the books of his *Reflections* here when this was an important Roman outpost. But Esztergom is best known as the residence of Magyar kings in the twelfth and thirteenth centuries and the seat of the primate of the Hungarian Catholic church.

The largest cathedral in Hungary (390 feet long) was built here on Castle Hill (Várhegy) between 1822 and 1860. An earlier church had been built on this spot by

St. Stephen, Hungary's first king, in 1010. Today the cathedral's treasury includes numerous works of art, including a thirteenth-century gold cross upon which the kings of Hungary took their oaths.

The Museum of the Stronghold of Esztergom, adjoining the cathedral, contains fragments of a royal palace that had been destroyed during the Turkish occupation and nearly forgotten until this century, when large-scale excavations were undertaken. The palace was begun in 972 by St. Stephen's father, but its most glorious period came in the late twelfth century during the reign of King Béla III.

The Christian Museum of Esztergom (Keresztény Múzeum; Berényi Zsigismond út. 2) contains one of Hungary's most important fine arts collections. It includes excellent examples of medieval Italian and Hungarian paintings, fine Flemish and French tapestries, and a remarkable fifteenth-century altar.

Esztergom actually sits on a narrow side channel of the Danube, separated from the main stream by a long island connected to the city by bridges.

BEST EN ROUTE

Hotels in the Danube Bend area are relatively simple places, charging about $15 or $20 a night for a double room with breakfast. There are a number of excellent camping sites along the route, including one on Pap Island, near Szentendre, which accommodates up to 1,000 campers. For restaurants, expect to pay $10 to $12 for a dinner for two without drinks, wine, or tip.

DOBOGÓKŐ

Nimród Szálló Hotel – A modern hotel with 75 rooms set high in the woods of the Pilis Mountains. The restaurant serves game in season. Reservations are advised (phone: 336-508).

VISEGRÁD

Hotel Silvanus – A modern, well-designed hotel on top of a mountain with a good restaurant and bar. On Mt. Visegrád (phone: 136-063).
Önkiszolgáló Etterem – A good self-service restaurant near the Danube. Rév út.

ESZTERGOM

Fürdő Szálló – An 89-room hotel near the spa and swimming pools. It has a restaurant and bar and central heating. Bajcsy Zsilinszky út. 14 (phone: 147).
Hotel Volan-Tourist – A small hostelry in the center of town run by one of the country's tourist agencies. Some of its rooms have showers. József A. tér 2 (phone: 271 or 705).
Úszófalu Halászcsárda – A good fish restaurant on the island, at the corner of Szabad Május Sétány and Táncsis Mihály út.

Lake Balaton

The sandy beaches of Lake Balaton, where water temperatures range from 69 °F (21°C) to 81°F (27°C) in the summer, attract a solid stream of vacationers, both Hungarian and foreign, from May to September. Since World War II, the Hungarian government has developed the area around Balaton — Central Europe's largest lake — into a mass recreation center; the 122-mile (197-km) shoreline is virtually one continuous resort.

The southern shore is generally flat, with only an occasional steep hill overlooking the lake, and the water is extremely shallow, making it an ideal beach for families with small children. The north shore is characterized by a chain of long-extinct and now eroded volcanoes. Gently undulating vineyards cover the basalt hills, producing the grapes for some of the finest wines of Hungary. The area is also known for its effervescent mineral springs.

If you don't like crowds, it is best to visit the lake area in early spring or fall — rates are cheaper then, too. There are good rail connections for most of the larger resort towns, and in summer there are frequent fast trains from Budapest. The following route, beginning and ending in Budapest, explores the various resort areas around the lake.

BUDAPEST: For a detailed report of the city and its hotels and restaurants, see *Budapest,* THE EUROPEAN CITIES.

En Route from Budapest – The outskirts of Budapest give way to undulating hills as you travel southwest on Highway 70. The Brunswick Mansion, in a beautiful old park at Martonvásár, about a half-hour from Budapest, is preserved in the memory of Ludwig von Beethoven, who composed some of his important works while visiting here in the early 1800s. Beethoven concerts are given in the park during the summer, and there is a Beethoven Museum.

Almost one-third of Velencei Lake, which begins some 6 miles (10 km) beyond Martonvásár, is thick with reeds and dotted with swampy, marshy islets. In spring and autumn its grassy knolls are stopping places for scores of thousands of migrating birds, including rare waterfowl. The 6-mile-long lake is a rapidly developing holiday resort, with good beaches, yachting facilities, hotels, restaurants, and camping sites, particularly along the southern shore near Gárdony and Agárd. The northern shore attracts anglers, hunters, and other sportsmen. It is also possible to drive directly to Székesfehérvár from Budapest on the M7 motorway.

SZÉKESFEHÉRVÁR: During the Middle Ages, when it was called Alba Regia, this town was a thriving royal seat where Hungarian kings were crowned and, later, buried. Today, it is an important industrial center in the Meadowland (Mezöföld), where three-fourths of the population is engaged in agriculture. Most of the medieval town was destroyed during the Turkish occupation (1543–1688). However, a number of interesting buildings remain in the inner city. The main square of the inner town is Szabadság tér, where you will find the seventeenth-century baroque Town Hall, the former Zichy Palace, with its attractive rococo and baroque interior, and the Garden of Ruins (Romkert). This open-air museum of ruins is on the site of extensive excavations of a former cathedral, where Hungarian kings were crowned, and a former royal palace.

The King Stephen (István Király) Museum, at the corner of Gagarin tér and Népköztársaság, has interesting exhibits of local archaeology, history, and folklore.

Siófok, the biggest tourist center on Lake Balaton, is about an hour's drive from Székesfehérvár on the M7 motorway — or somewhat longer if you follow Highway 70 through a number of small towns.

SIÓFOK: The shores of Lake Balaton are virtually one long string of beach resorts, but Siófok is the largest town on the southern shore and is continually expanding to take in neighboring communities. It has the most sophisticated tourist operations, some of the best beaches, and crowded facilities from Easter till the season ends.

Although the obvious attraction of Siófok is its long sandy beach, there are a few interesting churches and an excellent riding academy nearby. There is also an open-air theater in Dimitrov Park and many pleasant garden restaurants in which to relax. The

IBUSZ office here can even arrange for you to take a cooking class with a chef from one of the top resort hotels.

There are ferries to the north shore peninsula of Tihany from Siófok's Szántód Harbor. Inland from the lake, on Highway 65 at Ságvár, are interesting ruins of a fortified Roman camp, dating from the third century.

En Route from Siófok – The shore road winds through numerous resort towns, but at Balatonföldvár a road south leads to Kőröshegy, where many of the original features are retained in a fifteenth-century, single-naved Gothic church, despite restoration work in the eighteenth century. The taverns here are good places to sample the regional wine and listen to gypsy music.

After carefully negotiating several dangerous sudden curves through the town of Balatonszemes, the shore road reaches Fonyód, the site of Stone and Bronze Age settlements and now a busy resort area. At Balatonkeresztúr, Highway 7, which has paralleled the lake since Zamárdi, veers south, and Highway 71 serves the north shore.

KESZTHELY: The largest of the lake towns, Keszthely has been a municipality since the early fifteenth century. Its charming old streets create a pleasant ambience, and there are a number of interesting sights to divert you from the pleasures of the beaches. The Georgicon (Georgicon út.) was founded in 1797 and was the first agricultural college established on the European continent. The Helicon Library, in the former palace of Count Georges Festetics, contains over 80,000 volumes as well as valuable antiquities and art. The Balaton Museum (Kossuth Lajos and Museum streets) has interesting historical and ethnographical exhibits.

Héviz, the most famous spa in Hungary, with its own warmwater lake and indoor and outdoor thermal baths, is a few miles west of here.

En Route from Keszthely – The shore road passes through the Badacsony, a district of basalt terraces where lava from long-extinct volcanoes has created bizarre rock formations. The area also is known for its fruit growing and for the excellence of its vineyards. The ruins of Szigliget Castle, dating from the thirteenth century, stand on a hill just west of the town of Badacsony.

Beyond Balatonszepezd, a favorite retreat of artists and writers, a mile-long road leads up a hillside to Zánka, where there is a fisherman's lodge in the woods and a thirteenth-century church that was remodeled in the baroque style in 1786. Medieval pageants are sometimes held in summer in the fifteenth-century castle in Nagyvázsony, a town about 10 miles (16 km) farther north.

TIHANY: The small peninsula of Tihany, a series of hills covered with poplar and acacia trees and the scent of lavender, is one of the loveliest spots on Balaton. Its long history as a stronghold can be read in the remains of a 3,000-year-old earthenwork fortification and in Celtic and Roman ruins. A beautiful yellow abbey church with twin spires stands on a hill overlooking the peninsula. The museum here has the richest exhibits of art and local history on Balaton.

There is excellent fishing in Lake Belsö, high on a hill above Balaton — in effect, a lake within a lake; and the villagers' unusual thatch-roofed houses of dark gray volcanic tufa add charm to the landscape. Government institutes have been set up on the peninsula to study its wealth of geological and botanical rarities.

BALATONFÜRED: One of the oldest and most renowned health resorts in the area, Balatonfüred is the last large town on Lake Balaton. There are several large, new hotels here, an attractive poplar-lined promenade along the lake, and an inviting central park. There is also a classical Round (Kerek) Church, built in the 1840s on Jókai út. Yachting races are frequently held here, and the harbor is the busiest on Lake Balaton.

In the main square, Gyógytér, there is a colonnaded pavilion built over the bubbling waters of a volcanic spring. In all, the town has 11 medicinal springs that have been attracting those seeking cures, particularly for heart and nerve disorders, for decades.

En Route from Balatonfüred – The shore road can be followed through a dozen or so small communities around the lake back to a connection with the M7 motorway or Highway 70 to return to Budapest. Another alternative is to take Highway 73 north from Balatonfüred into the Bakony hills to Veszprém before heading back to Budapest.

VESZPRÉM: Built on five hills, this picturesque town of cobblestone streets, old gateways, and arches is Bakony's cultural and economic center. It is an old settlement rich in historical monuments. The Vár (Castle) Museum, in the Heroes' Gate (Hösi Kapu) near Vöröshadsereg Square, contains old weapons, armor, and historical documents. The eighteenth-century baroque Episcopal Palace (Tolbuhin út. 12) is next to the early Gothic Gizella Chapel, built in the thirteenth century.

The Bakony Museum, in Lenin Park on Kálvária Hill, has exhibits that detail the Bakony region's history, customs, and crafts.

BEST EN ROUTE

Lake Balaton is Hungary's most popular resort, so hotel reservations should be made well in advance if you plan to visit during the summer. A double room will cost between $20 and $45 per night, depending on the month and resort chosen. All the hotels listed are open from May to September unless otherwise noted. It is also possible to rent cottages or apartments on the lake, and IBUSZ can arrange for the rental of sailboats that can sleep four at $200 to $400 per week. Restaurants range in price from $25 and up for a dinner for two in the expensive range; around $15 in the moderate; and $10 and under, inexpensive. Prices do not include drink, wine, and tip.

The wines of the Balaton region, particularly the spicy white ones, are justly famous. Among the best are the Badacsony Blue Stalk (Badacsonyi Kéknyelü), Gray Friar (Badacsonyi Szürkebarát), and Riesling (Badacsonyi Rizling). The food specialty is the perch-pike–type fish *fogas*.

SIÓFOK

Balaton Hotel – On the lake with a private beach. All rooms have balconies, and the hotel has a nightclub and an espresso bar. Petőfi Sétány 9 (phone: 1-0655). Moderate.

Európa Hotel – Lakeshore setting and private beach. A restaurant and an espresso bar are among the hotel's amenities. Petőfi Sétány 17 (phone: 1-1400). Moderate.

Hungária Hotel – Balconied rooms, private beach, restaurant, and bar. Petőfi Sétány 13 (phone: 1-0677). Moderate.

Napfény Hotel – Small, family-type hotel near the beach, with balconied rooms. Petőfi Sétány 2 (phone: 1-1408). Inexpensive.

Fogas Restaurant – Excellent food in a garden setting. Váradi tér. Moderate.

Ménes Csárda – Very good — and very spicy — local specialties are served in this restaurant, actually a restored old stable decorated with antique folk art. In Szántód, about 6 miles (10 km) west of Siófok on the main highway to Balatonföld-vár. Moderate.

KESZTHELY

Helikon Hotel – Facing the beach. Spa facilities, restaurant, bar, tennis courts, and yacht marina. Balatonpart (phone: 1-1330). Expensive.

Fishermen's Inn (Halász Csárda) – Fish specialties. South of Keszthely on the lakeshore (phone: 1-2751). Moderate.

Helikon Tavern – Good food and wine, and gypsy music. About 5 miles (8 km) east of town. Moderate.

TIHANY

Tihany Hotel – Private beach, tennis, riding, and water skiing; nightclub, espresso bar, and restaurant. Rév út. 3 (phone: 4-4091). Expensive to moderate.

Fogas Csárda – Excellent fish dishes served on a terrace or in one of four dining rooms. Gypsy music. Off Hwy. 71. Expensive to moderate.

BALATONFÜRED

Annabella Hotel – Picturesque surroundings on the lakeshore; private beach, restaurant and terrace, and espresso bar. Open May to October. Beloiannisz út. 25 (phone: 4-0110). Expensive.

Marina Hotel – On the lake with a private beach; restaurant with gypsy music, espresso bar, health club, nightclub. Open May to October. Széchenyi út. 26 (phone: 4-0821). Expensive.

The Great Hungarian Plain

The Great Hungarian Plain (Nagy Alföld), east of the Danube, is the heart of Hungary and one of Europe's richest larders. During the past century, the thousands of acres of the drifting sand and needle grass that characterized this desert plain, called the *puszta,* have been transformed into lush orchards and vineyards, and modern machinery now cultivates the corn and wheat fields.

But the government has taken steps to preserve the heritage of the rural Hungarian peasant, long romanticized by poets and painters: the isolated whitewashed crofts, the special *puszta* gray cattle and horse herds, the traditional arts and crafts. They can still be seen in places such as the National Park of Hortobágy.

This circular route from Budapest takes you to some of the most important towns of the area of the Great Hungarian Plain sometimes referred to as Little Cumania and to some of its art centers. Most of the towns are on main railway lines and can be visited on a train journey through the region. There are also bus connections.

BUDAPEST: For a detailed report on the city and its hotels and restaurants, see *Budapest,* THE EUROPEAN CITIES.

    En Route from Budapest – About an hour's drive southeast on the E15 motorway, Highway 40 to the south takes you to Cegléd, an old peasant community that was the birthplace of István Tömörkény, one of the great chroniclers of peasant life. The Kossuth Lajos museum (Rákóczi út. and Marx K. utca) contains the patriot's death mask. Farther south is Nagykőrös, the center of a rich market-gardening region famous for its Kőrös Morello cherries and other fruit. A splendid morning market is held here.

KECSKEMÉT: This is the hometown of Zoltán Kodály, the famous composer of modern music who also collected and wrote about Hungarian folk music. And this sprawling town itself seems to blend two worlds.

Since World War II, Kecskemét has become an important food-processing center, and modern housing estates have replaced many single-story dwellings. But the old peasant architecture can be seen along Bánk Bán and János Hoffman streets. The secessionist town hall on Kossuth tér is, perhaps, the most characteristic building. Its inner walls and corridors are decorated with folk themes and brightly colored flower motifs. A bit southwest of the square, behind the 16-story county council building, is a unique double-gated peasant house with a fine veranda. Beautiful examples of shepherds' cloaks and embroidered clothing of the region are on display at the Katona József Muzeum, on the Katona József promenade.

An artists' colony, where many of Hungary's best painters and sculptors of the twentieth century have worked, is in a large park on Mártírok út., southeast of the center.

The Kecskemét area is famous for its apricots and apricot brandy, called *barack,* and a grape harvest (Kecskeméti Szüret) is held each September. In odd-numbered years there is a Kecskemét Folk Music Meeting of singers and musicians and the International Kodály Seminar for music teachers; an International Creative Camp of Musicians takes place every July.

The Kecskemét riding school, just outside the city on Highway 44, has excellent sport and jump horses selected from the famous stud farms of the *puszta.*

En Route from Kecskemét – Heading south on the E5 motorway you reach Kiskunfélegyháza, an important cultural center of Kiskúnság (Little Cumania). The Kiskun Muzeum has a good archaeological collection and an interesting penology display.

A road to the west of town will take you to the Kiskunság National Park and its major section, the Bugacpuszta. The gray cattle and branch-horned *racka* sheep of the region graze here in pastures surrounded by trees, marshes, and sand dunes. The Shepherd Museum, a glass-walled, circular building resembling a Mongolian jurta tent, has displays that detail the old nomadic way of life and of animal breeding in the *puszta.* An refurbished old inn nearby provides an ideal setting for sampling Hungarian specialties and regional wines.

Another detour off the E5 motorway, this one to the east just before you reach Szeged, leads to Fehértó, a well-known bird sanctuary near Lake Fehér, the home of red heron, ducks, and other fish-eating birds. (Permission to visit must be obtained in advance.)

One of the typical sights of the Great Hungarian Plain is storks nesting in the chimneys of farmhouses along the road.

SZEGED: The economic and cultural center of the southern region of the Great Hungarian Plain straddles the Tisza River near the Yugoslavian border. The present town was laid out after a devastating flood just over 100 years ago, but Szeged has a long, rich history.

It was occupied by the Ottoman Empire for 144 years until the end of the seventeenth century, and it was plundered and burned in 1704 in retaliation for its support of the freedom struggle against the ruling House of Hapsburg of Austria. During the war of independence from the Hapsburgs, Szeged was, for a short time, the capital of the country. During the great Tisza flood of 1879, the town was destroyed once again.

The central town square, Széchenyi tér, has a pleasant promenade of old plane trees and is lined by a number of various public buildings. A few blocks south is the impressive Dóm tér, a square surrounded by arcaded buildings of dark red brick and dominated by the twin-spired Votive Church at its center. The neo-Romanesque church has the second largest organ in Europe (the largest is in Milan's cathedral). Part of the huge square is the site of the Szeged Open-Air Theater, where the Szeged Festival (Szegedi Szabadtéri Játékok) of opera, drama, and ballet is held every year in July and August. Hungary's finest Greek Orthodox Serbian church, known for its outstanding iconostasis, is on the north side of the square.

Szeged is famous for its salami products, beautifully embroidered slippers, and a delicious fish soup, *szegedi halászlé.* In Tápé, an outer district of the town noted for the artistic mats woven by its women, villagers have retained their picturesque folkways and dress. A collection of folk dress and everyday articles can be seen at Vártó út. 2.

Traditional as well as newer styles of pottery are made in workshops at Hódmező-vásárhely, a small town 16 miles (25 km) northeast of Szeged on Highway 47. The Tornya Museum there has interesting archaeological and ethnographical collections.

En Route from Szeged – About halfway to Baja on Highway 55 you can turn north on Highway 53 to reach Kiskunhalas, home of the famous Halas lace, *halasi csipke*. You can see the lacemakers at work at the Cottage Industry Cooperative, and the Lace House (Csipkeház) has a large exhibit of the fine craft that has won the town a worldwide reputation.

BAJA: This picturesque town on the banks of the Danube and Sugovica rivers has numerous islands with sandy lidos and fine parks, lovely old churches, and an artists' colony in a former nobleman's mansion at Arany János út. 1. The folklore and folk art collections of the Türr István Museum (Béke tér) are typical of the region.

KALOCSA: This town, 21 miles (34 km) north of Baja on Highway 51, is one of the most important centers of folk art in Hungary. The women of the town are famous for the primitive, ornamental painting with which they decorate the walls of their homes and for the designs they paint on furniture and door panels. The finest examples of their work can be seen at the Népművészetiház (Tompa Mihály út. 1–3), housed in the same building as the Folk Art Cooperative, where some of these "painting women" work with outsiders interested in learning this folk art.

In quaint little villages nearby, you can often see whitewashed houses strung with garlands of the red peppers that are grown in the area and are used to make fine Hungarian paprika.

Northeast of Kalocsa is Kiskőrös, hometown of the nineteenth-century revolution-ary poet Sándor Petőfi.

The highway back to Budapest parallels the Danube, passing through Dunapataj, a village near pleasant Szelidi Lake, and through two towns where the poet Petőfi lived and worked — Dunavecse and Szalkszentmárton.

BEST EN ROUTE

First-class hotel accommodations are limited, but prices are relatively low. At the places mentioned, a double room with bath and breakfast will cost about $26 to $30 a night. Meals are also quite inexpensive in the towns of the Great Hungarian Plain. Dinner for two, with a local wine, will cost between $10 and $12 at most good restaurants.

KECSKEMÉT

Hotel Aranyhomok – This five-story modern hotel on one of Kecskemét's central squares is the best in the area. It has a large restaurant and garden, a coffee shop, and a bar. Széchenyi tér 2 (phone: 20-011).

Szélmalom Inn – This restaurant is housed in a replica of the traditional white-washed windmills of the Great Hungarian Plain. Just outside town on the E5 motorway.

SZEGED

Hungária Hotel – Near a shady park on the bank of the Tisza River, next to the Szeged National Theater. All rooms have baths. Komócsin Z. tér 2 (phone: 10-855).

International 1st Class Camping Site and Motel – Dorozsmai út. 2 (phone: 61-255).

Alabárdos Restaurant – Oksola út. 13.

Exploring Iceland

An extended trip to Iceland is a strange blend of culture shock and geological field trip. Though this country might be the world's largest small town (there are only 225,000 people on the whole island, and half of them live in Reykjavik), the natives are among the most sophisticated of Europeans, aware of the latest in both fashion and culture. Though Iceland has the oldest republic in the world (founded by Norse wanderers in AD 960), the country is a geological infant, still growing steadily from fissures, lava flows, earthquakes, and volcanoes.

In the North Atlantic between the Denmark Strait to the west and the Norwegian Sea to the east, Iceland is 190 miles from north to south and 300 miles from east to west. Because it's partially ringed by the warm currents of the Gulf Stream, the island is habitable — barely. Its weather is abruptly changeable, and its terrain is unlike any other country on Earth. More than 10% glacier and 10% lava, it's a land of hot and cold. The word "geyser" is Icelandic, and geothermal water is everywhere. Some of this naturally hot water has been harnessed, and one hot spring, Deildartunguhuer, has been so pressurized and heated by the Earth's interior turbulence that boiling water flows through it at 40 gallons per second. Amazingly, this boiling water flows completely naturally, close to the Arctic Circle, in the Land of the Midnight Sun. There are volcanic eruptions on an average of one every 5 or 6 years, but the Icelanders have started to adapt to even this. (In 1973, when a volcano erupted on the inhabited island of Heimaey, the entire population was evacuated in a matter of hours. Though the eruption lasted from January to May, Icelandic scientists were able to cool and reroute the lava flows with ocean water so that most of the town was saved and the harbor left open.)

The countryside is hauntingly beautiful, with an almost treeless landscape of stark lava fields, awesome glaciers, lakes, mountains, and a fjord-indented coastline. There are rivers in Iceland, but they aren't navigable because of their breakneck currents caused by a combination of rainfall and melting glaciers that also leave the riverbeds strewn with debris. The price of this stark, natural beauty is the need to import almost all raw materials and staples from wood to fruit to fuel. Iceland raises sheep and cattle (also reindeer have been imported and bred); lamb is the staple in the Icelanders' diet. The life here is hard, but the people of Iceland have one of the longest life expectancies in the world.

Outside Reykjavik, the capital, there's not too much in the way of town life. A ring road around the island was completed in 1974, but if you want to travel north, it's best to fly to Akureyri, the northern capital of 12,300 staunch citizens who live on Arctic banks and make wry New Englanders seem like outgoing Texans.

Because of its need to import almost everything, Iceland is very expensive — from cabs to meals to hotels — but a trip here can be a special experience, one in which you can't help both marveling at the people and becoming keenly aware of the power and life of the Earth itself.

REYKJAVIK: Many people stop over here on transatlantic flights, but few have the foresight to stay and explore Iceland's capital and commercial and maritime hub. A good place to start an exploration is the Austurvöllur, the quiet central square at the intersection of Kirkjustraeti and Posthusstraeti. This was the reputed home site of Iceland's first settler, a Norwegian Viking named Ingólfur Arnarson, who arrived in 874. The republic's early history was not all rosy — Iceland was long dominated by both the Norwegians and the Danes. In the nineteenth century, however, there was a successful independence movement led by Jón Sigurdsson, Iceland's national hero, whose statue stands here in the grassy quadrangle. The city surrounds this square with neat, multistoried buildings topped with red, white, and green roofs, all scrupulously crisp and clean. On the various adjacent edges of the square are the imposing Parliament House, the stone Cathedral of Reykjavik, and the large *Hotel Borg.* Also near the square is the Tjörn, the town pond and summer home for many wheeling Arctic terns.

It's an easy city to walk around in, and though the signs are generally incomprehensible, most of the people speak English. The Thjodminjasafnid is the national cultural museum (at the corner of Sudurgata and Hringbraut), where you'll also find the national museum of art. Even before the Norse, Irish monks came to Iceland as early as the eighth century. After the establishment of the Althing (the governing body) in 930, art flourished and Icelandic literature — the most sophisticated writings of the Middle Ages — is still preserved in illuminated manuscripts. You'll find a sampling of the precious "saga" manuscripts at the Manuscript Institute of Iceland (Arnagardur), an unassuming modern building. Both these museums are part of the University of Iceland. In nearby Laugardalur you can take a swim and sauna in the city's open-air pool, naturally heated year-round by hot springs.

A circle route from Reykjavik east can, in 1 day, encompass the country's most famous natural and historic attractions: the Geysir hot spring area, the Gullfoss waterfall, and Thingvellir, the site of the ancient parliament. There aren't that many roads, but it's still a good idea to get a clear map and trace your route before you start east from the capital through Hellisheidi to Hveragerdi.

HVERAGERDI: This town is important for its many greenhouses, which Iceland depends on year-round for such warm-weather crops as tomatoes, bananas, and grapes. The greenhouses are heated entirely from the active hot springs of the area. Continue past the towns of Selfoss, Hraungerdi, and Húsatoftir, where you turn north to Flúdir. You can stop at the Skalholt Cathedral here, where there are outdoor concerts on summer Sunday afternoons.

THE GREAT GEYSIR AND THE GULLFOSS: Continue north to two of the most famous natural sights in Iceland. The world "geyser" originated with the Icelandic Great Geysir, a sprouting hot spring that gives its name to similar springs all over the world. The original only rarely performs now, but nearby is another old regular known as Strokkur.

Another 16 miles (26 km) east is the Gullfoss, the Golden Waterfall. Considered to be one of the world's most beautiful, this fall plunges down a series of cascades into a deep gorge of the Hvítá River. Now return west across the Brúará River, past Middalur, to the Laugarvatn Lake area. This is a deep glacial lake and a popular resort area, with hotels, campsites, an indoor swimming pool, and a steambath built directly over the hot springs.

THINGVELLIR: From Laugarvatn, continue west across Lyngdalsheidi to Thingvellir. This Plain of National Assembly, or Althing, was named for the country's first open-air legislative assembly, which was established here in AD 930. The Icelandic Parliament had its roots in these annual 2-week summer confabs, which were attended by tribal chieftains from throughout the country. Thingvellir is starkly and beautifully situated on an immense lava plain intersected by rock fissures and surrounded by a craggy distant horizon. To the northeast is an extinct shield volcano, Skjaldbreidur, at the northern end of Lake Thingvallavatn. Since there are few visible remains of the early meetings, it's best to visit Thingvellir with a knowledgeable guide, but even on your own, you can savor the peacefulness here. You can camp at one of the sites in the surrounding national park.

From here travel south to Úlfljótsvatn Lake and the Ljosafoss waterfall via the Thrastalundur woods. You drive alongside the Sogid River, popular with the salmon-fishing set, and head south past Ingólfsfjall Mountain. The secondary road rejoins the main route (just west of Selfoss), which takes you back to Reykjavik.

BEST EN ROUTE

Everything in Iceland is expensive. There's no getting around this. A cup of coffee can cost as much as $1.50, a short cab ride, $3 or $4. The best food and lodgings are in Reykjavik. The ptarmigan (called *rjupa* here) is very good; it's served in a delicious sauce called *rjupusosa*. There is no tipping in Iceland.

REYKJAVIK

The Borg Hotel – A traditional, high-ceilinged hotel, which opened in 1930, upon the millennial of the founding of the Althing. It's quiet, stylish, and right on Austurvöllur Square. Pósthússtraeti 11 (phone: 1-1440). Expensive.

Holt Hotel – Tucked away on a quiet residential street, this hotel has what many consider the city's best restaurant. Bergstadastraeti 37 (phone: 2-1011). Expensive.

The Naust – A seafood restaurant in a former fish warehouse — what could be more atmospheric? It has a small dance floor and very good food. The *Naust* is very popular with the residents. Vesturgata 6-8 (phone: 1-7759). Expensive.

Exploring Ireland

Whether you come for the salmon and trout that jump onto your line; to share a "jar" at a pub while you listen to traditional music played on pipe and fiddle and old tin whistle; to clamber over craggy mountains or ponder prehistoric monuments; to capture the varied greens of the landscape on canvas or film; to rent a cottage and write a novel; or to visit relatives or make new friends, your welcome in Ireland will be warm.

The Republic of Ireland, across the narrow Irish Sea from England, has few natural resources, but it has two that make it a "little bit of heaven" for travelers: enchanting beauty and charming, friendly people. Since it must import more than it can export, Ireland depends heavily on income from tourism.

It may be the lyricism that first attracts people to this island on the western fringes of Europe — all those songs about the "lilt of Irish laughter" and the way place names roll off the tongue: the Gap of Dunloe, the River Liffey, Galway Bay, Kilkenny and Kildare. The Irish seem born with a love of language, and the poet-philosopher has always been the real king of Ireland, even in ancient times when poets or seers called *fili* preserved Celtic laws and history orally. This is the land that produced the towering artistry of William Butler Yeats, James Joyce, and Samuel Beckett (never mind that the latter two had to leave the country to find full expression). And though Beckett may write in French, there is no doubt he is Irish. Today, Ireland gives special tax breaks to artists and writers.

Although English is the everyday language of most people in the Republic, Irish, a form of Gaelic, is actually the national language. Irish was, in fact, the vernacular outside the cities and larger towns until the early nineteenth century. But with the establishment of a national system of schools, English spread to a point where today there are only pockets of Irish-speaking people. You are more likely to see the Irish language than hear it; public signs frequently are posted in both English and Irish.

Many of the people who believe that the Irish language is an essential part of Irish nationality also work to preserve national games and dances and other riches of Ireland's Celtic past. The best way to hear traditional music and song and to see Irish dancing is to attend one of the frequent sessions held by the more than 200 branches of Comhaltas Ceoltoiri Eireann, the central organization for the promotion of these arts. An important 3-day festival of traditional music and song, the All-Ireland Fleadh, is held on the last weekend of August each year in a different town.

The Celts came to this island from Central Europe sometime after 600 BC, but it is believed that there were inhabitants here as early as 6000 BC. Ireland has the richest concentration of prehistoric monuments in Western Europe, including numerous megaliths known as dolmens. Most often they are three huge boulders standing upright to support a heavy capstone, and they usually mark an ancient burial site.

The prehistory that has been preserved in Ireland's epic tales, legends, and poetry is a marvelous mixture of myth and fact. There are story cycles dealing with kings — some of them belonging to history, others to legend — like the Fenian cycle, which tells of the deeds of the giant Finn MacCool and his band of warriors, the Fianna. There are stories of the Little People, leprechauns and the like, who, according to folklore, were related to the Tuatha De Danann, an early Irish race with magical powers driven underground by Celtic Milesians, the predecessors of the current Irish, said to come from Spain. It is, perhaps, a measure of how integral fairies and spirits are to the Irish culture to note that this country's greatest poet, William Butler Yeats, once devoted himself to a study of Irish folklore and an extensive classification of the Little People.

When St. Patrick brought Christianity to Ireland in the fifth century, he found an island country of small, separate kingdoms united in language and culture. The development of the church in Ireland along monastic rather than ecclesiastic lines reflects to some extent the development of the country itself. In its early days there were no towns or villages, just cottages scattered over the countryside.

Norsemen raided the island repeatedly from the ninth century until their defeat in 1014 at Clontarf, near Dublin, by the high king Brian Boru. The defeat did not promote Irish unity, however, because Boru died soon after, and when his sons initiated wars over the division of his lands, it ultimately gave the Normans, newly arrived in England, an opportunity to land troops in Ireland.

During the next 700 years, the Norman and then Tudor conquests spread over the whole of Ireland. Irish landlords were systematically supplanted by English and Scottish settlers, many of whom were Protestant. Ulster became the stronghold of these settlers, and that northeastern province grew different in character from the rest of the island. With the parliament in the hands of the British-Protestant minority, stiff penal laws were enacted to deprive Catholics and dissenters of civil and religious rights.

Inspired by the American and French Revolutions, followers of Wolf Tone and other leaders challenged the British in 1798, but the uprising was crushed, and in 1801, Ireland became part of the United Kingdom. The great potato famine (1845–48) added to the miseries of the Irish people. Farmers whose crops failed were evicted by their landlords, and during a 5-year period, the country lost a million people to starvation and an equal number to emigration, which many saw as the only hope for a decent life. Such extreme conditions led to the formation of the Irish Republican Brotherhood in 1858 and a renewed sense of Irish nationalism.

In 1914, Parliament passed a Home Rule bill for Ireland (that Protestants in the north opposed), but 2 years later Patrick Pearse and James Connolly led the Easter Uprising, proclaiming Ireland a Republic. Although the rebels only held out a week, the British aroused the feelings of the whole country

by executing 15 of the leaders. At the next general election, 73 of 105 seats
in the Irish parliament were won by a militant independence party called Sinn
Fein. These Sinn Fein members met in Dublin on January 21, 1919, to issue
a declaration confirming the Republic proclaimed in 1916 and to constitute
themselves as the National Parliament (Dail).

The attempt by the British to suppress the parliament and the military wing
of republicanism, the Irish Republican Army (IRA), led to a guerrilla war
for independence, euphemistically referred to as the time of "troubles." Britain granted dominion status to the Irish Free State, but Northern Ireland had
the option to get out, and the country was partitioned. In 1937, a new
constitution declaring Ireland to be a sovereign, independent, democratic
state was approved by plebiscite.

The ultimate reunification of the Republic with Northern Ireland is still a
major goal of many Irish Catholics. The Irish parliament has outlawed the
IRA, but that organization has continued its campaign of violence in England
and Northern Ireland, with financial aid from US citizens, since hostilities
broke out over demands for just treatment of Catholics in Northern Ireland.
Since 1969, thousands of people have been killed and injured in the fighting
in Northern Ireland. But although there has been some minor terrorist activity in the Republic, there is little likelihood a visitor will encounter any
unpleasantness.

The Republic of Ireland is only a bit larger than the state of West Virginia.
At its widest east-west point it is 171 miles across, and at its greatest north-
south length it stretches 302 miles. Mild winds from Europe and the warm,
damp air from the Gulf Stream along its west coast in the Atlantic Ocean
combine to keep the weather mild. Temperatures rarely drop to freezing
during the winter, and summer temperatures range from 57°F (14°C) to 61°F
(16°C), but can reach 70°F (21°C) to 75°F (24°C) at times. Except for a strip
along the east coast, the country receives some rain at least 200 days a year.
This climate is responsible for one of Ireland's more outstanding features: its
remarkable verdant beauty.

Ireland's natural beauty should be explored leisurely. Do it by car if you
must, but consider the alternatives. Go on foot along the stone-walled lanes
wherever they may lead or take a small map and compass and wander
through the woodlands. There are over 100 centers throughout the country
that rent bicycles and provide maps and time estimates for excursions. Or rent
a horse-drawn caravan and travel the byways in the tradition of the tinkers,
Ireland's itinerant repairmen (get information from the Irish Tourist Board).

The range of accommodations in Ireland is one of the most varied in
Europe. There are hotels in castles, in fine old Georgian mansions, in farmhouses, and in old inns. You can also stay in private homes that offer bed and
breakfast or rent your own Irish cottage in five counties: Mayo, Clare, Tipperary, Limerick, and Galway (information is available from the Irish Tourist
Board or Rent an Irish Cottage, Ltd., Shannon Airport House, Shannon
International Airport, County Clare, Ireland).

The routes we have outlined are designed to afford maximum exposure to
the wonders of Ireland. The initial route takes you along the coast from
Dublin to Cork through the Wicklow Mountains, the pretty villages and rich

farmland of County Wexford and County Waterford, to Blarney Castle and Ireland's second largest city. The second route, from Cork to Killarney, traverses an area of lakes and mountains long celebrated for its beauty by poet and painter alike. It is a fisherman's paradise and a golfer's heaven as well, so it should come as no surprise that it is the area of Ireland most overrun by tourists in the summer.

From Killarney to Galway, our third route passes through the rich agricultural area of the Midwest Counties, along the lovely River Shannon and on to the starkly beautiful Cliffs of Moher and the gray rock of the Burren country and then to Galway Bay. From Galway, our fourth route takes in the rugged Aran Islands, then heads north through the melancholic Connemara Mountains to Sligo and Yeats country. The final route, from Sligo to Donegal, travels through a rugged area dominated by limestone hills — the Ireland of myth and legend.

Southeast Ireland: Dublin to Cork

A scenic 160-mile (256-km) coastal route can take you from Dublin to Cork in 4½ leisurely hours. But to savor the changing moods and character of the Irish scene you must meander. The route you should consider to get a feel for southeast Ireland wanders over more than 250 miles (400 km) in seven counties; it snakes south from Dublin through Wicklow, Wexford, and Waterford, angles north to take in the countryside of Kilkenny, arcs west into legendary Tipperary, and veers south again to Cork and the coast. Ideally, this tour should be spread over 3 days.

It will seem incredible, but a mere half-hour's drive from the city center of Dublin brings you to the splendid isolation of the Wicklow Mountains. Here, great valleys with melodious names like Glenmalure, Glendalough, Imaal, Clara, and Avoca wind through heather-covered hills. Uncrowded roads pass unforgettable sights — a high waterfall, an ancient monastic settlement, a splendid estate.

To the south lies the friendlier, less dramatic landscape of County Wexford; fertile farmland is served by picturesque villages and the historic, narrow-streeted town of Wexford itself. Just to the west is Waterford, a name synonymous with the fine crystal whose renown has tended to overshadow the scenic beauty of the county. Thirty miles (48 km) north of Waterford is ancient Kilkenny, the town dominated by magnificent Kilkenny Castle along the River Nore. The rich pasturelands of Tipperary and the Golden Vale continue into Cork. It is quiet scenery, without the brooding grandeur of the west; rolling hills rise behind ancient towns; Norman castles sit on riverbanks shared with roofless, ruined abbeys.

The suggested stopping points in a 3-day tour are Wexford, Waterford, Kilkenny, or Cashel. If your schedule allows only 2 days for the route, skip Kilkenny.

DUBLIN: For a detailed report on the city and its hotels and restaurants, see *Dublin,* THE EUROPEAN CITIES.

En Route from Dublin – The coast road from Dublin leads past two famous resorts: Dun Laoghaire (pronounced "dunleary"), on the south shore of Dublin Bay, a residential town on a magnificent harbor; and Sandycove, the site of the Martello Tower where James Joyce once lived, today open to the public as a Joyce museum. Continuing to Dalkey and Killiney, one enters George Bernard Shaw territory. Shaw had a cottage on Dalkey Hill that he described as commanding "the most beautiful view in the world." Just before Bray, make a right turn onto Route T7 (marked Wexford) and drive inland. Another right turn takes you through hills into a wooded hollow where you come upon Enniskerry, one of the prettiest villages in Ireland, renowned for the estate of Powerscourt.

ENNISKERRY: Near the village, signs point the way to Powerscourt, one of Ireland's great estates. Its beautiful Georgian mansion was gutted by fire in 1974, but its substantial skeleton attests to its former grandness. Also remaining are 14,000 acres of resplendent grounds, including gardens with rare shrubberies along the River Dargle; a deer park; and the 400-foot Powerscourt Waterfall, the highest on these islands. (The gardens are open from St. Patrick's Day to October; small admission charge.)

From Powerscourt, driving through the Wicklow Hills, you come to Roundwood, the highest village in Ireland, and just beyond is Laragh, the gateway to Glendalough.

GLENDALOUGH: This deep glen, set in the Wicklow Mountains between two lakes, is a very special place with a very romantic history. In the sixth century, when St. Kevin came to Wicklow in search of tranquillity, he found it here. But the hermit's sanctity attracted so many disciples that, almost unwittingly, he founded a great monastery that eventually became one of the most renowned centers of learning in Europe. The visitor today sees the remains of many buildings from the ninth through the thirteenth century, including a perfect example of a Round Tower. There are wonderful nature trails in the valley's forest park.

En Route from Glendalough – Following Route T61, you pass through the densely wooded vales of Clara and Avoca. (The latter is the beauty spot where the Avonmore and Avonbeg rivers join to form the River Avoca. Here the poet Thomas Moore wrote his hymn to the vale, "The Meeting of the Waters.")

Heading back to the coast, you come to Arklow, an important fishing port and boatbuilding center. *Gypsy Moth III,* the yacht that took Sir Francis Chichester around the world, was built in an Arklow shipyard.

At Arklow, pick up N11 into County Wexford, through the towns of Gorey and Ferns, to Enniscorthy.

ENNISCORTHY: In a picturesque part of the Slaney Valley, this small town clings to steeply sloping ground along both banks of the river. The object of many attacks throughout history, including seizure of the lands by Oliver Cromwell and his forces in the seventeenth century, this was the site of a famous rebellion against the British in 1798. The insurgents made their last stand on Vinegar Hill, at the eastern end of the town, and were forever commemorated in the ballad "Boulavogue."

Enniscorthy Castle, dating from the sixteenth century, is excellently preserved and now devoted to a folk museum. St. Aidan's Cathedral is a fine example of neo-Gothic architecture, made all the more impressive by its commanding site overlooking the River Slaney.

WEXFORD: Also on the River Slaney, along its estuary, is hilly Wexford, settled in 850 by the Vikings, who gave it its name, Waesfjord ("the harbor of the mud flats"). The Normans took the town in the twelfth century and founded Selskar Abbey, where Henry II of England spent Lent of 1172 in penance for the murder of Thomas à Becket. The ruins of the abbey are a tourist attraction, as is the Bull Ring, in the center of town, where bullfights were staged for the Norman nobles. In 1649 Cromwell captured

Wexford, massacred the townspeople, and destroyed 13 churches in a grand, 3-day orgy of antipopery self-righteousness. The house where he stayed is now a Woolworth's store. Other historic Wexford houses, dealt with more fairly by fate, include the birthplace of Sir Robert McClure, the Arctic explorer who discovered the Northwest Passage, and the home of Lady Wilde, mother of Oscar Wilde.

The best way to see the town is on one of the daily walking tours organized by members of the Old Wexford Society (tours are offered for free, although contributions are always welcome; detailed information is available at the tourist office on Crescent Quay, phone: 2-3111). In October, Wexford holds an acclaimed opera festival, including a program of exhibitions, concerts, recitals, and films.

From Wexford, take Route N25 to New Ross.

NEW ROSS: On a hill overlooking the River Barrow, New Ross is the home of lovely St. Mary's Abbey, a relic of Norman times. Five miles (8 km) east, on L159, is the John Fitzgerald Kennedy Memorial Park, a splendid arboretum commemorating President Kennedy, whose ancestors came from nearby Dunganstown. Try the *New Ross Galley* — the restaurant on a boat — where you can combine a good meal with a superb cruise between New Ross and Waterford.

WATERFORD: Route N25 leads to Waterford, another former Viking settlement. Reginald's Tower, a fortification built by Reginald the Dane in 1003, is now a museum. Beautiful eighteenth-century Christ Church Cathedral is also a tourist attraction (open Monday, Wednesday, and Friday afternoons in the summer). Above all, the city is famous for the crystal that bears its name, and a visit to the Waterford glass factory is a must. The original plant opened in 1783, and the fine glass, exported throughout the world, quickly made its reputation. There was a 100-year hiatus in production when the industry as a whole went into decline, but in 1951 the factory reopened and has since outgrown its buildings several times. Today the company employs 2,000 people and hosts an average of 3,000 visitors a week who watch the batch mixers, pot fillers, and master blowers in action (open Mondays through Fridays; closed the first 2 weeks in August; children under 12 not admitted; phone: 3311).

From Waterford take Route N9 to Kilkenny.

KILKENNY: This ancient and historic city is dominated by two beautifully preserved major buildings. The thirteenth-century Cathedral of St. Canice marks the spot of an even older monastery from which the city grew, and a climb up Round Tower beside the cathedral offers fine views of the city and surrounding countryside. Dominating the view and everything else in sight is the magnificently preserved Norman palace on the banks of the River Nore, Kilkenny's second treasure. Before the Normans came, the city was the capital of the kingdom of Ossory. In the fourteenth century, the existing Ossory palace was taken over — and then taken apart — by the Normans, who raised in its place the castle that has stood, defiant of time, ever since. Across the road, in its former stables, is the Kilkenny Design Workshop, where government-subsidized artisans create models for industrial and consumer products, developing Irish designs in various media including silver, copper, textiles, and pottery. Visitors are not allowed in the workshops, but splendid showrooms sell products from jewelry to full-fashioned garments. As in Wexford, there are marvelous walking tours of the city. Ask at the tourist office at Shee Alms House, Rose Inn St. (phone: 2-1755).

Take Route T6 going south from Kilkenny and join T37 at Ballymack, continuing to Cashel in County Tipperary.

CASHEL: Dominating the market town that bears its name is the Rock of Cashel — Cashel of the Kings — the history of which spans sixteen centuries. From the fourth century, the kings of the province of Munster were crowned on this 300-foot limestone rock and had their palace here. St. Patrick preached Christianity on the site in 450. In the twelfth century, King Murtagh O'Brien gave his palace to the Church and began a period of great ecclesiastical building. Even the now roofless buildings retain their grandeur, but Cormac's Chapel, still roofed, is a gem of twelfth-century Hiberno-Romanesque architecture (open daily; small admission charge). The lovely Queen Anne deanery, built for the archbishop in the eighteenth century, is now a hotel — *The Cashel Palace* — with a fine restaurant. Craft shops flourish on Cahir Road. Outstanding are *Rossa Pottery*, where they make delicate glazed objects, and *Shanagarry Weavers*. There is excellent trout fishing on the River Suir (permits can be obtained at the tourist office, Town Hall). From Cashel, Route N8 leads south to Cahir.

CAHIR: Cahir Castle, dominating the Suir, is one of the largest and most splendid medieval castles in Ireland. Restored, it is open to the public.

En Route from Cahir – Follow Route N8 out of Cahir to Mitchelstown and N73 to Mallow. To the left rise the Knockmealdown Mountains; on the right are the Galtees. The rich fishing waters of the Blackwater make Mallow a popular angling and hunting center. From Mallow, N20 goes south to Cork city.

CORK: The name Corcaigh means "marshy place," an apt description of its state for centuries after St. Finbarre founded a monastery here in the sixth century where Cork University now stands. (Cork's patron saint is honored in the lovely neo-Gothic Protestant cathedral of St. Finbarre.) Today the city straddles the two branches of the River Lee without getting its feet wet, only to be expected in a city of 120,000 people, the Republic's second largest metropolitan area. Cork's excellent shopping center offers many goods. Major department stores are on Patrick Street; one of the best is *Munster Arcade*. Small shops and boutiques abound on Princess and Oliver Plunkett streets. The Cork Craftsman's Guild (Patrick St.) was organized to foster the merchandizing of crafts. Walking-tour maps are available from the tourist office (Grand Parade). The city also has an active cultural life: a drama festival in March, the International Choral Festival in April-May, and the Cork International Film Festival in September. There is a good ballet company, operatic society, and theater company. The Cork Literary and Scientific Society is the oldest of its kind in Ireland; its Historical and Archaeological Society is renowned.

Two trips from Cork should not be missed, one to Blarney Castle and the other to Kinsale.

BLARNEY: Route L60 leads to Blarney, only 6 miles (10 km) away. Few people in the English-speaking world have not heard of the Blarney Stone, which is said to confer the gift of eloquence on all who kiss it. The gift is well earned, however, for the stone juts out just under the battlement, which means you have to lie on your back far above a sheer drop and, with a guide holding your legs, stretch to your utmost to touch lips to stone. The view of the pretty castle park from the tower is better than the kiss. Both castle and park are open daily. The small village of Blarney, attractive in its own right, boasts a craft shopping center offering high-quality products at reasonable prices.

KINSALE: With its narrow streets, tall houses and stormy history, this attractive little town 17 miles (27 km) south of Cork is a requisite stop for lovers of good food — "the culinary capital of Ireland." There is, for the town's size, an extraordinary range of really top-class restaurants whose proprietors have banded together in a Good Food Circle that holds an annual Gourmet Festival.

BEST EN ROUTE

The southeastern region has some very good hotels and restaurants and a great many that are fair to mediocre. The listing here considers only the best in both accommodations and cuisine.

Expect to pay $50 or more per night for a double in one of the hotels or inns listed as expensive; from $35 to $50 in the moderate range; under $35 in those places listed as inexpensive. Meals at even the best restaurants are reasonable. We have categorized as expensive a meal for two that costs $40; $20 to $30 falls into the moderate range; and you can have quite good meals for as little as $10 to $20 for two in inexpensive

spots. Reservations for hotels are a must everywhere during the tourist season and at
other times when there are special festivals.

WEXFORD

White's Hotel – This topnotch, centrally located hotel has 55 rooms (50 with bath
or shower). The restaurant is competent, and there is a good quick-service grill.
The seafood is particularly good. Abbey St. (phone: 2-2311). Moderate.

Talbot Hotel – Although it is generally considered quite nice, the quality of the
rooms does vary. There are 111 rooms, only 87 with bath or shower. The hotel's
sports complex includes squash courts and an indoor heated swimming pool.
Trinity St. (phone: 2-2566). Moderate.

Killiane Castle – Kathleen Mernagh runs this gracious guesthouse set on 230 acres.
Both rooms and apartments are available, and there's a seventeenth-century tower
on the grounds. Off the Rosslare Harbour Rd., Drinagh (phone: 2-2272). Inexpensive.

NEW ROSS

Galley Cruising Restaurant – This intriguing restaurant on a boat prepares fresh
produce with appealing flair, but much of the appeal is the cruise itself —
a long munch through the New Ross–Waterford River valleys. Bridge Way
(phone: 2-1723). Moderate.

WATERFORD

Ardree Hotel – With its imposing position high above Waterford, the 100 spacious
rooms of this modern hotel all have views over the city. The bar is pleasant; the
restaurant is only adequate, and you will probably want to eat out. Ferrybank
(phone: 3-2111). Moderate.

Tower Hotel – Centrally located beside historic Reginald's Tower, this pleasant
hotel has 81 rooms that are particularly well furnished. The big dining room is
very good and the standard of service is high. The Mall (phone: 7-5801). Moderate.

KILKENNY

Newpark Hotel – This comfortable and modern hotel with attractive decor is known
for its friendly service. There are 45 rooms, 38 with bath. The dining room is small
but quite good. Castlecomer Rd. (phone: 2-2122). Moderate.

CASHEL

Cashel Palace – This elegant Queen Anne building, formerly an archbishop's
residence, is set amid beautiful formal gardens in the town center. It has 20 rooms
with bath. Its restaurant is quite good. Main St. (phone: 6-1411). Expensive.

CAHIR

Earl of Glengall – This restaurant serves tasty pub lunches and more formal dinners
at very reasonable prices. Its cuisine is Irish and Continental. The Square (phone:
4-1115). Expensive to moderate.

Kilcoran Lodge – A few miles outside Cahir, on the right side of the Mitchelstown
Road, this former shooting lodge is a charming country hotel on the slopes of the
Galtee Mountains. It has 22 rooms, 14 with bath. The cuisine in the airy dining
room is good (phone: Cahir 261). Moderate.

MALLOW

Longueville House – This 18-bedroom Georgian mansion overlooks the lovely
River Blackwater, where guests may fish. The restaurant features home-grown
produce superbly cooked by the owner. Reservations essential (phone: 2-7156).

CORK

Arbutus Lodge – Although it is an elegant mansion amid gardens overlooking the city and river, it is considered a grade B hotel because its 20 rooms are on the small side with minuscule bathrooms. There is a patio and bar for summer lunch. Famous for its cuisine, the restaurant is run by food and wine enthusiasts for enthusiasts. Montenotte (phone: 50-12-37). Expensive.

Jury's Hotel – It has 140 comfortable, modern rooms, all with bath, radio, and TV. The *Vintage Room* is an elegant dining room with fine cuisine; the *Coffee Dock* is also pleasant. Western Rd. (phone: 96-63-77). Expensive.

Silver Springs Hotel – This modern hotel is at the edge of the city center. Many of its 72 rooms have a fine view over the city. The dining room, however, is only fair. Glanmire Rd. (phone: 50-75-33). Expensive.

Imperial Hotel – This grande dame in the city center has an air of faded grandeur, but it is being refurbished. Some of the 80 rooms are splendid; others are in need of a face-lifting. The dining room offers very competent international cuisine; the grill is less satisfactory. South Mall (phone: 96-53-33). Expensive to moderate.

Oyster Tavern – This is a traditional chophouse and an inner-city favorite. The whitebait and sole are memorable. Busy, so you may have to wait in the bar, which is pleasant. Market La., off Patrick St. (phone: 22-71-61). Moderate.

KINSALE

White Lady Inn Hotel – The hotel has only 10 rooms, none with bath. But its restaurant in this restaurant town is great. A member of the Good Food Circle, it has an excellent choice of fish and steaks. During high season there is nightly entertainment. Lower O'Connell St. (phone: 7-2381). Moderate.

The Blue Haven Hotel – This is a small, cozy hotel, with 12 rooms, 1 with bath. Here again, the dining room is the big attraction. Fresh produce and seafood dishes are the specialty of the house. The wood-paneled bar has log fires going; emphasis is on personal service. Pearce St. (phone: 7-2209). Moderate to inexpensive.

The Vintage – This vine-covered, beamed little restaurant stands in a winding street near the harbor. The cooking is French, with particular emphasis on local produce. Closed Tuesdays and Wednesdays November to February. Main St. (phone: 7-2502). Expensive to moderate.

Skippers Restaurant and Wine Bar – Another member of the Kinsale Good Food Circle, this intimate restaurant specializes in seafood. Closed Mondays. Near the pier fronting on Lower O'Connell St. (phone: 7-2664). Moderate.

Southwest Ireland: Cork to Killarney

Artists and writers have for centuries celebrated the beauty of the Kingdom of Kerry, where the majesty of Ireland's highest mountains contrasts starkly with its romantic glens and the splendor of the rugged coastline gives way to glorious lakes and luxurious forests. It is a landscape of infinite variety and constantly changing colors. Basically, the mountainous southern part of Kerry consists of the three large peninsulas of Beara, Iveragh, and Dingle; the smaller northern part is an area of undulating plain that stretches as far as the Shannon estuary. Along the coast, sandy bays alternate with cliffs and rocky headlands; the inland scenery includes the beautiful lakes of Killarney.

But scenic beauty is by no means Kerry's only attraction. Its many coastal resorts, climbable mountains, excellent fishing waters, good golf courses, and a wealth of ancient monuments make the southwest a paradise for sight-seeing or sports-loving travelers.

There are lively, cheerful towns where pub regulars have formed semi-formal singing groups, small fishing towns where the lilt of the ancient Irish tongue is on most lips, remote and lovely places where time has stood still.

This route concentrates on Kerry's great peninsulas: Beara, which it shares with Cork; Iveragh, famous as the Ring of Kerry, the complete scenic circuit around the peninsula; and Dingle, the most northerly promontory, which stretches 30 miles west from the low-lying country around Tralee to mountain ranges that turn to wild, deserted hills and lead to magnificent coastal scenery. You should allow 3 days and nights for the tour. If your time is limited, make sure you don't miss the Ring of Kerry, roughly a 110-mile (176-km) round trip from Killarney. To see it leisurely will take most of 1 day.

CORK: For a description of the city, see the previous route.

En Route from Cork – Route T29 takes you along the north bank of the River Lee and passes through the picturesque villages of Dripsey, with its woolen mills, and Coachford.

MACROOM: This thriving market town, worth a quick visit, is set amid a large Irish-speaking district, and on market day Irish can be heard everywhere. The ruined castle, reached via the market square, stands at the center of town.

En Route from Macroom – Go back 1 mile (1.6 km) on the Cork road, T64, and turn left for Inchigeelagh. Past Inchigeelagh the road hugs the north bank of the long and lovely Lough Allua. But the minor road along the south bank is even more beautiful, so that's the one you should take. Make a right turn 3.7 miles (6 km) beyond Ballingeary, where the sign reads: Gougane Barra.

GOUGANE BARRA: The mountain-encircled lake of Gougane Barra, source of the River Lee, is where St. Finbar, the founder of Cork, had his hermitage in the sixth century. It has a splendid forest park with extensive nature trails.

Return to T64. Continue southwest as the road descends via Keimaneigh Pass and the Ouvane Valley to Ballylickey and Glengarriff.

GLENGARRIFF: The name means "the rough glen" and is only partially true of this lovely village on the Beara Peninsula snuggled into a deeply wooded glen. There is nothing rough about this glen, and sheltered as it is from any harsh winds, the village has a justly famous reputation for mild weather and tropical vegetation. Some of the plants and trees that flourish here are arbutus, eucalyptus, fuchsia, rhododendron, and blue-eyed grass. There is excellent sea and river fishing in and around the town, and bathing is good along the nearby coves, one of which, Poulgorm ("blue pool"), is a picturesque spot with a fine view — just a 2-minute walk from the village post office. There are tennis courts, a golf course, and unlimited terrain for riding and walking.

En Route from Glengarriff – If pressed for time, continue directly to Kenmare via N71. Otherwise follow the spectacular Healy Pass road, which is 17 miles (27 km) longer. From Glengarriff this follows L61 along the south coast of mountainous Beara, the least-frequented of the three great southwestern peninsulas. At the foot of the Caha Mountains is Adrigole village. Hungry Hill, from which Daphne du Maurier took the title of her novel, looms to the northwest. At the schoolhouse in Adrigole turn right when you come to the sign: Healy Pass.

HEALY PASS: This road, opened in 1931, was built at the direction of Tim Healy, the first governor-general of the Irish Free State. It climbs to a height of 1,084 feet as it crosses the Caha Mountains, the border between County Cork and County Kerry, and provides magnificent views over Sheep's Head and Mizen Head to the south and Kenmare River and the mountains of the Iveragh Peninsula to the north.

LAURAGH: The Healy Pass road descends to join the scenic sea road, L62, at Lauragh. Close to this village is the estate of Derreen House, whose beautiful subtropical gardens are open to visitors Sunday, Tuesday, and Thursday afternoons; April through September. Not far from Lauragh are the Cloonee Lakes, stocked with salmon and sea and brown trout. Route L62 continues along the coast to Kenmare.

KENMARE: This small town, at the head of the Kenmare River where the Roughty River meets the sea, has the mild climate common to the south coast. It is an excellent center from which to tour both the Beara and Iveragh peninsulas. There is bathing in the sheltered coves west of the town, salmon and brown trout fishing, and boating in the bay. Kenmare is also noted for its lacemaking; a famous point lace is made and exhibited at the convent of the Poor Clare nuns. Other sites of interest include a ring of prehistoric stones, called the Druid's Circle, about one-quarter mile southwest of town, and St. Finan's Holy Well nearby, which is reputed to have healing powers.

Kenmare is the site for the Fruits de Mer Festival (usually held in September), which features deep-sea fishing, seafood exhibitions and banquets, and a wide range of entertainment.

The most direct road to Killarney is Route T65(N71), over the mountains to Molls Gap, via Ladies View, a lookout point with a panoramic view of the wonderful lakes of Killarney before entering the city. A more circuitous route is the famous Ring of Kerry road that encircles the Iveragh Peninsula by way of Templenoe and Parknasilla. Take N70 from Kenmare.

PARKNASILLA: Renowned for its lush vegetation, this estate is the grounds of the beautiful *Great Southern Hotel,* a favorite holiday place of George Bernard Shaw.

SNEEM: This pretty town, where the Dutch royal family has vacationed, lies amid equally pretty scenery at the head of the Sneem River estuary. There is very good fishing here: Brown trout, salmon, and sea trout abound in the river and nearby mountain lakes. You'll want to stop at the *Blue Bull* — a quite pleasant country pub and restaurant — if only for a quick drink to see its collection of art by contemporary Irish artists. An anomaly in the collection is the death mask of James Joyce.

STAIGUE FORT: Beyond Sneem, the Ring of Kerry road winds inland for a few miles through wild scenery, meeting the coast again at Castlecove, a peaceful retreat near a fine sandy beach. Here, make a right turn at a small sign: Staigue Fort. About 1.5 miles (2.5 km) north are the imposing ruins of a circular stone fort, which could date back as far as 1,000 BC, that is one of Ireland's finest archaeological remains. Its rough stones are held in place without mortar.

CAHERDANIEL: Back on the coast road, past Westcove, is the village of Caherdaniel, near the shore of Derrynane Bay. In the vicinity is the curious hermitage of St. Crohane, hewn out of solid rock. About a mile away is another unmortared stone fort. Nearby is Derrynane House, once the home of Daniel O'Connell, "the Liberator," who gained the emancipation of Irish Catholics in 1829. The house, now restored, contains a museum with O'Connell's personal possessions and furniture. The house is part of Derrynane National Historic Park, with a nature trail through fine scenery. It is open to the public all year.

En Route from Caherdaniel – Route N70 climbs to a height of 700 feet at the Pass of Coomakista and offers a superb view. While the inland mountains rise sharply — to 1,600 feet — on one side, the lonely Skellig Rocks can be seen on the other in the open Atlantic. Skellig Michael bears the remains of a sixth-century monastery; it can be reached on a calm day from Portmagee. On the descent from

Coomakista, Ballinskelligs Bay comes into view, with the village of Waterville nestling in its curve.

WATERVILLE: This small, unspoiled village lies between the Atlantic and beautiful Lough Currane on the eastern shore of Ballinskelligs Bay. On the east and south, mountains rise from Lough Currane, reaching 2,000 feet on the east side; in the lake itself float several islands, and in addition to Currane, there are many smaller lakes in the vicinity. With all this water, Waterville is a famous angling center almost by default, and no aquatic pursuit is ignored. There is boating, bathing from the fine sandy beach on the bay shore, and, for resolute landlubbers, golfing on a championship course.

En Route from Waterville – Follow either the coastal Route N70 back to Caherdaniel and on to Glenbeigh or take one of the splendid mountain roads to Glencar and Glenbeigh. The latter is recommended. At New Chapel Cross, 1.5 miles (2.5 km) outside Waterville, leave N70 for an unclassified road to the Pass of Ballaghisheen. At a point between Bealalaw Bridge and Lough Acoose, a left turn leads to Caragh Lake and descends to rejoin N70 at Caragh Bridge. A right turn continues to Killorglin, famous for its Puck Fair (every August the town holds a 3-day festival during which a goat is enthroned as King Puck to preside over a cattle, sheep, and horse fair. Shops are open day and night. Thousands of people come from all parts of Kerry). From Killorglin, take T67 to Killarney. A left turn leads to Glenbeigh.

GLENBEIGH: At the entrance to a semicircle of mountains known as the Glenbeigh Horseshoe, where the Behy River flows into Dingle Bay, the town nestles at the foot of Seefin Mountain (1,621 feet). The scenery here is magnificent, and the circuit of hills from Seefin to Drung Hill (the horseshoe) is one of Kerry's finest mountain walks, with glacial corries and lakes throughout and fabulous trout fishing in innumerable rivers and lakes.

En Route from Killorglin – Follow N70 to Castlemaine, where L103 takes you into the Dingle Peninsula, a thriving center of Gaelic language and culture, rich in archaeological remains. This peninsula has been the setting for movies and should be familiar to filmgoers who have seen *Ryan's Daughter.*

INCH: Not far from the head of Dingle Bay, on the south side of the peninsula, lies the sheltered seaside resort of Inch. Its name to the contrary, the town is a 4-mile strip of firm golden sand that provides excellent bathing. The beach is backed by dunes that have yielded evidence of very early habitations.

DINGLE TOWN: The peninsula's chief town lies at the foot of a steep slope on the north side of the harbor and is bounded on three sides by hills. It was the main port of Kerry in the old Spanish trading days, and in the reign of Queen Elizabeth I it was important enough as an outpost to merit a protective wall. It has always been a fishing town; deep-sea fishing facilities are excellent. There is also good bathing and pony trekking into the surrounding hills. It is the gateway to the West Kerry Gaeltacht, the Irish-speaking district, and a good base for extended exploration of this rich area.

En Route from Dingle – The road continues to Ventry, with its delightful beach. To the right of the road beyond Ventry are signs for "beehive huts." These lead to groups of small stone buildings shaped like beehives, constructed without mortar on a corbel principle. They generally served as monks' cells in early Irish monasteries. Since the ancient method of construction is still in use, it is often difficult to distinguish the old from the recent.

The road from Dingle continues to Slea Head at the tip of the peninsula, where the view of the Blasket Islands, the westernmost point in Europe (except for Iceland), is spectacular.

THE BLASKETS: This is a group of seven islands in the Atlantic. The largest, the Great Blasket, is about 4 miles long and .75 mile wide. Now uninhabited, it used to be known as "the next parish to America" when it had a village settlement. The

Blaskets were inhabited from prehistoric times by an Irish-speaking community that gradually thinned out until, in 1953, the last islanders moved to the mainland. Many islanders were exponents of the art of Seanachai, or storytelling. Three books have been written about island life: *Twenty Years A-growing,* by Maurice O'Sullivan; *The Islander,* by Thomas Crohan; and *Peig,* by Peig Sayers — all Blasket islanders. Boats to the Blaskets can be hired in Dunquin, north of Slea Head.

En Route from Slea Head – The road continues through Dunquin and Ballyferriter. About 1.5 miles (2.5 km) northeast is Gallerus Oratory, one of the best-preserved ninth-century buildings in Ireland. Although it is built of unmortared stone, it is completely watertight after more than 1,000 years.

Return to Dingle via Ballyferriter. To get to Tralee, go over the Conair (also called Connor) Pass if it's a clear day. Driving this road demands great care; it should be avoided in bad weather. Leave Dingle by the unclassified road marked Conair Pass, climbing northeasterly between the Brandon and Dingle mountains. At the summit (1,500 feet) is a breathtaking view: the bays of Brandon and Tralee to the north, Dingle Bay and Dingle town to the south, and the lakes in the deep valley to the left. The road then winds down along the base of great cliffs and ultimately goes through a valley of boulder-strewn wilderness. In the town of Camp, take adjoining T68 for Tralee.

TRALEE: This friendly, busy trading center is one of the most active towns in southern Ireland. There is salmon and trout fishing in its rivers, excellent deep-sea fishing, a choice of superb beaches, sailing, skin diving, riding, and golf. Throughout the summer, the Ashe Memorial Theatre is the scene of Siamsa (pronounced "she-amsa"), a folk theater that brings to life, through mime, music, song, and dance, the customs of the Irish countryside. Inquire for details at the tourist office (32 the Mall; phone: 2-1288). The Irish Ballet Company also performs here regularly. The greatest attraction of the town, however, is undoubtedly the Festival of Kerry at the end of August. This week-long event is described as "the greatest free show on earth." Its highlight is the crowning of the Rose of Tralee, the loveliest Irish girl in the world. Throughout the festival the town is brilliantly lit; every street is the scene of some outdoor entertainment or sporting event.

KILLARNEY: This city is one of the major destinations of most visitors, in good part because of the unrivaled beauty of its location. Three main lakes are in a broad valley stretching south between mountains: Nearest town is the Lower Lake, the largest of the three; the peninsula of Muckross separates it from the Middle Lake, which is connected with the Upper Lake by a narrow strait called the Long Range. The lakes are surrounded by luxuriant woods of oak, arbutus, birch, holly, and mountain ash, among which grow ferns, mosses, and other plants. Besides the three main lakes, there is Lough Guitane, 4 miles southeast, and innumerable small tarns hidden in the folds of mountains and in rockbeds. Around Killarney the effects of the Ice Age are everywhere; ice-smoothed rocks abound in the glens and among deep grooves and channels carved by glacial action.

Part of Killarney's lake district lies within the 11,000-acre Bourne Vincent Memorial Park, once a private estate and in 1932 presented to the government, which promptly made it a national park. Muckross House, a nineteenth-century manor, is now a folk museum with a blacksmith, weaver, potter, and harness maker at work.

South of the city is the Gap of Dunloe, a magnificent gorge that runs for 4 miles between Macgillicuddy's Reeks and the Purple Mountains. Killarney tours, especially the journey through the gap, must be made on ponies, by pony trap, or on foot. In the park, horse-drawn jaunting cars are available. The gap tour includes a boat ride that, in turn, requires some shooting of rapids to traverse the three lakes.

Not the least of the area's attractions is Killarney itself, a lively town dominated by the beautiful nineteenth-century Catholic Cathedral of St. Mary in New Street. There are two championship golf courses nearby and a racetrack.

BEST EN ROUTE

The southwest is the most visited area in Ireland. That means that hotels of all degrees from luxurious to plain are plentiful, but rooms are always in demand. Book well in advance, and expect to pay somewhat more than in other parts of Ireland. The good news is that the hotels in the area are excellent (the one exception is Tralee, where neither accommodations nor restaurants warrant a lot of enthusiasm, but where the pubs are simply wonderful) and well versed in dealing with excited and overawed visitors. Many activities associated with the southwest — pony treks and fishing, long hikes in the mountains and deep-sea expeditions — can be arranged through hotels.

There is a wide range of prices in the hotels and restaurants. Certainly there are many lovely bed and breakfast hotels, with extremely reasonable rates, but for the luxurious resorts that are scattered around the route (an example might be the *Europe* in Killarney), rates can jump to $75 a night for a double in the middle of summer. That's still cheap compared to an international hotel in Stockholm, but for Ireland it's pricey.

In general, expect to pay around $60 per night for a double in those places listed as expensive; from $40 to $60 in the moderate range; and under $40 in the inexpensive. A restaurant listed as expensive will charge as much as $40 for a meal for two; between $20 and $35 in the moderate range; and under $20 for two in the inexpensive category. Prices don't include wine, drinks, or tips.

KENMARE

Park Hotel – More like being offered the hospitality of a friend's fine old country estate than staying at a hotel. The 50 rooms and suites are individually decorated with lovely pieces (in one room is a sleigh bed; in another, a four-poster), and everywhere elegance is enhanced by typical Irish warmth. The formal yet friendly atmosphere prevails in the dining room as well, where the kitchen turns out admirable Continental cuisine. Next door is a nine-hole golf course, and riding stables and salmon fishing are nearby (phone: 41200). Expensive.

Kenmare Bay Hotel – During the Fruits de Mer festival, the hotel can be very busy. It has 68 airy and modern rooms, a pleasant bar, and a good restaurant. Closed January and February. Sneem Rd. (phone: 4-1300). Moderate.

The Purple Heather Bistro – Seafood is a specialty of the house, with meals served in the comfortable bar. Closed Sundays and late October to March. Henry St. (phone: 4-1016). Moderate.

Riversdale House – The 40 rooms here (all with bath) are large but sparsely furnished. The premises, however, are modern. The dining room fare is quite good, as is the service (phone: 4-1299). Moderate.

PARKNASILLA

Great Southern Hotel – One of George Bernard Shaw's favorite vacation spots, this beautiful hotel on a lush estate is splendid all around. There are 60 rooms with bath, a private golf course for guests, a heated indoor swimming pool, and fishing or boating on the bay. The cuisine is superb (phone: 4-5122). Expensive.

SNEEM

The Blue Bull – A combination pub and restaurant, the place serves good food wherever you eat it, but the pub grub is extra good, and that's rare. The restaurant's food is French provincial. The premises serve as a kind of art gallery, specializing in modern art by Irish artists. Pub open year-round; restaurant closed October to April. S Square (phone: 4-5231). Moderate.

WATERVILLE

Waterville Lake Hotel – This deluxe resort lies in a setting of unparalleled beauty on the shores of lovely Lough Currane within a stone's throw of the sea. Completely refurbished in 1985, it has 32 rooms, 18 luxurious suites, and a fine restaurant. Other amenities include an 18-hole championship golf course, heated indoor pool, thermal spa pool, sauna, and solarium. Open May through September (phone: 4133).

GLENBEIGH

The Towers Hotel – The 22 recently refurbished rooms with bath are fairly comfortable, but the real glory of the hotel is its superb restaurant. Although *The Towers* was recently sold, it is expected that the high standards here will be maintained. Closed November to March (phone: 12). Expensive.

The Glenbeigh Hotel – Here the beauty is in the gardens. There are 18 Old World rooms, 11 with bath, and the restaurant is good (phone: Glenbeigh 4). Expensive to moderate.

DINGLE

The Sceilig – This modern hotel has 80 comfortable rooms and a heated outdoor swimming pool. The restaurant is particularly good for seafood. Closed November to mid-March (phone: 5-1144). Moderate.

TRALEE

Earl of Desmond – This 52-room hotel, too, is modern and is about a mile outside town. The restaurant is fair (phone: 2-1299). Expensive.

Ballygarry House Hotel – This recently refurbished country inn with private garden has 16 individually decorated rooms, all with private bath, and a Continental restaurant. Leebrook (phone: 2-1233). Moderate.

The Brandon Hotel – It is centrally located and modern, with 162 rooms with private bath, dining room, coffee shop, and nightclub (phone: 2-1311). Moderate.

Tralee Bay – In the lovely seaside town of Castlegregory, 14 miles (22 km) from Tralee, is this small — 13 rooms, 6 with bath — hotel, of modest decor but warm atmosphere. Castlegregory (phone: 3-9138). Moderate.

Tralee Pubs – *The Oyster Tavern,* The Spa, west of Tralee (phone: 3-6102).
The Brogue Inn, Rock St. (phone: 2-2126).
The Pig & Whistle, Rock St. (phone: 2-1894).
The Abbey Inn, Bridge St. (phone: 2-2084).
The Bridge Inn, Bridge St. (phone: 2-1827).
The Tavern, Boherbue (phone: 2-1161).

KILLARNEY

Killarney Great Southern Hotel – The oldest hotel in town has 180 comfortable rooms, but some in the modern wing are smallish. The public rooms are very elegant. The dining room is splendid (phone: 3-1262). Expensive.

The Europe – Like its name, this hotel is more European than Irish. (It is German-owned, which may explain it.) With a marvelous location on the shore of one of the Killarney lakes, it has all the amenities of a luxury hotel — a heated indoor pool in a health complex that includes a sauna. The 168 rooms vary in size and degree of luxury. The hotel has two restaurants: The main dining room and a more intimate second room are good but not wildly exciting. Closed December, January, and February. Fossa (phone: 3-1900). Expensive.

Dunloe Castle – This is a sister to the *Europe,* and is not an old Irish fortress but a modern hotel. (The actual Dunloe Castle is on the grounds, however.) The *Dunloe Castle* is somewhat smaller than the *Europe,* with 140 rooms, and other amenities include a heated indoor pool, sauna, tennis courts, and croquet. Open April through October. Beaufort (phone: 4-4111). Moderate.

Aghadoe Heights – This modern hotel is small — 55 rooms that are less than luxurious but make up for it with fine lake views. The service is friendly. The restaurant is quite good. Aghadoe (phone: 3-1766). Moderate.

Ross – In the center of town, this family-owned and -run hotel is warm, relaxed, and friendly. The restaurant is simple, but good, and the service pleasant. There are 42 rooms, 26 with bath. Killarney (phone: 3-1855). Moderate.

The Midwest Counties: Limerick and Clare

Limerick is a county of rolling grassland south of the River Shannon estuary. It is a rich agricultural area, particularly in the east, where it is known as the Golden Vale. The majestic Shannon drains the fertile pasturelands, making them ideal for dairy farming. This is countryside with a quiet beauty: Low hill ranges dot the plains; small towns rise here and there, each with its ruined castle or abbey and ancient bridge. Some of Ireland's best fox hunting is in this county, home also of many stud farms.

The huge Shannon estuary separates Limerick from County Clare to the north. Clare provides a stark contrast to the rural beauty of Limerick. Stone is the keynote of the landscape; it predominates everywhere. Along the west coast, spectacular slate and limestone cliffs drop to the incoming Atlantic, forming a coast of spectacular bluffs. To the north this rugged coast rises nearly 700 feet above the sea in the sheer Cliffs of Moher. Inland rises the Burren, a vast series of limestone terraces that shelter many caves and underground streams and a confusing profusion of both Arctic and Mediterranean vegetation, neither of which is usually found in these latitudes.

Limerick is the gateway to the Irish Republic for travelers landing at Shannon International Airport, only 15 miles away (in County Clare), 30 minutes by car or bus. Many tourists are routed to the south or northwest from Dublin via Limerick. The Dublin to Limerick leg is 123 miles (198 km), about 3½ hours' driving time.

The following route starts at Killarney, going generally north, with some backtracking and detours. It can be done in 2 days with time planned for one of the medieval Shannon castle banquets. The overnight stay could be in Limerick or Ennis.

KILLARNEY: For a description of the city, see the previous route.

En Route from Killarney – You have a choice of two equally pleasant routes: through Listowel, Tarbert, and Askeaton — the Limerick road along the Shannon — or the inland route through Newcastle West and Adare. You can also combine the routes to see the most interesting parts of each. The route that follows is a combination: the estuary road to Askeaton, turning inland at Askeaton to Adare.

Leave Killarney on N22 for Tralee. Continue on N69 through literary Listowel, where a writers' conference is held for a week every June, with performances of plays by Kerry authors and literary get-togethers. About 11 miles (18 km) north, at Tarbert, is the 60-mile-long estuary of the River Shannon. At the dairy town of Glin, you enter County Limerick. Glin is the site of beautiful eighteenth-century Glin Castle, which has a craft shop and tearoom. Askeaton is another picturesque old town with some notable ruins: Fifteenth-century Askeaton Castle straddles the steep banks of the River Deel; a Franciscan friary stands on the banks of the river, and in its Protestant cemetery are the chancel and belfry of St. Mary's Church.

From Askeaton, turn off the main road onto L36, going inland through Rathkeale, a busy market town. On the way out of town, on the right, are the ruins of the thirteenth-century Augustin priory of St. Mary's.

At Rathkeale, turn east onto N21. About 7 miles (11 km) northeast is the enchanting village of Adare, its thatched cottages and lichened medieval churches surrounded by woods on the River Maigue. The finest of the monastic ruins here is the fifteenth-century Franciscan friary on the estate of the earl of Dunraven, the nineteenth-century manor house and the grounds of which are open to the public. Among other noteworthy ruins are the fourteenth-century Adare Castle, thirteenth-century Trinitarian Abbey (incorporated into the town's Catholic church), and the fourteenth-century Augustin priory, now part of the town's Protestant church. Route N21 continues northeast to Limerick, about 11 miles (18 km).

LIMERICK CITY: The fourth largest city in Ireland (pop. 145,000) offers an appropriately engaging introduction to the country for those many, many visitors who begin journeys here after the short half-hour trip in from Shannon Airport. Limerick is a major port, an inevitable product of its enviable position on the River Shannon; and while the city has a reputation for industry, those it is most famous for are all amiably light: traditional Limerick lace, still produced here; wonderfully cured hams and bacon; salmon fishing; and flour milling.

Limerick is a city of wide streets, handsome Georgian houses, and impressive public buildings such as the Custom House and the Town Hall.

This gracious architecture hardly reflects its violent history. It was occupied by the Danes in the ninth century and taken by the Anglo-Normans toward the end of the twelfth century. In 1210, King John ordered the building of a strong castle and Shannon Bridge to control the crossing point of the river. In later centuries the city walls were extended for security. In the seventeenth century the city was torn between revolts by the Irish who seized the city and sieges by the English to bring them to their knees. The Treaty of Limerick in 1691 was to end hostilities and grant political and religious liberty to the Irish and the Catholics, but repeated violations of the treaty forced thousands into exile. The Treaty Stone, on which the pact was signed, stands on Thomond Bridge near King John's Castle; beside the castle is twelfth-century St. Mary's Cathedral. This Church of Ireland structure is architecturally interesting; inside is an unusual collection of fifteenth-century misericords, oak carvings from choir stalls. Remnants of the old city walls, bearing the marks of cannon, can be seen near St. John's Hospital. Also worth a visit is the Limerick lace collection in the Good Shepherd Convent (Clare St.).

But as befits a city that is the major gateway to Ireland, contemporary Limerick has a great deal to offer visitors besides its ancient sites. A roster of activities includes racing three times weekly at the city track; salmon and trout fishing at Castleconnell, 8 miles (13 km) away, and brown trout and grilse fishing on the River Mulcair, 4 miles (6.5 km) away; horse racing at Greenpark on Lower Killarney Road and Limerick Junction, 21 miles (33 km) out of town; golf at Ballyclough and at Castletroy, 3 miles (5 km) away; and swimming and boating on the River Shannon.

En Route from Limerick – As soon as you leave the city on N18 going west, you are in County Clare. Some 12 miles (20 km) from Limerick you pass *Bunratty*

Castle. This splendidly restored fifteenth-century castle is open to the public daily, as is the park on the castle grounds, where visitors can see typical Shannon houses through the ages and watch traditional skills such as candle making, bread baking, and iron forging. Raucous medieval banquets — food and entertainment — are held nightly in the castle. These require reservations through Shannon Castle Tours (phone: 6-1444, 6-1788).

Beyond the castle, just before the road turns north, N19 branches off to the left to Shannon Airport. Continuing on N18 to Ennis, another 12 miles (19 km), you pass through Newmarket-on-Fergus.

ENNIS: Friendly, narrow-streeted Ennis is County Clare's capital. It is a progressive business and marketing center, but of greater interest to the visitor are the remains of several abbeys in and around town: Ennis Abbey, built in the thirteenth century and remodeled through the fifteenth century, a mixture of architectural styles; Clare Abbey, a twelfth-century Augustin priory; and Killone Abbey, from the same period.

En Route from Ennis – Take Route T70 west through hilly Ennistymon, where the little river Cullenagh falls in cascades through the town center. Here join T69 to get to Lahinch, a resort with a mile-long beach, excellent for bathing and surfing. There is an indoor entertainment center for the unpredictable Irish weather and a challenging golf course, and periwinkles and dilisk are sold in twists of newspapers along the promenade. Route L54 in Lahinch leads to the fishing village of Liscannor and 3 miles (4.8 km) west (a sign indicates the turnoff) are the Cliffs of Moher, one of the outstanding features of County Clare. Rising nearly 700 feet above the sea and extending about 5 miles along the coast, they provide magnificent views — especially from O'Brian's Tower (a short climb from the car park) at their northern end. From here you can see the Aran Islands to the north and, on a clear day, across Galway Bay all the way to Connemara.

LISDOONVARNA: Ireland's only surviving spa is in the hilly Burren country of north Clare, 5 miles (8 km) from the sea. The spa's waters come from sulfur and iron springs that contain iodine and magnesium, beneficial in certain cases of rheumatism and arthritis. The Spa Centre is open from Easter to October; it has saunas, sun lounges, mudbaths, and facilities for massage as well as beauty therapy. There is also a café on the premises.

En Route from Lisdoonvarna – Several routes crisscross the Burren (meaning "great rock"), the strange lunar-like region of bare, silvery limestone hills, caves, underground waterways, and "turloughs" (intermittent lakes, sometimes called disappearing lakes because the water is absorbed by the porous limestone, acting like a drain). Though naked and treeless, the Burren is a naturalist's delight because of its rare, low-growing flora, such as Irish orchid and blue spring gentian, scattered over rock and sod. There are about 500 ring forts, or *caher,* where inhabitants of the Burren lived in about 600 BC. The most spectacular of these is Caherdoonerish, 600 feet up on Black Head with 18-foot walls and a view of the Aran Islands.

Just outside Ballyvaughan, you can stop to see the impressive stalactites in Aillwee Cave (open to the public). At Rinn Point in Ballyvaughan, there is shore fishing for flatfish and mullet, while the bay affords bottom fishing for bass, flounder, and dogfish.

From Ballyvaughan, continue on N67 through Kinvara, which has a long, sandy beach at Traught Strand, and on into County Galway, past *Dun Guaire,* another castle in which medieval banquets are held. At Kilcolgan turn left onto N18 for Galway city.

Beyond Kilcolgan is Clarinbridge, the heart of oyster country and the scene of Ireland's annual oyster festival in September. Route N18 leads to Oranmore where it becomes N6 into Galway city.

BEST EN ROUTE

Perhaps because County Limerick and County Clare are close to Shannon International Airport, the area offers unusual accommodations along with the somewhat hokey entertainment-cum-restaurant fare offered as medieval castle banquets. If you hate crowds, avoid the banquets, particularly the one at *Bunratty Castle; Dun Guaire* is a little more intimate as medieval banquets go, but that's not going very far. Don't make the mistake, however, of writing castles completely off your itinerary. Only 8 miles (12.8 km) from Shannon Airport is *Dromoland Castle*, one of the finest hotels (and arguably the best) in Ireland. The Irish do this sort of thing extremely well (there are about eight of these castle hotels in Ireland) and if you want to spend the money, *Dromoland Castle* is a unique experience.

Price ranges for hotels, including castles, are $90 and up for a double, very expensive; $65 to $80, expensive; $40 to $60, moderate; below $40, inexpensive. For restaurants: about $65 for two, expensive; $30 to $55, moderate; under $25, inexpensive. Prices don't include wine, drinks, or tips.

ADARE

Dunraven Arms – It's hard to say which is more beautiful: the ivy-covered old-world hotel or its location on Adare's cottage-lined main street. Both are lovely. The hotel has 25 bedrooms, all with bath. It also has a very good restaurant. Main St. (phone: 9-4209). Moderate.

LIMERICK

Dromoland Castle – For true luxury, you must go outside Limerick to Newmarket-on-Fergus, about 16 miles (26 km) (8 mi/13 km from Shannon Airport). *Dromoland Castle* is one of Ireland's castle hotels. Unadulterated luxury prevails in its public rooms and most of its 67 bedrooms. Since it is really a resort, it offers extras within its spacious grounds, like golf, riding, tennis, shooting, and fishing. The dining room is formal, as befits a palace, and its cuisine is excellent. Newmarket-on-Fergus (phone: 7-1144). Very expensive.

Jury's – Just over the bridge from the Limerick city center, this modern hotel has 100 well-appointed rooms. Its *Copper Room* is a particularly good restaurant. There is also a quick-service grill. Ennis Rd. (phone: 5-5266). Expensive.

Limerick Inn – A few miles outside town is this modern, reasonably comfortable hotel with 133 rooms and an efficient staff. Its restaurant and grill are considered above average. Ennis Rd. (phone: 5-1544). Moderate.

Shannon Shamrock Inn – This Paddy Fitzpatrick hotel has 100 rooms, a heated indoor pool, a sauna, a French/Irish restaurant, and a bar. It's next to Bunratty Castle and Durty Nellie's pub. About 10 miles from Limerick in Bunratty (phone: 6-1177). Moderate.

La Picola Italia – This recently opened restaurant has a comprehensive menu of very good Italian fare along with a romantic atmosphere and friendly service. Open daily from 6:30 PM to midnight. 52 O'Connell St. Moderate.

Bunratty Castle – If you like your meals with pizzazz, a medieval castle banquet may be your thing. Along with the sumptuous all-Irish meal, which you eat without silverware as did the medievals, you get songs and recitations by castle maidens, who also pour the mead (that's the brew of honey and apple our Irish forebears met the muse with). By reservation: Shannon Castle Tours (phone: 6-1788).

ENNIS

Old Ground – This ivy-clad, centrally located hotel is gracious and old-fashioned. It has 63 bedrooms and a competent restaurant. O'Connell St. (phone: 2-8127). Moderate.

LAHINCH

Aberdeen Arms – If you want to stay somewhere cheerful and close to the sea, this is the hotel for you. All of its 48 rooms have baths. The bar serves periwinkles rather than peanuts, and the restaurant offers some very fine seafood. Open April to October (phone: 8-1100). Moderate.

BALLYVAUGHAN

Gregan's Castle – Since the spa of Lisdoonvarna has only mediocre hotels, it is advisable to come to this lovely antique-filled manor house at the foot of Corkscrew Hill and overlooking the Burren country and Galway Bay. There are 16 cozy bedrooms, 12 with bath. Open March through October (phone: 7-7005). Moderate.

KINVARA

Dunguaire – This castle serves more intimate, but not less fun, medieval banquets than *Bunratty*. The food is Irish and good; the entertainment "literary" — featuring recitations from the work of famous Irish writers such as Yeats. Call Shannon Castle Tours (phone: 6-1788) for reservations.

KILCOLGAN

Raftery's Rest – In the heart of oyster country, you won't find better oysters and seafood generally than in this country pub with restaurant. And it's cheaper than most of its kind. At the junction of Routes N67 and N18 (phone: 8-6175).

Moran's Oyster Cottage – This popular stop vies with *Raftery's* for the "best oysters" designation. What makes it attractive above and beyond the food is its old-world air and grassy setting on the shores of Galway Bay. People love to sit outside or lounge on the grass in the summer months. The Weir (phone: 8-6113). Expensive.

Paddy Burke's Oyster Inn – The winner of the 1977 National Bar Food competition, this internationally famous oyster tavern offers quality bar food along with its Cordon Bleu fare in the restaurant. It has a warm relaxed atmosphere. Clarinbridge (phone: 8-6107). Inexpensive.

The Irish West:
Galway to Mayo to Sligo

Galway is a large county divided into two contrasting regions by the expanse of Lough Corrib. To the west, lying between the lake and the Atlantic, is Connemara — a region of scenic grandeur dominated by the rocky mountain range known as the Twelve Bens. Connemara — with a kaleidoscope of mountain and valley, lake and stream, bog and sea — has inspired many painters. They've painted the sparkle of water in deep valleys, tiny whitewashed cottages, great castles on the shores of calm and wooded lakes, fields the size of pocket handkerchiefs, and splendid forested estates. The region east of Lough Corrib is more subdued; it is a fertile limestone plain, partially covered with bogs, that extends to the Galway-Roscommon border and the River Shannon.

The people of Connemara and of the Aran Islands, west of Galway Bay, are an ancient people with ancient ways. They still fish the wild seas in their frail boats called *curraghs,* pasture their sheep on the green and golden mountainsides, and speak mostly Irish, the language of the Celts. Galway city lies south of the lake. It is an important tourist center and the gateway to the scenic areas of the county.

GALWAY CITY: On Galway Bay at the mouth of the River Corrib, Galway is a busy seaport, a thriving city with good hotels and stores and a fine university.

The Magnata mentioned by Ptolemy in the second century AD is thought to have been Galway. The city evolved from a fort built in 1142, then was seized by the Anglo-Normans, who converted it into a walled town by the thirteenth century, a powerful western stronghold. While they isolated themselves from the native Irish population, the Normans engaged in active trading with the rest of the world. Much of their commerce was with Spain, and some intermarriage occurred, which accounts for the dark hair and coloring of many Galway people and the Iberian influence in some of the city's architecture.

Since historic Galway is compact, with narrow streets, it is best seen on foot; walking-tour maps, with an interesting path through old Galway clearly laid out, are available at the tourist office; Eyre Sq. (phone: 6-3081). There are several sights that should not be missed. Lynch's Castle (Shop St.) is a fine old mansion and the four-teenth-century Church of St. Nicholas (Lombard St.) is supposed to be the last place Christopher Columbus worshipped before sailing for America. Near the fish market is the Spanish Arch leading to Spanish Parade, so named because it was the favorite promenade of Spanish merchants. The Salmon Weir Bridge spanning the River Corrib draws many visitors during the spawning season, when hundreds of salmon can be seen stacked on the riverbed waiting to leap upriver to their spawning grounds in Lough Corrib.

Since Galway is the gateway to Gaelic country, it is only fitting that an authentically Irish — that is, Gaelic — entertainment should flourish here. The folk theater, Taibhd-hearc (pronounced "tive" — to rhyme with "dive" — "yark"), operates year round on Middle Street (phone: 2024). It puts on special variety shows with music and dancing, called *Seoda,* for visitors three times a week in July and August.

Several summer events attract big crowds and fill hotels and guesthouses nearby: the 5-day Galway races in July and August; the week-long Galway oyster festival in September; and an annual ceremony called the Blessing of the Sea at the beginning of the herring season. During festival weeks the town is jammed and accommodations are impossible to find; reservations are a must.

West of the city, on Route L100, close to the shore of Galway Bay, is Salthill, a resort suburb of pastel-painted houses and a long boardwalk with a stunning view. Thirty miles out to sea from Galway are the three Aran islands — Inishmore, the largest with 7,635 acres; Inishmaan; and Inisheer. These rugged and barren chips of land immortal-ized in Robert Flaherty's film *Man of Aran* offer an interesting side trip. You can reach the islands by boat from Galway in 3 hours or by air in 20 minutes. Flight and boat schedules as well as booking information for both transportation and accommodations for an overnight stay on the islands are available at the tourist office.

On the islands you will be transported back in time to a primitive way of life. The language is Irish, and some of the people still wear homespun clothing. You can watch the islanders create soil from sand and seaweed to grow feed for their livestock and meager produce for themselves; fishermen put out to sea in *curraghs* (boats made of narrow strips of wood and tarred canvas no different from those their ancestors used); and the women spin and weave their own clothing.

If you go for the day, you can tour the island in a jaunting car. If you stay overnight, you can wander the rocky paths in splendid isolation or explore the ancient ruins — forts and churches.

Boats from Galway land at Kilronan, the main town on Inishmore. To get to the smaller islands, take a *curragh* from Kilronan.

En Route from Galway – North on the main road is Sligo, about 57 miles (92 km) away. Our route, designed to cover as much as possible in 1 day and still see the outstanding sights of Connemara, is roughly twice that distance. Good bases for extended exploration are Cashel, at the head of Bertraghboy Bay on the west coast, and Clifden, farther up the coast on the edge of the Atlantic. Both towns have good hotels.

Leave Galway on N59, going northwest a few miles until you come to Moycullen. On the left side of the road is a Connemara marble factory where you can observe marble being worked — shaped, ground, carved, and polished. Both the plant and a shop that sells finished objects are open daily. Continuing on N59, you are actually parallel to Lough Corrib, but you don't see the lake until you get to Oughterard, a lovely trout and salmon angling center.

From Oughterard, N59 curves west through Maam Cross and passes the shores of some of Connemara's lovely lakes — Lough Shindilla, Oorid Lough, beautiful Lough Glendalough at Recess, and Lough Derryclare. This stretch of road has some of the best scenery in Connemara, with the lakes on one side and the Twelve Bens looming majestically ahead. The mountains are conical, with precipitous slopes distinctively colored by lichens and mosses.

Beyond Recess, the first turn to the left is L102, marked Carna. Take this road for about 5 miles (8 km) to an unmarked right turn, which leads to Cashel.

CASHEL: This little angling resort is beautifully situated on the waters of Bertraghboy Bay. Cashel (not to be confused with the town in County Tipperary) is little more than the superb *Cashel House Hotel,* where French President Charles de Gaulle vacationed in 1969, a year before his death; another hotel, a post office, a school, and a couple of shops — and that's it. The town is idyllic for the gardens that thrive in this wooded, sheltered bay amid peace and quiet. There is also ample opportunity for outdoor activities, from freshwater and sea fishing to horseback riding and mountain climbing.

The next stop on our route is less than 5 miles (8 km) west on L102.

ROUNDSTONE: A charming fishing village with whitewashed houses overlooking a tranquil harbor, Roundstone is known for its fine beaches, particularly Dog's Bay, a magnet for naturalists and geologists interested in studying foraminiferans — unusual, large-shelled amoeboid protozoa. Towering over the village is isolated Urrisbeg Mountain, which provides a splendid view of the surrounding lake-dotted countryside and the splendid, irregular coastline.

En Route from Roundstone – Continue around the promontory on coastal Route L102, known as "the brandy and soda road" because of the bracing quality of the air. It passes through Ballyconneely on the remote shores of Ballyconneely Bay, the westernmost point on the road. There are glorious beaches everywhere, including the lovely Coral Strand on the shores of Mannin Bay. Deep-sea fishing can be arranged in many villages along the way.

CLIFDEN: The main town of Connemara, Clifden is an ideal center for exploring the glorious scenery of the region. The busy little town nestles on the edge of the Atlantic against a superb backdrop of mountains. The Connemara Pony Show held here each August attracts buyers from throughout the world.

En Route from Clifden – Route N59 leads north to Moyard and then west through Letterfrack to the romantic Kylemore Pass, a beautiful valley dominated by the nineteenth-century castellated mansion *Kylemore Abbey,* now a girls' school run by Benedictine nuns; they also manage a pottery and restaurant open to visitors.

Beyond Kylemore, the road follows the southern shore of Killary Harbour, a magnificent fjordlike arm of the sea that runs inland between steep mountains rising like enormous walls. Near the head of Killary Bay is the village of Leenane, another angling resort and an excellent center for mountain climbing. The Killary craft shop offers light, homemade snacks, such as soups, sandwiches, and scones.

From Leenane, take Route L100 into County Mayo. Go past the Asleagh Falls, heading west on the north shore of Killary Harbour, where the road turns inland and the landscape alternates between dramatic lakefront and brooding mountains. At Louisburgh, near the coast, the road becomes Route T39, going east to Westport. Along the way is Ireland's "holy mountain," Croagh Patrick, an isolated cone-shaped peak rising 2,510 feet from the shore of Clew Bay and one of the most conspicuous features of western Ireland's landscape. On this mountain, St. Patrick is said to have fasted 40 days during Lent in 441, praying that Ireland would never lose the Christian faith. According to tradition, he summoned all venomous creatures in Ireland to the summit and then cast them out. (To this day there are no snakes in Ireland.) Every year, on the last Sunday in July, thousands of pilgrims — many barefooted — climb the mountain before dawn. Throughout the day, masses are celebrated in the little chapel at the top.

WESTPORT: The town is charmingly laid out on an arm of Clew Bay in a hollow surrounded by trees and groves. In recent years, it has become a deep-sea fishing center, and the annual June festival draws many fishermen. The main tourist attraction, however, is Westport House, a beautiful estate less than 2 miles (3 km) miles from town. The fine Georgian mansion overlooking the bay is the home of the marquess of Sligo (open to the public April through mid-October). The house is a treasure of fine paintings, silver, Waterford glass, and exhibits of historical interest. There is also a small zoo on the grounds.

En Route from Westport – There are a number of routing alternatives from Westport. If you want to base yourself for several days in a fairy-tale setting in County Mayo, you must stay at *Ashford Castle* in Cong, roughly halfway between Galway and Westport, on the north shore of Lake Corrib. The thirteenth-century fortress, the former home of the Guinness family, is now a luxury hotel with elegant rooms and suites overlooking either the lake, the River Cong, or the landscaped gardens that stretch over several hundred acres. It is a sporting paradise — for hunting, fishing, golf, and tennis.

From Westport to Sligo you have a choice of routes. If you're pressed for time, take N60 east 11 miles (18 km) to Castlebar, a small bustling town in the heart of the limestone plain; continue on N5 to Charlestown and join N17 going northeast until you bump into N4, which will take you into Sligo. This route is roughly 53 miles (85 km).

A more scenic alternative from Castlebar is Route L134 north to Pontoon, a picturesque angling resort between Lough Conn and the smaller Lough Cullen, both of which are full of salmon and trout. Cross the isthmus between the lakes and continue north to Ballina, County Mayo's largest town (pop. 6,000), on the salmon-rich River Moy.

From Ballina, take shore Route T40 into County Sligo through Enniscrone and Easkey. Join the main Sligo road, N4, at Ballisodare.

BEST EN ROUTE

The best accommodations in the northwest can be very good (and very expensive), such as the *Great Southern Hotel* in Galway, the two Cashel hotels, or *Ashford Castle*, probably the best castle hotel in Ireland. But as you head north there will be fewer and fewer hotels worth noting, and fine restaurants are few and far between. The price range for a double room in the area's hotels is $55 and up, expensive; $30 to $45, moderate; below $30, inexpensive. For a meal for two: $45 and up is considered expensive; $30 to $45, moderate; under $30, inexpensive. Prices don't include wine, drinks, or tip.

GALWAY CITY

Great Southern Hotel – This is by far the most gracious hotel in Galway. The 120 bedrooms are comfortable, but it's well worth staying here just to dine in the *Claddagh Grill* or to savor its spectacular view over the city. There is also a swimming pool and sauna complex. Eyre Sq. (phone: 6-4041). Expensive.

Ardilaun House – Once the stately home of an aristocratic scion, the building and grounds still retain a patrician aura. It's hidden away among trees and shrubs on Taylor's Hill, the best address in town. Salthill (phone: 2-1433). Expensive.

Anno Santo – For those who prefer the quiet life, here is a classy, intimate place with a relaxed atmosphere. Specify private bath. Threadneedle Rd., Salthill (phone: 2-2110). Moderate.

OUGHTERARD

Currarevagh House – Owner-managed, this small atmospheric country house is set like a jewel amid wooded surroundings on the shores of Lough Corrib. The 15 rooms (only 11 with bath) are old-fashioned but comfortable. Open only from April to October. Reservations essential. Four miles (6 km) north of Oughterard, (phone: 8-2313). Moderate.

CASHEL

The Zetland – This fine hotel is small, with 15 good rooms, 13 with bath. Closed November through February (phone: Galway 8 or 34). Expensive.

Cashel House – This Georgian country house, where Charles de Gaulle vacationed, has 29 bright, pleasant bedrooms, 27 with bath. Its dining room fare, cooked by the owner, is so superb that even the French president raved. Closed November through February (phone: Galway 9). Expensive to moderate.

CLIFDEN

Abbeyglen – The proprietor sees to it that the hotel is warm and friendly and that the cuisine is of a high standard. There are 42 rooms, 40 with bath, and a heated outdoor swimming pool. Closed December through February (phone: Clifden 33). Moderate.

Celtic Hotel – This hotel, too, promises a friendly atmosphere. It has 20 rooms, a small bar, and a particularly pleasant restaurant with imaginative menus and good, fresh, home-cooked food. Main St. (phone: Clifden 115). Moderate.

Crocknaraw House – Six miles (10 km) from Clifden is another country house hotel with a quiet atmosphere, 10 rooms (6 with bath), beautiful grounds, and fine food. Closed November through March. Moyard (phone: Moyard 9). Moderate.

LEENANE

Peacocks – A sort of Celtic bazaar with a big bar for booze and fast grub, a more sedate sit-down restaurant with good fare, and a shop with all the stereotypical Emerald Isle souvenirs. You can even stay overnight. Maam Cross (phone: 8-2306). Moderate.

WESTPORT

Westport Ryan's – You do not have a great choice here. This hotel is the best, which isn't saying much. There are 56 rooms with very thin walls. Not a good place to fall into, or out of, love. The rest is modern and efficient but featureless. The restaurant is adequate. The hotel was formerly called Jury's (phone: 2-5811). Expensive to moderate.

Newport House – If you go out of town 7.75 miles (12.5 km) from Westport, there is a delightful, rambling Georgian mansion set in its own wooded estate. It has everything the town hotels don't have: 21 great rooms and delicious cuisine. Newport (phone: 4-1222). Expensive to moderate.

CONG

Ashford Castle – This thirteenth-century castle is considered by many to be Ireland's finest castle hotel. Beside Lough Corrib in beautiful grounds, it has 77 rooms and suites with views of the lake or the gardens. The rooms are beautifully appointed, as are the public rooms, with their views over the landscaped gardens. It is a fairy-tale castle, splendidly run. The superb cuisine often features the day's catch of fish. It is possible to dine at the castle even if you aren't staying there, but reserve well in advance. Ashford Castle (phone: 2-2644). Expensive.

The North: Sligo to Donegal

The northwest is rugged country. County Sligo is a healthy mix of mountain, lake, and coastal scenery. In the western part, the Ox Mountains form a background to the coastal plain, while north of Sligo town the landscape is dominated by steep-sided, flat-topped limestone hills. The low-lying coast is fringed by sandy beaches and low cliffs.

Sligo is extraordinarily rich in archaeological remains and places associated with the heroes and heroines of the ancient Irish epics and sagas. Inextricably linked to this area and its Celtic tradition is the poet William Butler Yeats. His poems, particularly the early ones, create a haunting picture of ancient Ireland, the Ireland of myth and legend, and you won't regret having his cadences and images in your mind's eye when you come to Sligo.

Donegal, the most northerly county in the Republic, extends along much of the northwest coast. It is one of the wildest, loveliest, and most remote parts of Ireland, with distinctive scenery — a bay-indented coast, great areas of blue and purple mountains, deep wooded glens, and many lakes. All kinds of stone, from cave-riddled limestone to mixtures of igneous rocks, make up the foundation of the land and give the scenery its form and color.

SLIGO TOWN: Although Sligo is northwest Ireland's most important town, its population is only 14,000. It is picturesquely situated on the estuary of the Garravogue River on a wooded plain between Lough Gill and the sea. If the lake, with its scattered islands, is not one of Ireland's loveliest, it is most certainly its most famous, immortalized by one of Yeats's best-known poems, "The Lake Isle of Innisfree." The town itself contains some fine buildings, the most notable being the thirteenth-century Dominican friary, Sligo Abbey. Although the building was sacked in 1641, the ruins — a nave, choir, and central tower — are magnificent. From June to August, guided walking tours of Sligo leave every day at 11 AM from the tourist office (Stephen St.; phone: 071-2436).

Sligo is an excellent angling center for game fish. There are fine beaches close to town at Strandhill and Rosses Point. The latter also has a splendid golf course.

A short tour of Yeats country should certainly include a trip along the shore of Lough Gill. Three-hour boat tours leave from Doorly Park (Riverside Quay).

Another site that should not be missed is the archaeologically rich area west of town, bounded by its main natural feature, the Hill of Knocknarea (1,078 feet), on whose summit Ireland's ancient warrior queen Maeve reputedly lies buried beneath an immense cairn. Between Knocknarea and Sligo town is Carrowmore, the "graveyard of the giants," a site containing the greatest concentration of megalithic burial stones in Ireland.

En Route from Sligo – Route N15 goes north through Bundoran and Ballyshannon — wild country scarcely touched by time, where small whitewashed, thatch-roofed cottages huddle together against the fierce Atlantic gales and where Irish is the vernacular. A few miles from Sligo, the road passes Ben Bulben, known as the "table mountain" for its curious shape. On its slopes, 1,730 feet high, the great warrior and ill-starred lover of Irish myth — Diarmuid — met his death; and at its base is buried Yeats, who celebrated Diarmuid's exploits in poetry. Yeats's grave by the little Protestant church in Drumcliffe lies exactly as he had willed it in his 1938 poem "Under Ben Bulben." The tombstone bears the poem's famous last stanza: "Cast a cold eye/On life, on death /Horseman, pass by!"

Farther along the coast is Bundoran in County Donegal, a popular resort on the south shore of Donegal Bay. Bundoran has a fine bathing beach with a promenade, excellent freshwater and sea fishing, and a championship golf course. It also has one of the best views in the area: the Sligo-Leitrim Mountains to the south, the Donegal hills to the north, and, along the beach, a range of cliffs carved into fantastic shapes by the waves.

A few miles up the coast is the lively hilly town of Ballyshannon, on the banks of the River Erne, reputedly the oldest settlement in Ireland. According to tradition, Parthalon, a Scythian, settled on the islet Inis Saimer in the Erne estuary at Ballyshannon in 1500 BC.

A short detour along L24 from Ballyshannon leads to one of Donegal's most spectacular bathing and surfing beaches, a 3-mile-long strand surrounded by gentle hills at Rossnowlagh. Return to N15 to continue to Donegal town.

DONEGAL TOWN: This thriving market town at the head of Donegal Bay and the mouth of the River Eske is an excellent touring center because of its location where the main roads from Derry, West Donegal, and Sligo converge. *Magees,* which manufactures the celebrated Donegal tweed, is in the town, and its mills are open to the public. Visitors can watch the distinctive technique of close weaving and the use of the plant dyes that produce the tweeds' famous heather tones. The retail store is on the Diamond, the central square; the factory is on Milltown (phone: Donegal 5). The imposing ruin of sixteenth-century Donegal Castle stands on the bank of the River Eske near the Diamond. South of the town are the remains of the fifteenth-century Donegal Abbey.

En Route from Donegal – Take Route N56 west to Killybegs, one of Ireland's most important fishing ports on a fine natural harbor. Killybegs is noted also for the greatly valued carpets that carry its name. These carpets are hand-knotted in a fine flat weave. They are made to order, often with special patterns, for important public places; the White House, Buckingham Palace, and Dublin Castle all have Killybegs carpets in their ceremonial rooms. The craft of hand knotting in pattern goes back to fifth-century Persia. Visitors can watch this old process today in the Killybegs plant, Donegal Carpets Ltd. (phone: Killybegs 21).

From Killybegs, continue on T72A west to Carrick, a good starting place for the ascent of Slieve League (1,972 feet) and for exploring the magnificent cliff scenery of the adjoining coast. In Carrick, make a 2-mile (3.2-km) detour south to Teelin. From here, a mountain track leads over Carrigan Head to the secluded Lough O'Mulligan and the sheer cliffs of Bunglass, which rise out of the water to a height of 1,024 feet. The view from the point, named Amharc Mor ("the great view"), lives up to its name: It is among the most magnificent in Donegal. Experienced climbers can go farther along the cliff edge to One Man's Pass, a narrow ledge with a precipice of more than 1,800 feet on one side, dropping sheer down to the sea, and on the other an almost equally precipitous escarpment falling down to a lonely mountain lake. From there it is not far to the summit of Slieve League, at 1,972 feet the highest maritime cliff in Europe, against whose base the Atlantic hurls powerful crashing waves. The path along the mountaintop is very rough and dangerous.

Retrace your steps from Teelin to Carrick and continue west on T72A to Glencolumbkille.

GLENCOLUMBKILLE: In the heart of the Irish-speaking area of South Donegal, this glen runs into the hills from Glen Bay. Many houses dot its slopes in surroundings at once peaceful and strikingly picturesque. On the north side rises the cliff of Glen Head. The coast has splendid rock scenery and there is a beautiful beach, and it is a popular family vacation spot. Glencolumbkille is rich in monuments dating from pre-Christian times as far back as 5,000 years ago.

Adjacent to the holiday village is a remarkable folk village recreation of cottages representing different periods of Irish life, furnished with historically correct objects down to the smallest utensils. An energetic Catholic priest, Father James McDyer, founded a cooperative here, and due to his efforts, there is now a flourishing industry, including a fish processing plant, a factory that manufactures electrical parts, and a knitting mill. Handmade Irish sweaters can be purchased here at some of the lowest prices in the country.

En Route from Glencolumbkille – An unclassified road leads to Ardara. This road rises to spectacular Glengesh Pass at 900 feet, then plunges in a steep descent to the valley below. Ardara, in a pretty valley at the mouth of the River Owentocher and Loughros More Bay, is another important center for the manufacture of Donegal homespun tweeds. Route N56 leads north to the Gaelic districts of Dungloe and Gweedore. In Gweedore, make a left turn along L32 until you meet T72, which will take you to Bloody Foreland, the cliff that takes its name from the warm, ruddy color of its rock in the setting sun.

Route T72 curls eastward along the coast to Gortahork, near Ballyness Bay. For the traveler who wants to spend several days in the area, the town of Gortahork, with *McFadden's* hotel and fine restaurant, is a good center for touring the north — to Melmore Head, Horn Head, Fanad Head, and the Inishowen Peninsula with Malin Head, the northernmost point in Ireland. This northland of the Republic consists of spectacular peninsulas ringed by misty, craggy, windswept cliffs rising straight from the water, with dramatic views of the boundless Atlantic Ocean broken by numerous islands and headlands.

If you are pressed for time, take N56 from Gortahork to Letterkenny, the principal town of County Donegal, which overlooks Lough Swilly where the River Swilly empties into the lake. From here there is a selection of routes across the interior of the county to the east coast, all of them passing through superb mountain scenery. Route N56 descends through the twin towns of Stranorlar, where it joins N15, and Balleybofey through the wild and lonely Barnesmore Gap back to Donegal town.

Donegal town is 138 miles (222 km) from Dublin through the inland counties and 176 miles (283 km) from Shannon Airport.

BEST EN ROUTE

Because the north country has spectacular vistas, so do many of the hotels (the vistas are often better than the accommodations themselves). But the north has come a long way, and things are getting better all the time. Still, because hotels and restaurants are rather isolated and some are fairly small, it is necessary to make reservations. Expect to pay $55 and up for a double room in the expensive range; $30 to $45 in the hotels we list as moderate; under $30 in the inexpensive category. For meals, $45 for two is expensive; $15 to $20, moderate; under $15, inexpensive. Prices don't include wine, drinks, or tip.

SLIGO

The Sligo Park – Not elegant, this is a cheerful, modern, friendly hotel. Its 60 rooms are bright and spacious. The dining room is quite good (phone: 3291). Moderate.

The Yeats Country Ryan – With a motor hotel like this, one must rave about its magnificent location and let it go at that. The setting is indeed beautiful, just a few minutes from the splendid beach at Rosses Point. The hotel itself is modern, with 79 adequate rooms. The restaurant is also adequate. Rosses Point (phone: 7-7211). Moderate.

ROSSNOWLAGH

The Sand House – Another spectacular beachside setting marks this hotel. Of its 40 rooms (all with bath), many overlook the sea. The public rooms are elegantly furnished. The entire place exudes a feeling of peaceful rest. The dining room is good, and golf course adjoins the hotel. This is surfing territory, and surfboards are available at the hotel (phone: 6-5777). Moderate.

DONEGAL TOWN

Hyland Central Hotel – Although the hotel is homely and standing squat in the center of town, it gets unreserved recommendations from those who have stayed in its 59 comfortable rooms. The cuisine is very good. The Diamond (phone: 2-1027). Moderate.

The Abbey Hotel – Also in the town center, this pleasant hotel has 40 rooms, 28 with bath. The good food in the dining room and the generally warm, friendly service make up for its deficiencies. The Diamond (phone: 14). Moderate to inexpensive.

GLENCOLUMBKILLE

The Glenbay – An informal warm-hearted place with a fine view over the Atlantic. The dining room has its ups and downs. Overall, however, the food is good. The location is beautiful, about 1.5 miles (2.4 km) southwest of Glencolumbkille in Malinmore (phone: Glencolumbkille 3). Inexpensive.

GORTAHORK

McFaddens – If a hotel can ever be described as sociable, this is it. There are 35 rooms (7 with bath). It has a good reputation for food. Main St., Gortahork (phone: 3-5267). Moderate.

Port-na-Blagh – In another fine location on a cliff overlooking Sheep Haven Bay, this is called a welcoming hotel for its friendliness. It has 58 comfortable rooms, 29 with bath. The seafood is particularly good. Port-na-Blagh (phone: 3-6129). Moderate.

Exploring Italy

Italy has played a prime role in forming Western European culture, but paradoxically, the modern nation of Italy, established in 1870, is still in the process of coming into its own. The dual nature of its history is both a burden and a blessing. As Italy experiences the growing pains of a young industrial power, its progress is undermined by political turbulence and strife. And always there is its history to contend with. Not since the glorious age of Rome, when the city was the core of a world empire, has Italy experienced such peace and prosperity. And not since the Renaissance have its artistic and cultural achievements attained such great heights.

This heritage is one of which the Italians are justly proud. The brightest jewels of the Renaissance still glow in Italy — the Foundling Hospital by Brunelleschi in Florence that revolutionized architectural design; the anatomically accurate portrayal of the human form in works by Leonardo da Vinci; Raphael's lifelike Madonnas; and Michelangelo's monumental Sistine Chapel ceilings in Rome.

This rich heritage is one of the major forces unifying the Italian people. Italians take pride in the national treasure of their cultural legacy. This, their common language, and their religion (97% of all Italians are Roman Catholics) are what Italians share, whether they come from Milan, Rome, or Palermo.

Italy's boot-shaped peninsula covers 116,318 miles, stretching from the mainland of southern Europe 745 miles into the seas of the Mediterranean, with 5,280 miles of coast. The country has a confusing maze of borders — France on the northwest, Switzerland and Austria to the north, Yugoslavia to the northeast, the Ligurian Sea to the northwest, the Tyrrhenian Sea to the west, the Mediterranean Sea to the southwest, the Ionian Sea to the southeast, and the Adriatic Sea on the east. This country of coasts and water is strung out on a frame of mountains: the highest peaks are in the Alps of the north — Mont Blanc at 15,771 feet and the Matterhorn at 15,205 feet; but along the spine of country run the Apennines, a rocky backbone that goes the entire length of the Peninsula. The climate varies with the topography. Along the seacoast, winters are temperate and summers are hot. In the mountains, summer days are warm, nights cool, and winters cold and snowy.

As the climate varies with topography, so do the economics. The south — rocky, devoted to sheepherding and olive growing — is ravished by poverty. The north, comprising a vast plain drained by the Po River, is far richer, with great industrial centers, such as Milan, Genoa, and Turin, and agricultural areas devoted to rice, wheat, and especially grapes, which find their way into a variety of fine Italian wines.

Italy is the home of some 56 million people, 92% of whom live in its cities.

Throughout history, Italians have been urban animals, viewing cities as centers of culture and civilization and settling them with great energy and ingenuity. Even agricultural workers tend to live in cities or towns, preferring to travel long distances to the fields rather than live in them. Some three million people live in Rome, the capital and Italy's major cultural and historical center. In Rome is Vatican City, an independent enclave in which the pope is sovereign. Other major cities are Florence, Milan, Turin, Venice, Genoa, Naples, and Palermo, Sicily. Ethnic and linguistic minorities comprise less than 5% of Italy's population. Of these, the major groups live in border regions: Slovenes in Friuli-Venezia Giulia, German speakers in Trentino-Alto Adige, and French speakers in Valle d'Aosta. Some inhabitants of Calabria and Sicily speak Greek and Albanian dialects.

Some of these different groups are actually descended from people who inhabited the country during Italy's long and complicated history. Recorded civilization in Italy dates back to around 2000 BC, when the peninsula was settled by fair, blue-eyed Ligurians, ancestors of the Latins. Around the ninth century BC, the Greeks sailed to Italian shores, and Italy became a setting for the myth of Ulysses and other legends. The Greeks settled southern Italy and Sicily during the eighth century BC, establishing colonies of city-states known as Magna Graecia. The Greek civilization thrived in the sixth and fifth centuries BC, declining in the fourth century BC. While the Greeks were colonizing the south, the Etruscans, a highly artistic civilization from Asia Minor, settled central Italy.

In the third century BC, the Romans conquered Italy and established a great empire from Rome. Julius Caesar reigned during the first century BC; his conquest of France — Gaul — made Rome supreme over much of the barbaric as well as the civilized world. Under Caesar, Roman culture flourished, enriched by an infusion of Greek elements. After Caesar's assassination, his nephew Octavian (later known as Augustus) succeeded him and instituted the Pax Romana, a 200-year period of peace when the Roman Empire was as powerful as it would ever be. At the end of the second century AD, the bishop of Rome gained supremacy as the head of the new Christian religion.

And yet Rome declined in the years following the Pax Romana, and Italy was torn apart by invading groups. For a brief period it was reunited when Charlemagne was named Holy Roman Emperor in 800, but the ensuing century saw the country disintegrate into conflicting groups seeking control of provincial kingdoms. Italy was ravaged by battles between different city-states until Napoleon came to power in the early nineteenth century.

Despite this internal strife, Italian civilization and culture reached its peak during the Renaissance, in the fifteenth and sixteenth centuries. The independent city-states established a delicate balance of power, and rich patrons such as the Medici family of Florence supported the arts. The humanistic secular atmosphere encouraged worldly life and human endeavor. This age spawned some of the greatest artists of Western civilization — Leonardo da Vinci, a genius in many fields, the personification of the Renaissance man (1452–

1519); Michelangelo (1475–1564); Raphael (1483–1564); and the architect Brunelleschi (1377–1466).

Napoleon annexed large sections of Italy, including Rome, in the early nineteenth century. A long tradition of disunity and foreign domination brought about the Risorgimento, the movement for political unity in Italy, that gathered broad support under the popular leader Giuseppe Garibaldi. Italy was finally united under King Victor Emmanuel II in 1870.

The country was ruled as a monarchy and joined the Allies in World War I. Benito Mussolini rose to power during the early 1920s and ushered in one of the darkest periods in Italy's history. Il Duce, a leader of the National Fascist party, promised a vague program of order at home and greater prestige abroad, though what he actually delivered was a totalitarian state controlled by the militia. Mussolini formed an alliance with Hitler and fought against the Allies during World War II. Under his rule, the National Racial Code was implemented, and more than 10,000 Italian Jews were killed in Nazi concentration camps. The Italian Resistance Movement fought Mussolini and the Nazis, but their reprisals took a heavy toll on Italy. Large parts of the country were in ruins, 400,000 people were killed, hundreds of thousands were left homeless, and the economy was sharply disrupted. Mussolini was captured by partisans in 1945 and executed.

The experience of World War II and fascism deeply scarred Italy. Though the country was declared a republic in 1946, during the postwar era Italy has been seriously divided by exteme political differences. Dozens of governments have risen and fallen since the war. The leading parties are the Centrist Christian Democrats and the Italian Communist Party. Their diametrical opposition to one another contributes to the rampant factionalization of Italian politics. Neither party has managed to gain a clear majority. In the most recent national election the Christian Democrats won by a slim margin, and currently govern in coalition with other Centrist and Center-Left parties.

From the early 1970s to 1982, terrorist acts aimed at political leaders and wealthy industrialists plagued the country, along with strikes and double-digit inflation. Today, political violence has fallen sharply, but Italy still has many problems. In part, these are caused by the staggering socioeconomic discrepancy between the rich industrial north and the poorer, rural south. Until the past decade, this gap caused great internal migrations from south to north and village to city. At present, the biggest economic problems are widespread unemployment among Italian youth and ongoing inflation, caused by massive government deficits and dependence on dollar-expensive imported raw materials. Though Italy is ranked as the seventh industrial power of the non-Communist world, its economy is underdeveloped in many respects. Structural imbalances, an inefficient administrative system, and political fragmentation have made it difficult to proceed with economic and social reforms.

Family ties are particularly strong in Italy. Although divorce was introduced a decade ago, so far relatively few Italians have made use of it. It is common for offspring to live at home until they marry, and often married couples unable to find affordable housing will remain with one set of parents. Feminism has made some minor inroads, but the number of women who pursue careers is still lower than in most other Western countries. While children are highly valued, economic considerations, birth control availability, and an extremely liberal abortion law have led to a declining birth rate. Nevertheless, enduring traditions and widespread frustration with a malfunctioning government have strengthened the family as the root of Italian society.

Italians are opera lovers, passionate soccer fans, and avid filmgoers. Neorealism in cinema, which has had a profound influence on contemporary film, was developed in Italy. This movement aimed to portray real life in films by setting them in the streets with nonprofessional casts. Luchino Visconti's *Ossessione,* Vittorio de Sica's *Bicycle Thief,* and Roberto Rossellini's *Open City* exemplify this movement. In the 1960s and 70s, Italian cinema moved away from neorealism. The films of Federico Fellini became increasingly surreal, and Michelangelo Antonioni explored existentialist themes. A younger generation led by Bernardo Bertolucci produced films of social and political comment. In recent years, Italian cinema has been dominated by the genre known as "commedia all'italiana," light comedies with an ironic, bittersweet edge.

The area in which Italian differences shine most brightly is food. The concept that most people carry of Italian food is hopelessly limited. Italy is made up of 18 different regions, each with its own distinct cuisine. The best way to enjoy the delights of Italy's regions is to eat your way through them, sticking to regional specialties and experimenting with new dishes rather than going for a known quantity. In the Piedmont, for example, Italy's mountainous northwest corner, the cuisine has been deeply influenced by France and Switzerland. Specialties are exquisite whole truffles and *grissini,* crisp breadsticks, as well as the Turin cheese, *fontina,* that is used in a fondue-like dish called *fonduta.* In late summer and early fall a favorite Piedmont dish is the huge, fresh mushroom called *porcini;* for dessert have *zabaglione,* the rich whipped pudding made of egg yolks, sugar, and Marsala wine.

Milan, the capital of the Lombardy region, sits on a vast marshy plain north of the Po River better suited to rice and cattle than to wheat and olive trees. Thus rice and butter, rather than pasta and oil, are the basis of Lombardy cuisine. Its most famous dish is *cotoletta milanese,* a thin scaloppine of fine Lombardy veal lightly breaded. A favorite dessert is *panettone,* a brioche-like cake stuffed with fruit. Another good dessert is a pear with Gorgonzola cheese.

Tuscany cuisine centers around finely grilled and spitted meats in such dishes as *bistecca fiorentina, capretto* (suckling kid), and *cinghiale* (boar). Rich soups are popular, such as the *zuppa di verdure* (vegetable soup) and *acquacotta* (literally, "cooked water," a mixture of bread, broth, pasta, vegetables, eggs, and cheese so thick that it can be eaten with a fork).

Sicilian cuisine is based on seafood, and tuna, sardines, mullet, octopus, porgy, and salt cod are likely to turn up at any meal. Sicily is the home of *cannelloni,* however, the wonderful squares of noodles rolled into tubes and filled with ricotta cheese and ground meat that are now popular worldwide. And delicious salads, using much eggplant, are ubiquitous. *Caponata* is a cold salad that incorporates onions, olives, celery, and capers; *melanzane alla trapanese* is fried eggplant seasoned with rosemary, tomato puree, and garlic.

Italians eat their main meal in the afternoon around 1 PM. The meal follows a traditional pattern; however, most menus are à la carte, so you can order as much or as little as you want. The opening course is generally antipasto, a mixed platter of cold hors d'oeuvres — cooked vegetables, salami, and prosciutto — or another appetizer. Soup or pasta follows and you can eat pasta in any of its various forms — macaroni (in soup or on a plate), spaghetti, lasagna, or vegetable soup. The entrée consists of meat — veal or chicken are best, or fish in coastal areas — accompanied by a green salad or vegetable. Sauces vary widely but tend toward butter and garlic in the north and tomato bases in the south. Drink Italian wines with the main course. The fruit course follows — peaches, apricots, grapes, or figs, depending on the season; the final course is *dolci,* or sweets, anything from rich Italian pastries to *gelato,* ice cream, or *sorbetto,* refreshing ices. Try some espresso, strong Italian coffee served with lemon or a touch of anisette. Though Italian cuisine is rich in variety, it is usually hearty and tasty. Wherever you are in Italy, it's hard to go wrong.

In the following pages we outline ten driving routes that cover Italy's major areas of interest, from the Alps along the country's northern border with France and Switzerland, the Italian Riviera, to the islands of Sicily and Sardinia in the Tyrrhenian Sea. The routes are by no means comprehensive, but they offer an introduction to the incredible diversity and the awesome beauty of the Italian countryside and the people. The routes are the Lombardy Lake region from Milan to Sirmione and the Italian-Swiss border to the Po Valley; Emilia, through the Po Valley and western Apennine Mountains from Milan to Ferrara; the Piedmont and Val d'Aosta from Entreves to Turin through the foot of the Alps; the Italian Riviera; the Dolomites from Bolzano to Trento, passing through the eastern Alps near the Austrian border; rugged, central Tuscany from Florence to Cortona through the Apennine Mountains; Campania on the southwestern coast around Naples and Paestum; Calabria, the southern toe of Italy's boot; and Sicily and Sardinia.

The Lombardy Lakes

The northwestern border of Italy and Switzerland — rent by the jagged peaks of the Alps and laced together again by a healing series of spectacular, deep lakes — has been a play area since the Romans conquered Gaul and Cicero set up a summer house on Lake Como. The Lombardy lakes were originally formed by the same glaciers that cut the peaks and valleys of the nearby Alps into such fine relief, but Lombardy itself is a great deal larger than just its lake area. Below this stitching of lakes spread 9,000 square miles of gradually flattening land, flowing around Milan from the foothills of the Alps to the green fertile plains of the Po River valley.

Once the center of Roman Gaul, Lombardy suffered a long and turbulent history, during which it was inexorably caught between the forces of northern and southern Europe. Buffeted between one ruling power and another for centuries, it came under the influence of the German Empire, the bishops of Milan, and Venice, France, and Austria. During the Middle Ages, Lombardy was controlled by powerful families, often cultured and worldly and almost always unprincipled and ruthless. As a result the Lombardy heritage includes as much German and French medieval art and architecture as home-grown bloodshed and mayhem.

The dynasties lost their power to Venice in the fifteenth century, only 100 years before a French invasion swept Lombardy into the Austrian Hapsburg empire. It joined the new Italian kingdom in 1860. Much of this history is revealed in the accumulation of architecture around the lakes, from Roman ruins to elegant eighteenth-century villas. The area's warm climate and fertile soil are responsible for the wide variety of luxuriant Mediterranean flowers, cypress trees, and other flora.

Since Milan is the most central Lombardian city, easily accessible to major highways, it is here that the 5-day route begins. The trip first takes you north toward Lake Maggiore and magnificent views of the distant Alps, along lakeside roads to Lake Lugano and a brief visit to the Swiss town of Lugano. Heading back toward Italian Lombardy again, the route travels down to Lake Como, then cuts across the plains and valleys, past several resort towns, in a southeastern direction. On the last segment of the trip, more time is spent in the cities themselves. Bergamo, the two-tiered city; Brescia, a commercial center; and Garda, site of Italy's largest lake, are some of the stops made on the final portion of the trip.

MILAN: For a detailed report on Milan, and its hotels and restaurants, see *Milan,* THE EUROPEAN CITIES.

En Route from Milan – Pass the industrial suburbs of Lainate and Saronno, where the flat plains around the city begin to give way to mountainous terrain. In the Valley of Olona, surrounded by mountain peaks, lies the town of Castiglione Olona. The art treasures of Olona are the work of the medieval Cardinal Branda Castiglione, who embellished his hometown with Renaissance houses for himself and his relatives and his cathedral with a famous series of frescoes by Renaissance artist Masolino de Panicale. See the Castiglione Mansion and its small church in the main square.

VARESE: This is now a center of Italy's shoe industry, but its pleasant hillside surroundings have made it popular as a summer resort as well. From the gardens of the eighteenth-century Palazzo Comune (City Hall) you get a fine view of the distant Alps, and at nearby Villa Mirabella there is a good museum of prehistoric finds in the lake district.

LAVENO: Commanding an outstanding view of Lake Maggiore, the second largest and what some regard as the most beautiful of the Italian lakes, Laveno is now known primarily for its ceramic industry.

From here take a steamer over to the famous lakeside town and resort of Stresa on the Piedmontese side of the lake, 21.5 miles (34.5 km) away.

STRESA: On the edge of the Pallanza Bay, Stresa abounds in eighteenth-century villas and gardens, many of them now luxurious hotels. Among the villas worth noting are Villa Ducale, the Villa Pallavicini, and the Villa Vignola.

En Route from Stresa – Continue north on the lakeside road to Luino, a small industrial town and resort near the mouth of the Tresa River, which runs into the lake. At Ponte Tresa you are on the tip of Lake Lugano, more than half of which is in Italian-speaking Switzerland. Lake Lugano is wilder than Lake Maggiore, with a more exotic beauty. From Ponte Tresa, itself half Swiss, follow the lakeside frontier to Porto Ceresio for the 70-minute ferry ride to Lugano, Switzerland.

LUGANO: Lugano was ceded to the Swiss by Milan in the early sixteenth century and has remained so despite Italy's attempts to regain it in 1798. Lugano seems modern until you reach the heart of the old city, which is entirely Italian. On via Cattedrale is the sixteenth-century cathedral, with some excellent early frescoes and a Renaissance tabernacle. In the old city is Villa Favorite, one of the finest private art collections in the world, collected by Baron Heinrich Thyssen-Bornemisza, with works from the sixteenth through the eighteenth century and some later French Impressionists.

The boat between Lugano and Porto Ceresio stops at Campione d'Italia, a tiny medieval town on the Italian side of the lake that has been the birthplace of artists and sculptors since the early Middle Ages and now has one of Italy's four legal casinos.

The road south backtracks to Varese, from which Route 342 leads to Como on beautiful Lake Como.

COMO: Originally settled by the Romans, this ancient city on the southern tip of Lake Como has for centuries been the home of Italian silk manufacturing. Of greater interest to the visitor is the wealth of its architecture, much of which is clustered around the piazza del Duomo, where the lovely Pretorian palace known as Il Broletto (1215) stands next to the Palazzo del Comune of the same period and the Duomo, begun in Renaissance Gothic style in 1396 and finished by baroque artists in 1770. Along via Vittorio Emanuele visit the fine Romanesque church of San Fedele.

CERNOBBIO: This lakeside resort, right next to Como, is dominated by the magnificent sixteenth-century Villa D'Este, once the home of the powerful dukes of Ferrara, now a hotel. The villa stands near a beautiful park on the shores of Lake Como.

En Route from Cernobbio – Before you leave the western end of Lake Como, you can drive around the lake to Varenna or take a steamer directly to Bellagio, leading to the southbound portion of the route. The extra drive of approximately 48 miles (78 km) around the lake is well worth the trip.

GRAVEDONA: This is the principal town on Lake Como's northern shore and one of the three cities that remained independent from the Middle Ages to the late sixteenth century. In the town center stands the massive square Palazzo Gallio and the small twelfth-century Church of Santa Maria del Tiglio.

BELLAGIO: The town of Bellagio, sometimes called the Pearl of the Lake, sits at the point where the main part of Lake Como intersects with the leg commonly called Lake Lecco. The narrow streets and ancient buildings make for a lovely, relatively easy walk, full of every sort of diversion. There's a bathing beach beside the Villa Serbelloni, in the middle of town, and the lovely gardens at the Villa Melzi are worth a visit — especially for the marvelous view across the lake toward Tremezzo.

LECCO: The western branch of Lake Como is also known as Lake Lecco, named for this industrial town at its southern tip. Lecco is also the scene of the famous novel *I Promessi Sposi,* by Alessandro Manzoni, whose eighteenth-century villa still stands in the area.

BERGAMO: The two-tiered city of Bergamo, straddling a hill overlooking the Lombardy plain, is divided into a modern, busy lower center and a silent, medieval upper one. The Lower City, Città Bassa, was almost entirely built in 1924 by the main architect of the Fascist period, Piacentini. Visit the Palazzo dell'Accademia Carrara, with a worthwhile collection of Italian furniture of the sixteenth and seventeenth centuries. It also has a good collection of Rubens, Van Dyck, and Clouet.

The Upper City, Città Alta, is reached by a funicular that drops its passengers in piazza Mercato delle Scarpe, inside the medieval walls of the old city. Bergamo was originally an Etruscan city; then it became a Roman town, a Lombard duchy, and finally part of first the Venetian and then the Austrian dynasties. At the heart of the Città Alta is the Piazza Vecchia amid a breathtaking collection of medieval buildings including the severe twelfth-century Palazzo della Ragione and its massive tower. Through the archways of the palace, you can see the cathedral square, with the fifteenth-century Cappella Colleoni, whose façade is a striking composition of colored marbles and delicate carving. The Romanesque basilica Santa Maria Maggiore, to which the chapel is attached, was begun in the twelfth century. Also on the square is the small fourteenth-century baptistry (which was once inside the basilica) and the cathedral, which has a nineteenth-century façade. Make your way back to Piazza Mercato delle Scarpe, from which Via Rocca leads off to the medieval lookout post, La Rocca, in the middle of a spacious park. From its height you will have a glorious view of the surrounding Bergamasque valleys.

En Route from Bergamo – Cross the industrial Seriana Valley via the tiny sulfur bath resort of Trescore Balneario and the neighboring spa of Gaverina. Stop in the principal resort of Lovere when you reach Lake d'Iseo, one of the smallest and least developed of the Lombardian lakes. The road from Lovere to Sornico is the most scenic along the lake's western bank.

BRESCIA: Badly bombed during World War II, this commercial and industrial city on Lake d'Iseo has been largely restored so that its Renaissance and medieval piazza and buildings are visible once again. Its central piazza della Vittoria is one of the few comparatively modern constructions. Also visit the original Roman center of the city and the Capitoline Temple, which dates to AD 72 and houses examples of Roman art.

From Brescia take Route 45B through Rezzato and Tormini to Lake Garda.

LAKE GARDA: This is the largest and most spectacular of the Italian lakes. Its northern shores are surrounded by wild mountain scenery while the broader southern part of the lake lies in lower, softer green countryside. Most famous of its lakeside resorts is Gardone Riviera, where the Fascist poet Gabriele D'Annunzio lived and died at the Vittoriale degli Italiani, a curious complex of memorials, gardens, and memorabilia, all collected by D'Annunzio himself and left as a museum for future generations.

BEST EN ROUTE

Endearing, gracious, and elegant hotels and inns are found throughout the Lombardy lakes region. Fine restaurants that serve excellent, classic European country cooking are also a hallmark of the area. Expect to pay $80 or more per night for a double room at those hotels we've categorized as expensive; between $60 and $75 at hotels in the moderate category; under $55, inexpensive. Expect to pay $60 or more for a meal for two at expensive restaurants; between $45 and $55 at restaurants in the moderate category; under $40, inexpensive. Prices do not include drinks, wine, or tip.

VARESE

Ristorante Lago Maggiore – This well-run restaurant serves some of the finest examples of Lombardian cuisine — fillet steaks with cream truffles, roast meat, and game. The selection of wines is excellent. Closed Sundays. Via Carrobbio 19 (phone: 23-11-83). Expensive.

Il Sole – Very good food and a beautiful lakeside view are the double attractions of this restaurant. Another plus is that it has its own beach facilities. Closed Tuesdays and January. About 14 miles (27 km) north of Varese in Ranco (phone: 96-95-07). Expensive to moderate.

STRESA (PIEDMONT)

Grand Hotel et des Iles Borromees – This baroque, turreted villa is a quintessential luxury hotel. Its well-furnished, spacious rooms all have private baths. It has a private beach on Lake Maggiore, an incomparable view, superb gardens, swimming pool, and restaurant. 67 Lungolago Umberto (phone: 3-0431). Very expensive.

Villa Aminta – Less extravagant, this nonetheless has tennis courts, tasteful gardens, a private beach, and a good restaurant. Closed from November through mid-March. 123 Via Nazionale del Sempione (phone: 3-1197). Moderate.

Hotel du Park e Villa Pineta – This secluded hotel stands in a lovely garden. Closed mid-October through March. Via Gignous 1 (phone: 3-0335). Moderate.

Ristorante L'Emiliano – Despite its rather somber decor, the culinary repertoire — fillet steak with truffles, grilled fish, perfectly cooked vegetables, mushrooms in season, and a select choice of wines — is heartwarming. Closed Tuesdays and from mid-November to mid-December. Corso Italia 48 (phone: 3-1396). Expensive.

LUGANO (SWITZERLAND)

Hotel Bellevue au Lac – This spacious hotel stands in a garden overlooking Lake Lugano and the surrounding mountains. It has a swimming pool, car park, and a good restaurant. Closed from mid-October to mid-March. Riva Caccia 10 (phone: 54-33-33). Expensive to moderate.

Hotel de la Paix – Somewhat more modest, this hotel has a good swimming pool and enviable views of the lakes and mountains. Closed in January. Via Cattori 18 (phone: 54-23-31). Moderate.

Ristorante Bianchi – This traditional and warm restaurant of top quality is in old Lugano. Specialties include cold antipasto and veal dishes. Via Pessina (phone: 22-84-79). Expensive to moderate.

CERNOBBIO

Grand Hotel Villa d'Este – In a modernized sixteenth-century villa at a lakeside park, it has a swimming pool, tennis courts, a golf course, and a very good restaurant. Via Regina 40 (phone: 51-14-71). Very expensive.

Hotel Asnigo – This comparatively less lavish hotel has a delightful garden, good views of the lake, and an adequate restaurant. Closed from November through mid-March. About 1 mile (2 km) north of town, at Piazza Santo Stefano (phone: 51-00-62). Inexpensive.

Ristorante Terzo Crotto – This is one of the best restaurants on Lake Como for northern cuisine — a wide variety of soups, excellent meat, fresh mushrooms, truffles, wild strawberries, and blueberries in their respective seasons. Closed Thursdays and November. Via Volta 21 (phone: 51-23-04). Moderate.

COMACINA ISLAND

Locanda dell'Isola Comacina – Set on the only sizable island in Lake Como, at the end of a winding, narrow path, this place features a menu that hasn't changed in nearly 40 years. And why should it, when the feast served up includes "Smuggler's Trout" (perfectly grilled fish splashed with olive oil), pressed roast chicken, a huge antipasto (the marinated carrots are especially delicious), and a dessert of homemade vanilla ice cream atop fresh orange slices, doused in banana liqueur. Comacina Island, Lake Como (phone: 55083). Expensive.

BERGAMO

Excelsior San Marco – This first-class hotel has 150 rooms, all with private bath and air conditioning. There's also a good restaurant (closed Fridays). Piazza Repubblica 6 (phone: 23-21-32). Expensive.

Hotel del Moro – The restaurant at this unpretentious hotel is excellent. Largo Porta Nuova 6 (phone: 24-29-46). Moderate.

Ristorante La Pergola – This traditionally elegant restaurant in the old part of Bergamo serves delicious food and has a very good selection of wines. Try the tasty fish ravioli, mushroom soup, and especially the homemade sweets. Closed Sundays and August. Borgo Canale 62 (phone: 22-33-05). Expensive.

Ristorante Taverna del Colleoni – In a sixteenth-century palace in the old quarter, this place serves traditional dishes with imaginative variations. *Polenta* (maize pudding) with fried egg and white truffles, fresh mushrooms, truffles, smoked ham, and meat are all delicious. Pasta dishes are light and appetizing. Closed Mondays and August. Piazza Vecchia 7 (phone: 23-25-96). Expensive.

Ristorante La Vendemmia – Exquisitely prepared Bergamasque dishes — smoked goose breast, local salami, and cheese fritters — are served in the garden of this seventeenth-century house, weather permitting. Closed Mondays. Via Fara 17 (phone: 22-11-41). Expensive.

Emilia

Stretching from the southern end of the flat and fertile Po Valley and the western Apennine Mountains north of Tuscany, Emilia only came into existence as a region in 1860 with the unification of Italy. The name originates from the Roman road, the via Emilia, which runs in a straight line from Milan to Rimini on the Adriatic coast; it was built by Aemilius Lepidus to connect the Roman Empire with its newly acquired northern European lands. Since that time, the road has been responsible for much of the region's trade development and was an important communication line throughout the various Roman and medieval conflicts that swept through Emilia's cities and countryside. During World War II, it was used by the Allied forces occupying Italy.

Emilia is a small region, but its culture and customs are the product of twenty centuries of densely packed history. Most of its cities — Parma, Bologna, Ferrara — were medieval and Renaissance duchies or principalities and are replete with architectural memorials of long and eventful histories. But it is a rich area to visit for more than its history, for a good part of its cultural distinction is expressed in its cuisine, the richest cooking in Italy. Bologna is known as Bologna the Fat, and for good reason. Emilia is where *tortellini,* those delicious pasta packets filled with meat or vegetables, and *tagliatelle,* golden flat egg noodles, are served wrapped in dense *ragù Bolognese,* the traditional meat sauce made with pork, beef, chicken livers, vegetables, butter, and cream. Here is where *mortadella* (the grandfather of American bologna) and salami originated. And here is where Parma, one of Italy's most beautiful cities, inspired delectable Parma ham and world-famous Parmesan cheese.

Although pork is the most popular meat in Emilia, veal is deliciously transformed in Bologna to create *lombatini di vitello* — veal chops wrapped in prosciutto with a cream sauce. The major wines of the region are the frothy Lambrusco and a fruity red called Sangiovese.

It is also a region of geographic contrast — mountainous in the west, where the Apennines shoot down central Italy; flat in the northeast, where a broad expanse of flatlands surrounding the huge Po River cradles some of Italy's best agricultural soil. In the mountains south of Bologna, the Emilian capital, ancient watchtowers still stand atop nearly inaccessible peaks; they were built by medieval warlords to keep constant vigil for enemies approaching in the strife-torn region. These strategic towers were used again by the Allies in the last war.

A logical starting place for a 4-day tour of this region is on the northwestern tip, where the via Emilia connects Milan to the town of Piacenza. Caught between the Po River and the Apennine foothills, Piacenza is an important trade center. It also offers a first glimpse of the medieval Gothic and Roman-esque styles of art and architecture found throughout the cities on this route. Heading south, the other major cities on the route include Parma; Modena, a well-endowed agricultural area as well as an artistic center claiming one of the finest galleries in the country; Bologna, a major hub of commerce and learning, renowned for its ancient university; and Ferrara, a former cultural enclave for artists, writers, and philosophers, now turned toward agriculture and industry.

MILAN: For a detailed report, see *Milan,* THE EUROPEAN CITIES.

PIACENZA: The original Roman city is long gone, destroyed by invading barbarian tribes at the dissolution of the Roman Empire, but much of the medieval town that flourished from the twelfth century remains, even though Piacenza today is thoroughly modern, caught up in the production of methane gas from the rich fields buried beneath the flatlands of the Po River valley. Wheat, hemp, and maize are traded here in a thriving agricultural market, but the old city, centered around piazza Cavalli, captures the essence of medieval Emilia as well as any town in the region. Dominated by two statues of medieval rulers belonging to the Farnese family, which held the duchy of Piacenza from the sixteenth to the eighteenth century, the piazza is surrounded by the graceful Gothic Palazzo del Comuni, known as Il Gotico, on one side. On the other side stands the thirteenth-century Church of San Francesco, at the beginning of via Venti Settembre, which ends in front of the Duomo, a rather majestic cathedral in Lombardian-Romanesque style built between the twelfth and thirteenth centuries.

En Route from Piacenza – Travel on the via Emilia through pleasant green countryside to Salsomaggiore, the second largest spa town in Italy. It has saline waters, which are good for rheumatism, as well as the natural sulfur pools in nearby Tabiano.

PARMA: In the middle of the vast plain south of the Po River, Parma is acclaimed for its architectural beauty and gastronomic delights. It abounds with excellent restaurants, so when exploring, stop in almost any section of town for a satisfying meal. Pork meat cuts in Emilia are generally the most famous in Italy; in Parma, the specialty is prosciutto, which, combined with Parmesan cheese, often garnishes many dishes.

Despite heavy bombing in the last war, Parma still retains much of its splendor as the former capital of the duchy of Farnese. The old center of the town is piazza Garibaldi, bounded by the governor's palace, clock tower, and the town hall. More spectacular, however, is the group of buildings of the ecclesiastical authorities and their interior frescoes, particularly the design by Correggio of the Assumption of the Virgin Mary on the roof of the cupola in the Romanesque Duomo. From the via del Duomo it is a short walk to piazza Marconi and the Church of Madonna dell Steccata, a majestic sixteenth-century church damaged by bombs in the last war but admirably restored. Next, visit the Palazzo della Pilotta, one of the unfinished buildings begun during the reign of the dukes of Farnese. It's now a museum, with exhibits spanning the city's history from prehistoric times to the late Renaissance as well as collections from ancient Egypt and the Far East. Equally interesting is the National Gallery, with rooms devoted to Emilian artists, especially the school established in Parma by Correggio, and Italian artists from other regions from the fourteenth, fifteenth, and sixteenth centuries.

MODENA: Originally a Roman colony, this city fell under the control of powerful ducal dynasties in the early Middle Ages, later passing to Austrian dominion. The medieval period proved the strongest influence on Modena's artistic development and today remains the dominant presence in the city's role as a center of art.

For a rich sampling of Gothic and Romanesque design, begin a city tour at the cathedral in the piazza Grande. Begun in 1099 and finished three centuries later, its architecture is mainly early Gothic while inside frescoes and statues date from the fifteenth century. Outside the cathedral, notice the tall, graceful Lombardian bell tower known as the Ghirlandina, the city's best-known monument. Going down the via Emilia, be sure to stop at the Palazzo dei Musei, which houses one of Italy's finest art galleries.

BOLOGNA: You would not be a hopeless romantic to see something of the fate of all Italy in the varying fortunes of this city. Built by the Etruscans (who called it Felsina), it was conquered by the Gauls, invaded by the Romans, sacked by northern tribes during the dissolution of the Roman Empire, and finally, in the twelfth century, plunged into the interminable internecine warfare of the Guelphs and Ghibillines, who represented no ideology beyond their allegiance to various personalities and vague identification with pro- and antipapal forces. It was not until the Guelphs prevailed in the middle of the thirteenth century that Bologna came to full flower and the form of the city as it exists today was established — red slate roofs, long arcades, distinctive elliptical domes. During this period the university — the oldest in Europe, founded in 1076 — flourished, and in the sixteenth century, when the city became associated with several ruling families (of whom the Bentivoglio were the most famous), the city became a center of art, literature, and learning. Today Bologna is a Communist town, the core of the famous industrial Red Belt that crosses Italy from Tuscany through Emilia.

In the center of town is the traffic-free piazza Maggiore, where three Gothic structures stand within a few steps of one another. The Palazzo Comunale is the most complicated, a group of palaces incorporated into one beautifully proportioned complex. It houses a small but fine municipal art collection of works by some of the finest Renaissance and eighteenth-century artists. A similar architectural plan, involving seven separate churches of different periods joined together, exists at the Church of Santo Stefano complex. This consists of the eleventh-century Church of the Crucifix, the octagonal Church of the Holy Sepulcher (where St. Petronius is buried), and the Church of St. Peter and St. Paul. Several other small chapels and churches are housed in this medieval complex as well.

FERRARA: To reach this city, you finally leave the via Emilia at the Bologna highway junction and head north. Autostrada A15 takes you to new Emilian territory — one of very green countryside dotted with vines and trees. Ferrara itself sits on drained and filled-in marshland. It is now an agricultural and industrial center that once flourished as a commercial and cultural stronghold during the Renaissance. As an independent duchy under the dukes of Este and their rich courts, it was a haven for some of the most highly talented artists, philosophers, humanists, and writers of the age.

When you arrive, first visit the Castello Estense, a fortress with massive corner towers and a surrounding moat built in the fourteenth and fifteenth centuries. Many of the inside rooms are open to the public — some with majestic interiors and frescoed ceilings. The castle chapel and dungeons are open as well. Nearby is the twelfth-century Romanesque-Gothic cathedral and marble bell tower facing the thirteenth-century Palazzo Comunale, which had to be restored in 1924. Along via Scandiana visit the fourteenth-century Palazzo Schifanoia, which the fabled dukes used for their many amusements. Now a museum, its interior walls are frescoed with scenes from the life of Duke Borso D'Este. A short distance away, in the via Settembre, stands the unfinished but splendid Renaissance Palazzo di Ludovico il Moro, now an archaeological museum full of Etruscan and Roman treasures.

BEST EN ROUTE

In Emilia you'll find some pleasant if not outstanding hotels and some truly splendid restaurants. Expect to pay $70 or more per night for a double room at those hotels categorized as expensive; between $50 and $65 at hotels in the moderate category; under $45, inexpensive. Expect to pay $60 or more for a meal for two at those restaurants we've classified as expensive; between $40 and $50 at restaurants in the moderate category; under $35, inexpensive. Prices do not include drinks or tip.

PARMA

Park Hotel Stendhal and Ristorante La Pilotta – The most elegant hotel in town stands in a small square in the old quarter. The restaurant is closed during August and on Sundays. Piazzeta Bodoni 3 (phone: 20-80-57). Expensive.

Park Hotel Toscanini and Ristorante al Torrente – Somewhat less fancy than the *Stendhal,* this hotel in the center of town has a very good restaurant. The restaurant is closed Mondays and August. Viale Toscanini 4 (phone: 2-9141). Expensive to moderate.

Hotel Bristol – Although the quarters are modest, the atmosphere is certainly pleasant. Strada Garibaldi 73 (phone: 20-80-37). Moderate.

Restaurant Angiol d'Or – Here you'll find excellent beef and veal dishes. Closed Tuesdays, Wednesdays, and August. Via Scutellari 1 (phone: 2-2632). Moderate.

La Filoma – The decor is not as lavish as that of the *Angiol d'Or,* but the stuffed veal and *tortelli alla parmigiana* make up for it. Closed weekends. Via 20 Marzo 15 (phone: 3-4269). Moderate to inexpensive.

MODENA

Ristorante Fini – Roast meat is brought to your table and carved to your liking at this excellent, elegant restaurant. Closed Mondays and Tuesdays. Reservations recommended. Largo San Francesco (phone: 22-33-14). Expensive to moderate.

Oreste – Considerably less ornate than the *Fini,* it serves terrific pasta and poultry. Closed on Wednesdays and in July. Piazza Roma 31 (phone: 24-33-24). Expensive to moderate.

Bianca – This simple and homey trattoria serves delicious Modenese dishes, and is extremely popular — mainly because Bianca herself has been running its kitchen for the last 35 years. Closed Sundays and August. Via Spaccini 24 (phone: 31-15-24). Moderate.

Da Enzo – This is where to find the best traditional Italian cuisine. Specialties include pheasant with polenta and homemade tortellini. Closed Saturdays and August. Via Coltellini 17 (phone: 22-51-77). Moderate to inexpensive.

BOLOGNA

Hotel Garden – As its name suggests, this agreeable building is surrounded by greenery and flowers. It has a restaurant and parking area. Via delle Lame 109 (phone: 52-22-22). Expensive to moderate.

Hotel Roma – In the traffic-free zone, it is centrally located, quiet, and has its own garage. Via d'Azeglio 9 (phone: 27-44-00). Moderate.

Ristorante Al Pappagallo – This well-known, traditional establishment is known for its fillet steak cooked in flaky pastry. Closed in August. Piazza Mercanzia 3 (phone: 23-28-07). Expensive.

Dante – Fine food and a delightful, elegant atmosphere. Reservations a must. Closed Mondays and the first half of August. Via Belvedere 2 (phone: 22-44-64). Expensive.

Ristorante Grassilli – Reservations are advisable at this small restaurant where green gnocchi and risotto alla chef are the specialties. Closed on Wednesdays and in July. Via del Luzzo 3 (phone: 22-29-61). Expensive to moderate.

FERRARA

Ripagrande Hotel – This elegant, new hotel occupies a Renaissance palazzo. The decor is a striking blend of antique and modern, and the rooms on the upper levels have a lovely rooftop view. Good bar and restaurant. Via Ripagrande 21 (phone 3-47-33). Moderate to expensive.

Hotel Astra – A centrally located hotel with first-class accommodations and a good restaurant. The restaurant is closed Wednesdays and August. Viale Cavour 55 (phone: 2-62-34). Moderate.

Hotel Europa – Although it's on the main street, it has a secluded garden and a parking area. Corso Giovecca 49 (phone: 3-3460). Moderate to inexpensive.

Buca San Domenico – The pizza here is the best in town, but there are also many other good dishes. Closed Mondays and July. Piazza Sacrati 22 (phone: 3-70-06). Moderate.

Grotta Azzurra – A popular place specializing in northern Italian cuisine. Closed Sundays and July. Piazza Sacrati 43 (phone: 3-73-20). Moderate to inexpensive.

Ristorante Vecchia Chitarra – This unpretentious place serves solid Ferrarese cooking. Closed Tuesdays. Via Ravenna 11 (phone: 6-2204). Moderate to inexpensive.

Piedmont and the Val d'Aosta Region

Piedmont, the northwesternmost region of Italy, is one of the shortest routes on our tour of the country. As its name implies, it lies mostly at the foot of the Alps, which surround it on three sides, and is only a few miles from the French border. Its eastern portion is within the outer limits of the great Po River valley.

This route also includes the adjacent region of Val d'Aosta, formed by valleys surrounded by the high peaks of Mont Blanc, the Matterhorn, and Mt. Rosa in the north and Gran Paradiso in the south. Governed by private council, this politically autonomous region stretching from Courmayeur to

Pont St. Martin consists of small French-speaking mountain villages closely bound by mountain traditions and customs. The mountains surrounding Val d'Aosta are interspersed with medieval castles and sophisticated resorts, many open year-round for skiing.

A tour of both regions begins at Entrèves, where a modern tunnel connects France and Italy. It continues south through Courmayeur and other Val d'Aosta resorts until it enters Piedmont territory. The final portion of the trip is spent in Turin, the capital of Piedmont and an industrial and cultural center.

Piedmont, with access to France, played an important role in Rome's control of its empire, and there are important ruins from the Imperial Age at Aosta, Susa, and Turin. But its richest period was under the dukes of Savoy, from the sixteenth through the nineteenth century. The House of Savoy filled Turin with Renaissance, baroque, and rococo palaces and the countryside with castles and hunting lodges such as Stupinigi (now a museum of decorative arts) and sanctuaries such as La Superga. In the nineteenth century, Piedmont was the moving force behind the unification of Italy under the House of Savoy.

In 1861 Turin ceased being the capital of the region and the entire area turned from politics to industrial and resort operations. Today the Turin area has become one of the chief industrial zones of the country, supported by Fiat, Olivetti, and other major corporations, while the mountain areas, particularly the Val d'Aosta, have developed into prosperous resorts for both winter and summer sports.

From Roman times, Piedmont's strategic position — guarding one of the main approaches to Italy from northern Europe — has been its source of power. Hannibal is known to have crossed the Alps here in the third century BC (with elephants in tow), and in 1800 Napoleon I led his army over the Great St. Bernard Pass. Today a tunnel under the same pass assures year-round entry from Switzerland to Italy and the 7.5-mile (12-km) tunnel under the Mont Blanc range carries very heavy international traffic from France. Both tunnels lead to Aosta, from which Autostrada A5 runs to the north Italian plain. There are several other transalpine passes through this region that are open only in summer, including Little St. Bernard, the Mont Cenis, and Mont Genèvre from France, and the Simplon from Switzerland.

ENTRÈVES: The first in a series of mountain resorts that mark the Piedmont–Val d'Aosta range, Entrèves best serves the area as a base of operations.

You can travel by cable car from Entrèves across four different sections of the Mont Blanc range (the highest in Europe) to Chamonix in France. At its summit of 15,771 feet above sea level, the Mont Blancs open to a sensational panorama of peaks and glaciers — but go only in good weather, otherwise the view is badly obstructed.

Another scenic excursion can be made to the head of the Val Ferret as far as Arnouva. If you are really energetic, hike the mule track to the Pre' de Bar, about .5 mile (1 km), an alpine rise 6,767 feet above sea level with superb views of the surrounding peaks.

COURMAYEUR: This village in the upper Dora Baltea Valley, 3 miles (5 km) from

Entrèves, is the largest resort in the Val d'Aosta. Originally a fashionable summer resort, it is now also popular for winter skiing, with 66 hotels and 30 lifts, cable cars and tows, nightclubs, discotheques, and all the usual resort paraphernalia.

AOSTA: The regional capital of Val d'Aosta and the Italian connection for the Great St. Bernard Pass road into Switzerland, Aosta is an ancient town, founded by the Romans in 25 BC. It combines interesting Roman remains (the Arch of Augustus, the Pretorian Gate, sections of the Roman walls and theater), with evidence of a prosperous medieval society. The latter gave rise to the Church of Sant' Orso, founded in the tenth century. Its cloister, cathedral, and apse towers were built over a period of three centuries. Aosta is also the starting point for the Gran Paradiso National Park, a nature preserve comprising the Cogne and Valsavarenche valleys.

CERVINIA: Once a summer pasture for cattle from nearby villages, Cervinia is now a completely modern center, with 40 hotels, 21 ski lifts, cable cars and tows, skating rinks, bobsled runs, bowling alleys, swimming pools, and saunas. Towering to the north is the Matterhorn and to the west the Jumeax precipices, making it one of the most beautifully situated resorts in the Val d'Aosta. It is a year-round resort, with winter skiing, summer hiking excursions into near and far mountains (including the Matterhorn and Preithorn), and spectacular views anytime.

The town, however, is not cheap, but within the reasonable to expensive price range, you'll find a wide selection of hotels.

CHAMPOLUC: At the foot of the Preithorn and the western peaks of the Monte Rosa massif, this town is a popular winter sports resort, but it's even more pleasant and quiet in the summer. Hotels here are unpretentious and set amid refreshing pine forests or atop mountain slopes.

GRESSONEY VALLEY: Within this valley are a number of year-round resorts, the main ones being Gressoney St. Jean and Gressoney La Trinite. Either one can serve as a starting point for a climb up Monte Rosa, at 15,203 feet the second highest peak in the Alps.

En Route from Gressoney Valley – Beyond Pont St. Martin, the two main southbound highways, the A5 and the SS26, leave the mountain region of the Val d'Aosta and enter Piedmont proper, marked by the more level area of the north Italian plain. The SS26 runs to Chivasso, where it forms a junction with SS11 for Turin. This route is not advisable since it runs through the northern suburbs of Turin, generally congested with very heavy traffic. Instead, take A5, which leads to the city's north end.

TURIN (TORINO): The capital of the Piedmont region, Turin is one of the great industrial centers of Italy, with a population of 1,200,000. Founded by the Romans, it didn't acquire prominence until the sixteenth century, when the reigning dukes of Savoy filled Turin with fine baroque palaces and churches. These now stand in the old section of town, the heart of which is the piazza Castello, a handsome, arcaded square with the former Royal Palace at the north end and the Palazzo Madama on the east. Parts of the Palazzo Madama are Roman, parts medieval, though the elegant facade on the piazza is a baroque addition of the eighteenth century. On the northeast side of the piazza is the Opera (Teatro Regio), also with a baroque facade but with an ultramodern interior, the product of a 1973 restoration. One of the liveliest city streets is the arcaded via Roma, which leads to the piazza San Carlo, a cultural and commercial haven that contains the great Egyptian Museum and the Galleria Sabauda, both in the baroque Palace of the Academy of Sciences.

Near the riverbanks in the east is the most peculiar edifice, which has become the emblem of the city. Known as Mole Antonelliana, it was originally a synagogue built in 1863. Its tower ends in a spire 548 feet high and now serves as a lookout point.

Farther east is the Po River, lined with handsome and fashionable residential buildings. Upstream is Valentine Park, laid out in 1830 with an imitation medieval castle and an exhibition village. The park's modern exhibition center is the site of the annual Automobile Show; farther upstream is the Automobile Museum, with a good collection of antique cars. On the city's west side is the Gallery of Modern Art (via Magenta), well worth a stop.

Since the traffic problem in Turin is particularly bad and parking is a great problem, it is best to tour the city on foot. Also, it's advisable to take rooms in hotels that have garages or reserved parking lots.

For a gastronomically rewarding excursion on the outskirts of Turin, drive to Alba, a small town in the hilly country known as Le Langhe, the center of one of the great wine-producing regions of Italy.

Since Turin is at the center of a network of highways leading in all directions, it's a convenient starting point for trips throughout Italy and to France. Main roads lead to the Riviera, Genoa, Florence, Rome, Milan, and the Italian lakes.

BEST EN ROUTE

Accommodations in the Piedmont and Val d'Aosta range from elegant to rustic. Expect to pay $85 or more per night for a double room at those hotels classified as expensive; between $60 and $75 for a double room at hotels in the moderate category; under $60, inexpensive. Resort prices can increase by 30% in the ski season. Expect to pay $70 or more for a meal for two at those restaurants categorized as expensive; between $50 and $60 in the moderate category; under $45, inexpensive. Prices do not include drinks, wine, or tip.

ENTRÈVES

Hotel Pilier d'Angle – This modest, 12-room hotel in the middle of the village has a pleasant garden and restaurant (phone: 8-9129). Inexpensive.

Hotel Astoria – This reasonably priced, centrally located establishment has 26 rooms, a garden, and a restaurant. There is a garage. Closed mid-September to mid-December, May through June. À la Palud N (phone: 8-9910). Inexpensive.

Hotel Val Veny – Beyond the town limits, with a dazzling view of Mont Blanc, this 20-room hotel is open only in the summer. Only five of the rooms have private baths. There is a garage. About 2.5 miles (4 km) from Entrèves on the Val Veny road (phone: 8-9904). Inexpensive.

Hotel Portud – Most of the 38 rooms have private baths. Although the view isn't quite as spectacular as that at the *Val Veny*, it is quite pretty. This hotel, too, is only open in the summer. At Portud, 4 miles (6 km) on the Val Veny road (phone: 8-9920). Inexpensive.

Maison de Filippo – A charming, rustic village restaurant, this is a good place for hearty, filling fare. Closed in June, November, and on Tuesdays (phone: 8-9968). Expensive to moderate.

Restaurant la Clotze – This place serves some of the best Piedmontese cooking around; it also has a fine view of Mont Blanc. Closed Wednesdays and from mid-June to mid-July. About 4 miles (6 km) from Entrèves on the Ferret road at Plampincieux (phone: 8-9928). Moderate.

COURMAYEUR

Hotel Palace Bron – Overlooking the village from a relatively isolated location, its striking surroundings help to compensate for its out-of-the-way setting. It has 29 rooms, many with views of the lovely garden and grounds. Closed October to mid-December, May through June. Plan Gorret 37 (phone: 84-25-45). Expensive.

Hotel Royal E Golf – Facilities at this classy 80-room hotel include a heated swimming pool, garden, and restaurant. Closed September through November,

May through June. In the center of town, at Via Roma 83 (phone: 84-36-21). Expensive.

Hotel Cresta et Duc – Open from December through April and from June through September, this is a comfortable 38-room hotel. Via Circonvallazione 7 (phone: 84-25-85). Moderate to inexpensive.

Restaurant Vieux Pommier – In the center of town, this restaurant is closed during October and on Mondays except in high season. Piazzale Monte Bianco 25 (phone: 84-22-81). Moderate.

Restaurant K2 – Although it's named after the second highest mountain in the world (climbed in the 1950s by a Courmayeur citizen), this is a down-to-earth establishment on the road to Mont Blanc that serves well-prepared dishes. Closed Mondays, and in May, June, and November. Villair (phone: 84-24-75). Moderate.

AOSTA

Hotel Valle d'Aosta and Grill le Foyer – *Valle d'Aosta* is the name of the modern, 102-room hotel with garage amid gardens. *Grill le Foyer* is the restaurant, closed Tuesdays and November. Corso Ivrea 174 (phone: 4-1845). Expensive to moderate.

Rayon de Soleil – This comfortable, 32-room hotel is on a broad avenue in the center of town. Its restaurant is closed on Fridays. Viale Gran San Bernardo (phone: 36-22-47). Moderate to inexpensive.

CERVINIA

Hotel Cristallo – In addition to 96 well-appointed rooms, you will find tennis courts, a covered swimming pool, and a garage. Closed September through November and May through June. In the center of town (phone: 94-81-25). Expensive.

Residence Cieloalto – This modern 80-room hotel has both indoor and outdoor swimming pools, tennis courts, and a garage. In the center of town (phone: 94-87-55). Expensive.

Hotel Chalet Valdotain – Set amidst quiet countryside, with a good view of Lac Bleu, this unpretentious 35-room hotel is closed in May, October, and November. About 1 mile (2 km) from town at Lac Bleu (phone: 94-94-28). Moderate.

Restaurant Pavia – Here is good, plentiful fare in a friendly environment. Closed on Thursdays, mid-May to mid-July, and from September 15 through November. In the village (phone: 94-90-10). Moderate.

Restaurant La Grotta – This is another good restaurant in the center of town. Closed Thursdays (phone: 94-94-92). Moderate.

CHAMPOLUC

Anna Maria – In a pine forest, this 20-room charmer is only open from mid-June through mid-September. Full board is included with the price of a room (phone: 30-71-28). Moderate.

Genzianella – Splendidly situated in a mountain valley, this 20-room hotel offers simple accommodations. Closed in October. At St. Jacques (phone: 30-71-56). Inexpensive.

TURIN (TORINO)

All hotels have parking facilities or garages.

Jolly Hotel Principi di Piemonte – One of the leading hotels in town, its 105 rooms have air-conditioning and it has a good restaurant. Via Gobetti 15 (phone: 51-96-93). Expensive.

Turin Palace – Continental breakfast is included with the price of one of its 125 rooms, but there is no restaurant. Via Sacchi 8 (phone: 51-55-11). Expensive.

Jolly Ambasciatori – This is the largest hotel in town. Its 203 rooms are air-conditioned and it has a restaurant. Corso Vittorio Emanuele 104 (phone: 5752). Expensive.

Sitea Grand Hotel – Recently renovated, this hotel offers excellent service, comfortable rooms, and a central location. Via Carlo Alberto 35 (phone: 55-701-71). Expensive to moderate.

Rex – A centrally located 65-room hotel, it serves Continental breakfast but, again, has no restaurant. Via Pomba 25 (phone: 51-72-02). Moderate.

Alexandra – The best thing about this modern, 50-room hotel is its site on the Dora River. Lungo Dora Napoli 14 (phone: 85-83-27). Moderate.

President – Centrally located, this 72-room hotel has a lovely terrace and enclosed garden. Service is courteous, and the atmosphere is pleasantly friendly. Via Antonia Cecchi 67 (phone: 85-95-55). Moderate.

Restaurant del Cambio – A historical restaurant with classic Victorian design, its cuisine matches the ambience. The house specialties are fondue with truffles, pot roast in Barolo, and mixed boiled meats. Closed in August and on Sundays. Piazza Carignano 2 (phone: 54-66-90). Expensive.

Restaurant Al Gatto Nero – The specialties are Florentine steak, grilled fish, and meat. There is an excellent wine cellar. Closed in August and on Sundays and Mondays at noon. Corso Filippo Turati 14 (phone: 59-04-14). Expensive.

Restaurant Villa Sassi – Set in an eighteenth-century villa with a large garden, this luxurious, fashionable restaurant has 12 rooms with private bath for overnight stays. Closed during August, Sunday evenings, and on Mondays. Across the River Po, Traforo del Pino 47 (phone: 89-05-56). Expensive.

Vecchia Lanterna – For classic Piedmontese food — risotto with Barolo, agnolotti (a kind of pasta) stuffed with duck, and saddle of venison — make a reservation to dine here. Closed in August, Saturdays at noon, and all day Sunday. Corso Re Umberto 21 (phone: 53-70-47). Expensive.

Tastevin – This elegant restaurant serves specialties such as risotto with Spumante, lamb with balsamic vinegar, and, for dessert, zabaglione with Barolo. Closed Sundays and August. Corso Siccardi 15 (phone: 54-56-40). Moderate to expensive.

Montecarlo – The mixed menu here offers classic Italian dishes and nouvelle cuisine concoctions like duck with blueberries. Closed Sundays and August. Via San Francesco da Paola 37 (phone: 54-12-34). Moderate.

Tre Galline – A classic Piedmontese trattoria in the city's historic quarter, it enjoys a solid reputation. Closed Mondays and August. Via Bellezia 37 (phone: 54-68-33). Moderate.

The Italian Riviera

The Italian Riviera stretches in an arc across the northwestern part of the Mediterranean coast of Italy, bordered by France on the west and Tuscany on the east; its apex is just west of Genoa. The Riviera is traversed by two main roads: the via Aurelia and the Autostrada, both running an average distance of 164 miles (265 km). The Autostrada generally runs a few miles inland from the coast, with exits for the most important towns. Since the coast is mountainous and generally very steep, the views are often spectacular, although sometimes interrupted by tunnels. In fact, take caution when driving in high winds along roads that pass over gulleys, especially when issuing from tunnels. The via Aurelia runs entirely along the shoreline, passing straight through coastal towns and villages. Although picturesque in spots, the road is narrow and twisting and the traffic usually heavy. The best plan is to take the Autostrada, exiting only at the places you wish to visit.

The warm climate, clear air, and scenic mountain backdrop of the Italian Riviera have made it one of Europe's leading resorts. It is wise, therefore — and during the high summer season essential — to make hotel reservations well in advance. The best seasons for the Riviera are spring (March through June), autumn (mid-September through October), and possibly Christmas week (although it is too cold for swimming). July and August are best avoided because of the crowds, noise, and heavy traffic. Each town has a tourist information office, generally called Azienda di Turismo or Pro Loco, that can provide detailed information on hotels, restaurants, sites, and activities.

There are two border crossing points from France. The Autostrada is reached from Monte Carlo or Menton (an extension from Nice is under construction), with the actual border in the middle of a tunnel. Passport and customs control is on the Italian side of the tunnel. The French shore road runs into the Italian via Aurelia at Ponte San Ludovico, just outside Menton. Border formalities for tourists are usually perfunctory, but on weekends and during the high season lines can be long. If you travel on the shore road, stop directly after the border crossing to visit the Balzi Rossi caves, where traces of prehistoric human habitation have been discovered. Also explore the Hanbury Gardens of La Mortola, one of the most famous botanical gardens in Europe. From here you can join the Autostrada at the Ventimiglia exit and either stop in the town — set, in part, on a hill with narrow streets and Roman remains — or continue directly to Bordighera.

BORDIGHERA: This is one of the older resort towns of the Riviera, patronized in the late nineteenth century by the English and by various European royalties. The Italian Riviera was settled not by Latins but by Ligurians, a fair northern race, and like many Ligurian towns, Bordighera consists of an older center on a hill with a newer section along the shore. Between the two are villas, hotels, and beautiful gardens centered along the old Roman road. Bordighera is famed for its palm trees and has held a monopoly for the supply of palms to the Vatican for Palm Sunday since 1586.

Many of the large hotels in town, which in the past catered to dowager duchesses and retired Indian major generals, are now closed or turned into apartment houses, but a few still exist in their original form. Bordighera has 100 hotels, so there are plenty of others to choose from.

SAN REMO: This is the largest resort on the Riviera, with a resident population of over 60,000 that is at least quintupled by summer tourists. It is a noisy, overcrowded, and overbuilt town whose major attraction is the Municipal Casino, where you can win a fortune or (more likely) lose your shirt at roulette, baccarat, and other games of chance. You can also get a very fine (but expensive) dinner in the casino restaurant. There are dozens of restaurants, pizzerias and snack bars in town; for recreation try sailing, water skiing, golf (an 18-hole course can easily be reached by cable car), and shopping.

Several excursions can be made from San Remo. The best is to Monte Bignone, which offers a superb view over the coast and a nearby pine forest. It can be reached by either road or cable car. Another worthwhile trip is to the artist colony at Bussana Vecchia, an old town destroyed by an earthquake in 1887 and abandoned until the 1950s, when it was taken over by a group of artists who settled among the ruins.

En Route from San Remo – Beyond San Remo, for the next 30 miles (48 km) or so, the coast isn't particularly interesting, and it is a good section to cover on the Autostrada until you reach the Andora exit and there rejoin the coastal road, following the signs for Laiguelia and Alassio. (There is a bad section of road around Cape Mele with alternating one-way traffic.)

LAIGUEGLIA: This small resort at the southern end of the Bay of Alassio has a good beach and several hotels. A picturesque old town, it also has many fine old houses and a large baroque church.

ALASSIO: This is one of the oldest resort towns on the Riviera and, despite a good number of unaesthetic modern buildings, it is still quite attractive, with a fine sandy beach over 1.5 miles long. The old town along the beach consists of one narrow street (now a pedestrian zone) with shops, taverns, restaurants, and cafés. The town hills rise steeply into the villa district, which has many gardens laid out by the original winter residents, mostly English. The tennis club in town hosts international tournaments, and, at Garlenda (11 mi/18 km distant), an excellent 18-hole golf course, with a country club and bungalows for rent. Good skiing is available at Monesi, about 31 miles (50 km) away, making Alassio a year-round resort. The high season, though, is from April to the end of September.

Alassio is an excellent base from which to explore the churches and ancient monuments of nearby villages. Stop at Moglio, Vegliasco, and Testico, all within a distance of 12 miles (20 km).

ALBENGA: Once an important Roman port, Albenga is now a busy market town for the produce of the hinterland (fruit, particularly peaches, and early vegetables). Visit the Roman Naval Museum, with the remains of a Roman ship sunk in Albengan waters in the first century BC.

From Albenga you can take an interesting excursion inland through the Aroscia Valley past Villanova, an ancient walled town, to Ortovero, a region famous for the red Pigato wine. You can continue on through the pleasant countryside to Ponte di Nava, where you'll find the object of this jaunt, *Beppe's,* a fine restaurant specializing in snails, game, trout, and, in season, raspberries. Before turning back, visit Ormea, a pretty summer resort; Garessio, known for its mineral springs; and, finally, the romantic village of Castelvecchio.

The shore road from Albenga is unattractive, and it is advisable to transfer to the Autostrada as far as Genoa.

GENOA (GENOVA): The greatest port in northern Italy and the main outlet for the "Industrial Triangle" (Turin, Milan, and Genoa), this city (pop. 800,000) rises like an amphitheater from its semicircular port into the hills above the city. Surrounding the harbor is the oldest (medieval) section, with steep and narrow streets and arcades and medieval houses and churches (a total of about 400). Above the port is Renaissance Genoa, consisting of fine palaces built by rich Genoese merchants, once the rivals of the Venetians in cultivating trade with the East. Then, on the higher slopes and in the flat area to the east, is modern Genoa, with wide streets and boulevards, squares and public gardens. Still higher is the Circonvallazione a Monte, a panoramic boulevard winding in and out among the hills, with fine views over the city. The layout of the city is very confusing since it follows no recognizable plan: The visitor would be well advised to buy a city map, available at any newspaper kiosk. Fortunately, the principal sights and monuments are well marked.

The sixteenth and seventeenth centuries saw a flurry of artistic activity in this wealthy shipping city. The impetus was provided by a number of Flemish artists — Rubens and Van Dyck, among them — who were invited to come to the city to work for wealthy merchant families, primarily making portraits. To form an image of what the city was like in this grand period, stroll down via Garibaldi (known as via Aurea before last century), lined with sixteenth-century palaces of elaborate design. The frescoes and gallery of Palazzo Cataldi, the art gallery in Palazzo Bianco (with fine collections of Genoa's adopted Flemish sons), and the antiques in Palazzo Doria Tursi tell reams about the life in Renaissance Genoa.

For one of the best panoramas of the city, take a cable car from Largo della Zecca up to the Righi.

Genoese cuisine features a number of specialties, such as *trenette al pesto* (noodles and a sauce flavored with basil, garlic, and pine nuts); fish *ravioli;* a vegetable pie known as *torta pasqualina* (Easter pie); *cappon magro,* a mixed salad of vegetables and fish with a mayonnaise sauce (very rich); and, of course, fish of all kinds.

En Route from Genoa – From Genoa, continue east on the Autostrada until you reach Camogli, a picturesque small port with tall houses, a favorite residence for sea captains. On the second Sunday in June, a gigantic fish fry is held here.

Continue on the Autostrada to the Rapallo exit, where you get on the shore road leading to Santa Margherita and Portofino on the Tigullo Gulf, one of the most scenic sections of the Riviera. Rapallo itself is grossly overbuilt. It has 65 hotels, a yacht harbor, and a 9-hole golf course. The beaches are barely adequate, but many of the better hotels have swimming pools.

SANTA MARGHERITA LIGURE: This is the best resort in the Tigullo area since it is neither overbuilt nor underdeveloped — perfect for a comfortable stay. The resort has 38 hotels, some situated on the waterfront or overlooking the sea and others above the town, with a view.

PORTOFINO: This is considered by many to be the "pearl" of the Italian Riviera. Originally a small fishing village enclosed in a bay, it has grown into a very exclusive (and expensive) resort, retaining its original atmosphere and charm by very stringent zoning regulations. Take a walk to the lighthouse past the church of San Giorgio for a fine view over the whole bay (total walking time is 1 hour). And don't miss the nearby hamlet of San Fruttuoso, reached by motorboat in 20 minutes.

En Route from Portofino – To reenter the main roads, you must backtrack to Rapallo. Beyond Rapallo, the Autostrada runs almost entirely inland until it reaches the La Spezia exit and continues into Tuscany.

The via Aurelia follows the coast, past Chiavari and Sestri Levante; then it, too, moves inland, climbing through fine scenery to the Bracco Pass. The coast from here to La Spezia is very steep, rugged, and very beautiful, but until a new road (370) is completed to Monterosso, its Cinque Terre (five towns — Monterosso, Vernazza, Corniglia, Manarola, and Riomaggiore), the most unspoiled part of the whole Riviera, are difficult to reach. These are small fishing and wine-growing towns clinging to the rocky coast and are more easily reached by train or from La Spezia on the finished portion of the shore road. (The railroad works its way mostly through tunnels, but each town has a station.)

LERICI: Sailing back from a visit to Leigh Hunt in Pisa, headed for his home in Lerici on the Gulf of Spezi, Percy Bysshe Shelley was capsized and drowned here in 1822; his body, found washed ashore, was burned in a funeral pyre by his wife and companions. This romantic and tragic event has marked this attractive little town ever since, drawing both historians and simple romantics to spend some time here. Lerici acts as a stop on the Riviera route, though short excursions to Tellaro, Montemarcello, and Bocca di Magra on the estuary of the Magra River are possible from here.

BEST EN ROUTE

Since the Italian Riviera is a resort area, you will find many fine hotels and restaurants, and high seasonal prices. Expect to pay $70 or more per night for a double room at those hotels categorized as expensive; between $50 and $65 at those places in the moderate category; under $45, inexpensive. Expect to pay $55 or more for a meal for two at those restaurants categorized as expensive; between $35 and $45 at a restaurant in the moderate category; under $30, inexpensive. Prices do not include drinks, wine, or tip.

MORTOLA INFERIORE

Hotel Eden – In keeping with its name, the 21-room hotel's most gracious feature is its garden. Open from April through mid-November. Via Aurelia (SS 1) (phone: 3-9431). Moderate to inexpensive.

Ristorante La Mortola – Specialties at this international restaurant are scampi with mustard sauce and crêpes Suzette. Closed from November until early December, Monday evenings, and Tuesdays. On SS 1 opposite the Hanbury Gardens (phone: 3-9432). Expensive to moderate.

BORDIGHERA

Grand Hotel Capo Ampelio – This old, established, 104-room hotel is set in a park with a swimming pool and restaurant. It has recently been remodeled. Closed mid-October through mid-December. Via Virgilio 5 (phone: 26-43-33). Expensive to moderate.

Grand Hotel del Mare – Another 104-room hotel that stands in a park, this one is distinguished by its beach. It also has a swimming pool. Closed from mid-October through mid-December. Via Aurelia, about 1 mile (2 km) from town (phone: 26-22-01). Expensive.

Le Chaudron – This charming restaurant offers very good Italian and French cuisine. Try the spaghetti with lobster and the irresistible homemade desserts. Closed Mondays and from mid-November to mid-December. Piazza Bengassi 2 (phone: 26-35-92). Expensive to moderate.

Hotel Jolanda – The peaceful atmosphere of the villa district around this 49-room hotel makes it a relaxing place to spend a few days. Closed from mid-October until early December. Corso Italia 85 (phone: 26-13-25). Moderate.

Hotel Astoria – Not as lavish as the *Jolanda,* this hotel in the villa district has 24 rooms and a garden. Closed November to mid-December. Via Tasso 2 (phone: 26-29-06). Moderate.

Ristorante La Reserve Tastevin – The menu contains an interesting selection of Mediterranean specialties. Closed Mondays and from October 26 to December 23. Via Arziglia 20 (phone: 26-13-22). Moderate.

Ristorante Chez Louis – An eclectic assortment of tasty Italian and French cuisine characterizes the culinary repertoire. Closed in November and on Tuesdays. Corso Italia 28 (phone: 26-16-02). Moderate.

Ristorante Romano – Here, the accent is on pasta and other Italian dishes. Closed Wednesdays. Piazza del Popolo 15 (phone: 26-16-82). Moderate.

SAN REMO

Hotel Royal – Many of the 140 rooms in this classic luxury hotel overlook the beach or surrounding park. There are a heated swimming pool and tennis courts. Closed from October through mid-December. Corso Imperatrice 74 (phone: 7-9991). Expensive.

Hotel Méditerranée – Near the yacht harbor, it has 70 rooms, a swimming pool, and fragrant gardens. Closed November through mid-December. Corso Cavallotti 76 (phone: 7-5601). Expensive.

Hotel Astoria–West End – This 93-room hotel is set among spacious gardens near the sea. Corso Matuzia 8 (phone: 7-0791). Expensive.

Grand Hotel Londra – Set in a park, this 127-room hotel has a heated swimming pool. Closed October through mid-December. Corso Matuzia 2 (phone: 7-9961). Expensive.

Hotel Résidence Principe – If you plan to stay in town for a while, consider booking one of the 52 rooms in this residential hotel, with very pretty gardens, swimming pool, and a lovely view. Closed November to mid-December. Via Asquasciati 48 (phone: 8-3565). Moderate.

Hotel Villa King – Although not deluxe, this 21-room hotel is pleasant, in a shady garden. Closed from mid-October through mid-December. Corso Cavallotti 92 (phone: 88-01-67). Moderate to inexpensive.

Hotel Villa Maria – This 19-room hotel's most attractive feature is its flower garden. Corso Nuvoloni 30 (phone: 88-28-82). Inexpensive.

Hotel Europa e Pace – More than half the 78 rooms in this unpretentious but comfortable hotel have private baths. Many have windows overlooking the sea. Corso Imperatrice 27 (phone: 7-0605). Inexpensive.

Ristorante Casinò – You won't have to gamble on the high quality of food or service here. Ranking epicures rate both as consistently superb. Corso Inglesi in the Municipal Casinò (phone: 7-9901). Expensive.

Ristorante Pesce d'Oro – House specialties are *lasagne al pesto,* fish soup, and grilled scampi. As seating capacity is limited, reservations are essential. Closed in June and on Mondays. Corso Cavallotti 272 (phone: 6-6332). Expensive.

Da Giannino – Simplicity and good taste characterize this restaurant; owner and chef Mrs. Gasperini prepares some very fine fish and squid dishes. Try one of the local Ligurian wines. Closed Sundays, the first half of July, and the first half of December. Lungomare Trento e Trieste 23 (phone: 7-0843). Expensive.

Ristorante U'Nostromû – Here you'll find excellent risotto and well-prepared fish. Closed in November and on Wednesdays. Piazza Sardi 2 (phone: 8-0767). Moderate.

Osteria del Marinaro – You will find any number of fish dishes (but only fish) on the menu. Reservations are essential. Closed Mondays. Via Gaudio 30 (phone: 8-9478). Moderate.

LAIGUEGLIA

Hotel Laiguelia – This restored old mansion on the shore has 55 rooms. Closed from November through March. Piazza Libertà 14 (phone: 4-9001). Moderate.

Hotel Splendid – Aptly named, this establishment has 42 well-appointed rooms, many of which overlook the beach. There is also a swimming pool. Closed November through March. Piazza Badarò 4 (phone: 4-9325). Moderate.

Hotel Beau-Sejour – Many of the 32 rooms in this converted palace overlook the hotel's private beach. Closed November through March. Piazza Cavour 8 (phone: 4-9019). Inexpensive.

Hotel Residence Paradiso – Some of the 32 units at this unpretentious hotel have kitchenettes. Via dei Pini 1 (phone: 4-9285). Inexpensive.

ALASSIO

Grand Hotel Diana – Although some of the 55 rooms have beachside balconies, those at the back of the hotel are noisy. In addition to a private beach, there are a swimming pool, sauna, and restaurant. Closed November through mid-March. Via Garibaldi 110 (phone: 4-2701). Expensive.

Grand Hotel Méditerranée – It overlooks the sea of the same name, with its own beach. Of its 82 rooms, 74 have private baths. Closed from November through March. Via Roma 63 (phone: 4-2564). Expensive to moderate.

Hotel Regina – Although not a lavish hotel, 31 of its 39 rooms have private baths.

Closed from November through February. Via Garibaldi 220 (phone: 4-0658). Moderate.

Hotel Lido – This substantial, 52-room hotel is on the beach. Closed from mid-October through March. Via 4 Novembre 9 (phone: 4-0158). Moderate to inexpensive.

Ristorante La Vigna – Be sure to make reservations before heading for this popular terrace restaurant. Closed Wednesdays. At Solva (phone: 4-3301). Expensive.

La Palma – Don't miss the special fish soup and the wonderful *pasta al pesto* served here. Reservations necessary. Closed Tuesdays and mid-October to mid-December. Via Cavour 5 (phone: 4-0314). Expensive to moderate.

Cafe Roma – You can easily while away a few hours at this pleasing café with adjoining snack bar. Closed Mondays. Via Dante (phone: 4-0168). Moderate.

Ristorante Excelsior – This is a good place to sample French and Italian cuisine. Closed Wednesdays. Via Robutti 6 (phone: 4-0454). Moderate.

GENOA (GENOVA)

There are more than 200 hotels, many in each price range, and innumerable restaurants and pizzerias in the Genoa area.

Hotel Colombia-Excelsior – A member of the luxury Excelsior chain, this 171-room hotel has a fine restaurant. Via Balbi 40 (phone: 26-18-41). Expensive.

Hotel Plaza – As you might expect, this 100-room establishment is in the most fashionable part of town, near the Piazza Corvetto, and has a classy restaurant. Via Martin Piaggio 11 (phone: 89-36-42). Expensive.

Hotel Savoy Majestic – While not as elegant as the former two places, the 116 rooms here are extremely comfortable. The restaurant is also very good. Via Arsenale di Terra 5 (phone: 26-16-41). Expensive.

Hotel Eliseo – This modest 34-room hotel is centrally located. Via Martin Piaggio 5 (phone: 88-02-10). Moderate.

Hotel Astoria – Although this simple hotel near the Brignole railroad station does not have its own restaurant, 60 of its 74 rooms have private baths. Piazza Brignole 4 (phone: 87-33-16 or 87-39-91). Moderate.

Ristorante del Mario – Classic Genoese cooking and a wide choice of good wines. Reservations advised for dinner. Closed Saturdays and August 5 to 25. Via Conservatori del Mare 33 (phone: 29-84-67). Expensive to moderate.

Vittorio Al Mare – This seaside restaurant with a beautiful view specializes in fish and risotto dishes. Closed Mondays. Belvedere Firpo 1, at Boccadasse (phone: 31-28-72). Moderate.

Ristorante Nino – This place serves Ligurian and Piedmontese specialties. Closed Mondays and July. Salita del Fondaco 20 (phone: 20-58-84). Moderate.

Ristorante La Polveriera – You can reach this garden restaurant with its romantic view of the city via the Righi funicular. It specializes in Ligurian cuisine. Closed Mondays and Tuesdays. Via Parco del Peralto 30 (phone: 21-56-77). Moderate.

CAMOGLI

Hotel Cenobio dei Dogi – Its gardens overlook the 88-room hotel's private beach and the bay. It also has a tennis court, swimming pool, and restaurant. The restaurant is closed on Fridays and January 7 through February. Via Cuneo 34 (phone: 77-00-41). Expensive.

Ristorante Da Gai – On the waterfront, it serves only fresh fish cooked in a variety of ways. Closed Thursdays and January. Piazzetta Colombo (phone: 77-02-42). Expensive to moderate.

RAPALLO

Grand Hotel Bristol – Many of the 91 rooms in this well-maintained hotel overlook the gardens, private beach, and heated swimming pool. There is also a restaurant. Via Aurelia Orientale 369 (phone: 5-0216). Expensive.

Rapallo Eurotel – This good, 64-room hotel has a garden, swimming pool, and restaurant. Via Aurelia Occidentale 22 (phone: 6-0981). Moderate.

Hotel Riviera – The 26 rooms all look out to sea. There is a good restaurant. Closed from November through mid-December. Piazza 4 Novembre (phone: 5-0248). Moderate.

Da Ardito – This popular restaurant has maintained its high standards for the last 50 years. It serves tasty regional dishes and wonderful local wines. Closed Tuesdays. Via Canale 9, Dan Pietro di Novello (phone: 5-1551). Moderate to inexpensive.

Ristorante Monique – Here, too, you'll find imaginative fish and seafood dishes. Closed Tuesdays and January 20 to February 20. Lungomare Vittorio Veneto 6 (phone: 5-0541). Moderate.

SANTA MARGHERITA LIGURE

Hotel Imperial Palace – In a spacious park, this luxury 108-room hotel has a heated swimming pool and a restaurant. Via Pagana 19 (phone: 8-8991). Very expensive.

Grand Hotel Miramare – Many of the 71 rooms face the private beach. There is also a garden, heated swimming pool, and a restaurant. Via Milite Ignoto 30 (phone: 8-7014). Expensive.

Hotel Laurin – Near the harbor, it has 41 rooms, a swimming pool in a garden, and a restaurant, *La Broche.* Closed from November through Christmas. Corso Mancini 3 (phone: 8-9971). Expensive.

Hotel Metropole – Most of its 48 rooms have private baths. Its garden overlooks a private beach. Closed November through mid-December. Via Pagana 2 (phone: 8-6134). Moderate.

Hotel La Vela – This remodeled old villa overlooking the bay has 16 rooms, a garden, and a restaurant. Corso Cuneo 4 (phone: 8-6030). Moderate.

Ristorante Bassa Prora – On the waterfront, its specialty is fresh fish and seafood. Closed Monday evenings and mid-September to mid-October. Via Garibaldi 7 (phone: 8-6586). Moderate.

Ristorante La Paranza – This is another fine fish restaurant. Closed Thursdays, and mid-January to mid-February. Via J Ruffini 46 (phone: 8-0686). Moderate.

Ristorante Beppe Achilli – Here you'll find a wide selection of roast meats and fowl. Closed Wednesdays and December. Via Bottaro 29 (phone: 8-6516). Moderate.

PORTOFINO

Hotel Splendido – The most fashionable, exclusive hotel in town has 65 rooms, a heated swimming pool, and tennis courts. Reservations are essential at the restaurant. Closed December through February. On the hillside above the village (phone: 69-51-51). Very expensive.

Piccolo Hotel – Smaller than the *Splendido* and considerably less extravagant, this 26-room hotel has a garden, parking area, and an outdoor restaurant. Closed from November through February. On the hillside above the village, below the *Splendido* (phone: 6-9015). Moderate.

Hotel Nazionale – On the harbor, it has 56 rooms and a restaurant (phone: 6-9138). Expensive.

Hotel Eden – This economical 9-room hotel is in the center of the village, and also has a restaurant (phone: 6-9091). Inexpensive.

Ristorante Il Pitosforo – On the waterfront, it serves some of the best fresh fish and seafood in town. Closed in January and February and on Tuesdays. On the harbor (phone: 6-9020). Very expensive.

LERICI

Hotel Shelley e delle Palme – Most of the 53 rooms overlook the bay. Lungomare Biaggini 5 (phone: 96-82-04). Moderate.

Ristorante La Calata – Lerici's finest fresh fish can be sampled here, on the waterfront. Closed Tuesdays and November. Via Mazzini 7 (phone: 96-71-43). Moderate.

Ristorante Golfo dei Poeti – Another good seafood restaurant with a nautical atmosphere. Closed Tuesdays. Via Mazzini 19 (phone: 96-74-14). Moderate.

Hotel Byron – This comfortable, 17-room hotel also overlooks the water. Lungomare Biaggini 25 (phone: 96-71-04). Moderate.

The Italian Dolomites

One of Europe's most beautiful and striking mountain ranges is the Italian Dolomites, part of the eastern Alps, from the central northern region of the Trentino–Alto Adige east to the Veneto region and the Piave River, both only a short distance from the Austrian border. The range continues south to the fringe of the fertile Po Valley. It is the home of some of Italy's most popular ski resorts, including Cortina d'Ampezzo and Ortisei.

The Dolomites have a fascinating geological history. Their unique formations of pinnacles and sheer rocks are the result of huge prehistoric eruptions from the sea that covered the area millennia ago. Sea fossils are found in the highest peaks, and Stone Age and Iron Age implements have been found in the Alps overlooking Bolzano, indicating that the Dolomites may have been one of the earliest inhabited areas in Europe.

The geologic structure of these mountains — limestone and porphyry — give them their famous rose-pink hue that deepens to an almost fiery red at sunset. Most towns in the Dolomites are a delightful mixture of Roman ruins, medieval fortifications and castles, early medieval buildings decorated with frescoes, and baroque churches. The Dolomites stand at a European crossroads, the meeting point of different peoples, languages, and cultures; and they have become battlegrounds innumerable times, from invasions by Roman legions and Emperor Charlemagne's campaigns to battles between the Austrian Empire and the Italian states. At the end of the ruthless conflicts of World War I, much of the Dolomites were handed over to Italy by Austria, and so Alto Adige — South Tyrol until 1918 — though Italian, is predominatly German-speaking.

The climate is typical of mountainous regions throughout Europe — snow on high ground from November to April, spring rain through June, and hot, sunny weather in the summer — though summer is infamously unpredictable, with sudden rains and fogs likely anytime.

To see as much as possible, one must zigzag through the Dolomites, stopping for cable car climbs or walks through interesting towns. The route described below begins at the Brenner Pass, on the Italy-Austria border, at the Italian town of Bolzano in the eastern Dolomites and follows a very crooked and irregular path until it returns to its starting point. By following it, you will have meandered completely through the eastern portion of the mountains, stopping in such towns as Bressanone, Ortisei, Brunico, Cortina, and San Martino di Castrozza. To cover the western part of the Dolomites, you again begin at Bolzano, but this time travel in the opposite direction, following the twisted southbound route to Trento. Each portion takes a few days, so allow a total of about 6 days. One encouraging factor: The Dolomites have one of the most efficient and dense networks of mountain roads in Europe and offer a wide variety of accommodations at every level.

BOLZANO: An important gateway to northern Europe in ancient times, Bolzano, called Bozen by its German-speaking population, reflects a predominantly Austrian character in its language and culture. It is the traditional capital of the Alto Adige area of the Dolomites.

The old center of Bolzano is entirely Tyrolean (the Alto Adige region was Austrian-controlled South Tyrol until 1918). The thirteenth-century Gothic cathedral stands in piazza Walther. Medieval arcades flank the narrow main street, along which modern shops have been built. This long street runs into the market square at piazza delle Erbe. Visit the Museo dell'Alto Adige, which houses a rare collection of local wooden sculptures and paintings, and cross the Isarco River for a short walk to the tiny, picturesque village of Gries. Don't miss its charming Gothic parish church.

En Route from Bolzano – For one of the less frequented, romantic routes to the Dolomites, take the northbound road 508 for 41.5 miles (67 km) to Vipiteno and explore the lonely medieval castles of Roncolo, Novale, and Sarentino on the way.

BRESSANONE: One of the most charming Alto Adige towns, Bressanone claims an eclectic combination of Gothic, Renaissance, and baroque architecture. Its thirteenth-century cathedral cloister and the tiny chapel with a fresco of St. Christopher are worth a visit, but even if you see nothing else here, you must stop at the *Hotel Elefante,* a beautifully preserved sixteenth-century building with original furnishings and one of the best restaurants in the Dolomites.

ORTISEI: At the foot of the grassy slopes of the Alpe di Siusi, Ortisei is a summer and winter resort. It's the chief town of the Val Gardena, one of the most romantic valleys of the Dolomites, carpeted with wild flowers that attract hikers every spring. A 6-minute cable car ride from the town takes you to the upper slopes of this range, opening up to incomparable views of the neighboring Catinaccios (or Rosengartens) and the long, pointed outline of the Sassolungo (Langkopf) Mountain.

En Route from Ortisei – Drive for 6 miles (10 km) to Selva di Val Gardena, a skier's and climber's paradise. Travel past the resort of Arabba, then head north through the Val Badia, yet another Dolomite ski valley and one of the few places where the ancient language of Ladino (a derivative of Latin) is still spoken.

BRUNICO: The capital of the Prusteria Valley and almost entirely Austrian in character, Brunico is famous for the spacious and gentle slopes that surround it. It is dominated by the Tyrolean castle of Bishop Bruno of Bressanone, built in 1251, but the area's greatest attraction is a half-hour's walk away — the breathtaking panorama from the Plan di Corones.

En Route from Brunico – Follow Route 49 toward the Lake of Misurina, one of the most romantic spots of the Dolomites. Near the lake are the Tre Cime di Lavaredo Mountains, a popular Dolomite climb. Follow Route 48 to Auronzo di

Cadore. You are now in the Veneto region, a more sparsely populated area of the Dolomites.

CORTINA D'AMPEZZO: In a sheltered basin surrounded by pine forests and some of the most spectacular Dolomite peaks, Cortina is probably the best-known and best-loved mountain resort in the entire Dolomites. It offers a huge variety of ski runs as well as walking and climbing trails and is well supplied with hotels and restaurants in every category.

SAN MARTINO DI CASTROZZA: This is not merely another popular ski resort. San Martino di Castrozza, surrounded by tall peaks and pine-wooded slopes, is a local scenic wonder. Pale di San Martino, the group of Dolomite pinnacles that dominate the city, are famous for their intense rose-pink glow at sunset. There are many available chalet-style hotels, typical of the region.

En Route from San Martino di Castrozza – Travel north past Predazzo and Moena and on to Vigo di Fassa, the capital of the lovely Fassa Valley and another Ladino-speaking area. To complete the eastern portion of the trip, follow Route 241 back toward Bolzano. It leads into the famous strada delle Dolomitti, the most popular Dolomite road. Make a few short stops along the strada at the Passo di Costalunga, the small Lake of Carezza (Karersee), whose water, for geological reasons, is a deep siena red. The route then descends into the wild, romantic Ega Valley. After passing beneath the main Brenner Pass highway, you are back in Bolzano.

Here again is your starting point, but this time for a trip through the western Dolomites, which lie primarily in the Trentino region. These are marked by local mineral spring waters that course through the lake and mountain areas and by architectural monuments of the medieval and Renaissance ages. You begin this western Dolomite route with Merano.

MERANO: This old-fashioned spa town is typical of Trentino's special charm. Its inner core is small, quaint, and Tyrolean while the outer town is marked by massive, somber, nineteenth-century Austrian hotels.

CLES: This pretty, medieval village in the heart of Val di Non was once the home of the Clesio family, medieval rulers whose ancestral castle dominates the town. A small Renaissance parish church also stands in the village center.

MADONNA DI CAMPIGLIO: Now one of Italy's biggest mountain resorts, Madonna di Campiglio offers countless excursions in summer and winter into the two ranges — Brenta and Adamello. Although mountain climbing in this region is geared to veteran hikers, there are several less challenging trails for beginners.

En Route from Madonna di Campiglio – As you head toward Trento, the road winds through some of the most attractive countryside of the region. You will come upon the spa center of Comano, the romantic lake and castle at Toblino, Lake Santa Massenza (which runs through the tiny spa town of Vigolo Baselga), and the peaceful lakeside village of Terlago.

TRENTO: Only 18.5 miles (30 km) south of Bolzano, this city served, for the same strategic reasons as its northern neighbor, as an important Roman town on the Brenner Pass. In the years following Roman rule, Trento fell into relative obscurity, but it once again gained fame in the mid-sixteenth century as the seat of the famous Council of Trent, held by Church authorities to consolidate Church power and curtail abuses in the face of the Protestant Reformation. Trento has always been Italian in character and language, despite its position in Austrian territory until 1918.

Some city highlights include the via Belenzani, one of Trento's most beautiful streets, lined with Venetian and Renaissance palaces with frescoed exterior walls; the baroque Church of San Francisco Saverio; and Trento's most celebrated monument — Il Castello di Buon Consiglio (the Castle of Good Counsel) — the original dwelling place of the bishops of Trentino–Alto Adige, built in the thirteenth century.

BEST EN ROUTE

Grand old Tyrolean hotels, inns, and converted castles stand on mountainsides and in the center of town in this part of the country. Expect to pay $70 or more per night for a double room at those places categorized as expensive; between $50 and $65 at hotels in the moderate category; under $45, inexpensive. Hearty country fare and local wines are served in any number of pleasant restaurants. Expect to pay $60 or more for a meal for two at those restaurants categorized as expensive; between $40 and $50 at restaurants in the moderate category; under $35, inexpensive. Prices do not include drinks or tip.

BOLZANO

Hotel Grifone-Greif – There are some beautiful furnishings on the large landings and in the upstairs reading rooms at this traditional Austrian hotel on the central piazza. The restaurant is excellent. Piazza Walther 7 (phone: 2-7056). Expensive.

Hotel Luna-Mondschein – This is a somewhat less refined but nonetheless characteristically Tyrolean hotel with a garden and a restaurant specializing in local cuisine. Via Piave 15 (phone: 2-5642). Expensive to moderate.

Hotel Scala-Stiegle – On the edge of the old town, this old-fashioned Tyrolean hotel has gardens, a swimming pool, and a restaurant. Via Brennero 11 (phone: 4-1111). Moderate.

Ristorante Castel Guncina – After months of restoration, a small Tyrolean castle has been converted to a restaurant where original and classic cooking is presented with a full complement of local wines. Closed Mondays. Via Miramonti 9 (phone: 4-6161). Moderate.

BRESSANONE

Hotel Elefante – In a secluded corner of town with a garden and a heated swimming pool, the inside of this hotel has changed little for the past 400 years except for essential modernizations such as heating. It's filled with genuine sixteenth-century furnishings. Closed mid-November through February. Via Rio Bianco 4 (phone: 2-2288). Expensive to moderate.

Hotel Corona d'Oro – More modest by comparison, this hotel in the old, porticoed center of town has a modern, pleasantly furnished restaurant where simple Tyrolean dishes, wine, and beer are served. Goldene Krone, via Fienili 4 (phone: 2-4154). Moderate to inexpensive.

Ristorante L'Elefante – This elegant restaurant serves local cuisine prepared with great care and the freshest ingredients. Try the house specialty, *Piatto Elefante* — a mountainous variety of cold meats served with appropriate sauces. Closed Mondays. Via Rio Bianco (phone: 2-2288). Moderate.

ORTISEI

Hotel Aquila-Adler – This hotel and restaurant have a garden, tennis court, swimming pool, and garage (phone: 7-6203). Expensive to moderate.

Hotel Sole – Only 5 minutes by cable car from Ortisei, it offers food and simple accommodations with spectacular views. Sonne in the Alpi di Siusi (phone: 7-6377). Moderate to inexpensive.

SELVA DI VAL GARDENA (WOLKENSTEIN)

Hotel Tyrol – One of Selva's chalet-style hotels has some of the most superb views of the Dolomites. The restaurant is known for good country food and friendly service. Closed from October through mid-December and from mid-April through mid-June (phone: 7-5270). Expensive to moderate.

Hotel Dorfer – This small, relatively isolated hotel has a private garden and a decent restaurant. Closed October through mid-December and May through mid-June (phone: 7-5204). Moderate to inexpensive.

BRUNICO (BRUNECK)

Hotel Royal Hinterhuber – Set on a hill with an impressive, wide-angle view of the surrounding valleys, this hotel has gardens, tennis courts, swimming pool, parking area, and a fine restaurant. Closed mid-October to mid-December and mid-April to mid-May. Nearly 2 miles (3 km) southeast of Brunico (phone: 2-1221). Expensive to moderate.

Hotel Andreas Hofer – Pinewood walls and typical Tyrolean furniture are the most distinctive decorative features of this modern hotel. Fresh mushrooms in season are the chef's specialty. Closed the first half of December. Via Campo Tures 1 (phone: 8-5469). Inexpensive.

AURONZO DI CADORE

Hotel Auronzo – Because it is in the less-populated, less-developed eastern Dolomites, this small hotel in a pinewood park is a good place for a quiet, relaxing few days. Closed from mid-September through mid-June. Via Roma 32 (phone: 9215). Moderate to inexpensive.

Hotel Al Lago – A pretty little hotel above Santa Caterina Lake, it has quite a good restaurant. Closed from October through May. Via Piave 14 (phone: 9314). Inexpensive.

CORTINA D'AMPEZZO

Hotel de la Poste – This luxury, chalet-style hotel has spacious rooms and a well-known restaurant. Closed October 20 to December 20. Piazza Roma 14 (phone: 4271). Expensive.

Hotel and Ristorante Capannina – Although not a luxury hotel, it is well situated and has one of the best restaurants in town. The Venetian and Tyrolese cooking is superb, as is the selection of wines. Closed from October through mid-December and from mid-April until July. Via della Stadio 11 (phone: 2950; hotel; 2633, restaurant). Expensive to moderate.

Hotel Franceschi – In addition to a restaurant, it has tennis courts, a parking area, and a fine garden. Closed mid-April to mid-June and October to December 20. Via Cesare Battisti 86 (phone: 2601). Expensive to moderate.

Hotel Menardi – This little hotel on the northern outskirts of town has a pleasant restaurant and a private garden from which you can see the Dolomites. Closed from October through mid-December and from April until July. Via Majon 110 (phone: 2400). Moderate to inexpensive.

SAN MARTINO DI CASTROZZA

Hotel San Martino – Recently modernized and enlarged, this is actually one of the oldest hotels in the area. Most of its rooms have retained their balconies, from which you can see the entire valley. A swimming pool, tennis court, and restaurant round out the facilities. Closed from mid-September through mid-December and from mid-April through June (phone: 6-8011). Moderate to inexpensive.

Hotel Rosetta – Not as lavish as the *San Martino,* it, too, maintains an aura of classy tradition and has a garden, parking area, and restaurant. Closed mid-September throughout mid-December, and mid-April through June. (phone: 6-8056). Inexpensive.

Birreria Drei Tannen – This lively, elegant little restaurant serves hearty mountain food and local wine at tables set around a fireplace; dinner only. Closed mid-September to mid-December and mid-April through June (phone: 6-8325). Expensive to moderate.

MERANO

Ristorante Andrea – Here you'll find well-prepared Tyrolean cuisine in a friendly atmosphere. Via Galilei 44 (phone: 3-7400). Closed Mondays and mid-January to mid-March. Expensive to moderate.

MADONNA DI CAMPIGLIO

Golf Hotel – This large country hotel has a 9-hole golf course, garden, and parking area. Service is friendly and efficient. The restaurant is excellent. Closed April through June and September through December. Campo Carlo Magno (phone: 4-1003). Expensive.

Hotel Caminetto – The gardens at this comfortable hotel overlook the Dolomites, and the restaurant serves well-cooked Tyrolean meals. Closed from April to mid-July and from September through November (phone: 4-1242). Moderate.

TRENTO

Hotel Villa Madruzzo – This converted eighteenth-century villa has comfortable rooms and a pretty garden. Nearly 2 miles (3 km) east of town in Cognola (phone: 98-62-20). Moderate to inexpensive.

Chiesa – The menu features appealing local specialties, and the pasta is particularly good. Closed Mondays. Via San Marco 64 (phone: 98-55-77). Moderate.

Ristorante Port 'Aquila – Standing behind the walls of a castle, it specializes in Trentino meat and game dishes and good wines. Closed Sundays and August. Via Cervara 66 (phone: 2-6139). Moderate to inexpensive.

Tuscany

Extending from the snow-capped Apennines north of Florence to south of the Maremma marshland, Tuscany is probably Italy's wealthiest region. Its riches lie in a cultivated diverse land that has prospered since the early Etruscan, Roman, and later medieval periods, with a gastronomical discipline that rivals the finest on the continent. But even more important, Tuscany's art, architecture, and age-old traditions reflect an illustrious history now deeply embedded in its modern culture. Some of its cities and villages number among the oldest in central Italy.

Tuscany derives its name from the Roman Tuscia. Its original inhabitants were the pre-Roman Etruscans, a peaceful, progressive, and artistic people whose origins are obscure, but who spread through an area of Italy between Naples and the northern Po Valley. Eventually overrun by the Romans in 40 BC, the heart of Etruscan civilization — the land between the Tiber and Arno rivers — became a province of the Roman Empire. The Etruscans were wise in agricultural ways, and it's undoubtedly to them that Tuscany owes its reputation as a producer of some of the best wine and food in Europe.

Despite modernization in the past few decades, Tuscany holds fervently to its medieval past. Every year long-standing traditions — such as a thirteenth-century horse race, the Palio, in Siena; a Saracen jousting tournament in Arezzo; and a medieval football game in Florence — are reenacted by Tuscans, all of which allow them to remember their roots and relive their past.

The logical starting point for a Tuscan itinerary is Florence, the leading cultural and shopping hub of the region. Slightly west of central Italy, the Tuscan route curves under the cross-country sway of the Apennines. It travels seaward to Pisa, then inland and south to Siena, down toward the marshlands of Maremma, and finally northeast to Arezzo and Cortona, 50 miles (80 km) south of Florence. Between the large cities, it passes through mountaintop villages, seafaring towns, and sites of ancient ruins. This is a route on which one could tarry happily for weeks, but properly organized, it can be covered in about 4 or 5 days, hitting the highlights and getting a feel for the area and its people. From Florence (for a complete report on the city, see *Florence,* THE EUROPEAN CITIES), the route goes to Lucca, where the tour really begins.

LUCCA: Striking because of its unusual architectural character, Lucca is marked by a mixture of styles that date from the sixth century. The town is surrounded by sixteenth-century ramparts, and a short walk shows a predominance of Romanesque and Pisan influence. Visit the huge eighteenth-century piazza Napoleone at the center of town, the National Art Gallery of Lucca, and a cathedral begun in the sixth century, which stands in the lush green piazza di San Martino.

Also a rich architectural center famous for its olive oil, Lucca's market comes alive every morning. Townspeople crowd the vast squares surrounding the Church of St. Michele.

PISA: An important Italian port in the early Middle Ages, Pisa was a much-sought-after center of trade until 1405, when it became a Florentine city. Recognizable from afar for its fabled leaning tower, Pisa is a delight of Romanesque architecture. Her builders and stone carvers were among the finest of the Renaissance period.

When you enter Pisa, head for the piazza del Duomo, where the famous tower stands beside a cathedral and baptistry, richly decorated with carving by the Pisano family. The tower itself was begun by Bonanno Pisano in 1174 and, despite the sinking foundations, was completed in 1350. It's worth climbing up to the top, for the tower affords a panoramic view of the entire city. Visit the nearby Campo Santo, a twelfth-century cemetery built by the Crusaders, and its surrounding Gothic galleries.

En Route from Pisa – Turn inland on Route 67, past the industrial town of Pontedera, and veer off at San Miniato Basso to visit the art-filled hilltop town of San Miniato. There, from a castle above the town's twelfth-century cathedral, you can look out over the whole Arno Valley. From San Miniato, take a minor road south through unspoiled vineclad Tuscan hills past the villages of Casastrada, Mura, and Il Castagna. Continue for 31 miles (50 km) to San Gimignano, the town of medieval towers. Looking out from the hilltops of this city, it might as well be the fourteenth century. The lookout posts built for prestige by noblemen during the early medieval wars still offer magnificent views of the surrounding valley Col d'Elsa. Leaving San Gimignano on the main Siena highway (Route 68), turn left and drive through the characteristic wine country of the Chianti Valley to Poggibonsi, a wine trading town. From there, turn south for the last 15.5 miles (25 km) to Siena.

SIENA: After Florence, Siena has probably the richest artistic heritage in Tuscany. An important agricultural town, the medieval spirit of Siena is almost entirely preserved. Originally an Etruscan city later taken over by the Romans (who named it Sena

Julia), it was a much-contested territory through the medieval wars between the Italian states. After many vicissitudes, including the plague in 1348, Siena became part of the Duchy of Tuscany in 1559.

The city is laid out over three hilltops surrounded by walls. Begin a tour of Siena at the piazza del Campo, the heart of the city and the scene of the famous Palio, when each of the former medieval districts is represented by a horse and bareback rider in a mad race around the piazza. The Palio, held on July 2 and August 16 every year, is the highlight of a festival carried out with color and fervor by the Sienese — not as a staged tourist attraction, but as a celebration of their heritage.

In the sloping piazza del Campo stands the graceful Gothic town hall with its bell tower, accessible to the public. Then make your way to the piazza del Duomo, where the cathedral dedicated to St. Catherine, the city's patron saint, stands on a raised marble platform. Visit the baptistry, which seems to form the crypt of the cathedral, and browse through the Pinacoteca Nazionale — the art gallery at Palazzo Buonsignori — for a fundamental knowledge of Sienese art.

Walking along the narrow streets of via di Città and Via Banchi di Sopra, both of which skirt the piazza del Campo, you will come to the Chigi Saracini Palace. Now a music academy, it houses some beautiful Renaissance apartments displaying a gallery of Tuscan paintings, open to the public upon request. Along the same row is the Loggia dei Mercanti, the merchants' center, which once served as the center of commerce. Farther along are the piazza Salimbeni and its four palaces, built over a period from the thirteenth to the sixteenth century. The palace designs reflect the progression of architectural styles over the years from the medieval to the Renaissance and finally the baroque.

You can spend days in Siena simply wandering through the medieval streets soaking in the atmosphere of the city. It's also one of the greatest wine centers in Italy. For some of the best Chianti around, buy a bottle at Siena's *Cantina Sociale,* and for some excellent cooking, frequent the local trattorias. You can stay at hotels converted from Renaissance palaces or in the outlying country overlooking the Chianti hills.

En Route from Siena – Take the Porta S. Marco and Route 73 for Grosseto, 58 miles (94 km) away. This route is in complete contrast to the gentle, vineclad hills of central Tuscany. Sparsely populated, wild and uncultivated, this is an introduction to the Maremma marshland. Travel past the small villages en route until a vast panorama opens out over the Maremma plains to the sea and the Argentario Peninsula. This gives way beyond Grosseto, the capital of Maremma, to green coastal plains until it reaches the forests and green hills of the national park known as the Uccellina.

UCCELLINA: The home of the original flora and fauna of Maremma, the Uccellina National Park features grasslands and beaches. One example of an Uccellina beach, and generally characteristic of the Tuscan shoreline, is Marina di Alberese, where a long stretch of white sand faces the edge of a pine forest. You can arrange visits to the park through the office some 3 miles (5 km) away in the village of Alberese.

Out of the Maremma region grew an unusual heritage when it became famous in the eighteenth century as a kind of "Wild West" of Italy. Herds of cattle and wild horses ran free through the plains, and cattle rustlers and bandits abounded.

SATURNIA: A tiny village on a hilltop, it's surrounded by countryside of Etruscan necropolises. In the village lie the remains of a Roman road, the via Claudia, as well as a reconstructed twelfth-century castle. Named Aurinia by the Etruscans, the later name of Saturnia is said to be derived from the Roman god Saturn. In the valley below the village swirl the steaming sulfur springs of the Terme di Saturnia.

En Route from Saturnia – From Saturnia take the road for Sovano and Sorano, two special villages atop hills of tufo — the soft red earth of Etruria — surrounded by Etruscan tombs. Transfer to the Roman road, the via Cassia, then turn north for the first time along the route, leaving the Etruscan hills behind and heading back for the fertile green of central Tuscany. Along this final segment of the drive you'll come across many small towns in medieval settings. Follow the turns on the highway that lead to Route 327, and follow it until you reach the town of Arezzo.

AREZZO: The Romans called it Arretium — a town that lies in the middle of olive- and vine-covered hills in a valley where the Chiana and Arno rivers meet. At the center of town is the sloping piazza del Popolo, beautifully proportioned and containing the thirteenth-century People's Palace and Church of St. Francis. On the opposite side of the piazza sits the Merchants' Loggia — a long spacious arcade used in the Middle Ages as a local market and for trade. The piazza is also the scene of the annual Joust of the Saracen — a reliving of a medieval tournament on horseback. The target of the joust is the effigy of a Saracen set on a swiveling pole and balanced on one side with a spiked iron ball.

From the piazza, walk through the old quarter of town to the Ponte Solesta, which spans the Tronto River. Across the bridge is a magnificent view of the town, with its medieval towers and churches.

CORTONA: On the border of Tuscany and Umbria, atop a hill clustered with olive trees and vineyards, Cortona is like a step back in time to the early Renaissance. Secluded and silent, the walled city consists of steep narrow streets that open onto uneven piazzas. Its cathedrals and palaces display paintings and other artwork, and the Palazzo Pretorio (Casali) houses a rich Etruscan museum.

BEST EN ROUTE

In this part of Italy you will find some very pretty hotels and reasonably priced restaurants where regional cuisine is nothing less than a fine art. Expect to pay $70 or more per night for a double room at those hotels categorized as expensive; between $50 and $65 in the moderate category; under $45, inexpensive. Expect to pay $55 or more for a meal for two at those restaurants classified as expensive; between $35 and $45 at restaurants in the moderate category; under $30, inexpensive. Prices do not include drinks, wine, or tip.

LUCCA

Ristorante Buca di San Antonio – This place offers some of the best Lucchese cooking in town, served in a friendly atmosphere. Risotto and game dishes are specialties. Closed Mondays and Sunday evenings and the last 2 weeks of July. Via della Cervia 1/5 (phone: 5-5881). Moderate.

Antico Caffe delle Mura – Here you'll find more typical Lucchese country cooking, such as rich vegetable soups and boiled meats. Balvardo Santa Maria 2 (phone: 4-7962). Moderate.

PISA

D'Azeglio – A small, first-class hotel with inviting decor and good service. Piazza Vittorio Emanuele 11 (phone: 50-03-10). Expensive to moderate.

Hotel Arno and Ristorante da Antonio – This hotel and restaurant near the banks of the Arno are within walking distance of the National Museum. Piazza della Repubblica (phone: 2-2243). Inexpensive.

Ristorante Buzzino – Here is some of the best Pisan cooking, especially mixed grilled fish and roast veal with herb and mushroom sauce. Chianti wines are plentiful and excellent. Closed Tuesdays and November. Via Cammeo 44 (phone: 2-7013). Expensive.

Ristorante Sergio – Despite its unpretentious surroundings, this place overlooking the Arno River serves plentiful Pisan food and wine. Closed Sundays and from

July 15 to August 16. Lungarno Pacinotti 1 (phone: 4-8245). Expensive to moderate.

SAN GIMIGNANO

Hotel La Cisterna and Ristorante La Terrazza – In a medieval town square, this 47-room hotel is known for its large, wooden-balconied rooms overlooking the valley that surrounds this quiet hilltop town. The restaurant on the top floor serves excellent Tuscan cuisine. Closed Tuesdays and mid-November to mid-March. Piazza della Cisterna (phone: 94-03-28). Expensive to moderate.

SIENA

Park Hotel – Set in a beautiful park on the outskirts of town, this elegant fifteenth-century villa has tennis courts, a heated pool, spacious rooms, and a fine restaurant. Via di Marciano 16 (phone: 4-4803). Very expensive.

Hotel Garden – This pleasant, 64-room hotel has gardens, swimming pool, and a restaurant. Via Custoza 2 (phone: 4-7056). Moderate to inexpensive.

Hotel Chiusarelli – At the edge of the old city, this hotel has a restaurant, a small garden, and a parking area. Viale Curtatone 9 (phone: 28-05-62). Inexpensive.

Ristorante Grotta Santa Caterina – You'll find a wide selection of Siena Chianti wines at this characteristically medieval tavern. Closed Mondays. Via della Galluzza 26 (phone: 28-22-08). Moderate to inexpensive.

Ristorante Mariotti–da Mugolone – Hearty meals are served in a simple setting. Closed Thursdays and June 5–20. Via dei Pellegrini 8 (phone: 28-32-35). Inexpensive.

SATURNIA (GROSSETO)

Hotel Terme di Saturnia – This large, peaceful, country hotel has a natural sulfur swimming pool, putting green, horseback riding, tennis courts, and a good restaurant (phone: 60-10-61). Expensive to moderate.

CORTONA

Hotel San Luca and Ristorante Tonino – Here, the setting is undeniably charming — on the fringe of a medieval town with tranquil, rural surroundings. The restaurant is closed Tuesdays and November 1–20. Piazza Garibaldi (phone: 60-37-87). Expensive to moderate.

Villa Guglielmesca – Overlooking Cortona, this villa serves finely prepared dishes (phone: 60-33-65). Inexpensive.

Campania

Campania has long lured enthusiastic visitors with its spectacular natural splendors, its unparalleled wealth of archaeological excavations and historic monuments, and its people, who have cheered the world with their music and their food.

Two picturesque gulfs (Naples and Salerno), three promontories (Phlegrean Fields, the Sorrento Peninsula, and Cilento), a massive volcano (Vesuvius), a forest-covered mountain at the edge of the blue Tyrrhenian Sea (Mt. Faito), and several romantic islands (Capri, Ischia, and Procida) are sufficient reason to tour this region. Add to this plenitude one of the greatest concentrations of archaeological excavations in the world — at Pompeii, Herculaneum, and Paestum, as well as others scattered around the region at other points — unforgettably romantic towns of historical and mythological importance such as Sorrento, Amalfi, Ravello, Positano, and Naples itself, and the region becomes a journey of compulsive interest.

Dominated by the cities of Naples, Amalfi, and Sorrento, the area consists primarily of three sections, each with a splendor of its own. There's the Bay of Naples in the north, a volcanic area with steaming natural hot springs first used by the ancient Romans as thermal spas; a series of three romantic islands off the coast of Naples, including the international resort of Capri; and the Amalfi Coast, the picturesque rocky mountain region winding along the Tyrrhenian Sea from Sorrento to the Gulf of Salerno.

Vesuvius, one of the few volcanoes in Europe still active, stands poised between the northern and southern edges of the Campanian route. Its fiery lava, which buried Pompeii and Herculaneum in AD 79, has not erupted with force since 1944. However, the twin peaks still emit trails of smoke at periodic intervals.

The November 23, 1980, earthquake that devastated vast parts of Campania struck the interior Apennine zone in the southeast, leaving the coast practically untouched. Thus, the islands and the popular Amalfi Coast were spared damage. In Naples, several buildings received dangerous cracks and two collapsed altogether, but the major hotels and restaurants were not harmed and are functioning normally. The Pompeii ruins were closed temporarily for repairs but have reopened to tourists. Sorrento suffered some minor damage, and the few hotels that were affected merely used the situation to their advantage and did some repainting and renovating.

The route begins in Naples, the regional capital and the center for fascinating tours to the volcanic region.

NAPLES: For a complete report on the city, see *Naples*, THE EUROPEAN CITIES.

En Route from Naples – While based in Naples, take an excursion to the eerie Phlegrean Fields, a steamy volcanic zone of dark, violent beauty about 12.5 miles (20 km) from the city. It extends along the Gulf of Pozzuoli on a promontory from Cape Posillipo to Cape Miseno. Visit the still-semiactive crater of Solfatara near Pozzuoli, then continue to the Lake Avernus crater, regarded by the ancients as the entrance to the Underworld. Continue on to Baia, noted for its ancient Roman baths, and Cape Miseno. The cape has wonderful views of the islands of Ischia and Procida. From Cape Miseno, travel up the outer edges of the promontory to the ruins of Cumae, an eighth-century Greek colony, where Virgil's verses were written in the Cave of the Sibyl. Then drive the 15.5 miles (25 km) to Pompeii. If time is a factor, do a combined Pompeiian-Herculaneum day tour. Of the two Roman cities buried in the AD 79 eruption of Vesuvius, the latter is the more interesting. Its patrician villas are more elegant and less thoroughly excavated. If, however, you have time to do the whole thing properly — and it's worth making time — start with the excellent National Museum in Naples the day before, where the majority of the Pompeii treasures are exhibited, and at the sites use the guidebooks published by Libreria dello Stato called *Pompeii* and *Herculaneum*.

Take a trip to Vesuvius itself, now a desolate and barren landscape overlooking the Bay of Naples and the rest of Campania.

THE ISLANDS: There is frequent ferryboat and hydrofoil service between the islands of Capri, Ischia, and Procida and the mainland cities as well as helicopter transport from the Naples-Capodichino Airport to Capri and Ischia. Even on a limited schedule, spend at least a day on Capri, and if time is no problem, visit Ischia as well. Procida is the least attractive of the three islands — it's very volcanic, with four craters and black sand.

CAPRI: The gem of the bay, sunny Capri (pronounced *kah*-pree) was a favorite resort for the Phoenicians and ancient Romans as it is today for international jetsetters and day-trippers. It is not, however, a swimmer's paradise; there are few beaches on Capri's dramatic, almost inaccessible coastline. Its villages consist of small public squares, villas and white houses, set amid varied subtropical vegetation. Visit the towns of Capri and Anacapri, the Marina Piccola and Marina Grande, and the famous Blue Grotto sea cave. Also, stop at the ruins of Villa Jovis (one of the many resorts of ancient Tiberias) and the Villa San Michele at Anacapri, celebrated by Alex Munthe. Spectacular views of the Faraglioni (rock inlets) are seen from the Punta di Tragara belvedere.

ISCHIA: Twice the size of Capri but half as crowded, Ischia is of volcanic origin (its source, Mt. Epomeo, hasn't erupted in nearly seven centuries, and its slopes now produce the renowned Epomeo wine). Sandy beaches, thermal hot springs, and lush green scenery all contribute to the fast-growing popularity of this Emerald Isle, as it is known. Porto d'Ischia is the charming island harbor town, south of which is Ponte d'Ischia (named for an Aragonese-built bridge), the site of a fifteenth-century castle. Casamicciola and Lacco Ameno are favorite resorts, and Sant'Angelo is one of the island's several picturesque fishing villages.

AMALFI COAST (COSTA AMALFITANA): Stretching from Sorrento to Salerno along the gulf of that name, the Amalfi Coast is one of the most spectacular drives on any Italian route. On a peninsula, the northern portion around Sorrento has been exploited in recent years, but the southern half of the peninsula remains a romantic paradise — sun-warmed rocks and terraced gardens, lemon and olive groves overlooking sparkling blue bays and coves, flowered promontories and secret beaches. In *The Immoralist* André Gide says that the road from Sorrento to Ravello "was so beautiful that I had no desire . . . to see anything more beautiful on earth."

Although the Amalfi Coast actually begins at Sorrento, a couple of preliminary stops en route make the drive from Naples more interesting. Pick up the Autostrada del Sole (A3) as far as Castellammare di Stabia, less than 31 miles (50 km) from Naples, which was, like Pompeii and Herculaneum, destroyed by Vesuvius in AD 79. Then, take the scenic road (SS145) that curves around the northern coast of the peninsula and stop a short distance farther at Vico Equense. It offers good views of the coast, inexpensive boat service to Capri, and delicious pizzas, sold, like textiles, by the yard — actually, by the meter. Look for a large sign, "Pizza al Metro," towering over some of the town's cliff-hanging white houses.

SORRENTO: Tourists return time and again to Sorrento, a legendary resort amid beautiful gardens. It features several architectural points of interest, including the main Duomo, the churches of Carmina and Sant'Antonio, the fourteenth-century Correale Palace, and the lovely Casa Veniero.

En Route from Sorrento – Be prepared for a treacherous slice of highway that continues clear around the mountains until you reach Positano. To avoid the entire scene, drive back north to Gragnaro (famous for its red wine) and take an inland route to Positano.

POSITANO: John Steinbeck once described Positano as "a dream place that isn't quite real." Its white houses and terraced gardens cling gently to slopes that roll into the sea, all around a picturesque port dotted with small fishing boats.

During the tenth century, it was one of the most important mercantile cities in the world, but more recently it has become a refuge for writers and artists, who derive inspiration from its natural and architectural settings. Positano is a particular favorite among the younger set, not only because its vertical architectural plan makes frequent climbing necessary in daily living, but also because its fashions center around original and inexpensive boutique wear designed by local artisans. These items, which are displayed temptingly along narrow cobblestone streets, set the fashion pace for summerwear throughout Italy.

En Route from Positano – The road continues past many fishing villages and Saracen towers — once the haunts of pirates — perched on peaks and reefs above the sea. The cliffside corniche then passes over the great gorges of the Valley of Furore and carves into the rocky walls of the Lattari Mountains east to Amalfi.

AMALFI: A Moorish-looking town with white houses and a curiously Oriental church, Amalfi was originally an important maritime republic loyal to Byzantium. Its greatest period of prosperity was during the eleventh century, when the Amalfi Navigation Tables, the oldest maritime code in the world, regulated shipping in the entire Mediterranean.

RAVELLO: This is by far the most picturesque spot along the Gulf of Salerno. When you arrive in Ravello, first visit the Villa Rufolo, the home of Richard Wagner, then stroll through the gardens of the Villa Cimbrone to the belvedere for a spectacular view of the monasteries of Sant'Antonio and Santa Chiara and the entire gulf. Ravello's cathedral has a fine set of bronze doors and two famous pulpits.

PAESTUM: This is one of the finest sites of Italy, set in the seaside mountains, with the city's three Greek temples standing nobly among asphodel, oleander, and aromatic herbs. The temples and surrounding ruins are made of limestone, centered around the Temple of Neptune and the Temple of Ceres. In fact, the Temple of Neptune is more likely to have been dedicated to Hera, but in any case it is one of the best-preserved temples in Europe, dating from the fifth century BC. Don't miss the relatively new museum, particularly the Diver's Tomb and themetopes of Thesauros from the sanctuary of Hera Argiva. (Always check opening and closing times with a hotel porter in town; they are notoriously unreliable and unpredictable.)

If returning to Rome by car, pick up the Autostrada via Nola, bypassing Naples, at Salerno.

BEST EN ROUTE

Some of the most truly charming hotels and restaurants in Italy are tucked away in Campania. Expect to pay $70 or more per night for a double room at the hotels categorized as expensive; between $50 and $65 in the moderate category; under $45, inexpensive. Expect to pay $55 or more for a meal for two at those restaurants classified as expensive; between $35 and $45 in the moderate category; under $30, inexpensive. Prices do not include drinks or tip.

LUCRINO (LAKE AVERNUS)

La Ninfea – On a lake that was once part of the Bourbons' hunting reserve, this restaurant is renowned for the preparation of fresh fish. Closed Tuesdays and from September 15 to June 15. Via Italia 1 (phone: 866-1326). Expensive to moderate.

CAPRI

Quisisana e Grand Hotel – Recently acquired by German radio-TV magnate Max Grundig, this deluxe, 130-room hotel caters to a well-heeled, well-traveled crowd. It has tennis courts and a swimming pool. Closed November through March. Via Camerelle 2 (phone: 837-0788). Expensive.

Hotel Punta Tragara – Designed by master French architect LeCorbusier, it has a splendid view of the Faraglioni (offshore needle rocks). In addition to antique furnishings in the 41 rooms, it has a swimming pool, spa baths, and hydromassages. Closed October 15 through March. Punta Tragara, 57 Via Tragara (phone: 837-0844; 837-7790). Expensive.

Scalinatella – An elegant, small hotel overlooking the sea. Closed November to March 15. Via Tragara 8 (phone: 837-0633). Expensive.

Hotel Luna – The garden terraces at this lovely and comfortable 48-room hotel have a fine offshore view of the Faraglioni. The interior decor is tasteful, service is good, and there is a swimming pool. Closed November through March. Via Matteotti 3 (phone: 837-0433). Expensive.

Flora – A 14-room hotel with romantic appeal but no restaurant. Closed November through March. Via Serena 26 (phone: 837-0211). Moderate.

Villa Krupp – With 12 rooms, this family-style inn overlooks the gardens of Augustus and the sea. Viale Matteotti 12 (phone: 837-0362). Inexpensive.

La Canzone del Mare – This pleasant afternoon restaurant on the beach is a favorite with swimmers and sunbathers, who come for a relaxing meal and a drink before the restaurant closes at dusk. The specialty of the house is fresh fish. Reservations suggested. Closed October to Easter. Marina Piccola (phone: 837-0104). Expensive.

La Pigna – This well-run restaurant is frequented by yachtsmen and owners of neighboring villas. A few minutes' walk from the center of town on the road to Marina Grande. Closed Easter, October, and Tuesdays in low season. Via Lo Palazzo 30 (phone: 837-0280). Expensive to moderate.

La Capannina – A rather chic restaurant sporting a Michelin star. Specialties are fish and pasta. Try the green gnocchi with salmon and the *penne* with eggplant. Closed Wednesdays (except in August), and November through March. Via le Botteghe 14 (phone: 837-0732). Expensive to moderate.

Da Luigi – Another place that's usually full of yachtsmen since it's accessible by sea. Considered one of the top restaurants on the island. Lunch only. On the road of the Faraglioni (phone: 837-0591). Expensive to moderate.

Da Gemma – Not far from the piazzetta, this convenient restaurant with a pleasant outdoor terrace is another of Capri's most favored restaurants for many different dishes. Reserve. Closed Mondays and November. Via Madre Serafina 6 (phone: 837-0461). Moderate.

Casina delle Rose – Stick to the local dishes, especially the fish, and avoid the international selections. Closed from November to mid-March and on Tuesdays during spring and fall. Via Vittorio Emanuele 29 (phone: 837-0200). Moderate.

ISCHIA

Hotel L'Albergo della Regina Isabella e Royal Sporting – A deluxe, supercomfortable 133-room spa, recently acquired by the excellent CIGA chain, it has a swimming pool, beach, tennis court, and gardens. Closed November through March. Piazza S. Restituta 4 at Lacco Ameno (phone: 99-43-22). Expensive.

Excelsior – This extravagantly decorated 67-room Excelsior chain hotel is noted for its excellent service. The building is set among landscaped gardens with a swimming pool and a nearby beach. Closed mid-October to mid-April. Via Gianturco 3 (phone: 99-10-20). Expensive.

Jolly – With 200 comfortable rooms, this hotel at Porto Ischia features thermal spa treatments. There is also a swimming pool and an excellent restaurant. Closed January and February. Via de Luca 42 (phone: 99-17-44). Expensive.

Grand Hotel Punta Molina – An elegant 88-room hotel overlooking the sea with lovely gardens and a swimming pool. Closed November through April. Lungomare Telese già Colombo (phone: 99-15-44). Expensive to moderate.

Bristol Palace – This 36-room hotel has a private beach and gardens. Closed November through March. Via Marone 10 (phone: 99-21-81). Moderate.

Moresco – An old Spanish-style building smothered in bougainvillea. It has 63 rooms, a swimming pool, tennis courts, gardens, and a solarium. Closed November through February. Via Gianturco 16 at Punta Molino (phone: 99-11-22). Moderate.

Pensione La Villarosa – This charming, family-style, 37-room villa has a splendid garden fragrant with gardenias. It is known for friendly, personal service and comfort. Closed November through March. Via Gigante 3 (phone: 99-24-25). Inexpensive.

Damiano – The specialty is fish in this modern-looking restaurant with a glass-enclosed terrace. Reservations recommended. Closed October through March. Via Nuova Circonvallazione in Porto Ischia (phone: 98-30-32). Expensive to moderate.

Gennaro – It has a central location and authentic island decor, and it's known for its fish soups and antipastos. Closed Tuesdays and November to mid-March. Via Porto 66 in Porto Ischia (phone: 99-29-17). Moderate.

Ristorante Di Massa – The specialties of the house are honest Ischitana dishes — fresh fish and rabbit *(coniglio)*. Closed during winter and on Tuesdays. Via Seminario 29, Ischia Porto (phone: 99-14-02). Moderate.

GULF OF NAPLES COAST

Hotel Le Axidie – The 29 balconied rooms have delightful views of the sea. It occupies a former monastery and is furnished with antiques. On the grounds are a swimming pool and beach. Marina Equa, Vico Equense (phone: 879-8181). Expensive to moderate.

Da Gigino – Pizzas are sold by the meter in a spacious, open-air garden in the center of town. Via Nicoteria 10 (phone: 879-84-26). Inexpensive.

SORRENTO

Hotel Excelsior Grand Hotel Vittoria – This old-fashioned 125-room Excelsior chain hotel is surrounded by orange and lemon groves. The panoramic terraces overlook well-kept grounds with a swimming pool. An elevator whisks you down to the hotel's private beach. Pizza Tasso 34 (phone: 878-1900). Expensive

Parco dei Principi – This 100-room hotel occupies a Bourbon family villa with a stupendous park and a view of the gulf. It, too, has a swimming pool and beach. An excellent hotel, especially for the price. Via Rota 1 (phone: 878-2101). Expensive to moderate.

President – Set high on a bluff amid a pine grove overlooking the bay, this 82-room hotel has a swimming pool and gardens outside Sorrento on Colle Parise. Closed November through March. Via Nastro Verde (phone: 878-2262). Moderate.

Hotel Imperial Tramontano – This 104-room hotel is in the heart of town, yet surrounded by nice gardens. Many of the rooms overlook the gulf and beach, and there is a swimming pool. Closed December through March. Via Veneto 1 (phone: 878-1940). Moderate.

Bristol – This pleasant, 130-room hotel has a swimming pool, restaurant, and a terrace with a beautiful view of the gulf. Via Capo 22 (phone: 878-4522). Moderate.

Bellevue Syrene – A converted eighteenth-century villa, this 50-room hotel is particularly recommendable. In addition to its charming setting, it has an elevator to a private beach. 5 Piazza della Vittoria (phone: 878-1024). Inexpensive.

Minerva – Somewhat out of the way, it's worth it because of its lovely position on the sea. With only 50 rooms, this family-style pension has charm and a good restaurant, *La Minervetta*. Via Capo 30 (phone: 878-1011). Inexpensive.

La Tonnarella – This unpretentious 11-room pension on the outskirts of town overlooks the sea, and has a hilltop restaurant in a lemon- and oleander-filled garden. Closed November to March. Via Capo 31 (phone: 878-1153). Inexpensive.

La Favorita o' Parruchiano – This authentic Sorrentine restaurant serves fresh local cheeses — *trecce, burielli* — vegetables, and fish. Try the very good fish soup. Closed on Wednesdays during winter and spring. Corso Italia 71–73 (phone: 878-1321). Moderate.

La Pentolaccia – A pleasant restaurant in the heart of old Sorrento, it's renowned for its seafood and Neapolitan music in the background. Closed Tuesdays. Via Fuorimura 8 (phone: 878-5077). Moderate to inexpensive.

Antico Francischiello – Cheerful and hospitable, with genuine local cooking. Closed Tuesdays except in summer. You'll find *Antico Francischiello* in Massalubrense on Via Villazzano 27, about 4 miles (6 km) from Sorrento (phone: 877-1171). Moderate.

POSITANO

Hotel San Pietro – Built into a cliff next to the sea, this 46-room hotel has an elevator to a private beach, a swimming pool, and tennis courts. Closed November through March. Less than 1 mile (2 km) south of town (phone: 87-57-39). Expensive.

Hotel Le Sirenuse – Author John Steinbeck stayed in one of the 65 rooms of this converted eighteenth-century villa, now a superb hotel with a good swimming pool and view of the sea (phone: 87-50-66). Expensive.

Poseidon – The 50 rooms in this elegant establishment offer a lovely view of the sea and coastline. Swimming pool. Closed October 15 through April. Via Paitea 148 (phone: 87-50-14). Expensive.

Miramare – This 14-room hotel has a distinctive warmth despite its small size. Closed mid-November to mid-March. Viatrara Gencino (phone: 87-50-02). Expensive to moderate.

Palazzo Murat – The eighteenth-century palace of Gioacchino Murat (a king of Naples and Napoleon's brother-in-law) has been tastefully restored with some period furniture and wood-beamed ceilings. All of the 28 rooms have a certain magic, but especially those overlooking the courtyard filled with purple bougainvillea. Closed October through March. 9 Via dei Mulini (phone: 87-51-77). Moderate.

Casa Albertina – A small and attractive family-run hotel with personal service. All rooms have terraces overlooking the sea. Via della Tavolozza 4 (phone: 87-51-43). Moderate to inexpensive.

La Bougainville – In the center of town, this 14-room hotel is clean and convenient (phone: 87-50-47). Inexpensive.

Buca di Bacco – This is traditionally Positano's favorite restaurant of the yachting crowd. Try the fish and you might well understand why. Closed October 16 to March 24. Opposite the port (phone: 87-56-99). Expensive to moderate.

La Cambusa – A very good restaurant that gets better all the time. *La Cambusa* goes so far as to employ its own fishermen, and it also turns out Positano's best spaghetti with zucchini (the town's most characteristic dish) and an excellent fish soup. A lovely veranda overlooks the piazzetta and the beach (phone: 87-54-32). Moderate.

Chez Black – A favorite of bathers taking a lunch break. Try the spaghetti with clams or the mixed fish fry. Via del Brigantino 19 (phone: 87-50-36). Moderate.

Da Vincenzo – Less glamorous than some others but a favorite of Positanese. Local cuisine is featured, including lots of fresh vegetables and baked pasta. Up the hill on the Casa Soriano curve (ask anyone). Inexpensive.

AMALFI

Excelsior Grand Hotel – This modern, efficient, 85-room member of the Excelsior chain has a beach, swimming pool, and gardens. Closed November through March. 5 kilometers outside Amalfi in Pogerola (phone: 87-13-44). Expensive to moderate.

Albergo Cappuccini – An old monastery converted into a splendid 48-room hotel. High on a cliff, it has sensational views of the coast. Also a solarium and a private beach. Via Annunziatella 46 (phone: 87-10-08). Moderate.

Luna e Torre Saraceni – This converted thirteenth-century convent has 42 rooms, lovely cloisters, and a swimming pool (phone: 87-10-02). Moderate.

Santa Caterina – This 42-room hotel stands atop a cliff with an elevator leading to a beach. There is a saltwater pool, also (phone: 87-10-12). Moderate.

Miramalfi – This place also has an elevator to the beach, swimming pool, and 44 rooms (phone: 87-12-47). Moderate.

Belvedere – It's cut into a cliff so that the series of terraces appear to be growing downward. Naturally, it overlooks the sea, with dazzling views from its 33 rooms. And it has a swimming pool (phone: 87-12-66). Moderate.

Da Gemma – A homey trattoria featuring outdoor dining in summer. Seafood specialties include spaghetti with clams and linguine with scampi. Good local wines. Closed Thursdays. Salita Fra Gerardo Sasso 9 (no phone). Moderate to inexpensive.

La Caravella – This place serves genuine southern Italian home-style cooking at bargain prices. What more could you ask for? Closed Tuesdays and November. Via Camera 12 (phone: 87-10-29). Inexpensive.

RAVELLO

Palumbo al Confalone – This utterly romantic nineteenth-century villa, built on the ruins of the twelfth-century Confalone, is perched 1,200 feet above the Amalfi Drive. Its fine restaurant offers specialties like *fusilli al gorgonzola* and *crostini* of mozzarella. Be sure to have lunch in the beautiful garden overlooking the Gulf of Salerno — a special delight. Via Toro 28 (phone: 85-72-44). Moderate.

Caruso Belvedere Hotel – Formerly the eleventh-century Palazzo D'Afflitto, it has been transformed into a delightful, 26-room hotel with a good restaurant. Via Toro 50 (phone: 85-71-11). Moderate to inexpensive.

Rufolo – This 29-room hotel has splendid gardens, a swimming pool, and an excellent restaurant (phone: 85-71-33). Moderate to inexpensive.

Parsifal – Not as elegant as the others but nonetheless tasteful, this 20-room hotel is in a section of a thirteenth-century convent. Closed October through March. Piazza Fontana (phone: 85-71-44). Inexpensive.

Caruso Belvedere – Founded in 1903, this restaurant is deservedly famous. It produces its own wines and a curious house soufflé — half lemon, half chocolate. Not only is the food delicious, the setting is gorgeous. Closed Tuesdays during winter. Via Toro 50 (phone: 85-71-11). Moderate.

Compa' Cosimo – Home cooking, Ravello style — fresh fish and vegetables. Specialties include minestrone and bean soup. Closed Mondays. Via Roma (phone: 85-71-56). Moderate to inexpensive.

Calabria

Calabria, the sunny toe in the boot that is Italy, is a strangely beautiful land. It is neither the average tourist's idea of southern Italy (as all sun, song, and smiles) nor is it the strictly dreary picture of a depressed people in a depressed part of the Mezzogiorno forever brooding on their not-insignificant problems. Calabrians have the knack — learned perhaps out of necessity — of living reality rather than worrying about it.

It's a land rich in natural scenery, from the rugged, vineclad slopes of the northern Sila Mountains to the coastal beaches at the southern tip of the Tyrrhenian Sea. A warm climate produces an abundance of olive, lemon, and orange groves as well as bergamots, figs, and chestnuts that dot the mountains and central plains. But it's more the picturesque towns and the old-fashioned warmth of the Calabrians that set this region of Italy apart.

This is a land of hospitable people who welcome visitors with genuine cordiality, a jug of wine, a home-cooked meal, and a zest for living. Tradition is elemental to the Calabrians and embraces all areas of life. These southern Italians are also a superstitious people, celebrating their many religious feasts with pagan rites and wailing laments reminiscent of ancient Greece — no surprise in an area once known as Magna Graecia.

The region is divided into three provinces named after their capital cities: Cosenza, the inland section in the north; Catanzaro, farther south, near the eastbound Ionian coast; and Reggio di Calabria, at the tip of the toe, separated by only a narrow strait from Sicily.

If you're making your first visit to Calabria, we suggest driving from central Italy. Although you can fly to Lamezia Terme or Reggio di Calabria and rent a car there, the 248-mile (400-km) drive from Salerno (403 mi/650 km from Rome) on the Autostrada del Sole (A3) is unforgettable. You'll wind through some of Italy's most spectacular scenery: through tunnels carved out of the mountains, with views of medieval hill towns, pine forests, and glistening sea below.

The Autostrada extends into Reggio di Calabria in southern Italy, but there is an alternative in Route 18. You can pick that up by leaving the Autostrada at Lagonegro for Praia a Mare. Remember, though, that in the south of Italy, points of interest are much more widely separated than in the north, and driving is very difficult except for stretches of Route 18, which follow the coast quite closely.

You begin the Calabrian portion of this trip in Praia a Mare, at the northern edge of the region. The route proceeds down the coastline, making several stops along the way at resort beaches and inland medieval towns. The part of the coastline that best captures the essence of Calabria is the Costa Viola (Violet Coast) in the southern province of Reggio. The Costa Viola extends some 31 miles (50 km) from Gioia Tauro to Santa Trada, just north of the provincial capital of Reggio di Calabria. Named for the violet hue that the land and turquoise Tyrrhenian Sea take on at sunset, the Costa Viola consists of a strip of small towns and sandy beaches, the latter interrupted by dramatic cliffs and grottoes. Many of the beaches are accessible only by boat, and the larger ones have only recently been provided access with roads and are indiscriminately dotted with pensioni and trattorie.

While the towns of this region have been reconstructed in a rather nondescript fashion following the 1908 earthquake, each still has its classic *corso* (main street), which provides the setting for the ritual evening *passeggiata* (promenade) and a favorite café or bar on the main piazza where townspeople gather to exchange gossip over a coffee, ice cream, or pastry.

From the Costa Viola you drive to Reggio di Calabria, the most modern city of the region, and continue inland toward the eastern coast and the Ionian Sea. There you'll find Italian towns still rich in Greek heritage as well as remnants of medieval architecture.

En Route from Salerno – On the drive south toward Costa Viola from the beginning of Route 18, make your first stop at Paria a Mare or at Diamante, a bit farther along. Either provides a fine introduction to the province of Cosenza, with its wooded plains and beaches, many of which are becoming popular as year-round resorts. H. V. Morton's *A Traveller in Southern Italy* noted: "From Pizzo southward there is an additional clarity in the air, a bluer sea, beautiful clouds . . . one thinks a landscape like this could produce only poets and artists."

Continue right around the cape (Capo Vatico) past Nicotera (where wonderful terra-cotta masks are made — they ward off evil spirits), returning to Route 18 south. Now you begin the itinerary along the Costa Viola, with the first stop at Gioia Tauro.

GIOIA TAURO: Although this town is not a spectacular entry to the Costa Viola, it does boast some magnificent olive trees on the Plain of Gioia, said to be the oldest and largest in Europe, supposedly dating back to the time of Christ.

PALMI: Beyond the silvery flicker of olive groves along the coastline, the road suddenly opens to the largest of Palmi's sandy beaches, La Tonnara. At the southernmost point of the beach, on a rock jutting out of the sea, stands a solitary ancient olive tree. When the town council declared it Palmi's symbol a few years ago and began fertilizing and doctoring it, *l'olivo* suddenly wilted, demanding to be left once again to its own resources.

Like its symbol, Palmi thrives when left to follow its natural course. Physically lush subtropical plants and uncultivated flora — jasmine, bougainvillea, prickly pears, and of course the bergamots — fill the air with a sweet fragrance; culturally, Palmi's inhabitants continue to follow ancient beliefs and customs. You'll find living proof of the latter at the Calabrian Folklore Museum, which has fine collections of old and new masks from Seminara, Greek-style ceramics from the Ionian coast, pastoral art from the Aspromonte, and a number of religious and superstitious objects used to ward off evil spirits.

Before leaving Palmi, don't miss a trip up to the top of Mt. St. Elia, "the balcony over the Tyrrhenian." The magnificient view includes Mt. Etna and Messina in Sicily, the Aeolian islands, and the Calabrian coast as far north as Cape Vatican. And be sure to take a drive to La Marinella, a tiny fishermen's cover, Palmi's bathing beach before the road to La Tonnara was built some 20 years ago. It's not a very comfortable pebble beach, but the area is good for snorkeling.

BAGNARA: South of Palmi, beyond the famous Zibibbo vineyards clinging to rocky terraces that descend toward the sea, you reach the swordfishing center of the Costa

Viola. Activity hasn't changed in this town since the days of the early Greeks. Life centers around the capture, sale, and preparation of swordfish, at least between April and late July or August, when the fish come to spawn from colder Arctic waters. The fishermen harpoon the swordfish by hand as they did in ancient times.

Once ashore, the heavy catch is carried on the heads of the *bagnarote* (women of Bagnara) to the market for sale. Many are also exported to the larger cities and show up in restaurants throughout Italy. (They appear as *pescespada* on the menu.)

Swordfish serves as the main diet staple for the southern Calabrians nearly four months a year; it is cooked in so many different ways that no one seems to tire of the meaty morsels. Most often, they are grilled and dowsed with *salmoriglio,* a tasty sauce of garlic, oregano, and olive oil.

SCILLA: As you drive south on the coastal highway with the Aspromonte mountains to the left, the dramatic indented coastline on the right suddenly gives way to the huge rock of Scilla, recalling the myth of Scylla and Charybdis, which inspired poets from Homer to Schiller.

The town named for the rock of Scilla again brings to mind the ancient Greeks and their ancient rituals. This is never more evident than in Scilla's picturesque fishermen's quarters, known as the Chianalea. Here, a narrow cobblestone road lines the houses rooted to the famous rock. Fishermen's wives sit on small chairs outside their doorways when the swordfish aren't running, mending the great nets that provide their livelihood. When walking through the area, stop for lunch in a typical Scillan-house-turned-restaurant, *Da Glauco.*

Before you even begin to approach Chianalea, you come upon an impressive medieval castle, seemingly sculpted out of the rock of Scilla itself. The foundations date from 493 BC, only it now hosts a youth hostel — one of the best of its kind — and a discotheque. This, as well as the grand terrace of the main town square, is worth a visit. Now a favorite promenade for residents and tourists, the terrace overlooks the rooftops of the old town and the beautiful sandy Sirens Beach.

SANTA TRADA: The Costa Viola ends with this town, the peninsula's closest point to Sicily and the planned site of a gigantic bridge that will eventually connect the two. The treacherous tidal currents of the Strait of Messina recall the plight of the ancient mariners. In fact, the currents are so strong and the water so cool that swimming between here and Reggio is nothing less than exhilarating, although the calm lukewarm waters between Palmi and Scilla are generally preferable.

VILLA SAN GIOVANNI: From this point there is frequent car ferry and hydrofoil service across the strait to Messina. Similar transport to Messina is also available regularly from Reggio, making a day trip to Taormina, only 31 miles (50 km) from Messina, almost irresistible.

REGGIO DI CALABRIA: A modern city almost entirely rebuilt following the earthquake of 1908, Reggio di Calabria is the gateway to Sicily. Although surrounded by a somewhat unattractive coastal shelf and numerous factories. Reggio has its high points. These include an elegant seaside boardwalk (Lungomare Marina) and the interesting National Museum (piazza de'Nava 26), housing artifacts from the archaeological excavations in the region — especially of the early Greek and Roman civilizations — and the recovered and restored bronzes of Riace.

GERACE: You'll recognize Gerace well before you arrive, perched high on a sharp rock overlooking Locri. This solemn medieval town has a richness of art treasures unequaled in the region.

LOCRI: Your arrival in Locri itself may be less inspiring, since this flat modern town is more reminiscent of the dry and dreary Far West than of any Greek city you've ever seen. Don't despair. Drive a few miles south to the ruins of the ancient city of Epizephyrii. Take care not to miss the Greek-Roman theater at Portigliola, a fair hike from the Antiquarium, or museum, at the entrance to the ruins.

En Route from Locri – Rather than retrace your route across the rugged Aspromonte mountain chain, if it's early enough in the day, you can return to Reggio and the Costa Viola by driving clear around the "toe" on Highway 106 along the Ionian or Jasmine Coast. This will take you past the Bovalino Marina on the slopes of the Aspromonte, Capo Spartivento, and the picturesque locality of Pentidattilo. While this area is particularly enticing for its traditional Indian summer during September and October, the months of June through August are more interesting for the student of folk customs. During this time feasts are celebrated in towns throughout the area, many concluding with elaborate fireworks displays.

BEST EN ROUTE

Accommodations in Calabria tend to be somewhat more rustic than those in other parts of Italy. Expect to pay $70 or more for a double room at those hotels categorized as expensive; between $50 and $65 at those in the moderate category; under $40, inexpensive. Restaurants serve generous portions of southern Italian cooking. Expect to pay $55 or more for a meal for two at those restaurants categorized as expensive; between $35 and $45 in the moderate category; under $30, inexpensive. Prices do not include drinks or tip.

GIOIA TAURO

Euromotel – This simple roadside hotel has adequate accommodations. Rte. 111, about 2 km southeast of the city (phone: 5-2083). Moderate.

Il Buco – Northern Italian dishes, primarily from Emilia, share the menu with local cuisine. Via Lomoro (phone: 5-1512). Moderate to inexpensive.

PALMI

Arcobaleno – This small hotel is on the road between Palmi and the Taureana beach and has a restaurant, swimming pool, and tennis courts. Contrada Taureana (phone: 4-6315). Moderate.

Centro Residenziale Costa Viola – Run by priests, this quiet countryside summer hotel becomes a study center during the winter. The rooms have a lovely sea view. Localita Torre (phone: 2-2016). Inexpensive.

South Paradise – A hotel run by emigrants from Australia, it stands on Pietrenere beach (phone: 4-6278). Inexpensive.

Garden – Traditionally considered the town's first hotel because it is the oldest, this is actually undeserving of any accolades that are not contingent on age. Piazza Losardo 9 (phone: 2-3645). Inexpensive.

Oscar – In the heart of town, this hotel offers a more modern alternative to the *Garden.* Via Roma (phone: 2-3293). Inexpensive.

Miami – Although not as sophisticated as its name suggests, it is found on a big local beach, Tonnara (phone: 4-6343). Inexpensive.

La Lampara – Rustic in atmosphere, it serves excellent fish dishes, especially *involtini di pescespada* (swordfish) in season. Lido Tonnara (phone: 46-332). Moderate to inexpensive.

Pizzeria La Margherita – Specialities here are *pizza alla pioggia* and homemade whole wheat pasta in anchovy sauce. Across the road from the northern end of the Tonnara beach (no phone). Moderate to inexpensive.

La Marinella – Salvatore's special pasta with tomato sauce, local *pecorino* (sheep's milk cheese), and good fresh fish are your best culinary bets here. Marinella cove (no phone). Moderate to inexpensive.

Pinewood Pizzeria – Pizza is served under pine trees at St. Elia (phone: 2-2926). Inexpensive.

SCILLA

La Sirene – This hotel-restaurant on the beach serves fresh fish al fresco, near the sea. It has only seven rooms. On the beach. Via Nazionale 57 (phone: 75-40-19). Inexpensive.

Da Glauco – A typical house-turned-restaurant with a magnificent terrace overlooking the fishermen's houses, the port, and the Mediterranean, its extra special dish is Signora Pontillo's spicy dried tomatoes and pickled eggplant antipasto. At the left end of the via Chianalea (no phone). Moderate to inexpensive.

Alla Pescatora – Run by a former fisherman, it serves fine seafood. Closed Tuesdays and December 20 to January 4. Via Colombo 32 (phone: 75-41-47). Inexpensive.

VILLA SAN GIOVANNI

Castello Altafiumara – This restored castle by the sea has tennis courts and a swimming pool. Near Villa San Giovanni-Cannitello (phone: 75-90-61). Moderate.

Piccolo Hotel – Simply, the best hotel in town. Piazza Stazione (phone: 75-14-16). Moderate to inexpensive.

REGGIO DI CALABRIA

Grand Hotel Excelsior – One of the deluxe Excelsior chain, this is *the* hotel in the capital. Piazza Independenza (phone: 2-5801). Moderate.

Primavera – A simple but comfortable hotel with 52 rooms. Via Pentimele 177 (phone: 47-081). Inexpensive.

Bonaccorso – This restaurant near the station rates a Michelin star for its fine pasta and boiled meat. Closed Fridays and from mid-July to mid-August. Via Bixio 11 (phone: 96-048). Moderate.

Conti – Although its ratings have fallen somewhat (it once held one Michelin star), this is still one of the best restaurants for local antipasto, macaroni, and fish. The carafe wine, Pellaro, is excellent. Closed Mondays, except in August. Via Giulia 2 (phone: 2-9043). Moderate to inexpensive.

GERACE

Fagiano Bianco – Unless you are traveling with a group, you may find this lovely cantina closed, but the same food is served at the bar on the main square, where a few tables are set outdoors in fine weather. *Antipasto della casa* and wine are excellent here. Piazza Central (no phone). Inexpensive.

LOCRI

Motel Faro – If you want to spend some additional time exploring the Greek-Roman theater of Locri, you'll find these accommodations convenient. Portigliola, on Rte. 106 (phone: 36-10-15). Inexpensive.

Sicily

The largest island in the Mediterranean (10,207 square miles), Sicily is probably the least "Italian" of Italy's regions. Because of its strategic position between Europe, Africa, and Asia, Sicily has been invaded, conquered, and settled by many people in the last 3,000 years. Each group left traces of its civilization, both in the character of the Sicilians and in the architectural remains of its town churches, temples, and villas.

Originally part of Magna Graecia (Greater Greece), Sicily (and Siracusa, on the southeastern coast, in particular) was a great cultural center until it fell to the Romans and became an exploited colony. With the fall of the Roman Empire, Sicily became open territory, invaded by a succession of armies from barbaric northern tribes and Saracens to Byzantines. Finally, in the eleventh and twelfth centuries, the Normans brought a period of political peace to the island, and Sicily became an autonomous state whose power extended halfway up the Italian peninsula. Beginning in the thirteenth century, however, it fell back under foreign rule, to be controlled by France, Spain, and the Bourbon kings of Naples until the arrival of Garibaldi, who began his campaign for the unification of Italy in Sicily. The island became part of Italy in 1860.

While by nature an agricultural land, Sicily has in the last 20 years or so developed some industry in the form of oil refineries and chemical plants. The island's natural wealth, though, lies in its citrus fruits, olives, and vineyards, with the most fertile land on the slopes of Mt. Etna. Europe's only active volcano, Mt. Etna at 9,840 feet dominates eastern Sicily.

A common means of access to Sicily is by ferryboat or hydrofoil from the southern tip of the mainland at Reggio di Calabria or Villa San Giovanni across the Strait of Messina. This brings you to the starting point of the Sicilian route at the northeastern end of the island. The route zigzags along coastal roads and inland highways, covering the island in a fragmented, but often-traveled pattern that covers the most interesting towns and villages.

When visiting Sicily, try to arrive in spring or early fall; the climate is closer to that of North Africa than Europe, so it is advisable to avoid the intense heat of July and August.

MESSINA: The main port of Messina, founded by the Greeks in the eighth century BC and occupied by the Carthaginians and then the Romans, was rebuilt after the disastrous earthquake of 1908 and again after the bombardments of World War II.

Perhaps Messina's most unusual feature is a curious mechanical and astronomical clock, the biggest in the world, built in Strasbourg and brought to the town in 1933. Housed in the bell tower of the town's thirteenth-century Norman cathedral, the mechanism activates various carved figures, and evangelical scenes move into an intricate series of acts at midday that lasts for almost an hour. The clock and cathedral are in the central piazza del Duomo. Just east of the cathedral is the church of the Annunziata dei Catalani, another Norman construction, and at the end of viale della Liberta is the National Museum, with a choice selection of Renaissance and post-Renaissance art.

TAORMINA: Twenty centuries ago this tiny, well-developed resort town (with only 5,000 full-time residents) was popular with the Greeks and Romans. It gained international fame early in the twentieth century, when it was rediscovered by a group of English and German aesthetes. The draw has always been the same: its mild year-round climate and its spectacular position overlooking the bay and the rocky coast below. Best of all, in spite of the quite heavy tourist traffic in the summer, the town has lost none of its historical charm.

The first stop on any tour of Taormina should be the Greek theater, carved out of a natural cavity on the hillside and dominated by the smoking peak of Mt. Etna in the distance. It must be the most dramatic setting for a theater in the world. It is still used for modern productions of Greek tragedy as well as for summer festivals.

In the central piazza Vittorio Emanuele stands Palazzo Corvaia, the site of Sicily's parliament in the fourteenth century, though the present building is about 100 years older than the original.

Stroll down the nearby corso Umberto, the main shopping street, to piazza 9 Aprile, a terrace surrounded by cafés where you can sit and enjoy a local almond wine aperitif and incomparable view of the bay. Farther along is the medieval convent of San Domenico, now one of the most beautifully situated hotels in Taormina. At the end of Corso Umberto is a tiny funicular station where a cable car takes you down to the beach of Mazzaro in the summer.

In addition to restaurants and hotels, Taormina is also full of nightclubs where Sicilian folklore is reenacted in song and dance by local groups.

CATANIA: Repeatedly destroyed and rebuilt after violent eruptions of Mt. Etna, Catania is a thriving commercial center originally founded as a Greek colony in the eighth century BC. Since the last eruption of Etna to affect Catania was in 1693, the old city center has a seventeenth- and eighteenth-century air. In the heart of the city, at the piazza del Duomo, stands the symbol of Catania — an elephant sculpted out of lava with an obelisk on its back. To the left of this structure is the Chierici Palace; nearby, a small river flows from its underground course along the slopes of Etna.

Catania serves not only as an economic and architectural center but as the starting point for a trip to the top of Mt. Etna. This takes at least half a day (preferably morning) and requires appropriate dress — heavy mountain shoes and some warm clothing. Leave the city along the long, straight main street, via Etnea, which takes you through a landscape of burned-out craters and lava rocks past a mountain hotel (at 20 mi/33 km) to a cable car to the top, central crater. There you will see a large sea of magma heaving and bubbling with sulfur fumes. It is advisable to take along a guide from town. Make sure to start your trip back to town at least 2 hours before sunset.

En Route From Catania – Follow Route 114 some 42 miles (70 km) south, passing as you do the bridge over the River Simeto, where English and American troops fought bitterly against the Germans and Italians at the beginning of the Allied advance through Italy in 1943. Several war cemeteries dot the area.

SIRACUSA: More than any other Sicilian town, Siracusa shows archaeological evidence of the ancient Greek and Roman civilizations. Although now it has the air of a quiet provincial town, Siracusa was once a major cultural and political center on a par with Rome, Athens, and Carthage. One of the many legends surrounding it involves a Roman attack by sea and an ingenious defense planned by Archimedes, a native of Siracusa. He devised a system of setting fire to the enemy Roman ships by means of reflecting sun rays onto their sails. Siracusa was eventually captured by the Roman fleet, however, and Archimedes killed. Excavations around both Siracusa and Ortigia, the island site of the city's original settlement, now reveal much of its early Greek and Roman foundations.

Before you explore the city's archaeological remains, visit the archaeological museum at the piazza del Duomo. It is one of the most important museums in Italy and necessary for a basic knowledge of Sicily's history and prehistory. In its collection is the magnificent Greek statue, Venus Anadiomene — *Venus from the Sea* — discovered in 1804. The archaeological zone stands behind the present city. Its main highlight is the Greek theater, probably the largest and most complete monument of its type in the ancient world left to us. Sculpted out of rock probably in the third century BC, the theater found frequent use in its main patron at the time, Aeschylus, a prolific playwright. Under his influence, Siracusa saw the birth of Greek drama. The theater is still used today for performances of Greek plays.

Opposite the Greek theater stands the Ara di Ierone II, a huge altar built for public sacrifices. From here it is a short walk to the Roman amphitheater, constructed in the third and fourth centuries BC for the spectacle of Christians fighting lions. Although now planted with cypress and oleander trees, you can still clearly see traces of the original structure.

AGRIGENTO: Its hillside position on the southern coast overlooking the surrounding valley and sea earned for Agrigento the praise of the ancient Greeks and the poet Pindar, who named it "the most beautiful city of mortals." It is the site of the Valley of Temples, a magnificent complex of temples and impressive columns built in the fifth and sixth centuries BC as well as the birthplace of both the ancient philosopher-scientist-priest Empedocles and the modern playwright Luigi Pirandello.

PALERMO: The capital of Sicily and the seat of the regional Sicilian government, Palermo was known by the Greeks as Panorum — all port — for its gulf location, and today it still ranks as the most important seaport on the island.

Architecturally, Palermo is divided into a modern north side and an historic south side. The core of the old quarter is a crossroads known as the Quattro Canti di Città — the Four Songs of the City — bound by a group of baroque buildings built in 1609. Nearby is the piazza Pretoria and a sixteenth-century fountain, decorated by statues of pagan gods and nicknamed piazza della Vergogna — Square of Shame.

Many of the beautiful palaces and churches for which Palermo is often recognized are of Norman design. This is true of the Church of the Martorana (piazza Bellini) and the cathedral along corso Vittorio Emanuele (a street flanked by baroque palaces). The latter houses five royal tombs.

BEST EN ROUTE

In Sicily you will find a number of luxury hotels, converted historic villas, and many smaller, simpler hotels. Expect to pay around $70 or more for a double room at those hotels categorized as expensive; between $50 and $65 at those in the moderate category; under $45, inexpensive. Fish and seafood are the major ingredients in Sicilian cooking, and you can sample them at quite a few good restaurants. Expect to pay $55 or more for a meal for two at those restaurants categorized as expensive; between $35 and $45 at those in the moderate category; under $30, inexpensive. Prices do not include drinks or tip.

MESSINA

Alberto – The most elegant restaurant in town, it serves such delicacies as spaghetti *en papillote.* Closed Sundays and August 5 to September 5. Via Ghibellina 95 (phone: 71-07-11). Expensive to moderate.

Ristorante Pippo Nunnari – This pleasantly rustic place, decorated with antiques, is ideally suited for an introduction to Sicilian cooking. *Pasta alla Norma* (pasta with tomato sauce topped with slices of eggplant), *pescespada* (swordfish), available in May and June, and the Sicilian dessert *pignolata* are served along with robust Sicilian wines. Closed Thursdays and July 1–15. Via Ugo Bassi 157 (phone: 293-8584). Moderate.

TAORMINA

Hotel San Domenico Palace – A convent during a previous incarnation, its spacious rooms, furnished in antiques, were formerly monastic cells. Low entrances and thick walls help cool the interiors during oppressively hot summers. It has a swimming pool, parking area, and a restaurant. Piazza San Domenico 5 (phone: 2-3701). Expensive.

Grande Albergo Capotaormina – This large, modern hotel has a private beach, a swimming pool, and a well-run restaurant. Closed December through February. Capo Taormina (phone: 2-4000). Expensive.

Villa Le Terazze – This restaurant near the cathedral serves good Sicilian as well as Continental cuisine. Closed Mondays and November through March. Corso Umberto 172 (phone: 23-913). Expensive to moderate.

Hotel Timèo – Standing next to the Greek Theater, this old villa has been transformed into a tastefully decorated hotel with turn-of-the-century charm. Via Teatro Greco 59 (phone: 2-3801). Expensive to moderate.

Villa Saint Andrea at Mazzarò – Overlooking a small bay, this comfortable little hotel has its own private beach, a colorful garden, and a restaurant. Closed from November through mid-March (phone: 2-3125). Expensive to moderate.

Ristorante Il Pescatore – Taormina's best restaurant stands against a hill above the rocky bay. The simple but well-chosen menu mainly features fish. Closed Mondays and November through February. Mazzaro, about 4 km outside the city (phone: 2-3460). Moderate.

CATANIA

La Siciliana – This family-style restaurant has a garden for outdoor dining. The menu includes traditional Sicilian dishes like roast kid and mixed fish grill as well as heady regional wines. Closed Sunday evenings and Mondays. Viale Marco Polo 52/A (phone: 37-64-00). Expensive to moderate.

Pagano – A homey, casual restaurant near the courthouse, it serves a wide variety of Sicilian specialties. Closed Sundays and August. Via de Roberto 37 (phone: 32-27-20). Moderate.

SIRACUSA

Grand Hotel Villa Politi – This converted nineteenth-century villa surrounded by gardens was one of Winston Churchill's favorite vacation spots. Near the archaeological zone, it has a good restaurant, a swimming pool, and tennis courts. Via M. Politi 2 (phone: 3-2100). Expensive to moderate.

Ristorante Jonico a Rutta e Ciauli – This is one of the few places in Sicily where the meat is as delicious as the fish. The restaurant's terrace has a great view of the sea and cliffs. Closed Tuesdays and the first half of September. Riveria Dionisio il Grande 194 (phone: 6-5540). Moderate.

PIAZZA ARMERINA

Jolly Hotel – This comfortable, unassuming hotel in the center of town is known for its good restaurant. Via Altacura (phone: 8-1446). Moderate.

Hotel Selene – Smaller and considerably more modest, the restaurant here is adequate. Viale General Gaeta 30 (phone: 8-2776). Inexpensive.

AGRIGENTO

Hotel Villa Athena – Built at the turn of the century, this charming hotel has a swimming pool, a garden, an excellent restaurant, and a great view over the Valley of Temples. The restaurant, one of the best in Sicily, serves meals where the Arab culinary influence is noticeable. Via dei Templi (phone: 2-3833). Moderate.

Taverna Mosé – Traditional Sicilian cuisine in a pleasant atmosphere. Closed Mondays and August. Contrada San Biagio 6 (phone: 26-778). Moderate.

PALERMO

Villa Igiea Grand Hotel – This classic Sicilian villa stands on a private beach and has a swimming pool and tennis courts. Both the hotel and its restaurant are renowned for excellent service. Via Belmonte 43 (phone: 54-37-44). Expensive.

Excelsior Palace Hotel – A comfortable, recently renovated hotel near the fashionable Via della Libertà. Via Marchese Ugo 3 (phone: 26-61-55). Moderate.

Grande Albergo delle Palme – This large, old-fashioned hotel has an appropriately seductive touch of decadence and is centrally located. Via Roma 398 (phone: 58-39-33). Moderate.

Ristorante Charleston – One of Sicily's most famous restaurants because of the consummate excellence of its cuisine, this must be visited in order to appreciate its high reputation. Closed Sundays and mid-June to mid-September. In the summer, *Charleston* has a branch at the Mondello Beach, which serves excellent fish and wonderful dessert. Piazzale Ungheria 30 (phone: 32-13-66). Expensive.

Ristorante Gourmand's – One of Palermo's most popular restaurants, it serves classic Sicilian cuisine. Closed Sundays. Via della Libertà 37/e (phone: 32-34-31). Expensive to moderate.

Ristorante La Scuderia – Traditional Sicilian dishes are prepared with love and imagination in this modern establishment on the outskirts of town. You can dine in the garden. Closed Sundays. Viale del Fante 9 (phone: 52-03-23). Moderate.

A'Cuccagna – A lively trattoria serving good regional food. Closed Sundays. Via O. D. Granatelli 21/A (phone: 58-72-67). Moderate.

N'Grasciata – Good home cooking is found at this typical dockside trattoria off the beaten tourist track. Try the *bottarga* (pressed tuna eggs) by itself or as a sauce for pasta. Via Tiro a Segno 12 (phone: 23-09-47). Moderate to inexpensive.

Casa del Brodo – This small tavern becomes the gathering place of Sicilian men and women of letters in the evenings. You can get regional soup and pasta dishes according to the season and sometimes grilled fish, meat, and good local wine. Vicolo Paterna 5 (no phone). Inexpensive.

Sardinia

Floating in the Tyrrhenian Sea 115 miles from Italy's western coast and 130 miles from Africa's northern coast lies the rugged, sunwashed island of Sardinia. Originally inhabited in Neolithic times, Sardinia had an early history of invasion by Phoenician and Punic forces who, in addition to warfare, brought the island trade, language, writing, and, of course, art, of which many examples are on exhibit today in the capital city, Cagliari. In the later Roman-Punic wars, Sardinia was conquered by the military forces of the Roman Empire. During the Middle Ages and Renaissance, Sardinia was the object of intense rivalry between various Italian city-states, and its relationship to the rest of Italy was only resolved when it joined the unification in 1860 as a region. Here, on the tiny island of Caprera off Sardinia's northern shore, Giuseppe Garibaldi is buried.

With a population of about 1.5 million, Sardinia is one of the most sparsely populated Italian regions, although it is the second largest island in the Mediterranean. Its people have been firmly planted on their home ground for centuries and are something of a race apart from Italian mainlanders and even the Sicilians, whose island has also been crossed and conquered continuously through the centuries. Sardinians are a hardy, withdrawn, but hospitable people. They believe strongly in an independent economy based on agriculture and fishing, despite the gradual development of industry on the island.

For those who live off the land, life is hard even today, and the sight of a lonely shepherd eking out a living on some stony hilltop is still fairly common. Once Sardinia was the main supplier of timber for the Italian mainland; now the land is bare, covered by olive trees, juniper, myrtle, cactus, asphodel, and wild roses, the odor of which covers the island in spring.

There are still few roads in Sardinia and not more than half a dozen large towns on its 9,300 square miles. These few towns, though, are invested with a history that makes them well worth visiting. And for those interested in prehistoric ruins, stone dwellings called *nuraghi* abound.

Start your tour of the island in Cagliari, and drive along the western coast past fishing villages, new resorts, and coal mining towns until you reach the unspoiled northern tip of the island at Santa Teresa. Then head back south to Cagliari, but this time along the eastern coast, Smeralda Costa, a one-time haven for jetsetters. The trip forms a complete loop in approximately 5 days.

CAGLIARI: The city can be reached by the daily car ferry from Civitavecchia, a few miles north of Rome. Cagliari is to all appearances a modern town and a busy port. It has an old center, however, surrounded by thirteenth-century walls built by the Pisans. When you enter the medieval core of the town, explore the cathedral and then walk to the Terrazza Umberto I — all that is left of a sixteenth-century Spanish fortification. The terrace offers a splendid view of the harbor and nearby pine forests. Be certain to visit the Roman amphitheater, Sardinia's largest Roman monument, and the Botanical Gardens, with its display of Mediterranean and tropical plants.

En Route from Cagliari – Before beginning the northward climb up the Sardinian coastline, drive south for 31 miles (50 km) to Nora. En route you pass Sarroch and Villa St. Pietro, and nearby *nuraghe* colonies. These groups of small, circular stone structures are considered to be the earliest signs of civilization on the island. Nobody has yet determined whether they indicate dwelling places, burial grounds, or fortifications. Nearby is the Church of Sant'Efisio, honoring the patron saint of Cagliari. It's enlivened by a colorful traditional religious procession every May.

SAN ANTIOCO: This ancient port is now connected by a bridge to the Sardinian mainland. In its old center (where a Genoese dialect is still spoken), visit the museum of ancient artworks and the nearby necropolis of Sulcis. Its long sandy beaches and spectacular rocky coastline are an added attraction. From the port of San Antioco, take the car ferry for the 40-minute ride to Caroforte on the neighboring island of San Pietro.

SAN PIETRO: Lined with beaches and undulating rock-hewn inlands, Isola San Pietro is the tuna center of Sardinia. Here the killing of huge tunafish, called mattanza, during May and June is a major event and provides, along with agriculture, one of the island's main sources of income. From San Pietro's Caroforte take the ferry to Porto Vesme (an hour's crossing) and continue to Iglesias, 18 miles (30 km) inland.

IGLESIAS: This is the capital of the coal mining area and the home of a museum for other mineral specimens found in Sardinian soil. Its architecture reflects a Spanish influence, evident in the town's two Gothic cathedrals.

ORISTANO: Along the Gulf of Oristano and the mouth of the River Tirso, this town survived centuries of foreign invasion. Remains of its original medieval defense walls — the Porta Manna — stand in the central piazza Roma. In town, visit the Antiquarium Arborense, a museum containing archaeological findings from the Neolithic age.

THARROS: Originally a Carthaginian, then a Roman port, this town was probably abandoned around the eleventh century. Its ruins reveal something of each age, from

Punic waterworks and temples, to Roman baths and houses, to early Paleo-Christian churches and a Jewish temple.

BOSA: On one of the hills surrounding the fishing village of Bosa Marina, this small town at the mouth of the Temo River is dominated by the medieval castle of Serravalle. Primarily Spanish in character, the town's residential section is replete with sixteenth- and seventeenth-century facades and wrought-iron balconies. About 1 mile (1.6 km) outside town stands the Church of San Pietro Extramuros, the oldest Romanesque church in Sardinia, built in the eleventh century.

ALGHERO: Set amid olive and eucalyptus trees, Alghero combines a long stretch of beachland with an old town center clearly Catalanian Spanish in character. Many Catalán customs are practiced here to this day.

On your tour, follow the ancient defense walls until you near the town center, then walk toward the stocky round tower, Torre Sulis, for a splendid view of the surrounding coast. It's worth taking a side trip by boat across the bay to Capo Caccia and the Grotte di Nettune, a series of underground caves that have, over the ages, formed crystalline stalactites and stalagmites. Much of the grotto is yet unexplored.

En Route from Alghero – Travel north to the prehistoric (Bronze Age) necropolis of Anghelu Ruiu in the heart of Sardinian wine country (Tenuta dei Pini). From the necropolis, continue north to Sassari.

SASSARI: This is Sardinia's second capital, founded in the eleventh century by coastal inhabitants seeking a more secure dwelling place inland. A relatively independent locality, its citizens are renowned for their courage in resisting the Austrians in World War I.

Sassari's history is best traced by a visit to the National Museum. It contains archaeological findings from prehistory to the Middle Ages as well as some fine examples of Sardinian art and craftsmanship. Walk through town past the Fonte Rosello (Spanish fountain) built in 1605 and the remains of the medieval defense walls and towers. Climb the steep slope of corso Vittorio Emanuele II to the Church of Santa Maria di Bethlehem, with its Romanesque facade and baroque interior. This church houses the concluding ceremonies of Sassari's Feast of Candles procession, which is held on August 14 to commemorate the end of an outbreak of the plague in 1580.

CASTELSARDO: Tourist development in Castelsardo hasn't spoiled the loveliness of this one-time fishing village. The remains of a medieval castle on a high rock overlooking the town still offer an unparalleled view of the Costa Paradiso to the north and the Gulf of Asinara to the west and southwest, and the old part of the town with its steep winding streets and sixteenth-century cathedral still stands intact. Castelsardo is also known for craftsmanship, especially basketwork made from the fronds of the dwarf palm trees that abound in the area.

En Route from Castelsardo – Take a leisurely drive north from Castelsardo to Santa Teresa, enjoying the Costa Paradiso, with its red cliffs and fantastic rock formations jutting into a vivid blue sea. The ride is 37 miles (60 km) on route 200.

SANTA TERESA GALLURA: Santa Teresa, on the farthest northern tip of Sardinia, is another small fishing village developed for tourism but still unspoiled. Surrounded by sheltered bays, it's an ideal stopping place. A trip also should be made to the Capo Testa Peninsula, about a half mile (1 km) outside town, and its amazing rock formations. From there, Corsica appears to be only a stone's throw away.

En Route from Santa Teresa Gallura – As you travel around the northern cap of Sardinia, the coastal road brings you to a pair of islands — Palau and Capo Orso, opposite the archipelago of La Maddalena — that are barren, but beautiful. Accompanied by many other islands surrounding the archipelago, these are rich fishing grounds and renowned tourist spots. One of the most famous islands nearby is Caprera, where Garibaldi is buried. The southbound route along the eastern coast of Sardinia now begins.

COSTA SMERALDA: Called a millionaire's playground, Costa Smeralda (the Emerald Coast), on the northeastern edge of Sardinia, has been transformed in the last 10 years by the Aga Khan into one of the most fashionable resorts in Europe. Hotels built in a rustic style border private secluded bays (*Cala di Volpe* is an example), and fishing villages have been transformed into quaint towns with cafés, restaurants, and boutiques. Stop in Porto Rotondo, with its terrace overlooking the huge harbors, and neighboring Porto Cervo.

For a taste of the local cuisine, it is more advisable, and probably cheaper, to go to Olbia, 9 miles (15 km) south of Porto Rotondo.

OLBIA: One of the main ports that connect Sardinia to Italy, Olbia is surrounded by a ragged coastline and picturesque little islands dotted here and there in the gulf.

NUORO: Almost devoid of monuments, churches, or remains that mark its origins, Nuoro is nevertheless worth an overnight stay just to see something of the wild interior of Sardinia. On a hill, it overlooks a vast expanse of woodland and barren mountains, favorite grounds for hunters. It is also the hometown of two of Sardinia's greatest writers — Sebastiano Satt, poet, and Nobel Prize winner Grazia Deledda, whose house is now preserved as a tiny museum on via Deledda.

En Route from Nuoro – This final portion of the Sardinian route takes you along southeastern coastal roads and then inland to Cagliari. You pass through a wide, green, and prosperous valley until you reach Oliena, at the bottom of a craggy mountain, the Sopromonte, famous for its vineyards. Continue on to Tortoli and Arbatax, resort towns renowned for their beauty.

Continue south through the coastal plains of Sardinia, past several *nuraghe* excavations, and on to Nuravera, an agricultural town, once surrounded by orange groves, now surrounded by a few discretely placed tourist hotels. On Route 125, turn inland for the last 39.5 miles (64 km) to Cagliari, where the road winds through forests and mountain gorges to the Quartu Sant'Elena, a suburb of Cagliari. There, some interesting fifteenth-century Sardinian paintings are displayed in the parish church. Returning to Cagliari proper, there should be time for a last Sardinian meal before the night ferry leaves for Civitavecchia.

BEST EN ROUTE

Accommodations on Sardinia range from sleek coastal resorts to simpler establishments, but all share a greater or lesser proximity to the sea. Expect to pay $90 or more per night for a double room at those places categorized as expensive; between $70 and $85 at those in the moderate category; under $65, inexpensive. Expect to pay $50 or more for a meal for two at those restaurants categorized as expensive; between $35 and $45 at restaurants in the moderate category; under $30, inexpensive. Prices do not include drinks or tip.

CAGLIARI

Ristorante Dal Corsaro – Fresh and imaginatively cooked lobster, eel, shrimp, and fish are all well worth trying. There are also traditional Sardinian meat dishes and a large selection of robust Sardinian wines. Service is competent and friendly. Closed Tuesdays and from December 22 to January 4. Viale Regina Margherita 28 (phone: 66-43-18). Moderate. (During the summer this restaurant opens another branch at Poetto.)

Ristorante Sa Cardiga e Su Schironi – The front of this small, unpretentious restaurant is a bar and grocery store; the back houses a homey restaurant with good local wine and food. Closed Sundays and December. Viale Pula 74 (phone: 7-1652). Inexpensive.

ISOLA SAN PIETRO

Hotel Riviera – This small hotel is distinguished by its impressive position on a hill that affords dramatic views of the rocky coast (phone: 8-4004). Moderate to inexpensive.

ORISTANO

Il Faro – Considered this city's best restaurant, specialties here include spaghetti with *bottarga* (pressed tuna eggs), *penne* (tubelike pasta) with pecorino cheese, and mixed fish grill. Closed Sundays, the first half of January, and the second half of July. Via Bellini 25 (phone: 70-002). Expensive to moderate.

La Forchetta d'Oro – Fish features prominently on the menu, especially the Sardinian *bottarga*. Its terrace and garden contribute to the restaurant's popularity. Closed Sundays and the last half of August. Viale Armando Diaz 8 (phone: 7-0462). Moderate.

ALGHERO

Il Pavone – Great soups, antipastos, risottos, and seafood are served at this small, family-run restaurant. Many think it's the best in town. Closed Wednesdays and January. Reservations suggested. Piazza Sulis 3/4 (phone: 97-95-84). Expensive to moderate.

Uccio Ristorante del Mare – All the local specialties — spaghetti with squid, sea bass, lobster, and crab — are available, as are the best local wines. Closed Tuesdays and November. Via Minerva 16 (phone: 97-92-38). Moderate to inexpensive.

Ristorante Le Lepanto – This warm, traditional restaurant faces the sea. When available, fresh lobster is the house specialty. Caviar is usually on the menu. Via Carlo Alberto 135 (phone: 97-91-59). Moderate to inexpensive.

SANTA TERESA GALLURA

Hotel Shardana – This secluded hotel and restaurant have a private beach, swimming pool, garden, and tennis courts. Although its isolation is now threatened by encroaching development, its position on the sea is still lovely. Closed November through March. Capo Testa (phone: 75-40-31). Expensive to moderate.

Hotel Li Nibbari – In a field between the main road and the rocky Santa Teresa beach, this quiet, comfortable hotel has a good restaurant. Closed October through May. About 1 mile south of town (phone: 75-44-53). Moderate to inexpensive.

Ristorante Canne al Vento da Brancaccio – The owners of this simple restaurant are also farmers, which accounts for the freshness of the meat and cheese. The wine selection is very good. Closed Saturdays and October through November 15. Via Nazionale 9 (phone: 7-4219). Inexpensive.

COSTA SMERALDA

Cala di Volpe – Owned by the Aga Kahn, this extravagant hotel has served as a background for James Bond movies and is the jet set headquarters on Sardinia. The 125 rooms are rustic in decor but luxurious in appointments. Open May through September (phone: 9-6083). Very expensive.

Cervo – A large, elegant hotel, with a freshwater pool. Closed November through mid-March. Porto Cervo (phone: 9-2003). Expensive.

Le Ginestre – This 64-room hotel has a restaurant and a freshwater pool and is a short walk from a small beach. It's a good choice if you don't care about being directly on the water. Closed October through mid-April. Porto Cervo (phone: 9-2030). Moderate.

Lu Stazza – Here's where to sample Sardinian specialties like *maloreddus* (dumplings with a tomato and sausage sauce) and *porcetto al mirto* (suckling pig roasted on a spit and served on a bed of myrtle leaves). On the road from Porto Cervo to Arzachena (no phone). Moderate.

OLBIA

Ristorante La Tana del Drago – The nearby Golfo degli Aranci keeps this place well supplied with fresh fish. Closed Mondays and November. About 1 mile (2 km) northeast of town (phone: 2-2777). Moderate.

Ristorante Gallura – This small, humble restaurant serves traditional Sardinian dishes. Rooms are available, too. The restaurant is closed Fridays. Corso Umberto 145 (phone: 2-4648). Moderate.

NUORO

Hotel E.S.I.T. – This place offers genuine hospitality and home-cooked food. Monte Ortobene, about 5.5 miles east of town (phone: 3-3108). Moderate.

Hotel Grazia Deledda – The largest hotel in town, it has a fine restaurant where service is good, as is the cooking. Via Lamamora 175 (phone: 3-1257). Moderate to inexpensive.

Ristorante Fratelli Sacchi – Here you'll find a limited but well-prepared menu. Pasta with asparagus and roast wild boar are house specialties. Rooms are available. Closed Mondays and February. Monte Ortobene (phone: 3-4030). Moderate to inexpensive.

ARBATAX

Ristorante Speranza – Traditional food is served within view of the eastern Sardinian coast. Twenty rooms, some with private baths, are available (phone: 6-7248). Inexpensive.

Exploring Liechtenstein

Liechtenstein is not the obscure, lunch-stop country it's often made out to be. Almost three times the size of Bermuda, it's a fairy-tale land of medieval castles, lush Rhine meadows, ivy-clad chalets, vineyards, and quaint villages clinging to the Alps. Although Liechtenstein borders Switzerland and Austria and is quite close to one of the most popular tourist circuits in Europe, this 62-square-mile principality of 25,000 residents still has the virtue of being off the beaten track of most travelers.

The country is ruled by Prince Franz Josef II Maria Alois Alfred Karl Johann Heinrich Michael Georg Ignatius Benediktus Gerhardus Majella, the Twelfth Ruling Prince of Liechtenstein, Duke of Troppau, Duke of Jägerndorf, Count of Reitberg, and Knight of the Golden Fleece; in contrast to the pomp of his name and titles, the prince, one of the wealthiest men in Europe, dresses casually and drives around in his own medium-priced car. He and the royal family live in the thirteenth-century castle perched about 300 feet above Vaduz, the country's main city. The prince presides over a land that has been continuously inhabited for more than 5,000 years. In the late 1600s, a wealthy Austrian, Prince Liechtenstein, bought out two bankrupt counts with property in the Rhine Valley and created the principality in 1719.

Today, it is an industrialized nation producing an array of items from pharmaceuticals to false teeth, yet its factories are virtually impossible to find because they're in low-profile buildings in vineyards, polluting neither the air nor the water. Liechtenstein's people — none of whom is unemployed — enjoy one of the highest standards of living in the world, pay very low taxes, and take in a per capita export revenue of about $14,000 annually.

There are several ways to get to Liechtenstein: A 5-minute drive or a train ride from Buchs, Switzerland, brings you to the village of Schaan, and it's a half-hour drive from Feldkirch, Austria. Both Buchs and Feldkirch are stops on the Paris-Innsbruck-Vienna express; local trains on the same route stop at three Liechtenstein villages — Schaan, Nendeln, and Schaanwald. A convenient and enjoyable entry route is the hour-long train ride from Zurich on the Zurich-Milan line. The train glides through spectacularly beautiful Swiss countryside along the western shores of the Zürichsee and Walen lakes to the medieval Swiss town of Sargans. A 15-minute ride by the Swiss Postbus or by taxi takes you from one of the oldest democracies in the world to Vaduz, the capital of monarchal Liechtenstein, one of the last remnants of the Holy Roman Empire.

Vaduz is a convenient base for successive explorations of the northern lowlands, eastern mountain region, and southern Rhine Valley; this 50-mile (80-km) route takes about 2 or 3 days of leisurely travel. If you enter from Switzerland, you won't have any border-crossing headaches because Liechtenstein and Switzerland have the same currency and customs authority. If you enter from Austria, Switzerland's formalities apply. The people of the principality speak the Swiss brand of German.

VADUZ: Most of the highlights in Vaduz (pronounced va-dootz) are in the tiny main street area (the Städtle). Head for the Liechtenstein National Tourist Office (Städtle 37) and arm yourself with free brochures and guides and a detailed map of the principality (about $5). There are two major attractions in the same building as the tourist office: the Prince's Art Gallery and the Liechtenstein Post Office Museum. The art gallery is packed with priceless objets d'art, including one of the most impressive Rubens collections in the world. In addition, there are Rembrandts, Botticellis, Pieter Brueghels, and Van Dycks. Many of the paintings are reproduced on Liechtenstein's postage stamps, which can be seen (and purchased) in the Post Office Museum. The museum is known to philatelists the world over, as the stamps are among the most decorative and valuable in the world. Right next door is the National Museum. Get your passport stamped with the impressive crown insignia at the museum's boutique on the first floor. The museum has local artifacts dating from the Iron Age and a vast collection of medieval weapons, sculptures, and paintings.

The boutiques, souvenir shops, and sidewalk cafés in this area are worth a browse. You can find good buys in leather and wooden handicrafts, local wine, art books, chocolates, and domestic liqueurs. Treat yourself to the local grilled game meats, soufflés, and hearty stews served at one of Europe's most celebrated restaurants, in the *Hotel Real,* next door to the tourist office. Felix Real, the owner-chef, and his brother, Emil Real, who operates the posh *Park Hotel Sonnenhof* (in a mountainside vineyard half a mile away on Mareestrasse), learned how to cook in their native Italy. They perfected their skills at *Maxim's* of Paris, and have been catering to royalty ever since; they were part of the culinary team at the erstwhile Shah of Iran's multimillion-dollar bash at Persepolis in 1972.

No visit to Vaduz is complete without a trip to the palace, and the most enjoyable way to get there is by taking a leisurely, 20-minute stroll up a wooded footpath from the tourist office. Or take a bus from the Städtle or rent a bicycle (from Hans Melliger). Although the castle itself is not open to the public, the terraces and rolling meadows around it are perfect picnic spots, and the elevation provides a panoramic view of Vaduz, the Rhine Valley, and the surrounding Alps. You can drive, cycle, or take the postbus (the Swiss Rail Pass is good on them) from Vaduz north to Schellenberg, the next community. It's a half-hour trip.

SCHELLENBERG: Sprawled over wooded hills and lush meadowlands, this community has several archaeological sites dating back to the New Stone Age. In addition, the partially restored ruins of two medieval castles are worth a visit. If you take a walk along the marked Eschnerberg mountain trail, you'll see the historic areas as well as the beautiful woods. The next community to the south — the villages of Mauren and Schaanwald — is virtually in another era.

MAUREN and SCHAANWALD: Bordered by gentle meadows to the south and west and mountains to the east, Mauren and Schaanwald are two villages about a mile apart. Archaeological excavations in Mauren have unearthed the remains of a Roman bath and warehouse dating from the second century. The village has a beautiful parish church and a vicarage erected in 1787. The most popular attraction here, however, is the bird sanctuary–nature path that extends from Mauren east to Schaanwald. From Schaanwald, head west about 3 miles (5 km) to Gamprin-Bendern.

GAMPRIN-BENDERN: The Rhine flows gently past this area of rolling pastures and picture-postcard farmhouses. Here are the remains of a church built around 500 AD and a large building constructed after the Reformation that today serves as a vicarage;

the church and vicarage, on a hilltop, can be seen from afar and are favorites with visitors and photographers. It's about a mile southeast to the next area.

ESCHEN and NENDELN: The village of Eschen was first documented in the Carolingian estates registry (c. 831), but excavations reveal that it was inhabited as far back as 5000 BC. Visit the prehistoric settlements of Malanser and Schneller in Eschen, and the medieval Holy Cross, St. Sebastian, and Rochus chapels in Nendeln. Then take the road leading up through Eschen to the posh neighborhood of Schönbühl and view the houses of the most desirable residential area in Liechtenstein. From Nendeln drive south along the twisting mountain road, about 3 miles (5 km), to Planken.

PLANKEN: This little village of about 220 persons was settled in the thirteenth century. The dialect used here is drastically different from that of the rest of the Rhine Valley, as are the culture, cuisine, and costumes of the residents. It's a beautiful village of meadows and quaint inns. The views of the mountains, villages, and the Rhine Valley are excellent from the road south to Schaan.

SCHAAN: Two miles (3 km) north of Vaduz, this village of trim gardens, flower-decked homes, cafés, and colorful shops features a twelfth-century Romanesque church and an imposing eighteenth-century chapel. Return to Vaduz and head south about 3 miles (5 km) to Triesen, where you can begin exploring the Liechtenstein Alps.

TRIESEN: At the foot of the Alps and on the Rhine, Triesen was once inhabited by Roman nobility as a result of its convenient location. Especially interesting are the Roman-era section of the village (the Oberdorf) and the Maria and St. Mamerten chapels.

En Route from Triesen – Several hiking paths fan out to the Liechtenstein Alps and south across the Rhine Valley into Switzerland. From Triesen take the excellent road north into the mountains. After twisting and turning for about 4 miles (6 km), the road arrives at the idyllic village that gives the community its name.

TRIESENBERG: The residents of this tiny village dress in colorful costumes and build their wooden homes in a decorative, regional style that's been in vogue since 1300. At its altitude of 3,600 feet, Triesenberg seems nailed to the side of the Alps and commands an excellent view of the misty Rhine Valley below and the Alpine pine forests behind the village. Here you may see chamois and deer darting out of the woods or view the cattle, sporting enormous bells, grazing in the lush meadows.

En Route from Triesenberg – The Rhine and Samina valleys are connected by a 2,800-foot mountain tunnel. Excellent roads and cross-country hiking trails (the distances are usually marked in approximate walking times) zigzag through the Samina. Even if you're pressed for time, instead of proceeding directly east and up to Malbun, give yourself another hour or two and make your way via Masescha, Gaflei, and Steg.

MASESCHA: A quaint hamlet, 4,100 feet high and about 2 miles (3 km) north of Triesenberg, Masescha provides a breathtaking panorama and Theodul's Chapel, a restored medieval monument. If you want to spend some time hiking or mountain climbing, Gaflei, about a mile farther north, is a good bet. One of several mountain paths starting here is the Prince's Climb (Furstensteig), which follows a high ridge between the Rhine and Samina valleys; originating at 4,900 feet, the path weaves around several peaks up to an altitude of 7,000 feet. From Gaflei, there's an excellent road as well as several mountain paths to Steg, where you can visit the chapel of St. Wendelin, honoring the patron saint of shepherds. From Steg the road meanders southeast along the icy Malbuner Bach about 2 miles (3 km) before reaching Malbun.

MALBUN: At the base of a bowl of mountains, Malbun is rapidly becoming one of the most popular winter ski centers in the eastern Alps. Take the chair lift up to the Bettlerjoch Peak at 6,900 feet; in summer the *Liechtenstein Alpine Club (Pfalzerhütte)* operates a restaurant and provides accommodations at the Bettlerjoch. If you have time, hike from Malbun to the Sareiserjoch border pass into Austria; this adventurous jaunt takes about 2 hours. From Malbun, head back down the road to Triesen and proceed south into Balzers.

BALZERS: Amid rolling meadows, vineyards, and medieval castles, Balzers is reputed to be the home of the fictional Heidi. The area is dominated by the impressive Gutenberg Castle, built on a prehistoric mound; from 1314 to 1824 it belonged to the Hapsburgs. Near the castle and worth visiting are the Mariahilf and St. Peter chapels, the parish church, and the old vicarage. Another attraction here is the Elltal nature preserve and its collection of rare Alpine flora. Balzers also hosts summer opera and theater performances that draw audiences from all over Europe.

BEST EN ROUTE

One good reason for spending time in Liechtenstein is that the prices of its hotels and restaurants are generally more reasonable than those of Switzerland. We've rated hotels charging from $65 to $115 a night for a double room with bath as expensive; from $35 to $65 as moderate; and under $35 as inexpensive. Many of Liechtenstein's best restaurants are in the hotels.

VADUZ

Parkhotel Sonnenhof – This is possibly one of the best small hotels in Europe. The cuisine is regional and French and prepared by celebrated chef Emil Real. The dining room is open to hotel guests only. Reservations recommended. Mareestr. (phone: 2-1192). Expensive.

Hotel Real – This establishment features hearty and well-prepared regional cooking. Städtle (phone: 2-2222). Expensive to moderate.

Hotel Engel – This small hotel serves French cuisine in its dining room. Open daily. Städtle (phone: 2-1057, 2-1186). Moderate.

Landhaus Vaduzerhof – In the heart of town, this small hotel serves regional cuisine. Reservations are recommended in summer. Closed November through February. Zollstr. (phone: 2-4664, 2-2140). Inexpensive.

ESCHEN-NENDELN

Hotel Engel – Lamb and venison are the specialties in this hotel's popular restaurant. Closed Wednesdays. Reservations recommended. 9491 Nendeln (phone: 3-1260). Moderate.

PLANKEN

Hotel Saroya – Small and homey, it's one of the best deals in the principality. Closed Wednesdays. Reservations recommended in summer. 9494 Planken (phone: 3-1584). Inexpensive.

SCHAAN

Hotel Dux – There's an excellent restaurant in this hotel serving Swiss, French, and regional cuisine. The house specialty is fondue. Closed August through January. 9494 Schaan (phone: 2-1727). Moderate.

TRIESEN

Hotel Meierhof – Fish dishes are the specialty in this establishment's excellent restaurant. Reservations recommended. 9495 Triesen (phone: 2-1836, 2-2836). Moderate.

Motel in Liechtenstein – Here's another place where you can sample fine local seafood while staying at a good hotel. Closed November and December. Reservations recommended in summer. 9495 Triesen (phone: 2-2666). Moderate.

TRIESENBERG

Hotel Martha Bühler – The terrace restaurant of this inn offers a fine view. Open daily. Reservations necessary. 9497 Triesenberg (phone: 2-5777). Moderate.

GAFLEI

Tourotel Gaflei – Swiss, French, and regional fare are served in this large hotel. Open daily. Reservations recommended. 9497 Gaflei (phone: 2-2091). Moderate.

MALBUN

Alpenhotel Malbun – Here's a good, moderately priced, medium-sized hotel that serves both Continental and local food. Closed November to mid-December. Reservations recommended. 9497 Malbun (phone: 2-1181). Moderate.

Exploring Luxembourg

Bordered by France, Germany, and Belgium, the Grand Duchy of Luxembourg calls itself "the green heart of Europe," for fully one-third of the country's 999 square miles is still unspoiled forest. Although it is slightly smaller than Rhode Island, Luxembourg has a topography that ranges from the Moellerdall area in the rugged Ardennes Mountains (Little Switzerland) to lush farmland. Flowers are everywhere. Fields are sprinkled with wild poppies, daisies, clover, and buttercups — the perfect Impressionist landscape. White and purple lilacs outline the roadways, and in early summer the hillsides blaze with yellow gorse bushes. Storybook villages nestle beside peaceful rivers. Castles — some restored and others in ruins — cap the mountaintops.

Luxembourg's hotels and inns are clean and relatively inexpensive, and its restaurants serve a cuisine that combines the subtleties of French cooking with the heartiness of German food. The local white wines are fresh, light, and tart, and they are drunk with both fish and meat (red wines are not produced here).

The nation's history is dense with traces of all the armies that have marched across Europe. Once part of the Roman Empire, the country has been manipulated by dukes and dictators, princes and potentates, knights and nobles. France, Spain, Prussia, Bohemia, and the Netherlands have all had their fingers in its political pie, and for hundreds of years Luxembourg was involved in one alliance, treaty, or confederation after another. Twice in this century, the country has been invaded by Germany, but peace and relative prosperity have reigned since the Allies liberated the area in September 1944. Today, Luxembourg is a constitutional monarchy with a bicameral legislature. The upper chamber is appointed by the monarch; the lower house is elected by popular vote. The present ruler is the Grand Duke Jean, who is married to the Princess Josephine Charlotte of Belgium.

With a population of 360,000, Luxembourg is one of the few nations with a declining birth rate, low unemployment, and virtually no poverty; its gross national product is estimated to be the equivalent of $3 billion. Roman Catholicism is the prevalent religion, but the country also has Protestant and Jewish communities.

Iron mining and steel production are the major industries, followed by banking. Agriculture, including the cultivation of grapes, and cattle raising are also important, and a number of major US corporations have subsidiaries in Luxembourg. Tourism is an increasingly valuable revenue producer (Luxembourg entertains 2 million visitors per year); the country's appeal to those who love camping and hiking is on the upswing.

Most international travelers arrive at Luxembourg Airport in Luxembourg City. (For years the city was the European gateway for millions of Americans taking advantage of Icelandair's low-cost transatlantic flights, but vacationers are now urged to stay and see the country.) A valid passport is the only document required for citizens of the US and most other nations. There's a national tourist office in Luxembourg City (pl. d'Armes), at Findel Airport, at the Air Terminus (near the railway station), and in many other towns.

Using Luxembourg City as a base, you can easily reach any other part of the country within hours, and all of Luxembourg can be covered without strain in a week to 10 days. It's a good idea to spend several nights in smaller towns like Echternach and Vianden to experience the charm of their small inns and hotels and the distinctly medieval atmosphere of the country; in these villages you'll find rebuilt feudal battlements, ancient abbeys, and patrician houses in quiet, verdant settings. You'll find an interesting mixture of Gallo-Roman and Germanic cultural influences as well as three major languages: German, French, and Luxembourgeois (a combination of the other two). It's customary to speak French with waiters.

LUXEMBOURG CITY: Luxembourg's over-1,000-year-old capital has an exciting location: The oldest part of the city is actually a high plateau whose steep cliffs plunge into the beautifully landscaped valleys of the Alzette River. Ninety-eight old and modern bridges connect this central plateau to other parts of the city on surrounding hills and plateaus. If you suffer from vertigo or acrophobia, proceed cautiously as you cross the dizzying bridges or the steep precipices.

Winding around the edge of Luxembourg City's central plateau is the celebrated Promenade de la Corniche, a walkway offering breathtaking views of the city. For centuries this area was a fortress of great strategic importance. Although the military fortifications were dismantled from 1867 to 1883, the Casemates — a 13-mile network of underground passages — remain just below the promenade; cut into the solid rock of the plateau, they could shelter thousands of soldiers. Exploring these dark and damp tunnels can be fun for the nimble (enter at place de la Constitution). As you stroll through the old city, take note of the Renaissance Grand Ducal Palace constructed in the sixteenth to eighteenth century (rue de la Reine), and the Foreign Ministry, built in 1751 (rue Notre-Dame) adjoining the Cathedral of Notre-Dame (1613–21), with its fine sculptures and crypt. The National Museum (rue de la Boucherie) features interesting archaeological and sculpture exhibits; it's open every day except Monday. Place d'Armes, in the heart of the city, is a popular public square with outdoor cafés and a bandstand for concerts.

Just east of the city is the US Military Cemetery at Hamm. Over 5,000 American Third Army soldiers who died during the Battle of the Bulge are buried here. Later, when General George S. Patton was killed in an automobile accident, he, too, was buried here.

MONDORF-LES-BAINS: Southeast of Luxembourg City, on the French border, is Luxembourg's famous spa. In a spacious public park, it is renowned for its foul-tasting but supposedly curative waters. The warm water has been used to treat rheumatism, liver, and gall bladder problems, and it is a powerful laxative when imbibed. The park has a large, lovely rose garden. The town also boasts a new casino, *Casino 2000.*

ECHTERNACH: This medieval village lies along the Sauer River on Luxembourg's eastern border; its name means "the place where horses are brought to drink." Across the river is Germany and the mountains that once held the Siegfried line between France and Germany from 1933 to 1938. (You can still see the bunkers on the hill.) Heavily damaged during World War II, Echternach has been meticulously restored. The Town Hall, which dates from 1328, is the centerpiece of the charming main square. Nearby, beside the river, is the imposing Benedictine Abbey that was founded in the seventh century by a Northumbrian monk, St. Willibord, whose remains are buried in the crypt of the abbey's basilica. Among the abbey's treasures are its impressive twelfth-century frescoes and the brilliant, modern, stained-glass windows. The basilica is the terminus of the famed dancing procession, held every Whittuesday (usually in mid-May). Religious in origin — it is an act of penance, an expression of pious fervor — the event is celebrated by the entire village. Swaying, jumping, and dancing, the crowd moves through the streets as a haunting repetitive tune is played, paying homage to the English saint.

LITTLE SWITZERLAND: Hiking is a top sport throughout Luxembourg, but nowhere is it better — or more beautiful — than in the Moellerdall (Miller's Dale) section of the Ardennes that's also known as Little Switzerland. Just a few minutes north of Echternach, it comes as a complete surprise. After parking your car, you walk through gently rolling fields into a forest, and suddenly you're on a narrow path leading up and down through deep gorges, across bubbling streams, and beside (and through) enormous bolders. The whole area is dense with the kinds of tall straight trees Cézanne loved to paint. Although the area isn't as wild as it looks and the main hiking path is only about 2 miles long and fairly well defined, you're strongly advised to have either a guide or a very good map of the area. Comfortable clothes and hiking boots are also musts.

VIANDEN: This village on the Our River (an extension of the Sauer) near the German border, a short drive north of Echternach and the Little Switzerland area, is one of Europe's more romantic spots. A charming small bridge arches over the river, connecting the two parts of the town, and a formidable castle stands guard high on an overhanging hill. The narrow streets — parts of which date from the ninth century — slope down to the river, where graceful promenades line both banks. Next to the bridge is the little house where French writer Victor Hugo spent part of his exile.

BOURSCHEID AND DELANNOY (CLERVAUX): Two of Luxembourg's most interesting castles lie just northwest of Vianden; you can stay there and visit both castles in a day's outing, driving out one way and returning another. Bourscheid, an eleventh-century walled castle, is perched on a mountaintop overlooking the hills, valleys, and waters of the Ardennes region. The extensive ruins here are restored. The eleventh-century Delannoy Castle, home of Franklin D. Roosevelt's ancestors, stands in the center of Clervaux, another charming village surrounded by mountains. Three important permanent exhibits are housed in Delannoy Castle: photographer Edward Steichen's Family of Man collection, scale models of Luxembourg's medieval castles, and a Battle of the Bulge display. If you're particularly interested in the battle, you can visit the Battle of the Bulge Museum in Wiltz; the town has numerous monuments and remnants of World War II.

BEST EN ROUTE

This small country has a fairly wide range of hotel prices. The nightly cost of a double room with bath or shower can range from $25 to $75. Accommodations priced from $55 to $75 are called expensive; those from $45 to $70 are termed moderate; and those going from $25 to $40 are rated inexpensive. Restaurant prices range from $50 and up for a dinner for two in places listed as expensive; around $30 for those in the moderate category; and $12 in the inexpensive category. Prices do not include drinks, wine, or tip.

LUXEMBOURG CITY

Hotel Cravat – Luxembourg's most elegant hotel overlooks the Petrusse Valley. 29 blvd. Roosevelt (phone: 2-19-75). Expensive.

Le Royal – In the heart of the historic old city, this thoroughly modern hotel is complete with swimming pool, sauna, and solarium. 12 blvd. Royal (phone: 4-1616). Expensive.

Hotel Intercontinental Luxembourg – Recently built, this hotel in Europa Park is just minutes away from the center of town. A wide range of services are available for both the business and vacation traveler, including a complete health club with indoor pool. Rue Jean Engling, Dommeldange (phone: 4-3781). Expensive.

Aerogolf-Sheraton – This ultramodern hotel near the airport — it's totally soundproof — has fine cuisine. Its top-floor *Cockpit Bar* features excellent light entertainment. Rte. de Trèves, Senningerberg (phone: 3-45-71). Expensive.

Holiday Inn – Luxembourg's largest hotel (260 rooms) — and one of its newest — is on the "new plateau" near the European Parliament and European Court of Justice buildings and the Trade Fair Building. It overlooks the old part of the city. Rue de Fort Niedergrunewald, Kirchberg (phone: 43-77-61). Expensive.

Hotel Eldorado – This small, modern hotel near the railway station has an excellent restaurant. 7 pl. de la Gare (phone: 48-10-71). Moderate to inexpensive.

La Poêle d'Or – Opposite the Grand Ducal Palace, this restaurant serves delicious French food; start with quail eggs and then have one of the veal dishes. 20 rue du Marché-aux-Herbes (phone: 4-0813). Moderate.

EHNEN (near MONDORF-LES-BAINS)

Hotel Simmer – This old inn on the Moselle River has long been famous for fine food: Try their pâté, stuffed Luxembourg trout, and Charlotte russe. 117 rte. du Vin (phone: 7-6030). Inexpensive.

ECHTERNACH

Bel-Air Hotel – A winding road leads you up to this lovely, secluded inn above the river. Surrounded by its own park, the *Bel-Air* has a gracious dining room and a delightful cocktail lounge. 1 rte. de Berdorf (phone: 72-93-83). Expensive.

Grand Hotel – On the Sauer River overlooking the hills of Germany and the old Siegfried Line the *Grand* is a modern hotel with small but well-designed rooms and large modern bathrooms. Excellent cuisine is served on the enclosed porch facing the river. 27 rte. de Diekirch (phone: 72-96-72). Moderate.

VIANDEN

Hotel Heintz – A historic landmark, the *Heintz* is a superb small hotel. Once part of the adjoining medieval Trinitarian monastery, it's a delightful place presided over by the warm and expansive Madame Hansen; Margaret Truman, US Ambassador Perle Mesta, and Beatrice Patton have all stayed here. Each room is individually decorated. And the food is excellent; a typical meal might consist of ham or mushroom quiche, smoked tongue with Béarnaise sauce, beans wrapped in bacon, raspberry sherbert with whipped cream, and a carafe of the house wine. 55 Grand'-rue (phone: 8-4155). Inexpensive.

WILTZ

Du Vieux Château – This elegantly decorated restaurant features a terrace and à la carte meals. 1 Grand'rue (phone: 9-6018). Moderate.

Hotel du Commerce – Although this appears to be just an average tavern, the food is memorable. Don't miss the tender, succulent broad beans and the remarkable homemade ice creams. 9 rue des Tondeurs (phone: 9-6220; 9-5670). Inexpensive.

Exploring the Maltese Islands

The sun-drenched Maltese Islands — an archipelago comprising the main island of Malta, its smaller sister island of Gozo, the islet of Comino, and two large rocks, Cominotto and Fifla — are near the very center of the Mediterranean some 60 miles south of Sicily. Because of their strategically important location, the islands have always attracted foreign powers; as a result, they possess a wealth of history out of all proportion to their size. From megalithic temples and Roman ruins to the Arab city of Mdina, from religious traditions dating back to AD 60, when St. Paul is said to have been shipwrecked here, to the enormous artistic achievements of the Knights of St. John of Jerusalem in the sixteen, seventeenth, and eighteenth centuries, Malta's successive occupants have left behind a rich cultural tapestry set against a backdrop of honey-colored hills and azure sea. Nevertheless, the tiny nation, now an independent republic within the British Commonwealth, has remained intensely individualistic. Its 320,000 inhabitants have managed to combine a cosmopolitan attitude with a strong sense of tradition and national pride; along with their own basically Semitic language, nearly all Maltese speak English, Italian, and often French as well. Today, Malta is an ideal vacation spot, offering a near-perfect Mediterranean climate, superb beaches and lovely harbors, a fascinating variety of architectural and historical treasures, and a genuinely warm and welcoming people.

Driving on Malta and Gozo can be a challenge, particularly for Americans. Driving is on the left-hand side and there are no highways, just plenty of good, tarmac roads. Since the total area of Malta and Gozo is barely 119 square miles (Malta itself is only 14 miles long), and the actual distance between points of interest is very short, you may be tempted to jog rather than drive, but the steep, hilly roads of both islands will soon dispel such notions.

Our route starts out at Malta's capital, Valletta, proceeds inland to the ancient walled city of Mdina, and crosses finally, after several short but interesting detours, to the town of Marfa at the northwest tip of the island, from which point you can take the ferry for a 1- or 2-day visit to Gozo.

VALLETTA: The island's capital was built by Jean de la Valette, grand master of the Order of Knights of St. John, after the epic siege by the Turks in 1565. Rising dramatically from the water, in one wide sweep, the city dominates the island's historic Grand Harbor, one of the finest natural ports in Europe.

Although Valletta today is a mixture of old and new, the city retains much of its original baroque flavor. You will have no trouble exploring the town on foot; it is only about 1,000 yards long and is built in a regular grid around the main street, now called

Republic Street, where many of the better shops are found. Also on Republic Street is the National Museum of Archaeology in the sixteenth-century Auberge de Provence, one of seven inns built by the Knights of St. John of Jerusalem. Inside, important collections of prehistoric pottery, statuettes, stone tools, and ornaments recovered from Malta's many prehistoric sites are exhibited. Farther along Republic Street is St. John's Co-Cathedral, historically and artistically one of the most important monuments on the island. Completed around 1578, it was designed by Gerolamo Cassar, chief engineer of the Order, who was also responsible for building much of Valletta itself. Each of the cathedral's chapels was allotted to a national group of the Order and each is notable in its own way. Caravaggio's masterpiece *The Beheading of St. John* hangs in the oratory. The Palace of the Grand Masters, an imposing edifice built around two courtyards off Palace Square, was also designed by Cassar. Many of the State apartments are decorated with friezes depicting episodes from the history of the Order. Running along the back of the building is the Armoury, two halls containing a fine collection of arms and armor.

The National Museum of Fine Arts (South St.) is in an eighteenth-century palace; it houses paintings, sculpture, furniture, and objects connected with the Order of St. John. A section of the museum is reserved for works by Maltese artists. Also worth a visit is the Manoel Theatre (Theatre St.), built as a court theater in 1731 and now one of the oldest in Europe. From the Upper Barrakka Gardens, on the edge of the city, you are rewarded with a magnificent view of Grand Harbor and, across the harbor, the ancient cities of Vittoriosa, Cospicua, and Senglea. The best way to explore the harbor and the Three Cities, as they are called, is in one of Malta's brightly colored *dghajjes* (pronounced "dicers"), or water taxis, available for hire at the Old Customs House.

As you leave Valletta, and its suburb of Floriana, take a look back at the city's once-formidable sixteenth-century fortifications. Built to resist attack from non-European invaders, they served most recently to shelter the Maltese population from the determined bombing of Hitler's Luftwaffe.

En Route from Valletta – South of the city in the village of Paola is the Hypogeum, an underground monument built around 2400 BC and consisting of a system of caves, passages, and cubicles cut from the rock.

Guided tours are available. Nearby, at Tarxien, are three well-preserved historic temples discovered in 1915.

MDINA: Towering upon a 700-foot plateau, Mdina was once part of a Roman town built in 218 BC. According to tradition, it was here that St. Paul converted the Roman Governor Publius to Christianity and consecrated him the first bishop of Malta. In AD 870 the Arab conquerors walled up a small section of the plateau and named it Mdina, the Arab word for a walled city. When Arab rule ended in 1090, Count Roger of Sicily started a building program within the city walls, and between that time and the coming of the Knights of St. John, Mdina was the capital of Malta. Today it is also known as Citta Vecchia, the Old City, and is the finest and best-preserved city on the island. Historically the home of the Maltese nobility and the archbishopric, it has retained its Maltese flavor and has remained virtually unchanged for centuries. No cars are allowed in the city, so park outside the ramparts.

On entering the city, you come straight to St. Publius Square, which is dominated by the baroque facade of the Cathedral of St. Peter and St. Paul, built on the site of an older church in 1694. The Cathedral Museum houses such treasures as the painting of the Madonna and Child attributed to St. Luke, who was shipwrecked in Malta with St. Paul; a flagon by Cellini; engravings by Dürer; and the cross carried to Godfrey of Bouillon in the first crusade to Jerusalem in 1099. The Vilhena Palace, on the right of the square, now houses the Museum of Natural History. Follow Villegaignon Street to the city's northern bastion, which offers superb views of the island.

En Route from Mdina – Across the moat from Mdina is the suburb of Rabat, famous for its catacombs and the island's only remaining Roman villa.

To the south lies Verdala Castle, a traditional medieval palace designed by Cassar in 1586 as a summer palace for the Grand Master Verdale. The palace grounds, known as the Buskett Gardens, served as hunting grounds in the days of the knights. Today they are the scene of the Mnarja, the traditional folk festival held on the weekend before June 29. Horse, mule, and donkey races are held during the day, while folk singing, feasting, and dancing go on all night.

MOSTA: This is the site of the church of St. Mary, known as the Rotunda. A massive structure built in 1860, it boasts the third largest dome in the world.

En Route from Mosta – The north road leads to St. Paul's Bay, where St. Paul is said to have been shipwrecked. To the northeast stands Mellieha, towering on a high ridge overlooking Ghadira Bay. Here, in a grotto, is the church where St. Luke is supposed to have taken shelter and painted the Madonna.

After skirting the spectacular beach of Ghadira Bay, the road winds up the hills to Cirkewwa, where, twice daily, a ferry carries people, cars, and provisions to the sister island of Gozo.

GOZO: This is the legendary isle of Calypso, from which Ulysses found it so difficult to tear himself away. The Maltese like to say that a sea divides the islands of Malta and Gozo, although in reality they are only about 4 miles apart. In fact, Gozo does have a character all its own, noticeable the moment you set foot there. The tiny island, only 9 miles long and 4.5 miles wide, seems immune to the passage of time; it is sleepy and rural, greener than Malta, a bit more picturesque, and more dominated by its hilltop villages, with their quiet squares.

En Route from Mgarr – It is only a 5-minute ride from the port of Mgarr to the capital, Victoria, but you can make a short detour to visit the village of Xaghra, with its subterranean caves full of stalactites and stalagmites. A short walk brings you to the famous Ggantija Temples, which date back some 4,500 years.

VICTORIA (RABAT): The center of communications for the island, this is nonetheless a quiet, charming town. The Citadel (Gran Castello) was the medieval capital and is built much like Mdina, on a hill overlooking the surrounding countryside. The town has a modest but graceful cathedral, which, instead of a dome, has a clever perspective painting that simulates one. Victoria's quaint Old Town centers around its main square, It-Tokk. In the early evening it is filled with people strolling, talking, and drinking the good local wine.

En Route from Victoria – Just north of the road leading to San Lawrenz is the Basilica of Ta' Pinu, a simple, lovely church that has become a center for pilgrimage. To the west, along the coast, is the Inland Sea and Window, a natural pebbly bathing pool with crystal-clear water and sheer cliffs hanging over it dramatically. Heading north from Victoria, in a few minutes you arrive at Marsalforn, which, in summer, is a popular seaside resort and, in winter, a quiet fishing village. Also on the north coast is Calypso's Cave, with its magnificent view over the red sands of Ramla Bay.

COMINO: Only 1 mile square, Comino has one hotel, no cars, and, needless to say, an authentic get-away-from-it-all atmosphere. The boat trip from Malta takes 20 minutes and operates in the summer.

BEST EN ROUTE

Malta is a resort, and some of the best hotels still have an upper-crust British Empire flavor to them. The lodgings aren't cheap by Italian standards (Malta's nearest neighbor), except for hotels offering off-season packages. Among the restaurants, however, the competition is fierce; consequently many good meals are available on romantic seaside terraces or in atmospheric Arabian cafés for reasonable prices. There are restaurants on Malta with Chinese, Mexican, Italian, Viennese, and British menus. The best dishes, though, are local. Much of the meat is shipped frozen from Australia, but the rabbit is fresh and cooked over an open fire in a stew called Stuffat Tal Fenek. The seafood dishes made from fresh Mediterranean catches are also excellent. Many hotel restaurants advertise a per-head flat rate that's usually a good deal.

VALLETTA-FLORIANA

Grand Hotel Excelsior – A deluxe, old-world hotel with all the modern luxuries. Great Siege Rd., Floriana (phone: 62-36-61). Expensive.

RABAT-MDINA

Xara's Palace – If you're staying inland, this might be an interesting place to pick. It doesn't have much in the way of facilities (it's not even air-conditioned), but it drips with atmosphere. St. Paul's Sq., Mdina (phone: 67-40-01). Moderate.

ST. PAUL'S BAY

Mistra Village – A modest seaside hotel, actually part of a chain but mostly notable for its restaurant, the *Ir-Razzet Grill*. Good food is cooked over an open fire. Xemxija Hill (phone: 57-39-44). Moderate.

SLIEMA–ST. JULIANS

Dragonara – There are more hotels in the Sliema area than anywhere else on the island. This is the fanciest one, in the heart of the resort area, and has it all — private beach, heated pool, TV, private parks, a romantic setting. St. Julians (phone: 3-6421). Expensive.

Cavalieri – Has everything the *Dragonara* has but for a little less money. Spinola Rd., St. Julians (phone: 3-6255). Expensive.

Hole in the Wall – A great seafood place that doesn't open until 7 PM and closes all day Sunday. Try the scampi or the dendici. 32 High St., Sliema (phone: 3-6110). Moderate.

Sharmila – For a fancy meal, this is the place; the *St. Moritz* overlooks Spinola Bay. Seafront, St. Julians (phone: 3-9246). Expensive.

Il-Fortizza – This place is a little too commercial and touristy, but the building is interesting and the food is generally good. The specialty is fresh fish in good Italian sauces. Tower Rd., Sliema (phone: 3-6908). Moderate.

GOZO

Hotel Ta' Cenc – The only deluxe hotel on Gozo, it's out of the way but relaxing. Sannat (phone: 7-6819). Expensive.

Exploring Monaco

The principality of Monaco, although one of the smallest states in Europe, is, at the same time, one of the most famous because of its wealth and glamour. Today's Monaco is a mixture of old and new, with sleek modern buildings next door to the pastel stucco and tile of traditional French Mediterranean architecture. The emphasis everywhere is on sumptuous elegance. Yachts of the rich and famous fill the port, the shops display the wealth one dreams of — vintage wines, rare jade and ivory, costly jewels, couturier clothes and furs. Tourists, dazzled by the display, may sometimes forget that Monaco, with its rare climate and its turbulent history, has other resources besides man-made riches.

The climate is much like Southern California's: Winters are mild; summers warm, with little rain. The vegetation, too, is like Southern California's, with orange and lemon trees, palms, and live oaks. The water temperature of the Mediterranean is ideal for swimming. The only drawback is the beaches, all rock in their natural state. The few sand beaches here are all man-made, and Monaco's most exclusive stretch of beach is actually just over the border, in France.

Monaco is ruled by the Grimaldi family, one of whose ancestors (Francesco Grimaldi, a Ligurian nobleman immortalized as Malizia, the Cunning One) wrested control of the territory from the Republic of Genoa in 1297. For more than a hundred years, the family fought Genoa to maintain control of its conquest, and once that matter was settled, it still had to contend with other occupying foreign powers — Spain from 1524 to 1641, France from 1641 to 1814. When the Grimaldis regained sovereignty in 1814, Monaco was larger than it is today and included the cities of Roquebrune and Menton, which separate the principality from the Italian border. These two cities grew discontented under the yoke of Monaco and seceded in 1848, reducing the state to its present size.

Modern Monaco, with an area of only 468 acres, is divided into four parts: Monaco (the old city); Monte Carlo (the new city); La Condamine (the port); and Fontvieille (the industrial district, where Monaco brews its own beer). But, in comparison to tourism, industry is of minor importance to Monaco. The tourist business was given a major overhaul by the present ruler, Prince Rainier III, and his American wife, Princess Grace, formerly the actress Grace Kelly, who died in 1982. Modern hotels and convention centers have been built. Monaco maintains extensive public tennis courts and an 18-hole golf course, and the harbor, of course, offers superb sailing and water skiing.

Among special events are the Monte Carlo Rallye in January and the famous Grand Prix auto race in late May. The summer months are enlivened by the International Fireworks Festival, and early December, by the International Circus Festival. The Monte Carlo Philharmonic Orchestra can be heard practically year-round; the Monte Carlo Opera's season is from January through March.

Although Monaco is a sovereign state, with its own postage stamps (favorites with collectors) and car license plates, it is politically bound to France. There are no formalities crossing the border — you may not even realize when you've done it. And French money is the medium of exchange.

Because Monaco is so small, you don't need a car. There is a good internal bus system, which also takes side trips to some interesting neighboring towns. But if you prefer to be independent, you can rent a car from a number of international agencies.

You'll have no language problem in Monaco. English is widely spoken, and lots of English books and magazines are available at newsstands and bookstores.

MONACO

GRAND CASINO: A world-famous landmark. Even if you're not a gambler, you shouldn't miss the casino, where the legend of glamorous Monaco really began. The secession of Menton and Roquebrune reduced the revenues as well as the size of the principality, and when Prince Charles III came to the throne in 1856, he took up his father's idea of opening a gambling casino like the fashionable and successful one at Baden-Baden. A casino was built and struggled along until 1862, when the prince hired an expert manager, François Blanc, who had run the casino in Bad Homburg. Blanc hired boats and carriages to bring people from up and down the coast to Monaco's casino. At the same time, he spurred construction nearby of Monaco's first luxury hotel, the *Hôtel de Paris*. Through Blanc's efforts, the casino became fashionable and by 1869 was bringing in such large sums that the prince was able to abolish all taxes for his citizens. In 1878 Charles Garnier, the architect of the Paris Opera House, was commissioned to design the casino building you see today.

Stop for a minute in front of the casino to absorb the drama of the setting: the sea in the background; lush gardens; the building itself, with its copper roof enhanced by a green patina; and always, the coming and going of elegant limousines and sports cars carrying glamorous patrons from all over Europe. When you enter, you can go as far as the American Room and White Salon (slot machines and American-style games) without restriction, though you may have to show a passport to prove you're 21. A passport and an entrance fee are required for the European gaming rooms, such as the Touzet Rooms and Salons Privés. Most rooms open daily at either 10 AM or 3 or 4 PM.

PRINCE'S PALACE: With its crenellated tower sporting a rather incongruous clock and its Louis XIV cannons complete with neat stacks of cannonballs piled like apples in a market, the palace looks like an operetta castle, perfect for a miniature monarchy. At the sentry boxes, the guard changes each day precisely at 11:55 AM. The picture is so quaint you may not wish to risk destroying the illusion by going inside.

You can go inside, however, from July through September. You'll see the Court of Honor, surrounded by mainly seventeenth-century frescoes, the State Apartments, and the Throne Room. Admission charge.

EXOTIC GARDEN: A cactus garden, but much more, this was a project of Prince Albert I. It clings to the side of a cliff at the western approach to Monaco, more than 300 feet above the sea. The inclination of the cliff provides protection from northern winds and maximum exposure to the winter sun, so the 9,000 species of cacti and succulents from semi-arid climes around the world thrive as well here as in their native habitats. Equally impressive is the view, a sweeping one that embraces the whole principality.

Within the garden, at the base of the cliff, are the Observatory Caves. Although today you're most likely to notice the stalagmites and stalactites, at one time the caves housed prehistoric man, whose bones have been found here. You can take a guided tour of the caves, but note that the climb up and down totals 558 steps. If this seems too much, the nearby Museum of Prehistoric Anthropology safeguards what has been found on the site (and elsewhere in the principality and environs). Open daily; a single admission fee covers the garden, caves, and the museum.

OCEANOGRAPHIC MUSEUM: Not only a museum, but a working scientific research institute, this was another brainchild of Prince Albert I, called the "scholar prince" because of his passionate interest in oceanography. Prince Albert wanted a museum to house the results of his scientific expeditions around the world and to promote the science of oceanography. The building on the rock of Monaco, at the edge of a sheer drop, was a bold construction for the time. Pillars had to be built from sea level to support the building, and the rocks below had to be hollowed out to let in sea water for the aquarium. Though the work began in 1899, the inauguration did not take place until 1910.

Start your visit on the lowest level, with the aquarium. It's one of the finest in Europe — not surprising when you learn that the director of the museum is Jacques-Yves Cousteau. On the ground floor are zoological exhibits, skeletons of large marine mammals, and specimens that Prince Albert brought back from his travels. The top floor is perhaps the most interesting. Here are kept Prince Albert's whaleboat, nineteenth-century brass navigational instruments, and, in complete contrast, ultramodern diving equipment. Open daily; there is an admission charge.

OUTSKIRTS

LA TURBIE: Take the winding Route de la Turbie from Monaco to the Grand Corniche, and turn west (5 mi/8 km). This is the highest of the three corniches, offering spectacular views of coast and mountains. Built by Napoleon on the site of the ancient Roman Aurelian Way, its highest point is at La Turbie, 1,475 feet above Monaco.

The town is best known for its Roman relic, the Trophy of Augustus. It is worth a visit because there are only two structures of this kind still standing (the other is in Romania). The Trophy was built in 6 BC to commemorate Augustus Caesar's victory over the Gallic tribes of the region. The round pillar originally stood 160 feet high. On the base was engraved a list of the 44 conquered tribes, and above, between Doric columns, were statues of the generals who took part in the campaign. The top was surmounted by a statue of Augustus himself, flanked by two prisoners. A large part of the monument was destroyed by the Lombards in the sixth century, and villagers took much of the fallen stone for their houses. Now it is being restored.

You can climb up on the ruins for some spectacular views and interesting camera shots. If you'd rather, go to the terraces below the Trophy, where you have a panoramic view of Monaco and can see down the coast as far as Bordighera, Italy.

End your visit with the Trophy Museum. The display includes a model of the Trophy in its original form as well as interesting photographs of the restoration, much of which was sponsored by an American, Edward Tuck. The Trophy and museum are open daily. There is a small charge.

ROQUEBRUNE: Take the Grand Corniche east 4 miles (about 7 km). At the *Vistaëro Hotel,* stop to enjoy the view from this building perched right at the edge of a cliff.

The medieval village of Roquebrune is clustered around the oldest castle in France; you should be sure to see it for its very evocative picture of life in the Middle Ages. The village is typical of the medieval architecture all along this coast. The streets are narrow and steep; some are actually stairways, or vaulted passages. The buildings are made of rough stone with red tile roofs. The doors and windows are small to conserve heat in winter and keep the houses cool in summer.

Start from the place de la République, once the advance defense post for the castle.

Walk along the rue Raymond-Poincaré to the place des Deux-Frères, up the rue Grimaldi, then left into rue Moncollet. Here you see medieval residences cut right into the rock. Guests of the castle were accommodated here.

The castle itself was built at the end of the tenth century by Conrad I, count of Ventimiglia, for defense against the Saracens. Its ownership was bounced back and forth among Italy, Monaco, and France. It was used as a fortress, a manorial home, and even a prison under the French directorate.

Start your visit in the great Ceremonial Hall. The well in the center was fed by rainwater, a vital detail in this dry countryside. You'll also see the niche for the lords' throne, a fifteenth-century mullioned window, and, slightly lower, a storeroom. Climb the stairs to the three upper levels. On the first are a small guardroom, the former prison, and the archers' dormitory. On the second are the lords' living quarters, bedrooms, dining room, and kitchen with a primitive bread oven. These rooms have been restored and furnished. From the top level — the artillery platform — there's a glorious view of the red-roofed village, with Monaco and the Mediterranean beyond.

Roquebrune is a pleasant spot for lunch. You can also find some attractive handicrafts by artisans in Roquebrune — colorful pottery, and trays and salad bowls made of olive wood.

You can return to Monaco via Cap Martin. Take the Grande Corniche to the Moyenne Corniche, then go east to D52, where you will cut back west. D52 winds among the magnificent villas of the aristocracy (Empress Eugénie of France once lived here) before joining the Corniche Inférieure, which takes you back to Monaco through Monte Carlo Beach.

EZE-VILLAGE: Take the Moyenne Corniche about 5 miles (8 km) east. It's a better road than the Grand Corniche, but more crowded and less scenic. A cliff-perched town, like Roquebrune, Eze-Village has winding streets, a cactus garden, and a sweeping view of the Mediterranean from the ruins of the castle. It's less historic than Roquebrune, but has two gourmet restaurants. Eze is also a good place to buy locally made copper and enamel jewelry.

BEST EN ROUTE

Expect to pay $100 and up per night for a double room in hotels listed as expensive; $60 and up for those in the moderate category; and under $60 for those in the inexpensive category. Restaurants range in price from $60 and up for a dinner for two in the expensive category; $30 to $60 in the moderate; and less than $30 in the inexpensive category. Prices usually include service charges, but not drinks or wine.

Hôtel de Paris – Like the casino across the square, its contemporary, this is a historic landmark that is *the* address in Monaco. It has 300 luxuriously refurbished rooms as well as the regal Salle Empire dining room and a swank rooftop restaurant that are among Monaco's best. Pl. du Casino (phone: 50-80-80). Expensive.

Hermitage – Opened in 1899, it still looks like a fit setting for a turn-of-the-century grand duke. A winter garden, a restaurant with belle époque decor and food to match, and 200 luxurious rooms. More sedate than the bustling Hôtel de Paris. Sq. Beaumarchais (phone: 50-67-31). Expensive.

Loews Monte Carlo – An ultra-modern polygon right at the edge of the water, with 600-plus rooms, its own American-style casino, swimming pool, disco, nightclub, and several so-so restaurants. Av. des Spélugues (phone: 50-65-00). Expensive.

Monte Carlo Beach – One of two Monaco hotels right on a beach. Small (50 renovated rooms) and charming (the terracotta-roofed building dates from 1928), it's east of town at the exclusive Monte Carlo Beach Club (phone: 78-21-40). Expensive.

Beach Plaza – The other hotel on a private beach, this one is modern, with some 300 air-conditioned rooms, swimming pools, and an open-air grill restaurant. 22 av. Princesse-Grace (phone: 30-98-80). Moderate.

Mirabeau – Elegant, yet less expensive than the other Société des Bains de Mer hotels (Hermitage, Paris, Monte Carlo Beach). This is in a modern high-rise, with its own pool, restaurants, and 100 rooms. 1 av. Princesse-Grace (phone: 30-90-01). Moderate.

Alexandra – There are 55 rooms with bath or shower in this modest hotel. No restaurant. 35 bd. Princesse-Charlotte (phone: 50-63-13). Inexpensive.

Terminus – These 54 rooms with bath or shower, TV, and radio are near the train station. Two restaurants. 9 av. Prince-Pierre (phone: 30-20-70). Inexpensive.

Le Bec Rouge – Fans of its classic cuisine and elegant air consider it the best in town. The blinis with smoked salmon or caviar are a specialty. Closed January. 11 av. de Grande-Bretagne (phone: 30-74-91). Expensive.

La Calanque – The maritime decor suggests the specialty here: fine seafood. Closed Sundays and mid-March to mid-April. 33 av. St.-Charles (phone: 50-63-19). Expensive.

Grill de l'Hôtel de Paris – A panoramic rooftop location, excellent *grillades*, a remarkable wine list, and exquisite raspberry soufflés all conspire to make it memorable. Closed Mondays and most of January. Pl. du Casino (phone: 50-80-80). Expensive.

Le Stanc – New and already top-notch. You'll consume exquisitely refined cuisine while surrounded by a wonderful collection of antique toys. Closed Sundays and Mondays. 18 blvd. des Moulins (phone: 50-63-37). Expensive.

Polpetta – This café specializes in Italian and southern French cuisine. Closed Tuesdays and mid-January to mid-February. 2 rue Paradis (phone: 50-67-84). Moderate.

Le Pistou (Loews Monte Carlo) – On the hotel roof and serving specialties of Provence — lamb with a sauce of vegetables and garlic; local cheeses. Closed early January to mid-February. Av. des Spélugues (phone: 50-65-00). Inexpensive.

Nightclubs – Although Monaco's nightlife has traditionally been monopolized by the *Casino of Monte Carlo* (phone: 50-69-31), you can also try your luck at the casino in *Loews Monte Carlo* (phone: 50-65-00) or at the one in the *Monte Carlo Sporting Club,* open summer only. Then squander your winnings or drown your sorrows at Régines lively nightspots — *Jimmy'z* and *Parady'z,* both in the sporting club (phone: 30-71-71). In winter, *Jimmy'z* moves to the pl. du Casino (phone: 50-80-80).

ROQUEBRUNE

Le Roquebrune – This is the place to go if you have the urge for a delicious bouillabaisse. Closed November and Wednesdays out-of-season. 100 Corniche Inférieure (phone: 35-00-16). Moderate.

Les Lucioles – Delightful view of the sea from an open terrace, and fixed-price menu. Closed Thursdays and from November to March. 12 pl. de la République (phone: 35-02-19). Inexpensive.

EZE-VILLAGE

Château de la Chèvre d'Or – In a restored medieval manor house overlooking the sea, the cuisine is classic French. Closed Wednesdays and from mid-November to mid-February. On the Moyenne Corniche at Rue Barri (phone: 41-12-12). Expensive.

La Couletta – Classic French cuisine, with especially fine sauces. Closed Mondays and December 1 through January 31. Pl. de Gaulle (phone: 41-05-23). Expensive.

Exploring the Netherlands

The Netherlands is a small country — smaller than most American states — and can be crossed by car in a couple of hours. Packed into this tiny area, however, is an astonishing diversity of things to see and do. The country's compactness, combined with its excellent freeway system, is handy for visitors since most points on the recommended tour routes can easily be reached in day trips from Amsterdam.

The unique geography of the Netherlands has shaped the country's history and the character of its people. Named for its unusually low (nether) geographic location — all of western Holland is below sea level — the Netherlands has risen literally from the sea to become an affluent, intriguing nation. During the last Ice Age, a great glacier shaped much of Holland into flat land. As the climate warmed and the glaciers melted, millions of tons of melting ice increased the water level of the North Sea (bordering the Netherlands on the west), causing the sea to inundate these low-lying lands. The land was not flooded evenly, because sand dunes acted as natural breakwaters and this brought about the development of lagoons and swamps. Much of the Netherlands is land reclaimed from the sea by various advanced draining techniques. The Dutch were pioneers of dike building and drainage canals, and their history is a continuous battle with the sea over which they have triumphed. On lands that were once flooded stand the country's greatest cities — Amsterdam, Rotterdam, and The Hague. Perhaps the Dutch people's constant struggle with water — exemplified by the mythical Dutch boy who stuck his finger in the leaking dam and saved his town from flooding — have made them tenacious and successful. What they have accomplished with almost negative natural resources is proof of their success. Well-designed cities with stunning architecture, neat polder fields of the rural landscape, and the enduring works of art of the Netherlands's Golden Age, the seventeenth century, are among the spoils for the native and the traveler.

Wherever you go, stop first at the local VVV tourist office for information. VVVs are located in practically every town and village, as well as major frontier posts and railway stations. Each VVV specializes in its own region though most also carry the standard literature on the rest of the country issued by the National Tourist Office. These brochures, maps, and pamphlets are the best local guides. The Dutch automobile association, ANWB, has the best detailed road maps, and also publishes a large number of specialized touring maps on different themes and regions. You can pick up maps at the ANWB office in The Hague (Wassenaarseweg 220) or in Amsterdam (Museumplein 5). Falk-Verlag also publishes a multilingual road map of the country, available from any newsstand.

As you enter towns and cities, follow the *Centrum* signs to reach the center. *Doorgaand Verkeer* indicates the route for through traffic.

Our first route leads you through Randstad, where the major cities are concentrated. Though the cities are quite close together, they offer remarkable diversity, from the well-preserved old town of Haarlem to the extremely modern-looking Rotterdam. The Northern Netherlands route takes in the typical Dutch polder landscape of the North Holland province, and heads over the immense Enclosing Dike, which contains the North Sea. The Southern Netherlands route passes through the most geographically varied area of the country, through moors and forests, and the hill country of north Brabant and Limburg — the most French of the country's provinces. The last itinerary takes in the eastern region where medieval castles and fortified towns lie amidst forests and purple heathland.

The Randstad:
From Amsterdam to Rotterdam

This region, much of it below sea level, exemplifies Holland's compact diversity. Although the *Randstad* refers to a sort of supercity bounded by Amsterdam, Utrecht, Rotterdam, and The Hague, the greatest distance between any two of these cities is a mere 47 miles (75 km), from Amsterdam to Rotterdam. No four cities, as their inhabitants are quick to point out, could be more different. Nor is it the intention of planners that the four simply expand until they merge in an unbroken mass of concrete. Though this area is the most industrialized and densely populated in the country (60% of Holland's inhabitants live here), villages, farms, and rural and recreational areas are carefully preserved to maintain the variety and livable quality of the megapolis. All the sophisticated attractions of modern urban life can be found here, as well as miles of unbroken flower fields, lush pastures with grazing cows, and small historic towns. The route leaves Amsterdam on the Haarlemmerweg, which becomes the N5 state highway leading to Haarlem, and winds its way south through the bulb fields to Leiden, The Hague, Delft, and Rotterdam.

HAARLEM: This 900-year-old town has one of the country's best-preserved historic centers. An important city when Amsterdam was only a sleepy fishing village, Haarlem is still remembered for its heroic resistance during Holland's 80-year revolt against Spain, when it was besieged in 1572 for 7 months and finally largely destroyed, along with much of the population.

Haarlem's central square is the medieval Grote Markt, ringed by a number of noteworthy buildings including the fourteenth-century Stadhuis (town hall), originally a hunting lodge of the counts of Holland; the ornate Renaissance Meat Market, built in 1603 (now a museum); and the Grote Kerk or Church of St. Bavo constructed between 1390 and 1520. The church is also known for its Müller organ, built in 1738.

With 68 registers and 5,000 pipes, the organ has lured the likes of Mozart and Handel to Haarlem. Every June, it is the centerpiece of an annual improvisation competition that draws top organists from all over the world. From the beginning of April until mid-October, public concerts are given on Tuesday evenings and Thursday afternoons. Also of special interest is the Frans Hals Museum (Groot Heiligland 62), originally a home for old men built in 1608. On spring and summer evenings, romantic candlelight concerts are performed in the museum. Haarlem is the starting point of the annual spring flower parade through the bulb district, which takes place on the fourth Saturday in April at 10 AM.

    En Route from Haarlem – A short detour 6 miles (10 km) west leads to Zandvoort, a popular resort, with its 5.5 miles of sandy beaches (including a nudist beach). The town is also the site of Holland's Grand Prix race circuit, as well as one of the country's three casinos.

    Just outside of Heemstede you'll find the Heemstede Cruquius Museum, Cruquiusdijk 27 and 32, one of the three original steam-driven pumping stations that drained the immense Haarlem Lake from 1849 to 1852. Today the area is the location of the Schiphol international airport, 13 feet below sea level and probably the only airport in the world built on the site of a naval battle. The teahouse next to the museum is a handy place for a break.

    At the world's largest flower auction in Aalsmeer some 7 million cut flowers are sold daily (except weekends) in the 75-acre auction hall (Legmeerdijk 313). Tours are available between 8 and 11 AM. Arrive early to see the operation at its blooming best. On the first Saturday in September, Aalsmeer is the starting point of the world's biggest floral parade, which travels to Amsterdam and back. Floats are on view in the auction halls the days before and after the parade.

    Nieuw-Vennep is the modern site of the famous Bols Company (Lucas Bolsstraat 7). After more than four centuries in business, this is the world's oldest distiller of liqueurs.

    In April and early May, Holland's vast bulb fields are in brilliant bloom. If you visit at this time, take a minitour by turning south at Hillegom toward Lisse, and follow the signposted flower route. In Lisse, don't miss the Keukenhof (Stationsweg), a spectacular 70-acre garden featuring some 7 million bulbs and 5,000 square yards of greenhouses, open only during the blooming period.

    A train/bus/entry ticket package is available from most Dutch railway stations.

LEIDEN: Dating from Roman times, Leiden is one of Holland's oldest towns. For a long time, it was also one of the most important. It is the site of the country's first university, established in 1575 in recognition of the town's heroic role in the revolt against Spain. Part of the university is still housed in the former convent chapel (Rapenburg 73), where it has been since 1581. The lifting of the siege of Leiden in 1574 is celebrated every year on October 3. America's Pilgrim ancestors took refuge here from 1608 to 1620 and you should not miss the chance to visit the Pilgrim Fathers Documents Center (Boisotkade 2a) or the restored St. Pieter's Church where they worshiped. For a light lunch, try some Dutch-style pancakes, which come in a variety of flavors, at the *Oude Leyden* (Steenstraat 51).

THE HAGUE: This city of half a million, third largest in the Netherlands and the country's political capital and seat of government (Amsterdam is the official capital), provides an excellent capsule illustration of the varied character of the Randstad.

    As befits a major world capital housing more than 60 foreign embassies, The Hague is a smart, sophisticated, and cosmopolitan city, known for its beauty, elegance, and stateliness. The city contains three royal palaces, and retains a distinctively regal air. The daily business of government is carried on in the historic Binnenhof (Inner Court) complex of buildings in the ancient heart of the city, dominated by the magnificent 700-year-old Ridderzaal (Knights' Hall). It was here that the village of Die Haghe grew up around a hunting lodge built by the count of Holland in the thirteenth century. Summer offers special treats. The imposing fifteenth-century Church of St. Jacob or Grote Kerk (the Kerkplein), features carillon concerts at noon on Mondays, Wednesdays, and Fridays while the mansion-filled and tree-lined Lange Voorhout is turned into an open-air antique market every Thursday. The Mauritshuis Museum (Plein 29), a seventeenth-century palace housing one of the world's best collections of paintings from the Dutch school, is also close by.

An entirely different side of The Hague is presented by the city's lively seafront, Scheveningen, which has long been one of Europe's major resorts and has recently undergone a complete renovation. Features include an attractive promenade and pier, a nudist beach, and the newest of Holland's three casinos in the landmark *Kurhaus Hotel.*

The Hague has more than a score of museums. Principal among these is the Gemeente (City) Museum (Stadhouderslaan 41), with its collection of modern art and rare musical instruments (special concerts are sometimes performed on them). The Panorama Mesdag (Zeestraat 65b) has the world's largest painting, completed in 1881 depicting Scheveningen life at the time. The Gevangenpoort (Prison Gate) Museum (Buitenhof 33) is a medieval horror chamber with torture rooms and instruments still intact. Other notable museums include the Costume Museum (Lange Vijverberg 14), with period costumes and furniture, and the Museum Scheveningen (Neptunusstraat 92), illustrating the history of Scheveningen as a fishing village.

The Hague is best known for its unique miniature city, Madurodam, five acres of meticulously crafted reproductions of real structures done on a scale of 1:25. Everything works, too, from the 2-mile railway network to the canal locks and harbor fire boats. Nearly 50,000 tiny lights come on at dusk. At Haringkade 175 in the Scheveningse Bosjes woodland park, Madurodam is open from April through September.

Other Hague sights include the Royal Residence at Huis ten Bosch Palace, the home of Queen Beatrix, on the Bezuidenhoutseweg in the Haagse Bos (Hague Woods), and the Peace Palace, Carnegieplein, a gift of the American millionaire philanthropist Andrew Carnegie and now the site of the International Court of Justice.

With its many woods and parks, The Hague also lays claim to the title of Holland's greenest city. Worthy of special attention are the nineteenth-century Japanese Garden, Clingendael Park, open during the blooming season from about mid-May to mid-June, and the world-famous rosarium in the 50-acre Westbroekpark in the Scheveningse Bosjes.

The Hague's unique combination of city, woodland, seaside, and dunes, is reflected in the wide range of recreational facilities available. Greyhounds race at Clingendael on the Rijksstraatweg, and the horses run at Duindigt in Wassenaar, Waalsdorperlaan 29a. Nearby Duinrell has a campground, recreational area, and amusement park, where you can even ski on artificial slopes (and snow) in the wintertime. You can swim year-round in the new glass-covered surf pool on the Promenade in Scheveningen, as well as in the ocean, and go deep-sea fishing or take a North Sea cruise from Rederij Jacq. Vrolijk, Doorniksestraat.

Special Hague events include the ceremonial opening of Parliament on the third Tuesday in September, when the queen sets out in her golden coach, and the week-long annual North Sea Jazz Festival in July, which attracts top performers from all over the world. Vlaggetjesdag (Flag Day), celebrated late in May when the colorfully bedecked herring fleet sets out from Scheveningen for the first catch of the new season, also belongs in this category, but declining herring stocks have made its future somewhat uncertain.

DELFT: This 725-year-old town with its architecturally splendid 300-year-old center is best known outside of Holland for the famous pottery that has become synonymous with its name. The Porceleyne Fles (Rotterdamseweg 196) is the only factory that still makes Delftware in the traditional way (others churn out machine-made imitations). You can watch the company's 300 artists painting the entirely handmade Delft Blue.

To the Dutch, Delft is most important for its historical associations. William the Silent of Orange, the country's founding father and precursor of the present royal family, was assassinated here in 1584. Some bullet holes from that attack can still be seen in the walls of the beautiful fifteenth-century Prinsenhof Museum (Agathaplein), William's residence at the time. The museum itself is devoted primarily to the history of Delft and the Netherlands's long struggle for independence from Spain.

Delft is the traditional burial place of the royal family. Tombs are not on public view, but you can visit the mausoleum of William at the New Church, on the Markt, built in 1496.

ROTTERDAM: Holland's second largest city, with a population of about 600,000, Rotterdam once rivaled Amsterdam in beautiful old buildings but was devastated by a Nazi air raid in 1940. Rotterdam was rebuilt and is today an extremely modern city — well designed and attractive. Air and light sometimes seem to have been used as purposefully as glass and steel in its reconstruction. The broad 1¼-mile pedestrian shopping precinct, Lijnbaan, is an attraction in its own right. The 600-foot Euromast (Parkhaven 20) is worth a visit for its panoramic restaurant, café, and observation tower, and an airborne ship's bridge manned by retired officers who are happy to explain the instruments.

Don't miss the opportunity to tour the large, modern port complex by boat from Spido at the Willemsplein. Greenery is well provided for by the beautiful Kralingse Bos woodland park, and the Boymans-van Beuningen Museum (Mathenesserlaan 18–20) is a fine modern art museum. The highly respected Rotterdam Philharmonic Orchestra, under the leadership of James Conlon, offers the best in classical music at the Doelen Concert Hall, Schouwburgplein 50. The Doelen also hosts a number of special cultural activities, including the International Poetry Festival every June.

Rotterdam is not all modern, however. Miraculously spared the Nazi bombs was the historic port of Delfshaven, from which America's founding Pilgrim fathers sailed on the first leg of their voyage to the New World in 1620. A painstaking 20-year project restoring Delfshaven's 110 buildings was completed in 1980, and many of these now belong to artists and practitioners of traditional crafts. Of special interest is the Guild House of the Sack Carriers who unloaded the ships (Voorstraat 13–15), where you can buy at bargain prices new pewter objects cast in original seventeenth- and eighteenth-century molds and watch how they are made. De Dubbelde Palmboom historical museum (Voorhaven 12) is devoted to old crafts. If you want to see the Pilgrim Fathers' Church, call first or check next door at Voorstraat 18 (phone: 010-774-156). A special commemoration service is held there every Thanksgiving Day.

Close to Rotterdam is Kinderdijk, with Holland's greatest concentration of windmills. On Saturday afternoons July and August, weather permitting, all 19 mills are turning.

Also outside of Rotterdam is the town of Gouda; its Cheese Market is held in the seventeenth-century weigh house in the central Markt on Thursday mornings from 9:30 AM to noon, June 30 to August 31. Nearby is Holland's oldest (1448) and most beautiful town hall, which lures marriage-minded couples from all over the country. On a selected evening in mid-December, the entire square is illuminated by candlelight until the magnificent town Christmas tree, a gift from Norway, is switched on. Carol singing and a concert in the church follow.

BEST EN ROUTE

In the Hague, expect to pay $70 and up for a double room in the expensive range, $40 to $60 in the moderate range, and under $50 in the inexpensive category. In Amsterdam there's a wider variety of good standard accommodations at moderate prices. Dinner for two should cost from $30 to $40 in expensive restaurants, from $10 to $25 in those listed as moderate, and under $10 in the inexpensive ones. Prices do not include drinks or wine.

THE HAGUE

Kurhaus Hotel – Originally opened in 1885, this historic hotel was completely rebuilt and reopened in 1979. Dominating the seaport resort area of Scheveningen, the hotel has a classical facade that is an exact replica of the original. Inside, there's a luxurious modern hotel, centered around a vaulted dome reception area with old paintings and inlaid mosaics. The most elegant of the Netherlands' three casinos is here along with a first-class French restaurant and two bars. Adjacent to the hotel is an all-weather recreation center with a pool, sauna, and solarium. Kurhausplein 1 (phone: 070-520-052). Expensive.

Westbroekpark – This restaurant is in an open glass pavilion in the middle of a beautiful park. You can dine on French specialties while looking at the hundreds of roses growing outside. Try the four-course Golden Rose menu. From June to September, dining is outside in the midst of a blaze of color. Reservations recommended. Kapelweg 35 (phone: 070-546-072). Moderate.

ROTTERDAM

Atlanta Hotel – This four-star hotel in the town center opposite City Hall offers all modern amenities. Aert van Nesstraat 4 (phone: 010-11-04-20). Expensive to moderate.

DELFT

De Prinsenkelder – Set in a medieval cellar with Gothic arches, old wood, and antique tables, this atmospheric restaurant specializes in French cuisine. Its specialty menus change weekly. Reservations recommended. Schoolstraat 11 (phone: 015-121-860). Expensive.

The Northern Netherlands

This 155-mile (248-km) route travels through the typical Dutch polder landscape of North Holland province, across the immense Enclosing Dike, which holds back the North Sea, into Friesland, the Netherlands's most unusual province. North Holland is characterized by its flat, rustic meadowlands reclaimed from the sea and sprinkled with church spires and thatch-roofed farmhouses, but it also possesses dreamy fishing villages, as well as the country's most beautiful beaches.

Friesland, particularly the Wadden Islands just off the coast, is a nature-lover's paradise, containing one of Europe's most important bird sanctuaries and wildlife preserves, as well as the country's best facilities for water sports. With its own language, history, and cultural traditions, passionately clung to by the majority of its half-million residents, Friesland gives the impression of being more of a mini-republic than a Dutch province. Its history is in fact older than Holland's; so fierce were the early Frisians, that even the Roman legions were unable to subdue them. The Frisians literally built their country with their bare hands, doggedly constructing huge mounds of earth called *terpen* to protect them from the sea. More than 100 million cubic yards of earth (the equivalent of 21 Great Pyramids) were shifted this way. The Frisians, who also have a sense of humor, have made something of a joke out of their legendary pride and stubborn independence by issuing passports. Pick one up at one of the tourist offices. They make intriguing souvenirs, and also offer valuable reductions on many attractions.

ZAANDAM: Just outside of town is De Zaanse Schans, a village constructed in 1948 from threatened historic mills and houses that were transported to the site and painstakingly reassembled. It is now a living museum occupied by families, but the windmills — as well as an antique clock museum and an old bakery — are open to the public. In town, at Krimp 24, you can see the cottage where the eccentric Russian Czar, Peter the Great, disguised as a shipyard worker, stayed while on a state visit in 1697. In nearby Koog a/d Zaan (Museumlaan 18) is a windmill museum with models demonstrating how the mills work.

En Route from Zaandam – The stretch of coastline a few miles west of the route is among the most unspoiled in the country. There is a magnificent 12,500-acre dune reservation with entrances at the villages of Wijk aan Zee, Heemskerk, Castricum, Bakkum, Egmond, and Bergen. The last village is an artists' colony.

ALKMAAR: This picturesque town is especially famed for its cheese market on the central Waagplein. On Friday mornings at 10 AM in the spring and summer, a colorful 350-year-old tradition continues as the cheeses are auctioned off and carried to the fourteenth-century weighing house by members of one of Europe's few surviving medieval guilds.

HOORN: Like others along what was once the Zuider Zee, this historic port town on the shore of Lake Ijssel has adopted tourism and water sports since being cut off from the ocean. Summer is the season for a folklore market that gives demonstrations of traditional crafts, and the historic triangle tour, which includes a trip by steam train to Medemblik, and by boat to Enkhuizen. Nearby, the Zuiderzee Museum, a reconstructed — and inhabited — village of 130 homes and shops, depicts the area's turn-of-the-century fishing culture. If you're hungry, get off the train at the stop for *De Nadorst,* a restaurant in a thatch-roofed 350-year-old farmhouse specializing in hearty local dishes.

The villages of Marken and Volendam, where the locals still wear traditional costumes (mainly as a draw for tourists), and the little-changed seventeenth-century cheese town of Edam, lie 12.5 miles (20 km) south of Hoorn. A rather strange museum in Edam (Wowneerstraat 8) is in a sixteenth-century house that has a cellar that actually floats; at different times, the house has been occupied by a man famed for his beard, which reached down to his toes and back up to his shoulders; a woman nearly 9 feet tall; and another man who weighed over 500 pounds! Exhibits focus on them and other local curios.

En Route from Hoorn – At Den Oever you may like to make a side trip by heading 16 miles (25 km) to Den Helder, where you can catch a ferry to Texel, the largest and most popular of the Wadden Islands. Although Texel is swamped with campers in the summer, all of the islands are beautiful and undeveloped.

Back en route, you cross the Afsluitdijk, a massive 12-mile-long dike separating the North Sea from freshwater Lake Ijssel. Stop at the monument, 4 miles (6 km) from Den Oever and climb up for a view of the surrounding water. If this dike ever springs a leak, it'll take much more than a boy's finger to plug it up.

A short way up the coast is the seaport town of Harlingen, originally a Norman settlement, now a jumping-off point for the attractive islands of Vlieland and Terschelling. Cars are banned from Vlieland.

Franeker features an unusual working planetarium (Eise Eisingastraat 3) with a model, created by a craftsman in 1781, that demonstrates the solar system as it was known in the eighteenth century. A short way off the road at the next junction at Dronrijp is Winsum, the center of a uniquely Frisian sport — pole-vaulting over canals. Developed from the practical need of a means of crossing the canal-laced fields, this sport is interesting because most of the contestants end up in the water rather than on the far bank. Championships are held on Saturdays in August.

LEEUWARDEN: Built on three *terpen,* this city is the capital and heart of Friesland. The notorious spy, Mata Hari, was born here. A statue of her stands on the Korfmakerspijp. The house she grew up in is now occupied by the Museum of Frisian Literature (Gröte Kerkstraat 28). The Fries Museum (Turfmarkt 24) has English-speaking guides who provide some insight into the history and culture of this unique province. The Princessehof Museum (Gröte Kerkstraat 11) has an excellent ceramics collection, including many one-of-a-kind pieces. From the sixteenth-century Oldehove Tower (Oldehoofster Kerkhof), you can view the city in the summer. The *Taveerne De Waag,* in the weigh house, built in 1568, is an interesting place to eat.

Another unique form of recreation that is rapidly gaining in popularity with tourists is *wadlopen* — walking through the shallows. The Wadden Sea between the mainland and the islands is so shallow that it is actually possible to walk to three of the islands when the tide is out. Organized treks are an absolute must for birdwatchers. They require a day, an experienced guide, suitable clothing and equipment, and some advance planning. Departures are from Holwerd or Wierum on the coast to the north. For information contact the VVV in Leeuwarden (Stationsplein 1; phone: 05100-32224). The hamlet of Hoogebeintum stands on the highest (40 feet) *terp* in the province. To view the thirteenth-century church get the key from the minister.

SNEEK: This popular yachting center is the site of a major international regatta in August. In the lake district, Friesland is Holland's prime location for all water sports.

SLOTEN: This walled town with a population of 700 is the smallest in Friesland. Resembling a movie set, this popular center for water sports is worth seeing.

En Route from Sloten – In Wolvega there's a statue of the founding father of New York, Peter Stuyvesant, who was born in the adjoining community of Weststellingwerf.

Zwarlendijkster: Between the villages of Een and Bakkeveen are these preserved fortifications dating from 1593, on which Stuyvesant based New York's defenses. It was this first wall that gave Wall Street its name. The wooded area is an attractive place to walk or bicycle. From here you can easily return to Leeuwarden via Drachten or extend your tour by continuing north to the university city of Groningen, and looping back down to Amsterdam through a few pastoral provinces.

BEST EN ROUTE

Expect to pay $70 and up for a double room in an expensive hotel, $40 to $60 in the moderate range, and about $35 in the inexpensive category. Dinner for two should cost $30 to $40 in the restaurants listed as expensive, $10 to $20 in those listed as moderate, and under $10 in the inexpensive. Prices do not include drinks or wine.

LEEUWARDEN

Oranje Hotel – This modernized, reasonably priced hotel in the center of town has 80 rooms and a good restaurant specializing in typical Dutch food. Stationsweg 4 (phone: 058-126241). Moderate.

GROUW

Hotel Oostergoo – Cozy, simple but comfortable, this 24-room hotel on the lake about 6 miles (10 km) from Leeuwarden has a restaurant serving Dutch food and fish specialties. Nieuwe Kade 1 (phone: 05662-1309). Moderate to inexpensive.

The Southern Netherlands

This 225-mile (360-km) route, bordered by Belgium to the south, passes through the most geographically varied part of the Netherlands, from the estuaries and islands of Zeeland (Sea Land) on the North Sea coast, through the moors and forests of North Brabant, to the hill country — the only hill country in Holland — of Limburg province in the southeastern pocket between Germany and Belgium. These last two, the country's Catholic provinces, are notorious among their sterner Protestant brethren for the annual carnival madness that sweeps the southeast for 3 days in February. The festivities, which include parades, colorful costumes, street music, round-the-clock opening of cafés, and general hysteria, are at their most frenetic in the larger towns, particularly Bergen op Zoom, Den Bosch, Breda, and Maastricht. North Brabant and Limburg are the least Dutch of the country's provinces, with closer cultural, historic, religious, and geographical links to the south. Limburg in particular has a distinctive French flavor.

ROTTERDAM: For a complete description of Rotterdam, see *The Ranstad: From Amsterdam to Rotterdam.* Then, head west to the old fortified town of Brielle, the first town to go over to the Protestant cause after being taken by privateers in the service of William the Silent on April 1, 1572. The event is celebrated every year on this date.

STELLENDAM: On the night of January 31, 1953, freak conditions combined to fulfill the worst of Dutch nightmares. Some 300 miles of dikes stretching from Rotterdam southward were overwhelmed by a raging North Sea, resulting in the flooding of 4.5% of the nation's total land area, and the deaths of nearly 2,000 people. The Dutch answer to this disaster was the daring Delta Plan. Begun in 1955 and only now approaching completion, this engineering feat closes off the huge estuaries dividing Zeeland, transforms two of them into freshwater reservoirs and recreation areas, and eliminates more than 400 miles of coastline. Most of the time you travel through Zeeland, you will be driving over water. These roads, linking the formerly isolated province to the rest of the country, were created by the Delta Plan. The Delta Expo (Spuisluizen), which explains and illustrates this immense project, is open year-round and well worth a visit.

En Route from Stellendam – The route passes through a region that has become an important center for water sports, with its beach resorts, campgrounds, dunes, and woods, and its excellent facilities for sailing, fishing, wind surfing, and so on. Zierikzee and Veere are particularly attractive towns. An intriguing place to eat or stay in Veere is *De Campveerse Toren,* originally part of the town fortifications and now a monument. It has also been an inn since 1558 and was selected by William of Orange for his wedding feast, which is the Dutch equivalent of "George Washington slept here."

MIDDELBURG: The completely reconstructed medieval center of this small provincial capital won the title of "model center" during Europe's Architectural Heritage

Year, and some of Holland's most interesting old buildings are to be found here. Most famous is the abbey dating from 1120, with its complex of churches, a 1,280-foot tower known as Long John that can be climbed in the summer, a museum depicting Zeeland's history and culture, and a distinctive restaurant done in period décor. If you find the wealth of architectural treasures somewhat overwhelming, visit Miniature Walcheren (Molenwater) where they are all meticulously reproduced on a scale of 1:20. In the summer you can tour the city by horse-drawn tram or attend a Thursday market with locals in regional costume. Surrounded by lovely countryside and coastline, Middelburg is a good place in which to stay over.

    En Route from Middelburg – At the seafront city of Vlissingen, you can lie on the beach and watch an incessant stream of passing ships making their way to and from the major Belgian port of Antwerp. A steam train in Goes makes daily tours of the region in the summer. The old center of Bergen op Zoom, on the Ooster Schelde inlet from the sea, is worth a stop.

BREDA: Principal sights of this historic town, beautifully situated amidst moors and woodlands, are the market square and Grote Kerk on the Grote Markt, and nearby Breda Castle, originally dating from 1350. The castle has been the home of the Royal Military Academy since 1828. Though not open to the public, the castle is the place where the Dutch signed New Amsterdam (later rechristened New York) over to the British in 1667. Breda hosts a popular 1920s-style jazz festival every May, and on Saturdays from April through September there is a curiosities and crafts market on the Havermarkt. The VVV (Willemstraat 17) conducts a historic-mile walking tour of the center in the summer.

    About 12.5 miles (20 km) north of Breda lies the unique marshland nature preserve of Biesbosch, a fisherman's and bird-watcher's paradise of tangled creeks and waterways. Boat tours of the area are available in summer from Zilvermeeuw Cruises (Weitjes 3) in the tiny village of Drimmelen, near Made, site of Europe's largest inland yacht harbor. The *Biesbosch Restaurant* has fish specialties and provides an unrivaled view of the watery terrain (open from Easter until mid-October).

TILBURG: This town is a handy jumping-off point for a number of interesting side trips. If you pass town and turn right toward Hilvarenbeck, you will come to the turnoff for the Beekse Bergen amusement and safari park. In the summer you can take a steam train from Tilburg's Station West to the crazy-quilt village of Baarle-Nassau, which has two of nearly everything, including mayors. Many of the residents cross the international frontier between Holland and Belgium every time they go from one room of their homes to another. About 7.5 miles (12 km) north of Tilburg on the road to Waalwijk is the enchanting fairy-tale park Efteling (at Kaatsheuvel), as well as Europe's biggest amusement park. The Autotron in Drunen, between Waalwijk and 's-Hertogenbosch, has a fine collection of antique cars.

's-HERTOGENBOSCH: This mouthful, usually known by the more manageable name Den Bosch, is the provincial capital of North Brabant. So taken with the city was the fifteenth-century painter Hiëronymus Bosch, that he adopted it as his last name. His ardor was understandable, as Den Bosch is especially famed for its romantic antique center. Its market square (markets are on Wednesday and Saturday mornings) and the fourteenth-century St. Janskerk cathedral are among Europe's most beautiful. Even the VVV, housed in a small thirteenth-century castle (Markt 77), is an attraction in this surprising city.

    Weight-watchers can eat in peace at the medieval *Dry Hamerkens* (Hinthamerstraat 57), which features calorie-conscious menus as well as fuller selections. Just outside of town in neighboring Vught on the E9 south is an impressive restaurant housed in the sixteenth-century Maurick Castle, complete with drawbridge.

    En Route from 's-Hertogenbosch – In Eindhoven (Noord Brabantlaan 1A), you can visit Evoluon, the giant Philips Electronics Company's futuristic salute to technology, housed in a distinctive, nonflying saucer. This dazzling exhibition includes all kinds of fascinating gadgets with which to play.

From here you can drive direct to Maastricht on E9, or take the more leisurely alternative — E3 east to Venlo on the German border, and south from there. This route passes through Limburg's loveliest countryside, dotted with churches and castles. The landscape actually resembles the popular (and largely prewar) picture many people have of Europe. On the way to Venlo detour north via Venray to the village of Overloon, the site of a unique and disturbing war museum (Museumpark 1), which includes a 35-acre park still littered with the battered tanks, field guns, and other weapons left behind after the 3-week Battle of Overloon. Closed Saturdays and Sundays.

MAASTRICHT: Dating originally from pre-Roman times, this provincial capital is Holland's oldest city. Maastricht was besieged 21 times; 9 of the 100 castles of Limburg province are located here, as well as a myriad of historical monuments. One of Europe's finest restaurants, *Château Neercanne,* is in Holland's only terraced castle. The 40,000-bottle wine cellar is kept at optimal temperature in a grotto beneath the castle. For a lighter touch in haute cuisine, try *Au Coin des Bons Enfants.* Its French owners are particularly well known for their seasonal specialties, including wild game.

The heart of Maastricht is its central square, 't Vrijthof, ringed by numerous cafés and monuments including the tenth-century St. Servaas Church, and *In Den Ouden Vogelstruys,* a café opened in 1312. A good place for a snack, the café is said to be the oldest in Holland. The stone bridge spanning the Maas River, constructed in 1298, is even older.

A unique sight nearby is the 120-mile network of man-made tunnels beneath nearby St. Pietersberg hill, 2 miles south of the city. Begun by the Romans in search of marl for building stone, the tunnels have also provided a handy refuge during the city's frequent times of trial. Parts of this subterranean realm date from the French occupation of 1794 and include a World War II treasure room, where Rembrandt's immortal *Night Watch* was preserved from the Nazis. Note the signatures of Sir Walter Scott and Napoleon, among countless others, on the tunnel walls. Enter via Châlet Bergrust, Luikerweg 71.

VALKENBURG: This hill town is a popular vacation spot among the Dutch. Approximately 40 more miles of tunnels lie beneath the ruins of Holland's only hilltop castle. Several entrances lead to a coal-mine museum, a mysterious underground lake, and an exact replica of the Roman catacombs. Above ground is the country's third casino at Odapark.

HEERLEN: The Thermen Museum (Coriovallumstraat 9), built over an excavated Roman bath in this ancient town, contains many indigenous Roman artifacts.

VAALS: At 1,000 feet, this is the highest point in the Netherlands and the meeting point of Holland, Belgium, and Germany.

BEST EN ROUTE

Expect to pay $70 and up for a double room in the expensive range, $40 to $60 in the moderate range, and about $35 in the inexpensive category. Dinner for two should cost $30 to $40 in the restaurants listed as expensive, $10 to $20 in those listed as moderate, and under $10 in the inexpensive. Prices do not include drinks or wine.

VEERE

De Campveerse Toren – Close to Middelburg, this historic inn has 19 rooms as well as a restaurant, specializing in fish dishes, that has been catering to tourists for five centuries. Kade 2 (phone: 01181-291). Expensive to moderate.

VLISSINGEN

Grand Hotel Britannia – This pleasant seaside hotel has 35 rooms. Its restaurant offers local fish specialties, and lovely wide-angle views of ships sailing to and from foreign ports of call. Blvd. Evertsen 244 (phone: 01184-13255). Moderate.

WITTEM

Kasteel Wittem – This 12-room hotel-castle dates originally from the tenth century and is on its own private grounds. Inside there's a Michelin star–rated restaurant. Wittemmerallee 3 (phone: 04450-1208). Expensive to moderate.

GULPEN

Kasteel Neubourg – This moated castle, surrounded by woods, features 25 spacious rooms and a French restaurant. Closed in January and February. Rijksweg 1 (phone: 04450-1222). Expensive.

Utrecht and the East

Of special interest to nature lovers, this 109-mile (175-km) route passes through some of Holland's loveliest countryside, from the forests and purple heathland of the 240-square-mile Veluwe nature preserve with its wild deer and boar, to the farmlands and great country estates of bordering Achterhoek. With a turbulent history stretching back to Roman times, this area is rich in castles and fortified towns, and has some of the best-preserved medieval structures in the country.

En Route from Amsterdam – Take the A1/E35 to Hilversum where you pick up the A27 to Utrecht. This takes you past Muiden on the former Zuider Zee, a popular water sports center famous for its thirteenth-century castle, and moat-ringed Naarden, a beautifully preserved old fortress town. On the opposite side of Hilversum are the Loosdrecht Lakes, a major center for water sports and recreation.

UTRECHT: Founded by the Romans in 47 AD, this ancient city is the geographic and historical center of the Dutch nation. Today it has a population of about 234,000 and is Holland's fourth largest city. Worthy of special attention is the medieval city center and the unique canalside wharves and cellars (now shops and cafés) lining the Nieuwegracht and Oudegracht. At the heart of the old center is the Domplein, a square containing one of the country's most magnificent cathedrals. Work on the church was begun in 1254, and required over 250 years to complete. The 350-foot tower, constructed separately and completed in 1382, is the tallest in the Netherlands.

Utrecht is also the convergence point of the Dutch railway system and there is a fascinating railway museum in a former station (Johan van Oldebarneveltlaan 6), exhibiting old steam locomotives and models. The Music Box Museum (Achter de Dom 12) has a collection of mechanical music-makers dating back to the eighteenth century, ranging from singing birds and a violin-and-piano playing monstrosity, to musical chairs and street organs. The Centraal Museum (Agnietenstraat 1) contains historical displays, including an authentic Viking ship. Take a short side trip to the village of Haarzuilens and the spectacular De Haar Castle, set in an artificial lake amidst grounds modeled after Versailles (3 mi/5 km on E9 toward Amsterdam). The castle is still occupied, but parts of it are frequently open to the public.

En Route from Utrecht – A slight detour to Soest on the road leading through De Bilt and Bilthoven leads past Soestdijk Palace (actually a seventeenth-century hunting lodge), home of the former Queen Juliana.

AMERSFOORT: This town has walls, four city gates, and double moats still ringing it, as well as a wealth of architectural treasures within its medieval center. The *Lamme Goetsack* (Lieve Vrouwestraat 4), an antique restaurant in a sixteenth-century house in the old center, features traditional Dutch cuisine.

APELDOORN: From here you can tour the wooded Veluwe region by steam train. Trains leave in the summer (daily, except Saturdays) from Stationsplein 13A. The museum at Het Loo Palace (Koninklijk Park 1) was formerly the Royal Residence and includes many displays on the royal family.

HOGE VELUWE: In the center of this national park in a lovely woodland setting, you'll find the Kröller-Müller Museum, with its outstanding collections of modern art and sculpture. *De Koperen Kop* is a restaurant in the park, where you can watch the deer being fed. Pick up a map of the park at the entrance.

ARNHEM: This attractive town had the misfortune to be the scene of Operation Market Garden, a serious defeat in 1944 of the British airborne troops, which was portrayed in the film *A Bridge Too Far.* Important mementos of that heroic and desperate battle are the Airborne Cemetery at nearby Oosterbeek, and the Airborne Museum in Grote Hartensteyn in the same town. The nearby twelfth-century Doorwerth Castle houses a hunting museum. Immediately north of the city at Schelmseweg 89 is the 100-acre Openlucht (Open-Air) Museum, in which actual farms, mills, and homes have been reconstructed to give a complete picture of traditional Dutch country life. There's also a costume museum, and a zoo and safari park, where you can drive or take a minitrain through 60 acres of free-roaming lions, giraffes, and other beasts of the wild. A pleasant place for a meal is the farm restaurant *Boerderij Rijzenburg* at nearby Schaarsbergen, also an entrance to the Hoge Veluwe.

ACHTERHOEK: Extending eastward from the Veluwe, this is a protected, rustic region of farms, woodlands, and great country estates. The VVV in Zutphen, 16 miles (26 km) from Arnhem on the A48, has maps for do-it-yourself bike tours through the castle-filled countryside.

BEST EN ROUTE

Expect to pay $70 and up for a double room in the expensive range, $40 to $60 in the moderate range, and about $35 in the inexpensive range. Dinner for two should cost $30 to $40 in the restaurants listed as expensive, $10 to $20 in those listed as moderate, and under $10 in the inexpensive. Prices do not include drinks or wine.

ARNHEM

Groot Warnsborn – Surrounded by forest, this lovely 29-room former manor house is only a few minutes from the center of town. Features include a French restaurant with seasonal menus. Bakenbergseweg 277 (phone: 085-455-751). Expensive.

HEELSUM

Klein Zwitserland – Just west of Arnhem, this 63-room chalet-style hotel also has an indoor pool, a sauna, a solarium, tennis courts, bike rentals, and miniature golf on the premises; horseback riding is available nearby (phone: 08373-19104). Expensive.

De Kromme Dissel – This attractive restaurant is noted for its candle-lit, old world ambience. Klein Zwitserlandlaan 5, Heelsum (phone: 08373-19104). Expensive.

Exploring Norway

The Kingdom of Norway stretches along the western edge of the Scandinavian peninsula, bordering Sweden, Finland, and Russia to the east. Norway has a 1,700-mile coastline on the North Atlantic, raggedly indented with inlets, fjords, peninsulas, and islands. Because the coast is so well sheltered, and most of the country's land area is so rocky and mountainous, Norwegians have taken to the sea since prehistoric times. In the ninth century, Norway's Vikings developed ocean-based marauding into a way of life.

Today's Norway numbers only 4 million people — half of the population of New York City — rattling around over a spacious 149,158 square miles. The country is not particularly urban, and the major cities would be considered large, pleasant villages by most countries' standards. Oslo, the capital and biggest of the towns, has a population of less than half a million; Bergen (pop. 207,200) is an important cultural center, famous for its beautiful fjords; Trondheim (pop. 134,600) is a major center for trade, shipping, and industry; Stavanger (pop. 91,900) is another industrial outpost, handling fish processing, shipbuilding, and pumping Norway's North Sea oil. Other large towns include Kristiansand, Drammen, Skien, Tromsø, and Ålesund, and Bodø.

Norway is a constitutional monarchy, ruled by King Olav V and his cabinet, plus a prime minister, storting (parliament), and supreme court. The present independent government was installed in 1905, although the apparatus of state has been developing since the early nineteenth century, heavily inspired by the constitutions and ideals of the American and French revolutions.

Possibly the most important question on the minds of all those who have never been to Norway is: What is a fjord? A fjord is a long, narrow inlet of the sea, with very steep, nearly parallel sides that extend below the surface of the water. A land area with a fjord looks like a macrocosmic cheesecake from which a long, narrow slice has been cut. Norway's Sognefjord runs over 100 miles inland from the North Sea, with walls that plunge 4,000 feet to the ocean floor. The sight from the top of the fjord of tons of ice-blue water roaring and foaming between the rocky walls is one of the most spectacular wonders in nature.

About one quarter of Norway's land area is above the Arctic Circle, yet the climate of Oslo averages only about 12° colder than that of New York. The North Atlantic drift keeps Norway's harbors free of ice.

Rivers like the Glomma and the Rana run through the mountains and valleys, and provide much hydroelectric power. One quarter of the country is forested, and the timber industry is big. Fish is exported all over the world;

iron, nickel, and aluminum are mined; manufacturing is the biggest single employer, services second, employing about one quarter of the working population each. About one tenth of the work force is in agriculture, and another tenth in trade. Norway's merchant fleet is the seventh largest in the world, with over 1,600 ships, and unlike the official merchant leader, Liberia, Norway's fleet is manned mostly by natives of the country. Tankers, cargo vessels, fishing boats, and passenger vessels, all privately owned and run, are important to the country's balance of payments.

Most Norwegians are of Scandinavian stock — like the Swedes — but in the county of Finnmark in the north live Lapps and Finns. There are two official languages, *bokmål* ("book language"), the language of literature and wealth, a vestige of Danish rule, and *nynorsk,* a language developed by a nineteenth-century nationalist, based on rural dialects. Both *bokmål* and *nynorsk* are used in the media, but *bokmål* still prevails. In the far north, Lapp also is spoken.

Considering Norway's rough-hewn and beautiful countryside, it isn't too surprising that Norwegians are very outdoors-oriented. Like the Swedes, they have a reputation for having blond hair, robust health, and good looks. They do a lot of walking, as befits a country where distances are great, roads are often rough, and fuel is expensive. The population density is scant, and even cities are laid out with lots of elbow room. Oslo is touted by the city fathers as one of the biggest cities in Europe, since it covers 175 square miles, including vast areas of farmland and forest.

Norwegians get used to snow in winter, and are less likely to burrow inside when the weather is cold than people from warmer climates. The word *ski* is Norwegian. Both cross-country and downhill skiing are avidly pursued by large numbers of people, and a Nordic specialty is ski-jumping. In the last 50 years, Norway has won more Olympic gold medals in Nordic skiing than any other country. Speed skating also has a long tradition and strong following. Soccer, as in the rest of Europe, is the biggest organized sport. Popular indoor activities include boxing, gymnastics, and ballroom dancing.

The arts in Norway are encouraged by heavy state subsidies, particularly in film and book publishing. One of the most striking examples of government-sponsored art is the 150-piece sculpture park near Oslo by Gustav Vigeland, built at the city's expense. Norway has produced artists of international renown: painter Edvard Munch, composer Edvard Grieg, and dramatist Henrik Ibsen. It is interesting to note that a brooding, death-obsessed spiritualism pervades the work of the nation's three greatest cultural figures. Some say the stark seasonal contrasts in the land of the midnight sun have a profound effect on the national psyche. The actress Liv Ullmann was also born in Norway.

Norwegian folk art is highly practical, using fine handwork in the making of furniture, embroidery, weaving, and silver. The expression *arts and crafts* is based on the Scandinavian concept of *brukskunst;* Norway has several museums devoted to applied art.

The area of Norway was just an agglomeration of small Viking kingdoms until Harald Haarfagre ("fair hair") united them at the end of the ninth century, based on the model of a northern British kingdom he had recently pillaged. Missionaries from Britain brought Christianity to Norway in the tenth and eleventh centuries.

Leif Eriksson, a Viking émigré living in Iceland, became the first European to reach America, touching down in Newfoundland in AD 1000. The Vikings established settlements in the Northeastern US — some say they got as far south as Maine and Massachusetts.

Norway prospered as an independent country until the plague set in in 1349 and wiped out half the population. The German Hanseatic League assumed Norway's trade in Bergen and the rest of the country slipped into 400 years of Danish rule. Sweden took over Norway when Denmark was defeated with its ally Napoleon in 1814. During the nineteenth century, 880,000 Norwegians emigrated elsewhere, mostly to the US. In 1905, the nation finally broke off from the Swedes and set up their own kingdom, appointing Carl, the second son of the king of Denmark, who took the Norwegian name Haakon VII. Haakon's son Olav took the throne at his father's death in 1957.

Norway stayed neutral in World War I, although half her merchant fleet was sunk. The Nazis invaded in World War II, and installed concentration camps, political executions, and economic disaster. The king and most of the fleet escaped; Norwegian ships were vital to Allied operations in the North Atlantic, and Norwegians at home sabotaged the German occupiers courageously and ruthlessly. The leader of the collaborationist forces in Norway, Vidkun Quisling, whose name has come to be a synonym for *traitor*, was executed at the war's end, with the expulsion of the Germans.

Since World War II, Norway's wealth of trade, industry, and cheap hydroelectric power have given her citizens one of the highest standards of living in Europe, and with the discovery of large oil and gas deposits off the North Sea coast, her future looks stable, even in a worldwide energy crisis.

Over 80% of Norway's land area is taken up by mountains and forests. Norway is somewhere you go to see natural beauty, rather than the marvels of civilization: mountains, valleys, fjords, moors, lakes, forests, and waterfalls, and, in general, the absence of other people. The weather is often beautiful, just right for as brown a tan as you can get anywhere, but be ready for rain — make good use of clear days.

There are two routes below for exploring Norway. The first begins in Oslo, possibly the least hectic capital city in Europe, and winds down the Oslofjord and up the other side through prime beach and sun country, cuts west through pine-scented forests to the barren Telemark plateau, and finishes in a burst of fjords and flowers in Bergen, on the Atlantic coast. The second route is a 1,000-mile adventure to the point farthest north on the continent of Europe, beginning by road in Trondheim, switching to a coastal steamship from Bodø to Tromsø to take you through the sheer cliffs of the western islands, and finishing again by car to the barren North Cape, far above the Arctic Circle.

Oslo to Bergen

This scenic route begins with the calm and pastoral capital of Norway. Oslo, a city of a mere 448,700 inhabitants and many clapboard houses, farms, and forests, is also the seat of the Norwegian parliament. From here, you'll drive down the Oslofjord, west to the rococo church in Kongsberg, and over across the Telemark, where you'll find farms, beautiful stave churches, and barren heaths. The last stop is Norway's pride, fjord-bound Bergen, a graceful eleventh-century city that has played host to Viking, merchant, and warships, art, and industry in its 1,000-year history.

Another way to travel this route is via the Bergen-Oslo railway. Providing a dramatic 280-mile (451-km) day trip across Norway's rooftop, this classic line spans desolate Hardanger plateau, far above the timber line, 6,000-foot mountains, and the old alpine and cross-country ski resorts of Geilo and Voss. You can make reservations in advance at one of the branches of the Norwegian National Tourist Office in the US.

OSLO: For a complete report on the city and its restaurants and hotels, see *Oslo*, THE EUROPEAN CITIES.

En Route from Oslo – Along the coast south of Tønsberg on the Brunlanes Peninsula are good beaches and quiet coves for swimming and sailing, from Stavern to Nevlunghavn. The shoreline twists and turns on itself often, creating many protected beaches along the small towns in the area. The waters are quite warm in July and August. Take Route 8 through Larvik north toward Kongsberg; you'll be driving along the Laagen River through a valley of cornfields and bright red and white farmhouses.

KONGSBERG: Kongsberg, "the king's mountain," was founded by King Christian IV when silver was discovered here in 1624. The city flourished and became the second largest in Norway, and declined as the silver output fell in the nineteenth century. The last mine was abandoned in 1957. The eighteenth-century rococo church in Kongsberg is worth seeing; its exterior is unprepossessing brick, with a copper cupola, but inside all is rich and elaborate. The ceiling is covered with paintings and hung with crystal chandeliers; the pulpit, altar, choir balcony, and organ are carved with great enthusiasm, and painted in golds and blues. There are three tiers in the gallery, and box seats for the king and lesser dignitaries. Kongsberg is now a major ski area, with three T-bars, five giant slalom courses, and touring trails, as well as a ski school. The abandoned silver mines are also worth a visit, and the town runs a special little railway into the hills for sight-seers.

TELEMARK: West of Notodden begins the country of Telemark, a wild, often barren area of mountains, valleys, and plateaus that stretch all the way to the fjord district. The first inhabitants here were hunters; small, single-family farms followed, in the style of the American prairie. It is thought that skiing was invented here. The towns and villages exist mostly in the south and east; this is the prime area for a characteristic feature of rural Norwegian architecture, the *stabbur* or storehouse. In a countryside of individual farms, there was no town warehouse in which to store grain, so a story was added to each house to tuck away surplus for the lean years. Much care was lavished on the building and ornamentation of these houses, from elaborate wall hangings to beautifully carved joists and furniture, intricate "rose painting" on walls, doorways, clocks, and pottery. Many *stabbur* in Telemark are open to visitors, so sample two or three as you drive through.

As you proceed west, you'll pass through more valleys, farms, and villages, and by quite a few roadside cafés. At Haukeliseter there's a summer ski school.

At Eidsborg, south of E76, is a fine example of a stave church, nestled on a hill. The outside walls of a stave church are covered with a sheath of hand-carved tiles that overlap each other like the leaves of an artichoke, giving the whole building the look of a single, living plant. Note the elaborate wood carvings on the columns in the doorway and the interior.

The route now cuts through the heart of the Hardangervidda, a nearly uninhabited plateau of lakes and moors, where the elevation is about a mile. Several thousand years ago, a glacier came through here, ripping away everything in its path, leaving the wet, mossy, treeless landscape you see before you. Lakes, boulders, heather, and an awesome bleakness extend left and right until you arrive at the fjords.

LOFTHUS: Turn north onto E47 toward the industrial town of Odda and the Sørfjorden. The road skirting the precipice is both narrow and scenic, burrowing through mountains, and passing over towering waterfalls. The hamlet of Lofthus, which is past Odda on the eastern edge of the fjord, was a favorite retreat of Edvard Grieg. The place has a mystical peacefulness; it is surrounded by snow-capped mountains and the Folgefonn glacier in the distance, and crowded with blossoms in the summertime.

   En Route from Lofthus – Continue up to Kinsarvik, and take the ferry across the mouth of the Sørfjorden to Kvanndal, on the western edge of the great Hardanger Fjord. Drive south along the fjord toward Bergen, as waterfalls spawn rainbows, and mountains rest against each other like the backs of huge sleeping animals. This is the most spectacular region of what is considered by some the most scenic country in the world. Once you arrive in Bergen and find a place to roost, you must, without fail, drive, ferry, and walk through as much of this titanically beautiful region as possible. The best time to go is May and early June, when the fruit trees are in bloom.

BERGEN: Looking like a crowded gingerbread village, Bergen sits in a harbor under Mount Fløyen, protected and hidden from the North Sea by a peninsula. It is one of Norway's most worldly, cultural, and physically beautiful cities.

Vikings used to set out for England, Europe, and Iceland from the coves around Bergen. The city was founded in 1070 by King Olav the Peaceful, who thought it would make a good center for trade with Europe and northern Norway. He was right: It was so good that in 1350 a collection of Hansa merchants from Germany moved to Bergen and grabbed control of the city's trade, making Bergen their colony. The Germans held on for 200 years, making the port into a major trading center of the Hanseatic League and the richest city in Norway. Finally, in 1559, the Danish authorities trained their guns on the Hanseatic buildings and offered the Germans citizenship or oblivion; some left, and some became Norwegians. The Hanseatic Museum in town is a reconstructed sixteenth-century Hansa merchant's house, smelling of cool wood in some rooms, and dried cod in others. Norwegian cod was an important item of trade for Catholic Europe, as it often provided Friday's dinner. At the museum you can also see the scales the merchants used for weighing goods — one scale for buying, and another for selling. The wharf in the Bryggen section of town is where trade went on. Now, painters, weavers, and artisans have their workshops in the restored medieval wooden houses.

Overall Bergen has an eighteenth-century grace, with a skyline of close-packed mansard roofs punctuated by church steeples. The best view of the city is from the funicular that goes up Mount Fløyen (1,050 feet), which operates until midnight. At the summit is a restaurant, surrounded by paths that lead through lakes, flowers, pine, and heather.

In late May and early June is the Bergen International Festival, featuring music, drama, opera, ballet, and folklore. A lot of the music, understandably, is by local hero Edvard Grieg, and concerts are held every day at Grieg Hall in town, and out at his old residence in the suburb of Hop, a pastoral Victorian estate on a lake. World-renowned conductors and soloists are featured. Concerts are also held at Haakonshallen and St. Mary's Church. Plays are performed at Den Nationale Scene — Ibsen predominates — and folk plays and dances take place outdoors.

Haakonshallen and St. Mary's Church are both worth seeing in their own rights; the thirteenth-century hall was badly damaged in World War II when a German ship carrying nitroglycerin blew up in the harbor, but the restoration of the massive medieval construction was well done. The Romanesque Mariakirke (St. Mary's Church) is considered Norway's most beautiful church, with an intricately carved and painted baroque pulpit, donated by the Hansa in the sixteenth century.

With the wealth brought in by trade, art was sure to follow, and industrialist Rasmus Meyer's private collection of paintings, drawings, and furniture is probably the best in Norway outside of the Oslo National Gallery. Meyer lived from 1858 to 1916, and his particular zest was for native Norwegian painters: lots of Munch, of course, plus Nikolai Astrup, Harriet Backer, Gerbard Munthe, and J. C. Dahl.

BEST EN ROUTE

Hotels along this route are rather expensive, from $50 to $100 for a double or single room at a luxury, tourist hotel, which provides meals, entertainment, and bars. Guesthouses, which are smaller and may not have a private bath or shower, cost from $12 to $20, and are scattered throughout villages and towns. All you have to do is ask at a local tourist information center, or flag down a passing Norwegian. If you prefer, you can camp out on one of the many campgrounds in the countryside for from $2.50 to $8 a night; chalets can be rented for $85 to $225 a week, and there are a number of youth hostels, mostly open during the summer season, for $5 to $8 a night (bring a sleeping bag). Again, tourist information centers in the villages can direct you. The Royal Norwegian Automobile Club huts are offered to all AAA members: For further information contact KNA, Parkveien 68, Oslo 2 (phone: 56-26-90).

Telephone numbers for some of the hotels listed below are unavailable at present: Make reservations through a local SAS office or travel agent.

KONGSBERG

Grand – The best hotel in the city; provides small comfortable rooms and good meals. In the middle of town (phone: 73-20-29). Expensive.

BERGEN

Hotel Norge – This 241-room luxury hotel offers double and single rooms, private baths, restaurant, garden summer cafés, disco, and bars. Ole Bulls Plass 4 (phone: 323000). Expensive.

SAS Royal Hotel – It's a 250-room, first-class hotel. In the Bryggen section of the harborfront. Restaurant, café, nightclub, and bar (phone: 31-80-00). Expensive.

Neptun – This 99-room hotel just completed modernizing most of its rooms to include baths. Walckendorffsgate 8 (phone: 32-60-00). Expensive.

Rosenkrantz – This 83-room hotel is small, comfortable, and offers private baths. Also a popular nightspot. Rosenkrantzgt 7 (phone: 31-50-00). Expensive.

Park Pension – A converted townhouse near the university. Running water; not all rooms have private bath, but it's a good buy. Reserve well in advance. Parkveien 22 and Harald Harfagersgate 35 (phone: 32-09-60). Inexpensive.

Holbergstuen – An old-world tavern on the second floor of the building; big old armchairs, beams along the ceilings. Try the fish fillet with prawns, mushrooms, and asparagus. Torgalmenning 6 (phone: 31-80-15). Moderate.

Trondheim to the North Cape

This is a trail for the adventurous. We don't mean that it's physically danger-ous, but that it requires an active spirit and a zest for exploration. It's an expedition to the Nordkapp, the northernmost point in Europe. You must go in June, July, or August, so the roads will be clear of snow, and so you can see the midnight sun. The north of Norway is big, wild, and exotic, but no one can tell you what the beautiful sights are. Here, you write your own guidebook and judge each towering cliff, deep-blue lake, and clump of flower-ing heather with your own eyes.

Start your trip in a rented car from Trondheim, the capital of the province of Trøndelag, at the threshold of the Arctic. Founded in the tenth century, Trondheim is now a commercial city, and the seat of one of Norway's biggest universities. You'll be taking the Arctic Highway (E6) north from here through lakes and river valleys past Mosjøen and Mo-i-Rana to cross the Arctic circle into the land of the midnight sun at the top of a barren plateau.

At Bodø, you'll hop on the coastal steamer, which will take you between the sheer cliffs of the Lofoten and Vesterålen islands to Tromsø, the oil boom town, and launching base for many North Pole expeditions. Pick up a car here for the rest of your own expedition: A ferry will carry you across the last strait to Honningsvåg, so you can drive to the North Cape, and look down on all of Europe.

Another way to explore this part of the Norwegian coast is to take the express steamer from Bergen to Kirkenes — 1,500 miles, 6 days one-way or 11 days round-trip. The steamer calls at about 30 fishing villages and towns, including Trondheim, Bodø, Lofoten and Vesterålen, Hammerfest and Hon-ningsvåg. The northeastern terminus, Kirkenes, is on the Russian border, where the Iron Curtain isn't much more than a chainlink fence. The steamers are small and clean, with ample deck space, hearty buffet-style meals, and a bar. Dress is informal; the sea air, invigorating; and the scenery, breathtaking.

TRONDHEIM: Trondheim is home of one of Norway's major technical universities and a big trading town, exporting timber, fish, and farm products, and a major ship-builder and transportation center. Trondheim is a pleasant and useful city, but not spectacular looking. Its buildings draw on a tradition of the ordinary from the nine-teenth and twentieth centuries: solid stone office buildings and glass-and-steel cheese-boxes. There are also some old narrow streets of small, pastel-colored wooden houses.

Trondheim's Nidaros Cathedral, built for St. Olav, has attracted pilgrims from all over Europe. It was badly battered during the Reformation, and a lot of the Gothic-Romanesque hybrid that stands now is twentieth-century restoration work. Norway's Gustav Vigeland, creator of the mammoth sculpture garden in Oslo's Frogner Park, carved the gargoyles and grotesques for the head tower and north transept. Behind the cathedral is the restored Knight's Hall of the twelfth-century Archbishop's Palace. From here, late-Viking-age kings ruled Norway's Christianized colonies in Britain, Iceland, and Greenland. (Unfortunately, it was partially destroyed in a 1983 fire and is closed.)

Make your way to the Ringve Museum of Musical History in a manor house in the eastern suburbs. During the tours, the guide plays the well-preserved instruments from time to time: spinets, harpsichords, and pianos, and some vintage string and wind instruments as well. On the walls all around are paintings and photographs of famous composers and musicians.

Two of the best features of present-day Trondheim are the fish market on the docks and the fruit stands in the Torvet (marketplace).

En Route from Trondheim – Just north of the city in the Stjørdal Valley, near the village of that name, is the ruin of the fortress of Hegra Festning, built in 1910 as a bulwark against the Swedes (the border is 49 miles to the east). The fort became a symbol of the Norwegian Resistance in World War II when a German force was badly mauled trying to take it in 1940. Peace has taken the fort since then; bushes and flowers are now crowding the barbed wire, gun ports, and blasted walls; the view of the surrounding hills and the valley 1,000 feet below is splendid. Wild strawberries, raspberries, and blueberries grow in the vicinity.

In the village of Hegra, on the other side of the valley, are the Leirfall rock carvings, one of the most prolific sites in Norway, chiseled in 500 BC. They are said to be the religious art of an agricultural civilization, designed to increase fertility; they are symbolic and simple of line, showing stylized ships, and people and animals, some with erect phalluses — as well as circles, dots, swastikas, and footprints. Move on up the highway through the low, wooded Lake Snåsa region; you'll pass near Børgefjell National Park on the right.

About 60 miles (96 km) north of Mo-i-Rana you cross the Arctic Circle in the valley of the great, green Rana River; snow-covered bluffs 4,000 feet high lie to the left and right as you climb to the top of an empty plateau, and into the land of the midnight sun (66°32'N). The line of the Arctic is marked by a stone monument; there is a post office offering Arctic Circle postmarks nearby, and a café with the inevitable souvenir shop.

The countryside following the circle, near Rognan, is some of the most spectacular you will see along this route: The road passes high above the Saltdalsfjord, which is sometimes covered with a light mist, past snow-covered mountains hulking behind.

BODØ: Bodø is the capital of Nordland province; the sun doesn't go down here from June 1 to July 12. It's warm, considering the latitude, sitting at the mouth of the Vestfjorden, sheltered by the Lofoten Islands. Add to this the opportunities that lurk everywhere for fishing, climbing, bird watching, or just walking around gaping at the scenery, and you can understand why tourists by the droves come here to soak up the midnight sun. Do not miss the famous cathedral, built in 1956: The tall bell tower is separate from the rest of the structure; the main roof is copper, the outer walls concrete, and the inside wonderfully large and airy, with a high ceiling, reddish-brown woodwork, hand-made wall hangings, and delicate stained-glass windows at each end of the building.

Burned and bombed to the ground at the beginning of WWII, Bodø has long since recovered its position as a leading fishing and Arctic communications center. Visitors can try their hand at fishing at Saltstraumen, the world's most powerful maelstrom, 20 miles outside town. Millions of gallons of water rush through the narrow passage, guaranteeing catches of cod, halibut, and salmon. No license is required; rent tackle at any Bodø shop.

LOFOTEN AND VESTERÅLEN: Now begins the marine portion of your expedition to the Nordkapp; turn in your rented car and claim your bunk on the coastal steamer at Bodø to make the 24-hour passage to Tromsø, threading through the steep cliffs and fishing villages of the Lofoten and Vesterålen islands. The steamer is a functional ship, a cargo and mail vessel that can also take about 200 passengers. It's not the *QE2*, but it's clean, it's only for 24 hours, and you'll get more of the incredible scenery than you could playing chemin de fer on some cushy cruise ship. The islands present a wall of snow-capped mountains and cliffs that rise suddenly from the shore to heights of 2,000 to 3,000 feet. It's particularly dramatic as the steamer slips into a narrow strait between two peaks and seems about to be swallowed in their immense shadows. Faster, but equally scenic transport is provided by deep-sea catamarans which turbo-propel passengers from Bodø to Tromsø in just under 8 hours.

TROMSØ: Disembark at Tromsø and pick up your car. An ancient whaling capital, Tromsø was also base of operations for North Pole explorers and polar bear hunters; much of its frontier-style atmosphere has been retained, and it's now something of a boom town. Tromsø has doubled in size to about 47,000 in the past decade with the advent of a medical school and regional hospital specializing in Arctic ailments. All the establishments in town — restaurants, brewery, pubs, and pizzerias — claim to be the world's northernmost. Worth a look are the local museum devoted to Arctic exploration; the aquarium; and the Arctic Cathedral, whose design is reminiscent of an iceberg. The cable car affords a bird's-eye view of Tromsø and its fjord, where in WW II, the German battleship *Tirpitz* was finally sunk by British bombers.

En Route from Tromsø – Your last leg in this trek is the shortest, about 280 miles (448 km), over dry plateau, as the Arctic Highway winds around fjords and inlets, and passes a few villages. Lyngen Fjord between Tromsø and Alta is thoroughly alpine, with jagged peaks and hairpin turns. Alta is little more than an airport and a trading town. Before turning north, consider a day trip south through Europe's deepest canyon and up across the plateau to Kautokeino, the major center for the nomadic Lapp reindeer herders. The Lapps congregate here to trade and worship, and have built a church and a hotel in the style of a Lapp hut. The town silversmith, whose shop you can visit, makes jewelry in ancient Lapp designs. If you plan to spend the night, the modern lodge on the bluff overlooking town is more expensive, but also quieter and more comfortable than the Lapp hotel in the valley.

Back in Alta, continue north to Hammerfest, the world's northernmost incorporated town. Stop at the town hall to join the Royal and Ancient Society of Polar Bears, testifying to your northerly adventure. From here you can take an excursion boat directly to the North Cape, or you can drive and ride the ferry up to Honningsvåg, the largest fishing port in Norway.

The first man to reach the North Cape is said to have been a Viking named Ottar, who sailed around it in 880 AD, bound for the White Sea. England's King Alfred the Great met Ottar and had his story of the voyage "beyond the known world" set down in writing. The account sits in the British Museum today.

Another 21 miles (34 km) will bring you from Honningsvåg to the black cliff that Ottar signed exactly 1,100 years ago. The British Museum probably won't keep your tour diary, but you certainly will; and the Nordkapp post office will also issue you a special certificate testifying to the fact that you've been there, and mail your postcards to boot.

The sun shines continuously here from May 14 to July 30; the most beautiful sight, however, is in early August, when the sun dips below the horizon for a few minutes of night, in a spectacular glow of red and purple.

BEST EN ROUTE

Hotels in the Arctic Circle region all run about the same price (between $40 and $75, double or single rooms), which we call expensive. Some exceptions to this are listed. Most offer private baths and/or showers, plus other amenities offered in luxury hotels. Make reservations beforehand.

TRONDHEIM

Britannia Hotel – Above all, well run. Has a kind of medieval-modern air; rooms are large and comfortably furnished; the hotel has its own garden and restaurant — the food is good — and there are fountains and palm trees in the middle of it. Dronningensgt 5 (phone: 07-53-00-40). Expensive.

Naustloftet Fish Restaurant – The upstairs overlooks the fjord, and is done up like an old boathouse inside: wooden implements, copper kettles, and captain's chairs. As you might expect, fish is the thing to get, wiggling-fresh from the sea. There is a café on the ground floor. Prinsens Gate 42 (phone: 07-52-18-25). About $24 for dinner.

Vertshuset Tavern – A wooden tavern, built in 1739. Mountain-style cooking (smoked ham, diced meat, salami, mutton with garnishes) and also more conventional food. Near the Folk Museum (phone: 07-52-09-32). About $17 for dinner. Closed January 7 to March 15.

BODØ

SAS Royal – This 15-story, 194-room hotel is the largest in the city, and offers private baths and showers, restaurant, nightclub, bars, and disco. Storgaten (phone: 081-24-100). Expensive.

Grand – A 52-room hotel that offers baths and showers, double and single rooms, and a dining room. Storgaten 3 (phone: 081-20-000). Moderate.

Fonix – An elegant little café that uses sterling silver utensils, but has low prices for lunch. The fish fillets would melt in your mouth. Near the Tourist Information Center. About $4 for lunch; dinner is more.

LOFOTEN AND VESTERÅLEN

For the 24-hour steamer trip from Bodø to Tromsø, you must reserve a berth 2 to 3 months in advance in the summer season. A couple can reserve a private cabin, but singles room with strangers of the same sex. Bergen Line, 505 Fifth Ave., New York, NY 10017 (phone: 212-986-2711). The cost for a cabin is from about $85 to $96 per person, not including meals.

TROMSØ

SAS Royal – One block from the steamer pier, this large (207 rooms) and convenient hotel has a fine harbor view and several restaurants. Sjøgata 7 (phone: 083-83-606 or 86-550). Expensive.

Grand Nordic Hotel – There are 136 rooms, several restaurants, and many other comforts. Storgaten 44 (phone: 083-85-500). Expensive.

Polar Hotel – This one has 64 comfortable rooms. Groennegate 45 (phone: 083-29-544). Moderate.

Saga – A simpler hotel, *Saga* has a cafeteria and about 50 rooms, most with showers. Near the harbor. Richard Withsplass 2 (phone: 083-81-180). Moderate.

Peppermøllen and Fiskekrogen – Here you can sup on fresh, well-prepared fish, reindeer, and grouse. Storgaten 42.

A note on northerly nightlife: – *Charly's,* at the *SAS Royal,* and *Boccaccio,* at

Storgaten 84, are the biggest and best nightclubs. The latter is run by a Texas-bred Norwegian. At *Ølhallen*, the beer hall in the basement of the brewery on Storgaten, you can swap stories with fishermen and polar bear hunters.

HONNINGSVÅG

SAS Nordkapp hotell – This 120-bed hotel provides food and private baths and/or shower. Centrally located on the harborfront (phone: 084-72-333). Expensive.

Exploring Poland

One of the most fascinating things about Poland is that it is both a Roman Catholic and a Communist country. The Polish Workers' Party (Polska Zjednoczona Patria Robotnicza — PZPR) is economically and militarily aligned with the Soviet Union. Yet, Polish churches overflow with worshipers on Sundays and holy days; as much as 95% of Poland's 35 million people are, at least nominally, Roman Catholic.

Indeed, the most momentous occasions in recent Polish history were the visits by the first Polish pope, John Paul II, to his homeland in June 1979 and June 1982. Relations between the church and the government have varied from open conflict to mutual tolerance since the Communists assumed power after World War II. But, seeing a pope officially welcomed by the government here seemed less an anomaly than it would have in any other Communist country. From almost the very beginning of the country's 1,000-year history, Roman Catholicism has been virtually synonymous with Polish nationhood.

The Poles are descended from tribes of Western Slavs who were unified in the tenth century by a plains-dwelling tribe, the Polanie, in order to resist increasing invasions from the west by Germanic tribes. In 966, Duke Mieszko I put the new state under the protection of the Holy Roman Empire and accepted Christianity for himself and his people.

Most of Poland lies in the north European plain. It stretches south from the Baltic Sea to the Sudety and Carpathian mountains, which separate it from Czechoslovakia. It is bordered by East Germany on the west; and the Soviet Union on the east. Temperatures are higher than normal for Poland's latitude, but weather conditions vary from region to region. Winters can be severely cold, and there are frequent showers in summer. However, pleasant warm weather continues through October.

Prevailing winds and tidal action have resulted in few good harbors along the Baltic coast, but they have created wonderful long sandy beaches that attract tens of thousands of vacationers to the 325-mile seacoast. Below the sand dunes and forests of the coastal belt, there is a stunning postglacial region of thousands of lakes and heavily wooded hills rich in wildlife. Poland has 12 natural parks and some 500 wildlife preserves. The wild European bison is protected here, along with chamois, bear, moose, and the swift, dun-colored tarpan, one of the smallest horses in the world.

The central lowlands are mostly flat and, although they do not have the richest soils, are the most extensively cultivated areas. About 48% of Poland's 35 million people live in rural areas. Many Poles own and work their own land, but mechanization has been slow. In general, industrial development has been emphasized at the expense of agriculture. The foothills region paralleling the two mountain ranges along the southern border contains most of the country's mineral wealth and its best agricultural land. It is the most industrialized and most heavily populated area of the country.

The mountains themselves are not particularly rugged, except in the High Tatra range of the Carpathian Mountains, and have long been populated by farmers and shepherds. Outdoor activities, the beauty of the scenery, and the charm of local folk art, particularly wood carving, make the mountains an important tourist destination.

The borders of modern Poland are strikingly similar to those of the first Polish state, although the country's history has been one of constant struggle to hold its own against larger, more aggressive neighbors. At one point — from 1795 to 1918 — Poland ceased to exist as an independent state, having been partitioned by Austria, Prussia, and Russia. During that 123-year period, the Roman Catholic faith served as an element of cohesion and unity for the Polish people.

The most ruinous period for Poland, after it was restored as a republic in 1918, occurred when the country was invaded and quickly conquered by the Germans in 1939. Poland remained under foreign occupation for 6 years, during which time the devastation and loss of life was, perhaps, the worst suffered by any of the war's victims. Cracow alone among its cities escaped massive destruction, and 6 million Poles — half of them Jews — were killed in Nazi extermination camps. Today, these camps, such as Auschwitz, are maintained as museums, constant reminders of the war's horrors.

Jews had been welcomed as immigrants early in the fourteenth century during the reign of Casimir III, one of Poland's greatest rulers, and before World War II, they constituted 10% of the population. Many of the survivors of the war emigrated to Israel following an anti-Semitic campaign in 1968. It is estimated that there are less than 10,000 Jews in Poland today.

After the war, Poland made an extraordinary effort to rebuild its cities and restore monuments and buildings important to its past. In Gdańsk, a whole district of tall, narrow, Gothic houses was reconstructed, reviving the charm and grace of the big port city. The recent completion of the Royal Palace in Warsaw fulfilled a 30-year dream of Poles everywhere, including 7 million Americans of Polish origin. Contributions, both large and small, from many of these Polish-Americans helped sustain the restoration work at the palace.

The strong spirit of Polish nationalism can be traced to the fact that the country's population is extremely homogeneous; 98% of the people are ethnically Polish. They are proud of their heritage and their heroes: Nicholas Copernicus, whose theories about the universe provided the foundation for modern astronomy; Marie Skłodowska-Curie, whose research with her husband led to the discovery of radium; Frederick Chopin, whose mazurkas and polonaises seem to embody the Polish spirit; and, the newest pope of the Roman Catholic Church — the former Karol Cardinal Wojtyla of Cracow. The religious shrine of Our Lady of Częstochowa, Cracow — Poland's second largest and loveliest city — and the breathtaking Tatras draw hundreds of thousands of visitors to southern Poland each year. The route south from Warsaw through heavily industrialized Upper Silesia to the medieval beauty of Cracow and beyond to the serenity of the mountains where centuries-old traditions of farmers and herdsmen are intact offers the traveler a continuum of Polish history. By car, the route from Warsaw to Częstochowa is about 135 miles (216 km), from Częstochowa to Cracow approximately 50 miles (80 km), and from Cracow to Zakopane, some 66 miles (106 km). There are also rail connections.

WARSAW: For a detailed report on the city and its hotels and restaurants, see *Warsaw*, THE EUROPEAN CITIES. The capital is the usual point of departure for tours to other parts of Poland.

CZĘSTOCHOWA: The huge monastery complex on top of Jasna Góra Hill has dominated this drab Warta River town since Paulist monks founded it in 1382. The monastery is the focal point of a religious cult devoted to Our Lady of Częstochowa, the so-called Black Madonna.

Each year, enormous numbers of pilgrims come to pay homage to the sacred portrait of the madonna, said to have been painted by St. Luke. The portrait, with its darkened paint, hangs over an exquisite altar of wrought silver and ebony wood in a chapel in the monastery church. More than 100,000 people take part in the main pilgrimage each year on St. Mary's Day in mid-August. Over the centuries, monarchs and others seeking blessings from Our Lady of Częstochowa have donated priceless art, jewelry, and heirlooms to swell the monastery's treasury. Many of the offerings are on permanent exhibition. You can also visit the monastery library, which contains some 20,000 valuable documents and records pertaining to Polish history.

Częstochowa itself is the chief town of Poland's largest iron-ore mining region. Since World War II there has been extensive urban and industrial development here.

En Route from Częstochowa – Heading south on E16, you pass some of the region's iron-ore mines before reaching Siewierz, where you can visit the ruins of the medieval castle of the Bishops of Cracow who once ruled here. Katowice, the capital of the Upper Silesia industrial region, is a modern industrial center and home of the renowned Grand Symphony Orchestra of the Polish radio. The route continues south to Tychy, a popular resort center on Lake Poprocanskie, then turns east to Oswiecim, site of the largest Nazi concentration camp of World War II.

Some 4 million people, most of them Jews, were killed at the three camps operated here from 1940 to 1945. The site of the Auschwitz and Birkenau camps has been made into a national museum. Pictures of the victims, the gas chambers where they died, and the enormous display cases containing their personal belongings — even hair shorn from prisoners and destined to be sold as pillow stuffing — are a chilling reminder of the grisly crimes committed here. A film of Auschwitz and the starving prisoners who were still alive the day the camp was liberated is shown at the museum several times a day.

CRACOW: Cracow is almost everyone's favorite Polish city. Travelers destined for the Tatra resorts to the south almost always stay here longer than they had planned. Unlike Warsaw and other Polish cities, Cracow was untouched by bombs and other massive destruction during World War II. Its medieval charm is still apparent on every tree-shaded street.

Poland's second-largest city has recently attracted international attention because this is the see Karol Cardinal Wojtyla served before becoming Pope John Paul II, the first Roman Catholic pope from a Communist country.

Wawel Hill, with its fortified castle and cathedral, dominates the skyline, while Rynek Główny, one of the largest town squares in Europe, is the center of city life.

The hill was first fortified to defend a crossing of the Vistula River beneath it. The stately Gothic cathedral was built from 1320 to 1364, and by the time of King Casimir the Great (1333–1370), Wawel was the center of state authority and culture. In the sixteenth century, King Sigismund the Old had a beautifully proportioned Renaissance palace built as his residence. The north wing was later renovated in accordance with the baroque spirit.

Although the royal court was moved to Warsaw in 1609, Wawel remained the place of coronation of Polish kings, and even when Poland was occupied by the Austrians, it was a national treasure that symbolized the country's independence. During World War II, the Nazis had plans to blow up the castle and the cathedral, but a surprise offensive by the Russian army prevented this wanton destruction.

You enter the castle through an arcaded courtyard that is now used for open-air concerts. The castle's 71 rooms are high and airy and richly appointed. Among its treasures is a collection of 136 rare, sixteenth- and seventeenth-century Flemish tapestries. The Chamber of Deputies has an unusual coffered ceiling that features heads carved and painted in the sixteenth century to represent members of the royal court. Another chamber is covered entirely in Spanish leather, which has been embossed and hand-painted with fine designs.

The elaborate tomb of St. Stanislaus, Poland's patron saint, stands in the middle of the nave of the adjacent cathedral, and two chapels are particularly noteworthy. These are: the Chapel of the Holy Cross, decorated with colorful, fifteenth-century frescoes, and Sigismund Chapel, in which red marble tombs are set strikingly against white marble walls. An eleventh-century crypt, incorporated from an earlier cathedral on this site, is crammed with the tombs of kings, queens, bishops, and Polish national heroes.

Splendid old mansions of noblemen and merchants are clustered on streets at the bottom of Wawel Hill. Grodzka street leads right to the main town square, but along the way there are dozens of narrow passageways between shops that open onto tiny courtyards with workshops and balconied houses.

Most of the buildings in the main square were built between the fourteenth and sixteenth centuries. The huge white and brown Clothier's Hall (Sukiennice) was built in the fourteenth century, but was renovated in the Renaissance style in the sixteenth century. Always a center of commerce, the building now contains dozens of small craft and souvenir shops on the ground floor and houses the Gallery of Polish Painting, with a fine collection of eighteenth- and nineteenth-century work on the second floor.

The Church of the Virgin Mary (Mariacki), opposite the Clothier's Hall, is best known for the magnificent altarpiece carved over 500 years ago by Wit Stosz in late Gothic style. This medieval triptych of life-sized figures in gold raiment depicts the assumption of the Virgin Mary. A series of fourteenth-century stained-glass windows above the triptych take up its themes and colors.

Diagonally across the square from the church is the old town hall tower, the only reminder of the town hall that was demolished in 1820. The tower houses a branch of the National Museum, and its dungeon has been turned into a wine cellar.

The red brick of St. Florian's Gate, the Barbican, and some town walls and towers are all that remain of the medieval fortifications that protected old Cracow. Today the limits of the older parts of the city are marked by a green belt of gardens, known as Planty.

Another important landmark is the Jagiellonian University, founded in 1364 by King Casimir the Great and one of the oldest centers of learning in Europe. A prized possession in its museum is the world globe on which Copernicus first acknowledged America. The country is indicated by the words, "America New Discovery." Today, some 50,000 students study at the university.

Europe's second oldest synagogue, built in the fourteenth century for exiled Spanish Jews, is on ul. Szeroka in the old Jewish quarter. The interior is being refurbished by the government. During the war, the Nazis desecrated the synagogue, using it to stable horses.

There were about 40,000 Jews in Cracow before the war; today there are perhaps 2,000. Remu'h Synagogue, nearby at ul. Szeroka 24, is where services are held for the remaining Cracow Jews. In a cemetery near the synagogues, there is a lovely memorial: Pieces of desecrated tombs with Hebrew words and carved decorations have been fashioned into a wall resembling a great stone collage.

Cracow boasts a long and rich theater tradition. The eight repertory theaters here are well known for the quality of their productions. One of the best is Helena Modrzejewska Stary Theater (ul. Jagiellonska 1) and almost every première at its branch, Kameralny Theater, is of national interest. The J. Stowacki Theater (pl. św. Ducha 1), which shares the premises with the Cracow Opera House, also is of high repute.

In even-numbered years, the International Biennale of Graphic Arts is held here. Works of art by contemporary artists and folk artists are on view and for sale at branches of *Cepelia,* the folk arts and crafts cooperative, and *Desa,* antique and art shops. Some of the *Cepelia* branches are at ul. Karmelicka 12; Sukiennice, ul. Szewska 22; Rynek Główny 7; and pl. Mariacki 1. *Desa* branches include the B Gallery, ul. Bracka 2; Modern Art Gallery, Nowa Huta-Osiedle Kościuszkowskie, pavilion 1A; and Contemporary Art Gallery, ul. św. Jana 3.

For general tourist information, check with the Wawel Tourist Information and Advertising Center (ul. Pawia 8). Excursions can be arranged through various tourist offices, including Orbis, the Polish Tourist Office (al. Puszkina 1) in the *Orbis-Cracovia Hotel.*

ZAKOPANE: This charming town, nestled between the Gubalowka Ridge and the towering Tatras, is an extremely popular, always lively holiday center. In winter, skiing is an important added attraction, but all year round, it is the beauty of the mountains and valleys and the rich folk culture preserved by the highlanders that draw Poles to Zakopane.

Fir, beech, and spruce grow in the subalpine woods of the Tatras. As you go higher, there are spruce forests and stone pine, dwarf mountain pine, and alpine pastures with little vegetation. Edelweiss and stone pine are among the 260 species of plants here, and the region is a natural habitat for lynx, marmot, chamois, brown bear, various deer, and, sometimes, the golden eagle.

The town itself is a museum of regional folk culture. The wooden gingerbread houses are similar to Norwegian stave churches, but more complicated in design. The lacy look of the carved facades is reminiscent of Victorian valentines. Against the backdrop of pine forests and snow-peaked mountains, these homes seem most idyllic. At the lower end of ul. Krupówski near Kościeliska, there are a small mid-nineteenth-century church, several typical highlanders' houses, and a cemetery where nearly every monument is a masterpiece of folk art. The local museum (dr. Tytus Chalubinski Tatrzanskie Museum; ul. Krupówski 10) includes a reconstruction of a highlander's cottage interior, specimens of plants, birds, and animals native to the Tatras, and a collection of local costumes. Tea Cottage (ul. Bulwary Stowackiego 39) is another museum with typical regional flavor.

Many men of the area still wear white woolen trousers with distinctive black and red embroidery called *parzenica,* and richly embroidered, capelike outer garments, known as *cucha,* to the delight of the tourists. In the outdoor market, country women sell hand-knitted mohair cardigans, the primitive leather moccasins worn by highland people, and special local cheeses.

There are horse carriages available to take you to the surrounding areas, such as the village of Jaszczurówka, where a small wooden church stands as an almost perfect example of elaborate Zakopane architecture, and Harenda which has an eighteenth-century church built of squared larch trunks.

For a magnificent panorama of the town and the Tatras, you can take a chair lift from near the *Orbis-Kasprowy Hotel* to the top of Gubałowka Hill. At Kuźnice, a little more than 2 miles (3 km) north of Zakopane, there is a funicular to Kasprowy Wierch (6,451 feet), the region's most famous ski mountain. There are ski routes down to Zakopane and to Kuźnice.

The Dolina Biatego Valley, where the crystal Bialy Potok stream flows through steep crags, is just a 15- or 20-minute walk from the center of Zakopane.

Local restaurants serve such regional specialties as braised boar, elk, and rabbit, and night-time entertainment in Zakopane ranges from folk music and dancing to discotheque.

BEST EN ROUTE

Hotel rooms may be hard to come by at the height of the tourist season, and impossible to get at Częstochowa during the August pilgrimage. If you can book one, a double will cost from $55 to $70 a night at an expensive hotel; $40 to $55, at a moderately priced one; and $30 to $40 at an inexpensive hotel.

In Zakopane, the Tatry Regional Tourist Economy Enterprise (ul. Kosciuszki 23A) can arrange accommodations in private homes in the area.

Dinner for two with wine, at an expensive restaurant, will cost $25 to $35; at a moderately priced restaurant, $15 to $25; and at an inexpensive one, as little as $5.

CZĘSTOCHOWA

Orbis-Patria – A modern, medium-sized hotel on the main avenue to Jasna Góra. It is also one of the best places for food, either in its restaurant or nightclub. ul. Starucha 1 (phone: 4-7001). Expensive.

CRACOW

Orbis-Holiday Inn – Although all Orbis hotels in Cracow are listed as first-class, this one is several shades better than the rest for its decor, restaurant, and general ambience. It also has a swimming pool. However, it is a 10-minute bus ride or a 5-minute drive to Rynek Głowny. ul. Marsz. Koniewa 7 (phone: 37-50-44). Expensive.

Orbis-Cracovia, – ul. Puszkina 1 (phone: 22-86-66). Expensive.

Staropolska Restaurant, – ul. Sienna 4. Expensive to moderate.

Orbis-Francuski, – ul. Pijarska 13 (phone: 22-51-22). Moderate.

Europejski, – ul. Lubicaz 5 (phone: 5-5863). Moderate.

U Wentzla Restaurant, – Rynek Głowny 18. Moderate.

Balaton Restaurant, – ul. Grodzka 37. Moderate.

Dniepr Restaurant, – ul. 18 Stycznia 55. Moderate.

Krak – The best camping site near Cracow. ul. Radzikowskiego 99 (phone: 7-5840). Inexpensive.

ZAKOPANE

Orbis-Kasprowy – Beautifully situated on a mountainside, this hotel is only a 10-minute walk from town. Each room has a terrace with a lovely view. Rooms are small, but modern and bright. The restaurant is attractive and serves excellent food. Polana Szymoszkowa (phone: 40-11-20). Expensive.

Orbis-Giewont, – ul. Kosciuszki 1 (phone: 20-11-15). Expensive to moderate.

Gazda, – ul. Zaruskiego 1 (phone: 50-11-15). Moderate.

Jedruś Restaurant, – ul. Świerczewskiego 5. Moderate.

Watra Restaurant, – ul. Zamoyskiego 2. Moderate.

U Wnuka – This café is housed in an old inn that has typical regional decor. Inexpensive.

The best campground in the Zakopane area is located on ul. Zeromskiego (phone: 2256). Inexpensive.

Exploring Portugal

To most people Portugal means either Lisbon — the sophisticated capital city, rich in monuments, museums, and churches — or the Algarve — famed vacation area, with its congenial mixture of sea, beaches, luxurious hotels, and varied cuisine. However, beyond Lisbon's city limits and away from the southern shore lies a country of ancient towns, walled villages, and captivating scenery.

Portugal's history goes back 3,000 years, to the time when Greek and Phoenician traders established settlements here. Later, Portugal became part of the Roman Empire (the country was then known as Lusitania), and many remains of the Roman occupation survive. Following the decline and fall of Rome, Portugal was subject to invasions by Visigoths from the north and by Moors from the south. By the mid-twelfth century, Portugal had emerged as a nation with its own culture and language, and by the fifteenth century it held title to the most extensive empire in the world. Though the empire has disappeared, the past is still very much alive among Portuguese people today. The handicrafts, colorful costumes, festivals and dances, and splendid restoration of historic buildings reflect a cultural heritage almost unchanged in spite of much evidence of modern progress.

Portugal is rectangular-shaped, bordered on the north and east by Spain and on the south and west by the Atlantic Ocean. With an area of some 35,553 square miles, Portugal is a relatively small country. Its major cities are Lisbon (pop. 782,266) and Oporto (pop. 310,437). The landscape encompasses a wide variety of contrasts — the lush green valley of the Minho River, the rugged mountains of the Tràs-os-Montes region, the steep-hilled vineyards of the Alto Douro, and the Beira flat coast. In the south the pale gold wheat fields and olive and cork groves of the Alentejo give way to the cosmopolitan resorts of the Algarve, where beaches and imposing cliffs are washed by the warm waves of the Gulf Stream.

The summer's heat is moderated along the coast by sea breezes. Days can be quite hot but the temperature drops in the evening. Winters are mild and snow is seldom seen except in the high mountains. The climate is most pleasant for driving trips in the spring and fall, but travel in the southern region is also comfortable during the winter.

Road development is somewhat rudimentary — partly macadamized, partly cobbled limestone bricks, and seldom wider than two lanes except for the fast superhighways in and out of Lisbon and Oporto. Road signs are fairly obvious, but travelers should be equipped with a handbook of Portuguese phrases and a Michelin road map. While driving watch out for donkeys and oxen. They were on the roads long before the automobile and are still there. Gasoline is expensive, but Portugal is still a bargain in other respects, relative to most European countries. Well-maintained hotels and *pousadas* (government-owned inns) as well as excellent restaurants are found throughout the country. Accommodations are generally good and plumbing is modern and clean. Tap water is considered safe to drink but most people prefer bottled mineral water. Grapes are grown in many areas and the regional wines are excellent. When dining out, request the house wine if one is available.

Two weeks is sufficient to travel around most of Portugal. Our first route originates in Lisbon and heads north through Oporto, the second largest city; from here it loops around the mountainous northern region to Guimarães, the cradle of the Portuguese nation, and Vila Real, home of Mateus wine. The next route starts in Lisbon, circles around the central region taking in the towns of Elvas, Estremoz, and Évora, which are rich in historic sites. The last itinerary focuses on the Algarve, Portugal's southern coast and beach resort area.

The Northern Coastal Region and Western Mountains

This route covers a lot of territory, temporally as well as geographically, starting at the modern capital of Lisbon, traveling through Oporto, industrial center and second-largest city, to Guimarães, birthplace of Portugal's first king.

The route from Lisbon to Oporto in the western part of the country along N1 is heavily trafficked. Though the route links Portugal's most densely populated areas, it passes through small towns, forests, farms, woods, olive groves, and a few popular beach resorts on the Atlantic. Many of the highlights of the route are architectural — the extravagant mountaintop castle built by Fernando II between 1846 and 1850 in Sintra; the imposing marble monastery in Mafra built in 1717 for King João V; the walled town of Óbidos; and the splendid abbey Mosteiro de Santa Maria, which contains the tombs of two ill-fated lovers of the fourteenth century. Ranging even farther back you can see the ruins of Conimbriga, the most important Roman settlement on the Iberian Peninsula.

Leaving Oporto, the route heads north, then east and south, circling through the mountainous northern region. The road is a little bumpy, but not unacceptably so. It links small fishing villages, and then travels along the Minho River, Portugal's northernmost natural border with Spain. Highlights along the way are Braga, an ancient city founded by the Romans with monuments from the twelfth century through ornate eighteenth-century baroque styles. Guimarães and Vila Real, home of the famous Mateus wine, are set amidst the deep vales and terraced mountain vineyards of the great port wine producing region.

LISBON: For a detailed report on the capital, its hotels and restaurants, see *Lisbon,* THE EUROPEAN CITIES. Depart from Lisbon on N249 in the direction of Queluz and drive 17.5 miles (28 km) to Sintra in the verdant hills of the Serra da Sintra. Stop off in Queluz for a look at its eighteenth-century pink rococo palace, surrounded by formal gardens. Sometimes described as Portugal's Versailles, the palace was built by Pedro III for his "mad queen" Maria. It is now used to house visiting dignitaries, and the former palace kitchen — with its giant spits, marble tables, and walk-in fireplace — is now a charming restaurant.

SINTRA: Nestled on the northern slope of the mountain, the old town is notable for its palaces and elegant mansions with ivy- and lichen-covered walls. Many days of the year, a mist envelopes the peak, giving the town an eerie, fairy-tale atmosphere. Sintra so entranced Lord Byron that he remained there to write. For centuries the town was a favored summer residence of Portuguese kings and royal families. The Paço Real on the main square was built by João I in the fourteenth century on the ruins of a fortress that had been taken from the Moors in 1147 by Portugal's first king, Afonso Henriques. Above the town looms the Castelo dos Mouros (Moorish Castle), a monumental structure dating from between the seventh and ninth centuries. On the mountaintop, reached by a steep ascent, the Palácio da Pena, built by Queen Maria II's consort, Ferdinand Saxe-Coburg-Gotha, with the help of German architect Baron Eschwege from 1840 to 1850, is an extravagant example of the work of a wildly creative imagination, comparable to Ludwig II's castles in Bavaria. The delightful Monserrate Gardens on N375, designed by Francis Cook in the nineteenth century, display over 3,000 floral and botanical specimens.

On the winding streets, you'll find shops selling antiques and handicrafts. A twice-monthly Sunday antique market attracts many browsers and buyers to the tiny adjacent village of São Pedro, N9.

En Route from Sintra – Before N247.3 winds into the forest, make a stop at Convento dos Capuchos, a sixteenth-century monastery with its cells and rooms carved out of rock in the hillside. Make a slight detour to Cabo da Roca for a spectacular view of cliffs, coast, and sea. Its lighthouse marks the westernmost point in Europe. Retrace to Sintra and pick up N9 to Mafra.

MAFRA: The imposing marble Mosteiro rises from the road without preamble. Erected in 1717 for King João V by German architect Fredrich Ludwig, the great edifice contains a monastery, basilica, palace, and once housed a school of sculpture. Its library houses 20,000 volumes of seventeenth- and eighteenth-century works on theology, geography, and military theory. The facade alone demands attention with its baroque decorations, columns, statuary, and ornate belfries. You can purchase lovely pale blue and white pottery in the shops facing the monastery or just 3 miles away in the town of Sobreiro, where it is made.

En Route from Mafra – At Torres Vedras, 21 miles (34 km) along N9, you'll see distant windmills outlined on the rolling hilltops, vineyards, and apple and pear orchards set out in neat fields. At Bombarral, 16 miles (26 km), take N8 7 miles (11 km) to Óbidos.

ÓBIDOS: This walled town is dominated by the old castle's keep and towers. Taken from the Moors in 1148 by Afonso Henriques, the little city so captivated Queen Isabella in 1228, that her consort, King Dinis, presented it to her. Pass through the double-arched gateway, follow the narrow main street to Igreja de Santa Maria, and park below in the square. Proceed on foot to Igreja de São Tiago where a path on the left leads to the ramparts. On the right is the *Pousada do Castelo,* once the royal palace. The serene dining room inside serves a pleasantly formal lunch. Shops in town offer a wealth of handicrafts: lace, embroidered tablecloths, basketry, fashionable heavy knitted sweaters. Don't miss the octagonal church standing alone in a field below the town. Built by Phillip II of Spain, it contains a fourteenth-century onyx statue of a black virgin which resembles the Black Virgin of Monserrat in Spain.

En Route from Óbidos – Caldas da Rainha, on N8, is a large commercial center noted for its spa dating back to 1485. It was founded by Leonor, the Spanish wife of King Dinis, who believed in the curative power of its waters. The city's hospital and park still bear her name. Traditional regional ceramics are on sale in the town's shops and factories, and an annual ceramics fair draws large crowds.

Veer left at Alfeizerão and head for São Martinho do Porto, a typical beach resort. From the promenade you can see an unusual saltwater lake connected to the ocean through a rift between high coastal cliffs. If you like quiet beaches with good fishing and clean water, try Foz do Arelho Beach on a small, pine-covered peninsula, just 2 miles from Caldas.

A short drive north on N242 leads to the famous fishing port of Nazaré, where the beach is lined with brightly painted, high-prowed fishing boats. Nazaré has recently become a rather touristy beach resort, but some customs survive: Men still wear traditional plaid shirts and black caps, and women, black capes. They still dance the *vira* — a spirited folk dance — and cook their tasty fish stew, *caldeirada*. For an excellent view, drive or take a funicular to the Sítio, a section in town perched high above the beach. There is a spectacular view from the belvedere, and on the cliff just below you can see a hoof print. According to legend, it was made by the horse of Portuguese nobleman Dom Fuas Roupinho, who accidentally rode off the cliff while pursuing a deer. He prayed to Our Lady of Nazaré and was saved; in gratitude he built the little Chapel of Memory, which is perched on the cliff. *Mar e Sol* or *Riba Mar* serve good meals along the seaside. Though the shops appear rather touristy, they sell handsome hand-knit fishermen's sweaters at moderate prices.

ALCOBAÇA: Constructed by Cistercian monks in 1178, the Mosteiro de Santa Maria is one of Portugal's most splendid abbeys. The building has been altered and restored but the interior retains its uplifting spaciousness. The church contains the flamboyant Gothic styled tombs of Inês de Castro and Dom Pedro, ill-fated lovers of the fourteenth century. (Inês was murdered by a group of noblemen to prevent King Dom Pedro from marrying her. The enraged king executed them in revenge, after forcing them to pay homage to her dead body dressed in the garb of a queen.) In the cloister you can visit the monks' kitchen with its enormous chimneys and marble tables; a stream of the River Alcoa flows underneath this kitchen. In the Middle Ages the stream provided fresh fish for the royal table. On the Rossio, the sweeping square before the abbey, the distinctive pottery and ceramics of the region are displayed for sale.

BATALHA: A masterpiece of Portuguese Gothic and Manueline (after Manuel I, during whose reign the transition from Gothic to Renaissance styles gave birth to an original artistic form of decoration in Portugal) styles, the town's church is an awesome monument. Embellished with flying buttresses, turrets, and tracery, it was erected between 1402 and 1438 to commemorate the victorious battle of Aljubarrota, which ended Castilian domination of Portugal. The stark, soaring interior of the nave is offset by a richly decorated cloister and lavabo. The small Founder's Chapel contains the tombs of King João I, Queen Philippa of Lancaster, and their children, most notably Prince Henry the Navigator. Guided tours give access to an unfinished section of chapels. The square adjacent to the monastery is lined with small shops and cafés.

FATIMA: A side trip can be made from Batalha to Fatima — a distance of 20 miles (32 km) — the world-famous shrine where the Virgin Mary appeared in 1917 to three shepherd children. The pilgrimages on May 13th and October 13th often bring crowds of a million pilgrims from all over the world. The town has several hotels.

LEIRIA: This pleasant town is just 7 miles (11 km) from Batalha on rt. 1. In its center on a volcanic hill stands the Castelo, built in 1135 by Afonso Henriques, from which you have a panoramic view of the picturesque old town and the charming countryside. Leiria is most appealing for an stroll at twilight — when the old streets and houses seem to blend with the modern. A festival held during the last 2 weeks of March features exhibitions and folk dancing. Another worthwhile side trip can be taken to Marinha

Grande, 8 miles (13 km) from Leiria. This glassmaking center was founded around 1730, and the glass factory was built by the Stephens brothers, Englishmen who later donated it to the state. You can visit the glass museum and the factories.

En Route from Leiria – The main road to Coimbra, N1, leads through 45 miles (72 km) of farms, olive trees, and pine woods. About 9 miles (14 km) below Coimbra, an archaeological dig has uncovered traces of a Roman town, Conimbriga, inhabited first by Celts in Neolithic times. You can see the remains of what was once the most important Roman settlement on the Iberian Peninsula. Guided tours are available.

COIMBRA: Beginning as a Roman settlement, suffering invasions by barbarians and Moors, taken by Christians in 1064, Coimbra finally came into its own as a cultural and artistic center after the founding of its famed *universidade* in 1290. Climb the steep narrow cobbled way through the old town to the university courtyard for a tour of the ancient buildings. The magnificent Biblioteca is decorated in carved and gilded baroque-styled wood with intricately painted ceilings; it contains an enormous collection of old books. The Ceremonial Hall hung with portraits of the kings of Portugal and the beautiful Manueline ornamented chapel are still in use today. A former episcopal palace nearby holds the Museu Machado de Castro (Rua de Borges Carneiro) where one is led from room to room by French-speaking guides determined to explain everything about each of the collections' gold objects, sculptures, paintings, and ceramics. The basement displays ancient relics and marble busts of Romans. Also worth visiting are: the twelfth-century cathedral, Sé Velha, with its flamboyant Gothic altarpiece; the sixteenth-century Mosteiro de Santa Cruz and its lovely Manueline cloister; a twelfth-century Cistercian convent, Mosteiro de Celas; and across the river on N110.2, Convento de Santa Clara-a-Nova. Children will enjoy the nearby Portugal dos Pequenos, a beautifully constructed village with replicas of all the country's famous buildings scaled down to a child's size.

En Route from Coimbra – Follow N1 18 miles (28 km) to Luso, a lovely spa situated in the midst of forested rolling hills. An olympic-sized swimming pool in the gardens behind *Grande Hotel das Termas* is open to the public for a small fee.

BUÇACO: Take the winding road through Buçaco Forest, a park founded in 1628 by Carmelite monks. In the center of the forest a royal hunting lodge, built from 1888 to 1907 by Carlos I, has been transformed into the *Palace Hotel*. This incredible structure was designed in a pastiche of Manueline styles and is highly ornamented. A table on the round elaborately decorated porch overlooking the gardens provides an enchanting setting for lunch or dinner. Adjacent to the hotel stands a seventeenth-century Carmelite monastery, chapel, and cloister open to visitors. The olive tree in the driveway marks the spot where Wellington tied up his horse on the eve of winning a great victory over French invaders in 1810. The well-maintained forest has a myriad of trails for good hiking.

En Route from Buçaco – Retrace through Luso to Mealhada to pick up N1 north. Along the way you'll see numerous shops carrying copper and brass wares. On the road from Buçaco there are more than a dozen restaurants which specialize in *leitão a bairrada* (suckling pig roasted on a spit) accompanied by a variety of regional vegetables. Also offered is a champagne-like wine called *Espumante* — both white and red — which is delicious when chilled. If you have time turn off at Águeda for a side trip to Aveiro. This coastal fishing village, inhabited since the eleventh century, is crisscrossed by lagoons and canals and surrounded by weedy marshes and sand flats. Fishing, seaweed gathering, and ceramic and china manufacturing are the chief industries.

Some 34 miles (54 km) farther up the coast on N109 is the popular resort, Espinho. Featuring a vast swimming pool complex, facilities for all water sports, a fine golf course, clay pigeon shooting, and a casino, Espinho is purely for fun.

N109 leads into the superhighway approach to Oporto, the second largest city in Portugal.

OPORTO: Its history dating back to the eighth century BC, the region known as Portucale was given to Henri of Burgundy in 1095 as part of the dowry of Princess Teresa. Developed as an important trading center with northern Europe, the area of Portucale eventually gave its name to the entire country after figuring prominently in the struggle for independence. Renamed Oporto, it became the base of the Portuguese shipping fleet, which evolved into a formidable maritime power.

Cross the River Douro via Ponte Dom Luis I; the lodges of Vila Nova da Gaia, storehouses of the world famous port wine, lie below the bridges. Narrow streets, heavy traffic, and many one-way signs contribute to the difficulties the driver may encounter in trying to find the way to the central parking location, Praça do Hamberto Delgado. The easiest, most comfortable way to see this tightly built industrial town is to take a Cityrama Bus tour, which will include a stop at the wine center across the Douro. Principal places of interest include the twelfth-century catedral, Terreiro da Sé; the Igreja de São Francisco, a Gothic church with a richly decorated interior (Rua Infante Dom Henrique); and the Museu Soares dos Reis (Rua de Dom Manuel II), where the exhibits include early paintings, sculpture, pottery, and religious works of art. Many shops display silver, gold, and filigree jewelry, leather goods, and locally made ceramics. Some of the best restaurants are *Portucale, Orfeu, Escondidinho,* and the *Comercial.* Everyone drinks the various ports, plain and iced, and the *vinho verde* house wines.

En Route from Oporto – The N14 heads north 20 miles (32 km) through vineyards and cornfields to Vila Nova de Famlicão, where you pick up N103 to Barcelos. This attractive town is known for its painted rooster, which has become a popular symbol of Portugal. According to legend, a pilgrim from Galicia, Spain, was staying at the home of a Barcelos judge when the house was robbed. He was unjustly accused of the crime and sentenced to hang. He asked to see the judge who was at dinner and eating a rooster. The pilgrim said to the judge: "May that rooster rise up and crow if I am innocent." It did, and he was set free. Barcelos has a lively Thursday market where you can buy handmade rugs, laces, ceramics, brightly enameled figurines, as well as housewares and blue jeans. The ruined Ducal Palace houses an archaeological exhibit and ceramics museum. The 17 miles (27 km) along N14 to Viana do Castelo is a lovely drive. The entire region is known for its good hunting and fishing as well as for its fairs and religious pilgrimages. A list of these activities is available at the Portuguese Tourist Office.

VIANA DO CASTELO: This fishing port and holiday resort is nicely situated, with a seascape, river bank, and hillside. One of the most famous festivals in the country, Festa da Nossa Senhora da Agonia, is held here each year during the third week of August, when the townspeople don their colorful embroidered costumes to take part in the activities. A former eighteenth-century palace, the Museu Municipal (Rua Manuel Espregueira) houses a fine exhibit of tiles, furniture, pottery, and ceramics. The Praça da República has sixteenth-century buildings and the Igreja da Misericórdia, which are worth a look. Follow the signs for Santa Luzia, up a winding road through pine and eucalyptus, to the Basilica of Santa Luzia for a dazzling view of the entire region.

En Route from Viana do Castelo – Follow Hwy. 203 along the Lima River to Ponte de Lima, a town with a Roman bridge and many sixteenth- and seventeenth-century manor houses. Some of these — the Conde de Aurora, for example — are open to the public. For dinner, try lamprey stuffed with rice, a regional specialty.

VALENÇA: In spite of strong fortifications, this town of old stone houses and cobblestone streets was once at the mercy of Spanish invaders. The thirteenth-century castle at the far end of town has been handsomely reshaped into a modern inn, *Pousada de*

São Teotónio. The seventeenth-century ramparts open on an incomparable view of the Minho Valley and the Spanish mountains beyond. Shops in town carry a good selection of sweaters and embroidered bedspreads.

En Route from Valença – Passing through the gate, turn left down the hill to N101, then it's 11 miles (18 km) to Moncão. This walled town is an attractive base from which to explore the Peneda-Gerês National Park. The National Forest Department can arrange guided excursions through the park, so you can see its many wild horses and boars. Nearby at Bretiandos and Briteiros there are pre-Celtic ruins. A comfortable inn, *Albergaria Atlántico,* has a decent dining room with a nice view. There is also a nice *pousada, Pousada de São Bento,* at Caniçada at one of the entrances to Peneda-Gerês National Park.

The N101 now begins its journey 46 miles (73 km) south to Braga. Take a look at the stately mansion of Brejoeira, before the ascent on the shady mountain road, and stop off in Ponte da Barca to sample its white, dry, "green" wines.

BRAGA: Founded in the fifth century by the Romans, conquered by Visigoths and Moors, this ancient city has developed into a visibly prosperous industrial center. Liberated from the Moors by King Ferdinand of Léon in 1040, Braga came under the influence of the church soon after when the Archepiscopal See was established here. Over the centuries many monuments, churches, and palaces were erected by the bishops; in the eighteenth century Braga became the center of baroque art in Portugal. The highly decorated twelfth-century Sé Catedral contains a museum of sacred art and the tombs of its founders, Henri of Burgundy and Dona Teresa. Among the buildings of notable architectural design are the Antigo Paço Episcopal church overlooking the Jardim de Santa Barbara, the nearby town hall, and the thirteenth-century castle and keep. Many of the old buildings are artfully lit in the evenings. A religious festival is held during Holy Week, and the Nativity of St. John is celebrated for 3 days starting on June 23. Every Tuesday there is a market on the edge of town where you can buy handcrafted articles from artisans of the region. *Terraço* is a popular restaurant.

En Route from Braga – Some 3 miles (5 km) from Braga on N103.3, the baroque steps appear which lead to the eighteenth-century sanctuary of Bom Jesus do Monte. This curious stairway is adorned with chapels and statuary depicting figures from the Passion. Mount the steps as the pilgrims do or reach the top by funicular or motor car for a spectacular view from the church plaza.

Take N101 south to Guimarães.

GUIMARÃES: This attractive, busy town is known as the cradle of the Portuguese nation. Foundations for the village were begun in the tenth century with the construction of a monastery. In 1095 the village was presented to Henri of Burgundy by his father-in-law Alfonso VI, king of León and Castile. The great Castelo, whose keep dates from the tenth century, was the birthplace of Afonso Henriques who became the first king of Portugal. Nearby is the tiny Romanesque church of St. Michael and beyond, the fifteenth-century palace of the dukes of Bragança. Visit the Romanesque Igreja Nossa Senhora da Oliveira and its cloister exhibition, Museu Alberto Sampaio. Just below the town park lies the Igreja São Francisco whose interior flaunts an ornately carved and gilded baroque altar; old tiles decorate the walls of the chancel. Walk to the old section of town on the Rua Santa Maria, lined with fourteenth- and fifteenth-century houses. Hand-embroidered linens are a speciality of this area.

En Route from Guimarães – This 22-mile (35-km) stretch of N101 to Amarante is populated by lacemakers whose wares are spread out at the side of the road. After crossing the Tamega River, turn left onto N15, which wends slowly up into the stern but grand Serra do Marão. Halfway (18 mi/29 km) to Vila Real, you'll come across the *Pousada de São Gonçalo,* a good place for a lunch break.

VILA REAL–MATEUS: Proceed through Vila Real, following the signs for Murça and Sabrosa on N322 to Mateus, home of the famous wine. At the Mateus Manor, visit the imposing eighteenth-century baroque residence, so familiar from the label on Mateus bottles. Still owned by the counts of Vila Real, the manor contains old Portuguese furnishings, family portraits, and cases full of mementos, memorabilia, toys, and personal effects. Access to the chapel and gardens is given but you can only view the vineyards from a distance.

En Route from Vila Real – There are a few alternatives from here. If you have a flexible schedule, the N2 north of Vila Real links notable spa towns — Vidago, with its parks and woodland; and Chaves, an old town with a Roman bridge, seventeenth-century ramparts, a castle with a fourteenth-century keep, and a spa.

A longer drive on N15 from Vila Real ambles through a vast mountain region for 86 miles (138 km) to Bragança, whose walled medieval city and towering twelfth-century castle keep dominate the lower modern town. Just outside the town is the *Pousada São Bartolomeu,* pleasant for an overnight stay.

If your time is more limited, continue on N2 into the deep vales and terraced mountain vineyards of the great port wine producing region. Cross the Douro River at Régua, and wind your way through the valley where the grape vines cling to the nearly perpendicular terraced hillsides that drop down to the river to Lamego.

LAMEGO: This is a neatly arranged town of sixteenth- and eighteenth-century houses. The Cortes, a representative body of nobles, clergy, and townspeople, met here in 1143 to acknowledge Afonso Henriques as king of Portugal and implement the royal right of succession to the throne. In the Museu de Lamego, a former eighteenth-century bishop's palace, early paintings, tapestries, and sixteenth- to eighteenth-century tiles are on display. Several churches of note are the Sé, which dates from the twelfth century; the Igreja do Desterro, with fine interior decoration (ask for admission at 148 Calçada do Desterro); and the Santuario Nossa Senhora dos Remédios, a baroque edifice whose impressive staircase is embellished with an unusual arrangement of pinnacles and ornamental tiling. Lamego is also known for its smoked ham and all kinds of sausages.

VISEU: Farther south on N2 is this important agricultural and crafts center. Sixteenth-century residences and eighteenth-century balconied townhouses line the narrow streets of the old section. The cathedral on the Praça da Sé has an interesting cloister and gallery of sacred art. Also worth a look is the Museu Grão Viseu, which contains paintings from the sixteenth-century Viseu school and representative works of old and new Portuguese art.

En Route from Viseu – The best route to complete the circle to Oporto is N16 west to N1 north at Albergaria-a-Velha and straight on to Oporto (84 mi/134 km). Otherwise you can head south to Tomar along N2, N234, N1, and N110, where you can pick up the central route at its northernmost point.

BEST EN ROUTE

Expect to pay $65 and up for a double room per night in a hotel in the expensive category, $30 to $40 in the moderate, and $25 to $30 in the inexpensive category. A dinner for two people will cost $30 and up in the expensive range, about $20 in the moderate, and $15 in the inexpensive range. Prices do not include drinks, wine, or tips.

SINTRA–SÃO PEDRO

Hotel Palácio dos Seteais – This former eighteenth-century palace is set in a beautiful park and garden. The 18 rooms are exquisitely furnished and decorated. An elegant dining room serves international and regional cuisine; there is also a bar. Rua Barbosa du Bocage 8, on N375 (phone: 923-3200). Expensive.

Solar de S. Pedro – Good Portuguese and international fare are served in attractive and comfortable surroundings. Closed Wednesdays. Praça D. Fernando II, 12, S. Pedro de Sintra (phone: 923-18-60). Moderate.

Galeria Real – Above an antique shop, this appealing dining room serves excellent regional and French dishes. Reservations. Rua Tude de Sousa, on N9 (phone: 923-1661). Moderate.

Cafe Solar dos Mouros – Decorated in Moorish style with beautiful tiles and a fountain, this restaurant is just off the square. R. Consig. Pedroso 2 (phone: 923-1706). Moderate.

ÓBIDOS

Pousada do Castelo – Originally a sixteenth-century palace, this inn on the ramparts has a regional décor, six rooms, and a rustically elegant dining room with country and international cuisine; bar. Reservations recommended. Paço Real (phone: 9-5105). Moderate.

Estalagem do Convento – Delightfully converted convent has antique-styled furnishings and 13 rooms. The beamed-ceiling dining room specializes in regional fare. Reservations recommended. Rua Dr. João de Ornelas (phone: 9-5217). Moderate.

SÃO MARTINHO DO PORTO

Hotel Parque – This spacious mansion-style hotel has 44 rooms in a garden setting. Only breakfast is served; no restaurant. Av. Marechal Carmona (phone: 9-8108). Inexpensive.

NAZARÉ

Hotel da Nazaré – A modern 50-room hotel with bar. Largo Afonso Zuquete (phone: 4-6311). Inexpensive.

Hotel Praia – This modern hotel is on a main street near the beach; 40 rooms. Breakfast only. Av. Vieira Guimarães 39 (phone: 4-6423). Inexpensive.

Mar Bravo – It has regional fare and good seafood (but expensive), plus a panoramic view to recommend it. Praça Sousa Oliveira (phone: 4-61-80). Moderate.

LEIRIA

Hotel Euro-Sol – Nicely landscaped, this attractive modern hilltop hotel has an outdoor pool, an exceptional top-floor dining room, and a bar; 54 rooms. Rua D. José Alves Correia da Silva (phone: 2-4101). Moderate.

Estalagem Claras – Good regional cooking is available at this simple inn. Av. Heróis de Angola 42 (phone: 2-2373). Inexpensive.

BATALHA

Estalagem do Mestre Afonso Domingues – This sparkling, gracious inn near Batalha's Church — one of Portugal's most renowned monuments — has 21 rooms, air-conditioning, and a pleasant dining room. Reservations recommended. Batalha (phone: 9-6260). Inexpensive.

COIMBRA

Hotel Astoria – Old-fashioned comfort amid 1930s decor is the advantage of this conveniently located hotel. There's a quiet dining room and a bar. Av. Emidio Navarro 21 r/c. (phone: 2-2055). Moderate.

Dom Pedro – Good regional and international cuisine is served at this elegantly rustic restaurant. Av. Emidio Navarro 58 (phone: 2-9108). Moderate.

LUSO

Grande Hotel das Termas – Surrounded by gardens and parks, this large resort hotel has 157 rooms, a spacious dining room, and a bar — all newly decorated. Facilities include a huge outdoor pool, spa, tennis, casino, and nightclub. Open from June till mid-October. In town (phone: 9-3450). Moderate.

Estalagem do Luso – This lovely guesthouse has seven artfully furnished rooms and a dining room. Rua Dr. Lúcio Pais Abranches (phone: 9-3114). Moderate.

BUÇACO

Palace Hotel do Buçaco – Surrounded by forest, park, and gardens, this magnificent ex–royal hunting lodge features Manueline decorations, fine furniture, 70 luxurious bedrooms, and a splendid dining room; bar. Floresta do Buçaco (phone: 9-3101). Expensive.

AVEIRO

Pousada da Ria – This balconied inn overlooking the lagoon and town has 10 comfortable rooms, swimming pool, a dining room with regional cooking, and bar. Torreira-Murtosa (phone: 4-6132). Inexpensive.

ESPINHO

Praiagolfe – This modern beach hotel has 199 air-conditioned rooms, restaurant, bar, nightclub, and a large outdoor pool; golf course adjacent. Rua 6 (phone: 92-06-30). Moderate.

OPORTO

Hotel Infante de Sagres – An oasis in the midst of a busy city, this luxury hotel has 84 pleasant rooms, a grand dining room with attentive service, and elaborately decorated lounges. Praça D. Filipa de Lencastre 62 (phone: 2-8101). Expensive.

Hotel Porto Atlántico – This supermodern complex out of the city center has 58 air-conditioned rooms, indoor and outdoor pools, shops, and restaurants. Rua Afonso Lopes Vieira 66, off E5 (phone: 69-49-41). Moderate.

Portucale – This excellent restaurant on the 13th floor of Albergaria Miradouro offers splendid views and international and regional cuisine. Reservations. Rua da Alegria 598 (phone: 2-7861). Expensive.

Comercial – This complex has two restaurants and a bar. International and regional cuisine is served in the attractive ground-floor restaurant; a good selection is available in *Taverna do Infante* below. Rua Infante Dom Henrique 77 (phone: 2-2463). Moderate.

VIANA DO CASTELO

Hotel do Parque – This modern hotel overlooking the Lima River has inviting grounds, spacious lounges, a heated pool, a rooftop restaurant with regional and international cuisine, and a bar; 120 rooms. Praça da Galiza (phone: 2-4151). Moderate.

Hotel de Santa Luzia – High above town, this 42-room hotel surrounded by a park and gardens has an old-world atmosphere and modern amenities — heated pool, tennis courts, excellent restaurant, terrace with a stunning view, and a bar. Monte de Santa Luzia (phone: 2-2192). Moderate.

VALENÇA

Pousada de São Teotónio – This modern inn at the edge of a walled town has 16 nice rooms, an airy dining room, good food, and a bar. The terrace has a gorgeous view. Valença do Minho (phone: 2-2252). Inexpensive.

BRAGA

Hotel de Turismo – This modern hotel conveniently located on a main street has a spacious interior, 93 air-conditioned rooms, a pool, bar, and shops. Av. da Liberdade (phone: 2-7091). Moderate.

Do Elevador – This quiet little hotel above the city provides enchanting night views; 25 rooms. Food is served. Bom Jesus do Monte (phone: 2-5011). Inexpensive.

Inácio – This popular restaurant has stone walls, rough beams, and tasty regional cooking. Campo das Hortas 4 (phone: 2-2335). Moderate.

CANIÇADA

Pousada de São Bento – This new stone-walled inn has spectacular views, 10 rooms with rustic decor, a dining room with good, hearty, regional cooking; outdoor pool. Cerdeirinhas-Soengas Caniçada (phone: 5-7190). Inexpensive.

GUIMARÃES

Jordão – Below the Jordão cinema, this spacious, busy restaurant serves a variety of international and regional dishes. Av. Afonso Henriques 62 (phone: 4-0198). Moderate.

VIDAGO

Vidago Palace Hotel – This pleasant hotel has a tranquil atmosphere, park grounds, pool, tennis, golf course; 122 rooms. Breakfast is served. Parque (phone: 9-7356). Inexpensive.

LAMEGO

Estalagem de Lamego – Set in a pretty park, this small inn has 7 rooms and a pleasant dining room. On N2 (phone: 6-2162). Inexpensive.

VISEU

Hotel Grão Vasco – Near the old section of town, this modern hotel has 89 rooms, lovely lawns and trees, and a swimming pool. The dining room serves regional and international cuisine; bar. Rua Gaspar Barreiros (phone: 2-3511). Moderate.

O Cortiço – Probably the most famous restaurant in Portugal, it's noted for robust regional cooking, and friendly, lively service. Spread over several nearby addresses, a table in this restaurant is always found even on the busiest nights. Rua Nova 36, 47, 64 (phone: 2-3853). Moderate.

Central Portugal

This route originates in Lisbon and loops around central Portugal through an area of rolling plains criss-crossed by rivers and known for cork and olive oil production. The bold reds of the stripped tree trunks along the way attest to the wealth of cork growing here. Central Portugal offers much of interest. In Tomar the magnificent Convento de Cristo, a fortified castle and convent, blends styles of architecture from the twelfth through seventeenth centuries. Next, the route swings through Marvão, a medieval village, and through three of Portugal's most engaging towns: Elvas, where a fifteenth-century aqueduct still carries water to the town; Estremoz, whose artisans are famous for their pottery figurines of people and animals; and Évora, where you can see a Roman temple dating from the second century.

LISBON: For a detailed report on the capital, its hotels and restaurants, see *Lisbon,* THE EUROPEAN CITIES. From Lisbon pick up E3, then N3 for the 49-mile (79-km) trip to Santarém.

SANTARÉM: Founded in 10 BC by Iberian King Abidis, taken from the Moors in 1147 by Afonso Henriques, Santarém was once the royal residence. This busy little district capital is now the center of bull breeding for Portugal's bullfighting season. The Igreja de São João de Alporão (Rua Serpa Pinto) serves as an archaeological museum with a diverse assortment of Arabian and Romanesque objects, sculpture, coats of arms, and the flamboyant Gothic tomb of the Count of Viana. The fourteenth-century Gothic Igreja da Graça has a particularly attractive interior, but permission for entry must be obtained from the Turismo (Rua Capelo).

En Route from Santarém – Cross the Tagus River on N368 for Alpiarça in order to visit the lovely Museu Casa dos Patudos, former residence of José Relvas, statesman and art patron. The collection includes seventeenth- and nineteenth-century tapestries and carpets, china, paintings, and furnishings. Follow N118 to N243, recrossing the Tagus to N365. Turn onto N113 for the 35 miles (56 km) to Tomar.

TOMAR: Founded by the Order of the Templars on the River Nabão, this town is crowned by the magnificent Convento de Cristo. The Templars started building the fortified castle and convent in 1160 but construction was not completed until the seventeenth century. This beautiful monument combines several styles of architecture with the Salamancan entrance, the rotunda modeled after the Holy Sepulcher in Jerusalem, the Italian Renaissance cloister, and the fanciful Manueline window seen from an upper terrace of the Cloister Santa Barbara. Halfway down the hill from the convento, there is a good view from the plaza of the Renaissance Capela de Nossa Senhora da Conceicão. The fifteenth-century Igreja de São João Baptista (Praça República) has a Manueline belfry and a notable interior. Tomar has a lovely city garden with a lagoon for boating and an old water mill.

En Route from Tomar – The village of Abrantes has a ruined castle-fortress with a splendid view from its belvedere.

CASTELO DE VIDE: This is an appealing spa town of prehistoric origins with whitewashed houses and winding alleys. The Castelo, rebuilt in 1299 and restored in 1710, provides a marvelous view from its keep. The old Judiaria quarter has many houses with interesting Gothic doorways.

MARVÃO: Firmly established atop a rough hill sits the medieval village of Marvão, a stronghold fought over during the civil war of 1828–1834. Follow signs to Marvão-Beria, wending up the steep incline to the rampart gateway. Either park outside the walls or drive to Pillory Square. Walk to the summit, enter through four gateways, and climb the stairs to the parapets leading to the castle keep. *Pousada de Santa Maria* is a simple friendly inn with a dining room overlooking a panorama of mountains and the Spanish border.

PORTALEGRE: Once a center of tapestry manufacturing and silk production, the seventeenth- and eighteenth-century mansions of this attractive town attest to past prosperity. Notable buildings include the cathedral, Largo da Sé, and the tapestry workshops in the old Jesuit monastery (Rua Fernandes).

ELVAS: The great Aqueduto da Amoreira joins the impressive ramparts of this old village and carries water to the inhabitants as it has since the fifteenth century. Turn into the viaduct gateway and proceed to the mosaic-tile, tree-lined Praça da República. Walking around this area, you can see the Igreja de Nossa Senhora da Assuncão with its imposing marble chancel, the tile-faced Igreja Nossa Senhora da Consolação, and the castle in the northwest corner of the ramparts, which dates from Moorish times. The military bastion of Forte de Nossa Senhora da Graça on a hill north of the town and the Forte de Santa Luzia to the south complete the fortifications.

ESTREMOZ: This old hilltop village of red-roofed white houses rises from the plains. The ancient cobbled streets, thirteenth-century keep, tiled castle chapel, seventeenth-century walls, and Igreja Santa Maria's collection of primitive paintings are of greatest interest. The village is a fine place for an evening walk.

The artisans of Estremoz, a well-known pottery center since the sixteenth century, are especially recognized for their unusual pottery figurines depicting people and their animals in scenes of everyday life. You'll also see beautiful objects made of marble from the local quarries.

ÉVORA: This town is one of the oldest settlements of the Iberian Peninsula. Follow the "centro" signs and park on the Praça do Giraldo or continue on to the *Pousada dos Lóios* and park there. The second-century Templo Romano is one of the few reminders of the Roman past in Portugal. Evora was a center of learning in the fifteenth century. Its old university — now a public high school — has an *aula magna* (large assembly hall) entirely covered with seventeenth-century tiles. The Sé is particularly interesting for its variety of architectural styles and adornments and for the contents of the treasury. This rich collection includes ecclesiastical objects and old illuminated books and manuscripts. The Museu Regional, adjacent to the Sé in a former sixteenth-century episcopal palace, houses ancient sculpture and primitive paintings. The venerated sixteenth-century Igreja de São Francisco (Praça 28 de Maio), built in the Gothic Manueline style, has a chapel constructed of bones. This oddity was conceived by a Franciscan monk as an incentive for his fellow brothers to meditate on the transitory nature of life. *Cozinha de Sto. Humberto* is a good restaurant.

En Route from Évora – From here you can complete the circle by returning to Lisbon or heading south for the Algarve. If you are returning to Lisbon, go via Setubal to Palmela and Sesimbra for visits to their three castles, for swimming and deep-sea fishing, and for splendid views from the Arrabida Mountains. The entire Arrabida Peninsula once belonged to the dukes of Palmela, but it is now a national park. Its flora is unique in Europe, comparable to Corsica and the Ardennes.

SETUBAL: For centuries an important commercial port, Setubal is located at the mouth of the Sado River, which is noted for its extensive beds of giant oysters. The Castelo de São Filipe, built during Spanish domination, sits above the city and is now a fine *pousada.*

Just across the water and easily reached by car ferry or hovercraft is the Troia Peninsula with 20 miles of fine sand beaches for swimming, surfing, and skin diving. A new tourist complex with hotels, nightclubs, modern shops, and a golf course has just been opened. The Troia Peninsula is steeped in history and legend — ruins of a Roman fish factory and chapel have been excavated.

PALMELA: Located 6 miles (10 km) above Setubal in a region famous for its Muscatel wines, Palmela has a royal residence and a twelfth-century fortress, recently transformed into a splendid 25-room *pousada.*

SESIMBRA: At the southern foothills of the Arrabida Mountains facing south on a wide bay lies Sesimbra, which combines the charm of an old fishing village with the amenities of a modern tourist resort. Its very good fish restaurants specialize in grilled red mullet, sea bass, and sardines. If you prefer to catch your own dinner, rent a boat with a professional guide at the docks. The ruins of Sesimbra Castle, overlooking the town, were once a Moorish stronghold.

En Route from Sesimbra – Stop off in Vila Fresca de Azeitão, home of Lancers rosé wines and, more importantly for wine buffs, the home of one of Europe's finest sweet dessert wines — Fonseca's Setubal Muscatel. You can sample both at the Lancers rosé winery and at the company's old wine cellars down the road where Setubal Muscatels are aged.

BEST EN ROUTE

Expect to pay $50 and up per night for a double room in a hotel in the expensive category, $35 to $40 in the moderate, and $20 and under in the inexpensive category. A dinner for two people will cost $30 and up in the expensive range, about $20 in the moderate, and $15 in the inexpensive range. Prices do not include drinks, wine, or tips.

SANTARÉM

Alcaide-Mór – This restaurant has pleasant food and atmosphere at the right price. Rua Luis de Camoes 26 (phone: 2-3117). Inexpensive.

TOMAR

Hotel dos Templários – Set on landscaped grounds next to a river park, this modern hotel has 84 air-conditioned rooms with balconies, swimming pool, tennis, very good food, and a bar. Reserve odd-numbered rooms for fabulous evening views. Largo Cândido dos Reis (phone: 3-3121). Moderate.

Pousada de São Pedro – Overlooking Portugal's largest reservoir, this quiet inn has 16 rooms, a dining room with views of the dam and Zêzere River. Castelo do Bode, on N358 (phone: 3-8159). Inexpensive.

MARVÃO

Pousada de Santa Maria – Perched on a mountain side in an ancient walled town, this inn has nine small neat rooms, country-style décor, and a dining room offering wide views, simple regional cooking, and a bar. Marvão (phone: 9-3201). Moderate.

ELVAS

Pousada de Santa Luzia – Just off the main road stands this attractive air-conditioned inn with 11 rooms, and an inviting dining room serving fine regional and international cuisine; bar. Av. de Badajoz, on N4 (phone: 2-2194). Moderate.

ESTREMOZ

Pousada da Rainha Santa Isabel – Set in a medieval palace in the old town, this grand luxury hotel has 23 large rooms with canopied beds, a lofty dining room with excellent food, a bar, and an inner patio. Largo Dom Diniz (phone: 2-2618). Moderate.

ÉVORA

Pousada dos Lóios – This elegantly restored convent still has many original details, and 28 compact, attractively furnished rooms. The dining room built around the cloister serves regional food prepared according to old convent recipes. There's also a breakfast room and a bar. Largo Conde de Vila Flor (phone: 2-4051). Expensive.

BEJA

Luís da Rocha – This busy, simple restaurant serves decent food at modest prices. Rua Capitão João Francisco de Sousa 63. Inexpensive.

SETÚBAL

Pousada de São Filipe – Built within old castle walls, this rustically furnished inn has 15 rooms, a dining room serving regional specialties, and a bar. Setúbal (phone: 2-3844). Moderate.

Caranguejus – This bright modern restaurant specializes in seafood. Closed Mondays. Av. Alexandre Herculano 62A (phone: 2-9263). Inexpensive.

PALMELA

Pousada de Palmela – Located in an imposing twelfth-century castle that stands on the crest of a high hill, it offers a spectacular view of the sea and the countryside. There is a restaurant and a bar. 2950 Palmela (phone: 235-1226). Expensive.

SESIMBRA

Hotel do Mar – Built into the side of the hill and overlooking the beach, this 119-room hotel has a commanding view plus a swimming pool, bars, and other comforts. Rua dos Combatentes do Ultramar (phone: 22-33-26). Moderate.

Hotel Espadarte – A 79-room hotel right on the beach, convenient for fishing. Esplanada Comandante Tenreiro (phone: 223-3189). Moderate.

The Algarve

The Algarve has been a favorite holiday area with Europeans for many years. Beach-loving Americans recently have begun vacationing on the southern coast of Portugal. Fine sandy beaches, edged by gigantic sandstone cliffs, offer long stretches of untrammeled shore, as well as tiny hidden coves. Strung along the coast are luxury hotels and attractive first- and second-class establishments. But the Algarve has not suffered from uninhibited development; in addition to the resort complexes there are small fishing villages and simple residential areas.

The best of many worlds is available in the Algarve, from sophisticated nightlife to seaside solitude. The sports enthusiast will find excellent facilities for tennis, golf, riding, fishing, water skiing, and boating. The shoppers will find a wide selection of fine handcrafted articles — pottery, embroidery, knitwear, and jewelry. Festivals take place throughout the year. There are many excellent restaurants that serve seafood and regional specialties as well as international cuisine.

The best time to visit the Algarve is from the end of January, when the almond trees are in blossom, through the summer until the end of October. But the Algarve is really a year-round resort, as the weather is never very cold by European standards.

The route traced below follows the coast from Vila Real de Santo António in the east to Cabo de São Vincente in the west along N125 for a distance of some 100 miles (160 km). The two-lane road is not a coastal route — in order to reach the beach resorts turn off at the sign for each destination. Although little byways sometimes lead from one beach settlement to another, they are often poorly marked and surfaced.

The most interesting features of the Algarve lie west of Portimão. Here the landscape softens into tree-covered rolling hills with small farms. You pass little painted donkey carts on the road and catch glimpses of the sea. As you approach the turnoff for Sagres, N268, the terrain becomes more rugged. At this spectacular route's end lies the famous school of Henry the Navigator.

PRAIA DE MONTE GORDO: A long flat stretch of beach and several first-class hotels make this town a great place to vacation. The early-fourteenth-century ruined castle of the Knights of Christ is an interesting historical site in Castro Marim, west on N125.6.

TAVIRA: This fishing village is built on both shores of the Rio Séqua. A Greek settlement in 380 BC, the town was later conquered by the Goths and Moors. The foundations of the bridge date from Roman times and there is a ruined thirteenth-century castle.

OLHÃO: Founded by fishermen in the eighteenth century, life in this town of pale houses revolves around its fish market.

FARO: The capital of the Algarve was an important Moorish city, taken by Afonso III in 1249 to end Arab domination in Portugal. The old town, surrounded by ancient houses and parts of the defensive walls, has two museums and the Sé (Largo de Sé), the interior of which is decorated with seventeenth-century tiles. In the Ethnological Museum an English-speaking guide gives explanations of the historical and folkloric displays. The Museu Maritimo, in the old office of the captain of the port on the Doca (marina), exhibits model ships and fishing boats.

LOULÉ: High in the hills above Faro, this little center of handicrafts is a good place to shop for pottery, brassware, copper, basketry, and so on.

ALMANSIL-VALE DO LOBO: This lovely recreation area is the location of one of the Algarve's most illustrious resort hotels, *Dona Filipa*. There's also a well-designed residential area. *La Réserve* is a good place to dine.

QUARTEIRA: Once a quiet fishing village, this is now a busy, fast-growing resort town with a superb beach. Among the best restaurants are *O Elegante* and *Isidoro*.

VILAMOURA: This highly-developed vacation and tourist center stretches from the sea to N125. Vilamoura has a large yacht marina and an excellent golf course.

ALBUFEIRA: Called the St.-Tropez of the Algarve, this large resort town has a Moorish ambience that belies its diverse resort activities and sophisticated nightlife. The last town to be taken from the Moors in 1250, there is nothing left here of historical value but it is pleasing to walk around town or watch the return of the fishing boats and explore the caves and grottoes along the beach. There's good shopping for handicrafts and antiques.

ARMAÇÃO DE PERA: This old fishing village lies between sandstone cliffs. You can take boat excursions to the caves and grottoes along the shore.

LAGOA: This typical Algarvean market town was founded in the fifteenth century on the site of a much earlier Roman settlement. Shopping is the highlight at this crafts center; you can also visit the Lagoa winery. *Togi* is an inviting hilltop restaurant with a spectacular view of the sea.

SILVES: This ancient hill town was once the Moorish capital of the Algarve. All that remains of that time is the impressive restored castle-fortress. The parapets command a panoramic view and in the evenings the lighted battlements are a memorable sight. The thirteenth-century Gothic cathedral, Santa Maria, contains the remains of a Moorish mosque and tombs presumed to be those of Crusader soldiers.

PORTIMÃO: The largest fishing town on the Algarve has lots of activity, many tourists, and heavy traffic. The approach to the port from the bridge across the Arade River opens up a captivating view of the bay with its boats and quays. The town itself is pleasant for walking and there are many good shops on the Rua Santa Isabel and the Rua do Comércio. Just southeast, before crossing the bridge, is the seaside village of Ferragudo, a small fishing hamlet with a ruined sixteenth-century castle. There are several luxury hotels along the beach in Praia da Rocha and Praia dos Três Irmãos. For the best in golfing, head to the fine *Penina Golf Hotel* in Penina.

LAGOS: Founded by the Carthaginians in 350 BC, this is the most attractive harbor town on the Algarve. The walls around the old section are traces of Roman occupation. From this port, the caravels of Henry the Navigator embarked on many voyages of exploration and discovery. The seventeenth-century Forte do Pau da Bandeira still dominates the harbor. The chapel of Igreja de Santo António off the Rua Henrique C. Silva has a baroque interior with much gilded statuary and a painted trompe l'oeil ceiling. Adjacent to the chapel is a museum containing extensive folkloric and archaeological exhibits and sacred art. The Igreja São Sabastião (Rua Conselheiro J. Machado) has some features of artistic merit including a Renaissance door and tiled walls. Shops sell antiques, brass and copperware, and embroidery. For excellent dining try the distinctively decorated *Pouso do Infante*.

Stop off at Ponta da Piedade, a colorful site of caves, beach, and sea, west of town.

En Route from Lagos – The landscape from Lagos to Sagres on N125 becomes grandly severe, supporting a handful of tiny villages ending abruptly at Vila do Bispo. Turn left onto N268 for a few kilometers; you'll come to a right turn leading to the lighthouse overlooking Cabo de São Vicente — allegedly the landing place of the boat containing the martyred body of St. Vincent.

SAGRES: On this windy, solitary headland, Prince Henry established a navigation school in the fifteenth century, which enabled the Portuguese to maintain naval supremacy for almost two centuries. The old school building and residence is now a hostel. From the clifftops, you can do some challenging fishing or watch the boats as they trawl the deep for a rich variety of fish. The area is a very dramatic land's end.

BEST EN ROUTE

Expect to pay $85 and up per night for a double room in a hotel in the expensive category, $40 to $65 in the moderate, and $35 and under in the inexpensive category. A dinner for two people will cost $40 and up in the expensive range, about $35 in the moderate, and $15 in the inexpensive range. Prices do not include drinks, wine, or tips.

MONTE GORDO

Hotel Alcazar – This attractive, modern, air-conditioned hotel has 95 rooms, a restaurant, bar, and pool. Rua de Ceuta (phone: 4-2181, 4-2141). Moderate.

Hotel Vasco da Gama – This comfortable beach hotel has 182 rooms and suites, a spacious restaurant, bars, a pool, and tennis. Av. Infante Dom Henrique (phone: 4-2321). Moderate.

TAVIRA

Eurotel – In a beautiful setting with a sea view, this hotel has 80 rooms, a dining room, pool, and tennis. Quinta das Oliveiras (phone: 2-2041). Moderate.

SÃO BRAZ DE ALPORTEL

Pousada de São Braz – Set in the hills north of Faro this inn has 21 rooms, a dining room, and bar. São Braz de Alportel (phone: 4-2305). Moderate.

FARO

Hotel Eva – On the marina, this popular modern hotel has 150 air-conditioned rooms, a top-floor dining room, rooftop terraced swimming pool, nightclub, and bars. The hotel runs a courtesy bus service to the beach. Av. da República (phone: 2-4054). Moderate.

Al Faghar – Fine Portuguese cooking and atmosphere are served up in large doses. Reserve a table in the balcony window. Rua Tenente Valadim 30 (phone: 2-3740). Moderate.

Casa de Lumena – This attractive ex–family mansion has outdoor patio dining and a varied Portuguese menu. Reservations. Praça Alexandre Herculano 27 (phone: 2-2028). Moderate.

ALMANSIL–VALE DO LOBO

Hotel Dona Filipa – This superbly run and maintained hotel overlooking the beach has 129 attractive air-conditioned rooms with large balconies, a terrace with pool, and tennis courts. The dining room has fine Continental cuisine and excellent service. A buffet lunch is served in a terrace area. There's a lively bar, an inner patio, and a golf course next to the hotel. Make reservations well in advance. Vale do Lobo (phone: 9-4141). Expensive.

O Elegante – This restaurant on the waterfront offers first-class Portuguese food. Closed Tuesdays. Reservations. Av. Infante de Sagres (phone: 6-5339). Expensive.

Isidoro – This spacious dining room, done in nautical decor, overlooking the sea, serves good seafood and regional dishes. Av. Infante de Sagres (phone: 6-5219). Moderate.

VILAMOURA

Hotel Dom Pedro – Close to the beach, this modern attractive hotel has 260 air-conditioned rooms with balconies, a swimming pool, tennis, golf course, and bar. Vilamoura (phone: 6-5412). Expensive.

Vilamoura Golf Hotel – This extensive resort complex includes 40 villas, 52 hotel rooms and suites, a restaurant, bars, shops, and a spacious pool. In town (phone: 6-5321). Moderate.

ALBUFEIRA

Hotel da Balaia – Surrounded by green lawns on a cliff overlooking the beach, this modern hotel is nicely designed with balconied rooms, an inviting dining room, a luncheon terrace, bar, a large swimming pool, and boutiques; 12 family villas and 180 rooms. Praia Maria Luisa (phone: 5-2681). Expensive.

António Catuna – This popular, rustically decorated restaurant serves regional specialties. Closed Sundays. Reservations recommended. Rua B (phone: 5-2050). Moderate.

A Ruína – On the edge of Fishermen's Beach in an old building, this restaurant has very fresh fish and a terrace bar with a marvelous view. Rua Cais Herculano (phone: 5-2094). Moderate.

Borda d'Água – A few kilometers east of Albufeira, this attractive restaurant overlooking the beach serves excellent seafood and Continental dishes. Closed Mondays. Reservations recommended. Open June–September. Praia da Oura (phone: 5-2045). Moderate.

ARMAÇÃO DE PERA

Vilalara – Luxurious resort village, 2 kilometers west of town, has 65 beautifully furnished apartments and villas, appealing indoor and outdoor restaurants, pool, tennis, bar, and private beach. Armação de Pera (phone: 5-5333). Expensive.

Hotel do Garbe – This first-class, clifftop hotel has 103 rooms and suites, and a dining room and terraced pool overlooking the beach. Also has bar and shops. Av. Marginal (phone: 5-5187). Moderate.

PORTIMÃO

The Old Tavern – Good English and Continental dishes are served in an old Portuguese atmosphere. Closed Saturdays. Reservations recommended. Rua Júdice Fialho 43 (phone: 2-3325). Moderate.

PRAIA DA ROCHA

Hotel Algarve – This establishment has unique Moorish-inspired modern decor and furnishings, 200 air-conditioned rooms and suites, a giant pool set amidst green lawns and gardens. There's also an intimate grill room and bar, and a dining room with a sea view; nightclub and shops. Probably the best first-class hotel buy in the Algarve. Av. Tomás Cabreira (phone: 2-4001). Expensive.

PRAIA DOS TRÊS IRMÃOS

Hotel Alvor Praia – This hotel has are 241 lovely air-conditioned rooms and suites. The sparkling split-level dining room has an international menu and an outdoor buffet lunch. There's a spectacular beach setting, a large pool, tennis, fishing, excursion boat, shops, bar, and a nightclub. Praia dos Três Irmãos (phone: 2-4020). Expensive.

PENINA

Hotel do Golf da Penina – One of the most exciting golf resorts in the world, the 27-hole championship course was designed by Henry Cotton. Facilities include a driving range, tennis courts, and a huge pool with sun decks and bar. There are 215 air-conditioned rooms and suites, nicely decorated lounges, dining room, grill room, and bar with dancing. Penina Portimão (phone: 2-2051). Expensive.

LAGOS

Hotel de Lagos – This first-class, 150-room hotel has a fine restaurant and runs regular buses to the beach for guests. Rua Nova da Aldria (phone: 6-2011). Moderate.

Alpendre – This well-staffed first-class restaurant has an extensive menu and full service. Closed Wednesdays. Reservations recommended. Rua António Barbosa Viana 17 (phone: 6-2705). Moderate.

Lagosteira – Under the same management as *Alpendre,* this restaurant specializes in seafood. Closed Tuesdays. Reservations recommended. Rua 1 de Maio 26 (phone: 6-2486). Moderate.

SAGRES

Hotel da Baleeira – This simple, comfortable hotel is extremely popular because of its prime seaside location. The 114 rooms look out on the sea. There is also a saltwater pool, a bar, and a pleasant dining room with smashing views. In town (phone: 6-4212). Moderate.

Pousada do Infante – On the cliffs with an incredible view, this attractive inn has 15 rooms, a dining room with a sea view, and a terrace. In town (phone: 6-4222). Moderate.

A Tasca – This fishermen's restaurant serves good seafood and regional dishes. In town (phone: 6-4177). Moderate.

Exploring Romania

Romania is an eastern European country of some 91,700 square miles that's bordered by Russia to the north, the Black Sea to the east, Hungary and Yugoslavia to the west, and Bulgaria to the south. The population has risen to over 22 million (Romania has the highest growth rate in Eastern Europe) of which the largest concentration (something over 2 million) is in the capital city of Bucharest.

There are three major historic and geographic areas in Romania. Walachia is on the flat Danube plain in the south. The Danube itself is a natural southern border with Bulgaria, and historically the river brought trade and culture to the valley from the west. Bucharest sprang up here as a major center of government and industry. The Danube flows into the Black Sea and below the river delta there stretches the only Romanian seacoast, primarily a resort area with many beaches. There is a major seaport at Constanta.

North of the Danube plain the country is fairly mountainous. Transylvania is a belt of Alpine massifs and forests that cross the midsection of the country. Traditionally allied with Walachia, the area has had a turbulent history of being overrun, from time to time, by various hordes — the Germanic and Magyar from the west and the Ottoman from the south.

The northern sector of the country is known as Moldavia, a historically independent state in the Carpathian Hills with its own folk traditions and culture. It wasn't until the mid-nineteenth century, when Walachia and Moldavia were unified, that Romania took on its present shape. Neutral during World War I, a fascist regime gained power in Romania at the beginning of World War II, but in 1944 the government was overthrown and the new leaders joined the advancing Russian armies against Germany. Today Romania is a Soviet ally, though an outspoken and independent one, and because of its Romance language and Danubian culture Romania remains one of the most Western of all the European Communist states.

The first route in Romania starts with a tour through Bucharest, the spacious and leisurely capital city with parks and lakes, and then takes you north to Braşov, a well-preserved medieval city in the heart of Transylvania. The second route is a tour of the famous monasteries of Bukovina, a small area up near the Russian frontier and the historic seat of the Moldavian monarchy. These beautifully frescoed, medieval folk churches, though rarely toured, were awarded the Pomme d'Or by FIJET (The International Federation of Tourism Journalists and Writers).

Bucharest and Braşov:
A Trip into Transylvania

This isn't so much a road tour as it is a visit to two urban centers, Bucharest for its own merits and Braşov not only for itself but also as a base for sight-seeing. The two cities are separated by about 105 miles (168 km) of good road, which passes through countryside in transition. By the roadside there are endless groups of athletes in fashionable warm-up suits (there's a long list of famous Romanian sports heroes from Nadia Comăneci to Ilie Nastase and the whole country is very sports conscious), but in the more rural areas you can still see groups of women laundering the week's wash in the local streams. There are also cows, healthy-looking water buffaloes, and herds of geese being driven alongside the route. You can buy native handmade clothes with beautiful embroidery from roadside vendors.

Bucharest is a flat and friendly city on the northern Danube plain, but as you drive north to Braşov you rise into the Transylvanian Alps where the skiing is good and the winter resorts are plentiful.

BUCHAREST: Bucharest is a city of wide streets, spacious parks, and leisurely walks down tree-lined and flowered boulevards. There aren't very big crowds of sight-seers anywhere because there aren't any really world-renowned sights to see, but the city does offer a mix of old-world Eastern flavor with that of a modern, thriving, Communist state. The nightlife in Bucharest isn't very exciting, but there are some nightclubs, an opera, live theater, evening shows of the Romanian State Circus, a surviving Yiddish Theater, and lots of old American movies. During the daytime, the city is a bustling combination of avid shoppers, hearty food, and relaxing lakeside cafés. There is a strong European tone here as the Romanian language is one of the Romance tongues rather than one of the slavic-sounding languages spoken by most of Romania's neighbors. For a city on the same latitude as Detroit there is an amazing amount of vegetation and it's all well cared for.

The city as it stands today is only about five hundred years old, but the area was a population center since the Stone Age. Originally called the Dîmbovița Citadel, it was renamed Bucharest in 1459 by none other than Vlad the Impaler, more universally known as Dracula, who actually did do much toward unifying his country. There has been an active city planning office here since the end of World War I and the old-city buildings are venerated and well kept. Since World War II there has been a building boom in both high-rise residences and government meeting halls that seem to fit in comfortably among all the older structures.

The nicest walk in town is out to the lakeside Herăstrău Park on the north side where you'll find the village museum with exhibits of recreated peasant households. From the cafés you can sit and watch small boats and sailing yawls cross the lake against the green backdrop of poplar-lined banks. Several times a year there are also international festivals held here.

The nicest trip out of town is 9 miles (14 km) through the western parks and forests to the elegant Mogosoaia Palace (1702) of Prince Constantin Brâncoveanu. Now a museum housing medieval art and artifacts, the building itself overshadows its contents. It's a formal building built on the scale of a Venetian palazzo with ornately arched colonnades, a stately close-cropped garden, and a quiet reflecting pond.

There's an abundance of starchy food here, the most common of which is *mamaliga,* a cornmeal affair that conjures up a cross-breeding of mush and home fries. *Brinza* is a white cottage-cheesy item and *ciorba* is a national soup that comes in many colors and flavors. The Romanians are most at home with fish dishes and if you stick to carp and sturgeon you can't go wrong. If you need meat the *mititei* (skinless sausages blistered over an open fire with a flavor that will keep you alert) are the best bet.

The Romanian wine industry is in a rebuilding phase and the local vintages are noted for having great potential. *Cotnari* is a very good white wine generally served after the main course and it vies with *Tuica,* a plum brandy, as the popular evening drink.

BRAŞOV: From Bucharest, drive north on Route 1 (E15) to this early medieval city at the foot of Mount Tîmpa in the Transylvanian Alps. The road takes you along the Prahova and Timis river valleys and passes through old Dacian settlements (founded as early as 70 BC) that are now winter ski spas. Braşov is a red-roofed town with winding streets, small squares, and a cable car ride up the mountainside that lets you absorb all the views. It's now one of the nation's chief industrial centers, but you wouldn't guess it after a walk through town. The town hall dates from the 1300s and the Black Church houses, behind its imposing Gothic facade, a collection of Oriental rugs.

The best day trip from Braşov is up into the Carpathian Mountains to the resort town of Poiana Braşov and the Bran Castle. The Bran is mistakenly touted as Dracula's home base but in truth Vlad only occasionally vacationed there (generally depending on how much of a lead he had on his pursuers). Still the castle is worthy of a visit. It's on a green hill with thick fortified walls, dramatic peaked towers, and comfortable and inviting interiors. Poiana Braşov (also called "Sunny Glade") is a wonderful stop for summer hikes or winter skiing and skating. The restaurants here feature hot and homemade Dacian goodies all cooked over open fires.

BEST EN ROUTE

Expect to pay anywhere between $50 and $65 (and up) per night for a double in hotels we've listed as expensive, between $25 and $35 for those in the moderate category, and under $25 for those listed as inexpensive. Meals are a much better deal. Most restaurants charge about $12 for even the most lavish, three-course extravaganza for two. Of course, you can still feed yourself in Romania, stand-up style, with good, nourishing stuff for under $4 for two. Prices do not include wine, tips, or drinks.

BUCHAREST

The Inter-Continental Hotel – This is the kind of centrally located hotel that tries to offer you everything in one place. There are at least two of everything here — restaurants, bars, conference halls. There's also a swimming pool and sauna. Bălcescu Bd. 4 (phone: 14-04-00). Expensive.

Bucureşti – Conveniently situated in the center of Bucharest, this deluxe 800-room hotel is the city's newest. Along with two restaurants, the hotel boasts two swimming pools, a sauna, and a gym. Calea Victoriei 63-76 (phone: 15-45-80). Expensive to moderate.

Capşa – This is an old meeting place for local artists and the food is excellent. If you don't want to try the local specialties you can opt for Continental mainstays. The desserts are special. Edgar Quinet Str. 1 (phone: 13-44-82). Moderate.

Pescărus – This is a beautiful terrace restaurant, overlooking the lake, that serves international cuisine. You can eat leisurely and watch the boats. It's a bit overpriced but still affordable. Herăstrău Park (phone: 16-30-95). Moderate.

BRAŞOV

Carpati – This is the hotel of choice in Braşov. It's very fancy with big comfortable rooms and a restaurant with really good food. Gh-Gheorghiu-Dej Bd. 9 (phone: 4-2840). Hotel: expensive; restaurant: moderate.

Cerbul Carpatin (near the Carpati hotel) – This is possibly the only true Transylvanian nightclub in the world. It's not the Copa, but there is music and dancing, and the people are polite. Moderate.

POIANA BRAŞOV

Sura Dacilor – This restaurant, with an A-frame structure that dates from the 1500s and looks both handmade and sturdy, is surrounded by grassy mountain walks. You can smell good things as soon as you enter. In the middle of town. Moderate.

The Moldavian Monasteries: Bukovina

Bukovina is a small tract of land in the northern Carpathian foothills that gradually rise from the Siret River valley farther north and east. The area, in the northeast corner of Romania, is a Moldavian reservation of beautiful mountain scenery with knobby, green-carpeted hills spotted with dense fir stands. The local Moldavians still sport their traditional dress whites, and the almost total lack of English-speaking people (except for tour guides) makes a trip here adventurous. Bukovina is not heavily toured and it's not really convenient to any place that is. There's minimal nightlife, absolutely no water skiing, and few wines of distinction. However, the International Federation of Tourist Journalists and Writers (FIJET) found Bukovina worthy of its prestigious Pomme d'Or award in 1975. This is because there are five churches and monasteries here, with exterior walls covered in frescoes, that are like no other structures in the world.

The buildings are all relatively simple and took months rather than generations to build. They are, however, the epitome of folk architecture built to an unwieldy and large scale that makes them look from a distance like squat, one-story bungalows. It is only when you approach them that you realize how enormous they are. They have few windows and are covered by peaked-cap roofs that descend steeply and then suddenly bow out, creating wide eaves over thick walls, the outsides of which are covered with artwork. Virtually every facade is bathed in color with frescoes depicting the bible, classical philosophy, and local folklore — a historic library of pictograms.

Moldavian history's medieval golden era was overseen by its greatest monarch, Stephen the Great, who, though he never rated a title higher than prince, reigned from 1457 to 1504. Because of the turbulence of the times and the violence of the populace, the length of Stephen's reign was unheard of (and even today ranks with Joe DiMaggio's 56 consecutive, safely hit-in games as a feat of longevity). He was a master tactician who encouraged cultural pursuits, and all the churches were built during his era or shortly thereafter. He is credited with the development of the Moldavian style, which is a blending of rough hewn, by-hand building techniques (that were at the same time structurally primitive and colorfully folksy) with the far more sophisticated architectural concepts of the southern Byzantine and the European Gothic. The frescoes on the church walls served the dual purposes of being a showcase for the area's unified cultural expression and a schoolroom, teaching history and religion to a predominantly illiterate constituency. These priceless frescoes have been preserved outside although exposed to the elements for almost 500 years. Their colors are so rich and true that the blue on the sides of the Voronet Church has been give a name of its own, Voronet blue. Though the art world has many times attempted to copy it, this blue has never been accurately duplicated in its authentic richness.

It's best to plan your tour with the Romanian Tourist Board in Bucharest where you can arrange to hire an English-speaking guide, if you like, or just get a good road map of Bukovina and wander on your own.

SUCEAVA: This town of 50,000 is the major hub of the area and the jumping-off point for any tour of the monasteries. Suceava is 270 miles (432 km) from Bucharest and you can cover the distance in 1 hour by plane or 6 hours by train (you can also arrange for a car and driver in Bucharest), or you can drive the distance yourself in a day. This was the seat of Moldavian power from 1388 to 1564 and you can still see the vestiges of the medieval citadel — which was often attacked but never conquered, not even by the Ottoman armies commanded by Mohammed II after they overran Constantinople.

There are several interesting churches in town but since the rest of the route is predominantly architectural, your time here would be better spent browsing the more secular folkwares — mostly spin-offs of the handmade fabrics and local pottery industries — that Bukovina is famous for. In the *Princely Inn* you'll find the Folk Art Museum, which houses a restoration of the interior of an authentic peasant house, and exhibits of national costumes, dolls, masks, wedding regalia, and carpets.

The monasteries are spread out over the 56 miles (90 km) or so directly west of Suceava and if you want to make all five stops you'd better plan on a day out and a day back. If you want to spend less time make sure to route yourself carefully so that you don't get lost and find night falling in a town where nobody speaks a language you can understand and it takes you an hour to find out that there aren't any hotels in the vicinity. Driving northwest out of Suceava on Route 2, turn left at Milisăuti and you'll soon come to Arbore, the first of the famous churches.

ARBORE: This is the smallest and the simplest of the churches. Though the interior is only dimly lit, the outside walls are covered with frescoes that tell the story of the Genesis and also depict the lives of the saints. The predominant color here is green and there are five distinct shades of it that mix with reds, blues, and yellows. In the courtyard there are two stone slabs with fifteen even gouges that the artists used for holding and mixing their paints. The best-preserved works are on the western wall and the buttressing. Unlike most primitive wall painting there is an abundance of detailing here involving the use of perspective, animated figures, and literal facial expressions.

SUCEVITA: Continuing west from Arbore you hit the town of Solca and turn north through Clit to Marginea. From there it's only another 6 miles (9 km) west to Sucevita. The monastery here is surrounded by thick stone walls and guarded by five imposing towers. There are more frescoes here than at any of the other churches and they are everywhere, inside and out, except on the western wall where the painter fell off his scaffold and died. (Legend has it that the wall was left blank as a tribute to him.) In addition to the religious paintings there are also portraits of Sophocles, Plato, and Aristotle along with more Eastern images from the *Arabian Nights*. The village of Sucevita is one of the most picturesque in all of Romania — the houses' verandahs have carved wooden pillars, and townfolk dress in national costumes.

MOLDOVITA: About 18 miles (29 km) west of Sucevita on Route 17A you'll find the commune of Vatra Moldovitei in the shadow of the Rarău mountain. Moldovita has another large monastery in the center of the town. The paintings here have a less religious flavor. The most striking series is of the siege of Constantinople with detailing that outlines the entire city. There's a museum here where you can see engraved and painted furniture including Prince Petru Rares's black ornamental throne. The manicured grounds are neatly laid out with flagstone paths that run from fortification to castle to church.

If you continue south you'll come to the town of Cimpulung Moldovenesc where you might consider stopping the night before returning east to Suceava on the southern half of the route.

VORONET: Driving east along the Moldova River on Route 17 you pass through the towns of Vama, Moldidu, and Frasin, stopping at Gura Humorului (18 mi/30 km from Cimpulung) where you can go north to the Humor Monastery or south to the Voronet. The Voronet is the most famous and the oldest of the monasteries (1488) and was built by Stephen the Great himself. Called the Sistine Chapel of the East, the paintings here were the innovators of a style that took from the Byzantine art of the south and mixed with it a more Gothic flavor. The building itself is the most elegant of all these structures, more involved and animated with rows of repeating pilasters capped by round arches, crenolated friezes, and round windows. The famous blue is breathtaking and the paintings, especially those of the Last Judgment, are simultaneously humane and barbaric with pretty women, musicians, and people being torn apart by wild beasts.

HUMOR: Less than 4 miles (6 km) north of Gura Humorului, the Humor Monastery is the last of the churches. It was built in 1530 and is unique in that it has a large open verandah, arched on three sides. It's also interesting to note that in one of the frescoes here the devil is portrayed as a woman. From here it's only another 22 miles (35 km) back to Suceava on Route 17.

BEST EN ROUTE

Expect to pay anywhere between $50 and $65 (and up) per night for a double in hotels we've listed as expensive, between $25 and $35 for those in the moderate category, and under $25 for those listed as inexpensive. Meals are a much better deal. Most restaurants charge about $12 for even the most lavish, three-course extravaganza for two. Of course, you can still feed yourself in Romania, stand-up style, with good, nourishing stuff for under $4 for two. Prices do not include wine, tips, or drinks.

SUCEAVA

Arcasul – You might be a little wary of a place that brags about its parking lot, but if you've just driven 8 hours from Bucharest, you'll find the *Arcasul* is just what the doctor ordered. Besides comfortable rooms with big, soft beds, it's also got a bar and a good restaurant. Mihai Viteazul Str. 4–6 (phone: 1-0944). Moderate.

Căprioara Restaurant – Just outside of town in the Adîncata forest you'll find the rustic *Căprioara Chalet*. Beautiful surroundings for some good Moldavian fare of strong goulashes and brandy to wash everything down. 5 miles from Suceava. Moderate.

SUCEVITA

Sucevita – Close to the monastery, this first-class inn has a restaurant that's small but has great food. The people will make you feel like you are Prince Stephen's long lost brother-in-law. Moderate.

The Black Sea Coast

The Romanian coastline on the Black Sea stretches for about 150 miles from the Danube delta at the Russian border all the way south to the Bulgarian frontier. Roughly 165 miles (266 km) east of Bucharest, this area can be reached by plane in about half an hour or by train or car in about 3 hours. (You ferry across the Danube at the midpoint in the trip.) Sandy beaches and fancy resorts line the coast; the unpolluted and tideless sea assures delightful swimming. And should you tire of toasting yourself on the Black Sea's strands, you can drive into Constanta for a shot of civilization or cruise into the Danube Delta for a whiff of wilderness.

CONSTANTA: Romania's main port city occupies the site of the ancient citadel, Tomis, founded by Greek merchants during the sixth century BC. The city is a mix of the early Greek, the Roman (Ovid was exiled here and there's a square named after him with a pensive statue of the famous poet), and the Eastern Byzantine (there's a mosque here with an Arabian mosaic dome and a lighthouse-like minaret). Part of the sand here is flanked by a hedge and tree line that combines with the ornate facades of the older buildings to give this resort an older flavor.

THE DANUBE DELTA: The 2,500-year-old town of Tulcea is 77 miles (123 km) north of Constanta on Route 22, where the Danube trisects and fans into its delta. The Greeks called the city Aegyssus and the Danube Delta Museum chronicles their coming and going. The town is now the main departure point for tourists who want to take river cruises into the delta to see the nature preserve. The land is wildly beautiful here: marshes crisscrossed by canals and brooks; islands bristling with rushes and reeds; clumps of trees sheltering otters, foxes, wildcats, and boars. During migratory periods, over 300 species of birds nest in the delta.

BEST EN ROUTE

The hotel and restaurants listed below are moderately priced, that is, accommodations will probably run about $30 per night, dinner, about $12.

CONSTANTA

Continental – An adequate downtown hotel that offers a private bath, telephone, and TV in every room. Bd. Republicii 20 (phone: 1-5660).

Casa Cu Lei – This restaurant is an architectural monument, and each of its dining rooms has a different structural design — Brancovan (a Romanian subdivision), Venetian, and Spanish. It's worth having a meal here simply for the atmosphere. Dianei Str. 6.

Cazino – An ornate restaurant on the sea wall (you can't miss it) with huge, round, arched windows, an eating terrace on a promontory stretching out over the water, and fine food.

Exploring San Marino

Every year thousands of tourists discover the spectacular beauty and quaint charm of San Marino. This oldest and smallest republic in the world lies 11 miles (18 km) from the Adriatic coast of north central Italy. With a population of 21,500 and an area of 23 square miles, San Marino borders the regions of Emilia Romagna to the north and the Marches to the south.

As you travel southwest toward the republic from the coastal town of Rimini, the dominant feature of San Marino dramatically comes into view: Mount Titanus, at a height of 2,475 feet, with its three towering peaks. The mountain and surrounding hills are the territory of San Marino, its towns consisting of the capital of the same name and eight smaller villages or "castles." The climate is temperate with summer temperatures that rarely exceed 80°F (26°C).

The city of San Marino, on top of Mt. Titanus, offers a vast and varied panorama, overlooking the Apennines to the south, expansive plains and hills to the north, and the brilliant blue Adriatic to the east. On a clear day you can catch a glimpse of the Yugoslav coast, 156 miles away.

Inside the city are interesting historical sites and colorful remnants of the republic's long past. The best local tourist map can be obtained from the Consulate General of San Marino, 400 Madison Ave., New York, NY 10017 (phone: 212-753-1300). You can find a less-detailed version of this map in the Michelin green guide to Italy.

San Marino dates back almost 1700 years to the arrival of a Christian stonecutter named Marinus. Fleeing the religious persecution of the Roman Emperor Diocletian, Marinus sought out the secluded safety of Mt. Titanus. Here he built a chapel, and, with a companion named Leo, began a saintly life. Other Christians soon followed him, giving rise to a community founded in freedom. San Marino has struggled ever since to maintain its freedom and in recent years has maintained political neutrality. The republic extends protection to refugees from all over the world. Sadly, San Marino was bombed during World War II, despite its proclaimed neutrality.

Today its economy is based on industry, tourism, and some farming. Coining its own money and supporting an army, the republic also obtains revenue from the sale of postage stamps, which have considerable philatelic value.

San Marino is accessible by bus, car, and even helicopter. The year-round bus service from Rimini leaves frequently from the Piazza Giulio Cesare and arrives at the Stazione Autobus di Linea. In summer a helicopter service connects Rimini with Borgo Maggiore, a market town one mile from the capital. From there, you can reach San Marino via a dramatic cable lift ride. The nearest airports are at Miramare di Rimini (9 mi/14 km away), and Forlì (38 mi/60 km away). The nearest train station is in Rimini. Travel by car is scenic on the four-lane highway from Rimini, though you can also reach the border along other well-paved but more sinuous routes. (The best road map for driving in the area is the Michelin map of Italy and Switzerland.)

The border is marked by a banner proclaiming, in Italian, a "Welcome to the Ancient Land of Liberty." A passport is not needed to enter, and there is no customs control, despite the customs station.

Within minutes you are in Serravalle, the most populated suburb. Here you see evidence of industrial growth alongside one of the country's oldest and best-kept castles. Since the bestowal of Serravalle to San Marino in 1463, the republic's territory has not been increased by a single inch. Not even Napoleon's offer to extend its borders in 1797 was accepted. Since 1963 Serravalle's town hall has been the site of the International Competition of Extemporary Art.

Continuing along the winding road, you will see Domagnano, another of San Marino's eight "castles," to the left before arriving at Borgo Maggiore.

BORGO MAGGIORE: A market town established in the twelfth century, and worth a stop. Originally known as Mercatale, this town has held a market every Wednesday since 1244. The Piazza Anita Garibaldi, so named in honor of the brief stay of the hero's wife, remains practically unchanged. The town's medieval appearance contrasts sharply with the modern Sanctuary of the Blessed Virgin of Consolation.

From Borgo Maggiore you can reach San Marino by foot along the shortcut called the Costa, by car, or by cable lift.

SAN MARINO: Proceeding along the highway, you enter the city through St. Francis' Gate, begun in the fourth century as a monastery door. To the side you will see the convent and church of St. Francis — founded in 1361, this is the oldest and most artistic in the country. Note the fourteenth-century windows. The cloister houses a museum and art gallery.

From this point San Marino can be toured most enjoyably on foot. The view from the peaks is well worth the walk, and you can begin your ascent along the Via Antonio Orafo.

A worthwhile stop is the nearby Valloni Palace on Via Giosuè Carducci, off the Piazzetta del Titano. Here are found the state archives with documents dating from 885, as well as the government library and museum (in which you will find paintings), the Garibaldi Museum, and archaeological items. Via Carducci ends with the Porta della Rupe, the gate through which you will enter the city if you take the shortcut from Borgo Maggiore. To continue your ascent, return to the Piazzetta where you might want to stop and enjoy the displays of colorful earthenware for which San Marino is known.

It is a short walk up the hill to Piazza Garibaldi and the government stamp office.

Leading off to the right is Via Melchiorre Delfico, the heart of the Jewish community, whose presence is documented as far back as the fourteenth century.

Continue along the Via XXV Marzo to the Piazza della Libertà, the largest and most elegant of San Marino's squares. You are only a few steps from the mountain shelf and a spectacular view. The statue in the middle of the square is a nineteenth-century statue of liberty. If you're hungry, try *La Taverna,* where the decor is rustic, but the food is good. Or maybe you'd just like to relax at one of the outdoor tables while you sip some excellent local Moscato or San Giovese wine.

When you're ready to move on, stroll over to the Gothic-style Government Palace dominating the square. You might want to arrive in time for the changing of the guards; you can get information on the time from the Tourist Office on nearby Via Bellucci.

The Government Palace houses many works of art as well as symbols of the republic's long past, including a bust of Abraham Lincoln. It is also in this palace that the government bodies meet.

Continue on Via Bellucci to a small, nameless street that leads you along a charming path to the Basilica of San Marino.

Built in neoclassic style, the basilica houses commemorations of several significant historical figures, including the founding saint whose mortal remains are buried under the altar.

From the Basilica, follow the alleyways through the oldest quarter of the city to the first of the three castles, or "feathers" as they are poetically called. This castle, known as the Rocca or Guaita, dates back to the eleventh century. The caves below house a prison still in use today. Enjoy the splendid view!

The Rocca is joined by a watch path to the second castle, the Fratta or Cesta, on the highest point of Mt. Titanus. The fifth-century pentagonal tower houses the San Marino Museum of Firearms.

Continue along the path through the violets and sea breezes to the third tower, the Montale. This narrow, graceful structure goes back to the twelfth century. Inside is housed another prison, 25 feet deep.

From the Montale you begin to come back down the slope passing the Kursaal, or Congress Palace, a modern building in which the contemporary International Biennial Painting Exhibition is held.

Turn back toward the city following Via Lungomonte XXVIII Luglio. You will note the modern buildings and, just up the hill, tennis facilities, all evidence of a modern age in this most ancient of states.

You can see San Marino at its traditional best during its colorful holidays. On the first of each April and October, the ornate ceremony of investiture of the newly elected captains regent is held. Each year, on September 3, in celebration of Saint's Day and the founding of the republic, the crossbow competition is held, complete with Renaissance costumes. Another historic holiday is June 4.

BEST EN ROUTE

Expect to pay $40 or more per night for a double room in hotels rated as expensive; $30 to $40 in those listed as moderate; and under $30 in inexpensive hotels. A meal for two will cost between $20 and $40 at *Ristorante Diamond*.

SAN MARINO

Grand Hotel San Marino – The most comfortable hotel in San Marino, this place also offers a beautiful view of the Apennines. It has 54 rooms, each with private shower or bath, and garage. Closed from December to February. Via Lungomonte (phone: 99-24-00). Expensive to moderate.

Hotel Titano – A very pleasant hotel with a terrace restaurant looking out on the mountains. It has 54 rooms, nearly all with private bath or shower. Closed December to February. Via XXV Marzo (phone: 99-10-07). Moderate.

Hotel Tre Penne – A simple hotel with 17 rooms, half with private bath or shower. Closed January and February. Via G. Simone delle Penne (phone: 99-24-37). Inexpensive.

La Grotta – A charming little hotel with 14 rooms, all with private bath, and a pleasant restaurant. Via M. Delfico (991-214). Inexpensive.

Ristorante Diamond – The best restaurant in the town — also has several rooms for guests, each with private shower or bath. The building is quite unusual in that it's been dug out of rock. Closed December to February. Via XXV Marzo (phone: 99-10-03). Moderate.

Exploring the Soviet Union

The Soviet Union is the Communist Revolution and the incredible beauty of Russian churches and religious icons. It is the music of Peter Ilyich Tchaikovsky and Nikolai Rimsky-Korsakov, space exploration, and the art treasures of the Hermitage. It is Stalin's purges, vodka and caviar, a *troika* ride across the snow in bitter cold, and the warmth of a family gathering around the samovar. It is a parade of intellectual and religious dissidents, the "Song of the Volga Boatman," the voices of Leo Tolstoy and Fyodor Dostoyevsky, and the Kremlin bells ringing out across Red Square. It is borscht and ballet, balalaikas and bureaucracy.

The Union of Soviet Socialist Republics (USSR) is the world's largest country. It stretches some 6,800 miles (10,880 km) from the Baltic Sea in the west to the Bering Strait, which separates it from Alaska, in the east, and extends north-south nearly 3,000 miles (4,800 km.). Its 8.65 million square miles represent more than one sixth of the earth's total land mass, covering the eastern half of Europe and the northern third of Asia. Winters can be long and severe, and the short growing season and insufficient rainfall have hindered agricultural development.

This vast country comprises 15 separate union republics, and its quarter-billion people represent more than 100 ethnic groups — although Russians, Ukrainians, and Belorussians make up about half the total. Russian is the official language, but the use of local minority languages is encouraged.

The so-called European part of the USSR, ranging from the country's western borders to the Ural Mountains, is the area of densest population and the area most frequented by tourists. We also have included the several southern countries of the Transcaucasus between the Baltic and Caspian seas, which, though less often visited, offer a most interesting look at a section of the USSR influenced more by the Middle East than Europe.

The tensions between west and east were important in shaping the history of this country, which from the ninth century to 1922 was known as Russia.

The eastern Slavic tribes who lived in this area from earliest times were relatively peaceful, but were preyed upon often by Asian and Germanic tribes. In the ninth century the Viking Varangians were invited by the Novgorod Republic to come and restore order; their reign lasted until the seventeenth century. Meanwhile, Orthodox religion, adopted from the Byzantine Empire, was introduced in Kievan Russia, and was to remain a dominant theme of Russian life until the Bolshevik Revolution proclaimed official atheism in this century.

The Tatar invasions began in the thirteenth century. Russia was conquered and held in bondage for some 250 years until the State of Muscovy became strong enough, under Ivan the Great, to break the Mongol stranglehold. It was during the Tatar period that the institution of serfdom took hold.

Sixteenth-century Russian history was dominated by Ivan the Terrible who built a powerful united state, but also imposed a reign of terror. A period of strife and upheaval followed his death. Then Michael Romanov, the first of the dynasty that would rule Russia for over 300 years, was elected czar. Peter the Great, the first powerful Romanov, came to the throne at the end of the seventeenth century. He introduced Western customs, culture, and technical achievements that transformed his country from a backward principality to a powerful empire. But neither he nor Catherine the Great, widow of his grandson and the next powerful Russian ruler, dealt with the system of serfdom that enslaved tens of thousands of Russian peasants. Russia's most famous serf rebellion, the Pugachev revolt, occurred during her reign.

In the wake of the French Revolution and the Napoleonic wars, a wave of liberalism spread over Europe, but the czars of imperial Russia continued to run their country like a private estate. When Czar Alexander I died in 1825, there was an abortive revolution known as the Decembrist uprising, which, although it was crushed, became a symbol for liberals, radicals, and revolutionaries for the remainder of the century. After Russia was defeated by the French and British in the Crimean War, Czar Alexander II found it practical to issue a proclamation freeing the serfs, but the evils of the system continued. When the czar was killed by a terrorist's bomb in 1881, any gains that had accrued to the peasants were lost and a reactionary attitude had set in that would dominate the remaining years of Russian czardom.

Still, the nineteenth century had been an extraordinary one for the arts in Russia. Literature flourished, beginning with Alexander Pushkin, and including Nikolai Gogol, Ivan Turgenev, Dostoyevsky, and Tolstoy. In music, Russia produced Tchaikovsky, Modest Moussorgsky, Alexander Borodin, and Rimsky-Korsakov. Toward the end of the century, there was a flowering of the dramatic arts with the plays of Anton Chekhov and the staging of Konstantin Stanislavsky. And by the early twentieth century, Russia had become preeminent in ballet.

At the turn of the century, however, the conditions of the peasants deteriorated further in the wake of a staggering depression and Russia's defeat in the Russo-Japanese War. When a peaceful group of workers and their families tried to petition the czar for relief, the militia opened fire on them. This massacre, known as Bloody Sunday, was the first act of violence in the 1905 Revolution, which led to the establishment of a more democratic form of constitutional monarchy. However, Russia's entry into World War I imposed further hardships on the country. In March 1917, a bourgeois democratic revolution brought down the entire structure of czardom, and a provisional government was formed. Then, on November 7, the Bolsheviks, V.I. Lenin's Communist Party, replaced the provisional government with the first Soviet state. A full-scale civil war raged until 1922, when the Red Army emerged victorious and Russia became the Union of Soviet Socialist Republics.

After Lenin died, the Soviet leadership passed to Joseph Stalin, and the country moved into a period of rapid industrialization and collectivization of agriculture. Stalin was a ruthless leader in absolute control of the Communist Party. When he purged the party of those he considered unworthy of membership, they were not merely expelled; they were executed.

Economic development was interrupted by World War II, in which the Soviet Union was allied with Britain, France, and the United States. The people of the Soviet Union suffered extraordinary losses during the war. Huge areas of the country were destroyed, and some 20 million soldiers and civilians were killed. Following the war, Soviet power extended into neighboring countries of Eastern Europe, and by 1946, the Cold War between the Soviet states and the western powers was a fact of life.

After Stalin's death, his excesses were denounced by Nikita Khrushchev, who, as premier, preached peaceful coexistence with the West. But his tenure also saw the widening of an ideological rift between the USSR and mainland China, which lessened Soviet influence in some parts of the world. Khrushchev retired into obscurity in 1964. He was succeeded by Leonid Brezhnev who has presided over a period of détente with the West.

The Soviet Union is different things to different people. In truth, it is neither a workers' paradise nor an authoritarian land of automatons. Where it fits on such a continuum is something for individual assessment. But for the tourist willing to set preconceptions aside for the duration, this big important country has much to offer. It has a splendid cultural history and an impressive record of modern technical and scientific achievement.

Traveling in the quiet countryside provides the perfect opportunity to meet and get to know people. A surprisingly high percentage of Soviet citizens speak English, German, or French. For the most part, they will be proud of their country and interested in yours. You may learn more about the Soviet Union from such personal encounters than from any other aspect of your trip.

The following routes have been designed to introduce you to some of the interesting places in the European part of the USSR, and to permit you to experience the cultures of several different ethnic groups. The first route, down the mighty Volga River from Kazan to Rostov-on-Don, provides a window on the history of Russia. The second route is actually an exploration of two of the Soviet Union's most important cities — Kiev and Odessa — which introduces you to the Ukrainian culture. For rest and relaxation, we have provided a tour of Black Sea resorts. This route takes you from Yalta in the Crimea along the eastern shore to Sukhumi in Soviet Georgia. Our last tour from Batumi on the Black Sea coast through snow-peaked Caucasus Mountains to Ordzhonikidze will acquaint you with the several nationality groups in Georgia.

The Volga

The Volga is a river the size and strength of Russia itself, a waterway that crosses a continent, a river the Russians call "mother." Tourists who travel its route by steamer come closer to feeling the spirit of the Russians. The timeless atmosphere of quaint rural villages and the old world is juxtaposed with the modern technology of hydroelectric installations and automobile plants. The Volga is a mighty river: 2,300 miles long, from Volgoverkhvoye northwest of Moscow to Astrakhan, a delta city on the Caspian Sea.

Since earliest times, the Volga has carried Finns, Slavs, Turks, Mongols, and Tatars; Jews, Christians, and Moslems, all seeking trade and conquest. In 1552, Ivan the Terrible opened the Volga to the Russians by defeating the Kazan Tatars. The most recent conflict over the Volga came from Hitler and the German army. During the months between August 1942 and February 1943, the Nazis ravaged Stalingrad (now Volgograd) in an unsuccessful attempt to subdue Russia and reach the oil-rich Caspian.

Today, the Volga region hosts thousands of tourists from around the world each year. This river route takes you from Yaroslavl to Kazan, Ulyanovsk, Volgograd, and Rostov-on-Don, 900 miles (1,440 km) to the south. You can reach Kazan by plane, train, or car. Intourist can arrange the Volga River cruise for you. The entire Kazan to Rostov-on-Don trip takes 11 days, but you may select a shorter itinerary. Cruise boats provide complete accommodations, including meals and lodging.

KAZAN: The capital of the Tatar Autonomous Republic is also the cultural center of the Tatars (or Tartars), one of the many nationalities of the USSR. The city dates from the fifteenth century. It was the center of a typical medieval Moslem state with many internal conflicts, as well as struggles with the Russians. In 1552, Czar Ivan the Terrible and the Russian army captured Kazan. Today, the city is half Russian and half Tatar.

A good place to begin a tour of the city is the Kazan Kremlin (Pervomaiskaya pl.), which dates from the fifteenth and sixteenth centuries. The Kremlin, near where the Kazanka River enters the Volga, is an architectural monument with marvelous towers and churches. There is an impressive panorama of the Kremlin from the Spassky (Spasskaya) Tower. Across the square from the Spassky Tower is the Tatar State Museum with a good collection of information about the Volga region. Near Lake Kazan there are two imposing eighteenth-century mosques: Mardzhani, open for services (ul. Nasiri 17) and Apanayevskaya (ul. Nasiri 29).

During the nineteenth century, the University of Kazan (ul. Lenina 18) was a center of liberal ideas in eastern Russia. V.I. Lenin-Ulyanov was expelled from law school here in 1887 for taking part in student riots. Today there is a statue of Lenin as a student in front of the university. There is also a Lenin Monument in Svodbody pl., the main square of Kazan.

An important collecting and processing point for Russian furs, Kazan is a major rail junction and one of the largest industrial centers in the Volga basin.

The main shopping center is ul. Bauman. Musa Dzhalil Opera and Ballet Theater is in Svodbody pl. and the puppet theater is at ul. Lukovskova 21. You can relax in Gorky Park on ul. Ershova or at the zoo and botanical gardens, ul. Taktasha 112.

En Route from Kazan – By boat, the trip to Ulyanovsk takes about 12 hours. The boat passes through the Kuybyshev Reservoir and valleys, where, depending on the season, you may see fruit trees in bloom or fields of wheat, sunflowers, or potatoes. Coriander is grown and processed in one of these valleys. Approaching Ulyanovsk, you pass the popular bathing beach on Paltsensky Island, which can be reached by boat from Ulyanovsk.

ULYANOVSK: This small city on a high hill on the Volga-Sviyaga watershed was called Simbirsk until 1924, when it was renamed for its most famous son: Vladimir Ilich Ulyanov, known to the world as V.I. Lenin. Lenin was born here on April 22, 1870.

The Lenin Museum (ul. Lenina 48), which contains mementos of Lenin's youth, is in the house where the family lived in the 1880s before Lenin left to attend the University of Kazan. Nearby a huge Lenin Memorial Complex, including the house in which he was born, his grammar school, and other buildings associated with his life, was opened in 1970 to commemorate the 100th anniversary of Lenin's birth. A statue of Lenin as a schoolboy is in front of the railway station.

There are a number of interesting old, low, wooden houses along the narrow streets of the city. The main shopping street is ul. Goncharov.

En Route from Ulyanovsk – The journey to Volgograd takes about 36 hours by boat, but is full of fascinating sights. Shortly after leaving Ulyanovsk, you pass Vinnovskaya Grove, a popular recreation park.

If you made the river journey in the mid-60s and come back today, you will be struck by how much the Volga bears witness to Soviet progress. The former town of Stavropol, south of the Kuibyshev Reservoir and Hydroelectric Plant, has become the new city of Togliatti. This new industrial center was renamed for a former leader of the Italian Communist Party when the Volga Automobile Factory was built and equipped in cooperation with the Italian firm, Fiat. Excursions to Togliatti can be made by hydrofoil from Ulyanovsk. Nearby you can see the Lenin Hydropower Works.

Now the Volga winds around the Zhiguli Mountains. Forests and small settlements of Russian vacation homes, *dachas,* line the banks.

VOLGOGRAD: Historically, this city has been important as a southern outpost to protect Russia from invasions. It was founded in the sixteenth century as the fortress town of Tsaritsyn to guard the Volga route.

The city made its greatest mark on history during the period in which it was called Stalingrad (1925–1961) by handing the German army one of its most significant defeats of World War II. Stalingraders fought the Nazis house to house for a full year until Soviet troops could encircle and defeat them. The Victory Monument to the heroism of Stalingrad's people, on the ancient Mamaev Kurgen hill, is one of the most moving war monuments ever built: Scenes of battle are depicted on the steps leading up from Lenin Prospekt. An eternal flame burns in the circular Hall of Military Glory. Slogans of the street-fighters are carved into the walls, and the names of all the war dead are inscribed on mosaic plaques.

Volgograd stretches along the river for 43 miles. It is the administrative and economic center of the lower Volga region.

There is a planetarium on ul. Yuri Gagarin, a circus on ul. Volodarsky, a musical comedy theater on the Central Quay, and a puppet theater at Lenin Prospekt 15. Shopping is concentrated in the area around the city's center, Fallen Fighters Square (Pavshikh Bortsov pl.) and the Alleya Geroyev.

En Route from Volgograd – The boat goes west here through the canal connecting the Volga with the River Don.

To reach the Don, your boat passes through a number of locks and the Tsimlyansk Reservoir, which feeds the canal and irrigates the steppe.

ROSTOV-ON-DON (Rostov-na-Dony): If you have come the entire way from Kazan, you may notice the difference in the appearance of this southern city, the gateway to the Caucasus. The area of Rostov-on-Don beyond the central Theater Square (Teatralnyi pl.) was once the Armenian town of Nakhichevani, and the houses here are typically low, old Armenian dwellings.

Rostov-on-Don became a city in 1797, having grown up around a fortress built to defend Russia from the Turks. Its importance as a port city and trade center was enhanced by the completion of the Volga-Don Canal in 1952.

Shopping and museums are along ul. Engelsa. There are four theaters, a racecourse, a regional philharmonic orchestra, a bathing beach, a sports stadium, and several parks here.

Some 42 miles (67 km) to the east in the industrial town of Taganrog on the Axov Sea, you can visit the Chekhov Museum in the house where the great Russian writer and dramatist was born.

Moscow is about 2 hours by plane from Rostov-on-Don, if you are at the end of your tour. On the other hand, it is a good starting place for a tour of the Black Sea coast. You can also return to Moscow by way of Kiev.

BEST EN ROUTE

Hotel prices throughout the USSR are related to your travel plan, the season, and the class of accommodations you choose, rather than the individual hotels. For Western tourists, lodging is at least as expensive here as in major American cities. Economy options do not usually exist, except for camping.

Restaurants generally open in late morning and close by midnight. Reservations are not usually necessary and prices are relatively low, compared with costs for similar meals in the US.

The cuisine of the Volga region is wholesome and hearty. You might begin your meal with an array of hot and cold appetizers called *zakusky*. Baked fish stuffed with buckwheat groats, and *solyanka*, a fish stew made tart with salted cucumbers and olives, is a delicious entrée.

KAZAN

Kazan Hotel and Restaurant – With Intourist office, ul. Bauman 9 (phone: 2-0091).
Tatarstan Hotel and Restaurant – ul. Bauman 86 (phone: 2-4324).
Parus Restaurant – On a houseboat near Lenin Bridge (Lenina Most).
Vostok Restaurant – ul. Kuybysheva 13.
Mayak Restaurant – ul. Dekabristov 185.

ULYANOVSK

Venets Hotel and Restaurant – With Intourist office, ul. Sovietskaya 15 (phone: 9-4320).
Volga Hotel and Restaurant – ul. Goncharov (phone: 1-4577).

VOLGOGRAD

Volgograd Hotel and Restaurant – Pavshikh Bortsov pl. (phone: 37-72).
Intourist Hotel and Restaurant – ul. Mir, 14 (phone: 33-45-53).
Leto Restaurant – Open during the summer months in the City Garden.
Mayak Restaurant – On the Volga Embankment.

ROSTOV-ON-DON

Moskovskaya Hotel – With Intourist office, ul. Engelsa 62 (phone: 6-5391).
Rostov Hotel – Budyonovsky Prospekt 59 (phone: 6-0198).
Tsentrainy Restaurant – ul. Engelsa 36.
Volgodon Restaurant – ul. Beregovaya 31.
Teatralny Restaurant – Open in summer; in Oktyabrskoi Revolutsii Park.

Kiev and Odessa

Two of the most important cities in the USSR are located in the Ukrainian Soviet Socialist Republic, which lies between Russia, to the east, and the satellite countries of Poland, Czechoslovakia, Hungary, and Bulgaria, to the west. Kiev is the third-largest city in the USSR, and Odessa, on the Baltic Sea, is one of its major ports.

The Ukraine slopes down from the Carpathian Mountains in the west to rolling hills with beautiful oak and beech forests, and broad plains where the soil is rich and black. It is well developed agriculturally, as well as industrially, and is sometimes referred to as the "breadbasket" of the USSR.

Although the sentiment for Ukrainian nationalism has remained strong, Ukrainians have long been considered junior partners in governing the USSR. Leonid Brezhnev, the General Secretary of the Soviet Communist Party, was born here and held important party posts in the Ukraine earlier in his career. Khrushchev, Russian by birth, was a party official here and carried out Stalin's purges in the Ukraine.

Kiev is some 532 miles (851 km) southwest of Moscow. It can be reached by plane, train, or road. Odessa, almost due south of Kiev — about 303 miles (485 km) — is also linked by rail, air, and road, and can be reached by sea. You can sail between Kiev and Odessa on the Dnieper River.

KIEV: The capital and cultural center of the Ukraine is a picturesque city that grew up on a series of wooded hills overlooking the Dnieper. Poplar and chestnut trees along the streets soften the effect of the rather undistinguished buildings built after World War II. Parks and gardens make up nearly 60% of Kiev.

Before the Golden Horde, led by a successor of Ghengis Khan, destroyed the city in 1240, Kiev had been the leading East Slav principality. Christianity had been introduced to Russia through Kiev in the tenth century. After 300 years of repeated invasion by Lithuanians, Crimean Tatars, and Poles, the Ukraine was united with Russia in 1654. Kiev suffered severely during World War II; only one fifth of its prewar population was found alive when Kiev was liberated from the Nazis in 1943.

The oldest monument in the city is the Golden Gate (Zolotye Vorota), built in 1037 as the main entrance to the city at Bolshaya Podvalnaya and Volodimirska streets. St. Sophia Cathedral (Sofinsky Sabor) with its 13 cupolas and impressive interior frescoes and mosaics is nearby at ul. Volodimirska 24. It is now a state museum.

One of the most fascinating places in Kiev is the Monastery of the Caves (Perchersakaya Lavra; ul. Sichneve Povstannya 211), which was founded in 1051 by two monks. This complex of churches, cathedrals, and monuments was built in and around a series of caves on the high right bank of the Dnieper. Mummified bodies of monks can be seen in the tombs of the Nearer Caves, also known as St. Anthony's Caves (Blizhshie Pechory). Just outside the monastery is the Church of the Redeemer of the Birchwood (Tserkov Spasa-na-Berestove), where Yuri Dolgaruki, founder of Moscow, and other princes of Kiev are buried.

Pushkin and Gogol are among the Russian writers who lived in Kiev for a time, and

Taras Shevchenko, the poet and artist looked upon as the father of the Ukrainian national literature, was born here. You may visit the house in which he was born (Shevchenko Lane 8a), and the Shevchenko Museum (Shevchenko Prospekt 12) houses his art and literary work. (A memorial park has been established where this great figure of Ukrainian romanticism is buried, about 92 miles (147 km) down river from Kiev near the town of Kanev. The trip can be made by boat.)

To sample the rich Ukrainian culture, visit the Museum of Ukrainian Art (ul. Kirova 29), which includes the work of Ukrainian artists from the fifteenth to nineteenth centuries, and Soviet Ukrainian artists. Examples of handiwork and folk art, such as the intricately painted eggs called *krashenki,* dating from the sixteenth to the twentieth centuries, are displayed in the Historical Museum (ul. Volodimirska 2).

Kiev is a wonderful city to explore. The park on Volodimirska provides a marvelous view of the river, and the promenade along the Dnieper is a wonderful place for a summer evening stroll. The city's most popular bathing beach, on Trukhaniv Island in the river, can be reached by a footbridge, Parkovyi Most. There are several theaters, a horse-racing track, a circus, and numerous parks. Shopping is concentrated near Kreshchatik Prospekt, but there also is an interesting outdoor market at ul. Vorovskov 17, and a large covered market, Bessarabka, on Shevchenko Prospekt.

Besides the usual forms of public transportation — trams, subway, buses, and trolleys — Kiev has a funicular railway connecting Vladimir's Hill Park (Volodimirska Girka) with the lower town.

ODESSA: Although a settlement and port had flourished here on the north shore of the Black Sea for centuries, Odessa itself is a relatively young city. It was built by order of Catherine the Great after the Russian army captured the entire region from the Turks in 1789. Its favorable location and special privileges granted by the czar enabled the city to quickly become one of the greatest ports in Russia.

The magnificent, wide, granite steps of the Potemkin Staircase, which lead up from the embankment, present an impressive entrance to the city for visitors arriving by sea. The staircase is named for the well-known battleship *Potemkin,* whose sailors mutinied, then stormed up the steps to join Odessa workers in an unsuccessful attempt at revolution in 1905. There are several monuments to the men of the *Potemkin* in the city.

Odessa withstood a 69-day siege by the Nazis during World War II. Later, along with Leningrad, Volgograd, and Sevastopol, Kiev was accorded the title of Hero City by the decree of the Praesidium of the Supreme Soviet. Intourist can arrange tours of the catacombs, hundreds of miles of caves in the area that served as hiding places for World War II partisans (as well as revolutionaries and criminals, at other times).

Primorsky Prospekt, at the top of the Potemkin Staircase, is a main street and popular seaside promenade; the heart of the city is October Revolution Square (Oktyabrskoi Revolutsii pl.). Poplars, chestnuts, and white acacia trees grow along the avenues.

The facade of the five-domed Assumption (Uspensky) Cathedral (Sovietskoi Armyiyi) is a combination of Russian and Byzantine styles. The Opera House (ul. Lastochkina 8) has an Italian Renaissance facade and resembles the Vienna opera house. You can trace the history of the people who have lived along the north coast of the Black Sea through exhibits at the Archaeological Museum (Kommunarov pl.).

For entertainment, there are several theaters, a concert hall, a circus, and a horse-racing track. There are several excellent bathing beaches, including one in Shevchenko Park, and numerous spas along the coast.

From Odessa, many tourists visit the Crimea and the resorts along the eastern coast of the Black Sea.

BEST EN ROUTE

As elsewhere in the Soviet Union, the price of hotel accommodations is related to the season, the class of accommodations you choose, and your travel plan, rather than to individual hotels. For Western tourists, lodging is at least as expensive here as in major American cities. Economy options usually do not exist, except perhaps for camping facilities.

Restaurants open in late morning and usually close by midnight. Reservations are not generally required and prices are relatively low, compared with what similar meals cost in the US.

You must, of course, try chicken Kiev in Kiev, though you will find it in Odessa as well. Beef stroganoff and various concoctions of ground meat mixtures, called *kotlety*, are good entrées, while *blini* — thin, rolled pancakes stuffed with cheese, meat, or vegetable fillings — make good snacks or entrées. The best tortes and sweetcakes in the USSR are baked in the Ukraine.

KIEV

Dnieper Hotel and Restaurant – ul. Kreschchatik 2 (phone: 26-65-69).
Intourist Hotel and Restaurant – ul. Lenina 26 (phone: 24-52-46).
Moskva Hotel and Restaurant – ul. October Revolution 4 (phone: 29-28-04).
Ukraina Hotel and Restaurant – Shevchenko Prospekt 5 (phone: 21-73-35).
Abkhazia Restaurant – ul. Kreschchatik 42.
Metro Restaurant – ul. Kreschchatik 19.
Dynamo Restaurant – ul. Kirova 3.

ODESSA

Odessa Hotel – Possibly the best hotel in the USSR. Primorsky Prospekt 11 (phone: 22-50-19).
Krasnaya Hotel – ul. Pushkinskaya 15 (phone: 22-72-20).
Yuzhny Restaurant – ul. Khalturin 12.
Ukraina Restaurant – ul. Karl Marx 12.

Georgia

Georgia, from the subtropical climes of its Black Sea coast to the snow-peaked Caucasus Mountains, is one of the most delightful and least explored areas of the USSR. In few other corners of the world are the trade and migration routes of the past better represented by the present than in the Georgian Soviet Socialist Republic.

Mountain and valley communities settled by various nationalities throughout the centuries cling tenaciously to their identities, resisting assimilation. These groups — Imeretians, Abkhazians, Svanetians, Kabards, Ossetians, Daghestanians, and others — speak dozens of different languages and dialects, in some cases unintelligible to their nearest neighbors. They are Moslem, Christian, and Jew, though their religion now is not emphasized. The predominant language of the region is Georgian; the official language is Russian.

This route takes you from Batumi on the Black Sea — only miles from Turkey — to Tbilisi, the capital of Georgia, and north through the highest points of the Caucasus Mountains to Ordzhonikidze. The route is only about 341 miles (546 km) long, but it leads through rugged mountains, narrow valleys, and over winding roads. The scenery, cuisine, and friendly people will more than compensate for the inconvenience of the terrain.

BATUMI: Magnolias, palms, and other subtropical trees grace this important resort and port city on the Black Sea close to the Turkish border. Situated along one of the best bays of the Black Sea, Batumi's beaches of sand and small pebbles attract sun-worshipers from April to November. Extension of an oil pipeline from Baku in the early part of this century made Batumi part of the oil export trade, increasing its importance as a port.

Batumi's location has led to its occupation at various times by Romans, Greeks, Byzantines, and Turks. For 300 years before it was placed under Russian authority in 1878, Batumi had been dominated by the Turks. During that time, the local population was forced to adopt Islam. The Muslim Georgians are called Ajars and Batumi is the capital of the Ajar (Atchar) Autonomous Republic.

You can still discern the Oriental and Moslem character of the city in parts of the old town, and the Mosque (ul. Chkalov 6) is open for services. The local museum (ul. Dzhinzaradze 4) has an interesting exhibition of national costumes; there are also a circus, an aquarium, and several theaters. The Summer Theater, built in the Georgian style in 1948, is in Primorsky Park, adjacent to a wide beach. Another pleasant green space is the 45-acre Young Pioneers' Park.

For shopping, there is a market and a department store on ul. Chavchavadze. The many small cafés throughout the city are good places to sample the mouthwatering Georgian cuisine.

En Route from Batumi – There's a good beach less than 4 miles (6 km) north of Batumi at Makhindzhauri. The name means "place of the maimed," which refers to the Georgian Christians who were tortured into accepting Islam by the Turks. A little farther along the coast is the Green Cape (Zelyoni Mys) resort; the botanical garden here is said to be the most beautiful in the USSR.

The route inland to Gori passes through a valley where collective farms cultivate tea and tangerines, and bamboo grows beside the road. The valley ends at Dioknisi, where you pass over a low range of mountains to Adigeni. A road to the north takes you to a mineral springs resort, Abastumani (4,255 feet). Continuing on the main road, you come to Akhaltsikhe (Ahalcihe), a town famous for an old fortress and its silver filigree. About 37 miles (60 km) farther east is Borzhomi, another warm springs resort. There's a sixth-century monastery here, and numerous spas and vacation homes in the area.

About 24 miles (38 km) to the southeast is a ski resort, Bakuriani (5,415 feet), but you'll need to make reservations well in advance if you plan to stop here.

Returning to the main road, you pass through Khashuri (Haøuri) and then Kareli, where you begin to see the high peaks of the Caucasus in the distance.

GORI: This is the town where Stalin was born in 1894. There are ruins of a twelfth-century fortress, Goris-Tsikhe, on a hill overlooking the town, but the town itself dates from the sixteenth century.

Gori was inhabited by refugee Armenians in the twelfth century, and later occupied by Turks, Georgians, and Persians, until it was taken by Russia in 1801. An earthquake in 1920 severely damaged the town.

On a hill above the right bank of the River Kura, opposite Gori, there is a sixteenth-century church dedicated to St. George, Goris-Dzhavri Monastery. According to legend, it was founded by Queen Tamara in thanksgiving to the saint for rescuing her favorite falcon.

En Route from Gori – A very poor road along the Kura River east of Gori leads to the ancient cave town of Uplis-Tsikhe (also known as Troglodite Town), which was inhabited before the time of Christ. The town was organized in tiers, and the houses, streets, and markets are distinguishable today. North of the town, by another very bad road, is the village of Didi Ateni, which has an important Georgian monument: the seventh-century Sioni Church, decorated with tenth-century frescoes.

Heading toward Tbilisi, the capital of Georgia, the scenery begins to change from lush, wooded slopes to barren, almost monotonous cliffs above the raging Kura.

TBILISI: There is a distinctly Mediterranean flavor to this city of olive-skinned Georgians, Azearbaijan peasants, Asian Kurds, and others. Food, drink, and celebration are integral parts of the spirit of Tbilisi and its million inhabitants. On the right bank of the Kura, since ancient times Tbilisi has been a key point on the trade routes from the Caspian to the Black Sea, and from Armenia across the Caucasus to Russia.

The city is bounded on the west by Mt. David (Mtatsminda Mountain), on the east by the Makhat Range, and on the south by the Sololax. It was built on a series of hills in the fifth century on the right bank of the river. This old part of town, or *stary gorod,* is a series of narrow, winding streets where the houses seem to hang from the hills. The Georgian word *tbili* means warm, and the city has long been known for its warm sulphur springs, some of which are still active along the banks of the river. You can visit some of the bathhouses in the old town. The oldest is the Erekle Bath (ul. Bannaya and ul. Akhundova).

There are a number of interesting churches in the city and the Georgian Art Museum (ul. Ketskhoveli 1) has an excellent collection of icons, frescoes, china, and Georgian paintings. The Georgian State Philharmonic Concert Hall is at Plekhanov Prospekt 123. This is the home of the Georgian national dance ensemble, which has won an international reputation, as well as the home of the State Symphony Orchestra and other musical groups. There are a number of other important theaters here, including the Georgian Puppet Theater (Rustaveli Prospekt 37).

Several farmers' markets selling fresh produce and, occasionally, crafts of the province dot the city. Rustaveli Prospekt is the main street and the place for shopping. *Tsitsinatella* (Rustaveli 23) is a hard-currency shop, and handicrafts are on sale at *Art Salon* (Rustaveli 19). The city's largest park is atop Mount David, 1187 feet above the town. You'll find the *Funicular Restaurant* on the top floor of a three-story house in the park.

Average temperatures here in July and August are well above 90°F (32°C).

MTSETA (MTSKHETA): A short distance north of Tbilisi is the cradle of Georgian culture — the ancient capital of Mtseta on the slopes of the holy Mt. Kartli. According to legend, the Sveti Tskhoveli Cathedral here is built on the spot where the robe that Christ had worn to his crucifixion was rediscovered in 328 AD. It supposedly had been brought here by a Jew who had won it when lots were drawn for Christ's garments. The present version of the cathedral is a perfect example of fifteenth-century Georgian architecture. This is also the city of St. Nina's good works and miracles, and the main church of the Samtavra Convent is dedicated to her. Near the convent is an ancient cemetery that was used from the Iron Age until the eleventh century.

En Route from Mtseta – The Georgian Military Highway north through the Caucasus to Ordzhonikidze wanders through some of the most beautiful landscape in the Soviet Union. The highway follows the Aragvi River through the villages of Natakhtari and Zhinvali where you can see the ruins of castles and watchtowers.

From Tzilkani, Mt. Kazbek begins to appear intermittently in the distance. After you pass through Ananuri, known for its sixteenth-century fortress, the road becomes more winding. Pasanauri, at the confluence of the Black Aragvi and the White Aragvi (3,335 feet), is an area of alpine meadows, wild game, and river trout. From Mleti, the road begins a steep ascent via sharp curves around what seem to be perpendicular rock walls. The views are spectacular as you approach Gudauri, where snow is often still deep in June. You reach your highest point at Krestovi Pass (7,700 feet), where avalanches are a problem at certain times of the year.

As you descend toward Ordzhonikidze, you pass through the town of Kazbegi in the shadow of Mt. Kazbek's snowy peak (16,545 feet). The road follows the Terek River down to Gveleti through the Daryal Gorge to Lars and Balta, and finally to Ordzhonikidze (2,345 feet), the capital of the North Ossetian Autonomous Republic.

ORDZHONIKIDZE (ORDŽONIKIDZE): Lime trees and nineteenth-century houses line the main street — Mir Prospekt — of this strategically located town, north of the snow-covered Caucasus Mountains. The town originally was called Vladikavkaz, which means "mistress of the Caucasus," but was renamed in 1931 in honor of Grigory Ordzhonikidze, a prominent Communist and statesman.

On both sides of the River Terek and protected by rocky cliffs, Ordzhonikidze is especially important because of its position on the Georgian Military Highway, which leads south through the mountains to Tbilisi. At the entrance to the highway, at Tbilisskoye Chaussee, there is a 79-foot granite obelisk in memory of the 17,000 Red Army soldiers who lost their lives in battles with the White Guard during the civil war of 1919.

Exhibitions at the local museums and performances at the Ossetian Music and Drama Theater (Naberezhnaya 18) will give you a good picture of Ossetian life. For typical food and a view of the city, try the *Mountain Eagle (Gorny Orel)* restaurant on the slopes of Mt. Lysaya about 7 miles (11 km) from town.

BEST EN ROUTE

Hotel prices have more relationship to the travel plan or class you opt for and the season, than they do with the hotel. Lodging for all Western tourists is at least as expensive in the USSR as in major American cities, and economy options usually do not exist, except when camping. Most restaurants open in late morning and close at 11 PM or midnight. Reservations are usually not necessary for restaurants along the route, and prices are relatively inexpensive.

The most famous Georgian dish is *shasklik:* skewered bits of meat — frequently lamb — marinated in pomegranate juice. A good snack or entrée is the unsweetened pastry filled with meat, cheese, or cabbage, called *porozhki. Kachapuri* is a delicious cheese-filled pie which varies a bit, according to local traditions within the region. A good baked egg, cheese, and meat dish is called *cheezhi-peezhi.* The favorable climate means that many fresh vegetables are available year-round. When available, caviar from the Caspian Sea and trout from Armenia are prized delicacies.

BATUMI

May Day Hotel – ul. Karl Marx 45 (phone: 9-7380).
Intourist Hotel – ul. Ninoshvili 11 (phone: 9-7331).

TBILISI

Iveria Hotel – With an Intourist office. ul. Inashvili 6 (phone: 99-70-89).
Intourist Hotel and Restaurant – Rustaveli Prospekt 7 (phone: 83-28-81).
Tbilisi Hotel and Restaurant – Rustaveli Prospekt 13 (phone: 99-07-98).

Aragvi Restaurant – Naberezhnaya.
Daryal Restaurant – Rustaveli Prospekt 22.

ORDZHONIKIDZE

Intourist Hotel – Mira Prospekt 19 (phone: 3-2552).
Kavkaz Hotel – ul. Vatutin 47 (phone: 3-4926).
Gorny Orel Restaurant – Mt. Lysaya, about 7 miles (11 km) from town.
Terek Restaurant – Mir Prospekt 32.
Otdykh Restaurant – In Hetagurov Park.

Black Sea Resorts

The seaside towns and holiday resorts along the Black Sea are almost perfect places to strike up acquaintances with Soviet citizens, who vacation here too. It's easy to begin a casual conversation on the beach or in the relaxed atmosphere of an outdoor café. Actually, vacationers here are an international lot. In addition, many foreigners come to take cures; the area is renowned for its mineral spas.

The resort towns of the Crimea and the eastern coast of the sparkling blue Black Sea are all the more beautiful because the Caucasus Mountains serve as their backdrop. The scenery varies from rocky cliffs to sloping foothills lush with subtropical vegetation, and rare and unusual plants flourish in the marvelous climate.

Cool water temperatures and the high salt content make swimming in the Black Sea an exhilarating experience, and most of the beaches are composed of pebbles and small stones. Nonetheless, many vacationers prefer Black Sea resorts to those of the Mediterranean, which is connected to the Black Sea by the Bosphorus. The climate along the Caucasian coast is similar to that of the French Riviera, which is why some people call this area the Soviet Riviera. Temperatures are a few degrees cooler on the Crimean coast.

A visit to the Black Sea is most enjoyable if made in a leisurely fashion, with stops at various resorts. The entire trip can be done by Black Sea steamer or by car, or in combination with the air service between Adler on the Caucasian coast and Simferopol in the Crimea.

YALTA: All passenger ships sailing to the Crimea and the Caucasus stop at Yalta, a charming resort town that lies in a natural amphitheater formed by mountains as high as 4,500 feet.

Yalta is best known to Westerners as the scene of the 1945 conference between US President Franklin D. Roosevelt, British Prime Minister Winston S. Churchill, and Soviet Premier Josef Stalin, during the last stages of World War II. The conference was held at Livadia, the former residence of the czars, a few miles east of Yalta.

One of the special attractions in Yalta is the Chekhov Museum (ul. Kirova 112) in the two-story, white house in which the great Russian writer lived during the last 6 years of his life. It was here that Chekhov wrote two of his most brilliant plays, *The Cherry Orchard* and *The Three Sisters.*

Another favorite tourist stop is the Wine Tasting Hall (ul. Litkins 1) where talks on Crimean wine production are followed with free samples of the product. The wine-making center of the Crimea is just northeast of the city at Massandra. Beyond Massandra, off the road to Simferopol, is the 80,000-acre Crimean Game Preserve. Guided tours can be arranged through the Intourist office at your hotel. The Nikitsky Botanical Garden, near the seashore east of Yalta, contains the world's largest rose garden with over 1,600 varieties.

Yalta was first mentioned in chronicles in the early twelfth century. Once a colony of Genoa, it was under Turkish domination for centuries until it became part of Russia at the end of the eighteenth century. Another hundred years later, it had become a popular resort. There are scores of sanatoriums along the coast, including dozens in Yalta itself. It is estimated that over a million people vacation in this area each year. The best bathing beach in the Crimea is Golden Beach (Zolotoi Plyazhm), southwest of Yalta between Livadia and Miskhor. Alupka, a bit farther to the southwest, is one of the most beautiful resort towns in the Crimea. Its Vorontsov Palace, surrounded by a 100-acre park here, was designed by Edward Blore, one of the architects of Buckingham Palace.

East from Yalta, you can visit Feodosiya, famous in the thirteenth century as a slave market town, and Kerch, an industrial center and fishing base on the Kerch Straits. There is a railroad from Kerch across the straits to the Caucasian coast. You can also travel to the Caucasian coast from here by boat.

En Route from Yalta – There are car ferries and passenger boats to take visitors from the Crimea to the Greater Sochi coast, and air connections between Simferopol and Adler, just south of Sochi. If you prefer, it is possible to drive around the Sea of Azov, from the Crimea to Zhdanov, Rostov-on-Don, and Krasnodar and pick up the coastal route at the port city of Novorossysk.

As you head south, the road passes between bays and beaches to the west and the foothills of the Caucasian Mountains on the east. The first village of note is Gelendzhik, one of the oldest settlements on the Black Sea coast. Burial monuments over 4,000 years old have been found in this area. The coast road gradually climbs to about 2,625 feet, then, after cutting through the Mikhailov Pass, descends to Archipo-Ossipovka at the mouth of the Vulcan River.

Tuapse, an important port that handles crude oil that is piped here from the northern side of the Caucasus, is the last good-sized town before entering Lazarevskoye, the northernmost district of greater Sochi. Ashei, a pleasant little seaside resort just north of the village of Lazarevskoye, is known for its excellent beaches and the nearby mountains which are popular with climbers.

The Memedoo Gorge in the Ashei range near Lazarevskoye has a number of small waterfalls and grottoes.

The village of Dagomyss, just north of Sochi, is well known as a terminus for hiking routes through the Caucasian State Preserve. From a park on the western slopes of Mt. Armyanka, there are stunning views of the Greater Sochi area, the sea, and the mountains.

SOCHI: This is the most important resort in the USSR. Sheltered by mountains, which seem to descend right into the sea, Sochi is favored by a climate similar to that of Nice or San Remo, and is considered the heart of the Soviet Riviera.

Although there was a fortress here in the mid-nineteenth century, the town didn't begin to grow until the area's potential as a health resort, because of its mineral springs, was recognized in 1893. By 1909, the first of the grand spa hotels had been opened; today there are nearly 60 and most of the 250,000 people who live in greater Sochi are employed in some facet of the health or holiday industry. About 2 million people visit greater Sochi each year.

Spectacular panoramas of the town, the sea, and the mountains are available from an observation tower atop Mt. Bolshoi Akhun, about 14 miles (22 km) from the center of Sochi. The viewing platform stands 2,155 feet above sea level, and there is a restaurant nearby. Bus 39 from the Riviera section of the city goes to the mountain-top.

The 25-acre Riviera Park, with its charming outdoor cafés, scores of sports grounds, and an open-air theater, is the center of Sochi life. Kurortny Prospekt, the main street, runs south from the park, paralleling the sea. A 114-foot spire with a star on top, on the roof of the main seaport building, provides an unusual landmark for boats miles at sea.

The public beaches are south of the center of the town.

Some of the sanatoriums that have been built on the hills and cliffs have funicular railways or elevators. One of the most beautiful of these is the Ordzhonikidze Sanatoria, which was built in Italian Renaissance style during the 1930s. The interior was decorated in traditional Russian style by local artists.

In addition to the beautiful mimosas, oleanders, magnolias, and palms that grow along Sochi's streets, there are specimen trees and shrubs from all over the world in the local Dendarium (Kurortny Prospekt 74).

Traces of prehistoric man have been found in some of the caves of the Caucasus. Two, Vorontsovskiye and Kudepstinskiye, are near Sochi, but they should only be visited with an experienced guide.

Other short excursions can be made to the Agur waterfalls near old Matsesta, to the yew and boxtree grove on the eastern side of Mt. Akhun in the Caucasian National Preserve, and to one of the large tea plantations in the area.

En Route from Sochi – About 13 miles (20 km) south of Sochi is the town of Khosta, famous for its health treatment centers and as a hiking station. Then comes Adler, where the central airport for the entire region is located. An extensive drainage system has helped turn Adler, once merely marshland, into a sunny, subtropical garden noted for its health spas and campgrounds.

As you leave the Krasnodar region and enter Abkhazia, an autonomous republic that is part of Soviet Georgia, you may sense differences in the language and culture. The first Abkhazian resort you encounter is Gagra where, thanks to its marvelous climate, roses bloom in winter. If you leave the coast road, heading northeast, you can visit Lake Ritsa, at 2,860 feet above sea level one of the most beautiful in the Caucasus. The drive, about 38 miles (60 km), takes you through a deep canyon and past forests of spruce, pine, and beech.

Back on the road south, the beaches become more sandy and less pebbly, as you approach Sukhumi. One of the most beautiful beaches on the entire coast is at Gudauta, about 27 miles (43 km) north of Sukhumi.

SUKHUMI: The city seems to be one big park: its avenues lined with lovely laurels, palms, and Himalayan cedars; its gardens rich with eucalyptus, citrus, and banana trees. There is a botanical garden (ul. Chavchavadze 18) with rare and unusual flowers, and the plants in the 80-acre forest-park on the slopes of Sukhumi Hill have been selected so that the garden is always in bloom.

Sukhumi, which lies between the mouths of the Gumits and Kelasuri rivers, is the capital of Abkhazia. The settlement was built by the Romans in about the second century, and was one of the chief slave markets on the Black Sea under the Turks, before Abkhazia freed itself with the help of Russia. There are a number of interesting ruins, including the eleventh-century castle of King Bagrat in the southeastern part of the city. A short distance from the castle ruins is Shrom Cave, a wonderland of stalactites and stalagmites.

Another unusual attraction is the monkey-breeding farm maintained on the slopes of Mt. Trapetsaya under the auspices of the Academy of Sciences of the USSR. The animals, primarily baboons and macaques, are used for scientific research purposes.

Many visitors to the Black Sea resort areas end their trip here, but it is also a starting point for tours of the Georgian Soviet Socialist Republic.

BEST EN ROUTE

The price of your accommodations has less to do with the hotel you choose than with the travel plan or class you select, or whether you visit the Black Sea by cruise ship. Lodging for all Western tourists is at least as expensive in the USSR as in major American cities, and there are not many economy options, other than camping.

Most restaurants open late in the morning and close at 11 PM or midnight. Reservations may be advisable at the better restaurants in the most popular resort areas. Food prices are relatively low.

Some of the best renditions of Russian, Ukrainian, and Caucasian food are found in Black Sea restaurants. Sample the beef Stroganoff, chicken Kiev, and Caucasian *shashlik* (skewered lamb). The semitropical climate means fruit and fresh vegetables are available all year-round. And dairy products such as the fetalike *sulguni* cheese, sour cream or *smetana,* and yogurt, called *matsoni,* are excellent.

YALTA

Oreanda Hotel – Less than 100 feet from the shore, along the seaside Promenade. ul. Lenina 35/2 (phone: 2-2794).
Tavrida Hotel and Restaurant – ul. Lenina 13 (phone: 2-3284).
Yalta Restaurant – ul. Botkinskaya 18.
Ukraina Restaurant – Promenade 34.

SOCHI

Camellia Hotel and Restaurant – Kurortny Prospekt 91 (phone: 99-03-97).
Magnolia Hotel and Restaurant – Kurortny Prospekt 50 (phone: 99-56-72).
Primorye Restaurant – ul. Chernomorskaya 10.
Noviye Sochi Restaurant – ul. Vinogradnaya.
Akhun Restaurant – On the slopes of Mt. Bolshoi Akhun.

SUKHUMI

Sinop Motel – Tbilisskoye Highway.
Abkhazia Hotel and Restaurant – ul. Frunze 2 (phone: 3311 or 3391).
Aragvi Restaurant – Mira Prospekt 67.
Amza Restaurant – Sukhumskaya Gora, on Sukhumi Hill.

Exploring Spain

Spain has marvelous beaches, castle-hotels, glorious art, stirring music, sophisticated cities, excellent food, wonderful wines, joyous religious festivals, and the drama of the bullfight. There are items of the highest-quality leather and lace for the shopper, as well as unique low-priced souvenirs. There are cultural differences that add special interest to the various regions; and there are churches of astounding beauty.

It is a country whose various layers of civilization can be seen in monuments, architecture, and art: dolmens and cave paintings from prehistoric times; the horseshoe shape of arches which tell you the Moors were here; Romanesque and Gothic churches from the European Christian period; lavishly ornamented cathedrals from Spain's own golden age; and magnificent paintings by a parade of geniuses from El Greco in the sixteenth century to Velázquez in the seventeenth, Goya in the eighteenth, and Picasso in our own century.

In short, Spain seems almost to have been designed with the tourist in mind. Unfortunately, it has done so well in luring holiday-makers from less sunny climes that the character of some areas, particularly along the Costa del Sol, is hardly Spanish at all.

A total 194,883 square miles in area, Spain occupies most of the Iberian Peninsula, which lies to the south of France between the Atlantic Ocean and the Mediterranean Sea and is separated from north Africa by the Strait of Gibraltar. (Much smaller Portugal, along the west coast, shares the peninsula.) Spain is the third-largest country in Europe after the USSR and France, and is more mountainous than any other European country except Switzerland. It also has 2,475 miles of coastline, and it is possible to ski in the Sierra Nevada, less than 50 miles from the Costa del Sol.

Provinces near the Pyrenees are green and lush, with meadows and fields bordered by trees and hedges. A high (2,000-foot), dry plateau, the *meseta,* dominates central Spain, its brown earth sometimes awash with golden cereal grains; and, to the south, along the Mediterranean, the land supports vineyards and olive groves, as well as lemon and orange trees. Except in the higher reaches of the mountains, temperatures remain relatively high throughout the year in Spain. In the southeast, for instance, temperatures range from 55°F (13°C) to 60°F (15°C) in January. The extreme south is the hottest in summer, with thermometers registering above 100°F (38°C) in some places.

When Phoenicians first came to Spain in the eleventh century BC, they found Iberian tribes already living in the eastern parts of the country. It was the Phoenicians who gave the name Hispania to the peninsula, known to them as "Land of Rabbits." Greeks, Celts, Carthaginians, Romans, and Visigoths also invaded the country before the Moors conquered Spain in AD 711 and imposed an Islamic culture. Christianity had spread across Spain as early as the first century AD; eventually there ensued a 700-year Christian campaign to reconquer Spain. It was not until the late fifteenth century that King Ferdinand and Queen Isabella were able to drive the last enclave of Moors from Granada and unite Spain.

Isabella and Ferdinand had instituted the cruel court of the Inquisition to discover and punish converted Jews and later Muslims, who were insincere. Christians also were investigated for heresy. The court lasted until 1834. In the same year as the reconquest of Granada, the Catholic monarchs expelled all Jews who would not convert. Interestingly, the year was 1492, and across the Atlantic Ocean, Christopher Columbus, outfitted by the same monarchs, was opening a new era for Spain by discovering America.

By the sixteenth century, Spain was a major colonial power. Spanish conquistadores plundered Latin America in search of gold and silver and declared the New World to be part of Spain. Precious minerals were shipped to the homeland by galleons, and Spain's naval prowess became so great that its fleet was known as the Invincible Armada until its defeat, in 1588, by Great Britain. Spain's subsequent military losses in the Thirty Years' War, which ended in 1643, further contributed to its decline as a powerful nation.

During the nineteenth century, Spain suffered a series of internal conflicts, which were, in essence, protests against foreign monarchy. The three Carlist wars, which actually revolved around pretenders to the thrones, finally resulted in the creation of a republic in 1873, but it lasted only one year before the monarchy was restored. At the same time, Spain's Latin American colonies were struggling for autonomy, and Cuban independence at the end of the Spanish-America War in 1898 spelled the end of the Spanish overseas empire.

The bitter division between monarchists and republicans continued well into the twentieth century. In 1923, King Alfonso XIII appointed a military dictator, who was so unpopular with the masses that he was forced into exile. The king finally abdicated to avoid a civil war. But when the elections that followed produced a socialist republican majority and the government initiated reforms, it engendered such right-wing opposition that civil war erupted. Francisco Franco, who had led the victorious Nationalist forces, became dictator of Spain. Under his regime, Spain remained neutral in World War II. Political dissent in Spain was suppressed and civil liberties were stifled until Franco's death in 1975, at which time Juan Carlos ascended the throne and undertook a policy of liberalization.

Our seven Spanish routes are: northern Spain along the Cantabrian seacoast from the Basque country west to Santiago de Compostela; Castile, which passes through central Spain's most important historic cities; the Costa del Sol, with Spain's most famous resort towns; the more rugged Costa Brava, along the northern Mediterranean coast to the French border; Andalusia, which has retained more Moorish traditions than any other part of Spain; the Canary Islands, off the northwest coast of Africa; and the Balearic Islands.

Note: If you have always dreamt of castles in Spain *(paradores),* you can now make reservations easily through Marketing Ahead, Inc., 515 Madison Ave., New York, NY 10022 (phone: 212-759-5170). Information is also available at the Spanish National Tourist Office in the US (see *Sources and Resources,* GETTING READY TO GO).

Northern Spain

The north coast of Spain extends from the Basque Mountain range, which abuts the foothills of the Pyrenees, to the country's most westerly reaches on a little ledge above Portugal. This tour begins in the Basque country, follows the coast to La Coruña, and then turns inland to the south to end in Santiago de Compostela, the spiritual capital of Spain.

The Basque region, which resembles the lower-Alpine section of Austria, deserves special attention because the Basque people are very possibly the oldest surviving ethnic group in Europe. (They predate the ancient Iberian tribes of Spain.) The Basques have a strong sense of political and cultural autonomy and, when waxing most poetic, claim direct descent from Adam and Eve via the lost city of Atlantis. Most serious scholarship on the Basques offers no definitive answers as to their ethnic origins, and early Basque history remains something of a mystery.

The Basque language is not believed to be Indo-European in origin; it is something of a linguistic missing link, thought to date from the very beginning of the use of language itself. Non-Latins, the Basques are fair-skinned and live in both Spain and France. Their motto "Four Plus Three Equals One" refers to the four Spanish and three French Basque provinces, and the desire for political independence and autonomy.

Our route begins on the Basque part of the coast, due north of Pamplona, at Fuenterrabía, a resort town near the French border and just south of Biarritz. It continues to the charming city of San Sebastián, a major Basque city and a world-renowned summer resort. Following the coast through lovely old Spanish towns like Santillana del Mar, the route includes such natural wonders as the Picos de Europa mountain range, with snow-capped peaks as high as 8,688 feet and the *rías* of northwest Spain, which are inlets similar to the fjords of Norway and the lochs of Scotland. The final stop is Santiago de Compostela, a fascinating historical city that has been a shrine for a thousand years, the destination for pilgrims honoring the Apostle St. James, who is buried there.

FUENTERRABÍA: This popular seaside resort and fishing port has steep streets and tiny houses with flower-bedecked, wrought-iron balconies. Because of its strategic position near the frontier, it was the target of attack by the French for centuries. Each September 8, Fuenterrabía celebrates the feast of Our Lady of Guadalupe, who is said to have saved the town after a 2-month siege by the French in 1638. The town is also noted for its excellent seafood.

PASAJES DE SAN JUAN: This village is best reached via Pasajes de San Pedro; launches cross regularly. Pasajes de San Juan is a tiny town with brightly painted houses squeezed together, rowing clubs, good restaurants, and a central plaza of unparalleled charm. Notice how the freighters and tankers entering the straits dwarf the quayside houses. French author Victor Hugo lived and worked here during his exile in the winter of 1843; his house (San Juan 59) is open to the public.

SAN SEBASTIÁN: On three hills, cut by the Urumea River, and graced with the lovely scallop-shaped bay, the Bahía de la Concha, beautiful San Sebastián with its sandy beaches is one of the major summer resorts of Europe, playground of the wealthy and aristocratic inhabitants of Madrid. It's also a major Basque city. Although the old town (Parte Vieja) at the foot of Mount Urgull was destroyed by fire in 1813, it has been rebuilt — narrow streets and all — and is worth exploring, especially at about 8 PM, when the bars and restaurants of its central square, Plaza de la Constitución, are crowded. The balconies around this charming square have numbers because they were ringside seats for bullfights once held here.

The San Telmo Museum, on the Calle Coro at the foot of Mount Urgull, is set in a sixteenth-century Renaissance monastery, and has interesting Basque memorial crosses, an ethnographic exhibit, and strange old Basque headdresses. You can drive to the top of Mount Urgull for a fine view of the town and the bay from the public park at the top. The building there is a military museum.

Also be sure to stroll along the Paseo Nuevo, the wide promenade that encircles Mount Urgull and offers fine vistas of the bay and the sea beyond. For a truly spectacular panorama of the city, the bay, and the sea, drive 3 miles (4 km) west along the Concha beach to Mount Igueldo.

The Basque country, but particularly San Sebastián, is a place where good eating assumes major importance. The city has a Gastronomic Academy and very exclusive all-male eating societies that sponsor eating contests, but the flair for good eating spills over into the local restaurants, the most modest of which is likely to serve outstanding food. Seafood is especially good here.

During the summer season San Sebastián holds a 2-week music festival, an international film festival, and a folklore festival called Basque Week. The posh casino is a traditional highlight. For further information about San Sebastián, contact the tourist office, Andia 13 (phone: 42-17-74).

GUERNICA: Heading west from San Sebastián along the Cantabrian coast road, you reach the town of Guernica, whose wretched decimation during the Spanish Civil War (2,000 died in 3 hours) has been immortalized by Picasso in one of his greatest paintings. (The original canvas, which once hung in New York's Museum of Modern Art, has now been returned to Spain for display in the Casón del Buen Retiro — part of the Prado — in Madrid.) The town has been rebuilt in traditional style. A few miles farther west, the beach at Baquio is worth a stop.

BILBAO: Although this is one of the more famous towns in northern Spain, there isn't much to see unless you happen to come during the early August bullfights. Then you will see some serious animals, feisty matadors, and a spirited festival. Bullfight critics and the matadors themselves stay at the *Ercilla,* Ercilla 37 (phone: 443-8800).

SANTANDER: This region of Old Castile is the geographical, cultural, and ethnic section of Spain just to the west of the Basque country. During the summer it is exceptionally crowded with tourists, particularly archaeological scholars exploring the Stone Age Caves at Altamira.

Proceeding to the town of Santander on Route 50, you'll find many good reasons for stopping here. These include: Sardinero Beach, the Santander Summer Music Festival, and the International University Menéndez y Pelayo on Calle de Rubio. The town is divided into an old section — much of which was wiped out during a tornado more than 30 years ago — and a new area near the harbor devoted to shops and restaurants.

SANTILLANA DEL MAR: This is a lovely, beautifully preserved old Spanish town renowned for its Collegiate Church, which dates from the twelfth century; here the relics of St. Juliana (Santillana is a contraction of Santa Juliana) are enshrined. See the Romanesque church with its magnificent sarcophagus honoring the saint and the impressive cloisters, memorable for their capitals, which were carved by a master craftsman during the twelfth century. Also noteworthy are the town's old patrician houses, dating from the fifteenth to seventeenth centuries, particularly the Villa House, now an inn, with its semicircular balconies, and the houses along the Calle de las Lindas and the Calle del Río. (The latter street has a stream running down its center.)

En route from Santillana del Mar – Continue west and you will reach the massive Picos de Europa Cordillera mountain range, where breathtaking gorges have been carved by the mountain streams. These spectacular snow-capped mountains rise between Santander and Oviedo, and their highest peak is 8,688 feet. A good place to stay between Santander and Oviedo is the typically Spanish resort town of Llanes. From here, if you wish, you can catch a glimpse of the mountains, by taking a detour of 11 miles (18 km) to Covadonga, turning south just before the town of Cangas de Onis. Here a shrine was erected in a most dramatic mountain setting, commemorating the reconquest of Spain from the Moors, which began in Covadonga in 722. The road is steep and narrow, but passable.

OVIEDO: Oviedo is the capital of Asturias, a regional entity that was originally a separate kingdom. Known primarily as a mining region, Asturias has a rugged seacoast, a mountainous interior that has been compared to the Swiss Alps, and a natural greenness of exceptional depth and intensity. Salmon and trout, deer and mountain goat populate the Asturian streams and mountains. The coastal villages produce ample seafood. The Oviedo market held daily in the Plaza de Daoiz y Velarde and the Cathedral Square are the main attractions in this small town. Don't miss the matchless twelfth-century sculpted columns at the Cámara Santa church, where the gold and silver items in the treasury are also very fine and very old (ninth century).

En Route from Oviedo – Continuing along the coast, you enter the region of Galicia in the northwest corner of the Iberian Peninsula. Because of its geographic isolation, Galicia has remained the least developed part of Spain. Its ocean waters are sparkling clean, but there are few tourist accommodations. Life in Galicia is very basic, and its fishermen battle daily with poverty and the dangers of the sea.

An unusual geographic feature here is the *rías* — inlets similar to the sea lochs of Scotland, the fjords of Norway, and the abers of Brittany. The Rías Altas extend along the north coast from Ribadeo to La Coruña and the Rías Bajas continue along the west coast from La Coruña to Pontevedra.

On this route you might want to look for the *cetarías,* seafood pounds, where lobsters and other crustaceans can be bought alive. Nearby open-air restaurants will cook and serve your acquisitions.

The area is also known for the Ribeiros wines; the red is very dark and fruity; the white champagnelike; there's also a light, bubbly cider.

LA CORUÑA: This town, from which Philip II's Armada set sail in 1588 to be defeated by England's Drake and Hawkins, is now called the San Sebastián of Galicia for its lovely beaches. The town itself is also charming, with its medieval walls and its second-century Roman lighthouse, the Hercules Tower, which still functions.

Along the harbor in the park of San Carlos are the eighteenth-century San Anton and San Carlos forts. The old section of La Coruña, called La Ciudad (the City), has lovely cobbled streets and little squares like the Plaza de Santa Bárbara. The cafés in the old part of town are social centers, and the Plaza Maria Pita is a good place for eating, drinking, and strolling.

SANTIAGO DE COMPOSTELA: Santiago's only rivals are Rome and Jerusalem, and the shrine here attracts pilgrims from all over the world. Santiago is the contraction for *San Diego,* or St. James. A legend says that St. James the Apostle landed here to proselytize and then died in Judea at the hands of Herod. His body was buried here, lost, and rediscovered by a miracle wrought in the ninth century. It is said that the night sky showered stars upon his grave to reveal its whereabouts to the faithful. The name *compostela* refers to the land *(campo)* of stars *(estrellas)*. St. James is still honored by pilgrimages in years when his holy day falls on a Sunday, usually every 5, 6, or 11 years; the next year is 1993. The famous Way of St. James (El Camino de Santiago), extending from Paris through Pamplona, Burgos, and León to Santiago, and marked with monasteries and churches, is one of the world's oldest tour routes; one early guidebook dates from 1130.

The center of attraction in Santiago is the cathedral, built during the eleventh through thirteenth centuries. It can be seen from plazas on all sides, the chief of which is the Plaza de España or del Obradoiro. The magnificent Obradoiro facade is a 1750 baroque creation by Fernando Casas y Novoa. Richly ornate, it is sculpted in a blend of straight and curved lines characteristic of the baroque style. Be sure to see the wonderful twelfth-century Romanesque Door of Glory, the Romanesque Goldsmith's Door, and the seventeenth-century Holy Door — all of which are inside the cathedral.

Santiago (pop. 93,000) is also the site of one of Spain's earliest universities. The student quarter and the old neighborhood between the cathedral and the university are the most popular strolling and dining areas in town. The summer music school, headed by Andrés Segovia, the great guitarist, is another attraction.

Explore the Plaza del Obradoiro fronting the cathedral and the Plaza de la Quintana at its east end, and wander along such medieval streets as the Rúa Nueva, Calle del Franco, and Rúa del Villar. On the western side of town is the Paseo de la Herradura, a pleasant promenade along a wooded hill, which offers a fine view of the cathedral and, the city.

The annual festival of Santiago de Compostela is celebrated on July 25, with grand processions and much feasting. At this time, be sure to make hotel reservations in advance. For more information about the city, contact the Tourist Office, Rúa del Villar 43 (phone: 58-40-81).

BEST EN ROUTE

Expect to pay $45 or more for a double room in those hotels we've categorized as expensive; between $30 and $45 at a hotel in the moderate category; under $30, inexpensive.

Basque gastronomy is a high art, renowned throughout the world. Here, you will find several restaurants of supremely high caliber where every meal is truly unforgettable. Expect to pay $45 or more for a meal for two at those restaurants we've categorized as expensive; between $25 and $45 for a meal for two in the moderate category; under $25, inexpensive. Prices do not include drinks, wine, or tips.

FUENTERRABÍA

Parador Nacional El Emperador – This should be your first stop in Spain as you cross the border from France. Not only is the Basque cooking good, but this former medieval castle cum fortress with real cannonball holes in the facade has an interesting art gallery. Plaza de Armas (phone: 64-21-40). Moderate.

Kulluxka-Zeria – This genial place serves fish and seafood prepared according to Basque recipes. San Pedro 19–23 (phone: 64-27-80). Moderate.

PASAJES DE SAN JUAN

Txulotxo – Here you'll find a splendid selection of Basque seafood and fish dishes. Closed during October and on Tuesdays. San Juan 66 (phone: 35-66-09). Moderate.

Casa Cámara – Renowned as one of the most important centers of new Basque cooking, the cuisine here features natural ingredients with traditional and innovative recipes. Lobster dishes are the house specialty. San Juan 79 (phone: 35-66-02). Expensive.

SAN SEBASTIÁN

Hotel de Londres y de Inglaterra – Standing on the beach, the *Londres* is all wood on the inside, complete with creaking floors and elevators. An incomparable old-world establishment. Zubieta 2 (phone: 42-69-89). Moderate.

Arzac – The high priest of the new Basque cuisine, owner-chef Juan Mari Arzak has won Spain's National Gastronomy Prize. His river crabs with truffles and lobster sauce, pastries, apple pudding with strawberry cream, and mousse are considered among the most delectable culinary creations in the country. Closed June, November, Sunday nights from December through May, and on Mondays. Alto de Miracruz 21 (phone: 27-84-65). Expensive.

Recondo – Farm-fresh produce enhances the rich meat and fish dishes. Closed Wednesdays. On the road to Igueldo (phone: 21-29-07). Expensive to moderate.

Casa Paco – Another bastion of new Basque cooking, it is known for its sea bream, baby eels, and anchovies. Av. 31 de Agosto 28 (phone: 42-28-16). Moderate.

Aldanondo – This unpretentious chophouse has a distinct rural sporting flavor. Euska-Erria 6 (phone: 42-28-52). Moderate.

Akelarre – Delicate Basque and French cuisine carefully prepared and served in a lovely setting atop Monte Igueldo. Barrio Igueldo (phone: 21-20-52). Moderate.

GUETARIA

Kai Pe and Kaia – *Kai Pe,* upstairs, and *Kaia,* downstairs, serve some of the best seafood on the Basque coast. From the *Kaia,* you can see the port, across the Gulf of Vizcaya, all the way to Biarritz, France. The Txacoli, bottled by Txomin Echaniz for *Kai Pe,* is a special white wine made from bitter grapes on the hillsides overlooking the sea. The restaurant is on the port. General Arnao 10 (phone: 83-24-12). Expensive to moderate.

GUERNICA

Zimela – This simple restaurant is a good place for a filling meal. Carlos Gangoiti 57 (phone: 685-1012). Moderate to inexpensive.

BILBAO

Hotel Ercilla – Crossing the time warp from old-world style to new-world comfort, this is the traditional favorite of matadors and bullfight critics. Ercilla 37 (phone: 443-8800). Moderate.

Carlton – Adequate, although hardly luxurious lodging, this is a pleasant alternative to the *Ercilla,* which might well be full during the bullfight season in August. Moyua 2 (phone: 416-2200). Moderate.

Excelsior – Another good choice for comfortable sleeping quarters in Bilbao. Hurtado de Amézaga 6 (phone: 415-3000). Inexpensive.

Guria – Here, you'll find some prized Basque delicacies prepared according to traditional recipes. Codfish and steak are house specialties. Closed Sundays. Barrencalle Barrena 8 (phone: 415-0434). Very expensive.

Gredos – Though not as lavish as *Guria,* this restaurant offers traditional Basque dishes at reasonable prices. Closed mid-July to mid-August. Alameda de Urquijo 50 (phone: 443-5002). Moderate to inexpensive.

SANTANDER

Mar de Castilla – A fine seafood restaurant along the port with a good harbor view. Estación Marítima (phone: 21-34-44). Expensive to moderate.

Casa Valentin – Fish and seafood are served in a more modest setting at lower cost. Isabel II, 19 (phone: 22-70-49). Inexpensive.

DIRECTIONS / Spain   1193

SANTILLANA DEL MAR

Parador Nacional Gil Blas – This converted medieval villa provides smashing accommodations in a remarkable natural setting, near the prehistoric Altamira caves. Plaza Ramón Pelayo II (phone: 81-80-00). Moderate.

Altamira – Since the *Parador* has limited rooms for guests, this is the number-one alternate choice in town. It's nowhere nearly as spectacular, but quite charming. Calle Canton 1 (phone: 81-80-25). Inexpensive.

LLANES

Don Paco – This is a comfortable Spanish-style resort hotel, modest and quiet, with 42 rooms with baths. Posada Herrera (phone: 40-01-50). Inexpensive.

Montemar – Similar to the *Don Paco,* this place has a cafeteria and 40 rooms. Genaro Riestra (phone: 40-01-00). Inexpensive.

OVIEDO

Hotel de la Reconquista – Is unquestionably the best place for an overnight stop in Oviedo. Calle Gil de Jaz (phone: 24-11-00). Inexpensive.

Casa Fermin – Oviedo's most notable restaurant is acclaimed for its venison in season, from October through March, and Asturian codfish. San Francisco 8 (phone: 21-24-59). Expensive to moderate.

Principado – Traditional Asturian cooking. The desserts and pastries here are especially good. San Francisco 6 (phone: 21-77-92). Moderate to inexpensive.

RIBADEO

Parador Nacional – Built on a less monumental scale than the other *paradores,* this is nonetheless a well-kept government-run hostelry. Its restaurant, which serves Galician dishes — boiled ham with greens, fresh fish, empanada (fish or meat pie) — has a fine reputation. Amadeo Fernandez (phone: 11-08-25). Moderate.

LA CORUÑA

El Rápido – The best selection of seafood in the city, as well as some Galician dishes, both complemented by Ribeiro and Albariño wines. Estrella 7 (phone: 22-42-21). Expensive.

Fornos – Here you'll find well-prepared regional dishes and a good selection of hearty local wines. Olmos 25 (phone: 22-16-75). Moderate.

VILLALBA

Parador de los Condes de Villalba – Between La Coruña and Santiago, this 6-room hotel is set in a vine-covered medieval tower and furnished with antiques. Its fine restaurant specializes in *zarzuela,* assorted fish, and *fillaos,* custard rolled in crêpes. Valeriano Valdesuso (phone: 51-00-11). Moderate.

SANTIAGO DE COMPOSTELA

Hostal de los Reyes Católicos – This magnificently decorated fifteenth-century building is one of the most memorable inns in northern Spain. Plaza del Obradoiro (phone: 58-22-00). Very expensive.

Peregrino – If the *Hostal* is fully booked, you won't be disappointed at the quality of this elegant old hotel. Rosalia de Castro (phone: 59-18-50). Moderate.

Don Gaiferos – This restaurant is renowned as one of the very best in town. Closed the first two weeks in February and on Sunday nights. Rúa Nueva 23 (phone: 58-38-94). Expensive to moderate.

El Franco – This is a fine restaurant specializing in Galician cuisine. Av. del General Franco 28 (phone: 58-12-34). Expensive to moderate.

Castile

Although the term *Castile* is used to denote a region embracing 15 provinces in the mountainous central plateau, the area is actually divided into two — Old Castile (Castilla La Vieja) and New Castile (Castilla La Nueva). New Castile, the geographic center of Spain, comprises the provinces of Cuenca, Ciudad Real, Guadalajara, Madrid, and Toledo. Old Castile lies to the north of the Guadarrama and Somosierra mountain ranges of the Cordillera Central and includes the provinces of Ávila, Burgos, Segovia, Soria, Palencia, Valladolid, León, Zamora, Salamanca, and Santander.

Our itinerary takes you from Madrid south to Toledo, then northwest to Ávila with a side trip to Salamanca, then northeast to Segovia, Valladolid, and Burgos. From Burgos, you can continue northeast to Pamplona, site of the bull run immortalized by Ernest Hemingway in *The Sun Also Rises.*

MADRID: For a complete report on the capital and its hotels and restaurants, see *Madrid,* THE EUROPEAN CITIES. Two small Castilian towns that you might consider visiting before beginning our tour are Aranjuez and Chinchón, both within about 30 miles of Madrid.

On Route NIV, Aranjuez is famous for its spring strawberries and asparagus. Its cool shady boulevards and plazas draw many a Madrid family for Sunday promenades. Aranjuez's main sites of interest are the Royal Palace (El Palacio), begun by Felipe II; the Sailor's House (Casa de Marinos), which housed the royal boats; the Prince's Garden; and the Farmer's House (Casa del Labrador). This romantic town inspired the haunting, lyrical *Concierto de Aranjuez,* by composer Joaquin Rodrigo, which has been interpreted by many jazz artists, Miles Davis among them.

The central plaza of Chinchón is one of the best-known small-town squares in central Spain, and is the site of bullfights during the summer season.

The best way to begin our tour of Castile is to head south from Madrid on Route N401 for 44 miles (70 km) to Toledo.

TOLEDO: Master artist El Greco's painting *View of Toledo* depicts this sixteenth-century city standing atop green, windswept hills, under fiercely tormented stormy skies. Whether or not you happen to catch similar climatic forces at work during your visit, you will be inspired anyway by the beauty of Toledo's palaces, private houses, and courtyards, as well as the view of the city itself from the Circunvalación road which runs parallel to the Río Tajo.

A center of Spanish civilization from as far back as the eighth-century Moorish era, Toledo has enough important sites to keep anyone engrossed for a good number of days. Overlooking the city, near the banks of the Río Tajo stands the Alcázar, a fortress that once housed El Cid, the Lord Champion of the eleventh century whose valor and heroic exploits were the subject of Spain's first epic poem, *El Poema del Cid,* written in the early twelfth century. El Cid was the subject of quite a few poems, tales, and plays through the ages. One of the most famous is the French seventeenth-century playwright Corneille's neoclassic interpretation of the Spanish hero's life, *Le Cid.* The reconstructed Alcazar is open daily (the original building was destroyed during the Civil War) and houses the museum of the Spanish Civil War.

The cathedral, at Arco de Palacio, in the center of the city, dates from the thirteenth century and contains ornate artwork, sanctuaries, chapels, and bell towers, representing literally hundreds of years of devoted, inspired craftsmanship. You can ascend the bell tower, where an eighteenth century bell is still in use.

Saint Thomas Church (Iglesia Santo Tomé), at Angel Santo Tomé, houses El Greco's famous painting *The Burial of the Conde de Orgaz.* A few blocks away, on Paseo del Tránsito and the corner of Calle Reyes Católicos, is the fourteenth-century synagogue El Tránsito (it no longer functions as a Sephardic Jewish house of worship). During the Inquisition, the synagogue became a church and the Jews who prayed there became Christians. Many of those who failed to convert fled the country. Part of the synagogue houses a museum that is open daily and contains Sephardic religious articles.

The El Greco House and Museum (Casa y Museo del Greco) is the former abode of the sixteenth-century artist and contains some of his paintings and memorabilia. It is across and up the street from the synagogue.

From Toledo, take Route 403 northeast to Ávila.

ÁVILA: This city was one of the strongholds of the reconquest of Spain from the Moors by the Christians, a 700-year conflict that finally ended in 1492 when King Ferdinand and Queen Isabella seized Granada and united Spain. Standing at almost 4,000 feet above sea level, the city is famous for its walled battlements. You can get the best view of the walls from the western section of the city, where they overlook the Río Adaja. Guided tours of some sections of the wall and walks along several sentry paths are available, or you can freely roam the parapets. The battlements at Ávila are considered to be among the best existing examples of medieval fortifications. The cathedral at the foot of Calle Tostado; the Deanery Museum (Casa de los Deanes), containing Flemish and Spanish art; and the Convent of St. Teresa of Ávila are the main sites in town.

Not far from Ávila stands El Escorial, a palace and monastery constructed by King Felipe the Second, in a near-record 21 years. An austere, classical monument, it achieves a rare architectural consistency and contains paintings by Bosch, El Greco, and Velázquez, among others, in addition to its remarkable library and crypt.

En Route from Ávila – If you wish to make a side trip to Salamanca, you can simply follow Route 501 northwest. Salamanca is a university town with a Plaza Mayor, which is more elaborate than the one in Madrid. You can walk around the city's major sites in about 3 hours; these include the university, the new and old cathedrals, and the Patio de las Escuelas, a square near the university. Surrounding Salamanca is an agricultural region where bulls are raised and tanned to produce Spanish leather. From Salamanca, you may return to Ávila, or take the new highway to Villacastín or San Rafael and follow Route NV1 to Segovia.

SEGOVIA: In the city's main square, in 1474, Queen Isabella was proclaimed monarch of Castile. Other Segovia sites are the Roman aqueduct and fourteenth-century alcázar (palace) with nineteenth-century modifications. In the center of town stands a late Gothic cathedral and Romanesque churches. On the road south of Segovia you'll find the stone bridge that Ernest Hemingway described as a steel bridge and used as a setting in his novel, *For Whom the Bell Tolls.*

Continue on Route 601 from Segovia to Valladolid.

VALLADOLID: A university city, Valladolid claims to speak the purest Castilian Spanish. The house of sixteenth-century author Miguel de Cervantes, who wrote *Don Quixote* and who is known as the father of the modern novel, is located near the Plaza Zorrilla, just off Calle Miguel Iscar. The other important sites in town are the cathedral; the sixteenth-century cloisters of San Gregorio College (Colegio San Gregorio); the Archaeological Museum (Museo Arqueológico) containing Roman artifacts; and the university (Universidad de Valladolid).

Take N620 to Burgos.

BURGOS: It was in Burgos, the tenth-century capital of Castile, that Francisco

Franco was declared the *caudillo* (military commander) in 1936. The city holds a permanent place in Spanish military history, and none other than El Cid, the eleventh-century warrior who became a legend, is buried in the Burgos Cathedral. In fact, the cathedral — with its slender, openwork spires — is the main reason for stopping here. After the cathedrals of Toledo and Seville it is the third largest in the country, dating as far back as the thirteenth century. Other sections were added in the fourteenth, fifteenth, and sixteenth centuries. Guided tours of the cathedral are conducted daily; it's on Calle Laín Calvo in the center of town.

En Route from Burgos – The wheat fields and lush pine woods that surround Burgos were the inspiration for poet Antonio Machado. After Spain's loss of her last colonial possessions in the Spanish-American War, Machado and a group of writers, called the Generation of '98, turned to celebrate the most characteristically Spanish (really Castilian) countryside. A visit to the town of Soria on Route 234 will acquaint you with the pastoral landscape. Some fine examples of Romanesque architecture can be seen here, and there are interesting, burnt sienna-colored houses built by successful sheep farmers and a sixteenth-century cathedral. Northeast of Soria on Route N111 are the ruins of the city of Numantia, whose citizens chose to starve rather than to capitulate to the Romans in 133 BC.

Stay on Route N111 all the way to Pamplona.

PAMPLONA: Not actually in Castile, this city in the province of Navarre is one of the most famous in Spain. In his novel, *The Sun Also Rises,* Ernest Hemingway wrote about the annual Festival of St. Fermín (Fiesta de los Sanfermines) during which the bulls are allowed to run through the streets in the early morning hours. The afternoon bullfights are among the most spectacular in the world. The festival takes place from July 6 to July 20. The city's main sites are the fourteenth-century cathedral and the Navarre Museum (Museo Navarro), housing murals and religious sculpture.

BEST EN ROUTE

Decent and frequently even sumptuous accommodations at reasonable prices can be found throughout Castile, especially if you are fortunate enough to obtain a room in one of the government-run *paradores* or *albergues nacionales.* But you need to make reservations months in advance. Contact the Spanish National Tourist offices in the United States. Expect to pay between $30 and $40 for a double room in a hotel listed as moderate; under $30, inexpensive.

Castilian restaurants provide gracious, aristocratic atmosphere as well as fine cuisine. Expect to pay $45 or more for a meal for two at those restaurants we've listed as expensive; between $20 and $45 at those restaurants in the moderate category; under $15, inexpensive. Prices do not include drinks, wine, or tips.

TOLEDO

Parador Nacional Conde de Orgaz – A low, two-story hotel commanding a sweeping view of the city, this is generally considered to be one of the most stunning *paradores* in the national chain. The restaurant serves international as well as Castilian cuisine. The rooms have air-conditioning. Cerro del Emperador (phone: 22-18-50). Moderate.

Carlos Quinto – If the *Parador* is fully booked, this is a fine alternative in the center of town. Trastamara (phone: 22-21-00). Moderate.

Maravilla – This is another good, centrally located hotel. It, too, is definitely worth considering if you can't get a room at *Conde de Orgaz.* Barrio Rey 7 (phone: 22-33-00). Moderate.

Hostal de Cardenal – Unquestionably the best restaurant in town, it is set in an old house that once served as a cardinal's residence. It has a lovely garden with trees and 27 rooms. Paseo Recaredo 24 (phone: 22-08-62). Expensive.

Chirón – This restaurant is known for the splendid scenery and surroundings. The building stands across the Puerta de Chambron entryway through the city's walls overlooking the Río Tajo. Paseo Recaredo 1 (phone: 22-01-50). Moderate.

Venta de Aires – This is another leading restaurant with a tree-filled garden and charming location. Circo Romano 25 (phone: 22-05-45). Moderate.

ARANJUEZ

Casa Pablo – This pleasant Castilian restaurant serves local asparagus and strawberries. Almíbar 20 (phone: 891-1451). Moderate to inexpensive.

CHINCHÓN

Mesón Cuevas del Vino – The best restaurant in town is in an old mill. Benito Hortelano 13 (phone: 894-0206). Moderate to inexpensive.

ÁVILA

Parador Nacional Raimundo de Borgoña – This grand old building was actually an eleventh-century palace where Raymond of Burgundy (Raimundo de Borgoña) lived during a military crusade against the Moors. The exterior of the castle is bleached white stone; inside, whitewashed walls and tiled floors are artistically furnished. Marqués de Canales y Chozas (phone: 21-13-40). Moderate.

Parador Nacional Gredos – In an old lodge with a new wing added in 1975, it stands in a wooded section of a plateau with excellent views of the Gredos mountain peaks, about an hour from Ávila. Inside, the atmosphere is similar to a hunting lodge. Freshly caught trout is the dining room's specialty. Navarrendonda de la Sierra (phone: 34-80-48). Moderate.

El Rastro – This old inn has been converted into a charming restaurant. Plaza del Rastro 4 (phone: 21-12-19). Moderate.

SALAMANCA

Parador Nacional Tordesillas – This is a modern inn set in pleasant rural surroundings. Although not quite as dramatic as the reconverted-castle *paradores,* it offers very good accommodations at exceptionally reasonable cost. On the Salamanca-Valladolid road in Tordesillas (phone: 77-02-51). Moderate.

SEGOVIA

Albergue Nacional de Villacastín – One hour's drive from the city of Segovia, this is a modern, unpretentious lodge with dining facilities. Government-run, as are the *paradores,* it is somewhat more humble but still an excellent value. On Route 110 southwest of Segovia in Villacastin (phone: 10-70-00). Moderate.

Parador Nacional – This is a new parador with a four-star (first-class) rating. It has a fine view of the city from its hilltop location and is only a 5-minute walk from town (phone: 43-04-62). Moderate.

Mesón de Cándido – Segovia's finest restaurant, set in a fifteenth-century house, specializes in Castilian delicacies — roast suckling pig, lamb roast, veal chops, and a special soup made according to the master chef's recipe. Plaza Azoguejo 5 (phone: 42-81-02). Moderate.

Duque – This noted restaurant is *Cándido*'s main rival, serving typically Castilian food. Cervantes 12 (phone: 43-05-37). Moderate.

VALLADOLID

Mesón de la Fragua – Of the many restaurants and cafés around Plaza Mayor, this is the best. Paseo Zorrilla 10 (phone: 33-71-02). Moderate.

BURGOS

Landa Palace – This splendid castle-hotel has a very fine restaurant that turns out delicious French dishes along with equally appetizing local specialties. Madrid-Irun Hwy. (phone: 20-63-43). Expensive to moderate.

SORIA

Parador Nacional Antonio Machado – The contemporary building looks out toward the mountains and the Río Duero Valley. The dining room is noted for its Castilian game dishes and rich Rioja wines. Parque del Castillo, Soria (phone: 21-34-45). Moderate.

The Costa del Sol

The Costa del Sol is Spain's answer to Acapulco and Rio de Janeiro: miles upon miles of high-rise hotels, condominiums, bungalows, and campsites overlooking the azure Mediterranean. In fact, it is one of Europe's most developed and most popular beach resort areas. Many people look upon the Costa del Sol as an international playground rather than part of Spain. Some argue, incontestably, that the original character of the area — dry, hilly land sprinkled with whitewashed cottages — has been changed forever by the resorts that provide accommodations, nightlife, and other recreational services for tourists — about six million every year.

The Costa del Sol extends from Almería on the easternmost part of the southern Mediterranean Coast to Algeciras, 236 miles to the west. The center of the coast is the city of Málaga, an important but polluted port. Both Algeciras and Málaga have ferries connecting Spain with Tangiers, Morocco, and Ceuta, Spanish Morocco. In the 84 miles (134 km) between Málaga and Algeciras are the most developed (and crowded) of the Costa del Sol resort towns — Torremolinos, Fuengirola, and Marbella. Along this stretch of road (or beach) you are more likely to hear Swedish, German, French, Arabic, and English spoken than Spanish.

Though not always so named, the Costa del Sol has been attractive to foreign visitors ever since the Phoenicians landed on its shores in about the sixth century BC. They were followed by the Greeks, Romans, and Moors. The Moorish influence, although considerably more visible in the inland villages, can still be seen along the coast. Fortresses and the ruins of guard towers stand on cliffs near the sea. In contrast to the modern, white high-rises that line much of the dry, hilly coast are villages of whitewashed cottages and colorful gardens.

The best time of year to visit is around March and April, before the hordes descend. The temperatures tend to be in the 60s F with clear, sunny skies. In the summer, the mercury climbs into the 80s and 90s F, but because the heat is dry and breezes from the Mediterranean cool the air, few hotels other than expensive ones have air-conditioning.

Although you can plan to visit every resort along the Costa del Sol, we recommend that you choose one spot as a base and make 1- or 2-day trips to other towns. In any case, Route 340 runs the entire length of the Costa del Sol and all you need do is follow it.

ALMERÍA: Just outside of town, the Almería desert contains some of the world's most famous sand dunes. Certainly, they are among the most filmed — *Lawrence of Arabia, The Good, the Bad, and the Ugly,* and *Reds* were made here, to name a few. Residents claim that so many film crews have drifted through town over the years, that they no longer remember the titles of the movies that were (and are) being made. In the 60s, Almería was known to thousands of young people who were on the road in Europe as the place where you could make a few bucks as an extra in a Western. All you had to do was join the Spanish actors' union, sign on with a film company, and be willing to spend 8 or 9 hours in the sweltering heat dressed as a cowboy or Indian. You can find out which movies are being filmed in the neighborhood by stopping in at the offices of Almantur, the official tourist promotion board on the Carretera de Málaga (phone: 23-48-59). The people in the office will give you maps directing you to the film locations in the area.

In town, the main place of interest is the alcazaba, an old Phoenician castle that was converted into a fortress by the Moors. The site of music festivals during the second half of August, the alcazaba stands on a hill. You can't miss it.

The cathedral is another building that has lived through various incarnations. Originally a mosque, it was Christianized in the sixteenth century; however, architecturally, it has retained something of a Moorish character.

ALMUÑECAR: This town — one of those clean coastal villages that smell of orange blossoms — dates back to the Phoenicians who called it Sexi. But don't get your hopes up. Although the nearby beaches of San Cristóbal, Punta del Mar, La Herradura, and Berenguel can be as sexy as the bodies languishing on them at the moment, Almuñecar itself offers only a Roman aqueduct and a Moorish fortress as sight-seeing attractions. As in Almería, the fortress here, too, is called the alcazaba.

NERJA: When Bob Dylan wrote the song *Subterranean Homesick Blues* back in the 1960s, chances are he was not thinking of Nerja. But, chances are the song's title will immediately spring to mind as you approach the caves for which this little town is world famous. Discovered by two youngsters who were poking around the countryside in 1959, the caves were opened to the public in 1960. Since then, visitors have come to wander through the mazes, gazing at the underground waterfalls, crypts, and the stalactites and stalagmites that adorn ceilings and floors, and are lit by multicolored lights. Adjoining the caves is an anthropological museum with prehistoric paintings said to be 20,000 years old. A music and dance festival is held in the caves every year, during the first 2 weeks in August.

Apart from its caves, Nerja is known for a natural promontory overlooking the Mediterranean called El Balcón de Europa (the Balcony of Europe). If it sounds like a promising title for a best-selling novel, perhaps you'll be inspired to start writing after contemplating the stunning seascape.

This is also a good town for festivals. In addition to the music festival in August, there is a procession of boats honoring the Virgin of Carmen on July 16, a series of parades with fireworks honoring San Isidro (St. Isidore) on May 15, and a 4-day bash in honor of Nerja's patron saint, from October 9 through October 12.

   En Route from Nerja – Take an interesting side trip to the village of Frigiliana, only 3 miles (5 km) inland from Nerja in the surrounding Almijara mountains. This tiny Andalusian town (pop. 2,160) of winding streets, red tile–roofed cottages, tropical flowers, and enchanting views of the neighboring mountains and valleys may be declared a national monument in order to protect it from possible ravishment by twentieth-century developers.

MÁLAGA: The center of the Costa del Sol is known as the place that gave the world sweet Málaga wine. The vineyards that produce the wine grapes cover the hills on the outskirts of town. You can sample Málaga wine at any one of the small *bodegas* (taverns) in the center of town.

In addition to its prized vineyards, Málaga has a few other spots of interest. Overlooking the city, the Gibralfaro Castle spreads along a reddish cliff covered with ivy and cypress trees. The castle dates back to the Phoenician times, and has Moorish modifications that were added in the eighth century. The castle adjoins the alcazaba where the Arab monarchs resided during the eleventh century. (It now contains an archaeological museum, which is open daily.) They are both on a hilly park accessible by Calle Mundo Nuevo or Calle Victoria to Ferrandiz.

Málaga's cathedral a sixteenth-century building with a truncated bell tower, has an ornate interior. The adjoining museum is open daily. The cathedral, not surprisingly, is on the Plaza de la Catedral.

The Fine Arts Museum (Museo de Bellas Artes), housed in an old palace (San Agustín 6), contains an eclectic collection of Roman artifacts; Moorish art; and paintings by El Greco, Murillo, and Picasso, a native son of Málaga. (Picasso's birthplace is at Plaza de la Merced 16).

To get a feeling for Málaga, take a carriage ride along the Paseo del Parque, a promenade near the waterfront lined with tropical gardens and sidewalk cafés. Or, amble down Calle Marques de Larios, Málaga's main shopping street. At the Plaza de Toros, at the end of the Paseo del Parque, you can take a guided tour and get a glimpse of what goes on behind the scenes of a bullfight. The most important bullfights of the year take place on Easter Sunday, during the Corpus Christi festivities in June, and during the first week in August. For more information about bullfights and other events, contact the Tourist Information Office, Marques de Larios 5 (phone: 21-34-45).

Málaga is an excellent jumping-off point for trips to Africa. The ferry and hydrofoil to Tangiers and Ceuta (Spanish Morocco) leave from the Estación Marítima along Muelle Heredia. (Note that the ferry and hydrofoil service operates year-round, except when waters are too turbulent.)

TORREMOLINOS: This is the busiest resort on the Costa del Sol. At one time (less than 25 years ago, in fact), Torremolinos was a quiet little fishing village visited by handfuls of European tourists. You would never know it to look at the place today: White high-rise hotels and apartment complexes line the coast. Many have tennis courts and swimming pools. Along the town's streets are restaurants, supermarkets, nightclubs, discotheques, and boutiques. Nearby is a golf course, the National Golf Parador, and the 20-acre Tivoli Amusement Park. And of course there is always the Mediterranean.

In the summer, Torremolinos is jam-packed with tourists from all over the world. In November, when the Benalmádena Film Festival is held in Torremolinos, the town is even more hectic than at peak season, if that's possible.

BENALMÁDENA COSTA: Although it is difficult to see where Torremolinos ends and Benalmádena Costa begins because the scenery is the same, Benalmádena has a somewhat more subdued atmosphere and a less frenetic nightlife than the super-resort next door. A new casino with a nine-story apartment complex has opened at Torrequebrada outside Benalmádena.

FUENGIROLA: A family resort area of seaside villas and campsites overlooking the sea, Fuengirola is quieter than Torremolinos or Benalmádena. Here you'll find pleasant little beach cafés, bars, and quiet coves as well as wide, white stretches of sand. Overlooking Fuengirola is a tenth-century Moorish castle, Sohail. A few miles north of the coast, in the hills, Lew Hoad, a former Wimbledon tennis player, runs a tennis camp called Rancho de Tenis. The 18-hole Mijas golf course is nearby.

MARBELLA: The most chic of the towns along the Costa del Sol, Marbella is also the most expensive and has retained more of its traditional architecture than any of its neighbors. Many oil sheiks and movie stars have homes here, and the prices in the picturesque little bistros and designer boutiques reflect it. Not far from Marbella are several golf courses: Golf Río Real/Los Monteros, designed by Robert Trent Jones; Golf Nueva Andalucía; Aloha Golf; Golf Guadalmina; and Golf Atalaya Park.

NUEVA ANDALUCÍA: This community is actually a section of Marbella. It has a smashing marina — Puerto José Banus, where hundreds of yachts from all over the world dock. Nueva Andalucía is also the home of the Costa del Sol's first casino at Club de Playa Torre del Duque, which offers roulette (European and American), blackjack, baccarat, chemin de fer, and punto y bancca. The casino is part of a leisure complex also containing four swimming pools, a nightclub, three bars, and three restaurants.

ESTEPONA: Although developers are starting to build here, Estepona has managed so far to retain its traditional character, with fishermen, goatherds, and farmers living as they have for centuries. Not far from Estepona is the Robert Trent Jones–designed Club de Golf Sotogrande.

ALGECIRAS: Most people don't really get acquainted with this sleepy little port on the southernmost peninsula of Spain. Although it has a few hotels, it is mostly known for its port, from which ferries leave for Tangiers, Morocco, and Ceuta, Spanish Morocco. The people in Algeciras are very friendly and the town market is a fascinating bustling center of peddlers, greengrocers, and butchers.

BEST EN ROUTE

The Costa del Sol has 250,000 hotel beds, ranging from comfortable to elegant. There are apartment houses, hostels, inns, *paradores* (inns owned by the Spanish government), and government-run campsites that cater primarily to families with recreational vehicles or large tents. The biggest bargain here might be renting a villa, condominium, or apartment. Ask a travel agent or write Ms. Sara Burns, Urbanization Los Monteros, Marbella, or Sr. Carlos M. Gil, Costa del Sol Tourist Board, PO Box 298, Palacio de Congresos, Torremolinos (Málaga). Expect to pay $100 or more for a double room at places listed as very expensive; $65 to $100 is expensive; between $30 and $60 is moderate; under $30, inexpensive.

Service, atmosphere, and presentation of food are almost always pleasant on the Costa del Sol. Expect to pay more than $50 for a meal for two at those restaurants listed as expensive; between $25 and $50 at those restaurants in the moderate category; under $25, inexpensive. Prices do not include drinks, wine, or tips.

ALMERÍA

Gran Hotel – There's no shortage of hotels in Almería; there is, however, a shortage of *good* hotels. *Gran Hotel,* a modern, clean building overlooking the harbor, is the best. Av. Reina Regente, 4 (phone: 23-80-11). Moderate.

NERJA

Parador Nacional de Nerja – This two-story building has a landscaped garden and overlooks the beach. There is a swimming pool and a restaurant serving international as well as local cuisine. Playa de Burriana (phone: 52-00-50). Moderate.

MÁLAGA

Málaga Palacio – A large, curving, Miami-style beachfront hotel, it has three swimming pools, a sauna, two tennis courts with night lighting, restaurant, and nightclub. Cortina del Muelle 1 (phone: 21-51-85). Moderate.

Parador Nacional Gibralfaro – With only 12 rooms in its luxuriously appointed interior, this inn is constantly booked. The terrific location — overlooking the sea next to Gibralfaro Castle — makes the restaurant and bar popular spots. Reservations required (phone: 22-19-02). Moderate.

Skorpio – Near the *Gibralfaro,* with a view of the sea, this air-conditioned restaurant serves *paella,* refreshing gazpacho, and seafood. It also has 28 rooms and a parking garage. Closed Sundays. Ventaja Alta (phone: 25-84-94). Moderate.

Antonio Martín – This simple restaurant near the harbor serves fresh fish, seafood, and, of course, *paella.* Air-conditioned, it has a view of the harbor. Paseo Marítimo 4 (phone: 22-21-13). Moderate.

Casa Pedro – This is your best bet for a hearty seafood meal served up in an unpretentious locale alongside the ocean. At El Palo beach just outside of the city on the road to Almería Quitapenas 4 (phone: 29-00-13). Inexpensive.

TORREMOLINOS

Parador Nacional del Golf – Contemporary in design and situated on an 18-hole golf course, this is a 40-room newcomer to the *parador* chain. In addition to a beachfront location, it has a swimming pool and a restaurant. The *Parador* is actually halfway between Málaga and Torremolinos (phone: 38-12-55). Moderate.

Melía Torremolinos – This 281-room resort complex is one of the largest on the Costa del Sol. A member of the Spanish Melía hotel chain, it offers everything from two nightclubs to Sunday morning mass. And it's about 5 minutes' walk from the beach. Av. de Montemar (phone: 38-05-00). Moderate.

Camping Torremolinos – If you're traveling on a budget, but would like to be close to Torremolinos's nightlife and social scene, this is a good alternative to costly hotels. How much you actually have to rough it depends on the kind of RV, camper, or tent you bring; facilities include a swimming pool and showers. It's about a 10-minute walk to the beach. On the highway between Torremolinos and Benalmádena (no phone). Inexpensive.

Casa Guaquín – This is a family-run restaurant in every sense; the owner's family even catches the seafood served. Closed Thursdays and December. Carmen 37, Playa Carihuela (phone: 38-45-30). Moderate.

La Chalana – Continental dishes share the menu with Spanish *paella* and fresh fish. Closed from November to mid-December and on Tuesdays. Paseo Marítimo (phone: 38-49-56). Moderate.

Hong Kong – Egg roll addicts can get their fix here, Torremolinos-style and Cantonese cooking is generally pretty good. Closed during the first 3 weeks of November. Cauce (phone: 38-41-29). Inexpensive.

Portofino – This terrace that has been built on the beach serves seafood that couldn't taste any fresher if you caught it yourself. Playa Montemar (no phone). Inexpensive.

El Cangrejo – This is another good place for fish and seafood. Bulto 25 (phone: 38-04-79). Inexpensive.

FUENGIROLA

Camping Playa de la Butibamba – Despite its unlikely sounding name, this campsite is on a quiet stretch of beach near a cluster of villas. The sites are a bit too close together for privacy, but if you just want some place to sleep, it is quite adequate. On the highway between Fuengirola and La Debla (no phone). Inexpensive.

Casa Zafra – Unmistakably nautical in atmosphere, the inside of this seafood restaurant has been built to resemble a ship. Perla 6 (no phone). Expensive to moderate.

Van Gaalen's – Right on the beach, this restaurant has good, fresh seafood. Closed Mondays and November (phone: 47-56-94). Moderate.

Don Bigote – Another restaurant noteworthy for its decor, this place has a pleasantly rough-hewn Andalusian country air. Spanish cuisine is served. Francisco Cano 41, Los Boliches (phone: 47-50-94). Moderate.

La Langosta – This is another fine seafood restaurant. Closed December through mid-January and on Mondays. Francisco Cano 1 (phone: 47-50-49). Moderate.

China – For hefty Indonesian meals or old-fashioned Cantonese dishes, this restaurant can't be beat. Ramón y Cajal 27 (phone: 47-29-93). Moderate to inexpensive.

MARBELLA

Hotel Puente Romano – These sun-drenched, palm-studded villas lounge beside the Mediterranean. Each of the 200 airy rooms has a private terrace. Four restaurants, tennis courts, and a *Regine's* disco. Carretera Cadiz, Km. 184 (phone: 77-01-00). Very expensive.

Hotel Los Monteros – A 168-room complex of three buildings spread over the grounds of a former estate, it has five swimming pools, ten tennis courts, a golf club, horseback riding, beachfront, and lots of trees. Carretera de Cádiz, Km. 194 (phone: 77-17-00). Very expensive.

Marbella Club – This dazzling, sleek, newly expanded resort brought Marbella its fame. Here you can rub elbows with the jet set — if you're willing to pay for it. Carretera de Cádiz (phone: 77-13-00). Expensive to moderate.

NUEVA ANDALUCÍA

Golf Hotel Nueva Andalucía – A sparking white building set among floral gardens, this 21-room hotel is close to three Robert Trent Jones–designed golf courses. Equipment can be rented and lessons are available. There is a heated pool, dining room, shopping arcade, and discotheque. Nueva Andalucía (phone: 78-03-00). Expensive to moderate.

ALGECIRAS

Camping Costasol – A hilly plot of land given over to tents and campers, its main blessing is its proximity to a stretch of beach offering a fine view of the Rock of Gibraltar. It's about a 20-minute bus ride from town on the Carretera Cádiz-Málaga (no phone). Inexpensive.

Marea Baja – The menu here offers a large variety of fish and seafood entrées, and ice cream crêpes for dessert. Closed Sundays. Trafalgar 2 (phone: 66-36-54). Inexpensive.

The Costa Brava

The Costa Brava (wild coast) forms the twisted, tortuous, rocky northeastern shoreline of Spain. Unquestionably the country's most rugged coast, as well as its shortest, the Costa Brava's granite cliffs rise out of the sea in such jagged forms that they appear to have been chewed out of the earth by a sea monster with serrated teeth. The cliffs shelter a plethora of bays, coves, inlets, vest-pocket beaches, and traditional whitewashed villages.

Technically, the Costa Brava extends from Blanes — an industrial town about 40 miles north of Barcelona — to Port-Bou, a fishing village 95 miles farther north, perched on the border between Spain and France. Despite its fierce name, the Costa Brava is a popular vacation spot and boasts more hotels and guest houses than any other single area of Spain.

As recently as the mid-1950s, the Costa Brava attracted primarily painters and poets. Contemporary surrealist Salvador Dalí was one of the first major artists to settle into a villa at Port Lligot, Cadaqués, near the French border. But in the late 1950s and early 1960s, this relatively unknown coast was besieged by British tourists in search of bargain vacation areas. And before long, many scenic nooks and crannies were being developed into jazzy resorts.

Although its popularity with twentieth-century foreign guests is a relatively recent phenomenon, the Costa Brava was first visited by Phoenician sailors around the eleventh century BC. Greeks, Romans, Carthaginians, and Moors followed. Along the coast can be seen some of the structures left by these peoples — Phoenician ruins at Rosas, remnants of a Greek edifice at Ampurias, and the Moorish alcazaba (fortress) at Tossa del Mar, to name but a few.

The Costa Brava is also dotted with structures such as towers, walls, castles, and monasteries that were erected much later — during the Middle Ages, between the fifth and fifteenth centuries AD, as defenses against the ravages of pirates and privateers who regularly preyed on coastal settlements.

These days, visiting the Costa Brava is immeasurably safer. Especially as far as weather is concerned. Hardly a cloud passes overhead during the dry, hot summers between May and September, when temperatures are generally in the 80s F. Winters, though moist, are mild enough to support miles of umbrella pines, acres of cork trees, and groves of olive and fig trees. In fact, the so-called wild coast is anything but that when it comes to climate — the average annual temperature is a comfortable 60°F.

Yet it is precisely this gentleness of climate that accounts for one of the biggest problems you are likely to face when visiting the Costa Brava — overcrowding. Be sure to make reservations well in advance or you might find yourself hopelessly stranded, without any place to sleep.

There is one other thing to keep in mind. Unforgettably dramatic though they are, the roads are dangerous. If you are at all faint-hearted on the road, you should not attempt to drive here. If you do, do not allow your attention to wander, even for a few moments. Be particularly alert on the single lane, north-south road between Lloret de Mar and San Felíu de Guixols, and between Cadaqués and Port-Bou, where dozens of hairpin turns skirt the seacoast. One saving grace here is the relatively short distances between towns, which means you can get off the road reasonably quickly. In addition, plenty of buses ply the route and any hotel concierge can provide you with an updated schedule.

BLANES: About 40 miles (64 km) north of Barcelona, the southernmost town of the Costa Brava is hardly the most compelling. Blanes's 300-yard-long, relatively flat beach is lined with a strip of aging white apartment buildings and hotels. The permanent population of 16,000 swells considerably during the summer when sailors are drawn to the decent anchorages in the harbor and the yacht club. Tourist information is available at the town hall (phone: 33-03-48).

LLORET DE MAR: While Lloret de Mar is only now being discovered by Americans, it has been a favorite bargain vacation spot with European tourists for many years. The accommodations here are generally quite adequate and inexpensive.

The wide, half-moon-shaped, sandy beach is good for swimming, but it gets so crowded between July and September that Jones Beach looks spacious by comparison.

Lloret's fine seaside promenade, Paseo de Mosén Jacinto Verdaguer — known as Cinto Verdaguer to Lloretans — is a palm-lined boulevard whose trees cast gentle shadows on the people eating and drinking at its outdoor cafés. But you really have to adore crowds to appreciate it.

On the other hand, about 2 miles (3 km) south is the lovely little beach and bay of Santa Cristina, just off the Blanes-Lloret road, a golden stretch of sand amid greenery and volcanic outcroppings. And in the opposite direction, just another 2 miles (3 km) north of Lloret, is Playa de Canyelles, one of the most beautiful sections of the Catalán coast. The beach is divided in half by El Corquinyoli, a massive rocky ridge. If there's any isolation in the vicinity of Lloret, you may still find it here. For tourist information, contact the town hall (phone: 33-47-35).

TOSSA DE MAR: An 8-mile (13-km) drive from Lloret de Mar along the edge of the sea brings you to one of the most popular resorts on the Costa Brava, the gleaming white town of Tossa de Mar. The old quarter of town (Vila Vella) predates even the Roman civilization. Surrounded by walls constructed later, in the twelfth century, it is guarded by a Moorish alcazaba. (For a very special photograph, try shooting from one of the three ancient towers' arches.)

The town's main beach is exceptionally crowded, but you can find some measure of seclusion on El Codolar behind Vila Vella. If there are still too many people for your liking, try Playa Llorell about 2 miles (3 km) south of town.

We've already mentioned the crush of visitors the Costa Brava area experiences. Beautiful little Tossa de Mar is a case in point: Of the 49 hotels in town, only 17 have more than 100 rooms, and the rest are smaller. Don't expect to be able to be ushered into a room during July and August. You'll have better luck during April, May, September, and October, before and after the height of the season when the weather can still be relied upon to be pleasant.

Tourist information is available at the town hall (phone: 34-01-08).

SANT FELÍU DE GUIXOLS: This small town stands about 15 miles (24 km) north of Tossa de Mar along one of the meanest stretches of coastal road imaginable. Located at the edge of a shimmering, sheltered bay, long favored by fishermen, San Felíu was the site of a Benedictine monastery in the eleventh century. Although the monastery no longer exists, you can still see some of the ruins on the side of the road. Its fine beach, cafés, and bullring make this another very popular resort. Tourist information is available from the town hall (phone: 32-03-80).

S'AGARÓ: If you're traveling on a budget, it's a good idea to stay in San Felíu and spend a day or two visiting the haute monde of the Costa Brava barely 2 miles (3 km) to the north. But if you want a real taste of luxury and you can afford it, head for S'Agaró right away.

With a teeming population of about 200 permanent residents, the village is the summer residence of many Spanish and foreign luminaries. A model of meticulous, strictly enforced city planning codes, S'Agaró's contemporary residential community is the brainchild of architect José Ensesa, who wanted to create the perfect seaside resort. Many visitors to S'Agaró believe he accomplished his task. A walk along the Paseo de Ronda will give you a good idea of the success and extent of the planning — the Paseo is lined with gardens, fountains, statuary, and chalets, ending at lovely Playa Concha. Not bad for a village the size of a postage stamp.

BAGUR: The principal cove in this town is Aiguablava, or blue water, in the local Catalán dialect. Although it is appropriately named, it is nonetheless rivaled by neighboring coves Cala Fornells and Cala de Sa Tuna. Just north of town, Sa Riera is an unusual beach on the open seas. When the winds come from the south, the water is calm and transparent, but when the winds come from the north, the sea boils over the rocks. Sa Riera beach cannot be seen from the road; you must walk down a series of steps through the trees to a concrete balcony built on a granite shelf. From here, another set of steps leads down to the sand and rock outcroppings. For quiet seclusion, few places can compare with Sa Riera.

AMPURIAS: While antiquities of Roman origin are almost commonplace in Spain, Phoenician ruins are a rarity. But here in Ampurias you can visit an archaeological zone containing Phoenician ruins from the sixth century BC as well as those from a later (first century BC) Roman settlement. The Phoenician community, called Emporion, was uncovered in 1908 and is almost fully excavated. A walk through the restored ruins alone is worth the trip to the Costa Brava, since it gives you an idea of what daily life was like 2,500 years ago. Artifacts from both Phoenician and Roman sites are on display inside the Archaeological Museum building, where audio tapes provide a full explanation of the rise and fall of both civilizations. It is exceptionally well done and should not be missed.

ROSAS: Known for its sparkling bay and docks where fishermen sell their daily catch from the decks of their boats, Rosas, too, expands well beyond its 7,000 permanent residents during the summer months when the long beach is practically wall-to-wall people. For a bit more privacy, visit the nearby coves: Canyelles Petites, Canyelles Grosses, Monjoy, and Joncais. Tourist information is available at town hall (phone: 25-73-31).

En Route from Rosas – Although not widely known, the town of Figueras is home to the Dali Museum, a converted castle housing many works of the surrealist painter who lives in nearby Cadaqués. We're not sure which is more impressive: the gigantic canvases or the 50-foot-high glass ceiling. But it's definitely worth a side trip.

CADAQUÉS: This is undoubtedly a special corner of Spain. Although only several hours' drive from Barcelona, Cadaqués is worlds apart in time and tempo. This little town is pure Catalán, and its austere character reflects the fact that its residents must daily extract their living from the relentless sea. The home of the town's most famous resident, Salvador Dali, is an obvious exception. The painter's estate, formed of adjoining cottages, is marked by gigantic egg-shaped ornaments and projects a completely different lifestyle and attitude. Although your first impression of Cadaqués may be of the stark contrast between the dark, brooding mountains and the tiny, pretty white houses, one look at Dali's whimsical garden will lighten your mood.

Dali is not the only artist to make his home here. Since the late 1940s Cadaqués has been an artists' retreat colony. Perhaps because of its relative inaccessibility, the town has retained its tranquillity and has not yet been transformed by tourism.

PORT-BOU: Nestled at the foot of the Pyrenees mountains that meet the Mediterranean in a horseshoe-shaped embrace of land and sea, Port-Bou stands on the Spanish-French border. This busy little fishing village has, in addition to the quiet beach within the horseshoe-shaped cove, two nearby beaches: Cala Tres Plagetas and El Piño.

BEST EN ROUTE

As this is one of the most developed resort areas of Spain, you can find all manner of accommodations, from luxury hotels to more modest places. Expect to pay $50 or more for a double room at hotels we've classified as expensive; between $30 and $50 at those hotels listed in the moderate category; and under $30, inexpensive.

The Costa Brava has quite a few restaurants that serve well-prepared Mediterranean cuisine in naturally beautiful surroundings. Expect to pay $50 or more for a meal for two at those restaurants we've listed as expensive; between $25 and $50 at those restaurants in the moderate category; under $25, inexpensive. Prices do not include drinks, wine, or tips.

BLANES

Patacano – After three generations of serving fish and seafood, this restaurant has expanded to accommodate its substantial clientele. Closed Mondays in winter. Paseo del Mar 12 (phone: 33-00-02). Moderate.

LLORET DE MAR

Dex – A smallish hotel on the beach, it has a swimming pool, hairdresser, and bingo. And it is quite reasonably priced. Juan Llaverías (phone: 36-42-66). Inexpensive.

Helios Lloret – Centrally located on the beach, this, too, has a swimming pool. Fernando Agulló 86 (phone: 36-51-08). Inexpensive.

Garbi Park – Yet another beachfront establishment, but without frills. Urbanización Garbi, Av. Nuestra Sra. de Loreto (phone: 36-54-82). Inexpensive.

El Trull – Near the beach, with a pretty view of the seacoast, this restaurant has a swimming pool. Urbanización Playa Canyelles (phone: 36-49-28). Moderate.

Roca Grossa – This restaurant, which also has a swimming pool, caters to a discriminating international clientele. Closed from mid-October through mid-March. Urbanización Roca Grossa (phone: 36-51-09). Moderate.

TOSSA DE MAR

Gran Hotel Reymar – The largest hotel in town has a great view of the sea, landscaped gardens, beachfront, fishing facilities, swimming pool, and a nightclub. Pets are allowed. There is a doctor on the premises. Rooms have air-conditioning. Mar Menuda (phone: 34-03-12). Moderate.

Hotel-Restaurante Maria Angela – Not far from the sea on the main promenade, this simple, pleasant hotel has central heating in rooms, an unusual feature for the Costa Brava, and an outdoor café. Portal Nou 3 (phone: 34-03-58). Inexpensive.

Castell Vell – Within the ancient walled city, this picturesque little place serves good regional cuisine. Closed from October through March. Plaza Roig y Soler 1 (phone: 34-10-30). Moderate.

Bar Sa Muralla – This old, whitewashed building tucked among the houses close to the wall serves lunch and drinks under colorful umbrellas. Paseo del Mar (no phone). Inexpensive.

SANT FELÍU DE GUIXOLS

Eldorado Petit – This is a good place to sample freshly caught fish and seafood. Rambla Vidal 11 (phone: 32-10-29). Expensive.

Club Náutico – One flight up, it affords a view of the harbor and serves Mediterranean cuisine. Paseo del Mar (phone: 32-06-63). Expensive to moderate.

Amura – Another good restaurant with an interesting view. Closed from October through March. Plaza San Pedro 1 (phone: 32-10-35). Moderate to inexpensive.

S'AGARÓ

Hostal de la Gavina – It is unquestionably one of the most luxurious hotels in the country, with prices to match. Perched on a cliff with two beaches below, it has two tennis courts lit for night playing and offers guest privileges at a nearby golf course. The highlight of the white, Spanish mission-style building is its dining room, where evening meals are served by candlelight. Plaza de la Rosaleda (phone: 32-11-00). Very expensive.

BAGUR

Cap sa Sal – Yet another cliffside resort that appears to have sprung quite naturally from the gray rock jutting into the blue sea, it has two swimming pools, a health club with sauna, tennis courts, motorboats, water skiing, six restaurants, and four bars. Cala de Aiguafreda (phone: 62-21-00). Expensive.

Parador Nacional Aiguablava – The site of this government-run inn is sublime, but its construction must have been an act of sheer courage. It straddles a promontory 150 feet above a sheltered sliver of beach, accessible by weather-beaten granite steps. The water is ideally suited for swimming, snorkeling, and scuba diving. But the food in the dining room is mediocre. Reservations required 6 months in advance. Contact the Spanish National Tourist Offices in the US. Punta d'es Mut (phone: 62-20-58). Expensive to moderate.

CADAQUÉS

Rocamar – Although not on the beach, its pretty gardens offer some compensation. So do the swimming pool, tennis courts, and discothèque. The rooms have central heating. Dogs are allowed on the premises. Dr. Bartomeus (phone: 25-81-50). Moderate.

Playa Sol – A quieter establishment with fewer entertainment facilities, this one is located on a good beach. Playa Pianch (phone: 25-81-00). Moderate.

Campsites – No fewer than 90 government-run campsites cover the coast between Blanes and Port-Bou. That's about one for every mile. Some have swimming pools and recreation rooms. Others occupy choice beachfronts. All of them are jammed during July and August, probably because they are very inexpensive. For information, contact the Spanish National Tourist Office in the US.

Es Baluard – Here you'll find some of the finest Mediterranean cooking in town. While you're not likely to find Salvador Dali having a meal, you might well catch a glimpse of his neighbors. Riba Nemesio Llorens 2 (phone: 25-81-83). Moderate.

Don Quijote – This charming little restaurant has a terrace filled with flowers. Av. Caridad Seriñana (phone: 25-81-41). Moderate.

PORT-BOU

L'Ancora – Comfortably decorated with old country furnishings, this place serves French and Spanish cuisine. Closed during November and on Tuesdays. Paseo de la Sardana 4 (phone: 39-00-25). Moderate to inexpensive.

Andalusia

The Andalusian region is, in a very real way, the heart of Spain. Indeed, Andalusia is home to that which most people think of as Spanish: the flamenco, a flamboyant music and dance that's so identified with the Gypsies of Granada and Seville; Spain's many famous matadors — El Cordobés, Manolete, and Lagartijo; the traditional orange blossom–draped, white-washed cottages clinging precariously to rocky hillsides; and the stunning Moorish palace and garden complex, the Alhambra.

A mountainous region in the southern part of the country, Andalusia comprises eight provinces: Almería, Cádiz, Córdoba, Granada, Huelva, Jaén, Málaga, and Seville. The Sierra Morena, Sierra Nevada, and Sistema

Penibética mountain ranges take up large sections of the interior. Much of the land is given over to the cultivation of olives, oranges, sunflowers, and grapes. Andalusia is bordered on the west by the Gulf of Cádiz, on the south by the Strait of Gibraltar, and on the southeast and east by the Mediterranean Sea. Andalusia's major cities are Córdoba, Granada, and Seville.

The recorded history of the region dates back to the arrival of the Phoenicians between the eleventh and fifth centuries BC. Around the same era, the Celts, who migrated south from northern Europe, intermarried with the native Iberian residents; their offspring, the Celtiberians, are the ancestors of the present-day Spanish. Around the turn of the millenium, the Romans arrived, bringing their culture, politics, and philosophy. They built cities at Italica (Seville), Córdoba, and Baelo-Claudia, as well as roads, aqueducts, and monuments. The Romans were followed by the Christian Visigoths around the fifth and sixth centuries AD, who were, in turn, vanquished by the Moors in AD 711. The Moorish era is known as the golden age of Andalusia. During this period, the region was the seat of an independent caliphate that thrived while the rest of the European continent remained in the Dark Ages. The most important Andalusian monuments — the Mezquita of Córdoba, the Giralda of Seville, and the Alhambra of Granada — date from this epoch.

In 1492 the Moslem empire in Spain, already reduced to the kingdom of Granada, was conquered by the Catholic monarchs Ferdinand and Isabella. In the same year, the adventurer Christopher Colombus set off from Cádiz, an Andalusian port, to discover the New World.

Nowadays, people from the New World travel to discover Andalusia. The best time to visit is in March and April, when the temperatures are in the 60s and 70s F (15° to 21°C) and it is not yet crowded. June, July, and August are peak months. It tends to rain in the winter.

Our tour starts in Córdoba, and heads southwest to Seville and Jerez de la Frontera, before winding northeast through the mountains to Ronda and Granada. If you are driving remember that the countryside is very rugged and so are the roads.

CÓRDOBA: Founded by the Romans in 151 BC, it was a city popular with Julius Caesar, Pompey, and Agrippa. Both Senecas were born here. Ruins of Roman walls and a Roman stone bridge reconstructed by the Moors still span the Río Guadalquivir. The former capital of Moorish Spain during the eighth century, it was governed as a separate emirate until the tenth century when the Caliphate of Córdoba was established. During the tenth-century reign of Abderramán II, the city had 500,000 inhabitants and some 300 mosques. It was at that time one of the leading cities in Europe and also one of the leading cities of the Moslem world. Today, the population numbers only 255,000, but in many areas of the town the mystery of the Córdoban past is still very much alive.

While you are in Córdoba, be sure to see La Mezquita, a masterpiece of Moorish–early Spanish architecture that was first a mosque, then a cathedral. During the eighth century, the Moslems shared the mosque with the Christians. After passing through the Patio of the Orange Trees (Patio de los naranjos) you enter a forest of columns — alabaster, jasper, and marble — topped by ocher and tan horseshoe arches. The columns come from as far away as North Africa where they were taken from Roman, Visigoth, and Phoenician ruins. One testimony to the size of the mosque is the fact that the Christians built a full-sized cathedral in its center after Córdoba was reconquered in 1236. La Mezquita is open daily (Cardenal Herrero).

Surrounding La Mezquita is the oldest part of the city. Called the Judería, it contains the Jewish quarter to the northwest. On Calle Judíos, there is a fourteenth-century synagogue with segregated men's and women's sections. Nearby, on Calle Averroes and Calle Judíos, is a patio where flamenco dancers perform during the summer months. Across the street from the synagogue is the Municipal Museum (Museo Municipal) which contains early Córdoban artifacts, and the Taurino Museum (Museo Taurino) which has articles that belonged to some of Córdoba's major matadors — Lagartijo, Manolete, Machaco, Currita, and El Cordobés.

Along the banks of the Río Guadalquivir, the Alcázar, a group of splendid Moorish gardens of pools, towers, fountains, and terraces, is open daily. If you are a fan of Don Quixote's, be sure to visit Plazuela del Potro, where an inn mentioned in the classic novel by Cervantes is still standing.

About 4 miles (6 km) west of town is the Medina Azahara, the remains of a Moorish city built in the tenth century. It's worth a side trip, especially for the pleasant country-side surroundings.

Although you can shop for souvenirs in the area around La Mezquita, the only really worthwhile items are Córdoba leather and filigree silver. There are plenty of little cafés where you can sip coffee and relax.

The Office of Tourist Information is at Hermanos G. Murga 13 (phone: 22-12-05). Now take the NIV southwest to Seville.

SEVILLE: According to legend, Seville was founded by Hercules the Greek. Although the city shares a similar pattern of earlier history with Córdoba, Seville came into its own after the Christian reconquest of Andalusia in the thirteenth century. The cathedral contains some of the treasure that Spanish conquistadores brought back from the New World.

The cathedral and Alcázar complex (Av. Queipo de Llano) is the most impressive site in the city. The fifteenth-century cathedral is the third largest in the world, after St. Peter's and St. Paul's, and the largest gothic structure in the world. Like the Cathedral of Córdoba, it is built on the site of a former mosque adjoining a Patio of the Orange Trees. All that remains of the original mosque is a statuesque 322-foot Moorish tower, La Giralda, which is now the symbol of Seville. After touring the opulent fifteenth- and sixteenth-century interior of the Cathedral, take the exit called Puerta de los Naranjos which opens onto the patio. Walk to the Puerta Oriente, across a plaza, and you will find yourself at the Alcázar, the Moorish fortress that was modified by the Christians in the fourteenth century to resemble the Alhambra in Granada.

After touring the Alcázar, have lunch at the *Hostería del Laurel* (Plaza de las Venerables 5), where none other than Don Juan is supposed to have eaten before or after he went a-wooing. It's still in service and the food is quite good.

After lunch, why not take a walk through the Barrio de Santa Cruz, or down Calle Sierpes, the main street reserved for pedestrian traffic. Be sure to spend some time strolling through Parque María Luisa along the banks of the Río Guadalquivir and Av. María Luisa, and take a boat ride at the Plaza de Espana. After such a pleasant afternoon, you'll know why Bizet's *Carmen* and Rossini's *The Barber of Seville* are set here.

Unlike Córdoba, Seville has maintained its prominence as the spiritual center of Andalusia. In fact, the best time to visit Seville is during Semana Santa (Holy Week), and during the weeks following Easter until the *fería* (folkfair) in April. During this time many holy images are paraded through the streets; the religious processions are world famous. Reservations often are made a year in advance.

Route E25 will take you south to Jerez de la Frontera.

JEREZ DE LA FRONTERA: The town that first gave the world sherry is still producing it. Guided tours are conducted through Jerez's wine cellars with wine sampling offered afterward. You can buy sherry on the spot if any particular brand appeals to you. If you imbibe a bit more sherry than you're accustomed to, be sure to spend the night in Jerez before tackling the roads to Ronda, as they twist around cliffs and are difficult to navigate. You can also rent a chauffeured car or take an organized bus tour.

En Route to Granada – Set in the hills of the Serranía de Ronda, one of the oldest cities in Spain, Ronda is divided into two sections by a gorge more than 50 feet deep. South of the gorge is the old Moorish section with its narrow, curving streets and alleyways. In this part of town is found the Palace of the Moorish King (Casa del Rey Moro); the Cathedral of Santa María la Mayor, which was a mosque in an earlier incarnation; and the Moorish baths. The Plaza de Toros is said to be the place where Pedro Romera started modern bullfighting in the eighteenth century. The best way to see Ronda is on foot. The splendid views of the surrounding hills and the gorges are truly impressive. Don't expect the Rondeños to welcome you with wide open arms; they are less exuberant than their other Andalusian neighbors. This may have something to do with the fact that the Serranía de Ronda used to be a refuge for bandits and *contrabandistas*.

You can get to Ronda from Jerez by heading east on Route 342. This road continues to Granada but it is a tortuous, time-consuming route. Scenic, yes; but you'll probably spend so much time praying that you won't enjoy the views. Alternatively, you can take Route 344 south to Fuengirola and follow the coastal route (340) through Málaga to Motril, heading north on Route 323 to Granada. It gets you there without the agony.

GRANADA: To most people, Granada is synonymous with the Alhambra, a lavish fortress-palace-garden complex built on a mountain overlooking the city. Built by the Nasrid royal family (an Islamic group that fought the Christians in the thirteenth century), the Alhambra is one of the best preserved of all Moorish palaces in the world. It consists of three main areas: the Alcazaba and watch tower that date back to the ninth century; the Alhambra itself; and the Generalife, or summer gardens. Within the Alhambra is the fourteenth-century palace, which has many spacious courtyards and patios decorated with mosaic arches, fountains, columns, and gardens. A visit to the Alhambra is a dazzling, sensual experience: color, texture, sound, and smell intermingle.

Down the hill from the Alhambra, on Calle San Jeronimo in the Cathedral quarter, is the Royal Chapel (Capilla Real), where the Catholic monarchs Ferdinand and Isabella are buried on the site of their victory over the Moors.

Opposite the Alhambra, the hilly Albaicín neighborhood is an intriguing maze of cottage-lined streets and patio gardens that sprout, like miniature Generalifes, in the middle of each house. The Sacromonte, at the summit of Albaicín, has some Gypsy caves where flamenco dances are performed. Be forewarned that they are overpriced; the shows in town are usually at least as good (if not better) and much less expensive.

For a list of reputable flamenco clubs and information on festivals, contact the Office of Tourist Information, Pavaneras 19 (phone: 22-10-22).

In winter, from November to May, you can ski at Solynieve ski center at Sierra Nevada, a few miles from Granada. Facilities include a chair lift, eight ski lifts, and two cable cars. For details, see the Tourist Office listed above.

BEST EN ROUTE

Hotels range from modern to historic *paradores* (government-owned inns). Expect to pay $65 or more for a double room at those places we've listed as expensive; between $30 and $60 for a room in the moderate category; under $30, inexpensive.

Andalusian restaurants are known for their pretty flowers, music, and artistic presentation of food that add sparkle to the atmosphere. Expect to pay over $50 for a meal for two at those restaurants we've listed as expensive; between $25 and $50 at those restaurants in the moderate category; under $25, inexpensive. Prices do not include drinks, wine, or tips.

CÓRDOBA

Melía Córdoba – What it lacks in charm, it makes up for in modern amenities and a super convenient location right in the center of town. It has a nightclub, bar, dining room, swimming pool, and a shopping arcade. Jardines de la Victoria (phone: 29-80-66). Moderate.

Parador Nacional de la Arruzafa – On the outskirts of town, this is not in a historic building, but rather in a fairly ordinary looking, relatively recent structure. The dining room serves game in winter and gazpacho with almonds in summer. Av. de la Arruzafa (phone: 27-59-00). Moderate.

Residencial Maimónides – A small hotel right across the street from La Mezquita offers modest accommodations and the most scenic location in town. In the old section. Torrijos 4 (phone: 47-15-00). Moderate to inexpensive.

Caballo Rojo – Córdoba's leading restaurant serves Andalusian gazpacho, tortillas, and Valencian paella. Cardenal Herrero 28 (phone: 47-53-75). Moderate.

El Churrasco – Various cuts of steak are served with potatoes, rice, and/or eggs. Closed during August and on Thursdays. It's located one flight up at Romero 16 (phone: 29-08-19). Moderate to inexpensive.

SEVILLE

Hotel Doña Maria – Directly across the street from the cathedral in the Barrio de Santa Cruz, this small, four-star hotel has received good reviews from just about everyone who's crossed its threshold. Don Remondo 19 (phone: 22-49-90). Moderate.

Hotel Inglaterra – Another top-rate, contemporary hotel in the center of the city, behind the town hall. Many of its comfortable rooms have large balconies. It's a short walk from here to the cathedral and Calle Sierpes. A good buy for Seville. Plaza Nueva 7 (phone: 22-49-70). Moderate.

Parador Nacional Alcázar del Rey Don Pedro – A low, long building, standing on a hill about half an hour from Seville, it was designed to be a replica of a Moorish castle. It has a restaurant, bar, and swimming pool. Carmona (phone: 14-10-10). Moderate to inexpensive.

Hostería del Laurel – After touring the Alcázar, have lunch where the infamous Don Juan dined. Plaza de los Venerables 5 (phone: 22-02-95). Moderate.

Oriza – One of the fanciest restaurants in town, this is a favorite of the local aristocracy and visiting European epicureans. Closed Sundays. Betis 61 (phone: 27-95-85). Moderate.

Río Grande – Here, wide terraces flank the riverbanks and the architecture of the building is lovely in its own right. Betis 70 (phone: 27-83-71). Moderate.

Mesón Don Raimundo – In a former convent with antique furnishings, this restaurant has plenty of atmosphere and good seafood. Closed Sunday nights. Argote de Molina 26 (phone: 22-33-55). Expensive to moderate.

El Burladero – Handsomely decorated with tiled ceilings and wood paneling, it's very popular with the Spanish. Start with *angulas de Aguinaga,* baby eels, or gazpacho, then have meat, poultry, game, or paella. Service, food, and wine are excellent. Canalejas 1 (phone: 22-29-00). Moderate.

JEREZ DE LA FRONTERA

Gaitán – Prepared with savory herbs, the Andalusian stews and soups served here are complemented by delicious original dishes and tempting desserts. Closed Sunday nights, Mondays, and August. Gaitán 3 (phone: 34-58-59). Moderate to inexpensive.

GRANADA

Parador Nacional de San Francisco – This one tops the list of *paradores*. Located in a restored fifteenth-century section of the Alhambra itself, it is booked solid throughout the year. Reservations are required 8 months in advance. Alhambra (phone: 22-14-93). Moderate.

Alhambra Palace – If you cannot get a room in the *Parador* and still want to stay near the Alhambra, this might be the solution. It, too, stands on the Alhambra hill. The decor tends to be more of a Hollywood interpretation of Moorish splendor, but it does have pleasant rooms and some great views of the Alhambra or the city. Peñapartida 1 (phone: 22-14-68). Moderate.

Washington Irving Hotel – Named for the American writer whose *Tales of The Alhambra* helped rekindle foreign interest in the place, this hotel is close to the Alhambra and offers decent, inexpensive accommodations. Paseo de Generalife, 2 (phone: 22-75-50). Moderate to inexpensive.

Torres Bermejas – This is the best restaurant in town for Andalusian cuisine. Closed Sundays. Plaza Nueva 5 (phone: 22-31-16). Moderate.

Colombia – Next door to the Alhambra, meals are served to the background accompaniment of flamenco guitarists. Closed Sundays. Antequeruela Baja (phone: 22-74-34). Inexpensive.

Cunini – Granada's most prominent fish restaurant also features seafood flown in from the coast. Pescadería 9 (phone: 22-37-27). Inexpensive.

The Canary Islands

A cluster of seven major and six minor islands in the South Atlantic, the Canary Island archipelago lies about 65 miles (104 km) off the northwest coast of Africa. Spread across the 28° north latitude line, just four degrees north of the Tropic of Cancer, the Canaries have a springlike climate throughout the year — in the 70s F (21°–31° C). The major islands are Tenerife, Gran Canaria, Fuerteventura, La Gomera, Hierro, and La Palma, also known as "the green island" because of its comparatively heavy rainfall and the intense green of its forests.

Although legends suggest that the Canary Islands are the remains of the lost continent of Atlantis, history indicates that the first recorded visit occurred during the first century AD. According to Roman historian Pliny the Elder, it was Juba II, at that time King of Mauritania, who was the first tourist of note to visit the Canary Islands. In those days, the islands were called Canariae Insulae, which, in the original Latin, means "dog islands." So, when Juba II stepped off the royal barge, he was greeted by a pack of large, snarling dogs. According to Pliny (the only available source), Juba hastily retreated to Mauritania.

It wasn't until the late fifteenth century that Spain claimed the seven cone-shaped volcanic islands and renamed them Las Canarias after a variety of finch that live in the trees. We don't know what happened to the original Latin dogs for which the islands were named 1,400 years earlier, but we do know that the archipelago became greatly sought after. The two main islands, Gran Canaria and Tenerife, were finally conquered by Kind Ferdinand and Queen Isabella in 1496.

Not much is known about the original inhabitants, the Guanche cave dwellers who were decimated by the Spanish armies, bubonic plague, locust-induced famine, and volcanic eruptions. A tall, blond, light-skinned, blue-eyed people, the Guanche are believed to have been descended from a mixture of Viking, African, Berber, and Phoenician stock. According to archaeologists, who have unearthed ceramic and leather artifacts, the Guanche were monotheistic and mummified their dead.

The present-day Canary Islanders are a pacific, friendly, artistic people who make their living farming, fishing, and producing handicrafts, as well as by working at various jobs in the modern resort developments. Though only recently discovered by American tourists, the Canary Islands have long been popular with vacationing Europeans. The quaint villages of white cottages with red roofs sprinkled throughout the mountainous interior of the volcanic islands make the Canary Island archipelago inviting to travelers who enjoy exploring unusual places and discovering the distinctive character of each island.

GRAN CANARIA

As you fly into Gando International Airport, south of Gran Canaria's capital, Las Palmas, the island looks like Mt. Everest rising from the Sahara. As you descend, the stark, rugged landscape becomes greener and soon you can distinguish banana trees, coffee groves, sugarcane, almond trees, and tomato farms. Each village is actually an oasis.

LAS PALMAS: The capital city of this 922-square-mile island is a duty-free port; Europeans from all over the Continent flock here for the bargains in furs. Two well-known furriers with shops in half a dozen European cities, *Voula Mitsakou* (Luis Morote 28, at the junction of Calle Sagasta and Av. General Vives) and *Kanellopoulos* (Sagasta 46) charge 30% to 50% less for their leopard, sable, ermine, and other skins in Las Palmas than in their other branches. In addition to the furriers, you will find plenty of shops selling Chinese silks, Indian marble, cameras, tape recorders, liquor, shoes, clothing, jewelry, and souvenir items. Bargaining or "negotiation," as it is otherwise called, is highly appropriate, but you have to be good at it to best the Indian, Pakistani, and Lebanese merchants who own most of the stores. It is a good idea to know the prices of items you are considering before you actually buy. And if you're in the market for a camera, be sure you know the exact model number: It can make a big difference in price.

Las Palmas covers a strip of seafront on the northwest tip of the island. A natural depression in the coastline has provided a sheltered bay for the beach called Playa de las Canteras. The rocky breakwater, shaped rather like an arm, extends almost around the bay and makes it as calm as a lake. Running parallel to the beach, the 2-mile (3.2-km) Paseo de las Canteras promenade boasts numerous restaurants: Swedish, Italian, Chinese, Finnish, Mexican, Indian, German, and Spanish, as well as a few of the sit-down or stand-up, fast-food variety. In addition, there are many bars, cafés, and bistros.

The rhythm of life in Las Palmas is determined by the sun. Visitors often spend the day lying in the sun from 8 or 9 AM until 4 or 5 PM. Then, in the cool of the evening, they head for the outdoor cafés, shops, restaurants, and bars of the Paseo. Shops remain open until dusk, about 9 PM. If clouds or mist interfere with the sun, people stroll or shop — but only until the sun reappears.

Sometimes people go for a walk in Parque Santa Catalina where Canarian families often come for their evening strolls. It's very pleasant, as local guitarists play impromptu serenades for passersby. To get to the park, walk along Calle Padre Cueto four blocks to Castillo, then head right along Castillo for two blocks. (By the way, the park, and everywhere else in the Canary Islands, is safe for visiting at night.)

The public market is a good place for taking photographs of people engaged in the ordinary everyday commerce of buying and selling foodstuffs and other provisions. It occupies an entire block at the corner of Calles Néstor de Torre and Galicia. From the Paseo, walk up Calle Thomas Miller, the street with the statue of the dolphin. Take it straight to the market.

Doramas Park (Parque Doramas) contains a zoo, swimming pool, and an unusual model of a Canarian village designed by local painter Néstor de la Torre. The park is easy to get to: Any bus traveling along Calle León y Castello at Parque Santa Catalina also goes to Parque Doramas. After a visit to the park, the *Bodegon* restaurant is a good place to taste Canarian food. But watch out; first encounters with Canarian food can be explosive. The ubiquitous sauce called *mojo picón* is a falso amigo (false friend). Its seemingly benign aroma belies its true nature. *Mojo picón* is not just a hot sauce, it's an incendiary concoction of chili peppers, garlic, oil, vinegar, salt, and pepper. But don't hesitate to order either the *cazuela canario* or *sancocho de pescado,* a fish casserole and stew, respectively. Try them both — they're delicious.

TEJEDA: About 25 miles (40 km) southwest of Las Palmas along narrow, mountain roads stands the petrified forest, which the Spanish poet Unamuno (1864–1936) called a "petrified storm." It stands about 4,800 feet above sea level amid a bleak, awesome, volcanic landscape. Be sure to take advantage of the sensational lookouts *(miradores)* along the route. Bus excursions and English-speaking taxi drivers also cover this route. The concierge at any hotel will help you arrange transportation.

MASPALOMAS: On the southern edge of Gran Canaria, about 35 miles (56 km) from Gando Airport, lies an ocher strand of beach, Playa del Inglés, that curves around a palm-fringed lagoon, looking like a setting from *The Arabian Nights.* Just 1 mile to the west of the Maspalomas lighthouse, Playa Pasito Blanco has a deep-water harbor with a marina where deep-sea charters can be hired. There is an 18-hole golf course at *Maspalomas Oasis*, a new resort.

PUERTO RICO: Just 20 miles (32 km) west of Maspalomas, this apartment-condominium complex is great for families and couples who want to spend a month, a summer, or the entire year in a setting complete with marina, beach, swimming pools, restaurants, shopping, nightclubs, and playgrounds. The complex is pretty big, but the design of the community is not overwhelming. You can find out about booking space in Puerto Rico from the Tourist Office in Las Palmas or at Spanish National Tourist Office in the US. (This area is not particularly recommended for singles.)

SAN BARTOLOMÉ DE TIRAJANA: Another day trip from Las Palmas or Maspalomas takes you to this town at the bottom of a huge crater at the foot of the central mountains. At 6,500 feet, the snow-capped Pozo de las Nieves ridge is the highest point on the island. It's a 2-mile (3.2-km) hike, straight up, from San Bartolomé to the peaks.

TENERIFE

Just 20 minutes by air from Las Palmas, Tenerife, with 1,235 square miles, is the largest of the Canary Islands. (It can also be reached by flights from Madrid in a little over 2 hours.) Lusher, with more forest, colorful vegetation, and a somewhat higher rate of rainfall, Tenerife is called the island of "eternal spring." It is also the archipelago's main agricultural center. Most vegetables grown in the Canaries come from Tenerife's soil.

SANTA CRUZ DE TENERIFE: A duty-free port, the capital of Tenerife is more Spanish in character and aesthetically more pleasing than Las Palmas. However, it has no beaches of which to speak and is primarily a city of shops. The streets bounded by Calle del Castillo, Valentín Sanz, Emilio Calzadillo, and the ocean form a square within which are literally hundreds of shops selling everything. As in Las Palmas, the Indian, Pakistani, Lebanese, and Spanish shopkeepers are willing to negotiate but they are not about to give anything away. Calle del Castillo is closed to traffic from the Plaza de España to the park at the end of the street. Plaza de España is noteworthy because of its memorial and monument to the men of Tenerife who died in World War II. Due to its height, the monument can be seen from quite a distance, so try to use it as a directional marker as you head into the shopping district, which is almost always jammed with hordes of shoppers.

PLAYA LAS TERESITAS: With barren volcanic cliffs for a backdrop, this beach, about 10 minutes from the center of town along the road to San Andrés, resembles a moonscape. In fact, you would think you were swimming in a moon crater if the moon had water. Only ¼ mile long and about 150 yards wide, the beach is totally protected from the open Atlantic by a stone jetty. You can reach the beach by taking a bus from the Plaza de España.

OROTAVA: One of Tenerife's most compelling sites, Orotava is located across the neck of the island from Santa Cruz and overlooks Puerto de la Cruz, 1,000 feet below. This is the best place to shop for indigenous crafts. Be sure to visit the *Artesanía* (Calle San Francisco), one of a national chain of arts and crafts centers established by the Spanish government. It is in an old house with a flower-filled patio. Here you will find the delicate *calado*, drawn-thread embroidery, used for everything from handkerchiefs to tablecloths, manufactured by women working at wooden looms. The women speak English and they are glad to answer questions. In addition to local crafts, ceramics from Seville and leather from Barcelona are also on sale.

The annual Corpus Christi festival in June is a celebration of the religious fervor, energy, and artistry of the people of Orotava. Before the festival's procession, the town's squares and streets are covered with carpets of brilliant flowers and colorful sand designs. The largest and most intricate sand carpet is laid on the Plaza del Ayuntamiento, across town from the *Artesanía*. On other streets around town carpets made from hundreds of thousands of flower petals — bougainvillea, dahlias, geraniums, carnations — as well as crushed leaves and pine needles depict a variety of biblical scenes. Although the Feast of Corpus Christi is at its most colorful in Orotava, it is celebrated throughout the Canaries, floral carpets and all.

PICOS DEL TEIDE: There are few places on earth where you can explore volcanic craters. Even fewer give you the chance to stand more than 2 miles above sea level and look in all directions, unhindered. El Pico del Teide, a crater more than 40 miles in circumference and more than 6,600 feet above sea level, is one of those rare places. Just beyond the crater stands the highest mountain in Spain, El Teide, at 12,500 feet. Parque Nacional Las Cañadas del Teide has a cable car to the top of the mountain. The 15-minute ride to the summit is breathtaking enough to make even the most avid photographers gaze at the scenery and forget about taking pictures. When there are few clouds, the six other major Canary Islands and the coast of Africa are clearly visible. At dawn, the sun touching the mountains creates splendid shadows that blend with the different shades of lava and ash. The stillness and barrenness is intensely moving.

PUERTO DE LA CRUZ: Considering that Puerto de la Cruz has no beach worthy of its name, it is reasonable to wonder why it is the major tourist center of the Canaries. Put simply, Puerto is pure resort — an enclave of shops, hotels, restaurants, bars, and discos. There is hardly anything else. The town has been given over to strolling, shopping, and eating. To compensate for no beach, clever architects and engineers have built sea-water pools, promenades, man-made lakes, and lounging areas into and around the rocky volcanic outcroppings that extend offshore for hundreds of yards.

The best way to get to know Puerto is on foot. A walk through the most interesting part of town should begin at Plaza de Concejil on Calle Generalísimo Franco. Head right on Calle de Santo Domingo, then left on Calle de San Telmo. San Telmo, the main drag, runs along the waterfront. It's an elegant street with a bevy of fine shops and hotels to match. Follow San Telmo until it becomes Avenida de Colón and runs parallel to Playa de Martiánez. Take it to Calle Agular y Quesada, then back to the Plaza.

Puerto de la Cruz is about a half-hour bus or car ride from the Los Rodeos Airport near Santa Cruz de Tenerife.

LANZAROTE

An eerie, burnt-out island punctuated by hundreds of extinct volcanoes, Lanzarote is the most physically astonishing of the Canaries. Its scenery is so unusual that people who fly in from Tenerife or Las Palmas always describe the place as unforgettable.

ARRECIFE: The island's capital is actually a fishing town with an airport. Two castles, San Gabriel and San José, stand guard on a hill. Arrecife itself is not particularly interesting, but a drive north to Teguise, the former capital set on top of an extinct volcano, gives you a splendid view of some of the smaller Canaries: La Graciosa, Montaña Clara, Alegranza, Roque del Este, and Roque del Oeste. The highlight of Teguise is Guanapay Castle, perched on top of the cone. Not far from Teguise, the Verdes Cave tunnels more than 3 miles inside the Corona Volcano. Near the cave, at Jameos del Agua Lagoon, is a brand-new nightclub.

Heading into the interior from Arrecife takes you through the terrace farms of La Gería. Here, farmers spread over their fields a layer of fine volcanic ash, which absorbs the nightly dew and provides moisture for the plants. Out of this bizarre agricultural technique, sumptuous melons, watermelons, figs, onions, tomatoes, and grapes are grown. The grapes are fermented to produce Malvasía wine.

Continuing west farther into the interior of the mountain brings you to Montaña de Fuego, the most stunning of the island's natural attractions. From the top of the mountain, you can see hundreds of extinct volcanoes in the surrounding countryside. The summit is accessible by camel; you ride in chairs slung over either side of the hump. Camel processions leave from Arrecife for the 2-hour trip.

Heading south from Arrecife you will find the Tías resort development, which can accommodate 1,000 visitors in small hotels, cottages, and apartment houses. There is a marina with deep-sea fishing charters available. At the southernmost tip of the island is Playa Blanca, which is, as its name suggests, a white beach.

LA GRACIOSA

To the north of Lanzarote, this tiny, 17-square-mile island has one small mountain, la Montaña de las Agujas. La Graciosa has two fine beaches, Caleta del Sebo and Conchas.

FUERTEVENTURA

Fuerteventura has the longest shoreline of any of the islands, with plenty of spacious, empty beaches. If you really want total seclusion, this is a good spot for it. Playa de Jandía at the southern end of the island and Gran Tarajal have good fishing: Sardines, swordfish, and tuna are quite plentiful and easily caught. The capital, Puerto del Rosario, has an airstrip and not much else.

LA PALMA

Known as "the green island," La Palma covers 457 square miles. Its capital, Santa Cruz de la Palma, slopes along the eastern side of a crater called La Caldera de Taburiente.

Approximately 17 miles in circumference, La Caldera is ringed with pine trees and has been declared a national park. You can explore it to a depth of 2,500 feet. The city itself has some sixteenth-century buildings, including the Church of San Salvador and the Ayuntamiento (city hall); a natural history museum containing aboriginal artifacts; and traditional village architecture, featuring ornately hand-carved balconies protruding from the second and third stories of adjoining whitewashed cottages.

At the southernmost tip of the island is the vineyard district of Fuencaliente. To the north of the capital is the verdant forest of Los Tilos where the thick tropical vegetation includes giant ferns.

Although facilities and services for tourists are not as well developed as in Gran Canaria or Tenerife, La Palma does attract good numbers of Europeans who prefer quiet vacations.

LA GOMERA

The craggy seacoast and mountainous terrain of this island have made transportation difficult. To compensate, the islanders have developed over the years a system of communication based on whistling, with which they can "speak" to each other from hilltop to valley.

About 20 miles (32 km) from Tenerife's Playa de los Cristianos (in southern Tenerife), La Gomera is the site of the Church of the Asunción where Columbus and his crews heard mass before setting off for parts unknown. The house in which he lived, called the Casa de Colón, is now a museum. The Torre del Conde, an old fortress, has been declared a national historic monument.

Apart from San Sebastián, the capital, and the whistling Gomera islanders themselves, the island has several banana plantations, orchards, a fishing village called Playa Santiago, and a good, tawny beach on Valle Gran Rey.

HIERRO

The smallest major island of the archipelago (less than 167 square miles), Hierro is called "the island of iron." It is the harshest of all, with black volcanic soil, steep massifs, deep craters, and barren mountains. Around 5,000 of the island's 7,000 residents live in the capital, Valverde. Valverde is the central town of an agricultural area where wine is the major product. In the southern part of Hierro, there is good fishing at La Restinga.

BEST EN ROUTE

With plenty of hotels to choose from, the choices listed below represent those that have some particularly appealing quality — location, service, or aesthetic design. Expect to pay $60 or more for a double room at those places in the expensive category; between $30 and $50 at a hotel in the moderate category; under $30, inexpensive.

Restaurants in the Canary Islands span the culinary spectrum from sleek international dining spots to funky regional places where you can sample local cooking. Expect to pay $50 or more for a meal for two at those places we've categorized as expensive; between $25 and $45 at those restaurants in the moderate category; under $25, inexpensive. Prices do not include drinks, wine, or tips.

GRAN CANARIA

Santa Catalina – Of Las Palmas' more than 100 hotels, this one has the most intriguing atmosphere. An imitation Moorish palace standing in the middle of the flowers of Parque Doramas, it has a large swimming pool, miniature golf, shopping arcade, and fireplaces in the public rooms. It compares favorably with the more modern establishments. Parque Doramas (phone: 24-30-40). Expensive.

Reina Isabel – This is the only hotel right on the beach at Las Palmas. Relatively modern in decor and furnishings, its facilities include a fine restaurant, swimming pool (with adjoining disco), beachfront nightclub, and solarium. It has a very good reputation as a place that appeals to a discriminating clientele. Alfredo L. Jones 40, Paseo Playa de las Canteras, Las Palmas (phone: 26-01-00). Moderate.

Maspalomas Oasis – The center of the action, this is a very busy, large resort complex popular with European tour groups. It has a nightclub, golf course, horseback riding, tennis, health club, shopping arcade, and a number of other facilities. Playa de Maspalomas (phone: 76-01-70). Moderate.

Hotel Tamarindos – Although far from the fashionable, sophisticated cities of Europe, this hotel rivals the best of them in decor, grounds, and amenities. Its two swimming pools and beach make it a good place for simple lounging in the sun. There is even a full buffet alongside one of the swimming pools, several bars, and a disco. On the hillside across the highway, the huge, white, cast-concrete object with a pole in its center is a sundial — a gift from the Swedish people. And you can set your watch by it. Playa San Agustín, Las Retamas (phone: 76-26-00). Moderate.

La Pardilla – This campsite with a capacity for 200 tents, has a swimming pool and most of the necessary facilities. It is closed in January. Located on the autopista about 6 miles (10 km) south of Telde (no phone). Inexpensive.

Temisas – This one is relatively small as campsites go, but then so is the demand. It's built to accommodate about 50 tents. For food, beverages, and other supplies, Aguimes is the closest town. In Temisas (no phone). Inexpensive.

Guantanamo – At Mogán, or more specifically, on the beach at Puerto de Mogán, this campsite is about 90 miles (144 km) from Las Palmas. Although it can accommodate 50 tents, food, beverages, and other supplies are not available on the site. But if you're interested in spending your time on the beaches of the south coast or visiting Cruz de Tejeda, this is your best bet. In Guantanamo (no phone). Inexpensive.

San Agustín Beach Club – The best restaurant on the island is resplendent with African decor amid a strikingly contemporary setting. It's renowned for top-notch international cuisine. Closed during May and June. San Agustín, Plaza de los cocoteros 2 (phone: 76-03-70). Moderate.

Nanking – It's a long way from the China Sea to the Mediterranean, but the Cantonese culinary influence has nonetheless weathered the tide. Many people's first choice as the best Chinese restaurant in town, this is certainly one of the most popular. Its air-conditioned interior is undoubtedly a factor, along with the food. José F. Roca 11, Las Palmas (phone: 26-98-70). Moderate.

La Guanchía – Classical Basque dishes are served along with imaginative original creations. Wines are from La Rioja and Lanzarote. Closed Sundays. Luis Atúñez 25 (phone: 23-44-43). Moderate.

Bogedón – This is our favorite place for Canarian food. Try the seafood here; specialties include *cazuela canario* (fish casserole) and *sancocho de pescado* (fish stew). Parque Doramas, Las Palmas (no phone). Moderate.

Puerto Rico – This decent little restaurant serves local food, particularly fish and seafood. On the beach at Playa Mogán, Puerto Rico (no phone). Inexpensive.

TENERIFE

Mencey – Somewhat faded but nonetheless charming, this old yellow building has retained some of its former grandeur despite modernization. Set in splendid gardens, it was remodeled several years ago. Rooms have been refurbished and a new wing with motel-type units has been added. Facilities include two swimming pools, tennis courts, bar, and a poolside buffet. Av. José Naveira 38, Santa Cruz (phone: 27-67-00). Moderate.

Semiramis – Puerto's futuristic centerpiece must be seen to be believed. Imaginative architecture makes it appear to be built from top to bottom, running down a mountain. All rooms overlook the ocean and have refrigerators; some have kitchens. It also has two swimming pools, tennis courts, a lounge area with games, and a good dining room. Urbanización La Paz, Puerto de la Cruz (phone: 38-55-51). Moderate.

Parador Nacional de las Cañadas del Teide – Ideal for catching the sunrise over the Picos del Teide. In fact, your hosts won't allow you to oversleep. The new wooden inn is modeled after a Swiss chalet with a swimming pool and a lounge with a fireplace. The inn is surrounded by nature-trails. Reservations required well in advance. Orotava (phone: 33-23-04). Inexpensive.

San Felipe – A convenient, comfortable establishment with a freshwater swimming pool, tennis courts, and a nightclub featuring flamenco dancers. But we think that the service could be spiffier, especially in the huge dining room. Av. de Colón 13, Puerto de la Cruz (phone: 38-33-11). Moderate.

Parque San Antonio – If you want to get away from the madding throngs of tourists in Puerto de la Cruz, but wish to be close enough to the center of town to make quick forays, consider this as your first choice for accommodations. Tucked away in a veritable botanic garden all its own, it is merely 5 minutes by bus from the center of town. Rey 1, Arenas, Puerto de la Cruz (phone: 38-49-08). Inexpensive.

La Riviera – Snazzy Continental cuisine is the hallmark of this chic, tastefully decorated restaurant. Closed from mid-August through mid-September and on Sundays. Rambla Generalísimo Franco 155, Santa Cruz de Tenerife (phone: 27-58-12). Moderate.

El Pescado – The name means "the fish" and that's what you'll find on the menu, prepared in a variety of intriguing ways. Closed from May through September and on Wednesdays. Av. Venezuela 3, Puerto de la Cruz (phone: 38-26-06). Moderate.

Mesón del Teide – In Las Cañadas National Park, its unparalleled location on the 2,000-foot mountain El Portillo makes this worth the trip, even if you only sip a glass of wine and snack on a sandwich. La Orotava (no phone). Inexpensive.

LANZAROTE

Hotel Las Salinas – Looking like a giant spacecraft newly touched down in a tropical paradise, it offers 310 modern rooms, each with a private terrace facing seaside. Outdoor delights such as tennis, diving, and sailing abound, as do indoor pleasures — restaurants, bars, massage, sauna, cinema, and disco. Costa Teguise (phone: 81-30-40). Expensive.

Arrecife Gran Hotel – Although standing smack in the middle of a village, there is no way this contemporary resort could be considered to be in the center of the action. Its most astounding feature is a restaurant on an island in the middle of a small lake that can only be reached by boat. It also has a pool, cheerful dining room, and lots of flowers. Av. Mancomunidad (phone: 81-12-54). Moderate.

Castillo de San José – Located in the bottom of a medieval castle that is now a contemporary art museum, this is one of the most beautiful restaurants on the island. One mile (2 km) northeast of Arrecife on the road to Las Caletas (phone: 81-23-21). Moderate.

Casa Salvador – Tucked away in one of the quieter corners of the island, this lovely seafood restaurant stands right on the beach. Playa Blanca de Yaiza (no phone). Moderate to inexpensive.

El Diablo – Another dramatically located restaurant, it stands amid the volcanic mountains of the interior. It is only open for lunch. Montaña del Fuego, Tinajo (phone: 84-00-57). Inexpensive.

Abdon Betancort – Family-style cooking is done as the clientele watches. Closed Sundays and October. Canalejas 54 (phone: 81-05-22). Inexpensive.

FUERTEVENTURA

Parador Nacional Fuerteventura – Standing on the edge of the ocean, this brand-new, modern *parador* is the most splendid hotel on the island. Puerto del Rosario, Urb. Playa Blanca (phone: 85-11-50). Expensive.

LA PALMA

Parador Nacional de Santa Cruz – This is another sparkling new addition to the national chain. It, too, rates top marks. Av. Maritima, Santa Cruz de la Palma (phone: 41-23-40). Moderate.

LA GOMERA

Parador Nacional de la Gomera – This comfortable, pleasant little hotel is part of the national chain. La Horca (phone: 87-11-00). Moderate.

The Balearic Islands

The Balearic Islands lie 90 miles southeast of Barcelona in the Mediterranean Sea. The major section of the archipelago consists of two pair of islands: Majorca and Minorca, and Formentera and Ibiza. Many smaller islands of lesser significance complete the archipelagic structure. Of the four major islands, Majorca (whose name means "the larger") is the largest, best known, and best equipped for tourism. Minorca (whose name means "the smaller") receives fewer foreign visitors and, consequently, has retained its tranquil, seaside communities. Ibiza is home to jetsetters, artists, and pseudo-artists, of whom Howard Hughes' self-proclaimed biographer Clifford Irving is probably the most famous. Formentera is undoubtedly the most secluded of the four islands.

The Balearic Mountains are thick with ancient fig and olive trees while the beaches are shaded by evergreens. The surrounding seas are exceptionally calm and clear despite the prevailing winds.

The Balearic language is a dialect of Catalán, the language of Cataluña, the Barcelona region of mainland Spain. Catalán is a Romance language that resembles Provençal French with some vestiges of colonial Latin as spoken in the Roman Empire.

Remnants of human habitation date from the Bronze Age. Located in different parts of the islands are large stone pyramids, thought to be Bronze Age tombs, called *talayots.* Later Balearic islanders were mercenaries and seamen in the armies and navies of Rome and Carthage. The Moors reigned from AD 902 until 1229 when the Aragonese reconquest converted the Balearics into a prosperous center of Mediterranean trade. In the sixteenth century, Spain's attention shifted to the New World and the Balearics fell into the hands of the Turks and the Barbary pirates, whose influence can still be seen in the walls and watchtowers of Majorca.

During the eighteenth century, Father Junípero Serra set forth from the

Balearics, where he was born, to found the string of missions along the California coast known as El Camino Real, or the Mission Trail. In the nineteenth century, composer Frédéric Chopin and his mistress, author George Sand, chose Majorca as their island retreat.

Twentieth-century visitors find that May, early June, and September are the best months for a quiet, relaxing visit. The weather is sparkling clear, with temperatures in the 70s and 80s° F (21°–26°C). July and August are the most intense, active months. The Balearic Islands have a climate temperate enough for year-round water sports: sailing, swimming, diving, and deep-sea fishing for sole, perch, and bream. There is a racetrack in Palma, the capital of Majorca, and plenty of golf courses and tennis courts.

MAJORCA

PALMA DE MALLORCA: Incredible though it sounds, between June and September, the airport of Palma, the Balearics' and Majorca's capital, handles more transients than New York's John F. Kennedy Airport. With thousands of hotel rooms and hundreds of restaurants, Palma is one of the world's busiest resort centers.

The Bay of Palma is protected from the wind and weather by the Puig Mayor mountain range which lies to the northwest of the city. Palma Nova and Magaluf beaches are the only two sandy areas to the west of Palma, although there are hotels along the sheer coastline. To the east of the city, although there is less protection, there are miles of excellent beaches and resorts known as the Playas de Palma. With 282,000 residents, the city of Palma contains almost half of the island's population.

Known as the Ciutat de Mallorca after the liberation from the Moors in 1229, the town was colonized by Jews and Genoese and subsequently prospered. James II and his successors were able to build majestic Gothic buildings and Italian-style villas. Mansions were erected in the fifteenth and sixteenth centuries by descendants of merchants and landed gentry. The typical Mallorcan casa (inner patio with marble columns) developed in the eighteenth century can be seen in many parts of Palma.

The heart of the city is the wide promenade, or *rambla,* known as the Borne (open market).

In the old part of town east of the Borne are shops that specialize in crafts, filigree, embroidery, world-famous pearls, and glasswork. A morning walk might begin at the town hall (Ayuntamiento) at 2 Plaza Cort. Here you'll find the Van Dyck painting *The Martyrdom of San Sebastián* hanging on the first floor. Continue one block south to Santa Eulalia Church (Iglesia Santa Eulalia). Across the street stands the Casa Vivot, one of the best examples of eighteenth-century Palma townhouses with an inner court and paintings by Breughel, Ribera, and others. At Plaza San Francisco, San Francisco Church contains the tomb of Ramón Llull, famed Doctor Illuminatus, philosopher and humanist of cosmopolitan thirteenth-century Majorca. One block south of the Plaza, Casa Palmer is a fine example of sixteenth-century Gothic and Renaissance architecture. The Moorish Baths, intact from the era of the Caliphate, can be found on Paseo Umjuay. Liberally sprinkled along this route are cafés and saloons for late breakfasts and early aperitifs.

Casa Oleza (Calle Morey 2) is another example of the famous Mallorquín patios or interior courtyards. The Oleza patio is an extraordinarily well balanced composition which includes an iron-topped well, typical wide arches, and short marble columns supporting a balcony.

To the west of El Borne are the three palaces: Palacios Morell, on Calle San Cayetano; Palacio Sollerich, on the Borne itself, with one of the best patios in the city; and Palacio Montenegro, on the street of the same name.

Other important sights include the cathedral; the Spanish Pueblo (Pueblo Español), which includes exact reproductions of famous houses representing different regions, epochs, and architecture from all parts of Spain; La Almudaina, a Moorish fortress located just off Plaza de la Reina; La Lonja, a fifteenth-century structure built by Guillermo Sagrera to house an exchange; the fishing neighborhood of Puig San Pere; and Bellver Castle, overlooking Palma in Parque Bellver.

For maps and brochures about places of interest, hotels, and restaurants, contact the Tourist Information Office at the airport (phone: 26-08-03) or Av. Jaime Tercero 10 (phone: 21-22-16) in the center of town.

With 250 miles of coast broken into dazzling coves, inlets, and beaches, Majorca has much to explore. Because the narrow roads snaking around cliffs with precipitous drops are a legitimate driving hazard, we recommend that you hire a chauffeured car with an English-speaking guide to get to the fishing villages, resorts, and other sites of interest described below. The classic seascapes and mountain scenery deserve to be enjoyed fully, and if you are unused to the surprisingly rugged dips and turns of the roads, chances are you will be too preoccupied with safety to savor the sights. From Palma, there are five distinct touring routes: (1) from Palma north to Valldemosa, Deya, and Sóller; (2) from Palma north to Manacor and the caves; (3) from Palma northeast to Pollensa and Formentor; (4) from Palma to the eastern coves; and (5) from Palma to the southwest peninsula.

PALMA TO SÓLLER: The 46-mile (74-km) Valldemosa-Deya-Sóller tour is a relaxed, 1-day trip from Palma. Valldemosa and Deya may be seen in the morning with a late lunch at the Puerto de Sóller. You can stop for coffee in the mountain pass on the road back to Palma.

Valldemosa's main attraction is the Carthusian monastery in which George Sand and Chopin passed the winter of 1838–1839. Beyond Valldemosa the road runs along thousand-foot cliffs to San Marroig. The former resident, Archduke Luis Salvador, here had a fine view of the Foradada, a famous rock with a donutlike perforation.

The village of Deya is surrounded by hills and evergreen forests. Known for its large colony of British artists and bohemians, Deya perches loftlike over the sea. Below the village is a stream outlet, tiny cove, Cala Deya, and beach.

The town of Sóller lies a few miles inland from the port. The road back to Palma over the Alfabia Sierra offers excellent views of the sea and sunset to the west.

PALMA TO THE DRACH CAVES (CUEVAS DEL DRACH): The second recommended route through Manacor, Artá, and the Drach Caves covers 109 miles (175 km), about 3 hours' driving time. Manacor is 30 miles (48 km) from Palma. From the city of Manacor, it is a short distance to Porto Cristo and the caves. Las Cuevas del Drach consist of four chambers of polychromatic pools and stalactite columns spreading over a distance of just over 1 mile. The tour takes 90 minutes and costs about $2. Other caves can be found in Artá and in the city of Manacor. In fact, the Artá caves are said to have inspired Jules Verne to write *Journey to the Center of the Earth*.

Also on this route are found the *talayots,* megalithic stone structures thought to be Bronze Age burial markers. The village of Capdepera is the site of a fortress high over the Mediterranean. Cala Ratjada is a fishing town with small streams and ocean beaches. On the way back to Palma, you can stop at the town of Petra, birthplace of Junípero Serra (1713–1784), the Franciscan monk whose Californian and Mexican missions developed into San Diego, Monterey, and San Francisco.

PALMA TO FORMENTOR: The third route, to Cape Formentor, northernmost point of the island, covers between 109 and 124 miles (175 and 198 km), passing through Pollensa and Alcudia, and other points of interest along the way. You can stop at Selva to see the San Lorenzo church; at Campanet to see the caves; and at Alcudia where old Roman ramparts and a Roman theater still stand. Puerto de Pollensa is a well-entrenched artists' colony with a sheltered bay and fine harbor. Stop in at the museum of the painter Anglada Camerasa, which features the island's most representative artists. Puerto de Pollensa has become home to many Europeans and Americans; you can purchase a cottage for around $30,000 or rent one for anywhere between $200 and $400 a month.

The road from Puerto de Pollensa to Formentor passes one genuinely overwhelming vista after another. The best places to stop for a look are Es Colomer Belvedere lookout and the Cape Formentor lighthouse. The golf course in Formentor is made all the more challenging by the constant winds.

PALMA TO EASTERN COVES: The fourth route, which covers the coves or *calas* of the island's east coast, is a 100-mile (160-km) run with stops at Campos, Felanitx, Porto Colom, Cala Mitjana, Cala D'Or, Porto Petro, and Cala Santañyi. For a shorter trip, proceed directly to Santañyi and spend the day visiting only the Calas of Santañyi, Figuera, and Llombarts.

PALMA TO SOUTHWEST PENINSULA: The fifth and last route is a Palma-Palma Nova-Paguera-Andraitx-Estallenchs-Bañalbufar-Esporlas-Palma circuit of 56 miles (90 km). The southwest coast has a fine selection of beaches and the island's most intense concentration of hotels. Santa Ponsa, Cala Fornels, Camp de Mar, Puerto de Andraitx, Estellenchs, and Bañalbufar are the main sites of interest.

MINORCA

Minorca, the second-largest Balearic Island, measures 258 square miles, numbers just under 50,000 inhabitants, and is less tourist-oriented than Majorca. The British occupation of the islands during the eighteenth century left discernible traces in the architecture: guillotine windows, rocking chairs, folding wing Pembroke-style tables, and stand-up clocks with Queen Anne inlay work. The heathlike countryside, swept by the north wind, is lightly wooded, with wind-bent wild olive trees, low stone walls, and small fields.

Cows and sheep provide the basis for the island's two main industries, shoes and cheese. Mayonnaise owes its name and discovery to Mahón, the island's largest city (pop. 20,000).

Minorca is a place where people go to spend a few weeks or months, as opposed to Majorca, which caters to shorter-term vacationers. Developments such as Binibeca and Punta Prima near Mahón, and Cabo Dartuch near Ciudadela, Minorca's second-largest city, usually offer lodgings for periods of weeks, rather than days.

The spots to visit on the island of Minorca include Ciudadela and Mahón on the western and eastern ends, respectively; Cabo de Caballerias and Fornells to the north; and Cala de Santa Galdana to the south. Mercadal is in the approximate center of the island and was once the site of the island government. Monte Toro, the island's highest point and a religious sanctuary, is 2 miles (3 km) from Mercadal.

Minorca can be reached by air from Palma or Barcelona. The island's airport is at Mahón. Boat service connects Ciudadela to Palma and Alcudia, Mallorca. The Tourist Information Center is in Mahón at Plaza de la Constitución 13 (phone: 36-37-90).

MAHÓN: A gleaming little port that somehow manages to retain an innately unobtrusive air, Minorca's largest city has one of the best sheltered harbors in the Mediterranean with excellent anchorages. The main site of interest is the Finca San Antonio, former residence of British Admiral Nelson. About one mile from town near Trepuco village stand several *talayots*.

CIUDADELA: Minorca's second-largest city is surrounded by exceptionally fine beaches: Cala Santandria, Algañares, Cala Blanca, and Cala Blanes. Boiled lobster with mayonnaise sauce and Mahón cheese with sausages are the tastiest local dishes.

FORNELLS: At first glance this is merely a modest fishing village standing in a grove of evergreens, but its appearance masks its popularity as a resort.

IBIZA

The 320-square-mile island of Ibiza lies 70 miles southwest of Palma de Mallorca. Ibiza rose to prominence in the Mediterranean region during the years of Carthaginian hegemony (seventh century BC), and to this date, the predominant influence in the island's architecture is North African.

Accessible by air from Barcelona, Madrid, Palma, and Valencia, or by sea from Barcelona, Palma, Valencia, and Alicante, Ibiza attracts a well-heeled, international crowd who tend to stay on the island for months or years at a time.

IBIZA: The island's capital is separated into an upper town (Dalt Vila) and a harbor by an ancient sixteenth-century wall. Sights in the Dalt Vila include: the Las Tablas Gateway, the cathedral, and the Archaeological Museum containing Punic ruins excavated from Ibizan sites. The town is compact and you should find these special places easily. From the belfry in the Dalt Vila, there is an excellent view of the town and port. The Tourist Information Office is at Vara de Rey 2 (phone: 30-19-00).

The Marina Quarter explodes into sound and color as you enter from the sedate Dalt Vila. Every afternoon (except Wednesdays), the narrow streets are packed with portable shops where vendors sell nearly everything — shell and silver jewelry, watercolors, leather goods, terra-cotta figurines, and other items — and music blasts from the innumerable indoor-outdoor pubs featuring exotic mixed drinks and even more exotically garbed waiters and waitresses.

Ibiza's most popular beaches are Ses Figuretas, Talamanca, and Playa D'En Bossa. Several of Ibiza's beaches have gone "naturalist" (nude), although there is some shedding of bikinis on nearly all of them. About 12 miles (19 km) west of the city of Ibiza, the town of San Antonio Abad overlooks the thousand-foot rock island, the Vedrá. The Santa Inés church, which has been declared a national monument, sits atop ancient catacombs.

FORMENTERA

Formentera — whose name means "the wheat island," from the Latin "frumentum" — is the smallest of the Balearics, covering 60 square miles. Lying 11 miles south of Ibiza, it is significantly more tranquil than the other three Balearic Islands. With 3,500 year-round inhabitants, it also attracts considerably fewer tourists.

Boat service across the Es Freus channel connects La Sabina, Formentera's harbor, with Ibiza. The tiny capital of the island, San Francisco Javier, has a population of around 800 and is a cluster of sparkling white cottages. Topographically, the island consists of a string of beaches with Berberia Cape on the southern end of the island and La Mola Cape, guarded by a lighthouse, on the eastern end. Pine forests and salt flats take up much of the interior.

Although Formentera is a great place for relaxing by the sea or participating in water sports, there is no nightlife to speak of.

BEST EN ROUTE

Hotel prices are comparable with those along the Costa del Sol. You can expect to pay $50 or more for a double room at those places we've listed as expensive; between $30 and $50 for a double room in a hotel we've classified as moderate; under $30, inexpensive.

There are literally dozens of restaurants in Majorca, the largest and busiest island, but considerably fewer restaurants of note on Minorca, Ibiza, and Formentera. Expect to pay $50 or more for a meal for two at those restaurants we've categorized as expensive; between $25 and $50 at those restaurants in the moderate category; under $25, inexpensive. Prices do not include drinks, wine, or tips.

MAJORCA

Formentor – In a pine grove, its extensive gardens, terraces, swimming pool, anchorage, and overall environment make it the most luxurious of the island's hotels. Playa de Formentor (phone: 53-13-00). Expensive.

Victoria – Not as fancy as *Son Vida,* but a good choice on the western side of Palma's bay. Joan Miró 125 (phone: 23-43-42). Expensive.

Son Vida – This converted palace, about 4 miles (6 km) from Palma on the road toward Andraitx, stands on a hill with splendid views of the bay, city, and mountains. Activities include swimming, golf, tennis, boating, and horseback riding. Dinner in the baronial dining room is a long, drawn-out affair. Castillo de Son Vida, Palma (phone: 45-10-11). Expensive.

Daina – Large enough to have spaciousness, yet small enough to know you're here, this excellent hotel commands a view of Pollensa's Bay. Atilio Boven 2, Puerto de Pollensa (phone: 53-12-50). Moderate to inexpensive.

La Caleta – The most elegant of the capital's many restaurants serves Continental and Mediterranean food. Federico García Lorca 19, Palma (phone: 23-27-51). Expensive.

El Puerto – This notable seafood restaurant serves excellent food. Paseo de Sagrera 3, Palma (phone: 22-11-04). Moderate.

Casa Sophie – Here the French cuisine is exquisite. Closed December and on Sundays. Apuntadores 24, Palma (phone: 22-60-86). Moderate.

Jardin Chino – As its name, "Chinese Garden," suggests, this is Palma's finest Chinese restaurant. Plaza Mediterraneo 2, Palma (phone: 23-00-53). Moderate.

Mi Vaca y Yo – This roadside *tavernita* serves hearty meals of typical Mallorquín cuisine. Playa de Canyarnel, Capdepera (no phone). Moderate.

La Tablita – This is another little restaurant in a tiny pocket of the island. Cala Ratjada (no phone). Moderate.

Club Náutico – Here you can get fresh seafood and fish in a nautical atmosphere. Muelle Viejo, Pollensa (phone: 53-10-10). Moderate.

Restaurant La Lonja – This restaurant prepares the finest bouillabaise with fresh lobster on the island. Dique Muelle Viejo Pollensa (phone: 53-00-23). Moderate.

Estación Marítima Stay – This is *the* place for succulent crab creations, other seafood dishes, and the most potent Irish coffee on Majorca. Malecón del Puerto Pollensa (phone: 53-00-13). Moderate.

Restaurant Becfi – Argentinian *parrillada* (barbecued mixed grill) and lobster are the specialties. Closed Mondays. Av. Anglada Camarasa 9, Pollensa (phone: 53-10-40). Moderate.

Petit Celler Carnete – This is the best restaurant in the center of town. Cetre 5, Sóller (no phone). Moderate to inexpensive.

Ca'n Pacienci – Start a meal here with the tomato soup (made with fresh cream) or a pâté, then try the stuffed chicken or one of the traditional Mallorquín dishes. Carretera del Puerto, Pollensa (phone: 53-07-87). Inexpensive.

Casa Gallega – Although the Balearic Islands are a long way from the northwest corner of mainland Spain, this place specializes in Galician cuisine. Pueyo 6, Palma (phone: 22-11-41). Inexpensive.

Celler Sa Premsa – *Celleres* (cellars) and *tavernitas* (taverns) serve Mallorquín food, primarily combinations of pork *(lechona),* fresh fish, seafood, plenty of squid, and paella. This is a favorite. Plaza Obispo Berenguer de Palou 8 (phone: 22-35-29). Inexpensive.

Celler Ca Vostra – This is one of the best *tavernitas* in Pollensa. Camino Alcudia, Pollensa (phone: 53-15-46). Inexpensive.

Celler El Puerto – This is a good place for a hefty seafood lunch. Plaza Almirante Oquendo 22, Pollensa (no phone). Inexpensive.

MINORCA

Port Mahón – Best hotel in Mahón. Fort de l'Eau, Paseo Marítimo (phone: 36-26-00). Moderate.

Rocamar – For good seafood, especially typical Minorcan *caldereta* (lobster stew), this is a good choice. Cala Fonduco (phone: 36-56-01). Moderate.

Chez Gaston – Here you can get Continental dishes along with fresh fish and seafood. Conde de Cifuentes 13 (phone: 36-00-44). Inexpensive.

El Greco – This is another good place for Mediterranean fare. Doctor Orfila 49, Mahón (phone: 36-43-67). Inexpensive.

D'Es Port – This little café on the docks serves boiled lobster with mayonnaise sauce and Mahón cheese with sausages. Cuidadela (no phone). Inexpensive.

Casa Diego – Near *D'es Port,* this place features similar local fare at bargain prices. Ciudadela (no phone). Inexpensive.

Mare Nostrum – For a generous Minorcan meal, visit this restaurant on the beach. Playa Santandria (no phone). Inexpensive.

Ses Set Voltes – This is another "find" on the beach. Playa Santandria, Ciudadela (no phone). Inexpensive.

Casa Riera – For fresh fish and seafood, this is the best in town. Plaza Generalísimo 7, Fornells (no phone). Inexpensive.

IBIZA

Ses Figueres – One of the smaller Ibiza hotels, *Ses Figueres* has splendid views of the bay. On Talamanca beach, it is a modest establishment that offers excellent value. Playa de Talamanca, Ibiza (phone: 30-13-62). Inexpensive.

Marblau – A truly fine hotel in relaxed, shady surroundings. Its 15 rooms have windows overlooking the sea. Los Molinos (phone: 30-12-84). Inexpensive.

Campsites – The Spanish government operates three campsites on Ibiza: *San Antonio* at San Antonio Abad; *Florida* at Santa Eulalia del Río; and *Cala Bassa* at Bahía de San Antonio. For information contact the Spanish National Tourist Office in the US.

Dalt Vila – In the sedate upper town, this place serves hearty Mediterranean meals. Plaza Luis Tur 3 (phone: 30-55-24). Moderate.

Marblau – A seafood restaurant near the marina, it has a splendid view of the sea and neighboring islands. It also rents rooms. Los Molinos (phone: 30-12-84). Moderate.

FORMENTERA

Hostal Capri Voramar – This quiet hotel on Es Pujols beach, protected from the wind by Cape Punta Prima, looks across the water to Ibiza. It's restaurant is one of the best on the island for seafood and fresh fish. Playa Es Pujols (phone: 32-01-20). Inexpensive.

Sa Volta – Here, you will find good local food in a pleasant environment. Es Pujols (phone: 32-01-21). Moderate.

Exploring Sweden

The images of Sweden that are universally recognized are a kind of code to this complex Scandinavian culture. Fierce, bearded Vikings; healthy, blond youths; dense silent forests; sparkling blue lakes and crystalline fjords — the fascination of a visit is learning just how these particular images have come to represent Sweden, and in what ways they are a true picture. As always, the truth will prove twice as fascinating as anything you could imagine.

As in any country, history and culture start with geography. Occupying the eastern half of the Scandinavian Peninsula, the country shares borders with Norway to the west and Finland to the northeast. The more populous southern third of the country juts into the Baltic Sea; the northern end creeps over the Arctic Circle. Parts of Sweden are still glacier-bound; several thousand years ago, *all* of Sweden was covered with ice. However, for the most part, Sweden's landscape is now speckled with lakes and carpeted with meadows and forests. Sweden has a temperate climate with warm summers and cold winters. The generally poor soil and rocky terrain have led Swedes to turn to forestry, mining, and steel production for their major industries.

The earliest settlers in Sweden appeared in about the third century BC; these people were mostly farmers and fishermen. Many years later, in the first century AD, a seafaring tribe, that turned to plunder and trade, grew very powerful and began to control what is now Sweden. This tribe — the Svea, forefathers of the Vikings — initiated trade, as well as conflict, with parts of Europe and Britain. Sweden was well situated for trade and as it became more lucrative, the Hanseatic League became interested in the country. Soon several German merchants came to live in Visby, a prosperous walled town on the island of Gotland, and in Stockholm, which was then a port and fortress on Lake Mälaren. By the fourteenth century, the Hansa merchants controlled Sweden; in an effort to resist the Hanseatic influence, Norway, Sweden, and Denmark joined together as the Union of Kalmar. The center of government for this union was in Denmark. Eventually the Swedes began to resent even the Danish rule, and in the sixteenth century Gustavus Vasa, a Swedish noble, led a rebellion. In 1523, victorious, he was elected king, and thereafter the influence of the Hanseatic League waned.

For several hundred years, until the early nineteenth century, Swedish kings were constantly at war with their neighbors, including Germany, Denmark, Poland, Finland, and Russia. As a result, Sweden annexed as well as lost many territories in Europe, Scandinavia, and even America. In 1809 Sweden enacted a series of reforms, making the king a ceremonial figurehead and conferring the powers of government on an elected parliament. Later in the nineteenth century, Sweden declared itself a neutral country, a policy that remained in effect throughout the two world wars.

The Swedish Welfare System was born during the depression of the 1930s and grew up during and after World War II. Basically a system for the redistribution of income, the plan attempts to provide every Swede with a minimum and satisfactory standard of living — food, housing, education, and medical care. The price tag for these humane policies is a staggering 50% to 80% personal income tax.

Sweden leads the world in the exploration and experimentation with design. Based on the concept that functional things must also be graceful, Swedish design has influenced or changed the appearance of many everyday items, such as furniture, glassware, ceramics, or textiles.

A strong folkloric heritage provides Sweden with rich cultural texture. In the summer numerous festivals are held, for which men and women don their native costumes and dance around traditional Maypoles — made of detailed wrought iron or wood and decorated with intertwined sprigs of flowers and forest greenery. In the Dalarna region, *spelmanslag* (fiddlers) often entertain at the festivals, playing ancient folk tunes and ballads.

Our tours of Sweden each offer you a taste of new and old Sweden: the Dalarna and Värmland route runs through dense forests and medieval towns; the Gothenburg route takes you north from Sweden's second largest city and maritime capital through the fishing villages and along the dramatic fjords of Sweden's granite coastline; the historic walled city of Visby is the highlight of the Gotland route; and the Lapland route ventures into one of the last unspoiled and uncivilized areas on earth — the Lapp wilderness.

Dalarna and Värmland

The trip up from Stockholm northwest to Mora and back down to Karlstad covers roughly 520 miles (832 km) and takes you through the Swedish heartland provinces of Dalarna and Värmland. The route meanders through seemingly unending forests that break unexpectedly to reveal breathtaking lake expanses. The roads occasionally rise, resting at overlooks where the landscape unfolds beneath you in long, floating lines. The major towns are clustered around the two great lake districts, Siljan in Dalarna and the Fryken group in Värmland.

The dense Dalarna forests were first cut back for settlement in the sixteenth century, when rich veins of iron ore and copper were discovered and mined under the leadership of King Gustav Wasa. The Dalarna route from Stockholm takes you first to the mining town of Falun and then on to the picturesque Siljan Lake towns of Leksand, Rättvik, and Mora, where you turn south for Värmland. As you travel, you'll notice the landscape changes: the deep forests and weathered wooden sheds of Dalarna give way to Värmland's wide verdant fields and country villas.

Värmland has been home to some of Sweden's "greats": famous writers Erik Gustaf Geijer and Selma Lagerlöf (a 1909 Nobel laureate in literature), as well as John Ericsson who, after emigrating to New York, changed the concept of sea power with his design for the USS *Monitor,* the first successful iron-clad warship. From Mora you can plunge farther west and then south to the Fryken Lake towns of Torsby, Sunne, and Arvika. Or you can follow the Klarälven River directly south through Ransäter to Karlstad, the major city of Värmland on the vast Vänern Lake.

STOCKHOLM: For a detailed report on the city and its hotels and restaurants, see *Stockholm,* THE EUROPEAN CITIES. The great city of Stockholm originated as a modest thirteenth-century Viking fortification built on an island where Lake Mälaren meets the Baltic Sea. As was often the case, the military installation grew into a civilized center of art and commerce, but Stockholm's transition was perhaps more dramatic than that of other cities that developed in this way. Far from the usual random urban sprawl, Stockholm spread over 14 islands into one of the most beautiful and certainly the most ordered city in the world. Stockholm is the home of the Swedish monarch, but the real ruler of the city is design. Streets, buildings, and squares are preserved with religious respect. Trees are judiciously planted along cobbled boulevards, and flower urns are artistically arranged in quiet plazas flanked by pastel-colored three- and four-story buildings capped with elegant and varied entablatures — a stepped arch on one house, a rounded, baroque detail on another, and a rose-windowed gable on a third. The Swedish design concept is evident everywhere and is typified in glassware that developed from involved Venetian decoration into the simpler Scandinavian look of utility with no loss of grace. Utility and grace are carried through from town plan to individual buildings to the furniture inside the buildings and finally to the people themselves.

En Route from Stockholm – Falun is a 3- or 4-hour drive from Stockholm on Route 70 and the largest town in Dalarna. The main point of interest here is the Falun Copper Mine that's been in operation since the Vikings forged swords and shields — long before Sweden was even a country. This mine was the Renaissance world's major source of copper, and places like Versailles were roofed with its output. There's a tour of the mine that takes you down an elevator to the winding shafts and cavernous spaces below. While here, note the rock wall autographed by touring royalty and the massive 650-foot timber wall — a marvel of carpentry and probably the highest wooden edifice in the world.

SILJAN LAKE TOWNS: Lake Siljan is a blue glacial lake surrounded by lush evergreen forests and towns that look much as they did in the early Middle Ages.

From Falun, you can either proceed directly to Lake Siljan on Route 80 or double back onto Route 70, where the first lake town you come to is Leksand, a thriving, woodsy resort. On the first Sunday in July there's a boat race here that's a hotly contested national event. The vessels used are called "church boats" and they look like mastless, mini, Viking ships. They widen from a sharp prow and sit low in the water as they glide across the lake, each propelled by 20 oarsmen dressed to the nines in native finery. (The boats don't sit idle the rest of the year, so if you can't get there for the race, don't be surprised to see them actually transporting residents back and forth to church.) After the race, there's a folk-dance festival replete with *spelmän* — fiddlers dressed in the traditional high black socks, white shirts, and ornate black vests with red piping. There's also an annual folk miracle play, *Himlaspelet (The Road to Heaven),* that's performed outdoors every summer. The lakeside museum exhibits folk works painted by wandering peasant artists who went door to door, depicting religious scenes on the residents' ceilings. The biblical heroes in these paintings are invariably clothed in Dalecarlian costume. The local brew is called Maywine and at the various festivals it's imbibed by the bucket.

If you prefer a thorough and organized view of the lake towns, you can pick up a boat lake tour at Rättvik, only 7.5 miles (12 km) from Leksand. If you just want a quick but comprehensive peek at the region, there's an old wooden tower (just outside of town at Vidablick) that you can climb for free. From the top you can reconnoiter at will. Rättvik also has a new cultural center with a library and two museums as well as a preserved farm complex called Gammelgård. Many of the wooden structures here were built in the sixteenth century with incredible care and skill. The tongue and grooving at the corners is so perfectly executed it looks as if the beam ends were machined. The original shingles look more durable than space-age plastics and the fences are marvelously designed to adapt to changing terrain.

Mora is the last lake town and the last stop in Dalarna. It's the finishing point of the Wasa Ski Race, the longest cross-country skiing competition in the world, annually attracting more than 10,000 entrants who challenge the grueling 53-mile run. Like the other Siljan towns, Mora celebrates the past in summer festivals and Maypole dancing. The most famous of all Swedish painters, Anders Zorn (1860–1920), lived here and many of his portraits are on display in the Zorn Museum along with Scandinavian sculpture, furniture, textiles, and other examples of local crafts. You can also visit the Zorn Gardens and explore the artist's home and studio. There's another lakeside open-air museum here which depicts the indigenous rural life of the Middle Ages. Just east of Mora in the town of Nusnäs you can watch craftsmen fashioning the traditional Dala Horse souvenirs that are sold all over the country.

En Route to Karlstad – There are many small destinations in Värmland that take you off the main southern route along the Klarälven River that you pick up at Stöllet. Instead of heading directly south to Karlstad, you can cut back north and take a canoe trip through beautiful scenery at Sysslebäck. The fishing here is great and you can rent tackle along with your canoe. If you head west from Stöllet, you hit Route 234, which you can take south through the Fryken Lake towns of Torsby — a traditional Norwegian/Swedish trading center — and Sunne — the nearest town to the two mansions associated with Selma Lagerlöf, who is perhaps Sweden's most famous author and her home in the town of Mårbacka, just east of Sunne, is now a museum. Ten minutes south of Sunne is the Rottneros Manor, which she used as a model for the Ekeby mansion in her best-known work, *The Saga of Gösta Berling.* Rottneros Manor is now a sculpture park and garden — one of the most beautiful spots in all of Sweden, displaying the works of many prominent Scandinavian artists. As a last stop on this Värmland detour, you might want to continue southwest to Arvika, a small town of 16,000 on the Glafsfjorden Lake where you can take a boat tour of the area or listen to a summer concert at the Ingesund Music College. This lake area is wonderful for hiking and there are more than 125 miles of marked trails across fields, along lakeshores, and through forests.

RANSÄTER: If you drive directly south from Stöllet along the Klarälven River on Route 62, "The Pilgrim's Way," you go through the prosperous and quiet little river town of Ransäter, the home of dramatist Erik Gustaf Geijer. In midsummer, the *Värmlänningarna,* a Swedish *Romeo and Juliet,* is performed outdoors. His home is also open to the public.

The village surrounding the open-air theater is an example of more affluent country habitats, dating back to the time when timber cut from the area started fetching good prices in Great Britain during the end of the industrial revolution. The timber was used for props in English coal mines. It was floated down the Klarälven River, and even today tug boats with half-mile-long batches of timber in tow slowly descend the river to Karlstad — the main city of the province — where the timber is processed.

KARLSTAD: This is the capital of the province and the home of the Värmland Museum, which has exhibits of textiles, painting and crafts, as well as historic displays. The museum is centrally located in a manicured park on Sandgrundet. The Marieberg

Forest is the town's other large park; here you can see a show at the open-air theater, or dance at one of the music pavilions. Karlstad is a commercial center and the main northern port on the Vänern, the largest lake in Western Europe. The port itself is on the Klarälven River and you can take a tour boat at Residenstorg for a leisurely sail around the city's waterways. Just outside of town in Skutberget and Örsholmsbadet are lakefront open-air baths.

From Karlstad, you can take an interesting side trip to Filipstad, 25 miles (40 km) to the northeast. Filipstad is the birthplace of John Ericsson and you can visit his home and mausoleum (at different spots to the north and east of town). As we have said, Ericsson migrated to Brooklyn, New York, where he became an ironmonger and builder. At the outbreak of the American Civil War he implemented a visionary plan to combine the new diesel engine with a screw propeller for the design of the Union's iron-clad ship, the *Monitor.* This ship soundly defeated the Confederate iron-clad entry, the *Merrimack,* winning Ericsson an honored place in naval history. In 1890, the US Navy returned his body to Filipstad where it was entombed and the mausoleum was built.

BEST EN ROUTE

Hotels in Sweden aren't nearly as expensive as they used to be because of the devaluation of the Swedish krona. A number of hotels offer special weekend discounts and low summer rates. An expensive hotel can run anywhere from $50 to $100 per night. The moderate establishments charge $25 to $50 and the inexpensive places go from $15 to $25. It's wise to make reservations in advance or to use the Swedish hotel "cheque" system whereby reservations for your next stop are made by the hotel management at your present stop. This can be arranged through any travel agent.

LEKSAND

Tre Kullor – A quaint guesthouse in a farmlike setting. Everything here is on a really personal basis. The food is not only homemade and good, but there's probably more of it than you can eat. There's a sauna in the basement and a beautiful cherry tree in the front yard. Hjortnàsvagen 2 (phone: 0247-11350). Moderate.

MORA

Mora Hotell – A small, clean hotel with 92 neat, comfortable rooms. It's easy to find in the center of town (phone: 0250-11750). Expensive to moderate.

KARLSTAD

Stadshotellet – This stately 140-room hotel is in a large yellow building overlooking the river. You can sit in the nearby café, play tennis or golf nearby, or take a dip in the pool. Kungsgatan 22 (phone: 054-115220). Expensive to moderate.

Gothenburg and the West Coast

The west coast of Sweden, with Gothenburg at its center, is very popular with Scandinavian vacationers but often neglected by international tour operators. This is surprising because the scenic coastal strip combines most of the features the foreign visitor looks for in a typical Scandinavian vacation.

South of Gothenburg is an almost continuous ribbon of sandy beaches and summer resorts, but this trip takes you in the opposite direction — north, toward the Norwegian border. You follow a craggy, granite coastline that breaks up into skerries toward the sea and opens into fjords and lakes toward the land. The whole coast is dotted with tiny isolated fishing villages and peaceful yacht harbors tucked away in rocky coves.

The area attracts many visitors from Scandinavia and northern Europe during the summer months (June through August), yet once away from the busy camping sites and major highways you enter an intimate, peaceful world of great natural beauty that seems untouched by modern industrialization.

Many visitors live the nomadic life in trailer homes or under canvas at the many camp sites. Youth hostels, rented summer chalets, or fishermen's cottages are ideal accommodations for overseas visitors. They're plentiful and reasonably priced.

One interesting aspect of this route is its flexibility. You can head directly up the map to the Norwegian border or meander in and out of the windswept coastal indentations, stopping at any fjord or island that catches your eye. You'll find the drive is at least 200 miles (320 km) long and probably longer if you do a lot of island and fjord hopscotching. You'll also find that the dramatic coastal roadside scenery is as much of an attraction as the stops along the way.

GOTHENBURG: Though this is the principal seaport of Scandinavia and the home of some of Sweden's major industrial concerns, don't make the mistake of hurrying through here without pausing to get acquainted with this friendly unsophisticated city of 700,000. Despite being Sweden's second major city, with a busy downtown commercial area, Gothenburg has a relaxing pace and there are plenty of entertainment spots for the tourist to mix with the native.

The city was founded in the early seventeenth century as a Dutch colony (King Gustav Adolf II granted its first charter in 1621), but has also drawn on the influence of Germans and English over the ensuing centuries. Gothenburg quickly reveals itself to be a garden city with well-kept canals, parks, and botanical gardens like Trädgårdsföreningen and Botaniska Trädgården. Take a Paddan boat canal tour that takes you under 20 bridges to soak in the Dutch influence, and the short boat excursion to Älvsborg Fortress to learn about the great naval battles of the seventeenth century between Swedish and Danish forces.

Kronhuset (Kronhusgatan) is the oldest building in Gothenburg and has a museum recording the history of the city, as well as reconstructions of turn-of-the-century shops. Sjöfartsmuseet, or Maritime Museum (Stigbergstorget), displays ship models from Viking times to the present and richly illustrates the maritime traditions of this major port.

The main drag in Gothenburg is Kungsportavenyn, referred to as simply Avenyn (Avenue). It's a wide, tree-lined boulevard with cafés, shops, elegant buildings, and nightclubs. There are restaurants that serve Italian, Scottish, German, and Chinese fare, and even a smattering of American fast-food favorites. The cafés here are the best places in town to sit and watch people go by — during the day, the shoppers and tourists, and during the evening, the local young folk who cruise up and down, finally congregating at the Poseidon Fountain in the Götaplatsen, the large square at the end of the avenue. At one side of the fountain is the Stadsbiblioteket (library), where you can check on the progress of your favorite baseball team or get the latest on the US political scene by looking at one of the American newspapers available in the reading room.

The Gothenburg Art Gallery, also in the Götaplatsen, has an amazingly good collection of modern art including work by Cézanne, Van Gogh, Rodin, and Picasso. There's also work by modern Scandinavian masters like Anders Zorn, Edvard Munch, and Carl Milles.

One place you should not pass up on your visit here is the Feskekörka, or fish church, next to the fish market in Gothenburg Harbor. The church, built about 100 years ago, resembles any other normal Lutheran church until you step inside — and discover it's actually a fish market, filled with some 20 booths where merchants offer for sale every kind of seafood, from lobsters to herring, fresh and smoked salmon, eels, sole, flounder, crabs, shrimp, and many others. An auction is held at the harbor every morning at 7 AM for the day's fresh catches.

In order to plan your route up the coast in detail, you might want to stop at the Gothenburg Tourist Office (Kungsportsplatsen 2; phone: 100740). To start your trip north, you leave town on the main highway, E6, and after a short drive along the Göta River valley, you get off the main road and enter Kungälv, a 1,000-year-old town with a turbulent history.

KUNGÄLV: A merchant town occupied this site as early as the tenth century. Three hundred years later, the location had gained significance strategically as a border stronghold between Norway and Sweden (the present border runs more than a hundred miles to the north), and work began on the impregnable Bohus Fortress. This mighty stronghold was subjected to many sieges through the centuries but was never taken by force of arms. The ruined structure still stands proud and impressive, jutting up amid the trees on a now placid island.

Across the river in the old part of the town, around Västra Gatan, are several interesting old wooden buildings, mainly from the eighteenth century, and an exquisite church dating from 1679, which has a richly adorned baroque interior.

Leaving Kungälv, avoid the main highway and make your way northwest on winding country roads, heading for Tjuvkil and the Instö car ferry across to the island of Koön. From here there is a small passenger-only ferry to Marstrand, a yachting harbor and fashionable summer resort on a small wooded island dominated by the seventeenth-century Carlsten Fortress.

MARSTRAND: Herring fishing made this island village a prosperous one during the sixteenth century, but then the lucrative herring shoals moved away and there followed a history of mixed fortunes with periodic devastation by fire and pestilence. Today, the picturesque white-walled timber buildings and crooked alleyways belie this troubled past, never more so than on international regatta days in July or August, when tall-masted yachts swarm the quayside and suntanned visitors stroll the waterfront.

En Route from Marstrand – Make your way back to the mainland and, still keeping to the small country roads, follow the winding coast north until you reach Stenungsund, less than an hour's drive away. Here you sweep to the left and up onto the impressive Tjörn Bridges, spanning three beautiful sounds and linking the mainland with the idyllic islands of Tjörn and neighboring Orust. The Tjörn bridges are a tourist attraction in themselves, offering a splendid vantage point for panoramic views over rocky, heatherclad isles and often a colorful procession of yachts passing through the sound below.

On the seaward fringes of Tjörn Island, there is a fairy-tale world of refreshingly unsophisticated fishing communities such as Rönnäng and Skärhamn, where red timber cottages huddle together on rocky headlands or perch precariously on tiny skerries. Rows of stockfish are hung out to dry on large tent-shaped racks, and pleasure boats and round-hulled fishing vessels line the wooden jetties. The area is also rich in Stone Age relics. The northern edge of Tjörn Island is linked by bridge to the neighboring island of Orust, where you can explore more ancient relics and quaint fishing villages, notably the lobster harbor, Mollösund, tucked away on a peninsula in the southwest corner of the island.

Continue to the northwest corner of Orust to Ellös, where a car ferry transports you across to Rågårdsvik on the island of Skaftö. Head north across the island to the attractive seaside resort of Fiskebäckskil where you can stroll at the harbor, enjoy a swim, fish, sail, or try the 9-hole golf course.

From Fiskebäckskil a regular car ferry service takes you to Lysekil.

LYSEKIL: Once the center of the local stone-quarrying industry, this small village of 7,000 is now a popular resort and yacht harbor with many diversions for the summer tourist. By day you can enjoy tennis or swimming, and at night, the area's many restaurants and discos. Boat excursions for sea fishing or general exploration in the surrounding waters are available at the harbor.

At Brastad, some 10 miles (16 km) north, stop to view the remarkable ancient rock carvings, then follow Route 162 again, turning left onto Route 163 at Hallinden. Proceed to a fork in this highway, and turn left toward the coast again in the direction of Åby and Kungshamn.

KUNGSHAMN: Kungshamn and neighboring Smögen are two of the finest and most interesting fishing ports on this coast. Kungshamn has a modern fishing harbor and if you stay until evening you can watch the shrimp auction and afterward enjoy a fresh seafood supper. Nearby Smögen can be reached by way of the Smögen Bridge, and is a lovely, picturesque fishing hamlet with quite an international atmosphere in summer. Stroll the long wooden quayside lined with timber boathouses and souvenir shops and admire the elegant pleasure craft and rugged fishing vessels crowding every inch of mooring space. Fishing trips are arranged to go out to the best fishing grounds in the archipelago for whiting, cod, and mackerel.

En Route from Kungshamn – Follow the coast road north past fjords, wide bays, and rocky inlets until you join Route 163 again at Bottne Fjord. Drive north through Hamburgsund and Fjällbacka until you reach Grebbestad. This route shows the rugged, sculptured coastline at its best and all along the way there are places where you can linger awhile for some angling or bathing.

A couple of miles east of Grebbestad lie Tanum and Tanumshede, the best known of all Sweden's rock-carving sites. The strange figures and symbols you see here were carved in the granite rock some 3,000 years ago and are still legible. The most impressive of the carvings is at Fossum and depicts a battle scene.

The route continues north on main Route E6, reaching the Norwegian border at the Svinesund Bridge, some 60 miles (96 km) from Oslo.

BEST EN ROUTE

Expect hotels in Sweden to be priced as high as those in the US. Very expensive hotels, which carry single and double suites, run anywhere from $75 to $120 a night. More moderate in price are those first-class tourist hotels with full accommodations (private baths in most; in some you may have to opt for a bathroom in the corridor); these run $40 to $75, single or double room. Other hotels, smaller in size, can run from $30 to $65 (moderate), and $25 to $40 (inexpensive). Reservations are recommended.

There's a hotel cheque system available covering all of Sweden, with 36 hotels participating from this part of the coast. Advance booking is made for the first hotel of your stay and reservations for your next overnight stop are made on arrival at each hotel along your route. The system also provides various discounts. Consult the Swedish Tourist Board, 75 Rockefeller Plaza, New York, NY 10019 (phone: 212-582-2802), for details on hotel cheque systems. Detailed information on Swedish summer chalets is available from the Gothenburg Tourist Board, Booking Service, Kungsportsplatsen 2, S-411 10 Gothenburg, Sweden (phone: 031-100 760), or Inter Holiday AB, Lilla Kungsgatan 1, 411 08 Gothenburg, Sweden (phone: 13-67-57).

GOTHENBURG

SAS Park Avenue Hotel – 320-room property offers banquet facilities, bar, restaurant, sauna, and secretarial services (if you need them), among other amenities. Kungsportsavenyn 36–38 (phone: 17-65-20). Very expensive.

Hotel Windsor – Smaller, 83-room hotel offers a bar and English-style restaurant. Kungsportsavenyn 6 (phone: 17-65-40). Expensive.

KUNGÄLV

Hotel Fars Hatt – A pleasant hotel in a convenient location. Torget 442 00 (phone: 0303-10970). Moderate.

MARSTRAND

Alphyddan – A modest 37-room hotel in the center of this small island town. Långgatan 6, 440 30 (phone: 0303-61200). Moderate.

LYSEKIL

Hotel Lysekil – A 50-room hotel with a restaurant and a nightclub. Rosvikstorg 453 00 (phone: 0523-11860). Moderate.

TANUMSHEDE

Tanums Gestgifveri – An old country inn that serves very good food and is an ideal overnight spot for soaking in the historic ambience of this ancient region, the site of strange rock carvings estimated to be over 3,000 years old. On Route E6 (phone: 0525-29010). Expensive to moderate.

Gotland

In the time of the Vikings, Gotland was the gateway to Scandinavia. It's Sweden's largest island, off the east coast in the Baltic, and, because of its location, it was historically the guardian of the peninsula. It began as a strategic military base for a succession of Viking kings bent on plundering the lands to the east (now Russia) and later became a trading point and cultural center. The history of Gotland is still visible all over the island in Stone Age cave dwellings, Viking runes (large stones inscribed with colorful pictures), and medieval churches.

After the decline of the Vikings and the development of more civilized methods of international trade, Visby, Gotland's main city, became the center of the Hanseatic League, a Germanic trade association. In the thirteenth century the burghers of Visby built an intricate limestone wall modeled on the effective Roman civil defense perimeters. As the town grew prosperous with trade, the people built an affluent city within the wall, out of the marble and the sandstone they found in abundance on their flat, fertile island.

Gotland was civilized long before the Swedish mainland and became one of the wealthiest and most powerful states in Europe, but in 1361 Danish King Valdemar Atterdag invaded. (Legend has it that the king's lover, the treacherous daughter of Visbian Nils the Goldsmith, opened the city gate and let the Danes in.) In any case, Visby fell and never regained its imperial stature.

Today Gotland is a land of beaches, spas, and sailing, with a beautiful landscape and a warmer climate than the rest of Sweden so that, aside from tourism, farming is the mainstay of the island's economy. Gotland is 78 miles long and 25 miles wide with plenty of room for Gotland sheep — a black-wooled variety — to graze all year round. In the Lojsta Hajd woodland you can also see the Gotland Russ ponies, small and temperamental from inbreeding, but unusual looking and still friendly.

Geologically, the most remarkable features of this island are the "marine stacks" — nature's own sculptures of stone, formed by eroding winds and waters — that give Gotland's lovely sandy beaches a character all their own. The stacks are formed at the stony edges of the slopes leading to the sandy beaches.

You enter Gotland through Visby. In the summer, there are car ferries from Nynäshamn, Oskarshamn, and Västervik on the mainland, and from Grankullavik on the island of Öland. If you bring your own car, make sure to book tickets well in advance as the auto berths are often sold out. Even without a car, advance booking is required since the summer ferries are usually packed with travelers. Flights are available to Visby airport from Stockholm, Arlanda, Norrköping, and Kalmar.

VISBY: This is one of the oldest cities in Sweden and its wall alone would make it worth the trip. The wall is about 2 miles long and when first built was capped by 44 towers with crenellated turrets and long, thin archer's windows. Each tower is also a gateway. Inside the walls you can see gleaming whitewashed stone houses with shiny red-tile roofs; the city has a sort of southern European look. Eventually, Visby grew too large for its surrounding wall and was forced to build up, around, and over itself. It's now a town of romantic arches and alleyways with clinging vines and bushes growing out of every wall cranny. The red roofs are punctuated by stepped gables, and bicycles are the preferred mode of transportation over the cobbled streets. Visby has been called the city of roses and there are colorful blossoms everywhere. The Almedalen old harbor, lifted by land augmentation over the centuries, has been transformed into a botanic oasis with many varieties of flowers.

There are 92 churches on Gotland and only one of them was built after 1350. Some of them are in ruins but there's still more stained glass here than anywhere else in Scandinavia. At the church of St. Nicolaus, an outdoor play is put on every summer portraying the life of one of Visby's local saints. A more vivid glimpse into the past, however, is outside the wall at the Galberget (hanging mound), which was a raised medieval execution area whose stone gallows you can still examine.

Visby is also a tourist town with good restaurants, shops to browse through, and comfortable hotels. If you want to rent a bicycle, ask at the tourist office, Strandgatan 9 (phone: 0498-10982). They'll also tell you where you'll find the best sailing, skin diving, and surf.

   En Route from Visby – The Väte, a fourteenth-century stone church, is 18 miles (29 km) south of Visby on Route 142.

   From Väte, the route continues along the highway into the Lojsta Hajd woodlands — the home of the Gotland ponies. Half wild, half domestic, the ponies are left to roam around for 3 years before they are rounded up to be broken in.

   Turning east at Fide, you pass the Etelhem Church, go through the village of

Hemse, and arrive at Holmhällar fishing village on the southeastern tip of Gotland.

HOLMHÄLLAR: The beaches around Holmhällar are splendid, and here samples of the typical marine stacks can be seen. You'll also find several caves with stalagmites like frozen curtains of stone, formed by millennia of dripping water seeping through the limestone bedrock.

Farther south, the Hoburgen man — a marine stack shaped like a head — marks the island's southernmost point. The view across the Baltic is breathtaking.

En Route from Holmhällar – Returning north to Visby along the coast, stop over at Kronvald fishing village. According to legend, it was here that invading Danes landed. Back in Visby, you can head north on the island, but avoid the uppermost part of Gotland, which is a restricted area.

The Lummelunda caves and the Lummelunda geological museum, a 20-minute drive north along the coast of Visby, are recommended sites, as is a drive across the island to Slite. Beaches at Slite are excellent, and the Slite Strandbad beach, on a little island off the harbor, is especially enjoyable.

BEST EN ROUTE

Just because you're off the mainland doesn't mean hotel prices will be lower. On the contrary, they're about the same as on previous routes: $48 to $100 (very expensive), $35 to $71 (expensive), $25 to $61 (moderate), and $17 to $37 (inexpensive). Every hotel has double and single rooms, and it's not a bad idea to reserve beforehand, especially during the summer months.

You can also rent private rooms and cottages on the island. Contact Gotlandsresor AB, Box 2081, 621 02 Visby (phone: 0498-19010).

VISBY

Visby – A 92-room hotel that has two restaurants, the *Guldkanten* and *Oskar* (with nightly entertainment in summer) and a sauna. Strandgatan 6 (phone: 0498-11925). Expensive.

HEMSE

Hemse – A 20-bed hotel that is small but pleasant, and has a restaurant. Storgatan, 620 12 Hemse (phone: 0498-80151). Moderate.

Lapland

For many travelers, Lapland, sprawling across the wild regions of Arctic Scandinavia, has the same sort of fascination usually reserved for remote, exotic destinations like Samarkand, Tibet, and Katmandu.

There is indeed a certain romance about an area still unconquered by man and civilization, a domain of awesome proportions where reindeer roam free and fast-disappearing wildlife such as the bear and golden eagle still hold their own. Man has made but small inroads here: The nomadic Lapps, who are believed to have migrated to Scandinavia from Russia, accepted the hardy lifestyle that Arctic conditions imposed in making this their home, following the migratory reindeer herds. In recent decades, the quest for iron ore and the need for electrical power generated by the mighty rushing rivers has given rise to industrialization in the wilderness. It is the development of modern towns like Kiruna that has made conventional tourism possible in these parts. Of course, along with modernization comes the breaking down of old traditions and it isn't uncommon now to see snow mobiles during reindeer round-ups and Lapps wearing blue jeans instead of their ancient colorful outfits fashioned almost entirely of reindeer hides.

When contemplating a vacation trip, bear in mind that the unique rewards of travel in these regions, the joy of experiencing vast tracts of unspoiled nature and of living under the midnight sun, must be paid for in the form of a few discomforts. Your accommodations may be a well-equipped but simple mountain chalet instead of a luxury hotel, and you might suffer a few insect bites if you forget your repellent, but this doesn't mean that you have to be an athlete and outdoorsman to venture this way. Time your visit, however, during the warm summer months of June, July, and August, and possibly even May and September — temperatures at this time are warmer than those in winter.

The route takes you through a landscape where birch-clad valleys and vast pine forests give way to mountain plateaus, waterfalls, river rapids, and primeval moss-covered fens; where herds of reindeer follow age-old migratory paths, swimming bravely across broad rivers to reach their mountain grazing lands; where the fisherman, naturalist, and amateur photographer have more excitement in one week than friends back home might experience in a lifetime.

The numerous rivers of the region snake down in valleys from the mountainous northwest to spill out finally into the Gulf of Bothnia. Roads tend to follow these river valleys, each ribbonlike highway reaching up into the mountains and, in some cases, winding as far as the Norwegian coast. Each road is a tour route in its own right. They pass fish-rich lakes, vast national parks, snow-capped mountain ranges, and Arctic tundra. Fittingly, each road has a romantic name, like the Blue Road, Way of the Four Winds, the Midnight Sun Road, or the Linné Route.

Your tour route, designed to give you a varied and, as far as possible, complete picture of these northern wilds, traces a winding path northward into the mountains.

For the most part, the roads are modern with hard metal surfaces, but in some of the more remote stretches, you may find yourself driving on well-kept dirt roads.

Our starting point is Luleå, the Baltic port that can be reached by regular air service, railroad, or by main highway E4 from Stockholm, an ideal gateway into the region. At the tourist office here, Nordkalottresor/Norrlands Turistråd (Kungsgatan 5, phone: 0920-69885), you can collect a useful information brochure covering Swedish Lapland. From Luleå, follow Route 97 northwest and you will soon pass the garrison town, Boden. Keen golfers may wish to enquire about the local 9-hole course, one of the world's most northern golf courses and one of the very few where you can tee off by the light of the midnight sun. At Boden turn left and drive southwest on Route 356 heading for Älvsbyn some 30 miles (48 km) farther on — a market town on the Pite River deservedly known as the "land of the rapids." At Älvsbyn, turn right onto Route 374, traveling northwest to Storforsen, Europe's largest unrestricted waterfall and last untamed giant rapids. See the Pite River crash and rumble its way at breakneck speed down the hillside, falling 252 feet over a stretch of 3 miles. There is a forestry museum here with tar-works and charcoal stacks in operation so you can see what a Swedish lumber camp looked like in days gone by.

Leaving Storforsen, you continue northwest through lake-dotted open moorland, passing over the Arctic Circle (there's little more than a signpost to mark the crossing), and finally reaching the Lapp center of Jokkmokk.

JOKKMOKK: Here at the Lapp museum you will receive your first insight into the rich and colorful culture of the hardy, nomadic Lapps. The museum displays more than 1,200 Lapp objects, including life-size old storehouses, folk costumes, sleighs, delicately carved wooden utensils, and an array of exquisite silver jewelry. From now on you will become increasingly aware of your presence in the wild domain of the Lapps and their precious reindeer, for you are certain to meet them face to face from time to time during your tour. Since the reindeer herds are nomadic and unpredictable, it is not possible to set dates and places when and where you can see the migration or the summer musters. It's possible to get help and guidance from a friendly Lapp, but don't make the mistake of insulting these taciturn folk by approaching them as some sort of curiosity or tourist attraction. They are a proud people whose labor is honest and whose lifestyle is hard, a nomadic race who are making the difficult transition into twentieth-century civilization as their native region, Lapland (an area that cuts across Scandinavian national boundaries), becomes less and less remote. Today, there are only 40,000 Lapps left in Scandinavia, 15,000 of whom live in Sweden.

After you visit the museum, call at the tourist office to collect your Polar Certificate recognizing your crossing of the Arctic Circle, and then take a look at the Gamla Kyrkan (The Old Church), a small timbered building dating from 1753 (damaged by fire in 1972).

The county of Jokkmokk contains the vast, wild, and unforgettably beautiful national parks, Sarek, Padjelanta, and Stora Sjöfallet. These provide a worthwhile detour for the experienced outdoorsman through the last true wilderness in Europe. The 100 glaciers and 20 towering peaks of these wild preserves are the haunt of the osprey, loon, wild goose, and golden eagle. The stepping-off point for hiking expeditions into Sarek National Park lies about 80 miles (128 km) northwest of Jokkmokk along highway 805 at Kvikkjokk. Here you can pick up the famous King's Trail, a hiking route laid out by the Swedish Touring Club and marked by cairns. There are mountain chalets at suitable intervals along the route, but don't attempt this hike unless you know what you're doing.

En Route from Jokkmokk – Take Highway 97 north for about 30 miles (48 km), crossing the Lule River and reaching Porjus, a community developed in conjunction with the hydroelectric project harnessing the Porjus Falls. East of Porjus is the Muddus National Park, an area of virgin pine and spruce forest, untouched swamplands, and undulating granite mountains. Muddus is a nature reserve for bear, elk, marten, and weasel, and the home of many rare migratory birds. Unfortunately, this is also wild country, difficult to penetrate and more for the avid bird-watcher and naturalist than the conventional tourist, although some trails have been laid out with raised wooden duckboards to improve accessibility.

Continue on Highway 97 for about another 30 miles (48 km) and you enter Gällivare, passing Thunder Mountain, which rises some 2,699 feet above sea level.

GÄLLIVARE: This is a flourishing mining community and trading center where you will have much to do: join one of the daily tours to the nearby iron mines at Malmberget; visit the local museum at Vasara with 2,000-year-old skis on display; and view the eighteenth-century Ettore Church. A modern building here of considerable interest to the tourist is Björnfällan (The Bear Trap), a 54-square-foot log cabin said to be the largest in the world, built with 80 tons of stone and 230,000 feet of timber, most of which is 400-year-old gray pine. The building acts as a service center for a holiday village of log cabins clustered in the surrounding countryside, and it contains two saunas, a swimming pool, meeting rooms with open fires, shops, and restaurant. From Gällivare, there are connections by taxi flight using light aircraft to Tjuonajokk, Miekak, and Rastojaure mountain fishing camps, where grayling, char, and salmon trout provide the challenge for the keen angler. Gällivare airport has daily scheduled air service to Stockholm.

En Route from Gällivare – Follow Highway 98 north through moorland and forest, passing scenic lakes and rivers. After some 50 miles (80 km) you reach Svappavaara. Those who feel in need of a little big-city luxury and home comfort can continue another 30 miles (48 km) west to Kiruna, a mining town with modern accommodations. Here you can get a wonderful meal of local delicacies such as white grouse (*ptarmigan*) followed by cloudberries and cream for dessert. Kiruna also has tours into the world's biggest underground mine, which extracts up to 30 million tons of iron ore annually.

For those who decline the luxury of the Kiruna detour, the tour route turns east at Svappavaara and then north at Vittangi. From here it's 65 miles (104 km) to Karesuando, a church village on the border of Sweden and Finland. The road is through a tundra region of countless lakes and rivers where the subsoil is permanently frozen. From here the lunatic fringe may choose to continue northward via Kautokeino and Alta in Norway all the way up to North Cape, a magnificent precipice that marks the northernmost tip of Europe. Another alternative is to follow Route E78 southeast into Finland. Our less ambitious but nonetheless spectacular route proceeds northwest from Karesuando on Route E78 — the beautiful "Way of the Four Winds," running parallel with the Könkämä River along the Swedish-Finnish border.

Seventy miles (112 km) farther on as you climb steadily into an alpine region, you cross the border into Norway at Siilastupa, finally reaching Skibotn on the Lyngen Fjord. Your first breathtaking glimpse of the awe-inspiring fjord, its sheer rock walls rising nearly vertically, unbroken but for the odd frothy waterfall crashing into the still waters below, tells you have reached the rocky, skerried coastline of northern Norway. Follow the road southwest along the scenic fjord passing Kvesmenes, where you might join a deep-sea fishing trip to the shark waters of the Arctic Ocean. On either side of the Lyngen Fjord rise the ragged peaks of the Lyngen Alps, spewing impressive blue white glaciers right down to the surface of the water. The faces of the glaciers sparkle like diamonds in the sun. Leaving the fjord, follow Route E78 looping northwest onto a large peninsula toward the Arctic fishing port of Tromsø.

TROMSØ: Your first impression of Tromsø — apart from the obvious beauty of its coastal setting and backdrop of blue mountains — will be the lush green vegetation that contrasts strongly with the Arctic tundra you have recently passed through at similar latitudes. The rich flora and mild climate on this coast are explained by the Gulf Stream that washes warm currents onto these northern shores.

Tromsø is the largest city in northern Norway (see *Exploring Norway*, DIRECTIONS) often called the gateway to the Arctic because of the many expeditions that have set out from here. Take the 2½-hour sight-seeing tour that leaves from the *SAS Royal Hotel*, showing you the best of Tromsø Island, on which most of the city is situated, and the town museum, which traces the history of the region from the Stone Age through Viking times and up to the present. The museum also has a section devoted to Lappish ethnography. At the end of the tour you are dropped near the cable car ride up to Storsteinen Mountain, where you receive a sweeping panoramic view over the green city, its wide fishing harbor, and the gentle mountains beyond. Here in Tromsø is your chance to enjoy the more conventional tourist pursuits of a shopping spree and an evening out.

Your route ends in Tromsø but there are possibilities to continue south along the coast passing the fishing harbor of Narvik and the wild and beautiful Lofoten Islands. Taking this route, it is also possible to enter Sweden again at Graddis and follow the "Silver Road" via Arjeplog and Arvidsjaur back to our starting point, Luleå.

BEST EN ROUTE

Accommodations are sparse in Lapland, and in the same price range as the previous routes: $48 to $105 (very expensive), $35 to $71 (expensive), $25 to $61 (moderate), and $17 to $27 (inexpensive). Again, make reservations before you come.

GÄLLIVARE

Björnfällan – Holiday village of a very high standard has log cabins and a service center that includes saunas, swimming pool, meeting rooms with open fires, shops, and a cafeteria (phone: 0970-14560). Make reservations with your travel agent. Expensive.

KIRUNA

Hotel Ferrum – This 170-room hotel provides rooms with private baths, dining room and dancing. In town (phone: 0980-18600). Expensive.

TROMSØ (NORWAY)

SAS Royal Hotel – This 270-room hotel has excellent accommodations, private baths, and a very good restaurant. Sjogata 7 (phone: 083-56000). Very expensive.

Exploring Switzerland

Switzerland is small, but there is probably not one square mile that does not contain some beauty or interest. The variety of its scenery is enormous and almost everything is within easy reach. Switzerland's people are also incredibly diverse: Four ethnic and linguistic groups — German, French, Italian, Romansh — maintain their characteristics, culture, and independence under the aegis of one central government. Not only do the 26 cantons (states) guard their individual rights fiercely (until 1848 some had even their own money), but so does every community within the cantons. This is why it's possible to pay twice as much in taxes in one village as in another a mile away.

Geographical or historical necessity played less of a part in the formation of the Confederatio Helvetica (Swiss Confederation) than did the will of the people. In prehistoric times most of the territory was inhabited by Celts (the Helvetians were one of the main Celtic tribes). Later it was ruled by the Romans, who brought cultural and economic prosperity, and then it was overrun by Germanic tribes. The latter included the Alemanns, who settled in what is today the German area of the country, and the Burgundians, who settled in the French. In feudal times the territory was part of the Holy German Empire, and was later ruled by princely families or bishops, who often fought each other for supremacy. It was against the Hapsburgs that the original three forest cantons (Uri, Schwyz, Unterwalden) rebelled, and they eventually formed an alliance, marking the birth of the nation in 1291. It did not happen as dramatically as the famous legend of William Tell has it, but the spirit of freedom was the same, and Tell and his apple are still revered today. (This story of Swiss nationhood arose in the fifteenth century and was made world-famous by the German poet Schiller in the eighteenth century. It tells of a conspiracy, solemnly sworn among representatives of the three cantons, to overthrow the evil Bailiff Gessler, who had subjected the archer Tell to his famous ordeal.) One by one, all the cities and cantons joined or were acquired by the confederation; the last one was Jura in 1979.

The country is now ruled by a federal government, similar to that of the US, which wields executive and legislative power. The executive branch is controlled by a federal council consisting of seven members and headed by a president serving a one-year term. Since the head of the council is also the country's president, most Swiss don't know who their government's chief executive is for a given year.

You will generally find the Swiss very friendly and helpful. In most hotels, there is always somebody who speaks English. The best times for motoring are June, September, and October, when the high passes are open but the roads aren't clogged with travelers. Despite the changeable weather, any time is good — in recent years, for example, November has been a particularly beautiful month for touring the mountains. Roads are good, but the German Swiss tend to be cautious (and very law-abiding) drivers. Road numbers exist only on maps and not on road signs. Also, note that a fine is imposed if you are caught driving on any Swiss highway without the special car sticker that is used in lieu of tolls. Rental cars usually have these stickers; if you're driving into Switzerland, they are available for about $1 at border crossings.

, The best maps are *Switzerland for Leisure,* put out by Kümmerly and Frey, and the Michelin regional maps. For local city maps, ask at the tourist offices. The best quick-reference source is the green Michelin guidebook, *Switzerland;* for statistics and general information, there's a small red paperback, also called *Switzerland,* which is published yearly by Kümmerly and Frey. The *Swiss Hotel Guide,* available at the tourist offices, is also helpful.

The four itineraries described below take you through the most important regions and cities, giving a good cross-section of the country. Three of the four routes originate in Zürich, the largest city and industrial and financial center of Switzerland. The Zürich to Geneva route passes through some of Switzerland's most historic towns, including Murten and Fribourg. The Zürich to Lugano route travels the high Swiss Alps, running through mountain passes famous for their breathtaking scenery. Another routing from Zürich to Lugano, via the Engadine, cuts through the heart of Swiss tourism, with stops at Bad Ragaz and St. Moritz, the famous health spas. The last route, Bern to Montreux, is typical of diverse Switzerland: It connects the Alps with Lake Geneva and en route you will savor subtropical vegetation as well as glacial vistas.

Zürich to Geneva

This itinerary, which stresses culture and cities, is more idyllic and peaceful than the mountain routes. Starting with Zürich, the route goes west along the Rhine to Basel, then proceeds southwest through the country's oldest mountain range, the Jura (where the language changes from German to French), then to the basin of the Biel and Neuchâtel lakes and gentle, pastoral countryside, to its climax, radiant Lake Geneva with its crown of Alps. The trip includes stops in culturally vibrant Basel; charming Neuchâtel; the "museum town" of Murten; historic Fribourg; enchanting Gruyères; and the university town of Lausanne. Any season is good for this 260-mile (416-km) route. Count on doing it in 3 fairly leisurely days; it's possible to do it in 2 by leaving out some museums.

En Route from Zürich – Take the scenic (and actually shorter) Route N7, which passes the airport and proceeds along the Rhine, which is not yet navigable here. Tiny Kaiserstuhl, just off the main road, is worth a short stop, as it has kept its medieval look. Across the old bridge is Germany. After Zurzach, which features a spa with hot springs, the Aare — the largest all-Swiss river — joins the Rhine in a picturesque confluence at Koblenz. All along the other side of the Rhine loom the Gothic towers of small German towns. Soon after pretty Laufenburg, the road divides; head for Rheinfelden, with its old spa and famous brewery. From here take Route 3 to Augst, site of the impressive ruins of Augusta Raurica, the oldest Roman settlement on the Rhine. Much has been restored, and you can see some of the artifacts found — including silver plates decorated with mythological details — on display at the museum. It's only a few more minutes from here to Basel.

BASEL: Although it's Switzerland's second city (after Zürich) in terms of population and business, Basel is first in culture — a traditional patron of the arts. Of Celtic Roman origin, the city later was ruled by a prince-bishop for over 1,000 years. (This explains the bishop's staff in Basel's coat of arms.) The town joined the Swiss Confederation in 1501, and became Protestant soon after. It has always had major importance as a port (the Rhine is navigable from here on down) and as a road junction, especially after the river's first bridge, the Mittlere Brücke, was built in 1225. It remained the only one to span the Rhine for centuries, and it still stands.

It's easy to get lost in Basel, so park in the center of town and do your exploring on foot. A walk along the Obere Rheinweg, a promenade following the Rhine's right bank, will give you a good overall picture of old Basel; it's also nice to take the ferry across. On the other side of the Rhine is the twelfth-century cathedral (Münster), which provides another fine panorama of the town from its twin Gothic towers. Nearby you'll find some interesting patrician townhouses. The town hall, on Market Square (still the site of a daily market), is an impressive sixteenth-century sandstone building that's adorned with frescoes.

And, of course, there are the museums. The Fine Arts Museum (Kunstmuseum, St. Albangraben), one of the most remarkable of its kind in the world, features the Amerbach collection. It includes outstanding examples of early German and Flemish art and the largest group of paintings by the Holbein family assembled anywhere. (Amerbach was a friend of the Holbeins.) There are also French impressionist works and modern abstracts. The Cherry Orchard Museum (Kirschgarten, Elizabethenstrasse 27), housed in a lovely old patrician mansion, has period furniture, magnificent porcelain, antique watches, and a delightful exhibition of old toys. It also contains a substantial part of the collection of the Historical Museum; the latter is set in the Gothic Barfüsser church, on Barfüsserplatz.

This Week in Basel, a booklet published by the Tourist Office, provides an excellent suggested walking tour of the old town, complete with a map. While you're here, stop at "three-countries corner," a spot marked by a spire, where the Swiss, German, and French borders all converge, and take in the excellent view of the port and city from the terrace (reachable by elevator) of the Swiss Navigation Companies' silo. And be sure to sample the local cookie specialty, *basler leckerli.* In addition, you can take in a free concert, given in a number of different churches year-round. It's a good idea to visit Basel on the Monday after Ash Wednesday, for that's when the town really comes alive in an annual carnival called *Fasnacht.*

En Route from Basel – Take the road parallel to Route 18 south; just off the road and near Basel's city limits is Arlesheim, with its charming baroque church and famous Silberman organ. On a mountain overlooking this town is the fortress-like Goetheanum, the center of the Anthroposophical Society. The structure was built according to exacting esoteric rules — for example, no right angles. Goethe's scientific theories strongly influenced the movement, and his plays are often performed here.

At Laufen, you enter the pastoral Jura range. The region becomes French-speaking as you drive along the Birs River to Delémont, former summer residence of the prince-bishops of Basel. The lovely baroque palace is the seat of the new Jura government. Nearby is Courfaivre, with its remarkable modern stained-glass windows created by Fernand Léger in the village church.

Continuing on Route 18, you'll pass through the most unspoiled section of the Jura, the Franches Montagnes; as you ride the high plateau, it's easy to feel on top of the world. Here are lovely natural parks, pastures with grazing horses (this is the major horse-breeding region), low farmhouses, and little inns that serve good local trout and ham. At Le Roselet (off Les Emibois) you can visit a home for old horses. La Chaux de Fonds is the center of Swiss watch manufacturing, and there is a truly fabulous underground watch museum: On view in specially lit sections is the world's most comprehensive collection of timepieces, from sundials to atomic clocks (Musée International d'Horlogerie, 21 rue des Musées). A scenic mountain pass road ascends to Vue des Alpes, where there's a lookout point at 4,209 feet. On clear days the panorama of the Bernese Alps and Mont Blanc is overwhelming. Descending toward Lake Neuchâtel, you come to Valangin, a charming little town with an old castle that's now an interesting regional museum. From here, it's a short ride to Neuchâtel, a honey-colored university town on a peaceful lake.

NEUCHÂTEL: Some claim that the purest French in the world is spoken in this aristocratic city; after the eleventh century, it belonged successively — and by inheritance — to the House of Orléans and the king of Prussia. The intellectual and cultural heritage can be felt in a walk through the old town, especially in the twelfth-century University Church and the castle. The Ethnographic Museum is outstanding for its Egyptian and African collections and thematic display rooms (St. Nicolas 4). The Museum of Art and History features ingenious automatons invented in the eighteenth century (rue des Beaux-Arts).

En Route from Neuchâtel – Cross the canal connecting the Neuchâtel and Biel lakes north of the city, and head for Murten, located on the far side of the lake of the same name.

MURTEN (MORAT): This enchanting town is a museum in itself, having retained most of its medieval ramparts and towers. A historic battle was fought here in the fifteenth century between the Swiss Confederates and the army of the duke of Burgundy, and it's still commemorated today. A walk around the ramparts provides picturesque views of the old roofs, the lake, and the castle. Main Street (Hauptstrasse) displays a pleasing harmony of design, with its arcaded, geranium-covered houses, fountains, and city gate; a row of restaurants and cafés makes it even more inviting. It's a short drive southeast to Fribourg.

FRIBOURG: You enter one of the most picturesque and interesting cities of the country through an old gate; strangely, it's often bypassed by tourists. Its river, the Sarine, is a true dividing line between the French and German parts of Switzerland. Fribourg is a historical Roman Catholic bastion, and the site of a renowned Catholic university established in 1889. Founded in 1157, the city was ruled by different families until it joined the confederation in 1481. Several major religious orders, such as the Franciscans, Cistercians, and Jesuits, have settled here in the course of centuries.

The Franciscan Church (Église des Cordeliers, rue de Morat), completed in the thirteenth century and rebuilt in the eighteenth century, retains its original chancel and stalls, as well as its splendid St. Anthony altarpiece, painted by two artists whose signatures were red and white carnations. In addition, bridges on the winding Sarine offer marvelous views of the town. The river itself swirls around Fribourg's unusual spurlike rock formations. You should also see the Gothic towers and elaborately decorated interiors of St. Nicholas' Cathedral; the turrets and belfry of the sixteenth-century town hall; and the excellent collection of sculpture, furniture, and jewelry housed in the elegant Museum of Art and History (all on rue de Morat).

En Route from Fribourg – Continue along the pretty, man-made Lake Gruyère; for a more scenic route, don't take the freeway or the main road, but the smaller one that goes via Marly and Corbières (stop at the bridge for a good view) through regions of pastoral scenery where folklore is still alive. Then proceed via Broc directly to Gruyères.

GRUYÈRES: This hilltop town, definitely one of the route's highlights, appears to be preserved against time — it could be the setting for fairy tales. Cars are prohibited within the town's walls for a good part of the year, so leave yours in one of the lots on the outskirts. Then take a leisurely stroll down the wide, cobblestone main street that's lined with old houses, observing the house on the left with the gracefully carved sixteenth-century window frames. Proceed up to the castle, the former abode of the benevolent counts of Gruyères, and view the collection of tapestries, furniture, and medieval war booty housed in the impressive fifteenth-century edifice. Gruyères is, of course, an excellent place to sample fondue; also try the local heavy cream with berries. In the morning, pay a visit to the cheese factory at the bottom of the hill and watch the product being made. Later, there's an audio-visual show.

En Route from Gruyères – Head north to Bulle, featuring the Gruërien Museum, with its fine collection of regional costumes and furniture. Next, turn south to Châtel St. Denis on the same road, and begin the magnificent descent to Lake Geneva; from here the road to Blonay is more scenic and less direct. The lake begins to come into view here, with the grandiose high Valais Alps providing a beautiful backdrop. Whether you come from the Blonay road or Route 12, you end up near Vevey, a pleasant resort that's the headquarters of the Nestlé Company. The Wine Growers Fraternity displays models of its costumes dating back to the last century in the Old Vevey Museum. Although the new freeway to Lausanne is particularly scenic, it's still better to drive there through the vineyards on the specially marked Wine Route (Route de Vignoble) through old villages like Chexbres, Riez, and Grandvaux. On this route, you'll drive along narrow roads, passing old castles (many of which are privately owned), and small pubs and inns that serve regional specialties and their own home-grown white wine. The lake is always in view, and the drive is especially beautiful in late fall when the vineyards turn yellow. Several wine caves are open to visitors. Take the lake road at Lutry and enter Lausanne by way of the port of Ouchy.

LAUSANNE: The route climbs steeply from Ouchy to the old town of this youthful, upbeat university city. Recent excavations of Neolithic skeletons have dated habitation of the area to the Stone Age, and part of the late Roman city of Lousonna has been unearthed slightly west of here. Starting with its consecration in 1275, however, the cathedral has been the center of town and is closely connected with its history.

It is the most beautiful Gothic building of Switzerland with its picturesque towers, sculptured doors, and relief work; a museum containing some of its treasures recently opened in the splended Bishops's Palace next to it. An unusual, fascinating collection of works by mentally deranged artists, donated to the city by the French painter Jean Dubuffet, is nicely exhibited in an eighteenth-century palace (Collection d'Art Brut, Château de Beaulieu, avenue de Bergières). From the center of town, take a funicular down to Ouchy, a bustling port with lovely views of Lake Geneva and the mountains. Stop into one of the cozy pubs here and sample the *raclette* — a toasted cheese specialty served with potatoes and pickles.

En Route from Lausanne – Take Route 1 toward Geneva; you'll pass through Morges, a pleasant little town with an excellent view of the lake's widest point, as well as the Vaud Military Museum, which displays arms and uniforms dating back to 1798. Nyon is worth a stop.

NYON: This delightful port, lined with flowers, served Caesar as a base for his Helvetian couriers, and it still bears some traces of Roman times; for example, the god Attis is represented on Caesar's Tower here. The new Roman Museum, built on the ruins of a recently discovered Basilica, is considered the best of its kind in the country. Open daily, closed for lunch. The town's ramparts are also worth seeing.

En Route from Nyon – Before reaching Geneva, you may find a stop at Coppet enjoyable; this town features the chateau where Germain de Staël, a Swiss novelist, lived after Napoleon's affections for her cooled. It's elegantly furnished in Louis XVI style, and has some fine portrait paintings. The best way to enter Geneva is along the lake. (For more information see *Geneva*, THE EUROPEAN CITIES.)

BEST EN ROUTE

Although we haven't listed them, there are many small inns in the Jura region that offer good local food and acceptable accommodations. The ratings given below are based on the price of a double room for two with bath and/or shower during high season (usually January to December in establishments on this route). If the cost of accommodations exceeds $85, we've called it expensive. The moderate price range is $40 to $85, and rooms we've called inexpensive go for less than $40 for a night. Expect to pay $60 and up for a dinner for two in the expensive range, from $30 to $45 in the moderate, and around $20 in the inexpensive range. Prices do not include drinks and wine; the tip is included.

BASEL

Hotel Three Kings (Drei Konige) – The oldest luxury hotel in the country, the *Three Kings* boasts a historic guestlist — from emperors to authors. It's directly on the Rhine and has excellent rooms and a good restaurant on the terrace. Blumenrain 8 (phone: 25-52-52). Expensive.

Hotel Krafft am Rhein – In the Klein (small) Basel section, this hotel has a fine view of the cathedral. Rheingasse 12 (phone: 26-88-77). Moderate.

Restaurant Bruderholz – In recent years, this elegant establishment has become one of Switzerland's finest. Outside the center of town, it specializes in French food. Bruderholzallee 42 (phone: 35-82-22). Expensive.

Restaurant Schloss Binningen – This delightful sixteenth-century château has genuine antiques (the owner's hobby); it also features a garden, a terrace, and excellent food. It's in the suburb of Binningen. Closed Sunday evenings and Monday at noon. Schlossgasse 5 (phone: 47-20-55). Expensive to moderate.

Café Bachmann – A traditional café with outstanding pastry and good light snacks, the *Bachmann* overlooks the Rhine at Mittlere Bridge. Closed Sundays. Mittlere Brücke (phone: 25-41-52). Moderate.

Restaurant Kunsthalle – The favorite of many artists, this place is lively and has good food. Closed Sundays. Steinenberg 7 (phone: 23-42-33). Moderate.

Zum Goldenen Sternen – The oldest pub in Switzerland. St. Albanrheinweg 70 (phone: 23-16-66). Inexpensive.

NEUCHÂTEL

Hotel Beaulac – Modern hotel beautifully situated on the lake harbor. Quais Léopold Robert et du Port (phone: 25-88-22). Moderate.

Maison des Halles – This popular restaurant is in an ancient building in the old town. Place des Halles (phone: 24-31-41). Moderate to inexpensive.

MURTEN

Hôtel Restaurant Le Vieux Manoir – Set right on the lake with its own private beach, this slightly pretentious hotel has pleasant rooms and an excellent restaurant. Closed January and February. 3280 Meyriez-Morat (phone: 71-12-83). Expensive to moderate.

Hotel Adler – This establishment features a charming restaurant with a flowery terrace — the specialty is warm ham. Hauptgasse (phone: 71-21-34). Inexpensive.

GRUYÈRES

Hostellerie des Chevaliers – Just outside the village walls, this charming modern hotel has a fine view. 1663 Gruyères (phone: 6-1933). Moderate.

Hôstellerie de St. Georges – The windows of this charming, antique-furnished, old inn face the open country below. There's a big terrace, and an elegant, cozy Rôtisserie with excellent food. 1663 Gruyères (phone: 6-2246). Inexpensive.

Le Chalet – This cozy, rustic restaurant is near the castle. It serves fine fondue and other specialties. 1663 Gruyères (phone: 6-2154). Moderate.

LAUSANNE

Le Château d'Ouchy – This romantic hotel in a twelfth-century fortress is right on the lake. Place du Port (phone: 26-74-51). Expensive to moderate.

Hôtel La Résidence – Combining two charming old villas, *La Résidence* has a modern interior. 15 place du Port (phone: 27-77-11). Expensive to moderate.

Hôtel de Ville-Crissier – Managed by chef Fredy Giradet, this restaurant serves simply the best food in Switzerland — and perhaps in the world! Plan to stop here for a leisurely meal, but be sure, however, to make reservations far in advance — for dinner, several months before; for lunch, several weeks before. 1 route d'Yverdon, Crissier (phone: 34-15-14). Expensive.

La Grappe d'Or – This is the best restaurant in town for both food and atmosphere; its specialty is meat grilled over a wood fire. Closed Sundays. Cheneau de Bourg 3 (phone: 23-07-60). Expensive.

Aux Trois Tonneaux – Here you can find an inexpensive café as well as a more elegant restaurant; both are intimate and good. 18 rue de Grand-Saint-Jean (phone: 22-02-66). Moderate to inexpensive.

COPPET

Hôtel du Lac – This enchanting small hotel on the lake has elegant rustic rooms, an outstanding restaurant, and a garden. 1296 Coppet (phone: 76-15-21). Expensive to moderate.

Zürich to Lugano via the Four Passes

This, the most scenically spectacular route, with one dramatic highlight after another, takes you zigzagging from north to south through the geographical and historical center of Switzerland, covering eight cantons. The views are often breathtaking: sparkling lakes, snowy peaks, flowery chalets, and pastures with bell-tinkling cows. Although the route is primarily scenic and historical, Lucerne and Lugano offer some points of cultural interest. The Four Passes portion of the trip is possible only in June through October and is closed for the rest of the year; it's advisable to travel here in good weather only. Spend at least 3 days on this 233-mile (373-km) route. You can do it in 2 days if you leave Lucerne out, but even then it would be impossible to absorb everything. It's best to start on the Four Passes circuit in the morning, driving with the sun at your back wherever possible.

En Route from Zürich – You leave Zürich (for more information, see *Zürich,* THE EUROPEAN CITIES) on the heavily traveled road to Switzerland's most popular tourist town, Lucerne, then drive along the strangely shaped, highly scenic Lake Lucerne, through the sanctuary of the country, where William Tell shot his legendary apple and the Swiss Confederation started in 1291. (It will help you enjoy all the spots of historical interest on this route to read Schiller's *William Tell* or a synopsis of it.) You gradually ascend on newly built, excellent roads into the highest Swiss Alps. The route makes a rough circle through three of the mountain passes, proceeding up and down through frequent hairpin curves and great scenery, and then continues south on the fourth, the St. Gotthard Pass road. This was developed in the thirteenth century after the frightening Schöllenen Gorge was conquered. It has since become a vital artery for tourist trade and military use. By the way, the St. Gotthard Pass is a favorite maneuver area of the Swiss army, and in spring and fall you are bound to see soldiers. Population is scarce and life extremely difficult in these high regions, but you never have to drive too long before you spot an inn, small village, or service station. On the Gotthard Pass you cross the great north-south divide and the scenery soon becomes different; this is also a weather divide and you often pass from clouds into brilliant sunshine. (Strangely, it is seldom the other way around.) The route continues down the Leventine Valley along the Ticino River, which gave its name to the canton, and passes through vineyards, past campaniles and places with Italian names — it's like a different country, though it has been part of Switzerland since 1803. After Bellinzona, the first sturdy palm trees appear and beautiful Lugano is close by. Although the roads are excellent throughout, they're narrow at certain points; at times, they widen into freeways. There's a great deal of traffic in summer and on weekends, so try to avoid it. And don't rush. A rule of the mountain roads is that the ascending car has the right of way, though on this route roads are wide enough for two.

Take the main road to Lucerne along the pleasant, verdant Sihl Valley. The freeway after Sihlbrugg eliminates a slow and uninteresting stretch between Baar and Zug. (If time permits, a short detour to Zug is worthwhile, for its placid lake and charming old town.) The main road is nothing special, but it gets you to Lucerne in about an hour.

LUCERNE: This most photographed Swiss city is truly beautiful, even in the bad weather, which it often has. Once a modest fishing village, it became famous and rich as the bridgehead of the important Gothard route, opened in the thirteenth century. In 1332, it was the first city to join the Swiss Confederation, then consisting of only the three original cantons. Parts of impressive fortifications, like the Musegg tower and wall, are still standing. The Reformation, which swept most of sixteenth-century Switzerland, never succeeded in Lucerne, which remains today a Roman Catholic bastion. The yearly mid-August Music Festival is one of the most important in Europe. Lucerne deserves several days, but if you only have time for the main sights, start with the town symbol: the famous Kapellbrücke, a covered bridge that spans the Reuss River. Along with the flanking Water Tower (Wasserturm), the bridge served as a fortification against attack. The inside partitions of the bridge are graced with 120 paintings, done in the sixteenth to eighteenth centuries, which illustrate Lucerne's history. The tower served as a lookout point, a prison, and an archives, and now belongs to the Artillery Club. Other important sights of Lucerne's old town section are the town hall (with its historical museum) on Kornmarkt Square, Weinmarkt Square with its lovely painted houses and Renaissance fountain, and the Spreuerbrücke, a covered bridge which has macabre Death Dance paintings. A walk along the lakeshore quais is also interesting, but another famous Lucerne sight, the Lion Monument (Löwendenkmal, Denk-malstr.), could be left out without much loss. The Glacier Garden (Gletschergarten) next to it is interesting, with its Ice Age glacier potholes and giant stones; there's also a museum containing prehistoric specimens, the first relief map of Switzerland, and some furnishings of old Lucerne. The Cathedral Hofkirche (Leodegarstr.) has an especially atmospheric courtyard, with tombstones in the walls. The Swiss Transport Museum (Verkehrshaus, Lidostr.) is much more interesting than its name indicates: There's a lively exhibition of the development of ships, trains, cars, and planes displaying the oldest specimen of each. The museum also has a marvelous model of the Swiss railway crossing the Gothard, with 12 trains simultaneously in motion. Also on the premises is the Hans Erni House, containing works by the famous Lucerne artist. The Richard Wagner Museum is in the southern suburb of Tribschen (in an idyllic villa with a lovely view about 2 miles from Lucerne). The composer lived here for years and wrote some of his major works. Letters, photographs, and Wagner's original scores can be seen at the museum. The villa also houses an interesting collection of old musical instruments from all over the world. (In winter, it's closed Mondays, Wednesdays, and Fridays.)

Shopping is easy and seductive: Watches and clocks, jewelry, handicrafts, embroidery, and souvenirs all can be bought. Most of the shops are around Schwanenplatz or on the way to the cathedral. To find the largest selection of jewelry, pay a visit to *Bucherer* (Schwanenpl. 5). Nearby, you'll also find a good place to shop for embroidery: *Sturzenegger* (Schwanenpl. 7). Souvenirs also abound near the Lion Monument.

If you spend an evening in Lucerne, don't miss the night boat; it's garish but fun, and the view of the brightly lit town alone makes the trip worthwhile. You can have a fondue dinner or just wine on board, and dance to live folk music. For the best view of the town, have a drink in the pleasant garden of *Hotel Château Gütsch* (Kanonenstr.); the cafés along the Reuss near the Kapellbrücke are also nice stops.

En Route from Lucerne – Drive along Lake Lucerne (also called Vierwaldstättersee, or the Lake of the Forest Cantons), with its several distinct branches ("as a handkerchief waving goodbye in four different directions," a poet said), to Meggen. There's an interesting modern church right off the main road. Don't be put off by its exterior: The transparent marble walls inside are wonderful, especially in sunshine. You'll pass Merlischachen and its steep wooden houses with their first floors elevated high above the ground; these houses, accessible only by stairs, are typical of this region. Here also is the Astridchapel, built where Queen Astrid of Belgium had a fatal car accident in 1935. Küssnacht, a little town with an important role in early Swiss history, features *Hotel Engel,* a most remarkable historic building on its main square. Only a mile outside town, on Road 2, is the famous Hohle Gasse; park your car and walk the short sunken road where, according to the legend, William Tell waited to kill Bailiff Gessler. There's a small chapel at the end of the road commemorating his success. Road 2 continues on the shore of Lake Zug to Arth and Goldau, under the slopes of Mount Rigi, with extraordinary views all along, then passes charming little Lauerzer Lake. The Schwanau Island is a good place to stop for lunch or a drink beneath the ruins of a former fortress. You have to ring the bell on shore for a boat to pick you up. From here, it's only 3 miles (5 km) to Schwyz, which is not on the main road, but worth a short visit. (The fast freeway from Arth bypasses Lauerz.)

A more scenic and longer road from Küssnacht to Schwyz follows the sometimes rocky shores of the lake on the "Lucerne Riviera," where flowers blossom early in the season, through the resort areas of Weggis and Vitznau. Vitznau has Europe's oldest rack-and-pinion railway to Mount Rigi. Built by its inventor in 1871, the railway still has over 95% of its original cog racks; the ride up the steep slope is filled with wonderful views. Several lakeshore restaurants along the way specialize in fish. A high, rocky road leads to Gersau, a tiny sovereign republic for 500 years (1390–1800); the lake is deepest here, and has lovely underwater scenery.

If you want to leave Lucerne out of your itinerary, you can proceed directly from Zürich on the freeway to Arth and Schwyz or Brunnen; it's also very scenic.

SCHWYZ: This town provided Switzerland with its name and flag, and its Archive of Federal Charters (off Bahnhofstr.) preserves the original Covenant of Confederation of 1291. The sixteenth-century town hall, in picturesque Town Hall Square (Rathauspl.) has paintings of historical scenes on its exterior walls. Schwyz, a predominantly Catholic town, supplies the Vatican with some of the Swiss Guard.

BRUNNEN: Many famous guests, including Queen Victoria and Richard Wagner, have visited this old-fashioned resort. It used to be a shelter from the ferocious *föhn* storms, which can whip up the water into 400-foot spouts. Across the lake is Treib, another old storm refuge and a traditional asylum for fugitives. It was the meeting place of the first Confederation of Switzerland; you can still see the first house of parliament, the parlor of a local inn.

En Route from Brunnen – The magnificent Axenstrasse is a road hewn in rock high above the fjordlike Urner Lake (still part of Lake Lucerne), and for 10 miles the view of the steep wild shores across, the deep blue water below, and the Alps ahead is unforgettable. In season, the traffic is quite heavy, but the scenery compensates for everything. Several lookout points between Brunnen and Sisikon provide views of historic Rütli Field, where the representatives of the original cantons took a solemn oath of independence from the Hapsburgs, according to Schiller. Each year, on August 1, speeches and celebrations are held here in commemoration of a national holiday. After Sisikon, a tunnel replaces the open mountain road — it's safer for cars, but takes away the view. Leave your car at the south end of the tunnel and walk along the old road, a perfect place to take pictures. The William Tell Chapel (Tellskapelle) commemorates another dramatic event in the Tell legend: Held captive on his enemies' boat, Tell took advantage of a sudden storm and leaped to shore. A short, steep path leads down to the chapel from the roadside parking area. The lake ends at Flüelen and you can continue on the new freeway or drive through Altdorf, the small capital of Uri Canton (one of the original three) and see the statue of William Tell in the main square. Erected in 1895, it has since been made famous by its representation on Swiss postage stamps. Both roads follow the Reuss Valley and slowly start to climb the St. Gotthard massif. If you're interested in trains, drive through Erstfeld; the model in the Lucerne Transport Museum is based on the busy railroad station here (see *Lucerne*).

AMSTEG: This is the last village before the big climb starts, and if you haven't stopped yet, the *Hotel Stern and Post* is ideal; it has served as a stopover for travelers on stagecoaches and other vehicles for over 150 years.

En Route from Amsteg – The smooth new freeway takes you up to Wassen effortlessly. There's a remarkable waterfall, Pfaffensprung, nearby, but you have to park off the old road before Wassen to see it; the cascading waters produce some marvelous rainbows as they hit the rocks. From Wassen, take the old road to Göschenen; this should give you a good idea of how difficult it was to build a road up the Gotthard massif 600 years ago. Göschenen's lively railroad station is found at the north end of the two tunnels that convey trains and cars through the pass. From here, you can get a good view of the Upper Dammastock ice field. Next you pass through the Reuss Valley with its smooth, granite walls culminating in a legendary bottleneck, The Schöllenen Gorge. This defile made the development of a route southward through the Gotthard Pass impossible until the thirteenth century, when a road was driven through the gorge. The new road diminishes the contemporary traveler's feeling for the eeriness of the place. To recapture some of that awe, park your car near Devil's Bridge (Teufelsbrücke) and take a short walk on the old road. The bridge itself replaced another bridge here, which, according to legend, was built with the aid of the Devil, who asked to be paid with the soul of the first creature to cross it. The result angered the Devil a great deal — the creature turned out to be a goat. The enraged Devil then heaved a huge stone into the valley; one of the large rocks a short distance before the gorge is called the Devil's Stone.

After the gorge, head for Andermatt, a popular ski resort and a true crossroads of the Alps. The Furka and St. Gotthard roads have their junction here. Driving back to Wassen, you get a completely different view of the scenery than you had on the way to Andermatt. At Wassen, take the Susten road going west, unless it is afternoon and the light is against you.

The Susten Road, finished in 1945, was the first Swiss mountain road built especially for motorists. As it starts its steady climb, the route presents an interesting view of the jagged crests of a group of mountains called the Five Fingers. Driving through the upper hairpin bends, you'll see the panorama widen to a final view of the valley. Before you reach the tunnel through the road's crest, you can stop and survey the peaks from a viewing table. Walk to the road's highest point — 7,411 feet — from the large parking lot at the tunnel's west end. The view for the next few miles is the most magnificent the route offers: You'll see an arctic landscape at the foot of the Stein glacier, including a small lake complete with miniature icebergs. You can park at several road bends to enjoy views of the steep descents (from the Susten Pass Hotel a short "glacier road" leads even deeper into ice, snow, and rocks). After passing through some fertile valleys, you'll reach Innertkirchen, where you can pick up the Grimsel Road; the ancient *Tännler Inn*, just before the junction, is a good place to rest.

The Grimsel Road first passes through some pastoral scenery that's dominated by huge escarpments. (The avalanches are fierce here in the winter.) Then the views become more and more Dantesque — enormous granite rocks, slabs, and walls polished smooth and shiny by glacier action. Park your car for a view of the spectacular Handegg Waterfall cascading into a narrow gorge. Next, after a small, turquoise lake, you'll see the surrealistic Lake of Grimsel — an elongated reservoir created by two dams. The steep upward bends provide the best view of the lake; at the road's crest there's another small lake where a battle between the Austrians and the French took place in 1799. From here you can turn down to Gletsch, where the Furka Road begins, and catch a first glimpse of the Rhône glacier.

Although Gletsch itself consists of only a few houses, it's a good place to view the constantly receding glacier. Today, the glacier isn't in the basin, but photos of 100 years ago show it reaching the valley. This is where the Rhône, one of the longest rivers of Europe, starts its course. As you climb the Furka, every bend supplies another view of the glacier; the best one is just before the *Hotel Belvedere*. Even though it's disappointingly gray and dirty on the surface because of the heavy flow of traffic, the glacier is still impressive. Stop at the *Belvedere*, which is defunct as a hotel, but still has a snack restaurant. There's enough parking space, and it's the best point to view the panorama of the Bernese and Valais Alps. But the main attraction is the ice grotto that's cut into the glacier: Its transparent walls glitter with an unbelievable bluish light as the sun comes through the crevasses. A few miles beyond is the highest point of the Furka Pass, measuring 7,975 feet, with the Galenstock peak hovering above. The road skirts the Alps descending, first gently, then steeply, toward Realp, providing a sweeping view of the barren valley below.

If you don't want to make another stop at Andermatt, turn off at Hospenthal (marked by an old watchtower) to pick up the Gotthard Road. After a few steep turns, the scenery becomes desolate; the road's crest at 6,919 feet has rocks and glacial ponds that are very uninviting. The pass owes its name to a chapel of the patron saint that was built here in about 1300. From here, you can take either the new freeway through the tunnel and viaduct, or the smaller, steeper, somewhat more scenic one through the Tremola, with its view of the Leventine Valley below, to Airolo, a tunnel exit station and tourist resort. Take Route 2 from here.

The Leventine Valley is not very interesting compared to all you have already seen, but the driving's quite fast. Rough stone houses, chestnut trees, and the campaniles of the Ticino River area appear; there are several rushing waterfalls and, a little farther on, vineyards. Giornico has a remarkable Romanesque church, San Nicolao, and charming houses off the main road. You may want to stop at Bellinzona.

BELLINZONA: This administrative center of Ticino Canton has guarded the valley for centuries with three old castles. One of them, Castello Montebello, now houses the excellent historical and archaeological City Museum. Castello di Sasso Corbaro has a beautiful view and a café.

En Route from Bellinzona – The plain widens and soon Route 2 starts a steep but short climb up Monte Ceneri and offers wonderful glimpses of the Lago Maggiore below. It's about 10 minutes to Lugano from here. For a more scenic approach, take the exit marked "Lugano and Paradiso."

BEST EN ROUTE

Accommodations on this route tend to be more costly from mid-June through September, and drop off — sometimes significantly — from November through March. We've assigned an expensive rating to hotel rooms costing $100 to $140 in high season. Accommodations are moderate if they run from $70 to $95. And we've rated rooms inexpensive if they cost $50 to $65. Rates are for a double room with a shower. Restaurant prices range from $60 and up for a dinner for two in places listed as expensive, $35 to $50 in those listed as moderate, and around $20 in the inexpensive category. Prices do not include drinks and wine; tips are included.

LUCERNE

Grand Hotel National – Known for its comfortable and luxurious rooms with views of Lake Lucerne, the hotel also has a popular Viennese café with a terrace that's open in summer months. Haldenstr. 4 (phone: 50-11-11). Expensive.

Palace Hotel – Lucerne's other high-quality hotel, the *Palace* also has very comfortable accommodations with lake views. Haldenstr. 14 (phone: 50-22-22). Expensive.

Hotel Balances and Bellevue – Situated on the Reuss River in old town, the *Balances and Bellevue* is furnished with antiques. It's closed from November to March. Weinmarkt (phone: 51-18-51). Expensive to moderate.

Hotel and Restaurant Wilden Mann – Owned by the same family for over 100 years, this establishment has small but very charming rooms, and is located in an ancient house. Its tavern has excellent food. Major credit cards. Bahnofstr. 30 (phone: 23-16-66). Moderate.

Hotel Château Gütsch – Featuring a fabulous view from its hillside perch, the *Gütsch* has a good restaurant in a rustic setting, and serves drinks and snacks in its garden. Since it's a bit difficult to find the place at first, the hotel runs a private cable car from the center of town. Kanonenstr. (phone: 22-02-72). Moderate.

Hotel Eden – This gracious, well-located hotel, offering many rooms with balconies, is an excellent value. Open year-round. Haldenstr. 47 (phone: 51-38-06). Inexpensive.

Hotel Pickwick – This informal little hotel on the river in old town has an amusing custom: Each patron gets an apple at night. Breakfast vouchers for a nearby restaurant are supplied on request. (Since it's difficult to find the entrance, ask at the *Pickwick Club.*) Rathausquai 6 (phone: 51-59-27). Inexpensive.

Old Swiss House – This famous restaurant near the Lion Monument has lovely rustic decor and serves Swiss and international cuisine. Major credit cards. Löwenpl. 4 (phone: 51-61-71). Expensive to moderate.

Zum Raben – Housed in a medieval building in Old Town, this is one of Lucerne's newest and best restaurants. It is owned and run by cookbook author Marianne Kaltenbach, who presents delicious, inventive dishes. Major credit cards. Kornmarkt (phone: 51-51-35). Expensive.

MERLISCHACHEN

Restaurant Motel Swiss Chalet – This touristy but very attractive motel-restaurant on the main road serves good snacks. Rte. 2, Merlischachen (phone: 37-12-47). Moderate. The attached, charming *Schloss Hotel* is directly on the lake.

KÜSSNACHT

Gasthof Engel – This hotel, a splendid example of old local architecture, is where the Helvetian Confederation held its sessions from 1423 to 1712. Küssnacht (phone: 81-10-57). Moderate.

LAUERZERSEE

Restaurant Insel Schwanau – In a highly romantic setting on a tiny island after which it's named, this restaurant serves good food. You must ring the bell on the lakeshore to be picked up by a boat. It's closed in the winter. No credit cards. Insel Schwanau (phone: 21-17-57). Moderate.

BRUNNEN

Hotel Waldhaus Wolfsprung – This small chalet hotel is set in a forest and has a private beach. It's closed in the winter. Axenstr. (phone: 32-11-73). Inexpensive.

ALTDORF

Hotel Goldener Schlüssel – This establishment is located in a charming historic house in the center of town. 6460 Altdorf (phone: 2-1002). Moderate to inexpensive.

AMSTEG

Hotel Restaurant Stern and Post – A comfortable old stagecoach inn, the *Stern and Post* features excellent food and wood-paneled, antique-filled rooms. 6474 Amsteg (phone: 6-4440). Moderate.

INNERTKIRCHEN

Gasthof Tännler – This hotel is in a lovely old farmhouse. Although the rooms are comfortably appointed, they don't have separate baths. Susten Pass Road, Innertkirchen (phone: 71-14-27). Inexpensive.

Zürich to Lugano
via the Engadine

This 204-mile (325-km) route contains scenery that's dotted with architectural jewels, and takes you through the center of Swiss tourism, the Canton

Grisons (Graubünden). Romansh, a language stemming from Illyrian and Latin, is still spoken here; sections of the canton once formed part of ancient Rhaetia, a province of the Roman Empire. The Rhaetians resisted both the Celts (who, in pre-Roman times, occupied all of present Switzerland except Grisons) and the Germanic tribes, who came after the Romans. Rhaetia completely controlled the north-south Alpine crossings before the Gothard Pass was opened. Ruled by feudal lords and bishops, the Rhaetians formed an alliance with three other groups in the fifteenth century. Wars, Hapsburg rule, and more wars typify the ensuing history of the area, and the many castles and ruins are vivid signs of this. The canton joined the Swiss Confederation in 1803, but Romansh officially became the country's fourth national language in 1938. Swiss German is also spoken here. Although the passes of the route are open year-round, September is perhaps the best time to take the trip because the special light of the Engadine is most evident then. Spring, when you can see the overwhelming contrast of snowy Grisons with blossoming Ticino, is also a good time to go. Though it's almost as mountainous, this route has scenery that's quite different than that of the central Alps — it's less forbidding, and has more color and variety. Starting again from Zürich in the north, you drive southeast, passing by Lake Walensee, to Chur, the artistic, cultural, and administrative center of the canton; then you climb through spruce-covered mountains to the ancient Roman Julier Pass and descend into the extraordinary Engadine Valley. Here are Switzerland's most famous resorts, including St. Moritz, the queen of them all. From here, the route proceeds down to warmer regions and chestnut groves, dipping briefly into Italy along Lake Como, and turns back into Switzerland's Tessin (Ticino), a cheerful canton that has retained its Lombardian culture since becoming part of Switzerland in 1803.

Although the roads are always excellent, on weekends they're usually crowded. This is a perfect route for seeing the high mountains in winter, as most other crossings are closed, and the skiing is unequaled anywhere. Your car will need winter equipment into late spring. Spend at least 3 days and 2 nights — and preferably more. And don't miss Grison's culinary specialties of *bündnerfleish* (paper-thin slices of air-dried beef that are eaten with the fingers) and rich, delicious nutcake; with a glass of wine, the two make a perfect light meal.

En Route from Zürich – Drive along the freeway running adjacent to Lake Zürich; there's a lovely view of the lake and the distant mountains. Traffic gets very heavy at Lake Walensee, but the grand scenery of sheer rocks, waterfalls, and the characteristically jagged peaks make up for it. The lake is treacherous, with sudden storms that take their toll in damages each year. The fortress of Sargans, visible from afar, looms over this important medieval trading route. Soon afterward is Bad Ragaz — the best-known health spa in the country: Its mineral waters have been in use since the eleventh century. (In the old days, patients were lowered down with ropes to springs located a little farther on in the Tamina Gorge.) It has elegant hotels, lovely parks, and an 18-hole golf course. Next is Maienfeld, a charming, sleepy little town with beautiful patrician houses. The valley here follows the Rhine, the longest river in Europe, as it flows down the Alps. And the pastures are "Heidi country" — they served as the setting for the famous book.

CHUR: Recent excavations here date the city back to 3000 BC. After the Roman period, Chur was a center of Christianity. Walk the narrow streets of the enchanting old town with its medieval houses, and after crossing under an old gate, climb the steps to the cathedral; there's a famous Gothic triptych inside, as well as a pre-Christian sacrificial stone, near the altar. The splendid baroque Bishop's Palace (*Hof*), next to the cathedral, is still the bishop's residence. The *Hofkellerei*, a pub in the Bishop's Palace, is a good place for some *bündnerfleish* or other refreshments. The Rhaetian Museum, set in a seventeenth-century mansion on Hofstrasse, has many prehistoric, Roman, and medieval treasures.

En Route from Chur – Leaving Chur, Route 3 climbs steeply, offering a wonderful view of the city and its many spires. The road leads through scented, moss-covered woods to Lenzerheide, a popular resort with one of the most unusual hotels, *Guarda Val;* the hotel's Alpine barns make it worth a stop, even if you don't spend the night. In Lenz (Lantsch), the language changes from German to Romansh and road signs are bilingual. The village itself has an interesting cemetery with ornate iron crosses. This lovely drive through meadows, rounded hillsides, distant chapels, and sweeping views steeply descends toward Tiefencastel, in the Albula Valley. A white church tower marks Tiefencastel, but the real attraction is the Carolingian church of St. Peter of Mistail, built in AD 926. Ask townspeople for directions to the church; they'll also tell you where to get the key if the church is closed. Castle ruins dot the slopes along the road from here, reminders of a turbulent past; you'll pass through Savognin (a resort with three notable baroque churches), to the Marmorera Dam Reservoir, which has flooded two tiny hamlets. Bivio has a jewel of a Catholic church with Renaissance and baroque interiors. The ancient Roman Septimer road branches off from here, and is open only to hikers. The austere Julier Pass, 7,494 feet, used by the Romans, is still the main entrance to the Engadine. Its Latinate name recalls the important role of the Romans in the early Swiss history — two roadside markers are parts of a former Roman temple. From the final steep bends of the now-descending road there's a wonderful panorama of almost the entire Engadine valley. Its clear sky, beautiful lakes, charming architecture, and extraordinary scenery justify its fame. Excursions in the valley are easily taken; Silvaplana is the first village in the Engadine, and a few minutes away is glittering St. Moritz.

ST. MORITZ: The town itself is disappointing, as its urban streets and houses are without charm or character. But the lacustrine setting, excellent climate, mineral spas, and jet-set guests have made it famous. The Mauritius Springs have been in use here for about 3,000 years. Don't miss the Engadine Museum (on the road to the baths), a delightful reconstruction of local architectural styles, including typical *sgrafitti* (plaster decorations) and a wide-ranging collection of furniture, illustrating the domestic life of farmers, bishops, and lords. The Segantini Museum contains works of the Engadine's most famous painter, Giovanni Segantini, an Italian of the late nineteenth century. Winter is the best time for celebrity watching, and the *Palace Hotel* is a good place to do it — its *King's Club* is a center of nightlife here. For more moderate fare, try the charming *Chesa Veglia* for tea or dinner. Or check out the excellent nutcake at *Café Hanselmann.* In the winter, skiing is superb, snow and sun almost guaranteed; and, at sporting events and on the slopes, you can rub elbows with active and inactive royalty and movie stars who generally have their own homes up here. There are opportunities for dozens of excursions and walks, but there are two things you should do even if you have little time at your disposal: a cable car ride up Muottas Muragl, 8,084 feet, for a spellbinding view of the upper Engadine Valley, and a walk along the Sils Lake on a well-kept footpath. On the latter walk, stop at the Italian-speaking hamlet of Isola for delicious, homemade cheese and a drink. The

German philosopher Friedrich Nietzsche spent much time around here, and his house in Sils is now a small museum. A ride up the Corvatsch, 10,840 feet, from Silvaplana takes you to eternal snow and summer skiing. In season, there are many cultural events in St. Moritz, featuring famous artists. Golf, horseback riding, tennis, swimming (in pools, because the lakes are too cold), sailing, and windsurfing are also available.

En Route from St. Moritz – After driving along the Silvaplana and Silser lakes you come to the Maloja Pass, which is not really a pass at all (as it's lower than St. Moritz), but the upcoming sharp drop and curving steep road make it look like one. At the peak of the road, opposite the *Maloja Kulm Hotel,* there's a beautiful lookout over the Bergell Valley ahead. This valley has its very own characteristics: It's still alpine but has undeniably southern traits that become more and more pronounced with every turn. Sections of the old Roman road interlace it.

In Vicosoprano, a medieval tower attached to the town hall was a prison and torture chamber used for witch trials in the sixteenth century. (If it's closed, ask at the office.) A short detour to Soglio is a must: Taking the narrow, winding road through chestnut groves, you reach this spectacular little village on a ledge, with its palaces of the once powerful and still prominent Salis family. The best known of the palaces, the charming *Hotel Palazzo Salis,* has a romantic garden. There's also a magnificent view from the little cemetery. At Castasegna, the Alpine vegetation is left behind as you cross into Italy, and vineyards and fruit trees appear, and the architecture becomes distinctly southern. After Chiavenna, take the narrow principal road along the western side of Lake Como toward Como and Lugano; although the road periodically has heavy traffic, the lake is beautiful. At Menaggio take Road 340 right — watch for the tricky turnoff, it's easy to miss — to Lake Lugano (Italians call it Lago di Ceresio) and into Switzerland again. The lake is narrow and finger-shaped here, and there are steep, wooded, roadless slopes on the other side. Located near Lugano, between the principal road and the lake, is Gandria, a charming village that's worth a side trip.

GANDRIA: Explore the village by climbing up and down its steps, going under its arches, and walking between its old arcaded houses. It has many boutiques and is a typical artist's village. Sit on the terrace of a café hanging out over the water, and gaze at rows of pastel houses rising directly from the lake. The Smuggler's Museum, in an original hideaway on the other side of the lake, is approachable by boat only. Boats usually leave twice a day from Gandria.

En Route from Gandria – At Castagnola the bay opens out and you get the full visual impact of Lugano, one of Switzerland's most picturesque towns.

LUGANO: This cultural center of Ticino is ideal for a spring or fall sojourn. It features a palm tree–lined lakeshore promenade, arcaded streets, sunny piazzas with cafés, and the beautiful old church of Santa Maria degli Angioli with its famous sixteenth-century frescoes. The main artistic attraction is the Villa Favorita, a splendid private art collection of European masters in the owner's residence on Castagnola Road (open weekends only). A 10-minute funicular ride from the Paradiso quarter up Monte San Salvatore provides a fabulous circular panorama of lakes and Alps. You can get an even more sweeping view from Monte Bré on the other side of Lugano. It's possible to drive there via a very narrow, very steep road, but it's easier to take the funicular from Cassarate Road. Boat trips on the lake run frequently and are highly recommended. In the Italian village of Campione, 10 minutes away by boat or car, the casino has recently added craps and blackjack.

BEST EN ROUTE

Accommodations on this route can be costly, especially in famed resorts and health spas like St. Moritz and Bad Ragaz. Hotels that charge $130 to $200 and up for a double room with shower for a night get an expensive rating; extremely elegant resorts, like the *Palace, Suvretta, Kulm,* and *Carlton* hotels in St. Moritz, are considerably more expensive. Accommodations ranging from $75 to $130 are moderate, and those costing below $75 for two for a night in high season are rated inexpensive. Restaurants range in price from $65 and up for a dinner for two in places listed as expensive, $30 to $55 in those listed as moderate, and around $20 in the inexpensive category. Prices do not include drinks and wine; the tip is included.

BAD RAGAZ

Quellenhof – This is the most elegant hotel in the spa. It's closed in the winter. 7310 Bad Ragaz (phone: 9-0111). Expensive.

Im Schloss Ragaz – A small château with a few charming rooms, the *Ragaz* also has several modern bungalows. It's in a large park and has a swimming pool. 7310 Bad Ragaz (phone: 9-2355). Moderate.

CHUR

Hotel Stern – This 300-year-old inn serves outstanding cuisine, including Grisons specialties. Reichsgasse 11 (phone: 22-35-55). Moderate to inexpensive.

Hofkellerei – In the Bishop's Palace, this old pub features regional furniture and serves local specialties. Hof 1 (phone: 23-32-30). Moderate to inexpensive.

LENZERHEIDE

Hotel Guarda Val – This hotel provides all the modern comforts despite its rustic, Alpine, barnlike exterior. Its enchanting restaurant is set on a big terrace. Coming down from Chur, turn right as you enter Lenzerheide. Lenzerheide-Sporz (phone: 34-22-14). Moderate.

ST. MORITZ

Badrutt's Palace Hotel – It looks like a gingerbread castle, situated on a hillside with lake and mountain views, and draws a jet set crowd. They come for the luxurious rooms (270 in all), the spacious French restaurant, the renowned wine cellar, the fitness center, and, presumably, for that seductive well-pampered feeling. 7500 St. Moritz (phone: 21101). Very expensive.

Suvretta House – "What the *Palace* strives for, the *Suvretta* has already achieved," says one guest. This very exclusive hotel attracts old money. A nine-story castle of a building, it is off the beaten track — a self-sustaining resort with its own ski school and private lift, not to mention two bowling alleys and an award-winning restaurant. 7500 St. Moritz (phone: 21121). Very expensive.

Hotel Steffani – This cozy family hotel in the center of town serves Grisons specialties in its restaurant. 7500 St. Moritz (phone: 2-2101). Moderate.

Chesa Veglia – This is a restaurant-café with a delightful Grisons interior. 7500 St. Moritz (phone: 3-3596). Moderate.

Café Hanselmann – This popular watering hole serves the best cakes in town. 7500 St. Moritz (phone: 3-3864). Moderate.

SILVAPLANA

Hotel La Staila – A small hotel in an historic old house, *La Staila* is a good value. 7513 Silvaplana (phone: 4-8147). Inexpensive.

SOGLIO

Hotel Palazzo Salis – In one of the old town palaces, this establishment affords a very exclusive atmosphere, even if the comfort isn't always perfect. There's a small garden and a good restaurant. It's closed in winter. In high season, reservations are recommended. 7649 Soglio (phone: 4-1208). Inexpensive.

LUGANO

Hotel Splendide Royal – Featuring old-world elegance, modern comfort, and excellent service, this hotel has rooms with fabulous terraces on the lake. A good value. Riva Caccia 7 (phone: 54-20-01). Expensive to moderate.

Hotel Restaurant Ticino – In an old Tessin palazzo, the *Ticino* has a nice little terrace; the rooms surround a charming inside patio. It's closed in the winter. No credit cards. Piazza Cioccaro 1 (phone: 22-77-72). Moderate to inexpensive.

Ristorante Antico – Featuring a vine-covered terrace overlooking the lake, this hotel has a handful of rooms without separate baths. It's closed in the winter. Gandria (phone: 51-48-71). Inexpensive.

Bern to Montreux

Starting in Bern, the capital of Switzerland and one of Europe's loveliest towns, this 184-mile (294-km) route first proceeds east and south to the mountainous Bernese Oberland, and then into the unique Valais region, ending up in Montreux, a popular resort on Lake Geneva. Count on 3 days for the tour; the best time to see Valais is in October, when its colors are most beautiful. This route combines scenic, historical, and cultural attractions, and is passable all year round. To climb to the eternal snows of the impressive Jungfrau, however, you have to take a special train.

Although you'll see some lovely pastoral scenery, replete with flowers and clear blue lakes, in the Bernese Oberland, it's the Alpine triumvirate of Eiger, Mönch, and Jungfrau that make the area exceptional. With Interlaken as the jumping-off point, this is one of the world's most famous mountain recreational spots. The upper Rhône Valley, forming part of the canton of Valais, is an altogether different world. Isolated from the rest of the country by the steep mountains, its warm climate and abundant vegetation make it reminiscent of Provence; indeed, the Valais is Switzerland's main wine-growing region. Ruins and castles dot the slopes, and numerous museums and churches bear witness to the canton's historical importance. And the amazing lateral valleys, ascending quickly to more than 6,000 feet, should definitely be explored.

The Bernese and Valais people share a similar history; the region was ruled successively by Celts, Romans, Germanic tribes, and the Holy Roman Empire. Then came the rapid expansion of German-speaking Bern, which eventually dominated more than one-third of present Switzerland. The Valais, where the Romans first settled, was later divided between German and French influence and today the eastern part is still German and the western part French. Napoleon temporarily annexed Valais for France and began building the Simplon Pass Road (a passage already used by the Romans), but he did not live to see it in use.

BERN: Built on a peninsula of the winding Aare River, this enchanting capital has kept its character intact. The duke of Zähringen established the city in 1191 on his thickly wooded hunting ground. It was agreed that the first animal caught on a particular hunt would supply the new city with its name; when the creature turned out to be a bear, the duke dubbed the town Bärn, from which its present name derives, and placed a bear on its coat of arms. In 1353 Bern joined the confederation and later became extremely powerful because of its aggressive expansionist policies. The canton has tenaciously held onto its annexed territories, and Jura was only just recently able to break away. In 1848 it was chosen the seat of the federal government, replacing Zürich.

The arcaded streets of Bern's old town are the city's true main attraction, featuring the Gothic and baroque facades of homes that are often incredibly luxurious inside. (Take a look at the houses on Junkerngasse, for example — it's the city's most prestigious street address.) In 1405, the wooden houses of the old town were completely destroyed by fire; but by the eighteenth century, they were completely rebuilt in the yellow green sandstone you see here today. Modern Bern simply grew up around the older city, and the aristocratic tradition contrasts nicely with a youthful spirit that also characterizes this university town. Somewhat typically, recently discovered medieval fortifications are structurally integrated with an underground passage in the main railroad station, and explanatory notes have been supplied. All of old Bern's significant sights are within walking distance of each other, and the Tourist Office provides an excellent map of the center of town.

Walk to the Nydegg Bridge for a good view of the irregular group of roofs atop the houses at the bend of the Aare River; as a result of a law quite unusual for the symmetry-minded Swiss, these domiciles could not be built at the same size and height. A few steps across the bridge, you'll find the Bear Pit (Bärengraben), which houses a number of the city's symbolic animals. Across the bridge in the opposite direction, and a short distance down Junkerngasse, the high tower and flying buttresses of the Cathedral of St. Vincent (Münster) come into view. The main portal of this impressive Gothic church features several old statues (some of them still painted) depicting aspects of the Last Judgment and dating from the beginning of the sixteenth century. And if you don't mind climbing the 254 steps to the tower's platform, you'll be rewarded with an excellent panorama of the town and the Bernese Alps. Farther west, you'll find the Clock Tower (Zytglocke), first built in the twelfth century and restored in the sixteenth; at regular intervals during the day, large groups of people cluster to view the mechanical jesters, bears, and kings perform at 4 minutes before the hour in the tower of the astronomical clock.

The dignified, domed Parliament Building is in the Florentine Renaissance style, and one of its regular guided tours can provide some idea of the workings of Swiss government. Every Tuesday and Saturday, there's a lovely flower market in front. Walk along the high Kirchenfeldbrücke for a different view of town around the Parliament Building.

The museums of Bern are worth a separate trip; the Fine Arts Museum (Kunstmuseum), for example, has the largest collection of works by Paul Klee, a native of Bern, and a great number of modern French paintings (Hodlerstr.). The Kunsthalle houses temporary exhibitions of the latest in international art (Helvetiapl.). The Bernese Historical Museum features booty from the Burgundian wars and from other expansionist escapades, including arms, standards, tapestries, and manuscripts, as well as beautiful furniture from later periods (Helvetiapl.). Others are the Natural History Museum (Bernastr.) with its imaginative display of animals in natural surroundings; the Swiss Alpine Museum (Helvetiapl.), which has models of early alpinism and skiing, and reliefs of the Alps; and the Swiss Postal Museum, in the same building as the Alpine Museum, with one of the largest permanent stamp collections of the world. The National Library has one of the most extensive Bible collections anywhere (Hallwylstr.).

Cellars are as characteristic as arcades in the old town, and they now serve mainly as art galleries, boutiques, theaters, and restaurants. One of the most interesting cellar attractions is the oldest wine tavern of Bern, the Klötzlikeller (Gerechtigkeitgasse 6). Bern's nightlife is surprisingly vibrant, featuring dozens of pubs and nightclubs. It was at the city beach, right under the Parliament windows, that the first topless bathers appeared, igniting a national controversy.

En Route from Bern – The autobahn goes directly to Thun, but if you have time and the weather is good, take the lovely country road via Riggisberg, with its checkerboard fields and wide vistas. On summer afternoons, you can see a most extraordinary private collection of old textiles at the Abegg Foundation in Riggisberg. A short distance east of the freeway, at Kiesen, is an interesting cheese museum with a reconstruction of a workroom and a multilingual audio-visual show. Soon comes Thun, an attractive town on the lake of the same name; its medieval castle has a historical museum containing impressive tapestries, as well as a toy collection. Take the road along the scenic north shore through the resorts of Hilterfingen and Gunten, sometimes passing high over the cold, blue green lake that's one of the country's favorite spots for sailing. Interlaken is highly overrated and not really worth a stop, unless you're interested in the souvenir shops or the especially good pastry served at *Café Schuh;* continue to Grindelwald, a bustling resort village in a glacier with the Alps' Eiger peak hovering above it.

JUNGFRAU (VIRGIN): This is the only one of the three peaks that non–mountain climbers can reach. Count on a minimum of a half-day for the railway climb up to the 11,336-foot Jungfraujoch, the "saddle" of the mountain. In good weather, the high transportation price (around $50 per person minimum) is justifiable, but don't bother taking the trip at all if the visibility is questionable. The train ride itself provides spectacular rocky views, lookout stops, and multilingual explanations. Besides the incredible panoramas to be seen from its terraces, the Jungfraujoch features summer skiing, dog-sled riding, and mountain climbing. The Aletsch glacier — the largest in the Alps — can be seen from here. It's also possible to take the train back to Lauterbrunnen, site of a grand waterfall, on the other side of the mountain.

En Route from Grindelwald – Head back to Interlaken and proceed along the south side of Lake Thun (not on the freeway) to picturesque Spiez, which has a lovely view from the railroad station. From here you begin the journey into the Kander Valley, heading south on the main road toward Kandersteg; the route, narrow at first, passes under steep peaks. Then it widens, and weather-beaten, carved wooden houses with large roofs come into view. Stop at Blausee, a small jewel of a lake with extraordinary clear, blue water set in a moss-covered forest; there's a trout hatchery here, and *Restaurant Blausee,* which serves trout specialties. Soon you'll reach Kandersteg, a small resort, where a railway takes cars through the Lötschberg Tunnel in about 15 minutes; from Goppenstein on the other side, a narrow road leads down to Route 9, and the wide, sunny Rhône Valley. (If you're interested in a pilgrimage to the Matterhorn, you can reach Zermatt — closed to autos — via a train from Täsch, which is over an hour's drive south from Goppenstein.) Turning west, you'll soon reach Sierre, the first stop in Valais.

SIERRE: The language changes from German to French within this lovely town, reputed to be the sunniest in Switzerland. In *Château de Villa,* an old castle under huge trees, there's a combination museum and restaurant, serving excellent *raclette* (a Valais cheese specialty) and wine from local vineyards. A unique pewter museum opened in 1978 in the former *Hôtel Château Bellevue.*

En Route from Sierre – Proceeding west on Route 9, just before Sion, you'll reach St. Leonard, site of the largest subterranean lake in Europe.

SION: The two peaks which dominate this 2,000-year-old town give it a sense of history. The ruins of a medieval stronghold rest atop the hill called Tourbillon, and a fortresslike church, completed in the fifteenth century, crowns the Valère peak. The latter structure, Notre Dame de Valère (Our Lady of Valère), is well worth the climb; park your car in the lot between the two hills. An excellent panorama of the lower Valais can be viewed from the terrace. Inside, there are splendid seventeenth-century stalls with panels that portray scenes from the life of Christ, and the oldest functioning organ in the world (built in 1390). Each year, international organ concerts are held here. The attached museum contains Romanesque furniture that belonged to the bishops of Sion and Valais embroidery and lace. In town, the magnificent Supersaxo mansion, built in 1505, features a wooden ceiling with a huge rose depicting the Nativity. A short distance away is the seventeenth-century town hall (Hôtel de Ville, rue de Grand Pont) with its richly ornamented wooden door. Also interesting is the 3,500-piece glass collection on display at the Archaeological Museum (Grange à l'Eveque at Majoria).

For an outstanding view of Sion, drive 5 miles (8 km) to Savièse, an ancient-looking mountain village. Sion itself is a good place to start from in exploring the valleys that extend south below the Rhône. These are typified by extreme, rocky landscapes graced with small barns and chalets; two that are particularly interesting are the Hérens and Hérémence valleys.

HÉRENS AND HÉRÉMENCE VALLEYS: Cross the Rhône south from Sion, and take one of the secondary roads that climbs the steep ledge toward Vex, where Dent Blanche, one of the highest peaks in Switzerland, comes into view. From Vex, the road passes high over a stream and later through a tunnel underneath the Pyramids of Euseigne — bizarre, crowned columns formed by the erosion of the rock. The valley narrows and deepens as the road ascends to Evolène, a pleasant mountaineering resort known for its tall, wooden houses filled with flowers. Women of this village still wear local costumes. Head back for Euseigne and drive up from there through the desolate, eerie scenery of the Hérémence Valley. The road ends at the enormous Grand Dixence Dam; a height of 935 feet makes it the tallest dam in the world. Completed in 1966, it's the most formidable construction task yet undertaken by the Swiss. An elevator ascends from the parking lot to water level, and there's a walking path along the top. Return to Sion on the route that passes through the villages of Hérémence and Salins.

En Route from Sion – Take Route 9 until just beyond Ardon, then turn right onto the secondary road through the vineyards; you'll pass through small wine-growing communities like Chamoson, Leyron, and Saillon, which are protected by sunbaked rocky slopes. Saillon features the ruins of an impressive castle as well as picturesque old houses. In this region, you can visit wine caves, and small inns serve local food. At Martigny, take Route 9 again, following the Rhône as it turns sharply north. St. Maurice, the capital of Valais under the Romans, is worth a stop. Take a guided tour of the church's treasury, one of the most opulent in the Christian world; among the items on view here are a gold casket decorated with pearls and cameos, and a golden ewer that reputedly belonged to Charlemagne.

Farther north, near Bex, you can stop for a gourmet meal at *Rôtisserie St. Christoph,* a restaurant and motel set in a medieval fortress. Aigle, renowned for white wine, features a fifteenth-century castle with a Wine and Salt Museum. Continue along the freeway for the best view of Montreux.

MONTREUX: Cypresses, fig trees, magnolias, climbing vines, and other Mediterranean forms of vegetation flourish in Montreux, Lake Geneva's most popular resort; its climate is mild all year long. Musical events — including an annual jazz festival — have, in recent years, enlivened the quiet atmosphere here.

Walk through old Montreux, with its interesting houses and crooked streets, along a lovely promenade by the lake, to the terrace of the local church. From here you can get a good view of the towers of Château Chillon, about 2 miles south. The fortress on Chillon rock was initially constructed in the ninth century to defend the major road to Italy, but its present form dates from the thirteenth century. Its recurrent use as a prison was made especially famous by Byron's poem "The Prisoner of Chillon."

Montreux also offers other attractive side trips: The spectacular train ride to the Rochers de Naye, for example, shouldn't be missed. The trip affords excellent views of Lake Geneva, the Alps, and the Jura. And for more entertainment, Lausanne is only 20 minutes away.

BEST EN ROUTE

There are some good budget accommodations on this route; a number of hotels charge as little as $40 for a double room with shower for a night. Hotels charging $90 to $130 and up in high season are expensive. Those asking $60 to $90 are moderate. We've rated those establishments charging $40 to $60 as inexpensive. Restaurants range in price from $50 and up for a dinner for two in those places listed as expensive, from $35 to $55 in those listed as moderate, and about $20 in the inexpensive category. Prices do not include drinks and wine; the tip is included.

BERN

Hotel Bellevue Palace – This is where visiting kings and queens stay. Have a drink on the terrace for the view and atmosphere. Kochergasse 3 (phone: 22-45-81). Expensive.

Hotel Schweizerhof – Next to the railroad station, this very comfortable hotel has genuine antique furnishings that have been collected by its owners, the Gauer family. Schweizerhoflaube 11 (phone: 22-45-01). Expensive.

Hotel Goldener Adler – In the heart of old town, this beautiful old inn provides adequate comfort and a friendly, family atmosphere. Gerechtigkeitsgasse 7 (phone: 22-17-25). Inexpensive.

Schultheiss-Stube – The best restaurant in town is in the *Hotel Schweizerhof;* it's cozy, and has superb food. Schweizerhoflaube (phone: 22-45-01). Expensive.

Hotel City Mövenpick – A modern, cozy establishment, across from the railroad station, the *Mövenpick* serves a good breakfast buffet. Bubenbergpl. (phone: 22-53-77). Moderate.

Kornhauskeller – Set in a cellar (once a granary) this lively place specializes in *berner platte,* an assortment of boiled meats and sausage served with sauerkraut that's much lighter than it sounds. A brass band entertains at night. Closed Mondays. Kornhauspl. (phone: 22-11-33). Moderate.

Restaurant Schlüssel – This small place is popular because of its good food. Rathausgasse 72 (phone: 22-02-16). Moderate to inexpensive.

Klötzlikeller – Over 300 years old, the *Klötzlikeller* is a wine tavern that serves snacks. Closed mornings and Sundays. Gerechtigkeitsgasse 62 (phone: 22-74-56). Inexpensive.

Nightclubs – *Mocambo,* Aarberggasse 61 (phone: 22-15-51), and *Chikito,* Neuen-
gasse 28 (phone: 22-26-80), are the best, offering daily floor shows.

GRINDELWALD

Grand Hotel Regina – One of the best in the Bernese Oberland, the *Regina* is quite
luxurious and serves excellent food. The hotel is closed in November. 3818 Grindelwald (phone: 54-54-55). Expensive.
Hotel Spinne – This modern hotel has a casual atmosphere. It's closed in November.
3818 Grindelwald (phone: 53-23-41). Moderate.

BLAUSEE

Restaurant Blausee – In a fabulous setting on Blue Lake, this restaurant offers
trout specialties. It's closed in winter. 3717 Blausee (phone: 71-16-41). Moderate.

SIERRE

La Grotte – As its name implies, this small hotel is built into the rocks, on the shore
of the lake. It's closed in November. 3960 Sierre (phone: 55-46-46). Inexpensive.
Relais du Manoir – This restaurant, run by local wine growers, serves and sells
outstanding wines; a few local food specialties, including *raclette,* are also available. It's set in the sixteenth-century *Château de Villa.* 3960 Sierre (phone: 55-
18-96). Moderate.

SION

Caves de Tous Vents – Set in a thirteenth-century wine cellar, with a big garden
outside, this restaurant serves excellent Valais specialties. It's closed Mondays.
Rue des Châteaux (phone: 22-46-84). Moderate.
Hotel Continental – This small modern hotel has an exceptionally good restaurant.
The pub specializes in cheese dishes. 116 rue de Lausanne (phone: 22-46-41).
Inexpensive.

BEX

Rôtisserie and Motel St. Christoph – Rustically attractive, the *St. Christoph* serves
charcoal-grilled specialties. It's set in a small medieval fortress; all rooms have
individual terraces and exits to the garden. 1880 Bex-les-Bains (phone: 65-29-79).
Hotel, inexpensive; restaurant, expensive to moderate.

MONTREUX

Hôtel Montreux Palace – If you want to splurge, here's luxury. 100 Grand-Rue
(phone: 63-53-73). Expensive.
Hôtel Eden au Lac – Recently renovated, the *Eden* retains its turn-of-the-century
charm. There's a garden right on the lake, where luncheon buffet is served. Except
for the week of the jazz festival, it is usually quiet. 11 rue du Théâtre (phone:
63-55-51). Expensive.
Hotel Europe – This typical old "grand hotel," with a lovely lake view, is a very
good value, though it's sometimes overrun with groups. Avenue des Alpes 15
(phone: 63-45-41). Inexpensive.
La Vieille Ferme – It's a charming farm, very rustic, slightly out of the center of
town, in Montreux-Chailly, and it serves local specialties. Try their *raclette* —
to country music. Closed Mondays (phone: 64-64-64). Moderate.
Caveau Suisse – In this lively discothèque, with its cozy, rustic atmosphere, you
can also dine. It's in the center of old Montreux. 40 rue de la Gare (phone:
63-16-62). Moderate.

Exploring Yugoslavia

The Socialist Federal Republic of Yugoslavia is the remarkable conglomeration of 6 republics, 5 to 6 major languages, and the culture of a dozen different empires from all over world history. Stretched across the Adriatic Sea between Europe and Asia, the area has been ruled and changed for a time by everybody from the ancient Celts to the Ottomans; from the marauding Goths to the stately Austrians; and from Jove to Mohammed to Jesus Christ. Monuments of the different empires are in every part of the country.

In Yugoslavia, you'll find that the language, festivals, costume, religion, and cooking style change wherever you go. The land of Yugoslavia is surprisingly varied over its 99,000 square miles. There are the snowy Julian Alps in the north and the warm Adriatic coast in the south, with its 1,000 offshore islands. Dense forests in several regions still harbor bear, wolves, wild boar, and deer; and the central plains are as low, flat, and lush as medieval Flanders. Hills or mountains cover most of Yugoslavia except for the north central region; rail and road transportation are not very extensive or sophisticated yet. The interior is full of large, clear lakes and warm mineral springs. The two biggest rivers are the Sava and the Danube, which meet at Belgrade.

Yugoslavia is governed by its Communist Party, which came to power with Russian aid after World War II, but the state is tolerant of religion, linguistic diversity, and a degree of local autonomy. Marshal Tito pulled Yugoslavia away from the USSR's influence in 1948 and forged his own alliances.

Yugoslavians travel freely at home and abroad. The press is subject to self-censorship, but there is easy access to foreign publications of all kinds in the major cities.

Belgrade is the capital and the center of commerce, industry, and communications. The main cultural centers are Zagreb, Dubrovnik, and Ljubljana; Skopje is an important industrial town. Other large cities include Split, Novi Sad, Rijeka, Sarajevo, and Titograd.

About one-third of the population works in agriculture, the rest in urban industry. Although the nation is becoming more urban and cosmopolitan, the different ethnic groups in Yugoslavia have a powerful folk tradition, which you will notice wherever you go: Dances, folklore plays, and mystical pageants are celebrated in every region and are taken quite seriously.

Roads in Yugoslavia have improved considerably in recent years. The Adriatic Highway (Jadranska Magistrala) runs along the coast, and is one of the most scenic roads on the Continent. Another major route is the Ibar Highway (Ibarska Magistrala), which runs from Belgrade to Skopje in the east. These two routes link up with a number of lateral roads.

We've laid out three routes for exploring Yugoslavia. The most popular is the coastal route, which begins near Trieste, Italy, and winds south along the

Adriatic Sea through the cities of Portoroz, Opatija, Rijeka, Zadar, Split, and Dubrovnik. This coastal area is full of beach resorts, Roman ruins, steep bluffs, cultural festivals, and fine seafood. The second trek begins in Podkoren, in the Julian Alps in northwestern Yugoslavia. Bring your skis. You will drive south through mountains to Ljubljana and Zagreb and on to the capital city of Belgrade. Belgrade has over 30 museums and galleries, hosts symphonies, opera companies, and film festivals, and serves cuisine of every nationality. The third route starts 3 miles from the Greek border and winds north through Macedonia, where you can stop for Turkish mosques, Byzantine frescoes, and Bohemian folk festivals, and for fishing and swimming at lakefront resorts. The route continues through Pristina to Belgrade.

Trieste to Dubrovnik

Guiding a reader on an auto tour of the Yugoslav Adriatic is different from giving advice on an artistic, historical, or skiing tour. There are no complicated directions; after the first 25 miles (40 km), you'll be going southeast on the Adriatic Highway (Jadranska Magistrala), overlooking the incredibly blue Adriatic Sea — if the water isn't on your right, you took a wrong turn. The areas along the coast are quite diverse, but we're only going to mention a few spots in any detail, since your reasons for driving the coast are probably going to be the same all the way along — sun, sand, and sea — and you'll know them when you find them. The wonderful thing about this coast is that you'll stumble on what you're looking for everywhere. So, this tour will give you some idea of what you're passing through, tell you about some interesting sights, and give you some broad tactics on where to find your piece of sand.

The most important advice is this: The resort cities are crowded at high season — June, July, and August — so if you want privacy and you don't want to spend too much money, go to the small village beaches (which are as beautiful as any), and stay at pensions or private houses. Then go into town to take your pulse-quickening excitement whenever you're ready for it. If you can travel in May, September, or October, you'll find the tourist population comparatively low, and your lodging costs likewise: Prices drop up to 50% in those months, and the climate is just as fine as at high season.

The northern half of this journey, from Trieste to Zadar, goes over a predominantly rocky shoreline, with good pebble beaches. South of Zadar is where the lush Mediterranean vegetation begins, with palm, pine, and hibiscus. Throughout, the beaches are lovely and the weather quite dependably sunny and warm except for a few months in winter, when it sometimes rains. The coastline is among the most jagged in Europe. If you measured its length as the crow flies, it would be 390 miles (628 km); when you follow the contours of all the bays, inlets, and peninsulas, the coast measures 1,125 miles (1810 km). You will be driving along the coast, following nearly its every twist, for a total of 530 miles (852 km).

Yugoslavia's Adriatic coast is known for its nudist colonies; this is more or less the center for organized nudism, or "naturism," in southern Europe.

Generally speaking, nudism is a very health-oriented, bring-the-kids kind of lifestyle. The philosophy is that clothes give us dirty minds; most nudist camps are notoriously nonsexual. Naturist resorts are open to anyone, and there are at least 30 well-known ones between Trieste and Ulcinj; some are near large cities, some near small villages, and many on islands. If you don't need a lot of fancy facilities, every seaside village has its own informal nude bathing area.

Over the millennia, sailors, conquerors, and adventurers have left behind their houses, their ships, and their descendants to stay along the Adriatic coast and its islands. However, many of the 1,000 islands off the coast are still inhabited only by seagulls and moss; this applies to many in the Kornati chain off Zadar. Perhaps you'll take some time out to visit a timeless desert island away from your car and your hotel, and listen to the silence.

The route begins in the Slovenian greenery around Trieste at the Lipica horse farm, breeding ground of the proud Lipizzaner horses, and descends to the seaside for a taste of Austro-Hungarian grandeur near the old resorts of Portoroz and Opatija. You will see the Roman forum of Pula, still in use, sample two sets of sun-soaked islands, and watch the coast go greener and more lush as you drive south. The pandemonium of Rijeka and Zadar may dizzy you, and Diocletian's palace in Split will certainly awe you; for relief, you can poke along the beach in small Dalmatian villages. The last stop is the cultural and Bohemian capital of the coast, Dubrovnik, where you can, particularly during the summer season, take in the best art, music, and nightlife the twentieth century has to offer, inside the walls of a sixteenth-century town. You may want to take your trip farther down the coast, and there are some suggestions for places to see.

TRIESTE: Get on the highway northeast toward Sezana, to cross the border into Yugoslavia just before you reach that town. The approach from Trieste brings you into Yugoslavia's Republic of Slovenia, an area ruled by the German nobility from the time of Charlemagne until World War I. Slovenia was the lush, hilly playground of the Austro-Hungarian Empire, with grand, lakefront resorts.

LIPICA: Off the highway past Sezana is the four-century-old horse farm at Lipica, the original stud farm of the Lipizzaner horse, founded in 1580 by Archduke Charles of Austria. Lipica supplied the horses for the Austrian cavalry and the famous Spanish riding school of Vienna. All this wouldn't be half so interesting, except that they'll let you ride them. For the rest of your days, you'll probably never ride such a thoroughly blue-blooded, beautiful, well-brought-up horse. There is instruction available if you need it, and for spectators there are shows in the indoor riding ring.

En Route from Lipica – Continue east on the road to Divaca, where you will intersect a highway; turn south toward Kozina and go beyond it about 20 miles (32 km), until you meet up with the road you will follow the rest of this trip, the Adriatic Highway.

Go south to Portoroz, the largest and best-known seaside resort in Slovenia; flowers grow in abundance in this former old-world bastion — Portoroz means "Port of Roses." Sailing and parachuting competitions, cultural events and folklore plays take place here in the summer. In the neighboring town of Seca, there is a permanent outdoor exhibit of stone sculpture called "Forma Viva."

Stop at Piran, on a peninsula about 5 minutes outside Portoroz. This is an old Mediterranean town with narrow streets, and small churches with Renaissance and baroque paintings. Piran's city walls are still standing, as is a fragment of a Byzantine wall.

PULA: From Portoroz the highway continues down the coast to Pula, a major coastal city built on an ancient Illyrian settlement dating from the fifth century BC. It became a Roman colony; the Roman amphitheater in Pula, which seats 23,000, has lasted better than the one in Rome. Pula's amphitheater is still in use: The annual Festival of Yugoslav Films (among other events) is held here. Other Roman buildings include a first-century temple to the Emperor Augustus, and the fourth-century Hercules gates. Close to Pula is Medulin, a small seaside village with good beaches.

En Route from Pula – The road continues through a number of fishing villages. From one of them, Brestova, you can get a car ferry to the resort islands of Cres and Losinj; more on the resort islands below.

OPATIJA: Opatija, at the foot of Mount Ucka, 40 miles (64 km) along the coast, was a popular resort among the Austro-Hungarian nobility. Its streets still have a nine-teenth-century air, with elegant shops, and luxury hotels with formal gardens; they also have casinos. For culture, you can see a play at Opatija's summer theater.

En Route from Opatija – Near Opatija is the medieval village of Volosko. A sand walk stretches along the beach for 6 miles, and goes through the nearby fishing villages of Ika and Icici.

RIJEKA: From Opatija it is 10 miles (16 km) to Rijeka, the largest Yugoslavian port, at which all ship, railway, and bus routes leading to this part of the Adriatic coast converge. It has museums, art galleries, theaters, a library, a university, a Benedictine church, and a Croation fortress from the Middle Ages built by the Frankopans, the former ruling family of Croatia.

En Route from Rijeka – From Rijeka to Split, 240 miles (386 km), the coastal highway affords spectacular views of the sea, Kvarner Bay, and various coves, villages, and islands. At the entrance of the Bay of Bakar is the town of Kraljevica, and its early baroque castle. Nearby is the *Uvala Scott* hotel complex and "vacation village."

Krk is the largest island in Kvarner Bay, and the largest in the Adriatic, with sand and pebble beaches, and lush vegetation. Near the *Uvala Scott* hotel complex, there is a new bridge connecting Krk with the coast. There are ancient forts and medieval castles as well.

Crikvenica, 9 miles (14 km) from Kraljevica, is a famous seaside resort and medical center that uses *thalassotherapy* — treating ailments ranging from nervous tension to heart disease with sea water. The small resort of Selce is 2 miles (3 km) from Crikvenica; 4 miles (6 km) farther on is Novi Vinodolski, with a sandy beach.

RAB and LOŠINJ: The island of Rab, in Kvarner Bay between Krk and Pag, is one of the sunniest regions in Europe, with abundant foliage and a mild climate. The main town is Rab, which was an ancient Greek and then a Roman settlement; at times it becomes a crowded bathing resort. Four bell towers rise above the town walls. In the town is a fourteenth-century palace and the seventh-century church of St. John.

Lošinj is farther out in the bay, beyond the island of Cres, and is extraordinarily green, but is also crowded at peak times.

PAG: The island of Pag, famous for its fine (and expensive) sheep's-milk cheese, is just as pretty as the more touristy islands, but more rural, and with fewer hotels and facilities. If you don't mind staying in a pension, you can avoid the crowds here.

ZADAR: Zadar is the southernmost point of the Kvarner Bay area. Besides being an ancient place, settled well before the first century — with surviving buildings, gates, and other relics of the Roman Empire — Zadar is the center of twentieth-century, bustling, hard-and-fast tourism for the northern half of the coast. There's an airport just north of town, rail service toward the east, and ferry and hydrofoil service leading from Zadar to everywhere. It's not a quiet place. There are lots of high-rise hotels, pleasure boats, and populous beaches. There is also a lot of functional activity on the water: Fishing is done with nets from small boats.

If you feel adventurous, hire a water taxi or a fisherman to take you out to one of the uninhabited Kornati islands, which are set aside as a national park, for the day or the week or longer — making sure to make arrangements for being picked up. You might consider renting a boat yourself in town; you can leave your car with the boat rental people. This could be the most exhilarating part of your trip; it's not often in this life you can rule your own island in the sea. If you have a tent, you can camp out on the sand under the stars for as long as you like. The undisturbed sound of lapping waves is good for the spirit. Come with supplies, though; there's no fresh water anywhere. If you prefer to sight-see with a group, there are regular excursions to the islands from Zadar.

Stop by the town's museums and treasuries — it's had an interesting past — and visit the ninth-century church of St. Donat.

En Route from Zadar – About 40 miles (64 km) south of Zadar is Sibenik, founded in the tenth century at the estuary of the Krka River. Take a tour of the port by boat; the view of Sibenik's white-domed medieval and Renaissance palaces from the water is grand. You might also take an excursion to Skradin to see the waterfalls of the Krka River.

Primosten is 5 miles (8 km) south of Sibenik, a small peninsula town. Lodging is found mainly in private houses, although a new hotel complex is nearby. There is also a nudist beach.

Do not fail to see Trogir, a "museum town" on an island about 20 miles (32 km) before Split. The animals in the carvings and reliefs of the cathedral of St. Lovro are so vivid they look as if they may drool on you at any moment. There is one ancient Roman relief, the Diety and Petronius, and several medieval buildings, including the cathedral, the Lucic Palace, and the Pamfogna Palace.

SPLIT: Split, on the opposite end of the peninsula from Sibenik, is one of the two or three towns on the Adriatic you shouldn't miss. The present administrative center of the region of Dalmatia, it was founded in the fourth century AD by the Roman emperor Diocletian as his retirement home. The titanic palace and enclosed town he had built make up the old quarter of modern Split. The palace has four gates: gold, silver, iron, and bronze. The chambers are so huge that many of them were made into entire houses in later years; the corridors are now streets in the old town. Symphony concerts, opera, dance performances, and plays take place inside the walls, and the palace basement is the site for several art and historical galleries.

In the town that grew up outside the walls, there is a sixteenth-century synagogue and cemetery. Generally speaking, the new quarter is a resort town, with hotels, heated swimming pools, and a good supply of places to go.

You can book an excursion from Split to the inland town of Sinj, where the Alka medieval jousting tournament is held every August, featuring knights on horseback.

En Route from Split – Along the coast from Split to Dubrovnik, 134 miles (214 km), is an area of shimmering blue coves, sandy and pebbled beaches sheltered by pine trees, and balmy offshore islands, all overlooked by the 5,000-foot peaks of the coastal mountains; it is known as the Makarska Riviera, and is the most lush and sunny area on the Adriatic. In this Makarska region are the towns of Brela, Baska Voda, Makarska, Tucepi, and Podgora, and the fishing villages of Drasnice, Igrane, Zivogosce, Drvenik, and Zaostrog.

SOUTHERN ISLANDS: The islands in this southern end of the coast are the main tourist attractions in Yugoslavia. The most popular ones as well as those less traveled are characterized by a consistently warm, sunny climate, good beaches, thick vegetation, and ancient forts and dwellings.

Brac, a popular island, has extensive pine woods in its hills, good for walking. At Bol is the baroque church Gospa od Kamena and a beautiful sandy beach called Zlatni Rat (Golden Cape).

Hvar is a year-round resort that welcomes many tourists. The main town, also called Hvar, has the oldest theater in Europe, built in 1612; performances are still held there. Hvar's hotel managers are so confident of the weather there, they say that from November through March their guests will pay no rent for any day the temperature goes below freezing, or if it snows or fogs over; they allow 50% off if it rains more than three hours, providing guests stay at least 7 days.

Korcula claims Marco Polo as a native son. The town of Korcula has its own cathedral, built between the thirteenth and sixteenth centuries, which contains paintings by Tintoretto and Bassani.

Mljet is an out-of-the-way spot, very wild and forested, and is considered the most beautiful of these islands. It has two hotels, lots of private houses with rooms for rent, and a national park. Mljet is definitely for the slightly adventurous.

Solta (near Split) is also off the beaten track, and consequently never gets very crowded. There are lots of boarding houses where you can stay and get to know the islanders.

DUBROVNIK: The city of Dubrovnik, the last stop on your trek, looks like the same powerful, grandiose, and magnificent city it was in the sixteenth century. Formerly the Free Republic of Dubrovnik, it was a center of art and commerce, and gaudy rival to another city-state on the Adriatic, Venice. Now Dubrovnik, preserved in its medieval splendor, is considered the most beautiful city in Yugoslavia.

Seen from above, the roofs of the city make up a sea of red orange tile, dotted with the white domes of a few particularly grand edifices. The buildings are constructed on a huge scale, with rows of pillars and sweeping arches, imperious towers, gorgeous stonework facades, and momentous fortifications bristling with cannons. And, of course, there are fountains, courtyards, gardens, and bell towers. Particularly awesome buildings are the Doge's Palace, Onofri's Fountain, and the baroque church of St. Vlaho.

The first thing to do when you get into town is to get a view of the whole place — by walking around the city on top of its thick walls, which will take you about 2 hours. You might want to take a cable car tour as well, to see the bright colors of the landscape from above.

Dubrovnik's summer festival, from mid-July to late August, brings in world-class performers of symphonic and chamber music, opera, ballet, drama, and folklore to play in the palaces, gardens, and courtyards.

Nightlife in Dubrovnik is either bohemian, cosmopolitan, expensive, or, frequently, all three. The city has several superb restaurants (see *Best en Route*) and a gambling casino.

Dubrovnik's synagogue, on Zudioska (Jewish) Street, is the third oldest in Europe. The Maritime Museum has artifacts and historical background on the city's sixteenth-century heyday; there tends to be a museum or gallery on just about every corner.

The island of Lokrum is a particularly good (and popular) bathing spot and park just south and east of the town's mainland. If you feel up to it, you can pick your way through the foliage to the Adriatic side of the island for a more private swim. There is a nudist beach on Lokrum known for its nonplatonic atmosphere.

En Route from Dubrovnik – You may feel like going down the coast from Dubrovnik all the way to the Albanian border. Besides stopping along the way at whatever little beach grabs your fancy, we recommend you visit Cavtat, which has ancient Greek and Roman monuments, and one of the swankiest hotels on the coast; Herceg-Novi, with its lovely flower gardens; Igalo, Yugoslavia's best-known spa; Budva, founded in the fourteenth century BC, with Greek and Roman monuments and long, sandy beaches; Sveti Stefan, a tiny medieval village on an island connected to the mainland by a causeway, converted entirely into expensive deluxe tourist housing; and Ulcinj, with a long and inviting sandy beach.

BEST EN ROUTE

Accommodations for two people in an expensive place will cost $100; moderate, $15–$60; inexpensive, $15–$25. The restaurants we list below are all in the expensive category, by Yugoslav standards — which means $6–$15 per person for dinner, including wine.

PORTOROZ

Bernardin Hotel complex – Comprising the *Bernardin*, the *Grand Emona*, and the *Villas Park*. Splashy, angular, modern hotels, embracing a small marina. Portoroz 66320 (phone: 7-5271). Expensive to moderate.

OPATIJA

Kvarner Hotel – Turn-of-the-century European, with banquet halls, chandeliers, and flowered terraces facing the sea. Good Continental food and entertainment every night. Park 1, Maja, 51410 Opatija (phone: 71-12-11). Moderate.

ISLAND OF KRK

Haludovo – A deluxe hotel built as a Mediterranean fishing village with red tile roofs; constructed originally as a playground by *Penthouse* magazine, now open to the public. Malinska, Krk (phone: 88-55-66). Moderate.

SPLIT

Lav – The name means "lion," and it's the best hotel in the Split area, albeit rather ultramodern and concrete. It's 6 miles south of Diocletian's palace. 58000 Split (phone: 55-14-44). Moderate.
Dioklecijan Restaurant – On a ship anchored in the port. Go for *Dalmatinska pasticada* (marinated beef stew), and local fish and other seafood.

DUBROVNIK

Babin Kuk Holiday Park – This complex contains 4 ultramodern hotels, designed by Durrell Stone, the architect of the Kennedy Center in Washington DC. Every conceivable facility is available; the *Dubrovnik President* is the most elegant. 50001 Dubrovnik (phone: 2-2999). Expensive.
Croatia Hotel – Tucked into the cliffs overlooking the Adriatic in the tiny town of Cavtat, near Dubrovnik. As good as anything in the city. 50210 Cavtat (phone: 78-022). Expensive.
Libertas – Multitiered modern structure built into the side of a hill on the beach. Overlooks the city ramparts and the sea; has its own pool, sauna, solarium, restaurant, and nightclub. Lavcevicera 1, 50000 Dubrovnik (phone: 2-7444). Expensive.
Excelsior – On the water, with one of the best views of the walled city of Dubrovnik. An old grand dame of a hotel, popular with Americans. 3 Fran Supila, 50000 Dubrovnik (phone: 23-566). Moderate.
Konavski Dvori – 20 minutes south of the old city. Try the freshwater trout or the lamb-on-the-spit.
Madmaison – A French restaurant in an ancient townhouse inside the walled city.
Orsan – A 15-minute drive north from Dubrovnik, and probably the best restaurant in Yugoslavia. A converted peasant house made of stone. Famous for seafood.

SVETI STEFAN

Sveti Stefan Hotel – A sixteenth-century fishing village and pirate stronghold, turned deluxe hotel. It completely occupies a small island, connected by a causeway to the mainland. All cars are parked on shore. The cottages' exteriors were preserved intact, and given plush, air-conditioned innards. 81315 Sveti Stefan (phone: 4-1333; 4-1013). Expensive.

Milocer Hotel – The former residence of the queen of Montenegro, with a mansion and six villas. Has its own beautiful pebble beach, with mountains and a pine forest as a backdrop. 81315 Sveti Stefan (phone: 4-1013). Moderate.

Podkoren to Belgrade

This tour of the heartland begins in the Julian Alps, which are shared by Italy, Austria, and Yugoslavia, in the Yugoslav mountain town of Podkoren. Bring your skis or your hiking clothes, and prepare to take in some heavenly Alpine air. You will visit inland natural beauties such as the Martuljk waterfalls, Lake Bled, and the limestone caves at Postojna. Plan to spend some time at Lake Bled for swimming, rowing, fishing, or skating, depending on the season. As the elevation drops, you'll tour the cultural centers of Ljubljana and Zagreb, where we recommend you see what sports the natives are playing and what concerts they're attending — and also, where they've been going to church for the past 700 years or so. There's an optional side trip to the Plitvice Lakes National Park that would add about 160 miles (256 km) to your total; the Plitvice Lakes form a natural staircase of 16 cascading lakes.

A long drive through a forest full of wild animals such as foxes, elk, grouse, and wild boar ensues after Zagreb, followed by the green fertile plains. This grain belt of Slavonija is a good place to meet rural people and get a sense of what it's like to live away from the shrillness of cities; it's exhilarating to get attuned to a place where time does not seem man-made.

Belgrade, the capital, is the end of the journey, the city with the most hustle and bustle in Yugoslavia. Here in the center of Yugoslav industry, commerce, and communication, you can get the best possible sense of what Yugoslavia thinks it's about; everything from industrial fairs to film festivals is held in Belgrade; there are gypsy street-singers in Skadarlija, the bohemian and theater district; buy a souvenir from a sidewalk craftsman.

PODKOREN: Start at the mountain town of Podkoren, near the Austrian border on Route E94, a main tourist road, and drive south through the blue green Julian Alps at 2,700 feet. If you ski, you can stop at the winter resort at Ratece-Planica, where there are ski slopes, five jumps, and lifts; there are several other resorts in the area: Kranjska Gora (one of Yugoslavia's most developed winter sports centers), Mount Vitranc, and Gozd Martuljk. If you don't know how to downhill ski, this might be a good time to cross-country ski or learn how — it's not hard to pick up, and there can't be many better spots in the world to begin. Near Gozd Martuljk are the huge Martuljk waterfalls at the foot of Mount Spik, and the Pericnik waterfall at Mojstrana. There are several hiking trails passing through these Slovenian mountains, one extending all the way from the Baltic Sea in northern Europe to Yugoslavia's

Adriatic. The water of the nearby Sava River is a brilliant metallic blue, and the air is Alpine-clear.

BLED: The mountain resort of Bled is 25 miles (40 km) in from Podkoren, sitting on Lake Bled in a valley surrounded by the snow-capped Alps. The castle of the bishops of Brixen (eleventh century), overlooking the lake from a sheer cliff, has been converted into a museum and inn. Lake Bled's waters are restricted to bathing and rowing (no motorboats to break the peace), and skating and curling in the winter. In the area are hunting grounds, fishing spots, tennis courts, riding facilities, and Yugoslavia's only 18-hole golf course.

En Route from Bled – A detour of 19 miles (30 km) to the southeast will bring you to Lake Bohinj, another mountain lake area good for skiing and hiking.

LJUBLJANA: About 55 miles (88 km) down from Podkoren is Ljubljana (pronounced "lyoob-lyana"), the capital of the Republic of Slovenia, and the cosmopolitan and economic center of the state as well. Expositions, concerts, festivals, exhibits, and major sporting events (basketball, hockey, soccer, Ping-Pong) all take place here. Ljubljana's museums are particularly worth a look; the National Museum is one of the oldest in Europe. The city's architecture spans the fifteenth to twentieth centuries, with many baroque buildings and 30-story modern monoliths.

En Route from Ljubljana – Worth a detour is a visit to the Postojna Caves in Postojna, where in towering chambers of limestone, the dripping water has formed shapes in stalactites and stalagmites, more magnificent and improbable than anything in Minimal Art. Take E93 from Ljubljana, it's just a 40-minute drive to get there.

Highway E94 out of Ljubljana passes through woods, with no intersections. At 39 miles (63 km) south of the city is a turnoff for Novo Mesto, on the Krka River, where you can go swimming or trout fishing. Back on the main highway you will reach the thirteenth-century castle of *Otocec*, on an island in the Krka. Like many Yugoslav monuments, the castle is now a hotel and restaurant.

The mountains give way to hills and wide river valleys between Ljubljana and the next major Yugoslav city, Zagreb, 93 miles (148 km) away. This region has several spas dedicated to treating a wide range of complaints, from neuralgia to heart disease: Dolenjske Toplice, Smarjeske Toplice, and Cateske Toplice are on or near the main highway. Most spas offer the use of their hotels and hot springs to the healthy as well as the sick.

You will cross the Slovenia-Croatia border on E94 about 16 miles (25 km) from the Croatian capital of Zagreb, Yugoslavia's second-largest city and its artistic center.

ZAGREB: Zagreb comprises what is now really three cities: the Upper Town (Gornji Grad), the oldest part of Zagreb, with many buildings from the thirteenth century; the Lower Town (Donji Grad), built at the turn of the nineteenth century; and New Zagreb (Novi Zagreb), built since World War II, very stark and square, with wide parking lots. The Upper and Lower towns are protected as national monuments.

Zagreb is an important locale on the world cultural circuit: Major opera companies and symphonies play here, and the International Festival of Contemporary Music takes place in Zagreb every other year; *I Solisti di Zagreb* is one of the world's foremost chamber groups; every second year Zagreb hosts the World Festival of Animated Cartoons; and every year in July is the International Folklore Festival. A permanent exhibition of so-called "Hlebine School of Native Painters" is centered in Zagreb at the Gallery of Primitive Art. A visit will give you some idea of this movement. And while you're here, check out any of Zagreb's numerous other museums, galleries, and private collections.

Make sure you see the Croatian National Theater, at night, if possible, for its sturdy, majestic exterior and beautiful music-box interior: plush red seats, inlaid wooden booths, huge fresco ceiling, and splendid chandelier.

. Zagreb's churches are well worth a tour: St. Mark's, a thirteenth-century church, has medieval coats of arms in mosaic on its tile roof; St. Stephen's Cathedral has intricate stonework towers, over 300 feet high, and thick fortifications.

As Yugoslavia's most culturally sophisticated city, Zagreb has the country's most cosmopolitan nightlife; some streets are cobblestone, and the cafés and restaurants have an old-world Austro-Hungarian style.

In the city environs there are more things to do: In the immediate vicinity are enough woods for walking, hunting, and fishing. Marshal Tito's birthplace in Kumrovec, 28 miles (45 km) away, is done up as a museum dedicated to him — it looks rather Early American, with the exposed cross-beamed ceiling and a rough-hewn rocking cradle in the corner.

At Belec, 22 miles (35 km) from the city, is a baroque church decorated inside with carvings and figurines of diabolical inventiveness, with an altar like a three-dimensional Hieronymus Bosch painting.

En Route from Zagreb – If you have the time, it is worth a side trip to the Plitvice Lakes National Park, 80 miles (128 km) south of Zagreb. Take E96 out of the city, and when the road forks at Karlovac — 30 miles (48 km) on — turn due south (towards Tusilovic); the road signs will direct you as you get near. Plitvice Lakes form a natural staircase of 16 blue green lakes, each cascading down into the next in the middle of a virgin forest. There are hotels near the park and quite a few tourists.

. It is 240 miles (384 km) from Zagreb to Belgrade on the main highway, which passes through dense forests, on the Slavonian plains, populated principally by elk, grouse, wild boar, and hunters. The Srem plains follows, the most fertile cropland in Yugoslavia. If you're sick of castles by now, you won't find many here — only sugar beets, green hills, and rustic farm folk who might have stepped out of a painting by Pieter Breughel the Elder.

BELGRADE: Belgrade is the capital of Serbia as well as Yugoslavia's capital and largest city (pop. 1.4 million) and its center of commerce and communication. The Celts were the first to settle it in the fourth century BC, building a fortress on the white rocks overlooking the mouth of the rivers Sava and Danube; Belgrade means "White City." The fort of Kalemegdan now stands on that spot, built on the Celtic foundations, but that is nearly all of Belgrade's tumultuous past that remains — the city has been razed to the ground by invaders 36 times since its founding. The last was during World War II, so most of Belgrade was built since then in a bleak, socialist-modern style, although some sections of nineteenth-century Mittel European grandeur and Turkish exotica did survive.

As the center of government and industry, Belgrade is the site for various business expositions. At various times of year are the Salon of Automobiles, the Technical Fair, the Fashion Fair, the Book Fair, and numerous others.

International festivals of film, music, and theater are held in Belgrade as well; the tourism offices in Yugoslavia are always happy to supply details.

Belgrade's National Museum has a huge collection, and it is definitely worth a trip for a view of Yugoslavia's crazy-quilt heritage — Illyrian and Celtic tools, Greek and Roman busts, Bulgarian swords, Byzantine icons, Turkish jewelry, and works by Serbian and European painters up to the twentieth century. There is a Museum of Modern Art as well, and an Ethnographical Museum. At Mount Avala, 12 miles (20 km) from town, is a monument to the Unknown Soldier by Yugoslavia's best-known sculptor, Ivan Mestrovic.

Visit the nineteenth-century Bohemian quarter of the city, Skadarlija, when you go to the theater, for a taste of old-world style. There are cafés, Belgrade's best restaurants, cabarets, gypsy street-singers, open-air theaters, and folk dancing. In the summer the street is lined with food stands and the stalls of artists and craftsmen.

BEST EN ROUTE

Accommodations for two people in an expensive place will run $38–$104; moderate, $15–$60; inexpensive, $15–$25. The restaurants we've listed below are all in the expensive category, by Yugoslav standards — which means $6–$15 per person for dinner, including wine.

BLED

Grand Hotel Toplice – A beatifically elegant hotel on Lake Bled in the Julian Alps, with crisp mountain air, damask sofas, Persian rugs, and finely tailored guests. You can go swimming, fishing, or hunting nearby. 20 Cesta Svobode, PO Box 41, 64260 Bled (phone: 7-7222). Moderate.

Blejski Grad – The oldest tavern in the city, with heavy, rustic wooden furnishings. The cooking is Viennese style.

LJUBLJANA

Holiday Inn – Yes, really. In Europe, *Holiday Inns* are fancy places; this is Yugoslavia's first. In the middle of town, with a full-size swimming pool on the roof (phone: 21-14-34). Moderate.

ZAGREB

Esplanade – An art deco masterpiece, with huge rooms, crystal chandeliers, and black marble walls. Good service, and painstaking nineteenth-century elegance. Mihanoviceva 1, 41000 Zagreb (phone: 51-22-22). Expensive.

Zagreb Intercontinental Hotel – Considered the best hotel in Yugoslavia. Square, glassy, and modern, with Yugoslav native paintings on the walls. Big rooms, and its own swimming pool and health club. Krsnjavoga 1, Zagreb (phone: 44-34-11).

Gradski Podrum – The name means "the city cellar," and to enter you descend from the street, finding yourself in a large restaurant that preserves its intimacy by the use of partitions. Continental cooking, elegant atmosphere, and crisp service.

Opera Rooftop – At the *Zagreb Intercontinental Hotel.* Inside there is a certain pretentiously overblown elegance, but still, the huge sweeping windows give you nice views of the new and old cities. Try the prune-garnished Dalmatian pot roast, or the Bosnian stew served in earthenware pots.

BELGRADE

Moskva – Considered by some to be Belgrade's best. In the middle of town; has several duplex suites with a common window lighting both levels. Balkanska Br. 1, 11000 Belgrade (phone: 68-62-55).

Belgrade Inter-Continental Hotel – Belgrade's newest deluxe hotel, conveniently located next to the Sava Convention Center. M. Popovica, 11000 Belgrade (phone: 13-47-60).

Tri Sesira – "The Three Hats," in the Bohemian or Skadarlija section. Spicy Serbian food and mellow Gypsy music.

PLITVICE LAKES

Lika – Tucked away in the park itself. Homemade bread and brandy, local trout and cheese, and lamb on the spit.

Bitola to Belgrade

This is a short tour of some of Yugoslavia's most famous art treasures, found in the churches, mosques, monasteries, and excavated towns of Macedonia and Serbia. This eastern part of the country was ruled, in order, by the Greeks, Romans, Byzantines, Serbian medieval kings and Turks. The Greeks and Romans contributed marble statues and tile mosaics; the Byzantines and Serbians covered the walls of their churches with religious frescoes; and the Turks, forbidden to represent life in art, built magnificent mosques and forts decorated inside with abstract patterns. If you like art, you should visit here, because you won't see these objects in the original anywhere else — no museum in New York or Chicago can ever remove and borrow the frescoes of Sopocani, or the floor from the Imperial Mosque of Pristina, or the mosaic water nymph from the bath in the Roman town at Gamzigrad. And besides, these objects are in their original setting, where the original purpose is a little nearer to the observer's reach than it could be hanging on a wall in a strange city.

You will start at the ruins of the ancient Greek city of Heraclea near Bitola, Yugoslavia, and finish at Belgrade, traversing the works of the Byzantine and Turkish empires en route. Some of the locations are far-flung; monasteries in particular tend to be secluded; the beautiful lake and mountain settings should make up for the inconvenience of reaching some of them. All of the sites are well known and well marked.

July and August are the peak months for folk festivals; ask the government Tourist Office for a listing for this region if you are interested.

BITOLA: We begin 3 miles (5 km) from the border of Greece, near the Yugoslav city of Bitola, in the Republic of Macedonia. About 1.9 miles (3 km) south of town are the ruins of the ancient Greek city of Heraclea, which was an important commercial and strategic center linking Constantinople to the Adriatic coast. Particularly beautiful are the mosaic tile floor in the foundations of the basilica uncovered there, and the life-size marble statues. At the end of July in Bitola is a folk festival called St. Elia's Days, which features songs and dances from all over Yugoslavia.

En Route from Bitola – Proceed West on E5S, a main tourist highway, toward Ohrid. About 15 miles (24 km) along this road, take the left-hand turnoff and head for the church of St. George in Kurbinovo, near the town of Pretor on the eastern shore of Lake Prespa. The church itself is rather unassuming, but the frescoes inside, painted in 1191, are striking — take note particularly of the Assumption and the Annunciation.

OHRID: Go back up to the main highway and continue to Ohrid, the city on the shores of Lake Ohrid. The church of St. Sophia in Ohrid is the most famous and sumptuous medieval monument in Macedonia, built in the eleventh and fourteenth centuries. When the Turks moved in, they covered up the church's dramatic frescoes with mortar — since images of life are forbidden in Islam — but these were carefully uncovered in the 1950s. The Ascension is particularly expressive: note the dour, attentive angels in the friezes, crouching in a background of quiet green and blue.

There are brilliantly colored frescoes at another Ohrid monument, the Church of St. Clement, including an athletic angel in the Annunciation who is about to touch Mary in midstride.

En Route from Ohrid – Take a detour south along Lake Ohrid towards St. Naum's monastery on the Albanian border. The lake will be on your right, and a national park on your left. Take the opportunity to go for a swim in the clear waters and a hike in the park. St. Naum's, when you reach it, is extraordinary for its beautiful setting on the lake, and the state of its preservation. Drive the 19 miles (30 km) back north to the main highway and take it all the way to Skopje.

SKOPJE: Skopje, Macedonia's capital, was badly damaged in an earthquake in 1963, so most of its buildings are modern. Ironically, Skopje was founded in 518 by refugees from the ancient town of Scupi (3 miles from present-day Skopje), which had just been destroyed by an earthquake; they named the new settlement after their hometown.

There is much to see, despite both quakes, in Skopje and its environs. A magnificent medieval footbridge spans the River Vardar, and is still very much in use. The great Mustafa-pasha Mosque and the Daut-pasha bath were built in the fifteenth century by the Turks.

The church of St. Panteleimon in Nerezi (just south of the city) is the place to see, if you see no other church in Macedonia. The fresco of St. Damian, painted in 1164, is remarkable for its somber dignity in color composition and graceful lines. Experts rank the Lamentation, the Nativity, the Visitation, and the Transfiguration as among the finest in Byzantine art.

Marko's Monastery, properly called the Church of St. Demetrius (fourteenth century), is just south of Nerezi, and has frescoes of biblical subjects not conventionally treated in ecclesiastical art. A moving example is Rachel's Tears.

En Route from Skopje – Head north on E27 out of Skopje toward Pristina. Just short of Pristina is the Monastery at Gracanica (thirteenth to fourteenth centuries); the stones making up the structure are red and yellow, giving the effect of gold. The top of the building has rows of ascending arches and towers, gathering to one pinnacle tower on the roof — it is considered the most beautiful early Serbian building anywhere. The frescoes inside are perfectly preserved, displaying in lively fashion the horrors and glories of this world and the next, sort of an illustrated Dante.

The Roman ruins of Ulpiana, near Gracanica, contain mosaics, tombstones, and a basilica.

PRISTINA: Pristina is the capital of the Province of Kosovo (an autonomous province of Serbia), and is a mixture of old Eastern architecture with ultramodern. The most important monument is the Imperial Mosque, built in 1461 by Sultan Mehmet II; there are also several nineteenth-century Turkish buildings standing in the town. The collection in the Museum of Kosovo tells the Oriental history of the town in detail.

NOVI PAZAR: Go northwest out of Pristina on E27 toward Titova Mitrovica, following the road past that town to Novi Pazar. Novi Pazar is also being built up in modern style, but the Alem-Altum Turkish mosque (sixteenth century) is worth seeing.

The real attraction is 10 miles (16 km) west of the town in the hills at Sopocani. The monastery there was built in 1265 by King Uros I to house his own tomb. The frescoes of Sopocani, with those of Nerezi, are said to be the best in Byzantine art. Using yellow, green, violet, and gold leaf (which has by now peeled away), the artist here painted with great feeling the nobility and tragedy of man. See in particular the Dormition of the Virgin and the saints' portraits.

KRALJEVO: Take the highway north out of Novi Pazar to Kraljevo, to see the restored monastery of Zica, painted bright earthen red, as it was in medieval times. Built from 1208 to 1220, it was here at the seat of the archbishopric of Serbia that the medieval Serbian kings were crowned. The remaining frescoes here are few, but of beautiful quality and color.

The Kalenic Monastery near Kraljevo is constructed with graceful and detailed relief in its arches; its architecture is among the best in the Serbian style.

En Route from Kraljevo – Get on the highway east for a final stop before Belgrade. About 22 miles (35 km) after the town of Krusevac, after the highway has turned north and converged with the highway from Nis, take an eastward turnoff (toward Romania) and drive until you get to the town of Zajecar, just shy of the Bulgarian border. Near town are the excavations of the late Roman fortress of Gamzigrad (third and fourth centuries). There you will find the palace ruins, a huge Roman bath, and mosaics with a grace, sumptuousness, and eroticism that will refresh you.

Gaze at the splendid city gates of Gamzigrad, which no longer keep anyone in or out; whenever you feel ready, get back on the highway west toward Paracin and the Danube, and turn north to Belgrade and civilization, where the Gamzigrads of the future wait their turn.

BEST EN ROUTE

OHRID

Desaret – A new hotel on Lake Ohrid, with a wooden Macedonian-style exterior (which might look Scandinavian to Western eyes). (Phone: 2–4040.) Moderate: ranges from $33 to $36 for two, per night, depending on the season.

Inex Gorica Hotel – The best restaurant in the region, which serves Ohrid trout — found only in Lake Ohrid. Expensive by Yugoslav standards: $6–$15 for dinner, including wine.

Index

11134585
ISBN 0-395-39398-1